AFRICAN AMERICAN LIVES

African American Lives

GENERAL EDITORS

Henry Louis Gates Jr.

Evelyn Brooks Higginbotham

*W. E. B. Du Bois Institute for African and
African American Research, Harvard University*

*in association with the
American Council of Learned Societies*

OXFORD
UNIVERSITY PRESS

2004

OXFORD
UNIVERSITY PRESS

Oxford New York

Auckland Bangkok Buenos Aires Cape Town Chennai
Dar es Salaam Delhi Hong Kong Istanbul Karachi Kolkata
Kuala Lumpur Madrid Melbourne Mexico City Mumbai
Nairobi São Paulo Shanghai Taipei Tokyo Toronto

Copyright © 2004 by Oxford University Press, Inc.

All *American National Biography* entries © 2004 by the American Council of Learned Societies.
"Prince Whipple" entry based on a chapter previously published in *Black Portsmouth* © 2004 by Mark
Sammons and Valerie Cunningham, used by permission of University Press of New England.

Published by Oxford University Press, Inc.
198 Madison Avenue, New York, New York 10016
http://www.oup.com

Oxford is a registered trademark of Oxford University Press

Library of Congress Cataloging-in-Publication Data

African American lives / edited by Henry Louis Gates, Jr. and Evelyn
Brooks Higginbotham.
p. cm.
Includes bibliographical references (p.) and index.
ISBN 0-19-516024-X (hardcover : alk. paper)
1. African Americans—Biography. I. Gates, Henry Louis. II.
Higginbotham, Evelyn Brooks, 1945-
E185.96 .A446 2004
920′.009296073—dc22
2003023640

Printing number: 9 8 7 6 5 4 3 2 1

Printed in the United States of America
on acid-free paper

Editorial and Production Staff

Acquiring Editor
Casper Grathwohl

Project Editor
Martin Coleman

Editorial Assistant
Ryan Sullivan

Copy Editors
Janet Bale
Mary L. Gillaspy
Marcia Merryman Means
Neil Schlager

Proofreaders
Carol Holmes
Melodie Monahan
Neil Schlager
Ryan Sullivan

Art Coordinator
Sarah Feehan

Indexer
Katharyn Dunham

Compositor
Laserwords

Manufacturing Coordinator
Chris Critelli

Designers
Joan Greenfield (interior)
Nora Wertz (jacket)

Editing, Design, and Production Director
John Sollami

Director of Editorial Development
Timothy J. DeWerff

Publisher
Karen Day

CONTENTS

*A*frican American Lives tells many stories and yet one. Its six hundred and eleven biographies span more than four centuries, presenting the lives of men and women whose backgrounds and achievements are as varied as their talents, skills, and knowledge. Taken together these lives of distinction attest to the integral character of African Americans to the life of this nation—to their abiding influence on American culture and institutions. *African American Lives* presents this history through a mosaic of individuals, some known throughout the world and others all but forgotten. We chose to include both familiar and unfamiliar names in the belief that history is more than the coherent account of important national events and social movements and that it is more than great ideas and works of art. The contours and content of history are shaped by people's lives, their personal choices and circumstances, individual uniqueness and creativity. Large events and small ones are brought about by ordinary people, for even the greatest of us is but an individual, while the least of us—as can be seen frequently in *African American Lives*—may have a profound effect on the course of world events.

African American Lives is the first publication of a much larger project, the *African American National Biography*, produced jointly by Harvard University's W. E. B. Du Bois Institute for African and African American Research and Oxford University Press. The project is modeled after the superb twenty-five volume *American National Biography* (1999), published by Oxford in collaboration with the American Council of Learned Societies—indeed, 257 entries in the current volume are reprinted from *ANB*. Taking *African American Lives* as its core, the *African American National Biography* will expand to eight volumes containing approximately 6,000 biographies and will thus illuminate the broad sweep of African American biography more fully than ever before, giving us an even greater appreciation of the roles played by African Americans in history.

The study of history itself has changed considerably since the 1970s when Rayford Logan and Michael R. Winston edited the *Dictionary of American Negro Biography* (1982), the first scholarly and comprehensive biographical reference work on African Americans. At the time of the *DANB*'s publication, African American women's history as well as the history of the civil rights and Black Power movements had just begun to emerge as vibrant fields of study. Attention to popular culture has provided greater insight into the lived experience of people who did not necessarily leave a written record. In the past three decades, historical methodology came increasingly to look upon new types of evidence, such as slave testimony and oral interviews, and to adopt interpretive frameworks that focused on indigenous movements, specifically the agency and social activism of local people rather than national leaders. The many changes in scholarship have brought to light an abundance of names remembered only by generations long gone.

Choosing some six hundred biographies to reflect so much history in a single volume proved a daunting task in itself. Our goal was to include not simply the greatest, the most deserving, or the most famous African Americans, but a selection that is representative of the broad range of African American experience. To accomplish this, we sifted through a database of over 11,000 names, solicited the advice of experts in many fields, and found ourselves in innumerable fascinating conversations. If the result of that process, as printed in this book, provokes further discussion among readers as to who should or should not be included, then it has served an important function already, because lively debate is an important tool for achieving understanding.

Reading through these biographies, one gets a sense of the interplay of the lives and careers of the subjects and of the breadth and depth of history behind their actions and ideas. As an example, let us follow through *African American Lives* the web of interconnections stemming from a single event—one that took place on 1 December 1955. **Rosa Parks** is rightly famed for refusing to give up her seat that day to a white rider on a bus in Alabama, but she did this neither on a whim nor alone. She was a protégée of the NAACP field secretary **Ella Baker**, and like **Septima Clark**, she had trained carefully to be an effective activist at the Highlander Folk School in Tennessee. Subsequent to her arrest, she worked with **Jo Ann Robinson, E. D. Nixon, Martin Luther King Jr.**, and many others to organize the Montgomery bus boycott. Parks's refusal to give up her seat was itself no innovation, but rather drew upon a long history of similar protest. In 1947 **Bayard Rustin** was dragged from the front of a bus in Chapel Hill, North Carolina, and sentenced to thirty days on a chain gang; a few years earlier, before breaking the color barrier in major league baseball, **Jackie Robinson** was court-martialed—and acquitted—after refusing to move to the back of a segregated military bus. **Benjamin Jefferson Davis Jr.** was arrested in the early 1920s for sitting in the Jim Crow section of an Atlanta trolley car. The legality of the "separate but equal" doctrine itself was established by the infamous Supreme Court decision stemming from the arrest of **Homer Plessy**, who sat deliberately in a "whites only" railway coach in Louisiana in 1892 to challenge that principle. And there were similar protests before that: the career of **Ida B. Wells-Barnett** as both an activist and a journalist began in 1883 when she refused to leave a first-class ladies' car on the Chesapeake, Ohio, and Southwestern Railway; the Reconstruction congressman **Robert Brown Elliott** lobbied successfully for a bill to ban discrimination in public transportation in the 1870s; twice, in 1868 and 1866, **Mary Ellen Pleasant** sued a San Francisco streetcar company for not allowing her to ride; in 1866 in Philadelphia **George Moses Horton** protested with a poem entitled "Forbidden to Ride on the Street Cars"; in 1864 **Sojourner Truth** won in court the right to ride the streetcars in Washington, D.C. In 1855 **James W. C. Pennington** successfully challenged a New York City law prohibiting African Americans from riding inside a horse-drawn car. When **Sarah Parker Remond** was ejected from her seat in a place of public entertainment in Salem, Massachusetts, in 1853, she sued for reparations and won. There have been many others, but, as far as we know, the pioneer of such action was **David Ruggles**, who refused to give up his seat in a New Bedford, Massachusetts, railway car in 1841, only a year after the railway was established there. Of such connections is African American history made.

Like those named above, many of the subjects in *African American Lives* can be described as activists, but this book is not merely a collection of biographies of civil rights workers and politicians. *African American Lives* covers the full panoply of life for almost five centuries. In 1528, **Esteban**, the first African known to have stepped onto the North American continent, began his epic journeys across the South and Southwest, eventually becoming a Zuni deity after his death. African American history has continued ever since, and to represent that history in this book you will find at least the following:

138 writers and journalists

136 activists

90 slaves

81 politicians, government workers, judges, and lawyers

77 musicians

66 ministers, preachers, rabbis, and other religious workers

66 educators

50 athletes and sports figures

40 actors, performers, directors, and filmmakers

31 doctors, nurses, and medical workers

28 artists and photographers

23 business people and entrepreneurs

20 military personnel

16 scientists

11 philanthropists

10 dancers

9 frontiersmen, pioneers, and cowboys

8 inventors

8 explorers

7 aviators and astronauts

2 legendary figures

1 elephant hunter

If these numbers, incomplete as they are, add up to more than 611 (they actually add up to 918), that is because people are not easily classifiable and thus many must be included in more than one category. We all live varied, complex lives, and the subjects in *African American Lives* reflect that complexity to the fullest.

We have chosen to include in *African American Lives* the biographies of living subjects as well as dead. Many biographical dictionaries include only deceased subjects, and that certainly makes the writing, editing, and updating easier. However, much of importance has taken place in the past century, and the historical record would be seriously skewed if many undeniably significant people were left out of *African American Lives* simply because they are still alive. **Martin Luther King Jr., Medgar Evers**, and **Eldridge Cleaver** are gone, but **James Meredith, Angela Davis, Jesse Jackson**, and many others are still with us. The story of the struggle for civil rights in the latter half of the twentieth century is best appreciated through the lives of all of these and more. **Alvin Ailey**, too, has died, but **Katherine Dunham, Arthur Mitchell**, and **Bill T. Jones** have not; taken together, their careers brightly illuminate our understanding of the African American contribution to modern dance. **Jimi Hendrix** is dead, though many of those who paved the way for his success live on; perhaps we need mention only **B. B. King, Chuck Berry**, and **Bo Diddley**.

Every attempt has been made in *African American Lives* to include relevant family information. Typically, the first paragraph gives birth and death dates, the names and occupations of the parents, if these are known, and information about the subject's early life and education. The course of African American history, especially in earlier periods, has been such that in many cases dates, parentage, and family connections are difficult to determine. In order to make such connections explicit, the mother's maiden name has been given, where possible, so as to identify both sides of the family. This use of the maiden name is not meant to imply anything about the parents' marital status.

Cross-references throughout *African American Lives* make it easier to trace the web of contemporaneous and historical relationships that give structure to African American history. The first time anyone whose biography appears in *African American Lives* is named in the text of another biography, the name is printed in small capitals. For example, the biography of **Malcolm X** includes references to MARCUS GARVEY, ELIJAH MUHAMMAD, MARTIN LUTHER KING JR., MUHAMMAD ALI, FANNIE LOU HAMER, CORETTA SCOTT KING, ADAM CLAYTON POWELL JR., JAMES BALDWIN, LOUIS FARRAKHAN, OSSIE DAVIS, ALEX HALEY, and SPIKE LEE. If any of these cross-references piques your interest or curiosity, you can simply turn to that entry to find out more about the person.

However, you do not necessarily need to know the name of a particular person in order to explore *African American Lives*. An index of subjects classified by their occupations or areas of renown will help you to find, for example, slaves and abolitionists, explorers and adventurers, civil rights workers, preachers and other religious figures, writers and journalists, artists and actors, dancers and musicians. A thematic index allows you to look up organizations, places of importance, and other significant topics. There you will find references to the NAACP, CORE, SNCC, SCLC, the Black Arts Movement, the Universal Negro Improvement Association (UNIA), the maritime underground railroad, and even the M Street School/Paul Laurence Dunbar High School, in Washington, D.C., where more than twenty of the subjects in *African American Lives* taught or were educated.

The biographies in *African American Lives* are also supplemented by several appendices. There are listings of all African American members of Congress and federal judges. There are also lists of winners of the NAACP Spingarn Medal, and all African American recipients of the Presidential Medal of Freedom, Nobel Prizes, Pulitzer Prizes, the National Medal of Arts, the National Humanities Medal, and the Congressional Medal of Honor. Names in boldface type in these appendices identify those for whom there is a biography in the book.

We are pleased to make available in a single volume these biographies of people who have significantly shaped our history. Some of them, like **Jim Beckwourth** and **Mae Jemison**, literally blazed trails to new frontiers. Others, like **Moses Roper, Ellen** and **William Craft**, and **Henry Box Brown**, found new pathways to freedom. Their successors labored long and hard to broaden those pathways, to pave them and make them smoother, as we see in the lives of **Mary McLeod Bethune, Jo Ann Robinson**, and **Roy Wilkins**. Many others have taught us, lifted our spirits, entertained us, and even amazed us with their skills as educators, writers, artists, dancers, and athletes. We hope that *African American Lives* will serve as more than just a reference book–that it will provide its readers with the same insights, understanding, and pleasures that we have gained from editing it.

—Henry Louis Gates Jr.
—Evelyn Brooks Higginbotham
   Editors

*A*frican American Lives owes its existence to an extraordinary collective effort. Our heartfelt appreciation goes out to all who contributed to making this book a reality. There would, of course, be no book, without the research and scholarship of more than 400 persons who wrote the biographical entries. The generosity of Oxford University Press and the American Council of Learned Societies was crucial to our endeavor. Oxford University Press underwrote the funding of the *African American National Biography (AANB)* project, and the American Council of Learned Societies permitted us to reprint biographies from the *American National Biography*.

Yet just as *African American Lives* tells many individual stories, its publication speaks to the specific roles and skills of various individuals. From the very beginning we benefited from the assistance of Richard Newman. A treasure trove of African Americana, Richard offered precise and insightful answers to any question about African Americans both prominent and obscure. Although he did not live to see the publication of this book, Richard Newman's influence is pervasive, not only in the four biographies that he wrote and in the many details he contributed to others, but also in the very shape and spirit of the project as a whole.

Karen C. C. Dalton has been a tremendous asset to this project from its inception. Karen aided us in organizing the entire *AANB* staff, and she continues to support the staff through her incomparable administrative skills. She has contributed concretely to this volume by selecting much of the artwork and photographs and advising on the rest, as well as by writing an entry.

We owe an inestimable debt to John K. Bollard, the Managing Editor of *AANB* for his unstinting efforts and unwavering commitment. We thank him most of all for the high standards he set for himself, his staff, and the project as a whole as he oversaw the selection of entries, coordinated the search for contributors, read through and edited the entire text, and communicated with the editors, the contributors, and the editorial and production staff at Oxford University Press. No one worked harder to make this book possible.

The *AANB* Associate Editors Sholomo B. Levy, Steven J. Niven, and Lisa E. Rivo are the lifeblood of the project. They wrote many of the entries in addition to soliciting expert contributors to write hundreds more. Months were spent in their going through submissions with fine-tooth editorial combs to eliminate errors before polishing the text to a high sheen. The quality of this book owes much to their scholarship, their skills as writers and editors, and to their energy and unflagging dedication.

Members of the Editorial and Advisory Boards provided valuable service in selecting names for inclusion, recommending contributors for entries, and reviewing completed entries. Particular thanks go to Vincent Carretta, Bruce Kellner, and Ingrid Monson for their advice, editorial care, and their time in various conversations about the project.

Indeed many scholars and experts have willingly provided advice and labor in their various fields. We are particularly grateful to Professors David Wilkins and Charles Ogletree of the Harvard University Law School for helping to choose entries in the legal professions. Judge Ann Claire Williams on the Seventh Circuit Court of Appeals assisted in identifying federal judges for inclusion. The Very Reverend James Munroe, Dean of Christ Church Cathedral, Springfield, Massachusetts, graciously advised on Episcopal clergy and on church history and procedure. Professor Christine Shelton of Smith College made invaluable suggestions regarding women in sports and reviewed our choices with considerable care. Professor William Oram and Professor Emeritus Dennis Hudson, both of Smith College, and Professor Margaret G. Lloyd of Springfield College were more than generous with their time, recommending contributors and discussing the parameters of the entire project. Michael C. Vazquez, Executive Editor of *Transition*, has been readily available for resolving editorial and procedural questions.

Thanks go, as well, to the curators, archivists, and contributors who helped us locate photographs and artwork, especially Ray Doswell, Curator of the Negro Leagues Baseball Museum, Kansas City, Missouri, Karen O'Brien, Collections Manager of the University of Michigan Museum of Anthropology, Kisha Tandy, Assistant Curator of Social History, Indiana State Museum, and Brian Turner of the Florence (Massachusetts) Historical Society, and Tritobia Hayes-Benjamin, Director, Howard University Gallery of Art.

Administrative and practical support was provided by Sandra B. Walker, Lisa Gregory, Joanne Kendall, Mai Huynh, Nicole Maskiell, Jill Roszhart, Saran Kaba, and the entire staff of the Harvard University Department of African and African American Studies. The project research assistants, Lisa E. Brooks and Chikwendu Reginald Mbawuike, and our intern David-Andrew Wallach willingly undertook tedious but necessary tasks, such as data entry, library research, tracking of manuscripts, and clerical upkeep.

The *AANB* database of more than 11,000 names was compiled by Lisa E. Rivo with the tireless assistance of Paul Hana, Eddie Bruce, and Philip Choy. Technical support and maintenance of our computer systems has been ably and efficiently provided by Shannon Brantley, Sharon Rogge, Linwood Webster, and the staff of the Harvard University Faculty and Staff Computer Support Services. We are also grateful to Scott Haywood and Daniel Martinez for the care and upkeep of the *AANB* offices.

Finally we must acknowledge once again our sincere gratitude to Oxford University Press. We are particularly grateful to Casper Grathwohl, Publisher of the Reference section, for his vision and inspiration, and for his material and emotional commitment to this project. We could not have completed this book without Oxford representatives Timothy DeWerff, John Sollami, Abigail Powers, Sarah Feehan, Ryan Sullivan, and especially Martin Coleman, the Project Editor who oversaw with care and patience the considerable task of fitting all the bits and pieces of this book into a seamless whole.

DIRECTORY OF CONTRIBUTORS

Lloyd Ackert
Thomas, Vivien Theodore

Martha Ackmann
Jemison, Mae; Stone, Toni

Philip N. Alexander
Branson, Herman Russell

Eric Anderson
White, George Henry

Stephen W. Angell
Singleton, Benjamin; Turner, Henry McNeal

Michael A. Antonucci
Dixon, "Big" Willie James; Gibson, Althea; Payton, Walter

Donald S. Armentrout
Jones, Absalom

Felix L. Armfield
Jones, Eugene Kinckle

Lillian Ashcraft-Eason
Michaux, Lightfoot Solomon

Deborah F. Atwater
Kelly, Sharon Pratt

Allan D. Austin
Delany, Martin Robison

Reid Badger
Europe, James Reese

David R. Bains
McGuire, George Alexander

William J. Baker
Owens, Jesse

Beth Bates
Lampkin, Daisy Elizabeth Adams

Alexander Battles
Foxx, Redd

Annemarie Bean
Sissle, Noble

E. H. Beardsley
Murray, Peter Marshall

Michael J. Beary
Demby, Edward T.

William K. Beatty
Williams, Daniel Hale

Chris Bebenek
Belafonte, Harry; Jones, James Earl

H. Kenneth Bechtel
Bouchet, Edward Alexander

Silvio A. Bedini
Banneker, Benjamin

Gregory Bell
Graves, Earl; Johnson, John; O'Neal, Stanley; Parsons, Richard Dean; Raines, Franklin Delano

Christopher Benfey
Rillieux, Norbert

Barbara Bennett Peterson
Stockton, Betsey

Adam Biggs
Brooks, Walter Henderson

Roger Biles
Dinkins, David N.

Dedra McDonald Birzer
Esteban

R. J. M. Blackett
Chester, Thomas Morris; Day, William Howard

Charles Blancq
Bolden, Buddy

Sterling Bland
Mars, James; Parker, William

DeAnne Blanton
Williams, Cathay

Maxwell Bloomfield
Jones, Scipio Africanus

John K. Bollard
Stagolee

Henry Warner Bowden
Grimké, Francis James

Rob Bowman
Brown, James

William H. Brackney
Tindley, Charles Albert

Dennis Brailsford
Molyneaux, Tom

Stacy Braukman
Davis, Angela Yvonne

Jonathan Brennan
Caesar, John

Ian Brookes
Cole, Nat King; Marsalis, Wynton

Cecil Brown
Stagolee

Joseph A. Brown
Gregory, Wilton

T. Dennis Brown
Blakey, Art

Elizabeth Brown-Guillory
Childress, Alice

Dickson D. Bruce
Grimké, Archibald Henry

Robert Burke
Dunjee, Roscoe

Cynthia A. Callahan
Petry, Ann

Penelope Campbell
Russwurm, John Brown

Patricia Canson-Griffith
Chisholm, Shirley

Brycchan Carey
Equiano, Olaudah

Charles W. Carey Jr.
Dunbar, Paul Laurence; Julian, Percy Lavon

Richard Carlin
Handy, W. C.

Rodney P. Carlisle
Lynch, John Roy

Glenda Carpio
Smith, Bessie

Vincent Carretta
Gronniosaw, James Albert Ukawsaw

Clayborne Carson
*Abernathy, Ralph; King, Martin Luther,
Jr.; Malcolm X*

Steven R. Carter
Hansberry, Lorraine Vivian

Floris Cash
Matthews, Victoria Earle

Faye A. Chadwell
Carter, Eunice Hunton

Aimee Lee Cheek
Langston, John Mercer

William Cheek
Langston, John Mercer

Samuel Christian
Dandridge, Dorothy

Thomas Clarkin
Bunfche, Ralph Johnson

Kathleen N. Cleaver
Newton, Huey P.

William J. Cobb
Pickens, William; Randolph, A. Philip

Johnetta B. Cole
Simmons, Ruth J.

James Lincoln Collier
Ellington, Duke

Lisa Gale Collins
Lawrence, Jacob Armstead

Mary F. Corey
Coker, Daniel

Angelo Costanzo
Hammon, Briton

Prudence Cumberbatch
Mfume, Kweisi

Maceo Crenshaw Dailey
Moton, Robert Russa

Karen C. C. Dalton
Baker, Josephine

Cyprian Davis
Healy, Eliza; Rudd, Daniel

John Davis
Blind Tom

Nina Davis Howland
Wharton, Clifton Reginald

Jared N. Day
Payton, Philip A., Jr.

Mary De Jong
Smith, Amanda Berry

David M. Dean
Holly, James Theodore

Thomas F. DeFrantz
Williams, Bert, & George Walker

Theodore C. DeLaney
Chavis, John

Dennis C. Dickerson
Cannon, George Dows

Robert M. Dixon
Massey, Walter Eugene

Marty Dobrow
*Abdul-Jabbar, Kareem;
Griffith-Joyner, Florence*

Julyanne E. Dodson
Lee, Jarena

Davison M. Douglas
Robinson, Jackie

Lynn Downey
Pleasant, Mary Ellen

Ronald P. Dufour
Jackson, Mahalia

Sandy Dwayne Martin
Varick, James

Gerald Early
*Ali, Muhammad; Flood, Curt;
Foster, Rube*

Alice Knox Eaton
*Brown, William Wells; Dunbar-Nelson,
Alice; Hopkins, Pauline Elizabeth*

Margaret E. Edds
Wilder, Douglas

Thomas Edwards
Carson, Ben

Marta Effinger
Jones, Madame Sissieretta Joyner

Douglas Egerton
Turner, Nat; Gabriel

Walter Ehrlich
Scott, Dred

Harry J. Elam
*O'Neal, Frederick Douglass; Parks,
Suzan-Lori*

William G. Elliott
Blake, Eubie

Kent Engelhardt
Parker, Charlie

Lia Epperson
Alexander, Sadie Tanner Mossell

Paul A. Erickson
Cobb, William Montague

John R. Ernest
Hughes, Louis

Jean Fagan Yellin
Jacobs, Harriet

Duncan F. Faherty
Hammon, Jupiter

Caroline M. Fannin
Bullard, Eugène Jacques

SallyAnn H. Ferguson
West, Dorothy

Robert Fikes
Murphy, Isaac

Roy E. Finkenbine
Douglass, Frederick; Nell, William Cooper

Jennifer Fleischner
Keckly, Elizabeth Hobbs

Pamela M. Fletcher
Bannister, Edward Mitchell

Frances Foster
Garnet, Henry Highland

Rayvon David Fouché
Latimer, Lewis Howard

Virginia C. Fowler
Giovanni, Nikki

Thomas Fox
Amos, Harold

Dewey Franklin Mosby
Tanner, Henry Ossawa

John C. Fredriksen
Flipper, Henry Ossian

Lisa D. Freiman
Delaney, Beauford; Saar, Betye

Gary Frost
Temple, Lewis; Woods, Granville T.

C. Dale Gadsden
Mitchell, Arthur

Julie Gallagher
Hedgeman, Anna Arnold

Vanessa Northington Gamble
Jefferson, Mildred Fay

Larry Gara
Still, William

Eric Gardner
Greenfield, Elizabeth Taylor

Marybeth Gasman
Johnson, Charles Spurgeon

David Barry Gaspar
Walcott, Derek

James Gavin
*Jackson, Michael; Jones, Quincy;
Vaughan, Sarah*

Elshaday Gebreyes
Jones, Bill T.

Andy Gensler
Johnson, Francis; Wonder, Stevie

Larry R. Gerlach
Robeson, Paul

Paula Giddings
Wells-Barnett, Ida B.

Jenifer W. Gilbert
McKissick, Floyd Bixler

Freda Scott Giles
Bubbles, John

Glenda Gill
Waters, Ethel

Glenda E. Gilmore
Smalls, Robert

Jacqueline Goggin
Woodson, Carter Godwin

Lewis Gordon
West, Cornel

Sara Graves Wheeler
Johnson, Mordecai Wyatt

Stanton Green
Mays, Willie

Robert M. Greenberg
Hayden, Robert Earl

Farah Jasmine Griffin
Holiday, Billie; Marshall, Paule

David R. Griffiths
Robinson, John C.

Pamela Grundy
Washington, Ora

Betty Kaplan Gubert
Farmer, James

Lawrence Gushee
Oliver, King

Susan Gushee O'Malley
Baker, Ella Josephine

Antoinette Handy
Anderson, Marian

Jon M. Harkness
Fuller, Solomon Carter

Richard Harmond
Delany, Bessie, and Sadie Delany

Leonard Harris
Locke, Alain Leroy

Robert L. Harris
*Barnett, Claude Albert; Wesley,
Charles Harris*

Trudier Harris
Terry, Lucy

William C. Harris
Bruce, Blanche Kelso

Jim Haskins
Bricktop

Samuel A. Hay
Davis, Ossie; Dee, Ruby

Robert C. Hayden
*Chinn, May Edward; Hinton, William
Augustus; Wright, Louis Tompkins*

Tanu Henry
Davis, Benjamin O., Jr.

Leslie L. Heywood
Coachman, Alice; Stokes, Louise

F. Michael Higginbotham
Edwards, Harry Thomas

Darlene Clark Hine
Bethune, Mary Jane McLeod; Parks, Rosa

Peter P. Hinks
Walker, David

Graham Hodges
Williams, Peter, Jr.

Graham Russell Hodges
Cornish, Samuel Eli; Ruggles, David

James Holmberg
York

Thomas C. Holt
Du Bois, W. E. B.

Maureen E. Honey
Earley, Charity Adams

Olive Hoogenboom
Greener, Richard Theodore

John Hope Franklin
Williams, George Washington

Gerald Horne
Davis, Benjamin Jefferson

Alton Hornsby
Young, Andrew Jackson, Jr.

John R. Howard
Carter, Robert Lee

Sharon Howard
Hutson, Jean Blackwell

Ron Howell
Sharpton, Al

Mark A. Huddle
Roper, Moses; Thompson, John

Karen Jean Hunt
Remond, Sarah Parker

M. Thomas Inge
Herriman, George Joseph

John N. Ingham
Merrick, John; Walker, Madame C. J

J. Susan Isaacs
Johnson, Joshua; Pippin, Horace

Cassandra Jackson
Harper, Frances Ellen Watkins

David Jackson
Height, Dorothy; Howard, Perry Wilbon

Eric R. Jackson
Frazier, E. Franklin; Pinchback, P. B. S.

Gregory S. Jackson
Bibb, Henry Walton

Portia P. James
McCoy, Elijah

Kenneth R. Janken
*White, Walter Francis; Logan, Rayford
Whittingham*

Régine Jean-Charles
Poitier, Sidney

Paul Jefferson
Reid, Ira De Augustine

Randal Jelks
Mays, Benjamin E.

McKay Jenkins
Ashe, Arthur

Clifton H. Johnson
Cullen, Countée

David Joyner
Waller, Fats

Betty Kaplan Gubert
Schomburg, Arthur Alfonso

Janis F. Kearney
O'Leary, Hazel R.

Ann T. Keene
Jordan, Barbara

Tammy L. Kernodle
Smith, Willie Mae Ford

Joseph D. Ketner
Duncanson, Robert S.

Jason King
*Cosby, Bill; Parks, Gordon, Jr.;
Washington, Denzel*

Patricia Miller King
Cass, Melnea Agnes Jones

Stacy Kinlock Sewell
Remond, Charles Lenox

Elise K. Kirk
Norman, Jessye; Price, Leontyne

Amy H. Kirschke
Douglas, Aaron

Edward Komara
Patton, Charley; Waters, Muddy

Isaac Kramnick
Lawrence, Margaret Morgan

David Krasner
Cook, Will Marion

Edward L. Lach Jr
*Higginbotham, A. Leon, Jr.; Young,
Coleman; Brown, Charlotte
Eugenia Hawkins*

Gaynol Langs
Rudolph, Wilma

Maria Lauret
Walker, Alice Malsenior

Daniel J. Leab
Still, William Grant

Theresa Leininger-Miller
Barthé, Richmond; Reason, Patrick Henry

Larry Lester
Pickett, Bill

Deborah Levine
Elders, M. Joycelyn

Alan Levy
Burleigh, Henry Thacker

Eugene Levy
Johnson, James Weldon

Sholomo B. Levy
*Ali, Noble Drew; Angelou, Maya; Baraka,
Amiri; Davis, Sammy, Jr.; Farrakhan,
Louis Abdul; Father Divine; Ford, Arnold
Josiah; Fortune, T. Thomas; Franklin, C.
L.; Franklin, John Hope; Garvey, Amy
Euphemia Jacques; Gordy, Berry, Jr.;
Henson, Matthew Alexander; Himes,
Chester Bomar; Hope, John; Johnson,
William H.; Jordan, Vernon; King, B. B.;
Lorde, Audre; Matthew, Wentworth
Arthur; Reverend Ike; Toomer, Jean;
Wilson, August; Woods, Tiger*

Rita Liberti
Miller, Cheryl

Richard C. Lindberg
du Sable, Jean Baptiste Pointe

Lili Cockerille Livingston
Ailey, Alvin

Mamie E. Locke
*Bell, James Madison; Hamer, Fannie Lou
Townsend; Plessy, Homer Adolph*

Kip Lornell
Dorsey, Thomas Andrew

Spencie Love
Drew, Charles Richard

John A. Lucas
Hubbard, William DeHart

Ralph E. Luker
*Haley, Alex; Hurston, Zora Neale; Johns,
Vernon Napoleon; Steward, Theophilus
Gould; Young, Whitney Moore, Jr.*

Michael Maiwald
Thurman, Wallace

Devona A. Mallory
Marrant, John

Lawrence H. Mamiya
Muhammad, Elijah

Kenneth R. Manning
*Hill, Henry Aaron; Just, Ernest Everett;
Matzeliger, Jan Earnst; Poindexter,
Hildrus Augustus; Turner, Charles Henry*

Charles H. Martin
Herndon, Angelo Braxton

Mia Mask
Goldberg, Whoopi

John E. Mason
Berry, Chuck

Julian Mason
Chesnutt, Charles Waddell

Robert Mason
*Coleman, William T., Jr.; Morrow,
E. Frederic*

Jay Mazzocchi
Healy, James Augustine

David McBride
*Berry, Leonidas Harris; White, Augustus
Aaron, III*

Timothy P. McCarthy
Cardozo, Francis Louis

Barbara McCaskill
Craft, William, and Craft, Ellen

Bill McCulloch
Broonzy, Big Bill

Christine G. McKay
Harrington, Oliver W.

Jean McMahon Humez
Jackson, Rebecca Cox

Linda O. McMurry
*Carver, George Washington; Work,
Monroe Nathan*

Genna Rae McNeil
Houston, Charles Hamilton

Ronald E. Mickens
*Imes, Elmer Samuel; Wilkins, J.
Ernest, Jr.*

Kristie Miller
De Priest, Oscar Stanton

Frederick V. Mills
Allen, Richard; Bragg, George Freeman, Jr

Richard Mizelle
Blackwell, David; Sotcher, David

Phil Montesano
Bell, Philip Alexander

James Ross Moore
Mills, Florence

Marcyliena Morgan
Shakur, Tupac Amaru

Robert C. Morris
Wright, Richard Robert, Sr.

Wilson J. Moses
Crummell, Alexander

William F. Mugleston
Garvey, Marcus; Love, Nat; Washington, Booker T.

William Nash
Williams, John Alfred

Ellis Nassour
Mabley, Moms

Daniel A. Nathan
Lacy, Sam

Marc Anthony Neal
Charles, Ray; Franklin, Aretha

Francesco L. Nepa
Morton, Ferdinand Quintin

Leroy Nesbitt
Slowe, Lucy Diggs

Cynthia Neverdon-Morton
Terrell, Mary Eliza Church

Gerald G. Newborg
Thompson, Era Bell

Pamela Newkirk
Rowan, Carl Thomas; Whitaker, Mark

Richard Newman
Brown, Henry Box; Grace, Charles Emmanuel; Haynes, Lemuel; Healy, Patrick Francis

Steven J. Niven
Bates, Daisy Lee; Berry, Halle Maria; Bradley, Thomas; Calloway, Cab; Chamberlain, Wilt; Clark, Kenneth Bancroft; Fauset, Crystal Bird; Garvey, Amy Ashwood; Hyman, Flora "Flo"; Johnson, Jack; Jones, Bill T.; Laveaux, Marie; Liston, Sonny; Louis, Joe; McDaniel, Hattie; McDonald, Gabrielle Kirk; Meredith, James Howard; Moses, Robert Parris; Murray, Albert; Onesimus; Otabenga; Powell, Colin; Rainey, Ma; Rice, Condoleezza; Rustin, Bayard Taylor; Schuyler, George Samuel; Scottsboro Boys; Sheppard, William Henry; Simpson, O. J.; Thomas, Clarence

Terence J. O'Grady
Hendrix, Jimi

Stephen Ochs
Cailloux, André

James O'Toole
Healy, Michael

Nell Irvin Painter
Truth, Sojourner

June O. Patton
Laney, Lucy Craft

Barry Lee Pearson
Broonzy, Big Bill

William H. Pease & Jane H. Pease
Steward, Austin

Nan Peete
Harris, Barbara

Lara Pellegrinelli
Fitzgerald, Ella

James L. Penick
Railroad Bill

Burton W. Peretti
Basie, Count

Linda M. Perkins
Coppin, Fanny Jackson

Jeffrey B. Perry
Harrison, Hubert Henry

Marilyn Elizabeth Perry
Parsons, Lucy

Bernard L. Peterson
Bailey, Pearl; Fetchit, Stepin

Sarah K. A. Pfatteicher
Crumpler, Rebecca Davis Lee

J. Alfred Phelps
James, Daniel, Jr.

Betty E. Plummer
Durham, James

Fritz Polite
Robinson, Eddie

Carol Polsgrove
Forman, James

Constance Porter Uzelac
Coleman, Bessie; Porter, James Amos

Deborah Post
Keith, Damon Jerome

Wendell Pritchett
Weaver, Robert Clifton

Bernadette Pruitt
Washington, Margaret Murray

Sarah J. Purcell
Hull, Agrippa

Howard N. Rabinowitz
Elliott, Robert Brown

Albert J. Raboteau
Thurman, Howard W.

Arnold Rampersad
Ellison, Ralph Waldo

Ann Rayson
Baldwin, James; Larsen, Nella

Mark A. Reid
Lee, Spike

James A. Riley
Bell, Cool Papa

Lisa E. Rivo
Beckwourth, Jim; Brown, Hallie Quinn; Catlett, Elizabeth; Cole, Johnnetta Betsch; Cole, Rebecca; Davis, Benjamin Oliver, Sr.; Dove, Rita Frances; Dunham, Katherine Mary; Fuller, Meta Vaux Warrick; Jackson, Shirley Ann; Jones, Lois Mailou; Jordan, June; Kitt, Eartha Mae; Lewis, Edmonia; Micheaux, Oscar; Morgan, Garrett Augustus; Parks, Gordon, Sr.; Puryear, Martin; Rose, Edward; Savage, Augusta; VanDerZee, James Augustus Joseph; Walker, Maggie Lena; Wilson, Harriet E.; Winfrey, Oprah

Hildred Roach
Joplin, Scott

Edward Rodman
Burgess, John Melville

Noliwe Rooks
Malone, Annie Turnbo

Rosetta E. Ross
Edelman, Marian Wright; Norton, Eleanor Holmes; Tubman, Harriet

Jacqueline Anne Rouse
Clark, Septima P.

Hazel Rowley
Wright, Richard

Rob Ruck
Paige, Satchel

John Runcie
Coltrane, John William

Thaddeus Russell
Gaye, Marvin; Hall, Prince; Washington, Harold

Nichole T. Rustin
Mingus, Charles, Jr.

John Daniel Saillant
Paul, Nathaniel

Frank A. Salamone
Drake, St. Clair, Jr.

Mark J. Sammons
Whipple, Prince

David Sanjek
Diddley, Bo

Xiomara Santamarina
Freeman, Elizabeth

Monica Saunders
Lewis, Oliver

Todd L. Savitt
Lynk, Miles Vandahurst

Elizabeth D. Schafer
Cesar

N. Elizabeth Schlatter
Basquiat, Jean-Michel

Roger A. Schuppert
Brawley, Benjamin Griffith; Ruffin, Josephine St. Pierre

Loren Schweninger
Bayley, Solomon; Gibbs, Mifflin Wistar

Billy Scott
Hill, Mary Elliott

Laine A. Scott
Grimké, Angelina Weld

Freda Scott Giles
McKay, Claude

Michael N. Searles
Nigger Add

Milton C. Sernett
Bryan, Andrew; Cary, Lott; George, David; Liele, George; Loguen, Jermain Wesley

Stephanie Shaw
Staupers, Mabel Doyle Keaton

Joan Sherman
Horton, George Moses

John C. Shields
Wheatley, Phillis

Alyn Shipton
Gillespie, Dizzy

Kenneth L. Shropshire
Robinson, Sugar Ray

Tiwanna M. Simpson
Vesey, Denmark

Lyde Cullen Sizer
Bowser, Mary Elizabeth

Cherise Smith
Sleet, Moneta, Jr.

David Lionel Smith
Northup, Solomon

Erin A. Smith
Fauset, Jessie Redmon

Maureen M. Smith
Smith, Tommie; Williams, Venus, and Serena Williams

Robert C. Smith
Jackson, Jesse L., Sr.; Lewis, John; Rangel, Charles

Valerie Smith
Morrison, Toni

Frances Smith Foster
Albert, Octavia Victoria Rogers

David F Smydra
Bond, Julian; Brown, Jim; Horne, Lena; Jordan, Michael; McLendon, Johnny; Pryor, Richard; Reed, Ishmael; Ross, Diana; Russell, Bill; Scott, Wendell

Richard Sobel
Chenault, Kenneth Irvine

Jack Sohmer
Armstrong, Lil

Gabriel Solis
Monk, Thelonious

Albert B. Southwick
Taylor, Major

Jocelyn Spragg
Harold Amos

Kimberly Springer
Cooper, Anna Julia Haywood; Evers-Williams, Myrlie

Lucia C. Stanton
Hemings, Sally

John Stauffer
Smith, James McCune

Robert Stepto
Brown, Sterling Allen

Rodger Streitmatter
Trotter, William Monroe

James D. Sullivan
Brooks, Gwendolyn

Terrie F. Sultan
Marshall, Kerry James

Marcia G. Synnott
Burroughs, Nannie Helen

John Szwed
Davis, Miles

Theodore Taylor
Brown, Jesse Leroy

Yuval Taylor
Grimes, William

Rosalyn Terborg-Penn
Quarles, Benjamin Arthur

Herman E. Thomas
Pennington, James William Charles

Kenneth F. Thomas
Calloway, Ernest

Kathleen Thompson
Bass, Charlotta

J. Mills Thornton
Nixon, Edgar Daniel; Robinson, Jo Ann

Sarah Thuesen
Shepard, James Edward

Timothy N. Thurber
Brooke, Edward; Wilkins, Roy

Frank Tirro
Armstrong, Louis

W. S. Tkweme
Brown, H. Rap

Barbara B Tomblin
Johnson-Brown, Hazel

Edgar Allan Toppin
Scott, Emmett Jay

Steven C. Tracy
Johnson, Robert; Hooker, John Lee; Hughes, Langston; Jefferson, Blind Lemon

Brian Turner
Askin, Luther B.

Mark Tushnet
Marshall, Thurgood

Wayne J. Urban
Bond, Horace Mann

Peter Valenti
Aaron, Hank

Constance Valis Hill
Lane, William Henry; Robinson, Bill

Cassandra Veney
Robinson, James Herman; Robinson, Randall

Sudhir Alladi Venkatesh
Wilson, William Julius

Elizabeth Zoe Vicary
Henson, Josiah; Payne, Daniel Alexander

Melissa Vickery-Bareford
Aldridge, Ira Frederick; McClendon, Rose

Keith Wailoo
Blackwell, David; Satcher, David

Peter Wallenstein
Delany, Bessie and Sadie; Hastie, William Henry; Murray, Pauli; Powell, Adam Clayton, Jr.

Ronald Walters
Brown, Ron

Harry M. Ward
Attucks, Crispus

Henry Warner Bowden
Tanner, Benjamin Tucker

Michael Salim Washington
Bechet, Sidney Joseph; Coleman, Ornette

Eleanor F. Wedge
Bearden, Romare

Eric Weisbard
Little Richard

Kimberly Welch
Blyden, Edward Wilmot

Dennis Wepman
Carmichael, Stokely; Cinqué

Martha Wharton
Elaw, Zilpha; Foote, Julia A. J.; Prince, Nancy; Stewart, Maria W.

Melanye White Dixon
Jamison, Judith

Stephen J. Whitfield
Till, Emmett Louis

David Wiggins
Lewis, Carl

Carolyn Williams
Grimké, Charlotte Forten

Clarence G. Williams
Lee, Raphael Carl

Kenneth H. Williams
Revels, Hiram Rhoades

Lee Williams
Caliver, Ambrose

Vernon J. Williams
Nabrit, Samuel Milton

Clint C. Wilson
Abbott, Robert Sengstacke

Dreck Wilson
Abele, Julian Francis; Williams, Paul Revere

Wayne Wilson
DeFrantz, Anita L.

Julie Winch
Douglass, Sarah Mapps; Forten, James

Michael R. Winston
Miller, Kelly

Kari J. Winter
King, Boston

Charles K. Wolfe
Lead Belly

Jennifer Wood
Johnson, John Rosamond; Johnson, Robert L.; Lewis, David Levering; Motley, Constance Baker

Nan Elizabeth Woodruff
Blackwell, Unita Z.

Barbara Woods
King, Coretta Scott

Richard Wormser
Morton, Jelly Roll

Donald R. Wright
Cuffe, Paul

Thomas J. Wyly
Sullivan, Leon Howard

Shirley J. Yee
Cary, Mary Ann Camberton Shadd

Natalie Zacek
Evers, Medgar

Jacob Zumoff
Cleaver, Eldridge; Seale, Bobby

Entries drawn from *American National Biography* are indicated by asterisks

Aaron, Hank
Abbott, Robert Sengstacke*
Abdul-Jabbar, Kareem
Abele, Julian Francis
Abernathy, Ralph
Ailey, Alvin*
Albert, Octavia Victoria Rogers*
Aldridge, Ira Frederick*
Alexander, Sadie Tanner Mossell
Ali, Muhammad
Ali, Noble Drew
Allen, Richard*
Amos, Harold
Anderson, Marian*
Angelou, Maya
Armstrong, Lil*
Armstrong, Louis*
Ashe, Arthur*
Askin, Luther B.
Attucks, Crispus*
Bailey, Pearl*
Baker, Ella Josephine*
Baker, Josephine
Baldwin, James*
Banneker, Benjamin*
Bannister, Edward Mitchell
Baraka, Amiri
Barnett, Claude Albert
Barthé, Richmond*
Basie, Count*
Basquiat, Jean-Michel*
Bass, Charlotta
Bates, Daisy Lee
Bayley, Solomon
Bearden, Romare*
Bechet, Sidney Joseph
Beckwourth, Jim
Belafonte, Harry
Bell, Cool Papa
Bell, James Madison*
Bell, Philip Alexander
Berry, Chuck
Berry, Halle Maria
Berry, Leonidas Harris
Bethune, Mary Jane McLeod*
Bibb, Henry Walton*
Blackwell, David
Blackwell, Unita Z.
Blake, Eubie*
Blakey, Art*

Blind Tom
Blyden, Edward Wilmot*
Bolden, Buddy*
Bond, Horace Mann*
Bond, Julian
Bouchet, Edward Alexander*
Bowser, Mary Elizabeth
Bradley, Thomas
Bragg, George Freeman, Jr.*
Branson, Herman Russell
Brawley, Benjamin Griffith*
Bricktop*
Brooke, Edward
Brooks, Gwendolyn*
Brooks, Walter Henderson*
Broonzy, Big Bill*
Brown, Charlotte Eugenia Hawkins*
Brown, H. Rap
Brown, Hallie Quinn
Brown, Henry Box
Brown, James
Brown, Jesse Leroy
Brown, Jim
Brown, Ron
Brown, Sterling Allen*
Brown, William Wells
Bruce, Blanche Kelso*
Bryan, Andrew*
Bubbles, John
Bullard, Eugène Jacques*
Bunche, Ralph Johnson*
Burgess, John Melville
Burleigh, Henry Thacker*
Burroughs, Nannie Helen*
Caesar, John
Cailloux, André
Caliver, Ambrose
Calloway, Cab
Calloway, Ernest
Cannon, George Dows
Cardozo, Francis Louis*
Carmichael, Stokely*
Carson, Ben
Carter, Eunice Hunton*
Carter, Robert Lee
Carver, George Washington*
Cary, Lott*
Cary, Mary Ann Camberton Shadd*
Cass, Melnea Agnes Jones*
Catlett, Elizabeth

Cesar*
Chamberlain, Wilt
Charles, Ray
Chavis, John*
Chenault, Kenneth Irvine
Chesnutt, Charles Waddell*
Chester, Thomas Morris*
Childress, Alice
Chinn, May Edward*
Chisholm, Shirley
Cinqué*
Clark, Kenneth Bancroft
Clark, Septima P.
Cleaver, Eldridge
Coachman, Alice
Cobb, William Montague*
Coker, Daniel*
Cole, Johnnetta Betsch
Cole, Nat King
Cole, Rebecca
Coleman, Bessie*
Coleman, Ornette
Coleman, William T., Jr.
Coltrane, John William
Cook, Will Marion*
Cooper, Anna Julia Haywood
Coppin, Fanny Jackson*
Cornish, Samuel Eli*
Cosby, Bill
Craft, William, and Craft, Ellen
Crummell, Alexander*
Crumpler, Rebecca Davis Lee*
Cuffe, Paul
Cullen, Countée*
Dandridge, Dorothy*
Davis, Angela Yvonne
Davis, Benjamin Jefferson*
Davis, Benjamin O., Jr.
Davis, Benjamin Oliver, Sr.
Davis, Miles
Davis, Ossie
Davis, Sammy, Jr.
Day, William Howard*
Dee, Ruby
DeFrantz, Anita L.
Delaney, Beauford
Delany, Bessie, and Sadie Delany*
Delany, Martin Robison
Demby, Edward T.
De Priest, Oscar Stanton*

Diddley, Bo
Dinkins, David N.
Dixon, "Big" Willie James
Dorsey, Thomas Andrew*
Douglas, Aaron
Douglass, Frederick*
Douglass, Sarah Mapps*
Dove, Rita Frances
Drake, St. Clair, Jr.*
Drew, Charles Richard*
Du Bois, W. E. B.*
Dunbar, Paul Laurence*
Dunbar-Nelson, Alice
Duncanson, Robert S.*
Dunham, Katherine Mary
Dunjee, Roscoe
Durham, James*
du Sable, Jean Baptiste Pointe*
Earley, Charity Adams
Edelman, Marian Wright
Edwards, Harry Thomas
Elaw, Zilpha
Elders, M. Joycelyn
Ellington, Duke*
Elliott, Robert Brown*
Ellison, Ralph Waldo
Equiano, Olaudah
Esteban
Europe, James Reese*
Evers, Medgar*
Evers-Williams, Myrlie
Farmer, James*
Farrakhan, Louis Abdul
Father Divine
Fauset, Crystal Bird*
Fauset, Jessie Redmon*
Fetchit, Stepin*
Fitzgerald, Ella
Flipper, Henry Ossian*
Flood, Curt
Foote, Julia A. J.
Ford, Arnold Josiah
Forman, James
Forten, James*
Fortune, T. Thomas
Foster, Rube
Foxx, Redd*
Franklin, Aretha
Franklin, C. L.
Franklin, John Hope
Frazier, E. Franklin*
Freeman, Elizabeth
Fuller, Meta Vaux Warrick
Fuller, Solomon Carter*
Gabriel*
Garnet, Henry Highland
Garvey, Amy Ashwood
Garvey, Amy Euphemia Jacques
Garvey, Marcus*
Gaye, Marvin*

George, David*
Gibbs, Mifflin Wistar*
Gibson, Althea
Gibson, Josh
Gillespie, Dizzy
Giovanni, Nikki
Goldberg, Whoopi
Gordy, Berry, Jr.
Grace, Charles Emmanuel*
Graves, Earl
Greener, Richard Theodore*
Greenfield, Elizabeth Taylor*
Gregory, Wilton
Griffith-Joyner, Florence
Grimes, William
Grimké, Angelina Weld*
Grimké, Archibald Henry
Grimké, Charlotte Forten*
Grimké, Francis James*
Gronniosaw, James Albert Ukawsaw
Haley, Alex*
Hall, Prince*
Hamer, Fannie Lou Townsend*
Hammon, Briton
Hammon, Jupiter*
Handy, W. C.*
Hansberry, Lorraine Vivian*
Harper, Frances Ellen Watkins
Harrington, Oliver W.*
Harris, Barbara
Harrison, Hubert Henry*
Hastie, William Henry*
Hayden, Robert Earl*
Haynes, Lemuel*
Healy, Eliza*
Healy, James Augustine*
Healy, Michael
Healy, Patrick Francis*
Hedgeman, Anna Arnold
Height, Dorothy
Hemings, Sally*
Hendrix, Jimi*
Henson, Josiah*
Henson, Matthew Alexander
Herndon, Angelo Braxton
Herriman, George Joseph*
Higginbotham, A. Leon, Jr.*
Hill, Henry Aaron*
Hill, Mary Elliott*
Himes, Chester Bomar
Hinton, William Augustus*
Holiday, Billie
Holly, James Theodore*
Hooker, John Lee
Hope, John
Hopkins, Pauline Elizabeth
Horne, Lena
Horton, George Moses
Houston, Charles Hamilton*
Howard, Perry Wilbon

Hubbard, William DeHart*
Hughes, Langston*
Hughes, Louis
Hull, Agrippa*
Hurston, Zora Neale*
Hutson, Jean Blackwell
Hyman, Flora "Flo"
Imes, Elmer Samuel*
Jackson, Jesse L., Sr.
Jackson, Mahalia*
Jackson, Michael
Jackson, Rebecca Cox*
Jackson, Shirley Ann
Jacobs, Harriet*
James, Daniel, Jr.
Jamison, Judith
Jefferson, Blind Lemon*
Jefferson, Mildred Fay
Jemison, Mae
Johns, Vernon Napoleon*
Johnson, Charles Spurgeon
Johnson, Francis
Johnson, Jack
Johnson, James Weldon*
Johnson, John
Johnson, John Rosamond
Johnson, Joshua*
Johnson, Judy
Johnson, Mordecai Wyatt*
Johnson, Robert*
Johnson, Robert L.
Johnson, William H.
Johnson-Brown, Hazel
Jones, Absalom*
Jones, Bill T.
Jones, Eugene Kinckle
Jones, James Earl
Jones, Loïs Mailou
Jones, Madame Sissieretta Joyner
Jones, Quincy
Jones, Scipio Africanus*
Joplin, Scott
Jordan, Barbara*
Jordan, June
Jordan, Michael
Jordan, Vernon
Julian, Percy Lavon*
Just, Ernest Everett*
Keckly, Elizabeth Hobbs
Keith, Damon Jerome
Kelly, Sharon Pratt
King, B. B.
King, Boston
King, Coretta Scott
King, Martin Luther, Jr.*
Kitt, Eartha Mae
Lacy, Sam
Lampkin, Daisy Elizabeth Adams
Lane, William Henry*
Laney, Lucy Craft*

Smith, Willie Mae Ford
Stagolee
Staupers, Mabel Doyle Keaton
Steward, Austin*
Steward, Theophilus Gould*
Stewart, Maria W.
Still, William*
Still, William Grant*
Stockton, Betsey*
Stokes, Louise
Stone, Toni
Sullivan, Leon Howard
Tanner, Benjamin Tucker*
Tanner, Henry Ossawa*
Taylor, Major
Temple, Lewis
Terrell, Mary Eliza Church*
Terry, Lucy*
Thomas, Clarence
Thomas, Vivien Theodore
Thompson, Era Bell*
Thompson, John
Thurman, Howard W.
Thurman, Wallace*
Till, Emmett Louis*
Tindley, Charles Albert*
Toomer, Jean
Trotter, William Monroe*
Truth, Sojourner*
Tubman, Harriet

Turner, Charles Henry*
Turner, Henry McNeal*
Turner, Nat
VanDerZee, James Augustus Joseph
Varick, James*
Vaughan, Sarah
Vesey, Denmark
Walcott, Derek
Walker, Alice Malsenior
Walker, David*
Walker, Madame C. J.*
Walker, Maggie Lena
Waller, Fats
Washington, Booker T.*
Washington, Denzel
Washington, Harold*
Washington, Margaret Murray
Washington, Ora
Waters, Ethel
Waters, Muddy*
Weaver, Robert Clifton
Wells-Barnett, Ida B.
Wesley, Charles Harris
West, Cornel
West, Dorothy
Wharton, Clifton Reginald*
Wheatley, Phillis*
Whipple, Prince
Whitaker, Mark
White, Augustus Aaron, III

White, George Henry*
White, Walter Francis
Wilder, Douglas
Wilkins, J. Ernest, Jr.
Wilkins, Roy
Williams, Bert & George Walker*
Williams, Cathay
Williams, Daniel Hale*
Williams, George Washington*
Williams, John Alfred
Williams, Paul Revere
Williams, Peter, Jr.*
Williams, Smokey Joe
Williams, Venus
Wilson, August
Wilson, Harriet E.
Wilson, William Julius
Winfrey, Oprah
Wonder, Stevie
Woods, Granville T.
Woods, Tiger
Woodson, Carter Godwin*
Work, Monroe Nathan*
Wright, Louis Tompkins*
Wright, Richard
Wright, Richard Robert, Sr.*
York
Young, Andrew Jackson, Jr.
Young, Coleman*
Young, Whitney Moore, Jr.*

AFRICAN AMERICAN LIVES

A

AARON, HANK

(5 Feb. 1934–), baseball player and executive, was born Henry Aaron in the Down the Bay section of Mobile, Alabama, the third of eight children of Herbert Aaron and Estella (maiden name unknown). His parents had left the Selma, Alabama, area during the Depression for greater opportunity in Mobile's shipbuilding industries. In 1942, as the family grew and Down the Bay became more crowded with wartime job seekers, the Aarons moved to a rural suburb of Toulminville. Working as a boilermaker's apprentice, Herbert Aaron suffered through the frequent layoffs that plagued black shipyard workers before wartime demand dictated full employment. Ever resourceful, Herbert Aaron bought two lots in Toulminville, hired carpenters to frame out the roof and walls of a house, and set about with his family to find materials to finish the property. The Aarons continued to live

in the house even as Henry achieved superstardom.

Making balls from such scavenged materials as tape and tin cans and using them by himself or in frequent games with his playmates, young Henry loved baseball. His younger brother Tommie became a professional player, later joining Hank on the Milwaukee Braves in 1962. While the big leagues were still a dream, Henry was developing the skills and techniques of success by tossing bottle caps into the air and hitting them with a broomstick. This regimen encouraged him to hit with his weight shifted to his front foot, a stance that resulted in the consistently good contact between ball and bat that set him apart from other hitters. From his earliest playing days, players and coaches wondered at the size and strength of Aaron's wrists. Henry's notable qualities were not limited to his batting stance, however. Herbert Aaron had instilled in his son qualities of pride, determination, and respect exercised

without attracting attention. Henry later recounted that, when he left home to play baseball, his father told him that "Nobody would want to hear what I had to say until I proved myself" (Aaron and Wheeler, 17).

After JACKIE ROBINSON broke the color barrier in the major leagues in 1947, the thirteen-year-old Henry skipped school to listen to Brooklyn Dodgers broadcasts on a pool-hall radio. Five years later he left Alabama for Indiana to play for the Indianapolis Clowns in the Negro American League. Aaron's world expanded even further when the Major League Boston Braves purchased his contract from the Clowns in 1952. Having just missed out on signing WILLIE MAYS, the Braves front office acted quickly with Aaron, and sent him to their Class C Northern League farm team in Eau Claire, Wisconsin. Despite bouts of homesickness and the difficulties of playing shortstop in the minor leagues, he fared well in Eau Claire. He hit .336 to finish second in the league, earning a trip to spring training in 1953 with the parent Braves club, now moved to Milwaukee. Reassigned to second base, Aaron was sent to the Class A Sally League team in Jacksonville after manager Ben Geraghty learned that he was willing to become the first black player in the league. Along with outfielder Horace Garner and shortstop Felix Mantilla, Aaron integrated the deep South league. Geraghty respected and supported Aaron, who hit a league-leading .362 and won the Most Valuable Player award. That winter, he began playing the outfield.

During the summer of 1953, Aaron met Barbara Lucas and enjoyed spending time with her family. The couple married on 6 October, and a daughter was born a year later. Four other children followed.

When Braves left fielder Bobby Thomson broke his leg during spring training for the 1954 season, Aaron was given the opportunity to start in his

Aaron gets a hug from his mother after breaking Babe Ruth's record with his 715th home run. The prized ball is held by Tom House, the Braves's pitcher who caught it in the Atlanta bullpen. © Bettmann/CORBIS

place. He responded by hitting .280 and winning the job permanently. Clearly, the Braves had a bona fide major leaguer. During that first season, the Braves traveling secretary Donald Davidson began calling Henry "Hank," and the name stuck. At the end of the season, Aaron requested a change from the number five he had been wearing, and in 1955 he began wearing number forty-four, the number he made famous.

Aaron performed well in 1955 and even better in 1956, when he hit .328 and won the National League batting title. Disappointment dominated his mood at season's end, however, when the Braves lost the pennant to the Dodgers in the final series. Determined to win the pennant his team had lost the previous year, Aaron had, arguably, his best year ever in 1957. Hitting a dramatic home run to win the pennant and playing solidly as the Braves defeated the New York Yankees to take the World Series, he won the National League's Most Valuable Player award.

Many observers wondered why Aaron, although the best hitter in baseball, was not regarded as an American superstar, as were Mickey Mantle and Willie Mays. The issue is complex. Mantle's great popularity during the period might be attributed to his racial identity as a white man and to the greater opportunity for publicity afforded to those who played in New York. Mays enjoyed far greater adulation than Aaron, perhaps because of his more outgoing personality. At least part of the answer seems to lie in Aaron's personality: quiet, steady, workmanlike, balanced. Such steadfastness shouts no claims, calls no attention to itself. It exists; it endures.

Hank played well season after season and his home run totals accumulated, but the Braves suffered increasingly lean years following their glory days in Milwaukee, particularly after the club moved to Atlanta in 1966. Although Aaron experienced racist attitudes and behavior all his life, the tenor of abuse shifted once it was realized he had a chance to break Babe Ruth's career home run record. For some whites, the idea of a black man replacing Ruth as the home run king was too much to bear.

Pressures multiplied. Divorced from his first wife early in 1971, he married his second wife, Billye Williams, widow of the civil rights activist Dr. Sam Williams, late in 1973. During the 1973 season he hit a remarkable forty home runs in only 392 at bats, but threats on Aaron and his family increased. The FBI assigned agents to accompany Billye and the children. Aaron was often forced to eat by himself, and after he had received a particularly venomous death threat, he warned teammates not to sit next to him in the dugout. Somehow, though, he managed to concentrate on the game that he loved. Hank's friend Congressman JOHN LEWIS suggests that "Hank was shattering something. Sometimes I believe that maybe some force or some power gives you that extra ounce of grace" (Tolan, 169). Perhaps the example of his father and Jackie Robinson and the words of MARTIN LUTHER KING JR. gave Aaron the power to use his bat as his voice in overcoming racism in the United States.

Aaron broke Ruth's record on 8 April 1974, with his 715th home run. He increasingly used his place in the spotlight to press for greater equality, and in Atlanta he spoke his mind with increasing force. Buoyed when Frank Robinson became the first black manager in Major League Baseball in 1975, Aaron stressed the need for more African American managers and executives. However, Atlanta's chilly reaction to his push for black front-office candidates led Aaron to endorse a trade to the American League Milwaukee Brewers in 1975. After two seasons, he retired with 755 home runs.

In 1977 Braves owner Ted Turner hired Aaron as an executive with responsibilities in the Braves farm system—the network of affiliated minor league teams that provides players for the major league team. As a Braves executive, Aaron served as an advocate for African American candidates and worked to eliminate racial barriers in sports, in part through partnerships with the NAACP, Operation PUSH, and Big Brothers/Big Sisters. He continues to work with such activists as ANDREW YOUNG and JESSE JACKSON in establishing baseball, as not only America's national pastime, but also as a leading force in creating a more just society.

FURTHER READING

Baseball-related documentation and clippings files relating to Hank Aaron's career are housed in the archives of the National Baseball Hall of Fame in Cooperstown, New York.

Aaron, Hank, with Furman Bisher. *Aaron, r.f.* (1968; rev. ed. as *Aaron*, 1974).

———, with Lonnie Wheeler. *I Had a Hammer: The Hank Aaron Story* (1991).

Poling, Jerry. *A Summer Up North: Hank Aaron and the Legend of Eau Claire Baseball* (2002).

Tolan, Sandy. *Me and Hank: A Boy and His Hero, Twenty-Five Years Later* (2000).

—PETER VALENTI

 ABBOT, ROBERT SENGSTACKE
(28 Nov. 1868–29 Feb. 1940), newspaper publisher, was born Robert Abbott in Fort Frederica, St. Simons Island, off the coast of Savannah, Georgia, the son of Thomas Abbott and Flora Butler, former slaves who operated a grocery store on St. Thomas Island. Thomas Abbott died the year after Robert was born, and Robert's mother moved to Savannah, where in 1874 she married John Herman Henry Sengstacke. Sengstacke was the son of a German father and a black American mother and, although born in the United States, was reared in Germany. He returned to the United States in 1869 and pursued careers in education, the clergy, and journalism. In the latter role Sengstacke became editor of the *Woodville Times*, a black community weekly newspaper that served Savannah-area residents. Abbott's admiration for his stepfather inspired him to add the name Sengstacke to his own and to attempt to become a publisher in his own right.

Abbott's first newspaper job was as a printer with the white-owned *Savannah Echo*. He soon decided to obtain a college education; after attending several other institutions, Abbott enrolled at Hampton Institute in Virginia in 1889 at the age of twenty-one. Hampton, founded by the Congregationalists and supported by northern philanthropists, was both a trade school and an academic institution for African Americans. Abbott completed training as a printer in 1893, then culminated his undergraduate career with a bachelor's degree in 1896, after nearly seven years at Hampton. His experience there included opportunities to hear two charismatic black speakers, FREDERICK DOUGLASS and IDA B. WELLS-BARNETT, who influenced him to seek a leadership role in the development of civil rights for black Americans. After graduating from Hampton, Abbott moved to Chicago, where in 1899 he earned a law degree from Kent College of Law, the only black in his class of seventy students. Abbott, however, was never admitted to the bar. For the next few years he tried to establish a career as a lawyer in several midwestern cities without success; eventually he returned to Woodville to teach in a local school.

In 1905, at the age of thirty-seven, Abbott returned to Chicago and began publication of his own newspaper, the *Chicago Defender*. He chose Chicago as the base for his paper because of its large black population (more than thirty thousand), though at the time the black newspaper field in Chicago was extremely crowded, with three established local weeklies and the availability of two other well-respected journals, the *Indiana Freeman* and the *New York Age*. The title "Defender" represented his pledge that the paper would defend his race against the ills of racism.

Abbott's first number of the *Defender* was virtually a one-man production operated from rented desk space in a real estate and insurance office with furnishings that included a folding card table and a borrowed kitchen chair. But with an initial investment of twenty-five cents (for paper and pencils) and the help of his landlady's teenage daughter, he was able to launch a publishing enterprise that became one of the most influential newspapers in the United States. Within ten years the *Defender* was the nation's leading black newspaper, with an estimated circulation of 230,000.

Despite his early exposure to the printing trade and newspaper publishing, Abbott was seen by many of his contemporaries as an unlikely candidate for success as a newspaperman. He was not an articulate speaker, but he had a strong talent for gathering rumor, hearsay, and other information and turning them into human-interest stories. Abbott also proved a master at upstaging his competitors. Proclaiming his paper to be "the only two-cent weekly in the city" and

focusing front-page coverage on sensational and crime news, Abbott steadily increased his paper's readership. The *Defender*'s most significant contribution, however, was perhaps its crusade to encourage black migration from the former slave states of the South to Chicago and other midwestern cities.

The campaign, launched during World War I, was instrumental in bringing thousands of blacks to the North in search of better jobs, housing, and educational opportunities. For Abbott the migration was part of a plan to increase the *Defender*'s circulation and give him an opportunity to penetrate the black readership markets in the South. Several southern cities so resented the effectiveness of the *Defender*'s campaign that they banned its distribution. The *Atlanta Constitution* wrote that the migration cost the South "her best labor" force and that the region's economy suffered greatly. It has been estimated that nearly thirty-five thousand blacks moved to Chicago from the founding of the *Defender* in 1905 to 1920, more than doubling the city's African American population.

An indirect result of the heavy influx of black migrants to Chicago was a race riot in 1919 that highlighted the tensions between whites and blacks in the city. Abbott was appointed to the Commission on Race Relations, charged with determining the causes of the riot. Although the commission's report implicated the *Defender*'s strong stance for black civil rights as a contributing factor in the riots, Abbott signed the document.

The *Defender* was a fearless champion for the cause of racial equality for African Americans. Abbott enumerated his policies as the elimination of racial prejudice in the United States, the opening of trade union membership to blacks, black representation in the president's cabinet, equal employment opportunities for blacks in the public and private sectors, and black employment in all police forces nationally. He also sought the elimination of all school segregation and the passage of federal civil rights legislation to protect against breakdowns in desegregation laws at the state level as well as to extend full voting rights to all Americans. These policies found a ready

market, and the *Defender*'s growth during World War I allowed it to open and maintain branch offices in several major U.S. cities as well as one in London. During the war Abbott publicly asked why blacks should fight for the United States on foreign battlefields while being denied basic rights at home, a stance that provoked investigations by the federal government. In 1918, just two months short of his fiftieth birthday, Abbott married Helen Thornton Morrison; they had no children.

In the decade following World War I, the *Defender*'s circulation began to fall with the arrival of a new competitor, the *Chicago Whip*, and the onset of the Depression years. The *Defender* generally supported Republican politics, although in 1928 Abbott opposed Herbert Hoover in favor of the Democratic candidate Alfred E. Smith. During the 1930s, perhaps because of the 1919 riots and the impact of the Depression, the *Defender* took a more moderate stance regarding racial matters. The period also took a personal toll on Abbott, and he suffered several financial reversals. By 1935 circulation had declined to seventy-three thousand. After his mother died in 1932, Abbott began to travel extensively and attempted during the mid-1930s an ill-fated venture into magazine publishing with *Abbott's Monthly*.

Following a costly divorce from his first wife in 1932, Abbott married Edna Brown Dennison in 1934 but soon fell into ill health. In 1939 he gave control of the *Defender* to his nephew John H. Sengstacke, son of his half brother Alexander. Abbott died at his home in Chicago the following year. He left behind a newspaper that had pioneered new territory for the black press, becoming the first national paper to have an integrated staff and to be unionized. In 1956, under John Sengstacke's leadership, the *Defender* became a daily newspaper, soon to become the flagship publication of the nation's largest black newspaper chain.

FURTHER READING

Abbott's papers are in the *Chicago Defender* Archives in Chicago.
Ottley, Roi. *The Lonely Warrior* (1955).
Wolseley, Roland E. *The Black Press U.S.A.* (1971; 2d ed., 1990).
—CLINT C. WILSON

ABDUL-JABBAR, KAREEM (16 Apr. 1947–), basketball player, was born Ferdinand Lewis Alcindor, the son of Ferdinand Lewis "Al" Alcindor, a police officer with the New York Transit Authority, and Cora Alcindor, a department-store price checker. The almost thirteen-pound baby arrived in Harlem one day after the major league debut of JACKIE ROBINSON in Brooklyn; as with Robinson, fiercely competitive athletics and the struggle against racial injustice would define much of his life.

From a young age, Alcindor was introspective and intense. He had an artistic sensibility, drawn in part from his father, a stern and silent cop who played jazz trombone and held a degree from Juilliard. An only child in a strictly Catholic household, he moved from Harlem at age three to the Dyckman Street projects on the northern tip of Manhattan, a racially mixed,

middle-class community. In third grade he was startled to see a class photo that featured him not just towering over his classmates as expected, but standing out by the color of his skin. "Damn, I'm dark and everybody else is light!" Alcindor recalled thinking years later (Abdul-Jabbar, *Giant Steps*, 15). In fourth grade, his parents shipped him to an all-black boarding school outside Philadelphia, where he was taunted for his intellectual leanings. But in his one year at Holy Providence School, he developed street toughness and also launched his first hook shot, a weapon that would become his aesthetic and athletic trademark.

Back in New York from fifth grade on, Alcindor began to grow into his coordination. By eighth grade, he was a sinewy six feet, eight inches; by tenth grade, he was a seven footer with astonishing agility. At Power Memorial, an all-boys Catholic school where his teams lost only one game in his final three years, Alcindor never fit neatly into the

jock stereotype. He read widely, joined the debate team, and began to frequent New York's jazz clubs. On the court, though, the Renaissance man reigned. His game was at once graceful and ferocious. Coach Jack Donohue opened up the world for his sensitive star, bringing him to NBA games at Madison Square Garden. There the coach pointed with particular reverence to the inspired and unselfish play of Celtics center BILL RUSSELL. Donohue's influence was not completely positive, however. At half-time of an unusually lethargic performance during Alcindor's junior year, the fiery coach tore into his prodigy, telling him he was acting "just like a nigger!" (*Sports Illustrated*, 27 Oct. 1969). The wound from that remark festered for many years.

That summer Alcindor's growing awareness of racism sharpened when he participated in the journalism workshop of the Harlem Youth Action Project. At one point he covered a press conference by MARTIN LUTHER KING JR., a moment commemorated in a photograph in *Jet* magazine. He also witnessed five days of rioting in Harlem after a white policeman shot a black teenager. "Right then and there I knew who I was and who I had to be," he said in a *Sports Illustrated* profile (31 Mar. 1980). "I was going to be black rage personified, black power in the flesh."

The summer of 1964 also proved defining in his association with WILT CHAMBERLAIN. Eleven years Alcindor's senior and established (along with his rival Russell) as the dominant big man in the NBA, Chamberlain took the high school kid under his considerable wing. He loaned Alcindor jazz albums, invited him to his apartment to play hearts, and ferried him in his Bentley up to Saratoga to watch Chamberlain's prize thoroughbreds run. At one point the two played a memorable game of H-O-R-S-E, a matchup of trademark hook shots by Alcindor and fadeaways by Chamberlain that would have been captured on film in a better world.

After another scintillating high school season, Alcindor enrolled at the University of California, Los Angeles (UCLA), winner of the last two national championships. Although NCAA rules then forbade freshmen to play varsity sports, Alcindor served immediate notice by scoring thirty-one points and leading

Kareem Abdul-Jabbar makes his trademark shot, the skyhook, described by Bill Russell as "the most beautiful thing in sports." Corbis

the freshman team to an emphatic fifteen-point victory over the storied varsity. The next year, under the dignified tutelage of coaching legend John Wooden, Alcindor launched a collegiate career for the ages. In his very first game he broke the school scoring record with fifty-six points. He earned three consecutive All-America honors, leading the Bruins to three straight national titles and a glittering record of 88–2. Having reached his full height of seven feet, two inches, Alcindor had become a complete player. A menacing shot blocker, he intimidated on defense, and his devastating hook shot and ferocious inside moves were almost impossible to stop. So powerful was his impact on the game that the NCAA outlawed the dunk after his freshman year (though it was reinstated ten years later).

Never satisfied with a one-dimensional life, Alcindor broadened his horizons by studying martial arts with Bruce Lee, and by reading *The Autobiography of MALCOLM X.* Having dismissed what he considered to be the repressive Catholicism of his childhood, he developed a deep connection to Islam. After his junior year in the summer of 1968, he studied in a New York mosque and became a devout follower of Hamaas Abdul-Khaalis. That same summer, Alcindor decided to boycott the Olympic Games, refusing to play for a country that, he felt, denied fundamental rights and respect to black people. He publicly supported the "black power" salutes of sprinters TOMMIE SMITH and John Carlos on the medal podium in Mexico City, earning him a mound of hate mail when he returned to UCLA for his senior year.

In 1969, shortly before he graduated with a BA in History, Alcindor polished off his college basketball career with a 37-point, 20-rebound performance in UCLA's victory over Purdue in the NCAA championship game. He became the first pick in the NBA draft, selected by the Milwaukee Bucks, an expansion team that had managed a grim 27–55 record in its first season. For six years he toiled in Milwaukee, a period marked by brilliance on the court and tumult off it. Averaging 28.8 points per game, he won Rookie of the Year honors in 1969–1970 and sparked the Bucks to a dramatic turnaround with a 56–26 record. Perhaps never before or

since has one person's impact on a professional team been so profound. The next year, teaming with newly acquired Oscar Robertson, Alcindor led his team to an NBA championship. Though criticized by the media as an aloof giant, his impact on the game was undeniable. He averaged 31.7 points and 16 rebounds per game, and earned the first of six Most Valuable Player (MVP) awards, a figure unmatched in NBA annals.

His connections to Islam and Abdul-Khaalis became increasingly public. The religious mentor chose Alcindor's bride in 1971 (Habiba Brown) and the name Kareem Abdul-Jabbar (meaning "generous and powerful servant of Allah"), which became legal a few months later. In one off-season, the NBA's most dominating player studied Arabic at Harvard; another year he traveled to the Middle East. In 1972–1973 he was followed by NBA security guards after six of Abdul-Khaalis's relatives, including four of his children, were murdered by Black Muslim extremists. (A few years later Abdul-Khaalis was sentenced to forty years in jail for his involvement in a hostage-taking incident, during which a reporter was killed.)

On the court Abdul-Jabbar's excellence was undiminished (MVP awards again in 1972 and 1974), but off-court strains were evident. He separated from his wife shortly after the birth of his first daughter in 1973, though they later had two more children. (He subsequently had two additional children with other women.) Abdul-Jabbar had a falling out with Chamberlain over the latter's claim in an autobiography that black women were sexually inferior and his public support of President Richard Nixon. Then in the 1974–1975 season, Abdul-Jabbar got poked in the eye and responded by slamming his fist into a backboard support, breaking two bones in his hand, and taking him away from the game, his oasis. At year's end, the Bucks accommodated his demands for a trade, shipping him to the Los Angeles Lakers in return for four players.

Abdul-Jabbar's first years back in California were marked by more of the same: overpowering play (MVP awards in 1976 and 1977) coupled with a brooding court mien that earned him few friends. In the first game of the 1977–1978 season, he was widely criticized for responding to an elbow by Milwaukee's Kent Benson with

a devastating punch that sidelined Benson with a concussion and Abdul-Jabbar with another fractured hand. Increasingly, the game's best player was regarded as an outcast. "No man is an island," opined the legendary *Los Angeles Times* columnist Jim Murray, "but Kareem gave it a shot."

In time, though, Abdul-Jabbar found his way back to shore, an American life that had a decided second act. In 1979–1980 the Lakers added rookie point guard Magic Johnson, whose on-court exuberance was contagious. That year, with Abdul-Jabbar again earning MVP honors, the Lakers captured the NBA title. The Lakers became the dominant team of the 1980s, winning five titles with a stylish, fast-breaking brand of basketball known as "Showtime." In various ways Abdul-Jabbar seemed to soften. He displayed a deft comic touch in the 1980 movie *Airplane,* which opened up film and television roles for him in coming years. In 1983 he was visibly moved when fans around the country sent him jazz records after his treasured collection was destroyed in a house fire. Later that year he published *Giant Steps,* an unusually candid and cathartic autobiography. On the court he seemed almost impervious to age. In 1983–1984 he became the league's all-time leading scorer, eclipsing Chamberlain's record, appropriately enough, with his trademark shot, now widely known as a skyhook—"the most beautiful thing in sports," according to Bill Russell (*Time,* 20 Feb. 1989). Abdul-Jabbar seemed downright exuberant in 1984–1985 as the Lakers defeated the Celtics in the NBA Finals. Even pushing forty, bald and begoggled, he remained a force, helping the Lakers become the first repeat champions of the NBA in nineteen years in 1987 and 1988. So durable was he that when he played in his nineteenth and final All-Star game in 1989, he was older than seven of the twenty players in the accompanying NBA Legends Classic. When he finally retired a few months later, he had played more games, scored more points, and blocked more shots than anyone in league history. "In my opinion," the regal John Wooden said, "he is the most valuable player in the history of the game."

In his retirement, Abdul-Jabbar took to writing, including a highly reflective account of his final season, *Kareem,* and a history book, *Black Profiles in Courage* (1996), written with Alan Steinberg. He started a jazz label and remained involved in television and motion pictures. He initially professed a desire to stay away from basketball, but in a variety of broadcasting and coaching roles, including one year as an assistant coach for a high school team on an Apache Indian reservation, he began another long, graceful arc to the hoop.

FURTHER READING

Abdul-Jabbar, Kareem, with Peter Knobler. *Giant Steps* (1983).
———, with Mignon McCarthy. *Kareem* (1990).
———, with Stephen Singular. *A Season on the Reservation* (2000).

Smith, Gary. "Now, More Than Ever, a Winner," *Sports Illustrated* (23 Dec. 1985).
                                    —MARTY DOBROW

ABELE, JULIAN FRANCIS (21 Apr. 1881–18 Apr. 1950),

architect, was born in Philadelphia, Pennsylvania, the eighth of eleven children of Charles Sylvester Abele and Mary Jones, a washerwoman and milliner. Charles Able changed the spelling, although not the pronunciation, of his surname to Abele after mustering out of the Union army following the end of the Civil War. Charles, who worked as a carpenter and laborer at the U.S. Treasury Customs House, a sought-after patronage job, and as a porter, died when Julian was twelve. Mary Jones Abele was a descendant of ABSALOM JONES, the first African American Protestant Episcopal priest. Julian and his siblings were fourth generation Philadelphians and were expected by their parents to achieve recognition, marry well, and assume their rightful place in Olde Philadelphia society. Julian's oldest brother, Robert, was one of the first African American graduates of Hahnemann Medical College and a cofounder in 1907 of Mercy Hospital, the only Philadelphia hospital which would accept African Americans. Julian's oldest sister, Elizabeth, was a calligrapher and his sister Mary taught in a private school prior to marrying. His brothers Charles Jr. and Joseph worked as a sign maker and electrical engineer, respectively. His brother Ernest was considered a ne'er-do-well inventor, and Frederick, according to his grand niece, was "a little off the bean." Another brother, Harry, died as an infant, while two other brothers, Harry II and Thomas, died in their twenties. Julian was raised in a home where the fine arts were appreciated and family members knew the difference between a finale and a finial. Although Charles Jr. was the wealthiest family member, Robert inherited leadership of the family after his father's death. He paid Julian's tuition so his younger brother could pursue his dream to become an architect.

Abele followed his sisters and brothers to the Institute for Colored Youth (ICY), a private, preparatory school founded and supported by Philadelphia Quakers. ICY's principal, FANNY COPPIN, whose educational innovations included fostering close relationships between faculty and students, mentored Julian personally, encouraging his ambition to become an architect and counseling him to enroll in the recently organized Pennsylvania Museum School of Industrial Art (PMSIA) after his 1897 graduation from ICY. During a period when the Franklin Institute and the School of Design for Women, both in Philadelphia, refused to enroll African Americans, Abele was admitted to the PMSIA without objection, and in 1898 he became one of the school's first recipients of a certificate in architectural design. Abele continued his architectural training at the University of Pennsylvania School of Architecture, where he won the respect of his peers and several awards for design and rendering and was also elected president of the Architectural Society. In 1902 he graduated with a BS in Architecture, becoming the school's first African American graduate and the second African American to earn a degree in Architecture, following Robert Robinson Taylor, an 1898 graduate of the Massachusetts Institute of Technology.

Abele's training included a continuing relationship with Philadelphia's T-Square Club, a professional organization founded in 1883 by thirteen Philadelphia architects. Admitted while a student at the University of Pennsylvania, Abele was the club's only African American member. In 1901, while a fourth-year student at the University of Pennsylvania, he had been awarded the T-Square Club Prize for superior performance. Thereafter Abele consistently earned first-place mentions, beating out more experienced architects in the club's annual competitions, which were held until 1925. Abele also showed his work at the architecture clubs of Pittsburgh and Toronto and at the Architectural League of New York.

While still a student, Abele was listed as an architect in the Philadelphia city directory, and until 1903 he worked evenings for noted Philadelphia architect Louis C. Hickman. Soon after graduation, Abele went to Spokane, Washington, to design a house for his sister, Elizabeth Abele Cook, and her husband, John F. Cook. Already one of the most formally educated architects in the Commonwealth of Pennsylvania, he took the evening architectural design course offered by the Philadelphia Academy of Fine Arts, receiving a certificate in May 1903. Abele spent the next few years in Europe. And while he was not, as has been claimed, a graduate of L'Ecole des Beaux-Arts in Paris, he did travel throughout France and Italy, later exhibiting sketches completed during his European sojourn. On his application for membership in the American Institute of Architects, Abele listed travel to England, France, Germany, Switzerland, Italy, and Spain.

Abele's ribbon-winning, pen-and-ink sketches revealed a talented draftsman who "could delineate shadows with a grease pencil in so subtle a way that the observer got the impression of far more detail than Abele had actually drawn" (Maher, 372). Deeply fearful that an injury to his right hand would destroy his livelihood, Abele taught himself to draw with his left hand. Abele was also a landscape painter.

In 1906 Horace Trumbauer, known for the design of elegant mansions, hired Abele as a junior architect, making Abele the first African American architect employed by a white-owned firm. When he was promoted to senior designer two years later, Abele became responsible for siting buildings, collaborating with Trumbauer in choosing architectural styles, and creating the "look" for all commissioned buildings. Abele remained with Trumbauer until 1950, contributing to the design of more than two hundred buildings, twenty-one of which are listed on the National Register of Historic Places.

After Trumbauer's death in 1938, Abele became head of the firm and, for the first time, was able to sign his own name to designs.

A lifelong Francophile, Abele was a smart dresser and a sports and symphony fan. He shunned the spotlight, preferring, either by temperament or necessity, to remain in the background. On 6 June 1925 Abele married Parisian Marguerite Bulle, a graduate of the Paris Conservatoire of Music. After nine years of marriage and three children, Marguerite ran off with a Polish émigré singer.

Under Trumbauer, Abele designed lavish homes, including Whitemarsh Hall (1916), a 150-room limestone home for Edward Stotesbury, a banker and Philadelphia's wealthiest citizen; Shadow Lawn (1927), a West Long Beach, New Jersey, mansion for Hubert Parson, the president of F.W. Woolworth & Company; and Marly (1931) in Washington, D.C., for Dodge Brothers Motor Company heiress Delphine Dodge Baker. Abele designed the New York mansion of James Buchanan Duke, president of both the American Tobacco Company and the Southern Power Company, a building that is now New York University's Graduate Institute of Fine Arts. Trumbauer's firms largest and most important work was commissioned by Duke for Duke University; Abele designed eleven Georgian-style buildings on the east campus and thirty-eight Gothic-style buildings on the west campus. While this represented more buildings than Henry Ives Cobb designed for the University of Chicago, Ralph Adams Cram designed for Princeton University, or Robert Robinson Taylor designed for Tuskegee Institute, there is no evidence that Abele ever set foot on Duke University's campus.

Abele contributed to the design of the Philadelphia Museum of Art, and after Trumbauer's death, he played a key role in the completion of the building. Typically, until recently, histories of Widener Library at Harvard University, which was designed by the firm of Horace Trumbauer, made no mention of Abele, one of the building's chief architects.

Julian Abele died on 18 April 1950 after suffering his second heart attack. He was buried in Eden Cemetery in Collindale, a Main Line suburb of Philadelphia, near the mausoleums for Charles Eishenlohr, Peter Widener, and Thomas Develon Jr. that Abele had designed. The Corinthian-colonnaded Free Library of Philadelphia, which Abele designed in 1917, can be seen from his gravesite.

FURTHER READING

Adams, Michael. "A Legacy of Shadows," *Progressive Architecture* (Feb. 1991): 85.

Bond, Max. "Still Here: Three Architects of Afro-America–Julian Francis Abele, Hilyard Robinson and Paul R. Williams," *Harvard Design Magazine* (Summer 1997).

Maher, James. *Twilight of Splendor* (1975).

Tatman, Sandra L., and Roger W. Moss, eds. *Biographical Dictionary of Philadelphia Architects: 1700–1930* (1985).

Wilson, Dreck Spulock, ed., *African American Architects: A Biographical Dictionary 1865–1945* (2003).

—DRECK SPURLOCK WILSON

ABERNATHY, RALPH

(11 Mar. 1926–17 Apr. 1990), clergyman and civil rights leader, was born David Abernathy near Linden, Alabama, the tenth of twelve children of farm owners Will L. Abernathy and Louivery Bell Abernathy. Abernathy spent his formative years on his family's five-hundred-acre farm in rural Marengo County in southwestern Alabama. His father's economic self-sufficiency and industry spared the family from most of the hardships of the Great Depression.

"We didn't know that people were lining up at soup kitchens in cities all over the country," he would recall in his autobiography, *And the Walls Came Tumbling Down* (Abernathy, 6). Along with other family members, he attended Hopewell Baptist Church, where his father served as a deacon, and decided early to become a preacher, a commitment strengthened by a conversion experience at the age of seven. Abernathy attended high school at all-black Linden Academy, a Baptist-affiliated institution. Having little exposure to whites during his childhood, he remembered being "relatively unaware of racism or segregation" (Abernathy, 28).

In 1944 Abernathy was drafted into the armed services and enlisted as Ralph David Abernathy, a name given to him by his sister Manerva that he would use publicly for the rest of his life. Promoted to the rank of sergeant in the army, Abernathy served with his unit in France during the closing months of World War II, and he did not see combat before Germany's surrender. A bout of rheumatic fever prevented him from accompanying his unit to the Pacific theater, where, he later heard, nearly all of his comrades were killed in a battle on a Japanese-held island.

Returning to Alabama, Abernathy enrolled at Alabama State College in Montgomery. Elected president of the student council during his sophomore year, he led a strike against poor food in the student dining hall and

Ralph Abernathy gives the victory sign from a police van after his arrest in Washington, D.C., during the Poor People's Campaign in June 1968.
© Bettmann/CORBIS

the following year led another protest against substandard student housing. In 1948 Abernathy also chose the occasion of Mother's Day following his mother's death (his father had died several years earlier) to announce before the Hopewell congregation his call to the ministry. Soon afterward, he was ordained. He graduated from Alabama State College in 1950 with a BS in Mathematics. After serving briefly as a radio disc jockey during the summer of 1950, he spent a year in graduate studies in sociology at Atlanta University.

While in Atlanta, Abernathy attended a service at Ebenezer Baptist Church, where he heard a sermon by MARTIN LUTHER KING JR., who was finishing his summer duties as his father's assistant before returning to his studies at Pennsylvania's Crozer Theological Seminar. "I stopped to shake his hand and comment on his sermon," Abernathy later wrote. "At that meeting we both recognized in one another a kindred spirit" (Abernathy, 89).

Abernathy returned to Montgomery to become dean of men at Alabama State, while also serving as minister of a small congregation at Eastern Star Baptist Church in Demopolis. Soon afterward, however, he accepted a call from Montgomery's hundred-year-old First Baptist Church. In 1952 Abernathy married Juanita Odessa Jones of Uniontown, Alabama, a teacher at the Monroe County Training School in Beatrice, Alabama. The following year, the first of the couple's four children was born.

In 1954 King moved to Montgomery to assume the pastorate of Dexter Avenue Baptist Church, and the Abernathys quickly formed ties with King and his wife, CORETTA SCOTT KING: "Because of Jim Crow we could only have dinner at home. So the four of us had dinner every night, with Coretta preparing the meal one evening, Juanita the next. And usually conversations among the four of us would last way beyond midnight" (Abernathy, 129). According to Abernathy, the two preachers and their wives discussed plans to turn Montgomery "into a model of social justice and racial amity," but they did not begin to implement these plans until ROSA PARKS was arrested on 1 December 1955 for refusing a bus driver's order to give up her bus seat to a white man (Abernathy, 129). The next day,

E. D. NIXON, a local NAACP leader and a Pullman car porter, called Abernathy to seek his help in rallying support for a bus boycott initiated by JO ANN ROBINSON of the Women's Political Council in Montgomery. Abernathy took the lead in mobilizing the city's black clergy and other local residents.

After the boycott got off to a successful start on 5 December, Abernathy became program chairman of the newly organized Montgomery Improvement Association (MIA)—a name he later took credit for suggesting—and King was elected the MIA's president. As the boycott continued during the following year, Abernathy became a key figure in the movement. He often spoke at mass meetings, sometimes giving fulsome introductions of King, who would later describe Abernathy as "my closest associate and most trusted friend" (King, *Autobiography* [1998], 64). Abernathy was one of more than one hundred boycott leaders arrested in February 1956 for violating Alabama's antiboycott statute. The willingness of the indicted leaders to go to Montgomery's jail to be arrested demonstrated their resolve and proved to be a turning point in the boycott. After King's conviction in March was appealed, the trials of Abernathy and the other defendants were postponed by a continuance. In November the U.S. Supreme Court ruled that bus segregation in Montgomery was illegal, and in the following month Abernathy joined King in riding the city's first desegregated bus.

In January 1957 Abernathy was among a group of black ministers who gathered in Atlanta to organize a regional group to sustain and expand the bus protests that had occurred in Montgomery and other southern cities. Although he was called away from the meeting owing to the bombing of the First Baptist Church and his parsonage, he returned to form an organization that eventually became the Southern Christian Leadership Conference (SCLC). King became president and Abernathy secretary-treasurer of the new group.

Abernathy accompanied King to most of the subsequent major events of the southern civil rights struggle, joining him in jail during the key campaigns in Albany, Georgia, in 1961 and 1962 and Birmingham, Alabama, in 1963.

A year after King moved from Montgomery to Atlanta in order to be closer to SCLC's headquarters in that city, Abernathy followed him and, at King's urging, became pastor of Atlanta's West Hunter Street Baptist Church in August 1961. Abernathy shared King's firm commitment to nonviolence and traveled with him to Oslo, Norway, in 1964 to attend King's Nobel Peace Prize acceptance ceremony. In 1965 Abernathy was named at King's request to the new position of vice president at large of SCLC, clarifying his status as King's successor.

Abernathy continued to work closely with King during the Poor People's Campaign of 1968 and was at the Loraine Motel in Memphis when an assassin killed King on 4 April. Abernathy was the first person at King's side. He knelt down and tried to comfort the dying King while cradling his head: "Martin. It's all right. Don't worry. This is Ralph. This is Ralph."

After the assassination, Abernathy assumed the presidency of SCLC and continued the Poor People's Campaign. He later admitted, however, that he lacked many of King's attributes: "I didn't have as many degrees as he did and I didn't have his polish. In addition, my skin was darker, a more important factor in dealing with the white press than anyone would dare admit" (Abernathy, 499). The Resurrection City encampment of antipoverty protesters in Washington, D.C., could be sustained only until July 1968, when Abernathy and the remaining protesters were arrested. He served twenty days in jail. After this setback, Abernathy continued as SCLC's president, but the group's effectiveness declined as many of King's former associates departed. In 1977 Abernathy left SCLC to make an unsuccessful run to represent an Atlanta district in the U.S. House of Representatives.

Abernathy's post-SCLC years were marked by continued outspokenness on civil rights issues and some controversy. In the 1980s, he broke ranks with most black leaders to support Ronald Reagan's presidential candidacy. "Reagan promised me that he would make a jobs program a top priority for his administration," he later explained. When Abernathy's autobiography was published in 1989, he again sparked controversy by confirming reports of King's "weakness for women" (Abernathy, 470). Abernathy denied rumors that King had interracial affairs, saying "He was never attracted to white women and had nothing to do with them, despite the opportunities that may have presented themselves" (Abernathy, 472). But he suggested that on the night of King's assassination, King may have been involved in a sexual assignation and argued with another lover. Members of King's family and some of his former SCLC associates publicly rebuked Abernathy, who defended himself by insisting that King's dalliances had already been revealed. The year following the publication of his autobiography, Abernathy died at the age of sixty-four.

FURTHER READING

Some of Ralph Abernathy's papers are included in the Southern Christian Leadership Conference collection, Library and Archives of the Martin Luther King Jr. Center for Nonviolent Social Change, Atlanta, Georgia. Portions are available on microfilm.

Abernathy, Ralph David. *And the Walls Came Tumbling Down* (1989).

Branch, Taylor. *Parting the Waters: America in the King Years, 1954–63* (1988).
———. *Pillar of Fire: America in the King Years, 1963–65* (1998).
Garrow, David J. *Bearing the Cross: Martin Luther King, Jr., and the Southern Christian Leadership Conference, 1955–1968* (1986).

Obituary: *New York Times*, 18 Apr. 1990.
—CLAYBORNE CARSON

AILEY, ALVIN

(5 Jan. 1931–1 Dec. 1989), actor, dancer, and choreographer, was born in Rogers, Texas, the son of Alvin Ailey, a laborer, and Lula Elizabeth Cliff, a cotton picker and domestic. Before Ailey was a year old, his father abandoned the family, leaving them homeless for close to six years. During that time Ailey and his mother made their way, often by foot, across the unforgiving terrain of the impoverished and bitterly racist Brazos Valley in southeastern Texas to seek shelter with relatives and find work in nearby fields.

A bright, curious child, Ailey joined his mother in the cotton fields as soon

as he could carry a sack. He reveled in the sights and sounds of the gospel choirs and worshipers that he witnessed in the black Baptist churches of his youth. Ailey also became acquainted with the less pious side of life through those who spent Saturday nights dancing, drinking, and fighting in roadside bars and dance halls where blues musicians played over the constant drone of passing trains. Ailey had a photographic memory that allowed him to recall the body language of the people he saw in both bars and churches, memories he later drew on in his work.

In 1937 Ailey and his mother moved to Navasota, Texas, where they lived with Amos Alexander, a local black businessman. Alexander treated Ailey as a son and provided him with the only secure family environment he would experience. Ailey relished the stability of living in one place, eating regularly, going to the same school, and worshiping at the True Vine Baptist Church, but he developed a deep sense of obligation to Alexander and felt inferior to Alexander's own children. Ailey's 1961 autobiography, *Knoxville: Summer 1915*, is a moving account of his life in Navasota.

In 1942 Ailey's life changed dramatically. His mother moved to Los Angeles, determined to get one of the thousands of jobs being created by West Coast aircraft factories gearing up to handle the demands of World War II. Before his mother was hired as a night-shift worker for Lockheed, she and Ailey lived in a white section of the city, where she worked as a domestic and he attended a previously all-white school. Ailey's status as the only black student in the school reinforced his feelings of insecurity and inferiority. His love for dance was sparked by a class field trip to see Sergei Denham's Ballet Russe de Monte Carlo in 1943. Ailey had seen vaudeville shows, revues, and theater productions, but after seeing the Ballet Russe he attended as many dance events as he could. Among them was a presentation of the KATHERINE DUNHAM company. Dunham's spectacular productions of African and Caribbean dance styles had a tremendous influence on Ailey's concept of dance, theatricality, and the unique expressionism of ethnic dance.

In 1971, in his virtuoso solo *Cry*, Ailey immortalized his reaction to attending a white school and watching

In 1958, Alvin Ailey founded the Alvin Ailey American Dance Theatre in New York City. Ailey choreographed an important body of work, including such signature pieces as Revelations *and* Blues Sweet, *that celebrated black worship and music and other African American themes in dance.* New York Public Library

his mother scrubbing floors and hanging out laundry for white families. This piece, the first significant work created by Ailey for JUDITH JAMISON, was Ailey's tribute to his mother and "all black women—especially our mothers." Ailey always paid homage to his cultural heritage, and he created works based on experiences from different moments of his life. Of the seventy-nine works he created during his lifetime, his least successful dealt with subjects not drawn from his own experiences.

After moving to a racially mixed section of Los Angeles, Ailey attended Jefferson High School, which drew students of black and Hispanic heritage. He excelled in foreign language studies and distinguished himself as a gymnast. Intent on becoming a foreign language teacher, he entered the University of California, Los Angeles, in 1948 as a foreign language major.

By that time, however, he had started formal dance training under Lester Horton at the urging of high school friend Carmen de Lavallade. A white man, Horton had founded the first multiracial dance company in America and developed his own modern dance technique. The breadth of movement and expression supported by the Horton technique appealed to Ailey. He also was intrigued by Horton's ability to fuse elements of theater and stagecraft in his works.

Ailey made his professional debut in Horton's company in 1950. He continued working toward his college degree until he decided to join Horton as a full-time dancer and teacher of the Horton technique. Late that year Horton died. With support from de Lavallade and veteran Horton dancers James Truitte and Joyce Trisler, Ailey took over the artistic reins of the company, ran the school, and began to choreograph.

Ailey and de Lavallade were cast in the 1955 Twentieth Century–Fox motion picture *Carmen Jones*, directed by Herbert Ross. After filming was completed in 1954, Ross paired them in the Broadway-bound Truman Capote show *House of Flowers*. Their Broadway debut catapulted Ailey and de Lavallade into the limelight, but they continued to appear with Horton's company. Until 1960, Ailey remained an integral part of the effort to keep the company alive.

Living in New York City, Ailey studied dance with, among others, Martha Graham, Doris Humphrey, Donald McKayle, Karel Shook, and Charles Weidman. He also studied acting under Stella Adler. As a dancer Ailey moved with the power and grace of a lion. His physical strength, riveting presence, and ability to make movement appear to spring from within rather than as a result of the choreography set him apart from his peers. His total immersion in the roles he performed defined his approach to choreography and attracted gifted dancers to his productions.

Ailey's success on Broadway as a dancer and actor garnered him numerous theater awards and a secure future in musicals and theater. During this period, in addition to *House of Flowers*, Ailey appeared in *The Carefree Tree* (1955), HARRY BELAFONTE's 1956 production of *Sing, Man, Sing*, and LENA HORNE's 1957 *Jamaica*, the latter choreographed by Jack Cole. In 1958 Ailey drew on his memories of Saturday nights at the roadside bars to create

the dance *Blues Suite*, which captured the parade of emotions experienced by people unable to escape the drudgery of hapless lives. Two years later he brought the charismatic Baptist preachers, fire-and-brimstone sermons, and gospel spirituals of his church to life in his signature masterpiece, *Revelations*. Noted for its spontaneity, *Revelations* has proven its universal appeal to audiences around the world. As a result, it remains the cornerstone of his company's outstanding repertory. Ailey also appeared off-Broadway as an actor in *Call Me by My Rightful Name*, with Robert Duvall and Joan Hackett, and *Two by Saroyan*, and he made his Broadway debut in an acting role as Claudia McNeil's son in the 1962 production of *Tiger, Tiger, Burning Bright*.

Throughout his Broadway career Ailey never lost sight of his goal to establish a multiracial dance company with a repertoire representing the past and future of American modern dance and the unique qualities of black cultural expression. Ailey used the fees he earned on Broadway to fund his own company and recruited several Broadway dancers to join the Horton dancers he was assembling to create a concert group.

In 1958 Ailey presented the Alvin Ailey American Dance Theater in concert at New York City's Ninety-second Street YM-YWHA. Public and critical response was excellent and inspired Ailey and his dancers to continue building the company. To keep his dancers together, Ailey provided food and shelter when they were unable to find work between concert engagements. He also ran the company by himself, getting bookings, taking care of production details, promoting the troupe, and handling the company finances out of a shoebox. As financially strapped as the company was, Ailey refused to limit the company and its audiences to an all-Ailey repertoire. He often crossed the color line to empower those who shared his dream of establishing a dance company without racial limitations.

In 1960 the premiere of Ailey's *Revelations* created a sensation in the dance world, and the company's future began to take shape. That year Robert Joffrey commissioned Ailey to create a work for his ballet company, which brought Ailey in touch with the Joffrey company's

backer, Rebekah Harkness. Harkness established a nonprofit foundation to sponsor broadly diverse projects within the field and cooperated with the U.S. Department of State Cultural Exchange Program to generate international recognition of American cultural achievements. The success of Ailey's *Feast of Ashes*, inspired by Federico García Lorca's *The House of Bernarda Alba* and set to an original Carlos Surinach score, put him in good stead with Harkness. Impressed by Ailey's fusion of dance styles and aware of the financial gridlock his company was in, Harkness allocated foundation funds to send Ailey's company on its first foreign tour.

In 1963 Harkness established the Harkness Ballet under the artistic direction of George Skibine. Ailey was invited to restage *Feast of Ashes*, which remained the property of the new company, and he was commissioned to create a new work for the company's inaugural season. As usual, Ailey applied the fees he earned to his own company. Although Harkness's wealth reinforced Ailey's personal insecurities, his commitment to his own company enabled him to accept her largesse.

Ailey's company ran out of money during its appearance at the First World Festival of Negro Arts in Dakar, Senegal, in 1966. Ailey managed to get his dancers to Barcelona, Spain, where his *Macumba*, set to Harkness music, was scheduled to premiere. Within a few hours of their arrival in Barcelona, Ailey had arranged for his dancers to be absorbed into the Harkness Ballet for the remainder of its European tour.

Although several of Ailey's dancers immediately found jobs with other companies, several joined the Harkness company for its summer workshop in Rhode Island. Jamison and Morton "Tubby" Winston stayed on for its subsequent American tour, but only Winston remained with the ballet company after Ailey's company resumed operation following a brief period of reorganization.

Ailey's relationship with Harkness remained strong, and his company continued to receive support from her foundation. Ailey always credited her for giving his company the opportunity to survive long enough to gain an international following in the world of dance.

With the exception of its brief period of reorganization, the Alvin Ailey American Dance Theater continued to build audiences around the world and offer more performances a year than any other American dance company. According to Jamison, whom Ailey named his successor before his death, the company covered most of its budget from almost year-round touring engagements in the United States and abroad.

Despite Ailey's achievements and enormous contributions to the world of dance, he remained unable to put aside his insecurities and accept his success. As a result, he felt undeserving of the many honors and awards that he received during his lifetime. His most significant awards included a Dance Magazine Award in 1975, the Spingarn Medal of the National Association for the Advancement of Colored People in 1976, the Capezio Award in 1979, the United Nations Peace Medal in 1982, the Samuel H. Scripps American Dance Festival Award in 1987, and a Kennedy Center award in 1988. The anxiety he felt over accepting awards often triggered long spells of depression and self-destructive behavior.

In 1980 Ailey was diagnosed as a severe manic-depressive during his hospitalization after he created a public disturbance. Although he continued to create significant new works for his company and others, Ailey began turning over his responsibilities for running the main company, its affiliated school, and a student repertory ensemble to others. However, he remained involved with developing an interactive, multidisciplinary summer workshop for inner-city children with interests in the arts.

Ailey, who never married, died in New York's Lenox Hill Hospital surrounded by his mother; Jamison; Sylvia Waters, director of the Alvin Ailey Repertory Ensemble; and Masazumi Chaya, assistant artistic director of the Alvin Ailey American Dance Theater.

FURTHER READING

Ailey's archive is housed at the Alvin Ailey American Dance Center in New York City.

Ailey, Alvin, with Peter Bailey. *Revelations* (1995).

Jamison, Judith, with Howard Kaplan. *Dancing Spirit* (1993).

West, Cynthia S'thembile. "Alvin Ailey: Signposts of an American Visionary." *African American Genius in Modern Dance* (1993).

Obituaries: *New York Times*, 2 Dec. 1989; *Dance Magazine*, Feb. 1990.
—LILI COCKERILLE LIVINGSTON

 AL-AMIN, JAMIL ABDULLAH. *See* Brown, H. Rap.

 ALBERT, OCTAVIA VICTORIA ROGERS (24 Dec. 1853–1890?), author and activist, was born in Oglethorpe, Georgia, the daughter of slaves. Details of her life are sketchy. Little is known of her parents or her childhood beyond the date and place of her birth and the fact that she was born into bondage; thus, it is particularly intriguing that in 1870, only five years after the Thirteenth Amendment abolished slavery and one year after Atlanta University opened, seventeen-year-old Octavia was among the 170 students enrolled at that institution. Most of the little we know of her life comes from *The House of Bondage* (1890), the book that made her famous. From that source we learn that in 1873 she was teaching in Montezuma, Georgia, when she met fellow teacher A. E. P. Albert. They married in 1874 and had one daughter.

Sometime around 1877 Albert's husband was ordained as a Methodist Episcopal minister, and the family moved to Houma, Louisiana, and later to New Orleans. It is not clear whether Octavia Albert ever worked professionally again. Most likely she did not, as it was rare for school systems, especially in the South, to employ married women, and because her husband quickly assumed a social prominence that would have discouraged her from being a wage earner.

A. E. P. Albert became a religious and political leader, held a degree in theology, was a trustee of New Orleans University, and served as editor of the *South-Western Christian Advocate*. As befitted her social position, Octavia Albert vacationed with her family at resorts such as the Bay St. Louis in Mississippi, attended lectures and

Octavia V. R. Albert collected interviews with former slaves in The House of Bondage, *realistically describing their lives both before and after emancipation.* Schomburg Center

receptions, and generally participated in the religious reform efforts deemed proper for a minister's wife. However, it is clear that she was not content with these activities, but she made her home a center of activity where people of all classes and conditions were welcome to study the Bible, learn to read and write, and discuss current events.

It was from just such community involvement that the idea was born for *The House of Bondage*. Albert's sympathies and interests had been increased by the frequent conversations she had with elderly former slaves, including Charlotte Brooks, who discussed with Albert her slavery experiences in Virginia and Louisiana. Albert announced that she intended to write Charlotte Brooks's story in—as closely as possible—Brooks's own words. Years later Albert stated, "My interest in, and conversations with, Aunt Charlotte, Aunt Sallie, Uncle John Goodwin, Uncle Stephen, and the other characters represented in this story led me to interview many other people [who gave] me additional facts and incidents about the colored people, in freedom as well as in slavery" (Albert, 120).

The full title of Albert's book reveals the grandness of her project: *The House of Bondage; or, Charlotte Brooks and Other Slaves: Original and Life-Like, as They Appeared in Their Old Plantation and City Slave Life; Together with*

Pen-Pictures of the Peculiar Institution, with Sights and Insights into Their New Relations as Freedmen, Freemen, and Citizens. Some months after her death, Albert's *House of Bondage* was serialized in the *South-Western Christian Advocate*; it proved so popular that "letters poured in upon the editor from all directions, urging him to put it in book form" (Albert, v). The volume was published posthumously in 1890. The scope of Albert's project, covering rural and urban slavery and using oral testimonies, distinguishes her work from other studies of the period. In the 1880s slavery had once more become a popular topic for many writers, but most were of the so-called Plantation School, which considered the South a place of chivalry and slavery a benevolent, paternalistic institution. At the same time, many contemporary publications and politicians justified racial discrimination and increased violence against African Americans on the grounds that former slaves harbored deep hostility and plans for revenge and were without morals, self-discipline, or ambition. Declaring that "none but those who resided in the South during the time of slavery" (Albert, 1) could testify accurately to its horror, Albert set out to set the record straight by publishing interviews with former slaves, by describing their condition after slavery, and by celebrating the achievements they and their descendants had won despite great and increasing odds.

According to historian John Blassingame, Albert was one of only a handful of experienced interviewers in the country and also "one of the most interesting" (Blassingame, lxi) in the country. Fascinating stories of slave life unfold in the dialogue between Albert and the interviewers. The major narrative is that of Charlotte Brooks; the half-dozen other extended accounts and the multitude of incidents in the lives of others they knew or had heard about serve primarily to supplement or emphasize the material that Brooks provides. Albert uses poetry, songs, speeches, and other material for documentation, for context, and for texture. Although she intended her work to combat negative stereotypes, Albert also emphasized another goal. It was vital, she argued, that the story of those who survived slavery and those who overcame racial

oppression be treasured and transmitted to "our children's children," not only to set the record straight but to inspire African Americans. Her book posits "education, property, and character" as the "trinity of power" by which African Americans could gain their rightful places in society (Albert, 127).

FURTHER READING

Foster, Frances Smith. Introduction to Octavia V. Rogers Albert, *The House of Bondage* (1988).

Blassingame, John, ed. *Slave Testimony: Two Centuries of Letters, Speeches, Interviews, and Autobiographies* (1977).

Majors, Monroe. *Noted Negro Women* (1893).

—FRANCES SMITH FOSTER

ALDRIDGE, IRA FREDERICK (24 July 1807–10 Aug. 1867), actor, was the son of Daniel Aldridge, a minister, and Lurona (maiden name unknown). Although certain historical accounts record that Aldridge was born in Senegal, Africa, and was the grandson of the Fulah tribal chieftain, modern biographical scholarship has established that he was born in New York City. It is possible that he could claim Fulah ancestry, but his lineal descent from tribal royalty is unconfirmed. Extant evidence concerning Aldridge's life is sketchy, conflicting, or exaggerated, possibly owing in part to the aggrandizements of theatrical publicity.

As a young boy, Aldridge attended the African Free School in New York City. Although Aldridge's father intended for him to join the clergy, Aldridge showed an early attraction to the stage, excelling at debate and declamation. Around 1821 Aldridge tried to perform at Brown's Theatre (also known as the African Theatre), but his father forced him from the stage. English playbills later stated that Aldridge came via the African Theatre, New York, so Aldridge must have circumvented his father's objections before the theater was closed in 1823. Recognizing the slim prospects for an African American actor in the United States at a time of strong prejudices against blacks, Aldridge made plans to immigrate to England.

European audiences embraced Ira Aldridge as one of the greatest tragedians of his time. In this portrait painted by Henry Perronet Briggs around 1830, the "African Roscius" is depicted as Othello, one of Aldridge's best-known roles. National Portrait Gallery, Smithsonian Institution/Art Resource, NY

Aldridge became a dresser to the English actor Henry Wallack, who was performing in New York. Henry Wallack's brother, James, then employed Aldridge as a personal attendant while on passage to Liverpool. J. J. Sheahan, a friend of Aldridge's, wrote that James Wallack had planned to sponsor Aldridge and make money off his engagements, but when Wallack told a reporter that Aldridge was his servant, the two went their separate ways. (The often repeated account that Aldridge became the personal attendant of the British classical actor Edmund Kean and accompanied him back to England has been proved false.) Aldridge arrived in England in 1824, and although he announced his return to the United States a number of times throughout his career, he never went home.

Although it has been generally accepted that Aldridge made his debut in England in 1826 as Othello, playbills show that his first major engagement in London was at the Royal Coberg Theatre on 10 October 1825 under the name Mr. Keene. Aldridge, also dubbed the "African Roscius," acted under this name until around 1832. In his debut Aldridge played the royal slave Oroonoko in *The Revolt of Surinam*. During this engagement he also played in *The Ethiopian* and *The Libertine Defeated*. That the engagement was a success for Aldridge is evident in a playbill announcing his appearance in *The Negro's Curse*, a play written expressly for him. His biographers suggest that Aldridge rose to leading roles so quickly in part because of the novel appeal of having a "Man of Colour" in the cast. During the early part of Aldridge's career, many reviewers doubted the ability of a black actor, saying, for example, "Owing to the shape of his lips it is utterly impossible for him to pronounce English in such a manner as to satisfy the unfastidious ears of the gallery" (*The Times* [London], 11 Oct. 1825). Nonetheless, Aldridge was popular with audiences.

The prejudiced criticism demonstrated in the London press made it difficult for Aldridge, despite his popularity with the public, to establish a career in the city. He turned, therefore, to the English provinces, where he developed his craft over the next twenty-five years. In his first provincial engagement

at Brighton, he played Oroonoko and, for the first time on record, Othello, making no great impression. He toured Sheffield, Halifax, Manchester, Newcastle, Edinburgh, Lancaster, Liverpool, and Sutherland. His repertoire consisted of *Othello, Oroonoko, The Slave, The Castle Spectre, The Padlock*, and *The Revenge*. *Othello* and *The Padlock* remained in his repertoire until his death.

In 1829 Aldridge appeared in Belfast, with Charles Kean playing Iago to Aldridge's Othello and Oroonoko to his Aboan. In 1830 Aldridge played his first "white" role, Captain Hatteraick in *Guy Mannering*, using white makeup and a wig. Afterward, Aldridge regularly played white roles, such as Shylock in *The Merchant of Venice* and Rob MacGregor in *Rob Roy*. In 1833 Aldridge played Dublin and for the first time crossed paths with Edmund Kean. Playing in an overlapping engagement, Kean saw Aldridge in the role of Othello and afterward recommended him to the Royal Theatre at Bath, a prestigious provincial playhouse. Within three weeks Aldridge opened at Bath with his regular repertoire.

In 1833 Aldridge was invited to appear at the Theatre Royal Covent Garden, where he opened as Othello to Ellen Tree's Desdemona. The London press, however, was still unwilling, on the whole, to accept a black leading actor at its major theaters. A few critics found his performance commendable, but most agreed that Covent Garden was no place for a "curiosity" such as Aldridge. He had been scheduled to appear in two other roles at Covent Garden, but the performances were canceled for reasons that remain unclear. It is believed that the threats of critics perhaps convinced the Covent Garden manager, Pierre Laporte, that the "novelty" was not worth the financial risk. Whatever the reason for the cancellation, Aldridge's achievement is recorded by his biographers, who commented that his performance at Covent Garden "will forever be red-letter days in the history of world theatre and human progress, for . . . a lone Negro from an enslaved people challenged the great white actors in the very heart of their Empire" (Marshall and Stock, 135).

Rejected by London for a second time, Aldridge returned to the provinces

for many successful years. In 1852 he began his first tour of the Continent. His success in Europe was unequaled by any other in his career. His first tour through Belgium, Hungary, Germany, Austria, and Poland lasted three years. In 1857 he toured Sweden, and afterward he continually toured the Continent, including Russia, until his death, returning to England periodically to play the provinces. It was on his first tour that he added the roles of Macbeth, King Lear, and Richard III to his repertoire and received great honors from the princes of Europe. The king of Prussia awarded him the Gold Medal of the First Class for Art and Sciences; in Vienna the emperor presented him with the Medal of Ferdinand; and he was made an honorary member of the Hungarian Dramatic Conservatoire in Hungary, the Imperial and Archducal Order of Our Lady of the Manger in Austria, and the Imperial Academy of Beaux Arts in St. Petersburg. After he played the major cities of Europe to royalty and accolades, it is no wonder that Aldridge preferred to tour Europe rather than the small provincial theaters of England. The racism in the United States and, to a lesser extent, England, was not present in other European countries at the time. As a result, Aldridge thrived in continental Europe, which judged him by his ability on the boards rather than by the color of his skin. In 1858, however, Aldridge finally found success at the Lyceum Theatre in London and in 1863 was granted British citizenship.

His biographers credit Aldridge with being "the first to show that a black man could scale any heights in theatrical art reached by a white man—and recreate with equal artistry the greatest characters in world drama" (Marshall and Stock, 335). Known for his versatility, Aldridge played both the greatest tragic characters of Shakespeare and the melodramatic slave characters of his early career with dexterity. A physically impressive man, Aldridge was known for his strong, clear voice and a style more realistic than that used by his contemporaries—so realistic that accounts by actors mention that Aldridge caused them to forget that they were on a stage, and the play became "naked, shattering reality." He was known as well for personalizing his roles, especially Othello; he studied and interpreted his roles with little consideration for the traditional interpretation. When he was abroad, he acted in English, while his supporting cast used the native language. One Russian actor who worked with Aldridge, Davydov, said that "his mimicry, gestures, were so expressive that knowledge of the English language for the understanding of his acting was not needed at all" (V. N. Davydov, *Razkaz o Proshlom* [1930], 98).

Aldridge was married twice, although we know very little about his wives. His first wife, the Englishwoman Margaret Gill, whom he married in 1832, died in 1864. He married his second wife, the countess Amanda Paulina von Brandt of Sweden, in 1865. Aldridge and his second wife had five children, one of whom died in infancy. Aldridge died in Lødz, Poland, while on his way to perform in St. Petersburg.

FURTHER READING

Hill, Errol. *Shakespeare in Sable* (1990).

Malone, Mary. *Actor in Exile: The Life of Ira Aldridge* (1969).

Marshall, Herbert. *Further Research on Ira Aldridge: The Negro Tragedian* (1970).

Marshall, Herbert, and Mildred Stock. *Ira Aldridge: The Negro Tragedian* (1958).

Obituary: *The Times* (London), 18 July 1867.
—MELISSA VICKERY-BAREFORD

ALEXANDER, SADIE TANNER MOSSELL

(2 Jan. 1898–2 Nov. 1989), attorney and civil rights activist, was born Sadie Tanner Mossell in Philadelphia, Pennsylvania, the youngest of three children of Aaron Albert Mossell Jr., an attorney, and Mary Louise Tanner. In 1899 Mossell's father deserted the family and fled to Wales. During elementary school Sadie and an mother divided their time between Mossell's grandparents' home in Philadelphia and an aunt and uncle's home on the campus of Howard University in Washington, D.C. When her mother returned to Pennsylvania, Mossell remained under the care of her aunt and uncle in Washington until she graduated from M Street High School.

Mossell entered the University of Pennsylvania in the fall of 1915 and majored in education. Her years as a student in an institution with so few women students and even fewer African Americans were extremely challenging. Yet, with her family's financial and emotional support, she prospered academically and graduated with honors in three years. In 1918 she received her BS from Pennsylvania's School of Education. While her grades were high enough to gain her admittance to Phi Beta Kappa, the university did not select her for this honor for over fifty years.

Mossell completed her graduate work at the University of Pennsylvania, earning an MA in Economics in 1919 and being awarded the Frances Sargent Pepper Fellowship in Economics, one of five grants awarded to women in the Graduate School of Economics. On 15 June 1921 Mossell became the first African American woman in the United States to earn a PhD in Economics. Despite her academic accomplishments, Mossell could find no suitable work as an educator, since even the Philadelphia high schools refused to employ African American teachers. She faced similar roadblocks in the business world. Mossell was forced to go to North Carolina, where she worked for the black-owned North Carolina Mutual Life Insurance Company in Durham as an assistant actuary.

Although she first met Raymond Pace Alexander while they were both students at the University of Pennsylvania, she did not marry him until after he completed his education. In 1920 Raymond became the first black graduate of the University of Pennsylvania's Wharton School of Finance and Commerce and graduated from Harvard Law School in 1923. The two were married on 29 November 1923 at the Tanner home in North Philadelphia.

Feeling unsatisfied with a life of domesticity, Alexander decided to go to law school. In 1924 she became the first black woman to enroll at the University of Pennsylvania School of Law. As in previous years, Alexander continued to face challenges stemming from the racist and sexist attitudes harbored by the law school administration, students, and outside institutions. In 1926 she became one of the first two black student contributors and associate editors elected to the *University of Pennsylvania Law Review*. The dean

Sadie Tanner Mossell Alexander received her PhD in Economics in 1921.
University of Pennsylvania Archives

of the law school, however, refused membership to any black woman. He eventually relented when Alexander received the support of a faculty member. In 1927 Alexander became the first black woman to graduate from the University of Pennsylvania School of Law, to gain admission to the Pennsylvania Bar, and to practice law in Pennsylvania. Alexander entered practice at her husband's law firm, making Raymond and Sadie Alexander one of the first husband and wife legal teams in the United States. Such a partnership afforded her a smoother transition into the profession than would have been possible on her own.

At her husband's suggestion, Alexander arranged to be admitted to Orphans' Court in Philadelphia shortly after her admission to the Pennsylvania bar. Orphans' Court cases afforded Alexander the opportunity to gain more trial experience than most female lawyers, of any race, in Philadelphia. She argued appeals before the full Orphans' Court bench, the Pennsylvania Supreme Court, and the United States District Court. She developed expertise in probate law, divorce, and domestic relations matters and became the firm's expert on estate and family law. In addition to her legal work, Alexander served in local government. In 1928 she became the first black woman to be appointed assistant city solicitor in Philadelphia. She served until 1930 and again from 1934 to 1938. She continued to work even after she became pregnant, giving birth to two daughters, Mary Elizabeth in 1934 and Rae Pace in 1936.

Alexander was also active in the John Mercer Langston Law Club. The organization was formed in 1925 as an alternative to the Philadelphia Bar Association, which prohibited any significant participation by African Americans. In 1932 Alexander, the only woman in the law club, helped to form a legal aid bureau to assist African Americans who could not afford to hire lawyers.

For years Alexander worked with her husband—who specialized in civil rights and criminal defense cases—to combat racial discrimination and segregation in Philadelphia movie theaters, hotels, and restaurants. They helped to draft the 1935 Pennsylvania state public accommodations law, which prohibited discrimination in public places. Later Alexander advocated for the integration of the University of Pennsylvania's faculty and the U.S. military.

Alexander was instrumental in the development of the National Bar Association (NBA), formed in 1925 as an alternative to the American Bar Association, which excluded blacks from membership. As one of the few female members of the organization, Alexander labored to highlight the role of black women in the law. She published a study on the status of African American women lawyers and found that the overwhelming majority of black women admitted to practice at the time were actively engaged in the law. Alexander was elected national secretary of the NBA on 26 November 1943 and remained in office until 1947.

Alexander became the first black woman appointed to a presidential commission when President Harry S. Truman selected her as a member of his Committee on Civil Rights in 1946. In 1948 the committee issued *To Secure These Rights*, a report on the need for more adequate means to protect civil rights. The report provided recommendations for increasing civil rights protections for all Americans, regardless of race, religion, or national origin. These recommendations became the basis for future civil rights policies and legislation, including the desegregation of the armed forces.

In addition to her duties as assistant city solicitor, Alexander played an active role in Philadelphia civic affairs. She served as a member of the Philadelphia Fellowship Commission from 1949 to 1965 and as its chairperson from 1965 until 1968. Alexander also chaired a special subcommittee charged with ensuring that a new version of the city's charter would contain provisions to safeguard equal opportunity and fair treatment in the city's administration. In 1952 Alexander drafted a portion of the charter that provided for the formation of the Philadelphia Human Relations Commission (HRC) and was subsequently appointed to be one of the nine commissioners on the HRC, which investigated allegations of employment discrimination in Philadelphia.

In 1959 Alexander opened her own law practice soon after her husband was appointed Philadelphia's first black judge. She continued to specialize in domestic relations and often took on clients who could not afford to pay her, considering such pro bono work "as much my duty as I consider it the duty of a physician to serve a dying patient" (Nier, 59). She worked diligently in her solo practice until 1974, when she joined the Philadelphia firm of Atkinson, Myers, and Archie as counsel.

In 1979 President Jimmy Carter appointed Alexander chair of the White House Conference on Aging. Throughout her life she remained active with a number of civil rights and social action organizations. She continued contributing to public life until 1983, when she was diagnosed with Alzheimer's disease. Alexander succumbed to this and other maladies at the age of ninety-one.

For over half a century, Alexander excelled as a pioneering lawyer, feminist, and civil rights activist by opening many of the doors of opportunity that were closed to African American women of her era. She "knew well that the only way [to] get that door open was to knock it down" (Hill, 80). In doing so, she dismantled racial and gender constructs of her time and created a new identity for women and African Americans by using the law as a tool for social change.

FURTHER READING

Sadie Alexander's papers are housed in the University of Pennsylvania Archives and Records Center in Philadelphia, Pennsylvania.

Hill, Ruth Edmonds. *The Black Women Oral History Project* (1991).

Mack, Kenneth W. "A Social History of Everyday Practice: Sadie T.M. Alexander and the Incorporation of Black Women into the American Legal Profession, 1925–1960," *Cornell Law Review* 87, no. 1405 (2002).

Nier, Charles Lewis. "Sweet Are the Uses of Adversity: The Civil Rights Activism of Sadie Tanner Mossell Alexander," *Temple Political and Civil Rights Law Review* 8, no. 59 (1998).

Segal, Geraldine R. *Blacks in the Law: Philadelphia and the Nation* (1983).

Smith, J. Clay, Jr. *Emancipation: The Making of the Black Lawyer 1844–1944* (1993).

Obituaries: *New York Times* and *Philadelphia Inquirer*, 3 Nov. 1989.

—LIA B. EPPERSON

ALI, MUHAMMAD

(17 Jan. 1942–), world champion boxer and political activist, was born Cassius Marcellus Clay Jr. in Louisville, Kentucky, the eldest of two sons raised by Cassius Clay Sr., a sign painter and something of a frustrated artist, and Odessa Grady, a domestic. Young Clay began to take boxing lessons at the age of twelve because someone had stolen his bicycle and he was determined to exact revenge against the perpetrators. He never discovered who stole his bike, but he did blossom as a young fighter, taking instruction from the Louisville policeman Joe Martin. His brother, Rudolph Arnette Clay (Rudolph Valentino Clay in some sources and later Rahaman Ali), also took up boxing, but, lacking his brother's talent, never became a significant presence in the sport.

Clay became a gym rat, feeling that he could succeed in boxing as he never could in school. Although he showed no special ability in his first few years, he was extraordinarily determined. He was indeed a poor student, graduating from Central High School with a D-minus average, ranking 376 in a class

Muhammad Ali defeats Sonny Liston for the heavyweight title in a first round knockout, 1965. Library of Congress

of 391. But he became one of the most impressive amateur boxers in the country, winning six Kentucky Golden Gloves championships. He was the National Amateur Athletic Union (AAU) champion in 1959 and 1960 and won a gold medal as a light heavyweight in the 1960 Rome Olympics, although he almost did not go to the Olympics because he was afraid to fly.

His boyish good looks and his outgoing personality, combined with the gimmicks of his poetry and his good-natured bragging, made Clay famous after the Olympics, and he received a great deal more media attention than most amateur fighters. He turned professional immediately after returning from Rome and was managed by a syndicate of seven Louisville businessmen. He was skillfully guided by the wily veteran trainer Angelo Dundee, who did not try to change Clay's unorthodox style, which had always

infuriated most of the old heads of boxing. Clay, like most highly touted young fighters, won all of his early fights against either second- or third-rate opponents or noted fighters whose skills had deteriorated, like Archie Moore. His most difficult fight of this "contender" stage was against Doug Jones, in which Clay won a ten-round decision, although many at ringside thought he lost the fight. With his constant bragging, his poetry, and his zany antics, he won a national following, even appearing briefly in the 1962 film version of Rod Serling's *Requiem for a Heavyweight*.

At six feet, three inches tall and over two hundred pounds, Clay astonished sportswriters with his hand and foot speed, his reluctance to punch to the body, his ability to defend himself while holding his hands at his waist, and his insistence on avoiding punches by moving his head backward instead of to the side. Clay modeled much of

his style after his idol, the welterweight and middleweight champion SUGAR RAY ROBINSON. No heavyweight before Clay ever possessed such speed, quickness, or grace, and he attracted many people to boxing who would normally have had little interest in the sport, simply because they were enthralled with his style.

On 25 February 1964 in Miami, Clay fought as an underdog for the heavyweight title against SONNY LISTON, a former convict. Liston was thought to be virtually invincible because of his devastating one-round knockouts of the former champion Floyd Patterson, the last heavyweight champion to weigh less than two hundred pounds. So few thought that the bragging Clay had a chance that rumors circulated that he would not even show up for the fight. Most thought the young braggart had no punch and no chin and would barely be able to withstand the hard-punching Liston. Clay, for his part, had been harassing Liston during most the period before the fight, taunting him by calling him "the Bear" and "ugly" and banging on Liston's front door in the early morning hours, demanding that he fight him then and there. The weigh-in ceremony the morning of the fight was part theater of the absurd and part screwball comedy. Clay, wearing a robe that said "Bear Hunting," seemed as if he wanted to attack Liston and gave the appearance of being completely out of control. It was all an act on Clay's part to gain a psychological edge over his opponent.

More ominous, from the perspective of the fight's promoters and most of the general public, were rumors coming out of Miami that Clay was being seen with MALCOLM X, the charismatic minister of the Nation of Islam (NOI). This was probably the most feared and misunderstood religious sect of the time and certainly one of the most militant black organizations to emerge since the Depression. Clay had already joined the controversial group, but he did not announce his membership until after the fight with Liston. In part this was because he did not want the fight cancelled as the result of his religious conversion and in part because the Muslims did not want to be overly embarrassed by his defeat, which nearly all in the organization thought would happen, including the group's leader,

ELIJAH MUHAMMAD. Malcolm X however was confident that Clay would win. He convinced the young boxer that the fight was a jihad, a symbolic war, both political and religious, between the crescent and the cross or between the black man who was for his people and the black man who represented white interests. The jihad image was a psychological device that Clay (and in many cases, his opponents) used to dramatize virtually all the major fights of his career, turning them into contesting forms of black political propaganda.

Clay stunned the sporting world by defeating the aging Liston fairly easily in seven rounds. After the fight Clay announced that he had not only joined the NOI but that he had a new name, Muhammad Ali. The response from the boxing establishment, the sporting press, and the white public generally was hostile, even vitriolic. The NOI was largely seen, mistakenly, as an antiwhite hate group, something analogous to the Ku Klux Klan. Although there had been a few black jazz musicians who had converted to Islam, most of the public, black and white, knew little about the religion, and the NOI's highly racialized version of Islam further distorted the perceptions of most Americans. Never was an athlete so pilloried by the public as Ali was. Most sports journalists ridiculed his religion and refused to call him by his new name. The former champion Floyd Patterson went on a personal crusade against the NOI in his fight with Ali on 22 November 1965, which Patterson lost. Patterson later became one of the few fighters to defend Ali publicly during his years of exile. No black athlete since the reign of JACK JOHNSON (1908–1915), the first black heavyweight champion, so enraged most whites and not a few blacks with his opinions and the way he chose to live his life.

He won a rematch with Sonny Liston in Lewiston, Maine, on 25 May 1965 in a bizarre first-round knockout, just two months after Malcolm X was gunned down in Harlem; yet these were soul-wrenching times for Ali because a scandal surrounding Elijah Muhammad had separated Ali from Malcolm X at the time of his mentor's assassination. Ali, probably one of the most unpopular fighters in history, spent most of the next year beating George Chuvalo in

Toronto, Henry Cooper in London, and Karl Mildenberger in Germany. He also defeated Ernie Terrell in Houston, one of his few American fights during this period.

While Ali was abroad, the Selective Service changed his draft status from 1-Y (unfit for military service because of his low score on army intelligence tests) to 1-A (qualified for induction). Many saw this change as a direct response to intense negative public opinion concerning Ali's political views and the result of the escalation of the Vietnam War. In fact, after the Gulf of Tonkin incident, the passing score on the army intelligence tests was lowered, so that many other men besides Ali were affected. Ali refused to serve in the military on the grounds that it violated his religious beliefs. (Elijah Muhammad had served time in prison during World War II for refusing to enter the armed services and for sympathizing with the Japanese. Wallace Muhammad, son of Elijah, also served time for refusing military service.)

In 1967 Ali was convicted in federal court of violation of the Selective Service Act and sentenced to five years in prison. He was immediately stripped of his boxing title, and every state athletic commission stripped him of his boxing license. For the next three and a half years, Ali, free on bond while appealing his case (which he eventually won on appeal to the U.S. Supreme Court on a technicality), was prohibited from boxing. He spoke on college campuses, became a darling of the antiwar movement, and inspired black athletes and activists such as the sports sociologist Harry Edwards, who tried to organize a black boycott of the 1968 Olympics. The medal-winning track stars TOMMIE SMITH and John Carlos gave clenched-fist salutes during the playing of the National Anthem at those Games and were promptly sent home.

In 1970, with public opinion strongly against the Vietnam War and aided by growing black political power in several southern state governments, Ali was given a license to fight in Georgia. He returned to the ring on 26 October and defeated Jerry Quarry in three rounds. Although he was still a brilliant fighter, the long layoff had eroded his skills to some degree. He took far more punishment in the ring when he

returned than he had before his hiatus. This was to have dire consequences for him as he grew older.

Ali had his biggest, most competitive and commercially successful fights in the 1970s. On 8 March 1971 he lost to the undefeated Philadelphian Joe Frazier in a close fifteen-round decision at Madison Square Garden in New York City, in what was the richest, most publicized sporting event in American history. The fight was so brutal that both men were hospitalized afterward, Frazier for several days. It was Ali's first defeat. He won the North American Boxing Federation title, a significant but lesser honor than the world's championship, in July 1971. He lost again in March 1973 against the former marine Ken Norton in a twelve-round decision in which Ali's jaw was broken. Ali regained his North American Boxing Federation title from Norton in a highly disputed twelve-round decision six months later.

In January 1974 he fought Frazier again at Madison Square Garden. It was a nontitle match, as Frazier had lost his title to George Foreman. This time Ali won a close twelve-round decision. Ali finally regained the title in Kinshasa, Zaire, on 30 October 1974, when he knocked out Foreman in the eighth round of a fight where he was a decided underdog, most of the public thinking that Ali, at thirty-two, had passed his prime. Ali used a technique he called "Rope-a-Dope," where he leaned against the ropes and permitted Foreman to punch away at him; this approach, punctuated by Ali's punishing flurries at the end of each round, eventually fatigued the heavy-fisted younger champion. Ali was to use the technique in later fights, when he was too lazy to train, thus taking increasingly great punishment in the ring.

After regaining the title, Ali was lionized in the United States and enjoyed incredible popularity around the world. He became not only the most famous American Muslim but also the most famous Muslim anywhere and was the most photographed and publicized black man in history. He appeared in a film version of his life—*The Greatest* (1977)—based on his 1975 autobiography (edited by TONI MORRISON), joining JACKIE ROBINSON and JOE LOUIS as black athletes who starred in versions of their life stories on the screen. Ali also appeared on television programs and commercials. He even beat Superman in a special 1978 oversized issue of that comic. Part of this adulation and acceptance stemmed from the fact there was a general shift in attitude on the part of white sportswriters and the white public, but Ali himself tended to be less doctrinaire in his political and religious views as he grew older. And he was always gregarious and funny, something that lessened some of the white public's venom against him even when Ali was most demonized. Sometimes, his denigration of black opponents and his bragging seemed shrill and tasteless, as if he himself had grown weary of the act. He eventually embraced Wallace D. Muhammad's more ecumenical form of Islam when the NOI split into two factions following the death of Elijah Muhammad in 1975.

On 15 February 1978 an out-of-shape, uninspired Ali lost his title again to a young former marine and Olympic champion from St. Louis named Leon Spinks. Ali, however, managed to regain his title by beating Spinks on 15 September of the same year. In 1979, weary of the ring wars, his reflexes shot, his legs gone, and his appetite for competition slaked, Ali retired from the ring, only to do what so many great, aged champions do: come back. On 2 October 1980 Ali unsuccessfully challenged the heavyweight champion and his former sparring partner Larry Holmes, enduring a savage beating over ten rounds. His next fight was a ten-round decision loss to Trevor Berbick on 11 December 1981. After the Berbick fight, Ali retired for good, with a professional record of fifty-six wins, thirty-seven by knockout, and five losses. He was elected to the Boxing Hall of Fame in 1987.

Even before his retirement from the ring, Ali's speech was becoming slurred. After retirement he seemed to age, moving slowly and speaking with a thick tongue, his speech almost incomprehensible. He also suffered bouts of palsy. There is some debate as to whether Ali has Parkinson's disease or a Parkinson-like deterioration of his neurological system. Was this condition caused by the punishment he took in the ring in the later years of his

career? It can certainly be safely said that his illness was aggravated by his ring career. Today, although Ali leads a very active life, doing magic tricks, signing autographs, giving out copies of the Koran, traveling, and appearing at various public events, including, most famously, the lighting of the Olympic flame at the 1996 Games in Atlanta, he walks slowly and rarely talks.

Ali's private life was turbulent. He has married four times: to Sonji Roi (1964–1965), Belinda Boyd Ali (1967–1976), Veronica Porsche Ali (1977–1986), and his current wife, Lonnie Ali, whom he married in 1986. He also had numerous affairs when he was younger. He has nine children, including one adopted son. Interest in Ali has been rekindled in recent years thanks to the Academy Award–winning documentary *When We Were Kings* (1996) and *Ali*, a Hollywood feature film released in 2001. Books continue to be written about him, and he has probably been the subject of more photographic books than any athlete in the twentieth century.

It is impossible to overestimate Ali's importance not only as a gifted athlete who dominated his sport for nearly two decades and helped make sports a multimillion-dollar television enterprise but also as a religious and political presence in American popular culture. He clearly made white America more aware not only of Islam but also of the growing militancy of black people who were discontent with the status quo. Ali clearly symbolized in the 1960s and 1970s the fact that blacks were redefining their relationship with whites as they were redefining themselves. Ali came to represent racial pride, strong religious principles, and youthful exuberance.

FURTHER READING

Early, Gerald, ed. *The Muhammad Ali Reader* (1998).

Hauser, Thomas. *Muhammad Ali: His Life and Times* (1991).

Kram, Mark. *Ghosts of Manila: The Fateful Blood Feud between Muhammad Ali and Joe Frazier* (2001).

Mailer, Norman. *The Fight* (1975).

Oates, Joyce Carol. *On Boxing* (1987).

Olsen, Jack. *Black Is Best: The Riddle of Cassius Clay* (1965).

Plimpton, George. *Shadow Box* (1977).

Remnick, David. *King of the World: Muhammad Ali and the Rise of an American Hero* (1998).

Sheen, Wilfred. *Muhammad Ali* (1975).

Torres, Jose. *Sting like a Bee: The Muhammad Ali Story* (1971).

—GERALD EARLY

ALI, NOBLE DREW

(8 Jan. 1886–20 July 1929), religious leader and founder of the Moorish Science Temple, was born Timothy Drew, the son of former slaves, in North Carolina. Much of his life is shrouded in mystery that he and his followers helped to create. He was apparently orphaned and claimed at various times that he was raised by Cherokee Indians and that he was a descendant of Bilali Mohammed, a heroic African Muslim Sufi who had been enslaved in the United States. Without parents and with little formal education, Drew may have joined a traveling circus and been influenced by such extravaganzas as the Barnum and Bailey pageant "The Wizard Prince of Arabia." He further claimed that at the age of sixteen he was taken by a gypsy woman to North Africa and there studied with a Moroccan mystic in the Essene Schools. As a test of his wisdom and worthiness, he was placed inside an Egyptian pyramid and miraculously found his way out, proving to all that he was a prophet. Having passed this test, he relates that he embarked on a pilgrimage to Mecca, where the sultan Abdul ibn Said gave him the name "Ali" and the sheiks presented him with a charter to teach Islam in America to those people of African descent who had been robbed of their true identity.

While much of Ali's biography may be fabricated, the story contains clues to his actual development and the origin of the ideas he would eventually propagate. His tale of exotic world travels, in fact, may describe an intellectual journey; the books he read and the people he encountered supplied the content of his eclectic ideology. Since he was born in the South after Reconstruction, it is reasonable to assume that his lot was similar to that of the four million black people of the period: poor and uneducated, with little opportunity for improvement. Thus, at an early age, Ali came to believe that the way to change one's future is to change one's

Noble Drew Ali (center), in the cultural garb that he pioneered, stands before the Moorish Science Temple of America. Schomburg Center

past. In this way, Ali set the stage for future black cultural movements to reinterpret history as a means of racial empowerment.

The evidence suggests that Ali migrated north—as did nearly half the black population of the South between 1890 and 1930. He settled in Newark, New Jersey, where he worked as a railway expressman, attended Masonic lodges, worshipped with proselytes of a new Islamic sect called the Ahmadiyya Muslim Community, and joined the Theosophical Society, which included Mohammed Alexander Russell Webb, a prominent American convert to Islam and a proponent of Eastern religious thought. In 1913 Noble Drew Ali founded a congregation, the Canaanite

Temple, in Newark. He claimed that before starting this organization he had met with Theodore Roosevelt at the White House, informed the president of his plan to convert "the Negro," and assured him that black Muslims would be loyal American citizens. According to Ali, Roosevelt responded by saying "Getting Negroes to accept Islam will be about as easy as getting horses to wear pants" (Evanzz, 62–63). There is no independent record that such a meeting ever took place.

By the 1920s the essential elements of Ali's doctrine had begun to coalesce. From the Judeo-Christian tradition, he emphasized the importance of Ruth, a Moabite woman who converted to Judaism and became a maternal ancestor

of Jesus Christ. Morocco, Ali argued, was the ancient land of the Moabites, who, he believed, had olive skin tones like the blacks of America. Therefore, he proposed the term "Moorish American" as a replacement for "Negro," which did not connect a people with any particular land, language, religion, or history. "Asiatic Blackman," which he also coined, expanded the presumed ancestral homeland of black people from sub-Saharan Africa to include lands and peoples from the Middle East to India. From his limited knowledge of Islam, Ali found a god for the Moorish people in Allah.

The garb and ceremonies that Ali developed for his movement were influenced by the black Masonic tradition in America begun by PRINCE HALL in 1784. Modern observers who did not understand the historical context or cultural importance of these innovations often ridiculed the ceremonial dress, headwear, handshakes, passwords, and symbols that Ali used. Actually, such practices were quite common in both white and black lodges and secret societies. African Americans often took these organizations seriously, believing that such groups held the answers to questions about their true identity. Ali's experimentation with garb and culture prefigures the Black Power movement's adoption of African garb in the 1960s as a form of political expression.

In 1927 Ali codified his basic beliefs and published them as *The Holy Koran of the Moorish Science Temple*, also known as the *Circle Seven Koran*. While most of this text is derived from other wisdom literature, he introduced a number of practices, such as a diet that excluded meat and prohibitions on smoking and alcohol, that distinguished his movement from others of the time.

After several splits, power struggles, and doctrinal differences, Ali moved his headquarters to Chicago in 1925 and began referring to his growing organization as the Moorish Holy Temple of Science. In 1928 it was renamed the Moorish Science Temple of America (MSTA); by that time it had more than thirty thousand members with seventeen branches in fifteen states and operated many small businesses. The addition of "America" in the title indicated that members of this group were trying to forge a kind of patriotic black nationalism that incorporated their American identity. Those who joined the organization were issued identity cards that described the bearer's nationality as "Moorish American." The card also read, "I am a citizen of U.S.A." There are reports of MSTA members who brandished these cards at white people as if to say, "I know who I am."

Noble Drew Ali taught that black people in America had had an intact Moorish culture, complete with a flag and tribal appellations. He claimed that these cultural markers were taken away after the American Revolution in order to subordinate black slaves to their white masters. Allegedly, Ali confronted President Woodrow Wilson with this

information and demanded the return of the Moorish flag and the right of black people in America to add Bey and El to their surnames.

Ali's appointment of women to leadership positions within the organization was remarkably progressive. During the restructuring of the MSTA in 1928, M. Whitehead-El (also known as Dove-El) was made a "grand sheikess" over one congregation in Chicago and then elevated to the position of governor of several temples under her jurisdiction. Black women of this time were rarely given similar positions within black Christian denominations, and women within Islamic sects were traditionally excluded from such roles. Ali also supported changes that made the MSTA a more democratic organization and ultimately led to the local election of certain officers, many of whom were women. By the late 1920s the MSTA had become a political force in Chicago and played an important role in the election of OSCAR DE PRIEST to the U.S. House of Representatives in 1928, the first African American elected from a northern state.

Ali's demise and the subsequent decline of the MSTA coincided with the murder of Sheik Claude Greene. When Sheik Greene, who had publicly challenged Ali's management of the organization, was found murdered in his office at Unity Hall in March of 1929, Ali was immediately indicted as an accomplice to the crime—even though he and his wife, Pearl Jones Ali, were not in the city at the time of the assassination. Shortly after being released from police custody, Noble Drew Ali died at his home. While newspapers reported the cause of death as tuberculosis, members of the MSTA speculated that he had succumbed to injuries inflicted by the police or that MSTA members loyal to Greene had killed him.

Noble Drew Ali did not have any known heirs, but he left a legacy of African American interest in Islam that survived in the MSTA, in orthodox Sunni Muslim sects, and in other black nationalist organizations. He had a profound influence on W. D. Fard and ELIJAH MUHAMMAD, who were both members of the MSTA before they established the more militant Nation of Islam. Today, African Americans constitute one of the largest segments

of the Muslim population in the United States.

FURTHER READING

The MSTA maintains a private archive of its material at its headquarters in Chicago. Primary documents about Noble Drew Ali also can be found in the files on the MSTA at the headquarters of the Federal Bureau of Investigation (also called the "Noble Drew Ali" file).

Clegg, Claude Andrew, III. *An Original Man: The Life and Times of Elijah Muhammad* (1997).

Evanzz, Karl. *The Messenger: The Rise and Fall of Elijah Muhammad* (1999).

Lincoln, C. Eric. *The Black Muslims in America* (1961).

Marsh, Clifton. *From Black Muslims to Muslims* (1996).

Turner, Richard Brent. *Islam in the African-American Experience* (1997).

Wilson, Peter Lamborn. *Sacred Drift: Essays on the Margins of Islam* (1993).

—SHOLOMO B. LEVY

ALLEN, RICHARD

(14 Feb. 1760–26 Mar. 1831), American Methodist preacher and founder of the African Methodist Episcopal church, was born into slavery to parents who were the property of Benjamin Chew of Philadelphia. He and his parents and three additional children were sold in 1777 to Stokely Sturgis, who lived near Dover, Delaware. There he attended Methodist preaching events and experienced a spiritual awakening. Allen, his older brother, and a sister were retained by Sturgis, but his parents and younger siblings were sold. Through the ministry of Freeborn Garretson, a Methodist itinerant preacher, Sturgis was converted to Methodism and became convinced that slavery was wrong. Subsequently, Allen and his brother were permitted to work to purchase their freedom, which they did in 1780.

The next six years Allen worked as a wagon driver, woodcutter, and bricklayer while serving as a Methodist preacher to both blacks and whites in towns and rural areas in Maryland, Delaware, Pennsylvania, and New Jersey. By attending Methodist instructional meetings between 1777 and 1780, Allen became an exhorter and then a licentiate as early as 1780. After the American War of Independence, he traveled extensively in Delaware, Maryland, New Jersey, and Pennsylvania. In December 1784 he and Harry Hosier were the only two black preachers to attend the Christmas Conference in Baltimore, where the Methodist Episcopal Church was organized. He probably saw the Methodist leaders Thomas Coke, Bishop Francis Asbury, Richard Whatcoat, and Thomas Vasey at the conference. During 1785 he traveled the Baltimore circuit with Whatcoat.

At one point Asbury, the leader of American Methodism, invited Allen to become his traveling companion, an offer Allen accepted. In 1786 he preached to interracial groups of Methodists in Radnor, Pennsylvania, and at St. George's Church, Philadelphia. Assigned to preach at predawn meetings, Allen often preached four or five times a day and organized evening prayer groups. Unpaid by the church, he supported himself and later his family as a shoemaker. He married Flora (maiden name unknown) in 1791 and, after his first wife's death, was married a second time, in 1805, to Sarah (maiden name unknown). Allen and his second wife had six children.

In February 1786, while he was in Philadelphia, Allen organized a prayer-meeting society of forty-two members. His concern was to find and instruct "his African brethren," few of whom attended public worship. Noting the need for a place of worship for African Americans, he and his colleagues ABSALOM JONES, William White, and Dorus Ginnings found their efforts to meet this need opposed by the leadership of St. George's Church. In November 1787 black members of St. George's Church were pulled away from prayer and asked to leave, so Allen and Jones and their associates withdrew. Renting an unused store, Allen and Jones, with the help of Benjamin Rush and Robert Ralston, raised funds for a new building, which in 1794 became the St. Thomas African Episcopal Church of Philadelphia, the first independent black church in North America.

Allen, who remained a Methodist, purchased an abandoned blacksmith shop, moved it to Sixth Street near Lombard, and had it renovated. On 29 June 1794 Bishop Asbury dedicated the building as a church. For years Allen and

his congregation thought the property, called Bethel Church, was theirs, only to be informed by successive elders at St. George's that Bethel Church was within their charge. In 1816, however, the Pennsylvania Supreme Court confirmed the independent existence of Bethel, and official contact between the two churches ceased.

Aware of friction between black and white Methodists in other places, Allen sent invitations to African churches to form an ecclesiastical organization. On 9 April 1816 sixty delegates from five black congregations met at Bethel Church and agreed to confederate. The result was the formation of the African Methodist Episcopal (AME) Church. Allen, who had been ordained deacon by Bishop Asbury in 1799, was ordained elder on 10 April 1816 and the next day was consecrated as bishop. The first *Discipline* was published in 1817, and the new organization's first General Conference was held in Philadelphia on 9 July 1820, with Bishop Allen presiding. For Allen, the Methodist emphasis on the simplicity of the Gospel, expressed through discipline and community, pointed the way to freedom from sin and physical slavery as well. His life and career, and the founding of Bethel Church, embodied this development and confirmed his role as a leader in the forefront of the black church movement.

Early in 1797 Allen, Jones, and JAMES FORTEN SR. led black Philadelphians to petition the national government for the first time to revoke the Fugitive Slave Act of 1793 and to end slavery. In 1814, when it was feared that Philadelphia would be attacked by the British, Allen, Jones, and Forten raised the Black Legion of 2,500 men. Although Allen did not initially oppose voluntary emigration of blacks, as promoted by the American Colonization Society (formed in 1817), he came to see that large-scale emigration of free blacks would result in the abandonment of their brethren to slavery. In *Freedom's Journal* (2 Nov. 1827), Allen declared colonization a mistake. In 1830 he presided over the first meeting of the National Negro Convention Movement, which provided a structure for black abolitionism and organized the American Society of Free Persons of Color.

Allen led and participated in the formation of many organizations for

the betterment of his people. The Free African Society established 12 April 1787 was the first black institution with the characteristics of a benevolent and reform organization. In 1795 a day school was operational in Bethel Church, and on 26 October 1796 the founding of a First Day school, or Sunday school, and a night school was reported. In 1804 Allen led in the creation of the Society for Free People of Color for Promoting the Instruction and School Education of Children of African Descent. From 1818 to 1820 he served as book steward of the Book Concern of the AME church. The creation of the Free Produce Society of Philadelphia, on 20 December 1830, was also his work. He chaired the first National Negro Convention from 20 to 24 September 1830, which was held at Bethel Church. In 1831 the address to the First Annual Convention of the People of Colour was signed by the Reverend Allen, in his role as president and senior bishop of the AME Church. In 1794 Allen and Jones had been cited by the mayor of Philadelphia for their services to the sick and dying during the yellow fever epidemic of 1793. Allen died in Philadelphia, but his contributions to religion, education, and culture live on in such institutions as the Allen Temple, Cincinnati, Ohio; Allen University, Columbia, South Carolina; and the Richard Allen Center for Culture and Art, opposite Lincoln Center, New York City.

FURTHER READING

Allen, Richard. *The Life, Experience and Gospel Labors of the Rt. Rev. Richard Allen* (1960).

George, Carol V. R. *Segregated Sabbaths: Richard Allen and the Emergence of Independent Black Churches 1760–1840* (1973).
Nash, Gary B. *Forging Freedom: The Formation of Philadelphia's Black Community, 1720–1840* (1988).
Raboteau, Albert J. "Richard Allen and the African Church Movement" in *Black Leaders of the Nineteenth Century* (1988).
Wesley, Charles H. *Richard Allen, Apostle of Freedom* (1935).

—FREDERICK V. MILLS

AMOS, HAROLD

(7 Sept. 1918–26 Feb. 2003), scientist and educator, was born in Pennsauken,

New Jersey, the second of nine children, to Howard R. Amos Sr., a Philadelphia postman, and Iola Johnson, who had been adopted by and worked for a prominent Philadelphia Quaker family who schooled her with their own children at home. This family remained lifelong friends of Iola and kept the young Amos family well supplied with books, including a biography of Louis Pasteur, which piqued Harold's interest in science the fourth grade. Both Howard and Iola expected their children to be serious about their education and to excel academically. Harold, along with his siblings, took piano lessons and remained a competent amateur pianist. He also gained a reputation as an excellent tennis player.

Harold received his early education in a segregated school in Pennsauken, then graduated first in his class from Camden High School, in New Jersey. He later recalled that his love of teaching was awakened by the "wonderful teachers" that he had from first through twelfth grade. After graduation in 1936, Harold attended Springfield College in Springfield, Massachusetts, on a full academic scholarship at a time when few such scholarships were offered to African Americans. Amos graduated summa cum laude in 1941, with a major in biology and a minor in chemistry. The following year he worked as a graduate assistant in the biology department at Springfield College, until he was drafted into the U.S. Army, where he served in the Quartermaster Corps as a warrant officer, personnel. He spent close to two years in England before the invasion of France and then served on the continent until he was discharged in February 1946.

In the fall of 1946 Amos enrolled in the biological sciences graduate program at Harvard Medical School (Division of Medical Sciences), earning an MA in 1947 and a PhD in Bacteriology and Immunology in 1952, becoming the first African American to earn a PhD from the division. After spending a year as a Fulbright Fellow at the renowned Pasteur Institute in Paris, where he worked with molecular biologist Georges Cohen, Amos returned to Harvard Medical School. With the exception of three subsequent sabbatical periods in France, he remained at Harvard for close to fifty years, rising through the ranks

as a faculty member in the Department of Bacteriology and Immunology (now Microbiology and Molecular Genetics). Amos was made a full professor in 1969, named the Maude and Lillian Presley Professor of Microbiology and Molecular Genetics in 1975, and became professor emeritus in 1988. As chair of his department from 1968 to 1971 and again from 1975 to 1978, Amos was the first African American to head a department at Harvard Medical School. He was known particularly for his interest in and encouragement of students and young faculty.

In his role as chairman of the Division of Medical Sciences at Harvard Medical School from 1971 to 1975 and from 1978 to 1988, Amos provided creative, forward-looking leadership with fairness and diplomacy. The door to his office was almost always open, and he welcomed drop-in visitors. For decades of students and faculty, Amos personified the Division of Medical Sciences. He was an effective, inspiring, and inexhaustible supporter of all students, especially minorities, in science and medicine, and served, often in leadership positions, on numerous boards and advisory committees dedicated to these interests. Among others, Amos sat on the board of directors of the Josiah Macy Jr. Foundation, the Minority Medical Faculty Development Program Advisory Committee of the Robert Wood Johnson Foundation, the National Cancer Advisory Board, the President's Cancer Panel, and the Massachusetts Division of the American Cancer Society. As part of his interest in expanding the participation of minorities in research, he was an early advocate of the National Institute of Health's programs for minority college students.

Early in his career Amos intended to pursue research as an *E. coli* microbiologist, but, upon realizing that it was a field already crowded with competent senior scientists, he decided to study animal viruses and animal cells in culture. He was particularly interested in cells that could become malignant when infected with animal viruses and in sugar metabolism in cells. The body of scientific work that Amos carried out was eclectic in its scope and in the questions he asked, but it can be characterized as uncovering many facets

of metabolism and of understanding how cells function and influence organisms. Amos pioneered approaches to studying how proteins and RNA in cells are affected by nutrients, including glucose, and hormones, such as insulin, from outside the cell.

Amos used cells in culture to understand how molecules get into cells and how entry is regulated during cell starvation or in plentiful conditions. He was particularly interested in how these influences controlled metabolism of RNA, work he did at an early time in the history of RNA biology. His work provided valuable information to other investigators, who studied the normal and abnormal control of cell division and how this could provide insights into understanding cancer. Major laboratories around the world were influenced by the careful and dependable work that he published. Between 1953 and the mid-1980s he was an author on over seventy scientific papers.

Amos was legendary for the continual contributions that he made to the work of his colleagues, his own students, and to untold numbers of other students with whom he talked and worked. He had a prodigious memory and an unusually creative approach, and he always asked insightful questions and offered clear suggestions to a myriad of other scientists who were fortunate enough to cross his path. In this way he created an aura of old-fashioned intellectualism in its best sense, and he contributed, behind the scenes, to literally thousands of scientific papers by other authors who directly benefited from his input. By reaching such a broad group of scientists—in terms of their levels of training or profession, their institutions, and the types of biological science they pursued—Amos helped usher in modern biology and modern biologists.

Amos described teaching as one of his primary responsibilities, and he was always accessible, quick to offer words of praise and encouragement, advice, and support. Even during his graduate school days, Amos was praised for his devotion to and competence as both a teacher and a mentor. He followed his students' careers and personal lives with enthusiasm, regularly communicating with countless medical and graduate students, many of whom held important positions in a broad range of fields, long after they had graduated. He had an unusual ability to capture people's strengths and to help develop them.

Amos never married but had a large circle of devoted friends, drawn from all walks of life and representing many phases and interests of his own life. He was well known as an enthusiastic Francophile, enjoyed using his fluent French, and appreciated French literature, music, and cuisine. Amos was a gracious and attentive host, organizing dinners at interesting restaurants or at his farm near Kezar Falls, Maine, to which he invited people whom he thought would enjoy meeting each other.

Amos was the recipient of numerous awards, including several honorary doctoral degrees, the Centennial Medal of the Harvard Graduate School of Arts and Sciences (2000), the first Charles Drew World Medical Prize from Howard University (1989), and the National Academy of Sciences' highest honor, the Public Welfare Medal (1995). He was named a Fellow of the American Academy of Arts and Sciences (1974), and elected to the American Association for the Advancement of Science (1991) and the Institute of Medicine of the National Academy of Sciences (1991). A modest man, few of his colleagues were aware of the full range of honors he had received.

Upon the occasion of his retirement from Harvard Medical School at the age of seventy, he noted that he "had to get back to work to try to do something useful with these few remaining years" (letter, October 1989). He accepted the position as the first national director of the Minority Medical Faculty Development Program (MMFDP) of the Robert Wood Johnson Foundation, serving until 1994. He developed a reputation for keeping in contact with and encouraging the MMFDP Fellows and their family members long after their tenure in the program, and for seeking alternative positions for applicants who were not awarded fellowships. Amos wrote to a friend less than a year before his death that he was "still working full-time in the lab and writing two manuscripts" on glycerol metabolism in mammalian cells (letter, March 2002). Amos died

in Boston on 26 February 2003, shortly after suffering a stroke.

Harold Amos broke many barriers during his lifetime, in the scientific insights he directly and indirectly made possible, in his teaching and mentoring, and in his administrative contributions. Wherever he served, he was chosen because of his superior credentials. Amos's personable and accessible style in all aspects of his life and work succeeded in blending highly competitive academic work with the highest level of cultural appreciation and enjoyment, all with a profound degree of attention to collegiality and friendship.

FURTHER READING

Amos's 1972–2003 papers are housed at the Countway Library of Medicine, Harvard Depository of Rare Books.

Beecher, H. K. *Medicine at Harvard: The First Three Hundred Years* (1977).

Obituaries: *Boston Globe*, 4 Mar. 2003; *Harvard University Gazette*, 6 Mar. 2003.
—THOMAS O. FOX
—JOCELYN SPRAGG

ANDERSON, MARIAN
(17 Feb. 1897–8 Apr. 1993), contralto, was born in Philadelphia, Pennsylvania, the daughter of John Berkeley Anderson, a refrigerator room employee at the Reading Terminal Market, an ice and coal dealer, and a barber, and Anne (also seen as "Annie" and "Anna," maiden name unknown), a former schoolteacher. John Anderson's various jobs provided only a meager income, and after his death, before Marian was a teenager, her mother's income as a laundress and laborer at Wanamaker Department Store was even less. Still, as Anderson later recalled, neither she nor her two younger sisters thought of themselves as poor. When Marian was about eight, her father purchased a piano from his brother; she proceeded to teach herself how to play it and became good enough to accompany herself. Also as a youngster, having seen a violin in a pawnshop window, she became determined to purchase it and earned the requisite four dollars by scrubbing her neighbors' steps. When

she attempted to teach herself this instrument as well, she discovered that she had little aptitude for it.

Anderson joined the children's choir of Union Baptist Church at age six. Noticing her beautiful voice and her ability to sing all the parts, the choir director selected her to sing a duet for Sunday school and later at the regular morning service; this was her first public appearance. Later she joined the senior choir and her high school chorus, where occasionally she was given a solo.

While she was still in high school, Anderson attempted to enroll at a local music school but was rejected with the curt statement, "We don't take Colored." She applied and was accepted to the Yale University School of Music, but a lack of finances prevented her from enrolling. Although she was not the product of a conservatory, Anderson was vocally prepared by Mary Saunders Patterson, Agnes Reifsnyder, Giuseppe Boghetti, and Frank La Forge. Over the years she was coached by Michael Raucheisen and Raimond von zur Mühlen, and she also worked briefly (in London) with Amanda Aldridge, daughter of the famous black Shakespearean actor IRA ALDRIDGE. Boghetti, however, had the greatest pedagogical influence.

Anderson's accompanists (with whom she enjoyed excellent relationships) were the African Americans Marie Holland and William "Billy" King (who, for a period, doubled as her agent), the Finnish pianist Kosti Vehanen, and the German pianist Franz Rupp. Between 1932 and 1935 she was represented by the Arthur Judson Agency and from 1935 through the remainder of her professional life by the great impresario Sol Hurok.

One of the happiest days of Anderson's life was when she called Wanamaker to notify her mother's supervisor that Anne Anderson would not be returning to work. On another very happy occasion, in the late 1920s, she was able to assist in purchasing a little house for her mother in Philadelphia. Her sister Alyce shared the house; her other sister, Ethel, lived next door with her son James DePreist, who became a distinguished conductor.

For many, including critics, an accurate description of Anderson's singing voice presented challenges.

Marian Anderson at the Lincoln Memorial, where she sang to an audience of 75,000 on Easter, 1939, after being barred from Constitution Hall because she was black. © CORBIS

Because it was nontraditional, many simply resorted to the narrowly descriptive "Negroid sound." Others, however, tried to be more precise. Rosalyn Story, for example, has described Anderson's voice as "earthy darkness at the bottom... clarinet-like purity in the middle, and... piercing vibrancy at the top. Her range was expansive—from a full-bodied D in the bass clef to a brilliant high C" (Story, 38). Kosti Vehanen, recalling the first time he heard Anderson's "mysterious" voice, wrote, "It was as though the room had begun to vibrate, as though the sound came from under the earth.... The sound I heard swelled to majestic power, the flower opened its petals to full brilliance; and I was enthralled by one of nature's rare wonders" (Vehanen, 22). Reacting to his first encounter with Anderson's voice, Sol Hurok wrote, "Chills danced up my spine.... I was shaken to my very shoes" (Story, 47).

In 1921 Anderson, who was by then a well-known singer at church-related events, won the National Association of Negro Musicians competition. Believing that she was ready for greater public exposure, she made her Town Hall (New York City) debut in 1924. Disappointed by the poor attendance and by her own performance, she considered giving up her aspirations for a professional career. The following year, however, she bested three hundred other singers to win the National Music League competition, earning a solo appearance with the New York Philharmonic at Lewisohn Stadium.

In 1926, with financial assistance from the Julius Rosenwald Fund, Anderson departed for Europe for further musical study. After returning to the United States, she gave her first concert at New York City's Carnegie Hall in 1930. That same year she gave her first European concert, in Berlin, and toured Scandinavia. In 1931 alone she gave twenty-six concerts in fifteen states. Between 1933 and 1935 she toured Europe; one of her appearances was at the Mozarteum in Salzburg, where the renowned conductor Arturo Toscanini uttered the memorable line "Yours is a voice such as one hears once in a hundred years" (Anderson, 158). Another exciting experience took place in the home of the noted composer Jean Sibelius in Finland. After hearing Anderson sing, he uttered, "My roof is too low for you" and then canceled the previously ordered coffee and requested champagne. Sibelius also honored Anderson by dedicating his composition *Solitude* to her.

Anderson's second Town Hall concert, arranged by Hurok and performed on 30 December 1935, was a huge success. A one-month tour of the Soviet Union was planned for the following year but ended up lasting three months. Anderson was a box-office sensation as well in Europe, Africa, and South America. Her seventy U.S. concerts in 1938 still stand as the longest and most extensive tour for a singer in concert history. Between November 1939 and June 1940 she appeared in more than seventy cities, giving ninety-two concerts. Her native Philadelphia presented her with the Bok Award in 1941, accompanied by ten thousand dollars. She used the funds to establish the Marian Anderson Award, which sponsors "young talented men and women in pursuit of their musical and educational goals."

During 1943 Anderson made her eighth transcontinental tour and married the architect Orpheus H. Fisher of Wilmington, Delaware. The marriage was childless. In 1944 she appeared at the Hollywood Bowl, where she broke a ten-year attendance record. In 1946, six hundred editors in the United States and Canada, polled by *Musical America*, named Anderson radio's foremost woman singer for the sixth consecutive year. Anderson completed a South American tour in 1951 and made her television debut on the *Ed Sullivan Show* the following year. Her first tour of Japan was completed in 1953, the same year that she also toured the Caribbean, Central America, Israel, Morocco, Tunisia, France, and Spain.

Anderson sang the national anthem at the inauguration of President Dwight D. Eisenhower in 1957, and between 14 September and 2 December of that year she traveled thirty-nine thousand miles in Asia, performing twenty-four concerts under the auspices of the American National Theater and Academy and the U.S. State Department. Accompanying Anderson was the journalist Edward R. Murrow, who filmed the trip for his *See It Now* television series. The program, which aired on 30 December, was released by RCA Records under the title *The Lady from Philadelphia*. In 1958 Anderson served as a member of the U.S. delegation to the General Assembly of the United Nations. Three years later she sang the national anthem at the inauguration of President John F. Kennedy, appeared in the new State Department auditorium, and gave another concert tour of Europe. Her first tour of Australia was a highlight of 1962.

In early 1964 Hurok announced Marian Anderson's Farewell Tour, beginning at Constitution Hall on 24 October 1964 and ending on Easter Sunday 1965 at Carnegie Hall. The momentousness of the event was reflected in Hurok's publicity: "In any century only a handful of extraordinary men and women are known to countless millions around the globe as great artists and great persons.... In our time there is Marian Anderson." After the tour she made several appearances as narrator of Aaron Copland's *Lincoln Portrait*, often with her nephew James DePreist at the podium.

Although in her own lifetime Anderson was described as one of the world's greatest living contraltos, her career nonetheless was hindered by the limitations placed on it because of racial prejudice. Two events, in particular, that illustrate the pervasiveness of white exclusiveness and African American exclusion—even when it came to someone of Anderson's renown—serve as historical markers not only of her vocal contributions but also of the magnificence of her bearing, which in both instances turned two potential negatives into resounding positives.

In 1938, following Anderson's numerous international and national successes, Hurok believed that it was time for her to appear in the nation's capital at a major hall. She previously had appeared in Washington, D.C., at churches, schools, and civic organization meetings and at Howard University, but she had not performed at the district's premiere auditorium, Constitution Hall. At that time, when negotiations began for a Marian Anderson concert to be given in 1939 at the hall owned by the Daughters of the American Revolution, a clause appeared in all contracts that restricted the hall to "a concert by white artists only, and for no other purpose." Thus, in February 1939 the American who had represented her country with honor across the globe was denied the right to sing at Constitution Hall simply because she was not white.

A great furor ensued, and thanks to the efforts of First Lady Eleanor Roosevelt and Secretary of the Interior Harold Ickes, the great contralto appeared the following Easter Sunday (9 April 1939) on the steps of the Lincoln Memorial before an appreciative audience of seventy-five thousand. She began the concert by singing "America" and then proceeded to sing an Italian aria, Franz Schubert's "Ave Maria," and three Negro spirituals—"Gospel Train," "Trampin'," and "My Soul Is Anchored in the Lord." Notably, she also sang "Nobody Knows the Trouble I've Seen." Commemorating the 1939 Lincoln Memorial concert is a mural at the Interior Department; it was formally presented in 1943, the year that Anderson made her first appearance in Constitution Hall, by invitation of the Daughters of the American Revolution and benefiting United China Relief.

The second history-making event came on 7 January 1955, when Anderson made her debut at the Metropolitan Opera House in New York, becoming the first black American to appear there. Opera had always interested Anderson, who tells the story in her autobiography of a visit with the noted African American baritone HARRY BURLEIGH, during which she was introduced to and sang for an Italian gentleman. When she climbed the scale to high C, the man said to Burleigh, "Why sure she can do Aida," a traditionally black role. On her first trip to England, Anderson had visited a teacher who suggested that Anderson study with her, guaranteeing that she would have her singing Aida within six months. "But I was not interested in singing Aida," Anderson wrote. "I knew perfectly well that I was a contralto, not a soprano. Why Aida?"

The international press announced Anderson's pending debut at the Met in October 1954. As the educator and composer Wallace Cheatham later noted, the occasion called for the most excellent pioneer, "an artist with impeccable international credentials, someone highly respected and admired by all segments of the music community" (Cheatham, 6). At the time there was only one such person, Marian Anderson. About Anderson's debut, as Ulrica in Giuseppe Verdi's *Un Ballo in Maschera, Time* magazine (17 Jan. 1955) reported that there were eight curtain calls. "She acted with the dignity and reserve that she has always presented to the public.... Her unique voice—black velvet that can be at once soft and dramatic, menacing and mourning—stirring the heart as always."

Anderson was a recipient of the Spingarn Medal (from the NAACP), the Handel Medallion (from New York City), the Page One Award (from the Philadelphia Newspaper Guild), and the Brotherhood Award (from the National Conference of Christians and Jews). She was awarded twenty-four honorary doctorates and was cited by the governments of France, Finland, Japan, Liberia, Haiti, Sweden, and the Philippines. She was a member of the National Council on the Arts and a recipient of the National Medal of Arts; in 1978 she was among the first five performers to receive the Kennedy Center Honors for lifetime achievement.

Several tributes were held in the last years of Anderson's life. In February 1977 the musical world turned out to recognize Anderson's seventy-fifth (actually her eightieth) birthday at Carnegie Hall. On 13 August 1989 a gala celebration concert took place in Danbury, Connecticut, to benefit the Marian Anderson Award. The concert featured the recitalist and Metropolitan Opera star JESSYE NORMAN, the violinist Isaac Stern, and the maestro Julius Rudel, conducting the Ives Symphony Orchestra. Because Anderson's residence, "Marianna," was just two miles from the Charles Ives Center, where the concert was held, the ninety-two-year-old grand "lady

ANGELOU, MAYA

from Philadelphia" was in attendance. The Public Broadcasting Service (PBS) television station affiliate WETA prepared a one-hour documentary, *Marian Anderson*, which aired nationally on PBS on 8 May 1991. Anderson died two years later in Portland, Oregon, where she had moved to live with her nephew, her only living relative.

Many actions were taken posthumously to keep Anderson's memory alive and to memorialize her many accomplishments. The 750-seat theater in the Aaron Davis Arts Complex at City College of New York was named in her honor on 3 February 1994. The University of Pennsylvania, as the recipient of her papers and memorabilia, created the Marian Anderson Music Study Center at the Van Pelt–Dietrich Library. Of course, her greatest legacy is the singers who followed her. As the concert and opera soprano LEONTYNE PRICE, one of the many beneficiaries of Anderson's efforts, said after her death, "Her example of professionalism, uncompromising standards, overcoming obstacles, persistence, resiliency and undaunted spirit inspired me to believe that I could achieve goals that otherwise would have been unthought of" (*New York Times*, 9 Apr. 1993).

FURTHER READING

Anderson's papers and memorabilia are housed at the Van Pelt–Dietrich Library at the University of Pennsylvania.

Anderson, Marian. *My Lord, What a Morning* (1956).

Bogle, Donald. *Brown Sugar: Eighty Years of America's Black Female Superstars* (1980).
Cheatham, Wallace. "Black Male Singers at the Metropolitan Opera," *Black Perspective in Music* 16, no. 1 (Spring 1988): 3–19.
Sims, Janet. *Marian Anderson: An Annotated Bibliography and Discography* (1981).
Southern, Eileen, ed. *Biographical Dictionary of Afro-American and African Musicians* (1982).
———. *The Music of Black Americans: A History*. 2nd ed. (1983).
Story, Rosalyn. *And So I Sing* (1990).
Vehanen, Kosti. *Marian Anderson: A Portrait* (1941; repr. 1970).

Obituaries: *New York Times* and *Washington Post*, 9 Apr. 1993.
—ANTOINETTE HANDY

 ANGELOU, MAYA
(4 Apr. 1928–), writer, poet, and performer, was born Marguerite Annie Johnson in St. Louis, Missouri, the second of two children of Bailey Johnson, a doorman and a naval dietician, and Vivian Baxter Johnson, a card dealer who later became a registered nurse. Her parents called her "Rita," but her brother, Bailey, who was only a year older, called her "My Sister," which was eventually contracted to "Maya." When Maya was three years old, she and Bailey were sent to Stamps, Arkansas, to live with their paternal grandmother, Annie Henderson, whom Maya often referred to as "Mother."

Mrs. Henderson was a strong, independent black woman who owned a country store, in which Maya lived and worked. Maya was a bright student and an avid reader; she absorbed the contradictory messages of love emanating from the Christian Methodist Episcopal Church and of hatred, revealed in the pervasive mistreatment of blacks by their white neighbors. In 1935 Maya returned to live with her mother in Chicago, until it was discovered that the eight-year-old had been raped by her mother's lover, Mr. Freeman, in whose care she was often left. Freeman was murdered, probably by Maya's uncles, after she testified in court. The trauma of the attack, the trial, and the misplaced guilt she felt for the death of the man who had abused her trust caused Maya to withdraw into an almost complete silence. She was sent back to Arkansas, where for the next four years she rarely spoke. By reading literature and poetry to her, Mrs. Bertha Flowers, a local, sophisticated black woman with impressive elocution, helped renew a love of language in a girl many believed to be mute.

At the age of thirteen Maya was at the top of her class when she and Bailey went again to live with their mother, who had by then moved to San Francisco. She attended George Washington High School and studied dance and drama at the California Labor School. She spent a summer with her father, but violent quarrels with his girlfriend compelled Maya to run away, preferring to live in an abandoned van for a month. In 1944 she temporarily dropped out of

school and got a job as a streetcar conductor (becoming the first black woman in San Francisco to hold that position). As an adolescent she was almost six feet tall, insecure, desperate for affection, and confused about her sexuality. In this emotional state, she began an intimate relationship with a male acquaintance and became pregnant at the age of sixteen. Yet with indomitable determination she returned to school and graduated one month before giving birth to her only child, Clyde.

Angelou's journey to adulthood became the basis of her first and most celebrated autobiographical novel, *I Know Why the Caged Bird Sings* (1970), which was nominated for a National Book Award and named from a line in the poem "Sympathy," by PAUL LAURENCE DUNBAR. This book was soon followed by *Gather Together in My Name* (1974), which continues her odyssey. Angelou takes the reader through her postwar years as a single mother working as a cook at a Creole café in San Diego. She attempted to join the army and tried to retreat to Arkansas, the place of past comfort, only to learn that as an adult her lack of racial deference endangered her and those she loved. In 1947 her early efforts to become an entertainer led her into a world of drug use. During this period she became a madam for two lesbian demimondaines, and an abusive relationship with a man briefly plunged her into a life of prostitution. The narrative ends at the close of the 1940s with Angelou pulling her life together, as the religiously inspired title implies.

In 1950 Angelou began a three-year marriage to a former Greek sailor, Tosh Angelos ("Angelou" is a variant of his name), recounted in her third autobiographical volume, *Singin' and Swingin' and Gettin' Merry Like Christmas* (1976). Her singing and dancing career began to show promise when she became a calypso performer at the Purple Onion in San Francisco. This led to bookings in Chicago and ultimately at the Village Vanguard in New York. She moved to New York to study dance with Pearl Primus and in 1954 landed a role in the George Gershwin opera *Porgy and Bess*, which toured Europe until 1955. When she returned to the United States, her career was progressing, but her failed marriage

26

and frequent separations from her son evoked troubling memories of her own childhood. The book ends on a note of reconciliation and redemption as she sets out with her son on a Hawaiian cruise.

A fourth volume, *The Heart of a Woman* (1981), begins shortly after her return from Europe, when an old friend brings BILLIE HOLIDAY to Angelou's small San Francisco apartment for lunch. In this passage Angelou's skills as a writer are particularly evident. She recalls events with astonishing detail and relates them in an authentic and compelling style as her prose shifts between Standard English and the black vernacular she summons when its effect is most appropriate. Her ear for the particular speech patterns of her characters is evident in her re-creation of Billie Holiday's sassy and salty manner. These lively narrative qualities are sustained as the scene shifts to Brooklyn, where she moved in 1957 to appear in the off-Broadway play *Calypso Heatwave*. While in New York she joined the Harlem Writers Guild, whose members included JAMES BALDWIN, PAULE MARSHALL, and John Henrick Clarke. This intellectual environment nurtured her literary interests and shaped her political activism. In 1960 she played a leading role in staging *Freedom Cabaret*, a revue she wrote to raise money to help MARTIN LUTHER KING JR. and the civil rights movement.

A few months later BAYARD RUSTIN nominated her to become the northern coordinator for the Southern Christian Leadership Conference. She held this position for a few months, but in May 1961 she was offered the role of White Queen in Jean Genet's Obie Award–winning play *The Blacks*, which had a cast that included JAMES EARL JONES and Cicely Tyson. However, soon after the production began, she left because of a monetary dispute with the director. Angelou's common-law husband at the time, the South African freedom fighter Vusumzi Make, did not want his wife to work, insisting that "no wife of an African leader can go on the stage" (Angelou, *The Heart of a Woman*, 205). Angelou found out that Make could not support the family without her income shortly before their move to Cairo, Egypt, in late 1961, when she discovered that they were being evicted from their Manhattan apartment.

In Cairo, Angelou became disillusioned by the chauvinism of black nationalists and defied her controlling, philandering husband by taking a job as the associate editor of the *Arab Observer*, an English-language newspaper. In 1963 she left Make and moved to Accra, Ghana, where she worked for the University of Ghana and became an editor of the *African Review* and a contributor to the *Ghanaian Times* and the Ghanaian Broadcasting Company. She arranged the itinerary for her friend MALCOLM X during his visit to Ghana, and she enjoyed a close relationship with the family of W. E. B. DU BOIS, who had expatriated from the United States to live in Ghana some years earlier. Angelou returned to the United States in 1966 to continue her career in the theater; however, James Baldwin urged her to pursue her writing. Angelou's final autobiographical volume, *All God's Children Need Traveling Shoes* (1986), recounts her sojourn in Africa and brings us to the verge of her literary stardom.

DAVID LEVERING LEWIS has argued that Angelou's work is prominent within a grand tradition of African American autobiography extending from the slave narratives of FREDERICK DOUGLASS and HARRIET JACOBS, through the early modern memoirs of BOOKER T. WASHINGTON and the somewhat fictionalized autobiography of ZORA NEALE HURSTON, to the contemporary *Autobiography of Malcolm X*. While she incorporates the elements of triumphalism that one typically finds in the slave narratives and some of the determined individualism of the Horatio Alger genre, Angelou mingles Brer Rabbit savvy with resilient love to produce books that reveal harsh realities about race and gender in American life.

Most of her literary acclaim focuses on her autobiographies but Angelou has also published nine volumes of poetry, including *Just Give Me a Cool Drink of Water 'forel Diiie* (1971), which was nominated for a Pulitzer Prize, and the noteworthy *And Still I Rise* (1978), which contains the very popular title poem and the often recited "Phenomenal Woman." In addition, she received a Tony Award nomination for her role in the Broadway play *Look Away* in 1973 and an Emmy Award nomination for her performance

in Alex Haley's *Roots* in 1977. She became the first woman and the only African American to read a poem at a presidential inauguration when President Bill Clinton invited her to read "On the Pulse of Morning" in 1993. Two years later she was one of the few women to speak at LOUIS FARRAKHAN's Million Man March, where—despite her own unhappy relationships—she affirmed her hope for the black family.

When her eight-year marriage to the British builder Paul Du Fue ended in divorce in 1981, Angelou moved to North Carolina, where she became the Reynolds Professor of American Studies at Wake Forest University. She has remained a prolific writer, performer, and speaker well into her seventies.

FURTHER READING

Angelou, Maya. *All God's Children Need Traveling Shoes* (1986).
———. *Gather Together in My Name* (1974).
———. *The Heart of a Woman* (1981).
———. *I Know Why the Caged Bird Sings* (1970).
———. *Singin' and Swingin' and Gettin' Merry Like Christmas* (1976).

Bloom, Harold, ed. *Modern Critical Views: Maya Angelou* (1999).
Lupton, Mary Jane. *Maya Angelou: A Critical Companion* (1998).

—SHOLOMO B. LEVY

ARMSTRONG, LIL

(3 Feb. 1898–27 Aug. 1971), jazz pianist, composer, and singer, was born Lillian Hardin in Memphis, Tennessee, the daughter of Dempsey Hardin, a strict, churchgoing woman who disapproved of blues music. Nothing is known of her father. At age six Lil began playing organ at home, and at eight she started studying piano. In 1914 she enrolled in the music school of Fisk University in Nashville, taking academic courses and studying piano and music theory. After earning her diploma, around 1917 she joined her mother in Chicago, where she found work demonstrating songs in Jones' Music Store. Prompted by her employer, in 1918 Hardin became house pianist for the clarinetist Lawrence Duhé's band at Bill Bottoms's Dreamland Ballroom, where she played with the cornetists "Sugar Johnny"

Smith, Freddie Keppard, and KING OLIVER; the trombonist Roy Palmer; and other New Orleans musicians. Because she was still a minor, her mother picked her up every night after work.

In January 1920 Hardin joined a second Oliver-led band, and in May 1921 she went to San Francisco with Oliver's Creole Jazz Band for a six-month job at the Pergola Dance Pavilion. Hardin then went back to Chicago and a job at the Dreamland, resuming her former position with Oliver in the summer of 1922. In late August, LOUIS ARMSTRONG joined Oliver's group as second cornetist. Shortly thereafter Armstrong and Hardin began courting. However, while working at the Dreamland, she had married a singer named Jimmie Johnson, whose infidelities soon proved grounds for divorce. Eager to help free Armstrong from his own ill-advised first marriage, Hardin arranged divorces for both of them in 1923, and they were married in February 1924. They had no children. In 1923 King Oliver's Creole Jazz Band recorded thirty-seven performances, on which the pianist was limited to a strictly subordinate role in the rhythm section.

Even before they were married, Lil had begun trying to make Louis more sophisticated in his manners and dress, as well as urging him to leave Oliver. Louis, however, remained adamantly loyal to Oliver until mid-1924, when the band broke up following a long midwestern tour. Months of Lil's prodding had taken their toll, and, finally convinced that he should seek better avenues to showcase his own talent and reap its reward, Louis gave Oliver notice. In September he was offered a featured position in Fletcher Henderson's orchestra at the Roseland Ballroom in New York. In October, Lil followed her husband east but soon returned to Chicago to lead her own band at the Dreamland. During this period, Louis Armstrong's reputation grew far beyond what it had been in Chicago, but by early November 1925 he was ready to leave New York, primarily because Lil wanted him to come home. By this time she was enjoying a successful run with her Dreamland Syncopators and encouraged the owners to pay a higher salary

than usual to bring in Louis as a featured attraction.

Between November 1925 and December 1927 Lil Armstrong appeared on all of the Louis Armstrong Hot Five and Hot Seven recordings, forty-four titles in all. She also led one Hot Five date under her own name (as Lil's Hot Shots) in May 1926 and participated, along with Louis, on sessions with Butterbeans and Susie, Alberta Hunter, and the Red Onion Jazz Babies. In July 1926 she also recorded with the New Orleans Bootblacks and the New Orleans Wanderers. In early 1929 she recorded with Johnny Dodds in both trio and sextet settings.

Although her command of the piano was marred by limited technique, swift, unswinging time, and a paucity of melodic ideas, Lil Armstrong was nevertheless a highly productive composer of jazz songs. It is difficult to ascertain exactly which songs she wrote independently of Louis Armstrong, but it can be assumed that she played an important role in transcribing and arranging certain melodic themes that he invented. Among the Hot Five and Hot Seven numbers for which she is given full or partial credit are "I'm Gonna Gitcha," "Droppin' Shucks," "King of the Zulus," "Jazz Lips," "Struttin' with Some Barbecue," "Hotter than That," and "Knee Drops." She also contributed "Gate Mouth," "Too Tight Blues," "I Can't Say," "Perdido Street Blues," "Papa Dip," and "Mixed Salad" to the 1926 Bootblacks and Wanderers sessions as well as "Pencil Papa," "Heah Me Talkin'," and "Goober Dance" to Dodds's 1929 dates. However, it must be said that her own contributions on piano, whether as soloist or accompanist, are invariably the least interesting elements of these recordings.

During the late 1920s Lil bought an eleven-room home in Chicago and real estate on Lake Michigan's Idlewild resort, properties she retained throughout her life. When Lil's job at the Dreamland ended in the spring of 1926, Louis joined Carroll Dickerson's orchestra at the Sunset Café while Lil worked in Hugh Swift's band and later toured with Freddie Keppard. During this time Lil also studied at the Chicago Musical College, and, after earning a degree in teaching, she studied at the New York College of Music,

where she received her postgraduate degree in 1929.

Louis, who had started philandering while he was in New York, was beginning to tire of Lil's constant jealousy and pressure for him to better himself commercially. He began a serious relationship with another woman, Alpha Smith, around 1928. After numerous arguments with her husband, who had at last become successful, Lil finally sued for legal separation in August 1931, retaining her properties and receiving a considerable cash allowance. She eventually granted him a divorce and also won a suit against him for the rights to the songs they had co-composed. Lil never remarried, and she kept all relevant Louis Armstrong memorabilia, including letters, photos, and his old cornet, until her death.

Through the mid-1930s Lil Armstrong led both all-female and all-male bands of varying sizes in the Midwest, sometimes under the billing of Mrs. Louis Armstrong and Her Orchestra. She also broadcast regularly and appeared as a soloist in the *Hot Chocolates* and *Shuffle Along* revues. From 1936 Lil Armstrong lived in New York and worked as a house pianist for Decca Records, between 1936 and 1940 leading small jazz groups with such featured sidemen as Joe Thomas, J. C. Higginbotham, Buster Bailey, and Chu Berry. She also provided the accompaniments for the singers Blue Lu Barker, Rosetta Howard, Alberta Hunter, Frankie "Half Pint" Jaxon, Peetie Wheatstraw, and others and participated in jazz dates under the leadership of Red Allen, Johnny Dodds, and Zutty Singleton. She emerges as a vivacious and entertaining singer on her own Decca recordings of 1936–1940. Among her compositions from this period are "My Hi-De-Ho Man," "Brown Gal," "Just for a Thrill," "Born to Swing," "Let's Get Happy Together," and "Everything's Wrong, Ain't Nothing Right." In late 1940 Armstrong returned to Chicago, where she worked throughout the next decade as a soloist in many local venues.

In early 1952 Armstrong went to Paris, where she recorded in a trio with SIDNEY BECHET and Zutty Singleton and also under her own name in 1953 and 1954. She worked primarily as a soloist in Paris but also spent some time in

London before returning in the late 1950s to Chicago. In December 1960 she recorded with Franz Jackson's band and in September 1961 led her own group for an album in the Riverside label's *Chicago: The Living Legends* series. In late October 1961 she participated in the telecast of *Chicago and All That Jazz*, an all-star jazz concert segment of NBC's *Dupont Show of the Week*. Little is known of Armstrong's activities after this point, but she probably continued appearing in clubs in Chicago and environs. Following Louis Armstrong's death in July 1971, a memorial concert was staged in his honor on 27 August at Chicago's Civic Center, and it was during her performance at this event that Lil Armstrong suffered a fatal coronary.

FURTHER READING

In 1960 or 1961 an oral interview with Lil Armstrong titled *Satchmo and Me* was released as Riverside RLP12–120.

Dahl, Linda. *Stormy Weather* (1984).

Giddins, Gary. *Satchmo* (1988).

Jones, Max, and John Chilton. *Louis: The Louis Armstrong Story 1900–1971* (1971; rev. ed., 1988).

Placksin, Sally. *American Women in Jazz* (1982).

Unterbrink, Mary. *Jazz Women at the Keyboard* (1983).

Obituary: *New York Times*, 28 Aug. 1971.

Discography:

Bruyninckx, Walter. *Swing Discography, 1920–1988* (12 vols., 1985–1989).

Rust, Brian. *Jazz Records, 1897–1942* (1982).
—JACK SOHMER

ARMSTRONG, LOUIS

(4 Aug. 1901–6 July 1971), jazz trumpeter and singer, known universally as "Satchmo" and later as "Pops," was born in New Orleans, Louisiana, the illegitimate son of William Armstrong, a boiler stoker in a turpentine plant, and Mary Est "Mayann" Albert, a laundress. Abandoned by his father shortly after birth, Armstrong was raised by his paternal grandmother, Josephine, until he was returned to his mother's care at age five. Mother and son moved from Jane Alley, in a violence-torn

slum, to an only slightly better area, Franklyn and Perdido streets, where nearby cheap cabarets gave the boy his first introduction to the new kind of music, jazz, that was developing in New Orleans. Although Armstrong claims to have heard the early jazz cornetist Buddy Bolden when he was about age five, this incident may be apocryphal. As a child, he worked odd jobs, sang in a vocal quartet, and around 1911 bought a used cornet with his savings. He dropped out of school and got into trouble; in 1913 he was placed in the New Orleans Colored Waifs' Home for Boys, where Peter Davis, the music instructor, gave Armstrong his first formal music instruction. He left the home in June 1914. Although he was remanded to the custody of his father, he soon went to live with his mother and younger sister, Beatrice, whom Armstrong affectionately called "Mama Lucy."

As a teenager, Armstrong played street parades, associated with the older musicians, and held various jobs, including delivering coal with a mule-drawn coal wagon. In his second autobiography, *My Life in New Orleans*, he relates the importance of these years in his development, particularly the influence of KING OLIVER:

At that time I did not know the other great musicians such as JELLY ROLL MORTON, Freddy Keppard,...and Eddy Atkins. All of them had left New Orleans long before the red-light district was closed by the Navy and the law [1917]. Of course I met most of them in later years, but Papa Joe Oliver, God bless him, was my man. I often did errands for Stella Oliver, his wife, and Joe would give me lessons for my pay. I could not have asked for anything I wanted more. It was my ambition to play as he did. I still think that if it had not been for Joe Oliver jazz would not be what it is today (99).

In 1918 Armstrong married Daisy Parker and began his life as a professional musician. Between November 1918 and August 1922 he played cornet at Tom Anderson's club as well as in the Tuxedo Brass Band, in Fate Marable's band on Mississippi River excursion paddle-wheel steamers, and incidentally in several New Orleans cabarets. His musical associates during these years were Oliver, Warren "Baby" Dodds, Johnny Dodds, Johnny St. Cyr,

Honore Dutrey, George "Pops" Foster, and Edward "Kid" Ory.

Armstrong's rise to prominence began with his move to Chicago in August 1922, when Oliver invited him to come to the Lincoln Garden's Cafe as second cornet in Oliver's Creole Jazz Band. This group defined jazz for the local Chicago musicians and stimulated the development of this music in profound ways. Armstrong's first recordings were made with Oliver in 1923 and 1924; "Riverside Blues," "Snake Rag," "Mabel's Dream," "Chattanooga Stomp," and "Dipper Mouth Blues" are some of the performances that preserve and display his early mature work.

In 1924 Armstrong divorced his first wife and that same year married the pianist in Oliver's band, Lillian Hardin (LIL ARMSTRONG). She encouraged him to accept an invitation to play with the Fletcher Henderson orchestra at the Roseland Ballroom in New York City. Armstrong's impact on this prominent name band was phenomenal. His solo style brought to the East a tonal power, creative virtuosity, and rhythmic drive that had not been a regular aspect of the Henderson band's performance practice. Armstrong's influence on Henderson, himself an arranger and pianist, and two of his fellow band members, in particular, the arranger and saxophonist Don Redman and the saxophone virtuoso Coleman Hawkins, was partially responsible for the development of a new jazz idiom or style—swing. During his fourteen months with Henderson, Armstrong participated in more than twenty recording sessions and left memorable solos on "One of These Days," "Copenhagen," and "Everybody Loves My Baby," on which he cut his first, brief, vocal chorus. While in New York, Armstrong also recorded with Clarence Williams's Blue Five, a small combo that included the already famous saxophonist SIDNEY BECHET, and with the star blues singers MA RAINEY and BESSIE SMITH. With Henderson, Armstrong played trumpet, but in these small-group sessions he returned to cornet. For another two years he continued to use both instruments but finally retired his cornet for the brighter, more-focused sound of the trumpet.

Despite his growing stature among the jazz community, Armstrong was still but a sideman when he returned to Chicago in 1925. He immediately became the star of his wife's band at the Dreamland Cafe and soon joined Erskine Tate's orchestra at the Vendome Theater. In November 1925 he made his first recordings as a leader with a pickup group of old associates he called the "Hot Five"—his wife, Lil, on piano; Kid Ory on trombone; Johnny Dodds on clarinet; and St. Cyr on banjo. These recordings of the Hot Five and the Hot Seven (with the addition of bass and drums) are towering monuments of traditional jazz. "Cornet Chop," "Gut Bucket Blues," "Heebie Jeebies," "Skid-Dat-De-Dat," "Big Butter and Egg Man," "Struttin' with Some Barbecue," "Hotter Than That," and several others are numbered among the classics of this style, have entered the standard repertory, and continue to be studied and performed regularly. In these recordings Armstrong established his eminence as a cornet and trumpet virtuoso and an unparalleled improviser, composer, and jazz vocalist. Melrose Brothers published notated transcriptions of some of his solos in 1927 immediately after the appearance of these recordings; these may be the first transcriptions from recorded performances ever published. The significance of this series of recordings is summarized by Gunther Schuller in his study *Early Jazz*:

The smooth rhythms of the earlier improvisations give way to stronger, contrasting, harder swinging rhythms. Double-time breaks abound. Melodic line and rhythm combine to produce more striking contours. This was, of course, the result not only of Armstrong's increasing technical skill, but also of his maturing musicality, which saw the jazz solo in terms not of a pop-tune more or less embellished, but of a chord progression generating a maximum of creative originality.... His later solos all but ignored the original tune and started with only the chord changes given (Schuller, 102–103).

Armstrong's association with Earl Hines in 1927 led to another series of pathbreaking recordings in 1928, most notably "West End Blues," with a reconstituted Hot Five, and "Weather Bird," a trumpet and piano duet. In "West End Blues," Armstrong not only achieves an unprecedented level of virtuosity but also displays the beginnings of motivic development in jazz solos. In "Weather Bird," Hines and Armstrong partake in a rapid exchange of antecedent-consequent improvised phrases that set a pattern for future jazz improvisers who "trade fours and twos."

In 1929 Armstrong moved with his band from Chicago to New York for an engagement at Connie's Inn in Harlem. The floor show used a score by FATS WALLER that became a Broadway success as *Hot Chocolates* and featured an onstage Armstrong trumpet solo on "Ain't Misbehavin'." He also pursued many other endeavors, going into the recording studio to front his own band with Jack Teagarden and playing and singing in Luis Russell's group, which also featured the Chicago banjoist and guitar player Eddie Condon. Armstrong's singing style was unique in American popular music, especially when it was first presented to listeners on a broad scale through recordings of the 1920s.

One of his first vocal accomplishments was to introduce an improvisatory vocal-instrumental mode of singing called "scat singing" in his recordings of "Heebie Jeebies" and "Gully Low Blues" of 1926 and 1927, respectively. Although this method of singing nonsense syllables was common in New Orleans and had been used by others, it was Armstrong's recordings that were credited with the invention of this new device and that influenced hosts of later jazz singers. Contrasting with the classically oriented popular-song vocalists of the day, with the shouting-and-dancing stage singers of ragtime and minstrelsy, and with the loud and lusty belters of the classic blues, Armstrong's natural technique brought a relaxed but exuberant jazz style and a gravelly personal tone to popular singing. His 1929 recordings of "I Can't Give You Anything but Love" and "Ain't Misbehavin'" achieved great popular success. Armstrong continued to sing throughout his career and reached a pinnacle of popular success in 1964 when his recording of "Hello Dolly" became the best-selling record in America, moving to number one on the popular music charts.

From 1930 to the mid-1940s Armstrong was usually featured with a big band. In 1935 he joined forces with Joe Glaser, a tough-minded businessman who guided his career until 1969. Armstrong divorced Lil Hardin, marrying Alpha Smith in 1938. He later divorced her and was married a fourth and final time in 1942 to Lucille Wilson. He had no children with any of his wives. After World War II, Armstrong returned to performing with a small ensemble and played a concert in New York's Town Hall, with "Peanuts" Hucko (clarinet), Bobby Hackett (trumpet), Jack Teagarden (trombone), Dick Cary (piano), Bob Haggart (bass), and Sid Catlett (drums), that inaugurated a new phase in his career. After the success of this "formal concert," Armstrong began to tour with a band labeled his "All Stars," ensembles of approximately the same size but with varying personnel selected from the ranks of established, well-known jazz musicians. Through Glaser's efforts, Armstrong and his All Stars became the highest-paid jazz band in the world. They toured successfully, sparking a renewed interest in Armstrong's recordings and earning him a place on the cover of *Time* magazine on 21 February 1949.

Throughout his long career Armstrong, as trumpeter, remained the leading figure among classic jazz musicians and rode many waves of public and financial success, but his historical impact as a jazz instrumentalist lessened as new styles developed and younger musicians looked elsewhere for leadership. Still, his solo trumpet playing remained superlative while other phases of his career, such as singing, acting, writing, and enjoying the fruits of his celebrity, gained prominence as time passed. Between 1932 and 1965 he appeared in almost fifty motion pictures, including *Rhapsody in Black and Blue* (1932), *Pennies from Heaven* (1936), *Every Day's a Holiday* (1937), *Doctor Rhythm* (1938), *Jam Session* (1944), *New Orleans* (1946), *The Strip* (1951), *High Society* (1956), *Satchmo the Great* (1957), *The Beat Generation* (1959), *When the Boys Meet the Girls* (1965), and *Hello Dolly* (1969). Beginning with broadcasts in April 1937, he was the first black performer to be featured in a network radio series, and he appeared as a guest on dozens of television shows starting in the 1950s.

Often unjustly criticized for pandering to the racist attitudes that prevailed in the venues where he performed, Armstrong was, in fact, a significant leader in the struggle for racial equality in America. He was a black artist whose work blossomed contemporaneously with the other artistic and intellectual achievements of the Harlem Renaissance and an important personage who spoke publicly in protest and canceled a U.S. State Department tour in 1957 when Governor Orval Faubus of Arkansas refused to let black children attend a public school. Armstrong firmly believed in equal opportunity as a right and in personal merit as the only measure of worth, and he was one of the first black jazz musicians to perform and record with white musicians (Hoagy Carmichael, Tommy Dorsey, Jack Teagarden, Bud Freeman, and Bing Crosby, among others). His artistry was such that he became a role model not only for black musicians but also for numerous aspiring young white musicians, most notably Bix Beiderbecke, Jimmy McPartland, Bobby Hackett, and Gil Evans.

Informally he became known as an "Ambassador of Goodwill," and Ambassador "Satch" toured Europe and Africa under the sponsorship of the Department of State during the 1950s. Armstrong amassed many honors in his lifetime—medals, stamps in his honor from foreign countries, invitations from royalty and heads of state, and critical awards such as the annual *Down Beat* Musicians Poll—but none seemed to hold greater significance for him than returning to his birthplace, New Orleans, in 1949 as King of the Zulus for the annual Mardi Gras celebration. Even though ill health plagued him in his last few years, Armstrong continued to work, appearing on television and playing an engagement at the Waldorf-Astoria Hotel in New York City during the last year of his life. He died in his home in Corona, Queens, New York.

Louis Armstrong and but three or four others are preeminent in the history of jazz. His importance in the development of this art form has gained greater, almost universal recognition in the years since his death as scholars and musicians reevaluate his contributions as a soloist, composer, bandleader, and role model. The measure of his impact on the social history of twentieth-century America also seems to be greater now as he gains recognition for his contributions to the Harlem Renaissance, for his actions as a thoughtful spokesperson for black Americans, as a significant writer of autobiography, as an entertainer of stature, and as a singer responsible for the development of major trends in American popular and jazz singing. His most accomplished biographer, Gary Giddins, wrote in *Satchmo*:

Genius is the transforming agent. Nothing else can explain Louis Armstrong's ascendancy. He had no formal training, yet he alchemized the cabaret music of an outcast minority into an art that has expanded in ever-widening orbits for sixty-five years, with no sign of collapse (26).

FURTHER READING

The papers of Louis Armstrong are preserved in the Louis Armstrong Archive at Queens College of the City University of New York, and virtually all of his recordings, some oral history material, and other related documents are at the Institute of Jazz Studies at Rutgers University in Newark, New Jersy.

Armstrong, Louis. *Satchmo: My Life in New Orleans* (1954).
———. *Swing That Music* (1936).

Collier, James Lincoln. *Louis Armstrong: An American Genius* (1983).
Friedwald, Will. *Jazz Singing: America's Great Voices from Bessie Smith to Bebop and Beyond* (1990).
Giddins, Gary. *Satchmo* (1988).
Gourse, Leslie. *Louis' Children: American Jazz Singers* (1984).
Jones, Max, and John Chilton. *Louis: The Louis Armstrong Story 1900–1971* (1971; rev. ed., 1988).
Schuller, Gunther. *Early Jazz: Its Roots and Musical Development* (1968).
———. *The Swing Era: The Development of Jazz 1930–1945* (1989).

Obituary: *New York Times*, 7 July 1971.

Discography
Westerberg, Hans. *Boy from New Orleans: A Discography of Louis "Satchmo" Armstrong* (1981).

—FRANK TIRRO

ASHE, ARTHUR

(10 July 1943–6 Feb. 1993), tennis player, author, and political activist, was born Arthur Robert Ashe Jr. in Richmond, Virginia, the son of Arthur Ashe Sr., a police officer, and Mattie Cunningham. Tall and slim as a young boy, Ashe was forbidden by his father to play football; he took up tennis instead on the segregated playground courts at Brookfield Park, near his home. By the time he was ten years old he came under the tutelage of a local tennis fan and physician from Lynchburg, R. Walter Johnson. Johnson had previously nurtured the talents of ALTHEA GIBSON, who became the first African American to win Wimbledon, in 1957 and 1958, and his second protégé would prove no less successful.

Johnson was an exacting coach; he had his charges practice hitting tennis balls with broom handles to develop their hand-eye coordination. But his lessons extended beyond tennis; he also helped the young Ashe navigate an often hostile, segregated South. Johnson and Ashe's father (his mother died when he was six) instructed Arthur in the manners, discipline, and grace that would mark his carriage within and without the nearly all-white tennis world. When Arthur was fifteen, Johnson tried to enter him in an all-white junior tournament sponsored by the Middle Atlantic Lawn Tennis Association and held at Richmond's Country Club of Virginia, but the club refused his application. As a result, Ashe, who was ranked fifth in his age group in the country, was unable to earn a ranking from his own region.

In 1958 Ashe reached the semifinals in the under-fifteen division of the junior national championships. Soon afterward a tennis coach from St. Louis, Richard Hudlin, offered to take Ashe under his wing, and after completing his junior year in high school in Richmond, Ashe accepted. He moved in with Hudlin and his family and completed his schooling at Sumner High School in St. Louis, the alma mater of the African American comedian and activist Dick Gregory. In 1960 and 1961 Ashe won the U.S. junior indoor singles title.

After graduating from high school, Ashe accepted a tennis scholarship to the University of California at Los Angeles (UCLA), where he became an All-American, led his college team to the National Collegiate Athletic Association championship, won the U.S. Hard

Arthur Ashe makes a return during the men's singles title match against Jimmy Connors at Wimbledon, 1975. © Bettmann/CORBIS

Court Championship, and was named to the U.S. Davis Cup team. While at UCLA, he also spent time training with the tennis legends Pancho Segura and Pancho Gonzalez, who helped him develop the powerful serve and volley game that would become, along with his sheer athleticism, Ashe's trademark.

In 1965, while still in college, Ashe was ranked third in the world, and he beat the Australian Roy Emerson in five sets to win the Queensland championships at Brisbane, Australia. Graduating from UCLA in 1966 with a degree in Business Administration, Ashe entered a Reserve Officer Training Corps camp and finished second in his platoon for overall achievement at the end of the six-week course. He attained the rank of first lieutenant, serving in the military from 1967 to 1969. During this time he continued playing tennis, winning the U.S. Clay Court Championships in 1967. In 1968, while still an amateur and still in the U.S. Army, he defeated Tom Okker to win the first U.S. Open, one of the two most prestigious tennis tournaments in the world; with this victory he was ranked first in the world. Numerous wins followed, including three Davis Cups, the World Championships of Tennis in 1975 (a year in which he again became the world's highest-ranked player), and two additional Grand Slam championships—the Australian Open in 1970 and Wimbledon in 1975. At Wimbledon he became the first African American man to win at the All-England Club, beating Jimmy Connors. Ashe also won the doubles titles at the French, Australian, and Wimbledon championships.

John McPhee, whose book *Levels of the Game* (1969) chronicled Ashe's match with Clark Graebner, his opponent in the semifinal of the 1968 U.S. Open, considered Ashe a competitive genius. "Even in very tight moments, other players thought he was toying with them," McPhee wrote later in an appreciation piece in the *New Yorker* after Ashe's death. He continues:

They rarely knew what he was thinking. They could not tell if he was angry. It was maddening, sometimes, to play against him. Never less than candid, he said that what he liked best about himself on a tennis court was his demeanor: "What it is is controlled cool, in a way. Always have the situation under control, even if losing. Never betray an inward sense of defeat." And of course he never did—not in the height of his athletic power, not in the statesmanship of the years that followed, and not in the endgame of his existence.

Over the course of his career Ashe earned more than $1.5 million, becoming the sport's first black millionaire and one of his era's most visible African American athletes. Several companies, including Coca-Cola and Philip Morris, hired him to promote their products, and he worked for ABC television and HBO as a sports commentator. Ashe married Jeanne Marie Moutoussamy in 1977, and they had one daughter, Camera Elizabeth. In 1979, at the age of thirty-six, Ashe suffered a heart attack, which forced him to undergo bypass surgery and retire from playing competitive tennis. Still, one year after his operation he became the first and only African American to be named captain of the U.S. Davis Cup team, a position he held until 1985. Under his leadership the team won the international competition in 1981. In 1985 he became the first African American man elected to the International Tennis Hall of Fame.

Throughout his career and afterward Ashe spent considerable time and energy working for civil and human rights. He wrote eloquently about his complex position as a world-renowned success in a field dominated by whites; even as his moderation appealed to whites, he was occasionally criticized by more vocal black activists. "There were times, in fact, when I felt a burning sense of shame that I was not with other blacks—and whites—standing up to the fire hoses and the police dogs, the truncheons, bullets and bombs that cut down such martyrs as Chaney, Schwerner, and Goodman, Viola Liuzzo, MARTIN LUTHER KING JR., MEDGAR EVERS and the little girls in that bombed church in Birmingham, Ala.," he was quoted as saying in *The Black 100: A Ranking of the Most Influential African Americans, Past and Present* ([1993], 363). "As my fame increased, so did my anguish. I knew that many blacks were proud of my accomplishments on the tennis court. But I also knew that many others, especially many of my own age or younger, did not bother to hide their indifference to me and my trophies or even their disdain and contempt for me."

In 1973, after three years of trying, Ashe had received an invitation to play in the previously all white South African Open; twelve years later Ashe, the longtime friend of the still imprisoned Nelson Mandela, was arrested in South Africa for protesting apartheid. In 1992 he joined a group of protesters who were arrested in Washington, D.C., for objecting to the treatment of Haitian refugees by the George H. W. Bush administration. Ashe's concern for fairness and human dignity extended beyond race. In 1974 he helped found the Association of Tennis Professionals, a players' union, and served as president until 1979. He later became a board member of the United States Tennis Association, chairman of the American Heart Association, and a board member for the National Foundation for Infectious Diseases.

Always a bookish, thoughtful man, Ashe cultivated a second career as a writer and sports historian. Through his research, he managed to trace his own roots back ten generations on his father's side to a woman who, in 1735, was brought from West Africa to Yorktown, Virginia, on the slave ship *Doddington*. Ashe's benchmark three-volume history of black athletes in America, *A Hard Road to Glory*, was published in 1988.

Ashe suffered a number of serious health problems that ended his playing career but barely seemed to slow him down. He had a second heart attack in 1983, followed by emergency brain surgery in 1988; after the last operation rumors began to spread about his infection with HIV, the virus that causes AIDS. Although he kept his illness secret for nearly a decade, Ashe was forced to admit his diagnosis publicly when, on 7 April 1992, the newspaper *USA Today* threatened to print the story as soon as it could be confirmed. Because Ashe did not officially acknowledge his illness to the newspaper, he was able to put off publication of the story for a day and to inform friends, family members, and health officials of his condition. On 8 April, the day after *USA Today*'s initial phone call, Ashe held a press conference to break the news himself, reporting that the virus had been transmitted during blood transfusions associated with his second heart operation in 1983. The event prompted a worldwide outpouring of grief and a squall of commentary about the conflict between the press's responsibility to report the news and an individual's right to privacy. That year he helped raise fifteen million dollars for the Arthur Ashe Foundation for the Defeat of AIDS, and in part for this work he was named Sportsman of the Year by *Sports Illustrated*.

Ashe's death in New York City provoked a sense of loss that extended far beyond the boundaries of the tennis world or the borders of the United States. A memorial service held at the Richmond governor's mansion of DOUGLAS WILDER, the first African American governor of Virginia, attracted thousands of admirers from around the world. Wilder said that Ashe's "leadership may not be confined to athletics and sports alone, for he was totally committed to improving the lives of those yet to enjoy the full fruition of rights and opportunities in this country" (*New York Times*, 7 Feb. 1993).

Ashe's passing was mourned by many who saw in his example an unusual dignity and elegance, even in the face of a terrible disease. "Why, when we knew Arthur Ashe's health was precarious, did the news of his death from pneumonia last Saturday hit us like a ball peen hammer between the eyes?" wrote Kenny Moore in a cover story in *Sports Illustrated*. "Why did the announcement of this gentle man's passing force even the raucous Madison Square Garden crowd at the Riddick Bowe–Michael Dokes fight into unwonted reflection, never quite to return to the fray? In part, surely, we reel because, even with AIDS and a history of heart attacks, Ashe didn't seem to be sick. He, of all men, hid things well. His gentility shielded us from appreciating his risk" (15 Feb. 1993, 12).

FURTHER READING

Ashe, Arthur, with Frank Deford. *Arthur Ashe: Portrait in Motion* (1975).
———, with Arnold Rampersad. *Days of Grace* (1993).
———, with Neil Amdur. *Off the Court* (1981).

—MCKAY JENKINS

Luther Askin, the earliest known black baseball player on an integrated team, photographed in his Nonotuck Fire Brigade uniform, c.1878. Collection of the Florence Business and Civic Association

 ASKIN, LUTHER B.
(26 Dec. 1843–6 Apr. 1929), the first African American to integrate baseball, was born in Pittsfield, Massachusetts, the second son of Nelson Askin and Sarah Lloyd. In 1844 Nelson Askin moved to Florence, a mill village in Northampton, Massachusetts, to open a livery. Across the road was the Northampton Association of Education and Industry, a utopian community whose ideals and practices ensured an integrated membership. Although the association disbanded in 1846, many members stayed in Florence, including SOJOURNER TRUTH and DAVID RUGGLES; their influence marked the village as a "sanctuary" for all, regardless of religion, class, or race. But in 1849, when Sarah Askin arrived in Florence with her six children, Nelson had already sold off parts of his property, and shortly thereafter the livery was seized by creditors. By 1850 Nelson had abandoned Sarah. From then on, Sarah took in washing to support her children, who at the earliest opportunity left school to find work.

Luther Askin worked for more than fifty years in a brush shop, rising to foreman, in itself an accomplishment. He was also a stonecutter, carpenter, fireman, and musician. But his principal accomplishment was to play first base, from 1865 to 1866, for the Florence

Eagle Base Ball Club. In 1872 Askin married Alice Lattimore of Moreau, New York. The couple remained in Florence for fifty-six years, raising five children. After Alice's death in 1928, Askin moved to Brooklyn to be with his daughters, where he died in 1929.

By every account, Askin led an unassuming life; the attention he received came about not from his own desire for recognition, but from an abiding need on the part of the people of Florence to celebrate the Eagle Base Ball Club. That Askin took pride in his seasons as an Eagle is evident, for his obituary lists his membership in the club before any other association. Yet no reference is made to his integration of the "Eagle nine." References to Askin's race can be found only in birth and census records or in accounts that address subjects other than the Eagles.

The papers of the Eagles' captain, Arthur G. Hill, show that he regarded Askin as "colored" (Hill, 1916). Although Askin's skin was light enough for his race to go unnoticed beyond the village, it is safe to assume that his teammates knew Askin's racial identify, as did most of Florence. Yet even in Florence the subject of Askin's integration of the Eagles went unmentioned for over a century. The reasons for this silence may be found in the shifting identity of the Askin family, some of whom were variously referred to as "colored," "black," "mulatto," and one of whom, by the 1900s, identified himself as "white."

The drawing of the color line in baseball had its roots in the game's origins. In the 1840s, when amateur clubs were formed in New York City, baseball was a gentlemanly activity engaged in by professional men of the upper middle class. In time, the dockworkers of Brooklyn formed their own ball clubs and introduced a greater degree of competition, often offending the older clubs, who regarded "rough play" with distaste. Before the Civil War, blacks and whites had little social contact, and therefore no overt effort was required to segregate ball clubs. Blacks were playing baseball "as early as whites," along separate, "roughly parallel lines" (Seymour, *People's*, 532).

After the Civil War, "base ball fever" swept down upon the northeastern United States, and hundreds of amateur

"nines" were formed. The limited pool of talent in Florence, with a population of only 1,400, partly explains why Catholics and Protestants, Irish mill workers, and Ivy League graduates played side-by-side. Also, the village's communitarian heritage, especially the Northampton Association, accounts for the heterogeneity of the Eagles. Even so, it would have been highly unusual for a black player to appear in "match games" arranged through invitations by clubs of adult white males. Yet this is what happened when Askin played for the Eagles.

The Eagles made their debut on 1 August 1865, defeating a team of Civil War veterans who called themselves champions of the "Army of the Potomac." In this, the Eagles' first official match, Askin played first base, qualifying him as "one of the original nine," and in most sources he is recognized as such.

The Eagles went undefeated from August 1865 to June 1866, and in each game Askin started at first base. The people of Florence had set their sights on winning the silver ball, a trophy symbolic of the championship of western Massachusetts. Crowds up to five thousand turned out; a pair of "sporting men" won seven hundred dollars at a single match, twice the annual salary of a millworker. The Eagles, who only the season before had taken the field barefooted and without uniforms, were altogether transformed. The club now wore fine uniforms, ordered balls for $3.50 apiece from New York, and had one hundred members, all of whom paid dues even if they did not play. It was as if the evolution of baseball had been compressed into the Eagles' first two seasons, transforming the game from a leisurely recreational activity to an intensely competitive sport.

On 9 June 1866, in the aftermath of the Eagles' first defeat (against the silver ball–champion Hampdens of Chicopee, no less), Askin was summarily dropped from the lineup. Whether the drive to win the silver ball brought about his demotion is difficult to say. All along, Askin was highly regarded for his fielding. In 1895 an anonymous player reminisced about Askin, calling him "Old Bushel Basket" because "the balls seemed to drop into his fingers and

stay there as if a basket had held them" (Sheffeld, 186). In that reminiscence, there is a perplexing reference to a "sickness" that had, in some unspecified fashion, impaired Askin's performance. Yet a few weeks after his demotion, Askin scored seven runs for the Eagles' "second nine," so he was not so sick that he could not play.

In 1867, the year after Askin was dropped from the Eagles, the Pythians, a black team from Philadelphia, tested the baseball color line by applying for membership in the National Association of Amateur Base Ball Players. The National Association responded by putting in place a written ban against blacks, thus codifying the separate racial lines along which amateur ball clubs had evolved. Professional baseball, beginning with the National League in 1876, made little effort to address this situation. With rare exceptions, most notably the Walker brothers, Fleetwood and Weldy, who played in the American Association in 1884, segregation in professional baseball was the norm.

For years to come, local fans cited the Eagles as the amateur ideal, for compared to the Florence lads, it was said that all professional teams fell short. Some Eagles were well placed to cultivate their legend, having prospered as businessmen, politicians, journalists, and judges. Celebrations were staged in 1915 and 1916, the golden anniversaries of the club's founding and reign as champions. On both occasions Askin, then in his seventies, spoke on the evolution of baseball to a more "scientific" game. His remarks were reported, but no mention was made of the anomaly of his inclusion at reunions of an all-white team, nor did Askin pose for photographs. Like many African Americans of his era, Askin may have been deferential to the point of invisibility; or he may have chosen not to risk calling attention to his son, Luther Benjamin Askin, a bandleader in Lowville, New York, who had been passing for white for years.

Askin remained an unacknowledged pioneer of baseball integration until 1999, when Jim Ryan, a Florence centenarian, in the course of contributing to a local baseball history, recalled that he and Askin had "talked baseball" during the 1920s. During these encounters, Askin, then in his eighties, spoke to

Ryan of his days with the Eagles. In reporting this, Ryan did not hesitate to identify the Askin family as black, for that was how the people of Florence had long regarded them. Other instances of integration in early baseball may yet be discovered, but finding them could be difficult, especially if a veil was drawn over the evidence, as with the Florence Eagles and Askin.

FURTHER READING

Papers that clarify the racial identity of the Askin family, especially the writings of Arthur G. Hill, are housed in the archives of the Florence Civic and Business Association, in Florence, Massachusetts.

Seymour, Harold. *Baseball: The Early Years* (1960).
———. *Baseball: The People's Game* (1990).
Sheffeld, Charles A. *History of Florence Massachusetts* (1895).
Turner, Brian. "America's Earliest Integrated Team?" in *The National Pastime* (2002): 81–90.
Turner, Brian, and John S. Bowman. *The Hurrah Game: Baseball in Northampton 1823–1953* (2002).

—BRIAN TURNER

ATTUCKS, CRISPUS

(c. 1723–5 Mar. 1770), probably a sailor, was the first to be killed in the Boston Massacre of 5 March 1770. Generally regarded to have been of mixed ancestry (African, Indian, and white), Attucks seems to have hailed from a Natick Indian settlement, Mashpee (incorporated as a district in 1763, near Framingham, Massachusetts).

While Attucks's life and background before the tragic event are uncertain, two reasonable conjectures stand out. First, he was a descendant of those Natick Indians converted to Christianity in the seventeenth century. One tribesman, John Attuck, was hanged on 22 June 1676 for allegedly conspiring with the Indian insurrection of that year. Second, it appears that Attucks may have once been a slave. The *Boston Gazette* of 2 October 1750 printed this notice: "Ran away from his Master, William Brown of Framingham on the 30th of September last, a mulatto Fellow, about twenty-seven years of age, named Crispus, 6

feet 2 inches high, short curled hair, his knees nearer together than common."

J. B. Fisher, who argues that Attucks had Indian blood, also claims that he became a crewman on a Nantucket whaler, owned by a Captain Folger, which was docked at the time of the Massacre in Boston harbor. A sailor, James Bailey, testified that the assaulting group, which Attucks headed, "appeared to be sailors." John Adams (1735–1826) said that Attucks "was seen about eight minutes before the firing at the head of twenty or thirty sailors in Cornhill.... He was a stout fellow, whose very looks were enough to terrify any person.... He was about forty-seven years old."

The Bostonians' wrath had long been building against the stationing of the Fourteenth and Twenty-ninth British regiments in the town. On the evening of 5 March, Attucks dined at Thomas Symmonds's victualing house and, learning of the commotion taking place at the customshouse on King Street, joined a group headed in that direction. It is said that he and others had earlier threatened British soldiers at Murray's barracks. Attucks and his

gang gathered cordwood sticks and wooden pieces from butchers' stalls, carrying these makeshift weapons over their heads as they approached the scene of the disturbance. John Adams, in remarks before the jury that tried the British soldiers for their role in the Massacre, stated that "Attucks appears to have undertaken to be the hero of the night, and to lead this army with banners." In his summation, Adams also said that "it is in this manner, this town has been often treated; a Carr from Ireland, and an Attucks from Framingham, happening to be here" to "sally out upon their thoughtless enterprises, at the head of such a rabble of negroes, &c., as they can collect together..." Testimony at the soldiers' trial differed over whether Attucks had grabbed for the bayonet of Private Hugh Montgomery, causing a struggle that resulted in the shooting. John Adams tried to portray Attucks as the instigator, "to whose mad behavior, in all probability, the dreadful carnage of that night is chiefly ascribed." Adams added that Attucks's group was a "mob whistling, screaming, and rending like an

Paul Revere's engraving of The Boston Massacre *in 1770 captures British soldiers firing on colonial protesters. African American dockworker Crispus Attucks was the first of five men to be killed and the first martyr of the American Revolution.*
© Bettmann/CORBIS

Indian yell." Some witnesses, however, testified that Attucks was killed while leaning on his cordwood stick. Two shots to his breast caused the fatality.

After the massacre, the bodies of Attucks and James Caldwell, the two nonresident victims, were brought to Faneuil Hall. On 8 March a funeral procession of ten to twelve thousand people and numerous coaches accompanied the hearses of Attucks and three other victims to Granary burial ground, where all four coffins were buried in one grave.

Captain Thomas Preston, the British officer of the day who commanded the squad that fired upon the civilians, and eight soldiers were tried before the Suffolk Superior Court in Boston from 27 November to 5 December 1770. Preston and six of his men were acquitted, including William Warren, who was charged specifically with killing Attucks; two others were found guilty of manslaughter and were branded on the thumb after pleading benefit of clergy.

Crispus Attucks, apparently of African and Indian ancestry, was the first martyr of the American Revolution. Later, black military companies were named for him. In 1888 the city of Boston and the state of Massachusetts erected on Boston Common a memorial to Attucks and the other massacre victims.

FURTHER READING

Fisher, J. B. "Who Was Crispus Attucks?" *American Historical Record* 1 (1872): 531–533.

QUARLES, BENJAMIN. *The Negro in the American Revolution* (1961).

Temple, Josiah H. *History of Framingham, Massachusetts, 1640–1885* (1887).

Wroth, L. Kinvin, and Hiller B. Zobel, eds. *Legal Papers of John Adams* (3 vols., 1965).

Zobel, Hiller B. *The Boston Massacre* (1970).

—HARRY M. WARD

B

 BAILEY, PEARL
(29 Mar. 1918–17 Aug. 1990), actress, singer, and entertainer, was born Pearl Mae Bailey in Newport News, Virginia, the daughter of the Reverend Joseph James Bailey and Ella Mae (maiden name unknown). Her brother Bill Bailey was at one time a well-known tap dancer.

While still in high school, Bailey launched her show business career in Philadelphia, where her mother had relocated the family after separating from Rev. Bailey. In 1933, at age fifteen, she won the first of three amateur talent contests, with a song-and-dance routine at the Pearl Theatre in Philadelphia, which awarded her a five dollar prize. In a second contest at the Jungle Inn in Washington, D.C., she received a twelve dollar prize for a buck-and-wing dancing act. After winning a third contest at the famed Apollo Theatre in Harlem, she began performing professionally—first as a specialty dancer or chorus girl with several small bands, including NOBLE SISSLE's band, on the vaudeville circuits in Pennsylvania, Maryland, and Washington during the 1930s, then as a vocalist with Cootie Williams and COUNT BASIE at such smart New York clubs as La Vie en Rose and the Blue Angel, and on the World War II USO circuit, during the 1940s.

Bailey made her Broadway debut as a saloon barmaid named Butterfly in the black-authored musical *St. Louis Woman*, which opened at the Martin Beck Theatre, 30 March 1946, and ran for 113 performances. Although the show was only modestly successful, she was praised for her singing of two hit numbers, "Legalize My Name" and "(It's) A Woman's Prerogative (to Change Her Mind)." For her performance, she won a Donaldson Award as the best Broadway newcomer. After several failed marriages, one to comedian Slappy White, Bailey married the legendary white jazz drummer Louis Bellson Jr., in 1952; they adopted two children. Their marriage was reportedly a happy one. In later years, she frequently sang with her husband's band, and at one time toured with CAB CALLOWAY and his band.

After appearing in supporting roles in two predominantly white shows in 1950–1951, Bailey's first Broadway starring vehicle was *House of Flowers* (1954), a Caribbean-inspired musical. Bailey played the part of Mme. Fleur, a resourceful bordello madam, whose house of prostitution in the French West Indies is facing hard times, forcing her to resort to desperate measures to save it. The show opened at the Alvin Theatre, 30 December 1954, and had a run of 165 performances. Despite what the *New York Times* (30 Dec. 1954) called "feeble material," she was credited with "an amusing style" and the ability to "[throw] away songs with smart hauteur."

Bailey's most important Broadway role was as the irrepressible Dolly Levi (a marriage broker who arranges a lucrative marriage for herself) in the all-black version of *Hello, Dolly!*, which opened at the St. James Theatre in November 1967 for a long run, sharing the stage with the original 1964 Carol Channing version. The black version provided tangible evidence that roles originally created by white actors could be redefined and given new vitality from the perspective of the African American experience. Lyndon Johnson, who had used the show's title song as his campaign theme song in 1964, changing the words to "Hello, Lyndon!," saw the show when it came to Washington and was invited, along with his wife Lady Bird, to join Bailey onstage for a rousing finale. For her performance, Bailey won a special Tony Award in 1968.

Bailey's most important film roles included *Carmen Jones* (1954), as one of Carmen's friends; *St. Louis Blues* (1958), as composer W. C. HANDY's Aunt Hagar; *Porgy and Bess* (1959), as Maria, the cookshop woman; *All the Fine Young Cannibals* (1960), as a boozing, over-the-hill blues singer; and *Norman...Is That You?* (1976), opposite comedian REDD FOXX, as estranged

Pearl Bailey in her first starring role on Broadway, as Madame Fleur in House of Flowers (1954), with her three flowers, left to right, Tulip (Josephine Premice), Pansy (Enid Mosier), and Gladiola (Enid Moore). © Bettmann/CORBIS

parents of a gay son. Her voice was also used for Big Mama, the owl, in the Disney animated film *The Fox and the Hound* (1981).

A frequent performer and guest on television talk shows beginning in the 1950s, Bailey also hosted her own variety series on ABC, *The Pearl Bailey Show* (Jan.–May 1971), for which her husband directed the orchestra while she entertained an assortment of celebrity guests. She also appeared on television in "An Evening with Pearl" (1975) and in a remake of *The Member of the Wedding* (1982), in the role of Berenice. Bailey released numerous albums and was also the author of several books, including two autobiographies, *The Raw Pearl* (1968) and *Talking to Myself* (1971), and *Pearl's Kitchen* (1973), a cookbook.

In 1975 Bailey was appointed as a U.S. delegate to the United Nations. Other honors and awards included a citation from New York City mayor John V. Lindsay; *Cue* magazine entertainer of the year (1969); the First Order in Arts and Sciences from Egyptian president Anwar Sadat; the Screen Actors Guild Award for outstanding achievement in fostering the finest ideals of the acting profession; and an honorary Doctor of Humane Letters from Georgetown University (1977). She later earned a degree in theology from Georgetown.

During the later years of her life, Bailey was hospitalized several times for a heart ailment. She also suffered from an arthritic knee, which was replaced with an artificial one just prior to her death. She collapsed, apparently from a heart attack, at the Philadelphia hotel where she was staying (her home was in Havasu, Arizona); she died soon after at Thomas Jefferson University Hospital in Philadelphia.

Bailey was best known for her lazy, comical, half-singing, half-chatting style, expressive hands, tired feet, and folksy, congenial philosophy of life, which endeared her to audiences both black and white. The *New York Times* obituary (18 Aug. 1990) called her "a trouper in the old theatrical sense," who had "enraptured theater and nightclub audiences for a quarter-century by the languorous sexuality of her throaty voice as well as by the directness of her personality." At her funeral, Cab Calloway, who had starred with her in *Hello, Dolly!*, said that "Pearl was love,

pure and simple love"; and her husband called her "a person of love," who believed that "show business" meant to "show love."

FURTHER READING

Bailey, Pearl. *The Raw Pearl* (1968).
———. *Talking to Myself* (1971).

Bogle, Donald. *Blacks in American Films and Television: An Illustrated Encyclopedia* (1988).
———. *Brown Sugar: Eighty Years of America's Black Female Superstars* (1980).
Peterson, Bernard L., Jr. *A Century of Musicals in Black and White: An Encyclopedia of Musical Stage Works by, about, or Involving African Americans* (1993).

Obituaries: *New York Times*, 18, 24, and 25 Aug. 1990.

—BERNARD L. PETERSON

 BAKER, ELLA JOSEPHINE (13 Dec. 1903– 13 Dec. 1986), civil rights organizer, was born in Norfolk, Virginia, the daughter of Blake Baker, a waiter on the ferry between Norfolk and Washington, D.C., and Georgianna Ross. In rural North Carolina where Ella Baker grew up, she experienced a strong sense of black community. Her grandfather, who had been a slave, acquired the land in Littleton on which he had slaved. He raised fruit, vegetables, and cattle, which he shared with the community. He also served as the local Baptist minister. Baker's mother took care of the sick and needy.

After graduating in 1927 from Shaw University in Raleigh, North Carolina, Baker moved to New York City. She had dreamed of doing graduate work in sociology at the University of Chicago, but it was 1929, and times were hard. Few jobs were open to black women except teaching, which Baker refused to do because "this was the thing that everybody figures you could do" (Cantarow and O'Malley, 62). To survive, Baker waitressed and worked in a factory. During 1929–1930 she was an editorial staff member of the *American West Indian News* and in 1932 became an editorial assistant for GEORGE SCHUYLER's *Negro National News*, for which she also worked as office manager. In 1930 she was on the board of

directors of Harlem's Own Cooperative and worked with the Dunbar Housewives' League on tenant and consumer rights. In 1930 she helped organize and in 1931 became the national executive director of the Young Negroes' Cooperative League, a consumer cooperative. Baker also taught consumer education for the Works Progress Administration in the 1930s and, according to a letter written in 1936, divided her time between consumer education and working at the public library at 135th Street. She married Thomas J. Roberts in 1940 or 1941; they had no children.

Beginning in 1938 Baker worked with the National Association for the Advancement of Colored People (NAACP), and from 1941 to 1946 she traveled throughout the country but especially in the South for the NAACP, first as field secretary and then as a highly successful director of branches to recruit members, raise money, and organize local campaigns. Among the issues in which she was involved were the antilynching campaign, the equal-pay-for-black-teachers movement, and job training for black workers. Baker's strength was the ability to evoke in people a feeling of common need and the belief that people together can change the conditions under which they live. Her philosophy of organizing was "you start where the people are" and "strong people don't need strong leaders." In her years with the NAACP, Baker formed a network of people involved with civil rights throughout the South that proved invaluable in the struggles of the 1950s and 1960s. Among the more significant of her protégés was the Alabama seamstress ROSA PARKS. Baker resigned from her leadership role in the national NAACP in 1946 because she felt it was too bureaucratic. She also had agreed to take responsibility for raising her niece. Back in New York City, she worked with the NAACP on school desegregation, sat on the Commission on Integration for the New York City Board of Education, and in 1952 became president of the New York City NAACP chapter. In 1953 she resigned from the NAACP presidency to run unsuccessfully for the New York City Council on the Liberal Party ticket. To support herself, she worked as director of the Harlem Division of the New York City Committee of the American Cancer Society.

In January 1958 BAYARD RUSTIN and Stanley Levison persuaded Baker to go to Atlanta to set up the office of the Southern Christian Leadership Conference (SCLC) to organize the Crusade for Citizenship, a voter registration program in the South. Baker agreed to go for six weeks and stayed for two and a half years. She was named acting director of the SCLC and set about organizing the crusade to open simultaneously in twenty-one cities. She was concerned, however, that the SCLC board of preachers did not sufficiently support voter registration. Baker had increasing difficulty working with MARTIN LUTHER KING JR., whom she described as "too self-centered and cautious" (Weisbrot, 33). Because she thought that she would never be appointed executive director, Baker persuaded her friend the Reverend John L. Tilley to assume the post in April, and she became associate director. After King fired Tilley in January 1959, he asked Baker once again to be executive director, but his board insisted that her position must be in an acting capacity. Baker, however, functioned as executive director and signed her name accordingly. In April 1960 the executive director post of SCLC was accepted by the Reverend Wyatt Tee Walker.

After hundreds of students sat in at segregated lunch counters in early 1960, Baker persuaded the SCLC to invite them to the Southwide Youth Leadership Conference at Shaw University on Easter weekend. From this meeting the Student Nonviolent Coordinating Committee (SNCC) was eventually formed. Although the SCLC leadership pressured Baker to influence the students to become a youth chapter of SCLC, she refused and encouraged the students to beware of SCLC's "leader-centered orientation." She felt that the students had a right to decide their own structure. Baker's speech "More Than a Hamburger," which followed King's and James Lawson's speeches, urged the students to broaden their social vision of discrimination to include more than integrating lunch counters. JULIAN BOND described the speech as "an eye opener" and probably the best of the three. "She didn't say, 'Don't let Martin Luther King tell you what to do,'" Bond remembers, "but you got the real feeling that that's what she meant" (Hampton and Fayer, 63). JAMES FORMAN, who became

director of SNCC a few months later, said Baker felt SCLC "was depending too much on the press and on the promotion of Martin King, and was not developing enough indigenous leadership across the South" (Forman, 216).

After the Easter conference weekend, Baker resigned from the SCLC, and after having helped Walker learn his job she went to work for SNCC in August. To support herself she worked as a human relations consultant for the Young Women's Christian Association in Atlanta. Baker continued as a mentor to SNCC civil rights workers, most notably ROBERT P. MOSES. At a rancorous SNCC meeting at Highlander Folk School in Tennessee in August 1961, Baker mediated between one faction advocating political action through voter registration and another faction advocating nonviolent direct action. She suggested that voter registration would necessitate confrontation that would involve them in direct action. Baker believed that voting was necessary but did not believe that the franchise would cure all problems. She also understood the appeal of nonviolence as a tactic, but she did not believe in it personally: "I have not seen anything in the nonviolent technique that can dissuade me from challenging somebody who wants to step on my neck. If necessary, if they hit me, I might hit them back" (Cantarow and O'Malley, 82).

After the 1964 Mississippi summer in which northern students went south to work in voter registration, SNCC decided to organize the Mississippi Freedom Democratic Party (MFDP) as an alternative to the regular Democratic Party in Mississippi. Thousands of people registered to vote in beauty parlors and barbershops, churches, or wherever a registration booth could be set up. Baker set up the Washington, D.C., office of the MFDP and delivered the keynote speech at its Jackson, Mississippi, state convention. The MFDP delegates were not seated at the Democratic National Convention in Washington, D.C., but their influence helped to elect many local black leaders in Mississippi in the following years and forced a rules change in the Democratic Party to include more women and minorities as delegates to the national convention.

From 1962 to 1967 Baker worked on the staff of the Southern Conference Education Fund (SCEF), dedicated to helping black and white people work together. During that time she organized a civil liberties conference in Washington, D.C., and worked with Carl Braden on a mock civil rights commission hearing in Chapel Hill, North Carolina. In her later years in New York City she served on the board of the Puerto Rican Solidarity Committee, founded and was president of the Fund for Education and Legal Defense, which raised money primarily for scholarships for civil rights activists to return to college, and was vice chair of the Mass Party Organizing Committee. She was also a sponsor of the National United Committee to Free ANGELA DAVIS and All Political Prisoners, a consultant to both the Executive Council and the Commission for Social and Racial Justice of the Episcopal Church, and a member of the Charter Group for a Pledge of Conscience and the Coalition of Concerned Black Americans. Until her death in New York City she continued to inspire, nurture, scold, and advise the many young people who had worked with her during her career of political activism.

Ella Baker's ideas and careful organizing helped to shape the civil rights movement from the 1930s through the 1960s. She had the ability to listen to people and to inspire them to organize around issues that would empower their lives. At a time when there were no women in leadership in the SCLC, Baker served as its executive director. Hundreds of young people became politically active because of her respect and concern for them.

FURTHER READING

Ella Baker's papers are in the Schomburg Center for Research in Black Culture of the New York Public Library.

Cantarow, Ellen, and Susan Gushee O'Malley. *Moving the Mountain* (1980).
Forman, James. *The Making of Black Revolutionaries* (1972).
Hampton, Henry, and Steve Fayer. *Voices of Freedom* (1991).
Ransby, Barbara. *Ella Baker and the Black Freedom Movement* (2003).
Weisbrot, Robert. *Freedom Bound* (1990).

Obituary: *New York Times*, 17 Dec. 1986.
—SUSAN GUSHEE O'MALLEY

 **BAKER, GEORGE.** *See* Father Divine.

BAKER, JOSEPHINE
(3 June 1906–10 Apr. 1975), dancer, singer, and entertainer, was born in the slums of East St. Louis, Missouri, the daughter of Eddie Carson, a drummer, who abandoned Baker and her mother after the birth of a second child, and of Carrie McDonald, a one-time entertainer who supported what became a family of four by doing laundry. Poverty, dislocation, and mistreatment permeated Baker's childhood. By the age of eight she was earning her keep and contributing to the family's support by doing domestic labor. By the time Baker was fourteen, she had left home and its discord and drudgery; mastered such popular dances as the Mess Around and the Itch, which sprang up in the black urban centers of the day; briefly married Willie Wells and then divorced him; and begun her career in the theater. She left East St. Louis behind and traveled with the Dixie Steppers on the black vaudeville circuit, already dreaming of performing on Broadway.

Baker's dream coincided with the creation of one of the greatest musical comedies in American theater, *Shuffle Along*, with music by EUBIE BLAKE and lyrics by NOBLE SISSLE. A constant crowd-pleaser with her crazy antics and frantic dancing as a comic, eye-crossing chorus girl, Baker auditioned for a role in the musical in Philadelphia in April of 1921, only to be rejected as "too young, too thin, too small, and too dark." With characteristic determination, she bought a one-way ticket to New York, auditioned again, and was rejected again, but she secured a job as a dresser in the touring company. On the road she learned the routines, and, when a member of the chorus line fell ill, she stepped in and became an immediate sensation. More than five hundred performances later, in the fall of 1923, the *Shuffle Along* tour ended, and Baker was cast in Sissle and Blake's new show, *Bamville*, later retitled and better known as *The Chocolate Dandies*.

When the musical opened in New York in March of 1924, Baker not only played Topsy Anna, a comic role straight out of the racist minstrel tradition, but also appeared as an elegantly dressed "deserted female" in the show's "Wedding Finale," foreshadowing the poised and polished performer of world renown she would become.

In the summer of 1925 Baker's dancing at the Plantation Club at Fiftieth Street and Broadway caught the eye of Caroline Dudley Reagan, a young socialite planning to stage a black revue in Paris in the vein of *Shuffle Along* or *Runnin' Wild*, the revue that introduced the Charleston in 1924. The company that came to be known as La Revue Nègre was long on talent, with such now legendary figures as the composer Spencer Williams, the bandleader and pianist Claude Hopkins, and the clarinetist SIDNEY BECHET, the dancer and choreographer Louis Douglas, and the set designer Miguel Covarrubias. Baker joined the troupe as lead dancer, singer, and comic. When the performers arrived in Paris in late September 1925, opening night at the Théâtre des Champs Elysées was ten days away. During that brief time the revue was transformed from a vaudeville show, replete with the stereotypes expected by a white American public, into a music-hall spectacle filled with colonialist fantasies that appealed to the largely male, voyeuristic Parisian audience.

When La Revue Nègre opened to a packed house on 2 October 1925, it was an instantaneous *succès de scandale*. First, Baker stunned the rapt onlookers with her blackface comic routine, in which, seemingly part animal, part human, she shimmied, contorted her torso, writhed like a snake, and vibrated her behind with astonishing speed. Then she provoked boos and hisses as well as wild applause when, in the closing "Dance sauvage," wearing only feathers about her hips, she entered the stage upside down in a full split on the shoulders of Joe Alex. Janet Flanner recorded the moment in the *New Yorker*: "Midstage, he paused, and with his long fingers holding her basket-wise around the waist, swung her in a slow cartwheel to the stage floor, where she stood like his magnificent discarded burden, in an instant of complete silence. She was an unforgettable female ebony

statue." Called the "black Venus" and likened to African sculpture in motion, Baker was seen both as a threat to "civilization" and, like *le jazz hot,* as a new life force capable of energizing a weary France mired down in tradition and in need of renewal.

Paris made "la Baker" a celebrity, embracing both her erotic yet comic stage persona and her embodiment of Parisian chic as she strolled the city's boulevards beautifully dressed in Paul Poiret's creations. Beginning in 1926 Baker starred at the oldest and most venerated of French music halls, the Folies-Bergère. Once again, she was a shocking sensation. Instead of the customary bare-breasted, light-skinned women standing in frozen poses onstage at the Folies, Baker presented the Parisian audience with a dark-skinned, athletic form clad in a snicker-producing girdle of drooping bananas, dancing the wildest, most electrifying Charleston anyone had ever witnessed. As the young African savage Fatou, she captured the sexual imagination of Paris.

In 1928, sensing that her public was beginning to tire of her frenetic antics, Baker left Paris. During an extended tour of European and South American cities with her manager and lover, Giuseppe "Pepito" Abatino, she studied voice, disciplined her dancing, and learned to speak French. However, Baker's reception in such cities as Vienna, Budapest, Prague, and Munich was not what it had been in Paris. Protests broke out in hostile reaction to her nudity, to jazz music, and to her foreignness. Baker also encountered for the first time the racism she thought she had left behind in America, the racism against which she would campaign onstage and off for the rest of her life. By the time she made her triumphal return to Paris two and a half years later, she had transformed herself into a sophisticated, elegantly attired French star.

In the 1930s Baker's career branched out in new directions. Singing took on new importance in her performances, and in her 1930–1931 revue at the Casino de Paris she perfected her signature song, "J'ai deux amours," proclaiming that her two loves were her country and Paris. She began recording for Columbia Records in 1930. She starred in two films, *Zou-Zou* (1934) and *Princesse Tam-Tam* (1935), whose story lines paralleled her rags-to-riches life. In the first film she is transformed from a poor laundress to a glamorous music-hall star and in the second from a Tunisian goat girl to an exotic princess. In the fall of 1934 she successfully tackled light opera in the starring role of Offenbach's operetta *La Créole*.

One year later, hoping to enjoy the success at home she had earned abroad, Baker sailed with Pepito to New York and began four months of preparation for the Ziegfeld Follies of 1936. The reviews of the New York opening in January took hateful aim at Baker's performance. Belittling her success abroad with the explanation that in France "a Negro wench always has a head start," the reporter remarked that "to Manhattan theatergoers last week she was just a slightly buck-toothed Negro woman whose figure might be matched in any night-club show, and whose dancing and singing might be topped practically anywhere outside of Paris." Critics, black and white, resented her performing only French cabaret material rather than "Harlem songs." Newspapers also reported that Baker personally was snubbed, refused entrance to hotels and nightclubs. Reactions to this discrimination varied, with some condemning her for "trying to be white." The columnist Roi Ottley of the *Amsterdam News*, on the other hand, praised her efforts to overcome Jim Crowism, saying that "she was just trying to live ignoring color." He recommended that "Harlem ... should rally to the side of this courageous Negro woman. We should make her insults our insults."

Disappointed by her reception in her homeland and saddened by the death from cancer of Pepito, Baker returned to Paris and to the nude revues at the Folies-Bergère. By then thirty years old, she wanted to marry and have children. She realized the first desire on 30 November 1937, when she wed Jean Lion, a rich and handsome Jewish playboy and sugar broker. After fourteen months of marriage, during which Baker did not become pregnant and Lion continued his wild ways, she filed for divorce, which was granted in 1942.

In June of 1940 German troops invaded Paris. Baker, who refused to perform either for racist Nazis or for their French sympathizers, fled to Les Milandes, her fifteenth-century château in the Dordogne, with her maid, a Belgian refugee couple, and her beloved dogs. Since September 1939 Baker had served as an "honorable correspondent," gathering information about German troop locations for French military intelligence at embassy and ministry parties in Paris. Once Charles de Gaulle had declared himself leader of Free France in a radio broadcast from London and called for the French to resist their German occupiers, Baker joined "résistance" and was active in it throughout World War II, working mostly in North Africa. For her heroic work she was awarded the Croix de Guerre, and de Gaulle himself gave her a gold cross of Lorraine, the symbol of the Fighting French, when he established headquarters in Algiers in the spring of 1943. Baker was a tireless ambassador for the Free France movement and for de Gaulle, performing for British, American, and French soldiers in North Africa and touring the Middle East to raise money for the cause. In recognition of the propaganda services she performed during this tour, she was made a sublieutenant of the Women's Auxiliary of the French Air Force. After the war de Gaulle awarded Baker the coveted Medal of Resistance.

Moving into the 1950s Baker harnessed her formidable energies behind two causes. The first was her own pursuit of racial harmony and human tolerance in the form of her "Rainbow Tribe." To demonstrate the viability of world brotherhood, with the orchestra leader Jo Bouillon, whom she had married in 1947, Baker adopted children of many nationalities, races, and religions and installed them at Les Milandes. In order to support the family that eventually numbered thirteen and to finance the massive renovation of the château and related construction projects, Baker returned to the stage. A quick trip to the United States in 1948 was as unsuccessful as the one twelve years earlier and left her convinced that, if possible, race relations there were even worse than before. This realization prompted Baker's second cause, the pursuit of civil rights for black Americans through the desegregation of hotels, restaurants, and nightclubs.

Traveling with a $250,000 Parisian wardrobe; singing in French, Spanish, English, Italian, and Portuguese; and performing with masterly showmanship, in 1951 Baker began an American tour in Cuba. When word of her success in Havana reached Miami, Copa City moved to book the star for a splashy engagement. Contract negotiations were long and difficult. Initiating what would become her standard demand with nightclubs, Baker insisted on a nondiscrimination clause. If management would not admit black patrons, she would not perform. The integrated audience for Baker's show at Copa City was the first in the city's history. Baker took her tour and her campaign against color lines from city to city—New York, Boston, Atlanta, Las Vegas, and Hollywood. And audiences loved her. *Variety* wrote, "The showmanship that is Josephine Baker's ... is something that doesn't happen synthetically or overnight. It's of the same tradition that accounts for the durability of almost every show biz standard still on top after many years."

The pinnacle of Baker's civil rights efforts was reached in August 1963 when she was invited to the great March on Washington. Dressed in her World War II uniform, Baker stood on the platform in front of the Lincoln Memorial and spoke to the crowd of thousands, blacks and whites, demonstrating for justice and equality: "You are on the eve of victory. You can't go wrong. The world is behind you." Baker was among those arrayed around Martin Luther King Jr. as he delivered his "I have a dream" speech. Certainly, for Josephine Baker, that day was a dream come true.

The remaining years of Baker's life were not tranquil. Given her extravagant spending and generosity, financial problems continued to plague her. Jo Bouillon finally despaired of trying to raise so many children or to impose any fiscal responsibility and left Baker. In 1968 Les Milandes was sold, and Baker, who barricaded herself in the house with her children, was evicted. Such setbacks notwithstanding, she continued to give comeback performances, astonishing crowds with her ability to rejuvenate herself the moment she stepped on stage, the consummate star. Her final performance in Paris to a sold-out house on 9 April 1975 was no exception.

The following day, just two months shy of her sixty-ninth birthday, Baker died of a cerebral hemorrhage brought on by a stroke. All of France mourned the passing of "la Joséphine." National television broadcast the procession of her flag-draped coffin through the streets of Paris and the funeral service at the Church of the Madeleine, where twenty thousand Parisians gathered to pay their respects.

In *Jazz Cleopatra: Josephine Baker in Her Time*, Phyllis Rose writes of Baker's "cabaret internationalism" as her "way of expressing a political position." A performer of consummate skill, Baker enthralled audiences for more than a half century. But personal adulation was not enough. Like PAUL ROBESON, HARRY BELAFONTE, LENA HORNE, BILL COSBY, and others, Baker put her prestige and popularity in the service of civil rights, racial harmony, and equality for all humanity.

FURTHER READING

Baker, Josephine, and Marcel Sauvage. *Les mémoires de Joséphine Baker* (1927).

——. *Les mémoires de Joséphine Baker* (1949).

Baker, Josephine, and Jo Bouillon. *Joséphine* (1976).

Colin, Paul. *Le tumulte noir* (1927).

Hammond, Bryan, and Patrick O'Connor. *Josephine Baker* (1988).

Rose, Phyllis. *Jazz Cleopatra: Josephine Baker in Her Time* (1989).

Obituary: *New York Times*, 13 April 1975.
—KAREN C. C. DALTON

BALDWIN, JAMES

(2 Aug. 1924–30 Nov. 1987), author, was born James Arthur Baldwin in Harlem, in New York City, the illegitimate son of Emma Berdis Jones, who married the author's stepfather, David Baldwin, in 1927. David Baldwin was a laborer and weekend storefront preacher who had an enormous influence on the author's childhood; his mother was a domestic who had eight more children after he was born. Baldwin was singled out early in school for his intelligence, and at least one white teacher, Orrin Miller, took a special interest in him. At

P.S. 139, Frederick Douglass Junior High School, Baldwin met black poet COUNTÉE CULLEN, a teacher and literary club adviser there. Cullen saw some of Baldwin's early poems and warned him against trying to write like LANGSTON HUGHES, so Baldwin turned from poetry to focus more on writing fiction. In 1938 he experienced a profound religious conversion at the hands of a female evangelist/pastor of Mount Cavalry of the Pentecostal Faith, which he later wrote about in his first novel, *Go Tell It on the Mountain* (1953), in his play *The Amen Corner* (1968), and in an essay in *The Fire Next Time* (1963). Saved, Baldwin became a Sunday preacher at the nearby Fireside Pentecostal Assembly.

In 1938 Baldwin entered De Witt Clinton High School in the Bronx; he graduated in 1942. There Baldwin was challenged intellectually and was able to escape home and Harlem. He wrote for the school magazine, the *Magpie*, and began to frequent Greenwich Village, where he met black artist BEAUFORD DELANEY, an important early influence. Torn between the dual influences of the church and his intellectual and artistic private life, Baldwin finally made a choice. At age sixteen he began a homosexual relationship with a Harlem racketeer and later said he was grateful

to the older man throughout his life for the love and self-validation he brought to the tormented and self-conscious teenager. As a preacher, Baldwin considered himself a hypocrite. At this same time, he discovered that David Baldwin was not, in fact, his real father and began to understand why he had felt deeply rejected as a child and had hated and feared his father. Fearing gossip about his homosexual relationship would reach his family and church, Baldwin broke with both the racketeer and the church. Now eighteen, he also moved away from home, taking a series of odd jobs in New Jersey and spending free time in the Village with artists and writers, trying to establish himself. He returned home in 1943 to care for the family while his stepfather was dying of tuberculosis. A few hours after his father's death, his youngest sister was born, named by James Baldwin, the head of the family. The Harlem riot of 1943 broke out in the midst of this family upheaval, all of which Baldwin described eloquently in *Notes of a Native Son* (1955).

After his father's funeral Baldwin left home for the last time, determined to become a writer. In 1944 he met RICHARD WRIGHT, who helped him get a Eugene F. Saxon Fellowship to work on his first novel, then titled "In My

James Baldwin, author of Go Tell It on the Mountain, *photographed in Paris in 1975.* © Sophie Bassouls/CORBIS SYGMA

Father's House." He gave part of the $500 grant to his mother and tried to start his literary career. Although Baldwin's first novel was rejected by two publishers, he began to have some success publishing book reviews and essays, establishing a name and a reputation. At the same time, he had difficulty extracting himself from the influence of Richard Wright, who became for Baldwin the literary father that he had to reject, as David Baldwin had been the punishing stepfather to be overcome. With what was left of the Rosenwald Fellowship he had received in 1948, Baldwin, frustrated by the fits and starts of his writing career and tired of America's racism, bought a one-way air ticket to Paris and left the United States on 11 November.

In Paris, Baldwin met writers such as Jean-Paul Sartre, Jean Genet, and Saul Bellow. He garnered notice as a critic with the essay "Everybody's Protest Novel," which came out in *Partisan Review* in 1949. Although mostly a critique of Harriet Beecher Stowe's *Uncle Tom's Cabin*, this was the first of a series of three essays in which Baldwin attacked his literary mentor, Wright. Baldwin followed with "Many Thousand Gone" in 1951 and, after Wright's death, "Alas Poor Richard" in 1961. But not until he took himself, his typewriter, and his BESSIE SMITH records to a tiny hamlet high in the Swiss Alps in 1951 did Baldwin begin to work in earnest on his first and best novel, *Go Tell It on the Mountain*. In this autobiographical family novel, fourteen-year-old John Grimes undergoes an emotional-psychological-religious crisis of adolescence and is "saved." *Go Tell It on the Mountain* explores the histories and internal lives of John's stepfather Gabriel, mother Elizabeth, and Aunt Florence, spanning the years from 1875 to the Depression and including "the Great Migration" from the South to Harlem. It was well received and was nominated for the National Book Award in 1954; Baldwin said in an interview with Quincy Troupe that he was told it did not win because RALPH ELLISON's *Invisible Man* had won in 1953 and America was not ready to give this award to two black writers in a row.

Baldwin won a Guggenheim grant to work on a second novel, published in 1956 as *Giovanni's Room*, about a homosexual relationship and with all-white characters in a European setting. Baldwin's American publisher turned it down for its honesty, so Baldwin had to publish *Giovanni's Room* first in London. It was a book Baldwin had to write, he said in an interview with Richard Goldstein, "to clarify something for myself." Baldwin went on to say, "The question of human affection, of integrity, in my case, the question of trying to become a writer, are all linked with the question of sexuality." The central character, David, a young American living in Paris, is forced to choose between his fiancée, Hella, and his male lover Giovanni. David rejects Giovanni, who is later tried and executed for the murder of an aging homosexual. Racked with guilt, David reveals his true homosexual nature and breaks his engagement, making Giovanni the injured martyr and moral pole in the novel.

Baldwin's first collection of essays, *Notes of a Native Son*, appeared in 1955. These autobiographical and political pieces made Baldwin famous as an eloquent and experienced commentator on race and culture in America. Here he says on his father's funeral,

This was his legacy: nothing is ever escaped. That bleakly memorable morning I hated the unbelievable streets and the Negroes and whites who had, equally, made them that way. But I knew that it was folly, as my father would have said, this bitterness was folly. It was necessary to hold on to the things that mattered. The dead man mattered, the new life mattered; blackness and whiteness did not matter; to believe that they did was to acquiesce in one's own destruction. Hatred, which could destroy so much, never failed to destroy the man who hated and this was an immutable law.

(Bantam ed. [1968], 94–95)

Baldwin returned periodically to the United States throughout the 1950s and 1960s, but never to stay. He first visited the South in 1957 and met MARTIN LUTHER KING JR. In 1961 he published the collection of essays *Nobody Knows My Name: More Notes of a Native Son*. By 1963 he was prominent enough to be featured on the cover of *Time* magazine as a major spokesman for the early civil rights movement after another collection of essays, *The Fire Next Time*, arguably Baldwin's most influential work, appeared. His first play, *Blues for Mr. Charlie* (1964), a fictionalized account of the 1955 Mississippi murder of fourteen-year-old EMMETT TILL, followed. In *The Fire Next Time* Baldwin effectively honed his prophetic, even apocalyptic rhetoric about racial tensions in America, fusing his themes of protest and love. During this period Baldwin had also published his third novel, *Another Country*, in 1962. His influence in national politics and American literature had reached a peak.

Another Country took Baldwin six years to complete; it eventually sold four million copies after a slow start with negative reviews. It is considered to be Baldwin's second-best novel. In it Baldwin portrays multiple relationships involving interracial and bisexual love through a third-person point of view. Again he looks for resolutions to racial and sexual tensions through the power of love. The characters, however, often have trouble distinguishing sex from love and sorting through their attitudes toward sex, race, and class. Though successful, the novel is somewhat unwieldy with nine major characters, dominated by black jazz drummer Rufus Scott, who commits suicide at the end of the first chapter. The conclusion leaves readers with the hope that some of these troubled characters can achieve levels of self-understanding that will allow them to continue searching for "another country" within flawed and racist America. As Nigerian writer Wole Soyinka wrote in 1989,

In the ambiguities of Baldwin's expression of social, sexual, even racial and political conflicts will be found that insistent modality of conduct, and even resolution, celebrated or lamented as a tragic omission—love.... James Baldwin's was—to stress the obvious—a different cast of intellect and creative sensibility from a Ralph Ellison's, a Sonia Sanchez's, a Richard Wright's, an AMIRI BARAKA's, or an Ed Bullins's. He was, till the end, too deeply fascinated by the ambiguities of moral choices in human relations to posit them in raw conflict terms. His penetrating eyes saw the oppressor as *also* the oppressed. Hate as a revelation of self-hatred, never unambiguously outward-directed. Contempt as thwarted love, yearning for expression. Violence as inner fear, insecurity. Cruelty as an inward-turned knife. His was an optimistic, grey-toned vision of humanity in which the domain of mob law and lynch culture is turned inside out to reveal a landscape of scarecrows, an inner content of straws that await the compassionate breath of human love.

(Troupe, 11, 17–18)

With the death of Martin Luther King Jr., and the change in the civil rights movement of the late 1960s from integrationist to separatist, Baldwin's writing, according to many critics, lost direction. The last two decades of his life he spent mostly abroad, particularly in France, which may have increased his distance from America in his work. In the essay collection *No Name in the Street* (1972), Baldwin discussed his sadness over the movement's waning. At the same time, he found himself the subject of attacks by new black writers such as ELDRIDGE CLEAVER, much like his own rejection of Richard Wright in the 1950s. *The Devil Finds Work* (1976) is Baldwin's reading of racial stereotypes in American movies, and *The Evidence of Things Not Seen* (1985), an account of the Atlanta child murder trials, was unsuccessful, although the French translation of this book was very well received. Baldwin also wrote a series of problematic novels in his later years: *Tell Me How Long the Train's Been Gone* (1968), *If Beale Street Could Talk* (1974), and *Just above My Head* (1979). In these novels Baldwin seems to go over the familiar ground of the first three novels: racial, familial, and sexual conflicts in flawed, autobiographical plots. He never again achieved the mastery of his first novel, *Go Tell It on the Mountain*, one of the key texts in all of African American literature and of American literature as a whole.

After Baldwin died on the French Riviera, his funeral was celebrated on 8 December 1987 at the Cathedral of St. John the Divine in New York, where MAYA ANGELOU, TONI MORRISON, AMIRI BARAKA, the French ambassador Emmanuel de Margerie, and other notables spoke and performed. Baldwin has generally been considered to be strongest as an essayist, though he published one outstanding novel, and weakest as a playwright because he became too didactic at the expense of dramatic art. His achievements and influence tended to get lost in the sheer productivity of his career, especially as his later work was judged not to

measure up to his earlier work. After his death scholars were able to look at Baldwin's contribution with perspective and a sense of closure, and his literary stature grew accordingly.

FURTHER READING

Baldwin's personal papers and manuscripts are in the James Weldon Johnson Collection, Beinecke Rare Book and Manuscript Library, Yale University; the Berg collection at the New York Public Library; and the Schomburg Center for Research in Black Culture of the New York Public Library, among other repositories.

Books by Baldwin not mentioned above include *Going to Meet the Man* (1965), *A Dialogue: James Baldwin and* NIKKI GIOVANNI (1971), *One Day When I Was Lost: A Scenario Based on* ALEX HALEY's *"The Autobiography of* MALCOLM *X"* (1972), *A Rap on Race* (with Margaret Mead [1973]), *Little Man, Little Man: A Story of Childhood* (1976), *Jimmy's Blues: Selected Poems* (1983), *The Price of the Ticket: Collected Nonfiction* (1985), and *Perspectives: Angles of African Art*, ed. James Baldwin et al. (1987).

Campbell, James. *Taking at the Gates: A Life of James Baldwin* (1991).
Gates, Henry Louis, Jr. "The Welcome Table [James Baldwin]" in *Thirteen Ways of Looking at a Black Man* (1997).
Leeming, David Adams. *James Baldwin: A Biography* (1994).
Porter, Horace A. *Stealing the Fire: The Art and Protest of James Baldwin* (1989).
Standley, Fred L., and Nancy V. Burt, eds. *Critical Essays on James Baldwin* (1988).
———, and Louis H. Pratt, eds. *Conversations with James Baldwin* (1989).
Troupe, Quincy, ed. *James Baldwin: The Legacy* (1989).
Weatherby, W. J. *James Baldwin: Artist on Fire* (1989).

Obituaries: *New York Times*, 2 Dec. 1987; *Washington Post*, 5 Dec. 1987; *New York Review of Books* 34 (Jan. 1988).

—ANN RAYSON

BANNEKER, BENJAMIN

(9 Nov. 1731–19 Oct. 1806), farmer and astronomer, was born near the Patapsco River in Baltimore County in what became the community of Oella, Maryland, the son of Robert, a freed slave, and Mary Banneky, a daughter of a freed slave named Bannka and Molly Welsh, a freed English indentured servant who had

been transported to Maryland. Banneker was taught by his white grandmother to read and write from a Bible. He had no formal education other than a brief attendance at a Quaker one-room school during winter months. He was a voracious reader, informing himself in his spare time in literature, history, religion, and mathematics with whatever books he could borrow. From an early age he demonstrated a talent for mathematics and for creating and solving mathematical puzzles. With his three sisters he grew up on his father's tobacco farm, and for the rest of his life Banneker continued to live in a log house built by his father.

At about the age of twenty Banneker constructed a striking clock without ever having seen one, although tradition states he may once have examined a watch movement. He approached the project as a mathematical challenge, calculating the proper sizes and ratios of the teeth of the wheels, gears, and pinions, each of which he carved from wood with a pocket knife, possibly using a piece of metal or glass for a bell. The clock became a subject of popular interest throughout the region and many came to see and admire it. The timepiece operated successfully for more than forty years, until his death.

After his father's death in 1759, Banneker continued to farm tobacco, living with his mother until she died some time after 1775. Thereafter he lived alone, his sisters having one by one married and settled in the region. They attended to his major household needs. His life was limited almost entirely to his farm, remote from community life and potential persecution because of his color, until the advent of new neighbors.

In about 1771 five Ellicott brothers of Bucks County, Pennsylvania, purchased large tracts of land adjacent to the Banneker farm and began to develop a major industrial community called Ellicott's Lower Mills (now Ellicott City, Maryland). They initiated the large-scale cultivation of wheat in the state, built flour mills, sawmills, an iron foundry, and a general store that served not only their own needs but also those of the region. They marketed their flour by shipping it from the port of Baltimore. Banneker met members of the Ellicott family and often visited the building sites to watch each structure as it was being erected, intrigued particularly by the mechanisms of the mills.

George Ellicott, a son of one of the brothers, who built a stone house near the Patapsco River, often spent his leisure time in the evenings pursuing his hobby of astronomy. As he searched the skies with his telescope, he would explain what he saw to neighbors who came to watch. Banneker was frequently among them, fascinated by the new world in the skies opened up by the telescope. Noting his interest, in 1789 young Ellicott lent him a telescope, several astronomy books, and an old gateleg table on which to use them. Ellicott promised to visit Banneker as soon as he could to explain the rudiments of the science. Before he found time for his visit, however, Banneker had absorbed the contents of the texts and had taught himself enough through trial and error to calculate an ephemeris for an almanac for the next year and to make projections of lunar and solar eclipses.

Banneker, now age fifty-nine, suffered from rheumatism or arthritis and abandoned farming. He subsequently devoted his evening and night hours to searching the skies; he slept during the day, a practice that gained him a reputation for laziness and slothfulness from his neighbors.

Early in 1791 Banneker's new skills came to the attention of Major Andrew Ellicott, George's cousin, who had been appointed by President George Washington to survey a ten-mile square of land in Virginia and Maryland to become the new site of the national capital. Major Ellicott needed an assistant capable of using astronomical instruments for the first several months of the survey until his two brothers, who generally worked with him, became available. He visited Ellicott's Lower Mills to ask George to assist him for the interim, but George was unable to do so and recommended Banneker.

At the beginning of February 1791 Banneker accompanied Major Ellicott to Alexandria, Virginia, the beginning point of the survey, and was installed in the field observatory tent where he was to maintain the astronomical field clock and use other instruments. Using the large zenith sector, his responsibility was to observe and record stars near

the zenith as they crossed the meridian at different times during the night; the observations were to be repeated a number of nights over a period of time. After he had corrected the data he collected for refraction, aberration, and nutation and compared it with data in published star catalogs, Banneker determined latitude based on each of the stars observed. He also used the transit and equal altitude instrument to take equal altitudes of the sun, by which the astronomical clock was periodically checked and rated.

Banneker had the use of Major Ellicott's texts and notes, from which he continued to learn, and spent his leisure hours calculating the ephemeris for an almanac for 1792. In April, with the arrival of Major Ellicott's brothers, Banneker returned to his home. He was paid the sum of sixty dollars for his services and travel. Ellicott was paid five dollars a day exclusive of room and board while his assistant surveyors were paid two dollars a day. Banneker still supported himself primarily with proceeds from his farm.

Shortly after his return home, with the assistance of George Ellicott and family, Banneker's calculations for an almanac were purchased and published by Baltimore printers Goddard & Angell as *Benjamin Banneker's Pennsylvania, Delaware, Maryland and Virginia Almanack and Ephemeris, for the Year of Our Lord, 1792 . . .*; a second edition was produced by Philadelphia printer William Young. The almanac contained a biographical sketch of Banneker written by Senator James McHenry, who presented Banneker's achievement as new evidence supporting arguments against slavery.

Shortly before the almanac's publication, Banneker sent a manuscript copy of his calculations to Thomas Jefferson, secretary of state, with a covering letter urging the abolition of slavery. Jefferson replied, "No body wishes more than I do to see such proofs as you exhibit, that nature has given to our black brethren, talents equal to those of the other colors of men, and that the appearance of a want of them is owing merely to the degraded condition of their existence. . . . No body wishes more ardently to see a good system commenced for raising the condition both of their body & mind to what it

ought to be." The exchange of letters between Banneker and Jefferson was published as a pamphlet by Philadelphia printer David Lawrence and distributed widely at the same time that the almanac appeared. Promoted by the abolitionist societies of Pennsylvania and Maryland, the almanac sold in great numbers.

Encouraged by his first success, Banneker continued to calculate ephemerides for almanacs that were published for the succeeding five years and sold widely in the United States and England. A total of at least twenty-eight editions of his almanacs were published, largely supported by the abolitionist societies. Although he continued to calculate ephemerides each year until 1804 for his own pleasure, diminishing interest in the abolitionist movement failed to find a publisher for them after the 1797 almanac.

Although he was not associated with any particular religion, Banneker was deeply religious and attended services of various denominations whenever ministers or speakers visited the region, preferring meetings of the Society of Friends. He was described as having "a most benign and thoughtful expression," as being of erect posture despite his age, scrupulously neat in dress. Another who knew him noted, "He was very precise in conversation and exhibited deep reflection." Banneker died in his sleep during a nap after having taken a walk early one Sunday morning a month short of his seventy-fifth birthday. He had arranged that immediately after his death, all of his borrowed texts and instruments were to be returned to George Ellicott, which was done before his burial two days later. During his burial in the family graveyard on his farm, his house burst into flames and was destroyed. All that survived were a few letters he had written, his astronomical journal, his commonplace book, and the books he had borrowed.

The publication of Banneker's almanacs brought him international fame in his time, and modern studies have confirmed that his figures compared favorably with those of other contemporary men of science who calculated ephemerides for almanacs. Long thought lost, the sites of Banneker's house and outbuilding have been the subjects of an archaeological excavation from which various artifacts have been recovered. Banneker has been memorialized in the naming of several institutes and secondary schools. Without the limitation of opportunity because of his regional location and the state of science in his time, Banneker would undoubtedly have emerged as a far more important figure in early American science than merely as the first black man of science.

FURTHER READING

Most of Banneker's personal papers, correspondence, and manuscripts are privately owned.

Bedini, Silvio A. *The Life of Benjamin Banneker* (1972).

Tyson, Martha Ellicott. *Banneker, the Afric-American Astronomer: From the Posthumous Papers of Martha E. Tyson* (1884).
—SILVIO A. BEDINI

One of the first African American painters to receive national recognition, Edward M. Bannister was known not only for landscapes and seascapes but also for portraits and genre works, such as The Newspaper Boy of 1869. Art Resource/Smithsonian American Art Museum, Gift of Jack Hafif and Frederick Weingeroff

 BANNISTER, EDWARD MITCHELL (c. 1826– 9 Jan. 1901), painter, was born in St. Andrews, New Brunswick, Canada, the son of Hannah Alexander, a native of New Brunswick, and Edward Bannister, from Barbados. While his birth date has generally been given as 1828, recent research has suggested that he was born several years earlier. After the death of his father in 1832, Edward was raised by his mother, whom he later credited with encouraging his artistic aspirations: "The love of art in some form came to me from my mother.... She it was who encouraged and fostered my childhood propensities for drawing and coloring" (Holland, *Edward Mitchell Bannister*, 17). His mother died in 1844, and Edward and his younger brother, William, were sent to work for a wealthy local family, where he was exposed to classical literature, music, and painting. Edward's interest in art continued, and an early biography of the artist reported that "the results of his pen might be seen on the fences and barn doors or wherever else he could charcoal or crayon out rude likenesses of men or things about him" (Hartigan, 71).

In the early 1850s Bannister settled in Boston, where he supported himself by working as a hairdresser. By 1853 he was employed by Madame Christiana Carteaux, a successful black entrepreneur who operated several beauty salons and sold her own line of hair products and who would later become his wife. Unable to persuade any of the local established artists to take a black man on as a pupil, Bannister studied art independently during this period. Despite these obstacles, he achieved some local recognition as a landscapist and portrait painter. In 1854 Dr. John V. DeGrasse, the first black doctor admitted to the Massachusetts Medical Society, gave Bannister his first commission, a harbor scene entitled *The Ship Outward Bound* (location unknown).

On 10 June 1857 Bannister and Carteaux were married, and by the following year Bannister had established himself as a full-time artist. His wife's financial and emotional support was critical to his success. As he recalled in later years, "I would have made out very poorly had it not been for her, and my greatest successes have come through her, either through her criticisms of my pictures, or the advice she would give me in the matter of placing them in public" (Holland, *Edward Mitchell Bannister*, 8). The couple was active in Boston's African American arts community and in the abolitionist movement. Bannister served as an officer of the Union Progressive Society and the Colored Citizens of Boston and was a delegate to the New England Colored Citizens Convention in 1859 and 1865.

In the 1860s Bannister began his professional artistic career in earnest. A listing in the Boston city directory identifies him as a portrait painter, and in 1862 he traveled to New York to study photography in order to enter into the lucrative daguerreotype business. Bannister advertised his services as a daguerreotypist in 1863 and 1864, but none of his photographs has been identified. During these years he also undertook his only formal art training, taking life-drawing classes at the Lowell Institute between 1863 and 1865 with the sculptor and anatomist Dr. William Rimmer. Few works survive from this period of Bannister's career, but his portraits of *Prudence Nelson Bell* (1864, private collection) and of *Robert Gould Shaw* (c. 1864, location unknown), the latter raffled to raise money for the families of black soldiers killed in the Civil War, are evidence both of his success as a portraitist and his ties to Boston's abolitionist and activist communities.

In 1869 Bannister left Boston and settled in Providence, Rhode Island, perhaps because of his wife's family ties to the area. He announced his professional arrival in the city by exhibiting two paintings, a portrait of the famous Boston abolitionist *William Lloyd Garrison* (location unknown) and *Newspaper Boy* (1869, National Museum of American Art [NMAA]), a sensitive portrait of one of the many young boys who sold papers on the streets of Boston. Although the racial identity of the fair-skinned child is uncertain, the painting is often discussed as one of Bannister's few known works dealing directly with African American subjects.

Upon moving to Providence, Bannister began to paint fewer portraits and more landscapes and sea scenes, the work for which he is primarily known today. While he never traveled to Europe, his work—like the work of many American painters—was strongly influenced by European art, particularly the landscape paintings of the Barbizon school. These loosely handled scenes of peasants and farm animals working in bucolic harmony touched a chord among many American landscape painters, and in works such as *Driving Home the Cows* (1881, NMAA) and *Hauling Rails* (1891, NMAA), Bannister created similarly idyllic images of pastoral landscapes. In *Haygatherers* (c. 1893, private collection), Bannister extended this poetic vision of rural life to a specifically American context, depicting African American women and children loading a cart with hay. The artist also painted many scenes of Rhode Island's coastline, which he observed from the decks of his small yacht, the *Fanchon*. In addition to his finished oil paintings completed in the studio, Bannister did many sensitively handled oil sketches and drawings, and these small works are among the freshest and most attractive of his works.

Like many nineteenth-century artists, Bannister viewed the depiction of the natural world as a spiritual endeavor. In a lecture delivered in 1886, he described

the artist's role as "the interpreter of the infinite, subtle qualities of the spiritual idea centreing [sic] in all created things, expounding for us the laws of beauty, and so far as finite mind and executive ability can, revealing to us glimpses of the absolute idea of perfect harmony" (Hartigan, 77).

Bannister came to national attention when his painting *Under the Oaks* (location unknown) was awarded a first-prize medal at the Centennial Exhibition in Philadelphia in 1876. The only other African American artist represented at the exhibition was EDMONIA LEWIS, whose life-sized sculpture, *Death of Cleopatra*, caused quite a sensation. Bannister had submitted his work without any biographical detail, and he later recalled the surprise of the awards committee upon learning of his racial identity: "Finally when I succeeded in reaching the desk where inquiries were made, I endeavored to gain the attention of the official in change. He was very insolent.... I was not an artist to them, simply an inquisitive colored man; controlling myself, I said deliberately, 'I am interested in the report that *Under the Oaks* has received a prize; I painted the picture.' An explosion could not have made a more marked impression. Without hesitation he apologized, and soon every one in the room was bowing and scraping to me" (Hartigan, 70). A Boston collector, John Duff, purchased the painting for fifteen hundred dollars, a substantial sum of money at the time.

This success led to increased demand for his work and to his visibility and prominence in the local Providence art world. Bannister served on the first board of the new Rhode Island School of Design (RISD) and was a founding member of the Providence Art Club. Officially chartered in 1880, the club served as a center for Providence's artistic community, hosting lectures and social events and mounting regular exhibitions in the spring and fall. Bannister showed his work at the club's exhibitions for the remainder of his career and served regularly on the executive committee. His work was purchased both by African American patrons, such as JOHN HOPE, George Downing Jr., and MADAME SISSIERETTA JONES, and by local white collectors, such as Isaac Bates and Joseph Ely.

While landscape and sea scenes remained Bannister's specialty, he made occasional forays into religious and history painting throughout his career. An account of Bannister's studio in the 1860s mentions a painting of *Cleopatra Waiting to Receive Marc Antony* (location unknown), and in the 1890s he painted several literary compositions, including a small oil sketch of *Leucothea Rescuing Ulysses* (1891, Newport Hospital, Rhode Island) and scenes from Edmund Spenser's *Faerie Queen*. Bannister's figure paintings are less confident in their execution than his landscapes, perhaps because of his lack of formal artistic training, but he continued to experiment artistically throughout his career. The late work *Street Scene* (late 1890s, Museum of Art, RISD), a brightly colored impressionist view of an urban thoroughfare, demonstrates Bannister's continued interest in experimenting with new styles and subjects even in the final years of his career.

Bannister died of a heart attack on 9 January 1901, while attending a prayer meeting at the Elmwood Street Baptist Church in Providence. In May of that year a memorial exhibition of his work, including 101 paintings, was mounted at the Providence Art Club. In the catalog the artist John Arnold recalled, "His gentle disposition, his urbanity of manner and his generous appreciation of the work of others made him a welcome guest in all artistic circles.... He was par excellence a landscape painter, the best our state has ever produced. He painted with profound feeling, not for pecuniary results, but to leave upon the canvas his impression of natural scenery, and to express his delight in the wondrous beauty of land, sea, and sky" (*Painters of Rhode Island*, 1996, 13).

FURTHER READING

Bannister's papers are at the Archives of American Art at the Smithsonian Institution, Washington, D.C.

Hartigan, Lynda Roscoe. *Sharing Traditions: Five Black Artists in Nineteenth-Century America* (1985).
Holland, Juanita. *Edward Mitchell Bannister, 1828–1901* (1992).
———. "To Be Free, Gifted and Black: African American Artist, Edward Mitchell Bannister" in *International Review of African American Art* 12.1 (1995).
—PAMELA M. FLETCHER

BARAKA, AMIRI

(7 Oct. 1934–), poet, playwright, educator, and activist, was born Everett Leroy Jones in Newark, New Jersey, the eldest of two children to Coyette Leroy Jones, a postal supervisor, and Anna Lois Russ, a social worker. Jones's lineage included teachers, preachers, and shop owners who elevated his family into Newark's modest, though ambitious, black middle class. His own neighborhood was black, but the Newark of Jones's youth was mostly white and largely Italian. He felt isolated and embattled at McKinley Junior High and Barringer High School, yet he excelled in his studies, played the trumpet, ran track, and wrote comic strips.

Graduating from high school with honors at age fifteen, Jones entered the Newark branch of Rutgers University on a science scholarship. In 1952, after his first year, he transferred to Howard University, hoping to find a sense of purpose at a black college that had eluded him at the white institution. It was at this point that a long process of reinventing himself first became evident; he changed the spelling of his name to "LeRoi" and told anyone who asked that he was going to become a doctor. Yet, he was more interested in pledging fraternities than getting good grades. In retrospect Jones blamed the college's "petty bourgeois Negro mentality" (*Autobiography*, 113) for his academic failure and came to regard black colleges as places where they "teach you to pretend to be white" (Watts, 22).

With his college ambitions dashed, Jones joined the air force in 1954, where he trained as a weatherman. He graduated at the top of his class and was stationed at Ramey Air Force Base in Puerto Rico. There he became an avid reader of Proust, Hemingway, Dostoyevsky, Sartre, and Camus. He subscribed to literary journals such as the *Partisan Review* and began to send his poems to publishers, who promptly rejected them. Jones claimed that his possession of left-leaning reading material was responsible for his dishonorable discharge from the military in 1957. Working as a stock clerk at the Gotham Book Mart in Manhattan, he resumed a friendship with Steve Korret, an aspiring writer in New York's Greenwich Village.

Through Korret, Jones was introduced to an avant-garde literary scene and a bohemian culture that profoundly altered his life. Allen Ginsberg, the doyen of the Beat poets of the 1950s, became a mentor after Jones wrote him a letter on toilet paper to show how hip he was. Charles Olson, a leader of the ultramodern Black Mountain poets, influenced his writing, and even LANGSTON HUGHES, who occasionally gave readings in the Village accompanied by bassist CHARLES MINGUS, encouraged him and nurtured a friendship that Jones cherished deeply. In 1958 Jones married, in a Buddhist temple, a white, Jewish woman, Hettie Cohen, the secretary of *The Record Changer*, a jazz magazine where Jones worked as the shipping manager. Together they had two children and published *Yugen*, a chic, though short-lived, literary magazine.

By the late 1950s Jones's poetry began to appear in such periodicals as *Naked Ear, Evergreen Review*, and *Big Table*, and in 1959 he founded a publishing company, Totem Press, which issued his first collection of poems, *Preface to a Twenty-Volume Suicide Note* (1961). Though his poetry at this point had a distinct blues idiom, it was not yet overtly political. That transformation was prompted by a visit to Cuba in 1960, where he saw artists as revolutionaries who advanced Cuban nationalism. This experience led him to view his own situation more critically. Soon after returning he began to write polemical essays such as "Cuba Libre," he became a street activist, and he urged his Beat peers to strive for greater political relevance in their work. Jones then demonstrated that he was a serious student of history and music with the publication of *Blues People: Negro Music in White America* (1963). RALPH ELLISON remarked that "the tremendous burden of sociology which Jones would place upon this body of music is enough to give even the blues the blues" (Justin Driver, *New Republic*, 25 Apr. 2002), but most critics regarded the book as an important contribution.

In 1963 Jones tried his hand at playwriting and discovered that here, too, he had the Midas touch. *Dutchman*, a play about a "black boy with a phony English accent" who has a fatal encounter with an attractive white woman on a New York City subway, won an Obie in 1964, and became a sensation in many circles; it continues to be performed, and established Jones's new persona as an American firebrand. The following year, while at a book party surrounded by his cohorts from the Village, Jones received word that MALCOLM X had been assassinated up in Harlem. He later remembered this moment as an epiphany in which he realized that he was in the wrong crowd: "I felt that I had been dominated by white ideas, even down to my choice of wife" (*Village Voice*, 12 Dec. 1980). He left his wife and moved to Harlem, where he established the Black Arts Repertory Theater-School and soon became a leading black nationalist.

Jones's only novel, *The System of Dante's Hell*, was published in 1965, and much of the poetry he wrote during this period was a repudiation of his earlier life and career. In "Black Dada Nihilismus" he wrote, "Rape the white girls. Rape / their fathers...choke my friends," and in "The Liar" he reasoned, "What I thought was love / in me, I find a thousand instances / as fear." In "Black Art" he lays out his criteria for black poetry in lines such as "Poems are bullshit unless they are / teeth.... We want poems / like fists beating niggers out of Jocks / or dagger poems in the slimy bellies / of the owner-jews," and he speaks of his verses as a "poem cracking steel knuckles in a jew-lady's mouth." Later, in an essay entitled "Confessions of a Former Anti-Semite," he acknowledged that during his "personal trek through the wasteland of anti-Semitism," his need to make an intellectual and political break with American liberals was unfortunately expressed as a venomous attack on Jews—who had earlier been his greatest liberal influences—and was often motivated by an unresolved anger towards his ex-wife. "Anti-Semitism," he wrote, "is as ugly an idea and as deadly as white racism" (*Village Voice*, 12 Dec. 1980).

The treatment of gays and homosexuality in Jones's work is highly problematic, as it is both complex and contradictory. Two of his early plays, *The Baptism*, set in a church, and *The Toilet*, set in a men's room, feature gay characters who can be interpreted sympathetically. According to Werner Sollors, "Homosexuality is viewed positively by Baraka both as an outsider-situation analogous to, though now also in conflict with, that of Blackness, and as a possibility for the realization of 'love' and 'beauty' against the racial gang code of a hostile society" (Sollors, 108). Ron Simmons argues that the gay tension is present in his work because Jones "never reconciled his homosexual past," a past that Jones alludes to in *The System of Dante's Hell* and ruminates about in "Tone Poem:" "Blood spoiled in the air, caked and anonymous. Arms opening, opened last night, we sat up howling and kissing. Men who loved each other. Will that be understood? That we could, and still move under cold nights with clenched-fists" (Simmons, 318). Jones concludes that race-conscious men could not safely sleep with men and be credible black nationalists. Yet, unlike ELDRIDGE CLEAVER, Jones did not see a contradiction in JAMES BALDWIN, who was explicit and unapologetic about his homosexuality. In "Jimmy!," a stirring eulogy to Baldwin he read at Baldwin's funeral in 1987, he credits Baldwin with starting the Black Arts Movement and pleads, "Let us one day be able to celebrate him like he must be celebrated if we are ever to be truly self determining. For Jimmy was God's black revolutionary mouth."

In 1966 Jones married Sylvia Robinson, a fellow poet. The following year he adopted the Swahili Muslim name Imamu Amiri Baraka (which means "spiritual leader, prince, blessed"), and she became Amina ("faithful") Baraka. Together they had five children. Baraka never fully embraced Islam as a religion and later dropped Imamu from his name. Rather he practiced "Kawaida," a form of cultural black nationalism that is an eclectic blend of Islamic, Egyptian, West African, and other traditions synthesized by Maulana Karenga, Baraka's mentor from about 1967 until Baraka became a Marxist in 1974. With the publication of *Home* (1966), especially the seminal essay "The Myth of 'Negro Literature,'" Baraka profoundly influenced a new generation of writers, including AUGUST WILSON, Haki Madhubuti, and Sonia Sanchez. As a political organizer in 1970, Baraka helped Kenneth Gibson to become the first black mayor of

Newark, New Jersey, where Baraka had returned to live, and he was a principal organizer of the National Black Political Convention in Gary, Indiana, in 1972.

While serving a forty-eight week sentence in a Harlem halfway house in 1979, following a domestic dispute and a conviction for resisting arrest, Baraka began writing his autobiography, in which he characterizes some of the earlier sexist, racist, and specious ideological reasoning of the Black Power movement as little more than "nuttiness disguised as revolution" (*Autobiography*, 387). After becoming a Third World Marxist, the pace of both his writing and his activism slowed over the next two decades, during which he taught at several colleges, including Yale University, Rutgers University (where he was denied tenure), and at Stony Brook University, where he retired as Professor Emeritus in 1999. He received the American Book Awards' Lifetime Achievement Award in 1989, and in 2002 he was named Poet Laureate of New Jersey. Yet controversy continued to dog him as the governor and state legislature introduced legislation to remove Baraka as laureate in reaction to his poem "Somebody Blew Up America," which alleges that Israel and President George W. Bush had foreknowledge of the September 11, 2001, terrorist attack against the World Trade Center in New York City.

FURTHER READING

Baraka, Amiri. *The Autobiography of Leroi Jones* (1984, rpt. 1997).

———. *The LeRoi Jones/Amiri Baraka Reader* (1999).

Simmons, Ron. "Baraka's Dilemma: To Be or Not to Be?" in *Black Men on Race, Gender, and Sexuality*, ed. Devon Carbado (1999).

Sollors, Werner. *Amiri Baraka/LeRoi Jones: The Quest for a "Populist Modernism"* (1978).

Watts, Jerry Gafio. *Amiri Baraka: The Politics and Art of a Black Intellectual* (2001).

—SHOLOMO B. LEVY

 BARNETT, CLAUDE ALBERT (16 Sept. 1889– 2 Aug. 1967), entrepreneur, journalist, and government adviser, was born in Sanford, Florida, the son of William Barnett, a hotel worker, and Celena

Anderson. His father worked part of the year in Chicago and the rest of the time in Florida. Barnett's parents separated when he was young, and he lived with his mother's family in Oak Park, Illinois, where he attended school. His maternal ancestors were free blacks who migrated from Wake County, North Carolina, to the black settlement of Lost Creek, near Terre Haute, Indiana, during the 1830s. They then moved to Mattoon, Illinois, where Barnett's maternal grandfather was a teacher and later a barbershop owner, and finally to Oak Park. While attending high school in Oak Park, Barnett worked as a houseboy for Richard W. Sears, cofounder of Sears, Roebuck and Company. Sears offered him a job with the company after he graduated from high school, but Barnett's mother insisted that he receive a college education. He graduated from Tuskegee Institute with a degree in Engineering in 1906. His maternal grandfather and BOOKER T. WASHINGTON, founder and head of Tuskegee Institute, were the major influences on Barnett's life and values. He cherished the principles of hard work, self-help, thrift, economic development, and service to his race.

Following graduation from Tuskegee, Barnett worked as a postal clerk in Chicago. While still employed by the post office, in 1913 he started his own advertising agency, the Douglas Specialty Company, through which he sold mail-order portraits of famous black men and women. He left the post office in 1915 and in 1918, with several other entrepreneurs, founded the Kashmir Chemical Company, which manufactured Nile Queen hair-care products and cosmetics. Barnett became Kashmir's advertising manager and he toured the country to market its products and his portraits. He helped to develop a national market for Kashmir and also pioneered the use of positive advertisements. Traditional advertisements featured an unattractive black woman with a message that others should use the company's products to avoid looking like her. In contrast, Barnett used good-looking black models and celebrities with positive messages about the beauty of black women. He visited local black newspapers to negotiate advertising space and discovered that they were desperate for national news but did not have the resources to subscribe to the established newswire services. Barnett recommended that the *Chicago Defender*, founded by ROBERT ABBOTT in 1905 and the most widely circulated black newspaper during the early twentieth century, establish a black news service. The newspaper rejected his proposal since it had enough sources for its own publication and feared harming its circulation by providing competitors with material.

In March 1919, with backing from Kashmir's board of directors, Barnett started the Associated Negro Press (ANP) in the company's office. In 1926 the Kashmir Chemical Company dissolved under legal pressure from Procter and Gamble, which made a similar line of products called Cashmere. Barnett was now free to devote his attention fully to ANP. During this era black newspapers published weekly, so ANP evolved as a mail service rather than as a wire service, thereby making it affordable to subscribers. Moreover, the major wire services did not offer much information about African Americans. Barnett began ANP with eighty subscribers, including almost all the black newspapers and several white papers. He charged $25 to join ANP and a monthly fee of $16 to $24, depending on whether newspapers received dispatches once or twice a week. Subscribers agreed to credit ANP for articles featured in their newspapers, to provide ANP with news about their communities, and to forfeit membership if they failed to pay for the service within sixty days.

The staff produced about seventy pages of copy a week, including news stories, opinion pieces, essays, poetry, books reviews, cartoons, and occasionally photographs; the copy was then mimeographed and sent to subscribers. It did not cost much to operate ANP. The service mined news stories from various sources, such as black newspapers, the white press, special correspondents, and news releases from government agencies, foundations, organizations, and businesses, creating one of the most comprehensive files of news stories about African Americans. Barnett wrote some of the stories himself under the pen name Albert Anderson, a

combination of his middle name and his mother's maiden name. Because subscribers usually were late in paying their fees, Barnett struggled to keep ANP afloat. Sometimes he took advertising space in the newspapers in lieu of news service fees. His companies, first Associated Publishers Representatives and later the National Feature Service, then sold the space to advertisers, offering advertisers lower rates than they would get if they placed advertisements directly with the newspapers.

In 1932 Barnett became one of the first graduates to serve on Tuskegee Institute's board of trustees. He also served as president of the board of trustees of Provident Hospital in Chicago, director of the Supreme Liberty Life Insurance Company, member of the Red Cross's national board of governors, and trustee of the Phelps-Stokes Fund. During the late 1920s and early 1930s he headed the Republican Party's publicity campaign for the black vote. Some of his ANP subscribers became upset by his stories that favored the Republicans. After Franklin D. Roosevelt's election to the presidency in 1932 and first lady Eleanor Roosevelt's growing popularity among African Americans, Barnett ended his relationship with the Republican Party.

Barnett married the popular concert singer and actress Etta Moten in 1934. She had three daughters from a previous marriage. Barnett managed her career until 1942, when she assumed the lead role in the Broadway show *Porgy and Bess* and began to require the attention of a full-time agent. Also in 1942, Barnett became special assistant to the secretary of agriculture, Claude R. Wickard, a position that he held with successive secretaries until 1952, when the Republicans regained the White House with the election of Dwight D. Eisenhower. During his tenure with the Department of Agriculture, Barnett was a strong advocate for black tenant farmers and sharecroppers and sought to make it possible for them to own land. He also tried to improve the condition of black farmers through federal aid for health, education, and insurance programs. He was particularly interested in strengthening black agricultural colleges.

During World War II, ANP employed eight people at its Chicago

headquarters and had almost two hundred subscribers. The news service opened an office in Washington, D.C., and later one at the United Nations in New York City. Barnett penned many articles about segregation in the military and pressed the federal government to accredit black journalists as war correspondents. His advocacy of racial equality played an important role in President Harry S. Truman's decision in 1948 to desegregate the military.

With an expanding African independence movement after World War II, Barnett secured more than one hundred African newspapers as subscribers to ANP. In 1959 he organized the World News Service to provide copy to subscribers in Africa. Barnett traveled to Africa more than fifteen times to solicit subscribers and to collect material for articles on black progress. He and his wife became avid collectors of African art and were much-sought-after speakers on Africa to African American civic, fraternal, and religious organizations. Although he had no formal training as a newsman, Barnett helped to develop a generation of black journalists. Most of his featured columnists wrote for the benefit of a large black audience rather than for pay.

With the rise of the civil rights movement during the late 1950s, many white newspapers began to cover the black community in the United States. News organizations started hiring black correspondents, most of whom had broken into the industry with ANP. Barnett had established a means for the black press to secure national and later international news about black people. ANP, with its motto "Progress, Loyalty, Truth," set professional standards for the black press and nurtured black journalists who were well prepared to move into mainstream media with the success of the civil rights movement. Increased competition, persistent financial problems, and failing health forced Barnett to close ANP and to retire in 1963. He made several more trips to Africa and began writing an autobiography. He died of a cerebral hemorrhage at his Chicago home.

FURTHER READING

The Archives and Manuscript Department of the Chicago Historical Society house Barnett's papers and ANP files. Most of this material is available on microfilm.

Evans, Linda J. "Claude A. Barnett and the Associated Negro Press." *Chicago History* 12, no. 1 (Spring 1983): 44–56.

Hogan, Lawrence D. *A Black National News Service: The Associated Negro Press and Claude Barnett, 1919–1945* (1984).

Silverman, Robert Mark. "The Effects of Racism and Racial Discrimination on Minority Business Development: The Case of Black Manufacturers in Chicago's Ethnic Beauty Aids Industry." *Journal of Social History* 31, no. 3 (Spring 1998): 571–597.

Obituary: *New York Times*, 3 Aug. 1967.
—ROBERT L. HARRIS JR.

BARTHÉ, RICHMOND

(28 Jan. 1901–6 Mar. 1989), sculptor, was born in Bay St. Louis, Mississippi, the son of Richmond Barthé and Marie Clementine Roboteau, a seamstress. His father died when Barthé was one month old. Barthé began drawing as a child and first exhibited his work at the county fair in Mississippi at age twelve. He did not attend high school, but he learned about his African heritage from books borrowed from a local grocer and publications given to him by a wealthy white family that vacationed in Bay St. Louis. This family, which had connections to Africa through ambassadorships, hired Barthé as a butler when he was in his teens; he moved with them to New Orleans. At age eighteen Barthé won first prize for a drawing he sent to the Mississippi County Fair. Lyle Saxon, the literary critic for the *New Orleans Times Picayune*, then attempted to register Barthé in a New Orleans art school, but Barthé was denied admission because of his race.

In 1924 Barthé began classes at the School of the Art Institute of Chicago, his tuition paid by a Catholic priest, Harry Kane. Living with an aunt, Barthé paid for his board and art supplies by working as a porter and busboy. During his senior year Barthé began modeling in clay at the suggestion of his anatomy teacher, Charles Schroeder. His busts of two classmates were shown in the Negro History Week exhibition. These works, along with busts of the Haitian general Toussaint-Louverture and the painter HENRY OSSAWA TANNER (first exhibited at a children's home in Gary, Indiana), were included in the Chicago Art League

annual exhibition in 1928, the year of Barthé's graduation.

Barthé achieved wide recognition for his bronze busts and figures in the 1930s and 1940s. Within a year after his move to New York City in February 1929, he completed thirty-five sculptures. He continued his education at the Art Students League with fellowships from the Rosenwald Foundation (1929–1930). Barthé's first solo exhibitions (favorably reviewed by the *New York Times*) were in 1934 at the Caz-Delbo Gallery in New York, the Grand Rapids Art Gallery in Michigan, and the Women's City Art Club in Chicago, followed by exhibitions in New York at Delphic Studios (1935), Arden Galleries (1939), DePorres Interracial Center (1945), International Print Society (1945), and Grand Central Art Galleries (1947). He also exhibited in numerous group shows at various institutions, including the Harmon Foundation (1929, 1931, and 1933), the New York World's Fair (1939), the Whitney Museum annual exhibitions (1933, 1940, 1944, and 1945), the Metropolitan Museum of Art's *Artists for Victory* (1942), and the Pennsylvania Academy of Fine Arts' annual exhibitions (1938, 1940, 1943, 1944, and 1948).

Many of Barthé's early works, such as *Masaai* (1933), *African Woman* (c. 1934), and *Wetta* (c. 1934), depict Africans. Barthé dreamed of visiting Africa, stating, "I'd really like to devote all my time to Negro subjects, and I plan shortly to spend a year and a half in Africa studying types, making sketches and models which I hope to finish off in Paris for a show there, and later in London and New York" (Lewis, 11), but he never traveled to the continent. Other works by Barthé, such as *Feral Benga, Stevedore*, and *African Man Dancing* (all 1937), were among the first sculptures of black male nudes by an African American artist.

In the mid-1930s Barthé moved from Harlem to midtown Manhattan for a larger studio and to be closer to major theaters, as many of his clients were theatrical celebrities. Among his portrait busts are *Cyrina* (from *Porgy and Bess*, c. 1934), *Sir John Gielgud as Hamlet* (commissioned for the Haymarket Theatre in London, 1937), *Maurice Evans as Richard II* (1938, now in the Shakespeare Theatre in Stratford, Connecticut), and *Katherine Cornell as Juliet* (1942). Barthé

Richmond Barthé's sculptures depicting African and African American themes garnered acclaim and success from the Harlem Renaissance on. The Blackberry Woman *of 1932, with its fluid sense, is characteristic of his bronzes.* Whitney Museum of American Art

later produced busts of other entertainers, such as *Josephine Baker* (1950) and *Paul Robeson as Othello* (1975).

Barthé's largest work was an eight-by-eighty-foot frieze, *Green Pastures: The Walls of Jericho* (1937–1938), which he completed under the U.S. Treasury Art Project at the Harlem River Housing Project. His other public works of art include portraits of Abraham Lincoln, in New York (1940) and India (1942); Arthur Brisbane, in Central Park; GEORGE WASHINGTON

CARVER, in Nashville (1945), and BOOKER T. WASHINGTON, at New York University (1946).

Many of Barthé's busts, such as *Birth of the Spirituals* (1941) and *The Negro Looks Ahead* (1944), are imbued with a calm spirituality. Barthé described his representational work as an attempt to "capture the beauty that I've seen in people, and abstraction wouldn't satisfy me.... My work is all wrapped up with my search for God. I am looking for God inside of people. I wouldn't find it in squares, triangles and circles" (Reynolds and Wright, 154). A strong believer in reincarnation, the artist often called himself an "Old Soul" who had been an artist in Egypt in an earlier life.

In the 1940s Barthé received numerous awards, beginning with Guggenheim fellowships in 1941 and 1942. In 1945 he was elected to the National Sculpture Society (sponsored by the sculptor Malvina Hoffman) and the American Academy of Arts and Letters. He also received the Audubon Artists Gold Medal of Honor and the James J. Hoey Award for interracial justice. The sculptor was also active in several artists' organizations: the Liturgical Arts Society, the International Print Society, the New York Clay Club, and the Sculptors Guild. He also had solo exhibitions at the South Side Art Center in Chicago (1942); the Sayville Playhouse on Long Island (1945); the Margaret Brown Gallery in Boston (1947); and Montclair Art Museum in New Jersey (1949).

In 1950 Barthé received a commission from the Haitian government to sculpt a large monument to Toussaint-Louverture; it now stands in front of the Palace in the Haitian capital, Port-au-Prince. In 1947 Barthé had moved to Jamaica, where he remained through the late 1960s. His most notable works from this time are the General Dessalines monument in Port-au-Prince (1952) and a portrait of Norman Manley, the prime minister of Jamaica (1956). The Institute of Jamaica hosted Barthé's solo show in 1959. In 1964 the artist received the Key to the City from Bay St. Louis. He then sculpted contemplative black male nudes, such as *Meditation* (1964), *Inner Music* (1965), and *Seeker* (1965).

Barthé left the West Indies in 1969 because of increasing violence there and spent five years traveling in Switzerland, Spain, and Italy. He then settled in Pasadena, California, and worked on his memoirs. In 1978 he had a solo exhibition at the William Grant Still Center in Los Angeles and was subsequently honored by the League of Allied Arts there in 1981. He died in Pasadena. Following his death, a retrospective was held at the Museum of African American Art (1990). Barthé's work toured the United States with that of Richard Hunt in the Landau/Traveling Exhibition *Two Sculptors, Two Eras* in 1992. His work, which was eventually collected by the Metropolitan and Whitney museums in New York City, the Smithsonian Institution in Washington, D.C., and the Art Institute of Chicago, among many others, continues to be featured in exhibitions and survey texts on African American art.

FURTHER READING

Lewis, Samella. *Two Sculptors, Two Eras* (1992).
Reynolds, Gary A., and Beryl J. Wright. *Against the Odds: African American Artists and the Harmon Foundation* (1989).

—THERESA LEININGER-MILLER

BASIE, COUNT

(21 Aug. 1904–26 Apr. 1984), jazz pianist, composer, and bandleader, was born William James Basie in Red Bank, New Jersey, the son of African American parents Harvey Lee Basie, an estate groundskeeper, and Lillian Ann Chiles, a laundress. Basie was first exposed to music through his mother's piano playing. He took piano lessons, played the drums, and acted in school skits. An indifferent student, he left school after junior high and began performing. He organized bands with friends and played various jobs in Red Bank, among them working as a movie theater pianist. In his late teens he pursued work in nearby Asbury Park, but he met with little success. Then, in the early 1920s, he moved to Harlem, where he learned from the leading pianists of the New York "stride" style, Willie "The Lion" Smith, James P. Johnson, Luckey

Roberts, and especially FATS WALLER, his exact contemporary.

Basie remained undecided between a stage or musical career. Until 1929 he alternately combined playing in Harlem nightclubs and theaters (on piano and organ) and touring with bands for vaudeville and burlesque troupes, which took him as far from New York as New Orleans, Kansas City, and Oklahoma. In Kansas City, during a layover in 1927 or 1928, Basie was stricken with spinal meningitis. After recovering, he worked solo jobs and eventually joined Walter Page's Blue Devils, a major regional dance band. The Blue Devils featured the southwestern boogie-woogie style of relatively spare blues-based melodies, effortless dance rhythms, and "swinging" syncopation (all hallmarks of the later Basie band style). Basie worked at devising arrangements for the band, assisted by trombonist-guitarist Eddie Durham. Basie's ability to read and write music improved over the years, but he continued to rely on staff and freelance arrangers. At this time Basie lost interest in the musical stage and dedicated himself to dance music.

Kansas City, a wide-open hub of speakeasies, gambling, and prostitution, offered an active job market for black musicians who specialized in the aggressively swinging southwestern (or Kansas City) blues style. While with the Blue Devils, Basie blended this style with his New York "stride" piano background, and in 1929 he was hired by Bennie Moten, who led the most successful Kansas City band of the time. Basie later called this move both the greatest risk and the most important turning point of his career. The Moten band toured extensively and played to large crowds in Chicago and New York.

About 1930, while working as Moten's second pianist and arranger, Basie married Vivian Wynn, but they soon separated and later divorced. Also in 1929 or 1930, he met a young chorus dancer, Catherine Morgan. She and Basie married in 1942 and had one daughter.

During a touring break in 1934, Basie took some Moten band musicians to Little Rock, Arkansas, for a longer-term job at a single location, after which the Moten band broke up. Back in Kansas City, Basie worked as a church organist and was preparing to join Moten's newest group when the bandleader died unexpectedly in 1935.

Since 1928 Basie had called himself "Count" in imitation of royal nicknames used by other Harlem musicians, but only on taking over the Moten band did he bill himself by that name. Basie soon had the best players from the Moten unit working for him at the Reno Club in Kansas City. This nucleus included trombonists Dan Minor and Eddie Durham, who was the band's chief arranger during its early years; tenor saxophonists Herschel Evans and Lester Young, a key innovator in jazz history; and the inimitable blues vocalist Jimmy Rushing.

To many listeners, however, the heart of the band was its superb rhythm section: on drums, Jo Jones, a keenly knowledgeable musician who revolutionized both big band and small group drumming; on guitar, Claude Williams, who was replaced in 1937 by Freddie Green (the mainstay of the Basie group for five decades); and on bass, Walter Page, former leader of the Blue Devils. These three men, in concord with Basie's own idiomatic piano work, synchronized their playing with unmatched skill, lightening and shading the driving, four-to-a-bar Kansas City beat, and infusing the band's ensemble play with supple, flowing, danceable rhythms.

In 1935 the white writer, critic, and record producer John Hammond heard a Basie radio broadcast and made arrangements to give the band national exposure. Expanding the group to thirteen men, Basie took his musicians to Chicago, where six of them made their first, classic recordings under the pseudonym (for contractual reasons) Jones-Smith, Inc. In New York City the band played at the Roseland Ballroom and recorded for Decca Records, with which the inexperienced Basie signed a demanding, long-term contract that paid no royalties. Included in the larger band's initial recordings was Basie's signature tune, "One O'Clock Jump," which featured the leader's slyly spare opening piano solo and the repeated, haunting melody played by the band. By this time Buck Clayton's often muted trumpet solos had become another of the band's features, while Ed Lewis on trumpet, Earle Warren on alto saxophone,

and Jack Washington on baritone saxophone anchored those instrumental sections. The band later formed an association with Columbia Records, which continued into the 1940s.

The Basie orchestra had come to New York City at the height of the big band era, but the group's relaxed, unembellished, freely swinging style reportedly puzzled those mostly white East Coast listeners who were enthusiasts of the strictly disciplined, thoroughly professional Benny Goodman orchestra. Hammond worked with Basie to tighten the band's section work and solo presentations. Such New York musicians as trombonists Dicky Wells and Benny Morton and trumpeter Harry Edison were hired. BILLIE HOLIDAY, who already had forged her own deeply personal jazz singing style, became the band's first woman vocalist, to be replaced a year later by Helen Humes. They each joined Jimmy Rushing, who solidified his position as the leading male blues singer of the big band era. The changes paid off in the late 1930s with successful stints at New York's Famous Door and Savoy Ballroom ("the home of happy feet"), followed by engagements in Chicago and San Francisco.

Basie later recalled that by 1940 "what that name [Count Basie] stood for now was me and the band as the same thing." The band undertook almost constant tours throughout the country and continued its prolific recording work. Among bandleaders Basie was matched only by DUKE ELLINGTON as a careful, tenacious master of a group of disparate individual artists. Both men were ambitious leaders who defined the basic sounds of their groups, and each of them was ready to step back and allow great freedom to their soloists. But although Ellington was a composer of major stature, Basie was the more successful in integrating his band into the lucrative, white-dominated entertainment industry of the 1940s through the 1970s.

With the start of World War II, Basie, like many other bandleaders, had to cope with myriad difficulties; some of these included restrictions on travel, the musicians' union's two-year recording ban, and above all the military draft's continual disruption of the band's roster. Basie again showed great skill in choosing talented replacements, at

different times bringing in trombonist J. J. Johnson, trumpeter Joe Newman, tenor saxophonists Lucky Thompson, Paul Gonsalves, and Illinois Jacquet, and drummer Shadow Wilson, among others. All through the 1940s the orchestra worked at choice locations such as New York's Ritz-Carlton and Philadelphia's Academy of Music, while it also maintained nearly continuous nationwide touring. After the recording ban was lifted at the end of 1943, the band resumed making records until the close of the decade. In addition, the Basie group was featured in several Hollywood films—*Reveille with Beverly, Crazy House,* and *Top Man* (all 1943)—and made frequent appearances on Kate Smith's national radio show.

Following the war Basie continued to revise personnel and shuffle arrangers; he allowed younger players like Wardell Gray on tenor saxophone and Clark Terry on trumpet to introduce a few new bebop ideas. But by the late 1940s the band had become relatively unadventurous. That development coincided with waning public interest in swing era orchestras, and in 1950 Basie was forced to disband.

Basie remained active for more than a year with a sextet that showcased Gray, Terry, and clarinetist Buddy DeFranco. In 1952, at the urging of singer Billy Eckstine, he assembled a new orchestra, which eventually would include Marshall Royal as first alto saxophonist and rehearsal director; the highly original trumpeter Thad Jones; tenor saxophonists Frank Foster, Frank Wess, Paul Quinichette, and Eddie "Lockjaw" Davis; Basie's longtime rhythm colleague Freddie Green; drummer Gus Johnson, soon replaced by Sonny Payne; and the blues and ballad singing of Joe Williams. Birdland, then the most thriving club for jazz in New York, served as an effective home base, though the band often played the Blue Note in Chicago and the Crescendo in Los Angeles as well.

This edition of the Basie orchestra placed new emphasis on arrangers and precisely played ensembles. Arrangers Neal Hefti, Ernie Wilkins, QUINCY JONES, and "the two Franks" (Foster and Wess) played key roles in making the band sound more appealing to a wider audience. The Basie orchestra now served a varied range of popular tastes, recording with celebrity singers such as Frank Sinatra and Tony Bennett, and featuring everything from Wild Bill Davis's crowd-pleasing arrangement of "April in Paris," to popular television theme songs, to jazz versions of rhythm and blues hits. In 1963 the Basie orchestra was featured in four best-selling albums, including two instrumental records arranged by Quincy Jones. Such popularity had not been attained by any big band since World War II, and, with rock music coming to dominate the record industry, it was a feat not to be duplicated.

Basie and his musicians had made the first of thirty successful European tours in 1954, and in 1963 they made the first of eight trips across the Pacific Ocean. Frequent national tours continued, usually reaching the West Coast twice each year. By 1961, when it performed at one of President John F. Kennedy's inaugural celebrations, the band had become part of America's official culture. Further appearances at the White House culminated in a reception for Basie in 1981, which celebrated a Kennedy Center honor for his contributions to the performing arts. In 1982 he was given a tribute, sponsored by the Black Music Association, at New York's Radio City Music Hall.

Six years earlier, in 1976, Basie suffered a heart attack that kept him away from the band for half a year. After returning, he continued the band's touring on a reduced schedule, while remaining active at work in the recording studios. But various illnesses further weakened him, and a year after his wife's death, he died in Hollywood, Florida.

Basie's unique ability to inspire a large jazz band with the rhythmic drive and ease of 1930s Kansas City small combos, to select and lead an ever-changing roster of talented and complementary musicians, to adapt to rapidly evolving and diverse musical tastes while maintaining artistic integrity, to integrate his band into the mainstream of American entertainment, and to give the band matchless worldwide exposure all show him to have been one of the major figures in twentieth-century American music.

FURTHER READING

Basie's memorabilia and papers are still in private hands, although they have been pledged to the Hampton University Library, Hampton, Virginia.

Basie, Count, with ALBERT L. MURRAY. *Good Morning Blues* (1985).

Dance, Stanley. *The World of Count Basie* (1980).
Schuller, Gunther. *The Swing Era* (1989).
Sheridan, Chris. *Count Basie: A Bio-Discography* (1986).

Obituary: *New York Times*, 27 Apr. 1984.
—BURTON W. PERETTI

 BASQUIAT, JEAN-MICHEL
(22 Dec. 1960–12 Aug. 1988), painter, was born in Brooklyn, New York, the son of Gerard Basquiat, an accountant originally from Haiti, and Matilde Andradas, of Puerto Rican descent. A precocious draftsman from childhood, Basquiat received little formal artistic training. The last school he attended was the experimental City-as-School program in Manhattan, where he befriended fellow artist Al Diaz.

Before quitting school altogether in 1978, Basquiat created SAMO (meaning "same old shit"), which was variously a pseudo-religion, a fictional logo, a nom de plume, and a persona. Basquiat and Diaz spray-painted original aphorisms with a copyright symbol next to the word SAMO on walls and in alleys in lower Manhattan. Their mock epigrams and mottoes included "SAMO as an end to mindwash religion, nowhere politics, and bogus philosophy," "SAMO saves idiots," and "plush safe he think, SAMO." Whereas other graffiti artists such as Fab 5 Freddy, Futura 2000, and Rammellzee painted multicolored and elaborately designed "tags" on subway cars and alleyways, Diaz and Basquiat focused on their concepts and text-based work rather than aesthetics. In the 11 December 1978 issue of the *Village Voice*, Basquiat and Diaz identified themselves as SAMO; soon thereafter, they parted ways.

Aside from his SAMO work, Basquiat drew and painted his own art on any available surface he could find, including refrigerator doors; he also made postcards and t-shirts, which he sold on the street. Using oil and acrylic paints, oil paint sticks, and collage materials, he blended roughly drawn visual elements and text. When asked about his subject matter, Basquiat responded that he painted "royalty, heroism, and the streets." Black male figures, skulls, crowns, and hobo symbols proliferated in his paintings. He sometimes included references to his personal heroes, such as musician CHARLIE PARKER and boxer JOE LOUIS, as well as art-historical

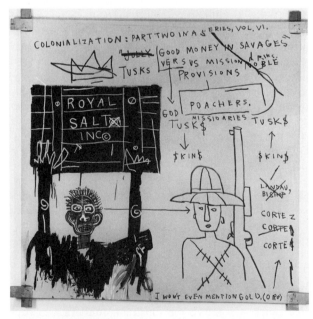

Native Carrying Some Guns, Bibles, Amorites on Safari, 1982, by Jean-Michel Basquiat, is six feet square, and done in acrylic, oil, and oil paintstick on canvas with exposed wood supports. The Hermes Trust (Isle of Man). Collection of Francesco Pellizzi

references such as Leonardo da Vinci's sketchbooks. Basquiat used words not as expanded captions but as crucial components in the composition and meaning of the work, sometimes repeating words or crossing them out, as in *Horn Players* (1983, Eli and Edythe L. Broad Collection, Los Angeles). In this painting, the artist painted Charlie Parker's name and the word "ornithology" (referring to the musician's nickname "the Bird") several times on the canvas, overlaid with more paint and next to his painted images of the musician. Basquiat once said, "I cross out words so that you will see them more; the fact that they are obscured makes you want to read them."

In 1980 Basquiat painted a large mural for his first group exhibition, the Times Square Show. Organized by Colab (Collaborative Projects Incorporated), the exhibition featured several artists early in their careers, including Jenny Holzer, Kenny Scharf, and Kiki Smith. The following year Basquiat took part in numerous exhibitions in New York, such as New York/New Wave at P.S. 1, along with artists Robert Mapplethorpe and Andy Warhol, and Beyond Words: Graffiti Based-Rooted-Inspired Works at the Mudd Club. The Galleria d'Arte Emilio Mazzoli in Modena, Italy, held Basquiat's first one-man exhibition in the spring of 1981.

In 1980 New York art dealer Annina Nosei began selling Basquiat's work and offered him her gallery basement to use as his studio. Despite this unusual arrangement (Nosci was criticized for having Basquiat "on exhibit"), she exposed Basquiat's art to several important collectors and gave him his first U.S. one-man exhibition in 1982. Although Basquiat changed dealers often in his short career, he maintained steady relationships with Los Angeles dealer Larry Gagosian and Bruno Bischofberger, who was based in Switzerland and was the artist's international representative.

Basquiat was the youngest artist in the prestigious Documenta 7 exhibition in Kassel, Germany (1982), and in the 1983 Biennial Exhibition at the Whitney Museum of American Art. The Museum of Modern Art included him in their International Survey of Recent Painting and Sculpture at MOMA (1983).

He continued to gain recognition when, in 1983, he became a close friend of Andy Warhol, who was also represented by Bischofberger. At the suggestion of the dealer, the two artists collaborated on several paintings in 1985. Warhol painted or silk-screened corporate logos such as those of GE and Arm & Hammer along with other images including Felix the Cat. Basquiat painted over and around Warhol's work with his repertoire of motifs and words. Their paintings, exhibited in New York at the Tony Shafrazi Gallery that same year, received mixed reviews. One *New York Times* critic wrote that Basquiat was an art world mascot and that Warhol used him to regain his own popularity. Warhol and Basquiat ended their friendship following the exhibition.

An article on Basquiat written by Cathleen McGuigan for the *New York Times Magazine* (10 Feb. 1985) exposed him to a popular audience but also posed questions about the consequences of an inflated art market on such a young career. Some critics claimed that Basquiat became more interested in making art that would satisfy his collectors than in creating innovative work. But many of his last works featured new developments, such as very dense accumulations of words and images, as in *Untitled (Stretch)* (1985, estate of the artist), or starkly powerful compositions, as exemplified by *Riding with Death* (1988, private collection), which shows a dark human skeleton riding a white skeleton of a horse.

Basquiat died of a drug overdose in New York at the age of twenty-seven. His death at such an early age commanded reflection in the art world, an environment where artistic ideals had been replaced by greed and the pursuit of fame due to a period of auspicious wealth and soaring art prices. Basquiat, who never hid his career aspirations, was hailed as the first African American art star. Bearing the burden of this title, he was sometimes viewed as an exotic novelty or as a traitor to his race in the predominantly white art world. But Basquiat refused to be labeled. He said, "I don't know if my being black has anything to do with my success. I don't think I should be compared to black artists but all artists."

Although not an organized movement, Basquiat and other painters

grouped as "neo-expressionists"—including Julian Schnabel, Georg Baselitz, and Susan Rothenberg—returned a sense of bravura and improvisation to painting that harked back to the abstract expressionists. Influenced by pop art, Basquiat's wordplay and use of signs and symbols aligned him with other postmodern artists, particularly those like Robert Longo who combined specific and sometimes edited images inspired by the mass media to convey meaning. Basquiat also maintained a very personal vision in his work, painting his heroes (boxers and jazz musicians), his artistic influences (da Vinci and Warhol), and episodes from his own life (drug use and racism) in his idiosyncratic style. His poetic means of combining text with imagery and social issues with personal experiences resonates in the work of several contemporary artists such as Glen Ligon and Lorna Simpson.

FURTHER READING

Basquiat, Jean-Michel, with Bruno Bischof berger. *Jean-Michel Basquiat* (1999).

Hoban, Phoebe. *Basquiat: A Quick Killing in Art* (1998).
Marshall, Richard, ed. *Jean-Michel Basquiat* (1992).
Tate, Greg. "Nobody Loves a Genius Child." *Village Voice*, 14 Nov. 1988: 31–35.
Wincs, Michael. "Jean-Michel Basquiat: Hazards of Sudden Success and Fame." *New York Times*, 27 Aug. 1988.
                    —N. ELIZABETH SCHLATTER

BASS, CHARLOTTA

(Oct. 1880–Apr. 1969), journalist, activist, and vice presidential candidate, was born Charlotta Amanda Spears in Sumter, South Carolina, the sixth of eleven children of Hiram Spears and Kate (maiden name unknown). The details of her childhood are unknown, but sometime before her twentieth birthday she went to live with her brother in Providence, Rhode Island, and began work at the *Providence Watchman*, selling ads and helping in the office. After ten years, suffering from exhaustion, she went for a rest to California on the advice of her doctor.

At the beginning of what was to have been a two-year stay, Spears went

Charlotta Bass became the first black woman to run for national office when she accepted the Progressive Party's nomination as candidate for vice president in 1952. Los Angeles Public Library

against her doctor's orders and took a job at the *Eagle*, a newspaper with a largely black readership. Her job was to sell advertising and subscriptions. However, when the newspaper's editor, John Neimore, became ill, he began to turn the operations of the *Eagle* over to Spears. When he died, the paper's new owner put Spears in charge, in May 1912. Spears continued to publish news of black society but increasingly dealt with social and political issues in the paper she renamed the *California Eagle*. Her commitment to righting the wrongs of society quickly became apparent.

In 1912 Joseph Bass joined the paper as an editor. Bass had been one of the founders of the *Topeka Plain Dealer*, and he shared Spears's concerns about injustice and racial discrimination. The two were soon married and ran the paper together for the next two decades. Among the targets of their passionate attacks was D. W. Griffith's film *The Birth of a Nation*, which perpetuated the worst kind of racial stereotyping in order to glorify the Ku Klux Klan. (The Klan tried to sue the paper for libel in 1925, but the suit was unsuccessful.) The Basses powerfully championed the black

soldiers of the Twenty-fourth Infantry who were unjustly sentenced in a 1917 race riot that took place in Houston, Texas. They also filled their newspaper with support for the SCOTTSBORO BOYS, nine young men who were framed and convicted of rape in Scottsboro, Alabama, in 1931. The Basses also strongly endorsed labor leader A. PHILIP RANDOLPH in his battle against racial discrimination in railroad employment.

Away from the newspaper, Bass helped found the Industrial Business Council, which fought discrimination in employment practices and encouraged entrepreneurship among black people. In an effort to defeat housing covenants in all-white neighborhoods, she formed the Home Protective Association. In 1919 she attended the Pan-African Congress in Paris, organized by W. E. B. DU BOIS, and during the 1920s was co-president of the Los Angeles chapter of MARCUS GARVEY's Universal Negro Improvement Association.

After Joseph Bass died in 1934, Charlotta Bass continued to run the *California Eagle* on her own. She also became more active in local and national politics. In 1940 the Republican Party

chose her as western regional director for Wendell Willkie's presidential campaign. Three years later she became the first African American member of the Los Angeles County Superior Court grand jury. In 1945 Bass ran for the L.A. city council as a "people's candidate" in a landmark election for black Angelenos. Although she lost the race, her progressive platform and powerful campaigning united diverse black organizations throughout the city's Seventh District. Her campaign also laid the groundwork for later, more successful, African American candidates, notably future L.A. city councilman and mayor TOM BRADLEY.

The immediate postwar years in the United States were marked by a growing demand for African American civil rights, which was met by an upsurge in Klan activity and other forms of racial violence. In her newspaper and in her political activities, Bass took an unyielding stand against these horrors. When blacklisting hit Hollywood, she spoke out in favor of the "Hollywood Ten," a group of screenwriters who had refused to testify before the House Un-American Activities Committee (HUAC) about alleged Communist infiltration of the film industry. She herself was called before the California equivalent of HUAC, the Tenney Committee, which she denounced as "fascist."

Believing that neither of the major parties was committed to civil rights, Bass left the Republican Party in the late 1940s to become one of the founders of the Progressive Party. Nearing the age of seventy, she campaigned heavily for the party's presidential candidate, Henry Wallace, in the 1948 election. Leaving the *California Eagle* in the early 1950s, she traveled to wherever she felt her voice might make a difference for the causes that she believed in. She went to Prague, Czechoslovakia, to support the Stockholm Appeal to ban the bomb at the peace committee of the World Congress. Like other members of the American Left at the time, notably PAUL ROBESON, she traveled to the Soviet Union and commented on its apparent lack of racial discrimination.

In 1950, she ran for California's Fourteenth Congressional District, but lost again. Bass nonetheless believed that her campaign had been successful in raising the issues she felt were important. This realization led her to accept the Progressive Party's nomination for vice president of the United States in 1952, making her the first black woman to run for national office. Bass was a consistent thorn in the side of her Republican opponent, Senator Richard Nixon, attacking him fiercely throughout the campaign. Her platform called for civil rights, women's rights, an end to the Korean War, and peace with the Soviet Union. By the early 1950s, however, the Progressive Party was perceived by many Americans to be too closely linked to the Communist Party. Some of those links were real; others the result of McCarthyite hysteria. Either way, Bass and her running mate fared poorly, even among African Americans in those states that allowed blacks to vote. Nationally, the Progressive Party won only 0.2 percent of the vote.

In 1960 Charlotta Bass wrote an autobiography entitled "Forty Years: Memoirs from the Pages of a Newspaper." During her years of retirement, she maintained a library in her garage for the young people in her neighborhood. It was a continuation of her long fight to give all people opportunities and education. She died in Los Angeles.

With remarkable dedication, Charlotta Bass used her role as editor of the oldest black-run newspaper on the West Coast to crusade against injustice and inequality. She may never have won an election, but, as she said in her 1952 campaign, "Win or lose, we win by raising the issues."

FURTHER READING

Bass's unpublished manuscript "Forty Years: Memoirs from the Pages of a Newspaper" is available at the Southern California Library for Social Studies and Research in Los Angeles and the Schomburg Center for Research in Black Culture of the New York Public Library.

Gill, Gerald R. "'Win or Lose—We Win': The 1952 Vice Presidential Campaign of Charlotta A. Bass," in *The Afro-American Woman: Struggles and Images* (1981).
Streitmatter, Rodger. *Raising Her Voice: African American Women Journalists Who Changed History* (1994).

Obituary: *Los Angeles Sentinel*, 17 Apr. 1969.
—KATHLEEN THOMPSON

BATES, DAISY LEE

(11 Nov. 1914–4 Nov. 1999), journalist and civil rights activist, was born Daisy Lee Gatson in Huttig, Arkansas, to parents she would never know. She may also have had four brothers. Bates learned as a child that three white men had attempted to rape her mother, who died while resisting them. Realizing that a black man in Arkansas could not successfully prosecute whites for murder, and fearing reprisals if he attempted to do so, Daisy's father left town shortly afterwards, leaving his infant daughter with friends Orlic and Susie Smith, who adopted her. Daisy enjoyed the close love and attention that came from being an only child, but the Smiths could not protect her from the most pernicious manifestations of white supremacy in Jim Crow Arkansas: verbal and physical abuse from whites, substandard education, and minimal economic opportunities. Her childhood was also scarred by the presence in town of one of her mother's murderers, though Daisy, the image of her mother, exacted a kind of revenge by staring at and haunting the man referred to in her memoirs as the "drunken pig."

At the age of fifteen she met twenty-eight-year-old Lucius Christopher "L.C." Bates, a journalist then working as an insurance agent. The couple courted for several years and married in 1942, moving to Little Rock, Arkansas, to establish the *Arkansas State Press*, a weekly newspaper for the black community. They had no children.

During World War II, the *State Press* exemplified the increasing determination of southern blacks to challenge their second-class citizenship. In 1942, for instance, its reporting of a white policeman's cold-blooded murder of a black soldier on the streets of Little Rock prompted white advertisers to withdraw their financial support of the paper in protest. The Bateses persisted in exposing police brutality, however, and by the end of the war the *State Press*'s campaigns had persuaded the Little Rock authorities to hire black policemen to patrol African American neighborhoods. The paper's crusading reputation greatly increased its circulation among blacks throughout Arkansas but also earned the Bateses the enmity of conservative whites. In 1946, for example, Daisy and L.C. were sentenced to ten days in prison for publishing an article criticizing the conviction of labor activists, but the couple was later

Daisy Bates (standing, second from left), with the Little Rock Nine, who integrated the Little Rock, Arkansas, Central High School against fierce opposition in 1957. Library of Congress

released on bond, and the Arkansas Supreme Court quashed their sentences.

In 1952 the Arkansas NAACP recognized Daisy Bates's tireless campaigning for civil rights by electing her its president, a post that placed her at the forefront of desegregation efforts two years later, when the U.S. Supreme Court delivered its *Brown v. Board of Education* decision. Commentators believed that Arkansas under Governor Orval Faubus, a racial moderate, might lead the region in compliance with the school desegregation ruling, and that progressive Little Rock would lead Arkansas. After 1955, however, the Court's implementation decree, *Brown II*, emboldened segregationist whites. *Brown II* required local authorities to desegregate with "all deliberate speed," a phrase that white-dominated school boards, including Little Rock's, interpreted as a signal to delay and obstruct integration. In 1956 Bates responded to white delaying tactics by urging readers of the *State Press* to support *Cooper v. Aaron*, an NAACP lawsuit recommending the speedy integration of the Little Rock schools.

In September 1957 the Little Rock school board finally unveiled its plan to enroll nine black students in the previously all-white Central High School, but even that token effort enraged whites. Working-class whites were particularly aggrieved that their children would be integrated while the children of wealthier whites would not. Tensions were raised further on the first day of classes, when Governor Faubus enlisted the Arkansas National Guard to surround the school. Warning that "blood would run in the streets" if blacks entered the building, Faubus had essentially used military force to deny the "Little Rock Nine" their constitutional right to attend an integrated school. Such defiance encouraged other whites to resist violently. Someone threw a rock through Bates's window, threatening dynamite next. And when one of the students, Elizabeth Eckford, attempted to enter the school alone, white mobs jeered at, spat at, and physically threatened the fifteen-year-old.

Throughout the tension, Daisy Bates served as the main adviser and confidante of the children and their parents. She paid for private bodyguards,

held strategy sessions in her home, tutored the children during the three weeks that the state of Arkansas refused to do so, and helped handle the demands of the world media. On 25 September 1957, after President Dwight Eisenhower had federalized the National Guard and sent one thousand Screaming Eagles paratroopers from the 101st Airborne Division to enforce the law, Bates escorted the students through the front door of Central High School. In the year that followed, she continued to act as a mentor for the students when they braved intimidation and assaults, and also when they fought back, as one student did when she emptied a bowl of hot chili on the head of a white youth who taunted her. Bates's defiance and the courage of the students earned them the NAACP's Spingarn Medal in 1958.

The successful, albeit minimal, integration of Central did not end conflicts between Bates and the Little Rock authorities. In October 1957 she resisted a local ordinance that required organizations to provide the city clerk with financial records and the names of staff and officers. Other municipalities used such information to harass and punish NAACP members, and Bates argued that compulsory disclosure of these records infringed citizens' rights to freedom of association. The local court duly convicted Bates of violating the ordinance in 1957, but that conviction was reversed in 1960 by a unanimous U.S. Supreme Court ruling, *Bates v. Little Rock*.

After the Little Rock crisis, Bates faded from the national spotlight but remained active in civil rights. She spoke at the 1963 March on Washington, worked in the Johnson administration's War on Poverty, and led a community revitalization project in rural Arkansas. In 1984 the University of Arkansas awarded her an honorary degree. Many other awards followed. The city of Little Rock named an elementary school in her honor in 1987, and she even carried the Olympic torch en route to Atlanta in 1996. She received her greatest honor posthumously, when President Bill Clinton, a fellow Arkansan and friend, awarded Bates and the Little Rock Nine the Congressional Gold Medal. As the Nine received their honors from the president in November 1999, Bates lay in state in the Arkansas Capitol, a few feet away from the spot

where Governor Faubus had predicted blood in the streets in 1957.

Popular histories of the civil rights era often depict Daisy Bates as the epitome of virtuous, nonviolent resistance and grace under pressure, largely on the strength of her brave, motherly shepherding of the Little Rock Nine. Indeed she was nonviolent in her approach, but she was also a realist. Her journalism was confrontational. She challenged police brutality and, from the time she learned of her mother's murder, found it "hard to suppress certain feelings, when all around you see only hate" (Tyson, *Robert F. Williams and the Roots of Black Power*, 153). Such feelings were not unreasonable given that the Ku Klux Klan raised three fiery crosses on her lawn and that white supremacists bombed her home several times. In 1959 she was at first equivocal about the case of Robert Williams, a North Carolina NAACP leader who advocated that blacks arm themselves in self-defense. After NAACP Executive Secretary WALTER WHITE promised Daisy an extra $600 a month to help the ailing *State Press*, however, she agreed to support White's campaign to censure Williams. That decision reflected Bates's pragmatism—white advertisers had withdrawn support from the *State Press*, and the paper would soon fold. Daisy Bates was certainly courageous, but like others in the civil rights movement—and like activists in all eras—she recognized that success often requires compromise.

FURTHER READING

There are three main manuscript sources for information on Bates. In 1966 she donated papers related to the Little Rock crisis to the State Historical Society in Madison, Wisconsin. Twenty years later, she donated papers to the Special Collections Library of the University of Arkansas in Fayetteville. For her tenure as president of the Arkansas NAACP, see the Papers of the NAACP in the Library of Congress, Washington, DC.

Bates, Daisy Lee. *The Long Shadow of Little Rock* (1962).

Kirk, John A. *Redefining the Color Line: Black Activism in Little Rock, Arkansas, 1940–1970* (2002).
Jacoway, Elizabeth, and C. Fred Williams. *Understanding the Little Rock Crisis* (1999).

Obituary: *New York Times*, 5 Nov. 1999.
—STEVEN J. NIVEN

BAYLEY, SOLOMON

(c. 1771–c. 1839), was born a slave near Camden, in Kent County, Delaware. Bayley wrote in his *Narrative* that his grandmother was a "Guinea woman" who had been transported from West Africa to Virginia when she was only eleven years old and sold to "one of the most barbarous families of that day." Despite this, she gave birth to fifteen children and "lived to a great age" (38). Bayley's mother had been born and raised with the same Virginia family. She had had several children with her husband, Abner, by the time her master and mistress died and one of their daughters and her husband moved to Delaware, taking the black family. A few years later Solomon Bayley was born, one of thirteen children.

Bayley grew to manhood in Kent County, Delaware. He took a slave named Thamar as his wife and they had two children. When the wife of the couple who owned them died, and her husband moved back to Virginia in 1799, Bayley and his family, along with his mother and father and siblings, were transported to Hunting Creek, which later became Alexandria, Virginia. Under Delaware law, slaveholders taking slaves out of the state were not permitted to put them up for immediate sale, but soon after they arrived the owner sold the entire family. Moreover, they were scattered in all directions, "some to the east, some west, north and south" (39). About one year after the sale, Bayley's father, brother, and sister were sold and taken to the Caribbean. His mother was more fortunate. She ran away with Bayley's infant brother, and made it to freedom in New Jersey.

In his reminiscence, Bayley explained that, shortly after arriving in Virginia, he began legal proceedings to secure his freedom. Not only did Delaware law prohibit his immediate sale, but a Virginia statute, passed in 1795, gave persons illegally detained as slaves the right to sue for their freedom. If they did not have enough money to launch a suit, they would be assigned counsel and allowed to sue *in forma pauperis* (as a poor person). "I employed lawyers," Bayley wrote, "and went to court two days, to have a suit brought to obtain my freedom" (2). Two days before the trial date, he was "taken up and put on board a vessel out of Hunting Creek, bound to Richmond." Jailed and cast into irons, he was "brought very low." After some time, he was put into one of three wagons owned by his new master and began a journey toward the mountains. "Now consider, how great my distress must have been," he later confessed, "being carried from my wife and children" (2).

At this point, Bayley decided to run away. Waiting for the right moment, he slipped off the wagon and hid in some bushes until the other wagons had passed. He then set out across the countryside heading back toward Richmond. Thinking he would surely perish, he ran at night and with the aid of "a dreadful wind," thunder, lightning, and rain, he avoided capture. Twice slave catchers with their trained hunting dogs came close, but the rain covered up his scent. From Richmond, Bayley made it to Petersburg, remaining there three weeks before going down the James River in a small boat with another runaway. When they reached Chesapeake Bay, his companion was detected, captured, and after trying to escape by jumping over the side of a boat, was bludgeoned to death with an oar. Bayley, however, escaped detection. Having instructed his wife if they were ever parted to run away and meet him at a specific location on the Eastern Shore (perhaps the farm of an antislavery white or free black family), Bayley miraculously found his wife and his two children. Together, they set out to the North and freedom.

When Bayley and his family returned to Kent County in 1799, the white man who had illegally sold him and his family in Virginia confronted Bayley and threatened to enslave him again; Bayley, in turn, threatened to take him to court. In the end the two compromised; if Bayley paid the man eighty dollars, a fraction of his market value, he would be allowed to go free. Bayley agreed, purchased himself, and finally, as he put it, "the yoke was off my neck" (18). In freedom, the ambitious and energetic Bayley learned the trade of coopering. With the demand for barrels high, and his wages higher than those of many whites, he was able to save enough to purchase his wife and children. He made his final purchase in 1813, buying his son, described by the auctioneer as a "likely young negro," for $360 and one shilling. Several white men, including one whom Bayley described as a "great man," assisted him, paying him for his security bond and asking another bidder to allow Solomon to purchase his son.

During the Second Great Awakening in the early nineteenth century, Bayley experienced a religious conversion. He joined the Methodist Episcopal Church, became one of its most devout members, and, when one minister suggested it was a sin not to sanctify his marriage in the eyes of God, he married his wife (he was in the process of purchasing her freedom at the time) in a church ceremony. Bayley felt so strongly about his new faith that he gave up working as a cooper because the wooden barrels he made were used for whiskey. Following his conversion, he became a farm laborer and spent a good deal of time as a lay preacher.

In 1820 Robert Hurnard, a British abolitionist visiting Delaware, heard stories about Bayley's remarkable escape and invited him to talk about his life. Upon his return to England, Hurnard wrote to Bayley, asking him to write a memoir and some letters about his life. Hurnard learned that Bayley had placed his two daughters, Margaret and Leah, "out in the service of respectable families" (vi) but they, along with his son, Spence, had died prematurely. Although advanced in life, Bayley enjoyed good health, as did his wife, who was four years older.

In 1824 Bayley's recollections were published in England, with Hurnard promising to "transmit the whole of the profits of the publication to America, for the benefit of the aged couple" (viii). Although disjointed and containing lengthy Biblical quotations, *A Narrative* gives the reader a rare glimpse into the life of a runaway slave in the late eighteenth century. It emphasizes Bayley's fear, anxiety, and the remarkable obstacles confronting runaways. It also reveals the treachery of greedy whites, as well as the sympathy and support of those whites opposed to slavery. It also shows the primary importance of the black family, Christianity, and the triumph of human spirit over adversity.

In one of his letters, the self-taught Bayley observed that, for some time, he had followed the career of the pan-Africanist PAUL CUFFE SR. and was himself considering leaving the United States. In 1827 Solomon and Thamar Bayley decided to emigrate to Liberia, a fledgling colony in West Africa. Before departing, Bayley obtained a letter of commendation from Willard Hall, a U.S. District Court Judge and leader in the Delaware colonization movement, a group of whites who offered assistance to free blacks who wished to settle in West Africa; Hall wrote that despite his "unfavorable age" (Bayley was about fifty-six) "his character stands high not only among his people of colour, but among the most respectable of our citizens." The two former fugitive slaves then boarded the brig *Doris* out of Baltimore, and, along with eighty other passengers, mostly from New York and Maryland, they set sail via Norfolk, Virginia, for Liberia.

During the period when the Bayleys arrived in the Liberian capital of Monrovia, there were clashes between native inhabitants and the approximately twelve hundred settlers, and newcomers were dying from "the fever," or malaria. Nonetheless, the Bayleys cleared a seven-acre plot and began cultivating a small farm on the outskirts of Monrovia, near the St. Paul's River. Solomon built a platform overlooking the river under a large tree, where, time permitting, he read and wrote. Following the death of his wife in 1833, Bayley published *A Brief Account of the Colony of Liberia*, which discussed the agricultural and commercial progress of the colony and the relationship between settlers and native Africans. He returned to the United States that year and visited a number of cities, but returned to Liberia, where he remarried and continued to farm, preach, and participate in community life until his death.

FURTHER READING

Bayley, Solomon. *A Narrative of Some Remarkable Incidents in the Life of Solomon Bayley, Formerly a Slave in the State of Delaware, North America* (1825).

Dalleo, Peter. "The Growth of Delaware's Antebellum Free African American Community" in *A History of African Americans of Delaware and Maryland's Eastern Shore*, ed. Carole Marks (1997).

Williams, William H. *Slavery and Freedom in Delaware, 1639–1865* (1996).

—LOREN SCHWENINGER

BEARDEN, ROMARE

(2 Sept. 1911–11 Mar. 1988), artist, was born Romare Howard Bearden in Charlotte, North Carolina, the son of R. Howard Bearden, a grocer, and Bessye Johnson. When Bearden was about four years old, the family moved to New York, settling in Harlem, where he went to public school and his parents developed a wide network of acquaintances among the Harlem jazz musicians and intellectuals of the day. His father later became an inspector for the New York Board of Health; his mother, a civic leader. Bearden finished high school in Pittsburgh, however, having lived there for a time with his grandmother. In 1932, after two years at Boston University, he transferred to New York University, where he created illustrations for the undergraduate humor magazine and earned a BS degree in Education in 1935. For the next two years he contributed political cartoons to the *Baltimore Afro-American*. Unable to find steady work, he enrolled at the Art Students League and studied drawing with the German emigré artist George Grosz in 1936–1937.

At about this time, Bearden joined the 306 Group, an informal association of black artists and writers—among

them JACOB LAWRENCE and RALPH ELLISON—who met in the studio of his cousin, the painter Charles Alston, at 306 West 141st Street. From 1938 to 1942, now beginning to paint, Bearden supported himself as a full-time caseworker with the New York City Department of Social Services, a job to which he returned after World War II. In 1940, at the Harlem studio of a friend, Ad Bates, Bearden exhibited some of the work he had completed over the past four years, including paintings in oil and gouache, watercolors, and drawings. Taking his own studio on 125th Street, located over the Apollo Theater, he began work on a series of paintings that evoked the rural South of his childhood. Typical of the series is *Folk Musicians* (1941–1942), painted in a bold and dramatic style with flat planes and simplified, colorful figures.

While serving with an all-black regiment in 1944, Bearden mounted a solo exhibition at the "G" Place Gallery in Washington, D.C., which brought him to the attention of the influential New York dealer Samuel Kootz. Bearden's first exhibition at the Kootz Gallery, in 1945, was devoted to the *Passion of Christ* series, a group of semiabstract, cubist-inspired watercolors on paper. The exhibition was highly successful in terms of reviews and sales; *He Is Arisen*, purchased by the Museum

In Romare Bearden's works, particularly his jazz- and Cubism-inspired collages, all aspects of African American life—from labor to love, rural to urban, domestic to public—are both particular and universal in nature. © Manu Sassoonian

of Modern Art in New York, was the first of Bearden's works to enter a museum collection. The following year, Kootz exhibited Bearden's painting *Lament for a Bullfighter*, inspired by García Lorca's poem "Lament for the Death of a Bullfighter." Inclusion of Bearden's works in the 1945 and 1946 annuals at the Whitney Museum of American Art in New York and in the Abstract and Surrealist American Art show held at the Art Institute of Chicago in 1948 further boosted his growing reputation.

In 1951 Bearden went to Paris on the GI Bill to study philosophy at the Sorbonne. In addition to meeting the cubist masters Pablo Picasso and Georges Braque, Bearden joined the circle of black artists and writers inspired by the concept of negritude. As he later admitted, however, the most significant thing he learned during his year in France was how to relate the black experience to universal experience. Between 1952, when he returned to New York, and 1954, the year he married West Indian dancer Nanette Rohan, Bearden devoted himself mainly to music; some twenty of the songs he wrote in this period were published and recorded. Bearden then returned to painting and set up a new studio in lower Manhattan, on Canal Street, where he and his wife lived for the rest of his life. (They had no children.) In 1961 he showed some of his now wholly abstract oil paintings in the first of several solo exhibitions at the Cordier & Ekstrom Gallery, his dealers from that year on.

Bearden, who had described art in the journal he began keeping in 1947 as "a kind of divine play" (Schwartzman, 217), was increasingly drawn to collage, a way of "playing" with assortments of materials to create a whole and a medium much employed by the cubists. He created his first signed collage, *Circus*, in 1961; three years later collage became his chief method of expression. The beginning of the civil rights movement and his participation in the discussions of the Spiral Group (which he cofounded in 1963) on the role of black artists in a time of new challenges coincided with this profound change in Bearden's art. In 1964 he created a series of small montages composed of fragments of reproductions cut from newspapers,

magazines, or postcards and pasted onto a paper backing; these assemblages were then photographed and enlarged. The resulting *Projections*, as Bearden titled them, were exhibited that year at Cordier & Ekstrom. Later, arranged in series by subject matter, they were developed into true collages. One such sequence, titled *The Prevalence of Ritual*, includes individual panels representing "The Funeral," "The Baptism," and "The Conjur Woman." Another collage series evokes Harlem street life, as in *The Dove*, a crowded assemblage of cutout figures set against a suggestion of city buildings. The bizarrely composite figures, the abrupt shifts in scale between heads and bodies, and the arbitrary spatial relationships convey the rich, kaleidoscopic variety of the scene. Other series recall the Harlem jazz world of the 1930s (*The Savoy*, for example) and southern life (the nostalgic *Train Whistle Blues*).

As Bearden developed his collage techniques into the 1970s, he began to incorporate more of his own painted touches, in acrylics or watercolors, as well as torn pieces of paper in various hand-painted colors and bits of fabric. Spaces were opened up and thus were easier to perceive. Coinciding with the start of annual visits to his wife's family home on Saint Martin, the artist's palette took on the lush colors of the Caribbean and the collage figures became overtly sensuous. One of these later collages, *The Block* (1971), a large six-panel composition, approached mixed-media work; with the accompaniment of taped gospel and blues music, children's voices, and actual street noises, it re-created the look, sounds, and "feel" of an urban street.

Besides working in collage, Bearden designed tapestries and posters; in 1968 he was represented in an international poster exhibition in Warsaw, Poland. He designed sets for the Alvin Ailey Dance Company in 1977 and continued to make prints, including the colored lithographs that illustrate a 1983 edition of the work of the Caribbean poet DEREK WALCOTT. He also created murals, such as *Quilting Time*, commissioned by the Detroit Institute of Arts and installed there in 1986. In it, the quilter and six onlookers form a frieze against a brilliantly hued tropical setting. The whole is a mosaic of

glass tesserae, so combined and colored as to suggest the molding of bodies and the textures and folds of fabrics.

A large traveling retrospective of Bearden's work, organized by the Mint Museum in Charlotte, North Carolina, in 1980 and concluding its tour at the Brooklyn Museum in 1981, capped Bearden's career. Also in 1980 he taught at Yale University, one of several temporary teaching posts he held during the course of his career. Represented in every major museum in New York City and in others throughout the country, he is considered to have transformed collage, generally regarded as a minor art form, into a forceful means of expression with universal appeal. His biographer called him "An artist for all seasons and for all humankind" (Schwartzman, 305).

In addition to *The Painter's Mind: A Study of Structure and Space in Painting*, written with his longtime friend, the artist Carl Holty (1969), Bearden wrote (with Harry Henderson) *A History of Afro-American Artists from 1792 to the Present*, which was posthumously published in 1993. He and Henderson also wrote a book for young readers, *Six Black Masters of American Art* (1972).

Part of Bearden's legacy consists of his multiple roles as teacher; as art director of the Harlem Cultural Council, to which he was appointed in 1964; as organizer of the landmark exhibition, the Evolution of Afro-American Artists: 1800–1950, held at City College of New York in 1967; and as cofounder, in 1969, of the Cinque Gallery in New York, a showcase for younger artists from various minority groups. For these contributions, Bearden was inducted into the National Institute of Arts and Letters in 1966; he was honored by his home state in 1976 as recipient of the Governor's Medal of the State of North Carolina, and he also was awarded the National Medal of Arts in 1987. The Pratt Institute (1973) and Carnegie-Mellon University (1975) awarded him honorary doctorates. He died in New York City.

FURTHER READING

The Schomburg Center for Research in Black Culture of the New York Public Library is the primary source of archival material relating to Bearden: photographs, his sketchbook and notebooks, and correspondence. The center also maintains a collection of his posters as well as examples of his other work. The Archives of American Art, in New York, houses the Romare Bearden Papers.

Campbell, Mary Schmidt, and Sharon F. Patton. *Memory and Metaphor: The Art of Romare Bearden, 1940–1987* (1991).
Igoe, Lynn M., with James Igoe. *250 Years of Afro-American Art: An Annotated Bibliography* (1981).
Schwartzman, Marvin. *Romare Bearden: His Life and Art* (1990).

Obituary: *New York Times*, 13 Mar. 1988.
—ELEANOR F. WEDGE

BECHET, SIDNEY JOSEPH (14 May 1897–

14 May 1959), clarinetist, soprano saxophonist, and composer, was the youngest of five sons and two daughters (three other children died in infancy) born to Omar Bechet, a shoemaker, and Josephine Michel in New Orleans, Louisiana. Bechet was raised as a middle-class Creole at the time when state law reclassified Creoles of color as Negro. The adoption of the black codes and de jure segregation had profound repercussions for the first generations of "ragtime" and jazz musicians in the Crescent City. Although Sidney spoke French in his childhood household and his grandfather, Jean Becher, was free and had owned property since 1817, Sidney Bechet identified himself as African American.

The Bechet family was decidedly musical. Sidney's father played the flute and trumpet for relaxation, and Sidney's brothers all played music as a hobby and developed skills in various trades for their vocations. Homer was a janitor and string bassist, Leonard a dentist and trombonist, Albert Eugene a butcher and violinist, Joseph a plasterer and guitarist. When he was only seven or eight years old, Sidney began playing a toy fife and soon began practicing on his brother's clarinet morning, noon, and night. He played in a band with his older brothers, but his family and other adult musicians quickly realized that Sidney was a prodigy whose technique outstripped that of some professionals.

Sidney's mother organized parties and hired professional bands to play in her home. When Sidney was just ten years old, she hired the great band of Manuel Perez (who sent the equally legendary Freddie Keppard as a substitute) to play for her oldest son's twenty-first birthday. George Baquet, the band's clarinetist, was late for the engagement, and Sidney, sequestered in another room, began playing his brother's clarinet as Baquet arrived. Sidney played well enough to cause Keppard to believe that it was Baquet warming up. As a result, Baquet began giving Sidney clarinet lessons. Bechet learned from him certain rudiments of clarinet playing, but he had already developed an unorthodox set of fingerings and refused to learn to read music. Bechet also studied with Paul Chaligny and Alphonse Picou. His most important influence, however, came from "Big Eye" Louis Nelson. Nelson did not play in the academic style and specialized in the rougher "uptown" styles of the black players. Another lasting influence was the opera, which his mother took him to listen to. He especially liked the tenors (his favorite was Enrico Caruso), and the heavy vibrato that characterized his playing was in part modeled after them.

As Bechet began to play with professional organizations in parades, picnics, dance halls, and parties, he did not attend school regularly, despite his family's admonitions, and he reportedly ignored their advice about learning a trade other than music. At age fourteen he joined the Young Olympians, and soon he was playing with all the notable bands of New Orleans, including those led by Buddy Petit and Bunk Johnson. Bechet's family worried about the boy's exposure to the seamier aspects of musicians' nightlife. Yet, in this setting, Bechet developed into a soft-spoken and charming fellow who was very attractive to women. He also became a heavy drinker with a very short fuse and sometimes displayed a violent temper. As a teenager he was jailed for a violent incident. This odd mixture of musical virtuosity, charm, and violence would follow Bechet throughout his adult life.

Bechet went to Chicago in 1918, where he quickly found work within the various New Orleans cliques that dominated the scene. There he met and played for NOBLE SISSLE, JAMES REESE EUROPE, and WILL MARION COOK. Bechet's virtuosity and his ear for melodies and harmony were such that he amazed all three of these bandleaders, despite his not being able to read music, a skill normally required for these orchestras. In 1919 Bechet joined Cook's Southern Syncopated Orchestra, which brought him to New York, where his talents were much in demand. He then went to the British Isles with Cook's orchestra. British audiences received the orchestra warmly, and many critics singled out Bechet's playing as noteworthy. The most important review came from the Swiss conductor Ernst Ansermet, who wrote, in what was the first truly insightful critical article on jazz, that Bechet was an "extraordinary clarinet virtuoso" and an "artist of genius."

While in England, Bechet bought a soprano saxophone. The soprano saxophone was used very little in jazz, in part because of the severe intonation problems it presents, especially in the early models. But Bechet had a strong embouchure and a highly developed vibrato that allowed him to express himself with the instrument, and his supremacy as the greatest soprano saxophonist in jazz was not challenged until JOHN COLTRANE took up the instrument years after Bechet's death. The saxophone was perfect for Bechet, as its brassier and louder projection facilitated his natural inclination to take the melodic lead, usually the prerogative of trumpeters in the jazz ensembles of the 1910s and 1920s.

Bechet's stay in London ended when he was charged with assaulting a woman. Bechet pleaded not guilty, as did his codefendant, George Clapham. The stories of the two defendants and the two women involved conflicted, and Bechet hinted that his troubles with the police in England had racial overtones. He was sentenced to fourteen days of hard labor and was then deported on 3 November 1922.

Upon his arrival in New York, Bechet began to work in the theater circuit. He joined Donald Heywood's show *How Come*, in which Bechet played the role of How Come, a Chinese laundryman who was also a jazz musician. He was later billed as the "Wizard of the Clarinet" in theater bookings under Will Marion Cook's leadership. Bechet also began his recording career in New York, through Clarence Williams, a shrewd talent scout who helped supply black talent to record companies eager to cash in on the blues craze that followed Mamie Smith's hit record "Crazy Blues." In 1923 Bechet recorded his soprano saxophone on "Wild Cat Blues" and "Kansas City Man Blues" on Okeh Records. These records were listened to by thousands and served as models of jazz phrasing and improvisation for young musicians, including the likes of Johnny Hodges, Harry Carney, and Lionel Hampton. Bechet's success led to other recordings, where he accompanied singers such as Sara Martin, Mamie Smith, Rosetta Crawford, Margaret Johnson, Eva Taylor, and Sippie Wallace. Bechet also began composing and made a big impression with his "Ghost of the Blues." He also wrote significant portions of *Negro Nuances,* a musical cowritten with Will Marion Cook and his wife, Abbie Mitchell. While the musical was not successful, Cook praised Bechet's compositions lavishly in the *Chicago Defender.*

In 1925 Bechet joined the *Black Revue,* featuring JOSEPHINE BAKER. The show took them to France, where they both became expatriates. Bechet continued working under the leadership of Noble Sissle and others. He also worked extensively in Germany, where he met Elisabeth Ziegler in 1926. He would eventually marry her in 1951, after both of them had married and divorced others. His original plans to marry Ziegler, after bringing her back to Paris in 1928, were spoiled. An argument between Bechet and the banjoist Gilbert "Little Mike" McKendrick began over a dispute about the correct harmonies to a song they had just played. By the end of the night the two were shooting at each other. Neither Bechet nor McKendrick was hit, but the pianist Glover Compton was shot in the leg, the dancer Dolores Giblins was shot in the lung, and an innocent bystander was shot in the neck. Bechet was sentenced to fifteen months in jail and was then deported.

He moved to Berlin and later returned to the United States after rejoining Noble Sissle's orchestra. In New York he led the New Orleans Feetwarmers with the trumpeter Tommy Ladnier. The group was short-lived, and Bechet briefly went into retirement from music and opened the Southern Tailor Shop in Harlem. In addition to tailoring, Bechet held jam sessions in the back room and cooked and served Creole cuisine. In 1934 Bechet returned to music once again at the behest of Noble Sissle. By the end of the 1930s the market for Bechet's style of jazz had lessened, but his cachet increased by the 1940s during the crest of the jazz revival. He played as either a bandleader or a star soloist throughout the United States. In 1949 he returned to Europe, eventually settling in France again, where he was the acknowledged patron saint of the European jazz revival. In 1951 he married Ziegler, with whom he lived for the rest of his life. He also had another home with a woman named Jacqueline, with whom he had a son, Daniel, in 1954. Bechet penned his most famous composition, "Petite fleur," in 1952, and in 1953 the Paris Conservatory Orchestra debuted his *La Nuit est une Sorcière,* a ballet in seven movements. With the help of two amanuenses, Joan Reid and Desmond Flower, Bechet also wrote *Treat It Gentle,* one of the most literarily ambitious jazz autobiographies.

Bechet, along with LOUIS ARMSTRONG, was among the first great jazz improvisers to liberate their solos from the rhythms and contours of the melody. Bechet's fame might have been even more widespread had the clarinet not fallen out of favor and the soprano saxophone been less obscure. He was the first to fashion legato melodies on the instrument and influenced such saxophone giants as Johnny Hodges and Coleman Hawkins. He died before two of his disciples on the instrument, Steve Lacy and John Coltrane, popularized the instrument in the 1960s.

FURTHER READING

Bechet, Sidney. *Treat It Gentle* (1960).

Chilton, John. *Sidney Bechet: The Wizard of Jazz* (1987).

Obituary: *New York Times,* 15 May 1959.
—SALIM WASHINGTON

BECKWOURTH, JIM

(26 April 1800?–1866?), mountain man, fur trapper and trader, scout, translator, and explorer, was born James Pierson Beckwith in Frederick County, Virginia, the son of Sir Jennings Beckwith, a white Revolutionary War veteran and the descendant of minor Irish aristocrats who became prominent Virginians. Little is known about Jim's mother, a mixed-race slave working in the Beckwith household. Although he was born into slavery, Jim was manumitted by his father in the 1820s. In the early 1800s, Beckwith moved his family, which reputedly included fourteen children, to Missouri, eventually settling in St. Louis. Some commentators suggest that Beckwith, an adventurous outdoorsman, was seeking an environment less hostile to his racially mixed family.

As a young teenager, after four years of schooling, Jim Beckwourth (as his name came to be spelled) was apprenticed to a blacksmith. Unhappy as a tradesman, he fled to the newly discovered lead mines in Illinois's Fever River region and then to New Orleans in search of greater adventure. Motivated by a lack of work and by the racism he encountered, Jim responded to a newspaper ad placed by the entrepreneurial fur traders Andrew Henry and William Henry Ashley. The ad called for "One Hundred MEN to ascend the Missouri to the Rocky Mountains"; Jim enlisted in 1824. The Ashley-Henry strategy, which Beckwourth emulated, combined direct beaver trapping with trading for furs at the Indian villages. He learned trapping and frontier skills alongside legendary mountain men Jedediah Smith and Jim Bridger, becoming a crack shot and expert bowie knife and tomahawk handler. Beckwourth was present at the first Mountain Man rendezvous at Henry's Fork on the Green River in 1825. He claimed to have been married briefly to two Blackfoot Indian sisters during this period.

While on a trapping expedition in the late 1820s, Beckwourth was captured by Crow Indians (Absaroke or Sparrowhawk people). How exactly Beckwourth came to live with the Crow remains unclear. During the years he lived with the tribe, Beckwourth became a valued Crow warrior and tribe member. He lived with a succession of Indian women and acknowledged one child, Black Panther or Little Jim. Beckwourth's tribal names—Morning Star, Antelope, Enemy of Horses, Bobtail Horse, Bloody Arm, Bull's Robe, and Medicine Calf—capture both the

The adventurer and explorer Jim Beckwourth. William Katz Collection

romance and the narrative value of his years living, hunting, and raiding with the Crow.

Leaving the tribe and the Ashley-Henry fur trading company behind in 1836, Beckwourth crisscrossed the Western frontier playing cards, prospecting, trapping, selling whiskey to Indians, stealing horses, brawling in saloons, and guiding settlers. Hired by the U.S. Army as a muleskinner, messenger, and scout during the Seminole War of 1837, he fought against the Seminole, a confederation of Native Americans and runaway slaves. Subsequently, Jim traveled the Southwest working as a fur trader and translator for Andrew Sublette and Louis Vasquez on the Santa Fe Trail and as a wagon loader at Bent's Fort in Taos. In 1842 Beckwourth opened a trading post with his current wife, Louise Sandoval, in what is presently Pueblo, Colorado. A few years later, abandoning yet another family, Beckwourth answered the siren call of California, where he survived as a horse thief (he claimed to have

stolen over two thousand horses), a letter carrier, and from 1846 to 1847 as a guide for the American forces during the conquest of California.

The discovery of gold in 1848 brought Beckwourth to the Sierra mining camps. But while most forty-niners panned for gold, Jim invested in a more lucrative gamble: a passable travel route through the rugged mountain terrain. In 1850 he located the Beckwourth Pass near present-day Reno, Nevada. Capitalizing on his discovery, Jim built a wagon road servicing settlers and gold rushers and established a ranch and trading post in what came to be known as Beckwourth, California. A charming and personable host, Jim briefly reinvented himself as a hotel and saloonkeeper. The pass, which in its heyday accommodated ten thousand wagons annually, remained popular until the railroad supplanted wagon travel in 1855.

In 1858 Beckwourth traveled east to St. Louis, Denver, and Kansas City, until gold was discovered near Pikes Peak, Colorado. Beckwourth and his latest

wife, Elizabeth Lettbetter, worked as shopkeepers in Denver, but Jim never quite adapted to city life; his marriage dissolved, and he subsequently married a Crow woman named Sue. The Colorado Volunteer Cavalry hired Beckwourth to locate Cheyenne and Arapaho Indian camps in 1864. Beckwourth's role in the subsequent Sand Creek Massacre permanently alienated him from the Indian tribes.

The facts of Beckwourth's life remain in contention. Even the year of his birth is debated among historians. Much of the historical perplexity is the result of obfuscations in the autobiography that Beckwourth dictated to Thomas D. Bonner in 1854. Most significantly, the autobiography omits any mention of Beckwourth's race. While it was Bonner who altered the spelling of the name "Beckwourth," Jim was responsible for confusing dates, omitting details, and lavishly embellishing the facts of his life, including his role in events, the number of rivals killed, money made, and battles waged. He may have taken as his own the heroic tales of other frontiersmen, including EDWARD ROSE, who lived with the Crow a generation before Beckwourth. The book, published in 1856, put into print stories Beckwourth had been spinning for years. Storytelling was a valued skill and an important part of the period's oral tradition, and Beckwourth had spent a lifetime fashioning elaborate narratives with himself as the hero. The book found a ready audience among armchair travelers fascinated and titillated by the exoticism and liberation of frontier stories. Once the inaccuracies of his text were revealed, however, Beckwourth was quickly labeled a liar. As a result, many early historians wrote him off as an unreliable and purposeful braggart, while others, fueled by racism, attacked him on the basis of his "mixed blood." Today, historians generally agree that much of the text's basic narrative can be believed and that it represents an invaluable documentary record.

An inveterate adventurer and explorer, Beckwourth looked and dressed the part. Dark-eyed, muscular, and taller than six feet, he often dressed in embroidered buckskin, Crow leggings, ribbons, earrings, and gold chains and wore his thick, dark hair loose to his waist or elaborately braided. Beckwourth was not, as has been claimed, completely illiterate. He spoke English with great skill, fluent French, some Spanish, and a number of Indian dialects. The elision of race in his autobiography has been compounded by numerous painted portraits that untruthfully depict him as very light-skinned and by the 1951 film *Tomahawk*, which cast Jack Oakie, a white actor, as Beckwourth.

Mystery still surrounds Beckwourth's death in Crow territory near the Bighorn River in 1866. While it is generally believed that he died of sickness or food poisoning, the rumor lingers that he was purposefully poisoned by the Crow after rejecting offers to rejoin the tribe.

FURTHER READING

Beckwourth, James P. *The Life and Times of James P. Beckwourth, Mountaineer, Scout, Pioneer, and Chief of the Crow Nation of Indians as told to Thomas D. Bonner* (1856).

Mumey, Nolie. *James Pierson Beckwourth: An Enigmatic Figure of the West, A History of the Latter Years of His Life* (1957).

Wilson, Elinor. *Jim Beckwourth: Black Mountain Man and War Chief of the Crows* (1972).

—LISA E. RIVO

 BELAFONTE, HARRY

(1 Mar. 1927–), singer, actor, activist, and producer, was born Harold George Belafonte Jr. in Harlem in New York City, the son of Harold George Belafonte Sr., a seaman, and Melvine Love, a domestic worker. Belafonte Sr. was an alcoholic who contributed little to family life, other than occasionally hitting his spouse, and the young Harry was brought up almost exclusively by his mother. Harold and Melvine, who were both from the Caribbean, had a difficult time adjusting to life in New York, and after the Harlem race riots of 1935, Melvine and her son moved to her native Jamaica, where Harry spent five years shielded from American racism. When World War II broke out, the Belafontes returned to Harlem. Hoping for better conditions, the family would often try to pass for white. With white relatives on both the mother's and father's sides, they were all fair-skinned enough to be taken for Greek, Italian, or even Irish. Duty bound, Belafonte joined local gangs, drafted to help defend his white enclaves from neighboring blacks.

Belafonte attended school in Harlem, but struggled with dyslexia; by ninth grade he had had enough and dropped out. Soon thereafter he enlisted in the U.S. Navy and was assigned to an all-black unit. Because of his race—and his temper—Belafonte was assigned as a munitions loader, one of the most dangerous jobs on the home front. "The men who were stuck with munitions loading were very bitter, very angry," he recalls. "In our bitterness and anger we went out and got drunk. We wanted to beat up everybody we met, including each other" (Eldridge, 117–118). When feeling less pugilistic, Belafonte discovered a passion for politics. He enjoyed sitting in on discussions of race and racism in the United States and labored to understand pamphlets and essays by W. E. B. Du Bois.

Belafonte met his first wife, Margurite Byrd, while his unit was stationed in Norfolk, Virginia. Byrd was studying psychology at the nearby Hampton Institute; she remembers their early relationship as "one long argument over racial issues" (Gates, 160). Belafonte and Byrd married in 1948 and had their first child, Adrienne, a year later. By this time, Belafonte had finished his tour of duty and moved his family to New York. Here, at Harlem's American Negro Theatre (ANT), Belafonte saw a play that sparked his interest in acting. With support from the GI Bill, he was soon enrolled in a workshop at the New School for Social Research, together with Marlon Brando, Tony Curtis, and Bea Arthur. Working as a janitor's assistant to help pay the bills, Belafonte volunteered backstage at the ANT. This quickly led to a role in a production of Sean O'Casey's *Juno and the Paycock*.

It was also at the ANT that Belafonte met SIDNEY POITIER, another black actor of Caribbean extraction, who became a lifelong friend and who, some say, stole Belafonte's career. The two were almost exact contemporaries and competed for many of the same roles. In a 1948 show called *Days of Our Youth*, Poitier was working as Belafonte's understudy. When Belafonte could not perform one night owing to his janitorial duties, Poitier filled in. A producer happened to be in the audience that evening and approached Poitier after the show. It was the actor's big break, the one that eventually landed him in Hollywood.

Belafonte soldiered on in the theater, but slowly began to turn his attention toward music. On a friend's suggestion he performed at amateur night at a midtown club called the Royal Roost and was immediately hired full time. His performance consisted of pop jazz standards, a repertoire Belafonte found less than edifying; after a year he called it quits. By this time he had saved up a tidy sum of money, and he used it to open a grill called the Sage in Greenwich Village. The restaurant folded after eight months, but during that time it had served Belafonte as a late-night rehearsal space. Belafonte began indulging his interest in folk music at the Sage, and, after it closed, he pursued his research at a more conventional venue, listening to field recordings in the Library of Congress.

In 1951 Belafonte brought his new act to the stage. Folk hardly seemed a promising genre at the height of the McCarthy era, when many of its left-leaning practitioners such as PAUL ROBESON and Pete Seeger were blacklisted, but success came quickly, with sell-out crowds at big-name clubs and a recording contract from RCA. Harry Belafonte's voice alone cannot account for his success, but combined with his stage persona—tight trousers, open shirt, and shiny, mocha skin—it wowed audiences. Belafonte sang the expected folk standards, but then veered off toward African, Caribbean, and even Hebrew songs like "Hava Nageela." (He claims most American Jews learned the tune from him.) In spite of his success, Belafonte suffered the same indignities as other black entertainers of the day and was routinely denied the right to eat or sleep at the same venues that paid dearly to book his act. But Belafonte was quick to have revenge; in 1954, after *Brown v. Board of Education* declared segregation unconstitutional, he cancelled his engagements in the South.

Belafonte released several folk albums, but it was not until 1956 that he fully embraced the Caribbean music that delighted his audiences. *Harry Belafonte—Calypso* proved an instant classic, and two songs in particular,

"The Banana Boat Song (Day-O)" and "Jamaica Farewell," topped the charts. Some claimed Belafonte had bastardized true Trinidadian calypso, but Belafonte was unapologetic about tailoring the music to American audiences. It was clearly an astute commercial move; in a year's time the album had sold 1.5 million copies, more than any previous record by a single artist.

As audiences grew and shows sold out, Belafonte resumed acting, taking roles in films and plays, including John Murray Anderson's Broadway revue *Almanac*, which earned him a Tony Award. Perhaps his most personally significant performance was in *Carmen Jones* (1954), an all-black film version of Georges Bizet's opera *Carmen* that also starred DOROTHY DANDRIDGE and PEARL BAILEY. Belafonte and Marguerite Byrd's second daughter, Shari, was born in 1954, but Belafonte's marriage ended in divorce in 1957. That same year he married Julie Robinson, a dancer with the KATHERINE DUNHAM Company, with whom he would later have a son, David, and a daughter, Gina. Initially, Belafonte's divorce slipped under the media's radar screen, but word of his remarriage eventually did get out, not least because his new bride was white.

Belafonte continued to act, including a role in 1957's *Island in the Sun*, a controversial tale of interracial love, but he found himself increasingly put off by Hollywood's ham-fisted attempts to deal with race. The scripts that came his way ranged from the shallow to the offensive, and Belafonte seemed unable to get any of his own ideas produced. In the 1960s he abandoned the cinema and engrossed himself in politics.

Belafonte had met MARTIN LUTHER KING JR. in 1956 during the Montgomery bus boycott and was immediately taken with King's passion and candor. At that first meeting, King seemed uncertain about the fate of the civil rights movement. He asked Belafonte for support, and over the next decade Belafonte lent his name and energy to the cause. He proved instrumental in rallying celebrities at home and abroad, forging political connections, and organizing fund-raisers. Belafonte also devoted large sums of his own money, heavily insuring King's life and bailing out activists arrested during sit-ins and protest marches. When King was jailed in Birmingham, it was Belafonte who led the charge to raise the fifty-thousand-dollar bail. His efforts earned him a place on the board of directors of King's Southern Christian Leadership Conference. Over the years of their joint involvement, Belafonte and King developed a close personal friendship, which lasted until King's death in 1968.

After the civil rights movement began to wane, Belafonte shifted his focus to Africa. His appointment by President John F. Kennedy as a cultural adviser to the Peace Corps in 1961 had first sparked his interest, and through the coming decades he devoted boundless energy to campaigns for development aid and human rights. Chief among these was the anti-apartheid struggle in South Africa, which consumed Belafonte in the 1980s. In 1987 the United Nations Children's Fund recognized his efforts and made him a goodwill ambassador, a position he has used to draw attention to famine, war, and the plague of AIDS.

Belafonte's activism often drew on his connections in the entertainment world. For a week in 1968 he guest hosted Johnny Carson's *Tonight Show*, turning light entertainment into politics with guests like Robert F. Kennedy and Martin Luther King Jr. In his anti-apartheid efforts, he worked to introduce exiled South African musicians like Miriam Makeba and Hugh Masekela to listeners in the United States, and in 1988 he released *Paradise in Gazankulu*, his own album of South African–themed music. In 1985 Belafonte took a similar approach to relief efforts for famine in Ethiopia. Inspired by pop stars from the British Isles who launched Band Aid in 1984, Belafonte was the driving force behind "We Are the World," an American effort in 1985 which raised over seventy million dollars in aid for Ethiopian famine victims.

Perhaps because his political and show-business interests have always been so entwined, Belafonte has never been forced to choose between the two. In the thick of the anti-apartheid movement, he resumed acting and found time to mount major concert tours. Earlier, at the height of the civil rights movement, Belafonte had begun what may be his most ambitious musical project, a series of records then called *Anthology of Negro Folk Music*. He wanted to showcase the richness and variety of the African American musical tradition with a collection that included work songs and spirituals, minstrel tunes and lullabies. But when recording was completed in 1971, the backers of the project, RCA and *Reader's Digest*, pulled out, citing lack of commercial prospects, and the tapes languished in RCA vaults. They were finally released in 2001 as *The Long Road to Freedom: An Anthology of Black Music* and were nominated for a Grammy Award for best historical album.

The release of *Long Road* topped off a flurry of show-business activity by Belafonte in the 1990s. In 1995 he starred in the independent film *White Man's Burden* and the following year played gangster Seldom Seen in Robert Altman's *Kansas City*. Plans were afoot for Belafonte to produce yet another picture with an unusual take on race—a film version of *Amos 'n Andy*, the long-running radio and television show that was criticized by the NAACP, among others, for perpetuating racist stereotypes, but which nonetheless enjoyed a substantial audience among African Americans from the 1920s to the 1950s.

Belafonte has also continued to play sold-out shows and has campaigned to raise awareness about prostate health among African American men and the need to curb gang violence. He provoked controversy, however, in a much-criticized 15 October 2002 appearance on CNN's *Larry King Live*, when he refused to apologize for his earlier denunciation of Secretary of State COLIN POWELL as President George W. Bush's "house slave." Powell called Belafonte's comments "an unfortunate throwback to another time and another place," but the entertainer insisted that the secretary of state was a "sell-out." Asked by King if the same term applied to CONDOLEEZZA RICE, Bush's national security advisor, Belafonte replied, "Yes. Absolutely. Absolutely. Even more so."

In the final analysis, Harry Belafonte remains difficult to pigeonhole either as an activist or as an entertainer, but it hardly seems worth the effort. Whether his greatest achievements have taken place onstage or off remains open to debate; his success in both arenas does not.

FURTHER READING

Eldridge, Michael. "Remains of the Day-O." *Transition* 92: 110–137.

Gates, Henry Louis, Jr. *Thirteen Ways of Looking at a Black Man* (1997).

Ward, Brian. *Just My Soul Responding: Rhythm and Blues, Black Consciousness, and Race Relations* (1998).

—CHRIS BEBENEK

BELL, COOL PAPA

(17 May 1903–7 Mar. 1991), baseball player and manager, was born James Thomas Bell in Starkville, Mississippi, the son of Jonas Bell, a farmer whose father was an American Indian, and Mary Nichols. James had six siblings, two sisters and four brothers, and said that his mother taught him to be an honest, clean-living man who cared about other people.

He was reared in the Oktoc community near Starkville and began playing pickup games on the local sandlots while attending the local school through the eighth grade. There was neither a high school nor gainful employment in his hometown, so in 1920 Bell moved to St. Louis, Missouri, to live with his older brothers and attend high school, completing two years before ending his formal education. Soon after arriving in St. Louis, he met Clarabelle Thompson, and they were married in September 1920. The marriage lasted seventy years but was childless.

The young husband worked for the Independent Packing Company and played baseball with the semi-pro Compton Hill Cubs and the East St. Louis Cubs. At this stage of his career, Bell was a promising, left-handed pitcher with a varied repertoire of pitches that included a screwball, a curve, and a knuckleball. He was scouted and signed in 1922 by the St. Louis Stars of the Negro National League for ninety dollars a month. In his rookie season he acquired the colorful nickname by which he was known forever afterward. In a crucial game situation, Bell struck out the great Oscar Charleston, the best hitter in the Negro Leagues at the time and a future Hall-of-Famer. Manager Bill Gatewood, impressed by the youngster's poise under pressure, applied the appellation "Cool Papa" to his protégé, and the name stuck.

In 1924, after an arm injury ended his pitching career, Cool Papa became a full-time outfielder, where he could use his incredible speed to the greatest advantage. He played a shallow center field and routinely demonstrated extraordinary range in the field by making sensational catches. A natural right-handed batter, he learned to switch-hit to better utilize his speed from the left side of the batter's box. He was so fast going from the batter's box to first base that if he bunted and the ball bounced twice, the fielders would say "Put it in your pocket" because there was no chance to get him out. When JACKIE ROBINSON played in the Negro Leagues with the Kansas City Monarchs, he was a shortstop, but knowledgeable observers knew that it was not his best position and that if he wanted to break into the major leagues he would have to change position. To demonstrate this to him, Cool Papa would hit ground balls to Robinson's right and beat the throw to first base.

Once clocked at twelve seconds circling the bases, Cool Papa is recognized as the fastest player ever to play the game. He was so swift that some players said that it looked like his feet did not even touch the ground. His incredible speed also made him an omnipresent base-stealing threat, and in 1933 he was credited with 175 stolen bases in a 200-game season. He sometimes took two bases on a bunt or scored from second base on a sacrifice fly.

While his speed was real, it was often exaggerated. SATCHEL PAIGE, the legendary pitcher and a skilled raconteur known to embellish stories, said that Cool Papa was so fast that he could turn off the light switch and be in bed with the covers pulled up to his chin before the room got dark. Cool Papa confirmed that he had demonstrated this skill but added a detail that Paige had conveniently omitted: the light switch was faulty, which resulted in a delay before the light went out. In later years, the boxer MUHAMMAD ALI claimed for himself the ability to perform the same feat.

During his ten seasons in St. Louis, Bell consistently batted well over .300, with his best year coming in 1926, when he batted .362, with fifteen home runs and twenty-three stolen bases in the eighty-five-game season; moreover, the Stars won Negro National League pennants in 1928, 1930, and 1931. Following the 1931 season, both the franchise and the league fell victim to the economics of the Great Depression and disbanded. With the demise of the league, the 1932 season was one of chaos, as players scrambled to earn a spot on the roster of a surviving solvent

Cool Papa Bell, the fastest man in baseball, could round the bases in 12 seconds.
National Baseball Hall of Fame

franchise. Cool Papa was no exception and played with three teams, the Detroit Wolves, the Kansas City Monarchs, and the Homestead Grays.

In 1933 he joined owner Gus Greenlee's Pittsburgh Crawfords, and for the next four years Bell continued to bat over .300 each season, as the Crawfords contended for the championship of the new Negro National League. In 1933 Greenlee, who was league president, claimed a disputed championship, and in 1934 the team again finished strong but missed the play-offs. In 1935 the Crawfords defeated the New York Cubans in a seven-game play-off for an undisputed title, and they repeated as champions in 1936. That season was interrupted when the league sent a select All-Star team to participate in the Denver Post Tournament, which they won with ease, as Bell batted .450 and topped the tournament in stolen bases. During each of his four seasons with the Crawfords, Bell was voted to start in the East-West All-Star game, where he always played centerfield and batted leadoff.

In 1937 Cool Papa left the Crawfords and spent the next five years in Latin America. In his first season he helped dictator Rafael Trujillo's All-Stars win the 1937 championship in the Dominican Republic. Bell later said that the players were told that if they didn't win the championship they would be executed. In 1938 he went to Mexico, where he remained for the next four seasons. After two years with Tampico, where he batted .356 and .354, he split the 1940 season between Torreon and Veracruz and had his best year in Mexico, winning the Triple Crown with a batting average of .437, twelve home runs, and seventy-nine RBI. He also led in hits with 167 and in triples with fifteen in the eighty-nine-game season, as Veracruz won the pennant. Cool Papa played with Monterrey in 1941 and ended with a .367 career batting average in the Mexican League.

During his long baseball career, Cool Papa supplemented his summer income by playing in integrated winter baseball leagues in California and Cuba. In California he had a .368 career batting average for a dozen intermittent winters between 1922 and 1945, and in 1933–1934 he led the league with a .362 batting average. In 1928 he played the first of three consecutive winters in Cuba

with Cienfuegas and batted .325, while leading the league in home runs, stolen bases, and runs scored. He returned to Cuba for the 1940–1941 season, playing with Almendares in his final season, to finish with a career .292 batting average in the Cuban winter league.

In 1942 Cool Papa returned to the United States, joined the Chicago American Giants of the Negro American League, and began a string of three additional appearances in the East-West All-Star game. In 1943 he joined the Homestead Grays, the dominant team in the Negro National League, and batted .356 as the Grays won the pennant and defeated the Negro American League's Birmingham Black Barons in the Negro World Series. In 1944 he batted .373, and the Grays defended their Negro League championship by defeating Birmingham in a Negro World Series rematch. The following year he batted .302, as the Grays won another pennant but were swept in the World Series by the Cleveland Buckeyes. Cool Papa's last year with the Grays was 1946, during which he batted .396. He later said that he had won the batting title that year but "gave" it to Monte Irvin to enhance his chances to play in the major leagues.

For the next four years Cool Papa was a playing manager with lesser teams, the Detroit Senators in 1947 and the Kansas City Stars, a farm team for the Monarchs, from 1948 through 1950. He finished his Negro Leagues career with a lifetime .341 batting average and also had a .391 average in exhibition games against major leaguers. In 1951 he became a part-time scout for the St. Louis Browns, until the franchise moved to Baltimore in 1954. After leaving baseball he worked as a custodian and night security officer at St. Louis City Hall until he retired around 1970.

In 1974 Cool Papa Bell was inducted into the National Baseball Hall of Fame in Cooperstown, New York. He died of a heart attack in St. Louis, Missouri in 1991, only a few weeks after his beloved wife, Clarabelle.

For a quarter-century, Bell showcased his exceptional speed and all-around excellence on baseball diamonds throughout the United States and Latin America, demonstrating that African Americans could compete successfully against white athletes. His career

contributed significantly to the eventual elimination of baseball's color line.

FURTHER READING

Holway, John. *Voices from the Great Black Base Ball Leagues* (1975).
Peterson, Robert. *Only the Ball Was White* (1970).
Riley, James A. *The Biographical Encyclopedia of the Negro Baseball Leagues* (1994).
—JAMES A. RILEY

BELL, JAMES MADISON (3 Apr. 1826–1902), abolitionist, poet, and lecturer, was born in Gallipolis, Ohio. His parents' identities are unknown. At age sixteen, in 1842, he moved to Cincinnati. While there, in 1848, he married Louisiana Sanderlin (or Sanderline), with whom he had several children, and also learned the plastering trade from his brother-in-law, George Knight. Bell worked as a plasterer during the day and attended Cincinnati High School for Colored People at night. Founded in 1844 by Reverend Hiram S. Gilmore, the school had a connection to Oberlin College and was said to have given impetus to the sentiment found in *Uncle Tom's Cabin* and the cause of human freedom. Through his studies Bell was thoroughly indoctrinated into the principles of radical abolitionism.

In 1854 Bell moved his family to Chatham, Ontario, Canada, feeling that he would be freer under the authority of the British government. While continuing his trade he became involved in political activities and met and befriended John Brown. As his ally, Bell raised money and enlisted men to support Brown's raid on Harpers Ferry. He probably was one of the last people to see Brown before the raid took place.

In 1860 Bell moved to San Francisco, California, where he became involved in the fight to ensure equal education for local black children. He also took a leading and active role at various state conventions protesting laws that discriminated against blacks. At one such convention, held by ministers of the African Methodist Episcopal (AME) Church, Bell addressed the subjects of the role of the church and its relationship to the state. He was an active member and steward of the AME Church in San Francisco. Although far removed from the battle-field, Bell worked as a crusader for abolition during the Civil War. Bell wrote some of his most rousing poems while living in California, including "Emancipation," "Lincoln," and "The Dawn of Freedom." His works were long, comprising as many as 950 lines, and were meant to be recited. Although Bell is known as a poet today, poetry came second to his activism during his lifetime.

Bell left California and moved to Toledo, Ohio, in 1865. He arrived at the time of emancipation and began to work with the freedmen, focusing his energies on the struggle for civil rights. Bell later went to Canada to visit his family and eventually moved them to Toledo. He continued to be active in the AME Church, serving as superintendent of the Sunday school and as a lay worker. Active briefly in Republican politics, Bell was elected as a delegate from Lucas County to the state convention and as a delegate at large from the state of Ohio to the Republican National Convention in both 1868 and 1872. He was a vocal and enthusiastic supporter of the nomination of Ulysses S. Grant at both conventions.

Bell traveled frequently, espousing doctrines on human liberty, enjoining blacks to use their freedom responsibly, and instructing freedmen in their political and civic duties, often reciting his long poems as the method of instruction. Bishop B. W. Arnett, a friend who worked with Bell in the church, often traveled with him as he gave public readings of his poetry and lectured on educational and legal rights for black Americans. According to Arnett, no one instructed people better or had a more imposing manner than Bell. "Many a young man who was not an honor to his race and a blessing to his people received the first spark of inspiration for true greatness" while listening to Bell's poems (Arnett, 10).

Bell addressed many issues in his poems, including slavery, war, emancipation, and Reconstruction, often referencing historical figures, such as John Brown, or events of historical significance. Although he tended to vary the lengths of stanzas, his poems have been described as "almost identical and dull" and "without any distinctive literary quality." Many of Bell's poems were published individually, though they were eventually compiled in Arnett's *The Poetical Works of James Madison Bell* (1901).

One of Bell's long poems, "The Progress of Liberty" (1866), was written for the third anniversary of the Emancipation Proclamation. Its 850 lines review the Civil War, the triumph of liberty, and the martyrdom of Abraham Lincoln:

> The bondsman's gloomy night has passed;
> The slavery of this land is dead;
> No tyrant's power, however vast,
> Can wake it from its gory bed.

It continues,

> Though slavery's dead, yet there remains
> A work for those from whom the chains
> Today are falling one by one;
> Nor should they deem their labor done,
> Nor shrink the task, however hard,
> While it insures a great reward,
> And bids them on its might depend
> For perfect freedom in the end.

Bell also used poems to encourage blacks to be model citizens:

> In this yourselves must take the lead;
> You must yourselves first elevate;
> Till then the world will ne'er concede
> Your claims to manhood's high estate.

In addition, Bell used his works—and the reading of them—to denounce laws and policies that he deemed to be detrimental to blacks. He is said to have triumphed in his "daring, vigorous satire of President Andrew Johnson" in the poem "Modern Moses, or 'My Policy' Man" (1867). Called Bell's "most inventive and readable work" because of its "shrewd humor and irony, concrete topicality and personal emotion" (Sherman, 192), the poem ridicules Johnson from a personal as well as political perspective. It portrays the president as a Judas who betrayed the people by vetoing the Freedman's Bureau Bill:

> Mark when that bill for the supply
> Of starving millions met his eye;
> A breadless, clotheless, houseless throng.
> Thus rendered by his nation's wrong.
> Does he the bill in haste receive
> And sign, their suff'rings to relieve?

He goes on:

> Then he in their deep hour of grief,
> Did them relieve and kept his vow;

> When with a dark and wrinkled brow,
> He stamped his veto on their prayer,
> And doomed the suppliants to despair.

In *From Slavery to Freedom*, historian JOHN HOPE FRANKLIN argues that the overwhelming acclaim of the poet PAUL LAURENCE DUNBAR probably overshadowed the works of Bell and other black poets of his era. If not for Dunbar's fame, Bell might have been more highly regarded as a poet during an age that was critical to the political, social, and cultural development of black Americans.

FURTHER READING

Arnett, Bishop B. W. *The Poetical Works of James Madison Bell* (1901).
Sherman, Joan R. *African American Poetry of the Nineteenth Century: An Anthology* (1992).

—MAMIE E. LOCKE

BELL, PHILIP ALEXANDER (1808?–25 April 1889), newspaper editor and civil rights activist, was born in New York City, the third of three children, to Alexander Bell and Letty (maiden name unknown). A stutterer, the young Bell turned to writing to express himself, honing his natural talents under the teachers at New York City's African Free School, an institution respected for such alumni as Shakespearean actor IRA ALDRIDGE and Episcopal priest and pan-Africanist ALEXANDER CRUMMELL. After finishing school, Bell set out to make journalism his life's work, hoping to use the press to advance black interests.

On 25 January 1831 Bell attended a meeting of the Colored Citizens of New York at the Boyer Lodge Room. The meeting's attendees rejected the idea of black colonization in Liberia, West Africa—a plan of the American Colonization Society—saying that blacks absolutely claimed "this country, the place of our birth, and not Africa, as our mother country." A few months later, Bell was one of New York's representatives at the First Annual Convention of the People of Colour, held in Philadelphia in 1831, to discuss colonization, the abolition of slavery, and ways of achieving equality for "every freeman born in this country." Bell attended a second Philadelphia convention in 1832, which revisited the previous year's proposal,

Philip A. Bell, newspaper publisher, campaigned actively for civil rights and workers' rights on both the East and West Coast. Schomburg Center

the resettlement of ex-slaves in Canada, instead of Liberia. Throughout his journalistic career, Bell regularly attended similar conventions as a delegate from New York or, later, from San Francisco.

As an activist and writer in 1837, Bell joined with Charles Ray to establish New York's *Weekly Advocate*, soon renamed the *Colored American*. Bell used the paper to underscore his basic themes: opposition to colonization, an end to slavery, and equal rights. After the paper's demise, he articulated the same themes in the Philadelphia *Elevator* and the New York *Anglo-African*. Not content with just writing his message, Bell also directed the New York Intelligence Office, where he helped escaped slaves to find work or to flee to Canada.

During the 1840s and 1850s, Bell had established himself as an important newspaperman and an advocate for East Coast blacks. Meanwhile, on the West Coast, California was undergoing transformation from a Mexican province to a state. Its new status encouraged free blacks and ex-slaves to migrate there, as did Bell's friend, the activist and future judge MIFFLIN WISTAR GIBBS. Sometime in 1859 or early 1860 Bell decided to move to San Francisco, California, arriving in 1860.

Almost immediately, Bell joined the black community's efforts to eliminate California state statutes that prevented blacks from testifying and acting as witnesses in court cases involving whites. To end such laws and to provide a voice for the community, Bell and Peter Anderson established the San Francisco *Pacific Appeal* in 1862. In one of his earliest editorials, Bell wrote, "Our paper is devoted to the interests of the Colored People of California and to their moral, intellectual and political advancement [and] ... will advocate their rights, their claims to humanity and justice; it will oppose the wrongs inflected on them." In another editorial, Bell assessed African American life:

Exiles in our native land, aliens in the country that gave us birth, outlaws for no crime, proscribed without offence, amenable to the laws without being protected by them, thus we stand, innocent victims of an unholy and unrighteous prejudice—truly our condition is most deplorable.

(*Pacific Appeal*, 12 April 1862)

Bell and Anderson soon disagreed over editorial policy, forcing Bell to quit the paper in July 1862. Bell remained in the newspaper business, however, as an agent for New York's *Anglo-African*, while continuing his effort to overturn the discriminatory testimony and witness laws. His struggle proved successful in March 1863, when Governor Leland Stanford signed a measure repealing these laws. For Bell, however, the struggle for rights did not stop there; African Americans needed equal education and the right to vote. To help achieve those ends, Bell established his own newspaper, the *Elevator*, in April 1865. Working in conjunction with the Colored State Convention of 1865, Bell and the delegates sent a petition to the California State Legislature requesting voting rights. When the California state senate tabled it, Bell responded, "We will continue to repeal slander and denounce injustice and oppression ... and fearlessly contend for our inalienable rights." In other *Elevator* editorials, Bell explained community goals succinctly:

To "set us right before the law."
To "give us the common right of citizens—in *political franchise*, in the school system."

To "give us in common with the other races, civil liberties" and "equal advantages with them in the development of common resources of the country."
To end the United States as exclusively a "white man's country."
To provide "equal laws for our safeguard and protection."

Bell spent considerable time from 1865 to 1867 working to gain the right to vote for African Americans, but then a new challenge emerged. For many years, black children in San Francisco had attended a separate elementary school, staffed by black teachers, in a building located on Broadway Street. In 1868 the San Francisco school board decided to close the school's Broadway building, replace its black teachers, and move the students to an inferior facility at the old Greenwich Street School. Bell responded that black teachers "feel an interest in the education of their race," and parents showed their resolve by boycotting the school. Of 209 school-age children, only twenty attended the Greenwich School. This equal-education fight dragged on for several years, until Bell convinced superintendent of schools James Denman to open a new school on Taylor and Vallejo streets. This much-improved facility, however, still did not satisfy Bell or the black parents. They pushed to have children attend the regular grammar and high schools in an integrated environment. Finally in 1875 the school board acquiesced, and both white and black students began attending the same schools.

The decade of the 1870s brought further changes and challenges. Once the federal government passed the Fifteenth Amendment, blacks in California could vote, but Bell realized that they also needed to become politically involved. Although he supported the Republican Party of Lincoln, Bell urged his readers to vote not for a party's candidate, but for the most qualified individual. In the late 1870s he warned African Americans to be wary of Denis Kearney's Workingmen's Party and its anti-Chinese platform, not because he was sympathetic to the Chinese, but because he feared repercussions for African Americans. In 1878 Bell supported the National Labor Party, and at its state convention in San Francisco, he held the position of sergeant-at-arms. Bell realized that the problems of workers—white, black, and Asian—overshadowed group identity; he simply wanted all workers to benefit from the land, and from economic, social, and political reforms through effective political leadership.

Philip Bell had other talents besides political activism. With his stuttering under control, he appeared as an actor in the Colored Amateur Company productions of *Ion* and *Pizarro*. As a literary critic, he wrote reviews of both white and black community productions of Shakespeare's *Richard III*, *As You Like It*, and *The Merchant of Venice*. In a review of the latter, Bell commented, "I have always sympathized with Shylock, have considered him 'more sinned against than sinning.'"

The late 1870s and early 1880s saw a still vigorous Bell continuing his efforts towards achieving equal rights and "elevating the character of our race." In the mid-1880s, however, his health began to decline, forcing him to retire. During his newspaper career Bell had made very little money, and since he never married or had children, he had to depend for his support on the charity of local women. Bell never fully regained his health, and he died in San Francisco in 1889. Judge Mifflin W. Gibbs described Bell as "proud in his humanity and intellectually great as a journalist," but perhaps the best summation of Bell's life comes in his own words, "Action is necessary. Prompt and immediate. Agitate! Agitate! Agitate!"

FURTHER READING

The best sources of information on the life and activities of Bell are the files of the New York *Colored American* and *Anglo-African* and the San Francisco *Pacific Appeal* and the *Elevator* newspapers.

Montesano, Philip M. *Some Aspects of the Free Negro Question in San Francisco, 1849–1870* (1973).

Penn, I. Garland. *The Afro-American Press and its Editors* (1891).

Obituary: *San Francisco Bulletin*, 26 and 27 Apr. 1889.

—PHILIP M. MONTESANO

 BENGA, OTA. *See* Otabenga.

 BERRY, CHUCK

(18 Oct. 1926–), singer, songwriter, and guitarist, was born Charles Edward Anderson Berry in St. Louis, Missouri, the fourth of six children of Henry William Berry, a carpenter and handyman, and Martha Bell Banks. The industrious Henry Berry instilled in his son a hunger for material success and a prodigious capacity for hard work, traits which were not entirely apparent in Berry as a youth. Martha Berry, a skilled pianist and accomplished singer, passed on to her son her love for music. By the time he was a teenager, however, Berry preferred jazz, blues, and the "beautiful harmony of country music" to his mother's Baptist hymns (Berry, 14).

Chuck Berry, who helped shape rock and roll and moved the guitar to center stage, 1956. Frank Driggs Collection

In 1944 Berry and two friends hatched an ill-considered plan to drive across the country to California. They soon ran out of money and committed a series of armed robberies in an attempt to return home. All three were arrested, convicted, and given ten-year sentences. In prison, Berry began to take music seriously, cofounding a gospel quartet and a rhythm and blues band popular with both black and white inmates. The quartet sang during services in the prison chapel and met with such success that prison officials allowed the group to sing for African American church congregations in Kansas City and St. Louis.

Berry was released on parole in 1947, and returned to St. Louis. In 1948 he married Themetta Suggs, with whom he had four children. While working menial day jobs, he studied guitar with Ira Harris, who laid the foundation of his guitar-playing style. The recordings of guitarists Charlie

Christian, T-Bone Walker, and Carl Hogan, who played in Louis Jordan's band further shaped his sound. NAT KING COLE, MUDDY WATERS, and Joe Turner were among the singers whose diverse styles he sometimes emulated. Berry's taste, although eclectic, was firmly rooted in both the urban blues and rhythm and blues of the era.

By 1952 Berry was playing regularly in local St. Louis clubs and had developed a reputation as a capable sideman, whose flamboyant stage presence and willingness to indulge in "little gimmicks," such as singing country and western songs, delighted audiences. Among those who noticed the rising bluesman was pianist Johnny Johnson, leader of a popular trio whose repertoire included blues, rhythm and blues, and popular songs. When one of Johnson's sideman was indisposed, Johnson asked Berry to sit in with the band at the Cosmopolitan Club in East St. Louis.

Audiences at the Cosmopolitan Club responded enthusiastically to Berry and the club's owner immediately asked Johnson to hire him permanently. Johnson readily agreed, explaining that Berry's showmanship "brought something to the group that was missin'" (Pegg, 25). Berry's performance with Johnson's trio on New Year's Eve 1952 marked the beginning of a remarkable musical collaboration that produced "Roll Over Beethoven" (1956), "School Day" (1957), and "Rock and Roll Music" (1957), which, more than any other songs, defined the new musical genre of rock and roll. Although Johnson helped to shape the melodies, and his powerful left hand supplied much of the songs' rhythmic drive, the men were not equal partners. The lyrics were Berry's alone, and he was the sole author of songs such as "Maybellene" (1955), his first hit, and "Johnny B. Goode" (1958), one of the most honored songs in rock and roll history.

Within a few years, Berry's role in the trio overshadowed Johnson's, and he began to look beyond St. Louis's African American nightclubs toward a wider audience. In 1955 he visited Chicago, hoping to build on his local success by signing a recording contract. The blues musician MUDDY WATERS, whom Berry met after a concert, directed him to Leonard Chess, who ran a small independent record company. Like many of the era's independent labels, Chess Records produced the African American music that major labels tended to ignore. Chess agreed to record "Maybellene," a song similar to the country and western novelties that Berry often sang, and "Wee Wee Hours," a standard blues tune.

"Maybellene" fired Leonard Chess's imagination. He knew that young white consumers, bored with the music that major labels produced, were searching for something new. Many had gravitated towards rhythm and blues, which, beyond its musical excellence, possessed the lure of the forbidden.

Independent labels courted this emerging market; and disk jockeys, such as Alan Freed, who began calling the music "rock and roll," expanded it. Chess believed that "Maybellene," with its fusion of country and western and rhythm and blues, was the perfect song for the times. It proved to be a dazzling success.

Like most of Berry's songs, "Maybellene" sold well to both whites and blacks. Like all of his songs, it was an exercise in "signifyin'," drawing on African American vernacular forms to speak, simultaneously, in more than one voice. While whites heard something both familiar and unexpected—a frenetic homage to country and western—African Americans heard an affectionate parody. The song reached number two on *Billboard* magazine's pop chart (the "white" chart) and number one on the rhythm and blues chart (the "black" chart). "Maybellene" amalgamated black and white musical styles, exalted cars, girls, and—implicitly—sex, and moved the electric guitar to center stage, creating a musical template that generations of rock and roll musicians would follow.

Determined to repeat the success of "Maybellene," Berry began the process of transforming himself from a competent bluesman into a brilliant rock and roller. With one eye on the cash register and the other on his growing legions of young white fans, he wrote songs that were, above all, marketable. Although producing great art was the least of his concerns, many of the songs that Berry wrote between 1955 and the early 1960s were nothing less than miniature masterpieces. His lyrics blended irony, parody, and literal-minded observation into a coherent whole. His music, while grounded in rhythm and blues, continued to draw on country and western and other popular forms.

In late 1959 and early 1960, Berry's string of successes ended when he was arraigned on two counts of having violated the White Slave Traffic Act (Mann Act), a federal statute. The federal prosecutor in St. Louis alleged that Berry had, on two separate occasions during concert tours, transported Joan Mathis Bates, a white woman in her late teens, and Janice Norine Escalanti, a fourteen-year-old Native American girl, across state lines for immoral purposes. When the case involving Bates went to trial, both she and Berry admitted to having had a consensual sexual relationship, and Bates added that she was in love with him. The jury acquitted Berry, noting that the charges involved a voluntary relationship between two adults.

The Escalanti case, however, ended in a conviction. The jury accepted Escalanti's testimony that she and Berry had engaged in consensual sexual relations on several occasions. The fact that the relationship was consensual had no impact on the charges; prosecutors were only required to prove that, after transporting Escalanti across state lines, Barry's behavior had been "immoral." While Berry denied that he had had a sexual relationship with Escalanti, he proved a nervous and unconvincing witness. The behavior of trial judge George Moore, who repeatedly interjected remarks of a racial nature into the proceedings, compounded Berry's difficulties. Berry appealed his conviction, arguing that Moore's hostile and prejudicial conduct had deprived him of a fair trial. A federal appellate court agreed, and sent the case back to the district court. However, in 1961 Berry was convicted a second time, and entered federal prison in 1962.

By the time Berry was released in 1963, his music had begun to sound old-fashioned. Even though songs that he wrote in prison, such as "Promised Land" (1964), rank among his best, his career as a recording artist was waning. Berry enjoyed a brief revival in 1972, when he scored his first number one hit on the pop chart with the trifling, double-entendre–filled "My Ding-A-Ling." Although he rarely recorded after this point, Berry continued to tour, often with great success, well into his seventies.

In 2000 Johnny Johnson sued Berry, claiming that he had never received credit for cowriting many of the songs that Berry recorded in the 1950s and that he had thereby been defrauded of millions of dollars in royalties. Parts of the case were dismissed in 2001, with the court ruling that it would be impossible for Johnson to prove that he had cowritten the songs. The court also noted that because so much time has passed, many potential witnesses had died and that the memories of others had faded. In addition, Johnson had admitted in the *St. Louis Post-Dispatch* that he spent much of the 1950s in an alcoholic fog, rendering his testimony suspect. Although the precise nature of the relationship between the two men is likely to remain disputed, Johnson's role was almost certainly that of an arranger of Berry's musical ideas.

In his later years, Berry accrued honors that acknowledged his central role in reshaping popular music. He is a member of the Blues Foundation Hall of Fame, the National Academy of Popular Music Songwriter's Hall of Fame, and, in 1986 he was among the first artists inducted into the Rock and Roll Hall of Fame.

FURTHER READING

Berry, Chuck. *Chuck Berry: The Autobiography* (1987).

Collis, John. *Chuck Berry: The Biography* (2002).

Pegg, Bruce. *Brown Eyed Handsome Man: The Life and Hard Times of Chuck Berry, an Unauthorized Biography* (2002).

Discography
Rothwell, Fred. *Long Distance Information: Chuck Berry's Recorded Legacy* (2001).
—JOHN EDWIN MASON

BERRY, HALLE MARIA (14 Aug. 1966–), film actress and model, was born in Cleveland, Ohio, the daughter of Jerome Berry, a hospital attendant, and Judith Hawkins, a psychiatric nurse. Her father, an

alcoholic, abandoned the family when she was four, leaving her mother to raise Halle and her sister Heidi, first in predominantly black inner-city Cleveland and later in that city's white suburbs. Berry's childhood was troubled, in part because of the economic hardship of growing up in a single-parent household. But as the light-skinned child of an interracial couple—her mother was white, her father African American—she also endured racial taunts from both blacks and whites. Fellow students called her "zebra" and on one occasion left an Oreo cookie in her school locker. Berry never had any doubts about her own identity, however, and states on her Web site that her "race" is African American and English.

An extremely shy teenager, Berry craved acceptance from her peers and worked energetically to be the most active and popular young woman at her high school. As a cheerleader, editor of the school newspaper, an honor student, and class president, she appeared to have succeeded, but when fellow students accused her of stuffing the ballot box in the voting for prom queen, she was forced to share the title with a white student. Although this reversal suggested to Berry that whites would not accept a standard of beauty that included people of color, her success in beauty pageants suggested otherwise. By the mid-1980s an African American woman as flawlessly beautiful as Halle Berry could win Miss Teen Ohio and Miss Ohio. As a runner-up in the 1986 Miss U.S.A. pageant, Berry, then a student at Cleveland's Cuyahoga Community College traveled to London to represent the United States in Miss World, the leading international beauty contest. Although Miss Trinidad & Tobago won the title, Berry placed sixth and created a sensation by appearing in the "national costume" segment of the pageant wearing a skimpy bikini with strands of beads and shooting stars. The outfit was purported to express "America's advancement in space," but it drew the ire of other contestants such as Miss Holland, who wore the traditionally bulky and much less revealing Dutch costume with clogs.

Berry found participation in beauty pageants an ideal preparation for a career in Hollywood, since it taught

her how to lose and not be devastated. Considered too short at five feet six inches to be a runway model, she won bit parts in the television sitcoms *Amen* and *A Different World*, but she was rejected at her first audition for a major television role in *Charlie's Angels '88*. She did win a regular spot as a teenage model in 1989's short-lived sitcom on ABC, *Living Dolls*, but increasingly found that her stunning looks and beauty pageant past kept her from landing the serious acting roles she desired. A minor but critically praised role as a crack addict in SPIKE LEE's *Jungle Fever* (1991) signaled a change in her fortunes. That performance marked Berry's first, but by no means last, effort to overcome critics, including Lee himself initially, who could not envision her as anything less than glamorous. In preparation for the role, she interviewed drug addicts and refused to bathe for ten days before shooting. Her next role, as a radio producer on the prime-time soap opera *Knots Landing*, was much less gritty, but it did ensure greater exposure and led to a series of prominent appearances in the film comedies *Strictly Business* and *Boomerang* (1992) and the television miniseries of ALEX HALEY's *Queen* (1993).

In the 1990s Berry became one of the most bankable actors in Hollywood, appearing in popular, though not critically acclaimed movies such as *Fatherhood* (1993), *The Flintstones* (1994), and *Executive Decision* (1996). She received favorable reviews for these parts, but the praise—film critic Roger Ebert described her as "so warm and charming you want to cuddle her"—may have reinforced the view in Hollywood that she was best suited to light roles. At the same time, Berry's beauty and poise earned her an MTV award in 1993 for "most desirable female," an assessment shared by *People* magazine, which since 1992 has consistently listed her among the most beautiful and best dressed women in the world, and by the manufacturers of Revlon makeup, who named her their main spokesmodel in 1996. In an age of celebrity, when fashion has come to mean as much to the corporate world and consumers as films and television, such accolades have greatly enhanced Berry's fame, fortune, and clout. Indeed, in 2002 the *Wall Street*

Journal reported that the financially ailing Revlon Company was relying on a line of Halle Berry cosmetics as the primary means of halting its plummeting profits and share price.

Berry's growing fame and celebrity came at the price of endless media scrutiny. Her 1993 marriage to David Justice, a pitcher for the Atlanta Braves, delighted the tabloids, who printed scores of articles on the glamorous newlyweds, but the couple's troubled relationship and acrimonious divorce three years later was like manna from heaven for the *National Enquirer* and the *Star*. Though she continued to play an increasing variety of film roles, including a drug-addicted mother forced to give up her child to adoption by white parents in *Losing Isaiah* (1995), Berry's personal life provided greater publicity than her movies. In February 2000 a judge placed her on three years probation and ordered her to pay $13,500 in fines and perform 200 hours community service for leaving the scene of a traffic accident. Berry enjoyed better press in 2001, when she married singer Eric Benet and became stepmother to his daughter, India.

Her first leading role, as DOROTHY DANDRIDGE in the television drama *Introducing Dorothy Dandridge* (1999), gave Berry the critical success she had long craved and won her an Emmy Award for outstanding lead actress. As a longtime admirer of Dandridge, Berry co-produced the biopic and lobbied hard to publicize this HBO film about an African American actress renowned for her poise and beauty who suffered from depression and several unhappy and tempestuous relationships. Although Berry never faced the full force of Jim Crow segregation, she strongly identified with Dandridge's determination to broaden the diversity of roles open to women of color.

The parallel with Dandridge continues with Berry's performance in *Monster's Ball* (2001), when she became the first black woman to win the Academy Award for best actress; in 1955, nearly half a century earlier, Dandridge had been the first African American nominated in that category. Some critics ridiculed the speech in which Berry accepted her award in the name of "every nameless, faceless woman of color that now has a chance

because this door tonight has been opened." They noted that actresses like HATTIE MCDANIEL and Dandridge, let alone thousands of unsung women in the civil rights movement, had already given that door an almighty push. Yet Berry was hardly the first Oscar-winning actress—or actor, for that matter—to be overcome by gushing hyperbole in receiving their profession's highest award. Others, including the members of the Academy, praised her portrayal of a poor southern black woman struggling to raise a son after the execution of her husband, and her complex relationship with one of his white executioners. In the *Nation* Michael Eric Dyson, a prominent black academic, lauded Berry's bravery in using her speech to speak up for "ordinary brothers and sisters."

Berry's breakthrough in winning an Academy Award and the sharp criticisms of her acceptance speech capture nicely the ambiguities facing prominent African Americans at the beginning of the twenty-first century. Black American talents and achievements are recognized and rewarded by America's dominant culture as never before, yet that same culture continues to debate those successes in highly racialized ways.

FURTHER READING

Dyson, Michael Eric. "Oscar Opens the Door." *The Nation*, 15 Apr. 2002.

Farley, Christopher J. *Introducing Halle Berry* (2002).

Norment, Lynn. "Halle's Big Year." *Ebony*, Nov. 2002.

—STEVEN J. NIVEN

 BERRY, LEONIDAS HARRIS (20 July 1902– 4 Dec. 1995), physician and public service and church activist, was born on a tobacco farm in Woodsdale, North Carolina, the son of the Reverend Llewellyn Longfellow Berry, general secretary of the Department of Home and Foreign Missions of the African Methodist Episcopal (AME) Church, and Beulah Harris Berry. Leonidas acquired the desire to become a doctor at the age of five, when a distinguished-looking local doctor treated a small wound on his foot. The young boy was impressed by this "miraculous"

event. His aspiration to go to medical school intensified while he was attending Booker T. Washington High School in Norfolk, Virginia. In 1924 Berry graduated from Wilberforce University and went on to obtain the SB in 1925 from the University of Chicago. In 1930 he also received his medical degree from the University of Chicago's Rush Medical College. Berry continued his medical training, earning an MS in Pathology at the University of Illinois Medical School in 1933. He completed his internship at Freedmen's Hospital (1929–1930), one of the nation's first black hospitals, and then his residency at Cook County Hospital in Chicago (1931–1935).

For most of his career, Berry resided in Chicago, becoming a nationally and internationally recognized clinician. His practice and research were centered at Chicago's Provident, Michael Reese, and Cook County Hospitals. From 1935 until 1970 Berry was a mainstay of the physician staff at Provident. This institution, which had been founded by DANIEL HALE WILLIAMS, was one of the nation's leading black hospitals. In 1946 Berry became the first black physician admitted to the staff at Michael Reese. At Cook County he was the first black internist, rising from assistant to senior attending physician during his long affiliation with this institution (1946–1976). He also served as clinical professor in medicine at the University of Illinois from 1960 until 1975.

Beginning in the 1930s Berry developed into a leader in the emerging specialty of gastroenterology. This branch of medicine focuses on the physiology and pathology of the stomach and intestines as well as their interconnected organs, such as the liver, esophagus, gallbladder, and pancreas. Berry's clinical accomplishments were at the forefront of his specialty. He became an international authority on digestive diseases and the technique of endoscopy. Berry helped revolutionize his field when he became the first American doctor to employ the fiberoptic gastro-camera to examine the inside of the digestive tract. The use of this instrument became increasingly refined, enabling physicians to diagnose at much earlier stages various diseases, especially cancers, of the gastrointestinal organs. He invented the Eder-Berry gastrobiopsy scope, a device that made it possible to retrieve tissue samples from the stomach for microscopic study. This instrument has been exhibited at the Smithsonian Institution in Washington, D.C.

In addition to his extraordinary clinical achievements, Berry was a superb medical academician. During the course of his career, he authored or co-authored twelve books and eighty-four medical research articles and presented more than 180 medical lectures, exhibitions, and academic papers nationally and internationally. In 1941 Berry presented a research paper before the gastroenterology and proctology section at the American Medical Association's (AMA) annual convention in Cleveland, Ohio, the first time a black physician made a national presentation before this prestigious group.

The church activities and travels of Berry's father and mother deeply impressed him throughout his early life—so much so that Berry's autobiography, *I Wouldn't Take Nothin' for My Journey* (1981), was written primarily as a memoir dedicated to his parents and their lives. Even while achieving his clinical and academic successes, Berry, raised in the swirl of his parents' church work and community service, never lost touch with the traditional ideals of the black American community—ideals that emphasize charitable work and resistance to racial discrimination. He realized these ideals by expanding his duties and resources at the hospitals and medical schools where he worked, as well as by taking on leadership positions in AME Church and community organizations. From the early 1950s Berry served as president of the mostly black Cook County Physicians Association. He led a citywide movement to set up medical services for young drug addicts and to prevent the spread of drug addiction. His plan involved organizing medical counseling clinics and follow-up services for drug addicts—a plan that became a program that he administered for eight years with finances provided by the Illinois state legislature and the Illinois Department of Public Health.

In 1965 Berry served as president of the National Medical Association (NMA), the nation's premier organization established for black physicians. The highlight of his tenure was spearheading the NMA's activities to integrate the AMA. At this time the AMA still maintained segregated local chapters throughout the nation. In addresses to his NMA constituents, Berry described his disdain for this discriminatory barrier faced by black doctors. He called this practice "a senseless social embargo... against licensed and practicing physicians based upon a criterion of race in some [AMA] societies and tokenism in others" (Morais, 220). In order to place the NMA on higher ground regarding the integration of physician associations, at the August 1965 annual convention, the association passed Berry's proposal that the NMA recruit white physicians. At the convention's press conference, Berry stated his rationale clearly: "We cannot remain a segregated [medical] society when we are pressing for integration ourselves" (Morais, 196).

Under Berry's leadership the NMA next held a series of formal meetings with AMA officials and trustees. These meetings, which took place between September 1965 and August 1966, resulted in the adoption of several cooperative measures. First, the two organizations agreed to increase recruitment efforts to attract more black Americans into medical careers. Second, the AMA resolved to appoint more black members of the two organizations to high-standing councils and committees of the AMA. Finally, the AMA appointed a special committee of the AMA board of trustees to serve as a watchdog body to work against segregation in local chapters and physician practices. The committee contacted segregated local chapters to persuade them to comply voluntarily with the AMA's national resolutions prohibiting racial discrimination in local societies, hospitals, and medical care.

Berry also was a deeply committed "churchman" for the AME Church. He strove to use his church ties to work with other denominations on projects for community betterment. For example, for many years Berry served as the medical director of the Health Commission of the AME Church. In this capacity, in the mid-1960s he developed means to support the integration drive in Cairo, Illinois. In response to Ku Klux Klan activities and entrenched neighborhood poverty, local community activists in Cairo launched an antiracism campaign known as the Black United Front. Berry organized a "flying health service to Cairo" called the Flying Black Doctors to assist the Cairo activists. Berry's group of thirty-two physicians, nurses, and technicians flew down to Cairo and gave medical exams to some three hundred persons. The Cairo activities of the Flying Black Doctors attracted the attention of the national news media, including NBC's famed television news show, the Huntley Brinkle Report, with Chet Huntley and David Brinkley.

Berry liked to refer to himself as a "multidimensional doctor." In his autobiography he emphasizes that although he was a successful clinician, he was most pleased that he had never given in to the tendency to become too "circumscribed and perhaps obsessed with the pursuit of excellence in... matters purely medical" (405). Berry viewed his medical and public service achievements as much more than solo endeavors. Instead, he believed that they were the direct outgrowth of family and religious influences that stemmed from the slave communities of the pre–Civil War United States. In his autobiography Berry writes: "The success of my career [was] a high water mark in the destiny of the Berry family in its long odyssey through the generations. The strength of Afro-American culture to a great extent lies in the unique common bonds which tie together many [such] successful Black nuclear and multinuclear families in America" (Berry, 407). Berry and his extended family have left a permanent contribution at the highest levels of American and black American medical science and religious life.

FURTHER READING

The papers of Leonidas H. Berry, 1907–1982, are located in the Modern Manuscripts Collection, History of Medicine Division, National Library of Medicine, Bethesda, Maryland. There is also a body of Berry's personal papers at the Schomburg Manuscripts and Rare Books Collection, New York Public Library, New York City, under the title Leonidas H. Berry Papers, 1932–1988.

Berry, Leonidas H. *I Wouldn't Take Nothin' for My Journey: Two Centuries of an Afro-American Minister's Family* (1981).

Morais, H. M. *The History of the Negro in Medicine* (1968).

Obituary: *New York Times* (Late Edition), 12 December 1995.
—DAVID MCBRIDE

 BETHUNE, MARY JANE McLEOD (10 July 1875–18 May 1955), organizer of black women and advocate for social justice, was born in Mayesville, South Carolina, the child of the former slaves Samuel McLeod and Patsy McIntosh, farmers. After attending a school operated by the Presbyterian Board of Missions for Freedmen, she entered Scotia Seminary (now Barber-Scotia College) in Concord, North Carolina, in 1888 and graduated in May 1894. She spent the next year at Dwight Moody's evangelical Institute for Home and Foreign Missions in Chicago, Illinois. In 1898 she married Albertus Bethune. They both taught briefly at Kindell Institute in Sumter, South Carolina. The marriage was not happy. They had one child and separated late in 1907. After teaching in a number of schools, Bethune founded the Daytona Normal and Industrial Institute for Training Negro Girls in Daytona, Florida, in 1904. Twenty years later the school merged with a boys' school, the Cookman Institute, and was renamed Bethune-Cookman College in 1929. Explaining why she founded the training school, Bethune remarked, "Many homeless girls have been sheltered there and trained physically, mentally and spiritually. They have been helped and sent out to serve, to pass their blessings on to other needy children."

In addition to her career as an educator, Bethune helped found some of the most significant organizations in black America. In 1920 Bethune became vice president of the National Urban League and helped create the women's section of its Commission on Interracial Cooperation. From 1924 to 1928 she also served as the president of the National Association of Colored Women. In 1935, as founder and president of the National Council of Negro Women, Bethune forged a coalition of hundreds of black women's organizations across the country. She served from 1936 to 1950 as president of the Association for the Study of Negro Life and History, later known as the Association for the Study of Afro-American Life and History. In 1935 the National Association for the Advancement of Colored People awarded Bethune its highest honor, the Spingarn Medal. She received honorary degrees from ten universities, the Medal of Honor and Merit from Haiti (1949), and the Star of Africa Award from Liberia (1952). In 1938 she participated along with liberal white southerners in the annual meetings of the Southern Conference for Human Welfare.

Bethune's involvement in national government began in the 1920s during the Calvin Coolidge and Herbert Hoover presidential administrations, when she participated in child welfare conferences. In June 1936 Bethune became administrative assistant and, in January 1939, director in charge of Negro Affairs in the New Deal National Youth Administration (NYA). This made her the first black woman in U.S. history to occupy such a high-level federal position. Bethune was responsible for helping vast numbers of unemployed sixteen- to twenty-four-year-old black youths find jobs in private industry and in vocational training projects. The agency created work-relief programs that opened opportunities for thousands of black youths, which enabled countless black communities to survive the Depression. She served in this office until the NYA was closed in 1944.

During her service in the Franklin D. Roosevelt administration, Bethune organized a small but influential group of black officials who became known as the Black Cabinet. Prominent among them were WILLIAM HENRY HASTIE of the Department of the Interior and the War Department and ROBERT WEAVER, who served in the Department of the Interior and several manpower agencies. The Black Cabinet did more than advise the president; they articulated a black agenda for social change, beginning with demands for greater benefit from New Deal programs and equal employment opportunities.

In 1937 in Washington, D.C., Bethune orchestrated the National Conference on the Problems of the Negro and Negro Youth, which focused on concerns ranging from better housing and health care for African Americans to equal protection under the law. As an outspoken advocate for black civil rights, she fought for federal anti–poll tax and anti-lynching legislation. Bethune's influence during the New Deal was further strengthened by her friendship with First Lady Eleanor Roosevelt.

During World War II, Bethune was special assistant to the secretary of war and assistant director of the Women's Army Corps. In this post she set up the first officer candidate schools for the corps. Throughout the war she pressed President Roosevelt and other governmental and military officials to make use of the many black women eager to serve in the national defense program; she also lobbied for increased appointments of black women to federal bureaus. After the war she continued to lecture and to write newspaper and magazine columns and articles until her death in Daytona Beach, Florida.

Urged by the National Council of Negro Women, the federal government dedicated the Mary McLeod Bethune Memorial Statue at Lincoln Park in southeastern Washington, D.C., on 10 July 1974. Bethune's life and work provide one of the major links between the social reform efforts of post-Reconstruction black women and the political protest activities of the generation emerging after World War II. The many strands of black women's struggle for education, political rights, racial pride, sexual autonomy, and liberation are united in the writings, speeches, and organization work of Bethune.

FURTHER READING

Holt, Rackman. *Mary McLeod Bethune: A Biography* (1964).
Ross, B. Joyce. "Mary McLeod Bethune and the National Youth Administration: A Case Study of Power Relationships in the Black Cabinet of Franklin D. Roosevelt." *Journal of Negro History* 60 (Jan. 1975): 1–28.
Smith, Elaine M. "Mary McLeod Bethune and the National Youth Administration" in *Clio Was a Woman: Studies in the History of American Women* (1980).

Obituary: *New York Times*, 19 May 1955.
—DARLENE CLARK HINE

BETHUNE, THOMAS. *See* Blind Tom.

BIBB, HENRY WALTON

(10 May 1815–1854), author, editor, and antislavery lecturer, was born into slavery on the plantation of David White of Shelby County, Kentucky, the son of James Bibb, a slaveholding planter and state senator, and Mildred Jackson. White began hiring Bibb out as a laborer on several neighboring plantations before he had reached the age of ten. The constant change in living situations throughout his childhood, combined with the inhumane treatment he often received at the hands of strangers, set a pattern for life that he would later refer to in his autobiography as "my manner of living on the road." Bibb was sold more than six times between 1832 and 1840 and was forced to relocate to at least seven states throughout the South; later, as a free man, his campaign for abolition took him throughout eastern Canada and the northern United States. But such early instability also made the young Bibb both self-sufficient and resourceful, two characteristics that were useful against the day-to-day assault of slavery: "The only weapon of self defense that I could use successfully," he wrote, "was that of deception."

In 1833 Bibb met and married Malinda, a slave on William Gatewood's plantation in nearby Oldham County, Kentucky, and the following year she gave birth to Mary Frances, their only child to survive infancy. At about this time Gatewood purchased Bibb from the Whites in the vain hope that uniting the young family would pacify their desire for freedom. Living less than ten miles from the Ohio River, Bibb made his first escape from slavery by crossing the river into Madison, Indiana, in the winter of 1837. He boarded a steamboat bound for Cincinnati, escaping the notice of authorities because he was "so near the color of a slaveholder," a trait deemed undesirable by prospective slave buyers and for which he endured prolonged incarcerations at various slave markets.

Bibb situated this first escape historically as "the commencement of what was called the underground railroad to Canada." Less than a year after achieving freedom, Bibb returned to Kentucky for his wife and daughter. He was captured and taken to the Louisville slave market, from which he again escaped, returning to Perrysburg, Ohio.

In July 1839 Bibb once more undertook to free his wife and child. Betrayed by another slave, Bibb was again taken to Louisville for sale; this time his wife and child accompanied him on the auction block. While awaiting sale, Bibb received the rudiments of an education from white felons in the prison, where he was forced to work at hard labor for a summer. Finally, a speculator purchased the Bibbs for resale at the lucrative markets of New Orleans. After being bought by Deacon Francis Whitfield of Claiborn Parish, Louisiana, Bibb and his family suffered unimaginable cruelty. They were physically beaten and literally overworked to the point of death, and they nearly perished for lack of food and adequate shelter. Bibb attempted two escapes from Whitfield, preferring that his family risk the perils of the surrounding Red River swamps than endure eighteen-hour days in the cotton fields.

The final escape attempt resulted in Bibb's permanent separation from his family in December 1840. First staked down and beaten nearly to death after his capture, Bibb was then sold to two professional gamblers. These men took him through Texas and Arkansas and into "Indian Territory," where they sold him to a Cherokee slave owner on the frontier of white settlement in what is probably present-day Oklahoma or southeastern Kansas. There Bibb received what he considered his only humane treatment in slavery. Because he was allotted a modicum of independence and respect, and because he was reluctant to desert his master, who was then terminally ill, Bibb delayed his final escape from slavery by a year, departing the night of his master's death. He traveled through wilderness, occasionally stumbling onto Indian encampments, before crossing into Missouri, where his route took him east along the Osage River into Jefferson City. From there he traveled by steamboat through St. Louis to Cincinnati and on to freedom in 1841.

In Detroit in the winter of 1842, Bibb briefly attended the school of the Reverend William C. Monroe, receiving his only formal education. Bibb's work as what he called an "advocate of liberty" began in earnest soon after his final escape from slavery; for the next decade he epitomized the black abolitionist, making his voice heard through lectures, a slave narrative, and the independent press. Like his contemporaries FREDERICK DOUGLASS, WILLIAM WELLS BROWN, and WILLIAM and ELLEN CRAFT, Bibb was among a first generation of African American fugitives from the South who used their firsthand experience in slavery as a compelling testimony against the atrocities of the southern institution.

Although his highly regarded *Narrative of the Life and Adventures of Henry Bibb, An American Slave* was not published until the spring of 1849, Bibb began telling the story of his life before antislavery crowds in Adrian, Michigan, in May 1844. His story proved so poignant in its depiction of human suffering and endurance, so heroic in its accounts of ingenious escapes, and so romantic in its adventures in the territories of the West that the Detroit Liberty Association undertook a full-scale investigation to allay public incredulity, an unprecedented response to a nineteenth-century slave narrative. Through correspondence with Bibb's former associates, "slave owners, slave dealers, fugitives from slavery, political friends and political foes," the committee found the facts of Bibb's account "corroborated beyond all question."

Lecturing for the Michigan Liberty Party, Bibb was sent to Ohio to speak along the north side of the Mason-Dixon Line, a region notorious for its proslavery sympathies. Bibb returned to the South one final time in the winter of 1845 in search of his wife and daughter. While visiting his mother in Kentucky, Bibb learned that his wife and daughter's escape from certain death on Whitfield's plantation came at the expense of their marriage; Malinda had been forced to become the mistress of a white southerner. In 1848, on a sabbatical from lecturing, Bibb met and married Mary E. Miles, an African American abolitionist from Boston. It is not known whether they had children. With the passage of the 1850 Fugitive Slave

Law, the Bibbs fled to Sandwich, western Canada, where, in January 1851, Henry and Mary established the *Voice of the Fugitive*. This publication was a biweekly antislavery journal that reported on the condition of fugitives and advocated the abolition of slavery, black colonization to Canada, temperance, black education, and the development of black commercial enterprises.

With the aid of the black abolitionists JAMES T. HOLLY and J. T. Fisher, Bibb organized the North American League, an organization evolving out of the North American Convention of Colored People, held in Toronto and over which Bibb presided in September 1851. The league was meant to promote colonization to Canada and to serve as the central authority for blacks in the Americas. Although the league survived but a few short months, Bibb continued to work toward colonization, encouraging Michigan philanthropists a year later to help form the Refugee Home Society—a joint-stock company for the purpose of acquiring and selling Canadian farmland to black emigrants—to which Bibb attached his journal as its official organ. Tension among prominent black Canadians, however, brought about the society's demise. Bibb died in Windsor, Ontario, Canada, without realizing his vision for an African American colony.

FURTHER READING

Andrews, William L. *To Tell a Free Story: The First Century of Afro-American Autobiography, 1760–1865* (1988).

Hite, Roger W. "Voice of a Fugitive: Henry Bibb and Ante-bellum Black Separatism." *Journal of Black Studies* 4 (Mar. 1974): 269–284.

QUARLES, BENJAMIN. *Black Abolitionists* (1969).

Ripley, C. Peter, ed. *The Black Abolitionist Papers*, vols. 3–4 (1985, 1991).

Silverman, Jason H. *Unwelcome Guests: Canada West's Response to American Fugitive Slaves, 1800–1865* (1985).

—GREGORY S. JACKSON

BLACKWELL, DAVID

(24 Apr. 1919–), mathematician and professor, was born David Harold Blackwell in Centralia, Illinois, the oldest of four children, to Grover Blackwell, a locomotive mechanic for the Illinois Central Railroad, and Mabel Johnson. Although much of Blackwell's hometown was segregated, he attended an integrated elementary school. He first became interested in mathematics in high school where, although not particularly interested in algebra or trigonometry, he immediately took an interest in geometry—the scientific study of the properties and relations of lines, surfaces, and solids in space. Later in his life Blackwell credited his high school geometry instructor for showing him the beauty and the usefulness of mathematics. He joined his high school's mathematics club where his instructor pushed students to submit solutions to the *School Science and Mathematics Journal*, which published one of Blackwell's solutions. It was with geometry that Blackwell first began to apply mathematical methods and formulas to games such as "crosses" in order to determine the probability of winning for the first player.

When Blackwell entered college at the age of sixteen, he intended at first to become an elementary school teacher. In 1938 he earned an AB degree from the University of Illinois at Urbana-Champaign and went on to receive an AM in 1939 and a PhD in 1941. Here, his interest in probability and statistics emerged and flourished. His dissertation, written under the direction of Joseph L. Doob, was entitled "Some Properties of Markoff Chains." When he completed the PhD, Blackwell was only twenty-two years old and was only the seventh African American to receive a PhD in Mathematics.

After completing the PhD, Blackwell accepted a Rosenwald Postdoctoral Fellowship at the Institute for Advanced Study in Princeton, prompting outrage from some in the university community who vehemently opposed the appointment of an African American to this position at Princeton, which had not yet even enrolled African American students. The University's president, Harold D. Dodds, admonished the institute for making such an appointment against the wishes of the university community and sought unsuccessfully to block Blackwell's appointment.

Perhaps because of his experience in the Ivy League, Blackwell seemed to be aware of the limited opportunities for African American scholars in higher academia, and with the exception of an application and interview at the University of California at Berkeley, he applied for faculty positions at only historically black colleges and universities. After one year at Princeton he took short-term professorships at Southern University in Baton

David Blackwell, an innovator in statistical analysis, game theory, and mathematical decision-making. Schomburg Center

Rouge, Louisiana, and Clark Atlanta University.

In 1944 Blackwell joined the faculty of Howard University as an assistant professor at a time when the Washington, D.C., institution was a mecca for black scholars, including the historian RAYFORD W. LOGAN, the philosopher ALAIN LOCKE, and the sociologist E. FRANKLIN FRAZIER. Shortly after arriving at Howard, Blackwell married Ann Madison, and in just three years he had risen to the rank of full professor and chairman of the mathematics department.

At Howard, Blackwell also launched his career as a widely recognized and honored researcher in mathematics. Hearing a lecture and attending a subsequent meeting with the well-known statistician Abe Girshick stimulated Blackwell's interest in statistics and sequential analysis. Even while teaching and chairing the Department of Mathematics at Howard, Blackwell published over twenty research papers in mathematical statistics. Between 1948 and 1950 his interest in the theory of games—the method of applying logic to determine which of several available strategies is likely to maximize one's gain or minimize one's loss in a game or military solution—was revived by three summers of work at the Rand Corporation. Blackwell became particularly interested in the art of dueling with pistols and in determining the most statistically advantageous moment for a dueler to shoot. In the midst of the cold war, such statistical analyses of games became useful and pertinent for the federal government in thinking about U.S. military strategy, and Blackwell's work and Blackwell himself became a leader in the field of statistical analysis and game theory. In 1950–1951 Blackwell spent one year as a visiting professor of statistics at Stanford University.

All of Blackwell's work in game theory (including the art of dueling and the statistical analysis of bluffing as a strategy in poker) culminated in 1954 when he and Abe Girshick jointly wrote *Theory of Games and Statistical Decisions*. This book served as a mathematical textbook for students in statistical decision functions. Building upon the prior works of John von Neumann and A. Wald in the statistical and conceptual aspects of decision theory and theory of games, Blackwell and Girshick developed new and innovative concepts of mathematical decision making that were later used in military tactics, the business world, and engineering.

By the time of the book's publication in 1954, Blackwell's career was rising rapidly. Shortly after he gave an address on concepts of probability at the International Congress of Mathematicians in Amsterdam, he was offered and accepted a position as professor of statistics at the University of California at Berkeley. Serving as chair of the Berkeley statistics department from 1957 to 1961, Blackwell continued to be a prolific academic writer, publishing over fifty articles in the field of statistical analysis. Prominent appointments and accolades soon followed. In 1955 he was elected president of the Institute of Mathematical Statistics, and later served as president for the International Association for Statistics in Physical Sciences and the Bernoulli Society, and vice-president of the International Statistical Institute, the American Statistical Association, and the American Mathematical Society.

In 1965 Blackwell became the first African American named to the National Academy of Sciences (NAS), a body used by the federal government and other agencies to investigate, experiment, and report on scientific matters. (Remarkably, nearly three decades later in 1996, *The Journal of Blacks in Higher Education* found that Blackwell had been joined by only two further black inductees at the NAS, the chemist PERCY LAVON JULIAN and the sociologist WILLIAM JULIUS WILSON). In 1979 Blackwell received the prestigious von Neumann Theory Prize from the Operations Research Society of America for his work in dynamic programming, and in 1986 Blackwell received the R.A. Fisher Award from the Committee of Presidents of Statistical Societies. All of these awards and prizes acknowledged the continued relevance of his research in statistical analysis and game theory. In addition to being known as one of the world's best mathematicians, his scholarly work and professional activities have brought Blackwell honorary degrees from Howard, Harvard, Yale, the University of Illinois, Carnegie-Mellon, the University of Southern California, Michigan State, Syracuse, Southern Illinois University, the University of Warwick in England, and the National University of Lesotho. Blackwell retired from Berkeley in 1989, although he remains on the faculty as professor emeritus and continues to publish in mathematical journals. Blackwell has also advised over fifty graduate students. Blackwell's legacy in teaching and researching, and the path-breaking trail he made for African Americans in the mathematics field, makes him one of this century's most notable figures in this highly specialized area.

FURTHER READING

Blackwell, David, et al. *Theory of Games and Statistical Decisions* (1954).

DeGroot, Morris H. "A Conversation with David Blackwell." *Statistical Science*, Feb. 1986: 40–53.

Guillen, Michael. "Normal, against the Odds." *New York Times*, 30 June 1985.

Martin, Donald A. "The Determinacy of Blackwell Games." *Journal of Symbolic Logic*, Dec. 1998: 1565–1581.

"The Mathematics of Poker Strategy." *New York Times*, 25 Dec. 1949.

"National Academy of Sciences: Nearly as White as a Posh Country Club in Alabama." *Journal of Blacks in Higher Education* (Summer 1996): 18–19.

—KEITH WAILOO
—RICHARD MIZELLE

BLACKWELL, UNITA Z.

(18 Mar. 1933–), civil rights activist and mayor, was born in Lula, Mississippi, the daughter of sharecroppers in Coahoma County, Mississippi. Her father had to leave Mississippi when he refused to obey his plantation owner's order to send his young daughter Unita to the fields to pick cotton. He found work in an icehouse in a neighboring state. Her mother was illiterate and determined that her children would learn to read and write. In the Mississippi Delta, everyone was required to pick and chop cotton, and the schools closed down to allow for this work except for two or three months a year. Consequently, Unita Blackwell and her sister took the ferry across the Mississippi River to West Helena, Arkansas. She lived with her aunt

for eight months of the year and attended Westside Junior High School, where she completed the eighth grade. Later, she received her high school equivalency diploma. Blackwell spent her younger years picking cotton—as much as three hundred bales a day. After she married, she and her husband went to Florida to pick tomatoes and work in a canning plant. She moved to Mayersville, Mississippi, in 1962 and picked cotton, while her husband worked for U.S. industries.

In 1964 she became a field worker for the Student Nonviolent Coordinating Committee under the supervision of STOKELY CARMICHAEL. She was in charge of voter registration in the Second Congressional District in Mississippi, and, along with seven other people, she registered to vote in Issaquena County. She became a close friend of FANNIE LOU HAMER, and they both became founding members of the Mississippi Freedom Democratic Party (MFDP), formed in 1964 to challenge the white supremacist Democratic Party in Mississippi. Along with Hamer, Blackwell was an MFDP delegate to the 1964 Democratic national convention in Atlantic City. Members of the MFDP challenged the seating of the all-white delegates from Mississippi, and Blackwell, Hamer, and others testified before the credentials committee. When Hamer presented her famous testimony before the committee, President Lyndon Johnson called a press conference to prevent television coverage of the powerful and inspirational speaker from Mississippi. After much political wrangling, the MFDP was awarded only two delegate seats, which the members refused.

In the summer of 1965 the MFDP marched on the state legislature in Jackson to support Governor Paul Johnson's request that the legislators repeal Mississippi's discriminatory voting laws. Over half of the five hundred demonstrators were in their teens. Police arrested more than two hundred of the marchers, including Blackwell, placing them in the stockyards of the state fairgrounds, where many of the women were tortured. Blackwell herself was imprisoned for eleven days (USM oral history interview, 35–36).

Blackwell continued to press for change in the Delta. In 1965 she demanded that the school board provide decent facilities, teachers, and books for her son's school. The board refused to hear the demands, and Blackwell sued for desegregation of the schools in *Sharkey and Issaquena County Consolidated Line v. Blackwell*. The black principal followed the orders of the school board and refused to cooperate and, in Blackwell's view, left them with no alternative but to sue. "Desegregation of school was not one [of] our favorites" she recalled. "Our thing was to have good schools, didn't care what color they were.... We was asking for books; we was asking for fixing of the schools, that they would be just as nice" (University of Southern Mississippi oral history interview, 44). She won her case.

Undaunted by intimidation, Blackwell continued her struggle for justice. In the winter of 1965 and 1966 poor people in the Delta were hungry and cold. Indeed, two people froze to death. Conditions were made worse when planters evicted sharecroppers for registering to vote and participating in civil rights activities; the planters then saw to it that officials denied the evicted sharecroppers access to the federal food commodity program. With no food to eat and no place to live, sharecroppers formed the Mississippi Freedom Labor Union in January of 1965. The union launched a strike, and domestic workers, tractor drivers, and field hands walked off of their jobs all over the Delta.

As evictions and starvation continued, the union members Blackwell, Ida Mae Lawrence, and Isaac Foster, in the face of the federal government's refusal to answer their plea for help, decided to set up their own community and government. They led over seventy men, women, and children onto the empty Greenville Air Base, consisting of two thousand acres and three hundred buildings. There Blackwell eloquently expressed the goals of the group: "I feel that the federal government have proven that it don't care about poor people. Everything that we have asked for through these years has been handed down on paper. It's never been a reality. We the poor people of Mississippi is tired," she continued. "We're going to build for ourselves, because we don't have a government that represents us" (Grant, 501). A group of Air Police removed the squatters after thirty hours, but Blackwell and others had forced national attention on the dire poverty that many lived in and the limits of federal programs to address poor peoples' concerns.

Blackwell continued her efforts on behalf of poor people, becoming a national spokesperson on the issues of community economic development and low-income housing. In 1967, along with Hamer, Annie Devine, and Amzie Moore, she helped organize the Mississippi Action for Community Education Inc. (MACE) "to build and strengthen local human capacities and indigenous community development efforts" in the Mississippi Delta. MACE has trained local community organizers and leaders; conducts literacy, job training, career development, and arts education programs; and sponsors the Mississippi Delta Blues and Heritage Festival. In the late 1960s and early 1970s Blackwell worked with the National Council of Negro Women as a community-development specialist, establishing cooperative ventures in ownership of low-income housing. In 1983 she received a master's degree in Regional Planning from the University of Massachusetts at Amherst.

Blackwell has remained politically active on both a local and a national level. In 1976 she was elected mayor of Mayersville, becoming the first African American to hold mayoral office in Mississippi. In 1979 she attended President Jimmy Carter's Energy Summit at Camp David, and in 1984 she addressed the National Democratic Convention in San Francisco. In 1989 she chaired the National Mayor's Conference and, in 1991, the Black Women's Mayor's Conference. From 1976 to 1983 she was president of the U.S.-China Peoples' Friendship Association and traveled to China on numerous occasions. She has traveled extensively throughout Asia, Central America, and Europe.

In recognition of her achievements, in 1992 Blackwell was awarded the prized MacArthur Fellowship, also called the "genius" award, and the University of Massachusetts invited her to become the Eleanor Bateman Alumni Scholar. Her fighting spirit and faith in humanity persists. In 2000 she observed: "It seems like the whole century has been about overcoming. Fighting and then overcoming. You had women's suffrage, and apartheid and segregation. And we blacks lived in that lock-in, and somehow survived. How, I do not know. Nothing but a God I say. The whole era was full of hate, but we're trying to overcome it, and we're headed for something new, I just feel it. Maybe we are the group of people, the blacks in America, that brought everyone to their worst, and then to their best. Including ourselves" (UMASS Online Magazine).

FURTHER READING

The most extensive source of information on Mrs. Blackwell is her interview, located in the Civil Rights in Mississippi Digital Archive, McCain Library and Archives, University of Southern Mississippi. See also the Mississippi Action for Community Education Inc. web site, and UMASS Online Magazine (Winter 2000).

"My Whole World Was My Kinfolks." UMASS Online Magazine, Winter 2000.
"Mississippi Freedom Labor Union, 1965 Origins," and "We Have No Government," in Jo Ann Grant, ed. *Black Protest: History, Documents, and Analyses, 1619 to the Present*, 498–505.
Dittmer, John. *Local People: The Struggle for Civil Rights in Mississippi* (1994).
Mills, Kay. *This Little Light of Mine: The Life of Fannie Lou Hamer* (1993).
Payne, Charles. *I've Got the Light of Freedom: The Organizing Tradition and the Mississippi Freedom Struggle* (1995).

—NAN ELIZABETH WOODRUFF

BLAKE, EUBIE

(7 Feb. 1883–12 Feb. 1983), composer and pianist, was born James Hubert Blake in Baltimore, Maryland, the son of John Sumner Blake, a stevedore, and Emily Johnston, a launderer. His father was a Civil War veteran, and both parents were former slaves. While the young Blake was a mediocre student during several years of public schooling, he showed early signs of musical interest and talent, picking out tunes on an organ in a department store at about age six. As a result, his parents rented an organ for twenty-five cents a week, and he soon began basic keyboard lessons with Margaret Marshall, a neighbor and church organist. At about age twelve he learned cornet and buck dancing and was earning pocket change singing with friends on the street. When he

was thirteen, he received encouragement from the ragtime pianist Jesse Pickett, whom he had watched through the window of a bawdy house in order to learn his fingering. By 1898 he had steady work as a piano player in Aggie Shelton's sporting house, a job that necessitated the lad's sneaking out of his home at night, after his parents went to bed. The objections of his deeply religious mother when she learned of his new career were overcome only by the pragmatism of his sporadically employed father, once he discovered how much his son was making in tips.

In 1899 (the year SCOTT JOPLIN's famous "Maple Leaf Rag" appeared), Blake wrote his first rag, "Charleston Rag" (although he would not be able to notate it until some years later). In 1902 he performed as a buck dancer in the traveling minstrel show *In Old Kentucky*, playing briefly in New York City. In 1907, after playing in several clubs in Baltimore, he became a pianist at the Goldfield Hotel, built by his friend and the new world lightweight boxing champion Joe Gans. The elegant Goldfield was one of the first establishments in Baltimore where blacks and whites mixed, and there Blake acquired a personal grace and polish that would impress his admirers for the rest of his life. Already an excellent player, he learned from watching the conservatory-trained "One-Leg Willie" Joseph, whom he often cited as the best piano player he had ever heard. While at the Goldfield, Blake studied composition with the Baltimore musician Llewellyn Wilson, and at about the same time he began playing summers in Atlantic City, where he met such keyboard luminaries as Willie "the Lion" Smith, Luckey Roberts, and James P. Johnson. In July 1910 he married Avis Lee, the daughter of a black society family in Baltimore and a classically trained pianist.

In 1915 Blake met the singer and lyricist NOBLE SISSLE, and they quickly began a songwriting collaboration that would last for decades. One of their songs of that year, "It's All Your Fault," achieved success when it was introduced by Sophie Tucker. Sissle and Blake also performed in New York with JAMES REESE EUROPE's Society Orchestra. While Sissle and Europe were in the service

during World War I, Blake performed in vaudeville with Henry "Broadway" Jones. After the war Sissle and Blake formed a vaudeville act called the Dixie Duo, which became quite successful. In an era when blacks were expected to shuffle and speak in dialect, they dressed elegantly in tuxedos, and they were one of the first black acts to perform before white audiences without burnt cork. By 1917 Blake also had begun recording on both discs and piano rolls.

In 1920 Sissle and Blake met the successful comedy and dance team of Flournoy Miller and Aubrey Lyles, who suggested combining forces to produce a show. The result was the all-black *Shuffle Along*, which opened on Broadway in 1921 and for which Blake was composer and conductor. The score included what would become one of his best-known songs, "I'm Just Wild about Harry." Mounted on a shoestring budget, the musical met with critical acclaim and popular success, running for 504 performances in New York, followed by an extensive three-company tour of the United States. The show had a tremendous effect on musical theater, stirring interest in jazz dance, fostering faster paced shows with more syncopated rhythms, and paving the way in general for more black musicals and black performers. *Shuffle Along* was a springboard for the careers of several of its cast members, including JOSEPHINE BAKER, Adelaide Hall, FLORENCE MILLS, and PAUL ROBESON.

Sissle and Blake worked for ten years as songwriters for the prestigious Witmark publishing firm. In 1922, through Julius Witmark, they were able to join ASCAP (American Society of Composers, Authors, and Publishers), which did not at that time include many blacks. They also appeared in an early sound film in 1923, *Sissle and Blake's Snappy Songs*, produced by the electronics pioneer Lee De Forest. In 1924 they created an ambitious new show, *The Chocolate Dandies*. Unable to match the success of *Shuffle Along*, the lavish production lost money, but Blake was proud of its score and considered it his best.

The team returned to vaudeville, ending their long collaboration with a successful eight-month tour of Great Britain in 1925–1926. The two broke up when Sissle, attracted by opportunities in

Europe, returned to work there; Blake, delighted to be back home in New York, refused to accompany him. Over the next few years Blake collaborated with Harry Creamer to produce a few songs and shows; reunited with "Broadway" Jones to perform the shortened "tab show" *Shuffle Along Jr.* in vaudeville (1928–1929); and teamed with the lyricist Andy Razaf to write songs for *Lew Leslie's Blackbirds of 1930*, including "Memories of You," later popularized by Benny Goodman. After Lyles's death in 1932, Sissle and Blake reunited with Miller to create *Shuffle Along of 1933*, but the show failed, in part because of the Depression. The remainder of the decade saw Blake collaborating with the lyricist Milton Reddie on a series of shows, including the Works Progress Administration–produced *Swing It* in 1937, and with Razaf on several floor shows and "industrials" (promotional shows). Blake's wife died of tuberculosis in 1939, but despite his grief he managed to complete, with Razaf, the show *Tan Manhattan*.

During World War II, Blake toured with United Service Organizations shows and worked with other collaborators. In 1945 he married Marion Gant Tyler, a business executive and former showgirl in several black musicals. She took over management of his financial affairs and saw to the raising of his ASCAP rating to an appropriate level, enhancing their financial security considerably.

After the war, at the age of sixty-three, Blake took the opportunity to attend New York University, where he studied the Schillinger system of composition. He graduated with a degree in music in 1950. Meanwhile, the presidential race of 1948 stirred renewed interest in "I'm Just Wild about Harry" when Harry Truman adopted it as a campaign song. This resulted in a reuniting of Sissle and Blake and in a revival in 1952 of *Shuffle Along*. Unfortunately, the producers' attempts to completely rewrite the show had the effect of eviscerating it, and the restaging closed after only four performances.

Following a few years of relative retirement, during which Blake wrote out some of his earlier pieces, a resurgence of popular interest in ragtime in the 1950s and again in the 1970s thrust him back into the spotlight for the last decades of his life. Several

commemorative recordings appeared, most notably, *The Eighty-six Years of Eubie Blake*, a two-record retrospective with Noble Sissle for Columbia in 1969. In 1972 he started Eubie Blake Music, a record company featuring his own music. He was much in demand as a speaker and performer, impressing audiences with his still considerable pianistic technique as well as his energy, audience rapport, and charm as a raconteur. Appearances included the St. Louis Ragfest, the Newport Jazz Festival, the *Tonight Show*, a solo concert at Town Hall in New York City, and a concert in his honor by Arthur Fiedler and the Boston Pops in 1973, with Blake as soloist. In 1974 Jean-Christophe Averty produced a four-hour documentary film on Blake's life and music for French television. The musical revue *Eubie!*, featuring twenty-three of his numbers, opened on Broadway in 1978 and ran for a year. Blake was awarded the Presidential Medal of Freedom at the White House in 1981.

Blake's wife, Marion, died in June 1982; he left no children by either of his marriages. A few months after his wife's death, his hundredth birthday was feted with performances of his music, but he was ill with pneumonia and unable to attend. He died five days later in New York City.

Over a long career as pianist, composer, and conductor, Blake left a legacy of more than two thousand compositions in various styles. His earliest pieces were piano rags, often of such extreme difficulty that they were simplified for publication. As a ragtime composer and player, he, along with such figures as Luckey Roberts and James P. Johnson, was a key influence on the Harlem stride-piano school of the 1930s. In the field of show music, Blake moved beyond the confines of ragtime, producing songs that combined rhythmic energy with an appealing lyricism. Particularly notable was his involvement with the successful *Shuffle Along*, which put blacks back on the Broadway stage after an absence of more than ten years. Over his lifetime he displayed a marked openness to musical growth, learning from "all music, particularly the music of Mozart, Chopin, Tchaikovsky, Victor Herbert, Gershwin, Debussy, and Strauss," and, indeed, some of his less well known pieces show these influences. Finally, his role in later years as

an energetic "elder statesman of ragtime" provided a historical link to a time long gone as well as inspiration to many younger fans.

FURTHER READING

Blake's papers are at the Maryland Historical Society in Baltimore.

Jasen, David A., and Trebor Jay Tichenor. *Rags and Ragtime: A Musical History* (1978).
Kimball, Robert, and William Bolcom. *Reminiscing with Sissle and Blake* (1973).
Rose, Al. *Eubie Blake* (1979).
Southern, Eileen. *The Music of Black Americans: A History* (1971; 2nd ed., 1983).
—WILLIAM G. ELLIOTT

 BLAKEY, ART
(11 Oct. 1919–16 Oct. 1990), jazz drummer and bandleader, was born Art William Blakey in Pittsburgh, Pennsylvania, the son of Burtrum Blakey, a barber, and Marie Roddericker. His father left home shortly after Blakey was born, and his mother died the next year. Consequently, he was raised by a cousin, Sarah Oliver Parran, who worked at the Jones and Laughlin Steel Mill in Pittsburgh. He moved out of the home at age thirteen to work in the steel mills and in 1938 married Clarice Stuart, the first of three wives. His other wives were Diana Bates and Ann Arnold. Blakey had at least ten children (the exact number is unknown), the last of whom was born in 1986.

As a teenager Blakey taught himself to play the piano and performed in local dance bands, but he later switched to drums. Like many of his contemporaries, Blakey initially adapted the stylistic drumming techniques of well-known swing era drummers, including Chick Webb, Sid Catlett, and Ray Bauduc, to whom he frequently paid tribute. As a result, his earliest playing experiences away from Pittsburgh centered around ensembles fronted by well-known, big-band leaders.

Although some sources indicate Blakey first worked with the Fletcher Henderson Orchestra in 1939, it seems unlikely. Drummer Pete Suggs joined the Henderson band in June 1937 and remained with him until the group disbanded two years later, when Henderson became an arranger and pianist for the Benny Goodman band.

However, Blakey did join a newly formed Henderson band in the spring of 1943 after playing with Mary Lou Williams's twelve-piece band and briefly leading his own group at a small Boston nightclub in 1942.

During the early 1940s Blakey was assimilating the innovative bop drumming styles of Kenny Clarke and Max Roach, as evidenced by his selection as drummer for the Billy Eckstine big band organized in 1944. This group (with trumpeter DIZZY GILLESPIE as musical director) started at the Club Plantation in St. Louis and was among the first big bands to play bebop-influenced arrangements. Although somewhat unsuccessful as a commercial venture, the band rehearsed and recorded from 1944 to 1947. Blakey's playing with this ensemble indicates that regardless of the bebop bent of the repertoire, he played mainly late, swing-style drums. But it was during his tenure with Eckstine that Blakey came in contact with several major bop luminaries, including Gillespie, CHARLIE PARKER, MILES DAVIS, Dexter Gordon, and Kenny Dorham. His association with these musicians placed him firmly in the bop camp, where he remained throughout his career. After the dissolution of Eckstine's band, Blakey joined THELONIOUS MONK for the pianist's first Blue Note recordings in 1947; theirs was a complementary collaboration that continued off and on for the next decade. That same year Blakey organized a rehearsal band, the Seventeen Messengers, and in December made several recordings for Blue Note with his octet, Art Blakey's Jazz Messengers, which included Dorham on trumpet. This group was the first to bear the name through which Blakey would later become famous.

In 1948 Blakey made a brief, nonmusical trip to Africa, at which time he converted to the Islamic religion, changing his name to Abdullah Ibn Buhaina. By mid-1948 he had returned to the United States, recording once again with Monk that July and with saxophonist James Moody in October. The next year he joined Lucky Millinder's R&B–based band and recorded with him in February. Although Blakey never recorded under his Muslim name, several of his children share this name with him,

and later he was known to his musical friends as "Bu."

During the early 1950s Blakey solidified his bop drumming style by playing with well-known bop musicians such as Parker, Davis, Buddy DeFranco, Clifford Brown, Percy Heath, and Horace Silver. In the mid-1950s Blakey and Silver formed the first of the acclaimed Jazz Messengers ensembles that initially included Dorham, Hank Mobley, and Doug Watkins. When Silver left in 1956, Blakey retained leadership of the group that with constantly changing personnel became an important conduit through which many young, talented jazz musicians would pass. For the next twenty-odd years the Jazz Messengers's alumni comprised a list of virtual "who's who" in modern jazz, including Donald Byrd, Bill Hardman, Jackie McLean, Junior Mance, Lee Morgan, Benny Golson, Bobby Timmons, Mobley, Wayne Shorter, Curtis Fuller, Freddie Hubbard, Cedar Walton, Reggie Workman, Keith Jarrett, Chuck Mangione, McCoy Tyner, Woody Shaw, Joanne Brackeen, Steve Turré, WYNTON MARSALIS, and Branford Marsalis.

Despite impaired hearing, which ultimately left him deaf, Blakey continued to perform with the Jazz Messengers until shortly before his death in New York City. Throughout his dynamic and influential career he worked with nearly every major bop figure of the last half of the twentieth century, and his Jazz Messengers ensembles provided a training ground for dozens more. He was inducted into the *Down Beat* Jazz Hall of Fame in 1981, and the Jazz Messengers received a Grammy Award for Best Jazz Instrumental Group Performance in 1984. The group recorded several film soundtracks (mainly overseas) from 1959 to 1972, and a documentary film, *Art Blakey: The Jazz Messenger* (Rhapsody Films), containing interviews with Blakey and other musicians as well as performances by the Jazz Messengers, was released in 1988. Blakey also appears in a jazz video series produced by Sony called *Art Blakey and the Jazz Messengers: Jazz at the Smithsonian* (1982).

Blakey's recorded legacy spans forty years and documents his prodigious and prolific career as drummer and leader. His earliest big-band recordings with Eckstine (De Luxe 2001, 1944) demonstrate an advanced swing style

comparable to the best of the late swing era drummers. Although his early Monk recordings (*The Complete Blue Note Recordings of Thelonious Monk*, Mosaic MR4-101) are clearly bop-oriented, he retains some of his earlier swing characteristics. By the beginning of the 1950s, however, several of Blakey's well-defined playing characteristics emerge, including his heavy and constant high-hat rhythm and effective use of both bass drum and high-hat as additional independent rhythmic resources, which identify him as a progressive and influential bop drummer.

The Jazz Messengers' recordings are numerous and contain performances of varying degrees of success; however, Blakey's playing remains somewhat consistent, regardless of whom he is accompanying. The most impressive of the Messengers' playing is in a collection of recordings the group made in 1960 (*The Complete Blue Note Recordings of the 1960 Jazz Messengers*, Mosaic, MD6-141). Here, the group, consisting of Lee Morgan, Wayne Shorter, Bobby Timmons, Jymie Merritt, and Blakey, demonstrates exceptional talent and produces some of the Messengers' most memorable numbers, including Blakey's signature tune, "Night in Tunisia," composed by Gillespie. Later Messenger recordings with such notables as Jarrett and Mangione (*The Best of Art Blakey*, EmArcy 848245-2 CD, 1979) and the Marsalis brothers (*Keystone 3*, Concord CJ 196/CCD 4196, 1980), provide excellent examples of the continued influence Blakey's leadership had on the growth of jazz in the last quarter of the twentieth century.

The harshest criticism of Blakey's playing was directed at his loud, often overpowering drumming style, which developed in the 1950s and may have contributed to his early hearing loss. Nevertheless, he could also be a sensitive and unobtrusive drummer, as many of his ballad accompaniments demonstrate. Furthermore, his frequently recorded, unaccompanied, improvised drum solo pieces provide numerous examples of his imaginative and flashy, but somewhat musically misdirected, solo ability.

FURTHER READING

Goldberg, Joe. *Jazz Masters of the Fifties* (1965).
Harricks, Raymond, et al. *These Jazzmen of Our Times* (1959).

Stewart, Zan. "Art Blakey in His Prime." *Down Beat*, July 1985.

Taylor, Arthur. *Notes and Tones: Musician to Musician Interviews* (1977).

Obituary: *New York Times*, 17 Oct. 1990.

Discography

The Best of Art Blakey, EmArcy 848245-2 CD, 1979.

The Complete Blue Note Recordings of the 1960 Jazz Messengers, Mosaic, MD6-141, 1960.
—T. DENNIS BROWN

BLIND TOM

(25 May 1849–13 June 1908), pianist and composer, was born Thomas Greene Wiggins to Domingo Wiggins and Charity Greene, field slaves on the Wiley Jones Plantation in Harris County, Georgia. In 1850 Tom, his parents, and two brothers were auctioned off to General James Neil Bethune, a prominent attorney and anti-abolitionist newspaper publisher from Columbus, Georgia. The discovery two years later of the toddler, newly renamed Thomas Greene Bethune, blind from birth, possibly mentally impaired, and unusually captivated by random sounds, playing one of the general's daughters' piano pieces "totally 'stonished us," according to Charity (*New York Times*, 27 Nov. 1886).

The general, however, viewed Tom's unforeseen musical ability as an opportunity. Eulogized in 1895 as "almost the pioneer free trader in this country" and "the first editor in the south to openly advocate secession" (*New York Times*, 21 Jan. 1895), Bethune saw the potential for this helpless, prodigiously talented boy to become a symbol of what Bethune would argue were "sufficient reasons why we should keep our slaves as they are...a class of laborers...incapable of taking care of themselves, and controlled by individuals who are not only capable of taking care of them but interested in doing it" (*Corner Stone*, 3 Feb. 1859). Soon Tom would be even more valuable to him as a cash cow.

Ensuring Tom's musical success became Bethune's top priority. Otherwise uneducated, Tom began his piano studies under Mary, the eldest Bethune daughter. Her expertise was soon eclipsed, and more professionally recognized teachers were engaged. Tom's acute ear, phenomenal auditory memory, and natural keyboard facility allowed him to assimilate the repertoire they favored so quickly that in 1857 Bethune produced a debut for the eight-year-old at Columbus's Temperance Hall that led to numerous other concerts around the state of Georgia. But the death in May 1858 of Bethune's wife, Frances, and the increasingly active role the Georgia attorney was assuming in the emerging debate over states' rights made it impossible for the general to stay on as Tom's manager. So, in 1859, he leased Tom out for three years to the Savannah impresario Perry Oliver, whose savvy promotion of the pianist paid dividends well in excess of the fifteen thousand dollars Bethune received in return.

Trading on long-standing racial stereotypes and on the public's fascination with the freak show during this period, Oliver advertised Tom as "The Wonder Negro Child...whose feats at the piano baffle the most scientific and learned men in the land" (*New Orleans Times Picayune*, 5 Feb. 1861). Further fueling the carnival atmosphere was the incorporation of an onstage master of ceremonies, a by-request format, and a series of sensational pianistic and extra-musical stunts designed to shift attention away from the legitimate aspects of the boy's talent. Still guaranteed were concert performances rendered "with all the taste, expression, and feeling of the most distinguished artist" (*New Orleans Times Picayune*, 5 Feb. 1861) of compositions by Bach, Beethoven, Chopin, Gottschalk, Liszt, Mendelssohn, Meyerbeer, Rossini, Thalberg, Verdi, and even Wiggins himself, chosen by members of the audience off a list of eighty-two items drawn from the pianist's purported repertoire of seven thousand established

Blind Tom, pianist, composer, and slave, had a phenomenal memory for music and began giving concerts at the age of eight.

works. But these mainstream pieces increasingly gave way to a series of sensational pianistic and extra-musical stunts. Among these stunts were Tom's flawless re-creations of original compositions played moments earlier by a local pianist onstage; performances of complicated classical works with his back to the piano; on-the-spot improvisations of an accompaniment to any piece presented, even one he had never heard before; and simultaneous renderings of three different songs, one using the right hand, another using the left, and the third sung, each in a different key. Other program innovations were Tom's recitations of texts in foreign languages he could not even speak and famous political speeches of the era in the same rhythm and pitch pattern in which they were originally uttered. A final otherworldly touch was the verbal introduction by Tom of each of his own compositions in the third person.

Significant in this era before recordings was the deal Oliver cut in 1860 with Horace Waters in New York and Oliver Ditson in Boston to publish "Oliver Galop" and "Virginia Polka," the first of nineteen solo piano pieces by Wiggins to make it into print. On the surface, most of Tom's keyboard works come off as run-of-the-mill rehashings of nineteenth-century European dance and concert music—waltzes, gallops, a mazurka, a polka, a theme and variations, and a nocturne. A deeper probing, however, reveals in them sophisticated compositional materials and evocative imagery that offer a window onto Wiggins's unique and insular world. "The Rainstorm" (composed when Wiggins was just five years old), "Cyclone Galop," "Voice of the Waves," "Water in the Moonlight," and "Daylight" all grew out of Tom's documented fascination with sounds of nature. The hypnotic ostinato of mechanical devices, yet another of Tom's obsessions, was realized musically by him in both "Sewing Song: Imitation of a Sewing Machine" and "Battle of Manassas," Wiggins's signature piece. Based on a firsthand account by one of Bethune's sons of that important Confederate victory, "Manassas" employed tone clusters and mouthed effects, materials not adopted again by composers until the twentieth century.

Leading up to the Civil War, the annual revenue from Wiggins's concerts and the sale of his sheet music reached $100,000, equivalent today to $1.5 million per year, making Blind Tom undoubtedly the nineteenth century's most highly compensated pianist. Wiggins, of course, saw almost none of this money, as it was deposited directly into the Bethune bank account. So widespread had the pianist's reputation become under Oliver that in 1860 he gave a command performance for the president at the White House, the first African American to do so.

Traveling became so difficult after the beginning of the Civil War that in 1861 Oliver and Bethune were forced to void the final year of their contract. Wiggins, however, continued to give concerts south of the Mason-Dixon Line, ironically often arranged by Bethune for the benefit of the Confederate war machine. In response to Abraham Lincoln's 1863 Emancipation Proclamation, the general persuaded Wiggins's parents to sign an indenture agreement in 1864. This arrangement bound their son to his former owner for the next five years in exchange for "a good home and subsistence and $500 a year" for the parents and "$20 per month and two percent of the net proceeds" for Tom (*Cincinnati Daily Commercial*, 20 June 1865). It was at this time that "Blind Tom," the stage name assigned to Wiggins, first appeared in broadsides and newspapers advertising his concerts.

The Confederate surrender in 1865, however, opened the door for Bethune's guardianship to be challenged. That year, in fact, a habeas corpus petition was filed against Bethune in a Cincinnati court, not by Tom's parents but by Tabbs Gross, a former slave turned show business promoter, known publicly as "the Barnum of the African Race." The six-day trial, covered nationally in the press, culminated on 26 June 1865 in a controversial verdict leaving Wiggins in the care of General Bethune.

Blind Tom's only tour of France and England, the following year, earned his handlers an additional $100,000 and written testimonials by Ignaz Moscheles and Charles Hallé, the first praise of Tom's ability from pianists of international repute. That year, too, the French physician and educator Edouard

Seguin included a profile of Blind Tom's behavior in his seminal work on autism, *Idiocy and Its Treatment by the Physiological Method* (1866). Whether Wiggins had a mental disorder is a question that may never be fully answered.

Increasingly dependent on income from Tom's concerts after the war, Bethune decided in 1868 to move his immediate family and Tom to a more centrally located base of operations in Warrenton, Virginia, just forty miles southwest of Washington, D.C. The general's indenture contract with Wiggins's parents was soon to expire, but with Domingo recently dead and Charity still living in Georgia, no one was present to object when, in 1870, Bethune had a Virginia probate judge declare Tom mentally incompetent and name Bethune's son John as Wiggins's new legal guardian.

In 1875 John Bethune, acting as Wiggins's manager, moved with Tom to New York City, where in 1882 John married Eliza Stutzbach, owner of the boardinghouse he and the pianist shared in Greenwich Village. The bloom was soon off the rose, and in 1884 annulment proceedings were initiated against the bride, characterized in John's will as "a heartless adventuress who sought to absorb my estate" (*New York Times*, 23 Mar. 1884). Before any resolution could be worked out, John Bethune was accidentally killed while attempting to board a moving train in Wilmington, Delaware.

The repercussions for Wiggins were enormous. Eliza Bethune, finding that she had been frozen out of her deceased husband's will, persuaded Tom's mother to file a second habeas corpus petition in 1885 against General Bethune, with the understanding that, should Charity prevail, guardianship of Tom would be turned over to Eliza herself. Exactly that improbable scenario played out when, on 30 July 1887, Judge Hugh L. Bond, a federal judge in Baltimore, extricated Thomas Wiggins from the thirty-eight-year custody of Bethune and his immediate family.

Reports that Wiggins lapsed into a self-imposed semiretirement for the last twenty years of his life, as a silent protest against his forced separation from his former owner, appear exaggerated. Clearly, he was distraught over the new arrangement, but he continued to give concerts, albeit not at the same tireless pace as before, and to compose new pieces for publication, their copyright now assigned to Eliza Bethune. Wiggins's occasional absence from the stage, however, did spawn both rumors of his death, most notably in the 1889 flood of Johnstown, Pennsylvania, and the appearance of various Blind Tom impersonators on the nascent vaudeville circuit. Retired in 1908 and well on his way to musical obscurity, Wiggins suffered a stroke and died at age fifty-nine in Hoboken, New Jersey, where he had moved from Manhattan with Eliza in 1903. His body was taken to the Evergreens Cemetery in Brooklyn for burial in a grave that remained unmarked until 1 July 2002. Blind Tom may have been the first in a long line of black musicians, including many of the bluesmen that followed him, to have been canonized and exploited in life and marginalized and all but forgotten in death.

FURTHER READING

Jay, Ricky. *Learned Pigs and Fireproof Women* (1986).

Riis, Thomas L. "The Legacy of a Prodigy Lost in Mystery." *New York Times*, 5 Mar. 2000.

Southall, Geneva Handy. *Blind Tom, the Black Pianist-Composer, Continually Enslaved* (1999).

Obituary: *New York Times*, 16 June 1908.

Discography

John Davis Plays Blind Tom (Newport Classic Ltd. NPD 85660).

—JOHN DAVIS

BLYDEN, EDWARD WILMOT (3 Aug. 1832–12 Feb. 1912), educator, diplomat, and advocate of Pan-Africanism, was born on the island of St. Thomas, part of the present-day Virgin Islands, the son of Romeo Blyden, a tailor, and Judith (maiden name unknown), a school-teacher. The family lived in a predominantly Jewish, English-speaking community in the capital, Charlotte Amalie. Blyden went to the local primary school but also received private tutoring from his father. In 1842 the Blydens left St. Thomas for Porto Bello, Venezuela, where Blyden showed his

Edward Wilmot Blyden, Liberian diplomat and an early proponent of Pan-Africanism. Library of Congress

facility for learning foreign languages. By 1844 the family had returned home to St. Thomas. Blyden attended school only in the morning, and in the afternoons he served a five-year apprenticeship as a tailor. In 1845 the Blyden family met the Reverend John P. Knox, a famous white American minister who had assumed pastorship of the Dutch Reformed Church in St. Thomas, where the Blydens were members. Knox quickly became Blyden's mentor and encouraged his academic studies and oratorical skills. Because of Knox's influence, Blyden decided to become a clergyman, an aspiration his parents supported.

In May 1850 Blyden accompanied Mrs. John Knox to the United States and attempted to enroll in Rutgers Theological College, which was Reverend Knox's alma mater, but was refused admission because he was black. Blyden's attempts to gain admission to other theological colleges also failed. During this time he met important white Presbyterian clergymen, such as John B. Pinney, Walter Lowrie, and William Coppinger, who became his lifelong supporters. All three men were involved with the American Colonization Society. They convinced Blyden to go to Liberia, which had become an independent nation in 1847.

Blyden left the United States for Liberia on 21 December 1850 and arrived at Monrovia on 26 January 1851. Initially, he worked as a part-time clerk for a merchant and resumed his studies at Alexander High School, a new Presbyterian institution headed by the Reverend D. A. Wilson, a graduate of Princeton Theological Seminary. Blyden's intellectual abilities impressed Wilson, who then persuaded Knox to support Blyden as a full-time student. By 1853 Blyden was a lay preacher, and by 1854 he was a tutor at his high school and acted as principal during Wilson's frequent absences due to illness. Blyden published one of the first of his many provocative pamphlets on African affairs, *A Voice from Bleeding Africa*, in 1856, the year he married Sarah Yates, the mulatto niece of B. P. Yates, the vice president of Liberia. Their marriage was an unhappy one, though they had two children. Blyden blamed his marital troubles on his wife's loyalty to what he termed the "mulatto clique" that dominated Liberian politics. However, other important reasons for the marriage's collapse were financial problems due to Blyden's insufficient income and his wife's disinterest in her husband's intellectual pursuits. In 1858 he was ordained a Presbyterian minister, succeeding Wilson as principal of Alexander High School.

Throughout the 1860s and 1870s Blyden became intensely involved in the educational and political affairs of Liberia. In 1861 he was appointed Liberian educational commissioner and traveled to the United States and Britain on a lecture and fund-raising tour. He encouraged African Americans to immigrate to Liberia, "back home to the Fatherland," where he contended they could live free from slavery and racial inequality. From 1860 to 1871 he taught classics at Liberia College; he was also the Liberian secretary of state (1864–1866). In 1871 Blyden was forced to leave Liberia temporarily for Sierra Leone after a coup d'état against the Edward Roye administration (1870–1871) endangered his life. He returned to Liberia in 1872 to become principal of Alexander High School again, a post he held until 1878. As the Liberian ambassador to the Court of St. James's in Britain from 1877 to 1879, Blyden unsuccessfully tried to win financial support for Liberia from Britain. He then served as president of Liberia College (1880–1884) and was minister of the interior (1880–1882). In 1885 he ran unsuccessfully for president of Liberia, though he had left the country to live in Sierra Leone.

From the late 1880s to the early 1900s Blyden wrote his most important work on Pan-Africanism, *Christianity, Islam, and the Negro Race* (1887), and maintained his diplomatic and educational commitments. The Liberian government again appointed him ambassador to the Court of St. James's in 1892, and he served as a special envoy to London and Paris in 1905. From 1901 to 1906 he was director of Mohammedan education in Sierra Leone. Poor and frail, he underwent an operation for an aneurysm in the knee at the Royal Southern Hospital in Liverpool, England, in 1909. His friends in the Colonial Office in London helped secure a small pension for him in 1910. He died in Sierra Leone two years

later. His funeral service represented the unity he tried to forge among Africans during his lifetime: it was a Christian service in which Muslim men bore his coffin from his residence. His long career as an educator, diplomat, and proponent of Pan-Africanism attracted scholarly attention from African, Caribbean, and African American historians, biographers, and political scientists.

FURTHER READING
Cole, Julius Ojo. *Edward Wilmont Blyden: An Interpretation* (1935).
Esedebe, P. *Pan Africanism: The Idea and the Movement, 1776–1963* (1982).
Lynch, Hollis. *Edward Wilmont Blyden: Pan-Negro Patriot* (1967).
Moses, Wilson. *The Golden Age of Black Nationalism, 1850–1925* (1978).
—KIMBERLY WELCH

BOLDEN, BUDDY

(6 Sept. 1877–4 Nov. 1931), jazz musician, was born Charles Joseph Bolden in New Orleans, Louisiana, the son of Westmore Bolden, a drayman, and Alice Harrison. Although Bolden is one of the earliest known figures in the development of jazz in New Orleans, there was little factual information about him until the publication in 1978 of Donald M. Marquis's *In Search of Buddy Bolden*. In this admirable piece of investigative research, Marquis dispels much of the rumor that had grown around Bolden's life in New Orleans and establishes him as an important member of the founding generation of jazz musicians. Marquis confirms that Bolden was not a barber and did not own a barbershop, as popularly believed, although he apparently spent considerable time at barbershops, which served as musicians' meeting places, where information on jobs could be exchanged. Nor did he edit a "scandal sheet" called the *Cricket*. He did drink a lot, played a loud cornet, and was eventually committed to an asylum for erratic behavior resulting from chronic alcoholism.

Like most other New Orleans musicians of that period, Bolden pursued a part-time career performing jazz (then called ragtime). Not until

1902 did city directories begin listing him as a "musician." Before that year he was identified as a "plasterer" and resided in his family's uptown home on First Street in New Orleans. Sufficient documentation and testimony exist to verify that in about 1895 Bolden became active as a cornetist and bandleader at various indoor and outdoor locations in New Orleans. These venues included Lincoln and Johnson parks, Longshoreman's Hall, and Tulane University in the uptown area; the Milneburg and West End resorts on Lake Pontchartrain; the Masonic Hall in Algiers; the Fairgrounds Race Track; and a number of "social clubs" whose halls lined the Perdido–South Rampart Street area. The period from 1897 to 1906 marked the prime of Bolden's tenure as a jazz musician—a time when he enjoyed a sort of preeminence among other players for his boldness and audacity and the barrelhouse nature of his music.

Essentially an "uptown" musician, Bolden had limited contact with the more learned downtown musicians and performed primarily for black audiences. As an untutored musician with little if any formal education, and as one who played mostly by ear, he made music of the "rough blues" variety used to accompany the "slow drag" and other enticing dances of prostitutes. The downtown Creoles called it "honky tonk" music, and Bolden's repertoire was reputed to be particularly coarse. According to Marquis, it appealed "especially to a liberated, post–Civil War generation of young blacks." One number in particular, "Buddy Bolden's Blues," also known as "Funky Butt," was popular enough to cause Union Sons Hall (a location where Bolden's band frequently played) to be commonly referred to as Funky Butt Hall in his honor.

The principal difficulty in assessing the musical contributions of Bolden stems from the total absence of audio recordings. Although he was active during a period when early recordings were being made, no cylinders or records of his playing are known to exist. The search for a cylinder allegedly made by Bolden and his band in the late 1890s, and first reported by one of Bolden's sidemen, Willie Cornish, to the *Jazzmen* editor Charles Edward

Smith in 1939, proved fruitless. The only photograph (the original now lost) of Bolden shows him with a six-piece ensemble that included cornet, trombone, two clarinets, guitar, and string bass. Nonetheless, legendary accounts abound of his playing and bandleading and even his lifestyle.

As his celebrity as a cornetist and bandleader grew, so did his appetite for high living. Even as early as 1895 he had become a "ladies' man," known to have consorted with the sporting crowd and prostitutes, one of whom, Hattie Oliver, gave birth to his illegitimate son. Their common-law marriage lasted only a few years, and in 1902 Bolden met Nora Bass and entered into a second common-law marriage that produced his only daughter. The Boldens' domestic environment was anything but tranquil, as contemporary police records and testimony from family members attest. Early in 1906 Bolden began suffering severe headaches, fits of depression, and episodes of violent behavior—all apparently related to his excessive drinking. An attack on his mother-in-law on 27 March, during which he struck her in the head with a water pitcher, led to his arrest and detainment by police, initiating the only apparent newspaper coverage he was to receive during his lifetime. Continued episodes of depression and violent behavior left him in a deranged state that placed him in conflict with many of his former musical cohorts as well as members of his family. Finally, in April 1907, having been confined to the house of detention, Bolden was moved to the state hospital for the insane in Jackson, Louisiana. There he lived out the remaining twenty-four years of his life, separated from his family and largely forgotten for the role he had played as one of the earliest identifiable jazz pioneers.

FURTHER READING

Marquis, Donald M. *In Search of Buddy Bolden* (1978).

—CHARLES BLANCQ

![icon] **BOND, HORACE MANN**
(8 Nov. 1904–21 Dec. 1972), college professor and administrator, was born in Nashville, Tennessee, the son of James Bond, a Congregationalist minister, and Jane Alice Browne, a graduate of Oberlin College and a schoolteacher. Horace Bond's paternal grandmother, Jane Arthur Bond, was a slave who raised two sons by herself. These two sons, Bond's father and his uncle, Henry, both earned college degrees and embarked on professional careers. Three of Bond's four siblings earned college degrees, and his cousins on his father's side also distinguished themselves academically. This family achievement was important to Horace Bond, because it exemplified the way in which numerous scholars of his generation were nurtured within the African American community. He published a book on the family origins of African American scholars near the end of his life, *Black American Scholars: A Study of Their Beginnings* (1972).

Bond was an intellectually precocious child. He was educated at schools attached to colleges and universities in towns where his father served as a minister—Talladega, Alabama, and Atlanta, Georgia. He finished high school at the age of fourteen at the Lincoln Institute in Shelbyville, Kentucky. He then attended Lincoln University (Pennsylvania) and graduated at the age of eighteen in the class of 1923. He stayed on at Lincoln for a year as a teaching assistant, attended graduate school for a summer at Pennsylvania State College (now Pennsylvania State University), and earned master's (1926) and doctoral (1936) degrees from the University of Chicago. Bond married Julia Washington in 1929; they had three children. Their second child, JULIAN BOND, became famous as a member of the student civil rights movement in the 1960s and served as a Georgia state legislator.

Bond's major field was education, and he specialized in both the history of education and the sociology of education in his graduate studies. He served on the faculties of Langston University in Oklahoma (1926–1928), Alabama State College in Montgomery (1928–1929), Fisk University in Nashville (1929–1931), and Dillard University in New Orleans (1932–1935). He also was chairman of the education department at Fisk and the founding academic dean at Dillard. In the first two decades of his academic career he was closely associated with the Julius Rosenwald Fund and its president, Edwin Embree. In part because of this relationship, he was chosen as president of Fort Valley (Georgia) State College in 1939. He served in that position until 1945, when he became president of his alma mater, Lincoln University. Bond remained as president of Lincoln until 1957, when he resigned amid controversy over a plan to increase the number of white students at the institution;

Horace Mann Bond (right), with W. E. B. Du Bois (left), E. Franklin Frazier, his daughter Jane Marguerite, and his son Julian Bond. Courtesy of Julian Bond

his relations with older, white faculty, many of whom had taught him as an undergraduate and had difficulty seeing their former student as their superior; and his frequent trips away from campus. He then moved to Atlanta University, where he served as dean of the School of Education for five years and then as director of its Bureau of Educational and Social Research. He retired in 1971 and died in Atlanta one year later.

Bond was the author of six books and numerous articles. In the 1920s he published articles critical of the racial bias in tests assessing intelligence quotient (IQ). His two most enduring books were published in the 1930s, *The Education of the Negro in the American Social Order* (1934), a study of the inferior conditions in black schools and colleges, and *Negro Education in Alabama: A Study in Cotton and Steel* (1939), an economic interpretation of educational conditions for blacks in Alabama. His articles from the 1930s until the end of his life were published in both academic and popular journals, and he made numerous speeches to black church and civic groups in his later years. His scholarly output was a lifelong concern for Bond, but it diminished in the 1940s and 1950s as he took on the duties of a college president. Bond worked as a historian for the National Association for the Advancement of Colored People as it prepared a legal brief answering historical questions asked by the U.S. Supreme Court in deliberating the famous *Brown v. Board of Education* (1954) school desegregation case.

Bond became particularly interested in Africa and Africans in the late 1940s, and he took nearly twenty trips to that continent in the 1940s and 1950s. He was a founder of the American Society for African Culture and was active in numerous groups that advocated cooperation between Africans and African Americans. He developed the Institute for African Studies at Lincoln University and made sure that African students were welcome at Lincoln and were supported financially whenever possible. In this regard he built on a long-standing commitment of Lincoln to Africa and Africans. Bond was especially interested in Liberia, Nigeria, and Ghana. During Bond's university presidency, the Gold Coast

(later called Ghana) political leader and Lincoln alumnus Kwame Nkrumah was awarded an honorary doctorate from Lincoln.

During his career Bond carefully balanced concern for personal survival and professional advancement with a pursuit of social and political activism on behalf of his race that often risked reprisals. He was a representative of the middle generation of African American intellectuals that followed the generation of W. E. B. DU BOIS and BOOKER T. WASHINGTON of the early twentieth century and preceded the civil rights activists of the 1960s. He was one of the first of his race to be recognized for his professional academic accomplishments and also was one of the first to head an institution of higher learning.

FURTHER READING

Bond's papers are in the Archives and Manuscripts Division, University of Massachusetts (Amherst) Library.

Urban, Wayne J. *Black Scholar: Horace Mann Bond, 1904–1972* (1992).
———. "The Black Scholar and Intelligence Testing: The Case of Horace Mann Bond." *Journal of the History of the Behavioral Sciences* 25 (1989): 323–334.
———. "Philanthropy and the Black Scholar: The Case of Horace Mann Bond." *Journal of Negro Education* 58 (1989): 478–493.
Williams, Roger. *The Bonds: An American Family* (1971).

—WAYNE J. URBAN

 BOND, JULIAN
(14 Jan. 1940–), activist and politician, was born Horace Julian Bond in Nashville, Tennessee, the second of three children of HORACE MANN BOND, a college professor and administrator, and Julia Washington, a librarian. Although the family lived near Macon, Georgia, where Horace was president of Fort Valley State College, Julia insisted on driving to Nashville, Tennessee, to secure better hospital care for Julian's birth. This pride in the Bond lineage can be traced through four generations: Jane Arthur Bond, Julian's great-grandmother, had been a slave who raised two sons fathered by her white master. Her first son was the Reverend James Bond, an educator and

preacher in Tennessee and Kentucky; his son, Horace, held professorial and administrative posts at five colleges and universities before fathering Julian. In 1943 Horace Bond called upon his colleague W. E. B. DU BOIS (who was in Fort Valley at the time to deliver a speech) to participate in a small ceremony for young Julian's benefit. "With champagne and mock solemnity, [they] decreed that Julian Bond should follow in their footsteps" (Williams, 181).

Horace Bond became president of Lincoln University, the oldest black college in America, but Julian did not seem destined to follow the path that had been laid for him. He approached grammar school fecklessly, frustrating the teachers who spotted his charismatic intelligence. He scored the highest in his class on a sixth-grade reading test, and his mother later quipped that he "never opened a book since" (Williams, 184). Nonetheless, when Bond finished eighth grade, he was recruited by George School, a Quaker preparatory school in eastern Pennsylvania. His inconsistent academic record continued—though by all accounts he was quite popular—and he required a year more than the standard four to graduate. Apart from athletic accolades on the diving and wrestling teams, Bond's most steady success came in literature, and in 1957 he enrolled at Morehouse College as an English major.

His academic performance was lackluster, but Bond's extracurricular activities reflected a thoughtful mind at work. Bond had become a dedicated poet by this point, and his poetry was published in multiple anthologies while he was still an undergraduate. (LANGSTON HUGHES would anthologize Bond's poems in *New Negro Poetry U.S.A.* in 1964.) He also founded a literary journal and took summer classes at Boston University.

On 1 February 1960 four black college students integrated a lunch counter in Greensboro, North Carolina. A few mornings afterward, Bond was in an Atlanta drugstore, skipping compulsory chapel, when an acquaintance rushed in with news of the sit-in. He implored Bond to help him do something similar in Atlanta. Bond agreed, mostly just to end the conversation. That afternoon a student meeting was held, and before he knew it Bond had helped found the Committee on Appeal for Human Rights. COAHR bought a full-page advertisement in Atlanta's newspapers, taking the city government to task for limiting African American employment to menial positions and for not proportionally representing the black community on the city's police force.

Whites were aghast at the discontent brewing in their city. They were further taken aback when COAHR rapidly organized sit-ins at public buildings, lunch counters, and restaurants. When Morehouse students departed for summer vacation, Bond and a handful of others remained. When students returned in the autumn, they faced two lines of registration on the first day: one for class and one for upcoming demonstrations. Bond would later describe COAHR as a "masterpiece of precision"—it was well funded and mobilized thousands of volunteers, and every project was planned with intricate forethought of strategic gain. But the organization did have its opponents: the *Daily World*, Atlanta's only African American newspaper, criticized COAHR for being too confrontational. Bond and his colleagues consequently raced to publish their own paper, the *Atlanta Inquirer*. First as a reporter and eventually as managing editor, Bond helped diversify the movement's outreach methods and establish critical media contacts as he honed his public demeanor.

In 1961, under the combined strain of working for COAHR, editing the *Inquirer*, and his engagement to a Spelman coed, Alice Clopton, Bond withdrew from Morehouse halfway through his senior year. By then the Student Nonviolent Coordinating Committee (SNCC) had emerged as a catalyst in the civil rights movement, and it hired Bond as its communications director. He married Clopton later that year (they would eventually have five children) and proceeded to work for SNCC until 1965, when the Georgia legislature reapportioned voting districts as a gesture toward reeling in decades of racial gerrymandering. A newly created West End district in Atlanta became the logical place for an African American candidate. Bond was reluctant, but his fellow SNCC worker JOHN LEWIS urged him to run. Initially campaigning as a publicity move, Bond soon became

absorbed in the effort, introducing himself to voters door-to-door; he won with 82 percent of the vote.

Shortly before Bond took his seat, a reporter called him to inquire what he thought about SNCC's recently released statement condemning the Vietnam War. The reporter covertly taped the conversation, in which Bond supported the statement. The political backlash was intense. The legislature accused him of giving "aid and comfort to the enemies of the United States and the enemies of Georgia" and by a tally of 184-12 refused to seat him. Two years and two elections later—both of which Bond won—the U.S. Supreme Court overturned the legislature's action.

In 1968 Bond again challenged Georgia politicos by heading a rival delegation to the Democratic National Convention, one that more accurately represented Georgia's racial demographics. When his delegation successfully won its place in the convention, Bond was approached about the nomination for vice president. Although he was, at twenty-eight, seven years too young to hold office, Bond still kept his name on the ballot while the first few states voted. He then withdrew when the point had been made: African Americans were a vital force in the Democratic Party, as signaled by the first African American nomination for vice president.

Bond rode the crest of his popularity for over a decade. In 1969, when the National Association for the Advancement of Colored People (NAACP) honored Du Bois by dedicating his childhood home as a memorial park, they called on Bond to give the address. In reference to Du Bois's proclamation of the color line as the twentieth century's most looming problem, Bond opined that problems had worsened. They now included "the new colonization of people, both here and abroad, the new imperialism practiced by Western democracy, and the continuing struggle of those who have not against those who have" (Williams, xiv). Simultaneously with his tenure in the Georgia legislature, Bond completed his degree at Morehouse in 1971; became a coveted speaker; and published *A Time to Speak, A Time to Act* (1972), a volume of essays on race and politics. In 1974 he moved

from the House of Representatives to the Senate, and in 1976 he waged a short-lived campaign for president of the United States before bowing out because of insufficient funds.

Bond's tendency to impress upon people the possibility that he was still an underachiever continued to resurface. When Jimmy Carter won the 1976 presidential election, his administration invited Bond to join them in Washington. Bond refused, but whether he did so out of pride, fear of shouldering more responsibility, or simple disagreement with Carter only he could say. He found himself a political outsider, and his performance in the Georgia legislature increasingly began to resemble the scholastic effort of his youth. Bond was chastised for apathy toward racial causes and excessive absenteeism in the legislature, and when he ran for the U.S. House of Representatives in 1986 against his former SNCC comrade John Lewis, his opponent conducted a spirited campaign that vanquished Georgia's former political prodigy. Within the next couple of years Clopton would accuse Bond of cocaine use (though she quickly retracted the charge) and divorce him. Bond's mistress and purported drug dealer was sentenced to over twenty years in prison, and Bond was later named in a paternity suit that he eventually conceded.

In the late 1980s and through the 1990s Julian Bond rededicated himself to his strength: communications. He narrated the civil rights documentary *Eyes on the Prize* (1987) for the Public Broadcasting System; continued hosting the nation's preeminent television show on black politics, *America's Black Forum*; and wrote a syndicated column. Bond also reentered academia, accepting a visiting professorship at Harvard in 1989 and joining the faculties of both the University of Virginia and American University shortly thereafter. In 1990 he married Pamela Horowitz, a lawyer from Washington, D.C. Bond continued his speaking tours and professorial work and in 1998 was elected chair of the NAACP board of directors.

FURTHER READING

Neary, John. *Julian Bond: Black Rebel* (1971).
Williams, Roger M. *The Bonds: An American Family* (1972).

—DAVID F. SMYDRA JR.

BOUCHET, EDWARD ALEXANDER

(15 Sept. 1852–28 Oct. 1918), educator and scientist, was born in New Haven, Connecticut, the youngest of four children of William Francis Bouchet, a janitor, and Susan Cooley. Part of New Haven's black community, the Bouchets were active members of the Temple Street Congregational Church, which was a stopping point for fugitive slaves along the Underground Railroad. During the 1850s and 1860s New Haven had only three schools that black children could attend. Edward was enrolled in the Artisan Street Colored School, a small (only thirty seats), ungraded school with one teacher, Sarah Wilson, who played a crucial role in nurturing Bouchet's academic abilities and his desire to learn.

In 1868 Bouchet was accepted into Hopkins Grammar School, a private institution that prepared young men for the classical and scientific departments at Yale College. He graduated first in his class at Hopkins and four years later, when he graduated from Yale in 1874, he ranked sixth in a class of 124. On the basis of this exceptional performance, Bouchet became the first black student in the nation to be nominated to Phi Beta Kappa. In the fall of 1874 he returned to Yale with the encouragement and financial support of Alfred Cope, a Philadelphia philanthropist. In 1876 Bouchet successfully completed his dissertation on the new subject of geometrical optics, becoming the first black person to earn a PhD from an American university as well as the sixth American of any race to earn a PhD in Physics.

In 1876 Bouchet moved to Philadelphia to teach at the Institute for Colored Youth (ICY), the city's only high school for black students. ICY had been founded by the Society of Friends because African Americans had historically been denied admittance to Philadelphia's white high schools. Members of the ICY board of managers like Cope, Bouchet's Yale benefactor, believed firmly in the value of a classical education and were convinced that blacks were capable of unlimited educational achievement. In 1874 Cope had provided forty thousand dollars to establish a new science program at ICY,

and soon thereafter recruited Bouchet to teach and administer the program.

Although Philadelphia was as segregated as any southern city, it offered a supportive environment for a man of Bouchet's abilities. The city's black population, the largest in the North, had made considerable progress in education during the decades preceding his arrival. As early as 1849 half the city's black population was active in one or more of the many literary societies established by the black community. After the Civil War the ICY played an important role in training the thousands of black teachers that were needed throughout the country to provide freedmen with the education they sought.

Bouchet joined St. Thomas's Church, the oldest black Episcopal church in the country, served on the vestry, and was church secretary for many years. The bishop also appointed Bouchet to be a lay reader, which gave Bouchet the opportunity to take a more active part in church services. Bouchet took his scientific interests and abilities beyond the ICY into the broader black community, giving public lectures on various scientific topics. He was also a member of the Franklin Institute, a foundation for the promotion of the mechanic arts, chartered in 1824. Bouchet maintained his ties with Yale through the local chapter of the Yale Alumni Association, attending all meetings and annual dinners.

By the turn of the century, a new set of ICY managers emerged, more receptive to the industrial education philosophy of BOOKER T. WASHINGTON than to academic education for blacks. In their efforts to redirect the school's programs, the all-white board fired all the teachers, including Bouchet, in 1902 and replaced them with instructors committed to industrial education.

Over the next fourteen years Bouchet held five or six positions in different parts of the country. Until November 1903 he taught math and physics in St. Louis at Sumner High School, the first high school for blacks west of the Mississippi. He then spent seven months as the business manager for the Provident Hospital in St. Louis (November 1903–May 1904), followed by a term as a United States inspector of customs at the Louisiana Purchase Exposition held in St. Louis (June 1904–October

1906). In October 1906 Bouchet secured a teaching and administrative position at St. Paul's Normal and Industrial School in Lawrenceville, Virginia. In 1908 he became principal of Lincoln High School of Gallipolis, Ohio, where he remained until 1913, when an attack of arteriosclerosis compelled him to resign and return to New Haven. Undocumented information has Bouchet returning to teaching at Bishop College in Marshall, Texas, but illness once again forced him to retire in 1916. He returned to New Haven, where he died in his boyhood home at 94 Bradley Street. He had never married or had children.

Bouchet had the misfortune of being a talented and educated black man who lived in a segregated society that refused to recognize his particular genius and thus hindered him from conducting scientific research and achieving professional recognition. Segregation produced isolation as Bouchet spent his career in high schools with limited resources and poorly equipped labs. Even with Bouchet's superior qualifications, no white college would have considered him for a position on its faculty. Completely excluded from any means of utilizing his education and talent, Bouchet languished in obscurity. The ascendance of industrial education also served to limit his opportunities, since his academic training in the natural sciences made him unattractive as a candidate at the increasing number of black institutions that adopted a vocational curriculum.

The absurdity of the claims made by some proponents of vocational education concerning the innate inability of blacks to undertake an academic education could not have been more obvious to Bouchet. From his own accomplishments and those of his students, it never occurred to Bouchet that blacks could not master the fields of classical education or excel in science. In the face of personal setbacks and a changing public mood on black education, Bouchet maintained his standards and never altered his educational ideals.

FURTHER READING

Some of Bouchet's writings and those of his classmates are available in the Yale University Manuscripts and Archives, Sterling Memorial Library.

"Edward A. Bouchet, Ph.D." *Negro History Bulletin* 31 (Dec. 1968).

Mickens, Ronald E. "Edward A. Bouchet: The First Black Ph.D." *Black Collegian* 8, no. 4 (Mar.–Apr. 1978).

Perkins, Linda M. *Fanny Jackson Coppin and the Institute for Colored Youth, 1865–1902* (1987).

Obituary: *Bulletin of Yale University, Obituary Record of Yale Graduates, 1918–1919,* no. 11 (1919).

—H. KENNETH BECHTEL

 BOWSER, MARY ELIZABETH

(1839?–?), Union spy during the Civil War, was born a slave on the Richmond, Virginia, plantation of John Van Lew, a wealthy hardware merchant. Very little is known about her early life. Upon Van Lew's death in 1843 or 1851, his wife and daughter, Elizabeth, manumitted his slaves and bought and freed a number of their family members, Mary among them. Like most of their former slaves, Mary remained a servant in the Van Lew household, staying with the family until the late 1850s. Noting her intellectual talent, Elizabeth, a staunch abolitionist and Quaker, sent Mary to the Quaker School for Negroes in Philadelphia to be educated.

Mary returned from Philadelphia after graduating to marry Wilson Bowser, a free black man. The ceremony was held on 16 April 1861, just days before the Civil War began. What made the ceremony so unusual was that the parishioners of the church were primarily white. The couple settled outside Richmond. There is no record of any children. Even after her marriage, Bowser was in close contact with the Van Lew family, clearly sharing their political goals. As a result, their wartime record was very much intertwined, and information about Bowser can be gleaned through the records of Elizabeth Van Lew.

Despite her abolitionist sentiments, Elizabeth Van Lew was a prominent figure in Richmond. Shunned by many before the war began, her loyalty to the Union during the war earned her further enmity. Unlike other spies, Van Lew used this enmity as a cover for her serious efforts on behalf of the Union. Adopting a distracted, muttering personae, she was dubbed "Crazy Bet." During the war, Van Lew helped manage a spy system in the Confederate capitol, went regularly to the Libby Prison with food and medicine, and helped escapees of all kinds, hiding them in a secret room in her mansion.

Perhaps Van Lew's most trusted and successful source of information was Mary Bowser. Like Van Lew, Bowser had considerable acting skills. In order to get access to top-secret information, Bowser became "Ellen Bond," a slow-thinking, but able, servant. Van Lew urged a friend to take Bowser along to help out at functions held by Varina Davis, the wife of the Confederate president, Jefferson Davis. Bowser was eventually hired fulltime, and worked in the Davis household until just before the end of the war.

At the Davis's house, Mary worked as a servant, cleaning and serving meals. Given the racial prejudice of the day, and the way in which servants were trained to act and seem invisible, Mary was able to glean considerable information simply by doing her work. That she was literate, and could thus read the documents she had access to—and, in that way, better interpret the conversations she was hearing—could only have been a bonus. Jefferson Davis, apparently, came to know that there was a leak in his house, but until late in the war no suspicion fell on Mary.

Richmond's formal spymaster was Thomas McNiven, a baker whose business was located on North Eighth Street. Given his profession, he was a hub for information. His bakery was an unexceptional destination for his agents, and McNiven was regularly out and about town, driving through Ricmond making deliveries. When he came to the Davis household, Mary could daily—without suspicion—greet him at his wagon and talk briefly. In 1904, just before he died, McNiven reported his wartime activities to his daughter, Jeannette B. McNiven, and her nephew, Robert W. Waitt Jr., chronicled them in 1952. According to McNiven, Bowser wass the source of the most crucial information available, "as she was working right in the Davis home and had a photographic mind. Everything she saw on the rebel president's desk, she could repeat word for word. Unlike most colored, she could read and write. She made a point of always coming out to my wagon when I made deliveries at the Davis' home to drop information" (quoted in Waitt, Thomas McNiven Papers).

By the last days of the Confederacy, suspicion did fall on Mary—it is not known how or why—and she chose to flee in January 1865. Her last act as a Union spy and sympathizer was an attempt to burn down the Confederate White House, but this was not successful.

After the war ended, the federal government, in an attempt to protect the postwar lives of its Southern spies, destroyed the records—including those of McNiven's and Van Lew's activities—that could more precisely detail the information Bowser passed on to General Ulysses S. Grant throughout 1863 and 1864. The journal that Bowser later wrote chronicling her wartime work was also lost when family members inadvertently discarded it in 1952. The Bowser family rarely discussed her work, given Richmond's political climate and the continuing attitudes toward Union sympathizers. There is no record of Bowser's postwar life, and no date for her death.

Bowser is among a number of African American women spies who worked on the Union side during the Civil War. Given the nature of the profession, we may never know how many women engaged in undercover spy operations, both planned and unplanned. HARRIET TUBMAN is the most well known, especially for her scouting expeditions in South Carolina and Florida that resulted in the freedom of hundreds of slaves. In 1995 the U.S. government honored Mary Elizabeth Bowser for her work in the Civil War with an induction into the Military Intelligence Corps Hall of Fame in Fort Huachuca, Arizona.

FURTHER READING

Coleman, Penny. Spies! *Women in the Civil War* (1992).

Forbes, Ella. *African American Women During the Civil War* (1998).

Kane, Harnett T. *Spies for the Blue and Gray* (1954).

Lebsock, Suzanne. *A Share of Honor: Virginia Women 1600–1945* (1984).

Van Lew, Elizabeth. *A Yankee Spy in Richmond: The Civil War Diary of "Crazy Bet" Van Lew*, ed. David D. Ryan (2001).
—LYDE CULLEN SIZER

BRADLEY, THOMAS

(29 Dec. 1917–29 Sep. 1998), mayor of Los Angeles, was born in a log cabin on a cotton plantation near Calvert, in Robertson County, Texas, the son of Lee Thomas Bradley and Crenner Hawkins, sharecroppers. Calvert had thrived in the late nineteenth century, buoyed by the cottonseed industry and the Southern Pacific Railroad, but its economy had declined by the time of Thomas's birth. Life for sharecroppers like the Bradleys was precarious—little better, in fact, than it had been for Lee's father, a slave in the Carolinas. They knew the certainty of picking cotton for eighteen hours a day and the annual uncertainty of the price of that cotton. Heavily indebted to white landlords, Lee and Crenner struggled to provide their family with vital necessities, such as food and health care; five of their children died in infancy. Like many southern blacks in the 1920s, the Bradley family saw only one answer to the restrictions of Jim Crow: migration, first to Dallas; then briefly to Arizona, where even the six-year-old Tom picked cotton for a while; and, finally, in 1924, to Los Angeles.

The Bradleys struggled in their new home. Unable to find steady employment in Los Angeles, Lee served as a crewman on Pacific Coast ocean liners. Crenner found work as a maid, and Tom's elder brother dropped out of school to work on farms in Orange County. Even so, as a boyhood friend of Tom's recalled, the Bradleys "were poorer than a lot of folks were poor" (Sonenshine, 59). His parents' enforced absences left Tom as the de facto head of the household. As a teenager, he had to balance the family budget, negotiate sibling rivalries, and take care of his handicapped younger brother, experiences that he would later draw upon as a politician. Although Crenner relied heavily on Tom, she was also determined that her son, a studious child, should take advantage of the educational opportunities available to him in the Los

Tom Bradley is sworn in as mayor of Los Angeles by a former Chief Justice of the U.S. Supreme Court, Earl Warren, in 1973. © Bettmann/CORBIS

Angeles school system. A combination of academic success and prowess on the track brought him to Polytechnic High School, one of the best schools in the city. As one of the few black students at Poly, and one of the poorest, Tom faced discrimination, but he quickly earned a reputation as a mediator, often called on by the administration to ease tensions among the diverse student body. Those skills and his high profile as the captain of the track team and as a star football player helped Tom win his first political campaign, as president of the Poly Boys' League. They also helped him win a full athletic scholarship to the University of California, Los Angeles (UCLA) in 1937.

Bradley thrived at UCLA. He continued to star on the track and also played football on a team that included the future baseball legend JACKIE ROBINSON. Fraternity politics occupied much of Bradley's time in college; his membership in Kappa Alpha Psi helped him create a network of black professionals who would later back his political ambitions. Bradley continued to help his family in the summertime by shoveling scrap iron, gardening, and working as a photographer for the comedian Jimmy Durante. That connection to Hollywood would later prove invaluable in Los Angeles politics. In 1940, his junior year, Bradley took

the Los Angeles Police Department (LAPD) entrance exam, placed near the top, and decided to leave UCLA to join the police force. With a steady income of $170 a month, Bradley felt secure enough to propose marriage to Ethel Arnold, a fellow member of the New Hope Baptist Church; they married in May 1941. Tragically, their first child died the day she was born, the Bradleys' first wedding anniversary. Two daughters were born later.

Although Bradley had broken racial barriers at UCLA with ease, the LAPD presented a far greater challenge. Only three of his seventy-one colleagues at the police academy and one hundred of the four thousand members of the force were black, a situation that changed little in Bradley's twenty years on the force. By the time he resigned in 1961, Bradley had risen to lieutenant, the highest rank held by an African American on the force at that time. Bradley did much to improve race relations, most notably in his role as head of the LAPD's community-relations detail. Bradley's superiors, however, resisted his efforts to bolster the image of the force in nonwhite neighborhoods. In 1960 Police Chief William Parker vetoed Bradley's unilateral decision to integrate the radio cars in his division. That reversal undermined the lieutenant's authority and also suggested that reform of the LAPD—and the city's other racist institutions—would have to come from outside.

After Bradley resigned from the police force, he became increasingly active in the Democratic Party, and in 1961 he was elected city councilman for Los Angeles's ethnically diverse Tenth District, defeating his white opponent by a two-to-one margin. The Tenth District did not include Watts, but when that neighborhood rebelled against police brutality, overcrowding, and high unemployment in August 1965, Bradley emerged as the leader of all Angelenos opposed to the policies of Mayor Sam Yorty and Chief Parker. Parker inflamed black opinion by blaming the riots on "monkeys in a zoo." Yorty was less offensive, but equally inaccurate, in reproaching "Communists for agitating Negroes with propaganda over past police brutality" (Payne and Ratzan, 73).

Bradley knew from his own experience on the force that police brutality was no myth, and over the next four years he became the most visible critic of the LAPD excesses and the most vocal proponent of increased federal and local efforts to improve equal economic opportunity. In 1969 Bradley challenged Yorty for the position of mayor. The election was racially divisive, though most of the mud was flung by Yorty, who disingenuously, but successfully, linked the moderate Bradley to militants such as the Black Panther ELDRIDGE CLEAVER. Bradley chose not to respond in kind, a stance that some commentators viewed as a tactical error. In a rematch in 1973 Bradley won easily. Yorty again tried to paint his opponent as an extremist, but this time Bradley responded with a television campaign that highlighted his police experience and charming, far-from-militant demeanor. Bradley energized his base of African American voters, made gains among Asians and Latinos, and won over significant sections of the city's white business community, most notably in Hollywood. Yorty had misread the electoral dynamics of an increasingly diverse Los Angeles.

Over the next twenty years Bradley tried to govern the city as inclusively as he had run his campaign; this was no easy task, given the city's rapid growth and the increasing diversity of its population. In his first term in office Bradley attempted to redevelop the crumbling downtown of Los Angeles. He skillfully deployed state and federal funds to bring jobs to depressed neighborhoods, but the antitax crusade of the late 1970s wreaked havoc with any meaningful effort to use government to solve the city's problems. In 1978 Californians approved Proposition Thirteen, a referendum measure that cut property taxes and drastically reduced the revenues available to local governments. Given that Bradley had already cut property taxes in 1976, the revenue loss proved devastating to those impoverished Angelenos most dependent on government services. Downtown business leaders, however, were delighted by what they saw as Bradley's fiscal rectitude and worked closely with him in the late 1970s and 1980s on his three flagship projects: revitalization of the downtown business district, expansion of the Los Angeles International Airport, and bringing the Olympic Games to the city in 1984. The latter undertaking was particularly rewarding to Bradley, the UCLA track star who, as a child, had read avidly about the ancient Games and who, as a teenager, had peered through the L.A. Coliseum fence to catch a glimpse of the 1932 Olympians. Despite a Soviet boycott, the Los Angeles Olympics, the first privately funded games, proved to be a resounding commercial success. That year Bradley was the recipient of the NAACP's Spingarn Medal.

Bradley succeeded in diversifying the city workforce, but the deep-rooted racism of the LAPD proved intractable. After 1978 he faced a formidable foe in Daryl Gates, the new police chief. In the 1980s a rash of police shootings and beatings of minorities provoked anger in the black community, not only at Gates but also at Bradley for failing to fire him. Constitutionally, however, the mayor did not have the power to do so. The 1991 police beating of a black motorist, Rodney King, videotaped by a bystander and later relayed worldwide on television, however, was the final straw for Bradley, who worked behind the scenes to remove Gates. The acquittal of King's attackers in 1992 was an "outrage," Bradley told a news conference.

Many of the citizens of South Central Los Angeles agreed. Within hours of the acquittal, the city experienced its greatest civil unrest since the Watts riot. More than fifty people were killed, four hundred were injured, and seventeen thousand were arrested. Property damage amounted to one billion dollars. In his last year in office, Bradley worked hard to bring the city's fractious communities together. Although all races had participated in the riots, relations between African Americans and Korean Americans were particularly fraught, since many of the black rioters had targeted Korean shopkeepers. While Bradley had his share of political disappointments, notably his defeat in two gubernatorial campaigns in 1982 and 1986 and a 1989 financial disclosure scandal, the South Central riots would remain the low point of his career. Bradley had earned a law degree at Southwestern University while still a policeman, and on leaving office in 1993 he practiced law until he suffered a heart attack and a stroke in 1996. He died of a heart attack two years later in Los Angeles.

Mourners at Bradley's funeral recalled his electoral victories and losses and agreed upon his warmth, courtliness, and charm. Bradley's abiding legacy, however, was an ability to craft and to maintain for two decades a broad, multiracial, and ideologically diverse political coalition in one of the world's most fragmented cities.

FURTHER READING

The Mayor Tom Bradley Administrative Papers (1973–1993) at the Department of Special Collections of the UCLA Library provide the most comprehensive introduction to his five terms as mayor and include some materials on his earlier career. The UCLA Oral History Program, also at the Department of Special Collections of the UCLA Library, has interviews with Bradley and many of his contemporaries in Los Angeles and California politics.

Davis, Mike. *City of Quartz: Excavating the Future in Los Angeles* (1992).
Payne, J. Gregory, and Scott C. Ratzan. *Tom Bradley: The Impossible Dream* (1986).
Sonenshine, Raphael J. *Politics in Black and White: Race and Power in Los Angeles* (1993).

Obituaries: *New York Times* and *Los Angeles Times*, 30 Sept. 1998.

—STEVEN J. NIVEN

BRAGG, GEORGE FREEMAN, JR.

(25 Jan. 1863–12 Mar. 1940), Episcopal clergyman, was born in Warrenton, North Carolina, the son of George Freeman Bragg Sr. and Mary Bragg (maiden name unknown). He was two years old when the family moved to Petersburg, Virginia, where he studied at the elementary school and at St. Stephen's Parish and Normal School. His family helped found St. Stephen's Church for Negroes in 1867. At age six he was employed as a valet by John Hampden Chamberlayne, editor of the *Petersburg Index*. In 1879 he entered a school founded by Major Giles B. Cooke, a former chaplain on Robert E. Lee's staff; the school had become a branch of Virginia Theological Seminary. The next year he was suspended for not being "humble" but was appointed a page in the Virginia legislature by the Readjuster Party. After a severe case of typhoid fever and a period of teaching school in 1885, he returned to his theological studies at Cooke's school, renamed the Bishop Paine Divinity and Industrial School. He was ordained deacon on 12 January 1887 and priest on 19 December 1888 by Bishop Francis M. Whittle. He married Nellie Hill in 1887; they had four children.

Bragg's parish ministry began in 1887 at St. Luke's Church in Norfolk, Virginia, where within four years he built a new church and rectory, renovated a school, organized the Holy Innocents (which became Grace Church), and founded the Industrial School for Colored Girls. After becoming rector of St. James First African Church in Baltimore, Maryland, in 1891, he opened St. James Mission in Portsmouth, Virginia. Under his leadership, St. James Church became self-supporting, purchased a rectory, and built a new church. By 1931 there were five hundred communicants, and the church made annual charitable contributions of a thousand dollars. At least four young men entered the priesthood under Bragg's guidance. In addition, he established the Maryland Home for Friendless Colored Children and was associated with St. Mary's Home for Boys and St. Katharine's Home for Little Girls. For thirty-five

George Freeman Bragg Jr. (seated), with two of his sons, also clergymen. University of North Carolina at Chapel Hill Libraries, Rare Book Collection

years he was general secretary of the Conference of Church Workers among Colored People and a special chaplain to the bishop of the diocese of Maryland.

Beyond his service within his denomination, Bragg performed many duties. In 1884 he was honorary commissioner to the New Orleans Exposition. Virginia's governor Fitzhugh Lee appointed him a curator to the Hampton Normal and Agriculture Institute in 1887. He also served as chaplain to the second battalion of Virginia Colored Militia. In Maryland he was on the board of managers for the House of Reformation for Colored Boys and a member of the State Inter-Racial Commission. He started the Committee of Twelve, a group of black leaders, including BOOKER T. WASHINGTON and W. E. B. DU BOIS, that campaigned against the Poe Amendment, designed to disfranchise blacks in Maryland. He led the fight to have Negro teachers assigned to Negro schools in Baltimore. In 1905 he joined the Niagara Movement, a forerunner of the NAACP, and became a supporter of Du Bois, its founder.

Bragg's early association with the *Petersburg Index* had generated a lifelong interest in journalism. At age nineteen he had begun publishing the

Virginia Lancet, a pro-Republican paper involved in Virginia politics. In 1886 he founded a new paper, the *Afro-American Churchman*, published, he said, in the interests of the Colored Episcopal church. Also that year he founded the *Afro-American Ledger*, which he later merged with the *Baltimore Afro-American*. The *Church Advocate* served for many years as the unofficial organ of the Conference of Church Workers among Colored People and was filled with biographical sketches of clergy, histories of local black Episcopal churches, and commentary on the continuing struggles of blacks in the Episcopal Church. In later years it served as a parish paper for Bragg's church. The *Maryland Home* was a monthly, published to promote the Maryland Home for Friendless Colored Children.

Some of his published works, all of which contain biographical data, are *The Colored Harvest in the Old Virginia Diocese* (1901), *Afro-American Church Work and Workers* (1904), *The Story of Old St. Stephen's, Petersburg, Va.* (1906), *The First Negro Priest on Southern Soil* (1909), *Bond Slave of Christ* (1912), *Men of Maryland* (rev. ed., 1925), *The Pathfinder ABSALOM JONES* (1929), and *Heroes of the Eastern Shore* (1939). A major work still of prime importance is *History of the Afro-American Group of the Episcopal Church* (1922). Many of these volumes were printed on Bragg's own printing press, under the imprint of the Church Advocate Press.

Race relations would be improved, Bragg believed, by morally sensitive, educated people of both races, and he did not hesitate to denounce racial discrimination within his own denomination. Petitions for his selection to the episcopate were made in 1911 and 1917, but he was not elected. He died in Baltimore.

FURTHER READING

Bragg's papers are in the Schomburg Center for Research in Black Culture of the New York Public Library, the Moorland-Spingarn Research Center, Howard University, Washington, D.C.; and Virginia State University, Petersburg.

Brydon, George M. *The Episcopal Church among the Negroes of Virginia* (1937).
Burkett, Randall K., et al., eds. *Black Biography, 1790–1950: A Cumulative Index* (3 vols., 1991).
Suggs, Henry L., ed. *The Black Press in the South* (1983).

—FREDERICK V. MILLS

BRANSON, HERMAN RUSSELL (14 Aug. 1914–

7 June 1995), physicist, educator, and academic administrator, was born in Pocahontas, Virginia, the son of Harry P. Branson, a coal miner, and Gertrude Brown. In 1928, after several years at his local elementary school, Herman enrolled at Dunbar High School in Washington, D.C., one of the nation's preeminent black secondary schools. He was encouraged in this move by a young black physician, William Henry Welch, who practiced in Pocahontas and who rented lodgings from young Branson's grandmother.

At Dunbar, Branson was introduced to studies in Latin, advanced mathematics, and other disciplines to which he would not have been exposed in his local high school. After graduating as valedictorian in 1932, he enrolled at the University of Pittsburgh with a view to studying medicine, partly because his

great-uncle had been trained as a physician there. Branson completed the premedical program in two years and still found time to immerse himself in a wide range of science courses. "Physics could answer more questions than any other science," he later recalled, "so I decided physics was what I'd go into—but I really liked biology and chemistry, so as an undergraduate I took almost enough for a major in four fields: biology, chemistry, math, and physics" (Manning interview).

When the University of Pittsburgh turned down his application to the medical school in 1934—they had no intention of admitting blacks at the time, he was convinced—he transferred to all-black Virginia State College, where he majored in physics, graduating summa cum laude in 1936. His eclectic mix of scientific interests as an undergraduate foreshadowed the versatile, interdisciplinary character of his later research.

In 1936 Branson enrolled as a doctoral student in physics at the University of Cincinnati. He chose Cincinnati in part because he had relatives with whom he could live in the city, but also because the university had an excellent physics department, including faculty member Boris Podolsky, known for his work in quantum mechanics. Podolsky was a primary mentor, but Branson—still intent on shaping his program in multidisciplinary ways—took courses in other fields as well, for example with Harris Hancock, a mathematician specializing in the theory of elliptic functions. Branson earned a PhD in Physics in 1939, and that year he married Corolynne Gray of Cincinnati; they had two children, Corolynne Gertrude and Herman Edward, both physicians.

His first academic appointment was at Dillard University, where he served as instructor in mathematics and physics from 1939 to 1941. Part of that period was spent as a Rosenwald Fellow in physics at the University of Chicago; the Rosenwald fellowships had been established by the Julius Rosenwald Fund in 1936 to support advanced study for "Negroes of unusual talents and abilities in any field of work." In 1941 Branson was appointed assistant professor of

physics and chemistry at Howard University; he was assistant professor of physics, 1942–1944, professor of physics, 1944–1968, and department head, 1955–1968.

At Howard, Branson embarked on a lifelong commitment to improving science education for African Americans. He developed a physics undergraduate major and a graduate program there in the 1940s, when physics in black colleges and universities was thought of primarily as a service course for premedical majors, rather than as a discipline in its own right. In 1942 and 1943 he published several articles on blacks in science and technology, particularly addressing issues relating to research, education, and the war effort, as in "The Role of the Negro College in the Preparation of Technical Personnel for the War Effort" (*Journal of Negro Education* 11 [July 1942]); "Physics Training for the Negro Student" (*American Journal of Physics* 10 [Aug. 1942]); and "Contribution of Natural Sciences to the Development of Attitudes" (*Quarterly Review of Higher Education Among Negroes* 11 [Jan. 1943]). After the war he continued to address the role of blacks in the sciences and published two notable articles: "The Negro in Scientific Research" (*Negro History Bulletin* 15 [Apr. 1952]), and "The Negro Scientist" (in *The Negro in Science,* ed. Julius H. Taylor [1955]).

The next decade was a time of remarkable productivity in Branson's scientific research as well. He pioneered the use of integral equations in describing processes in biological systems, published as "A Mathematical Description of Metabolizing Systems" (*Bulletin of Mathematical Biophysics* 8 [1946]; 9 [1947]). He was also among the first to use radioactive phosphorus (^{32}P), mathematical methods, and electron microscopy in the study of sickle cell anemia blood cells (*Science* 115 [25 Jan. 1952]). Another innovative line of research brought him to the intersection between biology and information theory. He calculated, for example, the information content of several protein molecules in "Information Theory and the Structure of Proteins" (in *Information Theory in Biology,* ed. Henry Quastler [1953]).

Most important of all, and least recognized, is his contribution to early discoveries about the structure of proteins. In the late 1940s, working as a National Research Council senior fellow with Linus Pauling and others at the California Institute of Technology, Branson helped discover the "alpha-helix," the first clear vision of three-dimensional order in proteins. He established and solved the relevant spatial equations and demonstrated the hydrogen-bonded helical structure of certain amino acids. The "alpha helix," announced in a paper coauthored by Branson, Pauling, and Robert B. Corey, "The Structure of Proteins: Two Hydrogen-Bonded Helical Configurations of the Polypeptide Chain" (*Proceedings of the National Academy of Sciences* 37 [1951]), ranks as one of the most important discoveries in the history of biology in the twentieth century, anticipating the helical structure of DNA. Pauling was awarded the Nobel Prize in Chemistry for the achievement in 1954, while Branson's role has been all but forgotten.

After nearly three decades at Howard University, Branson served as president of Central State University, Wilberforce, Ohio, from 1968 to 1970, and of Lincoln University, from 1970 to 1985. His leadership at these two historically black institutions reflected his ongoing commitment to educational opportunity for African Americans. In the spring of 1970 he led a group of fifteen black college and university presidents to a White House meeting with President Richard Nixon, laying out the frustration felt by blacks nationwide toward the administration's policies; Nixon responded with a 30 percent increase in federal aid for historically black educational institutions.

Following his retirement as president of Lincoln University in 1985, Branson directed the Pre-College Science and Mathematics Program at Howard University, bringing high school seniors into mentoring relationships with professional scientists. He worked hard throughout his career to raise public awareness about the role and potential of scientific careers for blacks. "The civil rights struggle is quite a recent thing," he said in a 1966 interview, "and until we provide Negroes with suitable opportunity from the time they are born, we are not going to have as many Negro physicists as numerically we should" (Branson, 70). An early critic of "black studies" as a discrete academic discipline, he feared that such programs would emphasize emotion at the expense of intellectual rigor and distract attention from more practical goals.

In 1969 Branson became a cofounder of the National Association for Equal Opportunity in Higher Education and from 1970 to 1973 he served as its president. He was elected to membership in the Institute of Medicine, National Academy of Sciences in 1975. His stellar accomplishments over a life of service distinguished him as both a scholar and administrator.

FURTHER READING

Important archival sources for Branson's career may be found in the Moorland-Spingarn Research Center at Howard University, the Julius Rosenwald Fund Archives in the Fisk University Library Special Collections, Nashville, Tennessee, and in the Lincoln University Archives, Lincoln University, Pennsylvania. Oral histories conducted by Kenneth R. Manning in 1976 are held at the Massachusetts Institute of Technology. There is no published biography.

Hodes, Bernard. "The Negro in Physics—An Interview with Herman Branson." *Physics Today* 19 (Sept. 1966): 72–73.

Obituaries: *New York Times*, 13 June 1995; *Jet*, 26 June 1995.

—PHILIP ALEXANDER

 BRAWLEY, BENJAMIN GRIFFITH (22 Apr. 1882– 1 Feb. 1939), educator and author, was born in Columbia, South Carolina, the son of Margaret Saphronia Dickerson and Edward McKnight Brawley, a prosperous Baptist minister and president of a small Alabama college. Brawley was an exceptionally bright boy, and the family's frequent moves never interfered with his learning. Up until the third grade he was tutored at home by his mother, but he also attended schools in Nashville, Tennessee, and Petersburg, Virginia. During summers, when he was not studying the classics, Latin, and Greek at home, he earned money by doing odd jobs, working on a tobacco farm in Connecticut or in a printing office. One summer he drove a buggy for a white doctor—and studied Greek while the doctor was out. At age twelve he was sent to Virginia to be tutored in Greek and he also studied the language with his father.

By age thirteen Brawley had excelled so much in his studies that he was sent to the preparatory program at Atlanta Baptist College (later Morehouse College). He was surprised and disappointed on his arrival to note that most of the older students there knew nothing of classical literature, much less Greek or Latin. His classmates were equally surprised to find such a young man in their midst, but they soon discovered just how valuable an asset he was. Aware of his intellectual and grammatical prowess, they brought their compositions to him before passing them on to their instructors. Brawley excelled outside the classroom as well. He played football, managed the baseball team, and cofounded the school newspaper, the *Athenaeum* (later the *Maroon Tiger*), for which he wrote numerous articles and poems. Brawley is also said to have initiated the first debate among African American colleges when his Morehouse team challenged another group from Talladega College.

In 1901 Brawley graduated with honors from Atlanta Baptist College and immediately took a teaching position, for five months at thirty-five dollars a month, in a one-room school in Georgetown, Florida, but then, in 1902, he took a teaching job at his alma mater, where he stayed until 1910. During his years at Atlanta Baptist College, he also earned his BA (1906) from the University of Chicago and his MA (1908) from Harvard by taking mostly summer courses. Then he accepted a professorship at Howard University and while teaching there met Hilda Damaris Prowd, who became his wife in 1912. They had no children. After only two years at Howard, he returned to Atlanta Baptist, where, in addition to teaching, he became the college's first dean and where his teaching techniques became legendary.

Brawley considered teaching to be a divine profession that should be used to bring students "into the knowledge of truth," the success of which depended as much upon the efforts of the teacher as on those of the student.

He expected of his students the same high academic and moral standards that he had learned as a child, and he stressed that teaching should take into account the whole student—his or her physical, emotional, economic, and moral background. Brawley would commonly make students memorize long passages from classical literature, and he returned any compositions with even the slightest degree of sloppiness or imprecision, marking them with terse comments like "Too carelessly written to be carefully read" (Parker, *Phylon* [1949], 18). A traditionalist first, last, and always, Brawley was also dissatisfied with the state of education in the country, which emphasized materialism and innovation rather than rote learning.

Although Brawley still earned his primary living as a teacher, he also began to turn seriously toward another profession. He had written articles for his school paper and other publications for several years, but from 1921 on he produced at least ten books and about one hundred newspaper and magazine articles, book reviews, editorials, and other efforts. Whether he was writing about African American life and culture, as in *A Social History of the American Negro* (1921), or more literary topics, as in *A New Survey of English Literature* (1925), Brawley stressed two major themes: first, that literature must rest on a sound artistic and moral basis and, second, that it should present not just the struggles of individuals and races, but "a mirror of our hopes and dreams" as well (*The Negro Genius* [1937], 196). He was particularly saddened that most novels and short stories about African Americans that came out of Harlem and other places in the 1920s depicted characters as comic or appealed to readers' lower natures. "We are simply asking," he wrote in *The Negro Genius*, "that those writers of fiction who deal with the Negro shall be thoroughly honest with themselves" (206). Only by strict adherence to these high ideals, Brawley believed, could the lot of his own race be improved and race relations be dealt with honestly.

In 1920, after many years at Morehouse, Brawley went to the African Republic of Liberia to conduct an educational survey. Shortly after his return in early 1921, he followed in his father's footsteps and became an ordained Baptist minister at the Messiah Congregation in Brockton, Massachusetts. After only a year, however, he found the congregation's type of Christianity not to his liking and resigned. Brawley returned to teaching, first at Shaw University in North Carolina, where his father, by then in failing health, taught theology, and then, in 1931, at Howard, where he stayed until the end of his life. In 1936 he published *PAUL LAURENCE DUNBAR: Poet of His People*. He died at his home in Washington, D.C., from complications following a stroke.

Brawley's impeccable academic credentials and high standards earned him the respect of almost all his students, although that respect was shown in unusual ways. One story goes that a student came to class carrying under his arm a bundle wrapped in newspaper, which everyone assumed was laundry. Instead, the student had carefully wrapped his essay in the bundle to be sure that it met Brawley's exacting standards. Brawley's techniques, coupled with his difficulty in abiding by any standards other than his own, earned him his share of criticism, but far more often than not they achieved desirable results.

FURTHER READING

The Brawley papers are at the Moorland-Spingarn Research Center at Howard University. A complete bibliography of Brawley's published works appears in *North Carolina Historical Review* 34 (Apr. 1957), 165–175.

Parker, John W. "Benjamin Brawley and the American Cultural Tradition." *Phylon* 16 (1955), 183–194.
"Phylon Profile XIX: Benjamin Brawley—Teacher and Scholar." *Phylon* 10 (1949), 15–24.
Price, Charlotte S. *Richard Le Gallienne as Collected by Benjamin Griffith Brawley* (1973).

Obituary: *New York Times*, 7 Feb. 1939; *The Crisis* 46 (1939).

—ROGER A. SCHUPPERT

BRENT, LINDA. *See* Jacobs, Harriet.

BRICKTOP (14 Aug. 1894–31 Jan. 1984), entertainer and nightclub operator, was born in Alderson, West Virginia, the daughter of Thomas Smith, a barber, and Hattie E. (maiden name unknown), a domestic worker. Christened Ada Beatrice Queen Victoria Louise Virginia, because her parents did not wish to disappoint the various neighbors and friends who offered suggestions for naming her, Bricktop received her nickname because of her red hair when she was in her late twenties from Barron Wilkins, owner of a nightclub called Barron's Exclusive Club in Prohibition-era Harlem.

Bricktop's father died when she was four, and her mother moved with the children to Chicago to be near relatives. Hattie Smith worked as a domestic in Chicago, and her children attended school. Bricktop showed early musical talent and interest in performing. She made her stage debut as a preschooler, playing the part of Eliza's son Harry in a production of *Uncle Tom's Cabin* at the Haymarket Theatre. As an adolescent, she had the opportunity to perform onstage again when she was hired as part of the chorus for a show at the Pekin Theatre. She quit school at age sixteen to pursue a career as an entertainer, first touring with (Flournoy) Miller and (Aubrey) Lyles, a well-known black comedy team.

After the Miller and Lyles show folded, Bricktop toured with a variety of black vaudeville acts across the northern half of the United States. In the early 1920s she returned to Chicago and worked as a saloon performer at Roy Jones's and the Cafe Champ, owned by heavyweight champion JACK JOHNSON. In 1922 she went to Harlem, where she worked in Connie's Inn, among other nightclubs, and received her nickname. In 1924 she was invited to work in Paris at Le Grand Duc, a tiny club in Montmartre managed by EUGÈNE BULLARD, an African American pilot who had distinguished himself during World War I in the French Foreign Legion and the Lafayette Escadrille.

Never a great song stylist, Bricktop attracted the attention of white Americans in Paris because of her charming personality and her ability to make them feel at home. T. S. Eliot wrote a poem for her. F. Scott Fitzgerald liked to say, "My greatest claim to fame is that I discovered Bricktop before Cole Porter." But it was her discovery by Porter, who later wrote the song "Miss Otis Regrets" for her, that put the imprimatur of acceptance upon her. Under Porter's aegis, Bricktop became a darling of the American celebrity set in Paris. By the fall of 1926, Bricktop had opened the first Bricktop's nightclub in Paris, catering to such American luminaries as Fitzgerald, Elsa Maxwell, Tallulah Bankhead, Ernest Hemingway, and Barbara Hutton, and to international celebrities like the Aga Khan. "Everybody belonged, or else they didn't bother coming to Bricktop's more than once," she wrote in her autobiography.

A succession of Bricktop's nightclubs followed, both in Paris and, in the summertime, at Biarritz, where Bricktop claimed to have cradled the romance of the Duke of Windsor and the American divorcée Wallis Simpson. Among the careers she nurtured was that of the British-born black singer Mabel Mercer.

The stock market crash in the United States in October 1929 had no effect, at first, on the "gay" life in Paris. In December 1929 Bricktop married Peter Ducongé, an African American saxophonist from New Orleans, and the two purchased a country home in Bougival, outside Paris. Childless, each led an independent life, as well as sharing a life together. Some years after their marriage, however, Peter had an affair with a young African American singer whom Bricktop had taken under her wing in Paris. On learning of her husband's infidelity, Bricktop refused to sleep with him again, although she never divorced him. He died in 1967.

In 1939, as war in Europe and the invasion of France seemed imminent, the Duchess of Windsor (the former Wallis Simpson) and Lady Mendl (Elsie de Wolfe) helped Bricktop escape from Paris to New York, where her friend Mabel Mercer had already relocated. Mercer managed to find a niche as a singer in New York cabarets, but Bricktop's special talents as a self-described "saloonkeeper par excellence" went unappreciated. Bankrolled by the tobacco heiress Doris Duke, she relocated to Mexico City, where she

successfully ran clubs until the war in Europe was over. In 1943 she converted to Catholicism and remained a devout Catholic for the rest of her life.

Returning to Paris in 1950, she found her old stomping grounds much changed, as was the clientele. After trying and failing to revive the prewar atmosphere, Bricktop removed to Rome, where on the Via Veneto from 1951 to 1965 she re-created the feeling of the old Bricktop's for a new celebrity crowd, primarily American film stars. The romance of Richard Burton and Elizabeth Taylor first made the gossip columns when they were seen together at the Rome Bricktop's during the filming of *Cleopatra*. To Bricktop her career in Rome was secondary to the golden years in Paris, and she never fully accepted the Hollywood film stars as the nouveau royalty.

When Bricktop's older sister Blonzetta became ill in 1965, Bricktop returned to Chicago to nurse her and, after her death, went back to straighten out her affairs. Blonzetta left Bricktop a substantial inheritance. In her early seventies, Bricktop moved to Los Angeles, returned briefly to Europe, and then in 1970 settled in New York City. She made a recording of "So Long, Baby" with Cy Coleman, briefly ran a club owned by Huntington Hartford and then one called Soerabaja, and appeared from time to time at clubs in Chicago, at the Playboy Club in London, and at "21" in New York. Ill health caused her to cease working in 1979.

In August 1983 Bricktop published her autobiography, *Bricktop*, written with Jim Haskins. Five months later she died in New York City. To the end she was a lady of the dawn who drank only champagne and expected a rose from every male visitor.

FURTHER READING

Bricktop's papers are in the collection of the Schomburg Center for Research in Black Culture of the New York Public Library.

Boyle, Kay, and Robert Altman. *Being Geniuses Together, 1920–1930* (1968).

Haskins, Jim. *Mabel Mercer: A Life* (1968).

Obituary: *Rolling Stone*, 29 Mar. 1984.

—JIM HASKINS

BROOKE, EDWARD

(26 Oct. 1919–), lawyer and U.S. senator, was born Edward William Brooke III in Washington, D.C., to Edward Brooke Jr., an attorney for the Veterans Administration, and Helen Seldon. Growing up in an integrated middle-class neighborhood, Brooke readily absorbed his mother's instruction to respect others and treat all people equally. The Brookes lived relatively free from much of the racism endured by other African Americans. "We never felt hated," his mother recalled (Cutler, 14). Brooke attended Dunbar High School, an elite public school with many middle-class and upper-class African American students and then went on to Howard University, where he became president of the school's chapter of the Alpha Phi Alpha fraternity and earned his bachelor's degree in 1941. Following the bombing of Pearl Harbor later that year, Brooke was drafted into an all-black combat unit in the army. He served in many roles, including as a defender of those who had been court-martialed. His tour of duty during World War II took him to Africa and to Italy, and he earned a Bronze Star for leading an attack on a military battery. While in Italy he met his wife, Remigia Ferrair-Scacco, who had served in the underground resistance against the Nazis. The couple married in 1947 and later had two daughters.

Brooke enrolled in law school at Boston University in 1946. He became editor of the law review during his final year of school and went on to earn LLB and LLM degrees. Brooke then practiced law in the Roxbury area of Boston, where he witnessed firsthand the problems African Americans faced regarding housing, education, employment, and health care. At the same time, he worked as legal counsel for the local chapter of the NAACP and served on the board of directors of the Greater Boston Urban League. He lobbied the state legislature for the elimination of segregation in the state's National Guard units and worked on an appeal to the U.S. Supreme Court to outlaw segregation in railroad dining cars. Brooke was also very active in the AMVETS, an organization for World War II veterans, and in 1956 he

Edward W. Brooke receives the NAACP's Spingarn Medal from NAACP Director ROY WILKINS, *as Senator Edward Kennedy looks on, 1967.* © Bettmann/CORBIS

served as the National Judge Advocate for the group.

In 1950 Brooke's friends persuaded him to run for the state legislature. A Republican in a heavily Democratic state, he lost the election and vowed never to run for office again, in part because his wife was upset over campaign talk about their mixed marriage. He nonetheless ran for the legislature two years later but lost again. Brooke narrowly lost another election in 1960, this time for secretary of state for Massachusetts. Although he had failed in his quest for political office, Brooke won the respect of numerous leaders in the state's Republican Party and soon accepted an appointment to the Boston Finance Commission. He quickly earned a reputation as a tough crime fighter as he exposed corruption in several city agencies, including the police department.

In 1962 Brooke was elected as Massachusetts attorney general, becoming the first African American ever to win such a statewide position. He first won a difficult primary battle, overcoming strong objections from Republican leaders concerning his liberalism and inexperience, and then went on to win the general election by appealing to white voters on the strength of his personal charm and his record with the Boston Finance Commission. As would be the case throughout his career, Brooke resisted attempts to label him a "black" politician. He commented, "I'm the lawyer for the five million citizens of Massachusetts, not for its...Negroes" (Cutler, 117). He did not ignore racial matters, however. While in office Brooke filed a brief in support of a fair housing law and helped draft legislation to forbid employment discrimination by businesses and unions. A firm believer in gradual change through legal means, he clashed with civil rights leaders over their plans to have students boycott school for a day, which would have violated the state's truancy laws, to protest de facto segregation in Boston.

Brooke's triumph as an African American in an overwhelmingly white state propelled him into national Republican debates in 1964. Like other liberal Republicans, Brooke grew alarmed at the conservative movement's efforts to nominate Arizona Senator Barry Goldwater, who had voted against the 1964 Civil Rights Act, as the party's presidential candidate that year. Attending the Republican convention in San Francisco, Brooke urged the party to adopt a strong civil rights plank and seconded the nomination of Governor William Scranton of Pennsylvania, a more moderate candidate on race and other issues, for president. Goldwater withstood the Scranton challenge, and Brooke, like several other northeastern liberals, refused to support the Arizonan that fall. Although Goldwater suffered a crushing defeat in November, Brooke was overwhelmingly reelected as Massachusetts attorney general.

Two years later Brooke won election to the U.S. Senate. The victory marked him as the first black senator since Reconstruction and as the first African American to win a senate seat by popular vote. As conservatives gained influence within the Republican Party nationally, Brooke continued to support many of President Lyndon Johnson's social-welfare Great Society programs. Brooke even attacked Johnson on occasion for doing too little to combat poverty, and in 1966 he published his views on racial and economic problems facing black Americans in *The Challenge of Change*. He also became deeply involved in debates over the future of the Republican Party. Although he once again refused to make his race an issue, Brooke urged the party to broaden its appeal beyond white, middle-class suburbanites by reaching out to African Americans and other minorities. Many political pundits saw him as a leader who could bring at least some of the black vote back to the party of Abraham Lincoln. Soon after his election, there was speculation among some Republicans, as well as in the media, that Brooke would make an excellent choice for the Republican vice-presidential nomination in 1968.

Brooke was at the center of debates over the racial violence of the mid- and late 1960s. Following enormously destructive riots in the summer of 1967 in Newark, New Jersey, and Detroit, Michigan, President Johnson chose Brooke to serve on his Advisory Commission on Civil Disorders (also known as the Kerner Commission). Brooke toured several riot-torn areas and firmly rejected conservative claims that the riots were the result of communist influence or a conspiracy among radical black leaders. Instead, he insisted that the riots stemmed from social and economic problems related to jobs, housing, education, and health care. At the same time, Brooke held to his beliefs in integration and peaceful change. He worried that the media gave too much attention to more radical black leaders, such as STOKELY CARMICHAEL, and he rejected Black Power, calling it "a turn in the wrong direction" (Cutler, 197). In 1968 Brooke worked closely with Senator Walter Mondale of Minnesota, a liberal Democrat, on behalf of the Fair Housing Act.

During the late 1960s and early 1970s Brooke regularly criticized Richard Nixon's civil rights policies. He blasted the president for his early approach to school desegregation in the South and for not following through on his promise to promote economic development in the inner cities through "black capitalism." Worried that Nixon was too eager to appeal to white southerners and suburbanites, Brooke played a prominent role in successful efforts to defeat Nixon's nominations of the conservatives Clement Haynsworth and G. Harrold Carswell to the Supreme Court. He also opposed the nomination of William H. Rehnquist out of concern about his right-wing views on civil rights, though the Senate confirmed Rehnquist.

Brooke won reelection in 1972 but lost six years later, in part because of press revelations that he had lied about his personal finances in a deposition related to his divorce that year from his wife. In 1979 he became head of the National Low-Income Housing Coalition, resumed practicing law in Virginia, and married Anne Fleming. The couple had one son, Edward W. Brooke IV. In 2002 Brooke developed breast cancer and launched an effort to alert men to the dangers of this rare disease among men. A recipient of the NAACP's Spingarn medal for black achievement in 1967, Brooke symbolizes the post–World War II rise of African Americans to prominent political positions, as well as his generation's faith in integration and working through established political and legal channels to achieve change.

FURTHER READING

Edward Brooke's papers are in the Library of Congress, Washington, D.C.

Cutler, John. *Ed Brooke: Biography of a Senator* (1972).

—TIMOTHY N. THURBER

BROOKS, GWENDOLYN

(7 June 1917–3 Dec. 2000), poet and novelist, was born Gwendolyn Elizabeth Brooks at her grandmother's home in Topeka, Kansas, the daughter of David Anderson Brooks, a janitor, and Keziah Wims Brooks. When she was two months old, the family settled in Chicago, where she would live the rest of her life. Brooks and her brother had a sheltered upbringing in a cheerful, orderly household. (She would later draw on memories of those years for her poem "a song in the front yard" [1945].) At Forrestville Elementary School, where she learned that light skin and fine hair were valued, this shy child with dark skin and coarse hair felt socially isolated. Her mother, however, encouraged her interest in writing, and Brooks published her first poem in *American Childhood* magazine in 1930.

Later, to escape further isolation at a mostly white high school, she transferred to an all-black school; finally, at the somewhat more integrated Englewood High School, she found a peer group and teachers who encouraged her writing. From then on, she was constantly publishing—in national periodicals and regularly in Chicago's African American newspaper, the *Defender*. With her mother's encouragement, she showed her work to the poets JAMES WELDON JOHNSON, whom she found cold and distant, and LANGSTON HUGHES, with whom she established a long friendship.

Her family struggled financially during the Great Depression, but the year she finished high school Wilson Junior College opened with a low tuition that made it possible for her to earn an associate's degree. After college Brooks endured a series of dead-end jobs, including a humiliating position as a domestic; she later fictionalized that experience in her poem "Bronzeville Woman in a Red Hat" and in a chapter of her novel *Maud Martha*. She also worked several months for a charlatan spiritual healer operating out of the Mecca Building, a once fashionable apartment building that had decayed into a tenement; her experiences therein would later become the basis of her long narrative poem "In the Mecca." Active in the Youth Council of the NAACP, she

cofounded a club for young black artists and writers. Through the NAACP, she met fellow poet Henry Blakely, whom she married in 1939; they had two children. Blakely died in 1996.

Brooks's mature style developed after 1941, when she and her husband joined a South Side poetry workshop run by the white socialite Inez Cunningham Stark. Brooks credited Stark with introducing her to the artistic possibilities available in poetic form and forcing her to submit her work to more rigorous aesthetic judgment. She began winning poetry contests, and book publishers encouraged her to develop more poems about African American life. The title of her first book, *A Street in Bronzeville* (1945), refers to the *Defender*'s name for the African American section of Chicago. The book includes some of her most admired poems, such as "The Sundays of Satin-Legs Smith," a portrait of a Bronzeville dandy; "The Mother," a bold and compassionate poem about abortion; and two poems that present African American perspectives on World War II, "Negro Hero" and "Gay Chaps at the Bar."

Working on poetry, fiction, and book reviews while her son attended school, Brooks wrote *Annie Allen* (1949), which loosely follows the life of the title character, an intelligent, sensitive African American woman. The centerpiece is the poem "The Anniad"; the title alludes to Virgil's ancient epic the *Aeneid*, and the language strives for Virgilian complexity, suggesting the extraordinary heroism and ingenuity it takes to get through an ordinary life. For that book she became the first African American to receive a Pulitzer Prize.

Ironically, as Brooks was receiving high literary honors, her family was having trouble finding suitable housing. The tiny apartments they lived in are described in many of her poems. Housing for African Americans in Chicago was then limited to one area on the South Side; it had expanded very little over the decades, while its population had increased, nearly doubling in the 1940s. Part of her motivation for writing a novel, therefore, was to earn enough of an advance to be able to put a down payment on a house. The resulting autobiographical novel, *Maud Martha* (1953), is now considered a classic of African American literature, with its intimate, affectionate, and sometimes infuriated view of urban African American life in mid-century, before the rise of the civil rights movement. It portrays, through a series of lyrical scenes and frequent linguistic play, the childhood and young adulthood of an African American woman in Chicago.

Brooks's next collection, *The Bean Eaters* (1960), took an explicitly political turn with such poems as "The Ballad of Rudolph Reed," about the tragic result of a black family's move into a white neighborhood. Her most popular and most often reprinted poem, "We Real Cool," in eight short, infectiously rhythmic lines, introduces seven dropouts bragging about their wild lives despite their expectation of early death. She came to consider this poem her most successful combination of artistry with popular appeal, since, with its clarity and catchiness as well as its frequent inclusion in anthologies, it has spoken to an unusually broad audience.

In 1963 Brooks was offered a teaching position at Chicago's Columbia College. Throughout the 1960s and 1970s she would go on to teach also at Elmhurst College, Northeastern Illinois University, and the University of Wisconsin at Madison, among other schools. Brooks identified 1967 as the turning point in her career. Attending a Black Writers Conference at Fisk University, she was impressed by the contrast between the formal respect for her and the enthusiasm for the more radical AMIRI BARAKA. That striking contrast indicated to her a shift in African American culture from liberal integrationism toward a more militant black nationalism. Returning home, she was asked by the writer and community organizer Walter Bradford to lead a workshop for some members of the Blackstone Rangers street gang who were interested in writing. Although she eventually turned that workshop over to Bradford, she started meeting with black college students (including Don L. Lee [later Haki R. Madhubuti] and Carolyn Rodgers) for workshops in her home. Both these groups resisted Brooks's attempts to teach traditional poetic forms and high cultural aesthetics, insisting rather on a populist aesthetic in tune with their radical politics.

Also in 1967 Brooks read at the dedication of a mural depicting African American cultural heroes, including herself. Afterward, some of her workshop students led her into a local bar, where they gave an impromptu poetry reading, much to the appreciation of the patrons. The literary ambitions of the gang members and the warm reception of the tavern customers opened Brooks's eyes to an audience she had neglected. The events of that year initiated her commitment to the Black Power movement and black cultural nationalism, as well as to the Black Arts Movement, which in the late 1960s and early 1970s encouraged black artists and writers to reject European-derived aesthetics and the production of works for white audiences in favor of African and African American themes and forms for a specifically African American audience.

In 1968 she succeeded Carl Sandburg as poet laureate of Illinois, and, using her own funds, she established an award for young writers in the state. That same year Harper and Row, Brooks's publisher since 1945, brought out the collection *In the Mecca*, which includes her narrative poem set in the Mecca Building, as a tribute to martyred heroes such as MALCOLM X and MEDGAR EVERS, and a sequence of poems about the Blackstone Rangers. Starting with *Riot* (1969) she published new work only with black presses. Dudley Randall's small but influential Broadside Press in Detroit began publishing chapbooks of her new poetry, two anthologies she edited, and her unconventional autobiography *Report from Part One* (1972). Rather than providing a straightforward narrative of her life, the latter volume offers a collage of anecdotes, comments on her own and others' writing, interviews, photographs, and commentary on her work by other writers. She would publish other chapbooks and the collection *To Disembark* (1981) through Madhubuti's Third World Press and her own imprints.

In 1969 she and her husband separated, and she felt a renewed sense of freedom. She traveled on her own to East Africa, an experience that influenced her sense of American blacks as Africans in the New World. It was during this period that she wrote the

first volume of her autobiography and began editing an annual periodical, *The Black Position* (1971–1974). Her mother, however, encouraged Brooks and her husband to reconcile, which they did in 1973; in part to celebrate that reunion, they traveled together to Ghana.

In 1976 Brooks became the first black woman elected to the National Institute of Arts and Letters. She was appointed poetry consultant to the Library of Congress in 1985. By this point, however, much of her early work, except for *Selected Poems* (1963), was out of print, so she self-published her collected works, *Blacks* (1987). Over the years, she received numerous awards, including over fifty honorary doctorates. She died in Chicago.

With passion, clarity, and rich literary craft, Brooks's writings present and comment on urban African American life in the mid- to late twentieth century. As the struggle for racial justice heated up, she became a more overtly political public figure. She was the most prestigious African American poet of her generation, so her conversion in the late 1960s to a radical black politics was an important endorsement of that position. Her decision to publish only with black presses restricted the audience for her later work, but it made concrete her commitment to African American readers and cultural institutions. She successfully married political engagement with the highest quality of artistry and in the latter part of her career sought to present poetry as a cultural practice available to everyone, not just the literary elite. A major figure in American poetry, she used her personal prestige to support and inspire young black writers and to establish publishing institutions that would serve the specific cultural interests of African Americans.

FURTHER READING

Brooks's papers are at the Bancroft Library, University of California, Berkeley.

Brooks, Gwendolyn. *Report from Part One* (1972).
——. *Report from Part Two* (1996).

Bodlen, B. J. *Urban Rage in Bronzeville: Social Commentary in the Poetry of Gwendolyn Brooks* (1998).
Kent, George E. *A Life of Gwendolyn Brooks* (1990).
Melhem, D. H. *Gwendolyn Brooks: Poetry and the Heroic Voice* (1987).

Mootry, Maria K., and Gary Smith, eds. *A Life Distilled: Gwendolyn Brooks, Her Poetry and Fiction* (1987).

Wright, Stephen Caldwell, ed. *On Gwendolyn Brooks: Reliant Contemplation* (1996).

Obituary: *New York Times*, 4 Dec. 2000.
—JAMES D. SULLIVAN

 BROOKS, WALTER HENDERSON

(30 Aug. 1851–6 July 1945), clergyman, temperance leader, and poet, was born in Richmond, Virginia, the son of Albert Royal Brooks and Lucy Goode, slaves. Brooks's father, an enterprising slave, owned his own "snack house" and a livery business that brought him into contact with some of Virginia's wealthiest citizens, including his wife's owner, the German consul Daniel Von Groning. Albert Brooks purchased his wife's freedom in 1862 for eight hundred dollars. Still a slave, Walter Brooks at age seven was sold to the Turpin & Yarborough tobacco firm. He woefully recalled his time there, writing: "It was all I could do to perform the task assigned to my little hands. What I do remember is that I stood in mortal fear of 'the consequences' of failing to do what was required of me." When the Richmond manufacturer fell victim to wartime economic decline, Brooks was allowed to reside with his mother and began working in hotels, boardinghouses, and restaurants. In his youth he acquired the doctrines that served as the foundation for his life's work. He learned temperance from his pastor, the Reverend Robert Ryland, who taught songs at Christmas to curb the consumption of "egg-nog and the drinking of wine in countless homes," and Brooks's parents instilled "lessons of uprightness and sobriety."

After the Union victory in the Civil War, Brooks worked to make a place for himself in the world. In 1866 he entered the preparatory program at Lincoln University, a Presbyterian school founded for African Americans in Pennsylvania. He obtained his college degree in 1872 and one year later earned his theological degree. He joined the Ashmun Presbyterian Church in Lincoln in 1868. When he returned to Richmond after graduation, he changed denominations and was baptized into the First African Baptist Church. In 1874

he married the pastor's daughter, Eva Holmes; they had ten children.

Between 1874 and 1876 Brooks worked with the American Baptist Publication Society as a Sunday school missionary in Virginia. He gained national attention for his views on temperance when he addressed the society at its anniversary meeting in Philadelphia in 1875. His speech, entitled "Facts from the Field," sparked controversy when he "drew a picture of the drinking habits of preachers" in an effort to illustrate the critical need for temperance. That same year Brooks became the chaplain of the Anti-Saloon League of the District of Columbia. He retained this position until 1882.

Brooks's greatest legacy came from his work as a Baptist minister. In 1876 he was formally ordained into the ministry and a year later became pastor of the Second African Baptist Church of Richmond. In 1880 he briefly returned to his missionary work, but by 1882 he had accepted the pastorate of the Nineteenth Street Baptist Church in Washington, D.C. Over the next sixty-three years Brooks established a national reputation. He assisted John W. Cromwell in creating the Virginia Historical and Literary Society and for a time served as vice president in the Bethel Literary and Historical Association in Washington, D.C. Brooks was a trustee of NANNIE BURROUGHS's National Training School for Women and Girls and the Virginia Theological Seminary and College in Lynchburg, Virginia. He supported the black women's club movement, and in 1896 his church was the site of the foundational meeting of the National Association of Colored Women.

Brooks played an important role in efforts to build and maintain a national black Baptist convention. He was chairman of the American National Baptist Convention's Bureau of Education, a black organization founded in 1886, and he continually mediated relationships with national white Baptist conventions. In 1889 the American Baptist Publication Society, in an effort to increase black participation, agreed to accept literary contributions from Brooks and two of his colleagues for its regular publication. The society, however, reneged on its offer when its southern white contingency voiced

opposition. The society opted instead to create a special publication for black clergymen, the *Negro Baptist Pulpit*. Although Brooks authored an article for that volume, he and his colleagues were infuriated by this palliative act and predicted that it would typify future relations. Further difficulties led eventually to the formation of a black-controlled denominational body, the National Baptist Convention, U.S.A., in 1895.

Brooks's intellectual capabilities and dedication earned him recognition as an exceptional scholar. He wrote a number of essays on the history and development of black Baptist organizations and their relationships with white Baptists. For the *Journal of Negro History* he wrote "The Evolution of the Negro Baptist Church" (Jan. 1922) and "The Priority of the Silver Bluff Church and Its Promoters" (Apr. 1922). For the *Crisis* he wrote "Unification and Division among Colored Baptists" (May 1925). In his work with the Bethel Literary and Historical Association, he offered a "severe but eloquent criticism" of FREDERICK DOUGLASS's lecture "The Philosophy and History of Reform" that "occasioned a battle royal between him and Mr. Douglass, in which 'Greek met Greek' with vigorous onslaught and heroic defence [*sic*]." Brooks was a member of the American Negro Academy and a lifelong member of the Association for the Study of Negro Life and History, where he worked closely with CARTER G. WOODSON.

Brooks's first wife died in 1912, and three years later he married Florence H. Swann. Following Florence's death, he married Viola Washington in 1933. Late in his life Brooks established himself as a poet. Two books of his poetry were published, *Original Poems* (1932) and *The Pastor's Voice* (1945). His poems thematically reflect his lifelong concerns for temperance, faith in God, and racial progress.

Brooks, like many black clergy of his time, used the church and his role as pastor for purposes that extended beyond the sacred. He was uncompromising in his struggle to promote education and the use of Christian morals as means to improve the quality of life for black Americans. As racial segregation gained legal precedent and race-related violence reached new heights, Brooks fought for equality and clung to a faith in the American creed that was second only to his faith in God.

FURTHER READING

Brooks's granddaughter Evelyn Brooks Higginbotham, Harvard University, possesses some of his papers, including a 1935 autobiographical piece, "Memories of a Life Time," some untitled autobiographical notes, and a genealogical "History of the Brooks Family."

Higginbotham, Evelyn Brooks. *Righteous Discontent: The Women's Movement in the Black Baptist Church, 1880–1920* (1993).

Moss, Alfred A. *The American Negro Academy* (1981).

Washington, James Melvin. *Frustrated Fellowship: A Black Baptist Quest for Social Power* (1986).

Woodson, Carter G. Introduction to Watter Brooks, *The Pastor's Voice* (1945).

Obituaries: *Journal of Negro History* 30 Oct. 1945; Washington, D.C., *Evening Star*, 8 July 1945.

—ADAM BIGGS

BROONZY, BIG BILL

(26 June 1893?–15 Aug. 1958), blues singer and guitarist, was born William Lee Conley Broonzy in Scott, Bolivar County, Mississippi, the son of Frank Broonzy and Nettie (or Mittie) Belcher, former slaves who became sharecroppers. One of at least sixteen children, including a twin sister, he lived in Mississippi until age eight, when his family moved to Arkansas, near Pine Bluff, to try sharecropping there. As a youngster he made violins out of cornstalks, learning music from an uncle, Jerry Belcher, and a local musician known as See See Rider. He and a friend began playing homemade instruments to entertain local children, though always out of sight of his parents—stern Baptists who frowned on secular music. The parental disapproval eased, however, when he graduated to a real instrument (supposedly bought for him by a white patron) and began earning money as a musician. When he was twelve, the family moved to Scotts Crossing, Arkansas, where he continued to play, mainly for white dances.

In 1912, however, he joined the Baptist Church, briefly putting music aside to try his hand at preaching. In 1914 (some accounts say 1916) he married a fellow church member, seventeen-year-old Guitrue (or Gertrude) Embria, who allowed him to take up music again, he said later, because it paid more than preaching. In 1918 he was drafted, serving with an army supply company in France. Returning to Arkansas, he grew dissatisfied with life in the South. In early 1920 he left his wife and went to Chicago, where he eventually found work as a Pullman railroad sleeping-car porter. He took guitar lessons from Papa Charlie Jackson, a recording artist who introduced him to the Paramount Records executive J. Mayo Williams. After an unproductive session for Paramount in 1926, Broonzy and the guitarist John Thomas cut four sides in late 1927 and early 1928, launching Broonzy on one of the most prolific recording careers in blues history.

Through the 1930s and 1940s he recorded hundreds of sides for a dozen labels, including the most important blues labels of that era: Bluebird, Columbia, OKeh, and Vocalion. He recorded both as a solo artist and in small-combo formats. He became active on Chicago's house-party circuit and then the tavern and club scene as it developed in the late 1930s and 1940s, working with such artists as Memphis Minnie and John Lee "Sonny Boy" Williamson.

As early as 1938 he began making inroads on a new market, participating in John Hammond's *From Spirituals to Swing* programs at Carnegie Hall in New York City—possibly the first appearance of a Mississippi-born blues musician in concert format. He also worked New York's Cafe Society nightclub in 1939 and 1940. In 1941 and 1942 he toured with a Mississippi protégé, the vocalist Lil Green, until she started singing with big rhythm-and-blues bands. On tour in Houston, Texas, Broonzy married a "Creole woman," Rosie Syphen, who returned with him to Chicago, where he plunged back into a steady schedule of club work. They had five children.

Although World War II interrupted his recording career, the interruption apparently did not cause a major financial blow. Partly because he recorded under contract to the music publisher

Lester Melrose, not to any specific labels, Broonzy received little more than session fees as a recording artist. He once claimed that he earned a total of only two thousand dollars for the hundreds of songs he had recorded. As a result, even during his tenure as the nominal king of Chicago blues, he always worked nonmusical jobs on the side.

Broonzy returned to the recording studio in 1945, working in a new band format as he tried, with diminishing success, to keep pace with the postwar rhythm-and-blues sound. In 1947 the folklorist Alan Lomax brought Broonzy to New York, along with Memphis Slim and Sonny Boy Williamson, for a Town Hall concert. The next day, Lomax supervised a recording session at which the three blues artists, identified by pseudonyms (Broonzy's was "Natchez"), played music and talked candidly about life in the South. That session, like the *From Spirituals to Swing* concert, marked another stage in Broonzy's shift from racial/ethnic recording star to interpreter of blues for white audiences.

By the 1950s African American popular musical tastes had passed Broonzy by, and his recordings were more of a documentary or folk music nature. In 1950 and 1951 he briefly left the Chicago blues scene and took a job as a janitor at Iowa State University, where he learned to read and write. Returning to music, Broonzy looked more and more to the predominantly white folk revival audiences for work—for example, touring with the Chicago critic and oral historian Studs Terkel's program *I Come for to Sing*. He also looked to overseas markets and was one of the first artists to bring traditional American blues to British, European, Australian, African, and South American audiences in the 1950s. He appeared in several films and, with his newly acquired literacy, became the first Delta artist to be credited with an autobiography, *Big Bill Blues* (1964), a compilation of anecdotes, tall tales, and recollections originally written as letters to the Belgian enthusiast Yannick Bruynoghe. On tour in England in 1957, Broonzy was forced by health problems to return to Chicago, where he was diagnosed with lung cancer. He died in Chicago.

Big Bill Broonzy's performing career spanned five decades, taking him from the Deep South to Chicago and on to

Bluesman Big Bill Broonzy in 1957.
Terry Cryer/CORBIS

Europe, where he became one of the first and most effective ambassadors for American blues. As a recording artist, he recorded over 250 songs—many of them his own—prior to World War II and hundreds more in the postwar era. He also played as a sideman at countless sessions for other artists. As an instrumentalist, he could handle down-home finger picking or single-string electric styles, and, even late in his career, he could flash techniques that dazzled the guitar-oriented folk-music audience. Although he ended his career singing protest songs and other folk material in coffeehouses and cabarets, Broonzy was the central character in the first generation of Chicago blues musicians and spent most of his adult life performing blues, ragtime, hokum, and pop material for the so-called race market. Because he was one of the first blues artists to work successfully for white audiences, though, Broonzy helped shape the way several generations thought about the blues. Perhaps his most enduring musical influence was on a host of young, white British blues aficionados, notably John Mavall, Eric Clapton, and Jimmy Page, who in the 1960s sparked a blues-inspired "British invasion" of America. Broonzy was elected to the Blues Foundation Hall of Fame in Memphis, Tennessee, in 1980.

FURTHER READING

Broonzy, Bill. *Big Bill Blues: Big Bill Broonzy's Story as Told to Yannick Bruynoghe* (1964).

Harris, Sheldon. *Blues Who's Who: A Biographical Dictionary of Blues Singers* (1989).
Lomax, Alan. *The Land Where Blues Began* (1993).

Discography
Dixon, Robert M. W., and John Godrich. *Blues and Gospel Records: 1902–1943*, 3rd ed. (1982).
Leadbitter, Mike, and Neil Slaven. *Blues Records 1943–1970: A Selective Discography*, vol. 1 (1987).
Oliver, Paul, ed. *The Blackwell Guide to Blues Records* (1989).

—BILL MCCULLOCH
—BARRY LEE PEARSON

BROWN, CHARLOTTE EUGENIA HAWKINS

(11 June 1883–11 Jan. 1961), educator, was born Lottie Hawkins in Henderson, North Carolina, the daughter of Edmund H. Hight, a brick mason, and Caroline Frances Hawkins. Accounts vary as to whether her father and mother separated before or after her birth, and it is also unclear whether her parents ever married. After her mother married Nelson Willis, Lottie (as she was called until she changed her name to Charlotte Eugenia in high school) relocated with nineteen members of her extended family to Massachusetts in 1888. By joining the widespread migration of African Americans, the family hoped to enjoy greater economic opportunities and a better life. After settling in Cambridge, her stepfather worked odd jobs to support the family, while her mother boarded African American Harvard students, operated a laundry, and babysat. Hawkins began her elementary education at the Allston School in Cambridge, where she befriended two of Henry Wadsworth Longfellow's daughters and excelled in her studies. She also attended Baptist Sunday school, where at the age of twelve she organized a kindergarten department.

Hawkins then attended Cambridge English High and Latin School. During her senior year she met and made a favorable impression upon the former president of Wellesley College Alice Freeman Palmer. Although Hawkins wanted to attend Radcliffe in order to gain the best possible preparation for

a teaching career, her mother urged her to enter teaching immediately. As a compromise, Hawkins entered the Salem Normal School (later Salem State College) in 1900. Having spotted Palmer's name in the school catalog, Hawkins wrote to her in search of advice; her inquiry gained her a letter of recommendation and an offer of financial assistance from Palmer.

A second chance encounter at the beginning of Hawkins's second year at Salem determined the course of her life. After meeting a representative of the American Missionary Association on a train between Salem and Cambridge, she decided to accept an offer to return to her native state and operate a school for the association. Leaving Salem before graduating (she later received credit for her work in the South and was awarded a diploma), she traveled south by train and arrived in McLeansville, North Carolina. After walking four miles to the community of Sedalia, she boarded with a local minister and on 12 October 1901 welcomed fifteen children to the poorly maintained one-room shack that was the Bethany Institute.

Although Hawkins was accepted by the community and encouraged by her accomplishments during the five-month school term, her future in Sedalia looked bleak when the association moved to close all its smaller schools at the end of the school year. Undaunted and determined to complete her work in the community, Hawkins rejected an offer from the association to teach elsewhere and returned north with the goal of raising sufficient funds to open her own school.

Upon returning to Cambridge, she approached Palmer for assistance, only to find her benefactress in poor health and bereft of her fortune. Palmer did, however, provide her with the names of several possible financial contributors. After soliciting funds from these people, Hawkins traveled to the resort community of Gloucester, Massachusetts, where she gave dramatic recitations and musical performances to raise money. She returned to Sedalia with less than four hundred dollars and, with that money and a donation of fifteen acres of land and an old blacksmith shop, she opened the school on 10 October 1902.

The school, which was named the Palmer Memorial Institute the following summer in honor of her recently deceased mentor, soon became a success story. Inspired by and patterned after BOOKER T. WASHINGTON's Tuskegee Institute, Palmer in its early years emphasized basic instruction and manual training. Students were responsible for daily chores and farm work as well as academics. The school filled a dire need in a state in which educational opportunities for African Americans were few. (No teacher-training institutions existed until the 1930s, and there was no public schooling in the Sedalia area until 1937.) Fund-raising was a constant concern; fortunately, wealthy northerners, such as Charles W. Eliot (who also served as the president of the first board of trustees), Seth Low, and Galen S. Stone, were generous in their support. The American Missionary Association added its resources in 1924, and Hawkins's own fund-raising efforts resulted in a permanent endowment of $250,000.

Despite her many commitments, Hawkins did not neglect her own intellectual development. She took summer and regular courses at Simmons College, Temple University, and Harvard University. It was at the latter that she met Edward S. Brown, whom she married in June 1911. Although he initially returned with Hawkins to Sedalia and taught at Palmer, he left after five years to teach at a similar school in South Carolina, and the marriage ended in divorce. Charlotte Hawkins Brown, though childless, raised several nieces and nephews at her on-campus home, the Canary Cottage. One of her nieces, Maria Hawkins Ellington, became a singer and later married NAT KING COLE.

The Palmer Institute eventually grew to three hundred acres in size and shifted its academic emphasis; in its latter years it became a preparatory school with a focus on high school—and junior college–level instruction. While Brown's students remained central in her life, she also engaged in professional activities and social activism. She helped found the North Carolina State Federation of Negro Women's Clubs in 1909 and also served as its president (1915–1936). While she was president, the federation purchased and maintained the Efland Home for Wayward Girls in Orange County, North Carolina; it was the only institution of its type for African American women in the state.

Charlotte Hawkins Brown's interest in interracial harmony led to her work in founding the Commission on Interracial Cooperation in 1919. That same year she published *Mammy: An Appeal to the Heart of the South*, a fictional indictment of the treatment of African Americans during slavery. Fully supportive of civil rights, Brown chafed under the restrictive racial atmosphere of her day and frequently challenged established Jim Crow standards. She refused to ride in segregated elevators and was sometimes ejected from "whites only" Pullman berths. Nonviolent in outlook, she occasionally resorted to lawsuits in order to challenge the discriminatory practices that she encountered during her travels. Despite her outspoken nature, Brown was a firm believer in the social graces. She constantly sought to inculcate manners as well as education into her students and published *The Correct Thing to Do, to Say, and to Wear* in 1941 as a guidebook in this area.

Brown remained busy throughout her life. She was named in 1940 to the North Carolina Council of Defense—one of the first African Americans so nominated—and also served as a member of the Executive Committee of the Home Nursing Council of the American Red Cross during World War II. Although she retired as president of Palmer in October 1952, she retained the post of director of finance until 1955. She died in Greensboro, North Carolina, after a lingering illness.

Charlotte Hawkins Brown is remembered for her pioneering efforts at Palmer Memorial Institute. Given early advantages of education and upbringing, she returned to her native state to provide educational opportunities for her fellow African Americans at a time when those opportunities were not readily available. She succeeded against often overwhelming odds in creating a preparatory school that provided hundreds of students with opportunities for a better life. Although Palmer Institute closed because of financial problems in 1971, its graduates are Brown's greatest legacy.

FURTHER READING

The papers of Charlotte Eugenia Hawkins Brown are held at the Schlesinger Library of Women in America at Radcliffe College, Cambridge, Massachusetts. Additional material on Brown and on Palmer Institute is available at the Charlotte Hawkins Brown Museum and Historic Site in Sedalia in the W. C. Jackson Library at the University of North Carolina at Greensboro and in the North Carolina Historical Room at the Greensboro Public Library.

Marteena, Constance Hill. *The Lengthening Shadow of a Woman: A Biography of Charlotte Hawkins Brown* (1977).

Wadelington, Charles W., and Richard F. Knapp. *Charlotte Hawkins Brown and Palmer Institute: What One Young African American Woman Could Do* (1999).

Obituary: *New York Times*, 12 Jan. 1961.
—EDWARD L. LACH JR.

 BROWN, H. RAP (4 Oct. 1943–), militant political activist and religious leader, was born Hubert Geroid Brown in Baton Rouge, Louisiana, the youngest child and second son of Eddie C. Brown, a laborer for Esso Standard Oil, and Thelma Warren, a teacher. According to his own account, Brown was a rebel from the earliest days against the color biases of his community as well as the authoritarianism and Eurocentric curricula of the schools in Baton Rouge. He identified with youth street culture and its heroes, whose verbal and physical jousting he extolled in his 1970 memoir *Die Nigger Die!* His facility at signifying or "playing the dozens" earned Brown the "Rap" sobriquet that he was to carry throughout the first phase of his public career.

Brown attended Southern University in Baton Rouge from 1961 to 1963 but dropped out to pursue his growing interest in the civil rights movement. Following his brother Ed, whose social activism was also lifelong, he moved to Washington, D.C., and became active in the Nonviolent Action Group (NAG), an affiliate of the Student Nonviolent Coordinating Committee (SNCC), composed largely of Howard University students. Although Brown never enrolled at Howard, he participated increasingly in the group's meetings and demonstrations and became deeply involved in SNCC activities. He worked with the Mississippi Summer Project and in 1966 was appointed director of the Greene County Project in Alabama, part of the group's campaign to organize black voters and elect black candidates.

Brown was elected chairman of SNCC in 1967, succeeding STOKELY CARMICHAEL at a time when the organization's community-organizing programs were on the wane and as the mainstream media had begun to denounce SNCC's turn to Black Power. Brown's incendiary rhetoric—"They're scared of me with this .45, wait till I get my atomic bomb!" (from the film *King: From Montgomery to Memphis,* 1970)—alienated many of SNCC's former liberal allies, but his denunciations of government racism and corruption struck a chord with disillusioned young African Americans. So, too, did Brown's approving remarks about the July 1967 Detroit riots, in which he urged blacks to stop "trying to love that honky to death ... shoot him to death, brother. Cause that's what he's out to do to you" (Sitkoff, *Struggle for Black Equality,* 217).

Many commentators, especially whites, understood the "burn, baby, burn" refrain of one of Brown's speeches as an unqualified call to violence. However, his political philosophy was less nihilistic than that phrase might suggest. In fact, Brown stated in that speech in Cambridge, Maryland, that "if America don't come around, we going to burn it down, brother. We going to burn it down, brother, if we don't get our share of it." America, then, could prevent violence by radically redistributing wealth and resources. Yet if violence were to come, Brown reminded his audience—and the journalists and politicians who denounced him for his militancy—that, "violence is as American as cherry pie."

Brown's tenure as SNCC chairman was hampered by numerous arrests and indictments on a variety of charges. His effectiveness was severely undermined by constant litigation. The most consequential of these legal troubles arose out of an uprising in Cambridge, Maryland, where authorities charged him with incitement following his speech there in July 1967. The federal government also charged Brown with unlawful interstate flight to avoid prosecution, violation of the National Firearms Act, arson, and violation of the terms of his bond. Although many of these charges would ultimately be dropped, Brown spent much of his twelve-month tenure as SNCC chairman behind bars. Brown was also appointed the Black Panther Party's minister of justice in 1968, though, with his own legal troubles and SNCC duties, this was largely a titular office. Brown went underground in 1970 rather than stand trial for the incitement to riot charges, and little is known of his activities at that time. He resurfaced in October 1971, when he was captured along with three others in the aftermath of an armed holdup of a New York City nightclub. Although it was not part of the legal defense, supporters claimed that this robbery was directed at drug dealers, whose illegal and immoral profits from exploiting the black community were to be used for the movement. If true, such actions were in line with those of the Black Liberation Army, whose members engaged in similar activities, often with equally unsuccessful results. In any case, Brown, who converted to Islam while imprisoned in the Tombs and changed his name to Jamil Abdullah al-Amin, was convicted of armed robbery and assault with a deadly weapon and sentenced to five to fifteen years in prison. He was paroled in 1976 and moved south, where he lived quietly as the owner of a small neighborhood store in Atlanta's West End. Al-Amin eventually became the imam of a small Muslim community in Atlanta, and in 1993 he published a book of sermons entitled *Revolution by the Book: The Rap Is Live.* His community earned a reputation as a positive force in lowering the incidence of street crime in the neighborhood. However, the group, and al-Amin in particular, seemed to be targets of numerous investigations by police agencies over the years. (During his later murder trial, Atlanta police would accuse them in the press of involvement in a dozen unsolved murders in the neighborhood.) Perhaps the most bizarre episode was a 1995 charge of attempted murder, in which the police alleged that al-Amin shot at a man walking down the street for no apparent reason. This well-publicized case was later dropped when the supposed victim denied that al-Amin was his attacker and later joined the *masjid,* or mosque. Federal authorities also tried to tie members of the *masjid* to the 1993 World Trade Center bombing in New York City, with much press attention. Eventually two *masjid* members were convicted of gunrunning.

On 16 March 2000, two Atlanta police officers, who stated that they were seeking to arrest al-Amin on charges of driving a stolen car and impersonating a police officer, approached his house at ten thirty at night. Both were shot; one was killed. The survivor claimed to have shot his assailant, and a blood trail seemed to confirm his story. Al-Amin was the prime suspect. He fled to Alabama, where he was captured several days later, uninjured and proclaiming his innocence. There were sensational headlines across the country about the bloodthirsty former Black Panther cop killer, while an international campaign supporting al-Amin's right to a fair trial was mounted. Nonetheless, an all-black Fulton County jury found him guilty of murder in March 2002 and sentenced him to life without parole.

Al-Amin's story is unsettling, bizarre, and tragic. He is painted by opponents of social change as a violent murderer with a history of involvement in active violence. His supporters cite a legacy of FBI repression of black activists leading to his ultimate fate as a prisoner for life. Yet al-Amin's SNCC activities, as well as his later leadership of a religious community, clearly display a commitment to humanistic concerns at odds with his status as a convicted murderer.

FURTHER READING

Al-Amin, Jamil Abdullah. *Die Nigger Die!: A Political Autobiography* (1970, 2nd ed. 2002).

Carson, Clayborne. *In Struggle: SNCC and the Black Awakening of the 1960s* (1981).
—W. S. TKWEME

 BROWN, HALLIE QUINN (10 Mar. 1845?– 16 Sept. 1949), elocutionist, educator, women's and civil rights leader, and writer, was born in Pittsburgh, Pennsylvania, the daughter of Thomas Arthur Brown, a riverboat steward

Hallie Q. Brown, elocutionist and educator. Duke University

and express agent, and Frances Jane Scroggins, an educated woman who served as an unofficial adviser to the students of Wilberforce University. Thomas Brown was born into slavery in Frederick County, Maryland, the son of a Scottish woman plantation owner and her black overseer. Brown purchased his freedom and that of his sister, brother, and father. By the time of the Civil War, he had amassed a sizable amount of real estate. Hallie's mother, Frances, was also born a slave, the child of her white owner. She was eventually freed by her white grandfather, a former officer in the American Revolution.

Both of Hallie's parents became active in the Underground Railroad. Around 1864, the Browns and their six children moved to Chatham, Ontario, where Thomas worked as a farmer and Hallie began to show a talent for public speaking and performance. The Browns returned to the United States around 1870, settling in Wilberforce, Ohio, where Hallie and her youngest brother enrolled in Wilberforce University, an African Methodist Episcopal (AME) liberal arts school and the first four-year college owned and operated by African Americans in the United States.

Wilberforce was at that time under the direction of the AME bishop DANIEL ALEXANDER PAYNE, America's first black college president and a Brown family friend.

Brown graduated with a BS from Wilberforce University in 1873. (The university later gave Brown two honorary degrees, an MS in 1890 and a doctorate in Law in 1936.) Shortly after graduation Brown moved to the South, beginning what would become a lifelong commitment to education and to the advancement of disenfranchised women and African Americans. For more than a decade, in plantations and public schools from Yazoo, Mississippi, to Columbia, South Carolina, Brown taught literacy skills to black children and adults denied education during slavery.

Attracted to its combination of education with entertainment, Brown had joined the Lyceum movement in 1874. The Lyceum, a nineteenth-century movement that fostered adult education in the arts, sciences, history, and public affairs through traveling programs of lectures and concerts, brought Brown's eloquent lectures to a wide audience in the South and Midwest. By the early 1880s Brown was touring with the Lyceum full time. She continued her elocution training at the Chautauqua Lecture School from which, in 1886, she graduated at the top of her class, having completed several summer sessions.

As Brown's eminence and reputation grew, so did her job prospects. From 1885 to 1887 she served as dean of Allen University in Columbia, South Carolina, the first black college in South Carolina, founded in 1870. In 1887 Brown returned to Ohio, where for the next five years she taught in the Dayton public schools and at a night school she founded for migrant African American adults recently relocated from the South. The Tuskegee Normal and Industrial Institute brought Brown to Alabama from 1892 to 1893 to serve as lady principal, or dean of women, under the direction of BOOKER T. WASHINGTON.

Brown's lasting dedication to Wilberforce University began in 1893, when she was hired by her alma mater as professor of elocution. Brown would remain a part of the Wilberforce community, as an English and elocution teacher, trustee, and fund-raiser, until her death. Shortly after her appointment, however, Brown

suspended her classroom teaching duties in favor of a series of extensive lecture tours of Europe.

Brown left for Europe in 1894 and remained on tour for much of the next five years. She quickly became an internationally lauded lecturer and performer, speaking on the themes of African American culture, temperance, and women's suffrage. Enamored audiences flocked to experience Brown's lectures on topics like "Negro Folklore and Folksong" and her recitations of the works of PAUL LAURENCE DUNBAR and other African American authors. Brown was a featured speaker in London at the Third Biennial Convention of the World's Woman's Christian Temperance Union in 1895 and a representative to the International Congress of Women held in London in 1899. Having been introduced to the royal family via letter by FREDERICK DOUGLASS in 1894, Brown performed for Queen Victoria on several occasions, even joining the monarch for tea at Windsor Castle and as a guest during the Jubilee Celebration in 1899. Brown was made a member of the exclusive Royal Geographical Society in Edinburgh, and in 1895 she helped form the first British Chautauqua, a Lyceum-style touring educational program, in North Wales.

Brown returned to teaching full time at Wilberforce around the turn of the century but visited Europe once again in 1910 as a representative to the Woman's Missionary Society of the AME Conference held in Edinburgh. For Brown, this trip marked the culmination of over ten years of work with the AME Church and validated her role in the church outside of her association with Wilberforce University. In 1900 Brown had campaigned for the job of AME secretary of education. Although she failed to get the appointment, she remained committed to expanding the role of women in the church. Brown remained in Britain for seven months, raising enough money for Wilberforce to build a new dormitory. Still popular as a lecturer, Brown gave a command performance for King George and Queen Mary and was a dinner guest of the Princess of Wales.

While Brown is remembered for her achievements as an elocutionist, it is her vision of a nationally organized African American women's community that has secured her place in history. Brown was a pioneering force in the formation of the black women's club movement, the development of which saw the establishment of schools, scholarships, museums, elder-care facilities, and political institutions.

Concerned that the achievements of African Americans would be omitted from the exhibitions at the 1893 World's Fair and Columbian Exposition in Chicago, Brown petitioned for a seat on the Board of Lady Managers, the planning committee presiding over the U.S. exhibits. "For two hundred and fifty years the Negro woman of America was bought and sold as chattel," Brown argued. "Twenty-five years of progress find the Afro-American woman advanced beyond the most sanguine expectations. Her development from the darkest slavery and grossest ignorance into light and liberty is one of the marvels of the age.... What more is needed? Time and equal chance in the race of life" (*The World's Congress of Representative Women*, May Wright Sewall, ed., 1894). The Board denied Brown's request, explaining that only individuals representing organizations could participate. Provoked by her exclusion and motivated to set up a national organization devoted to and run by black women, Brown cofounded the Colored Women's League of Washington, D.C. Two years later Brown's organization merged with JOSEPHINE ST. PIERRE RUFFIN's Boston Women's Era Club, becoming the National Federation of Afro-American Women, which was later renamed the National Association of Colored Women (NACW).

Brown served as national president of the NACW from 1920 to 1924 and as honorary president until her death. During her tenure at the NACW, Brown took a leadership role in two projects: the creation and maintenance of a memorial at the former home of Frederick Douglass in Washington, D.C., and the establishment of the Hallie Q. Brown Scholarship Loan Fund for the education of black women, a national program open to college students and postgraduate women, that allots generous loans to be repaid with no interest.

In addition to her work with the NACW, Brown played major roles in several other African American and women's organizations. She served as president of the Ohio State Federation of Colored Women's Clubs from 1905 to 1912 and worked as an organizer for the Women's Christian Temperance Union. Brown lent her support and oratorical skill to a variety of issues. In 1922 she lobbied President Warren Harding and several key U.S. senators in support of a federal antilynching law and worked with the NAACP in its efforts to defeat a national bill outlawing interracial marriages. On another occasion, in an incident reported in the *New York Times*, Brown arrived in Washington, D.C., for the 1925 All-American Musical Festival of the International Council of Women and found the auditorium segregated. In a biting speech condemning the council's racist policy, Brown threatened a boycott by the festival's black performers if segregation continued. When her demands were not met, many of the audience members joined the two hundred black performers in a boycott of the program.

Brown was also engaged in mainstream political organizations. An ardent Republican, she spoke in support of local, state, and national candidates in Ohio, Pennsylvania, Illinois, and Missouri. Brown's Republican activities increased in the 1920s and 1930s, during which time she labored on behalf of the National League of Women Voters and as vice president of the Ohio Council of Republican Women. In 1924 Brown emerged on the national stage, addressing the Republican National Convention in Cleveland. Speaking in support of Warren Harding's nomination, Brown took the opportunity to discuss issues of significance to African Americans. After the convention, Brown directed the Colored Women's Activities at the Republican national campaign headquarters in Chicago and the new National League of Republican Colored Women, which adopted the slogan "We are in politics to stay and we shall be a stay in politics."

Concurrent with her teaching, lecturing, and organizing, Brown worked as a writer, essayist, and anthologist. She published several collections of speeches and prose, including *Bits and Odds: A Choice Selection of Recitations* (1880), *Elocution and Physical Culture* (1910), *First Lessons in Public Speaking* (1920), *The Beautiful: A True Story of Slavery* (1924), *Our Women: Past, Present and Future* (1925), and *Tales My Father Told*

(1925). She often wrote of the power and complexity of black America's relationship to language, frequently using black vernacular speech in her writing, and of the importance of African American heritage, family history, and culture. In 1926, when Brown was in her seventies, she published her best-known book, *Homespun Heroines and Other Women of Distinction*, a collection of sixty biographies of black women born in North America between 1740 and 1900.

"Miss Hallie," as Brown was known at Wilberforce, remained active until her death in 1949, near age one hundred. Her legacy continues through the scholarship fund that bears her name; the good works of the Hallie Quinn Brown Community House in St. Paul, Minnesota; and the Hallie Q. Brown Memorial Library at Wilberforce University, a facility that includes a collection of books by and about African Americans.

FURTHER READING
Brown's unpublished papers are held at the Hallie Q. Brown Memorial Library at Wilberforce University in Wilberforce, Ohio.

Davis, Elizabeth Lindsay, ed. *Lifting as They Climb* (1933, 1996).
Majors, M. A. *Noted Negro Women: Their Triumphs and Activities* (1893).
—LISA E. RIVO

BROWN, HENRY BOX
(1815?–?), escaped slave, was born on a plantation in Louisa County, Virginia, to unknown parents. As a youth, Brown lived with his parents, four sisters, and three brothers until the family was separated and his master hired him out at age fifteen to work in a tobacco factory in Richmond, Virginia. Brown's autobiography illuminates the vicissitudes of slave life but does not recount any further major events in his own life other than his marriage around 1836 to Nancy, the slave of a bank clerk, with whom he had three children. But in August 1848 Brown's master reneged on an earlier promise and sold his wife and children away from him. Betrayed by his master and separated forever from his beloved family, the formerly mild-mannered Brown resolved to liberate himself from "the bloody dealers in the bodies and souls of men."

Depicted in a lithograph from 1850, Philadelphia abolitionists release Henry "Box" Brown from the crate in which he had himself shipped from slavery in Virginia to freedom. Library of Congress

In response to Brown's prayerful search for a way to freedom, "an idea," he reported, "suddenly flashed across my mind." Brown's revelation was that he have himself nailed into a wooden box and "conveyed as dry goods" via the Adams Express Company from slavery in Richmond to freedom in Philadelphia (Brown, 57–58). This plan was carried out with the assistance of two friends, a white abolitionist, Dr. Samuel A. Smith, and James Caesar Anthony Smith, a free black. A wooden box, complete with baize lining, air holes, a container of water, and hickory straps, was constructed by a carpenter, who measured it precisely to hold Brown's five-feet, eight-inch, two-hundred-pound body. The crate was addressed to Dr. Smith's friend, William Johnson, an abolitionist on Arch Street in Philadelphia and marked "this side up with care." On 29 March 1849, at four o'clock in the morning, the box was loaded on a wagon and delivered to the depot, and Brown began his historic, twenty-seven-hour, 350-mile odyssey, some of it upside down and all of it in danger.

The box with its human content eventually found its way to the Anti-Slavery Committee's office on North Fifth Street in Philadelphia. A small, nervous group, including WILLIAM STILL, the African American conductor of Philadelphia's Underground Railroad, pried open the lid to reveal, in "my resurrection from the grave of slavery," the disheveled and battered Henry Brown, who arose and promptly fainted (Brown, 62). Revived by a glass of water, he proceeded to sing Psalm 40, which includes the line "Be pleased, O Lord, to deliver me" (Psalms 40:13 [AV]). Discovering a flair for the dramatic, he immediately took the name "Box" to celebrate his new identity as well as his escape.

Brown went on the antislavery public-speaking circuit in the Northeast. Not only did he have a powerful story to tell, he also found other ways to exploit the lecture platform. Brown seems to have possessed a natural stage presence. He sang songs, including Psalm 40, and he cleverly adapted to his own purposes a popular song of the day, Stephen Foster's 1848 ballad "Uncle Ned." The original text begins:

Dere was an old Nigga, dey called him
    Uncle Ned—
He's dead long ago, long ago!
He had no wool on de top ob his head—
De place where de wool ought to grow.

Chorus:
Den lay down de shubble and de hoe,
Hang up de fiddle and de bow;

No more hard work for poor old Ned—
He is gone whar de good Niggas go.

Brown's version begins:

Here you see a man by the name of
    Henry Brown,
Ran away from the South to the North,
Which he would not have done but they
    stole all his rights,
But they'll never do the like again.

Chorus:
Brown laid down the shovel and the hoe,
Down in the box he did go;
No more slave work for Henry Box Brown,
In the box by *Express* he did go.

Not only is Brown's revision witty and entertaining, it also is a window into his mind. He used a song everyone knew, a song with racist lyrics, stereotypical images, and a condescending attitude, all set in a sentimentalized South. Brown subverted the norms and values of a white supremacist society, turning Uncle Ned upside down, as it were, by replacing negative representations with positive ones.

Another way the imaginative and entrepreneurial Brown broadened the appeal and effect of his performance was through the addition of a large didactic panorama, "The Mirror of Liberty," which consisted of thousands of feet of canvas, divided into scores of panels painted with scenes depicting the history of slavery. Josiah Wolcott, a white Massachusetts artist, designed and painted it, perhaps with the assistance of other artists. Brown recruited Benjamin F. Roberts, an African American activist from Boston, to write an accompanying lecture, "The Condition of the Colored People in the United States." To dramatize its message, the panorama showed alternating scenes, one a traditional and romanticized American view and the next an image of the cruelty of slavery—a whipping post, for instance—in the same place. Just as Brown's version of "Uncle Ned" turned a popular ballad into a protest song, so the "Mirror of Liberty" transformed idealized American myths into the realities of a slave society.

It is not known whether Box Brown solicited an author to tell his story or whether he was approached by abolitionists; in either event, Brown submitted his life to Charles Stearns for presentation to the world. A nephew of Brook Farm's Utopian founder, George Ripley, Stearns was a militant antislavery activist. Though earlier a pacifist, he had participated so ardently in the violent struggle between pro-slavery and anti-slavery factions in Kansas during the late 1850s known as "Bleeding Kansas" that he lost his pacifism. In Boston in 1849 Stearns published his *Narrative of Henry Box Brown who Escaped from Slavery Enclosed in a Box 3 Feet Long and 2 Wide Written from a Statement of Facts Made by Himself. With Remarks upon the Remedy for Slavery. By Charles Stearns.* The book's problem was Stearns's "Remarks." As well as appearing in a separate essay, they permeated the entire text with Stearns's dogmatic ideology and arrogant and opinionated style.

Brown's personal response was to edit or, more likely, to have the book heavily edited at the first opportunity. Most of Stearns's overblown rhetoric was simply excised. With the passage of a stronger fugitive slave law in 1850, the North was legally obliged to participate in the recapture and return of runaways. Skirting the threat of arrest in Providence, Rhode Island, Brown immediately left for England. A second edition of his autobiography, with a Manchester 1851 imprint, appeared with a new title: *Narrative of the Life of Henry Box Brown Written by Himself.* Brown was forced to leave the United States, even the free North, before he could find his own voice.

In England, Brown repeated his American successes, and, if some reports are to be believed, his life and lifestyle continued to change, taking him even further away from the simple and pious person he had been in Richmond. A critic complained from England that Brown was indulging in tobacco, strong drink, gambling, and fancy clothes and that "he have got it into his head to get a wife or something *worst*" (Brown, xxix). Brown then disappeared from view, with hints that he married an English woman and moved to Wales. Brown began his life in anonymity and, at least so far as we now know, ended it in the same way. For a short interval, however, he was celebrated as the brave and creative man who mailed himself to freedom.

FURTHER READING

Brown, Henry Box. *Narrative of the Life of Henry Box Brown Written by Himself* (1851, reprinted 2002 with an Introduction by Richard Newman).
—RICHARD NEWMAN

BROWN, JAMES

(3 May 1933–), rhythm-and-blues singer, was born James Joe Brown Jr. in a country shack just outside Barnwell, South Carolina, to Joe Gardner and Susan Behlings. His father did various jobs, while nothing is known about his mother's occupation. Brown was raised in extreme poverty, and his parents separated when he was four; two years later he went to live with his great-aunt, Minnie Walker, in Augusta, Georgia.

Brown's father often sang blues songs in the evening, and when Brown was four, his father gave him a ten-cent harmonica. His earliest years were spent tap dancing in the street for spare change. He claims to this day that his formidable sense of rhythm stems from such humble beginnings. A self-taught musician, Brown began to play organ at the age of eight and later acquired a rudimentary knowledge of bass, guitar, saxophone, and trumpet. At eleven Brown won his first talent contest as a singer, and a year later he formed a group he called the Cremona Trio. In those same years Brown was involved in petty crime, shoplifting and stealing car batteries and hubcaps to obtain money for school clothes and food. In 1948, at the age of fifteen, he was caught stealing cars for the second time and was sentenced to eight to sixteen years in the Georgia Juvenile Training Institute in Rome, Georgia, thus ending his formal schooling at the seventh grade. Nicknamed Music Box, Brown formed a gospel quartet in prison.

In 1952, Brown was paroled and went to live in Toccoa, Georgia. There he joined a group formed by Bobby Byrd, whom Brown had met during a baseball game while he was still in prison. Byrd's group originally sang gospel and was known as the Gospel Starlighters. Just before being joined by Brown, they had switched to singing rhythm and blues and consequently had changed their name to the Avons. They would soon be known as the Flames and eventually as James Brown and the Famous Flames. As word of the group's incredibly intense live shows spread throughout the South, they were summoned to Macon, Georgia, by LITTLE RICHARD's manager, Clint Bradley, after Richard became a national star in 1955.

A year later Ralph Bass signed Brown and the Famous Flames to

James Brown, who became "The Godfather of Soul," performing with the Famous Flames in 1964. Library of Congress

Cincinnati-based King Records, their releases appearing on the subsidiary Federal label. Legend has it that upon hearing the demo recording of "Please Please Please," King's owner, Syd Nathan, fired Bass. Nathan could not believe that anyone would want to buy a record that consisted of six straight eight-bar verses, each of which was made up solely of one bar after one bar call-and-response patterns between Brown and the Flames. What Nathan did not understand, Brown knew from playing the song night after night in concert. Audiences would go crazy over the heightened emotion Brown conveyed, using numerous gospel-derived vocal devices. It took several months, but eventually "Please Please Please" reached the number-six position on *Billboard*'s R&B charts. Brown's debut effort and later singles, such as 1958's "Try Me" and 1960's "Think," were, along with early efforts by RAY CHARLES and Sam Cooke, the first examples of what would become known as soul music.

In 1962 Brown suggested that he wanted to record a live album at the Apollo Theater in New York. Long billed as "The Hardest Working Man in Show Business," Brown was positive that a recorded version of his legendary show would sell in significant numbers. When Nathan refused to finance the recording, Brown paid for it himself. Upon its release in 1963, *Live at the Apollo* climbed all the way to number two on *Billboard*'s LP charts. Such success was pretty well unprecedented for black artists and totally unheard of for live albums.

As the 1960s unfolded and Brown enjoyed a string of successes, American society underwent momentous changes. The civil rights movement had successfully brought about legal desegregation, but as the end of the decade approached most African Americans still found themselves the last hired and first fired, being paid less money than white workers for the same labor, living in inferior housing and sending their children to substandard schools.

As this reality slowly made itself manifest, the mood of black America began to change. In 1966 during the JAMES MEREDITH march in Mississippi, STOKELY CARMICHAEL popularized the phrase "Black Power." A year earlier

the predominantly black neighborhood of Watts in Los Angeles had burned in the first of the modern-day race rebellions. In 1967 Newark, New Jersey, and Detroit, Michigan, would also burn. This new militancy no longer asked for equality, nor did it seek to achieve such equality by adopting mainstream (i.e., "white middle class") standards of deportment. Rather, black Americans were encouraged to celebrate and embrace everything black and to assume and demand equality. Inspired by the belief that "black is beautiful," many African Americans began to explore their historical and psychological connections to their African motherland. While some blacks adopted African names and wore African garb, many more began to sport an "Afro" or "natural" haircut.

This re-Africanization of black culture was also reflected in popular music, most radically in the development of funk by James Brown. In the simplest terms, Brown, beginning in 1967 with "Cold Sweat," de-emphasized melody and harmony (for example, by having whole sections of a song with no chord changes and by delivering the lyrics in a voice closer to speaking than singing) while privileging rhythm (by employing more complex syncopated figures and using several different rhythmic patterns simultaneously, creating interlocking grooves). This reconstruction of Brown's music could be interpreted as de-emphasizing parameters favored by white American society while highlighting sub-Saharan African characteristics; this was, in effect, re-Africanizing the music, thus paralleling the re-Africanization of African American society at large at the time.

Brown could be a temperamental and demanding bandleader—his trombonist Fred Wesley once noted that "James was bossy and paranoid" (quoted in Ward, 392). But when it came to performance, Brown was often able to submerge his ego in pursuit of a more democratic, communal sound. Notions of community and solidarity are connoted in "Cold Sweat" in a number of ways. Throughout the performance Brown utters any number of vocables judiciously placed within the rhythmic matrix. In doing so, he projects himself as part of the band rather than as a separate, somehow special, more important front man.

Similarly, he can be heard during the performance calling out such things as "Maceo, Maceo," "Give the drummer some," "Bernard, come on and help him out; play that thing." In this way, Brown conveys a sense of community. He explicitly *names* those who are contributing, recognizing their intrinsic value as individuals and the equality implicit in *collectively* unleashing the spiritual magic of the performance. "Cold Sweat" ends after seven and a half minutes with an extraordinary section in which Brown seems to be shredding his larynx while singing, "I can't, I can't, I can't, I can't stop, I can't stop, I can't stop singing." The effect is cathartic. Brown thus demonstrates an exceptional level of commitment that is not lost on his audience. It is as if he has no choice in the matter.

Within a year Brown had connected funk lyrically to the newly emergent black consciousness, specifically with the song "Say It Loud, I'm Black and I'm Proud." Around that time he made clear that he was "totally committed to black power, the kind that is achieved not through the muzzle of a rifle but through education and economic leverage" (quoted in Ward, 392). Brown believed in the bootstraps philosophy of BOOKER T. WASHINGTON, and like the 1960s civil rights activists JAMES FORMAN and FLOYD MCKISSICK, in 1972 he supported Richard Nixon, whose presidential platform advocated "black capitalism," in the form of federal loans to small black businesses.

Significantly, "Black and Proud" would be Brown's last Top Ten pop hit until 1985's "Living in America." Conversely, this was the beginning of his greatest success on the R&B charts. Between 1968 and 1974 Brown had forty-one R&B hits, thirty-two of which went to the Top Ten. This is extraordinary testimony to the meaning he held for the black community in the United States at the time. It would appear that as Brown's music became understood as more African, it was encoded or at least decoded by blacks and whites as having a value and aesthetic system that was largely outside the experience of most white Americans. Consequently, most white Americans found little they could relate to while, in direct contrast, black Americans embraced funk as one of the most meaningful expressive forms of the time. Brown's music also found a huge audience in Africa in the late 1960s and early 1970s, influencing the Nigerian star Fela Kuti, among other exponents of Afrobeat.

At the same time that Brown was personally dominating the R&B charts in the United States, he built up a stable of artists in his revue whom he recorded for King, Polydor, and his own People label. Among the most successful of these side projects were Vicki Anderson, Lyn Collins, Bobby Byrd, and his backing group, the JB's. Brown seemed to be an endless source of funky grooves, writing hits for himself and his stable of artists while developing legendary bands that included such luminaries as Bootsy Collins, Fred Wesley, Maceo Parker, Pee Wee Ellis, and the drummers Melvin Parker, Jabo Starks, and Clyde Stubblefield.

In the 1980s Brown and funk music fell out of fashion, only to be resurrected and revered by decade's end, owing to the inordinate number of times his earlier hits were sampled by many prominent rap artists. Despite a troubled personal life, Brown endured. He was married three times and rumors of spousal abuse were frequent. So too were his run-ins with the law, for drugs or gun possession, tax evasion, and assault. In one incident, in September 1988, police pursued Brown through South Carolina and Georgia and arrested him on a count of arrest and battery with intent to kill and a series of traffic offences. Sentenced to six years in prison, Brown was released on probation in February 1991. In 1998 Brown was convicted of another drug-related offense and arrested for domestic violence in 2004.

Brown has continued to tour, record, and earn the numerous accolades that might be expected of an elder statesman. He received the Grammy Lifetime Achievement Award in 1992 and was inducted into the Rock and Roll Hall of Fame in 1996. In 2003 he received a Kennedy Center Honor for his achievements and influence in popular music. He was even, in March 1997, recognized by the State Legislature of Georgia, a body not hitherto known for its funkiness. A joint House and Senate resolution declared him "the

minister of the new super heavy funk," and credited James Brown with bringing "a spark of energy and excitement to an otherwise listless U.S. music scene."

FURTHER READING

Brown, James, and Bruce Tucker. *James Brown: The Godfather of Soul* (1986).
Brown, Geoff. *James Brown: A Biography* (1996).
Rose, Cynthia. *Living in America: The Soul Saga of James Brown* (1990).

—ROB BOWMAN

BROWN, JESSE LEROY (13 Oct. 1926–4 Dec. 1950), the first black U.S. Navy pilot, was born in Hattiesburg, Mississippi, the son of John Brown, a sharecropper, and Julia Lindsey, a schoolteacher. The family worked from sunup to sundown and lived in a typical, unpainted, pine-board house with one story and a tin roof. Behind the house were a well, an outhouse, chicken and hog pens, and a vegetable garden. John Brown was a deacon in the Baptist church, where the family worshiped each Sunday.

Young Jesse fell in love with flying at age six, when his father took him to an air show, and he marveled at the white wing walkers, parachute jumpers, and acrobatic tricks performed by the pilots of the biwinged aircraft. His father didn't have the two dollars to let his son ride in a cockpit that day, but by the time he was seven Jesse was reading *Popular Aviation* magazine by kerosene lamp late into the night. Jesse was also fascinated by movies of World War I dogfights between American and German planes and decided that he wanted to be a fighter pilot. Whenever a plane from the dirt strip at nearby Palmer's Crossing flew overhead, the youngster would wave at it with his straw hat and yell, "That's where I'm going to be someday."

On Saturday afternoons Jesse could usually be found hiding near the dusty forty-foot-wide, five-hundred-yard runway at Palmer's Crossing. Though he was repeatedly chased away by Corley Yates, the field manager and mechanic, nothing could stop Jesse from watching the biplanes rush down the runway. This war between Corley Yates and Jesse Brown went on for years.

Jesse Leroy Brown in the cockpit of a Corsair fighter. Naval Historical Foundation

Brown's school in Lux, Mississippi, consisted of only one room with eight rows of benches. Students from first grade to eighth grade assembled each day, batting bugs in summer and shivering in winter. The powerful influence of their mother ensured that all five Brown boys were excellent students. In 1938, when Jesse was one bench from finishing Lux, he began to deliver the *Pittsburgh Courier*, a black newspaper that one day ran a long article about the black man's struggle to enter military aviation. Reading it, twelve-year-old Jesse was furious at General Hap Arnold, chief of the U.S. Army Air Corps, who said, "Negro pilots cannot be used in our present Air Corps since this would result in having Negro officers in command of white enlisted men." When the *Courier* editorialized that there was a white belief that black men didn't have "the brains or fortitude or aptitude to fly military planes," Jesse cut the article out, nailed it to the wall over his bed, and then wrote a letter to President Franklin Roosevelt asking why black pilots were excluded from the air corps.

Brown attended Eureka High School, making "A" grades, playing football and basketball, and starring in track. Graduating in 1944, he chose to enroll that September at Ohio State University, against the advice of his principal and friends, who wanted him to enroll in a black college in Mississippi. Brown wanted to test his abilities, however, and was prepared to withstand prejudice at the predominantly white university. He majored in engineering and joined the track team, but as always his great interest was flying. There was a navy V-5 program at the university, and Brown took the entrance exam after being told that no African American had ever entered Selective Flight Training. Three years later, having passed all tests, he prepared for entry into the Naval Air Training Command in Glenview, Illinois, by looking into a mirror and yelling at himself, "Nigger! Nigger! Nigger!" After two weeks of training, Brown made his solo flight in a dual cockpit "Yellow Peril" Stearman, a navy training biplane, executing three perfect landings.

Although his officer instructors often derided him, and though he almost flunked out of the arduous Pre-Flight School at Ottumwa, Iowa, because he couldn't swim, Brown persisted. Though Glenview had been tough, it was easy compared to Pre-Flight, where Brown confronted every possible physical and mental test, the final being in a Dilbert Dunker to simulate an open ocean crash. His preflight instruction then continued at the Pensacola, Florida, Naval Air Station, where he flew a single-wing SNJ trainer to prepare for carrier landings. As the only African American among six-hundred-odd white midshipmen, Brown felt enormous pressure and often faced outright hostility from his instructors. One vowed, "No nigger is going to sit his ass in the cockpit of a Navy fighter." Each day was a struggle, and twice he had to appear before a special board to save his existence at Pensacola because of aerial mistakes.

Brown got some relief from the strain and loneliness when he married nineteen-year-old Daisy Pearl Nix in October 1947, even though that was forbidden by training regulation. If the union were discovered, he would be headed back to Lux within twenty-four hours. He found a home for Daisy in Pensacola through the church. He could talk to her, and they could discreetly meet. Brown struggled on the ground and in the air but finally made his first carrier landing on the USS *Wright* in the Gulf of Mexico on 17 June 1948, flying an SNJ trainer. After five landings, the *Wright*'s loudspeaker rasped, "Midshipman Brown qualified." On 21 October, Brown, flying a Hellcat fighter, a super aircraft of its day, won his gold wings at Jacksonville Naval Air Station. The public information office put out a press release: *First Negro Naval Aviator*, along with a photo. *Life* magazine published his picture. But Daisy Brown, still hidden from the navy,

and in her fourth month of pregnancy, couldn't perform the traditional pinning on of his wings.

In mid-January 1949, less than a month after the birth of his daughter, Pamela, Brown left for Quonset Point, Rhode Island, for his first assignment as a fighter pilot with Squadron 32 on the USS *Leyte*. On 26 April he was sworn into the navy as an ensign, and he began flying a Bearcat three to five hours a day. Later that year he began flying a Corsair, the navy's "killer" aircraft of World War II. Since they no longer needed to hide their marriage, the Browns also rented a house in Quonset Point and entered the social life of the air station. It was the happiest time in Brown's life. In June 1950, however, North Korea invaded South Korea, and President Harry Truman decided to take America into the Korean War.

On 4 December 1950 the carriers *Leyte* and *Philippine Sea* were stationed off the northeast coast of North Korea. For three desperate days Brown and his fellow pilots had been ordered to provide maximum air support, day and night, to fifteen thousand U.S. Marines fighting their way along the bloody, body-strewn, ice-bound road to Hungnam, North Korea. More than one hundred thousand Chinese troops surrounded the marines. That morning Brown dressed quickly in long johns, coveralls, a sweater, a rubber antiexposure suit, and fleece-lined boots and gloves and proceeded to his Corsair. He headed for the infamous Chosin Reservoir and the bloody road where marines were dying around the clock. Arriving over land, Brown and his flying partners dropped to five hundred feet to search for targets. As Brown and his comrades passed overhead, Chinese troops lying on their backs unseen in the snow fired upward. When a bullet hit Brown's fuel line, his wingman, Thomas Rudner, flying close by, walked him through the safety procedures they had learned in flight school. Meanwhile, U.S. planes began circling the area, ready to use every single bit of firepower to keep the communists at bay. It did not matter to Brown's fellow pilots that his skin was black. He was simply a gallant shipmate and friend.

Brown crashed uphill, out of control. With his plane skidding over the frozen ground, only his harness kept him from

being a punching bag, as the huge engine and four-bladed propeller broke off and careened away, leaving a tangle of steel and wires in the cockpit. His fellow pilots kept circling, watching for a sign of life. Finally, Brown opened the canopy, which had jammed on impact, and waved, but he could not climb out. A piece of steel had jammed his knee in that narrow space, and escape was impossible.

Tom Rudner then made a decision against all combat regulations, one that could have earned him a court-martial for destroying a navy aircraft. He decided to risk his own life and crash land, hoping he could help before Brown's two-hundred-gallon gas tank exploded. Rudner put his Corsair down as close as possible to Brown's plane, knowing that the enemy troops on the rise might shoot both of them. Talking to Brown continually, Rudner packed snow into the area of the smoke and used his own radio to call in a helicopter. Rudner kept talking to Brown while the injured pilot drifted in and out of consciousness. At one point Brown said to Rudner, "Cut my leg off," but Rudner could not. Nor could Charlie Ward, the pilot of a Sikorsky rescue helicopter, because night had fallen, making it impossible for him to see.

A few minutes later, Brown told Rudner, "Tell Daisy how much I love her." He then took a shallow breath, and as his head slumped down on his chest, Rudner and Ward wept.

Aboard the *Leyte* there was shock and disbelief. The African American stewards on board ship had carefully made Brown's bunk each morning and made sure he got the best meals. They wept bitterly as a bugle played taps and marines fired volleys off the stern. Hudner persuaded Captain Sisson, his commanding officer, that Brown would not have approved a mission to recover his dead body if it meant risking the lives of others. Sisson therefore ordered two divisions to give Jesse Brown a "warrior's funeral." Within an hour seven Corsairs (six loaded with napalm), piloted by Brown's friends, took off for Somong-ni. Arriving there, one fighter dropped down to make a run over the two aircraft. The sun was out, and the sky was blue. Brown sat in his cockpit, snow dusting his hair. Then six aircraft loaded with napalm rose to ten thousand feet while the seventh continued to climb, almost straight up, and the radios connecting them heard, "Our Father who art in heaven, hallowed be Thy name." In roaring dives, the Corsairs released their napalm pods, and Brown vanished in sheets of fiery red.

FURTHER READING

Taylor, Theodore. *The Flight of Jesse Leroy Brown* (1998).

—THEODORE TAYLOR

 BROWN, JIM
(17 Feb. 1936–), athlete, actor, and activist, was born James Nathaniel Brown on St. Simons Island, Georgia, to Theresa and Swinton Brown, a one-time boxer, who abandoned Theresa and their son two weeks after his birth. A couple of years later Theresa departed for Long Island, New York, to take a domestic job, leaving Jim to be raised by his great-grandmother and grandmother, the latter an alcoholic. By 1944 Theresa had saved enough money to send for Jim, and they were reunited in Manhasset, Long Island, for the first time in six years. Despite the usual friction of being the new kid—he was once accused by his peers of fighting dirty—Brown eventually distinguished himself athletically. He gained the attention of a local policeman, who lent Brown keys to the high school gym so that the youth could organize Police Boys' Club games whenever he and his friends wanted to play.

At Manhasset High School, Jim became a starter on the football team at the age of fourteen; he also played basketball, track, and baseball. By the end of his senior year he had tallied thirteen varsity letters, earning All-State honors in all but baseball; he averaged thirty-eight points per game in basketball (including a high game score of fifty-five) and 14.9 yards per carry in football. A self-proclaimed "gang warlord" in high school, Brown managed to keep himself on the academic honor roll and graduated in 1953 with more than forty athletic scholarships from which to choose.

Brown decided instead upon Syracuse University in upstate New York. Syracuse had not offered him a

Jim Brown in his final season with the Cleveland Browns (1965).
© Bettmann/CORBIS

scholarship, but a family friend secured enough support from Manhasset businessmen to bankroll his freshman year, confident that he would quickly play his way into a scholarship. He did not accomplish this until his sophomore year, when a teammate's injury opened up a spot for him on the football team. It was a breakout year, as he also scored fifteen points per game in basketball, ran track, and played lacrosse for the first time. In track he competed in the decathlon, placing fifth nationally. Though this was good enough to qualify for the 1956 Olympics, Brown declined, because he felt it was dishonest to devote too much time to anything other than his scholarship sport, football. Altogether he would earn ten letters in three years across four sports; he was named All-American once in football and twice in lacrosse. In the latter sport, he became the first African American to play in the storied North-South game, though he only needed to play part of it to account for half of the North's output, scoring five goals and assisting on two, in a 14–10 victory.

Graduating with a degree in Physical Education, Brown planned to pursue coaching when his athletic career was over. In the meantime, he ignored repeated advances from major league baseball teams, as well as the Syracuse Nationals in basketball, and he declined a three-year, $150,000 deal offered by a Syracuse promoter to become a professional boxer. He finally decided on a $15,000 deal with the Cleveland Browns of the National Football League (NFL).

As a fullback in 1957 Brown led the league in rushing, totaling 942 yards and leading Cleveland to the Eastern Division Championship while picking up Rookie of the Year honors. The following year he increased his yardage per carry by 1.2 yards to 5.9, scored eighteen touchdowns, and was named Player of the Year. He never missed a game due to injury, and he became such a dominating presence in his sport that he headed a players' revolt against Cleveland's coach, Paul Brown, in 1962. Paul Brown was subsequently fired, and the team's new coach for

1963, Blanton Collier, better utilized his star by designing plays that granted Brown more running room along the line of scrimmage. Brown responded with his best season by collecting more than a mile in total yards (1,863 at 6.5 yards per carry) and scoring fifteen touchdowns; he performed similarly the next year, and Cleveland won the NFL Championship. In 1965, Brown's final season, he averaged more than five yards per carry for the third consecutive year, scored twenty-one touchdowns, and took home his second Most Valuable Player award. He played in the Pro Bowl every single year and led the league in rushing for eight of his nine seasons.

The following autumn, however, saw Brown in Europe, filming a lead role in *The Dirty Dozen* (1967), a big-budget Hollywood picture about American convicts who become highly trained World War II soldiers. He had already appeared two years earlier in *Rio Concho* (1964), and when the Cleveland Browns owner Art Modell threatened to cut him if he did not report to training camp immediately, Brown retired to devote his full energies to a movie career. For *100 Rifles* in 1969 Brown was paid $200,000 and starred opposite Raquel Welch, with whom he filmed the first love scene between a black man and a white woman ever captured in a Hollywood picture. These three movies, along with *Ice Station Zebra* (1968), were his most successful mainstream projects.

As Brown made the transition from football star to movie star, the press became increasingly concerned with his personal life, particularly after his marriage to Sue Jones ended in the late 1960s. The couple, who had married in 1958, had three children. Brown, a regular on the Hollywood social scene, had numerous encounters with the L.A. Police Department—almost all of them involving questionable behavior by both parties—culminating in Brown's arrest when his girlfriend fell from a second-floor balcony during a domestic dispute, though she never pressed charges. A year later Brown was arrested for felonious assault in a hit-and-run traffic incident; the case was dismissed during trial. In 1978 he was found guilty of misdemeanor battery for punching a player on a golf course, and in 1986 he was again arrested in a domestic dispute, though again the charges were dropped.

In the 1960s and 1970s Brown commenced a number of charitable endeavors, most of which centered around the Black Economic Union, a collective of African American business owners dedicated to pooling and recommitting their wealth to projects such as teenage education, job training, and rehabilitation. In 1971 he was inducted into the NFL Hall of Fame, though nearly twenty years later he would threaten to withdraw on behalf of historically neglected black players. (Brown would eventually be inducted into the College Football Hall of Fame and the Lacrosse Hall of Fame, as well.) He continued making movies such as the "blaxploitation" films *Slaughter* (1972) and *Slaughter's Big Rip-Off* (1973) and the all-black western *Take a Hard Ride* (1975), but they failed to match his earlier commercial successes. In the early 1980s Brown started a movie production company, Ocean Productions, with his friend RICHARD PRYOR, but Pryor soon fired him.

In 1973 the Buffalo Bills's O. J. SIMPSON broke Brown's rushing record for a single season, and in 1984 Brown's career rushing record fell to the Chicago Bears' WALTER PAYTON. But Brown's athletic legacy was already established, and four years later he founded the Amer-I-Can Program Inc., a nonprofit organization dedicated to reaching gang members and prisoners; in 1992 Amer-I-Can played an essential role in securing a truce between L.A.'s rival gangs, the Bloods and the Crips. By 2000 Amer-I-Can had spread to twelve cities and built a reputation for developing innovative strategies to rehabilitate prisoners and troubled youths. Brown's own troubles with the authorities continued, however. He was sentenced to three years probation in October 1999 for smashing the car of his second wife, Monique Brown, and in 2002 he served four months in prison for refusing to undergo court-ordered domestic violence counseling. Brown appeared in a few more Hollywood productions, most notably as a defensive coordinator in Oliver Stone's football epic, *Any Given Sunday* (1999). It was an ironic turn for an offensive player of whom one opponent had said, "the best way to tackle Brown is to hold on and wait for help."

FURTHER READING

Brown, Jim, with Myron Cope. *Off My Chest* (1964).

———, with Steve Delsohn. *Out of Bounds* (1969).

Toback, James. *Jim: The Author's Self-Centered Memoir on the Great Jim Brown* (1971).

—DAVID F. SMYDRA JR.

BROWN, RON (1 Aug. 1941–3 Apr. 1996), was born Ronald Harmon Brown at Freedmen's Hospital in Washington, D.C., the son of William Brown, who worked for the Federal Housing and Home Finance Agency, and Gloria Elexine Carter. The Browns moved to Harlem, New York, in 1947, and Ron grew up in the famed Theresa Hotel, where his father was manager. JOE LOUIS was a frequent guest, and gave young Ron the nickname "Little Brown." Ron showed his entrepreneurial skills at an early age by getting autographs of Louis, SUGAR RAY ROBINSON, and other celebrity guests at the Theresa and selling them for five dollars each to his friends. His parents, both graduates of Howard University, set Ron on a solid path to join the black middle class, which became, in many ways, the social network that would make possible many of his achievements. As a child, he met various politicians, including DAVID DINKINS, Congressman CHARLES RANGEL, and other notables, many of whom became his supporters in his adult life. He was the only black student at the Hunter College elementary school, and he graduated from the Rhodes School, a private preparatory school, in 1958.

Brown attended Middlebury College in Vermont and was the first African American inducted into Sigma Phi Epsilon fraternity—an action which cost the Middlebury chapter its charter in the national organization. After graduating with a BA in Political Science in 1962, he married Alma Arrington, a recent graduate of Fisk University from New York. The couple had two children. Brown entered the U.S. Army as a second lieutenant, serving abroad in Germany and Korea, where he was promoted to captain. But rather than continuing a military career, he left the service in early 1967 and began working for the National Urban League (NUL) while pursuing a law degree in the evenings at the St. John's University Law School in New York, graduating in 1970. Motivated in part by the feeling that he had missed being involved in the civil rights movement that was the focus of so much of the African American community in the 1960s, Brown chose to work with the NUL because it was a leading social service and civil rights organization.

Brown began at the NUL as an assistant to Malcolm Puryear, deputy director to executive director WHITNEY YOUNG. Brown's talent was noticed and he rose quickly within the organization. When VERNON JORDAN assumed the role of president and CEO of the NUL after Young's death in 1971, Brown was promoted to general counsel. In October 1973 he was appointed director of the NUL's Washington bureau, which was responsible for maintaining relations with politicians on Capitol Hill and members of the business community in the task of managing the League's agenda. Because of his effectiveness in this role, the League appointed him as liaison for its Commerce and Industry Council.

In 1980, Brown, who had been a district leader of the Democratic party in Westchester County, New York, in 1971, became increasingly interested in national politics and left the National Urban League to join Senator Edward Kennedy's presidential campaign as deputy manager. After Kennedy's unsuccessful presidential bid, the Senate Judiciary Committee hired Brown as its chief counsel, making him the first African American staff director of a major congressional committee. After the Senate passed to Republican control in 1981, Brown took a position at Patton, Boggs and Blow, a prestigious Washington lobbying and law firm. Brown's clients at the firm included Japanese electronics firms, the government of the autocratic Haitian leader Jean-Claude "Baby Doc" Duvalier, and a number of major domestic companies. In 1987 the firm made him a partner.

Brown continued to combine party political work with his lobbying activities, and in 1981 he became general counsel to the Democratic

National Committee (DNC). He also was a prominent supporter of JESSE JACKSON's historic presidential bid in 1988, and Jackson invited Brown to serve as director of convention affairs for his presidential campaign. Increasingly, Jackson relied on Brown, rather than on his official campaign manager, as his key strategist in the run up to the Democratic National Convention in Atlanta. After Michael Dukakis became the Democratic presidential nominee at that convention in July 1988, Brown played a key role in cementing a relationship between Dukakis and Jackson, winning the respect of both the establishment and insurgent wings of the Democratic Party. At the convention, Brown also secured for himself a seat on the Party's national executive.

The experience and contacts he made in unifying the often fractious Democratic Party gave Brown the confidence to run for the post of DNC chairman in January 1989. Upon his election in February, he became the first African American to serve in that position. Brown and his staff, especially his political director, Paul Tully, prepared the Democrats to compete in the 1992 election by creating a "coordinated campaign" in which the national party worked closely with state party campaigns. This approach worked to the advantage of the Democratic presidential nominee, Bill Clinton, who campaigned without a strong national organization. Brown's direction of the DNC was also central in building national support for Clinton after his nomination. His choice of New York City as the party's convention site proved controversial, however, because Brown also served on the board and held stock in a company that had just won a $210 million dollar waste treatment contract from the city. Despite such negative publicity, Brown's political and business contacts in New York proved invaluable in helping the Clinton campaign gain access to one of the largest media and financial markets in the country.

Bill Clinton, who often acknowledged that he would not have become president of the United States without Brown's help, appointed Brown as secretary of commerce in 1993. Again, Brown was the first African American to hold that position. Although he

had hoped to become secretary of state, Brown settled enthusiastically into his new role, becoming one of the most vigorous secretaries of commerce in history. Believing that he could "really realize something for the American people," he traveled extensively throughout the country and around the globe to boost the standing of American business, securing numerous lucrative agreements for U.S. businesses abroad. During his tenure, a time of rapid economic growth, U.S. exports increased by over twenty-five percent.

Brown was not without his critics. He came under considerable attack from congressional Republicans who claimed that his trade missions favored Democratic Party supporters. In response, he stressed the bipartisan makeup of his delegations and their success in winning contracts for American firms and jobs for American citizens. Brown was particularly sensitive to the historical exclusion of minority firms and vigorously promoted expanded opportunities for minority businesses. But liberal groups like Common Cause were also critical of Brown's close ties to large corporations. The New York Times—hardly part of any vast right-wing conspiracy—ran a series of editorials in 1993 criticizing Brown's lack of full disclosure of his business interests.

Brown was cleared of the bribery charges leveled against him in 1993, but in 1995 Attorney General Janet Reno initiated an investigation into claims that he had submitted misleading financial disclosures and that his son Michael had been paid by an Oklahoma company in order to gain influence with his father. However, while on a trade mission to Dubrovnik, Croatia, in April 1996, a plane carrying Brown and his delegation of twelve executives of major corporations and fourteen U.S. government employees crashed during a storm in the mountains of Bosnia. At the time of his death, Ron Brown was considered by many to be the most powerful African American in the country.

FURTHER READING

Brown, Tracey L. *The Life and Times of Ron Brown* (1998).

Holms, Steven A. *Ron Brown: An Uncommon Life* (2001).

Obituary: *New York Times*, 4 April 1996.
—RONALD WALTERS

 BROWN, STERLING ALLEN (1 May 1901–13 Jan. 1989), professor of English, poet, and essayist, was born in Washington, D.C., the son of Sterling Nelson Brown, a minister and divinity school professor, and Adelaide Allen. After graduating as valedictorian from Dunbar High School in 1918, Brown matriculated at Williams College, where he studied French and English literature and won the Graves Prize for an essay on Molière and Shakespeare. He graduated from Williams in 1922 with Phi Beta Kappa honors and a Clark fellowship for graduate studies in English at Harvard University. Once at Harvard, Brown studied with Bliss Perry and, most notably, with George Lyman Kittredge, the distinguished scholar of Shakespeare and the ballad. Kittredge's example as a scholar of both formal and vernacular forms of literature doubtlessly encouraged Brown to contemplate a similar professorial career, though for Brown the focus would be less on the British Isles than on the United States and on African American culture, in particular. Brown received his MA in English from Harvard in 1923 and went south to his first teaching job at Virginia Seminary and College at Lynchburg.

Brown's three years at Virginia Seminary represent much more than the beginning of his teaching career, for it was there that he began to immerse himself in the folkways of rural black people, absorbing their stories, music, and idioms. In this regard, Brown is usefully likened to two of his most famous contemporaries, ZORA NEALE HURSTON and JEAN TOOMER (with whom Brown attended high school). Like Hurston, Brown conducted a kind of iconoclastic ethnographic fieldwork among southern black people in the 1920s (she in Florida, he in Virginia) and subsequently produced a series of important essays on black folkways. Like Hurston and Toomer, Brown drew on his observations to produce a written vernacular literature that venerated black people of the rural South instead of championing the new order of black life being created in cities in the North. And like Toomer, in particular, Brown's wanderings in the South represented not just a quest for literary material but also an odyssey in search of roots more meaningful than what seemed to be provided by college in the North and black bourgeois culture in Washington. After Virginia Seminary, Brown taught briefly at Lincoln University in Missouri and Fisk University before beginning his forty-year career at Howard University in 1929.

Brown's first published poems, many of them "portraitures" of Virginia rural black folk, such as Sister Lou and Big Boy Davis, appeared in the 1920s in *Opportunity* magazine and in celebrated anthologies, including COUNTÉE CULLEN's *Caroling Dusk* (1927) and JAMES WELDON JOHNSON's *Book of American Negro Poetry* (1922; 2nd ed., 1931). When Brown's first book of poems, *Southern Road*, was published in 1932, Johnson's introduction praised Brown for having, in effect, discovered how to write a black vernacular poetry that was not fraught with the limitations of the "dialect verse" of the PAUL LAURENCE DUNBAR era thirty years earlier. Johnson wrote that Brown "has made more than mere transcriptions of folk poetry, and he has done more than bring to it mere artistry; he has deepened its meanings and multiplied its implications." Johnson also showed his respect for Brown by inviting him to write the *Outline for the Study of the Poetry of American Negroes* (1931), a teacher's guide to accompany Johnson's poetry anthology.

The 1930s were productive and exciting years for Brown. In addition to settling into teaching at Howard and publishing *Southern Road*, he wrote a regular column for *Opportunity* ("The Literary Scene: Chronicle and Comment"), reviewing plays and films as well as novels, biographies, and scholarship by black and white Americans alike. From 1936 to 1939 Brown was the Editor on Negro Affairs for the Federal Writers' Project. In that capacity he oversaw virtually everything written about African Americans and wrote large sections of *The Negro in Virginia* (1940). The latter work led to his being named a researcher on the Carnegie-Myrdal Study of the Negro, which generated the data for Gunnar Myrdal's classic study, *An American Dilemma: The Negro Problem and Modern Democracy* (1944). In 1937 Brown was awarded a Guggenheim Fellowship, which afforded him the opportunity to complete *The Negro in American Fiction* and *Negro Poetry and Drama*, both published in 1937. *The Negro Caravan: Writings by American Negroes* (1941), a massive anthology of African American writing, edited by Brown with Ulysses Lee and Arthur P. Davis, continues to be the model for bringing song, folktale, mother wit, and written literature together in a comprehensive collection.

From the 1940s into the 1960s Brown was no longer an active poet, in part because his second collection, "No Hidin' Place," was rejected by his publisher. Even though many of his poems were published in the *Crisis*, the *New Republic*, and the *Nation*, Brown found little solace and turned instead to teaching and writing essays. In the 1950s Brown published such major essays as "Negro Folk Expression," "The Blues," and "Negro Folk Expression: Spirituals, Seculars, Ballads and Work Songs," all in the Atlanta journal *Phylon*. Also in this period Brown wrote "The New Negro in Literature (1925–1955)" (1955). In this essay he argued that the Harlem Renaissance was, in fact, a New Negro Renaissance, not a Harlem Renaissance, because few of the significant participants, including he himself, lived in Harlem or wrote about it. He concluded that the Harlem Renaissance was the publishing industry's hype, an idea that gained renewed attention when publishers once again hyped the Harlem Renaissance in the 1970s.

The 1970s and 1980s were a period of recognition and perhaps of subtle vindication for Sterling Brown. While enduring what was for him the melancholy of retirement from Howard in 1969, he found himself suddenly in the limelight as a rediscovered poet and as a pioneering teacher and founder of the new field of African American studies. Numerous invitations followed for poetry readings, lectures, and tributes, and fourteen honorary degrees were bestowed on him. In 1974 *Southern Road* was reissued. In 1975

Brown's ballad poems were collected and published under the title *The Last Ride of Wild Bill and Eleven Narrative Poems.* In 1980 Brown's *Collected Poems*, a volume edited by Michael S. Harper, was published in the National Poetry Series. Brown was named poet laureate of the District of Columbia in 1984.

Brown had married Daisy Turnbull in 1927, possibly in Lynchburg, where they had met. They had one child. Brown was very close to his two sisters, who lived next door in Washington. They cared for him after his wife's death in 1979 until Brown entered a health center in Takoma Park, Maryland, where he died.

Brown returned to Williams College for the first time in fifty-one years on 22 September 1973 to give an autobiographical address and again in June 1974 to receive an honorary degree. The address, "A Son's Return: 'Oh Didn't He Ramble'" (*Berkshire Review* 10 [Summer 1974], 9–30; reprinted in Harper and Stepto, eds., *Chant of Saints* [1979]), offers much of Brown's philosophy for living a productive American life. At one point he declares, "I am an integrationist... because I know what segregation really was. And by integration, I do not mean assimilation. I believe what the word means—an integer is a whole number. I want to be in the best American traditions. I want to be accepted as a whole man. My standards are not white. My standards are not black. My standards are human." Brown largely achieved these goals and standards. His poetry, for example, along with that of LANGSTON HUGHES, forever put to rest the question of whether a written art based on black vernacular could be resilient and substantial and read through the generations. Despite his various careers, Brown saw himself primarily as a teacher, and it was as a professor at Howard that he felt he had made his mark, training hundreds of students and pioneering those changes in the curriculum that would lead to increasing appreciation and scrutiny of vernacular American and African American art forms. In short, Brown was one of the scholar-teachers whose work before 1950 enabled the creation and development of American studies and African American studies programs in colleges and universities in the decades to follow.

FURTHER READING

Brown's papers are housed at Howard University, chiefly in the Moorland-Spingarn Collection.

Gates, Henry Louis, Jr. *Figures in Black: Words, Signs, and the "Racial" Self* (1987).

Gabbin, Joanne. *Sterling A. Brown: Building the Black Aesthetic Tradition* (1985).

Jones, Gayl. *Liberating Voices: Oral Tradition in African American Literature* (1991).

Stepto, Robert. "'When de Saints go Ma'chin' Home': Sterling Brown's Blueprint for a New Negro Poetry." *Kunapipi* 4, no. 1 (1982): 94–105.

———. "Sterling Brown: Outsider in the Renaissance" in *Harlem Renaissance Revaluations* (1989).

Obituary: *New York Times*, 17 Jan. 1989.

—ROBERT STEPTO

 BROWN, WILLIAM WELLS (Mar. 1815– 6 Nov. 1884), slave narrator, novelist, playwright, historian, and activist, was born in Lexington, Kentucky, the son of a slave mother, Elizabeth, and George Higgins, the white half-brother of Brown's first master, Dr. John Young. As a slave, William was spared the hard labor of his master's plantation, unlike his mother and half-siblings, because of his close blood relation to the slave-holding family, but as a house servant he was constantly abused by Mrs. Young. When the family removed to a farm outside St. Louis, Missouri, William was hired out in various capacities, including physician's assistant, servant in a public house, and waiter on a steamship. William's "best master" in slavery was Elijah P. Lovejoy, publisher of the *St. Louis Times*, where he was hired out in the printing office in 1830. There William acquired some education, though not literacy.

William's work on the steamship opened his eyes to the idea of freedom, since he observed the comings and goings of free people every day. His abuses at the hands of a drunken master, Major Freeland, who amused himself by tying his slaves in the smokehouse and burning tobacco at their feet in a game he called "Virginia play," persuaded William to seek freedom for himself and his family as soon as an opportunity arose. Perhaps William's most formative year in slavery was 1832, when he was

William Wells Brown gained recognition for his autobiographical slave narrative published in 1847, the account of his travels in Europe published in 1852, and his novel, Clotel; or, the President's Daughter: A Narrative of Slave Life in the United States *(1853). University of North Carolina at Chapel Hill Libraries*

hired out to James Walker, who ran boatloads of slaves down the Mississippi River to the lucrative New Orleans slave markets. During this year William observed firsthand the deepest degradations and cruelties of the slave trade, detailed in his later writings, as families were separated and unruly slaves were tortured and killed. William himself took part in preparing slaves for auction by darkening the gray hair of older slaves and arranging the slaves in happy scenes of dancing and card playing.

On his return to St. Louis in 1833, at the urging of a sister, William made his first attempt at escape, crossing the river into Illinois with his mother in a stolen skiff. After ten days of traveling at night and sleeping during the day, William and his mother continued their journey in daylight, only to be retrieved by slave catchers within a few hours. Once again William's near relation to his master saved him from being sent to the New Orleans slave market, unlike his mother, and he was ultimately sold to a steamship owner. Within a few months William escaped again, walking off the ship into the city of Cincinnati, choosing the date of 1 January 1834, as his first day of freedom. During his walk north William added "Wells Brown" to his name, in honor of the Quaker who helped further his escape and nursed him through illness brought on by exposure.

As a free man based in Cleveland, Brown quickly got work as a steamship steward on Lake Erie, helping as many as sixty-nine slaves escape to Canada during one seven-month period. Brown also married Elizabeth Schooner in the summer of 1834; their first child, a daughter, was born in the late spring of 1835 but died several months later. Two more daughters, Clarissa and Josephine, were born to the couple in 1836 and 1839, respectively. In 1836 the Browns moved to Buffalo, New York, where Brown continued his participation in the Underground Railroad and became a leader of the local black community's temperance organization. During this busy period Brown devoted himself to the cause of abolition and quickly acquired literacy.

In the mid 1840s Brown moved to Boston without Elizabeth, taking their daughters with him to be educated at a boarding school in New Bedford while he traveled as an antislavery lecturer. In 1847 he published the *Narrative of William Wells Brown, a Fugitive Slave, Written by Himself*, which went through numerous editions in both the United States and England, surpassed in popularity only by one other slave narrative, that of FREDERICK DOUGLASS, published two years earlier. Brown also published *The Anti-Slavery Harp: A Collection of Songs for Anti-Slavery Meetings* (1848). That same year, his last master in slavery, Enoch Price, offered to buy Brown's freedom for $325, an offer that Brown widely publicized, along with his refusal. He wrote, "God made me as free as he did Enoch Price, and Mr. Price shall never receive a dollar from me or my friends with my consent" (Heermance, 15). This refusal necessitated Brown's removal to Europe, which he arranged in 1849 as a delegate to the International Peace Congress in Paris. At the congress, Brown was warmly received by Alexis de Tocqueville and Victor Hugo, among

other European luminaries. Brown achieved great renown as an antislavery lecturer throughout Great Britain, and he was also a frequent contributor to several British newspapers. In 1851, after his wife's death, his two daughters joined him in England, and in 1853 he published the first travel memoir by an African American, *Three Years in Europe*.

In 1854 he added to his list of firsts by publishing the first novel by an African American, *Clotel; or, The President's Daughter*. In this novel Brown fictionalizes the relationship between Thomas Jefferson and the slave SALLY HEMINGS through the story of their daughter and draws on his experiences as a firsthand observer of the slave trade in his detailed accounts of slaves being "sold down the river" and in auction scenes. Elegantly written and sentimental in the style of the day, *Clotel* is a sprawling, heavily plotted novel that sold relatively well and established Brown as the first African American man of letters. Brown was clearly entranced with its themes, for he continued working on the novel for years, publishing new versions in 1860, 1864, and 1867.

Also in 1854 Brown was persuaded to let friends buy his freedom so he could return to the United States and continue his work in the abolition movement. He maintained his literary output during this period, updating his *Narrative* and *The Anti-Slavery Harp* and expanding his travel narrative under the title *The American Fugitive in Europe* (1855). In 1856 he wrote his first play, *The Doughface Baked; or, How to Give a Northern Man a Backbone*, another first for African American writers in a new genre. The play satirized the Reverend Nehemiah Adams of Boston, who defended slavery; the written text for this play is lost. Brown's play *The Escape; or, A Leap for Freedom* (1848) achieved more renown through public readings, though no record exists of either play being staged fully. In 1860 Brown married Anna Elizabeth Gray, with whom he had one daughter, Clotelle, in 1862.

Brown's lifelong interest in medicine, begun under slavery, led him to study on his own in England and the United States, and in 1864 he treated the wife of the abolitionist William Lloyd Garrison. Around this time he began writing

"M.D." after his name to indicate that he was actively practicing medicine, medical school not being a requirement during this period. He maintained an office for the purpose for over a decade in the 1860s and 1870s, though he clearly divided his time among many other endeavors, chiefly his writing and a renewed dedication to the temperance cause. During the Reconstruction period, Brown advocated temperance for free African Americans as essential for elevating their condition. While lecturing in the South for the temperance cause in 1871, Brown narrowly escaped death at the hands of the Ku Klux Klan.

In the 1860s Brown turned to yet another genre of writing, publishing his first work of history in 1863, *The Black Man, His Antecedents, His Genius, and His Achievements*, which consisted of fifty-four biographical sketches of African Americans "designed to reduce white 'colorphobia'" (Ellison and Metcalf Jr., 4). He also published a detailed account of black soldiers in the Civil War, *The Negro in the American Rebellion* (1867). He continued his output of historical works with *The Rising Son* (1873), a wide-ranging study of blacks in the United States, Africa, and the Caribbean. His last publication was an expanded autobiography entitled *My Southern Home; or, The South and Its People* (1880). He died in Boston.

William Wells Brown remains an enduring figure in African American history and literature for his writing, his activism, and his remarkable story of survival and triumph over slavery, illiteracy, and systemic racism. He was well regarded in his own time in the United States and Europe, and his writing, particularly his depiction of the slave trade in the various versions of his novel *Clotel*, retains a sharpness of wit and pointed observation for twenty-first century readers.

FURTHER READING

Brown, William Wells. *Narrative of William Wells Brown, a Fugitive Slave, Written by Himself* (1847) in *From Fugitive Slave to Free Man: The Autobiographies of William Wells Brown*, ed. William L. Andrews (1993).

———. *My Southern Home; or, The South and Its People* (1880), in Andrews (see above).

Ellison, Curtis W., and E. W. Metcalf Jr. *William Wells Brown and Martin Delany: A Reference Guide* (1978).

Farrison, William Edward. *William Wells Brown: Author and Reformer* (1969).

Heermance, J. Noel. *William Wells Brown and Clotelle: A Portrait of the Artist in the First Negro Novel* (1969).

Whelchel, Love Henry. *My Chains Fell Off: William Wells Brown, Fugitive Abolitionist* (1985).

—ALICE KNOX EATON

 BRUCE, BLANCHE KELSO (1 Mar. 1841–17 Mar. 1898), black political leader and U.S. senator during the Reconstruction era, was born in Farmville, Virginia, the son of Polly (surname unknown), a slave. The identity of his father is unknown, but he took the surname of the man who owned his mother before he was born. His childhood as a slave on a small plantation, first in Virginia, then briefly in Mississippi, and finally in Missouri did not significantly differ, as he later recalled, from that of the sons of whites. This relatively benign experience in slavery perhaps owed a great deal to the fact that he was the light-skinned favorite of a benevolent master and mistress. He shared a tutor with his master's son and thus obtained the education that prepared him for later success. During the Civil War, despite the benevolence of his owner, he fled to freedom in Kansas, but after slavery was abolished he returned to Missouri, where he reportedly established the first school in the state for blacks, at Hannibal.

After the war Bruce briefly attended Oberlin College in Ohio, but following the passage of the Reconstruction Acts of 1867, which provided for black political equality in the former Confederate states, he moved to Bolivar County in the Mississippi Delta. Soon after his arrival, the district commander appointed him a voter registrar in neighboring Tallahatchie County. He also organized plantation blacks into the new Republican Party and soon attracted the attention of state party leaders.

When the first Mississippi legislature under the new order met, Bruce was elected sergeant at arms of the state senate. A man of magnificent physique and handsome countenance and possessed of impeccable manners, Bruce won the support of white Republicans like Governor James Lusk Alcorn as well as blacks. In 1871 he won election to the joint office of sheriff and tax collector of Bolivar County. The Republican state board of education also appointed him county superintendent of education. He virtually created the biracial but segregated system of education in the county and secured the support of whites for it. In all of these positions he gained a reputation for financial integrity.

Bruce also invested in land and within a decade had attained the status of planter. In 1872 he was named to the board of levee commissioners for a three-county district—a group with the power to raise revenue and build embankments in the Delta region. Bruce's political and financial success and his promotion of labor stability among black workers had the effect of moderating the opposition of conservative planters to Republican control in Bolivar County.

By 1874 Bruce's fame had spread beyond the Delta. His political skill and his moderation had won him support from all factions of the Mississippi Republican Party. In February the legislature elected him to the U.S. Senate by a nearly unanimous vote, which included the support of a few conservative Democrats. In March 1875 Bruce took his seat in the Senate, becoming the nation's second black senator and the first black to be elected to a full term. In the Senate he served on four committees, including the important select committees on Mississippi River improvements and on the Freedmen's Bank. As chairman of the latter committee, he led the effort to reform the management of the institution and provide relief for depositors. But a Bruce-sponsored Senate bill to obtain congressional reimbursement for black victims of the bank's failure did not pass. He also spoke out against a Chinese exclusion bill and for a more humane Indian policy. Bruce took these positions primarily because of the harsh implications that such a racist, exclusionist policy had for blacks.

Bruce's main interest in the Senate was the defense of black rights in the South at a time when state and local Republican governments were replaced by hostile conservative ones. Although he was usually unobtrusive in attempting to persuade Congress, and specifically its Republican members, to enforce the Reconstruction amendments to the Constitution, he became passionate in denouncing the violence and intimidation that characterized the Mississippi election of 1875, overthrowing Republican rule.

Despite bitter setbacks for blacks during this period, Bruce remained committed to the Reconstruction goal of black assimilation into American society with all of the rights of whites. He opposed both of the organized efforts at black migration of the late 1870s, the Kansas Exodus and the Back-to-Africa movement. He did so on the grounds that neither destination had much to offer blacks and that the rights of the race could yet be achieved in white America. His prestige among blacks suffered considerably because of his opposition to emigration. In 1878 he married Josephine B. Wilson, the daughter of a prominent black dentist of Cleveland, Ohio; they had one son. After their marriage and the couple's acceptance into white Washingtonian society, Bruce became largely insulated from the black masses.

During his last years in the Senate he devoted much of his time to Republican Party affairs and black education. In Mississippi he joined with two other black leaders, John R. Lynch and James Hill, to dominate the state Republican organization, gaining important federal patronage for his supporters. In promoting black education, he advanced the self-help doctrine, which ultimately became associated with BOOKER T. WASHINGTON.

With the Democrats in control of the state legislature, Bruce made no effort to obtain reelection to the U.S. Senate. After the expiration of his term in 1881, he continued to live in Washington but retained his plantation in Mississippi. He also continued to participate in national Republican politics and was a popular speaker on behalf of black education. In 1881 President James Garfield appointed Bruce register of the U.S. Treasury, and he continued to hold the office during Chester A. Arthur's administration. In 1884–1885 he served as director of the black exhibits in the Industrial Cotton Centennial Exposition held in New Orleans. These exhibits focused on the material progress that blacks had made since Emancipation. In 1896 he received strong support for a seat in William McKinley's cabinet, but he had to settle for his previous position of register of the Treasury. Bruce died of diabetes in Washington, D.C.

FURTHER READING

The Blanche K. Bruce Papers are held at the Rutherford B. Hayes Presidential Center Library, Fremont, Ohio. Howard University Library, Washington, D.C., also has a collection of Bruce papers, including letters.

Gatewood, Willard B. *Aristocrats of Color: The Black Elite, 1880–1920* (1990).

Harris, William C. "Blanche K. Bruce of Mississippi: Conservative Assimilationist" in *Southern Black Leaders of the Reconstruction Era* (1982).

—WILLIAM C. HARRIS

 BRYAN, ANDREW
(1737–6 Oct. 1812), clergyman, was born at Goose Creek, South Carolina, about sixteen miles from Charleston. His slave parents' names are unknown. GEORGE LIELE, the itinerant African American Baptist minister from Savannah, Georgia, baptized Bryan in 1782. Bryan married Hannah (maiden name unknown) about nine years after his conversion. Jonathan Bryan, Andrew's master and a New Light Presbyterian sympathetic to the evangelical movement in the South, allowed him to exhort both blacks and whites. About 1790 a white landowner allowed Bryan to build a wooden shed on the outskirts of Savannah at Yamacraw. There Bryan held religious meetings for African Americans, both slave and free, between sunrise and sunset. When white opposition arose, Bryan and his hearers retreated to the nearby swamp to conduct their religious activities.

The evangelical revivals fostered by the Second Great Awakening drew blacks and whites together into common religious circles. In 1788 Abraham Marshall, a white Baptist clergyman, ordained Bryan, baptized about fifty of his followers, and organized them into a congregation known as the Ethiopian Church of Jesus Christ. By strict Baptist rules, the constitution of the church was an irregular act, since a council of Baptist clergy was not involved. Nevertheless, the Ethiopian Church of Jesus Christ became a center of Baptist activity among African Americans in the Savannah region.

During the British occupation of Savannah, whites, fearful of slave insurrection, imprisoned Andrew and his brother Sampson. While defending himself before the city magistrates, Andrew Bryan, according to a report in the *Baptist Annual Register*, "told his persecutors that he rejoiced not only to be whipped, but *would freely suffer death for the cause of Jesus Christ.*" Jonathan Bryan arranged for the release of Andrew and Sampson and allowed Andrew to resume worship services in a barn on his estate at Brampton. A Savannah court ruled that the congregation could hold meetings between sunrise and sunset, which it did without significant opposition during the next two years. By 1790 Bryan's church had 225 full communicants and about 350 converts. Renamed the First African Baptist Church, it became a member of the predominantly white Georgia Baptist Association, which had decided that Marshall's irregular action in organizing the congregation was justifiable, given the circumstances.

In 1794, with financial assistance from influential whites, Bryan purchased a plot of land in Savannah for a permanent church building. In 1795 Jonathan Bryan died, and his heirs allowed Andrew to purchase his freedom for fifty pounds sterling. Bryan's congregation prospered, growing to over seven hundred members by 1800. In that year Bryan wrote the English Baptist John Rippon, publisher of the *Baptist Annual Register.*

With much pleasure, I inform you, dear Sir, that I enjoy good health, and am strong in body, at the age of sixty-three years, and am blessed with a pious wife, whose freedom I have obtained and an only daughter and child who is married to a free man, tho' she, and consequently under our laws, her seven children, five sons and two daughters, are slaves. By a kind Providence I am well provided for, as to worldly comforts, (tho' I have had very little given me as a minister) having a house and lot in this city, besides the land on which several buildings stand, for which I receive a small rent, and a fifty-six acre tract of land, with all necessary buildings, four miles in the country, and eight slaves; for whose education and happiness, I am enabled thro' mercy to provide.

The First African Baptist Church sponsored the formation of a daughter congregation, the Second African Baptist Church, in 1799. Second African eventually sponsored the organization of the Ogeechee or Third African Baptist Church. At the time of Bryan's death, First African Baptist had 1,458 members. Andrew Marshall, Bryan's nephew, succeeded him as pastor. The First African Baptist Church, with its roots in the work of Liele and Bryan in the Savannah region and the preaching of DAVID GEORGE on the Galphin plantation at Silver Bluff, Georgia, has been called the first independent African American Baptist church in North America. Recent research has uncovered earlier Baptist slave congregations, but Bryan and First African remain important in early black Baptist history. When Bryan died in Savannah, the white Savannah Baptist Association eulogized him, declaring, "This son of Africa, after suffering inexpressible persecutions in the cause of his divine Master, was at length permitted to discharge the duties of the ministry among his colored friends in peace and quiet, hundreds of whom, through his instrumentality, were brought to a knowledge of the truth as 'it is in Jesus.'"

Andrew Bryan pioneered in efforts to plant the Christian faith under the Baptist banner among fellow blacks in the post–Revolutionary War era. Though not without opposition, he enjoyed a surprising degree of religious freedom during the evangelical renaissance in the South. After the insurrections led by DENMARK VESEY in 1822 and NAT TURNER, a fellow Baptist, in 1831, the white South severely restricted black preaching. Nevertheless, the seeds sown by Bryan and others during the earlier decades matured. Historically, more African Americans, slave and free, have belonged to Baptist churches in the South than to any other denomination.

FURTHER READING

The principal sources of information on Bryan are the occasional Baptist almanacs, known as the *Baptist Annual Register*, edited and published by John Rippon, the English Baptist, in the early 1790s and republished in "Letters Showing the Rise and Progress of the Early Negro Churches of Georgia and the West Indies," *Journal of Negro History* 1 (Jan. 1916): 69–92.

Davis, John W. "George Liele and Andrew Bryan, Pioneer Negro Baptist Preachers." *Journal of Negro History* 3 (Apr. 1918): 119–127.

Sobel, Mechal. *Trabelin' On: The Slave Journey to an Afro-Baptist Faith* (1979).

Washington, James M., Jr. *Frustrated Fellowship: The Black Baptist Quest for Social Power* (1986).

—MILTON C. SERNETT

 BUBBLES, JOHN

(19 Feb. 1902–18 May 1986), dancer, singer, entertainer, and actor, was born John William Sublett in Louisville, Kentucky. His parents' names are not known. His early childhood was spent in Indianapolis, Indiana, where his family was part of a touring carnival; by the age of seven, John was performing on the stage, participating in amateur contests as a singer. Accounts differ as to when he returned to Louisville and when he met his vaudeville team partner, Ford Lee "Buck" Washington. Some sources list their ages as ten and six, respectively, while others list them as thirteen and nine. The team began working professionally by 1915 as "Buck and Bubbles," an act combining music and comedy.

They would remain together for nearly forty years, originally combining Washington's talents as a pianist with Sublett's as a singer; when his voice changed, Sublett turned to tap dancing as his primary talent. As they developed their act, the two took odd jobs to help support themselves and their families. While employed as ushers in the gallery at the Mary Anderson Theater in Louisville, they worked on their act after hours and were seen by the theater's manager. When an opening in the program arose, Buck and Bubbles were hired to perform, but they had to appear in blackface, posing as white minstrels, since the theater did not allow African American acts on the stage. An audition for a touring show, *The Kiss Me Company*, ensued and Sublett became Washington's legal guardian so

that Buck would be allowed to tour at such a young age.

In September 1919 the duo reached New York and played without blackface at the Columbia Theater on Forty-seventh Street, across from the mecca of vaudeville, the Palace. The act was an immediate success, becoming one of the few black acts to tour on the Keith, Orpheum, and other white vaudeville circuits. African American acts were primarily relegated to the Theater Owners Booking Association (TOBA or "Toby"), which circulated acts to theaters in African American communities. According to Bubbles, "We were easy to book because we didn't conflict with most acts. Nobody wrote for us or gave us lines. We thought funny and that's the way it came out onstage" (Smith, 59). Buck and Bubbles became the first African American act to be held over at the Palace, the first to play Radio City Music Hall, and only the second to be featured in the Ziegfeld Follies in 1931, after headlining in Lew Leslie's *Blackbirds of 1930*.

In 1927 RCA Victor made test recordings of Buck and Bubbles that were not released. From nine sides recorded for Columbia between 1930 and 1934, only two were released: "He's Long Gone from Bowling Green" and "Lady Be Good." The duo made recordings in London in 1936, and there is reportedly a solo album released by Bubbles, *From Rags to Riches*. In 1935 George Gershwin cast Bubbles as the original Sportin' Life in *Porgy and Bess*. Washington was also in the cast, as "neither took a job without the other being hired" (*Variety* Obituary, 110). Later, Buck and Bubbles became the first African Americans to perform on television, in New York in 1939. The team became popular in Europe as well, touring extensively.

Buck and Bubbles' performances on film began in 1929 with a series of Pathé comedy shorts: *Black Narcissus, Fowl Play, In and Out, Darktown Follies, High Toned,* and *Honest Crooks*. These were followed by *Night in a Niteclub* (1934), *Calling All Stars* (1937), *Varsity Show* (1937), and *Atlantic City* (1944). In 1943, billed as John W. Sublett, rather than John Bubbles, as he was more popularly known, he performed the featured role of Domino Johnson in MGM's *Cabin in the Sky*, the all-black

cast musical starring ETHEL WATERS, LENA HORNE, and Eddie "Rochester" Anderson. Sublett won critical acclaim for his solo number, "Shine," a song written by DUKE ELLINGTON, which some critics perceive as a subtle, incisive protest against racism. Other film appearances include *I Dood It* (also known as *By Hook or by Crook*, 1943), *Laff Jamboree* (1945), *Mantan Messes Up* (1946), and *A Song Is Born* (1948).

After Washington's death in 1955, Bubbles continued as a solo performer until 1967, when a stroke left him partially paralyzed and sent him into semiretirement. In 1955 he appeared in the German film *Solang' es hübsche Mädchen gibt*, released in the United States as *Beautiful Girls* (1958). Bubbles is among the legendary tap dancers featured in the film documentary *No Maps on My Taps* (1979). He was also the first African American entertainer to appear on *The Tonight Show Starring Johnny Carson*. Some of his other major television appearances include *The DuPont Show of the Week* (1961), *The Lucille Ball Show* (1962), and *The Belle of 14th Street* (1967), a vaudeville re-creation conceived for Barbra Streisand. As a solo act, he appeared regularly with Danny Kaye, Judy Garland, and Anna Maria Alberghetti. During the 1960s he toured Vietnam with Bob Hope and earned the Award of Merit from the U.S. government. There was little work after 1967, but in 1979 George Wein called upon Bubbles to sing at the Newport Jazz Festival. In 1980 Bubbles returned to the New York stage in *Black Broadway*, a musical review, and was honored by the American Guild of Variety Artists (AGVA) with a lifetime achievement award. That same year a recording of excerpts from *Porgy and Bess*, by Leontyne Price and William Warfield, featuring Bubbles as Sportin' Life, was released by RCA Victor.

Bubbles, often described as "the father of rhythm tap," which was also known as "jazz tap," changed the face of tap dance. When he was eighteen years old, he was laughed out of the Hoofers Club, a Harlem gathering place where the foremost tap dancers in the nation openly challenged and competed against each other. This event served to heighten his drive to be acknowledged as a dancer and sent him into intensive practice. At that time, tap dancers stayed on their toes and included a great deal of "flash," or gymnastic virtuosity, in their acts. Bubbles pared down his body movement and added his heels to his tap combinations, creating more syncopated rhythms while exhibiting mastery in the speed and complexity of the steps he improvised.

Soon, dancers came to his shows to try to copy his style. Bubbles frustrated them by changing his steps with each performance. "Double over-the-tops," a difficult figure-eight pattern, and "cramp rolls," a complex sequence of heel-toe combinations, were among his signature innovations. His style is said to have prepared the way for the rhythms of bebop jazz. Hollywood called upon Bubbles to tutor Fred Astaire, Eleanor Powell, and Ann Miller, among other renowned dancers. In the words of Fayard Nicholas, of the famed Nicholas Brothers dance team, "What you used to see Fred Astaire do in the movies, Bubbles had done long before." Bubbles's last appearance as a performer occurred in 1980 at a tribute to George and Ira Gershwin at the Kennedy Center Library. A cerebral hemorrhage took his life at his home in Baldwin Hills, near Los Angeles, California.

FURTHER READING

Goldberg, Jane. "John Bubbles: A Hoofer's Homage," *Village Voice*, 4 Dec. 1978.
Smith, Bill. *The Vaudevillians* (1976).

Obituaries: *New York Times*, 20 May 1986; *Variety*, 21 May 1986; *The Annual Obituary: 1986*.

—FREDA SCOTT GILES

BUHAINA, ABDULLAH IBN. *See* Blakey, Art.

BULLARD, EUGÈNE JACQUES (9 Oct. 1895– 12 Oct. 1961), combat pilot, was born Eugene James Bullard in Columbus, Georgia, the son of William Octave Bullard, a laborer and former slave, and Josephine Thomas. Both parents were of African American and Creek Indian descent. In 1906 Bullard, the seventh of ten children, ran away from home,

ending his formal education. He lived for a time with a band of gypsies, who taught him to ride racehorses. He then worked as a horse handler, jockey, and laborer in several southern states. Bullard gained the respect of several employers by his quiet insistence on treatment with dignity and equality, an ethos instilled in him by his father and strengthened by his sojourn with the tolerant, English-born gypsies.

Early in 1912, Bullard made his way to Norfolk, Virginia, where he stowed away on a freighter bound for Europe. Set ashore in Aberdeen, Scotland, Bullard worked his way south, joining a traveling vaudeville troupe, Freedman's Pickaninnies, in Liverpool later that year. There he also trained as a prizefighter and won his first fight, on points, in early 1913. A good but not exceptional fighter, Bullard fought under the auspices of African American welterweight champion Aaron Lester Brown, "the Dixie Kid." On 28 November 1913, Bullard first fought in Paris, achieving a twenty-round win not reported in local boxing papers. Bullard discovered in Paris his ideal milieu, where people of all races and nationalities found acceptance and equal opportunity. The following spring, after touring the Continent with Freedman's Pickaninnies, Bullard settled in Paris. Adept at languages, he earned his living both as a fighter and as an interpreter for other fighters. At about this time he began to use the Francophone version of his name, Eugène Jacques Bullard (pronounced Bull-*ar*).

In August 1914 war broke out in Europe. On 19 October 1914, shortly after his nineteenth birthday, Bullard enlisted in the French Foreign Legion. He saw action as a machine gunner in some of the bitterest fighting on the Western Front. Following crippling losses along the Somme in April 1915, three Foreign Legion regiments were consolidated into one.

Late that summer, Bullard's father wrote to the U.S. secretary of state, pleading that his son, not yet twenty, be "freed at once and sent home" from the war. "He must have made a mistake when he enlist [*sic*]," William Bullard wrote, and enclosed a document certifying that his son's birth date as recorded in their family Bible was 9 October 1895. (In his autobiography,

Bullard himself several times gave his birth year as 1894, from which has stemmed ongoing confusion.) The American ambassador in Paris was notified of the elder Bullard's request, but since under French law a nineteen-year-old was not underage, neither the American nor the French government took further action (Lloyd, 41–42).

After heavy fighting in the Champagne region in autumn 1915, Bullard and other surviving Legionnaires were transferred to regular French regiments, Bullard to the 170th Infantry, a crack unit known to the Germans as the "swallows of death." Early in 1916, the 170th was sent to Verdun, a sector notorious for its savage fighting, and in March of that year Bullard sustained a crippling thigh wound, for which he received the Croix de Guerre.

Unable to continue ground fighting, Bullard transferred to aviation gunnery. His recuperation complete, he began training in October 1916, soon transferred to fighter pilot training, and on 5 May 1917 received pilot's license number 6950 from the Aéro Club de France. Moving on to advanced pilot training, in August Bullard was assigned to squadron 93 of the Lafayette Flying Corps, a group of American fighters under French command. With squadrons 93 and 85, Bullard flew at least twenty missions over the Verdun sector. He reported shooting down at least two enemy planes; as happened to other flyers, however, there was no corroborating evidence, so these were not scored as official "kills."

A competent pilot appreciated by his comrades, Bullard nevertheless was abruptly removed from aviation and returned to the 170th Infantry as a noncombatant. Circumstantial evidence suggested that, while other pilots of the Lafayette Flying Corps were transferred to the American Army Air Corps, Bullard was remanded because of his race. The United States would not commission an African American aviator until 1942.

Bullard was discharged from the military on 24 October 1919, nearly a year after the armistice. Since his war wounds prevented serious resumption of his boxing career, he instead became a jazz drummer and later was central to the management of Le Grand Duc, one of the most noted Parisian jazz clubs between the wars. Ada Louise Smith, known as BRICKTOP, first headlined there before opening her own Montmartre club. The roll call of musicians and guests at Le Grand Duc included the most celebrated names in Paris in the 1920s. Bullard also became the proprietor of Gene Bullard's Athletic Club and owner of another celebrated jazz club, L'Escadrille, in the 1930s.

In 1923 Bullard married Marcelle Straumann, daughter of a socially prominent family. The couple had two daughters and also a son, who died in infancy. Bullard's deep commitment to his businesses was incompatible with his wife's society interests. They separated after eight years and divorced in 1935; Bullard retained custody of his two daughters.

At the outset of World War II, Bullard assisted French counterintelligence by reporting information gleaned from the conversations of Nazi visitors to his establishments. When Germany invaded France in May 1940, Bullard, with many others, left Paris to fight. Unable to reach the 170th Infantry to the east, Bullard volunteered with the 51st Infantry at Orléans. After he was severely wounded in June, his French commanding officer, who had also been his superior at Verdun, ordered him to flee south, fearing that Bullard would be executed if captured. Making his way overland to Spain, Bullard eventually reached New York, medical treatment, and involvement with Charles de Gaulle's Free French movement. During and after the war, Bullard lived in Harlem and was active with New York's French community. He returned briefly to France in 1950–1951, while unsuccessfully seeking compensation for the loss of his Parisian businesses. At the invitation of the French government, he assisted at the relighting of the eternal flame at the Arc de Triomphe in 1954. In 1959 he was made a chevalier of the Legion of Honor, France's highest award; he received fifteen medals in all from the French government. Bullard died in New York and is buried in the French War Veterans' plot, Flushing Cemetery, Queens, New York.

For many years after World War I, the conventional stance of American authorities was that blacks did not have the mettle or the intellect to fly. In France, Bullard was widely recognized as an athlete, war veteran, and leader in Parisian expatriate society. However, his achievement in daring to train and fly as a combat pilot was given little recognition in the United States until well after his death. In 1989, Bullard was inducted into the Georgia Aviation Hall of Fame. He is depicted on the noteworthy "Black Americans in Flight" mural at the St. Louis International Airport, dedicated in 1990. A memorial bust at the Smithsonian Institution's National Air and Space Museum was unveiled in 1991, and on 14 September 1994, Bullard was posthumously commissioned as a second lieutenant in the U.S. Air Force.

FURTHER READING

Correspondence and manuscript relating to the writing of Bullard's unpublished autobiography are part of the Louise Fox Connell Papers, Schlesinger Library, Radcliffe College, Cambridge, Massachusetts. The text of Bullard's autobiography, *All Blood Runs Red: My Adventurous Life in Search of Freedom* (completed 1961) is in the possession of Bullard's daughter and grandson.

Carisella, P. J., and James W. Ryan. *The Black Swallow of Death* (1972).
Cockfield, Jamie H. "All Blood Runs Red." *Legacy: A Supplement to American Heritage* (Feb./Mar. 1995): 7–15.
Lloyd, Craig. *Eugene Bullard: Black Expatriate in Jazz-Age Paris* (2000).
Stovall, Tyler. *Paris Noir: African Americans in the City of Light* (1996).

Obituaries: *New York Times*, 14 Oct. 1961; *New York Amsterdam News*, 21 Oct. 1961.
—CAROLINE M. FANNIN

BUNCHE, RALPH JOHNSON

(7 Aug. 1904– 9 Dec. 1971), scholar and diplomat, was born in Detroit, Michigan, the son of Fred Bunch, a barber, and Olive Agnes Johnson. His grandmother added an "e" to the family's last name following a move to Los Angeles, California. Because his family moved frequently, Bunche attended a number of public schools before graduating first in his class from Jefferson High School in Los Angeles in 1922. He majored in Political Science at the University of California, Southern Branch (now University of California, Los Angeles [UCLA]), graduating summa cum laude and serving as class valedictorian in 1927. He continued his studies in political science at Harvard, receiving his MA in 1928, and then taught at Howard University in Washington, D.C., while working toward his PhD at Harvard. In 1930 he married Ruth Ethel Harris; they had three children. Bunche traveled to Europe and Africa researching his dissertation and received his PhD from Harvard in February 1934.

Concerned with the problems facing African Americans in the United States, Bunche published numerous articles on racial issues and the monograph *A World View of Race* (1936). He and his colleague John P. Davis organized a 1935 conference called "The Status of the Negro under the New Deal," at which Bunche criticized the Franklin D. Roosevelt administration and the New Deal. He was also involved in the creation of the National Negro Congress, an attempt to bring white Americans and African Americans of different social and economic backgrounds together to discuss race matters. In the final years of the decade Bunche contributed research and reports to a Carnegie study on American race relations headed by the sociologist Gunnar Myrdal. The resulting work, *An American Dilemma: The Negro Problem and Modern Democracy*, published in 1944, was a landmark study of racial conflicts in the United States.

The rise of totalitarianism in Europe and the outbreak of war in 1939 worried Bunche, who feared that a Nazi victory in Europe would spur the growth of fascism in the United States, with disastrous consequences for African Americans. In 1941 he entered public service, accepting a position as a senior analyst in the Office of the Coordinator of Information (later the Office of Strategic Services). As head of the Africa Section, Bunche urged his superiors to approach the problem of postwar decolonization of European holdings in Africa. His proposal was rejected, and he transferred to the Department of State in 1944.

Bunche served as an adviser to the American delegations at the conferences in Dumbarton Oaks and San Francisco concerning the creation of the United Nations (UN). Recognized for his contributions on colonial and trusteeship policies, he was appointed a member of

Ralph Bunche, winner of the 1950 Nobel Peace Prize, photographed by Carl Van Vechten in 1951. Library of Congress

the U.S. delegation to the 1945 meeting of the Preparatory Commission of the UN and the first session of the UN General Assembly in 1946. In April 1946 Bunche took a temporary position on the UN Secretariat as director of the trusteeship position. The temporary position became permanent, and he served on the UN Secretariat for the remainder of his life.

In 1947 Bunche was appointed to the UN Special Committee on Palestine. He drafted both the majority report, which recommended a partition of the territory between Palestinians and Jews, and the minority report, which called for the creation of a federal state. The UN General Assembly accepted the partition plan, and Bunche was named the principal secretary for a commission designed to oversee its implementation. With the outbreak of war in 1948, Bunche was appointed as an assistant to the UN mediator, Count Folke Bernadotte. Following Bernadotte's assassination in September of that year,

Bunche became the acting mediator. He successfully negotiated armistice agreements between Israel and several Arab states and was awarded the 1950 Nobel Peace Prize for his efforts.

Bunche's commitment to the UN did not prevent him from speaking out against racial discrimination in the United States. In 1949 he turned down a position as assistant secretary of state, noting that he did not want to experience the blatant discrimination against African Americans that existed in the nation's capital. Bunche was appointed an undersecretary general for special political affairs in 1954. With the outbreak of the Suez crisis in 1956, he was again called upon to use his diplomatic skills in a Middle Eastern conflict, and he organized the UN Emergency Force that was responsible for peacekeeping activities in the region. His Middle East experience prepared him for the difficulties he faced in 1960, when he organized and commanded both the military and civilian branches of the UN peacekeeping force sent to the Congo. He

again directed a peacekeeping force when conflicts erupted on the island of Cyprus in 1964.

Bunche continued to press for the civil rights of African Americans. Although he still hoped for a society free from racial division, the civil rights conflicts of the late 1960s troubled him greatly. He participated in the 1965 march from Selma to Montgomery with MARTIN LUTHER KING JR. However, Bunche found himself under attack from leaders such as STOKELY CARMICHAEL and MALCOLM X, who argued that he had served white society and abandoned his African heritage. In turn, Bunche denounced the separatist agenda of the Black Power movement. Health problems, many related to diabetes, slowed him in the final years of his life. He died in New York City.

During his lifetime Bunche garnered international recognition and numerous awards for his UN service, including the U.S. Medal of Freedom in 1963. Although his position earned him the derision of many civil rights leaders in the 1960s, he was dedicated to the cause of African American civil rights throughout his career. By using his diplomatic skills in the service of the UN, he promoted the cause of peace in a world that sorely needed men of dedication and ability in this area.

FURTHER READING

Bunche's papers are at the Library of the University of California, Los Angeles, and the United Nations Archives in New York City. A smaller collection is at the Schomburg Center for Research in Black Culture of the New York Public Library.

Keppel, Ben. *The Work of Democracy: Ralph Bunche, Kenneth B. Clark, Lorraine Hansberry, and the Cultural Politics of Race* (1995).

Rivlin, Benjamin, ed. *Ralph Bunche: The Man and His Times* (1990).

Urquhart, Brian. *Ralph Bunche: An American Life* (1993).

—THOMAS CLARKIN

BURGESS, JOHN MELVILLE (11 Mar. 1909– 24 Aug. 2003), Episcopal bishop, was born in Grand Rapids, Michigan, the second son of Theodore Thomas Burgess, a train porter, and Ethel Inez

The Burgess Window at Grace Episcopal Church in Vineyard Haven, Massachusetts, depicting Bishop Burgess (right) and ABSALOM JONES. Window by Lyn Horey Studio Inc./Photo by Robert Schellhammer

Beverly, a kindergarten schoolteacher. He attended the public elementary school and Central High School in Grand Rapids, Michigan. In his boyhood he worked as a newsboy, took piano lessons, and was an acolyte at St. Phillip's Episcopal Church. In his teenage years he worked for a construction company, and while attending the University of Michigan he supported himself as a waiter and dishwasher. He graduated with a degree in Sociology in 1930.

Bishop Burgess was one of the first black graduates of the Episcopal Theological School in Cambridge, Massachusetts, where, in 1934, he received his Master of Divinity degree. In 1938 he was called to St. Simon Cyrene Episcopal Church, in Lincoln Heights, Ohio. At an Episcopal Church Conference for Colored Church orkers in 1944 he met

Whis wife, Esther Taylor, and they married the next year in her home parish in 1945 in Fredericton, New Brunswick, Canada. They subsequently had two daughters, Julia and Margaret. Burgess served as chaplain at Howard University from 1946 to 1956. In 1951 he became the first black canon at Washington Cathedral in Washington, D.C., while retaining his position at Howard.

He reached other milestones in the Episcopal Diocese of Massachusetts, as when he became archdeacon of Boston and superintendent of the Episcopal City Mission in Boston, assuming both roles in 1956. In 1962, he became the first black Episcopal priest to be popularly elected as suffragan bishop of the Diocese of Massachusetts within the regular order of the Episcopal Church. EDWARD T. DEMBY was the first African American Episcopal bishop, but before

Burgess black bishops had been elected to serve only black people or had been elected and appointed to Haiti or Liberia by the House of Bishops. In 1969 Burgess again made history as the first black elected as a diocesan bishop in the Episcopal Church, serving in that capacity from 1970 until his first retirement in 1975. During his tenure in Boston, Burgess was at the forefront of revitalizing urban ministry, confronting racism in public education, supporting efforts toward prison reform, and fighting the restoration of the death penalty. He provided significant leadership as an ecumenical leader in a coordinated effort to maintain peace in the early stages of the rancorous Boston school desegregation crisis. Burgess successfully built bridges between the black and white communities. He played a significant role as the president of the Black Ecumenical Commission, an organization formed by black clergy and laity of predominantly white denominations. Inspired in part by the national effort spearheaded by JAMES FORMAN and the Black Economic Development Committee, the commission secured, in 1971, more than three million dollars from their denominations in response to a demand for reparations on the local level. This was one of the few positive responses to the so-called Black Manifesto for Reparations for Slavery.

Bishop Burgess also remained a very popular figure in his diocese, with reforms designed to increase lay participation in the decision-making structure of the church. He also modeled shared leadership with the Right Reverend Ben Arnold, who was elected suffragan bishop of Massachusetts in 1972. Together they reformulated the urban mission strategy of the diocese and pioneered efforts to establish links with community-based social activists. The latter initiative became institutionalized as the Burgess Urban Fund by the Episcopal City Mission, which was created in honor of Burgess's retirement. This grant program was influential in swaying the philanthropic community in Boston to redirect their giving to grassroots organizations committed to economic development, housing, and racial reconciliation.

Bishop Burgess also drew attention to the importance of supporting community-based programs in the other twenty-one cities in the Diocese of Massachusetts. A strong supporter of lay ministry, he expanded the diocesan staff to include competent laymen and laywomen in the areas of Christian education, finance, and children's ministries. He also instituted many reforms in the diocesan structure to increase its efficiency. For example, he restructured the moribund archdeaconry system into a much more representative district system, thereby increasing the size of the Diocesan Council. At the end of his tenure the Diocese of Massachusetts was a much more inclusive diocese.

In 1976 Burgess and his wife moved to New Haven, Connecticut, where he served as bishop in residence and then as interim dean of the Berkeley Divinity School at Yale University. Using New Haven as his base, he continued an active ministry for many years, serving as assistant bishop in several dioceses and as a missionary presence in the Netherlands Antilles (Curaçao). In 1990 he and Esther retired to their summer home in West Tisbury, Massachusetts, on Martha's Vineyard.

These highlights of his career hardly do justice to the breadth and depth of his influence within the national Episcopal Church and the Anglican Communion. While he will be remembered for these achievements, Burgess gained his keen sense of social justice and his zeal to combat racism and violence during his early ministry at St. Phillips and St. Simon Cyrene at the height of the Depression. The brutal tactics used by the automobile industry to disrupt the formation of an integrated United Auto Workers Union and the struggles of the poor families in his congregations in coping with discrimination, the Depression, and the advent of World War II engendered in him the necessary sensitivity to be an effective chaplain at Howard University and a strong advocate for social justice from the pulpit of the National Cathedral in Washington, D.C.

While the bulk of his career was focused on institutional leadership and social policy, Burgess remained a deeply spiritual man. Before his marriage he had taken vows with the Order of the Holy Cross. This deep spiritual well, coupled with his practical experience, made him a powerful preacher and advocate in every cause that he undertook. Even in his retirement he brought those skills to bear in helping stabilize the fledgling black caucus within the Episcopal Church, the Union of Black Episcopalians. As a result of his leadership, both local and national church positions, lay and clerical, have been opened to black Episcopalians across the board.

Burgess also wrote many articles on social justice, urban ministry, and black preaching. In his *Black Gospel/White Church* (1982), he places in context some of the great sermons preached by black clergy during 192 years of black history in the Episcopal Church, melding a sharp critique of racism in the church with a keen social analysis of the role that black Episcopalians have played in the church and in society.

By opening the doors to the highest level of decision making in the Episcopal Church, Burgess paved the way for such African American notables as Bishop John Walker of Washington, D.C.; BARBARA HARRIS, the first woman elected bishop in the Anglican Communion; and some fourteen other black diocesan and suffragan bishops in the Episcopal Church. All of these people and countless others owe much to his courage, foresight, and perseverance. The length of his career is itself a testimony to the strength of his call and the inspirational leadership that he provided for all people of goodwill in the church.

Burgess's career spanned a period of considerable social change in the United States. Clearly, he understood the priorities of economic and social justice and was able to articulate and exemplify practical ways in which the church could be an effective instrument in the struggle for justice on many fronts. His leadership lent credibility and momentum to the ecumenical movement that was attempting to find its way in the mid-twentieth century, and undoubtedly he helped realize the dreams of those early black priests and laypeople whose faithfulness to a church that scorned them laid the foundation for future change. He was much sought after as a mentor to aspiring clergy of all colors and seen as a role model for black clergy and laity who sought careers at higher levels of institutional management in the life of the church.

This has left a lasting legacy in the church and the world including over twenty bishops of color and many laypeople in significant management positions at both the national and diocesan levels of the church. And, finally, his ministry became the model for effective leadership for blacks in society and helped encourage the aspirations and contributions of people like Senator EDWARD BROOKE, Justice THURGOOD MARSHALL, and Margaret Bush Wilson of the NAACP. These and countless other black Episcopalians looked up to and admired Burgess as a trailblazer for blacks in the Episcopal Church and as a champion of social justice and world peace.

FURTHER READING

Obituaries: *Boston Globe* and *New York Times*, 27 Aug. 2003.

—EDWARD W. RODMAN

BURLEIGH, HENRY THACKER (2 Dec. 1866–12 Sept. 1949), composer and spiritual singer, was born in Erie, Pennsylvania. Little is known about his parentage. When he was a boy, his excellent singing voice made Harry, as he was known, a sought-after performer in churches and synagogues in and around his hometown. In 1892, having decided on a career in music, Burleigh won a scholarship to the National Conservatory of Music in New York City. His matriculation coincided with the arrival of the Czech composer Antonín Dvořák, who taught there for four years. Dvořák, who was intensely interested in indigenous American music, found a valuable resource in the young Burleigh, who sang for him various African American spirituals. From Burleigh, Dvořák first heard "Go Down, Moses," "Roll, Jordan, Roll," "Were You There," "Swing Low," and "Deep River." When Dvořák set an arrangement of Stephen Foster's "Old Folks at Home," he dedicated it to Burleigh.

Buoyed by Dvořák's interest, Burleigh was further encouraged by what he interpreted to be fragments of these spirituals in Dvořák's famous *New World Symphony*. Some analysts agreed, but others took exception to this interpretation. An aesthetic dispute quickly took on political overtones. "Nothing could be more ridiculous than the attempts that have been made to find anything black . . . in the glorious soulful melody which opens the symphony," opined one New York critic. "Nothing could be more white. . . . Only a genius could have written it." While a few figures in the outwardly refined world of concert music had expressed some appreciation of African American traditions, Burleigh saw how readily this attitude could yield to prejudices that were ultimately no different from the racism he had encountered throughout his life. Burleigh never forgot the lesson. Indeed, when his own compositions first came before New York critics in the late 1890s, the composer encountered the same perverse efforts to reduce art to racial categories. One critic, admitting Burleigh's quality, proclaimed that "in his excellent songs [Burleigh was] more white than black."

Despite the sincere appreciation he received from such a luminary as Dvořák, Burleigh was wary of the white-dominated music world because of its bigotry and its tendency to place music into racial categories. He was also uncomfortable with the growing popularity of minstrelsy and jazz in the early twentieth century, for he feared that African American musical traditions could too easily be caricatured and mocked. Minstrel songs, he declared, "are gay and attractive. They have a certain rhythm, but they are not really music. The mistake [in capitalizing on their appeal] was partly the fault of the Negroes, partly the result of economic pressure."

Burleigh would never compromise his art, as he was sensitive to how easily it could be miscast and distorted. At the same time, though, he never abandoned the ideal that the cultural store he could bring forth in his singing and song-writing had a universality and hence a potential to transcend identities and labels. The spiritual, he felt, provided "the accent that is needed, a warm personal feeling which goes directly to the heart of the people." It had meaning as an articulation not only of African American culture but of the general human experience, particularly of the great human yearnings for freedom and universality, illustrated by what Burleigh

believed to be the two most profound stories in scripture—those of Moses and of the Resurrection. To Burleigh, the spirituals embodied these profound sentiments. Dvořák's response to them revealed how they could resonate in the soul of another musically sensitive person who was as yet unacquainted with any component of American culture. During World War I Burleigh found this point further underscored when a song he wrote called "The Young Warrior" became a popular marching tune among troops in the Italian army.

While working as a notator and editor in a New York publishing house, Burleigh continued to compose, almost exclusively as a songwriter, and throughout his life he sang. He became a celebrated performer of spirituals in several New York churches and compiled and published the first full anthology of African American religious music. He died in New York City in relative obscurity, but his music has been posthumously rediscovered and appreciated.

FURTHER READING

Simpson, Anne K. *Hard Trials: The Life and Music of Henry T. Burleigh* (1990).
Southern, Eileen. *The Music of Black Americans: A History* (1971).

—ALAN LEVY

 BURROUGHS, NANNIE HELEN (2 May 1879–20 May 1961), school founder, was born in Orange, Virginia, the daughter of John Burroughs, a farmer and itinerant Baptist preacher, and Jennie Poindexter, a cook and former slave. After moving to Washington, D.C., with her mother in 1883, Burroughs graduated in 1896 with honors in business and domestic science from the Colored High School on M Street. When racial discrimination barred her from obtaining a position either in the Washington, D.C., public schools or the federal civil service, Burroughs worked as a secretary, first for the Baptist *Christian Banner* in Philadelphia and then for the National Baptist Convention's Foreign Mission Board. She moved to Louisville, Kentucky, in 1900, when the Board's headquarters relocated there, and she stayed in Louisville until 1909. Studying business

Nannie Burroughs helped to found the National Training School for Women and Girls in Washington, D.C., in 1909 and served as its president until 1961. Library of Congress

education, she organized a Women's Industrial Club for black women, which evolved into a vocational school.

In 1900 Burroughs helped found the separate Woman's Convention, an auxiliary to the National Baptist Convention, and she served for forty-eight years as its corresponding secretary. Recruiting about 1.5 million black women—more than 60 percent of the entire convention's membership—the Woman's Convention was a congress of delegates from local churches, district associations, and states. It promoted charity work and home and foreign missions. Burroughs, who had spoken eloquently on "Women's Part in the World's Work" to the First Baptist World Alliance in London in 1905, also edited the *Worker*, a quarterly missionary magazine, which she began in 1912 and then revived in 1934, with the support of the white Woman's Missionary Union of the Southern Baptist Convention.

Burroughs also convinced the Woman's Convention to found the National Training School for Women and Girls, Incorporated (NTS), which opened on 19 October 1909 in Lincoln Heights, Washington, D.C. Serving as school president until her death,

Burroughs raised money, primarily among black women, to pay off the six-thousand-dollar purchase price. NTS also received some support from the white Woman's American Baptist Home Mission Society. The school's title did not include the word "Baptist," since it admitted young women and girls of all religious denominations. Enrollment rose to between 100 and 150 students, who could choose either the trade school or the seminary; the latter offered four divisions: seventh and eighth grades, a four-year high school, a two-year normal school, and a two-year junior college. By 1934 more than two thousand girls and women from the United States, the Caribbean, and Africa had taken academic, domestic science, trade, social service, and missionary training courses. To pay for their education, some students worked on campus, while others were domestic servants during the summer. By 1960 the school's physical plant had expanded from one to nine buildings and from six to thirteen acres.

Keenly aware of the limited employment opportunities for black women, Burroughs emphasized preparing students for employment as ladies' maids and laundresses. Domestic work, she believed, should be considered professional and even unionized. Burroughs inculcated a creed of racial self-help through her "three Bs—the Bible, the bath, and the broom: clean life, clean body, clean house." Students were trained to become respectable workers by being pious, pure, and domestic. But instead of being submissive, they were to become proud black women, inspired by a required course in African American history and culture. In 1927 Burroughs presented a paper to the Association for the Study of Negro Life and History on "The Social Value of Negro History." Under her leadership, NTS served as a center for African American community organizations and hosted the 1923 convention of the International Council of Women of the Darker Races. Burroughs, who participated with black clubwomen in memorializing the Anacostia home of FREDERICK DOUGLASS, was active in the NAACP and served in the 1940s, along with MARY MCLEOD BETHUNE, as one of two black women vice presidents on its national board.

Burroughs fought for thirty years for NTS's independence. When the National

Baptist Convention of the United States of America Inc., its new name after an internal division in 1915, charged that the school lacked a valid charter, Burroughs proclaimed, "This is God's hill," entrusted to her "and to the Negro Baptist women of America" for the black women of the world. The National Baptist Convention withdrew support from the school in June 1938 and urged that the Woman's Convention also sever its connections. Although the National Baptist Convention voted in 1939 to dismiss Burroughs from the Woman's Convention, the women rallied behind her. She continued to serve as corresponding secretary during the years when the school had no official financial support. In 1939 its charter legally incorporated several changes adopted earlier: the self-perpetuating board of trustees changed its name to the National Trade and Professional School for Girls, the board was streamlined, and the property was conferred to the Woman's Convention. The school began a fundraising campaign, since insufficient funds had caused it to close from 1935 to 1938. In 1947 new leaders of the National Baptist Convention formally endorsed the school, and in 1948 the Woman's Convention elected Burroughs president. Renamed in her honor in 1964, the school was designated a National Historic Landmark in 1991.

Burroughs spoke out on many contemporary political and social issues, for which she was put under surveillance by the federal government in 1917. She argued that until black men and women freely exercised their Fifteenth Amendment voting rights, they could not stop lynching and racial discrimination. Forming networks with other activist women such as Mary McLeod Bethune and MAGGIE LENA WALKER, Burroughs chaired the National Association of Colored Women's (NACW) Anti-Lynching Committee, was a charter member of the Anti-Lynching Crusaders, and belonged to the Commission on Interracial Cooperation's Women's Division. A regional president of the NACW, Burroughs chaired its Citizenship Department, which encouraged women to organize citizenship groups. She founded and became president of

the short-lived National Association of Wage Earners, whose purpose was to affiliate working women with the NACW clubwomen. Burroughs, president of the National League of Republican Colored Women, was appointed in 1932 by President Herbert Hoover to chair a committee reporting on African American housing at the President's Conference on Home Building and Home Ownership. During the Depression she assisted families in the nation's capital by helping to set up a medical clinic, convenience store, and the farming, canning, and hairdressing operations of the self-help Cooperative Industries Inc.

In 1944 Shaw University in Raleigh, North Carolina, conferred on Burroughs an LLD, and in 1958 the Washington chapter of the Lincoln University Alumni Association honored her at its annual Founders Day Banquet. She never married. Burroughs died in Washington, D.C. The District of Columbia honored her by naming 10 May 1975 the first Nannie Helen Burroughs Day.

Although contemporaries compared her to BOOKER T. WASHINGTON because of her advocacy of industrial education, she accepted neither black subservience to whites nor female subordination to male authority. Indeed, she told African American men to "glorify" black women for their many family and community contributions and not treat them as "slaves and servants" (*Pittsburgh Courier*, 23 Dec. 1933). Fighting brilliantly and stubbornly for the Woman's Convention, the National Training School, and for racial pride, Burroughs became a powerful role model for future generations.

FURTHER READING

Burroughs's papers are in the Library of Congress.

Barnett, Evelyn Brooks. "Nannie Burroughs and the Education of Black Women" in *The Afro-American Woman: Struggles and Images*, eds. Sharon Harley and Rosalyn Terborg-Penn (1978).
Easter, Opal V. *Nannie Helen Burroughs* (1995).
Harrison, Earl L. *The Dream and the Dreamer* (1956; repr. 1972).

Obituary: *Washington Post*, 21 May 1961.
—MARCIA G. SYNNOTT

C

CAESAR, JOHN

(?–17 Jan. 1837), African Seminole (Black Seminole) leader, warrior, and interpreter, was born in the mid-eighteenth century and joined the Seminole nation in Florida, one of the many groups of African Seminole Indians who fought to maintain an autonomous and independent nation. There are few written records to reveal the early life histories of the many escaped Africans and American Indians in the maroon communities across the Americas, and Caesar's life proves no exception. By the time his exploits were recorded in U.S. military records, Caesar was well acculturated to Seminole life and politics, and thus he had likely been a long-time member of the Seminole nation. His work as an interpreter between Native Seminoles and the U.S. military, however, reveals his early upbringing among English-speaking Americans. He grew up in a time of intense conflict between the Seminoles and European colonists, and had become a seasoned war veteran by the time of the Second Seminole War (1835–1842). Like many African Seminole women and men, Caesar had a spouse living on one of the local plantations, alongside the St. Johns River.

During the First Seminole War (1817), Caesar was a prominent leader who conducted raids on neighboring plantations and sought out runaway slaves and free African Americans to join the Seminole nation. He was closely associated with Seminole leader King Philip (Emathla), and together the two men battled the soldiers of the U.S. government during two wars. Acknowledged by U.S. military leaders and local plantation owners as a brilliant and powerful foe, Caesar followed a strategy of developing ties with enslaved African Americans on plantations in the St.

Johns River area, using these relationships to acquire supplies and recruit slaves to join the African Seminole resistance.

African Seminoles like Caesar had a complex political and social relationship with Native Seminoles. The escape of slaves from plantations was encouraged by the early Spanish colonists who were in competition with English colonies over Florida territory. Although some Native Seminoles held African Seminoles as slaves, especially in the nineteenth century, African Seminoles had significant autonomy and political influence, particularly as the maroon nation grew in size and strength. There was significant intermarriage and cultural exchange among the various local communities which included African Seminoles, Native Seminoles, free and enslaved African Americans, and members of various Native American nations who joined forces with the Seminoles. Although some African Seminole slaves faced a form of slavery comparable to that practiced by European American plantation owners, others were adopted into Seminole clans, enslaved for a limited period of cultural adaptation to the new nation, and could marry and have children who would be free citizens of the nation. Caesar, like most African Seminoles, adopted the language and many of the cultural traditions of his Native Seminole counterparts, and African Seminoles brought their own African cultural traditions as well, which had a significant influence on the development of Seminole culture. Because African Seminoles were faced with the threat of enslavement on southern plantations, many served as fearless leaders in the Seminole wars against the United States in order to prevent the defeat of the Seminole nation. Many Native Seminoles also had their lives inextricably linked with those of African Seminoles due to intermarriage, and were unwilling to abandon their African Seminole

family and friends to slave traders and plantation owners.

There were many other influential African Seminoles, including John Horse and Abraham, the latter serving as the chief associate, adviser, and interpreter to Seminole chief Micanopy. Like his counterpart Abraham, Caesar was the head adviser and interpreter to a Seminole chief, King Philip, father of Wild Cat and leader of the St. Johns River Seminoles. Caesar and Abraham worked together to sow the seeds of discontent among plantation slaves in Florida, and to develop relationships with free blacks and slaves who would assist in re-supplying the war effort. Caesar was successful in convincing numerous African slaves to join the Seminoles in their struggle for freedom.

In December 1835, with the beginning of the Second Seminole War, Caesar and King Philip attacked and destroyed numerous St. John's sugar plantations. Slaves joined the Seminoles in further attacks, which continued into 1836. The Second Seminole War lasted for nearly seven years, and was characterized by the perspective of General Thomas Jesup, who declared: "This, you may be assured is a negro and not a Indian war" (Thomas S. Jesup Papers, The University of Michigan, Box 14). African Seminoles, Native Seminoles, and escaped African slaves fought together in battles that cost the U.S. military dearly.

The incident for which Caesar is perhaps best known occurred in early March 1836. General Gaines and his troops were suffering the effects of a lengthy siege by the Seminole warriors, when Caesar unexpectedly arrived at Gaines's campsite to announce that the Seminoles wished to discuss a cease-fire agreement. Gaines agreed, and the parties met the next day in a series of discussions, with Caesar and Abraham serving as interpreters. Caesar's role in initiating the negotiations remains a matter of debate; in any case, the talks ended abruptly with the arrival of General Clinch, whose advance forces fired on the Seminole participants. Although Gaines claimed a victory after his troops' withdrawal, the Seminoles gained strategic advantages with the cease-fire holding long enough for the Seminoles to regroup and reinforce their position.

With the arrival of General Thomas S. Jesup in late 1836, the war took on a new and disturbing dimension, with Osceola's fighters pushed back into King Philip and John Caesar's St. Johns River territory. Caesar organized runaway slaves and a number of Native Seminoles into small bands of warriors, and attacked the plantations just outside St. Augustine. Caesar's attacks were effective, and to strengthen his position he went on raiding parties to acquire horses. On 17 January 1837, he and his men were discovered attempting to steal horses from the Hanson plantation, and that evening, as they sat around their campfire, they were attacked by Captain Hanson's men, who killed three warriors, including Caesar.

Caesar's untimely death did not diminish the importance and influence of his life. His effectiveness at recruiting slaves from the plantations forced the U.S. military to negotiate over the issue of African Seminoles, and this resulted in the removal of African Seminoles alongside Native Seminoles, rather than their immediate re-enslavement on southeastern plantations. He was a major leader in a powerful maroon nation, which offered a unique opportunity for autonomy and freedom for Africans and American Indians who dared to escape plantations and European American colonial oppression. Caesar served as a potent symbol of an alternative vision for both African Americans and American Indians, that of merging cultures and political alliances. The two communities combined forces, and this new alliance proved a powerful and convincing tool in the hands of John Caesar, an African Seminole visionary, warrior, and political strategist.

FURTHER READING

Mulroy, Kevin. *Freedom on the Border* (1993).
Porter, Kenneth. *The Black Seminoles* (1996).
—JONATHAN BRENNAN

CAILLOUX, ANDRÉ

(25 Aug. 1825–27 May 1863), first black soldier to die in the Civil War, was born in Plaquemine Parish, Louisiana, the son of André Cailloux, a slave skilled in masonry and carpentry, and Josephine Duvernay, a slave of Joseph Duvernay. On 15 July 1827 young André was baptized in St. Louis Cathedral in New Orleans.

After the death of Joseph Duvernay in 1828, Joseph's sister, Aimée Duvernay Bailey, acquired André Cailloux and his parents and brought them all to New Orleans. There André likely learned the cigar-maker's trade from his half-brothers, Molière and Antoine Duvernay, the freed sons of his mother, Josephine, and her master Joseph Duvernay. After he was manumitted by his mistress in 1846, Cailloux married another recently freed slave, Félicie Coulon, on 22 June 1847. Cailloux adopted Félicie's son, Jean Louis, and the couple had four more children, three of whom survived into adulthood.

Cailloux and his wife moved into the ranks of the closely-knit New Orleans community of approximately eleven thousand free people of color (*gens de couleur libre*, Creoles of color, or Afro-Creoles). African or Afro-French/Spanish in ancestry, French in culture and language, and Catholic in religion, free people of color occupied an intermediate legal and social status between whites and slaves within Louisiana's tripartite racial caste system. Denied political rights, free people of color nevertheless could own property, make contracts, and testify in court. They constituted the most prosperous and literate group of people of African descent in the United States, with a majority earning modest livings as artisans, skilled laborers, and shopkeepers, while a few enjoyed greater wealth. Some free people of color owned slaves, either for economic reasons or as a way of bringing together family members. Although most free people of color were of mixed race, they ran the gamut of phenotypes. Cailloux, for example, bragged of being the blackest man in New Orleans.

By the mid-1850s Cailloux, who had learned to read and write, had become a respectable, independent cigar maker. He resided in a Creole cottage worth

about four hundred dollars, and purchased his slave mother, reuniting his family. Cailloux had his children baptized in the Catholic church, and sent his two sons to *L'Institution Catholique des Orphelins dans l'Indigence* (*Institute Catholique*), a school run by Afro-Creole intellectuals influenced by the inclusive and egalitarian ethos of the 1848 French Revolution. Cailloux's peers elected him an officer of *Les Amis de l'Ordre* (the Friends of Order), one of the numerous mutual aid and benefit societies established by free people of color during the decade. These provided forums in which people of color could exercise leadership and engage in the democratic process.

By the late 1850s, however, the legal, social, and economic position of free people of color had deteriorated, and in 1861, Cailloux sold his cottage at auction. After the Civil War began, free people of color answered the governor's request that they raise a militia regiment by forming the Defenders of the Native Land, otherwise known as the Louisiana Native Guards Regiment. They did so out of fear of possible reprisals if they failed to respond positively, and in the hope of improving their circumstances. Mutual aid and benefit societies formed themselves into companies for service in the regiment. Cailloux, for instance, assumed the rank of first lieutenant in Order Company. Louisiana officials, however, intended the regiment more for show than for combat.

When Confederate forces abandoned the city of New Orleans to Federal forces in late April 1862, the Louisiana Native Guards disbanded. In August 1862, however, U.S. General Benjamin F. Butler, suffering from a shortage of troops and fearing a Confederate attack on the city, authorized the recruitment of three regiments of free people of color, the first units of people of African descent formally mustered into the Union Army. While the field grade officers were white, the company officers were free people of color.

Cailloux received a commission as captain in the First Regiment. He quickly raised a company of troops, the majority of whom were Catholic free men of color drawn from the city's Third District, where he worked and attended meetings of *Les Amis de l'Ordre*. But despite a formal directive that restricted enlistments to free men,

Cailloux also welcomed runaway slaves, both French and English speaking. He no doubt shared the hope expressed by Afro-Creole activists in the pages of their newspaper *L'Union*, that military service would give blacks a claim to citizenship. Gentlemanly, athletic, charismatic, and confident, the thirty-eight-year-old Cailloux cut a dashing figure, belying the stereotype of black servility and inferiority.

Cailloux and the men of the Native Guards, however, faced daunting challenges. They suffered discrimination and abuse at the hands of white civilians, soldiers, and their own national government. In the field, they found themselves consigned primarily to guard duty or to backbreaking manual labor. To make matters worse, General Nathaniel P. Banks, Butler's successor, determined to purge the Native Guard Regiments of their black officers.

Yearning to prove themselves in combat, Cailloux and two regiments of the Native Guards received their chance on 27 May 1863 at Port Hudson, Louisiana, one of two remaining Confederate strongholds on the Mississippi River. There Cailloux's company spearheaded an assault by the First and Third Regiments against a nearly impregnable Confederate position. As the Native Guards approached to within about two hundred yards of the entrenched Confederate force, they encountered withering musket and artillery fire and the attacking lines broke. Cailloux and other officers attempted to rally their men several times. Finally, in the midst of the chaos, Cailloux, holding his sword aloft in his right hand while his broken left arm dangled at his side, exhorted his troops to follow him. Advancing well in front, he led a charge. As he reached a backwater obstacle, he was struck and killed by a shell. The remaining Native Guards retreated, as did Union forces all along the battle line that day. Cailloux's body lay rotting in the broiling sun for forty days until the surrender of Port Hudson on 8 July 1863.

Cailloux's heroics encouraged those supporting the cause of using black troops in combat. *L'Union* declared that Cailloux's patriotism and valor had vindicated blacks of the charge that they lacked manliness. To memorialize Cailloux, Afro-Creole activists orchestrated a public funeral in New Orleans presided over by the Reverend Claude Paschal Maistre, a French priest recently suspended by the archbishop of New Orleans for advocating emancipation and the Union cause. Emboldened by Cailloux's heroism, blacks, both slave and free, asserted their growing political consciousness. They packed the city's main streets in unprecedented numbers as the military cortege bearing Cailloux's casket made its way to St. Louis Cemetery Number 2. Maistre eulogized Cailloux as a martyr to the cause of Union and freedom; northern newspapers gave extensive coverage to his death and funeral; George H. Boker, a popular poet, memorialized Cailloux in his ode, *The Black Captain*; and Afro-Creole activists in New Orleans elevated him to almost mythic status, invoking his name in their campaign against slavery and on behalf of voting rights.

In October 1864 delegates to the National Negro Convention literally wrapped themselves in Cailloux's banner. With the First Regiment's bloodstained flag hanging in a place of honor, numerous speakers invoked Cailloux's indomitable spirit and heroism and launched a nationwide campaign for black suffrage through the creation of the National Equal Rights League. Both in life and in death, André Cailloux, whose surname means "rocks" or "stones" in French, served to unite and inspire people of color in their struggle for unity, freedom, and equality.

FURTHER READING

Edmonds, David C. *The Guns of Port Hudson: The Investment, Siege, and Reduction*, 2 vols. (1984).

Ochs, Stephen J. *A Black Patriot and a White Priest: André Cailloux and Claude Paschal Maistre in Civil War New Orleans* (2000).

———. "American Spartacus." *American Legacy*, Fall 2001, 31–36.

Wilson, Joseph T. *The Black Phalanx* (1890).

Obituary: New York Times, 8 Aug. 1863.

—STEPHEN J. OCHS

 CALIVER, AMBROSE

(25 Feb. 1894–29 Jan. 1962), educator, college administrator, and civil servant, was born in Saltville, Virginia, the youngest child of Ambrose Caliver Sr.

Little is known about his parents, but very early in his life he and his two siblings moved to Knoxville, Tennessee, where they were raised by an aunt, Louisa Bolden. Bolden, a widowed cook who took in boarders to make ends meet, allowed Caliver to accept a job at a very young age. According to one account, the young Caliver was working in a coal mine by the time of his eighth birthday. Early employment, however, did not prevent him from attending school regularly. After receiving an education from Knoxville's public school system, he enrolled at Knoxville College, where he obtained his BA in 1915. He eventually earned an MA from the University of Wisconsin (1920) and a PhD from Columbia University (1930).

After graduating from Knoxville, Caliver immediately sought employment as an educator. In 1915 he married his childhood sweetheart, Rosalie Rucker, and they both took various teaching jobs, first in Knoxville and then in El Paso, Texas. By 1917 they had returned to Tennessee, where they received faculty positions at Fisk University in Nashville. Caliver's acceptance of the position at Fisk was significant, because he became one of the few black faculty members hired on campus. Caliver began working at Fisk during one of the most tumultuous points in the university's history. Under the leadership of Fayette A. McKenzie, Fisk gained the unwarranted reputation of being out of touch with the African American population. Caliver assisted in changing this perception. An ardent believer in the industrial and manual arts, he encouraged Fisk's students to take woodshop and other courses that would teach them how to work with their hands. Caliver believed that these skills would not only benefit the students financially but also make them assets to the local black community. According to one observer, one of Caliver's more memorable moments at Fisk was when he drove a bright red wagon that his students had made in his workshop across the platform during a university assembly.

Fisk administrators soon recognized the talent of their young faculty member and quickly gave him other responsibilities. In a continuing effort to strengthen the school's ties to the local black community, Caliver organized the

Tennessee Colored Anti-Tuberculosis Society. Serving four years as the organization's director and chair of its executive committee, Caliver sought to increase awareness and prevent the spread of the disease among Tennessee's African American population. His other major administrative appointments at Fisk included a spell as university publicity director in 1925, and as dean of the Scholastic Department the following year. In 1927 Caliver was appointed Fisk's first African American dean of the university (1927).

Fisk only briefly enjoyed Caliver's services as dean. Two years after his appointment, he took a one-year leave from his duties to complete the requirements for his doctorate at Columbia University. Caliver never returned to his position at Fisk. Shortly before his graduation, he received two job offers—one for a faculty position at Howard University and, shortly afterward, another for a position at the U.S. Office of Education. In 1930 he accepted the latter job and became the Office of Education's Specialist in Negro Education. It was in this post that Caliver made what is arguably his most lasting contribution to African American education.

During his tenure in the U.S. Office of Education, Caliver participated in numerous studies and published several articles and monographs dealing with the status of African American education. These works included the pamphlets *Bibliography on the Education of the Negro* (1931), *Background Study of Negro College Students* (1933), and *Rural Elementary Education among Negro Jeanes Supervisors* (1933). Some of his monographs during this period were *The Education of Negro Teachers in the United States* (1933), *Secondary Education for Negroes* (1933), and the *Availability of Education to Negroes in Rural Communities* (1935). Caliver was also instrumental in creating the National Advisory Committee of the Education of Negroes. This group, consisting of many leading educators from across the United States, sought to discuss the problems and develop programs to enhance black education. Hoping to benefit the greatest number of African Americans, the organization tended to focus on issues in secondary schools,

such as poor facilities and inadequate materials, rather than on inadequacies in African American institutions of higher learning.

The study of secondary schools undoubtedly contributed to what Caliver saw as the greatest problem facing black education: adult illiteracy. According to some estimates, approximately one quarter of the 12.6 million African Americans were illiterate. Caliver was determined to place this issue in the national spotlight. To accomplish this, he reached out to prominent African American organizations and leaders and encouraged them to take a more active role. Caliver also called for the preparation of instructional materials, the creation of teacher-training workshops, and the development of adult-education programs at historically black colleges and universities. He oversaw the creation of several readers to increase literacy. These readers, "A Day with the Brown Family," "Making a Good Living," and "The Browns Go to School." not only increased literacy skills but also emphasized family living, thrift, and leisure activities.

In addition to his contributions to adult education, Caliver also succeeded in utilizing radio as a tool for education and instilling racial pride. In 1941, with funding from such philanthropic groups as the Julius Rosenwald Fund, he created *Freedom's People*, a nine-part series examining African American life, history, and culture. From September 1941 through April 1942, the National Broadcasting Company broadcast the program, one of the first of its kind devoted exclusively to African Americans. *Freedom's People* taught its listeners not only about famous black historical figures but also about the contributions of blacks in the areas of science, music, and industry. The program featured guest appearances by some of the most prominent African Americans of the day including JOE LOUIS, A. PHILIP RANDOLPH, and PAUL ROBESON.

For the next two decades Caliver's efforts in adult education and literacy increased. From 1946 to 1950, he directed the Office of Education's Literacy Education Project, and in 1950 he became the assistant to the commissioner of education. By 1955 Caliver

was the chief of the Office of Education's Adult Education Section. This new appointment, along with his election as the president of the Adult Education Association of the United States six years later, contributed to his reputation as one of the most ardent crusaders against illiteracy in the federal government. Ambrose Caliver died in January 1962, still working as diligently as he had in his youth. At the time of his death he was moving forward with plans to expand and increase the services of the Adult Education Association of the United States.

FURTHER READING

Daniel, Walter G., and John B. Holden. *Ambrose Caliver: Adult Educator and Civil Servant* (1966).

Wilkins, Theresa B. "Ambrose Caliver: Distinguished Civil Servant." *Journal of Negro Education* 31 (Spring 1962): 212–214.

Obituary: *Washington Post*, 2 Feb. 1942.

—LEE WILLIAMS JR.

 CALLOWAY, CAB
(25 Dec. 1907–18 Nov. 1994), popular singer and bandleader, was born Cabell Calloway III in Rochester, New York, the third of six children of Cabell Calloway Jr., a lawyer, and Martha Eulalia Reed, a public school teacher. In 1920, two years after the family moved to the Calloways' hometown of Baltimore, Maryland, Cab's father died. Eulalia later remarried and had two children with John Nelson Fortune, an insurance salesman who became known to the Calloway children as "Papa Jack."

Although he later enjoyed a warm relationship with his stepfather, the teenaged Cab had a rebellious streak that tried the patience of parents attempting to maintain their status as respectable Baltimoreans. He often skipped school to go to the nearby Pimlico racetrack, where he both earned money selling newspapers and shining shoes and began a lifelong passion for horse racing. After his mother caught him playing dice on the steps of the Presbyterian church, however, he was sent in 1921 to Downingtown Industrial

Cab Calloway, propelled to stardom with his exuberant "Minnie the Moocher," was photographed by Carl Van Vechten, 1933. Library of Congress

and Agricultural School, a reform school run by his mother's uncle in Pennsylvania. When he returned to Baltimore the following year, Calloway recalls that he resumed hustling but also worked as a caterer, and that he studied harder than he had before and excelled at both baseball and basketball at the city's Frederick Douglass High School. Most significantly, he resumed the voice lessons he had begun before reform school, and he began to sing both in the church choir and at several speakeasies, where he performed with Johnny Jones's Arabian Tent Orchestra, a New Orleans–style Dixieland band. In his senior year in high school, Calloway played for the Baltimore Athenians professional basketball team, and in January 1927 he and Zelma Proctor, a fellow student, had a daughter, whom they named Camay.

In the summer after graduating from high school, Calloway joined his sister Blanche, a star in the popular *Plantation Days* revue, on her company's midwestern tour, and, by his own account,

"went as wild as a March hare," chasing "all the broads in the show" (Calloway, 54). When the tour ended in Chicago, Illinois, he stayed and attended Crane College (now Malcolm X University). While at Crane he turned down an offer to play for the Harlem Globetrotters, not, as his mother had hoped, to pursue a law career, but instead to become a professional singer. He worked nights and weekends at the Dreamland Café and then won a spot as a drummer and house singer at the Sunset Club, the most popular jazz venue on Chicago's predominantly African American South Side. There he befriended LOUIS ARMSTRONG, then playing with the Carroll Dickerson Orchestra, who greatly influenced Calloway's use of "scat," an improvisational singing style that uses nonsense syllables rather than words.

When the Dickerson Orchestra ended its engagement at the Sunset in 1928, Calloway served as the club's master of ceremonies and, one year later, as

the leader of the new house band, the Alabamians. His position as the self-described "dashing, handsome, popular, talented M.C. at one of the hippest clubs on the South Side" (Calloway, 61) did little to help his already fitful attendance at Crane, but it introduced him to many beautiful, glamorous, and rich women. He married one of the wealthiest of them, Wenonah "Betty" Conacher, in July 1928. Although he later described the marriage as a mistake, at the time he greatly enjoyed the "damned comfortable life" that came with his fame, her money, and the small house that they shared with a South Side madam.

In the fall of 1929 Calloway and the Alabamians embarked on a tour that brought them to the mecca for jazz bands of that era, Harlem in New York City. In November, however, a few weeks after the stock market crash downtown on Wall Street, the Alabamians also crashed uptown in their one chance for a breakout success, a battle of the bands at the famous Savoy Ballroom. The hard-to-please Savoy regulars found the Alabamians' old-time Dixieland passé and voted overwhelmingly for the stomping, more danceable music of their rivals, the Missourians. The Savoy audience did, however, vote for Calloway as the better bandleader, a tribute to his charismatic stage presence and the dapper style in which he outfitted the Alabamians.

Four months later, following a spell on Broadway and on tour with the pianist FATS WALLER in the successful *Connie's Hot Chocolate* revue, he returned to the Savoy as the new leader of the Missourians, renamed Cab Calloway and His Orchestra. In 1931 the band began alternating with DUKE ELLINGTON's orchestra as the house band at Harlem's Cotton Club, owned by the gangster Owney Madden and infamous for its white-audiences-only policy. Calloway also began a recording career. Several of his first efforts for Brunswick Records, notably "Reefer Man" and "Kicking the Gong Around," the latter about characters in an opium den, helped fuel his reputation as a jive-talking hipster who knew his way around the less salubrious parts of Manhattan. Although he denied firsthand experience of illicit drugs, Calloway did admit to certain vices—fast cars, expensive clothes, "gambling, drinking, partying [and] balling all through the night, all over the country" (Calloway, 184).

It was 1931's "Minnie the Moocher," with its scat-driven, call-and-response chorus, that became Calloway's signature tune and propelled him to stardom. The most prosaic version of the chorus had Cab calling out, "Hi-de-hi-de-hi-di-hi, Ho-de-ho-de-ho-de-ho" or, when the mood took him, "Oodlee-odlyee-odlyee-oodle-doo" or "Dwaa-de-dwaa-de-dwaa-de-doo," while his orchestra—and later the audience—responded with the same phrase. Calloway recalled in his autobiography that the song came first and the chorus was later improvised when he forgot the lyrics during a radio broadcast. The song's appeal was broadened in 1932 by its appearance in the movie *The Big Broadcast* and in a Betty Boop cartoon short, *Minnie the Moocher*. Radio broadcasts from the Cotton Club and appearances on radio with Bing Crosby made Calloway one of the wealthiest entertainers during the Depression era. The Calloway Orchestra embarked on several highly successful national tours and in 1935 became one of the first major black jazz bands to tour Europe.

Although the Calloway Orchestra was arguably the most popular jazz band of the 1930s and 1940s, most jazz critics view the bands of Duke Ellington, Louis Armstrong, and COUNT BASIE as more musically sophisticated. ALBERT L. MURRAY's influential *Stomping the Blues* (1976) does not even mention Calloway, although it does list several members of his orchestra, including the tenor saxophonist Chu Berry and the trumpeter DIZZY GILLESPIE, who joined the band in 1939 and left two years later, after he stabbed Calloway in the backside during a fight. With the drummer Cozy Cole and the vibraphonist Tyree Glenn, the Calloway Orchestra showcased its rhythmic virtuosity in several instrumentals, including the sprightly "Bye Bye Blues" and the sensual "A Ghost of a Chance," both recorded in 1940.

It was, however, Calloway's exuberant personality, his cutting-edge dress style—he was a pioneer of the zoot suit—and his great rapport with his audiences that packed concert halls for nearly two decades. In the 1940s he was ubiquitous, appearing on recordings,

radio broadcasts of his concerts, and in movies such as *Stormy Weather* (1943), in which he starred with LENA HORNE, BILL "BOJANGLES" ROBINSON, KATHERINE DUNHAM, and FATS WALLER. In 1942, he hosted a satirical network radio quiz show, "The Cab Calloway Quizzicale." Calloway even changed the way Americans speak, with the publication of *Professor Cab Calloway's Swingformation Bureau* and *The New Cab Calloway's Hepsters Dictionary: Language of Jive* (1944), which became the official jive language reference book of the New York Public Library. The *Oxford English Dictionary* credits Calloway's song "Jitter Bug" as the first published use of that term.

The end of World War II marked dramatic changes in Calloway's professional and personal lives. In 1948 the public preference for small combos and the bebop style of jazz, pioneered by Gillespie, among others, forced Calloway to break up his swing-style big band. One year later Calloway divorced Betty Conacher, with whom he had adopted a daughter, Constance, in the late 1930s, and married Zulme "Nuffie" McNeill, with whom he would have three daughters, Chris, Lael, and Cabella. His career revived, however, in 1950, when he landed the role of Sportin' Life in the revival of George Gershwin's *Porgy and Bess* on Broadway and in London and Paris. The casting was inspired, since Gershwin had modeled the character of Sportin' Life on Calloway in his "Hi-de-hi" heyday. From 1967 to 1970 he starred with PEARL BAILEY in an all-black Broadway production of *Hello Dolly!*, and in 1980 he endeared himself to a new generation of fans, with his performance of "Minnie the Moocher," in the film *The Blues Brothers*, with John Belushi and Dan Aykroyd. That role led to appearances on the television shows *The Love Boat* and *Sesame Street* and on Janet Jackson's music video "Alright," which won the 1990 Soul Train award for best rhythm and blues/urban contemporary music video.

In June 1994 Calloway suffered a stroke at his home in White Plains, New York, and died five months later at a nursing home in Hockessin, Delaware. President Bill Clinton, who had awarded Calloway the National Medal of the Arts a year earlier, paid tribute to him as a "true legend among the musicians of this century, delighting generations

of audiences with his boundless energy and talent" (*New York Times*, 30 Nov. 1994). Calloway, however, probably put it best when he described himself in his autobiography as, "the hardest jack with the greatest jive in the joint."

FURTHER READING

Calloway's papers are held at Boston University.

Calloway, Cab, and Bryant Rollins. *Of Minnie the Moocher and Me* (1976).

Schuller, Gunther. *The Swing Era: The Development of Jazz, 1930–1945* (1989).

Obituary: *New York Times*, 20 Nov. 1994.
—STEVEN J. NIVEN

CALLOWAY, ERNEST

(1 Jan. 1909–31 Dec. 1989), labor activist, journalist, and educator, was born in Heberton, West Virginia, the son of Ernest Calloway Sr.; his mother's name is unknown. The family moved to the coalfields of Letcher County, Kentucky, in 1913, where Calloway's father, "Big Ernest," helped organize the county's first local chapter of the United Mine Workers of America. The Calloways were one of the first black families in the coal-mining communities of eastern Kentucky, and Ernest was, by his own description, "one of those unique persons...a black hillbilly." Calloway attended high school in Lynchburg, Virginia, but ran away to New York in 1925 and arrived in the middle of the Harlem Renaissance. He worked as a dishwasher in Harlem until his mother fell ill, when he returned to Kentucky at age seventeen and worked in the mines of the Consolidated Coal Company until 1930. During the early 1930s he traveled as a drifter around the United States and Mexico.

Calloway came to the end of his resources at a tent colony near the small town of Ensenada in the Baja Mountains of Mexico in 1933. There he had a frightening hallucinatory experience that changed his life. "Damnedest experience that whole night," he later recounted to an interviewer. "I think this was the first time that, the morning after getting out of those mountains and that frightening experience, the first time that I really began thinking about myself and about people and what makes the world tick." He returned to the coal mines of Kentucky determined to move beyond a drifter's existence.

Inspired by his strange experience in the mountains, Calloway submitted an article on marijuana use to *Opportunity*, the magazine of the National Urban League, in 1933. *Opportunity* rejected it, and, sadly, a copy of it did not survive. The magazine did ask him to write another article, however, on the working conditions of blacks in the Kentucky coalfields. He submitted the second article, "The Negro in the Kentucky Coal Fields," which appeared in March 1934. This article resulted in a scholarship for Calloway to Brookwood Labor College in New York, a training facility for labor organizers founded by the pacifists Helen and Henry Fink and headed by A. J. Muste. Moreover, the article began Calloway's long involvement with labor issues.

From 1935 to 1936 Calloway worked in Virginia and helped organize the Virginia Workers' Alliance, a union of unemployed Works Progress Administration workers. He helped organize a conference in 1936 to ally the labor movement with the unemployed—groups organized by socialists, communists, Trotskyists, and unemployment councils. After turning down an offer to recruit African Americans into a front group for the U.S. State Department and its intelligence services, Calloway moved to Chicago in 1937. There he helped organize the Red Caps, as railway station porters were known, and other railway employees into the United Transport Employees Union. He also helped write the resolution creating the 1942 Committee against Discrimination in the Congress of Industrial Organizations (CIO). When the first peacetime draft law came into effect in 1939, Calloway was among the first African Americans to refuse military service as a protest against race discrimination. Although the case received national publicity, it was never officially settled, and Calloway never served in the Jim Crow U.S. Army.

Calloway's career in news journalism began when he joined the National CIO News editorial staff in 1944. Two years later he married DeVerne Lee, a teacher who had led a protest against racial segregation in the Red Cross in India during World War II. DeVerne Calloway later served as the first black woman elected to the state legislature in Missouri. She did much to increase state aid to public education, improve welfare grants, and reform the prison system in the state.

In 1947 Calloway received a scholarship from the British Trade Union Congress to attend Ruskin College in Oxford, England, where he spent a year. He then returned to the United States and began working with Operation Dixie, the CIO's southern organizing drive in North Carolina. Because of a dispute over organizing tactics in an attempt to unionize workers at R. J. Reynolds Tobacco Company, Calloway left the CIO in 1950 and returned to Chicago. Harold Gibbons of the St. Louis Teamsters union enlisted him to establish a research department for Teamsters Local 688 in St. Louis, which was at that time one of the most racially progressive union locals in the nation.

In the 1950s Calloway played a pivotal role in civil rights and labor activism in St. Louis. In 1951, three years prior to the U.S. Supreme Court's school desegregation decision in *Brown v. Board of Education*, Calloway advised Local 688 on a plan to integrate the St. Louis public schools; the St. Louis Board of Education rejected the Teamsters proposals. The St. Louis branch of the NAACP elected Calloway president in 1955. Within the first two years of his presidency, membership grew from two thousand to eight thousand members. He led successful efforts to gain substantial increases in the number of blacks employed by St. Louis taxi services, department stores, the Coca-Cola Company, and Southwestern Bell. Under his leadership, the group helped defeat a proposed city charter in 1957 that did not include support for civil rights.

Calloway's political involvement included serving in 1959 as campaign director for the Reverend John J. Hicks, who became the first black elected to the St. Louis Board of Education. Calloway also directed Theodore McNeal's 1960 senatorial campaign. McNeal won by a large margin, becoming the first black elected to the Missouri Senate. In 1961 Calloway worked as the technical adviser for James Hurt Jr. in his successful campaign as the second black to be elected to the St. Louis school board. He also helped his wife, DeVerne, win her historic spot in the Missouri legislature in her first bid for public office.

In 1961 the couple began publishing *Citizen Crusader*, later named *New Citizen*, a newspaper covering black politics and civil rights in St. Louis. It provided Calloway with a larger platform for his writing than anything had previously. During this period he developed a passion for explaining in numbers and tables the arithmetic of African American political power in St. Louis. The newspaper lasted until November 1963, but even after it stopped publishing, the Calloways continued to produce newspapers, including one entitled *Truth*, in support of their political allies. As a testament to the effectiveness of these papers, in 1964 supporters of Barry Goldwater published their own version of *Truth*, complete with an identical masthead, solely to take a stand against a local Democratic Party candidate endorsed by the Calloways' *Truth*.

Calloway worked with the Committee on Fair Representation in 1967 to develop a new plan for congressional district reapportionment. Supported by black representatives in the Missouri legislature and a coalition of white Republicans and Democrats, the plan created a First Congressional District more compatible with black interests. In 1968 Calloway filed as a candidate for U.S. Congress in the new district but was defeated in the Democratic primary by William Clay, who became the first black elected to the U.S. Congress from Missouri.

In 1969 Calloway lectured parttime for St. Louis University's Center for Urban Programs. He became an assistant professor when he retired as research director for the Teamsters in June 1973 and, later, Professor Emeritus of Urban Studies at St. Louis University. From his modest roots, Calloway pursued a multifaceted life, all the while creating a record of thoughtful reflections on public events and history over a lifetime of change. He suffered a disabling stroke in 1982 and died after a series of additional strokes. His name is still spoken with reverence in his hometown and among people familiar with his work.

FURTHER READING

Ernest Calloway's papers, as well as those of DeVerne Calloway, are in the Western Historical Manuscript Collection–St. Louis at the University of Missouri–St. Louis.

Burnside, Gordon. "Calloway at 74." *St. Louis Magazine*, March 1983.
Bussel, Robert. "A Trade Union Oriented War on the Slums: Harold Gibbons, Ernest Calloway, and the St. Louis Teamsters in the 1960s." *Labor History* 44, no. 1 (2003): 49–67.
Cawthra, Benjamin. "Ernest Calloway: Labor, Civil Rights, and Black Leadership in St. Louis." *Gateway Heritage*, Winter 2000–2001, 5–15.

—KENNETH F. THOMAS

 CANNON, GEORGE DOWS (16 Oct. 1902–31 Aug. 1986), physician and political activist, was born in Jersey City, New Jersey, the son of George E. Cannon and Genevieve Wilkinson. His father was a prominent and politically connected physician who graduated from Lincoln University in Pennsylvania and the New York Homeopathic Medical College. His mother, a teacher, was descended from a leading Washington, D.C., family that was free before the Civil War. Cannon and his sister, Gladys, grew up in an eighteen-room red brick house on a main Jersey City thoroughfare where their parents regularly received a retinue of prestigious visitors, including BOOKER T. WASHINGTON, numerous doctors from the all-black National Medical Association, and several Republican Party officeholders. Cannon greatly admired his father and emulated his professional and political involvements.

At his father's alma mater, Lincoln University, a Presbyterian institution, Cannon performed acceptably but without academic distinction. He scored well enough in his premedical courses, however, to be eligible for medical school upon graduation from Lincoln in 1924. Cannon gained admission to Columbia University's College of Physicians and Surgeons through the intervention of his father, who knew the president of the university. Despite enduring racially prejudiced professors, Cannon completed his freshman year with passing grades on all of his exams. His father's accidental death in April 1925 kept him from classes for a short time. Although Cannon fulfilled all of his class and laboratory assignments, his brief absence became a pretext for the dean to fail him in all of his courses. Cannon believed that racial prejudice and the manner of his admission had stirred a dislike for him. Because the Howard and Meharry medical schools would not admit him during the following fall, he entered Howard's graduate school to study for a master's degree in Zoology with the famed ERNEST EVERETT JUST. Impressed with Cannon's proficiency and saddened by his sorrowful experience at Columbia, Just recommended him to Rush Medical College in Chicago. Though the staff at Rush was less racist than that at Columbia, Cannon and the other black student, LEONIDAS BERRY, were told that each had been admitted so that the other one would not be lonely. Nonetheless, Cannon excelled in his work and made up for the lost time resulting from his ouster at Columbia. He was diagnosed with tuberculosis, however, during the final month before graduation. Treatment at a sanatorium in Chicago for nearly two years preceded his reentry to Rush. He earned the MD degree on 18 December 1934 after an internship at Chicago's all-black Provident Hospital. Continued health problems put Cannon into the Waverly Hills Hospital, a Louisville, Kentucky, sanatorium from 1934 through 1936, where he received treatment and pursued a medical residency. In the meantime, he had married his college sweetheart, Lillian Mosely, on 25 December 1931. The uncertainties surrounding his health compelled the couple to forgo parenthood, and they never had children.

Despite Cannon's fragile health, he vigorously developed as a leading New York City physician. He did not want to be bound to Harlem Hospital for staff privileges, so he tried throughout the late 1930s and 1940s for admittance to other hospitals. He was accepted on the staff of the Hospital for Joint Diseases in 1944. At the Triboro Tuberculosis Hospital, a racist physician, who opposed his appointment, eventually died and thus cleared the way for Cannon's appointment in 1947. He also gained privileges to treat and admit patients at the hospital for the Daughters of Israel. Cannon still encountered racist roadblocks at other facilities. He targeted hospitals with religious affiliations to admit black physicians to their staffs. Catholic, Episcopal, and Presbyterian hospitals rebuffed him. In the latter case, his membership at St. James Presbyterian Church in Harlem did not matter. At Lutheran Hospital a sympathetic white colleague made Cannon his substitute in the x-ray department, but hospital authorities overruled him. Jewish hospitals were more receptive. Mt. Sinai Hospital initially brought in Cannon as an assistant adjunct radiologist. Over time his radiology training at Triboro and his success at Mt. Sinai earned Cannon the respect he deserved among his black and white peers.

Cannon engaged in other struggles for black professionals and patients. He belonged to the integrated Physicians Forum, an alternative organization to the racially restrictive county medical societies and their parent group, the American Medical Association (AMA). Forum doctors focused on health care for the disadvantaged and fought racism in medical institutions. In Harlem he joined the Upper Manhattan Medical Group, a branch of the Health Insurance Plan of the City of New York, which rendered services through a prepaid health delivery system. Through the Physicians Forum, Cannon challenged the fee-for-service payment practice that most AMA doctors preferred. The improvement of conditions at Harlem Hospital also drew Cannon's attention. As president of the all-black Manhattan Central Medical Society and chairman of its Subcommittee on Health and Hospitals, Cannon exerted pressure upon city officials, who then corrected the lack of x-ray equipment, the absence of psychiatric services, and the inadequate number of surgeons to perform tonsillectomies. They also pressed city officials to open to blacks all municipal nursing schools beyond the two at Harlem and Lincoln hospitals.

Though a maverick Democrat, Cannon did not hesitate to form coalitions with radicals, including communists. As chair of the Non-Partisan Citizens' Committee in 1943 and 1945, he backed the successful candidacy of BENJAMIN

JEFFERSON DAVIS JR., a Communist, as Harlem's representative to City Council. Cannon himself was asked to run for city council and the state senate, both positions that he could have easily won. Whenever his party seemed too passive on civil rights matters, he supported candidates from other political groups. In 1948, for example, Henry A. Wallace, the Progressive Party presidential candidate, in Cannon's opinion, was a stronger advocate for civil rights than either Governor Thomas E. Dewey, the Republican, or President Harry Truman, the Democrat. Hence, Cannon became the Chairman of the Harlem Wallace-for-President Committee. Cannon held that it was possible to work with communists and Progressives on matters of race. Though he eschewed radical ideologies, Cannon's involvement with the Physicians Forum and its efforts for government-guaranteed health care and his political cooperation with radicals suggested to zealous anticommunists that Cannon's political sympathies were suspect. He was an enemy of Russia, he often said. Nonetheless, anyone who wished to work with him on black advancement was always a welcome ally.

Cannon's affiliations with the NAACP and the NAACP Legal Defense Fund (LDF) complemented his political activism. He served as the chairman of the life membership campaign for the New York state NAACP, and between 1956 and 1966 he held the same position for the national organization. At a dinner that he attended with Vice President Richard M. Nixon, Cannon planned to challenge the future president to buy an NAACP life membership. Before Cannon could successfully press his point, a black Nixon supporter said that the vice president should not pursue this symbolic action. Cannon, however, never forgot Nixon's affront to the NAACP. In 1962 Cannon became the secretary of the LDF, a position he held until 1984. Hence, during the height of the civil rights movement, he sided with the integrationist thrust of the NAACP and the LDF. The Black Power movement never drew support from Cannon.

His social and political activism extended to higher education. In 1947 Cannon became an alumni trustee of Lincoln University in Pennsylvania and later chairman of the board of trustees. His Lincoln classmate HORACE MANN

BOND had become in 1946 the first black president of the university, and each believed that Lincoln could become a model for racially integrated higher education. Though Cannon did not share Bond's intense zeal for African studies and forging stronger connections with emerging African nations, both understood that training leaders in various professions for both sides of the Atlantic was a crucial mission for their institution. Cannon developed positions on the role of faculty, continuation of the theological seminary, the need for greater alumni support, and the necessity of confronting the hostility of whites in neighboring Oxford, Pennsylvania. Cannon's frequent and detailed correspondence with Bond and his several successors showed a deep involvement in the affairs of Lincoln University that lasted through the 1980s. When Lincoln became the principal trustee of the Barnes Foundation, a repository of priceless modern art in suburban Philadelphia, Cannon delved into another area of educational and cultural affairs that further distinguished his alma mater.

When Cannon died in 1986, his Rush classmate Leonidas H. Berry eulogized Cannon and observed that his fragile health gave him a special empathy for his patients and motivated his extensive efforts for the uplift of African Americans. He lived to be an octogenarian despite diagnoses that belied the possibility for such a long and consequential career.

FURTHER READING

The George D. Cannon Papers are held at the Schomburg Center for Research in Black Culture of the New York Public Library. See also the George D. Cannon Files, Horace Mann Bond Papers, Lincoln University, Pennsylvania.

James, Daniel. "Cannon the Progressive." *New Republic*, 18 Oct. 1948.

—DENNIS C. DICKERSON

 CARDOZO, FRANCIS LOUIS (1 Feb. 1837– 22 July 1903), minister, educator, and politician, was born in Charleston, South Carolina, the son of a free black woman (name unknown) and a Jewish father. It is uncertain whether Cardozo's father was Jacob N. Cardozo,

the prominent economist and editor of an anti-nullification newspaper in Charleston during the 1830s, or his lesser-known brother, Isaac Cardozo, a weigher in the city's customhouse. Born free at a time when slavery dominated southern life, Cardozo enjoyed a childhood of relative privilege among Charleston's antebellum free black community. Between the ages of five and twelve he attended a school for free blacks, then he spent five years as a carpenter's apprentice and four more as a journeyman. In 1858 Cardozo used his savings to travel to Scotland, where he studied at the University of Glasgow, graduating with distinction in 1861. As the Civil War erupted at home, he remained in Europe to study at the London School of Theology and at a Presbyterian seminary in Edinburgh.

In 1864 Cardozo returned to the United States to become pastor of the Temple Street Congregational Church in New Haven, Connecticut. That year he married Cathcrine Rowena Howell; they had six children, one of whom died in infancy. During his brief stay in the North, Cardozo became active in politics. In October 1864 he was among 145 black leaders who attended a national black convention in Syracuse, New York, that reflected the contagion

Francis L. Cardozo became the first black state official in South Carolina during Reconstruction. Library of Congress

of rising expectations inspired by the Civil War and emancipation.

In June 1865 Cardozo became an agent of the American Missionary Association (AMA) and almost immediately returned to his native South Carolina. His brother Thomas Cardozo, the AMA's education director, was accused of having an affair with a student in New York, and Francis Cardozo replaced him while also assuming the directorship of the Saxton School in Charleston. Within months the school was flourishing under his leadership, with more than one thousand black students and twenty-one teachers. In 1866 Cardozo helped to found the Avery Normal Institute and became its first superintendent.

Unlike many South Carolinians of mixed race, Cardozo made no distinction between educating blacks who were born free and former slaves, nor did he draw conclusions, then common, about intellectual capacity based on skin color gradations. Instead, he was committed to universal education regardless of "race, color or previous condition," a devotion he considered "the object for which I left all the superior advantages and privileges of the North and came South, it is the object for which I have labored during the past year, and for which I am willing to *remain* here and make this place my home."

Despite the fact that he claimed to possess "no desire for the turbulent political scene," Cardozo soon found himself in the middle of Reconstruction politics. In 1865 he attended the state black convention in Charleston, where he helped draft a petition to the state legislature demanding stronger civil rights provisions. In 1868, following the passage of the Reconstruction Acts by Congress, he was elected as a delegate to the South Carolina constitutional convention. From the onset he was frank about his intentions, "As colored men we have been cheated out of our rights for two centuries and now that we have the opportunity I want to fix them in the Constitution in such a way that no lawyer, however cunning, can possibly misinterpret the meaning."

Cardozo wielded considerable influence at the convention. As chair of the Education Committee, he was instrumental in drafting a plan, which was later ratified, to establish a tax-supported system of compulsory, integrated public education, the first of its kind in the South. Despite his support for integration, however, he also understood the logic articulated by black teachers of maintaining support for separate schools for blacks who wanted to avoid the hostility and violence that often accompanied integration. Consistently egalitarian, he opposed poll taxes, literacy tests, and other forms of what he called "class legislation." Moreover, he fought proposals to suspend the collection of wartime debts, which he thought would only halt the destruction of "the infernal plantation system," a process he deemed central to Reconstruction's success. In fact, Cardozo argued, "We will never have true freedom until we abolish the system of agriculture which existed in the Southern States. It is useless to have any schools while we maintain the stronghold of slavery as the agricultural system of the country." Thus, he called for a tripartite approach to enfranchisement: universal access to political participation and power, comprehensive public education, and reform initiatives that guaranteed equal opportunity for land ownership and economic independence.

After the convention, Cardozo's career accelerated. A "handsome man, almost white in color . . . with . . . tall, portly, well-groomed figure and elaborately urbane manners" (Simkins and Woody), Cardozo played a central role in the real efforts to reconstruct American society along more democratic lines. In 1868 he declined the Republican nomination for lieutenant governor in the wake of white claims of Reconstruction "black supremacy." Later that year he was elected secretary of state, making him the first black state official in South Carolina history, and he retained that position until 1872. In 1869 Cardozo was a delegate to the South Carolina labor convention and then briefly served as secretary of the advisory board of the state land commission, an agency created to redistribute confiscated land to freedmen and poor whites. In this capacity, he helped to reorganize its operations after a period of severe mismanagement and corruption. As secretary of state, he was given full responsibility for overseeing the land commission. In 1872 he successfully advocated for the immediate redistribution of land to settlers and produced the first comprehensive report on the agency's financial activities. By the fall of 1872, owing in large part to Cardozo's efforts, over 5,000 families—3,000 more than in 1871—had settled on tracts of land provided by the commission, one of the more radical achievements of the Reconstruction era.

In 1870, the same year that the federal census estimated his net worth at an impressive eight thousand dollars, Cardozo was elected president of the Grand Council of Union Leagues, an organization that worked to ensure Republican victories throughout the state. His civic activities included serving as president of the Greenville and Columbia Railroad, a charter member of the Columbia Street Railway Company, and a member of the Board of Trustees of the University of South Carolina. Some sources report that he enrolled in the university's law school in October 1874; however, no evidence exists that he ever received a degree.

From 1871 to 1872 Cardozo was professor of Latin in Washington, D.C., at Howard University, where he was considered for the presidency in 1877. In 1872 and 1874 he was elected state treasurer, vowing to restore South Carolina's credit. During his first term as treasurer he oversaw the allocation of more money than had been spent "for the education of the common people by the government of South Carolina from the Declaration of Independence to 1868, a period of ninety-two years" (Cardozo, *The Finances of the State of South Carolina* [1873], 11–12). In the words of one conservative newspaper editor, Cardozo was the "most respectable and honest of all the state officials." Despite his longstanding reputation for scrupulous financial management, he was accused in 1875 of "misconduct and irregularity in office" for allegedly mishandling state bonds. Though he claimed reelection as treasurer in 1876, he officially resigned from the office on 11 April 1877. Subsequently tried and convicted for fraud by the Court of General Sessions for Richland County in November 1877, Cardozo was eventually pardoned by Democratic governor Wade Hampton before his sentence, two years in prison and a fine of four thousand dollars, was commuted.

Following the ascendancy of the new Democratic government and the final abandonment of Radical Reconstruction in 1877, Cardozo moved in 1878 to Washington, D.C., and secured a clerkship in the Treasury Department, which he held from 1878 to 1884. Returning to education in the last decades of his life, he served as principal of the Colored Preparatory High School from 1884 to 1891 and from 1891 to 1896 as principal of the M Street High School, where he instituted a comprehensive business curriculum. A prominent member of Washington's elite black community until his death there, Cardozo was so revered by his peers, black and white, that a business high school opened in 1928 was named in his honor.

FURTHER READING

The Francis L. Cardozo Family Papers are held at the Library of Congress. *Proceedings of the 1868 Constitutional Convention of South Carolina* (Charleston, 1868) help to locate Cardozo's ideas within the context of Reconstruction debates. The *Twentieth Annual Report on the Educational Condition in Charleston, American Missionary Association* (1866) contains Cardozo's assessment of black education in the aftermath of the Civil War.

Foner, Eric. *Reconstruction: America's Unfinished Revolution, 1863–1877* (1988).
Holt, Thomas. *Black over White: Negro Political Leadership in South Carolina during Reconstruction* (1979).
Richardson, Joe M. "Francis L. Cardozo: Black Educator during Reconstruction." *Journal of Negro Education* 48 (1979): 73–83.
Simkins, Francis, and Robert H. Woody. *South Carolina during Reconstruction* (1932).
Sweat, Edward F. "Francis L. Cardozo— Profile of Integrity in Reconstruction Politics." *Journal of Negro History* 44 (1961): 217–232.
—TIMOTHY P. MCCARTHY

CARMICHAEL, STOKELY (29 June 1941–

15 Nov. 1998), civil rights leader, later known as Kwame Ture, was born Stokely Standiford Churchill Carmichael in Port-of-Spain, Trinidad, British West Indies, the son of Adolphus Carmichael, a carpenter, and Mabel (also listed as May) Charles Carmichael, a steamship line stewardess and domestic worker. When he was two, his parents immigrated to the United States with two of

their daughters. He was raised by two aunts and a grandmother and attended British schools in Trinidad, where he was exposed to a colonial view of race that he was later to recall with anger. He followed his parents to Harlem at the age of eleven and the next year moved with them to a relatively prosperous neighborhood in the Bronx, where he became the only African American member of the Morris Park Dukes, a neighborhood gang. But although he participated in the street life of the gang, he had more serious interests. "They were reading funnies," he recalled in an interview in 1967, "while I was trying to dig Darwin and Marx" (quoted in Parks, 80). A good student, he was accepted in the prestigious Bronx High School of Science. When he graduated in 1960 he was offered scholarships to several white universities, but a growing awareness of racial injustice led him to enroll in predominantly black Howard University in Washington, D.C. Impressed by the television coverage of the protesters at segregated lunch counters in the South, he had already begun to picket in New York City with members of the Congress of Racial Equality (CORE) before he entered college in the fall of 1960.

Carmichael became an activist while still in his first year at Howard, where he majored in philosophy. He answered an ad in the newsletter of the Student Nonviolent Coordinating Committee (SNCC), a student desegregation and civil rights group, and joined the first of the interracial bus trips known as Freedom Rides organized in 1961 by CORE to challenge segregated public transportation in the South. He was arrested for the first time when the bus reached Mississippi. He was jailed frequently in subsequent Freedom Rides, once serving a forty-nine-day term in Mississippi's Parchman Penitentiary.

After graduating in 1964, Carmichael joined SNCC full time and began organizing middle-class volunteers of both races to travel into the South to teach rural blacks and help them register to vote. From his headquarters in Lowndes County, Mississippi, he was credited with increasing the number of black voters of that county from 70 to 2,600. Lacking the support of either the Republican or the Democratic Party, he created the all-black Lowndes County

Freedom Organization, which took as its logo a fierce black panther. Growing impatient with the willingness of black leaders to compromise, he led his organization to shift its goal from integration to black liberation. In May 1966 he was named chairman of SNCC.

In June of that year, after JAMES MEREDITH's "March Against Fear" from Memphis to Jackson had been stopped when Meredith was shot, Carmichael was among those who continued the march. On his first day, he announced his militant stand: "The Negro is going to take what he deserves from the white man" (Sitkoff, 213). Carmichael was arrested for trespass when they set up camp in Greenwood, Mississippi, and after posting bond on 16 June he rejoined the protesters and made the speech that established him as one of the nation's most articulate spokesmen for black militancy. Employing working-class Harlem speech (he was equally fluent in formal academic English), he shouted from the back of a truck, "This is the 27th time I've been arrested, and I ain't going to jail no more. The only way we gonna stop them white men from whuppin' us is to take over. We been saying freedom for six years and we ain't got nothing. What we gonna start sayin' now is Black Power!" (Oates, 400). The crowd took up the refrain, chanting the slogan over and over.

The term "Black Power" was not new with Carmichael—RICHARD WRIGHT had used it in reference to the anticolonialist movement in Africa, and ADAM CLAYTON POWELL JR. had used it in Harlem—but it created a sensation that day in Mississippi, and Carmichael instructed his staff that it was to be SNCC's war cry for the rest of the march. The national press reported it widely as a threat of race war and an expression of separatism and "reverse racism." ROY WILKINS, leader of the NAACP, condemned it as divisive, and MARTIN LUTHER KING JR. pleaded with Carmichael to abandon the slogan. But although King persuaded SNCC to drop the use of "Black Power" for the remainder of the march, the phrase swept the country. Carmichael always denied that the call for black power was a call to arms. "The goal of black self-determination and black self-identity—Black Power—is full participation in the decision-making processes affecting the lives of black people and the recognition of the virtues in themselves as black people," he wrote in his 1967 book, written with Charles V. Hamilton, *Black Power: The Politics of Liberation* (47).

In August 1967 Carmichael left SNCC and accepted the post of prime minister of a black militant group formed by HUEY P. NEWTON and BOBBY SEALE in 1966, the Black Panther Party, which took its name from the symbol Carmichael had used in Mississippi. As its spokesman he called for the Southern Christian Leadership Conference (SCLC), the NAACP, and the Nation of Islam to work together for black equality. That year he traveled to Hanoi to address the North Vietnamese National Assembly and assure them of the solidarity of American blacks with the Vietnamese against American imperialism. In 1968 he married the famous South African singer Miriam Makeba; the couple had one child.

Carmichael remained with the Black Panthers for little more than a year, resigning because of the organization's refusal to disavow the participation of white radicals, and in 1969 left America for Africa, where he made his home in Conakry, capital of the People's Revolutionary Republic of Guinea. By then completely devoted to the cause of socialist world revolution emanating from a unified Africa, he became affiliated with the All-African People's Revolutionary Party, a Marxist political party founded by Kwame Nkrumah, the exiled leader of Ghana then living in Guinea as a guest of its president Sekou Touré. Carmichael changed his name, in honor of his two heroes, to Kwame Ture, and toured U.S. colleges for several weeks each year speaking on behalf of the party and its mission of unifying the nations of Africa. Divorced in 1978, he married Guinean physician Marlyatou Barry; the couple had one son. His second marriage also ended in divorce.

During the 1980s Ture's message of Pan-Africanism inspired little interest in the United States, and the attendance at his public appearances fell off. As *Washington Post* reporter Paula Span noted shortly before his death, "Back in the United States, there were those who felt Ture had marginalized himself, left the battlefield. His influence waned with his diminished visibility, and with the cultural

and political changes in the country he'd left behind." He also came under criticism for anti-Semitism because of his persistent attacks on Zionism. A collection of fourteen of his speeches and essays published in 1971, *Stokely Speaks: Black Power Back to Pan-Africanism*, included such inflammatory assertions as "The only good Zionist is a dead Zionist," and was attacked in the press. The bulletin of the Anti-Defamation League of B'nai B'rith criticized his campus addresses, calling him "a disturbing, polarizing figure" who caused hostility between blacks and Jews.

In 1986, two years after the death of his patron Sekou Touré, Ture was arrested by the new military government on charges of subversive activity, but he was released three days later. Despite the continued fragmentation of Africa and the diminished influence of Marxism, he never lost his faith in the ultimate victory of the socialist revolution and the fall of American capitalism. To the last he always answered his telephone "Ready for the revolution," a greeting he had used since the 1960s. In 1996 he was diagnosed with prostate cancer, with which he believed he had been deliberately infected by the FBI. Despite radiation treatment in Cuba and at New York's Columbia-Presbyterian Medical Center during his last year, he died of that disease in Conakry.

Kwame Ture left a mixed legacy. His provocative rhetoric was widely opposed by black leadership: Martin Luther King Jr. decried his famous slogan as "an unfortunate choice of words," and Roy Wilkins condemned his militant position as "the raging of race against race." But Ture's childhood friend Darcus Howe wrote of him in a column in *The New Statesman* (27 Nov. 1998), "He will be remembered by many as the figure who brought hundreds of thousands of us out of ignorance and illiteracy into the light of morning."

FURTHER READING

Carmichael, Stokely, with Ekwueme Michael Thelwell. *Ready for Revolution. The Life and Struggles of Stokely Carmichael (Kwame Ture)* (2003).
Carson, Clayborne. *In Struggle: SNCC and the Black Awakening of the 1960s* (1981).
King, Martin Luther, Jr. *Where Do We Go from Here: Chaos or Community?* (1967).
Oates, Stephen B. *Let the Trumpet Sound: The Life of Martin Luther King, Jr.* (1982).
Parks, Gordon. "Whip of Black Power." *Life*, 19 May 1967, 76–82.
Sitkoff, Harvard. *The Struggle for Black Equality, 1954–1980* (1981).
Span, Paula. "The Undying Revolutionary." *Washington Post*, 8 Apr. 1998.
Van Deburg, William L. *Modern Black Nationalism: From Marcus Garvey to Louis Farrakhan* (1997).

Obituary: *New York Times*, 16 Nov. 1998.
—DENNIS WEPMAN

 CARSON, BEN
(18 Sept. 1951–), pediatric neurosurgeon, was born Benjamin Solomon Carson in Detroit, Michigan, the son of Robert Carson, a minister of a small Seventh-Day Adventist church, and Sonya Carson. His mother had attended school only up to the third grade and married at the age of thirteen; she was fifteen years younger than her husband. After his father deserted the family, eight-year-old Ben and his brother, Curtis, were left with their mother, who had no marketable skills. Sonya worked as a domestic when such jobs were available, and she struggled with bouts of depression, for which, at one point, she had herself admitted to a psychiatric hospital. Despite her disabilities, she became the biggest factor in determining Ben's later success, which she and Ben attribute to divine intervention.

Except for two years in Boston, Ben grew up in a dangerous and impoverished neighborhood in Detroit. Initially, he did so poorly in school that by the fifth grade even he classified himself as "the class dummy." In part, his difficulties resulted from a failure to detect his need for eyeglasses. Nevertheless, when Sonya noticed the poor academic performance of her two sons, she instituted insightful strategies, curtailing their play activities and television viewing and demanding that the boys read two books each week and write reports on them for her to review—despite the fact that she could barely read herself. (Later she, too, went on to college.) Her stern intervention was also accompanied by positive reinforcement. When she learned of Ben's nascent interest in medicine, she said reassuringly, "Then, Bennie, you will be a doctor" (Carson, *Gifted Hands*, 27). Her parenting techniques catapulted Ben from the bottom of the fifth grade to the top of his seventh grade class.

Ben then became a normal teenager, desiring both stylish clothes and acceptance from his peers. As a result of this shift in his priorities, his grades plummeted from As to Cs, and he even confronted his mother angrily because she would not buy the fashionable clothes that he craved. She devised a scheme for him to manage the household expenses with her salary, saying that the remaining money could be used to buy the things he wanted. When Ben began this exercise, he was astounded and wondered how she made ends meet, because the money was gone before he had paid all the bills. Ben learned an invaluable lesson; he appreciated his mother's tenacity, curtailed his sartorial demands, and focused once again on his studies.

As a teenager Ben had a volatile temper, and at fourteen he attempted to stab a friend with a pocketknife simply because the boy would not change the radio station. Ben believes that it was through divine providence that his knife struck only his friend's belt buckle. This experience initiated another transformation in his life. He began to pray for help controlling his anger, he avoided trouble outside school, and he ended up graduating third in his class.

During Carson's freshman year at Yale University, he writes, "I discovered I wasn't that bright" (*Gifted Hands*, 73), and he wondered if he had what it would take to succeed in the highly competitive premed program. Aubrey Tompkins, the choir director of the Mt. Zion Seventh-Day Adventist Church, encouraged him and helped him regain his confidence. In retrospect, Carson wrote that "the church provided the stabilizing force I needed" (*Think Big*, 65). After receiving his BA in 1973, Carson entered the University of Michigan School of Medicine, where he studied with Dr. James Taren, a neurosurgeon and dean, who advised his students, when confronted with the choice of whether or not to operate, to "look at the alternatives if we do nothing" (*Think Big*, 65). This statement has resonated throughout Carson's professional career as a neurosurgeon. Another of his teachers, Dr. George Udvarhelyi, impressed upon him the importance of understanding the patient as much as the patient's diagnosis. Through this

advice, Carson developed the gentle bedside manner of a good country doctor. In 1975 Carson married Lacena "Candy" Rustin; they subsequently had three sons.

Carson received his MD in 1977 and fulfilled his residency at Johns Hopkins University School of Medicine, where he was often mistaken for an orderly—despite the fact that he wore the white lab coat that should have identified him as a doctor. Carson was not only undaunted by such prejudice, he actually thrived on debunking racial stereotypes. From 1982 to 1983 he served as chief resident in neurosurgery at Sir Charles Gairdner Hospital in Australia before Dr. Donlin Long recommended and engineered his appointment as chief of pediatric neurosurgery at Johns Hopkins. At the time of his appointment, Carson was only thirty-three years old and already considered a rising star in his field.

Carson gained international renown and made medical history in 1987, when he led a surgical team of seventy people in a twenty-two-hour operation that successfully separated the seven-month-old Binder twins, who were joined at the skull. In 1994 he performed a similar operation on conjoined South African girls, one of whom died during the operation and the other two days later; three years later he successfully separated six-month-old Zambian boys. Performing approximately four hundred operations per year in his pediatric unit, Carson is often called upon to assist surgeons all over the world.

In July of 2003 Carson was an assisting surgeon in a widely publicized attempt to separate twenty-nine-year-old Iranian sisters, joined at the backs of their heads, who themselves decided that a fifty-fifty chance that one or neither would survive the operation was better than continuing to live in a conjoined state, where they could not pursue their individual and distinct interests. Following the failure of this operation and the deaths of both sisters, Carson determined not to perform any more such operations on adults.

In August 2002, Carson successfully underwent surgery himself for prostate cancer, which had not metastasized. Throughout this ordeal, just as in surgery with his patients, Ben Carson

relied on his faith and the will of God to carry him through.

In addition to his practice, Carson has written numerous articles for medical journals; an autobiography, *Gifted Hands: The Ben Carson Story* (1990); and two motivational books, *The Big Picture* (1999) and *Think Big* (1992). He has been an outspoken champion of such issues as racial diversity, affirmative action, and health care reform. In 1994 Carson and his wife founded the Carson Scholars Fund, which offers scholarships to encourage children to take an interest in science, math, and technology and to balance the attention given to sports and entertainment with an appreciation of academic achievement.

FURTHER READING

Carson, Ben. *The Big Picture: Getting Perspective on What's Really Important in Life* (1999).
———. *Gifted Hands: The Ben Carson Story* (1990).
———. *Think Big: Unleashing Your Potential for Excellence* (1992).
—Thomas O. Edwards

CARTER, EUNICE HUNTON (16 July 1899–25 Jan. 1970), attorney, was born in Atlanta, Georgia, the daughter of Canadian-born William Alphaeus Hunton, an executive with the Young Men's Christian Association (YMCA), and Addie Waites, a field-worker with the Young Women's Christian Association (YWCA) in Europe. Carter's parents had three other children, but only Carter and her younger brother lived to adulthood. After the race riots of 1906, Carter's family left Atlanta for Brooklyn, New York, where Carter attended public schools. When her mother went to Strasbourg, which was at that time in Germany, to study at Kaiser Wilhelm University from 1909 to 1910, Carter accompanied her.

Carter attended Smith College in 1917, graduating cum laude with a BA and an MA in 1921. Her master's thesis was titled "Reform of State Government with Special Attention to the State of Massachusetts." Following in her parents' footsteps, Carter went into public service. For eleven years she was

Eunice Carter worked internationally for equal rights for women. Archival Research International/Double Delta Industries Inc. and Pike Military Research

employed as a social worker with family service agencies in New York and New Jersey. In 1924 she married Lisle Carter, a Barbados native and dentist who practiced in New Jersey. The couple had one child.

Eunice Carter took occasional classes at Columbia University, finally committing herself to night classes at the Fordham University law school, where she completed her LLB in 1932. She was admitted to the New York bar in 1934. That same year she made an unsuccessful bid for a seat in the New York state assembly. Between 1935 and 1945 she belonged to the National Association of Women Lawyers, the National Lawyers Guild, the New York Women's Bar Association, and the Harlem Lawyers Association. She served as secretary of the Committee on Conditions in Harlem after the riots there in spring of 1935.

An Episcopalian and a Republican, Carter began a private practice after law school and also started her active career in social organizations. In August 1940 an *Ebony* article listed Carter as one of seventy known Negro women who had become lawyers since 1869 ("Lady Lawyers," 18). Carter remained in private practice only briefly before William C. Dodge hired her to be a prosecutor for New York City magistrate's or criminal courts. As a prosecutor, Carter tried many cases against prostitutes, most of which she did not win. Because the same bail bondsman and lawyer represented these women, Carter suspected that a bigger organization was controlling prostitution. She told her boss, who dismissed her suspicions. However, Thomas Dewey, a special prosecutor investigating organized crime, took her suspicions seriously and eventually hired Carter as an assistant district attorney. She became part of a team that Dewey organized to investigate rackets and organized crime, particularly as it involved "Dutch" Schultz (Arthur Flegenheimer). She is also acknowledged for developing valuable evidence in the case against "Lucky" Luciano. Because of Carter's skills, in 1941 Dewey named her head of a Special Sessions Bureau overseeing juvenile justice. Eventually supervising more than 14,000 criminal cases per year, Carter served as a trial prosecutor until 1945.

Carter then returned to private practice and greater involvement in civic and social organizations and the movement for equal rights for women. She was a charter member, chairperson, trustee, and member of the Executive Board of the National Council of Negro Women (NCNW), founded in 1935 by MARY MCLEOD BETHUNE and twenty other women. Carter was also a member of the Roosevelt House League of Hunter College, and was active in the National Board of the YWCA (1949), the YWCA's administrative committee for its Foreign Divisions, the Panel on Women in Occupied Areas under Communism, and the Association of University Women. In 1945, as the chair of the NCNW's committee of laws, Carter, with her close associate Mary McLeod Bethune, attended a San Francisco conference that organized the United Nations. She was also very active in the local YWCAs of Harlem and Manhattan. Carter served as the secretary of the American Section of the Liaison Committee of International Organizations and the Conference on the Group of U.S. National Organizations; as a consultant to the Economic and Social Council for the International Council of Women (1947); as the chairperson of the Friends of the NAACP; as the vice president of the Eastern Division of the Pan-Pacific Women's Association and the National Council of Women of the U.S. (1964); and as the cochair of the YWCA's Committee on Development of Leadership in Other Countries. In 1954 Carter visited Germany to serve as an adviser to the German government on women in public life. In 1955 she was elected to chair the International Conference of Non-Governmental Organizations of the United Nations. She was also a trustee of the Museum of the City of New York and a member of the Urban League. Carter retired from law in 1952. She died in New York City.

FURTHER READING

The following collections contain information on Carter: a vertical file on Carter in the Woodruff Library of the Atlanta University Center; the National Council of Negro Women papers at the National Archives for Black Women's History in Washington, D.C.; and the Eunice Carter portrait collection in the New York Public Library Research Library.

Berger Morello, Karen. *The Invisible Bar: The Woman Lawyer in America, 1638 to the Present* (1986).

Obituaries: *New York Times*, 26 Jan. 1970; *New York Amsterdam News*, 31 Jan. 1970; *Jet*, 12 Feb. 1970.

—FAYE A. CHADWELL

CARTER, ROBERT LEE (11 Mar. 1917–), attorney and federal judge, was born in Careyville, Florida, the youngest of eight children of Robert Carter and Annie Martin. Shortly after his birth, Robert's family joined tens of thousands of blacks migrating from the rural South to the big cities of the North, seeking a better life. Within months of settling in Newark, New Jersey, his father died, leaving his mother a widow at age thirty-nine and the sole support of a large family. Working as a domestic by day and taking in laundry at night, she managed to keep the family together.

Carter excelled as a student, encouraged by his mother, who hoped he would train to be a minister. In his teen years she moved the family to East Orange, New Jersey, to escape the increasing decay and desperation of Newark during the Great Depression. Graduating from East Orange High School in 1933, he entered Lincoln University in Pennsylvania on a scholarship. Upon graduating in 1937, Carter entered Howard Law School and came to the attention of its dean, WILLIAM HENRY HASTIE, and THURGOOD MARSHALL, who had preceded Carter at both Lincoln and Howard. After graduation from Howard in 1940, Carter attended Columbia University on a Rosenwald Fellowship, emerging on the eve of war with a master's degree in Law.

When America entered World War II, Carter enlisted in the racially segregated army as a private and was sent to a military base in Georgia. There he encountered pervasive racial segregation and a demeaning, dismissive racial contempt. Black soldiers were confined to menial labor rather than being trained for combat or behind-the-lines technical support. Although he was accepted to Officers' Candidate School, his career as a second lieutenant proved tumultuous. He brought charges against two white enlisted men who had made racial slurs, insisted upon entering the officer's club at his base, and refused to live off base, as other blacks did. The matter came to a head when Carter successfully defended a black soldier accused of raping a white woman by establishing that she was a prostitute who had consented to the engagement. Charges brought

against him in retaliation resulted in an administrative discharge that would have made him again subject to the draft. His Howard Law School mentor, William Hastie, a civilian aide to the secretary of war, Henry Stimson, intervened, however, to secure an honorable discharge.

Carter left the army in 1944 and returned to the practice of law as assistant counsel to Thurgood Marshall, then the lead attorney for the NAACP's Legal Defense Fund (LDF). At that time racial segregation remained firmly entrenched by law and custom in the South and was sustained by custom and habit in much of the rest of the country. The "separate but equal" doctrine of *Plessy v. Ferguson* (1896) still guided judicial thinking and enjoyed popular support. Few could have expected that Carter, Marshall, and a handful of young lawyers working from a small set of offices near the New York Public Library would, within a decade, persuade the U.S. Supreme Court to overturn *Plessy*.

In the postwar years the NAACP challenged segregation along a number of fronts, including housing, transportation, and schools. Carter played an increasingly prominent role in these cases. On 3 April 1950 he found himself standing before the U.S. Supreme Court engaged in an oral argument in *McLaurin v. Oklahoma*. George McLaurin, a black man, had applied to graduate school at the University of Oklahoma. Claiming to uphold the "separate but equal doctrine," the university had assigned McLaurin a separate table on the library's mezzanine, a table in a corner of the cafeteria, and a seat just outside the classrooms where his courses were taught. Carter argued that the practice effectively denied McLaurin an equal education. On 5 June 1950 the Supreme Court handed down its decisions in *McLaurin* and in *Sweatt v. Painter*, a Texas Law School case that Thurgood Marshall had argued. Both Carter and Marshall won, delivering a fatal blow to segregation at the level of graduate and professional training.

The LDF's efforts to dismantle segregation at the level of elementary and secondary education would prove more difficult. In 1950 Carter suggested gathering evidence of the damaging psychological effects of segregation on black children. Although the idea was met

with skepticism by some of his colleagues, Carter found an ally in the psychologist KENNETH B. CLARK, who had developed experiments in which children selected and assigned characteristics to black and white dolls. Their results suggested that black children held negative perceptions of black dolls, the dolls that looked like them. Carter brought Clark and other social scientists into the legal struggle as it moved through the lower courts toward the Supreme Court.

In the spring of 1951, accompanied by the LDF's Jack Greenberg, Carter journeyed to Topeka, Kansas, where Oliver Brown and other black parents were suing in federal court to integrate their elementary schools. Carter called Clark and other psychologists to the stand to testify that the races did not differ in intelligence and that segregation injured black children emotionally and psychologically. When Judge Walter Huxman ruled against the parents, *Brown v. Board of Education* of Topeka, Kansas, was joined with cases from South Carolina, Virginia, and Delaware. All challenged school segregation, and all were to be decided by the Supreme Court at the same time.

In December 1952 Carter, Marshall, and other LDF attorneys stood before the Supreme Court to argue the school segregation cases. Under tough questioning from some of the justices, Carter contended that the segregation laws of Kansas denied Linda Brown her constitutional right to an equal education. With the death of Chief Justice Fred Vinson, a decision was delayed, and the cases were scheduled to be argued again before the new chief justice, Earl Warren, in December 1953. On 17 May 1954 the Supreme Court handed down its landmark decision in *Brown v. Board of Education*: it ruled unanimously that state-imposed racial segregation in the schools was unconstitutional.

The ruling provoked fierce opposition from southern whites. Alabama, for example, passed legislation requiring the NAACP to make its membership list public. Disclosure would have exposed members to intimidation or worse. To protect southern blacks' First Amendment rights, Carter, who was general counsel for the NAACP from 1956 to 1968, argued *NAACP v. Alabama* before the Supreme Court in 1958. In June of that year the Supreme

Court ruled in Carter's favor, declaring that the free-speech rights of NAACP members would be violated if their names were made public and they were thereby exposed to threats from die-hard segregationists.

Over the span of his career with the NAACP, Carter won twenty-one of twenty-two cases argued before the Supreme Court. He had always had a scholarly bent and in 1968 took a one-year appointment as a Fellow with the Urban Center at Columbia University. This was followed by a period in private practice. In 1972 Richard Nixon nominated him to the federal bench as a judge with U.S. District Court, the Southern District of New York. On the bench Carter presided over a range of cases, including those involving business executives charged with white-collar crimes and cases in which members of organized crime stood accused of violent offenses. The country's continuing struggle for racial justice also engaged him, and he reflected in 1989 that the conservative public policies of the 1970s and 1980s had resulted in a racial climate that was bleaker than any he could recall. Under Chief Justice William Rehnquist, he wrote, the Supreme Court "has embarked on a studied program to return the Fourteenth Amendment's due process and equal protection clauses and the federal civil rights law to the empty formalistic readings these provisions received before 1938" (85).

Carter recognized, however, that he and other more liberal minded members of the federal judiciary, such as A. LEON HIGGINBOTHAM, CONSTANCE BAKER MOTLEY, and DAMON KEITH, could still promote a form of jurisprudence based on the egalitarian principles exemplified by Brown. In 1998 Carter wrote an important opinion in Prey v. New York City Ballet, stating that lawyers hired by an employer to investigate claims of sexual harassment may have to make their findings known to the complainants. In October of 2000 he handed down a decision ordering the Sheet Metal Workers union to pay more than two million dollars in back wages to minority workers against whom it had discriminated. Along the way he also held adjunct faculty positions at New York University Law School and

the University of Michigan Law School and published extensively.

If Carter had merely argued *McLaurin*, his name would be in the history books. If he had simply argued for bringing the insights of psychology to the fight against discrimination, he would be remembered. If he had only argued *Brown*, he would be celebrated. And if he had merely had a thirty-year distinguished career on the federal bench, he would be honored. That he did all of these things and more speaks to Carter's extraordinary faith in using the American constitutional system to overcome the pernicious legacy of segregation and racial inequality.

FURTHER READING

Information on Carter's work for the NAACP Legal Defense Fund can be found in the NAACP Papers in the Manuscript Division of the Library of Congress.

Carter, Robert L. "Thirty-five Years Later: New Perspectives on Brown" in *Race in America: The Struggle for Equality*, eds. Herbert Hill and James E. Jones Jr. (1993), 83–96.

Greenberg, Jack. *Crusaders in the Courts* (1994).
Kluger, Richard. *Simple Justice* (1975).
—JOHN R. HOWARD

CARVER, GEORGE WASHINGTON (c. 1864–5 Jan. 1943), scientist and educator, was born in Diamond (formerly Diamond Grove), Missouri, the son of Mary Carver, who was the slave of Moses and Susan Carver. His father was said to have been a slave on a neighboring farm who was accidentally killed before Carver's birth. Slave raiders allegedly kidnapped his mother and older sister while he was very young, and he and his older brother were raised by the Carvers on their small farm.

Barred from the local school because of his color, Carver was sent to nearby Neosho in the mid-1870s to enter school. Having been privately tutored earlier, he soon learned that his teacher knew little more than he did, so he caught a ride with a family moving to Fort Scott, Kansas. Until 1890 Carver roamed around Kansas, Missouri, and Iowa seeking an education while supporting himself doing laundry, cooking, and homesteading.

In 1890 Carver entered Simpson College in Indianola, Iowa, as a preparatory student and art major. Convinced by his teacher that there was little future in art for a black man, he transferred the next year to Iowa State, where he was again the only African American student. By the time he received his master's degree in Agriculture in 1896, Carver had won the respect and love of both faculty and students. He participated in many campus activities while compiling an impressive academic record. He was employed as a botany assistant and put in charge of the greenhouse. He also taught freshmen.

The faculty regarded Carver as outstanding in mycology (the study of fungi) and in cross-fertilization. Had he not felt obligated to share his knowledge with other African Americans, he probably would have remained at Iowa State and made significant contributions in one or both of those fields. Aware of deteriorating race relations in the year of *Plessy v. Ferguson* (1896), he instead accepted BOOKER T. WASHINGTON's offer in 1896 to head the agricultural department at Tuskegee Normal and Industrial Institute in Macon County, Alabama. Carver brought both his knowledge and professional contacts to Tuskegee. Two of his former teachers, James Wilson and Henry C. Wallace, became U.S. secretaries of agriculture, as did Wallace's son, Henry A. Wallace. All three granted Department of Agriculture aid to Tuskegee and provided access to such presidents as Theodore Roosevelt and Franklin D. Roosevelt.

Carver's strong will led to conflicts with the equally strong-willed Washington over Carver's incompetence at administration. His contacts and flair for teaching and research protected Carver from dismissal. In both his teaching and his research, his primary goal was to alleviate the crushing cycle of debt and poverty suffered by many black farmers who were trapped in sharecropping and cotton dependency. As director of the only all-black agricultural experiment station, he practiced what was later called "appropriate technology," seeking to exploit available and renewable resources. In the classroom, in such outreach programs as farmers' institutes, a wagon equipped as a mobile school, and in agricultural bulletins,

Botanist George Washington Carver at Tuskegee Institute, 1940.
© Bettmann/CORBIS

Carver taught how to improve soil fertility without commercial fertilizer, how to make paints from native clays, and how to grow crops that would replace purchased commodities. He especially advocated peanuts as an inexpensive source of protein and published several bulletins containing peanut recipes.

Carver never married, but he came to regard the Tuskegee students as his "adopted family." He was a mentor to many, providing financial aid and personal guidance. Devoutly religious in his own way, he taught a voluntary Bible class on campus.

At the time of Washington's death in 1915, Carver was respected by agricultural researchers but was largely unknown to the general public. Long in the shadow of Washington, Carver became the heir to the principal's fame after being praised by Theodore Roosevelt at the funeral. In 1916 he was inducted into the Royal Society for the Arts in London. Then the peanut industry recognized his usefulness. In 1921 a growers' association paid his way to Washington, D.C., so that he could testify at congressional tariff hearings, where his showmanship in displaying peanut products garnered national publicity. In 1923 Atlanta businessmen founded the Carver Products Company, and Carver won the Spingarn Medal

of the National Association for the Advancement of Colored People. The company failed but obtained one patent and much publicity. In 1933, for example, an Associated Press release overstated Carver's success in helping polio patients with peanut oil massages. Carver became one of the best-known African Americans of his era.

His rise from slavery and some personal eccentricities—such as wearing an old coat with a flower in the lapel and wandering the woods at dawn to commune with his "Creator"—appealed to a wide public. Advocates of racial equality, a religious approach to science, the "American Dream," and even segregation appropriated Carver as a symbol of their varied causes. Carver made some quiet, personal stands against segregation, but he never made public statements on any racial or political issues. Thus his name could be used for contradictory goals. He relished the publicity and did little to correct the exaggerations of his work, aside from humble protestations regarding his "unworthiness" of the honors that came in increasing numbers.

Though some of this mythology was unfortunate, Carver served as a role model to African Americans and as a potent force promoting racial tolerance among young whites. The Commission on Interracial Cooperation and

the Young Men's Christian Association sent him on lecture tours of white campuses in the 1920s and 1930s. On these occasions Carver converted many who heard his lectures to the cause of racial justice. To them Carver was no "token black" but a personal friend and confidant. Indeed, many people who met Carver, Henry Ford among them, were made to feel they were "special friends."

Carver never earned more than $1,200 a year and refused compensation from peanut producers. Nevertheless he was able to accumulate almost $60,000 because he lived in a student dormitory and spent very little money. In 1940 he used his savings to establish the George Washington Carver Foundation to support scientific research—a legacy that continues at Tuskegee University. He died three years later in Tuskegee. Although his scientific contributions were meager relative to his fame, Carver did help hundreds of landless farmers improve the quality of their lives. And his magnetic personality and capacity for friendship inspired and enriched countless individuals.

FURTHER READING

Most of Carver's papers are at the Tuskegee University Archives in Alabama.

Holt, Rackham. *George Washington Carver: An American Biography* (1943; rev. ed., 1963).
Kremer, Gary R. *George Washington Carver in His Own Words* (1987).
McMurry, Linda O. *George Washington Carver: Scientist and Symbol* (1981).
—LINDA O. MCMURRY

CARY, LOTT (c. 1780– 10 Nov. 1828), Baptist preacher and missionary to Africa, was born on a plantation in Charles City County, Virginia, thirty miles from Richmond, the son of slave parents (names unknown). His grandmother Mihala had a strong influence on Lott's early religious development. He married around 1800 and, with his first wife (name unknown), had two children. Lott's master sent him to Richmond in 1804 as a hired slave laborer. He worked in the Shockoe Tobacco Warehouse first as a laborer and then as a shipping clerk. (The spelling of Cary's name as "Carey" is probably due to confusion in some primary sources with the well-known English Baptist, the Reverend William Carey. Lott Cary, however, signed his name as "Cary.")

Cary attended the predominantly white First Baptist Church, as did other blacks in Richmond. He experienced conversion in 1807 after hearing a sermon on Jesus and Nicodemus. Allowed to earn money by selling waste tobacco, Cary purchased his freedom and that of his two children in 1813. His wife had died by this time. Anxious to study the Bible, Cary enrolled in a night school taught by William Crane. There he learned to read, write, and do elementary arithmetic. His studies allowed him to assume greater responsibilities at the tobacco warehouse and achieve more economic independence; he eventually rose to the position of foreman with a salary of eight hundred dollars per year. He remarried about 1815; with his second wife (whose name also is unknown) he had one child.

Cary felt called to the Christian ministry and began to hold meetings for Richmond's African American residents. The First Baptist Church licensed him around 1814 after a trial period. Contemporaries credited him with extraordinary abilities as an extempory speaker. Cary's strong interest in foreign mission work began when he heard Crane report on the plans of the American Colonization Society (ACS) for establishing colonies of African Americans in West Africa and conducting Christian missions. Cary sought to arouse interest in Africa among fellow blacks in Richmond and, along with Crane, was instrumental in organizing the Richmond African Baptist Missionary Society in 1815. Because of white opposition to unregulated black organizations in the wake of the insurrection of GABRIEL in 1800, Crane, one of the white members of First Baptist, served as president of the missionary society. Cary was recording secretary.

Cary developed an even stronger interest in going to Africa as a Christian missionary after the visit of Luther Rice to Richmond in 1817. He sought support from the white Baptist General Missionary Convention. When asked why he should want to leave America for the uncertainties of Africa, Cary said:

"I am an African, and in this country, however meritorious my conduct, and respectable my character, I cannot receive the credit due to either. I wish to go to a country where I shall be estimated by my merits, not by complexion; and I feel bound to labor for my suffering race" (Gurley, 148). The Baptist Board of Foreign Missions and the ACS endorsed Cary in 1819. The ACS had been organized in December 1816 by whites who were interested primarily in removing blacks (especially free blacks) to West Africa; most ACS members did not oppose slavery as an institution. Cary's reservations concerning the policies of the ACS apparently were overshadowed by his desire to see Africa and conduct mission work there. He served the ACS without pay.

Cary and a group of twenty-eight colonists, plus a number of children, departed from Norfolk, Virginia, onboard the brig *Nautilus* bound for Sierra Leone in January 1821. Before leaving America, Cary and six other colonists, including his close friend Colin Teague, organized a missionary Baptist church. As he boarded ship Cary told those who had assembled to see the *Nautilus* off, "It may be that I shall behold you no more on this side of the grave, but I feel bound to labor for my brothers, perishing as they are in the far distant land of Africa. For their sake and for Christ's sake I am happy in leaving all and venturing all" (Gurley, 149). The Richmond African Baptist Missionary Society gave seven hundred dollars to support Cary. This was the first effort by black Baptists in America to do mission work in Africa.

After a voyage of forty-four days, Cary and the other colonists arrived at Freetown, Sierra Leone, which the British government had taken over in 1808 for the settlement of "Liberated Africans" whom the British navy freed from captured slave ships. Agents of the ACS had urged the U.S. government to establish a freed-slave colony on Sherbro Island, down the coast from Freetown, but when Cary arrived in 1821 no provisions had been made for them. The new arrivals were required to cultivate farms and do other labor in Sierra Leone. Soon after their arrival, Cary's second wife died of tropical fever, leaving him to care for three children. While in Sierra Leone, Cary

did missionary work among the Vai tribe at Cape Grand Mountain.

By December 1821 arrangements had been made for the purchase of land from King Peter, the principal chief around the cape, for another settlement. This later became part of the Republic of Liberia. In early 1822 Cary and his family moved to Mesurado (now Cape Monrovia). Jehudi Ashmun, a representative of the ACS, served as colonial agent of the colony of about 130 members, and Cary acted as health officer and inspector. In addition to assisting Ashmun in defense of the colony against the forces of King Peter, who was resentful of the colony's expansion, in 1822 Cary established a Baptist church in Monrovia that grew to about seventy members by 1825. Known as Providence Baptist, the church had its nucleus in the missionary congregation Cary and fellow Baptists had organized before leaving the United States. Cary also established a day school in Monrovia, which was moved to Cape Grand Mountain in 1827 but eventually closed because of insufficient funding.

In 1823 conflict developed between the earliest colonists and Ashmun, who attempted to redistribute town lots because of the arrival of additional settlers. The controversy escalated to the point where some colonists were charged with sedition and stealing rations. Although Cary initially opposed Ashmun, he mediated the dispute between the disgruntled colonists and the governing authorities. Liberia was established with a permanent government in 1825 as a colony of the United States; Ashmun became governor. Cary was elected vice agent of the colony in September 1826. When Ashmun became ill and left for the United States in March 1828, the entire administrative responsibility of the colony fell into Cary's hands. After Ashmun's death in August 1828, Cary was appointed governor of the more than twelve hundred settlers of Liberia.

In late 1828 a native group known as the Bassa, with whom the colonists had been having periodic conflict, robbed a factory at Digby, a settlement north of Monrovia. Cary called for a show of force by the settler militia. On 8 November 1828 he was making cartridges in the old agency house when a candle was accidentally upset.

The ammunition exploded. Seriously injured, Cary died two days later; he was buried in Liberia. A monument was later erected that bore the inscription "Lott Cary's self-denying, self-sacrificing labors, as a self-taught Physician, as a Missionary and Pastor of a Church, and finally as Governor of the Colony, have inscribed his name indelibly on the page of history, not only as one of Nature's Noblemen, but as an eminent Philanthropist and Missionary of Jesus Christ." In 1897 black Baptists in America organized the Lott Cary Foreign Missionary Convention in honor of Cary's pioneering labors in Liberia.

FURTHER READING

Fitts, Leroy. *Lott Carey: First Black Missionary to Africa* (1978).
Gurley, Ralph Randolph. *Life of Jehudi Ashmun, Late Colonial Agent in Liberia, with an Appendix Containing Extracts from His Journal and Other Writings, with a Brief Sketch of the Life of the Rev. Lott Cary* (1835).
Taylor, James B. *The Biography of Elder Lott Cary* (1837).

—MILTON C. SERNETT

 CARY, MARY ANN CAMBERTON SHADD
(9 Oct. 1823–5 June 1893), African American educator, journalist, editor, and lawyer, was born in Wilmington, Delaware, the daughter of Abraham Doras Shadd and Harriet Parnell. Although she was the eldest of thirteen children, Mary Ann Shadd grew up in comfortable economic circumstances. Little is known about her mother except that she was born in North Carolina in 1806 and was of mixed black and white heritage; whether she was born free or a slave is unknown. Shadd's father was also of mixed-race heritage. His paternal grandfather, Jeremiah Schad, was a German soldier who had fought in the American Revolution and later married Elizabeth Jackson, a free black woman from Pennsylvania. Abraham Shadd had amassed his wealth as a shoemaker, and his property by the 1830s was valued at five thousand dollars. He was a respected member of the free black community in Wilmington and in West Chester, Pennsylvania, where the family had moved sometime in the 1830s, and

he served as a delegate to the American Anti-Slavery Society in 1835 and 1836.

Mary Ann Shadd continued her family's activist tradition by devoting her life to the advancement of black education and the immediate abolition of slavery. As a youth she attended a private Quaker school for blacks taught by whites, in which several of her teachers were abolitionists. During the 1840s she taught in schools for blacks in Wilmington, West Chester, New York City, and Norristown, Pennsylvania. When passage of the Fugitive Slave Act of 1850 endangered the freedom of free blacks as well as fugitive slaves, Shadd joined the faction of black abolitionists who promoted the controversial cause of voluntary black emigration to Canada. This movement illustrated the depth of disillusionment with the United States that had developed among many blacks since the 1840s. Angered and disappointed in the continued tolerance of slavery and the upsurge of violence against free blacks, a faction of black activists broke from the American abolitionist organization and from those black abolitionists who preferred to stay and fight oppression in the United States.

Between 1850 and 1860 approximately forty thousand blacks fled to southern Ontario. Shadd found employment in 1851 as a teacher of blacks in Windsor, Ontario, and was later joined by several members of her family. Shadd taught school and became a fervent spokeswoman for the emigration movement. Like most teachers in the black settlements, she had to struggle to keep her schools open, facing such obstacles as inadequate supplies, ramshackle school buildings, inclement weather, and the frequent outbreak of cholera and measles.

In addition to teaching, Shadd was a talented writer. One of the most important enterprises was her participation with the Reverend Samuel Ringgold Ward in the founding in 1853 of the *Provincial Freeman*, a newspaper dedicated to promoting the interests of Canadian blacks, in Toronto, Ontario. The *Provincial Freeman* functioned as Shadd's vehicle for promoting Canada as a haven for the oppressed and for condemning the United States. In addition, she wrote extensively on the topics of temperance, antislavery,

anti-colonization, black education, and women's rights.

Shadd also used the podium effectively for promoting her ideas, despite the resistance she often encountered against women who engaged in the traditionally male activity of public speaking. After much debate, for example, she was given the opportunity to address the all-male delegation at the Eleventh Colored National Convention in Philadelphia in 1855. One man in the audience noted that her eyes were "small and penetrating and fairly flash when she is speaking." He described her as a "superior woman…however much we may differ with her on the subject of emigration." At another engagement, an observer praised her as "a woman of superior intellect, and the persevering energy of character." On her lecture trips, however, she often found the platform closed to women. While in Rockford, Illinois, she wrote to her brother Isaac that the citizens were "so conservative…as not to tolerate lectures from women." In both her writings and her speeches, Shadd spoke her mind, often roundly criticizing leading black men in the United States and Canada for providing inadequate support for Canadian black communities.

Her outspoken and candid manner often brought her into conflict with other black Canadian activists during the 1850s over such issues as the appropriate means for funding black schools and for raising money to help newly arrived blacks. Her most publicized feud was with HENRY BIBB and Mary Bibb, American-born free black activists who had helped in the establishment of the black settlement in Windsor the year before Shadd arrived. What began as a disagreement over policies escalated into a bitter personal feud between Shadd and the Bibbs that was well publicized in their rival newspapers and in Shadd's lengthy correspondence with George Whipple, secretary of the American Missionary Association. In his *Voice of the Fugitive*, Bibb chastised her for criticizing him, calling her unladylike, while Shadd described him as "a dishonest man."

The Bibbs favored all-black schools sponsored by the Canadian government, but Shadd sought to break down all racial barriers, favoring privately funded schools that made no distinctions about color. Although she encouraged black parents to make concerted efforts to sustain the schools, finding the necessary funds was a formidable barrier. Shadd finally was forced to appeal to the American Missionary Association for assistance.

Shadd also criticized the activities of the Refugee Home Society, an organization that Henry Bibb had started in 1850 to distribute land, clothing, and money to black refugees. Shadd accused Bibb of corruption and of perpetuating a "begging scheme." According to Shadd, who charged that corrupt agents pocketed the money, few such resources actually went to the refugees. She argued further that too much assistance would prevent black settlers from becoming self-reliant.

Her marriage in 1856 to the widower Thomas F. Cary, a barber and bathhouse proprietor from Toronto, did not prevent her from continuing to write, lecture, and teach. When at home in Chatham, she worked on the newspaper and cared for Thomas Cary's three children. They had two children of their own, one in 1857 and another in 1860. Shadd Cary continued to lecture and write for the *Provincial Freeman*. She also operated her school until 1864. During the Civil War she traveled to the United States to help recruit soldiers for the Union army. In 1869 Mary Ann Shadd Cary, by then a widow, moved to Washington, D.C., with her two children. Later, she lived with her older daughter, Sarah E. Cary Evans, a schoolteacher. Between 1869 and 1871 she began her studies in law at Howard University but stopped for unknown reasons. She resumed her studies in 1881 and received her degree in 1883, the only black woman in a class of five, although there is no evidence that she actually practiced law. She also continued her support for women's rights. In 1878 she delivered a lecture at the annual National Woman Suffrage Association Conference. She died at home in Washington.

Mary Ann Shadd Cary stands as one of the most significant, yet least recognized abolitionists who worked on behalf of black emigration and the sustenance of black settlements in Canada. At the same time, her lifelong challenge of racism and sexism made Cary an important figure in the struggle for racial and sexual equality during the nineteenth century.

FURTHER READING

Manuscript collections on the life of Mary Shadd Cary are in the Moorland-Spingarn Library at Howard University in Washington, D.C., and the Ontario Black History Society in Toronto.

Bearden, Jim, and Linda Jean Butler. *Shadd: The Life and Times of Mary Ann Shadd Cary* (1977).
Sterling, Dorothy, ed. *We Are Your Sisters: Black Women in the Nineteenth Century* (1984).

—SHIRLEY J. YEE

 CASS, MELNEA AGNES JONES (16 June 1896– 16 Dec. 1978), civic leader and civil rights activist, was born in Richmond, Virginia, the daughter of Albert Jones, a janitor, and Mary Drew, a domestic worker. Seeking broader employment and educational opportunities, the Jones family moved to Boston, Massachusetts, when Melnea was five years old. Her mother died when she was eight, and she and her two sisters were entrusted to the care of an aunt, Ella Drew. After one year at Girls' High School in Boston, she was sent to St. Francis de Sales Convent School, a Roman Catholic school for black and Indian girls in Rock Castle, Virginia. There household management was taught in addition to the academic curriculum; she graduated as valedictorian of her class in 1914.

When she returned to Boston, she was unable to find work as a salesgirl because of her race. Instead, she was employed as a domestic worker until her marriage to Marshall Cass in December 1917; she resumed domestic work during the Depression, when her husband lost his job as a dental laboratory technician. The marriage lasted until his death in 1958. The couple had three children.

While her husband was serving in World War I, Cass moved in with her mother-in-law, Rosa Cass Brown, who introduced her to community and church activities and persuaded her of the importance of the vote for women. At Brown's urging, Cass became a leader in the local suffrage movement and also joined the NAACP.

In the 1920s Cass joined the Kindergarten Mothers, later renamed the Friendship Club, of the Robert Gould Shaw House, in the heart of the black community in Boston's South End. With other neighborhood mothers, she raised money for Shaw House. Cass served twice as president and also as secretary of the Friendship Club. The group established the first nursery school in the black community, which became a model for later day care centers. The motto she selected for the Friendship Club, "If we cannot do great things, we can do small things in a great way," exemplified Cass's personal philosophy.

Her work at Shaw House started Cass on a lifetime of community service. She served as secretary, vice president, president, and chairman of the board for the Northeastern Region of the National Association of Colored Women's Clubs and in the 1960s was vice president of the national organization. During World War II, she was one of the organizers of Women in Community Services; in the 1960s she was community resources chairman and was active in recruiting girls for the Job Corps. In 1949 she was a founder and charter member of Freedom House, a private social service and advocacy agency, initiated by Muriel S. Snowden and Otto Snowden to aid and develop the black community. In the 1950s she joined the Women's Service Club and was its sixth president, serving for seventeen years, during which time she oversaw the development of the Migrant Service Program and the initiation, in 1968, of a federally funded homemaker training program. It was said of Cass that "it would be difficult to find a single successful black individual in Boston who hadn't been given a boost by her"; indeed, she was available to lend a helping hand to every individual in need, whatever his or her station in life.

The city of Boston began to call upon Cass's talents in the 1950s when she was appointed the only female charter member of Action for Boston Community Development, an agency that was established to help people displaced by urban renewal and that later administered the city's poverty program; she served as its vice president for eight years, retiring in 1970. For ten years she was a member of the Board of Overseers of Public

Welfare for the city of Boston, an advisory group to the mayor and the Welfare Department.

Throughout her adult life, Cass was a leader in the struggle against racial discrimination. She participated in A. PHILIP RANDOLPH's drive to organize the sleeping car porters. In 1933, nearly twenty years after she was denied employment as a salesgirl, she joined demonstrations led by WILLIAM MONROE TROTTER to get Boston department stores to hire blacks. The next year she demonstrated in favor of the hiring of black doctors and nurses at Boston City Hospital. For many years she was on the board of the Boston YWCA but left the organization in 1951 because of its discriminatory practices; she rejoined years later only after many policy changes had been made. A life member of the NAACP, she served in many capacities in the Boston branch and held the presidency from 1962 to 1964, when the NAACP organized demonstrations against the Boston School Committee and held sit-ins to support desegregation and protest inequality in the curriculum for black children. She continued the tradition started by William Monroe Trotter of annually laying a wreath in honor of CRISPUS ATTUCKS, and she successfully lobbied for Boston to observe the birthday of FREDERICK DOUGLASS.

In her seventies, Cass became a spokesperson for the elderly, serving as president of the Roxbury Council of Elders, chairperson of the Mayor's Advisory Committee for Affairs of the Elderly (1975), and chairperson of the Massachusetts Advisory Committee for the Elderly (1975–1976). National recognition came in 1973 when Elliott Richardson appointed her to represent consumers' Medicare interests on the National Health Insurance Benefits Advisory Council.

Patriotic and church organizations also benefited from her participation. Among other affiliations and offices, as state president of the United War Mothers of America, she was the first black woman to hold that office in a national patriotic organization. She was also the first woman, black or white, elected state president of the Gold Star and War Parents of America. At St. Mark Congregational Church in Roxbury she was a charter member of the Mothers' Club and chaired the

Social Action Committee. In 1967 she was the first woman to deliver a sermon for Woman's Day from the pulpit of the Ebenezer Baptist Church in Boston.

On many occasions, the community expressed its appreciation for her contributions. As early as 1949 the Friendship Club of Shaw House gave a banquet in tribute to her "efficient leadership, wise counsel, dependability, and fair judgment." In 1966 Mayor John Collins proclaimed 22 May "Melnea Cass Day," and more than 1,000 people attended a salute to the "First Lady of Roxbury." In 1974, at the recommendation of the Massachusetts State Federation of Women's Clubs, she was named Massachusetts Mother of the Year, and in 1977 she was designated one of seven "Grand Bostonians." Several facilities were named in her honor: the Melnea A. Cass Metropolitan District Commission Swimming Pool and Skating Rink (1968), the Melnea A. Cass Clarendon Street Branch of the YWCA (1976), and Cass House, a mixed-income apartment development (1989). Malnea A. Cass Boulevard opened in Boston in 1981.

At age seventy-nine Cass expressed the philosophy that had guided her life of service: "I am convinced that my life belongs to the whole community, and as long as I live, it is my privilege to do for it whatever I can, for the harder I work the more I live" (funeral program, St. Mark Congregational Church). She died in Boston. "By doing many small things in a great way" she had improved life for Boston's black community and won the respect and admiration of Bostonians of all races.

FURTHER READING

Melnea Cass's papers are kept at the Northeastern University Libraries in Boston, Massachusetts. Her oral history recorded with Tahi L. Mottl in 1977 is published in *The Black Women Oral History Project*, ed. Ruth Edmonds Hill, vol. 2 (1991). The original tapes and two folders of newspaper clippings and memorabilia are in the files of the Black Women Oral History Project, Schlesinger Library, Radcliffe College, Cambridge, Massachusetts.

Hill, Ruth Edmonds. "Melnea Cass "First Lady of Roxbury" in *Notable Black American Women*, ed. Jessie Carney Smith (1992).

Obituaries: *Boston Globe*, 20 Dec. 1978; *Bay State Banner*, 21 Dec. 1978.

—PATRICIA MILLER KING

CATLETT, ELIZABETH (15 Apr. 1915–), sculptor, printmaker, and teacher, was born Alice Elizabeth Catlett to Mary Carson, a truant officer, and John Catlett, a math teacher and amateur musician who died shortly before Elizabeth's birth. Elizabeth and her two older siblings were raised by their mother and paternal grandmother in a middle-class neighborhood of Washington, D.C. Encouraged by her mother and her teachers at Dunbar High School to pursue a career as an artist, she entered Howard University in 1931, where she studied with African American artists James Lesesne Wells, LOÏS MAILOU JONES, and JAMES A. PORTER. After graduating cum laude with a BS in Art in 1935, Catlett taught art in the Durham, North Carolina, public schools before beginning graduate training at the University of Iowa in 1938. Under the tutelage of artist Grant Wood, Catlett switched her concentration from painting to sculpture and undertook the study of African and pre-Columbian art. From Wood, Catlett gained a respect for disciplined technique, and when he encouraged her to depict subjects derived from

Elizabeth Catlett's Homage to My Young Black Sisters (1968). © Elizabeth Catlett/Licensed by VAGA, New York, NY

her own experience, she focused on African American women and the bond between mother and child, themes that would occupy her for a lifetime. Catlett received the University of Iowa's first MFA in 1940, and the following year *Mother and Child* (1940, limestone), a component of her thesis project, won first prize in sculpture at the American Negro Exposition in Chicago.

After a summer teaching at Prairie View College in Texas, Catlett was hired as head of the art department at Dillard University in New Orleans in 1940. The following summer, while in Chicago studying ceramics at the Art Institute of Chicago and lithography at the Southside Community Art Center, Catlett met artist Charles White. The couple married later that year and eventually settled in Harlem, New York, in 1942, where they thrived as part of the area's African American creative community. Catlett continued her studies at the Art Students League and with sculptor Ossip Zadkine. She taught at the Marxist-based Jefferson School, and sat on the arts committee of one of the largest Popular Front organizations in Harlem. Catlett's job as promotional director of the George Washington Carver School, a community school for working people, brought her into contact with working-class and poor people for the first time. As her politics crystallized, so too did her commitment to depicting the reality and courage of working Americans and to producing work for African American audiences. In 1945 she was awarded a grant from the Rosenwald Fund to produce a series depicting black women. The renewal of the grant for the next year allowed for the completion of the innovative series *The Negro Woman*, fifteen linoleum cuts documenting the epic history of African American women's oppression, resistance, and survival. An integrated narrative of text and prints, the series depicts historic figures SOJOURNER TRUTH, HARRIET TUBMAN, and PHILLIS WHEATLEY along with images of field hands, washerwomen, segregation, and lynching.

Fellowship funds also brought Catlett and White to Mexico in 1946, where in addition to finishing *The Negro Woman* series, Catlett hoped to resuscitate her failing marriage. Although the couple returned to New York and filed for divorce several months later, this first trip to Mexico proved pivotal for Catlett

both professionally and personally. In early 1947 she returned to Mexico City, where she had befriended a circle of Mexican artists that included Diego Rivera, Frida Kahlo, and David Alfaro Siqueiros. Soon after, she made Mexico her permanent residence and joined the printmaking collective, Taller de Grafica Popular (TGP), or The People's Graphic Art Workshop, through which she had produced *The Negro Woman* series. The TGP supported progressive and nationalist causes through graphic materials that communicated directly with the primarily illiterate public. Attracted to the workshop's creatively collaborative environment and its engagement with audiences, Catlett made the TGP her artistic home for the next decade. It was in 1947, as well, that Catlett met and married Mexican artist Francisco Mora. Between 1947 and 1951, the couple had three children, Francisco, Juan, and David, and remained TGP members until 1966.

In Mexico Catlett found a vital environment for politically committed art, which had become less permissible in the United States by the late 1940s, especially after the establishment of the House Un-American Activities Committee in 1947. From her arrival in Mexico until the mid 1950s, Catlett focused on printmaking, primarily lithography and linoleum prints, inexpensive mediums that are easily reproduced. Topical and populated with both Mexican and African American families and workers, Catlett's print work during this period is graphically bold, combining elements of expressionism and Soviet social realism with a visual vocabulary drawn from Mexican and African sources.

When her youngest child entered kindergarten in 1956, Catlett returned to sculpture, although she continued to make prints. Shortly after her arrival in Mexico, Catlett had studied ceramic sculpture and pre-Columbian art with Francisco Zuniga and in the mid-1950s she studied woodcarving with Jose L. Ruiz. In 1958, Catlett became the first woman professor of sculpture at Mexico's National School of Fine Arts, and a year later she became head of the department, a position she held until her retirement in 1976.

Catlett had arrived in Mexico a highly educated and technically sophisticated artist with a developed style. In Mexico, her sculptures continued

to feature simple and fluid forms with few embellishments and a reverence for materials. Whether in marble, onyx, bronze, terra cotta, or woods, her sculptures are concerned with volume and space. They convey a sense of monumentality even in small and medium-size pieces. The influence of Henry Moore, Jan Arp, and Constantin Brancusi can be seen in her smooth and highly polished surfaces and organic forms. But while they flirt with abstraction, her sculptures remain figurative. Representations of ethnicity and the female body, specifically images of motherhood and the body of the black woman, Catlett's pieces continually revisit themes and compositions of earlier works.

At the National Conference of Negro Artists in 1961, Catlett delivered a keynote address that called for politically engaged art: "We must search to find our place, as Negro artists, in the advance toward a richer fulfillment of life on a global basis. Neither the Negro artist nor American art can afford to take an isolated position" (*Fifty-Year Retrospective*, 20). The speech raised her profile within the art community but also increased pressure from the U.S. State Department, which identified her as an "undesirable alien." Catlett became a Mexican citizen in 1962 and found herself barred from the United States until 1971, when she was finally granted a visa to attend her first solo exhibition in the United States, held at the Studio Museum in Harlem. Beginning with her initial Mexican exhibition in 1962, there was steady demand for her work in both Mexican and American exhibitions, and after the Studio Museum exhibition, she regularly received solo shows, seventeen in the 1970s alone, mostly in the United States.

Through the Black Arts Movement and the women's movements of the 1960s and 1970s, Catlett renewed her interest in American politics and themes and, in turn, her work drew attention from intellectuals and curators in the United States. Her sculptural and print works from this period comment directly on topical issues, including the imprisonment of ANGELA DAVIS in *Freedom for Angela Davis* (1969, serigraph) and race riots in *Watts/Detroit/Washington/Harlem/Newark* (1970, hand colored linocut). Catlett's support of black nationalism can be seen in such works as *Homage to My Young Black Sisters* (1968, cedar), *MALCOLM X Speaks for Us* (1969, color linocut), *The Torture of Mothers* (1970, color lithograph), *Negro es Bello* (1968, lithograph), which includes renderings of Black Panther buttons, *Homage to Black Women Poets* (1984, mahogany), *Black Unity* (1968, mahogany), represented by a clenched fist on one side and a pair of faces on the other, and *Target* (1970, bronze), a bust of a black man as seen through the cross-hairs of a gun sight. Catlett's commitment to the Black Arts Movement included exhibiting at black institutions where her work would be seen by African American audiences.

Upon her retirement from teaching in 1976, Catlett and Mora, who died in February 2002, moved to Cuernavaca, Mexico. In 1982 she took a second apartment in New York and began spending more time teaching and lecturing in the United States. Catlett continued to produce work through the 1980s, 1990s, and into the new century. Her work has been included in every major exhibition of black artists from the 1960s to the present, and she has received numerous exhibitions, awards, and commissions in Mexico, the United States, and Europe. Recently called the "dean of black American female artists" by the *New York Times*, Catlett has received six honorary doctorates and honors from a host of institutions, including the cities of Atlanta, Cleveland, Little Rock, Philadelphia, Dallas, and Washington, D.C., the Philadelphia Museum of Art, and the National Council of Negro Women. In September 2002, the Cleveland Museum of Art mounted *Elizabeth Catlett: Prints and Sculpture*, a major exhibition spanning the artist's sixty-year career.

FURTHER READING

Catlett's papers are held at the Amistad Research Center, Tulane University, New Orleans.

Hampton University Museum. *Elizabeth Catlett, Works on Paper, 1944–1992* (1993).
Herzog, Melanie. *Elizabeth Catlett: An American Artist in Mexico* (2000).
Lewis, Samella. *The Art of Elizabeth Catlett* (1984).
Neuberger Museum of Art. *Elizabeth Catlett Sculpture: A Fifty-Year Retrospective* (1998).

—LISA E. RIVO

CESAR (c. 1682–?), slave and medical practitioner who developed primitive pharmaceuticals, is thought to have been born in Africa or the Caribbean and transported to the southern colonies as a slave. He might instead have been born into slavery in South Carolina. (His name is often spelled Caesar.) The names of his parents are unknown. He may have been the descendant of skilled medicine men, who transferred medical knowledge from their native cultures to the colonies, sharing drug recipes and folk remedies that used herbs and roots, or of slave midwives, who had performed cesarian sections in Africa and taught other slaves that procedure.

Cesar might also have had Native American Indian ancestors, because many Carolina slaves had intermarried with native tribes. Southern Native Americans were known for their potent herbal remedies. Slave physicians either were self-taught or acquired some training from fellow slaves or masters, and they became celebrities within their communities for their healing powers. Their reputations boosted their social rank, and whites became aware of their "curative knowledge."

Cesar was well known in his community for his use of roots and herbs as an antidote to poison. His pharmaceutical prowess attracted the attention of colonial leaders, and his successes were preserved in colonial records. The 24 November 1749 journal of the South Carolina Commons House of Assembly in Charleston noted that a "Member acquainted the House that there is a Negro Man named Caesar belonging to Mr. John Norman of Beach Hill, who had cured several of the Inhabitants of this Province who had been poisoned by Slaves." The legislator stated that Cesar "was willing to make a Discovery of the Remedy which he makes Use of in such Cases for a reasonable Reward." The following day the assembly appointed a committee to investigate the claim and "report what Reward the said Negro Man Caesar shall merit for his Services." By Wednesday, 29 November, the assembly "Ordered that Doctor Glen and Doctor Brisband be added to the Committee who were appointed to . . . examine into

the Services lately done by a Negro Man called Caesar . . . who have it in charge to desire the Aid and Observations of any skilful Physicians they shall think fit."

Committee member Mr. Austin delivered a report to the clerk, which was read to the legislators. William Miles had informed the committee that his sister and brother had been poisoned and that Cesar had saved their lives. Miles's son had recently been poisoned and "wants Caesar to his Relief." Other testimonials included "Henry Middleton, Esq., [who] believed he was poisoned and after two doses was cured. His overseer had also been cured." A Mr. Sacheverell "informed the Committee that Caesar had undertaken to cure a Man who was violently afflicted with Fits, and, in Appearance, will effect it."

Cesar's master, John Norman, told the committee that "to his Knowledge, Caesar had done many Services in a physical Way, and in particular had frequently cured the Bite of Rattle Snakes, and never knew him to fail in any one Attempt." Norman elaborated that "Caesar had been frequently called upon as a Doctor in many Cases by the Neighbours," mentioning an "Instance to the Committee of a Negro Man that had been cured of the Yaws by Caesar when he had been twice salivated, and was covered with an intire [*sic*] Scab from Top to Toe." The committee noted that "another Point Caesar is very famous in is the Cure of Pleurisies many of which he had undertaken to the Knowledge of Mr. Norman which had had very deadly symptoms."

Cesar was then asked "on what Conditions he would discover his Antidotes, and such other useful Simples as he was acquainted with," and he replied "that he expected his Freedom, and a moderate Competence for Life, which he hoped the Committee would be of Opinion deserved one hundred Pounds Currency per Annum." Cesar told the Assembly that "he proposed to give the Committee any satisfactory Experiment of his ability they please, as soon as he should be able to provide himself with the necessary ingredients."

The committee supported Cesar's request, suggesting that "he shall have his Freedom, and an annual Allowance of one hundred pounds for Life with such a further Allowance for any other useful Discovery he may make to the Public as this House shall think fit." The house approved the committee's recommendation and "Resolved that this House will make Provision for Payment to the said John Norman of the appraised Value of the said Negro Caesar." Cesar was appraised by four people, two nominated by the house and two by Norman. On 7 December 1749 the house issued a statement "that upon due Consideration of all the Advantages the said Negro Slave Caesar (aged near sixty-seven Years) might be of to the Owner by his knowledge and Skill may be worth the Sum of five hundred Pounds Current Money of South Carolina," which the public treasurer was ordered to pay "immediately" and also "advance the Sum of fifty Pounds to be paid to the Negro Man named Caesar."

The house also requested that the *South Carolina Gazette* print Cesar's prescription for public use, which appeared in the 14 May 1750 issue. Most historians consider this the first publication of a medical cure developed by an African American; the person who actually wrote the instructions is unknown but probably was Cesar's master, an assemblyman, a local doctor, or the printer. One year later, issue number 877 of the *South Carolina Gazette*, dated 25 February to 4 March 1751, stated, "There having been so great a Demand for our Gazette of the 14th of May 1750, (wherein was published, by Order of the Commons House of Assembly, the Negro Caesar's Cure for Poison) that none were left in a short time, 'tis hoped the Re-publication of that Cure, may not be unacceptable at this Time."

Cesar described the symptoms of poisoning and revealed how he prepared his cure for poison, which called for boiling the "roots of Plantane and wild Hoar-hound, fresh or dried," and straining it. "Of this decoction let the patient take one third part three mornings fasting successively, from which if he finds any relief, it must be continued, 'till he is perfectly recovered," Cesar prescribed. "During the cure, the patient must live on spare diet, and abstain from eating mutton, pork, butter, or any other fat or oily food." He advised that they boil goldenrod roots with sassafras and "to this decoction,

after it is strain'd, add a glass of rum or brandy, and sweeten it with sugar, for ordinary drink." For fevers that accompany poisoning, he suggested a wood-ash mash.

For rattlesnake bites, Cesar told physicians to "take of the roots of Plantane or Hoarhound, (in summer roots and branches together) a sufficient quantity, bruise them in a mortar, and squeeze out the juice, of which give as soon as possible, one large spoonful: if he is swell'd you must force it down his throat." He noted that "this generally will cure; but if the patient finds no relief in an hour after, you may give another spoonful which never fails." He also recommended that "to the wound may be applied, a leaf of good tobacco, moisten'd with rum."

Cesar's cures became well known and were also published, probably near the time of his death, in 1789 at Philadelphia, and in the 1792 *Massachusetts Magazine*. They were also mentioned in William Buchan's *Domestic Medicine* (1797), which noted that Cesar's detailed description "was in the grand tradition of Sydenham, the great English clinician of the seventeenth century." Cesar's work provided a foundation for future black physicians, including James Derham, considered the first African American doctor, who practiced in New Orleans after the American Revolution, and an unknown man described as "a Doctor among people of his color" in the 22 June 1797 issue of the Charleston, South Carolina, *City Gazette and Daily Advertiser*. Cesar's career preceded by a century and a half the acceptance of African Americans into U.S. medical schools.

FURTHER READING

Primary source material on Cesar can be found in *The Colonial Records of South Carolina: The Journal of the Commons House of Assembly March 28, 1749–March 19, 1750*, ed. J. H. Easterby, vol. 9 (1962).

Curtis, James L. *Blacks, Medical Schools, and Society* (1971).
Morais, Herbert M. *The History of the Afro-American in Medicine* (1976).
Numbers, Ronald L., and Todd L. Savitt. *Science and Medicine in the Old South* (1989).
Savitt, Todd. *Medicine and Slavery: The Diseases and Health Care of Blacks in Antebellum Virginia* (1978).

—ELIZABETH D. SCHAFER

CHAMBERLAIN, WILT (21 Aug. 1936–12 Oct. 1999), basketball player, was born Wilton Norman Chamberlain in Philadelphia, Pennsylvania, the sixth of nine surviving children born to William Chamberlain, a janitor and handyman, and Olivia Ruth Chamberlain, a domestic maid and cook. Although Chamberlain claimed in his 1973 autobiography that he was born measuring twenty-nine inches in length, much above average, he later stated that at birth "there was absolutely nothing special about me. I was a little over twenty-two inches long" (Chamberlain, 1991, 25). At any rate, young Wilton was always the tallest in his grade school classes and became known as the "Big Dipper" or "Dip," both of which he preferred to "Wilt the Stilt," a nickname later coined by a journalist. He was also among the most athletic students, participating as a nine-year-old in 1946 in the famed Penn Relays near his West Philadelphia home.

When he entered Overbrook High School in 1951, Chamberlain, by then six feet, seven inches tall, continued his interest in track and field, excelling at sprints, the high jump, and the shot put. Although he dreamed of participating in the Olympics as a decathlete, Chamberlain increasingly focused on basketball, a sport that had just begun to allow blacks in its professional ranks and which offered greater financial rewards for his talents. Overbrook won fifty-eight of the sixty-one games in which he played, one of those rare losses coming when West Catholic High School assigned four defenders to guard him. Chamberlain's height and strength certainly gave him an advantage over most opponents, but it was his ball-handling skills and athleticism that enabled him to dominate the highly competitive Philadelphia high school leagues. He developed into an excellent dribbler and passer and, contrary to his later reputation, a highly reliable free-throw shooter. In one game, he scored a remarkable ninety points, a figure that he would surely have repeated in other games had his coach not benched the star center to prevent embarrassing opponents. Nonetheless, in his three seasons at Overbrook, Chamberlain set a statewide scoring record of 2,252 points.

however, the Boston Celtics defeated the Warriors, even though Chamberlain outscored and outplayed the Celtic's BILL RUSSELL, the dominant defensive player of that era.

The Russell-Chamberlain rivalry endured throughout the 1960s. Chamberlain usually edged Russell in terms of individual scoring, but Russell's Celtics invariably defeated Chamberlain's teams. Chamberlain followed his amazing rookie season by breaking his own scoring and rebounding records in 1960–1961, averaging 50.4 points a game. Increasingly, Chamberlain stood out as a scoring phenomenon on an otherwise lackluster Warriors team, most famously amassing one hundred points against the New York Knickerbockers in 1962, a record unlikely to be broken. Most teams found that the only way to stop him was to foul him, a particularly useful tactic, given his relatively poor (.511) performance at the foul line; Chamberlain's 5,805 missed free throws will almost certainly remain an NBA record. More impressively, given his powerful physical presence and aggressive reputation on and off the court, Chamberlain never fouled out from a game.

Although Chamberlain's scoring feats declined in his final years in the NBA, his efforts for the Philadelphia 76ers in 1966–1967 and the Los Angeles Lakers in 1971–1972 finally earned him accolades as a great team player and his only NBA championship rings. In 1966–1967, he ranked third in the league in assists, a rejoinder to those critics and fellow players who viewed him as selfish. Indeed, Chamberlain had a highly driven ego and an even higher conceit regarding his considerable abilities, qualities that did not endear him to fellow players with equally large egos but somewhat lesser talents. He also believed that because of his greater size and strength, fans and fellow players did not credit his achievements as much as they should have. "Nobody roots for Goliath," he famously complained. On the Lakers team in the 1971–1972 season, Chamberlain adopted an uncharacteristic defensive role and, playing with a broken hand in the finals, again won the NBA's MVP award. He retired one season later and in 1978, his first year of eligibility, was elected to the NBA Hall of Fame.

Unlike many professional athletes, Chamberlain enjoyed his retirement more than his playing career. He

Wilt Chamberlain comes up against his perennial rival BILL RUSSELL, *1966.* Library of Congress

Chamberlain also excelled at the University of Kansas, though his performance did not quite match the unrealistic expectations that national journalists had raised about his prospects. In 1957 he led Kansas to the National Collegiate Athletic Association (NCAA) championship game and was selected as Most Valuable Player (MVP) of the tournament, even though his side lost in triple overtime to North Carolina. That loss devastated Chamberlain, who showed much less intensity in his junior season. He found life in segregated Lawrence, Kansas, uncomfortable, suffered racial abuse from opposing fans, and missed crucial games after an opponent kneed him in the groin. He especially resented an NCAA rule change that prohibited offensive goaltending and thus prevented the seven foot, one inch player from guiding his teammates' shots into the basket. A scandal involving improper payments of at least twenty thousand dollars further clouded his college career. Although Chamberlain received no official censure, the NCAA later placed Kansas on probation for buying him a Cadillac.

Forgoing his senior year at Kansas, Chamberlain joined the Harlem Globetrotters in New York City in 1958. He loved the showmanship of players like Meadowlark Lemon and claimed that he learned more from his one year on tour with the Trotters than from three years at Kansas. In that year—the happiest in his life, he stated in 1974—he improved his outside shooting, a consequence of being switched from his normal position of center to guard. He also began a love of foreign travel when the Globetrotters undertook a tour of Europe, including the first visit to the Soviet bloc by an American sports team, and were granted audiences with the Soviet leader Nikita Khrushchev and Pope John XXIII.

In 1959 Chamberlain joined his hometown Philadelphia Warriors and transformed the team's fortunes within a season. He established nine National Basketball Association (NBA) scoring records that season, including the highest average for both points and rebounds, and was voted Rookie of the Year, All-Star MVP, and the league's MVP. In that season's play-offs,

pursued several other sports—most successfully, volleyball—although his former professional status prohibited his dream of appearing in the Olympics. Chamberlain also sponsored a women's track team, Wilt's Wonder Women. His second autobiography, *A View from Above* (1991), gained him notoriety for his claim to have slept with twenty thousand women, but it also depicts a man with a lively intelligence, a fierce competitive edge, and rather traditionalist tastes. He reminisces about home cooking and NAT KING COLE and regrets the arrival of vast sports arenas and shopping malls. This memoir, albeit somewhat rambling, deals humorously with his celebrity and with shorter people's reactions to his height. Although he remained physically active throughout the 1990s, he also began to suffer from heart disease and died, apparently of a heart attack, in his Los Angeles home.

In the 1960s Chamberlain's notoriety and his scoring records helped build the national audience for what had been a minor sport. Later basketball stars, such as Magic Johnson and MICHAEL JORDAN, may have been better liked, but none matched Chamberlain's dominance in both scoring and rebounding.

FURTHER READING

Chamberlain, Wilt. *A View from Above* (1991).
Chamberlain, Wilt, with David Shaw. *Wilt: Just Like Any Other 7-Foot Black Millionaire Who Lives Next Door* (1974).

Deford, Frank. "Doing Just Fine, My Man." *Sports Illustrated*, 18 August 1986.
Libby, Bill. *Goliath: The Wilt Chamberlain Story* (1977).

Obituary: *New York Times*, 13 Oct. 1999.
—STEVEN J. NIVEN

CHARLES, RAY

(23 Sept. 1930–) singer, bandleader, and entrepreneur, was born Ray Charles Robinson in Albany, Georgia, the son of Bailey Robinson, a day worker, and Aretha (maiden name unknown). Charles's younger brother and only sibling drowned at age four. By the age of seven Charles had lost his sight to glaucoma and was sent to the State School for the Blind and Deaf in St. Augustine, Florida, where he remained

until his mother's death when he was fifteen. It was during his time at the school for the blind, which was segregated by race, that he received formal piano lessons and learned to read braille. After his mother's death, he set out on his own, traveling and working as a musician around Jacksonville, Florida.

Charles's earliest influences as a musician were the jazz and blues pianist Charles Brown and the pianist and singer NAT KING COLE. His ability to learn the styles of both musicians allowed him to gain work in clubs where audiences were familiar with their music. Sensing the need to branch out beyond Florida, Charles moved to Seattle, Washington, at the age of eighteen. In Seattle, Charles formed a band, the McSon trio, and made his first recording, his own composition, "Confession Blues," on the Swing Time label owned by Jack Lauderdale, who encouraged Charles to move to Los Angeles in 1950. In Los Angeles, Charles recorded two more singles for Swing Time before he began to tour nationally with the guitarist Lowell Fulson. Charles eventually became Fulson's musical director. In 1952 Charles signed with the Shaw Agency and began to tour nationally as a solo artist. On the strength of his second single, "Baby Let Me Hold Your Hand," Charles was signed to a recording

contract by Ahmet Ertugen, the founder of Atlantic Records. Charles's first release for the label was "It Should Have Been Me" (1952).

Charles's early recordings with the Atlantic label favored the styles of Charles Brown and Nat Cole—styles that had earned him a minor reputation as a rhythm-and-blues artist. But it was with the single "I've Got a Woman," backed by "Come Back Baby," that Charles began to exhibit the innovative style that would become the foundation of soul music. At the core of Charles's innovation was his use of chords and rhythms drawn from black gospel music to write and record music that had distinctly secular themes. "I've Got a Woman," for example, was based on "Let's Talk about Jesus," a gospel hit for the Bells of Joy in 1951. Follow-up recordings by Charles, like "A Fool for You" (1955) and "Drown in My Own Tears" (1955), also adhered to Charles's "soul" strategy, but "Hallelujah, I Love Her So" in May of 1956 became his first crossover hit.

As Charles's new style became popular, he began to face criticism from black ministers and gospel audiences. The genius of his burgeoning style was his intuitive understanding that the "Saturday night sinner" and the "Sunday morning saved" were often one and the same. The addition of doo-wop girls

Ray Charles crosses both musical and racial boundaries to bring his music to a wide range of audiences. Library of Congress

called the Raeletts accentuated a feeling of call and response, the verbal interaction common between a black minister and his choir. By the time Charles scored with the gospel-frenzied "What'd I Say," a top-ten pop single in 1959, he had inspired legions of followers, many of whom, like Sam Cooke and ARETHA FRANKLIN, went directly from the black church to the pop charts.

Much of Charles's early success was rooted in his ability to master many musical genres, most notably jazz, rhythm and blues, and soul. After Charles and his band made a successful appearance at the 1958 Newport Jazz Festival, Atlantic capitalized on his growing popularity with the recording *The Genius of Ray Charles* (1959), which included the pop standards "Don't Let the Sun Catch You Crying," "Come Rain or Shine," "It Had to Be You," and the big-band romp "Let the Good Times Roll." The album was the last that Charles recorded for the label, though there were subsequent releases of previously recorded music. In November 1959 Charles signed with ABC-Paramount, which offered a larger advance on future royalties, a higher rate of royalties, and ownership of his own master recordings. Charles had mixed success with his first two singles for ABC-Paramount, but with the third release he achieved his biggest hit ever.

Hoagy Carmichael's "Georgia on My Mind" (1960) was an old ballad that sentimentally recalls the American South. Charles infused the song with his unique soulful style and in the process made it one of his signature tunes. The song went to number three on the pop charts and earned Charles the first two of twelve Grammy Awards from the National Academy for the Recording Arts and Sciences. The following year Charles achieved his first number-one pop song and another Grammy with Percy Mayfield's "Hit the Road Jack."

The success of "Georgia on My Mind" signaled a new direction in Charles's recording career. Always fascinated by country-and-western musicians, Charles finally recorded a full-fledged country song, Hank Snow's "I'm Moving On," toward the end of his tenure at Atlantic. This was followed by Charles's groundbreaking *Modern Sounds in Country and Western Music* in April 1962. Though ABC-Paramount was fearful that

Charles would lose his core fan base, Charles scored his second number-one pop single with "I Can't Stop Loving You." Despite the label's initial concerns, the song also topped the R & B charts for sixteen weeks. So successful was *Modern Sounds in Country and Western Music* that Charles released a follow-up in late 1962. *Modern Sounds in Country and Western Music 2* included versions of Hank Williams's "Your Cheating Heart" and the popular standby "You Are My Sunshine."

When Charles released *Ingredients in a Recipe for Soul* in 1963, it was clear that he had so successfully integrated so many genres into his repertoire that it was no longer possible to label his music simply jazz, soul, or country and western. Ray Charles was becoming widely known as a song stylist, as evidenced by the success of his renditions of tracks like "That Lucky Old Sun" and "Ol' Man River," both from *Ingredients in a Recipe for Soul*, and the singles "Without Love (There Is Nothing)" and "Busted," a top-five single on both the pop and R & B charts. In 1964 Charles was arrested for drug possession in Boston. He received a five-year suspended sentence, kicked his twenty-year heroin addiction, and miraculously continued his music career unabated. Although taste in popular music changed during the 1960s, with the appearance of Motown and British groups like the Rolling Stones and the Beatles, Charles continued to make quality recordings in his own style. He even covered "Yesterday" and "Eleanor Rigby" by the Beatles on his recordings *Listen* (1967) and *A Portrait of Ray* (1968). Charles also began to record themes for Hollywood films, the best known being "The Cincinnati Kid" (1965) and "In the Heat of the Night," the latter from the 1967 film starring SIDNEY POITIER. The film's soundtrack was arranged by Charles's old friend QUINCY JONES, whom he had met when he moved to Seattle in 1948. Charles's "Here We Go Again," released in 1967, was his last major crossover recording until the late 1980s.

Although Charles largely remained on the periphery of the civil rights movement as a recording artist, preferring to provide financial assistance privately, he did offer his political vision on *A Message from the People* (1972). This album includes versions of STEVIE WONDER's "Heaven Help Us All," JAMES WELDON

JOHNSON's "Lift Every Voice and Sing" (often referred to as the "Negro National Anthem"), and Dick Holler's "Abraham, Martin and John." The recording also features a stirring version of "America the Beautiful" that was re-released as a single in 1976 to coincide with the U.S. bicentennial celebration. Charles also earned a Grammy Award in 1975 for his rendition of Wonder's politically charged "Living for the City."

Charles recorded regularly with little fanfare throughout the late 1970s and early 1980s, though he was feted with awards and acknowledgements. In 1981 he was awarded a star on the Hollywood Boulevard "Walk of Fame." He was among the first inductees into the Rock Hall of Fame in 1986, and in 1979 the state of Georgia declared his version of "Georgia on My Mind" the official state song. Charles released his autobiography *Brother Ray*, written with David Ritz, in 1978. He had a bit of a renaissance in the mid-1980s, making popular recordings with the country artists Willie Nelson ("Seven Spanish Angels"), George Jones ("We Didn't See a Thing"), and Hank Williams Jr. ("Two Old Cats like Us"). In 1989 he teamed again with Quincy Jones to record "I'll Be Good to You," with Chaka Khan. The song reached number one on the R & B charts. Charles earned his twelfth Grammy Award in 1993 for "A Song for You." Popular cameos on *Sesame Street* and commercial endorsements for Pepsi Cola kept his music and image firmly embedded in the minds of generations of Americans.

Ray Charles was married twice and has nine children, but his music always took precedence over all other activities. Throughout his career Charles has maintained an intense touring schedule, not simply for the economic benefit but also to bring various styles of black music to audiences that may have otherwise remained unfamiliar with them. Charles's influence on American popular music has perhaps been rivaled only by figures like DUKE ELLINGTON, B. B. KING, and JAMES BROWN, all of whom toured well into their sixties and seventies, each holding up the banner for the particular brand of popular music he is best known for. Charles's remarkable ability to draw from many styles of popular music made it possible for him to cross—and thereby diminish—musical, racial, political, and geographical barriers.

FURTHER READING

Charles, Ray, with David Ritz. *Brother Ray* (1978).

Lydon, Michael. *Ray Charles: Man and Music* (1998).
Wexler, Jerry, and David Ritz. *Rhythm and Blues: A Life in American Music* (1993).
—MARK ANTHONY NEAL

CHAVIS, JOHN (1763–

13 June 1838), Presbyterian minister and teacher, was born in Granville County, North Carolina; the names of his parents are unknown. He grew up as a free black near Mecklenberg, Virginia. By his own account, Chavis was born free and was a Revolutionary War army veteran. Details of his military service and the events of his life immediately following the war are not known, but he began his studies for the Presbyterian ministry in 1792 at the age of twenty-nine. According to an apocryphal account, one planter had a wager with another that it was impossible to educate a black man. In order to settle their dispute, they sent Chavis to the College of New Jersey (now Princeton University). More than likely, Chavis's religious fervor and potential for scholarship attracted the attention of Presbyterian leaders in Virginia, who believed a black clergyman might do a better job of evangelizing slaves and free blacks than white ministers.

During his three years at the College of New Jersey, Chavis studied under the private tutelage of the college president, John Witherspoon, who often instructed one or two black students and several Native Americans as well. Chavis's studies in New Jersey ended when Witherspoon died in 1794. The next year he resumed studies at Liberty Hall Academy (now Washington & Lee University) in Lexington, Virginia, also a Presbyterian school. Chavis completed his studies there in 1799, and when it licensed him to preach in early 1800, the Lexington Presbytery expressed hopes that he would serve the blacks of the community.

After leaving the Lexington Presbytery in 1801 Chavis served the Hanover, Virginia, Presbytery before going to work under the supervision of the Synod of Virginia in 1804. Ultimately, he also preached in Maryland and North Carolina. At the beginning of each new assignment, Presbyterian leaders admonished Chavis to focus his efforts on the evangelization of slaves and free blacks, but his preaching attracted large numbers of whites and hardly any blacks. In 1883 one white North Carolinian remembered Chavis as a "venerable old Negro preacher," who was "respected as a man . . . familiar with the proprieties of social life, yet modest and unassuming, and sober in language and customs." Southern white admirers seemed to look beyond his race, while slaves and free blacks were unable to identify with one of their own who sounded and behaved like a white man.

By 1807 Chavis had opened a small school and devoted almost all of his attention to that endeavor. During the school's first year of operation he taught both white and black children together, but some white parents objected. The next year he advertised daytime classes for white students and evening classes for blacks. At different times, Chavis operated his school in Chatham, Wake, Orange, and Granville counties of North Carolina, and it attracted prominent white students, including the sons of the state's chief justice Leonard Henderson; James Horner, who later founded the Horner School in Oxford, North Carolina; Charles Manly, who later served as the state's governor; Willie P. Mangum, a prominent Whig senator; and Abram Rencher, who became governor of New Mexico.

Chavis charged low tuition rates, which kept his school full while providing ample money for his own support and that of his wife. By March 1828 he was able to boast that the enrollment had reached sixteen. The small, orderly school ran for about thirty years before political developments forced it to close. The 1831 insurrection of NAT TURNER created a climate of fear and distrust among white southerners that resulted in severe restrictions on the black population. The North Carolina legislature passed a law that prevented blacks from preaching or teaching, thus creating economic hardships for Chavis.

By 1832 the sixty-nine-year-old Chavis turned to the Orange, North Carolina, Presbytery for support. After careful study, the Presbytery resolved to take up a collection for his support. The sums forwarded to Chavis were never sufficient, and there is evidence that he found his situation extremely embarrassing. In 1833 he hoped to earn money for himself by publishing an essay entitled "The Extent of the Atonement," but he needed the Presbytery to pay publication costs. Many other religious leaders had already written on the subject, and the Presbytery decided that such an essay would not be interesting enough to sell. Chavis continued to depend on them for charity throughout the remainder of his life. From October 1834 to April 1835 the Presbytery expended $81.95 for his support, but the sum was not always as generous. In the fall of 1835, when the Orange Presbytery divided, the new Roanoke Presbytery assumed Chavis's support. In 1837 it resolved to pay him fifty dollars annually.

John Chavis retained a close personal relationship with his former student, Senator Willie P. Mangum, and advised him to reject the demands of the abolitionists during the mid-1830s. His position on slavery was cautious because he feared for the plight of masses of black people who would face homelessness and uncertain futures. Chavis did not want them to be more miserable than they already were. His position seems startling, but no one was any more aware of the difficulties of living free than this impoverished man, who constantly depended on the charity of whites for support.

John Chavis died in North Carolina sometime between the April and October 1838 meetings of the Presbytery. At the October meeting, they resolved to continue support for his widow.

FURTHER READING

The Papers of Willie P. Mangum, in the Manuscript Collection of the University of North Carolina Library, contain letters that Chavis wrote to Mangum.

Berlin, Ira. *Slaves without Masters: The Free Negro in the Antebellum South* (1974).
FRANKLIN, JOHN HOPE. *The Free Negro in North Carolina, 1790–1860* (1943).
Kaplan, Sidney, and Emma Nogrady Kaplan. *The Black Presence in the Era of Revolution*, rev. ed. (1989).
Shaw, G. C. *John Chavis, 1763–1838* (1931).
—THEODORE C. DELANEY

CHENAULT, KENNETH IRVINE (2 June 1951–),

lawyer and corporate leader, was born in Mineola, New York, to Hortenius Chenault, a dentist and a Morehouse and Howard University graduate, and Anne N. Quick, a dental hygienist and Howard alumna. The second of three brothers and one sister, Ken grew up in middle-class, mostly white Hempstead, Long Island, and attended the innovative, private Waldorf School in Garden City through twelfth grade. Although both his parents had graduated top in their classes, Kenneth was at first a middling student. He improved academically and became class president and captain of the track and basketball teams. He also avidly read biographies of famous people, including FREDERICK DOUGLASS, W. E. B. DU BOIS, and Winston Churchill.

Starting Springfield College on an athletic scholarship, he transferred under the mentorship of Waldorf's Peter Curran to Bowdoin College in Maine. There he joined two dozen black pioneers at the all-male (until 1972) and predominantly white elite college, graduating in 1973 with a BA in History, magna cum laude. He told a friend, "I've got to get into the system to help my people. If I get in, I can help somebody else" (*Ebony*, July 1997). Attending Harvard Law School, he became moot court champion and received a JD in 1976 (when he also got an American Express Gold card), joining the Massachusetts bar five years later. In 1977 Chenault married Kathryn Cassell, a Tufts University political science major and New York University law student who became a United Negro College Fund lawyer. They live in New York State with two sons, Kenneth Jr. and Kevin.

Chenault became an associate with the New York corporate law firm of Rogers & Wells from 1977 to 1979. Without an MBA, in 1979 he joined a Boston business-consulting firm, Bain & Co., which familiarized him with large corporations, executives, and business strategies. Among his Bain mentors was a Harvard Law School classmate, the son of a former Michigan governor and a future Massachusetts governor, W. Mitt Romney, who takes credit for hiring Chenault, saying, "He was able to process a lot of conflict... cut

through the confusion... arrive at very powerful... recommendations and then see them through to their implementation" (*Ebony*, July 1997).

In 1981 Chenault was hired as director of strategic planning for American Express Company in New York City, whose "membership has its privileges" branding of "charge" cards (payable monthly) versus credit cards (revolving payment) differentiated it from Visa and MasterCard. In 1983 he was promoted to vice president of Merchandise Services, a foundering division that he reorganized from a $150-million to a $500-million department. In 1984 he became general manager of Merchandise Servicess and senior vice president of AmEx Travel-Related Services (TRS), with green, gold, platinum, and travelers' checks lines. In 1986 he became executive vice president and general manager of the platinum/gold card division. Under his leadership AmEx became the fifth-leading direct marketer as he upscaled Merchandise Servicess to produce 20 percent yearly growth. But the old-line company, founded in 1850 and offering "charge cards" to compete with Diners Club since 1958, initially resisted his innovations.

In 1987 AmEx finally introduced for current members a credit card, Optima, to compete with Visa and MasterCard. While the company anticipated that existing AmEx members would be creditworthy, in fact, Optima defaults were twice as high as predicted, and company profits dropped. Although the Optima problems were not Chenault's responsibility, he recognized that AmEx was "arrogant and felt entitled" to customer patronage (*Current Biography*, 1998), and he instituted innovations such as linking cards to frequent flyer mileage. In 1988 Chenault became executive vice president of the Consumer Card and Financial Services Group, again producing record growth. *Black Enterprise* named him among the twenty-five "most powerful black executives in corporate America." In 1990 his listing appeared in *Who's Who in America* and in 1992 *Who's Who among Black Americans*.

In 1990 Chenault became president of AmEx Consumer Card and Financial Services groups, and by 1991 he managed relations with all firms accepting AmEx cards. Then he faced the "Boston Fee Party," a revolt of one hundred

restaurant owners unhappy with unresponsive AmEx treatment and steep transaction fees (3.5 percent vs. 2 percent for Visa and MasterCard). Chenault negotiated selective fee reductions for electronic transactions to keep the merchants as AmEx vendors and maintain the company's competitive position. He also began extending and downscaling the brand by reaching mass markets at Kmart, Sears, and Wal-Mart.

In 1993, when Harvey Golub became CEO, Chenault became president of American Express USA, and his attention to consumer trends and developments in computer technology improved AmEx's position. He increased company offerings to sixty co-branded cards. Merchants doubled to sixty thousand, with transaction fees of 2.7 percent. In 1994 the Optima True Grace card (later ended) was introduced, along with cards for groups like college students and seniors, though AmEx's share of card transactions fell from 22.9 percent in 1990 to 15.9 percent in 1996.

In 1995 Golub named Chenault vice chairman of AmEx. Early in his term Chenault had to "restructure" by laying off 15,800 jobs to cut three billion dollars in costs, and he was recognized within the company as having handled the layoff professionally. Employment rose to 73,620 in 1997. In 1996 he became head of TRS International, and in 1997 AmEx market share rose for the first time in ten years. Even though AmEx faced falling share prices, card members grew to 54.3 million in 1998. In 1998 Visa still dominated the industry at 54 percent, with MasterCard at 28 percent, and AmEx at 13.7 percent, though antitrust efforts against Visa and MasterCard promised to reduce their market share.

In February 1997 Golub named Chenault president and chief operating officer, designated him heir apparent "as the primary internal candidate to succeed" as CEO when Golub retired in 2004, and placed Chenault on the company board. When it appeared that Chenault might become the first African American to run one of America's largest corporations, he remarked that it would be "naïve and untrue to say that race is not a factor in our society" but at AmEx, "I have been totally judged on my performance" (quoted in Jessie Smith, *Notable Black American*

Men, [1992], 192). In December 1998 *Business Week* ran a cover story on "The Rise of a Star."

In May 1999 Golub announced that Chenault would become CEO in 2001 when Golub stepped down three years early to enable his successor to increase his responsibilities within the company. In September 1999 Chenault became Black Enterprise Corporate Executive of the Year and appeared in *International Who's Who*. Although FRANKLIN DELANO RAINES became the first black CEO of a Fortune 500 company in 1999, Chenault would become the first black CEO of a Dow Jones blue chip firm.

In January 2001 Chenault became AmEx CEO and, in April, chairman of the twenty-two-billion-dollar enterprise. Early on he faced a financial crisis over write-offs of junk bonds. Soon after, he ably managed from afar the crisis at AmEx after the September 11 attack on the World Trade Center, evacuating the company headquarters in the nearby World Financial Center and helping 500,000 stranded cardholders by increasing credit limits. At an emotional meeting, he took command of comforting a shocked staff. "Ken epitomizes two attributes I think will be important here," said Golub. "One is courage and the other is composure" (*Business Week*, 29 Oct. 2001). Not long afterward, Chenault stood at George W. Bush's side at "ground zero," stressing the need to improve security at airports and public sites, and he appeared with Mayor Rudolph Giuliani and Governor George Pataki on requests for federal funds to rebuild the city. In 2001 *Fortune* named him one of the fifty most powerful African American executives.

Following his philosophy that "part of being a leader is pulling people from disparate backgrounds together" and that minorities, "more than others, must give back to help our community and to ease the way of those who will follow" (Chenault, 11–12), Chenault is on the boards of Junior Achievement, the New York Medical Center, Bowdoin College, the NCAA, and the ARTHUR ASHE Institute for Urban Health. He was also named Corporate Arts Patron by the Harlem Studio Museum. Chenault belongs to the American Bar Association and the Council on Foreign Relations, and he has served on the boards of the Brooklyn Union Gas Company, IBM,

and Quaker Oats. He received honorary degrees from Adelphi, Bowdoin, Howard, Morgan State, Notre Dame, and SUNY Stony Brook. A team builder who shattered the glass ceiling, Chenault exemplifies his own dictum that "as barriers against us fall, we must not fail to move forward" (Chenault, 13).

FURTHER READING

Chenault, Kenneth. "Control What You Can: Your Own Integrity, Your Own Performance" in *Take a Lesson: Today's Black Achievers on How They Made It and What They Learned along the Way*, ed. Caroline Clarke (2001).

Byrne, John, and Heather Timmons. "Tough Times for a New CEO." *Business Week* 29 Oct. 2001.
Heberling, Michael E. *Modern Day CEOs: The Good, the Bad, and the Ugly* (2001).
Pierce, Ponchitta. "Kenneth Chenault, Blazing New Paths in Corporate America." *Ebony*, July 1997.

—RICHARD SOBEL

CHESNUTT, CHARLES WADDELL (20 June 1858–15 Nov. 1932), writer, was born in Cleveland, Ohio, the son of Andrew Jackson Chesnutt, a horse car driver, and Ann Maria Sampson. His parents were free African Americans who had left Fayetteville, North Carolina, in 1856 to escape the oppressiveness of life in a slave state and its sparse opportunity. They were married in Cleveland in 1857. During the Civil War, Chesnutt's father served four years as a teamster in the Union army, but the family returned to Fayetteville in 1866 because A. J. Chesnutt's father, Waddell Cade (a local white farm owner—the name Chesnutt came from A. J.'s mother, Ann), helped his son establish a grocery store there. Young Charles helped in the store and over the years heard many things there about southern life and folkways that he recorded or remembered and that later became part of or informed his writings. Charles attended the Howard School, which existed through the efforts of local black citizens and the Freedmen's Bureau, but after his father lost his store and moved to a nearby farm, Charles was forced at age fourteen to change his role in the school from that of eager pupil to pupil-teacher

in order to help with family finances. He continued to read widely in various fields, especially in literature, thereby further educating himself.

Chesnutt began teaching in Charlotte, North Carolina, in 1872 and in the summers in other North and South Carolina communities. In the fall of 1877 he returned to Fayetteville to work in the new state normal school there. The following summer he married one of the school's teachers, Susan U. Perry, and the first of their four children was born the following spring. Though Chesnutt became principal of the normal school at age twenty-two and continued to study various subjects regularly, he felt restricted in opportunities and intellectually isolated in the post–Civil War South. In 1883 he used his self-taught ability to take shorthand at two hundred words per minute to escape, first to New York for a few months and then to Cleveland, where he was joined by his family in April 1884. He lived there the rest of his life.

In Cleveland, Chesnutt worked as an office clerk and court reporter, passed the Ohio bar exam in 1887 (with the highest grade in his group), and established a prosperous legal stenography firm, eventually after several moves acquiring a fourteen-room home. More importantly, he worked at becoming a writer. He had been moving in that direction for some time, and in 1872 a

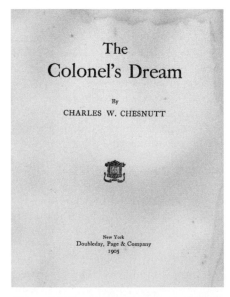

Chesnutt's The Colonel's Dream, *(1905)*. University of North Carolina

local weekly Negro newspaper had published his condemnation of the reading of dime novels. The growth of his interest in literature and his ambition to become a writer are reflected in numerous entries in his journals during the 1870s and 1880s, especially as he became more and more aware of what had been written and was being written about the South and black people, subjects about which he felt confident of his own better knowledge and understanding. His journal entry for 29 May 1880 spoke of a purpose for his intended writing that would improve the South and all of its people. It included the declaration, "I think I must write a book." However, before he would accomplish that goal there were to be years of sketches, tales, and stories, beginning in 1885 published in various periodicals, including eventually such widely known magazines as *Family Fiction, Puck*, the *Overland Monthly*, the *Crisis*, the *Southern Workman*, the *Century*, the *Outlook, Youth's Companion*, and various newspapers in some of the nation's larger cities.

Chesnutt's most important breakthrough came with the publication of his tale "The Goophered Grapevine" in the *Atlantic Monthly* for August 1887. Although the editors did not then know the author's race, this was the first piece of short fiction published by an African American in a magazine with such prestige as to easily put the work before the majority of American readers. Chesnutt would publish short fiction and articles (both usually concerning racial matters) for much of the rest of his life, but very much tapering off after the early part of the twentieth century.

"The Goophered Grapevine" was the first of three of his stories in the *Atlantic Monthly* that focused on conjuring as an important aspect of black folklife. This is revealed in post–Civil War tales about earlier times in the Fayetteville area told by Uncle Julius, a shrewd and likable character who uses the stories to his own advantage and along the way also reveals much about what slavery meant in the daily concerns of its victims, of which he had been one. These three tales and four other Uncle Julius tales became Chesnutt's first book, *The Conjure Woman*, published by Houghton Mifflin (1899). In these stories Chesnutt broadened the range of racial realism in American literature, and all of

his five volumes of fiction would deal with various facets of racial problems, with strong focusing on the experiences and points of view of his African American characters, though his concerns were always for both blacks and whites in American society and particularly in the South.

The stories of his second book of fiction, *The Wife of His Youth and Other Stories of the Color Line*, also published by Houghton Mifflin (1899), are in most ways quite different from the conjure stories and illustrate the variety of Chesnutt's skill and art. They are more contemporary and less rural and folk oriented, with more focus (sometimes ironically) on middle-class African Americans, especially those with light skin color. About half of these stories are set in North Carolina, and about half in Ohio. As its title suggests, this book intended to demonstrate the complex difficulties and sensitivities of those who (like Chesnutt himself) were of obvious racially mixed blood in societies both north and south, in which they aspired to rise even in the face of uncertainties about how that would be viewed. Chesnutt had very light skin and few Negroid features. He wrote about respect and injustice from personal concern and experience. These stories are sometimes tragic and sometimes comic, as he tried to write from a balanced and whole view of racial phenomena he had observed at close hand. Various reviews called attention to Chesnutt's presentation of African American characters in other than stereotypes and his making them of real interest and concern as individual human beings. Notable among such reviews was high praise from William Dean Howells in the *Atlantic Monthly* for May 1900, which took note of both of Chesnutt's volumes of fiction and of his biography of FREDERICK DOUGLASS (1899) in the Beacon Biographies Series. Howells also identified Chesnutt with various well-known contemporary writers of realistic fiction whom Howells championed.

On 30 September 1899 Chesnutt had closed his stenography business in order to pursue writing full time. In the autumn of 1900 Houghton Mifflin brought out *The House behind the Cedars*, the first of three novels Chesnutt would publish. It is a fuller and more straightforward exploration of

some of the miscegenation themes that had been found in his second volume of stories. The primary setting of the novel is the Fayetteville area, and it focuses on the emotional and practical (and sometimes tragic) difficulties of relatively white African Americans who chose to pass as white in the post–Civil War South. Although Chesnutt himself chose not to pass even though he could have, he knew those who had done so and understood and sympathized with their motives. Another novel, *The Marrow of Tradition*, followed from Houghton Mifflin in October 1901. This work, with his largest cast and most complicated plot, also is set in North Carolina. It is based on the riot that occurred in Wilmington in 1898 when white supremacists took over the city government with accompanying violence against blacks. In addition to having concerns with racial justice, as had his first novel, this book also has some focus on the aspirations of African Americans who choose to participate in the more highly respected professions. However, this work is even more interracial, its principal characters are white, and there is more direct criticism of the white population. While Howells praised the straightforwardness of the novel's moral concerns, he was disturbed by its bitterness. It did not sell well enough for Chesnutt to continue his attempt to succeed as a full-time author, and he reopened his stenography business before the year was over.

While disappointment and the need to gain financial stability slowed Chesnutt's literary aspirations, he did publish one more novel. Another North Carolinian, Walter Hines Page, while an editor at Houghton Mifflin had praised Chesnutt's accuracy of local color and had assisted his progress. Now Page persuaded Chesnutt to leave Houghton Mifflin, even though his relations with that firm had been good, and in September 1905 (the year in which Thomas Dixon's racially negative novel *The Clansman* was a bestseller) Page's firm (Doubleday, Page & Company) brought out *The Colonel's Dream*. Its protagonist, a former Confederate officer, returns to his southeastern North Carolina hometown and proposes a plan to bring it out of the economic hardships caused by the Civil War and its aftermath. He is willing to invest his own resources, but the plan is rejected because of greed and racial prejudice in the community. Reflecting Chesnutt's continuing loving concern for the area where he had spent his formative years, this book is dedicated to "the great number of those who are seeking, in whatever manner or degree... to bring the forces of enlightenment to bear upon the vexed problems which harass the South."

However, the various-faceted message for the South (and the country as a whole) that pervades Chesnutt's fiction and nonfiction, particularly concerning economic and social justice in relation to race, was not being accepted by those for whom it was most intended. He now turned his efforts more to other aspects of his life, among them his family, his business, and his involvement in several cultural organizations in Cleveland. One of these was the prestigious bibliophilic Rowfant Club, which refused membership to this nationally respected author three times before finally admitting him in 1910. His satiric "Baxter's Procrustes" (*Atlantic Monthly*, June 1904) is based on that club, and many think it is his best-written story. His career as a writer resulted in his publishing between 1885 and 1931 sixty-one pieces of short fiction (including those in the two volumes); one biography; thirty-one speeches, articles, and essays; seven poems; and three novels. Also, he left unpublished a sizable correspondence, one play, six novels, fifty-three essays and speeches, eighteen short stories (most of which have now been published by Render), three journals, and one notebook.

Chesnutt's published fiction, particularly his five books, was his most important accomplishment both artistically and in his attempts to improve social (particularly racial) relations. However, in addition to his fiction, his early work as an educator, his stenographic work in Cleveland, and his other writings, he also was active in various other pursuits that gave him pleasure, visibility, influence, reputation, and opportunity. He put his concerns, his knowledge of the law, and his respected reputation and personality to good use in speaking out on political and legal matters locally and nationally, particularly when they concerned the rights of African Americans. Early in his career as a writer he had

made the acquaintance of George Washington Cable and through this association had joined in the efforts of the Open-Letter Club, a project of several persons interested in and knowledgeable about the South to provide accurate information about that region and racial matters. Chesnutt was an active member of the National Association for the Advancement of Colored People (NAACP) in Cleveland and nationally, and there was mutual respect between him and both BOOKER T. WASHINGTON and W. E. B. DU BOIS. Though these two leaders took somewhat different approaches to the problems of African Americans and how best to solve them, Chesnutt saw merit in some aspects of the positions of both men and said so publicly, but also spoke up when he disagreed with them. He was a member of the General Committee of the NAACP and of Washington's Committee of Twelve for the Advancement of the Interests of the Negro Race. He addressed immediate socioeconomic problems and in various ways tried to promote awareness of and concern over the racial situation in America (particularly in the South—William Andrews has referred to his three novels as a New South trilogy). Chesnutt felt that the racial situation was undermining American democracy and that solutions to it would require sensitive understanding, ethical and moral conscience, and courage. In both his fiction and nonfiction his view of the proper future for African Americans was for gradual assimilation of them into the mainstream of American life through education and hard work. His three daughters and his one son all graduated from well-known colleges, and he lived to see them established in their chosen endeavors and moving into that mainstream, as he had in his way before them.

Though the major part of Chesnutt's literary career ended with the publication of *The Colonel's Dream* in 1905, respect for him as a pioneering writer continued. Among the recognition given him was an invitation to attend Mark Twain's seventieth birthday party at Delmonico's in New York in 1905 and membership in the National Arts Club in 1917. In 1913 Wilberforce University gave him an honorary degree, and in 1928 he was awarded the NAACP's prestigious Spingarn Medal for his "pioneer

work as a literary artist depicting the life and struggle of Americans of Negro descent, and for his long and useful career as scholar, worker and freeman of one of America's greatest cities." That same year *The Conjure Woman* was republished by Houghton Mifflin in a special edition with a foreword by the literary critic and leader in racial concerns Joel Spingarn. In 1926 the committee to choose the first recipient of the newly established Harmon Foundation Award for the work of an African American writer during the preceding year recommended that the chronological stipulation be waived and the first award be given to Chesnutt to acknowledge his pioneering work and his continuing example to other African American writers. This was not allowed, and unfortunately Chesnutt never knew of this acknowledgment of high esteem from a distinguished panel of his literary peers both black and white.

Chesnutt was the first important African American writer whose primary genre was fiction and the first African American writer to be published primarily by major publishers and major periodicals. Writing and publishing during times that were not very socially, politically, or legally favorable to African Americans in general, Chesnutt wrote fiction to provide entertainment and to call attention to racism and social injustice, especially for middle-class light-skinned blacks and working-class blacks in small towns and the rural South. He believed that the sources of as well as the solutions to their problems were in the South, so he wrote about the South and in ways that he intended to be more accurate, realistic, and better than those of others using similar subject matter. He purposefully dealt with topics regarding racial problems, such as miscegenation, which he felt other southern writers were avoiding or mistreating. In doing this he used various literary devices, including accurate dialect and details of local color and black life, satire, humor, irony, pathos, and even first-person point of view for nonblack characters. However, while he wrote with unblinking truth and obvious strong social purpose, he also wrote without rancor and with attention to and faithful portrayal of both sides of problems, creating a variety of memorable characters. He especially hoped to counter the too often derogatory and stereotypical portrayal of black characters and to make readers more aware of the positive and often complex humanity and variety of African Americans, the mistreatment of minorities and their need for greater social justice, and the fallibility of human nature.

Sylvia Render has pointed out that Chesnutt promoted American ideals in popular American forms and in accord with accepted contemporary literary standards, and was published by very reputable firms. However, after his death his works were generally underread and undervalued until attention to them revived in the 1960s. In his Spingarn Medal acceptance Chesnutt said, "I didn't write my stories as Negro propaganda—propaganda is apt to be deadly to art—but I used the better types [of Negroes], confident that the truth would prove the most valuable propaganda." A few months later he wrote to JAMES WELDON JOHNSON, "I wrote the truth as I saw it, with no special catering to anybody's prejudices." He died in Cleveland.

FURTHER READING

The most important sources for unpublished Chesnutt writings and related materials are the Chesnutt collection of the Cravath Library at Fisk University and the Chesnutt papers at the Library of the Western Reserve Historical Society, Cleveland.

Andrews, William L. *The Literary Career of Charles W. Chesnutt* (1980).

Chesnutt, Helen M. *Charles Waddell Chesnutt: Pioneer of the Color Line* (1952).

Ellison, Curtis W., and E. W. Metcalf Jr. *Charles W. Chesnutt: A Reference Guide* (1977).

Heermance, J. Noel. *Charles W. Chesnutt: America's First Great Black Novelist* (1974).

Keller, Frances Richardson. *An American Crusade: The Life of Charles Waddell Chesnutt* (1978).

Render, Sylvia Lyons. *Charles W. Chesnutt* (1980).

—JULIAN MASON

 CHESTER, THOMAS MORRIS (11 May 1834– 30 Sept. 1892), lawyer and Civil War correspondent, was born in Harrisburg, Pennsylvania, the son of George Chester and Jane Maria (maiden name unknown), restaurateurs. When, as a young man of eighteen, Chester decided

to emigrate to Liberia, he wrote Martin H. Freeman, his former teacher at the Avery Institute in Pittsburgh, that his passion for liberty could no longer "submit to the insolent indignities and contemptuous conduct to which it has almost become natural for the colored people dishonorably to submit themselves." It was a bold assertion of independence for one who had come of age in a household long associated with the anticolonization sentiments of radical abolitionism. But the country's willingness to appease southern interests, symbolized by the passage of the Fugitive Slave Law in 1850, persuaded Chester, sometime before his 1853 graduation, to emigrate.

Anxious to recruit the son of such a prominent black family, leaders of the Pennsylvania Colonization Society led Chester to believe that he could complete his education in Monrovia. But the colony could not meet his needs, and within a year Chester was back in the United States where, with the support of the New York Colonization Society, he attended Thetford Academy in Vermont from 1854 to 1856. Following graduation Chester returned to Monrovia, where he became active in politics and published and edited the short-lived *Star of Liberia*, which appeared intermittently between 1859 and 1861. He also taught school at the new settlement of Robertsport and in Monrovia. During this period he made frequent trips back to the United States, under the auspices of the Colonization Society, to promote emigration to Liberia.

Continued troubles with political rivals in Monrovia persuaded Chester in 1861 to return to the United States where he continued to work for the cause of colonization. Abraham Lincoln's Emancipation Proclamation prompted him to delay his return to Liberia in early 1863. Chester headed the recruitment drive in central Pennsylvania for the two black Massachusetts regiments but ceased his activities when it became clear that blacks would not be appointed officers. Before resigning the civilian appointment, however, Chester became the first black to be given a captaincy in the Pennsylvania state militia when he raised a company to help defend the state capital against Confederate forces in the weeks before Gettysburg.

In 1864 Chester was employed by John Russell Young, editor of the Philadelphia *Press*, as a war correspondent attached to the Army of the James. He was the first and only African American to report on the war for a major daily newspaper. Chester's dispatches provide the most sustained accounts of black troop activity around Petersburg and Richmond in the last year of the war. He reported on the contributions of black troops to the war effort, sent moving accounts of the death and carnage of battle, and, with a rakish sense of humor, provided glimpses into camp life. Chester was one of the first reporters to enter Richmond, and with some bravado and a touch of irony he wrote his next dispatch seated in the chair of the Speaker of the Confederate House of Representatives. Chester remained in Richmond until June 1865, reporting on efforts to rebuild the city and on the activities of the African American community.

In 1866 Chester was commissioned by the Garnet League, the Harrisburg chapter of the Pennsylvania Equal Rights League, to undertake a fund-raising tour of Britain and the Continent. Even before his assignment with the *Press* Chester had been thinking of studying law in England and in 1863 had briefly visited London, where he made invaluable contacts in abolitionist circles. The tour was a rousing personal success although it is unclear exactly how much money he raised. During his visit to Russia, Chester was introduced to the royal court by Cassius M. Clay, U.S. minister to St. Petersburg. Chester was invited to join the annual review of the imperial guard and to dine with the royal family.

At the conclusion of his mission Chester applied and was admitted to Middle Temple, London, where he studied law from 1867 to 1870. In April 1870 he became the first African American to be called to the English bar. A few weeks later Chester argued his first case in the hallowed halls of the Old Bailey, defending a shoemaker charged with murder. Although all the evidence pointed to the defendant's guilt, Chester's skillful cross-examination saved his client from the gallows. The accused was sentenced instead to ten-year's penal servitude.

A few months after his return to the United States in mid-1870, Chester decided to settle in New Orleans, having been impressed with the level of black political power in the city. By the time of his arrival in 1871, the Republican Party was immobilized by factionalism and violence. On 1 January 1872, in the streets of New Orleans, Chester was shot (but not seriously wounded) by members of one of the political factions.

In 1873 Chester was admitted to the Louisiana bar, the first black man to be admitted according to contemporary news accounts, and he played a prominent role in many of the civil rights suits brought by blacks under the state's new antidiscrimination laws. In May 1873 he was commissioned a brigadier general in the Louisiana state militia by Governor William Kellogg. The militias had been formed by Republican administrations to fill the void left by departing federal troops. Two years later Kellogg appointed Chester superintendent of public education for the First Division, which included areas around New Orleans. The following year Chester was moved to head the Fifth Division with offices in Delta, Madison Parish. Chester retained both the rank of brigadier general and the position of superintendent until the return to power of the Democrats in 1876.

With the aid of powerful friends in Pennsylvania, particularly members of the Cameron family, Chester was appointed U.S. commissioner for New Orleans in 1878, a position he held for almost two years. In December 1882 he was sent, as an assistant to the U.S. attorney for the Eastern District of Texas, on a special mission to investigate political violence in the area. But disputes with Washington over payments for expenses led to the termination of his appointment before he had completed his investigation.

Chester married Florence Johnson, twenty-one years his junior, in 1879. Little else is known of his life except that in 1884 he was named president of the North Carolina Wilmington, Wrightsville and Onslow Railroad, a company established by African Americans to build a rail system connecting the towns to important markets in Virginia. The plans never materialized, and

Chester returned to his law practices in Louisiana and Pennsylvania. Chester died at his mother's home in Harrisburg of an apparent heart attack.

Chester was fiercely independent, driven by what he called "self respect and pride of race." As he told many audiences at home and abroad, he was descended from a long line of independent black men and women who had openly defied all forms of racial restrictions. In Liberia his work as editor and teacher contributed to the social and political life of Robertsport and Monrovia. In the United States he sought to push the country toward realizing the dream of full equality for all its people.

FURTHER READING

Letters from and about Chester are in the American Colonization Society papers at the Library of Congress; in the Simon Cameron papers, Historical Society of Dauphin County, Pennsylvania; in the Massachusetts Historical Society; in the archives of the Society of the Middle Temple, London; in Records of the General Agent (record group 60) at the National Archives; and in the Jacob C. White papers at the Moorland-Spingarn Library, Howard University.

Blackett, R. J. M. *Thomas Morris Chester: Black Civil War Correspondent* (1989).

—R. J. M. BLACKETT

CHILDRESS, ALICE

(12 Oct. 1916–14 Aug. 1994), playwright and actress, was born in Charleston, South Carolina, and brought up in Harlem, New York, by her grandmother, Eliza Campbell White. Although Alice's grandmother had little or no formal education, she had an natural creative spirit, and fostered in her granddaughter a thirst for knowledge and an appreciation for the arts by exposing her to museums, galleries, libraries, theater, and concerts. She also encouraged Alice to role-play and create stories and skits, many of which grew out of Wednesday-night testimonials at Harlem's Salem Church. These testimonials, Alice later realized, allowed poor people in their community to relieve themselves of

burdens linked to race, class, and gender biases.

Alice lived on 118th Street between Lenox and Fifth Avenues and attended Public School 81 and the Julia Ward Howe Junior High School. She enrolled in Wadleigh High School, but dropped out after two years, forced to earn a living after the death of both her grandmother and mother in the early 1930s. Primarily self-taught, Alice worked as an assistant machinist, photo retoucher, domestic worker, salesperson, and insurance agent, jobs that tied her to working-class people who later found their way into her writing.

Unfulfilled by these odd jobs, Alice reinvented herself, gravitating toward theater because of her love of dialogue. In the 1930s she formed alliances with Harlem actors and won cameo roles in plays. During this time she met and married Alvin Childress. Best known for his role as Amos Jones in the 1950s show *Amos 'n Andy*, Alvin Childress one of the first African American actors to star on television. In 1935 a daughter, Jean, was born. The couple soon divorced but maintained a professional relationship throughout the 1940s, working side by side in the American Negro Theater (ANT), a training ground for black artists, including SIDNEY POITIER, OSSIE DAVIS, RUBY DEE, Frank Silvera, Hilda Simms, Canada Lee, and Earle Hyman. Childress developed as an actress, director, and playwright at the ANT from 1941 to 1952. After work in several ANT productions, Childress starred on Broadway from 1944 to 1954 in *Anna Lucasta*, a play by Philip Yordan first staged at the ANT and costarring Alvin, Canada Lee, and FREDERICK O'NEAL. The play ran for 957 performances and earned Childress a Tony Award nomination.

While at the ANT, Childress responded to a call for more plays by, for, and about blacks. In 1949 she directed and starred in her first one-act play, *Florence*. One of Childress's major accomplishments during her tenure with the ANT was her role in the early 1950s in initiating guaranteed pay in advance for union off-Broadway contracts in New York. Childress's *Just a Little Simple* (based on the short story collection *Simple Speaks His Mind* by

LANGSTON HUGHES) and *Gold through the Trees* (1952) were the first plays written by black woman to be produced professionally and performed by unionized actors.

In 1955 Childress made theater history when she became the first African American woman to win an Obie Award, with *Trouble in Mind* (1955), which she directed off-Broadway at the Greenwich Mews Theater. In July 1957 she married musician Nathan Woodard, with whom she collaborated on several creative projects. In 1966 Childress was awarded a two-year appointment to the Radcliffe Institute for Independent Study (now the Mary Ingraham Bunting Institute) at Harvard University, where she became friendly with playwrights Lillian Hellman and Tillie Olsen. While at Radcliffe she wrote *Wedding Band: A Love/Hate Story in Black and White*, a play about interracial love and the racism of laws barring marriage between blacks and whites.

In 1972 Childress and Joseph Papp codirected the *Wedding Band* for the New York Public Theater's Shakespeare Festival. Two years later she adapted *Wedding Band* for television. Childress's other plays include *String* (1969), *Wine in the Wilderness* (1969), *Mojo: A Black Love Story* (1970), *The World on a Hill* (1974), *When the Rattlesnake Sounds* (1975), *Let's Hear It for the Queen* (1976), a piece she wrote for her only grandchild, Marilyn Alice Lee, *A Portrait of* FANNIE LOU HAMER (1978), *Sea Island Song*, renamed *Gullah* (1977 and 1981), and *Moms: A Praise Play for a Black Comedienne* (1986), based on the life of MOMS MABLEY. In an attempt to improve the quality of the lives of African Americans, Childress's plays underscore themes affecting the lives of American blacks: the need for self-determination and self-definition, the destructiveness of stereotypes, and the need for more creative, positive images.

Childress, who had spoken out against injustices in her column in *Freedom*, a newspaper edited by PAUL ROBESON, and in the *Baltimore Afro-American* (collected in *Like One of the Family: Conversations from a Domestic's Life* [1956]), became increasingly committed to the issue of poverty in America after her travels to Russia, China,

and Ghana in the 1970s. She raised the social issues of poverty, addiction, child abuse, and racism in her fiction as well as in her dramatic works. Childress wrote a number of books, including three novels for young adults, *A Hero Ain't Nothin' but a Sandwich* (1973), which she later adapted as a screenplay; *Rainbow Jordan* (1981); and *Those Other People* (1989). Her novel for adults, *A Short Walk* (1979), traces black experiences in America from the MARCUS GARVEY movement through the 1940s. Like her plays, Childress's novels incorporate black history and emphasize the importance of relying upon ancestors for strength and guidance.

Childress garnered many honors, particularly for *Rainbow Jordan* and *A Hero Ain't Nothin' but a Sandwich*, which won a National Book Award nomination, the Lewis Carroll Shelf Award, and an American Library Association award for Best Young Adult Book. Childress was the recipient of the first Paul Robeson Award for Outstanding Contributions to the Performing Arts, a Radcliffe Alumnae Graduate Society Medal for Distinguished Achievement, a Lifetime Career Achievement Award from the Association for Theatre in Higher Education in 1993, and election to the Black Filmmakers Hall of Fame.

Childress's contributions to American life and letters are significant. Her novels created a much-needed space in American literature to view the dangers awaiting black adolescents in a hostile world. Her plays underscored her belief that black adults, too, were at great risk from the destructive forces in a racist society. She was an activist who saw a need for change and worked tirelessly both inside and outside of the theater to revolutionize American society. Childress, who died of cancer in 1994, wrote successfully for the American stage for over four decades and served as a major link in the development of African American theater.

FURTHER READING

Betsko, Kathleen, and Rachel Koenig, eds. *Interviews with Contemporary Women Playwrights* (1987).
Brown-Guillory, Elizabeth. *Interview with Alice Childress, SAGE: A Scholarly Journal on Black Women* (1987).
Bryer, Jackson R., ed. *The Playwright's Art: Conversations with Contemporary American Dramatists* (1995).
Jennings, La Vinia Delois. *Alice Childress* (1995).
Jordan, Shirley M., ed. *Broken Silences: Interviews with Black and White Women Writers* (1993).

Obituary: *New York Times*, 19 Aug. 1994.
—ELIZABETH BROWN-GUILLORY

CHINN, MAY EDWARD

(15 Apr. 1896–1 Dec. 1980), physician and cancer researcher, was born in Great Barrington, Massachusetts, the daughter of William Lafayette Chinn, a former slave who had escaped to the North from a Virginia plantation, and Lulu Ann Evans, a domestic worker. William Chinn had unsteady employment because of racial discrimination, but occasionally worked at odd jobs and as a porter. Raised in New York City, May Chinn was educated in the city's public schools and at the Bordentown Manual Training and Industrial School (N.J.), and she attended Morris High School in New York. A severe bout with osteomyelitis of the jaw plagued her as a child and required extensive medical treatment. Though her family's poverty forced her to drop out of high school in the eleventh grade for a factory job, she scored high enough on the entrance examination for Teachers' College at Columbia University a year later to be admitted to the class of 1921 without a high school diploma.

Chinn's early ambition was to be a musician. Despite the family's poor economic situation, her parents financed piano lessons that gave her some professional opportunity in music as a young adult. For several years in the early 1920s she was a piano-accompanist for the famed singer PAUL ROBESON, and she initially majored in music education at Columbia. She was the only African American and female in her music classes, and ridicule from one professor caused her to abandon music for study in the sciences. The switch to science, combined with her childhood experience of being treated for osteomyelitis, led to her decision to become a medical doctor. After graduating from Columbia with a BS degree in 1921, she was admitted to the Bellevue Hospital Medical College (now New York University Medical College) and in 1926 became its first African American woman graduate. In 1926 she was one of the first three African Americans to be accepted as interns at New York City's public Harlem Hospital. (The other two were men.)

Upon completion of her internship Chinn faced the "color" barrier confronted by all African American physicians; she could not gain admitting privileges for her patients at any hospital in New York City. She opened an office in a brownstone on Edgecombe Avenue in Harlem next to the Edgecombe Sanatorium, a private hospital owned and operated by a group of black physicians. In return for living and office space, she answered all-night emergency calls at the sanatorium. During the 1930s she studied dermatology and gynecology at the Post-Graduate Hospital Medical School in New York, and in 1933 she received an MS degree in Public Health from Columbia University.

Chinn's interest in cancer research was elicited by the clinical experience of seeing so many patients in advanced stages of the disease, and this led to the development of a "fanatical preoccupation" in understanding and treating cancer. No hospital in New York City would allow her to do cancer work because of her race, but she was unofficially allowed to work with resident physicians at Memorial Hospital and was instructed in how to perform biopsies. Between 1928 and 1933 she studied cytological methods for the diagnosis of cancer under George Papanicolaou, developer of the Pap Smear test for cervical cancer. African American physicians in Harlem, having learned of her connection at Memorial and her training and clinical experience there, began to send her specimens for biopsies. In 1944 she was appointed to the staff of the Strang Clinic affiliated with Memorial and New York Infirmary Hospital. While working at the Strang Clinic over the next twenty-nine years, she helped to devise ways to detect cancer in asymptomatic patients. Her evaluation of patients' family histories to detect cancer in the early stages was recognized as a significant approach to cancer understanding and treatment at the time.

Over the course of her 52-year career Chinn became a legend in Harlem. She was one of a handful of pioneering African American women in medicine in the mid-1920s through the 1930s and 1940s who overcame barriers of race and gender in medical school, in postgraduate training, and in gaining hospital appointments. In addition to her family medical practice and cancer work, she was a clinician and medical adviser in New York State Department of Health–supported day care centers in New York City (1960–1977) and a staff member of the New York Infirmary for Women and Children (1945–1956). As the physician assigned to escort fifty severely handicapped persons of the St. Jeanne Valois Guild of New York City to Paris, Lourdes, and Rome in 1961, she was granted a special audience with Pope John XXIII and in 1978 served as a medical consultant to 100 refugees from southern Africa who were attending colleges throughout the United States. After her retirement from private practice in 1977, Chinn continued to work in three Harlem day care centers sponsored by the state department of health.

Chinn's cancer research and clinical practice was recognized by her election as a member of the New York Academy of Sciences in 1954, and in 1957 she received a citation from the New York City Cancer Committee of the American Cancer Society. She was elected to the Society of Surgical Oncology in 1958, became a Fellow of the American Geriatrics Society in 1959, and was elected to medical membership of the American Society of Cytology in 1972 and as a Life Member of the American Academy of Family Physicians in 1977. In 1975 she was a founder of the Susan Smith McKinney Steward Medical Society, named for the first African American woman licensed to practice medicine in the state of New York. Chinn received a Teachers' College Distinguished Alumnus Award from Columbia University in May 1980 and an honorary doctor of science degree from New York University in June 1980. She died while attending a reception in Avery Hall at Columbia University.

FURTHER READING

Chinn's papers are housed in the Schomburg Center for Research in Black Culture of the New York Public Library.

Brozan, Nadine. "For a Doctor at 84, a Day to Remember." *New York Times*, 17 May 1980.
Davis, George. "A Healing Hand in Harlem." *New York Times Magazine*, 22 Apr. 1979.
Hill, Ruth Edmonds, ed. *The Black Women Oral History Project* (1991).

Obituary: *New York Times*, 3 Dec. 1980.
—ROBERT C. HAYDEN

 CHISHOLM, SHIRLEY (30 Nov. 1924–), U.S. congresswoman, was born Shirley St. Hill in Brooklyn, New York, the eldest daughter of Charles St. Hill, a laborer born in British Guiana (now Guyana), and Ruby Seale, a seamstress born in Barbados. Shirley's first three years were spent in Brownsville, a predominately Jewish area of Brooklyn. Finding the wages for unskilled factory work insufficient to care for three children properly, the St. Hills sent their three daughters to Barbados, where they lived with their maternal grandparents on the family farm. Shirley credits her grandmother Emily Seale with instilling in her a strong character and determination.

The girls returned to Brownsville in 1934, after their mother gave birth to another daughter. Despite the social and financial hardships of the Depression, Ruby encouraged her children to respect the values of civility, thrift, poise, humility, education, and spirituality, though the sisters endured a substantial amount of teasing in the neighborhood for upholding these values and the sense of decorum and respectability that their parents expected of them. Charles St. Hill's influence on Shirley's political development was also profound. His support for MARCUS GARVEY and his pride in his labor union were frequent dinner table discussion topics, and in her autobiography Chisholm recalls that she went to listen to many black nationalist orators with her father.

In 1936 the family moved to the Bedford-Stuyvesant area of Brooklyn, where the Caribbean and southern black residents constituted about half of the population. Unaccustomed to the animosity blacks faced in that neighborhood, Shirley felt the sting of racial epithets for the first time. During this time she also became aware of racial discrimination, when her father's workdays in a burlap bag factory were inequitably reduced. As a result, Ruby was forced to find work as a domestic, leaving Shirley with the responsibility of looking after the home and caring for her younger sisters. Shirley entered Girls High School in 1939 but was still guarded closely by her parents. Shy and self-conscious because of her West Indian accent, she became a voracious reader, maintained superior marks in school, and was elected vice president of a girl's honor society. Determined to pursue a career in teaching, one of the few career options available to black women at that time, Shirley entered Brooklyn College in September of 1942. Motivated by her increasing awareness of the racism at the college, she shed her shyness, joined the debating society, and began to speak out on racial issues. She also became active in the HARRIET TUBMAN Society for Negro History and formed Ipothia, a sorority for black women. Believing that "service is the rent we pay for the privilege of living on this earth" (a phrase also attributed to MARIAN WRIGHT EDELMAN), Shirley St. Hill volunteered with the Urban League and the NAACP, in hospitals, and at a home for the aged. While still in college, she publicly challenged the mostly Irish-American organization that ran Brooklyn's old Seventeenth Assembly District for ignoring issues of concern to African Americans, even though two-thirds of the district's constituents were black.

Despite graduating cum laude in 1946, Shirley had difficulty finding work, and she resented that whites with lesser qualifications appeared to have better job opportunities. Eventually hired as a classroom teacher at Mt. Calvary Child Care Center in Harlem, she later became the center's director. Concurrently she enrolled in the master's program in early childhood education at Columbia College, where she met fellow student and private investigator Conrad Chisholm, whom she married in 1949. Conrad Chisholm eventually became an investigator for the City of New York and was by her side through most of her political career until their divorce in 1977.

In 1953 she became director of the Friends in Need Nursery School in Brooklyn, but moved on after one year to become the director of the Hamilton-Madison Child Care Center on Manhattan's Lower East Side. By 1959 she had become a program consultant for the New York City Division of Day Care, but she continued her community work in Bedford-Stuyvesant, setting up youth programs for children, petitioning for better postal service and sanitation, and serving on the board of directors of the Albany Houses public housing project. Through these activities she became involved with New York's political clubs, which were organized by state assembly districts. In 1953 Chisholm joined with her political mentor Wesley McD. "Mac" Holder to help elect the first black judge in Brooklyn's history. Through that effort, the Bedford-Stuyvesant Political League (BSPL) was launched, and Chisholm remained active in this club as well as the regular Democratic organization. In 1958 Chisholm unsuccessfully challenged Mac Holder for the presidency of the BSPL, which caused a schism between them for ten years.

Chisholm was inactive on the political scene for two years following her loss to Mac Holder, but she soon returned to politics to help form the Unity Democratic Club. The primary goal of this club was to oust the white political machine of the Seventeenth Assembly District. Victorious in this mission, Unity became the official Democratic club for the district, and in 1964 Unity nominated Chisholm to fill a vacated seat in the New York State Assembly. She was elected to the assembly, but her victory was marred by her father's death during the campaign.

Chisholm soon earned a reputation in Albany as a maverick who voted her conscience and frequently went against the party line. During her tenure, she introduced more than fifty bills into the legislature, of which eight passed. The most notable of these was her creation of the SEEK (Search for Education, Elevation and Knowledge) program, which enabled financially disadvantaged students to attend college. She also was a powerful advocate of extending unemployment insurance coverage to domestic employees and of providing state aid to day-care centers.

Determined to beat the political machine that had emerged in Brooklyn's newly created black-majority Twelfth District, Chisholm ran for Congress in 1968. Reuniting with Mac Holder, she campaigned with the slogan "Fighting Shirley Chisholm—Unbought and Unbossed." Emergency surgery for a stomach tumor caused Chisholm to lose some early ground to her opponent, the civil rights activist JAMES FARMER. Finding, however, that there were two and a half women for every man on the voter-registration rolls, Chisholm garnered the support of women's organizations. Her fluency in Spanish also attracted the Hispanic vote, thus providing an ultimately victorious block against her Republican opponent.

As a freshman representative to the Ninety-first Congress in 1969, Chisholm asked to be assigned to the House Education and Labor Committee. Instead, she was assigned to the Committee for Rural Development and Forestry, whose agenda was totally unrelated to the needs of her urban district. After failing in her attempts to enlist the support of more senior representatives, she defiantly approached the Speaker's dais to protest the assignment. Again, her diligence paid off, and she was reassigned to the Committee on Veterans Affairs. In 1971 she secured a seat on the powerful House Education and Labor Committee, which enabled her to focus on the economic and educational issues of greatest relevance to her constituents.

Chisholm became increasingly well known on Capitol Hill for her straightforward criticism of cozy bipartisan politics and the seniority system. In the late 1960s, the tap of Chisholm's trademark stiletto heels struck a dissonant chord in the boys club atmosphere of the U.S. Congress. Her unabashed and uncompromising liberalism also stood out, even in that relatively liberal era. She fought passionately for greater racial and gender equality, demanded a lowering of the voting age, spoke out against the Vietnam War, and supported the National Association for the Repeal of Abortion Laws. In 1970 Chisholm headed a coalition of women's groups to raise bail for a jailed Black Panther Party member.

Chisholm gained national recognition in January 1972, when she announced her intention to run for the presidency of the United States. Inspired by the young people with whom she maintained constant contact, she campaigned in six states while continuing to attend to her duties in Washington and Brooklyn. She did not receive the support of the Congressional Black Caucus, however, which severely dented her chance of winning the Democratic nomination. But her impressive showing of 151 votes to George McGovern's 1,415 constituted the largest number of convention votes cast for a female candidate in U.S. party political history.

Continuing to serve in the House of Representatives, Chisholm emerged as a powerful advocate for fair housing programs and the educational rights of the poor and racial minorities. Her most significant legislative achievement came in the mid 1970s, when she successfully led the opposition in Congress to President Ford's veto of federal support for state daycare services. By the time Chisholm retired from Congress in 1982, however, she had become less of a maverick, and, as a member of its Rules Committee, even something of a Capitol Hill insider.

She has subsequently held faculty appointments at Mount Holyoke College, Massachusetts, where she taught politics and women's studies from 1983 to 1987, and at Spelman College in Atlanta, Georgia, where she was a visiting scholar in 1985. Chisholm is the author of two autobiographies, *Unbought and Unbossed* (1970) and *The Good Fight* (1973), and in 1984 she cofounded the National Political Congress of Black Women. In 1993 President Bill Clinton asked her to serve as U.S. Ambassador to Jamaica, but she

declined the appointment for health reasons. Chisholm lives in Florida with her second husband, Arthur Hardwick, whom she married in 1977.

Shirley Chisholm will be remembered as the woman warrior of American politics and as a champion for underrepresented Americans. CHARLES RANGEL and KWESI MFUME, who followed her into Congress, attained greater political clout on Capitol Hill. JESSE JACKSON earned more votes and delegates in his 1984 and 1988 campaigns for the Presidency. In each of these cases, however, their task was made easier by the precedents and the example set by Shirley Chisholm.

FURTHER READING

Chisholm, Shirley. *The Good Fight* (1973).
———. *Unbought and Unbossed* (1970).

Gill, LaVerne McCain. *African American Women in Congress: Forming and Transforming History* (1997).
Hicks, Nancy. *The Honorable Shirley Chisholm, Congresswoman from Brooklyn* (1971).
—PATRICIA E. CANSON

CINQUÉ (c. 1814–c. 1879), slave mutineer, was born Sengbe (also spelled Singbe and Sengbeh) Pieh in the village of Mani, in the Mende territory of Sierra Leone, Africa, the son of a rice farmer. His mother died when he was young, and at about the age of twenty-five he lived with his father, his wife, and his three children. One day while working alone in his rice field, he was seized by four members of the Vai tribe, often employed by Europeans to capture slaves for the market. He was taken to Lomboko, an island at the mouth of the Gallinas River on the coast of Sierra Leone, where he was purchased by Pedro Blanco, a Spanish slave trader, for sale in Cuba. He remained in Lomboko for three months in chains before Blanco filled the ship that was to transport him to Havana.

Slavery was still legal in Cuba, but the trans-Atlantic trade in slaves had been abolished by international treaties in 1820. When Cinqué arrived he was thus technically contraband, but once landed he was legally a slave and was housed with many other recently

transported Africans. Within ten days, he was purchased, along with forty-eight other able-bodied African men, by one of the leading Spanish dealers in Cuba, José Ruiz, who paid $450 each for them. Ruiz and a companion, Pedro Montes, who had made the more modest purchase of four children all under twelve years of age, loaded their fifty-three slaves on the schooner *Amistad* on 28 June 1839 and set sail for Puerto Príncipe, a short distance from Havana. Each slave had been provided with a false Spanish passport in case of search by English authorities while in transit.

Alarmed by the cruel joke of the ship's cook, who communicated to the slaves that they were to be killed and eaten by the crew, Cinqué found a nail while exercising on deck and picked the lock on his iron collar. On the third night out, he freed his fellow slaves, all but three of whom were from Mende territory and spoke the same language. Arming themselves with machetes being shipped to the sugar plantations for cutting cane, the slaves quickly killed the cook and Ramón Ferrer, the captain. The two remaining crew members disappeared, presumably drowned trying to swim for shore. The mutineers, under Cinqué's command, then ordered their former owners Ruiz and Montes to steer the ship back to Africa. Montes, who had been a sea captain, was put at the helm and told to head into the rising sun, but the Spaniard reversed the course every night in hopes of being picked up and freed by Americans or Cubans. This zigzag route continued for sixty-three days, during which ten of the Africans died. At last on 26 August, the need for food and water forced Cinqué to order a landing at the next island they saw, which proved to be Long Island, New York.

The vessel was immediately seized by U.S. Navy officers, and on 29 August the mutineers were arrested for piracy and murder. Ruiz and Montes were set free; they demanded the return of the ship and its cargo, including the slaves, as their property. Because New York was a free state, Coast Guard Lt. Thomas Gedney, who had seized the schooner, had the *Amistad* towed to Connecticut, where slavery was still legal, hoping to claim it and its forty-three surviving slaves as salvage. The Africans, including the four children, were jailed in New Haven

Philadelphia abolitionist Robert Purvis commissioned this portrait by Nathaniel Jocelyn of Cinqué or Sengbe, the leader of the rebellion on La Amistad in 1839.
William K. Sacco/Courtesy of The New Haven Colony Historical Society

while the courts undertook to clarify the local, national, and international issues involved. Lt. Gedney sued for possession of the boat and all its cargo; Ruiz brought a separate suit for the return of his human property; and because Cuba was a possession of Spain, the Spanish government demanded that the slaves be returned to Havana to be tried for murder. President Martin Van Buren, seeking to maintain good diplomatic relations with Spain, supported the claim.

The trial of the Africans in the Circuit Court in Hartford on 17 September 1839 became a national sensation. The proslavery southern states opposed the freeing of the slaves, recognizing the threat to the institution on which their economy depended, and abolitionists in the north saw the case as an opportunity to promote their cause. The handsome, charismatic leader of the mutiny became a hero in the northern press, where his name took the form Cinqué (variously spelled Cinquè, Cinquez, or Cinquenzo, and sometimes embellished with the

forename Joseph), and his status in Africa was elevated to royalty. William Cullen Bryant's poem "The African Chief," published in the *Emancipator* on 19 September 1839, said of him, "A prince among his tribe before, / *He could not be a slave*" (italics in the original). In the meantime, the Africans were kept in the New Haven jail, where they were given English lessons and instruction in Christianity. To help defray the costs of their incarceration, they were exhibited to the curious for twelve and a half cents a look. Both dignified and congenial, the Black Prince, as Cinqué was often called in the newspapers, cheerfully consented to perform native dances and turn somersaults on the lawn.

Lewis Tappan, a founder of the New York Anti-Slavery Society, organized an *Amistad* Committee to help free the prisoners and hired the prominent constitutional lawyer Roger Sherman Baldwin for their defense. Baldwin argued that they were not legally slaves but "kidnapped Africans" and that their

mutiny was justified by "the inherent right of self defense." Cinqué delivered a speech so dramatically in his native Mende that it moved the audience even before it was translated for them. The Circuit Court found in favor of the Africans and ordered them freed. The Spanish government protested the decision and persuaded Secretary of State John Forsyth to direct the district attorney to appeal the case. President Van Buren issued an executive order to have the defendants transported to Cuba immediately if the appeal succeeded, thus preventing an appeal by the Africans. When the Federal District Court affirmed the Circuit Court's decision in January 1840, the government appealed again; in February of the next year the case was carried to the U.S. Supreme Court. The seventy-three-year-old former president John Quincy Adams, long an ardent supporter of abolition, was persuaded to join the defense, and his legendary eloquence carried the day. On 9 March, after trials that had dragged on for eighteen months, the Africans were once again declared free to return to Africa.

As the government refused to pay the costs of repatriation, several of the Africans went on a speaking tour, organized by the *Amistad* Committee, to raise money for their trip. Speaking in Mende, Cinqué was said to possess "a very graceful and animated manner" and became a popular spokesperson for the abolitionist cause. By November the mutineers, now reduced by death to thirty-five, had raised enough money for the long journey and embarked for Sierra Leone. They arrived in January 1842, accompanied by missionaries planning to establish a mission in Komende (spelled Kaw-Mendi in American sources), near Freetown. Cinqué continued inland to Mani in search of his family but, according to most reports, never saw them again. Little is known of his life after returning to Africa, but some accounts report that he made himself a powerful and prosperous chief among his people and even engaged in slave trading. Other versions have him returning to the mission to serve as an interpreter or returning there only in the last week of his life to die and be buried in the mission cemetery.

The leader of the only successful slave rebellion in American history,

Cinqué set in motion a legal battle that was to provide an important precedent in American and international law. The *Amistad* case helped to establish the authority of the courts, and it constituted what historian Howard Jones described as "an historic milestone in the long struggle against slavery and for the establishment of basic civil rights for everyone, regardless of color."

FURTHER READING

The principal collections of material related to Cinqué and the *Amistad* case are the Amistad Research Center in New Orleans, Louisiana; the Amistad collection of the New Haven Colony Historical Society Library in Connecticut; and the National Archives in Washington, D.C.

Baldwin, Simeon E. *The Captives of the Amistad* (1886).
Barber, John Warner. *A History of the Amistad Captives* (1840; repr. 2000).
Jones, Howard. *Mutiny on the Amistad: The Saga of a Slave Revolt and Its Impact on American Abolition, Law, and Diplomacy* (1987; repr. 1998).

—DENNIS WEPMAN

CLARK, KENNETH BANCROFT (24 July 1914–),

psychologist, was born in the Panama Canal Zone, the son of Jamaican immigrants Miriam Hanson Clark and Arthur Bancroft Clark. In 1919, Miriam left her husband and brought Kenneth and his sister Beulah to New York City. He attended public schools in Harlem, which were fully integrated when he entered the first grade, but were almost wholly black by the time he finished sixth grade. Kenneth's mother, an active follower of MARCUS GARVEY, encouraged her son's interest in black history and his academic leanings, and confronted his guidance teacher for recommending that Kenneth attend a vocational high school. A determined woman, active in the garment workers' union, Miriam Clark persuaded the authorities to send Kenneth to George Washington High, a school with a reputation for academic excellence. In 1931 he won a scholarship to attend Howard University in Washington, D.C.

Clark attended Howard at time of great academic and ideological ferment on campus. The faculty, arguably the

Kenneth B. Clark, whose "doll test" was cited in the famous 1954 Brown v. Board of Education *case, demonstrated the psychological harm segregation causes to children.* Library of Congress

greatest "dream team" of black academics ever assembled, included the philosopher ALAIN LOCKE, the political scientist RALPH BUNCHE, and the sociologist E. FRANKLIN FRAZIER. CHARLES HAMILTON HOUSTON and WILLIAM HENRY HASTIE taught at Howard Law School in those years, and numbered THURGOOD MARSHALL among their students. As editor of the *Hilltop,* the college newspaper, Clark immersed himself in the intellectual and political debates on campus and in 1935 was arrested for protesting segregation at the restaurant inside the U.S. Capitol building. Since Congress contributed to Howard's funding, several administrators proposed expelling the arrested students, but they were reprieved when Clark's mentor, Ralph Bunche, threatened to resign if such actions were taken. Clark graduated in 1931, remained at Howard to pursue a Master of Science degree, and taught in the Psychology Department at Howard for a year. He then moved to New York to pursue a PhD in Psychology at Columbia University, where his adviser discouraged him from choosing a "racial" topic for his dissertation for fear that it might harm his job chances. Clark's 1940 PhD, the first awarded to an African American at Columbia, was titled "Some Factors Influencing

the Remembering of Prose Materials." He taught briefly at Hampton Institute, a black college in Virginia, and in 1942 became the first black instructor appointed to the faculty of the City College of New York.

By then, Clark had begun collaborating on a study of racial self-identity in childhood with Mamie Katherine Phipps, a fellow Howard graduate whom he had married in 1938. They had eloped—Howard prohibited its undergraduates from marrying—and would later have two children, Kate, born in 1942, and Hilton, born a year later. Mamie Phipps had begun her study of children's perception of race in a class taught by her future husband at Howard and completed her dissertation on that topic at Columbia in 1943. Five years later, the Clarks established the Northside Center for Child Development. The Center provided a full range of psychological consulting and testing services for children, the first such agency in Harlem, and also carried out studies of racial self-identity in children.

One of these studies, now known simply as "the doll test," was to play a critical role in the NAACP's battle to end segregation. In the test, black children, aged 3–7 years old, were shown four identical dolls, two of them colored brown and two colored white, and asked to identify them as Negro or white. Three quarters of the children identified the dolls correctly. The psychologists then asked the children to give them the doll that they "liked best," or that looked "bad," or that is "a nice color," or that was most like themselves. Most of the black children studied expressed a preference for the white dolls, and rejected the black dolls; some did so in tears. The tests suggested to the Clarks that racial prejudice—and racial self-hatred—was fixed at an early age, and that only early intervention could prevent further psychic damage. In 1951, ROBERT L. CARTER of the NAACP's Legal Defense Fund (LDF) read of the Clarks' doll studies, and urged him to serve as an expert scientific witness in their efforts to outlaw segregated schooling. Clark carried out the doll tests among black children in Clarendon County, South Carolina, one of the four cases later consolidated in *Brown v. Board of Education*. As in the previous tests, the majority of black children in the Clarendon study identified with the white dolls and rejected the black ones. Clark also served as the expert psychological witness in the South Carolina, Virginia, and Delaware cases that formed part of *Brown*. More importantly, he acted as a liaison between the LDF and academics who submitted to the Court a legal brief outlining the psychological and sociological evidence of segregation's harmful impact on children. In May 1954, Chief Justice Earl Warren wrote for a unanimous Court in *Brown* that segregation was inherently unequal. Footnote 11 of that opinion cites the work of Kenneth B. Clark as evidence that segregation "retarded the educational and mental development of Negro children." Warren added that such psychological knowledge had not been available to the Court in 1896 when it had rendered its "separate but equal" ruling in *Plessy v. Ferguson*. The Justices' acceptance of psychological and social scientific testimony was unprecedented, and provoked controversy, though mainly among those who already opposed integration.

After *Brown*, Clark attempted to bring the psychological arguments made famous in that decision to a broader audience. The results were mixed. His 1955 book, *Prejudice and Your Child*, sold poorly, but Clark was much more successful as a public intellectual. He appeared in *Commentary* and other liberal journals, and the national media anointed him *the* black academic, much as it had anointed his friend JAMES BALDWIN as *the* black writer, and MARTIN LUTHER KING JR. as *the* civil rights leader. By 1963, when King, Baldwin, and thousands of lesser-known protestors had forced white Americans to look more deeply at the problems of racism, a second edition of *Prejudice and Your Child* found a larger audience. So, too, did Clark in a public television series, *The Negro and the Promise of American Life*, in which he interviewed the three most prominent African Americans of that era: Baldwin, King, and MALCOLM X. (Clark was a confidant of both King and Malcolm, and arranged the brief, but symbolic, meeting between the two leaders in 1964.) The interviews, published as *The Negro Protest* (1963), expressed Clark's belief that the United States had failed to live up to the promise of *Brown*. He envisioned only two ways in which America could avoid the racial explosions that would result from that unfulfilled promise: "One would be total oppression; the other total equality" (Keppel, *The Work of Democracy*, 138).

In the 1960s, Clark believed that latter goal was still possible. Harlem Youth Opportunities Unlimited (HARYOU), a grassroots anti-poverty project which Clark founded, was influential in the growing intellectual and public policy debate about poverty. The project envisioned job training schemes, preschool "academies," and a network of self-governing community councils dedicated to fighting poverty. Many of those programs were replicated in President Johnson's War on Poverty; HARYOU's pre-school academies, for example, served as the model for Head Start. Clark's experiences with HARYOU informed his most widely read book, *Dark Ghetto* (1965). He argued that America's inner cities were "colonies," exploited by the broader society's lack of interest in the educational, psychological, and economic well-being of African Americans. Until the nation responded to the institutionalized pathology of the ghetto with radical reforms, Clark concluded, America would "remain at the mercy of primitive, frightening, irrational attempts by prisoners in the ghetto to destroy their own prison"

(quoted in Keppel, *Work of Democracy*, 159). Though some in the civil rights movement criticized the book's emphasis on black victimhood, others, notably black power advocates such as STOKELY CARMICHAEL, were influenced by *Dark Ghetto's* discussion of African Americans' "colonial" status.

Clark did not advocate the separatist solutions offered by Carmichael, but America's retreat from the cause of racial justice in the 1970s and 1980s left him profoundly pessimistic about the future of civil rights. In 1990, he feared that the United States would never eradicate racism or achieve true integration. Looking back at the 1950s and 1960s, he shuddered at "how naïve we all were in our belief in the steady progress racial minorities would make through programs of litigation and education." Clark reflected that his life had been a "series of glorious defeats" (Clark, "Racial Progress and Retreat," 18).

Though it is true that the United States has far to go in achieving full integration, Dr. Clark's self-assessment seems unnecessarily negative. As the NAACP recognized in awarding him the Spingarn Medal in 1961, Clark's work as a psychologist was instrumental in the *Brown* decision, which set in motion an invigorated civil rights movement in the 1960s. It is also not insignificant that in 1970–1971 Clark served as the first black president of the American Psychological Association and also received that organization's Gold Medal Award for "contributions by a psychologist in the public interest." Kenneth Clark served that public interest by arguing persistently, with dignity and passion, that only radical change could eradicate the deep-rooted scars of racism in American Society.

FURTHER READING

Clark's papers are in the Library of Congress. Oral Histories of Kenneth and Mamie Phipps Clark are located in the Columbia University Oral History Program Collection in New York City.

American Psychologist Vol. 57, No. 1 (2002).
Clark, Kenneth B. "Racial Progress and Retreat" in Herbert Hill and James E. Jones Jr., *Race in America: The Struggle for Equality* (1993).
Keppel, Ben. *The Work of Democracy: Ralph Bunche, Kenneth B. Clark, Lorraine Hansberry, and the Cultural Politics of Race* (1995).

Kluger, Richard. *Simple Justice* (1977), chapter 14.

Markowitz, Gerald, and David Rosner. *Children, Race, and Power: Kenneth and Mamie Clark's Northside Center* (1996).

—STEVEN J. NIVEN

CLARK, SEPTIMA P.

(3 May 1898–15 Dec. 1987), educator, activist, and community leader, was born Septima Poinsette in Charleston, South Carolina, the second child of Peter Porcher Poinsette, a caterer, and Victoria Anderson, who took in laundry. Peter Poinsette emerged from slavery free of animosity or a spirit of rebellion but determined to serve others, to educate his children, and to follow Jesus Christ with a passion. Victoria Anderson Poinsette, who was born free and at one point lived in Haiti with relatives, boasted that she had never been a servant to any white family. Septima's parents met and married in Florida, later relocating to Charleston.

Septima graduated from Avery Institute in Charleston in 1916 and began teaching on Johns Island. She quickly learned that the educational season on the island was determined by the agricultural contracts between sharecroppers and landowners and that illiteracy and poverty contributed to a system akin to slavery. The children could only attend school in the brief period when they were not needed to plant or harvest. But the young people were aware of the world beyond Johns Island, and they wanted to learn to read and write in order to escape what they saw as a limited future. They came to her at night to learn to read and write, as did adults hoping to participate in church and fraternal functions. Poinsette came to see the clear discrepancy between the educational facilities for blacks and whites on the island; while she and another teacher looked after 130 students crammed into the crumbling Promiseland School, a nearby, neatly whitewashed school catered to only three white students. The white teacher at that school earned nearly three times Poinsette's salary.

In 1919 Poinsette returned to Charleston to teach at Avery Institute and became involved in a successful movement by the NAACP to secure black teachers for the public school

Septima Clark with ROSA PARKS *at the Highlander Folk School, an important training center for the civil rights movement.* Highlander Research and Education Center

system of the city of Charleston. While at Avery in 1920, she married Nerie Clark, a navy cook, with whom she had two children—Victoria, who lived for twenty-three months, and Nerie Clark Jr. Her in-laws became instrumental in the guardianship of Nerie Jr. after Nerie Sr. died in 1925, and Clark sought work in the public schools of Ohio, North Carolina, and South Carolina.

In 1929 Clark returned to Columbia, South Carolina, to work in the public schools. She also worked closely with the NAACP, which was pursuing a lawsuit to equalize the salaries of black and white public school teachers, and volunteered at a literacy program for black soldiers at nearby Camp Jackson. She joined with the Federated Women's Club and other civic groups in Columbia in developing a home for delinquent girls, creating an orphanage for black children, and assisting the elderly. Clark was accepted into Columbia's black society and also its social activities, and she earned her BA from Benedict College and her MA from the Hampton Institute. In 1947 she returned to Charleston to care for her elderly mother.

Clark then resumed teaching in the greater Charleston area and became involved in the activities of the black branch of the YWCA. Her work with the YWCA raised the problem of the lack of recreational facilities and

opportunities for the city's black girls and boys. It also brought her notoriety, since she befriended the ostracized Judge Waties Waring and Elizabeth Waring, prominent white Charlestonians who were shunned by most whites and some blacks due to their support of civil rights and social reform. Clark also resumed her work with the Charleston branch of the NAACP, and her refusal to deny her membership in that organization resulted in the Charleston school district firing her from her teaching job.

Clark learned of the Highlander Folk School in 1952 when a fellow YWCA worker encouraged her to attend the interracial institute in Monteagle, Tennessee. Clark attended Highlander during the summers of 1953 and 1954, excited to find a place in the South where progressive whites and blacks could meet and engage in dialogue about race. In 1954 and 1955 workshops on the *Brown* I and *Brown* II public school desegregation decisions brought civil rights leaders from across the South to Highlander to discuss how to work to implement the Supreme Court's rulings. By the summer of 1955 Clark began to focus on voting rights and brought activists from Charleston and the neighboring islands to Highlander with her. Among them was a former student, Esau Jenkins, from Johns Island, who had attempted to register fellow islanders to vote and wanted assistance in mobilizing his community. After Highlander sponsored an adult literacy program under Clark's and Jenkins's direction on Johns Island, neighboring islands sought to establish their own citizenship schools to prepare black residents for registering and voting.

When Tennessee authorities forced Highlander to close in 1959, its citizenship school program and its foundation support was picked up by the Southern Christian Leadership Conference (SCLC). Under the direction of Clark, Dorothy Cotton, and ANDREW YOUNG, the school was relocated to the McIntosh Center in southern Georgia. Along with Young and Cotton, Clark began a journey across the South informing black communities of the program and identifying candidates to attend a week-long workshop in citizenship and public policy. These graduates then returned to their respective communities to establish citizenship schools, which helped African Americans pass the literacy tests required to vote in many southern states.

From 1960 to 1970 Clark worked with the SCLC in implementing citizenship programs that helped thousands of African Americans across the South. She also worked with other civil rights groups, like SNCC, in preparing citizens to register to vote. Following the passage of the Civil Rights Act in 1964 and especially after the 1965 Voting Rights Act, Clark personally witnessed the impact of the citizenship program on the political empowerment of black southerners. Many blacks who sought political offices following 1965 had been affiliated with some aspect of the citizenship program, as these schools enhanced the political and social progress of blacks in the deep South.

In 1970 Clark retired from the SCLC and conducted workshops for the American Friends Service Committee, organized day-care sites, raised funds for scholarships, and became a sought-after speaker on civil and women's rights. In her latter years she began to review her position as a woman in the movement and the contributions of women, realizing how seldom they were recognized or appreciated. Clark was elected to the same school board that had fired her years earlier, and she began receiving a plethora of national and regional awards, an honorary degree from the College of Charleston in 1978, and South Carolina's highest award, the Order of the Palmetto, in 1982.

On 15 December 1987 Clark, freedom fighter, educator, and community crusader, died in Charleston, South Carolina. By insisting an African Americans' citizenship rights, she helped pave the way for the 1965 Voting Rights Act and the subsequent upsurge in black political mobilization in the South.

FURTHER READING

The Septima P. Clark Papers are held in the Special Collections department of the Robert Scott Small Library, College of Charleston, Charleston, South Carolina.

Clark, Septima P. *Echo in My Soul* (1962).

Brown, Cynthia S., ed. *Ready from Within: Septima Clark and the Civil Rights Movement* (1991).
McFadden, Grace J. "Septima P. Clark and the Struggle for Human Rights" in *Women in the Civil Rights Movement, Trailblazers and Torchbearers, 1941–1965*, eds. Vicki Crawford, Jacqueline A. Rouse, and Barbara A. Woods (1993).
Rouse, Jacqueline A. "'We Seek to Know...In Order to Speak the Truth': Nurturing Seeds of Discontent—Septima Clark and Participatory Leadership" in *Sisters in the Struggle, African American Women in the Civil Rights, Black Power Movement*, eds. Bettye Collier Thomas and V. P. Franklin (2001).

Obituary: *New York Times*, 17 Dec. 1987.
—JACQUELINE A. ROUSE

CLEAVER, ELDRIDGE (31 Aug. 1935–1 May 1998), Black Panther Party leader, was born Leroy Eldridge Cleaver in Wabbaseka, Arkansas, the third child of six born to Leroy Cleaver, a nightclub pianist and waiter, and Thelma (maiden name unknown), an elementary schoolteacher and janitor. After a brief stay in Phoenix, Arizona, the family moved in 1947 to East Los Angeles, where Leroy Cleaver, often abusive and violent towards Eldridge and his mother, eventually abandoned them. Soon afterwards, Eldridge was arrested for the first time, for stealing a bicycle, and from 1949 until 1966 he spent most of his time in reform school and prison. At one reform school in 1950, he briefly converted to Roman Catholicism—less out of religious conviction, he later recalled, than because at that school most Catholics were black or Latino and most Protestants were white. In 1952 he was returned to reform school after being caught selling marijuana.

In 1954, at age eighteen, Cleaver was convicted on a felony charge of selling marijuana and sent to prison. He would eventually spend time in Soledad, San Quentin, and Folsom prisons, and while he was incarcerated he began to take an interest in politics. The national controversy about *Brown v. Board of Education* (1954), the Supreme Court ruling outlawing school segregation, Cleaver recalled, "awakened me to my position in America and I began to form a concept of what it meant to be black in white America" (*Soul on Ice*, 3). When a white guard tore down a picture of a white woman Cleaver had pinned up in his cell and told him instead to post up a picture of a black woman, he became interested in how black men internalized racist standards of white beauty. The 1955 murder of EMMETT TILL, a young black boy from

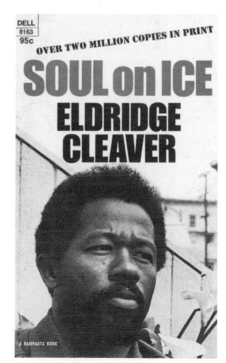

Eldridge Cleaver, Black Panther Party minister of information, published his best-selling Soul on Ice *in 1968. McGraw Hill*

Chicago who was brutally killed in Mississippi for "wolf whistling" at a white woman, only increased Cleaver's obsession, especially when he found himself attracted to the woman in question after seeing her photograph. "Somehow," he writes in *Soul on Ice*, "I arrived at the conclusion that, as a matter of principle, it was of paramount importance for me to have an antagonistic, ruthless attitude towards white women" (13). At this time, Cleaver later recalled, he believed that rape, especially against white women, was a political act.

Meanwhile, in 1958 Cleaver was arrested for the attempted rape of a nurse and again sent to prison. There he read voraciously, including works by Thomas Paine, Voltaire, Karl Marx, and RICHARD WRIGHT. He also joined the Nation of Islam, whose most prominent spokesman, MALCOLM X, had been, like Cleaver, a petty criminal who discovered radicalism and black nationalism in prison. When Malcolm split with the black Muslims, Cleaver supported him, and when Malcolm was killed in 1965—and supporters of the Nation of Islam were suspected—Cleaver began to write in order to "save myself" (25) from the profound confusion caused by this traumatic event. His lawyer, Beverly Axelrod, took these essays, in which he most clearly articulated, and rejected, his earlier position on rape, to the editor of the liberal, Catholic *Ramparts* magazine, and they were later published in *Soul on Ice*.

In November 1966 Cleaver was paroled, in part because his writings had attracted the support of literary stars like Norman Mailer, and he became a writer and editor for *Ramparts*. At about the same time, Cleaver met HUEY NEWTON and BOBBY SEALE, who had founded the Black Panther Party in Oakland in 1966. Influenced by revolutionaries in China, Cuba, Algeria, and Vietnam, the Panthers blended black nationalism with socialism and propounded a militant struggle for black rights, an end to police brutality, and the right of armed self-defense. Cleaver joined the Panthers, becoming their minister of information (or propaganda chief), and under his direction, they developed a savvy propaganda image, notably in his now-famous slogan, "If you're not part of the solution, you're part of the problem." In May 1967 the police arrested Seale,

Cleaver, and some thirty other Panthers in Sacramento for protesting a bill that would have outlawed carrying a loaded weapon. Five months later, after the police arrested Newton for killing an Oakland police officer, Cleaver helped organize the famous "Free Huey" campaign. This campaign, which convinced many that Newton was a political prisoner, dramatically increased awareness of the Panthers as it drew thousands of people to demonstrations. In December, Cleaver married fellow Panther Kathleen Neal.

The year 1968 proved to be a fateful one for Cleaver. His prison essays were published as *Soul on Ice*, whose imagery and anger won him considerable literary fame. Maxwell Geismar writes in the introduction that Cleaver "rakes our favorite prejudices with the savage claws of his prose until our wounds are bare, our psyche is exposed, and we must either fight back or laugh with him for the service he has done for us" (10). But both the local police and the national FBI continued their harassment of the Panthers. Seeking to destroy the militant organization, FBI director J. Edgar Hoover directed a campaign of infiltration, repression, and violence that eventually left most Panther leaders dead, in jail, or in exile. In April, Cleaver was involved in a Panther shoot-out in Oakland in which he and a police officer were wounded and Panther Bobby Hutton, aged seventeen, was killed. In response, the state revoked Cleaver's parole. In mid-June a California Superior Court justice released Cleaver from jail, calling him a "model parolee" victimized for his "undue eloquence in pursuing political goals." During this period Cleaver ran for U.S. president on the radical, California-based Peace and Freedom Party ticket. Shortly before he was due to return to jail in late November, he jumped his fifty-thousand-dollar bail, and on Christmas day, arrived in Cuba. For the next seven years Cleaver remained in exile in Cuba, North Korea, North Vietnam, China, Algeria, and, finally, France. In exile Eldridge and Kathleen Cleaver had a son, Maceo, in 1969, and a daughter, Joju, in 1970.

In Algeria, Cleaver helped organize an international office for the Panthers, though his time in exile coincided with the organization's disintegration as a result of both massive government repression and internal dissension. On the West Coast, Seale and Newton, who had been released from prison in 1970,

promoted community programs such as free breakfasts for children. Cleaver, more influential on the East Coast, emphasized the Panthers' militancy and the rhetoric of self-defense and revolution. In 1971 the Panthers expelled Cleaver, who, with Katherine, then organized the short-lived Revolutionary People's Communication Network. The Algerian government, interested in closer ties to the U.S., was growing uncomfortable with Cleaver's presence. Cleaver in turn became disillusioned with the Algerian government when it returned money donated to it by left-wing hijackers. In 1974, with the assistance of the French president, Valery Giscard d'Estaing, Cleaver established legal residency in France. Soon thereafter he began to move to the right of the political and religious spectrum and reverted to Christianity after having a spiritual vision. In 1975, in a deal with the FBI, Cleaver returned to the United States to stand trial for the charges arising out of the 1968 shoot-out in Oakland. Eventually, the charges for attempted murder were dropped, though he was placed on probation for assault and sentenced to 1200 hours of community service. By this time Cleaver had renounced his former radicalism and had become a born-again Christian, claiming that his travels in exile had made him appreciate American democracy and fear communism. In 1984 he declared that "I have taken an oath in my heart to oppose communism until the day I die."

In the late 1970s and early 1980s Cleaver seemed to flounder. As an attention-getting business venture, he developed the so-called Cleaver Sleeve—men's trousers with an exaggerated codpiece. For many, this symbolized the former Panther's decline. No longer an important African American spokesman, he had become a self-parody, trying to capitalize on his earlier fame and his emphasis (in his early prison writings) on his own sexuality as a political force. In 1985 his marriage ended in divorce. He was involved with various religious groups, including his own "Eldridge Cleaver Crusades," a hybrid synthesis of Islam and Christianity he called "Christlam," the Reverend Sun Myung Moon's Unification Church, and the Mormons.

Cleaver attempted to explain his political metamorphosis in *Soul on Fire* (1978), and he ran unsuccessfully for public office several times. In 1984 he supported Ronald Reagan's bid for reelection and ran as an independent against the veteran African American Democratic congressman Ron Dellums. Two years later Cleaver sought the Republican nomination for the U.S. senate seat in California, but again failed. His continued political marginalization was accompanied by a growing addiction to cocaine and in 1988 he was sentenced to probation after being convicted of cocaine possession and burglary. In 1992 he was again arrested for cocaine possession, although the charges were thrown out because the police had improperly arrested him. In 1994 he almost died from a severe blow on the head after an attack by another addict. Cleaver's response to this was to turn once again to evangelical Christianity.

In the late 1990s Cleaver's health declined, and he was diagnosed with both prostrate cancer and diabetes. In May 1998 he died of a heart attack in suburban Los Angeles, where he had been working as a diversity consultant at a private college. For a moment in the mid to late 1960s, Eldridge Cleaver's star burned more brightly than any of his contemporaries in the black nationalist movement. The sometimes bizarre political and personal meanderings of his later career cannot detract from the achievement of *Soul on Ice*, which conveyed on the written page the anger and resentment of young, urban blacks that exploded in the race rebellions of Watts, Detroit, and Newark.

FURTHER READING

Cleaver, Eldridge. *Soul on Fire* (1978).
———. *Soul on Ice* (1968).

Rout, Kathleen. *Eldridge Cleaver* (1991).

Obituaries: *New York Times* and *Washington Post*, 2 May 1998.

—JACOB ZUMOFF

COACHMAN, ALICE

(9 Nov. 1923–), track-and-field athlete, was the fifth of ten children born to Fred "Doc" and Evelyn Coachman in Albany, Georgia. She was primarily raised by her great-grandmother and maternal grandmother and endured the difficulties of impoverishment. As a child, she participated in music and dance and was active in sports. Like many other African American women, she competed in basketball and track in junior high, where she came to the attention of Coach Henry E. Lash at Madison High School.

It was at this point that Coachman made a leap and became part of what was fast becoming a track-and-field dynasty when she transferred to the Tuskegee Institute in Tuskegee, Alabama, where she was trained by the renowned coach Cleveland Abbott. Founded by BOOKER T. WASHINGTON in 1881 as a teacher's college, Tuskegee was one of the first black institutions to embrace women's athletics, and Abbott's team dominated the national track scene for decades, winning fourteen national outdoor titles, nine consecutively. When Coachman graduated from high school, she stayed at the Tuskegee Institute and obtained a certificate in tailoring in 1946. In 1947 she transferred to Albany State College, having earned the nickname the "Tuskegee Flash." From 1939 to 1948 she competed in the high jump, 50-meter dash, 100-meter dash, and many relay teams. At Tuskegee she won ten consecutive national outdoor high-jump titles. In 1946 she was the first African American selected for the All-American team.

Coachman joined the 1948 U.S. Olympic team along with eight other black women—nine of twelve women on the Olympic track-and-field team were African American that year. This stood in marked contrast to the 1932 and 1936 Games, when the black sprinters LOUISE STOKES and Tidye Pickett were included in the team, but not selected to run. At the 1948 London games, Coachman competed in the high jump with severe back pains caused by a twisted ovary, but nevertheless she won the gold medal on her first jump. Coachman jumped 5 feet, 6 $\frac{1}{4}$ inches, a feat that was both an Olympic and an American record. She was the first African American woman to win a gold medal. Audrey Patterson of Tennessee State, another black college with a standout women's track-and-field program, won a second Olympic medal when she got a bronze in the 200 meters. Coachman and Patterson were the only American track-and-field women to earn medals.

When Coachman returned home, she was honored with a parade, recognition dinners, and a meeting with President Harry S. Truman. Still, given American's deep segregation and racism, Coachman was not allowed to speak at the ceremony in her honor at the segregated Albany Municipal Auditorium in Georgia. Coachman felt the weight of her responsibility to excel, later saying that "if I had gone to the Games and failed, there wouldn't have been anyone to follow in my footsteps" (McElroy, 14). Her gold medal performance, along with Patterson's bronze medal, served to legitimate the start-up track programs at black schools. Her achievement was a great source of pride to black America, struggling under segregation and moving toward civil rights.

Although Coachman turned in a superlative performance at the 1948 Olympics and received a lot of attention in the years immediately following her win, her name quickly faded from public conversations. Track, like basketball, which had held great public interest in the 1920s and early 1930s, was by mid-century considered a "masculine" sport unsuited to properly feminine athletes. Stereotypes of race and gender intersected in devastating ways at this time and no doubt had an effect on Coachman's life. Women who competed in track were ridiculed as "muscle molls" or amazons, and it was a common view that women who succeeded in this sport were not "normal" women.

African American women, including Coachman, withstood this kind of ridicule and prevailed to occupy a central place in track and field. They stepped up to the challenge when middle-class white women had largely backed down, and they began a tradition of national and international excellence that continues to this day. Track participation was a double-edged sword for African American women. On the one hand, performances like Coachman's or those of Mae Faggs and WILMA RUDOLPH a little later demonstrated that African American women could excel at an endeavor valued by American culture: winning medals in an increasingly nationalistic Olympic games. On the other hand, because these achievements were in a "masculine" sport, it reinforced racist and sexist stereotypes of black women as less "feminine" than middle-class white women.

Because of her age and perhaps because of a growing dominant cultural ambivalence toward women's participation in track and field, Coachman retired from competition in 1948 and focused on her education. She received a degree in Home Economics and Science from Albany State College in 1949. She became the first black female athletic champion to sign a product endorsement for a multinational corporation, Coca-Cola, in 1952. For many years Coachman taught physical education and trained other women athletes, first at a high school in Albany, Georgia. She also taught at Southern Carolina State College, Albany State College, and Tuskegee High School. Now retired, she lives with her second husband, Frank Davis, in Alabama.

Coachman established the Alice Coachman Track and Field Foundation in 1994, a nonprofit organization for young athletes and retired Olympians. Despite the stigmatization of women's participation in track and field in mid-century, Coachman's legacy has opened the way for beloved American track stars, such as Evelyn Ashford, FLORENCE GRIFFITH-JOYNER, Gwen Torrance, Gayle Devers, Jackie Joyner-Kersee, and Marion Jones. Coachman has been honored with memberships in eight halls of fame, including the National Track and Field Hall of Fame, the Georgia Sports Hall of Fame, and the Albany Sports Hall of Fame.

FURTHER READING

Cahn, Susan K. *Coming on Strong: Gender and Sexuality in Twentieth-Century Women's Sport* (1994).

Emerson, A. D. *Olympians against the Wind: The Black American Female Difference* (1999).

McElroy, Kathleen. "Somewhere to Run" in *Nike Is a Goddess: The History of Women in Sports* (1998).

Vertinsky, Patricia, and Gwendolyn Captain. "More Myth Than History: American Culture and Representations of the Black Female's Athletic Ability." *Journal of Sport History* 25, no. 3 (1998): 532–561.

—LESLIE HEYWOOD

 ## COBB, WILLIAM MONTAGUE

(12 Oct. 1904–20 Nov. 1990), physical anthropologist and anatomist, was born in Washington, D.C., the son of William Elmer Cobb, a printer, and Alexzine Montague. Experiencing racial segregation in education, he graduated in 1921 from Dunbar High School, an elite college-preparatory school for African

Americans. Cobb attended Amherst College, where he pursued a classical education in arts and sciences, graduating in 1925. After graduation he received a Blodgett Scholarship to study biology at Woods Hole Marine Biology Laboratory in Massachusetts. There he met Howard University biologist ERNEST EVERETT JUST and decided to attend Howard University's College of Medicine. At the time, Howard was undergoing a transformation as its first African American president, MORDECAI JOHNSON, attempted to place the university under greater African American control. Showing great academic promise, Cobb was groomed to become a new member of the faculty. After receiving his medical degree in 1929, he was sent to Cleveland for postgraduate study at Western Reserve University.

Even before he could read, Cobb had been intrigued by pictures of human biological variation, or "race." At Western Reserve he pursued this interest by studying anatomy and the emerging discipline of physical anthropology under T. Wingate Todd, who amassed one of the two most extensive research collections of human skeletons in the United States, the Hamman-Todd Collection. Cobb spent two years at Western Reserve, earning a doctoral degree in 1932 on the basis of a thesis that inventoried skeletal material available for anthropological study in the United States. He was the first and, until the early 1950s, the only African American to earn a PhD in Physical Anthropology.

In 1932 Cobb returned to Howard University as professor of anatomy, intent on establishing a skeletal collection for the use of African American scientists. He prepared more than seven hundred skeletons from cadavers and compiled documentation on three hundred more. Through his efforts, the Cobb Collection at Howard grew to become comparable to the Hamman-Todd Collection and the Terry Collection at the Smithsonian Institution—an irreplaceable resource for studying the remains of Washington's poor from the Great Depression. Such skulls were particularly valuable because they provided a unique record of past states of sickness and health.

During his early years on the Howard faculty, Cobb continued to work on skeletal collections. His work resulted in

important publications on the craniofacial union, showing how the cranial portion of the skull grows relatively fast and remains stable after birth, while the facial portion grows relatively slowly and can be modified by the environment. He also undertook a massive study of cranial suture closure, showing that it is an unreliable estimator of skeletal age. In the 1930s many Americans believed that the emerging preeminence of African American sprinters and broad-jumpers in Olympic competition was due to racial anatomy. Cobb refuted this view by carefully measuring African American Olympic athletes and comparing their measurements to European-American and African American skeletal averages. JESSE OWENS's measurements, for example, turned out to be more "typical" of European-Americans than of African Americans, showing that racial biology and behavior are not fixed. This important finding had broad application outside athletics.

Cobb believed that African Americans represented a population whose physical and intellectual vigor had been enhanced by the evolutionary bottleneck of slavery. Slave-traders had selected superior physical specimens to transport to the Americas, and of these, only the strongest had survived the new diseases and brutal labor they encountered there. Considering the social barriers, their achievements were extraordinary. Furthermore, he believed that African Americans were highly adaptable and would become more genetically varied as social barriers to racial mixing crumbled. These views were intended to counteract prevailing views that African Americans were inferior because they had been insufficiently exposed to European American culture.

Cobb also undertook to show how racism and segregation were exacting a biological toll on African Americans and, through the added cost of separate and unequal health care, a financial toll on all Americans. He worked diligently for the racial integration of American hospitals and medical schools. To this end, he created the Imhotep National Conference on Hospital Integration, which met annually from 1957 through 1963, ending with the passage of the 1964 Civil Rights Act. Cobb was invited to attend the formal signing of the 1965 Medicare Bill, which the conference had promoted. On the subject of race, he published many articles in both popular and scientific journals, especially the *Journal of the National Medical Association*, which he edited for twenty-eight years. Among his associates in the integration effort were RALPH BUNCHE and W. E. B. DU BOIS. He was among the first physical anthropologists to direct the resources of that discipline toward social problems.

Cobb graduated from Howard in the same year that the American Association of Physical Anthropologists was founded; he contributed actively to the association in its formative years and was its president (1957–1959). As Cobb matured professionally, he rose to prominence in other anthropological and medical organizations, serving as president of the National Medical Association (1964–1965) and the National Association for the Advancement of Colored People (1976–1982). He chaired the department of anatomy at Howard University College of Medicine from 1949 until 1969, when he became distinguished professor, then distinguished professor emeritus in 1973.

Cobb was accomplished in the arts as well as science, playing violin and reciting literature and poetry, often in class. He was remembered by associates as a well-rounded Renaissance man. Later in life, his humanistic side flourished as he philosophized about the duality of human nature. Cobb presented his last professional paper in 1987. In his lifetime he received more than one hundred awards, published more than one thousand articles, and taught several thousand students. He died in Washington, D.C.

FURTHER READING

Documents relating to Cobb, including transcripts of interviews, are in the Moorland-Spingarn Research Center at Howard University.

Rankin-Hill, Lesley M., and Michael L. Blakey. "W. Montague Cobb (1904–1990): Physical Anthropologist, Anatomist and Activist." *American Anthropologist* 96, no. 1 (1996): 74–96.

Obituary: *American Journal of Physical Anthropology* 92 (1993): 545–548.

—PAUL A. ERICKSON

 COKER, DANIEL

(1780?–1835?), a founder of the African Methodist Episcopal church, author, and educator, was born a slave in Frederick County, Maryland, the son of Susan Coker, a white indentured servant, and Edward Wright, a black slave belonging to the same plantation owner whose name is unknown. Daniel Coker was educated with his master's son, who refused to go to school without his slave. When Coker was in his early teens he escaped to New York City where he joined the Methodist Church and was ordained as a lay minister.

Empowered by his education and ordination, Coker returned to Maryland in 1801 to become the first African American teacher at the African Academy, a school founded by the Baltimore Abolition Society for the education of free blacks. He was the first black licensed minister in Baltimore, and the spiritual leader of an independent prayer meeting formed by black Methodists dissatisfied with their position within the white Methodist church. But because the twenty-one-year-old Coker was still legally a slave, he was forced to remain in hiding until a Quaker abolitionist purchased and freed him. In 1806 Coker founded the Daniel Coker School, which by 1810 had an enrollment of one hundred fifty African American students.

In 1810 Coker wrote *A Dialogue between A Virginian and An African Minister*, generally considered the first published antislavery tract written by an African American. In this pamphlet, Coker exposed the failure of white Methodists to address the evils of slavery and refuted the notion that the Bible defended the institution. "But the question," Coker argued, "is concerning the liberty of a man. The man himself claims it as his own property. He pleads (and I think in truth) that it was originally his own; and he has never forfeited, nor alienated it; and therefore, by the common laws of justice and humanity, it is still his own."

In 1814, responding to the continued failure of Baltimore's white Methodists to grant ministries or autonomy to African American Methodists, Coker led the trustees of the black Methodist congregation in withdrawing entirely

from the white Methodist Church and in buying their own church.

During this time, Coker frequently communicated with the Reverend RICHARD ALLEN, another African American Methodist minister, whose struggles to form a separate black church in Philadelphia paralleled Coker's efforts in Baltimore. Coker's "Sermon Delivered Extempore in the African Bethel Church in the City of Baltimore," delivered on 21 January 1816, was a response to Allen's labors on behalf of black Methodism in Philadelphia.

In 1816 Baltimore's black Methodists met with their brethren from Pennsylvania, New Jersey, and Delaware and combined their separate churches into a single denomination, the African Methodist Episcopal Church. Richard Allen was elected chairman of the convention with Coker as vice-chairman. Because Coker was one of the few participants who could read and write, the task of drafting the convention's resolutions fell to him.

After Coker and Allen were both elected bishops, Allen insisted the new denomination needed only one and, according to many accounts, offered to resign. In a second election on 11 April 1816, Allen was chosen sole bishop. Coker was made pastor of Bethel, Baltimore's AME church, but for unknown reasons he was expelled from the AME within two years and reduced to a life of itinerant preaching.

Inspired by an earlier meeting with PAUL CUFFE SR., a pathbreaking black businessman and ship builder who had come to Baltimore in 1812 seeking support for his plan to transport free blacks to Sierra Leone, Coker allied himself with the American Colonization Society. In 1820 Coker set out for Sierra Leone in the company of Samuel Bacon and John P. Bankson representing the federal government and Samuel Crozer, an agent for the colonization society and eighty-three black emigrés. Envisioning himself as a Christian pilgrim, Coker kept a detailed record of the voyage, later published in Baltimore as the *Journal of Daniel Coker, A Descendant of Africa, from the Time of Leaving New York in the Ship Elizabeth, Capt. Sebor, On a Voyage for Sherbro, in Africa, in Company with Three Agents and about Ninety Persons of Colour* (1820). In the new settlement's early days, Coker served as a justice of the peace, held church services, and acted as a mediator between the white agents and black emigrants. The initial optimism of the voyagers was soon eroded by torrential rains, malaria, and polluted water. Within months, the U.S. government and ACS agents had died, leaving Coker in charge of the struggling settlement. But Coker's close ties with the white agents before their deaths undermined his authority with the surviving black settlers, and when they moved to their permanent settlement in Liberia in 1821 they left him behind. In 1821 Coker's wife, Maria (d. 1824), and his three sons sailed from Baltimore and joined him in Sierra Leone.

In 1822 the governor of Sierra Leone made Coker the superintendent of Hastings, a village that functioned as a repatriation center for West Africans retrieved from coastal slave traders after the abolition of the slave trade. In Hastings, Coker continued to preach, eventually seceding from the AME Church and founding the West African Methodist denomination. He died in Sierra Leone.

The trajectory of Coker's life is salient, in part, because it intersected with a number of important institutions—slavery, the AME, and the American Colonization Society. But it is the power of his voice as one of a small number of literate African Americans in the early national period that remains his most potent legacy. "May the time speedily come," Coker wrote in his Baltimore sermon, arguing for the formation of a separate black church, "when we shall see our brethren come flocking to us like doves to their windows. And we as a band of brethren, shall sit down under our own vine to worship, and none to make us afraid."

FURTHER READING

Because there is no biography of Daniel Coker, his own writings remain the richest source of information about his life and thought. The *Journal of Daniel Coker* is available on microfilm at the New York Public Library. Coker's second *Journal* written in Africa and covering the period from April 1821 to September 1821 is in the Library of Congress, Manuscripts Division.

Aptheker, Herbert. *A Documentary History of the Negro People in the United States*, vol. 1 (1973).

Coan, Josephus R. "Daniel Coker: Nineteenth-Century Black Church Organizer, Educator, and Missionary." *Journal of the Interdenominational Theological Seminary* 1 (1975): 17–31.

—MARY F. COREY

COLE, JOHNNETTA BETSCH (19 Oct. 1936–), anthropologist, educator, and college president, was born in Jacksonville, Florida, the second of three children to Mary Frances Lewis, an English teacher, and John Thomas Betsch Sr., an insurance executive. Johnnetta grew up in one of Florida's most prominent African American families; her great-grandfather, Abraham Lincoln Lewis, co-founded the Afro-American Life Insurance Company, Florida's first insurance company. An ambitious and civic-minded businessman, Lewis established several black institutions, including the colored branch of the public library, the Lincoln Golf and Country Club, and the seaside resort known as American Beach, the only beach allowing blacks in north Florida. Johnnetta's childhood was shaped by competing influences: her supportive family and community, and the racist attitudes and institutions of the Jim Crow South. Educated in segregated public and private schools, Johnnetta credits the influence of her teachers and her family friend MARY MCLEOD BETHUNE with encouraging her educational and moral development. Her family's active participation in civic works was fostered by strong ties to the church and a fundamental belief in community service, an attitude voiced by A. L. Lewis, and often repeated by Johnnetta as "Doing for others is just the rent you gotta pay for living on this earth."

Johnnetta excelled academically and entered Fisk University at the age of fifteen. A year later she joined her older sister Marvyne at Oberlin College in Ohio, where she switched her concentration from medicine to the social sciences. After receiving a BA in Sociology in 1957, she began graduate work at Northwestern University in Chicago, Illinois. Under the tutelage of anthropologist Melville Herskovitz, who had taught KATHERINE DUNHAM two decades earlier, Johnnetta earned an MA (1959) and a PhD (1967) in Anthropology. In a 1993 *Chicago Tribune* interview, she attributed her academic success in part to her family and friends back home: "It was wonderful to listen to old black folk who had not been educated themselves, say: 'Look at sister. Just look at sister. She is getting all that education.'" While at Northwestern, she met Robert Cole, a white graduate student in economics from Iowa. Over the objections of both their families, the couple married in 1960, and had three sons, David, Aaron, and Ethan Che. They divorced in 1982.

In 1970, after several years teaching anthropology and directing the black studies program at Washington State University, Cole was offered a tenured position at the University of Massachusetts, Amherst. She remained at UMass for the next thirteen years, during which time she taught anthropology and played a key role in establishing a black studies program. She served for a time as associate provost and was asked to head a panel that proposed university-wide curricula reform. In 1983 she took a teaching position at Hunter College in New York City, where she also directed the Latin American and Caribbean studies program.

Cole became one of the most influential figures in higher education when, in 1987, she became the first African American female president of Spelman College, a women's liberal arts school in Atlanta and one of the most prestigious of the nation's historically black colleges and universities. Founded in 1881 by two white Christian missionary women from New England, Spelman has graduated several generations of black women, including ALICE WALKER, and MARIAN WRIGHT EDELMAN. Cole's appointment, already a noteworthy affair, proved a sensation when, on the weekend of her inauguration, Camille and BILL COSBY donated $20 million to Spelman, setting the tone—and expectations—for her administration. Cole met the challenge, dramatically raising both the college's financial holdings and its public profile. Cole later estimated that she spent half of her time at Spelman raising money. The return on her investment was unmistakable. During her presidency, the college's endowment increased from $41 million to $143 million. Cosby's gift, the largest ever personal donation to a black college or university, and Cole's leadership encouraged a million dollar donation from OPRAH WINFREY, followed in 1992 by a $37 million gift from the DeWitt Wallace Fund, the largest donation ever made to a black college. The college's visibility received an additional boost when Cosby modeled Hillman College, the fictional setting for his *Cosby Show* spin-off, *A Different World*, after Spelman. The television show, which ran from 1987 to 1993, filmed its exterior shots on campus, introducing Spelman to millions of Americans each week. In 1992, *U.S. News and World Report* ranked Spelman the top liberal arts college in the South.

With the money she raised, Cole built up Spelman's physical plant, endowed scholarships and professorships, and established a mentoring program matching students with executives at local companies. She opened the Office of Community Service, making service central to Spelman's mission. Cole, who managed to teach an anthropology class each year, was known for her accessibility and visibility on campus, and when she nicknamed herself "Sister President," the students immediately embraced the title, and their president. Her success at Spelman was due in part to her interdisciplinary approach to scholarship and governance and to her experience articulating the practical and theoretical needs of emerging programs in black studies and women's studies. She introduced a clear set of priorities: building job networks for black women, introducing community service into leadership training, and expanding the notion of diversity to include differences *within* African American and women's communities. Cole embodied each of these efforts, fashioning a public identity that combined elements and attitudes from different worlds. Moving easily between the Southern black vernacular of her childhood and a formal academic speaking style, Cole is equally comfortable in the classroom and the boardroom. Even her fashion choices challenge the prevailing image of the woman in the gray-flannel suit: "Johnnetta includes at least one detail that defies conformity— a carved ivory Janus-faced pendant, made as the emblem of a Liberian secret society; a

cowrie-studded belt; or fabric handwoven by a friend" (Bateson, 25–26).

Shortly after arriving at Spelman in 1987, Cole married public health administrator Arthur J. Robinson Jr. and became stepmother to his two sons. Johnnetta and Art had been childhood playmates who, after forty years, were reunited when news of Cole's appointment prompted Art to look up his old friend. In 1992 she was honored with an appointment to President-elect Bill Clinton's transition team. As cluster coordinator for education, labor, and the arts and humanities, she was responsible for the review of the Department of Education budget, personnel, and programs. Soon after her appointment, however, she was subjected to attacks that her supporters likened to McCarthyism. Allegations that she was a pro-Communist, pro-Cuban, pro-Palestinian radical effectively bumped her from the list of candidates under consideration for education secretary.

In 1997 after serving for ten years, Cole resigned as president of Spelman. When asked about Cole's decision, Bill Cosby, perhaps overdramatically, told the *Atlanta Journal Constitution*, "I'm not happy. To me it's as if DIZZY GILLESPIE, MILES DAVIS, SARAH VAUGHAN, Carmen McRae, and ELLA FITZGERALD had all died on the same day." In 1998 she returned to teaching, taking a position at Emory University, and in 2002 put off retirement plans in order to accept the presidency of the financially beleaguered Bennett College in Greensboro, North Carolina, the only remaining black women's college in the nation other than Spelman.

Cole's scholarly work, which includes fieldwork studies in Cuba, Haiti, Grenada, Liberia, and the United States, has contributed rigorous analyses of race, gender, and labor to the field of cultural anthropology. Through her teaching and publishing, she has bridged disciplines, bringing together scholars from anthropology, African American studies, women's studies, African studies, and Latin American studies. She has written and edited numerous books, beginning with *Anthropology for the Eighties: Introductory Readings* (1982). Her many trips to Cuba resulted in *Race Towards Equality* (1986), and she broke new ground in women studies with *All American Women: Lines That Divide,*

Ties That Bind (1986). Another anthology, *Anthropology for the Nineties: Introductory Readings* (1988), continues to be used in the classroom and beyond. During her reign at Spelman, Cole produced *Conversations: Straight Talk with America's Sister President* (1993), and *Dream the Boldest Dreams: And Other Lessons of Life* (1997), two folksy books directed at a general audience. In 2003 she returned to scholarly publication with *Gender Talk: Sexism, Power, and Politics in the African American Community*, co-written with Beverly Guy-Sheftall.

Cole's charisma and innovative approaches to problem solving have made her a popular choice for appointments to both corporate and nonprofit boards. She has sat on the boards of directors of Merck and Company, Home Depot, and Coca-Cola, where she was the first female board member in the company's history. She has served as a trustee of several colleges and universities and in leadership positions at the Rockefeller Foundation, the Martin Luther King Center for Nonviolent Social Change, the Points of Light Foundation, the Feminist Press, the United Negro College Fund, and the American Council on Education. She has been awarded more than forty honorary degrees and has received dozens of honors from a wide range of organizations.

When *Essence* magazine asked Cole in 1997 to describe her goals, she replied, "I dream I come onto campus and on top of Rockefeller Hall...every inch of space is covered with young women flapping their arms, convinced they can fly. We must make these young African American women believe they indeed can fly, can do the impossible."

FURTHER READING

Cole, Johnnetta. *Conversations: Straight Talk with America's Sister President* (1993).

Bateson, Mary Catherine. *Composing a Life* (1989).

—LISA E. RIVO

 COLE, NAT KING
(17 Mar. 1917?–15 Feb. 1965), pianist and singer, was born Nathaniel Adams Coles in Montgomery, Alabama, the son of the Reverend Edward James

Nat King Cole in concert. © Bettmann/CORBIS

Coles Sr., a Baptist minister, and Perlina Adams Coles, choir leader and organist at her husband's church. The family, which included Nat's brother, Edward Jr. ("Eddie") and sisters, Eddie Mae and Evelyn, moved to Chicago when Nat was about four years old, where his brothers Isaac ("Ike") and Lionel ("Freddie") were born. All the Coles children demonstrated musical talent, each playing piano and organ at their father's services and singing in the church choir. Nat was especially precocious, capable at the age of four of a two-handed rendition of "Yes, We Have No Bananas" on the family piano. From the age of twelve he received formal piano training.

Nat grew up on Chicago's South Side, the heartland of Prohibition jazz culture, and attended Wendell Phillips High School. Grounded in gospel at home, he was enthralled by Chicago's jazz milieu, which influenced his organ playing in church; his father often admonished him to "tone it down." During this formative period of his

musical development, he was listening avidly to jazz emanating from nightclubs, often from the alleys outside. Both Earl "Fatha" Hines, then playing a residency at Chicago's Grand Terrace ballroom, and Teddy Wilson were significant influences. In about 1935 Nat abandoned school to concentrate on his musical career. While still a teenager, he organized two jazz groups: a big band, the Rogues of Rhythm, and a quintet, Nat Coles and His Royal Dukes. Drawing on Hines's band style, these groups played at school dances and other local venues. (Some speculated that Nat had illicitly acquired arrangements from the Hines book, the catalog of band arrangements that constituted its unique repertory.) Nat Coles's big band later challenged Hines's band to a "cutting contest" at the Savoy Ballroom (a competition between bands vying to outperform each other with the result determined by the audience), and, remarkably, Cole's band won.

In 1936 Nat's brother Eddie assembled the Solid Swingers with musicians

from the old big band and Nat as pianist. The new band obtained a six-month residency at Chicago's Club Panama and recorded, with little recognition, four sides for Decca's "race records" Sepia Series (a category of recordings marketed specifically to a black audience). In the same year Nat and Eddie toured with the revue *Shuffle Along*. On tour Nat met Nadine Robinson, a dancer in the show, and they were married in Ypsilanti, Michigan, in 1937. When the show eventually folded, in Long Beach, California, Nat and Nadine remained there.

The employment prospects for black musicians in Los Angeles were bleaker than in Chicago, and Nat later described the impecunious circumstances in which he "played every beer joint from San Diego to Bakersfield." He took such work as he could find, usually as a soloist, playing, as one biographer put it, "in joints with out-of-tune pianos, keys that didn't work, and audiences that didn't listen" (Gourse, 25). At other times he would "sit in" with jazz musicians with whom he was beginning to establish a significant local reputation. It was at this time that he wrote what would become one of his trademark songs, "Straighten Up and Fly Right," with a lyric derived from one of his father's sermons.

In 1937 Nat formed a trio with the guitarist Oscar Moore and the double bassist Wesley Prince (later Jimmy Miller), called King Cole and His Swingsters and, subsequently, the King Cole Trio marking his name change from "Coles" to "Cole." Such a combo was quite unusual at a time when the big bands of the Swing Era held sway, especially since the band excluded drums and featured electric guitar. The trio secured a residency at the Swannee Inn in Los Angeles, and it was there that Cole began to sing, apparently in response to audience requests. He made several significant recordings in the early 1940s, including a trio session in 1942 with Lester Young (tenor saxophone) and Red Callender (bass). From 1943 he recorded for the fledgling Capitol label. What made these recordings so distinctive was the trio's intensely responsive interplay, especially between Cole and Moore, and the tightly driven sense of swing behind Cole's elegantly felicitous piano. In addition to the trio's instrumental performances, Cole's role as a vocalist became increasingly prominent on recordings such as "Straighten Up and Fly Right" (1943), "(Get Your Kicks on) Route 66" (1944), "Sweet Lorraine" (1944), and "It's Only a Paper Moon" (1944). With the postwar rise of the starring vocalist, Cole switched emphasis from jazz pianist to "stand-up" singer. Cole, the "accidental" vocalist, possessed a warm baritone with a dark-grained timbre, an immaculate enunciation, and a seemingly effortless naturalism conveying intimacy and charm.

With "The Christmas Song" (1946), what was by then virtually an obligatory vocal was accompanied by a lavish orchestral arrangement that typically characterized the trio's subsequent sound, exemplified on such recordings as "I Love You (for Sentimental Reasons)" (1946), "Nature Boy" (1948), and "Mona Lisa" (1950). These records, all number-one hits, signaled a shift away from Cole's trio jazz toward luscious orchestral ballads. Cole's record sales for Capitol were so great that the company's new tower building was known as "the house that Nat built." More hits in a similar vein followed, including "Unforgettable" (1951), "When I Fall in Love" (1957), and "Let There Be Love" (1962), and much of Cole's work during this period was produced with arrangements by Billy May, Nelson Riddle, and Gordon Jenkins. The trio consequently became sidelined and eventually disbanded in 1955. Cole intermittently returned to a trio format, notably for the album *After Midnight* (1957), with John Collins (guitar), Charlie Harris (bass), and Lee Young (drums).

Cole divorced Nadine in 1948, having met Maria (Marie) Hawkins Ellington, a singer. Nat and Maria were married by the Reverend ADAM CLAYTON POWELL JR. at Harlem's Abyssinian Baptist church that same year. They had a daughter, Natalie Maria ("Sweetie"), in 1950 and later adopted another, Carol ("Cookie"). In 1959 they adopted a son, Nat Kelly, and in 1961 they had twin daughters, Timolin and Casey. Maria was often credited, or criticized, for her influential role in the subsequent direction of her husband's career.

Cole also appeared in several films in the 1950s, notably as himself in the biographical short *The Nat King Cole Story* (1955) and as the composer W. C. HANDY in *St. Louis Blues* (1958). In 1956 Cole became one of the first black performers to star in his own television series, *The Nat King Cole Show*, but despite favorable ratings, sponsors were reluctant to back a black performer, and, consequently, the show soon failed. He had already met racial prejudice in his career. In 1949 he bought a house in the exclusively white Hancock Park district of Los Angeles, where residents attempted to oust him, and in 1956 racist agitators assaulted him onstage at a concert in Birmingham, Alabama. Nevertheless, Cole could appear aloof from or at odds with civil rights activism, and he was criticized for complacency, especially as a highly successful crossover star reluctant to have his career tainted by any association with racial politics. For some, however, he had merely adopted a different strategy to militancy though his demonstrable commitment to racial equality went largely unpublicized. A heavy smoker throughout his life, Cole died of lung cancer at St. John's Hospital in Santa Monica, California.

Cole's standing remains anomalous and comprises two conflicting reputations. He was an extraordinarily innovative jazz pianist whose influential trio work played a vanguard role in validating small-group jazz, often denigrated as "cocktail lounge" music. With the trio's demise, however, this reputation became largely eclipsed by his spectacular popularity in the commercial mainstream. To his detractors, Cole had reneged on jazz and betrayed his talent as an instrumentalist for facile success as a pop singer. Certainly, Cole is now better known for his voice than his piano playing, and his recordings are more frequently categorized as "easy listening" than as jazz, a view that, unfortunately, traduces some of Cole's most distinctive popular recordings. Nevertheless, many would agree with Oscar Moore's "jazz epitaph" for Cole, reported in *Down Beat*: "I never thought Nat would become really important as a *singer*. To me, the cat was always a crazy piano player" (25 Mar. 1965).

FURTHER READING

Cole, Maria, with Louie Robinson. *Nat King Cole: An Intimate Biography* (1971).

Epstein, Daniel Mark. *Nat King Cole* (1999).
Gourse, Leslie. *Unforgettable: The Life and Mystique of Nat King Cole* (1991).
Haskins, James, with Kathleen Benson. *Nat King Cole: The Man and His Music* (1986).
"Nat 'King' Cole, 1917–1965." *Down Beat* 32, no. 7 (25 Mar. 1965): 14.

Obituary: *New York Times*, 16 Feb. 1965.

Discography
Teubig, Klaus. *Straighten Up and Fly Right: A Chronology and Discography of Nat "King" Cole* (1994).

—IAN BROOKES

COLE, REBECCA

(16 Mar. 1846–14 Aug. 1922), physician, organization founder, and social reformer, was born in Philadelphia, Pennsylvania, the second of five children all listed as "mulatto" in the 1880 U.S. census. Her parents' names are not known. In 1863 Rebecca completed a rigorous curriculum that included Latin, Greek, and mathematics at the Institute for Colored Youth, an all-black high school.

In 1867 Cole became the first black graduate of the Women's Medical College of Pennsylvania and the second formally trained African American woman physician in the United States. Dr. Ann Preston, the first woman dean of a medical school, served as Cole's preceptor, overseeing her thesis essay, "The Eye and Its Appendages." The Women's Medical College, founded by Quaker abolitionists and temperance reformers in 1850 as the Female Medical College of Pennsylvania, was the world's first medical school for women. By 1900 at least ten African American women had received their medical degrees from the school.

After completion of her MD, Cole was appointed resident physician at the New York Infirmary for Indigent Women and Children, a New York City hospital founded in 1857 by America's first woman physician, Elizabeth Blackwell, her sister, the surgeon Emily Blackwell, and Marie Zakrzewska, a German- and American-trained doctor. Cole worked as a "sanitary visitor," making house calls to families in slum neighborhoods and giving practical advice about prenatal and infant care and basic hygiene.

In the early 1870s Cole practiced medicine for a short time in Columbia, South Carolina, before taking a position as superintendent of the Government House for Children and Old Women in Washington, D.C. She then returned to Philadelphia, serving as superintendent of a shelter for the homeless until 1873, when she co-founded the Women's Directory Center. The center offered free medical and legal services to poor women, and according to its charter, programs aiding in "the prevention of feticide and infanticide and the evils connected with baby farming by rendering assistance to women in cases of approaching maternity and of desertion or abandonment of mothers and by aiding magistrates and others entrusted with police powers in preventing or punishing [such] crimes" (quoted in Hine, 113).

A sought-after lecturer on public health, Cole boldly countered W. E. B. Du Bois's claim that high mortality rates for blacks were due to an ignorance of hygiene. In an article published shortly before the turn of the century in *The Woman's Eye*, a clubwoman's journal, Cole argued that the spread of disease within the African American community was due to the unwillingness of white doctors to take proper medical histories of black patients.

Until the mid-nineteenth century, American medicine had been essentially unregulated. Doctors underwent less training than ministers and did not need a license to practice. Women benefited from the ease with which proprietary medical schools were given charters; between 1860 and 1900, nineteen medical schools for women were founded. During this same period, the number of women physicians rose from fewer than 200 to more than 7,000, or around 5 percent of American doctors (a percentage not surpassed until the 1970s). American women, of course, had long been practicing healing, as had African Americans of both genders. The earliest known African American physician was James Durham, a slave born in 1762. The first African American to receive a formal medical degree, James McCune Smith, did so in Scotland in 1837. Ten years later, David J. Peck became the first black to get an MD from an American medical school.

In 1890, 909 African American physicians were in practice, of these 115 were women, including Rebecca Cole. Beginning with Rebecca Crumpler, America's first black woman doctor, these pioneers composed one of the earliest groups of African American professional women. Despite the dual barriers of race and gender, many of these women worked outside their private practices in helping underserved populations of women and children and blacks barred from segregated facilities. Often denied privileges at existing institutions, these trailblazers established an array of health care institutions. In 1881 Susan Smith McKinney Steward co-founded a black hospital, the Brooklyn Women's Homeopathic Hospital and Dispensary. Eight years later, Caroline Still Wiley Anderson, the daughter of abolitionist William Still, co-founded the Berean Manual Training and Industrial School in Philadelphia. After years of treating patients at her home, Matilda Arabella Evans established the first African American hospital in Columbia, South Carolina. Lucy Hughes Brown and Sarah Garland Jones founded black hospitals and training schools in, respectively, Charleston, South Carolina, and Richmond, Virginia. The first woman to practice medicine in Alabama, Hallie Tanner Dillon Johnson, daughter of Benjamin Tucker Tanner and sister of Henry Ossawa Tanner, established a dispensary and nurses' training school while serving as resident physician at Tuskegee Institute.

By the last decades of Cole's career, however, the number of African American women physicians declined dramatically. The 1920 U.S. census lists only sixty-five African American women physicians. The professionalization and standardization of medicine further marginalized blacks and women, who were generally excluded from key organizations. Coeducation, which resulted in the closure of scores of women's schools and training facilities, further curbed the number of women physicians and dismantled much of the institutional and intellectual infrastructure that had supported late-nineteenth-century women doctors. Male African American doctors weathered these changes fairly well, as they now had access to a number of black medical schools and

hospitals; in 1920 black male doctors numbered 3,885.

In 1922, Rebecca Cole died after fifty years of practicing medicine. Her career and the contributions of the first wave of black women physicians illustrate that had opportunities been available, black women might have further invigorated the practice of medicine with their collaborative and community-based approach to health care.

FURTHER READING

Hine, Darlene Clark. "Co-Laborers in the Work of the Lord" in Ruth Abrams, ed. *"Send Us A Lady Physician": Women Doctors in America* (1985).

Wells, Susan. *Out of the Dead House: Nineteenth-Century Women Physicians and the Writing of Medicine* (2001).

—Lisa E. Rivo

 COLEMAN, BESSIE
(26 Jan. 1892–30 Apr. 1926), aviator, was born Elizabeth Coleman in Atlanta, Texas, the daughter of George Coleman, a day laborer of predominately Indian descent, and Susan (maiden name unknown), an African American domestic and farmworker. While Bessie was still very young, the family moved to Waxahachie, Texas, where they built a three-room house on a quarter-acre of land. She was seven when her father left his family to return to the Indian Territory (Oklahoma). The Coleman household was Baptist, and Bessie was an avid reader who became particularly interested in Booker T. Washington, Harriet Tubman, and Paul Laurence Dunbar. After finishing high school, she studied for one semester at Langston Industrial College, in Langston, Oklahoma.

Between 1912 and 1917 Coleman joined her two brothers in Chicago, where she studied manicuring at Burnham's School of Beauty Culture and worked at the White Sox Barber Shop. She supplemented her income by running a chili parlor on the corner of Twenty-fifth and Indiana avenues. In 1917 she married Claude Glenn. It was during this time that her brother Johnny related World War I stories to her about women flying planes in France. She decided that this would be her ambition.

Bessie Coleman, the first black woman aviator, 1923. © Underwood & Underwood/CORBIS

Coleman was rejected by a number of American aviation schools because of her race and sex. ROBERT ABBOTT, the founder of the *Chicago Defender*, a newspaper dedicated to black interests, suggested that she study aviation in France; she left the United States in November 1920. With Abbott and banker Jesse Binga's financial assistance, she studied at the School of Aviation run by the Caudron Aircraft Manufacturing Company in Le Crotoy. She later trained in Paris under a French pilot who reportedly shot down thirty-one German planes in World War I. Coleman's plane of choice was the 130-horsepower Nieuport de Chasse.

On 15 June 1921 Coleman received her pilot's license, number 18310, the first awarded to an American woman by the French Federation Aeronautique Internationale, and she became the only licensed African American woman pilot in the world. She returned to the United States in September 1921 but went back to Europe to study in Germany, where she received the first flying license granted to an American woman. She returned to the United States in August 1922.

With her goal of obtaining a pilot's license fulfilled, Coleman then sought to become an accomplished stunt and exhibition pilot. Barnstorming was the aviation fashion of the day, and Coleman decided to become part of these aerial acrobatics. United States air shows were attended by thousands of people. Sponsored by Abbott and Binga, Coleman made her first air show appearance at Curtiss Field in Garden City, Long Island, New York, during Labor Day weekend 1922 flying a Curtiss aeroplane. She then appeared at an air show at Checkerboard Airdrome in Chicago on 15 October. By this time Coleman had purchased three army surplus Curtiss biplanes.

Coleman's third exhibition was held in Gary, Indiana, where she met David Behncke, the founder and president of the International Airline Pilots Association, who became her manager.

The Gary exhibition was supervised by Reynolds McKenzie, an African American real estate dealer. There Coleman made a parachute jump after a white woman changed her mind.

On 4 February 1923, while Coleman was flying from municipal flying field in Santa Monica, California, to Los Angeles on her first exhibition flight on the Pacific Coast, her Curtiss JN-4 "Jenny" biplane engine failed, and she plunged 300 feet to the ground. The airplane was completely demolished, and Coleman had to be cut from the wreckage. During her recuperation she went on the lecture circuit and resumed flying as soon as she was able. Newspapers reported that she planned to establish a commercial passenger flight service.

Using Houston as her base, Coleman performed at air shows in Columbus, Ohio; Waxahachie and Austin, Texas; Memphis, Tennessee; and Wharton and Cambridge, Massachusetts. She thrilled crowds and became widely known for her flying outfit, which consisted of a pilot's cap, helmet, and goggles, a Sam Browne belt, long jacket and pants, white shirt and tie, and high boots. In 1924 Coast Firestone Rubber Company of California hired Coleman to do aerial advertising.

While recuperating from another airplane accident, which occurred during a race from San Diego to Long Beach, Coleman reflected on her third goal, opening the field to African Americans by establishing an aviation school in Los Angeles. She lectured to church and school groups and attended private dinners, speaking on the opportunities for blacks in aviation. She appeared in a number of documentary news films, and Coleman reportedly was scheduled to appear in *The Flying Ace*, billed as the "greatest airplane mystery thriller ever made"; it was produced in 1926 and featured an all-black cast.

In late April 1926 Coleman was in Florida at the invitation of the Negro Welfare League of Jacksonville to perform in an air show in Orlando for the annual First of May celebration. When the Orlando Chamber of Commerce informed her that African Americans would not be allowed to view her performance, she refused to participate in the show until "the Jim Crow order had been revoked and aviators had been sent up to drop placards letting the members of our race know they could come into the field" (Marjorie Kritz, "Bessie Coleman, Aviator Pioneer," undated leaflet, U.S. Department of Transportation). William D. Wills, Coleman's publicity agent and mechanic, flew her Jenny plane from Texas because local agencies would not rent a plane to a black person. Mechanical problems had occurred during the flight from Texas, and on the morning of Friday, 30 April, at Paxon Field, during a practice run, after the plane had been in the air only twelve minutes and had reached 3,000 feet, Wills, who was at the instruments, attempted to complete a nosedive, but the plane did not right itself. Though safety conscious, Coleman apparently had failed to secure her seat belt or wear a parachute. "Brave Bessie" was catapulted out of the plane and fell to her death. The plane continued in a downward spiral and crashed; Wills was also killed. Members of the Eighth Regiment of the Illinois National Guard served as pallbearers at Coleman's funeral in Chicago.

Coleman's place in aviation history is secure. In 1929 William J. Powell, author of *Black Wings* (1934), organized the Bessie Coleman School in Los Angeles. Bessie Coleman Aero Clubs, which promoted interest in aviation within the African American community, soon sprang up all across the United States, and the *Bessie Coleman Aero News*, a monthly periodical edited by Powell, first appeared in May 1930. On Labor Day 1931 the Bessie Coleman Aero Club sponsored the first all-black air show in the United States. Every Memorial Day African American aviators fly over her gravesite at Lincoln Cemetery in Chicago in single-file nose low to allow women passengers to drop flowers on her grave. Chicago mayor HAROLD WASHINGTON proclaimed 26 April 1986 Bessie Coleman Day. Also in 1986 the Federal Aviation Administration created the Bessie Intersection, located forty miles west of Chicago's O'Hare Airport, in her honor. She is included in a monument to African American aviators, *Black Americans in Flight*, at Lambert-St. Louis International Airport. On 27 April 1994 a U.S. Postal Service Bessie Coleman commemorative stamp was issued. She continues to be an inspiration to young African American women.

FURTHER READING

Freydberg, Elizabeth. *Bessie Coleman: The Brownskin Lady Bird* (1994).

Patterson, Elois. *Memoirs of the Late Bessie Coleman, Aviatrix; Pioneer of the Negro People in Aviation* (1969).

Rich, Doris L. *Queen Bess: Daredevil Aviator* (1993).

Obituary: *Chicago Defender*, 8 May 1926.
—CONSTANCE PORTER UZELAC

COLEMAN, ORNETTE

(19 Mar. 1930–), jazz innovator, saxophonist, composer, and trumpeter, was born Randolph Denard Ornette Coleman, in Fort Worth, Texas, the youngest of four children of Randolph Coleman, a cook, mechanic, and baseball player, and Rosa (maiden name unknown), a clerk and seamstress. Ornette's early life was marked by family tragedy: his oldest brother, Allen, died in the 1940s; his oldest sister, Vera, died as an adolescent; and his father died when Ornette was only seven. His surviving sister, Truvenza Coleman Leach, was a trombonist and vocalist who performed under the name Trudy Coleman.

Ornette began playing the alto saxophone in 1944 after his mother purchased an instrument with the agreement that he would get a job. A year later, at age fifteen, he began to play professionally. The saxophonists Dewey Redman and Prince Lashay and the drummer Charles Moffett were among the first musicians with whom Coleman played, and they remained close collaborators throughout his career. Coleman, who was primarily self-taught, developed an unorthodox approach to music that marked his entire progress as an improviser and composer. He took an extraordinarily fluid approach to tonality, which he incorporated into his enigmatic "harmolodic" theory of music. Coleman's idiosyncratic sense of intonation dates from his earliest studies of the saxophone, when he "realized that you could play sharp or flat in tune" (Litweiler, 25).

Most of Coleman's early employment was in gutbucket honky-tonks, which were often fronts for gambling houses where violence was frequent. These gigs were lucrative, and Coleman, who

Ornette Coleman, innovative and often enigmatic saxophonist, 1960. Library of Congress

made as much as one hundred dollars a week, became his family's primary wage earner. He also added to his technical knowledge of music while at I. M. Terrell High School (where the saxophonists King Curtis and Sonny Simmons were classmates) and with instruction from his cousin, James Jordan, and a local tenor sax hero, Red Connors (who, according to Coleman, once bested Lester Young in a jam session). Under Connors's tutelage, Coleman learned bebop compositions and switched to tenor sax. As an R&B saxophonist, Coleman was a honker in the style of Big Jay McNeely, delighting audiences with his squealing and screaming saxophone and gyrating body. The ecstatic blues voice Coleman developed in these early performances remained an important part of his artistry.

Coleman grew dissatisfied with the limitations of Fort Worth. His discomfort was not just in music; his overall aesthetic sensibility was out of step with his environs. One night, while playing alto in Red Connors's band at a gig in a white establishment, Coleman strayed from the melody of "Stardust" and was shouted down by a patron. Coleman later recalled another hostile encounter in Forth Worth: "I had a beard and my hair was thicker than it is now [it was also straightened and long] and this fellow came up to me and said, 'Say, boy, you can really play saxophone. I imagine where you come from they call you mister, don't they?... It's an honor to shake your hand because you're really a saxophone player—but you're still a nigger to me'" (Spellman, 93–94).

In 1949 Coleman left Fort Worth to tour with a minstrel band led by "Silas Green from New Orleans." The tour was a disaster. Coleman found the show's uninspired repertoire full of "white Dixieland tunes," the comedians "like Uncle Tom minstrels," (Spellman, 99–100) and the venues even more violent than those in Fort Worth. Worse, the band hated the way he played. After sharing his musical ideas with the other saxophonist, Coleman was fired, accused of trying to make the other horn player into a bebop musician. Stranded in Natchez, Mississippi, by happenstance, Coleman made his first recordings (now lost) in 1949 of rhythm and blues. He then joined R&B singer Clarence Samuel's band. While in this band, Ornette was led outside by a young woman, ostensibly to meet some admirers, only to be beaten and kicked by several huge men who also smashed his horn, apparently because his playing offended them. But Coleman's playing attracted staunch admirers from among New Orleans's elite musicians, including Ellis Marsalis, (father of WYNTON MARSALIS), Alvin Batiste, and Edward Blackwell. Coleman next joined Pee Wee Crayton and landed in Los Angeles in 1950, where he stayed until 1959.

In Los Angeles, Coleman developed a group sound with a group of musicians that included Blackwell, Don Cherry, and Billy Higgins, all of whom later accompanied him to national attention. He supported himself with odd jobs and care packages from his mother while studying music theory and rehearsing his compositions with sympathetic musicians. In 1954 he married the poet Jayne Cortez, and two years later their son, Ornette Denardo, was born. The marriage ended in divorce in 1964, though they had separated six years earlier. (Denardo, who began recording and performing with his father when he was only ten years old, took over management of his father's business, Harmolodic Inc., in 1983.) Coleman's music was highly controversial, and he found few opportunities for performance, but with the help of the bassist Red Mitchell, Coleman made his first recordings as a band-leader in 1958 for Contemporary Records.

John Lewis, leader of the Modern Jazz Quartet, became an ardent supporter of Coleman's music and used his influence to have Coleman and his protégé, Don Cherry, participate in the Lenox School of Jazz during the summer of 1959, where he gained other enthusiastic and influential supporters, including the composer Gunther Schuller and the jazz critic Martin Williams, who saw to it that Coleman's group was booked at the important Five Spot Café in New York City. The two-week engagement at the Five Spot was extended to two months. Coleman's performances quickly became the stuff of legend, attracting many important musicians, artists, and critics, some of whom proclaimed Coleman a genius and the most original saxophonist since CHARLIE PARKER; others thought that he was a charlatan.

Coleman was suddenly in demand for performances and recordings. His position as one of the handful of bona fide jazz innovators was solidified by 1961 after the release of several recordings with his quartet. He reached a new height of notoriety and controversy with a groundbreaking recording, *Free Jazz*, featuring two quartets playing simultaneously. This recording gave its name to the Free Jazz movement, which includes Coleman, JOHN COLTRANE, Cecil Taylor, and Albert Ayler among its preeminent exponents.

When Coleman realized that he was earning less money than white artists who drew smaller audiences, he tripled his fees, effectively pricing himself out of work. In 1962, at the height of his popularity, Coleman withdrew from the professional music scene, although he occasionally sat in with musicians whom he admired, including John Coltrane, who paid Coleman for lessons in his harmolodic theory. Coleman also taught himself to play the violin and the trumpet, which he showcased upon his return to performing and recording in 1965. Coleman's increased virtuosity on the alto saxophone and the fact that he learned to play the trumpet and violin almost completely without recourse to conventional techniques led many erstwhile detractors to recognize his unusual creativity.

In the 1970s and 1980s Coleman's scope as a composer and bandleader widened. In an attempt to gain work permits in England as a concert musician rather than as a jazz musician, Coleman began writing music for chamber groups and eventually for symphony orchestras. His most important symphonic work is *Skies of America* (1972); his most celebrated chamber piece, "The Country That Gave the Freedom Symbol to America," premiered at the *Festival d'Automne* in Paris in 1989. In 1972 Coleman visited Nigeria, and the following year he recorded with the Master Musicians of Joujouka in the Moroccan Rif Mountains. This music avoids clichés, crosses musical and cultural boundaries, and demonstrates Coleman's ideal of subsuming the soloist in the ensemble performance. Based upon this experience, he formed a new band, Prime Time, that featured the guitarist James "Blood" Ulmer, and the bassist Jamaladeen Tacuma. Prime Time included a doubled rhythm section (bass, drums, guitar, and keyboards) and used rock textures, country-and-western rhythms, funk grooves, and anything else Coleman found useful. In many ways this electric, eclectic band covered some of the same ground as MILES DAVIS did with his various fusion bands.

Coleman has continued to perform with musicians from different nations and traditions and to incorporate dancers, rappers, video artists, contortionists, and even body piercing into his shows. He was voted Artist of the Year in *Down Beat*'s 1998 International Critics Poll and has received numerous honors, including induction into the *Down Beat* Jazz Hall of Fame (1969) and the French Order of Arts and Letters (1998), two fellowships from the Guggenheim Memorial Foundation (1967, 1972), and one from the MacArthur Foundation (1994).

FURTHER READING

Litweiler, John. *Ornette Coleman: A Harmolodic Life* (1992).
MacRae, Barry. *Ornette Coleman* (1988).
Spellman, *Black Music, Four Lives* (1973).
Wilson, Peter Niklas. *Ornette Coleman: His Life and Music* (1999).

Discography
Cuscuna, Michael, and David Wild. *Ornette Coleman 1958–1979: A Discography* (1980).
—SALIM WASHINGTON

COLEMAN, WILLIAM T., JR. (7 July 1920–), lawyer

and public official, was born William Thaddeus Coleman Jr. in the Germantown district of Philadelphia, Pennsylvania, the son of William Thaddeus Coleman, a social worker, and Laura Beatrice Mason. His was a middle-class family with many of its members engaged in teaching, social work, and the church. Coleman attended an all-black elementary school in Germantown and a predominantly white high school, in which he was one of seven African American students.

Having harbored an ambition since childhood to be a lawyer, Coleman entered Harvard Law School in 1941 after graduating with a BA degree summa cum laude from the University of Pennsylvania. Wartime service in the U.S. Army Air Corps interrupted his legal studies, which he completed in 1946 by gaining his LLB degree magna cum laude, first in his class. He married Lovida Hardin in 1945; they would have three children. On leaving Harvard after an additional year of study, Coleman discovered that Philadelphia law firms refused to employ an African American, regardless of his qualifications, and he secured employment instead as law secretary to a judge on the Court of Appeals for the Third Circuit.

In 1948 Coleman became a Supreme Court clerk to Justice Felix Frankfurter. He was the first African American to hold such a position. At the end of his clerkship, Frankfurter wrote Coleman, "What I can say of you with great confidence is what was Justice Holmes's ultimate praise of a man: 'I bet on him'" (Kluger, 293). With employment in Philadelphia law firms still closed to him, Coleman then moved to New York City and joined the only multiracial practice on Wall Street, Paul, Weiss. In 1950 he began a long association with the NAACP Legal Defense and Educational Fund (LDF) when THURGOOD MARSHALL recruited him as a member of the team working on the school desegregation cases. Coleman's knowledge of Frankfurter was invaluable, but so was more generally the "cold-eyed counsel" (Kluger, 292) which he offered Marshall as a close adviser. He was, for example, skeptical of the LDF's reliance on the use of the social-science findings of KENNETH B. CLARK and others to prove

the harm of segregation. In 1955 he also advocated, though with some reluctance, that the LDF support the argument in favor of a gradual implementation of the Supreme Court's school desegregation decision the previous year in *Brown* v. *Board of Education*.

In 1952 Coleman joined what would later become Dilworth, Paxson, Kalish, Levy & Coleman as the first African American member of a white law firm in Philadelphia; he became a partner in 1966. His expertise involved corporate law and antitrust litigation, particularly in connection with transportation. The success he enjoyed in law brought invitations to join the board of mass-transit operations, airline corporations, and other major concerns.

Continuing his work for the LDF, Coleman defended civil rights activists at the height of the freedom struggle, including sit-in protesters and freedom riders. He acted as cocounsel on *McLaughlin* v. *Florida* (1964), in which he successfully argued that state laws against interracial cohabitation were unconstitutional. Outside his LDF work, and following his involvement in earlier efforts that had ended in failure, in 1965 Coleman represented the Commonwealth of Pennsylvania in a lawsuit against Girard College in Philadelphia, which practiced segregationist policies; the suit was fully and successfully concluded in 1968. Less successful was the outcome of an LDF case concerning the need for interdistrict desegregation plans to tackle racial disparities in schools. The 4–4 vote of the Supreme Court in the case *Richmond School Board* v. *Virginia Board of Education* (1973) left standing the decision of the lower court against interdistrict plans. Coleman became LDF president in 1971.

Coleman was a Republican with a probusiness philosophy, a position unusual within the LDF. He began his career as a public official in 1959 when President Dwight Eisenhower named him to the President's Commission on Employment Policy, designed to increase minority representation in the civil service. In 1964 he was appointed senior consultant and assistant counsel to the Warren Commission, which investigated the assassination of President John F. Kennedy. Coleman accepted other public appointments, including membership of the National

Commission on Productivity and the Phase II Price Commission during the Nixon administration. In 1973, however, he declined an invitation from Attorney General Elliott Richardson, with whom he had worked when both were Frankfurter's clerks, to become Watergate special prosecutor.

In March 1975 Coleman became the second African American to be appointed a member of a presidential cabinet, when Gerald Ford named him as secretary of transportation. At the Department of Transportation he was a pioneer in seeking to create an integrated national policy, releasing in 1977 what the *Washington Post* described as "a remarkable study on trends and choices in transportation" (23 Jan. 1977). His successor, Brock Adams, decided not to follow the course suggested by this report, however. Many other initiatives by Coleman faced difficulties due to the conflict between Congress and the White House that characterized the Ford administration as a whole. Coleman advocated the development of user fees to reduce the sector's reliance on government subsidy, but Congress declined to cut transportation appropriations, as much as doubling the levels of expenditure recommended by the administration. An example of this conflict involved the railroad industry, with Congress maintaining subsidies to an extent considered unwise by Coleman. Other key decisions taken by Coleman at Transportation included his determination that automobile manufacturers should not be required to install air bags, fearing consumer opposition to government interference; his approval of landings by supersonic airplanes at U.S. airports; and his support for the construction of two deep-water ports in the Gulf of Mexico to facilitate oil imports by supertanker.

Following Ford's defeat by Jimmy Carter, Coleman returned to private practice with the firm O'Melveny & Myers, while continuing his work on civil rights cases, acting as LDF chair from 1977 to 1997. His most high-profile case was not directly on behalf of the LDF, however. In *Bob Jones University* v. *United States* (1983), Chief Justice Warren Burger invited him to speak for the defendant when the Reagan-era Department of Justice decided to support the plaintiff. Coleman successfully argued before the Supreme Court that it was permissible for the Internal Revenue Service to withhold tax exemptions from private educational institutions, like Bob Jones University, that practiced racially discriminatory policies. Coleman's opposition to the Reagan administration in the case underscored his increasingly critical view of the Republican Party's approach to race.

One of the most influential lawyers in the nation who over many years made significant contributions to the protection of civil rights, as well as to public life more generally, Coleman received the Presidential Medal of Freedom in 1995.

FURTHER READING

Greenberg, Jack. *Crusaders in the Courts: How a Dedicated Band of Lawyers Fought for the Civil Rights Revolution* (1994).
Kluger, Richard. *Simple Justice: The History of "Brown v. Board of Education" and Black America's Struggle for Justice* (1975).

—ROBERT MASON

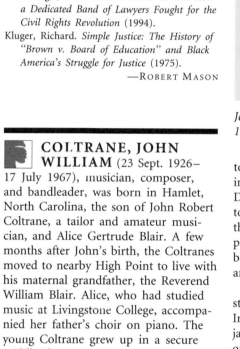

COLTRANE, JOHN WILLIAM (23 Sept. 1926–17 July 1967), musician, composer, and bandleader, was born in Hamlet, North Carolina, the son of John Robert Coltrane, a tailor and amateur musician, and Alice Gertrude Blair. A few months after John's birth, the Coltranes moved to nearby High Point to live with his maternal grandfather, the Reverend William Blair. Alice, who had studied music at Livingstone College, accompanied her father's choir on piano. The young Coltrane grew up in a secure middle-class environment in which both religion and music were highly valued. At age twelve he began studying alto horn, then the clarinet, and joined the High Point Community Band. From the outset, Coltrane practiced constantly, a pattern that he sustained throughout his life. By 1942 he was playing clarinet and alto saxophone in his high school band.

After graduating from high school in 1943, Coltrane moved to Philadelphia, where he worked as a laborer in a sugar-refining factory and studied saxophone at the Ornstein School of Music. He made his professional debut in 1945, and in August of that year was drafted into the U.S. Navy. He was posted

John Coltrane, whose cutting-edge style changed the face of jazz improvisation, 1962. Library of Congress

to Hawaii, where he played clarinet in naval marching and dance bands. Discharged in 1946, Coltrane returned to Philadelphia, resumed his studies at the Ornstein School, and made a living playing saxophone in rhythm-and-blues bands. This was the beginning of a long and thorough musical apprenticeship.

Coltrane developed his distinctive style in a variety of musical contexts. In 1947 and 1948 he toured with the jazz-influenced rhythm and blues group of Eddie "Cleanhead" Vinson, playing tenor saxophone for the first time. In 1949 he joined the influential DIZZY GILLESPIE Big Band and stayed with Gillespie when the band was reduced to a sextet. Coltrane made his recording debut with Gillespie in 1950. In 1952 and 1953 Coltrane was back on the rhythm and blues circuit with Earl Bostic, and in 1953 he joined the Johnny Hodges band. By 1955 Coltrane had developed an identifiable style that combined technical virtuosity with a unique tone. His potential was recognized by the trumpeter MILES DAVIS, who invited the saxophonist to join his quintet in 1955. This band was one of the key jazz

groups of the mid 1950s and joining it transformed Coltrane's career. The quintet toured widely and recorded frequently, and the consequent exposure enhanced his reputation. Within a week of joining Davis in the autumn of 1955, Coltrane married Naima Austin, becoming stepfather to her daughter, Syeeda.

By March 1957, Coltrane's alcohol abuse and heroin addiction had so affected his reliability that Davis dismissed him as a permanent member of the group, but Coltrane continued playing intermittently with Davis until 1960. In the ensuing nine months Coltrane rid himself of his addictions and completed his musical apprenticeship with a lengthy residency at the Five Spot Café in New York as part of the THELONIOUS MONK Quartet. Monk pushed Coltrane to the limit of his creativity. His lengthy solos were characterized by a persistent, relentless, rapid-fire outpouring of notes, to which the description "sheets of sound" would subsequently be applied. Coltrane's music was evolving rapidly. At the end of his gig with Monk, he rejoined Miles Davis as part of a sextet that included Cannonball Adderley. This group recorded two seminal albums,

Milestones (1958) and, with Bill Evans in the band, the more subtle and atmospheric *Kind of Blue* (1959).

By early 1960 it was clearly time for Coltrane to leave Davis and form his own band. Coltrane had been recording prolifically under his own name since the mid-1950s, initially for Prestige and then for the much more influential Atlantic label. Important albums like *Giant Steps*, recorded in 1959 and consisting entirely of Coltrane compositions, and *Coltrane Jazz*, recorded later that same year, further enhanced his reputation, raised his profile, and prepared the way for the launch of his solo career. The John Coltrane Quartet was formed as a permanent unit in April 1960.

The personnel of the band fluctuated during 1960, but when pianist McCoy Tyner and drummer Elvin Jones joined the group, Coltrane had the nucleus of the classic quartet that would be at the heart of his musical existence for the next five years. Bassist Jimmy Garrison joined in 1961, the same year in which Coltrane signed a lucrative contract with Impulse Records. The Impulse years produced a rich and diverse musical legacy including an album of ballads, sessions with DUKE ELLINGTON and with the singer Johnny Hartman, as well as the larger ensemble used on *Africa/Brass,* which reflected the influence of African rhythms and Indian concepts of improvisation.

However, the music with which Coltrane and the quartet were more usually associated was exemplified by the sessions recorded live at the Village Vanguard in New York in November 1961. On *Chasin' the Trane*, Coltrane, spurred on by the ferocious, fragmented, polyrhythmic drumming of Elvin Jones, unleashed an impassioned fifteen-minute solo full of honks, screams, and tonal distortions. This aspect of Coltrane's music met with a mixed reception among both audiences and critics. Some hailed him as an innovator, every bit as important as LOUIS ARMSTRONG in the 1920s or CHARLIE PARKER in the 1940s. Others, expecting nothing more demanding than renditions of Coltrane's commercially successful and relatively accessible 1960 recording of *My Favorite Things*, were appalled by what they heard and dismissed it as "anti-jazz" and "musical nonsense."

There was also disagreement concerning the extramusical significance of Coltrane's music. Some critics sought to link him with those younger African American musicians who, influenced by the ideas of the 1960s Black Power movement, identified their art as a revolutionary black music through which they could express their pain, their anger, and their condemnation of American society. Coltrane's position on issues of this kind was ambivalent. Arguably, if his music had any extramusical content, it lay in its visionary, spiritual quality rather than in any sociopolitical sensibility. It was no coincidence that, by the mid 1960s, Coltrane was releasing albums with titles like *Meditations, Ascension,* and *A Love Supreme.* Elvin Jones confirms that Coltrane's music "wasn't any protest against anything. John was all love. Everything that he did was out of his love for music, and his love for people" (*Jazz Journal* 28. 4 [1975], 4–5). This same love led Coltrane to record his composition *Alabama* following the death of four young African American girls in a 1963 bombing incident in a Birmingham, Alabama, church. The piece is a lament for the children, and its mood of sadness and desolation constitutes an eloquent response to their death.

In December 1964 the quartet recorded the four-part suite *A Love Supreme.* The suite, a testament to the continuing richness of their musical creativity and empathy and an expression of Coltrane's religious beliefs, received almost unanimous critical praise and rapidly became Coltrane's most celebrated album. In 1965 *Down Beat* magazine named *A Love Supreme* Record of the Year in both its Readers' poll and its International Critics' poll. Coltrane also won awards in the Tenor and Soprano Saxophone categories, was elected to the magazine's Hall of Fame, and named as Jazzman of the Year. Rather than rest on his laurels and exploit his fame, Coltrane moved the creative goalposts. In June 1965 he recorded *Ascension*, on which the quartet was augmented by such leading avant-garde players as Archie Shepp and Pharoah Sanders. The eleven-strong ensemble played a forty-minute piece in which uncompromising solos alternated with overpowering group improvisation, without much in the way of rhythm, melody, or harmony to anchor it.

Coltrane continued to explore the outer limits of improvised music. This musical policy, and a decision to expand the quartet, was not to the liking of all the original group members. McCoy Tyner left the band in December 1965, followed by Elvin Jones in March 1966. For the next year Coltrane recorded and toured with a group in which Jimmy Garrison remained on bass, with Pharoah Sanders on saxophone and Rashied Ali on drums. The piano chair was taken by Coltrane's partner, Alice McLeod, who became his second wife in August 1966, following his divorce from Naima. Between 1964 and 1967 the couple had three sons.

At the age of forty, Coltrane had found happiness in his personal life and was still at the height of his creative powers. He had completed a remarkable musical journey, from rhythm and blues via bebop to the cutting edge of the contemporary avant-garde movement. A series of duets he recorded with Rashied Ali in February 1967, subsequently issued as *Interstellar Space,* show his tenor playing to be as fierce and uncompromising as ever, but there is also a serenity and lyricism to the music. Whether this was a pointer to the future, or simply another episode in the juxtaposition of anguish and tranquillity evident in so much of Coltrane's music, remains uncertain. John Coltrane died of liver cancer in the Huntington Hospital in Huntington, Long Island.

Since his death, no single figure has dominated the jazz scene the way Coltrane did in the 1960s. He remains one of a select group of jazz musicians who evolved artistically throughout their careers and whose personal growth and development moved the music forward in significant ways. Into the twenty-first century Coltrane's influence remains profound. Long before the term "world music" came into vogue, Coltrane had shown the way by absorbing elements of Indian and African music. His move away from a chordal to a scalar approach helped change the face of jazz improvisation. His unsurpassed instrumental technique and his remarkable ability as an improviser have inspired generations of jazz musicians. Coltrane is dead, but lives on in his remarkable legacy of recorded work and in his continuing influence on the contemporary jazz scene.

FURTHER READING

Porter, Lewis. *John Coltrane: His Life and Music* (1998).

Priestley, Brian. *John Coltrane* (1987).

Thomas, J. C. *Chasin' the Trane: The Music and Mystique of John Coltrane* (1975).

Obituary: *New York Times*, 18 July 1967.

Discography

Fujioka, Yasuhiro. *John Coltrane: A Discography and Musical Biography* (1995).

—JOHN RUNCIE

COOK, WILL MARION

(27 Jan. 1869–20 July 1944), composer and librettist, was born in Washington, D.C., the son of John Hartwell Cook, a professor of law at Howard University, and Marion Isabel Lewis, a sewing instructor. He received classical violin training at the Oberlin Conservatory of Music (1884–1887). For approximately the next decade he presumably studied violin and composition with the German violinist Joseph Joachim at the Hochschule für Musik in Berlin (1888–1889?), and he continued harmony and counterpoint training under Antonìn Dvořák and John White at the National Conservatory of Music in New York City (1893–1895?).

Cook was a prolific composer whose instrumentals and songs were closely related to the craze for cakewalking and two-stepping. His first musical success began with the show *Clorindy, the Origin of the Cakewalk* (1898), which he originally wrote for the vaudevillian comedians BERT WILLIAMS and GEORGE WILLIAM WALKER, although it was first performed with Ernest Hogan in the lead. This landmark production departed from the minstrel tradition in two ways: first, by employing syncopated ragtime music; and second, by introducing the cakewalk to Broadway audiences. The show, which opened at the Casino Roof Garden Theatre in New York, emerged along with Bob Cole's *A Trip to Coontown* as one of the first all-black shows to play in a major Broadway theater, and Cook became the first black conductor of a white theater orchestra. The author JAMES WELDON JOHNSON noted that Cook "was the first competent composer to take what was then

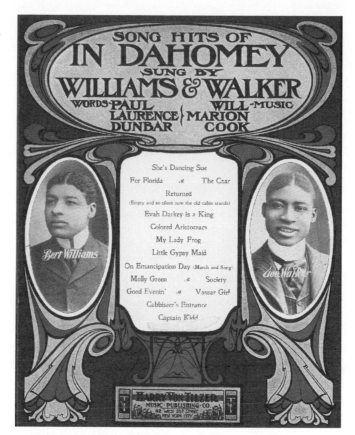

Talented musician, conductor, and composer Will Marion Cook wrote the music for In Dahomey, *a hit musical performed in 1902 by comedy team* BERT WILLIAMS *and* GEORGE WALKER. Duke University

known as rag-time and work it out in a musicianly way" (*Black Manhattan*, 103). The show's star, Abbie Mitchell, became Cook's wife in 1899. They were divorced in 1906, but continued to work together in show business; they had two children.

Clorindy presented songs that countered minstrel stereotypes. Whereas many of the tunes, notably "Hottes' Coon in Dixie" and "Who Dat Say Chicken in Dis Crowd?," continued in the minstrel tradition, others, such as the choral "On Emancipation Day" and the hauntingly lyrical "Ghost Ship" (unpublished), were stirring tunes that reflected black pride and the pain of middle passage. The production played throughout the summer of 1898 at the Casino in New York. After a brief but successful tour the show was incorporated into the Williams and Walker Company as part of their vaudeville routine.

In the first decade of the twentieth century Cook emerged as an original, if sometimes erratic, genius of

musical comedy. He teamed with PAUL LAURENCE DUNBAR, Alex Rogers, Joe Jordan, Williams and Walker, Jessie A. Shipp, Cecil Mack, JAMES ROSAMOND JOHNSON, and James Weldon Johnson to produce some of the most popular musical shows, vaudeville, and hit tunes. Cook's next three productions, *The Casino Girl* (1900), *The Policy Players* (1900), and *Jes Lak White Fo'ks* (1900), failed to duplicate his *Clorindy* success, but his fortunes turned upward when he created the music for Williams and Walker's *In Dahomey* (1902–1905), *Abyssinia* (1906–1907), and *Bandana Land* (1907–1909). *In Dahomey* opened successfully in New York, establishing the Williams and Walker Company as the premier black musical comedy troupe for the remainder of the decade. In addition, the show toured throughout Great Britain during the 1903–1904 season.

In 1910 Cook formed the New York Syncopated Orchestra, which toured the United States that same year. He also formed the orchestra known as the Clef

Club in 1912, a group of black musicians and entertainers. Both the Syncopated Orchestra and the Clef Club performed a mixture of Cook's music, as well as popular and classical music. His most popular songs, along with those from *Clorindy*, were "Swing Along," a satiric choral piece on relations between blacks and whites, "Mandy Lou," "Red, Red Rose," "Exhortation: A Negro Sermon," "Brown Skin Baby Mine," "Darktown Is Out Tonight," "Nobody Knows the Trouble I See," and "The Rain Song." In 1918 Cook moved his Syncopated Orchestra to Europe, and he was largely instrumental in creating the vogue for black musicians there and in England.

Cook's classical musical education proved a mixed blessing. Endowed with tremendous talent, his refusal to tolerate racism in the white world and show business egos in his own circles alienated him from many friends and colleagues. During the last two decades of his life Cook's productivity declined, but he did compose *In Darkydom* (1914) and fragments of a Negro folk opera called *St. Louis Woman* (1929). He also wrote spirituals, such as "Troubled in Mind" (1929), and during World War II he and his son Will Mercer Cook composed patriotic songs.

Abbie Mitchell referred to him as "a giant in experience, a sincere student of music in spite of all statements to the contrary, notwithstanding his eccentricities, his erratic temperament, which in later years caused him many disappointments, much poverty, loss of influence, contacts and friends and a deep sorrow" (Mercer Cook Papers). He died in New York City's Harlem Hospital.

FURTHER READING

Valuable sources of information on Cook include the Mercer Cook Papers, Moorland-Spingarn Research Center, Howard University; the Theatre Museum, London; the Music Division, Library of Congress; and the Billy Rose Theatre Collection at the New York Public Library for the Performing Arts, Lincoln Center.

Johnson, James Weldon. *Black Manhattan* (1930).
Peterson, Bernard L. *A Century of Musicals in Black and White* (1993).
Riis, Thomas L. *Just before Jazz* (1989).

————. *More than Just Minstrel Shows* (1992).
Sampson, Henry T. *Blacks in Blackface* (1980).

Obituary: *New York Times*, 21 July 1944.

—DAVID KRASNER

 COOPER, ANNA JULIA HAYWOOD (10 Aug. 1858?– 27 Feb. 1964), educator, writer, and activist, was born Anna Julia Haywood in Raleigh, North Carolina, to Hannah Stanley, the slave of George Washington Haywood, who was probably Anna's father. Anna exhibited a love of books and a gift for learning early in her childhood. Hannah was hired out as a nursemaid to a successful local lawyer, whose family most likely assisted her daughter in learning to read and write. Most important, however, was Anna's mother herself, who although illiterate, encouraged her daughter's education.

In 1867 Anna was one of the first students admitted to St. Augustine's Normal School and Collegiate Institute, a recently founded Episcopal school for newly freed slaves. At age nine she found herself tutoring students older than herself and decided to earn her teaching credentials. At St. Augustine's Anna first confronted the gender imbalance in education, challenging the exclusion of women from courses in theology and classics. In 1877, at the age of nineteen, Anna married George A. G. Cooper, a theology student and teacher at St. Augustine's who was fourteen years her senior. Social mores of the time barred married women from teaching, so Cooper gave up her budding teaching career. When George died two years later, however, Anna felt free to continue her teaching career.

Proficient in classics and mathematics, she enrolled in Oberlin College in Ohio in 1881 and was awarded a tuition scholarship. Cooper took on the mantle of "race woman," defending and advocating for blacks, and demanded the inclusion of women in the "gentlemen's course." Cooper earned a BA from Oberlin in 1884, placing her, along with MARY CHURCH TERRELL, among the first four African American women to earn a bachelor's degree. She followed this with an MS in Mathematics in 1887.

After a brief teaching stint at Wilberforce University in Ohio and a year

Anna Julia Haywood Cooper, principal of the renowned M Street High School in Washington, D.C. University of North Carolina at Chapel Hill Libraries

teaching at her alma mater, St. Augustine, Cooper was invited in 1887 by the superintendent of Colored Schools in Washington, D.C., to join the faculty at Washington Colored High School (soon after renamed the M Street Colored H.S. and, in 1916, Paul Laurence Dunbar H.S.). In Washington, Cooper and Mary Church (Terrell), who also took a teaching position at the school, boarded in the home of, and were influenced by the Pan-Africanist clergyman, ALEXANDER CRUMMELL.

In 1892 Cooper published *A Voice from the South by a Black Woman of the South*, a collection of essays widely acknowledged as the first black feminist treatise. Cooper held the view that black women were especially suited for raising the status of the black community, more so than black men. Cooper's perspective was unique in the vehemence of her assertion that "only the BLACK WOMAN can say 'when and where I enter…the whole *Negro race enters with me*'" (Cooper, 31). She became widely known on the lecture circuit, espousing many of the themes of the black club women's movement, such as education and culture as beacons on the path to black self-improvement. Cooper also helped edit *The Southland*, a magazine founded in 1890 by Joseph C. Price.

In 1892 Cooper cofounded the Colored Women's League to encourage black women's collective approach to the race's problems. As the Colored Women's League corresponding secretary, she addressed the World's Congress of Representative Women in Chicago in 1893. Her comments during a special session titled "The Intellectual Progress of Colored Women of the United States Since Emancipation" addressed the need for inclusiveness in tending to the needs of a broad range of women.

In 1900 Cooper served on the executive committee of the first Pan-African Conference in London, and she was one of two women invited to address the conference. She was certainly understating her role when she described herself simply as a globetrotter. She was the first and only woman elected to the American Negro Academy, an organization of artists and scholars dedicated to the publication of works in defense of the race, and whose members included PAUL LAURENCE DUNBAR, KELLY MILLER, ALAIN LOCKE, ARTHUR SCHOMBURG, WILLIAM PICKENS, W. E. B. DU BOIS, FRANCIS J. GRIMKÉ, Alexander Crummell, and CARTER G. WOODSON. In 1902 Cooper became principal of M Street High School. This position was not without its challenges from the elites of Washington, D.C. Cooper transformed the school into one of the best for black students. Contrary to BOOKER T. WASHINGTON's educational philosophy of vocational and industrial training, Cooper insisted on a college preparatory curriculum for her students. Her insistence on this curriculum was met with resistance, and her leadership of M Street was challenged by disagreement over the appropriate educational course for black students. In 1902–1903 Du Bois delivered a speech at the M Street School critical of the school's timidity toward expansive curricula. In response, advocates of the Washingtonian perspective spurred what became known as "the M Street High School Controversy." The school board levied an array of charges against Cooper in order to discredit her.

As Annette Eaton, a former M Street student explained, Cooper's tenure as principal fell victim to race and gender politics in Washington, D.C. Eaton noted the obstacles Cooper faced, pointing out that the white power structure clearly took issue with Cooper's audacity in preparing black students for college and believing that black students could easily match white students' achievement. Eaton also observed that the sexism Cooper encountered stemmed from three main causes: her ambition to succeed beyond the role of principal, her status as a married (though widowed) woman in a profession, and gossip regarding Cooper's rumored relationship with a male boarder, John Love, in her home.

Cooper had taken in John Love and his sister as foster children after they were orphaned. Both Love and his sister continued to board with Cooper as adults, along with four other female teachers. Although theirs was a close relationship, scholars speculate that Cooper declined Love's later marriage proposal, perhaps owing to the age difference or to the impropriety of marriage after being Love's guardian. The confluence of the school board's racism and the community's sexist views of her personal life—two forms of discrimination about which Cooper was quite vocal—forced her resignation as principal of M Street in 1906, after a year of disparaging testimony. Though hounded out of the position of principal, Cooper returned to the school to teach Latin four years later.

Cooper's industriousness in Washington, D.C., was not limited to her role as principal. Impervious to segregationist policies, Cooper helped found, in 1905, the Colored Women's YWCA and, in 1912, the Colored YMCA. Black women's clubs were instrumental in establishing YWCA branches in areas where there were no support services for black women moving from rural, southern communities to the North. Upon the death of her half-brother in 1915, Cooper adopted his five grandchildren, interrupting the doctoral studies at Columbia University that she had begun in 1911. After enrolling the children in boarding school in 1924, Cooper left for Paris to complete her degree at the University of Paris. She finished her dissertation, "The Attitude of France toward Slavery in the Revolution," in 1925 and, at age sixty-seven, became the fourth African American woman to receive a PhD.

After retiring from teaching at Paul Laurence Dunbar in 1930, Cooper became the second president of Frelinghuysen University, an educational institution for black adults founded in 1917. Cooper paid tribute to the role her mother played in her educational achievement by creating the Hannah Stanley Opportunity School, annexed to Frelinghuysen. Despite Cooper's many efforts to keep it open, Frelinghuysen, with economic problems and loss of accreditation, became the Frelinghuysen Group of Schools for Colored Working People, with Cooper as registrar, until it closed in the 1950s. Cooper maintained a scholarly writing life until her death at the age of 105 in Washington, D.C. A consummate race woman, Cooper serves as an examplar "of what one black women can do if given access to the halls of academe" (Henry Louis Gates Jr., *Norton Anthology of African American Literature*, 554).

FURTHER READING

Cooper's papers are housed in the Moorland-Spingarn Research Center, Howard University, Washington, D.C.

Cooper, Anna Julia. *A Voice from the South: by a Black Woman of the South*, with an introduction by Mary Helen Washington (1988).
———, Charles Lemert, and Esme Bhan, eds. *The Voice of Anna Julia Cooper: Including a Voice from the South and Other Important Essays, Papers, and Letters* (1998).

Hutchinson, Louise Daniel, and Anacostia Neighborhood Museum. *Anna Julia Cooper: A Voice from the South* (1982).
Johnson, Karen Ann. *Uplifting the Women and the Race: The Lives, Educational Philosophies, and Social Activism of Anna Julia Cooper and Nannie Helen Borroughs* (2000).
White, Deborah Gray. *Too Heavy a Load: Black Women in Defense of Themselves, 1884–1994* (1999).

—KIMBERLY SPRINGER

 COPPIN, FANNY JACKSON (1837– 21 Jan. 1913), educator, civic and religious leader, and feminist, was born a slave in Washington, D.C., the daughter of Lucy Jackson. Her father's name

Fanny Jackson Coppin, the first female principal of the prestigious Institute for Colored Youth in Philadelphia.
University of North Carolina

and the details of her early childhood are unknown. However, by the time she was age ten, her aunt Sarah Orr Clark had purchased her freedom, and Jackson went to live with relatives in New Bedford, Massachusetts. By 1851 she and her relatives had moved to Newport, Rhode Island, where Jackson was employed as a domestic by George Henry Calvert, a descendant of Lord Baltimore, the settler of Maryland. Jackson's salary enabled her to afford one hour of private tutoring three times a week. Near the end of her six-year stay with the Calverts, she briefly attended the segregated public schools of Newport. In 1859 Jackson enrolled at the Rhode Island State Normal School in Bristol. In addition to the normal course, she also studied French privately. Funded by her aunt Sarah and scholarships from Bishop DANIEL ALEXANDER PAYNE of the African Methodist Episcopal (AME) Church and Oberlin College, Jackson was able to enroll in the ladies department of Oberlin in 1860. She also helped to pay for her education by working during her years at Oberlin. By 1861 Jackson transferred into the collegiate department at Oberlin, where she distinguished herself and actively participated in student life. Her outstanding academic achievements resulted in her being chosen as the first African American student teacher of Oberlin's preparatory department. In addition, Jackson was chosen as

class poet and graduated in 1865 with an AB degree, becoming the second African American woman in the nation to receive such a degree.

After graduating from Oberlin, Jackson accepted the position of principal of the female department of the prestigious Institute for Colored Youth (ICY) in Philadelphia. Founded by the Society of Friends in 1837 as a high school for African Americans, the ICY offered a preparatory department, separate secondary-school departments for males and females, and a teacher training course. Jackson's ability as a teacher and as a principal was immediately recognized by the Quaker managers as well as the African American community. Her skills in public speaking and elocution were reflected in the improved speaking of the female students. By the end of her first year, the enrollment of the girls' secondary school nearly doubled from forty-two to eighty, and the school reported fewer dropouts. By 1869, when Ebenezer Bassett, the principal for the entire school, was appointed U.S. minister to Haiti by President Ulysses S. Grant, Jackson was promoted to head the entire school. This promotion was extremely significant because no woman at this time headed a coeducational institution that had both male and female faculty.

Immediately after Jackson became principal of the ICY, many changes that reflected her educational and personal philosophies began to appear at the school. She believed that if respect were given to students it would be returned by the students to the teachers. Thus, she abolished corporal punishment at the school. Academic performance at the school was so high that the institution averaged thirty visitors a week in 1869. Jackson also believed in fostering close relationships between the faculty, students, managers, and parents. She began sending monthly conduct papers to parents to inform them of their children's character, attendance, and recitations. Monthly meetings were also held with parents of ICY students. Managers began sponsoring teas for the school's upper-level students and teachers to stimulate conversation and fellowship. Her devotion to the ICY was so great that she remained as principal for the next twenty-one years.

In 1878 Jackson began a regular column titled "Women's Department" in the *Christian Recorder*, the newspaper of the AME Church. Through her column she was able to reach African American women of all income levels. She reported the achievements of women in education, employment, and other areas and also discussed cases of discrimination against black women. Jackson was always concerned about gender discrimination as well as racial discrimination and stressed to her female readers that they should pursue the same professions and occupations as men and not simply enter traditional female-dominated fields. In 1881 Jackson married Levi Jenkins Coppin, an AME minister at least fifteen years her junior.

Coppin's greatest contribution to the ICY was the establishment of an industrial department. She was stimulated to take action after visiting the Centennial Exposition in Philadelphia (1876), which emphasized education and national progress; she was particularly impressed by the exhibition of the Moscow Imperial Technical School's Victor Della Vos, who demonstrated his newly developed approaches to the teaching of the mechanical arts. She became acutely aware of the need to prepare African American youth for an increasingly industrial nation, and so she began to campaign for a department of industrial arts at the ICY. Her idea, though, was a hard sell. The Quaker managers did not want to incur additional expenses for expansion of the institution, and African Americans were apprehensive about what was being proposed by Coppin. Many of the leading families in Philadelphia who sent their children to the ICY had a tradition of classical education and affiliations with prestigious literary societies, and they were reluctant to embrace a form of education that appeared more practical in nature. Nevertheless, the industrial department finally opened in 1889, although it failed to offer the advanced classes that Coppin had proposed, such as mechanical drawing and engineering. Instead, the department offered only carpentry, bricklaying, shoemaking, printing, and plastering for men, and millinery, dressmaking, and cooking for women. By 1892 typing and stenography were added to the curriculum. The industrial department was a great success. As the only institution in Philadelphia to offer industrial training for African Americans, the ICY had eighty-seven students enrolled in the new department and 325 on a waiting list just two months after the department opened.

During Coppin's tenure as principal of the ICY, her normal students were so sought after that most were able to pass teacher examinations and secure employment successfully after only two years in secondary school. By 1890 three-fourths of the African American teachers in Philadelphia and Camden, New Jersey, were ICY graduates. Many of the institute's students also pursued the professions.

In addition to her school work, Coppin was extremely active in the African Methodist Episcopal Church. She was elected president of the local Women's Mite Missionary Society and later became national president of the Women's Home and Foreign Missionary Society. In addition, she was on the board of managers of the Home for the Aged and Infirm Colored People in Philadelphia for over thirty years (1881–1913), and she was elected vice president of the National Association of Colored Women in 1897.

In 1902 Coppin retired from the institute and accompanied her husband, who had been elected bishop of the Fourteenth Episcopal District of South Africa in 1900, to Capetown. They returned to Philadelphia in the spring of 1904. Bishop Coppin was then appointed to the Seventh Episcopal District, which encompassed South Carolina and Alabama. Coppin, who had frequently traveled with her husband, made the trip to South Carolina; however, the South African trip had severely impacted her health, and by 1905 her health had deteriorated to such an extent that she was primarily confined to her Philadelphia home for the remaining years of her life. She died in Philadelphia.

FURTHER READING

Primary documents concerning Coppin's Oberlin years are available in the Oberlin College Archives. Documents from her years as principal at the ICY are available at the Friend's Historical Library, Swarthmore College.

Coppin, Fanny Jackson. *Reminiscences of School Life, and Hints on Teaching* (1913; repr. 1987, 1995).

Perkins, Linda M. *Fanny Jackson Coppin and the Institute for Colored Youth, 1865-1902* (1987).

Obituary: *Philadelphia Tribune*, 1 Feb. 1913.
—LINDA M. PERKINS

 CORNISH, SAMUEL ELI (c. 1795–6 Nov. 1858), clergyman and newspaper editor, was born in Sussex County, Delaware, the son of free black parents. Cornish was educated after 1815 in Philadelphia, where he studied for the ministry with John Gloucester, pastor of the First African Presbyterian Church. During Gloucester's illness, Cornish served as minister to the church for a year. In this brief tenure Cornish learned much about the tenuous finances of black churches, knowledge that would serve him later. Cornish gained a probationary license to preach from the Presbyterian synod in 1819. He then spent six months as missionary to slaves on Maryland's Eastern Shore, where his license gave him greater credibility than most black preachers enjoyed. In 1821 he moved to New York City, where he worked in the blighted ghetto around Bancker Street and organized the first black Presbyterian congregation in New York, the New Demeter Street Presbyterian Church. Ordained in 1822, Cornish preached at New Demeter until 1828, while itinerating among blacks in New York and New Jersey. In 1824 he married Jane Livingston; they had four children.

In 1827 Cornish and JOHN BROWN RUSSWURM established *Freedom's Journal*, the first black newspaper in the United States. The editors combined local news and black history with condemnations of slavery and colonization. After several months, Cornish resigned to devote more time to his ministry. Russwurm operated the newspaper until he left abruptly for Africa in 1829. The same year, Cornish initiated *Rights of All*, which lasted less than a year. Eight years later, Cornish became editor of the *Colored American*, remaining in that post until 1839.

In his newspaper editorials, ministry, and personal life, Cornish emphasized the importance of education, hard work, thrift, and agricultural labor for the progress of African Americans. He first advocated agriculture for black uplift in 1827 in the *Colored American*. He offered to distribute two-thousand acres of land on the banks of the Delaware River in New Jersey to blacks willing to leave the city to become independent farmers. Vehemently opposed to colonization, in 1840 he coauthored with Theodore S. Wright a lengthy diatribe against the American Colonization Society entitled *The Colonization Scheme Considered, in Its Rejection by the Coloured People—in Its Tendency to Uphold Caste—in Its Unfitness for Christianizing and Civilizing the Aborigines of Africa and for Putting a Stop to the African Slave Trade.*

Cornish was a key participant in many of the reform movements of the antebellum period, serving as agent for the New York African Free Schools (1827–1829), member of the executive committees of the American Anti-Slavery Society and the New York State Vigilance Committee, manager of the American Bible Society (1835) and Union Missionary Society (1842), and a founder, executive committee member, and vice president of the American Missionary Society (1848–1858). A founder of the New York City Phoenix Society for mutual aid and education of urban blacks, Cornish had an active role in the early black national convention movement.

Cornish often disagreed with his colleagues. Although an organizer of the American Moral Reform Society, he left it because he felt it acted too slowly on racial issues. While active in the New York City Vigilance Committee, he opposed the controversial methods of one of its leaders, DAVID RUGGLES. In 1838 Ruggles used the pages of the *Colored American* without Cornish's permission to accuse a black New York City landlord of slave trading. A resulting lawsuit for libel threatened the financial viability of the newspaper. Cornish blamed Ruggles for the incident, which badly divided the local antislavery community. In 1840 he forced Ruggles to resign as head of the New York State Vigilance Committee.

In the late 1830s and 1840s Cornish took a number of controversial positions. He objected to William Lloyd Garrison's anticlerical tone and left the American Anti-Slavery Society for the American and Foreign Anti-Slavery

Society. Later he left the AFASS over its support of the Liberty Party because it would not back black political candidates. In 1839 he opposed the formation of an antislavery political party. In the late 1840s he disagreed strongly with the development of exclusively black conventions and political activity because he did not believe in racially separate movements. He disdained the Pan-African movement of the 1850s because of its support of colonization.

Cornish's Presbyterian affiliation caused problems for him. As the denomination grew more conservative and identified with colonization projects, Cornish sought refuge as an activist minister. In addition to his tenure at New Demeter, Cornish was pastor of Gloucester's Philadelphia church from 1831 to 1832 and in 1843 ministered to the activist Negro Presbyterian Church in Newark. In 1845 he organized and pastored the Emmanuel Church in New York City, where he remained until 1847.

In his personal life, Cornish suffered discrimination and tragedy. Although he regarded New York City as his home, racial discrimination against his children forced his departure in 1838 for Belleville, New Jersey, and then in 1840 for Newark. Cornish outlived his wife and three of his children. In 1855 he moved to Brooklyn, where he died. Despite his individualized politics and membership in a conservative denomination, Cornish sustained black abolitionist institutions while pioneering black journalism.

FURTHER READING

Cornish's papers can be found in C. Peter Ripley et al., eds., *The Black Abolitionist Papers*, microfilm ed. (1981–1983).

Pease, Jane H., and William H. Pease. *Bound with Them in Chains: A Biographical History of the Antislavery Movement* (1972).
Swift, David Everett. *Black Prophets of Justice: Activist Clergy before the Civil War* (1989).
—GRAHAM RUSSELL HODGES

COSBY, BILL

(12 July 1937–), actor and comedian, was born William Henry Cosby Jr. in Germantown, Philadelphia, the son of William Henry Cosby Sr., a U.S. Navy mess steward, and Anna Pearl Cosby. Many of the vicissitudes of Cosby's childhood in the poverty-stricken Richard Allen housing projects would be transformed later into fodder for his hilarious comedy routines and television shows. As a youngster, Cosby worked many hours shining shoes and performing menial tasks at a local grocery. He attended the Germantown High School for Gifted Students, where he was elected captain of the track and football teams.

At age nineteen, Cosby dropped out of school and enlisted in the U.S. Navy, in which he served for four years (1956–1960). During his stint in the navy, he managed to earn his high school equivalency diploma through correspondence and studied physical therapy. In 1960, with four years of military service under his belt, Cosby received a scholarship to the College of Education at Temple University in Philadelphia, where he majored in physical education. At Temple, Cosby earned a living as a bartender at local nightclubs. Inspired by comedy pioneers like Mel Brooks and Carl Reiner—and having always casually told jokes to friends and teammates—Cosby decided to try his hand as a comedian. In 1962, after he had appeared at various coffeehouses in Philadelphia, the Gaslight Café in New York's Greenwich Village booked Cosby for an engagement. He received a glowing review in the *New York Times*. Encouraged, Cosby began polishing and honing his act with the help of his friend Roy Silver, who would eventually become his manager.

In 1962 Cosby dropped out of school to focus more intensely on the comedy circuit. On 25 January 1964 he married Camille Hanks, and the couple had five children: Erika, Erinn, Ennis, Ensa, and Evin. Cosby made his television debut in 1965 on the *Tonight Show* with Johnny Carson. The appearance brought him headlining engagements at popular nightclubs nationwide, including the Hungry I in San Francisco, Mr. Kelly's in Chicago, the Flamingo in Las Vegas, and Harrah's at Lake Tahoe.

In sharp contrast to the explicit, anti-authoritarian routines of such contemporaries as George Carlin and RICHARD PRYOR, Cosby's comedic style avoided cursing. He gained a reputation for his congenial anecdotes about everyday foibles and family issues. A master storyteller with a strong gift for physical comedy and exaggerated impersonations, Cosby became known as "the Negro comedian who doesn't use racial material" (Cohen, 64). He would record eighteen comedy records over the course of his career, including *Bill Cosby Is a Very Funny Fellow* (1963), *To Russell, My Brother Whom I Slept With* (1968), and *My Father Confused Me, What Should I Do?* (1977). These records captured the spirit of his live comedy routines, selling twelve million copies and, over time, earning him eight Grammy awards.

Cosby's flair for comedy brought him to the attention of the television producer Sheldon Leonard, who cast him, as Alexander Scott, opposite the white actor Robert Culp in the NBC adventure-comedy series *I Spy* (1965). Playing a Temple University graduate and a Rhodes Scholar able to speak seven languages, Cosby became the first black actor to land a continuing role in a network series. He won three Emmy awards during the show's immensely popular three-year run. His national visibility garnered him a weeklong stand-up engagement at the Apollo Theater in Harlem, and in 1969 he took home his fourth Emmy for *The Bill Cosby Special*. A lifelong aficionado of black music and himself a jazz musician, Cosby became the president of the Rhythm and Blues Hall of Fame in 1968.

In the following years Cosby struggled to maintain a hit on network television. He starred as a physical education teacher Chet Kincaid on *The Bill Cosby Show* (1968), which ran to lukewarm reviews for three years. In 1972 Cosby launched a comedy-variety show called *The New Bill Cosby Show*, which lasted only a year, until May 1973. A short-lived sitcom, *Cos* (1976), was excoriated by critics. In 1973 he fared substantially better by creating and providing voice-overs for a cartoon series, *Fat Albert and the Cosby Kids*. Set in an inner city junkyard, the humorous show aimed to teach children creative solutions for everyday problems and ran for nearly eleven years.

In the 1970s Cosby cultivated his interests in education and child psychology to earn his bachelor's degree in Sociology from Temple University and a master's and doctorate in Education from the University of Massachusetts. He made guest appearances on children's television shows, such as *The Electric Company, Captain Kangaroo*, and *Pinwheel*. He launched a film career, starring in movies like *Hickey and Boggs* (1972), *Mother Jugs and Speed* (1976), *California Suite* (1978), and *The Devil and Max Devlin* (1981). Alongside his friend SIDNEY POITIER, Cosby starred in several successful crime-caper films: *Uptown Saturday Night* (1974), *Let's Do It Again* (1975), and *A Piece of the Action* (1977). In 1982 he starred in a feature film version of his comedy act, *Bill Cosby: Himself*.

In 1984 Cosby created the comedy series *The Cosby Show* for NBC. The show followed the life and times of the obstetrician Heathcliff "Cliff" Huxtable; his wife, Claire, a lawyer; and their five children. Buoyed by sharp writing and universal story lines, the show broke all Nielsen records to emerge as the top-rated family show for most of its eight-year run. Winning numerous Emmy awards and NAACP Image awards, *The Cosby Show* helped revitalize the stagnant sitcom genre in the early 1980s.

The success of *The Cosby Show* also triggered long-standing debates about the direction of black representation in the media. Many critics felt that the show's vision of black upward mobility was little more than a fairy tale that misdirected popular attention away from the increasing socioeconomic and political decline of African Americans in the Reagan era. Cosby's stated goal in representing upwardly mobile African Americans was to show that "we have the same kinds of wants and needs as other American families" (Smith, 165).

The Cosby Show received a massive syndication deal in 1988 and is still seen regularly on television. In 1988 Cosby also produced a television spin-off about life in an all-black college, called *A Different World*. Although his feature films during this period, such as *Leonard Part VI* (1988), *Ghost Dad* (1990), and *Meteor Man* (1993), were critically lambasted, Cosby would emerge as a literary powerhouse with successful books on family, aging, and relationships, such as *Fatherhood, Time Flies*, and *Love and Marriage*.

Cosby was recruited in the 1980s as a product spokesman for several major companies, including General Foods and Kodak. Along with his wife, the comedian also emerged as a humanitarian

when he donated $20 million to Spelman College—the largest contribution ever given to a university. Among his other charitable contributions were $1.3 million to be divided among Fisk University in Nashville, Tennessee, Florida A&M, Howard University in Washington, D.C., and Shaw University in Raleigh, North Carolina, as well as $325,000 to Central State University in Wilberforce, Ohio. In the 1990s he became part owner of the New Jersey Nets basketball team. Cosby was drawn into the deal by the team's sponsorship of a trust fund benefiting inner-city youth. One of the highest paid African American performers, Cosby also announced his intention to buy NBC in the 1990s, which did not come to fruition.

Cosby's television ventures in the 1990s pale in comparison to the success of *The Cosby Show*. A remake of the Groucho Marx game show *You Bet Your Life* was a flop in 1992. *The Cosby Mysteries*, patterned after Angela Lansbury's *Murder She Wrote*, received a lukewarm response in 1994. In that same year Cosby appeared in the television movie *I Spy Returns*. Somewhat more successful was *Cosby* in 1996, a sitcom that placed the comedy legend in more familiar environs. Playing a retiree living in Queens, he was reunited with Phylicia Rashad, the actress who had played his wife on *The Cosby Show*. In 1996 Cosby appeared with Robin Williams in the film *Jack*, and in 2000 he produced *Men of Honor*, a movie starring Cuba Gooding Jr. as Carl Brashear, the first African American U.S. Navy diver. Cosby's easy rapport with children came to the fore in two television shows, *Kids Say the Darnedest Things*, which he hosted in 1998, and *Little Bill* (1999), for which he was executive producer.

Cosby's popular image was dented somewhat in the late 1990s, when a woman named Autumn Jackson claimed to be his illegitimate daughter and demanded money from him. Cosby admitted publicly that he had an affair in 1974 with Jackson's mother, Shawn Thompson Upshaw, and that he had been paying her money to remain quiet about the relationship. Nonetheless, the comedian denied paternity—even agreeing during the trial to take a paternity test. Jackson refused. She was later convicted of extortion. Then, in

1997, Cosby's twenty-seven-year-old son, Ennis, part of the inspiration for the character Theo in *The Cosby Show*, was murdered in Los Angeles by a man attempting to rob him. The man was later arrested and convicted.

In 2002 NBC ran a reunion special of *The Cosby Show* that brought the cast together in celebration of the longevity and good humor of a comedy legend. Beyond his well-documented—and much-needed—ability to make people laugh, however, Bill Cosby's greatest legacy may well be in his charitable contributions. In addition to providing several historically black colleges with much needed funds, Cosby and his wife Camille have established one of the world's greatest private collections of African American art. The Cosbys' collection is intended to end the neglect of black artists, including JACOB LAWRENCE, HENRY OSSAWA TANNER, ELIZABETH CATLETT, and AUGUSTA SAVAGE, who were ignored or marginalized in their own time. In 2001 David Driskell, curator of the collection, published *The Other Side of Color: African American Art in the Collection of Camille O. and William H. Cosby, Jr.* (2001).

FURTHER READING

Adler, Bill. *The Cosby Wit: His Life and Humor* (1986).

Cohen, Joel H. *Cool Cos: The Story of Bill Cosby* (1969).

Latham, Caroline. *Bill Cosby for Real* (1985).

Rosenberg, Robert. *Bill Cosby: The Changing Black Image* (1991).

Smith, Ronald L. *Cosby: The Life of a Comedy Legend* (1997).

Discography

The Best of Bill Cosby (Warner Bros. 1798)

More of the Best of Bill Cosby (Warner Bros. 1836)

20th Century Masters: The Millennium Collection: The Best of Bill Cosby (MCA 112610)

—JASON KING

CRAFT, WILLIAM (1824–28 Jan. 1900), and **ELLEN CRAFT** (1826–1891), escaped slaves, abolitionists, teachers, entrepreneurs, and autobiographers, were born into slavery in antebellum central Georgia. William recalled little of his father and mother, who, along with a brother and

Ellen Craft posed as a prosperous southern gentleman to escape north. William Loren Katz Collection

a sister, were sold away "at separate times, to different persons" by his first master, a merchant named Craft (Craft, 8). Ellen was the daughter of Maria, a mixed-race slave, and James Smith, a white planter from Clinton, Georgia. Like her mother, Ellen was raised as a house servant until she was given, at age eleven, as a wedding present to her white half-sister Eliza, the wife of Robert Collins, a wealthy businessman and railroad builder in Macon, Georgia. While Ellen was serving as a lady's maid and seamstress in the Collins mansion, William was brought to Macon by a bank officer named Ira Taylor.

William was much in demand for his carpentry skills, as his first master had apprenticed him to learn this trade. Like other male slaves in urban areas who possessed specialized knowledge, he was "hired out," in this case to work for a white carpenter in town. He waited tables to earn his board and handed over a monthly percentage of his pay to Taylor while pocketing the rest. An accomplished seamstress, Ellen may have saved money from handiwork produced at night after her required duties were done. By the late 1840s both had attained physical mobility, economic self-sufficiency—and for William, a rudimentary reading ability—assets that proved crucial to their success in their escape from slavery.

William and Ellen met around 1846 and quickly fell in love. They agonized, however, over their inability to live together and to procure a Christian marriage. They were equally troubled by the dismal prospects for any children they might have. So long as Ellen remained

enslaved, the Crafts' children would suffer the brutalities of slavery—unrelenting and unrequited toil, crowded and unsanitary living conditions, whippings, perhaps rape by the master, and the auction block. By 1848 the couple had decided to escape to the North.

They strategically planned to make their escape during the Christmas holidays, when it was customary for slaveholders to relax surveillance of their "property," releasing their slaves from work for several days. The vigilance of the "paterollers"—who patrolled the countryside and monitored the activities of bound and free blacks traveling between plantations—also eased during the holidays. Fear of recapture, separation, punishment, and sale, however, must have weighed heavily on the couple, who were well aware of whites' anxieties about unchaperoned blacks. The Crafts' justifiable fears would have been heightened by the tense atmosphere of suspicion that resulted from such slave uprisings as those led by NAT TURNER in Virginia in 1831 and by DENMARK VESEY in Charleston, South Carolina, in 1822.

The Crafts thus decided to increase their prospects for success by using camouflage, a timeworn yet often effective diversion for runaways. Ellen took advantage of her light-skinned complexion by posing as a chronically ill, albeit prosperous, southern gentleman named William Johnson. She cut her hair, put on a suit and spectacles, layered bandages around her face to conceal her beardless chin, hung her arm lifelessly in a sling to avoid having to write, and topped the whole costume with an elegant, status-announcing beaver hat. William was darker in skin

color and facial features, so they devised for him to accompany his "master" as a slave valet. Under the ruse of seeking treatment for "Johnson's" various ailments, the couple conspired to travel to Philadelphia, where slavery was outlawed. After William obtained a pass from his master on the pretext of accompanying Ellen to visit her dying mother, they were ready.

On 20 December 1848, as southern protocol demanded, they boarded separate compartments on the same Macon-to-Savannah railroad that Ellen's current owner had built. On Christmas Day, after a few near exposures and close calls, they arrived in Philadelphia. The Crafts arrived in Boston several weeks later, in January 1849. Unlike other escaped slaves who fled at night following the North Star, lived off berries, and held close to riverbeds and ditches, William and Ellen Craft had traveled openly up the eastern seaboard, tempting fate with overnight stays at hotels swarming with southern planters.

For two years the Crafts were the darlings of northern abolitionists. They settled in Boston, the center of the American antislavery movement, where they lived in the dynamic African American enclave on Beacon Hill. The Crafts became sought-after participants at abolition meetings throughout New England, although in keeping with social convention, Ellen rarely spoke. They were familiar figures at the African Meeting House at Eight Smith Court (known around Boston as "the Black Faneuil Hall"), and at the integrated Charles Street AME Church. William was elected vice president of the League of Freedom, a group organized to protect fugitive slaves. In their private life, the Crafts established a model Victorian household. Possessed of an endearing shyness and delicacy, Ellen remained home but also earned a little "by the needle." White union members blocked William from plying his carpentry trade, but he sustained a modest used furniture business. This must have further romanticized him to Boston abolitionists, who well remembered black abolitionist DAVID WALKER's used clothing business located decades earlier on Brattle Street in Cambridge.

The Crafts were surrounded by a pantheon of notables, including ROBERT HAYDEN, the businessman, former slave, and Underground Railroad conductor who temporarily boarded the couple in his home; WILLIAM WELLS BROWN, the fugitive slave and novelist, who coached the pair for public appearances; the historian WILLIAM COOPER NELL; the lawyer and integration and antislavery activist Robert Morris; and the influential white reformers William Lloyd Garrison and Lydia Maria Child, who covered the couple extensively in their widely circulating newspapers the *Liberator* and the *National Anti-Slavery Standard*. At the peak of the Crafts' celebrity, Robert Hayden opened his home to celebrate at last the couple's Christian marriage.

Passage of the Fugitive Slave Law by Congress in September 1850 revealed the illusory quality of the Crafts' peaceful lives. In the North, fugitive and free blacks alike had always been imperiled by bounty hunters who abducted them back to the prison-house of slavery with impunity. With the Fugitive Slave Law, however, the federal government itself mandated extradition of escaped slaves to their owners, and punished those who harbored runaways with imprisonment and stiff fines. The Reverend Parker's biracial Vigilance Committee posted handbills on 24 April 1851 warning Boston's black citizens to "Keep a Sharp Look Out" for human "HOUNDS" engaged in "KIDNAPPING, CATCHING AND KEEPING SLAVES". The Crafts' owners issued a warrant for their arrest and sent two men, John Hughes and Willis Knight, to confiscate the now-famous couple. Thus began a cat-and-mouse chase during which William and Ellen lived separately and were moved frequently from one safe house to another. Bostonians largely resisted Hughes and Knight, hurling trash and epithets, and even jailing them, and Hughes and Knight eventually quit in fear and exasperation and returned to Georgia. The damage to the Crafts' sense of security was irreparable, however, and in November 1851 they sailed to Liverpool, England, by way of a packet from Halifax, Nova Scotia.

The couple bought a home in 1857 on Cambridge Road in Hammersmith, a suburb west of London, and traveled throughout England and Scotland, lecturing against slavery. The Crafts were active in benevolent groups such as the London Emancipation Society

and the British and Foreign Freedman's Aid Society, and they hobnobbed with transatlantic reformers such as Harriet Martineau and SARAH PARKER REMOND. British abolitionists raised money to enroll them in the experimental Ockham School, which combined manual training with a liberal arts education. At the London World's Fair in 1851, the Crafts staged a silent antislavery protest in the American exhibit and scandalized their former countrymen by walking arm-in-arm with white abolitionists. When a rumor began circulating that Ellen wanted to return to the South, she responded with an open letter in the antislavery press, asserting, "I had much rather starve in England, a free woman, than be a slave for the best man that ever breathed upon the American continent" (*Anti-Slavery Advocate* [Dec. 1852], 22). The culmination of the Crafts' overseas fame was the publication in 1860 of *Running 1,000 Miles for Freedom*, their recollection of bondage, escape, and pursuit by slave catchers in the North. In 1865 some of the proceeds from the book financed bringing Ellen's mother from post–Civil War Georgia to England.

While the Crafts were thankful to their "antislavery friends" for spiriting them to safety in England and for supporting them while they found their bearings, they were determined to be self-reliant. William tried several business schemes and twice sailed to Benin for prolonged visits in unsuccessful moves to end slavery there, to open an African mission school, and to establish trade links with Britain. After the Civil War ended, homesickness and their concern for the newly freed slaves inspired another move. The Crafts returned to the United States with their two youngest children, Ellen and Alfred, and their oldest son, Charles, then a teenager. Their two middle children, William Jr. and Brougham, briefly remained in England for their educations.

After a triumphant reunion with Boston friends in 1869, the Crafts returned to Georgia after nineteen years in exile. After a school they had opened in South Carolina was burned down by the Ku Klux Klan, William, in 1871, began raising money from Bostonians for the Woodville Cooperative Farm School, an Ockham-style school and plantation in Ways Station, Georgia, outside Savannah. Five years later after

the Crafts were accused by white neighbors of misspending funds and keeping sloppy records, they lost contributors. William sued for libel in Boston, but lost the case. The school closed in 1878. Ellen, who spent her last years with her daughter in Charleston, South Carolina, died in 1891. She was buried on the grounds of the Woodville Cooperative Farm School. After his wife's death, William struggled to make his mortgage payments amid lowering crop prices and escalating Jim Crow policies. In 1899 the banks repossessed his land and he died a year later in Charleston.

The Crafts' story has been imaginatively used by a number of authors, including their contemporaries William Wells Brown (in *Clotel*, 1853) and Lydia Maria Child (in *The Freedman's Book*, 1865), and Harriet Beecher Stowe, borrowed heavily from the Crafts' saga for plot and characterization in *Uncle Tom's Cabin* (1852). During the Harlem Renaissance, poet and playwright Georgia Douglas Johnson revisited the Crafts' story in her work. The Crafts' descendants, continuing the couple's commitment to racial advancement, became influential leaders and professionals. Many of the Boston places frequented by the Crafts have been designated national historic sites on the African American Heritage Trail. In London a plaque commemorates the site where these tireless "campaigners against slavery" once lived, on a street now called "Craft Court."

FURTHER READING

Letters from William and Ellen Craft are housed in the National Archives in Washington, D.C., and in the Boston Public Library's Anti-Slavery Manuscripts Collection.

Craft, William, and Ellen Craft. *Running 1,000 Miles for Freedom: The Narrative of William and Ellen Craft* (1860).

Blackett, R. J. M. *Beating Against the Barriers: The Lives of Six Nineteenth-Century Afro-Americans* (1986).

———. *Building an Antislavery Wall: Black Americans in the Atlantic Abolitionist Movement, 1830–1860* (1983).

McCaskill, Barbara. "'Yours Very Truly': Ellen Craft—The Fugitive as Text and Artifact," *African American Review*, Winter 1994.

Sterling, Dorothy. *Black Foremothers: Three Lives* (1988).

STILL, WILLIAM. *The Underground Rail Road* (1872).

—BARBARA MCCASKILL

CRUMMELL, ALEXANDER

(3 Mar. 1819–10 Sept. 1898), clergyman, activist, and Pan-Africanist, was born in New York City, the son of Charity Hicks, a freeborn woman of Long Island, New York, and Boston Crummell, an African of the Temne people, probably from the region that is now Sierra Leone. Boston Crummell had been captured and brought to the United States as a youth. The circumstances of his emancipation are not clear, but it is said that he simply refused to serve his New York owners any longer after reaching adulthood. Boston Crummell established a small oyster house in the African Quarter of New York. Alexander Crummell received his basic education at the African Free School in Manhattan. In 1835 he traveled to Canaan, New Hampshire, along with his friends Thomas Sidney and HENRY HIGHLAND GARNET, to attend the newly established Noyes Academy, but shortly after their arrival the school was destroyed by local residents angered by its policy of integration. He resumed his education at the Oneida Institute, in upstate New York. Later, rejected by the General Theological Seminary of the Protestant Episcopal Church in New York City for purely racial reasons, Crummell sought out private instruction from sympathetic clergymen in Providence and Boston, attended lectures unofficially at Yale University, and was elevated to the status of deacon in 1842.

Crummell was ordained a priest in 1844, but there were few among the Episcopal clergy who accorded him the respect due his office. As a young pastor in Providence, Rhode Island, during 1841 and 1842, he began to show the stubbornness, pride, and intellectual toughness that were his prime temperamental traits. Sometime in 1841 he married Sarah Mabitt Elston. Their first child was born and died during the scant year the Crummells spent in attempting to develop a congregation in Philadelphia in 1844. They later had at least five children. The young couple moved to New York in 1845 but was continually dogged by poverty, hunger, and racial discrimination.

Crummell had participated in the antislavery movement from the time he was a boy, when he worked in the New York offices of the American Anti-Slavery Society. He was the New England correspondent for the *Colored American* in the early 1840s and participated in the convention movement among black Americans. Crummell belonged to that faction of black activists who identified themselves as "race men," working through separate organizations for the specific interests of people of African descent.

After a fire in 1847 Crummell went to England to raise funds for a new church by lecturing on the antislavery circuit. With the support of distinguished British philanthropists, he established a fund for the church, but he also set up a separate fund to support his apparently long-standing ambition to study at Oxford or Cambridge. Crummell's experiences in England were comparatively pleasant despite poverty, illness, and the minor humiliations and thoughtless condescensions he and his family occasionally experienced. He was admitted to Queens' College, Cambridge, though his studies were disrupted by ill health, the difficult pregnancies of his wife, and the death of one of his children. He was further distracted by his travels on the antislavery circuit, which extended far from Cambridge. While uncompromisingly militant in his opposition to slavery, he did not present himself as an authority on the conditions of the slaves, often preferring to focus his lectures on the problem of "caste" encountered by the free black community.

Crummell was awarded the bachelor's degree by special examination in the spring of 1853. Early that summer, he surprised many of his supporters when he left for Liberia, West Africa, as a missionary under the financial sponsorship of the Protestant Episcopal Church. Crummell's opposition to colonization was well known, but he explained that he wished to bring up his children "amid the political institutions of black men."

Crummell's prickly disposition and contentious temperament were not improved by the rigors of frontier life. He suffered from heart ailments, fevers, varicose veins, and "liver complaint." Nonetheless he demonstrated tremendous energy, often embarking on long treks into the bush, working variously as a farmer, preacher, schoolmaster, politician, and small businessman, and toiling over vitriolic lucubrations regarding his enemies. He quarreled constantly and bitterly with his bishop, John Payne, a white man from Virginia, accusing him of color prejudice and condescension. Payne accused Crummell of conspiring to usurp his authority and of refusing to work with the native population. It is said, however, that Crummell was an effective preacher before native audiences and that, as administrator of the agricultural school at Cape Palmas, he met with remarkable success.

Although Crummell claimed he had no political ambitions, it is clear he hoped to have an influence on the political philosophy and intellectual life of the society. He envisioned a career as a scholar statesman and pinned his hopes on the new college that was to be erected in Monrovia. His cultural ideals and political ideology were revealed in speeches delivered in Liberia over the next decade. "The Relations and Duty of Free Colored Men in America to Africa" (1860) is an excellent illustration of his Christian black nationalist sentiments. Another essay, "The Responsibility of the First Fathers of a Country for Its Future Life and Destiny" (1863), reveals Crummell's vision of himself as a founding father of the republic. Crummell's uplift ideology was consistent with ideas expressed in the Constitution of the African Civilization Society drafted by American black nationalists in 1861 and anticipated the aims of MARCUS GARVEY's Universal Negro Improvement movement of the 1920s.

Crummell's marriage was never a happy one, and he was frequently alienated from his wife and children. At the time of her death in 1878, Sarah was living separately from him in New York. Crummell's dealings with associates, both clerical and lay, went no better than his domestic affairs during these years. He nonetheless continued to produce letters, sermons, and public addresses in a style both graceful and strong, which are among the most polished examples of African American literature in the nineteenth century.

In 1861 and 1862 Crummell toured and lectured widely in the United States on behalf of the American Colonization Society and in support of the nascent Liberia College. Upon his return to Liberia he was appointed to the professorship of English and moral philosophy at Liberia College. Crummell was not happy with the supervisory requirements of a professor's life, and he had differences with the college president, J. J. Roberts. He left the college for several months in 1865, claiming the need to look after the fortunes of his daughters, who were studying at Oberlin College in Ohio, but he also used the occasion to embark on another speaking tour in the United States, and on his return, he was relieved of his professorial duties.

Frustrated in his ambitions, Crummell submitted to the discipline of the church hierarchy and turned his attention to missionary work outside Monrovia. He published occasional letters in the Episcopal journal, *Spirit of Missions*, describing his preaching and travels in the backcountry. Crummell was committed to a policy of educating and intermarrying with the native population. He supported the assimilationist policies of President Edward James Roye, opposing Roberts and the Republican Party, whom he denounced as a "venal mulatto elite" dedicated to keeping the natives in a permanently inferior status. In 1871, when Liberia experienced its first coup, led by the Roberts faction, Roye was assassinated, and Crummell fled the country.

In 1872 Crummell became rector of St. Mary's Church in Washington, D.C. Seven years later he established the congregation of St. Luke's, which he served until his retirement in 1894. During this time, he was often embroiled in ecclesiastical controversies but continued to write on a variety of social and religious issues. His essay, "The Black Woman of the South: Her Neglects and Her Needs" (1883), outlines a program of moral and industrial education for the masses of poor black women to compensate for the ravages of slavery, anticipating the issues addressed by MARY CHURCH TERRELL, president of the National Association of Colored Women. Always an advocate of strong central government in the tradition of Alexander Hamilton and John Jay, he was critical of the democratic principles of Thomas Jefferson. In an undated sermon written in the 1880s, he expressed the opinion that "the nation's existence is endangered by insane political excitements." He believed it was the destiny of African Americans to offer a conservative balance to the radical tendencies of certain European immigrant groups.

Crummell was married in 1880 to Jennie Simpson, who played an active role in his church and social life. After his retirement from St. Luke's, Crummell was granted a lectureship at Howard University. He served as president of the Colored Minister's Union of Washington, D.C., worked actively in the Episcopal Church on behalf of its African American membership, and traveled and lectured widely. His address "The Solution of Problems, the Duty and Destiny of Man" at Wilberforce University in 1895 was a call for ceaseless intellectual struggle. In *The Souls of Black Folk* (1903), W. E. B. DU BOIS recalled the impression Crummell made at Wilberforce: "Instinctively I bowed before this man, as one bows before the prophets of the world. Some seer he seemed, that came not from the crimson Past or the gray To-come, but from the pulsing Now" (216).

In 1897 Crummell founded the American Negro Academy, an institution opposed to the educational policies of BOOKER T. WASHINGTON and committed to the vindication of the African race through scholarly publication. Although Crummell was an advocate of industrial education, he was just as strong a proponent of classical studies, the social sciences, and the liberal arts. The American Negro Academy program reflected Crummell's dedication to the development of independent black institutions, the promotion of stable nuclear families, and the development of individual character.

Crummell remained intellectually active until his death at Red Bank, New Jersey. His essays and addresses provide a unique if somewhat sardonic perspective on nineteenth-century intellectual life. Crummell published three books during his lifetime: *The Future of Africa* (1862), *The Greatness of Christ and Other Sermons* (1882), and *Africa and America* (1891). The best summation of his racial chauvinism is his sermon on "The Destined Superiority of the Negro" (1877). While Crummell contributed substantially to the African American protest tradition, it would diminish the importance of his legacy to view him primarily as a racial protest writer. His writings, for the most part addressed to black audiences, are most often concerned with the relationship of human nature to the concept of authority, the

importance of traditions and institutions to human existence, and the defense of literary culture.

FURTHER READING

Crummell's sermons have been preserved in the collections of the Schomburg Center for Research in Black Culture of the New York Public Library. Collections of his letters are held in the Archives of the Episcopal Church in Austin, Texas, Cuttington University College in Liberia, the Library of Congress, and the Jay Family Papers at Columbia University.

Moses, Wilson J. *Alexander Crummell: A Study of Civilization and Discontent* (1989).
Oldfield, John. *Alexander Crummell and the Creation of an African American Church in Liberia* (1990).
Rigsby, Gregory. *Alexander Crummell: Pioneer in Nineteenth-Century Pan-African Thought* (1987).

Obituary: *Colored American*, 24 Sept. 1898.
—WILSON J. MOSES

CRUMPLER, REBECCA DAVIS LEE (8 Feb. 1831–9 Mar. 1895), physician, was born in Delaware, the daughter of Absolum Davis and Matilda Webber. Little is known of her early life, except that she was raised in Pennsylvania by an aunt who was often sought out by sick neighbors and whose kind attention to the sufferings of others had a great impact on her appreciative and impressionable niece. By 1852 Crumpler had moved to Charlestown, Massachusetts (near Cambridge), and for the proceeding eight years worked as a nurse for various doctors there. Her lack of formal training did not distinguish her from other nurses at the time, as the first U.S. school for nurses did not open until 1873. In 1860, bearing letters of recommendation from her physician-employers, Crumpler sought admittance to the MD program at New England Female Medical College (NEFMC). The first black medical school in the United States would not open until 1868, and in antebellum America medical school administrators routinely denied entrance to blacks, both male and female. Yet the trustees of New England Female Medical College admitted Crumpler to their four-year medical curriculum in 1860.

In 1860 only about 300 of the 54,543 physicians in the United States were women with medical degrees. None were black women. American physicians were only gradually finding medical degrees necessary to their work; many still trained in apprenticeships, and most states had no licensing requirements. No records remain of Crumpler's first three years at NEFMC or of the struggles she may have endured to gain admittance or to remain enrolled. Her later writings give no indication that she was aware of her status as the first black woman MD in the United States; indeed, until the late twentieth century, scholars had assigned that distinction to REBECCA COLE, who received her degree from the Woman's Medical College of Pennsylvania in 1867, three years behind Crumpler. It seems likely that Crumpler attended medical school less to enable her to practice as a physician than to improve her nursing skills. She would later argue, for example, that "woman should study the mechanism of the human structure...before assuming the office of nurse" (Crumpler, 3).

On 24 February 1864 Crumpler and her two white classmates, Mary Lockwood Allen and Elizabeth Kimball, came before the four faculty members to undergo their final, oral examinations. Each candidate had had at least three years of preparatory coursework, written a thesis, and paid her graduation fees, all standard for the time. At the conclusion of the exam, the faculty voted to recommend Crumpler and her two classmates to the board of trustees, but they recorded some hesitation with regard to Crumpler's recommendation. "Deficiencies" in Crumpler's education and what the faculty regarded as her "slow progress" in medical school led the faculty to note that "*some* of us have hesitated very seriously in recommending her." In spite of their reservations, the faculty deferred to "the wishes of the Trustees & the present state of public feeling," suggesting that the faculty had felt pressured to pass Crumpler. The minutes of that meeting offer no further explanation. It is possible that the doctors for whom Crumpler had worked before entering medical school had put pressure on the faculty. Nevertheless, on 1 March the trustees conferred the "Doctress of Medicine" degree upon Crumpler, whom the trustees identified as "Mrs. Rebecca Lee, negress." According to NEFMC

statistics, in this period only about 35 percent of all women who attended the college completed the degree program. With Crumpler's graduation, the number of NEFMC graduates totaled forty-eight women. The college would close in 1873 without graduating another black woman. At around the time of her graduation she married Arthur Crumpler, but further details about him or their marriage are unknown except that Arthur outlived Rebecca.

Crumpler remained in Boston after graduation to practice and for a time sought additional training at an unspecified location in the "British Dominion." She specialized in caring for women and children, particularly poor ones. At the end of the Civil War she moved to Richmond, Virginia, to do what she considered "real missionary work," treating black patients through an arrangement with the Freedmen's Bureau (Crumpler, 3). Many southern blacks, particularly former slaves, found themselves without medical care after leaving the plantation. The resulting need led Crumpler and other black physicians to offer such care; it also encouraged many more blacks to seek formal medical training. White missionary groups as well as black community groups were instrumental in founding, in the late nineteenth century, the first black medical schools in the United States. Yet despite the need for them, black practitioners were not usually welcome in the postwar south. There is some indication that Crumpler herself was not well received in Richmond. One source suggests that "men doctors snubbed her, druggists balked at filling her prescriptions, and some people wisecracked that the M.D. behind her name stood for nothing more than 'Mule Driver' " ("Outstanding Women Doctors," *Ebony*, May 1964, 68).

By 1869 Crumpler had returned to Boston, where she practiced with "renewed vigor," perhaps because she felt more at home in the community where she had been trained. She lived, for a time at least, at 67 Joy Street on Beacon Hill, then a predominantly black neighborhood. By 1880 she and her husband had moved to Hyde Park, Massachusetts, where the residents apparently were less in need of her services. She appears not to have been in active practice in 1883, the year she

published *A Book of Medical Discourses* to advise women on medical care for themselves and their children. That she dedicated the volume to mothers and nurses seems a further indication that she viewed her medical training primarily as preparation for her nursing work. According to her death certificate, she died in Fairview, Massachusetts, still a resident of Hyde Park. Although much of Rebecca Lee Crumpler's life remains hidden, and in spite of her exclusion from most histories of American medicine, many have drawn inspiration from her achievements, as evidenced by the name of one of the first medical societies for black women: the Rebecca Lee Society.

FURTHER READING

Records of Crumpler's education at NEFMC are held at the Boston University Archives. A meager bit of information on her is available at the Archives and Special Collections on Women in Medicine at the Medical College of Pennsylvania, gathered as part of the Black Women Physicians Project.

Crumpler, Rebecca. *A Book of Medical Discourses in Two Parts* (1883).
Wells, Susan. *Out of the Dead House: Nineteenth-Century Women Physicians and the Writing of Medicine* (2001).
—SARAH K. A. PFATTEICHER

CUFFE, PAUL
(17 Jan. 1759–7 Sept. 1817), Atlantic trader and early African colonizationist, was born on Cuttyhunk Island off southern Massachusetts, one of ten children of Kofi (later Cuffe) Slocum, a freed slave originally from West Africa's Gold Coast, and Ruth Moses Slocum, a Wampanoag Native American, both farmers. Kofi Slocum's Quaker master freed him in the mid-1740s and, although he was excluded by race from membership in the Society of Friends, Kofi and Ruth Slocum lived by Quaker principles—hard work, frugality, and honesty. This diligence paid off in the 1766 purchase of a 116-acre farm in Dartmouth, Massachusetts, on Buzzard's Bay. At his death in 1772 Kofi bequeathed the farm to his sons Paul and John.

Taking his father's African name, Cuffe, and respecting his dual (Native American and African American) identity,

Engraved in 1812, this silhouette of Paul Cuffe Sr. and his brig, Traveler, commemorates the voyage he and a crew of nine black sailors made to Sierra Leone seeking land where American blacks could be repatriated. National Portrait Gallery, Smithsonian Institution/Art Resource, NY

the self-educated Cuffe sought his fortune at sea. Whaling was open to men of any race, so Paul worked on Atlantic whalers during his adolescent years. From this, he turned to maritime trading and, during the American Revolution, he was briefly jailed for running the British blockade of the colonies. When Massachusetts passed new tax levies in 1780, Cuffe joined his brother and five other Dartmouth free blacks in a petition protesting their "having No vote or Influence in the Election with those that tax us" because of being "Chiefly of the African Extraction" (Thomas, 9–10). He was jailed again, but his persistence brought reduction of the Cuffe brothers' tax debt in 1781. Two years later Cuffe married Alice Pequit, a Pequot Indian from Martha's Vineyard; by the end of the century the couple had seven children. He built a school to insure that racial discrimination would not deny his children and others a formal education.

Through the 1790s and into the 1800s Cuffe invested in a gristmill and store but he amassed his considerable wealth through maritime ventures. He worked closely with the Rotch family of New Bedford, Massachusetts, owners of a bank and financiers of whaling operations; he bought and built ships, developing his own maritime enterprise that involved trading the length of the U.S. Atlantic coast, with trips to the Caribbean and Europe; and he developed contacts around the Atlantic rim. For business partners as well as crew, he preferred his extended family of blacks and Native Americans.

Cuffe became aware of African colonization through the intellectual circles he encountered during his travels along the Atlantic coast. Since 1787 British philanthropists had been working to build a settlement of former slaves in Sierra Leone, on Africa's west coast, and British and American acts to end Atlantic slave trading in 1808 focused greater attention on the effort. Cuffe grew to share a belief with philanthropists on both sides of the Atlantic that slave trading had damaged Africa's moral foundation, but that African American colonists could bring Christianity to "uplift" African populations and in time replace the trade in humans with a commerce lucrative to the colonists and their supporters in the United States and Great Britain. He thus developed a plan to transport moral, religious, and industrious blacks across the Atlantic to begin the process of development while he worked to persuade people in the United States to support the effort.

To test the feasibility of such an effort, early in 1811 Cuffe loaded his brig, Traveller, with merchandise from Philadelphia and sailed to Freetown, Sierra Leone, his first voyage to Africa. Although English merchants profiting from the trade with Sierra Leone disapproved of Cuffe's intervention and worked against his designs, he ended his visit confident that African Americans could establish a prosperous colony in Africa. After venturing to Liverpool to gain British support for his "civilizing mission," Cuffe returned to Freetown. Late in 1811 he founded the Friendly Society of Sierra Leone, a cooperative black organization intended to encourage "the Black Settlers of Sierra Leone, and the Natives of Africa generally, in the Cultivation of their Soil, by the Sale of their Produce" (Harris, 55). Black colonists, English philanthropists, and the British government voiced approval.

Cuffe hoped to send at least one vessel each year to Sierra Leone, transporting African American settlers and goods to the colony and returning with marketable African products. As he talked about the venture in the United States, he stimulated black feelings of Pan-Africanism and brought new energy to African American thinking on emigration. The timing was not good, however. Because war with Great Britain was imminent, the U.S. House of Representatives refused Cuffe permission to trade with the British colony. He was forced to wait out the War of 1812, tending to family, business, and religious matters while urging the government to end the war and open trade. Once the war ended, Cuffe put his plans into action. On 10 December 1815 he sailed for Africa's west coast on the Traveller with a commercial cargo and thirty-eight African Americans, twenty of them children, intent on making a new life in Sierra Leone. This constituted the first, black-initiated "back to Africa" effort in U.S. history.

Cuffe failed to profit from the venture, but he obtained land for the settlers, and his enthusiasm for colonization grew. With racial tensions rising in the United States, as poor whites reacted to competition from growing numbers of free blacks, Cuffe believed still more strongly that only in Africa, away from white animosity, could African Americans "rise to be a people" (Thomas, 119). He soon was pressing for the United States to free its slaves and then colonize them on land they could own in Africa. It was an expensive proposition that, in the end, neither free blacks nor Cuffe and his supporters could finance. Ironically, as Cuffe's enthusiasm for colonization was growing, so was that of some white Americans, many with less philanthropic motives. Their new American Colonization Society, with government backing, would establish in 1821 the West African settlement for American free blacks that eventually would become the nation of Liberia. Cuffe did not live to witness that effort. In 1817, after a period of deteriorating health, he died at his Massachusetts farm.

W. E. B. Du Bois and Marcus Garvey are considered among the major advocates of Pan-Africanist thinking in the United States for their early-twentieth-century recognition of the transatlantic plight of persons of African descent. A full century earlier, Paul Cuffe had courageously advocated this position and had taken the first concrete steps towards its realization. For this reason,

Cuffe should be recognized as one of the fathers of American Pan-Africanism and one of the most successful black entrepreneurs of his generation.

FURTHER READING

Most of Paul Cuffe's letters and logs are housed in the New Bedford, Massachusetts, Free Public Library and the Old Darmouth (Massachusetts) Historical Society.

Harris, Sheldon H. *Paul Cuffe: Black America and the African Return* (1972).
Thomas, Lamont D. *Rise to Be a People: A Biography of Paul Cuffe* (1986).
Wiggins, Rosalind Cobb, ed. *Captain Paul Cuffe's Logs and Letters, 1808–1817: A Black Quaker's "Voice from Within the Veil"* (1996).

—DONALD R. WRIGHT

CULLEN, COUNTÉE

(30 May 1903?–9 Jan. 1946), poet and playwright, was the son of Elizabeth Thomas Lucas. The name of his father

Countée Cullen called upon African American writers to create a representative race literature, but not be restricted to racial themes. Photographed by Carl Van Vechten, 1941. Library of Congress

is not known. The place of his birth has been variously cited as Louisville, Kentucky, New York City, and Baltimore, Maryland. Although in later years Cullen claimed to have been born in New York City, it probably was Louisville, which he consistently named as his birthplace in his youth and which he wrote on his registration form for New York University. His mother died in Louisville in 1940.

In 1916 Cullen was enrolled in Public School Number 27 in the Bronx, New York, under the name of Countee L. Porter, with no accent on the first "e." At that time he was living with Amanda Porter, who generally is assumed to have been his grandmother. Shortly after she died in October 1917, Countee went to live with the Reverend Frederick Asbury Cullen, pastor of Salem Methodist Episcopal Church in Harlem, and his wife, the former Carolyn Belle Mitchell. Countee was never formally adopted by the Cullens, but he later claimed them as his natural parents and in 1918 assumed the name Countée P. (Porter) Cullen. In 1925 he dropped the middle initial.

Cullen was an outstanding student in every school he attended. He entered the respected, almost exclusively white, Dewitt Clinton High School for boys in Manhattan in 1918. He became a member of the Arista honor society, and in his senior year he received the Magpie Cup in recognition of his achievements. He served as vice president of the senior class and was associate editor of the 1921 *Magpie*, the school's literary magazine, and editor of the *Clinton News*. He won an oratorical contest sponsored by the film actor Douglas Fairbanks and served as treasurer of the Inter-High School Poetry Society and as chairperson of the Senior Publications Committee. His poetry appeared regularly in school publications and he received wider public recognition in 1921 when his poem, "I Have a Rendezvous with Life," won first prize in a citywide contest sponsored by the Empire Federation of Women's Clubs. At New York University, which Cullen attended on a New York State Regents scholarship, he was elected to Phi Beta Kappa in his junior year and received a bachelor's degree in 1925. His poems were published frequently in the school magazine, *The Arch*, of which he eventually became poetry editor. In 1926 he received a master's degree from

Harvard University and won the *Crisis* magazine award in poetry.

When Cullen's first collection of poetry, *Color*, was published in 1925 during his senior year at New York University, he had already achieved national fame. His poems had been published in *Bookman, American Mercury, Harper's, Century, Nation, Poetry*, the *Crisis*, the *Messenger, Palms*, and *Opportunity*. He had won second prize in 1923 in the Witter Bynner Undergraduate Poetry Contest sponsored by the Poetry Society of America. He placed second in that contest again in 1924 but won first prize in 1925, when he also won the John Reed Memorial Prize awarded by *Poetry* magazine.

Color received universal critical acclaim. ALAIN LOCKE wrote in *Opportunity*: "Ladies and Gentlemen! A genius! Posterity will laugh at us if we do not proclaim him now. COLOR transcends all of the limiting qualifications that might be brought forward if it were merely a work of talent" (Jan. 1926). The volume contains epitaphs, only two of which could be considered racial; love poems; and poems on other traditional subjects. But the significant theme—as the title implies—was race, and it was the poems dealing with racial subjects that captured the attention of the critics. Cullen was praised for portraying the experience of African Americans in the vocabulary and poetic forms of the classical tradition but with a personal intimacy. His second volume of poetry, *Copper Sun*, published in 1927 also by Harper and Brothers (the publisher of all his books), won first prize in literature from the Harmon Foundation. There are fewer racial poems in this collection than in *Color*; however, they express an anger that was not so pronounced in the earlier volume. The majority of the poems in *Copper Sun* deal with life and love and other traditional themes of nineteenth-century poetry.

Cullen edited the October 1926 special issue of *Palms* devoted to African American poets, and he collected and edited *Caroling Dusk* in 1927, an anthology of poetry by African Americans. Cullen was by this time generally recognized by critics and the public as the leading literary figure of the Harlem Renaissance. Gerald Early in *My Soul's High Song* (1991) said, "He was, indeed, a boy wonder, a young handsome black Ariel ascending, a boyish, brown-skinned titan who, in the early and mid-twenties, embodied many of the hopes, aspirations, and maturing expressive possibilities of his people."

Cullen said that he wanted to be known as a poet, not a "Negro poet." This did not affect his popularity, although some Harlem Renaissance writers, including LANGSTON HUGHES, interpreted this to mean that he wanted to deny his race, an interpretation endorsed by some later scholars. A reading of his poetry reveals this view to be unfounded. In fact his major poems, and most of those still being printed in anthologies, have racial themes. Cullen expounded his view in the *Brooklyn Eagle* (10 Feb. 1924):

If I am going to be a poet at all, I am going to be POET and not NEGRO POET. This is what has hindered the development of artists among us. Their one note has been the concern with their race. That is all very well, none of us can get away from it. I cannot at times. You will see it in my verse. The consciousness of this is too poignant at times. I cannot escape it. But what I mean is this: I shall not write of negro subjects for the purpose of propaganda. That is not what a poet is concerned with. Of course, when the emotion rising out of the fact that I am a negro is strong, I express it. But that is another matter.

From 1926 to 1928 Cullen was assistant editor to CHARLES S. JOHNSON of *Opportunity* (subtitled "A Journal of Negro Life"), for which he also wrote a feature column, "The Dark Tower." On the one hand, in his reviews and commentaries, he called upon African American writers to create a representative and respectable race literature, and on the other insisted that the African American artist should not be bound by race or restricted to racial themes.

The year 1928 was a watershed for Cullen. He received a Guggenheim Fellowship to study in Paris, the third volume of his poetry, *The Ballad of a Brown Girl*, was published, and, after a long courtship, he married Nina Yolande Du Bois. Her father, W. E. B. DU BOIS, the exponent of the "Talented Tenth" concept, rejoiced at bringing the young genius into his family. The wedding, performed by Cullen's foster father, was the social event of the decade in Harlem. After a brief honeymoon in Philadelphia, Cullen left for Paris and was soon joined by his bride. The couple experienced difficulties from the beginning. Finally, after informing her father that Cullen had confessed that he was sexually attracted to men, Nina Yolande sued for divorce, which was obtained in Paris in 1930.

Cullen continued to write and publish after 1928, but his works were no longer universally acclaimed. *The Black Christ and Other Poems*, completed under the Guggenheim Fellowship, was published in 1929 while he was abroad. His only novel, *One Way to Heaven*, was published in 1932, and *The Medea and Some Poems* in 1935. He wrote two books for juveniles, *The Lost Zoo* (1940) and *My Lives and How I Lost Them* (1942). His stage adaptation of *One Way to Heaven* was produced by several amateur and professional theater groups but remained one of his several unpublished plays. Critics gave these works mixed reviews at best.

Cullen's reputation as a writer rests on his poetry. His novel is not an important work, and it received little attention from the critics. He rejected so-called jazz and free-style as inappropriate forms of poetic expression. He was a romantic lyric poet and a great admirer of John Keats and Edna St. Vincent Millay. While his arch traditionalism and lack of originality in style had been seen in *Color* as minor flaws, they came to be viewed as major deficiencies in his later works.

Cullen's fall from grace with the critics had little effect on his popularity. He remained much in demand for lectures and readings by both white and black groups. In 1931 alone he read his poetry and lectured in various institutions in seventeen states and Canada. Some of his poems were set to music by Charles Marsh, Virgil Thomson, William Schuman, William Lawrence, Margaret Bonds, and others. However, even though he continued to live with his foster father, royalties and lecture fees were insufficient income for subsistence. He searched for academic positions and was offered professorships at Sam Huston College (named for an Iowa farmer, not the Texas senator), Dillard University, Fisk University, Tougaloo College, and West Virginia State College. There is no clear explanation of why he did not accept any of the positions. In 1932 he became a substitute teacher in New York public schools and became a full-time teacher of English and French at Frederick Douglass Junior High School in 1934, a position he held until his death (caused by complications of high blood pressure) in New York City, and where he taught and inspired the future novelist and essayist JAMES BALDWIN.

Cullen married Ida Mae Roberson in 1940, and they apparently enjoyed a happy married life. Cullen's chief creative interest during the last year of his life was in writing the script for *St. Louis Woman*, a musical based on Arna Bontemps's novel *God Sends Sunday*. With music by Harold Arlen and lyrics by Johnny Mercer, *St. Louis Woman* opened on Broadway on 30 March 1946. Although the production was opposed by WALTER WHITE of the National Association for the Advancement of Colored People and some other civil rights activists as an unfavorable representation of African Americans, it ran for four months and was revived several times by amateurs and one professional group between 1959 and 1980.

On These I Stand, a collection of poems that Cullen had selected as his best, was published posthumously in 1947. The 135th Street Branch of the New York Public Library was named for Cullen in 1951, and a public school in New York City and one in Chicago also bear his name. For a few brief years Cullen was the most celebrated African American writer in the nation and by many accounts is considered one of the major voices of the Harlem Renaissance.

FURTHER READING

Countée Cullen's personal papers are in the Amistad Research Center at Tulane University and the JAMES WELDON JOHNSON Collection in Beinecke Library at Yale University.

Early, Gerald, ed. *My Soul's High Song: The Collected Writings of Countee Cullen, Voice of the Harlem Renaissance* (1991).
Ferguson, Blanche E. *Countee Cullen and the Negro Renaissance* (1966).
Perry, Margaret. *A Bio-Bibliography of Countée P. Cullen, 1903–1946* (1971).
Shucard, Alan R. *Countee Cullen* (1984).

Obituaries: *New York Herald Tribune*, 10 Jan. 1946; *New York Times*, 10 and 12 Jan. 1946; *Negro History Bulletin* 14 (Feb. 1946): 98.

—CLIFTON H. JOHNSON

D

DADDY GRACE. *See* Grace, Charles Emmanuel.

DANDRIDGE, DOROTHY (9 Nov. 1922– 8 Sept. 1965), movie actress and singer, was born Dorothy Jean Dandridge in Cleveland, Ohio, the daughter of Cyril Dandridge, a Baptist minister, and Ruby Jean Butler, a movie and radio comedian. Dorothy, a child entertainer, was in and out of school while her mother directed and choreographed her two children in a sister vaudeville act. The "Wonder Kids" performed in Cleveland's black Baptist churches and toured throughout the South for five years.

In the early 1930s Ruby, whose husband had left her just before Dorothy's birth, moved her family to the Watts section of Los Angeles, California, to further their careers in show business. The Wonder Kids recruited another girl, Etta Jones, and formed a singing group called the Dandridge Sisters. In 1937 the act was sold to Warner Bros. for a movie called *A Day at the Races*. The Dandridge Sisters also made appearances at the Cotton Club in Harlem, New York, and toured with DUKE ELLINGTON, CAB CALLOWAY, and Jimmie Lunceford.

The outbreak of World War II interrupted the Dandridge Sisters' international tour and initiated their demise. Around this time Dorothy Dandridge met Harold Nicholas, who was one of the famous dancing Nicholas Brothers, and in 1942 they were married. In 1945 Dandridge's only child was born, and Harold immediately deserted his family because their child was severely brain damaged. In later years Dandridge teamed up with both Rose Kennedy and Jacqueline Kennedy Onassis in an effort to help the mentally

Dorothy Dandridge, the first black actor nominated for an Academy Award in a starring role, in 1955. Library of Congress

challenged under the auspices of the Joseph P. Kennedy Jr. Foundation.

Dandridge's first important film role was Queen of the Jungle in Columbia Pictures' *Tarzan's Peril* (1951). Dore Schary of MGM then hired Dandridge to play a compassionate black schoolteacher in *Bright Road*, costarring HARRY BELAFONTE. During this time, Dandridge began her nightclub and concert engagements. In 1951 bandleader Desi Arnaz agreed to temporarily employ Dandridge in his act at the Hollywood Mocombo. This appearance

compelled Maurice Winnick, a British theatrical impresario, to offer Dandridge an engagement at the Cafe de Paris in London. The next year the Chase Hotel in St. Louis, Missouri, which had never employed a black performer to entertain in its dining room, booked her for an engagement. Dandridge informed the management that she would not perform unless blacks were allowed to obtain reservations and be permitted to use the main entrance. These conditions were agreed upon by the hotel management, and a table was reserved for black members of the National Association for the Advancement of Colored People on opening night.

The most memorable and award-winning screen performance for Dandridge was in the title role of *Carmen Jones* (1954) produced by Otto Preminger in association with Twentieth Century–Fox. *Carmen Jones* costarred PEARL BAILEY and Belafonte. In 1955 Dandridge became the first black actor to be nominated for an Oscar in a starring role and the first black woman to take part in the Academy Awards show, presenting the Oscar for film editing. Dandridge also won a Golden Globe Award of Merit for Outstanding Achievement for the best performance by an actress in 1959. Dandridge's international acclaim led Twentieth Century–Fox to offer her a three-year contract that was the first and most ambitious offer given to a black performer by that studio. During the same year, Dandridge became the first black headliner to appear at the Waldorf-Astoria Hotel in New York City.

During the 1950s Dandridge starred in several films for Twentieth Century–Fox, Columbia Pictures, and foreign film companies. *Island in the Sun* (1957), with James Mason, Joan Fontaine, and Belafonte, was Hollywood's first major interracial film and was a box office success. In *Tamango* (1959), Dandridge portrayed an African slave in love with a white ship captain, played by Austrian actor Curt Jurgens. She costarred with SIDNEY POITIER in *Porgy and Bess* (1959). In addition to her film credits, Dandridge appeared on several television shows during the 1950s including "The Mike Douglas Show," "The Steve Allen Show," and "The Ed Sullivan Show." In November 1954 she also appeared on the cover of *Life* magazine, making history as the first black to do so.

In 1959 Dandridge married Jack Dennison (or Denison), a white restaurateur and nightclub owner; the marriage ended in divorce in 1962. In 1961 Dandridge costarred in a film with Trevor Howard, titled *Malaga*. Dandridge's last concert appearances included engagements in Puerto Rico and Tokyo. Her death was reported as the result of acute drug intoxication, an ingestion of the antidepressant

Tofranil, at her apartment in West Hollywood, California.

A retrospective article in the *Los Angeles Herald Examiner* lamented that Dandridge's passing meant "the ceasing of exquisite music...she walked in beauty...regal as a queen." In her lifetime Dandridge was named by a committee of photographers as one of the five most beautiful women in the world. She was an international celebrity who believed in breaking down barriers to achieve racial equality. Dandridge realized that a black male could become a big star without romantic roles, but a sexy black actress like her was limited because the American public was not ready for interracial romance on the screen. On 20 February 1977 Dandridge, the first black leading lady, was posthumously inducted into the Black Filmmakers Hall of Fame at the annual Oscar Micheaux Awards presentation in Oakland, California. Vivian Dandridge, her sister, accepted the award. In December 1983 Belafonte, Poitier, and others petitioned to secure a star on the Hollywood Walk of Fame for Dandridge, a trailblazer for blacks in the American film industry.

FURTHER READING

There is a clippings file in the Billy Rose Theatre Collection, New York Public Library for the Performing Arts, Lincoln Center.

Dandridge, Dorothy, with Earl Conrad. *Everything and Nothing: The Dorothy Dandridge Tragedy* (1970).

Agan, Patrick. *The Decline and Fall of the Love Goddesses* (1979).
Bogle, Donald. *Dorothy Dandridge: A Biography* (1999).
Mills, Earl. *Dorothy Dandridge* (1999).

Obituary: *New York Times*, 8 Sept. 1965.
—SAMUEL CHRISTIAN

DAVIS, ANGELA YVONNE (26 Jan. 1944–), radical activist, scholar, and prison abolitionist, was born in Birmingham, Alabama, to Frank and Sally Davis. Her father, a former teacher, owned a service station, and her mother was a schoolteacher. Both had ties to the NAACP and friends in numerous radical

groups, including the Communist Party. When Angela was four years old, her family moved from a housing project to a white neighborhood across town. The experience of being the only African Americans surrounded by hostile whites taught Davis at a young age the ravages of racism. Indeed, during the mid- to late 1940s, as more black families began moving into the area, white residents responded with violence, and the neighborhood took on the unenviable nickname "Dynamite Hill." Davis's racial consciousness was further sharpened by attending the city's vastly inferior segregated public schools.

As a junior at Birmingham's Parker High School, at the age of fourteen, Davis applied to two programs that could get her out of Alabama: early entrance to Fisk University, where she wanted to pursue a degree in medicine, and a program sponsored by the American Friends Service Committee to attend an integrated high school in the North. After much deliberation and with the encouragement of her parents, she opted for the latter, and in 1959 she moved to New York City. Davis lived with a leftist Episcopalian priest and his wife in Brooklyn and each day went to the Elisabeth Irwin High School on the edge of Greenwich Village. Stimulated intellectually and politically, she read the *Communist Manifesto* for the first time and later recalled that it hit her "like a bolt of lightning" (Davis, 109). During this time Davis also began going to meetings of an organization called Advance, a Marxist-Leninist student group affiliated with the Communist Party, as well as attending the lectures of the historian Herbert Aptheker at the American Institute for Marxist Studies.

Although her interest in radical theory did not wane during her college years at Brandeis University in Waltham, Massachusetts, it was tempered by what she viewed as the complacency of the student body there. One of only three African Americans in her freshman class in the fall of 1961, Davis often felt alienated and alone, but she eventually befriended a handful of international students. In the midst of white middle- and upper-class political apathy, she forged ahead in her own pursuit of knowledge and experience outside the confines of Brandeis. During the summer of 1962 she traveled to Helsinki, Finland, to participate in the Eighth World Festival for Youth and Students. She spent 1963–1964, her junior year, in France and, upon her return, began an intense intellectual relationship with the German-born Marxist philosopher Herbert Marcuse.

After receiving a BA in French Literature in 1965, Davis entered the University of Frankfurt in West Germany to pursue a PhD in Philosophy. During her two years there, she followed a pattern that marked her entire career, combining intensive study with political activism. In Frankfurt, Davis joined numerous socialist student groups and regularly participated in protests and demonstrations. But as she watched, from across the Atlantic, the civil rights movement in the United States take a dramatic turn away from nonviolence and toward black power and black nationalism, she yearned to be involved in what she referred to in her autobiography as the Black Liberation Movement. Davis left West Germany for the University of California, San Diego, where Marcuse was teaching. There she worked with the Black Panther Political Party (which was not affiliated with the Black Panther Party for Self-Defense, led by ELDRIDGE CLEAVER, BOBBY SEALE, and HUEY NEWTON) and a fledgling Los Angeles branch of the Student Nonviolent Coordinating Committee (SNCC). In 1969, however, she left both groups after being frustrated by their ideological infighting, sexism, and anticommunism and officially joined the Communist Party. She became a member of a cell in Los Angeles known as the Che-Lumumba Club (named after Che Guevara, the Latin American revolutionary, and Patrice Lumumba, the radical Congolese independence leader).

Davis's activism made her well known among southern Californian leftists, but she did not achieve national or international attention until the late 1960s, when two events catapulted her into the spotlight. Indeed, they would secure for Davis the near mythic status, depending on one's political perspective, of an iconic hero or the country's most dangerous subversive. The first episode occurred in 1969, when the Board of Regents of the University of California, supported by Governor Ronald Reagan,

fired Davis from her teaching position at University of California at Los Angeles, where she had received a non-tenure-track appointment in the philosophy department while completing her PhD. They cited a 1949 law prohibiting the hiring of Communists in the state university system. After months of legal wrangling, the board finally voted in June 1970 not to extend her appointment to a second year. Davis filed an appeal, but the controversy was soon overshadowed by the defining moment in her life as a political activist, the Soledad Brothers case.

In February 1970 George Jackson, John Clutchette, and Fleeta Drumgo, three African American inmates at the Soledad prison in north-central California, had been indicted for the murder of a white prison guard. The lack of evidence or witnesses to the crime, which had occurred during a melee inside prison walls, led many to believe that this was yet another example of the entrenched racism within the justice system, a perversion of the very system that was designed to protect American citizens, and a frame-up. Angela Davis quickly became a leader in the Soledad Brothers Defense Committee and soon developed a close relationship with Jackson, the most visible of the three, whose letters from prison would be published in 1971. On 7 August 1970, Jackson's younger brother Jonathan entered a courtroom in Marin County, pulled out a machine gun, and allegedly demanded the release of the Soledad Brothers. With the help of three San Quentin inmates who were present in the courtroom, Jackson took the judge and four other people hostage. Before they could get away, guards opened fire; in the ensuing gun battle Jonathan Jackson, two prisoners, and the judge were killed.

Less than ten days later a Marin County judge issued a warrant for the arrest of Angela Davis on one count of murder and five counts of kidnapping. According to the warrant, two of the guns used in the escape attempt were registered to Davis, which made her an accomplice. Thus began a high-profile manhunt, which included Davis's appearance on the FBI's Ten Most Wanted list and a cavalcade of press coverage, in which she was nearly universally described

as a "black militant," "black radical," or "militant black Communist." She was finally caught in a Manhattan Howard Johnson's on 13 October 1970 and imprisoned in a Greenwich Village jail for women. Davis was soon extradited to California, where her trial began in January 1971. Eighteen months later, during which time an international movement to "Free Angela Davis" flourished, she was acquitted on all charges.

Although Angela Davis would never again reach this level of notoriety, she was instantly enshrined in the pantheon of legendary African American freedom fighters, and she continued to wage a political and intellectual battle against all forms of inequality for decades after her imprisonment. In the classroom, as a professor at San Francisco State and, beginning in 1991, the University of California, Santa Cruz; on the campaign trail, as a candidate for vice president on the Communist Party ticket in 1980 and 1984; and on the lecture circuit, as an outspoken critic of the U.S. prison system and its basis and role in the institutional perpetuation of racial and economic inequality, Davis remained a vibrant and vital voice on the political left during a period of ascendancy of conservatism in the United States.

Davis published numerous books and articles, including her own autobiography in 1974 and a study of the interconnectedness of gender, racial, and economic oppression, *Women, Race, & Class*, in 1981. During the 1990s she appeared at rallies and demonstrations across the country, on issues ranging from the Million Man March, to the campaign to free Mumia Abu-Jamal from prison, to the ballot initiative against affirmative action in California. By the early years of the twenty-first century Angela Davis was leading the fight against what she termed the "prison industrial complex," calling for the abolition, rather than merely the reform, of prisons in the United States. Ever a lightning rod for controversy and a voice of true radicalism, this struggle was no less compelling for its unpopularity—something to which Davis had long been accustomed.

FURTHER READING

Davis, Angela. *Angela Davis: An Autobiography* (1974).

Aptheker, Bettina. *Morning Breaks: The Trial of Angela Davis* (1975).

Gates, Henry Louis, ed. *Bearing Witness: Selections from African American Autobiography in the Twentieth Century* (1991).

—STACY BRAUKMAN

DAVIS, BENJAMIN JEFFERSON (8 Sept. 1903–22 Aug. 1964), Communist Party leader, was born in Dawson, Georgia, the son of Benjamin Davis Sr., a publisher and businessman, and Willa Porter. Davis was educated as a secondary-school student at Morehouse in Atlanta. He entered Amherst College in 1922 and graduated in 1925. At Amherst he starred on the football team and pursued lifelong interests in tennis and the violin. He then attended Harvard Law School, from which he graduated in 1928. He was a rarity—an African American from an affluent family in the Deep South; however, his wealth did not spare him the indignities of racial segregation. While still a student at Amherst, he was arrested in Atlanta for sitting in the white section of a trolley car. Only the intervention of his influential father prevented his being jailed. As he noted subsequently, it was the horror of Jim Crow—the complex of racial segregation, lynchings, and police brutality—that pushed him toward the political left.

After graduating from Harvard, Davis was well on his way to becoming a member of the black bourgeoisie. He worked for a period at a black-owned newspaper, the *Baltimore Afro-American*, and in Chicago with W. B. Ziff, who arranged advertising for the black press. He then returned to Georgia, where he passed the bar examination and opened a law practice.

At this point an incident occurred that led to Davis's joining the Communist Party (CP). ANGELO HERNDON, a young Communist in Georgia, was arrested under a slave insurrection statute after leading a militant demonstration demanding relief for the poor. William Patterson, a black lawyer and Communist who led the International Labor Defense, recruited Davis to handle Herndon's case. Through discussions with his client, Davis decided to join the party in 1933.

As Davis was joining the CP, those African Americans who could vote were in the process of making a transition from voting for Republicans to voting for the Democratic party of Franklin D. Roosevelt. The GOP—particularly in the South, where Davis's father was a Republican leader—was pursuing a "lily-white" strategy that involved distancing itself from African Americans, who had been one of its staunchest bases of support; simultaneously, Roosevelt's "New Deal" promised relief from the ravages of the Great Depression.

Davis did not favor the Democrats, because in the South they continued to lift the banner of Jim Crow. His joining the CP was not unusual, given the times: many prominent African American intellectuals of that era—LANGSTON HUGHES and PAUL ROBESON, for example—worked closely with the Communists, not least because theirs was one of the few political parties that stood firmly in favor of racial equality. Moreover, the Soviet Union and the Communist International, which it sponsored—unlike the United States and its European allies—stood firmly in favor of the decolonization of Africa. Davis felt that capitalism was inextricably tied to the slave trade, slavery, and racism itself, and that socialism was the true path to equality.

Davis handled the trial of Herndon, and after the case went to the U.S. Supreme Court, with another lawyer dealing with the appeal, his client was freed. Davis went on to serve as a lawyer in the case of the SCOTTSBORO BOYS, African American youths charged falsely with the rape of two white women. They too were eventually freed because of decisions by the high court—after many years and many appeals—but Alabama then retried and convicted them.

Threats on Davis's life and the CP's desire to provide a more prominent role for him led to his moving to New York City in the mid-1930s. There he worked as journalist and editor with a succession of Communist journals, including the *Harlem Liberator*, the *Negro Liberator*, and the *Daily Worker*. At that last paper, he worked closely with the budding novelist RICHARD WRIGHT, with whom he shared a party cell; in this Communist organizational unit, Davis had the opportunity to comment on and shape some of Wright's earliest writings.

At its zenith during the 1930s, the Communist Party in New York State had about twenty-seven thousand members, of whom about two thousand were African Americans. Davis played a key role in the founding of the National Negro Congress, which had been initiated by the Communists; for a while the NNC included leading members of the National Association for the Advancement of Colored People (NAACP), the labor leader A. PHILIP RANDOLPH, and the Reverend ADAM CLAYTON POWELL JR.

Davis developed a close political relationship with Powell, a New York City councilman. When Powell moved on to represent Harlem in the U.S. House of Representatives, he anointed Davis as his successor. Davis was duly elected in 1943 and received a broad range of support, particularly from noted black artists and athletes such as BILLIE HOLIDAY, LENA HORNE, JOE LOUIS, Teddy Wilson, and COUNT BASIE. He received such support for a number of reasons. There were his qualifications—lawyer, journalist, powerful orator, and organizer. There was also the fact that at this time both the Democrats—who were influenced heavily by white Southerners hostile to desegregation—and the Republicans were not attractive alternatives for African Americans. Moreover, in 1943 the United States was allied with the Soviet Union, which had led to a decline in anticommunism, a tendency that in any event was never strong among African Americans.

On the city council Davis fought for rent control, keeping transit fares low, and raising pay for teachers, among other measures. He received substantial support not only from African Americans but also from many Jewish Americans, who appreciated his support for the formation of the state of Israel and for trade unions. In 1945 he was reelected by an even larger margin of victory. By the time he ran for reelection in 1949, however, the political climate had changed dramatically. The wartime alliance with the USSR had ended, and in its place there was a cold war internationally and a "Red Scare" domestically. Supporting a Communist now carried a heavy political price;

simultaneously, many of Davis's African American supporters were now being wooed by the Democratic administration of President Harry Truman.

During his race for the presidency in 1948, Truman was challenged from the left by Henry Wallace, nominated by the Progressive Party. Because Wallace received the support of such African American luminaries as Paul Robeson and W. E. B. Du Bois, there was fear among some Democrats that Truman's support from black voters would be eroded; in a close race this could mean victory for Republican candidate Thomas Dewey. Furthermore, Truman found it difficult to portray his nation as a paragon of human rights in its cold war struggle with the Soviet Union when blacks were treated like third-class citizens. Those pressures led Truman to put forward a civil rights platform in 1948 that outstripped the efforts of his predecessors in the White House. The Democrats succeeded in helping to undermine electoral support for Wallace and for Davis. Not only was Davis defeated in his race for reelection to the city council in 1949; he was also tried and convicted, along with ten other Communist leaders, of violating the Smith Act, which made the teaching or propagation of Marxism-Leninism a crime. After the U.S. Supreme Court in 1951 upheld these convictions in *Dennis v. United States*, Davis was jailed in federal prison in Terre Haute, Indiana, from 1951 to 1955. While there, he filed suit against prison segregation; *Davis v. Brownell*, coming in the wake of the 1954 High Court decision invalidating racial segregation in schools (*Brown v. Board of Education*), led directly to the curbing of segregation in federal prisons. After his release from prison, Davis married Nina Stamler, who also had ties to the organized left; they had one child, a daughter.

Davis's final years with the CP were filled with tumult. In 1956, in the wake of the Soviet intervention in Hungary, the revelations about Stalin's brutal rule aired at the Twentieth Congress of the Soviet Communist Party, and the Suez War, turmoil erupted in the U.S. party. Davis was a leader of the "hardline" faction that resisted moves toward radical change spearheaded by "reformers." Some among the latter faction wanted the

Communists to merge with other leftist parties and entities and become a "social democratic" organization, akin to the Socialist Party of France; others did not want the Party to be identified so closely with Moscow. There were those who disagreed with Davis's opposition to the actions of Israel, Britain, and France during the Suez War. Some felt that Davis's acceptance of the indictment of Stalin was not sufficiently enthusiastic; still others thought that Davis and his ideological allies should not have backed the Soviet intervention in Hungary. These internal party squabbles were exacerbated by the counterintelligence program of the Federal Bureau of Investigation that was designed, in part, to disrupt the party and ensure that it would play no role in the nascent civil rights movement.

When MARTIN LUTHER KING JR., the Atlanta minister and civil rights activist, was stabbed by a crazed assailant in New York City in 1958, Davis rushed to the hospital and provided blood for him. The Davis-King tie led J. Edgar Hoover to increase the FBI's surveillance of the civil rights movement. But as the civil rights movement was blooming, the Communist Party was weakening. Nevertheless, during the last years of his life Davis became a significant and frequent presence on college campuses, as students resisted bans on Communist speakers by inviting him to lecture. The struggle to invite Communists to speak on campus was a significant factor in generating the student activism of the 1960s, from the City College of New York to the University of California at Berkeley.

By the time Davis died in New York City, the Party was a shadow of its former self. His life showed, however, that African Americans denied equality ineluctably would opt for more radical solutions, and this in turn helped to spur civil rights reforms. African slaves had been an early form of capital and a factor in the evolution of capitalism; that a descendant of African slaves became such a staunch opponent of capitalism was, in that sense, the closing of a historical circle.

FURTHER READING

Davis's papers, including the unexpurgated version of his memoir, are at the Schomburg Center for Research in Black Culture of the New York Public Library.

Davis, Benjamin Jefferson. *Communist Councilman from Harlem: Autobiographical Notes Written in a Federal Penitentiary* (1969).

Foster, William Z. *History of the Communist Party of the United States* (1968).
Herndon, Angelo. *Let Me Live* (1937).
Horne, Gerald. *Black Liberation/Red Scare: Ben Davis and the Communist Party* (1994).

Obituaries: *New York Times*, 24 Aug. 1967; *Worker*, 1 Sept. 1967.

—GERALD HORNE

DAVIS, BENJAMIN O., JR. (18 Dec. 1912–4 July 2002), was born in Washington, D.C., the son of the U.S. army's first black general, BENJAMIN O. DAVIS SR., and his wife, Elnora Dickinson. Davis spent most of his childhood living on different military bases. By the time he entered high school, his family had settled in Cleveland, Ohio, where he attended a predominantly white school. At his high school, he began to prove his leadership ability, winning elections for class president. After high school, he enrolled in Cleveland's Case Western Reserve University and later the University of Chicago, before he was accepted in 1932, through the influence of the congressman OSCAR DEPRIEST, into the United States Military Academy at West Point.

At West Point, which discouraged black cadets from applying at the time, Davis faced a hostile environment and routine exclusion by his peers. His classmates shunned him and only talked to him when it was absolutely necessary. No one roomed with him, and he ate all of his meals in silence. Although he faced less humiliation, perhaps, than the black West Point cadets before him, such as the academy's first black graduate, HENRY O. FLIPPER, Davis remembered his four difficult years at West Point as a time of solitude and loneliness that, in spite of its struggle, prepared him for life in and outside of the military. The anonymously written statement about Davis in the 1936 *Howitzer*, the West Point yearbook, alludes obliquely and evocatively to his experience and presages his later success, "The courage, tenacity, and intelligence with which he conquered a problem

209

Benjamin O. Davis Jr., shown here in training as one of the renowned Tuskegee Airmen, led the first regiment of African American pilots. Library of Congress

incomparably more difficult than Plebe year won for him the sincere admiration of his classmates, and his singleminded determination to continue in his chosen career cannot fail to inspire respect wherever fortune may lead him." His endurance and subsequent success in the military permanently opened the doors of the prestigious military academy to African Americans.

Davis graduated in the top 15 percent of his class, becoming one of the two African American line officers in the U.S. Army. The other was his father. Shortly after his graduation from West Point, Davis married Agatha Scott. Davis was commissioned as a second lieutenant upon graduation and, because of his high class standing, should have been able to choose which branch of the military he wanted to join. But when he applied to be an officer in the Army Air Corps, he was denied. The military was not ready to send a black officer to lead an all-white squadron. Instead, he was assigned to the all-black Twenty-four Infantry Regiment at the segregated Fort Benning Army Base and

charged with a variety of inconsequential duties. He was even barred from the officers club at Fort Benning, an insult he later described as one of the worst he suffered during his service in the military.

In 1940, as the U.S. prepared for World War II, there was growing public support for increased African American participation in the war. In an effort to address those concerns and simultaneously reach out to African American citizens as he prepared for the upcoming election, President Roosevelt promoted Benjamin O. Davis Sr. to brigadier general, the highest post ever held by any African American in the U.S. Army. He also established a training program for black pilots at Tuskegee Institute (now Tuskegee University) in Alabama that prepared African Americans to join the Air Corps on an experimental basis. Davis entered this program with eleven other officers, a group that later attracted national attention and became known in history as the Tuskegee Airmen. During the program, Davis became the first black

officer to fly solo in an army aircraft, and he received his wings in March 1942. About a year later, with the rank of lieutenant colonel, Davis was charged with leading the first African American regiment of pilots, the 99th Pursuit Squadron. Although he and the unit he commanded felt prepared to advance to the frontlines of battle, some senior military officers discouraged the idea of blacks fighting in the war, believing their tactical and judgmental abilities were inferior, and the 99th was assigned routine non-combat missions in North Africa. In Washington hearings, Davis fiercely defended his men before both Pentagon and War Department authorities.

Near the end of 1943, Davis was promoted to colonel and assigned to a larger black unit, the 332nd Fighter Group, commonly called the Red Tails. With the 332nd, Davis arrived in Ramitelli, Italy, in January 1944, where his unit set out to disprove the widely accepted notion that blacks were inferior soldiers and airmen. Upgraded from the P-40 War Hawk aircraft the unit had flown in North Africa to the highly sophisticated P-47 Thunderbolt and P-41 Mustang fighter planes, on 9 June 1944, the unit accomplished its most noted military mission. Escorting B-24 bombers to targets in Munich, Germany, Davis led thirty-nine Thunderbolts in a battle with one hundred German Luftwaffe planes that resulted in the downing of six German planes. Following this action, Davis was awarded the Distinguished Flying Cross for leadership and bravery.

Under the command of Colonel Davis, his squadron carried out more than 15,000 missions, shot down 111 enemy aircraft, and destroyed another 150 on the ground, losing only 66 aircraft of their own. More remarkably, Davis's unit carried out 200 successful escort missions without a single casualty. In a highly classified report issued shortly after the war, U.S. General George Marshall declared that black soldiers were just as capable of fighting, and equally entitled to serve their country, as white soldiers.

After the war, President Truman, impressed and influenced by the shining performance of Davis and his unit, issued Executive Order 9981 requiring the integration of the armed forces.

Davis was appointed to posts at the Pentagon and served again as Chief of Staff in the Korean War, when he led an integrated unit. In 1954 he was promoted to brigadier general and in 1965 earned the three stars of lieutenant general. Davis was the first African American in any branch of the military to climb to that rank. He later served in the Philippines as commander of the Thirteenth Air Force, followed by a position as commander of the United States Strike Command in Florida. He retired in 1970 after leading the Thirteenth Air Force unit in Vietnam. Other military decorations include the Silver Star, Legion of Merit with two oak leaf clusters, the Air Medal with four oak leaf clusters, the Air Force Commendation Medal with two oak leaf clusters, and the Philippine Legion of Honor.

After his retirement from the military, Davis became director of public safety in Cleveland under that city's first black mayor, Carl Stokes, though Davis soon quit because he could not abide the deal-making that occurred in municipal government and his by-the-book military style clashed with Stokes's tolerance for civil disobedience exhibited by some black extremist groups. He later accepted a position with the Department of Transportation as Assistant Secretary of Transportation for Environment and Safety, where he directed the bureau's anti-hijacking and anti-theft initiatives. He was instrumental in passing the 55 miles per hour speed limit set to save lives and gas. In 1998 President Clinton promoted Davis to full general.

Benjamin O. Davis Jr.'s rise to prominence followed in the remarkable path of his father's career accomplishments. But his clear sense of purpose, evidenced by a record of professional advances in spite of blatant racism and legalized segregation, tell the story of a soldier not only inspired by his father's career, but also determined to triumph on his own over all the odds stacked against him. Davis became one of the earliest notably honored African American military officers, breaking down racial barriers with honor, discipline, and an unflinching will.

FURTHER READING

Davis, Benjamin O., Jr. *Benjamin O. Davis, Jr. American: An Autobiography* (2000).

Marvis, B., and Nathan I. Huggins, eds., *Benjamin Davis, Sr. and Benjamin Davis, Jr.: Military Leaders.* (1996).

Obituary: *New York Times*, 7 July 2002.
—TANU T. HENRY

DAVIS, BENJAMIN OLIVER, SR. (28 May 1880–26 Nov. 1970), U.S. Army officer, was born in Washington, D.C., the youngest of three children of Louis Patrick Henry Davis, a messenger for the U.S. Department of the Interior, and Henrietta Stewart, a nurse. Benjamin attended the Lucretia Mott School, one of Washington's few integrated schools, and then the segregated M Street High School. Impressed in his interactions with Civil War veterans and black cavalrymen, Benjamin joined the M Street Cadet Corps, earning a commission in the all-black unit of the National Guard for his senior year.

Although he had taken courses at Howard University during his senior year of high school, and despite his parent's objections, Davis chose a military career over college. He enlisted during the Spanish-American War in 1898 and joined the all-black Eighth U.S. Volunteer Infantry in Chickamauga, Georgia. A year later Davis reenlisted in the regular army. He served with the all-black Ninth Cavalry in Fort Duchesne, Utah, and quickly advanced to sergeant major, the highest rank for an enlisted soldier. In 1901 he underwent two weeks of officers' exams, becoming, along with John E. Green, one of two black candidates to earn a commission at a time when Charles Young (West Point class of 1889) was the only African American officer in the U.S. armed forces. Other than Young, West Point's only other black graduates, HENRY O. FLIPPER (class of 1877) and John Alexander (class of 1887), were, respectively, dishonorably discharged and dead. The next African American to graduate from West Point was Davis's son, in 1936.

General Benjamin O. Davis Sr. surveys operations in France, 1944. © CORBIS

Davis's first service as a commissioned officer was with the Ninth Cavalry in the Philippines, after which he was transferred to the Tenth Cavalry in Fort Washakie, Wyoming. He returned to Washington in 1902 to marry his childhood friend Elnora Dickerson. In 1905, following the birth of the couple's first child, Olive, and his promotion to first lieutenant, Davis was made professor of military science and tactics at Wilberforce College in Ohio. After serving as military attaché to Liberia from 1909 to 1911, Davis was reassigned to the Ninth Cavalry at Fort D. A. Russell, Wyoming. Davis's next detail, patrolling the United States–Mexican border in Arizona, necessitated sending his family to Washington within a year of the birth of his son, BENJAMIN O. DAVIS JR., in 1912. Following his promotion to captain in 1915, Davis returned to Wilberforce and to family life. The reunion, however, was short-lived; Elnora died in 1916 several days after the birth of their third child, Elnora.

When Davis was assigned the command of a supply troop in the Philippines in 1917, he sent his children to live with his parents in Washington. Two years later he married Sadie Overton, a Wilberforce teacher. After World War I, Davis, now a lieutenant colonel, taught at Tuskegee Institute in Alabama from 1920 to 1924. His next assignment was as instructor of the 372nd Infantry of the Ohio National Guard, a newly reorganized all-black unit. After four years, he was again transferred to Wilberforce for a year.

Davis became increasingly frustrated with teaching posts that undervalued his expertise and with assignments incommensurate with his rank. While the army routinely promoted Davis, he was assigned to noncombat positions, where he would not be in command of white personnel. He had spent World War I far away from the action and was repeatedly denied opportunities for more active duty. "I am getting to the point where I am beginning to believe that I've been kept as far in the background as possible," Davis wrote to Sadie in 1920 (Fletcher, 54). Adding to his dissatisfaction was the social ostracism the Davises encountered from other military families. Davis was certainly aware that, in 1920 alone, more

than seventy black World War I veterans had been lynched.

In 1930 Davis was promoted to colonel, becoming not only the highest ranking African American soldier in U.S. history, but—because John Green had retired in 1929—the *only* black officer in the U.S. Army. Despite repeated efforts to land a leadership position, Davis was reassigned to the Tuskegee classroom from 1930 to 1937. Davis's first high-profile appointment as colonel—escorting mothers and widows of slain World War I soldiers to European cemeteries in the summers of 1930 through 1933—was the result of self-promotion. "Let a colored officer," he successfully lobbied, "look after colored gold star mothers.... As you know I have traveled over the battlefields. I have a speaking knowledge of French" (Fletcher, 71). After another brief transfer to Wilberforce, Davis was finally put in charge of troops in 1938, when he was appointed regimental commander and instructor of the all-black 369th National Guard Infantry in New York City. Davis spearheaded the conversion of this service unit to an antiaircraft regiment, a move received by the black community as an indication that blacks could and should serve in all branches of the military.

In October 1940 Davis was promoted to brigadier general, becoming the first African American general. The timing of Davis's appointment, by President Franklin D. Roosevelt, just days before the 1940 presidential election, reflects pressure from African American leaders. When Davis's name did not appear on the list of proposed promotions circulated in September, the African American press responded—"Pres. Appoints 84 Generals, Ignores Col Davis" headlined the *New York Age*.

Roosevelt had signed the Selective Training and Service Act (1940), establishing the first peacetime draft in U.S. history, and although it included an antidiscrimination clause and the potential for expanded roles for African American soldiers, the legislation maintained segregation. Agitation by African American leaders, especially A. PHILIP RANDOLPH, helped secure Davis's promotion and other changes, including the establishment of a flight training program at Tuskegee (launched in January 1941), the appointment of

Judge WILLIAM HENRY HASTIE as civilian aide to the Secretary of War, and the inclusion of an African American on the Selective Service board.

Davis retired in June 1941 but was immediately recalled to active duty and assigned to the Office of the Inspector General in Washington, D.C., as an adviser on racial matters. As was often the case, racial discrimination began close to home. Davis arrived at his new office to find two colonels refusing to make room for his desk. Because there were no facilities for blacks at the state department, Davis ate lunch at his desk while he worked to support the promotion and improve the morale of black soldiers. Davis investigated complaints of racial discrimination, including the assignment of inferior officers to black units, the banning of black soldiers from army base facilities, and incidents of racial violence. Although appointed a member of the War Department's Advisory Committee on Negro Troop Policies in 1942, Davis's recommendations—which included assigning African American officers to command black troops, discontinuing the policy of segregating blood and plasma, gradually removing black soldiers from southern posts, better supervision and racial integration of military police, desegregating base entertainment facilities, and instituting a mandatory course on racial relations and black history—were routinely omitted from final committee reports.

At the end of 1944, in response to a severe shortage of combat soldiers, Davis, then adviser to General Dwight D. Eisenhower, drafted a plan using black soldiers as replacements in all-white units. Although Eisenhower refused Davis's suggestion of assigning soldiers based on "need not color," he allowed black soldiers to be grouped into replacement platoons for white companies. Davis's job included the production of public relations and educational materials related to issues of race, the most significant of which, *The Negro Soldier* (1944), was produced by the U.S. Army film unit run by Frank Capra. This film, which includes references to the history of African American soldiers and prominent blacks, was shown to all incoming soldiers. Davis was instrumental in arranging for the film to be released to the general public and for the production of a sequel, *Teamwork* (1946).

The longer he lived abroad, the more vocal became Davis's opposition to the army's segregationist policies. In a memo dated 9 November 1943, he lamented the difficulties facing the black soldier "in a community that offers him nothing but humiliation and mistreatment.... The Army, by its directives and by actions of commanding officers, has introduced the attitudes of the 'Governors of the six Southern states' in many of the 42 states" (Redstone Arsenal Historical Information papers). Davis was clear in his testimony before a 1945 congressional committee: "Segregation fosters intolerance, suspicion, and friction" (Fletcher, 147). Davis's unprecedented visibility—there was even a story about both Benjamin Sr. and Jr. in *True Comics* in 1945—drew fire from those who criticized what they considered Davis's accommodationist approach to combating disrimination within the army.

In 1945 Davis was awarded the Distinguished Service Medal for his work "on matters pertaining to Negro troops." A year later he was reassigned to the Office of Inspector General and focused on the army's postwar policy regarding black soldiers. The results of integrating the replacement program were encouraging; of the 250 white soldiers queried, 77 percent answered "Yes, have become more favorable towards colored soldiers since having served in the same unit with them" (U.S. Army report, 3 July 1945).

At a ceremony presided over by President Harry S. Truman in the White House Rose Garden, Davis retired on 14 July 1948 after fifty years of service. Twelve days later, President Truman issued Executive Order 9981, which established "equality of treatment and opportunity for all persons in the armed services without regard to race, color, religion or national origin." The last racially segregated unit was abolished in 1954. Davis, who died of leukemia, is buried in Arlington National Cemetery. In 1997 a commemorative U.S. postage stamp was issued in his honor.

FURTHER READING

The papers of Benjamin Oliver Davis Sr. are held by Mrs. James McLendon of Chicago.

Fletcher, Marvin E. *America's First Black General* (1989).

—LISA E. RIVO

DAVIS, MILES (26 May 1926–28 Sept. 1991), trumpeter, band leader, and composer, was born Miles Dewey Davis III in Alton, Illinois, the son of Miles Davis II, a dentist, and Cleota H. Henry, both from Arkansas. When Miles was one year old, his family moved to a multiracial neighborhood in East St. Louis, Illinois, where his father prospered, buying a farm in nearby Millstadt. Young Miles first studied trumpet with Elwood C. Buchanan and Joseph Gustat, the principal trumpeter with the St. Louis Symphony Orchestra, and he soon found work in local dance bands.

Caught up in the new music called bebop, Davis left for New York City after graduation and enrolled in the Juilliard School of Music, where he was exposed to the music of such composers as Hindemith and Stravinsky, and where he studied trumpet with William Vacchiano, principal trumpeter with the New York Philharmonic. Davis's nights were spent in the clubs on Fifty-second Street, where he first saw his heroes, CHARLIE PARKER, BILLIE HOLIDAY, Eddie Davis, and Coleman Hawkins, and soon began to perform with them. At a time when other trumpet players were emulating DIZZY GILLESPIE's bravura runs into the upper register and high-speed improvising, Davis cultivated an elegant soft tone and a deliberative approach. His solos were filled with space—pauses and phrasing that let the rhythm section be heard—and he abandoned the fast vibrato that most trumpet players favored. Such a spare approach led some to hear what he was attempting as amateurish, the efforts of a second-rate musician, but many of his contemporaries appreciated his individuality.

In 1945 Irene Cawthorn, Davis's high school sweetheart, was pregnant with their first child, and she joined him in New York during his second semester at Juilliard. He left school the next fall to join Charlie Parker's quintet, and played and recorded with them off and on for the next few years. When Parker

and Dizzy Gillespie left for the West Coast in 1946, Davis followed them and joined the Benny Carter Orchestra, then went back East with the Billy Eckstine Orchestra, a large bebop band filled with the music's finest players. It was while in the Eckstine Orchestra that Davis first began to use cocaine and heroin.

Now recognized as an innovator in bebop, Davis began to explore other ways of playing, and he made musical change his defining feature. In 1948, with the help of arranger and composer Gil Evans, he withdrew from the heat of bebop to develop the chamberlike music of a nine-piece group. Later dubbed the "Birth of the Cool" band, the group was, paradoxically, modeled on the somber, understated Claude Thornhill Orchestra, a white dance band. Almost immediately afterward, Davis formed a quintet that abandoned the aesthetics of cool and formulated what some call "hard bop," a music that intensified elements of bebop. Almost single-handedly, Davis had set into motion two warring styles that have been the subject of critical debate ever since.

After a trip to Paris in 1949, where he met writers and avant-gardists Boris Vian and Jean Paul Sartre, and fell in

Miles Davis in a pensive moment during a recording session at Fontana Records, c. 1973. © Hulton-Deutsch Collection/CORBIS

love with Juliette Greco, doyenne of the French bohemian world, Davis began making a number of important records in the 1950s with younger innovators such as Sonny Rollins and ART BLAKEY. In 1955 Davis put together a quintet with the innovative saxophonist JOHN COLTRANE, drummer Philly Joe Jones, bassist Paul Chambers, and pianist Red Garland. This popular group produced a series of recordings for Prestige Records, including *Relaxin'* (1956) and *Steamin'* (1956). The quintet's stylish mix of bebop lines and show tunes came to define jazz in the 1950s and in years to come. In a move that paid off handsomely, Davis recorded with this band for Columbia Records while still on contract at Prestige. Columbia released *'Round About Midnight* (1956) as soon as his contract with Prestige had expired.

Columbia had big plans for Davis and promoted him as both a bebopper who had played with Charlie Parker and as a romantic figure who could play for a larger audience. After a few experimental recordings that blended classical and jazz music, released as *The Birth of the Third Stream* (1956), Davis followed with a series of albums that caught the public's fancy. *Miles Ahead* (1957) paired him again with arranger Gil Evans, and extended the Birth of the Cool idea into a larger instrumental setting. *Porgy and Bess* (1958) was next, with Evans's lush settings providing Davis the popular platform he had been seeking. For *Sketches of Spain* (1959–1960), Evans turned to compositions by Joaquim Rodrigo, Manuel de Falla, and Spanish folk melodies, allowing Davis to display the dramatic elements of his playing, and producing a jazz record that simultaneously gestured towards classical, world, and mood music. When the French film director Louis Malle asked Davis to improvise the score for his film *Ascenseur pour l'échafaud* in 1957, the results were so successful that Davis undertook additional film music work, scoring music for *Siesta* (1987), *The Hot Spot* (1990), and most notably *A Tribute to JACK JOHNSON* (1970).

Outside these side projects and recordings with large groups, Davis continued to work nightly with his quintet. In 1958 he added

alto saxophonist Julian "Cannonball" Adderley and pianist Bill Evans to the group, and in 1959 they recorded *Kind of Blue*, a largely improvised album of pieces based on modes rather than chord progressions. This turned out to be Davis's most popular record, and possibly the best-selling jazz record of all time.

Just as Davis had disregarded the conventional wisdom on what jazz should sound like, he also rejected nostalgia, adulation, and the cultivation of fans. Dressed in designer suits, Davis left his *Playboy*-inspired house on New York's Upper West Side and drove to gigs in his Ferrari. Once on the bandstand, he refused to announce songs or introduce musicians, ignored applause, and when not playing, either turned away from the audience or left the stage. By refusing even a smile, Davis gained a certain magisterial distance, an air of nobility that reversed a century of performance haunted by the obsequiousness of minstrelsy. He would soon insist that the white female models who routinely adorned jazz album covers in the 1950s be replaced by black models, and more often than not it was his own face staring emotionless into the camera.

All this was part of what drew crowds to Davis's performances. He gained a sympathetic following among beats and hipsters. His persona and his onstage naturalism made him an exemplar for Method actors like James Dean, Dennis Hopper, and Marlon Brando. The Davis enigma was compounded by his silence about his work, both to the public and to his musicians, whom he seldom rehearsed or instructed about playing. On the rare occasions when Davis did speak, contradictions abounded. He might declare his allegiance to African American culture, and denounce white music, and then hire white musicians or proudly declare that he had learned to phrase on trumpet from listening to Frank Sinatra and Orson Welles. He would praise popular black performers like Sly and the Family Stone and JIMI HENDRIX, but just as quickly announce that he was studying the works of the Polish classical composer Krzysztof Penderecki and planning to record an instrumental version of Puccini's *Tosca*. His political views were complex and contradictory.

Too much the hipster to espouse causes in depth, Davis nonetheless sometimes played for leftist political rallies, and often spoke forcefully on the subject of white control of the entertainment business.

Davis's stylish dress and modish lifestyle gave him a visibility that other jazz musicians never achieved, and made him popular in the world of show-business. He traveled widely, made a great deal of money, and married or lived with a number of women, most of whom were in show business, including dancer Frances Taylor and actress Cicely Tyson. In addition to music, Davis had a number of interests that endlessly fascinated his audience. A friend of the welterweight champion Johnny Bratton, Davis trained as a boxer, and he raised horses, which he entered into competitions. He appeared on screen in the television series *Miami Vice* (1984) and in such films as *Dingo* (1991), and late in life he took up painting, working collaboratively with another painter, in effect improvising collectively.

There were times when the facts of Davis's social life threatened to overwhelm his music. Although he overcame heroin, other addictions plagued him for most of his life and contributed to his ongoing illnesses and physical ailments, including recurring nodes on the larynx (that led to his distinctive growl), diabetes, sickle-cell anemia, heart attacks and strokes, a degenerative hip, gallstones and ulcers, and what was rumored to be AIDS. In 1959 Davis's picture—his head bandaged, blood streaming down his tailored khaki jacket, a policeman leading him by handcuffs—appeared in newspapers. After refusing a policeman's order to move along from in front of New York City's Birdland club, Davis had been beaten over the head with a nightstick. Charges against Davis were ultimately dropped, but the message of the event was clear to many—the beatings received by civil rights demonstrators in the deep South were also a danger in the North, even for the most famous of black Americans.

In the 1960s Davis tried various new combinations of musicians, eventually putting together an exceptional quintet composed of Wayne Shorter on saxophone, Herbie Hancock on piano, Ron Carter on bass, and Tony Williams on drums. This group was abstract and earthy, traditional and free at the same time, and intensely rhythmic and full of melodic invention. Records such as *E.S.P.* (1965), *Miles Smiles* (1966), and *Nefertiti* (1967) redefined what jazz was capable of becoming.

Davis had always forced his audience to catch up with him, but now he went even further, adding electric piano and hinting at rock rhythms and tone color on *Filles de Kilimanjaro* (1968). He followed with *In a Silent Way* (1969), another shift in thinking. *In a Silent Way* was a surprisingly long, soft, and dreamlike work, closer to Ravel than to post-bop or rock, a purely textual piece, more sonic than improvisational. Davis now counted on the editing of producer Teo Macero to shape his work, and the two next recorded *Bitches Brew* (1969–1970), an album whose sound, production methods, cover art, and two-LP length signaled that Miles Davis—and jazz—were in motion again. Most critics and fans heard this music as Davis's foray into a new hybrid jazz-rock, although he saw it as a new way of thinking about improvisation and the role of the studio. Recordings Davis made in the mid-1970s, including *On the Corner* (1972) and *Dark Magus* (1974), were so richly textured with electronics and underpinned by funk rhythms that they became even harder to categorize—Psychedelic jazz? Free rock?

Davis's illnesses and addictions led to a breakdown in 1975, and he withdrew into the darkness of his house for the next four years. With the help of friends and lovers, he began to recover and play again, and in 1979 he formed a series of rock-inflected groups that made a series of uneven records, such as *Star People* (1982–1983) and *You're Under Arrest* (1984–1985). Breaking with Evans and Macero in 1986, Davis began to record the synthesizer-driven albums, like *Tutu* (1986–1987) and *Amandla* (1988–1989), that made him an international superstar. Although these studio recordings show Davis as restrained and often being led through the paces by producers, his live recordings from this period, such as *Live Around the World* (1988–91), were spirited reinventions. His final recordings, including *Miles and Quincy Live at Montreux* (1991), which he recorded with QUINCY JONES, were a

return to his old style. An effort at hip hop (*Doo-Bop*) was not completed before his death in Santa Monica, California, in 1991.

FURTHER READING

Davis, Miles, with Quincy Troupe. *Miles: The Autobiography* (1989).

Carr, Ian. *Miles Davis: The Definitive Biography* (1998).
Chambers, Jack. *Milestones: The Music and Times of Miles Davis* (1998).
Szwed, John. *So What: The Life of Miles Davis* (2002).
Tingen, Paul. *Miles Beyond: The Electric Explorations of Miles Davis, 1967–1991* (2001).

Obituary: *New York Times*, 6 Oct. 1991.

Discography
Lohmann, Jan. *The Sound of Miles Davis: The Discography* (1992).

—JOHN SZWED

DAVIS, OSSIE

(18 Dec. 1917–), writer, actor, and director, was born in Cogdell, Georgia, the oldest of four children of Kince Charles Davis, an herb doctor and Bible scholar, and Laura Cooper. Ossie's mother intended to name him "R.C.," after his paternal grandfather, Raiford Chatman Davis, but when the clerk at Clinch County courthouse thought she said "Ossie," Laura did not argue with him, because he was white.

Ossie was attacked and humiliated while in high school by two white policemen, who took him to their precinct and doused him with cane syrup. Laughing, they gave the teenager several hunks of peanut brittle and released him. He never reported the incident but its memory contributed to his sensibilities and politics. In 1934 Ossie graduated from Center High School in Waycross, Georgia, and even though he received scholarships to attend Savannah State College and Tuskegee Institute he did not have the minimal financial resources to take advantage of them. Instead, he spent a year clerking at his father's pharmacy in Valdosta, Georgia, before hitchhiking to Howard University, in Washington, D.C. Ossie spent the next four years at Howard, but he did not receive a

degree, as he had taken only the classes that appealed to him. However, at Howard, Ossie met the poet and scholar STERLING BROWN, who introduced him to the work of LANGSTON HUGHES and COUNTÉE CULLEN. Brown, Ossie later wrote, showed him that the "interest of my people was at stake, and I could only be a hero by serving their urgent cause. The Struggle opened a new chapter in my imagination" (Davis and Dee, 74–75). ALAIN LOCKE, his Howard theater teacher, began by introducing him to the world of black drama and ended up, according to Ossie, "giving me my life."

Another early influence on Ossie was Eldon Stuart Medas, leader of a West Indian student bull-session group at Howard, who showed Ossie how to love English poets and playwrights and how to use them to win political arguments. As Ossie was preparing to leave Howard in 1939, he attended the 16 April concert given by MARIAN ANDERSON on the steps of the Lincoln Memorial. This event, he later reflected, "married in my mind forever the performing arts as a weapon in the struggle for freedom.... It reminded me that whatever I said and whatever I did as an artist was an integral part of my people's struggle to be free" (Davis and Dee, 86–87).

Davis moved to Harlem at the suggestion of Locke, who recommended that the budding playwright apprentice himself to Dick Campbell, founder and artistic director of the ROSE MCCLENDON Players (RMP). At the RMP, Davis learned the fundamentals of acting and stagecraft and appeared in four plays between 1939 and 1941, including *BOOKER T. WASHINGTON*, a play by William Ashley starring Dooley Wilson. Davis later said of the RMP that "it cultivated and serviced the Harlem Community with high-grade entertainment that gave Negroes a chance to see their own lives...[and gave] Negro actors, stage managers, set designers, and assorted technicians, a chance to learn and practice their craft under the best instruction" (Davis, "The Flight from Broadway," 15).

In 1942 Davis's career was interrupted when he was drafted during World War II; he served as a medic in Liberia until 1945, after which he returned to New York, where the director Herman Shumlin cast him as the lead in Robert Ardrey's play *Jeb*. The drama, the story of a returning African American veteran who faces down the Ku Klux Klan to marry his girlfriend, costarred RUBY DEE. Davis and Dee appeared together again later that year in the national tour of *Anna Lucasta* and in 1948 at the Lyceum Theater in *The Smile of the World*. The couple married in 1948 and had three children: Nora, Guy, and Hasna.

Although Davis performed in fifteen plays between 1948 and 1957—including Marc Connelly's *Green Pastures* (1951) and *Jamaica* (1958) opposite LENA HORNE on Broadway, for which he received a Tony Award nomination—he thought of himself principally as a playwright. Since 1939, however, he had been struggling to complete "Leonidas Is Fallen," the story of a slave hero—modeled after the slave revolt leaders GABRIEL, DENMARK VESEY, and NAT TURNER—who dies fighting for his freedom. Davis hoped to create a "new kind of drama," different from contemporary black musical comedies and adaptations. During this period, Davis attended meetings of the Young Communist League in Harlem, paying close attention to the political speakers but also to the writers, from whom he hoped to find literary, as well as political, solutions. Davis never became a Communist, but he eventually became a playwright, with help from a playwriting class at Columbia University in 1947.

When Davis replaced SIDNEY POITIER opposite Dee in *A Raisin in the Sun*, it encouraged him to finish his play, *Purlie Victorious* (1961), which Davis described as the "adventures of Negro manhood in search of itself in a world for white folks only," that revealed "a world that emasculated me, as it does all Negro men . . . and taught me to gleefully accept that emasculation as the highest honor America could bestow" (Davis, "Purlie Told Me!" 155–156). In 1963 Davis adapted the play into a film, *Gone Are the Days*, in which he and Dee starred. In 1970 he retooled the play as a musical for Broadway, *Purlie*, which was nominated for a Tony Award for Best Musical.

Davis's film and television work began in 1950 with the film *No Way Out*, in which he starred with Dee. Over the next fifty years, working with many of America's best filmmakers

and performers, he appeared in more than one hundred film and television projects, including *The JOE LOUIS Story* (1953); *The Cardinal* (1963), directed by Otto Preminger; *The Hill* (1965), directed by Sidney Lumet; *A Man Called Adam* (1966), featuring SAMMY DAVIS JR., Cicely Tyson, and LOUIS ARMSTRONG; *The Scalphunters* (1968), directed by Sidney Pollock; *Let's Do It Again* (1975), directed by Sidney Poitier and starring Poitier and BILL COSBY; *Harry and Son* (1984), directed by Paul Newman; and *I'm Not Rappaport* (1996), costarring Walter Matthau. Davis has maintained a particularly rich creative relationship with the filmmaker SPIKE LEE, appearing in *School Daze* (1988), *Do the Right Thing* (1989), *Jungle Fever* (1991), *Malcolm X* (1992), and *Get on the Bus* (1996).

In addition to his many television guest appearances, Davis has had recurring roles in a number of television series, including the detective drama *The Outsider* (1967); *B. L. Stryker* (1989–1990), opposite Burt Reynolds; *Evening Shade* (1990–1994); and *The Promised Land* (1996). He has starred in numerous television dramas and miniseries, including many African American–themed works, such as *Roots* (1979), which also featured Dee; *Don't Look Back: The Story of Leroy "SATCHEL" PAIGE* (1981); and *King* (1978), in which he played Martin Luther King Sr. Davis's writing credits include *For Us the Living: The MEDGAR EVERS Story* (1983), which he cowrote with MYRLIE EVERS-WILLIAMS for American Playhouse, and three children's books: *Just like Martin* (1992) about MARTIN LUTHUR KING JR.; *Escape to Freedom: A Play about Young FREDERICK DOUGLASS* (1978), winner of the Jane Addams Children's Book Award and the American Library Association's CORETTA SCOTT KING Award; and *Langston, a Play* (1982).

In 1970 Davis directed his first film, *Cotton Comes to Harlem* (1970), an adaptation of CHESTER HIMES's detective novel about an armed robbery at a Back-to-Africa rally in Harlem. The commercial success of *Cotton*, for which Davis also wrote the screenplay and several songs, paved the way for what became known as the "blaxploitation" films of the 1970s. Although he was wary of many of the blaxploitation films, Davis agreed with the critic

Clayton Riley that they constituted "part of a stage of development for a number of people" (Riley, "On the Film Critic," *Black Creation*, 1972, 15), and he agreed to direct the film adaptation of J. E. Franklin's play *Black Girl* in 1972. Davis chose the project—about a high school dropout who dreams of becoming a ballet dancer but settles for dancing in a bar—in order to demonstrate to Hollywood and to black filmmakers, in particular, that black film could be both entertaining and reflective of the lives of real African Americans. In the early 1970s Davis directed *Kongi's Harvest* (1971), *Gordon's War* (1973), and *Countdown at Kusini* (1976), which he also wrote, and he established the Third World Cinema Corporation, a New York–based production company that trained African Americans and Latinos for film and television production jobs.

In 1980 Davis and Dee founded their own production company, Emmalyn II Productions Company. Together they produced and hosted three seasons of the critically acclaimed PBS television series *With Ossie and Ruby* and three years of the *Ossie Davis and Ruby Dee Story Hour*, a radio broadcast for the National Black Network. The couple has participated, separately and together, in the creation of numerous documentary and nonfiction projects, including *Martin Luther King: The Dream and the Drum*; *Mississippi, America*; and *A Walk through the 20th Century with Bill Moyers* for PBS. In 1998 they cowrote an autobiography, *With Ossie and Ruby: In This Life Together*. In 2002 Davis completed a new play, *A Last Dance for Sybil*, which ran in New York starring Dee.

Davis and Dee's commitment to civil rights and humanitarian causes has been central to their life and work. They have labored to introduce staged productions and readings into schools, unions, community centers, and, especially, black churches, because they were repositories "of all we thought precious and worthy to be passed on to our children" (Davis and Dee, 253). In the 1950s they risked their careers by stridently resisting Senator Joseph McCarthy's blacklisting activities. Highly active and visible during the civil rights movement, they served as masters of ceremonies for the 1963 March on Washington, and in

1964 they helped establish Artists for Freedom, which donated money to civil rights organizations in the name of the four little girls killed in Birmingham, Alabama. Davis's stirring eulogy at the 1965 funeral of MALCOLM X flawlessly articulated black America's loss: "Malcolm had stopped being a 'Negro' years ago. It had become too small, too puny, too weak a word for him. Malcolm was bigger than that. Malcolm had become an Afro-American and he wanted—so desperately—that we, that all his people, would become Afro-Americans too.... Malcolm was our manhood, our living, black manhood! This was his meaning to his people. And, in honoring him, we honor the best in ourselves." Davis and Dee's political work continued unabated over the next decades.

In addition to their many individual honors, Davis and Dee have jointly received the Actors' Equity Association PAUL ROBESON Award (1975), the Academy of Television Arts and Sciences Silver Circle Award (1994), and induction into the NAACP Image Awards Hall of Fame (1989). In 1995 they were awarded the National Medal of Arts by President Bill Clinton, and in 2000 they received the Screen Actors Guild's highest honor, the Life Achievement Award.

FURTHER READING

Davis, Ossie. "Purlie Told Me!," *Freedomways* (Spring 1962).
———. "The Flight from Broadway," *Negro Digest* (April 1966).
Davis, Ossie, and Ruby Dee. *With Ossie and Ruby: In This Life Together* (1998).
—SAMUEL A. HAY

DAVIS, SAMMY, JR.

(8 Dec. 1925–16 May 1990), singer, dancer, and actor, was born in Harlem, New York, the first of two children of Sammy Davis Sr., an African American vaudeville entertainer, and Elvera Sanchez, a Puerto Rican chorus dancer. Sammy's paternal grandmother, "Mama Rosa," raised him until he was three years old, when his father, who had separated from Elvera, took his son with him on the road. Within a few years, the child's role grew from that of a silent prop to that of a show-stealing singer and dancer, the youngest member of the Will Mastin Trio, featuring Sammy Davis Jr.

Fellow performers were the only family Sammy knew, and the world of the theater was the only school he ever attended. He was billed as "Silent Sam, the Dancing Midget" to hide him from truant officers and child labor investigators. After a period during which the group could not find work or shelter, Davis's father thought about returning the boy to his grandmother, only to discover that the young ham had already become addicted to the stage, the spotlight, and the adulation of approving audiences. In retrospect, Davis said he had "no chance to be bricklayer or dentist, dockworker or preacher" (Early, 4). By age seven he had made his film debut in the comedy *Rufus Jones for President* (1933), in which he played the title role of a little boy who falls asleep in the lap of his mother, played by ETHEL WATERS, and dreams that he is elected president of the United States.

During the Depression, Davis traveled on the "Chitlin' Circuit," a network of clubs that hired black acts to fill the time between performances by white headliners. Black entertainers had only a few minutes on stage and were prohibited from speaking directly to the audience; therefore, they often used a rapid variety of singing, dancing, and joking to hold the audience's attention. This eclectic quality came to define Davis's career. He believed it made him a superior entertainer; some critics believe he might have done better to focus on singing or dancing. Thus while Davis mastered several vocal and dance styles, nailed a number of impersonations, and played the drums, trumpet, vibes, and other instruments, he never developed his own style. BILL "BOJANGLES" ROBINSON, STEPIN FETCHIT, MOMS MABLEY, and REDD FOXX were among Davis's early influences, but he made the transition from vaudeville to Vegas, from burlesque to Broadway more easily than any of his predecessors and became one of the first "crossover"

Sammy Davis Jr. with fellow "Rat Pack" members Dean Martin and Frank Sinatra following a Carnegie Hall benefit for MARTIN LUTHER KING JR. in 1961. © Bettmann/CORBIS

African American celebrities in the United States.

Groucho Marx saw Davis perform at the Hillcrest Country Club and said, "This kid's the greatest entertainer," and then turned to Al Jolson, who was seated at his table, and remarked "and this goes for you, too" (Levy, 49). Davis's big break, however, occurred in 1941, when the Will Mastin Trio was performing in Detroit as an opening act for Frank Sinatra. Sinatra was so impressed by the fifteen-year-old entertainer that he used his growing fame to help Davis get some of the recognition and respect he deserved. Later Sinatra, too, would say that Davis was the greatest performer he had ever seen, because he could "do anything except cook spaghetti" (*Boston Globe*, 17 May 1990).

Davis's promising career was briefly interrupted when he was drafted into the U.S. Army, serving from 1943 to 1945. Although his unit at Fort Warren, Wyoming, was integrated, Davis suffered racial discrimination and beatings. After basic training, Davis was placed in Special Services, where he entertained enlisted men along with George M. Cohan. Throughout his life, Davis was determined to use his talent to make audiences love him even if they hated him. For him, performance was not only a way of transcending racial barriers, it was a means of gaining acceptance and distinguishing himself. As he wrote, "If God ever took away my talent I would be a nigger again" (Early, 20–21). Yet he realized that his success was Pyrrhic, that "being a star has made it possible for me to get insulted in places where the average Negro could never hope to go and get insulted" (Curt Schleir, "The Public Acclaim and Private Pain of Sammy Davis Jr.," *Biography*, 4.2 [Feb. 2000], 88).

After leaving the army, Davis made his first recording with Capitol Records and was named Most Outstanding New Personality of 1946 by *Metronome* magazine. The Will Mastin Trio regrouped and began opening for Mickey Rooney in Las Vegas in 1947 and the following year for Frank Sinatra in New York. These engagements led to television appearances on Eddie Cantor's *Colgate Comedy Hour* and the *Ed Sullivan Show*. By the early 1950s Davis had enough clout to force the integration of many of the hotels at which he performed. In 1954 his career could have ended when his car smashed into another vehicle while driving from Las Vegas to California. Davis lost his left eye in the accident, but within ten months he was back on stage performing with an eye patch—and, because of the publicity, he was bigger than ever.

In 1956 Davis played the lead in the Broadway musical *Mr. Wonderful*, in 1958 he appeared opposite EARTHA KITT in the film *Anna Lucasta*, and in 1959 he played Sporting Life in the film version of George Gershwin's *Porgy and Bess*. Beginning with *Ocean's Eleven* (1960), Davis made six films as part of a group of jet-setting actors dubbed the "Rat Pack," including Frank Sinatra, Tony Curtis, Dean Martin, Peter Lawford, and Joey Bishop. During this period, Davis's flashy jewelry, ostentatious dress, and characteristic jive talk made him the epitome of "hip" and, along with MILES DAVIS, the king of the "Cool Cats."

Controversy was an inseparable part of Davis's popularity. In an effort to quell rumors about his relationships with white women, Davis rushed into a marriage with Loray White, an African American dancer, in 1958. The marriage lasted only a few months. His highly publicized conversion to Judaism, which began sincerely with Rabbi Max Nussbaum after his accident and was based on an affinity he felt with the Jewish people, was suspected by some of being an indication of his desire to escape his blackness by assimilating into another culture. His relationship with the black community became more problematic after his 1960 marriage to the Swedish actress May Britt, with whom he had one child, Tracey, and adopted two, Mark and Jeff. Despite the fact that Davis was a strong supporter of the civil rights movement and a generous contributor to black charities—qualities that helped him earn the NAACP's Spingarn Award in 1969—his lifestyle was an easy target for the militants of the 1960s, and his embrace of Republican President Richard M. Nixon in 1972 brought his loyalties into question. Drinking, drug use, and his associations with people in the adult film industry and in satanic cults gave Davis a reputation that he both flaunted and regretted.

Davis was a top draw as a nightclub performer, earning fifteen thousand dollars for a single performance and as much as three million dollars a year, yet he always spent more than he earned. When his accountant expressed concern about his profligate spending, Davis bought him a gold watch with the inscription, "Thanks for the advice." Although he had become a solo act by the 1960s, he continued to share his salary with his father and Will Mastin for many years thereafter. In 1965 he was nominated for a Tony Award for his performance in *Golden Boy*, and in 1966 he briefly hosted his own television program, the *Sammy Davis Jr. Show*. He also appeared as a guest star on such popular shows as *Lawman* (1961), *Batman* (1966), *I Dream of Jeannie* (1967), and *The Mod Squad* (1969–1970). His appearance on *All in the Family* (1972) set a Nielsen ratings record, and on several occasions he was a substitute host on *The Tonight Show*.

In 1970, two years after his divorce from May Britt, Davis married the African American dancer Altovise Gore and adopted another son, Manny. His recording "Candyman" hit the top of the chart in 1972, and other hits, such as "Mr. Bojangles," "That Old Black Magic," and "Birth of the Blues," kept him in constant demand. His activities slowed during the 1980s as Davis struggled with various kidney and liver ailments and a hip replacement. President Ronald Reagan presented him the Gold Medal for Lifetime Achievement from the Kennedy Center for the Performing Arts in 1987.

Davis played his final role, as an aging dancer, in the movie *Tap* (1989), with his protégé Gregory Hines. He died the following year of throat cancer. He left three autobiographies, twenty-three films, and two dozen recordings to entertain future generations.

FURTHER READING

Davis, Sammy, Jr. *Hollywood in a Suitcase* (1980).
———. *Why Me?* (1989).
———. *Yes I Can* (1965).

Early, Gerald. *The Sammy Davis, Jr., Reader* (2001).
Haygood, Wil. *In Black and White: The Life of Sammy Davis, Jr.* (2003).
Levy, Shawn. *Rat Pack Confidential* (1998).

Obituaries: *New York Times*, 17 May 1990; *Rolling Stone*, 28 June 1990; *Ebony*, July 1990.

—SHOLOMO B. LEVY

DAY, WILLIAM HOWARD (16 Oct. 1825–2 Dec. 1900), educator and editor, was born in New York City, the son of John Day, a sailmaker, and Eliza Dixon, a seamstress. J. P. Williston, an inkmaker from Northampton, Massachusetts, first met Day during a visit to a school for black children in New York City. Williston was so impressed with the young student that he persuaded Day's mother to allow him, a white man, to adopt her son. Day spent five years in Northampton, where he attended school and was apprenticed as a printer at the *Hampshire Herald*. Refused admission to Williams College because of his race, Day enrolled at Oberlin College in Ohio (1843–1847). Soon after graduating, he was hired by the *Cleveland True Democrat* as a reporter, compositor, and local editor. He later published and edited the *Aliened American* (1853–1854), which aimed to promote education and defend the rights of African Americans. It was also the mouthpiece of the state's Negro Convention Movement, in which Day was a leading figure. Day married fellow student Lucy Stanton in 1852; one child was born to the marriage.

Five years out of college, Day organized a meeting in Cleveland to honor surviving black veterans of the Revolutionary War and the War of 1812. It was in part a memorial to his father, a sailor in the War of 1812 who had died tragically in 1829, and also partly an expression of Day's conviction that such valor in the defense of the nation was grounds enough to be recognized as citizens. "We ask for liberty; liberty here—liberty on Chalmette Plains—liberty wherever floats the American flag," Day wrote. "We demand for the sons of the men who fought for you, equal privileges" (*Cleveland True Democrat*, 9 Sept. 1852). The struggle for equal rights dominated Day's life.

The failure of his newspaper and increasing discrimination prompted Day and his family to join the growing number of African Americans emigrating to Canada. There he became involved in John Brown's preparations for the 1859 attack on Harpers Ferry, printing Brown's constitution in an isolated shack outside St. Catharines. Day was in Britain raising money for the fugitive slave settlement at Buxton, Ontario, when the attack occurred. He spent the next four years in Britain lecturing against slavery and working with the African Aid Society, an organization formed to support the efforts of MARTIN R. DELANY, HENRY HIGHLAND GARNET, Robert Campbell, and other advocates of African American emigration to the west coast of Africa. By the time of his return to the United States in 1863, Day's marriage had fallen apart because of what he considered to be irreconcilable differences. It is difficult to determine what these differences were, but it is clear that Day's long absences from home must have been a contributing factor. William and Lucy Day were finally divorced in 1872, after years of wrangling. A few months later Day married Georgie Bell of Washington, D.C.; he had no children with his second wife.

After returning to the United States, Day settled in New York City, devoting most of his time to working with the American Freedmen's Friend Society, a black-led freedmen's aid organization, and as lay editor of the *Zion Herald*, the organ of the African Methodist Episcopal Zion Church. In 1867 he was named by the Freedmen's Bureau as superintendent of schools for the freedmen of Maryland and Delaware. Day used this office to promote education, to support the construction of schools, and to work with local associations to increase educational opportunities for the freedmen. In spite of local and state opposition, Day reported significant growth in schools built and in attendance. Day lost his job in 1869 when the Freedmen's Bureau reorganized its local offices.

In 1872 Day moved to Harrisburg, Pennsylvania, after purchasing a local newspaper, *Progress of Liberty*, and changing its name to *Our National Progress*. Published simultaneously in Harrisburg and Philadelphia; Wilmington, Delaware; Camden, New Jersey; and New York City, Day saw the paper as both a regional and a national mouthpiece of African Americans. Despite its wide circulation, the paper ceased publication in 1875 largely on account of difficulties brought on by the economic depression of 1873. Day ran unsuccessfully for the Harrisburg School Board in 1873; five years later he became the first African American to be elected to the board. He remained a member for the rest of the century with the exception of brief periods in the 1880s when he refused renomination. In 1891 the board unanimously elected Day its president, a position he held until 1895. He finally retired from the board in 1899, ending an involvement in education lasting more than fifty years.

Day was a prominent force in central Pennsylvania Republican circles. His active involvement in the 1872 campaign led to his appointment to a clerkship in the state auditor general's office. But frustration with token appointments and the continued corruption of the state Republican machine under Simon Cameron led Day to break with the party in 1878. He temporarily threw his support to the Democrats but was back in the Republican fold in 1881. Although he remained an active supporter of the party, Day never again regained his place of prominence, nor was he, or any other black Pennsylvanian during Day's lifetime, ever nominated to significant office.

After his return from Britain in 1863, Day had become actively involved in the AME Zion Church. His parents' home had served as a meeting place for the fledgling denomination in the 1820s, and Day had been baptized by JAMES VARICK, the first bishop of the church. By 1870 Day was unquestionably the most prominent member of the denomination in Pennsylvania. He was named secretary-general of the national body in 1876 and presiding elder of the Philadelphia and Baltimore Conference in 1885. As elder he supervised a district that included Washington, D.C., and parts of Pennsylvania, Maryland, and Delaware. He was later appointed secretary of the board of bishops.

Day, a contemporary observed, was "one of the grandest and most refined men of this country regardless of race" (*Harrisburg Telegraph*, 14 Apr. 1898). It was a fitting tribute to a man who had spent all of his adult life promoting the cause of freedom and equality in the United States. Day died in Harrisburg as a result of a series of strokes.

FURTHER READING

A few letters from or about Day can be found at the American Missionary Association

Papers, Amistad Research Center, New Orleans; the Anti-Slavery Collection, Cornell University Library; Bureau of Refugees, Freedmen and Abandoned Lands, National Archives; the Leon Gardiner Collection, Pennsylvania Historical Society; the Gerrit Smith Papers, Syracuse University Library; and in *Black Abolitionists Papers, 1830–1865*, microfilm edition, reel 11.

Blackett, R. J. M. *Beating against the Barriers: Biographical Essays in Nineteenth-Century Afro-American History* (1986).
Simmons, William J. *Men of Mark: Eminent, Progressive and Rising* (1887).
Stutler, Boyd B. "John Brown's Constitution," *Lincoln Herald* 50–51 (1948).
Wheeler, B. F. *Cullings from Zion's Poets* (1907).

Obituary: *Harrisburg Telegraph*, 3 Dec. 1900.
—R. J. M. BLACKETT

DEE, RUBY (27 Oct. 1924–), actress and writer, was born Ruby Ann Wallace in Cleveland, Ohio, the third of four children of teenage parents, Gladys Hightower and Edward Nathaniel Wallace, a Pullman car porter. After Gladys ran off to follow a preacher, the couple divorced in 1924, and Edward married Emma Amelia Benson, a former schoolteacher, who lived in New York City. Emma, whom Ruby called "Mother," reared the Wallace children in Harlem, New York, where family lessons included picketing white-owned Harlem businesses that refused to hire African Americans.

Ruby graduated from Hunter College High School in 1939 and entered Hunter College, in New York City. Her professional theater career began in 1940 during her sophomore year, when the writer and director Abram Hill cast her in his social satire, *On Strivers Row* (1940) at the American Negro Theater (ANT), which he had cofounded with FREDERICK DOUGLASS O'NEAL and Austin Briggs-Hall earlier that year. Over the next few years Ruby appeared in five other ANT plays, including Hill's powerful indictment of white racism and exploitation, *Walk Hard* (1944). In 1941 she married Frankie Dee Brown, a midget and well-off liquor salesman, whom she divorced in 1945 because of his obsessive jealousy. Dee's busy personal and professional life took its toll

OSSIE DAVIS *and Ruby Dee starred together in Robert Ardrey's play* Jeb, *about a returning veteran who confronts the Ku Klux Klan, 1946.* Library of Congress

on her academic work. After flunking out of school, she was reinstated and graduated from Hunter in 1944.

Dee made her Broadway debut in the original production of *South Pacific* in 1943 and replaced ALICE CHILDRESS in the Broadway production of *Anna Lucasta* the next year. In 1945 Dee played the female lead in Robert Ardrey's play *Jeb*, the story of a returning African American veteran who faces down the Ku Klux Klan to marry his girlfriend; the part of Jeb was played by OSSIE DAVIS. Davis and Dee appeared together again later that year in the national tour of *Anna Lucasta* and in 1948 at the Lyceum Theater in *The Smile of the World*. The couple married in 1948 and had three children: Nora, Guy, and Hasna.

In 1959 Dee opened in the original cast of LORRAINE HANSBERRY's Broadway play *A Raisin in the Sun*, first opposite SIDNEY POITIER and later opposite her husband. Despite her reservations about the role—"It seemed that I'd been playing that same character, more or less, in almost everything I'd done" (Davis and Dee, 281)—Dee received great notices. In the mid-1960s, when she starred as Kate in *Taming of the Shrew* and Cordelia in *King Lear*, Dee became the first African American woman to play lead roles at the American Shakespeare Festival. During her illustrious theater career, Dee won an Obie Award for playing Lena opposite JAMES EARL JONES in Athol Fugard's off-Broadway play *Boesman and Lena* (1970) and a Drama Desk Award for *Wedding Band* (1973), a play by Alice Childress. Other theatrical highlights include her starring role in the 1988 Broadway comedy *Checkmates* opposite Paul Winfield and the role of Laura in *The Glass Menagerie* at the Arena Stage in Washington, D.C., in 1989.

Like her husband, Dee was committed to increasing the black presence among television and film crews. She had found it particularly ironic that 1950's *No Way Out*, the story of a wounded racist robber who does not want to be treated by a black intern, "deliberately barred [blacks] from participation in this image-making business" (Davis and Dee, 199). In addition to her stage work, Dee began appearing in film in the late 1940s, including *The Fight Never Ends* (1949), with JOE LOUIS playing himself; *The JACKIE ROBINSON Story* (1950), in which she played Rachel Robinson opposite Jackie Robinson playing himself; *Edge of the City* (1957); *St. Louis Blues* (1958), with NAT KING COLE, EARTHA KITT, CAB CALLOWAY, and ELLA FITZGERALD; *A Raisin in the Sun* (1961), reprising her role as Ruth; *The Balcony* (1963); *The Incident* (1967); *Up Tight* (1968), set in a Cleveland slum after the death of MARTIN LUTHER KING JR.; *Buck and the Preacher* (1972), directed by Poitier and costarring HARRY BELAFONTE; *Go Tell It on the Mountain* (1985), based on the book by JAMES BALDWIN; and two SPIKE LEE films, *Do the Right Thing* (1989) and *Jungle Fever* (1991).

For her work on television, Dee has been nominated for an Emmy Award seven times. She won an Emmy for *Decoration Day* (1990) and a Cable ACE Award for her performance in *Long Day's Journey into Night*. She played recurring characters on both *Guiding Light* (1967) and *Peyton Place* (1968–1969) on television and has appeared in such television dramas as *I Know Why the Caged Bird Sings* (1979), adapted from MAYA ANGELOU'S memoir; *To Be Young, Gifted, and Black* (1981); *The James Mink Story* (1996); *The Court Martial of Jackie Robinson* (1990); *Zora Is My Name*, about ZORA NEALE HURSTON, which she cowrote; and *Having Our Say: The Delany Sisters' First Hundred Years* (1999), in which she appeared as BESSIE DELANY. Dee has written several books, including *Glowchild and Other Poems* (1972); *My One Good Nerve* (1999),

which she turned into a one-woman show; and two children's books, *Two Ways to Count to Ten* (1988), winner of a Literary Guild Award; and *Tower to Heaven* (1991).

Davis and Dee have been working together—on stage, film, and television as performers, writers, and producers—for almost sixty years. In 1980 they founded their own production company, Emmalyn II Productions Company, and over the years produced both a television and a radio series, as well as numerous documentary and non-fiction projects. The couple has also worked together in civil rights and humanitarian causes, on the small and large scales. In the 1950s they risked their careers by stridently resisting Senator Joseph McCarthy's blacklisting activities. Their roles came to national attention when they served as masters of ceremonies for the 1963 March on Washington. The following year they helped establish Artists for Freedom, which donated money to civil rights organizations in the name of the four little girls killed in Birmingham, Alabama. Dee helped organize a summit of "prominent black leaders in the Struggle...[so that they] could meet in an informal atmosphere, talk, map strategy without press participation, without cameras" (Davis and Dee, 307). Dee often worked behind the scenes, helping establish Concerned Mothers, which raised money for Betty Shabazz and her children after the death of Shabazz's husband, MALCOLM X. She and Davis have been active in supporting the NAACP Legal Defense Fund and sickle-cell-disease research. They also campaigned for the release of Mumia Abu-Jamal, on death row since 1982 for killing a Philadelphia policeman, and protested civil rights abuses, including the killing of Amadou Diallo by New York police.

In addition to their many individual honors, Davis and Dee have jointly received the Actors' Equity Association PAUL ROBESON Award (1975), the Academy of Television Arts and Sciences Silver Circle Award (1994), and induction into the NAACP Image Awards Hall of Fame (1989). In 1995 they were awarded the National Medal of Arts by President Bill Clinton, and in 2000 they received the Screen Actors Guild's highest honor, the Life Achievement Award.

FURTHER READING

Davis, Ossie, and Ruby Dee. *With Ossie and Ruby: In This Life Together* (1998).
—SAMUEL A. HAY

DeFRANTZ, ANITA L.

(4 Oct. 1952–), Olympic rower and administrator, was born in Philadelphia, Pennsylvania, to Robert David DeFrantz, a social worker, YMCA administrator, and local school board member, and Anita Page, a speech pathologist and university professor. When DeFrantz was eighteen months old, her family moved to Indiana, living first in Bloomington and then Indianapolis.

DeFrantz was greatly influenced by her family's history of social and political activism. Her grandfather, Faburn Edward DeFrantz, was executive director of the Senate Avenue YMCA in Indianapolis from 1916 until 1952. Under his leadership, the Senate Avenue Y's "Monster Meetings" became an important forum over a span of several decades for the examination of issues affecting African Americans. They were public educational gatherings that brought to town such African American luminaries as W. E. B. DU BOIS, LANGSTON HUGHES, PAUL ROBESON, A. PHILIP RANDOLPH, JACKIE ROBINSON, ROY WILKINS, and THURGOOD MARSHALL. DeFrantz's parents met in the late 1940s as students at Indiana University. Her father was president of the campus NAACP chapter. Her mother was among the first group of African Americans to integrate student housing at the university.

DeFrantz's early athletic accomplishments were modest. As an elementary school student, she swam at Indianapolis's Frederick Douglass Public Park Pool and participated in local competitions. She attended Shortridge High School in Indianapolis. Although active in several extracurricular activities such as madrigal, band, orchestra, Quill and Scroll, and thespians, she did not play a sport.

A high school friend who graduated a year before DeFrantz and went to Connecticut College encouraged DeFrantz to apply to the college. She did so and was accepted. DeFrantz played basketball during her freshman year.

In the fall of her sophomore year, she discovered rowing. One day on campus, she spotted a strange-looking boat in front of the student union. When DeFrantz, who was nearly six feet tall, asked what it was, the college rowing coach told her it was for rowing, adding, "You'd be perfect for it" (Thomas, 1).

After graduating from college with honors in 1974, DeFrantz enrolled in law school at the University of Pennsylvania. She chose to attend the university primarily because the Vesper Boat Club, a training center for elite rowers, was located in Philadelphia. While in law school, DeFrantz trained for rowing three times a day and held a part-time job working from 10:00 p.m. to 6:00 a.m. at Philadelphia police headquarters interviewing defendants before their bail hearings.

Training under the tutelage of coaches at Vesper, she made her first national rowing team in 1975. That year she competed in the world championships, in the four-oared shell, at Nottingham, England, finishing fifth. The following year, 1976, was the first year that women competed in Olympic rowing. DeFrantz made the United States team as a member of the women's eight-oared shell. The team won a bronze medal at the Montreal Olympic Games.

After the Olympic Games, DeFrantz spent the fall of 1976 working at the Center for Law and Social Policy, in Washington, D.C. She completed law school in 1977 and was admitted to the Pennsylvania State Bar later that year.

She continued rowing with the goal of winning a gold medal at the 1980 Moscow Olympic Games. DeFrantz was a member of every United States national team between 1975 and 1980. She won a silver medal at the 1978 world championships, competed in world championship finals four times, and won six national titles. She supported herself financially by working as a staff attorney for the Juvenile Law Center of Philadelphia from 1977 to 1979, and then from 1979 to 1981 as a pre-law adviser and director of the Third World Center at Princeton University.

The 1970s also marked the beginning of DeFrantz's involvement in sports governance. Fellow athletes elected her to the United States Olympic Committee Athletes Advisory Council in 1976, a position she held until 1984. She become

a member of the United States Olympic Committee (USOC) board of directors in 1976 and joined the committee's executive board in 1977.

President Jimmy Carter's call for an American boycott of the 1980 Moscow Olympic Games in response to the Soviet Union's 1979 invasion of Afghanistan proved to be a pivotal event in DeFrantz's life. In April 1980 the USOC, under strong pressure from the Carter administration, voted against sending a team to Moscow. The decision outraged DeFrantz, who was considered a leading contender for the 1980 Olympic team. She argued that the federal government had never provided any financial support for athletes' training and that individual athletes should have the right to decide for themselves whether to compete in Moscow. She led a group of eighteen other athletes, one coach, and one administrator who filed a suit in United States District Court in April 1980 seeking to overturn the USOC decision. The suit failed, but it caught the attention of the International Olympic Committee (IOC), which in July 1980 awarded DeFrantz the Bronze Medal of the Olympic Order for her stand.

DeFrantz's defense of athletes' rights also attracted the attention of Peter Ueberroth, the president of the Los Angeles Olympic Organizing Committee. Ueberroth offered her a job developing the plan for the three Olympic villages used at the 1984 Games. She began at the committee in 1981, became the committee's vice president for Olympic Villages, and ran the day-to-day operations of the Olympic Village at the University of Southern California during the Games.

The 1984 Games generated a surplus of $223 million. Approximately $93 million of the surplus was used to establish the Amateur Athletic Foundation (AAF) of Los Angeles, a nonprofit corporation devoted to developing youth sports in Southern California. DeFrantz joined the foundation staff in 1985. In 1987 the board of directors elected her president. Under DeFrantz's leadership, the AAF invested more than $100 million in youth sports through grant making and self-initiated programs designed primarily to meet the needs of

young people historically underserved by private and public sports programming.

While still a staff member of the AAF in 1986, DeFrantz was elected to the IOC. She became the first African American and only the fifth woman elected to the organization. In 1992 the IOC elected DeFrantz to its executive board. Two years later she became the first woman elected vice-president in the committee's 103-year history. DeFrantz, however, was unsuccessful in her attempt in 2001 to win the IOC presidency.

Throughout her tenure on the IOC, DeFrantz has been a leading advocate of expanding the Olympic program to include more female athletes and more events for women. She became chair of the newly formed IOC Working Group on Women and Sport in 1995. The influence of DeFrantz and other advocates of gender equity in international sports was reflected in the changing composition of the Olympic Games. At the 1984 Los Angeles Games, two years before DeFrantz's election, women competed in sixty-two events and comprised 23 percent of all athletes. At the 2000 Sydney Games, there were 132 events for women, who made up 38.2 percent of all athletes.

Membership in the IOC provided DeFrantz entry to a variety of other international sports posts from the 1990s forward. She was vice president of the International Rowing Federation, a member of the executive committee of the Atlanta Committee for the Olympic Games, a member of the Board of Trustees for the Salt Lake Olympic Organizing Committee, and an arbitrator for the Court of Arbitration for Sport.

DeFrantz occupies an unusual, if not unique, position as an administrator of two distinctly different types of sports organizations. She is a member of several elite national and international sports governing bodies. At the same time, DeFrantz runs a foundation committed to youth sports. She is best known as an Olympic leader, a role she fulfills on a volunteer basis. Her actual vocation, however, is the development of community-based sports programs for children and teenagers. This dual identity, combined with her reputation as an advocate of women's sports and her visibility as an African American woman in sports administration, an arena dominated by white men, has earned DeFrantz a variety of awards and recognitions. These include the *Ladies Home Journal* 100 Most Important Women in America, 1988; NAACP Legal Defense and Educational Fund's Black Woman of Achievement Award, 1988; Women's Sports Foundation's Billie Jean King Contribution Award, 1996; *The Australian Magazine* 100 Most Powerful Women in the World, 1997; and *The Sporting News* 100 Most Powerful People in Sports, 1991–1999.

FURTHER READING

The most detailed account of Anita L. DeFrantz's life is an oral history transcript available at the Amateur Athletic Foundation sports library in Los Angeles.

Harvey, Randy. "Is She the Most Powerful Woman in Sports?" *Los Angeles Times Magazine*, 30 June 1996.

Jones, Charisse. "She Offers a Sporting Proposal," *Los Angeles Times*, 17 Dec. 1989.

Moore, Kenny. "An Advocate for Athletes," *Sports Illustrated*, 29 Aug. 1988.

Thomas, Emory, Jr. "Inside Moves: Former U.S. Medalist Emerges as Quiet Force in the Olympic Arena," *Wall Street Journal*, 28 June 1996.

—WAYNE WILSON

DELANEY, BEAUFORD

(30 Dec. 1901–26 Mar. 1979), painter, was born in Knoxville, Tennessee, the eighth of ten children, to Delia Johnson, a domestic worker, and John Samuel Delaney, a Methodist minister. Beauford attended the segregated Knoxville Colored High School, from which he graduated with honors. As a teenager, he met a local artist, Lloyd Branson, who painted impressionist-style landscapes and portraits. For several years Beauford worked for Branson as a porter in exchange for art lessons and began creating representational landscapes and portraits of local Knoxville blacks. Recognizing the young artist's talent, Branson pushed him to pursue formal art studies in Boston and helped finance his education.

In September 1923 Delaney left Knoxville for Boston, where he attended the Massachusetts Normal Art School (now Massachusetts College of Art), studying portraiture and academic traditions. He took classes at the Copley Society, the South Boston School of Art, and the Lowell Institute, and he copied original works of art at the Museum of Fine Arts, the Isabella Stewart Gardner Museum, and the Fogg Art Museum in Cambridge, refining his skills as a draftsman. Gradually, Delaney became fascinated by more modern work, especially that of the impressionist painter Claude Monet, which he saw in a retrospective mounted just after the artist's death in 1926. Monet's late water lily paintings provided an important example of abstract brushwork, light, and color that would prove critical to Delaney's later expressionistic painting.

Delaney arrived in New York City in November 1929 during the height of the Harlem Renaissance and settled in Greenwich Village, where he lived in several different apartments during his twenty-three-year stay. During the early 1930s Delaney supported himself doing traditional pastel and charcoal portraits of dancers and society. He also began producing more experimental works, sketching and painting people in the streets of Greenwich Village and Harlem, using erratic line and bright color. Delaney credited this stylistic shift to his New York environment. "I never drew a decent thing until I felt the rhythm of New York," he explained. "New York has a rhythm as distinct as the beating of a human heart. And I'm trying to put it on canvas. . . . I paint people. People—and in their faces I hope to discover that odd, mysterious rhythm" (*New York Telegraph*, 27 Mar. 1930).

Newspaper critics increasingly recognized Delaney's work, and in February 1930 the Whitney Studio Gallery included three of his oil portraits and nine pastel drawings in a group exhibition. The Whitney offered him work as a caretaker, gallery guard, and doorman, and in return he received a studio in the basement for two years. Delaney continued his studies with the Ashcan school artist John Sloan and the American regionalist artist Thomas Hart Benton at the Art Students' League in New York. In late 1930 he began a series of pastel and charcoal drawings of famous African American jazz musicians, including DUKE ELLINGTON, ETHEL WATERS, and LOUIS ARMSTRONG.

During the Works Progress Administration era, Delaney worked as an assistant to Charles Alston on his Harlem Hospital mural project but found himself drawn to European modernists, such as Cézanne, Gauguin, Van Gogh, and the fauves. He also loved the American modernists, including John Marin, Alfred Stieglitz, Arthur Dove, Georgia O'Keeffe, and Stuart Davis, and saw their work often at Stieglitz's gallery, An American Place. As art sales were slow during the Depression, Delaney earned money teaching art classes at various Greenwich Village schools and at an adult education project in Brooklyn.

In addition to experiencing the racial injustices of the time, Delaney also struggled with his homosexuality. Moreover, he began to suffer long bouts of depression and paranoia aggravated by alcoholism, and these illnesses plagued him throughout the remainder of his life.

In 1934 Delaney began exhibiting in the Washington Square Outdoor Exhibit, and his work became increasingly expressionistic, using distortion, heightened color, and manipulated perspective to create psychologically and spiritually charged paintings. During 1938 Delaney had two solo exhibitions of portraits, at the Eighth Street Playhouse in New York and Gallery C in Washington, D.C., and in October 1938 *Life* magazine featured him as "one of the most talented Negro painters." Delaney became a close friend of the writer JAMES BALDWIN in the early 1940s, and this pivotal friendship lasted throughout Delaney's life, providing companionship and intellectual camaraderie. Over the years Delaney painted roughly twelve portraits of Baldwin, including *Dark Rapture* (1941) and *James Baldwin* (1965).

During the 1940s Delaney's psychological problems and economic circumstances worsened, and, according to many of his notes, his paintings became a kind of salvation, a means of escaping the difficult realities of his daily life. Delaney's commitment to modernism and abstraction intensified, and the influence of European artists, particularly the postimpressionists and the fauves, can be seen in many works of this period, including *Can Fire in the Park* (1946), *Green Street* (1946), and *Washington Square* (1949). By the late

1940s Delaney had become an established expressionist painter in the New York art scene. He received positive reviews when he showed in two group exhibitions at Roko Gallery in 1949, and the following year he was given a solo exhibition there.

In 1950 Delaney won a two-month fall fellowship at the Yaddo writers and artists' community in Saratoga Springs, New York. While there, he read extensively and began thinking seriously about traveling to Paris, where many African American artists were working and living in exile. He returned to Yaddo in November 1951 and, after dispersing his paintings, sailed for Paris on 28 August 1953. Delaney settled in the Montparnasse section of Paris, going to many galleries, and frequenting the Musée d'Art Moderne, the Orangérie, and the city's many galleries. In Paris he found a circle of expatriate artists that included his dear friend James Baldwin, painters Larry Calcagno, Larry Potter, and Bob Thompson, and photographer Ed Clark.

While some of his paintings during this time were purely abstract, such as *Abstraction* (1954), others reflect Delaney's travels in Europe. In 1954 he exhibited at the Salon des Réalités Nouvelles in the Musée d'Art Moderne and the Ninth Salon at the Musée des Beaux Arts. By the fall of 1955 he had left Montparnasse for the suburb of Clamart. Still supporting himself through sporadic painting sales and generous contributions from friends, Delaney could not afford psychiatric treatment and suffered ongoing bouts of depression and paranoia that affected his ability to work. When he could concentrate, he vacillated between large-scale abstraction and figuration. In *Composition 16* (1954), Delaney's canvas glows with thick, swirling, intensely colored green, red, and yellow impasto surrounding a central glowing yellow light. *Self-Portrait* (1961) demonstrates the same fascination with light and gestural brushwork, integrated with an expressive likeness of the artist. The most important works to come out of his Paris years, however, were the allover abstractions, both the oil-on-canvas paintings and a series of gouache works on paper, which he showed in three important solo exhibitions at Galerie Paul Facchetti in 1960, the Galerie Lambert in 1964, and the Galerie Darthea Speyer in 1973.

In the summer of 1961 Delaney traveled to Greece. During the trip he was plagued by taunting, threatening voices that eventually led to his hospitalization, a subsequent suicide attempt, and then temporary institutionalization. His patron, Darthea Speyer, the cultural attaché at the American Embassy in Paris, arranged for his return to Paris. Eventually, Delaney's friends began to urge him to get professional psychological help, and he briefly rested at La Maison du Santé de Nogent sur Marne outside Paris. Afterward he stayed with Madame du Closel, a French art collector, and her husband. Delaney soon came under the care of a psychiatrist, Dr. Ferdiere, who specialized in depression and who diagnosed Delaney with acute paranoia. During this period Delaney created a series of quickly executed gouache works on paper that he called Rorschach tests, some done at his doctor's request. Delaney's final years in Paris were spent in a studio at rue Vercingetorix, where he was supported mainly by the du Closels. Despite his doctor's warnings, he drank sporadically, nullifying the effects of his antipsychotic medication. Delaney spent his final years institutionalized in St. Anne's Hospital for the Insane in Montparnasse, where he died in 1979.

FURTHER READING

Leeming, David. *Amazing Grace: A Life of Beauford Delaney* (1998).
———, and Robert Rosenfeld Gallery. *Beauford Delaney Liquid Light: Paris Abstractions, 1954–1970* (1999).
Long, Richard, and Studio Museum of Harlem. *Beauford Delaney: A Retrospective* (1978).

Obituaries: *New York Times*, 1 Apr. 1979; *Le Monde*, 5 Apr. 1979; *International Herald Tribune*, 6 Apr. 1979.

—LISA D. FREIMAN

DELANY, BESSIE (3 Sept. 1891–25 Sept. 1995), and **SADIE DELANY** (19 Sept. 1889–25 Jan. 1999) were born Annie Elizabeth Delany and Sarah Louise Delany in Raleigh, North Carolina, the daughters of Henry Beard Delany, an educator and Episcopal bishop, and Nanny James Logan. Bessie was to become a dentist, and Sadie a schoolteacher; late in life,

they gained fame for their published reminiscences. Descended from a mix of black, American Indian, and white lineages, the sisters grew up in a family of ten children in Raleigh on the campus of St. Augustine's, the African American school where their father, a former slave, served as priest and vice principal. The sisters graduated from St. Augustine's (Sadie in 1910 and Bessie in 1911) at a time when few Americans, black or white, were educated beyond grammar school. "We had everything you could want except money," recalled Bessie. "We had a good home, wonderful parents, plenty of love, faith in the Lord, educational opportunities—oh, we had a privileged childhood for colored children of the time" (*Smithsonian*, Oct. 1993, 150).

After completing their studies at St. Augustine's, both Sadie and Bessie went on to teaching jobs in North Carolina. Their father had strongly urged his daughters to teach, since he was unable to finance further education at a four-year college. He also advised them to make their own way, warning them against accepting scholarships that would obligate them to benefactors. Bessie took a job in the mill town of Boardman, while Sadie became the domestic science supervisor for all of the black schools in Wake County. Although she received no extra salary, Sadie also assumed the duties of supervisor of black schools in the county. Both sisters were shocked by the conditions their students lived in. Bessie later said in the sisters' joint memoir, *Having Our Say: The Delany Sisters' First 100 Years* (1993), that she found the families in Boardman "poor and ignorant" (89). Sadie remarked that her students' families in Wake County were "in bad shape" and that they "needed help with the basics" and "didn't know how to cook, clean, eat properly, or anything" (81). She therefore concentrated her efforts on teaching sanitation, hygiene, and food preparation. She also convinced many of her charges to continue their education.

In 1916 Sadie moved to Harlem in New York City and enrolled at Pratt Institute, then a two-year college. After graduating in 1918 she enrolled at Columbia University, where she earned a BS in 1920. She returned to North Carolina briefly with the intention of helping her people but, discouraged by the pervasive Jim Crow system, soon returned to Harlem. She encountered racism in New York but concluded that the North "was an improvement over the South" (107). She began teaching in an elementary school in Harlem in 1920, and for several years she also ran a candy business. In 1925 she received her master's degree in education from Columbia. Beginning in 1930, she taught at Theodore Roosevelt High School, a white school in the Bronx. Having skipped the interview because she feared her color would cost her the job, Sadie stunned school officials on the first day of school; but as she later observed, "Once I was in, they couldn't figure out how to get rid of me" (120). With her appointment, Sadie became the first African American in New York City to teach domestic science at the high school level.

In 1918, after teaching for a short time in Brunswick, Georgia, and taking science courses at Shaw University in Raleigh, Bessie joined her sister in New York, where she enrolled the following year in the dentistry program at Columbia University. She completed her DDS in 1923 and became only the second black female dentist licensed in the state of New York, with a practice in Harlem. She was well known there as "Dr. Bessie" and her office was a meeting place for black leaders, including JAMES WELDON JOHNSON and E. FRANKLIN FRAZIER. During the Depression of the 1930s she found herself twice evicted from her office, but she persisted in her work.

During their childhood the Delany sisters had encountered the segregation and the discrimination of the Jim Crow South and the threat of violence that underlay the system. Bessie remembered the first time she faced segregation when, as a child in the mid-1890s, she found she could no longer go to the park that she had previously played in, and she also recalled experimenting with drinking the water from a "whites only" fountain and discerning no difference in its taste. Yet, like her sister, she found that in the North, too, restrictions and dangers hemmed her in. Bessie's closest brush with the Ku Klux Klan came not in the South, however, but on Long Island.

Neither Bessie nor Sadie ever married. Nanny Delany had urged her daughters to decide whether they were going to marry and raise families or have careers. As Bessie said years later, it never occurred to anyone that a woman could have both a family and a profession, and the sisters decided on careers. Bessie and Sadie lived together for nearly eight decades in New York City and then in nearby Mount Vernon, and they were surrounded by family members. All but one of their siblings settled in Harlem, and after their father's death in 1928 their mother lived with them. The sisters were devoted to their mother, and it was largely to please her that after World War II they left Harlem and moved to a cottage in the north Bronx. In 1950 Bessie gave up her dental practice to care for their mother full time. After their mother's death in 1956, the sisters moved to Mount Vernon, where they purchased a house in an all-white neighborhood. Sadie retired in 1960. Sadie was amiable by nature, having broken the color barrier in the New York City public schools through craft instead of confrontation. By contrast, Bessie was feisty and contentious, accustomed to speaking her mind. "We loved our country," she observed, "even though it didn't love us back" (60). Asked her impression of the Statue of Liberty when she first entered New York harbor, she replied that it was important as a symbol to white immigrants but meant nothing to her. Regarding her experience at Columbia University, she noted: "I suppose I should be grateful to Columbia, that at that time they let in colored people. Well, I'm not. They let me in but they beat me down for being there! I don't know how I got through that place, except when I was young nothing could hold me back" (115).

The Delany sisters might have escaped notice by the wider world had they not in 1993 coauthored a best-selling memoir with the assistance of Amy Hill Hearth. *Having Our Say: The Delany Sisters' First 100 Years* had its origins in an essay that Hearth had written for the *New York Times* on the occasion of Bessie's one-hundredth birthday. So enthusiastic were readers' responses to the article that Hearth continued her interviews and produced the book. Published when Bessie was 102 and Sadie was 104, *Having Our Say* offered a perceptive, witty review of the sisters' lives through the previous century.

As Hearth observed in her introduction to the book, it was meant less as a study of black history or of women's history than of American history, but the sisters' age, race, and gender combined to provide a tart perspective on the past. These two black women spoke of their strong family, the racism and sexism that could have thwarted them, and their triumphs. They spoke of their experiences as teachers in the segregated South, their participation in the mass migration of African Americans from the South to the urban North, and—although more briefly—their recollections of the Harlem Renaissance in the 1920s and the Great Depression of the 1930s. *Having Our Say* remained on the *New York Times* best-seller list—first in hardback and then as a paperback—for seventy-seven weeks.

By the time Bessie Delany died aged 104 at her Mount Vernon home in 1995, *Having Our Say* had sold nearly a million copies in hardback or paper and had been translated into four foreign languages. Reviewers were generally enthusiastic about the book, but an unsigned commentary in the *Women's Review of Books* in January 1994 questioned the role of Amy Hill Hearth as a white woman selectively pulling together the recollections of two elderly black women. Such criticisms did not, however, diminish the popular appeal of the sisters' story, which was adapted as a Broadway play in 1995 and as a television movie in 1999, starring Diahann Carroll as Sadie and RUBY DEE as Bessie. That same year Sadie Delany died in Mount Vernon, aged 109.

FURTHER READING

The Delany family papers are at St. Augustine's College, Raleigh, North Carolina.

Delany, Sarah L., and A. Elizabeth Delany, with Amy Hill Hearth. *Having Our Say: The Delany Sisters' First 100 Years* (1993).
———. *The Delany Sisters' Book of Everyday Wisdom* (1994).
Delany, Sarah L., with Amy Hill Hearth. *On My Own at 107: Reflections on Life without Bessie* (1997).

Obituaries: Bessie Delany: *New York Times* and *Washington Post*, 26 Sept. 1995; Sadie Delany: *New York Times*, 26 Jan. 1999.

—RICHARD HARMOND
—PETER WALLENSTEIN

DELANY, MARTIN ROBISON (6 May 1812–24 Jan. 1885), political activist, doctor, newspaper editor, and author, was born in Charles Town, Virginia (now West Virginia), son of Samuel Delany, a slave, and Pati Peace, the free daughter of free and African-born Graci Pearce. In 1822 Pati fled with her children to Chambersburg, Pennsylvania; Samuel joined her in 1823 after purchasing his freedom.

In 1831 in Pittsburgh, Delany studied history, geography, literature, and political economy, informally, with Lewis Woodson and Molliston M. Clark. Here Delany began his restless, wide-ranging advocacy of African American political rights, cultural self-reliance, and independent enterprise. Opposed to physical and "servile" work, Delany apprenticed himself to a white doctor in 1833. During his time in Pittsburgh he joined or helped found several African American antislavery, temperance, historical, literary, and moral reform societies. When

Pennsylvania rescinded black suffrage in 1839, Delany explored the Mexican part of Texas, where slavery was illegal and blacks could become citizens. However, usurping American slaveholders were moving in, and Delany returned to Pittsburgh, ending his first attempt to find or found a nation for himself and his people.

In 1843, by now an established "cupper and leecher" (a person who drew blood for medicinal purposes), Delany married Catherine A. Richards, daughter of a once-wealthy mixed-race businessman. Unusually, they named their six surviving sons after prominent black heroes; their daughter, symbolically, Halle Amelia Ethiopia.

In August 1843, Delany launched the *Mystery*, a weekly newspaper that argued against slavery and for equality between the races. In 1847, now a recognized leader and an officer in his Freemason's Lodge, Delany impressed the abolitionists William Lloyd Garrison and FREDERICK DOUGLASS. Garrison wrote to his wife

(16 Aug. 1847) that Delany was "Black as jet,... a fine fellow of great energy and spirit." Promised a wider editorial field, Delany joined the staff at Douglass's forthcoming *North Star*. For a year and a half he promoted the newspaper, lectured, attended meetings, described and criticized the conditions and attitudes of black people from Detroit to Delaware, and wrote editorials on black political possibilities from Canada to Cuba. But by July 1849, his domestic reports turned pessimistic and he resigned a poor man from the financially strapped *North Star* and returned again to Pittsburgh.

Concluding that the Fugitive Slave Law section of the Compromise of 1850, which commanded Americans to return slaves fleeing to the North, also threatened to reenslave free blacks, Delany was moved to bolder assertions of his rights. Delany took recommendations from seventeen doctors to Harvard Medical School, where he was allowed to study for one term before a majority of white students petitioned that he be expelled. Delany made his way home by lecturing to black audiences on the physiological superiority of blacks to whites. Back in Pittsburgh, Delany moved his family to a section called Hayti, practiced medicine, and also served as principal of the Colored School.

Delany began to travel further afield. The 1851 North American Convention of Colored Freemen in Toronto, which resolved to encourage American slaves to come to Canada instead of going to Africa, took him to Canada. Then in April 1852 a settlement of free blacks in Nicaragua elected Delany "Mayor of Greytown..., civil governor of the Mosquito Reservation and commander in chief of the military forces of the province" (Ullman 139). A lack of funds stranded him in New York City, but there he hurriedly cobbled together the first book-length, antisentimental, sociopolitical report on "free" African Americans: *The Condition, Elevation, Emigration, and Destiny of the Colored People of the United States, Politically Considered* (1852). Sketches of contributions to the nation from 104 blacks were surrounded by reminders of white repression, condescension, and black dependence, leading to bold anticolonizationist, black-nationalist, pro-black–led emigrationist arguments and conclusions. Appearing, however, only a month after Harriet Beecher

Published in 1865, this hand-colored lithograph of physician and editor Martin Robison Delany marks his promotion to major, making him the highest ranking African American in the American military. Hulton/Archive by Getty Images

Stowe's *Uncle Tom's Cabin*, Delany's book received little attention.

Almost a year later, Delany criticized Douglass for commending Stowe's efforts while neglecting Delany's attempts to reshape black political discourse. By 1853 Delany was well along in composing his long fiction, *Blake*, but before its appearance, he published his "Origin and Objects of Ancient Freemasonry," a pamphlet claiming that Africans were the founders of the order and demanding white acceptance or rejection. He organized an opposition National Emigration Convention in Cleveland, Ohio, following Douglass's often-praised "We will fight it out here" Colored National Convention in Rochester, New York, in 1853. Delany's keynote address at the Cleveland convention sharpened the emigrationist arguments he had introduced in *Condition*.

Despite being honored in Pittsburgh for his efforts in an 1854 cholera epidemic, Delany moved his family to largely black Chatham, Canada, in 1856. Two years later, he arranged a meeting between African Americans and the militant white abolitionist John Brown, while also attempting to raise money to explore Africa. The U.S. Supreme Court's 1857 DRED SCOTT decision denied African Americans full citizenship rights and stated that, even in the North or in the new free territories, blacks were "beings of an inferior order" with "no rights which the white man was bound to respect." The ruling led several prominent black leaders to contemplate leaving the United States, as Delany had done, and encouraged some African Americans to plan emigration to Canada, Haiti, Central America, and Africa.

Delany's fiction found a publisher in January 1859, when the new monthly *Anglo-African Magazine* began printing twenty-six chapters of *Blake, or the Huts of America: A Tale of the Mississippi Valley, the Southern United States, and Cuba*. The work deliberately challenged earlier representations of slaves and free blacks. Not a novel, its freer form sampled several genres and offered a wide-ranging, conversational, song-and-verse-infused mix of imagined and real-world situations, characters, and observations. Its daring but careful hero prepared blacks to revolt against their oppressors from Texas to Dahomey in

Africa. In July, the tale's printing was suspended because its author was in Africa. Delany explored Liberia before going on to present-day Nigeria, where he and his fellow explorer, Robert Campbell, negotiated an agreement with several chiefs allowing African American emigrants the right to settle on arable land.

Delany subsequently spent seven months in England, where he raised interest in and money for his African emigration project. He returned to Canada on the eve of the American Civil War and published American and English versions of his *Official Report of the Niger Valley Exploring Party* (1861). Although he continued to encourage American blacks to consider emigration, he discovered in 1862 that white British missionaries and colonialists had undermined his African plans. Stymied again, Delany returned to writing. He simplified *Blake's* dialect transcriptions and a complete version appeared in the *Weekly Anglo-African* newspaper between November 1861 and June 1862. Unfortunately, the May 1862 issues have been lost, and only seventy-four of the promised eighty chapters survive. The last available words portentously warn: "'Woe be unto those devils of whites, I say!'" (*WAA*, 26 Apr. 1862).

The Emancipation Proclamation of January 1863 opened up the prospect of full citizenship for African Americans, and immediately Delany began recruiting for black regiments across the North. Around that time he moved his family to a new home near Wilberforce College in Ohio. In February 1865 he became the first black major to be assigned a field command when he was commissioned as a major in the 104th United States Colored Troops. Although the war was soon over, Delany continued to serve the unionist and abolitionist cause by taking a position with the Freedmen's Bureau.

For three years, Delany lectured and encouraged blacks in South Carolina, where African Americans were in the majority, to gain education, land, and a level of self-respect and political power that had been impossible under slavery—or even in the antebellum North. He brokered formal and informal contracts between blacks and whites, poor landholders, even-poorer workers, and racially prejudiced Northerners

and Southerners. In 1868 he was a delegate to the democratically innovative South Carolina State Constitutional Convention.

Delany also continued to write. From war's end through 1871, he wrote essays on the failures of southern political leadership during the war, the economic hopes for freedmen, and the racist neglect of a once glorious African culture in Egypt. His writings also examined the rights and duties of citizenship, and ways in which Northern capital, Southern land, and black workers might make a better United States.

During these busy years, Delany worked with Frances Rollin on *Life and Public Services of Martin R. Delany* (1868, reprinted in 1883), one of few nineteenth-century biographies of an African American. However, the book's optimistic prediction of improved circumstances for Delany and other blacks did not materialize. Stubbornly, he persistently sought to establish for himself a respectable position, but was unsuccessful in his campaign to serve as U.S. Consul to Liberia. In 1870 he worked for the South Carolina Bureau of Agricultural Statistics, and the following year he opened a real estate agency. From 1870 to 1872 Delany worked tirelessly, yet unprofitably, for the Republican Party as an honorary state militia member, before resigning because he had discovered rising corruption within that organization.

In 1873 and 1874, Delany, then a poorly paid federal customs clerk, courted southern whites while seeking a law requiring fair political representation of both races. He ran for lieutenant-governor of South Carolina as an independent Republican, but lost a close election. Behind local pressure, the state's last Republican governor appointed Delany as a trial justice (justice of the peace) in 1875. A year later, Delany supported a white Democrat, Wade Hampton, for governor and was reappointed as a trial justice through 1878. By then, Reconstruction, and the possibility of full black citizenship, had nearly ended. Late in 1877 Delany became involved with the Liberian Exodus Joint Stock Steam Ship Company, whose emigration ventures soon failed. Defeated there and in South Carolina, he headed north.

In 1879, Philadelphia's Harper & Brothers published Delany's *Principia of Ethnology: The Origin of Races and Color*, a Biblically-inspired swan song asserting the eternal and essential differences between blacks and whites. From 1880 through 1883 Delany worked at various civil service jobs around Washington, D.C., and in 1884 he joined a Boston firm with offices in Central America. Falling ill, he returned to Ohio and died in the home of his self-reliant, much-respected wife.

FURTHER READING

Levine, Robert S. *Martin Delany, Frederick Douglass, and the Politics of Representative Identity* (1997).
Ullman, Victor. *Martin R. Delany: The Beginnings of Black Nationalism* (1971).

—ALLAN D. AUSTIN

 DEMBY, EDWARD T.
(13 Feb. 1869–14 Oct. 1957), the first African American Episcopal bishop elected to serve in the United States, was born Edward Thomas Demby V and raised in Wilmington, Delaware, the eldest child of freeborn parents, Edward T. Demby IV and Mary Anderson Tippett. Young Edward was tutored by his uncle, "Professor" Eddy Anderson, for the majority of his primary and secondary school years. Anderson was the headmaster of a private high school located behind Ezion (Northern) Methodist Episcopal Church, a hub of Wilmington's black community.

After leaving Wilmington, Demby embarked on an educational odyssey that encompassed Philadelphia's prestigious Institute for Colored Youth, followed by Centenary Bible Institute (now Morgan State University) in Baltimore, Howard University in Washington, D.C., Wilberforce University in Ohio, and National University in Chicago. He usually taught in some capacity to support himself through college and operated more than one private academy in the course of his studies. By 1894 he was an ordained African Methodist Episcopal clergyman teaching theology at Paul Quinn College in Waco, Texas.

In 1895, while serving as dean of Paul Quinn, Demby converted to the predominately white Episcopal Church and immediately began a process leading to the priesthood. He was first a catechist, or lay reader, responsible for churches in Denver and rural West Tennessee, then a deacon in West Tennessee, and finally a priest in West Tennessee. When he was examined for the priesthood, he caused a sensation. The examiners were flabbergasted at Demby's command of sacred languages and overall intellectual prowess. Afterwards, they felt compelled to admit that "no one" could have done better on certain parts of the examination. As for Demby, he was already mindful of the possibility of one day becoming a bishop, and he did not want it said that he was given any shortcuts by reason of his color. Demby credited himself for being the first African American to operate a school that offered correspondence courses in sacred languages.

After the death of his first wife, Polly Alston Sherrill, Demby transferred to St. Augustine's, Kansas City, where in 1902 he married Antoinette Martina Ricks, a graduate of the first nursing class of Freedmen's Hospital, Howard University, and the head nurse at Freedman's Hospital in Kansas City.

Over the next five years, Demby served as a priest to churches in Cairo, Illinois, and Key West, Florida. In both cases he strove to reach large migrant populations via the parochial school adjacent to each church. At St. Michael's in Cairo, he discovered that Polly's Tuskegee background was especially effective in drawing attention to the school. However, while he served at St. Peter's in Key West, Demby no longer identified with Tuskegee. In 1907, at the zenith of the debate between W. E. B. DU BOIS and BOOKER T. WASHINGTON over the direction of African American education, Demby publicly condemned Washington's philosophy of industrial education. He said it was not in the best interests of African Americans and personally attacked Washington for being overly manipulative toward blacks and overly servile toward whites.

Simultaneously, Demby published letters regarding the election of black bishops to serve in the United States, a volatile issue confronting the 1907 General Convention of the Episcopal Church. It was a choice between two plans. The first, called the missionary district plan, called for the organization of black churches into missionary districts that would, in turn, elect black representatives to general conventions and be represented by black bishops in the national House of Bishops. Black missionary bishops and their delegates would enjoy political equality in exchange for wholesale segregation of the church, especially in the South. The second plan, called the suffragan bishop plan, would not have written segregation into church law, but would have allowed each diocese to elect suffragan (assistant) bishops to supervise black ministries in the same diocese. Suffragans would be under the authority of white bishops. They would have rights to the floor, but no vote in the House of Bishops. Like the Conference of Church Workers among the Colored People, the primary black advocacy group in the Episcopal Church, Demby preferred the missionary district plan for its autonomy and the vestige of equality it guaranteed. Ultimately, the general convention passed the suffragan plan into law.

Also in 1907, Demby moved back to Tennessee. His chief calling was Emmanuel Church in Memphis, but he served in many locations. He organized and supervised black missions in the Memphis area, served as dean and archdeacon of Tennessee's black Episcopalians, and supervised the establishment of Hoffman–St. Mary's Industrial Institute, the flagship of black education in Episcopal Tennessee. He was a leader in several religious, civic, and charitable groups in Memphis and considered himself an emissary to the white community.

In 1917 the dioceses in Arkansas, Texas, New Mexico, Oklahoma, Missouri, and Kansas elected Demby the nation's first black bishop. Although he was appointed to the Diocese of Arkansas, the bishops of the Province of the Southwest intended that Demby supervise black ministries throughout the region. However, by the time he was consecrated in 1918, dissenting black churches and their bishops had effectively reduced his jurisdiction to a mere handful of small churches in Arkansas. In addition, he had no official residence and no salary. Thus began a ministry Demby described as "making bricks without straw."

From 1918 to 1931 Demby confined his administrative duties primarily to Arkansas as he struggled for funds and credibility. As of 1922 the national church began appropriating additional funds for his operating expenses, and it finally began paying him a meagre salary. However, these appropriations enabled Demby to establish Christ Church Parochial and Industrial School in Forrest City, Arkansas, and recruit teachers to staff it. Likewise, he was able to recruit priests to fill pulpits in Arkansas and Oklahoma. The self-sufficient black church became his creed, and in 1930 he announced a ten-year plan to transform Arkansas's five black churches into independent parishes. Meanwhile, the 1925 general convention, realizing that Demby's jurisdiction had been heavily compromised at the outset, contemplated relocating him or reducing his appropriations. Inspired, or perhaps shamed, by these developments, the bishops of the Southwest made greater use of his ministry. Likewise, the church's black clergy, who had never been reconciled to Demby's second-class bishop status, began, nonetheless, to rally to his defense and grant him greater recognition. As for Demby, he toured the Southwest, as well as the rest of the country, preaching, marrying, and burying, and otherwise promoting black Episcopal missions. He found soliciting especially difficult, as he was by nature not a fund-raiser; rather, he believed that viable ministries engendered their own support. Nevertheless, he pressed on with nationwide canvasses in 1921 and 1927, and the situation was much improved in Arkansas by the end of the decade.

Demby's ministry in Arkansas and the Southwest was never the evangelical success he expected, and after 1932 it was even less so. The cause, aside from the general economic decline of the Great Depression, was the Newport incident of May 1932, when the annual convention of the Episcopal Diocese of Arkansas elected a bishop at Newport, Arkansas. In August, Demby and his white allies protested the racist conduct of that convention, and especially the election. As a result, the House of Bishops overturned the Arkansas election. The protest, however, inspired retaliatory acts by the offended parties, acts that had negative repercussions for Demby's ministry. By 1934 his situation was very ambiguous.

As Demby became more of a bishop in name only, he turned his energies upon the national church and the greater issue of black ministries in general. He was appointed a member of the church's Joint Commission on Negro Work, and, as such, influenced the general convention of 1940, which made several landmark decisions with regard to the status of African Americans in the Episcopal Church. Most importantly, Demby made the keynote speech, defeating yet another attempt to enact the missionary district plan. This event signaled the end of the plan and the demise of segregation as acceptable church policy. Diocese by diocese, institution by institution, the Episcopal Church desegregated itself over the next fifteen years.

Demby retired from his post in 1938 and spent the remainder of his life serving individual churches in Kansas, Pittsburgh, and Cleveland. He also traveled the country and spoke at events with a biracial theme. He died in Cleveland in 1957 and was eulogized as someone who could eradicate racism by sheer good example, if that were possible.

FURTHER READING

The Demby Family Papers can be found at the Schomburg Center for Research in Black Culture, New York Public Library.

Beary, Michael J. *Black Bishop: Edward T. Demby and the Struggle for Racial Equality in the Episcopal Church* (2001).
Lewis, Harold T. *Yet with a Steady Beat: The African American Struggle for Recognition in the Episcopal Church* (1996).
Shattuck, Gardiner H., Jr. *Episcopalians and Race: Civil War to Civil Rights* (2000).
—MICHAEL J. BEARY

DePRIEST, OSCAR STANTON (9 Mar. 1871–12 May 1951), politician, was born in Florence, Alabama, the son of Martha Karsner, a part-time laundress, and Neander R. DePriest, a teamster and farmer. His father, a former slave, joined the Republican Party. After a neighbor's lynching, the family moved to Salina, Kansas, in 1878. Young Oscar had sandy hair, blue eyes, and a light complexion and often fought over racial slurs made in his presence. After two years at Salina Normal School, he left home at seventeen, settling in Chicago. He apprenticed as a house painter and by 1905 had a successful contracting and real estate business. In 1898 he married Jessie L. Williams; they had one child.

DePriest was elected Cook County commissioner in 1904 and 1906 because he delivered a bloc of African American voters from the city's Second and Third wards for the Republican Party. He educated his constituency about city and county relief resources but lost the 1908 nomination over a dispute with First District congressman Martin B. Madden. For the next few years he maneuvered among various factions, sometimes supporting Democrats over Republicans. He reconciled with Madden and backed white Republican candidates for alderman against African Americans running as independents in 1912 and 1914.

In 1915 the growing African American community united to elect DePriest to the city council. Significant support came from women, who had won the municipal ballot in 1913. As alderman, he introduced a civil rights ordinance and fought against job discrimination. Indicted in 1917 on charges of taking a bribe from a gambling establishment, DePriest claimed the money as a campaign contribution. He was successfully defended by Clarence Darrow but was persuaded not to run again. He campaigned as an independent in 1918 and 1919 but lost to black Republican nominees. In the 1919 race riots, his reputation was revived when, armed with pistols, he drove twice a day to the stockyards to supply his community with meat.

The riots helped DePriest renew ties to the Republican mayor, William Hale Thompson, and he was a delegate to the 1920 Republican National Convention. In 1924 he was elected Third Ward committeeman. His help in Thompson's 1927 election won DePriest an appointment as assistant Illinois commerce commissioner. In the 1928 election he again ran successfully for Republican delegate and Third Ward committeeman. That same year he supported the renomination of Congressman Madden, who died shortly after the primary, and used his influence with the Thompson faction of the Republican party to win the nomination for Madden's seat. After he was nominated, he was indicted for alleged gambling connections and vote fraud, charges that his supporters maintained were politically motivated. DePriest refused to withdraw and won the election to represent the predominantly black First District. The case against him was subsequently dismissed for insufficient evidence.

DePriest became the first African American to serve in the U.S. Congress in twenty-eight years and the first from a northern state. He considered himself "congressman-at-large" for the nation's twelve million black Americans and promised to place a black cadet in West Point, fight for enforcement of the Fourteenth and Fifteenth amendments, and secure work relief for the unemployed. But he vowed to "represent all people, both black and white."

While denying that he sought "social equality," DePriest used his position to secure the rights of citizenship for African Americans. When his wife's attendance at First Lady Lou Hoover's traditional tea for congressional wives in 1929 created controversy, DePriest used the publicity to promote a fund-raiser for the National Association for the Advancement of Colored People (NAACP). He was much in demand as a speaker, urging audiences to organize and to vote, even in the South, where threats were made against his life. Although the Great Depression, which began shortly after his arrival in Congress, lured his constituents toward the Democrats, he won reelection in 1930 and 1932. He opposed federal relief, preferring state and local measures.

DePriest sponsored a number of bills to benefit his constituents, including pensions for surviving former slaves and appropriations for African American schools in the District of Columbia. His most important legislative victory was an amendment to the 1933 bill creating the Civilian Conservation Corps barring discrimination based on race, color, or creed. After the infamous 1931 SCOTTSBORO BOYS case in which nine young African American men were sentenced to death after being convicted on questionable evidence by an all-white jury of raping two white women, DePriest called for a law to enable a trial to be transferred to another jurisdiction if the defendant was deemed not likely to get a fair trial. Warning that the

country would suffer if one-tenth of its population were denied justice, he said, "If we had a right to exercise our franchise . . . as the constitution provides, I would not be the only Negro on this floor." The bill died in the Judiciary Committee, as did his proposal for an antilynching bill. He also fought unsuccessfully to integrate the House of Representatives restaurant, where he was served, but his staff was not.

By 1934 DePriest faced charges that his party was doing little to help African Americans hard hit by the depression, and he lost to Arthur W. Mitchell, the first African American Democrat elected to Congress. DePriest was vice chairman of the Cook County Republican Central Committee from 1932 to 1934, a delegate to the Republican National Convention in 1936, and alderman from the Third Ward in 1943–1947. He lost the 1947 election for alderman, partly because of charges of cooperating with the Democratic mayor. He continued in the real estate business with his son Oscar DePriest Jr. and died at his home in Chicago.

Skillful at organizing a coalition of black voters and using this bloc to pressure the dominant white political machine, DePriest was the forerunner of many local African American politicians in the latter part of the twentieth century. His six years in Congress enabled him to raise black political consciousness. Kenneth Eugene Mann, writing in the *Negro History Bulletin* in October 1972, noted that DePriest "took advantage of his opportunities and frequently created them."

FURTHER READING

The Arthur W. Mitchell Papers at the Chicago Historical Society have material on DePriest. For DePriest's speeches and resolutions in Congress, see the *Congressional Record*, 71st to 73d Congresses.

Christopher, Maurine. *Black Americans in Congress* (1971; repr. 1976).
Grossman, James R. *Land of Hope: Chicago, Black Southerners, and the Great Migration* (1989).
Ragsdale, Bruce A., and Joel D. Treese. *Black Americans in Congress 1870–1989* (1990).

Obituaries: *New York Times* and *Chicago Tribune*, 13 May 1951; *Chicago Defender*, 19 May 1951.

—KRISTIE MILLER

 DIDDLEY, BO
(20 Dec. 1928–), guitarist, songwriter, and musical innovator, was born Otha Ellas Bates in McComb, Mississippi, the only child of Ethel Wilson, a sharecropper in her teens, and Eugene Bates. He was raised with a number of other children by Ethel's first cousin, Gussie McDaniel. When McDaniel's husband died in 1934, the family moved to Chicago as part of the Great Migration, and the young boy's surname was changed to McDaniel to allow him to enter the public school system. There, he received the name Bo Diddley, an appellation whose origin has been variously explained by an array of stories. (Diddley himself claims not to know the origin, and downplays a possible connection to the diddley bow—a single string attached to a wall or house frame and played with a bottleneck slide or nail—stating that he never played one.) Diddley showed an aptitude for music early on; he studied the violin from the age of eight until he was fifteen under a classical instructor, O. W. Frederick, at the Ebenezer Missionary Baptist Church. He also took up drums, and he received his first guitar on his twelfth birthday. Owing to his large hands, he was not able to treat the fretboard delicately and came to approach the instrument something like a drum set, driving material forward by virtue of rhythm rather than melody. He began his first band, a trio named the Hipsters and later the Langley Alley Cats, after he dropped out of high school, and he supported his musical endeavors by working in a grocery store and a picture frame factory, in addition to being an elevator operator.

Songwriting came early and easily to Diddley, who wrote his first piece, "I Don't Want No Lyin' Woman," at age sixteen. In an effort to counteract the noise in the venues where he performed, Diddley built an amplifier by hand. He intuitively understood from the start that his style would conjoin volume and rhythm, and therefore, early on, he enlisted the assistance of a neighbor, Jerome Green, on maracas to underscore the beat. Together with Green, harmonica player "Billy Boy" Arnold, and others, Diddley established a reputation in the local clubs of Chicago.

Bo Diddley with his trademark hat and square guitar. Corbis

The sound they produced proved to be unique, for Diddley amalgamated a body of musical practices that originated in the rhythms of the church, the percussive speech patterns of the street, and the "shout mode" that harked back to drum-playing traditions in Africa. He combined that rhythmic approach along with a declamatory style in his vocals that prefigured rap. Acutely aware of his innovations, Diddley routinely objected to efforts to label this sound or to single out its influences: "Guys kind of piss me off trying to name what I'm doing, and you know, they don't want to accept what I tell them, so they want to use their own thing so they can title it. But I do know what it is, and a lot of times I tell people I don't, I just play it. But I know" (Chess, CH3-19502, 1990, 7). No matter what the source or the name of his musical style, Diddley etched a singular path by making his band stress rhythm over melody, and he frequently employed repetitious, often childlike words, drawn from street games or from the verbal one-upmanship associated with signifying, words used more for their sound than their sense. Diddley developed a "shave-and-a-haircut—two bits" sequence of rhythmic accents that audiences indelibly associate with his music. In 1946, he married Ethel Mac

Smith and they had two children before the marriage ended in divorce.

In order to break into the record business in 1955, Diddley, still performing under the name Ellas McDaniel, made a demonstration record of two songs: "Uncle John" and "I'm a Man." He took them to several local companies, including the black-owned Vee Jay Records, that turned him down. He then turned to Chess Records, owned by Leonard and Phil Chess. Established in 1947, the label initially made its mark with blues, recording such titans of the genre as MUDDY WATERS, Howlin' Wolf, and Little Walter. The Chess brothers were on the lookout for artists who could sell to a broad, not necessarily racially segregated audience. They were about to succeed with CHUCK BERRY, and they heard in McDaniel something that could be as marketable.

Inadvertently, while performing "Uncle John," the group proclaimed, "Bo Diddley." At first, Leonard Chess worried that this name might defame blacks. When he was assured it would not, the title of the track became "Bo Diddley," and a career was launched. Both sides of the single took off, and within weeks they occupied the number one and two spots on the *Billboard* jukebox charts as well as rising on the

Billboard list of what disk jockeys were playing. These songs clearly appealed to both black and white listeners, and therefore, in the parlance of the music business, they "crossed over."

A string of successful singles followed, including "You Don't Love Me" (1955), "Mona" (1957), and "You Can't Judge a Book by the Cover" (1962). Diddley consolidated his success with a riveting stage presence. His homemade square-shaped guitar and boosted amplification captivated audiences, as did the manner in which his behavior mirrored the sexual braggadocio of his lyrics. He strutted across the stage like the legendary bluesman CHARLEY PATTON, playing his guitar with his teeth, behind his back, over his head, and between his legs. He further upped the ante by adding, on more than one occasion, a female second guitarist, giving her such names as Lady Bo and the Duchess.

However, despite the galvanizing nature of his material and performance, Diddley's rise to the top of the charts was brief. With the appearance of the Beatles in the United States in 1964, many black artists associated with early rock and roll fell out of favor or were treated condescendingly as objects of nostalgia. Diddley continued to record for the Chess label until 1974, yet few of his albums or singles achieved commercial success.

Lamentably, Diddley found himself not only toppled from the charts but also convinced that he never received his due financial reward, either from Chess Records or from the companies that subsequently owned their recordings. He was relegated to Oldies venues for much of the 1970s, 1980s, and early 1990s, even though countless musicians and writers applauded his material and credited its influence upon rock and roll. Some of his songs became part of the permanent repertoire of American popular music, but the concrete rewards for that achievement were few.

Slowly, the tide turned. Tributes on the part of younger musicians led to renewed media exposure. Diddley appeared in the Eddie Murphy film comedy *Trading Places* (1983) and in a 1989 Nike commercial with the sports figure Bo Jackson. Honorific organizations across the musical spectrum honored him. Diddley was inducted into the Rock and Roll

Hall of Fame in 1987, and received the *Guitar Player* magazine Lifetime Achievement Award in 1990 and the Pioneer Award from the Rhythm and Blues Foundation in 1996. He accepted a lifetime achievement award at the 1998 Grammy Awards and was inducted into the Grammy Hall of Fame.

But awards do not pay the bills, and Diddley continued to perform into his seventies to keep his legacy alive. The influence and magnitude of that achievement cannot be underestimated. He codified a rhythm that has become an indelible feature of American vernacular music. His guitar style can be heard in genres as broad as rock and roll and heavy metal, and his use of technology to augment the impact of his material set in motion popular music's long-standing attachment to volume. Diddley's musical influence is clearly seen in the careers of such performers as Elvis Presley, Buddy Holly, and the Rolling Stones. Furthermore, his playful and yet sophisticated use of language and his declamatory delivery have made him one of the forefathers of rap.

FURTHER READING

Cohodas, Nadine. *Spinning Blues into Gold: The Chess Brothers and the Legendary Chess Records* (2000).

Palmer, Robert. *Rock and Roll: An Unruly History* (1995).

White, George R. *Bo Diddley: Living Legend* (1998).

Discography:
The Chess Box (CH3-19502).

—DAVID SANJEK

 DINKINS, DAVID N.

(10 July 1927–), mayor of New York City, was born David Norman Dinkins in Trenton, New Jersey, the first of two children of William H. Dinkins, a barbershop owner and real estate agent, and Sally (maiden name unknown), a domestic worker and manicurist. David's parents divorced when he was six years old, and he lived briefly with his mother after she moved to Harlem, New York City, although he soon returned to Trenton to live with his father and stepmother, Lottie Hartgell, a high school English teacher.

After graduating from high school in Trenton, Dinkins became one of the first African Americans to serve in the U.S. Marine Corps, and he graduated magna cum laude in 1950 from Howard University, where he majored in mathematics. He graduated from Brooklyn Law School in 1956 and practiced law in New York City until 1975. Dinkins and his wife, the former Joyce Burroughs, whom he married in 1953, have two children.

Dinkins became involved in politics through his wife, the daughter of a Democratic ward leader in Harlem. He served one term in the New York state assembly, two years as president of the New York City Board of Elections, and ten years as the city clerk. When his close friend Percy Sutton resigned as Manhattan borough president in 1977, he encouraged Dinkins to try for the position. After three unsuccessful attempts, Dinkins was elected borough president in 1985. A quiet, unassuming politician throughout his long and generally undistinguished public career, he managed, even as Manhattan borough president, to remain largely invisible to New York City voters.

Known as a stolid and courtly gentleman, but certainly not a dynamic or forceful leader, the sixty-two-year-old Dinkins surprised the political experts with his decision to challenge the incumbent mayor Edward Koch in 1989. The deterioration of race relations in New York City during the Koch years had accelerated during Koch's third term, and the local black press called for the election of the city's first black mayor. The racial unease plaguing the city intensified in the months preceding the August 1989 primary election, and Koch's responses to racially charged incidents seemed increasingly inadequate to many African Americans. Dinkins spoke about the need for racial rapprochement and promised to be a healer; he won the primary election with 50.8 percent of the vote to Koch's 42 percent.

In the general election that followed, the Republicans fielded a strong candidate in Rudolph Giuliani, a well-known federal prosecutor who had indicted a long list of Mafia dons, crooked politicians, and corporate embezzlers. Giuliani conducted an aggressive campaign, promising New Yorkers a tough law-and-order

administration, while Dinkins continued to emphasize his ability to bring the city together, to calm the roiling racial seas that seemed to be pounding the city from all sides. On 7 November 1989 a slender majority of the New York City electorate provided Dinkins with a 47,000-vote victory margin out of 1.9 million votes cast.

New York City's finances had been balanced over a precipice for decades, and Koch left his successor no shortage of worrisome dilemmas. The city's first black mayor inherited a billion-dollar deficit, with even greater fiscal problems on the horizon, as contracts would soon expire for 360,000 municipal employees. City officials counted 75,000 homeless in New York City, only 35,000 of whom found shelter nightly, and the city needed 250,000 more housing units. Schools, social agencies, and the health-care system lacked adequate resources. The closing of bridges, highways, and streets, as well as the frequent explosion of water mains, gave the impression that New York City's aged infrastructure was collapsing. Throughout his administration, Dinkins had to grapple with the intractable problem of how to balance the city's budget, satisfy the business community's demand for fiscal responsibility, and still find the resources to offer the costly social programs that much of his constituency and his own liberal beliefs demanded—all at a time when the federal government had reduced its largess to cities and the nation's economy remained mired in recession.

While struggling from year to year to manage the city's nettlesome financial problems, Dinkins also had to respond to a series of violent incidents that threatened to undermine the racial comity he had promised to nurture. On 18 January 1990, just seventeen days after Dinkins assumed office, an altercation between a Haitian American resident of the Flatbush section of Brooklyn and the Korean American owners of a neighborhood grocery store heightened racial tensions in the city. African Americans, led by AL SHARPTON, initiated a boycott of the store that lasted nearly a year and, as violence between blacks and Asians increased in Flatbush, critics accused Dinkins of being insensitive to the Asian immigrants.

The following year, three days of rioting erupted in the Crown Heights section of Brooklyn after a car driven by a Hasidic Jew accidentally struck and killed a black girl and seriously injured her brother. In retribution, an angry gang of black youths murdered a rabbinical student. The mayor tried unsuccessfully to mediate between African Americans and Hasidim in Crown Heights. Jewish leaders excoriated Dinkins for what they saw as his lack of impartiality, while African Americans praised him for what they considered his restraint.

More criticism came over the mayor's handling of yet another racial disturbance, a clash between police and Dominican immigrants in the upper Manhattan neighborhood of Washington Heights. Despite Dinkins's frequent attempts to cool angry passions, five days of rioting followed in Washington Heights. In the aftermath of the disturbance, the Policemen's Benevolent Association charged that the mayor had proved too tolerant of rioters and had expressed excessive criticisms of the police.

In 1993 Rudolph Giuliani easily secured the Republican nomination for mayor and launched an aggressive campaign that hammered constantly at a single theme—in four years, Dinkins had repeatedly demonstrated his inability to manage the myriad affairs of the complex city. Giuliani characterized the Dinkins administration as ineffective and wasteful, and the mayor himself as inept and unresponsive to whites, Latinos, and Asians. The result of such mismanagement, charged the former prosecutor, was evident in the deterioration of the quality of life in New York City, and no more so than in the escalating crime rate that had become a major focus of editorial comment in the press.

Dinkins ardently defended his record in city hall, attributing persistent economic problems to forces outside mayoral control. If racial tensions had risen nearly to the boiling point, Dinkins asserted, his administration had kept the lid on. New York City, he argued, had experienced no massive outbreak comparable to the riots in Los Angeles in 1992, following the announcement that Los Angeles police officers had been exonerated in the beating of Rodney King. Dinkins lost the vote for reelection by a narrow margin, receiving 48.3 percent of the vote to Giuliani's 50.7 percent, and thus became the first black mayor of a major U.S. city to relinquish the office after just one term.

Dinkins's mayoralty produced an ambiguous legacy. Because of New York City's preeminence among the nation's urban places, his election constituted a landmark in U.S. politics. Unlike successful black candidates in other large cities with black electoral majorities, Dinkins triumphed in 1989 in a city where blacks composed just 25 percent of the population. The *New York Times* recognized Dinkins's achievement, calling his election "a political coming of age" for African Americans (2 Jan. 1990). The lack of success of his reelection campaign in 1993 resulted from a perception that a courtly and cautious man had failed to effectively manage the city's affairs. His failure to solve New York's fiscal woes bespoke the difficulties facing a host of black mayors who arrived in city halls at a precarious time of urban retrenchment, suburban expansion, and dwindling resources. Yet by 1992 Dinkins had brought the city from massive deficits to a budget surplus and his community-policing programs resulted in a steady decrease in crime. However, his failure to convince voters of his ability to deal fairly and evenhandedly with all ethnic groups and races in New York City proved to be a serious shortcoming, in part because of the intense scrutiny inevitably applied to black mayors when issues of race relations arise.

FURTHER READING

Biles, Roger. "Mayor David Dinkins and the Politics of Race in New York City" in *African-American Mayors: Race, Politics, and the American City*, eds. David R. Colburn and Jeffrey S. Adler (2001).
Siegel, Fred. *The Future Once Happened Here: New York, D.C., L.A., and the Fate of America's Big Cities* (1997).
—ROGER BILES

 DIXON, "BIG" WILLIE JAMES (1 July 1915–29 Jan. 1992), blues musician, composer, and arranger, was born in Vicksburg, Mississippi, to Daisy McKenzie and, putatively, her husband Charlie Dixon. Willie was one of seven surviving children (out of fourteen). It is likely that Anderson "A. D." Bell, whom Willie Dixon called his stepfather, was actually his biological father, as records show that Daisy and Charlie Dixon finalized divorce proceedings in 1913. As a youth Dixon worked in his mother's restaurant as well as spending time in Vicksburg's barrel houses and juke joints. Along with his mother's interest in reading and writing poetry, contact with blues legends such as CHARLEY PATTON and Eurreal Wilford "Little Brother" Montgomery led Dixon to begin writing songs of his own.

The search for work and his own wanderlust put Dixon on the road at a young age. Arrested while traveling as a hobo through Clarksdale, Mississippi, and sentenced to thirty days on the Charles Allen Prison Farm, Dixon escaped to Memphis, Tennessee, on the back of a mule. Freight trains carried him north until he reached his sister in Chicago in 1929. Between 1926 and 1936 Dixon found his way to New York City, Ohio, Florida, and numerous hobo jungles throughout the South. He even shipped out to Hawaii, mistakenly boarding a vessel bound for the islands while he was cleaning ships.

Despite these adventures, it was back in Vicksburg that Dixon's career as a musician and songwriter began to take shape. When in Mississippi, he sold song lyrics to country and western musicians and sang bass with the Union Jubilee Singers, a gospel quartet. This group's popularity brought singing engagements around Mississippi and led to regular appearances on WQBC radio, doing weekly live broadcasts from the station's Vicksburg studios.

Always large for his age, as Dixon matured he approached three hundred pounds and began training seriously as a boxer. Fighting under the name James Dixon, he won the 1936 Illinois Golden Gloves in the heavyweight division. However, Dixon's professional boxing career was put on hold when he drew a suspension for brawling outside the ring. Soon afterward, the musician Leonard "Baby Doo" Caston persuaded Dixon to focus his energies on music full-time.

With Caston's help, Dixon left boxing behind. Not only did Caston make Dixon's first bass from an oil can and a strand of wire, he also introduced

Dixon to people in the music business. When the musicians' union recording ban of 1936–1937 was lifted, Dixon played bass at his first recording session with Caston and a vocal group called the Bumping Boys. In 1939 Caston and Dixon returned to the studio as members of the Five Breezes, cutting eight tracks that were released on Bluebird, RCA's "race record" label. (Race records were those produced or marketed with African American consumers in mind.)

The association with Caston and the other members of the Five Breezes established Dixon on the Chicago music scene. He moved about town, selling song sheets or printed copies of his version of the folk rhyme "The Signifying Monkey." He became a fixture at the many music clubs on Maxwell Street and also played at Martin's Corner on the city's West Side. However, Dixon's run of good fortune came to an abrupt end when the United States entered World War II following the Japanese attack on Pearl Harbor in December 1941. In 1942, he was literally pulled off the stage and arrested as a draft resister. Refusing military service, he was, like BAYARD RUSTIN and other conscientious objectors, imprisoned and became entangled in a lengthy court battle. In his memoir, *I Am the Blues*, Dixon stated, "I wasn't going to fight nobody.... I told them I didn't feel I had to go because of the conditions that existed among my people" (54). He served ten months for resisting the draft, and was released in 1944.

After the war Dixon and Caston reunited, forming a vocal trio along with Ollie Crawford. Calling themselves the Big Three (after Churchill, Roosevelt, and Stalin), the group had a run of hit records in the mid-1940s, including "The Signifying Monkey." White audiences embraced the Big Three's swing-oriented pop sound, and the group toured extensively throughout the Midwest. Even as the trio enjoyed their success, Dixon tired of the traveling and the musical direction the group was taking. In order to spend more time with his wife, Marie, and their eleven children, he began hiring himself out to Chicago studios when his touring schedule allowed.

During the late 1940s Chicago experienced a blues renaissance, as raw, down-home sounds were electrified in small clubs and bars on the South Side. As this music found the ears of black audiences in Chicago and around the country, a number of independent record producers sought to cash in, including Leonard and Phil Chess. Late in 1948, after watching Dixon perform in late-night jam sessions on Forty-seventh Street, Leonard Chess offered the bass player studio work for an upcoming session with the bluesman Robert Nighthawk. This began a relationship between Dixon and Chess that was, if nothing else, extremely productive for the former and very profitable for the later. Using Dixon's feel for the music as their guide, the Chess brothers, who were minor players in the race record market in the late 1940s, became hit makers in short order.

Throughout the 1950s and 1960s Dixon wrote, arranged, and played the music that made Chess Studios an assembly line of hits that topped both the blues chart and the R&B (rhythm and blues) charts. Artists such as MUDDY WATERS, Howlin' Wolf, and Little Walter drew from Dixon's extensive songbook, recording tunes such as "Hoochie Coochie Man," "Little Red Rooster," "Back Door Man Spoonful," "You Shook Me," and "Wang Dang Doodle." While at Chess, Dixon became a contributor to the foundation of rock and roll, playing bass and doing studio work in sessions with CHUCK BERRY and BO DIDDLEY. Dixon also served as an A&R (artist and repertoire) man, finding new talent for the Chess brothers. He was instrumental in ushering into the Chess empire the next wave of hit makers, including Otis Rush and Buddy Guy. Working through his own Yambo label, Dixon also promoted the recording careers of Koko Taylor, Lucky Peterson, and the Five Blind Boys of Mississippi.

Dixon toured overseas during the late 1950s and early 1960s, helping to awaken interest in the blues on an international scale. By playing in Europe and Great Britain, as well as at American folk festivals, he contributed to the so-called blues revival and witnessed his songs pass to a new generation of musicians. British acts including the Rolling Stones, Led Zeppelin, and Eric Clapton, as well as American rockers

such as the Grateful Dead and The Doors, had hits with his songs. However, these musical transfers were not without complications. After Leonard Chess's death in 1969, Dixon took legal action to regain the rights to his songs from Arc Music, the Chesses' publishing company. In 1977 he reached an out-of-court settlement, after which the rights were transferred to his Ghana Publishing Company. Soon afterward Dixon filed a successful suit for copyright violation against Led Zeppelin for their recording of "Whole Lotta Love."

As a statesman and steward of the blues, Dixon continued to perform and record in his later years. He was honored with numerous awards and citations, including the Blues Ink Lifetime Achievement Award and the W. C. HANDY Award. Despite health complications due to diabetes, Dixon worked to establish the Chicago public schools "Blues in the Schools" program and the Blues Heaven Foundation, a nonprofit organization dedicated to assisting older blues performers and providing scholarships to young musicians. He died in Burbank, California.

FURTHER READING

Dixon, Willie, with Don Snowden. *I Am the Blues: The Willie Dixon Story* (1989).

Flanagan, Bill. "Willie Dixon." In *Written in My Soul: Rock's Greatest Song Writers Talk about Their Music* (1986).

Wynn, Ron. "Blues Perspective." *Living Blues* 103 (May–June 1992).

Obituary: *Chicago Tribune*, 30 Jan. 1992.
—MICHAEL A. ANTONUCCI

 DORSEY, THOMAS ANDREW (1 July 1899– 23 Jan. 1993), blues performer, gospel singer, and composer, was born in Villa Rica, Georgia, the son of Thomas Madison Dorsey, a preacher, and Etta Plant Spencer. Dorsey's mother, whose first husband had died, owned approximately fifty acres of farmland. Dorsey lived in somewhat trying circumstances as his parents moved first to Atlanta and Forsyth, Georgia, and then back to Villa Rica during the first four years of his life. In Villa Rica the Dorsey family settled into a rural lifestyle supported by marginal farming that was slightly mitigated by his father's pastoral duties.

Though economically pressed, Dorsey's parents found enough money to purchase an organ, and it was on this instrument that their young son began to play music at around six years of age. Dorsey was exposed not only to the religious music that pervaded his home but also to the secular music—especially the emerging blues tradition—that encompassed the music universe of a young black American growing up in rural Georgia in the early twentieth century. His experience with secular music came through his friends as well as his uncle Phil Plant, who picked the guitar and wandered across southern Georgia as a bard. His mother's brother-in-law Corrie M. Hindsman, a more respectable member of the local black establishment, gave Thomas a rudimentary formal music education, including singing out of the shape-note hymnals and learning some of the antebellum spirituals.

In 1908 the family moved to Atlanta after Dorsey's parents finally tired of the lack of opportunities available to black Americans living in rural Georgia. Both worked at a variety of menial jobs while the elder Dorsey occasionally also worked as a guest preacher. Atlanta's higher cost of living meant a decline in social and economic status, however, and young Thomas dropped out of school after the fourth grade. He slowly became part of the commercial music scene that revolved around Decatur Street and the Eighty-one Theater in particular. By his mid-teens Dorsey was regularly working as a pianist at the clubs and at local Saturday night stomps, house parties, and dances sponsored by organizations such as the Odd Fellows.

For three years, between the summers of 1916 and 1919, Dorsey shuttled between Atlanta and Chicago in search of more lucrative and steady musical employment. He was principally a blues pianist who occasionally performed with small combos that played jazz, and well into the early 1920s Dorsey was still struggling to survive on his meager earnings from music. Although he attended the 1921 National Baptist Convention in Chicago (his Uncle Joshua invited his nephew to accompany him) and after the convention became music director of Chicago's New

Hope Baptist Church, Dorsey remained committed to the secular world. He was in a good position to cash in on this music when the blues records of BESSIE SMITH, Alberta Hunter, and MA RAINEY gained popularity in the mid-1920s. For several years he served as Rainey's pianist and arranger, touring the country playing tent shows and vaudeville stages. In 1928 he teamed with Tampa Red, and they soon had a hit with "It's Tight Like That"; until 1932 the duo earned a steady living playing on stage and recording for the Vocalion label. Dorsey also worked as a music demonstrator in Chicago music stores from 1928 on and as an arranger and session organizer for Brunswick and Vocalion records.

Dorsey's personal life had changed in August 1925 when he married Nettie Harper, who had recently arrived in Chicago from Philadelphia. He was given to occasional bouts with depression, and his marriage helped to stabilize him. When these periods descended upon him he turned not only to Nettie but also to his own religious upbringing. As early as 1922 Dorsey began publishing sacred songs in addition to blues. His 1926 composition "If You See My Savior, Tell Him That You Saw Me," came during one of his depressive periods and is perhaps the first "gospel blues" piece ever published. Dorsey pioneered this genre by combining sacred lyrics with the harmonic structure and form of the popular blues songs. In 1928 Dorsey met and mentored seventeen-year-old MAHALIA JACKSON, one of the first singers he knew who was able to combine the emotional feeling of blues with the sentiments of his new gospel songs.

Almost exactly seven years after their marriage, Nettie died in childbirth, followed within a day by their infant son, their only child. Dorsey fell into deep melancholy that lasted for months. He finally started to climb out of his depression by writing "Take My Hand, Precious Lord," and from that point until his own death Dorsey devoted his life to gospel performing, composing, and organizations. During the decade after his wife's death, Dorsey worked tirelessly to promote gospel music, first in Chicago and then across the United States.

As early as a year before Nettie's passing Dorsey had been turning more

and more of his attention to the sacred music realm. He founded and helped to direct the first gospel choir at Chicago's Ebenezer Baptist Church in late 1931. One year later Dorsey, along with gospel singer Sallie Martin, was instrumental in establishing the National Convention of Gospel Choirs and Choruses, formed in response to the steadily growing number of gospel choruses. These proved to be popular, though controversial, innovations within the black-American church. The old-line, more conservative mainstream church members proved resistant to change; they protested the showmanship that accompanied these groups' programs and were appalled by the clapping, highly syncopated rhythms, choreographed movement, and overt emotionalism that Dorsey instilled in the gospel choruses with which he worked. While sometimes troubled by criticism, Dorsey was undeterred. His final major contribution during this early period was to open the Thomas A. Dorsey Gospel Songs Music Publishing Company. This fledgling company sold thousands of copies of early gospel songs for ten cents apiece, disseminating them mainly at local churches and the early annual meetings of the National Convention of Gospel Choirs and Choruses.

Dorsey worked tirelessly over the next two decades in service to the growth of gospel blues and the organizations that he helped found. He traveled across the country teaching workshops, leading choruses, and occasionally singing, all the while retaining his Chicago base. He published scores of sacred songs during this period, including "There'll Be Peace in the Valley" (1938), "Hide Me in Thy Bosom" (1939), "Ev'ry Day Will Be Sunday By and By" (1946), and "I'm Climbing Up the Rough Side of the Mountain" (1951). In 1940 he married Kathryn Mosley, with whom he had two children, and in the 1960s and 1970s he served as an assistant pastor at the Pilgrim Church.

Slowed by age and the desire to stay closer to his Chicago home, Dorsey became less prolific over the last four decades of his life, composing fewer than twenty songs. Throughout his life Dorsey remained proud of his work in blues and of his guidance of Mahalia Jackson early in a career that eventually touched millions of Americans, black and white. By the late 1950s pop singers Pat Boone and Elvis Presley had underscored Dorsey's impact on modern gospel music through their influential recordings of "Peace in the Valley" and other Dorsey-inspired compositions. The 1982 documentary film *Say Amen, Somebody* pays warm tribute to Dorsey and other gospel pioneers. During the final years of his life Dorsey became recognized as the patriarch of the gospel blues movement, which he lived to see from its inception to its widespread acceptance. After several years of severely diminished health, he died in Chicago.

FURTHER READING

Dixon, Robert M. W., and John Godrich. *Blues and Gospel Records, 1902–1943* (1982).
Harris, Michael. *The Rise of Gospel Blues—The Music of Thomas Andrew Dorsey in the Urban Church* (1992).

Obituary: *New York Times*, 25 Jan. 1993.
—KIP LORNELL

DOUGLAS, AARON

(26 May 1899–2 Feb. 1979), artist and educator, was born in Topeka, Kansas, the son of Aaron Douglas Sr., a baker from Tennessee, and Elizabeth (maiden name unknown), an amateur artist from Alabama. Aaron had several brothers and sisters, but he was unique in his family in his singular drive to pursue higher education. He attended segregated elementary schools and then an integrated high school. Topeka had a strong and progressive black community, and Aaron was fortunate to grow up in a city where education and social uplift were stressed through organizations such as the Black Topeka Foundation. He was an avid reader and immersed himself in the great writers, including Dumas, Shakespeare, and Emerson. His parents were able to feed and clothe him but could offer him no other help with higher education. When he needed money to pursue a college degree, he traveled via rail to Detroit, where he worked as a laborer in several jobs, including building automobiles. It was hard work, but it increased his desire to attend college.

Upon his return to Topeka, Douglas decided to attend the University of Nebraska and arrived ten days into

Painter and graphic artist Aaron Douglas executed several murals depicting African American life and history, including The Song of the Towers, *the fourth panel in a mural series dated 1934 and titled* Aspects of Negro Life. *Schomburg Center*

the term with no transcripts in hand. This was the first in a series of steps he made to educate himself and improve his artistic skills. The chairman of Nebraska's art department realized Douglas's potential and agreed to accept him on the condition that his transcripts would follow. At Nebraska, Douglas discovered the writings of W. E. B. DU BOIS and found inspiration in them. By 1921 he was a constant reader of *Crisis* magazine, and later, *Opportunity*, and he began to seriously consider the nation's racial situation. Douglas graduated from Nebraska with a BFA in 1922 and accepted a teaching position at Lincoln High School in Kansas City, Missouri, where he was one of only two black faculty members. In 1925, after seeing a special issue of *Survey Graphic* magazine, which focused on Harlem and featured a portrait of black actor Roland Hayes on its cover, Douglas decided to quit his job and pursue his dream of

working as a full-time artist. Hoping for wider artistic opportunities and contact with a larger black community, Douglas moved to Harlem in 1925. While he was full of dreams, Douglas had very few connections in New York.

Only days after his arrival, *Crisis* editor W. E. B. Du Bois hired him to work in the magazine's mail room and to help illustrate the magazine. Du Bois, who had been editing *Crisis* for fourteen years, was struggling against the competition, *Opportunity* magazine, published by the National Urban League. Needing a stronger visual message, Du Bois turned to Douglas, commissioning bold covers, prints, and drawings to accompany essays, stories, and editorials expressing Du Bois's vision of what African Americans should know about the world around them, and what causes they should support. In 1927 Douglas was made art director at *Crisis*. When Douglas had started work at *Crisis*, he had also been hired by JAMES WELDON JOHNSON to illustrate for *Opportunity* magazine. Douglas soon found himself in the unique, and pleasant, position of having two major publications vying for his talents. Through his *Crisis* connections, Douglas met Bavarian artist Winold Reiss, who offered him a scholarship to study with him in his New York atelier, where Douglas immersed himself in the study of black life. Douglas was soon noticed by other patrons, and he quickly became one of the most sought-after illustrators of the Harlem Renaissance, receiving commissions to illustrate magazines and book covers as well as to execute a number of private commissions and public murals.

From his earliest Harlem paintings and prints, Douglas developed a strong commitment to establishing an African American identity tied to an African past, a history and identification encouraged by both Du Bois and ALAIN LOCKE. Douglas was drawn to African art even while he knew very little about it. As one of the key visual spokesmen for what became known as the Harlem Renaissance, Douglas used the art of the Ivory Coast, Ethiopia, and Egypt to establish a firm connection between African Americans and African culture. As he wrote to his future wife, Alta Sawyer, in 1925:

We are possessed, you know, with the idea that it is necessary to be white, to be beautiful. Nine times out of ten it is just the reverse. It takes lots of training or a tremendous effort to down the idea that thin lips and a straight nose is the apogee of beauty. But once free you can look back with a sigh of relief and wonder how anyone could be so deluded.

(Kirschke, 61)

Douglas married Alta in 1926. Over the years the couple's Harlem home became a central meeting place for the artists and writers of the Harlem Renaissance. Meanwhile, Douglas's illustrations, full of race pride and African heritage, had wide distribution and were seen across the country, in libraries, schools, social clubs, beauty parlors, and homes. He also provided artwork for other magazines, including *Theatre Arts Monthly*, as well as for numerous books. Douglas produced covers and interior illustrations for some of the Harlem Renaissance's

most significant literary achievements, including Alain Locke's *New Negro*, WALLACE THURMAN's *The Blacker the Berry*, Paul Morand's *Black Magic*, James Weldon Johnson's *God's Trombones*, COUNTÉE CULLEN's *Caroling Dusk*, and CLAUDE MCKAY's *Banjo*, and several works by LANGSTON HUGHES. Douglas was moved by the artistic milieu in which he worked, especially the literature of the time, written by his friends, which, along with his own work, described black life. Douglas's work articulated the black experience in Harlem in the 1920s and 1930s, including the tremendous output of visual arts and music, and the effects of discrimination and the Depression. Douglas offered a unique visual style, which combined elements of American and European modernism, including cubism, orphism, precisionism, and art deco patterning, with a strong Pan-Africanist vision. His linoleum cuts, pen and ink drawings, oils, gouaches, and frescos forged a distinct combination of modernist elements.

In 1928 Douglas and Gwendolyn Bennett became the first African American artists to receive a fellowship to study at the Barnes Foundation in Merion, Pennsylvania. Douglas's one-year fellowship was followed, in 1931, by a year of study in Paris at the Academie Scandinave, where he met African American painters HENRY OSSAWA TANNER and Palmer Hayden.

In addition to his work as an illustrator, Douglas was a painter, particularly of portraits. He was interested in murals and received several mural commissions, including a mural at the Harlem branch of the YMCA, the College Inn in Chicago, and Bennett College in South Carolina. His most innovative project—created for Cravath Hall Library at Fisk University in Nashville, Tennessee, in 1930—was a massive cycle of murals celebrating philosophy, drama, music, poetry, and science, as well as African and African American culture. Restoration of these murals in 2003 revealed orphist-like geometric circles and abstract papyrus-topped columns, as well as four murals that had been covered for decades. One mural depicts Africans left behind as their family members and friends are taken away, never to be seen again. The mural cycle chronicles the history of blacks from Africa and

slavery, to their triumphant release from servitude through education. Ambitious in its Pan-Africanist vision the mural includes elements drawn from Egypt, West Africa, and the Congo. In the 1960s Douglas entirely repainted the Fisk murals with a much brighter, bolder palette. In 1934 Douglas completed *Aspects of Negro Life*, four large mural panels sponsored by the WPA for the Countée Cullen Library at 135th Street (now the Schomburg Center for Research in Black Culture). Like the Fisk murals, these panels illustrate life in Africa before enslavement, through the years of slavery, emancipation, and into the African American present. Douglas offered hope even in the Depression, through creativity, music, and culture.

The Fisk mural commission led to Douglas's return to the university in 1937, where he established the university's first art department, remaining as chair of the department for over thirty years, until his retirement in 1966. In 1944, after years of part-time graduate work, he earned his MA from Columbia University Teacher's College. He taught and worked as an artist well into his seventies and considered his work as an educator at Fisk to be his greatest accomplishment. Douglas, whose work influenced countless artists with its unique vision of African American identity linked to a Pan-Africanist vision, died in Nashville in 1979.

FURTHER READING

Douglas's papers are held in the Fisk University Special Collections, Nashville, Tennessee, and at the Schomburg Center for Research in Black Culture of the New York Public Library.

Kirschke, Amy Helene. *Aaron Douglas: Art, Race and the Harlem Renaissance* (1995).

Obituary: *New York Times*, 22 Feb. 1979.

—AMY HELENE KIRSCHKE

DOUGLASS, FREDERICK (Feb. 1818–20 Feb. 1895), abolitionist, civil rights activist, and reform journalist, was born Frederick Augustus Washington Bailey near Easton, Maryland, the son of Harriet Bailey, a slave, and an unidentified white man. Although a slave, he spent the first six years of

This early photograph of Frederick Douglass shows the strength of character and determination that made him the most influential African American of the nineteenth century and the most powerful voice for the abolition of slavery and for equal rights. Corbis

his life in the cabin of his maternal grandparents, with only a few stolen nighttime visits by his mother. His real introduction to bondage came in 1824, when he was brought to the nearby wheat plantation of Colonel Edward Lloyd. Two years later he was sent to Baltimore to labor in the household of Hugh and Sophia Auld, where he remained for the next seven years. In spite of laws against slave literacy, Frederick secretly taught himself to read and write. He began studying discarded newspapers and learned of the growing national debate over slavery. And he attended local free black churches and found the sight of black men reading and speaking in public a moving experience. At about age thirteen he bought a popular rhetoric text and carefully worked through the exercises, mastering the preferred public speaking style of the time.

Literacy and a growing social consciousness made Frederick into an unruly bondsman. In 1833, after being taken by master Thomas Auld to a plantation near St. Michael's, Maryland, he organized a secret school for slaves, but it was discovered and broken up

by a mob of local whites. To discipline Frederick, Auld hired him out to a local farmer who had a reputation as a "slave breaker." Instead he became increasingly defiant and refused to allow himself to be whipped. Hired out to another local farmer, he again organized a secret school for slaves. Before long, he and his pupils had plotted to escape to the free state of Pennsylvania, but this too was discovered. Expecting further trouble from Frederick, Auld returned him to Baltimore in 1836 and hired him out to a local shipyard to learn the caulking trade. Taking advantage of the relative liberty afforded by the city, Frederick joined a self-improvement society of free black caulkers that regularly debated the major social and intellectual questions of the day.

After an unsuccessful attempt to buy his freedom, Frederick escaped from slavery in September 1838. Dressed as a sailor and carrying the free papers of a black seaman he had met on the streets of Baltimore, he traveled by train and steamboat to New York. There he married Anna Murray, a free black domestic servant from Baltimore who had encouraged his escape. They soon

settled in the seaport of New Bedford, Massachusetts, where Frederick found employment as a caulker and outfitter for whaling ships, and began a family; two daughters and three sons were born to the union in a little more than a decade. At the urging of a local black abolitionist, he adopted the surname Douglass to disguise his background and confuse slave catchers. He also joined the local African Methodist Episcopal Zion Church and became an active lay leader and exhorter.

Soon after arriving in New Bedford, Frederick Douglass was drawn to the emerging antislavery movement. He began to read the *Liberator*, a leading abolitionist journal edited by William Lloyd Garrison, and to attend antislavery meetings in local black churches, occasionally speaking out about his slave experiences. His remarks at an August 1841 convention of the Massachusetts Anti-Slavery Society on Nantucket Island brought him to the attention of Garrison and other leading white abolitionists. Society officials, impressed by Douglass's eloquence and imposing presence, hired him as a lecturing agent. Over the next two years, during which time he moved his family to Lynn, Massachusetts, he made hundreds of speeches for the society before antislavery audiences throughout New England and New York State. In 1843 he joined other leading abolitionist speakers on the One Hundred Conventions tour, which sought to strengthen abolitionist sentiment in upstate New York, Ohio, Indiana, and western Pennsylvania. His oratorical skills brought him increasing recognition and respect within the movement. But antislavery lecturing was a hazardous business. Douglass and his colleagues were often subjected to verbal assaults, barrages of rotten eggs and vegetables, and mob violence. And, as a fugitive slave, his growing visibility placed him in constant danger of recapture. He had to conceal or gloss over certain details in his life story, including names, dates, and locations, to avoid jeopardizing his newfound freedom.

Douglass's growing sophistication as a speaker brought other difficulties in the mid-1840s. At first, his speeches were simple accounts of his life in bondage. But as he matured as an antislavery lecturer, he increasingly sought to provide a critical analysis of both slavery and northern racial prejudice. His eloquence and keen mind even led some to question whether he had ever been a slave. As Douglass's skills—combined with his circumspection—prompted critics to question his credibility, some white abolitionists feared that his effectiveness on the platform might be lost. They advised him to speak more haltingly and to hew to his earlier simple tale. One white colleague thought it "better to have a *little* of the plantation" in his speech (McFeely, 95).

Douglass bristled under such paternalistic tutelage. An answer was to publish an autobiography providing full details of his life that he had withheld. Although some friends argued against that course, fearing for his safety, Douglass sat down in the winter of 1844–1845 and wrote the story of his life. The result was the *Narrative of the Life of Frederick Douglass, Written by Himself* (1845). The brief autobiography, which ran only to 144 pages, put his platform tale into print and reached a broad American and European audience. It sold more than thirty thousand copies in the United States and Britain within five years and was translated into French, German, and Dutch. Along with his public lectures, "the *Narrative* made Frederick Douglass the most famous black person in the world" (David W. Blight, ed., *Narrative of the Life of Frederick Douglass* [1993], 16).

Although the *Narrative* enhanced Douglass's popularity and credibility, it increased the threat to his liberty. He was still a fugitive slave—but now one with a best-selling autobiography. Antislavery colleagues advised Douglass to travel to Britain to elude slave catchers, also hoping that his celebrity would mobilize British abolitionists to bring international pressure against American slavery. He sailed in August 1845 and remained abroad twenty months, lecturing to wildly enthusiastic audiences in England, Scotland, and Ireland. Douglass broadened his reform perspective, grew in confidence, and became increasingly self-reliant during this time. English antislavery friends eventually raised the funds necessary to purchase his freedom from the Aulds and permit his return home. They also collected monies to allow him to begin his own antislavery newspaper in the United States. In December 1847 Douglass moved his family to Rochester in the "burned-over district," a center of reform activity in upstate New York. There he launched the weekly reform journal *North Star*, which promoted abolitionism, African American rights, temperance, women's rights, and a host of related reforms. Like his later journalistic ventures, it was well written and carefully edited and carried Douglass's message to an international audience. While it served as a personal declaration of independence, it initiated an ever-widening rift between Douglass and his Garrisonian colleagues, who sensed that they were losing control of his immense talent.

Douglass's movement away from Garrisonian doctrine on antislavery strategy also signaled his growing independence. Unlike Garrison, who viewed moral suasionist appeals to individual conscience as the only appropriate tactic, Douglass was increasingly persuaded of the efficacy of politics and violence for ending bondage. He attended the Free Soil Convention in Buffalo in 1848 and endorsed its platform calling for a prohibition on the extension of slavery. In 1851 he merged the *North Star* with the *Liberty Party Paper* to form *Frederick Douglass' Paper*, which openly endorsed political abolitionism. This brought a final breach with the Garrisonians, who subjected him to a torrent of public attacks, including scandalous charges about his personal behavior. Nevertheless, Douglass endorsed the nascent Republican Party and its moderate antislavery platform in the elections of 1856 and 1860. At the same time, he increasingly explored the possibilities of abolitionist violence. As early as 1849 Douglass endorsed slave violence, telling a Boston audience that he would welcome news that the slaves had revolted and "were engaged in spreading death and devastation" throughout the South (Benjamin Quarles, *Allies for Freedom* [1974], 67). After passage of the Fugitive Slave Act of 1850, which put the federal government in the business of capturing and returning runaway slaves, he publicly urged resistance to the law, with violence if necessary. And he became active in the Underground Railroad, hiding numerous fugitives in his Rochester home and helping them on the way to Canada West (now Ontario). Douglass's growing attraction to violence is evident in his 1852 novella, *The Heroic Slave*, generally considered to be the first piece of African American fiction, which glorified the leader of a bloody slave revolt. Later in the decade Douglass became involved in the planning for John Brown's 1859 raid at Harpers Ferry, Virginia, and secretly helped raise funds for the venture, although he thought it ill conceived. When the raid failed, he fled to Canada East (now Quebec), then on to England, fearing arrest on the charge of being Brown's accomplice. He returned home in 1860, disillusioned about African American prospects in the United States and planning to visit Haiti in order to explore the feasibility of black settlement there.

The coming of the Civil War revived Douglass's hopes. From the beginning of the conflict, he pressed President Abraham Lincoln to make emancipation a war goal and to allow black enlistment in the Union army. After Lincoln issued his Emancipation Proclamation in January 1863, Douglass spoke widely in support of the measure. Believing that military service might allow black men to demonstrate their patriotism and manhood, winning greater equality as well as helping to end slavery, he recruited for the Massachusetts Fifty-fourth Colored Infantry, the first African American regiment organized in the North. His stirring editorial "Men of Color, to Arms" was often reprinted in northern newspapers and became a recruiting poster. Nevertheless, Douglass was disgusted by the government's failure to keep its recruiting promises and met with Lincoln to protest discrimination against black troops. Before long, the War Department offered him a commission to enlist and organize African American regiments among the slaves fleeing to Union lines in the lower Mississippi Valley. He stopped publication of *Douglass' Monthly*, which he had begun in 1859, and waited. But the commission never came, and Douglass, refusing to go South without it, continued to lecture and recruit in the North. As the war wound toward a conclusion in 1864–1865, he worked to shape public memory of the war and the character of the peace. He reminded audiences that the conflict had been fought to abolish slavery; it would only be successful, he argued, if the former slaves were granted equal citizenship rights with other Americans.

The end of the war and the Thirteenth Amendment outlawing slavery posed a crisis for Douglass. After a quarter of a century as the preeminent black abolitionist, he wondered if his career was at an end. But he soon recognized that important work remained to be done. In an 1865 speech to the American Anti-Slavery Society, many of whose white members were calling to disband the society, he forcefully argued that "the work of Abolitionists is not done" and would not be until blacks had equal citizenship rights with other Americans. Although he vigorously supported the Fourteenth Amendment and other civil rights statutes, he believed that a meaningful Reconstruction required two essential elements: keeping the old leadership elite from returning to power in the South, and giving the freedmen the vote. Putting the ballot in the hands of black men, he argued, would prove the key to uplifting and protecting African American rights. When President Andrew Johnson refused to endorse these principles in an 1866 meeting with Douglass, the race leader became one of his most vocal critics. He lobbied hard for passage of the Fifteenth Amendment, even at the cost of a breach with many friends who opposed the measure unless it also granted women the vote.

The 1870s were a "time of troubles" in Douglass's life. An 1872 fire destroyed his Rochester home and the files of his lengthy journalistic endeavors. He moved his family to Washington, D.C., where two years earlier he had purchased the *New National Era*. Through careful editorial guidance, he attempted to shape the weekly into a mouthpiece for the race. But persistent financial troubles forced him to stop publication of the paper in 1874. That same year Douglass was named president of the Freedman's Savings Bank, a federally chartered savings and lending institution created to assist the economic development of former slaves. He soon found that the bank was in severe financial distress; it was forced to declare bankruptcy in a matter of months. These two failed ventures cost Douglass

thousands of dollars and some public respect. Other black leaders increasingly criticized his alleged moderation on key race questions, his devotion to American individualism (most clearly seen in his oft-repeated lecture, "Self-Made Men"), and his unswerving loyalty to the Republican Party. They openly attacked his failure to criticize the party's abandonment of the Reconstruction experiment in 1877.

The end of Reconstruction dashed Douglass's hopes for a meaningful emancipation. Even so, he never abandoned the fight for African American rights. And he still regarded the Republican Party as the likeliest vehicle for black advancement. A skilled practitioner at "waving the bloody shirt"—linking Democrats with slavery and the Confederacy—he campaigned widely for Republican candidates during the 1870s and 1880s. Partisanship brought rewards. President Rutherford B. Hayes appointed Douglass as the U.S. marshal for the District of Columbia (1877–1881), and President James A. Garfield named him the district's recorder of deeds (1881–1886). These offices made him financially secure. But changing family circumstances unsettled his personal life. His wife, Anna, died in 1882. Two years later he married Helen Pitts, his white former secretary. This racially mixed marriage stirred controversy among blacks and whites alike; nevertheless, it failed to limit Douglass's influence.

Douglass was not lulled into complacency by partisan politics. He pressed Republicans as forcefully as ever on issues of concern to the African American community, while continuing to campaign for party candidates. President Benjamin Harrison rewarded him with an appointment as U.S. minister to Haiti (1889–1891). In this capacity he became an unwitting agent of American expansionism in the Caribbean, unsuccessfully attempting to negotiate special shipping concessions for American business interests and the lease of land for a naval base at Môle St. Nicholas. He eventually resigned his post and returned home in disgust.

Douglass continued to claim the mantle of race leader in the 1890s. He denounced the wave of disfranchisement and segregation measures spreading across the South. He threw much of

his energy into the emerging campaign against racial violence. Between 1892 and 1894 he delivered "Lessons of the Hour"—a speech attacking the dramatic increase in black lynchings—to dozens of audiences across the nation. He personally appealed to Harrison for an antilynching law and used his position as the only African American official at the 1893 World's Columbian Exposition to bring the issue before an international audience. He had just returned from another lecture tour when he died at his Washington home.

The most influential African American of the nineteenth century, Douglass made a career of agitating the American conscience. He spoke and wrote on behalf of a variety of reform causes: women's rights, temperance, peace, land reform, free public education, and the abolition of capital punishment. But he devoted the bulk of his time, immense talent, and boundless energy to ending slavery and gaining equal rights for African Americans. These were the central concerns of his long reform career. Douglass understood that the struggle for emancipation and equality demanded forceful, persistent, and unyielding agitation. And he recognized that African Americans must play a conspicuous role in that struggle. Less than a month before his death, when a young black man solicited his advice to an African American just starting out in the world, Douglass replied without hesitation: "Agitate! Agitate! Agitate!" (Joseph W. Holley, *You Can't Build a Chimney from the Top* [1948], 23).

FURTHER READING

Personal papers, including letters, manuscript speeches, and the like, are in the Frederick Douglass Collection at the Library of Congress.

Douglass, Frederick. *Life and Times of Frederick Douglass* (1881; rev. ed., 1892).
———. *My Bondage and My Freedom* (1855).
———. *Narrative of the Life of Frederick Douglass, Written by Himself* (1845).
The Frederick Douglass Papers: Speeches, Debates, and Interviews, ed. John W. Blassingame (5 vols., 1979–1992).
Life and Writings of Frederick Douglass, ed. Philip S. Foner (5 vols., 1950–1975).

Andrews, William L., ed. *Critical Essays on Frederick Douglass* (1991).
Blight, David W. *Frederick Douglass' Civil War: Keeping Faith in Jubilee* (1989).

Martin, Waldo E., Jr. *The Mind of Frederick Douglass* (1984).

McFeely, William S. *Frederick Douglass* (1991).

Preston, Dickson J. *Young Frederick Douglass: The Maryland Years* (1980).

QUARLES, BENJAMIN. *Frederick Douglass* (1948).

Voss, Frederick S. *Majestic in His Wrath: A Pictorial Life of Frederick Douglass* (1995).

Walker, Peter F. *Moral Choices: Memory, Desire, and Imagination in Nineteenth-century American Abolition* (1978).

—ROY E. FINKENBINE

DOUGLASS, SARAH MAPPS (9 Sept. 1806–8 Sept. 1882), abolitionist and educator,

was born in Philadelphia, Pennsylvania, the daughter of Robert Douglass Sr., a prosperous hairdresser from the island of St. Kitts, and Grace Bustill, a milliner. Her mother was the daughter of Cyrus Bustill, a prominent member of Philadelphia's African American community. Raised as a Quaker by her mother, Douglass was alienated by the blatant racial prejudice of many white Quakers. Although she adopted Quaker dress and enjoyed the friendship of Quaker antislavery advocates like Lucretia Mott, she was highly critical of the sect.

In 1819 Grace Douglass and philanthropist JAMES FORTEN SR. established a school for black children, where "their children might be better taught than...in any of the schools...open to [their] people." Sarah Douglass was educated there, taught for a while in New York City, and then returned to take over the school.

In 1833 Douglass joined an interracial group of female abolitionists in establishing the Philadelphia Female Anti-Slavery Society. For almost four decades, she served the organization in many capacities. Also active in the antislavery movement at the national level, she attended the 1837 Anti-Slavery Convention of American Women in New York City. The following year, when the convention met at Philadelphia's ill-fated Pennsylvania Hall, which in 1838 was burned by an anti-abolitionist mob, she was elected treasurer. She was also a delegate at the third and final women's antislavery convention in 1839.

Douglass repeatedly stressed the need for African American women to educate themselves. In 1831 she helped organize the Female Literary Association of Philadelphia, a society whose members met regularly for "mental feasts," and on the eve of the Civil War she founded the Sarah M. Douglass Literary Circle.

Throughout the 1830s Douglass wrote poetry and prose under the pseudonyms "Sophanisba" and "Ella." Her writings—on the blessings of religion, the prospect of divine retribution for the sin of slavery, the evils of prejudice, and the plight of the slave—were published in various antislavery journals, including the *Liberator*, the *Colored American*, the *Genius of Universal Emancipation*, and the *National Enquirer and Constitutional Advocate of Universal Liberty*.

During the 1830s and 1840s Douglass was beset by financial problems. Her school never operated at a profit, and in 1838, deciding she could no longer accept the financial backing of her parents, she asked the Female Anti-Slavery Society to take over the school. The experiment proved unsatisfactory, however, and in 1840 she resumed direct control of the school, giving up a guaranteed salary for assistance in paying the rent. In 1852, now reconciled with the Quakers, she closed her school and accepted an appointment to supervise the Girls' Preparatory Department of the Quaker-sponsored Institute for Colored Youth. From 1853 to 1877 she served as principal of the department.

For more than forty years Douglass enjoyed a close friendship with abolitionists Sarah Grimké and ANGELINA WELD GRIMKÉ. After an uneasy start, the relationship between the daughters of a slaveholding family and the African American teacher deepened into one of great mutual respect. Sarah Grimké, fourteen years Douglass's senior, eventually became her confidante. After her mother's death in 1842 left Douglass as unpaid housekeeper to her father and brothers, Grimké sympathized with her: "Worn in body & spirit with the duties of thy school, labor awaits thee at home & when it is done there is none to throw around thee the arms of love."

In 1854 Douglass received an offer of marriage from the Reverend William Douglass, a widower with nine children and the minister of Philadelphia's prestigious St. Thomas's African Episcopal Church. Grimké considered him eminently worthy of her friend. He was a man of education, and his remarks about her age and spinster status were only proof of his lively sense of humor. As for Douglass's apprehensions about the physical aspects of married life, the unmarried Grimké assured her, "Time will familiarize you with the idea." The couple was married in 1855. The marriage proved an unhappy one. On her husband's death in 1861, Douglass wrote of her years "in that School of bitter discipline, the old Parsonage of St. Thomas," but she acknowledged that William Douglass had not been without his merits.

In one respect, marriage gave Douglass a new freedom. A cause she had long championed was the education of women on health issues. Before her marriage, she had taken courses at the Female Medical College of Pennsylvania. In 1855 she enrolled in the Pennsylvania Medical University and in 1858 embarked on a career as a lecturer, confronting topics that would have been considered unseemly for an unmarried woman to address. Her illustrated lectures to female audiences in New York City and Philadelphia drew praise for being both informative and "chaste."

Through the 1860s and 1870s Douglass continued her work of reform, lecturing, raising money for the southern freedmen and -women, helping to establish a home for elderly and indigent black Philadelphians, and teaching at the Institute for Colored Youth. She died in Philadelphia.

As a teacher, a lecturer, an abolitionist, a reformer, and a tireless advocate of women's education, Sarah Mapps Douglass made her influence felt in many ways. Her emphasis on education and self-improvement helped shape the lives of the many hundreds of black children she taught in a career in the classroom that lasted more than a half-century, while her pointed and persistent criticism of northern racism reminded her white colleagues in the abolitionist movement that their agenda must include more than the emancipation of the slaves.

FURTHER READING

A number of letters to and from Douglass are in the Weld-Grimké Papers at the University of Michigan and the Antislavery Manuscripts at the Boston Public Library. Douglass's role in the antislavery movement is documented in the records of the Philadelphia Female Anti-Slavery Society at the Historical Society of Pennsylvania and in the published proceedings of the three national women's antislavery conventions held between 1837 and 1839.

Barnes, Gilbert H., and Dwight L. Dumond, eds. *Letters of Theodore Dwight Weld, Angelina Grimké, and Sarah Grimké, 1822–1844* (2 vols., 1934).

Sterling, Dorothy, ed. *We Are Your Sisters: Black Women in the Nineteenth Century* (1984).

Winch, Julie. *Philadelphia's Black Elite: Activism, Accommodation, and the Struggle for Autonomy, 1787–1848* (1988).

—JULIE WINCH

DOVE, RITA FRANCES

(28 Aug. 1952–), writer, was born in Akron, Ohio, the second of four children of Ray A. Dove, the first black scientist in the tire industry, and Elvira Elizabeth Hord. Rita, who attended public school, read voraciously and began writing plays and stories while in elementary school. Selected as one of the most outstanding high school graduates in the nation, she visited the White House as a Presidential Scholar in 1970, after which she enrolled at Miami University in Oxford, Ohio, graduating summa cum laude with a BA in English in 1973.

She spent the next year as a Fulbright Scholar at the University of Tübingen in West Germany. Although Dove's presence drew attention from the locals—"Most Germans don't consider it impolite to stare, so they simply gawked at me or even pointed" (Taleb-Khyar, 350)—the German language had a lasting impact on her work. "German," Dove explained, "has influenced the way I write: I have tried to re-create in poems the feeling I had when I first began to speak the language—that wonderful sensation of being held hostage by a sentence until the verb comes along at the end" (Steffen, 168).

Upon her return to the United States, Dove began graduate study at the prestigious Writers' Workshop at the University of Iowa, earning an MFA in 1977. While in Iowa, Rita met the German writer Fred Viebahn. The couple married in 1979 and have one daughter. In 1981 Dove began

teaching creative writing at Arizona State University in Tempe, where she remained until 1989, when she became Professor of English at the University of Virginia in Charlottesville. Almost immediately, Dove began to win grants and fellowships, including a National Endowment for the Humanities (NEH) award that allowed her to serve as a writer in residence at the Tuskegee Institute in 1982.

In the late 1970s Dove's poems appeared in a number of magazines and anthologies, and she published several chapbooks, including *Ten Poems* (1977) and *The Only Dark Spot in the Sky* (1980). Dove's first book of poetry, *Yellow House on the Corner* (1980), treats both private, everyday events—a first kiss, family dinners—and the historical events of slavery. Referring to her second collection of poems, *Museum* (1983), Dove revealed, "One of my goals with that book was to reveal the underside of history, and to represent this underside in discrete moments" (Taleb-Khyar, 356).

Dove explored these themes further in her next poetry collection, *Thomas and Beulah* (1986), based on the lives of her maternal grandparents. Consisting of two parts—the first written from

Thomas's point of view, the second from Beulah's—the poems cleverly undercut the idea of a single historical narrative by offering alternative versions of the same events. In preparing the book, Dove interviewed her mother, read transcripts of Works Progress Administration interviews, studied the history of black migration, and listened to blues recordings. "What fascinates me," Dove explained, "is the individual caught in the web of history" (Taleb-Khyar, 356). Critics agreed, and *Thomas and Beulah* earned a Pulitzer Prize in 1987.

Dove's other publications include the poetry collections *Grace Notes* (1989), *Selected Poems* (1993), *Mother Love* (1995), *Evening Primrose* (1998), and *On the Bus with Rosa Parks* (1999); a collection of short stories, *Fifth Sunday* (1985); a novel, *Through the Ivory Gate* (1992); and a play, *The Darker Face of the Earth* (1994), which employs elements of Greek tragedy in a story set on an antebellum slave plantation in South Carolina.

In 1993 Dove became the youngest person and the third African American appointed Poet Laureate Consultant in Poetry at the Library of Congress, a position she held through 1995. As

Rita Dove, who served as the U.S. Poet Laureate from 1993 to 1995.
© Christopher Felver/CORBIS

Poet Laureate, Dove organized lectures and conferences, poetry and jazz evenings, and brought local Washington, D.C., students and Crow Indian children to the Library of Congress to read their poetry and be recorded for the National Archives. She presided over high-profile cultural events, including the 1994 commemoration of the two-hundredth anniversary of the U.S. Capitol, and the unprecedented gathering of Nobel laureates for the Cultural Olympiad in Atlanta, Georgia, in 1995. "I'm hoping that by the end," Dove told reporters, "people will think of a poet laureate as someone who's out there with her sleeves rolled up, not sitting in an ivory tower."

Ever since Dove began singing and playing cello in elementary school, music has been the companion of and inspiration for her poetry. As she explained,

My youth was filled with musical language: the acid drawl of an uncle spinning out a joke; the call-and-response of the AME church; jump rope ditties and BESSIE SMITH on the phonograph; the clear ecstasy of Bach and the sweet sadness of BILLIE HOLIDAY. Buoyed by this living cushion of sound, I began to write.

(*Essence*, 1995)

In the 1990s Dove produced several major musical collaborations, beginning with *Umoja—Each One of Us Counts*, commissioned by the 1996 Atlanta Olympic Summer Games. Her other large-scale productions include *Singin' Sepia* (1996), *Grace Notes* (1997), and *The Pleasure's in Walking Through* (1998), a collaboration with John Williams.

Writers, like musicians, Dove reminds her students, must study and practice. Dove revises incessantly, putting her poems through as a many as fifty or sixty drafts. In the years before she had family and public obligations, she wrote for up to eight hours each day. For Dove, writing is a combination of serendipity and puzzle solving, and her working methods encourage detours and tangents. "When I'm working on poems, I'm reading all the time," she revealed, "I just go to the bookshelf almost like a sleepwalker" (Taleb-Khyar, 363). She also relies on notebooks she has filled over the years with fragments of language: snippets of conversations,

words, ideas, images, even grocery and "to do" lists.

While she is interested in character and plot, Dove is generally more interested in the way stories are told than in the stories themselves. As a child, Dove challenged herself to write novels composed of words from school spelling lists; later, she found the same thrill in crossword puzzles. "I think my puzzle fetish has something to do with the way poems are constructed. Words start to reverberate by virtue of their proximity to one another. That's a spatial thing as well as a temporal one" (Steffen, 169). When it comes time to put a draft away, Dove uses an intuitive filing system that eschews organization by subject, date, or title. Instead, she files by color, by how a poem "feels" to her.

Coming of age after the peak of the Black Arts Movement, Dove subscribes to a less polarized, more inclusive, approach to writing and to race than poets one or two decades her senior, such as AMIRI BARAKA, JUNE JORDAN, AUDRE LORDE, and NIKKI GIOVANNI.

When I was growing up, I did not think in terms of black art or white art or any kind of art; I just wanted to be a writer. On the other hand, when I became culturally aware...it was exciting to recognize heretofore secret aspects of my experience—the syncopation of jazz, the verbal one-upsmanship of signifying or the dozens—not only to acknowledge their legitimacy, but to see them transformed into art.

(Steffen, 169)

Dove found herself less beholden to the collective, and more interested in the individual, her intimate relationships, and daily life. "I could do nothing else but describe the world I knew—a world where there was both jazz and opera; gray suits and blue jeans, iambic pentameter and the dozens, Shakespeare and [JAMES] BALDWIN" (*Essence*, 1995).

In addition to more than a dozen honorary doctorates, Dove has been honored with many awards, including the Duke Ellington Lifetime Achievement Award, the Charles Frankel Prize awarded by the NEH, the Heinz Award in the Arts, the Academy of American Poets' Lavan Younger Poet Award, and fellowships from the Mellon and Rockefeller Foundations. She has

served on the advisory or editorial boards of the Associated Writing Programs, the MacDowell Colony, the Thomas Jefferson Center for Freedom of Expression, *Callaloo*, and *Ploughshares*, and her media appearances include interviews on all major television networks, collaborations with public television, and a visit to *Sesame Street*. She is also a sought-after speaker and panel member and has served on juries for the Walt Whitman Award of the Academy of American Poets, the National Book Award, the Ruth Lilly Prize, and the Pulitzer Prize.

The power of language to transform and alter perception is at the heart of Dove's literary enterprise. "Poetry at its best..." she holds, "nudges the body awake. Poetry resonates and transforms by injecting us with the palpable pleasure of language: Words impress their contours on the tongue, and we breathe with the heartbeat and silences of the line tugging against the sentence as it wraps its sense around the instinctual axis" (*Ploughshares*, Spring 1990).

FURTHER READING

Harrington, Walt. "A Narrow World Made Wide," *Washington Post Magazine* (7 May 1995).

Rubin, Stan Sanvel, and Earl G. Ingersoll. "A Conversation with Rita Dove," *Black American Literature Forum* (Autumn 1986).

Steffen, Therese. *Crossing Color: Transcultural Space and Place in Rita Dove's Poetry, Fiction, and Drama* (2001).

Taleb-Khyar, Mohamed B. "An Interview with Maryse Conde and Rita Dove," *Callaloo* (Spring 1991).

—LISA E. RIVO

DRAKE, ST. CLAIR, JR. (2 Jan. 1911–15 June 1990), anthropologist, was born John Gibbs St. Clair Drake Jr. in Suffolk, Virginia, the son of John Gibbs St. Clair Drake Sr., a Baptist pastor, and Bessie Lee Bowles. By the time Drake was four years old his father had moved the family twice, once to Harrisonburg, Virginia, and then to Pittsburgh, Pennsylvania.

The family lived in a racially mixed neighborhood in Pittsburgh, where Drake grew to feel at ease with whites.

His strict Baptist upbringing gave him a deep understanding of religious organizations. His father also taught him to work with tools and to become an expert in woodworking, a skill Drake later employed in his field research.

A trip to the West Indies in 1922 with his father led to major changes in Drake's life. Rev. Drake had tried to instill in his son a deep respect for the British Empire, but the sight of the poverty in the Caribbean led the reverend to abandon his support of racial integration and convert to MARCUS GARVEY's ideas in favor of racial separation and a return to an African homeland for the black diaspora. He quit his pastorship and went to work as an itinerant organizer for Garvey. The young Drake was to trace his interest in anthropology to this trip with his father.

While his father worked for Garvey as an organizer and was constantly away from home on trips, Drake and his mother moved to Staunton, Virginia. In contrast to his Pittsburgh experiences, Drake encountered the caste system in full force in Virginia. These experiences led him to an appreciation of the radical African American poets of his day, particularly LANGSTON HUGHES, COUNTÉE CULLEN, and CLAUDE MCKAY. They also led him to combine action with study.

After graduating with honors from Hampton Institute in Hampton, Virginia, in 1931, Drake worked with the Society of Friends on their "Peace Caravans." These caravans worked for racial harmony and civil rights. Once again Drake met with whites in a common cause as an equal. He continued to work with the Quakers while teaching at one of their boarding schools. For a time he considered becoming a member of the Society of Friends; however, the realization that there was still prejudice in such a liberal group kept him from converting to the religion.

Drake decided to study anthropology in an effort to better understand the roots of human behavior. After teaching high school at the Christianburg Institute in Cambria, Virginia, from 1932 to 1935, he became a research assistant at Dillard University in New Orleans. There he combined his field research with action, joining the Tenant Farmers Union and the Farmers Union in Adams County, Mississippi. By his own accounts in "Reflections on Anthropology and the Black Experience," these periodic forays into activism nearly cost him his life. On one occassion, he and follow workers barely escaped a lynch mob. Drake recounts another incident where he was badly beaten and left unconscious.

After a year at Columbia University in 1936, Drake entered the University of Chicago in 1937 on a Rosenwald Fellowship. There he met the sociologist Horace Clayton and joined his research under the auspices of the Public Works Progress Administration (WPA), specializing in the African American church and the urban black population. This work became the basis for his contributions to *Black Metropolis* (1946), which he jointly authored with Horace B. Cayton. Drake married sociologist Elizabeth Dewy Johns in 1942; they had two children.

During World War II, Drake became actively involved in the struggle of African Americans for equality. He concentrated his efforts on the conflict in northern war industries and housing. He worked with various African American organizations for which he gathered hard data, joined in work actions, and served on various war boards concerned with presenting African American grievances to the federal government. While gathering data for *Black Metropolis*, Drake worked in a war plant and experienced inequality firsthand. Drake grew bitter at his fellow citizens who so enthusiastically fought fascism abroad but were unwilling to combat it in the United States. In response to these experiences Drake joined the merchant marine, in which he believed he would not encounter the same prejudice and segregation that he might have in the U.S. armed forces.

Following his discharge from the service, Drake completed his PhD in Anthropology at the University of Chicago in 1946 and accepted a position teaching at Roosevelt College that same year. Drake worked extensively in Africa, teaching in both Liberia and Ghana. In 1961 he developed a training program for Peace Corps volunteers in Africa. Over the years he was a personal adviser to many African leaders, including Kwame Nkrumah in Ghana and various high officials in Nigeria. However, as military rule steadily replaced civilian rule in the 1960s, Drake left Africa, refusing to work with dictators.

A prolific scholar, Drake focused his writing on racial concerns such as the problem of inequality, the plight of the urban poor, religion, race relations, and the relationship of African Americans to Africa. His major works include *Race Relations in a Time of Rapid Social Change* (1966), *Our Urban Poor: Promises to Keep and Miles to Go* (1967), and *The Redemption of Africa and Black Religion* (1970). He edited numerous journals and books and brought intellectuals together to discuss the issues of the day and propose actions to meet these problems.

In 1969 Drake moved to Stanford University, where he established the Center for Afro-American Studies, an Afro-American studies department that became a model for other universities. Drake refused to bow to the demand of radicals who wanted the department to be a center exclusively for black students, where others interested in African and Afro-American history would not be welcome. He refused to teach Afrocentric notions that saw Africans as the center of all civilizations and the inventors of all wisdom. He resisted the efforts of black militants outside and inside academia—STOKELY CARMICHAEL, James Turner at Cornell, Felix Okoye, and others—who believed that a person's skin color accredited or discredited him or her as an expert in African and Afro-American studies. Drake insisted on establishing his center on solid academic grounds.

Throughout his life, Drake showed personal integrity in working to achieve his goals of equality and respect for African Americans and their accomplishments. He founded the American Society for African Culture and the American Negro Leadership Conference on Africa in the early 1960s. He was never afraid to risk his life in pursuit of his goals. Drake died at his home in Palo Alto, California.

FURTHER READING

Some of Drake's manuscripts are in the collection of the Schomburg Center for Research in Black Culture of the New York Public Library.

Romero, Patrick W. *In Black America, 1968: The Year of Awakening* (1969).

Uya, Okon Edet. *Black Brotherhood: Afro-Americans and Africa* (1971).

Washington, Joseph R., Jr. *Jews in Black Perspective* (1984).

Obituary: *New York Times*, 21 June 1990.

—FRANK A. SALAMONE

DREW, CHARLES RICHARD

DREW, CHARLES RICHARD (3 June 1904–1 Apr. 1950), blood plasma scientist, surgeon, and teacher, was born in Washington, D.C., the son of Richard Thomas Drew, a carpet-layer, and Nora Rosella Burrell. Drew adored his hard-working parents and was determined from an early age to emulate them. Drew's parents surrounded their children with the many opportunities available in Washington's growing middle-class black community: excellent segregated schools, solid church and social affiliations, and their own strong example. Drew's father was the sole black member of his union and served as its financial secretary.

Drew graduated from Paul Laurence Dunbar High School in 1922 and received a medal for best all-around athletic performance; he also won a scholarship to Amherst College. At Amherst he was a star in football and track, earning honorable mention as an All-American halfback in the eastern division, receiving the Howard Hill Mossman Trophy for bringing the greatest athletic honor to Amherst during his four years there, and taking a national high hurdles championship. A painful brush with discrimination displayed Drew's lifelong response to it: after Drew was denied the captaincy of the football team because he was black, he ended the controversy by quietly refusing to dispute the choice of a white player. His approach to racial prejudice, as he explained in a letter years later, was to knock down "at least one or two bricks" of the "rather high-walled prison of the 'Negro problem' by virtue of some worthwhile contribution" (Love, 175). Throughout his life Drew, whether as a pioneer or as a team leader, helped others scale hurdles so they too could serve society.

While recuperating from a leg injury, Drew decided to pursue a career in medicine. He worked for two years as an athletic director and biology and chemistry instructor at Morgan College (now Morgan State University), a black college in Baltimore, Maryland, to earn money for medical school. There were few openings for black medical students at this time, but Drew was finally admitted to McGill University Medical School in Montreal, Canada. Despite severe financial constraints, he graduated in 1933 with an MDCM (doctor of medicine and master of surgery) degree, second in his class of 137. He was vice president of Alpha Omega Alpha, the medical honor society, and won both the annual prize in neuroanatomy and the J. Francis Williams Prize in Medicine on the basis of a competitive examination. Drew completed a year of internship and a year of residency in internal medicine at Montreal General Hospital. He hoped to pursue training as a surgery resident at a prestigious U.S. medical institution, but almost no clinical opportunities were available to African American doctors at this time. Drew decided to return to Washington, taking a job as an instructor in pathology at Howard University Medical School during 1935–1936.

Howard's medical school was then being transformed from a mostly white-run institution to a black-led one, through the efforts of Numa P. G. Adams, dean of the medical school, and the charismatic MORDECAI JOHNSON, Howard's first black president. Adams nominated Drew to receive a two-year fellowship at Columbia University's medical school.

No black resident had ever been trained at Presbyterian Hospital when Drew arrived at Columbia in the fall of 1938, but Drew so impressed Allen O. Whipple, director of the surgical residency program, that he received this training unofficially, regularly making rounds with Whipple. In the meantime, Drew pursued a doctor of science degree in medicine, doing extensive research on blood-banking, a field still in its infancy, under the guidance of John Scudder, who was engaged in studies relating to fluid balance, blood chemistry, and blood transfusion. With Scudder, Drew set up Presbyterian Hospital's first blood bank. After two years he produced his doctoral thesis, "Banked Blood: A Study in Blood Preservation" (1940), which pulled together existing scientific research on the subject. He became the first African American to receive the doctor of science degree, in 1940. In 1939 Drew had married Minnie Lenore Robbins, a home economics professor at Spelman College. They had four children.

Drew returned to Howard in 1940 as an assistant professor in surgery. In September of that year, however, he was called back to New York City to serve as medical director of the Blood for Britain Project, a hastily organized operation to prepare and ship liquid plasma to wounded British soldiers. He confronted

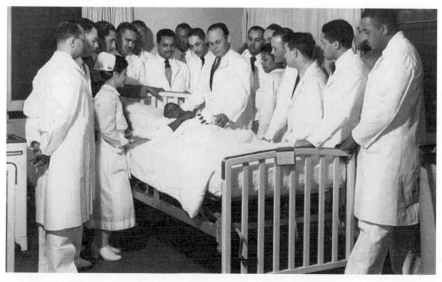

Dr. Charles Drew teaching at Freedmen's (now Howard) University Hospital. Moorland-Spingarn Research Center

the challenge of separating liquid plasma from whole blood on a much larger scale than it had ever been done before and shipping it overseas in a way that would ensure its stability and sterility. His success in this led to his being chosen in early 1941 to serve as medical director of a three-month American Red Cross pilot project involving the mass production of dried plasma. Once again Drew acted swiftly and effectively, aware that the model he was helping to create would be critical to a successful national blood collection program. Red Cross historians agree that Drew's work in this pilot program and the technical expertise he amassed were pivotal to the national blood collection program, a major life-saving factor during the war.

Soon after being certified as a diplomate of the American Board of Surgery, Drew returned to Howard in April 1941. In October he took over as chairman of Howard's Department of Surgery and became chief surgeon at Freedmen's Hospital, commencing what he viewed as his real life's work, the building of Howard's surgical residency program and the training of a team of top-notch black surgeons.

In December 1941 the United States entered the war, and the American Red Cross expanded its national blood collection program. It announced that it would exclude black donors, and then, in response to widespread protest, it adopted a policy of segregating the blood of black donors. Drew spoke out against this policy, pointing out that there was no medical or scientific reason to segregate blood supplies by race. (The Red Cross officially ended its segregation of blood in 1950.) His stance catapulted him into the national limelight: the irony of his being a blood expert and potentially facing exclusion or segregation himself was dramatized by both the black and white press and highlighted when he received the National Association for the Advancement of Colored People's Spingarn Medal in 1944.

A demanding yet unusually caring teacher, Drew stayed in touch with his students long after they left Howard. Between 1941 and 1950 he trained more than half the black surgeons certified by the American Board of Surgery (eight in all), and fourteen more surgeons certified after 1950 received

part of their training from him. In 1942 he became the first black surgeon appointed an examiner for the American Board of Surgery. Other responsibilities and honors followed: in 1943 he was appointed a member of the American-Soviet Committee on Science, and in 1946 he was elected vice president of the American-Soviet Medical Society. From 1944 to 1946 he served as chief of staff, and from 1946 to 1948 as medical director of Freedmen's Hospital. In 1946 he was named a fellow of the U.S. chapter of the International College of Surgeons; in 1949 he was appointed surgical consultant to the surgeon general and was sent to Europe to inspect military medical facilities.

Throughout this period Drew was struggling to open doors for his young black residents, who still were barred from practicing at most white medical institutions as well as from joining the American Medical Association (AMA) and the American College of Surgeons (ACOG). Throughout the 1940s he waged a relentless campaign through letters and political contacts to try to open up the AMA and the ACOG to black physicians; he himself joined neither.

While driving to a medical conference in Alabama, Drew died as the result of an auto accident in North Carolina. His traumatic, untimely death sparked a false rumor that grew into a historical legend during the civil rights movement era, alleging that Drew bled to death because he was turned away from a whites-only hospital. Drew's well-publicized protest of the segregated blood policy, combined with the hospital's refusals of many black patients during the era of segregation, undoubtedly laid the foundation for the legend that dramatized the medical deprivation Drew spent his life battling. Drew was a great American man of medicine by any measure; his extraordinary personality was best summed up by one of his oldest friends, Ben Davis: "I can never forget him: his extraordinary nobleness of character, his honesty, his integrity and fearlessness" (David Hepburn, *Our World* [July 1950]: 28).

FURTHER READING

The Charles R. Drew Papers are located in the Moorland-Spingarn Research Center of Howard University.

Love, Spencie. *One Blood: The Death and Resurrection of Charles R. Drew* (1996).
Wynes, Charles E. *Charles Richard Drew: The Man and the Myth* (1988).
Yancey, Asa, Sr. "U.S. Postage Stamp in Honor of Charles R. Drew, M.D., MDSc.," *Journal of the National Medical Association* 74, no. 6 (1982): 561–565.

Obituaries: *Journal of the National Medical Association* 42, no. 4 (July 1950): 239–246; *The Crisis* (Oct. 1951): 501–507, 555.
—SPENCIE LOVE

 **DREW, TIMOTHY.** *See* Ali, Noble Drew.

DU BOIS, W. E. B.
(23 Feb. 1868–27 Aug. 1963), scholar, writer, editor, and civil rights pioneer, was born William Edward Burghardt Du Bois in Great Barrington, Massachusetts, the son of Mary Silvina Burghardt, a domestic worker, and Alfred Du Bois, a barber and itinerant laborer. In later life Du Bois made a close study of his family origins, weaving them rhetorically and conceptually—if not always accurately—into almost everything he wrote. Born in Haiti and descended from mixed race Bahamian slaves, Alfred Du Bois enlisted during the Civil War as a private in a New York regiment of the Union army but appears to have deserted shortly afterward. He also deserted the family less than two years after his son's birth, leaving him to be reared by his mother and the extended Burghardt kin. Long resident in New England, the Burghardts descended from a freedman of Dutch slave origin who had fought briefly in the American Revolution. Under the care of his mother and her relatives, young Will Du Bois spent his entire childhood in that small western Massachusetts town, where probably fewer than two-score of the four thousand inhabitants were African American. He received a classical, college preparatory education in Great Barrington's racially integrated high school, from whence, in June

W. E. B. Du Bois, intellectual, scholar, editor, and civil rights activist, provided a leading voice in defining the struggle for civil rights in the twentieth century. © CORBIS

1884, he became the first African American graduate. A precocious youth, Du Bois not only excelled in his high school studies but contributed numerous articles to two regional newspapers, the Springfield *Republican* and the black-owned New York *Globe*, then edited by T. THOMAS FORTUNE.

In high school Du Bois came under the influence of and received mentorship from the principal, Frank Hosmer, who encouraged his extensive reading and solicited scholarship aid from local worthies that enabled Du Bois to enroll at Fisk University in September 1885, six months after his mother's death. One of the best of the southern colleges for newly freed slaves founded after the Civil War, Fisk offered a continuation of his classical education and the strong influence of teachers who were heirs to New England and

Western Reserve (Ohio) abolitionism. It also offered the northern-reared Du Bois an introduction to southern American racism and African American culture. His later writings and thought were strongly marked, for example, by his experiences teaching school in the hills of eastern Tennessee during the summers of 1886 and 1887.

In 1888 Du Bois enrolled at Harvard as a junior. He received a BA cum laude, in 1890, an MA in 1891, and a PhD in 1895. Du Bois was strongly influenced by the new historical work of German-trained Albert Bushnell Hart and the philosophical lectures of William James, both of whom became friends and professional mentors. Other intellectual influences came with his studies and travels between 1892 and 1894 in Germany, where he was enrolled at the Friedrich-Wilhelm III Universität (then

commonly referred to as the University of Berlin but renamed the Humboldt University after World War II). Because of the expiration of the Slater Fund fellowship that supported his stay in Germany, Du Bois could not meet the residency requirements that would have enabled him formally to stand for the degree in economics, despite his completion of the required doctoral thesis (on the history of southern U.S. agriculture) during his tenure. Returning to the United States in the summer of 1894, Du Bois taught classics and modern languages for two years at Wilberforce University in Ohio. While there, he met Nina Gomer, a student at the college, whom he married in 1896 at her home in Cedar Rapids, Iowa. The couple had two children. By the end of his first year at Wilberforce, Du Bois had completed his Harvard doctoral thesis, "The Suppression of the African Slave Trade to the United States of America, 1638–1870," which was published in 1896 as the inaugural volume of the Harvard Historical Studies series.

Although he had written his Berlin thesis in economic history, received his Harvard doctorate in history, and taught languages and literature at Wilberforce, Du Bois made some of his most important early intellectual contributions to the emerging field of sociology. In 1896 he was invited by the University of Pennsylvania to conduct a study of the seventh ward in Philadelphia. There, after an estimated 835 hours of door-to-door interviews in 2,500 households, Du Bois completed the monumental study, *The Philadelphia Negro* (1899). The Philadelphia study was both highly empirical and hortatory, a combination that prefigured much of the politically engaged scholarship that Du Bois pursued in the years that followed and that reflected the two main strands of his intellectual engagement during this formative period: the scientific study of the so-called Negro Problem and the appropriate political responses to it. While completing his fieldwork in Philadelphia, Du Bois delivered to the Academy of Political and Social Science in November 1896 an address, "The Study of the Negro Problem," a methodological manifesto on the purposes and appropriate methods for scholarly examination of the condition of black people. In March 1897, addressing the newly founded American Negro Academy in Washington, D.C., he outlined for his black intellectual colleagues, in "The Conservation of the Races," both a historical sociology and theory of race as a concept and a call to action in defense of African American culture and identity. During the following July and August he undertook for the U.S. Bureau of Labor the first of several studies of southern African American households, which was published as a bureau bulletin the following year under the title *The Negroes of Farmville, Virginia: A Social Study*. During that same summer, *Atlantic Monthly* published the essay "The Strivings of the Negro People," a slightly revised version of which later opened *The Souls of Black Folk* (1903).

Together these works frame Du Bois's evolving conceptualization of, methodological approach to, and political values and commitments regarding the problem of race in America. His conceptions were historical and global, his methodology empirical and intuitive, his values and commitments involving both mobilization of an elite vanguard to address the issues of racism and the conscious cultivation of the values to be drawn from African American folk culture.

After the completion of the Philadelphia study in December 1897, Du Bois began the first of two long tenures at Atlanta University, where he taught sociology and directed empirical studies—modeled loosely on his Philadelphia and Farmville work—of the social and economic conditions and cultural and institutional lives of southern African Americans. During this first tenure at Atlanta he also wrote two more books, *The Souls of Black Folk*, a collection of poignant essays on race, labor, and culture, and *John Brown* (1909), an impassioned interpretation of the life and martyrdom of the militant abolitionist. He also edited two short-lived magazines, *Moon* (1905–1906) and *Horizon* (1907–1910), which represented his earliest efforts to establish journals of intellectual and political opinion for a black readership.

With the publication of *Souls of Black Folk*, Du Bois emerged as the most prominent spokesperson for the opposition to BOOKER T. WASHINGTON's policy of political conservatism and racial accommodation. Ironically, Du Bois had kept a prudent distance from Washington's opponents and had made few overt statements in opposition to the so-called Wizard of Tuskegee. In fact, his career had involved a number of near-misses whereby he himself might have ended up teaching at Tuskegee. Having applied to Washington for a job shortly after returning from Berlin, he had to decline Tuskegee's superior monetary offer because he had already accepted a position at Wilberforce. On a number of other occasions Washington—sometimes prodded by Albert Bushnell Hart—sought to recruit Du Bois to join him at Tuskegee, a courtship he continued at least until the summer of 1903, when Du Bois taught summer school at Tuskegee. Early in his career, moreover, Du Bois's views bore a superficial similarity to Washington's. In fact, he had praised Washington's 1895 "Atlanta Compromise" speech, which proposed to southern white elites a compromise wherein blacks would forswear political and civil rights in exchange for economic opportunities. Like many elite blacks at the time, Du Bois was not averse to some form of franchise restriction, so long as it was based on educational qualifications and applied equally to white and black. Du Bois had been charged with overseeing the African American Council's efforts to encourage black economic enterprise and worked with Washington's partisans in that effort. By his own account his overt rupture with Washington was sparked by the growing evidence of a conspiracy, emanating from Tuskegee, to dictate speech and opinion in all of black America and to crush any opposition to Washington's leadership. After the collapse of efforts to compromise their differences through a series of meetings in 1904, Du Bois joined WILLIAM MONROE TROTTER and other Washington opponents to form the Niagara Movement, an organization militantly advocating full civil and political rights for African Americans.

Although it enjoyed some success in articulating an alternative vision of how black Americans should respond to the growing segregation and racial violence of the early twentieth century, the Niagara Movement was fatally hampered by lack of funds and the overt and covert opposition of Washington and his allies. Indeed, the vision and program of the movement were fully realized only with the founding of a new biracial organization, the National Association for the Advancement of Colored People (NAACP). The NAACP grew out of the agitation and a 1909 conference called to protest the deteriorating status of and escalating violence against black Americans. Racial rioting in August 1908 in Springfield, Illinois, the home of Abraham Lincoln, sparked widespread protest among blacks and liberal whites appalled at the apparent spread of southern violence and lynch law into northern cities. Although its officers made some initial efforts to maintain a détente with Booker T. Washington, the NAACP represented a clear opposition to his policy of accommodation and political quietism. It launched legal suits, legislative lobbying, and propaganda campaigns that embodied uncompromising, militant attacks on lynching, Jim Crow, and disfranchisement. In 1910 Du Bois left Atlanta to join the NAACP as an officer, its only black board member, and to edit its monthly magazine, the *Crisis*.

As editor of the *Crisis* Du Bois finally established the journal of opinion that had so long eluded him, one that could serve as a platform from which to reach a larger audience among African Americans and one that united the multiple strands of his life's work. In its monthly issues he rallied black support for NAACP policies and programs and excoriated white opposition to equal rights. But he also opened the journal to discussions of diverse subjects related to race relations and black cultural and social life, from black religion to new poetic works. The journal's cover displayed a rich visual imagery embodying the sheer diversity and breadth of the black presence in America. Thus the journal constituted, simultaneously, a forum for multiple expressions of and the coherent representation and enactment of black intellectual and cultural life. A mirror for and to black America, it inspired a black intelligentsia and its public.

From his vantage as an officer of the NAACP, Du Bois also furthered another compelling intellectual and political interest, Pan-Africanism. He had attended the first conference on the global condition of peoples of

African descent in London in 1900. Six other gatherings followed between 1911 and 1945, including the First Universal Races Congress in London in 1911, and Pan-African congresses held in Paris in 1919; London, Brussels, and Paris in 1921; London and Lisbon in 1923; New York City in 1927; and in Manchester, England, in 1945. Each conference focused in some fashion on the fate of African colonies in the postwar world, but the political agendas of the earliest meetings were often compromised by the ideological and political entanglements of the elite delegates chosen to represent the African colonies. Jamaican black nationalist MARCUS GARVEY enjoyed greater success in mobilizing a mass base for his version of Pan-Africanism and posed a substantial ideological and political challenge to Du Bois. Deeply suspicious of Garvey's extravagance and flamboyance, Du Bois condemned his scheme to collect funds from African Americans to establish a shipping line that would aid their "return" to Africa, his militant advocacy of racial separatism, and his seeming alliance with the Ku Klux Klan. Although he played no role in the efforts to have Garvey jailed and eventually deported for mail fraud, Du Bois was not sorry to see him go. (In 1945, however, Du Bois joined Garvey's widow, AMY JACQUES GARVEY, and George Padmore to sponsor the Manchester Pan-African conference that demanded African independence. Du Bois cochaired the opening session of the conference with Carvey's first wife, AMY ASHWOOD GARVEY.)

The rupture in world history that was World War 1 and the vast social and political transformations of the decade that followed were reflected in Du Bois's thought and program in other ways as well. During the war he had written "Close Ranks," a controversial editorial in the Crisis (July 1918), which urged African Americans to set aside their grievances for the moment and concentrate their energies on the war effort. In fact, Du Bois and the NAACP fought for officer training and equal treatment for black troops throughout the war, led a silent protest march down Fifth Avenue in 1917 against racism, and in 1919 launched an investigation into charges of discrimination against black troops in

Europe. Meanwhile, the unprecedented scope and brutality of the war itself stimulated changes in Du Bois's evolving analyses of racial issues and phenomena. *Darkwater: Voices within the Veil* (1920) reflects many of these themes, including the role of African colonization and the fundamental role of the international recruitment and subjugation of labor in causing the war and in shaping its aftermath. His visit to Liberia in 1923 and the Soviet Union in 1926, his subsequent study of Marxism, his growing awareness of Freud, and the challenges posed by the Great Depression all brought him to question the NAACP's largely legalistic and propagandistic approach to fighting racism. In the early 1930s Du Bois opened the pages of the *Crisis* to wide-ranging discussions of the utility of Marxian thought and of racially based economic cooperatives and other institutions in the fight against race prejudice. This led to increasing antagonism between him and his colleagues at the NAACP, especially executive director WALTER WHITE, and to his resignation in June 1934.

Du Bois accepted an appointment as chair of the sociology department at Atlanta University, where he had already been teaching as a visiting professor during the winter of 1934. There he founded and edited a new scholarly journal, *Phylon*, from 1940 to 1944. There, too, he published his most important historical work, *Black Reconstruction in America: An Essay toward a History of the Part Which Black Folk Played in the Attempt to Reconstruct Democracy in America, 1860–1880* (1935), and *Dusk of Dawn: An Essay toward an Autobiography of a Race Concept* (1940), his most engaging and poignant autobiographical essay since *Souls of Black Folk*. During this period Du Bois continued to be an active lecturer and an interlocutor with young scholars and activists; he also deepened his studies of Marxism and traveled abroad. He sought unsuccessfully to enlist the aid of the Phelps-Stokes Fund in launching his long-dreamed-of project to prepare an encyclopedia of black peoples in Africa and the diaspora. By 1944, however, Du Bois had lost an invaluable supporter and friend with the death of JOHN HOPE, the president of Atlanta University, leaving him

vulnerable to dismissal following sharp disagreements with Hope's successor.

Far from acceding to a peaceful retirement, however, in 1944 Du Bois (now seventy-six years old) accepted an invitation to return to the NAACP to serve in the newly created post of director of special research. Although the organization was still under the staff direction of Du Bois's former antagonist, WALTER WHITE, the 1930s Depression and World War II had induced some modifications in the programs and tactics of the NAACP, perhaps in response to challenges raised by Du Bois and other younger critics. It had begun to address the problems of labor as well as legal discrimination, and even the court strategy was becoming much more aggressive and economically targeted. In hiring Du Bois, the board appears to have anticipated that other shifts in its approach would be necessary in the coming postwar era. Clearly it was Du Bois's understanding that his return portended continued study of and agitation around the implications of the coming postwar settlement as it might affect black peoples in Africa and the diaspora, and that claims for the representation of African and African American interests in that settlement were to be pressed. He represented the NAACP in 1945 as a consultant to the U.S. delegation at the founding conference of the United Nations in San Francisco. In 1947 he prepared and presented to that organization *An Appeal to the World*, a ninety-four-page, militant protest against American racism as an international violation of human rights. During this period and in support of these activities he wrote two more books, *Color and Democracy: Colonies and Peace* (1945) and *The World and Africa: An Inquiry into the Part Which Africa Has Played in World History* (1947), each of which addressed some aspect of European and American responsibilities for justice in the colonial world.

As ever, Du Bois learned from and was responsive to the events and developments of his time. Conflicts with the U.S. delegation to the United Nations (which included Eleanor Roosevelt, who was also a member of the NAACP board) and disillusionment with the evolving role of America as a postwar world power reinforced his growing radicalism and refusal to be confined to a safe domestic agenda. He became a supporter of the leftist Southern Negro Youth Congress at a time of rising hysteria about Communism and the onset of the cold war. In 1948 he was an active supporter of the Progressive Party and Henry Wallace's presidential bid. All of this put him at odds with Walter White and the NAACP board, who were drawn increasingly into collusion with the Harry S. Truman administration and into fierce opposition to any leftist associations. In 1948, after an inconclusive argument over assigning responsibility for a leak to the *New York Times* of a Du Bois memorandum critical of the organization and its policies, he was forced out of the NAACP for a second time.

After leaving the NAACP, Du Bois joined the Council on African Affairs, where he chaired the Africa Aid Committee and was active in supporting the early struggle of the African National Congress of South Africa against apartheid. The council had been organized in London in the late 1930s by Max Yergan and PAUL ROBESON to push decolonization and to educate the general public about that issue. In the postwar period it, too, became tainted by charges of Communist domination and lost many former supporters (including Yergan and RALPH BUNCHE); it dissolved altogether in 1955. Having linked the causes of decolonialization and antiracism to the fate of peace in a nuclear-armed world, Du Bois helped organize the Cultural and Scientific Conference for World Peace in March 1949, was active in organizing its meetings in Paris and Mexico City later that year, and attended its Moscow conference that August. Subsequently this group founded the Peace Information Center in 1950, and Du Bois was chosen to chair its Advisory Council. The center endorsed and promoted the Stockholm Peace Appeal, which called for banning atomic weapons, declaring their use a crime against humanity and demanding international controls. During this year Du Bois, who actively opposed the Korean War and Truman's foreign policy more generally, accepted the nomination of New York's Progressive Party to run for the U.S. Senate on the platform "Peace and Civil Rights." Although he lost, his vote total ran considerably ahead of the other candidates on the Progressive ticket.

During the campaign, on 25 August 1950, the officers of the Peace Information Center were directed to register as "agents of a foreign principal" under terms of the Foreign Agents Registration Act of 1938. Their distribution of the Stockholm Appeal, alleged to be a Soviet-inspired manifesto, was the grounds for these charges, although the so-called foreign principal was never specifically identified in the subsequent indictment. Although the center disbanded on 12 October 1950, indictments against its officers, including Du Bois, were handed down on 9 February 1951. Du Bois's lawyers won a crucial postponement of the trial until the following 18 November 1951, by which time national and international opposition to the trial had been mobilized. Given the good fortune of a weak case and a fair judge, Du Bois and his colleagues were acquitted. Meanwhile, following the death of his wife, Nina, in July 1950, Du Bois married Shirley Graham, the daughter of an old friend, in 1951. Although the union bore no children, David, Shirley's son from an earlier marriage, took Du Bois's surname.

After the trial, Du Bois continued to be active in the American Peace Crusade and received the International Peace Prize from the World Council of Peace in 1953. With Shirley, a militant leftist activist in her own right, he was drawn more deeply into leftist and Communist Party intellectual and social circles during the 1950s. He was an unrepentant supporter of and apologist for Joseph Stalin, arguing that though Stalin's methods might have been cruel, they were necessitated by unprincipled and implacable opposition from the West and by U.S. efforts to undermine the regime. He was also convinced that American news reports about Stalin and the Soviet bloc were unreliable at best and sheer propaganda or falsehoods at worst. His views do not appear to have been altered by the Soviets' own exposure and condemnation of Stalin after 1956.

From February 1952 to 1958 both W. E. B. and Shirley were denied passports to travel abroad. Thus he could not accept the many invitations to speak abroad or participate in international affairs, including most notably the 1957 independence celebrations of Ghana, the first of the newly independent African nations. When these restrictions were lifted in 1958, the couple traveled to the Soviet Union, Eastern Europe, and China. While in Moscow, Du Bois was warmly received by Nikita Khrushchev, whom he strongly urged to promote the study of African civilization in Russia, a proposal that eventually led to the establishment in 1962 of the Institute for the Study of Africa. While there, he also received the Lenin Peace Prize.

But continued cold war tensions and their potential impact on his ability to travel and remain active in the future led Du Bois to look favorably on an invitation in May 1961 from Kwame Nkrumah and the Ghana Academy of Sciences to move to Ghana and undertake direction of the preparation of an "Encyclopedia Africana," a project much like one he had long contemplated. Indeed, his passport had been rescinded again after his return from China (travel to that country was barred at the time), and it was only restored after intense lobbying by the Ghanaian government. Before leaving the United States for Ghana on 7 October 1961, Du Bois officially joined the American Communist Party, declaring in his 1 October 1961 letter of application that it and socialism were the only viable hope for black liberation and world peace. His desire to travel and work freely also prompted his decision two years later to become a citizen of Ghana.

In some sense these actions brought full circle some of the key issues that had animated Du Bois's life. Having organized his life's work around the comprehensive, empirically grounded study of what had once been called the Negro Problem, he ended his years laboring on an interdisciplinary and global publication that might have been the culmination and symbol of that ambition: to document the experience and historical contributions of African peoples in the world. Having witnessed the formal détente among European powers by which the African continent was colonized in the late nineteenth

century, he lived to taste the fruits of the struggle to decolonize it in the late twentieth century and to become a citizen of the first new African nation. Having posed at the end of the nineteenth century the problem of black identity in the diaspora, he appeared to resolve the question in his own life by returning to Africa. Undoubtedly the most important modern African American intellectual, Du Bois virtually invented modern African American letters and gave form to the consciousness animating the work of practically all other modern African American intellectuals to follow. He authored seventeen books, including five novels; founded and edited four different journals; and pursued two full-time careers: scholar and political organizer. But more than that, he reshaped how the experience of America and African America could be understood; he made us know both the complexity of who black Americans have been and are, and why it matters; and he left Americans—black and white—a legacy of intellectual tools, a language with which they might analyze their present and imagine a future.

From late 1961 to 1963 Du Bois lived a full life in Accra, the Ghanaian capital, working on the encyclopedia, taking long drives in the afternoon, and entertaining its political elite and the small colony of African Americans during the evenings at the comfortable home the government had provided him. Du Bois died the day before his American compatriots assembled for the March on Washington for Jobs and Freedom. It was a conjunction more than rich with historical symbolism. It was the beginning of the end of the era of segregation that had shaped so much of Du Bois's life, but it was also the beginning of a new era when "the Negro Problem" could not be confined to separable terrains of the political, economic, domestic, or international, or to simple solutions such as integration or separatism, rights or consciousness. The life and work of Du Bois had anticipated this necessary synthesis of diverse terrains and solutions. On 29 August 1963 Du Bois was interred in a state funeral outside Castle Osu, formerly a holding pen for the slave cargoes bound for America.

FURTHER READING

Du Bois's papers are at the University of Massachusetts, Amherst, and are also available on microfilm.

Du Bois, W. E. B. *The Complete Published Works of W. E. B. Du Bois*, comp. and ed. Herbert Aptheker (1982).

Horne, Gerald. *Black and Red: W. E. B. Du Bois and the Afro-American Response to the Cold War, 1944–1963* (1986).

Lewis, David Levering. *W. E. B. Du Bois: Biography of a Race, 1868–1919* (1993).

———. *W. E. B. Du Bois: The Fight for Equality and the American Century, 1919–1963* (2000).

Marable, Manning. *W. E. B. Du Bois: Black Radical Democrat* (1986).

Rampersad, Arnold. *The Art and Imagination of W. E. B. Du Bois* (1976).

Obituary: *New York Times*, 28 Aug. 1963.

—THOMAS C. HOLT

DUNBAR, PAUL LAURENCE

(27 June 1872–9 Feb. 1906), author, was born in Dayton, Ohio, the son of Joshua Dunbar, a plasterer, and Matilda Burton Murphy, a laundry worker. His literary career began at age twelve, when he wrote an Easter poem and recited it in church. He served as editor in chief of his high school's student newspaper and presided over its debating society. While still in school, he contributed poems and sketches to the *Dayton Herald* and the *West Side News*, a local paper published by Orville Wright of Kitty Hawk fame, and briefly edited the *Tattler*, a newspaper for blacks that Wright published and printed. He graduated from high school in 1891 with the hope of becoming a lawyer, but, lacking the funds to pursue a college education, he went instead to work as an elevator operator.

Dunbar wrote and submitted poetry and short stories in his spare time. His first break came in 1892, when the Western Association of Writers held its annual meeting in Dayton. One of Dunbar's former teachers arranged to have him deliver the welcoming address, and his rhyming greeting pleased the conventioneers so much that they voted him into the association. One of the attendees, poet James Newton Matthews, wrote an article about Dayton's young black poet that received wide publication in the Midwest, and soon Dunbar was receiving invitations from newspaper editors to submit his poems for publication. Encouraged by this success, he published *Oak and Ivy* (1893), a slender volume of fifty-six poems that sold well, particularly after Dunbar, an excellent public speaker, read selections from the book before evening club and church meetings throughout Ohio and Indiana.

In 1893 Dunbar traveled to Chicago, Illinois, to write an article for the *Herald* about the World's Columbian Exposition. He decided to stay in the Windy City and found employment as a latrine attendant. He eventually obtained a position as clerk to FREDERICK DOUGLASS, who was overseeing the Haitian Pavilion, as well as a temporary assignment from the Chicago *Record* to cover the exposition. After a rousing Douglass speech, the highlight of the exposition's Negro American Day, Dunbar read one of his poems, "The Colored Soldiers," to an appreciative audience of thousands. Sadly, when the exposition closed, Chicago offered Dunbar no better opportunity for full-time employment than his old job as elevator boy, and so he reluctantly returned to Dayton. However, he did so with Douglass's praise ringing in his ears: "One of the sweetest songsters his race has produced and a man of whom I hope great things."

Dunbar's determination to become a great writer was almost derailed by a chance to pursue his old dream of becoming a lawyer. In 1894 a Dayton attorney hired him as a law clerk with the understanding that Dunbar would have the opportunity to study law on the side. However, Dunbar discovered that law no longer enthralled him as it once had; moreover, he found that working and studying left him no time to write, and so he returned to the elevator and his poetry. He soon had enough new poems for a second volume, *Majors and Minors* (1895), which was published privately with the financial backing of H. A. Tobey of Toledo, Ohio. This work contains poems in both standard English ("majors") and black dialect ("minors"), many of which are regarded as among his best. In 1896 William Dean Howells, at the time America's most prominent literary critic, wrote a lengthy and

Paul Laurence Dunbar, as shown in the frontispiece to his Lyrics of Sunshine and Shadow, *1905.* Library of Congress

nagging cough, perhaps the result of an abundance of heavy lifting in the dusty, drafty library combined with skimping on sleep while pursuing deadlines. Partly because of his success and partly because of ill health, he resigned from the library at the end of 1898 to devote himself full time to his writing.

In 1899 Dunbar published two collections of poems, *Lyrics of the Hearthside* and *Poems of Cabin and Field*, and embarked on a third reading tour. However, his health deteriorated so rapidly that the tour was cut short. The official diagnosis was pneumonia, but his doctor suspected that Dunbar was in the early stages of tuberculosis. To help ease the pain in his lungs, he turned to strong drink, which did little more than make him a near-alcoholic. He gave up his much-beloved speaking tours but continued to write at the same breakneck pace. While convalescing in Denver, Colorado, he wrote a western novel, *The Love of Landry* (1900), and published *The Strength of Gideon and Other Stories* (1900), another collection of short stories. He also wrote two plays, neither of which was ever published, as well as some lyrics and sketches. In the last five years of his life, he published two novels, *The Fanatics* (1901) and *The Sport of the Gods* (1901, in *Lippincott's*; 1902, in book form); two short story collections, *In Old Plantation Days* (1903) and *The Heart of Happy Hollow* (1904); eight collections of poetry, *Candle-Lightin' Time* (1901), *Lyrics of Love and Laughter* (1903), *When Malindy Sings* (1903), *Li'l Gal* (1904), *Chris'mus Is A-comin' and Other Poems* (1905), *Howdy, Honey, Howdy* (1905), *Lyrics of Sunshine and Shadow* (1905), and *Joggin' Erlong* (1906); and collaborated with Cook on another musical, *In Dahomey* (1902).

Dunbar had married writer Alice Ruth Moore (ALICE DUNBAR-NELSON) in 1898; they had no children. In 1902 the couple separated, largely because of Dunbar's drinking, and never reconciled. After the breakup Dunbar lived in Chicago for a while, then in 1903 returned to live with his mother in Dayton, where he died of tuberculosis in 1906.

Dunbar's goal was "to interpret my own people through song and story, and to prove to the many that after all we are more human than

enthusiastic review of *Majors and Minors*'s dialect poems for *Harper's Weekly*, a highly regarded literary magazine with a wide circulation. The review gave Dunbar's career as a poet a tremendous boost. Sales of *Majors and Minors* skyrocketed, and Dunbar, now under the management of Major James Burton Pond's lecture bureau, embarked on a national reading tour. Pond also arranged for Dodd, Mead and Company to publish *Lyrics of Lowly Life* (1896), a republication of ninety-seven poems from Dunbar's first two volumes and eight new poems. Howells, in the introduction to this volume, described Dunbar as "the only man of pure African blood and of American civilization to feel the negro life aesthetically and express it lyrically." The combination of Howells's endorsement and Dunbar's skill soon led

the latter to become one of America's most popular writers.

After the publication of *Lyrics of Lowly Life*, Dunbar went on a reading tour of England. When he returned to the United States in 1897, he accepted a position as a library assistant at the Library of Congress in Washington, D.C. Meanwhile, several national literary magazines were vying for anything he wrote, and in 1898 Dunbar seemed to have developed the golden touch. *Lippincott's Monthly Magazine* published his first novel, *The Uncalled*, which appeared in book form later that year; *Folks from Dixie*, a collection of twelve short stories that had been published individually in various magazines, also came out in book form; and he collaborated with WILL MARION COOK to write a hit Broadway musical, *Clorindy*. At this time he developed a

African." In so doing, he portrayed the lives of blacks as being filled with joy and humor as well as misery and difficulty. Dunbar is best known for his dialect poems that, intended for a predominantly white audience, often depict slaves as dancing, singing, carefree residents of "Happy Hollow." On the other hand, a great deal of his lesser-known prose work speaks out forcefully against racial injustice, both before and after emancipation, as in "The Lynching of Jube Benson," a powerful short story about the guilt that haunts a white man who once participated in the hanging of an innocent black. Perhaps his two most eloquent expressions of the reality of the black experience in America are "We Wear the Mask," in which he declares, "We wear the mask that grins and lies,.../We smile, but, O great Christ, our cries /To thee from tortured souls arise," and "Sympathy," wherein he states that "I know why the caged bird sings,.../It is not a carol of joy or glee, /But a prayer...that upward to Heaven he flings."

Dunbar was the first black American author to be able to support himself solely as a result of his writing. His success inspired the next generation of black writers, including JAMES WELDON JOHNSON, LANGSTON HUGHES, and CLAUDE MCKAY, to dream of and achieve literary success. Dunbar was celebrated and scrutinized by the national media as a representative of his race. His charm and wit, his grace under pressure, and his ability as a speaker and author did much to give the lie to turn-of-the-century misconceptions about the racial inferiority of blacks.

FURTHER READING

Dunbar's papers are in the archives of the Ohio Historical Society.

Gentry, Tony. *Paul Laurence Dunbar* (1989).
Martin, Jay, and Gossie H. Hudson, eds. *The Paul Laurence Dunbar Reader* (1975).
Williams, Kenny J. *They Also Spoke: An Essay on Negro Literature in America, 1787–1930* (1970).

Obituary: *New York Times*, 10 Feb. 1906.
—CHARLES W. CAREY JR.

DUNBAR-NELSON, ALICE

DUNBAR-NELSON, ALICE (19 July 1875–18 Sept. 1935), writer, educator, and activist, was born Alice Ruth Moore in New Orleans to Joseph Moore, a seaman, and Patricia Wright, a former slave and seamstress. Moore completed a teachers' training program at Straight College (now Dillard University) and taught in New Orleans from 1892 to 1896, then in Brooklyn, New York City, from 1897 to 1898. Demonstrating a commitment to the education of African American girls and women that would continue throughout her life, Moore helped found the White Rose Home for Girls in Harlem in 1898.

Moore's primary ambition, however, was literary, and she published her first book at the age of twenty, *Violets and Other Tales* (1895), a collection of poetry in a classical lyric style, essays, and finely observed short stories. The publication of Moore's poetry and photograph in a Boston magazine inspired the famed poet PAUL LAURENCE DUNBAR to begin a correspondence with her that led to their marriage in 1898. Her second book, *The Goodness of St. Rocque and Other Stories* (1899), a collection of short stories rooted in New Orleans Creole culture, was published as a companion volume to Dunbar's *Poems of Cabin and Field*, and their marriage was celebrated as a literary union comparable to that of Robert and Elizabeth Barrett Browning. The couple separated, however, in 1902, after less than four tumultuous and sometimes violent years, due in part to Paul's alcoholism. Paul Laurence Dunbar died of tuberculosis four years later. Although the couple never reconciled, Alice Dunbar expressed regret and outrage that his family did not inform her of his last illness, or even his death, which she learned of from a newspaper article.

In the fall of 1902 Alice Dunbar resumed her teaching career at Howard High School in Wilmington, Delaware. As an English and drawing instructor, then head of the English department, Dunbar also served as an administrator and directed several of her own plays at the school. Dunbar also pursued scholarly work at various institutions, including Columbia University and the University of Pennsylvania, ultimately completing an MA degree at Cornell University. A portion of her master's thesis on the influence of Milton on Wordsworth was published in the prestigious *Modern Language Notes* in 1909. In 1910 Dunbar secretly married a fellow Howard High School teacher, Henry Arthur Callis, although they soon divorced.

During this busy period of teaching, administration, and study, Dunbar also participated in the burgeoning black women's club movement, through which she delivered lectures on a variety of subjects, most commonly race, women's rights, and education. However, she achieved the most renown when speaking as the widow of Paul Laurence Dunbar. Like her late husband, she struggled with the preference among white audiences for Paul's "dialect" poetry, although she ably performed these works, along with his "pure English poems," which she preferred. Building on her work as a public speaker, Dunbar edited and published *Masterpieces of Negro Eloquence* (1914), a collection of Negro oratory from the pre- and post–Civil War era, designed to celebrate the fiftieth anniversary of the Emancipation Proclamation.

In 1916 Dunbar married Robert J. Nelson, a widower with two children, but maintained her association with her first husband by hyphenating her name. In *The Dunbar Speaker and Entertainer: The Poet and His Song* (1920), Dunbar-Nelson assembled a wider range of Negro oratory than in the political speeches of *Masterpieces of Negro Eloquence*, and included a large number of her husband's and her own poetry deemed suitable for performance, along with poetry, fiction, and speeches by JAMES WELDON JOHNSON, CHARLES W. CHESNUTT, and others. Dunbar-Nelson seems to have found her lifelong connection to her first husband both an asset, in furthering her writing and speaking career, and a burden, evidenced by several unsuccessful attempts to publish under a pseudonym.

Dunbar-Nelson's third marriage was satisfying both personally and professionally; as a journalist Nelson was supportive of Dunbar-Nelson's writing and political activities. Dunbar-Nelson combined her literary and political interests through the production and publication of *Mine Eyes Have Seen the Glory* (1918), a play promoting African American involvement in World

War I. She also toured the South for the Women's Committee for National Defense on behalf of the war effort and was active in the campaign for women's suffrage. She continued her political activism despite protests from her employers at Howard High, and in 1920 lost her job following an unsanctioned trip to a Social Justice conference in Ohio.

Relieved of her teaching duties, Dunbar-Nelson devoted herself more fully to political activism, and from 1920 to 1922 enjoyed a close collaboration with her husband through their publication of the liberal black newspaper, the *Wilmington Advocate*. She joined a delegation of black activists to meet with President Warren G. Harding in 1921, worked for passage of the Dyer Anti-Lynching Bill in 1922, and organized black women voters for the Democratic Party in 1924. As a member of the Federation of Colored Women, she cofounded the Industrial School for Colored Girls in Marshalltown, Delaware, and worked as a teacher and parole officer for the school from 1924 to 1928.

Dunbar-Nelson's journalistic and historical writings date from 1902, when she wrote several articles for the *Chicago Daily News*. In 1916 her lengthy historical work "People of Color in Louisiana" was published in *The Journal of Negro History*, and from 1926 to 1930 she was a newspaper columnist for the Pittsburgh *Courier* and the Washington *Eagle*. Many of her columns were syndicated by the Associated Negro Press, and her subjects ranged beyond the usual material considered suitable for women journalists, taking on political and social issues of the day, which she dealt with in a witty and incisive style. By contrast, many of Dunbar-Nelson's literary efforts, including four novels, went unpublished in her lifetime, although the best of them are now collected in a three-volume set, *The Works of Alice Dunbar-Nelson* (1988). Included are previously published and unpublished works of poetry, fiction, essays, and drama, which give evidence of Dunbar-Nelson's wide range of interests, both thematically and formally.

Dunbar-Nelson's exquisitely crafted fiction secures her position as a pioneer of the African American short story. Interestingly, her fiction and poetry,

which she considered the most "pure" from a literary point of view, deal only tangentially with the racial issues that so occupied her political and journalistic activities. In these works she focuses instead on issues of gender oppression and psychology, and evidences a frustration in her diary at the lack of interest from mainstream white publishers. The African American press was more receptive to her literary work, and between 1917 and 1928 Dunbar-Nelson published poems in *Crisis, Opportunity, Ebony and Topaz,* and other African American journals, enjoying a small heyday as a poet with the advent of the Harlem Renaissance.

In addition to recording her often frustrated literary ambitions, Dunbar-Nelson's diary, begun in 1921, offers a glimpse of her romantic relationships with both men and women, her lifelong worries about finances, and her struggle with traditional women's roles. Even in her mostly amicable relationship with Robert Nelson, Dunbar-Nelson objects to his insistence on her managing both household and professional duties, and she chafes at the regulation of her dress and makeup by male employers. The extant portions of the diary include the years 1921 and 1926–1931, and were published as *Give Us Each Day: The Diary of Alice Dunbar-Nelson* (1984).

In 1932 Robert Nelson received a political appointment to the Pennsylvania Athletic Commission and the couple moved to Philadelphia. Living in prosperity for the first time in her life, Dunbar-Nelson maintained an active social life among the black elite, including such luminaries as James Weldon Johnson, W. E. B. DU BOIS, LANGSTON HUGHES, Georgia Douglas Johnson, and MARY CHURCH TERRELL. No longer burdened by financial want, Dunbar-Nelson remained active in the last years of her life as a philanthropist and political activist. She died in Philadelphia of a heart condition.

Alice Dunbar-Nelson's life and work are testament to the diverse talents and activities of educated African American women of the late nineteenth and early twentieth centuries. As a light-skinned woman of mixed African, European, and Native American ancestry, Dunbar-Nelson was acutely sensitive to the resentment of both whites and darker-skinned African Americans, but also

occasionally passed for white in order to gain access to the racially segregated world of opera, museums, theater, and bathing spas. In much of her literary work, Dunbar-Nelson focused on nonracial themes, often creating white or racially ambiguous characters, but in her work as an educator, journalist, and activist, Dunbar-Nelson placed herself firmly within African American culture, where her contributions remain vital.

FURTHER READING

Dunbar-Nelson, Alice. *Give Us Each Day: The Diary of Alice Dunbar-Nelson,* ed. Gloria T. Hull (1984).

Hull, Gloria T. *Color, Sex, and Poetry: Three Women Writers of the Harlem Renaissance* (1987).

—ALICE KNOX EATON

 DUNCANSON, ROBERT S. (1821?– 21 Dec. 1872), painter, was born in Fayette, New York, the son of John Dean Duncanson, a carpenter and handyman, and Lucy Nickles. Robert's grandfather Charles Duncanson was a former slave from Virginia who was emancipated and around 1790 moved north. Perhaps because he was the illegitimate offspring of his master, Charles had been permitted to learn a skilled trade and later to earn his release from bondage. After the death of Charles, the Duncanson family moved west to the boomtown of Monroe, Michigan, on the tip of Lake Erie. There Robert, along with his four brothers, was raised in the family trades of house painting, decorating, and carpentry, a legacy of his grandfather's bondage. At the age of seventeen, after several years of apprenticeship, Robert entered into the painting trade with a partner, John Gamblin, advertising as "Painters and Glaziers."

For unknown reasons the painting partnership disbanded after only a year. Apparently Duncanson was not satisfied pursuing a trade and was determined to embark on a career as an artist. He moved to Cincinnati, the economic and artistic center of the United States west of the Appalachian Mountains and one of the major population centers of the free black population in the United States and a locus of abolitionist activity.

On account of the limited opportunities to learn the art of painting, Duncanson, like many American artists, was forced to teach himself art by painting portraits, copying prints, and sketching from nature. Seeking commissions to sustain his burgeoning artistic career, he became an itinerant painter, traveling regularly between Cincinnati, Detroit, and Monroe. The *Portrait of a Mother and Daughter* (1841) is Duncanson's earliest datable painting. The mannered and labored style of this portrait is typical among limners of this era but demonstrates considerable potential. This painting suggests the style of Duncanson's *Fancy Portrait*, which marked his exhibition debut in 1842. Within two years Duncanson painted his most impressive portrait of this period, *Portrait of William J. Baker* (1844). By the mid-1840s the artist's paintings improved considerably, prompting the *Detroit Daily Advertiser* to declare that "the young artist [paints] portraits...historical and fancy pieces of great merit" (2 Feb. 1846).

In 1848 Duncanson received his most important commission to date from the abolitionist minister, the Reverend Charles Avery, to paint *Cliff Mine, Lake Superior, 1848*. Duncanson's haunting image of the ravaged cliff resonates with metaphors of the destruction of nature and indicates his awareness of the Hudson River School–style of American landscape painting. This commission launched Duncanson into landscape painting and entrenched the artist in the network of abolitionist patronage that would sustain him throughout his career.

The commission from Avery resulted in Duncanson's emergence as the most significant African American artist of his generation and one of the primary Ohio River Valley landscape painters. In this fertile environment for landscape painting Duncanson's style improved dramatically to the point that in 1851 he created one of the landmark landscape paintings of the era, *Blue Hole, Flood Waters, Little Miami River*. His romantic landscapes emphasized themes of man in nature and were indicative of mainstream landscape painting of the era.

In 1853 Duncanson produced his only painting of an explicitly African American subject, *Uncle Tom and Little Eva*, after Harriet Beecher Stowe's novel *Uncle Tom's Cabin* (1852). The moment portrayed in the novel foreshadows Eva's death while she is teaching her slave, Tom, to read the Bible. For Duncanson this scene represented his belief in the potential for salvation from slavery through religious faith.

Duncanson's rise to artistic prominence prompted local arts patrons to sponsor his tour of Europe in 1853. Duncanson was the first African American artist to make the traditional "grand tour" of Europe. His art was enriched by the experience of Europe, which in his own words, "shed a new light over my path" (Spencer letters, 22 Jan. 1854, Newberry Library), as in his painting of ancient Roman ruins, *Time's Temple* (1854). After his return he produced a series of American landscapes, such as *Western Forest* (1857) and *Rainbow* (1859), that culminated in his recognition as "the best landscape painter in the West" (*Daily Cincinnati Gazette*, 30 May 1861).

As a free person of color Duncanson sympathized with his enslaved brethren and actively participated in abolitionist societies and their activities. In addition to receiving abolitionist patronage, on several occasions he donated paintings to support antislavery organizations. Notices of his work often appeared in the antislavery journals of the day, which championed his accomplishments and his contributions to African American society. In 1855 Duncanson collaborated with African American daguerreotypist James Pressley Ball on an antislavery panorama, *Mammoth Pictorial Tour of the United States Comprising Views of the African Slave Trade*, that toured the country.

Duncanson not only actively participated in antislavery activities, but many of his paintings also contained a veiled content that expressed the concerns of an African American artist living in the antebellum United States. At the end of the 1850s political concerns of the impending Civil War occupied the artist's thoughts. In response Duncanson created the most ambitious easel painting of his career, *Land of the Lotus Eaters* (1861). Duncanson's vast tropical landscape relates a tale from Homer's *Odyssey* that depicted dark-complexioned natives serving white soldiers. The painting evokes the evils of slavery and prophesies the forthcoming long and bloody civil conflict. Reviews of *Lotus Eaters* proclaimed the painting as Duncanson's masterpiece and noted his ambition to tour the painting in Europe. Exiling himself from the Civil War, the artist escaped in 1863 to Montreal, Canada, where he was eagerly received as a master American painter and "where his color did not prevent his association with other artists and his entrance into good society" (*Daily Cincinnati Gazette*, 24 Nov. 1865). By the time of his departure for England two years later, he had helped spawn the first native Canadian landscape painting school. Duncanson exhibited *Lotus Eaters* in Dublin, Glasgow, and London to great praise, with critics proclaiming him a "master" (*Art Journal*, 1866: 95).

While exhibiting *Lotus Eaters* in England, Duncanson took picturesque tours of the countryside, especially the Scottish Highlands. After his return to Cincinnati in 1867, with the laurels of international acclaim, Duncanson revealed his enchantment with the land and lore of Scotland in a series of landscapes that culminated his career. The last of these, *Ellen's Isle, Loch Katrine* (1871), is considered to be the pinnacle of his aesthetic and technical accomplishments. Inspired by Sir Walter Scott's epic poem *Lady of the Lake*, Duncanson depicted the island home of the Highland princess, Ellen Douglas, isolated on Lake Katrine. FREDERICK DOUGLASS had taken his surname from the Highland lord in Scott's poem, and W. E. B. DU BOIS fondly remembered the poem as the "sort of world we want to create for ourselves in America."

Tragically, at the same time Duncanson achieved his ultimate artistic success, he was suffering from a degenerative mental disorder. In the late 1860s he developed a severe dementia that led to extended periods of artistic inactivity and great difficulty in his personal life. By 1870 his condition had so worsened that it was painfully evident to his patrons and the public. He experienced dramatic swings in temperament and suffered from delusions, hallucinations, and violent outbursts. He had become a spiritualist and was convinced that he was possessed by the spirit of a past artist, a woman, who assisted him in the creation of his paintings such as *Ellen's Isle*. His psychotic behavior became so disruptive in 1872 that he produced little work that year. Somehow he managed to have enough paintings for an exhibition in Detroit that October. While hanging his paintings he suffered a seizure and collapsed, dying shortly thereafter. He had married twice. His first wife was Rebecca Graham, who died sometime before 1850. In around 1855 he married Phoebe (maiden name unknown).

Duncanson's remarkable artistic achievements and international reputation blazed the trail for subsequent African American artists and eased their passage and acceptance into the international cultural community. Shortly after his death Duncanson's work fell into obscurity. This unfortunate fate befell an artist whom the *Daily Cincinnati Gazette* regarded as the most important landscape painter working in the western United States and the key transitional figure in the emergence of the African American artist.

FURTHER READING

BEARDEN, ROMARE. *A History of African American Artists: From 1792 to the Present* (1993).

Ketner, Joseph D. *The Emergence of the African American Artist: Robert S. Duncanson, 1821–1872* (1994).

McElroy, Guy, and the Cincinnati Art Museum. *Robert S. Duncanson: A Centennial Exhibition* (1972).

Obituary: *Daily Cincinnati Gazette,* 28 Dec. 1872.

—JOSEPH D. KETNER

DUNHAM, KATHERINE MARY (22 June 1909–), dancer, choreographer, school founder, and anthropologist, was born in Chicago, Illinois, to Albert Millard Dunham Sr., an African American tailor and amateur jazz musician, and Fanny June Guillaume Taylor, a school administrator of French Canadian, English, Native American, and possibly African ancestry. The Dunhams lived in the predominantly white suburb of Glen Ellyn, Illinois, until Fanny's death when Katherine was four. Forced to sell the family home, Albert Dunham became a traveling salesman and sent Katherine and her older brother, Albert Jr., to live with relatives on the South Side of Chicago, where she was exposed to black vaudeville and blues performances.

Although Albert Sr. reunited the family after he remarried and purchased a dry cleaning store in Joliet, Illinois, he became increasingly unpredictable and violent. Katherine found an outlet in athletics and dance while attending public high school and junior college in Joliet. Hoping to extricate his sister from an unpleasant home situation that included Albert Sr.'s growing sexual interest in his daughter, Albert Jr. convinced nineteen-year-old Katherine to transfer to the University of Chicago, where he was studying philosophy on scholarship.

Dunham relished the independence and freedom she found in Chicago. Money was tight, but she managed to support herself working as a librarian and giving dance lessons. Dunham's

In a career spanning seven decades, Katherine Dunham has incorporated African-based cultural forms into contemporary dance worldwide. Photograph by Alfredo Valente; Library of Congress

ballet teacher, Madame Ludmila Speranzeva, took her to performances by the Isadora Duncan Dance Company and the Ballet Russe, and Albert Jr. introduced her to the theater crowd at the Cube Theater, which he cofounded. Inspired by Chicago's thriving African American intellectual scene, Dunham began hosting salon-style get-togethers, inviting a diverse group of artists, writers, performers, scholars, and social scientists, including choreographers Mark Turbyfull and Ruth Page, artist Charles Sebree, actor Ruth Attaway, ZORA NEALE HURSTON, BENJAMIN O. DAVIS JR., and Alan Lomax. Determined not to be a "polka dot," her term for a token black dancer, Dunham organized her own dance troupes, the first of which disbanded shortly after performing at the 1931 Chicago Beaux Arts Ball. Dunham featured her new troupe, the Negro Dance Group, two years later in a program commissioned by the 1933–1934 Chicago World's Fair.

All the while, Dunham had continued studying under Robert Redfield at the University of Chicago in one of the country's most innovative anthropology departments. Dunham's investigation into the role of dance in culture, a field she later called dance anthropology, dovetailed with the university's liberal humanist and interdisciplinary philosophy. Dunham was ahead of her time in seeing the possibilities in cross-pollinating her academic and performance work. With endorsements from Melville Herskovits, head of African Studies at Northwestern University, CHARLES S. JOHNSON, and Erich Fromm, Dunham applied successfully for a fieldwork scholarship from the Rosenwald Fund. In May 1935 she left for Jamaica, Martinique, Trinidad, and Haiti on a yearlong trip that proved fundamental to both her scholarly and performing careers.

Dunham wrote *Journey to Accompong* (1946) about her fieldwork in Jamaica, and the rituals of Martinique provided material for many choreographies. But it was Haiti and its African-based rhythms and movements that most affected Dunham. She documented the country's rich tradition of voodoo rituals, drumming, and sacred and secular dancing, and published two books devoted to Haiti, *Dances of Haiti* (1947) and *Island Possessed* (1969). In 1949 she purchased a villa near Port-au-Prince and began spending part of each year there.

Dunham received a BA in Anthropology from the University of Chicago in 1936 and immediately continued with graduate work at the University of Chicago and Northwestern University, eventually turning her research into *Dances of Haiti*. Although Dunham shifted focus to her performance career without completing a graduate degree, she remained devoted to anthropology, doing research in each country she visited, and serving as a visiting professor and lecturer at universities and anthropological societies worldwide.

In 1938 Dunham was appointed director of the Negro Unit of the Chicago branch of the Federal Theater Project, through which she choreographed dances for *Emperor Jones*, *Swing Mikado*, and *Run Lil' Chillun* and premiered her ballet *L'Ag'Ya*, based on her Caribbean research. The next year, Dunham was on Broadway in the 1939 labor union musical *Pins and Needles*. While in

New York she opened her first revue, *Tropics and Le Jazz Hot: From Haiti to Harlem* at the Windsor Theater to rave reviews. Back in Chicago, Dunham and her troupe spent evenings performing in nightclubs with DUKE ELLINGTON and days establishing a repertoire of programs that included "Rara Tonga," "Barrelhouse," and "Woman with a Cigar."

Dunham's revolutionary choreography blended Caribbean, South American, and African styles of movement and folk narrative with modern dance and ballet, leading the way for ALVIN AILEY's American Dance Theater and ARTHUR MITCHELL's Dance Theater of Harlem. By combining her interpretations of a dance lexicon drawn from African and Caribbean sources with a vocabulary of African American social dances such as "Cakewalk," "Ballin' the Jack," and "Strut," Dunham established black dance as an art form for the first time. A serious artist with popular appeal, Dunham created entertainment that was both academic and showbiz friendly, authentic, yet theatrical. In the 1950s European fashion houses even produced "Dunham" and "Caribbean" lines of clothing.

Soon after moving her troupe, now called the Katherine Dunham Dance Company, to New York City, Dunham's career soared to new heights when she starred on Broadway in the 1940 all-black musical *Cabin in the Sky*, which she choreographed with George Balanchine. Over the next twenty years, the Dunham Dance Company performed in sixty-nine countries, and Dunham choreographed one hundred dances and five revues, four of which were performed on Broadway. Dunham shows, including *Tropical Revue*, *Carib Song*, and *Bal Negre*, featured Caribbean and Latin American numbers, ballets often drawn from folk sources, and medleys of African American spirituals and social and plantation dances.

Between 1941 and 1948 the Dunham dancers toured throughout North America, and, beginning with their triumphant first visit in 1948, the company toured Europe annually, eventually adding North Africa, the Middle East, South America, Australia, and Asia to their schedule. Ever the anthropologist, Dunham "would collect 'something': a cultural expression, a movement, a local musician, or a dancer" in each location (Aschenbrenner, 147).

Following *Carnival of Rhythm* (1941), a short film made about the company, Dunham appeared in or choreographed several Hollywood films, including *Star-Spangled Rhythm* (1942), *Stormy Weather* (1943), *Pardon My Sarong* (1942), *Casbah* (1948), and *Mambo* (1954). She also became a television pioneer when, in 1940, her company was the first to perform an hour-long dance broadcast.

In 1941 Dunham married the white Canadian-born theater designer John Pratt, who worked as chief designer of Dunham's shows until his death in 1986. In 1951 the couple adopted Marie Christine Columbier, a four-year old French Martinique girl of mixed ancestry. (Dunham had been married briefly in the early 1930s to Jordis McCoo, a post office worker and part-time dancer.)

In 1945 Dunham opened the Dunham School of Dance and Theater in New York. Within a few years it had become the premiere training ground for African American dancers and a host of actors, including Butterfly McQueen, Marlon Brando, and James Dean. Dunham's mission was multifold: "To establish a well-trained ballet group. To develop a technique that will be as important to the white man as the Negro. To attain a status in the dance world that will give to the Negro dance student the courage really to study and a reason to do so. And to take Our dance out of the burlesque—to make of it a more dignified art" (Aschenbrenner, 110). The Dunham Method treated dance as part of a holistic enterprise involving the mind and spirit as well as the body. The school's faculty, which included Lee and Susan Strasberg, taught theater, literature, philosophy, music, and world cultures until it closed in 1955.

Financial pressures and arthritic knees forced Dunham to dissolve her company shortly after choreographing her last Broadway show, *Bambouche*, in 1962. The following year, she became the New York Metropolitan Opera's first black choreographer when she mounted a daring interpretation of *Aïda*, casting black performers as Egyptians before it became fashionable. In 1967, after a year spent choreographing for the National Ballet of Senegal, Dunham opened the Performing Arts Training Center (PATC) in East St. Louis, close to Southern Illinois University, where she taught until 1982. PATC offered classes in humanities, theater, dance, and martial arts, and its curriculum used dance to teach other subjects, such as reading, storytelling, and mathematics. In 1977 Dunham and Pratt opened the Katherine Dunham Dynamic Museum, a public facility that houses Dunham's art collection and materials documenting her career.

Dunham protested injustices throughout her career, particularly by challenging the racial segregation of hotels, restaurants, and rehearsal halls. When, over the objections of the U.S. State Department, she persisted in performing *Southland*, a ballet she choreographed that dramatized a lynching, the FBI mounted a campaign that financially damaged her company. In 1992 at the age of eighty-two, Dunham waged a forty-seven day hunger strike to protest the U.S. government's treatment of Haitian refugees.

In addition to a dozen honorary degrees, Dunham has received numerous awards including the Albert Schweitzer Music Award in 1979, a Kennedy Center Honors Award in 1983, the French Légion d'Honneur, the Southern Cross of Brazil, and several honors from the Haitian government. The author of numerous articles, Dunham published a childhood memoir *A Touch of Innocence* (1959) and a novel *Kasamance* (1967), set in Senegal. In 2000 the Library of Congress received one million dollars from the Doris Duke Foundation to collect and preserve materials relating to Dunham's legacy.

FURTHER READING

Dunham's papers are held at the Southern Illinois University in Carbondale.

Dunham, Katherine. *A Touch of Innocence* (1959).

Aschenbrenner, Joyce. *Katherine Dunham: Dancing a Life* (2002).
Beckford, Katherine. *Dunham: A Biography* (1979).

—LISA E. RIVO

 DUNJEE, ROSCOE
(21 June 1883–1 Mar. 1965), newspaper publisher and civil rights leader, was born in Harpers Ferry, West Virginia, the son of John William Dunjee, a former slave, and Lydia Ann Dunjee. The elder Dunjee, a Baptist minister, moved his family first to Minnesota and then to Oklahoma Territory in 1892. A library of fifteen hundred volumes was an important part of the family belongings and played a major role in Roscoe's education.

When his father died in 1903, Dunjee was left to care for his mother on their fruit and vegetable farm. He earned extra money by writing stories for local newspapers until he purchased a small printing plant in Oklahoma City in 1913. On 5 November 1914 he printed the first edition of the *Black Dispatch*, a paper targeting the growing black community in Oklahoma City, the state capital. Dunjee was criticized by local black leaders for using the word "Black" in the title of the paper. However, he dismissed such criticism as the opinions of people who were ashamed of their race.

From its inception, the *Black Dispatch* became the voice of the disenfranchised blacks of Oklahoma City. Through his editorials, Dunjee prodded readers to organize and fight for civil rights. In 1915, when Logan County election officials denied blacks the right to vote, Dunjee led the suffrage campaign. He publicized these injustices until the Supreme Court, in *Guinn v. United States*, struck down as unconstitutional Oklahoma's voting laws. This decision gave the fledgling National Association for the Advancement of Colored People its first national victory. Over the next half century, circulation of the *Black Dispatch* would reach a high of twenty-four thousand, with readers in every state and many foreign countries. One of Dunjee's young readers and newspaper carriers in the 1920s was the author RALPH ELLISON, whose father had been killed in an accident. Dunjee became a father figure to Ellison, who credited the publisher with inspiring his belief that civil rights could be obtained under the rule of American law.

In 1930 Dunjee rose to meet another challenge when GEORGE WASHINGTON CARVER, who had given a speech to the Oklahoma Association of Negro Teachers, was refused a ticket for a Pullman sleeping car on the Santa Fe Railroad. The incident spurred a series of attacks on Oklahoma's segregated public transportation laws and soon drew attention to the related problem of housing segregation in Oklahoma City. Dunjee raised money to fight ordinances that prevented blacks from living outside a small, overcrowded section of the city. He also organized mass public meetings to express the community's outrage. Soon, city leaders began to seek his counsel on race-related questions.

Public education was a subject dear to Dunjee's heart, for he recognized that a quality education was the key to economic opportunity for his people. He once asked an audience, "What goes on in a child's mind when he sings 'Sweet Land of Liberty' and at the same time remembers are libraries in his city or village that he cannot enter and other educational opportunities around him which he dare not attempt to utilize?" Dunjee also fought for equal funding for black schools in Oklahoma and publicly criticized state officials for leaving black schools without adequate funds to maintain buildings and pay teachers.

If a need existed in the black community in Oklahoma City, Dunjee was aware of it. He helped desegregate parks and swimming pools and raise the standard of medical care. Early on, he realized that the battle for civil rights would be won or lost in a courtroom. He had great respect for the law and American justice and pledged to hire the best lawyers he could find to carry on the battle. He personally sought out witnesses and established a defense fund for a young black man, Jess Hollins, sentenced to die for raping a white woman. In 1934 the U.S. Supreme Court used Hollins's case to end the practice of excluding blacks from Oklahoma juries.

Dunjee chartered Oklahoma's first NAACP chapter in 1914 and later became close friends with the NAACP lawyer THURGOOD MARSHALL, who advised him in legal situations and who came to Oklahoma to represent aggrieved blacks in several lawsuits. The most famous case was that of *Ada Lois Sipuel Fisher v. Oklahoma State Board of Regents* (1948). Fisher had been denied admission to the University of Oklahoma (OU) School of Law. Dunjee persuaded Fisher to become the plaintiff in a sweeping lawsuit that attacked the foundations of the segregated system of higher education in many southern states. Fisher had graduated with honors from Langston University and was well qualified for admission to the OU law school. However, in a much-publicized decision, the school's board of regents refused her, citing an antiquated discriminatory law that made it a misdemeanor in Oklahoma for white teachers to teach black students. Dunjee used his newspaper to raise funds to wage the battle. With Marshall as chief counsel, the Fisher case went to the Supreme Court, which ordered the state to provide Fisher a legal education equivalent to that of white Oklahomans. The Oklahoma leadership initially sidestepped this decision by setting up a sham law school in the basement of the state capitol solely for Fisher, who later attended the OU School of Law, graduated, and began a long and distinguished career as an educator and civil rights activist. Ironically, she was appointed in the 1980s as a member of the OU board of regents, the same body that had denied her admission decades earlier.

Where other papers equivocated, the *Black Dispatch* stated resolutely that in all matters of education "segregation is obvious discrimination." In 1948 Dunjee used the plight of George McLaurin to change the way black students were treated. McLaurin was forced by OU administrators to sit in a classroom alcove, where he could see the teacher but the white students could not see him. He also had separate eating and toilet facilities. Once again, Dunjee championed Marshall's legal efforts, which in 1950 resulted in a unanimous Supreme Court decision against OU for violating McLaurin's right to equal access to education. In its decision the court cited the Fourteenth Amendment and Oklahoma's own constitutional provisions for equal educational opportunities for all races.

Dunjee, who never married, died shortly before his eighty-second birthday. At his funeral, Marshall, who later that year became the first black member of the Supreme Court, said, "Roscoe Dunjee gave us inspiration to get the job done. He didn't wait for somebody else. He didn't back down, even when his own people said he was wrong." Although his vision and his brilliance can be clearly seen in the broad strokes of his editorial pen, the magnitude of Dunjee's contributions was not appreciated until years after his death. The extent to which he influenced the

course of Oklahoma history and of the struggle for civil rights is immeasurable.

FURTHER READING

Burke, Bob, and Denyvetta Davis. *Ralph Ellison: A Biography* (2002).
Burke, Bob, and Angela Monson. *Roscoe Dunjee: Champion of Civil Rights* (1998).
Miles-LaGrange, Vicki, and Bob Burke. *A Passion for Equality: The Life of Jimmy Stewart* (1999).

—BOB BURKE

 DURHAM, JAMES

(1 May 1762–?), physician, was born a slave in Philadelphia, Pennsylvania. His surname is sometimes spelled Derham. Despite his slave status, he learned basic reading and writing skills from his first owners, whom he described as Christians. Durham also received his medical training from his masters. At that period most American physicians acquired their medical education through the apprenticeship system. Durham began a form of apprenticeship at the age of eight, when he became the slave of John A. Kearsley Jr., a physician who taught him to compound medicines and to perform routine medical procedures. Durham later belonged to other doctors in Philadelphia, at least one of whom was a British sympathizer. This association with a Loyalist master probably explains why Durham later became the property of George West, a surgeon in the British Sixteenth Regiment.

Along with his new master, Durham performed amputations on wounded troops along the Eastern Seaboard. Smallpox and various febrile diseases wreaked havoc among the British troops in the colonies, and Durham and other medics also attempted to save the lives of men stricken with these diseases. In 1781 Spanish forces defeated the British at Pensacola, Florida, and carried Durham with their other spoils of war to Spanish-controlled New Orleans. There Robert Dow, a Scottish physician, purchased Durham.

For the next two years Durham, working under Dow's supervision, practiced medicine in the city's French Quarter. Their patients were probably victims of malaria, yellow fever, influenza, and many other

diseases common in eighteenth-century Louisiana. Although Durham had worked closely with the surgeon George West, it appears that he performed little if any surgery on Dow's patients.

Durham later described Dow as a good man, and there seems to have been mutual respect and admiration between slave and master. In April 1783 Dow permitted Durham, described as his faithful servant, to purchase his freedom for 500 pesos. Thereafter the two men enjoyed a close professional relationship for more than twenty years, during most of which Durham lived in New Orleans.

In 1788 Durham returned for about a year to Philadelphia, where he probably searched for family members and acquaintances whom he had not seen since before the Revolutionary War. During this sojourn he met America's foremost physician, Benjamin Rush. Like some of his peers, Rush was an early antislavery activist who wanted to meet talented blacks. At that time abolitionists believed that by publishing accounts of talented blacks and their achievements, they could counter arguments that slavery was justifiable on the grounds that Africans were intellectually inferior to whites. Through Rush's description of Durham, published in the *American Museum* (4 [July–Dec. 1788], 81–82), this former slave became well known in abolitionist circles.

Eighteenth-century Philadelphia was America's most sophisticated city, and Rush was able to introduce Durham to several prominent physicians and members of the Philadelphia College of Physicians and Surgeons. Durham was the first black medical practitioner most of them had encountered; moreover, he was certainly the first black man known to have appeared before an American medical society. Rush and Durham also talked at length about the diseases and medications used in Louisiana. Rush believed Durham was quite knowledgeable about the drugs of that time. He was also impressed with the former slave's fluency in French and Spanish.

In the spring of 1789 Durham was back in New Orleans, where he and Dow resumed their professional relationship. Their patients included some of the city's most prominent residents. It appears that Durham, like some other persons of color in early New Orleans, was not a victim of racial prejudice.

Durham remained in touch with Rush and corresponded with him over a period of sixteen years. In several letters he asked Rush to ship medical supplies to him and Dow, noting that on at least two occasions fire had destroyed their office and medical supplies. Durham, Rush, and Dow were familiar with the same medicines because all had studied under British physicians, and these medications were probably more readily available in Philadelphia than in New Orleans. Occasionally Durham sought advice from Rush regarding certain patients. The two men also exchanged views regarding the treatment of diseases such as yellow fever, which ravaged both Philadelphia and New Orleans during the 1790s.

That Rush respected Durham's expertise was evident when Rush read a paper written by the former slave before a session of the College of Physicians and Surgeons of Philadelphia. This treatise described a method used by Durham to treat "putrid sore throat," or diphtheria. It was one of the earliest medical papers written by an African American and was read before some of America's most respected physicians.

Durham experienced no difficulties with his medical practice in New Orleans until 1801, when Spanish authorities attempted to subject medical practitioners to restrictions not found under British colonial administration. The Spanish commissioners decreed that certain persons be forbidden to practice medicine in New Orleans until they had graduated from a medical school. Among those cited as a physician without the appropriate training was Durham. However, the commissioners agreed that Durham, even though he did not have formal training in medicine, could continue to treat diseases of the throat; apparently other members of his profession saw Durham as something of a specialist in this area.

Apparently Durham abided by this ruling; however, in a letter to Rush in 1802, he mentioned that he and Dow had encountered some cases of cowpox and wanted Rush's opinion regarding the most efficacious treatment. Possibly Durham had assumed some type of apprenticeship with Dow, working independently only when patients were stricken with diphtheria or some other ailment of the throat.

James Durham's correspondence with Rush ended in 1805. A few years earlier Durham had questioned Rush about the possibility of his practicing medicine elsewhere in the United States. When and whether he left New Orleans, however, remains a mystery, as do the date and place of his death.

FURTHER READING

Durham's letters to Rush are in the Benjamin Rush Papers, Manuscript Collection, Historical Society of Pennsylvania, Philadelphia; some appear in *Letters of Benjamin Rush*, ed. Lyman Butterfield, vol. 1 (1950), 497–498. He is mentioned in the Records of the Cabildo, New Orleans Public Library.

Morais, Henry M. *The History of the Afro-American in Medicine* (1976), 8–10.
Plummer, Betty E. "Letters of James Durham to Benjamin Rush," *Journal of Negro History* 65 (1980): 261–269.
Shryock, Richard H. *Medicine and Society in America: 1660–1860* (1960).

—BETTY E. PLUMMER

DU SABLE, JEAN BAPTISTE POINTE

(1745?–28 Aug. 1818), explorer and merchant, was born in San Marc, Haiti, the son of a slave woman (name unknown) and Dandonneau (first name unknown), scion of a prominent French Canadian family active in the North American fur trade. Surviving historical journals record the name of Jean Baptiste Pointe du Sable (Pointe au Sable by some accounts), a Haitian of mixed-race ancestry, as the first permanent settler of Chicago. In her 1856 memoir of frontier life in the emerging Northwest Territory, Juliette Kinzie, the wife of fur trader John Kinzie, makes note of the fact that "the first white man who settled here was a Negro." Several of the voyageurs and commercial men who regularly traversed the shores of southern Lake Michigan in the last decade of the eighteenth century kept accurate records of their encounters in journals and ledger books. One such entry describes du Sable as a "large man; a trader, and pretty wealthy."

Du Sable's pathway to economic reward in the emerging West began in Haiti many years earlier. Because of his race, du Sable was excluded from direct political participation but enjoyed the same basic rights as freedmen and thus was allowed social intercourse with the French settlers. There is no historical rendering of du Sable's activities prior to his departure from Santo Domingo. In general, though, his occupation seems to have been that of a trader. Accordingly, du Sable sailed from Haiti to pursue the dream of greater economic reward in a foreign land aboard the sloop *Susanne*. He arrived in New Orleans in 1764. Less than a year later du Sable completed a historic six-hundred-mile journey up the Mississippi River in the company of Jacques Clamorgan, a successful explorer and merchant who went on to become one of the first judges of the Court of Common Pleas in St. Louis. Du Sable's association with a man of Clamorgan's stature indicates that he was welcomed into a higher social class than one might normally expect of a man born to a slave woman in those times. There seems to have been less social rigidity in the western frontier, thus allowing du Sable to engage in commerce with the white settlers.

Du Sable staked a claim to eight hundred acres of farmland in Peoria and tended this property for several years until he made the decision to relocate to northeast Illinois in the land the Potawatomi tribe called "Eschecagou" (Chicago: literal translation, "land of the wild onions"). There du Sable founded the region's first commercial enterprise, a trading post on the marshy north bank of the Chicago River overlooking Lake Michigan. Juliette Kinzie's memoir provides some additional details of du Sable's holdings during this period. In addition to his "mansion" (measuring 22 × 40 feet), du Sable owned two barns, a horse mill, bakehouse, dairy, workshop, henhouse, and smokehouse. The inventory of farm equipment indicates that du Sable was harvesting wheat and cutting hay. To run such a busy trading operation and farming enterprise required that du Sable employ skilled labor. Undoubtedly many of his "employees" were Potawatomie Indians.

Du Sable cultivated a good relationship with the native peoples. For a time he lived among the indigenous tribe and took Catherine, the daughter of Potawatomie chief Pokagon, as his common-law wife. The marriage was formalized at Cahokia in 1788, but the union had been sanctioned by Indian tribal customs years earlier. The couple had two children.

The flourishing frontier outpost along the Chicago River was disrupted by the arrival of Charles-Michel Mouet de Langlade, a French nobleman and commercial trader, in 1778. De Langlade, whom midwestern historians consider to be the "father of Wisconsin," drove du Sable and his family from the region in order to claim the local trade and because of his racial enmity. Du Sable abandoned his claim and moved his family farther east. He took up residence in Michigan City, Indiana, but hostilities between the American colonists and the British government resulted in du Sable's arrest in August 1779. British regulars garrisoned at Fort Michilimackinac (Mackinac Island, Michigan) descended on du Sable's cabin adjacent to the River Chemin and removed him to their military encampment at Port Huron, north of Detroit.

Du Sable and his family were detained by the British for the duration of the American Revolution, a five-year period ending in approximately 1784. A report submitted by Lieutenant Thomas Bennett describes the circumstances of du Sable's arrest and subsequent confinement. "Corporal Tascon, who commanded the party, very prudently prevented the Indians from burning his home, or doing him any injury. The Negro, since his encampment, has in every respect behaved in a manner becoming to a man in his situation and his many friends who give him a good character." Du Sable fully cooperated with his captors and signaled his willingness to take charge of the Port Huron trading post after reports filtered back to Lieutenant Governor Patrick Sinclair that du Sable's predecessor, a Frenchman named Francois Brevecour, had badly mistreated the Indians. The "Pinery," as the British outpost and commissary was known, was maintained by du Sable until 1784, when historians believe that he returned to Illinois to reclaim his vacated properties following the cessation of war.

The Great Lakes region was fast becoming an important hub of commerce; much of the trade came from the Spanish settlements west of the Mississippi River. Thus, du Sable built and maintained a successful trading post at the mouth of the Chicago River.

Historians differ on the precise year du Sable started his business. However, journal accounts maintained by Hugh Heward, a Detroit commission agent, establish the presence of du Sable in Chicago on 10 May 1790. During this period du Sable supplied his customers with pork, bread, and flour in return for durable goods and cash. He lived in peace with the Indians, and the white traders passing through the region commented favorably on his character and business acumen.

These early observations describe the region's first settler as an honest man, fond of drink but well educated by contemporary standards. When du Sable sailed to Mackinac with his Indian companions in 1796, the British soldiers greeted him with a cannon salute as a token of esteem. It was a remarkable gesture indicative of his reputation and good character up and down the Great Lakes.

In May of 1800 Jean Baptiste du Sable disposed of his property for reasons not entirely clear. With certainty we can say that Chicago's first settler completed Chicago's first real estate transaction of any consequence when he sold the trading post to Jean La Lime, a French Canadian trapper from St. Joseph, for the sum of six thousand livres. The sale was witnessed by John Kinzie of Niles, Michigan (who in turn would purchase the estate from La Lime four years later in 1804), and was duly recorded in Detroit, the seat of government for the territory of Illinois.

We can only speculate about du Sable's motivations for wanting to leave Chicago. Perhaps his decision to vacate the region at this historic juncture had something to do with the arrival of the eastern settlers who were already pouring into this desolate marshland previously populated only by American Indians and wild animals. Fort Dearborn was erected in April 1803 to protect the interests of the white settlers from the native peoples. This frontier outpost would soon evolve into the city of Chicago.

Du Sable briefly returned to his farmland in Peoria and remained there for little more than a decade. It is believed that Catherine died in Peoria prior to June 1813, when du Sable retired to St. Charles, Missouri. In his declining years du Sable took great

precautions to ensure that he could live out the remainder of his life in comfort. He deeded his home in St. Charles to a granddaughter, Eulalie Baroda Denais, in return for her assurance that she would care for him and provide him with a proper burial in the local Catholic cemetery. Whether du Sable achieved these modest aims is less certain, but village records from St. Charles suggest that the venerable pioneer encountered serious financial setbacks late in life and was imprisoned as a debtor in September 1814. Du Sable died at his daughter's residence. No information is available concerning his financial condition at this time.

For many years afterward there was a self-conscious tendency on the part of Chicago chroniclers to deny Jean Baptiste Pointe du Sable credit for his role in the development of Chicago as the commercial hub of midwestern commerce. The fact of du Sable's race disturbed the nineteenth-century writers who touted the accomplishments of Chicago's original settlers in any number of civic boosterism tomes to appear during that era. His questionable lineage, his friendship with the American Indians, and his dealings with the English army during a time of war cast du Sable in an unfavorable light for many years. Not until 1935 and the opening of du Sable High School in Chicago was any significant honor accorded this man. In 1961 Margaret Burroughs founded the du Sable Museum of African American History on the city's South Side. Her museum remains a shrine to his memory.

FURTHER READING

What little we know of Jean Baptiste Pointe du Sable is gleaned from surviving journal accounts, most notably the *Journal of a Voyage Made by Mr. Hugh Heward to the Illinois Country*. A copy of the original manuscript is in the reference library of the Chicago Historical Society. See also the manuscript collection of the Wisconsin State Historical Society for materials covering the early settlement of Illinois Territory.

Cortesi, Lawrence. *Jean du Sable: Father of Chicago* (1972).
Quaife, Milo M. *Checagou: From Indian Wigwam to Modern City* (1933).
Sawyers, June Skinner. *Chicago Portraits: Biographies of 250 Famous Chicagoans* (1991).
—RICHARD C. LINDBERG

E

EARLEY, CHARITY ADAMS (5 Dec. 1917–13 Jan. 2002), commander of the only African American unit of the Women's Army Corps stationed in Europe during World War II, was born Charity Edna Adams, the eldest of four children. She was raised in Columbia, South Carolina, where her father was a minister in the African Episcopal Methodist Church. Her mother was a former teacher.

Adams graduated from Booker T. Washington High School in Columbia as valedictorian of her senior class and then from Wilberforce University in Ohio, one of the top three black colleges in the nation in the 1930s. She majored in Math and Physics and graduated in 1938. After returning to Columbia, where she taught junior

high school mathematics for four years, Adams enrolled in the MA program for vocational psychology at Ohio State University, pursuing her degree during the summers.

As a member of the military's Advisory Council to the Women's Interests Section (ACWIS), MARY MCLEOD BETHUNE, president of the National Council of Negro Women, had fought for the inclusion of black women in the newly formed Women's Army Auxiliary Corps (WAAC) in 1942. The dean of women at Wilberforce identified Adams as a potential candidate with both the education and the character to become a fine female officer. Intrigued by the possibilities of military service, Adams applied in June 1942 and in July 1942 she became the first of four thousand African American women to join

what became the Women's Army Corp (WAC). She was one of thirty-nine black women enrolled in the first officer candidate class at the First WAAC Training Center at Fort Des Moines in Iowa, where she was stationed for two and a half years, achieving the rank of major.

The armed forces were segregated in World War II, and Adams suffered indignities from those racist policies, but she handled them with great fortitude and tenacity. One of these incidents happened at Fort Des Moines when a white colonel upbraided her for visiting the all-white officers' club with a major who had invited her there. She was forced to stand at attention for forty-five minutes while the colonel scolded her for "race mixing" and told her that black people needed to respect separation of the races even if they were

Major Charity E. Adams (later Charity Adams Earley) inspects the first African American contingent of the Women's Army Corps assigned overseas, 1945. National Archives and Records Administration

EDELMAN, MARIAN WRIGHT

officers. Indignant, Adams never entered the officers' club again. Adams also encountered American segregation policies in England, where she commanded the only African American WAC unit to serve overseas, a postal unit stationed in Birmingham and then in France. The American Red Cross, working with the U.S. Army, pressured Adams to move her unit from integrated accommodations to a designated London hotel and sent her equipment to be used at a segregated recreational area. Adams refused the move and the equipment, insisting that her unit continue using its integrated facility, and she persuaded her troops not to change their lodgings.

Adams also battled occupational segregation within the army. African Americans were routinely assigned menial service jobs and denied access to office work or skilled jobs. Army labor requisitions for WAC personnel often were for administrative jobs, but these were regularly reserved for white women. In an effort to break down these barriers, Adams was sent to the Pentagon in 1943 along with the African American Major Harriet West, assistant to the WAC leader Oveta Culp Hobby, to increase quotas of black women in motor transport and other jobs. They received nominal support from the Pentagon, but racial discrimination in job assignments remained a problem throughout the war for both male and female African American soldiers.

As a black woman in uniform during the 1940s, Adams was subjected to the tensions confronting all black soldiers on the home front as well. On her first visit home to Columbia in December 1942, she accompanied her father to a meeting of the Columbia chapter of the NAACP, which he headed, to discuss the mistreatment of black soldiers by white military police at nearby Fort Jackson. Upon returning home, they discovered that the Ku Klux Klan had parked a line of cars in front of their house. Adams's father gave the family his shotgun to protect themselves while he went to the home of the NAACP state head, only to find that home similarly surrounded and the family was out of town. In her autobiography Adams recounts the tense night that followed, as she kept watch over the hooded Klan members until dawn, when they left.

Adams also describes an incident in 1944 at an Atlanta train station, when she was asked by two white military police to produce identification. Several whites in the segregated waiting room had cast doubt on her status as an army officer. Even though she was with her parents, this was a dangerous encounter for Adams. The previous year a black army nurse in Alabama had been beaten by police and jailed for boarding a bus ahead of white passengers, and three African American WACs stationed at Fort Knox, Kentucky, had been similarly beaten for failing to move from the white area of a Greyhound bus station. Despite the risk, Adams took charge by interrogating the MPs herself and demanding the name of their commanding officer so that she could file a report on them if they did not respect her rank. The MPs saluted and disappeared.

After the war Adams returned to Ohio State and completed her MA in 1946, after which she served as a registration officer for the Veteran's Administration in Cleveland, as manager of a music school at the Miller Academy of Fine Arts, and as dean of student personnel services at Tennessee Agricultural and Industrial State College and then at Georgia State College. On 24 August 1949, she married a physician, Stanley Earley Jr. Accompanying him to the University of Zurich, where he was a medical student, she learned German and took courses at the university and at the Jungian Institute of Analytical Psychology. Earley returned to the United States with her husband after he completed his training, and they had two children, a son and a daughter. The family settled in Dayton, Ohio, where she was actively involved in community affairs, serving on boards for social services, education, civic affairs, and corporations.

In 1989 Earley published a memoir of her wartime service, *One Woman's Army*. The courage and leadership Earley displayed in her pioneering role in the U.S. Army earned her an award for distinguished service in 1946 from the National Council of Negro Women and, decades later, a place on the Smithsonian Institution's listing of the most historically important African American women. In 1996 the Smithsonian's National Postal Museum also honored

Adams's wartime service. She died in Dayton at the age of eighty-three, having established a permanent place in history for her trail-blazing accomplishments in World War II.

FURTHER READING

Earley, Charity Adams. *One Woman's Army: A Black Officer Remembers the WAC* (1989).

Jones, Jacqueline. *Labor of Love, Labor of Sorrow: Black Women, Work, and the Family from Slavery to the Present* (1985).
Meyer, Leisa D. *Creating G.I. Jane: Sexuality and Power in the Women's Army Corps during World War II* (1996).
Putney, Martha. *When the Nation Was in Need: Blacks in the Women's Army Corps during World War II* (1992).

Obituary: *New York Times*, 22 Jan. 2002.
—MAUREEN HONEY

EDELMAN, MARIAN WRIGHT (6 June 1939–), civil rights attorney and founder of the Children's Defense Fund, was born Marian Wright in Bennettsville, South Carolina, to Arthur Jerome Wright, a Baptist minister, and Maggie Leola Bowen, an active churchwoman. Both parents were community activists who took in relatives and others who could no longer care for themselves, eventually founding a home for the aged that continues to be run by family members. The Wrights also built a playground for black children denied access to white recreational facilities, and nurtured in their own children a sense of responsibility and community service. As soon as Marian and her siblings were old enough to drive, they continued the family tradition of delivering food and coal to the poor, elderly, and sick. Arthur Wright also encouraged his children to read about and to revere influential African Americans like MARY MCLEOD BETHUNE and MARIAN ANDERSON (for whom Marian Wright was named).

Marian Wright experienced racial injustice from an early age, despite the efforts of her parents and other elders to protect their children from the harshest excesses of segregation. Maggie Wright was choir director, organist, and coordinator of church and community youth activities and could not always be with

264

Marian Wright Edelman, president of the Children's Defense Fund, whose mission since 1973 has been to "Leave No Child Behind." Corbis

her children; thus neighbors and parishioners often looked after the Wright children. Such communal parenting provided Edelman with a series of strong black female role models. These women, she later wrote, became "lanterns" for her childhood and adult life.

In 1956, two years after her father's death, Wright entered Spelman College in Atlanta, Georgia. There she met several people who became influential mentors, including the historian Howard Zinn, the educator and civil rights advocate BENJAMIN MAYS, and MARTIN LUTHER KING JR. At Spelman, she continued the deep religious commitment of her childhood. Her diaries from that time record her prayers, asking God to "help me do the right thing and to be sincere and honest," to "teach us to seek after truth relentlessly, and to yearn for the betterment of mankind by endless sacrifice" (Edelman, 61, 64). This centrality of faith to her daily life persisted throughout Wright's career. She later identified her life's work as a desire to emulate her mentors in "seeking to serve

God and a cause bigger than ourselves" (Edelman, 53).

During her junior year she received a Charles Merrill scholarship that provided a year of European study and travel to Paris, Geneva, and several Eastern Bloc nations. That experience, she wrote in her diary, changed her life. "I could never return home to the segregated South and constraining Spelman College in the same way" (Edelman, 43). Marian Wright was not alone. Inspired by the February 1960 sit-in protests at segregated North Carolina lunch counters, thousands of young black southerners began to actively resist Jim Crow. That spring Wright was arrested with other Atlanta students during a sit-in, and she helped develop a student document, "An Appeal for Human Rights," that was published in both the white-owned *Atlanta Constitution* and the *Atlanta Daily World*, a publication produced by, and primarily read by, African Americans. At Easter, she joined several hundred students, primarily from the South, at a gathering in Raleigh, North Carolina, initiated by ELLA BAKER of the Southern Christian

Leadership Conference. That meeting resulted in Wright's participation in the Student Nonviolent Coordinating Committee (SNCC).

In May 1960 Wright graduated from Spelman as class valedictorian and entered Yale University Law School that fall. Having abandoned her earlier plans of studying Russian literature or preparing for the foreign service, she now determined that mastering the law would best prepare her for assisting the black freedom struggle. While at Yale, Wright continued her civil rights commitment through the Northern Students' Movement, a support group for SNCC, and by visiting civil rights workers in Mississippi. During the summer of 1962, she traveled to the Ivory Coast under the Crossroads Africa student cultural exchange program founded by JAMES H. ROBINSON. After graduating from Yale in 1963, Wright spent one year preparing to become a civil rights attorney by working for the NAACP Legal Defense and Educational Fund in New York.

In 1964 Wright moved south to direct the LDF's activities in Jackson, Mississippi. She arrived during "freedom summer," a major voter-registration campaign that helped her forge relationships with ROBERT P. MOSES, FANNIE LOU HAMER, Mae Bertha Carter, UNITA BLACKWELL, and other civil rights leaders. Wright remained in Jackson for four years and became the first black woman admitted to the Mississippi bar. She also successfully supported continued federal funding for the Child Development Group of Mississippi (CDGM), one of the nation's largest Head Start programs. CDGM, founded as part of President Lyndon Johnson's War on Poverty, was strongly opposed by conservatives in Mississippi and the state's all-white Congressional delegation, who viewed the organization as too radical. To the extent that CDGM wanted to end poverty and inequality for all Mississippians, it *was* radical, indeed, revolutionary. Wright also filed and won a school integration lawsuit that began the process of fully desegregating Mississippi schools.

As a result of her civil rights practice and work for the poor in Mississippi, Wright testified before the U.S. Senate in 1967 about hunger and poverty in the state. Prompted by Wright's compelling testimony, Senator Robert Kennedy visited Mississippi to examine her assertions of extreme economic deprivation. Wright guided Kennedy on this fact-finding trip, which resulted in immediate federal commodity and, later on, in expansions of the federal food stamp program. Wright also encouraged Martin Luther King Jr. to launch the Poor People's Campaign, to dramatize the problems of poverty in America, and later served as an attorney for that effort following King's assassination in April 1968. That July, Wright married Peter Edelman, a prominent aide to Senator Kennedy. The couple had three sons, Joshua, Jonah, and Ezra.

Edelman moved to Washington in 1968 and continued her civil rights and antipoverty work through a Field Foundation grant that enabled her to found the Washington Research Project (WRP), a public-interest law firm that lobbied for child and family well-being, and for expanding Head Start and other anti-poverty programs. Three years later she moved with her husband to Boston, where she directed the Harvard Center for Law and Education from 1971 to 1973. In 1973 the WRP became the parent organization for the Children's Defense Fund (CDF), whose mission has been to "Leave No Child Behind." Under Edelman's presidency, the CDF has promoted a "healthy start," a "head start," a "fair start," a "safe start," and a "moral start" for all children. By tackling children's welfare, health care, and employment issues, as well as teenage pregnancy and adoption, the CDF became the nation's largest and most successful child advocacy organization. It has several local and state affiliates in many states. At its retreat center on a farm once owned by the *Roots* author ALEX HALEY in Clinton, Tennessee, the CDF focuses on Edelman's vision of transforming America by building a movement for children. CDF programs draw on the methods and lessons of the civil rights movement, for example, in the freedom school trainers program, which exposes young people to civil rights veterans and history. Those selected by the CDF to teach young adults are called Ella Baker Trainers, in honor of her role as a mentor for thousands of young activists like Marian Wright, Bob Moses, and STOKELY CARMICHAEL. The CDF's annual Samuel DeWitt Proctor Institute

also reflects Edelman's roots in the black church through its workshops, worship, singing, and inspirational preaching and teaching.

Edelman's tenacious defense of children's rights has earned her respect, opportunity, and honors. From 1976 to 1987 she chaired the Spelman College trustee board, becoming the first woman to hold that post. From 1971 to 1977 she served as a member of the Yale University Corporation, the first woman elected by alumni to this position. She has received numerous awards and honors, including the nation's highest civilian award, the Presidential Medal of Freedom, in 2000, a MacArthur Foundation Fellowship in 1985, the AFL-CIO Humanitarian Award in 1989, and honorary degrees from more than thirty colleges and universities. She has also been praised for several books on child advocacy and child rearing, including *Families in Peril: An Agenda for Social Change* (1987), *Stand for Children* (1998), and *Hold My Hand: Prayers for Building a Movement to Leave No Child Behind* (2001).

Edelman actively continues her CDF work, which remains as necessary today as when she founded the organization three decades ago. Her close friendship with her fellow Yale Law School graduate and CDF activist, Hillary Rodham Clinton, led to speculation that the CDF might wield considerable influence in the White House, when Clinton's husband, Bill Clinton, was elected president in 1992. However, in 1996 Edelman opposed President Clinton for supporting welfare reform legislation that she believed would worsen child poverty. Edelman has also criticized Clinton's successor, George W. Bush, who appropriated the CDF's "leave no child behind" motto as a campaign slogan but has shown little interest in backing up such rhetoric with meaningful legislation. Responding to President Bush's State of the Union address in 2002, Edelman stated:

The President's economic plan so far has favored the wealthiest one percent of Americans. This nation should not give another tax break to the wealthy or corporate America or make permanent existing tax breaks for the wealthiest individuals and companies until there are no more hungry, homeless, poor children. For the annual cost of what the President has already approved in

tax cuts to the top one percent of taxpayers, we could pay for child care, Head Start, and health care for all of the children who still need it—as proposed in the comprehensive Act to Leave No Child Behind.

("Statement by the Children's Defense Fund," 30 Jan. 2002, http://www.childrens-defense.org/statement_stateofunion.php.)

FURTHER READING

Edelman, Marian Wright. *Lanterns: A Memoir of Mentors* (1999).

Greenberg, Jack. *Crusaders in the Courts: How a Dedicated Band of Lawyers Fought for the Civil Rights Revolution* (1994).
—ROSETTA E. ROSS

EDWARDS, HARRY THOMAS (3 Nov. 1940–), federal judge, was born in New York City. Raised by his mother, Arline Ross, a psychiatric social worker, and his father, George F. Edwards, an accountant and state legislator, Edwards enjoyed a very close relationship with his maternal grandfather, a tax attorney, and two uncles who also were lawyers. His decision to attend law school after graduating with a BS degree from Cornell University in 1964 was due to his admiration of his grandfather and encouragement from his two uncles.

In 1962 Edwards entered the University of Michigan Law School, where he achieved a stellar academic record. He served as an editor of the *Michigan Law Review*, was selected for membership in the Order of the Coif, a legal honor society reserved for the top 5 percent of students, and received American Jurisprudence Awards for outstanding performance in labor law and administrative law. As a result of this record, Edwards earned a JD degree with distinction in 1965.

Edwards began his professional career as an associate attorney with the Chicago firm of Seyfarth, Shaw, Fairweather, and Geraldson, where he practiced law in the labor department from 1965 to 1970. Leaving the firm in 1970 to begin a teaching career at the University of Michigan Law School, he served as an associate professor of law from 1970 to 1973, and later as professor of law from 1973 to 1975. From January to June 1974 he was a visiting professor

Harry T. Edwards, chief judge of the District of Columbia Circuit. © Reuters NewMedia Inc./CORBIS

at the Free University of Brussels, participating in the Program for International Legal Cooperation. In 1975 Edwards began teaching at Harvard, where in 1976 he became only the third African American awarded tenure at Harvard Law School. While at Harvard, Edwards taught labor law, collective bargaining and labor arbitration, and negotiation and labor-relations law in the public sector. In 1977 Edwards rejoined the law faculty at the University of Michigan Law School. During his time at the university, Edwards also served as a member and then chair of the board of directors of AMTRAK, the largest passenger railroad company in the United States.

In 1980 President Jimmy Carter appointed Edwards to the U.S. Court of Appeals for the District of Columbia,

the most influential federal appeals court in the nation. Since joining the bench, Edwards has written hundreds of notable opinions, including decisions involving issues such as labor and employment, antitrust, administrative, tax, constitutional, civil rights, and criminal law. In his twenty-two years on the bench, Edwards developed a reputation for meticulous and thorough preparation for oral argument, as well as superbly crafted, tightly organized, and carefully annotated opinions.

In December 1982 Edwards was recognized by the *American Lawyer* as an Outstanding Performer in the legal profession for his judicial opinions in the area of labor law, and he continued to write important opinions in labor law in the 1990s. One such opinion was *Association of Flight Attendants, AFL CIO*

v. USAir, Inc. (1994) where the court was faced with the question of whether flight attendants employed by an airline that had been purchased by USAir were subject to the airline's collective-bargaining agreement with its own flight attendants. In his opinion, Edwards held that USAir's collective bargaining agreement did not apply to the new flight attendants because a "mere change in union representative had no effect on the status quo applicable to shuttle flight attendants." Thus the newly acquired flight attendants were able to adhere to the terms of their premerger collective bargaining agreement.

Edwards has been recognized for a series of articles regarding legal teaching and scholarship. In "The Growing Disjunction between Legal Education and the Legal Profession," in *Michigan Law Review* Vol. 91 (1) (1992), he argues that law schools are failing to educate students adequately by overemphasizing abstract theory at the expense of practical scholarship and pedagogy and that law firms are failing to ensure that lawyers practice law in an ethical manner. The article sparked a national debate among legal scholars and practitioners on the proper method of legal teaching and reform in law schools and law firms. Another of his articles, "The Effects of Collegiality on Judicial Decision Making," in *Pennsylvania Law Review* Vol. 151 (2003), explains how appellate judges decide cases. Edwards specifically refutes the common claim that the personal ideologies and political leanings of the judges on the District of Columbia Circuit are deciding factors in the ultimate holdings of the court. Despite his judicial duties, Edwards has also continued to influence students by teaching on a part-time basis at a number of law schools, including Harvard, Michigan, Pennsylvania, Georgetown, Duke, and New York University. Over the course of his teaching and judicial career, Edwards has found time to coauthor four critically acclaimed books: *Labor Relations Law in the Public Sector* (3rd edition 1985), *The Lawyer as a Negotiator* (1977), *Collective Bargaining and Labor Arbitration* (1979), and *Higher Education and the Law* (1979, annual supplements 1980–1983). He has also published numerous articles and pamphlets concerning issues in labor law, equal-employment opportunity, labor arbitration, higher education, alternative-dispute resolution, federalism, judicial process and administration, and comparative law.

Edwards became chief judge of the District of Columbia Circuit in 1994. During his seven-year stint as chief judge, he directed numerous automation initiatives at the court of appeals, oversaw a complete reorganization of the clerk's office and legal division, implemented case management programs that helped to reduce the court's case backlog and disposition times, and successfully pursued congressional support for the construction of an annex to the courthouse building. He also established programs to enhance communications with the lawyers who practice before the court, and received high praise from members of the bench, bar, and press for fostering collegial relations among the members of the ideologically divided court. In 2000–2001 Edwards presided over the court's hearings in *United States v. Microsoft*, the largest antitrust case in U.S. history. In this case, the court reviewed the legal conclusions regarding three alleged antitrust violations and the resulting remedial order imposed on Microsoft by the United States District Court for the District of Columbia. Edwards participated in the court's *per curiam* opinion that affirmed in part and reversed in part the district court's judgment that Microsoft violated section 2 of the Sherman Act.

In July 1996 the *American Lawyer* and the *Washington Legal Times* published personal profiles of Edwards, applauding his efforts in managing the District of Columbia Circuit as chief judge and in helping to bring collegiality to the court. Edwards stepped down from his position as chief judge in July 2001.

Edwards has served on numerous boards, including the board of directors of the National Institute for Dispute Resolution, the executive committee of the Order of the Coif, the executive committee of the Association of American Law Schools, and the National Academy of Arbitrators (as vice president). His numerous awards include the Society of American Law Teachers Award, recognizing distinguished contributions to teaching and

public service; the Whitney North Seymour Medal, presented by the American Arbitration Association for outstanding contributions; the 2001 Judicial Honoree Award presented by the Bar Association of the District of Columbia, recognizing significant contributions in the field of law; and eleven honorary JD degrees. He is a member of the American Law Institute, the American Judicature Society, and the American Bar Foundation. Edwards serves as a teacher/mentor at the Unique Learning Center in Washington, D.C., a volunteer program established to assist disadvantaged inner-city youth.

Married to Pamela Carrington-Edwards in 2000, Edwards has two children from a previous marriage to Ila Hayes Edwards.

Edwards begins his seminal article in the *Michigan Law Review* on legal education with a quotation from Felix Frankfurter, the former associate judge on the U.S. Supreme Court: "In the last analysis, the law is what the lawyers are," but this could also aptly apply to Edwards's professional career, for in the last analysis, the laws made by Edwards are what he is and what his life represents—a shining example of professionalism.

FURTHER READING

Edwards's papers have not been archived. Personal profiles of Edwards can be found in the July 1996 editions of the *American Lawyer* and *The Washington Legal Times*.

—F. MICHAEL HIGGINBOTHAM

EIKERENKOETTER, FREDERICK J. *See* Reverend Ike.

ELAW, ZILPHA

(c. 1790–?), evangelist and writer, was born near Philadelphia, Pennsylvania, to parents whose names remain unknown. In 1802, when Zilpha was twelve, her mother died during the birth of her twenty-second child, leaving Zilpha's father to raise the three children who

had survived infancy. Unable to support the family, her father sent her older brother to their grandparents' farm far from Philadelphia and consigned Zilpha to a local Quaker couple, Pierson and Rebecca Mitchel. Within eighteen months Zilpha's father died. Zilpha felt fortunate to stay with the Mitchels for the next six years, until she reached the age of eighteen.

Zilpha had enjoyed a close relationship with her father and was deeply grieved by his passing. The emotional turmoil associated with his death led her to a deeper contemplation of the state of her soul, though she felt that she had no religious instruction or direction to guide her through this period. Zilpha felt spiritually adrift between the public religious expressions she had witnessed as a young girl and the Quaker tradition where religious devotion was "performed in the secret silence of the mind" (Elaw, 54). Concerned about what she felt to be her increasingly impious behavior among the Mitchel children, Zilpha began to experience dreams and visions in which God or the archangel Gabriel warned her of her sinful ways and pressed her to repent before a promised cataclysmic end, when repentance would no longer be possible. When she was still a teenager, these dreams of damnation and her concerns about her feelings of guilt and sin led her to seek affiliation with the Methodists.

Conversion among the Methodists was a gradual process that Zilpha later compared to the dawning of the morning. That she marks her process in this way distinguishes her autobiography, *Memoirs of the Life, Religious Experience, Ministerial Travels, and Labours of Mrs. Elaw, An American Female of Colour* (1846), from many others in the spiritual autobiography genre, such as SOJOURNER TRUTH and JARENA LEE, in which the authors emphasize a single event or a miraculous series of distinctive incidents that worked an immediate and permanent change in the writer. Elaw, conversely, provides a model of slow but sure development over her adolescence and early adulthood.

In another vision Jesus appeared to Elaw as she wrote in her dairy and assured her that her sins had been forgiven. In 1808, at eighteen years of age, she "united [herself] in the fellowship of the saints with the militant church of Jesus on earth" (Elaw, 57), joining a local Methodist society. Conversion, study, church membership, baptism, and the new right to participate in Holy Communion transformed Zilpha's life. She gained a new self-confidence that she had not possessed before her revelation. The society became her family, God became her father, and Jesus became her brother and friend.

The spiritual reverie she enjoyed changed when she married Joseph Elaw in 1810. Joseph was not a born-again Christian. Zilpha's experience in this incompatible union served as the subject for one of the more powerful expositions in her narrative. She warns Christian women against marrying unbelieving men, suggesting that they would be more content to be drowned by a millstone hung about their necks for disobeying God's law. Pride, arrogance, and the independence of young women drove them to make marital choices without parental regulation, guardianship, and government, she argued. In her view, women ought to be subordinate to fathers and, upon marriage, to husbands. The "carnal courtship" was not marriage but fornication, and it promised to deceive and destroy the woman's spirit.

Elaw supported her opinion with scripture but, more convincingly, underpinned her discussion by describing the discord she suffered within her marriage. Joseph objected to Zilpha's zealous and public religious practice and pressed her to take in amusements that he enjoyed, like music and dancing in nearby Philadelphia. Although the temptation to lose herself in these amusements was great, she held fast to her convictions.

In 1811 the Elaws relocated to Burlington, New Jersey, where their daughter was born and where Joseph could ply his trade as a fuller until embargos during the War of 1812 prevented shipping exports. Elaw also attended her first camp meeting in New Jersey. Camp meetings, referred to in the subtitle of her narrative, were open-air religious revivals, often attended by hundreds of worshipers who traveled great distances to participate. These events were popular among the Methodists and provided extraordinary opportunities for women and African Americans to engage in preaching and religious leadership outside the monitored and regulated site of the church.

As Elaw described the meetings, the campgrounds often had segregated living spaces but integrated worship spaces. Consequently, after experiencing another sanctifying vision, Elaw involuntarily began to pray and preach publicly and gained a reputation for her evangelical power. At one camp meeting, she developed the desire to engage in a household ministry among families in her community, and she was endorsed in this enterprise by local Burlington clergy. Elaw maintained this "special calling" despite a chilly reception by some local black Methodist parishioners and the vigorous protests of her husband, who feared that she would be ridiculed.

Throughout her period of household ministry, Elaw struggled with a call to preach to a broader audience, with her divine mission at odds with her sense of feminine propriety. She continued to have dreams about a greater call, but she found little support for this vision as well. All thought of preaching ended for a time when her husband died on 27 January 1823. To support herself and her daughter, Elaw established a school, but closed it two years later, yielding to the call to preach. She placed her daughter with relatives and began to preach, for a while joining with Jarena Lee. Elaw's itinerant ministry took her through the mid-Atlantic and northeastern United States and even below the Mason-Dixon line in 1828 to Maryland and Virginia, preaching to blacks and whites, men and women, believers and nonbelievers. She remarked that she became a "prodigy" to those who heard and saw her. The confluence of her race, gender, and spiritual enthusiasm presented a singular spectacle to many whose fascination with her rendered them susceptible to her persuasive style and rhetoric.

In 1840 Elaw sailed to London, England, to preach and evangelize. She met with success there, but she continued to battle those who were not receptive to women preachers. Her narrative suggests that she intended to return to America in 1845, but no record of her return or activity in the United States exists after the publication of her narrative in 1846.

A notable feature of Elaw's narrative is the regularity with which she attributes her success to the combination of her race, gender, and salvation. Her narrative is modeled after Saint Paul's struggles and salvation, as detailed in his letters to the Christian churches in the New Testament. Taken as a whole, Elaw's narrative characterizes her race and gender as socially constructed "thorns" or burdens that, like Paul, she must endure. These "burdens" were the elements that rendered her a prodigy, or phenomenon to those who heard her preach. The confluence of her race, gender, and spiritual power were, in her understanding, elements of grace with which she had been blessed to do God's work.

Like many women active in preaching activities in the nineteenth century, Elaw traveled, spoke in an impassioned and inspired manner on the Bible, and wrote a narrative of her religious development as a guide to others, especially women, who might follow her path. She did not carry any official designation as a minister or preacher, but was recognized for her powerful and effective evangelism as an itinerant religious leader. As one of the earliest black women to claim the right to preach publicly, Elaw was a key figure in establishing the tradition of African American women religious leaders. This tradition continued throughout the nineteenth century in the work of such notable evangelists as JULIA FOOTE and AMANDA SMITH, and it laid the groundwork for the acceptance of such women as PAULI MURRAY and Bishop BARBARA HARRIS in ministerial roles in the late twentieth century.

FURTHER READING

Elaw, Zilpha. *Memoirs of the Life, Religious Experience, Ministerial Travels, and Labours of Mrs. Elaw, An American Female of Colour; Together with Some Account of the Great Religious Revivals in America* (1846).

Andrews, William L., ed. *Sisters of the Spirit: Three Black Women's Autobiographies of the Nineteenth Century* (1986).

—MARTHA L. WHARTON

ELDERS, M. JOYCELYN

(13 Aug. 1933–), physician, scientist, professor, public health official, and first African American surgeon general of the United States, was born Minnie Lee Jones in the small town of Schaal, Arkansas, the oldest of eight children of Curtis Jones, a sharecropper, and Haller Reed Jones. As a child, Jones performed the hard labor demanded of Arkansas farmers and their families, and she often led her younger siblings in their work on the small cotton farm. The family home was an unpainted three-room shack with no indoor plumbing or electricity, and there was no hospital or physician for miles around. Jones watched her mother give birth seven times without medical assistance; the only memory she has of a visit to a physician was when her father took a gravely ill younger brother twelve miles by mule to the nearest doctor.

Haller Jones was determined that her children would have more prosperous futures and instilled the importance of education in all of her children, sending them to school during the winter and constantly drilling them on reading skills during the summer months. Minnie Jones excelled at the small segregated Howard County Training School in Schaal, graduating as valedictorian at the age of fifteen. At the graduation ceremony a representative from the Philander Smith Methodist College in Little Rock awarded her a full scholarship. She almost was unable to accept, as transportation to Little Rock was too expensive and she was too valuable as a work leader in the fields. But the family managed with help from extended family and neighbors, and Jones began her college career in the fall of 1948.

At Philander Smith, Jones decided to pursue a career in science, hoping to work in a laboratory after college. Then, at an event arranged by her sorority, Delta Sigma Theta, she met Dr. Edith Irby Jones, the first African American medical student at the University of Arkansas. After hearing Edith Jones speak about her experiences there, she felt focused and inspired; Minnie Jones determined that she, too, would go to medical school and become a doctor. At about the same time, perhaps to demonstrate her newfound independence, she began to go by the name of Joycelyn, the middle name she had adopted during childhood.

Joycelyn Jones married a fellow student, Cornelius Reynolds, after graduation, and the couple moved to Milwaukee, Wisconsin, where Reynolds had secured employment. In Milwaukee, she worked as a nurse's aide at the veterans' hospital, where she learned of the Women's Medical Specialist Corps. The WMSC was a program in which the army trained college graduates as physical therapists and made them commissioned officers eligible for the GI Bill. Jones and Reynolds parted amicably in May of 1953, and Jones remained in the army for three years. She left when she had served enough time to pay for medical school at what is now the University of Arkansas for Medical Sciences, where she was the second black woman student to attend, after Edith Irby Jones.

In 1960, the same year she graduated from medical school, Jones met and married Oliver Elders, a high school basketball coach. She then completed an internship in pediatrics at the University of Minnesota and returned to the University of Arkansas for a residency in pediatrics with an emphasis on pediatric surgery. Elders came through at the top of her class and was named chief resident in her third year. Along the way, she had two children: Eric in 1963 and Kevin in 1965. After her year as chief resident, Elders decided on a career in academic medicine, serving simultaneously as a junior faculty member and completing a master's degree in Biochemistry. Elders ascended the professional ladder, achieving a full professorship and board certification in pediatric endocrinology in 1976. In all, Elders worked as a professor and practitioner of pediatric endocrinology for nearly twenty-five years and became especially renowned for authoring more than one hundred published papers and for her expert and compassionate treatment of young patients with diabetes, growth problems, and sexual disorders.

In 1987 Elders was appointed by then Arkansas Governor Bill Clinton to the position of director of the Arkansas Department of Health. She initially accepted with some misgivings about leaving her academic post, but she quickly became passionate about her new position. While in office, Elders and her team helped effect an impressive increase in the state health budget. They introduced a program to provide breast cancer screenings and provisions for funding around-the-clock in-home care for elderly and terminally ill patients, and they instituted programs to expand access to HIV testing and counseling services. Her policy initiatives for children resulted in a nearly 25 percent rise in immunizations and a tenfold increase in the number of early childhood screenings in the state. As director, Elders served on several presidential commissions on public health under President George H. W. Bush, and she was elected president of the Association of State and Territorial Health officers.

Elders was especially committed to lowering the teen pregnancy rate in Arkansas, at the time the second highest in the nation. In order to reduce the catastrophic public health consequences of such a high teen pregnancy rate, Elders and her team worked toward implementing a comprehensive health curriculum in the public schools, in which sex education would be a central topic. This would prove to be one of the most controversial acts of her administration, but Elders never backed down under pressure from her critics; she often commented that she felt she was in a unique position to help those in poor rural communities, having been raised in one, and that she would therefore not abandon the course she believed was right.

As director of the health department, Elders also worked toward establishing comprehensive health clinics in public schools. Because so many poor and rural communities in Arkansas lacked adequate health-care facilities, Elders and her staff reasoned that this would be the best way to expand access to preventive care measures, such as dental screenings and vaccinations. At the discretion of the local school board, these clinics could also be authorized to provide reproductive health counseling services and distribute condoms. Although the service was explicitly available only to students who had obtained their parents' permission, it touched off a heated national debate over the relative merits and dangers of distributing condoms in public schools, and Elders's policies became a regular target of critics nationwide.

In July 1993 Bill Clinton, by then president of the United States, appointed Elders to the position of surgeon general of the Public Health Services, and the U.S. Senate confirmed the appointment in September of the same year. Elders was the first African American and second woman appointed to this post, and, during her tenure, she served on a number of influential health policy committees and spoke widely on matters of public health. After only fifteen months as surgeon general, however, Elders was forced to resign over a public remark she had made at a United Nations World AIDS Day event. Following her presentation on school health clinics, a reporter asked her if she believed there should be any discussion of masturbation in high school health curricula. Elders responded, "I think it is part of human sexuality, and perhaps it should be taught."

Two weeks later, amidst a barrage of press coverage, Elders tendered her resignation and moved back to Little Rock. She returned to her academic post at the University of Arkansas Children's Hospital and a full schedule of public-speaking engagements, writing, and community and church involvement. Elders retired from her academic position in 1998, accepting an emeritus appointment. Since then she has lectured and published on those issues to which she has always been passionately dedicated: adequate health care for the poor, the importance of preventative health care, and the need for sex education in public schools.

FURTHER READING

Dr. M. Joycelyn Elders's personal papers are held privately in a storage facility in Little Rock, Arkansas.

Elders, Joycelyn, and David Chanoff. *Joycelyn Elders, M.D.: From Sharecropper's Daughter to Surgeon General of the United States of America* (1996).

—DEBORAH I. LEVINE

ELLINGTON, DUKE

(29 Apr. 1899–24 May 1974), jazz musician and composer, was born Edward Kennedy Ellington in Washington, D.C., the son of James Edward Ellington, a butler, waiter, and later printmaker, and Daisy Kennedy. The Ellingtons were middle-class people who struggled at times to make ends meet. Ellington's mother was particularly attached to him; in her eyes he could do no wrong. They belonged to Washington's black elite, who put much stock in racial pride. Ellington developed a strong sense of his own worth and a belief in his destiny, which at times shaded over into egocentricity. Because of this attitude, and his almost royal bearing, his schoolmates early named him "Duke."

Ellington's interest in music was slow to develop. He was given piano lessons as a boy but soon dropped them. He was finally awakened to music at about fourteen when he heard a pianist named Harvey Brooks, who was not much older than he. Brooks, he later said, "was swinging, and he had a tremendous left hand, and when I got home I had a real yearning to play."

He did not take formal piano lessons, however, but picked the brains of local pianists, some of whom were excellent. He was always looking for shortcuts, ways of getting effects without much arduous practicing. As a consequence, it was a long time before he became proficient at the stride style basic to popular piano playing of the time.

As he improved, Ellington discovered that playing for his friends at parties was a route to popularity. He began to rehearse with some other youngsters, among them saxophonist Otto "Toby" Hardwick and trumpeter Arthur Whetsol. Eventually a New Jersey drummer, Sonny Greer, joined the group. By age sixteen or seventeen Ellington was playing occasional professional jobs with these and other young musicians. The music they played was not jazz, which still was not widely known, but rags and ordinary popular songs.

He was not yet committed to music. He was also studying commercial art,

Duke Ellington photographed by GORDON PARKS SR. at the Hurricane Club in New York, 1943. Library of Congress

for which he showed an aptitude. However, he never graduated from high school, and in 1918 he married Edna Thompson; the following spring their son, Mercer, was born. Although later Ellington lived with several different women, he never divorced his wife.

He now had a family to support and was perforce drawn into the music business, one of the few areas in which blacks could earn good incomes and achieve a species of fame. Increasingly he was working with a group composed of Whetsol, Greer, and Hardwick under the nominal leadership of Baltimore banjoist Elmer Snowden. This was the nucleus of later Ellington bands. In 1923 the group ventured to New York and landed a job at a well-known Harlem cabaret, Barron's Exclusive Club. The club had a clientele of intellectuals and the social elite, some of them white, and the band was not playing jazz, but "under conversation music." Ellington was handsome and already a commanding figure, and the others were polite, middle-class youths. They were well liked, and in 1923 they were asked to open at the Hollywood, a new club in the Broadway theater district, soon renamed the Kentucky Club.

As blacks, they were expected to play the new hot music, now growing in popularity. Like many other young musicians, they were struggling to catch its elusive rhythms, and they reached out for a jazz specialist, trumpeter James "Bubber" Miley, who had developed a style based on the plunger mute work of a New Orleanian, "KING" OLIVER. Miley not only used the plunger for *wah-wah* effects but also employed throat tones to produce a growl. He was a hot, driving player and set the style for the band. Somewhat later, SIDNEY BECHET, perhaps the finest improviser in jazz at the time, had a brief but influential stay with the band.

Through the next several years the band worked off and on at the Kentucky Club, recording with increasing frequency. Then, early in 1924, the group fired Snowden for withholding money, and Ellington was chosen to take over. Very quickly he began to mold the band to his tastes. He was aided by an association with Irving Mills, a song publisher and show business entrepreneur with gangland connections. Mills needed an

orchestra to record his company's songs; Ellington needed both connections and guidance through the show business maze. His contract with Mills gave Ellington control of the orchestra.

As a composer, Ellington showed a penchant for breaking rules: if he were told that a major seventh must rise to the tonic, he would devise a piece in which it descended. His still-developing method of composition was to bring to rehearsal—or even to the recording studio—scraps and pieces of musical ideas, which he would try in various ways until he got an effect he liked. Members of the band would offer suggestions, add counterlines, and work out harmonies among themselves. It was very much a cooperative effort, and frequently the music was never written down. Although in time Ellington worked more with pencil and paper, this improvisational system remained basic to his composing.

Beginning with a group of records made in November 1926, the group found its voice: the music from this session has the distinctive Ellington sound. The first important record was "East St. Louis Toodle-Oo" (1926), a smoky piece featuring Bubber Miley growling over a minor theme. Most important of all was "Black and Tan Fantasy" (1927), another slow piece featuring Miley in a minor key. It ends with a quotation from Chopin's "Funeral March." In part because of this touch, "Black and Tan Fantasy" was admired by influential critics such as R. D. Darrell, who saw it as a harbinger of a more sophisticated, composed jazz. Increasingly thereafter, Ellington was seen by critics writing in intellectual and music journals as a major American composer.

Then, in December 1927 the group was hired as the house band at the Cotton Club, rapidly becoming the country's best-known cabaret. It was decided, for commercial purposes, to feature a "jungle sound," built around the growling of Miley and trombonist Joe "Tricky Sam" Nanton. About this time Ellington added musicians who would fundamentally shape the band's sound: clarinetist Barney Bigard, a well-trained New Orleanian with a liquid tone; saxophonist Johnny Hodges, who possessed a flowing, honeyed sound and quickly became the premier altoist in

jazz; and Cootie Williams, who replaced the wayward Miley and soon became a master of the plunger mute. These and other instrumentalists each had a distinctive sound and gave Ellington a rich "tonal palette," which he worked with increasing mastery.

Through the 1920s and 1930s Ellington created a group of masterpieces characterized by short, sparkling melodies, relentless contrasts of color and mood, and much more dissonant harmony than was usual in popular music. Among the best known of these are "Mood Indigo" (1930) and "Creole Love Call" (1927), two simple but very effective mood pieces; "Rockin' in Rhythm" (1930), a driving up-tempo piece made up of sharply contrasting melodies; and "Daybreak Express" (1933), an uncanny imitation of train sounds. These pieces alone won Ellington a major position in jazz history, but they are only examples of scores of brilliant works.

By now he had come into his own as a songwriter. During the 1930s he created many standards, like "Prelude to a Kiss" (1938), "Sophisticated Lady" (1932), and "Solitude" (1934). This songwriting was critically important, for, leaving aside musical considerations, Ellington's ASCAP royalties were in later years crucial in his keeping the band going.

It must be admitted, however, that Ellington borrowed extensively in producing these tunes. "Creole Love Call" and "Mood Indigo," although credited to Ellington, were written by others. Various of his musicians contributed to "Sophisticated Lady," "Black and Tan Fantasy," and many more. Though it is not always easy to know how much others contributed to a given work, it was Ellington's arranging and orchestrating of the melodies that lifted pieces like "Creole Love Call" above the mundane.

By 1931, through broadcasts from the Cotton Club and his recordings, Ellington had become a major figure in popular music. In that year the band left the club and for the remainder of its existence played the usual mix of one-nighters, theater dates, and longer stays in nightclubs and hotel ballrooms. Singer Ivie Anderson, who would work with the organization for more than a decade and remains the vocalist most closely associated with Ellington, joined him at this time.

In 1933 the band made a brief visit to London and the Continent. British critics convinced Ellington that he was more than just a dance-band leader. He had already written one longer, more "symphonic" piece, "Creole Rhapsody" (1931). He now set about writing more. The most important of these was "Black, Brown, and Beige," which was given its premiere at Carnegie Hall in 1943. The opening was a significant event in American music: a black composer writing "serious" music using themes taken from black culture.

Classical critics did not much like the piece. The problem, as always with Ellington's extended work, was that, lacking training, he was unable to unify the smaller themes and musical ideas he produced. Ellington, although temporarily discouraged, continued to write extended pieces, which combined jazz elements with devices meant to reflect classical music.

Additionally, beginning in 1936, Ellington recorded with small groups drawn from the band. These recordings, such as Johnny Hodges's "Jeep's Blues" (1938) and Rex Stewart's "Subtle Slough," contain a great deal of his finest work. Yet most critics would say that his finest work of the time was a series of concertos featuring various instrumentalists, including "Echoes of Harlem" (1935) for Cootie Williams and "Clarinet Lament" (1936) for Barney Bigard.

In 1939 the character of the band began to change when bassist Jimmy Blanton, who was enormously influential during a career cut short by death, and tenor saxophonist Ben Webster were added. Ellington had never had a major tenor soloist at his disposal, and Webster's rich, guttural utterances were a new voice for him to work with. Also arriving in 1939 was Billy Strayhorn, a young composer who had more formal training than Ellington. Until Strayhorn's death in 1967, a substantial part of the Ellington oeuvre was actually written in collaboration with Strayhorn, although it is difficult to tease apart their individual contributions. In 1940 Ellington switched from Columbia to Victor. The so-called Victor band of 1940 to 1942, when a union dispute temporarily ended recording in the

United States, is considered by many jazz critics to be one of the great moments in jazz. "Take the 'A' Train," written by Strayhorn, is a simple, indeed basic, piece, which gets its effect from contrapuntal lines and the interplay of the band's voices. "Cotton Tail" (1940) is a reworking of "I've Got Rhythm" that outshines the original melody and is famous for a powerful Webster solo and a sinuous, winding chorus for the saxophones. "Harlem Air Shaft" (1940) is a classic Ellington program piece meant to suggest the life in a Harlem apartment building and is filled with shifts and contrasts that produce a sense of rich disorder. "Main Stem" (1942) is another hard-driving piece, offering incredible musical variety within a tiny space. Perhaps the most highly regarded recording from this period is "Ko-Ko" (1940). Originally written as part of an extended work, it is based on a blues in E-flat minor and is built up of the layering of increasingly dissonant and contrasting lines.

By the late 1940s it was felt by many jazz writers that the band had deteriorated. The swing band movement, which had swept up the Ellington group in the mid-1930s, had collapsed, and musical tastes were changing. A number of the old hands left, taking with them much of Ellington's tonal palette, and while excellent newcomers replaced them, few equaled the originals. Through the late 1940s and into the 1950s there were constant changes of personnel, shifts from one record company to the next, and a dwindling demand for the orchestra. Henceforth Ellington would need his song royalties to support what was now a very expensive organization. In 1956 Ellington was asked to play the closing Saturday night concert at the recently established Newport Jazz Festival. At one point in the evening he brought tenor saxophonist Paul Gonsalves forward to play twenty-seven choruses of the blues over a rhythm section. The crowd was wildly enthusiastic; the event got much media attention, and Ellington's star began to rise again.

Through the late 1950s and 1960s Ellington continued to create memorable pieces, many of them contributed by Strayhorn, particularly the haunting "Blood Count" (1967). Also of value were a series of collaborations with Ellington by major jazz soloists from

outside the band, including LOUIS ARMSTRONG, Coleman Hawkins, and JOHN COLTRANE. Other fine works were Strayhorn's "UMMG," featuring DIZZY GILLESPIE; "Paris Blues" (1960), a variation on the blues done for a movie by that name; and an album tribute to Strayhorn issued as "...And His Mother Called Him Bill" (1967).

But by this time Ellington's main concerns were his extended works, which eventually totaled some three dozen. Many of these were dashed off to meet deadlines, or even pulled together in rehearsal, and are of slight value. Almost all suffer from the besetting flaw in Ellington's longer works, his inability to make unified wholes of what are often brilliant smaller pieces.

Although some critics today insist that much of this work is of value, it was not well reviewed outside the jazz press when it appeared. Among the most successful are "The Deep South Suite" (1946), "Harlem (A Tone Parallel to Harlem)," first recorded in 1951, and "The Far East Suite" in collaboration with Strayhorn and recorded in 1966.

To Ellington, the most important of these works were the three "Sacred Concerts," created in the last years of his life. They consist of collections of vocal and instrumental pieces of various sorts, usually tied loosely together by a religious theme. Although these works contain fine moments and have their admirers, they do not, on the whole, succeed. Duke Ellington's legacy is the short jazz works, most of them written between 1926 and 1942: the jungle pieces, like "Black and Tan Fantasy"; the concertos, like "Echoes of Harlem"; the mood pieces, such as "Mood Indigo"; the harmonically complex works, like "Ko-Ko"; and the hard swingers, such as "Cotton Tail." This work has a rich tonal palette. It uses carefully chosen sounds by his soloists; endless contrast not only of sound but of mood, mode, key; the use of forms unusual in popular music, like the four-plus-ten bar segment in "Echoes of Harlem"; and deftly handled dissonance, often built around very close internal harmonies. Although Ellington was not a jazz improviser in a class with Armstrong or CHARLIE PARKER, his body of work is far larger than theirs, more varied and richer, and is second to none in jazz. Ellington died in New York City.

FURTHER READING

Many Ellington papers and artifacts are housed in the Duke Ellington Collection, National Museum of American History, Smithsonian Institution. Additional materials are lodged in the Duke Ellington Oral History Project at Yale, the Schomburg Center for Research in Black Culture of the New York Public Library, and the Institute for Jazz Studies at Rutgers University.

Ellington, Edward Kennedy. *Music Is My Mistress* (1973).

Collier, James Lincoln. *Duke Ellington* (1987).
Dance, Stanley. *The World of Duke Ellington* (1970).
Ellington, Mercer, with Stanley Dance. *Duke Ellington in Person* (1978).
Jewell, Derek. *Duke: A Portrait of Duke Ellington* (1977).
Ulanov, Barry. *Duke Ellington* (1946).

Discography:
Aasland, Benny. *The "Wax Works" of Duke Ellington* (1979–).
Bakker, Dick M. *Duke Ellington on Microgroove* (1972–).
Massagli, Luciano, Liborio Pusateri, and Giovanni M. Volonté, *Duke Ellington's Story on Records* (1967–).

—JAMES LINCOLN COLLIER

ELLIOTT, ROBERT BROWN (11 Aug. 1842–9 Aug. 1884),

Reconstruction politician and U.S. Congressman, was born probably in Liverpool, England, of West Indian parents whose names are unknown. Elliott's early life is shrouded in mystery, largely because of his own false claims, but apparently he did attend a private school in England (but not Eton as he claimed) and was trained as a typesetter. It is likely also that in 1866 or 1867, while on duty with the Royal Navy, he decided to seek his fortune in America and jumped ship in Boston Harbor, without, however, taking out citizenship papers. All that is known for certain is that by March 1867 Elliott was associate editor of the *South Carolina Leader*, a black-owned Republican newspaper in Charleston. Shortly thereafter he married Grace Lee Rollin, a member of a prominent South Carolina free Negro family. The couple had no children.

During Reconstruction South Carolina's population was 60 percent black, and the state had many highly capable black leaders. Between 1867 and 1877, when state rule was formally restored, Elliott, a politically adept orator, developed into the major black spokesman and politician in South Carolina. He was one of the at least seventy-one black delegates to the 1868 Constitutional Convention, which drafted the most democratic constitution in South Carolina history. At the 1868 state Republican convention he was nominated for lieutenant governor but dropped out of contention after finishing third on the first ballot. That same year, while serving as the only black member of the five-man board of commissioners in Barnwell County, Elliott was elected to the South Carolina House of Representatives, where he became a very powerful player in state government. Almost elected as Speaker (placing second in the balloting), he was made chair of the committee on railroads and was appointed to the committee on privileges and elections, both very influential assignments. As assistant adjutant general of South Carolina, he even was placed in charge of organizing a militia. In 1870 Elliott was elected to the United States House of Representatives, defeating a white opponent in a district with only a slight black majority, and he was reelected by a wide margin two years later. Near the end of his second term he resigned in order to run again for the state house, winning easily. This time he did serve as Speaker from 1874 to 1876, when he was elected state attorney general. The next year, however, he was one of five Republicans removed from office following the Democratic takeover of Congress.

Elliott was even more influential within Republican Party ranks. A delegate to three national conventions (twice leading the delegation), he served as party chair in South Carolina for much of the 1870s and was permanent chair of most state nominating conventions.

In all of his political positions Elliott aligned himself with the Radical Republicans. At the state constitutional convention he led the successful opposition to both a literacy test for voters and a poll tax, as he well understood that they could later be used to keep blacks from voting. Also at the convention, he fought successfully to have invalidated all debts related to the sale of slaves. As a state representative, Elliott lobbied successfully for a bill to ban discrimination in public facilities and on public transportation. As a U.S. congressman, he gained some notoriety for a speech favoring federal suppression of the Ku Klux Klan and for his debate with former Confederate vice president Alexander Stephens over proposed legislation that subsequently became the Civil Rights Act of 1875. Also while in Congress he voted against the bill granting political amnesty to former Confederates. Elliott was nationally known by 1874, when black Bostonians asked him to give the oration at a memorial service for Radical senator Charles Sumner.

Despite Elliott's well-deserved reputation as a racial militant, his record is not that simple. For example, as a delegate to the 1868 constitutional convention he supported the creation of a public school system and compulsory school attendance but opposed integration. Elliott never seriously interested himself in the plight of rural or urban black workers, and as president of a state labor convention in 1869 he favored a permanent halt to the confiscation of planter land. Even a few of his Democratic critics acknowledged that Elliott's view of the role of the militia was more moderate than that of white governor Robert Scott, who saw it as an offensive and not a defensive force. In his speeches to black audiences, Elliott often expressed a belief in self-help as the means to political and economic empowerment.

Despite his moderate tendencies, Democrats insisted on seeing Elliott as an irresponsible hater of whites and as a troublemaker. White Carolinians, including some Republican enemies, categorized him as one of the state's major "corruptionists," a common and often unsubstantiated charge leveled against both black and white Radicals during Reconstruction. Although Elliott seems to have resisted small bribes and other minor enticements that some black and white politicians routinely accepted, his political career was not devoid of scandal. At least one financially lucrative deal made while he was on the state's powerful railroad committee was suspect; as assistant adjutant general he charged excessive fees; in addition to Republican Party funds he took state monies for his various lobbying efforts; and he distributed large sums of public as well as private money during election campaigns. Thus, even though a succession of law partnerships failed, Elliott maintained a high lifestyle and owned numerous city lots as well as an elegant three-story house in Columbia. Comparatively, however, the corruption of white governors Franklin Moses Jr., Daniel Chamberlain, and Robert Scott and U.S. Senator John Patterson was far more blatant, and Elliott, unlike several of his black and white contemporaries, was never indicted for any crime.

Elliott's reputation as a racial militant derived primarily from his successful efforts to increase black political participation, especially in terms of nominations to higher offices. In 1870, for example, as chair of the Republican nominating convention, Elliott made sure that black candidates were selected for three of the four congressional seats, that the candidate for lieutenant governor was black, and that overall blacks had greater influence in the party. These tactics angered white Republicans and Democrats alike, as did Elliott's shifting of allegiances so that his political support became the determining factor in important elections—especially gubernatorial elections. Elliott was not politically invincible, however, nor was he always successful in achieving his own political goals. Perhaps his most devastating defeat occurred in the bitter, three-way fight for the Republican nomination for the U.S. Senate in 1872.

As state chair, Elliott was in charge of the 1876 campaign and, despite the Democrats' widespread use of violence and intimidation, courageously spoke throughout the state. He hoped that his election as attorney general would prove to be a stepping-stone to the governorship, but the ouster of all Republican executive branch officeholders by the re-emergent Democrats in 1877 eliminated that possibility. Believing that the lack of Republican opposition would lead to dissension among Democrats, just as the absence of Democratic challengers had earlier produced divisions among Republicans, in both 1878 and 1880 Elliott, as chair, convinced party leaders not to run a statewide campaign. By 1880, however, Elliott had become

greatly discouraged, and in 1881 he led a delegation of black protesters who met with President-elect James Garfield. Asserting that black southerners were "citizens in name and not in fact" and that their rights were being "illegally and wantonly subverted," he appealed for federal help, which was not forthcoming.

Personal problems exacerbated Elliott's dire political outlook. Financial losses forced him to close his law office in 1879. His monthly salary as special inspector of customs in Charleston (a patronage position) was not enough to keep him from having to sell his house in order to pay off his debts. Continuing bouts with malaria and his wife's medical problems made his life even more difficult. A delegate to the Republican National Convention in 1880, Elliott was frustrated further by the defeat of his presidential choice, Secretary of the Treasury John Sherman. After eleven months in New Orleans as special agent of the Treasury, Elliott was fired for criticizing his boss and for supporting a losing political faction. A final law firm failed, and his health worsened. He died penniless in New Orleans of malarial fever.

Elliott was a charismatic and effective political leader who provoked outrage among whites and enthusiasm among blacks. What most outraged his opponents was Elliott's racial pride and his insistence on *demanding*, not asking, for his rights and the rights of black Americans. Persistently calling for the unprecedented expansion of national power in order to guarantee the fruits of Reconstruction while also urging blacks to be more worthy of the freedom they had won, Elliott was a precursor of many twentieth-century black leaders. Yet despite his reputation for political militancy, Elliott was always an ardent party man who believed that a strong Republican Party and Union constituted the best hope for racial equality.

FURTHER READING

Elliott's most important letters can be found in the South Carolina Governors Papers of Franklin Moses Jr., Robert Scott, and Daniel Chamberlain, South Carolina Department of Archives, and in the John Sherman Papers, Library of Congress.

Hine, William C. "Black Politicians in Reconstruction Charleston, South Carolina: A Collective Study," *Journal of Southern History* 49 (1983), 555–84.

Holt, Thomas C. *Black over White: Negro Political Leadership in South Carolina during Reconstruction* (1977).

Lamson, Peggy. *The Glorious Failure: Black Congressman Robert Brown Elliott and Reconstruction in South Carolina* (1973).

Rabinowitz, Howard N. *Race, Ethnicity, and Urbanization: Selected Essays* (1994).

—HOWARD N. RABINOWITZ

ELLISON, RALPH WALDO

(1 Mar. 1913?–16 Apr. 1994), novelist and essayist, was born in Oklahoma City, Oklahoma, the oldest of two sons of Lewis Ellison, a former soldier who sold coal and ice to homes and businesses, and Ida Milsaps Ellison. (Starting around 1940 Ellison gave his year of birth as 1914; however, the evidence is strong that he was born in 1913.) His life changed for the worse with his father's untimely death in 1916, an event that left the family poor. In fact, young Ralph would live in two worlds. He experienced poverty at home with his brother, Herbert (who had been just six weeks old when Lewis died), and his mother, who worked mainly as a maid. At the same time, he had an intimate association with the powerful, wealthy black family in one of whose houses he had been born.

At the Frederick Douglass School in Oklahoma City he was a fair student, but he shone as a musician after he

Ralph Ellison published Invisible Man *in 1952 and won the prestigious National Book Award the next year.* Archival Research International/Double Delta Industries Inc.

learned to play the trumpet. Graduating from Frederick Douglass High School in 1932, he worked as a janitor before entering Tuskegee Institute in Alabama in 1933. There his core academic interest was music, and his major ambition was to be a classical composer—although he was also fond of jazz and the blues. In Oklahoma City, which was second only to Kansas City as a hotbed of jazz west of Chicago, he had heard several fine musicians, including Lester Young, Oran "Hot Lips" Page, COUNT BASIE, and LOUIS ARMSTRONG. The revolutionary jazz guitarist Charlie Christian and the famed blues singer Jimmy Rushing both grew up in Ellison's Oklahoma City. However, classical music was emphasized at school. At Tuskegee, studying under William Levi Dawson and other skilled musicians, Ellison became student leader of the school orchestra. Nevertheless, he found himself attracted increasingly to literature, especially after reading modern British novels and, even more influentially, T. S. Eliot's landmark modernist poem, *The Waste Land*.

In 1936, after his junior year, Ellison traveled to New York City hoping to earn enough money as a waiter to pay for his senior year. Ellison never returned to Tuskegee as a student. Settling in Manhattan, he dropped his plan to become a composer and briefly studied sculpture. Working as an office receptionist and then in a paint factory, he also found himself inspired, in the midst of the Great Depression, by radical socialist politics and communism itself. He became a friend of LANGSTON HUGHES, who later introduced him to RICHARD WRIGHT, then relatively unknown. Encouraged by Wright, whose modernist poetry he admired, Ellison continued to read intensively in modern literature, literary and cultural theory, philosophy, and art. His favorite writers were Herman Melville and Fyodor Dostoyevsky from the nineteenth century and, in his own time, Eliot, Ernest Hemingway, and André Malraux (the French radical author of the novels *Man's Fate* and *Man's Hope*). These men, joined by the philosopher and writer Kenneth Burke as well as Mark Twain and William Faulkner, became Ellison's literary pantheon. (Ellison never expressed deep admiration for any black writer except—for a while—Wright. He

liked and was indebted to Langston Hughes personally but soon dismissed his work as shallow.)

In 1937, as editor of the radical magazine *New Challenge*, Wright surprised Ellison with a request for a book review. The result was Ellison's first published essay. Next, Wright asked Ellison to try his hand at a short story. The story, "Hymie's Bull," was not published in Ellison's lifetime, but he was on his way as an author. A trying fall and winter (1937–1938) in Dayton, Ohio, following the death of his mother in nearby Cincinnati, only toughened Ellison's determination to write. In 1938 he secured a coveted place (through Wright) on the Federal Writers' Project in New York, where he conducted research into and wrote about black New York history over the next four years. That year he married the black actress and singer (and communist) Rose Poindexter.

Slowly Ellison became known in radical literary circles with reviews and essays in magazines such as *New Masses*, the main leftist literary outlet. When he became managing editor (1942–1943) of a new radical magazine, *Negro Quarterly*, the lofty intellectual and yet radical tone he helped to set brought him more favorable attention. About this time Ellison came to a fateful decision. He later identified 1942 as the year he turned away from an aesthetic based on radical socialism and the need for political propaganda to one committed to individualism, the tradition of Western literature, and the absolute freedom of the artist to interpret and represent reality.

Facing induction during World War II into the segregated armed forces, Ellison enlisted instead in the Merchant Marine. This led to wartime visits to Swansea in Wales, to London, and to Rouen, France. During the war he also published several short stories. His most ambitious, "Flying Home" (1944), skillfully combines realism, surrealism, folklore, and implicit political protest. Clearly Ellison was now ready to create fiction on a larger scale. By this time his marriage had fallen apart. He and Rose Poindexter were divorced in 1945. The next year he married Fanny McConnell, a black graduate in drama of the University of Iowa who was then an

employee of the National Urban League in Manhattan.

With a Rosenwald Foundation Fellowship (1945–1946) Ellison began work on the novel that would become *Invisible Man*. (One day, on vacation in Vermont, he found himself thinking: "I am an invisible man." Ellison thus had the first line, and the core conceit, of his novel.) In 1947 he published the first chapter—to great praise—in the British magazine *Horizon*. In the following five years Ellison published little more. Instead, he labored to perfect his novel, whose anonymous hero, living bizarrely in an abandoned basement on the edge of Harlem, relates the amazing adventure of his life from his youthful innocence in the South to disillusionment in the North (although his epilogue suggests a growing optimism).

In April 1952 Random House published *Invisible Man*. Many critics hailed it as a remarkable literary debut. However, black communist reviewers excoriated Ellison, mainly because Ellison had obviously modeled the ruthless, totalitarian, and ultimately racist "Brotherhood" of his novel on the Communist Party of the United States. Less angrily, some black reviewers also stressed the caustic depiction of black culture in several places in *Invisible Man*. Selling well for a first novel, the book made the lower rungs of the best-seller list for a few weeks. Then, in January 1953, *Invisible Man* won for Ellison the prestigious National Book Award in fiction. This award transformed Ellison's life and career. Suddenly black colleges and universities, and even a few liberal white institutions, began to invite him to speak and teach. That year he lectured at Harvard and, the following year, taught for a month in Austria at the elite Salzburg Seminar in American Studies.

In 1955 he won the *Prix de Rome* fellowship to the American Academy in Rome. There he and his wife lived for two years (1955–1957) in a community of classicists, archeologists, architects, painters, musicians, sculptors, and other writers. While in Rome, Ellison worked hard on an ambitious new novel about a light-skinned black boy who eventually passes for white and becomes a notoriously racist U.S. senator, and the black minister who had reared the boy as his beloved son. He worked on this novel for the rest of his life.

Returning home, Ellison taught (1958–1961) as a part-time instructor at Bard College near New York City. This was followed by a term at the University of Chicago in 1961; two years (1962–1964) as a visiting professor of writing at Rutgers University in New Brunswick, New Jersey; and a year (1964–1965) as a visiting fellow in American Studies at Yale. During this time he published several important essays even as he toiled on his novel. In 1960 he published a short excerpt from his novel in the *Noble Savage*, a magazine that had been cofounded by Saul Bellow, a future Nobel Prize winner and close friend of Ellison's for some time.

Over the years Ellison was involved intellectually and personally with a wide range of major American scholars, critics, and creative writers. These included the philosopher Kenneth Burke, the critic Stanley Edgar Hyman, Bellow himself, the poet and novelist Robert Penn Warren, and the poet Richard Wilbur. Among blacks, his most important friendship for many years was with ALBERT L. MURRAY, a fellow student at Tuskegee in Ellison's junior year and later a professor of English there. Murray settled with his family in Harlem and published books about African Americans and the national culture. Starting in the 1960s Ellison was devoted to two institutions that honored achievement in the arts. The first was the American Academy and the National Institute of Arts and Letters. (Initially a member of the institute, he was elected later to the inner circle of excellence, the academy.) The other organization was the Century Association in mid-Manhattan, probably the most prestigious private club in the United States dedicated to the arts and literature.

As the years passed and his second novel failed to appear, Ellison's essays and interviews played a crucial role in furthering his reputation as an American intellectual of uncommon brilliance. His collection *Shadow and Act* (1964) reinforced this reputation. In it, Ellison insisted on the complexity of the American experience and the related complexity of black life. The black writer and artist, he insisted, should not be bound by morbid or negative definitions of the black experience but by a highly positive sense that cultural achievements such as the blues, jazz, and black folklore represent the triumph of African Americans over the harsh circumstances of American history—and a triumph of the human spirit in general. The Declaration of Independence, the U.S. Constitution, and the Bill of Rights were sacred documents authenticating the special promise of American and African American culture.

In 1965 a national poll of critics organized by a respected weekly magazine declared *Invisible Man* to be the most distinguished work of America fiction published since 1945. Other formal honors followed. However, the rise of Black Power and the Black Arts Movement about this time led to a backlash among younger, militant blacks against Ellison's ideas. Shunned at times on certain campuses, he was occasionally heckled or even denounced as an "Uncle Tom." Ellison was hurt by these assaults but remained confident about his values and insights. Moreover, the hostility of some younger blacks was offset by a host of honors. In 1966 he was appointed Honorary Consultant in American Letters at the Library of Congress, and the next year he joined the board of directors of the new Kennedy Center for the Performing Arts in Washington, D.C. At a crucial time in the rise of public television, he became a director of the Educational Broadcasting Corporation. In 1969 France made Ellison a *Chevalier dans l'Ordre des Artes et Lettres*. He also became a trustee of the New School for Social Research (now New School University) in New York and of Bennington College, in Vermont. Also in 1969 he received the highest civilian honor bestowed on a U.S. citizen, the Presidential Medal of Freedom.

From 1970 until 1979, when he reached the age of compulsory retirement, Ellison was Albert Schweitzer Professor of Humanities at New York University. Always interested in art—he and his wife collected African art as well as Western paintings and sculpture—he became a director of the Museum of the City of New York. In addition, he was a trustee of the Rockefeller-inspired Colonial Williamsburg Foundation in Virginia and a member of the Board of Visitors of Wake Forest University in Winston-Salem, North Carolina. He took these two last appointments as proof of important social change in the South, about which Ellison was sentimental because of the South Carolina and Georgia origins of his father and mother, respectively. In 1975 Oklahoma City honored him when he helped open the Ralph Ellison Branch of the city library system. President Ronald Reagan awarded him the National Medal of Arts in 1985.

The following year Ellison published his third book, *Going to the Territory*. Like *Shadow and Act*, this volume collected shorter pieces that reflected his unabated interest in the complex nature of black American and American culture. Vigorous to the end, Ellison died at his home in Manhattan. By this time he had seen his critics of the late 1960s and early 1970s decline in influence even as *Invisible Man* had become established as an American classic in fiction. After his death a succession of volumes have helped keep his reputation alive. These include his *Collected Essays* (1995), *Flying Home and Other Stories* (1996), and the novel *Juneteenth* (1999), all edited by John F. Callahan, who had been a trusted friend of Ellison's as well as a professor of American literature. Ellison's reputation rests on two remarkable books. As a novel of African American life, *Invisible Man* has no clear superior and very few equals to rival its breadth and artistry. With the exception of *The Souls of Black Folk* by W. E. B. DU BOIS, *Shadow and Act* is probably the most intelligent book-length commentary on the nuances of black American culture ever published.

FURTHER READING

The primary source of information on Ellison is the Ralph Waldo Ellison Papers in the Manuscripts Division of the Library of Congress, Washington, D.C.

Benston, Kimberly. *Speaking for You: The Vision of Ralph Ellison* (1987).
Graham, Maryemma, and Amjitjit Singh, eds. *Conversations with Ralph Ellison* (1995).
Jackson, Lawrence P. *Ralph Ellison: The Emergence of Genius* (2002).
Murray, Albert, and John F. Callahan, eds. *Trading Twelves: The Selected Letters of Ralph Ellison and Albert Murray* (2000).

O'Meally, Robert G. *The Craft of Ralph Ellison* (1980).

Obituary: *New York Times*, 17 Apr. 1994.
—ARNOLD RAMPERSAD

EQUIANO, OLAUDAH

(1745?–31 Mar. 1797), slave, writer, and abolitionist, was, according to his autobiography, *The Interesting Narrative of the Life of Olaudah Equiano, or Gustavus Vassa, the African*, born in the village of Essaka in Eboe, an unknown location in the Ibo-speaking region of modern Nigeria. Equiano recorded that he was the son of a chief and was also destined for that position. However, at about the age of ten, he was abducted and sold to European slave traders. In his narrative, Equiano recalls the Middle Passage in which "the shrieks of the women, and the groans of the dying, rendered the whole a scene of horror almost inconceivable" (58). Despite falling ill, Equiano survived the voyage and was taken first to Barbados and then to Virginia, where in 1754 he was bought by Michael Pascal, a captain in the Royal Navy. Pascal's first act was to rename the young slave Gustavus Vassa, an ironic reference to the Swedish freedom fighter and later king, Gustavus I Vasa (1496–1560). Documents make it clear that he went by the name of Vassa until the late 1780s.

However, two documents—his baptismal record of 1759 and a muster roll from 1773—call portions of Equiano's autobiographical account into question. Both documents record Equiano's place of birth as South Carolina. Given that Equiano's story after he left Virginia is verifiable historically, but that his preceding narrative is not, some scholars have argued that it is reasonable to conclude that he was indeed born in South Carolina, not Africa, and that the early parts of his *Narrative* were written as rhetorical maneuvers designed to bring attention to the horrors of the slave trade, maneuvers largely "based on oral history and reading, rather than on personal experience" (Carretta, 103). However, it is equally possible that at his baptism and on later occasions Equiano suppressed his African identity

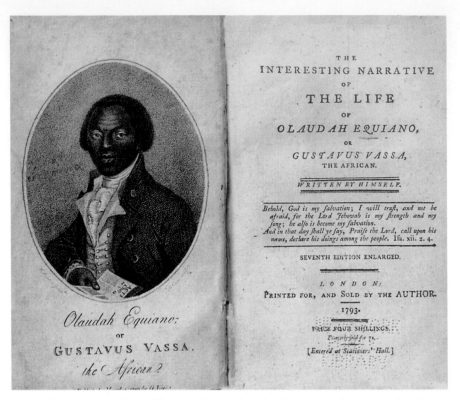

Olaudah Equiano published his autobiography, the first major slave narrative, in 1789, and became the first prominent black abolitionist. Schomburg Center

and claimed to have been born in South Carolina, only daring, or caring, to tell his real history later in life. Unless further evidence emerges, the truth may never be known.

Apart from minor disagreements about dates, which suggest Equiano inflated his age to make the story of his childhood seem more credible, the surviving historical evidence generally supports his autobiographical account from 1755 onwards. As a ten-year-old boy Equiano was taken to England and and then put aboard Pascal's warship, where he saw action in the French and Indian Wars. Equiano spent much time in London and suffered and recovered from smallpox and gangrene. Shipboard life gave him the opportunity to learn to read, write, and calculate, skills that later enabled him to work toward his own emancipation.

In December 1762 Equiano believed that he had earned his freedom, but in this he was deceived. Pascal swindled Equiano out of both his wages and his prize money, raised from selling captured goods, and sold him to a slave trader bound for Montserrat in the West Indies. There he was bought

by Robert King, a Quaker merchant, who employed Equiano as a gauger, a shipboard weights-and-measures officer. In this trusted position Equiano traveled in King's ships throughout the Caribbean and North America. He admired Philadelphia, but was badly beaten by a slave owner in Georgia. After witnessing many scenes of cruelty, Equiano "determined to make every exertion to obtain my freedom, and to return to Old England" (Equiano, 122). He obtained a promise from King that he would be manumitted if he could raise forty pounds (the equivalent of approximately four thousand dollars in 2003), the price King had paid for him. Starting with three pence (approximately two dollars in 2003), he began petty trading and gradually raised the money. After some negotiation, on 11 July 1766 in Monserrat Equiano's manumission papers were drawn up. "I who had been a slave in the morning, trembling at the will of another, now became my own master, and compleatly free. I thought this was the happiest day I had ever experienced" (137). Equiano had achieved his freedom legally, although it has been argued that by buying his way out of slavery he implicitly acknowledged its legitimacy.

Equiano's first paid employment was as an able-bodied seaman aboard King's ships. On one voyage he safely brought the ship home after the death of the captain. On another occasion he was instrumental in saving the crew after a shipwreck. In July 1767, frustrated at the "impositions on free negroes," especially in Georgia, where an attempt was made to kidnap him, he paid seven guineas (the equivalent of about $750 in 2003) for passage to London. On arrival, he was immediately paid the wages (also seven guineas) from his service in the Royal Navy. Meeting with Pascal he demanded, but was refused, his prize money. Over the winter he learned to play the French horn and, more usefully, how to dress hair.

A year of evening classes depleted his savings, and Equiano returned to sea as a steward. In Turkey he was impressed by Islam, but found Turkish rule in Greece oppressive; in Naples he witnessed an eruption of Vesuvius; in Portugal he observed the workings of the Inquisition; and in Jamaica he was reminded of the horrors of slavery. In May 1773, "roused by the sound of fame," he joined John Phipp's expedition to find a northwest passage to India. The expedition reached only as far as Spitzbergen (Svalbard) in Norway.

On his return to London, Equiano underwent a period of spiritual self-examination. In May 1774 he decided to move to Turkey and embrace Islam. He shipped as a steward aboard a merchantman bound for Smyrna (Izmir), but before sailing, the ship's cook, a former slave called John Annis, was kidnapped and forcibly sent to the Caribbean, a practice that had been declared illegal in 1772 after a campaign by the abolitionist Granville Sharp. After the incident, Equiano approached Sharp for help, and while their attempt to save Annis failed, the event put Equiano in touch with the emerging abolitionist movement in London. A second attempt to reach Turkey was aborted, and Equiano began to see his failure to reach the Islamic country as the work of providence. After much meditation and doubt, on 6 October 1774 he recorded his conversion to Christianity with the words "the Lord was pleased to break

in upon my soul with his bright beams of heavenly light" (190).

In 1775 Equiano joined a project to settle a colony on the Mosquito Coast (now Nicaragua). Some have argued that Equiano's official role—buying slaves for the colony—and his self-appointed role as missionary to the Mosquito Indians demonstrate his complicity in both the slave trade and European colonization. By June 1776 however, the colonists' "mode of procedure [became] very irksome" and he left the colony. On the return voyage he was imprisoned by a ship's captain who intended to sell him into slavery at Cartagena, but he made a daring escape and worked his passage back to London. Having "suffered so many impositions," he became "heartily disgusted with the seafaring life" and instead worked as a servant. In 1779 he applied to the Bishop of London to be ordained as a missionary to Africa, but was turned down. In 1784 Equiano returned briefly to sea and visited the newly formed United States where, in Philadelphia, he came into contact with a group of Quakers, led by Anthony Benezet, who had begun to speak out against slavery.

Returning to London in 1786, Equiano was appointed as commissary of stores and provisions to a project to resettle poor black Londoners to a new colony in Sierra Leone, making him the first black civil servant in British history. After complaining about "flagrant abuses," however, he was fired and, as he predicted, the project failed. Equiano then immersed himself in the campaign to abolish the slave trade, writing letters to the newspapers and, in March 1788, petitioning Queen Charlotte.

In May 1789 Equiano published his polemical autobiography, which quickly became a best-seller, going through nine British editions in his lifetime. An unauthorized edition was published in New York in 1791. Equiano publicized the book himself, undertaking an extensive lecture tour throughout the British Isles. Financially secure, on 7 April 1792 he married Susanna Cullen of Soham in Cambridgeshire, where they lived and had two daughters, one of whom survived to inherit an estate of £950 (approximately one-hundred thousand dollars in 2003). Equiano died in London in 1797; his place of burial is unknown.

By his own account, Equiano spent fewer than two years visiting regions now in the United States and, while he strongly asserted his African identity, he clearly came to regard England as his home. Yet his position in African American history and culture is important. As the author of the only substantial description of the Middle Passage written from a slave's point of view, Equiano provides an important point of connection between Africa and America. As the author of the first major slave narrative, his rhetorical style was widely emulated by many African American writers recounting their journey up from slavery. And as the first prominent black abolitionist, he offered a model for political activism that has remained relevant into the twenty-first century.

FURTHER READING

Equiano, Olaudah. *The Interesting Narrative and Other Writings*, ed. Vincent Carretta (2003).

Carretta, Vincent. "Olaudah Equiano or Gustavus Vassa? New Light on an Eighteenth-Century Question of Identity," *Slavery and Abolition* 20, no. 3 (1999).
Walvin, James. *An African's Life: The Life and Times of Olaudah Equiano, 1745–1797* (1998).

—BRYCCHAN CAREY

ESTEBAN (?–May 1539), explorer, enslaved North African, and the first representative of the so-called Old World to encounter peoples of today's American Southwest, was born in Azamor, Morocco. His career as an explorer began in 1528 with the journey to Florida of Pánfilo de Narváez.

This initial Spanish exploration of Florida ended in disaster. The Narváez expedition included four hundred men sailing on five ships. They departed Havana, Cuba, in April 1528 and reached present-day Tampa Bay on 1 May. There Narváez split his forces, ordering the ships to sail along the coast while he marched inward with three hundred men, searching for a fabled city of gold and its attendant riches. A series of attacks by natives reduced the Spanish forces, but they continued their explorations, reaching

Chakwaina, Esteban's mythical counterpart. University of Michigan Museum of Anthropology

Apalachen, principal settlement of the Apalachee people (located near present-day Tallahassee) by July 1528. Overwhelmed by native forces defended by highly skilled bowmen, the Spaniards fled south to the Gulf of Mexico in a vain search for their ships, which had returned to New Spain after a year of unsuccessful attempts to rejoin with Narváez. The Spanish explorers quickly constructed five barges out of palmetto fibers and horsehair and sailed west, mistakenly believing themselves closer to Mexico than to Cuba. For a month and a half, they sailed along the Gulf coast. Fierce storms off the Texas coast sank three of the five barges, but the barge carrying Esteban weathered the storm. In November 1528 the remnants of the Narváez expedition landed on a sandbar near present-day Galveston, Texas, which they named the Island of Ill Fate.

Esteban, Captain Andrés Dorantes (his master), Alvar Núñez Cabeza de Vaca, and thirteen other men managed to survive the winter. When spring approached, the men moved to the mainland. Soon thereafter, an encounter with Karankawa Indians resulted in their enslavement for five years until 1534. Twelve of the Spanish explorers did not survive their captivity. In 1534 the four remaining explorers, Esteban, Andrés Dorantes, Cabeza de Vaca, and Alonso del Castillo Maldonado, escaped from their captors. They traveled inland, where they encountered friendlier Indians, who believed them to be medicine men.

The four survivors quickly transformed themselves into "cultural brokers," learning various native languages and folkways to survive. Apparently, Esteban was particularly adept at learning languages, functioning as the group's interpreter and go-between. The four wandered from tribe to tribe throughout modern-day Texas and northern Mexico, presenting themselves as healers and religious figures, the "Sons of the Sun." According to one historian, their healing powers consisted mostly of prayers and theatrics, but included at least one surgery. The journey provided the four survivors with an unparalleled knowledge of native cultures, languages, wealth (or lack thereof), and of the region's topography.

This knowledge was highly prized when the quartet returned to Mexico City in July 1536, after wandering some fifteen thousand miles over the course of eight years. A chance encounter with Spaniards on a slaving expedition in northwestern Mexico ended the group's years of wandering. Dressed Indian-style and traveling with some six hundred native escorts, the four were barely recognizable as nonnatives.

Despite their truthful reports of very little wealth to be found among the northern indigenous tribes, the return of Esteban, Andres de Dorantes, Cabeza de Vaca, and Castillo Maldonado precipitated a flurry of excitement about the "northern mystery," as the Spanish termed the unknown lands to the north of Mexico. Plans for expeditions abounded, but such ventures could only proceed with the permission of the viceroy. And when it came to the possibility of an *otro Mexico*, another discovery with the same potential for wealth as the Aztec Empire, Viceroy Antonio de Mendoza had plans of his own. When the three European survivors refused to head an exploration venture, Mendoza purchased the slave Esteban, planning to send him in search of the Seven Cities of Cíbola, the fabled vast riches enjoyed by northern natives. For the sake of propriety, however, such an expedition could not be headed by a slave. Mendoza recruited a Franciscan friar, Marcos de Niza, to lead the expedition.

Esteban and Fray Marcos set out on their expedition to the north in 1539. By previous arrangement, Esteban ranged several days' journey ahead of the Franciscan. Also by previous agreement, Esteban left crosses of various sizes, which would indicate to Fray Marcos the magnitude of his findings.

Esteban maintained his "Son of the Sun" persona, using his skills as a linguist and a healer to ensure his safe passage through native lands. Indians later reported to members of the 1540 Coronado expedition that Esteban covered his sizeable frame with animal pelts and adorned his ankles and arms with bells, feathers, and pieces of turquoise. He soon gathered some three hundred native followers, both men and women, who trusted in his powers as a medicine man and showered him with gifts. He experienced no trouble until he reached the Zuni pueblo of Hawikuh, where, in response to his message that "he was coming to establish peace and heal them," elders warned him not to enter the village. A red and white feathered gourd rattle accompanying Esteban's message apparently angered the chief, who threw it to the ground, saying, "I know these people, for these jingle bells are not the shape of ours. Tell them to turn back at once, or not one of their men will be spared" (Gutiérrez, 39). Disregarding this warning, Esteban proceeded into the pueblo, where he was taken prisoner, and the village authorities tried to discern the reasons behind his arrival. According to one account, Esteban explained that other "children of the sun" would follow him, and then demanded wealth and women. These responses convinced the village elders that Esteban was a witch and a foreign spy, and as such, could not be allowed to live (Gutiérrez, 39–40). Other scholars have speculated that perhaps Esteban interrupted an important religious ceremony, or that the Zuni recognized Esteban as the advance flank of an invading force. If he were eliminated, an invasion or conquest might be avoided. According to Zuni oral tradition, Esteban behaved rudely toward the female members of the pueblo, incurring the wrath of the pueblo's men, who then killed him. Whatever the case, Esteban met his demise at Hawikuh in May 1539.

Noting the increasingly large crosses left for him, Fray Marcos viewed Hawikuh from afar, but with great anticipation. Word of Esteban's fate had reached him, and he was reluctant to journey any closer to the Zuni. So he took a long look at Hawikuh, as the bright sun beat down on its adobe apartments, making them gleam as if golden. Fray Marcos returned to Mexico City and to his benefactor, Viceroy Mendoza, reporting that Esteban's death had not been in vain, for he had found the fabled golden city of Cíbola. Eager to exploit such riches, the viceroy quickly organized another expedition to the north, to be led by Francisco Vásquez de Coronado accompanied by Fray Marcos. When Coronado reached Hawikuh, he found not a city of gold, but a village of mud huts and a people whose only recognizable wealth lay in a few stones of turquoise.

Esteban's appearance in Hawikuh must have made a lasting impression on the Zunis. Legends make Esteban the impetus for Chakwaina, a black ogre kachina, or spirit, who reflects the Pueblo oral tradition regarding the appearance of a black Mexican in their midst who represents both the Pueblo people's fears and the role Esteban played as the harbinger of European conquest.

FURTHER READING

Gutiérrez, Ramón A. *When Jesus Came, the Corn Mothers Went Away: Marriage, Sexuality, and Power in New Mexico, 1500–1846* (1991).

Hammond, George P., and Agapito Rey, eds. *Narratives of the Coronado Expedition, 1540–1542* (1940).

McDonald, Dedra S. "Intimacy and Empire: Indian-African Interaction in Spanish Colonial New Mexico, 1500–1800" in *Confounding the Color Line: The Indian-Black Experience in North America*, ed. James F. Brooks (2002).

Taylor, Quintard. *In Search of the Racial Frontier: African Americans in the American West, 1528–1990* (1998).

Weber, David J. *The Spanish Frontier in North America* (1992).

—DEDRA MCDONALD BIRZER

EUROPE, JAMES REESE

(22 Feb. 1880–9 May 1919), music administrator, conductor, and composer, was born in Mobile, Alabama, the son of Henry J. Europe, an Internal Revenue Service employee and Baptist minister, and Lorraine Saxon. Following the loss of his position with the Port of Mobile at the end of the Reconstruction, Europe's father moved his family to Washington, D.C., in 1890 to accept a position with the U.S. Postal Service. Both of Europe's parents were musical, as were some of his siblings. Europe attended the elite M Street High School for blacks and studied violin, piano, and composition with Enrico Hurlei of the U.S. Marine Corps band and with Joseph Douglass, the grandson of FREDERICK DOUGLASS.

Following the death of his father in 1900, Europe moved to New York City. There he became associated with many of the leading figures in black musical theater, which was then emerging from the tradition of nineteenth-century minstrelsy. Over the next six years, Europe established himself as a composer of popular songs and instrumental pieces and as the musical director for a number of major productions, including Ernest Hogan's "Memphis Students" (1905), John Larkins's *A Trip to Africa* (1904), Bob Cole and JOHN ROSAMOND JOHNSON's *Shoo-Fly Regiment* (1906–1907) and *Red Moon* (1908–1909), S. H. Dudley's *Black Politician* (1907–1908), and BERT WILLIAMS's *Mr. Load of Koal* (1909). During *Red Moon*'s run, he was involved with, but did not marry, a dancer in the company, Bessie Simms, with whom he had a child.

In April 1910 Europe became the principal organizer and first president of the Clef Club of New York, the first truly effective black musicians' union and booking agency in the city. So effectual was the club during the years before World War I that, as JAMES WELDON JOHNSON recalls in his memoir *Black Manhattan* (1930), club members held a "monopoly of the business of entertaining private parties and furnishing music for the dance craze which was then beginning to sweep the country." Europe was also appointed conductor of the Clef Club's large orchestra, which he envisioned as a vehicle for presenting the full range of African American musical expression, from spirituals to popular music to concert works. On 27 May 1910 he directed the one-hundred-member orchestra in its first concert at the Manhattan Casino in Harlem. Two years later, on 2 May 1912, Europe brought 125 singers and instrumentalists to Carnegie Hall for an historic "Symphony of Negro Music," featuring compositions by WILL MARION COOK, HARRY BURLEIGH, J. Rosamond Johnson, William Tyers, Samuel Coleridge-Taylor, and himself. It was the first performance ever given by a black orchestra at the famous "bastion of white musical establishment," and Europe returned to direct concerts there in 1913 and 1914.

In 1913 Europe married Willie Angrom Starke, a widow of some social standing within New York's black community; they had no children. Later that year, he and fellow Clef Club member Ford Dabney became the musical directors for the legendary dance team of Vernon Castle and Irene Castle until the end of 1915 when Vernon Castle left to serve in World War I. Irene Castle recalls in her memoir *Castles in the Air* (1958) that they wanted Europe because his was the "most famous of the colored bands" and because he was a "skilled musician and one of the first to take jazz out of the saloons and make it respectable." With the accompaniment of Europe's

James Reese Europe, regimental bandleader with the Fifteenth "Hellfighters" Infantry Regiment, brought live ragtime, blues, and jazz to Europe during World War I. National Archives

Society Orchestra, the Castles toured the country, operated a fashionable dance studio and supper club in New York City, and revolutionized American social dancing by promoting and popularizing the formerly objectionable "ragtime" dances, such as the turkey trot and the one-step. The most famous of the Castle dances, the fox-trot, was conceived by Europe and Vernon Castle after an initial suggestion by composer W. C. HANDY. As a result of his collaboration with the Castles, in the fall of 1913 Europe and his orchestra were offered a recording contract by Victor Records, the first ever offered to a black orchestra. Between December 1913 and October 1914 Europe and his Society Orchestra cut ten sides of dance music for Victor, eight of which were released.

In 1916 Europe enlisted in the Fifteenth Infantry Regiment of the New York National Guard, the first black regiment organized in the state and one of the first mobilized into federal service when the United States entered World War I in 1917. After encountering severe racial hostility while training in South Carolina, the infantry was sent directly to France and assigned to the French army. Europe, who held two assignments, bandmaster of the regiment's outstanding brass band and commander of a machine gun company, served at the front for four months and was the first black American officer to lead troops in combat in the Great War. The entire Fifteenth Regiment, which was given the nickname "Hellfighters," emerged after the Allied victory in November of 1918 as one of the most highly decorated American units of the war. Europe's band, which performed throughout France during the war, was the most celebrated in the American Expeditionary Force and is credited with introducing European audiences to the live sound of orchestrated American ragtime, blues, and a new genre called "jazz."

On 17 February 1919 the regiment and its band were given a triumphant welcome-home parade up Fifth Avenue, and Lieutenant Europe, hailed as America's "jazz king," was signed to a second recording contract; he and the band subsequently embarked upon an extensive national tour. Europe's career ended abruptly and tragically a few months later, however, when during the intermission of one of the band's concerts in Boston, he was fatally stabbed by an emotionally disturbed band member. Following a public funeral in New York City, the first ever for a black American, Europe was buried with military honors in Arlington National Cemetery.

Europe composed no major concert works, but many of his more than one hundred songs, rags, waltzes, and marches exhibit unusual lyricism and rhythmic sophistication. His major contributions, however, derive from his achievements as an organizer of professional musicians, a skilled and imaginative conductor and arranger, and an early and articulate champion of African American music. Through his influence on NOBLE SISSLE, EUBIE BLAKE, and George Gershwin, among others, Europe helped to shape the future of American musical theater. As a pioneer in the creation and diffusion of orchestral jazz, he initiated the line of musical development that led from Fletcher Henderson and Paul Whiteman to DUKE ELLINGTON. Without the expanded opportunities for black musicians and for African American music that Europe helped to inaugurate, much of the development of American music in the 1920s, and indeed since then, would be inconceivable.

FURTHER READING

Badger, Reid. *A Life in Ragtime: A Biography of James Reese Europe* (1995).

Charters, Samuel B., and Leonard Kunstadt. *Jazz: A History of the New York Scene* (1962).

Erenberg, Lewis A. *Steppin' Out: New York Nightlife and the Transformation of American Culture, 1890–1930* (1981).

Kimball, Robert, and William Bolcom. *Reminiscing with Sissle and Blake* (1973).

Riis, Thomas. *Just Before Jazz: Black Musical Theater in New York, 1890–1915* (1989).

Obituaries: *Chicago Defender*, 24 May 1919; *New York Times*, 12 May 1919.

—REID BADGER

EVERS, MEDGAR

(2 July 1925–12 June 1963), civil rights activist, was born Medgar Wiley Evers in Decatur, Mississippi, the son of James Evers, a sawmill worker, and Jessie Wright, a domestic worker. He was drafted into the U.S. Army in 1943 and served in the invasion of Normandy and the French campaign. After the war ended Evers returned to Mississippi, where he attended Alcorn Agricultural and Mechanical College, a segregated land-grant institution, from which he graduated in 1952 with a bachelor's degree in business administration. While at Alcorn he met a nursing student, Myrlie Beasley (MYRLIE EVERS-WILLIAMS), whom he married in 1951; the couple had three children.

After graduating from Alcorn, Evers spent several years working as a traveling salesman for the Magnolia Mutual Insurance Company, a business founded by, run by, and serving African Americans. His extensive travels through impoverished areas of Mississippi made him aware of the terrible poverty and oppression suffered by many black southerners and led him to become an active volunteer in the Mississippi chapter of the NAACP. His skill and enthusiasm did not pass unnoticed by the organization's leadership, and in 1954, after Evers's application to the University of Mississippi Law School was rejected on racial grounds, he was appointed to the newly created and salaried position of state field secretary for the NAACP, in Jackson.

Evers's duties as field secretary were originally bureaucratic—collecting, organizing, and publicizing information about civil rights abuses in Mississippi. However, his anger, aroused by the refusal of southern authorities to enforce the U.S. Supreme Court's landmark 1954 decision against segregation of public institutions, led him to more direct forms of action, sometimes to the dismay of the generally more conservative NAACP leadership. Evers did not shy away from high-profile activities; he helped to investigate the death of EMMETT TILL, a teenager murdered allegedly for having whistled at a white woman, and he served as an adviser to JAMES MEREDITH in his eventually successful quest to enroll as

Medgar Evers, whose murder became an important symbol of the civil rights movement, is shown on the program at his funeral. Corbis

the first black student at the University of Mississippi.

Evers's more aggressive style of leadership became evident in the early 1960s, when he helped to organize the Jackson Movement, an all-out attempt to end segregation in Mississippi's largest and most densely black-populated city. Throughout 1962 and 1963 Jackson's African American residents, under Evers's leadership, struggled for racial justice, focusing on the issues of integration of public schools, parks, and libraries and the hiring of African Americans for municipal offices and on the police force. Evers's tactics, which included mass meetings, peaceful demonstrations, sit-ins, and economic boycotts of segregated businesses and of the state fair, helped to unify Jackson's black community. His energy and diplomacy helped to resolve conflicts and create unity between radical youth groups and the more conservative organizations of middle-class adults and also attracted the participation of some moderate white Jackson residents. However, Evers's actions were perceived as antagonistic by many other white Jacksonians.

Shortly after midnight on 12 June 1963 Evers returned to his home after a Movement meeting and was ambushed in his driveway and shot to death. News of the murder spread rapidly through

Jackson's black community, and a riot was narrowly averted. Evers was buried with full military honors at Arlington National Cemetery, and the NAACP honored him posthumously with its 1963 Spingarn Medal.

A Federal Bureau of Investigation probe of Evers's murder led to the arrest of Byron de la Beckwith, a fertilizer salesman, avowed anti-integrationist, and member of a long-established Mississippi family. Beckwith was tried for the crime, but, despite the testimony of several witnesses who claimed that they had heard the accused boast of having shot Evers, he was found not guilty by an all-white jury. A retrial ended in the same verdict. In February 1994, however, a third trial, this time by a racially mixed jury, ended in Beckwith's conviction for Evers's murder and a sentence of life imprisonment.

Although his career as a political activist and organizer was cut short by his death, Medgar Evers became and has remained an important symbol of the civil rights movement. The brutal murder of a nonviolent activist shocked both black and white Americans, helping them to understand the extent to which areas of the Deep South tolerated racial violence. Evers's death was a crucial factor that motivated President John F. Kennedy to ask the U.S. Congress to enact a new and comprehensive civil rights law, an action that committed the federal government to enforcement of policies to promote racial equality throughout the United States. Evers's name has remained alive through the efforts of the NAACP's Medgar Evers Fund, which provides financial assistance for efforts to improve housing, health care, education, and economic opportunity for African Americans. A branch of the City University of New York was named Medgar Evers College in 1969. His widow, Myrlie Evers-Williams, served as interim president of the national NAACP in 1995.

FURTHER READING

Bailey, Ronald. *Remembering Medgar Evers* (1988).

Evers, Charles. *Evers* (1971).

Evers-Williams, Myrlie, and William Peters. *For Us, the Living* (1967).

Nossiter, Adam. *Of Long Memory: Mississippi and the Murder of Medgar Evers* (1994).

Salter, John R. *Jackson, Mississippi: An American Chronicle of Struggle and Schism* (1979).

Vollers, Maryanne. *Ghosts of Mississippi: The Murder of Medgar Evers, the Trial of Byron de la Beckwith, and the Haunting of the New South* (1995).

Obituary: *New York Times*, 13 June 1963.
—NATALIE ZACEK

EVERS-WILLIAMS, MYRLIE (17 Mar. 1933–), civil rights activist, was born Myrlie Beasley in Vicksburg, Mississippi, and was raised, following her parents divorce, by her grandmother, Annie McCain Beasley, and her aunt, Myrlie Beasley Polk. Both women were schoolteachers who encouraged young Myrlie in her educational pursuits through activities such as singing, public speaking, and piano lessons. Myrlie hoped to major in music in college, but neither of Mississippi's state schools for blacks, Alcorn A&M College or Jackson State, had such a major. In 1950 Myrlie enrolled at Alcorn, intending to study education and music. Only two hours after arriving on campus, however, she met MEDGAR EVERS, an upperclassman and army veteran seven years her senior. He soon proposed, and they were married on

24 December 1951. Following Medgar's graduation and Myrlie's sophomore year, the couple moved to Mound Bayou, Mississippi, where Medgar took a position as an insurance salesman with Magnolia Mutual Insurance, a black-owned company.

Myrlie Evers entered the civil rights movement through Medgar's work as the NAACP state field secretary for Mississippi. This was the beginning of a lifetime of work against segregation and racial violence against blacks. Medgar's appointment came in 1954, the same year as their daughter Reena Denise's birth and a year after the birth of their first child, Darrell Kenyatta. Son James Van Dyke was born in 1960. Myrlie Evers worked full time as a secretary in the NAACP Jackson office and the Everses worked tirelessly on the NAACP's agenda of securing voting rights, coordinating civil rights demonstrations, and desegregating public facilities. The Everses were also deeply involved in the quest to bring the murderers of EMMETT TILL to justice and in the efforts of JAMES MEREDITH in desegregating the University of Mississippi.

Due to their civil rights work and their direct confrontation with the white supremacist power elite, the Evers family lived under the constant threat of violence. The children were trained to take cover should gunfire erupt and Myrlie practiced the steps she would take if her husband were shot. In one incident, their home was firebombed while Medgar was away at a meeting, leaving Myrlie to put out the fire while in fear that the arsonists were still nearby. The violence reached its climax for the Evers family on 12 June 1963, when Medgar was killed by a sniper's bullet in front of their home. The Evers children dove for the floor as trained, as Myrlie ran outside and found her husband bleeding from a gunshot wound to the back. Although he was rushed to the hospital and admitted to the emergency room—after hospital officials vacillated on their segregation policy—Medgar Evers died an hour after the shooting.

At the scene of the murder the police retrieved a rifle with the fingerprints of Byron De La Beckwith, an outspoken racist and anti-integrationist. Beckwith was indicted twice but freed by deadlocked, all-white juries. Medgar's murder and the failure of the jury to

Myrlie Evers (later Evers-Williams) at a memorial service for her husband, MEDGAR EVERS, 1963. © Flip Schulke/CORBIS

convict Beckwith were catalysts in Myrlie Evers's quest for justice in the face of racial discrimination. Evers also credits her late husband with raising her racial awareness and pride in her race.

Though he believed Mississippi would be the best place to live were Jim Crow segregation ever abolished, Medgar always thought California would be a good place to raise their children. A year after Medgar's murder and the subsequent trials, Evers and her three children moved to Claremont, California. She cowrote a book about her husband, *For Us, the Living* (1967), and gave speeches for the NAACP. In the book Evers details the tensions and emotions she felt as she grew from a sheltered Mississippi childhood into civil rights activism alongside Medgar in the virulently racist South.

Evers experienced several life changes upon moving to California. She enrolled in Pomona College, graduating with a BA in Sociology in 1968. She then served as assistant director of planning and development for the Claremont College system. She also ran for Congress in 1969. Though she lost the race, it was the first time she explicitly stepped out of her murdered husband's shadow, changing her political ticket from "Mrs. Medgar Evers" to "Myrlie Evers." In 1975 Evers married Walter Williams, a longshoreman and union organizer who died of prostate cancer in 1995.

In step with her lifetime of activism and achievements, Evers-Williams accomplished two firsts. Los Angeles Mayor TOM BRADLEY appointed her to the city's Board of Public Works, making her the first black woman to serve in that capacity. Evers-Williams served on the board from 1988 to 1990, comanaging a million-dollar annual budget. In 1995 Evers-Williams became the first woman to serve as chair of the board of the NAACP. Before leaving the position in 1998, Evers-Williams helped recuperate the organization's image, which was damaged by her predecessors, who left the organization four million dollars in debt.

Evers-Williams remained determined to see Beckwith brought to justice. In addition to trips back to Mississippi to track Beckwith's whereabouts, Evers-Williams continued to search for evidence that would spur a new trial.

After Jackson reporter Jerry Mitchell unearthed documents proving the long-suspected collusion between government officials and white supremacists, Evers pressured Mississippi prosecutors to move for a new trial. In 1994, more than thirty years after the assassination, Beckwith was finally convicted of Medgar Evers's murder and sentenced to life in prison, opening the door to the prosecution of other old civil rights cases. In 1996, *Ghosts of Mississippi*, a film directed by Rob Reiner, dramatized the events surrounding the final Beckwith trial. WHOOPI GOLDBERG played Evers-Williams in the film, which centered on prosecutor Bobby DeLaughter's quest to bring Beckwith to trial in 1994.

In 1999 Evers-Williams published an autobiography, *Watch Me Fly: What I Learned on My Way to Becoming the Woman I Was Meant to Be*. She has received seven honorary doctorates and awards from the NAACP, the U.S. Congressional Black Caucus, and the League of Women Voters. In 1988 she established the Medgar Evers Institute, which works to encourage a better understanding of human rights. The Institute's Archive and Justice Center are based in Jackson, Mississippi, while the Oregon State University Medgar Evers Institute Fellowship Center is based in Bend, Oregon, where Evers-Williams lives.

FURTHER READING

Evers, Mrs. Medgar, with William Peters. *For Us, the Living* (1967).

Evers-Williams, Myrlie, with Melinda Blau. *Watch Me Fly: What I Learned on My Way to Becoming the Woman I Was Meant to Be* (1999).

Hampton, Henry, and Steve Fayer. *Voices of Freedom: An Oral History of the Civil Rights Movement from the 1950s through the 1980s* (1991).

—KIMBERLY SPRINGER

F

FARMER, JAMES

(12 Jan. 1920–9 July 1999), founder and national director of the Congress of Racial Equality (CORE), civil rights activist, and educator, was born James Leonard Farmer Jr. in Marshall, Texas, the son of James Leonard Farmer (known as "J. Leonard"), a Methodist minister and the son of ex-slaves, and Pearl Houston Farmer, who had been a teacher. Farmer's father, who earned a doctorate of religion from Boston University, was one of the first blacks in Texas to hold a PhD. When Farmer was six months old the family, which included an older sister, moved to Holly Springs, Mississippi, where his father had accepted teaching and administrative posts at Rust College. Able to read, write, and count by the age of four and a half, Farmer was accepted into the first grade. The family soon moved again, as Professor Farmer joined the department of religion and philosophy at Samuel Houston College in Austin, Texas.

Farmer's outstanding academic and oratorical skills won him a four-year scholarship, and at the age of fourteen he entered Wiley College in Marshall. He was fortunate in his mentor, the poet Melvin B. Tolson. Farmer was captain of the debating team and president of his fraternity. After his graduation in 1938, he enrolled at Howard University in Washington, D.C., to study for the ministry. Among others, the staff at Howard included STERLING BROWN, RALPH BUNCHE, CARTER G. WOODSON, BENJAMIN MAYS, and, most notably, HOWARD THURMAN. Poet, philosopher, and preacher, Thurman introduced Farmer to Mohandas K. Gandhi's philosophy on the use of nonviolence to effect social change. At this time Farmer became the part-time student secretary for the Fellowship of Reconciliation (FOR), a Quaker pacifist organization.

During his years at Howard's School of Religion, Farmer focused on the interrelatedness of religion, economics,

James Farmer, director of the Congress of Racial Equality, leading a demonstration at the New York World's Fair, 1964. Library of Congress

and race, and he wrote his master's thesis on this theme. As a result of his studies, Farmer decided not to be ordained, as the racial segregation in all denominations was repugnant to him. Close to graduation in 1941 when his father asked him what he then planned to do, he replied, "Destroy segregation." Asked how, Farmer told him it would involve mass mobilization and the use of Gandhi's principles.

Farmer began the grand mission of his life by continuing to work at FOR, first in Chicago, giving antiwar speeches there and in other midwestern cities. In Chicago he used Gandhi's technique for the first time to integrate a coffee shop where Farmer and a friend had been refused service. With added insult, they had been asked to pay one dollar for a nickel doughnut and had had their money thrown to the floor. In May 1942 they returned with a group of twenty-eight others and staged a sit-in that succeeded.

At this time, under the auspices of FOR, Farmer cofounded CORE (Committee of Racial Equality). The acronym came before the name, to indicate its purpose: that racial equality is the core of a just society. In little over a year CORE had chapters in New York, Philadelphia, Detroit, Seattle, and Los Angeles. Its appeal was broad because CORE had always stressed its interracial aspect, mirroring the belief that the "race problem" concerned all Americans, black and white. At its second annual convention in 1944, "Committee" became "Congress," reflecting its rapid growth. Peak membership came in the 1960s when CORE had eighty-two thousand members in 114 chapters. But Farmer described their efforts during the 1940s at integrating housing, banks, amusement parks, and barber shops as "a flea gnawing on the ear of an elephant" (Farmer, 153), for the lack of publicity CORE received.

In 1945 Farmer worked as a union organizer for furniture workers in the South. He also recruited college students for the League for Industrial Democracy, a socialist organization; organized and led strikes for the New York arm of AFSCME (American Federation of State, County, and Municipal Employees); continued to participate in CORE's activities; and became program director for the National Association for the Advancement of Colored People (NAACP), under the leadership of ROY WILKINS. In 1945 Farmer married Winnie Christie; they had no children and divorced the following year. In 1949 he married Lula Peterson; they had two daughters.

In February 1961 Farmer took the helm of CORE, the organization he had founded, as its first national director. "The dream that made our hearts beat since 1942 was in 1960 a reality," Farmer recalled in his autobiography. The Montgomery Bus Boycott of 1956 had been successful, and a lunch counter sit-in, which four students in Greensboro, North Carolina, staged on 1 February 1960, soon became the catalyst for the formation of the national Student Nonviolent Coordinating Committee (SNCC).

In May 1961 Farmer launched the Freedom Rides to the South to end desegregation in interstate transportation and in station waiting rooms. A participant as well as CORE's director, Farmer faced terrifying episodes, and he was in a Louisiana jail on the day of the March on Washington in 1963. The demands for civil rights were answered with bus and church burnings and beatings by mobs and police. The violence escalated into the murders of CORE members James Chaney, Andrew Goodman, and Michael Schwerner in Mississippi in 1964. Such violence, coming a year after the Birmingham church bombing, in which four young girls died, and the murder of MEDGAR EVERS, motivated civil rights workers to challenge the idea of nonviolence, as well as the large role played by whites within CORE. The preference for more confrontational action undermined Farmer's tenure, and he resigned in 1966.

Farmer then taught at Lincoln University in Pennsylvania and at New York University. In 1968 he ran for a Brooklyn congressional seat but lost to SHIRLEY CHISHOLM. President Richard Nixon appointed Farmer assistant secretary in the Department of Health, Education, and Welfare in April 1969. "Chaf[ing] in the ponderous bureaucracy and long[ing] for my old role as advocate, critic, activist," Farmer resigned in December 1970. During the 1970s he worked with the Council on Minority Planning and Strategy, a think tank, and with organizations of public employees that made mortgage loans for integrated housing.

In 1985, despite failing eyesight, Farmer completed and published his autobiography, *Lay Bare the Heart*. He then taught history at Mary Washington College in Fredericksburg, Virginia, where he died.

To an enormous degree, James Farmer accomplished the goal he set for himself at the age of twenty-one, to "destroy segregation." His vision and energy challenged the social status quo and eliminated many injustices in American life. As Farmer summed up, "In movement days . . . the grasping at liberty . . . ennobled life for this nation" (Farmer, 351).

FURTHER READING

The James Farmer Papers are at the Center for American History at the University of Texas at Austin. Tapes relating to his run for Congress in 1968 are held at the Schomburg Center for Research in Black Culture of the New York Public Library.

Farmer, James. *Lay Bare the Heart* (1985).

Sklansky, Jeff. *James Farmer: Civil Rights Leader* (1992).

Obituaries: *New York Times*, 10 July 1999; *Jet*, 26 July 1999.

—BETTY KAPLAN GUBERT

FARRAKHAN, LOUIS ABDUL (11 May 1933–), leader of the Nation of Islam, was born Louis Eugene Walcott in the Bronx, New York City, to Sarah Mae Manning, a native of St. Kitts, who worked as a domestic. Farrakhan's biological father was Manning's husband, Percival Clarke, a light-skinned Jamaican cab driver. By the time young Louis was born, however, Manning had left Clarke and was living with Louis Walcott. Manning hoped her baby would be a girl and have a dark complexion like herself and Walcott. Nevertheless, when the child was born male and with a light complexion, she named him Louis and listed Walcott as the father (Magida, 10). Walcott stayed with the family during their move to the Roxbury section of Boston in 1937, but departed shortly thereafter.

Raising two young children alone during the Depression was difficult, but Sarah Mae kept her boys from harm and attended to their cultural as well as material needs. At the age of six Louis started violin lessons. He later studied with a Jewish instructor, among others, and became a local prodigy, appearing on the *Ted Mack Amateur Hour* at the age of sixteen. Louis was also an altar boy and choir member at St. Cyprian's Episcopal Church. Next to the church stood Toussaint L'Ouverture Hall, formerly the Boston headquarters for black nationalist MARCUS GARVEY, one of Louis's childhood heroes. Louis was an exceptionally bright student whose academic promise earned him a place at the prestigious Boston Latin School. Not comfortable in those elite surroundings, Louis transferred to the English High School, where black students were still in the minority, but where he could thrive academically and shine as a popular track star.

He had dreams of attending the Juilliard School, but by his teen years Louis's taste in music had broadened to include calypso, and he wondered if he might not more easily become the next HARRY BELAFONTE than a black Jascha Heifetz. Thus, when the all-black Winston-Salem Teacher's College offered him an athletic scholarship, he left for North Carolina—quite unprepared for the racism and segregation he would encounter. Although there were seven female students for every male student at the college, Louis was in love with Betsy Ross, a young, black Roman Catholic woman back in Roxbury. By the summer following his sophomore year, Betsy was pregnant with the first of their nine children. College had been a disappointment, so instead of returning to campus in September 1953, he married Betsy at St. Cyprian's. For the next few years, Louis supported his family and pursued a career as a calypso entertainer.

His melodic voice, suggestive lyrics, provocative dancing, and colorful outfits paid tribute to his West Indian parentage and earned him the stage name "The Charmer."

While touring in Chicago as the feature performer with the Calypso Follies in February 1955, Louis was invited by a friend to attend a meeting of the Nation of Islam (NOI). When Louis arrived at the converted synagogue on Chicago's South Side, he was not impressed by the oratorical ability of ELIJAH MUHAMMAD, the organization's leader, thinking to himself, "This man can't even speak well" (Magida, 31). However, Muhammad's message of black nationalism and his powerful indictment of the white race for a litany of wrongs perpetrated against black people resonated profoundly in Louis's heart and mind. Back in Boston, MALCOLM X, the most dynamic and articulate of Muhammad's ministers, personally oversaw much of Louis's conversion and training. Louis X, as he was then known, rose quickly within the ranks of the Nation of Islam from acolyte to a captain of the Fruit of Islam, a security and fraternal auxiliary. In 1959 Louis X became the minister of Temple No. 11 in Boston, which was located in a building that had formerly been the Boston Rabbinical College. Apparently unaware that the property had changed hands, the city directory listed Louis X as "Rabbi Eugene L. Walcott."

Within five years Louis X had tripled the membership in the Boston mosque to approximately three hundred members, with many more sympathizers and supporters. Like W. D. Fard, the mysterious founder of the NOI who adopted much of the pseudo-Islamic teachings of NOBLE DREW ALI, Louis X propagated the doctrine that their unique form of Islam was the true religion of black people in America, who were, they believed, the lost tribe of Shabazz, and that the "white man" was the devil incarnate (Lincoln, 77–81). Louis X projected the organization's carefully cultivated image of black men who were proud and defiant, well dressed in their trademark bow ties, and able defenders of the black community. To their credit, the NOI was more effective than most rival organizations at rehabilitating criminals, helping drug addicts, and inculcating their particular values,

which prohibit drinking, smoking, and extramarital relations. Louis X drew on his artistic talents to aid in recruitment by recording songs such as "A White Man's Heaven Is a Black Man's Hell" and "Look at My Chains," and he wrote two plays: *The Trial*, which literally put the white race on trial for crimes against humanity, and *Orgena* ("A Negro" spelled backward).

In 1964, when Malcolm X informed his protégé that their leader, Elijah Muhammad, had fathered several children with his teenage secretaries, Louis X made it clear that if a conflict should emerge, he would side with Muhammad. When the split occurred that March, an internecine struggle ensued. In December 1964 Louis X published an article in *Muhammad Speaks* declaring Malcolm X a traitor and ominously announced, "The die is set, and Malcolm shall not escape.... Such a man as Malcolm is worthy of death." On 14 February 1965 Malcolm and his family narrowly escaped when their home was bombed; then on 21 February, Malcolm was fatally shot at the Audubon Ballroom in Harlem. Convicted of the murder were three members of the NOI, one of whom was connected to the Newark mosque where Louis X had been the morning of the assassination. Thirty years later, while not admitting to a direct role in the murder, Louis X acknowledged that his rhetoric contributed to a hostile atmosphere.

Three months after the assassination of Malcolm X, Muhammad gave Louis X the name Abdul Farrakhan and appointed him to lead Malcolm's Harlem mosque. Within two years Minister Farrakhan had risen to Malcolm's former position as national spokesman of the NOI. When Elijah Muhammad died of congestive heart failure in 1975, many expected Farrakhan to be named as his successor and were surprised to learn that Muhammad had chosen his fifth son, Wallace (now Warith) Muhammad to be the next supreme minister. Wallace restructured the NOI in an effort to bring its beliefs and practices in line with the majority of Sunni Muslims throughout the world, a move that required purging the organization of its racial ideology. In October 1976 the NOI was officially dissolved in order to give birth to the World Community of al-Islam, which

ultimately became the American Society of Muslims. Farrakhan, who had been transferred to the Chicago headquarters during the reorganization, believed these changes had gone too far, and in September 1977 he called on dissenting ministers and members to join him in restoring the NOI under his leadership.

The resurrection of the Nation of Islam began in a funeral home that Farrakhan purchased in Chicago. From that location he started the newspaper *Final Call* and began to buy properties liquidated by Wallace. In 1986 he purchased Elijah Muhammad's mansion in Hyde Park for $500,000, and in 1988 he acquired the flagship mosque of the NOI in Chicago, which he renamed Mosque Maryam. With a five-million-dollar, interest-free loan from Libyan leader Mu'ammar Gadhafi in 1985, Farrakhan launched a line of cosmetic products. The NOI also owns farmland and small businesses and broadcasts on several television and radio stations. Though Farrakhan succeeded in rebuilding the NOI, membership in the organization has never exceeded fifty thousand, and he did not come to national attention until the presidential campaign of JESSE JACKSON in 1984. Farrakhan was on the board of directors of Operation PUSH, Jackson's organization, and he traveled with Jackson to Syria that December to secure the release of U.S. Navy lieutenant Robert O. Goodman, an African American airman who had been shot down over Lebanon. Farrakhan received little publicity until Jackson's anti-Semitic reference to New York City as "Hymietown" was reported by the African American journalist Milton Coleman. Farrakhan responded with an oblique threat on Coleman's life and implied the existence of a Jewish conspiracy to perpetuate black subordination. Farrakhan and his spokesman, Khallid Abdul Muhammad, soon found themselves at the center of a firestorm of charges of anti-Semitism, denials, and countercharges.

Farrakhan has referred to Adolf Hitler as "a very great man" (later explaining he meant "wickedly great"), to the Jewish people as the "killer of all the prophets," and to Judaism as a "dirty religion" (Magida, 146–149). Because his remarks range from harsh but legitimate criticisms to ugly stereotyping, different constituencies champion or attack isolated aspects of his persona while ignoring that which does not fit the image they have of him. Farrakhan portrays himself as the paladin of unspoken truth—as with the publication of *The Secret Relationship between Blacks and Jews* (1991)—and his opponents portray themselves as defenders against a rising tide of black anti-Semitism. Farrakhan is aware that his obsession with Jews is unhealthy and easily exploited, but he says, "It's like I'm locked now in a struggle. It's like both of us got a hold on each other, and each of us is filled with electricity. I can't let them go, and they can't let me go" (Gates, 145).

The pinnacle of Farrakhan's influence was reached on 16 October 1995, when he convened the "Million Man March," a mass gathering of black men on the Washington Mall for a day of atonement. The goals of the march were introspective, focusing on accepting personal responsibility and healing the internal wounds of the black family, rather than hurling grievances at the government. The African American community was polarized between those who supported the objectives of the rally and those who would not participate as long as women were excluded and as long as Farrakhan refused to disavow his anti-Semitism. According to some estimates, a million men may indeed have attended. By all accounts the Million Man March far surpassed the size but not the influence of the 1963 March on Washington, and Farrakhan himself had much of the popularity but little of the stature of Dr. MARTIN LUTHER KING JR.; yet, he had undeniably tapped into a deep yearning in the souls of many black folk.

FURTHER READING

Alexander, Amy, ed. *The Farrakhan Factor* (1998).

Gates, Henry Louis, Jr. "The Charmer," in *Thirteen Ways of Looking at a Black Man* (1997).

Levinsohn, Hamlish Florence. *Looking for Farrakhan* (1997).

Lincoln, C. Eric. *The Black Muslims in America* (1961, rpt. 1973).

Magida, Arthur J. *Prophet of Rage: A Life of Louis Farrakhan and His Nation* (1996).
—SHOLOMO B. LEVY

 FATHER DIVINE
(? May 1879–10 Sept. 1965), religious leader and founder of the Peace Mission movement, was born George Baker in Rockville, Maryland, to George Baker Sr., a farmer, and Nancy Smith, an ex-slave who worked as a domestic with her three daughters before marrying Baker sometime in the 1870s.

Nancy, who had been owned by two Catholic masters, exposed her children to the Negro spiritual traditions of the Jerusalem Methodist Church in Rockville until she died in 1897.

Following his mother's death, George Baker gravitated to Baltimore, as did thousands of Negroes in search of a better life. He appears on the census of 1900 as a gardener, and he also found work on the docks, where he witnessed the crime and poverty of the destitute and was moved by a new message of ecstatic salvation emanating from dozens of storefront churches in the city. Baker, a dark, stout man with a high-pitched voice, impressed people with his earnest demeanor. He quickly rose from Sunday school teacher to evangelist. However, it was Baker's message, rather than oratorical skills or charisma, that ultimately distinguished him from any number of itinerate preachers. His message synthesized the teachings of evangelical churches with the "New Thought" ideology of Charles Fillmore and Robert Collier. Essentially a form of positive thinking, proponents of New Thought asserted that correct thinking, which Baker and others interpreted in a religious sense, could empower the believer to improve his or her circumstances. This notion contrasted sharply with the ritualistic or heaven-focused beliefs of many denominations, regardless of their form of worship. Baker's theology could be applied to solving earthly problems of poverty and racism. Indeed, he later referred to his centers as "heavens on earth."

The most striking element of Baker's message, that of his own divinity, gradually emerged after he attended the Azusa Street Revival, which gave birth to the Pentecostal movement in California during the spring of 1906. Baker returned to Baltimore convinced that he had been transformed to serve a higher purpose. The following year Samuel Morris entered Baker's church and proclaimed, "I am the Father Eternal!" (Weisbrot, 19). Morris was cast out by the congregation, who considered his words blasphemous, but Baker was intrigued by Morris's interpretation of 1 Corinthians 3:16, "Know ye not that ye are the temple of God, and the Spirit of God dwelleth in you?"(AV) as establishing the possibility of human divinity. For the next five years the two enjoyed a relationship in which

Louis Farrakhan speaking in 1985 as head of the Nation of Islam.
© Bettmann/CORBIS

Morris was "Father Jehovia, God in the Fathership degree" and Baker was "the Messenger, God in the Sonship degree" (Watts, 27). Later, John Hickerson, known as "Reverend St. John Divine Bishop," who claimed to speak fluent Hebrew and taught that all black people were descended from Ethiopian Jews, became the third member of their trinity.

In 1912 this divine partnership ended as Hickerson and Baker both began to question whether their own degree of divinity might equal or surpass that claimed by Father Jehovia. Hickerson went north to establish the Church of the Living God in New York City, and Baker went south, preaching in various towns until 1914, when he settled briefly in Valdosta, Georgia. There a group of irate husbands and clergy had Baker indicted on lunacy charges, arguing that claiming to be God and encouraging sexual abstinence even for married women was proof of his insanity. One local paper ridiculed him with the headline "Negro Claims to Be God." He was booked as "John Doe, alias God," indicating that he no longer used the name Baker. But neither on the witness stand nor in interviews did Baker appear to be one of the crazed lunatics that he and his followers were made out to be. The jury found Baker guilty but did not have him committed because he was not a threat to himself or others. Chastened by this experience and by an earlier clash with southern ministers that got him sixty days on a Georgia chain gang, Baker moved in late 1914 to New York City, where he established a religious organization that, for a while at least, kept a relatively low profile.

The prototype for the Peace Missions began in a quiet, middle-class neighborhood in Brooklyn in 1917 and then two years later moved to an affluent white suburb in Sayville, New York, where he was known as "Major Jealous Devine" before settling on the appellation "Father Divine." These missions were experiments in communal living. Residents and visitors entered a world in which race was considered not to exist; even the words "white" and "Negro" were barred from use. Gender distinctions were also treated as suspect, and adherents referred to "those who call themselves women" and "so-called men." Nor were distinctions recognized on the basis of class, title, or office; all identities were subordinate to being a follower of God. On 15 November 1931 Father Divine and ninety-three of his followers were arrested at their Long Island mission for disturbing the peace. The interracial composition of the movement drew the ire of Judge Lewis Smith, who considered race mixing ipso facto a disturbance of the peace. Father Divine, believing that he was being persecuted, refused to pay the five-dollar fine. When the fifty-six-year-old judge suddenly dropped dead three days after imposing a one-year sentence, Father Divine remarked, "I hated to do it." The conviction was later overturned, and the coverage in the black press brought Father Divine to national attention.

During the Depression Father Divine moved his base of operation to Harlem and opened an estimated 160 Peace Missions in the United States, Canada, and Europe. The movement even boasted of a postcard from China addressed to "God, Harlem, USA" that was promptly delivered to Father Divine. While the majority of his followers in New York were black migrants from the South and immigrants from the Caribbean, in other areas of the country, such as California, white membership may have risen as high as 70 percent. A number of Father Divine's wealthy followers contributed land, buildings, and large sums of money to the organization. Where other charities opened soup kitchens for the poor, Father Divine served lavish buffets twice daily, consisting of between fifty and two hundred menu items of the finest fare available. These centers operated on an honor system where the poorest dined for free and others paid as little as ten cents for a meal and two dollars a week for lodging. Critics have argued that Father Divine was merely pandering to the poor, simple, and ignorant, but according to one contemporary academic observer, "Eating is hardly ever advanced as a reason for having come into the movement" (Fauset, 63 n. 10). Father Divine referred to these banquets as "Holy Communions," and in the absence of any formal liturgy for the sect, the meals, songs, and testimonials formed the core of their religious activity.

Father Divine advanced bold political positions, calling for a minimum wage, limits on corporate wealth, the abolition of capital punishment, and the passage of antilynching legislation. He ran his organization through a series of secretaries, mostly women; there were no ministers or clergy other than Father Divine himself. Drinking, smoking, and sexual relations were strictly prohibited, while industry and financial independence were strongly encouraged. By the end of the Depression, the Peace Mission operated scores of businesses, several hotels, a large farming cooperative, a number of mansions, and two newspapers, *New Day* and *Spoken Word*. Yet, the Peace Mission did not pass a collection plate at their meetings, nor did they peddle healing merchandise or accept contributions from nonmembers. Those who lived at a mission center might be expected to donate their earnings to the movement, but Father Divine's propensity to share the wealth seems consistent with his philosophy of prosperity, rather than with the unalloyed avarice of a con artist.

During the 1940s membership in the Peace Mission movement declined rapidly from its height of about 50,000. The end of the Depression diminished Father Divine's appeal and relevance. Moving to his Philadelphia estate in 1942 to avoid a lawsuit, he became separated from his base of support. The death of his first wife, Peninnah, known as "Mother Divine," generated doubt about Father Divine's promise of everlasting life for the faithful. Father Divine's assertion that Peninnah was reincarnated in the form of his second wife, "Sweet Angel," a young, white Canadian whom he married in 1946, cast further suspicion on his omnipotence. He made few public appearances in the 1950s, and rumors of his failing health quickly spread. The man who would be God died of diabetes in 1965, but to a small band of stoic believers, he still exists in spirit.

The acquisition of great wealth and claims of divinity invite comparisons between Father Divine and DADDY GRACE, another flamboyant black minister of the period. However, the breadth of Father Divine's poverty programs, the extent of his political activism, and his use of theology to address social conditions suggest that he had more in common with MARCUS GARVEY as a colorful, complex, and important historical figure.

FURTHER READING

The papers of Father Divine are held by the Peace Mission in Philadelphia, Pennsylvania Many of his sermons, essays, beliefs, and writings of Father Divine are published in the Peace Mission's two newspapers, *Spoken Word* and *New Day*.

Fauset, Arthur Huff. *Black Gods of the Metropolis* (1971).

Watts, Jill. *God, Harlem U.S.A. The Father Divine Story* (1992).

Weisbrot, Robert. *Father Divine and the Struggle for Racial Equality* (1983).

Obituary: *New York Times*, 11 Sept. 1965.
—SHOLOMO B. LEVY

 FAUSET, CRYSTAL BIRD (27 June 1893– 28 Mar. 1965), legislator and activist, was born Crystal Dreda Bird in Princess Anne, Maryland, the daughter of Benjamin Bird, a high school principal, and Portia E. Lovett. Crystal's father died when she was only four, and her mother took over his principalship of the all-black Princess Anne Academy until her own death in 1900. An orphan by age seven, Crystal remained true to her parents' commitment to education. Ironically, her early loss probably improved the educational opportunities of a child born to Maryland's segregated Eastern Shore. Reared by an aunt in Boston, she attended public school, graduated from the city's Normal School in 1914, and taught for three years. She later earned a BS from Columbia University Teacher's College in 1931.

Her personal success notwithstanding, Crystal Bird came to realize that racial inequality was an American, rather than merely a southern, dilemma. In 1918, on the eve of the Great Migration, she began work as a field secretary for the Young Woman's Christian Association, organizing social programs for black women. Traveling throughout the nation, she began to make the connections between race, gender, and class that informed a lifelong crusade for justice.

Although the 1920s witnessed the emergence of a race-conscious "New Negro," Bird developed an enduring faith in interracial cooperation. Beginning in 1927 she worked with the interracial section of the American Friends Service Committee, whose purpose was to articulate to whites the needs and desires of African Americans. She continued this mission six years later, when she helped found Pennsylvania's Swarthmore College Institute of Race Relations.

The misery of the Great Depression convinced Crystal Bird of the need to ground interracial cooperation in political action. The sight of "long, patient bread lines opposite swank Central Park Apartments" persuaded her that the New Deal offered the best hope of change. Resident in Philadelphia since her marriage in 1931 to high school principal and political columnist Arthur Huff Fauset (they would have no children), she joined the Democratic Party just as it began to challenge that city's well-entrenched Republican machine. Addressing Democrats in 1935, she lashed out at the "orgy of Republican mismanagement" in Philadelphia's City Hall and pleaded that "living people be given a chance to live."

One year later Fauset made her mark in national politics, serving as director of colored women's activities for the Democratic National Committee. Although many blacks benefited from the New Deal, her work proved no easy task. In the previous election, most African Americans had remained loyal to the party of Abraham Lincoln, and segregated New Deal agencies threatened to keep them in the GOP column. Furthermore, Fauset had to counter the Republican charge that Franklin D. Roosevelt, who had at that time proposed no civil rights legislation, was beholden to southern Democrats. Nonetheless, Fauset reminded northern blacks that they too could wield the ballot to counter the white South. Using the trump card of first lady Eleanor Roosevelt, Fauset urged blacks to cast "sentimentality and tradition aside" in support of a "great humanitarian effort."

The 1936 campaign won Fauset plaudits, and two years later she won her party's nomination for a state legislative race. Promising to push for slum clearance, affordable housing, and fair employment legislation, she, along with two white Democrats, easily defeated three Republican candidates.

In the Philadelphia *Afro-American*, Fauset declared her election less a personal victory, than a "recognition of colored womanhood." In one sense that was true: African American women had mobilized throughout the city, boosting black participation as a whole, thereby increasing the Democratic vote. Yet Fauset had won election from West Philadelphia, then an ethnically diverse but predominantly white section of the city. The electoral returns suggest that both whites and blacks had voted the straight Democratic ticket. Community leaders who had recently initiated interracial forums on a variety of issues may also have encouraged white racial tolerance.

As the first black woman elected to a state legislature, Crystal Fauset emerged in the first rank of African American leaders. The *Crisis* magazine, black America's preeminent journal of opinion, heralded her victory on its cover. Likewise, black newspapers followed her speeches avidly, highlighting her appeal that black women actively engage in the making of history.

Yet that same national reputation may have convinced Fauset that she needed a broader stage. After barely a year, she left her Pennsylvania assembly seat to work as a race relations adviser for the state's Works Progress Administration. Then, in October 1941, she emerged as race relations adviser to the Office of Civilian Defense (OCD), a position vital to the coming war effort. Her duties included the coordination of nationwide OCD race programs, publicizing the African American role in the war effort, and promoting black participation in civil defense activities. In pursuing these goals, writer Roi Ottley noted, Fauset displayed "exceeding resiliency under pressure" (*"New World A-Coming": Inside Black America*, 264). As one of only two women in the black cabinet, she now also had the ear of Eleanor Roosevelt, an old friend from the Swarthmore Institute.

The year 1944 proved to be a turning point in Fauset's political and personal life. Going back to electoral politics, she resigned from the OCD to work full time for the Democratic National Committee. However, a tense relationship with the DNC's chairman, Robert E. Hannegan, provoked her to not only resign but also to endorse Republican

Thomas Dewey for president. Fauset attacked the Democratic chairman as "a dictator...not willing to deal democratically with Negroes." But critics suggested that frustrated ambition explained Fauset's decision. The staunchly Democratic Chicago *Defender* noted, for instance, that Fauset had failed to be appointed recorder of deeds in Washington, D.C. Whatever the reason, her defection prompted one further lifestyle change. Although she and Arthur Fauset had been separated for some time, her husband, a Democrat, filed for divorce a mere two days after she bolted to the GOP.

After World War II, Fauset continued to seek interracial cooperation but focused more on global issues. She helped found the United Nations Council of Philadelphia in 1945, attended the inaugural session of the United Nations in San Francisco, and coordinated programs to promote understanding between whites and people of color. But as African nations gained independence, she became more critical of her own nation's failures with regard to race, protesting in 1957 that a delegation to celebrate Ghana's independence did not include "a woman like myself...to represent the millions of slave mothers" who had built America.

Fauset died in Philadelphia, just a few short months before the passage of the Voting Rights Act, the zenith of the interracial cause to which she had dedicated her life.

FURTHER READING

Fauset left no consolidated manuscript collection, but much information can be gleaned from the many organizations for which she worked. The Archives of the YWCA (Young Women's Christian Association) in New York City and the Records of the American Friends Service Committee in Philadelphia contain materials pertaining to her early career. The Records of the Office of Civilian Defense, RG 171 of the National Archives, offer a wealth of information on Fauset's OCD activities.

"Mrs. Fauset Fails to Get D.C. Post, Bolts Demos," *Chicago Defender*, 16 Sept. 1944.
"Mrs. Fauset Sees Social Security of Mrs. Roosevelt in White House," *Washington Tribune*, 18 Oct. 1936.

Obituaries: *New York Times*, 30 Mar. 1965; *New York Amsterdam News*, 3 Apr. 1965.
—STEVEN J. NIVEN

FAUSET, JESSIE REDMON

FAUSET, JESSIE REDMON (27 Apr. 1882– 30 Apr. 1961), writer, editor, and teacher, was born outside Philadelphia, Pennsylvania, in Camden County, New Jersey, the daughter of Redmon Fauset, an African Methodist Episcopal minister, and Annie Seamon. Fauset was probably the first black woman at Cornell University, where she graduated Phi Beta Kappa with a degree in Classical and Modern Languages in 1905. She taught briefly in Baltimore before accepting a job teaching French and Latin at the famed all-black M Street (later Dunbar) High School in Washington, D.C. While teaching, Fauset completed an MA in French at the University of Pennsylvania (1919).

From 1912 to 1929 Fauset contributed numerous articles, reviews, poems, short stories, essays, and translations of French West Indian poems to the *Crisis*, the official publication of the National Association for the Advancement of Colored People. At the urging of its editor, W. E. B. DU BOIS, she moved to New York City to become the literary editor of the *Crisis* from 1919 to 1926. She was instrumental in discovering and publishing most of the best-known writers of the Harlem Renaissance, including LANGSTON HUGHES, CLAUDE MCKAY, JEAN TOOMER, and COUNTÉE CULLEN. In 1920–1921 Fauset also edited a monthly magazine for African American children called *Brownies' Book*. During this period Fauset and her sister made the apartment they shared in Harlem a salon where the black intelligentsia and their allies gathered to discuss art and politics.

Although she exercised substantial influence as a literary mentor, Fauset is best known for her writing. Her poetry appeared in the *Crisis* and was published in numerous anthologies. Her essays and articles run the gamut from Montessori education to international politics to travel essays about her experiences as a delegate to the second Pan-African Congress held in London, Brussels, and Paris in 1921. Her best-known essay, "The Gift of Laughter" (1925), is an analysis of the black comic character in American drama. Fauset is primarily known, however, for her four novels—*There Is Confusion* (1924), *Plum Bun* (1929), *The Chinaberry Tree* (1931),

and *Comedy: American Style* (1933)—all novels of manners centering on the careers, courtships, and marriages of the black professional classes, Du Bois's so-called talented tenth.

Fauset and fellow Harlem Renaissance writers WALTER WHITE and NELLA LARSEN, with whom she is frequently compared, were all galvanized into print by the 1922 publication of T. S. Stribling's *Birthright*, a best-selling novel about a mixed race Harvard graduate written by a white man. In a 1932 interview, Fauset remembered how she felt when *Birthright* was published: "Here is an audience waiting to hear the truth about us. Let us who are better qualified to present that truth than any white writer try to do so" (*Southern Workman*, May 1932, 218–219). *There Is Confusion* (1924) was her first attempt to present that truth. Du Bois called it "the novel that the Negro intelligentsia have been clamoring for" (*Crisis*, Feb. 1924, 162). It offered some refreshingly positive images of black characters: Joanna Marshall turns the street dances of African American children into a successful stage career; Peter Bye overcomes his bitterness toward the white branch of his family and becomes a surgeon; and Maggie Ellersley, a poor laundress's daughter, establishes her own lucrative chain of beauty shops.

Fauset traveled in Europe and studied French at the Sorbonne and the Alliance Française in Paris in 1925. She left her job as an editor at the *Crisis* in 1926 in order to find employment that would allow her more time for writing. Discrimination made it impossible for her to work in a New York publishing house, so she returned to teaching. From 1927 to 1944 she taught at a Harlem junior high school and DeWitt Clinton High School in New York City.

In 1929 Fauset published her second and best novel, *Plum Bun*, a story about light-skinned Angela Murray, who abandons her darker-complexioned sister to "pass" for white, initially seeking to marry a white man to gain access to power and wealth. Here Fauset turned nursery rhymes and the traditional romance plot to alternative uses, unveiling the complex ways in which racism and sexism make the happy endings such plots promise impossible for black women to achieve. In 1929 Fauset married Herbert E. Harris, an insurance executive. They had no children.

Fauset's third novel, *The Chinaberry Tree* (1931), explores issues of miscegenation, illegitimacy, and "respectability" as they are played out in a small New Jersey town. Only after white writer Zona Gale agreed to write an introduction to the novel testifying that blacks such as those Fauset depicted—middle-class, hard-working, "respectable" blacks—really existed did the publisher agree to go ahead with the book. Most white publishers and readers preferred black characters that did not challenge stereotypes—primitive, exotic characters displaying uninhibited sexuality in Harlem's slums—to Fauset's portraits of the black professional classes.

Fauset's final novel, *Comedy: American Style* (1933), explores the damage wreaked on the lives of a middle-class black family by the internalized racism of the mother. Olivia Cary's obsession with whiteness leads to the suicide of her dark-complexioned son, the unhappy marriage of her light-skinned daughter to a racist white man, and the emotional and material ruin that follow alienation from their community.

Fauset continued to travel extensively, lecturing on black writers to audiences of various types. She was visiting professor at Hampton Institute in 1949 and taught French and writing at Tuskegee Institute. She died in Philadelphia.

Fauset's literary reputation has experienced some dramatic turns. Initial reviews in both the black and the white press were generally positive. William Stanley Braithwaite, for example, called Fauset "the potential Jane Austen of Negro Literature" (*Opportunity*, Jan. 1934, 50). During the 1960s and 1970s, however, critics of African American literature preferred accounts of poverty and racial protest to Fauset's portrayals of the black elite. Robert Bone, labeling her novels "uniformly sophomoric, trivial, and dull," placed Fauset in the "Rear Guard" of the Harlem Renaissance, contrasting her conservatism with the more politically confrontational texts of younger writers. Feminist critics of the 1980s and 1990s, however, recuperated much of Fauset's work. Fauset's plots—dismissed by earlier critics as melodramatic, sentimental, and marred by coincidence—have been interpreted

anew as sites for investigating how class and race complicate the traditional romance plot. Given the structure of American society in the 1920s and 1930s—institutionalized racism and sexism and white control of publishing houses and patronage—Fauset's achievements as an important actor in Harlem literary culture and a theorist of gender, race, and power are particularly noteworthy.

FURTHER READING

Fauset manuscript materials are at the Moorland-Spingarn Research Center at Howard University.

Christian, Barbara. *Black Women Novelists: The Development of a Tradition, 1892–1976* (1980).
McDowell, Deborah. "The Neglected Dimension of Jessie Redmon Fauset" in *Conjuring: Black Women, Fiction, and Literary Theory*, eds. Marjorie Pryse and Hortense Spillers (1985).
Sylvander, Carolyn Wedin. *Jessie Redmon Fauset, Black American Writer* (1981).
Wall, Cheryl. "Jessie Redmon Fauset, 1882–1961" in *Gender of Modernism*, ed. Bonnie Kime Scott (1990).
Watson, Carole McAlpine. *Prologue: The Novels of Black American Women, 1891–1965* (1985).

Obituary: *New York Times*, 3 May 1961.
—ERIN A. SMITH

 FETCHIT, STEPIN

(30 May 1892 or 1902–19 Nov. 1985), actor, was born Lincoln Theodore Monroe Andrew Perry in Key West, Florida, the son of a cigar-maker. Little is known of his family or upbringing. He frequented racetracks as a boy, began working at age fourteen in carnivals and medicine shows as "Rastus, the Buck Dancer," and was jailed for larceny as a young man. Before going into movies, he danced in vaudeville as half of a team called "Step 'n' Fetchit, the Two Dancing Fools from Dixie," taking the name from a horse that Perry had bet and won on. After the act split up, Perry kept the name for his solo vaudeville act.

Fetchit's movie career was launched when he won the role of a stable boy in MGM's *In Old Kentucky* (1927), soon

followed by other bit parts, including a river pilot in the first film version of *Show Boat* (1929). However, it was in Fox Film Corporation's *Hearts in Dixie* (1929) that Fetchit established his movie reputation in the role of Gummy, a shiftless plantation lackey with a slack-jawed expression, bald head, lanky body, and slow-motion style of moving and speaking. This was the first of a long line of lazy, shuffling, whining, dim-witted black menials that Fetchit was to portray for Fox in more than forty films.

When black reporter Ruby Berkley Goodwin interviewed Fetchit for a 1929 *Pittsburgh Courier* article, she was surprised that Fetchit was "an energetic man with a collegiate look and a nervous quality that showed itself in his gesticulating and restless movements." In later years he was accused of perpetuating a negative racial stereotype, but he replied, "I was just playing a character, and that character did a lot of good" (*Los Angeles Times*, 20 Nov. 1985, 3). "If I hadn't broken that [door]," he said in a later interview, "all the things that BILL COSBY and SIDNEY POITIER have done wouldn't be possible. I set up thrones for them to come and sit on" (*New York Times*, 20 Nov. 1985, D31).

Among Fetchit's best-remembered feature films were those he made with Will Rogers, including *David Harum* and *Judge Priest* (both 1934). In *David Harum* Fetchit played a stable groom who is sold several times, along with a worn-out horse, in a classic comedy horse-trading scam. In *Judge Priest* he played a prisoner brought before the judge (Rogers) for chicken-stealing; afterwards, in the judge's personal custody, he is the constant target of his insults and physical abuse, but they develop a rather poignant friendship.

Fetchit made movies with Shirley Temple (*The Littlest Rebel*, 1935; *Dimples*, 1936), Spencer Tracy (*Marie Galante*, 1934), Don Ameche and Ann Sothern (*Fifty Roads to Town*, 1937). He also appeared in *Charlie Chan in Egypt* (1935), but his portrayal of Charlie's black servant as stupid and inarticulate was unsuitable, and he was replaced in following films.

By the early 1940s Fetchit had earned and squandered more than two million dollars. He tried to offset his degrading screen image by living the flamboyant lifestyle of a movie star; he owned

Known for his comic minstrel roles first in vaudeville and then in more than forty Hollywood films, Stepin Fetchit here waits to board a plane to a meeting of the NAACP in New York in 1934. © Bettmann/CORBIS

twelve cars (one a pink Rolls-Royce) driven by chauffeurs, fifty suits, and six homes staffed with Chinese servants. His lavish parties, public brawls, and involvement in a paternity suit were highly publicized. He was married and divorced three times and had two sons, one of whom committed suicide after allegedly killing three people in Pennsylvania in 1969.

By 1947 Fetchit had been dropped by Fox and declared bankruptcy. For the next few years he worked in nightclubs and made a few all-black films, including *Miracle in Harlem* (1947). In 1951, after a period of remorse and repentance, he was able to get a few movie roles, but by this time his stereotypical portrayals were no longer acceptable, and his film career could not be resuscitated.

In the late 1960s Fetchit became a part of boxer MUHAMMAD ALI's entourage and embraced the Black Muslim faith. In 1968, at the height of the civil rights movement, he was one of the subjects of a CBS television documentary, *Black History: Lost, Stolen or Strayed*, in which he was accused of creating and perpetuating unfavorable images of black people. In 1970 he sued CBS for defamation of character, asking damages of three million dollars, but a

federal judge dismissed the case in 1974 on the grounds that Fetchit was a public figure, and that only his role had been criticized, not the actor personally.

From 1977 to his final illness Fetchit resided at the Motion Picture and Television Country House in Los Angeles. He died of complications from pneumonia and congestive heart failure in the Motion Picture and Television Hospital in Woodland Hills, Los Angeles. His age at death was officially reported as eighty-three, although he had sometimes claimed to be ten years younger.

Fetchit's films are seldom shown today, and when they are, his scenes are usually cut to avoid offending African Americans; nonetheless, he should not be denied a place in film history. He received a special Image Award from the Hollywood Chapter of the NAACP in 1976 and was elected to the Black Filmmakers Hall of Fame in 1978, for his pioneering contributions. He was the first black man to be featured in a succession of films by a major studio. When he broke down the doors that had been closed to black performers, he made it possible for thousands of others to pass through.

FURTHER READING

Bogle, Donald. *Blacks in American Films and Television: An Illustrated Encyclopedia* (1988).

———. *Toms, Coons, Mulattoes, Mammies, and Bucks: An Interpretive History of Blacks in American Films* (1973).
Boskin, Joe. *Sambo: The Rise and Demise of an American Jester* (1986).
Cripps, Thomas. *Slow Fade to Black: The Negro in American Film* (1977).
Leab, Daniel J. *From Sambo to Superspade: The Black Experience in Motion Pictures* (1975).
—BERNARD L. PETERSON

FITZGERALD, ELLA

(25 Apr. 1917–15 June 1996), singer and songwriter, was born Ella Jane Fitzgerald in Newport News, Virginia, the only child of William Fitzgerald, a transfer wagon driver, and Temperance Williams, a laundress and caterer. Fitzgerald never knew her father; her mother married Joseph Da Silva, a Portuguese immigrant, when Fitzgerald was three years old. Following the tide of the Great Migration, the family moved north to Yonkers, New York. Fitzgerald's half-sister, Frances, was born there in 1923.

Fitzgerald's childhood is scantily documented; throughout her life she remained extremely reluctant to grant interviews and to reveal much about her early years in particular. She belonged to Bethany African Methodist Episcopal Church and received her education via various public schools, where she excelled in her studies. At some point she took a few private piano lessons and learned the rudiments of reading music. Singing and dancing were her early loves, and Fitzgerald would show off the latest steps to earn small change on neighborhood street corners and in local clubs. Her mother brought home records by Mamie Smith, the Mills Brothers, and white singing trio the Boswell sisters. Throughout her career Fitzgerald singled out Connee Boswell, leader of the group and a popular solo artist, as an important early musical influence.

After her mother died in 1932, Fitzgerald was allegedly abused by her stepfather and moved to Harlem to live with her mother's sister, Virginia. Like many other children during the Great Depression, she dropped out of school in the scuffle for economic survival. She

Ella Fitzgerald during a television appearance on the Dinah Shore Chevy Show *in 1959.* © Bettmann/CORBIS

worked running numbers and as a lookout for a local "sporting house," knocking on the door in warning if the police should be nearby. Unfortunately, she must have been caught. Through the family court system, Fitzgerald was sent to Public School 49 in Riverdale-on-Hudson, essentially an orphanage. Thus began a harrowing episode in her life that she never publicly acknowledged.

Overwhelmed with children—P.S. 49 was the only facility for blacks—Fitzgerald was transferred to the New York State Training School for Girls at Hudson, euphemistically labeled a reform school. In addition to the overcrowded and dilapidated quarters, the girls routinely endured beatings by male staff members. Punishments included shackles and solitary confinement (*New York Times*, 23 June 1996). After her release Fitzgerald joined Harlem's homeless.

In contrast to singer BILLIE HOLIDAY, for whom similar childhood traumas came to inform her tragic persona,

Fitzgerald apparently sought to excise these experiences from her memory. Instead she cultivated a guileless, happy-go-lucky image through her musical repertory and interviews, one that she perpetuated throughout her life. These traits had an added benefit; they formed a protective insulation that allowed her to negotiate the male-dominated musical culture she soon entered.

The story of Fitzgerald's victory at Apollo Theater's Amateur Night contest on 21 November 1934 has become the stuff of legend. She intended to compete as a dancer, but the presence of the Edwards Sisters, a well-known and glamorously attired dancing team, unnerved her. Instead she sang "Object of My Affection" and "Judy," songs she learned from Boswell's versions.

As her prize, Fitzgerald should have been given a week's engagement at the theater, but she looked so disheveled from living on the streets that the management would not allow it. A second win the following February, this time

at the Harlem Opera House, earned her a week-long spot with the Tiny Bradshaw Band. Her real break, however, came that spring with her gradual addition to the Chick Webb Orchestra. Already widely admired as a drummer and bandleader, the twenty-seven-year-old Webb craved popular success. His gamble on the young "girl singer" helped turn the band into a lucrative commercial venture that rivaled any such ensemble across the country.

Fitzgerald's career ushered in a new era for popular singers in which they were no longer ancillary performers in big bands, but rather powerful, independent artists. During the early swing era, singers were typically limited to one vocal chorus within a band's arrangement of a given song, and to one or two numbers during a live set. Webb however afforded Fitzgerald an unprecedented amount of the spotlight, and within months of joining the band, she dominated its recorded output. By 1937 she was given equal billing with Webb. Some three months after his death in June 1939 (Webb had battled tuberculosis of the spine), the group was rechristened Ella Fitzgerald and Her Famous Orchestra.

Her talents warranted the high profile. Already exhibiting the vocal ease, perfect intonation, and exuberant swing for which she became admired, Fitzgerald scored her first two hits in 1936: "Sing Me a Swing Song (And Let Me Dance)" and "(If You Can't Sing It) You'll Have to Swing It" (also known as "Mr. Paganini"). However, it was her refashioning of a children's nursery rhyme that made her the most popular singer in America, black or white, at a time when "race music" rarely crossed over into the mainstream. Fitzgerald cowrote "A-Tisket, A-Tasket" (1938) with arranger Al Feldman, later known as Van Alexander. She authored several other songs over the course of her career and was a member of the American Society of Composers, Authors, and Publishers (ASCAP).

Fitzgerald embarked on a solo career in 1942, but her popularity temporarily waned. Her repertory had been built on commercial dance band arrangements and "novelty" tunes subject to changing fashion. She was thought of as a pop singer rather than a jazz singer, categories she ultimately transcended.

Fitzgerald had always possessed an uncanny ear, and she began to pick up the new harmonic and rhythmic vocabulary of bebop being developed by musicians such as saxophonist CHARLIE PARKER and trumpeter DIZZY GILLESPIE. Scat singing, a kind of wordless vocal improvisation, had been part of Fitzgerald's performances since "You'll Have to Swing It." In that song, scat was considered nothing more than an entertaining gimmick, but Fitzgerald would be among the first singers to emulate the virtuosic bebop solo by "using her voice like a horn," a metaphor common among musicians. In such instances, the song was not a vehicle for storytelling or psychological drama, but rather a springboard that launched her own improvisational flights.

In fact, Fitzgerald counted among the rare musicians who made the stylistic transition from swing to bebop. She toured the South with Gillespie's big band in 1946 and found that jamming nightly with the instrumentalists honed her skills. Around this time, she added three staples to her repertory that became landmarks of vocal jazz: the wordless "Flying High," "Lady Be Good," and "How High the Moon," the source of the chord changes for Charlie Parker's "Ornithology." Fitzgerald consistently referenced Parker's melody in her performances, making her connection to bebop musically explicit.

Behind the scenes, Fitzgerald had met bassist Ray Brown, also on the road with Gillespie, and married him the following year. (He was her second husband; her 1941 union with Ben Kornegay was annulled when manager Moe Gale discovered the groom's criminal past.) The Browns adopted Fitzgerald's nephew, named Ray Jr., but the relationship could not bear their frenetic and often separate touring schedules. They divorced in 1953, yet continued to work together intermittently.

A new phase in Fitzgerald's career began in the 1950s through her association with impresario Norman Granz, an exceptional promoter of both jazz and racial equality. His *Jazz at the Philharmonic* (JATP) programs brought the music from clubs into concert halls, not only across the United States but also in Europe, Asia, and Australia, creating worldwide recognition for those musicians he presented. Fitzgerald toured

with JATP for the first time in 1949, and Granz became her manager in 1953. He liberated her from her longtime recording contract with Decca in 1955 to record for his own new Verve label.

Under Granz's direction she completed a series of groundbreaking "songbooks" dedicated to the work of individual composers and lyricists: Cole Porter (1956), Richard Rodgers and Lorenz Hart (1956), DUKE ELLINGTON (1957), George and Ira Gershwin (1959), and Harold Arlen (1961). With Fitzgerald's performances faithful to the original melodies and with little in the way of embellishment, the songbooks sought to elevate these works from Broadway theater, movie musicals, and dance halls to the status of art song. They further helped Fitzgerald cross over from jazz to general audiences, where she continued to break color barriers in exclusive clubs and other venues.

Granz sold Verve in 1960 but remained Fitzgerald's manager; she moved to the West Coast Capitol label in 1966. Although she attempted to keep up with the pop music of the day, singing songs by the Beatles, among others, she eventually realized that the time for covering other people's compositions was over, and returned to her tried-and-true repertory.

In the decades that followed, she continued to perform and record as much as her health allowed. Fitzgerald underwent open-heart surgery in 1986. Diabetes led to eyesight and circulatory problems, including the amputation of a toe in 1987 and both legs below the knees in 1993, shortly after she retired from performing. She died in her Beverly Hills home in 1996, the recipient of some thirteen Grammy Awards, eight honorary PhDs, the National Medal for the Arts, and a Kennedy Center award.

FURTHER READING

Ella Fitzgerald's music and business papers are housed at the Library of Congress.

Gourse, Leslie. *The Ella Fitzgerald Companion* (1998).
Nicholson, Stuart. *Ella Fitzgerald: A Biography of the First Lady of Song* (1993; additions 1996).
Pleasants, Henry. *The Great American Popular Singers* (1974).

Obituary: *New York Times*, 16 June 1996.

—LARA PELLEGRINELLI

 FLIPPER, HENRY OSSIAN (21 Mar. 1856– 3 May 1940), soldier and engineer, was born in Thomasville, Georgia, the son of Festus Flipper and Isabelle (maiden name unknown), slaves. During the Civil War and Reconstruction he was educated in American Missionary Association schools and in 1873 gained admission to Atlanta University. That year Flipper also obtained an appointment to the U.S. Military Academy through the auspices of Republican Representative James C. Freeman. He was not the first African American to attend West Point, as Michael Howard and James Webster Smith preceded him in 1870, but neither graduated. Flipper subsequently endured four years of grueling academic instruction and ostracism from white classmates before graduating fiftieth in a class of sixty-four on 14 June 1877. He was commissioned second lieutenant in the all-black Tenth U.S. Cavalry, and the following year recounted his academy experience in an autobiography, *The Colored Cadet at West Point* (1878).

Flipper enjoyed a brief but active military career. He was billeted at various frontier posts, including Forts Elliott, Concho, Davis, and Quitman in

Henry O. Flipper, the first African American to graduate from the United States Military Academy at West Point, in 1877. Schomburg Center

Texas, and Fort Sill, Indian Territory (now Okla.), and engaged in numerous engineering activities. This regimen included drainage of swamps at Fort Sill, building a wagon road from that post to Gainesville, Texas, and installing telegraph lines from Fort Elliott, Texas, to Camp Supply, Indian Territory. Flipper also distinguished himself in the 1880 war against the Apache Victorio and earned commendation from Colonel Benjamin H. Grierson. He was then posted as acting commissary of subsistence at Fort Davis in November 1881, when Colonel William R. Shafter accused him of embezzling $3,791.77 in missing commissary funds that were assumed to be stolen. A court-martial cleared Flipper of all charges but found him guilty of "conduct unbecoming an officer and a gentleman," and dismissed him from the service on 30 June 1882. For the rest of his life Flipper professed his innocence and ascribed the end of his military career to racial prejudice.

As a civilian, Flipper remained in the West for nearly half a century and distinguished himself in a variety of mining, engineering, and surveying work. Commencing in 1883, he functioned in northern Mexico as a cartographer for the Banco Minero and as chief engineer for several American mining concerns. Fluent in Spanish, Flipper became an authority on Spanish and Mexican land law, and in 1891 he represented Nogales, Arizona, in an important land grant case. His expertise convinced Justice Department officials to appoint him as a special agent in the court of private claims. In 1882 he published *Mexico Laws, Statutes, etc.*, which was long held as a definitive treatise on the subject.

Flipper returned to northern Mexico in 1901 and spent the next eleven years as resident engineer for a number of American mining companies. In this capacity he befriended Albert Fall, a future U.S. senator from New Mexico, with whom Flipper exchanged extensive correspondence during the Mexican Revolution. When Fall became secretary of the interior in 1921, he appointed Flipper as an assistant working on the commission tasked with locating, constructing, and operating railroads in Alaska. After Fall was implicated in the Teapot Dome scandal of 1923, Flipper left the Interior Department to work for an oil company in Venezuela

and compiled another significant work, *Venezuela Laws, Statutes, etc.* (1925). He returned to Atlanta in 1930 to reside with his brother, Bishop Joseph Flipper of the African Methodist Episcopal Church. Flipper died in Atlanta.

Flipper is best remembered as the first African American graduate of West Point and for the controversy surrounding his dismissal. However, his forty-eight-year career as an engineer established him as an important figure in western development. Furthermore, Flipper's impressive linguistic and legal credentials were valuable assets for the growth of mining industries in both the United States and Mexico. His civilian endeavors were all conspicuously marked by the high moral conduct and methodological problem solving imparted to him at West Point. Although he was denied vindication by the military while he was alive, in December 1976 the Department of the Army finally granted him a posthumous honorable discharge and a military reinterment. Furthermore, on 3 May 1977 a bust of Flipper was unveiled at West Point, signifying formal recognition from the institution that had so scorned him. Apparently, he never married.

FURTHER READING

Flipper's military correspondence is in RG 94, Records of the Adjutant General, National Archives. Scattered personal materials are in the Benjamin H. Grierson Papers, Texas Tech University, Lubbock; and the Frank H. Edmund Papers, U.S. Military Academy.

Black, Lowell D. *An Officer and a Gentleman* (1985).
Harris, Theodore D., ed. *Negro Frontiersman: The Western Memoirs of Henry O. Flipper* (1963).
Robinson, Charles M. *The Court-martial of Lieutenant Flipper* (1994).

—JOHN C. FREDRIKSEN

FLOOD, CURT

(18 Jan. 1938–20 Jan. 1997), baseball player and artist, was born Curtis Charles Flood in Houston, Texas, the youngest of six children of Herman and Laura Flood. In 1940 the family moved to Oakland, California. Flood's older brother, Carl, who had trouble with the

law from childhood, slipped into a life of crime. Flood, however, began playing midget-league baseball at the age of nine. George Powles coached the team and produced, besides Curt Flood, such players as Frank Robinson, Vada Pinson, Joe Morgan, and Jesse Gonder. The other factor that kept Flood out of trouble was encountering Jim Chambers, who encouraged his interest and development as an artist at Herbert Hoover High School in Oakland. Flood played baseball throughout his teenage years and became a promising athlete. However, he was small, weighing barely one hundred forty pounds and standing only five feet, seven inches tall as a senior in high school. Despite his diminutive stature, he was signed by the Cincinnati Reds in 1956 for a salary of four thousand dollars. He received no bonus for signing, but the contract was impressive for a working-class boy who had just graduated from high school.

As a minor league player in Tampa, Florida, Flood had to endure the racial taunts and slurs that other black ball players suffered when playing newly integrated baseball in the South. Having grown up on the West Coast, he had never encountered the uncompromising nature of southern segregation, and it was quite a revelation to him. The odds were not in Flood's favor of making it to the major leagues, but he hit .340 in his first year of professional baseball, including twenty-nine home runs. He briefly came up to play with the Reds at the end of the season—Flood was being groomed by the team to be a third baseman—but he had little future in that position with the organization. So, in 1957 Cincinnati traded Flood to the St. Louis Cardinals, who made him a centerfielder, a position he held for them for the next twelve years.

At the time Flood joined the Cardinals, they were geographically the southernmost major league team. Owned by August Busch Jr., who also owned the Anheuser-Busch brewing company, and who was, in many respects, predictably conservative, the team itself exhibited surprisingly liberal tendencies for its day. Minority and white players got along very well, and the team insisted on integrated accommodations for its players during spring training. Under managers Johnny Keane and Red Schoendienst, the team flourished on the field

Curt Flood, whose challenge of baseball's reserve clause eventually led to salary arbitration and the age of the free agent in sports. Baseball Hall of Fame

in the mid-1960s. With stars such as pitcher Bob Gibson, third baseman Ken Boyer, second baseman Julian Javier, first baseman Bill White, and outfielder Lou Brock, along with the outstanding play of Flood, who was not only a good hitter but one of the best defensive outfielders of his day, the Cardinals won the World Series in 1964, beating the New York Yankees. Adding outfielder Roger Maris and first baseman Orlando Cepeda, they won again in 1967, beating the Boston Red Sox. St. Louis went to the World Series again in 1968, but lost to the Detroit Tigers in seven games. Busch began to break up his championship team in 1968, and the Cardinals did not go the World Series again until 1982.

In October 1969, after a disappointing season for St. Louis, Flood, catcher Tim McCarver, and pitcher Byron Browne were traded to the Philadelphia Phillies. Flood was thirty-one years old in 1969, and the Cardinals thought, reasonably enough, that the outfielder's best years were behind him. Flood, shocked and disappointed by the trade and what he took to be the team's cavalier treatment of him, refused to accept it. At first he considered retiring. He had a lucrative business as a portrait artist in St. Louis and many other ties in the city. Moreover, he had heard that Philadelphia was a tough place for a black player to play, though the Phillies offered Flood a salary of ninety thousand dollars, a handsome sum at the time.

After thinking the matter over and talking with his friend Marian Jorgensen, Flood decided to sue Bowie K. Kuhn, Commissioner of Baseball, and the American and National Leagues over baseball's reserve clause, which prevented Flood from being able to negotiate with any team he wished that might desire his services. Flood presented his

case to his union, the Players Association, and its new executive director, Marvin Miller, who, though thinking the suit was ill timed and not likely to succeed, supported Flood. His fellow players simply wanted Flood's assurances that he was not challenging the league for racial reasons, which he insisted he was not. Former Supreme Court justice Arthur Goldberg represented Flood.

Flood was not the first player to challenge the reserve clause, which was established in the 1870s and made a player permanently the property of the particular team that possessed his contract; however, he became the most famous. Baseball owners argued that without the reserve clause, their leagues would have no stability, because players would simply move from team to team in order to leverage the highest salary. The history of early baseball actually supported this contention by the owners. However, the main reason for the reserve clause was to control player salaries by not permitting them to offer their services in an open market. The baseball team owners essentially argued that it was a monopoly that could not function successfully unless it completely controlled the freedom of its employees, a position supported by the U.S. Supreme Court, which had exempted professional baseball teams from antitrust laws in 1922.

Flood was facing long odds in his lawsuit. The public was decidedly against him, not feeling great sympathy for a man claiming to be a "slave" and being treated like "a consignment of goods" who was making ninety thousand dollars a year. Most sportswriters were similarly unsympathetic, as were the lower federal courts and the Second Circuit Court of Appeals. Flood lost his case and sat out the 1970 season. While appealing the case to the Supreme Court, he returned to baseball briefly, playing for the Washington Senators, which had made a deal with Philadelphia to get him. But Flood left the Senators after playing only thirteen games. He felt that he no longer had the desire or the ability to play, especially in the face of hostility from the baseball establishment, and he moved to Copenhagen, Denmark, where he spent most of the 1970s. He never played professional baseball again.

On 18 June 1972, the Supreme Court affirmed the Second Circuit's ruling by a vote of five to three. Even though the Court ruled against him, Flood had generated enormous publicity and discussion about the reserve clause. By the end of 1972 baseball owners agreed to salary arbitration, the beginning of the end of the reserve clause. In 1975 pitchers Andy Messersmith and Dave McNally challenged the reserve clause by working one year without a contract and then declaring themselves free agents. They won their case in labor arbitration, and the age of free agency had arrived.

Flood was right in calling himself "a child of the sixties." There was a strong element of protest and reform in his challenge. Other black athletes of the time, most notably MUHAMMAD ALI, openly defied society's expectations of them and challenged the businesses for which they worked. But the issue here, actually, transcends race and is more powerfully related to athletes being seen by the public as more than mere performers or machines, but as men and women with vital concerns about their well-being and with vital interests that they should be permitted to protect. It must be remembered that all Flood wanted was the right to offer his services to any major league team, the same freedom to move from one job to another that most Americans enjoy.

Flood, who had been a heavy smoker, died of throat cancer at the age of fifty-nine. He was survived by his wife, actress Judy Pace, and a child by a previous relationship. In 1998 Congress passed the Curt Flood Act, giving Major League Baseball players the same protection under antitrust laws that all other athletes enjoyed.

FURTHER READING

Flood, Curt (with Richard Carter). *The Way It Is* (1971).

Korr, Charles. *The End of Baseball As We Knew It: The Players Union, 1960–1981* (2002).
Miller, Marvin. *A Whole Different Ball Game: The Sport and Business of Baseball* (1991).
Will, George F. *Bunts* (1999).

—GERALD EARLY

 FOOTE, JULIA A. J.
(1823?–22 Nov. 1900), evangelist and writer, was born the fourth child of freed parents in Schenectady, New York. Little is known of her early life except what can be gleaned from her autobiography, *A Brand Plucked from the Fire* (1879). It is known that she had a brother and an elder sister. She never reveals her family surname, nor does she provide her full name in the text.

Julia's mother—unnamed in *Brand*, though deeply influential in Julia's life—was born a slave in New York and suffered under a cruel master and mistress. Though this is a traditional claim in texts grounded in the slave narrative tradition, as popularized by such accounts as those of FREDERICK DOUGLASS and SOJOURNER TRUTH, Foote (to use her married name) provides graphic detail to support her mother's claim of suffering. When Julia's mother refused her master's sexual advances and reported his behavior to her mistress, the master tied and whipped her. Then, he washed her back with salt water and would not permit her to change her clothing for a week. At the end of the week, realizing that she could not remove the clothing because it had stuck fast to her scabs, the mistress tore the fabric from the wounds, thus reopening them. For Julia, this episode exemplified the lack of an effective voice, the powerlessness, and the vulnerability of African American women struggling in servitude. Her father's youth was no less troubled. He had been born free, but was enslaved as a child. Julia's father eventually bought himself, Foote's mother, and her elder sister out of slavery.

Foote's family was religious, though not nearly as attentive to their faith as Julia would become. As a young couple, her parents joined the Methodist Episcopal church after a drowning scare. They professed their faith, but as Julia states, "They were not treated as Christian believers, but as poor lepers" (Andrew, 167). The sort of treatment they received is reflected in an incident that occurred in her parents' church. Normally, African American members of the congregation did not descend from the gallery to take communion until all the white members had been served. On one occasion, however, her mother and a friend, believing the white members were finished, had started for the communion table when two white women approached the table and reproached her mother saying, "Don't you know better than to go to the table when white folks are there?" Foote attributes the comment to the "fruits of slavery." Her mother's customary hesitance to move forward until whites had been served, and white expectation that their faith needs would be met before the faith needs of African Americans, was, in Foote's estimation, neither Christian nor humane. Nonetheless, her family continued to attend this church.

At ten years of age, denied access to school in Schenectady, Julia was sent to work for the Prime family, who lived in the local countryside. The Primes took an interest in Julia's intellectual and spiritual growth and secured a place for her in the local school. While she was attending this school, her teacher became involved in a sex scandal, murdered the woman who implicated him, and was publicly hanged. These events reinforced for Julia moral codes that became important elements of her faith as she grew.

Chief among these moral principles were honesty and integrity. While Julia served the Primes, another young person in their employ stole some cakes from their storage cellar. Unable to find the cakes, Mrs. Prime accused Julia of stealing and eating them. Julia protested but would not name the real culprit. Mrs. Prime, enraged because she believed Julia was lying, vowed to whip Julia until she told the truth. The next day, Mrs. Prime rode into town and purchased a whip with which she punished Julia. Early the next morning, Julia chopped the rawhide into little pieces, then walked directly back to her mother's home. When the Primes followed, Julia's mother, having herself experienced even harsher unwarranted punishment, spoke up in defense of her daughter's integrity, yet she had to send Julia back to work for the Primes. By recounting this event in her spiritual autobiography, Foote redeems her mother's integrity, defines a free mother's role in regard to her daughter, and marks herself as a woman acting directly on her own behalf.

In 1838, at fifteen, Julia joined the African Methodist Episcopal church. The gift of a Bible at this time heightened her desire to read more fluently. She read her Bible regularly, even when she was injured six months later and lost sight in one eye. As her spiritual knowledge deepened, Foote took great interest in the doctrines of sanctification and holiness. Though the pursuit of spiritual growth required that she disregard her mother's warnings against pursuing sanctification, thought by many to be available only to the elderly and infirm. Foote believed that her faith justified such acts and that she would be blessed, if not forgiven, for taking them.

At age eighteen Julia married George Foote, though he was not as devout a Christian as she. Since the young man was attempting to secure a position in the shipyards in Massachusetts, they moved to Boston, and Julia began a household ministry, visiting and praying with a few neighbors, including some who were on their deathbeds. Her religious work among her neighbors began to attract the attention of George's coworkers, who ridiculed him for having little control over his wife. Enraged by this turn of events, George threatened to send her home or to an asylum if she did not immediately stop her evangelical work. In the end, Julia persisted, and George signed on with a seagoing vessel. He subsequently died at sea, probably in the late 1840s.

Foote's household ministry was not the work she felt she had been called to do, though she hesitated to pursue the broader public ministry she felt was her calling. After a vision induced by a mysterious illness she feared terminal, she agreed to preach publicly, much to the chagrin of her pastor and noted abolitionist Jehiel C. Beman. Reverend Beman and members of his Boston congregation eventually excommunicated Foote, but Foote took her complaint to the African Methodist Episcopal Zion (AME Zion) Conference for a hearing. Disappointingly, her claim was never heard. Using the language of the *Dred Scott* case, Foote argued that in the denomination, women had no rights to express their faith as they felt called to declare it; moreover, male ministers should be bound to respect this calling in women just as they respected it in men.

In spite of her problems with the denominational hierarchy, Julia Foote's ministry enjoyed great success. She preached through New England, Ohio,

Canada, Michigan, and New York but was eventually forced to quit the work because she could no longer speak due to what she characterized as a "throat difficulty." She settled and worked in Cleveland, Ohio, for about a decade until she regained her voice in 1869. When she began to preach again, she associated herself with the Holiness movement then popular in the Midwest.

Foote's narrative, *A Brand Plucked from the Fire*, recounts the story of her journey toward spiritual development and provides a platform from which she revises the past, reaching toward a future of spiritual liberation. Little is known of her activities after 1879, until she became the first woman to be ordained a deacon in the AME Zion Church in 1894. In 1900, shortly before her death, she became the second woman to be named an elder in the denomination.

Foote's autobiography is a testament to human fortitude and religious faith. The debilitating effects of gender discrimination, particularly against women in the clergy, are a central theme of her writing. This well-crafted spiritual autobiography, with its evocation of traditional slave narratives, provides a model for African American women seeking to find their own voices in the generation after the abolition of slavery.

FURTHER READING

Andrews, William L., ed. *Sisters of the Spirit: Three Black Women's Autobiographies of the Nineteenth Century* (1986).
Collier-Thomas, Bettye. *Daughters of Thunder: Black Women Preachers and Their Sermons, 1850–1979* (1997).
Houchins, Sue, ed. *Spiritual Narratives* (1988).

—MARTHA L. WHARTON

FORD, ARNOLD JOSIAH (23 Apr. 1877–16 Sept. 1935), rabbi, black nationalist, and emigrationist, was born in Bridgetown, Barbados, the son of Edward Ford and Elizabeth Augusta Braithwaite. Ford asserted that his father's ancestry could be traced to the Yoruba tribe of Nigeria and his mother's to the Mendi tribe of Sierra Leone. According to his family's oral history, their heritage extended back

to one of the priestly families of the ancient Israelites, and in Barbados his family maintained customs and traditions that identified them with Judaism (Kobre, 27). His father was a policeman who also had a reputation as a "fiery preacher" at the Wesleyan Methodist Church where Arnold was baptized; it is not known if Edward's teaching espoused traditional Methodist beliefs or if it urged the embrace of Judaism that his son would later advocate.

Ford's parents intended for him to become a musician. They provided him with private tutors who instructed him in several instruments—particularly the harp, violin, and bass. As a young adult, he studied music theory with Edmestone Barnes and in 1899 joined the musical corps of the British Royal Navy, where he served on the HMS *Alert*. According to some reports, Ford was stationed on the island of Bermuda, where he secured a position as a clerk at the Court of Federal Assize, and he claimed that before coming to America he was a minister of public works in the Republic of Liberia, where many former slaves and early black nationalists settled.

When Ford arrived in Harlem, New York City, around 1910, he gravitated to its musical centers rather than to political or religious institutions, although within black culture, all three are often interrelated. He was a member of the Clef Club Orchestra, under the direction of JAMES REESE EUROPE, which first brought jazz to Carnegie Hall in 1912. Other black Jewish musicians, such as Willie "the Lion" Smith, an innovator of stride piano, also congregated at the Clef Club. Shortly after the orchestra's Carnegie Hall engagement, Ford became the director of the New Amsterdam Musical Association. His interest in mysticism, esoteric knowledge, and secret societies is evidenced by his membership in the Scottish Rite Masons, where he served as Master of the Memmon Lodge. It was during this period of activity in Harlem that he married Olive Nurse, probably around 1916, with whom he had two children before they divorced in 1924.

In 1917 MARCUS GARVEY founded the New York chapter of the Universal Negro Improvement Association (UNIA), and within a few years it had become the largest mass movement in African American history. Ford became the musical director of the UNIA choir, while Samuel Valentine was the president and Nancy Paris its lead singer. These three became the core of an active group of black Jews within the UNIA who studied Hebrew, religion, and history and held services at Liberty Hall, the headquarters of the UNIA. As a paid officer, Rabbi Ford, as he was then called, was responsible for orchestrating much of the pageantry of Garvey's highly attractive ceremonies. Ford and Benjamin E. Burrell composed a song called "Ethiopia," which speaks of a halcyon past before slavery and stresses pride in African heritage—two themes that were becoming immensely popular. Ford was thus prominently situated among those Muslim and Christian clergy, including GEORGE McGUIRE, chaplain general of the UNIA, who were each trying to influence the religious direction of the organization.

Ford's contributions to the UNIA, however, were not limited to musical and religious matters. He and E. L. Gaines wrote the handbook of rules and regulations for the paramilitary African Legion (which was modeled after the Zionist Jewish Legion) and developed guidelines for the Black Cross Nurses. He served on committees, spoke at rallies, and was elected one of the delegates representing the thirty-five thousand members of the New York chapter at the First International Convention of Negro Peoples of the World, held in 1920 at Madison Square Garden. There the governing body adopted the red, black, and green flag as its ensign, and Ford's song "Ethiopia" became the "Universal Ethiopian Anthem," which the UNIA constitution required be sung at every gathering. During that same year Ford published the *Universal Ethiopian Hymnal*.

Ford was a proponent of replacing the term *Negro* with the term *Ethiopian* as a general reference to people of African descent. This allowed the biblical verse "Ethiopia shall soon stretch out her hand to God" (Psalms 68:31 [AV]) to be interpreted as applying to their efforts, and it became a popular slogan of the organization. At the 1922 convention, Ford opened the proceedings for the session devoted to "The Politics and Future of the West Indian Negro," and he represented the advocates of Judaism on a five-person ad hoc

committee formed to investigate "the Future Religion of the Negro."

Following Garvey's arrest for mail fraud in 1923, the UNIA lost much of its internal cohesion. Since Ford and his small band of followers were motivated by principles that were independent of Garvey's charismatic appeal, they were repeatedly approached by government agents and asked to testify against Garvey at trial, which they refused to do. However, in 1925 Ford brought separate lawsuits against Garvey and the UNIA for failing to pay him royalties from the sale of recordings and sheet music, and in 1926 the judge ruled in Ford's favor. No longer musical director, and despite his personal and business differences with the organization, Rabbi Ford maintained a connection with the UNIA and was invited to give the invocation at the annual convention in 1926.

Several black religious leaders were experimenting with Judaism in various degrees between the two world wars. Rabbi Ford formed intermittent partnerships with some of these leaders. He and Valentine started a short-lived congregation called Beth B'nai Israel. Ford then worked with Mordecai Herman and the Moorish Zionist Temple, until they had an altercation over theological and financial issues. Finally, he established Beth B'nai Abraham in Harlem in 1924. A Jewish scholar who visited the congregation described their services as "a mixture of Reform and Orthodox Judaism, but when they practice the old customs they are seriously orthodox" (Kobre, 25). The Harlem chronicler JAMES VANDERZEE photographed the congregation with the Star of David and bold Hebrew lettering identifying their presence on 135th Street and showing Rabbi Ford standing in front of the synagogue with his arms around his string bass and with members of his choir at his side, the women wearing the black dresses and long white head coverings that became their distinctive habit and the men in white turbans.

In 1928 Ford created a business adjunct to the congregation, called the B'nai Abraham Progressive Corporation. Reminiscent of many of Garvey's ventures, this corporation issued one hundred shares of stock and purchased two buildings; it operated a religious and vocational school in one and

leased apartments in the other. However, resources dwindled as the Depression became more pronounced, and the corporation went bankrupt in 1930. Once again it seemed that Ford's dream of building a black community with cultural integrity, economic viability, and political virility was dashed, but out of the ashes of this disappointment he mustered the resolve to make a final attempt in Ethiopia. The Ethiopian government had been encouraging black people with skills and education to immigrate to Ethiopia for almost a decade, and Ford knew that there were more than forty thousand indigenous black Jews already in Ethiopia (who called themselves Beta Israel but who were commonly referred to as Falasha). The announced coronation of Haile Selassie in 1930 as the first black ruler of an African nation in modern times raised the hopes of black people all over the world and led Ford to believe that the timing of his Ethiopian colony was providential.

Ford arrived in Ethiopia with a small musical contingent in time to perform during the coronation festivities. They then sustained themselves in Addis Ababa by performing at local hotels and relying on assistance from supporters in the United Sates who were members of the Aurienoth Club, a civic group of black Jews and black nationalists, and members of the Commandment Keepers Congregation, led by Rabbi W. A. MATTHEW, Ford's most loyal protégé. Mignon Innis arrived with a second delegation in 1931 to work as Ford's private secretary. She soon became Ford's wife, and they had two children in Ethiopia. Mrs. Ford established a school for boys and girls that specialized in English and music. Ford managed to secure eight hundred acres of land on which to begin his colony and approximately one hundred people came to help him develop it. Unbeknownst to Ford, the U.S. State Department was monitoring Ford's efforts with irrational alarm, dispatching reports with such headings as "American Negroes in Ethiopia—Inspiration Back of Their Coming Here—'Rabbi' Josiah A. Ford" and instituting discriminatory policies to curtail the travel of black citizens to Ethiopia.

Ford had no intention of leaving Ethiopia, so he drew up a certificate of ordination (*shmecha*) for Rabbi Matthew that was sanctioned by the Ethiopian government, in the hope that this document would give Matthew the necessary credentials to continue the work that Ford had begun in the United States. By 1935 the black Jewish experiment with Ethiopian Zionism was on the verge of collapse. Those who did not leave because of the hard agricultural work joined the stampede of foreign nationals who sensed that war with Italy was imminent and defeat for Ethiopia certain. Ford died in September, it was said, of exhaustion and heartbreak, a few weeks before the Italian invasion. Ford had been the most important catalyst for the spread of Judaism among African Americans. Through his successors, communities of black Jews emerged and survived in several American cities.

FURTHER READING

The papers of Rabbi Ford are held largely in private collections; however, correspondence between Ford and Matthew is contained in the Rabbi Matthew Collection at the Schomburg Center for Research in Black Culture of the New York Public Library, along with other collections relating to Harlem's black Jews. Detailed records of Ford's efforts in Ethiopia are available at the National Archives, State Department Records for Ethiopia.

King, Kenneth J. "Some Notes on Arnold J. Ford and New World Black Attitudes to Ethiopia" in *Black Apostles: Afro-American Clergy Confront the Twentieth Century*, eds. Randall Burkett and Richard Newman (1978).

Kobre, Sidney. "Rabbi Ford," *The Reflex* 4.1 (1929).

Scott, William R. "Rabbi Arnold Ford's Back-to-Ethiopia Movement: A Study of Black Emigration, 1930–1935," *Pan-African Journal* 8.2 (1975).

—SHOLOMO B. LEVY

FORMAN, JAMES

(4 Oct. 1928–), civil rights leader and writer, was born in Chicago to Octavia Allen and Jackson Forman. He lived on a farm with his maternal grandmother in Marshall County, Mississippi, until he was six. Then his mother and step-father, John Rufus, who worked in the stockyards, took him back to Chicago, where he attended St. Anselm's—a Catholic school—and Betsy Ross Grammar School. As a teenager he discovered that John Rufus was not his biological father, and he met Jackson Forman, then a taxi driver. Graduating from Englewood High School in 1947, Forman studied at Wilson Junior College for one semester before he joined the air force, where he served for four years.

The year after his discharge in 1951, Forman started classes at the University of Southern California. One night when he emerged from the library, two Los Angeles police officers arrested him on suspicion of robbery and took him to jail, where he was beaten, subjected to brutal interrogation, and (he would learn later) to some form of electric shock. He was then taken to a state mental hospital. His first wife, Mary Sears, whom he had married after returning from service in Okinawa, helped get him transferred to the Veteran's Neuropsychiatric Hospital in Los Angeles. After his release he separated from Sears and moved back to Chicago. In the fall of 1954 he started classes at Roosevelt University in Chicago, where he became student government president, graduating in 1957.

He then spent a year as a graduate student in African affairs and government at Boston University.

After DAISY BATES helped nine black students to integrate Central High School in Little Rock in 1957, Forman obtained press credentials from the *Chicago Defender* to cover the start of their second year. By this time, Forman knew he wanted to be a writer. He also knew that he wanted to help build a mass movement for racial change. Influenced by India's Gandhi and Ghana's Kwame Nkrumah, he wrote a novel, *The Thin White Line* (unpublished), in which the northern protagonist uses nonviolence to organize a mass movement in the South. Planning to go south himself, in 1959 he took education courses at Chicago Teacher's College to qualify as a teacher; that same year he married Mildred Thompson, who joined him in his civil rights work.

After a wave of student sit-ins shook the southern status quo in the spring of 1960, Forman traveled to Fayette County, Tennessee, on behalf of an emergency relief committee formed by the Chicago chapter of the Congress of Racial Equality (CORE). Seeing himself

James Forman, former executive director of SNNC, lectures on the structure of American capitalism. © Bettmann/CORBIS

as "pamphleteer and historian of our cause" (Forman, 130), he supplied the African American press with articles on sharecroppers evicted from their homes for trying to register to vote. In Nashville, Tennessee, he participated in nonviolent demonstrations, and in Monroe, North Carolina, he supported local NAACP Chairman Robert Williams's challenge of a segregated swimming pool.

Forman had begun to envision an organization in which he and others would work full time building a civil rights movement, and he talked that idea over with students active in the Student Nonviolent Coordinating Committee (SNCC). SNCC had been a loose coalition formed by students involved in the sit-in movement. As SNCC made the transition in 1961 into an organization with full-time field-workers, Forman became its executive secretary. From this point on, he was closely involved with civil rights movement campaigns across the South. For the next five years, as SNCC's chief operational officer, Forman was responsible for raising and disbursing funds, providing legal help for SNCC staff in jail, getting coverage from the media, meeting with representatives of other civil rights organizations, and collecting affidavits to bring attention to brutality. With his eye on history, Forman insisted that staff turn in detailed field reports; as a result, the SNCC archives contain an unparalleled record of community organizing. JULIAN BOND, who worked closely with him, would later write Forman, "He molded SNCC's near-anarchic personality into a functioning, if still chaotic, organizational structure" (Forman, xi). Forman was not just working the phones. He spoke at mass meetings and walked picket lines. He faced police brandishing guns and went to jail for demonstrating.

The 1964 Mississippi Summer Project brought increasing pressure on SNCC by what Forman saw as an alliance of liberals and labor activists critical of SNCC's relations with organizations some considered communist. Losing his patience during the 1965 Selma campaign, Forman gave what SNCC chairman JOHN LEWIS called "one of the angriest, most fiery speeches made by a movement leader up to that point." Urging the

White House to bring Alabama Governor George Wallace to heel, Forman offered this threat in a Montgomery church: "I said it today, and I will say it again. If we can't sit at the table of democracy, we'll knock the fucking legs *off!*" (Lewis, 340).

In May 1966, weary of criticism of his role in the SNCC, which was torn by internal debates over excluding whites, Forman declined renomination as executive secretary. Increasingly, his attention was drawn to Africa, which he had several opportunities to visit, and he became SNCC's international affairs director in 1967. Frantz Fanon's *Wretched of the Earth* had strengthened his view of African Americans as colonized people and his acceptance of violence as a road to freedom. Never committed to nonviolence except as a tactic, Forman now spoke out in favor of armed self-defense and in 1968 he briefly held the title of minister of foreign affairs for the Black Panthers.

After he resigned from that position, Forman reemerged in the political limelight at the 1969 National Black Economic Development Conference held in Detroit by the Interreligious Foundation for Community Organization. Believing that class as well as race played a role in the oppression of blacks, Forman presented a Black Manifesto calling for a socialist revolution against capitalism. He demanded half a billion dollars from Christian churches and Jewish synagogues as reparations for the exploitation of African Americans in the slave trade. The money would be used to establish black-controlled media outlets, a southern land bank, and other institutions that would empower black people. The Manifesto urged delegates to disrupt churches to bring attention to their demands. On 4 May 1969, the day Forman had set for the disruption to begin, he walked up the aisle of Manhattan's Riverside Church, interrupting the morning communion service, to demand reparations. Many present did not stay to hear him, although later the minister, Dr. Ernest Campbell, expressed sympathy with the Manifesto's goals. Although some churches did donate funds to various institutions in response to the Manifesto, the results disappointed Forman.

By the winter of 1969–1970, SNCC had been disbanded, replaced by the

Student National Coordinating Committee, and Forman had lost his position as international affairs director. Already the author of one book, *Sammy Younge, Jr., The First Black College Student to Die in the Black Liberation Movement* (1968), he published *The Political Thought of James Forman* (1970) and *The Making of Black Revolutionaries* (1972). He subsequently earned a master's degree in African and Afro-American History from Cornell University (1983) and was awarded a PhD by the Union of Experimental Colleges and Universities (1985). His master's thesis appeared as a book, *Self-Determination and the African American People* (1984).

In the 1980s and 1990s Forman held a position as legislative assistant to the president of the Metropolitan Washington Central Labor Council (AFL-CIO) and taught at American University in Washington, D.C. Cancer diagnosed in the early 1990s undermined his health, but he continued his political activities, organizing support for District of Columbia statehood, working in Democratic presidential campaigns, and serving as president of the Unemployment and Poverty Action Committee and publisher of the Black America News Service. Among his projects since then has been a campaign for District of Columbia statehood. A collection of his writing, *The High Tide of Black Resistance and Other Political and Literary Writings*, appeared in 1994. Forman had two sons with his third wife, Constancia Romilly: James Forman Jr., a lawyer, educator, and writer, and Chaka Forman, an actor. His marriage to Romilly ended in divorce.

When *The Making of Black Revolutionaries* was republished in 1997, Julian Bond wrote in a foreword that without James Forman, "there would have been no SNCC, at least not the one that developed in the early 1960s" (Forman, xiii). Forman's work with SNCC endures not only in the lasting changes it engendered but also in the SNCC field reports and *The Making of Black Revolutionaries*—dramatic records of the movement he helped to build.

FURTHER READING

The Student Nonviolent Coordinating Papers, 1959–1972, are available on microform from UMI. Forman's correspondence is available at the Schomburg Center for Research in Black Culture of the New York Public Library.

Forman, James. *The Making of Black Revolutionaries* (1997).

Carson, Clayborne. *In Struggle: SNCC and the Black Awakening of the 1960s* (1995).
Greenberg, Cheryl Lynn, ed. *A Circle of Trust: Remembering SNCC* (1998).
Lewis, John, with Michael D'Orso. *Walking with the Wind: A Memoir of the Movement* (1998).

—CAROL POLSGROVE

 FORTEN, JAMES
(2 Sept. 1766–4 Mar. 1842), businessman and social reformer, was born in Philadelphia, Pennsylvania, the son of Thomas Forten, a freeborn sailmaker, and Margaret (maiden name unknown). James's parents enrolled him in the African School of abolitionist Anthony Benezet. When James was seven, his father died. Margaret Forten struggled to keep her son in school, but he was eventually forced to leave at age nine and work full time to help support the family. His family remained in Philadelphia throughout the American Revolution, and Forten later recalled being in the crowd outside the Pennsylvania State House when the Declaration of Independence was read to the people for the first time.

In 1781, while serving on a privateer, Forten was captured by the British and spent seven months on the infamous prison ship *Jersey* in New York harbor.

After a voyage to England in 1784 as a merchant seaman, Forten returned to Philadelphia and apprenticed himself to Robert Bridges, a white sailmaker. Bridges taught Forten his trade, loaned him money to buy a house, and eventually sold him the business. Inheriting most of Bridges's customers and establishing a reputation as a master craftsman in his own right, Forten prospered. His profits were invested in real estate, loans at interest, and eventually in bank, canal, and railroad stock.

In 1803 Forten married Martha Beatte, of Darby township, Delaware County, Pennsylvania. She died in 1804, and a year later he married Charlotte Vandine, a Philadelphian of European, African, and Native American descent. They had eight children. The Forten children, Margaretta, Harriet, Sarah, James, and Robert—along with Robert's daughter, CHARLOTTE L. FORTEN GRIMKÉ—were all active in the antislavery movement.

Forten's emergence as a leader in Philadelphia's black community coincided with his growing prosperity. Well-read and articulate, he was often called on to draft petitions and to chair meetings. In 1799 he joined other black citizens in petitioning for an end to the slave trade and for legislation to prevent the kidnapping of free people. When Congress refused to consider the petition, Forten wrote to thank the one man, George Thatcher of Massachusetts, who had spoken in its favor. The letter attracted considerable attention.

In 1813, responding to an attempt by the state legislature to restrict the rights of black Pennsylvanians, Forten published *Letters from a Man of Colour*. Attacking the proposed legislation, he cited Pennsylvania's reputation as a haven for the oppressed. He also objected strenuously to a law that would reduce all black people, including "men of property," to the status of felons.

Forten's role in the debate over African repatriation was pivotal. He was initially enthusiastic about the proposal of the African American shipowner PAUL CUFFE SR. to take American free blacks to Britain's colony of Sierra Leone. Forten had no intention of relocating, but he agreed with Cuffe that less fortunate members of the community might benefit from emigrating.

With the formation of the American Colonization Society (ACS) in 1816, Forten moved from support of African resettlement to outspoken opposition. At first, when approached by an officer of the ACS whom he knew to be a dedicated abolitionist, he gave the organization a qualified endorsement. When others in the ACS spoke of the need to deport free blacks to the new colony of Liberia because of their "pernicious" influence on the slaves, however, Forten expressed alarm. The leaders of the ACS repeatedly urged him to set an example by emigrating. They offered him incentives to begin a packet service between the United States and Liberia. Forten was unmoved, and for the rest of his life he remained one of the most vocal critics of the ACS.

Freeborn, Forten was a lifelong opponent of slavery, and he worked with two generations of white abolitionists.

He had many contacts with the "gradualists" in the Pennsylvania Abolition Society (PAS). He hired servants recommended by the PAS, sent his four sons to the PAS school, and even took into his home an African prince the society was educating. However, neither he nor any other African American was invited to join the PAS.

The extent of Forten's involvement in the antislavery cause changed with the emergence of the "new school" abolitionists in the early 1830s. William Lloyd Garrison became a close personal friend and often visited the Forten home. Forten advanced him money to begin publishing the *Liberator*. Thereafter he gave advice on sales and distribution and more money to tide Garrison over periodic crises. In 1832, when Garrison was preparing his *Thoughts on African Colonization*, Forten sent him his own collection of material on the ACS. He was elected a vice president of the new American Anti-Slavery Society and helped organize auxiliaries at the state and local levels.

Forten saw the abolition of slavery as one aspect of a moral crusade to transform society. Temperance, education, pacifism, and women's rights all had their place in his vision of America. In 1834 Forten and a group of like-minded black reformers founded the American Moral Reform Society, braving criticism from their own community that they were unrealistic, naive, and lacking in racial pride as they advocated the abandonment of terms of racial identification, promoted a sweeping reform agenda, and vowed to direct their efforts at all Americans, regardless of race.

In the last decade of his life Forten's faith in the power of reform to regenerate society was severely tested. As a wave of racial violence swept the country, he, his family, and the community institutions to which he belonged all came under attack, including mob violence and destruction of property. On several occasions he received death threats because of his opposition to colonization.

The violence was accompanied by an erosion of the civil rights of Pennsylvania's African Americans. In 1832 Forten and his son-in-law, Robert Purvis, protested a move by the state legislature to restrict the mobility of black Pennsylvanians. In 1838 Pennsylvania's constitution was revised. Blacks, regardless of wealth, were barred from voting, while most adult white men were enfranchised. On behalf of his community, Forten brought suit to establish his right to vote. After losing the case, he helped finance the printing of an appeal urging voters to reject the proposed constitution. Nevertheless, the constitution was ratified by a large majority.

In 1841 deteriorating health obliged Forten to curtail his business activities and his reform work. When he died in Philadelphia, the abolitionist press eulogized him, the local papers commented on the many prominent white merchants who attended his funeral, and the *African Repository*, the journal of the ACS, regretted that to the end he did not change his mind about colonization.

FURTHER READING

Forten's letters are in the Paul Cuffe Papers at the New Bedford Free Public Library, New Bedford, Massachusetts; the Antislavery Manuscripts at the Boston Public Library; the Historical Society of Pennsylvania; and the Pennsylvania Abolition Society.

Billington, Ray Allen. "James Forten—Forgotten Abolitionist," *Negro History Bulletin* 13 (Nov. 1949).

Douty, Esther M. *Forten the Sailmaker: Pioneer Champion of Negro Rights* (1968).

Nash, Gary. *Forging Freedom: The Formation of Philadelphia's Black Community, 1720–1840* (1988).

Ripley, C. Peter, ed. *Black Abolitionist Papers, 1830–1865* (1981).

Winch, Julie. *Philadelphia's Black Elite: Activism, Accommodation, and the Struggle for Autonomy* (1988).

—JULIE WINCH

FORTUNE, T. THOMAS
(3 Oct. 1856–2 June 1928), journalist and activist, was born Timothy Thomas in Marianna, Florida, the third of five children, to Emanuel and Sara Jane, slaves of Ely P. Moore. After emancipation his family took the name Fortune from that of an Irish planter, Thomas Fortune, whom Emanuel believed to be his father. Emanuel was elected to the Florida House of Representatives in 1868, where he served for three years until he was forced to leave Marianna as the reign of terror that drove

T. T. FORTUNE.

T. Thomas Fortune, publisher, editor, and the dean of the African American press. Ohio Historical Society/African American Museum

black office holders from power swept through Florida. Before his family joined him in Jacksonville, they lived in Tallahassee, where the young Fortune worked as a page in the state senate. During his four sessions there, Fortune developed a distrust of black and white politicians from both political parties. Though he spent only a few years at primary schools run by the Freedmen's Bureau, he acquired what he called "the book learning fever," which prepared him for his later literary activities.

Fortune's mother died in 1868, and his father, who worked as a carpenter, made wise investments in real estate that allowed him to provide for his children while remaining active in politics until his death in 1897. Fortune got his start in publishing as a printer's devil for the *Jacksonville Daily Union*. When the paper changed hands, Fortune found work at the post office until Congressman J. W. Purman secured

a position for him as a special inspector of customs in Delaware. However, Fortune believed that his true calling was to be found in the law, and in 1874 he enrolled at Howard University in Washington, D.C. Fortune had been largely self-educated, yet the polish of his prose outshone that of many of his credentialed peers. Thus, when the bank in which he had placed his savings for college collapsed, Fortune was able find work at a black newspaper, the *People's Advocate*, which earned him enough money during the day to study law at night.

Though Fortune never lost his interest in legal matters, he left Howard University to teach briefly in Florida before going to New York City in 1881 with his bride, Carrie C. Smiley. Of their five children, only Jessica and Frederick lived to adulthood. Fortune's first publishing job in New York was as a compositor for a white religious paper, the *Weekly Witness*. From there he worked as an editor for a black paper that began as the *Rumor* and became the *New York Globe* (1881–1884), the *New York Freeman* (1884–1887), of which he was the sole proprietor, and finally the *New York Age* in 1887, where he was both editor and co-owner. The power struggles, financial reorganizations, and management turnovers that led to so many name changes illustrate the constant battle to survive that Fortune waged during those years. He wrote over three hundred articles during his fifty-year career, but it was the editorials that he wrote between 1881 and 1907 that established his prominence during a bleak period for African American leadership between the decline of FREDERICK DOUGLASS and the rise of BOOKER T. WASHINGTON.

In the decades after the Civil War, the black press had grown from a few dozen antislavery organs to as many as five hundred papers; most were short-lived, weekly newsletters that espoused the positions of the Republican Party, to which the black electorate had been loyal. During an era famous for its "yellow journalism," Fortune attempted to run a truly independent and nonpartisan paper that was national in scope, original in content, and taken note of by the larger white media. He was a fiery critic, a witty satirist, and an astute analyst. As president and chairman of the executive council of the Afro-American Press Association during much of the 1890s, Fortune fought to raise the standards of his profession.

Booker T. Washington recognized Fortune's exceptional talent and hired him to ghostwrite *A Negro for a New Century* (1899) and *The Negro in Business* (1907); Fortune also wrote speeches for Washington and edited large sections of Washington's first autobiography, *The Story of My Life and Work* (1900). When Fortune finished working on the autobiography and noticed how little mention Washington had given to his service, he returned the manuscript with a note that read "I write in great sorrow and with wounded pride because I have tried to do so much to sustain you and your work and am grieved and pained to find it amounts to so little in the summing up" (Thornbrough, 209). Fortune remained loyal to Washington because he largely agreed with Washington's education and economic policies, though he advocated more militant positions on

civil rights than Washington was willing to endorse publicly. Nonetheless, Fortune often defended Washington against his most strident critics, explaining that Washington was a "conservative" while he himself was a "radical." At times Washington seemed to be sincere in trying to help Fortune, as in 1903 when he secured a special assignment for Fortune to study conditions in the Pacific for Theodore Roosevelt's administration. At other times Washington used his financial leverage to manipulate the *Age* as he had other Negro papers.

In December 1889 Fortune assembled in Chicago over one hundred delegates from across the country for the purpose of establishing the National Afro-American League to address African American political concerns. Thirty years before ALAIN LOCKE announced the birth of the "New Negro," Fortune wrote an article in the *Age* to mark

the death-knell of the shuffling, cringing creature in black who for two centuries and a half had given the right of way to white men, and proclaiming in no uncertain voice that a new man in black, a freeman every inch, standing erect and undaunted, an American from head to foot, had taken the place of the miserable creature. What does he look like? *He looks like a man!* He bears no resemblance to a slave, or a coward, or an ignoramus."

(*New York Age*, 21 Dec. 1889)

The league failed to attract sufficient popular or financial support to survive beyond 1894, but its spirit and much of its platform was adopted by the Niagara Movement (1905) led by W. E. B. DU BOIS and the NAACP (1909). Fortune did not join either of these organizations because of his qualified loyalty to Booker T. Washington, his personal animosity toward their leaders, and his conflicting view of how legal arguments should be framed. He did, however, hold the presidency of the rival National Afro-American Council from 1902 to 1904 before it, too, became defunct.

A leading advocate of women's rights, Fortune was present at the founding convention of the Federation of Afro-American Women in 1895, successfully urging the adoption of the appellation "Afro-American" rather than the more common "Negro" or "Colored." He also did much to advance the careers of journalists VICTORIA EARLE

MATTHEWS and IDA B. WELLS-BARNETT, who both worked at the *Age* at various times. Nor was Fortune afraid to take controversial positions within the black community: he condemned racism in the North as strongly as he did in the South; he supported the right of "manly retaliation," even though he did not advocate violence; and when Douglass was roundly criticized in 1884 for marrying Helen Pitts, a white woman, Fortune was one of the few black leaders to come to his defense. Similarly, Fortune found himself at odds with Bishop HENRY MCNEAL TURNER, who urged immigration to Africa; he clashed with EDWARD BLYDEN and ALEXANDER CRUMMELL, whose strand of black nationalism would have excluded people of mixed race, arguing instead that such distinctions would worsen racial conditions by creating a "color line in a color line"; and he railed against the creation of an educated Negro aristocracy of the kind implied by Du Bois's "Talented Tenth," warning that his race did not need another "swaggering pedagogue or a cranky homiletician."

In 1884 Fortune published *Black and White: Land, Labor, and Politics,* a scholarly treatise influenced by the writings of Karl Marx, in which Fortune called for a class alliance that would transcend race. This was followed by a historical work, *The Negro in Politics* (1885), and a volume of poetry, *Dreams of Life* (1905).

The dissolution of his marriage, his chronic financial woes, and increased drinking caused Fortune to suffer a mental breakdown in 1907. Though he managed to recover his health over the next several years, he lost control of the *Age* and with it an independent platform from which to express his ideas. He eked out a living as a freelance writer with several African American and white papers until 1923 when MARCUS GARVEY, who had recently been convicted of mail fraud, asked Fortune to become editor of the *Negro World,* even though he was not a member of the UNIA. Fortune held this post until he died of heart disease in 1928, having established a well-founded reputation as the dean of the African American press and providing a model of intellectual rigor and journalistic integrity.

FURTHER READING

A small collection of Fortune's papers and issues of his newspapers are available at the Schomburg Center for Research in Black Culture of the New York Public Library. His lengthy correspondence with Booker T. Washington is located in the Booker T. Washington Collection at the Library of Congress.

Thornbrough, Emma Lou. *T. Thomas Fortune: Militant Journalist* (1972).

—SHOLOMO B. LEVY

FOSTER, RUBE

(17 Sept. 1879–9 Dec. 1930), baseball player, manager, and entrepreneur, was born Andrew Foster in Calvert, Texas, the fifth child of Sarah (maiden name unknown) and the Reverend Andrew Foster, presiding elder of the Methodist Episcopal Church of Calvert. Growing up in a post-Reconstruction world of strictly enforced racial segregation backed by white terrorist violence, Andrew attended the segregated school in Calvert. As a boy Andrew had a knack for baseball, the most popular sport in America at the time. His father, a devout churchman, tried to discourage him from playing, but young Andrew persisted and even organized a team while he was still in grade school. Indeed, Andrew was so drawn to the game that he quit school after the eighth grade to pursue baseball as a career.

Foster started pitching for the Waco Yellow Jackets, becoming a star pitcher by the time he was eighteen. By 1902 he had a reputation for being a tough pitcher, with a fastball, curve, and screwball. That year he joined the Chicago Union Giants (most all-black teams at this time called themselves the Giants) and reputedly won fifty-one games, including a victory over the great white professional pitcher Rube Waddell, which is how Foster earned his nickname. As records for barnstorming black players were poorly kept, it is difficult to know exactly how many games Foster actually won. By this time Foster was officially part of the itinerant, rough-and-tumble world of the professional African American baseball player, a world not unlike that of the black professional prizefighter. Boxing was, like baseball, intensely popular at this time.

Rube Foster, a skilled pitcher and manager, formed the first Negro League in baseball. National Baseball Hall of Fame Library, Cooperstown, NY

Baseball in post–Civil War America was still developing and did not entirely resemble the modern game. By the 1880s, however, three strikes equaled a strikeout, four balls were a walk, leather gloves were regularly used, and pitchers could throw overhand. By 1889 something like today's Major League Baseball existed, with two leagues: the National League, founded in 1876, and the American Association, founded in 1882. The American League, which replaced the American Association, came into existence under the leadership of Ban Johnson in 1901. There were several other professional leagues, as well as a good number of barnstorming teams that traveled around challenging various local nines. Amateur baseball could be found everywhere in America, from company teams to college teams. Though some local teams, such as the Florence (Massachusetts) Eagles with their first baseman LUTHER ASKIN, were occasionally and quietly integrated shortly after

the Civil War, amateur baseball was officially segregated in 1867. By 1887 there were approximately twenty black players on professional teams. But on 14 July 1887 the Chicago White Stockings player-manager Cap Anson demanded that the opposing club from Newark not play its two black players, George Stovey and Fleet Walker. This was the beginning of the gentleman's agreement that was to keep African Americans, indeed, all black- or dark-skinned men, from playing in any of the established professional leagues until 1945, when the Brooklyn Dodgers signed JACKIE ROBINSON. There were teams that tried to get around the custom by saying that a player was Hispanic or Indian, but this rarely worked and, in any case, any dark-skinned Hispanic or Indian who was as dark as the average African American was not allowed to play professional baseball on the same field as whites. Since many black men had a passion as strong as whites for playing this game as professionals, they were forced to form their own teams and eventually their own leagues.

By the turn of the century, black teams were barnstorming units. They traveled around the country playing other teams, sometimes white, sometimes black. There were many disadvantages to this in selling black baseball to the public. First, players jumped from team to team during the season, willing to leave one team for another if they could get more money. Roster instability made it impossible for managers and team owners to rely on the players through a season. The second disadvantage was that teams were unable to claim the loyalty of fans in a particular location or to have a structured season of competition. The only answer to this confusion and disorganization was to form a league, but this was virtually impossible, although it was a dream of many of the early organizers of black baseball. The dreamers included, most notably, Sol White, whose 1907 book *The History of Colored Base Ball* is one of the most important accounts of black baseball before the formation of leagues.

Foster pitched for the Cuban X-Giants and the Philadelphia Giants. He also played in Cuba, a popular location for black ballplayers during the winter months. In 1907 Foster returned to Chicago to become the manager of the Chicago Leland Giants, establishing himself as a first-rate manager and transforming the Leland Giants into one of the most skilled black teams in the country. In 1911 Foster formed a partnership with John M. Schorling, the son-in-law of Charles Comiskey, owner of the Chicago White Sox. The team that Foster put together, the Chicago American Giants, became one of the powerhouse teams in black baseball history. Foster still pitched occasionally, but he concentrated on managing and general managing, and, although he was stern with his men, he was highly successful at putting together teams and getting the most out of his players. As a manager Foster was a master of "little ball": bunting, the hit-and-run, the steal, the sacrifice. Of course, this was before the age of the home run, and most teams tended to play this way, but Foster's team did it better than most.

Foster's problems with booking agent Nat Strong regarding scheduling games in the East and his interest in stopping bidding wars for top players eventually led him to form his own league in 1920. The first Negro League was formed in February 1920 at the YMCA in Kansas City and was made up of the Chicago American Giants, the Chicago Giants, the Detroit Stars, the St. Louis Giants, the Kansas City Monarchs, the Taylor ABCs, and the Cuban Stars. Foster became both the president and the treasurer of the league, and he continued to manage the Chicago American Giants as well. All of the Negro League owners were black except J. L. Wilkinson, who owned the Kansas City Monarchs and had previously owned the All-Nations, a team composed of African Americans, Mexicans, Indians, and whites. In 1923 Foster helped to form the Eastern Colored League, ensuring that the Negro Leagues would have the same structure as Major League Baseball. In 1924 the Negro World Series was introduced. With the league undercapitalized, still faced with having to play a great number of barnstorming games, and still facing booking obstacles, it was remarkable that Foster was able to establish a league and make it work. He thus became not just one of the greatest baseball men around, but also one of the most important black entrepreneurs in history.

Foster's autocratic rule created friction and enemies, and eventually he was forced to resign in 1925. He was also suffering from deteriorating mental health, partly induced by overwork, and by September 1926 he was in a state mental asylum in Kankakee, Illinois, where he died in 1930. Foster's body lay in state for several days before his burial in Chicago, the city in which he had achieved his greatest fame.

Foster was not only one of the greatest figures in black baseball but one of the most important men involved in professional baseball in the United States. Few men have been involved in as many facets of the game. Although records are incomplete, Foster was certainly one of the great pitchers of his era. He was also one of the great managers of the game, introducing sophisticated tactics and strategies. Foster recognized talent and knew how to motivate players and teach them how to play. His men played hard and they played to win at a time when black ballplayers and teams were often employed to clown around and degrade themselves in minstrel-type routines, particularly for white fans. In organizing the league, Foster was also one of the game's great general managers. He was flamboyant, competitive, a "race man," and a dreamer. Foster was elected to the National Baseball Hall of Fame in 1981.

FURTHER READING

Cottrell, Robert Charles. *The Best Pitcher in Baseball: The Life of Rube Foster, Negro League Giant* (2001).

Peterson, Ralph. *Only the Ball Was White: A History of Legendary Black Players and All-Black Professional Teams* (1970).

Ribowsky, Mark. *A Complete History of the Negro Leagues, 1884–1955* (1995).

Riley, James A. *The Biographical Encyclopedia of the Negro Baseball Leagues* (1994).

Rogosin, Donn. *Invisible Men: Life in Baseball's Negro Leagues* (1983).

Rust, Art. *Get That Nigger off the Field* (1976).

—GERALD EARLY

FOXX, REDD (9 Dec. 1922– 11 Nov. 1991), comedian, was born John Elroy Sanford in St. Louis, Missouri, the son of Fred Sanford, an electrician, and Mary Carson, a radio preacher and domestic worker. He spent his early childhood in St. Louis. After his father deserted the home in 1926, he and his mother moved to Chicago, where she worked for the vice president of the Chicago White Sox baseball team. While attending DuSable High School, he and two friends formed a washtub band, the Bon Bons. In 1939 the trio hopped a freight train to New York, where they met with sporadic success. Although they performed mostly on street corners and in subway stations, they occasionally appeared at the Apollo Theatre and on the *Major Bowes Amateur Hour*.

Friends nicknamed Sanford "Chicago Red" because of his red hair. He then added the surname Foxx in admiration of the baseball star Jimmie Foxx. He devised a distinctive spelling of the name he would be known by for the rest of his life: Redd Foxx.

In the mid-1940s Foxx married Eleanor Killebrew; they divorced in 1951. He was married three more times, in 1955 to Betty Jean Harris (divorced in 1974); in the mid-1970s to Yun Chi

Redd Foxx, in character as Fred Sanford from the 1970s television series Sanford and Son. © Bettmann/CORBIS

Chong (divorced in the late 1980s); and in 1991 to Kahoe Cho. He had no children.

In 1942 Foxx got his first regular job as a solo entertainer at Gamby's, a nightclub in Baltimore. He returned to New York in 1945 with a unique, polished act. Two years later he teamed with Slappy White and saw his salary rise from $5 to $450 a week. In 1952 Dinah Washington invited the duo to open for her in California. Foxx and White split up soon after that, but Foxx remained on the West Coast at the end of the engagement.

Foxx found the club scene in California even more segregated than on the East Coast. Still, he persevered in finding progressively larger venues and contracts, while supplementing his income with work as a sign-painter. In 1955 Dootsie Williams, the owner of Dooto Records, caught Foxx's act and approached him with the revolutionary idea of recording an album consisting only of stand-up comic material and devoid of novelty songs. Foxx's sexually suggestive material prevented radio stations from broadcasting the albums. Nevertheless, the "party albums," as

they would come to be known, were hugely popular in homes across the country. Foxx eventually recorded fifty-four party albums that together sold well over ten million copies.

Owing to the popularity of the party albums, Foxx's salary and his acceptance at white nightclubs increased. In the early 1960s two famous patrons in these venues advanced Foxx's career. Frank Sinatra heard him perform, settled his Dooto contract, and signed him to LOMA, a subsidiary of the newly formed Reprise label. In 1964 television host Hugh Downs saw Foxx at a club in San Francisco. Although television producers had been leery of Foxx's blue reputation, Downs booked him as a guest on the *Today* show. Foxx was a smash, and this appearance led to regular spots on talk shows such as *The Tonight Show* and *The Joey Bishop Show*, as well as appearances on television series such as *Mr. Ed*, *Green Acres*, and *The Addams Family*.

Along with his television success, Foxx appeared regularly in Las Vegas throughout the 1960s. In 1968, when ARETHA FRANKLIN failed to appear for an opening-night show, Foxx, the opening act, entertained the crowd for one hour and forty minutes. Bookers from the Hilton International Hotel who saw this performance were impressed enough to offer him a year-long, $960,000 contract.

Foxx broke into motion pictures in 1970, portraying an aging junk dealer in the United Artists release *Cotton Comes to Harlem*. This led directly to his title role in Norman Lear's adaptation of the British comedy *Steptoe and Son*, NBC's new television series *Sanford and Son*. It was an immediate hit. Foxx created the main character, Fred Sanford, named after his late brother. Foxx's portrayal of the irascible junkman who faked heart attacks—crying out "I'm coming, Elizabeth!" with the arrival of each "big one"—elevated him to his highest popularity. During the show's 1972–1977 run, Foxx was nominated for six Emmy Awards. Initially he had some degree of control over the show, but in 1977 he left it because of continual differences of opinion over the writing.

Although Foxx's talent was still bright, his luck was not. *The Redd Foxx Comedy Hour*, which premiered on ABC after Foxx left NBC, ran only for the

1977–1978 season. A revival of the Fred Sanford character, *Sanford* (NBC, 1980–1981), was also short-lived, as was *The Redd Foxx Show* (1986). Throughout this period Foxx continued to entertain crowds in Las Vegas; however, his lavish spending habits caught up with him in 1989, when the Internal Revenue Service forced him to sell off houses and cars to cover back taxes. In 1991 Foxx's luck was finally turning good again with the early success of another situation comedy, CBS's *The Royal Family*, but he died of a heart attack on the set, just weeks into the show's run.

Although Foxx will be remembered mainly for his work on *Sanford and Son*, his most lasting contribution is the invention of the stand-up comedy album. In his party albums he pioneered not only an innovation in record marketing but also freedom of speech in comedy. As a result, the voices of many other comedians were heard more widely in the homes of America.

FURTHER READING

Foxx, Redd. *Redd Foxx B.S.* (*Before Sanford)*, ed. Joe X. Price (1979).

Watkins, Mel. *On the Real Side: Laughing, Lying, and Signifying—The Underground Tradition of African American Humor that Transformed American Culture from Slavery to Richard Pryor* (1994).

—ALEXANDER BATTLES

FRANKLIN, ARETHA

(26 March 1942–) singer and pianist, was born Aretha Louise Franklin in Memphis, Tennessee, the daughter of the Reverend C. L. FRANKLIN, a prominent Baptist minister, and Barbara Siggers. Franklin was one of five children, including sisters Carolyn and Erma, brother Cecil, and half-brother Vaughn.

Franklin and her family settled in Detroit, Michigan, where her father, after a brief sojourn in Buffalo, New York, took over the New Bethel Baptist Church in 1948. Aretha Franklin was literally raised in the bosom of African American religious tradition and was thus the direct product of one of the most significant institutions in the African American community.

Aretha Franklin, "The Queen of Soul," whose song "Respect" became an anthem of the women's movement in the late 1960s, acknowledges her fans in a 1980 performance. © Hulton-Deutsch Collection/CORBIS

As a youth Franklin was intimately exposed to the artistry of the major black gospel performers of the era, including Sam Cooke (then of the Soul Stirrers), MAHALIA JACKSON, James Cleveland (who at one time during Franklin's youth was the Minister of Music at New Bethel), and Marion Williams and Clara Ward (both of the Clara Ward Singers). Ward was Franklin's most significant gospel influence. Franklin's father also exposed her to the music of jazz performers like pianists such as Dorothy Donegan, Oscar Peterson, and Art Tatum. Among the secular performers who profoundly affected Franklin was the rhythm and blues vocalist Dinah Washington. As a teenager Franklin began to travel with her father as the opening act for his gospel show. It was in Detroit's New Bethel Baptist Church, however, that the fourteen-year-old Franklin made her first recording. The live album was released by Chess Records in 1956, the same label that distributed her father's sermons.

By the age of eighteen Franklin had left Detroit for New York City. Though she was reportedly wooed by Sam Cooke, then an artist for RCA Records, and by BERRY GORDY JR.'s fledgling Motown label, the legendary producer John Hammond signed Franklin to record for Columbia Records. Hammond had been instrumental in the early career of BILLIE HOLIDAY, and it was with vocalists like Holiday, Dinah Washington, and BESSIE SMITH in mind that Hammond helped to craft Franklin's early recordings for the Columbia label. Franklin's initial recordings—*Aretha (with the Ray Bryant Combo)* (1961), *The Electrifying Aretha Franklin* (1962), and *The Tender, the Moving, the Swinging Aretha Franklin* (1962)—were produced by Hammond and Robert Mersey. The albums included "Blue Holiday" and "God Bless the Child." An accomplished pianist, Franklin was also featured as an instrumentalist on some of these albums. During this period Franklin married Ted White, who also became her manager.

Robert Mersey also produced *Laughing on the Outside* (1963) and *Unforgettable—A Tribute to Dinah Washington* (1964). The latter recording featured Franklin's renditions of some of Washington's best-known recordings, including "This Bitter Earth," "Evil Gal Blues," and "What a Difference a Day Makes." Though Franklin was served well by Hammond and Mersey, it was with Johnny Otis that her career finally exhibited some degree of consistency. Franklin never achieved broad, mainstream appeal during her tenure at Columbia Records (1960–1966), but her recordings with Otis, which included *Runnin' Out of Fools* (1964), *Yeah!!! In Person with Her Quartet* (1965), and *Soul Sister* (1966), positioned Franklin as a rhythm and blues artist, as opposed to a jazz or mainstream pop artist.

Franklin signed with Atlantic Records in 1967 and began a fruitful professional relationship with producer Jerry Wexler. Wexler's first instinct upon signing Franklin was to have her travel to the South and record at the legendary Fame Studios in Muscle Shoals, Alabama. On the evening of 24 January 1967 Franklin and a group of white rockabilly musicians laid down the basic tracks to "I Never Loved a Man (The Way I Love You)" and "Do Right Woman—Do Right Man," songs that changed the face of American pop music and began Franklin's ascent as one of the most influential musical artists in American history. Franklin's first four albums for Atlantic, *I Never Loved a Man the Way I Loved You* (1967), *Aretha Arrives* (1967), *Lady Soul* (1968), and *Aretha Now* (1968), established her as the most important black female vocal artist since Billie Holiday. The recordings contained a litany of hit singles such as "Respect," "Dr. Feelgood," "Baby, I Love You," "Chain of Fools," "(You Make Me Feel Like) A Natural Woman," and "Think" that are synonymous with the best music produced since the advent of the rock-and-roll era in the mid-1950s. It was in this period that Franklin became universally known as the "Queen of Soul." On the strength of "Respect," Franklin earned her first Grammy Award for Best R&B Vocal Performance, Female. She won the award every year between 1967 and 1974, totaling ten Grammy Awards during that time frame. Though Franklin never viewed her version of "Respect" as explicitly political, the passion with which she expressed her desire for respect, literally spelling out the word in the song's memorable breakdown, resonated within both the civil rights and burgeoning women's rights movements.

While Franklin still maintained a significant popular following, her subsequent body of work for Atlantic in the early 1970s was less commercial and more reflective of her maturing artistry. Her music during this period also reflected the end of her tumultuous marriage with Ted White, which ended in 1969, most notably in the song "All the King's Horses." This body of work was marked by the number of recordings written by Franklin and her sister Carolyn. Notable among these recordings are *Aretha—Live at the Fillmore West* (1971), *Young, Gifted and Black* (1972), and *Amazing Grace* (1972). Whereas *Live at the Fillmore West* gave witness to Franklin's wide appeal beyond soul music audiences (and provided a once in lifetime performance with RAY CHARLES on "Spirit in the Dark") and *Young, Gifted and Black* represented Franklin's most cogent statements on the political movement for which many believe her music is the soundtrack, *Amazing Grace* represented the most important musical statement of her career. Recorded live at the New Temple Missionary Baptist Church in Los Angeles, nearly fifteen years to the day that she stepped into Fame Studios, *Amazing Grace* reunited Franklin with James Cleveland and the black church traditions that birthed her. Highlights of

the recording include a ten-minute version of "Amazing Grace" and a stirring rendition of Clara Ward's "How I Got Over," with the legendary vocalist sitting in the audience.

During the 1970s Franklin had the opportunity to work with well-known black producers like QUINCY JONES and Curtis Mayfield, who produced *Hey Now Hey (The Other Side of the Sky)* in 1973 and *Sparkle* in 1976, respectively. The latter recording featured music written for the film *Sparkle* and featured "Giving Him Something He Can Feel," Franklin's last major hit for the Atlantic label. She married actor Glynn Turman in 1978 but their marriage ended six years later. Franklin signed with the Arista label in 1980. *Love All the Hurt Away* (1981), her second album for the label, took advantage of her star-turn in the film *The Blues Brothers* (1979), where she appeared as a soul-singing waitress. The project also featured a duet with George Benson on the title track.

In an effort to update her sound, Franklin was paired with young songwriters and producers Luther Vandross and Marcus Miller. Both *Jump to It* (1982) and *Get It Right* (1983) were moderate successes, but it wasn't until 1985, when she joined forces with Michael Narada Walden on *Who's Zoomin' Who?* with the song "Freeway of Love" that Franklin matched her commercial success of the late 1960s and early 1970s. Her follow-up recording, *Aretha* (1986), featured a duet with George Michael on the song "I Knew You Were Waiting," which became her first number one pop song since "Respect." In 1987 Franklin was inducted into the Rock and Roll Hall of Fame, becoming the first woman to achieve the honor. During this period she also returned to her gospel roots, recording *One Lord, One Faith, One Baptism* (1988). Franklin continued to record for the Arista label throughout the 1990s, notably pairing with hip-hop artist Lauryn Hill on the Grammy Award–nominated "A Rose Is Still a Rose" in 1998. She also received a Lifetime Achievement Award from the National Academy of Recording Arts and Sciences (NARAS) in 1994. At the 1998 Grammy Awards ceremony, Franklin performed the aria "Nessun Dorma" from Puccini's *Turandot*, filling in at the last moment for the famed

Italian tenor Luciano Pavarotti, who had taken ill less than an hour before his scheduled performance. Franklin also has the distinction of performing at inaugural celebrations for presidents Jimmy Carter (1977) and Bill Clinton (1993) and at the funeral for MARTIN LUTHER KING JR., where she sang "Amazing Grace."

Aretha Franklin remains the most celebrated black female singer ever. Her influence continues to be heard in artists like Miki Howard, Whitney Houston, and Mary J. Blige. Franklin's well-known moniker, "Queen of Soul," acknowledges that she has become one of the yardsticks by which black popular music is measured. Late in her career, Franklin's releases are still viewed as an event.

FURTHER READING

Franklin, Aretha, with David Ritz. *Aretha: From These Roots* (1999).
Bego, Mark. *Aretha Franklin: The Queen of Soul* (2001).
Ward, Brian. *Just My Soul Responding: Rhythm and Blues, Black Consciousness, and Race Relations* (1998).
Wexler, Jerry, and David Ritz. *Rhythm and Blues: A Life in American Music* (1993).
—MARC ANTHONY NEAL

FRANKLIN, C. L.

(22 Jan. 1915–27 July 1984), preacher, was born Clarence LaVaughn Pitman in Sunflower, Mississippi, to Elijah J. Pitman and Willie Ann Pitman, sharecroppers. Elijah served in Europe during World War I, returned to Mississippi briefly, and then departed. Shortly thereafter, Willie Ann married Henry Franklin, a farmer; the family took his name, and Franklin became Clarence's father. As a boy Clarence usually went to school from December to March, which was when he was not needed in the field. His mother took him and his stepsister, Aretha, to St. Peter's Rock Baptist Church, where he sang in the choir, and eventually became lead tenor. His father, religious but not a churchgoer, exposed Clarence to the blues idiom of BLIND LEMON JEFFERSON and other soulful musicians.

At the age of nine or ten Clarence attended a revival meeting and took his

FRANKLIN, C. L.

first step toward a career in the ministry when he joined the church. In the tradition of many black Baptist congregations in the South, he sat on the mourner's bench with the other initiates, gave a personal testimony (in his case without ecstatic exaltation), and was voted in by acclamation. Full-immersion baptism in a local river soon followed. As a teenager Clarence heard a sermon by Dr. Benjamin J. Perkins about the "doubting" apostle Thomas that prompted him to wonder if he, too, had a calling to preach. He described receiving a sign, a vision like the burning bush encountered by Moses, except that in his vision the walls of his room were ablaze without being consumed. From the flames came a voice saying, "Go and preach the gospel to all the nations" (Franklin, 9). He preached his first sermon at the age of fifteen or sixteen, but there was no congregation in the vicinity that needed a minister, particularly one so young and inexperienced. He became a migrant worker and itinerate preacher, working on farms from Mississippi to Michigan, picking everything from cotton to strawberries, and preaching at camp meetings and receptive congregations along the way. After a few years he returned to Mississippi, where his father, who needed help on his farm, told Clarence, "Now you have got to make up your mind whether you want to preach or plow" (Franklin, 13).

Clarence decided to devote himself to preaching and was ordained Reverend C. L. Franklin at St. Peter's Rock when he was only seventeen or eighteen years old. However, finding a congregation capable of supporting a minister during the Depression was very difficult. Many of the Negro churches throughout the South lacked the resources to engage a permanent minister. Hence, gifted black preachers sometimes worked a network of small congregations in order to sustain themselves. Franklin worked as a traveling preacher until he landed a temporary appointment at the County Line Baptist Church, where he learned painful lessons about the politics of church management that equipped him with skills that proved to be as valuable to his future success as his impressive oratorical ability. While visiting a congregation in Shelby during the late 1930s he met his wife, Barbara Siggers,

the church pianist. They had four children before her death in 1952.

Intellectually, Franklin demonstrated a passion for the life of the mind that was equal to his concern for the health of the soul. He studied theology at Greenville Industrial College and took a wide range of courses at LeMoyne College (now LeMoyne-Owen College), in Memphis, Tennessee. His scholarly manner distinguished him from many black preachers who had mastered the unique African American sermonic style, but who lacked Franklin's cerebral depth. Yet, unlike many seminary-trained clerics, Franklin's exegesis of scripture retained the fire associated with the black pulpit. In his view, "the mental can be spiritual, even more spiritual than the emotional" (Franklin, 16). In his version of "The Eagle Stirreth Her Nest," a traditional sermon that preachers had been adapting since the 1920s, Franklin vividly examines a difficult biblical metaphor with power and insight. In "The Twenty-Third Psalm," he breathes new life into a familiar passage by providing historical context while extracting contemporary relevance.

Some scholars have denigrated the oratorical style of Franklin and other black preachers, suggesting that their use of such rhetorical devices as call-and-response, repetition, syncopation, and the distinctive chant called the "hum" or "whoop" is nothing more than histrionics that only appeal to the emotions of uneducated listeners. Recent scholarship has shown, however, that the best black preachers combine these features into an interpretive style that emphasizes a theological relationship between a mighty God and an oppressed people that is particular to African Americans (LaRue, 19). Many aspects of this style are African in origin, and the hum, which Franklin reserved for his peroration, signifies a collective celebration and affirmation of what has been revealed in the sermon, rather than an academic summary of it. Gary Hatch's study of Franklin's homilies shows that he used narratives to "establish a series of relationships that appeal to the intellect and imagination as well as the emotions. These relationships constitute a type of 'poetic' logic in which reasoning is neither inductive nor deductive, but rather analogical" (Hatch, 228).

During his third year at LeMoyne College, Franklin accepted an offer to pastor the Friendship Baptist Church in Buffalo, New York. There he preached to a prosperous congregation while he studied at the University of Buffalo, but he soon found the environment both too cold and too conservative. In 1945 he spoke at the National Baptist Convention in Detroit. Representatives of the New Bethel Baptist Church in Detroit were so impressed that they invited him to lead their congregation. Over the next three decades, he brought that church from its location in a converted bowling alley to a beautifully renovated theater, and the congregation grew to more than two thousand members. He accomplished this by first acquiring a radio broadcast that attracted local listeners, and then in 1953 he signed a recording contract with Chess Records. Until that point Chess had only recruited musicians such as MUDDY WATERS, BIG WILLIE DIXON, and CHUCK BERRY. Franklin began touring the country with renowned gospel groups like the Dixie Hummingbirds and the Clara Ward Gospel Singers. Later he began touring with his own choir, which included his daughter, ARETHA FRANKLIN, who later achieved stardom as the "Queen of Soul." Over the course of his career, he produced seventy-six recordings of sermons and music that have sold millions of copies.

Throughout the 1960s Franklin was active in the civil rights movement. In 1963 he organized a march in Detroit, where his friend, MARTIN LUTHER KING JR., delivered an early version of his renowned "I Have a Dream" speech before it was heard nationally at the March on Washington. Franklin also worked to elect John Conyers to the U.S. Congress and COLEMAN YOUNG as the first black mayor of Detroit. His life was tragically cut short on 10 June 1979, when he was shot by burglars; he remained in a comatose state for five years before he died. As the quintessential black preacher, Franklin continues to influence, and perhaps even define, later generations of preachers. As Jeff Todd Titon observed, "Every African American preacher either has imitated him or has tried to avoid doing so" (Franklin, ix), and JESSE JACKSON has said that in the world of black

313

ministers, Franklin is regarded as "the Rabbi" of black preaching.

FURTHER READING

Franklin, C. L. *Give Me This Mountain* (1989).

Hatch, Gary Layne. "Logic in the Black Folk Sermon: The Sermons of Rev. C. L. Franklin," *Journal of Black Studies* 26:3 (1996).

LaRue, Cleophus J. *The Heart of Black Preaching* (2000).

Moyd, Olin P. *The Sacred Art: Preaching and Theology in the African American Tradition* (1995).

Obituary: *New York Times*, 28 July 1984.
—SHOLOMO B. LEVY

FRANKLIN, JOHN HOPE (2 Jan. 1915–)

historian, was born in Rentiesville, Oklahoma, the youngest of four children of Buck Colbert Franklin, an attorney, and Mollie Parker, an elementary school teacher. He was named after the famed educator JOHN HOPE, who had taught his parents in Atlanta, Georgia. When John's father had been ejected from a courtroom by a judge in Ardmore, Oklahoma, who refused to preside over a case argued by a "nigger," the family moved to Rentiesville, and then Colbert went alone to Tulsa in 1921 to establish his law practice. The family struggled and worried for his

Simmie Knox's portrait of Franklin.
Courtesy of the artist

safety after reading reports of the bloody race riot that took place in Tulsa that year. Colbert's office was burned down, but within a few years he had reestablished himself to the point where he could send for his family. Young John was an extraordinary student who won the local spelling bee for three consecutive years. Having been taught to read by his mother at age five, he also had begun to imitate his father's habit of reading or writing late into the night, despite the fact that the family had no electricity.

As a boy, Franklin developed a love for classical music and used money he earned from a paper route to attend local concerts. His parents declined to go with him, believing acceptance of the theater's Jim Crow seating arrangement to be a concession to segregation. As a teenager, he expected to follow in his father's footsteps and become a lawyer. Business was so slow during the Depression that when Franklin would stop by the office after school, his father would often have time to instruct him in classical Greek history and philosophy. Franklin was the valedictorian of his high school class and chose to attend Fisk University in Tennessee. Despite his tuition scholarship, he was forced to work several jobs to meet his living expenses. He took great satisfaction in remembering that an early English professor, who told him that he would "never be able to command the English language," later served on the committee that awarded him the prestigious Bancroft Prize for an article published in the *Journal of Negro History*. As president of the student body, he led a protest against the lynching of a black man near the campus and sent letters denouncing the practice to the mayor of Nashville and to President Franklin D. Roosevelt.

Academically, Franklin fell under the intellectual spell of Theodore S. Currier, a white, Harvard-trained historian who, over the course of four years, so imbued Franklin with a passion for history that it soon surpassed his interest in the law. After graduating from Fisk magna cum laude in 1935, Franklin was admitted to graduate school in the history department at Harvard University, but his parents, who had lost their home while he was in college, could not afford to send him. Professor Currier borrowed

the five hundred dollars Franklin needed to begin his studies.

In many ways Franklin's career mirrors that of his predecessor W. E. B. DU BOIS, who also attended Harvard after graduating from Fisk, except that Du Bois was required to enter as an undergraduate before being admitted to the graduate program. Franklin was the first African American from a historically black institution to enter the graduate history program directly; he completed the MA in only nine months while working odd jobs to sustain himself. He won fellowships to cover his tuition during the remaining years. While conducting research for his dissertation, Franklin had a chance meeting with Du Bois and was crushed by the elder scholar's condescension. The two men would later become respected colleagues, but Franklin often told the story of their first encounter as an example of the importance of humility among what Du Bois called the "talented tenth."

Franklin married his Fisk classmate, Aurelia E. Whittington, in 1940; they had one son, John. In 1941 Franklin received his PhD in History, and his dissertation was soon published as *The Free Negro in North Carolina, 1790–1860* (1943). During World War II he was denied a position as a historian with the War Department, even though white applicants with fewer academic credentials were accepted. From 1936 to 1956 he held faculty appointments at several historically black colleges, including Fisk, St. Augustine's College, North Carolina College, and Howard University.

He was living in Washington, D.C., and teaching at Howard while lawyers for the NAACP Legal Defense Fund were preparing to argue the *Brown v. Board of Education* case before the Supreme Court. THURGOOD MARSHALL asked Franklin to lead a group of scholars in documenting the historical portion of their brief. He also collaborated with CARTER G. WOODSON, known as the father of African American history, and scholars such as RAYFORD W. LOGAN, the chairman of Howard's history department, in promoting the work of the Association for the Study of Negro Life and History. His involvement in the civil rights movement, however, was not limited to the relative comfort of libraries. He prepared a program with the British Broadcasting Company called *The Briton's Guide to the March on Washington* in 1963, and in 1965 he joined some forty other historians in the Selma to Montgomery March.

Franklin wrote or edited some twenty books and over one hundred articles. His most significant contributions to the study of history are *The Militant South, 1800–1860* (1956) and *Reconstruction after the Civil War* (1961). These books place him in the revisionist vanguard that debunked the prevailing myths of the halcyon years of the Old South and the so-called tragic years of Reconstruction. Franklin replaced such interpretations with accurate descriptions of a brutal and bellicose society that was quick to go to war and to oppress large segments of its population because of racial difference. Franklin's most widely read book, *From Slavery to Freedom*, appeared in 1947 and has become a staple in the teaching of African American history. By 2003 it had gone through eight editions, had sold over three million copies, and had been translated into five foreign languages. *Black Leaders of the Twentieth Century* (1981), which he edited with August Meier, remains a highly regarded anthology. More recently, he coauthored with Loren Schweninger the prizewinning book *Runaway Slaves: Rebels on the Plantation* (1999).

In his reflective volume *Race and History* (1989), Franklin pays tribute to GEORGE WASHINGTON WILLIAMS, the nineteenth-century historian who wrote some of the first studies of black life and who, by insisting that he was not a "blind panegyrist of my race" (Franklin, *Race and History*, 44) set the highest professional standards for later historians. Among Williams's followers are Carter Woodson, BENJAMIN QUARLES, and Du Bois, whom Franklin considered to be the father of the broader field of African American studies.

Throughout his career, Franklin received offers to become dean and president of academic institutions for much higher pay than he earned as a scholar and teacher. He refused them all, assuming only the chairmanship of history departments. In 1956 he accepted the chairmanship of the all-white, fifty-two-member history department of Brooklyn College. The southern-born historian of the South measured the academic cost of the racism he experienced

in New York City in terms of the price it exacted in scholarship, surmising that in the time it took him to find a home in Brooklyn and a bank that would finance a mortgage, he could have written a small book. In 1964 he joined the history department of the University of Chicago, serving from 1967 to 1970 as chairman. Franklin also became the first African American to head a number of professional organizations: the American Studies Association (1967–1968); the Southern Historical Association (1970–1971); the United Chapters of Phi Beta Kappa (1973–1976), presiding during the organization's bicentennial; the Organization of American Historians (1974–1975); and the American Historical Association (1979–1980).

In 1982 Franklin became the James B. Duke Professor of History at Duke University, and in 1985 he joined the Duke Law School, where he served until 1992. He testified in 1987 before the Senate Committee on the Judiciary in opposition to the appointment of Robert Bork to the Supreme Court. He has received numerous honors. In 1995 Duke University established the John Hope Franklin Collection of African and African American Documentation and in 2001 the John Hope Franklin Center for Interdisciplinary and International Studies, along with the John Hope Franklin Humanities Institutes at the Center. In 1995 Franklin won the NAACP's highest honor, the Spingarn Medal, and President Bill Clinton awarded him the Presidential Medal of Freedom in the same year. Clinton also appointed Franklin in 1997 to lead a presidential commission on race. In 2002 Franklin received the Gold Medal of the Academy of Arts and Letters, and he has received over two hundred awards and honorary degrees during his distinguished career.

John Franklin has lectured throughout the world. In 2001 he collaborated with South African Archbishop Desmond Tutu in a PBS film, *Tutu and Franklin: A Journey Toward Peace*, in which the two of them counsel an interracial group of students from the United States, Senegal, and South Africa. Franklin, the consummate Renaissance man, remains engaged in numerous scholarly, civic, and horticultural

activities. His prominence in orchid culture has resulted in two orchids that bear his name: the *Phalaenopsis John Hope Franklin* and the *Brassolaelia Cattleya John Hope Franklin*.

FURTHER READING

Franklin, John Hope. "A Life of Learning" in *Race and History: Selected Essays 1938–1988* (1990).

Gates, Henry Louis, Jr., and Cornel West. "John Hope Franklin" in *The African American Century* (2000).

Meier, August. *Black History and the Historical Profession, 1915–80* (1986).

Thorpe, Earl E. *Black Historians: A Critique* (1971).

—SHOLOMO B. LEVY

FRAZIER, E. FRANKLIN

FRAZIER, E. FRANKLIN (24 Sept. 1894–17 May 1962), sociologist, was born Edward Franklin Frazier in Baltimore, Maryland, the son of James Edward Frazier, a bank messenger, and Mary E. Clark. Frazier's father had taught himself to read and write and until his death in 1904, stressed the usefulness of a formal education as a means of escaping poverty.

Young Frazier's interest in sociology began at an early age. It can be partly traced to James Frazier's attempt to make his children aware of the volatile atmosphere of race relations in Atlanta, Georgia, and Baltimore with daily discussions of articles and editorials from local newspapers. Despite the death of his father when Frazier was eleven years old, it appears that this process had a profound effect on Frazier's intellectual growth. He attended elementary and secondary school in Baltimore, and after graduating from Baltimore Colored High School in 1912, he attended, on scholarship, Howard University in Washington, D.C., graduating with honors in 1916. At Howard he subscribed to a vague socialist philosophy but, more importantly, demonstrated his mastery in languages, literature, and mathematics. He later taught these subjects at successive institutions: mathematics at Tuskegee Institute (1916–1917), English, French, and history at St. Paul's Normal and Industrial School in Lawrenceville, Virginia (1917–1918), and French and mathematics at Baltimore High School (1918–1919).

In 1919 Frazier entered the graduate program in sociology at Clark University (Worcester, Massachusetts), where, under the tutelage of Frank Hankins, he became skilled in the use of sociological methods and theories as objective tools in the examination of racial problems in American society. After receiving his MA in 1920, Frazier spent a year as a researcher at the New York School of Social Work (1920–1921) followed by a year at the University of Copenhagen in Denmark (1921–1922), where as a research fellow of the American Scandinavian Foundation, he studied that nation's rural folk high schools.

In 1922, back in the United States, Frazier married Marie Brown. Their union was childless. Earlier that same year he became director of the summer school session at Livingstone College in Salisbury, North Carolina. Until 1927 he also held a combined appointment as director of the Atlanta University School of Social Work and as instructor of sociology at Morehouse College in Atlanta. During these years Frazier published often and widely, more than thirty articles on such topics as the African American family, the activities of black business leaders, and the development of the African American middle class, until the appearance of "The Pathology of Race Prejudice" in the June 1927 issue of *Forum*.

Frazier's analysis of racial discrimination as a social pathology manifested in societal norms was highly controversial. Locals discovered the article with the appearance of several editorials in the Atlanta *Constitution* and the Atlanta *Independence* that condemned the findings revealed in the article. Not only did these editorials criticize Frazier's analysis, but they also questioned his intellectual abilities. Soon thereafter, the Fraziers began to receive harassing phone calls, death threats, and threats of being lynched. As a result of this violent atmosphere, and at the urging of friends, the Fraziers soon left the city.

From Atlanta, Frazier went to the University of Chicago as a graduate student and as a research fellow in the Department of Sociology. In 1929 he accepted a position as a lecturer in the sociology department at Fisk University in Nashville. After earning a PhD

in 1931, Frazier remained at Fisk, where he subsequently became a research professor of sociology in the Department of Social Science. In 1934 he became professor and head of the Department of Sociology at Howard University. He retired as professor emeritus of sociology in 1959 but continued to teach through both the African Studies Program at Howard and the School of Advanced International Studies Program at Johns Hopkins University until his death.

The black family—which Frazier viewed as a social unit that helped integrate its members into American society—and race relations in the United States, especially their negative impact on the development of the African American family, as well as the effects of urbanization on black family structure were all explored in Frazier's dissertation, published as *The Negro Family in Chicago* (1932). This pathbreaking book, which has been compared to W. E. B. Du Bois's classic study *The Philadelphia Negro* (1899), was followed by his book *The Negro Family in the United States* (1939). This book, which won the Anisfield Award in 1939 for the most significant work in the field of race relations, expanded on Frazier's earlier findings in Chicago and analyzed the various cultural and historical forces that influenced the development of the African American family from the time of slavery until the 1920s.

Frazier's most controversial book was *Black Bourgeoisie* (1957), an examination of the economic, political, and social behavior of the African American middle class as shaped by the experience of slavery and the forces of racial prejudice and discrimination. Frazier argued that the African American middle class had developed as a hybrid group. Lacking a solid economic base and subject to the same social marginality and isolation suffered by the African American population as a whole, the African American middle class tended to adhere to a set of values that differed from that of middle-class whites. More interested in high levels of consumption and status than in production and savings, the black bourgeoisie, Frazier concluded, tended to share the values and mirror the behavior of the white upper class rather than the white middle class. A Guggenheim

Fellowship awarded in 1939 enabled Frazier to extend his study of race relations and black family life to Brazil and the Caribbean. An ancillary interest in European and African relations was the focus of his *Race and Culture Contacts in the Modern World* (1957).

Frazier served as president of the District of Columbia Sociological Society and the Eastern Sociology Society and as vice president of the African Studies Association and the American Sociological Society (now the American Sociological Association). His election in 1948 as president of the American Sociological Society marked the first time that an African American had served as chief presiding officer of a national professional association. In 1955 he became an honorary member of the Gamma chapter of Phi Beta Kappa at Howard University. He died in Washington, D.C.

FURTHER READING

Franklin's papers are in the Moorland-Spingarn Research Center, Howard University.

Blackwell, James E., and Morris Janowitz, eds. "E. Franklin Frazier" in *Black Sociologists*.
Edwards, G. Franklin. "E. Franklin Frazier: Race, Education, and Community" in *Sociological Traditions from Generation to Generation*, eds. Robert K. Merton and Matilda White Riley (1980).
Odum, Howard. *American Sociology* (1951).
Platt, Anthony M. *E. Franklin Frazier Reconsidered* (1991).
Vlasek, Dale R. "E. Franklin Frazier and the Problem of Assimilation" in *Ideas in America's Cultures from Republic to Mass Society*, ed. Hamilton Cravens (1982).

Obituary: *New York Times*, 22 May 1962.

—ERIC R. JACKSON

FREEMAN, ELIZABETH (c. 1744–28 Dec. 1829), civil rights litigant, known as Mum Bett, was born a slave in Claverack, New York, most likely to African parents. Mum Bett and her sister were owned by the Dutch Hogeboom family in Claverack. At an uncertain date, the sisters were sold to the family of John Ashley, a judge in the Massachusetts Court of Common Pleas and a prominent citizen of Sheffield, Massachusetts. Little is known

Elizabeth "Mum Bett" Freeman's suit for liberty, argued and won by Thomas Sedgwick in 1783, significantly diminished the practice and effects of slavery in Massachusetts. In 1811 Susan Sedgwick painted Freeman's portrait in watercolors. Courtesy of the Massachusetts Historical Society

resolved that "Mankind in a State of Nature are equal, free and independent of each other, and have a right to the undisturbed Enjoyment of their lives, their Liberty and Property"—appealed to the law for the return of his slave, Mum Bett.

Instead of returning to the Ashleys, Mum Bett approached Theodore Sedgwick Sr., a lawyer she may have first met when he was working with Ashley on the Sheffield Declaration. Mum Bett convinced Sedgwick to represent her in suing for her freedom. Massachusetts's newly enacted 1780 state constitution had declared all men born free and equal, Mum Bett reasoned, and so her bondage must be illegal. Sedgwick agreed to take the case, which was joined by a man named Brom, another of Ashley's slaves. When curious interviewers subsequently asked her how she had arrived at that premise, perhaps presuming wrongly that an illiterate slave would not have any legal knowledge, she is reported to have said, "By keepin' still and mindin' things." By this she meant "when she was waiting at table, she heard gentlemen talking over the Bill of Rights and the new constitution of Massachusetts; and in all they said she never heard but that all people were born free and equal, and she thought long about it, and resolved she would try whether she did not come in among them" (Kaplan, 244). In this way Mum Bett, like many African Americans, was capitalizing on the hard-won knowledge she acquired as an exploited worker. On her own initiative, this Northern working woman tested Massachusetts's state constitution by claiming that its theory of men's equality made slavery illegal.

Sedgwick won the case, *Brom and Bett v. J. Ashley Esq.*, in 1781. A state court granted Mum Bett and Brom their freedom and required Ashley to pay them thirty shillings in damages. The case was subsequently hailed as a precedent-setting, landmark civil rights decision that helped diminish the practice and effects of slavery in Massachusetts, though scholars are quick to point out that technically speaking, slavery was not abolished in the state until 1866. At the time of the suit, Mum Bett is believed to have been the widow of a Revolutionary War veteran and the mother of one daughter, called Little

about Mum Bett's life with the Ashleys, but it probably resembled the life of many northern slaves during the eighteenth century. Most slaves lived in small households in close proximity to their owners and performed a wide range of tasks to support the North's diversified economy.

Mum Bett's decision to sue for freedom was sparked by an incident of cruelty that is prominent in accounts of

her life. When her mistress, Hannah Ashley, struck Mum Bett's sister "in a fit of passion" with a heated shovel, Mum Bett interposed and was struck instead. She "received the blow; and bore the honorable scar it left to the day of her death" (Swan, 52). After the incident, Mum Bett left the Ashleys and refused to return. John Ashley—who had, ironically, chaired the committee that drafted the 1773 Sheffield Declaration, which

Bett. After gaining her freedom, Mum Bett gave herself the surname "Freeman." The case brought Freeman and Sedgwick, who later became a judge and a senator, notoriety in their day and linked their names for posterity.

After the ruling, Freeman went to work for the Sedgwicks. Consequently, the most documented period of her life is time she worked for this prominent New England family. Freeman was remembered fondly, if somewhat paternalistically, by the Sedgwick children, Theodore Sedgwick Jr. and his sister, the writer Catherine Maria Sedgwick, for her skilled nursing, her long tenure as the family's loyal and faithful servant, and her spirited defense of the family's property during Shay's Rebellion in 1786. Freeman is buried in the Sedgwick family plot. Her tombstone reads, "She was born a slave and remained a slave for nearly thirty years. She could neither read nor write yet in her own sphere she had no superior or equal. She neither wasted time nor property. She never violated a trust nor failed to perform a duty. In every situation of domestic trial, she was the most efficient helper, and the tenderest friend. Good mother, farewell." Freeman inspired admiration from the family for her independent spirit. As Theodore Sedgwick Jr. related during an 1831 abolitionist speech in which he invoked Freeman's experience, "If there could be a practical refutation of the imagined superiority of our race to hers, the life and character of this woman would afford that refutation.... She had nothing of the submissive or subdued character, which succumbs to superior force.... On the contrary,...she uniformly...obtained an ascendancy over all those with whom she was associated in service" (Kaplan, 246).

Freeman is one of the most visible exemplars of often invisible, illiterate African Americans who contributed to black communities' challenges to racial inequality in the early republic. Their courageous efforts occurred well before the more famous ones of nineteenth-century black abolitionists such as FREDERICK DOUGLASS and SOJOURNER TRUTH. Though we know relatively little about Elizabeth Freeman, parallels exist between her life and that of Truth, another Northern black working woman. As an impecunious former

slave, before becoming renowned as an abolitionist, Truth did not hesitate to appeal to the courts for the return of her illegally sold son, despite her unlettered and lowly social status. In this way, Truth followed in Freeman's footsteps, both of them exemplifying a tradition of overlooked African American women who fearlessly claimed their inheritance of liberty as civic participants and contributors to national life.

Freeman eventually left the Sedgwick's employ and became a sought after nurse and midwife. She lived with her daughter in a house next door to Revolutionary War veteran AGRIPPA HULL. Elizabeth Freeman died a free woman in 1829. One of her great-grandchildren was W. E. B. DU BOIS, who was born almost forty years later in Great Barrington, Massachussetts, the town where her historic case was argued.

FURTHER READING

The Sedgwick family papers are available in a special collection at the Stockbridge Public Library, Stockbridge, Massachusetts.

Kaplan, Sidney. *The Black Presence in the Era of the American Revolution 1770–1800* (1973).
Martineau, Harriet. *Retrospect of Western Travel 2* (1838).
Nell, William C. *The Colored Patriots of the American Revolution* (1855, 1968).
Sedgwick, Theodore. *The Practicability of the Abolition of Slavery* (1831).
Swan, Jon. "The Slave Who Sued for Freedom." *American Heritage* 41 (Mar. 1990).
                                    —XIOMARA SANTAMARINA

 FULLER, META WARRICK (9 June 1877– Mar. 1968), sculptor, was born Meta Vaux Warrick in Philadelphia, Pennsylvania, the daughter of William H. Warrick and Emma Jones. Meta's great-grandmother, according to family lore, was an Ethiopian princess brought to the American colonies as a slave. Emma owned and operated several hairdressing parlors that catered to a white clientele. William owned a chain of barbershops and dabbled in real estate. Meta was ten years younger than her two siblings, William and Blanche. Through lessons and field trips to museums and concerts, the Warricks introduced their children to art and encouraged their creative endeavors.

Meta, who played the guitar, took dancing lessons, and sang in the church choir, exhibited an early talent for drawing.

After graduation from public high school in 1894, Meta won a three-year scholarship to the Pennsylvania Museum and School for Industrial Arts (now the Philadelphia College of Art). In 1897 her stay was extended when she was awarded a postgraduate scholarship to study sculpture. She graduated in 1899 with honors and took home first prize for best general work in modeling.

In 1899, following a generation of American artists who made pilgrimages to perfect their training and elevate their stature, Warrick left for Paris, which by the late nineteenth century had become the center of fine arts in the Western world. Paris later became the preferred destination for African American artists like WILLIAM H. JOHNSON, Hale Woodruff, and LOÏS MAILOU JONES, who were weary of America's racist and segregationist policies. The African American painter HENRY OSSAWA TANNER, a friend of Meta's uncle, had moved to Paris in 1891 and acted as her guardian during her stay in France. She studied at

Beginning in 1914 with this bronze, Ethiopia Awakening, *Meta Warrick Fuller created a number of sculptures embodying the struggles and aspirations of African Americans.* Schomburg Center

the Ecole des Beaux-Arts, the epicenter of academic art instruction, and, from 1900 to 1902, at the Academie Colarossi, where she met the American sculptor Augustus Saint-Gaudens.

In the summer of 1900 Warrick met W. E. B. DU BOIS, who was in Paris for the Universal Exposition. Du Bois took the young artist under his wing, escorting her to social events, introducing her to the city's literati, and encouraging her to adopt African American themes in her work. The next summer Warrick arrived at the house of sculptor Auguste Rodin with her sculpture *Secret Sorrow (The Man Eating His Heart)* under her arm. "Mademoiselle," Rodin is said to have exclaimed, "you are a sculptor. You have the sense of flow in your fingers." Encouraged by Saint-Gaudens and Rodin, Warrick began holding private exhibitions at her studio. In 1902 S. Bing mounted a one-woman show of her work at his prestigious gallery, L'Art Nouveau. Warrick's Parisian period culminated in 1903 when the Salon d'Automne exhibited *The Wretched*, a sculpture depicting seven figures in varying forms of human anguish. Traditionally trained in the academic style, Warrick was one of only a few women to study in Paris at the turn of the century. Emotional, expressive, and imbued with themes of death and sorrow, her Parisian work owes a great deal to Rodin and to the romantic realist sculptural style popular in late nineteenth-century France.

Upon her return to the United States in 1902, Warrick enrolled at the Pennsylvania Academy of Fine Arts, where she won the school's top award in ceramics. Encouraged by her success in Paris, she set up a studio in Philadelphia. Local dealers, however, failed to buy her work. Certain that her race was the reason behind their disinterest, Warrick turned to clients in Philadelphia's black community. Her re-engagement with the African American community resulted in an increase in black subjects in her work. In 1907 she became the first African American woman to receive a federal art commission when she was selected to produce a sculpture for the Negro Pavilion at the Jamestown Tercentennial Exposition. A depiction of the history of African Americans since settling in Jamestown in 1607, the tableau

was composed of fifteen pieces and one hundred and fifty figures.

In 1909 Warrick married SOLOMON FULLER, a neuropathologist and psychiatrist from Monrovia, Liberia, whose father was a repatriated former American slave. The newlyweds moved to Framingham, Massachusetts, over the objections of racist neighbors who organized a petition attempting to stop the Fullers from integrating the predominantly white suburb of Boston. A year later most of Fuller's work was destroyed in a fire that razed the Philadelphia warehouse where she was storing the contents of her studio. Devastated by her loss, which included almost all of her Parisian sculptures, Fuller shifted her focus to starting a family. Between 1910 and 1916 she bore three sons: Solomon Jr., Perry James, and William Thomas. Fuller eventually returned to sculpting, and she thrived in the Boston-area art scene. Critics have argued that Fuller's focus on domestic life, which was encouraged by her husband, kept her from becoming an internationally recognized artist.

It was Du Bois who both reignited Fuller's career and prompted her serious adoption of African American subject matter. In 1913, while editor of the *Crisis*, he commissioned a sculpture commemorating the fiftieth anniversary of the Emancipation Proclamation. In the resulting work, *Spirit of Emancipation*, an eight-foot-tall figural grouping, Fuller eschewed images of victimization and paternalism common to representations of slavery and featured instead a boy and girl with distinctly African features. The work exhibited a quieter, more stoic, and less emotionally wrought quality than her Parisian pieces. Inspired by Du Bois's Pan-African philosophy, Fuller emphasized the commonality of black Americans' heritage by mining African and African American themes and forms.

Fuller's sculpture, *Ethiopia Awakening*, marks a shift in African American representation. While Fuller's twelve-inch plaster prototype was produced as early as 1914, the final, life-sized bronze sculpture was unveiled in 1922 at the Making of America exhibit in New York City. Drawing from African and especially Egyptian sculptural forms, Fuller's figure, a standing female wearing the headdress of ancient Egyptian royalty,

emerges from mummy wrappings. The figure adopts the stillness, formality, and highly symbolic nature of Egyptian sculpture. Fuller departed, however, from traditional Egyptian sculptural imagery in insisting on frontality and by adding movement by turning her figure's head. As a statement of racial pride and anticolonialist protest, Fuller's image differs significantly from the work of contemporaries like Picasso, who appropriated African sculpture for its "primitivist" quality but removed it from its aesthetic and political contexts. Fuller, conversely, uses her image to connect black America to Africa, to the beauty of African women, and to the optimism of a new "awakening."

One of the first African American artists to draw heavily on African sculpture and themes, Fuller predated ALAIN LOCKE's call for artists to fashion a black aesthetic by turning to Africa, an idea codified in his 1925 essay "The Legacy of the Ancestral Arts." An important precursor to the Harlem Renaissance, Fuller led the way in style and content for the next generation of black artists. Although Fuller never lived in Harlem, she exhibited with and served as a juror for the Harmon Foundation. Fuller showed regularly at the Philadelphia Academy of Art and focused on themes relating to war, violence, and the search for peace. She received second prize for *Peace Halting the Ruthlessness of War* in a competition sponsored by the Women's Peace Party in 1915. Fuller's most significant works confronted the political and social climate of her time. Her 1919 sculpture, *Mary Turner (A Silent Protest Against Mob Violence)*, memorialized both the 1917 brutal lynching of Mary Turner, who was eight months pregnant, and the subsequent silent protest march organized by the NAACP in Harlem.

In 1929 Fuller built a studio near her home, which served as a salon where she entertained, taught classes, and mounted annual exhibitions. She celebrated the places and people that were important to her by creating sculptures for a host of local organizations, as well as busts of family, friends, and people she admired, including CHARLOTTE HAWKINS BROWN and Samuel Coleridge Taylor. She exhibited extensively in the Boston area, as well as at the 1936 Texas Centennial Exposition in Dallas, the AUGUSTA

SAVAGE Studios in New York, the 1940 Exposition of the Art of the American Negro 1851–1940 in Chicago, and the seventy-fifth anniversary of the Emancipation Proclamation exhibition held at the Library of Congress in Washington, D.C., in 1940.

In 1950, when her husband became blind as a result of diabetes, Fuller gave up her studio to care for him. Shortly after his death in 1953, she contracted tuberculosis and remained in a sanatorium for two years. Following her recovery she resumed work, donating the proceeds from her art to the civil rights movement and producing a series of sculptures of ten famous black women for the Afro-American Women's Council in Washington, D.C., in 1957. She continued honoring African American lives with works like *The Crucifixion* (1963), which eulogizes the four girls murdered in the 1963 Birmingham, Alabama, church bombing, and *Good Shepherd* (1965), dedicated to the clergymen who marched with MARTIN LUTHER KING JR.

Fuller died in 1968, and her ashes were dispersed off the coast of Martha's Vineyard, Massachusetts. Although she remained artistically active until her death at age ninety, a retrospective of her work was not mounted until 1984. The posthumous exhibition *An Independent Woman: The Life and Art of Meta Warrick Fuller* was held at the Danforth Museum of Art in her adopted city of Framingham.

FURTHER READING

Fuller's papers and photograph collection are held at the New York Public Library's Schomburg Center for Research in Black Culture.

Brawley, Benjamin Griffith. *The Negro in Literature and Art in the United States* (1929).
Driskell, David, ed. *Harlem Renaissance: Art of Black America* (1987).

—LISA E. RIVO

 FULLER, SOLOMON CARTER (11 Aug. 1872–16 Jan. 1953), neuropathologist and psychiatrist, was born in Monrovia, Liberia, the son of Solomon Carter Fuller, a coffee planter and Liberian government official, and Anna Ursala James.

His father, son of a repatriated former American slave, was able to provide a private education for his children at a school he established on his prosperous plantation. In the summer of 1889 young Solomon Fuller left home to return to the country where his grandfather had once been held in bondage. He sought higher education at Livingstone College in Salisbury, North Carolina, a college for black students founded ten years earlier.

Fuller graduated from Livingstone in 1893 with an AB and proceeded to pursue a medical degree at Long Island College Hospital in Brooklyn, New York. After one year he transferred to Boston University School of Medicine, where he received an MD in 1897. Although he was deeply disturbed by the racism he found in America, Fuller decided that he would not return to Liberia. Shortly after graduating he accepted an appointment as an intern at the Westborough State Hospital for the Insane, west of Boston. Two years later he was promoted to become the institution's chief pathologist, beginning a forty-five-year tenure at Westborough—twenty-two years as a pathologist and twenty-three as a consultant. In 1899 he also accepted a part-time instructorship in pathology at Boston University, where he quickly established a reputation as a talented teacher.

During these early years as a pathologist, Fuller took his room and board on the grounds of the Westborough State Hospital, which allowed him to spend long hours in the laboratory he directed. He concentrated on photography of extremely thin sections of brain tissue, employing great technical skill with microtome, microscope, and camera to search for connections between mental disorder and organic disease.

During the 1904–1905 academic year Fuller took a leave from his positions at Westborough and Boston and traveled overseas. At the University of Munich he studied under several prominent German medical scientists, including Alois Alzheimer, who would soon identify Alzheimer's disease. On a sightseeing trip to Berlin in 1905, Fuller worked up the courage to introduce himself to the famed immunologist Paul Ehrlich. Much to Fuller's surprise, Ehrlich was happy to have the company of the young American pathologist for the afternoon, and

the two continued their friendship by correspondence for years.

A few years after Fuller's return to Massachusetts, he had another brush with greatness. In 1909 Sigmund Freud was invited to give a series of five lectures at Clark University in Worcester, Massachusetts, not far from Westborough. Those lectures stand as a landmark in the history of American psychiatry, and Fuller was among the invited members of the audience. In the same year Fuller married Meta Vaux Warrick (META WARRICK FULLER), a woman of exceptional artistic talent whom he met when she happened to visit Westborough State Hospital. Meta's special gift was sculpture, and her works were often dramatic renderings of the black experience in America. In the years immediately surrounding the turn of the century, she had spent time in Paris and emerged briefly as an artistic sensation in the French capital when she won the admiration of Auguste Rodin, who said to her on their initial meeting, "My child, you are a sculptor; you have the sense of form in your fingers" (Velma J. Hoover, "Meta Vaux Fuller: Her Life and Art," *Negro History Bulletin* 40 (Mar.–Apr. 1977): 678). However, after returning home to Philadelphia, racial discrimination—and the traditional expectations of her upper-class black family—sapped much of the energy from Meta's artistic rise. When she met and married Fuller, Meta continued with her sculpture as an avocation and found some significant but limited success; she gave up the pursuit of her art as an all-consuming passion.

The newlyweds bought a house in Framingham, Massachusetts, roughly halfway between Boston University and Westborough State Hospital. Their initial welcome was not warm in the predominantly white community: some of the citizens circulated a petition in an unsuccessful attempt to prevent the black doctor and his wife from purchasing a house there. The Fullers managed to overcome—or at least to ignore—this insult and less overt manifestations of racism and went on to establish a comfortable home in Framingham, where they would raise three children and live out their days. Soon after their arrival in Framingham, Solomon Fuller began a private psychotherapy practice out of an office in his home, which added another layer of responsibility. Fuller's practice became large and included both white and black patients. His son recalled, "My father had great spiritual qualities. People came to him for a spiritual communion that was a refreshing, inspiring, and motivating experience.... My father had such a gracious, loving, radiant, and quieting personality that it had a great calming effect on his patients' problems" (Hayden and Harris, 27).

Although Fuller's private practice focused on psychiatric counseling, his research and teaching continued to center on neurology. He published a number of papers, including several on the disease named for his German mentor Alzheimer (Fuller is credited as having identified the ninth case of Alzheimer's disease in a 1911 publication). He also served for many years as the editor of the *Westborough State Hospital Papers*, an outlet for the publication of scientific work carried out by members of the hospital staff.

After twenty years of service at Boston University, in 1919 Fuller was named an associate professor of neuropathology; in 1921 his title was revised to associate professor of neurology. From 1928 until 1933 he functioned as the effective chair of the university's Department of Neurology. He retired in 1933, when a white assistant professor was promoted over him to a full professorship and officially named head of the department. Through his long years as a popular and respected teacher at Boston University, Fuller had never been placed officially on the school's payroll, although he had been paid for his services. The promotion of the junior colleague over him in 1933 was the final blow in a series of institutional indignities. On the occasion of his resignation, he stated with characteristic grace, "I regard life as a battle in which we win or lose. As far as I am concerned, to be vanquished, if not ingloriously, is not so bad after all." But he added, with understatement, "With the sort of work that I have done, I might have gone farther and reached a higher plane had it not been for the color of my skin" (Hayden and Harris, 22).

Soon after his retirement from Boston University, Fuller began to suffer increasingly from diabetes. By 1944 his eyesight had failed entirely as a result of the disease, and he was forced to end his long association with Westborough State Hospital. Although he lived his final decade in darkness, he continued to meet with a limited number of patients in his private psychiatric practice nearly until the time of his death in Framingham.

Fuller had returned to the country where his grandfather had begun life as a slave, and there he had won a high degree of professional success. His attainments might have been greater if his skin had been white, but in the place of some unrealized aspirations we are left with an impressive legacy of patience and perseverance.

FURTHER READING

Cobb, W. Montague. *Journal of the National Medical Association* 46 (1954): 370–72.
Hayden, Robert C., and Jacqueline Harris. *Nine Black American Doctors* (1976)

—JON M. HARKNESS

G

GABRIEL (1776–10 Oct. 1800), slave and revolutionary, was born near Richmond, Virginia, at Brookfield, the Henrico County plantation of Thomas Prosser. The identity of Gabriel's parents is lost to history, but it is known that he had two older brothers, Martin and Solomon. Most likely, Gabriel's father was a blacksmith, the craft chosen for Gabriel and Solomon; in Virginia, the offspring of skilled bondpersons frequently inherited their parent's profession.

Status as an apprentice artisan provided the young craftsman with considerable standing in the slave community, as did his ability to read and write (a skill perhaps taught to him by plantation mistress Ann Prosser). As Gabriel developed into an unusually tall young man, even older slaves looked to him for leadership. By the mid-1790s, as he approached the age of twenty, Gabriel stood "six feet two or three inches high," and the muscles in his arms and chest betrayed nearly a decade in Brookfield's forge. A long and "bony face, well made," was marred by the loss of two front teeth and "two or three scars on his head." His hair was cut short and was as dark as his complexion. Blacks and whites alike regarded him as "a fellow of courage and intellect above his rank in life."

During these years Gabriel married a young slave named Nanny. Little is known about her, including the identity of her owner and whether she had any children with Gabriel. It is likely that she lived on a nearby farm or tobacco plantation.

In the fall of 1798 Gabriel's old master died, and ownership of Brookfield fell to twenty-two-year-old Thomas Henry Prosser. An ambitious young man with a Richmond townhouse and a lucrative auction business, Prosser increasingly maximized his profits by hiring out his surplus slaves. Even the most efficient planters could not find enough tasks to keep their slave artisans occupied year-round, and many masters routinely hired out their craftsmen to neighboring farms and urban businessmen. Despite all of the work to be done at Brookfield, Gabriel doubtless spent a considerable part of each month smithing in and around Richmond. Though no less a slave under Virginia law, Gabriel enjoyed a rough form of freedom as his ties to young Prosser became ever more tenuous.

Emboldened by this quasi-liberty, in September 1799 Gabriel moved toward overt rebellion. Caught in the act of stealing a pig, a delicacy slaves used to supplement their meager diet, Gabriel refused to suffer his white neighbor's verbal abuse. Instead, he wrestled his tormentor to the ground and bit off the better "part of his left Ear." Under Virginia law, slaves were not tried as whites; instead they were prosecuted under a 1692 statute that established special segregated county tribunals known as courts of oyer and terminer composed of five justices of the peace. There was no jury and no route for appeal except to the governor. On 7 October Gabriel was formally charged with attacking a white man, a capital crime in Virginia. Although he was found guilty, Gabriel escaped the gallows through an ancient clause that, ironically, was now denied to white defendants. Slaves possessed the right of "benefit of clergy," which allowed them to escape hanging in favor of being branded on the thumb by a small cross if they were able to recite a verse from the Bible, an option available to Gabriel thanks to the Afro-Baptist faith of his parents. (There is no truth, however, to the Gilded Age myth that Gabriel was a messianic figure who wore his hair long in imitation of his hero Samson.)

Gabriel's branding and incarceration was the final indignity. By the early spring of 1800, his fury began to turn into a carefully considered plan to bring about his freedom—and the end of slavery in Virginia. As he explained it to his brothers Solomon and Martin, slaves from Henrico County would gather at the blacksmith shop at Brookfield on the evening of 30 August. As the small but determined band of insurgents—armed with crude swords fashioned from scythes—neared Richmond, it would split into three groups. The center column planned to swarm into Capitol Square and seize the guns stored in the building. Governor—and later U.S. President—James Monroe, slumbering in the adjacent executive mansion, was to be taken as a hostage but otherwise left unharmed. The other columns would set fire to Rocketts Landing, the warehouse district, as a diversion and then fortify the town. A small number of town leaders were to die, while most would live as hostages in order to force the Virginia elite to grant the rebels' demands, which included their freedom and an equitable division of city property. "Quakers, Methodists and French people," three groups who had earned a sometimes undeserved reputation as foes of slavery, were not to be harmed. The "poor white people," who had no more political power than did the slaves, "would also join" the rebels. If the town leaders agreed to Gabriel's demands, the slave general intended to "hoist a white flag" and drink a toast "with the merchants of the city."

Using their ability to hire their time away from their owners, Gabriel and his chief lieutenants contacted only those slaves whose talents and skills meant they had little contact with their owners. Recruiters moved north into Hanover, Goochland, and Caroline counties, while black mariners ferried word of the uprising down the James River to Petersburg, Norfolk, and Gloucester County.

The uprising, set to begin on the night of Saturday, 30 August, collapsed just before sunset on the appointed day when a severe thunderstorm hit southern Henrico. Creeks rose, washing away fragile wooden bridges and cutting off communications between Brookfield plantation and the city. Perhaps only a dozen slaves reached the blacksmith shop. The chaos of the storm convinced two Henrico house slaves, Tom and Pharoah, that the revolt could not succeed. They informed their owner of the conspiracy, and he hurried word to Governor Monroe in Richmond. As the militia closed in, Gabriel escaped south by way of the swampy Chickahominy River. After hiding along the James River for nearly two weeks, Gabriel decided to risk boarding the schooner *Mary*. Captain Richardson Taylor, a former overseer who had recently converted to Methodism, willingly spirited Gabriel downriver to Norfolk. There Gabriel was betrayed by Billy, a slave crewman who had heard of Monroe's three hundred dollar reward for Gabriel's capture. Returned to Richmond under heavy guard, Gabriel was found guilty of "conspiracy and insurrection." On 10 October 1800 the slave general died with quiet composure at the town gallows near Fifteenth and Broad. He was twenty-four. In all, twenty-six slaves, including Gabriel, were hanged for their part in the conspiracy. Another bondman allegedly hanged himself while in custody. Eight more rebels were transported to Spanish New Orleans; at least thirty-two others were found not guilty. Reliable sources placed the number of slaves who knew of the plot to be between five and six hundred.

Although the abortive uprising failed in its goals, southern whites were painfully aware that it was the most extensive and carefully planned slave plot yet devised in North America. In the aftermath, Virginia legislators labored to ensure that it would not be repeated. Intent on crushing black autonomy, the general assembly passed a number of laws abolishing black liberties, including the right to congregate on Sunday for religious services. After 1806 all manumitted slaves had twelve months to leave the state or be "apprehended and sold" back into bondage.

FURTHER READING

The trial records for Gabriel and his fellow conspirators are located in the Library of Virginia (Richmond). State newspapers covered the trials in great detail; the Richmond *Virginia Argus* and Fredericksburg *Virginia Herald* are especially useful. The papers of Thomas Jefferson and James Monroe, both in the Library of Congress, discuss the plot, as do the Tucker-Coleman Papers at the College of William and Mary; see also George Tucker's anonymous pamphlet, *Letter to a Member of the General Assembly of Virginia, on the Subject of the Late Conspiracy of the Slaves* (1801).

Aptheker, Herbert. *American Negro Slave Revolts* (1943).

Egerton, Douglas R. *Gabriel's Rebellion: The Virginia Slave Conspiracies of 1800 and 1802* (1993).

Mullin, Gerald. *Flight and Rebellion: Slave Resistance in Eighteenth-Century Virginia* (1972).

Schwarz, Philip J. *Twice Condemned: Slaves and the Criminal Law of Virginia, 1705–1865* (1988).

—DOUGLAS R. EGERTON

GARNET, HENRY HIGHLAND (23 Dec. 1815–12 Feb. 1882), minister, author, editor, and activist, was born near New Market, Maryland, to an enslaved couple then known as George and Henrietta Trusty. A few weeks after the death of their owner, Henry, his parents, his sister, and seven other relatives escaped to Wilmington, Delaware. Part of the Trusty family went to New Jersey, but George and Henrietta, having changed their surname to Garnet, continued on to New Hope, Pennsylvania, where nine-year-old Henry had his first days of formal education. In 1825 the family moved to New York City. Henry, along with his cousin Samuel Ringgold Ward (whose family were also fugitive slaves) and his neighbor ALEXANDER CRUMMELL, attended the African Free School. About 1830, while apprenticed to a Quaker farmer on Long Island, Henry was crippled in an accident. The intrepid fifteen-year-old returned to New York City and enrolled at Canal Street High School. In 1835 Garnet, with his school chums, Alexander Crummell and Thomas Sidney, moved to Canaan, New Hampshire, and enrolled at Noyes Academy. Their stay was brief because a white mob burned the school and fired shots into the boys' sleeping quarters. According to Crummell, Garnet saved their lives because he "quickly replied by a discharge from a double barreled shotgun" (Crummell, 280). The boys had to flee Canaan, but the next year they enrolled at the Oneida Institute in Whitesboro, New York. As his response to the Noyes attack indicates, Garnet did not conform to ideas of nonviolence and moral suasion as the only means of achieving an end. As a student involved in the abolitionist movement, however, he did try to use reason and persuasion in his letters that appeared frequently in the *Colored American*, sometimes under the pseudonym of "Sidney," in his speeches to groups such as New York City's Phoenix Society, and in his work with the Colored Young Men Organization that circulated petitions for equal rights to the New York state legislature. By 1840, when he graduated from Oneida, Henry Highland Garnet had already achieved a reputation as an impressive communicator and indomitable leader.

Garnet's first years after graduation were a period of intense activity and serious challenges. Between 1840 and 1841 he suffered the amputation of his leg, but this did not stop him from becoming a founding member of the American and Foreign Anti-Slavery Society, serving as pastor of the Liberty Street Presbyterian Church in Troy, New York, and gaining prominence as a leader in both the temperance movement and the Liberty Party. For a brief time he was employed by the American Home Missionary Society to do abolition and temperance work, but he resigned when the society objected to his increasingly radical politics.

Henry Highland Garnet, abolitionist and Pan-Africanist, c. 1881. National Portrait Gallery, Smithsonian Institution/Art Resource, NY

JAMES MCCUNE SMITH writes that Garnet's marriage in 1841 to Julia Ward Williams was "a most happy wedlock" (Smith, 32). Williams was herself no stranger to racial activism. She too had been a student at Noyes and before that had been enrolled at Prudence Crandall's school, which had also been shut down by racist attacks. Garnet admired her "as a good Christian and a scholar" and often acknowledged his wife as the source of ideas in his lectures. During their marriage Julia Garnet generally worked alongside her husband in such capacities as head of the Female Industrial School in Jamaica or as president of the Free Labor Bazaar in London. The couple had four children and adopted a young fugitive slave.

Garnet's radical politics and persuasive rhetoric made him a prominent but controversial leader in the state and national colored conventions of the 1840s. "An Address to the Slaves of the United States," which he offered for the endorsement of the 1843 convention in Buffalo, New York, is a particularly inflammatory example. Its beginning lines convey the tone and tenor of this remarkable document:

Brethren and Fellow-Citizens: Your brethren of the North, East, and West have been accustomed to meet together in National Conventions, to sympathize with each other, and to weep over your unhappy condition. In these meetings we have addressed all classes of the free, but we have never, until this time, sent a word of consolation and advice to you. We have been contented in sitting still and mourning over your sorrows, earnestly hoping that before this day your sacred liberties would have been restored. But, we have hoped in vain.

Arguing that it was "sinful in the Extreme" to "voluntarily" accept enslavement, Garnet declared it was their "solemn and imperative duty to use every means, both moral, intellectual, and physical" to obtain freedom and he evoked DENMARK VESEY, NAT TURNER, CINQUÉ, and Madison Washington as revolutionary role models. The speech scandalized more conservative delegates such as FREDERICK DOUGLASS, who reportedly delivered an hour-long tirade against advocating physical violence. When all was said and the vote taken, the endorsement failed by one vote.

Many of Garnet's speeches, including "An Address to the Slaves," were published in pamphlet form. He was also an active journalist who contributed articles to the *Colored American*, the *Voice of the Fugitive*, the *North Star*, and other periodicals, he served as agent for the *Palladium of Liberty* and the *Weekly-Anglo African*, and he edited two papers, the *Clarion* and the *National Watchman*.

In 1850 Garnet went to Great Britain to campaign on behalf of the Free-Produce movement, a segment of abolitionists who urged a boycott of all slave-made products. Garnet traveled extensively in England, Ireland, Scotland, and France, sometimes in the company of other antislavery lecturers such as JAMES W. C. PENNINGTON, JOSIAH HENSON, and Alexander Crummell. He was a delegate to the World Peace Congress in Frankfurt, Germany. In 1852 the United Presbyterian Church of Scotland employed Garnet as a missionary to Jamaica, where he served for about three years.

By 1856 Garnet was back in New York City as the pastor of the Shiloh Baptist Church, succeeding his former teacher and mentor, Theodore S. Wright. He quickly reestablished himself as a leader in African American communities and in some white abolitionist and religious circles. Garnet served on the executive council of the American Missionary Association, helped organize the Evangelical Association of Negro Ministers, and established an African American counterpart of the white Young Men's Christian Association. But it was his involvement with the African Civilization Society that provoked the greatest response before the Civil War.

Garnet's reasons for helping to found the African Civilization Society were quite complex. He had a sincere missionary zeal to convert masses of Africans to Christianity and his experiences in the freer societies of Europe and Jamaica probably made it more difficult for him to accept the persistence of slavery and racial discrimination in the United States. And he also believed that with selective emigration of skilled and industrious individuals, black people could "establish a grand center of Negro nationality, from which shall flow streams of commercial, intellectual, and political power which shall make colored people respected

everywhere" (Schor, 161). At first, leaders such as Frederick Douglass, WILLIAM WELLS BROWN, and George T. Downing vociferously denounced Garnet's project. Others, such as MARTIN R. DELANY, initially considered Garnet's plan competitive to their own emigration proposals. But by 1861 Douglass, Delany, and others had either endorsed Garnet's plan or stopped their public opposition. Then came the Civil War, and Garnet, like most African American leaders, turned his attention to supporting the Union army.

During the Civil War, Garnet recruited African American soldiers and served as a military chaplain. He moved to Washington, D.C., where he became pastor of the Fifteenth Street Presbyterian Church, a church with a congregation of prominent social activists. For example, the Contraband Relief Association, founded by ELIZABETH KECKLY, was based at Fifteenth Avenue Presbyterian. Garnet helped establish the Colored Soldiers Aid Society and various organizations to help the newly freed slaves.

After the war Garnet became the first African American invited to address the United States House of Representatives. He responded on 12 February 1865 with a sermon based upon Matthew 23:4 about the obligations of the advantaged to the disadvantaged. With citations that ranged from Plato, Socrates, Augustine, and Moses to Thomas Jefferson, Pope Leo X, General Lafayette, and William Ellery Channing (who had issued the invitation to speak), Garnet urged the legislators to "*Emancipate, enfranchise, educate, and give the blessing of the gospel to every American citizen*" [Italics his].

In 1868 Garnet served for a year as president of Avery College in Pittsburgh, Pennsylvania, then returned to his earlier position at Shiloh Presbyterian Church in New York. Around 1879, after the death of his first wife, Garnet married Sarah Smith Tompkins. He continued to agitate for equal rights in the United States and to espouse various Pan-Africanist plans, but his health and his political influence had declined precipitously. In 1881 his fondest hope was realized when he was appointed to a diplomatic post in Liberia. Garnet gave his farewell sermon on 6 November 1881 and sailed for Monrovia, where he died of a fever three months later.

Despite the early loss of a leg and countless other challenges, personal, political, and racial, the Reverend Henry Highland Garnet achieved international stature. In an acrostic published on 5 August 1865 in the *Weekly Anglo African*, he is summed up as a man "noble and earnest," "eloquent and faithful," and "a noble hero in the battle's shock."

FURTHER READING

Crummell, Alexander. "Eulogium on Henry Highland Garnet, D.D. Before the Union Literary and Historical Association; Washington, D.C., May 4th, 1882" in *Africa and America* (1969).

Ofari, Earl. *Let Your Motto Be Resistance: The Life and Thought of Henry Highland Garnet* (1972).

Schor, Joel. *Henry Highland Garnet: A Voice of Radicalism in the Nineteenth Century* (1977).

Smith, James McCune. "Sketch of the Life and Labors of Rev. Henry Highland Garnet" (1865).

—FRANCES SMITH FOSTER

Amy Ashwood Garvey, noted Pan-Africanist and proponent of women's activism, was the first wife of MARCUS GARVEY. Schomburg Center

GARVEY, AMY ASHWOOD

GARVEY, AMY ASHWOOD (18 Jan. 1897– 3 May 1969), Pan-African activist, was born Amy Ashwood in Port Antonio, Jamaica, to relatively prosperous middle-class parents. Her father was a successful caterer in Panama, and shortly after her birth Amy traveled with her brother and mother to live there. Amy returned to Jamaica in 1907 to be educated at the renowned Westwood Training College for Women, from which she graduated in 1914. It was there that the twelve-year-old first learned that her forebears had been taken forcibly from Africa by British traders and enslaved in Jamaica. Though frightened and angered to learn the horrors of the Middle Passage, Amy also became determined to learn more about her African roots. A visit to her elderly grandmother, who had been sold into slavery as a girl on the African Gold Coast, instilled in her a strong sense of pride in her Ashanti ancestors. She determined then that she had a mission "to help Africa and all her sons and daughters" (Martin, [1983], 224–225).

In 1914, at a debating society in Kingston, she met MARCUS GARVEY, a journalist and fellow Jamaican, who had recently returned from England. In Ashwood's account of their meeting, she and Garvey shared a "bond of comradeship" based on their common commitment to improving the conditions of black people in Jamaica and in the rest of the African diaspora. Toward that end Garvey launched the Universal Negro Improvement Association (UNIA) in Jamaica in July 1914 with Amy Ashwood as cofounder. Over the next two years she traveled extensively with Garvey as he tried to drum up support for the UNIA, which at that time espoused a mildly reformist program influenced by the self-help philosophy of BOOKER T. WASHINGTON. As secretary of the UNIA's Ladies' Division, Ashwood raised funds for the organization even after Garvey left for the United States in 1916. Shortly thereafter, however, Ashwood returned to Panama, in part because her parents disapproved of Garvey, who came from a more humble background than her own. Garvey continued to correspond with Ashwood, however, sending love letters to his "Josephine," which

he signed "your devoted Napoleon, Marcus."

When Ashwood reunited with Garvey in New York City in late 1918, the UNIA had adopted a more defiantly Pan-Africanist and anticolonialist philosophy. Garvey's powerful street-corner oratory and his newspaper, the *Negro World*, struck a chord with American blacks living in an era of intense racial violence. Hundreds were killed in race riots between 1917 and 1921. Thousands more returned from a war fought to make the world safe for democracy to find continued disenfranchisement in the South and poverty in the North. An efficient fund-raiser and a powerful speaker in her own right, Amy Ashwood again served as Garvey's partner in the UNIA, which by 1920 had hundreds of chapters worldwide and eventually became the largest international black movement in history. It was Ashwood who ensured that black women enjoyed prominent roles within local UNIA chapters. She also contributed to the *Negro World* and served as a director of the Black Star Line Steamship Corporation, which was intended to transport Garveyites wishing to return to Africa. Ashwood even thwarted an assassination attempt on Garvey in October 1919. On Christmas Day 1919 Ashwood married Garvey, and the couple held an elaborate reception for three thousand invited guests, before leaving for Canada with several UNIA officials, including Ashwood's maid of honor, Amy Jacques (AMY JACQUES GARVEY).

Ashwood's marriage to Garvey was short-lived and stormy. The couple shared their cramped Lenox Avenue apartment with Amy Jacques, Ashwood's brother Claudius, and another man, not an unusual arrangement in Harlem's crowded tenements. The major source of contention in the marriage was Garvey's determination that his new wife withdraw from her public role within the UNIA and that she subordinate her own goals to his more traditionalist view of a woman's proper place. Ashwood, very much an independent "new woman" of the 1920s, refused to alter her ways of public activism, public drinking, and maintenance of friendships with men other than Garvey. In March 1920 Garvey announced that he had separated from Ashwood, and in July he sought an annulment, accusing her of having affairs and of misappropriating UNIA funds. Ashwood denied the charges. Around this time Amy Jacques, already Garvey's private secretary, moved with him to a new apartment. Believing rumors that Garvey and Jacques had also begun an affair, Ashwood sued for divorce that August and moved to Canada. In her view, the relationship between Garvey and Jacques had been a double betrayal, since she had befriended Jacques in Jamaica and had introduced her to the UNIA and Garvey. Jacques, for her part, claimed not to have known Ashwood until 1918. In June 1922 Garvey won a divorce from his wife and married Jacques two months later. Amy Ashwood challenged the divorce in court and refused to sign the divorce decree.

In late 1922 Ashwood moved to London and immediately immersed herself in that city's cosmopolitan literary and political circles. She began working with a group of Nigerian students in the city to "promote African literatures, institutions, self-knowledge, welfare and a sense of duty to 'our country and race'" (Adi, 70). She also collaborated with Trinidadian calypso singer Sam Manning in the musical revues, *Hey, Hey!*, *Brown Sugar*, and *Black Magic*, touring England, the United States, and the Caribbean. In the 1930s she and Manning opened a nightclub in London that became a haven for Pan-Africanist intellectuals like C. L. R. James and George Padmore; it was also, James remarked, the only place in London that served good food. When Italy invaded Abyssinia in 1935, Ashwood and Padmore formed the International African Friends of Abyssinia (IAFA). Her skills as a public speaker and fund-raiser were also useful in the International African Service Bureau, an anticolonialist organization, in which she served alongside Jomo Kenyatta, later the first prime minister of an independent Kenya.

Ashwood's commitment to Pan-Africanism prompted several trips to Jamaica and the United States. In the early 1940s she attempted to found a school for domestic workers in her native land and also dabbled, unsuccessfully, in party politics. She had greater success assisting the 1944 Congressional campaign of ADAM CLAYTON POWELL JR., though her links to Powell and her friendship with PAUL ROBESON ensured the close attention of the FBI. She returned to London in 1945. That year, along with W. E. B. DU BOIS, she chaired the opening session of the Fifth Pan-African Congress, held in Manchester, England. Over the next two decades, several of the Congress's participants, notably Kenyatta and Ghana's Kwame Nkrumah, would lead their nations to independence.

Of greater significance to Ashwood herself, however, was her first trip to Africa. From 1946 to 1949 she traveled throughout West Africa, lecturing to women's groups and encouraging women's participation in decolonization efforts in Senegal, Nigeria, and Ghana. While in Ghana, she traveled to the Gold Coast, where she found her grandmother's birthplace and was officially welcomed as a member of the Ashanti people.

Ashwood maintained a hectic schedule in the 1950s. She invested, poorly, in several businesses in Africa and also traveled to the Caribbean to encourage women's activism there. In England she served as a social worker in Handsworth, Birmingham, and in Notting Hill, London. Both districts had large West Indian populations, most of them recent arrivals, who had been recruited in large numbers by British employers seeking cheap labor. When a race riot erupted in Notting Hill in 1958, Ashwood, who ran a community center in the district, led efforts to ease racial tensions and to ensure justice for blacks imprisoned following the riot.

In 1964 Ashwood moved back to Jamaica and arranged to return Marcus Garvey's body for burial as requested by the newly independent Jamaican government. Garvey had died in London in 1940, and the British authorities recognized her claim to be his widow, notwithstanding that Garvey had lived with Amy Jacques Garvey as his wife from 1922 until 1938. That year Jacques Garvey left her husband in London and returned to Jamaica. Ashwood spent her final days in Jamaica but journeyed to Harlem in 1968, where she praised the widespread adoption of the natural "Afro" hairstyle by black women and took great satisfaction in the renewed veneration of the Garveyites and the UNIA. She died, penniless, in Jamaica in May 1969.

Much more than Marcus Garvey's "Wife Number 1," Amy Ashwood enjoys a distinctive place in the history of Pan-Africanism, most notably in encouraging women of the African diaspora to play a significant role in the cause.

FURTHER READING

Amy Ashwood Garvey's papers are scattered in private collections in London, New York, and Kingston, Jamaica. See also the *Marcus Garvey and Universal Negro Improvement Association Papers*, ed. Robert A. Hill (1983–).

Adi, Hakim, and Marika Sherwood. "Amy Ashwood Garvey" in *Pan-African History: Political Figures from Africa and the Diaspora since 1787* (2003).

Martin, Tony. *Amy Ashwood Garvey: Pan-Africanist, Feminist, and Wife No. 1* (1988).

———. *The Pan-African Connection: From Slavery to Garvey and Beyond* (1983).

Stein, Judith. *The World of Marcus Garvey* (1986).

Taylor, Ula. "Intellectual Pan-African Feminists: Amy Ashwood Garvey and Amy Jacques Garvey" in *Time Longer than Rope: A Century of African American Activism, 1850–1950*, ed. Charles Payne and Adam Green (2003).

Yard, Lionel M. *Biography of Amy Ashwood Garvey, 1897–1969: Co-founder of the Universal Negro Improvement Association* (1990).

—STEVEN J. NIVEN

GARVEY, AMY EUPHEMIA JACQUES

(31 Dec. 1896–25 July 1973), journalist and Pan-Africanist, was born in Kingston, Jamaica, the daughter of George Samuel Jacques, a cigar manufacturer and landlord, and Charlotte Henrietta, a member of the Jamaican aristocracy. Amy's family traced their ancestry on the island back to John Jacques, a white property owner and the first mayor of Kingston. She grew up as part of the "brown elite," who were considered socially and economically superior to the black majority. After completing her secondary education at the exclusive Wolmers Girl's School, Amy worked in the law office of T. R. MacMillian for four years and had thoughts of becoming a lawyer. However, in April 1917 she left Jamaica for New York, arguing that the cooler climate would mitigate her recurring bouts of malaria.

Amy Jacques arrived in Harlem, the Mecca for ambitious Caribbean immigrants—particularly those animated by the new black nationalist philosophy of MARCUS GARVEY. In the summer of 1919 she attended a meeting of Garvey's Universal Negro Improvement Association (UNIA) at the six-thousand-seat headquarters, Liberty Hall. According to her account, after she peppered Garvey with some difficult questions about his program, he invited her into his office to continue their conversation. Noticing that his office was in a state of disarray, she offered her organizational services and soon become his private secretary, helping to plan, among other things, Garvey's lavish wedding to Amy Ashwood (AMY ASHWOOD GARVEY) on Christmas Day, where she served as the maid of honor. Jacques shared an apartment with Garvey and Amy Ashwood and two other men until Garvey separated from his wife in March 1920. She then moved to the same boardinghouse as Garvey, so that she would be "better protected at nights coming from meetings" (Garvey, 43). In July 1922 Garvey and Amy Jacques were married in Baltimore, shortly after his divorce from Amy Ashwood was granted.

Amy Jacques's prominence in the UNIA grew as Garvey's legal troubles began to mount and as popular and financial support for the organization began to wane. When Garvey was convicted on one count of mail fraud in June 1923, Amy Jacques became his most trusted spokesperson, his unofficial emissary, and the leader of the campaign to win his freedom. She first published a pamphlet about the trial called "Was Justice Defeated?", to demonstrate that Garvey was railroaded for his political beliefs. To correct what she and Garvey thought were distortions of his views, she then published two volumes of Garvey's speeches and articles in *The Philosophy and Opinions of Marcus Garvey* (1923, 1925). She took great liberty in selecting his least militant work and quietly omitted and added text where she thought appropriate. Some of the elected officers of the UNIA resented the influence that her ex officio status as Garvey's wife afforded her, but though she had been loath to assert herself publicly in the past, she now began to claim the mantle of his leadership.

Though never a dynamic speaker, Jacques was a gifted and prolific writer who used the printed word to give voice to issues of Pan-Africanism and the concerns of black women. When she became an associate editor of the *Negro World*, the main organ of the UNIA, in February 1924, she found a platform from which to express her ideas. T. THOMAS FORTUNE recognized her talent and encouraged her to write a new column in the paper, called "Our Women and What They Think." This column consciously avoided stories about women's fashions, celebrity gossip, and recipes, in favor of the more serious matters that would "prove that Negro women are great thinkers as well as doers." In articles such as "No Sex in Brains and Ability," Jacques wrote, "Some men declare that women should remain in the homes and leave professions and legislation to men, but this is an antiquated belief, and has been exploded by woman's competency in these new fields and further by the fact that their homes have not suffered by a division of their time and interest" (Taylor, 74).

Jacques advocated expanding women's roles beyond the domestic sphere, but she was not a feminist in the modern sense. Like early black female intellectuals FRANCES ELLEN WATKINS HARPER and MARY CHURCH TERRELL and fellow journalist IDA WELLS-BARNETT, Jacques wanted black women to achieve a social status equal to that of the white, middle-class women of her generation—despite the inherent contradiction posed between that Victorian vision and their simultaneous desire to have careers outside the home. In fact, in her article "Are Negro Women More Easily Satisfied than White Women?" she wrote "black women [would] come out of Miss Ann's kitchen, leave her washtub and preside over their own homes," if their men would "bring home the bacon" (Taylor, 84). By the time the column was discontinued in June 1927, Jacques had contributed nearly two hundred editorials and established an identity that was clearly distinct from her husband's.

In November 1927 Garvey was released from prison and deported to Jamaica. During his incarceration Jacques had come to feel that her role in his life had once again been reduced to that of a personal secretary, important only to carry out his instructions. Reflecting on a love poem that Garvey had sent to her and that waxed long about his suffering but hardly acknowledged the tremendous strain she was under, Jacques wrote, "What did he ever give in return? The value of a wife to him was like a gold coin—expendable, to get what he wanted, and hard enough to withstand rough usage in the process" (Garvey, 169).

Despite the fact that she had become a U.S. citizen the year before, she decided to join her husband in Jamaica in hopes of rekindling their relationship. When she arrived, they did not take the vacation he had promised; instead Garvey threw himself into his work, cashed in his life insurance policy to start a newspaper, the *Blackman*, and mortgaged their home and furniture to rent office space for the new UNIA that he intended to run from Jamaica. However, Garvey soon discovered that he had become persona non grata in many countries that either feared his populist rhetoric or yielded to American pressure. Once again Jacques was pressed into service as his representative to countries that barred him, and in 1929, when Garvey's leadership of the People's Political Party got him thrown into a Jamaican jail for three months for judicial contempt, it was Jacques who again came to the aid of her husband, who by then had been diagnosed with diabetes.

In 1930, after seven years of marriage, Jacques delivered their first son at home. Garvey was delighted by the news, rushed home to see them, and then returned to his office. By the time their second son was born in 1933, Jacques had become much more anxious about the family's precarious finances, worsened by the Depression, and she was greatly disappointed by Garvey's detachment as a husband and father. Garvey was singularly devoted to black liberation; "towards that purpose no one will ever stand in my way—no mother, no father, no wife, no sweetheart, no affiliation," he once said (James, 142). Feeling that the island of Jamaica had become his Elba, Garvey moved his family to London in 1935, where Jacques felt increasingly torn between her commitment to the movement and her responsibility to her children. Out of frustration, Jacques returned with the children to Jamaica in 1938 while Garvey was away on a speaking tour, never to see him again.

During their estrangement they communicated indirectly through the letters of their sons until Jacques received notice that Garvey had suffered a stroke in January 1940; this time she made no effort to be by his side. He died in June 1940 and his body remained in London until 1964, when Jacques found herself embroiled in a dispute with Amy Ashwood—who never accepted the legality of the 1922 divorce—over deciding Garvey's final resting place. Both women had competed for recognition as wife, widow, and political heir. Jacques created Garvey's African Communities League and often spoke in strangely spiritual terms of being led by Garvey, of speaking to him in her dreams, and literally declaring that "when I talk, I talk for Garvey" (Taylor, 225). Since Garvey left her no money and the promised pension from the UNIA never materialized, Jacques could rarely afford to travel, but she wrote incessantly to Pan-Africanists all over the world. She wrote a manifesto called *Memorandum Correlative of Africa, the West Indies and the Americas,* sent it to her former adversary W. E. B. DU BOIS, and hoped to attend the Fifth Pan-African Congress in Manchester, England in 1945. Unfortunately, she was unable to attend, so

George Padmore read excerpts from her manuscript.

Jacques became a writer for *The African: Journal of African Affairs,* and during the 1960s she traveled to Africa, met with Kwame Nkrumah, spoke out in defense of Patrice Lumumba, and was honored by MARTIN LUTHER KING JR. In 1963 she wrote *Garvey and Garveyism,* her memoir of the movement, and though she acknowledged the shortcomings of her personal relationship with Garvey, she remained deeply passionate about preserving his memory and their shared vision of Pan-Africanism until cancer slowed her activity. She died in 1973.

FURTHER READING

The papers of Amy Jacques Garvey are located in the Fisk University Special Collections, Nashville, Tennessee.

Garvey, Amy Jacques. *Garvey and Garveyism* (1963; rpt. 1978).

James, Winston. *Holding Aloft the Banner of Ethiopia* (1998).
Taylor, Ula Yvette. *The Veiled Garvey: The Life and Times of Amy Jacques Garvey* (2002).

Obituary: Jamaica Daily News, 7 Aug. 1973.
—SHOLOMO B. LEVY

 GARVEY, MARCUS
(17 Aug. 1887–10 June 1940), black nationalist, was born Marcus Moziah Garvey in St. Ann's Bay, Jamaica, the son of Marcus Moziah Garvey, a stonemason, and Sarah Jane Richards. He attended the local elementary school and read widely on his own. Difficult family finances forced him into employment at age fourteen as a printer's apprentice. Three years later he moved to Kingston, found work as a printer, and became involved in local union activities. In 1907 he took part in an unsuccessful printers' strike. These early experiences honed his journalistic skills and raised his consciousness about the bleak conditions of the black working class in his native land.

After brief stints working in Costa Rica on a banana plantation and in Panama as the editor of several short-lived radical newspapers, Garvey moved

to London, England, in 1912 and continued to work as a printer. The next two years there would profoundly mold his thoughts on black advancement and racial solidarity. He probably studied at the University of London's Birkbeck College; absorbed BOOKER T. WASHINGTON's philosophy of black self-advancement in his autobiographical *Up from Slavery*; and, perhaps most important, met Duse Mohammed Ali, a Sudanese-Egyptian who was working for African self-rule and Egyptian independence. Duse Mohammed published a small magazine, *Africa Times and Orient Review*. He allowed Garvey to write for the magazine and introduced him to other Africans. Garvey left London convinced that blacks worldwide would have to fend for themselves if they were ever to break the shackles of white racism and free the African continent from European colonial rule.

Back home in Jamaica in 1914, Garvey founded the Universal Negro Improvement and Conservation Association and African Communities League, usually known as the Universal Negro Improvement Association (UNIA). The UNIA would be the vehicle for Garvey's efforts at racial advancement for the rest of his life. His initial undertaking, a trade school in Jamaica, did not succeed, and in 1916 he took his organization and cause to the burgeoning "black mecca" of Harlem in New York City.

Over the next few years Garvey's movement experienced extraordinary growth for a number of reasons. With its slogan "One Aim, One God, One Destiny," the UNIA appealed to black American soldiers who had served abroad in World War I and were unhappy returning to a nation still steeped in racism. Harlem was a fortuitous location for Garvey's headquarters, with its sizable working-class black population, large number of West Indian immigrants, and the cultural explosion of the Harlem Renaissance in the 1920s. A Pan-African movement was already under way by the early 1920s, emphasizing the liberation of the African continent and black racial pride worldwide, and Garvey successfully tapped into this sentiment. Garvey himself was a gifted writer (using his weekly newspaper the *Negro World* as his mouthpiece) and a spellbinding orator in dazzling paramilitary garb.

Marcus Garvey (right), president of the UNIA, shown here with his deputy, George O. Marke (left), and Prince Kojo Tovalou-Houénou, c. 1924. Courtesy of Donna VanDerZee

Garvey's first marriage in 1919, to his secretary AMY ASHWOOD GARVEY, was an unhappy relationship that ended in divorce three years later. The couple was childless. In 1922 he married AMY JACQUES GARVEY, his new secretary. They had two sons.

By the early 1920s the UNIA had probably 65,000 to 75,000 dues-paying members with chapters in some thirty American cities, as well as in the West Indies, Latin America, and Africa. On various occasions Garvey claimed anywhere from two to six million members. Accurate membership figures are impossible to obtain, but unquestionably millions of other blacks were followers in spirit. Auxiliary organizations included the Universal Black Cross Nurses, the Black Eagle Flying Corps, and the Universal African Legion. The *Negro World* had a circulation of some fifty thousand.

In August 1920 the UNIA hosted a huge month-long international convention in New York City, with several thousand black delegates from all parts of the world, complete with uniforms, mass meetings, and parades. Garvey was named provisional president of a nonexistent but symbolically powerful "Republic of Africa." This latter move reflected Garvey's interest in the regeneration of Africa. He had already been exploring with the government of Liberia a UNIA construction and development project there and the potential for a back-to-Africa colonization movement for American blacks. Unfortunately, this undertaking foundered as his domestic businesses came into increasing difficulty.

Garvey's business enterprises were his proudest achievements and ultimately the source of his undoing. Inspired

by Booker T. Washington's support of black businesses, Garvey founded the Negro Factories Corporation to encourage black entrepreneurship in the United States and abroad. The corporation sponsored a number of small businesses in the United States, including a Harlem hotel and a publishing company.

The crown jewel of Garvey's enterprises was the Black Star Line, a steamship company founded in 1919 to carry passengers and trade among Africa, the Caribbean, and the United States. Garvey launched the line with his usual grandiose promises and a stock sale that raised more than $600,000 (at five dollars a share) the first year. What followed in the next twenty-four months was a tragic series of mishaps and mismanagement. The Black Star Line consisted of three aging, overpriced vessels that were plagued by mechanical breakdowns, accidents, and incompetent crews. The business side of the operation suffered from sloppy record keeping, inflated claims made to investors, and dishonest and possibly criminal practices on the part of company officers. One of the ships sank; another was auctioned off; the third was abandoned in Cuba.

Some of Garvey's critics, including many blacks, had begun to question his ethics, his business practices, and the whole UNIA operation. Notable among his black opponents was W. E. B. DU BOIS of the National Association for the Advancement of Colored People. Garvey's insistence on black nationalism ran counter to the NAACP's goal of full integration into American society. When Garvey associated openly with leaders of the white racist Ku Klux Klan and declared that the Klan was a better friend of his race than the NAACP "for telling us what they are, and what they mean, thereby giving us a chance to stir for ourselves," thousands of blacks were outraged.

In 1922 Garvey and three other Black Star Line officials were indicted by the U.S. government for using the mails fraudulently to solicit stock for the defunct steamship line. Ever the showman, Garvey used his trial for a flamboyant defense of himself and the larger cause of black advancement, striking a chord with at least some of his remaining followers, who saw him as a victim of white persecution. Unimpressed, the jury convicted Garvey (though not his codefendants), and he was sentenced to five years imprisonment. After a failed appeal to the U.S. Supreme Court, Garvey began his term in February 1925. That he was able to continue running the UNIA from his Atlanta jail cell was a tribute to his influence over his followers.

In 1927 President Calvin Coolidge commuted Garvey's sentence, and he was deported to Jamaica. The remainder of his life was a struggle to rebuild his movement. He attempted to rekindle his cause by getting involved in Jamaican politics but to no avail. He presided over UNIA conventions in Kingston in 1929 and Toronto in the late 1930s, but the grim realities of the Great Depression left most blacks with little interest and fewer resources to support movements such as his. He died of a stroke in London, where he had moved in 1935.

Obituaries of Garvey emphasized his business failures and portrayed him as an irrelevant relic from the past. His real achievement, however, was in creating the first genuine black mass movement in the United States and in extending that influence to millions of blacks abroad. He emphasized racial pride and purity, the proud history of his race, self-respect, and self-reliance. For his millions of poor and working-class American followers, Garvey's message of black pride and solidarity in the early 1920s came at a critical nadir of race relations. Such themes drew on the philosophy of Booker T. Washington as well as Du Bois, his sworn enemy. He was a harbinger of later black nationalist leaders such as MALCOLM X, STOKELY CARMICHAEL, and LOUIS FARRAKHAN. Garvey thus served as an important link between early twentieth-century black leaders and modern spokesmen. Moreover, he inspired modern African nationalist leaders, such as Kwame Nkrumah of Ghana and Jomo Kenyatta of Kenya, in their struggles against European colonialism.

FURTHER READING

Garvey's papers and materials from the UNIA can be found in the multivolume *Marcus Garvey and Universal Negro Improvement Association Papers*, ed. Robert A. Hill (1983–). Amy Jacques Garvey, ed., *Philosophy and Opinions of Marcus Garvey* (1968), is a collection of his early writings up to 1925.

Cronon, E. David. *Black Moses: The Story of Marcus Garvey and the Universal Negro Improvement Association* (1955).
Davis, Daniel S. *Marcus Garvey* (1972).
Garvey, Amy Jacques. *Garvey and Garveyism* (1963).
Martin, Tony. *The Emancipation of a Race* (1973).
Stein, Judith. *The World of Marcus Garvey: Race and Class in Modern Society* (1986).
Vincent, Theodore. *Black Power and the Garvey Movement* (1971).

Obituary: *New York Times*, 12 June 1940.

—WILLIAM F. MUGLESTON

GAYE, MARVIN (2 Apr. 1939–1 Apr. 1984), singer and songwriter, was born Marvin Pentz Gay Jr. in Washington, D.C., the son of Marvin Pentz Gay Sr., a Pentecostal minister, and Alberta (maiden name unknown), a domestic worker. The younger Marvin grew up in Washington, where he began his musical career by singing in the choir and playing organ at his father's church. At Cardozo High School in Washington, he played piano in a doo-wop group called the D.C. Tones. He left school after eleventh grade and enlisted in the U.S. Air Force. After a year of openly rebelling against his commanding officers and feigning mental illness, he was discharged in 1957 for inability to serve.

Gaye (as he later came to spell his name) then returned to Washington and formed a doo-wop group called the Marquees. In 1957 they recorded a single, "Wyatt Earp" and "Hey, Little School Girl," produced by blues singer and songwriter BO DIDDLEY, which failed commercially, and Gaye supported himself by working as a dishwasher at a whites-only drugstore lunch counter in Washington.

In 1958 Harvey Fuqua, a successful rhythm-and-blues singer and producer, hired the Marquees to replace his backup singers, the Moonglows. The newly formed Harvey and the Moonglows, moved to Chicago in 1959, touring the United States and making several recordings on the Chess Records label.

In 1960 Gaye and Fuqua moved to Detroit in an effort to sing with BERRY GORDY JR., founder of the fledgling Motown Records label. Soon after arriving in Detroit, Gaye was signed to the Motown label as a drummer for the label's star group, the Miracles. In 1961 Gordy agreed to produce an album featuring him as a singer, and *The Soulful Moods of Marvin Gaye*, which marked the official addition of the "e" to his last name, was the result. The album departed from other Motown recordings with its jazz-based sound. It was aimed at the "crossover" white market but failed commercially.

Urged on by Gordy, Gaye changed his approach to appeal to the growing black music market. In 1962 he wrote and recorded "Stubborn Kind of Fellow," a rhythm-and-blues dance song that failed to attract a significant white audience but reached the top ten of the R&B sales chart. "At that point I knew I'd have to travel the same road as all black artists before me—establish a soul audience and then reach beyond that," Gaye said. In 1962 Gaye performed in the first Motortown Revue, a traveling concert featuring Motown's top stars.

Gaye finally broke into the popular music charts in 1963 with "Hitch Hike," which he co-wrote and recorded as a Motown single. On Dick Clark's *American Bandstand* television show, he performed a new dance named after the song. His next single, "Pride and Joy," reached the top ten of the pop chart. Later that year Gaye married Anna Gordy, the subject of "Pride and Joy" and Berry Gordy's sister. The couple adopted a son, Marvin Pentz Gaye III, in 1965. Gaye's 1963 live album, *Marvin Gaye: Live on Stage*, cemented his position as a leading rhythm-and-blues performer.

Gaye scored various hits for Motown in the mid-1960s, including "How Sweet It Is" and "You're a Wonderful One" (1964), "Ain't That Peculiar" (1965), and "It Takes Two," performed with Kim Weston (1966). In 1967 Gaye began a recording partnership with Tammi Terrell, a young soprano brought into Motown to complement Gaye's smooth tenor. The pair recorded *United* (1967), which featured several hits, including "Ain't No Mountain High Enough" and "Your Precious Love." Over the next two years nine of their songs reached the pop and R&B charts, but the partnership ended

Marvin Gaye in performance in the 1980s. © S.I.N./CORBIS

message. The album also greatly broadened the form and content of black popular music. To the R&B palette established by Motown in the 1960s, Gaye added layers of string instruments, jazz-style horns, speaking voices, Latin percussion, and scat singing. The result was an extraordinarily lush and complex musical composition. The album was the most commercially successful of Gaye's career to that point. Three of its songs—"What's Going On," "Mercy Mercy Me," and "Inner City Blues"—reached the top ten on the R&B and pop charts. The album garnered Gaye a number of awards in 1971, including the *Billboard* Magazine Trendsetter of the Year, the *Cashbox* Magazine Male Vocalist of the Year, and the NAACP's Image Award.

Despite his renewed recording success, Gaye refused to perform live until 1 May 1972, four years after his last public performance, when he appeared at the Kennedy Center in Washington, D.C., as part of the city's Marvin Gaye Day. Later that year Gaye released *Trouble Man*, which served as the soundtrack for a film of the same name. *Trouble Man* contained only one vocal track, the title song, along with jazz instrumentals featuring Gaye on electronic keyboards, Trevor Lawrence on saxophone, and big-band arrangements by trombonist J. J. Johnson.

In 1973 Gaye moved to Los Angeles and released two albums, a duet with DIANA ROSS titled *Diana and Marvin*, which was a commercial failure, and *Let's Get It On*, a solo effort whose title track shot to number one on the R&B and pop charts. In another departure from Motown tradition, *Let's Get It On* presented an unabashed celebration of sex. The album was Gaye's greatest commercial success, selling more than five million copies. Shortly after the release of *Let's Get It On*, Gaye separated from his wife and moved into an isolated, semirural house in Topanga, California, with Janis Hunter, a sixteen-year-old girl. Gaye and Hunter had two children before they were married in 1977. Expanding on the success of *Let's Get It On*, Gaye performed in twenty cities on a national tour in the summer and fall of 1974.

In 1975 Gaye opened the Marvin Gaye Recording Studio in Hollywood and recorded *I Want You*, an album

when Terrell died of a brain tumor in 1970. During the late 1960s Gaye also recorded a number of hits as a solo artist, including the hugely successful "I Heard It through the Grapevine," which reached the top of the R&B and pop charts in 1969. By this point in his career, Gaye had mastered three distinct voices—a soothing midrange, a harsher, gospel-inflected shout, and a satiny falsetto.

Following the string of hits in the late 1960s, Gaye entered a reclusive phase in which for more than a year he refused to record or perform. During this time he trained rigorously in an attempt to join the Detroit Lions football team as a wide receiver. Fearing a lawsuit

if he were injured, in 1970 the team's ownership refused to give him a tryout. Gaye's musical experience during this period was limited to producing and writing material for a young R&B group called the Originals.

Gaye's greatest triumph as a musician came in 1971 with the release of *What's Going On*, which he wrote, produced, and performed. *What's Going On* broke several conventions for Motown, and for African American music in general. Written as a thematic suite, the album's lyrics decried American imperialism, urban poverty, police brutality, and ecological destruction, making it one of the first black mainstream recordings with an explicit protest

similar to *Let's Get It On* in its frank sexuality and smooth soul sound. Despite its cool reception by critics, *I Want You* sold more than one million copies. Gaye's 1976 performance at the London Palladium, which featured songs from throughout his career, was recorded and released in 1977 as *Marvin Gaye Live at the London Palladium*. The album included a studio-recorded disco track, "Got to Give It Up," which reached number one on the soul and pop charts.

Gaye's recording career took its strangest turn in 1978 with the release of *Here, My Dear*, an extended musical diatribe against his first wife, Anna, who had won a divorce ruling against him the previous year. Proceeds from sales of the album, which included the song "You Can Leave, but It's Going to Cost You," went to Anna as part of the divorce settlement. The settlement, along with an extravagant cocaine habit, several years of unpaid federal taxes, and a string of disastrous business investments, created a financial crisis from which Gaye never recovered. His 1979 tour was largely undertaken to repay enormous debts to musicians, his first wife, and the federal government. Forced to sell his house and many of his possessions, in 1980 Gaye lived in a van on a beach in Maui, Hawaii. That year his second wife divorced him. In 1981 a British promoter persuaded a reluctant Gaye to perform on a tour of England and Europe. After this tour Gaye remained in London, afraid to return to the United States and face prosecution for tax evasion.

That spring Gaye renounced his contract with Motown, severing a twenty-year relationship, and moved from London to Ostend, Belgium, where he and his son were supported by a Belgian businessman. Gaye signed a new recording contract with CBS Records in 1982 and released *Midnight Love*, his most successful album since *Let's Get It On*. "Sexual Healing," a reggae-style single from the album, remained number one on the soul charts for four months and made it to number three on the pop charts. The single sold more than one million copies, the album more than two million. This commercial success emboldened Gaye to return to the United States in the fall of 1982. He returned to Los Angeles and in January 1983, still struggling financially, moved

into his parents' home in the Crenshaw district of the city. That year Gaye won Grammy Awards for Best Male Vocal and Best Instrumental Performance in the rhythm-and-blues category for "Sexual Healing."

During the "Sexual Healing" national tour in the spring and summer of 1983, Gaye's cocaine addiction worsened and he developed severe paranoia and depression. Returning from the tour, he secluded himself in his parents' home for several months. On 1 April 1984, following a fight between the two men, Gaye was shot and killed by his father.

Gaye was one of the preeminent soul singers and composers of his generation. His versatile and silken voice and sensitive phrasing made him a singer without superior in the history of American popular music. A leading voice in the Motown sound of the 1960s, Gaye established himself as a virtuoso performer and composer in the 1970s, when his self-produced albums pioneered several new musical and lyrical forms in popular music.

FURTHER READING

George, Nelson. *Where Did Our Love Go: The Rise and Fall of the Motown Sound* (1985).
Ritz, David. *Divided Soul: The Life of Marvin Gaye* (1985; repr. 1991).

Obituaries: *New York Times*, 2 April 1984; *Rolling Stone*, 10 and 24 May 1984.
—THADDEUS RUSSELL

GEORGE, DAVID

(c. 1742–1810), lay preacher and émigré to Nova Scotia and Sierra Leone, was born on a Nottoway River plantation in Essex County, Virginia. His parents, slaves known as John and Judith, were of African origin and had nine children. While a youth David labored in the corn and tobacco fields and witnessed frequent whippings of other slaves, including his mother, who was the master's cook.

When he was about nineteen, George ran away to North Carolina, worked for a brief time, but was pursued and fled to South Carolina. He worked as a hired hand for about two years. After hearing that his first master was again pursuing

him, George escaped to Central Georgia where he hid among the Creek Indians. George became the personal servant of Chief Blue Salt, who later sold him to the Natchez chief, King Jack.

A trader with the white settlers, King Jack sold George to the Indian trader George Galphin of Silver Bluff, Georgia. Galphin sent George to work for John Miller, his agent. George mended deerskins and took care of Miller's horses until about 1766, when he went to live at Galphin's frontier trading post. Galphin, an Ulsterman who traded with the Creeks and Choctaws, treated George well.

About 1770 George married a woman known only as Phillis. Soon after his marriage he began attending slave prayer meetings led by a slave named Cyrus. George and his wife experienced conversion after hearing the preaching of GEORGE LIELE, the African American Baptist who conducted an itinerant ministry on plantations along the Savannah River. As a child, George had known Liele when the two were slaves in Virginia.

George and his wife were baptized about 1777 by Wait Palmer, a radical white Baptist who belonged to the Separate Baptist movement, which was zealously revivalistic, espousing the need for a "new birth." Liele encouraged George to preach with instruction from Palmer. Galphin employed a schoolmaster who, along with Galphin's children, taught George to read and write. Of learning these skills at the age of thirty, George later said, "The reading so ran in my mind, that I think I learned in my sleep . . . , and I can now read the Bible, so that what I have in my heart, I can see again in the Scriptures."

With assistance from Palmer, George organized a Baptist congregation on Galphin's Silver Bluff plantation that began with eight members; it expanded to about thirty members by 1778. During the revolutionary war, John Murray, Lord Dunmore offered emancipation to any slaves who sought sanctuary behind British lines. George went to Charleston. When the British evacuated Charleston in 1782, he and his family were among the Charleston refugees who went to New York City and then to Halifax, Nova Scotia.

Finding no opportunity to preach among blacks in Halifax, George settled in Shelburne. Because white justices, fearing civil disorder, would not let him preach in town, George had to content himself with a hut in the woods, where his preaching attracted whites as well as blacks. He soon had fifty members in what was only the second Baptist church organized in Nova Scotia. In 1784 recently disbanded British soldiers, resenting competition from free black laborers, attacked and destroyed many of their houses. George and his family fled to Birchtown. After six months George returned to Shelburne and regained possession of his old meetinghouse. During the next years he conducted missionary trips in the Maritime provinces. Though only a lay preacher, George was known for his rousing sermons and hymns and was responsible for the organization of seven Baptist churches in Nova Scotia before he left for Africa.

In 1791 Lieutenant John Clarkson of the British navy arrived in Nova Scotia to recruit Nova Scotia blacks for the British-sponsored "Free Settlement on the Coast of Africa" at Sierra Leone, West Africa. George was by now forty-eight years old, the father of six, the largest black landowner in Nova Scotia, and the pastor of two churches. He talked privately with Clarkson and became convinced of the merits of the Sierra Leone enterprise. On 15 January 1792 the George family departed Halifax for Cape Sierra Leone with about 1,200 other black Nova Scotians.

Soon after landing, George expressed his evangelical enthusiasm: "I preached the first Lord's Day (it was a blessed time) under a sail, and so I did for several weeks after. We then erected a hovel for a meeting-house, which is made of posts put into the ground, and poles over our heads, which are covered with grass." George led the formation of the first Baptist church in West Africa at Freetown, Sierra Leone. He and his members supported Clarkson when other settler factions challenged the authority of the British governor. In 1796, however, George opposed Governor Zachary Macaulay because Macaulay issued a decree that restricted the authority to perform marriages to the ordained clergy of the Anglican church and the governor. George was more moderate in his protest of British authority than some

Nova Scotians, as those who had come with Clarkson were known. More strident settlers called George "Macaulay's tool."

While in Sierre Leone, George did limited missionary work among the indigenous Temne. Conflict among the various ethnic groups prevented him from carrying out plans for establishing Baptist churches in areas outside those occupied by the colonists. George and Thomas Peters, another Nova Scotian, were the first unofficial members of the Sierre Leone Legislative Council. George traveled to Britain in December 1792, remaining six months visiting English Baptists and telling his story. After returning to Sierre Leone, George devoted himself to church work, especially as an advocate for the Baptists when opposition arose from Methodists in the colony. He died in Sierra Leone.

FURTHER READING

Bill, Ingraham E. *Fifty Years with the Baptist Ministers and Churches of the Maritime Provinces of Canada* (1880).

George, David. *Baptist Annual Register for . . . 1793*, 473–84.

Kirk-Greene, Anthony. "David George: The Nova Scotia Experience," *Sierra Leone Studies* 14 (1960): 93–120.

Walker, James W. St. G. *The Black Loyalists: The Search for a Promised Land in Nova Scotia and Sierra Leone, 1783–1870* (1976).

Wilson, Ellen Gibson. *The Loyal Blacks* (1976).
—MILTON C. SERNETT

 GIBBS, MIFFLIN WISTAR (17 Apr. 1823– 11 July 1915), businessman, politician, and race leader, was born in Philadelphia, Pennsylvania, the son of Jonathan C. Gibbs, a Methodist minister, and Maria Jackson. His parents were free blacks. His father died when Mifflin was seven years old, and his mother was an invalid. As a teenager, Mifflin attended the Philomathean Institute, a black men's literary society, and, like his brother Jonathan C. Gibbs (who would serve as secretary of state in Florida during Reconstruction), became a carpenter's apprentice, and subsequently a journeyman contractor. During the 1840s Mifflin Gibbs aided fugitive slaves by participating in local Underground

Mifflin W. Gibbs, politician, diplomat, businessman, and lawyer. Schomburg Center

Railroad efforts and worked with its famous conductor WILLIAM GRANT STILL. It was through this work that he became acquainted with the preeminent black abolitionist FREDERICK DOUGLASS, accompanying him on an 1849 tour of New York State.

During this tour, Gibbs learned that gold had been discovered in California, and he set out to find his fortune. Reaching San Francisco in 1850, he decided that more money could be made in business than in panning for gold. Consequently, along with a black partner, Peter Lester, Gibbs established a clothing and dry goods store. His business prospered, and he quickly became a well-known and successful entrepreneur. He also kept up his interest in the abolitionist movement, attending three state black conventions (1854, 1855, 1857) and in 1855 purchasing and becoming the editor of a local black antislavery newspaper, the *Mirror of the Times*.

During an economic recession in the United States in 1857–1858, Gibbs followed a new gold rush to Victoria, British Columbia, Canada, where he opened another store. He briefly returned to the United States in 1859 to marry Maria A. Alexander, a former Oberlin student who became the mother of their five children. During the next decade, Gibbs repeated his California business success in Canada by speculating in real estate, becoming the director of the Queen Charlotte Island Anthracite Coal Company, and building a wharf and railroad spur to transport coal. His business ventures brought him influence, and in 1866 he was elected to the first of two terms as a member of Victoria's Common Council. After the second term, however, disgruntled by the direction of local politics, he returned to the United States to complete a formal course in law at a business school in Oberlin, Ohio.

Touring the southern states to find a suitable location to establish a law practice, Gibbs settled in the rapidly growing town of Little Rock, Arkansas, in 1871. Beginning as a lawyer, he was later appointed county attorney, and in 1873 he won election as municipal judge of Little Rock, reportedly the first black man in the nation to be so honored. In 1875 when the Democrats returned to power, Gibbs lost the judgeship, but he quickly rose to prominence in the Republican Party, attending national Republican conventions and serving as a presidential elector for Arkansas in 1876 and as secretary of the Republican state central committee from 1887 to 1897. In 1877 he was appointed by President Rutherford B. Hayes as register of the U.S. Land Office for the Little Rock District of Arkansas. He served in the land office for twelve years, the last four as receiver of public monies. In 1897 he was appointed U.S. consul to Tamatave, Madagascar (1898–1901).

In 1901 Gibbs returned to Arkansas and the next year published *Shadow and Light, an Autobiography with Reminiscences of the Last and Present Century* (repr. 1968), a lively account of his life and times, with an introduction by the famous black leader BOOKER T. WASHINGTON. That Washington would introduce the book was no accident; Gibbs epitomized Washington's self-help philosophy. In Little Rock, Gibbs not only speculated in real estate but eventually owned a number of brick office buildings and rental properties. In 1903 Gibbs became president of the city's Capital City Savings Bank (it failed after five years) and later bought shares in several local companies while becoming a partner in the Little Rock Electric Light Company. He was also an active member of the National Negro Business League, founded by Washington to encourage entrepreneurship among blacks.

Although closely tied to the Republican machine in Arkansas, Gibbs fought for equal rights for blacks and supported emigration from the South as a cure for racial oppression (a radical stance in the late 1870s). After Theodore Roosevelt (1858–1919) summarily dismissed black soldiers accused of inciting a race riot in Brownsville, Texas, in 1906, Gibbs abandoned the Republican Party and endorsed Democrat William Jennings Bryan for the presidency. The common thread linking these diverse elements was Gibbs's commitment to what he termed "the progress of the race." Although he fought for equality and fair treatment, he believed that property acquisition and education were the keys to racial advancement and that African Americans should establish a skilled middle class in order to compete in the marketplace.

During the last decade of his life, using the income from his rental properties, Gibbs lived quietly and comfortably in Little Rock. After an illness of several months, he died at his home. He was survived by several notable children, among them Harriet Gibbs Marshall, who founded the Washington Conservatory of Music, and Ida Gibbs Hunt, who married William Henry Hunt, Gibbs's successor as U.S. consul to Madagascar. A man of education, talent, energy, and property, Gibbs had a remarkably varied career.

FURTHER READING

Dillard, Tom W. "'Golden Prospects and Fraternal Amenities,' Mifflin W. Gibbs's Arkansas Years," *Arkansas Historical Quarterly* 35 (Winter 1976): 307–333.

Obituaries: *Arkansas Gazette* and *Arkansas Democrat*, 12 July 1915; Washington *Bee*, 17 July 1915.

—LOREN SCHWENINGER

GIBSON, ALTHEA
(25 Aug. 1927–28 Sept. 2003), tennis champion and professional golfer, was born in Silver, South Carolina, the first of five children of Daniel Gibson and Annie Gibson, who worked as sharecroppers. The family moved to New York City in 1930, and Gibson grew up in Harlem. As a youth Gibson rejected rules and authority; a frequent truant, she dropped out of high school after one year. She did, however, enjoy competition, playing basketball and paddleball, and shooting pool. After Gibson won a 1941 Police Athletic League paddleball championship, Buddy Walker, a tournament official, suggested that she try playing tennis. With Walker's assistance, she began tennis lessons at Harlem's Cosmopolitan Club.

The following summer, Gibson was ready for tournament play. She won the 1942 New York State Open in the girls' division, a victory that began her rise through the ranks of the American Tennis Association (ATA), the governing body of black tennis in the United States. In 1944 and 1945 she won consecutive ATA girls' national championships. As an eighteen-year-old, Gibson qualified to play in the women's division in 1946. Despite losing in the finals of the women's singles competition, her play impressed Hubert A. Eaton and Robert W. Johnson, two southern physicians who were active in the ATA. Eaton and Johnson believed Gibson had the potential to become a world-class player. They felt that with proper training and instruction, she could break the color line, which had prohibited earlier black tennis players like LUCY DIGGS SLOWE and ORA MAE WASHINGTON from competing in tournaments sponsored by the United States Lawn Tennis Association (USLTA).

Following the advice of her friend the boxer Sugar Ray Robinson (whom she had met in a bowling alley) and his wife, Gibson left Harlem in 1946 and boarded at Eaton's home in Wilmington, North Carolina. She enrolled in Wilmington's segregated public high school and began training year-round on Eaton's private tennis court. During the summers, Gibson practiced her tennis at Johnson's home in Lynchburg, Virginia. She created a sensation on the ATA tournament circuit, capturing eight mixed doubles championships, with Johnson as her partner, and winning nine women's singles titles, including the first of her ten consecutive ATA woman's championships in 1947.

Gibson graduated from high school in 1949 and received an athletic scholarship to attend Florida A&M University (FAMU) in Tallahassee, where she played softball, volleyball, basketball, and

Althea Gibson on the way to becoming the first African American to win the women's singles championship at Wimbledon, 1957. Library of Congress

tennis. Before she arrived at the FAMU campus, she competed against white players in tournament action for the first time, at two indoor events sponsored by USLTA. Although she made it to the quarterfinals in both tournaments, Gibson did not receive invitations to play at outdoor tournaments because most major USLTA events were held at segregated country clubs, such as the West Side Tennis Club in Forest Hills, New York.

After Gibson was shut out of USLTA tournament play in the summer of 1949, Alice Marble, the winner of four U.S. Open titles and a former Wimbledon champion, wrote in support of Gibson's struggle to break the color line in tennis, just as JACKIE ROBINSON had ended baseball's color bar in 1947. In an editorial published in the July 1950 issue of *American Lawn Tennis*, Marble criticized the USLTA for its pro-segregation stance. The piece made an immediate impact, and Gibson entered several USLTA outdoor tournaments in the summer of 1950, including the USLTA National Clay Court and the Eastern Grass Court Championships. She also qualified to play in the USLTA National Championship tournament (now called the U.S. Open) at Forest Hills. On 28 August 1950 Gibson became the first African American to compete in this tournament, winning her first round match in straight sets, 6–2, 6–2. In the second round, she nearly pulled a stunning upset of the three-time Wimbledon champion, Louise Brough. With Gibson leading 1–6, 6–3, 7–6 and needing just one game to win, play was stopped because of severe weather. Brough rallied and won when play was resumed the next day. Gibson's performance in this and subsequent tournaments at Forest Hills established her as a fixture on the USLTA tour until her retirement from tennis.

Gibson continued to break racial barriers with each tournament appearance. In 1951 she became the first African American—male or female—to play on the grass courts of the All England Club at Wimbledon. She also captured her first international title that year, winning the Caribbean Open in Jamaica. By 1952 Gibson was ranked number nine among all American women tennis players. However, because tennis was an amateur sport during this era, after graduating from Florida A&M in 1953 she took a teaching position in the athletic department at Lincoln University in Jefferson City, Missouri. She struggled in the years following her graduation, and her tennis career appeared to stall. Gibson contemplated leaving the tour, but was convinced to continue by the tennis coach Sydney Llewellyn, with whom she began training in 1954. Her career was revitalized when she returned from playing a series of goodwill exhibition matches in Southeast Asia sponsored by the U.S. Department of State during the winter of 1955–1956.

As she approached thirty, Gibson began a remarkable tournament run in which she took eight Grand Slam titles between 1956 and 1958. This streak began with her first, and only, appearance at the French Open. On her way to capturing that tournament's women's title, 6–0, 12–10 over the defending champion, Angela Mortimer, Gibson also won the French doubles title with her partner, Angela Buxton. Pairing again with Buxton, she won her first women's doubles title at Wimbledon in June 1956. Before the year was over, Gibson claimed singles titles in the Italian Open and the Asian Championship, in addition to other international events, including the New South Wales, Pan American, and South Australian tournaments. With each new title and tournament appearance, a piece of the color line broke away.

Gibson was at the top of her game in 1957, the year in which she won the women's singles championship and defended her doubles title at Wimbledon. She later recalled that receiving her trophy from Queen Elizabeth II and shaking hands with her "was a long way from being forced to sit down in the colored section of the bus going into downtown Wilmington, N.C. (Obituary, *New York Times*, 29 Sept. 2003). When Gibson returned to New York City she was welcomed as a heroine, receiving the medallion of the city from Mayor Robert Wagner after a ticker tape parade. On 8 September 1957 she continued her pioneering career by becoming the first African American to win the U.S. Open, defeating Louise Brough in straight sets, 6–3, 6–2. This win was the first part of her clean sweep of the tournament, as she also captured the women's doubles with Darlene Hard and the mixed doubles championships with Kurt Nielsen. By year's end, Gibson was ranked as the number-one woman tennis player in the world and named Female Athlete of the Year by the Associated Press (AP), a first for an African American woman.

Gibson became a repeat winner of the AP Female Athlete of the Year award in 1958, successfully defending her Wimbledon singles title and taking a third straight doubles crown, this time with Maria Bueno. She also won her second straight U.S. National Championship at Forest Hills. Soon afterward Gibson retired from amateur tennis, leaving the tennis circuit with one hundred tournament victories.

Gibson kept her place in the public eye after her tennis career ended. She wrote her first autobiography, *I Always Wanted to be Somebody* (1958), recorded an album entitled *Althea Gibson Sings* (1958), and also appeared in the John Ford film *The Horse Soldiers* (1959) with John Wayne and William Holden. In 1960 she signed a $100,000 contract with the Harlem Globetrotters to stage tennis exhibitions in conjunction with Globetrotter appearances. However, this did not satisfy Gibson's competitive fire, and she began to explore the possibility of joining the newly constituted Ladies Professional Golfers Association (LPGA). By earning her tour card in 1964, Gibson broke another part of the color line by becoming the first

African American woman professional golfer. Although Gibson did not record any tournament victories while on the tour, she remained with the LPGA for seven years, playing in 171 tournaments. She briefly attempted a tennis comeback when Grand Slam tournaments were opened to both professionals and amateurs in 1968. She was inducted into the Tennis Hall of Fame in 1971.

Gibson, who married Will Darben in 1965, had settled in East Orange, New Jersey, upon her retirement from tennis. As well as coaching and teaching tennis, she also held a position in the East Orange Department of Recreation. In 1975 she was named New Jersey State Athletic Commissioner, becoming the first woman to serve in such a position anywhere in the United States. Gibson was honored for her groundbreaking accomplishments on and off court with numerous awards, including inductions to the International Women's Hall of Fame in 1980 and the International Women's Hall of Fame in 2002.

Althea Gibson died of respiratory failure in East Orange in September 2003. She was predeceased by Darben, and by her second husband, her former coach, Sydney Llewellyn. Gibson had no children. Her legacy continues to be carried out through the Althea Gibson Foundation, an organization founded to identify, encourage, and provide financial support for urban students seeking to develop their skills in tennis or golf. Her enduring significance lies in becoming the first African American to win Wimbledon, the world's premier tennis tournament. Gibson took great pride in that victory, which she viewed as the first ever world championship won by a black woman. That victory inspired a young Billy Jean King, who greatly admired Gibson's courage, and set a precedent for ARTHUR ASHE, who won the men's Wimbledon title in 1975. Gibson showed a particular interest in encouraging the relatively small cohort of African American women on the tennis circuit. Despite her failing health, she traveled to London in 1990 to cheer on Zina Garrison, the first African American to reach the Wimbledon finals since Gibson's last appearance in 1958. She also took great pleasure in the Wimbledon triumphs of VENUS AND SERENA WILLIAMS, who like her had grown up in poverty. "The crowds will love you," Gibson told Venus on one

occasion, reminding her, however, that it was important to "be who you are and let your racket do the talking" (Vecsey, D2).

FURTHER READING

Gibson, Althea, edited by Ed Fitzgerald. *I Always Wanted to Be Somebody* (1958).
Gibson, Althea, with Richard Curtis. *So Much to Live For* (1968).

Vecsey, George. "Gibson Deserved a Better Old Age," *New York Times*, 29 Sept. 2003, D2.
Wade, Virginia, with Jean Rafferty. *Ladies of the Court: A Century of Women at Wimbledon* (1984).

Obituary: *New York Times*, 29 Sept. 2003.
—MICHAEL A. ANTONUCCI

 ## GIBSON, JOSH

(21 Dec. 1911–20 Jan. 1947), baseball player, was born Joshua Gibson in Buena Vista, Georgia, the son of Mark Gibson, a sharecropper and steel mill worker and the son of former slaves, and Nancy Woodlock. Josh's two younger siblings, Jerry and Annie, were also children of this union. Around 1921 Josh's father left the uncertain work environment of southwestern Georgia and migrated north to Pittsburgh, Pennsylvania. After securing employment as a laborer with Carnegie-Illinois Steel, he arranged for his family to rejoin him. Josh had completed five years of elementary education in Georgia and enrolled at Allegheny Pre-Vocational School with the intention of becoming an electrician. After completing the ninth grade he left school for an apprenticeship in a Westinghouse Airbrake factory and began playing with a sandlot baseball team, the Pleasant Valley Red Sox. He then joined the semipro Pittsburgh Crawford Giants in 1928. In the spring of 1930 he married Helen Mason, but three months later she died in childbirth, while fraternal twins, Helen and Josh Jr., survived.

Gibson began his professional career when he was recruited by the Homestead Grays' player-manager, JUDY JOHNSON, in July 1930, after their catcher suffered a split finger. With Gibson as their regular catcher, the Grays capped a successful season by defeating the New York Lincoln Giants in a playoff for the Eastern Championship.

Josh Gibson slides into home during Negro Leagues East–West All-Star Game, 1944. © Bettmann/CORBIS

In the series Gibson batted .368 and hit three home runs, including a 460-foot drive at Yankee Stadium. A right-handed batter, he had extraordinary power and established himself as a superstar in his first full season, 1931. The press credited him with seventy-five home runs that year, although most were against semipro opposition, and the Grays again reigned as the best team in the east. In 1932 the Pittsburgh Crawfords owner, Gus Greenlee, raided the Grays, signing Gibson and other key players. With the flamboyant SATCHEL PAIGE pitching and Gibson catching, the Crawfords had one of baseball's stellar batteries, and for the next five years they were easily the finest team in the Negro Leagues.

In 1933 Gibson met Hattie Jones, and the couple soon established residence together. The first East-West All-Star game was played that year, and Gibson made the first of four straight all-star appearances. In those seasons he batted .464, .383, .440, and .457 and was the premier slugger in the Negro Leagues. In 1934 he was credited with sixty-nine home runs against all levels of opposition, and in the 1935 play-off against the New York Cubans for the Negro National League pennant, he hit .407 and smashed a dramatic

game-winning, two-run home run in the ninth inning of the final game. The 1935 Crawfords are considered to be the greatest team in the history of the Negro Leagues. In a postseason exhibition game that year, Gibson hit a home run off the white St. Louis Cardinals ace pitcher Dizzy Dean. Over his career Gibson would compile a .412 lifetime batting average against major leaguers. In 1936 the Crawfords won another pennant, and, during the season, Gibson and a select black all-star team were entered in the Denver Post Tournament and won the championship with ease.

In March 1937 Gibson was returned to the Homestead Grays in the biggest transaction in Negro Leagues history. Soon after signing with the Grays, he went to the Dominican Republic, where he led the league with a .453 batting average and powered the dictator Rafael Trujillo's All-Stars to the championship. Upon his return to the Grays, Gibson teamed with Buck Leonard to form a power tandem that the press dubbed the "Thunder Twins." Gibson was called the "black Babe Ruth," and the duo formed the nucleus of the Grays' "Murderers' Row" that in 1937 won the first of nine straight Negro National League pennants for the Grays.

In 1938 the media urged the major leagues to sign Gibson and other black stars, but to no avail. Around this time, Gibson and Leonard were called into the office of the Washington Senators' owner, Clark Griffith, and asked about their interest in playing in the major leagues, but despite their expressed confidence that they could make the team, Griffith told them, "Nobody wants to be the first." In 1938 the champion Grays made the first of two postseason tours of Cuba, with Gibson batting .347 in the series. Afterward he remained to play in the Cuban Winter League and powered Santa Clara to the championship, batting .356 and leading the league in home runs. One blast traveled an incredible 704 feet and is the longest home run in Cuban history.

In 1939 the Grays won their third straight pennant, Gibson recording a .440 batting average and a slugging percentage (the ratio of bases reached on hits to at bats) of 1.190. A postseason four-team tournament was held, with the Grays losing in the final round despite Gibson's pair of home runs. Gibson opted to spend the 1939–1940 winter in Puerto Rico as Santurce's playing manager, and he batted .380 while leading the league in home runs. He jumped to Venezuela for the 1940 season, but, when the league folded, he signed with Veracruz in the Mexican League, where he batted .467. Gibson returned to Veracruz for the entire 1941 season and led the league with thirty-three home runs and batted .374, as Veracruz repeated as champions. He then returned to Santurce in the Puerto Rican Winter League, where he led the league with a .480 batting average, a .959 slugging percentage, and thirteen home runs, to win the league's Most Valuable Player trophy. One of his home runs traveled over 600 feet and was the longest in the history of Puerto Rican baseball.

When the Grays' owner, Cum Posey, filed a ten-thousand-dollar lawsuit against Gibson for breach of contract and sought to take his house as compensation for alleged damages, a settlement was reached, and Gibson returned to the Grays for the 1942 season. With Gibson back in the fold, the Grays won another pennant, though the Kansas

City Monarchs swept them in the first Negro World Series between the Negro National League and the Negro American League. But as the result of alcoholic excesses and, possibly, drug abuse, Gibson's physical and psychological condition deteriorated during the season. This decline was apparent to many by the end of the year. In January 1943 he was committed to a hospital after suffering a nervous breakdown. He lapsed into a coma and was diagnosed with a brain tumor. Upon recovery, he decided not to have the tumor removed for fear that he might have permanent brain damage, and he did not inform the Grays of his condition. Gibson developed a relationship with Grace Fournier, a rumored drug addict whose husband was stationed overseas in the army, and her influence contributed to his continued debilitation. As his substance abuse worsened, Gibson's behavior became more erratic, and he was frequently hospitalized or committed to sanatoriums throughout the remainder of his life.

World War II was at its peak, but Gibson was ineligible for the draft because of bad knees from many years of catching, both summer and winter. Despite the problems in his personal life, he still maintained his high standard of performance, and the Grays won back-to-back Negro World Series from the Birmingham Black Barons in 1943 and 1944. In the 1943 World Series, Gibson hit a grand-slam home run, and, in the 1944 series, he batted .500 and also hammered a home run. By 1945 Gibson had lost some of his power, but he still batted .398 for the season, as the Grays won their ninth straight pennant but were swept by the upstart Cleveland Buckeyes in the Negro World Series. Gibson began the winter season in Puerto Rico, but he did not play well and was involved in another dark episode when he ran naked through a San Juan plaza and had to be physically subdued, after which arrangements were made for his return to Pittsburgh for a long rest.

The 1946 season was Gibson's last. A distinct difference was noticeable, both in his health and his playing skills. His defensive skills had eroded, and he could not even squat down behind the plate in a catcher's position. Observers were saddened to see what had happened to the once seemingly indestructible player. He suffered excruciating headaches and dizziness and was plagued by occasional disorientation, incoherence, and conversations with imaginary people. Two All-Star games were played that season, and, despite his debilitation, Gibson was the starting catcher in both games. The consistency of his power had diminished, but the potential was still present, and though he was only a shadow of his former self, Gibson retained his smooth swing and bashed several long home runs, including a 550-foot shot in St. Louis against the Cleveland Buckeyes.

By the end of 1946 Gibson was unable to care for himself and, after a weekend of intense headaches, he suffered a stroke and died at his mother's home in Pittsburgh only three months before JACKIE ROBINSON broke the major league color line. In 1972 Josh Gibson became the second player from the Negro Leagues, after Satchel Paige (1971), to be inducted into the National Baseball Hall of Fame at Cooperstown, New York.

FURTHER READING

Brashler, William. *Josh Gibson: A Life in the Negro Leagues* (1978).
Peterson, Robert. *Only the Ball Was White* (1970).
Ribowsky, Mark. *The Power and the Darkness: The Life of Josh Gibson in the Shadows of the Game* (1996).

Obituary: *Pittsburgh Courier*, 25 January 1947.
—JAMES A. RILEY

GILLESPIE, DIZZY

(21 Oct. 1917–6 Jan. 1993), jazz trumpeter, composer, and bandleader, was born John Birks Gillespie at Cheraw, South Carolina, the ninth and youngest child of James Gillespie, a brick mason, builder, and amateur musician, and Lottie Powe, a laundress. The earliest musical influences on Gillespie were the sounds of the town band, in which his father played and whose instruments were stored in the family home, together with the singing and hand clapping of the parishioners of the Sanctified Church a few doors away from his house. James Gillespie was cruel and sadistic, regularly beating his sons, but he died from an asthma attack when John was ten. Not long afterward, he was formally introduced to playing music by Alice Wilson, a schoolteacher at the Robert Smalls School in Cheraw. Growing up as the youngest child of a large single-parent family, John developed an early penchant for mischief, but music was a stabilizing influence in his life. After first playing trombone and then settling on trumpet, Gillespie joined a local amateur band of young musicians, playing for social events in and around Cheraw. He eventually won a music scholarship to the Laurinburg Institute, in Laurinburg, North Carolina.

Although the music tutor there, Philmore "Shorty" Hall, was a proficient trumpeter from Tuskegee College, Alabama, he had little time to pass on his knowledge to Gillespie, who consequently was largely self-taught, sharing his diligent trumpet practice routines with a cousin, Norman Powe, who later became a professional trombonist. In due course Gillespie also became a competent pianist, using the piano to help him understand harmony and developing the trick of playing the trumpet with his right hand while accompanying himself on the piano with his left.

Gillespie left the institute before graduating in 1935 and moved with his family to Philadelphia, where he joined the big band of Frankie Fairfax. This gave him a thorough musical apprenticeship, including touring throughout Pennsylvania and travels on the territory band circuit of the South and Southwest under the temporary leadership of the drummer Tiny Bradshaw. During his time in Fairfax's band, Gillespie acquired the nickname "Dizzy" for his occasionally outlandish behavior and frequent practical jokes, and he soon became popularly known by this name alone.

His contemporaries described Gillespie's early solos as redolent of LOUIS

Dizzy Gillespie, along with CHARLIE PARKER, was one of the innovators of bebop and a figurehead of modern jazz. His upswept trumpet, adopted in the 1950s, and his elastic cheeks made him instantly recognizable. Corbis

ARMSTRONG, but his trumpet-section colleagues Charlie Shavers and Carl Warwick introduced him to the stylistic innovations of Roy Eldridge. These became the dominant influences on Gillespie's playing, which he refined by studying Eldridge's work from records, broadcasts, and occasional live appearances in Philadelphia. In 1937 Shavers and Warwick persuaded Gillespie to move to New York City to join Lucky Millinder's orchestra, but when this plan fell through, Gillespie joined Teddy Hill's band and almost immediately set sail for a European tour that took him to France and Britain. Before leaving, Gillespie, at age nineteen, made his first records; his solo on Hill's "King Porter Stomp" reveals a remarkably mature player, already developing a style distinct from that of Eldridge.

During the Atlantic crossing, the trumpeter Bill Dillard coached Gillespie in the art of section playing. After appearances at the Moulin Rouge in Paris and the London Palladium, he returned to New York a seasoned big-band musician, continuing to work with Hill and with Edgar Hayes, Al Cooper, and the Cuban flutist Alberto Socarras. In 1939 he joined CAB CALLOWAY's orchestra, one of the most high-profile bands in jazz. This move brought Gillespie's playing to the attention of a large public. He not only recorded many solos with Calloway but also contributed arrangements to the band, including the innovative "Picking the Cabbage," which prefigured some of the rhythmic and structural devices he was to use in such later compositions as "A Night in Tunisia."

However, Gillespie found the endless routine of backing up Calloway's singing and dancing, and the relatively limited musical vocabulary of the majority of the music, to be highly restrictive. He fooled around onstage and played ever more daring solos that ventured into new harmonic directions, delivered at dazzling speed. Calloway disliked this "Chinese music," and matters came to a head in September 1941, when Calloway accused Gillespie of throwing a spitball on stage. Gillespie—innocent for once—responded by drawing a knife and stabbing his bandleader in the rear end. He was immediately fired.

Gillespie was one of a small number of African American musicians actively seeking to expand the vocabulary of jazz. In June 1940, in Kansas City, Gillespie had met CHARLIE PARKER, thus beginning their highly productive collaboration. In New York, Gillespie, Parker, and other young innovative players, including the drummer Kenny Clarke, who had worked with Gillespie in Hayes's orchestra, and the pianist THELONIOUS MONK, would jam after hours at such Harlem clubs as Minton's Playhouse and Monroe's Uptown House. These informal and experimental jam sessions allowed the musicians to play in small groups where they could develop their own personal styles and where they began to move jazz itself in a new direction. Unfortunately, because of a strike by the American Federation of Musicians in the early 1940s, these earliest forays into what came to be known as bebop are largely unrecorded.

The relationship of Parker and Gillespie developed further when both men played in the big band led by Earl Hines, during the first nine months of 1943. Together, Parker and Gillespie became figureheads of the new bebop movement, which drew together several revolutionary elements. Among their innovations, they employed unusual, often dissonant harmonies, such as ninths, elevenths, and thirteenths, as well as habitually flattening some regularly used intervals, such as fifths and sevenths. They also used brief thematic formulas to construct long, flowing melodic lines, often delivered at high speed, which ran over the conventional four- and eight-measure phrase lengths of popular songs, and they introduced cross-rhythms and uneven accents to the playing of rhythm accompaniments. If Parker was the mercurial, short-lived genius whose inspirational playing was the heart of the new style, Gillespie became its head, documenting their repertoire of new tunes, arranging and voicing them for small and large ensembles, and tirelessly teaching his contemporaries the necessary harmonic and rhythmic structures. As improvisers, the two were evenly matched, and Gillespie described Parker as "the other half of my heartbeat."

Gillespie first brought bebop to Fifty-second Street in New York, leading a band at the Onyx Club from late 1943 until early the following year. With Parker temporarily home in Kansas City, Gillespie worked with the saxophonists Lester Young, Don Byas, and Budd Johnson to develop the style. Later in 1944 he joined Billy Eckstine's orchestra, which marked an early attempt to transfer the new ideas to a large ensemble. However, it was the quintet that Parker and Gillespie led at the Three Deuces in New York, from the spring until the late summer of 1945, that cemented the principles of bebop, and the recordings they made together at that time capture the inspirational brilliance of their playing. Their repertoire included "Dizzy Atmosphere," "Groovin' High," and "Salt Peanuts."

After a short-lived attempt to launch his own big band in mid-1945, Gillespie went with Parker to California, a visit marred by Parker's growing drug dependence and unreliability. Gillespie returned to New York, subsequently launching a successful big band, which he led until the end of the decade, making numerous recordings and traveling to Europe in 1948. This group demonstrated how to transfer bebop to large groups successfully and introduced several new concepts, including the use of modal structures and Afro-Cuban rhythms, notably on "Cubano Be-Cubano Bop," a composition by Gillespie, the theorist George Russell, and the band's Cuban percussionist, Chano Pozo.

Gillespie's repertoire of songs became big-band standards, including "Things to Come" and "Algo Bueno," as well as light-hearted vehicles for the scat singing of Dizzy and the vocalists Joe Carroll or Kenny Hagood, such as "Oop-Pop-a-Dah." Most significantly, Gillespie's ebullient personality, ready wit, and show-business experience made this difficult new music palatable to large audiences, helped by the eccentric visual image he adopted, sporting a beret, horn-rimmed spectacles, and a goatee. Lampooned in the press, his fashions were adopted by many of the band's fans.

In the early 1950s Gillespie's big band ceased to be economically viable, and his wife, Lorraine Willis, whom he had married in 1940, encouraged him to abandon it. He temporarily experimented in rhythm and blues and with his own record label, Dee Gee. This was an unsuccessful period for him musically. Then, as the 1950s developed, his regular quintet with the pianist Wynton Kelly and the baritone saxophonist Bill Graham became a regular feature of the touring circuit, visiting Scandinavia, Germany, and France as well as traveling widely in the United States. In 1953 Gillespie took part in a celebrated reunion with Parker at Massey Hall in Toronto.

Gillespie continued to develop as a soloist, appearing from 1954 in Jazz at the Philharmonic concerts and on record for the entrepreneur Norman Granz, who was instrumental in helping Gillespie re-form his big band. This was when Gillespie adopted his trademark upswept trumpet, its bell angled upward at a forty-five-degree angle. Combined with his unusually puffed-out cheeks, he became one of the most visually distinctive figures in music.

Following tours on behalf of the U.S. State Department to the Middle East and South America, Gillespie kept his new big band going through 1956–1957, thereafter only returning to larger ensembles sporadically and preferring to tour regularly with his quintet. During the early 1960s Gillespie formed a productive partnership with the Argentinean composer Lalo Schifrin, performing "Gillespiana," a five-movement suite for trumpet and big band, at Carnegie Hall in March 1961. Schifrin worked as pianist in Gillespie's quintet and composed for the small group and larger forces, including "New Continent" in 1962.

By this time Gillespie was beginning to be regarded as a father figure of the jazz trumpet, gradually assuming the role that Louis Armstrong had previously enjoyed. Gillespie's solo touring for Granz and his group's appearances on the burgeoning festival circuit ensured his worldwide popularity. This became the pattern of his life for the next two decades: consistent touring with his quintet, solo appearances on disc and in all-star bands, and extension of his ambassadorial activities. The latter included, on one hand, being among the first American jazz players to visit Castro's Cuba and, on the other, appearing on *The Muppet Show*.

In his final years Gillespie adopted the tenets of the Baha'i faith. His last major musical venture in 1988 was to found his United Nation Orchestra, a big band that brought together musicians from North and South America and the Caribbean. After final quintet appearances at the Blue Note in New York during the summer of 1992, he became unable to play following the onset of pancreatic cancer. He died in Englewood, New Jersey, where he had lived for many years. He was survived by Lorraine and by his daughter, Jeanie Bryson, born in March 1958 to the songwriter Connie Bryson.

Gillespie's role as one of the principal architects of modern jazz has tended to be overlooked in favor of the achievements of Parker, who died in 1955. Gillespie's technical innovations in the speed and range of the trumpet, his codification of the harmonic structures and repertoire of bebop, and his role as mentor to generations of younger players made him an equally significant figure. In particular, he encouraged the careers of the trumpeters Lee Morgan, Jon Faddis, Claudio Roditi, and Arturo Sandoval and brought jazz to a vast international audience.

FURTHER READING

An oral history interview with Gillespie is in the Institute for Jazz Studies at Rutgers University, Newark, New Jersey. Some of his earliest autograph arrangements survive in the Cab Calloway Collection at the Mugar Memorial Library, Boston University.

Gillespie, Dizzy, with Al Fraser. *To Be or Not to Bop* (1980).

Gentry, Tony. *Dizzy Gillespie* (1991).
McRae, Barry. *Dizzy Gillespie: His Life and Times* (1988).
Shipton, Alyn. *Groovin' High* (1999, Rev. ed. with recordings list 2001).

Obituary: *New York Times*, 7 Jan 1993.

Discography
The French company Média 7 is issuing a comprehensive edition of Gillespie's output, including private recordings and broadcasts. Volumes 1–5 are MJCD 31, 41, 45, 86, and 110.
Dizzy's Diamonds (Verve 513875).
Dizzy Gillespie: The Complete RCA Bluebird Recordings (Bluebird 66528-2).
—ALYN SHIPTON

 GIOVANNI, NIKKI
(7 June 1943–), poet, lecturer, and educator, was born Yolande Cornelia Giovanni Jr. in Knoxville, Tennessee, the second of two daughters of Jones "Gus" Giovanni, a teacher and probation officer born in a small town in Alabama, and Yolande Cornelia Watson, a teacher and social worker from Knoxville. Shortly after Giovanni's birth, her family moved to Cincinnati, Ohio, to seek employment better than that available in the segregated South.

Giovanni was a quiet and somewhat introverted child, though unafraid to fight anyone who tried to bully her or her older sister, Gary. While Giovanni was still a toddler, her sister began calling her "Nikki," a name she was known by from then on. Although they were poor, her parents instilled in their children pride in who they were and a belief in their ability to become whatever they wanted. As Giovanni later wrote in "Nikki Rosa," "black love is black wealth." From her mother she learned the importance of dreaming, from her father the necessity of taking action to fulfill dreams. A bright, obedient child, Giovanni would frequently forget what she had been sent to the store to buy because her mind was caught up in daydreams. She loved to read and, early on, to write.

Giovanni's early education was at Oak Avenue School, a public school, and St. Simon's, an Episcopal school, both in suburbs of Cincinnati. After completing her first year of high school at Lockland High School, she moved to Knoxville to live with her grandparents, John Brown Watson and Emma Louvenia Watson. Giovanni developed a close relationship with her grandmother, the most important influence on her life, who taught her to be generous and to fight against racial injustice and inequality. These values inform her poetry as well as her life.

In 1960, after two years at Austin High School in Knoxville, Giovanni enrolled as an early entrant to Fisk University, her grandfather's alma mater. However, instead of the intellectual excitement she had anticipated, Giovanni found a conservative environment governed by inflexible rules. She immediately clashed with the dean of students, and by the end of her first semester had been expelled. For the next few years, she lived with her parents in Cincinnati. Recognizing the importance of finishing her undergraduate degree, and determined to do so at Fisk, she sought and gained re-admittance. Both Giovanni and the college had changed by 1964, and her experience this time was fruitful. She majored in history, revived the campus chapter of SNCC (Student Nonviolent Coordinating Committee), edited the school's literary magazine, enrolled in the writing workshops offered by writer in residence John Oliver Killens, and immersed herself in the rhetoric and ideas of the Black Power movement and the emergent Black Arts Movement. When she graduated from Fisk in January 1967, she had already started to publish small pieces, both prose and verse, in *Negro Digest*.

The death of her grandmother in March 1967 was a tremendous blow, but Giovanni channeled her grief into her writing, producing a substantial body of poems. After a short and unsuccessful stint at the University of Pennsylvania's School of Social Work, she moved to New York City in the summer of 1968. She borrowed money to privately print her first volume of poems, *Black Feeling Black Talk*. By the end of 1968, with money generated by the book's sales, she was able to self-publish her second volume, *Black Judgement*, which was distributed by Broadside Press. When the Master of Fine Arts program at Columbia University, in which she had enrolled, refused to accept these volumes as fulfillment of its writing requirements, she abandoned the program.

Giovanni's overnight success resulted from many factors. Her poems touched responsive chords in the thousands of people she read them to, whether chords of anger from "The Great Pax Whitie," chords of joy from "Beautiful Black Men," or chords of pride from "Ego Tripping." The oral quality of Giovanni's poetry, one of its distinctive features, gave it an appeal to people who did not typically like poetry, and many rap artists recognize her as the mother of rap music. In addition to the quality of her poetry, Giovanni's charisma and charm, together with her quick wit and waiflike appearance, drew people to her. For the next several years she appeared regularly on the black entertainment and talk show *Soul!* on WNET television, giving her a national audience rarely available to poets. When she became a single mother with the birth of her son, Thomas, in 1969, she seemed to embody women's liberation. People were shocked but also enamored.

Giovanni published her third volume of poetry, *Re: Creation*, with Broadside Press in 1970. That same year, she signed a contract with William Morrow, which published *Black Feeling Black Talk/Black Judgement* as one volume. Recognizing the publishing obstacles women face, she edited an anthology of poems by black women, *Night Comes Softly*. The following year, Bobbs-Merrill published her autobiography, *Gemini: An Extended Autobiographical Statement on My First Twenty-Five Years of Being a Black Poet*, which was nominated for a National Book Award. She also published a volume of poems for children, *Spin a Soft Black Song* (1971).

In 1971 Giovanni extended her appeal by releasing a recording of her poetry read with gospel music performed by the New York Community Choir. *Truth Is on Its Way* was introduced at a concert she performed with the choir at Canaan Baptist Church in Harlem before a crowd of 1,500. Despite the audience's enthusiastic reception, no one could have predicted the success of this album; within six months, *Truth* sold more than one hundred thousand copies and was played by radio stations across the country. More than any other single factor, *Truth* made Giovanni's poems almost as familiar to people as the hit songs they heard on the radio. Decades after the album's release, many people know the words to her poems, even though they may never have seen them in print.

In December 1971 Giovanni traveled to London to videotape a conversation with the writer James Baldwin for *Soul!* The Baldwin sessions aired on the program in December 1971 and were subsequently transcribed and made into the book *A Dialogue: James Baldwin and Nikki Giovanni* (1973). She began accumulating awards and honors, including an honorary doctorate from Wilberforce University. Giovanni maintained a busy lecture schedule, both to promote her poetry and to support herself and her son. Despite the sometimes frantic pace of her life, she continued to write, and in 1972 published *My House*, named one of the best books of 1973 by the American Library Association. *My House* turns away from the militant rhetoric characteristic of some of her early poems and explores themes related to language and female identity.

During the period 1972 to 1978, Giovanni engaged in a variety of activities. She became a consultant and regular contributor to the black news magazine *Encore*, and she gave public readings to large audiences throughout the country, including a sold-out performance at New York City's Philharmonic Hall. In addition, she published three volumes of poetry and a dialogue with the poet Margaret Walker, and released several more spoken-word albums. She continued to travel extensively, taking on an African lecture tour for the U.S. Information Agency.

Her father's stroke and subsequent diagnosis of cancer in 1978 brought Giovanni and her son back to Cincinnati, where she became the financial and emotional mainstay of the family. Her family responsibilities essentially ended what can be regarded as the first stage of her writing career. She had little time to write, and between 1978 and 1988 she published only three books, although one them was the remarkable *Those Who Ride the Night Winds* (1983),

in which she began to develop the poetic form characteristic of her later volumes.

In 1987 Giovanni accepted a faculty position at Virginia Tech in Blacksburg. Although she had held brief teaching appointments earlier in her career, the tenured position at Virginia Tech, which eventually evolved into a University Distinguished Professorship, was her first experience of stable employment. Once she settled into the position, Giovanni came to enjoy teaching, especially the time it gave her to think and to write. She published several new books, including *Racism 101* (1994), a book popular with college students.

Just as she had started to establish new directions for her career, however, Giovanni was diagnosed with lung cancer, and in January 1995 doctors told her she had about six months to live. Always a fighter, she traveled to Cincinnati for a second opinion, and remained to have successful surgery. Miraculously, the cancer did not spread.

Giovanni's encounter with cancer re-energized and refocused her imagination, and she entered another period of high productivity, publishing seven books between 1996 and 2002. Of these, three—*Love Poems* (1997), *Blues: For All the Changes* (1999), and *Quilting the Black-Eyed Pea* (2002)—won NAACP Image Awards, the awards of which she is proudest. Today, as much as when she started her career, Giovanni is a "poet of the people," drawing record audiences to her lectures and readings. These are matched by dozens of honors and awards, including twenty-two honorary doctorates. She continues to speak the truth as she sees it and to celebrate black people and black culture.

FURTHER READING

Nikki Giovanni's papers are housed in the Special Collections division of the Mugar Memorial Library at Boston University.

Giovanni, Nikki. *Gemini: An Extended Autobiographical Statement on My First Twenty-Five Years of Being a Black Poet* (1971).
———. "In Sympathy with Another Motherless Child (One View of the Profession of Writing)," in *Sacred Cows . . . and Other Edibles* (1988).
Fowler, Virginia C. *Nikki Giovanni* (1992).
Giddings, Paula. "Taking a Chance on Feeling," in *Black Women Writers (1950–1980)*, edited by Mari Evans (1983).

—VIRGINIA C. FOWLER

GOLDBERG, WHOOPI

(13 Nov. 1955–), actress and comedian, was born Caryn Elaine Johnson in New York City, the second of two children of Emma Harris, a sometime teacher and nurse, and Robert Johnson, who left the family when Caryn was a toddler. Caryn attended St. Columbia School, a parochial school located several blocks from the family's working-class neighborhood. New York provided a stimulating, multicultural environment that encouraged Caryn to reject the strictures of her Catholic education. By age eight, with the support of her mother, she began acting at the Hudson Guild in the Helena Rubinstein Children's Theater, and she also showed a precocious interest in ballet and music.

Caryn appeared in as many Hudson Guild productions as possible, but was less focused on her schoolwork. Her academic difficulties were exacerbated by dyslexia, though this was not diagnosed until later, and she dropped out of Washington Irving High School at age fourteen. Although Caryn's teenage insecurities were hardly atypical, she was particularly discouraged by the racism endemic in the career path that she hoped to follow: the movie industry. In Hollywood, a white standard of beauty predominated, and glamorous roles for black actresses had traditionally been reserved for light-skinned and lithe performers like DOROTHY DANDRIDGE and LENA HORNE. Caryn Johnson, however, was a brown-skinned beauty with full features of a type not yet acceptable to the entertainment industry's limited and racially determined ideas of beauty. But such racism did not deter her thespian ambitions, and she appeared in the chorus of the Broadway musicals *Jesus Christ Superstar* and *Hair*.

After leaving school, Johnson had an unexpected pregnancy and abortion, and she became, as she later explained, "chemically dependent on many things for many years." Later, the escapades, pain, and difficulties of this period became fodder for her stand-up comedy routines, finding their way into her one-woman show. Eventually, she entered treatment for substance abuse, and in 1973 she married her drug counselor, Alvin Martin. Their daughter, Alexandra, was born a year later, but the

Whoopi Goldberg in a moment of whimsy, 1985. Corbis

couple separated in the mid-1970s and Johnson moved with her young daughter to San Diego, California. There she worked as a beautician, funeral home hairstylist, and bank teller while performing in local theater groups. She was also, for a few years, on welfare before finding success at the San Diego Repertory Company, appearing in Berthold Brecht's *Mother Courage*, and with Spontaneous Combustion, an improvisational comedy group. Making her professional aspirations a reality required one more thing: to change her name, which she found boring, to a memorable moniker. She first chose "Whoopi Cushion" and then dropped Cushion for Goldberg, after her Jewish relatives.

In the late 1970s Goldberg moved to Berkeley, California, where she lived with her daughter and the playwright-performer David Schein. Performing at the Blake Street Hawkeyes Theater in 1982, she developed a one-woman play, *The Spook Show*, which she based on characters derived from life. The show included monologues spoken by a thirteen-year-old Valley Girl–surfer chick who uses a hanger to give herself an abortion, a seven-year-old black girl who pines for blue eyes, and Fontaine, a junkie with a PhD in Literature. Her performance and some of her characters were controversial; but more importantly, they were fresh, anarchic, and hilarious. Goldberg toured the United States and Europe with *The Spook Show* and in 1983 performed at the Dance Theater Workshop in New York, where the director Mike Nichols approached her about bringing the production to Broadway. Instead, Goldberg returned to San Francisco and mounted *Moms*, a one-woman show that she cowrote as a tribute to the vaudevillian MOMS MABLEY. A year later Goldberg returned to New York and to Nichols. Her debut on Broadway, in the newly renamed show, *Whoopi Goldberg*, won her Theatre World and Drama Desk awards, and in 1985 she received a Grammy Award for Best Comedy Recording.

In 1985 Goldberg made her film debut in Steven Spielberg's adaptation of ALICE WALKER's *The Color Purple*. Grossing over $80 million at the box office and earning an additional $50 million in home video rentals, the film was an unexpected commercial success. Its reception among African Americans was more controversial, however, as some black viewers believed that an African American filmmaker should have directed the movie; others took issue with what they deemed to be the material's unsympathetic depiction of black men. There was no such disagreement about Goldberg's strong, subtle performance, for which she received an Oscar nomination and a Golden Globe Award.

In addition to performing stand-up and touring with her one-woman show *Living on the Edge of Chaos*, Goldberg worked steadily in film and on television during the last half of the 1980s, although, with the exception of *Jumpin' Jack Flash* (1986), her films—*Burglar* (1987), *Fatal Beauty* (1987), *Clara's Heart* (1988), and *The Telephone* (1988)—were only marginal hits. Goldberg became a household name with *Ghost* (1990). The film grossed over $517 million worldwide and earned Goldberg an Academy Award for Best Supporting Actress, the second Oscar awarded to a black woman. (HATTIE MCDANIEL had won in 1939.) In 1992's *Sister Act*, Goldberg again struck box-office gold and won a second Golden Globe, although this time, Hollywood acknowledged, she carried the film.

Having proved her financial value, Goldberg began balancing her Hollywood film appearances in comedies such as *Made in America* (1993), *Eddie* (1996), and *The Associate* (1996) with roles in smaller, independent films, including *The Long Walk Home* (1990), a film about the 1955 Montgomery bus boycott; a hilarious role as a cop in Robert Altman's Hollywood satire *The Player* (1992); *Sarafina* (1992), a musical drama set in apartheid South Africa; *Corrina, Corrina* (1994), a 1950s period film in which she unexpectedly ends up as the romantic interest opposite the white actor Ray Liotta. She also appeared in *Boys on the Side* (1995), *How Stella Got Her Groove Back* (1998), and *Girl, Interrupted* (1999). In 1996 Goldberg portrayed MYRLIE EVERS-WILLIAMS, the wife of the slain civil rights leader MEDGAR EVERS, in the film *Ghosts of Mississippi*.

Goldberg's television career has been even more prodigious. In 1986, along with comedians Billy Crystal and Robin Williams, she began hosting the semi-annual live broadcast *Comic Relief*, a comedy showcase fund-raiser for the homeless, and in 1992 she launched a short-lived, self-titled, late-night talk show. As she became one of America's most recognizable cultural figures, Goldberg was increasingly tapped to host television tributes and to appear in cameos as "herself." She also appeared in her own HBO stand-up specials and had a recurring role (1988–1993) as Guinan on *Star Trek: The Next Generation*. Her pivotal role in the 1994 and 2002 *Star Trek* films further proved her popularity and crossover appeal. In 1994 Goldberg hosted the sixty-sixth annual Academy Awards, becoming the first black woman to preside over the Oscars since DIANA ROSS had cohosted in 1974. She returned to emcee the awards in 1996, 1999, and 2002. From 1998 until 2002, she was also executive producer and appeared as the center square of the Emmy Award–winning television game show *Hollywood Squares*.

Following her successful return to Broadway in 1997 as the lead in *A Funny Thing Happened on the Way to the Forum*, Goldberg expanded her theatrical activities, coproducing the Broadway revival of *Thoroughly Modern Millie* (2002) and *Harlem Song* (2002), a new musical by George C. Wolfe, and starring in and producing the Broadway revival of AUGUST WILSON's *Ma Rainey's Black Bottom* (2002), though the reviews for her performance were mixed.

Offscreen, Goldberg married David Claessen, a Dutch-born director of photography, in 1986, after her relationship with Schein ended in 1985. Goldberg's subsequent private relationship with the actor Ted Danson sparked public controversy after Danson performed in blackface at the Friar's Club roast of the actress in 1993. The following year she entered into a one-year marriage with the union organizer Lyle Trachtenberg, whom she met when he was unionizing the crew of *Corrina, Corrina*. From 1995 through 2000, she was involved with the actor Frank Langella.

The author of the best-selling *Book* (1997), Goldberg is the recipient of over forty awards, including six People's Choice awards, five Kid's Choice awards, and nine NAACP Image awards; she has garnered fourteen Emmy nominations and the 2001 Kennedy Center's Mark Twain Prize for American humor. Goldberg has been recognized as well for her humanitarian efforts on behalf of children, the homeless, human rights, substance abuse, and the battle against AIDS. (Her father died in 1993 from stomach cancer and complications from HIV infection.) In 1995 her hands, feet, and signature braids were pressed in cement outside Mann's Chinese Theater in Los Angeles, and in 2001, on her forty-sixth birthday, she received a star on Hollywood's Walk of Fame.

Despite being an African American woman in a white dominated industry, Goldberg has become a mainstay in American entertainment. An iconoclastic comedian and commentator, she uses humor both to critique and to amuse her audiences. Over the years, there has been a mixed response to her celebrity. Some film critics and historians argue that her asexual characters perpetuate the iconic stereotype of the black mammy in the white household, while others interpret her screen persona differently, viewing Goldberg as an iconoclastic figure and countercultural force. However, even Whoopi—whose name signifies both flatulence and love-making—has expressed frustration with the selective editing of sex scenes that have landed on the cutting room floor. Goldberg returned to television in 2003 with the sitcom *Whoopi*, in which she plays Mavis Rae, a one-hit wonder who now runs a small New York hotel. "Why not be active doing stuff that's still interesting to me? This was handed to me on a silver platter with no restrictions and no hassles. I have the ability to do the show I wanted to do" (*Jet*, 104, No. 18 [2003]). Critics have generally praised the show and have compared the prickly, politically incorrect Mavis Rae to the Archie Bunker character in the seventies sitcom *All in the Family*.

Often described as too fat, too funny, too noisy, and too rebellious, Whoopi Goldberg, who is willing to offend and to be offensive, has become what the critic Kathleen Rowe has termed an "unruly woman." In Broadway performances, movies, and television appearances, she has played defiant characters who overturn social hierarchies, cross racial boundaries, and subvert conventional authority.

FURTHER READING

Adams, Mary. *Whoopi Goldberg: From Street to Stardom* (1993).

Parish, James Robert. *Whoopi Goldberg: Her Journey from Poverty to Megastardom* (1997).

—MIA L. MASK

GORDY, BERRY, JR.
(28 Nov. 1929–), songwriter, entrepreneur, and filmmaker, was born in Detroit, Michigan, the seventh of the eight children of Berry Gordy Sr. and Bertha Fuller. After Reconstruction, Gordy's paternal grandfather, who was born a slave, managed to acquire 168 acres of land where he and his wife, Lucy Hellum, raised nine children, one of them being Gordy's father. Gordy's mother was of direct African descent on her father's side and of African and American Indian heritage on her mother's side. She was a schoolteacher in Sandersville, Georgia, and married Berry Gordy Sr. in 1918, when he returned from service in World War I.

In 1922 Gordy's parents left Milledgeville, Georgia, and settled in Detroit with their three oldest children. Unlike the majority of black migrants to the North, the Gordy's owned their own home. Seven years and five children later, Berry Jr. was born on Thanksgiving Day. The Gordys were a large, close-knit family, proud and middle class by the prevailing standards of the day. Until the Depression struck, Gordy's father and older siblings were industrious enough to supply the family with its material needs, working as laborers and selling ice and produce. By 1931, however, their financial situation was so desperate that the Gordy family had lost its home and, for a brief time, was forced onto the welfare rolls.

Gordy's Uncle B. A., Bertha's brother, gave him the only formal music lessons of his life. After only a year, Gordy tired of the monotony of learning scales when he discovered that he could play boogie-woogie and other popular styles by ear. By taking him to church three evenings a week and all day on Sunday, his parents exposed the young Gordy to soulful Negro spirituals and the stirring rhythms of black gospel, distinct influences on what would become the "Motown Sound."

The business work ethic was deeply ingrained in the Gordy children throughout their upbringing by both by their mother, who managed an insurance and real estate business, and by their father, who worked his way up from being an apprentice plasterer to running his own plastering business. Gordy's father purchased a commercial building on the corner of St. Antoine and Farnsworth, from which at various times the family operated businesses such as Gordy Contractors, Gordy Print Shop, Friendship Mutual Life Insurance Company, and a grocery store that bore the name of BOOKER T. WASHINGTON, the Negro leader who most emphasized economic development.

Young Gordy was a bright charmer who loved to be the center of attention. He was ambitious but impetuous and dropped out of Northeastern High School in his junior year to become a boxer. He had decent skills in the ring, but it was his fighting spirit and persistence that led to his appearance on the same card with JOE LOUIS in 1948, when the champ returned to Detroit to defend his title. Through sheer determination, Gordy eked out an unimpressive victory over his opponent in the featherweight division. By the time Gordy was drafted during the Korean War in 1951, he was already looking for some other occupation at which he might gain fortune and fame. When he returned from Korea in 1953, he had a GED and a new idea for a business.

Gordy's first foray into the music industry was as part owner of the "3-D Record Mart: House of Jazz." Gordy's father put up some of the money and Gordy's brother, George, invested on the condition that he be a partner. At this time Gordy was a jazz enthusiast; when patrons requested music by blues artists such as JOHN LEE HOOKER and B. B. KING, Gordy would try to persuade them to purchase music by bebop jazz artists like CHARLIE PARKER and MILES DAVIS. The record shop soon went out of business. However, Gordy learned two valuable lessons that guided him in the future: he did not like partners, and smart business decisions are as important as the music itself.

Over the next few years Gordy tried a number of jobs, from selling cookware to assembling cars at the Lincoln-Mercury plant. As he worked, he composed songs that he sent to magazines, entered in contests, and attempted to sell to performers appearing at local venues. Four of Gordy's enterprising siblings had established a photo concession at the Flame Show Bar and helped get a song written by Gordy and Tyran Carlo to Jackie Wilson, who recorded it as "Reet Petite" in 1957. With this triumph Gordy's confidence and determination grew.

Gordy and Carlo wrote four more hits for Wilson, including "To Be Loved," which later became the title of Gordy's 1994 autobiography. Gordy, however, was not content merely to hear his songs on the radio. By now a shrewd businessman, he realized that he could be much more successful if he owned the copyright for his songs and had his own record label to market them. In 1958 he took the first step toward realizing this goal by establishing a music publishing company, Jobete, named from the first two letters of Joy, Berry, and Terry, Gordy's children with his first wife, Thelma Coleman Berry. He married and divorced once more; ultimately, he fathered eight children with several women.

In order to finance his company, Gordy once again had to approach his family. Despite the fact that Berry Jr. had failed in his first venture, his family believed in him, and in January 1959 they lent him eight hundred dollars. With this money he rented an eight-room house at 2648 West Grand Boulevard, where he lived with his second wife, Raynoma Liles Gordy. Family, friends, and performers helped him to transform that house into "Hitsville USA," the first headquarters of Motown, the recording company he named after Detroit, the "Motor City." Motown would grow into a conglomerate that owned several record labels, a talent management agency, and a recording studio, with subsidiaries in the television and film industries.

Gordy's ability to identify, nurture, and retain talent for as long as he did was a major factor in Motown's success. He spotted Smokey Robinson when the latter was only seventeen. The two became lifelong friends and collaborators. Gordy signed "Little STEVIE WONDER" at the age of eleven, and he hired talented writers such as Brian Holland, Eddie Holland, and Lamont Dozier. He brought in Maxine Powell, who ran a finishing school, to give his young performers a clean-cut, professional, telegenic look. This allowed his artists to cross over onto the pop charts with unprecedented frequency. He hired Cholly Atkins, the famed dancer of the Cotton Club and Savoy Ballroom, to choreograph the signature steps of the Temptations, the Four Tops, and the Supremes. With these professionals added to a smart and loyal business staff, Gordy created a company that worked like a team and felt like a family.

In 1961 Gordy's young company had its first number-one hit when "Please Mr. Postman," by the Marvelettes, went to the top of the charts. At times as many as five of the Top-Ten songs on the *Billboard* charts were Motown productions. By the late 1960s Motown had become a virtual hit factory, producing top songs like cars rolling off an assembly line. This music was not merely commercially successful; it also won critical acclaim as Motown artists garnered Grammy Awards and other accolades while they dominated the charts. By 1972 Motown had become a powerful force in the record industry, with over one hundred Top-Ten songs, including thirty-one number-one hits.

In the early 1970s Gordy's interests began to move in other directions. In 1972 he moved the Motown headquarters to Los Angeles. He had experimented with a few television productions such as *Diana!* and a cartoon about the Jackson Five, but he wanted to take DIANA ROSS, his biggest star and love interest, to the big screen. *Lady Sings the Blues* (1973) was his first and biggest box-office smash. He had to put up the money himself before Paramount would agree to produce this film about the life of BILLIE HOLIDAY, which ultimately received five Academy Award nominations, including a Best Actress nomination for Diana Ross. This was followed by *Mahogany* (1975), which Gordy directed himself, *The Bingo Long Traveling All-Stars and Motor Kings* (1976), *Scott Joplin* (1977), *The Wiz* (1978), and *The Last Dragon* (1985).

While Motown's record sales from the 1970s and 1980s surpassed even

the remarkable figures of the 1960s, as new acts such as the Jackson Five and the Commodores reached ever-expanding audiences, the accomplishments of the 1960s remain unparalleled in terms of their cultural impact. Motown helped to define a generation through its music. By integrating American popular music to an unprecedented degree, Gordy helped to facilitate the social and political integration of the period. He also marketed some of the early recordings of speeches by MARTIN LUTHER KING JR. and readings by black poets, and he gave MARVIN GAYE and Stevie Wonder the creative freedom to produce such politically conscious albums as *What's Going On* (1971) and *Songs in the Key of Life* (1976), respectively, as well as the controversial anti-Vietnam War single by Edwin Star, "War" (1970).

In 1988 Gordy sold Motown Records to MCA and Boston Ventures for $61.9 million dollars. In 1997 he sold 50 percent of his Jobete Publishing Company, with its extensive music catalog, to EMI for $135 million dollars. In 2001 he endowed the Gwendolyn B. Gordy Fund to assist less-fortunate Motown artists, writers, and musicians. Gordy turned his eight-hundred-dollar investment into hundreds of millions of dollars; in the process, he created one of the largest and most influential black companies in history.

FURTHER READING

Gordy, Berry. *To Be Loved: The Music, the Magic, the Memories of Motown* (1994).

Abbott, Kingsley. *Callin' Out around the World: A Motown Reader* (2001).
Benjaminson, Peter. *The Story of Motown* (1979).
Early, Gerald Lyn. *One Nation under a Groove: Motown and American Culture* (1995).
Smith, Suzanne. *Dancing in the Street: Motown and the Cultural Politics of Detroit* (1999).
—SHOLOMO B. LEVY

GRACE, CHARLES EMMANUEL (25 Jan. 1881–12 Jan. 1960), better known as Daddy Grace or Sweet Daddy Grace or by his self-proclaimed title, Boyfriend of the

World, was one of the more flamboyant religious leaders of the twentieth century. He was born, probably as Marceline Manoel da Graca, in Brava, Cape Verde Islands, of mixed Portuguese and African ancestry, the son of Manuel de Graca and Gertrude Lomba. In the charismatic church that he founded and headed, however, he managed to transcend race by declaring, "I am a colorless man. I am a colorless bishop. Sometimes I am black, sometimes white. I preach to all races." Like many other Cape Verdeans, Grace immigrated to New Bedford, Massachusetts, around the turn of the century and worked there and on Cape Cod as a short-order cook, a salesman of sewing machines and patent medicines, and a cranberry picker.

Also known as Bishop Grace, he may have established his first church in West Wareham, Massachusetts, around 1919, but he achieved his early success in Charlotte, North Carolina, where he held evangelical tent meetings and attracted more than ten thousand followers in the 1920s. In 1927 in Washington, D.C., he incorporated the United House of Prayer for All People on the Rock of the Apostolic Faith. The phrase "All People" was said to indicate Grace's acceptance of the poor and disinherited who were unwelcome in more conventional churches. Grace established churches up and down the eastern seaboard, eventually numbering at least 500,000 people in some one hundred congregations in nearly seventy cities. Most, but not all, members were African American.

In person, Daddy Grace presented a dramatic figure with his shoulder-length hair; six-inch-long fingernails painted red, white, and blue; and gold and purple cutaway coats and chartreuse vests. A master of public pageantry and showmanship, he sponsored bands and parades, outfitted his followers in uniforms, and staged colorful outdoor mass baptisms in swimming pools or with fire hoses. He promoted band music and once asked, "Why should the devil have all the good times?" He was generally surrounded by adoring followers who pinned dollar bills to his robe as he walked slowly down the aisle of one of his churches.

Daddy Grace, charismatic founder of the United House of Prayer for All People.
Courtesy of Donna VanDerZee

Many nonfollowers thought Daddy Grace an exploitative religious fraud and confidence man. The alleged escapism of his church was widely criticized, and E. FRANKLIN FRAZIER, the Howard University sociologist, condemned the church for what he called its erotic dancing while disciples, mainly female, sang, "Daddy, you feel so good." Whatever spiritual or emotional satisfactions Daddy Grace provided his people, he also supplied apartment buildings, pension funds, retirement homes, burial plans, and church cafeterias that dispensed free food. He received a considerable income, invested heavily in real estate, and personally owned some forty residences. He bought the El Dorado on Central Park West in New York City, then the world's tallest apartment building. He purchased Prophet Jones's fifty-four-room mansion in Detroit, which he had repainted red, white, and blue to the consternation of the neighborhood. In 1938 he acquired the kingdom of heaven property in Harlem of another charismatic leader, FATHER DIVINE.

The money came not only from the offerings of the faithful members of the United House of Prayer for All People but also from the numerous Grace-sponsored moneymaking enterprises that manufactured and sold such products as soap, hair pomade, vitamins, and ice cream. Followers reportedly believed these products had special powers bestowed by Daddy Grace. Healing was an important element in the movement, and Grace was widely believed by the faithful to have curative powers, particularly via buttered toast from which he had taken a bite. His *Grace Magazine*, which sold for ten cents, was also thought to be restorative when touched to the body.

Daddy Grace fused elements from the holiness and Pentecostal religious traditions, but his church (often referred to as a sect) depended largely on his charisma. He did not himself actually assert the divinity his followers attributed to him. "I never said I was God," he once stated, "but you cannot prove to me I'm not." He did say, however, "If you sin against God, Grace can save you, but if you sin against Grace, God cannot save you," as well as "Grace has given God a vacation, and since God is on His vacation, don't worry Him." He delighted in pointing out how many times the word *grace* appears in the Bible and was fond of repeating the classic Protestant formula that salvation is by grace alone.

Grace's considerable wealth attracted several lawsuits. In 1957 Louvenia Royster, a retired Georgia schoolteacher, claimed that Daddy Grace had married her in New York in 1923 under the name of John H. Royster but had deserted her in 1928, leaving her with a daughter, now an adult. Grace responded that he was in the Holy Land at the time of the alleged marriage and had spent the night in question in the manger in which Jesus was born. The court dismissed her claim. Jennie Grace of New Bedford claimed that Daddy Grace had married her in 1909. She also was the mother of a grown daughter, whom she also said he had fathered. Whatever his relationships with these women, Daddy Grace apparently was the father of at least one child, a son, Marcellino V. Grace of Brentwood, Maryland.

The greatest legal difficulties came, however, after Grace's death, which occurred while he was visiting in Los Angeles. His finances were chaotic, and it was unclear what monies and property belonged to the church and what constituted his personal estate. There was some $25 million at issue, much of it in real estate but also including

$3 million in cash in seventy-five banks in fifty cities and diamond-studded keys to numerous safe deposit boxes. Thirty-six lawyers became involved in the litigation. The Internal Revenue Service put a lien of $5.9 million against the estate at his death, claiming he owed that amount in back taxes, but settled in 1961 for $1.9 million. Grace was buried in New Bedford.

A fierce internal struggle for succession ensued. Bishop Walter McCollough took over the United House of Prayer after winning a lawsuit against rival contender James Walton. Much less flamboyant than Grace, McCollough concentrated on consolidating the denomination, making it more traditionally Pentecostal, and building a substantial low-income housing project. He moved the church, he said, "from the storefront to the forefront."

FURTHER READING

Davis, Lenwood G. *Daddy Grace: An Annotated Bibliography* (1992).

Halter, Marilyn. *Between Race and Ethnicity: Cape Verdean American Immigrants, 1860–1965* (1993).

Manuel, Charles. "'Sweet Daddy' Grace?" in *Twentieth-century Shapers of American Popular Religion*, ed. Charles H. Lippy (1989).

Sevitch, Benjamin. "When Black Gods Preached on Earth: The Heavenly Appeals of Prophet Cherry, Daddy Grace, and Father Divine" in *Black Religious Leadership from the Slave Community to the Million Man March: Flames of Fire*, ed. Felton O. Best (1998).

Obituary: *New York Times*, 13 Jan. 1960.

—RICHARD NEWMAN

GRAVES, EARL (9 Jan. 1935–), entrepreneur and publisher, was born Earl Gilbert Graves in Brooklyn, New York, the oldest of the four children of Earl Godwyn Graves and Winifred Sealy, both the children of immigrants from Barbados. Earl's parents were very different people, yet both had characteristics that would influence his career. His father, an assistant manager at the Overland Garment Company, an apparel firm in New York City, was very serious and demanding, while his mother was outgoing and involved in a host of community activities. Earl has credited his work ethic, salesmanship,

and drive to his father and his involvement in various causes and organizations to the example of his mother.

Growing up, Earl always looked for opportunities to make money. At age six he sold Christmas cards to neighbors. Later, while attending Morgan State University in the early 1950s, Graves worked two jobs at once. Seeing the reluctance of local white florists to make deliveries on the predominantly black campus, he started a small business selling flowers. When Graves decided to major in economics at Morgan State, his decision was ridiculed; the corporate world was not considered a viable career option for African Americans. Undeterred, Graves continued in his course of study.

After graduating from Morgan State in 1957, Graves entered the army, became a paratrooper, and eventually rose to the rank of captain in the Nineteenth Special Forces Group, the Green Berets. In 1960, while in the service, he married Barbara Eliza Kydd. With children on the way, Graves left the army and the couple returned to Brooklyn, where he worked as a real estate agent. Graves, who had taken a real estate course in college, sold nine houses in his first three months.

Feeling the need to become more involved in politics, Graves wrote a letter to the Democratic National Committee (DNC) and was soon volunteering for the 1964 presidential campaign. His work with the DNC led to a job as an administrative assistant to the newly elected senator Robert F. Kennedy, a position he held for the next three years.

For the first time, Graves was exposed to extraordinary wealth and the power of money. If Kennedy wanted something, he was able to get it. Graves often recalled Kennedy's response when Graves informed him that former astronaut John Glenn, with whom the senator wished to speak, was on a rafting trip in Colorado. "Well, Graves," Kennedy exclaimed, "he won't be on the raft all day and when he gets off, I want to talk to him" (Graves, 119). Those in power, Graves learned, get things done. The larger lesson, a realization that drove the rest of Graves's professional life, was that money, above all other resources, can acquire the power to influence social and political causes.

After Robert Kennedy's assassination in 1968 many of his staffers were offered jobs or work-study grants, and Graves landed a seat on the advisory board of the Small Business Administration (SBA). The same year, he established the consulting firm Earl G. Graves Associates (later Earl G. Graves Limited), to advise corporations about economic development and urban affairs. Around this time Graves conceived the idea to create a newsletter that would chronicle the successes of, and issues relevant to, black businesspeople and also raise awareness of the importance of black consumer power. At the suggestion of the SBA's director, Howard Samuels, Graves decided to publish a full-fledged monthly magazine, and in August 1970 *Black Enterprise* was born.

In its early days *Black Enterprise* had trouble convincing much of corporate America that African Americans were interested in business. After all, out of three thousand senior-level executives at major corporations, only three were black. Potential advertisers questioned whether there were enough stories for *Black Enterprise* to tell, and they doubted the power of the African American market to buy the pricey items the big corporations produced. As a result, the magazine initially depended on the advertising of tobacco, liquor, and low-priced automobile companies. Financial support from other sectors, such as technology and securities industries and luxury car makers, took years of effort, with Graves leading the way, before big companies came to respect African American consumers. Despite these challenges, *Black Enterprise* was profitable by its tenth issue. By bringing stories and information to the marketplace that many mainstream media outlets had been ignoring, the magazine soon established itself as a premier magazine for African Americans. In 1973 the magazine introduced one of its most popular creations, the BE 100s, an annual list of the nation's largest black-owned businesses. By 2002 *Black Enterprise* had a circulation of 475,000 and annual revenues of over fifty-three million dollars.

In addition to *Black Enterprise* and *Black Enterprise's Teenpreneur*, launched in 2002, Earl G. Graves Limited publishes a host of print and electronic material, arranges high-profile conferences for black businesspeople, and sponsors the Greenwich Street Corporate Growth Fund, a venture capital fund that supports mid-sized black-owned businesses. While he has remained dedicated to the magazine, Graves's entrepreneurial spirit has not been limited to publishing endeavors. In 1990 he bought the bottling franchise Pepsi Cola of Washington, D.C. Graves sold the franchise back to the parent company in 1998 and remains active at Pepsi as the chairman of the company's Advisory and Ethnic Marketing Committee.

Because of his wide array of activities, Graves has become one of the most important champions of black capitalism. His book, *How to Succeed in Business without Being White* (1997), part autobiography and part career guide, made the *New York Times* and *Wall Street Journal* best-seller lists. Graves serves as a trustee or on the board of directors of many companies and organizations, including Aetna Foundation, Inc., AMR Corporation (American Airlines), Federated Department Stores, Inc., Rohm and Haas Company, Daimlerchrysler AG, the Steadman-Hawkins Sports Medicine Foundation, the Schomburg Center for Research in Black Culture, the Boy Scouts of America, Howard University, and the Committee for Economic Development. He has supported numerous causes, including his alma mater, Morgan State University, to which he donated one million dollars in 1995. Graves served as a civilian aide to the secretary of the U.S. Army from 1978 to 1980.

In addition to more than four dozen honorary degrees, Graves has received numerous awards and honors, including the Ronald H. Brown Leadership Award from the U.S. Department of Commerce, the NAACP Springarn Medal, induction into the Black College Hall of Fame, and election into the American Academy of Arts and Sciences. In 2002 he was appointed to the Presidential Commission charged with developing a plan for the establishment of a National Museum of African American History and Culture. Named one of the fifty most powerful and influential African Americans in corporate America by *Fortune Magazine* in

2002, Graves is widely sought after as a speaker.

Graves has taken steps to make sure that Earl G. Graves Limited lives long into the future. Each of his three sons has taken an active role in the company, though Graves remains chairman of the magazine he started decades ago. In August 2000, on its thirtieth anniversary, Graves quoted FREDERICK DOUGLASS in illuminating *Black Enterprise*'s efforts: "If there is no struggle, there is no progress.... This struggle may be a moral one or a physical one but it must be a struggle. Power concedes nothing without demand."

FURTHER READING

Graves, Earl G. *How to Succeed in Business without Being White* (1997).

Bell, Gregory S. *In the Black: A History of African Americans on Wall Street* (2001).
Edmond, Alfred, Jr. "Earl G. Graves: On the Record," *Black Enterprise* (Aug. 1995).
Weeks, Linton. "The Sweet Smell of Success," *Washington Post*, 17 June 1997.
—GREGORY S. BELL

GREENER, RICHARD THEODORE (30 Jan. 1844– 2 May 1922), educator, lawyer, and diplomat, was born in Philadelphia, Pennsylvania, the son of Richard Wesley Greener, a seaman who was wounded during the Mexican War while serving aboard the USS *Princeton*, and Mary Ann Le Brune. When he was nine, Richard and his parents moved to Boston but soon left for Cambridge, where he could attend "an unproscriptive school." Richard's father, as chief steward of the *George Raynes*, had taken his son on a voyage to Liverpool but then abandoned the sea in 1853 for the California gold fields. He "was taken sick, met with losses," and was never heard from again. When Richard was twelve years old, he left school to help support his mother. Although he quit one of his positions after an employer "struck" him, those whom he met while "knocking around in...different occupations" often helped educate him, sharing their libraries and tutoring him in French and Latin.

Greener's employer, Augustus E. Bachelder, helped finance Greener's

education. Following Bachelder's suggestion, Greener enrolled in the two-year college preparatory program at Oberlin College in Ohio (1862–1864), where he received "considerable practice in speaking and debating," but because of "some colorphobia, shown by...classmates" he returned to New England. In 1865 he graduated from Phillips Academy in Andover, Massachusetts, and then attended Harvard, whose president, Thomas Hill, was eager to experiment in educating an African American. Although Greener received the second prize for reading aloud that year, he had been conditionally admitted to college, because his background was uneven, and he especially lacked mathematical training. Because Hill wanted the experiment "fairly tried," Greener repeated his first year. At the end of his sophomore year he took the Boylston Prize for Oratory, and his senior dissertation, which defended the land rights of Irish peasants, won the first Bowdoin Prize for research and writing.

After becoming the first black person to graduate from Harvard College (1870), Greener later could not recall "many pleasant incidents" there, but he had done well scholastically and made friends with whom he felt at ease. Hailed as a member of the Negro intelligentsia, he began the decade as principal of the male department of the Institute for Colored Youth in Philadelphia (1870–1872) and ended it in the law department of Howard University, where he began teaching in 1877 and was dean from 1879 to 1880. In the interim he was principal of the Sumner High School in Washington, D.C. (1872–1873); associate editor of *New National Era and Citizen*, a publication for blacks; and a law clerk in the office of the attorney for the District of Columbia. He also taught Latin, Greek, international law, and U.S. constitutional history at the University of South Carolina (1873–1877). As acting librarian he rearranged and cataloged the university's books, completed a law degree there, and served on a commission to revise the state school system. In 1874 Greener married Genevieve Ida Fleet; five of their seven children reached adulthood. In 1876 Greener was admitted to the South Carolina bar and the next year to the bar of the District of Columbia, where he moved at the end of Reconstruction, when doors in South Carolina were suddenly closed to blacks.

Having left the South rather than surrender to white supremacists, Greener heartily endorsed the Windom Resolution (introduced in the U.S. Senate on 16 Jan. 1879 by William Windom of Minnesota) encouraging black migration out of the South (primarily to Kansas). Fearing that the federal government would not give southern blacks the protection they needed, Greener was the spokesman for a delegation of "representative colored men" who saw Windom and called for a special, but not legally exclusive black territory. Greener, who became secretary of the Exodus Committee, met in February with a group in Cincinnati and, along with Windom, took a central role in mid-April in organizing an Emigrant Aid Association in Washington. In December he went to Kansas to see firsthand the condition of new black settlers, who were called Exodusters. Disagreeing with FREDERICK DOUGLASS, the distinguished black abolitionist, who urged blacks to stay in the South, where their freedom would depend on "right" rather than "flight," Greener brilliantly answered Douglass's objections, taking them up one by one at a congress of the American Social Science Association held in September 1877 at Saratoga Springs, New York.

Greener had been a law professor at Howard University from 1877 to 1880 when the Board of Trustees temporarily disbanded its law department for lack of students. Having held two government clerkships before teaching at Howard and having in 1878 started a law firm, Cook & Greener, he continued his law practice, became a clerk in the office of the U.S. Treasury Department's first comptroller, and remained in demand as a speaker and writer.

In 1880 Greener became involved in the case of Johnson C. Whittaker, which divided the nation and led to the dismissal of the commandant of the U.S. Military Academy at West Point. While teaching at the University of South Carolina, Greener had helped secure Whittaker's appointment to West Point, after choosing him from among two hundred possibilities as the student most likely to succeed at the academy. Whittaker entered West Point in 1876 and was the roommate of HENRY O. FLIPPER,

who, in the following June, became the first black cadet to graduate from the academy. Helping Whittaker secure an education, just as his own benefactors had aided him, Greener kept in touch with his former student, who, on the morning of 6 April 1880, was found tied to his bed, bleeding and unconscious. Writing to Greener after he was accused of staging the attack and mutilating himself, Whittaker called it a "heinous plot engaged in by . . . cadets" and "sanctioned by the authorities."

Greener remained by Whittaker's side for most of the early inquiry and became a leading witness and assistant counsel in the court-martial that Whittaker demanded to clear his name (establishing the precedent that a West Point cadet is an officer of the U.S. Army). Because Greener had campaigned in six states for the Republican Party and was one of the thirty members of President James A. Garfield's Inaugural Executive Committee, he had access to important officials in both the departing Rutherford B. Hayes administration and the entering Garfield one. After army officers sitting on the court-martial found Whittaker guilty as charged, their decision was reviewed and overturned in March 1882 by Judge Advocate General David G. Swaim. Although, thanks to Greener, Whittaker was reinstated at West Point, Secretary of War Robert Todd Lincoln ordered him discharged for failing an examination he had taken immediately after his attack.

In 1884 Greener campaigned vigorously in eight states for the Republican Party and in 1885 was made chief examiner of the New York City Civil Service Board, a position he held until 1889. Also in 1885 he became a trustee of the Grant Monument Association and was elected its secretary (1885–1892). A personal friend of Ulysses S. Grant, whom he had met in 1868 at Harvard and to whom, during the Grant Administration, Greener had led four delegations of black and white supporters, Greener was proud to be the chief administrative official of Grant's monument association and remained a trustee for the rest of his life. A lover of art who had enjoyed browsing through books on monumental art in the libraries at Harvard, Greener considered himself "better posted [on the subject] than

any member of [the Grant Monument Association], and did not hesitate to attack . . . unworthy designs . . . foisted on the committee." After rejecting all proposals in the first competition, the association selected a design by John Hemenway Duncan from the second competition. "I was one of the first to point out the simplicity, dignity, and fitness of [Duncan's design]," Greener later noted, "as presenting the characteristics of the Conqueror of the Rebellion."

Greener was rewarded for campaigning for the Republican Party with a political appointment abroad. In January 1898 he turned down an appointment as consul to Bombay because of a bubonic plague epidemic there, and in July he became the first U.S. consul to Vladivostok, Russia, where he served until 1905. His tour of duty began as his country emerged as a world power from the Spanish-American War, and he witnessed both the completion of the Trans-Siberian railroad and the Russo-Japanese War. American newspapers often complimented Greener on the excellent performance of his duties and his help to American businessmen. Few people objected to his Japanese mistress (his marriage having been dissolved years earlier, after which his mixed-race wife and their children had passed as white). The Russians liked working with him, as did the British, who had him carry on their business when they were expelled from Vladivostok because of their pact with Japan. The Chinese decorated him with the Order of the Double Dragon for aiding war victims during the Boxer Rebellion in 1900.

But Greener's decoration for services to Japan during the Russo-Japanese War went to his successor, Roger Greene, whose name the Japanese confused with his. The U.S. State Department, where blacks were sometimes referred to as "coons," refused to rectify the situation. Dismissed from the post in 1905 on charges of bad habits and dereliction of duty, Greener requested a special investigation, which was carried out by his successor. The charges were not confirmed; apparently he had been confused with another Greener living in Vladivostok. Nevertheless, back in the United States, he was denied a personal hearing over his dismissal.

In 1906 Greener moved to Chicago, where he worked as a special agent for an insurance company and championed black rights in numerous letters to newspapers and in lectures. In July of that year he joined with W. E. B. Du Bois and others in the second convention of the Niagara Movement at Harpers Ferry, West Virginia. Although Du Bois and his backers, who later founded the NAACP, had formed the Niagara Movement to oppose the accommodationist philosophy of Booker T. Washington, Greener had hoped to make peace between the two black leaders. When his efforts failed, he backed Du Bois, ending a twenty-three-year friendship with Washington, and worked diligently for the NAACP.

Still brooding in 1912 over the Republican Party's treatment of him and other African Americans, Greener backed Woodrow Wilson for president and lived to see him reintroduce segregation into the federal bureaucracy. Greener, who died in Chicago, was perhaps the most gifted of those whom Du Bois called the "talented tenth" of African Americans. But the end of Reconstruction cut short his promising career as an educator in the South, and the seven years he was away in Russia lessened his impact on race relations in the United States during a crucial period.

Greener's second daughter, Belle, after concealing her identity, had a career equal to her talents, a privilege denied to her father. Claiming she was part Portuguese, she took "da Costa" as her middle name and removed the final "r" from her last name. Enjoying books and art, as her father did, Belle da Costa Greene steeped herself in the knowledge of rare books at Princeton University Library and in 1905, at the age of twenty-six, began working for the elder J. P. Morgan. With his backing and her own expertise, she became prominent in the world of rare books and manuscripts and was responsible for acquiring much of his collection. Long called "the soul of the Morgan Library," she was its director from 1924 to 1948.

FURTHER READING

Greener's papers, photographs (accompanied by a biographical leaflet), correspondence,

and writings are at the Schomburg Center for Research in Black Culture of the New York Public Library. His letters are also in the archives of Howard and Harvard universities.

Blakely, Allison. "Richard T. Greener and the 'Talented Tenth's' Dilemma," *Journal of Negro History* (Oct. 1974).

Stewart, Ruth Ann, and David M. Kahn. *Richard T. Greener: His Life and Work* (1980).

West, Emory J. "Harvard's First Black Graduates: 1865–1890," *Harvard Bulletin* (May 1972).

Obituary: *Chicago Daily Tribune*, 4 May 1922.

—OLIVE HOOGENBOOM

 GREENFIELD, ELIZABETH TAYLOR

(c. 1817–31 Mar. 1876), singer and teacher, known as the "Black Swan," was born a slave in or near Natchez, Mississippi. Her father may have been born in Africa, and her mother, Anna, was of mixed ancestry. Various sources offer no less than seven different birthdates between 1807 and 1824. Greenfield's use of "Taylor" rather than "Greenfield" in certain documents suggests that her parents used this surname, but little record of them survives.

When their owner, wealthy widow Elizabeth Holliday Greenfield, joined the Society of Friends and moved to Philadelphia in the 1820s, Elizabeth's parents were manumitted and emigrated to Liberia. Though records suggest her mother planned to return, Elizabeth never saw her parents again. She lived with her mistress until she was about eight years old and then rejoined her as a nurse/companion in about 1836; she seems to have lived with relatives in the interim. Several sources assert that Greenfield's mistress cared for her, and probate records show that her will called for an annuity to be paid to Greenfield. When her mistress died in 1845, though, her will was fiercely contested, and Greenfield received only a token sum.

Biographer Arthur LaBrew speculates that Greenfield began singing in church in the early 1830s. Though Quaker, her mistress seems to have approved of

Greenfield's musical aspirations, and a family friend (probably one of physician Philip Price's daughters) gave her some rudimentary instruction. Greenfield was singing at private parties by at least the mid-1840s, and LaBrew notes a performance in Baltimore around 1849 with black musician William Appo. By 1850 one Philadelphia directory listed her as a "music teacher."

In October 1851, Greenfield traveled to Buffalo, New York, supposedly to hear the "Swedish Nightingale" Jenny Lind. She impressed Electa Potter, wife of prominent Buffalo attorney Heman B. Potter, with both her voice and her carriage, and the Potters became her patrons. Their support and introductions to Buffalo's leading citizens led to a public performance on 22 October. Greenfield's "debut," which featured works by Bellini and Donizetti, was praised by Buffalo newspapers, and Greenfield, whom several reviewers compared favorably with Lind, was quickly dubbed the "African Nightingale." A comparison with another singer, "Irish Swan" Catherine Hayes, won out, though, and Greenfield became forever known as the "Black Swan."

The favorable press and promotion by Buffalo merchant Hiram Howard led to additional performances in Rochester and Lockport and an agreement with Colonel J. H. Wood, a promoter of mixed repute and sometime-associate of P. T. Barnum. Wood set up a tour in 1852 that took Greenfield across the North; she performed in over thirty cities, ranging from Boston and Providence to Chicago and Milwaukee. She also traveled to Ontario and to smaller abolitionist strongholds like Niles, Michigan. Her repertoire was similar to Lind's, and the press regularly compared the two. She also began to include popular American works like Stephen Foster's "Old Folks at Home." Praise for—and even amazement at—her vocal range, which reputedly encompassed over three octaves, was consistently tempered with comments emphasizing her lack of formal training; racist newspapers referred to her as the "African crow." Nonetheless, Greenfield filled theaters, and the tour was quite successful. After a brief rest, Greenfield made arrangements for

Elizabeth Taylor Greenfield, "The Black Swan," sang to packed audiences in both the United States and England before the Civil War. Schomburg Center

a performance in New York City and a tour of Great Britain, during which she would further her training. Buffalo citizens held a benefit concert on 7 March 1853 to help support her travel to Britain.

After the outpouring of support from both blacks and whites in Buffalo, Greenfield's time in New York City was both frightening and frustrating. The theater, Metropolitan Hall, was threatened with arson for featuring a black performer, its management barred blacks from attending, and Greenfield herself was refused entry to another theater to see Italian contralto Marietta Alboni. Still, her performance on 31 March attracted over two thousand people and cemented her celebrity. Soon after, Greenfield gave a second concert before an integrated audience specifically to benefit black charities.

Trouble followed Greenfield to Britain. Her British manager refused to advance her funds against future performances, and Greenfield struggled to meet basic expenses before finally withdrawing from her contract. She contacted the abolitionists Lord Shaftesbury and Harriet Beecher Stowe for aid, and they introduced her to Britain's abolitionist elite. The Duchess of Sutherland became Greenfield's patron, and Sir George Smart, composer to the Chapel Royal, began tutoring her. Greenfield's May 1853 performance at Stafford House, Sutherland's London home, led to several other performances. Sutherland and Smart eventually engineered a command performance for Queen Victoria on 10 May 1854. Victoria's praise—and her twenty-pound gift—did much to help Greenfield's spirits; however, she returned to the United States in July 1854.

Greenfield began touring the North soon after her return; in this second U.S. tour, and in her third in 1856, Greenfield returned to several of the cities from her first tour but also sought new venues—traveling as far south as Baltimore and performing more widely in Canada. Her 1854 tour included performances by Philadelphia tenor Thomas J. Bowers, known as the "colored Mario." Greenfield's 1856 tour was complemented by the 1855 publication of *The Black Swan at Home and Abroad*, a sixty-four-page promotional biography that heavily emphasized her early successes and her British tour. Greenfield's final extended tour in 1863 included mainly cities in the upper North.

After 1863, Greenfield gave occasional concerts, often to benefit African American causes. She regularly sang at events sponsored by the Civil and Statistical Association of the Colored People of Pennsylvania, including lectures by FRANCES ELLEN WATKINS HARPER and General O. O. Howard. LaBrew has also found evidence that she founded a "Black Swan Opera Troupe," which gave performances in Washington in 1862 and Philadelphia in 1866.

Between tours and after 1863, Greenfield lived in Philadelphia near her extended family. She achieved local note as a music teacher and is intermittently listed in city directories as a musician and a teacher (though one directory simply lists her occupation as "black swan"). Among her students, she counted Carrie Thomas, the leading soprano of the original Hampton Institute Singers, and Lucy Adger, whose family achieved local prominence for their talents. A devout Baptist, Greenfield also directed the choir and sang at Shiloh Baptist Church. Upon her death in 1876, Greenfield was eulogized in newspapers across the country.

Harriet Beecher Stowe said that had Greenfield received the education given her white peers "*no* singer of any country could have surpassed her" (*Sunny Memories of Foreign Lands*, vol. 2, 139). Given such talent, as well as her unprecedented international fame, her successes as a teacher, and her pioneering efforts to promote other black musicians, Greenfield was undoubtedly, as the author and activist MARTIN R. DELANY noted, among the most extraordinary persons" of the nineteenth century (*The Condition, Elevation, Emigration, and Destiny of the Colored People of the U.S.*, 102). In the early 1920s, several generations after Greenfield's death, Harry Herbert Pace established Black Swan Records, the first black-owned record label in the United States. Named in honor of the original Black Swan, the company issued the music of ETHEL WATERS and Fletcher Henderson.

FURTHER READING

Contemporary newspapers' coverage of Greenfield can be found in the microfilm collection *The Black Abolitionist Papers*, ed. C. Peter Ripley (1981).

Anonymous. *The Black Swan at Home and Abroad* (1855).

LaBrew, Arthur. *The Black Swan: Elizabeth T. Greenfield, Songstress: Biographical Study* (1969).

Riis, Thomas L. "Concert Singers, Prima Donnas, and Entertainers: The Changing Status of Black Women Vocalists in Nineteenth Century America" in *Music and Culture in America, 1861–1918*, eds. Michael Saffle and James R. Heintze (1998).

Story, Rosalyn. *And So I Sing: African American Divas of Concert and Opera* (1990).

Trotter, James Monro. *Music and Some Highly Musical People* (1878).

Obituary: *New York Times*, 2 Apr. 1876.

—ERIC GARDNER

GREGORY, WILTON

(7 Dec. 1947–), Roman Catholic priest, liturgical scholar, and bishop, was born Wilton Daniel Gregory, in Chicago, Illinois, the son of Ethel Duncan and Wilton Gregory Sr. The maternal side of Gregory's family was part of the Great Migration of African Americans after World War I, arriving in Chicago from Oxford, Mississippi. Soon after their arrival in the North, Gregory's maternal grandmother and her sister were enrolled at St. Benedict the Moor Boarding School in Milwaukee, Wisconsin, because their mother could not care for them and find work at the same time. While at St. Benedict the Moor,

Gregory's grandmother, Etta Mae Duncan, was baptized and received into the Roman Catholic Church. Even though she was not a practicing Catholic in her later life, she never lost her profound admiration and respect for the Catholic priests and nuns who provided her with a home and an education during those several years of her childhood.

Along with his two younger sisters, Gregory was raised in a single-parent home by his mother and grandmother after his parents divorced. In 1958, when the religious women who staffed St. Carthage Grammar School in Chicago made an aggressive effort to enroll neighborhood black children in the school, Etta Mae Duncan and Ethel Duncan Gregory placed all three children there. Wilton Gregory remembered his grandmother often exhorting her grandchildren to "get an education. They can't take that away from you" (private interview, 16 June 2003). Gregory began the sixth grade at St. Carthage Grammar School, and by the end of that academic year he was formally baptized and received into the Roman Catholic Church. Gregory attributes his attraction to the Catholic Church to the teachers and priests who staffed St. Carthage parish. After graduating from the eighth grade, he enrolled at Quigley Preparatory Seminary South, in the Archdiocese of Chicago, afterwards attending Niles College (now St. Joseph's College Seminary) of Loyola University in Chicago. He completed his theological studies for the priesthood at St. Mary of the Lake Seminary and was ordained a Roman Catholic priest for the Archdiocese of Chicago on 9 May 1973.

Gregory began an active priestly ministry after his ordination, serving as an associate pastor at Our Lady of Perpetual Help parish in Glenview, Illinois, teaching at Saint Mary of the Lake Seminary and assisting Cardinal John Cody in liturgical functions throughout the archdiocese. After three years of such service, Cardinal Cody released Gregory from his pastoral duties and sent him to begin graduate studies at the Pontifical Liturgical Institute ("Sant' Anselmo") in Rome, Italy. He earned his doctorate there in 1980 with a dissertation on "The Lector: Minister of the Word: An Historical and Liturgical

Bishop Wilton Gregory in 2001. Corbis

Study of the Office of the Lector in the Western Church."

Upon completion of his degree, Gregory returned to Chicago and to his position as a professor at the seminary. By this time Cardinal Joseph L. Bernadin had replaced Cardinal Cody as archbishop of Chicago. Gregory was ordained an auxiliary bishop for the Archdiocese of Chicago in December 1983, making him, at the age of thirty-six, the youngest bishop in the United States at that time. He has described his years as a bishop in Chicago as one of the great periods of his life and singled out Bernadin as "an extraordinary mentor, a beloved brother in Christ, and a devoted friend." Within a year of his ordination as bishop, Gregory became involved in the preparation of a document that would help define black Catholicism in the latter part of the twentieth century. Along with nine other black Catholic bishops, he published "What We Have Seen and Heard: A Pastoral Letter on Evangelization," in September 1984. This pastoral letter asserted that the black Catholic Church community—at that time, numbering over one-and-a-half million participants—had "come of age" and must be responsible for its own development and growth. The letter echoed the sentiments of Pope Paul VI in claiming that the black church had much to offer to the universal Catholic community and should no longer depend on missionary activity from other cultures for the spread and sustenance of faith.

In 1987 Gregory was chair of the Bishops' Subcommittee on Black Liturgy, which supervised the publication of another substantive contribution to black Catholic concerns. "In Spirit and Truth: Black Catholic Reflections on the Order of the Mass" carried liturgical reform into new areas of research and reflection. When the bishops' pastoral letter called for black Catholic initiatives in all aspects of religious life, the liturgy was central to their message. Gregory has stated that "as Catholics, our sacramental, ritual, life is our most precious heritage" (private interview). Once his administrative duties as bishop took up more and more of his focus and energy, Gregory devoted much of his love and care for liturgy in his preaching and presiding at rituals within his home dioceses and throughout the country, especially at regional and national gatherings of black Catholics.

In December 1993 Wilton Gregory made another sort of history within the Roman Catholic Church when he was appointed the seventh bishop of the diocese of Belleville, Illinois. The diocese of Belleville covers twelve thousand square miles in southern Illinois, from East St. Louis, Illinois, to Cairo, at the southernmost tip of the state, where the Ohio and Mississippi rivers meet. Gregory was the first African American cleric to be assigned to this 106-year-old diocese, with its even longer history of riots, lynchings, and systematic oppression of African Americans. In addition, upon his arrival Bishop Gregory had to confront a local crisis dealing with charges of sexual abuse among the clergy.

Restoring faith in the church, confronting racial abuses, and providing leadership for a demoralized clergy were priorities for Gregory during his early years as bishop in Belleville. He wrote a regular column, "What I Have Seen and Heard," for the diocesan newspaper, *The Messenger*, in which he addressed topics such as the death penalty, prison reform, euthanasia, and physician-assisted suicide. In 2000 Gregory funded and served as principal resource for a three-part video series on racism in the Catholic Church, *Enduring Faith: A Story of African American Catholics in America*.

In 1998 Gregory was elected vice-president of the United States Council of Catholic Bishops (USCCB), serving a three-year term, and was elected president in November 2001. He was the first African American bishop to serve as the coordinating administrator for the Catholic Bishops of the United States. In January of the following year, the *Boston Globe* began to publish a series of articles on sexual abuse among Catholic priests, and Gregory's tenure as president of the USCCB became almost entirely focused on that issue and its ramifications for the American Catholic Church.

In reflecting on his goals as president of the USCCB, Gregory once stated, "As bishop, as president of the conference, I hope I can get us to a point where we have a clear focus as to what must be done [about this scandal], and a means to accomplish it" (private interview), but he noted that it will take several generations for reconciliation to occur. "The reconciliation the church needs is not merely a reconciliation that is facile and quick, that is easy and too swiftly spoken . . . it involves the challenge of forgiving. Admission of guilt is only salvific when the response is 'you are forgiven'" (*Enduring Faith*). His personal anguish was summed up in his understanding, developed as a child in Chicago, that the Catholic Church should be at its best in caring for children. As he said, "If you love people's children, they will love you—that's what made this particular scandalous moment so devastating—because it was a violation of the children" (private interview).

Gregory has held on to a belief that in every crisis there is an opportunity for growth, and he maintains that the scandal that emerged during his time as bishop, both in Chicago and in Belleville, and that eventually erupted during his presidency presented just such an opportunity within the Roman Catholic Church. He summed up his optimism by saying, "I think that there is a new and healthy dialogue and relationship being established between clergy and laity. Something new is being born . . . what is being born is a new relationship with our laity who are educated, who are knowledgeable, whose love for the church is deep" (*Enduring Faith*).

FURTHER READING

Davis, Cyprian. *The History of Black Catholics in the United States* (1990).

———, and Diana L. Hayes, eds. *Taking Down Our Harps: Black Catholics in the United States* (1998).

—JOSEPH A. BROWN, S.J.

GRIFFITH-JOYNER, FLORENCE (21 Dec. 1959–21 Sept. 1998), track star, was born Delorez Florence Griffith in Los Angeles, California, the daughter of Robert Griffith, an electronics technician, and Florence Griffith, a seamstress. The seventh of eleven children, her parents divorced when she was four. Dee-Dee, as she was then known, grew up in a housing project in Watts, the site of race riots in the late 1960s. She described her family life as inwardly rich, though money was so tight she sometimes ate oatmeal for breakfast, lunch, and dinner. She developed her fashion sense from her mother, who taught her knitting and crocheting, and her grandmother, a beautician, who provided instruction on hair and nails. Though she was a quiet child, her fashion tastes betrayed a nonconformist streak: a gravity-defying braid thrust to the heavens in kindergarten, a pet boa constrictor wrapped around her neck as a teen.

Her speed was apparent at a young age. Nicknamed "Lightning" by one of her sisters, Florence was known to chase jackrabbits on visits to her father in the Mojave Desert. She began competing in meets with the SUGAR RAY ROBINSON Youth Foundation at age seven. In her early teens she twice proved a champion at the JESSE OWENS National Youth Games. After one such victory she earned congratulations from Owens himself.

The meeting did not seem to portend Olympic glory for Griffith, who spent most of her career in the shadow of others. Though she set records at David Starr Jordan High School, she couldn't beat fellow Los Angeles runner Valerie Brisco in championship meets. In college, first at California State University, Northridge, and then at UCLA, she worked with sprint coach Bob Kersee. In 1980 she just missed making the U.S. Olympic Team. Though she did manage an NCAA title in the

Florence Griffith-Joyner running with strength, grace, and confidence to win the 100-meter dash at the Olympics in Seoul, South Korea, 1988. © Duomo/CORBIS

Al's sister, Jackie Joyner-Kersee, was the world record holder in the heptathlon, and the wife of sprint coach Bob Kersee. This formidable foursome set its sights on the Seoul Olympics in 1988.

Competing in a white hooded bodysuit that seemed more Star Trek than track star, Griffith-Joyner took her familiar second place in the 200 meters in the World Championships in Rome in 1987. In the ensuing months, she intensified her training, sometimes pushing her workouts past midnight. She worked her hamstring and gluteal muscles for greater explosion out of the blocks. She adopted weightlifting advice from the new world record holder in the men's 100 meters, Ben Johnson of Canada. She claimed to have found a new ability to relax in competition, making her stride more efficient. Stronger and more focused than ever, she began to train in the sport's marquee race, the 100-meter dash, an event where she had almost no international experience.

Toting fourteen self-designed racing suits, she arrived in Indianapolis in mid-July for the U.S. Olympic Trials. Amid a midwestern heat wave that had track temperatures soaring well over one hundred degrees, she transformed into "Flo-Jo," a blazing beauty who put together some of the most breathtaking performances in the history of the sport. In one forty-eight-hour stretch she carved an indelible image: black mane flowing freely, neon nails clawing the humid air, perfectly made-up face locked in concentration, veins bulging to the surface, sculpted muscles surging relentlessly to the tape. Her outfits were "one-leggers"—dazzlingly hued spandex from shoulder to ankle with one beautifully defined leg laid bare, and brightly colored bikini briefs hugging her hips. Her speed was otherworldly. Four times she toed the line in the 100; four times she shattered Evelyn Ashford's four-year-old world record of 10.76. Though her initial heat of 10.60 was discounted because of excessive wind, the second heat of 10.49 set the standard far beyond her own lifetime. In shaving an almost incomprehensible .27 off the record (since the advent of electronic timing twenty years before, the mark had never been bested by even half that much), she provided one of track

200 meters in 1982 with a time of 22.39, her hopes for Olympic gold were dashed two years later in the Los Angeles Games when her 22.04 was only good enough for a close second, yet again, to Valerie Brisco-Hooks. That silver medal seemed to cement her status as a just-less-than-great performer, especially considering the boycott by Eastern European countries, which significantly diluted the field. Even her fashion statements didn't earn universal acclaim: her self-styled glistening bodysuits did result in a new nickname—"Fluorescent Flo"—but her

elaborately painted six-inch nails were cited as a reason for keeping her off the 400-meter relay, for fear that the baton pass could prove treacherous. For a while it looked like her running career might be over. She competed only sporadically, gained weight, and focused largely on her career—working in a bank by day and as a beautician at night. In time, though, she was lured back to the track, drawn by both an unquenched inner fire and an emerging family of track luminaries. In 1987 she married Al Joyner, the reigning gold medalist in the triple jump.

and field's most stunning moments—a time when perceived human limitations are torn asunder. It was commensurate with Roger Bannister's breaking the 4-minute mile in 1954, and Bob Beamon's awe-inspiring long jump of 29 feet, 2.5 inches in the Mexico City Games in 1968.

The record was hard to believe. Some doubted the accuracy of the wind gauge that registered 0.0, while a nearby gauge at the triple jump exceeded the legally allowed 4.47 miles per hour. Still, the stellar run was not completely out of context for the comet that had become Florence Griffith-Joyner. The next day she roared to victory in the semifinals and the finals in times of 10.71 and 10.61, both well within legal wind limits. In the 200 meters she won again, setting an American record of 21.77. That time had track enthusiasts salivating—as did her white lace bodysuit that she termed "athletic negligee."

In Seoul, the first Olympics in twelve years not to be softened by political boycott, Flo-Jo became a phenomenon the likes of which women's track had never known. Though she was required to wear the comparatively modest team uniforms, her speed was not compromised. She became the first U.S. woman ever to win four medals in the Olympics, garnering gold in the 100 (a wind-aided 10.54), the 200 (obliterating a nine-year-old world record in 21.34), and the 400 relay, and taking silver in the 1600 relay.

In a mere ten weeks, she had put a defining stamp on her sport and become, for a moment, the most widely recognized athlete in the world. She earned recognition from all corners: the Sullivan Award as the U.S. top amateur athlete, the Associated Press Female Athlete of the Year, even the top sports personality of the year from Tass, the Soviet News Service. She was deluged with endorsements, earning her yet another nickname—"Cash Flo." She graced covers of a wide variety of sports and fashion publications. Even *Ms.* magazine weighed in with a lengthy piece, referring to her as the "Siren of Speed."

It was not, however, a complete love-fest. Pointing to her huge improvement at twenty-eight, a relatively old age for a sprinter, and to her newly chiseled physique, some in the track community

accused her of using banned substances to supercharge her speed. The speculation was compounded by the fact that Ben Johnson, competing in the men's 100, had his gold medal and world record time of 9.79 stripped after testing positive for steroid use at Seoul. The fact that Flo-Jo passed every drug test she ever took, even submitting to especially rigorous testing in Seoul, did little to silence the critics. When she retired in February 1989 to concentrate on business interests, some felt she was merely ducking the random, out-of-meet testing that was being instituted in the sport. Always, she vehemently denied the allegations.

In the decade after her glittering performances, Flo-Jo poured herself into a variety of pursuits. She gave birth to a daughter, Mary Ruth, in 1990. She set up a foundation for underprivileged children and frequently returned to Watts to talk to kids. Designing new uniforms for the Indiana Pacers fueled her passion for fashion. She cochaired the President's Council on Physical Fitness. Occasionally she entertained comeback plans, targeting the 400 in the 1992 Olympics, and, rather quixotically, the marathon in 1996. She never ran an important race, though, after her blaze to glory in Seoul.

In 1996 she was hospitalized briefly after suffering a seizure on an airplane. Given a clean bill of health, she resumed her active schedule, which included writing the book *Running for Dummies.* She never lived to see its publication, however. At the age of thirty-eight she died in her sleep in the family's Mission Viejo home. The sudden death of an apparently healthy athlete revived allegations of steroid use. Autopsy results on Griffith-Joyner, however, revealed no evidence of banned substances. She died because of a vascular problem in her brain known as a "cavernous angioma," which apparently led to a seizure, causing her to asphyxiate in bed.

Griffith-Joyner took the world records in the 100 and 200 meters with her to the grave. She was not merely the fastest woman in the world or its most glamorous athlete. She provided a new definition of the possible for the American woman, a vision where speed and strength were compatible with sexiness, where being a fast female was nothing but a compliment.

FURTHER READING

Aaseng, Nathan. *Florence Griffith-Joyner: Dazzling Olympian* (1989).
Koral, April. *Florence Griffith-Joyner: Track and Field Star* (1992).
Stewart, Mark. *Florence Griffith-Joyner* (1996).

Obituary: *New York Times*, 22 Sept. 1998.
—MARTY DOBROW

GRIMES, WILLIAM

(1784?–1865?), slave and writer, was born in King George County, Virginia. His father was Benjamin Grymes, a wealthy Virginia planter; his mother was a slave of a neighbor, Dr. Steward, who was therefore William Grimes's first owner. Grimes (under three different names) served ten masters as a house servant, plantation worker, stable boy, and coachman in Virginia, Maryland, and Georgia. He was severely mistreated, more than once coming close to death from too much whipping. Grimes made a number of unsuccessful escape attempts: on one occasion he tried to break his own leg and on another pretended to starve himself. Cunning and combative, he several times induced his masters to sell him in order to improve his situation, with mixed results; he also entered into several bloody fights with other slaves. A superstitious man, he was frequently haunted by ghosts and was troubled by a woman he believed was a witch. But he also fervently embraced Christianity, from which he derived some solace.

Being light-skinned (he was at least three-quarters white), Grimes often passed as white at nighttime during his long residence in Savannah; this proved helpful to him in obtaining provisions for his final escape from slavery in about 1814. This he effected by hiding in a cotton bale onboard a ship bound for New York, after befriending some of the sailors. He then made his way to New Haven, Connecticut, having heard good things about the place from one of his former masters.

At first Grimes found it harder to be a freeman in Connecticut than to be a slave in Georgia. The employment he was able to procure demanded hard labor for little recompense. After saving about twenty dollars, he opened barber-shops in Providence, Rhode Island, and then New Bedford, Massachusetts, both of which closed within a few months. He had better luck in Litchfield, Connecticut, where he also let and traded horses and gigs. He nonetheless was involved in a number of court cases, including several in which he claimed to have been falsely accused of crimes, and his reputation suffered thereby. As he would later write in his autobiography, "It has been my fortune most always to be suspected by the good, and to be cheated and abused by the vicious" (60).

Grimes soon moved back to New Haven, where he waited on students, sold them groceries, and lent them money. By then, however, his last master knew where he was and sent a man to threaten to send him back to slavery if he did not buy his freedom. Grimes, at this point living in Litchfield, gave up everything he owned, including his house and land, for his freedom. He was, of course, happy to be free but also bitter about freedom's cost. "I would advise no slave to leave his master," he wrote. "If he runs away, he is most sure to be taken: if he is not, he will ever be in the apprehension of it" (67).

Now entirely destitute, with a wife, Clarissa Caesar, and children to support, he wrote his autobiography in 1824 and published and sold it the following year in the hope that the proceeds would ameliorate his condition. *Life of William Grimes, the Runaway Slave* was the first book-length autobiography of a fugitive American slave and thus inadvertently helped inaugurate a genre; it was also the longest autobiography of an African American yet written. While later slave writers almost invariably depicted a heroic triumph over adversity, Grimes remained unredeemed, fearful, bitter, and disconsolate. His book concludes with one of the most profound, chilling, and complex comments on American slavery to be found in any slave narrative: "If it were not for the stripes on my back which were made while I was a slave, I would in my will, leave my skin a legacy to the government, desiring that it might be taken off and made into parchment, and then bind the constitution of glorious happy *and free* America. Let the skin of an American slave, bind the charter of American Liberty" (68).

Grimes seems to have had no exposure to antislavery thought; yet his was the first black autobiography to refer to its author as a slave in its title, and it stands as a powerful indictment not only of southern slavery but also of northern anti-Negro discrimination. So, while Grimes pined for and praised freedom, he also stated, "I do think there is no inducement for a slave to leave his master and be set free in the Northern States" (67).

This is but one example of the apparent contradictions of Grimes's book. He professes the most profound religious faith, yet continually shows himself willing and ready to sin, and the virtue of forgiveness is noticeably absent in his narrative. He identifies as a black former slave, but he insistently repeats that he is three-quarters white. In the first sentence of his book he gives his year of birth and, still, at the end states, "I think I must be forty years of age, but don't know; I could not tell my wife my age" (68).

These contradictions probably arose from the difficulties Grimes had in defining himself, since that self had been heretofore defined by ten different owners. Throughout his book Grimes seems confused about how to present himself, for he was confronting a conundrum that every slave author faced: the necessity of asserting (or creating) an identity after having been robbed of one for most of one's life. Nowhere in the slave narrative tradition is this conundrum more evident than in Grimes's book, for no other slave autobiographer faced more difficulties in, and received less help in dealing with, his or her newfound freedom. As the slave narrative scholar William Andrews has noted, "Grimes's text signifies the possibility that the black self—as a unitive, knowable essence, as the locus of a usable past for its creators and sponsors—could not be recovered at all in the slave narrative.... The *Life* has stood as a loaded gun,... as much a threat to the literary system of autobiography as to the social system of slavery" (80–81).

After publishing his narrative, Grimes continued his peripatetic ways, making his home in Bridgeport, Norwalk, Fairfield, Stratford Point, and finally New Haven once more, where he remained for the rest of his life, "shaving heads,"

cleaning clothes, working at the colleges, and selling lottery tickets. In 1855, "being more than seventy years of age," he published a second edition of his autobiography, bringing it up to date with some humorous anecdotes and doggerel. No longer bitter or reproachful, he poked fun at himself, remarking that he had "often been called one of the most remarkable personages of modern times" (84). He had eighteen children, twelve of whom survived.

Grimes's pioneering book stands today as the most complex and disconsolate of all slave narratives, but it was little read until recently and had no discernible impact on the genre. Because it is untouched by abolitionist rhetoric, it is invaluable for fully understanding the psychological effects of slavery.

FURTHER READING

Grimes, William. *Life of William Grimes, the Runaway Slave* (1825, updated 1855).

Andrews, William. *To Tell a Free Story: The First Century of Afro-American Autobiography, 1760–1865* (1986).
Taylor, Yuval, ed. *I Was Born a Slave: An Anthology of Classic Slave Narratives* (1999).
—YUVAL TAYLOR

 GRIMKÉ, ANGELINA WELD (27 Feb. 1880– 10 June 1958), poet and teacher, was born in Boston, Massachusetts, the daughter of ARCHIBALD H. GRIMKÉ, an attorney and diplomat, and Sarah E. Stanley. Angelina's parents separated when she was very young, and she, an only child, was raised by her father. Her mother's absence undoubtedly contributed to Grimké's reverential treatment of maternal themes in her poetry, short stories, and especially her only published play, *Rachel* (1920). Her father dominated Angelina's life until his death in 1930. His continual insistence on her personal propriety and academic achievement seemed to inhibit his daughter's self-determination as much as it inspired her to make him proud of her.

Growing up in Boston, Angelina enjoyed a comfortable, middle-class life. Her distinguished family name gave her certain advantages, such as an education

Angelina Weld Grimké, whose Rachel: A Play of Protest *was the first play by an African American woman to be publicly staged.* Moorland-Spingarn Center

at better schools and frequent exposure to prominent liberal activists. But as the daughter of a white woman and a man of mixed ancestry, she was no stranger to racial tension. Her sensitivity to racism was further enhanced by her family's history. Angelina was named for her father's aunt, the social reformer Angelina Emily Grimké, who had campaigned for women's suffrage and for the abolition of slavery. Her father, the son of a slave, had dedicated his life to fighting prejudice. This heritage put enormous pressure on Angelina to carry on her family's tradition of embracing social causes. Timid and obedient as a child, she turned to writing as a release for her preoccupations: her need for a mother's attention, her diligence in living up to her father's expectations, and her inability to establish a lasting romantic partnership. Upon reaching adulthood, she remained introverted but began to use her writing as a public platform for denouncing racism.

In 1898 Angelina enrolled in the Boston Normal School of Gymnastics (which eventually became the Department of Hygiene at Wellesley College), graduating in 1902 with a degree in physical education. She then moved to Washington, D.C., where she taught physical education at the Armstrong Manual Training School, a vocational institution, until 1907. Apparently unhappy with both her duties and

her work environment, Grimké left Armstrong in order to teach English at the M Street High School, having prepared herself by taking summer courses in English at Harvard University from 1904 to 1910. Grimké remained at M Street until she retired from teaching in 1926.

Although Grimké wrote most prolifically between 1900 and 1920, her first published piece, a poem titled "The Grave in the Corner," appeared in the *Norfolk (Mass.) County Gazette* when she was only thirteen (27 May 1893). During her postsecondary studies, Grimké published more of her verse in the *Boston Transcript.* However, not all of her work was well received. The editor of the *Transcript*, Charles S. Hunt, rejected Grimké's poem titled "Beware Lest He Awakes" on the grounds that its "implied threat of a bloody rising on the part of the negro" was anachronistic. The poem, eventually published in *The Pilot* (10 May 1902), reflects the battle against racism that more typically characterizes Grimké's short fiction and her play *Rachel.* Another early poem, "El Beso," was published in the *Transcript* (27 Oct. 1909), accompanied by praise for Grimké's poetic talent.

Grimké's best-known poems include "To Keep the Memory of Charlotte Forten Grimké" (1915), about CHARLOTTE L. FORTEN GRIMKÉ, her aunt by marriage, "The Black Finger" (1923), "A Winter Twilight" (1923), "Tenebris" (1924), "For the Candlelight" (1925), "When the Green Lies over the Earth" (1927), and "Your Hands" (1927). These poems express her recurring themes of unfulfilled love and racial injustice or pay tribute to famous people. Other works feature tender depictions of children and mothers. A sense of despair pervades much of Grimké's verse, but only occasionally does her tone become strident or even moderately antagonistic. Her surviving manuscripts suggest that Grimké had, at one time, considered collecting her poetry into a volume tentatively titled *Dusk Dreams.* The project never materialized and the majority of Grimké's verse remains in holograph form among her personal papers. Much of this unpublished work consists of highly sentimental love poetry addressed to women by obviously female speakers. Some scholars have suggested that

these lesbian overtones kept Grimké from publishing verse that might have brought scandal to her family name.

Less varied in theme than her poetry, Grimké's prose and drama focus almost exclusively on lynching and the chagrin of African American motherhood. Her short stories "The Closing Door" (1919) and "Goldie" (1920) combine these two topics in an effort to shock white readers into realizing how prejudice and racially motivated violence contribute to the disintegration of the black family. Both stories appeared in the *Birth Control Review* and were widely perceived as advocating childlessness among African Americans. The heroines of these stories fervently desire to bear children, but they sacrifice their maternal longings in order to avenge and prevent persecution of blacks by whites. The young women make this decision after they lose friends and family members to lynch mobs. Likewise, the title character in Grimké's play *Rachel* breaks off her engagement and forswears motherhood when her "adopted" children come home in tears after having racist taunts hurled at them by white children.

Grimké is primarily regarded as a poet, yet her most celebrated work is her play *Rachel.* Written in three acts, the play depicts the struggle of a young black woman and her family in dealing with the racial prejudice that constricts their lives. Grimké unabashedly uses the story as a vehicle for antiracist propaganda, subtitling it "A Play of Protest." Even critics who have faulted Grimké's dramatic technique have been unable to deny the impact of her message. When the Drama Committee of the NAACP supported the original production of *Rachel* on 3 March 1916, Grimké became the first African American woman to have written a publicly staged drama. The play underwent at least two other stagings before its publication in 1920. It was not performed again for nearly seventy-five years, until its revival by the Spelman (College) Players in 1991.

Critics suggest that parts of *Rachel* are autobiographical. The title character's physical description matches that of Grimké. More significantly, Rachel's decision to forgo marriage and motherhood parallels a conscious choice made by Grimké. However, these similarities are largely superficial. Rachel abandons her dreams because of her heartbreak and anger over the racial injustice she sees affecting her loved ones. In contrast, Grimké's journals and poetry indicate that her homosexuality relegated her to a lonely and celibate life.

A second play, *Mara*, was discovered among Grimké's personal papers. It was apparently written in the wake of *Rachel*'s popularity, but no record exists of any performances or of Grimké's attempts to have it published.

Throughout her life, Grimké never enjoyed good health, which may explain in part why she eventually stopped teaching physical education in favor of English. A train accident led to a serious back injury in July 1911, and her retirement from teaching may have stemmed from physical incapacity. She nursed her father, who had retired to Washington, D.C., as he declined into death (1928 to 1930). She then moved to New York, where she spent the rest of her life in virtual seclusion. Her last significant publication was a selection of poems featured in COUNTÉE CULLEN's anthology *Caroling Dusk* (1927). After some thirty years of isolation, both artistic and social, Grimké died in New York in 1958.

For the most part, Grimké's published poems, stories, and her play enjoyed moderate acclaim during her lifetime. Although she lived geographically remote from the hub of the Harlem Renaissance, she earned recognition from her more prominent contemporaries, notably LANGSTON HUGHES and Cullen. She also attended literary gatherings in the Washington, D.C., home of her close friend and fellow poet Georgia Douglas Johnson. Yet compared with her peers, Grimké published relatively few works. Her renown may have suffered further due to her failure to produce a collection of her poems or any other sizable volume. When she withdrew from the literary world, her works faded into obscurity, where they remained until they regained scholarly interest in the late twentieth century. Grimké's resurgent eminence as a poet stems not only from her skillful imagery and lyricism but also from her unusual perspective as a woman of color who felt compelled to suppress her sexuality.

FURTHER READING

Grimké's papers are held at the Moorland-Spingarn Research Center of Howard University in Washington, D.C.

Hirsch, David A. Hedrick. "Speaking Silences in Angelina Weld Grimké's 'The Closing Door' and 'Blackness,'" *African American Review* 26 (1992), 459–474.

Hull, Gloria T. *Color, Sex, and Poetry: Three Women Writers of the Harlem Renaissance* (1987).

—LAINE A. SCOTT

GRIMKÉ, ARCHIBALD HENRY (17 Aug. 1849–25 Feb. 1930), scholar and activist, was born in Colleton County, South Carolina, near Charleston, the eldest of three sons of Henry Grimké, a lawyer and member of one of South Carolina's leading families, and Nancy Weston, a slave owned by Grimké. He was also a nephew, on his father's side, of the noted white southern abolitionists Sarah Grimké and Angelina Grimké Weld. Although Archibald was born a slave, Henry acknowledged him as his son. After Henry's death in 1852, his mother took him to Charleston, where, even though he was still legally a slave, he attended a school for free blacks.

This condition was to change with the coming of the Civil War, when, in 1860, one of Henry's adult white sons, from an earlier marriage, forced the Grimké brothers—Archibald, John, and FRANCIS J. GRIMKÉ—to work as household slaves. Archibald escaped in 1863, hiding in the home of a free Charleston family for the duration of the war.

Following Emancipation, the brothers enrolled in a school for freedpeople, where Archibald and Francis, in particular, caught the attention of the principal, the abolitionist Frances Pillsbury. She arranged for them to continue their education at Lincoln University in Pennsylvania. They entered in 1867 and succeeded notably. They also seem to have come to the attention of their aunts for the first time. Angelina Grimké Weld, living in Massachusetts, read an article about Lincoln in the *National Anti-Slavery Standard*, an abolitionist journal that continued to publish after the war. The Grimké

brothers were singled out for their talents, and Weld immediately suspected their connection with her family. She and her sister Sarah undertook the support of their newfound nephews. They enabled Francis to continue his education through Princeton Theological Seminary; he was to become a prominent Presbyterian minister, intellectual, and activist. They also helped support Archibald through Harvard Law School, from which he graduated in 1874. And they supported the youngest Grimké brother, John, but John did not do well and subsequently played little role in his older brothers' lives.

Following his graduation from Harvard, Archibald settled in Boston. In 1879 he married Sarah Stanley, daughter of a white abolitionist minister from Michigan, and on 27 February 1880 their daughter, ANGELINA WELD GRIMKÉ—destined to become a prominent poet and writer—was born. The marriage soon became stormy, partly but not entirely on racial grounds, and dissolved in 1883. Sarah Stanley Grimké pursued a successful career as a writer and lecturer on occultism until her death in San Diego, California, in 1898.

At the same time, Grimké became involved in politics as, aided by his

National Association for the Advancement of Colored People

70 Fifth Avenue
New York City

NATIONAL OFFICERS

President
MOORFIELD STOREY

Vice-Presidents
ARCHIBALD H. GRIMKÉ
REV. JOHN HAYNES HOLMES
BISHOP JOHN HURST
JOHN E. MILHOLLAND
MARY WHITE OVINGTON
OSWALD GARRISON VILLARD

EXECUTIVE OFFICERS

Chairman of the Board
MAJOR J. E. SPINGARN

O. G. VILLARD, Treasurer

DR. W. E. B. DU BOIS, Director
of Publications and Research

JAMES WELDON JOHNSON,
Field Secretary

BOARD OF DIRECTORS

Chairman, MAJOR J. E. SPINGARN, New York

Baltimore   Dr. F. N. Cardozo   New York   Rev. John Haynes Holmes
             Bishop John Hurst   Dr. V. Morton Jones
Boston   Joseph Prince Loud   Florence Kelley
             Moorfield Storey   Paul Kennaday
             Butler R. Wilson   John E. Milholland
Chicago   Jane Addams   Mary White Ovington
             Dr. C. E. Bentley   Arthur B. Spingarn
New Haven   George W. Crawford   Charles H. Studin
New York   Rev. Hutchins C. Bishop   Dr. John G. Underhill
             Dr. W. E. B. Du Bois

             New York   Oswald Garrison Villard
                         Lillian D. Wald
                         Dr. O. M. Waller
                         William English Walling
             Philadelphia Dr. William A. Sinclair
             Springfield Rev. G. R. Waller
             St. Louis   Hon. Charles Nagel
             Washington   Prof. George William Cook
                          Archibald H. Grimké
                          Charles Edward Russell

A pamphlet, "The Negro in Wartime, c. 1919, listing the officers and board of the NAACP, including Archibald Grimké, W. E. B. DU BOIS, and JAMES WELDON JOHNSON. Ohio Historical Society

aunts, he developed contacts with some of Boston's leading citizens. Identifying with the reform Republicans known as "mugwumps," he entered the public arena in 1883 as editor of the *Hub*, a party newspaper addressed to African American readers. He also involved himself in movements for women's rights and for labor and tariff reform. In about 1886 he began to rethink his Republican ties, believing that the party was taking African American constituents for granted. By 1887 he had followed many of his mugwump friends into the Democratic Party. Even as he engaged in politics, he began to show an interest in scholarship, writing well-received biographies of William Lloyd Garrison (1891) and Charles Sumner (1892).

In 1894 as a reward for his political efforts, Grimké was appointed American consul to the Dominican Republic under the second administration of the Democratic president Grover Cleveland. Grimké performed his duties well and enjoyed his time in the Dominican Republic, especially since it appeared to be a society untarnished by American-style racism. He was not entirely happy when the Republican administration of William McKinley replaced him with one of its own loyalists.

Returning to the United States, Grimké divided his time between Boston and Washington, D.C., where his brother Francis and Francis's wife, CHARLOTTE L. FORTEN GRIMKÉ, were leading figures. He also became active in the American Negro Academy, the scholarly society founded in 1896. Francis Grimké had been one of the founding members, along with such major figures as ALEXANDER CRUMMELL, KELLY MILLER, and W. E. B. DU BOIS. Archibald Grimké became a member in 1899 and assumed the organization's presidency in 1903, serving until 1919. Speaking and writing in a wide variety of settings, he displayed a growing interest in the economic and psychological dimensions of American racism, an interest he pursued for the remainder of his life.

At the same time, his career became intertwined with the increasingly virulent dispute between allies and opponents of BOOKER T. WASHINGTON. Like many, Grimké admired Washington's achievements but was angered by Washington's often conciliatory stance toward the racist policies and practices being put in place in turn-of-the-century America. As early as 1903 he was one of those leaders singled out by Du Bois in *The Souls of Black Folk* for their misgivings about Washington's programs and prominence.

Grimké occupied a complex place in the dispute over Booker Washington's leadership. He never came to share Washington's accommodationist approach to American racial problems and could even be said to have been at the cutting edge of creating an anti-Washingtonian ideology. Nevertheless, he spent several years closely affiliated with Washington and Washington's allies. In 1905 he signed on as District of Columbia correspondent, writing weekly columns for the *New York Age*, edited by Washington's ally T. THOMAS FORTUNE. Grimké's columns were fiercely independent, directly challenging Washington's leadership and ideas. Still, he worked with Washington and Washington's organization in a variety of ways.

During 1906 a number of factors began to drive him away from Washington's camp, and when the 1907 creation of the Niagara Movement by Du Bois, WILLIAM MONROE TROTTER, and others appeared to offer an alternative to Washington's machine, Grimké decided to join. Becoming, at the same time, editor of *Alexander's Magazine*, an important—and at one time Washingtonian—periodical, he used his position to champion the new movement.

The Niagara Movement was to undergo a major transformation over the next few years, especially as several important white reformers, also frustrated with Booker Washington's accommodationism, joined with Du Bois and others in contemplating the creation of an interracial organization to fight racial oppression. This was to result in the founding of the NAACP in 1910. Grimké was peripherally involved in the founding but actively involved in the association's activities. By 1913 he had become president of the Washington, D.C., branch and a member of the national board.

The D.C. branch was especially important to the NAACP. Woodrow Wilson had been elected president in 1912 and, upon assuming office, had instituted a thoroughgoing policy of segregation and discrimination in the federal government. As head of the D.C. branch, Grimké took on a major role in challenging those policies while trying to protect black federal employees from discriminatory treatment. These efforts were to become increasingly complex after April 1917, when the United States entered World War I. Grimké opposed the war—he was put under federal surveillance for a time—and was particularly incensed when Du Bois, in the NAACP's magazine the *Crisis*, urged African Americans to put aside their grievances to support the war effort. He was to be even more incensed when he learned that Du Bois had been offered a military commission to help address racial problems in the armed forces. He protested as a member of the national board and led the D.C. branch to condemn Du Bois bitterly.

After the war Grimké's career began to wind down. His work for the NAACP was widely appreciated, and he was awarded its highest honor, the Spingarn Medal, in 1919. At the same time, the national organization took on more of the lobbying activity that had previously been the province of the D.C. branch, lessening Grimké's role in such efforts. Plagued by ill health, he stepped down from the national board in 1923 and officially retired as president of the branch in 1925. His health failed in 1928, and he was bedridden for much of the time until his death, in Washington.

Although he was not as influential as Booker T. Washington or W. E. B. Du Bois, Grimké was an important figure. His significance was recognized, and occasionally resented, by his contemporaries, as he sought to carve out an independent place in a factional setting. Often prescient in his analyses of race relations, his life was itself a challenge to the simplistic, brutal racial environment of late nineteenth- and early-twentieth-century America.

FURTHER READING

Grimké's papers, along with those of his brother Francis Grimké and his daughter, Angelina Weld Grimké, are housed in the Moorland-Spingarn Research Center at Howard University in Washington, D.C.

Bruce, Dickson D., Jr. *Archibald Grimké: Portrait of a Black Independent* (1993).

Harlan, Louis R. *Booker T. Washington: The Wizard of Tuskegee, 1901–1915* (1983).

Lewis, David Levering. *W. E. B. Du Bois: Biography of a Race, 1868–1919* (1993).

Obituary: *Journal of Negro History* 15 (1930).
—DICKSON D. BRUCE JR.

GRIMKÉ, CHARLOTTE FORTEN

(17 Aug. 1837– 23 July 1914), educator, diarist, and essayist, was born in Philadelphia, Pennsylvania, the daughter of Mary Virginia Wood and Robert Bridges Forten, who were free blacks. Her father, a mathematician, orator, and reformer, was the son of wealthy sailmaker JAMES FORTEN SR., a leading African American activist in Philadelphia. Her mother, grandmother, and aunts had been among the founding members of the interracial Philadelphia Female Anti-Slavery Society (PFASS). Prominent figures such as abolitionist William Lloyd Garrison and Quaker poet and abolitionist John Greenleaf Whittier were friends of the Fortens. Whittier wrote a poem, "To The Daughters of James Forten."

Both privilege and misfortune marked the early life of Charlotte Forten. Although a very talented and well-educated man, Robert Forten never achieved financial stability. By the time he joined the family business, the sailmaking industry had been undermined by new steam-propelled vessels. Charlotte's mother died in 1840. Consequently, Charlotte spent most of her first years in the homes of her grandmother and of her aunt Harriet Forten Purvis, the wife of wealthy and mixed race Robert Purvis, who led the black reform community after James Forten died. Encountering a rapidly hardening racial climate, including mob violence and black disfranchisement in Pennsylvania, Purvis in 1842 moved his household from Philadelphia to the Quaker suburb of Byberry.

The inferior and segregated Pennsylvania schools prompted Robert Forten to send his daughter to Massachusetts to complete her education. In 1853 Charlotte was enrolled in the Higginson Grammar School in Salem. Following the examples of her aunts, particularly Margaretta Forten, a teacher, and Sarah

Louise Forten, who composed poetry, Charlotte decided to teach and to devote her skills to "elevate the race." After graduating from the Higginson School in February of 1855 and the Salem Normal School in July of 1856, she began teaching at the previously all-white Epes Grammar School of Salem.

In Massachusetts, Forten joined an expanding circle of abolitionists, including African Americans Charles Lenox Remond (in whose home she lived briefly) and his sister Sarah Remond, who were agents for the American Anti-Slavery Society, and white abolitionists Maria Weston Chapman and Lydia Maria Child, leading members of the Boston Female Anti-Slavery Society. This abolitionist community supported Forten's literary aspirations. In the *Liberator* Garrison published her "Poem for Normal School Graduates" in 1856. One of her last works, "Personal Recollections of Whittier," published in *New England Magazine* in 1893, honored the poet who had immortalized her aunts more than a half century earlier. Although Forten possessed a facility for writing and would continue to publish her poems and essays in reform and literary magazines for decades to come, her ambitions as a writer were never fully realized.

Forten has become best known for the diary she began in 1854. Consisting of four volumes that record her thoughts and experiences between 1854 and 1864 and a fifth volume covering the years from 1885 to 1892, Forten's journal provides valuable insight into the experiences of the black elite. Early diary entries reveal the struggle of a young woman of African ancestry in an era when the assumption of Anglo-Saxon superiority went virtually unchallenged. Measuring herself against European standards of beauty and morality led to feelings of inadequacy and depression, which probably influenced her physical health. Severe headaches and ongoing respiratory illness interrupted her work as a teacher between 1857 and 1862, during which time she traveled back and forth between Philadelphia and Massachusetts.

When she recovered sufficiently, Forten joined the ranks of "Yankee School Marms" who traveled to the Union-controlled Sea Islands of South

Carolina to educate erstwhile slaves left behind in large numbers by fleeing or absentee masters. Under the auspices of the Philadelphia Port Royal Relief Society, she became in 1862 the first African American teacher on St. Helena Island, working at a school conducted by the teacher and physician Laura Towne. Her writings from this period again reveal the tensions and contradictions in her life. She was, especially at first, enthusiastic about her mission, but her background—so very different from that of the population she served—sometimes limited her rapport with the Sea Islanders. Her relations with certain white colleagues, at the same time, were circumscribed by the racism that she suspected even some of the most well-disposed among them harbored. The death of her father, who had enlisted in the Union army and had been recruiting other African Americans, as well as her declining enthusiasm, ill health, homesickness, and poor living conditions, caused Forten to return to the North in May 1864. That same month and the next, *Atlantic Monthly* published her account of the Sea Islands.

From 1865 until 1870 Forten was secretary of the Teacher Committee of the New England Branch of the Freedmen's Union Commission in Boston, serving as a liaison between the teachers who labored among the newly freed people and their supporters in the North. In 1869 her translation of a French novel, Erckmann-Chatrian's *Thérèse; or, The Volunteers of '92*, was published. She spent the years 1870–1873 teaching, first at Robert L. Shaw Memorial School in Charleston and later at Summer High School, a black preparatory school in Washington, D.C. Turning to a profession newly opened to women during the Civil War era, she worked as a clerk in the Fourth Auditor's Office of the U.S. Treasury from 1873 until 1878, when she left to marry FRANCIS J. GRIMKÉ, a divinity student twelve years her junior. A short time before their marriage Francis Grimké had been ordained and appointed pastor to the Fifteenth Street Presbyterian Church in Washington.

Forten's marriage to Francis Grimké completed a unique circle of black and white abolitionists. Grimké, the son of wealthy planter Henry Grimké of

South Carolina and one of his slave women, Nancy Weston, was the nephew of two of the most famous white women abolitionists of the antebellum period, Angelina Emily Grimké and Sarah Grimké, who briefly had been members of PFASS, which the Forten Purvis women had helped found. Francis Grimké conducted the marriage ceremony, an interracial union, of FREDERICK DOUGLASS and his second wife, Helen Pitts.

The death a few months after the birth in 1880 of their only child, Theodora Cornelia, cast the only major shadow on the Forten-Grimké union. Illness plagued both at various times, and to improve his failing health, Francis Grimké was assigned to Jacksonville, Florida, where from 1885 to 1889 he was minister at the Laura Street Presbyterian Church. While in Jacksonville, Forten Grimké worked with the women of this church to provide social services for the local black community. She expanded these activities by becoming in 1896 a founding member of the National Association of Colored Women, which made major contributions to education, health, and other social services and to political activism, such as the antilynching campaign conducted by IDA B. WELLS-BARNETT.

After returning to Washington, Forten Grimké assumed additional family responsibilities by helping raise her husband's niece, ANGELINA WELD GRIMKÉ, the daughter of ARCHIBALD H. GRIMKÉ and Sarah Stanley, a white woman, who had proved unable to shoulder the burdens of an interracial family. In the 1890s Archibald and Angelina Weld Grimké became permanent members of the household of Francis and Charlotte Grimké.

In Angelina, Forten Grimké found both a focus for her maternal care and affection and an opportunity to nurture a literary talent. Living up to the family tradition of social activism, Angelina Weld Grimké used her talent to promote racial justice. In 1916 she wrote the play *Rachel*, a denunciation of the widespread lynching of that period and the first play written by an African American woman to be staged and performed, two years after the death of Forten Grimké.

After a long period of invalidism that left her bedridden for sixteen months, Forten Grimké died in Washington, D.C. Angelina Weld Grimké paid a final poetic tribute to her aunt in "To Keep the Memory of Charlotte Forten Grimké," which eulogized the "gentle spirit" who was both substitute mother and bearer of the family standard of political activism and intellectual endeavor.

FURTHER READING

The best source of information about Forten Grimké's life, character, and work are her diaries in the Moorland-Spingarn Research Center at Howard University, Washington, D.C.

Billington, Ray Allen, ed. *The Journal of Charlotte L. Forten* (1953).
Cooper, Anna J. *The Life and Writings of the Grimké Family* (1951).
Stevenson, Brenda, ed. *The Journals of Charlotte Forten Grimké* (1988).

—CAROLYN WILLIAMS

 GRIMKÉ, FRANCIS JAMES (4 Nov. 1850– 11 Oct. 1937), Presbyterian minister and civil rights activist, was born near Charleston, South Carolina, the son of Henry Grimké, a planter, and Nancy Weston, a biracial slave. As the second son of an unrecognized dalliance that was familiar to plantations such as Caneacres, young Grimké inherited his mother's status as servant. During the Civil War his white half brother sold him to a Confederate officer whom Grimké accompanied until the end of that conflict. The end of the war brought his manumission, and a benefactor from the Freedmen's Aid Society sent him to study at Lincoln University in Chester County, Pennsylvania.

Hard work and natural talent brought Grimké recognition on the campus. A newspaper account of the young scholar's outstanding record also attracted attention from his white aunts, Angelina Emily Grimké and Sarah Moore Grimké, who had been deeply involved in antislavery activities. After learning of the existence of a heretofore unknown nephew, the reformist sisters subsidized Grimké's education and remained in contact with him for the rest of their lives. After graduating from

Lincoln in 1870, Grimké studied law for a time (1870–1871, 1872–1873 at Lincoln; 1874–1875 at Howard University) but at length decided to enter the Presbyterian ministry. In 1878 he completed training at Princeton Theological Seminary and was ordained.

In 1878 Grimké accepted an invitation to become pastor of the Fifteenth Street Presbyterian Church in Washington, D.C., inaugurating a ministerial career that spanned more than half a century. That same year he married Charlotte Forten (CHARLOTTE L. FORTEN GRIMKÉ), whom he had first met at a freedman school. The couple had one child who lived for a scant few months in 1880. The city of Washington grew rapidly in the last quarter of the nineteenth century, and Grimké made his church an eminent part of that rapid development. His fame as a pulpit orator spread, and members of all denominations as well as people with diverse ethnic identities attended his sermons.

Health problems due to overwork soon intervened, however, and Grimké viewed as providential an invitation to serve a church in Florida in 1885. He followed a more relaxed routine at the Laura Street Church in Jacksonville for four years, but he was ready to return to Washington when his old church pleaded for his help in 1889. Thereafter he became an even more important figure in aesthetic and literary circles in the nation's capital. But more significant than recognition for erudition and genteel manners among the black elite, he developed a reputation for passionate advocacy in struggles for racial justice. As Jim Crow laws became more manifest and lynching increased, he moved from an accommodationist philosophy represented by BOOKER T. WASHINGTON to a more strident demand for government action in protecting the civil rights of black American citizens.

Grimké displayed powerful intellect and eloquence in his sermons. Using such standard components as biblical exposition and illustrative material from classical literature, he shaped most of his addresses into what he called "helpful" sermons. His preaching included ideas about salvation and proper doctrine, but it focused primarily on questions of social relevance. In Grimké's view the Christian ministry functioned essentially as a moral teacher, and he used contemporary issues to apply those lessons. In his day racial prejudice made itself known through lynchings, disfranchisement, and Jim Crow legislation, especially in the areas of education and public transportation. Grimké denounced those abuses and rallied African American leaders to fight racist discrimination. He repeatedly stressed self-improvement as a means of achieving equal rights with other segments of American society. He urged character formation, moral integrity, and education as elements that commanded respect. Through industriousness black citizens could, he argued, insist on parity with whites because they deserved it.

In the years around 1895 Grimké moved from being an accommodationist to being a gadfly, impatient at slow progress and insistent on faster change. He criticized Booker T. Washington for being too meek, and his prophetic ardor did not diminish with age. In 1913, for instance, he wrote Woodrow Wilson that he had hoped Wilson's "accession to power would act as a check upon the brutal and insane spirit of race hatred that characterizes certain portions of the white people of the country." After faulting the president for lack of vigor, he reminded him that "all class distinctions among citizens are un-American, and the sooner every vestige of it is stamped out the better it will be for the Republic." He finally retired from the pulpit in 1928 and lived another nine years before dying in Washington.

FURTHER READING

A collection of Grimké's personal papers, sermons, and addresses is housed in the library at Howard University in the District of Columbia.

Ferry, Henry J. "Patriotism and Prejudice: Francis James Grimké on World War I," *Journal of Religious Thought* 32 (1975): 86–94.

———. "Racism and Reunion: A Black Protest by Francis J. Grimké," *Journal of Presbyterian History* 50 (1972): 77–88.

Weeks, Louis B. "Racism, World War I and the Christian Life: Francis J. Grimké in the Nation's Capital," *Journal of Presbyterian History* 51 (1973): 471–488.

WOODSON, CARTER G., ed. *The Works of Francis James Grimké* (4 vols., 1942).

—HENRY WARNER BOWDEN

 GRONNIOSAW, JAMES ALBERT UKAWSAW

(c. 1710–c. 1773), was born Ukawsaw Gronniosaw, probably between 1710 and 1714 in Bournou (Bornu), a kingdom in what is now northeastern Nigeria. He was the youngest child of the oldest daughter of the king of Bournou. All that we know about James Albert Ukawsaw Gronniosaw is found in *A Narrative of the Most Remarkable Particulars in the Life of James Albert Ukawsaw Gronniosaw, an African Prince, as Related by Himself* (1772), one of the earliest "as-told-to" slave narratives recorded by a white amanuensis. According to this account, Ukawsaw Gronniosaw, spiritually dissatisfied with the animist faith in which he was raised, alienated himself from his friends and relatives by his constant questions challenging their faith in physical objects, as well as by his growing belief in the existence of an uncreated creator. Consequently, he became increasingly "dejected and melancholy."

When an African merchant from the Gold Coast invited the adolescent Gronniosaw to return with him to his home, more than a thousand miles away, Gronniosaw seized the opportunity. There, the merchant promised, Gronniosaw could play with boys his own age, and "see houses walk upon the water with wings to them, and the white folks." On arrival at the Gold Coast, however, the local king thought him a spy and decided to behead him. Affected by Gronniosaw's obvious courage in the face of death, the king relented, choosing to sell him into slavery rather than kill him. Rejected by a French slave trader because he was so small, Gronniosaw successfully implored a Dutch captain to buy him. On the voyage to Barbados, in a scene imitated in later slave narratives, Gronniosaw watched his new master reading, and thinking the book talked to the Dutchman, he held his ear close to it, hoping it would speak to him as well. He blamed his complexion for the book's silence.

A man named Vanhorn purchased him in Barbados and took him to New York City, where he was soon sold as a domestic slave to Theodorus Jacobus Frelinghuysen, a wealthy Dutch Reform clergyman in New Jersey and friend of the English evangelist George Whitefield. Introduced to Christianity by Frelinghuysen, and to reading by his schoolmaster, Peter Van Arsdalen, Gronniosaw experienced despair when he became convinced that his own sins were too great to deserve salvation. Around 1747, after reading the spiritual writings of John Bunyan and Richard Baxter, an attempt at suicide, and a three-day illness, Gronniosaw experienced his own spiritual rebirth when he recalled the words from the Bible, "Behold the Lamb of God." Gronniosaw's newfound happiness was quickly ended by the death of his master, who freed him in his will, and by recurrent spiritual doubts. As a free man Gronniosaw worked for various members of the Frelinghuysen family, all of whom, however, died within four years of the minister's death.

Having lost his friends in America, Gronniosaw decided to go to England and above all to Kidderminster, the birthplace of Baxter. Gronniosaw's reading and his experience in meeting Whitefield in New Jersey had convinced him that the English "people must be all *Righteous*." During the Seven Years' War, known in North America as the French and Indian War, debts forced Gronniosaw to work his way across the Atlantic, first as a cook on a privateer, and later as an enlistee in the Twenty-eighth Regiment of Foot. His lack of interest in money caused him to be cheated repeatedly. Landing at Portsmouth, England, near the end of 1762 brought Gronniosaw further disappointment when he discovered the English to be no more pious than Americans. Disillusioned, Gronniosaw went to London, where Whitefield found him housing. There he fell in love at first sight with an English weaver named Betty, who introduced him to the preaching of the eminent Baptist minister Dr. Andrew Gifford.

After about three weeks in London, Gronniosaw agreed to go to Holland at the request of some friends of his late master Frelinghuysen, to be examined about his experiences and his faith by several Calvinist ministers. While there, he was hired as a butler in the household of a very rich Amsterdam merchant, who treated him more as friend than a servant, and whose wife wanted Gronniosaw to marry her maid, an attractive young woman who had saved a good deal of money. But Gronniosaw chose to return to London after a year to be baptized by Gifford and to wed Betty, despite the objections of his English friends to his marrying such a poor widow. Although Betty normally earned a good living as a weaver, Gronniosaw and his wife and growing family soon fell on hard times because of the postwar economic depression. Through a series of Quaker contacts, Gronniosaw was able to find employment outside of London, first in Colchester, then Norwich, and later Kidderminster. Unfortunately, much of his work was seasonal, leading to long periods of deprivation and near-starvation during the winters, with the brief exception of the time spent in Norwich, where Betty was also able to find employment before their children contracted smallpox. They experienced the generosity of benefactors like Henry Gurney, a Quaker worsted manufacturer and banker in Norwich. But they also suffered the cruelty of an unnamed Baptist minister, Quakers, and an Anglican minister, all of whom refused to give a proper burial to one of Gronniosaw's daughters, who had died of fever in Norwich. His

Narrative closes with the "very poor Pilgrims" living in abject poverty in Kidderminster, their faith in God still intact.

Dedicated to Selina Hastings, Countess of Huntingdon, Gronniosaw's *Narrative* was first advertised in December 1772 in *Boddley's Bath Journal*. According to its preface, written by the countess's cousin, Walter Shirley, the *Narrative* "was taken from his own Mouth, and committed to Paper by the elegant Pen of a young LADY of the Town of LEOMINSTER." In 1809 the "young LADY" was identified, probably incorrectly, as Hannah More. By 1800, the *Narrative* had appeared in at least ten editions in England and America, as well as in a Welsh translation (1779) and serial publication in the *American Moral and Sentimental Magazine* in New York (1797).

The publication of Gronniosaw's *Narrative* in 1772 marked the beginning of the modern anglophone tradition of autobiographies written or dictated by slaves of African descent. As a foundational text, the *Narrative* contains many tropes, themes, character types, events, historical figures, and situations that reappear in various ways in subsequent writings by and about

African-British and African American figures. Perhaps most significantly, Gronniosaw's *Narrative* introduced in anglophone-African writing the trope of the "talking book," by which an illiterate African is introduced to the concept of reading. Although Paul Edwards first identified the trope in the narratives of Gronniosaw, JOHN MARRANT, Quobna Ottobah Cugoano, OLAUDAH EQUIANO, and John Jea, the significance of the relationship between literacy and freedom was subsequently developed at length by Henry Louis Gates Jr. in *The Signifying Monkey* (1988).

FURTHER READING

Gronniosaw, James Albert Ukawsaw. *A Narrative of the Most Remarkable Particulars in the Life of James Albert Ukawsaw Gronniosaw, an African Prince, as Related by Himself* (1772).

Costanzo, Angelo. *Surprising Narrative: Olaudah Equiano and the Beginnings of Black Autobiography* (1987).
Gates, Henry Louis, Jr. "The Trope of the Talking Book" in *The Signifying Monkey: A Theory of Afro-American Literary Criticism* (1988).

—VINCENT CARRETTA

H–I

HALEY, ALEX (11 Aug. 1921–10 Feb. 1992), writer, was born Alexander Palmer Haley in Ithaca, New York, the son of Simon Alexander Haley, a graduate student in agriculture at Cornell University, and Bertha George Palmer, a music student at the Ithaca Conservatory of Music. Young Alex Haley grew up in the family home in Henning, Tennessee, where his grandfather Will Palmer owned a lumber business. When the business was sold in 1929, Simon Haley moved his family to southern black college communities, including Alabama Agricultural and Mechanical College in Normal (near Huntsville), Alabama, where he had his longest tenure teaching agriculture. The three sons of Bertha and Simon Haley, Alex, George, and Julius, spent their summers in Henning, where, in the mid-1930s, grandmother Cynthia Murray Palmer recounted for her grandsons the stories of their family's history.

After graduating from high school in Normal, Alex Haley studied to become a teacher at Elizabeth City State Teachers College in North Carolina from 1937 to 1939. In 1939 he enlisted in the U.S. Coast Guard. Two years later Haley married Nannie Branch. They had two children. Haley spent twenty years in the coast guard, advancing from mess boy to ship's cook on a munitions ship, the USS *Murzin*, in the South Pacific during World War II. To relieve his boredom, he began writing, love letters for fellow shipmates at first, then romance fiction, which brought many rejection letters from periodicals such as *True Confessions* and *Modern Romances*. Finally, Haley sold three stories on the history of the coast guard to *Coronet*. In 1949 the coast guard created the position of chief journalist for him. Haley did public relations, wrote speeches, and worked with the press on rescue stories for the coast guard until he retired in 1959.

Failing to find other work and sustained by his military pension, Haley moved to Greenwich Village to work as a freelance writer in 1959. Casting about for his subject and voice, his early articles included a feature on Phyllis Diller for the *Saturday Evening Post*. Two articles for *Reader's Digest* were better indicators of Haley's future work. One was a feature on Nation of Islam leader ELIJAH MUHAMMAD; the other was an article about his brother George, who was the first African American student at the University of Arkansas law school in 1949 and would be elected to the Kansas state legislature in the 1960s. In 1962 *Playboy* hired Haley to produce a series of interviews with prominent African Americans: MILES DAVIS, Cassius Clay (MUHAMMAD ALI), JIM BROWN, SAMMY DAVIS JR., QUINCY JONES, LEONTYNE PRICE, and MALCOLM X. The last interview was the genesis of Haley's first important book, *The Autobiography of Malcolm X* (1965). Based on extensive interviews with the religious leader, the book was Haley's artistic creation and has won an important place in American biography. (Haley's manuscript of *The Autobiography of Malcolm X* is in private hands, but the publisher's copy is in the Grove Press Archive at Syracuse University.) His marriage to his first wife ended in 1964; that same year Haley married Juliette Collins. They had one child before their divorce in 1972.

Haley's second important book was even more his own story than *The Autobiography*. Recalling stories recounted to him by his grandmother twenty-five years earlier, Haley had begun research on his family's history as early as 1961. Backed by a contract from Doubleday, Haley began serious work on a book that was initially to be called *Before This Anger*. His research trips across the South took him to Gambia, West Africa, where a griot identified an ancestor as Kunte Kinte. In 1972 Haley founded and became the president of the Kinte Foundation of Washington, D.C., which sought to encourage research in African American history and genealogy. *Roots: The Saga of an American Family* (1976) finally appeared in the bicentennial year to great fanfare. A historical novel that invited acceptance as a work of history, it told the story of the family's origins in West Africa, its experience in slavery, and its subsequent history. A best-selling book that won a Pulitzer Prize, *Roots* had even greater impact when it was made into a gripping television miniseries. Broadcast by ABC in January and February 1977, it was seen, in whole or in part, by 130 million people. It stimulated interest and pride in the African American experience and had a much greater immediate impact than did *The Autobiography*.

In 1977, however, Margaret Walker brought suit against Haley for plagiarism from her novel *Jubilee*. Her case was dismissed. Subsequently, however, Haley reached an out-of-court settlement for $650,000 with novelist Harold Courlander, who alleged that passages in *Roots* were taken from his *The Slave*. Haley acknowledged that *Roots* was a combination of fact and fiction. By 1981 professional historians were challenging the genealogical and historical reliability of the book. A third lawsuit for plagiarism was filed in 1989 by Emma Lee Davis Paul. The symbolic significance of the linkage in *Roots* of the African American experience to its African origins for a mass audience continues to be important. Yet, by the time of Haley's death, renewed interest in Malcolm X and questions about the originality and reliability of *Roots* seemed to have reversed early judgments about the relative importance of the two books.

In 1988 Haley published *A Different Kind of Christmas*, a historical novella about the Underground Railroad. When he died in Seattle, Washington, Haley was separated from his third wife, Myra Lewis, and there were legal claims of more than $1.5 million against his estate. The primary claimants were First Tennessee

Bank, his first and third wives, and many creditors, including a longtime researcher, George Sims. The bank held a mortgage of almost one million dollars on Haley's 127-acre farm near Norris, Tennessee. His first wife claimed that their 1964 divorce was not valid, and his third wife claimed entitlement to one-third of the estate. The executor of Haley's estate was his brother George, who had been chief counsel to the U.S. Information Agency and chaired the U.S. Postal Rate Commission. George Haley concluded that the estate must be sold. In a dramatic sale on 1–3 October 1992, Alex Haley's estate, including his manuscripts, was auctioned to the highest bidder.

His novel *Queen: The Story of an American Family*, based on the life of his paternal grandmother, was published posthumously in 1993 and was the basis of a television miniseries that aired in February 1994. A second novel, *Henning*, which was named for the small community in West Tennessee where Haley lived as a child and is buried, remains unpublished.

FURTHER READING

Haley's early interviews for *Playboy*, research files on Malcolm X, and forty-nine volumes of *Roots* in various languages are at the Schomburg Center for Research in Black Culture of the New York Public Library. Manuscript and research material for *Roots* are at the University of Tennessee, Knoxville.

Haley, Alex. "Roots: A Black American's Search for His Ancestral African." *Ebony*, Aug. 1976, 100–102, 104, 106–107.

Bain Robert, ed. *Southern Writers: A Biographical Dictionary* (1979).
Nobile, Philip. "Uncovering Roots." *Village Voice*, 23 Feb. 1993, 31–38.
Taylor, Helen. "'The Griot from Tennessee': The Saga of Alex Haley's Roots." *Critical Quarterly* 37 (Summer 1995): 46–62.
Wolper, David L. *The Inside Story of TV's "Roots"* (1978).

Obituary: *New York Times*, 11 Feb. 1992.
                                —RALPH E. LUKER

 HALL, PRINCE (1735–4 Dec. 1807), Masonic organizer and abolitionist, was born in Bridgetown, Barbados, the son of a "white English leather worker" and a "free woman of African and French descent"; his birth date is variously given as 12 Sept. 1748 (Horton). He was the slave of William Hall, a leather dresser. At age seventeen, Hall found passage to Boston, Massachusetts, by working on a ship and became employed there as a leather worker. In 1762 he joined the Congregational Church on School Street. He received his manumission in 1770. Official records indicate that Hall was married three times. In 1763 he married Sarah Ritchie, a slave. In 1770, after her death, he married Flora Gibbs of Gloucester, Massachusetts; they had one son, Prince Africanus. In 1798 Hall married Sylvia Ward. The reason for the dissolution of the second marriage is unclear.

In March 1775 Hall was one of fifteen African Americans initiated into a British army lodge of Freemasons stationed in Boston. After the evacuation of the British, the black Masons were allowed to meet as a lodge and to participate fully in Masonic ceremonies, but full recognition was withheld. After a series of appeals, African Lodge No. 459 was granted full recognition in 1784 by the London Grand Lodge. Hall became the lodge's "worshipful master," charged with ensuring that it followed all the rules of the "Book of Constitution." He served in that position until his death.

During the revolutionary war, Hall worked as a skilled craftsman and sold leather drumheads to the Continental army. Military records indicate that he most likely fought in the war. During the war, Hall also agitated on behalf of abolition. In 1777 he and seven other African Americans, including three black Masons, petitioned the General Court to abolish slavery in Massachusetts so that "the Inhabitanc of these Stats" could no longer be "chargeable with the inconsistency of acting themselves the part which they condem and oppose in others." The petition was referred to the Congress of Confederation, but slavery was not abolished in Massachusetts until 1783.

Throughout the 1780s, Hall served as the grandmaster of the Masonic Lodge and owned and operated a leather workshop called the Golden Fleece. During that period he also emerged as a leading spokesman for black Bostonians. When Shays's Rebellion broke out in western Massachusetts in 1786, Hall and the African lodge offered to raise a militia of seven hundred black soldiers to assist the government in putting down the rebellion. "We, by the Providence of God, are members of a fraternity that not only enjoins upon us to be peaceable subjects to the civil powers where we reside," Hall wrote, "but it also forbids our having concern in any plot of conspiracies against the state where we dwell." The offer was turned down by the governor.

In 1787 Hall and seventy-two other African Americans, perhaps resentful of the state government's dismissive attitude toward them, signed a petition asking the state legislature to finance black emigration to Africa. "We, or our ancestors have been taken from all our dear connections, and brought from Africa and put into a state of slavery in this country," the petition stated, in marked contrast to the patriotic language of the petition on Shays's Rebellion. "We find ourselves, in many respects, in very disagreeable and disadvantageous circumstances; most of which must attend us, so long as we and our children live in America." This was the first public statement in favor of African colonization made in the United States. The legislature accepted the petition but never acted on it.

Shortly after the emigration petition, Hall drafted another petition to the Massachusetts legislature, this one protesting the denial of free schools for African Americans who paid taxes and therefore had "the right to enjoy the privileges of free men." In 1788 Hall drafted a petition, signed by twenty-two members of his lodge, expressing outrage at the abduction by slave traders of three free blacks in Boston. After a group of Quakers and other Boston clergy joined the call, in March 1788 the General Court passed an act that banned the slave trade and granted "relief of the families of such unhappy persons as may be kidnapped or decoyed away from this Commonwealth." Diplomatic actions obtained the release of the three captured freemen from the French island of St. Bartholomew. Hall and the African lodge organized a celebration for their return to Boston.

In 1792 Hall delivered a lecture on the injustice of black taxpayers' being denied free schools for their children. The lecture was published as *A Charge*

Delivered to the Brethren of the African Lodge on the 25th of June, 1792 (1792). After failing to convince the state government to provide education for black children, Hall in 1796 established a school for black children in his own house. He recruited two students from Harvard College to serve as teachers. In 1806 the school's increased enrollment prompted Hall to move it to a larger space at the African Society House on Belknap Street.

Hall died in Boston. The Prince Hall Masons, still the largest and most prestigious fraternal order of African Americans, was established one year after his death.

Hall was one of the most prominent and influential African Americans in the era of the American Revolution. As a leading spokesperson, organizer, and educator, Hall served as a principal agitator for abolition and for civil rights for black Americans in the period. He was also a pioneer in the establishment of fraternal organizations of African Americans at a time when such activities were deemed solely the province of whites.

FURTHER READING

Horton, James Oliver. "Generations of Protest: Black Families and Social Reform in Ante-Bellum Boston." *New England Quarterly* 49, no. 2 (June 1976).

Kaplan, Sidney. *The Black Presence in the Era of the American Revolution, 1770–1800* (1973).

Wesley, Charles H. *Prince Hall, Life and Legacy* (1977).

—THADDEUS RUSSELL

 **HAMER, FANNIE LOU TOWNSEND** (6 Oct. 1917– 14 Mar. 1977), civil rights activist, was born in Montgomery County, Mississippi, the twentieth child of Lou Ella (maiden name unknown) and Jim Townsend, sharecroppers. When Fannie Lou was two, the family moved to Sunflower County, where they lived in abject poverty. Even when they were able to rent land and buy stock, a jealous white neighbor poisoned the animals, forcing the family back into sharecropping. Fannie Lou began picking cotton when she was six; she eventually was able to pick three to four hundred pounds a day, earning a penny a pound. Because of poverty she was

forced to leave school at age twelve, barely able to read and write. She married Perry ("Pap") Hamer in 1944. The couple adopted two daughters. For the next eighteen years Fannie Lou Hamer worked first as a sharecropper and then as a timekeeper on the plantation of B. D. Marlowe.

Hamer appeared destined for a routine life of poverty, but two events in the early 1960s led her to become a political activist. When she was hospitalized for the removal of a uterine tumor in 1961, the surgeons performed a hysterectomy without her consent. In August 1962, still angry and bitter over the surgery, she went to a meeting in her hometown of Ruleville to hear JAMES FORMAN of the Student Nonviolent Coordinating Committee (SNCC) and James Bevel of the Southern Christian Leadership Conference (SCLC). After hearing their speeches on the importance of voting, she and seventeen others went to the courthouse in Indianola to try to register. They were told they could only enter the courthouse two at a time to be given the literacy test, which they all failed. On the trip back to Ruleville the group was stopped by the police and fined one hundred dollars for driving a bus that was the wrong color. Hamer subsequently became the group's leader. B. D. Marlowe called on her that evening and told her she had to withdraw her application to register.

Hamer refused and was ordered to leave the plantation. (Because Marlowe threatened to confiscate their belongings, Pap was compelled to work on the plantation until the harvest season was finished.) For a time, Hamer stayed with various friends and relatives, and segregationist night riders shot into some of the homes where she was staying. Nevertheless, she remained active in the civil rights movement, serving as a field secretary for SNCC, working for voter registration, advocating welfare programs, and teaching citizenship classes.

Hamer gained national attention when she appeared before the credentials committee of the 1964 Democratic National Convention in Atlantic City, New Jersey, on behalf of the Mississippi Freedom Democratic Party (MFDP), an organization attempting to unseat the state's regular, all-white delegation. Speaking as a delegate and co-chair of the MFDP, she described atrocities inflicted on blacks seeking the right to vote and other civil rights, including the abuse she had suffered at the Montgomery County Jail, where white Mississippi law enforcement officers forced black inmates to beat her so badly that she had no feeling in her arms. (Hamer and several others had been arrested for attempting to integrate the "white only" section of the bus station in Winona, Mississippi, during the return trip from a voter registration training session in

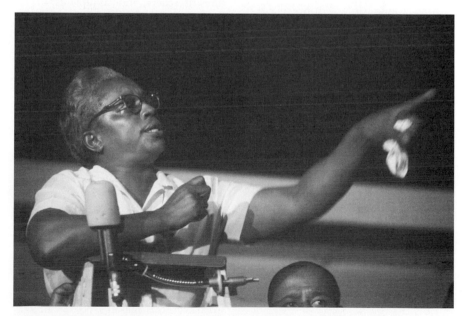

Fannie Lou Hamer speaking at a rally during the March Against Fear, 1966.
© Flip Schulke/CORBIS

South Carolina.) After giving her dramatic testimony, she wept before the committee. Although her emotional appeal generated sympathy for the plight of blacks in Mississippi among the millions watching on television, the committee rejected the MFDP's challenge.

That same year Hamer traveled to Ghana, Guinea, Nigeria, and several other African nations at the request and expense of those governments. Still, her primary interest was in helping the people of the Mississippi Delta. She lectured across the country, raising money and organizing. In 1965 she ran as an MFDP candidate for Congress, saying she was "sick and tired of being sick and tired." While many civil rights leaders abandoned grassroots efforts, she remained committed to organizing what she called "everyday" people in her community, frequently saying she preferred to face problems at home rather than run from them. In 1969 she launched the Freedom Farm Cooperative to provide homes and food for deprived families, white as well as black, in Sunflower County. The cooperative eventually acquired 680 acres. She remained active, however, at the national level. In 1971 she was elected to the steering committee of the National Women's political caucus, and the following year she supported the nomination of Sissy Farenthold as vice president in an address to the Democratic National Convention.

After a long battle with breast cancer, Hamer died at the all-black Mound Bayou Hospital, thirty miles from Ruleville. Civil rights leaders ANDREW YOUNG, JULIAN BOND, and ELEANOR HOLMES NORTON attended her funeral.

FURTHER READING

Hamer's papers are in the Amistad Research Center at Tulane University, the Mississippi Department of Archives and History, and the Wisconsin State Historical Society. Other papers and speeches are in the Moses Moon Collection at the National Museum of American History of the Smithsonian Institution and the Civil Rights Documentation Project at the Moorland-Spingarn Research Center at Howard University.

Dittmer, John. *Local People: The Struggle for Civil Rights in Mississippi* (1995).
Lee, Chana Kai. *For Freedom's Sake: The Life of Fannie Lou Hamer* (1999).
Mills, Kay. *This Little Light of Mine: The Life of Fannie Lou Hamer* (1993).
Payne, Charles M. *I've Got the Light of Freedom: The Organizing Tradition and the Mississippi Freedom Struggle* (1995).

Obituary: *Washington Post*, 17 and 19 Mar. 1977.

—MAMIE E. LOCKE

HAMMON, BRITON

(fl. 1747–1760), slave narrative author, wrote the earliest slave account published in North America. Practically nothing is known about him other than what he stated in the account of his life's events between 1747 and 1760. While living as a slave in New England in 1747, Hammon undertook a sea voyage that turned out to be a thirteen-year odyssey featuring numerous perils and repeated captures by American Indians and Spaniards. *A Narrative, of the Uncommon Sufferings, and Surprizing Deliverance of Briton Hammon, a Negro Man,—Servant to General Winslow, of Marshfield, in New-England, Who Returned to Boston, after Having Been Absent Almost Thirteen Years*, published as a fourteen-page pamphlet, was printed and sold in 1760 by Green and Russell, a Boston publishing firm that was bringing out popular Indian captivity narratives.

This remarkable story of sea adventures, treachery, and multiple captivities is believed to be the first autobiographical slave narrative on record. It is not clear whether Hammon's work was actually written by him. More than likely, it was dictated to a writer who faithfully transcribed the slave's spoken tale. The ungrammatical and plain style of the text and the lack of much editorializing in the main body of the account seem to indicate that Briton Hammon's words were written down almost exactly as he delivered them. However, the beginning and ending sections of the narrative do point to the probability that a white recorder stylistically embellished Hammon's work with traditional eighteenth-century religious statements and personal expressions of humility.

Hammon's journey commenced on the "25th Day of December, 1747," when, with his master's permission, the adventurous slave left Marshfield, Massachusetts, on a sea voyage. The next day he set sail from Plymouth on a ship bound for Jamaica and the "Bay" of Florida. After a month's journey, the ship arrived in Jamaica for a short stay and then sailed up the coast of Florida for the purpose of picking up "log wood." The vessel left Florida at the end of May, and in the middle of June it ran aground a short distance from shore, off "Cape-Florida." There, the captain's refusal to unload some of the cargo of wood so as to free the ship proved fatal. In two days' time a large group of Indians in canoes, flying the English colors as a ruse to trick the captain and his crew, attacked and murdered everyone on the ship except Hammon, who saved himself by jumping overboard. But the Indians soon took him out of the water, beat him, and told him they were going to roast him alive. However, much to Hammon's surprise, they treated him fairly well as their prisoner.

Hammon remained with the Indians for five weeks, until he managed to get to Cuba aboard a Spanish vessel whose captain he had previously met in Jamaica. The Indians pursued their escaped captive to Havana and demanded that he be returned to them. The governor of the island refused, but paid the Indians ten dollars to purchase Hammon. After working in the governor's castle for about a year, Hammon met up with a press gang that demanded he serve aboard a ship sailing to Spain. Upon his refusal, Hammon was put into a dungeon and held there for four years and seven months, during which time he tried without success to make the governor aware of his imprisonment.

Finally, through the efforts of friends, Hammon's situation came to the attention of the governor, who ordered him released and returned to his service. For the next several years Hammon worked for the governor in his castle and later for the bishop of Havana. During this time the long-suffering prisoner made three attempts to escape, and on the last one he succeeded. After a bit of difficulty he managed to be taken aboard an English ship that was about to sail for Jamaica and then on to London.

Upon his arrival in England, Hammon signed up for service on a succession of British naval vessels, one of which engaged in a battle with a

French warship. During this encounter he "was Wounded in the Head by a small Shot." After serving several months at sea, Hammon was discharged on 12 May 1759 to the Royal Hospital for Seamen at Greenwich, England, after "being disabled in the Arm." Hammon soon recovered, and over the next few months he worked as a cook on several ships. After suffering a bout of fever in London, Hammon signed aboard a vessel sailing for Boston. On the passage over the Atlantic Ocean he became delighted to learn that his "good Master" General Winslow, who had allowed Hammon to leave New England thirteen years before, was one of the passengers aboard ship. After the happy reunion, Winslow remarked that Hammon "was like one arose from the Dead, for he thought I had been Dead a great many Years, having heard nothing of me for almost Thirteen Years" (Hammon, 13).

At the ending of Hammon's narrative, he thanks the "Divine Goodness" for being "miraculously preserved and delivered out of many Dangers," and attests the fact that he has "not deviated from Truth" (Hammon, 14). The ending corresponds to the spiritual declaration at the beginning of his narrative, and both sections seem to be tacked on by someone else to give the story a religious framework. These, in addition to the many religious references Hammon himself inserts in his story, impart a spiritual autobiographical character to the work. The title of Hammon's book was similar to those of other published Indian captivity accounts, and at times his text seems to echo the phraseology and religious references of those accounts.

Hammon's work is believed to be the first of thousands of slave narratives written in America. His story follows the pattern of spiritual striving and of escape from physical captivity (in Hammon's case, Indian and Spanish bondage but not American slavery) that is an essential element of the many slave narratives that were published in the late eighteenth and early nineteenth centuries. In the immediate decades after Hammon's publication, there appeared several notable slave narratives including those by JAMES ALBERT UKAWSAW GRONNIOSAW (1772), OLAUDAH EQUIANO (1789), and Venture

Smith (1798). All that is known about Hammon's life after his return to New England in 1760 is that his short tale of captivity and escape became a well-known personal account in eighteenth-century America.

FURTHER READING

Hammon, Briton. *A Narrative, of the Uncommon Sufferings, and Surprising Deliverance of Briton Hammon, a Negro Man,—Servant to General Winslow, of Marshfield, in New-England, Who Returned to Boston, after Having Been Absent Almost Thirteen Years* (1760).

Andrews, William L. *To Tell a Free Story: The First Century of Afro-American Autobiography, 1760–1865* (1986).

Costanzo, Angelo. *Surprising Narrative: Olaudah Equiano and the Beginnings of Black Autobiography* (1987).

Foster, Frances Smith. *Witnessing Slavery: The Development of Ante-bellum Slave Narratives* (1979).

—ANGELO COSTANZO

HAMMON, JUPITER

(11 Oct. 1711–?), poet and preacher, was born on the estate of Henry Lloyd on Long Island, New York, most probably the son of Lloyd's slaves Rose and Opium, the latter renowned for his frequent escape attempts. Few records remain from Hammon's early life, though correspondence of the Lloyd family indicates that in 1730 he suffered from a near-fatal case of gout. He was educated by Nehemiah Bull, a Harvard graduate, and Daniel Denton, a British missionary, on the Lloyd manor. Except for a brief period during the revolutionary war, when Joseph Lloyd removed the family to Hartford, Connecticut, Hammon lived his entire life on Long Island, in the Huntington area, serving the Lloyds as clerk and bookkeeper. There is no surviving indication that Hammon either married or had children. The precise date of his death and the location of his grave remain unknown, although it is known that he was alive in 1790 and had died by 1806.

Hammon is best known for his skill as a poet and preacher. Early in the spiritual Great Awakening of the 1730s and 1740s he was converted to a Wesleyan Christianity, and his poems and sermons

reflect a Calvinist theology. Within the framework of these religious doctrines Hammon crafted a body of writing that critically investigates slavery. His first published poem, "An Evening Thought," appeared as a broadside on Christmas Day 1760. Imbedded within the religious exhortation is a subtle apocalyptic critique of slavery in which the narrator prays that Christ will free all men from imprisonment:

Now is the Day, excepted Time;
The Day of Salvation;
Increase your Faith, do not repine:
Awake ye every Nation.

The poem ends by calling on Jesus to "Salvation give" and to bring equality to all: "Let us with Angels share." Hammon couples a protest against earthly injustice with his religious conviction that all men are enslaved by sin.

Hammon's next publication, "An Address to Miss Phillis Wheatley," appeared in Hartford on 4 August 1778. The language of the poem offers PHILLIS WHEATLEY, then the most prominent African in America, spiritual—and thereby literary—advice. From the position of elder statesman Hammon attempts to correct what he sees as the pagan influences in Wheatley's verse:

Thou hast left the heathen shore;
Thro' mercy of the Lord,
Among the heathen live no more,
Come magnify thy God.

Psalm 34:1–3.

Typical of eighteenth-century American poetry, and primarily influenced by Michael Wigglesworth, Hammon's verse portrays America as a site for spiritual salvation since it is free of the corruption of the Old World. The poem seizes on biblical passages in order to fashion an argument that he hopes will convince Wheatley to write more religious verse. Hammon's next piece, *An Essay on the Ten Virgins*, advertised for sale in Hartford in 1779, is now lost.

Hammon exhorts his "brethren" to confess their sins and thus receive eternal salvation in his 1782 sermon *Winter Piece*. Its call to repentance and the proclamation of man's inherent sinfulness is consistent with other sermons of this era. Another prose essay, *An Evening's Improvement*, was printed in Hartford in 1783, and in it Hammon continues his protest against the institution of slavery. Published along with the sermon is Hammon's greatest poem, "A Dialogue, Entitled, the Kind Master and the Dutiful Servant," wherein he directly questions the unequal relationship between slave and master by emphasizing that before God, only sin divides Man:

Master
My Servant we must all appear,
And follow then our King;
For sure he'll stand where sinners are,
To take true converts in.
Servant
Dear master, now if Jesus calls,
And sends his summons in;
We'll follow saints and angels all,
And come unto our King.

The end of the poem disrupts the dialogue structure as the voice of the servant blends into that of the poet's. In the last seven stanzas Hammon instructs all in how to attain peace and harmony:

Believe me now my Christian friends,
Believe your friend call'd Hammon:
You cannot to your God attend,
And serve the God of Mammon.

Here Hammon argues that materialism (Mammon), a code for economic slavery, prohibits salvation because it leads an individual away from religious contemplation.

Hammon's final and most widely read piece, *An Address to the Negroes in the State of New-York*, was first printed in 1787 and then republished by the Pennsylvania Society for Promoting Abolition in 1806. In it Hammon speaks most directly against slavery. Within the body of his address Hammon argues that young African Americans should pursue their freedom even though he, at age seventy-six, does not want to be set free. Hammon calls for gradual emancipation: "Now I acknowledge that liberty is a great thing, and worth seeking for, if we can get it honestly; and by our good conduct prevail on our masters to set us free."

Hammon argues that earthly freedom is subordinate to spiritual salvation and that the need to be born again in the spirit of Christ overpowers all else, for in death "there are but two places where all go . . . white and black, rich and poor; those places are Heaven and Hell." Eternal judgment is what ultimately matters;

thus Hammon urges his fellow African Americans, in their pursuit of freedom, to seek forgiveness through repentance and to place spiritual salvation above mortal concerns.

Hammon remained unknown from the early nineteenth century until 1915, when literary critic Oscar Wegelin, who rediscovered Hammon in 1904, published the first biographical information on him as well as some of his poetry. Although Hammon apparently was not the first African American writer (evidence suggests he was predated by one Lucy Terry poem), his canon makes him one of America's first significant African American writers.

FURTHER READING

Blackshire-Belay, Carol Aisha, ed. *Language and Literature in the African American Imagination* (1992).
Inge, M. Thomas, et al., eds., *Black American Writers*, vol. 1 (1978).
O'Neale, Sondra A. *Jupiter Hammon and the Biblical Beginnings of African American Literature* (1993).
Ransom, Stanley Austin, Jr., ed. *America's First Negro Poet: The Complete Works of Jupiter Hammon of Long Island* (1970).
Wegelin, Oscar. *Jupiter Hammon: American Negro Poet* (1915).

—DUNCAN F. FAHERTY

HANDY, W. C. (16 Nov. 1873–28 Mar. 1958), blues musician and composer, was born William Christopher Handy in Florence, Alabama, the son of Charles Bernard Handy, a minister, and Elizabeth Brewer. Handy was raised in an intellectual, middle-class atmosphere, as befitted a minister's son. He studied music in public school, then attended the all-black Teachers' Agricultural and Mechanical College in Huntsville. After graduation he worked as a teacher and, briefly, in an iron mill. A love of the cornet led to semiprofessional work as a musician, and by the early 1890s he was performing with a traveling minstrel troupe known as Mahara's Minstrels; by mid-decade, he was promoted to bandleader of the group. Handy married Elizabeth Virginia Price in 1898. They had five children.

It was on one of the group's tours, according to Handy, in the backwater Mississippi town of Clarksdale, that he first heard a traditional blues musician. His own training was limited to the light classics, marches, and early ragtime music of the day, but something about this performance, by guitarist CHARLEY PATTON, intrigued him. After a brief retirement from touring in 1900–1902 to return to teaching at his alma mater, Handy formed his first of many bands and went on the road once more. A second incident during an early band tour cemented Handy's interest in blues-based music. In 1905, while playing at a local club, the Handy band was asked if they would be willing to take a break to allow a local string band to perform. This ragged group's attempts at music making amused the more professional musicians in Handy's band until they saw the stage flooded with change thrown spontaneously by audience members and realized that the amateurs would take home more money that night than they would. Handy began collecting folk blues and writing his own orchestrations of them.

By 1905 Handy had settled in Memphis, Tennessee. He was asked in 1907 by mayoral candidate E. H. "Boss" Crump to write a campaign song to mobilize the black electorate. The song, "Mr. Crump," became a local hit and was published five years later under a new name, "The Memphis Blues." It was followed two years later by his biggest hit, "The St. Louis Blues." Both songs were actually ragtime-influenced vocal numbers with a number of sections and related to the traditional folk blues only in their use of "blue" notes (flatted thirds and sevenths) and the themes of their lyrics. Many of his verses were borrowed directly from the traditional "floating" verses long associated with folk blues, such as the opening words of "St. Louis Blues": "I hate to see that evening sun go down." In the mid-1920s early jazz vocalist BESSIE SMITH recorded "St. Louis Blues," making it a national hit.

In 1917 Handy moved to New York, where he formed a new band, his own music-publishing operation, and a short-lived record label. He was an important popularizer of traditional blues songs, publishing the influential *Blues: An Anthology* in 1926 (which was reprinted and revised in 1949 and again after Handy's death in 1972) and *Collection of Negro Spirituals* in 1939. Besides his work promoting the blues, he also was a champion of "Negro" composers and musicians, writing several books arguing that their musical skills equaled that of their white counterparts. In 1941 he published his autobiography, *Father of the Blues*, a not altogether reliable story of his early years as a musician.

By the late 1940s Handy's eyesight and health were failing. In the 1950s he made one recording performing his blues songs, showing himself to be a rather limited vocalist by this time of his life, and one narrative recording with his daughter performing his songs. His first wife had died in 1937; he was married again in 1954, to Irma Louise Logan. He died in New York City. His autobiography was reissued after his death. In 1979 the W. C. Handy Blues Awards were established, to recognize excellence in blues recordings.

Handy may not have "fathered" the blues, as he claimed, nor did he write true "blues" songs of the type that were performed by country blues musicians. But he did write one of the most popular songs of the twentieth century, which introduced blues tonalities and themes to popular music. His influence on stage music and jazz was profound; "St. Louis Blues" remains one of the most frequently recorded of all jazz pieces.

FURTHER READING

Handy, W. C. *Father of the Blues: An Autobiography* (1941; repr. 1991).

Dickerson, James. *Goin' Back to Memphis: A Century of Blues, Rock 'n' Roll, and Glorious Soul* (1996).

Southern, Eileen. *The Music of Black Americans: A History* (1971; repr. 1983).
—RICHARD CARLIN

HANSBERRY, LORRAINE VIVIAN

(19 May 1930–12 Jan. 1965), playwright, was born in Chicago, Illinois, the daughter of Carl Augustus Hansberry, a real estate agent, and Nannie Perry, a schoolteacher. Throughout her childhood, Lorraine Hansberry's home was visited by many distinguished blacks, including PAUL ROBESON, DUKE ELLINGTON, and her uncle, the Africanist William Leo Hansberry, who helped

inspire her enthusiasm for African history. In 1938, to challenge real-estate covenants against blacks, Hansberry's father moved the family into a white neighborhood where a mob gathered and threw bricks, one of which nearly hit Lorraine. Two years later, after he won his case on the matter of covenants before the Supreme Court, they continued in practice. Embittered by U.S. racism, Carl Hansberry planned to relocate his family in Mexico in 1946 but died before the move.

After studying drama and stage design at the University of Wisconsin from 1948 to 1950, Hansberry went to New York and began writing for Robeson's newspaper *Freedom*. She also marched on picket lines, made speeches on street corners, and helped move furniture back into evicted tenants' apartments. In 1953 she married Robert Nemiroff, an aspiring writer and graduate student in English and history whom she had met on a picket line at New York University. Soon afterward, she quit full-time work at *Freedom* to concentrate on her writing, though she had to do part-time work at various jobs until the success of Nemiroff and Burt D'Lugoff's song "Cindy, Oh Cindy" in 1956 freed her financially to write full-time. She also studied African history under W. E. B. Du BOIS at the Jefferson School for Social Science.

In 1957 Hansberry read a draft of *A Raisin in the Sun* to Philip Rose, a music publisher friend, who decided to produce it. Opening on Broadway in 1959, it earned the New York Drama Critic's Circle Award for Best Play, making Hansberry the youngest American, first woman, and first black to win the award. This play about the Youngers, a black family with differing personalities and dreams who are united in racial pride and their fight against mutual poverty, has become a classic.

Although Hansberry enjoyed her new celebrity status, she used her many interviews to speak out about the oppression of African Americans and the social changes that she deemed essential. Her private life, however, remained painful and complex. Shortly after her marriage, her lesbianism emerged, leading to conflicts with her husband and within herself, difficulties exacerbated by the widespread homophobia that infected even the otherwise progressive social

Lorraine Hansberry, whose play A Raisin in the Sun *has become a classic of American drama.* Library of Congress

movements she supported. At some point amid her public triumph, she and Nemiroff separated, though their mutual interests and mutual respect later reunited them.

In 1960 she wrote two screenplays of *A Raisin in the Sun* that would have creatively used the cinematic medium, but Columbia Pictures preferred a less controversial version that was closer to the original. Accepting a commission from NBC for a slavery drama to commemorate the Civil War centennial, Hansberry wrote *The Drinking Gourd*, but this too was rejected as controversial. During this busy year she began research for an opera titled *Toussaint* and a play about Mary Wollstonecraft; started writing her African play, *Les Blancs*; and began the play that evolved into *The Sign in Sidney Brustein's Window*. In 1961 the film *A Raisin in the Sun* won a special award at the Cannes Film Festival.

In 1962 Hansberry wrote her post-atomic-war play, *What Use Are Flowers?*, while publicly denouncing the House Un-American Activities Committee and the Cuban "missile crisis" and mobilizing support for the Student Nonviolent Coordinating Committee (SNCC). The following year, she began suffering from cancer but continued her support for SNCC and, at JAMES BALDWIN's invitation, participated in a discussion about the country's racial crisis with Attorney General Robert Kennedy.

During 1964 she and Nemiroff divorced, but because of her illness they only told their closest friends and saw each other daily, continuing their creative collaboration until her death. She named Nemiroff her literary executor in her will. From April to October 1964 she was in and out of the hospital for therapy but managed to deliver her "To Be Young, Gifted and Black" speech to winners of the United Negro College Fund writing contest and to participate in the Town Hall debate on "The Black Revolution and the White Backlash." In October she moved to a hotel near the site of rehearsals of *The Sign in Sidney Brustein's Window* and attended its opening night. Despite its mixed reviews, actors and supporters from various backgrounds united to keep the play running until Hansberry's death in New York City.

FURTHER READING

The Hansberry Archives, which include unpublished plays, screenplays, essays, letters, diaries, and two drafts of an uncompleted novel, are held at the Schomburg Center for Research in Black Culture of the New York Public Library.

Carter, Steven R. *Hansberry's Drama: Commitment amid Complexity* (1991).
Cheney, Anne. *Lorraine Hansberry* (1984).
Nemiroff, Robert. *To Be Young, Gifted and Black: Lorraine Hansberry in Her Own Words* (1969).

—STEVEN R. CARTER

HARPER, FRANCES ELLEN WATKINS

(24 Sept. 1825–20 Feb. 1911) poet, novelist, activist, and orator, was born Frances Ellen Watkins to free parents in Baltimore, Maryland. Her parents' names remain unknown. Orphaned by the age of three, Watkins is believed to have been raised by her uncle, the Reverend William Watkins, a leader in the African Methodist Episcopal Church and a contributor to such abolitionist newspapers as *Freedom's Journal* and the *Liberator*. Most important for Watkins, her uncle was also the founder of the William Watkins Academy for Negro Youth, where she studied. A well-known and highly regarded school, the academy's curriculum included

elocution, composition, Bible study, mathematics, and history. The school also emphasized social responsibility and political leadership. Although Watkins withdrew from formal schooling at the age of thirteen to begin work as a domestic servant, her studies at the academy no doubt shaped her political activism, oratorical skills, and creative writing.

After leaving school, Watkins worked as a seamstress and as a child caretaker for a family who owned a bookstore. While in their employ, she continued her studies independently, reading liberally from her employers' book stock. Watkins's first poetry appeared in local newspapers while she was still a teenager. In 1846, at the age of twenty-one, she published her first book, a collection of prose and poetry entitled

Forest Leaves. No known copy of *Forest Leaves* has survived, though the scholar Frances Smith Foster has speculated that the volume probably contained poems and prose on subjects as varied as "religious values, women's rights, social reform, biblical history and current events" (Foster, 8).

Although Watkins had the advantage of a better education than that of many of her peers, she was not immune to the racial hostilities of the antebellum years. The Compromise of 1850 complicated the lives of Watkins and her family. Among the many components of this federal legislation was the Fugitive Slave Act, which required that all citizens participate in the recovery of slaves and imposed severe penalties on those who refused. The family lived in the precarious position of being free

Frances Ellen Watkins Harper, poet and novelist, campaigned for equal rights throughout much of the nineteenth century. Schomburg Center

blacks in Maryland, a slave state, at a time when federal legislation increasingly challenged black freedom. This undoubtedly shaped Watkins's feelings that all blacks—slave and free, wealthy or poor—had a duty to the welfare of their fellow African Americans, a theme that emerges frequently in her literature.

In 1850 Watkins's family was forced by local officials to disband their elite school for blacks and sell their home. Watkins moved to Ohio and began working as a teacher at the Union Seminary near Columbus. Why she chose to go to Ohio while some of her family members remained in Baltimore and others relocated to Canada is unknown. But in 1853 the state of Maryland forbade free blacks to enter the state. The penalty was enslavement. During this period in which Watkins was unable to return to her home state, a free black man was arrested and enslaved for entering Maryland. The man died soon after the ordeal. In a letter to WILLIAM STILL, Watkins cast this man's death as the beginning of her own commitment to abolitionism: "Upon that grave I pledged myself to the Anti-Slavery cause" (Still, 786).

Soon after this incident in Maryland, Watkins moved to Philadelphia, where she lived in a home that functioned as an Underground Railroad station, one of a series of homes used to assist fugitive slaves in their escape. While there, she published several poems in response to Harriet Beecher Stowe's *Uncle Tom's Cabin*: "Eliza Harris," "To Harriet Beecher Stowe," and "Eva's Farewell." The poems appear to have been widely circulated. "Eliza Harris" appeared in at least three national papers. Building on the pathos of Stowe's representation of the escape of the nearly white slave Eliza, Watkins makes the national implications of Eliza's condition explicit:

Oh shall I speak of my proud
    country's shame?
Of the stains on her glory, how give them
    their name?
How say that her banner in
    mockery waves—
Her "star spangled banner"—o'er millions
    of slaves?

                (Foster, 61)

In 1854 Watkins initiated her career as a public speaker in New Bedford, Massachusetts, delivering a lecture

entitled "The Education and the Elevation of the Colored Race." Soon after, she was enlisted as a traveling lecturer for the Maine Antislavery Society and became an admired and much sought after lecturer. In a letter that same year, Watkins reports lecturing every night of the week, sometimes more than once in a day, to audiences as large as six hundred people. In a period of six weeks in the fall of 1854 she gave thirty-three lectures in twenty-one cities and towns. Contemporary newspaper accounts describe her as an eloquent and moving speaker. The *Portland Advertiser*, for example, characterized her lectures by saying that "the deep fervor of feeling and pathos that she manifests, together with the choice selection of language which she uses arm her elocution with almost superhuman force and power over her spellbound audience" (Boyd, 43). Also in 1854 Watkins published *Poems on Miscellaneous Subjects*, which included poems on antislavery and equal rights. It appears that the publisher was confident that the book would be well received. Y. B. Yerrington and Sons of Boston published the book in Philadelphia and Boston. Both editions were reprinted in 1855, and by 1857 the publisher claimed that they had sold ten thousand copies of the book.

In 1860 Watkins married Fenton Harper, and together they purchased a farm outside Columbus, Ohio. The couple had a daughter, Mary. Although little is known about the marriage, Foster has described this period as a "semi-retirement" from Watkins's public life (18). Soon after her husband's death in 1864, Harper returned to New England and resumed her lectures. After the Civil War, she began lecturing in the South. She was particularly concerned with the future of the newly freed people. This trip would greatly influence Harper's literature. Three of her books, in particular, are concerned with Reconstruction efforts: a serialized novel, *Minnie's Sacrifice* (1869); a book of poetry, *Sketches of Southern Life* (1871); and her most famous novel, *Iola Leroy* (1896).

Significantly, the vision of a new nation that emerges in Harper's literature is not only one of racial equality but also one in which gender equality is represented as crucial to the fulfillment of the American creed of liberty. Harper participated in many

women's organizations, including the American Women's Suffrage Association, the National Council of Women, the Women's Christian Temperance Union, and the First Congress of Colored Women in the United States. Her status as both a woman and an African American, however, placed her in a complicated position, particularly as early white feminists, such as Susan B. Anthony and Lucretia Mott, used racist propaganda to assert the importance of women's suffrage over black male suffrage.

Harper, along with FREDERICK DOUGLASS, participated in the 1869 American Equal Rights Association meeting to debate the proposed Fifteenth Amendment, which would grant suffrage to black men. Harper supported the vote for black men: "When I was at Boston there were sixty women who left work because one colored woman went to gain a livelihood in their midst. If the nation could handle one question I would not have the black woman put a single straw in the way if only the men of the race could obtain what they wanted." (Boyd, 128). Harper continued her activism on behalf of African American and women's rights well into the 1890s, becoming the vice president of the National Council of Negro Women, which she had helped found in 1896.

Little is known about Harper between 1901 and her death in Philadelphia in 1911. Indeed, though she was a well-known public figure throughout much of the nineteenth century, many of the details of her life and work remain unknown. The rediscovery in the early 1990s of three of her novels—*Minnie's Sacrifice* (1869), *Sowing and Reaping* (1876–1877), and *Trial and Triumph* (1888–1889)—all published in the African Methodist Episcopal Church periodical the *Christian Recorder*, suggests that there is probably much more to know about the life and career of one of the most prolific and popular black writer of the nineteenth century.

FURTHER READING

Frances E. W. Harper's papers are housed at the Moorland-Spingarn Research Center of Howard University and at the Schomburg Center for Research in Black Culture of the New York Public Library.

Boyd, Melba Joyce. *Discarded Legacy: Politics and Poetics in the Life of Frances E. W. Harper 1825–1911* (1994).

Foster, Frances Smith. "Introduction" in *A Brighter Coming Day: A Frances Ellen Watkins Harper Reader* (1990).

Still, William. *The Underground Rail Road* (1872).

—CASSANDRA JACKSON

HARRINGTON, OLIVER W. (14 Feb. 1912–2 Nov. 1995), cartoonist, was born Oliver Wendell Harrington in New York City, the son of Herbert Harrington, a porter, and Euzenie Turat. His father came to New York from North Carolina in the early 1900s when many African Americans were seeking greater opportunities in the North. His mother had immigrated to America, arriving from Austria-Hungary in 1907, to join her half sister. Ollie Harrington grew up in a multiethnic neighborhood in the south Bronx and attended public schools. He recalled a home life burdened by the stresses of his parents' interracial marriage and the financial struggles of raising five children. From an early age, he drew cartoons to ease those tensions.

In 1927 Harrington enrolled at Textile High School in Manhattan. He was voted best artist in his class and started a club whose members studied popular newspaper cartoonists. Exposure to the work of Art Young, Denys Wortman, and Daniel Fitzpatrick later influenced his style and technique. About that time, toward the end of the Harlem Renaissance, he began to spend considerable time in Harlem and became active in social groups there. Following his graduation from Textile in 1931, he attended the National Academy of Design school. There he met such renowned artists and teachers as Charles L. Hinton, Leon Kroll, and Gifford Beal. During his years at the Academy, Harrington supported himself by drawing cartoons and working as a set designer, actor, and puppeteer.

In 1932 he published political cartoons and *Razzberry Salad*, a comic panel satirizing Harlem society. They appeared in the *National News*, a newspaper established by the Democratic party organization in Harlem, which folded after only four months. He then joined the Harlem Newspaper Club and was introduced to reporters such as Ted Poston, Henry Lee Moon, and Roi Ottley of the *Amsterdam News*, as well as Bessye Bearden of the *Chicago*

Cartoonist, journalist, and expatriate Oliver W. Harrington was best known for *Bootsie*, a cartoon character in an urban black community, and an African American aviator named *Jive Gray*. The Walter O. Evans collection

Defender and her son ROMARE BEARDEN. In 1933, Harrington submitted cartoons to the *Amsterdam News* on a freelance basis. During the next two years, he also attended art classes at New York University with his friend Romare Bearden. In May 1935, he joined the staff of the *News* and created *Dark Laughter*, soon renamed *Bootsie* after its main character, a comic panel that he would draw for more than thirty-five years. Harrington remarked that "I simply recorded the almost unbelievable but hilarious chaos around me and came up with a character" (*Freedomways* 3, 519).

When the Newspaper Guild struck the *News* in October 1935, Harrington, while not a guild member, supported the strike and would not publish his cartoons until it was settled. During the strike, he became friends with journalists BENJAMIN JEFFERSON DAVIS JR. (later a New York City councilman)

and Marvel Cooke, who were members of the Communist Party. While probably not a party member, he maintained active ties to the left from that time. Harrington soon returned to freelance work and taught art in a WPA program. Edward Morrow, a Harlem reporter and graduate of Yale University, and Bessye Bearden encouraged him to apply to the School of the Fine Arts at Yale, which accepted him in 1936. Supporting himself with his *Bootsie* cartoons (which he transferred to the larger circulation *Pittsburgh Courier* in 1938), scholarship assistance, and waiting on tables at fraternities, Harrington received a Bachelor of Fine Arts degree in 1940. He won several prizes for his paintings, although not a prestigious traveling fellowship at graduation, which he believed was denied him because of his race.

In 1942, after working for the National Youth Administration for a year,

Harrington became art editor for a new Harlem newspaper, the *People's Voice*, edited by ADAM CLAYTON POWELL JR. He also created a new comic strip, *Live Gray*. In 1943 and 1944 he took a leave from the *Voice* to serve as a war correspondent for the *Pittsburgh Courier*. While covering African American troops, including the Tuskegee Airmen, in Italy and France, he witnessed racism in the military to a degree he had not experienced before. In Italy he met WALTER WHITE, executive secretary of the National Association for the Advancement of Colored People (NAACP).

In 1946 White, who was attempting to strengthen the NAACP's public relations department following racial violence against returning veterans, hired Harrington as director of public relations. But by late 1947 the two had become estranged and Harrington resigned to become more active politically. With the *Bootsie* cartoons and book illustration work again his principal source of income, and after ending a brief wartime marriage, he joined a number of political committees in support of the American Labor Party and Communists arrested in violation of the Smith Act. In 1950 he became art editor of *Freedom*, a monthly newspaper founded by Louis Burnham and PAUL ROBESON. He also taught art at the Jefferson School for Social Sciences, a school that appeared on the Attorney General's list of subversive organizations. Informed of his ties to the school, the FBI opened a file on Harrington.

By early 1952, with some of his friends under indictment and others facing revocation of their passports, Harrington left the United States for France. Whether he had knowledge of the FBI investigation is unclear, but by the time he reached Paris, the Passport Office there had been instructed to seize his passport if the opportunity arose. Meanwhile, Harrington settled into a life centered around the Café Tournon with a group of expatriate artists and writers that included RICHARD WRIGHT and CHESTER HIMES. Himes called Harrington the "best raconteur I'd ever known." His *Bootsie* cartoons and illustration work continued to provide income and he traveled throughout Europe. For a short time, following a brief second marriage in 1955, he settled in England,

but he returned to Paris in 1956 as the Algerian War was worsening. The war divided the African American community, and Harrington became embroiled in a series of disputes with other expatriates. His visit to the Soviet Union in 1959 as a guest of the humor magazine *Krokodil* again attracted intelligence officials.

Saddened by the death of his close friend Richard Wright, and his income dwindling due to financial difficulties at the *Courier*, in 1961 Harrington traveled to East Berlin for a book illustration project and soon settled there for the remainder of his life. He submitted cartoons to *Das Magasin* and *Eulenspiegel* and in 1968 became an editorial cartoonist for the *Daily Worker*, later *People's Weekly World*. His press credentials enabled him to travel to the West, and many of his old friends, including Paul Robeson and LANGSTON HUGHES, visited him in East Germany. In 1972 Harrington returned for a brief visit to the United States; in the 1990s he visited more regularly. In 1994, after the publication of two books of his cartoons and articles raised interest in his work, he was appointed journalist-in-residence for a semester at Michigan State University. He died in East Berlin. He was survived by his third wife, Helma Richter, and four children: a daughter from his second marriage, a son from his third, and two daughters from relationships with women to whom he was not married. Harrington's complex personal life, as well as his politics, was sometimes a motive for his travels.

Harrington was often referred to as a "self-exile," but he never described himself that way. "I'm fairly well convinced that one is an exile only when one is not allowed to live in reasonable peace and dignity as a human being among other human beings" (*Why I Left America*, 66). Remembered as the premier cartoonist of the African American press for three decades and a central figure in the expatriate community in Paris in the 1950s, he battled racism through his art, his writings, and an alter ego named *Bootsie*.

FURTHER READING

Inge, M. Thomas, ed. *Dark Laughter: The Satiric Art of Oliver W. Harrington* (1993).
———. *Why I Left America and Other Essays* (1993).

Stovall, Tyler. *Paris Noir: African Americans in the City of Light* (1996).

Obituary: *New York Times*, 7 Nov. 1995.
—CHRISTINE G. McKAY

 HARRIS, BARBARA
(12 June 1930–), Episcopal bishop, was born Barbara Clementine Harris in Philadelphia, Pennsylvania, the middle child of Walter Harris, a steelworker, and Beatrice Price, who worked as a program officer for the Boys and Girls Club of Philadelphia and later for the Bureau of Vital Statistics for the Commonwealth of Pennsylvania. Barbara was born the day after St. Barnabas Day, and her family attended St. Barnabas Church; hence they named her Barbara.

Barbara graduated from the Philadelphia High School for Girls in 1948 and then attended the Charles Morris Price School of Advertising and Journalism. Upon completion of the program, she began a twenty-year career as a public relations consultant for Joseph V. Baker Associates, a black-owned national public relations firm headquartered in Philadelphia, eventually becoming president of the company. While in this office, she entered into a brief marriage, which ended in divorce. In 1968 Sun Oil recruited her as a community relations consultant. She stayed with Sun Oil for twelve years, rising to the position of manager of their public relations department. Her career was groundbreaking, and she worked hard to dismantle barriers for both women and African Americans in a predominately white male profession.

Harris, however, found her life's work not in the corporate world, but in the church. Always active in her church, she taught Sunday school and sang in the choir. She brought her friends to church with her no matter how late they had stayed out on Saturday night. She encouraged the parish of St. Barnabas to start a youth group and later initiated and took charge of a group for young adults. For fifteen years she volunteered with the St. Dismas Society, visiting prisons to conduct services on weekends and to counsel and befriend prisoners. During the summer of 1964 she helped register black voters in Mississippi, and the following year she took part in the march led by MARTIN LUTHER KING JR. from Selma to Montgomery, Alabama.

Even in the church Harris witnessed and experienced discrimination, and she came to recognize the need for change. In 1968 the General Convention of the Episcopal Church called a special convention in South Bend, Indiana, to address the concerns of African Americans in the church. As a direct result of the efforts of that convention, which Harris attended, the church began a long—and still unfinished—journey toward eliminating discrimination in the church.

In 1968 Harris transferred her membership to the more activist Episcopal Church of the Advocate in North Philadelphia. The rector, the Reverend Paul Washington, was a staunch fighter for justice who believed that the church should be the vehicle for transformation in the community. In the 1960s he hosted several controversial meetings, including an August 1968 Black Power convention that included such leading activists as STOKELY CARMICHAEL and H. RAP BROWN and that drew both thousands of people and the attention of the FBI.

On 29 July 1974 Harris led the procession into the Church of the Advocate for the controversial ordination into the priesthood of eleven women, "the Philadelphia Eleven." Two years later, after intense debate, the ordination of women as priests was sanctioned by the General Convention of the Episcopal Church. Harris soon began to hear the call to ordination herself. Because she could not just leave her career to attend seminary on a full-time basis, the Diocese of Pennsylvania made arrangements for her to attend classes at Villanova University from 1977 to 1979, and to study with clergy in the area. After several years she took the General Ordination Examinations required of all seminary graduates and passed with flying colors. She was ordained a deacon in 1979 and a priest in 1980.

After her ordination Harris served at the Church of the Advocate and then spent four years as priest in charge at the Church of St. Augustine of Hippo, in the Philadelphia suburb of Norristown, breathing new life into a congregation that had been moribund and on the verge of closing. During this period she also served as a chaplain to the Philadelphia County Prison, continuing her ministry to prisoners, giving particular attention to the "lifers," the longterm prisoners who seldom had visitors and were largely forgotten. In 1984 Harris became the executive director of the Episcopal Church Publishing Company. The primary publication of the company was *The Witness*, a liberal magazine with a history of speaking out on current issues. Harris proved to be a catalyst for the magazine's emphasis on issues of racism, sexism, classism, and heterosexism, both in the church and in society. Harris regularly contributed a hard-hitting, outspoken column entitled "*A Luta Continua*" ("The Struggle Continues"), which brought her to the attention of a national and international audience.

In the spring of 1987 the Diocese of Massachusetts held a conference on women in the episcopate, with many ordained women in attendance. Harris was one of the speakers and made a great impact on all those who were present. The following spring the diocese began the process of identifying those clergy who would stand for election later that year as suffragan bishop, an assistant to the diocesan bishop, and there was talk of adding women to the list of candidates. The Episcopal Church met in convention and tried to pass a resolution to appease those opposed to the election of a woman bishop, but when the Diocese of Massachusetts released the names of the candidates, Barbara Harris was one of two women on the list. That summer the Archbishop of Canterbury hosted the Lambeth Conference, a gathering of Anglican bishops held every ten years. There was much concern and debate over the Massachusetts election, for fear that electing a woman might cause a division in the Anglican Communion and endanger ecumenical relations with the Roman Catholic Church.

Harris went to the Lambeth Conference as a member of the press corps in her role with the Episcopal Church Publishing Company and was continually bombarded by participants and the other press members. To some she became a symbol of all that was wrong with the Episcopal Church, or at least with its "liberal" element. Objections to Harris's election were raised on a number of fronts—her nontraditional education and theological training, her status as divorced (an objection not raised in regard to males also being considered), her liberal social activism—but certainly the greatest impediment in the minds of many was simply the fact that she was a woman. The conference, however, ultimately allowed for the consecration of women by ruling that national churches had the right to choose their own bishops.

The Massachusetts election took place on Saturday, 25 September 1988, and Harris was stunned and surprised to be elected on the fifth ballot. Her strength and her faith were now going to be tested. The next step was for a majority of Episcopal dioceses to consent to the election. Although this was nominally a vote on whether the election was in accord with the church constitution, it was in reality based on the person and not the process. Harris's credentials, her qualifications, and her writings were again questioned. However, consent was obtained, and she subsequently got the necessary number of votes in the House of Bishops.

Harris was consecrated bishop on 11 February 1989. The day was glorious; Boston's Hynes Auditorium was packed with over eight thousand clergy and laypeople, representing the diversity and breadth of the Episcopal Church. As was expected, there were formal protests during the service. After the protests, Harris's mother walked over to her and said, "Don't worry, baby, everything will be all right. God and I are on your side." The Right Reverend Barbara Clementine Harris served as suffragan bishop in Massachusetts for over thirteen years, consistently carrying out her ministry of compassion, healing, and reconciliation and always speaking out for justice on behalf of the marginalized in our society. Harris has received sixteen honorary doctorate degrees from a broad range of colleges, universities, and seminaries and has traveled around the world sharing the good news. After retiring in November 2002, she agreed to serve part-time in the Diocese of Washington as an assisting bishop.

The debate over the role of women in the church grows quiet at times, but it has not gone away. The role of women was again called into question at the 1998 Lambeth Conference, which also saw heated discussions on homosexuality. The specter of schism in the Episcopal Church in the United States was again raised at the General Convention in 2003 in the debate over the confirmation of the openly gay canon Gene Robinson as bishop of New Hampshire. At the convention, Harris reminded those present of the similar fears felt in 1989 and pointed out that the Anglican Communion remains intact. Delivering a sermon in her home parish the day after her own election as bishop in 1988, Harris expressed in metaphor the significance of that event, a metaphor that, applied more broadly, captures the difficulty of bringing about change in the face of long-standing beliefs and attitudes: "A fresh wind is indeed blowing. We have seen in this year alone some things thought to be impossible just a short time ago. To some, the changes are refreshing breezes. For others, they are as fearsome as a hurricane."

FURTHER READING

Bozzuti-Jones, Mark Francisco. *The Mitre Fits Just Fine: A Story about the Rt. Rev. Barbara Clementine Harris, Suffragan Bishop, Diocese of Massachusetts* (2003).

—NAN PEETE

HARRISON, HUBERT HENRY (27 Apr. 1883–17 Dec. 1927), radical political activist and journalist, was born in Concordia, St. Croix, Danish West Indies (now U.S. Virgin Islands), the son of William Adolphus Harrison and Cecilia Elizabeth Haines. Little is known of his father. His mother had at least three other children and, in 1889, married a laborer. Harrison received a primary education in St. Croix. In September 1900, after his mother died, he immigrated to New York City, where he worked low-paying jobs, attended evening high school, did some writing, editing, and lecturing, and read voraciously. In 1907 he obtained postal employment and moved to Harlem. The following year he taught at the White Rose Home, where he was deeply influenced by social worker Frances Reynolds Keyser, a future founder of the NAACP. In 1909 he married Irene Louise Horton, with whom he had five children.

Between 1901 and 1908 Harrison broke "from orthodox and institutional Christianity" and became an "Agnostic." His new worldview placed humanity at the center and emphasized rationalism and modern science. He also participated in black intellectual circles, particularly church lyceums, where forthright criticism and debate were the norm and where his racial awareness was stimulated by scholars such as bibliophile ARTHUR SCHOMBURG and journalist John E. Bruce. History, free thought, and social and literary criticism appealed to him, as did the protest philosophy of W. E. B. DU BOIS over the more "subservient" one of BOOKER T. WASHINGTON. Readings in economics and single taxism and a favorable view of the Socialist Party's position on women drew him toward socialism. Then in 1911, after writing letters critical of Washington in the *New York Sun*, he lost his postal job through the efforts of Washington's associates and turned to Socialist Party work.

From 1911 to 1914 Harrison was the leading black in the Socialist Party of New York, where he insisted on the centrality of the race question to U.S. socialism; served as a prominent party lecturer, writer, campaigner, organizer, instructor, and theoretician; briefly edited the socialist monthly the *Masses*; and was elected as a delegate to one state and two city conventions. His series on "The Negro and Socialism" (*New York Call*, 1911) and on "Socialism and the Negro" (*International Socialist Review*, 1912) advocated that socialists champion the cause of the Negro as a revolutionary doctrine, develop a special appeal to Negroes, and affirm their duty to oppose race prejudice. He also initiated the Colored Socialist Club (CSC), a pioneering effort by U.S. socialists at organizing blacks. After the party withdrew support for the CSC, and after racist pronouncements by some Socialist Party leaders during debate on Asian immigration, he concluded that socialist leaders put the white "Race First and class after."

Harrison believed "the crucial test of Socialism's sincerity" was "the Negro," and he was attracted to the egalitarian practices and direct action principles of the Industrial Workers of the World (IWW). He defended the IWW and spoke at the 1913 Paterson

Hubert Henry Harrison, "The Father of Harlem Radicalism." Schomburg Center

Silk Strike with Elizabeth Gurley Flynn and "Big Bill" Haywood. Although he was a renowned socialist orator, and was described by author Henry Miller as without peer on a soapbox, Socialist Party leaders moved to restrict his speaking.

Undaunted, Harrison left the Socialist Party in 1914 and over the next few years established the tradition of street corner oratory in Harlem. He first developed his own "Radical Lecture Forum," which included citywide indoor and outdoor talks on free thought, evolution, literature, religion, birth control, and the racial aspects of World War I. Then, after teaching at the Modern School, writing theater reviews, and selling books, he started the "Harlem People's Forum," at which he urged blacks to emphasize "Race First."

In 1917, as war raged abroad, along with race riots, lynchings, and discrimination at home, Harrison founded the Liberty League and *The Voice*, the first organization and newspaper of the militant "New Negro" movement. He explained that the league was called into being by "the need for a more radical policy than that of the NAACP" (*Voice*, 7 Nov. 1917) and that the "New Negro" movement represented "a breaking away of the Negro masses from the grip of the old-time leaders" (*Voice*, 4 July 1917). Harrison stressed that the new black leadership would emerge from the masses and would not be chosen by whites (as in the era of Washington's leadership), nor be based in the "Talented Tenth of the Negro race" (as advocated by Du Bois). The league's program was directed to the "common people" and emphasized internationalism, political independence, and class and race consciousness. *The Voice* called for a "race first" approach, full equality, federal antilynching legislation, labor organizing, support of socialist and anti-imperialist causes, and armed self-defense in the face of racist attacks.

Harrison was a major influence on a generation of class and race radicals, from socialist A. PHILIP RANDOLPH to MARCUS GARVEY. The Liberty League developed the core progressive ideas, basic program, and leaders utilized by Garvey, and Harrison claimed that, from the league, "Garvey appropriated every feature that was worthwhile in his movement." Over the next few years Garvey would build what Harrison described as the largest mass movement of blacks "since slavery was abolished"—a movement that grew, according to Harrison, as it emphasized "racialism, race consciousness, racial solidarity—the ideas first taught by the Liberty League and *The Voice*."

The Voice stopped publishing in November 1917, and Harrison next organized hotel and restaurant workers for the American Federation of Labor. He also rejoined, and then left, the Socialist Party and chaired the Colored National Liberty Congress that petitioned the U.S. Congress for federal antilynching legislation and articulated militant wartime demands for equality. In July 1918 he resurrected *The Voice* with influential editorials critical of Du Bois, who had urged blacks to "Close Ranks" behind the wartime program of President Woodrow Wilson. Harrison's attempts to make *The Voice* a national paper and bring it into the South failed in 1919. Later that year he edited the *New Negro*, "an organ of the international consciousness of the darker races."

In January 1920 Harrison became principal editor of the *Negro World*, the newspaper of Garvey's Universal Negro Improvement Association (UNIA). He reshaped the entire paper and developed it into the preeminent radical, race-conscious, political, and literary publication of the era. As editor, writer, and occasional speaker, Harrison served as a major radical influence on the Garvey movement. By the August 1920 UNIA convention Harrison grew critical of Garvey, who he felt had shifted focus "from Negro Self-Help to Invasion of Africa," evaded the lynching question, put out "false and misleading advertisements," and "lie[d] to the people magniloquently." Though he continued to write columns and book reviews for the *Negro World* into 1922, he was no longer principal editor, and he publicly criticized and worked against Garvey while attempting to build a Liberty party, to revive the Liberty League, and to challenge the growing Ku Klux Klan.

Harrison obtained U.S. citizenship in 1922 and over the next four years became a featured lecturer for the New York City Board of Education, where Yale-educated NAACP leader WILLIAM PICKENS described him as "a plain black man who can speak more easily, effectively, and interestingly on a greater variety of subjects than any other man I have ever met in the great universities." In 1924 he founded the International Colored Unity League (ICUL), which stressed that "as long as the outer situation remains what it is," blacks in "sheer self-defense" would have to develop "race-consciousness" so as to "furnish a background for our aspiration" and "proof of our equal human possibilities." The ICUL called for a broad-based unity—a unity of action, not thought, and a separate state in the South for blacks. He also helped develop the Division of Negro Literature, History, and Prints of the New York Public Library, organized for the American Negro Labor Congress, did publicity work for the Urban League, taught on "Problems of Race" at the Workers School, was involved in the Lafayette Theatre strike, and lectured and wrote widely. His 1927 effort to develop the *Voice of the Negro* as the newspaper of the ICUL lasted several months. Harrison died in New York City after an appendicitis attack. His wife and five young children were left virtually penniless.

Harrison, "The Father of Harlem Radicalism," was a leading black socialist, the founder and leading force of the militant "New Negro" movement, and the man who laid the basis for, and radically influenced, the Garvey movement. During a heyday of black radicalism he was the most class conscious of the race radicals and the most race conscious of the class radicals. He critically and candidly challenged the ruling classes, racists, organized religion, politicians, civil rights and race leaders, socialists, and communists. During his life, though well respected by many, Harrison was often slighted. In death, his memory was much neglected, not least by "leaders" who had felt the sting of his criticism. He was, however, a political and cultural figure of great influence who contributed seminal work on the interrelation of race and class consciousness and whose book and theater reviews drew praise from leading intellectuals of the day. Historian J. A. Rogers stressed that "No one worked more seriously and indefatigably to enlighten his fellowmen; none of the Aframerican leaders of his time had a saner and more effective program—but others, unquestionably his inferiors, received the recognition that was his due."

FURTHER READING

Hill, Robert A., ed. "Hubert Henry Harrison" in *The Marcus Garvey and Universal Negro Improvement Association Papers*, vol. 1 (1983).

Jackson, John G. *Hubert Henry Harrison: The Black Socrates* (1987).

James, Portia. "Hubert H. Harrison and the New Negro Movement." *Western Journal of Black Studies* 13, no. 2 (1989): 82–91.

Perry, Jeffrey B., ed. *A Hubert Harrison Reader* (2001).

Samuels, Wilford D. "Hubert H. Harrison and 'The New Negro Manhood Movement.'" *Afro-Americans in New York Life and History* 5 (Jan. 1981): 29–41.

—JEFFREY B. PERRY

 HASTIE, WILLIAM HENRY (17 Nov. 1904– 14 Apr. 1976), civil rights attorney, law school professor, and federal judge, was born in Knoxville, Tennessee, the son of Roberta Childs, a teacher, and William Henry Hastie, a clerk in the U.S. Pension Office (now the Veterans Administration). He was a superb student and athlete. His father's transfer to Washington, D.C., in 1916 permitted

Hastie to attend the nation's best black secondary school, the Paul Laurence Dunbar High School, from which he graduated as valedictorian in 1921. He attended Amherst College, where he majored in mathematics and graduated in 1925, valedictorian, Phi Beta Kappa, and magna cum laude. After teaching for two years in Bordentown, New Jersey, he studied law at Harvard University, where one instructor adopted the custom of saying after asking a question of the class, "Mr. Hastie, give them the answer" (Ware, 30). He worked on the *Law Review* and earned an LLB in 1930.

Hastie returned to Washington, D.C., in 1930, passed the bar exam, and began his legal career as a practitioner and an educator. He joined the firm of CHARLES HAMILTON HOUSTON and Houston's father, William L. Houston, which then became Houston, Houston, and Hastie. He also joined the law faculty at Howard University, where his first students included THURGOOD MARSHALL and Oliver Hill. He took a year away to study again at Harvard, where he shared an apartment with his friend ROBERT WEAVER and earned his SJD in 1933. He returned to Howard, where, when he was working in Washington, he taught until 1946. At the same time he became active in civil rights. His students researched current civil rights cases, participated in rehearsals of arguments on those cases, and attended the Supreme Court to watch Hastie and other civil rights giants argue cases. In 1935 he married Alma Syphax; they had no children before they divorced. In 1943 he married Beryl Lockwood; they had two children.

Hastie believed that, in the pursuit of justice, people should "struggle as best they know how to change things that seem immutable" (Ware, 147). In 1933 he was a founding member in Washington, D.C., of the New Negro Alliance, part of the "don't buy where you can't work" movement of the 1930s. He took a case in which a local court issued injunctions against African Americans picketing at chainstore outlets that, though operating in black areas, hired only white clerks. He argued the case in trial court and in federal appeals court but lost both attempts. He was unavailable to argue the case before the Supreme Court, which, convinced by the arguments Hastie and other attorneys had mounted, ruled in *New Negro Alliance v. Sanitary Grocery Co.* (1938) that the Norris-LaGuardia Act barred injunctions against peaceful labor-related picketing.

A champion of equal opportunity and racial integration, Hastie worked with the National Association for the Advancement of Colored People (NAACP) on major civil rights cases elsewhere, among them the 1933 *Hocutt* case in North Carolina, in which a black applicant unsuccessfully challenged the white-only admissions policy of the University of North Carolina. He also participated in cases that sought equalization of teachers' salaries, including the 1939 *Mills* case in Maryland and the 1940 *Alston* case in Virginia, both of which the NAACP won. With Marshall he argued cases before the Supreme Court that secured victories against the white Democratic primary in *Smith v. Allwright* (1944) and against segregated interstate transportation in *Morgan v. Virginia* (1946). In 1945 he presided at a conference in Chicago on segregated housing that the NAACP called to plan litigation against the constitutionality of restrictive covenants.

A series of appointments with the federal government began in November 1933, when Interior Secretary Harold L. Ickes recruited Hastie as assistant solicitor. In that capacity Hastie helped draft the Organic Act of 1936 for the Virgin Islands, which established a fully elective legislature and broadened the electorate to include residents regardless of their property, income, or gender. Hastie, like Weaver, was an early member of what became known as President Franklin D. Roosevelt's "black cabinet." His performance at the Interior Department led to his appointment in March 1937 to a four-year term as district judge in the Virgin Islands, the first black federal judge in U.S. history. He resigned from his judgeship in early 1939 to become dean of the Howard Law School. He took leave of the deanship in June 1940 to become civilian aide to Secretary of War Henry L. Stimson, in charge of handling matters of race in the military. In 1942 President Roosevelt also named Hastie a member of the Caribbean Advisory Committee, to advise the Anglo-American Caribbean Commission, established to foster the wartime social and economic cooperation of British and U.S. possessions in the Caribbean. Though Hastie's work in the War Department earned him the title "father of the black air force" (Ware, 133), he resigned his position there in early 1943 in frustration over his limited effectiveness in curtailing racial segregation and discrimination in the military. For his efforts and his resignation over what he called the Army Air Force's "reactionary policies and discriminatory practices," he won the NAACP's Spingarn Award in 1943.

Hastie resumed his work at Howard University, and he presided at a rally in 1944 for a permanent Fair Employment Practices Committee. In 1946 President Harry S. Truman nominated him for the governorship of the Virgin Islands. The only African American who had previously served as governor of any U.S. jurisdiction was P. B. S. PINCHBACK, who served for a month as acting governor of Louisiana after being elected to the state senate during Reconstruction. Hastie had a rough time dealing effectively with public affairs in the islands, but he tried to enhance Virgin Islanders' self-government. He fostered a civil rights law that prohibited discrimination on the basis of race or color.

In 1948 Hastie briefly returned to the mainland, where he campaigned effectively in black communities in support of President Truman's reelection bid. In 1949 Truman appointed him to the U.S. Court of Appeals for the Third Circuit. Hastie took his seat as a recess appointment in December 1949, the first black federal judge with life tenure. Confirmed in 1950, he served as appeals judge until 1968, then as chief judge until he retired in 1971, and as senior judge thereafter. He wrote the decisions in more than four hundred cases. He was considered for a Supreme Court appointment as early as 1954 and as late as 1967, when President Lyndon Johnson nominated Hastie's former student Marshall instead.

A member of the Board of Directors of the NAACP Legal Defense and Educational Fund from 1941 to 1968, Hastie continued to give public lectures on civil rights. He also served on the Boards of Trustees of Amherst College and Temple University. Cool and suave, committed yet dignified, Hastie died in

Norristown, Pennsylvania. He excelled as a law school professor and dean, as a civil rights attorney and leader, and as a pioneer black officeholder in the federal government.

FURTHER READING

The William H. Hastie Papers at the Law School Library, Harvard University, are available on microfilm. The Beck Cultural Exchange Center in Knoxville, Tennessee, has a collection of Hastie's papers, books, and memorabilia and maintains a permanent Hastie exhibit. Other materials are at Howard University and in the NAACP Papers at the Library of Congress.

McGuire, Phillip. *He, Too, Spoke for Democracy: Judge Hastie, World War II, and the Black Soldier* (1988).

Rusch, Jonathan J. "William Henry Hastie and the Vindication of Civil Rights." *Howard Law Review* 21 (1978): 749–820.

Ware, Gilbert. *William Hastie: Grace under Pressure* (1984).

Obituaries: *New York Times* and *Washington Post*, 15 Apr. 1976.

—PETER WALLENSTEIN

HAYDEN, ROBERT EARL (4 Aug. 1913– 25 Feb. 1980), poet and teacher, was born Asa Bundy Sheffey in Detroit, Michigan, the son of Asa Sheffey, a steel-mill worker, and Gladys Ruth Finn. Early in his childhood, his parents separated and he was given to neighbors William and Sue Ellen Hayden, who also were black, and who reared and renamed him. Hayden grew up in a poor, racially mixed neighborhood. Extremely nearsighted, unathletic, and introverted, he spent much of his youth indoors reading and writing. When he was eighteen, he published his first poem. Hayden attended Detroit City College from 1932 to 1936; worked for the Federal Writers' Project of the Works Progress Administration (WPA) from 1936 to 1938; published his first volume of poetry, *Heart-Shape in the Dust*, in 1940; and, studying with W. H. Auden, completed an MA in English at the University of Michigan in 1944. In 1946 he began teaching English at Fisk University in Nashville, Tennessee.

During his twenty-three years at Fisk, he published four volumes of poetry: *The Lion and the Archer* (with Myron O'Higgins, 1948), *Figure of Time* (1955), *A Ballad of Remembrance* (1962), and *Selected Poems* (1966). These were years of demanding college teaching and creative isolation, but they were brightened by a Rosenwald Fellowship in 1947; a Ford Foundation grant to write in Mexico in 1954–1955; and the Grand Prize for Poetry in English at the First World Festival of Negro Arts in Dakar, Senegal, in 1966. At a writers' conference at Fisk, also in 1966, Hayden was attacked by younger blacks for a lack of racial militance in his poetry. Hayden's position, however, first articulated in 1948, was that he did not wish to be confined to racial themes or judged by ethnocentric standards. His philosophy of poetry was that it must not be limited by the individual or ethnic identity of the poet. Although inescapably rooted in these elements, poetry must rise to an order of creation that is broadly human and universally effective. He said, "I always wanted to be a Negro, or a black, poet...the same way Yeats is an Irish poet." He was trying, like Yeats, to join the myths, folk culture, and common humanity of his race with his special, transcendent powers of imagination. Hayden's Baha'i faith, which he adopted in the 1940s, and which emphasized the oneness of all peoples and the spiritual value of art, also helped sustain him as a poet. In the late 1970s he said, "today when so often one gets the feeling that everything is going downhill, that we're really on the brink of the abyss and what good is anything, I find myself sustained in my attempts to be a poet...because I have the assurance of my faith that this is of spiritual value and it is a way of performing some kind of service."

In 1969 Hayden joined the Department of English of the University of Michigan at Ann Arbor, where he taught until his death. During these years, he published *Words in the Mourning Time* (1970), *The Night-Blooming Cereus* (1973), *Angle of Ascent: New and Selected Poems* (1975), and *American Journal* (1978, rev. ed., 1982). He was elected to the American Academy of Poets in 1975 and appointed consultant in poetry to the Library of Congress in 1976–1978, the first African American to be selected.

Shifting from a romantic and proletarian approach in *Heart-Shape in the Dust* to an interest in rich language and baroque effects in *The Lion and the Archer*, Hayden's mature work did not appear until *A Ballad of Remembrance*. *Ballad* presents the first well-rounded picture of Hayden's protean subjects and styles as well as his devotion to craft. *Selected Poems* extends this impression and is followed by *Words in the Mourning Time*, which responds to the national experience of war, assassination, and racial militance in the late 1960s. Hayden's next volumes—*The Night-Blooming Cereus*, the eight new poems in *Angle of Ascent*, and *American Journal*—reveal an aging poet yielding to his aesthetic nature and his love of art and beauty for their own sake.

An obsessive wordsmith and experimenter in forms, Hayden searched for words and formal patterns that were cleansed of the egocentric and that gave his subjects their most objective aspect. Believing that expert craft was central, he rejected spontaneous expression in favor of precise realism, scrupulous attention to tone, and carefully wrought verbal mosaics. In Hayden's poetry, realism and romanticism interact, the former deriving significantly from his interest in black history and folk experience, the latter from his desire to explore subjective reality and to make poetry yield aesthetic pleasure. As Wilburn Williams Jr. has observed, "spiritual enlightenment in his poetry is never the reward of evasion of material fact. The realities of the imagination and the actualities of history are bound together in an intimate symbiotic alliance that makes neither thinkable without the other." Some of the major themes of Hayden's poetry are the tension between the tragic nature of life and the richness of the imagination, the past in the present, art as a form of spiritual redemption, and the nurturing power of early life and folk memories. His favorite subjects include the spirit of places, folk characters, his childhood neighborhood, and African American history.

In the debate about the purpose of art, Hayden's stance, closer to the aesthete than the propagandist, has exposed him to criticism. Yet the coalescence in Hayden's poetry of African American material with a sophisticated modernism represents a singular achievement in the history of American poetry. His poetry about black culture and history, moreover, reveals the deepest of commitments to his own racial group as well as to humanity as a whole.

Hayden was married in 1940 to Erma Morris, with whom he had one child. He died in Ann Arbor.

FURTHER READING

Hatcher, John. *From the Auroral Darkness: The Life and Poetry of Robert Hayden* (1984).
Williams, Pontheolla T. *Robert Hayden: A Critical Analysis of His Poetry* (1987).
—ROBERT M. GREENBERG

HAYNES, LEMUEL

(18 July 1753–28 Sept. 1833), Congregational minister, was born in West Hartford, Connecticut, the son of a black father and a white mother, both unknown, and both of whom abandoned him at birth. He was indentured at five months of age to a white family named Rose, through whom he absorbed strong Calvinist theology and evangelical piety. He was educated in the local schools, but, a serious and diligent child, he also taught himself by the light of the fireside at night; he later said, "I made it my rule to know more

Lemuel B. Haynes, Revolutionary War veteran, poet, and Calvinist preacher. Schomburg Center

every night than I knew in the morning." In 1783 he married Elizabeth Babbit, a white schoolteacher who had proposed to him; they became the parents of ten children.

Haynes fulfilled his indenture and came of age just as the American Revolution was beginning. He signed up as a Minuteman in 1774 and joined militia troops at Roxbury following the Lexington alarm. He joined the Continental army in 1776, marched to Ticonderoga, and was mustered out because he contracted typhus. Haynes remained a lifelong patriot, an admirer of George Washington, an ardent Federalist, and an outspoken critic of Jeffersonianism. He may even have been a member of the secretive Washington Benevolent Society.

Haynes who had poetic aspirations, is thought to be the author of a broadside poem (1774?) lamenting the death of Asa Burt, who was killed when a tree fell on him. He was the author of a patriotic ballad, "The Battle of Lexington" (1775?), which remained unpublished until 1985, after it was discovered by Ruth Bogin in the Houghton Library at Harvard. Although it demonstrates more sincerity than talent, the poem is not entirely without merit: "Freedom & Life, O precious Sounds / yet Freedome does excell / and we will bleed upon the ground / or keep our Freedom still."

Deciding on the ministry as a career, Haynes turned down an opportunity to attend Dartmouth College and instead studied privately with local ministers. He was licensed to preach in 1780, served the Granville, Connecticut, church for five years, and was ordained to the Congregational ministry on 9 November 1785 by the Association of Ministers in Litchfield County. Haynes was apparently the first African American ordained by a mainstream denomination in the United States. He moved to Torrington, Connecticut, where the congregation included the parents of John Brown. In the tradition of Jonathan Edwards and George Whitefield, Haynes was a New Light Congregationalist who favored revivalism but recognized and was critical of its excesses.

In 1788 Haynes became minister of the west parish in Rutland, Vermont, a conservative congregation he served for thirty years. An effective preacher, he was often invited to

speak at ordinations, funerals, and public events. He later recalled that he preached 5,500 sermons in Rutland, four hundred of them at funerals. He and the congregation remained a center of Calvinism in the midst of the Vermont frontier's rationalism of Thomas Paine and Ethan Allen.

In 1805 Haynes preached a sermon that made an impact far beyond his local circle. In the brief but witty response to visiting Universalist Hosea Ballou, Haynes satirically linked Ballou to the Garden of Eden's serpent, which, as the title of his homily claimed, also promised "Universal Salvation." The sermon was printed, and then reprinted, as late as 1865, until more than seventy editions had been issued throughout the Northeast.

Haynes's humor extended beyond religious satire. When the house of Reverend Ashbel Parmelee burned down, Haynes asked Parmelee if he had lost his sermon manuscripts in the fire. When Parmelee told him that he had, Haynes asked, "Well, don't you think that they gave more light than they ever had before?" Haynes once inadvertently walked into a hotel dining room where a private party was celebrating Andrew Jackson's election to the presidency. Handed a glass of wine and invited to offer a toast, Haynes lifted his glass to the new president and said "Andrew Jackson: Psalm 109, verse 8," then put down the glass and went on his way. When someone later looked up the Bible verse he discovered that it read "Let his days be few and let another take his office."

Eased out of the Rutland church when he was sixty-five, Haynes moved to Manchester, Vermont, where he became involved in a sensational murder case. Two brothers, Stephen and Jesse Boorn, were in prison, having been convicted of the murder of their mentally unstable brother-in-law, Russell Colvin. Colvin's body had not been found, but he had disappeared, and several clues (a found button, a bone unearthed by a dog) pointed to the brothers' guilt. Haynes befriended the Boorns and became convinced of their innocence. Colvin surfaced in New Jersey just before the brothers were to be executed and was brought back to Manchester in a moment of great local drama. Haynes wrote an account of the case, *Mystery Developed* (1820), which had all the shape of a short story, and he preached a sermon, *The Prisoner Released* (1820), which warned against convicting a person on the basis of circumstantial evidence. The British novelist Willkie Collins later read about the case and used the dead/alive theme in his story *John Jago's Ghost.* Haynes moved once again in 1822, serving the Granville, New York, church, just across the border from Vermont, until his death there.

Haynes has been remembered chiefly as a revolutionary war veteran and has even been omitted from some accounts of African American history, perhaps because he never lived among black people. Because his religious interests have long since been out of fashion, Haynes the theologian and preacher has been ignored, despite the remarkable publishing history of *Universal Salvation.* Haynes has often been criticized for his failure to speak out against slavery, but recent discoveries of Haynes material may alter that situation. In addition to Haynes's poem on Lexington, Bogin also found an unpublished manuscript, dating from about 1776, entitled "Liberty Further Extended." Composed by the young Haynes, probably while he was in the Continental army, it argues, on the basis of natural rights, for an expansion of the Revolution to encompass the liberation of the nation's African slaves. "Men were made for more noble Ends than to be Drove to market, like Sheep and oxen," Haynes wrote. "Even an affrican, has Equally as good a right to his Liberty in common with Englishmen." The incomplete manuscript was not published until 1983. A more recent discovery, by David Proper, reveals that Haynes preached the funeral sermon in 1821 for LUCY TERRY, the earliest known African American poet. A contemporary newspaper account states that Haynes read a poem that seems to be his own composition and that includes the lines "How long must Ethaopia's murder'd race / Be doom'd by men to bondage and disgrace?"

Haynes clearly was more race conscious than has been realized; he even identified himself, the author of "The Battle of Lexington," as "a young Mollato." In a Fourth of July speech in 1801 marking the twenty-fifth anniversary of American independence, Haynes contrasted European monarchy with American Republicanism and spoke of the plight of "the poor Africans among us." "What has reduced them to their present pitiful, abject state?" he asked. "Is it any distinction that the God of nature hath made in their formation? Nay, but being subjected to slavery, by the cruel hands of oppressors, they have been taught to view themselves as a rank of being far below others."

FURTHER READING

There is no collection of Haynes papers, but copies of his printed sermons and addresses are in the Congregational Library, Boston, Massachusetts; the American Antiquarian Society, Worcester, Massachusetts; Union Theological Seminary, New York City; and other depositories.

Newman, Richard. *Black Preacher to White America: The Collected Writings of Lemuel Haynes, 1774–1833* (1990).
———. *Lemuel Haynes: A Bio-bibliography* (1984).
Saillant, John D. "Lemuel Haynes and the Revolutionary Origins of Black Theology, 1776–1801." *Religion and American Culture* 2 (Winter 1993): 79–102.
—RICHARD NEWMAN

HEALY, ELIZA

(23 Dec. 1846–13 Sept. 1919), Roman Catholic nun, was born a slave in Jones County, Georgia, the daughter of Michael Morris Healy, a well-to-do plantation owner, and Eliza Clark, one of his slaves. Michael Morris Healy was a native of Ireland who had immigrated to Jones County near Macon, Georgia, where, after acquiring land and slaves, he became a prosperous planter. Eliza Clark had nine surviving children by Michael Healy, who acknowledged his children and carefully made provisions for their eventual removal outside of Georgia, where at that time, the manumission of slaves was virtually impossible.

Eliza Healy's mother died in the spring of 1850 and her father in the summer of the same year. By that time, her five older brothers and one older sister had already been sent north to be educated. The youngest three children, including Eliza, were successfully brought out of Georgia and sent to New York.

Although he was a Catholic, Michael Healy did not have his children baptized. In the North, however, several of the Healy children pursued vocations in their father's faith. The three youngest siblings, including Eliza, were baptized in New York in 1851. Their eldest brother, JAMES HEALY, was at that time a seminarian in Montreal. In 1854 in Paris he was ordained a priest for the Diocese of Boston and in 1875 became the second bishop of Portland, Maine, and the first African American bishop in the United States. Two other brothers also became Roman Catholic priests. PATRICK HEALY was ordained a Jesuit priest in 1865 and became president of Georgetown University in Washington, D.C., in 1874. A third brother, (Alexander) Sherwood Healy, served as a priest for the Diocese of Boston beginning in 1858. A fourth brother, MICHAEL HEALY, chose a secular path; he became a sea captain in the U.S. Revenue Cutter Service.

Both Eliza and her younger sister, (Amanda) Josephine, studied in schools operated by the sisters of the Congregation of Notre Dame in Montreal. At the same time, their older sister, Martha, was professed a nun in the same community in 1855. (Martha left the community with a dispensation from her vows in 1863.) After finishing her secondary education in 1861, Eliza, with Josephine, rejoined other members of the Healy family in the Boston area. About a dozen years later both sisters chose to lead the religious life.

Eliza was twenty-seven when she entered the novitiate of the congregation of Notre Dame in Montreal in 1874, and she made her first profession in 1876. Following the custom of the sisters of the Congregation of Notre Dame, she received the religious name of Sister Saint Mary Magdalen. In the beginning of her religious life, she taught in various schools operated by the Congregation of Notre Dame in Canada. She was superior of a convent for the first time in Huntington, Quebec, from 1895 to 1897, during which time her administrative gifts first became apparent. She returned to the mother house of the Sisters of Notre Dame in Montreal, where she was put in charge of English Studies and then served as a teacher in the Normal School from 1900 to 1903.

Sister Saint Mary Magdalen served longest at Villa Barlow in St. Albans, Vermont. From 1903 to 1918 she was superior and headmistress of the school, and during that time she completely restored and reorganized the school and community. The annals of the congregation recount the precarious financial situation at Villa Barlow when she took over; the community was almost ready to abandon the site: "She had to struggle against the parish and even the diocesan authorities. Her wisdom enabled her to unravel the complicated problems, to assure the resources, to pay the debts, and to make this... mission one of our most prosperous houses in the United States." Sister Saint Mary Magdalen also paid close attention to issues of health and hygiene for both the pupils and the sisters in her charge.

In 1918 she was sent to be superior of the Academy of Our Lady of the Blessed Sacrament on Staten Island, New York. In a few months she was able to improve the financial situation of the college, but her stay was brief. Her health declined rapidly, and she returned to the mother house in Montreal, where she died of heart disease the following summer.

Notices on Sister Saint Mary Magdalen by members of her community describe her as an indefatigable and somewhat demanding superior with a gift for business and organization. Her leadership qualities and her spirituality, such as her devotion to prayer, were especially remarked on by the sisters who had lived with her. Her relationship with the other sisters was described in the annals: "The sisters loved this superior, so just, so attractive, so upright!... she reserved the heaviest tasks for herself... in the kitchen, in the garden, in the housework.... She listened to everyone,... was equal to everything... spared herself nothing... so that nothing was lacking to make the family life [of the community] perfect."

While none of the Healy siblings ever spoke publicly about the issue of race, it remains at the heart of the family's story. Both Bishop Healy and his brother Alexander were visibly black, but Patrick Healy's racial identity was not well known outside of the Jesuit order. None of the priest brothers involved themselves with the black

Catholic community. In the same way, it seems that their gifted and dedicated sister lived out her life of leadership and service far removed from the world of her mother and the harsh circumstances faced by those of her mother's African heritage.

FURTHER READING

Information about Healy can be found in the archives of the Sisters of the Congregation of Notre Dame in Montreal, Canada.

Fairbanks, Henry G. "Slavery and the Vermont Clergy." *Vermont History* 27 (1959).
Foley, Albert S. *Bishop Healy: Beloved Outcaste* (1954).
———. *Dream of an Outcaste: Patrick F. Healy, S.J.* (1989).
O'Toole, James M. *Passing for White: Race, Religion, and the Healy Family, 1820–1920* (2002).

—CYPRIAN DAVIS

HEALY, JAMES AUGUSTINE

HEALY, JAMES AUGUSTINE (6 Apr. 1830– 5 Aug. 1900), Roman Catholic bishop, was born in Jones County, Georgia, the son of Michael Morris Healy, a planter, and his slave Eliza Clark. James's early years were spent in the insular world of Healy's 1,600-acre plantation. When he reached school age, James and his brothers Hugh and PATRICK HEALY were placed by their father in a Quaker school in Flushing, New York. Eventually all nine of the Healy siblings, including MICHAEL HEALY and ELIZA HEALY, left Georgia for the North.

In 1844 Healy and his brothers transferred to the College of the Holy Cross in Worcester, Massachusetts, a new Jesuit school established by Bishop John Bernard Fitzpatrick of Boston. Healy thrived in his new environment, excelling academically and experiencing a spiritual awakening that led to his decision to enter the priesthood in 1848. The Jesuit novitiate was in Maryland, a slave state, so with the help of Fitzpatrick, Healy in 1849 entered the Sulpician Seminary in Montreal, Canada. After receiving his MA two years later, Healy entered the seminary of St. Sulpice in Issy, France, where he worked toward becoming a professor of theology and philosophy. However, following the deaths of his parents in 1850

and of his brother Hugh in a freak accident in 1853, Healy felt called to return to the United States.

In Notre Dame Cathedral in Paris on 10 June 1854, Healy became the first African American to be ordained a Roman Catholic priest. He then returned to Boston, where he became an assistant pastor of the Moon Street Church and an administrator of the House of the Guardian Angel, a home for orphaned boys. Fitzpatrick soon brought Healy onto his staff and gave him the responsibility of organizing the chancery office. In June 1855 Healy officially became the first chancellor of the diocese of Boston, loyally serving Fitzpatrick and learning from him the subtleties of Catholic leadership in New England's anti-Catholic environment.

In 1857, after Fitzpatrick became ill, Healy took over many of the bishop's duties. Plans to build a new cathedral were delayed because of the Civil War, and in 1862 Healy became the rector of a makeshift cathedral that had been a Unitarian church. As the war climaxed, he helped found the Home for Destitute Catholic Children, bringing in the Sisters of Charity to run it in 1865.

After Fitzpatrick's death in 1866, the new bishop, John Joseph Williams, appointed Healy as the pastor of St. James Church, the largest Catholic congregation in Boston. If Healy was concerned that as a southerner of African descent he would be unacceptable to the predominantly Irish parishioners, he kept this concern to himself, and he soon won over the congregation through firm spiritual leadership and a tender affection for those in need. As one parishioner said, if Healy "had any such thing as an inferiority complex concealed about his person, his Irish congregation never discovered it, for he ruled them—and they were not easy to rule" (Foley, 109).

A highlight of Healy's years as the pastor of St. James was the establishment in 1867 of the House of the Good Shepherd, a refuge for homeless girls. However, his success as an apologist for the Catholic church before the Massachusetts legislature in March 1874 was perhaps his most impressive achievement. The legislature was considering the taxation of churches and other religious institutions, and Healy defended Catholic institutions—including schools,

James Augustine Healy was the first African American to become a Roman Catholic priest in 1854 and bishop in 1875. Holy Cross Special Collections

hospitals, and orphanages—as vital organizations that helped the state both socially and financially. He also eloquently condemned the laws that were already in place, which were generally enforced only on Catholic institutions.

Healy's success in the public sphere and his exemplary service as pastor of St. James led to his election by Pope Pius IX as the second bishop of Portland, Maine, in February 1875. Again he was concerned that the color of his skin would undermine his authority, particularly in regard to the fifty-two priests of the diocese. His fears, however, were never realized. Although Healy's personal history was the source of some intrigue and prejudice among his flock, his ability and pastoral excellence reduced the matter to a nonissue. He took firm control of the diocese, which covered all of Maine and New Hampshire and was growing rapidly

as a result of Irish and French Canadian immigration. Relying on the savvy of John M. Mitchell, a prominent local lawyer well schooled in Maine's political and social intricacies, Healy helped unify his parishes in an era when Catholics were often divided by ethnic differences.

Healy oversaw the founding of sixty parishes, eighteen schools (including American Indian schools), and sixty-eight charitable institutions within the diocese. In 1884, at Healy's suggestion, the diocese was divided by state lines, and a separate diocese of Manchester, New Hampshire, was established. Healy helped set up his former chancellor, Denis Bradley, as its first bishop. He also oversaw the establishment of the state's first Catholic college in 1886, as St. Mary's College in Van Buren opened its doors. Under Healy, dozens of religious congregations were established, many of French Canadian origin. By

1900 the Sisters of Mercy, the Sisters of the Congregation of Notre Dame, the Dominicans, the Marist Brothers, and the Christian Brothers were all established in various educational and institutional positions throughout the state.

While the quality of Healy's career proves that a person's race is not the essential characteristic by which he or she can be judged, his desire to avoid the issue led to several lost opportunities to condemn the sin of racism on a national stage. Even after the Third Plenary Council of Baltimore in 1884, which placed Healy on the newly formed Commission on Negro and Indian Missions, he refused to participate in organizations that were specifically African American. Three times, in 1889, 1890, and 1892, Healy declined to speak at the Congress of Colored Catholics. His legacy as the first African American Catholic bishop is at least partially diminished by this reticence.

Although Healy was haunted by racism throughout his life, he never allowed it to affect his duties. His graceful attitude toward the problem is exemplified by an encounter he had with a young parishioner during the sacrament of penance. The teenage girl, unaware that her confessor was Healy himself, admitted that she had "said the bishop was as black as the devil." Healy responded, "Don't say the bishop is as black as the devil. You can say the bishop is as black as coal, or as black as the ace of spades. But don't say the bishop is as black as the *devil!*" (Foley, 145).

Healy was a religious leader whose intelligence, spiritual conviction, and dedicated service inevitably defined him and created a devoted, if not wholly color-blind, following. He died in Portland, Maine.

FURTHER READING

Healy's papers are at the library of the College of the Holy Cross, Worcester, Massachusetts, the Archives of the Archdiocese of Boston, and the Archives of the Diocese of Portland, Maine.

Foley, Albert S. *Bishop Healy: Beloved Outcaste* (1954).
Lucey, William Leo. *The Catholic Church in Maine* (1957).
Merwick, Donna. *Boston Priests, 1848–1910: A Study of Social and Intellectual Change* (1973).

O'Toole, James M. *Passing for White: Race, Religion, and the Healy Family, 1820–1920* (2002).

Obituary: *Portland Express*, 6 Aug. 1900.
—JAY MAZZOCCHI

HEALY, MICHAEL

(22 Sept. 1839–30 Aug. 1904), Coast Guard officer and Alaska pioneer, was born Michael Augustine Healy in Jones County, Georgia, to Michael Morris Healy, an immigrant from Ireland, and Eliza Clark, a mixed-race slave owned by Michael Morris Healy. Michael was the sixth of nine surviving children born to his parents, who, though never legally married, maintained a common-law relationship for more than twenty years, neither one of them ever marrying anyone else. Michael Morris Healy was barred by Georgia law from emancipating either his wife or his children, but he treated them as family members rather than as slaves, even as he owned fifty other slaves. He was a successful cotton planter and amassed the resources to send his children north before the Civil War, which he did as each approached school age, beginning in 1844. The children exhibited a wide range of complexion, but most of them, including young Michael, were light-skinned enough so that anyone who did

Captain Healy, pictured here on USRC Bear, *was such a stern officer he was nicknamed "Hell-Roaring Mike."* Corbis

not know the family's story remained unaware of their racial heritage, presuming them to be white.

Michael followed his older brothers to the College of the Holy Cross in Worcester, Massachusetts, in 1850. They had flourished there, and three of them made the decision to become Catholic priests. JAMES HEALY, the first African American ordained as a Roman Catholic priest, eventually became the bishop of Portland, Maine; another, PATRICK HEALY, the first African American to earn a PhD and to be ordained a Jesuit priest, served as president of Georgetown University; (Alexander) Sherwood Healy, was the rector of the Cathedral of the Holy Cross in Boston. Two sisters, (Amanda) Josephine and ELIZA HEALY, became Catholic nuns, serving in convents and schools in the United States and Canada. Michael, however, had no interest in a religious career. Instead, he ran away from Holy Cross and by 1855 had found work in the maritime trades, serving on a succession of merchant vessels as a deckhand, mate, and, finally, second or first officer.

In September 1863 Healy enlisted in the United States Revenue Cutter Service (USRCS), the precursor of the modern-day Coast Guard. A year later he applied for an officer's commission, and, with the help of his brother James, who had connections among several important Republican politicians in Boston, he was appointed a second lieutenant. No mention of his racial background was made during the appointment process; had he been identified as having African American ancestry, he would almost certainly have been prevented from securing an officer's rank. Instead, officials of the USRCS were allowed to think that he was white. Shortly afterward, in January 1865, he married Mary Jane Roach, the daughter of Irish immigrants to Boston; they would eventually have one son.

For the next several years, Healy had a series of routine assignments on USRCS cutters based in Newport, Rhode Island; New Bedford, Massachusetts; and New York City, rising to the rank of first lieutenant. In the summer of 1874 he was assigned to the USRCS fleet based in San Francisco, charged with patrolling the waters off Alaska, which the United States had purchased from Russia a few years earlier. The

USRCS was the only government agency enforcing law and order in the northern Pacific, the Bering Sea, and the Arctic Ocean. Cutters made annual summer cruises in those waters, conducting basic exploration and scientific work, assisting commercial vessels, policing the whaling fleet, apprehending smugglers, and helping both settlers and natives. In March 1883 Healy was promoted to the rank of captain, becoming the first African American captain in the USRCS, a distinction he would not have claimed, and did not claim, for himself.

In 1886 Healy was given command of the ship *Bear*; the fame of the vessel and her captain grew steadily over the next decade as they went about their regular tasks. Exploration was high on the list. Twice, with the *Bear* anchored offshore, Healy sent exploring parties in launches upriver in search of overland routes to Alaska's northern slope. Although no practical routes were identified, the explorers catalogued much of the flora and fauna of inland Alaska for the first time, which Healy later published in two widely respected reports. Healy supervised efforts to protect wildlife, focusing particularly on attempts (not wholly successful) to prevent the overhunting of seals on the open seas. He provided regular assistance to the diminishing American whaling fleet concentrated above the Arctic Circle, which frequently entailed freeing whaling ships trapped in the ice and rescuing seamen stranded by shipwreck. Healy's contact with Inuit and Aleut natives culminated in his unusual plan to introduce domesticated reindeer into Alaska in the hope of improving native self-sufficiency. Beginning in 1891 he sailed repeatedly back and forth, buying reindeer from natives in Siberia who had been herding them for centuries, transporting the animals on the cutter, and establishing herds for the Alaska natives, among whom such herding had been unknown. By disrupting the illegal traffic in liquor and guns, Healy also attempted to curb the abuse of natives by white settlers from the United States.

Healy's endeavors earned him a wide reputation. Ask anyone in the Arctic "Who is the greatest man in America?," the *New York Sun* claimed in 1894, and the swift answer would be "Why, Mike Healy." His picturesque career was the stuff of novels, and, in fact, he appeared in a fictionalized but reasonably accurate portrayal in James Michener's bestselling 1989 book, *Alaska*. Eventually, however, Healy's stern, no-nonsense approach to law enforcement and his aggressive personality—for which he had been nicknamed "Hell-Roaring Mike"—proved his undoing. After several minor complaints were lodged against him, Healy was tried before a court-martial in San Francisco in 1890, charged with the cruel treatment of prisoners in his custody.

The trial became a rallying cry for temperance forces, who accused Healy of having been drunk at the time. While he was acquitted of all charges on that occasion, he was less fortunate six years later, when he was tried again, this time for abusive treatment of his own men and public drunkenness. At his 1896 trial Healy was found guilty. Although he could have been dismissed from the USRCS, his punishment was less severe. Instead, he was placed in the indeterminate status of "waiting orders," and he was made to suffer the embarrassment of being dropped to the bottom of the list of captains in the service, which was normally arranged by seniority. Neither in his trials nor in the newspaper accounts of them was his racial background raised as an issue; it apparently remained unknown, even to his opponents, who probably would have used it against him had they been aware of it.

Shortly after the turn of the century, Healy briefly achieved a kind of redemption when he was once again given command of USRCS ships. Healy retired from the service in the fall of 1903 and died the following summer. Today, his trailblazing position as the first black captain of the USRCS is celebrated, and in 1997 the Coast Guard commissioned an icebreaker named for him, recognizing that distinction. In his own lifetime, however, Healy exemplified the desire of some African Americans to pass in order to have successful careers in the white community.

FURTHER READING

Healy's logbooks and other records relating to his USRCS career are in the Coast Guard records at the National Archives and Records Administration, Washington, D.C.

O'Toole, James M. *Passing for White: Race, Religion, and the Healy Family, 1820–1920* (2002).
Strobridge, Truman R., and Dennis L. Noble. *Alaska and the U. S. Revenue Cutter Service, 1867–1915* (1999).

—JAMES M. O'TOOLE

HEALY, PATRICK FRANCIS (2 Feb. 1834– 10 Jan. 1910), Jesuit priest and university president, was born in Jones County, Georgia, the son of Michael Morris Healy, an Irish American planter, and Eliza Clark, an African American woman he had purchased. The senior Healy deserted from the British army in Canada during the War of 1812 and by 1818 had made his way to rural Georgia where he settled, speculated in land, and acquired a sizable plantation and numerous slaves. Healy acknowledged Eliza as "my trusty woman" in his will, which provided that she be paid an annuity, transported to a free state, and "not bartered or sold or disposed of in any way" should he predecease her. Healy also acknowledged his nine children by Eliza, although by state law they were slaves he owned, and he arranged for them to leave Georgia and move to the North, where they would become free.

After first sending his older sons to a Quaker school in Flushing, New York, Michael Healy by chance met John Fitzpatrick, then the Roman Catholic bishop coadjutor of Boston, who told him about the new Jesuit College of the Holy Cross opening in Worcester, Massachusetts. Patrick, along with three of his brothers, was enrolled in Holy Cross in 1844. A sister, Martha, was sent to the Notre Dame sisters' school in Boston. Patrick graduated in 1850, the year after his older brother JAMES HEALY was literally the first person to receive a diploma from the fledgling college. At Holy Cross the Healy brothers' race was fully known and generally accepted without incident. In one poignant letter, however, Patrick Healy wrote, "Remarks are sometime made which wound my very heart. You know to what I refer...I have with me a younger brother Michael. He is obliged to go through the same ordeal."

Although none of the Healy children were baptized until coming North,

In 1874 Patrick Francis Healy, the first African American Jesuit, became president of Georgetown University in Washington, D.C. Library of Congress

brothers James, Hugh, Patrick, and Sherwood were baptized at Holy Cross in 1844, and by 1851, all of the Healy children had been baptized. So it is not surprising that Patrick Healy decided to emulate his friends and protectors and enter the Society of Jesus. He matriculated at the order's novitiate in Frederick, Maryland, where his light skin apparently kept him from being identified as African American and thus in school contrary to the law.

After making his Jesuit vows in 1852, Healy taught at St. Joseph's College in Philadelphia and was then assigned back to Holy Cross, where he taught a variety of courses. In 1858 he was sent to Georgetown University in Washington, D.C., to continue his own studies in philosophy and theology, but soon he was abruptly reassigned to Rome, probably because his race had become an issue. His brother James, who had decided to enter the secular priesthood, attended the Sulpician seminaries in Montreal and Paris because it was not possible for a black person to be enrolled in an American school.

Patrick Healy's delicate health did not long tolerate the weather in Rome, so he was sent to the Catholic University of Louvain in Belgium. He was ordained to the priesthood on 3 September 1864 by Bishop Lamont in

Liége and then stayed on at Louvain to complete a doctorate in philosophy. He received his degree on 26 July 1865, apparently the first African American to earn a PhD. He returned to the United States the next year, after further spiritual training in France, and was assigned to teach philosophy at Georgetown.

Healy took his final vows as a Jesuit on 2 February 1867, the first African American to do so. If the illegitimacy of his birth made his ordination problematic, church officials overlooked this fact, as they did in the case of his brother James, who had become in 1854 the first African American ordained to the Roman Catholic priesthood. Patrick Healy moved quickly through the administrative ranks at Georgetown, becoming prefect of studies, or dean, and then vice president. When the president, the Reverend John Early, died unexpectedly in 1873, Healy was named acting president. Following confirmation by authorities in Rome, he was inaugurated the twenty-ninth president of Georgetown on 31 July 1874.

Patrick Healy's influence on Georgetown was so far-reaching that he is often referred to as the school's "second founder," following Archbishop John Carroll. Healy did, in fact, transform a small nineteenth-century college into a major twentieth-century university. He modernized the curriculum by requiring courses in the sciences, particularly chemistry and physics. He expanded and upgraded the schools of law and medicine. He centralized libraries, arranged for scholastic awards to students, and created an alumni organization. The most visible result of Healy's presidency was the construction of a large building begun in 1877 and first used in 1881. The imposing Healy Hall, with its 200-foot tower, contained classrooms, offices, and dormitories; its Belgian Gothic style was clearly reminiscent of Louvain. Paying for the building became somewhat problematic, however, when stories of Healy's race, never a secret, circulated through Washington.

Healy's influence extended beyond Georgetown as he mixed in the nation's capital with presidents of the United States and other government officials as well as the parents of Georgetown students. He served as head of the Catholic Commission on Indian Affairs. He preached often in Catholic churches in the Washington area, including St. Augustine's, an African American parish. He was present at the cornerstone laying of this church in 1874 and at the dedication of its new building in 1876. He spoke at congressional hearings in opposition to taxes on religious and educational institutions.

Healy's health was never robust, and he apparently suffered from epilepsy, which grew more serious with age. Upon the advice of his physician, he retired from the Georgetown presidency on 16 February 1882. Several assignments followed, but they existed largely in name only: St. Joseph's Church, Providence, Rhode Island; St. Lawrence Church, New York City; and St. Joseph's College, Philadelphia. In fact, in retirement he traveled extensively through Europe and the United States, often in the company of his brother James. He spent his last two years in the Georgetown infirmary, where he died, survived only by his sister ELIZA HEALY.

Patrick Healy's brothers and sisters led equally significant lives. James became bishop of Portland, Maine. (Alexander) Sherwood became a professor of moral theology and accompanied Boston archbishop John J. Williams to Vatican I as his personal theologian. Eliza became Sister Mary Magdalen, a superior in the Notre Dame sisters. MICHAEL HEALY, the only sibling not to follow a religious vocation, became "Hell Roaring Mike," captain of a U.S. revenue cutter in the Arctic and North Pacific.

FURTHER READING

Healy's papers, including his diaries, are in the Georgetown University Library.

Curran, Robert Emmett. *The Bicentennial History of Georgetown University*, vol. 1: *1789–1889* (1993).
Foley, Rev. Albert. *God's Men of Color* (1955, 1970).
O'Toole, James M. *Passing for White: Race, Religion, and the Healy Family, 1820–1920* (2002).

—RICHARD NEWMAN

 HEDGEMAN, ANNA ARNOLD (5 July 1899– 17 Jan. 1990), civil rights and women's rights activist, and government administrator was born Anna Arnold in Marshalltown, Iowa, to Marie Ellen Parker and William James Arnold II. The granddaughter of slaves, Anna grew up in Anoka, Minnesota. Her parents, particularly her father, stressed the importance of education, religion, and discipline. Anna attended Hamline University in St. Paul, Minnesota, from 1918 to 1922. She majored in English and pursued her studies with a passion that marked the way she lived her life. In 1919 she attended a lecture given by W. E. B. DU BOIS, who had just returned from the Pan-African Conference held in Paris. This was her initial exposure to the African freedom struggles.

In the spring of 1922 Arnold became Hamline University's first black graduate. Shortly afterward she boarded a train for Holly Springs, Mississippi, and began her teaching career at Rust College. On her trip to the South, she confronted the realities of the Jim Crow transportation system when she was forced to change trains halfway through the ride.

Rust College was a vibrant place, but its resources were stretched to the limit. During her two years in Holly Springs, Arnold began to grasp the devastating impact of racism. At the same time she learned about black history from Dr. J. Leonard Farmer, the dean of Rust College and the father of future civil rights leader JAMES FARMER. Frustrated by her inability to effect change, Arnold returned to the North in 1924, eager to work in a world she believed was more tolerant about race relations. But she quickly became disillusioned. Unable to secure a teaching position in a predominantly white school, Arnold realized that racism in the North was often more subtle, but just as devastating as it was in the South.

On the advice of a friend, Arnold sought a job with the YWCA and soon began work with the Negro branch in Springfield, Ohio. But she became increasingly angry about the way racism divided resources along the color line. Searching for a community and a place to belong, she made her way to the Northeast, first working at the Negro branch of the Jersey City YWCA and then settling in Harlem. She served as the Harlem YWCA's membership secretary and participated in the branch's stimulating cultural and educational programs. In 1933 she married Merritt Hedgeman, an interpreter and singer of black folk music and opera, and the couple made their home in New York City.

Ironically, the Depression enabled the relative newcomer to get a city administration job. Starting in 1934 she worked with the Emergency Relief Bureau (later the Department of Welfare), first as a supervisor and then as a consultant on racial problems. By the late 1930s Hedgeman had resigned from the Department of Welfare to assume the directorship of the Negro branch of the Brooklyn YWCA. Yet, even while she held that position, she organized the Citizens' Coordinating Committee to advocate for city jobs for black workers. Through her efforts and leadership, black New Yorkers secured the first 150 provisional appointments the city had ever given the black community.

In 1941 Hedgeman helped A. PHILIP RANDOLPH with his first March on Washington effort. As World War II drew to a close, Randolph asked Hedgeman to be executive director of the National Council for a Permanent Fair Employment Practices Commission (FEPC). She spoke at rallies with other civil rights advocates and led strategy meetings on how to move legislation through Congress. Despite the pressure to maintain the FEPC, Congress eliminated the program.

Hedgeman's work with the FEPC however, had attracted national attention. Congressman William Dawson of Chicago brought her on board the National Citizens for the Re-Election of President Truman campaign. For her commitment to the Democratic Party, she received a high-level federal appointment as assistant director of the Federal Security Agency, which later became the Department of Health, Education, and Welfare.

In 1953 Hedgeman traveled to India at the request of Ambassador Chester Bowles. She spent three months there as part of a social work delegation, and she lectured, met with students, and studied. Shortly after her return from India, President Eisenhower took office, and Hedgeman, a Democratic appointee, left Washington. Settling back in New York City, she immediately became involved in Harlem politics. Hedgeman

became the first African American in Mayor Robert F. Wagner Jr.'s cabinet in 1954. Her responsibilities included serving as the mayor's adviser and as a representative to the United Nations. In 1958 Hedgeman resigned from Wagner's administration and turned her energies to the private sector. She did not stay out of politics for long.

Local insurgents in the Bronx approached Hedgeman to run for the U.S. Congress in 1960. Although she was defeated in the primaries, she continued her activism locally and overseas. In July 1960 she flew to Ghana to deliver the keynote address for the First Conference of African Women and Women of African Descent. While there she met with African leaders Kwame Nkrumah and Patrice Lumumba.

Hedgeman aggressively pursued civil rights, again working closely with A. Philip Randolph as a major architect of the 1963 March on Washington. The only woman on a nine-member organizing committee, she challenged the male leaders, insisting that women be recognized for their tremendous contributions to the movement and that at least one woman be put on the official program.

As the Civil Rights Bill of 1964 made its way through Congress, Hedgeman, then the assistant director of the Committee on Race Relations for the National Council of Churches, helped coordinate the lobbying effort to get the stalled bill out of the Senate. Years of experience had taught her that the only hope of moving the president or Congress on race issues was through sustained public pressure.

In 1965 Hedgeman was asked to run for New York City council president. She suffered a defeat but maintained her commitment to electoral politics. In 1968 she ran for office one last time, for the New York State Assembly. Her opponent, incumbent CHARLES RANGEL, beat her in the primaries. Even as she fought for civil rights and pursued elected office, Hedgeman worked for women's equality. She was among the National Organization for Women's earliest members and served on its board of directors.

Hedgeman, who published autobiographies in 1964 and 1977, received an honorary doctorate from Hamline University and numerous awards for

her work on race relations. She died in Harlem Hospital in January 1990.

FURTHER READING

Hedgeman's papers are at the Schomburg Center for Research in Black Culture of the New York Public Library. The Schlesinger Library at Cambridge, Massachusetts holds a transcript of an unpublished interview conducted in 1978 as part of the Black Women Oral History Project.

Hedgeman, Anna Arnold. *The Gift of Chaos: Decades of American Discontent* (1977).
———. *The Trumpet Sounds: A Memoir of Negro Leadership* (1964).

Obituary: *New York Times*, 21 Jan. 1990.
—JULIE GALLAGHER

HEIGHT, DOROTHY

(24 Mar. 1912–) was born Dorothy Irene Height in Richmond, Virginia, the daughter of James Height, a building and painting contractor who became active in Republican politics, and Fannie Burroughs, a nurse and household worker, both twice widowed with children from earlier marriages. As a child, Dorothy loved to read, liked challenges, and always kept busy. When she was four, she and her family moved to Rankin, Pennsylvania, a small borough of Pittsburgh, during the Great Migration. Fannie participated in the black women's club movement through the Pennsylvania Federation of Colored Women's Clubs, and Dorothy recalled going with her mother to every state and national meeting and hearing the imperative of "uplifting the race."

Rankin was an ethnically diverse community, and Dorothy attended school with Germans, Croatians, Jews, Italians, Poles, and children of other ethnicities. Growing up, she generally experienced very little prejudice. Her first brush with racism, however, occurred when she was eight years old, when Sarah Hay, one of her Irish Catholic friends, refused to play with her one day because she was a "nigger." As she grew older, Dorothy would have other, more intense racist encounters. As a student, she proved to be exceptional. In addition to excelling at academics, she won several speech contests and had a passion for music, even cowriting the alma mater for her high school. She graduated from Rankin High School in June of 1929, after which she studied social work and psychology at New York University (NYU). While in college, Height worked as a proofreader for the *Negro World*, MARCUS GARVEY's widely circulated newspaper. In 1932, after just three years, she finished her BA and one year later earned an MA in Educational Psychology, also from NYU. Her college years paralleled the Harlem Renaissance and had allowed her to meet and hear presentations by W. E. B. DU BOIS, PAUL ROBESON, COUNTÉE CULLEN, LANGSTON HUGHES, and others.

After finishing college, Height began a long career as a social worker. Her first job, for which she was paid twenty dollars a month, was with the Brownsville Community Center in Brooklyn, where she addressed the community's high delinquency and unemployment rates. Soon after, she became an investigator for the Home Relief Bureau of the New York City Welfare Administration, earning twenty-seven dollars and fifty cents a week. She also worked with other community leaders to quell the Harlem riots of 1935. This riot began after a young African American stole a knife from a Harlem store. Rumors spread that he had been beaten to death, so crowds formed, accusing the white merchants of discrimination in employment and the police of brutality. The ensuing violence resulted in the death of three African Americans and the destruction of over two million dollars in property.

During this time Height worked with the United Christian Youth Movement of North America (UCYMNA), became president of the New York State Christian Youth Council, chaired the Harlem Youth Council, and attended the UCYMNA-sponsored World Conference on Life and Work of the Churches in Oxford, England, where she worked with BENJAMIN MAYS and his wife, Sadie. Over time Height's sphere extended to Africa, where she worked with Africans in Sierra Leone, Ghana, Nigeria, and Guinea. Eventually the U.S. State Department noticed her work and appointed her to its advisory panel on Africa.

Inspired by the Oxford conference, Dorothy helped organize the World Conference of Christian Youth, a global conference of young Christians held in Amsterdam in August 1939. Several months later Height resigned from the Home Relief Bureau and took a job as assistant executive director of the New York YWCA. The New York World's Fair brought thousands of young African American women to the city in 1939 in search of employment. In helping these young women, Height learned of the "Bronx slave market," where women waited on street corners for jobs as domestics, only to be exploited, physically and financially, by employers. Height fought, unsuccessfully, to have this practice abolished. She also fought to secure antilynching legislation, eliminate segregation in the armed forces, and reform of the criminal justice system.

At the third annual meeting of the National Council of Negro Women (NCNW), held in November 1937, Height met the NCNW's founder, MARY MCLEOD BETHUNE, and the keynote speaker, First Lady Eleanor Roosevelt. Shortly thereafter, Bethune appointed Height to the NCNW's resolutions committee, and in 1938 she worked with Roosevelt on the World Conference of Youth, held at Vassar College in Poughkeepsie, New York. Years later, in 1961, Height worked with Roosevelt again after President John F. Kennedy appointed her to the President's Commission on the Status of Women. As Height later recalled, "It was a privilege to know Mrs. Roosevelt and Mrs. Bethune, two extraordinary women" (93).

Height continued her work with the YWCA, taking a position as executive director of the PHILLIS WHEATLEY YWCA in Washington, D.C., in the fall of 1939. Five years later she returned to New York, becoming secretary for interracial education on the YWCA's national board, a position she felt would better allow her to "make a contribution to the national effort to end racism and segregation" (107). Height helped the YWCA adopt its first Interracial Charter in 1946, a very difficult task in light of the resistance on the part of many white southern YWCA branches. In 1965 she became the director of the YWCA's office of racial justice, a position she held until her retirement from the organization in 1977. In 2000 President Bill Clinton became the first recipient of the YWCA Dorothy I. Height Racial Justice Award.

Dorothy Height had joined the Delta Sigma Theta sorority in 1939. Two years later she became chair of its social action program, and from 1947 to 1956, she served as president of the sorority. Over the years she moved the Delta's annual convention from a church basement to the Kiel Auditorium in St. Louis, Missouri. Height developed the organization's Job Opportunity Project and began the Delta bookmobile project in Georgia, an effort that led the state to start providing rural and poor children with library services.

In 1957, two years after the death of Mary McLeod Bethune, Height became the NCNW's fourth president, a position she still holds at the beginning of the twenty-first century. Over the next four decades, under Height's leadership, the NCNW created the Bethune Museum and Archives, the first national archive on black women and published the organization's first book. She also established the annual Black Family Reunion Celebration and an anonymous debtors' program to help young black women with their finances; both programs were designed to strengthen the black family. The NCNW, which became tax exempt in 1966, confronted unemployment, hunger and malnutrition, the problems of poor housing and public health and participated in the March on Washington, voter education drives in the North, and numerous civil rights projects in Mississippi during the 1960s. Height herself participated in almost every major civil and human rights event, working closely with MARTIN LUTHER KING JR., ROY WILKINS, WHITNEY YOUNG, and A. PHILIP RANDOLPH among others.

In 1995 Height spearheaded the purchase of the NCNW's national headquarters, the historic Sears House on 633 Pennsylvania Avenue, in Washington, D.C. The NCNW, which includes more than four million women, shares its headquarters with the Dorothy I. Height Leadership Institute and the National Centers for African American Women. According to Height, the NCNW's "great strength has been that it builds leadership skills in women by emphasizing self-reliance, unity, and the commitment to working collaboratively" (271).

Height received the Citizens Medal Award from President Ronald Reagan in 1989 and the Presidential Medal of Freedom, the nation's highest civilian award, from President Bill Clinton in 1994. In her 2003 memoir, she reminded readers that while American leaders travel the world selling democracy and expressing concern for human rights, "many here at home still cannot enjoy the simplest benefits guaranteed by the Constitution because of endemic, institutionalized racism. Institutionalized racism is more than debilitating—it is disastrous for the nation. It is long past time to end it, completely, everywhere" (268–269).

FURTHER READING

Height, Dorothy. *Open Wide the Freedom Gates: A Memoir* (2003).

Giddings, Paula. *In Search of Sisterhood: Delta Sigma Theta and the Challenge of the Black Sorority Movement* (1988).
—DAVID H. JACKSON JR.

HEMINGS, SALLY

(1773–1835), slave and Thomas Jefferson's mistress, whose given name probably was Sarah, was born in Virginia, the daughter of the slave Elizabeth "Betty" Hemings and, allegedly, John Wayles, a merchant and planter. (Family members spell the surname both *Hemings* and *Hemmings*.) After Wayles's death in 1773, Betty Hemings and her children became the property of Thomas Jefferson and his wife, Martha Wayles Skelton Jefferson. From an early age Sally Hemings was a personal servant of Jefferson's daughter Mary (later Maria), whom she accompanied to France in 1787, when Sally was fourteen and Mary nine.

It is not known whether Sally, while in Paris, lived at Mary's convent school or at Jefferson's residence on the Champs-Elysées, where her brother James Hemings was *chef de cuisine*. Jefferson's expenditures during her two-year residence in Paris indicate that Sally received further training in the skills of a lady's maid, and she acted in that capacity for Jefferson's older daughter, Martha, when the latter began going out

in Parisian society in 1789. She intermittently received a small monthly wage during this period.

Jefferson, his two daughters, and his two slaves returned to Virginia at the end of 1789. Despite her long association with Jefferson's younger daughter, Sally Hemings remained at Monticello after Maria Jefferson's marriage and departure in 1797. Her son Madison Hemings remembered that she took care of Jefferson's chamber and wardrobe and did "such light work as sewing, &c." Jefferson's records reveal only that she was one of the "house-maids," that she bore six children, two of whom died as infants, and that, at Jefferson's death in 1826, she was still a slave, valued in the appraisal of his property at fifty dollars.

There is no certain information on Sally Hemings's status after Jefferson's death. It seems likely that she was unofficially freed by Jefferson's daughter Martha Randolph, whose 1834 will asked that "Sally" be given her "time." This may have been intended to legitimize an existing situation. She appears in an 1833 "List of Free Negroes & Mulattoes" with her son Madison, who recalled that his mother lived with him in Charlottesville until her death.

Madison Hemings, freed in Jefferson's will, related his life story to an Ohio journalist in 1873. It is this account, selectively accepted by historians, that contains most of what is known about the Hemings family. Hemings is the main source for the allegation that John Wayles was the father of Sally Hemings and five of her siblings. He also stated that he and his own brothers and sisters were Thomas Jefferson's children, the result of a relationship that began in Paris. When his account was published in 1873, the story of a possible sexual relationship between Jefferson and Sally Hemings had long been part of the public discourse. It had been transformed from local gossip to national news in the fall of 1802, when an article in the Richmond *Recorder* began, "It is well known that the man, *whom it delighteth the people to honor*, keeps, and for many years past has kept, as his concubine, one of his own slaves. Her name is sally." The author was James Thomson Callender, a disgruntled convert to the Federalist cause after his former heroes on the Republican side

failed to "reward" him with a postmastership. Other Federalist writers quickly incorporated the tale in their attacks on President Jefferson and his administration. Jefferson himself was silent on the issue. In accordance with his practice in regard to personal attacks, he never publicly denied a connection. One private letter, which might be interpreted as a denial, remains ambiguous. His own family members were consistent in their disbelief but made their denials privately.

For the rest of the century the allegation that the author of the Declaration of Independence kept his own children in slavery was taken up by critics of Jefferson's party, his region, and his country. Skeptical British travelers, highlighting the hypocrisy of the American experiment, repeated and embellished the story, and antislavery activists of the antebellum period used the relationship to emphasize the exploitation of the slavery system.

In the meantime, more quietly, a belief in their Jefferson ancestry passed from generation to generation of Sally Hemings's descendants. Their side of the story was first given wider circulation in 1974 in *Thomas Jefferson: An Intimate History* by Fawn M. Brodie, one of the very few Jefferson biographers to accept the Hemings-Jefferson connection. At the center of Brodie's psychological portrait is an enduring relationship between master and slave, romantic rather than exploitative. It is her version that captured and has held the public imagination since that time.

In the absence of solid evidence to prove or refute its existence, the possible relationship between Thomas Jefferson and Sally Hemings was the subject of vigorous and shifting debate for almost two centuries. The story became a convenient symbol for some of the anomalies of American history and complexities of American society, and African Americans in the twentieth century viewed its denial by historians as symbolic of the negation of oral traditions—often the only possible link to their ancestors in slavery. The results of DNA testing of Hemings and Jefferson descendants, published in the fall of 1998, strongly indicate, however, that Jefferson was the father of Hemings's youngest son, Eston, and perhaps all her known children. While the debate has turned to issues of family and master-slave relations, the findings have in effect deepened the enigma of Jefferson's character. Even more elusive, however, is the figure at the heart of the controversy, Sally Hemings herself.

FURTHER READING

Brodie, Fawn M. *Thomas Jefferson: An Intimate History* (1974).

French, Scot A., and Edward L. Ayers. "The Strange Career of Thomas Jefferson: Race and Slavery in American Memory, 1943–1993" in *Jeffersonian Legacies*, ed. Peter S. Onuf (1993).

Gordon-Reed, Annette. *Thomas Jefferson and Sally Hemings: An American Controversy* (1997).

Justus, Judith. *Down from the Mountain: The Oral History of the Hemings Family* (1990).

Peterson, Merrill D. *The Jefferson Image in the American Mind* (1960).

—LUCIA C. STANTON

HENDRIX, JIMI

(27 Nov. 1942–18 Sept. 1970), rock guitarist, singer, and songwriter, was born into a working-class black family in Seattle, Washington, the son of James Allen Ross Hendrix, a gardener, and Lucille Jetter. Named Johnny Allen Hendrix at birth by his mother while his father was in the service, his name was changed to James Marshall Hendrix by his father upon his return home. Self-taught as a left-handed guitarist from an early age, Hendrix played a right-handed guitar upside down, a practice he maintained throughout his life since it allowed for unusual fingering patterns and quicker access to tone and volume controls. His early influences ranged from jazz guitarist Charlie Christian to blues guitarists and honking rhythm and blues saxophone soloists. He attended elementary school in Vancouver, British Columbia, and Seattle and went to Garfield High School in Seattle. In his senior year, he left high school to become a paratrooper with the 101st Airborne Division of the U.S. Army.

At Fort Campbell, Kentucky, Hendrix formed a rhythm and blues band, the Casuals, with bassist Billy Cox, who would rejoin him years later at the height of his fame. Following his discharge from the army in 1962, he

moved to Nashville, where he played with some locally successful rhythm and blues groups and recorded a demonstration tape with the soul guitarist Steve Cropper, one of many guitarists to have an influence on Hendrix's maturing style. After a brief tour in 1963 with LITTLE RICHARD, Hendrix was in great demand as a sideman, performing with a number of established figures and groups such as Solomon Burke, Ike and Tina Turner, Jackie Wilson, B. B. KING, and, later, the Isley Brothers and Curtis Knight. In 1963–1964 Hendrix's guitar playing was increasingly influenced by traditional bluesmen such as ROBERT JOHNSON, T-Bone Walker, B. B. King, MUDDY WATERS, and especially Albert King, although the relatively few available recordings from this period reveal only that he was a fluent and idiomatic rhythm and blues guitarist and capable sideman.

Leading his own group, Jimmy James and the Blue Flames, in a Greenwich Village club in late 1965, Hendrix began to exhibit increasing signs of an original, even eccentric approach that incorporated feedback and other electronic sounds as an integral part of his style as well as overt sexual posturing and a further development of the showmanship techniques (such as playing his guitar behind his back and with his teeth) that he had displayed while touring with the Isley Brothers. Among the influences that took root in this period were Bob Dylan, whose mannered vocal style and sometimes mystical and visionary lyrics Hendrix admired, and the guitar playing of Mike Bloomfield, the inventive lead guitarist for the Paul Butterfield Blues Band and Bob Dylan.

Impressed by Hendrix's formidable technique, distinctive playing style, and charismatic stage presence, Chas Chandler, former bass guitarist of the British rock group the Animals, convinced Hendrix to return with him to England to launch a new career. Under Chandler's guidance, the new Jimi Hendrix Experience, also featuring bassist Noel Redding and virtuoso drummer Mitch Mitchell, quickly became a favorite on the British and European pop scenes, releasing its first single, "Hey Joe," in December 1966 and its first album, *Are You Experienced?* (Reprise 6267), in September 1967. Consisting mostly of original songs, the album was characterized by

extensive multitracking and electronic manipulation of sound (for example, phase shifting, tape reversed effects, and a variety of feedback sounds), the result of a collaboration between Hendrix and recording engineer Eddie Kramer. The album demonstrated that Hendrix's virtuoso guitar style had by this point successfully assimilated and adapted techniques from an unusually wide variety of sources ranging from soul guitarists to traditional and contemporary urban bluesmen and even jazz players such as Wes Montgomery. His vocal style had developed into a highly individualistic blend of mannerisms derived from blues, soul, and Dylan's half-spoken narrative style.

The *Are You Experienced?* album and associated singles did much to propel Hendrix to the forefront of the emerging British psychedelic rock movement, one of few black performers associated with that style. His popularity in the United States was guaranteed by his electrifying performance at the prestigious First International Monterey Pop Festival in June 1967, in which he burned his guitar and destroyed his equipment onstage.

Hendrix released his second album with the Experience, *Axis: Bold as Love* (Reprise 6281), in January 1968. This album exhibited an even more elaborate use of multitracking and electronic manipulation than the first, with some songs demonstrating more complex structures and more ambitious and visionary lyrics, some of which appear to have been inspired by drug experiences. In 1968 he was named artist of the year by both *Billboard* and *Rolling Stone* magazines.

Following this album, Hendrix began various attempts to expand the basic "power trio" format of the Jimi Hendrix Experience. The double album issued in September, *Electric Ladyland* (Reprise 6307), employed various other artists along with Redding and Mitchell and was the most intricately textured to date. Some songs, however, such as the hit single version of Dylan's "All along the Watchtower," showed an unusually straightforward, almost austere style, and others, such as "Voodoo Chile," suggested a return to the earlier urban blues style of Muddy Waters.

After the release of this album, Hendrix continually expressed the desire to shed his "psychedelic wizard" reputation and further develop his musical style, speaking on a number of occasions of his interest in jazz and his eagerness to perform with major jazz figures such as MILES DAVIS, who had shown some interest in Hendrix's music. Hendrix disbanded the Experience in 1969, envisioning a fluid "Electric Sky Church" made up of various musicians performing in different styles. His performance at the August 1969 Woodstock Festival, in which Billy Cox, a friend from his army days, replaced Noel Redding on bass, included a particularly dynamic and violent performance of the "Star Spangled Banner" that became famous as a demonstration of his unique guitar style. Under some pressure from black militants to make outspoken political statements, Hendrix shied away from active involvement in politics but did launch an all-black trio, the Band of Gypsys, featuring bass player Billy Cox and drummer/vocalist Buddy Miles, which in 1970 released an album of tracks (*The Band of Gypsys*, Capitol 0472) from a concert at the Fillmore East in New York City. But Hendrix remained dissatisfied, and the group quickly disbanded, with Hendrix walking offstage during a performance in early 1970. Hendrix was briefly rejoined by the original members of the Experience, but Noel Redding was soon replaced by Cox once again. In this period, Hendrix devoted considerable time to planning for and working in his new studio, Electric Lady Studios. His final live performances were erratic, with Hendrix sometimes appearing to be out of control or distant. He died in London in his sleep, asphyxiated following a presumably accidental overdose of sleeping pills. By then he had become a figure of gigantic proportions in the pop music world, not only as the first major black artist in the psychedelic style, but as a guitarist and composer whose work was considered strikingly original and distinctive.

Despite his great fame, his influence on later rock musicians was expressed more in terms of inspiration than direct imitation. Few if any of his followers appeared able to duplicate many of Hendrix's guitar-derived or studio-generated electronic effects with the finesse that he had demonstrated. His compositional approach was sufficiently

unique that his songs were largely inimitable as well. But the Hendrix legacy remains strong, if for no other reason than because he is seen as a musical free spirit who expanded the potential of the electric guitar and the boundaries of rock music in general in the late 1960s to a degree matched by few others.

FURTHER READING

Henderson, David. *Scuze Me while I Kiss the Sky: The Life of Jimi Hendrix* (1980).
Hopkins, Jerry. *Hit and Run: The Jimi Hendrix Story* (1983).
Knight, Curtis. *Jimi: An Intimate Biography of Jimi Hendrix* (1974).
Tarshis, Steve. *Original Hendrix* (1982).
Welch, Chris. *Hendrix: A Biography* (1972)

Obituary: *New York Times*, 19 Sept. 1970.
—TERENCE J. O'GRADY

HENSON, JOSIAH

(15 June 1789–5 May 1883), escaped slave and preacher, was born in Charles County, Maryland, on a farm owned by Francis Newman. As a child, Henson frequently saw his parents abused and severely beaten. On one occasion, as a punishment for defending his wife, Henson's father was sentenced to a physical mutilation that left him permanently scarred. Although he was raised without religion, Henson was immediately converted to Christianity after his first exposure to it at a revivalist camp meeting. As a young boy, he was sold to Isaac Riley.

Because of his unusual strength and intelligence, Henson was made superintendent of the farm at a young age. He managed the plantation well, doubling the annual crop production. One day, during an argument at a neighboring farm, Henson defended his master in an argument with the other plantation's overseer. In revenge, the overseer and three of his slaves waylaid Henson one evening soon afterward, beating him and shattering his shoulder blade. For the rest of his life, he could not raise his arms above shoulder level. At age twenty-two Henson married another slave (name unknown); they had twelve children.

Isaac Riley, the master of Henson's plantation, went bankrupt in 1825 and

was forced to sell his farm and to transfer his twenty slaves to his brother's farm in Kentucky. After making Henson swear to their safe passage, Riley entrusted him with the care of the slaves. The route to Kentucky took the party through Ohio, a free state, where many implored Henson to allow them their freedom, but Henson kept his word and brought them intact to their new owner. In 1828 Henson became a preacher for the Methodist Episcopal Church. He then attempted to buy his freedom from his owner. A price of four hundred dollars was settled on, but at the last minute the owner reneged on his agreement, deciding instead to sell Henson to a new owner in New Orleans. Journeying south with his master's son, who had instructions to transact some business and then to sell Henson before the return voyage, Henson's trepidation grew as he saw the terrible conditions in which slaves in the deep South lived. Midway through the journey, the master's son developed a serious fever, rendering him weak and helpless, and he begged Henson to bring him home safely. Though he could easily have deserted his young master and made a bid for freedom, Henson remained to escort the son back to his father. His loyalty met with neither reward nor gratitude. Henson's growing desire for freedom, augmented by outrage at this ingratitude, propelled him to escape with his wife and four young children in the summer of 1830. In two weeks he had reached Cincinnati, from there he sailed to Buffalo, New York, and, in October, he crossed the U.S. border into Canada.

Henson settled in Dresden, Ontario, near Lake St. Clair and south of the Sydenham River, and he became a preacher. His oldest son, then in school, taught him to read. Quickly establishing himself as a leader in the Afro-Canadian community, Henson made several trips back to the United States and across the Mason-Dixon line to help other slaves escape. During the Canadian Rebellions of 1837–1838 Henson served the British as a captain in a troop of Afro-Canadian volunteers. With the support of sponsors from England and America, Henson began laying the foundations for an Afro-Canadian community and industrial school. The British American

Institute, begun in 1842, encompassing two hundred acres of wooded land, was intended as a refuge for escaped slaves. However, the community never grew large or self-sufficient enough to survive, and by the end of the Civil War almost all of the colony's remaining members had returned to the United States. In 1849 Henson published his autobiography, *The Life of Josiah Henson, Formerly a Slave, Now an Inhabitant of Canada, as Narrated by Himself*. Reprinted in 1858, its name was changed to *Truth Stranger than Fiction: Father Henson's Story of His Own Life*, and the next edition was titled *"Truth Is Stranger than Fiction": An Autobiography of the Rev. Josiah Henson* (1879). Both later editions contain a foreword by Harriet Beecher Stowe.

On three journeys to England, in 1849, 1851, and 1876, Henson received much attention from members of high society there, including the archbishop of Canterbury. He was honored at a private party given in 1851 by Prime Minister Lord John Russell and invited by Lord Grey to travel to India to supervise cotton plantations. Soon after his return from England, Henson met Stowe. After *Uncle Tom's Cabin* was published in 1852, the public began to believe that Henson's life story was the basis for the character of Uncle Tom in the novel. Following the death of his first wife, Henson married a Boston widow. His final trip to England, a preaching and lecturing tour in 1876, was highlighted by Queen Victoria's personal gift of her photograph encased in a gold frame. Henson died in Dresden, Ontario.

Henson's life story is that of a daring early leader of slaves and escaped slaves, a man of high moral principles who endured great suffering. Although the British American Institute was small and unsuccessful, Henson's work as an ambassador to England for African Americans did much for their perception overseas. His greatest achievement was the example he offered of a man born into slavery, illiterate and handicapped by vicious physical abuse, who gained his freedom, learned to read, and became a preacher and a leader of a community of escaped slaves.

FURTHER READING

Pease, William, and Jane Pease. *Black Utopia: Negro Communal Experiments in America* (1963).

Stowe Harriet Beecher. *A Key to Uncle Tom's Cabin* (1853).

Winks Robin. *Blacks in Canada: A History* (1971).

Obituary: *New York Tribune*, 6 May 1883.
—ELIZABETH ZOE VICARY

HENSON, MATTHEW ALEXANDER (8 Aug. 1866– 9 Mar. 1955), Arctic explorer, was born in Charles County, Maryland, to Lemuel Henson, a sharecropper, and his wife, Caroline Gaines. As best as can be determined from the conflicting accounts of his life, Matthew's mother, Caroline, died when he was just two years old. His father then married Nellie, a neighbor with whom he already had a child. A few years later Lemuel died, leaving Matthew in the care of his abusive stepmother. Shortly after his eleventh birthday, Matthew left his five siblings and fled to Washington, D.C., where he worked for food and lodging at a restaurant owned by Janey Moore, whom he called "Aunt Janey." He may have attended the N Street School in Washington before a seaman known as Baltimore Jack captured his imagination with tales of adventure upon the high seas.

At age twelve Henson signed on as cabin boy on the *Katie Hines*, a three-masted sail and steam vessel. Over the next six years, the ship took Henson around the globe several times. During these voyages Captain Childs instructed Henson in reading, writing, history, and the nautical skills required for him to advance from cabin boy to able-bodied seaman. After Childs's death in 1883, Henson signed on to the *White Seal*, a Newfoundland fishing schooner, but he found the working conditions so vile and the attitude of the white crew so hostile that he sought alternative work on land. He lived in Boston, Providence, and New York City before becoming a clerk at Steinmetz and Son, a Washington, D.C., haberdashery. In the spring of 1887 Robert Peary, a young naval engineer, entered the store to buy a sun helmet. Peary was leading a party to map a canal route connecting the Atlantic and the Pacific through Nicaragua, and he asked if Henson would be interested in coming along as his "personal servant." Henson, whose thirst for adventure was as great as Peary's, accepted. This was the first of many voyages that Henson took with Peary over the next twenty-two years.

During seven months in the tropics of Nicaragua, a relationship of trust and respect developed between Henson and Peary. On their return from Nicaragua, Peary helped Henson get a job as a messenger at the League Island Navy Yard, which provided him not only with a steady income, but a pension as well, benefits that were difficult for Negroes to obtain. In April 1891 Henson married Eva Helen Flint, a member of Philadelphia's black middle class. He had financial security and a family, both of which he put at risk when he agreed to accompany Peary on a quest for the North Pole.

Henson accompanied Peary on seven Arctic expeditions. The first took place in 1891–1892, with the goal of traversing Greenland. They returned to Greenland in 1893–1895 to map the region but failed to reach the ice cap. The next two voyages, in 1896 and 1897, were expeditions to take a thirty-ton meteorite to the United States. During their longest polar expedition, from 1898 to 1902, Henson, who had recently divorced, entered into a relationship with an Inuit woman, Akatingwah, and they had a son, Anaukaq. The party returned to the United States without the grail they sought. They claimed to have set a new distance record of 87°6' N during a 1905–1906 attempt but were turned back by ice floes and water. Finally, a determined effort in 1908–1909 got Peary, at least, into the history books.

When they first set sail from Brooklyn in 1891, Henson had more experience at sea than any other member of the crew. Some of the white officers complained of Henson's "freedom and insolence." John Verhoeff, a southerner who expected subservience from Negroes, clashed with Henson so intensely that on one occasion Commander Peary's wife, Josephine Peary, suggested the two men simply "fight it out." Peary developed confidence in Henson's loyalty, dedication, and ingenuity, though he himself initially subscribed to the common stereotype that Negroes are better suited for warm climates. After their final mission, however, one member of the team, Donald MacMillan, stated flatly in *National Geographic* that Henson "went to the Pole with Peary because he was easily the most efficient of all Peary's assistants."

His intelligence, adaptability, and personal demeanor helped to make Henson indispensable to their mission. The Inuit called Henson *Mahri-Pahluk*, "the kind one." Henson himself writes that "I have been to all intents an Esquimo, with Esquimos for companions, speaking their language, dressing in the same kind of clothes, living in the same kind of dens, eating the same food, enjoying their pleasures, and frequently sharing their grief" (Henson, 4). Henson's close relationship with the Inuit was invaluable because they provided the expedition not only with labor and supplies, but also with knowledge and skills necessary for its very survival. For example, Europeans often used tents, whereas igloos provided better shelter and did not need to be transported. Similarly, explorers often wore woolen clothing and used Alpine skis, though the animal skins and shoes of the Inuit were more effective.

Henson was responsible for building the sledges and training the crews in their operation, engaging the Inuit who accompanied them and who manufactured their clothing, and even selecting the dogs. He participated in gathering scientific data, such as temperature and water depth, and he was cook, carpenter, hunter, and translator, as well as photographer—though most of his pictures were confiscated by Peary, who required all the members of his expeditions to sign nondisclosure agreements.

During their first voyage in 1891, Peary broke his leg and was almost completely dependent on Henson through the winter, when temperatures dropped to fifty degrees below zero. In 1898, during their fifth expedition, Peary lost eight toes to frostbite; Henson used his own body to warm Peary and saved his life by transporting him to safety. These were dangerous missions on which six men died; four Inuit died of Western diseases against which they had no immunity, Verhoeff mysteriously disappeared, and Ross Marvin was murdered by a member of his sledge crew. Under such extreme circumstances, Henson might best be described

as Peary's Arctic engineer, manager, and partner. However, the bonds of necessity that held the two together on the ice gave way to conventional divisions of race and class whenever they returned to "civilization."

After eighteen years of sacrifice and repeated disappointment, Peary, at age fifty-three and Henson, at forty-three, found themselves 175 miles from the top of the world with four Inuit—Ooatah, Egingwah, Seegloo, and Ooqueah. At intervals Peary had members of his crew return to base, leaving a cache of supplies for those who forged ahead. Henson suspected that Peary would ask him to trail behind on the last leg of the journey. Thus, on 6 April 1909, when Peary instructed him to stop just short of the North Pole, Henson claims that he inadvertently overshot his target and camped at the pole forty-five minutes before Peary arrived. Peary disputed this claim, and his relationship with Henson became much more distant after their return. Henson wrote that "for the crime of being present when the Pole was reached Commander Peary has ignored me ever since" (Henson, 151).

The recognition that Henson should have received for his role in the discovery was delayed in coming, first because of a spurious claim by Dr. Frederick Cook that he had beaten them to the pole, and then by lingering doubts that Peary miscalculated or fabricated his coordinates. But by all calculations the expedition reached an area that can be considered generally, if not precisely, the North Pole. Peary received numerous accolades and awards and was promoted to rear admiral, allowing him to retire with a pension of almost eight thousand dollars a year. In contrast, Henson found himself working as a handyman in a Brooklyn garage for sixteen dollars a week and moonlighting at the post office. His second wife, Lucy Jane Ross, had to work to supplement their income. Henson tried to make a living on the lecture circuit, and he published his autobiography, *A Negro Explorer at the North Pole* (1912), but there was little public interest in either.

BOOKER T. WASHINGTON and administrators at several black colleges held dinners or presented Henson with honorary degrees, and more than twenty years after his greatest accomplishment,

he was made an honorary member of the Explorers Club and an honorary member of the Academy of Science and Art of Pittsburgh. In 1913, by order of President William Howard Taft, Henson was given a position as a messenger at the U.S. Customs House in New York, which he held until the mandatory retirement age of seventy. However, repeated efforts to present Henson with a national medal of honor were blocked until 1944, when Congress authorized a medal honoring *all* the men of the Peary expedition. At Henson's funeral ADAM CLAYTON POWELL JR. asserted that the "achievements of Henson are as important as those performed by Marco Polo and Ferdinand Magellan." In 1988 Henson and his wife were reinterred at Arlington National Cemetery near the site of Robert Peary's grave.

FURTHER READING

The main body of Henson's papers is located in the Matthew Henson Collection at Morgan State University in Baltimore, Maryland.

Henson, Matthew. *A Negro Explorer at the North Pole* (1912).

Counter, S. Allen. *North Pole Legacy: Black, White & Eskimo* (1991).
Miller, Floyd. *Ahdoolo: The Biography of Matthew A. Henson* (1963).
Robinson, Bradley. *Dark Companion* (1947).

Obituary: *New York Times*, 10 Mar. 1955.
—SHOLOMO B. LEVY

 HERNDON, ANGELO (6 May 1913–9 December 1997), Communist organizer and political prisoner, was born in the tiny southern Ohio town of Wyoming, the son of Paul Herndon, a coal miner. His mother, Harriet, was of a mixed-race background and worked as a domestic. According to an early version of Herndon's autobiography, his name was recorded in the family Bible as Eugene Angelo Braxton Herndon. During Angelo's youth, the family experienced poverty, which grew worse after his father died. Fundamentalist Christianity helped family members endure such hard times, and at the age of nine Herndon underwent a deep religious experience and joined a local church. Shortly after he turned thirteen, Angelo and an older brother left home for Kentucky, where they worked in a coal mine for a while before heading farther south to Alabama.

Over the next several years Herndon found employment at various construction and mining sites in the Birmingham area, though he also encountered pervasive racism and witnessed the clear economic exploitation of African American workers. Upset by these degrading conditions, he became frustrated with the reluctance of black Alabamians to fight back against their mistreatment. As the teenager matured and developed a political consciousness, he came to view the emotional religion of his youth as an inadequate philosophy for the harsh realities of daily life. During the summer of 1930 Herndon attended an integrated rally held in Birmingham by the Unemployed Council, a national organization dominated by members of the Communist Party, and he was excited by the group's willingness to challenge white supremacy and economic inequality. A subsequent arrest by the local police convinced him that he had discovered the right path for himself and other African Americans. Toward the end of the summer, at the age of seventeen, Herndon formally joined the Communist Party. The new secular religion of Communism had replaced the fundamentalist Christianity of his youth.

The young convert eagerly plunged into a variety of Communist projects in Alabama, working tirelessly to organize miners and sharecroppers into unions and to develop a mass campaign around the nine wrongfully imprisoned SCOTTSBORO BOYS. His enthusiasm for the Communist cause did not go unnoticed by the authorities, however, and he was subjected to several additional arrests and beatings. Believing that such harassment lessened Herndon's effectiveness, the party reassigned him to Atlanta during the winter of 1931–1932, to revitalize the Unemployed Council there.

Soon after Herndon arrived in Atlanta, the city and county governments plunged into a deep financial crisis, endangering the area's limited relief program but also presenting the Communists with an excellent opportunity to attract members. As economic conditions steadily worsened during 1932, the Unemployed Council expanded its work among the jobless. In response to an announcement of further cuts in relief payments, Herndon successfully organized, on 30 June, an unprecedented protest by more than a thousand white and black workers in front of the Fulton County Courthouse. Unnerved by the demonstration, county commissioners immediately restored some of the previously eliminated funds. Meanwhile, the police department stepped up its surveillance of local radicals and eventually arrested Herndon on 11 July. Eleven days later a grand jury indicted him under an 1866 anti-insurrection law, which had revised an 1833 statute prohibiting slave revolts. Prosecutors specifically charged the young Communist with "attempting to incite insurrection against the state of Georgia," a capital offense. The severity of this charge clearly indicated that local officials viewed Herndon's interracial efforts as a dangerous threat to the existing social order.

In January 1933 Herndon received his day in court. He turned over the handling of his case to the International Labor Defense (ILD), which retained two local African American attorneys, BENJAMIN JEFFERSON DAVIS JR. and John Geer, to defend him. This bold but risky decision reflected Herndon's and the ILD's determination to confront white supremacy directly and unequivocally. During the trial, prosecutors tried to create an atmosphere of hysteria, warning that Communism directly threatened Georgia's political and economic stability. The prosecution specifically accused Herndon of circulating inflammatory literature and attempting to establish a radical movement whose ultimate aim was to overthrow the established government. Defense attorneys countered that there was no proof that the nineteen-year-old activist had taken any specific steps to organize an actual revolt and that the prosecution was based on fear of Communism and interracial cooperation. Herndon willingly took the stand to justify his actions. He told the jury that, in reality, he was being tried because he had dared to organize black and white workers together. The young defendant further argued that capitalism deliberately encouraged racism "in order to keep the Negro and white divided" (quoted in Martin [1976], 52). Finally, Herndon warned that although the state had the power to send him to prison, there would be more "Angelo Herndons to come in the future." His courageous but inexpedient testimony failed to impress the all-white, twelve-man jury, which found Herndon guilty and sentenced him to eighteen to twenty years in prison.

While Davis and Geer prepared an appeal to the state supreme court, the ILD launched a national mass campaign on behalf of Herndon, arguing that he was a political prisoner who had been unjustly convicted because of his radical beliefs. The ILD's persistence eventually built the case into a national cause célèbre. In May 1934 the state supreme court rejected the appeal. The ILD then recruited several specialists in constitutional law to argue the case before the U.S. Supreme Court. Meanwhile, Herndon remained behind bars in Atlanta until August 1934, when the ILD finally gained his release on bail.

Once he was free, Herndon embarked on several national speaking tours, increasing public awareness of his case. The ILD helped him compose a short autobiographical booklet describing his conversion to Communism and his trial, which the organization published under the title *You Cannot Kill the Working Class*. In May 1935 the Supreme Court turned down his appeal on technical grounds and sent the case back to the state courts. After Herndon surrendered to Georgia authorities, his lawyers initiated another round of legal maneuvers. In December a superior court judge unexpectedly ruled in Herndon's favor, temporarily striking down the insurrection law, but the state supreme court restored the conviction in June 1936.

While his attorneys prepared for another full hearing before the U.S. Supreme Court, Herndon remained free on a second bond and continued his public appearances in the North. With the assistance of a ghostwriter, he drafted a full-length autobiography, *Let Me Live*, which Random House released in early 1937. In April of that year Herndon finally received vindication. By a five-to-four vote, the U.S. Supreme Court declared the insurrection law, "as construed and applied," to be unconstitutional and overturned his conviction. In concluding that the Georgia statute was "an unwarranted invasion of the right of freedom of speech," the court moved closer toward acceptance of the so-called clear and present danger test for laws restricting First Amendment rights, an important constitutional shift.

His permanent freedom finally assured, Herndon returned to New York City, where he initially took a public role in many Communist activities and occasionally wrote articles for the *Daily Worker*. In 1938 he married Joyce M. Chellis, a native of Alabama. In the early 1940s he assisted RALPH ELLISON in founding and editing the short-lived *Negro Quarterly: A Review of Negro Life and Culture*. On two occasions he successfully thwarted efforts by New York City's selective service director to revoke his draft deferment. Like many other Communists, Herndon gradually became dissatisfied with the party during the war, and by the mid-1940s he had quietly left its ranks. He subsequently moved to Chicago and took a job as a salesman, discussing his past with only his closest friends. In 1967 he tentatively agreed to speak with a historian researching his trial but then changed his mind. Two years later the *New York Times* and Arno Press published a reprint of *Let Me Live*, as part of a series on African American history and culture. Despite revived interest in his earlier political activism, Herndon refused to make any public appearances, declined requests for interviews, and continued to live a very private life.

FURTHER READING

Herndon, Angelo. *Let Me Live* (1937).
———. *You Cannot Kill the Working Class* (1934).

Martin, Charles H. *The Angelo Herndon Case and Southern Justice* (1976).
———. "The Angelo Herndon Case and Southern Justice" in *American Political Trials*, ed. Michal R. Belknap (1994).
Thomas, Kendall. "'Rouge et Noir' Reread: A Popular Constitutional History of the Angelo Herndon Case" in *Critical Race Theory*, eds. Kimberle Crenshaw et al. (1995).

—CHARLES H. MARTIN

 HERRIMAN, GEORGE JOSEPH (22 Aug. 1880–25 Apr. 1944), cartoonist, was born in New Orleans, Louisiana, the son of George Herriman Jr., a tailor, and Clara Morel. There is uncertainty about Herriman's ethnic background. His birth certificate identified him as "Colored," his parents were listed in the 1880 New Orleans federal census as "Mulatto," but his death certificate noted that he was "Caucasian." During his lifetime, friends often thought he was Greek or French because of his Adonis-like appearance, and he has been called a "Creole." The family moved to Los Angeles when Herriman was a child, and his father opened a barbershop and then a bakery.

Herriman attended St. Vincent's College, a Roman Catholic secondary school for boys. When he finished school in 1897 he followed his artistic bent and began to contribute illustrations to the *Los Angeles Herald*. After the turn of the century he moved to New York City and began to contribute cartoons to *Judge*, *Life*, and other humorous periodicals and comic strips to various newspaper syndicates, including several sequential series such as *Musical Mose, Professor Otto and His Auto, Acrobatic Archie*, and *Two Jolly Jackies* for the Pulitzer Syndicate and *Major Ozone's Fresh Air Crusade, Alexander the Cat, Bud Smith*, and *Rosy Posy* for the World Color Printing Company. In 1902 he returned briefly to Los Angeles to marry Mabel Lillian Bridge, his childhood sweetheart; they had two children.

The great variety and skill of Herriman's numerous efforts soon attracted the attention of William Randolph Hearst, who hired him for several of his papers, including the *Los Angeles Examiner*. Herriman lived in Los Angeles from 1905 until 1910, when Hearst brought him back to New York City to draw for the *New York Evening Journal*. Here, Herriman created his first widely successful feature, which would become known as *The Family Upstairs*, a domestic comic strip about the Dingbat family and their noisy neighbors in the apartment above. On 26 July 1910 this study in urban paranoia was interrupted by the appearance of the family cat, which is hit in the head by a rock thrown by a mouse. Therein lay the genesis for

George Herriman, an African American cartoonist who concealed his racial heritage throughout his life, created the comic strip Krazy Katz. *The strip ran from October 1913 until the cartoonist's death in 1944.* Reprinted with special permission of King Features Syndicate

Herriman's most successful strip, *Krazy Kat*, which began as an independent feature on 2 July 1911.

In the world of *Krazy Kat*, Ignatz the Mouse is the object of Krazy Kat's affection, but instead of returning this love, Ignatz is disposed to hit the cat in the head with a brick. The cat naively believes that these clouts are meant as tokens of love. Meanwhile, the benevolent presence of Offissa Pup, himself in love with Krazy, operates to thwart Ignatz and keep the mouse behind jailhouse bars as much as possible. This situation of fully unrequited and androgynous love (Krazy's sex changes from time to time) is acted out against a surrealistic shifting background in the Arizona desert, while the characters speak a poetic dialogue and richly mixed dialect unique in literature outside the fiction of James Joyce or the poetry of E. E. Cummings. Both Cummings and T. S. Eliot wrote in praise of *Krazy Kat*, which has remained the most admired comic strip in newspaper history. No other strip has matched its genius in humorous whimsy, abstract style, and metaphoric power.

Several series of animated cartoons have been based on *Krazy Kat*, two stage ballets have been inspired by it, Jay Cantor has used the characters in a novel under the same title, and any number of modern artists have created paintings and sculptures in homage to Herriman. While Herriman produced *Krazy Kat* on a daily basis, he also created other comic strips, most notably *Baron Bean*, *Stumble Inn*, *Us Husbands*, and *Embarrassing Moments* (or *Bernie Burns*). He illustrated the anthologies of Don Marquis's columns about the poetic cockroach Archy and the feline vamp Mehitabel, giving an indelible visual stamp to the characters almost as endearing as Marquis's comic verse.

In 1922 Herriman settled permanently in Hollywood. He has been described as a handsome, slender, short man with twinkling gray eyes and curly black hair, given to wearing a Stetson hat. He once wrote of his creation, "Be not harsh with 'Krazy.' He is but a shadow himself, caught in the web of this mortal skein." A shy and private man, and more given to visual than verbal communication, he seldom commented on his art. He died in Los Angeles.

At the time of his death Herriman had penciled a week's worth of *Krazy Kat* comic strips, which were to remain uninked on his drawing board. Given the limited circulation of the feature by then, Hearst permanently retired the strip rather than allow other artists to continue it. Legend has it that *Krazy Kat* was a personal favorite of Hearst's, and no one could have imitated the Herriman style and whimsy, anyway. Like Pablo Picasso in painting, Herriman changed the visual style of his art form and influenced generations of cartoonists to come; like James Joyce in fiction, he stretched the traditional limitations of language; and like Samuel Beckett in drama, he captured the absurdities of efforts to communicate on the larger stage of life.

FURTHER READING

Inge, M. Thomas. *Comics as Culture* (1990).
McDonnell, Patrick, Karen O'Connell, and Georgia Riley de Havenon. *Krazy Kat: The Comic Art of George Herriman* (1986).
Marschall, Richard. *America's Great Comic-Strip Artists* (1989).
O'Sullivan, Judith. *The Great American Comic Strip* (1990).

—M. THOMAS INGE

HIGGINBOTHAM, A. LEON, JR. (25 Feb. 1928–14 Dec. 1998), jurist and civil rights leader, was born Aloysius Leon Higginbotham in Trenton, New Jersey, the son of Aloysius Leon Higginbotham Sr., a laborer, and Emma Lee Douglass, a domestic worker. While he was attending a racially segregated elementary school, his mother insisted that he receive tutoring in Latin, a required subject denied to black students; he then became the first African American to enroll at Trenton's Central High School. Initially interested in engineering, he enrolled at Purdue University only to leave in disgust after the school's president denied his request to move on-campus with his fellow African American students. He completed his undergraduate education at Antioch College in Yellow Springs, Ohio, where he received a BA in Sociology in 1949. In August 1948 he married Jeanne L. Foster; the couple had three children. Angered by his experiences at Purdue and inspired

by the example of Supreme Court Justice THURGOOD MARSHALL, Higginbotham decided to pursue a legal career. He attended law school at Yale and graduated with an LLB in 1952.

Although Higginbotham was an honors student at Yale, he encountered racial prejudice when he tried to find employment at leading Philadelphia law firms. After switching his sights to the public sector, he began his career as a clerk for Court of Common Pleas judge Curtis Bok in 1952. Higginbotham then served for a year as an assistant district attorney under future Philadelphia mayor and fellow Yale graduate Richardson Dilworth. In 1954 he became a principal in the new African American law firm of Norris, Green, Harris, and Higginbotham and remained with the firm until 1962. During the same period he became active in the civil rights movement, serving as president of the local chapter of the National Association for the Advancement of Colored People (NAACP); he was also a member of the Pennsylvania Human Relations Commission.

Between 1960 and 1962 Higginbotham served as a special hearing officer for conscientious objectors for the United States Department of Justice. In 1962 President John F. Kennedy appointed him to the Federal Trade Commission, making him the first African American member of a federal administrative agency. Two years later President Lyndon Johnson appointed him as U.S. District Court Judge for the Eastern District of Pennsylvania; at age thirty-six, he was the youngest person to be so named in thirty years. In 1977 President Jimmy Carter appointed him to the U.S. Federal Court of Appeals for the Third Circuit in Philadelphia. He became chief judge in 1989 and remained in the position until his retirement in 1993.

As a member of the federal bench, Higginbotham authored over 650 opinions. A staunch liberal and tireless defender of programs such as affirmative action, he became equally well known for his legal scholarship, with more than one hundred published articles to his credit. He also published two (out of a planned series of four) highly regarded books that outlined the American struggle toward racial justice and equality through the lens of the legal profession:

A. Leon Higginbotham, legal scholar and Chief Judge of the U.S. Court of Appeals for the Third Circuit in Philadelphia. Courtesy of Evelyn Brooks Higginbotham

first post-apartheid elections in South Africa in 1994, lent his counsel to the Congressional Black Caucus during a series of voting rights cases before the Supreme Court, and advised Texaco Inc. on diversity and personnel issues when the firm came under fire for alleged racial discrimination in 1996. In failing health, Higginbotham's last public service came during the impeachment of President Bill Clinton in 1998, when he argued before the House Judiciary Committee that there were degrees of perjury and that President Clinton's did not qualify as "an impeachable high crime." The recipient of several honorary degrees, Higginbotham also received the Raoul Wallenberg Humanitarian Award (1994), the Presidential Medal of Freedom (1995), and the NAACP's Spingarn Medal (1996). After he and his first wife divorced in 1988, Higginbotham married Evelyn Brooks, a professor at Harvard, and adopted her daughter. He died in a Boston hospital after suffering a series of strokes.

Although he never served on the Supreme Court, Higginbotham's impact on the legal community seems certain to continue. A pioneer among African American jurists, he also made solid contributions in the areas of legal scholarship, training, and civil rights.

FURTHER READING

Higginbotham's papers are held at the John F. Kennedy Presidential Library in Boston, Massachusetts. The Harvard University School of Law in Cambridge, Massachusetts, also maintains a file on Higginbotham. His career on the bench can be traced in issues 223 through 429 of the *Federal Supplement* (for his decisions on the district court) and in issues 560 through 983 of the *Federal Reporter*.

Bell, Derrick. "Judge A. Leon Higginbotham Jr.'s Legacy." *Rutgers Law Review* 53 (Spring 2001): 627–640.
Higginbotham, A. Leon. "An Open Letter to Justice Clarence Thomas from a Federal Judicial Colleague." *University of Pennsylvania Law Review* 140, no. 1005 (1992).
Ogletree, Charles, Jr., et al. "In Memoriam: A. Leon Higginbotham Jr." *Harvard Law Review* 112, no. 8 (June 1999): 1801–1833.

Obituaries: *New York Times, Philadelphia Inquirer,* and *Boston Globe,* 15 Dec. 1998.
—EDWARD L. LACH JR.

In the Matter of Color: Race and the American Legal Process, The Colonial Period (1978), in which he castigated the founding fathers for their hypocrisy in racial matters, and *Shades of Freedom: Racial Politics and Presumptions of the American Legal Process* (1996).

Higginbotham also taught both law and sociology at a number of schools, including the University of Michigan, Yale, Stanford, and New York University. He enjoyed a long relationship with the University of Pennsylvania, where he was considered for the position of president in 1980 before deciding to remain on the bench. Following his retirement in 1993, Higginbotham taught at Harvard Law School and also served as public service professor of jurisprudence at Harvard's John F. Kennedy School of Government. In addition, he served on several corporate boards and worked for the law firm of Paul, Weiss, Rifkind, Wharton, and Garrison in both New York and Washington.

Although most of his career was spent outside the public limelight, Higginbotham came to the forefront of public attention in 1991 when he published an open letter to Supreme Court nominee CLARENCE THOMAS in the *University of Pennsylvania Law Review*. Castigating Thomas for what he viewed as a betrayal of all that he, Higginbotham, had worked for, Higginbotham stated, "I could not find one shred of evidence suggesting an insightful understanding on your part of how the evolutionary movement of the Constitution and the work of civil rights organizations have benefited you." Although widely criticized for his stance, Higginbotham remained a critic of Thomas's after he joined the Supreme Court and later attempted to have a speaking invitation to Thomas rescinded by the National Bar Association in 1998.

In his later years Higginbotham filled a variety of additional roles. He served as an international mediator at the

HILL, HENRY AARON

(30 May 1915–17 Mar. 1979), chemist and businessman, was born in St. Joseph, Missouri, the son of William Anthony Hill II, the headwaiter at a local hotel, and Kate Anna Evans. Hill attended public elementary and secondary schools in St. Joseph and graduated from Bartlett High School in 1931. After completing his first year of college at Lewis Institute in Chicago (later a part of the Illinois Institute of Technology), he attended Johnson C. Smith University, an all-black institution in Charlotte, North Carolina. He graduated in 1936 with a BS cum laude in Mathematics and Chemistry.

Hill spent the 1937–1938 academic year as a special student at the Massachusetts Institute of Technology. The following year he studied at the University of Chicago, where he was one of two African American graduate students in the chemistry department. While the other black student, Warren Henry, went on to earn a PhD at Chicago (1941), Hill returned in 1939 to MIT to complete his doctoral work. The reason for this move is uncertain; it has been suggested that both Hill and Henry were in need of "work-study" assistance to carry them through the program and that the Chicago chemistry department was unwilling to support more than one African American student in this way.

Hill received a PhD in Chemistry from MIT in 1942. His work was supported by fellowships from the Julius Rosenwald Fund, a private foundation with a special interest in educational and other needs of African Americans. One of his mentors at MIT was the chemist James Flack Norris, whom Hill admired for his refusal to make an issue of race. According to Hill, Norris was "the first big man whom I met who was more interested in my ability to learn chemistry than in the identity of my grandparents."

Race proved to be a barrier, however, in the search for employment. Hill's job applications were declined by forty-five companies before North Atlantic Research Corporation in Newtonville, Massachusetts, hired him onto their staff in 1942 as a research chemist in charge of organic research. This job offer coincided with offers from several other firms, all of which occurred after the United States entered World War II. "The impenetrable barrier of race prejudice," Hill wrote to the Rosenwald Fund in 1942, "has been lowered under the pressure of the war effort, and some employers are accepting Negroes in the industries as laborers and even in the so-called professional positions." At North Atlantic, he helped develop water-based paints, protein fibers, rubber adhesives, surface coatings, firefighting foams, and several types of synthetic rubber. He became director of research in 1943 and company vice president in 1944 and held both positions until his departure in 1946 to join Dewey & Almy Chemical Company in Cambridge, Massachusetts, as a group leader in polymer research. During the war he worked for a brief period as a civilian chemist attached to the Office of Scientific Research and Development. He married historian Adelaide McGuinn Cromwell (later Gulliver) in 1943; they had one child.

In 1952 Hill cofounded National Polychemicals, Inc., a manufacturer of chemical intermediates used in elastomer and polymer production. He served as the company's assistant manager from 1952 to 1956 and vice president from 1956 to 1961, and was in charge of the company's technical operations in chemistry, engineering, research, and production. He resigned in 1961 to establish his own company, Riverside Research Laboratory, Inc., in Watertown, Massachusetts (later moved to Haverhill, Massachusetts), and was its president until his death. This enterprise provided research, development, and consulting services in the field of organic chemistry, particularly resins, rubbers, textiles, and plastics. Hill was the author of a number of related patents, including "manufacture of azodicarbonide" (1961), "barium azocarbonate as a blowing agent for high melting plastomers" (1963), and "urea-formaldehyde condensates" (1967).

A noted authority on polymer chemistry and fabric flammability, Hill was appointed in 1968 by President Lyndon B. Johnson to the National Commission on Product Safety, on which Hill served for two years. Thereafter, the focus of his work was on product liability and product safety. He devised and conducted tests for compliance with federal, state, and local safety standards. He was a consultant on product safety to various firms and testified in court as an expert witness in product liability cases—usually on behalf of plaintiffs injured by substandard products. Hill also served in 1969 as a member of the advisory council to the Subcommittee on Consumer Affairs of the U.S. Senate Committee on Commerce. He was a member of the National Motor Vehicle Safety Advisory Council (1970–1973, 1977) and chairman of its compliance committee, as well as a member of an evaluation panel of the National Bureau of Standards (1972–1976). In this latter stage of his career, he played an integral role in the modern consumer-rights movement.

Hill was active in the American Chemical Society. First elected to office in 1958, as chairman of the membership committee of ACS's Northeastern Section, he went on to play a prominent role in regional ACS affairs and served on the national council (beginning in 1964) and board of directors (1971–1978). In line with his evolving interest in community and consumer affairs, he became involved in labor, educational, and other issues of special concern to chemists and chemical engineers. He served, for example, as chairman of ACS's Committee on Professional Relations in 1968 and established an Economic Status Subcommittee and a Division of Professional Relations within ACS. Through these programs, he helped formulate guidelines that became a widely accepted protocol of employment and termination conditions for chemists and chemical engineers; in addition, he investigated periodic mass layoffs in the chemical industry and assisted in the resolution of employment problems faced by individual ACS members. Elected president of ACS in 1976, Hill was the first African American to hold this post.

Hill became a fellow of the American Association for the Advancement of Science in 1964. Other professional affiliations included memberships in the American Association of Textile Chemists and Colorists, New York Academy of Sciences, and American Institute of Chemists. He died in Haverhill, Massachusetts.

FURTHER READING

A file on Hill's work as a graduate student, along with related career information, is in the Julius Rosenwald Fund Archives, Special Collections Department, Fisk University, Nashville, Tennessee.

Manning, Kenneth R. "Henry C. McBay: Reflections of a Chemist" in *Henry C. McBay: A Chemical Festschrift: Proceedings of a Symposium in Honor of the First Martin Luther King, Jr., Scholar at the Massachusetts Institute of Technology*, eds. William M. Jackson and Billy Joe Evans (1994): 20.

Massie, Samuel P. "Henry A. Hill: The Second Mile." *Chemistry* 44 (Jan. 1971): 11.

Obituary: Chemical and Engineering News 57 (26 Mar. 1979): 6–7.

—KENNETH R. MANNING

HILL, MARY ELLIOTT

(5 Jan. 1907–12 Feb. 1969), organic and analytical chemist, was born in South Mills, North Carolina, the daughter of Robert Elliott and Frances Bass. Little is known about the early part of her life, except that she lived with her parents and two brothers in modest circumstances. After completing elementary and secondary education, she enrolled in Virginia State College in Petersburg, where during her sophomore year, she married Carl McClellan Hill, who in addition to being an honor student at Hampton Institute was also class president and an All-America guard on the school football team. Over the course of their 41-year marriage the couple had three children.

In 1929 Hill received a BS degree from Virginia State College Laboratory School, where from 1930 to 1937 she was instructor and critic teacher in high school sciences. As critic teacher, Hill advised other staff members, mediated conflicts or disagreements related to the attainment of teaching goals, familiarized herself with the most current books and teaching ideas, and suggested in-house changes, improvements, and course additions when appropriate. At various times between 1932 and 1936, while also teaching at the laboratory school, she taught chemistry at Hampton Institute, where from 1937 to 1940 she was a full-time faculty member and associate professor of chemistry.

Recognizing the practical benefits of advanced study, Hill enrolled in the Graduate School of Arts and Sciences at the University of Pennsylvania, where in 1941 she was awarded a master of science degree in analytical chemistry. For the next six years she was an instructor in chemistry at Dudley High School in Greensboro, North Carolina. Until about 1950 intractable racial barriers kept blacks from finding technical employment in the chemical industry or in academia outside of black colleges and universities. In the South during Hill's day, gifted black science students who did not aspire to medicine, dentistry, or agriculture were not encouraged to seek professional careers in science. The conventional wisdom was that unless a student's ambition was to teach in an all-black school, there was no work in science. This belief derived from the well known and widely publicized experiences of several world-class black scientists, such as chemist PERCY LAVON JULIAN, cell biologist ERNEST EVERETT JUST, and chemistry textbook writer Lloyd Ferguson. In the South, white college graduates with a doctoral degree in chemistry could choose to work in the chemical industry or to teach at either the high school or college level. For black graduate students with a similar degree, there were no such opportunities in the chemical industry, and teaching opportunities existed only in all-black high schools or colleges. If there were no vacancies in a college, the only options for the black PhD were to teach high school or switch fields.

In 1944, after serving one year as an assistant professor at Bennett College in Greensboro, Hill accepted a teaching position at Tennessee A & I College, a historically black college in Nashville now known as Tennessee State University, where for the next eighteen years she was an associate professor of chemistry; in 1951 she became acting head of the chemistry department. In 1962 her husband, who was dean of Tennessee A & I's School of Arts and Sciences, accepted the position of president of Kentucky State College in Frankfort, an historically black college. Relocating with him, Hill accepted a position as professor of chemistry. With her husband, she collaborated in the writing of *General College Chemistry* (1944), a textbook which Carl Hill coauthored with Myron B. Towns, and *Experiments in Organic Chemistry* (1954), a laboratory manual; the latter volume went through four editions. As an analytical chemist on her husband's research team, she was one of the coauthors of their forty-plus published papers.

Both a skilled classroom teacher and analytical laboratory chemist, Hill preferred the classroom because she enjoyed interacting with students, from whom she always demanded excellence. On the college campuses where she taught, Hill established and supervised student-affiliate chapters of the American Chemical Society, which influenced many African American students to consider careers in science and teaching. A conservative estimate is that at least twenty of her students became college professors. Her powerful influence on students is reflected in her having been designated as one of the top six chemistry teachers in the United States and Canada by the Manufacturing Chemists Association.

Until the early 1950s Europe, in particular Germany, was recognized as being the center of work in theoretical and experimental organic chemistry, the thrust of which is to create entirely new substances—preferably with commercial applications—out of existing raw materials. The break in scientific communication between German and U.S. chemists during World War II caused the American chemical industry to grow, and this led in the 1950s and 1960s to the ascendance of brilliant, creative, innovative chemists. Both Mary Hill and Carl Hill were in that category. Among other innovations the Hills used ketenes, which are highly reactive chemical substances with great potential as starting materials for creating new types of ethers, and for helping a chemist to better understand complex chemical reactions. In much of their work they used the then relatively new chemicals known as Grignard Reagents (named after the inventor, Nobel laureate Victor Grignard), which in controlled chemical reactions promote rearrangements of atoms to positions desired by the synthesis chemist and confirmed by an analytical chemist.

In her role as analytical chemist for her husband's research team, Hill pioneered efforts to create new methods, as well as to modify existing methods, of organic chemical analysis using such instruments as the ultraviolet spectrophotometer. She also established procedures for monitoring the progress of chemical reactions by determining the degree of solubility of reaction species in non-waterbased (nonaqueous) reaction systems. This ability to isolate, identify, and quantify such reaction products enabled synthesis chemists on her team, aided by the Grignard Reagents, to design new materials, including plastics.

The Hills were longtime, active members of St. Andrews Presbyterian Church in Nashville; Mary Elliot Hill was a member of the Women of St. Andrews, a church auxiliary, and also served for a time as church historian. She belonged to several professional and civic organizations, including Alpha Kappa Alpha National Honor Society, the American Chemical Society, the Tennessee Academy of Science, the National Institute of Science, and Beta Kappa Chi Sorority; she was also assistant editor of *The Bulletin*, the Beta Kappa Chi newspaper. After moving to Frankfort, she became an active member of the Women's Circle of the South Frankfort Presbyterian Church. She died in Frankfort and was interred at Norfolk, Virginia.

FURTHER READING

Davis, Marianna, ed. *Contributions of Black Women to America* (1982).
"Many Components Equal Mary Hill." Louisville *Courier-Journal*, 11 Oct. 1963.
Sammons, Vivian Ovelton. *Blacks in Science and Medicine* (1990).
Taylor, Jacques. *The Negro in Science* (1955).

Obituaries: (Frankfort) *Kentucky State Journal*, 12 Feb. 1969; *Norfolk Virginian-Pilot*, 13 Feb. 1969.

—BILLY SCOTT

HIMES, CHESTER BOMAR (29 July 1909– 12 Nov. 1984), writer, was born in Jefferson City, Missouri, the youngest of three sons, to professors Joseph Sandy Himes and Estelle Bomar. Himes believed that his surname derived from paternal ancestors who were skilled artisans owned by a Jewish slaveholding family named Heinz. The Bomar family claimed descent from an American Indian woman or African princess and an Irish overseer. Joseph Himes was sent to Claflin College in Orangeburg, South Carolina, where he studied blacksmithing. Himes's mother studied music at Scotia Seminary in Concord, North Carolina. After his parents married in 1901, they held a joint appointment at Georgia State College and then taught at a number of other colleges in the South, including Tuskegee Institute in Alabama. Chester sensed that the tension in his parents' marriage was a reflection of the struggle between white and black manifested in his mother's light complexion and his father's dark one. These perceptions, which were not shared by Chester's siblings, provide the backdrop for his novel *The Third Generation* (1954), and the themes of race, sex, and power recur throughout both his life and work.

When Himes was twelve years old, his brother Joseph nearly blinded himself in a chemistry experiment gone awry and was refused medical treatment at the local white hospital. After graduating from Glenville High School in 1926, Himes was working at a Cleveland hotel to earn money for college when he accidentally fell down an open elevator shaft, fracturing three vertebrae. He, too, was denied entry to a white hospital. Thus, when he entered Ohio State University in the fall, still wearing a back brace, he was scarred physically and emotionally. He had gained admission to the university in part because a grade of fifty-six he had received in one course was mistakenly recorded on his transcript as eighty-six; nevertheless, it was later found that he had the fourth highest IQ of any student entering that year. However, Himes was more interested in the illicit activities he found in the black underworld and in the superficial aspects of campus life than he was in his studies. At the end of his first semester, the highest grade he could muster was a C in English. The shady individuals he associated with later appeared as characters in his crime novels, but in 1927 keeping such company merely helped to get him expelled.

Back on the streets of Cleveland, Himes's delinquent behavior came to include soliciting prostitutes, gambling, and forging checks. His parents, who were going through a divorce, could not stop

Novelist Chester Himes, whose detective novels helped to pioneer a new genre of African American mystery writing. Library of Congress/Carl Van Vechten

his downward spiral—though his nearly blind brother was on his way to graduating magna cum laude from Oberlin College and earning a PhD. After two prior arrests in 1928, Himes was sentenced to twenty to twenty-five years in the Ohio State Penitentiary for an armed robbery he committed against a white couple. In 1930 the prison was engulfed in a fire that killed over three hundred inmates. Himes wrote a story about this tragedy called "To What Red Hell," which was published in *Esquire* in 1934. From then on, Himes considered himself a writer. His novel *Cast the First Stone* (1954) draws heavily on his prison experience, exploring the problems of crime and punishment and exposing the realities of prison life. *Run Man Run* (1966) presents the absurdity of the Negro condition as he saw it—a state of being imprisoned and paralyzed within a racist society.

A year after his release from prison in 1936, Himes married Jean Lucinda Johnson. During the Depression he found work as a laborer with the Works Progress Administration but was soon assigned to the Ohio Writer's Project, where he worked on a history of Cleveland and wrote an unsigned column for the *Cleveland Daily News*. During this period he met and befriended LANGSTON HUGHES, who assisted his writing career. In 1940 Himes and his wife moved to Los Angeles to work as butler and maid for the novelist Louis Bromfield, whom they hoped would help further Himes's career. When this did not happen, Himes found work in the shipyards and in war industry plants, while Jean found a position with slightly higher wages and status. His frustration with bigotry, liberals, union organizers, communists, and the Negroes he encountered at the NAACP, as well as his low opinion of women, found fictional representation in his most ambitious novels, *If He Hollers Let Him Go* (1945) and *Lonely Crusade* (1947).

A Rosenwald Fellowship allowed Himes to move to New York City in 1944 to write full-time. His work received mixed reviews and sold so poorly that when the money ran out, Himes sometimes worked as a caretaker or bellhop in order to survive. He separated from Jean in 1952 and began a series of relationships with white women—including a violent one with Vandi Haygood that became the basis for *A Case of Rape* (1984), first published in French in 1963. Himes wrote that "the very essence of any relationship between a black man and a white woman in the United States is sex" (Muller, 65). This sentiment gave both *The End of a Primitive* (1955), which Himes considered to be his best work, and the satirical *Pinktoes* (1961), a racial edge that was too unsettling for most Americans.

By the early 1950s Himes had become so disappointed with the United States that he went to Europe and became one of the many American expatriate writers living in Paris. RICHARD WRIGHT helped Himes make his European transition, assisting him professionally and introducing him to JAMES BALDWIN, though Himes considered Wright a rival as much as a friend and preferred to invite comparisons of his own work to Faulkner's. He lived a peripatetic existence in Europe, taking up with several women before meeting an English columnist, Lesley Packard, in 1958; the two were married in 1965. His writing career entered a new and unexpected phase when the French editor and translator Marcel Duhamel suggested that Himes write commercial detective novels. In 1958 his first attempt, *For Love of Imabelle*, won the French Grand Prix for the year's best detective novel.

At first, Himes considered his detective novels to be lucrative projects that he could churn out quickly in order to support his "serious" writing. He did not expect that *The Real Cool Killers* (1959), *The Crazy Kill* (1959), *The Big Gold Dream* (1960), *All Shot Up* (1960), and *Blind Man with a Pistol* (1969) would become as popular as they did. *Cotton Comes to Harlem* (1965) was made into a film directed by OSSIE DAVIS in 1970 and *The Heat's On* (1965) became the film *Come Back, Charleston Blue* in 1974. In Grave Digger Jones and his partner Coffin Ed Johnson, Himes created compelling characters who dispense their own brand of black justice and who have been compared to Dashiell Hammet's Sam Spade. With these books Himes helped to pioneer a new genre of African American mystery writing that continues with such writers as Walter Mosley and Nora DeLoach.

Himes lived the last sixteen years of his life in Spain, where he struggled with a variety of geriatric illnesses. He rarely visited the United States, but he never stayed any place in Europe long enough, or learned to speak any of the languages well enough, to consider Europe his home. In his final years, often writing in great arthritic pain, he finished two autobiographies, *The Quality of Hurt* (1972) and *My Life of Absurdity* (1976).

FURTHER READING

Some letters from Himes are located at the Beinecke Rare Book and Manuscript Library, Yale University.

Himes, Chester. *My Life of Absurdity* (1976).
——. *The Quality of Hurt* (1972).

Margolies, Edward, and Michel Fabre. *The Several Lives of Chester Himes* (1997).
Muller, Gilbert, H. *Chester Himes* (1976).

Obituary: *New York Times*, 14 Nov. 1984.
—SHOLOMO B. LEVY

HINTON, WILLIAM AUGUSTUS (15 Dec. 1883–8 Aug. 1959), physician and clinical pathologist, was born in Chicago, Illinois, the son of Augustus Hinton, a railroad porter, and Marie Clark; both parents were former slaves. His formal education was completed in Kansas City, Kansas, where his parents moved before

his first birthday. After attending the University of Kansas from 1900 to 1902, he transferred to Harvard College, where he received a BS in 1905.

Postponing a medical-school education because of lack of funds, Hinton taught the basic sciences at colleges in Tennessee and Oklahoma and embryology at Meharry Medical College between 1905 and 1909. While teaching at the Agricultural and Mechanical College in Langston, Oklahoma, he met a schoolteacher, Ada Hawes, whom he married in 1909; they had two daughters. During the summers Hinton continued his studies in bacteriology and physiology at the University of Chicago.

Hinton entered Harvard Medical School in 1909 and was awarded an MD in 1912. Scholarships and part-time work in the Harvard laboratories of Richard C. Cabot and Elmer E. Southard allowed him to attend medical school and support his family.

Because of racial discrimination, Hinton was prevented from gaining an internship in a Boston hospital. Unable to acquire the specialty training in surgery that he desired, he turned to the laboratory aspect of medicine. In 1912 he began working part time as a volunteer assistant in the department of pathology of the Massachusetts General Hospital. During the three years he spent at Massachusetts General after medical school graduation, he was asked to perform autopsies on all persons known or suspected to have syphilis. He also acquired a paid position as an assistant in the Wassermann Laboratory (the Massachusetts state laboratory for communicable diseases), based at the Harvard Medical School complex. (This laboratory had been named for August von Wassermann, who devised the first blood serum test for the detection of syphilis in 1906.) Southard was so impressed by Hinton's knowledge of syphilis that he arranged for him to teach its laboratory diagnostic techniques to Harvard medical students. Within two years of his medical school graduation, Hinton had published his first scientific paper on the serology of syphilis in Milton Joseph Rosenau's *Textbook of Preventive Medicine*.

In 1915, when the Wassermann Laboratory was transferred from Harvard to the Massachusetts Department of Public Health, Hinton was appointed assistant director of the Division of

Biologic Laboratories and chief of the Wassermann Laboratory. He served as the head of the Wassermann Laboratory for thirty-eight years. At the Peter Bent Brigham Hospital he observed both inpatients and outpatients, correlating serologic tests with the clinical manifestations and treatment of patients with syphilis. For twelve years, from 1915 to 1927, he immersed himself in the search for a more effective test for syphilis; the Wassermann test and others for syphilis yielded a high percentage of false positive results, and many doctors had lost confidence in the Wassermann test. Because the treatment of syphilis was long, painful, and dangerous, and it was a seriously debilitating disease, a more accurate test was badly needed.

In 1918 Hinton was appointed instructor of preventive medicine and hygiene at the Harvard Medical School, the beginning of a thirty-four-year teaching career at Harvard. In 1921 his instructional responsibilities were expanded to include bacteriology and immunology.

During the 1920s Hinton carried on intensive research on the pathology of venereal diseases. He was responsible for all syphilis testing in Massachusetts and had responsibility for the diagnosis of rabies for the State Division of Animal Husbandry. When Massachusetts established blood tests for syphilis as a requirement for marriage licenses and for mothers before birth, Hinton supervised the expansion of state laboratories from ten to 117. His laboratories also conducted research on tuberculosis and influenza for the state.

Hinton's signal, most important contribution to medical science came in 1927, when he perfected what was judged to be the most accurate and sensitive blood serum test for syphilis. His test drastically reduced the percentage of false positives. It also met the requirements of mass screening, quick results, simplicity, replicability, and unambiguity. For the next quarter of a century the Hinton test was universally used, replacing the Wassermann test. Even though the Hinton test was 98 percent accurate, Hinton was not completely satisfied, and he collaborated with John Davies in perfecting his test. By 1931 he had developed an improved version that could be done with smaller amounts of the patient's blood. The Davies-Hinton test

was adopted as the official test of the disease by the Massachusetts Department of Public Health. In 1934 the U.S. Public Health Service reported that its evaluation showed the Hinton test to be the best available, using sensitivity and specificity as evaluative standards.

In 1934 Hinton began writing his classic textbook, *Syphilis and Its Treatment* (1936). In this book, praised in both Europe and the United States, Hinton sought to provide "a clear, simple, relatively complete account of syphilis and its treatment for physicians, public health workers and medical students." The book became a standard reference in medical schools and hospitals. Documenting Hinton's years of research and "his experience in clinics with patients and the disease from their point of view," it is believed to be the first medical textbook written by an African American doctor.

Recognition came slowly and late to Hinton. In 1946 he was promoted to the rank of lecturer in bacteriology and immunology at the Harvard Medical School. Three years later, a year before he retired and twenty-two years after he had developed his first test for syphilis, he was elevated to the position of clinical professor—the first African American to attain the title of professor at Harvard.

Hinton was a member of the American Society of Clinical Pathologists, the Society of American Bacteriologists, the American Medical Association, and the American Association for the Advancement of Science, and a fellow of the Massachusetts Medical Society. In 1948 he was elected a life member of the American Social Science Association. He lectured frequently to the medical specialty groups of the National Medical Association. He contributed twenty-one medical-scientific articles to professional journals. He also served as a special consultant to the U.S. Public Health Service.

Hinton died in his home in Canton, Massachusetts. His legacy to American medicine was not forgotten. In 1974, fifteen years after his death, when the new State Laboratory Institute Building of the Massachusetts Department of Public Health in Boston was dedicated, it was named the William A. Hinton Serology Laboratory.

FURTHER READING

Cobb, W. Montague. "William Augustus Hinton, MD, 1883–." *Journal of the* *National Medical Association* 49 (Nov. 1957): 427–428.
Hayden, Robert C. "William A. Hinton: Pioneer against Syphilis" in *Eleven African American Doctors* (1992).

—ROBERT C. HAYDEN

HOLIDAY, BILLIE

(7 Apr. 1915–17 July 1959), vocalist and lyricist, was born Eleanora Fagan in Philadelphia, to a nineteen-year-old domestic worker, Sadie Fagan, and Clarence Holiday, a seventeen-year-old guitarist who would later gain fame as a member of the Fletcher Henderson Orchestra.

Shortly after giving birth, Sadie Fagan returned to her home in Baltimore with her newborn daughter in tow. During her youth in this gritty, working-class port town, the young Holiday would encounter two things that influenced her for the duration of her life: the criminal justice system and music. By the time she entered Thomas E. Hays Elementary School, Holiday was the stepdaughter of Philip Gough, who had married her mother on 20 October 1920. A tomboy, the future singer

Billie Holiday, nicknamed "Lady Day" by Lester Young, recorded over three hundred songs and set the standard for jazz singing in particular and American popular singing in general. © William P. Gottlieb, From the Library of Congress Collection

enjoyed playing stickball and softball with the boys in the neighborhood, and she loved the movies. These two forms of recreation, sports and film, helped to inspire the nickname by which she would become famous: Billie. Billie Dove was a popular film star of the day whom Holiday greatly admired. As a child, she began to sing popular blues songs around the house and in her neighborhood.

After her mother divorced Gough, Holiday was placed in the care of a neighbor while Sadie sought work elsewhere. Perhaps in an effort to protest her mother's absence, she began to skip school, and by January 1925 her truancy found her before the juvenile court. After finding Sadie Gough unfit to mother, the judge sent Holiday to the House of the Good Shepherd for Colored Girls, a home run by Catholic nuns. While there Billie was baptized. After a nine-month stay she was released in care of her mother, and the two moved into a small apartment about two blocks away from Sadie's new business venture, a small eatery. Sadie spent long hours at work, and the young Holiday was often left alone. On Christmas Eve 1926 Sadie came home from work to find her neighbor, Wilbert Rich, having sex with her daughter. Rich was arrested and charged with rape; Billie was sent, once again, to the House of the Good Shepherd. Rich was indicted on six counts of rape, but only found guilty of one. He served three months in prison.

After she was released, Billie never returned to school. Instead, she began to work in her mother's restaurant and in a local brothel. Her work at the brothel first involved only cleaning the white marble steps, running errands, and doing light cleaning in exchange for the opportunity to listen to the Victrola, but biographers agree that she eventually worked as a prostitute, a kind of "pretty baby" who also sang for the entertainment of the clientele. While at the brothel, she discovered the records of BESSIE SMITH and LOUIS ARMSTRONG, both of whom profoundly influenced her unique singing style. Other early influences were ETHEL WATERS and the Gregorian chant Holiday had heard at the House of the Good Shepherd.

In 1928 Holiday's mother moved to New York, settling in Harlem, and the following year, she sent for her teenage daughter. By May 1929 both mother and daughter had been arrested for prostitution, caught in a raid on a Harlem brothel. Holiday spent one hundred days in the penitentiary workhouse on Welfare Island (formerly Blackwell's Island, now Roosevelt Island). Upon her release she determined never again to work as a maid or a prostitute. She began singing in small clubs in Brooklyn and later in Harlem, soon moving to the more renowned Harlem clubs like Small's Paradise. Beginning her apprenticeship and advanced musical education, Holiday spent every waking hour with other musicians. In 1933 she was discovered by the young producer and aspiring impresario John Hammond, who heard her at a Harlem club called Covan's. He immediately wrote about her for a London-based jazz publication, *Melody Maker,* and later produced her first record, "Your Mother's Son-in-Law" and "Riffin' the Scotch," with Benny Goodman. She was eighteen years old. The following year Holiday met the tenor saxophonist Lester Young, with whom she had an immediate affinity.

In 1934 Holiday made her film debut in a DUKE ELLINGTON short, *Symphony in Black*, in which she sang "Saddest Tale," a slow blues. Holiday is riveting on film, but she made only one other, *New Orleans* (1947), with Louis Armstrong, playing a singing maid. Starting in 1935 Holiday recorded a number of sides with the gifted pianist Teddy Wilson. Some of the best of these featured Benny Goodman on clarinet, Roy Eldridge on trumpet, and Ben Webster (with whom Holiday had a brief and tumultuous affair) on saxophone. In the mid-1930s Joe Glaser, who managed Louis Armstrong, began to manage Holiday, and she began to get more work and greater exposure. He arranged for her to sing with the Fletcher Henderson Orchestra, one of the most popular big bands of the day. With the Henderson outfit, Holiday made a number of radio broadcasts, gaining exposure to a national audience. In the spring of 1937 she joined Buck Clayton and her good friend Lester Young, as well as the blues belter Jimmy Rushing, in the COUNT BASIE Orchestra; before long, she was on the road with the band. Basie gave her extraordinary freedom to stretch out musically and to cultivate her own style. She recorded for Columbia with members of the Basie outfit, especially Lester Young, but never with the entire orchestra. During this time, Lester Young gave Holiday the nickname "Lady Day," and she dubbed him "Prez." Life on the road was especially difficult for Holiday, as she faced firsthand the racism of the Jim Crow South. At one point she was encouraged by club owners to wear dark makeup so that Southern white audiences would not think she was a white woman singing with black musicians. By 1938 Holiday was no longer singing with the Basie Orchestra; she said she left because she was not paid enough.

When the white bandleader Artie Shaw heard that Holiday had left Basie, he offered her a job. She became one of the first black artists to join an all-white band. She traveled with Shaw throughout the country; although life on the road, with its constant confrontations with racial prejudice, proved to be more than Holiday wanted to handle. In New York, the owner of the Lincoln Hotel where she was performing with the Shaw band asked that Holiday take the service elevator. Although she had been thinking of leaving Shaw for some time, this proved to be the straw that broke the camel's back.

Fortunately, John Hammond brought her an offer that would change the direction of her career and in so doing make an indelible mark on the history of popular music. With Hammond's assistance, Holiday opened at Café Society, a new nightclub in Greenwich Village. Founded by Barney Josephson, the club not only presented racially mixed bands, but also had an integrated audience, making it unique in New York nightlife. It eventually became one of the favorite nightspots of bohemian intellectuals and political activists, as well as socialites looking for the thrill of something new.

During her tenure at Café Society, Holiday further shaped her style, both her singing and her visual presentation. A dramatic performer, she used each song as an opportunity to connect with her audience through a narrative that seemed almost personal. Here she began to sing the torch songs with which she would be identified throughout the rest of her career. She worked with smaller bands, including one led by Teddy Wilson. But most significantly, it was at Café Society that Holiday introduced

"Strange Fruit," a song written by Abel Meeropol as a protest against the practice of lynching. She often closed her performances with dramatic renditions of this song, after which she would leave the stage and refuse to return for an encore, and included it in her repertoire throughout her career. When her record company, Columbia, refused to record it, she sought out the independent record producer Milt Gabler, who arranged for her to record the song with his label, Commodore Records. With "Strange Fruit," Holiday came to the attention of a whole new audience of artists, activists, and intellectuals. She also came to the attention of the FBI when she began to sing what was also considered a political song, "The Yanks Aren't Coming." The recording of "Strange Fruit" marked the second stage of Holiday's career. From 1945 to 1950 Gabler recorded Holiday classics such as "Don't Explain," "Lover Man," and "My Man" on Decca, while also recording more blues- and jazz-oriented fare like "Fine and Mellow" and "Billie's Blues" for Commodore.

Holiday left Café Society to become the queen of Fifty-second Street, where the most important jazz clubs were located. During this time she was first arrested for possession of heroin, and in 1947 she was sent to the Federal Reformatory for Women at Alderson, West Virginia, where she served nine and a half months. It is said that she never sang a note while there. Upon her release, Holiday was denied her cabaret card and thus was unable to perform in jazz clubs where liquor was sold. A number of significant jazz artists fell prey to this law and found their livelihood severely limited. Limited in her club appearances, Holiday began singing in large halls. Shortly after her release from Alderson, she appeared before a wildly enthusiastic audience at Carnegie Hall on 27 March 1948.

From the time of her first arrest in 1947 until her death in 1959, Holiday would be harassed and haunted by law enforcement for possession and use of narcotics. She sometimes beat the charges, but they inevitably took their toll on the sensitive singer. She was arrested in May 1947 in Philadelphia, in January 1949 in San Francisco, in February 1956, again in Philadelphia, and, even as she lay on her deathbed in

New York in 1959, a guard was placed outside her hospital room.

In 1952 Holiday signed with Verve records. She began working with Norman Granz, who had helped to ensure the financial and critical success of ELLA FITZGERALD and Frank Sinatra, and hoped to do the same for Holiday. Granz surrounded her with major jazz talent and recorded her in the small jam-session atmosphere in which she thrived, using such musicians as Oscar Peterson, Ray Brown, Ben Webster, Jimmy Rowles, Benny Carter, and Harry Edison. In recordings of these sessions, one can hear the grain of her voice, and at times her songs are like recitations and incantations. Holiday's choices are thoughtful and original, and, as always, she makes every note count.

The album Lady in Satin, recorded in 1958, is perhaps one of Holiday's most controversial recordings. Critics disagree in their appraisals; gone is the youthful Holiday of the early Columbia sides and the fully mature singer-actress of the torch days. In her place is a woman looking back on some of her earlier material, reinterpreting it through the lens of a life that had been difficult but full, an artist wholly committed to her form.

Holiday died in New York from heart, kidney, and liver ailments, along with lung blockage, the unfortunate but inevitable consequence of decades of substance abuse. She was forty-four years old. She had been married twice, once to Jimmy Monroe and then to Louis McKay. She had no children.

Holiday recorded over three hundred songs, and set the standard for jazz singing in particular and American popular singing in general. She paved the way for the sophisticated black songstresses who followed her, but who have rarely matched her level of artistry or originality. Billie Holiday is undoubtedly one of the most important artists of the twentieth century, and her singular sound and distinctive approach to timing and phrasing, along with her iconographic life and image, have influenced not only other musicians, but poets, painters, novelists, and critical theorists.

FURTHER READING

Holiday, Billie, with William Dufty. Lady Sings the Blues (1956).

Clarke, Donald. Wishing on the Moon: The Life and Times of Billie Holiday (1995).
Gourse, Leslie, ed. The Billie Holiday Companion: Seven Decades of Commentary (1997).
Griffin, Farah Jasmine. If You Can't Be Free, Be a Mystery: In Search of Billie Holiday (2001).
Nicholson, Stuart. Billie Holiday (1995).
O'Meally, Robert. Lady Day: The Many Faces of Billie Holiday (1991).

Obituary: New York Times, 18 July 1959.

Discography
Billie Holiday: The Legacy (1933–1958), Sony (1991).
Billie Holiday: The Complete Decca Recordings, GRP Records (1991).
Billie Holiday: The Complete Billie Holiday on Verve 1945–1959, PolyGram Records (1993).
Billie Holiday: The Complete Commodore Recordings, GRP Records (1997).
Lady Day: The Complete Billie Holiday on Columbia 1933–1944, Sony (2001).
—FARAH JASMINE GRIFFIN

 HOLLY, JAMES THEODORE
(30 Oct. 1829–13 Mar. 1911), black emigrationist, missionary, and bishop, was born free in Washington, D.C., the son of James Overton Holly, a bootmaker, and Jane (maiden name unknown). At fourteen he and his family moved to Brooklyn, where he worked with his father. By 1848, while clerking for Lewis Tappan, an abolitionist, Holly became interested in the antislavery movement. In 1850 he and his brother Joseph set up as "fashionable bootmakers" in Burlington, Vermont, where both became involved with the growing debate over black emigration. James supported the American Colonization Society and Liberia, while Joseph believed that freed slaves should not have to leave the United States.

In 1851 Holly married Charlotte Ann Gordon (with whom he was to have five children) and moved to Windsor, Canada West (now Ontario), to coedit HENRY BIBB's newspaper Voice of the Fugitive. During his three years in the Windsor-Detroit area, Holly worked for the unsuccessful Refugee Home Society, ran the Amherstburg Emancipation Convention in 1851, and used the Voice to argue that emigration was the only solution for the problems of African Americans. He abandoned Roman Catholicism for the Protestant Episcopal Church, becoming a deacon in 1855 and a priest in 1856. Holly's new occupation, together with his devotion to the creation of a black nationality, set the course for his adult life.

While teaching grade school in Buffalo, New York, Holly was a delegate to the first National Emigration Convention in 1854 in Cleveland, Ohio. The next year, while representing both the National Emigration Board and the Board of Missions of the Protestant Episcopal Church, he visited Haiti to negotiate an emigration treaty and to locate a possible site for an Episcopal mission. Unsuccessful in both ventures, Holly settled in New Haven, Connecticut, where he taught school and served as priest of St. Luke's Church from 1856 to 1861. After participating in the 1856 National Emigration Convention, Holly traveled extensively to advocate African American emigration to Haiti. His lecture *Vindication of the Capacity of the Negro Race for Self Government and Civilized Progress*, published in 1857, proclaimed black pride and urged immigration to Haiti, a place of "far more security for the personal liberty and general welfare of the governed . . . than exists in this bastard democracy [the United States]." He also cofounded the Convocation of the Protestant Episcopal Society for Promoting the Extension of the Work among Colored People, a group whose goals included encouraging blacks to join the church and the emigration movement.

Convinced that free blacks needed white allies to support mass departure for Haiti, Holly corresponded in 1859 with Congressman Francis P. Blair Jr. about U.S. government aid for emigration. He also petitioned, unsuccessfully, the Board of Missions of the Episcopal Church to underwrite him as a missionary to Haiti. In 1860 Holly worked for the Scottish journalist and abolitionist James Redpath, the official Haitian commissioner of emigration. As an agent for the Haitian government, Holly lectured frequently in New England, New Jersey, and Pennsylvania and organized the "New Haven Pioneer Company of Haytian Emigrants." In 1861 Holly and 101 recruits moved to Haiti. As one colonist wrote home, "I am a man in Hayti where I feel as I never felt before, entirely free."

The initial year in Haiti proved to be disastrous for Holly's settlement. The rainy season brought fevers, fatalities, and then desertions. Among those who died were Holly's mother, his wife, two of their children, and thirty-nine others. Only Holly and a few followers remained on the island. In 1862, by then a Haitian citizen dedicated to the "regeneration and purification" of the Black Republic through the establishment of the Episcopal Church in Haiti, Holly returned to the United States. He hoped this trip would secure financial support from the General Convention of the Protestant Episcopal Church to establish a Haitian mission station. His request failed, but the American Church Missionary Society did agree to pay his salary in Haiti. In 1865 the Board of Missions of the Protestant Episcopal Church began minimal sponsorship of Holly's mission in Haiti, an arrangement that continued until 1911.

Holly hoped to replace Haiti's dominant Roman Catholicism with a national Episcopal church. In 1874 he became bishop of the Orthodox Apostolic Church of Haiti and was consecrated missionary bishop of Haiti at Grace Church, New York City. As the first black bishop of the Episcopal Church and as head of the Haitian Episcopal Church, he attended the Lambeth Conference in London in 1878. Recognizing education and good health to be important concerns of the church, Holly worked zealously to establish schools and medical institutions in Haiti. But fires and political upheaval hampered his efforts, and his overall church membership never exceeded a few thousand.

Although an infrequent visitor to the United States after 1861 (he made only seven trips in fifty years), Holly never lost interest in African Americans. He and his second wife, Sarah Henley, whom he married in 1862, sent nine sons to the United States for schooling. Holly also corresponded extensively with American blacks and published frequently on religious, political, and social issues in the *A.M.E. Church Review*.

While other emigration advocates of the mid-1800s spoke of leaving the United States but stayed, Holly spoke of leaving and actually left. Until his death in Port au Prince, Haiti, Holly never abandoned his belief that emigration was the only way for African Americans to improve their lives.

FURTHER READING

Holly's papers are in the Archives and Historical Collections of the Episcopal Church in Austin, Texas.

Dean, David M. *Defender of the Race: James Theodore Holly, Black Nationalist and Bishop* (1979).

Holly, James Theodore. "Vindication of the Capacity of the Negro Race for Self Government and Civilized Progress" in *Negro Social and Political Thought, 1859–1920: Representative Texts*, ed. Howard Brotz (1966).

Miller, Floyd J. *The Search for a Black Nationality* (1975).

—DAVID M. DEAN

HOOKER, JOHN LEE

(22 Aug. 1917?–21 June 2001), bluesman, was born near Clarksdale, Mississippi, on a large farm owned by his parents, William Hooker, a preacher as well as a farmer, and Minnie Ramsey. The fourth boy of ten to thirteen children, some of whom died in childbirth, Hooker's earliest musical experiences involved singing spirituals in the church where his father preached, though he resented both the enforced, backbreaking labor and the church singing on which his father insisted. When blues singer-guitarist Tony Hollins, who later recorded in 1941 and 1952, began courting Hooker's sister Alice, Hooker was enthralled by his musical performances. In fact, he acquired his first significant blues influence from Hollins, who gave him an old, beat-up guitar, which Hooker's father allowed him to keep even though the preacher dubbed it "the Devil" because of its secular lure. A Gypsy woman at a carnival told the young Hooker he would be famous all over the world, but he had little reason to dream that an illiterate African American boy from Mississippi would actually fulfill her prophecy, especially since his father would not even allow him to play the guitar in the house.

As Hooker reached adolescence, his mother and father separated, and Minnie began a relationship with sharecropper Will Moore. Unlike his brothers and sisters, young John Lee went to live with his mother and Moore, largely because Moore was also a guitar player and encouraged his stepson's playing. With a new Stella guitar, music lessons, and spiritual support provided by his stepfather, Hooker drew on the repertoires of Moore and his associates, Delta blues giant CHARLEY PATTON and Texan BLIND LEMON JEFFERSON. Excluded from work with Moore at country suppers, dances, and fish fries because of their violent ambience, Hooker ran away to Memphis around 1931, working both outside music and with gospel groups like the Big Six, the Fairfield Four, and the Delta Big Four. After a year Hooker arrived in Cincinnati, where his playing began to get wider public exposure. Some three years later he moved to Detroit, setting the stage for his emergence as a recording artist. At Henry's Swing Club, Hastings Street nightspots, and Lee's Sensation Bar, Hooker began establishing a reputation as an up-and-coming bluesman. Record store owner Elmer Barbee discovered Hooker and took him to Bernie Besman, a record distributor and owner of the Sensation label, who recorded four tunes by Hooker on 3 November 1948. The release on the Modern Records label of "Sallie Mae" and its B-side, "Boogie Chillun," a boogie in a groove that Hooker had learned from his stepfather Will Moore, provided Hooker with a smash hit and initiated a marathon series of recordings on both Modern and Sensation. A number of his hits became blues standards, including his version of Tony Hollins's "Crawling King Snake," "Hobo Blues," and "I'm in the Mood." During this time Hooker had three wives: Alma Hopes, to whom he was married for a few months in the early 1940s and by whom he had a daughter, Frances; Sarah Jones, with whom he lived for about one year; and Maude Mathis, whom he met in 1944 and to whom he stayed married until they divorced in 1971. They had five children: Diane, John Lee Jr., Karen, Robert, and Zakiya. He was also married briefly to Canadian Millie Strom in the late 1970s. Hooker continued to record for Modern until 1954; however, always on the lookout for moneymaking opportunities, he also recorded for the King, Regent/Savoy, Staff, Regal, Gone, Acorn/Chance, Chess, Deluxe, Gotham, JVB, Savoy, and Specialty labels,

becoming one of the most recorded blues performers of all time. He is also one of the most pseudonymously recorded bluesmen of all time, using such monikers as John Lee Booker, John Lee Cooker, Birmingham Sam and his Magic Guitar, Boogie Man, Delta John, Texas Slim, and Johnny Williams to disguise the fact that he was violating his contracts to record with different labels. These pseudonyms were superficial masks at best; Hooker's blues and boogie style is too deeply distinctive to deceive any but the most uninitiated and tone-deaf ear.

These early recordings are often considered Hooker's best. Playing alone on his electric guitar, he creates a stark world as a deep, Delta blues feeling passes through the alembic of his genius. Hooker can be both deeply traditional and spontaneously original, his deep and haunting voice moaning at times in unison with stark, jagged guitar lines and then pulsing into insistent, rhythmic action as his boogie rumbles sensually into place as a relief to the fierce isolation of his blues. The whispers and cries of his rich, baritone voice and the hammered chords and nervous rambling of his idiosyncratic guitar style are so individual that they sometimes render intensely personal to Hooker songs that were composed by other performers such as Roosevelt Sykes, Percy Mayfield, Charles Calhoun, and Sonny Boy Williamson. His duet and group recordings are somewhat less successful, since Hooker's creative approach to musical structure could befuddle all but the most sympathetic of backup musicians.

By 1955 Hooker had moved on to Chicago and the Vee-Jay label, owned by African American entrepreneurs Vivian Carter and Jimmy Bracken, who had previously struck gold with Jimmy Reed. The Vee-Jay years produced such hits as the oft-covered "Dimples" and "Boom Boom," as well as remakes of some of his earlier hits, and found Hooker frequently accompanied by bands in an attempt to update and commercialize his sound; even the pop-soul group the Vandellas provided backing vocals at one session. With recordings for Riverside, Fortune, Prestige, Atco, Galaxy, and Stax in between sessions for Vee-Jay in the 1955–1964 period, Hooker was a high-profile bluesman, both for the African American market and the

emerging "folk blues" audience of the early 1960s.

The "folk" and "rock" portions of Hooker's career began with appearances at the Newport Folk Festival in 1959 and 1960, when he began performing on acoustic guitar to match his new white audience's sense of what an "authentic" blues performer should sound like. His overseas appearance in 1962 with the Rhythm and Blues USA tour in England and Germany helped introduce Hooker to an international audience and instituted a new phase of his career, during which both his early recordings, which had generated a number of African American imitators, and his newer folk performances were copied by white electric blues bands such as Canned Heat and ZZ Top in America and the Animals and the Groundhogs in England. This set the stage for frequent American and European tours, appearances on the *Dick Cavett Show* (1969), *Midnight Special* (1974), and *Don Kirshner's Rock Concert* (1978), and, increasingly, recordings featuring white admirers among his accompanists. Highlights from this period include recordings with his cousin Earl Hooker (1969) and the blues-rock group Canned Heat (1970), who provided sympathetic accompaniment and increased Hooker's visibility through joint touring in 1970. An appearance in the *Blues Brothers* movie (1980), recordings with Hank Williams Jr. (1984), and a contribution to the soundtrack of *The Color Purple* (1985) acknowledged his status as an elder statesman of the blues and set the stage for the album *The Healer* (1989), which featured Carlos Santana, Los Lobos, and Bonnie Raitt and won several Grammy Awards, as did his last album of new recordings, *Don't Look Back* (1997). After the release of *The Healer*, Hooker became a staple of pop culture, appearing in advertisements and in videos on MTV, and collaborating on *The Hot Spot* movie soundtrack (1990) with MILES DAVIS. Increasingly fragile toward the end of his life, Hooker died in his sleep at his home in Los Altos, California.

John Lee Hooker is one of the great performers in the history of American music, and though his influence can be heard in the music of several successive generations, his primary importance still rests in his expression of the deepest human emotions in music of surpassing originality and beauty. Appropriately, he was one of the original performers inducted into the Blues Foundation's Blues Hall of Fame in 1980 and was inducted into the Rock and Roll Hall of Fame in 1991.

FURTHER READING

Fancourt, Leslie. *Boogie Chillun: A Guide to John Lee Hooker on Disc.*

Murray, Charles Shaar. *Boogie Man: The Adventures of John Lee Hooker in the American Twentieth Century* (2000).

Obrecht, Jas, ed. *Blues Guitar: The Men Who Made the Music. From the Pages of Guitar Player Magazine* (1993).

Obituary: *The Guardian* (U.K.), 23 June 2001.

Discography

Complete John Lee Hooker, 1948–1951 (vols. 1–4, Body and Soul 3057012, 3063142, 3067872, 3074242).

Ultimate Collection, 1948–1990 (Rhino 70572). *The Vee-Jay Years, 1955–1964.*

—STEVEN C. TRACY

HOPE, JOHN (2 June 1868–20 Feb. 1936), educator, was born in Augusta, Georgia, the son of James Hope, a wealthy white Scotsman who came to America in 1817, and Mary Frances Butts, who was born a slave in 1839. John's great-grandmother, Mary, had been raped by a Georgia planter at the age of sixteen and gave birth to John's grandmother, Lethea. She in turn had seven children by a neighboring slave owner, including John's mother, Mary "Fanny" Frances. As a young woman, Fanny became a housekeeper in the home of a prominent white physician, Dr. George M. Newton. Shortly after joining the household, Fanny became pregnant with the first of two children she had with Dr. Newton before his death in 1859. James Hope, a business associate of Dr. Newton's, then invited Fanny into his home. They lived openly as husband and wife and had four children, the third being John Hope.

In referring to the relationship between Thomas Jefferson and his slave SALLY HEMINGS, essayist Shelby Steele suggests that many slave women belonged to an invisible "companion class" to white men of power and wealth. This state of affairs marked John Hope's life in two important ways: in all outward appearances, John was white; but, having been raised in the bosom of the black community, he thought of himself as an African American and was determined to improve the lot of "his people."

John was only eight years old when his father died, and though his mother retained the house they lived in, the rest of the estate went to his father's white relatives or was mishandled by the executors of the will. Consequently, John grew up in the South during Reconstruction in a family with little financial means. He attended the Fourth Ward Colored School, a single structure housing the primary, intermediate, and grammar schools. The school was poorly financed and offered only a rudimentary curriculum, but the students there were fortunate to have motivated and highly trained teachers. John worked hard for average grades, and when he graduated from the eighth grade he decided to forgo high school; thus, at the age of thirteen it seemed that he had reached the end of his formal education.

For five years John worked as a wine steward and bookkeeper at Henson's Restaurant, a black-owned establishment in Augusta that excluded black patrons because its owner wanted to cater to a white clientele. John detested this policy, and the experience helped shape his attitude about intraracial bigotry among blacks. Equally profound was the religious conversion that John and his mother underwent in 1886. The Reverend John Dart, a young evangelist from Providence, Rhode Island, who became the pastor of Union Baptist Church, so moved John and his mother that they publicly confessed their sins, foreswore drinking, smoking, and card playing, and were baptized in the Savannah River.

It was Dart who persuaded John, at age eighteen, to attend Worcester Academy in Massachusetts. John worked at odd jobs to pay his tuition and suffered many economic privations, but he endured them all to graduate first in his class in 1890. That September he enrolled at Brown University in Providence, Rhode Island, expecting to pursue a career in the ministry. As in prep school, John worked at local restaurants to meet his expenses. He also wrote articles for the *Brown Daily*

John Hope, president of Morehouse College in Atlanta, Georgia, for twenty-five years, and one of the founders of Atlanta University. Atlanta University, Georgia/Blackstone Studios

Herald. The most popular social organizations on campus were the Brown fraternities. However, they had a "gentleman's agreement" not to admit persons of color. John was very familiar with "passing," the practice of some African Americans with very light complexions to pass for white, and he even knew family members who were passing. In 1893 he was invited by a friend to join an all-white fraternity on the tacit understanding that he would keep his black identity a secret. John indignantly refused. In later years, if people appeared to be confused about his race, John would proudly inform them that he was a "colored man."

Still deeply religious, John attended services at the black Pond Street Baptist Church on the west side of the city. There he cofounded a small literary club called the Enquirers, which sponsored social events and read works by PHILLIS WHEATLEY, FREDERICK DOUGLASS, and other African Americans. In this way John began to develop his leadership abilities and to create a more vibrant black community than the one he found on the campus of Brown University. By his senior year he had achieved a stellar academic record and was chosen to give the student address on Class Day in June 1894. His speech was entitled "Brown University," but his remarks were an uncritical recitation of the virtues of what he called a "superior Western Civilization." The faculty advisory committee was so taken with John's performance that the afternoon before commencement the chairman, Professor Appleton, offered John a position that they had secured for him at the *Providence Journal*. When John told them that he wanted to return to the South and work in the black community, they regarded his decision as a foolish waste of talent.

In the fall of 1894, Hope began his teaching career at Roger Williams University in Nashville, Tennessee. Four years later he became a professor of classics at Atlanta Baptist College, founded by white missionaries in a church basement in 1867 as Augusta Institute, a seminary for the training of black men. When Hope arrived in Atlanta with his wife, Lugenia Burns, there was only one other black professor on the faculty. The dominant model for black higher education had been set by Samuel Armstrong at Hampton Institute in Virginia and his protégé, BOOKER T. WASHINGTON, who established Tuskegee Institute in Alabama. Both institutions stressed industrial training and character development as their primary missions. In fact, Hope was sitting in the audience at the famous 1895 Atlanta Cotton States and International Exposition when Washington offered the following compromise on the race question: Negroes would not press for social or political equality as long as white society assisted them in their quest for economic and moral development.

Hope had great personal admiration for Washington and well understood the challenges of raising funds to support black education, yet he vehemently disagreed with Washington's philosophical approach to education and civil rights. At one of his first public speeches Hope asked rhetorically, "If we are not striving for equality, in heaven's name for what are we living" (Davis, 87). Hope's open dissent on this issue aligned him with W. E. B. DU BOIS, a close friend, and WILLIAM MONROE TROTTER, who formed the Niagara Movement in opposition to Washington. When Hope became the first black president of Atlanta Baptist College in 1906, he seized the opportunity to provide an alternative vision of black higher education, emphasizing classical training and preparation for professional occupations.

During Hope's twenty-five year tenure as president of Atlanta Baptist College, the institution changed its name to Morehouse College, its all-male student enrollment increased five-fold, and its faculty and academic curriculum were of the highest caliber. Hope managed to accomplish so much because, unlike Washington or Du Bois, he developed a leadership style that allowed him to speak forcefully on racial issues without alienating white supporters. While president of Morehouse, he played an active role in the NAACP, was a representative at the first "Amenia Conference" of African American leaders in 1916, attended the Pan African Congress in Paris in 1919, served on the board of the National Urban League, and was a president of the Association for the Study of Negro Life and History. Hope's crowning academic achievement was the role he played in the creation of the Atlanta University Center in 1929. Under this arrangement, Morehouse and Spelman Colleges would continue their undergraduate programs while Atlanta University supplied graduate studies in several academic disciplines. In 1931 Hope was unanimously elected president of Atlanta University, where he served until his death in 1936.

FURTHER READING

The John and Lugenia Burns Hope papers are stored at the Atlanta University Center Archives.

Davis, Leroy. *A Clashing of the Soul: John Hope and the Dilemma of African American Leadership and Black Higher Education in the Early Twentieth Century* (1998).
Torrence, Ridgely. *The Story of John Hope* (1948).

—SHOLOMO B. LEVY

 HOPKINS, PAULINE ELIZABETH (1859–13 Aug. 1930), novelist, journalist, and editor, was born in Portland, Maine, the daughter of Northrup Hopkins and Sarah Allen. She grew up in Boston and graduated from Girls High School. At age fifteen Hopkins won the first prize of ten dollars in gold for her essay, "The Evils of Intemperance and Their Remedy," in a contest sponsored by WILLIAM WELLS BROWN. At twenty Hopkins wrote the play *Slaves' Escape; or, The Underground Railroad* and played the lead role alongside other family members in the Hopkins Colored Troubadours. The production received favorable reviews; in tours around the northeastern United States, the play varied in length from four acts to three and was sometimes titled *Peculiar Sam; or, The Underground Railroad*. The Colored Troubadours also put on a variety of musical performances, and Hopkins was noted for her singing; indeed, she was once referred to as "Boston's Favorite Colored Soprano" (Shockley, 23). During her career as a performer in the 1880s, she wrote a second play, *One Scene from the Drama of Early Days*, based on the biblical story of Daniel in the lion's den; however, no record exists confirming that this play was ever produced. In order to support herself financially, Hopkins trained and worked as a stenographer in the 1890s. During this period she also delivered lectures on subjects in black history, such as Toussaint-Louverture. Hopkins rose quickly to prominence in 1900 with the publication of her novel, *Contending Forces: A Romance Illustrative of Negro Life North and South*, along with her work on one of the first journals owned and operated by African Americans, the *Colored American Magazine*. Both *Contending Forces* and the *Colored American* were published by the Colored Co-operative Publishing Company, and the novel was offered free to new subscribers of the magazine. As a cooperative venture, the *Colored American* stood out from its predecessors in African American publishing and from mainstream white magazines, and Hopkins became an active cooperative member, contributing both fiction and nonfiction, serving as editor of the Women's Department from 1901 to 1903 and later as literary editor in 1903. Indeed, Hopkins's writings appeared so often in the magazine that she sometimes used her mother's maiden name, Sarah Allen, or left her work unsigned, as in the case of her two series of biographies, "Famous Men of the Negro Race" and "Famous Women of the Negro Race." Hopkins also helped found the Colored American League in 1904, an organization that solicited support for the magazine, and she gave lectures throughout the United States to this end.

It is unclear what other roles Hopkins may have played throughout her tenure at the *Colored American* (1900–1904), or why she is listed as editor-in-chief on a single issue of the magazine (March 1904), but her editorial influence is undeniable. In addition to her own writing, she published works by William Braithwaite, BENJAMIN BRAWLEY, James D. Corrothers, and ANGELINA WELD GRIMKÉ. Most of the literary pieces represented were in the protest tradition; like many African American intellectuals of her era, including W. E. B. DU BOIS, Hopkins believed that literature could and should be used as a political tool. This belief is evident in *Contending Forces* and in her three novels serialized by the magazine, *Hagar's Daughters: A Story of Southern Caste Prejudice, Winona; A Tale of Negro Life in the South and Southwest*, and *Of One Blood; Or, the Hidden Self*. In these novels Hopkins drew on the popular traditions of her day, combining romance and suspense with history in complex plots of miscegenation under slavery and interracial marriage in the post–Civil War era. Response to her direct treatment of these themes was mixed, as it was for her contemporary, CHARLES W. CHESNUTT. Issues of passing and interracial relationships were more readily accepted as worthy of literary consideration a few decades later in the works of NELLA LARSEN, LANGSTON HUGHES, and JESSIE FAUSET, among others.

Indeed, Hopkins's willingness to articulate the difficult racial issues of her day certainly led to her departure from the staff of the *Colored American* in 1904, when the magazine was purchased by a supporter of BOOKER T. WASHINGTON. The new publishers changed the course of the magazine's mission, conforming closely to Washington's accommodationist views, which were anathema to Hopkins. A 1912 article in the African American journal *Crisis* reveals that Hopkins's unwillingness to accommodate the sensibilities of white financial supporters of the *Colored American* led to her resignation, and contemporary feminist critics also cite Hopkins's gender as a likely factor. Very few women, black or white, held positions of influence in the publishing world in the early twentieth century, and there is some evidence that several of her male contemporaries resented Hopkins's leadership role. Though she ostensibly left because of poor health, Hopkins's work was soon in print again, in her article "The New York Subway" (Nov. 1904) for *Voice of the Negro*. The *Voice* also published her series "The Dark Races of the Twentieth Century" (Feb.–July 1905).

Gender was assuredly a factor in Hopkins's inability to obtain steady work in the publishing industry after she left the *Colored American*. In 1905 she formed her own publishing company, P.E. Hopkins and Co., but probably due to lack of financial backing, the house released only one work, her pamphlet *A Primer of Facts Pertaining to the Early Greatness of the African Race*. She resumed her career as a stenographer and surfaced again briefly in the public eye in 1916, when she cofounded another magazine, *New Era*. Coedited by Walter Wallace, a former colleague on the *Colored American*, the new magazine resembled its predecessor (when under Hopkins's direction) in its mission and organization. *New Era* expressed great ambition in its commitment to uplift of the race, and included a wide range of journalistic writings, including history, essays, fiction, and a biography series explicitly described as a "sequel" to Hopkins's series for the *Colored American*. She also authored and printed the first installments of another serialized novel, *Topsy Templeton*, but the magazine folded after only two issues.

Little is known of Pauline Hopkins after the collapse of *New Era*. She was working as a stenographer at the Massachusetts Institute of Technology when she died from injuries suffered in an accidental fire at her home in 1930. Single throughout her life, she supported herself and, at times, her mother, through her work as a writer, editor, and stenographer. In her introduction to the first collection of essays on Hopkins, the literary critic Nellie Y. McKay stresses that "there is a need for a full-scale biographical project to fill in the large empty spaces surrounding [Hopkins's] life" (Gruesser, 18). Hopkins was certainly as prolific as any of her male contemporaries, including Charles Chesnutt and W. E. B. Du Bois; her frank discussion of miscegenation and her insistence on the rewriting of African American history prefigured themes and concerns that captured international attention during the Harlem Renaissance.

FURTHER READING

Hopkins's manuscripts are housed at the Fisk University Library in Nashville, Tennessee.

Gruesser, John Cullen, ed. *The Unruly Voice: Rediscovering Pauline Elizabeth Hopkins* (1996).

Johnson, Abby Arthur, and Ronald Mayberry Johnson. *Propaganda and Aesthetics: The Literary Politics of Afro-American Magazines in the Twentieth Century* (1979).

Shockley, Ann Allen. "Pauline Elizabeth Hopkins: A Biographical Excursion into Obscurity." *Phylon* 33 (1972): 22–26.

—ALICE KNOX EATON

 HORNE, LENA
(30 June 1917–), singer and actress, was born Lena Calhoun Horne in the Bedford-Stuyvesant neighborhood of Brooklyn, New York, the only child of Edna Scottron and Edwin "Teddy" Horne. Besides the extremely light-skinned Edna, only Horne's equally fair grandmother, Cora Calhoun Horne, was present at her birth, misleading the hospital staff into expecting a white baby, not the "copper-colored" child who was in fact born. The character of Horne's middle-class family was best embodied by her grandmother, an outspoken suffragist and member of the NAACP (in which she enrolled Horne at age two), and her uncle, Dr. Frank Smith Horne, an educator and occasional adviser to President Franklin D. Roosevelt. After the Hornes divorced in 1920, Edna pursued a mediocre performance career with the Lafayette Players, while Edwin, by most accounts a racketeer, moved to Pennsylvania. Horne accompanied Edna on her travels throughout the South, but eventually she settled with her grandmother in Brooklyn. When Horne was fourteen, Edna returned from a Cuban tour with a new husband, Miguel Rodriguez; now unwelcome among the black bourgeoisie of Brooklyn, the family moved to the Bronx.

In 1933 Edna arranged for her daughter to become one of ETHEL WATERS's chorus girls for the white audiences of Harlem's

Singer and actress Lena Horne signed a contract with MGM Studios which had an explicit clause that she would not play the stereotypical roles previously doled out to African Americans. Library of Congress

Cotton Club. Horne soon dropped out of school, abandoning her dream of becoming a teacher, in order to pursue a career as an entertainer. The gig at the Cotton Club was far from glamorous and required little but scant clothing, but over time Horne performed with the likes of BILLIE HOLIDAY, DUKE ELLINGTON, COUNT BASIE, and CAB CALLOWAY. She also earmarked a portion of her twenty-five dollar weekly wage for singing lessons. Horne, as well as many early critics, never maintained that she had a natural singing voice, but it responded tremendously to formal training.

At age seventeen Horne appeared briefly on Broadway, playing "Mulatto Girl" in a voodoo scene from *Dance with Your Gods* (1934). The show ran for only a couple of weeks, and Horne continued at the Cotton Club for another year. Despite some friction with the club's white management, Edna and

Miguel secured Horne's release to join NOBLE SISSLE's orchestra in Philadelphia, performing under the ostensibly more elegant pseudonym, Helena Horne. Touring eventually brought them through Pittsburgh, where her father Edwin was now managing a hotel; he and Horne reunited, and a year later she married one of his friends, Louis Jones. Nine years her senior and with no career prospects of his own, Jones's indulgent spending strained the marriage, yet the couple had two children in three years, Gail (1938) and Teddy (1940). Horne continued looking for work in show business, landing a role in the "quickie musical," *The Duke Is Tops* (1938); salary was delayed for the all-black cast, souring her first Hollywood experience. She then earned a coveted role in the Broadway revue *Blackbirds of 1939*, but the production lasted only nine performances. Despite the esteem she had

gained over four years of working clubs and fronting orchestras, along with film and stage work, Horne had not yet found her breakthrough gig. For a while she settled into domesticity; but in 1940 she separated from Jones and moved to New York, planning to get a foothold on her career and send for her children shortly.

In December of that year, her manager burst into a movie theater where Horne was enjoying the afternoon and implored her to audition for Charlie Barnett's band that same day. Barnett awarded her the job halfway through her first song, making her one of the first black women to sing lead with a white band. Her career hit full stride when she and Barnett recorded "Haunted Town" and "Good For Nothing Joe." But her personal life suffered. Jones had granted her full custody of Gail, but only occasional visitation rights with Teddy.

Soon Horne was appearing at the Apollo Theatre and Carnegie Hall, and in 1941 she began singing regularly at the Café Society Downtown, where she reportedly met WALTER WHITE and PAUL ROBESON on the same night. Their commitment to civil rights made a lasting impression on Horne, and when she was offered top billing at a Los Angeles club, White convinced her that she might be on the cusp of a larger accomplishment for African Americans as a whole. So in 1942 Horne left her boyfriend, the boxer JOE LOUIS, and moved to Los Angeles with Gail and a cousin, Edwina, who had been caring for her.

After a short singing stint at the Trocadero Club, Horne signed a seven-year contract with MGM which had an explicit clause that she would not play the stereotypical roles previously doled out to African Americans—thus paving the way to more dignified roles for other black actresses. But she lost her first role, a speaking part in *Thank Your Lucky Stars*, to Ethel Waters, because her skin was too light on film and any makeup bore too close a resemblance to blackface. She did receive a bit part in *Panama Hattie* (1942) that established the routine for most of her subsequent MGM films: Horne would appear in an evening gown, lean against a pillar, and sing in a single scene that could easily be deleted for southern theaters. But in 1943, when MGM gave her the lead in the all-black musical *Cabin in the Sky*, response was so positive that Twentieth

Century–Fox leased her for one picture, the BILL "BOJANGLES" ROBINSON musical *Stormy Weather* (1943). Horne sang the title track, and it remained her calling card throughout the rest of her career.

While filming *Stormy Weather*, Horne met Lennie Hayton, the white musical director who eventually worked on such hits as *Singin' in the Rain* and *Hello, Dolly*. Meanwhile, she continued at MGM, appearing in *I Dood It* (1943), *As Thousands Cheer* (1943), *Broadway Rhythm* (1944), *Two Girls and a Sailor* (1944) and *Ziegfeld Follies* (1946). Horne divorced Jones in 1944 and married Hayton in Paris in 1947, though the news was withheld until 1950. She had also become a World War II pinup girl and sang for the troops at American military bases. One story holds that at Fort Riley, Kansas, she spotted German prisoners of war with better seats than the African American soldiers, so she swept right past them and sang to the blacks in the back row.

Largely because of her connection with Paul Robeson, Horne was periodically blacklisted in Hollywood during the McCarthy witch hunts. She shifted her career back to the clubs and within a few years could command $12,500 per week. Horne appeared on television specials hosted by Ed Sullivan and Steve Allen and in 1956 was offered her first speaking role in a movie with whites, *Meet Me in Las Vegas*. The next year she recorded *Lena Horne at the Waldorf Astoria*, perhaps her most successful album. She appeared in her first starring role on Broadway, the wildly successful *Jamaica* (1957), but lost the leading role of the "mulatto" Julie in the movie *Showboat* to Ava Gardner, who, it turns out, ended up wearing the "Light Egyptian" blush that Max Factor had designed especially for Horne.

In the 1960s Horne increasingly involved herself in civil rights, on occasion working with JAMES BALDWIN, HARRY BELAFONTE, LORRAINE HANSBERRY, and Robert F. Kennedy. She participated in the March on Washington in 1963 and frequently raised money for civil rights organizations around the country. Hayton's death in 1971 had been preceded by Edwin's and Teddy's, both in 1970. Having lost the three men closest to her in less than two years, Horne retreated from the public eye; but she resumed performing a couple of

years later and collaborated with Tony Bennett in a 1974 Broadway show. In 1978 Horne played the good witch in *The Wiz*, a black version of the *Wizard of Oz* with DIANA ROSS and MICHAEL JACKSON. She was lauded with an honorary doctorate from Howard University in 1979, and that same year she put on a television special with Belafonte.

In 1981 Horne staged her most triumphant professional performance, the one-woman show *Lena Horne: The Lady and Her Music*. The pinnacle of the show came when she sang "Stormy Weather" twice, first as she had sung it in Hollywood almost forty years earlier, and then in the more fully matured and regal style of her current voice. *The Lady and Her Music* ran to 333 performances before touring in America and Europe for two years; it won a Tony Award, a citation from the New York Drama Critics Circle, and two Grammy Awards.

FURTHER READING

A collection of Lena Horne's papers is housed at the Schomburg Center for Research in Black Culture of the New York Public Library.

Horne, Lena, with Helen Arstein and Carlton Moss. *In Person: Lena Horne* (1950).
——, with Richard Schickel. *Lena* (1965).

Buckley, Gail Lumet. *The Hornes: An American Family* (1986).
Haskins, James, and Kathleen Benson. *Lena: A Personal and Professional Biography of Lena Horne* (1984).

—DAVID F. SMYDRA JR.

HORTON, GEORGE MOSES

HORTON, GEORGE MOSES (1797?–1883?), poet, was born in Northampton County, North Carolina, a slave of William Horton; the names of his parents are unknown. As a boy, he moved with his master's household to Chatham County, where he tended cows on the farm. Horton's teenage pleasures, he later wrote, were "singing lively tunes" and "hearing people read" (Horton, iv), and he taught himself to read, first learning the alphabet from an old spelling book. He acquired an extraordinary vocabulary and the forms, topics, and styles of his verse from reading the New Testament, Wesley's hymnal, and books given to him by University of North Carolina (UNC) students.

In his early twenties, now the slave of William's son, James Horton, George avoided the manual labor he disliked by walking eight miles from the farm to Chapel Hill on weekends to sell fruit and his poems. From about 1830 on, he hired his time from successive masters and lived on the university campus, earning his living as a professional poet and college servant. In about 1818 Horton married a slave woman surnamed Snipes with whom he had two children, a daughter, Rhody, and a son, Free Snipes.

During his early poetic career Horton composed verses in his head while plowing the fields—he could not write until about 1832—and dictated these love lyrics and acrostics to student customers who paid him twenty-five to seventy-five cents for each poem. He sold a dozen verses a week in this way for many years, until he found a benefactor, Caroline Lee Hentz, a poet and novelist. Mrs. Hentz inspired, copied down, and edited the verses Horton dictated. She had two of his poems published in the Lancaster (Massachusetts) *Gazette* (1828), and she probably transcribed the twenty-one verses for Horton's first book, *The Hope of Liberty* (1829). In the summer and fall of 1828 the New York *Freedom's Journal* published a few of Horton's poems along with editorials appealing for contributions for his manumission. In the same months, the Raleigh *Register* printed his poems, and with influential friends of the poet, such as the UNC president Joseph Caldwell and John Owen, governor of North Carolina, the *Register* campaigned for Horton's freedom. Money to buy the poet's freedom was to come from sales of *The Hope of Liberty*, but this historic volume earned scarcely any profit for its author and failed to generate enough funds to purchase his freedom.

Horton continued to earn three to four dollars a week from sales of his love poems, while he hired his time for twenty-five cents a week, gaining a substantial profit. His fame spread when *The Hope of Liberty* was reprinted in Philadelphia and Boston (1837–1838), and periodicals in the North and South published his verses in the 1840s. The first stanza of "On Liberty and Slavery" aptly describes his plight and illustrates his style:

Alas! and am I born for this,
To wear this slavish chain?

Deprived of all created bliss,
Through hardship, toil and pain!

In 1843 his new master, Hall Horton, a tanner and farmer of Chatham, raised the slave's hire fee to fifty cents, adding to other troubles. Horton's need to acclimate himself at age forty-six to a new young master, the death a few years earlier of his mentor, president Joseph Caldwell, the rise of pro-slavery sentiments and repressive legislation in North Carolina, and the pain of almost half a century in bondage all motivated Horton to try again to buy his freedom.

On 3 September 1844 Horton wrote an appeal to the abolitionist William Lloyd Garrison, who ten years earlier had printed Horton's "On Liberty and Slavery" in the *Liberator* (Mar. 29). Horton entrusted the mailing of this letter to the new UNC president, David L. Swain, who filed it among his papers. A year later the poet and his supporters circulated a subscription list in Chapel Hill for his new volume, *The Poetical Works* (1845). Even with the sales of this book of forty-four poems Horton could not accumulate sufficient funds to purchase his freedom, perhaps because some of his income went for drink. During the next fifteen years Horton continued to hire his time and survived as a poet, servant, odd-jobs man at the university, and part-time farm laborer.

In 1849 the Raleigh *Register* (Dec. 29) published Horton's spirited defense of American over foreign literature. In 1852 Horton wrote a letter begging David Swain to purchase him for $250 to alleviate his arduous eight-mile commute from the farm to Chapel Hill and promising to pay back Swain from sales of his poetry books. President Swain filed this letter, too (with a later appeal from Horton), and advised him to write to Horace Greeley. Horton wrote to Greeley in September 1852, asking for $175 "to remove the burden of hard servitude.... I am the only public or recognized poet of color in my native state or perhaps in the union, born in slavery but yet craving that scope and expression whereby my literary labor of the night may be circulated throughout the whole world." He added a poem, "The Poet's Feeble Petition," and entrusted the letter for mailing to David Swain, who again buried it in his papers. The slave would wait another dozen years for emancipation.

In his sixty-second year Horton delivered an oration, "An Address. The Stream of Liberty and Science. To Collegiates of the University of N.C. by George M. Horton the Black Bard" (1859). He spoke to freshman students, several of whom copied down parts of the "Address" as Horton rambled on. This chaotic twenty-nine-page manuscript reveals Horton's privations and need for liberty, and it includes visions of Judgment Day and a reborn world; fatherly advice to students, love, of knowledge and learning, and political opinions, including a prescient fear of the approaching bloody "dissolution of national union." Horton's voice sounds estranged and embittered, hopelessly resigned to his bondage. The slave's life in Chapel Hill became even more difficult after 1860; with the university depleted of students and resources by the Civil War, Horton lost the market for both his services and his poems.

On 17 April 1865 the Ninth Michigan Cavalry Volunteers entered Chapel Hill, and Horton found a patron in Captain William H. S. Banks. The twenty-eight-year-old Banks and the sixty-eight-year-old poet traveled in North Carolina with the Volunteers, going to Greensboro and Lexington in May, to Concord in June, and back to Lexington, where, on 21 July, Banks was released from service; then Banks and Horton journeyed to Raleigh. As he walked and camped some three hundred miles during three summer months, Horton composed ninety new poems for his third volume, which Banks got published in Raleigh as *Naked Genius* (1865). In *Naked Genius*, Banks solicited sales agents for a new book by Horton, "The Black Poet," but it was never published, and Banks soon abandoned Horton in Raleigh.

Few facts document the poet's last eighteen years. Probably in the winter of 1865–1866 he traveled to Philadelphia, Pennsylvania, where, on 31 August 1866, the Banneker Institute interviewed him, "a poet of considerable genius" (Stephen B. Weeks, "George Moses Horton: Slave Poet," *Southern Workman* [Oct. 1914], 576). *The Christian Recorder* (10 Nov. 1866) published his poem "Forbidden to Ride on the Street Cars," a protest against Philadelphia's segregated streetcars. The *African Repository* (Jan. 1867) printed his "Song for the Emigrant" and

noted that Horton had immigrated to Liberia. The *Repository* (Feb. and Mar. 1867) reported that fourteen persons from Philadelphia had been sent by the Pennsylvania Colonization Society on the trader *Edith Rose* from New York to Grand Bassa County, Liberia. They had sailed on 5 December 1866, arrived at Monrovia on 7 January 1867, and continued to Bexley a few days later. A "List of Emigrants for Liberia" describes Horton as sixty-eight years old, a tanner, and a Methodist, who could read and write. Later communiqués from the Philadelphia emigrants fail to mention Horton.

Collier Cobb, the head of the department of Geology at UNC, wrote in 1929 that he had "called on Poet Horton in Philadelphia in 1883, the very year in which he died." "I called him 'Poet,' which pleased him greatly," wrote Cobb in a letter to Victor Palsits, "and he told me that I was using his proper title." No other mention of Horton's presence or death appears in census or death records, periodicals, or archives after 1867.

Poet Horton lived in slavery for sixty-eight years. Although JUPITER HAMMON had been the first African American to publish a poem in 1760 and PHILIS WHEATLEY had been the first black person to publish a volume of poetry in 1773, Horton is the first African American poet whose work centers on the struggle for freedom. He was also the first African American to publish a book in the South, the only slave to earn a significant income selling his poems, and the only poet of any race to produce a book of poems *before* he could write. In recent years Horton has been honored by the founding of the George Moses Horton Society for the Study of African American Poetry (1996). He was inducted into the North Carolina Literary Hall of Fame in 1996 and the following year he was named "Historic Poet Laureate" of Chatham County.

FURTHER READING

Horton's letters and "An Address" are in collections of the University of North Carolina, Chapel Hill. Cobb's letter to Victor Paltsis is in the Schomburg Center for research in black culture of the New York Public Library.

Horton, George Moses. *The Poetical Works of George M. Horton, The Colored Bard of North Carolina, To Which is Prefixed The Life of the Author, Written by Himself* (1845).

Pitts, Reginald H. "'Let Us Desert This Friendless Place': George Moses Horton in Philadelphia—1866." *The Journal of Negro History* 80 (Fall 1995).

Sherman, Joan R., ed. *The Black Bard of North Carolina: George Moses Horton and His Poetry* (1997).

—JOAN R. SHERMAN

HOUSTON, CHARLES HAMILTON (3 Sept. 1895–22 Apr. 1950), lawyer and professor, was born in the District of Columbia, the son of William LePre Houston, a lawyer, and Mary Ethel Hamilton, a hairdresser and former schoolteacher. Houston graduated Phi Beta Kappa from Amherst College in 1915. After a year of teaching English at Howard University in Washington, D.C., he served during World War I as a second lieutenant in the 351st Field Artillery of the American Expeditionary Forces. Having experienced racial discrimination while serving his country, Houston "made up [his] mind that [he] would never get caught...without knowing...[his] rights, that [he] would study law and use [his] time fighting for men who could not strike back." He entered Harvard Law School in 1919, where he became the first African American elected as an editor of the *Harvard Law Review,* and in 1922 he earned an LLB cum laude. In 1922–1923 he studied for the doctorate in Juridical Science, becoming the first African American to be awarded the SJD at Harvard. Following an additional year of study with a concentration on civil law at the University of Madrid, Houston passed the bar examination for the District of Columbia in 1924. In that year he married Margaret Gladys Moran. They divorced in 1937, and Houston married Henrietta Williams, with whom he had one child.

Houston practiced law as a partner in the District of Columbia firm of his father (Houston & Houston; later Houston, Houston, Hastie & Waddy) from 1924 to 1950, with occasional leaves of absence. He also taught law and became an academic administrator at Howard University Law School, serving on its faculty from 1924 to 1935. His accomplishments at Howard were remarkable. From 1929 to 1935 he provided leadership during the transformation of the then nonaccredited evening school to a highly respected, full-time, American Bar Association–accredited day law school that enjoyed membership in the Association of American Law Schools. Directing the work of the law school as vice dean and chief administrative officer (1930–1935), Houston inspired the faculty and students with a sense of urgency and a spirit of boldness regarding the duty of African American lawyers as advocates of racial justice. Houston expounded a philosophy of "social engineering," which was grounded in the beliefs that law could be used effectively to secure fundamental social change in society and that the law was an instrument available to minority groups who were unable to use fully the franchise or direct action to achieve recognition of their rights and equality. Among his students during this period were Oliver Hill, William Bryant, and THURGOOD MARSHALL, each of whom would become distinguished civil rights litigators and the latter two of whom would achieve national renown as federal jurists.

Houston's civil rights advocacy primarily focused on achieving recognition of African Americans' equal rights under law through the elimination of legally enforced racial discrimination. He argued that the status of African Americans as an oppressed minority necessitated the "complete elimination of segregation" through a protracted struggle including a legal campaign supported by a "sustaining mass interest," with "leadership...develop[ing] from the aspirations, determinations, sacrifices and needs of the group itself." He served as the first full-time, salaried special counsel of the National Association for the Advancement of Colored People (NAACP) from 1935 to 1940. He proposed in 1934 and thereafter implemented a strategy for overturning the "separate but equal" precedent of *Plessy v. Ferguson* (1896) to the end that racial discrimination and segregation might be declared unconstitutional by the U.S. Supreme Court. In recognition of courts' reliance on *stare decisis* and of widespread racism, Houston developed a long-range strategy of building favorable precedents over time until a direct attack on segregation per se could be made based upon such precedents rather than following one proposed earlier by Nathan Margold to make an immediate attack on segregation. Houston's strategy was implemented by the NAACP and later its Legal Defense and Educational Fund under Thurgood Marshall's direction. While the NAACP and its Legal Defense Fund were concerned about various manifestations of racial discrimination, a special grant from the American Fund for Public Service was primarily devoted to funding cases involving discrimination in education because of its relation to the fundamental problem of white supremacy. According to Houston in 1935, "Apparent senseless discriminations in education against Negroes have a very definite objective on the part of the ruling whites to curb the young and prepare them to accept an inferior position in American life without protest or struggle."

As special counsel and later adviser to Thurgood Marshall, Houston emphasized for the sake of "effectiveness" both the importance of the use of African American lawyers and the commitment to a program of "intelligent leadership plus intelligent mass action." Houston worked with local African American attorneys and argued before the U.S. Supreme Court *Missouri ex rel. Gaines v. Canada* in 1938, the first major Supreme Court case in the groundwork laid for *Brown v. Board of Education* (1954), which declared segregation in public schools unconstitutional. He thereafter shaped with Marshall many of the essential legal precedents leading to *Brown,* including *Sipuel v. Oklahoma State Board of Regents* (1948), *McLaurin v. Oklahoma State Regents* (1950), and *Sweatt v. Painter* (1950). For African Americans in the Consolidated Parent Group of the District of Columbia, Houston initiated litigation against inequality in public schools, which under James Nabrit was later transformed and ultimately led to *Bolling v. Sharpe* (1954), the companion case to *Brown* declaring segregation in the District's public schools unconstitutional.

Houston's historical significance is chiefly derived from his role as strategist, legal counsel, and adviser in the struggle against racial discrimination in public education. It is noteworthy, however, that while he was among the first to emphasize the importance of training lawyers to change law and to participate in dissent regarding fundamental policy and practice of the government, he recognized that the judicial process was slow and not designed to change, but rather to uphold the status quo. Because of these "limitations," he cautioned those who would rely on the courts alone and encouraged African Americans to "do [their] own fighting and more of it by extra-legal means," that is, boycotts, demonstrations, and the like.

Houston's contributions to eliminating legal validation of racial discrimination extended into other areas, particularly the struggles for fairness in employment, housing, and the rights of the accused. He served, for a time, on the President's Fair Employment Practices Committee and in 1944 successfully argued before the U.S. Supreme Court in *Steele v. Louisville and Nashville Railroad* as well as *Tunstall v. Brotherhood of Locomotive Firemen and Engineers* the duty of fair representation regardless of race or union affiliation. In regard to housing discrimination, Houston assisted the NAACP in its preparation for *Shelley v. Kraemer* (1948) and was chief counsel before the U.S. Supreme Court in the companion case, *Hurd v. Hodge* (1948), in which the Court barred racially restrictive covenants in the states and the District of Columbia. With respect to the rights of persons accused of crimes, Houston litigated *Hollins v. Oklahoma* (1935) and *Hale v. Kentucky* (1938), in which the U.S. Supreme Court overturned the convictions and death sentences of African American defendants who had been tried by juries from which African Americans had been excluded on the basis of race.

An active participant in the civil rights struggle of African Americans beyond the courtroom, Houston engaged in a variety of expressions of political activism during his lifetime, including marching during the 1930s for the freedom of the SCOTTSBORO BOYS, writing a regular column of political commentary in the *Afro-American,* and testifying before Congress against lynching and other forms of racial injustice. His analysis and experiences compelled him in 1949 to urge African Americans

not simply to be "content...with...an equal share in the existing system," but to struggle to establish a system that "guarantee[d] justice and freedom for everyone."

Charles Hamilton Houston's grueling pace in the struggle for racial justice eventually resulted in a heart attack from which he died in Washington, D.C. He was buried in Lincoln Memorial Cemetery in Suitland, Maryland.

FURTHER READING

Letters and papers of Houston may be found in the records of the NAACP and the William L. Houston Family Papers in the Library of Congress, in the records of the Fair Employment Practices Committee at the National Archives, and in the Charles H. Houston vertical file, the Consolidated Parent Group Records, and the C. H. Houston Collection at the Moorland-Spingarn Research Center, Howard University.

Kluger, Richard. *Simple Justice* (1976).
McNeil, Genna Rae. *Groundwork: Charles Hamilton Houston and the Struggle for Civil Rights* (1983).
Segal, Geraldine. *In Any Fight Some Fall* (1975).
Tushnet, Mark. *The NAACP Legal Strategy against Segregated Education, 1925–1950* (1987).

Obituaries: *Afro-American,* 29 Apr. 1950; *Pittsburgh Courier,* 6 May 1950.

—GENNA RAE MCNEIL

 HOWARD, PERRY WILBON (14 Jan. 1877– 1 Feb. 1961), Republican politician and lawyer, was born in Ebenezer, Mississippi, the first of seven sons of Perry W. Howard Sr., a farmer and successful blacksmith, and his wife, Sarah. Both parents were former slaves. The only black family in Ebenezer, the Howards received sympathy from whites in the community, who respected their ambition, hard work, and frugality. Perry attended the Holmes County public schools before entering Alcorn A & M in 1891. He did not graduate but later earned his BA from Rust University, now Rust College, in Holly Springs, Mississippi, in 1899. He then served for one year as president of Campbell College, a small African Methodist Episcopal Church school in Jackson, Mississippi. He studied mathematics at Fisk

University in Nashville and was chair and professor of mathematics at Alcorn A & M until 1905. In 1904, while still at Alcorn, he earned a law degree from the Illinois College of Law in Chicago (now De Paul Law School) and was admitted to the Mississippi bar the following year.

In 1907 Howard married Wilhelmina Lucas of Macon, Mississippi, a Fisk graduate who taught in the literary department at Tuskegee Institute and the music department at Alcorn. The Howards had three children, but only two survived into adulthood. Howard was one of only twenty-four black lawyers practicing in Mississippi at the turn of the twentieth century, a period recognized by the historian RAYFORD W. LOGAN as the nadir of southern race relations, when African Americans suffered from segregation, disenfranchisement, and the ever-present fear of lynchings and racial violence. Whites did not seek the services of black lawyers and, since the state precluded African Americans from serving on juries, many blacks believed they would be given a fairer hearing if white lawyers represented them before white juries.

Howard's law practice, located in the center of Jackson's black business district, does not appear to have been profitable, but he compensated for this by serving as national chief counsel for the Elks and as president of the Mississippi Beneficial Life Insurance Company. Moreover, he worked as an officer for the Mississippi Negro Business League, the state affiliate of the National Negro Business League; became the first secretary and, later, president of the National Negro Bar Association; and was a trustee at Mississippi Utica Normal and Industrial Institute, a school designed after BOOKER T. WASHINGTON's Tuskegee model. (Howard, although he had received a liberal education at Fisk, was a staunch advocate of Washington and industrial education.)

That politics became Perry Howard's passion is no understatement. Early in his political career Howard was a protégé and political ally of Charles Banks. Banks, a businessman and Booker T. Washington's chief lieutenant for Mississippi, was the most powerful African American in the state. To some extent, whites accepted, and even encouraged, Howard's power and autonomy within the Mississippi Republican

Party. On one occasion the Ku Klux Klan even burned a cross on the lawn of Howard's white opponent to warn voters not to vote for the opponent. Because of Howard's political influence in the state, Republican President Warren G. Harding appointed him special assistant to the attorney general for the United States in 1921, making him the highest-paid African American working in the federal government. Howard moved to Washington, D.C., and lived there for the rest of his life, never again voting in Mississippi, though remaining an active force in the state's political life.

That same year, he joined one of Washington's leading black law firms, Howard, Hayes, and Davis (which became Cobb, Hayes, and Howard in 1935). Howard, James A. Cobb, and George E. C. Hayes all had strong political connections the Republican Party. Hayes had worked as the general counsel at Howard University, and Cobb had worked as a municipal judge for some years before joining the partnership. Thus, unlike a number of other black law firms that practiced only criminal law, Howard's firm branched out into municipal law, a more profitable area. The law firm also argued civil rights cases before the federal courts.

Except for 1920, Howard served as a Mississippi delegate to every Republican National Convention from 1912 to 1960, an era in which the white supremacist Democratic Party ruled the state's political life. Although there was a movement within the Republican Party to make its southern wing as "lily-white" as the Democrats, in 1919 Howard led a large contingent of African Americans to the Republican National Committee (RNC) meeting in St. Louis and to the Republican National Convention in Chicago in 1920, seeking recognition for his "black-and-tan" faction of the party. Both times he was defeated in his effort to be chosen as the Republican national committeeman for Mississippi by the forces of Michael J. Mulvihill, the white national committeeman from Vicksburg. However, in 1924 Howard successfully unseated Mulvihill at the national convention in Cleveland after Mulvihill refused to appoint any blacks to significant positions within the party. Howard thus became one of the first African Americans to serve on the RNC in the twentieth century. His position brought

along with it little more than prestige and patronage power, and even then the patronage most often went to white Democrats and very rarely to blacks.

Within a year of his election to the RNC, Howard became embroiled in controversy, which followed him throughout much of his public career. In 1925, when the Federal Bureau of Investigation and the Post Office Department uncovered widespread political corruption in Mississippi, Howard's political machine was accused of selling offices. Lesser postal positions allegedly went for up to $1,500, while more lucrative positions, such as U.S. marshal, postmaster, and revenue collector, went for as much as $2,500. Investigators also charged Howard with illegally soliciting campaign funds. Many people understood that Howard, more than any other Republican in Mississippi, controlled the party's appointments. Although the case was never proved in court, many observers presumed that Howard received most of the graft.

Howard, however, denied any wrongdoing and asserted that white supremacists, "lily-white" Republicans, and disappointed office seekers were out to get him. Despite Howard's denial, the chief examiner for the Justice Department recommended that the patronage charges against Howard be turned over to a grand jury and that Howard be fired from his appointed position for illegally soliciting campaign contributions. U.S. Attorney General John Garibaldi Sargent, however, did not act on these recommendations, and the FBI agents who conducted the investigation against Howard were either quietly reassigned or fired. Howard's behavior did not differ much from that of white politicians engaged in the business of patronage politics. Nonetheless, in 1929, after Howard had gone to trial twice, and with the prospect of a third trial, President Herbert Hoover's administration forced him to resign from his government post.

Black Mississippians criticized Howard for spending so much time away from his state. They contended that he rarely visited Mississippi after moving to Washington, that he made no effort to expand the black electorate in the Magnolia State, and that conditions for black Republicans were virtually the

same as they had been under white national committeemen. Several national black leaders also criticized Howard for joining southern whites in opposing the Dyer federal anti-lynching bill in 1922 and for opposing the formation of the Brotherhood of Sleeping Car Porters (BSCP), a group of black Pullman car porters trying to unionize. Although Howard had worked as a Pullman porter during his college years, when black porters attempted to unionize, he wrote a solicitous letter to the Pullman Company agreeing to help them resist the effort. Eventually, the company paid Howard to try to derail the movement. While Howard never denied being a paid agent for Pullman, he claimed that he opposed the black union effort because communists inspired it and black workers were about to destroy what he believed was their "amicable" relationship with the Pullman Company.

Both of Howard's allegations were spurious. A. PHILIP RANDOLPH, the leader of the BSCP, was a socialist, but also a vigorous anti-communist, and he called on President Calvin Coolidge to replace Howard with a black leader more representative of African American thinking. W. E. B. DU BOIS also criticized the Coolidge administration for allowing Howard to accept a fee from the Pullman Company while officially holding a governmental position. Randolph prevailed upon white Wisconsin Representative Victor L. Berger to investigate Howard's activities and ascertain if they warranted his removal from office. Other African American leaders, including JAMES WELDON JOHNSON, felt that Howard was an "Uncle Tom" who supported Pullman only because they paid him. Despite these criticisms, Howard kept his seat on the RNC until 1960. At that time he was eighty-three years old and the committee's ranking member. Perry Howard died in Washington the following year, after a very long career.

FURTHER READING

Jackson, David H., Jr. *A Chief Lieutenant of the Tuskegee Machine: Charles Banks of Mississippi* (2002).

Lisio, Donald J. *Hoover, Blacks, and Lily-Whites: A Study of Southern Strategies* (1985).

McMillen, Neil R. *Dark Journey: Black Mississippians in the Age of Jim Crow* (1990).

———. "Perry W. Howard, Boss of Black-and-Tan Republicanism in Mississippi,

1924–1960." *Journal of Southern History* 48.2 (May 1982).

Mollison, Irvin C. "Negro Lawyers in Mississippi." *Journal of Negro History* 15 (Jan. 1930).

Obituary: *New York Times*, 2 Feb. 1961.

—DAVID H. JACKSON JR.

HUBBARD, WILLIAM DeHART (25 Nov. 1903–23 June 1976), the first African American to win an individual Olympic Games gold medal, was born in Cincinnati, Ohio, the son of William A. Hubbard. Olympic historians know nothing of his father's occupation nor his mother's full name at the time of her marriage. After excelling in both academics and athletics at Walnut Hills High Schools between 1918 and 1921, Hubbard entered the University of Michigan. As a freshman he tied the school record in the 50-yard dash, set a school record of 24′ 6$\frac{3}{4}$″ in the long jump, and won two U.S. National Amateur Athletic Union (AAU) Championships in the long jump (24′ 5$\frac{1}{2}$′) and triple jump (48′ 1$\frac{1}{2}$″). He won All-American honors in 1922, and until his graduation in 1925, his exploits reserved for him recognition as the greatest combination sprinter-jumper of the 1920s.

Hubbard was a compact, 150-pound world-class sprinter, and no one before his time nor during his career was able to "run off" the wooden toeboard with the same speed as "King Hubbard." His speed and technique not only won him American, world, and Olympic honors, but he was the precursor of the even greater sprinter-jumpers of the next generation. The British expert, Colonel F. A. M. Webster, watched Hubbard, his speed, and jumping prowess and called Hubbard "a regular pinch of dynamite." Hubbard won AAU long jump titles six times, 1922–1927, "an astonishing achievement," wrote historian Roberto L. Quercetani. "His style included a run of less than 30 meters, a remarkable acceleration and a single, fast kick of the lead leg."

Hubbard qualified as an American Olympic team member for the 1924 Games in Paris; despite an injured leg, he won the gold medal with a 24′ 5$\frac{1}{8}$″

leap. Returning home to his studies and his athletics, Hubbard dominated the jumps and sprints at the prestigious National Collegiate Athletic Association (NCAA) Championships. He had won the 1923 NCAA jump title, and at the 1925 competition he literally hurled himself out of the sand pit with a world record leap of 25′ 10$\frac{7}{8}$″, having already won the 100-yard dash. The Associated Press release on 13 June 1925 shouted, "Hubbard approaches 26 feet, a long jump record that may stand for all time."

In 1926 Hubbard ran 100 yards in 9.6 seconds, tying the world record. He had recently graduated from Michigan, "one of only eight blacks in a class of 1,456" (Ashe, 79). Injuries plagued Hubbard, slowing him down so much that at the 1928 Olympic Games in Amsterdam he finished in eleventh place. His athletic career was finished, and with a degree in physical education, Hubbard accepted a position with the Cincinnati Recreation Department. For fifteen years he supervised Negro athletic leagues in that city and persisted in efforts to improve housing for blacks. In 1943 Hubbard moved to Cleveland and served as race relations adviser to the Federal Housing Authority, remaining in that position for many years. Hubbard died in Cleveland. His wife, Audrey, and three children survived.

FURTHER READING

ASHE, ARTHUR R. *A Hard Road to Glory: A History of the African American Athlete*, vol. 2 (1988), 78–79.

Mallon, Bill, et al. *Quest for Gold* (1984), 309–310.

Quercetani, Roberto L. *A History of Modern Track and Field* (1990), 73.

Webster, F. A. M. *Athletics of To-Day* (1929), 206–207.

Obituaries: *New York Times*, 25 June 1976; *Times* (London), 26 June 1976.

—JOHN A. LUCAS

HUGHES, LANGSTON (1 Feb. 1902?–22 May 1967), writer, was born James Langston Hughes in Joplin, Missouri, the son of James Nathaniel Hughes, a stenographer and bookkeeper, and Carrie Mercer Langston,

a stenographer. Left behind by a frustrated father who, angered by racism, sought jobs in Cuba and Mexico, and also left often by a mother searching for employment, Hughes was raised primarily in Lawrence, Kansas, by his maternal grandmother, Mary Langston. In 1915 he went to reside with his mother and stepfather, Homer Clark, in Lincoln, Illinois, later moving with them to Cleveland, Ohio.

Hughes spent the summers of 1919 and 1920 with his father in Mexico, writing his first great poem, "The Negro Speaks of Rivers," aboard a train on his second trip. By the time he entered Columbia University in September 1921, Hughes already had poems published in *Brownies' Book* and the *Crisis*. He left Columbia after one year, traveled as a dishwasher and cook's assistant on freighters to Africa and Holland and at Le Grand Duc in Paris, and later worked as a busboy in Washington, D.C. With financial help from the philanthropist Amy Spingarn, he entered Lincoln University in 1926 as an award-winning poet who had taken first place in an *Opportunity* contest and second and third places in a contest in the *Crisis* the year before. By the time he graduated in 1929, he had published two volumes of poetry, *The Weary Blues and Other Poems* (1926) and *Fine Clothes to the Jew* (1927), and had helped to launch the daring African American literary journal *Fire!!* He had also completed a reading tour in the South with the writer and anthropologist ZORA NEALE HURSTON, had become friends with other leading lights of the Harlem Renaissance, and had interested white socialites, artists, and patrons in his work.

For developing his artistic and aesthetic sensibilities, however, Hughes credited those people he dubbed admiringly as the "low-down folks." He praised the lower classes for their pride and individuality, that "they accept what beauty is their own without question." Part of the beauty that attracted him most was their music, especially the blues, which Hughes had heard as a child in Kansas City, as a teen in nightclubs in Chicago, Harlem, and Washington, D.C., on his trips through the South, and even as a young man in Europe. To Hughes, the blues were, as he wrote in "Songs Called the Blues" (1941), songs that came out of "black,

Langston Hughes occupies a place of central importance in twentieth-century African American literature and American literature generally. National Portrait Gallery, Smithsonian Institution/Art Resource, NY

beaten, but unbeatable throats." They were the sad songs of proud and wise people who, through the mixture of tears and laughter (often their response on hearing the lyrics) demonstrated a vivacity, wisdom, and determination. This inspired Hughes to attempt to capture the pulse and spirit of the blues tradition as a way of interpreting his people both to the rest of the world and to themselves. Hughes was galvanized by the music of his people, whether blues, jazz, or religious. The music provided him with themes, motifs, images, symbols, languages, rhythms, and stanza forms he would use in his writing throughout his career. As early as 1926, he was trying to schedule blues music as part of his poetry readings; in 1958 he recorded his poetry to the accompaniment of jazz groups led by Henry "Red" Allen and CHARLES MINGUS. At Hughes's funeral, a program of blues was performed.

At the beginning of his writing career, Hughes was encouraged by the writer and editor JESSIE FAUSET, W. E. B. DU BOIS, JAMES WELDON JOHNSON, one of the judges who awarded Hughes his first poetry prizes and later anthologized some of Hughes's work, and ALAIN LOCKE, whose 1925 issue of the *Survey Graphic*, later revised into the groundbreaking volume *The New Negro* (1925), included some of Hughes's work. Through both the intellectual leadership of the highbrows and the invigorating atmosphere provided by the low-down folks in Harlem, Hughes found himself encouraged and gaining in fame. Vachel Lindsay's praise in 1925 of poems left by his plate in the Wardman Park Hotel in Washington by a "busboy poet" precipitated a flurry of interest and brought Hughes a wider audience for his poetry. But it was arts patron Carl Van Vechten who gave Hughes's career its biggest boost in the

white world by taking Hughes's first book to Knopf and establishing contacts for Hughes that would serve him personally and professionally. Hughes repaid Van Vechten's assistance most directly with his support of and contributions to Van Vechten's novel *Nigger Heaven*; the two remained friends until Van Vechten's death in 1964.

At the end of her review of *The Weary Blues* in the *Crisis* in 1926, Fauset said of Hughes that "all life is his love and his work a brilliant, sensitive interpretation of its numerous facets." Not all reviews of Hughes's first book were so laudatory. Although the white press largely responded positively to Hughes's poetry, some black reviewers, seeking middle-class respectability from their "Talented Tenth" writers rather than Hughes's more realistic portrayal of the range of African American life, reacted negatively. They particularly opposed the blues and jazz poems of the opening section of the book. In his review in *Opportunity* in February 1926, the poet COUNTÉE CULLEN characterized the book as "scornful in subject matter" with "too much emphasis here on strictly Negro themes." Hughes naturally identified with the black masses, but at the same time he aligned himself with the modernist predilection for experimentation and frank treatment of themes previously banished from polite literature. Thus Hughes is both avantgardist and traditionalist in his approach to his art. Surely he must have appreciated Locke's review in *Palms* in 1926, which stated that some of the lyrics "are such contributions to pure poetry that it makes little difference what substance of life and experience they are made of." Clearly, however, the substance of life and experience of which they were made also was paramount to Hughes. The lives and dreams of African Americans found intimate expression in Hughes's poems, such as the heritage-laden "The Negro Speaks of Rivers," "Mother to Son," with its doggedly determined narrator, "To Midnight Nan at Leroy's," with its evocation of Harlem nightclub life, and the longingly hopeful "Dream Variation." The volume was an auspicious beginning that established Hughes's ideological and artistic leanings and conflicts that recurred amplified in his later work.

The responses to *Fine Clothes to the Jew* were even more extreme. Hughes realized that the book was, as he told the *Chicago Defender*, "harder and more cynical." He braced himself nervously for the reviews, encouraged by positive responses from Amy and Arthur Spingarn and GEORGE SCHUYLER. Again many black critics believed that Hughes had presented a cheap, tawdry portrait, far from the respectable Negro they longed to see in their literature. The "poet 'low-rate' of Harlem" the reviewer for the *Chicago Whip* dubbed him; "Sewer Dweller" sneered the headline of the New York *Amsterdam News* review; "piffling trash" pronounced the historian J. A. Rogers in the *Pittsburgh Courier*. Attacks on the short-lived *Fire!!* and Van Vechten's *Nigger Heaven*, which Hughes supported and for which he wrote blues lyrics following a lawsuit against Van Vechten for copyright infringement, compounded Hughes's embattled aesthetic consciousness at this time. However, Hughes continued undeterred, in spite of the volume's failure to sell well. In winter 1927, Alain Locke introduced Hughes to "Godmother" Charlotte Mason, an elderly, wealthy widow with a newfound interest in African American authors, who became his benefactor, offering both financial support and opinions about his work. After reading and lecturing in the South in summer 1927, during which he met up with Hurston in Biloxi, Mississippi, Fauset in Tuskegee, Alabama, and BESSIE SMITH in Macon, Georgia, Hughes returned to Harlem and the directive of Mason to write a novel, *Not without Laughter* (1930).

Initially Hughes and Mason got along well, but the artistic and social demands she made on him were at times stultifying, and even the stipend she provided placed him in uncomfortable surroundings that impeded his artistic progress. The social "upward mobility," the economic support for his mother and half brother Gwyn Clark, the free apartment, the patron-funded trip to Cuba—all were mixed blessings. After their relationship was ruptured in 1930, Hughes, hurt and angry, wrote about the situation in the poem "The Blues I'm Playing" (1934) and in the first volume of his autobiography, *The Big Sea* (1940). Winning the Harmon Foundation Prize in 1930 brought him welcome cash, and

he occupied some of his time by collaborating with Hurston on the play *Mule Bone* and traveling to Haiti, but the break with Mason was both psychologically and physically trying for Hughes.

Hughes dedicated *Not without Laughter* to his friends and early patrons, the Spingarns; his *Dear Lovely Death* was privately printed by Amy Spingarn in 1931. At the same time he was losing Godmother, difficulties with Hurston concerning *Mule Bone* put a chasm between them and a distrust of Locke, who was vying for Godmother's favor, separated Hughes from him as well. Hughes avoided dealing with these personal difficulties by going first to Florida, then Cuba, and on to Haiti, where he met with Haitian poet Jacques Roumain, who, inspired by Hughes, later wrote a poem titled "Langston Hughes" and received a letter of support from Hughes when he was sentenced to prison for alleged procommunist activity. Hughes, of course, had always identified with the masses, and he had a distinct influence on writers like Roumain and Nicolás Guillén, whom Hughes had inspired in 1929 to employ the rhythms of native Cuban music in his poetry. A 1931 reading tour partially sponsored by the Rosenwald Fund reintroduced Hughes to the rigid segregation and racism of the South, as did the much-publicized trial of the SCOTTSBORO BOYS. Hughes, the poet who initially had not been radical enough for the Marxist *New Masses* but who later published poems in that journal while at Lincoln, now began writing more controversial and directly political poems, such as "Christ in Alabama," which caused a furor that swelled his audience and increased sales of all his work.

In June 1932 he left for the Soviet Union with a group interested in making a film about race relations in America. Although the film, proposed by Soviet authorities and backed by the black communist James W. Ford, was never made, Hughes's travels in the Soviet Union showed him the lack of racial prejudice he longed for and a peasant class that he sought out and admired. Both *The Dream Keeper* and *Popo and Fifina*, children's books, were released to acclaim while he was in Russia. After visits to Japan, where Hughes was both questioned and put under

surveillance because he was a "revolutionary" just come from Moscow, and Hawaii, Hughes returned to wealthy arts patron Noel Sullivan's home in Carmel, where he worked on the short-story collection *The Ways of White Folks* (1934), which was published shortly before his father died in Mexico.

Hughes's interest in drama, as shown by his collaboration on *Mule Bone*, finally bore fruit with the 1935 production of his play *Mulatto* at the Vanderbilt Theater on Broadway and the Gilpin Players' 1936 production of *Troubled Island*. He received financial support from a Guggenheim Fellowship in 1935 and worked in Spain as a correspondent for the *Baltimore Afro-American* in 1937. Following the death of his mother in 1938, Hughes founded the Harlem Suitcase Theatre that same year, the New Negro Theatre in Los Angeles in 1939, and the Skyloft Players in Harlem in 1942. During this period he had plays produced in Cleveland, New York, and Chicago, among them *Little Ham* (1936), *Soul Gone Home* (1937), *Don't You Want to Be Free?* (1938), *The Organizer* (with music by James P. Johnson, 1939), and *The Sun Do Move* (1942), and he collaborated on a play with Arna Bontemps, *When the Jack Hollers* (1936). His experience with Hollywood, writing the script for *Way Down South* (1939), was a bitter disappointment. Still, Hughes managed to establish his importance as an African American dramatist and continued to write plays and libretti for the rest of his career.

The year 1939 found Hughes back in Carmel working on his autobiography, *The Big Sea*, which dealt with his life up to 1931. Positive response to the work was overshadowed by fevered excitement over RICHARD WRIGHT's *Native Son*, but Hughes did receive a Rosenwald Fund Fellowship at a point when his repudiation of his poem "Goodbye Christ" had turned some of his leftist friends against him. The Rosenwald money allowed Hughes to focus on writing rather than on financial matters. His blues-inflected *Shakespeare in Harlem* (1942) picked up where he had left off with *Fine Clothes to the Jew* in 1927 and provoked the same divided response as the earlier volume. Following an invitation to the writers' colony Yaddo, where he met Carson McCullers, Katherine Anne Porter, and Malcolm Cowley, he contacted the *Chicago Defender* about being a columnist and was hired. In 1943 Hughes created the beloved comic character Jesse B. Semple ("Simple"), the assertive and lively "low-down" hero who appeared in many of his *Defender* columns over the next twenty years. Also in 1943 he published the prose poem *Freedom's Plow* (introduced with a reading by Paul Muni, with musical accompaniment by the Golden Gate Quartet and later performed publicly by Fredric March) and *Jim Crow's Last Stand*, a leftist, patchwork book of poetry.

In 1945 Hughes began to work on lyrics for Elmer Rice's *Street Scene*, with music by Kurt Weill, which opened to strong reviews in 1947. Hughes, however, opted to work as a visiting writer in residence at Atlanta University that year, seeing his book of lyric poems *Fields of Wonder* released to mixed reviews and the publication of his translation, with Mercer Cook, of Roumain's *Masters of the Dew*. Receiving a regular salary from Atlanta and one thousand dollars from a National Institute and American Academy of Arts and Letters Award in 1946, plus royalties from *Street Scene*, provided him more financial stability, thus leaving time for him to edit with Bontemps a reissue of James Weldon Johnson's *Book of American Negro Poetry*. He was also able to publish a translation (with Ben Frederic Carruthers) of Nicolás Guillén's *Cuba Libre* and prepare another collection of poetry, *One-Way Ticket* (1949). A return to jazz- and blues-saturated poetry, this volume contains Hughes's celebrated "Madam" poems and the song "Life Is Fine," trumpeting perseverance and optimism. When the opera *Troubled Island* opened in 1949, Hughes was busy trying to find a publisher for the second volume of his autobiography and a new volume of poems. The production of *The Barrier* (1950), an opera based on the play *Mulatto*, yielded little money, though the collection of Simple stories *Simple Speaks His Mind* (1950) sold thirty thousand copies and received general critical acclaim. Hughes was becoming better known, and translations of his work and critical essays were appearing.

Yet as success loomed, Hughes's masterful jazz-imbued *Montage of a Dream Deferred* (1951), a book-length poem in five sections depicting the rhythms of bop, boogie, and blues of the urban African American experience in the context of continued deferment of the promises of American democracy, was critically panned. However, his short-story collection *Laughing to Keep from Crying* (1952) fared better with critics. Prolific throughout his career in multiple genres, Hughes began work on a series of children's books for Franklin Watts, which released *The First Book of Negroes* (1952), *The First Book of Rhythms* (1954), *The First Book of Jazz* (1955), *The First Book of the West Indies* (1956), and *The First Book of Africa* (1960). He also published other historical nonfiction works, *Famous American Negroes* (1954), *Famous Negro Music Makers* (1955), *A Pictorial History of the Negro in America* (with Milton Meltzer, 1956), *Famous Negro Heroes of America* (1958), *Fight for Freedom: The Story of the NAACP* (1962), and *Black Magic: A Pictorial History of the Negro in American Entertainment* (with Meltzer, 1967). The quality and success of these books established Hughes's importance as a popular historian of African American life. The second volume of his autobiography, *I Wonder as I Wander* (1956), emphasized Hughes's determination to survive and prosper, undaunted by the adversity and suffering he had faced in his travels in this country and around the world.

Nevertheless, Hughes found himself increasingly under the siege of McCarthyism and was forced to appear in March 1953 before Joseph R. McCarthy's Senate subcommittee, not to defend his poetry but to repudiate some of his zealous leftist activities and work. Hughes's Simple stories continued to draw positive critical response and pleased his readers, although the Simple collections, *Simple Takes a Wife* (1953), *Simple Stakes a Claim* (1957), *The Best of Simple* (1961), and *Simple's Uncle Sam* (1965) did not sell well. The play *Simply Heavenly* began a reasonably successful run in 1957, landing on Broadway and on the London stage. That same year his translation of *Selected Poems of Gabriela Mistral* appeared, followed in 1958 by his selection and revision of his writings, *The Langston Hughes Reader*, and in 1959 by *Selected Poems of Langston Hughes* and his rousing play *Tambourines to Glory*, which he had converted into a novel of the same title in 1958.

Certainly by the 1960s Hughes was an elder statesman of his people and a literary celebrity, adding to his publications stagings of his dramas, recordings, television and radio shows, and appearances at conferences (in Uganda and Nigeria and at the National Poetry Festival in Washington, D.C., in 1962), jazz clubs, and festivals. He received honorary doctorates from Howard University in 1963 and Western Reserve University in 1964. The poetry was still flowing, with *Ask Your Mama* (1961) and *The Panther and the Lash* (1967) demonstrating that Hughes's satiric and humanitarian impulses were undiminished, as were his dramatic juices, evidenced by the critical success of the gospel play *Black Nativity* (1961). Always eager to help younger writers, he edited *New Negro Poets: USA* (1964).

Indeed, the final years of his life were filled with activity: the production of his play *The Prodigal Son* (1965), a two-month State Department tour of Europe lecturing on African American writers, work on *The Best Short Stories by Negro Writers* (1967), and trips to Paris (with the production of *Prodigal Son*) and to Africa (as a presidential appointee to the First World Festival of Negro Arts), along with readings and lectures, filled his days. In the midst of this frenetic life, Hughes was admitted to the hospital with abdominal pains, later found to be caused by a blocked bladder and an enlarged prostate. Despite a successful operation, his heart and kidneys began to fail, and Hughes died in New York City.

Langston Hughes praised the "low-down folks" in the essay "The Negro Artist and the Racial Mountain" (*Nation*, 23 June 1926) for furnishing "a wealth of colorful, distinctive material" and for maintaining "their individuality in the face of American standardizations." Hughes's own life and career might be viewed in the same light. The variety and quality of his achievements in various genres, always in the service of greater understanding and humanity, and his specific commitment to depicting and strengthening the African American heartbeat in America—and to helping others depict it as well—gave him a place of central importance in twentieth-century African American literature and American literature generally. Hughes sought to change the way people looked not only at African Americans and art but also at the world, and his modernistic vision was both experimental and traditional, cacophonous and mellifluous, rejecting of artificial middle-class values, and promoting emotional and intellectual freedom. He demonstrated that African Americans could support themselves with their art both monetarily and spiritually. Hughes published over forty books in a career that never lost touch with the concerns of sharecroppers and tenement dwellers as it provided inspiration for not only African American writers but for all working people.

FURTHER READING

Hughes's papers are in the James Weldon Johnson Memorial Collection, Beinecke Rare Book and Manuscript Library, Yale University.

Berry, Faith. *Langston Hughes: Before and Beyond Harlem* (1983).
The Langston Hughes Review (1982–present).
Mikolyzk, Thomas A., ed. *Langston Hughes: A Bio-Bibliography* (1990).
Nichols, Charles, ed. *Arna Bontemps–Langston Hughes Letters, 1925–1967* (1980).
Rampersad, Arnold. *The Life of Langston Hughes*, vol. 1 (1986) and vol. 2 (1988).
Tracy, Steven C. *Langston Hughes and the Blues* (1988).

Obituary: *New York Times*, 24 May 1967.
—STEVEN C. TRACY

Louis Hughes, escaped slave, businessman, and nurse. University of North Carolina at Chapel Hill Libraries

HUGHES, LOUIS (1832– 19 Jan. 1913), author, businessman, and nurse, was born into slavery near Charlottesville, Virginia, the son of a white man and a black woman, possibly John and Susan Hughes. When he was about six years old, Louis was sold with his mother and two brothers to Dr. Louis, a physician in Scottsville, Virginia. When Dr. Louis died, young Louis was sold with his mother and brother to Washington Fitzpatrick, also of Scottsville, who soon sent him, then about eleven years old, to Richmond on the pretense of hiring him out to work on a canal boat. Parting with his mother at such a young age was difficult; even more difficult was his realization that he would never see his mother again. For Hughes this experience became the central symbol of the fundamental inhumanity of the system of slavery, a symbol to which he returns at key points in the autobiography that is

the sole source for most of the information on his life, *Thirty Years a Slave* (1897).

George Reid owned Hughes for a brief time after his arrival in Richmond; however, Reid sold Hughes because of the latter's frequent illnesses. Edmund McGehee, under whose ownership Hughes remained for the next two decades, purchased the young boy in November 1844. McGehee relocated Hughes to Pontotoc County, Mississippi, where he presented Hughes to his wife as a Christmas gift. In August 1850 McGehee sent Hughes to Memphis, Tennessee, to assist in the construction of a new house, in which Hughes would soon be established as butler and body-servant. Among Hughes's duties were the tasks of "working with medicine, giving it and caring for the sick" (Hughes, 2002, 57), an occupation to which Hughes would return years later following his escape from enslavement. While serving at the

new house in Memphis Hughes met his future wife, Matilda. Matilda was born on 17 June 1830 in Fayette County, Kentucky, and was purchased by McGehee in 1855. Louis and Matilda were married three years later, on 30 November 1858. The ceremony was held in the McGehee house parlor and presided over by the McGehee's parish minister, a rare privilege among the enslaved and proof of the couple's high status in the household. A year later Matilda gave birth to twins.

But while Hughes expressed his appreciation for McGehee's acknowledgment of the sanctity of marriage, he emphasized the limitations of McGehee's humanitarianism and the harshness of everyday life for himself and his wife. Hughes had tried to escape twice before his marriage and was severely punished after the second unsuccessful attempt. After their children were born, Matilda made her own desperate attempt to change her situation because she felt she was being forced to neglect them. She left with the twins and returned to Forrest's slave market, presenting herself to be sold again. Matilda was returned to the McGehees, who, according to Hughes, "beat her by turns" (Hughes, 2002, 78). The twins died six months later, weak from insufficient care. "Things continued in this way," Hughes reports, "until about June, 1862," when the McGehee family fled from advancing Union forces and Hughes was sent to the family plantation in Bolivar, Mississippi. After this forced separation from his wife, Louis was reunited with her in 1863 when he was sent to a family farm in Panola County, Mississippi.

The couple did not succeed in escaping from enslavement until close to the end of the Civil War. Before that time, after the outbreak of the Civil War, Hughes had made two more unsuccessful escape attempts. The first of these efforts, in the winter of 1862–1863, ended when Hughes was captured by Confederate soldiers. A few months later, Louis and Matilda tried to escape with another couple, but all were recaptured. Shortly after that, in the spring of 1863, the couple was sent with most of McGehee's other slaves to Alabama to be leased out to the state-run saltworks on the Tombigbee River, where Hughes and his wife remained for two years, and where Matilda gave birth to their daughter Lydia. Finally, on 26 June 1865, Hughes successfully escaped to Union-occupied Memphis. With the help of two Union soldiers, Hughes returned to Mississippi for Matilda and Lydia. They finally arrived in Memphis and their long-sought freedom on the Fourth of July 1865, which was after General Robert E. Lee's surrender at Appomattox Courthouse, but before they would otherwise have been freed.

After about six weeks in Memphis, the family moved to Cincinnati, Ohio, in August 1865, where Matilda hoped to find relatives. She was reunited with her mother and one of her sisters, and the family lived for a few months in Hamilton, Ohio. But they were determined to go to Canada, "as we regarded that as the safest place for refugees from slavery" (Hughes, 2002, 141), and so they traveled north through Detroit and entered Windsor, Ontario, Canada, on Christmas Day 1865. Louis and

Matilda secured positions at a hotel and remained there until the following spring, when Louis returned to Detroit in hope of earning higher wages. Following two years of working first as a waiter in Detroit and then on a steamboat, Hughes secured a position in a Chicago hotel, where he worked until 1868. During this time Hughes also attended night school. In Chicago he met John Plankinton, who offered Hughes a position in his new hotel in Milwaukee, Wisconsin. The Plankinton House was opened in September 1868, and Hughes's family, now enlarged by the recent birth of twins, was soon settled in what would be their permanent home. Sometime later, Hughes rediscovered his brother, from whom he had been separated since childhood, living in Cleveland, Ohio. He looked forward to a life "in which the joys of social intercourse had marvelously expanded" (Hughes, 2002, 147).

In Milwaukee, Hughes established himself as an enterprising businessman and a leader of the city's small African American community. In 1869 he was one of the founders of St. Mark's African Methodist Episcopal Church, a congregation in which the Hughes family remained prominent and active members. After a year's work at the Plankinton House, Hughes and his wife began to supplement their income with an independent laundry service. By 1874 their laundry work had increased so significantly that Hughes left the hotel to develop the growing family business. In the 1880s, though, Hughes returned to his earlier interest in caring for the sick and established himself as a nurse, his last and fondest professional enterprise. In his work as a nurse, Hughes traveled the country, going first to New Orleans and eventually as far as California and Florida.

While the events of his life make for a rich story of individual determination, religious faith, and familial devotion, Hughes's life, like so many others of the time, would have remained unknown had he not written the autobiography for which he is remembered. The book was copyrighted in 1896 and published by the South Side Printing Company in Milwaukee. Scholars disagree about whether Hughes wrote it himself or with the help of another person, but the book clearly represents Hughes's perspective on his many experiences. In

addition to relating the dramatic story of his life in and escape from slavery, Hughes presents a panoramic view of the South—including descriptions of various locales, agricultural methods and commerce, and southern society—as well as a revealing glimpse into post-emancipation life for African Americans in both the South and the North. By arranging for the independent publication of his narrative, Hughes freed himself "to write about his experience in the South and the North in his own way," and the story that he tells "identifies Hughes in several ways as more representative of the African American rank-and-file, both before and after slavery, than [FREDERICK] DOUGLASS or most of the other celebrated fugitive slaves whose antebellum narratives have dominated our understanding of what slavery was like" (Andrews, 9).

Matilda died on 7 October 1907, and Louis followed some years later on 19 January 1913. Before his death, his church published a history that included prominent attention to the Hughes family, and at his death, Hughes's status in the larger community was acknowledged in the form of obituaries in various Milwaukee newspapers.

FURTHER READING

Hughes, Louis. *Thirty Years a Slave: From Bondage to Freedom; The Institution of Slavery as Seen on the Plantation and in the Home of the Planter; Autobiography of Louis Hughes* (1897; reprinted in 2002).

Andrews, William L. "Foreword." *Thirty Years a Slave: From Bondage to Freedom; The Institution of Slavery as Seen on the Plantation and in the Home of the Planter; Autobiography of Louis Hughes* (2002).
Ash, Stephen V. *A Year in the South: Four Lives in 1865* (2002).
Stevens, Michael E. "After Slavery: The Milwaukee Years of Louis Hughes." *Wisconsin Magazine of History* 86 (Autumn 2002): 40–51.

—JOHN ERNEST

HULL, AGRIPPA

(1759–1848), Revolutionary War soldier, was born free in Northampton, Massachusetts, of unknown parentage. He was taken to Stockbridge, Massachusetts, at the age of six by Joab, an African American former servant to Jonathan Edwards. When Hull was eighteen years old, in May 1777, he enlisted to fight in the Revolutionary War as a private in General John Paterson's brigade of the First Massachusetts Regiment of the Continental army. Free blacks had been allowed by the Continental Congress to enlist in the army since January 1776, but each unit commander determined whether or not he would accept African American recruits.

Hull served as General Paterson's personal orderly for two years. He then attended General Tadeusz Kosciuszko, the Polish volunteer in the American cause, as an orderly for four years and two months. As an orderly, Hull performed a variety of personal and military duties for the generals, including serving as a surgeon's assistant in South Carolina in 1781. Hull was with Kosciuszko during battles from Saratoga, New York, through the campaign in the South and served with the general until the end of the war. When the Continental army was disbanded at West Point in the summer of 1783, Hull received a discharge signed personally by George Washington, the commander in chief, a document he prized for the rest of his life.

After the war, Hull returned to Stockbridge, Massachusetts, where he eventually owned a small plot of land. As was the case for many free African Americans in New England after the Revolution, Hull was on the economic margins of society, and he eked out a living from a variety of sources. He farmed his land, performed odd jobs around Stockbridge, and occasionally served as a butler and a major-domo to the local gentry.

However marginal his economic position, Hull was very much a part of town life in Stockbridge. The prominent Stockbridge resident and novelist Catharine Maria Sedgwick, whose family was friendly to Hull, called him "a sort of Sancho Panza in the village." He acquired a reputation for understanding the supernatural and was considered something of the town "seer."

Hull married twice and adopted at least one child. His first wife (whom he married sometime before 1790) was Jane Darby, a fugitive slave from Lenox, Massachusetts, whose master, Mr. Ingersoll, tried to seize her after she had married

Hull. After Jane Darby died, Hull married Margaret Timbroke. Sometime after the Revolutionary War, Hull adopted the daughter of Mary Gunn, a runaway slave from New York.

Like most Revolutionary War veterans, Hull was proud of his military service. When General Kosciuszko returned to the United States in 1797 after fighting for Polish independence, Hull traveled to New York to meet with him, and during this trip Kosciuszko directed the Ohio land granted to him by Congress to be sold to pay for a school for African Americans.

One of only several dozen African Americans who applied for Revolutionary War pensions, Hull received a veteran's pension from Congress, which he sought to have mailed to his home in 1828. Hull enlisted the help of Charles Sedgwick, who wrote to Acting Secretary of State Richard Rush for assistance with Hull's claim. Hull enclosed his discharge paper as proof of his service but worried that it might not be returned.

Slavery was outlawed by 1790 under the Massachusetts state constitution, but racial divisions in society persisted. Within a restrictive system of racial hierarchy, Hull used his good standing in the community of Stockbridge and his good humor to question the limitations of race. The town historian, Electa F. Jones, who knew Hull, recorded several anecdotes that reveal Hull's racial attitudes. For example, on one occasion he proclaimed: "It is not the *cover* of the book, but what the book *contains....* Many a good book has dark covers."

That Hull was a respected member of Stockbridge society by the end of his life in the 1840s is evidenced by two main facts. The historian Francis Parkman recorded his impressions of Hull after a visit to Stockbridge in 1844, declaring that Hull "looked on himself as father to all Stockbridge." Hull's respectability was also portrayed visually in 1844 in a daguerreotype photograph by Anson Clark, which was copied as an oil painting in 1848. The photograph and painting present an image of Hull as a distinguished, formally dressed old man staring out resolutely and grasping a cane firmly in his left hand. The oil painting of Hull, one of the few formal portraits of an African American Revolutionary War veteran, hangs in the Stockbridge Public Library.

Hull died in Stockbridge. His position in the Continental army was more distinguished than that of most African Americans who were allowed to serve, and as the orderly to generals, he witnessed some of the most important fighting of the war. Hull carried with him for the rest of his life the legacy of his important service to the revolutionary cause, which enhanced his pride as a free African American man. He stands as an extraordinary example of early African American military service and as a typical example of the free African Americans who carved a place for themselves in New England society between the Revolutionary War and the Civil War.

FURTHER READING

Some materials are available in the Agrippa Hull Collection in the Stockbridge, Massachusetts, Public Library.

Bradley, Patricia. *Slavery, Propaganda, and the American Revolution* (1998).
Jones, Electa F. *Stockbridge, Past and Present* (1854; repr. 1994).
Kaplan, Sidney, and Emma Nogrady Kaplan. *The Black Presence in the Era of the American Revolution* (1989).

—SARAH J. PURCELL

 HURSTON, ZORA NEALE (15 Jan. 1891–28 Jan. 1960), writer and anthropologist, was born Zora Lee Hurston in Notasulga, Alabama, the daughter of John Hurston, a Baptist minister and carpenter, and Lucy Ann Potts. John Hurston's family were Alabama tenant farmers until he moved to Eatonville, the first African American town incorporated in the United States. He served three terms as its mayor and is said to have written Eatonville's ordinances. Zora Neale Hurston studied at its Hungerford School, where followers of BOOKER T. WASHINGTON taught both elementary academic skills and self-reliance. Growing up in an exclusively black community gave her a unique background that informed and inspired much of her later work.

Much of the chronological detail of Hurston's early life is obscured by the fact that she later claimed birth dates that varied from 1898 to 1903.

Zora Neal Hurston published two important anthropological studies of African American and Caribbean folklore, as well as her most successful novel, Their Eyes Were Watching God, *in the mid-1930s.* Library of Congress/Carl Van Vechten

Most often she cited 1901 as her birth year, but the census of 1900 lists a Zora L. Hurston, born in 1891, as the daughter of John and Lucy Hurston. According to Zora Neale Hurston's later accounts, she was nine years old when her mother died, and, when her father remarried, she left Eatonville to be "passed around the family like a bad penny." At fourteen, she reported, she joined a traveling Gilbert and Sullivan theater company as maid and wardrobe girl. After eighteen months on the road, she left the company in Baltimore, Maryland. There Hurston worked in menial positions and studied at Morgan Academy, the preparatory school operated by Morgan College.

After she graduated from Morgan Academy in 1918, Hurston moved to Washington, D.C. She worked in a variety of menial positions and was a part-time student at Howard University from 1919 to 1924. At Howard, Hurston studied with ALAIN LOCKE and Lorenzo Dow Turner, who encouraged her to write for publication. Accepted as a member of Stylus, the campus literary club, she published her first short story, "John Redding Goes to Sea," in its literary magazine, the *Stylus*, in May 1921. Three years later CHARLES S. JOHNSON'S *Opportunity*, a major literary vehicle for writers of the Harlem Renaissance, published two of Hurston's stories, "Drenched in Light" and "Spunk." In these early stories she staked out a perspective characteristic of her later African American folktales. They celebrate the lives of ordinary black people who had little interaction with or sense of oppression by a white community.

In 1925, after winning an award for "Spunk," Hurston moved to New York City, where she joined other writers and artists of the Harlem Renaissance. As secretary and chauffeur to novelist Fannie Hurst, Hurston also gained access to contemporary white literary circles. In September 1925 she began studying at Barnard College on a scholarship. Nine months later Hurston, AARON DOUGLAS, LANGSTON HUGHES, and Wallace Thurman launched a short-lived, avant-garde magazine, *Fire!* Against the claim of older African American mentors, such as W. E. B. DU BOIS and Alain Locke, that a black writer was obliged to express a racial consciousness in the face of white hostility, they held that the creative artist's obligation was to give voice to the vitality of an African American culture that was more than simply a reaction to white oppression. Hurston's short story "Sweat" is the most important of her published essays and short stories in this period.

At Barnard, Hurston became a student of noted anthropologist Franz Boas. "Papa Franz," as she called him, encouraged Hurston's interest in the folklore of her people. Her first field research took Hurston to Alabama to interview a former slave, Cudjo Lewis, for CARTER G. WOODSON's Association for the Study of Negro Life and History. Her article "Cudjo's Own Story of the Last African Slaves," which appeared in the *Journal of Negro History* (1927), was marred, however, by plagiarism from Emma Langdon Roache's *Historic Sketches of the Old South*. When Hurston received a BA from Barnard in 1928, she was the first African American known to have graduated from the institution.

In 1927 Hurston married Herbert Sheen, a medical student with whom she had begun a relationship in 1921 when they were both students at Howard University. Four months after their marriage, however, Hurston and Sheen parted company, and they were divorced in 1931.

Hurston's literary career illustrates the difficult struggle of an African American female writer for support and control of her work. From 1927 to 1932 Hurston's field research was sponsored by a wealthy white patron, Charlotte Louise Mason. With that support Hurston made her most important anthropological forays into the South, revisiting Alabama and Florida, breaking new ground in Louisiana, and journeying to the Bahamas. Working in rural labor camps and as an apprentice to voodoo priests, she collected an anthropologist's treasure of folklore, children's games, prayers, sermons, songs, and voodoo rites. Yet, the hand that sustained was also the hand that controlled. Mason insisted that Hurston sign a contract that acknowledged the white patron's ownership of and editorial control over the publication of Hurston's research.

In the spring of 1930, Hurston and Langston Hughes collaborated in writing a play, *Mule Bone*. Only its third act was published, but in 1931 Hughes and Hurston quarreled over its authorship. When she claimed that its material was hers, he accused her of trying to take full credit for the play. The two authors never resolved their differences in the matter, but it seems clear that Hurston's anthropological research supplied the material to which Hughes gave dramatic form.

By the mid-1930s Hurston had begun to reach her stride. Her first novel, *Jonah's Gourd Vine*, was published in 1934. Its protagonist, John Buddy "Jonah" Pearson, is a folk preacher whose sermons display Hurston's mastery of the idiom. Indeed, the folk material threatens to overshadow the novel's characters and plot. Like her other work, the novel was also criticized for ignoring the effects of racial oppression in the South. In 1934, after a semester of teaching at Bethune-Cookman College in Daytona Beach, Florida, Hurston received a Rosenwald Fellowship and enrolled for graduate work in anthropology at Columbia University. Briefly in 1935–1936 she was employed as a drama coach by the Works Progress Administration (WPA) in New York. Hurston never completed a graduate degree, but she received Guggenheim field research fellowships for the 1935–1936 and 1936–1937 academic years. Her first major anthropological work, *Mules and Men*, appeared in 1935. It mined the rich lode of her research in southern African American folklore in the late 1920s and early 1930s. The Guggenheim fellowships took Hurston to Jamaica and Haiti to study Caribbean folk culture. Those studies produced her second major anthropological work, *Tell My Horse*, in 1938.

Now at the peak of her productive years, Hurston published her second major novel, *Their Eyes Were Watching God*, in 1937. Written in eight weeks, during which Hurston was recovering from a passionate romantic relationship, *Their Eyes Were Watching God* is the most successful of her novels artistically. Its heroine, Janie Starks, is a free-spirited woman who pursues her dream of emotional and spiritual fulfillment. Janie and her third husband, Tea Cake, like most of Hurston's folk subjects, enjoy their laughter and their sensuality even in their poverty. In her own life, however, Hurston was less successful in love. In 1939, after a year as an editor for the Federal Writers' Project in Florida and a year of teaching at North Carolina College in Durham, Hurston married Albert Price III, a WPA playground director who was at least fifteen years her junior. After eight months they filed for a divorce. There were attempts at a reconciliation, but the divorce became final in 1943.

Hurston's subsequent fiction was less successful artistically. *Moses, Man of the Mountain*, published in 1939, depicted the leader of the biblical exodus and lawgiver as a twentieth-century African American witch doctor. In 1942 Hurston published her autobiography, *Dust Tracks on the Road*. It was the most successful of her books commercially. As autobiography, however, it was an accurate portrait not of Hurston's life but of the persona she wanted the public to know: an ambitious, independent, even "outrageous" woman, with a zest for life unhindered by racial barriers. Yet her life became increasingly difficult. Arrested on a morals charge involving a retarded sixteen-year-old boy, Hurston was eventually cleared of the accusations. The African American press gave graphic coverage to the sensational nature of the case, and the publicity had a devastating effect on her career. Hurston's efforts to win funding for a field trip for research in Central America were frustrated until she received an advance for a new novel. In 1947 Hurston left the United States for the British Honduras, where she did anthropological research in its black communities and completed *Seraph on the Suwanee*, her only novel whose characters are white. Published in 1948, *Seraph on the Suwanee*'s portrait of Arvay Henson Meserve as a woman entrapped in marriage might have found a more receptive audience two decades earlier or two decades later.

By 1950 Hurston's failure to find a steady source of support for her work forced her to take a position in Miami as a domestic worker. There was a stir of publicity when her employer found an article in the *Saturday Evening Post* written by her maid. During the 1940s and 1950s, however, Hurston's essays were more likely to appear in right-wing venues, such as the *American Legion Magazine* or *American Mercury*, rather than the mainstream press. By then her celebration of African American folk culture and her refusal to condemn the oppressive racial climate in which it was nurtured had allied Hurston with forces hostile to the civil rights movement. A 1950 article titled "Negro Votes Bought" seemed to oppose the enfranchisement of African Americans. Four years later, in a letter to the editor of a Florida newspaper, which was widely reprinted, Hurston attacked the U.S. Supreme Court's decision in *Brown v. Board of Education* on the grounds that it undervalued the capacity of African American institutions to educate African American people and of African American people to learn apart from a white presence.

Throughout the 1950s Hurston worked intermittently as a substitute teacher, a domestic worker, and a contributor to a local newspaper, but she was ill and without a steady income. She spent much of her time writing and revising a biography of Herod the Great, but both the subject and the language of the manuscript lacked the vitality of her earlier work. Even after a stroke in 1959, Hurston refused to ask her relatives for help. She died in the county welfare home at Fort Pierce, Florida. After a public appeal for money to pay for her burial, Hurston was laid to rest in Fort Pierce's African American cemetery. In 1973 writer ALICE WALKER placed a granite tombstone in the cemetery, somewhere near Hurston's unmarked grave.

FURTHER READING

Material from Hurston's early career is scattered in collections at the American Philosophical Society Library, the Amistad Research Center at Tulane University, Fisk University's Special Collections, Howard University's Moorland-Spingarn Research Center, the

Library of Congress, and Yale University's Beinecke Library. The Zora Neale Hurston Collection at the University of Florida includes letters and manuscripts from her later years.

Davis, Arthur P. *From the Dark Tower: Afro-American Writers, 1900–1960* (1974).

Gates, Henry Louis, Jr., and K. A. Appiah, eds. *Zora Neale Hurston: Critical Perspectives Past and Present* (1993).

Hemenway, Robert E. *Zora Neale Hurston: A Literary Biography* (1977).

Newson, Adele S. *Zora Neale Hurston: A Reference Guide* (1987).

Sundquist, Eric J. *The Hammers of Creation: Folk Culture in Modern African American Fiction* (1992).

Turner, Darwin T. *In a Minor Chord: Three Afro-American Writers and Their Search for Identity* (1971).

Walker, Alice. "In Search of Zora Neale Hurston." *Ms.*, Mar. 1975, 74–79, 85–89.

Wall, Cheryl A. *Women of the Harlem Renaissance* (1995).

Obituary: *New York Times*, 5 Feb. 1960.
—RALPH E. LUKER

HUTSON, JEAN BLACKWELL

(7 Sept. 1914–4 Feb. 1998), librarian, archivist, bibliophile, and college professor, was born Jean Blackwell in Summerfield, Florida, to Paul O. and Sarah Myers. Her father was a commission merchant who operated a farm, buying and shipping produce. Her mother taught elementary school. At age four she moved to Baltimore, Maryland, her mother's hometown. Paul Blackwell remained in Florida and visited the family over the years. Jean was a very precocious child and a voracious reader. She graduated as valedictorian from Baltimore's Frederick Douglass High School in 1931. The prestigious secondary school gave her a love of black history, which was taught by Yolande Du Bois and May Miller, daughters of two famous black leaders, W. E. B. DU BOIS and KELLY MILLER. She met the poet and writer LANGSTON HUGHES, with whom she shared a lifelong friendship, and composer and pianist EUBIE BLAKE.

The Great Depression thwarted Hutson's original career goal of psychiatry. Instead, she spent three years at the University of Michigan, after which her mother persuaded her to transfer to Barnard College. In 1935 Blackwell

Jean Blackwell Hutson, chief of the New York Public Library's Schomburg Collection, with poet LANGSTON HUGHES. Schomburg Center

became the second black female graduate of Barnard; ZORA NEALE HURSTON was the first. Blackwell received a BA in English; the next year she received an MA from the Columbia School of Library Service and earned a teacher's certificate from Columbia University in 1941. In 1939 she married Andy Razaf, a song lyricist and FATS WALLER collaborator. The marriage ended in divorce after eight years.

Blackwell began her professional career in the New York Public Library from 1936 to 1939, when she left briefly to work as a high school librarian in Baltimore. Around 1947 she returned to the New York Public Library's Division of Negro Literature, the forerunner to the Schomburg Center, under the direction of ARTHUR SCHOMBURG. She remembered that "he arranged the books according to their color and size. So working late one night, I decided to rearrange them according to the Dewey Decimal System. When he discovered

what I had done the next day, he was so angry that he fired me. I was immediately banished from the Library." Her clash with Schomburg in her first position in the New York Public Library system resulted in her reassignment to a succession of branch libraries in the Bronx and Manhattan. She also worked at several branches in the central Harlem area. She returned to the Schomburg Collection in 1948 as curator, succeeding Dorothy Williams and Lawrence Reddick.

Jean Blackwell married John Hutson, a coworker, in 1952, and they adopted a baby girl. Her husband died in 1957, leaving Jean Blackwell Hutson a widow and single parent. Despite these personal tragedies, she persevered in her professional life, and under her guidance the Schomburg Collection thrived. *The Dictionary Catalog of the Schomburg Collection of Negro Literature and History* was published in 1962; two supplements and a microfilm copy made the holdings known to libraries throughout the world. During that same year Hutson became an associate adjunct professor in the history department of City College of New York, where she taught black history for almost ten years. During her tenure at the college she met President Kwame Nkrumah of Ghana while he was a student in New York City. At his urging, Hutson and his daughter spent the academic year 1964–1965 developing the African Collection at the University of Ghana.

Due to the deterioration of the 135th Street Branch Library, which had moved to the 136th Street former site of the mansion of A'lelia Walker's Dark Tower in 1941, Hutson began lobbying for a new building to protect the collection. With her help the Schomburg Corporation was established to raise funds and lobby for a new building. Hutson organized the corporation, lobbied politicians, and rallied the black community to preserve this heritage of their African descent. The Schomburg Collection had grown rapidly and became internationally known during the civil rights and Black Power movements of the 1960s. In 1951 the branch was renamed the COUNTÉE CULLEN Branch Library after the famous poet, teacher, and friend and neighbor of the library.

Through Hutson's marketing efforts on behalf of the Schomburg collection and her speaking with various politicians and organizations, the Schomburg began to receive private and New York City and State grants. In 1965 annual city funding from the North Manhattan Project resulted in the first budgetary increase for the collection since 1948. The Ford Foundation provided a grant in 1967. The first National Endowment for the Humanities (NEH) grant provided for an inventory of the collection, the first one that had been conducted in twenty-five years. Another NEH grant enabled the massive clipping file to be microfiched and made available to the world. In recognition of her diligence and attention to the collection, Hutson's title was changed from curator to chief of the Schomburg Collection. In 1972 the Schomburg Collection was transferred to the Research Libraries Division of the New York Public Library, becoming one of four research centers within the system, and renamed the Schomburg Center for Research in Black Culture. Finally, a grant from the federal government financed the construction of a new, climate-controlled building, designed by the black architect Max Bond. In the spring of 1980 Hutson was promoted to Research Libraries Assistant Director of Collection Management and Development for Black Culture. The new block-long facility opened in September 1980 at its new address, 515 Lenox Avenue, now Malcolm X Boulevard, between 135th and 136th Streets.

Throughout her career Hutson was active in numerous civic, social, professional and cultural organizations, including Delta Sigma Theta Sorority, the American Library Association, the African Studies Association, the NAACP, and the Urban League. Hutson was a founding member of the Black Academy of Arts and Letters and served as the first president of the Harlem Cultural Council. Her community service often benefited the Schomburg. For example, the collection received entire archives, manuscripts, photographs, or organizational records from the Harry A. Williamson Masonry Collection, the New York *Amsterdam News*, the Kurt Fisher Haitian Historical Documents, the Philippa Duke Schuyler family, and the Melville J. Herskovits African Art collection. She persuaded her old friends, the authors RICHARD WRIGHT and Langston Hughes, to donate their correspondence and manuscripts to the Schomburg.

A bibliography of Hutson's writings is included in *Nine Decades of Scholarship: A Bibliography of the Writings, 1892–1983, of the Staff of the Schomburg Center for Research in Black Culture.* They include her foreword to Roi Ottley and William J. Weatherby's *The Negro in New York: An Informal Social History* (1967) and the 1978 entry on the "Schomburg Center for Research in Black Culture," published in the *Encyclopedia of Library and Information Science.*

Hutson received many honors during her lifetime, including a Doctorate of Humane Letters from King Memorial College in Columbia, South Carolina. The Jean Blackwell Hutson Library Residence Program, University Libraries, at the State University of New York College at Buffalo offers a two-year post–Master of Library Science position.

Barnard College awarded its Medal of Distinction to Hutson in 1990, and Columbia University's School of Library Services honored her in 1992.

As an eightieth birthday tribute, the Schomburg Center celebrated Hutson's contributions during Heritage Weekend in January 1995 by naming the Jean Blackwell Hutson General Research and Reference Division in her honor. The division houses more than 150,000 volumes; the Schomburg Center itself provides access to more than five million items, all held under ideal environmental conditions.

Hutson died at Harlem Hospital on 4 February 1998. She worked at the Schomburg for thirty-two years, from 1948, when she was named curator there, until her retirement in 1980. Under her stewardship the Schomburg became the most comprehensive collection in the world of materials that document the history and culture of people of African descent. The collection includes not just materials about African Americans but covers the breadth of the African diaspora. Founded at the height of the Harlem Renaissance, the Schomburg's collections and exhibits have provided creative impetus to such important black artists as SPIKE LEE and ALEX HALEY and have made the production of numerous books, films, and documentaries possible.

FURTHER READING

Dodson, Howard, and Staff, Schomburg Center. *The Legacy of Arthur Alfonso Schomburg: A Celebration of the Past, A Vision for the Future.* New York Public Library, 1986.

Glendora Johnson-Cooper, "African-American Historical Continuity: Jean Blackwell Hutson and the Schomburg Center for Research in Black Culture" in *Reclaiming the American Library Past*, ed. S. Hildenbrand.

Schomburg Center for Research in Black Culture. *Jean Blackwell Hutson: An Appreciation* (1984).

Schomburg Center for Research in Black Culture/St. Philip's Episcopal Church. *A Memorial Tribute to Jean Blackwell Hutson: September 7, 1914–February 4, 1998*

Obituary: *New York Times*, 7 Feb. 1998.

—SHARON HOWARD

HYMAN, FLORA "FLO"

(31 July 1954–24 Jan. 1986), volleyball player, was born Flora Jean Hyman in Inglewood, California, to George W. Hyman, a railroad janitor and supervisor, and Warrene Hyman, the owner of the Pink Kitty Café. As a child Flo was self-conscious about her rapid growth—she stood six feet tall in junior high school—although her mother, who was also tall, encouraged her to be proud of her height and precocious athletic talent. Though she could have starred in basketball or track, in her sophomore year she took up volleyball, a game played primarily by affluent whites in nearby Redondo Beach, not by African Americans in working-class Inglewood.

In 1974 the strength and athleticism Hyman showed as a high schooler playing for the South Bay Spoilers earned her a place on the U.S. national volleyball team. That same year, University of Houston volleyball coach Ruth N. Nelson awarded her the first athletic scholarship ever awarded to a woman at the college; Hyman characteristically refused to accept the full amount of the award so that some of her teammates might also benefit. She studied mathematics and physical education and received several honors, most notably the 1976–1977 Broderick Sports Award from the Association of Intercollegiate Athletics for Women. In 1977, after being acclaimed the nation's top collegiate player and one of the world's outstanding players, Hyman decided to forgo her senior year to practice and play full-time for the U.S. national team in preparation for the 1980 Olympics. Under Dr. Arie Selinger, a demanding but inspirational coach, Hyman hoped that the United States could match the sport's most dominant nations, though unlike Japan, the Americans lacked major corporate sponsorship, and unlike China, they lacked state support and a talent pool of ten million players. Indeed, while basketball's WILT CHAMBERLAIN had vigorously promoted volleyball, most Americans ignored the sport, and the television networks showed no interest in broadcasting any women's team events. The American team made up for these deficiencies with a strong sense of camaraderie,

which was sorely tested when the United States withdrew from the 1980 Moscow Olympics to protest the Soviet Union's invasion of Afghanistan. The Americans' absence from Moscow denied the team a major stage upon which to display its talents, but the global volleyball community took note of Hyman's skills at the 1981 World Cup, where she was selected the tournament's outstanding player, and at the world championships in 1982, when she led the United States to the bronze medal.

American sports fans began to pay attention, too. At six feet, five inches tall, Hyman was the nation's most intimidating offensive player, able to spike a volleyball as fiercely and accurately as her contemporary, Julius Erving of the Philadelphia 76ers, dunked a basketball. On defense, her rangy, angular frame was initially a handicap, but she overcame her reluctance to throw her body to the floor when required and soon mastered the backcourt as well. According to sports journalist George Vecsey, Hyman was also one of the most charismatic athletes of her generation. Yet if Hyman's dominance in women's volleyball in the 1980s was as great as MICHAEL JORDAN's ascendancy in basketball a decade later, her celebrity and financial rewards never came close to those of even journeymen NBA players.

Buoyed by corporate sponsorship and the patriotic fervor that accompanied the 1984 Olympics in her hometown of Los Angeles, Hyman led the U.S. women to unprecedented public acclaim and a silver medal. Having devoted ten years of her life to volleyball—often cutting short the brief vacations she allowed herself—Hyman earned plaudits for her dominating performance and for her magnanimous praise of the gold-medal–winning Chinese team. Hyman made the most of the fame that the Olympics had granted her, joining civil rights leader CORETTA SCOTT KING, astronaut Sally Ride, and vice-presidential candidate Geraldine Ferarro at a women's rights rally during the 1984 elections.

American interest in women's volleyball proved fleeting, however, and Hyman returned to Japan, where she had begun to play professional volleyball for the Daiei team in 1982. By 1986 she had transformed Daiei, a struggling minor league team sponsored by

a supermarket chain, into a leading force in Japan's major volleyball league. Hyman remained a fierce competitor, though her coaching skills and ability to read the game now mattered as much as her play on the court. Indeed, to many it seemed fitting that Flo Hyman's final words were an exhortation to a teammate, uttered shortly before she collapsed near the end of a match in Matsue City, Japan, in late January 1986. Hyman died later that evening from what was first reported as a heart attack, but later announced as complications resulting from Marfan syndrome, an hereditary disorder that often leads to a fatal rupturing of the aorta. Hyman displayed one manifestation of the syndrome, her height, but did not suffer the more telling signs of the disorder, notably curvature of the spine or breastbone. As a consequence her condition was never diagnosed, though her death helped to publicize Marfan syndrome and has encouraged athletes and others at risk from the disorder to be tested. Hyman, who never married, was buried at Inglewood Park Cemetery in her hometown, and was survived by her father, who died three years later, and eight siblings. Her posthumous awards have been many: she was inducted into the Volleyball Hall of Fame in 1988 and named by USA Volleyball as the MVP for the years 1978–2002. She was also the first woman admitted to the University of Houston's Hall of Honor in 1998.

Flo Hyman typifies the new generation of women athletes who emerged in the 1970s and 1980s. They were the first beneficiaries of Title IX, federal legislation passed in 1972, which prohibited sex discrimination in college athletic programs that received federal funding. Indeed, in 1985 Hyman and basketball player CHERYL MILLER testified on Capitol Hill in support of strengthening Title IX. Hyman's open determination to win also reflected broad changes in American gender roles. Female athletes had always exhibited strength, power, and endurance, but now they began to celebrate those attributes, as well as the more traditionally accepted virtues of speed, skill, and grace. As Hyman put it in an interview with the *New York Times* in 1983, "Pushing yourself over the barrier becomes a habit.... If you want to win the war, you've got to pay the price" (Vecsey, S3). Her widely admired resolve and sportsmanship makes it fitting, therefore, that the Women's Sports Foundation established in 1987 an annual Flo Hyman Award to the female athlete who best exemplified over the course of her career Hyman's "dignity, spirit, and commitment to excellence."

FURTHER READING

Demak, Richard. "Marfan's Syndrome: A Silent Killer." *Sports Illustrated*, 18 Aug. 1986.

Vecsey, George. "America's Power in Volleyball." *New York Times*, 2 Oct. 1983.

Obituary: *New York Times*, 25 Jan. 1986.

—STEVEN J. NIVEN

IMES, ELMER SAMUEL (12 Oct. 1883–11 Sept. 1941), physicist, was born in Memphis, Tennessee, the son of Benjamin A. Imes, a minister, and Elizabeth Wallace. Imes attended school in Oberlin, Ohio, and the Agricultural and Mechanical High School in Normal, Alabama. Imes then enrolled at Fisk University in Nashville, Tennessee, where he received his BA in Science in 1903. Upon graduating, Imes accepted a position at Albany Normal Institute in Albany, Georgia, where he taught mathematics and physics. He returned to Fisk in 1910 and for the next five years worked toward an MS in Science while serving as an instructor in science and mathematics. After receiving his master's degree in 1915, Imes entered the University of Michigan's doctoral physics program, where he worked closely with Harrison M. Randall, who had recently returned from Germany. Randall had studied the infrared region of the spectrum in Friedrich Paschen's spectroscopy laboratory at Tübingen University.

For the next three years, Imes investigated the infrared spectrum of three diatomic molecules: hydrogen chloride (HCl), hydrogen bromide (HBr), and hydrogen fluoride (HF). Experimental and theoretical work had already shown that the molecular vibrational spectrum is quantized. Imes and Randall were interested in obtaining definitive evidence that the rotational spectrum was also quantized. In 1918 Imes received

his PhD and published his dissertation in a long article in the *Astrophysical Journal* (50 [1919]: 251–276). This work had a major impact on atomic physics: "In 1919, Randall and Imes published a single work that opened an entirely new field of research: the study of molecular structure through the use of high resolution infrared spectroscopy. Their work revealed for the first time the detailed spectra of simple-molecule gases, leading to important verification of the emerging quantum theory and providing, for the first time, an accurate measurement of the distances between atoms in a molecule" (Krenz, 12). Another view of Imes's research was presented by Earle Plyler in a 1974 speech at Fisk: "Imes' work formed a turning point in the scientific thinking, making it clear that quantum theory was not just a novelty, useful in limited fields of physics, but of widespread and general application."

Imes's results were immediately recognized by quantum scientists in both North America and Europe. In the two decades after its publication the paper was extensively cited in research papers and reviews on the rotational-vibrational spectra of diatomic molecules. Within a very short time, discussions of his work and his precision spectrum of HCl was incorporated into the standard textbooks on modern physics. Imes's experimental results also provided the first evidence for the existence of nuclear isotopics. This was shown by examining the doublet structure in his absorption band structure of HCl at 1.76 microns. This feature was interpreted to mean that two isotopes of chlorine were present.

As a black scientist holding a doctorate degree, Imes found his employment opportunities essentially limited to teaching at a black southern college or to seeking a position within industry or the federal government. For the next decade, Imes lived in and around New York City, where he was employed as an engineer and applied physicist. Imes's applied research and engineering activities resulted in four patents, each in the general area of measuring the properties of magnetic materials and the construction of instruments to conduct such tests. In 1920 Imes married NELLA LARSEN; they had no children. His own scholarly and literary interests, as well as his marriage to Larsen, one of

the better-known writers of the Harlem Renaissance, allowed him to associate with many members of the "Negro" intellectual and power elite, including W. E. B. DU BOIS, CHARLES S. JOHNSON, Arna Bontemps, LANGSTON HUGHES, AARON DOUGLAS, WALTER WHITE, and Carl Van Vechten. Many of these people would reappear in Imes's life in the 1930s as members of the Fisk University faculty or through some other strong connection to the institution.

In 1930 Imes was appointed chair of and professor in the physics department at Fisk, a position he held until his death. Imes initially devoted much of his time to the reorganization of the undergraduate physics curriculum and made preliminary preparations for the initiation of a full-fledged graduate program centered on research in infrared spectroscopy. Both Imes and his students were involved in several research projects; they used both X-rays and magnetic procedures to characterize the properties of materials and in the study of the fine structure of the infrared rotational spectrum of acetylene. Imes spent at least one summer at New York University carrying out experiments on magnetic materials, and he returned to the University of Michigan several summers to continue his research in infrared spectroscopy. He was active in three professional societies: the American Physical Society, the American Society for Testing Materials, and the American Institute of Electrical Engineers. Because of segregationist laws in the southern states he would only attend national meetings of these organizations when they were held in large northern cities or in Canada.

Imes felt that the students at Fisk, as well as his friends and colleagues, should be exposed to the general outline and themes of science. To this end he developed a course, "Cultural Physics," and wrote a rather large manuscript to be used for the course. In addition to his duties as chair, Imes did detailed work on the planning and design of a new science building, and he carried out extensive correspondence with other researchers, equipment designers, and equipment manufacturers. Imes was heavily involved in the general academic and social life of the university. He operated film equipment for various university clubs, participated in both the planning and execution of the Annual Spring Arts Festival, and served on various scholarship and disciplinary committees. One of his major concerns was the education and training of his students; several of them enrolled in graduate studies in physics at the University of Michigan.

Imes's marriage ended in 1933 when Larsen divorced him on the legal grounds of "cruelty." The couple had already been separated for a number of years, mainly because of her desire to pursue a writing career in New York. Imes died in New York City.

Throughout his career, Imes was held in high regard by his scientific colleagues. They immediately grasped the significance of the work he did at the University of Michigan showing that both the vibrational and rotational energy levels of molecules are quantized. His experiments also provided a precise set of data that could be used to make a critical test of the emerging quantum mechanics that was being formulated in Europe. Understood but never openly articulated during his lifetime was the fact that Imes's race had placed limitations on what he could achieve in science in America.

FURTHER READING

Imes's papers are located at Fisk University Library, Special Collections, the Carl Van Vechten Personal Collection, New York Public Library, and the JAMES WELDON JOHNSON Collection, Beinecke Library, Yale University.

Krenz, Gary D. "Physics at Michigan: From Classical Physics to Nuclear Research, 1888–1938." *LSA Magazine* 2 (Fall 1988): 10–16.

Obituary: Swann, W. F. G. *Science* 94 (1941): 600–601.

—RONALD E. MICKENS

J

JACKSON, JESSE L., SR.

(8 Oct. 1941–), civil rights leader, was born Jesse Louis Robinson in Greenville, South Carolina. His mother, Nancy Burns, was only sixteen years old when Jesse was born, and she was not married to Jackson's father, Noah Robinson. On 2 October 1943 Jackson's mother married Charles H. Jackson, a janitor, who adopted Jackson and gave him his name. In the course of his career, Jackson has frequently used the fact that he was born out of wedlock to a teenage mother to try to inspire young people to believe that no matter what their backgrounds they can "be somebody." At Greenville's Sterling High School, Jackson was a good student and an outstanding athlete. After gradua tion from high school, he accepted a football scholarship at the University of Illinois but left after a year. Jackson attributed his departure to the school's racist sports policy, stating that he could not play quarterback because it was a "whites only position."

Enrolling in 1961 at North Carolina Agricultural and Technical State University (A&T), an historically black college in Greensboro, Jackson became the school's star quarterback, head of his fraternity, and president of the student government. He was also a leader of the campus chapter of the Congress of Racial Equality (CORE), one of the leading national civil rights organizations in the 1960s. At age twenty-three he led demonstrations protesting segregation at Greensboro lunch counters and helped to organize a student civil rights group, the North Carolina Intercollegiate Council on Human Rights. Thus, from his high school and early college days, Jackson displayed the talents and ambition for leadership that were to character ize the rest of his life. Equally clear at this time was Jackson's intention to use those talents and ambitions in the cause of civil rights, which he has continued throughout his career. In 1962 he married Jacqueline Lavina Davis, a student from Fort Pierce, Florida. In the course of their marriage the Jacksons had five children. (In 1996 his oldest son, Jesse Louis Jackson Jr., was elected to the U.S. Congress from Chicago.)

In 1964 Jackson graduated from North Carolina A&T with a BA in soci ology and moved to Chicago to attend seminary. He had entered the min istry while in college, but he was not ordained into the Baptist clergy until 1968. Jackson enrolled in the Chicago Theological Seminary in 1965 and con tinued his civil rights activism, work ing for the Coordinating Council of Community Organizations, an umbrella association of Chicago civic and civil rights groups. Within a year Jackson had become director of the Coordinating Council. He dropped out of seminary to join the voting rights protests in Selma then being led by JOHN LEWIS of the Student Nonviolent Coordinating Com mittee (SNCC) and MARTIN LUTHER KING JR. of the Southern Christian Leadership Conference (SCLC). King was a strong-willed and gifted leader, and he surrounded himself with men of similar abilities, including RALPH ABERNATHY, ANDREW YOUNG, Hosea Williams, and Wyatt Tee Walker, among others. Viewing King as a hero and role model for activist ministry, Jack son desperately wanted to be a part of his inner circle. Within a year Jackson attained his goal when he was appointed national director of Operation Breadbas ket in 1967. Headquartered in Chicago, Operation Breadbasket was the northern arm of the largely southern-based SCLC. Modeled after a similar organization in Philadelphia led by LEON H. SULLIVAN, Breadbasket targeted and protested against businesses with discriminatory employment and contracting practices.

Operation Breadbasket thrived in Chicago under Jackson's leadership. The organization led highly visible boycotts against some of the city's leading businesses, sometimes resulting in employment opportunities for black workers and contracts for black

Jesse Jackson, civil rights leader and political activist, became the leading African American in the Democratic Party in the 1980s. © Jacques M. Chenet/CORBIS

entrepreneurs. Breadbasket's success made Jackson an influential figure in Chicago politics and enhanced his stature in SCLC's inner circle. That Jackson, considerably younger than the other SCLC leaders, could so quickly be placed in charge of SCLC's northern operations is testament to both his talents and his ambitions. Jackson was with King at the time of his assassination in Memphis in 1968 and claimed to have cradled the dying leader on the balcony of the Lorraine Motel, although the others present dispute this claim. Indeed, it was this dispute about Jackson's role at the time of King's death that initiated tensions between him and the SCLC leadership and that would eventually lead to Jackson's suspension and ultimate resignation from the organization. Mistrust of Jackson was reinforced when, against the explicit wishes of the King family and SCLC staff, he appeared the day after the assassination before the Chicago City Council and on national television in clothing that he claimed bore King's blood.

At the time of his death, King was in the final stages of planning the Poor People's Campaign—marches, demonstrations, and other protest activities designed to highlight the extent of poverty in America and to secure for the poor federally guaranteed jobs and income. Jackson, along with SCLC leaders James Bevel and Bernard Lafayette, had initially questioned the strategy and clarity of planning for the Poor People's March on Washington in internal SCLC deliberations. After King's death, however, he skillfully used the media and effectively stole the spotlight from Abernathy, King's designated successor, on the day of the national demonstration.

Undoubtedly, Jackson believed that he was better equipped to succeed King than Abernathy, and shortly after the Poor People's Campaign concluded, he asked the SCLC board to give him a higher position in the organization. The board refused. Sensing that Jackson was turning Operation Breadbasket into an autonomous organization, in 1971 the SCLC board asked Jackson to move Breadbasket to Atlanta, SCLC's national headquarters. Jackson refused. Later in the year the board suspended Jackson for sixty days because of alleged irregularities in the handling of Breadbasket funds. At this point Jackson resigned from SCLC and created Operation "PUSH"

(People United to Save Humanity) and named himself president. Operation PUSH (which in personnel was essentially Operation Breadbasket with a new name) continued Breadbasket's economic protests and boycotts, but it also began to engage in political protests and organizing. Jackson also established PUSH-EXCEL to encourage high performance by black schoolchildren. Adopting the self-styled characterization of the "country preacher," he traveled the country preaching moral responsibility, especially regarding sex during the teen years, out-of-wedlock childbearing, and the use of illegal drugs.

In 1972 Jackson made his first foray into national Democratic Party politics, cochairing an alternate delegation to the Democratic National Convention. Charging that the regular delegation headed by Mayor Richard J. Daley of Chicago had excluded minorities and women, Jackson played a major role in persuading the convention to oust the Daley delegation and replace it with the one he cochaired. In 1984 and again in 1988 Jackson ran for the Democratic nomination for president. He gained widespread support from black voters and Latinos, bringing significant numbers of new registrants into the Democratic Party. The excitement of his candidacy was felt largely in the Democratic primaries in 1984. He won in the District of Columbia and Louisiana, beating both the perceived frontrunner Walter Mondale, a former vice president, and Senator Gary Hart, and in Maryland he came in second, ahead of Hart. Jackson's performance at the primary level won him delegates to the 1984 Democratic National Convention, but with little support from the larger white electorate, he did not come close to winning the nomination. More important, however, was the popular acknowledgment of Jackson as the leading African American in the Democratic Party. In both the 1984 and 1988 elections he stood out as one of the party's leading advocates for liberal and progressive causes. He also established the Rainbow Coalition Inc., as a progressive, liberal adjunct to the Democratic Party. By the 1980s public opinion polls showed that blacks and whites alike perceived Jackson to be the preeminent African American leader.

Jackson also achieved international recognition as a "citizen diplomat,"

visiting countries in the Middle East, Latin America, and Africa. Pursuing conflict mediation, he negotiated the release of American prisoners of war in Syria and Yugoslavia and the release of political prisoners in Cuba. In the 1990s he called attention to the need for African American economic empowerment. He established the Wall Street Project to facilitate access by blacks and other minorities to investment capital, credit, and contracts and to help them secure positions as executives and board members in major American financial and corporate institutions. Unlike the economic empowerment strategy of Operation Breadbasket, the Wall Street Project relied on negotiations between elite power brokers, rather than mass boycotts and protests. The peripatetic Jackson, however, continued to lead demonstrations for causes that included not only civil rights but also the environment, women's rights, and workers' rights. In addition, he hosted *Both Sides*, a Sunday afternoon news talk program on CNN. In 1995 Jackson's Operation PUSH and his Rainbow Coalition were merged. The new organization, with Jackson as president, was called the Rainbow/PUSH Coalition.

Jackson's popularity and moral authority as a leader were undermined early in 2001 when the tabloid press revealed that he had fathered a child with Karin Stanford, a member of his staff who had written a book about his involvement in international affairs. The revelation of this extramarital relationship diminished Jackson's credibility, especially given the allegations of financial irregularities regarding his organizations' payments to his mistress and their child. He also lost his television talk show on CNN as a result of the affair.

According to a national survey conducted in 2000 by the Joint Center for Political and Economic Studies, Jackson had declined considerably in influence. The Joint Center's poll revealed Jackson with an 83 percent favorable to 9 percent unfavorable rating among blacks. In a 2002 poll the Joint Center found that Jackson's favorable rating among blacks had dropped to 60 percent, while his unfavorable rating had increased to 26 percent. By 2003 black scholars and commentators on African American politics were increasingly talking and writing about the "end of the Jackson era." And, in a move widely viewed as an attempt to displace Jackson as the preeminent African American leader, AL SHARPTON, a Jackson protégé, announced he was running for the 2004 Democratic Party presidential nomination.

From a historical perspective, it cannot be denied that Jesse Louis Jackson Sr. held sway over the minds and hearts of African Americans in the post civil rights era. During the 1980s and 1990s, at a time of declining civil rights gains, Jackson championed a spirit of protest that spoke to national and international human rights concerns, thus positioning himself as the most visible African American leader since Martin Luther King Jr. A 2000 poll of black political scientists asked them to list and rank the greatest black leaders of all time. Specifically they were asked to list in "rank order the five African Americans who, in your historical judgment, have had the greatest impact, for good or ill, on the well being and destinies of the African people in the United States" (Smith, 128). Of the ten greatest leaders, Jackson was the only living person on the list. He ranked number seven behind Martin Luther King Jr., W. E. B. DU BOIS, MALCOLM X, FREDERICK DOUGLASS, BOOKER T. WASHINGTON, MARCUS GARVEY, and THURGOOD MARSHALL, but ahead of IDA B. WELLS-BARNETT, MARY MCLEOD BETHUNE, FANNIE LOU HAMER, and ADAM CLAYTON POWELL JR. As one respondent in the poll wrote, "History will be very kind to him" (Smith, 133).

FURTHER READING

Frady, Marshall. *Jesse: The Life and Pilgrimage of Jesse Jackson* (1996).

Morris, Lorenzo, ed. *The Social and Political Implications of the 1984 Jesse Jackson Presidential Campaign* (1990).

Reed, Adolph. *The Jesse Jackson Phenomenon: The Crisis of Purpose in Afro-American Politics* (1986).

Smith, Robert C. "Rating Black Leaders." *National Political Science Review* 8 (2001): 124–138.

Stanford, Karin. *Beyond the Boundaries: Jesse Jackson in International Affairs* (1996).
—ROBERT C. SMITH

JACKSON, MAHALIA (26 Oct. 1911–27 Jan. 1972), gospel singer, was born in New Orleans, the daughter of John Jackson, a dockworker, barber, and preacher, and Charity Clark, a maid. Her mother died when Jackson was five, and she moved in with her mother's sister, Mahalia Paul, also known as Aunt Duke. She worked both for her aunt and for a local white family from an early age, and during the eighth grade (the last grade she attended before quitting school), she also worked as a laundress for five hours after school. She began to sing as a young child, particularly at the Mount Moriah Baptist Church, but she was also profoundly influenced by the BESSIE SMITH recordings her more worldly cousin Fred owned. However, Jackson was most powerfully shaped by her experiences with the Sanctified Church that was next door to her house. As she later noted, the church had no organ or choir. Members played drums, cymbals, and tambourines, and "everybody in there sang and they clapped and stomped their feet and sang with their whole bodies. They had a beat, a powerful beat, a rhythm we held on to from slavery days, and their music was so strong and expressive it used to bring the tears to my eyes" (Jackson, 32–33).

In 1928 Jackson moved to Chicago, where her aunts Hannah and Alice already lived. For a decade she supported herself by doing laundry for white families and working as a hotel maid. She joined the choir of the Greater Salem Baptist Church, which became her second home, and co-founded the "Johnson Gospel Singers" with another woman and three of the minister's sons. The group sang in churches for $1.50 a night, often traveling throughout Indiana and Illinois. Jackson herself sang in churches as far away as Buffalo, New York, and at revivals, homes, and hospitals, already employing the down-home, deeply emotive style that created a powerful tie with her audience and accentuated a sense of community. The larger black churches wanted nothing to do with this style at first, so she sang most often for storefront and basement congregations.

In 1935 Jackson met Isaac Hockenhull, a college-trained chemist who worked as a mail carrier. The two married in 1938; they had no children. For a time she traveled around the region selling cosmetics made from Hockenhull's own formulas, but by 1939 she had earned enough money from her singing to leave this and her other jobs and open an enterprise she named Mahalia's Beauty Salon. The business thrived, and she soon attached a flower shop, generating business for the latter at the many funerals at which she was invited to sing. While her commitment to religious singing grew, her husband wanted her to take voice lessons and become a

Mahalia Jackson, the matriarch of American gospel music. Library of Congress

concert singer; he urged her to pursue a role in an all-black production of *The Mikado*, but she refused. The two grew apart and divorced in 1943, although they remained lifelong friends.

In 1937 Jackson began to work with gospel composer THOMAS A. DORSEY, and she made her recording debut that year with "God's Gonna Separate the Wheat from the Tares," a song already punctuated with her trademark moans and growls. Dorsey became her champion, and she traveled widely, singing his songs at churches; he wrote "Peace in the Valley" for her in 1937 and served as her accompanist from 1937 to 1946. Realizing the uniqueness of her style, Dorsey encouraged Jackson to open her songs at a more tempered level, and to gradually build the excitement until the audience was ready for her uniquely celebratory climax: "In her deeply individualistic manner—running and skipping down the church and concert hall aisles, her eyes closed, hands tightly clasped, with feet tapping and body throbbing, all the while her voice soaring as if there were no walls to confine its spiritual journey—she was utterly possessed and possessing" (Schwerin, 62).

Jackson was a "stretch-out" singer who changed melody and meter as the spirit moved her. Her style borrowed from the "Baptist lining style," "a slow, languorous manner, without a regular pulse... that allowed the singer to execute each syllable by adding several extra tones, bending these added tones in myriad directions, and reshaping the melody into a personal testimony" (Boyer, 11). Thus her voice was at its most resonant and beautiful in slow hymns like "Just As I Am," sung with precise control and intense feeling. Her work with Dorsey also made Jackson a powerful presence in the city and raised the position of church singer to a new status; politicians frequently hired her to sing at funerals, an unprecedented "professionalization" of a sacred calling.

In 1945 Chicago broadcaster Studs Terkel brought new attention to Jackson when he played one of her recordings, "I'm Goin' to Tell God All about It One of These Days," over and over again on the air. Deeply impressed, Bess Berman signed her to a contract with Apollo Records in 1946, guaranteeing her ten thousand dollars a year. Her first four sides sold poorly, but her 1947 recording of "Move On Up a Little Higher" brought her royalties of $300,000 in the first year alone, earning her the title of "Gospel Queen." From 1946 to 1954 she recorded seventy songs for Apollo, and she commanded fees of one thousand dollars a night for appearances in New York and Chicago. Stung by dishonest promoters earlier in her career, she always insisted on being paid in cash on the day of her performance.

In 1950 the jazz historian and critic Marshall Stearns invited Jackson to perform at the Music Inn, near Tanglewood in Massachusetts, at a symposium on the history of jazz. Her appearance transformed her into an overnight national celebrity; she received dozens of offers to perform, appeared on *The Ed Sullivan Show*, and was appointed the official soloist for the National Baptist Convention. She also sang at the first of a series of Carnegie Hall concerts that broke all house records. Her 1952 recording of "I Can Put My Trust in Jesus" was awarded a prize by the French Academy of Music and led to her first European tour, with stops in England, Holland, Belgium, Denmark, and France. Although she collapsed in Paris six weeks after starting the tour, she received acclaim almost everywhere she sang, and her recording of "Silent Night" became a best-seller in Norway.

Courted by John Hammond, who was impressed by her rejection of the commercialization of gospel music, Jackson signed a lucrative contract with Columbia Records in 1953. She had her own radio show on a CBS station in Chicago in 1954, later converted to a half-hour television show. Although the reviews were excellent and the audience large, the network turned her down when she asked about taking the show national; they argued that they would never be able to get sponsors for the southern audience. And though she was often invited to appear on Chicago television, she found the experience frustrating, with arrangers trying to tone down her style and telling her how to sing her own songs. Even at Columbia, for which she recorded more than a dozen albums, producers filled her repertoire with "pop-gospel" songs like "A Rusty Old Halo," a "cute" crossover song, and burdened her with orchestras and choirs that only dampened the powerful impact of her impassioned voice. But Jackson enjoyed the popularity and the money, even as she complained that commercialization was compromising the music. And the results were not always disappointing; witness her 1955 recording of "Joshua Fit the Battle of Jericho," which clearly incorporates the battle against slavery into its meaning.

Jackson also toured widely during the 1950s, generally with her regular accompanist, Mildred Falls, and her cousin John Stevens. The three experienced the segregation that continued to curse the South, even while Jackson was enjoying huge commercial successes in the national white music market, and she soon immersed herself in the civil rights struggle. She appeared in Montgomery, Alabama, in 1956, for instance, when Reverend RALPH ABERNATHY asked her to sing at a ceremony honoring ROSA PARKS. And she personally experienced the racial hypocrisy of the North in 1957, when she bought a house on Chicago's South Side in a white neighborhood. Someone fired air rifle pellets into her living-room windows, and once again she found herself a national figure. The journalist Edward R. Murrow interviewed her on his *Person-to-Person* television show at her house, and for days crowds of people gathered outside in sympathy. She developed a close relationship with MARTIN LUTHER KING JR. In May 1957, at the Lincoln Memorial, she sang "I Been 'Buked and I Been Scorned" as part of a Southern Christian Leadership Conference Prayer Pilgrimage for Freedom. In 1959 she recorded "Great Gettin' Up Morning," highlighting the song's implicit attack on slavery. She was most proud of her participation in the August 1963 March on Washington, where she again sang "I Been 'Buked and I Been Scorned," beginning soft and gentle, then shouting for joy and leading the crowd in singing and clapping.

Jackson's involvement in the civil rights movement enhanced her career. After the Murrow interview she appeared on *The Dinah Shore Show*, the two singing a duet of the antiwar gospel song "Down by the Riverside." She appeared as guest star on most of the popular television variety shows of the decade, including those hosted by Bing Crosby, Perry Como, Steve Allen, Red Skelton, and Ed Sullivan. She even made a movie appearance in 1958 (albeit a somewhat embarrassing one) as a happy "colored" servant in the film *Imitation of Life*; racist typecasting was all too typical of Hollywood in the 1950s. And, of course, her singing continued to garner approval. DUKE ELLINGTON featured her on his 1958 recording of the "Black, Brown, and Beige" suite; for the studio version of "Come Sunday," Ellington had the lights turned out while Jackson sang by herself in the dark. Her national reputation was enshrined when she sang "The Star-Spangled Banner" at President John F. Kennedy's inauguration eve gala. In 1961 she enjoyed huge popular success on a European tour and made one of her very greatest recordings, "Elijah Rock," at a concert in Stockholm, Sweden, accompanied only by Falls on the piano.

Jackson's health began to deteriorate in 1963, and she was periodically hospitalized over the last years of her life for exhaustion and heart problems. Yet in 1964 she embarked on a hugely successful European tour that ended with a private papal audience in Rome and a longed-for visit to Jerusalem. That same year she married Sigmund Galloway; they had no children and divorced in 1967. That year she starred at the first-ever gospel concert at Lincoln Center. She appeared at the Newport Jazz Festival in 1970 and began another European tour in 1971, cut short by her last illness. She sang "Take My Hand, Precious Lord," at King's funeral, and sang at Robert F. Kennedy's funeral. She also expanded her business operations, establishing the "Mahalia Jackson Chicken System," eventually a chain of 135 stores, and continued to pursue her little-publicized charitable efforts through the Mahalia Jackson Scholarship Foundation, using her own money to send students to college. Jackson died in Evergreen Park, a Chicago suburb. She was buried in New Orleans and was commemorated at funerals both there and in Chicago, the latter attended by scores of dignitaries and marked by ARETHA FRANKLIN singing "Precious Lord."

By the end of her life, Jackson had immersed herself in business and real estate deals, and she seemed to spend more and more of her time meeting with accountants and lawyers. Her appearance fees were far beyond the reach of even prosperous churches to pay. But though purists attacked her

commercial concessions, she remained a regal, matriarchal presence in gospel and in American music in general. As the writer Anthony Heilbut noted, "All by herself, Mahalia was the vocal, physical, spiritual symbol of gospel music" (Heilbut, 57). Jazz, blues, and gospel enthusiasts found a common bond in her rhythmic energy and spiritual intensity. She was the first to carry gospel music beyond the black community, and she affected lives in an unparalleled personal way. Ellington noted that his encounter with Jackson "had a strong influence on me and my sacred music, and also made me a much handsomer kid in the Right Light." As Jackson herself stated in her autobiography, "There's something about music that is so penetrating that your soul gets the message. No matter what trouble comes to a person, music can help him face it" (184).

FURTHER READING

Jackson, Mahalia, with Evan McLeod Wylie. *Movin' On Up* (1966).

Boyer, Horace Clarence. Notes accompanying *Gospels, Hymns, and Spirituals* (Columbia Records, 1991).
Goreau, Laurraine. *Just Mahalia, Baby* (1975).
Heilbut, Anthony. *The Gospel Sound: Good News and Bad Times*, rev. ed. (1992).
Schwerin, Jules. *Got to Tell It: Mahalia Jackson, Queen of Gospel* (1992).

Obituary: *New York Times*, 28 Jan. 1972.

Discography
Jackson's most important recordings include her early sessions for Apollo Records. On Columbia the listener should begin with the 1991 compilation *Gospels, Spirituals, and Hymns*; also recommended are *Newport 1958* (1958) and *How I Got Over* (1976).
—RONALD P. DUFOUR

JACKSON, MICHAEL
(29 Aug. 1958–), singer, dancer, songwriter, pop and tabloid superstar, was born Michael Joseph Jackson in Gary, Indiana, a blue-collar town dominated by steel mills. His father, Joseph S. Jackson, a steelworker, and his mother, Katherine, were strict Jehovah's Witnesses. The couple had nine children—Maureen ("Rebbie"), Sigmund

("Jackie"), Toriano ("Tito"), Jermaine, Marlon, La Toya, Michael, Steven ("Randy"), and Janet—who grew up in poverty. The prohibitions of their religion were pushed aside in 1962 when Joseph, a frustrated singer, gathered Jackie, Tito, and Jermaine into a rhythm-and-blues act. The next year he added Michael, who was five.

The boys loved to sing, but Joseph became a demanding and controlling stage father who beat his children when they did not perform to his satisfaction. He pushed them mercilessly—especially Michael, the most talented. Even as a child Michael could dance like JAMES BROWN and sing with a soulful passion that quickly distinguished him from his brothers. Soon the boys were playing talent shows, nightclubs, and even strip joints. By 1966 Marlon had joined them. The next year they were signed to an Indiana label, Steeltown, as the Jackson Five. Michael soloed in a childlike voice on their first single, "Big Boy." The record was a local sensation that helped win them a deal with Motown in 1968. Their first four singles—"I Want You Back," "ABC," "The Love You Save," and "I'll Be There"—all made number one, an unprecedented coup.

The Jackson 5 became the hottest pop-soul-R&B group in show business. BERRY GORDY JR., Motown's owner, recognized that Michael had real star quality. Although the group continued to record together, Gordy began grooming Michael as a headliner, and throughout the 1970s Michael met and surpassed all expectations. In 1971 Jackson's first solo single, "Got to Be There," shot to number four. A 1972 follow-up, "Rockin' Robin," made number two. That summer Jackson scored his first of twelve number-one singles, "Ben," the title song of a horror film about an introverted boy whose best friend is his pet rat. In retrospect the song, sung with a moving sensitivity, seems an ominous portent of the lonely and confused fantasy world that Michael would later find himself inhabiting.

In 1975 the Jackson 5 began to break up when Jermaine refused to leave Motown after his brothers signed with Epic Records as The Jacksons. Michael's appearance as the Scarecrow in a lavish film version of *The Wiz* in 1978 starring DIANA ROSS became a springboard to his solo career. Although the film flopped, Michael formed a close relationship with the musical director, QUINCY JONES, who went on to produce the singer's fifth solo album, *Off the Wall* (1979). Where Jackson's previous albums had been weighted down by sappy love songs, *Off the Wall* was a glitzy blending of dance tracks, funk, and a higher grade of pop-soul ballads. It yielded four top-ten hits, two of which—the Grammy-winning "Don't Stop 'Til You Get Enough" and "Rock with You"—reached number one.

At his peak Jackson recorded *Thriller*, then the biggest-selling album in history, and made the cover of *Time*. His videos turned the MTV cable television channel into a worldwide phenomenon. Fred Astaire raved about his dancing. Black pop had never had a higher profile. Jackson had "taken us right up there where we belong," said his producer, Quincy Jones. "Black music had to play second fiddle for a long time, but its spirit is the whole motor of pop" (*Time* magazine, "Why He's a Thriller," March 19, 1984). Yet the so-called King of Pop would become as famous for his bizarre behavior as he was for his talent. The world saw a man-child so fragile that he seemed ever in danger of snapping.

Jackson had continued singing with his brothers until the release of *Thriller* in December 1982. The album was inspired by one of his fixations, the occult. Jackson wrote most of the songs; several had spooky themes, sweetened by irresistible dance rhythms and flashy production. The guest musicians Paul McCartney and Eddie Van Halen added extra star glitter. Seven of *Thriller*'s nine tracks made the top ten. "Billie Jean" and "Beat It" hit number one.

The album's success owed much to the videos that accompanied it, at a time when the genre was still new. The title song featured a conglomeration of dancing zombies. "Beat It," a statement against gang violence, recalled the schoolyard ballets of *West Side Story*. "Billie Jean," a tale of accused paternity, looked like a surreal horror film, with Jackson as a sinister, lurking presence. Jackson's innovations in promoting the *Thriller* album were so frequently emulated that he could be regarded as the most important pioneer of the modern music video. In 1983 Jackson performed on Motown's twenty-fifth-anniversary TV special where he introduced his

famous strutting-on-tiptoe "moonwalk" to an estimated forty-seven million viewers.

On 28 February 1984 *Thriller* won eight Grammy Awards. The next year Jackson and Lionel Ritchie teamed to write "We Are the World," an anthem for *USA for Africa*, an all-star hunger-relief album. Produced by Jones, the single raised fifty million dollars and won three Grammy Awards. Pepsi went on to offer Jackson a ten-million-dollar endorsement deal. Jackson, it seemed, had the magic touch—a notion perhaps reinforced by the single white sequined glove he wore in public.

But scandal soon began to overwhelm him. Jackson's skin was growing whiter, and rumors circulated that he was having his blackness bleached away, though the singer claimed he had vitiligo, a skin disease that leaves white blotches. Numerous attempts to alter his appearance through plastic surgery gave him a pale, gaunt, and strangely androgynous look. He started wearing surgical masks in public, ostensibly to keep out germs. Jackson seemed obsessed with staying a child. His best friends were either maternal figures—Jane Fonda, Diana Ross, Elizabeth Taylor—or children. He bought a huge ranch in Santa Ynez, California, and called it Neverland, after the magical place in *Peter Pan* where kids never grow up. Jackson filled Neverland with amusement park rides and preadolescents. The press gave him a new nickname: "Wacko Jacko."

In September 1987 he released a new album, *Bad*. It debuted at number one and yielded five number-one singles, "I Just Can't Stop Loving You," "Bad," "The Way You Make Me Feel," "Man in the Mirror," and "Dirty Diana." Jackson promoted *Bad* with the highest-grossing world tour of all time. *Bad*'s sales—an estimated eight million copies—seemed a letdown after the reported fifty-million-plus of *Thriller*. But that did not stop Sony from signing him, in March 1991, to a new contract—six more albums plus film projects and TV specials—for a reported $890 million.

A new album, *Dangerous* (1991), debuted at number one, as did its first single, "Black or White." But overall his sales were declining, even as his tabloid allure zoomed. In 1993, during the *Dangerous* tour, the family of a thirteen-year-old Neverland regular

charged Jackson with molesting the boy, who told his story in a deposition. Jackson countersued for extortion, while defending himself on TV; his only fault, he claimed, was "enjoying through [children] the childhood that I missed myself" (live interview, Dec. 22 1993). He ended up settling out of court, paying the family an estimated eighteen to twenty million dollars. Subsequently, Pepsi dropped him. A nineteen-month marriage (1994–1996) to Lisa Marie Presley, Elvis's daughter, was seen as a desperate scheme to save his image.

In 1994 Jackson released a double compact disc of old and new material: *HIStory: Past, Present and Future, Book I*. The album and a single, "You Are Not Alone," premiered at number one. In keeping with the Biblical grandiosity of the album's title, Jackson performed at the 1996 Brit Awards dressed as the Messiah and surrounded by worshipful children. The rock singer Jarvis Cocker stormed onstage in the middle of the song to protest the spectacle. More scandal erupted that year with the announcement that Debbie Rowe, his dermatologist's assistant, was carrying Jackson's baby. She married him on 14 November, and the couple had two children, Prince Michael Jackson Jr. and Paris Katherine Jackson. The couple divorced in October 1999. Jackson retained custody of Prince and Paris.

In 2001 Jackson was inducted into the Rock and Roll Hall of Fame. An all-star concert, televised from Madison Square Garden, celebrated the thirtieth anniversary of his first solo record. From there he returned to the front pages of the tabloids. A new solo album, *Invincible* (2001), debuted at number one but sank quickly, producing no hits. Blaming Sony for bad marketing, Jackson branded chairman Tommy Mottola a racist and the "devil." December 2002 found Jackson back in court, sued by a promoter for backing out of two millennium concerts. The singer gave near incoherent testimony, during which he revealed a nose caved in from a botched surgery. He was ordered to pay $5.3 million in damages.

Prince Michael II, his third child, had been born that year to an unnamed surrogate mother. Jackson nicknamed the boy "Blanket." On 19 November he stepped onto the terrace of his Berlin hotel suite to greet throngs of fans below. With TV cameras running, he dangled Blanket over the edge of the balcony, shocking people worldwide.

The most damaging exposé of all appeared in February 2003: the TV documentary *Living with Michael Jackson*, produced by the journalist Martin Bashir, who had gained Jackson's cooperation. Twenty-seven million American viewers got a hair-raising glimpse inside Neverland and heard Jackson admit that underage boys slept in his bed—platonically, he swore. Feeling betrayed, Jackson sold Fox TV a "rebuttal" documentary filled with home-movie footage that showed him in a highly favorable light. But the musical legend he had started building at age five seemed tainted beyond repair. In November 2003 further criminal charges of child molestation, made on the very day his latest recording was released, renewed the scandal and created another frenzy of criticism, commentary, and news-mongering.

Personal scandal and controversy diminished much of Jackson's popularity, but the eccentricity of his life cannot erase the unparalleled influence he had on the music industry—and thereby on American and even global culture—during the first twenty years of his career. He produced one of the best selling albums and music videos of all time in *Thriller*, he garnered the most number-one hits during the 1980s, and he holds the *Billboard* records for the most number-one hits by a male artist (thirteen) and the highest number of singles to enter at the top position.

FURTHER READING

Jackson, Michael. *Moonwalk* (1988).

Andersen, Christopher P. *Michael Jackson: Unauthorized* (1994).
Bishop, Nick. *Freak: Inside the Twisted World of Michael Jackson (from the Files of the National Enquirer)* (2003).
Taraborelli, J. Randy. *Michael Jackson: The Magic and the Madness* (1991).

—JAMES GAVIN

 JACKSON, REBECCA COX (15 Feb. 1795– 24 May 1871), itinerant preacher, religious writer, and Shaker eldress, was born a free African American in Horntown, Pennsylvania. According to sketchy autobiographical information, she was the daughter of Jane (maiden name unknown) Cox. No reference is made in her writings to her father, who probably died shortly after her birth. Rebecca Cox lived with her grandmother (never named) until she was between three and four years old, but by age six she was again living with her mother, who had remarried and was now called Jane Wisson or Wilson. Her stepfather, a sailor, died at sea the next year. At age ten, she was in Philadelphia with her mother and a younger sister and infant brother, the offspring, it seems, of a third marriage of her mother. Responsibility for caring for her younger siblings seems to have deprived Rebecca of the schooling her mother was somehow able to provide for the other children. Her mother died when she was thirteen, whereupon she probably moved into the household of her older brother Joseph Cox (1778?–1843), a tanner and clergyman eighteen years her senior.

The exact date of Rebecca Cox's marriage to Samuel S. Jackson is unknown, but it must have occurred before 1830, the year of her spiritual awakening and the year her autobiographical narrative begins. Apparently childless, she and her husband were living with Joseph Cox. She cared for her brother's four children and also worked as a seamstress, a relatively highly skilled and respected occupation for African American women at that time. Jackson had been brought up as a Methodist, presumably in the African Methodist Episcopal (AME) Church. Her brother Joseph was an influential preacher at the Bethel AME Church in Philadelphia but Rebecca and her husband apparently were not active church members prior to her spiritual awakening, which occurred during a violent thunderstorm. Her career as an independent preacher began shortly thereafter.

Carried on the waves of a religious revival, she soon moved from leading a small praying band to public preaching. She stirred up controversy within AME circles not only as a woman preacher, but also because she had come to believe that celibacy was a necessary precondition of a holy life. She insisted that she be guided entirely by the dictates of an inner voice, which she identified as the authentic voice of God. In her incomplete spiritual autobiography, which she began to write in the 1840s, perhaps using earlier journal entries as a source, Jackson recorded a wide variety of visionary experiences, dreams, and supernatural gifts, including a remarkable "gift of reading," or literacy, in direct response to prayer in 1831. This "gift" gave her independent access to the divine word and allowed Jackson to free herself from what she believed was censorship in the letters she dictated to her clergyman brother. She also recorded instances of healing, the gift of foresight, and the more mysterious "gifts of power," spiritual means of protecting herself from threats, both natural and human.

By the late 1830s Jackson had separated from her husband, broken with the AME Church, and successfully launched a career of itinerant preaching that took her throughout Pennsylvania, northern Delaware, New Jersey, southern New England, and New York State. Her first experience with religious communal life occurred during this period, when she became involved with a group of religious Perfectionists organized near Albany, New York, by a man named Allen Pierce in 1837. This group valued visions and revelations and acknowledged Jackson's gifts in this realm. In 1843, when the community dissolved, sixteen of them joined the nearby Shaker community at Watervliet.

Jackson visited the Shakers (the United Society of Believers in Christ's Second Coming) at this time and was attracted by their religious celibacy, their emphasis on spiritualistic experience, and their dual-gender concept of deity. In 1835 she had had a vision, which she believed was a "revelation of the mother spirit," and clearly was impressed by the sect's acknowledgment of the Holy Mother Wisdom as a "co-eternal" partner with the Almighty Father. With her younger disciple and lifelong companion, Rebecca Perot, Jackson lived in the Watervliet Shaker community from June 1847 until July 1851. The two women then returned to Philadelphia on an unauthorized mission to bring the truths of Shakerism to the African American community. In Philadelphia they experimented with seance spiritualism. In 1857 they returned to Watervliet, and after a brief second residence Jackson won the right to found and head a new Shaker "outfamily" in Philadelphia.

Little is known of the small Philadelphia Shaker family during the remainder of Jackson's life. Over the next twenty-five years, the family varied in size and was located at several different Philadelphia sites. There was always a core group of African American women, some living together in a single house. They supported themselves by daywork as laundresses and seamstresses and held religious meetings at night. In 1878 the Shaker historian Alonzo G. Hollister visited with his copy of the collected writings of Rebecca Jackson—based on manuscripts entrusted to the Shakers by Perot after Jackson's death—and at that time, the core group comprised about a dozen women, including at least one Jewish sister. A smaller number of men, including one or two white spiritualists, also were associated with the community. Perot and several other aging Philadelphia sisters retired to the Watervliet community by 1896, but Shaker records indicate that the community still existed in some form as late as 1908.

Jackson was one of a surprisingly large number of African American women preachers in the nineteenth century who mounted significant challenges to the exclusionary practices of established churches, using their claim to extraordinary, direct experience of the divine to carve out careers as religious leaders despite the patriarchal biases of their churches. More theologically radical than most, Jackson sought a perfectionist religion that would acknowledge a "mother divinity," at first using only her own religious experience as her guide but later incorporating the dual-gender godhead theology developed by Shakerism. Her permanent legacy, however, was not a new religious sect, but a remarkable body of visionary writing that writer ALICE WALKER has said "tells us much more about the spirituality of human beings, especially of the interior spiritual resources of our mothers, and, because of this, makes an invaluable contribution to what we know of ourselves" (Walker, 78).

FURTHER READING

Jackson's manuscript writings are in the Shaker collections of the Western Reserve Historical Society in Cleveland, Ohio, the Library of Congress, and the Berkshire Athenaeum at the Public Library in Pittsfield, Massachusetts.

Braxton, Joanne. *Black Women Writing Autobiography* (1989).

McMahon Humez, Jean. *Gifts of Power: The Writings of Rebecca Jackson, Black Visionary, Shaker Eldress* (1981).

Sasson, Diane. *The Shaker Spiritual Narrative* (1983).

Walker, Alice. *In Search of Our Mothers' Gardens* (1983).

—JEAN MCMAHON HUMEZ

JACKSON, SHIRLEY ANN (5 Aug. 1946–), physicist, chair of the U.S. Nuclear Regulatory Commission, and educator, was born in Washington, D.C., the second of four children, to George Jackson, a post office employee, and Beatrice Cosby, a social worker. In elementary school Shirley was bused from the Jackson's largely white neighborhood in northwest Washington to a black school across town. After the 1954 *Brown v. Board of Education* desegregation ruling and several years of "white flight" transformed the area into a predominantly black neighborhood, she attended the local Roosevelt High School, where she participated in an accelerated program in math and science. Shirley took college-level classes in her senior year, after completing the high school curriculum early, and she graduated as valedictorian in 1964. "As I was growing up," she recalled, "I became fascinated with the notion that the physical world around me was a world of secrets, and that science, as applied in direct experimentation, was the key that could unlock those secrets . . . experimentation was like a good mystery novel, a tangible, unfolding narrative of what made nature click" (Rensselaer Polytechnic Institute inaugural address, 11 Dec. 1998).

Jackson was supported in her educational pursuits by her parents and teachers, and when she left for the Massachusetts Institute of Technology (MIT) in 1964, she was sustained in part by a modest scholarship from her local church, the Vermont Avenue Baptist Church. More substantial financial aid came from the Martin Marietta Aircraft Company, the Prince Hall Masons, and later the National Science Foundation and the Ford Foundation.

When she entered MIT, Jackson was one of forty-three women in her freshman class of nine hundred, and one of fewer than a dozen African Americans in a university of more than eight thousand students. She excelled despite her isolation—some students refused to eat with her or let her join their study groups—and the specious "advice" of a professor who counseled, "Colored girls should learn a trade." "I chose a 'trade,'" Jackson reminisced in a 1997 keynote address to the National Technical Association; "I chose physics!" While at MIT, she volunteered at Boston City Hospital and tutored students at the Roxbury YMCA. Back on campus, she served at the behest of the president of MIT on the Task Force on Educational Opportunity, helped found the university's Black Student Union, and lobbied successfully for the increased admission of African American students. Her student activism drew attacks, some of which were violent, mostly from outside MIT. In South Boston she was shot at, spit on, and chased by whites.

Jackson's highest priority, however, was physics, and in 1968 she received a BS for her innovative work in solid-state physics. Although she was wooed by several prominent physics departments for graduate research, she remained at MIT, in part to encourage more African Americans to attend the school. Under the direction of James Young, the first black tenured physics professor at MIT, her research culminated in

Shirley Jackson, chair of the Nuclear Regulatory Commission and president of Rensselaer Polytechnic Institute.
Schomburg Center

a dissertation, "The Study of a Multi-peripheral Model with Continued Cross-Channel Unitarity," subsequently published in the *Annals of Physics* (1975). When Jackson received her PhD in Theoretical Elemental Particle Physics in 1973, she became the first African American woman to receive a PhD at MIT and the second African American woman to earn a PhD in Physics in the United States. Two years later she joined MIT's board of trustees, and in 1992 she became a lifetime trustee.

Jackson worked with a number of prestigious labs in the United States and Europe in the 1970s. As a research associate at the Fermi National Accelerator Laboratory in Batavia, Illinois, she studied hadrons (subatomic particles, including baryons and mesons, made up of quarks and gluons.) As a visiting scientist at the accelerator lab at the European Center for Nuclear Research in Geneva, Switzerland, she researched theories of strongly interacting elementary particles. In 1976 she was a visiting scientist at the Aspen Center for Physics in Colorado and lecturer in physics at the Stanford Linear Accelerator Center in Menlo Park, California.

From 1976 to 1991 Jackson conducted research for AT&T Bell Laboratories in Murray Hill, New Jersey, in theoretical physics, solid-state and quantum physics, and optical physics, focusing on polaron physics. Her explorations yielded improvements in the signal-handling capabilities of semiconductor devices, keeping Bell Labs in the forefront of electronic communications. While at Bell Labs, she served as president of the National Society of Black Physicists (1980–1982) and met physicist Morris Washington. The couple married in 1980, and a son, Alan, was born the next year. In 1991 Jackson joined the Department of Physics and Astronomy at Rutgers University, where she also served on the board of trustees. During her four years at Rutgers, she consulted for AT&T and continued serving on the New Jersey Commission on Science and Technology, to which she had been appointed in 1985.

In the mid 1990s Jackson served on advisory committees at the Department of Energy (DOE) and the National Nuclear Security Administration (NNSA), and in 1994 she was appointed to a task force to determine the future of the DOE National Laboratories. In 1995, when President Bill Clinton appointed her to chair the Nuclear Regulatory Commission (NRC), Jackson became the first woman and the first African American to head the federal agency. Jackson's introduction of risk-informed, performance-based regulations within the NRC and her crackdowns on nuclear power industry violations restored the NRC's credibility as a watchdog for nuclear safety while garnering respect from both environmentalists and nuclear energy proponents. Nicknamed the "Energizer Bunny," she served on two binational commissions led by Vice President Al Gore and spearheaded the formation of the eight-nation International Nuclear Regulators Association, for which she served as chair from 1997 to 1999.

In 1999 Jackson became the first black woman to head a major American research university when she was unanimously selected by the board of trustees as the new president of Rensselaer Polytechnic Institute (RPI) in Troy, New York, the nation's first degree-granting technological university. Hoping to transform RPI into a research and technology powerhouse, Jackson secured a $360 million gift, built a new leadership team, and oversaw extensive campus renovations, including plans for an $80 million biotechnology and interdisciplinary studies center and a $142 million electronic media and performing arts center. Some in the RPI community, however, balked at what they described as Jackson's inaccessibility and her autocratic leadership style.

Jackson continued to play a significant role in shaping public policy for science and technology by sitting on the advisory council of the Institute of the Nuclear Power Operations, on numerous committees at the National Science Foundation, and on the boards and on various committees of the National Research Council and National Academy of Sciences. Jackson also became a member of the National Advisory Council for Biomedical Imaging and Bioengineering, a research institute established in 2000 as part of the National Institutes of Health that advises the Department of Health and Human Services.

A proponent of public-private partnerships and of uniting research universities and corporate laboratories, Jackson sits on the board of directors of FedEx, AT&T, Marathon Oil Corporation, Medtronic, and BEST (Building Engineering and Science Talent), and she has served as a trustee of Lincoln University, Georgetown University, Rockefeller University, Associated Universities, Inc., and the Brookings Institution. Jackson is an elected member of the American Physical Society, the American Academy of Arts and Sciences, and the National Academy of Engineering, of which she was the first black woman member. She has received eighteen honorary degrees and numerous awards, including the New Jersey Governor's Award in Science, the Thomas Alva Edison Award, and induction into the National Women's Hall of Fame in Seneca Falls, New York, and the Women in Technology International Foundation Hall of Fame.

In 2004 Jackson became the president of the American Association for the Advancement of Science (AAAS), the world's largest general scientific society. "Today's rapid scientific and technological advances are posing 'knife-edge' questions," she told the AAAS in April 2003. "How can we derive maximum benefit from scientific discovery, for example, without unleashing maximum danger? It is up to the science and engineering community to lead us through these critical times."

FURTHER READING

Current Biography (1999).

Jenkins, Edward Sidney. *To Fathom More: African American Scientists and Inventors* (1996).

—LISA E. RIVO

JACOBS, HARRIET

(c. 1813–7 Mar. 1897), autobiographer and reformer, was born into slavery in Edenton, North Carolina, the daughter of Elijah, a skilled slave carpenter, and Delilah, a house slave. In her slave narrative *Incidents in the Life of a Slave Girl: Written by Herself* (1861), published under the pseudonym Linda Brent, Jacobs explained that although it was illegal, she learned to read and to spell at six, when, after her mother's death, she was taken in by her mistress. When Jacobs reached puberty this

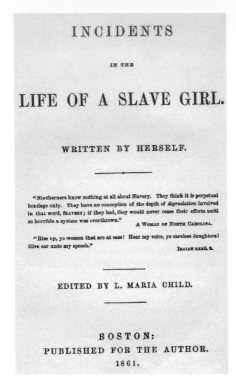

INCIDENTS

IN THE

LIFE OF A SLAVE GIRL.

WRITTEN BY HERSELF.

"Northerners know nothing at all about Slavery. They think it is perpetual bondage only. They have no conception of the depth of *degradation* involved in that word, SLAVERY; if they had, they would never cease their efforts until so horrible a system was overthrown."
A WOMAN OF NORTH CAROLINA.

"Rise up, ye women that are at ease! Hear my voice, ye careless daughters! Give ear unto my speech."
ISAIAH xxxii. 9.

EDITED BY L. MARIA CHILD.

BOSTON:
PUBLISHED FOR THE AUTHOR.
1861.

Incidents in the Life of a Slave Girl, 1861. University of North Carolina

mistress died, and she was willed to the woman's niece and sent into that child's home, where her new mistress's father subjected her to unrelenting sexual harassment. To save herself from concubinage, at sixteen she began a sexual liaison with a young white neighbor. (Called Mr. Sands in *Incidents*, he was Samuel Tredwell Sawyer, later a member of Congress.) This union produced a son and daughter. When she was twenty-one, her young mistress's father again threatened her with concubinage and, after she defied him, vowed to make her children plantation slaves. In June 1835 she ran away, hoping that instead of raising the children he would sell them and that their father would buy and free them. Her hopes were partially realized: the children were bought by their father, who permitted them to live with her grandmother, now a freedwoman, but he did not free them.

As a fugitive slave in the South, Jacobs hid for almost seven years in a tiny space under the roof of her grandmother's home. In June 1842 she escaped to Philadelphia. She was eventually reunited with her children in the North. In 1849 she joined an abolitionist circle in Rochester, New York. Jacobs wrote that after passage of the 1850 Fugitive Slave Law, she was sought by her North Carolina mistress but rejected an offer to buy her freedom: "The more my mind had become enlightened, the more difficult it was for me to consider myself an article of property; and to pay money to those who had so grievously oppressed me seemed like taking from my sufferings the glory of triumph" (*Incidents*, 199).

Despite her protest, in 1853 Jacobs was purchased from Mary Matilda Norcom Messmore by her New York employer, Cornelia Grinnell Willis, and she and her children were free from the threat of reenslavement. Persuaded to tell her story by Amy Post, a Rochester abolitionist and feminist friend, and after a futile attempt to enlist best-selling author Harriet Beecher Stowe as her amanuensis, Jacobs spent years writing her book. When she finished, the black writer and activist WILLIAM COOPER NELL introduced her to the white antislavery writer and activist Lydia Maria Child, who edited the manuscript and helped obtain financial backing from Boston abolitionists.

With the publication of *Incidents* in January 1861, Jacobs entered public life as "Linda, the slave girl." Praised in the black and reform press for its vivid dramatic power, her book appeared the following year in two London editions, one pirated. Renamed *The Deeper Wrong: Incidents in the Life of a Slave Girl, Written by Herself*, Jacobs's book won excellent reviews in mainstream newspapers such as the *Morning Star and Dial* (London), which heralded it as "the first personal narrative in which one of that sex upon whom chattel servitude falls with the deepest and darkest shadow described her own bitter experience" (10 Mar. 1862).

Had the Civil War not broken out, Jacobs might have followed other slave narrators onto the lecture platform. Instead, throughout the war and early postwar years she aided the "contraband," black refugees crowding behind the Union lines, by using her celebrity to raise money and supplies from northern sympathizers and to publish a series of newspaper reports on the condition of the refugees. In 1862 she did relief work in Washington, D.C.; the following year she and her daughter Louisa moved to Alexandria, Virginia, where with the help of the New England Freedman's Aid Society they established the Jacobs Free School.

Jacobs's philanthropic and reform efforts were acknowledged in 1864, when she was named to the executive committee of the Women's Loyal National League, headed by Elizabeth Cady Stanton and Susan B. Anthony. Jacobs and Louisa later continued their philanthropic work in Savannah, Georgia. In 1868 she sailed to London to raise money for an orphanage and old people's home. Welcomed by British reformers familiar with her *Deeper Wrong* and her newspaper reports from the South, Jacobs was successful at fundraising. Nevertheless, she recommended to her Quaker sponsors that the asylum not be built in Georgia, where the Ku Klux Klan was riding and burning.

When Jacobs returned to the United States with her daughter later in 1868 she retreated from public life. She moved first to Massachusetts and in 1877 to Washington, D.C., where, her health failing, she privately continued her work for the freed women and children.

Jacobs died of nephritis at her Washington home. She was eulogized by her longtime friend, Rev. FRANCIS J. GRIMKÉ, as "no reed shaken by the wind, vacillating, easily moved from a position. She did her own thinking; had opinions of her own, and held to them with great tenacity."

Incidents in the Life of a Slave Girl is the most important antebellum autobiography written by an African American woman. Although nineteenth-century readers recognized Harriet Jacobs as the pseudonymous "Linda," before the Harvard edition appeared in 1987 many twentieth-century scholars thought the book was white-authored fiction. Since then, it has been recognized as black-authored autobiography. Jacobs's pseudonymous slave narrative, which centers on her struggle against sexual oppression in slavery and on her efforts to win freedom, defied nineteenth-century taboos against women discussing their sexual experiences. Jacobs's public letters, published during the Civil War and Reconstruction, present a unique first-person account of the black war refugees and the freed people in the South.

FURTHER READING

Jacobs's papers are scattered in several collections. The most important are the Isaac and Amy Post Family Papers, University of Rochester, and the Dr. J. Norcom Papers,

North Carolina State Archives. Other sources include the Lydia Maria Child Papers (on microfilm); the Rochester Ladies' Anti-Slavery Society Papers, Clements Memorial Library, the University of Michigan; and the Julia Wilbur Papers, Haverford College.

Jacobs, Harriet. *Incidents in the Life of a Slave Girl*, ed. Jean Fagan Yellin (1987).

Andrews, William C. *To Tell a Free Story: The First Century of Afro-American Autobiography* (1986).

Foster, Frances Smith. *Written by Herself: Literary Production of African American Women, 1746–1892* (1993).

Garfield, Deborah M., and Rafia Zafar, eds. *Harriet Jacobs and Incidents in the Life of a Slave Girl* (1996).

Sterling, Dorothy, ed. *We Are Your Sisters: Black Women in the Nineteeth Century* (1984).

Yellin, Jean Fagan. *Women and Sisters* (1989).

—JEAN FAGAN YELLIN

JAMES, DANIEL, JR.

(11 Feb. 1920–25 Feb. 1978), U.S. Air Force officer, was born in Pensacola, Florida, the youngest child of Lillie Anna Brown, an educator, and Daniel James Sr., a laborer. Only six of the James's seventeen children were alive when Daniel was born. Considered "a gift" by his parents, Daniel began his education under the tutelage of his mother, who, disenchanted with the segregated Pensacola schools, opened her own school, the Lillie Anna James Private School. While Lillie Anna taught him arithmetic, patriotism, religion, English, spelling, physical education, literature, "good, common sense," and public speaking, his father stressed hard work, academic excellence, and perseverance in the face of racism.

Both parents provided homespun directives. According to his mother, there was an eleventh commandment: "Thou Shalt Not Quit. Prove that you can compete on an equal basis." Daniel's parents gave him the desire to succeed, the ability to enjoy the humor in life, and an appreciation of freedom and fair play, attributes that served him well. The drone of Navy aircraft flown from nearby Pensacola Naval Air Station helped mitigate the signs and realities of the Jim Crow South. The older

he became, the more Daniel watched the sky. As a teenager, he got to know the pilots at the local airfield, who took him up in old seaplanes and fighter aircraft in return for small chores.

At age thirteen Daniel left his mother's school and enrolled in Pensacola's Washington High School. Soon after, in a nod to his older brother Charles—a football star, college graduate, and teacher—Daniel announced that he would like to be called "Little Chappie—like my big brother!" (McGovern, 19).

Just before his high school graduation in 1937, Daniel's plans to attend college were nearly derailed by the death of his father. His mother and siblings, however, assured him that they would help with his tuition, and in September 1937 he enrolled at the Tuskegee Institute in Alabama. Unsure of his career goal, Daniel chose to major in physical education. Strong and more than six feet tall, he won acclaim as an athlete and student leader. His academic career, however, almost came to an end when he was expelled following a high-spirited escapade involving a few of his fellow students.

Luckily, he was saved when an experimental civilian flying training program at the college was instituted, to determine the feasibility of training African American men as military pilots under the government-sponsored Civilian Pilot Training Program. James qualified for training and began the career he had dreamed about, not only learning to fly but also teaching others in the Army Air Corps Aviation Cadet Program, some of whom would become members of the Tuskegee Airmen. In March 1942 he received a BS in Physical Education and completed his pilot training under the Civilian Pilot Training Program. He fell in love with Dorothy Watkins of Tuskegee, Alabama, in 1938. They married on 3 November 1942 and had two sons, Daniel III and Claude, and a daughter, Danice.

James enlisted in the Army Air Forces and was commissioned a second lieutenant in 1943. The military forces were rigidly segregated, and officers and enlisted men of color faced the tensions of racism in both civilian and military life. On one occasion James was arrested for staging a sit-in at a whites-only officers club. As the emcee of a

touring air force show called "Operation Happiness," James managed to get each base to desegregate their base theaters temporarily. When President Harry Truman declared racial segregation in the military illegal in 1948, it was exactly what Chappie James wanted to hear.

James completed fighter pilot combat training at Selfridge Field, Michigan. Assigned within the United States until September 1949, he was then stationed in the Philippines as a flight leader in the Twelfth Fighter Bomber Wing at Clark Field. In 1950 he was sent to Korea, where he flew 101 combat missions in F-51 and F-101 aircraft. On one day he was shot down, returned to his base aboard a marine tank, and then flew another mission. Upon his return to the United States in 1951, he was assigned to an all-weather jet fighter squadron (the Fifty-eighth Fighter-Interceptor Squadron). Against the backdrop of his stellar military work, he shone in community relations, which in 1954 garnered him the Massachusetts Junior Chamber of Commerce Young Man of the Year Award. Promoted to major in 1955, he became the first black officer to command an integrated 437th Fighter-Interceptor Squadron.

In 1957 he graduated from the Air Command and Staff College at Maxwell Air Force Base, Alabama, and became a staff officer in the Air Staff Division of the Deputy Chief of Staff for Operations. Transferred in July 1960 to the Royal Air Force Station at Bentwaters, England, he served first as assistant director of operations and then as director of operations for the Eighty-first Tactical Fighter Wing. He soon became commander of the Ninety-second Tactical Fighter Squadron and, later, deputy commander for operations for the Eighty-first Wing. In 1964 he was transferred to Davis-Monthan Air Force Base, Arizona, as director of operations with the 4453rd Combat Crew Training Wing. These assignments significantly broadened his expertise and experience with air force operations.

In 1966 James entered the Vietnam War as deputy commander for operations of the Eighth Tactical Fighter Wing, becoming vice commander for the wing in June 1967. He flew seventy-eight combat missions into North Vietnam against the most stubborn and dangerous defenses and was one of the leaders of the now famous Bolo MiG sweep, destroying seven Communist MiG-21s, the highest kill of any mission in that war. James was transferred to Florida and Eglin Air Force Base in 1967 and to Wheelus Air Base in Libya in 1969, where he commanded the 7272nd Fighter Training Wing. He became deputy assistant secretary of defense for public affairs in 1970 and principal deputy assistant secretary of defense in 1973.

Widely known for his speaking abilities, especially on the topics of Americanism and patriotism, James received notice both nationally and internationally. He was awarded the George Washington Freedom Foundation Medal twice in the 1960s and the Arnold Air Society Eugene M. Zuckert Award in 1970 for "outstanding contributions to Air Force professionalism" (quoted in Phelps, 345). The citation for this award recognizes him as a "fighter pilot with a magnificent record, public speaker, and eloquent spokesman for the American Dream we so rarely achieve" (Phelps, 345).

James was promoted to four-star general on 1 September 1975, becoming the first African American to hold the highest rank in the U.S. Air Force. In March 1977 he was assigned to the North American Air Defense Command as commander of the U.S. Air Force Aerospace Defense Command, with operational authority over American and Canadian strategic forces, a position that gave him the authority to initiate a nuclear attack. James retired from active service on 2 February 1978 and died less than one month later in the Air Force Academy Hospital, near Colorado Springs, Colorado.

FURTHER READING

Astor, Gerald. *The Right to Fight: A History of African Americans in the Military* (1998).

Dabbs, Henry E. *Black Brass: Black Generals and Admirals in the Armed Forces of the United States* (2nd ed. 1997).

McGovern, James R. *Black Eagle: General Daniel "Chappie" James, Jr.* (1985).

Phelps, Joseph A. *Chappie: America's First Black Four-Star General* (1992).

Rose, Robert A. *Lonely Eagles: The Story of America's Black Air Force in World War II* (1980).

Obituary: *New York Times*, 26 Feb. 1978.

—J. ALFRED PHELPS

 JAMISON, JUDITH
(10 May 1943–), dancer, educator, choreographer, and artistic director, was born in Philadelphia, Pennsylvania, the younger of two children of John Henry Jamison, a sheet-metal engineer, and Tessie Belle Brown. Judith's parents had left the racially segregated South during the great African American migration of the 1920s in search of a better way of life. Judith was born after the family had settled in the Germantown section of the city. The African American community in which she grew up built institutions that addressed the social, cultural, and political needs of its residents.

Judith's parents held high aspirations for their daughter and their son, John Henry Jr., and attendance at Mother Bethel African Methodist Episcopal Church was an integral part of family life. Judith's mother and father, who had met through their involvement in the church choir, made sure that their children were active in many youth groups. The Jamisons were a close-knit family with solid codes of behavior and a deep respect for critical thinking, education, and intellectual pursuits. Judith's upbringing included exposure to all the cultural institutions of the city and family outings to the opera, symphony, theaters, and museums. The Jamisons took advantage of black Philadelphia's rich cultural arts tradition, attending performances of the Dra Mu Opera Company and the Philadelphia Concert Orchestra, and participating in Heritage House Cotillions. Because both of her parents had once dreamed of becoming concert musicians, Judith studied piano and violin, and classical music filled the home.

Judith began formal dance classes at the age of six, when her mother enrolled her in the Judimar School of Dance, founded by Marion Cuyjet, a master ballet teacher who was prominent in the African American community. Judith was inquisitive, energetic, agile, and tall for her age, and dance became the perfect physical outlet. Hailed by her teacher as a prodigy, Judith displayed natural dance ability from the start. As a teenager, she studied ballet, tap, Caribbean, jazz, and modern dance and acrobatics with the teachers Delores Brown, John Hines, Joe Nash, Ernest Parham, and Anne Bernadino Hughes.

Judith progressed quickly and was given teaching responsibilities in addition to performing in numerous recitals. On occasion, she traveled with Cuyjet to study at professional dance studios in New York City. Judith's ballet debut was in 1959, at the age of fifteen, when she danced the role of Myrtha in *Giselle*.

After graduating from Germantown High School in 1962, Judith spent a year contemplating her future but never considered a dance career. In the early 1960s, at the suggestion of Cuyjet, she decided to attend Fisk University in Nashville, Tennessee. Judith's desire to dance was stronger than her interest in her academic studies, and after a year she returned home to the Philadelphia Dance Academy (presently known as the University of the Arts), with its dance curriculum that immersed students in ballet, modern dance, choreography, history, and notation. Judith augmented her studies by taking Horton technique at the studio of Joan Kerr, a noted Philadelphia modern dance teacher. She also attended a Philadelphia performance of the Alvin Ailey American Dance Theater (AAADT) while at the academy. The concert made a strong impression on her because of the virtuosic performances of ALVIN AILEY and one of his principal dancers, Minnie Marshall, and it was through this experience that she began to envision a career in dance.

In 1964 the choreographer Agnes de Mille discovered Jamison in a master class at the academy and invited her to come to New York to dance in American Ballet Theatre's (ABT) production of the *Four Marys*. She performed alongside the distinguished guest dancers Carmen de Lavallade, Cleo Quitman, and Glory van Scott. These black women were role models in a concert dance world slow to desegregate during a time of civil rights upheaval and the evolution of the Black Arts Movement. They followed in the path of KATHERINE DUNHAM and Pearl Primus by creating their own performance outlets in addition to supporting the work of emerging black choreographers with newly formed dance companies.

After Jamison's work with ABT ended, she found a temporary job at the World's Fair and then auditioned for the choreographer Donald McKayle for a HARRY BELAFONTE television special. She was not chosen for the production, but Alvin Ailey was present, noticed her potential immediately, and was quite taken with her statuesque beauty. In 1965 he invited her to join the second generation of AAADT, and she soon began one of the most celebrated dancers of the twentieth century.

Ailey and Jamison developed a close personal and professional relationship. He created many roles for her in major works, such as *Blues Suite* (1965), *Masekala Language* (1969), *Mary Lou's Mass* (1971), *Hidden Rites* (1973), and *The Mooche* (1975). She was known for her exquisite dancing style and majestic stage presence, with a performance delivery grounded in passion, lyricism, and spiritual fervor. In 1971 Ailey created his masterpiece *Cry*, which is dedicated to all black women, for Jamison to perform as a birthday present for his mother. The premiere was a definitive moment in Jamison's career, and the powerful performance and visual splendor moved the dance critic Clive Barnes to describe Jamison as "an African Goddess" (*New York Times*, 19 Nov. 1972). Her travels with AAADT took her throughout the United States and abroad, and the global exposure made her a sought-after guest performer with modern and ballet companies worldwide.

During the early years of her tenure with AAADT, Jamison met a fellow company member, the principal dancer Miguel Godreau. Born in Ponce, Puerto Rico, Godreau had attended New York's High School of Performing Arts and in 1967 joined Ailey's company. Four years later he and Jamison were married, but the union ended nine months later. In 1980, after fifteen years with AAADT, Jamison left to star in the hit Broadway musical *Sophisticated Ladies*. She maintained her association with the Ailey company and school and began developing her skills as a choreographer. In 1984 AAADT performed her first work, *Divining*, and in 1988 she returned to Philadelphia to form her own company, the Jamison Project. Her choreography, like Ailey's, is rooted in an African American aesthetic and uses a dance language that speaks to the universality of the human spirit.

Shortly before his death in 1989, Alvin Ailey asked Jamison to assume his duties as artistic director of AAADT. She disbanded the Jamison Project, returned to New York, and graciously accepted her charge to lead the company into

its fourth decade. She wanted to honor Ailey's mission to entertain, educate, and maintain a company dedicated to the preservation and enrichment of the American modern dance heritage.

Initially, her leadership role was extremely challenging. She inherited a company with mounting debt, but with the help of a new board of directors, a progressive fiscal plan was established. She made the difficult decision to release several veteran dancers and then added younger dancers to the company. Jamison maintained classic Ailey works as a staple of the repertoire and, with her eyes on the future, began showcasing more works by contemporary choreographers, such as Dwight Rhoden, Lynn Taylor-Corbett, Ronald K. Brown, Alonzo King, Jawole Willa Jo Zollar, Ulysses Dove, and Donald Bryd.

Jamison has evolved as a noted choreographer, adding several of her works to the AAADT repertoire, including *HERE. . . . NOW*, commissioned for the 2002 Cultural Olympiad; *Double Exposure*, for the Lincoln Center Festival (2000); *Echo: Far from Home* (1998); *Sweet Release* (1996); *Riverside* (1995); and *Hymn* (1993). She is the recipient of numerous awards and honorary doctorates; in 1999 she was chosen as a Kennedy Center honoree and in 2001 received the National Medal of Arts, the most prestigious award presented to artists in the United States.

Jamison's leadership has moved the AAADT organization to a position of financial stability and renewed artistic vitality. She has become a savvy businesswoman with adept public relations skills and an eloquent spokeswoman and ardent advocate for the arts in education. Affiliate programs that have flourished under Jamison's guidance include the AileyCamps for underserved youth, Arts-in-Education and Community Outreach, and the Ailey/Fordham University BFA degree program, which celebrated its first graduating class in 2002.

At the turn of the twenty-first century, Jamison spearheaded an ambitious campaign to build a permanent Manhattan home for AAADT that will serve as a testament to Ailey's vision of making dance accessible to all people. In 2004 it became the largest facility dedicated to dance in the United States. Jamison's journey from dancer, teacher, and choreographer to artistic director

has allowed her to emerge as one of the most influential contemporary visionaries in the performing arts.

FURTHER READING

Jamison, Judith. *Dancing Spirit: An Autobiography* (1993).

Dunning, Jennifer, with Howard Kaplan. *Alvin Ailey: A Life in Dance* (1996).

Haskins, James. *Black Dance in America* (1990).

Maynard, Olga. *Judith Jamison: Aspects of a Dancer* (1982).

White Dixon, Melanye. "Black Women in Concert Dance: The Philadelphia Divas" in *Black Women in America*, ed. Kim Marie Vaz (1995).

—MELANYE WHITE DIXON

JEFFERSON, BLIND LEMON (July 1897?– Dec. 1929), blues singer-guitarist, was born on a small farm near Wortham, Texas, the son of Alec Jefferson and Classie Banks, farmers. Because Jefferson was a poor, rural African American, few official documents exist to verify biographical details. Some researchers speculate that Jefferson, one of seven children, was born as early as 1880 (based on a studio portrait circa 1926 that reveals graying hair) and question the legend that he was blind from birth (printed in 1927 in *The Paramount Book of Blues*). Indeed, he may never have been totally blind, given stories about his ability to travel independently and to identify the denomination of paper money by its "feel."

One account dates Jefferson's performing career from around 1912, at parties and picnics and on the streets in Wortham, but he had moved to the streets, barrelhouses, and brothels of Waco and of the "Deep Ellum" area of Dallas by 1913. Around this time he may have worked as a wrestler and met singer-guitarist Huddie Ledbetter before LEAD BELLY, as the latter came to be known, went to prison in 1915. From that time into the 1920s, Jefferson remained the itinerant blues singer, hopping freights and traveling extensively, especially in many southern states, and playing at various social functions and, eventually, at house rent parties in Chicago. Around 1922 Jefferson married a woman named Roberta

Blind Lemon Jefferson, indisputably one of the most influential American musicians of the twentieth century. The Center for American History, The University of Texas at Austin

(last name unknown), later fathering a son, Miles, who also became a musician.

Jefferson's big career break came in 1925 when either Dallas dealer R. J. Ashford or pianist Sammy Price alerted J. Mayo Williams, manager of the "Race Artist Series" for Paramount Records, to Jefferson's talent. The peak years of the female vaudeville-blues artists were coming to an end by then. Paramount, seeking a followup to their success marketing male blues artist Papa Charlie Jackson, reaching the rural audience through their strong mail-order business, recorded Jefferson in Chicago in 1925. Though Jefferson was known as a blues performer, his first two recordings were spirituals, "Pure Religion" and "I Want to Be Like Jesus in My Heart." These were not issued until Jefferson had had four releases, and then under the thinly disguised pseudonym L. J. Bates. The name was also used for the 1928 release of his two other recorded religious songs, presumably because of Christians' antipathy to singers of what they sometimes termed Devil's music, the blues.

Jefferson's second session, circa March 1926, yielded his first two Paramount releases, the second of which, "Got the Blues"/"Long Lonesome Blues," garnered six-figure sales. Altogether Jefferson had eight Paramount releases in 1926, recording every few months for the next four years, and was

the company's premier blues artist for the rest of the decade. During those years Jefferson's ninety-four released sides (seven were unissued) on forty-three records reportedly sold in excess of one million copies. In 1927 his records were released at the rate of about one a month, and a special yellow and black label and photograph graced Paramount 12650, captioned "Blind Lemon's Birthday Record."

Jefferson's records enjoyed continuing popularity until and beyond the time of his death, despite his narrowing vocal range and the repetition of basic instrumental arrangements on many of his final recordings. Jefferson was officially listed as a porter living at Forty-fifth and State Streets in Chicago in 1928–1929, despite his continued popularity recording and performing. For example, he sang with a medicine show and with performer Rubin Lacy in Mississippi, where Jefferson reportedly refused twenty dollars to play a blues song because it was Sunday.

Jefferson died in Chicago under mysterious circumstances sometime in December 1929, possibly of a heart attack or exposure, or both, and perhaps abandoned by his chauffeur. There are various accounts left by various blues musicians. One story has an unknown woman cleaning out Jefferson's bank account and shipping his body to Mexia, Texas, while another has pianist Will Ezell accompanying his body for burial in the Wortham Negro Cemetery, in Freestone County, Texas, on New Year's Day 1930. A grave marker was finally placed in the cemetery and dedicated on 15 October 1967.

Jefferson is indisputably one of the most influential American musicians of the twentieth century. The primary catalyst for the recording of male blues performers, he provided a vocal and instrumental model for generations of blues, country, jazz, rhythm and blues, and rock performers. Emerging from the same milieu as Texas Alexander and Henry Thomas, two probably older performers who reflected the field holler and folk song traditions of Texas, Jefferson melded traditional songs and themes with a highly original, idiosyncratic style that galvanized his listeners. He combined high vocals with a percussive and complex polyrhythmic guitar style consisting of interspersed bass

runs and single-string treble riffs and arpeggios. His vast knowledge of traditional lyrics, increasingly modified by an original, poetic turn of mind, was so widely disseminated through recordings and appearances that his influence turns up in the work of blues performers of all styles and eras.

So great was Jefferson's popularity that many performers claim it a badge of honor to have seen, played with, or led him around on the streets. One who apparently did lead him, T-Bone Walker, adapted Jefferson's guitar style to an urbanized, large-band format that made Walker a seminal blues figure in the 1940s and shaped the guitar playing of B. B. KING. King recorded Jefferson's "Bad Luck Blues" and in turn became a major blues figure who influenced countless musicians. One of Jefferson's compositions, "Match Box Blues," has been recorded by blues artists, country performer Larry Hensely (1934), rockabilly's Carl Perkins (1955), and the Beatles (1964), among many others.

Immediately upon his death, Jefferson became a figure of mythical status. Reverend Emmet Dickinson's 1930 tribute compared him to Christ, while Walter Taylor and John Byrd's flip-side tribute also lamented his death, albeit in less grandiose terms. Roark Bradford's 1931 novel *John Henry* employed Jefferson as the archetypical blues singer/sage. But behind the mythologizing is the reality of his greatness—his originality, virtuosity, and intensity—recognized by literary artists such as LANGSTON HUGHES and STERLING BROWN, critics, and fans. He has entered the American consciousness to the extent that his face has appeared on T-shirts, sweatshirts, and matchbox covers. Jefferson is a member of the Blues Hall of Fame.

Blues performer Tom Shaw stated it simply: "He was the King."

FURTHER READING

Dixon, R. M. W., and John Godrich. *Blues and Gospel Records 1902–1942* (1982).
Evans, David. *Big Road Blues* (1982).
Groom, Bob. *Blind Lemon Jefferson* (1970).
Harris, Sheldon. *Blues Who's Who* (1979).

Discography
Complete Recorded Works in Chronological Order (vols. 1–4, Document DOCD 5017–5020).

—STEVEN C. TRACY

JEFFERSON, MILDRED FAY

JEFFERSON, MILDRED FAY (6 Apr. 1927–), physician and political activist, was born in Carthage, Texas, the only child of Millard Jefferson, a Methodist minister, and his wife, a schoolteacher whose maiden name was Roberts. Many aspects of Jefferson's life, including her mother's name and her early history, are difficult to determine, as she vigorously guards her privacy. However, a few sketchy details do emerge. In describing her childhood in Carthage, a small town in East Texas, Jefferson has noted, "My family never had any money as such, but they represented the top of the limited social structure in which we lived" (Merton, 125). Her mother's family, the Robertses owned property and donated the land for the Methodist church where Jefferson and her family worshipped. After graduating from the segregated schools of East Texas, Jefferson entered Texas College in Tyler, an institution established in 1894 by the Colored Methodist Episcopal Church. She received her BA in 1945.

Jefferson has stated that the motto "Decide what you want to do most, then set out to do it," has guided her life (Klemesrud, 44). This motto underscores the steely determination required for her to become a physician at a time when, according to the 1940 census, black women accounted for only 129 of the approximately 165,000 physicians in the United States. It is not known what prompted Jefferson's interest in medicine, but once she made her career choice, she pursued it passionately. After her graduation from Texas College, she moved to Boston to take premedical courses at Tufts University. In fall 1947 she became the first African American woman to enter Harvard Medical School, two years after it had admitted its first woman. In 1850 the medical school had admitted three black male students, including MARTIN R. DELANY, the black nationalist and later Civil War army officer. However, they were dismissed after just one semester after white students protested their admission.

When Jefferson entered Harvard Medical School, it was still uncommon for African Americans to receive their medical education outside of Howard University in Washington, D.C., or Meharry Medical School in Nashville, Tennessee. In 1948, 84 percent of the first-year black medical students enrolled at a black medical school attended either Meharry or Howard. Little is known about Jefferson's years at Harvard except that she received financial assistance from a Boston synagogue and graduated in 1951, eighty-two years after Edwin C. J. T. Howard was the first African American male to graduate from Harvard Medical School, and 169 years after the first white male to do so. Upon graduation, Jefferson applied for a residency in surgery at Boston City Hospital. At the time it was rare for any woman to pursue a residency in the male-dominated specialty of surgery. Not until 1968 did the American Board of Surgery certify a black woman, Dr. Hughenna L. Gauntlett. Four years later, two more African American women physicians, including Mildred Jefferson, received their board certification.

After completing her residency, Jefferson accepted a position as assistant clinical professor of surgery at Boston University Medical Center. She later became the first black woman elected to membership in the prestigious Boston Surgical Society. In 1963 she married Shane Cunningham, a real estate manager whom she met on a skiing trip to New Hampshire. Up until 1970 Jefferson lived quietly in Boston with her husband, maintaining her clinical practice and fulfilling her teaching responsibilities.

In 1970, however, Jefferson moved from the operating theater to the political arena when the annual meeting of the American Medical Association passed a resolution liberalizing sanctions against members who performed abortions. Jefferson joined a group of physicians who unsuccessfully opposed the resolution, which held that it was not unethical for physicians to perform abortions if the procedure were legal in their state. Upon her return to Massachusetts, Jefferson began what became a lifelong campaign against abortion. She helped establish the Value of Life Committee, an organization whose objective was to provide educational materials against abortion. However, the organization learned that it would have to have to enter a political struggle against abortion when in a November 1972 election, seventeen communities in Massachusetts voted in favor of a nonbinding referendum that liberalized abortion. Leaders of the committee, including Jefferson, decided to form a more activist organization, the Massachusetts Citizens for Life, a coalition of local pro-life groups.

Roe v. Wade, the 1973 United States Supreme Court decision that legalized abortion, provided a call to arms for pro-life activists and marked the rapid ascendancy of Jefferson to the national spotlight. In 1973 she joined the board of the National Right to Life Committee (NRLC) and within the year was named chairperson of the board. The primary objective of the NRLC was to ban abortion, but it also saw its mission to protect life before and after birth, especially for vulnerable populations. In January 1975 Jefferson served as an expert prosecution witness during the trial of Dr. Kenneth Edelin, an African American physician from Boston who had been charged with manslaughter for performing a third trimester abortion. The jury found Edelin guilty, but his conviction was later reversed by the Massachusetts Supreme Judicial Court.

Jefferson believes that life begins at conception and that abortions should not be performed under any conditions, including rape and incest. She has attributed her pro-life activism in part to her belief that abortion was tantamount to genocide for African Americans, and has claimed that "abortionists have done more to get rid of generations and cripple others than all of the years of slavery and lynching" (*Ebony*, April 1978, 88). Jefferson has also contended that it is her obligation as a physician to oppose abortion "because the Hippocratic oath represented a point at which the killing and curing function of the doctor was separated." Furthermore, she stated, "I know if I do not exercise my right as a physician to say 'no,' then maybe my silence will be interpreted as consent" (Timiraos). Jefferson sees herself not as an antiabortion activist, but as a pro-life one. "My objective is not to stop abortion," she has argued. "My objective is to restore the right to live to the Constitution. I am a right to life activist. I am not an anti-abortionist" (Blenkinsopp, "Speaker Clarifies Right to Life Movement," Harvard *Crimson*, 29 November 2001).

In June 1975, six months after her testimony in the Edelin trial, Jefferson was elected president of the NRLC, whose members were overwhelmingly white and Catholic. The election of Jefferson, a black Methodist woman, signaled the NRLC's intention to broaden its constituency and declare its autonomy from the Catholic Church. By 1978 the organization claimed approximately 2,800 chapters and one million members but, despite Jefferson's prominence, the organization remained predominantly white (Klemesrud, 44).

Jefferson emerged as an eloquent, politically astute, uncompromising, and formidable president. She crisscrossed the country advocating her views and did not hesitate to confront those who disagreed with them. Under her leadership the NRLC became a powerful political organization. It played a critical role in the 1976 passage through Congress of the Hyde Amendment, which prohibits federal Medicaid funding for abortion except when a woman's life is endangered. NRLC also launched its campaign for a Human Life Amendment to the U.S. Constitution that would prohibit all abortions. During Jefferson's presidency, the NRLC also established the NRLC Pro-Life Legal Action Project to fund legal strategies to reverse *Roe v. Wade*. Jefferson served three one-year terms as president of NRLC until political infighting forced her ouster in 1978 (Merton, 213).

Jefferson severed all her ties with the NRLC in 1980 but vigorously continued her activism in the pro-life movement, establishing her own organization, the Right-to-Life Crusade, of which she is president. She also remains active with Massachusetts Citizens for Life, the organization that she helped to found, and the Americans United for Life Legal Defense Fund. Jefferson's husband shared her pro-life views and participated in NRLC activities. However, by 1981 the couple, who had no children, had ended their marriage.

Jefferson's political activism has extended beyond the pro-life arena. She ran unsuccessfully in Massachusetts as a Republican candidate for the U.S. Senate in 1982, 1984, 1988, and 1990. In the 1990s she became chairman of the Citizens Select Committee on Public Health Oversight, which promotes moral education and abstinence. The committee grew out of Jefferson's opposition to the 1993 nomination of JOYCELYN ELDERS

as surgeon general, who was pro-choice. Jefferson has also become a popular speaker in conservative circles, speaking out against feminism, physician-assisted suicide, and secular humanism. *Conservative Digest* has called her one of the ten most admired conservative women.

In 2002 Jefferson emerged as a possible candidate for a position on a federal advisory committee on the protection of human subjects. The nomination arose as part of an effort of President George W. Bush to include fetuses under federal guidelines for human research. Although Jefferson was ultimately not named to the committee, her nomination demonstrates that she still continues to be an influential figure in conservative political circles.

FURTHER READING

Jefferson, Mildred F. "Introduction" in *Back to the Drawing Board: The Future of the Pro-Life Movement*, ed. Teresa R. Wagner (2003).

Klemesrud, Judy. "Abortion in the Campaign: Methodist Surgeon Leads the Opposition," *New York Times*, 1 March 1976, 44.

Merton, Andrew H. *Enemies of Choice: The Right-to-Life Movement and Its Threat to Abortion* (1981).

Sterling, Rosalyn P. "Female Surgeons: The Dawn of a New Era" in *A Century of Black Surgeons: The USA Experience*, ed. Claude H. Organ Jr. and Margaret M. Kosiba (1987).

Timiraos, Nick. "*Roe V. Wade* 30th Anniversary Prompts Conferences, Protests," *The Hoya* (24 Jan. 2003).
—VANESSA NORTHINGTON GAMBLE

 JEMISON, MAE

(17 Oct. 1956–), astronaut and physician, was born Mae Carol Jemison in Decatur, Alabama, the daughter of Charlie Jemison, a carpenter and roofer, and Dorothy Jemison, a teacher whose maiden name is unknown. After living the first three and a half years of her life in Alabama near the Marshall Space Flight Center, Mae moved to Chicago with her parents and older siblings, Rickey and Ada Sue. When her family experienced trouble with local gangs, they moved to another section of the city, where Mae immersed herself in her schoolwork. An avid reader,

she also was inspired by role models in the media, such as Lieutenant Uhura, a black woman astronaut portrayed by the actress Nichelle Nichols in the 1960s television series *Star Trek*. At a time when all astronauts were white and male, even a fictional character such as Lieutenant Uhura had a positive impact on Jemison. "A lot of times, fantasy is what gets us through to reality," Mae later said (Katz, 38). An outstanding student, active in student government and arts organizations, Mae excelled in science and graduated from Morgan Park High School in 1973.

She entered Stanford University at age sixteen, in part, she confessed, because of the renown of their football team. Unfortunately, Jemison did not feel entirely welcomed by the Stanford science faculty, whom she believed underestimated or ignored her. "The majority of physical science professors pushed me away," she later recalled (Jemison, 123). These chilly rebuffs did not deter her, however, and Jemison continued to study science and engineering while also enrolling in many African and Afro-American studies classes. She viewed her courses in the social sciences as vital, she recalled, "because I was unconsciously balancing the poor reception I often received in the science and engineering departments with the embrace of political science" (Jemison, 123). Jemison graduated in 1977 with a BS in Chemical Engineering.

After leaving Stanford, Jemison entered Cornell University Medical College (now Weill Cornell Medical College) in New York City. While in medical school, she also took modern dance classes in the city and became a great fan of the ALVIN AILEY dance troupe, particularly the dancer JUDITH JAMISON. During the summers between her second and third years in medical school, Jemison received a grant from the International Travelers Association and traveled to Cuba, Kenya, and Thailand, providing medical care. The experience deeply affected Jemison, whose attention to scientific and social concerns in the United States expanded to include international issues. She graduated with her medical degree in 1981 and returned to California as a medical intern at Los Angeles County/University of Southern California Medical Center in 1982.

Mae Jemison floats weightless in the Spacelab, 1992. © Roger Ressmeyer/CORBIS

From 1983 to 1985 Jemison served as the area Peace Corps medical officer in Sierra Leone and Liberia. She supervised the pharmacy and laboratory and established guidelines for public health and safety issues. She also collaborated with the National Institutes for Health and the Centers for Disease Control in the United States, researching hepatitis B vaccines and conducting studies of rabies and infectious diseases such as schistosomiasis, which is widespread in rural areas of Africa. She returned to the United States in 1985 to work as a general practitioner in Los Angeles.

Always curious and eager to embark on new paths, Jemison continued to take graduate classes in engineering while practicing medicine, and eventually she became interested in applying to the astronaut program of the National Aeronautics and Space Administration (NASA). Jemison found NASA's early prohibition on women astronauts "nonsensical" (Jemison, 171) and first applied to the astronaut corps less than a decade after the space agency began accepting female candidates in 1978.

NASA accepted Jemison on her second application, and she become one of fifteen astronauts selected from more than two thousand applicants. She was the first woman of color and the fifth African American astronaut in NASA's history. Beginning her training in August 1987, Jemison was part of the first class of astronauts to be selected after the 1986 *Challenger* accident. She told reporters that she was not daunted by the prospect of danger, but remained committed to the challenges of space exploration for the unique knowledge it provides. Dr. Joseph D. Atkinson Jr., a member of the astronaut board that selected Jemison and chief of NASA's Equal Opportunity Programs Office, was struck not only by Jemison's commitment to science but also by her social awareness. He found her scientific skill and sensitivity "to the social needs of the community" a formidable combination of abilities (Marshall, 54).

On 12 September 1992 Jemison rocketed into space aboard the space shuttle *Endeavor*. Her mission, STS 47, was a joint project of the United States and Japan. Jemison's duties as a mission specialist involved life-science experiments focusing on bone cell research and other technical assignments, including verification of the shuttle computer software in the Shuttle Avionics Integration Laboratory (SAIL). Among the personal objects Jemison elected to take on board with her were an Alvin Ailey dance poster, a statue from Sierra Leone, a certificate from Chicago schoolchildren pledging to improve their math and science skills, and a MICHAEL JORDAN jersey from the Chicago Bulls basketball team. Jemison noted that the items she brought along suggested that "space is a birthright for all of us on this planet" (Katz, 40). During her eight-day mission, Jemison orbited the earth 127 times and logged 190 hours, 30 minutes, and 23 seconds in outer space. Her first mission in space was also her last. After six years with the space agency, Jemison resigned from NASA the following year to start her own technology companies and explore teaching interests.

In 1993 Jemison founded the Jemison Group, Inc., a business that focused on, in her words, "integrating social issues with technology designs" (Jemison, 172). The Jemison Group has been involved in projects involving thermal electricity and the use of satellite-based telecommunications to facilitate health care in West Africa. A year later Jemison established The Earth We Share, an annual science camp, which attracts children aged twelve to sixteen from around the world. She also served as professor of environmental studies at Dartmouth College from 1995 to 2002 and, while at Dartmouth, founded another scientific research company, BioSentient Corporation, which investigates the application of techniques for controlling motion sickness and other medical problems.

In 2001 Jemison wrote an autobiography for young adults, *Find Where the Wind Goes*, in which she highlights episodes in her life that inspired or changed her. She has been involved in other media projects, including science programs on PBS and the Discovery channel. Fulfilling a childhood dream, she also appeared on *Star Trek: The Next Generation* during an episode entitled

"Second Chances." In 2004, Jemison is the A. D. White Professor at Large at Cornell University. She speaks on scientific literacy and the need to increase the numbers of women and minorities in science and technology.

Mae Jemison has been honored with awards from the National Women's Hall of Fame and the National Academy of Sciences Institute of Medicine. She holds honorary doctorates from Princeton University, Lincoln College (Pennsylvania), and Winston-Salem College (North Carolina). In 1999 she was selected as one of the seven most qualified women to be President of the United States by the White House Project, an organization which seeks to eliminate the glass ceiling for women in business and politics. Now residing in Houston, Texas, Jemison continues to work toward the understanding that scientific progress and social equity are inextricably linked.

FURTHER READING

Jemison, Mae. *Find Where the Wind Goes: Moments from My Life* (2001).

Atkinson, Joseph D., and Jay M. Shafritz. *The Real Stuff: A History of NASA's Astronaut Recruitment Program* (1985).
Katz, Jesse. "Shooting Star." *Stanford Today*, July/Aug. 1996.
Marshall, Marilyn. "Child of the 60s Set to Become First Black Woman in Space." *Ebony* 44 (Aug. 1989).

—MARTHA ACKMANN

JOHNS, VERNON NAPOLEON

(22 Apr. 1892–10 June 1965), Baptist pastor and civil rights pioneer, was born in Darlington Heights, near Farmville, Prince Edward County, Virginia, the son of Willie Johns, a Baptist preacher and farmer, and Sallie Branch Price. At age three, according to family tradition, young Vernon began preaching "on the doorstep or on a stump." Two years later he went with his older sister Jessie to a one-room school four miles from the Johnses' home. At seven, Vernon was kicked in the face by a mule. The injury scarred his left cheek, damaged his eyesight, and caused his left eyelid to twitch throughout his life. Johns later compensated for his weak eyesight by committing long passages of poetry and Scripture to memory.

For several years after 1902, Jessie and Vernon Johns attended the Boydton Institute, a Presbyterian mission school near Boydton, Virginia, but the death of their father in 1907 brought Johns back to the family farm. Two years later he was nearly killed by the horns of a bull. Shortly thereafter Johns left the family home to study at Virginia Theological Seminary and College in Lynchburg, where he received an AB in 1915. Admitted to the Oberlin School of Religion, Johns became the student pastor of a small Congregational church in Painesville, Ohio. While at Oberlin, Johns was offered a scholarship to Western Reserve Law School, but he felt that the ministry was his vocation. After giving the annual student oration at Oberlin's Memorial Arch in 1918, Johns received a BD from the Oberlin School of Religion and was ordained in the Baptist ministry.

In 1918 Vernon Johns began teaching homiletics and New Testament at Virginia Theological Seminary and became a graduate student in theology at the University of Chicago. Continuing to teach at the seminary, he became the pastor of Lynchburg's Court Street Baptist Church, where he served from 1920 to 1926. Economic self-help in African American communities was a persistent theme in Johns's ministry, and, at Court Street Church, he persuaded the men's Bible class to launch a grocery store. In 1926 Vernon Johns preached for the first of many times at Howard University's Rankin Memorial Chapel, became the first African American preacher to have a sermon, "Transfigured Moments," published in Joseph Fort Newton's *Best Sermons* series, and was named director of the Baptist Educational Center of New York City. A year later he married Altona Trent, the daughter of William Johnson Trent, the president of Livingstone College in Salisbury, North Carolina. Vernon and Altona Trent Johns became the parents of six children.

In 1929 Johns left New York to become president of Virginia Theological Seminary and College. In that capacity he founded an Institute for Rural Preachers of Virginia, which he conducted for ten years, and the Farm and City Club, which promoted economic ties between urban and rural African Americans. In 1933 Johns was pastor of

Holy Trinity Baptist Church in Philadelphia, Pennsylvania. He retired from the college presidency in September 1934 to his farm in Prince Edward County, where he lived until 1937. During those years Johns farmed, cut and sold pulpwood, operated a grocery store in Darlington Heights, and traveled, lecturing and preaching on the black church and college circuits. He launched the struggle to get school buses for African American students in Prince Edward County. Altona Trent Johns supplemented the family income by teaching public school in a one-room public school four miles from the family home.

In 1937 Johns became the pastor of First Baptist Church in Charleston, West Virginia. A former college president, the published pastor of an important African American congregation, and son-in-law of a college president, Vernon Johns seemed bound to a secure position in the African American elite. Yet he was rooted in the hard economic realities of Prince Edward County and grew contemptuous of the social pretense of the black bourgeoisie. As pastor of Charleston's First Baptist Church, he supplemented his income as a fishmonger. "I don't apologize for it," he later told students at Howard University, "because for every time I got one call about religion, I got forty calls about fish." It was a pattern Johns would repeat. In 1941 he returned to Lynchburg as pastor of Court Street Baptist Church.

In January 1948, months after Altona Trent Johns joined the faculty of Alabama State College in Montgomery, Vernon Johns was called as the pastor of that city's Dexter Avenue Baptist Church. He renewed his credentials as the publishing pastor of a leading African American congregation with an essay, "Civilized Interiors," in Herman Dreer's *American Literature by Negro Authors* in 1950, but he antagonized local white authorities with sermons such as "Segregation after Death," "It's Safe to Murder Negroes in Montgomery," and "When the Rapist Is White" and by summoning black passengers to join him in a protest of racial discrimination by walking off a bus in Montgomery.

In 1951, when his father-in-law became the first African American appointed to the Salisbury, North

Carolina, school board, Vernon Johns's sixteen-year-old niece, Barbara Johns, led African American students at R. R. Moton High School in Farmville, Virginia, in a boycott to protest conditions in Prince Edward County's schools. A month later attorneys for the National Association for the Advancement of Colored People filed suit to desegregate the county schools. That summer Barbara Johns left Prince Edward County to live with her aunt and uncle and spend her senior year of high school in Montgomery, Alabama. By then, however, Vernon Johns was antagonizing his own congregation's bourgeois sensibilities with sermons such as "Mud Is Basic" and by hawking produce at church functions. After four stormy years at Dexter Avenue, the deacons accepted one of Vernon Johns's resignation threats in the summer of 1952. Altona Johns left Montgomery for a position at Virginia State College in Petersburg, but her husband thought the deacons would relent and sequestered himself in the parsonage. When the trustees cut off its electricity, gas, and water in December 1952, Johns finally left Montgomery. In 1954 MARTIN LUTHER KING JR. took charge of Dexter Avenue Baptist Church.

Vernon Johns was never the pastor of a church again. From 1953 to 1955 he shuttled between his Prince Edward County farm, where he raised livestock, and his wife's home in Petersburg, where he became a mentor to Wyatt Tee Walker, the pastor of Gillfield Baptist Church. Between 1955 and 1960 Johns was director of the Maryland Baptist Center, but he was asked to resign after a public rebuke to white Baptist clergymen in Baltimore for their failure of nerve in race relations. Briefly in 1961 Johns edited and published *Second Century Magazine*. After preaching his last sermon, "The Romance of Death," in Howard University's Rankin Chapel, Vernon Johns died in Washington, D.C.

FURTHER READING

Branch, Taylor. *Parting the Waters: America in the King Years, 1954–63* (1988).
Evans, Zelia S., with J. T. Alexander, eds. *Dexter Avenue Baptist Church, 1877–1977* (1977).
Gandy, Samuel L., ed. *Human Possibilities: A Vernon Johns Reader, Including an Unfinished Ms., Sermons, Essays, and Doggerel* (1977).
Smith, Robert Collins. *They Closed Their Schools: Prince Edward County, Virginia, 1951–1964* (1965).

Obituary: *Jet*, 22 July 1965.

—RALPH E. LUKER

JOHNSON, CHARLES SPURGEON (24 July 1893–27 Oct. 1956), sociologist and college president, was born in Bristol, Virginia, the eldest of six children of Charles Henry Johnson, a Baptist minister, and Winifred Branch. Because there was not a high school for blacks in Bristol, he moved to Richmond and attended the Wayland Academy. In 1913 Johnson entered college at Virginia Union in Richmond, and graduated in only three years. While at college, Johnson volunteered with the Richmond Welfare Association, and one incident there had a profound impact on his future career. During the holiday season, while delivering baskets to needy people, he came across a young woman lying on a pile of rags, groaning in labor. Although none of the doctors in the area would help the young woman, Johnson persuaded a midwife to deliver the baby. He then tried to locate a home for the young woman, but those he approached shut the door in his face. Some families rejected the young woman because she was black and others because, in their eyes, she had sinned. Edwin Embree, Johnson's longtime friend, once noted that Johnson could not get the image of the young woman out of his mind and could not "cease pondering the anger of people at human catastrophe while they calmly accept conditions that caused it" (*Thirteen against the Odds* [1944], 214).

In 1916 Johnson moved north to pursue a PhD at the University of Chicago, which at that time employed some of the world's most prominent sociologists. It was there that he would meet his lifetime mentor, Robert E. Park. As a result of this relationship, many of Johnson's writings and approaches to race relations bear the mark of the eminent Chicago researcher. Johnson interrupted his studies to enlist in the military in 1918, but upon returning to Chicago a year later, he found himself in the middle of one of the most horrific race riots in U.S. history.

This incident sparked Johnson's involvement with the Chicago Race Relations Commission; as associate executive secretary for that body, he was largely responsible for the writing of *The Negro in Chicago: A Study of Race Relations and a Race Riot* (1922). With this publication, Johnson spearheaded a tradition of social science research that described changes in race relations as cycles of tension and resolution, largely caused by outside forces. Although partly based on the work of Park, Johnson's version of this sociological model envisioned a wider role for human intervention; in particular, he believed that government could influence this process. Johnson's work with the Chicago Race Relations Commission also introduced him to Julius Rosenwald, the Sears and Roebuck tycoon and creator of the Julius Rosenwald Fund (which assisted with the establishment of black schools in the South and provided scholarships to talented black intellectuals).

Johnson married Marie Antoinette Burgette on 6 November 1920. Johnson moved with his wife to New York City, where he became the director of research and investigations for the National Urban League. During this period he also edited the league's journal, *Opportunity*, and published short stories and poems by several prominent Harlem Renaissance authors, including, LANGSTON HUGHES, COUNTÉE CULLEN, AARON DOUGLAS, and ZORA NEALE HURSTON. Johnson also used his well-established connections to white philanthropists to secure financial support for black literature and art. In his view, promoting culture was a way of combating racism.

The sociologist Blyden Jackson, Johnson's colleague while he was attending Fisk University in Nashville, Tennessee, credits him with helping to "ease the transformation of more than one neophyte in the arts, like a Zora Neale Hurston, from a nonentity into a luminary of the Renaissance" (*Southern Review* 25.4 [1990], 753). Indeed, both Jackson and ALAIN LOCKE point to a 1924 dinner Johnson hosted in New York as one of the most important contributions to the Renaissance. With over three hundred people from both the white and black worlds in attendance (including Locke, JAMES WELDON JOHNSON, William

Baldwin III, JESSIE FAUSET, Countée Cullen, Albert Barnes, and W. E. B. DU BOIS), the event helped many black poets, artists, and writers find mainstream publishers and venues for their endeavors. For Johnson, events like this dinner were part of a carefully planned effort to improve opportunities for African Americans in the 1920s in ways that had not been possible during the nadir of race relations before World War I.

Near the close of the Renaissance in 1928, Charles Johnson returned south to Nashville to chair the Department of Social Sciences at Fisk University. Supported by a grant from the Laura Spelman Rockefeller Memorial, the department was set up with the idea that Johnson would be its leader. Armed with solid connections and ample funding, he brought many important individuals to the Fisk campus, including STERLING BROWN, James Weldon Johnson, HORACE MANN BOND, Robert E. Park, E. FRANKLIN FRAZIER, Arna Bontemps, and Aaron Douglas. Along with his colleagues in the social sciences, Johnson published widely. It was during this time that he produced some of his best known works, such as *Shadow of the Plantation* (1934), *Growing Up in the Black Belt* (1938), and *Patterns of Negro Segregation* (1942). Johnson also created an internationally renowned race relations institutes at Fisk, which brought together leaders, scholars, and ordinary citizens from throughout the United States and the world to discuss race relations in an integrated setting. Despite suffering extensive criticism locally, especially from the segregationist *Nashville Banner*, the institutes and Johnson's leadership drew great prominence to Fisk and to Johnson as an individual.

In 1946, at time when Fisk was experiencing a leadership crisis, its board of trustees considered selecting the first black candidate to lead the institution. Given his international stature and administrative skills, Johnson seemed like the most obvious candidate, but several of the alumni, including Fisk's most prominent graduate, Du Bois, spoke out vehemently against his selection. Johnson's close ties to philanthropy, including the Whitney, Ford, and Rosenwald foundations, made him suspect in their minds. For this group, the foundations were forever tainted by their previous efforts to promote an industrial curriculum at black colleges. Despite this

opposition, the financial needs of Fisk prevailed over ideology, and Johnson was inaugurated president in 1947; the board of trustees had recognized Johnson's success in advancing and improving Fisk's race relations institutes through his fundraising efforts and believed that he might similarly ensure progress for the university as a whole.

In his role as president, Johnson created the Basic College Early Entry Program. Although Johnson was a proponent of integration, he doubted that it would occur quickly and thus was inspired to initiate a program to nurture young black minds within the black college setting. The Basic College offered students a cohesive learning environment in which they benefited from the knowledge and experience of literary, artistic, and political figures that Johnson invited to campus in the years before his death in 1956. The program produced such figures as the Pulitzer Prize–winning author DAVID LEVERING LEWIS, HAZEL O'LEARY, energy secretary during the administration of President Bill Clinton, and Spelman College president JOHNNETTA COLE.

In addition to his university-related service, Johnson served as a trustee for the Julius Rosenwald Fund from 1933 to 1948, working specifically as the co-director of the fund's race-relations program. From 1944 to 1950 he acted as the director of the race-relations division of the American Missionary Association. Concurrently with his foundation work, Johnson conducted research for the federal government and worked as a cultural ambassador. As a member of the New Deal's Committee on Farm Tenancy, Johnson supported President Franklin Roosevelt's efforts to end poverty and racism in the rural South. After World War II, under the direction of President Harry Truman, Johnson was one of ten U.S. delegates for the first United Nations Educational, Scientific, and Cultural Organization (UNESCO) conference in Paris. And he assisted President Dwight Eisenhower by serving on the Board of Foreign Scholarships under the Fulbright-Hays Act.

Johnson spent a lifetime cultivating black scholarship, creativity, and leadership and used research and culture as tools to fight racism. As he grew older, however, the pressure generated by his many obligations began to take its toll:

his migraine headaches worsened, and he developed a heart condition. On 27 October 1956, on the way to a board meeting in New York, Johnson died of a heart attack on the train platform in Louisville, Kentucky, at age sixty-three.

Although Johnson's professional training and early practical experience in race relations were in the urban North, he chose to address race relations in the South, thereby differentiating himself from Du Bois and other black intellectuals. He was not a radical, but rather a diplomat who, through his collaborations, realized many of the ideas of thinkers more radical than he.

FURTHER READING

Charles S. Johnson's personal and professional papers are located in the Special Collections at Fisk University, Nashville, Tennessee.

Gasman, Marybeth. "W. E. B. Du Bois and Charles S. Johnson: Opposing Views on Philanthropic Support for Black Higher Education." *History of Education Quarterly* 42.4 (Winter 2002).
Gilpin, Patrick J., and Marybeth Gasman. *Charles S. Johnson: Leadership behind the Veil in the Age of Jim Crow* (2003).
Robbins, Richard. *Sidelines Activist: Charles S. Johnson and the Struggle for Civil Rights* (1996).

Obituary: *New York Times*, 28 Oct. 1956.
—MARYBETH GASMAN

 JOHNSON, FRANCIS (1792–6 Apr. 1844), bandleader, composer, multi-instrumentalist, and teacher, was probably born in Martinique, West Indies, to parents whose names are unknown. He settled in Philadelphia in 1809. While there is little historical record of Francis "Frank" Johnson's early life, it is known that three key figures helped young Francis hone his prodigious music skills: Matt Black, an African American bandleader from Philadelphia, P. S. Gilmore, "the father of the American band", and Richard Willis, the director of the West Point military band.

That Johnson played many instruments is clear from a student's observations of his studio, which housed "instruments of all kinds. . . . Bass drum, bass viol, bugles and trombones" (*A Gentleman of Much Promise: The Diary*

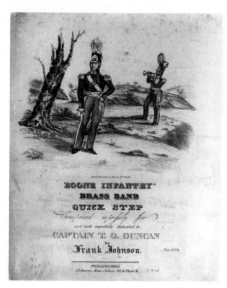

"Boone Infantry Brass Band Quick Step," 1844. Library of Congress

of Isaac Mickle 1837–1845, 196). While Johnson was an accomplished French horn player, he is best known as a virtuoso on both the violin and the Kent, or keyed bugle, which was used in orchestras and for martial music. The keyed bugle is much like a traditional bugle, but curved and with six keys that enable the instrument to cover a wide scale. Much American music in the antebellum period centered around military bands, with brigades often contracting their own ensembles. The War of 1812, in which African Americans fought, allowed blacks greater access to military bands. Johnson reportedly played in Matthew Black's band following the war and studied with Richard Willis before leading Philadelphia's Third Company of Washington Guards in 1815. By 1818, when Johnson was only twenty-six, he published *Six Setts of Cotillions.* These classical marches were the first music pieces ever to be published by an African American. Johnson's stature grew in Philadelphia—the burgeoning nation's cultural center—and he quickly became the city's best-known musician, playing concerts, balls, celebrations, and other social events for both the elite white society and the black community.

A passage from Robert Waln's *The Hermit in America* (1819) attests to Johnson's popularity: "[Johnson is the] leader of the band at all balls public and private, sole director of all serenades, acceptable and not acceptable; inventor-general of cotillions; to which add, a

remarkable taste in distorting a sentimental, simple, and beautiful song into a reel, jig, or country-dance" quoted in (Southern, 108). The historian Eileen Southern explains that the word "distorting" in this context is one of the first examples of "infusing the music with rhythmic complexities...and the transference of musical scores into actual sound" (113). That Johnson could change cotillions, waltzes, and quadrilles into popular music vernaculars such as reels, jigs and country dances makes plain his virtuosity. Taking such great liberties with genres suggests that Johnson may have been the first American musician to employ improvisational techniques, a practice that fomented future music revolutions.

By the 1820s Johnson became affiliated with several regiment bands, including the Washington Grays, the Philadelphia State Fencibles, and the First Troop Philadelphia City Calvary. During marches and parades, however, Johnson added drums and fife players to these bands, which consisted primarily of woodwinds, a French horn, and percussion. For dances, the band became Johnson's Celebrated Cotillion Band or Johnson's Fine Quadrille Band, employing woodwinds. In the 1830s, when brass instruments came to prominence in the United States, Johnson's band became a brass band.

When General Lafayette, the enormously popular Revolutionary War hero from France, returned to Philadelphia in 1824, Johnson received the honor of leading bands for the parades, balls, and celebrations. For the occasion, Johnson composed "Honour to the Brave" and "La Fayett's Welcome," as well as songs honoring Lafayette's battles, such as "Monmouth," "German Town," and "Yorktown."

We know Johnson was politically minded from at least two of his compositions. The first—"Recognition March on the Independence of Hayti, for the piano forte & flute. Composed expressly for the occasion and dedicated to President J. P. Boyer by his humble servant with every sentiment of respect"—was written in 1825 as a tribute to Haiti's independence from France, which stemmed from Toussaint-Louverture's slave revolt. Johnson's support for Boyer, the president of Haiti, makes it clear that Johnson, who was himself

from the French colonial territory of Martinique, supported independence for the colonies. Johnson announced his abolitionist politics by composing music to accompany the popular antislavery poem "The Grave of the Slave," written by the white Philadelphia socialite Sarah Forten.

In addition to playing for white patrons, Johnson played for numerous African American social functions, including balls, festivals, funerals, and church concerts in cities up and down the East Coast. During one of these trips in 1841, Johnson led a sacred music concert at the First African Presbyterian Church in Philadelphia, conducting Haydn's *Creation* with a fifty-piece orchestra. In the autumn of 1837 Johnson and four band members traveled to Europe, where they played a series of concerts in the major English cities. These performances are the very first record of any American touring Europe. The varied program included pieces by Mozart, arias by Rossini, and patriotic songs, all arranged by Johnson. During his six-month stay, Johnson was invited to perform for Queen Victoria, who allegedly presented Johnson with a silver bugle and for whom he later penned "Victoria Gallop."

On his travels Johnson was greatly influenced by European music. In addition to hearing Johann Strauss, he attended his first promenade concert in the tradition of Philippe Musard, who combined classical music with promenade in 1833. Upon returning to the United States in 1938, Johnson presented his own Concerts a la Musard, in Philadelphia. This was the first time such music had been performed in the United States. The concerts were enormously successful, attracting thousands of spectators. As an article in the *Detroit Free Press* declared, "It may be said without fear of contradiction that as a composer or musician, [Johnson] stands without peer" (23 Sept. 1893).

Johnson's most popular compositions included "Voice Quadrilles," "Philadelphia Grays' Quicksteps," and "Bird Waltz." Many of the songs used inventive methods, such as onomatopoeic devices. In "Voice Quadrilles" he instructed his band to laugh out loud and sing, and in "Bird Waltz" tweeting birds could be heard. "Sleigh Waltzes" featured the sounds of a blacksmith forging nails, a gleeful sleighing party, horses galloping, the cracking of whips, and the jingling of bells. Johnson taught students, and an informal Philadelphia school of music began to develop around him, which included the musicians William Appo, William Brady, Aaron J. R. Conner, James Hemmenway, Isaac Hazard, and Joseph G. Anderson.

Although Johnson was successful, he encountered racial discrimination throughout his career. Johnson, who was never able to perform in the American South, was once arrested and fined ten dollars "for being a free Negro with no license to be in Missouri." In 1821, despite Philadelphia's relatively tolerant reputation, white musicians in the Philadelphia Fencibles resigned over the inclusion of black musicians. Twenty years later, an 1843 *New York Tribune* story reported that one of Johnson's concerts in Pittsburgh had ended with an angry mob shouting "opprobrious epithets and hurling brick-bats, stones and rotten eggs."

Despite these indignities, Johnson held the first racially integrated concert on American soil in Philadelphia on 29 December 1843. He continued the practice until the spring of 1844, when he fell ill and died at the age of fifty-two. Johnson was buried with full honors at the St. Thomas African Church in Philadelphia. An editorial in the *Public Ledger* on 6 April 1844 lamented the great loss, stating, "It will be a long time before his place can be similarly filled."

Francis Johnson's trailblazing contributions to the American music canon are undeniable. He was the most popular musician in antebellum America, composing over two hundred pieces of music and playing before some of the world's greatest dignitaries. He introduced new music styles to America and was the first African American to publish music and to hold public formal band concerts. He was as well the first American of any color to tour Europe and to perform integrated musical concerts. That he was able to accomplish these extraordinary feats in the face of unbridled discrimination, while millions of his fellow African Americans were enslaved, is miraculous.

FURTHER READING

Southern, Eileen. *The Music of Black Americans: A History* (1997).

Discography

Hail to the Chief! American Political Marches, Songs, and Dirges of the 1880s (Sony Classical SFK 62485).
The Music of Francis Johnson & His Contemporaries: Early 19th Century Black Composer (Musicmasters 7029-2-C).

—ANDY GENSLER

JOHNSON, JACK

(31 Mar. 1878–10 June 1946), world boxing champion, was born Arthur John Johnson in Galveston, Texas, the eldest son of Henry Johnson, a janitor and former slave, and Tiny (maiden name unknown). Johnson landed in many schoolyard fights, usually returning home beaten, bruised, and crying unless his sister came to his defense. Only when his mother, the more dominant of his parents, threatened him with a worse whipping did he begin to fight back. After attending public school for six years, he assisted his invalid father and then drifted from one job to another, working as a horse trainer, a baker, and a dockworker, usually near Galveston, although his autobiography lists more exotic, far-flung locations. That memoir contains serial exaggerations and embellishments, many of which are repeated in the Tony- and Pulitzer Prize–winning stage play (1969) and later movie (1970), *The Great White Hope*.

Johnson also participated in "battle royals," in which he and eight or more black youths, often blindfolded, fought each other. The last youth standing won only a few coins. Such fights, staged for the amusement of whites, were intended to strip young African Americans of self-respect; for Johnson, however, they instilled a strong sense of grievance against a white power structure that tried to confine him. These bouts also led him into the realm of professional boxing. After several fights in Texas and Chicago, most of which he won, Johnson was matched in Galveston in 1901 against Joe Choynski, a veteran heavyweight from the golden era of Jewish-American boxing. Although Choynski was much slower than his nimble-footed challenger, he knocked the black fighter to the canvas with a right cross. Johnson remained there after a count of ten, at which point five

Texas Rangers climbed into the ring to arrest both boxers under a state law that prohibited prizefighting. The two men shared a cell for three weeks, during which time Johnson learned much about the art of boxing from his fellow prisoner. After his release, Johnson fought several bouts, mostly against black opponents, and in 1903 he defeated "Denver" Ed Martin on points to win the black heavyweight title.

The conventions of boxing did not prohibit fights across the color line, but following the lead of John L. Sullivan in 1885, all world heavyweight champions had refused to defend their title against blacks. Johnson was determined to end that restriction. Between 1905 and 1908 he defeated several white former champions with ease, approaching those bouts with an uncharacteristic savagery. A Philadelphia newspaper reported in 1905 that Johnson, at six feet, two inches and two hundred pounds, rendered Jack Monroe a "mass of palpitating gelatine" (Roberts, 43). Against black opponents Johnson emphasized speed, defensive counterpunching, and showmanship. However, he quickly tired of defeating black no-hopers and white has-beens, and in late 1906 he hired an ambitious white manager, Sam Fitzpatrick. With Fitzpatrick's backing, Johnson toured Britain and Australia in 1907, defeating several fighters and enhancing his reputation as a world heavyweight contender. The next year, he followed the reigning champion Tommy Burns to England and Australia, trying to goad him into a contest. Burns initially tried to avoid Johnson but was willing to abandon the principle of Jim Crow pugilism if the price was right. Thirty-five thousand dollars win, lose, or draw proved to be the right price.

On 26 December 1908 in Sydney, Australia, Johnson defeated Burns with a fourteen-round knockout to become the first-ever black world heavyweight champion. In each round he taunted the short, hard-punching Canadian, calling him "white as the flag of surrender," and inflicted a series of punishing right-hand uppercuts. Even the novelist and white supremacist Jack London reported from the ringside that it had been a contest between a grown man and a naughty child. "The Fight!—There was no fight!" London famously wrote (Ashe, 34).

White commentators took up London's call for the undefeated former champion Jim Jeffries to come out of retirement to restore the title to its rightful Anglo-Saxon provenance. After lengthy negotiations, Johnson faced Jeffries in what was billed as the "fight of the century" in Reno, Nevada, on 4 July 1910. Global interest was such that the fighters would share $100,000 in movie rights, ushering in a new era in boxing. Again, Johnson dominated the contest. His merciless uppercuts and jabs exposed the once invincible Jeffries for what he now was: an overweight, aging alfalfa farmer. The fight ended, mercifully for Jeffries, with a fifteenth-round knockdown. Johnson became the undisputed world champion and $110,000 richer, and Jeffries earned $90,000 for his considerable pains.

The full significance of the fight became clear the next morning, when newspapers reported a national wave of violence in which thirteen African Americans died and hundreds were injured. In some cases, blacks had fired guns and attacked whites, but most of the clashes involved whites exacting revenge for Johnson's victory. The violence reflected the rancorous, indeed rancid, atmosphere of the early-twentieth-century nadir in race relations, a time of white-on-black race riots and hundreds of lynchings of African Americans. In that respect, Johnson was merely a catalyst for preexisting white fears, though he took great pleasure in stoking and provoking those anxieties. He dressed flamboyantly, drank heavily, drove cars recklessly, taunted white boxers and spectators, and—most incendiary of all—flaunted a series of white lovers. In 1911 he married Etta Terry Duryea, a white woman. One year later, ostracized by her white friends and humiliated by beatings and what one biographer has called Johnson's "heroic infidelity," Duryea committed suicide, shooting herself in a room above his Chicago nightclub, the Café de Champion (Roberts, 140).

Like many famous and wealthy men, Johnson acted as though his money and celebrity placed him above the law. However, the world champion's skin color also attracted the attention of policemen, who arrested him for a string of offenses, usually involving reckless driving but most often for petty

transgressions. After being arrested for having Chicago license plates while driving in New York, Johnson complained, "Next thing somebody'll arrest me for bein' a brunette in a blond town" (Roberts, 126).

The champion's arrest in October 1912 was much more serious. He was charged under the Mann Act, a 1910 federal law that prohibited the transportation of women across state or national borders "for the purpose of prostitution, debauchery, or for any other immoral purpose." The Bureau of Investigation, forerunner of the FBI, charged that Johnson had abducted Lucille Cameron, a white woman who had worked as his secretary, as part of an interstate prostitution ring. The vigor with which the federal authorities pursued their case against Johnson was in inverse proportion to the evidence they gathered. Cameron refused to testify and married Johnson in 1912 or 1913, but that did not deter the Bureau, which found another white mistress, Belle Schreiber, to testify against him. The authors of the Mann Act had never intended to prosecute consensual sexual relations between an unmarried couple. Johnson's relationship with Schreiber may have been many things—tawdry, abusive, and maybe even "debauched" and "immoral" to some—but it did not violate the letter or the spirit of the law. Regardless of its flimsy evidence, the Bureau pursued the case and secured a conviction in May 1913, when twelve white male jurors found Johnson guilty and a judge sentenced him to one year in prison. Released on bond, he fled to Europe.

Johnson defended his world title three times in Paris and proved even more successful in maintaining his reputation as the world's most notorious carouser. Financial problems and the onset of World War I encouraged Johnson to sail for Central America, and in April 1915 he arrived in Havana, Cuba, to defend his title against Jess Willard. The 250-pound white Kansan absorbed heavy punishment in the early rounds but remained standing; in the twenty-sixth round he knocked out the champion. White commentators celebrated what they saw as the return of the natural racial order. Johnson, for his part, claimed—indeed, he swore to God and to his mother—that he had been promised fifty thousand dollars to throw

the fight. If so, he never received that payoff. Newsreel of the fight suggests a more prosaic explanation: the fitter, harder-hitting Willard had defeated the aging, poorly prepared Johnson.

After four years in Spain and Mexico, boxing, bullfighting, and squandering his fortune, Johnson surrendered to American authorities, serving one year in the federal penitentiary in Leavenworth, Kansas. Three years after his release in 1921, he divorced Lucille Cameron and married Irene Pineau. He briefly opened a nightclub, the Club De Lux, in Harlem in 1920, but money problems forced him to sell it to the New York gangster Owney Madden, who reopened it as the Cotton Club in 1923. After that, Johnson continued to box and perform in vaudeville shows, though the distinction between these activities became increasingly fine. In 1946 he lost control of his car near Raleigh, North Carolina, and died from his injuries.

Jack Johnson's life and legacy go far beyond the boxing ring. He was not only one of the greatest fighters ever but also a symbol of modernity, a movie-age celebrity, who was at once renowned and reviled in his native land and beyond. He embodied the greatest fears of early-twentieth-century whites, namely, that a hypersexualized "black beast" threatened the purity of white womanhood. For African Americans, Johnson presented more of a problem. Leaders like BOOKER T. WASHINGTON urged him to display more humility, fearing that the boxer's exuberant racial transgressions reflected badly on his race and might lead to even more violence against blacks. Yet for many blacks, Jack Johnson was a hero, a defiant forerunner of the assertive "New Negro" who emerged in the 1920s.

FURTHER READING

Johnson, Jack. *Jack Johnson—In the Ring—and Out* (1927); reprinted as *Jack Johnson Is a Dandy* (1969).

ASHE, ARTHUR R., Jr. *A Hard Road to Glory: A History of the African–American Athlete 1619–1918* (1988).
Roberts, Randy. *Papa Jack: Jack Johnson and the Era of White Hopes* (1983).
Sammons, Jeffrey T. *Beyond the Ring: The Role of Boxing in American Society* (1988).

Obituary: *New York Times*, 11 June 1946.

—STEVEN J. NIVEN

JOHNSON, JAMES WELDON

JOHNSON, JAMES WELDON (17 June 1871–26 June 1938), civil rights leader, poet, and novelist, was born in Jacksonville, Florida, the son of James Johnson, a resort hotel headwaiter, and Helen Dillet, a schoolteacher. He grew up in a secure, middle-class home in an era, Johnson recalled in *Along This Way* (1933), when "Jacksonville was known far and wide as a good town for Negroes" because of the jobs provided by its winter resorts. After completing the eighth grade at Stanton Grammar School, the only school open to African Americans in his hometown, Johnson attended the preparatory school and then the college division of Atlanta University, where he developed skills as a writer and a public speaker. Following his graduation in 1894 Johnson returned to his hometown and became principal of Stanton School.

School teaching, however, did not satisfy his ambitions. While continuing as principal Johnson started a short-lived newspaper and then read law in a local attorney's office well enough to pass the exam for admission to the Florida state bar. He also continued to write poetry, a practice he had started in college. In early 1900 he and his brother Rosamond, an accomplished musician, collaborated on "Lift Every Voice and Sing," an anthem commemorating Abraham Lincoln's birthday. African American groups around the country found the song inspirational, and within fifteen years it had acquired a subtitle: "The Negro National Anthem."

"Lift Every Voice and Sing" was not the only song on which the brothers collaborated. In 1899 the two spent the summer in New York City, where they sold their first popular song, "Louisiana Lize." In 1902 they left Jacksonville to join Bob Cole, a young songwriter they had met early on in New York, in the quickly successful Broadway song writing team of Cole and Johnson Brothers. Over the next few years Johnson was largely responsible for the lyrics of such hit songs as "Nobody's Lookin' but de Owl and de Moon" (1901), "Under the Bamboo Tree" (1902), and "Congo Love Song" (1903).

In 1906 Johnson's life took another turn when, through the influence of BOOKER T. WASHINGTON, Theodore Roosevelt appointed him U.S. consul to Puerto Cabello, Venezuela. In 1909 he moved to a more significant post as consul in Corinto, Nicaragua. A year later he returned to the United States for a brief stay in New York City, where he married Grace Nail, a member of a well-established African American family. They did not have children. In 1912 revolution broke out in Nicaragua. Johnson's role in aiding U.S. Marines in defeating the rebels drew high praise from Washington. He left the Consular Service in 1913; there would be, he felt, little opportunity for an African American in the newly elected Democratic administration of Woodrow Wilson.

Johnson maintained his literary efforts during this period. Several of his poems (including "Fifty Years," commemorating the anniversary of the Emancipation Proclamation) appeared in nationally circulated publications. In 1912 he published *The Autobiography of an Ex-Colored Man*, a novel whose central character, unlike Johnson, was light enough to "pass" as a white man; the book explores the young man's struggles to find his place in American society. Johnson returned to New York City in 1914, and he soon began a weekly column on current affairs for the *New York Age*, a widely distributed African American newspaper.

In 1917 Johnson joined the staff of the NAAC. He worked as field secretary, largely responsible for establishing local branches throughout the South and for increasing overall membership from 10,000 to 44,000 by the end of 1918. In 1920 Johnson became the NAACP's first African American secretary (its chief operating officer), a position he held throughout the 1920s.

Johnson was deeply committed to exposing the injustice and brutality imposed on African Americans throughout the United States, especially in the Jim Crow South. He labored with considerable success to put the NAACP on secure financial ground. He spent much time in Washington unsuccessfully lobbying to have Congress pass the Dyer Anti-Lynching Bill, legislation that would have made lynching a federal crime. Finally, Johnson was a key figure in making the NAACP a clearinghouse for civil-rights court cases; he collaborated closely with such noted attorneys as Moorfield Storey, Louis Marshall, and Arthur Garfield Hayes in a series of cases defending African American civil rights and attacking the legal structure of segregation. In all these efforts he worked closely with WALTER WHITE, whom he brought into the NAACP as his assistant and who succeeded him as secretary, and W. E. B. DU BOIS, the editor of *Crisis*, the NAACP monthly journal.

Johnson was probably better known in the 1920s for his literary efforts than for his leadership of the NAACP. He played an active role, as an author and as a supporter of young talent, in what has come to be called the Harlem Renaissance. Johnson urged writers and other artists to draw on everyday life in African American communities for their creative inspiration. He played the role of a father figure to a number of young writers, including CLAUDE MCKAY and LANGSTON HUGHES, whose often blunt prose and poetry drew condemnation from more genteel critics.

His own work during this period included a widely praised anthology, *The Book of American Negro Poetry* (1922), a volume that helped to give an identity to the "New Negro" movement. His continued interest in the African American musical tradition found expression in two collections of spirituals that he and Rosamond brought out: *The Book of American Negro Spirituals* in 1925 and *The Second Book of American Negro Spirituals* in 1926. A year later Johnson published his poetic interpretation of African American religion in *God's Trombones: Seven Negro Sermons in Verse*, a theme he first developed in "O Black and Unknown Bards" (1908). The year 1927 also saw the reissuing of *The Autobiography of an Ex-Colored Man*. Finally, Johnson published *Black Manhattan* (1930), the first history of African Americans in New York City.

In 1931 Johnson stepped down as secretary of the NAACP (though he remained on the association's board of directors) to become a professor at Fisk University. For the remainder of his life he spent the winter and spring terms in Nashville teaching creative writing and classes in American and African American literature. The rest of the year the Johnsons largely spent in New York City. He remained active as a writer, publishing *Along This Way*, his autobiography, in 1933 and *Negro Americans,*

What Now?, a work of social criticism, a year later. Johnson's unexpected death was the result of an automobile accident near Wiscasset, Maine.

Johnson took deserved pride in his accomplishments across a wide variety of careers: teacher, Broadway lyricist, poet, diplomat, novelist, and civil-rights leader. Though he suffered most of the indignities forced on African Americans during the Jim Crow era, Johnson retained his sense of self-worth; he proclaimed forcefully in *Negro Americans, What Now?* that "My inner life is mine, and I shall defend and maintain its integrity against all the powers of hell." The defense of his "inner life" did not mean withdrawal, but active engagement. Thus Johnson was a key figure, perhaps the key figure, in making the NAACP a truly national organization capable of mounting the attack that eventually led to the dismantling of the system of segregation by law.

Maintaining his "inner life" also led Johnson to write both prose and poetry that has endured over the decades. "Lift Every Voice and Sing," written a century ago, can still be heard at African American gatherings, and the title phrase appears on the U.S. postage stamp issued in 1988 to honor Johnson. *The Autobiography of an Ex-Colored Man* has remained in print since its reissue in the 1920s, and it holds a significant place in the history of African American fiction. *Along This Way*, also still in print after more than sixty years, is acknowledged as a classic American autobiography. Finally, *God's Trombones*, Johnson's celebration of the creativity found in African American religion, has been adapted for the stage several times, most notably by Vinnette Carroll (as *Trumpets of the Lord*) in 1963.

FURTHER READING

The bulk of Johnson's papers are held at the Beinecke Library, Yale University.

Johnson, James Weldon. *Along This Way: The Autobiography of James Weldon Johnson*, Sondra K. Wilson, intro. (2002).

Fleming, Robert E. *James Weldon Johnson* (1987).
Levy, Eugene. *James Weldon Johnson: Black Leader, Black Voice* (1973).
Price, Kenneth M., and Lawrence J. Oliver, eds. *Critical Essays on James Weldon Johnson* (1997).

Wilson, Sondra K., ed. *The Selected Writings of James Weldon Johnson*, 2 vols. (1995).
———. *In Search of Democracy: The NAACP Writings of James Weldon Johnson, Walter White, and* ROY WILKINS, *1920–1977* (1999).
—EUGENE LEVY

JOHNSON, JOHN

(19 Jan. 1918–), entrepreneur and publisher, was born Johnny Johnson in Arkansas City, Arkansas, the only child of Leroy Johnson, a sawmill worker, and Gertrude Jenkins, who worked odd jobs. He had a half sister named Beulah from Gertrude Johnson's previous marriage. Johnson's mother was his main source of encouragement. When he was eight years old, his father died in a sawmill accident. A year later his mother married James Williams.

The family lived in a caring but poor neighborhood, and Johnson attended the Arkansas City Colored School, which did not provide education beyond the eighth grade. Opportunities were limited for almost all African Americans; the adults were relegated to low-paying jobs. In his autobiography, *Succeeding against the Odds*, Johnson says that he noticed that the poor people worked in dirty overalls and sweated for a living, while the rich people wore suits, so he decided that his goal would be to work wearing a suit (Johnson and Bennett Jr., 45). His family saw a better chance to accomplish this goal in the North. In July 1933 the family moved to Chicago, Illinois, one of the many black families that moved from the rural South to the industrial North as part of the Great Migration.

For the family the economic promise of the big city faded fast. They had moved during the Great Depression, and soon after arriving Johnson's stepfather, mother, and sister were all unemployed. The family was forced to depend on welfare. While they struggled for money, Johnson, still a young teenager, enrolled in Wendell Phillips, an almost all-black high school. Because of a clerical error on his first day, he was designated a sophomore and thus skipped a year of school.

Chicago offered Johnson resources and new cultural opportunities. He spent hours at the public library reading about self-improvement and African American history. At school he got involved in a variety of extracurricular activities: he was elected class president of his junior and senior classes, he joined the French club, and was editor of the school newspaper. Because of his excellent school performance, he was the only student asked to speak at his commencement. Before the ceremony his teacher suggested that it was time for him to change his name as he entered adulthood. From then on, he decided he was to be known as John Harold Johnson. He graduated in 1936 and soon met an executive named Harry Pace who would change his life.

Harry Pace was the head of Supreme Liberty Life Insurance, a prominent company in Chicago. Johnson had admired the business executive and heard Pace speak at an Urban League luncheon. Johnson approached Pace and was soon working part time at Supreme Life. He began as an office worker making twenty-five dollars a month. Although the pay was low, it helped him accomplish two objectives. It allowed him to attend college at the University of Chicago with a partial scholarship, and it gave him his first exposure to African American businessmen. He loved the atmosphere so much that he dropped out of school in 1939 to work full time.

In 1941 Johnson married Eunice Walker, the daughter of a physician from Selma, Alabama. The couple would later have two children, John Jr., and Linda. Shortly after the wedding, Johnson came up with an idea for a business. This idea took shape when Harry Pace assigned Johnson to edit the company's employee magazine. The experience was so inspiring that Johnson decided to start his own magazine.

Johnson wanted to publish a black version of *Reader's Digest* and went to the First National Bank for a loan to fund his project. Within minutes he was escorted out by two security guards, who referred to him as "boy" (Dingle, 10). Johnson then went to wealthy members of the black community and even to ROY WILKINS, head of the NAACP. All of them advised Johnson to put his energies toward more promising ventures. Undeterred, he persuaded his mother to put up her new furniture as collateral for a five-hundred-dollar loan from the Citizens Loan Corporation. He then formed the Negro Digest

Publishing Company, and in November 1942 *Negro Digest* was born.

Johnson built his initial subscriber base by writing letters to Supreme Life policyholders. These efforts led to three thousand orders, but that was not enough to make a profit. To make more money, Johnson had to increase demand for his product. He went to distributing companies but was rebuffed because of their common belief that black products did not sell. To circumvent this obstacle, he told friends to go to newsstands and stores and ask for *Negro Digest*. Soon he received calls from dealers who were hearing about his magazine, and they ordered copies. With the help of word of mouth on the streets and advertisements in other outlets, circulation grew. Within a few months, the magazine was known throughout the nation. In 1943 Johnson persuaded first lady Eleanor Roosevelt to contribute a column to one issue. After it was published, circulation doubled overnight to 100,000 copies.

Johnson decided to expand his empire. Because a large number of African Americans were buying *Life* magazine, he decided to create a black picture magazine. The result of this idea was *Ebony,* which first hit the newsstands in November 1945. The magazine was successful immediately. In a strange way, however, it was too successful, because his magazines did not have enough corporate advertising to make them profitable. The more magazines he sold, the more he had to print, which meant more costs. So Johnson used tenacity, charm, and creativity to convince mainstream corporations that black consumers were worth their advertisements. It worked, and *Ebony* became extraordinarily profitable in a short time.

Eventually, *Negro Digest* outwore its welcome, and it was discontinued in 1951. After a few efforts to bring it back, publication ended in 1976. With *Ebony* as its foundation, the business was renamed Johnson Publishing Company in 1949, and it developed a number of other products to diversify its offerings. The most significant of these creations was *Jet,* a pocket-sized weekly magazine, and the *Ebony* Fashion Fair. Other offerings, such as *Tan Confessions* and *Ebony, Jr.,* were shortlived. Despite those occasional failures, Johnson Publishing has remained one of the nation's largest black-owned businesses for decades.

By 2002 *Ebony* had over twelve million monthly readers, and *Jet* had nine million readers. Johnson turned over the titles of chief executive officer and president to his daughter, Linda, who had graduated with an MBA from Northwestern University and worked in a number of roles for Johnson Publishing. (John Jr. had died in 1981 after a long bout with sickle-cell anemia.) Johnson remained the company's chairman.

In his autobiography, Johnson wrote that he hopes his example will stand as proof that "the Dream is still alive and well and working in America" (Johnson, 356). He will be remembered as one of the fathers of modern black capitalism. His publishing empire is the largest and most influential in African American history and its success helped to make the corporate world aware of the power of the African American market.

FURTHER READING

Johnson, John, and Lerone Bennett, Jr. *Succeeding against the Odds* (1989).

Dingle, Derek. *Black Enterprise Titans of the BE 100's: Black CEOs Who Redefined and Conquered American Business* (1999).
—GREGORY S. BELL

JOHNSON, JOHN ROSAMOND

(11 Aug. 1873–11 Nov. 1954), composer, performer, and anthologist, was born in Jacksonville, Florida, to Helen Dillet, the first black public schoolteacher in Florida, and James Johnson, the headwaiter at a local restaurant. He and his younger brother, JAMES WELDON JOHNSON, were raised in a cultured and economically secure home, a rarity for African Americans in the South in this era. Their mother read Dickens novels to them every night before bed, and they received music lessons from an early age. Indeed, John began playing the piano as a toddler. He went on to attend Atlanta University in Georgia, and his brother followed eight years later.

When Johnson graduated in 1899 from the New England Conservatory in Boston, where he had studied classical music, he realized that he wanted to explore the realm of musical comedy. He became a vocalist with Oriental America, an African American opera company whose productions differed from the pejorative, stereotypical representations of African Americans present in most theater at the time, often described as "coon" songs. Johnson retuned to Jacksonville to teach music lessons and assume the position of musical director in the public schools. He and his brother, who would become a prominent social activist, novelist, and diplomat, then left for New York to attempt to have their comic opera, *Toloso,* produced; this work satirized the sense of American imperialism after the Spanish-American War. While *Toloso* was never performed on Broadway, the Johnsons did meet a number of prominent people in the musical and theatrical industry in the process of trying to have their work brought to the stage.

Indeed, it was then that they met Robert Cole. The three men went on to collaborate as Cole and Johnson Brothers and created hundreds of popular songs, most notably "Under the Bamboo Tree" (1902) and "Congo Love Song" (1903). The team's first collaboration was "Louisiana Lize," a love song written in a new lyrical fashion, for which they earned fifty dollars. This song and the ones to follow marked a shift away from the burlesque and minstrel styles. Some of their songs (which featured titles like "I'll Love You, Honey, When the Money's Gone, But I'll Not Be with You" and "Ain't Dat Scan'lous") became best-sellers and were featured in numerous Broadway productions. The Johnson brothers' most famous collaboration, "Lift Every Voice and Sing," was created in 1900 to mark the anniversary of Abraham Lincoln's birthday. James wrote the lyrics and Rosamond wrote the music. The NAACP adopted it as the organization's official song, and it soon became known as the "Negro National Anthem."

Rosamond Johnson often set poetry to music, particularly the poetry of PAUL LAURENCE DUNBAR. The Johnsons also created musical comedies such as *The Shoo Fly Regiment* in 1906 and *The Red Moon* in 1908. Johnson also composed "The Belle of Bridgeport" (1900), "Humpty Dumpty" (1904), and "In Newport" (1904). He then collaborated with BERT WILLIAMS in "Mr. Load of

Koal" and soon found that the musical collaborations created by Cole and Johnson Brothers were being sung by such popular entertainers as Lillian Russell and George Primrose. Johnson studied with Samuel Coleridge-Taylor in London in the early 1900s, and when he toured Europe in the 1910s, he became one of the first African Americans to conduct a white orchestra when he directed the revue *Hello Paris*. He then returned to the United States to perform in vaudeville productions with Cole.

After Cole's death in 1911, Johnson became the musical director of the Hammerstein Opera House in London. Upon his return to the United States in 1914, he and his wife started a music school known as the Music School Settlement for Colored People. He had married Nora Ethel Floyd, one of his former piano students in Jacksonville, in 1913 in London. They had two children. Johnson toured across the country, singing spirituals with Taylor Gordon and covering the vaudeville circuit in the early 1920s. The Johnson brothers also edited collections of spirituals (*The Book of American Negro Spirituals* in 1925 and *The Second Book of American Negro Spirituals* in 1926). He performed on stage in the role of Lawrence Frasier in *Porgy and Bess* in 1935 and in *Mamba's Daughter* in 1939 and served as the musical director of *Emperor Jones*, starring PAUL ROBESON, in 1933, and *Cabin in the Sky* in 1935. Johnson spent the 1930s and 1940s as a music arranger and editor at a few publishing houses in New York and published hundreds of songs. He died at the age of eighty-one in New York City.

Johnson was an influential composer and performer who had a deep impact on the music and theater of New York from the beginning to the middle of the twentieth century. He and his brother will forever be remembered for giving the world "Lift Every Voice and Sing," but he should also be remembered as a prolific songwriter, singer, and anthologist. As talented as he was innovative, Johnson established new directions in both music and theater featuring African Americans, moving away from minstrelsy and toward productions that reflected his passion for musical comedy and his classical training in opera.

FURTHER READING

Johnson's papers are part of the Irving S. Gilmore Music Library at Yale University,

a collection of music, correspondence, and photographs that resides across the street from the archive of his brother, James.

Floyd, Samuel A., Jr., ed. *International Dictionary of Black Composers* (1999).
Johnson, James Weldon. *Along This Way* (1933).
Perry, Frank, Jr. "John Rosamond Johnson," in *Afro-American Vocal Music: A Select Guide to Fifteen Composers* (1991).
Woll, Allen. "The End of the Coon Song: Bob Cole and the Johnson Brothers," in *Black Musical Theatre: From Coontown to Dreamgirls* (1989).

—JENNIFER WOOD

JOHNSON, JOSHUA

(fl. 1795–1824), painter, was probably born in the West Indies. It is now generally believed by scholars of American art and history that Johnson was black and may have come to this country as a young man, probably as a slave. Johnson might be identified as the "negro boy" mentioned in the 1777 will of Captain Robert Polk of Maryland. This boy is thought to have been purchased by Polk's brother-in-law, the noted artist Charles Willson Peale. Stylistic resemblances between the work of Charles Willson Peale and Joshua Johnson are apparent. Unfortunately, very little documentation on Johnson exists and identification of his works is accomplished through provenance (mostly oral family tradition), and connoisseurship—observation of technique, subject matter, iconography, and style.

Johnson's artistic career spanned nearly thirty years, during which he worked only in Baltimore, painting portraits of many of its citizens. Like many artists of the period he more than likely also worked in a related field, such as sign painting or carriage painting, in order to make a living. It is likely that for most of his professional life he was a free man. If he had ever been a slave, he was evidently free by 19 December 1798, when he placed an advertisement for his services as a portrait artist in the *Baltimore Intelligencer*. A slave could not usually have advertised for clients in this manner, and in the advertisement he alluded to the difficulties of his life: "As a *self-taught genius*, deriving from nature and industry his knowledge of the Art; and having experienced many

Joshua Johnson became a prominent portrait painter with a largely white clientele. Pictured is the only signed painting attributed to Johnson, Sarah Ogden Gustin. National Gallery of Art, Washington, D.C.

insufferable obstacles in the pursuit of his studies, it is highly gratifying to him to make assurances of his ability to execute all commands, with an effect, and in a style, which must give satisfaction." He is listed as a "Free Householder of Coulour" in the 1816–1817 Baltimore city directory, and an 1810 census lists a Josa. Johnston as a "free negro." "Johnson" was on occasion spelled with a "t," and there is some disagreement among scholars as to whether "Johnson" is the correct form of the artist's last name. The only signed painting attributed to him (*Sarah Ogden Gustin*, National Gallery of Art, Washington, D.C.) shows it as "Johnson," while his advertisement spells his name as "Johnston," as does his signature on a 1798 petition for the paving of German Lane, where he lived.

Johnson was able to earn portrait commissions because of the growing wealth of Baltimore's citizenry. Colonial Baltimore attracted major capital investors in the 1780s; along with this growth came a certain cosmopolitan atmosphere. By 1800 a fifth of Baltimore's population was black, and nearly half of those persons were free, a very high percentage for the American South. The increasing popularity of Quakerism and Methodism in Maryland, both with strong anti-slavery stances, encouraged manumissions. Unfortunately, kidnapping for resale into slavery was a constant and real possibility, but safety in numbers helped somewhat, and Johnson, like many free blacks, initially chose to live in the poorer Fells Point area. However, he subsequently moved near the intersection of German and Hanover Streets, a wealthier neighborhood that boasted a number of abolitionists and no doubt provided many more clients. All but two of his approximately eighty known portraits are of white subjects.

Johnson spent his entire career in Baltimore, the only artist of the first quarter of the nineteenth century to do so. He is listed as a limner at eight different Baltimore addresses between 1796 and 1824, apparently never moving to other cities or towns in search of new clients. This consistency may in part be attributable to the difficulties he faced as a free black in a slave-owning society. Johnson often painted likenesses of his near neighbors. The majority of his late images are of working and middle-class Baltimoreans, while his early subjects reflect more upper-class individuals—members of prominent families, many of whom were also clients of the Peales (once again indicating an early connection to the Peale family).

Johnson probably did not maintain a painting studio, but like many artists of this period, he worked in his sitters' homes. Children constitute a particularly large percentage of his portrait subjects. He often posed them standing, and he used such decorative devices as fruit, books, and even butterflies. A painting of an unidentified girl shows the young subject holding a flower in one hand while she stands in front of greenery (Baltimore Museum of Art). Just under her other hand, an over-large butterfly sits on a bush. In another painting of a child, a young girl stands on a marble floor near a window with drapery pulled aside to reveal a hint of an exterior garden scene. (*Emma Van Name*, Whitney Museum of American Art, New York). Emma holds a strawberry in one hand and gestures to a wine glass nearly as big as she is filled with berries next to her. Johnson modeled the forms of the figure to indicate depth and created spatial relationships by using overlapping forms that moved back within the composition. His linear approach with thinly applied paint reflects knowledge

of, if not training by, Charles Willson Peale and indicates some awareness of European styles, though Johnson's works remain within the American folk tradition.

There are only two known portraits by Johnson of black sitters. These probably depict Abner (Bowdoin College Museum of Art, Brunswick, Maine) and Daniel Coker (American Museum in Britain, Bath, England), two dignitaries of the African Methodist Episcopal Church. The Daniel Coker identification is based on a comparison with a known portrait of him, while the identification of Abner Coker rests on its apparent pairing in size and composition with the other portrait and the professional relationship of the two men. There are few extant images of African Americans from this period, and these two portraits are respectful and dignified likenesses. A portrait of the Most Reverend John Carroll, first archbishop of Baltimore in 1808–1815, reflects Johnson's ties to the Catholic church, supported by baptismal and death records for his children. Stylistically the elongated eyes, thin paint, and crossed hands with book are all characteristic of Johnson's style.

Johnson's technical approach to painting was distinctive, helping with the identification of his works. Johnson stretched his canvases onto strainers with fixed corners using plain weave fabric that was tightly woven and quite textured. He apparently liked a colored ground, which ranged from gray to buff, and he painted with thin paint, making very few revisions. He would apply small areas of intense color that contrasted with the surrounding, more limited palette. His subjects, always portraits of individuals, place him squarely within the colonial tradition of American Art. Johnson's career parallels the development of painting in the colonies and he is significant within both African American history and the tradition of American art. The date of Johnson's death is unknown; he last appears in the Baltimore City Directory in 1824, in which he is listed as "Johnson, Joshua, portrait painter, Sleigh's Lane, S side E of Spring."

FURTHER READING

Very little archival documentation on Johnson exists, but both the Maryland Historical Society and the Abby Aldrich Rockefeller Folk Art Center have taken an interest in the artist.

Bearden, Romare, and Harry Henderson. *A History of African American Artists from 1792–present* (1993).

Pleasants, Dr. J. Hall. "Joshua Johnston: The First American Negro Portrait Painter." *Maryland Historical Magazine* 37, no. 2 (June 1942): 121–149.

Weekley, Carolyn J., et al. *Joshua Johnson: Freeman and Early American Portrait Painter* (1987).

—J. Susan Isaacs

 JOHNSON, JUDY
(26 Oct. 1899–15 June 1989), baseball player, manager, scout, and coach, was born William Julius Johnson in Snow Hill, Maryland, the son of William Henry Johnson, a seaman, boxing trainer, and athletic director, and Annie Lane. He was the youngest of three children, following his brother, Johnny, and his sister, Mary Emma. In 1905 or soon thereafter the Johnsons settled in Wilmington, Delaware, and William Henry secured a job as athletic director of the Negro Settlement House. He was skilled in the art of self-defense and taught the rudiments of boxing to both his youngest son and his daughter. Although Johnson hoped that his son

Judy Johnson, one of the greatest third basemen of his generation. National Baseball Hall of Fame

would become a prizefighter, the youth preferred playing sandlot football and baseball.

Baseball became young William's passion, and he played games in his neighborhood and the surrounding area, where his team would pass the hat and hope to get enough money to buy a couple of baseballs for the next game. His early equipment consisted of his father's hand-me-down glove that was falling apart from dry rot and street shoes with nailed-on metal spikes. He attended Frederick Douglass School and completed one year at Howard High School, both in Washington, D.C., before ending his formal education to take a job as a stevedore on the loading docks at Deepwater Port, across the Delaware River in New Jersey. He commuted to work and earned three dollars a week but continued to pursue the game he loved.

In 1918 he began playing semipro baseball with the Madison Stars of Chester, Pennsylvania. After the end of World War I he had a tryout with the Hilldale Daisies, a top black team in the Philadelphia suburb of Darby, Pennsylvania. (The team sometimes wore different uniforms and played as the Bacharach Giants in Atlantic City, New Jersey.) He played three games a week for five dollars per game, but it was clear that he was not yet ready to play at that level, and he soon returned to the Madison Stars, an unofficial farm team for Hilldale. Johnson was the Stars' shortstop until Hilldale, watching his progress, reacquired his contract in 1921 for a hundred dollars. William signed his first contract for $135 a month and acquired the nickname "Judy" because of his resemblance to an old-time baseball player named Jude Gans; he carried the name with him the rest of his life.

Hilldale's manager, Bill Francis, played third base, so Johnson was placed at shortstop, which was not his best position because of his restricted range. When John Henry Lloyd, a star shortstop himself, became Hilldale's manager in 1923, he moved Johnson to the hot corner (third base) and tutored him at the position, building his confidence. Johnson eventually became one of the best third basemen in the history of the Negro Leagues and always credited Lloyd with being instrumental in his success. He had good range, sure hands, and a strong and accurate arm. Although he was not fast afoot, Johnson was a smart, instinctive base runner. He batted right-handed and was a good line-drive hitter, with respectable extra-base power and an excellent batting eye. Having achieved professional success, he married Anita T. Irons, a schoolteacher, in 1923, and they had one daughter, Loretta, born in 1926. She would eventually marry Bill Bruton, a major league player.

In 1923 Hilldale became a charter member of the Eastern Colored League and won its first three pennants, with Johnson batting .391, .369, and .392 while playing a key role in the field. Johnson led the team in 1924 with a .341 batting average, but that year Hilldale lost in the first Negro World Series to the Negro National League champion, the Kansas City Monarchs, in a hard fought ten-game series. The same two teams met again in the 1925 Negro World Series, but this time Hilldale emerged victorious, winning four games against a single loss to reign as the Negro Leagues champions. Johnson batted only .250 but contributed some clutch hits to the victory. That was Hilldale's last pennant, but Johnson remained with the franchise through the 1929 season, batting .390 that year.

In addition to his success with Hilldale, Johnson played in winter baseball leagues. In 1924–1925 he played at West Palm Beach in the Florida Hotel League before taking the first of four winter treks to Cuba in 1926–1927, when he hit .374 for Alacranes. The next two winters Johnson played in Cuba, batting .331 and .341. He stayed home in the winter of 1929–1930 but returned for his last year in Cuba in 1930–1931 and finished with a lifetime Cuban batting average of .334.

Johnson left Hilldale in 1930 to become playing manager of a Pennsylvania team, the Homestead Grays. In July the Grays were playing the Kansas City Monarchs in Pittsburgh when the Grays' catcher suffered a split finger that forced him to leave the game. According to Johnson, he recruited young JOSH GIBSON, who was sitting in the stands as a spectator, to catch the remainder of the game. After being pressed into service as a replacement, Gibson became the regular catcher for the balance of the season and went on to become the greatest slugger in Negro Leagues history. At the end of the regular season the Grays defeated the New York Lincoln Giants in a ten-game play-off for the Eastern championship.

After only one season at the Homestead helm, Johnson returned to Hilldale as playing manager in 1931 until the team disbanded midseason in 1932. He then joined the Pittsburgh Crawfords, a dominant team in black baseball, and contributed batting averages of .332, .333, .367, and .315, respectively, from 1933 through 1936. During these years the Crawfords featured five future Hall of Famers: SATCHEL PAIGE, Josh Gibson, Oscar Charleston, COOL PAPA BELL, and Johnson himself. In 1933 the Crawfords' owner, Gus Greenlee, who was also league president, claimed a disputed Negro National League pennant, but the Crawfords then defeated the New York Cubans in a play-off, to win an undisputed 1935 championship; they repeated as champions in 1936. The 1935 team is considered by most baseball historians to be the greatest team in the history of the Negro Leagues.

During his tenure with the Crawfords, the inaugural East-West All-Star game was played in 1933. Johnson appeared in the game, getting a hit in his only time at-bat, and made another appearance in the 1936 East-West classic. During his years with the Crawfords the team played several postseason exhibition games against teams that included white major leaguers. In 1932 the Crawfords defeated Casey Stengel's All-Stars in five of seven games played, and two years later beat the St. Louis Cardinals and their star pitcher Dizzy Dean in three exhibition games. Johnson also played exhibition ball in Mexico in 1936 against major leaguers Rogers Hornsby and Jimmie Foxx. Johnson's career batting average against major leaguers was .263. In the spring of 1937 Gus Greenlee traded Johnson and Josh Gibson to the Homestead Grays for two mediocre players and $2,500, but Johnson chose to retire instead. He finished with a .309 career batting average in the Negro Leagues.

In retirement he lived near Wilmington in a two-story home in Marshalton, Delaware, that he had bought in 1934. He soon began coaching a local amateur baseball team, the Alco Flashes, and worked at a variety of jobs before returning to baseball. He was a supervisor for the Continental Can Company in Wilmington, operated a general store with his brother, drove a school bus, and worked in security at Mullins Department Store. In 1952 he was hired as a scout for the Philadelphia Athletics, and two years later he became the first black coach in the major leagues, when he went to spring training with the Athletics. His duties required that he also work with minor league clubs. While he was with the Athletics, the owner, Connie Mack, told Johnson that the reason he had not hired black players before JACKIE ROBINSON broke the color line was that "there were just too many of you to go in." Johnson scouted for the Milwaukee Braves in 1956 and for the Philadelphia Phillies in 1959.

Johnson finally retired in 1972 and was inducted into the National Baseball Hall of Fame in Cooperstown, New York, in 1975. Afterward, Wilmington's city government named the park where he had played in his youth in his honor, and a statue of Johnson was erected at the local minor league ballpark, home of the Wilmington Blues. After his wife, Anita, died in 1986, Johnson was never the same. The sadness of her death and the loneliness of her absence stayed with him until 1989, when he died of a stroke in Wilmington, Delaware.

During his career, Johnson starred on several of the Negro Leagues' top teams and earned recognition as one of the greatest third basemen, black or white, of his generation. His affiliation with major league franchises after the color line was eradicated helped younger generations of African Americans to make the transition to organized baseball.

FURTHER READING

Holway, John. *Black Ball Stars: Negro League Pioneers* (1988).

Peterson, Robert. *Only the Ball Was White* (1970).

Rendle, Ellen. *Judy Johnson: Delaware's Invisible Hero* (1994).

—JAMES A. RILEY

JOHNSON, MORDECAI WYATT (12 Jan. 1890– 10 Sept. 1976), university president and clergyman, was born in Paris, Henry County, Tennessee, the son of the Reverend Wyatt Johnson, a stationary engine operator in a mill, and Caroline Freeman. Johnson received his grammar school education in Paris, but in 1903 he enrolled in the Academy of the Roger Williams University in Nashville, Tennessee. The school burned in 1905, so Johnson finished the semester at the Howe Institute in Memphis. In the fall of that year, he moved to Atlanta to finish high school in the preparatory department of Atlanta Baptist College (renamed Morehouse College in 1913). There he completed a bachelor's degree in 1911. While at Atlanta Baptist, Johnson played varsity football and tennis, sang in various groups, and began his long career as a public speaker on the debating team.

After graduating, Johnson became an English instructor at his alma mater. For the 1912–1913 school year, he taught economics and history and served as acting dean of the college. During the summers, he earned a second bachelor's degree in the Social Sciences from the University of Chicago (1913). Johnson decided that he wanted to be a minister and enrolled in Rochester Theological Seminary. In seminary he was greatly influenced by Walter Rauschenbusch's theory of the Social Gospel, in which Christianity was responsible for economic and social change. While studying at Rochester he was a student pastor at the Second Baptist Church in Mumford, New York. He was granted a bachelor's of divinity degree in 1921 with a thesis titled "The Rise of the Knights Templars."

In December 1916 Johnson married Anna Ethelyn Gardner of Augusta, Georgia; they had five children. That year Johnson worked as a student secretary of the Young Men's Christian Association (YMCA). He traveled for one year in the Southwest, studying predominantly black schools and colleges. This effort resulted in the formation of the Southwestern Annual Student Conference.

Johnson was ordained in 1916 and received an assignment in 1917 to be the pastor of the First Baptist Church in Charleston, West Virginia. In his nine years in West Virginia, Johnson was responsible for organizing the Commercial Cooperative Society, the Rochdale

Mordecai Wyatt Johnson, the first African American president of Howard University. Schomburg Center

Cooperative Cash Grocery, and the Charleston branch of the National Association for the Advancement of Colored People (NAACP). Under his leadership, the membership of the local branch of the NAACP increased to one thousand in nine years. He also became active in the Negro Baptist Convention. By the time he left in 1926, Johnson was well known as a community activist and speaker. In 1921 he took a year of absence while he studied at Harvard. The following year, Johnson received a master's degree in Sacred Theology and gave the commencement address on postwar racism, titled "The Faith of the American Negro."

On 30 June 1926 Johnson was elected the thirteenth president of Howard University in Washington, D.C. Howard was chartered in 1867 out of the Freedmen's Bureau and was originally intended to be a theological seminary for African Americans and a normal school. By 1917 Howard and Fisk University were considered the only traditionally black schools offering a college-level education. When Johnson assumed the presidency of Howard on 1 September 1926, he had a broad vision for improvements to the university.

Johnson was the first African American to hold the presidency of Howard and came to office at a time when all other presidents of traditionally black colleges were white. Further, Howard was currently undergoing a time of controversy: Johnson's predecessor had been asked to resign, and the administration and the faculty sharply disagreed on a number of issues. Johnson sought to elevate the position of the professors by raising their salaries and providing tenure and security. During his tenure, he brought in professors with national reputations and a large number of African Americans with PhDs.

Johnson's priorities for improvements were explained in his Twenty-Year Plan, which called for educational and physical development. In 1926 the only two accredited schools at Howard were dentistry and liberal arts. During his years at Howard, Johnson doubled the number of faculty members, doubled the library resources, tripled the amount of laboratory equipment, and constructed twenty new buildings. Under Johnson, all of the schools and colleges became fully accredited. In addition, the university

enrollment increased by 250 percent and the budget grew from $700,000 to $8 million.

Johnson's most important contribution to Howard was fund-raising. He was not only successful at securing private donations and grants, but he also persuaded Congress to amend the charter of the university to provide annual appropriations on 13 December 1928. Between 1946 and 1960, Howard received an average of more than one million dollars annually. This added funding gave Howard an advantage over similar schools. For his work in gaining Howard annual federal funds, Johnson received the Spingarn Medal for Public Service in 1929. (The Spingarn Medal is the highest award given by the NAACP.)

Johnson retired in June 1960 and became president emeritus. Howard had been remade in his thirty-four-year tenure. The school had students from more than ninety countries. The professional schools in particular were impressive. Howard's medical school was producing half of the nation's African American doctors, and the law school was in the vanguard of civil rights, providing 96 percent of the African American lawyers.

After leaving Howard, Johnson served on the District of Columbia's Board of Education in 1962. In his three-year tenure, he was a vocal critic of the disparity between funding of predominantly white schools and black schools in the district. Johnson was also a member of several charitable organizations. He was on the National Council of the United Negro College Fund; vice chairman of the National Council for the Prevention of War; director of the American Youth Committee; a member of the Advisory Council for the National Youth Administration; a member of the National Advisory Council on Education; a member of the National Religion and Labor Board; and director of the National Conference of Christians and Jews. In addition, he was a strong advocate for nations under colonial control by countries such as Great Britain and France, and he was a member of the advisory council for the Virgin Islands. He was an early proponent of India's independence from Great Britain and often spoke on the topic. In one such lecture, he spoke at MARTIN LUTHER

KING JR.'s seminary, Crozer Theological Seminary in Philadelphia.

In 1969 Johnson's wife died. In April 1970 he married Alice Clinton Taylor King; they had no children. Howard University honored Johnson in 1973 by naming the administration building after him. His service was also recognized internationally: Ethiopia, Haiti, Liberia, and Panama all gave him awards for his achievements. Johnson died in Washington, D.C.

Johnson has been recognized for his excellent administrative skills and as "one of the great platform orators of his day." His involvement in civil rights and religious causes gained him notoriety. His organization and development of Howard University is remarkable. Johnson insisted on a quality faculty, high-caliber students, adequate funding, and sufficient facilities and laboratory equipment. These factors put Howard on a path for success. Johnson's contributions to Howard and his other causes have assured his legacy of improved educational opportunities for all.

FURTHER READING

Johnson's papers concerning Howard University are in the Moorland-Spingarn Research Center at Howard.

LOGAN, RAYFORD W. *Howard University: The First Hundred Years, 1867–1967* (1969).

McKinney, Richard I. *Mordecai—The Man and His Message: The Story of Mordecai Wyatt Johnson* (1998).

Winston, Michael R., ed. *Education for Freedom* (1976).

Obituaries: *New York Times* and *Washington Post*, 11 Sept. 1976.

—SARA GRAVES WHEELER

JOHNSON, ROBERT
(8 May 1911–16 Aug. 1938), musician, was born Robert Leroy Johnson in Hazelhurst, Mississippi, the son of Noah Johnson and Julia Major Dodds (occupations unknown). His mother was married at the time to another man, Charles Dodds Jr., who, because of an acquaintance's personal vendetta against him, had been forced to flee Mississippi for Memphis in 1907, changing his name to Charles Spencer. After his

mother eked out a living for two years working in migrant labor camps supporting Robert and his sister Carrie, she and her children joined Spencer, his mistress, and their children in Memphis in 1914. Eventually Julia left her children. Around 1918 Robert, an unruly, strong-willed child, also left Memphis, joining his mother and new stepfather, Willie "Dusty" Willis, in Robinsonville, Mississippi. Although Robert went to the Indian Lake School at Commerce, Mississippi, through the mid-1920s, eyesight problems both plagued him and provided him with an excuse to quit school. Johnson's favored instruments of his early teen years, Jew's harp and harmonica, were supplanted around 1929 by an interest in what became his primary instrument, the guitar, though he continued to play harmonica in a neck rack.

Johnson next began absorbing the sounds of other guitarists, developing his technique by listening in houses and juke joints to little-known locals like Harvey "Hard Rock" Glenn, Myles Robson, and Ernest "Whiskey Red" Brown, as well as now-legendary bluesmen CHARLEY PATTON and Willie Brown. After Johnson's marriage to Virginia Travis in 1929 ended in tragedy—both she and their baby died in childbirth in April 1930—he intensified his musical efforts, benefiting from the arrival of Eddie "Son" House in June 1930. House had recorded with Patton and Louise Johnson for Paramount Records, and it was House's furiously emotional performances that helped inspire some of Robert Johnson's best recordings. At the time, though, House and Brown often ran off the younger Johnson, an inexperienced neophyte who House claimed "made such a mess outta everything he played" (Calt and Wardlow, 43).

When Johnson left behind sharecropping and Robinsonville in search of his birth father and a musical vocation, he returned around 1931 to Hazelhurst, performing with mentor Ike Zinnerman in juke joints, writing down and practicing his songs in isolation in the woods, and playing on the courthouse steps during the day on Saturdays. In May 1931 Johnson married Calletta Craft, a woman ten years his senior, who showered him with attention, making his stay in southern Mississippi personally and musically fruitful, spurring a

newly confident Johnson to seek greener musical pastures. Deserting his family a short time later in Clarksdale, he headed back to Robinsonville to visit his mother and kin as well as to astonish House and Brown with his progress. After a couple of months he left this farming community for a performing base centered around Helena, Arkansas, though he traveled widely, playing in joints and levee camps in Mississippi, Arkansas, Tennessee, New York, and even in Canada. While around Helena, Johnson not only met Estella Coleman, who became his common-law wife, but also became a primary musical influence on her son, future recording artist Robert Lockwood Jr. In this period he also played with and inspired some of the Delta's greatest blues musicians, Sonny Boy Williamson II, Howlin' Wolf (Chester Burnett), Robert Nighthawk, and Elmore James among them.

By the middle 1930s Johnson was a popular Delta musician, albeit one with a reputation for drinking and womanizing. He was also ambitious, anxious to record as his old teachers Brown, Patton, and House had done. He auditioned for Jackson, Mississippi, music store owner and talent scout H. C. Speir, who passed Johnson's name on to ARC record label salesman/talent scout Ernie Oertle. Oertle took Johnson to radio station KONO facilities at the Blue Bonnet hotel in San Antonio, Texas, in 1936, recording two takes each of sixteen different songs on 23, 26, and 27 November. The success of Johnson's "Terraplane Blues," the title of which refers to a make of automobile, for the Vocalion label led to another session, in Dallas, where he recorded multiple takes of thirteen songs on 19 and 20 June 1937.

Riding the higher profile that "Terraplane Blues" brought him across the country, Johnson left the Delta with guitarists Calvin Frazier and Johnny Shines. They followed Highway 51 to St. Louis, Chicago, and Detroit and even played briefly in New York and New Jersey. Johnson proved to be an influential but elusive traveling partner, however, frequently departing unannounced, so the trio split, Frazier making a name for himself in Detroit, Shines, in Chicago. When Johnson produced no follow-up hits, ARC let his contract expire in June 1938 without recalling him to the

studio. On 13 August 1938, at a club where Johnson was performing outside Greenwood, Mississippi, called Three Forks, he drank some whiskey reputedly poisoned at the direction of a husband jealous of the attention that his wife and Johnson were paying to each other. Three days later Johnson died of pneumonia, just months before talent scout John Hammond intended to bring him to Carnegie Hall and probable acclaim at the Spirituals to Swing Concert in New York.

Johnson is a pivotal musician in the development of the blues. In many ways his work is a culmination of the work of Mississippi blues artists who preceded him and is a startling transformation of that material into a personal vision and style that defined the direction of post–World War II Chicago blues. The distinctive boogie figure that became his trademark, the famous bottleneck guitar intro to "I Believe I'll Dust My Broom," and the striking imagery of compositions such as "Cross Road Blues," "Sweet Home Chicago," "Love in Vain Blues," and "Hellbound on My Trail" influenced Williamson, Wolf, Nighthawk, James, and especially the young MUDDY WATERS (McKinley Morganfield), cementing his position as primary fountainhead of inspiration for artists whose work would lead blues and rock musicians like JIMI HENDRIX and the Rolling Stones back to Johnson's mesmerizing work. The sketchy nature of Johnson's biography before 1970 led to a good deal of mythologizing and misinformation, but his music has continued to startle listeners with its force and beauty. Chicago blues pioneer Muddy Waters called Johnson "one of the greatest there's ever been." British blues-rock performer Eric Clapton added reverently, "I have never found anything more deeply soulful than Robert Johnson. His music remains the most powerful cry that I think you can find in the human voice, really" (*Robert Johnson: The Complete Recordings*, 23). Longtime researcher Mack McCormack heard in Johnson's lyrics "a chilling confrontation with aspects of American consciousness. He is a visionary artist with a terrible kind of information about his time and place and personal experience." While Stephen Calt and Gayle Wardlow allow that among his contemporaries he was "conspicuous for his seediness, facial disfigurement...black derby," asserting that "only in his music did Johnson project anything but a prosaic figure," it is clear that, for many, Peter Guralnick's encomium—that Johnson was "certainly the most influential of all bluesmen"—is true (Calt and Wardlow, *Feel Like Going Home*, 54). He is a member of both the Rock and Roll Hall of Fame and the W. C. HANDY Awards Blues Hall of Fame.

FURTHER READING

Calt, Stephen, and Gayle Dean Wardlow. "Robert Johnson." *78 Quarterly* 1, no. 4 (1989): 40–51.

Guralnick, Peter. *Feel Like Going Home* (1999).
———. *Searching for Robert Johnson* (1988, 1998).

Pearson, Barry Lee, and Bill McCulloch. *Robert Johnson: Lost and Found* (2003).

Wald, Elijah. *Escaping the Delta: Robert Johnson and the Invention of the Blues* (2004).

Discography

Robert Johnson: The Complete Recordings, Columbia C2K 46222.

—STEVEN TRACY

JOHNSON, ROBERT L.

(April 8, 1946–), founder, chairman, and chief executive officer of Black Entertainment Television (BET), was born in Hickory, Mississippi, the ninth of ten children of Archie and Edna Johnson (a wood dealer and schoolteacher, respectively), but he spent most of his childhood in Freeport, Illinois. His father later became a factory worker and janitor. Robert Johnson, who is commonly known as Bob, was the only one of his siblings to attend college. He graduated with a BA degree in History from the University of Illinois in 1968. It was there that he met Sheila Crump, who would later become his wife. Johnson's interest in becoming an ambassador inspired him to earn an MA in Public Administration from the Woodrow Wilson School of Public and International Affairs at Princeton University in 1972. He then moved to Washington, D.C., and worked for both the Corporation for Public Broadcasting and Urban League. He went on to become the press secretary for Walter E. Fauntroy, the

congressional delegate for the District of Columbia. From 1976 to 1979, Johnson served as a lobbyist and then as the Vice President of Government Relations for the National Cable and Telecommunication Association, the main trade association of the American cable television industry.

At this point in his life, Bob Johnson had a revolutionary idea and very little money. His dream was to create the first cable network aimed at attracting African American viewers. With a $15,000 bank loan, Johnson approached John Malone, who was then the Chief Operating Officer of Tele-Communications Inc., the country's third-largest cable company at the time Malone invested $500,000 in the project and enabled Johnson and his wife to start Black Entertainment Television in 1979. The channel first aired at midnight on 8 January 1980, initially featuring reruns of comedies, infomercials, and old films before including music videos, which became a staple of the network. In 1991, BET became the first black-led company to be listed on the New York Stock Exchange, before going private in 1998. BET quickly became an African American icon. Johnson also created BET Holdings Inc., which entered the fields of publishing, film production, fashion design, and event production. BET expanded to include other channels such as BET International, BET Classic Soul, BET Hip Hop, BET Gospel, and BET Jazz, creating a cable empire of five channels reportedly reaching over seventy-five million homes. The BET Web site, BET.com, was a joint venture created by Microsoft, USA Networks, News Corporation and AT&T's Liberty Digital for $35 million in 1998. Through BET, Johnson created jobs for hundreds of African Americans in the television industry and provided a showcase for black artistic talent. Johnson sold BET in 1999, twenty years after its inception, to Viacom (the media conglomerate that owns CBS, Showtime, Nickelodeon, MTV, and Paramount Pictures) for nearly $3 billion in stock (over five times Johnson's initial investment), but he remains the chairman and CEO and he received $1.6 billion from the sale, making him the richest African American in the United States. Johnson has donated money to various charities, including

the United Negro College Fund and Howard University.

Johnson went on to create RLJ Companies and to buy restaurants, casinos, motion picture rights, and hotels. Out of the proposed merger of United and U.S. Airways, Johnson's goal was to own D.C. Air, the first major black-controlled American airline, but the airline merger was prevented by governmental intervention. Johnson is known as an ardent financial backer of the Democratic Party, but in 2002 he agreed to serve on the Social Security Commission under President George W. Bush. Johnson also initiated a million-dollar campaign to produce and air advertisements on BET to encourage viewers to vote. In 2003 he outbid basketball great Larry Bird to purchase the Charlotte Bobcats of the NBA and the Charlotte Sting of the WNBA for $300 million, making Johnson the first African American owner of a major sports franchise. His future plans include establishing the first national black-owned bank. He also owns one of the nation's largest collections of African American art, the Barnett-Aden Collection. Johnson serves on the boards of U.S. Airways, General Mills, the American Film Institute, and Hilton Hotels, as well as the board of governors for the Rock and Roll Hall of Fame in Cleveland and the Brookings Institute. Johnson is the recipient of the NAACP's Image Award and Princeton's Distinguished Alumni Award, and is listed in *Sports Illustrated* magazine's list of the 101 Most Influential Minorities in Sports. He also received *Broadcasting & CableMagazine*'s Hall of Fame Award. When he received *Cablevision Magazine*'s 20/20 Vision Award, the publication listed him as one of the twenty most influential people in the cable industry. Johnson and his former wife, Sheila, have two children.

Johnson's goal in creating BET was geared more toward economics than social policy, but his success in creating the network and using his financial power in such an impressive array of fields enabled him to break through numerous racial barriers and serve as a role model for many. Some critics fault BET's misogynistic rap videos and lack of original programming, as well as Johnson's sale of the company to the global media giant Viacom and his firing of the popular BET personality, Tavis

Smiley. It is Johnson's personal story, however, that merits acclaim. He went from a relatively humble background to amass unbelievable wealth by pursuing a dream. His life's accomplishments illustrate a remarkable example of perseverance, faith, and courage.

FURTHER READING

Pulley, Brett. *The Billion Dollar BET: Robert Johnson and the Creation of Black Entertainment Television* (2004).

Dingle, Derek T. *Black Enterprise Titans of the B.E. 100s: Black CEOs Who Redefined and Conquered American Business* (1999).

—JENNIFER WOOD

 **JOHNSON, WILLIAM H.** (18 Mar. 1901–13 Apr. 1970), artist, was born William Henry Johnson in Florence, South Carolina, the first of five children of Henry Johnson and Alice Smoot. From the moment of William's birth, neighbors speculated whether this light-skinned, wavy-haired child was the offspring of Henry Johnson, a dark-skinned laborer, and his wife, a woman with dark mahogany skin who worked as a domestic in the home of a prominent white family.

As a child, Johnson attended Wilson School, an all-black elementary school, where he exhibited an early interest in sketching. A teacher encouraged his talent by giving him supplies, and Johnson thought of becoming a cartoonist. However, as a youth he devoted most of his time to supplementing the meager family income as a pinsetter at a bowling alley, shoveling coal, and working at a laundry. Realizing that his opportunities for professional and artistic development were severely limited in a small, segregated southern town, Johnson boarded a train for New York City in 1918.

Upon his arrival in New York, Johnson lived on 128th Street in Harlem with his uncle, Willie Smoot. He found menial work in hotels and restaurants until the fall of 1921, when his drawings earned him a place at the National Academy of Design (NAD). Johnson excelled in his early studies and won a prize in a student competition for one of his drawings. During his second year Johnson fell under the influence of Charles Hawthorne, a new instructor

An artist of exceptional stylistic and expressive range, William H. Johnson employed a bold, "primitive" style to portray African Americans in the urban North and the rural South in the late 1930s and 1940s. Self-portrait, Smithsonian American Art Museum, Gift of the Harmon Foundation/Art Resource, NY

at the NAD, who fundamentally altered Johnson's perspective on art.

Hawthorne urged his students to seek inspiration from their subjects, to experiment with form, and to abandon the more subdued conservative palate in favor of vivid color and bold expression. During the summers from 1924 to 1926 Johnson studied with Hawthorne at the Cape Cod School of Art, doing odd jobs around the school to earn his tuition. He was usually the only black student in these settings, and he had a reputation for being reticent, even aloof, preferring to let his work speak for him. Hawthorne recognized Johnson's exceptional talent and encouraged him to go to Europe, cautioning him that in America "there is bound to be prejudice against your race (Powell, 37)."

It is widely believed that Johnson was denied the NAD's most coveted award, the Pulitzer Traveling Scholarship, in 1926 because of class and race prejudice. Hawthorne and others were so incensed by this apparent act of discrimination that they privately

raised the funds to support Johnson's study in France. Shortly after arriving in Paris, Johnson met the most renowned black painter of his generation, HENRY OSSAWA TANNER, who had long since made Paris his home. Johnson's European work from 1926 to 1932 focuses on the challenges of capturing landscapes and pastoral vistas rather than on human subjects. These paintings show an admiration for Paul Cézanne and the expressionist Chaim Soutine. Johnson often described what he was trying to express in his paintings as "primitivism." The art historian Richard Powell explains that Johnson's concept of primitivism "was not based on black culture itself, but rather on emotional and psychological interpretations of that culture" (Powell, 75).

In 1928 Johnson moved to Cagnes-sur-Mer in southern France. There he met the German expressionist sculptor Christoph Voll; his wife, Erna; and her sister, Holcha Krake, a ceramic and textile artist. Together this group traveled to Corsica, France, Germany, Luxembourg, and Belgium, visiting museums and sharing their work.

Anxious to find an audience for his growing body of work and hoping to live on the proceeds of his art, Johnson returned to America in 1929 and entered six of his pieces in the William E. Harmon Foundation competition. He won the Gold Medal, which came with a four-hundred-dollar cash award, and four of his paintings were selected for an exhibit, where they received favorable reviews. Johnson returned for a brief visit to Florence, South Carolina, where the local YMCA arranged a one-day show featuring more than one hundred paintings by their up-and-coming native son. On his return trip to New York City, Johnson stopped in Washington, D.C., where he stayed at the home of ALAIN LOCKE, a leading spokesperson for the Negro arts movement during the Harlem Renaissance. Locke became a mentor to Johnson, finding buyers for some of his paintings and introducing him to luminaries in the art and literary world.

In May of 1930 Johnson returned to Europe, married Holcha in June, and settled in the small Danish fishing village of Kerteminde. Many of Johnson's Scandinavian paintings, such as *Lanskab fra Kerteminde* (c. 1930–1932, National Museum of American Art [NMAA]) and *Sun Setting, Denmark* (c. 1930, NMAA), use vibrant color, thick paint, and strong brushwork reminiscent of the work of Vincent van Gogh. By the age of thirty Johnson had tried a variety of aesthetic approaches, from post-impressionism to European expressionism, yet, in his words, he had not found the "the real me." As he put it, "Europe is so very superficial. Modern European art strives to be primitive, but it is too complicated" (Powell, 69). Like Pablo Picasso and Paul Gauguin, who had incorporated African and Tahitian imagery into their work to great acclaim, Johnson planned a trip to North Africa for the spring of 1932. There, as he put it, "I might be the first at the same time primitive and cultivated painter the world has ever seen" (Turner and Dailey, 24).

Johnson and Holcha spent three months in Tunisia. They traveled to Kairouan, where Johnson painted a series of watercolors depicting the bustling markets, the towering minarets,

and the majestic mosque. When they returned to Denmark at the end of the summer, his paintings and her ceramics appeared in several local exhibitions, but Johnson sent the majority of his new work to the Harmon Foundation in New York, expecting that it would be exhibited and sold. The foundation managed to sell only two of Johnson's paintings in six years, owing both to their lack of effort and the contracting art market during the Depression. By the late 1930s the scourge of Nazi propaganda was spreading across Europe; Christoph Voll's work was discredited by the Nazis as "degenerate art," resulting in Voll's being fired from his teaching position in Germany. In November 1938, with these ominous clouds on the horizon, Johnson and Holcha sailed for New York.

Back in America, the Works Progress Administration had created the Federal Art Project (FAP). In May of 1939 Johnson was hired by the FAP and assigned to teach art at the Harlem Community Art Center. Two important developments emerged from this experience: Johnson again became part of the Black Arts Movement, surrounded by contemporaries like JACOB LAWRENCE and Gwendolyn Knight, and African Americans reappeared as the primary subject of his paintings.

During this period Johnson's paintings began to take on an Egyptian-like flatness, as can be seen in *Jitterbug (I)* (c. 1940–1941, NMAA), where the figures are animated on the canvas by bold colors and kinetic gestures. In addition, much of Johnson's American oeuvre contains explicit political messages, readily seen in *Chain Gang* (c. 1939, NMAA) and *Moon over Harlem* (c. 1943–1944, NMAA), which depicts acts of police brutality against Negroes; and his Fighters for Freedom series, which pays homage to such significant figures as FREDERICK DOUGLASS, HARRIET TUBMAN, and NAT TURNER.

Following Holcha's death from cancer in 1944, religious themes appear in Johnson's work with greater frequency, though his interest in spiritual subject matter was already well established. Johnson's own physical and mental state began to deteriorate rapidly after 1945. In 1946 he returned to Denmark, hoping to find the peace and happiness of an earlier time. However, Johnson's

behavior became increasingly erratic and confused, and he lived briefly as a vagrant on the streets of Copenhagen until it was determined that he suffered from an advanced case of syphilis-induced paresis. Johnson's European relatives sent him back to America, where he spent the rest of his life as an inmate at Central Islip State Hospital on Long Island. Johnson never painted again, and he died in 1970, oblivious to the growing critical acclaim of his work.

FURTHER READING

The papers of William H. Johnson are in two collections: William H. Johnson Papers, Archives of American Art, Smithsonian Institution, Washington, D.C., and William H. Johnson Papers, Smithsonian Institution Archives, Washington, D.C.

Breeskin, Adelyn D. *William H. Johnson* (1971).
Powell, Richard J. *Homecoming: The Art and Life of William H. Johnson* (1991).
Turner, Steve, and Victoria Dailey. *William H. Johnson: Truth Be Told* (1998).
—SHOLOMO BEN LEVY

JOHNSON-BROWN, HAZEL (10 Oct. 1927–), army general, nurse, and educator, was born Hazel Winifred Johnson, the daughter of Clarence L. and Garnett Johnson, in Malvern, Pennsylvania. One of seven children, she grew up in a close-knit family on a farm in West Chester, Pennsylvania. Although she was rejected from the local nursing program because of racial prejudice, Johnson persisted in her childhood dream of becoming a nurse and received a nursing diploma in 1950 from Harlem Hospital School of Nursing in New York City. Following graduation, she worked as a beginning-level staff nurse at Harlem Hospital's emergency ward and in 1953 went to the Veterans Administration Hospital in Philadelphia, quickly becoming the head nurse on a ward.

Two years later Johnson decided to join the army because, she said, "the Army had more variety to offer and more places to go" (Bombard, 65). She was commissioned as a second lieutenant in the U.S. Army Nurse Corps (ANC) and sent to Fort Sam Houston, Texas, for the medical Officer Basic Training Course. Johnson adjusted

Brigadier General Hazel Johnson-Brown, chief of the Army Nurse Corps. Army Nurse Corps Historical Collection, Office of the Surgeon General

quickly to military life, saying, "All that drilling...it was fun, going to school, going to classes" (Bombard, 67).

As a reserve officer on active duty, her first assignment was to the women's ward at Walter Reed Army Hospital in Washington, D.C., followed by duty as an obstetrical nurse with the 8169 Hospital, Camp Zama, Japan. Having already accumulated almost eighty credits toward her bachelor's degree in nursing, in 1957 she left the active army to serve in the U.S. Army Reserve while studying part time at Villanova University and working at the Veterans Administration hospital in Philadelphia. Johnson was subsequently accepted into the ANC RN Student program and completed her BSN degree in 1959.

Receiving a direct commission as first lieutenant in the regular army, Johnson returned to active duty in 1960 and was assigned to Madigan General Hospital at Fort Lewis, Washington, to care for a patient on a respirator. Johnson, who said, "My love for the OR started as a student," then completed the Basic Operating Room Nurse course at Letterman Army Medical Center at the Presidio in San Francisco and returned to Walter Reed in the operating room. In the summer of 1963 Johnson, by then a captain, was selected to attend Columbia University Teachers College, and in 1963 she completed her MA in Nursing Education with a minor in Medical Surgical Nursing. She then went back to

Letterman, where she taught the OR course from 1963 until 1966.

In 1966 Johnson was chosen to participate in a special project at the Forty-fifth Surgical Hospital in Texas, evaluating the first MUST (or Medical Unit, Self-Contained Transportable) hospital. Illness prevented her from deploying to Vietnam as the unit's OR supervisor and she went instead to Valley Forge General Hospital in Pennsylvania in October 1966 as the supervisor of Central Material Services. Then, in 1967, Johnson was promoted to major and became the first nurse to be a member of the staff at the army's Medical Research and Development Command. There she served as a project director for the Field Sterilization Equipment Development Project, reviewing procedures for field sterilization and developing new surgical equipment for army field hospitals. In 1969 she was promoted to lieutenant colonel.

After completing a three-year course of study toward her doctorate at Catholic University in Washington, D.C., Johnson became director and assistant dean at Walter Reed Army Institute of Nursing (WRAIN), University of Maryland School of Nursing, overseeing the last two classes to graduate from WRAIN. In the meantime, Johnson was working after hours on her dissertation, and in 1978 she was awarded her doctorate in Educational Administration from Catholic University.

That same year she went to Japan as assistant for nursing at the Eighth Army Command Office of the Surgeon and Chief, Department of Nursing, at the U.S. Army hospital in Seoul Korea. There she worked closely with the Korean Army Nurse Corps and Ewaha University School of Nursing students and, as the head nurse, traveled extensively to visit military health facilities in South Korea.

In 1979 Johnson was selected to be the sixteenth chief of the ANC and was promoted to the rank of brigadier general. She was the first chief to hold a doctorate, fourth chief to hold the rank of a general officer, and first black woman general in the history of the U.S. Army. "This achievement was not a straight road from her native Malvern, Pa.," the Surgeon General, Lt. Gen. Charles C. Pixley, said, "but was a road beset with obstacles and difficulties that could be overcome by extraordinary

dedication, enduring vitality and great moral courage." Johnson told newsmen, "For the nurse corps and my colleagues in nursing, I hope the criterion for selection didn't include race but competence" (*All Volunteer*, Feb. 1980). Competence, "integrity of purpose," and "honesty" in her job have been Johnson's lifelong goals. As chief of the ANC, Johnson initiated steps to include nursing in the Reserve Officer Training Corps (ROTC) scholarship program, established a summer clinical experience opportunity for ROTC nursing students, and published the first documented Standards of Nursing Practice for army nursing. Seeing a need for "research, writing, and publishing by nurses," Johnson encouraged the writing of an ANC history and continued education for army nurses, including the first Nursing Research Symposium. She also initiated the publishing of graduate education and military education requirements for all major positions for ANC officers and laid the foundation for a strategic planning conference to plan for the future of the corps.

Johnson retired from active duty in the army in 1983 to become the director of the government affairs division of the American Nurses Association and an adjunct professor at Georgetown University School of Nursing. In the 1980s Johnson married David B. Brown and in 1986 joined the faculty at George Mason University in Virginia as professor of nursing.

Among her many honors, Johnson-Brown has received the Evangeline C. Bovard Army Nurse of the Year Award, the Army Nurse of the Year Award from Letterman General Hospital, and the Daughters of the American Revolution's Nurse of the Year, Dr. Anita Newcomb McGee Award. Her military decorations include the Distinguished Service Medal, Army Commendation Medal with Oak Leaf Cluster, Meritorious Service Medal, and Legion of Merit. Johnson-Brown also holds honorary degrees from Morgan State University, the University of Maryland, and Villanova University.

When asked how she would like people to remember her, Johnson-Brown said, "Probably as a good person, one who tries to do the best job possible for the Corps and for the profession of nursing, and that I did try" (Bombard, 155).

FURTHER READING

The best account of Johnson-Brown's life is Lt. Col. Charles F. Bombard's 1984 oral history of the Army Nurse Corps, at the Center for Military History, Washington, D.C., which includes her curriculum vitae.

Carnegie, Mary Elizabeth. *The Path We Tread: Blacks in Nursing, Worldwide 1954–1994* (1995).

Samecky, Mary T. *A History of the U.S. Army Nurse Corps* (1999).

—BARBARA B. TOMBLIN

JONES, ABSALOM

(6 Nov. 1746–13 Feb. 1818), first black Protestant Episcopal priest, was born in Sussex, Delaware, the son of slave parents. He was a small child when his master took him from the fields to wait on him in the house. Jones was very fond of learning and was very careful to save the pennies that were given to him by ladies and gentlemen from time to time. He soon bought a primer and would beg people to teach him how to read. Before long he was able to purchase a spelling book, and as his funds increased he began to buy books, including a copy of the New

Absalom Jones, founder with RICHARD ALLEN of the St. Thomas's African Episcopal Church in Philadelphia in the early 1790s, was ordained the first black priest in the United States in 1804. Schomburg Center

Testament. "Fondness for books gave me little or no time for amusements that took up the leisure hours of my companions" (Bragg, 3).

When Jones was sixteen, his mother, five brothers and a sister were sold, and he was taken to Philadelphia by his master. There he worked in his master's store, where he would pack and carry out to customers' carriages goods that had been purchased. Gradually he learned to write and was soon able to write to his brothers and mother "with my own hand." In 1766 he began attending a Quaker-operated night school for blacks. When he was twenty-four, he married Mary (maiden name unknown), a slave woman. Shortly after the marriage, he arranged to purchase his wife's freedom. His wife's mistress agreed to a price of forty pounds, and Jones borrowed thirty pounds and the mistress forgave the remaining ten pounds. For the next eight years Jones worked almost every night until twelve or one o'clock to raise money to repay what he had borrowed.

By 1778 he had paid off the loan with which he had purchased his wife's freedom and made application to his owner to purchase his own freedom with some additional money that he had saved. This was not granted. Jones then bought a lot with a sizable house and continued to work and save his money. Again he applied to his master to purchase his freedom, and on 1 October 1784 he was granted manumission.

At this time the city of Philadelphia was alive with the spirit of the revolution and the ideal of universal freedom. In 1780 a law was passed that called for the gradual emancipation of the slave population. Also at this time a new religious movement was developing in the emerging United States. The Methodists were evangelicals within the Church of England who met in small groups to enhance their religious life. They were particularly strong in New York, Baltimore, and Philadelphia. On 24–25 December 1784, under the leadership of Thomas Coke and Francis Asbury, members of these Methodist societies met at Lovely Lane Chapel in Baltimore and organized the Methodist Episcopal Church as a new denomination separate from the Church of England. In the three large cities previously mentioned, numerous blacks

joined the Methodist church. Many of the free blacks of Philadelphia attended the mostly white St. George's Methodist Episcopal Church, as did Jones. Also among them was RICHARD ALLEN, who became the founder and first bishop of the African Methodist Episcopal Church. For a while the blacks and whites got along well at St. George's Church. As Methodism spread among the whites, the space occupied by black Methodists in the church building was more and more in demand by the increasing number of white congregants. The blacks were moved from place to place in the building as circumstances required. One Sunday morning in 1787 a number of blacks were seated together and had knelt for prayer. Jones, the leader of the group, was pulled from his knees, and the blacks were told to move to another place in the building. The entire group of blacks arose and walked out of the church never to return. This unpleasant episode was the occasion that prompted the first organization among free blacks of which there is any record.

On 12 April 1787 some of these black Methodists met in a home in Philadelphia and organized the Free African Society. Jones was the leader of the group, and Allen was one of the overseers. It was a benevolent and social reform organization at first. Episcopal bishop William White of Pennsylvania was a leader in the encouragement and support of the Free African Society. Gradually the Free African Society transformed itself into an "African Church" with no denominational ties. At a meeting held 21 July 1792, a resolution was adopted that appropriated money to purchase property on which to erect "a place of worship for this Society." The society erected a church building that was dedicated on 17 July 1794. Later in the year an election was held to determine with which denomination to unite. "There were two in favor of the Methodists, Absalom Jones and Richard Allen; and a large majority in favor of the Church of England. This majority carried" (Bragg, 9). Jones went with the majority, but Allen did not. On 12 August 1794 the African Church became St. Thomas Episcopal Church, the first black Episcopal church in the United States. It was formally received into the diocese of Pennsylvania on 12 October 1794.

At that October diocesan convention Jones was received as a candidate for holy orders in the Episcopal Church and was licensed as a lay reader. On 21 October 1794 he formally accepted the position of pastor of St. Thomas Church. At the diocesan convention on 2 June 1795, it was stipulated that St. Thomas Church was not entitled to send a clergyman or any lay deputies to the convention, nor was it "to interfere with the general government of the Episcopal Church." Jones was ordained a deacon on 23 August 1795 and then priest on September 1804, the first black to become a deacon or a priest in the Episcopal Church. From 1795 until his death, Jones baptized 268 black adults and 927 black infants. His ministry among blacks was so significant that he was called the "Black Bishop of the Episcopal Church." Jones died in Philadelphia.

FURTHER READING

The few extant Jones papers are in the Archives of the Episcopal Church, Austin, Texas.

Bragg, George F. *The Story of the First of the Blacks, the Pathfinder, Absalom Jones, 1746–1818* (1929).
Lammers, Ann C. "The Rev. Absalom Jones and the Episcopal Church: Christian Theology and Black Consciousness in a New Alliance." *Historical Magazine of the Protestant Episcopal Church* (1982): 159–84.
Lewis, Harold T. *Yet with a Steady Beat: The African American Struggle for Recognition in the Episcopal Church* (1996).
—DONALD S. ARMENTROUT

JONES, ADDISON. *See* Nigger Add.

JONES, BILL T.
(15 Feb. 1952–), dancer and choreographer, was born William Tass Jones in Bunnell, Florida, the tenth of the twelve children of Ella and Augustus Jones, migrant farm workers who traveled throughout the Southeast. The family became "stagnants" in 1959, when they settled in the predominantly white community of Wayland in the Finger Lakes region of upstate New York. There they harvested fruits and vegetables and also operated a restaurant and juke joint.

In childhood Jones navigated between the rural, southern black cultural values of his home life and the predominantly white middle-class world of his peers at school. Black English was spoken at home, white English in the classroom. That experience was not without its complications and, sometimes, pain, but Jones believed that it served him well as a performer by teaching him that the "world was a place of struggle that had to be negotiated" (Washington, 190). He did well at school, won awards for public speaking, directed a production of Arthur Miller's *The Crucible*, and starred on the track team. But Jones also cultivated an independent streak that one of his teachers, Mary Lee Shappee, encouraged. An outspoken atheist in a largely devout community, Shappee advised him, "There's something more than this" (Washington, 191).

Determined to find that "something," Jones entered the State University of New York at Binghamton in 1970 to study drama and prepare for a career on Broadway. He found himself increasingly isolated from fellow black students, however, believing that they viewed him as an "unauthentic, white dependent Negro" (Jones, 81). Although he had been in relationships with women in high school, he was also sexually attracted to men and was intrigued by a student group poster with the invitation "Gay?? Come Out and Meet Your Brothers and Sisters!!" At the consciousness-raising meeting, Jones confessed that coming out was especially difficult for him, because he was convinced that African Americans felt that being gay was the "ultimate emasculation of the black man" (Jones, 82).

During his second semester Jones met Arnie Zane, a Jewish Italian American photographer and drama student from Queens, New York. In 1971 Zane became Jones's first male lover, and the

Dancer and choreographer Bill T. Jones has infused the world of international contemporary dance not only with his own personal dance vocabulary but also with social concerns, such as HIV/AIDS, interracial relationships, and tolerance. © Lois Greenfield, 2003

couple began a personal and professional partnership that would last for seventeen years. Jones had begun dance lessons shortly before meeting Zane, but it was Zane who inspired his passion for dance. Jones enrolled in Afro-Caribbean and West African dance classes at Binghamton with the Trinidadian choreographer Percival Borde, participated in workshops on contact improvisation, and became grounded in the Cecchetti method of classical ballet. Martha Graham, who codified the language of modern dance, and Jerome Robbins, who choreographed *West Side Story*, were also influential in his development as a dancer.

During the early 1970s Jones and Zane lived a peripatetic, bohemian existence, first in Amsterdam and then in San Francisco, before returning to Binghamton in 1974. There the couple helped a fellow dancer, Lois Welk, revive her American Dance Asylum, supplementing their income with part-time jobs—Zane as a go-go dancer and Jones as a laundry worker. By 1976 Jones was beginning to achieve recognition in the dance world, receiving a Creative Artist Public Service Award for *Everybody Works / All Beasts Count*, a performance in which he spun around half naked in Central Park while shouting, "I love you" to the heavens in memory of two of his favorite aunts.

Determined to establish their own distinctive style, Jones and Zane rejected both the refined, regimented modernism that they believed characterized ALVIN AILEY's Dance Theater of Harlem and the cultural nationalist aesthetic of the Black Arts Movement. Instead, they developed an avant-garde approach influenced by Yvonne Rainier, a postmodernist choreographer and filmmaker known for her experiments with fragmented movements and for placing characters and narrative in radical juxtapositions. From the beginning of Jones and Zane's collaboration, reviewers noted that the bodies, movements, and personalities of the two dancers provided the most dramatic juxtaposition of all. As one early review noted: "Mr. Jones is black, with a long, lithe body, a fine speaking voice and a look of leashed hostility. Mr. Zane is white, short and chunky, with a buoyant, strutting walk and the very funny look of an officious floorwalker in a second-rate department store." (*New York Times*, 5 Apr. 1981). The couple also experimented with innovative locations for their performances—including the Battery Park Landfill in lower Manhattan—and often employed dancers who had little in the way of professional dance training. Looking back at their work in the late 1970s and early 1980s, Jones recalled that he and Zane "used to turn up our nose at refined technique. We thought it made for dead art. Instead, we'd look for the beauty in falling, running or in watching a large person jump" (*People*, 31 July 1989).

Jones and Zane left the American Dance Asylum in 1980, and the following year Jones appeared in *Social Intercourse: Pilgrim's Progress*, which was one of five pieces by promising new-comers selected for performance at the prestigious American Dance Festival in Durham, North Carolina. In that piece Jones improvised a solo with a monologue in which he paired seemingly paradoxical outbursts: I love white people / I hate white people; Why didn't you leave us in Africa? / I'm so thankful for the opportunity to be here; and I love women / I hate women. Jones's provocative style also ensured plenty of detractors, notably the *New Yorker*'s Arlene Croce, who described his work as narcissistic.

In 1982 Jones and Zane founded Bill T. Jones/Arnie Zane and Company, with Zane focusing mainly on directing and managing and Jones starring as the primary dancer. The company debuted the following year at the Brooklyn Academy of Music with *Intuitive Momentum*, a performance that drew on the martial arts, vaudeville, and social dance and which received positive reviews for the dancers' frenzied, acrobatic movements. The company won its first New York Dance and Performance Award (known as "Bessies") for their 1986 season at New York's Joyce Theater, and soon emerged as among the most popular and challenging troupes in the world of modern dance. In March 1988, however, with Jones at his bedside, Zane died of AIDS-related lymphoma. Jones, too, was diagnosed as HIV positive in the 1980s but remains asymptomatic. The couple's last collaboration, *Body against Body* (1989), includes Zane's photos, Jones's poetry and prose, performance scripts, and commentaries by dancers, critics, composers, and others.

Jones's career continued to flourish after his partner's death, and the company—which retained Zane's name—remained true to its founders' vision of an inclusive troupe that embraced different races, sexual orientations, and body shapes. Jones received a second Bessie in 1989 for *D-Man in the Waters*, and the following year, along with his sister Rhodessa Jones, he won an Isadora Duncan Dance Award (Izzy) for *Perfect Courage*.

Despite his growing fame, Jones continued to infuriate some reviewers, notably for *Last Supper at Uncle Tom's Cabin / The Promised Land* (1990), a multimedia work that ended with audience members joining the dancers on stage in taking off all of their clothes. Jones responded to those critics by noting that the nudity was the entire point of the piece. "In this polarized, sexually very confused city," he told the *New York Times*. "can we stand up as a group and not be ashamed of our nakedness?" (4 Nov. 1990). Even more controversial was *Still/Here* (1994), a work that addressed the subject of death and dying. The performance incorporated videotaped testimonies of a diverse range of people with terminal illnesses that Jones had collected at "Survival Workshops" that he had organized in several American cities. The *New Yorker*'s Arlene Croce dismissed the work as "victim art" and refused to attend the performance, provoking a firestorm of debate among Jones's many admirers and detractors.

The clearest answer to Jones's critics has been the steady flow of awards that he and his company continue to receive. These honors include a MacArthur Foundation award in 1994, a Laurence Olivier Award for Outstanding Achievement in Dance and Best New Dance Production for *We Set Out Early... Visibility Was Poor* (1999), a second Izzy for *Fantasy in C-Major* (2001), and a third Bessie for *The Table Project* and *The Breathing Show* (2001). In addition to choreographing more than fifty works for his own company, Jones has also received commissions for works for, among others, the Boston Ballet, the Berlin Opera Ballet, the Houston Grand Opera, and the Glyndebourne Festival in England. In 1995 Jones teamed up with the legendary jazz drummer Max Roach and the Nobel Prize–winning author TONI MORRISON to produce *Degga*, a collaboration of dance, percussion, and spoken word at the Lincoln Center's Serious Fun Festival. Perhaps the most significant and fitting of Jones's awards came in 2002, however, when the Dance Heritage Coalition of America named him an "Irreplaceable Dance Treasure."

FURTHER READING

Jones, Bill T., and Peggy Gillespie. *Last Night on Earth* (1995).

Gates, Henry Louis. *Thirteen Ways of Looking at a Black Man* (1997).

Washington, Eric K. "Sculpture in Flight." *Transition* 62 (1993).

—ELSHADAY GEBREYES
—STEVEN J. NIVEN

JONES, EUGENE KINCKLE (30 July 1885– 11 Jan. 1954), social welfare reformer, was the son of Joseph Endom Jones and Rosa Daniel Kinckle, a fairly comfortable and prominent middle-class black couple in Richmond, Virginia. Both his parents were college educated. Jones grew to maturity at a period in American history when the federal government turned its back on providing full citizenship rights to African Americans. Although the Civil War had ended slavery and the Fourteenth and Fifteenth Amendments to the U.S. Constitution had guaranteed blacks equal rights, state governments in the South began to erode those rights following the end of Reconstruction in 1877.

Jones grew up in Richmond at a time of racial polarization, and he watched as African American men and women struggled to hold on to the gains that some had acquired during Reconstruction. Like others in W. E. B. DU BOIS's "talented tenth," he saw education as the best means of improving his own life and of helping others, and he graduated from Richmond's Virginia Union University in 1905. He then moved to Ithaca, New York, to attend Cornell University, where, in 1906, he was a founding member of the nation's first black Greek lettered fraternity, Alpha Phi Alpha. He later helped found two other chapters at Howard University and at his alma mater, Virginia Union. He graduated from Cornell with a master's degree

in 1908 and taught high school in Louisville, Kentucky, until 1911. In 1909 he married Blanche Ruby Watson, with whom he went on to have two children.

In 1911 Jones began working as the first field secretary for the National Urban League (NUL), a social service agency for blacks that had been founded in New York City in 1910. By the 1920s he had superimposed the philosophy and organization of Alpha Phi Alpha upon the league, which was by that time dealing with the problems of poverty, poor housing, ill health, and crime that emerged during the first great black migration from the rural South to the urban North. He worked diligently to establish as many local branches as possible, believing that the concept of local branches would further the NUL's national agenda. Jones also placed key individuals in the directorships of local branches, which enabled him to be informed at all times of the conditions in black urban areas. In addition, he established fellowship programs to ensure that a larger pool of African American social workers would be available to tackle the problems that rural migrants faced in the burgeoning inner cities of the North. In 1923, along with the NUL's research director, the sociologist CHARLES S. JOHNSON, Jones helped launch *Opportunity*, a journal that addressed the problems faced by urban blacks but which also provided an outlet for a new generation of African American writers and artists, including AARON DOUGLAS and LANGSTON HUGHES.

In 1915 Jones and a group of other black social reformers founded the Social Work Club to address the concerns of African American social workers. This organization was short-lived, for by 1921 black social workers had become actively involved with the American Association of Social Workers. In 1925 the National Conference of Social Work elected Jones treasurer, making him the first African American on its executive board. Jones went on to serve the organization until 1933, by which time he had risen to the position of vice president of the National Conference of Social Work (NCSW). This post put him in a position of importance within the national structure of the social work profession. During Jones's tenure as an executive officer of the NCSW, he worked with other black

social workers to make white reformers aware—often for the first time—of the urban problems particular to African Americans.

In 1933 Jones became one of the leading black figures in Washington, D.C., when he took a position with the Department of Commerce as an adviser on Negro Affairs. Perhaps no single person matched Jones's efforts in delivering to African American communities the opportunities that became available to them through the federal government's newly initiated relief programs. While in Washington, he also served as the voice of the black community through the NUL and its local branches. In so doing, Jones came to personify the NUL in the 1930s, while he served along with MARY MCLEOD BETHUNE, ROBERT WEAVER, and WILLIAM HENRY HASTIE as part of President Franklin Roosevelt's so-called Black Cabinet.

By the time of Jones's retirement in 1940, the NUL had become a relatively conservative organization. A younger generation was rising to prominence, and many African Americans were no longer willing to wait as patiently for justice and their full citizenship rights as Jones and his contemporaries had been willing to do. However, Jones's handpicked successor, Lester B. Granger, continued in the more conservative style of leadership embraced by Jones. The NUL therefore did not engage in the direct methods of the modern civil rights movement until 1960, when WHITNEY YOUNG was appointed executive secretary. Jones died in New York after a short illness in January 1954.

Like other middle-class blacks, Jones felt a strong sense of responsibility for uplifting less fortunate members of his race. In that regard, his social views conformed with other turn-of-the-century African American social reformers, such as Du Bois, CARTER G. WOODSON, JAMES WELDON JOHNSON, IDA B. WELLS-BARNETT, and MARY CHURCH TERRELL. The accomplishments of these progressive era reformers have historically been ignored compared with those of their white counterparts, such as the settlement house leader Jane Addams. Scholars have recently begun to acknowledge, however, that African American middle-class activists like Jones led the early-twentieth-century social reform movement in black America, even though the middle-class ethos of these reformers did not exactly mirror that of the larger white society. Above all, Jones's tenure as executive secretary of the NUL showcases the achievements of early black social reformers. He also helped make the league an African American, and an American, institution.

FURTHER READING

Information on Jones can be found in the National Urban League Archives in the Manuscript Division of the Library of Congress, Washington, D.C.

Carlton-LaNey, Iris B., ed. *African American Leadership: An Empowerment Tradition in Social Welfare History* (2001).
Weiss, Nancy J. *The National Urban League, 1910–1940* (1974).
Wesley, Charles H. *The History of Alpha Phi Alpha: A Development in Negro College Life* (1929).

—FELIX L. ARMFIELD

JONES, JAMES EARL

(17 Jan. 1931–), actor, was born in Arkabutla, Mississippi, the only child of Robert Earl Jones, a prizefighter and actor, and Ruth Williams Connoly, a seamstress. James's parents parted ways in search of work before their son was born, and he was raised by his mother's parents, John and Maggie Connoly. He grew up on their farm, alongside seven children and two other grandchildren. From an early age James was put to work beside his aunts, uncles, and cousins, tending the livestock, hunting, and helping with harvests. At night Maggie Connoly would regale the family with lurid bedtime stories—tales of lynchings, hurricanes, and rapes. The Connolys knew that Mississippi schools offered their children little, and in 1936 they planned a move to Dublin, Michigan. Before the family left, John Connoly took James to his paternal grandmother's house in Memphis, but James refused to leave the car. He followed the family north later that year.

Soon after the move to Michigan, James began to stutter; he spoke only to his family, to the farm animals, and to himself. In grammar school he managed to get by on written work, and it was not until high school that someone sought to help him. An English teacher, Donald Crouch, pushed James to join the debate team. With practice, James proved a captivating orator and, by the end of high school, managed to overcome his stuttering in conversation, too. As he regained his powers of speech, he took to the classics Crouch taught and spent many an afternoon reading Shakespeare aloud in the fields.

At this time James's father was living in New York City and trying his hand at theater. When James announced to his uncle Randy that he, too, would be an actor, John Connoly pounced on his grandson and struck him in the back of the head. In 1949 James entered the University of Michigan on a Regents Scholarship and enrolled in premed classes, but the pull of the theater proved too strong; he began taking roles in school plays and spending his holidays in summer-stock productions.

Jones had joined the Reserve Officer Training Corps to help fund his education, and he abandoned school in 1953, just before graduation, convinced that he would shortly be killed in the Korean War. But the conflict cooled off that summer, and Jones spent his two years of service at the Cold Weather Training Command in Colorado. He enjoyed the strenuous work and the solitude of the Rockies, but when he told his commanding officer that he wanted to be an actor, he was urged to pursue theater before committing to military life. Jones finished his BA through an extension program and moved in with his father in New York. He enrolled in acting workshops at the American Theatre Wing, paying his way with funds from the GI Bill.

After twenty-four years of separation, Jones and his father did not get along well, and during one argument they nearly came to blows. But if the two did not bond as father and son, they came together over their shared passion. Late into the night, they would recite scenes from *Othello*. After six months Jones moved to the Lower East Side and continued his austere routine of workshops, auditions, and menial jobs. In 1957 he landed his first Broadway role as an understudy to Lloyd Richards in *The Egghead*. That same year he found more substantial work in Ted Pollock's play *Wedding in Japan*.

In the early 1960s off-Broadway theater offered a heady cocktail of new talent, edgy scripts, and rundown venues. Jones entered the fray as Deodatus Village in the 1961 production of Jean Genet's *The Blacks*, a savage and absurdist allegory of race relations written for an all-black cast. Critics at the *Village Voice* and the *New Yorker* swooned, and both singled Jones out for praise from a cast that included Cicely Tyson, Roscoe Lee Browne, Lou Gossett, and MAYA ANGELOU. Given the charged political climate and the play's violent language, performances were hard on audiences and performers alike, and Jones left the cast, to recover, some six times during the play's two-year run. In 1962 Jones earned several awards for his performances in *Moon on a Rainbow Shawl* and won an Obie as Best Actor in Off Broadway Theater for his work in *Clandestine on the Morning Line*. Throughout the 1960s Jones built a name for himself at the New York Shakespeare Festival and his 1964 title role in *Othello* won a Drama Desk Award for Best Performance. The following year, he received two Obies for his work in Othello and in Bertolt Brecht's *Baal*.

No role propelled his career, however, like his 1967 portrayal of Jack Jefferson, a character based on JACK JOHNSON, the first black heavyweight boxing champion, in Howard Sackler's play *The Great White Hope*. To prepare for the audition he began a brutal exercise regimen. Six feet, two inches tall, slimmed down to two hundred pounds, his head shaved and shiny, Jones landed the part, which earned him his first Tony Award and another Drama Desk Award. The play, which challenged and titillated audiences with its interracial love story, moved from the Arena Stage in Washington, D.C., to Broadway in 1968. Jones reprised the role two years later in Martin Ritt's film adaptation of the play, which costarred Jane Alexander and earned Jones an Oscar nomination.

SIDNEY POITIER urged Jones to avoid the stock parts film and television typically offered black actors. For several years Jones heeded the advice, but in 1964 he took a small part as a pilot in Stanley Kubrick's film *Dr. Strangelove.*

Jones also began to make inroads into the small screen. A 1965 stint on *As the World Turns* made him the first African American with a continuing role in a daytime soap opera. In 1967 Jones married Julienne Marie Hendricks, who had played Desdemona to his Othello in 1964. But Jones's growing success brought a new measure of instability to his life, and the marriage did not last.

On stage in 1970 Jones appeared in LORRAINE HANSBERRY's play *Les Blancs* and costarred with RUBY DEE in Athol Fugard's *Boesman and Lena*. He continued working in film and television throughout the early and mid 1970s. Highlights included playing the title role in *King Lear* on television in 1974 and appearing as the big screen's first African American president of the United States in *The Man* in 1972. In 1977 Jones was cast as PAUL ROBESON in the one-man show based on the life of the actor, singer, and activist who had once been feted for his magnetic stage presence, but wound up blacklisted as a result of his politics. Robeson died in 1976, and the play was meant to honor his career, but it, too, fell victim to censorship. Rallied by the actor's son, Paul Robeson Jr., the Ad Hoc Committee to End the Crimes against Paul Robeson charged that the play distorted Robeson's life. Theater after theater was picketed. After one of the last performances, Jones delivered a blistering indictment of the committee's antics. In 1979 Jones starred in the play's film adaptation directed by Lloyd Richards.

Jones, who continued his stage work in such plays as Fugard's *Master Harold and the Boys* and *Of Mice and Men*, has been known to stop mid-performance to shush members of the crew and the audience or to ask them in his round, resonant basso to "stop popping that fucking bubble gum!" (Jones, 334). His relationships with directors and writers have also been strained at times. In 1981 while preparing for a new production of *Othello*, Jones accused the director Peter Coe of turning Shakespeare's tragedy into a farce. In 1987's *Fences*, a father-son play about a poor black family, Jones butted heads with the playwright AUGUST WILSON. In spite of these clashes—or perhaps because of them—both plays won critical acclaim. *Othello* received a Tony for Best Revival, while *Fences* won Jones both a Tony and a Drama Desk for his performance.

In early 1982 Jones married Cecilia Hart. That December their son, Flynn Earl Jones, was born. To support his new family, Jones chose to spend more time in the unglamorous world of made-for-TV movies, bit parts, and voice-overs. The last came in droves after Jones lent his voice to the role of the archvillain Darth Vader in George Lucas's *Star Wars* films released in 1977, 1980, and 1983. Asked why he had agreed to provide the film's most evil character with a black voice, Jones replied that the work took two hours and paid seven thousand dollars.

Following *Fences*, Jones decided that he no longer had the energy for leading roles on the stage, which may account for his increased presence on the screen. In addition to his many featured roles on television, Jones appeared in a variety of films, including John Sayles's *Matewan* (1987), about coal miners struggling to form a union in Mingo County, West Virginia, in 1920. Jones worked in comedy as well, in such films as *Soul Man* (1986) and the Eddie Murphy vehicle *Coming to America* (1988). In 1989 he appeared as the reclusive, misanthropic writer in *Field of Dreams*, one the year's most popular films. Throughout the 1990s Jones appeared in films and on television at an astounding rate. He played Admiral Greer in the highly popular films *The Hunt for Red October*, *Patriot Games*, and *Clear and Present Danger*, based on the novels by Tom Clancy. Notable leading roles included the title role in the television series *Gabriel's Fire*, in which he starred for two seasons, and a priest accused of murder in the 1995 film version of Alan Paton's novel about South Africa, *Cry the Beloved Country*.

More and more, however, Jones is in demand simply as himself, as a host, presenter, and narrator. He voiced the animated characters King Mufasa in Disney's *The Lion King* (1994) and the long-silent Maggie on *The Simpsons*. A popular commercial pitchman, Jones and his distinctive voice have become part of American daily life, telling television viewers that they are watching CNN or thanking callers for using a Verizon pay phone. Instead of asking for autographs, fans beg Jones to record their answering machine messages. Over the last half century Jones has appeared in over two hundred films and television shows. For his work as an actor, Jones has won four Emmy awards, two Tony awards, two Obie awards, five Drama Desk awards, a Golden Globe award and a Grammy. A presidential appointee to the National Council on the Arts from 1970 to 1976, Jones has received five honorary doctorates and the NAACP Hall of Fame Image Award. In 1992 he was awarded the National Medal of Arts by President George Bush. While Jones's career displays a boundless range, depth, and energy, most of his fans see his legacy in more grandiose terms; he is, quite simply, the voice of America.

FURTHER READING

Jones, James Earl, and Penelope Niven. *James Earl Jones: Voices and Silences* (1993, 2002).

Bryer, Jackson R., and Richard A. Davison, eds. *The Actor's Art: Conversations with Contemporary American Stage Performers* (2001).

Gill, Glenda E. *No Surrender! No Retreat!: African American Pioneer Performers of Twentieth-Century American Theater* (2000).
—CHRIS BEBENEK

JONES, LEROI. *See* Baraka, Amiri.

JONES, LOÏS MAILOU (3 Nov. 1905–9 June 1998), artist and teacher, was born in Boston, Massachusetts, the second of two children of Carolyn Dorinda Adams, a beautician, and Thomas Vreeland Jones, a building superintendent. Loïs's father became a lawyer at age forty, and she credited him with inspiring her by example: "Much of my drive surely comes from my father—wanting to be someone, to have an ambition" (Benjamin, 4). While majoring in art at the High School of Practical Arts, Loïs spent afternoons in a drawing program at Boston's Museum of Fine Arts. On weekends she apprenticed with Grace Ripley, a prominent designer of theatrical masks and costumes. From 1923 to 1927 she studied design at the School of the Museum of Fine Arts and became one of the school's first African American graduates. Upon graduation, Loïs, who had earned a teaching certificate from the Boston Normal Art School, received a one-year scholarship to the Designers Art School of Boston, where she studied with the internationally known textile designer Ludwig Frank. The following summer, while attending Harvard University, she designed textiles for companies in Boston and New York. She soon learned, however, that designers toiled in anonymity, and so, seeking recognition for her creations, she decided to pursue a career as a fine artist.

The Jones family spent summers on Martha's Vineyard, the beauty of which inspired Loïs to paint as a child and where her first solo exhibitions, at age seventeen and twenty-three, were held. A retreat for generations of African American intellectuals, Martha's Vineyard exposed the young artist to career encouragement from the sculptor META WARRICK FULLER, the composer HARRY BURLEIGH, and Jonas Lie, president of the National Academy of Design. When she applied for a teaching job at the Museum of Fine Arts, administrators patronizingly told her to "go South and help your people." Jones did go to the South in 1928, but at the behest of CHARLOTTE HAWKINS BROWN, who offered her a position developing an art department at the Palmer Memorial Institute, an African American school in North Carolina. Two years later Jones was recruited by Howard University and remained on the faculty until her retirement in 1977.

For forty-seven years she taught design and watercolor (which was considered more appropriate to her gender than oil painting) to generations of students, including ELIZABETH CATLETT. "I loved my students," Jones told the Washington Post when she was asked about teaching. "Also it gave me a certain prestige, a certain dignity. And it saved me from being trampled upon by the outside" (1 Mar. 1978). Jones emphasized craftsmanship and encouraged each student's choice of medium and mode of expression. As a former student, Akili Ron Anderson, recalled, "Loïs Jones would punish you like a parent...but when you met her standards, when you progressed,

she loved you like your mother" (Washington Post, 26 Dec. 1995).

Jones remained committed to her own work and education, and she received a BA in Art Education magna cum laude from Howard University in 1945. In the 1930s she was a regular exhibitor at the Harmon Foundation, and from 1936 to 1965 she illustrated books and periodicals, including African Heroes and Heroines (1938) and the Journal of Negro History, for her friend CARTER G. WOODSON. After receiving a scholarship to study in Paris in 1937, Jones took a studio overlooking the Eiffel Tower, enrolled at the Académie Julien, and switched her focus from design and illustration to painting. France also precipitated a shift in her attitude. Feeling self-confident and liberated for the first time, she adopted the plein air method of painting, taking her large canvases outdoors onto the streets of Paris and the hills of the French countryside. With the African American expatriate artist Albert Smith and the French painter Emile Bernard as mentors, she produced more than forty paintings in just nine months. Jones's streetscapes, still lifes, portraits, and landscapes, typified by Rue St. Michel (1938) and Les Pommes Vertes (1938), illustrate a sophisticated interpretation of impressionist and post-impressionist style and sensibility.

African art and culture were all the rage during Jones's visit to Paris. Sketching African masks on display in Parisian galleries prepared her for what would become her best-known work, Les Fétiches (1938), a cubist-inspired painting of African masks that foreshadowed Jones's embrace of African themes and styles in her later work. In 1990, when the National Museum of American Art in Washington, D.C., acquired Les Fétiches, Jones responded: "I am very pleased but it is long overdue.... I can't help but think this is an honor that is 45 years late" (Washington Post, 7 Oct. 1994).

Even while the Robert Vose Gallery in Boston exhibited her Parisian paintings shortly after her return to the United States, Jones longed for the racial tolerance she had experienced in France. When she met Alain Locke upon her return to Howard, he challenged her to concentrate on African American subjects. And so began what Jones later

called her Locke period. Throughout the 1940s and early 1950s she continued to paint in a semi-impressionist style but increasingly depicted African American subjects, as in the character studies Jennie (1943), a portrait of a black girl cleaning fish; Mob Victim (1944), a study of a man about to be lynched; and The Pink Tablecloth (1944).

Jones began exhibiting more extensively, primarily in African American venues such as the Chicago Negro Exposition of 1940 and the black-owned Barnett Aden Gallery, although traditionally white venues also included her work. On occasion, Jones masked her race by entering competitions by mail or by sending her white friend Celine Tabary to deliver her work. Such was the case in 1941 when her painting Indian Shops, Gay Head (1940) won the Corcoran Gallery's Robert Wood Bliss Award. It was several years before the Corcoran knew that the painting was the product of a black artist.

In 1953 Jones married Louis Vergniaud Pierre-Noël, a Haitian artist she had met at Columbia University summer school in 1934. The couple, who had no children, maintained homes in Washington, Martha's Vineyard, and Port-au-Prince, Haiti, until Pierre-Noël's death in 1982. Shortly after their wedding Jones taught briefly at Haiti's Centre d'Art and the Foyer des Arts Plastiques. Haiti proved to be the next great influence on Jones's work. "Going to Haiti changed my art, changed my feelings, changed me" (Callaloo, Spring 1989). Character studies and renderings of the picturesque elements of island life soon gave way to more expressive works that fused abstraction and decorative elements with naturalism. Drawing on the palette and the diverse religious life and culture of Haiti, Jones incorporated voodoo gods, abstract decorative patterns, bright colors, and African elements into her paintings. Throughout the 1950s and 1960s she used strong color and flat, abstract shapes in a diverse range of works, including Bazar du Quai (1961), VeVe Voodou III (1963), and Paris Rooftops (1965).

In 1970–1971 Jones took a sabbatical from Howard and traveled through eleven countries in Africa, interviewing artists, photographing their work, and lecturing on African American artists.

Jones, who had spent the previous summer interviewing contemporary Haitian artists, used these materials to complete her documentary project "The Black Visual Arts." The bold, graphic beauty of African textiles, leatherwork, and masks resonated with her early fabric designs and provided a new vocabulary for her work, which now included collage as well as painting and watercolor. Once again, Jones visited museums and sketched African masks and fetishes, items increasingly significant in pieces like *Moon Masque* (1971) and *Guli Mask* (1972).

Throughout the 1970s and 1980s, inspired by Haiti and Africa and by the Black Arts Movement in the United States, Jones's work centered on African themes and styles.

Jones, who finally returned to Boston's Museum of Fine Arts in 1973 for a retrospective exhibition, had more than fifty solo shows. She received numerous awards and honorary degrees, including citations from the Haitian government in 1955 and from U.S. President Jimmy Carter in 1980. In 1988 Jones's artistic life came full circle when she opened the Loïs Mailou Jones Studio Gallery in Edgartown, Massachusetts, on Martha's Vineyard. At age eighty-four Jones assessed the key influences on her work: "So now...in the sixtieth year of my career, I can look back on my work and be inspired by France, Haiti, Africa, the Black experience, and Martha's Vineyard (where it all began) and admit: There is no end to creative expression" (*Callaloo*, Spring 1989). Loïs Mailou Jones died at age ninety-two at her home in Washington, D.C.

FURTHER READING

Jones, Loïs Mailou. *Loïs Mailou Jones: Peintures 1937–1951* (1952).

Benjamin, Tritobia Hayes. *The Life and Art of Loïs Mailou Jones* (1994).

Howard University Gallery of Art. *Loïs Mailou Jones: Retrospective Exhibition Forty Years of Painting, 1932–72* (1972).

National Center of Afro-American Artists and Museum of Fine Arts, Boston. *Reflective Moments: Loïs Mailou Jones Retrospective 1930–1972* (1973).

Obituaries: *Journal of Blacks in Higher Education,* Summer 1998; *Washington Post,* 12 June 1998.

—LISA E. RIVO

 JONES, MADAME SISSIERETTA JOYNER

(5 Jan. 1869–24 June 1933), classical prima donna and musical comedy performer, was born Matilda Sissieretta Joyner in Portsmouth, Virginia, less than four years after the abolition of slavery. Jones was the only surviving child of Jeremiah Malachi Joyner, an ex-slave and pastor of the Afro-Methodist Church in Portsmouth, and Henrietta B. Joyner, a singer in the church choir. Thus, she was exposed to music during her formative years. When she was six years old her family moved to Rhode Island where Sissieretta began singing in the church choir, which her father directed. Her school classmates were mesmerized by her sweet, melodic, soprano voice and nicknamed her "Sissy."

She began studying voice as a teenager at the prestigious Providence Academy of Music with Ada, Baroness Lacombe, an Italian prima donna. Not long afterwards, in 1883, when she was only fourteen, Sissieretta met and married David Richard Jones, a newspaperman who also served as her manager during her early years on stage. She also received more vocal training at both the New England Conservatory and the Boston Conservatory. After her first concert performance with the Academy of Music on 8 May 1888, the *New York Age* reported that Jones's "voice is sweet, sympathetic and clear, and her enunciation a positive charm. She was recalled after each number" (*The Black Perspective in Music*, 192). In an attempt to make her more palatable to white audiences, David Jones, who was himself of a mixed race background,

Lauded in Europe and America, but barred from singing at the Metropolitan Opera in New York because of her race, Madame Sissieretta Jones became the star of her own musical comedy troupe. Library of Congress

took his wife to Europe to have her skin lightened and to have some of her features altered.

Jones made her New York City debut in a private concert at the Wallack Theatre on 1 August 1888. She was already being compared to the Italian prima donna Adelina Patti, who was adored by audiences throughout the world. As a result, Jones was dubbed "Black Patti." She wanted her own identity but was forced to accept the nickname, which remained with her throughout her more than thirty-year career (Daughtry, 133).

In the early 1890s discussions ensued about possible appearances by Jones at the New York City Metropolitan Opera. She wanted very much to sing in a full-length opera at the Met. In the meantime, in 1891, she set out on a tour of the West Indies, where she was honored with numerous medals for her dynamic voice. After she returned to the United States, Jones appeared at Madison Square Garden in New York City in what was billed as an African Jubilee Spectacle and Cakewalk. Thousands listened to Jones, who was fluent in both Italian and French, sing selections from grand operas like Meyerbeer's *Robert le Diable* as well as her popular signature piece, "Swanee River." By 1892 she had already appeared at the White House three times as well as before European royalty. After performances at the Pittsburgh Exposition in 1893 and 1894, Jones became the highest paid black performer of her day.

Jones emerged as a celebrity and wanted to control her career. However, when she made this groundbreaking attempt in 1892, her manager, Major Pond, took her to court. There the judge ruled that she was ungrateful because she failed to appreciate how Pond was largely responsible for her accomplishments on the concert stage.

In New York City, Jones joined famed Czech composer Antonin Dvorak and his students from the National Conservatory of Music for a benefit concert in 1894. A *New York Herald* reporter said of the January concert, "Mme. Jones was an enormous success with the audience. To those who heard her for the first time she came in the light of a revelation, singing high C's with as little apparent effort as her namesake, the white Patti" (*The Black Perspective in Music*, 199). Both the

white and the black press continued to laud her as the "greatest singer of her race." Nevertheless, the opportunity to sing at the Metropolitan Opera was still denied to Jones because of her ethnicity. These racist restrictions inspired her to leave the concert stage behind.

At the turn of the century, black musical comedies, which were first called coon shows, drew huge crowds into the theaters. Black female performers entered musical theater around 1885. During the height of popularity for musical comedies, managers were in control and dictated what performers would do. Managers Rudolph Voelckel and John J. Nolan, who are often credited along with David Jones for luring "Black Patti" to musical theater, planned to make the former concert stage prima donna the star of her own musical black touring company.

On 26 September 1896 Black Patti's Troubadours made their debut in a mini-musical called "At Jolly Coon-ey Island: A Merry Musical Farce," cowritten by Bob Cole and William Johnson. "At Jolly Coon-ey Island" contained almost no plot. Rather, it was a revue that included classical music, vaudeville, burlesque, and skits performed by an enormous group of fifty dancers, singers, tumblers, and comedians. Black Patti's Troubadours were unique. Unlike other black companies, the Troubadours omitted the cakewalk, a popular, high-stepping dance, from their finale. Instead, an operatic kaleidoscope featuring Black Patti concluded the show. The Troubadours placed the spotlight on Black Patti, who stylishly appeared in tiaras, long satin gowns, and white gloves to perform selections from the operatic composers Balfe, Verdi, Wagner, and Gounod.

Black Patti's Troubadours, billed as the "greatest colored show on earth," was based in New York City but toured throughout the United States and abroad. Advertisements claimed the group traveled thousands of miles in the United States in a train car called "Black Patti, America's Finest Show Car." Jones was the central attraction in productions like *A Ragtime Frolic at Rasbury Park* (1899–1900) and *A Darktown Frolic at the Rialto* (1900–1901). Although it is unclear how much of Jones's actual earnings went to Voelckel and Nolan, two years after the establishment

of Black Patti's Troubadours, *The Colored American* reported that Jones commanded a salary of five hundred dollars per week. However, her husband was allegedly a gambler. His gambling, drinking, and misuse of their money led to the couple's divorce in 1899.

By 1900 Black Patti's Troubadours was solidly recognized as one of the most popular companies on the American stage. It helped to launch the careers of women like Ida Forsyne, Aida Overton Walker, and Stella Wiley. Many black performers, who began their careers with Black Patti, went on to experience success on their own. One might argue that their association with Jones, a highly respected, even revered performer, contributed to their later success.

As America's tastes began to change, the Troubadours adopted the name Black Patti Musical Comedy Company. Blacks began to view black musical comedies as negative depictions of their race, while whites began to turn their attention to other forms of entertainment. Some of the troupe's later productions were set in an African jungle. Jones played the queen in a 1907 production called *Trip to Africa*. She was included in the action of the comedy in a skit called "In the Jungles" for the first time in 1911. From 1914 to 1915 the operatic kaleidoscope no longer appeared in the Troubadours' program.

Jones made her final performance at New York City's Lafayette Theater in 1915. As the mother of two adopted sons, she moved back to Providence, Rhode Island, where she also cared for her ailing mother. When Jones became ill and fell into obscurity, she was forced to rely on assistance from the National Association for the Advancement of Colored People (NAACP). Sissieretta Jones died on 24 June 1933 at Rhode Island Hospital. She remains one of the most celebrated black performers of the late nineteenth and early twentieth centuries.

FURTHER READING

A press scrapbook on Jones is housed in the Moorland-Spingarn Collection, Howard University, Washington, D.C.

The Black Perspective in Music 4, no. 2 (July 1976).

Daughtry, Willia Estelle. "Sissieretta Jones: A Study of the Negro's Contribution to Nineteenth Century American Concert and Theatrical Life." PhD diss., Syracuse University, 1968.

Henricksen, Henry. "Madame Sissieretta Jones." *Record Research*, no. 165–166 (Aug. 1979).

Woll, Allen. *Black Musical Theatre: From Coontown to Dreamgirls* (1989).

—MARTA J. EFFINGER-CRICHLOW

 JONES, QUINCY

(14 Mar. 1933–), jazz musician, composer, and record, television, and film producer, was born Quincy Delight Jones Jr. on the South Side of Chicago, Illinois, the son of Sarah (maiden name unknown) and Quincy Jones Sr., a carpenter who worked for a black gangster ring that ran the Chicago ghetto. When Quincy Sr.'s mentally ill wife was institutionalized, he sent their sons, Quincy Jr. and Lloyd, to live in the South with their grandmother. In his autobiography Jones writes of growing up so poor that his grandmother served them fried rats to eat. By the age of ten he was living with Lloyd and their father in Seattle, Washington. "My stepbrother, my brother, and myself, and my cousin...we burned down stores, we stole, whatever you had to do," Jones said (*CNN Online,* "Q and A: A Talk with Quincy Jones," 11 Dec. 2001).

Modern jazz was Jones's way out. Inspired by the now legendary jazzmen who passed through Seattle in the 1940s, Jones began studying trumpet in junior high school. When COUNT BASIE brought a group to Seattle in 1950, Jones, then a teenager, approached one band member, Clark Terry, an acclaimed trumpeter, for lessons. "He's the type of cat, anything he wanted to do, he could've done," Terry said later in his autobiography.

Jones showed enough musical promise to win a scholarship to Schillinger House in Boston (now the Berklee School of Music), but he dropped out after a year to accept a place in the trumpet section of Lionel Hampton's band. In 1951, Hampton made a record of Jones's "Kingfish" and gave the teenager his first recorded composition. Thereafter, Jones settled in New York City, where he found work as an arranger for some of the biggest stars in jazz, including Count Basie, Cannonball Adderley, and Dinah Washington. In 1956 he hired an array of top musicians for his first album, *This Is How I Feel about Jazz.* "His

writing is not exploratory," writes jazz critic Leonard Feather. He wrote in his *New Encyclopedia of Jazz* about Jones's musical compositions, "Unlike many of the younger writers who have experimented with atonality and extended forms, he has remained within the classic jazz framework; his reputation rests mainly on brief compositions that combine the swinging big band feel of the better orchestras of the '30s with the harmonic developments of the '40s."

In May 1956 Jones joined the DIZZY GILLESPIE orchestra on a State Department–sponsored tour of the Middle East and South America. A year later he moved to Paris, where he studied with Nadia Boulanger, a conductor and composition teacher known for her illustrious expatriate pupils, including Aaron Copland and Virgil Thomson. Modern jazz was blossoming in Paris, and Jones became a producer-arranger for Disques Barclay, France's premier jazz label. In the fall of 1959 he became musical director of *Free and Easy,* a touring blues opera by Harold Arlen. Jones had assembled a big band for the show, and in September 1959 he took it on a European tour. The enterprise proved much too costly, and in 1960 it fell apart, leaving Jones deeply in debt.

Returning to New York, Jones was hired in May 1961 as an A&R ("Artist and Repertory") man at Mercury Records. After producing a number-one hit—Lesley Gore's teenage pop lament "It's My Party"—and other artistic and creative successes, he became vice president of the company in November 1964. It was reportedly the first time a black man had held such a high position in the U.S. record business. In addition to arranging and conducting for Frank Sinatra, Basie, SARAH VAUGHAN, and Peggy Lee, Jones was writing and recording his own albums.

Beginning with Sidney Lumet's *Pawnbroker* in 1964, Jones began composing film music, collaborating with many of the decade's seminal filmmakers, including Lumet, Sidney Pollack, Norman Jewison, Richard Brooks, and Paul Mazursky. He also teamed with the actor SIDNEY POITIER for six films during the 1960s and early 1970s. Jones's scores for such films as *The Pawnbroker, In Cold Blood* (1967), *In the Heat of the Night* (1967), *Cactus Flower* (1969), and *Bob & Carol & Ted*

& Alice (1969) introduced jazz, soul, and, later, funk into films, contributing to the increased sophistication and interrelatedness of music to popular film. Jones also played a part in bringing a new sound to TV with his scores for *Ironside* (1967–1975); *The BILL COSBY Show* (1969); *Sanford and Son* (1972–1977), starring REDD FOXX; and the miniseries *Roots* (1977), based on the book by ALEX HALEY and for which Jones won an Emmy.

Jones's affairs with a string of women, including Dinah Washington and Peggy Lee, had put a severe strain on his marriage to Jeri Caldwell, his white high-school sweetheart and the mother of his first child, Jolie. Married in 1957, the couple divorced nine years later. Jones quickly entered into a brief marriage with Ulla Andersson, a blonde model. In 1974 he married Peggy Lipton, star of TV's *Mod Squad.* The couple had two children and divorced in 1989.

In 1969 Jones moved to A&M, by which time he had made a nearly full-time shift toward commercial pop. The trumpeter MILES DAVIS had plunged into fusion, a new style of electric jazz-rock and Jones did the same in *Walking in Space* (1974), his first of several hit records that combined jazz, fusion, and funk. Jones continued his work as orchestrator, arranging the strings for Paul Simon's foray into pop-gospel and rhythm and blues, *There Goes Rhymin' Simon* (1973). But Jones remained loyal to the jazz musicians he loved and filled his orchestras with them. In 1973 he began a career in TV production with a gala special on the CBS network called *DUKE ELLINGTON...We Love You Madly,* featuring a cast that included Vaughan, Lee, Joe Williams, and Jones's boyhood friend RAY CHARLES, along with newer stars like Roberta Flack and ARETHA FRANKLIN.

Jones, who had worked on behalf of MARTIN LUTHER KING JR.'s Operation Breadbasket, helped organize Chicago's Black EXPO, an offshoot of Operation PUSH, with JESSE JACKSON in 1972. He later served on the board of PUSH and, much later, produced a talk show with Jackson, *The Jesse Jackson Show* (1990). Jones, who had begun seriously educating himself about black and African music, became increasingly committed to the historical preservation of African

American music. He helped establish the annual Black Arts Festival in Chicago and the Institute for Black American Music, which donated funds toward the establishment of a national library of African American art and music.

Jones's workaholic tendencies caught up with him in August 1974 when he suffered a near fatal brain aneurysm and underwent two major neurological surgeries. Once recovered, he returned to his career with the same fervor. In 1979 he produced MICHAEL JACKSON's solo album *Off the Wall*, which yielded four top-ten hits. In 1981 Jones left A&M and established the Qwest label at Warner Bros. Although he made his initial mark as a jazz arranger, producer, and bandleader, Jones became a household name by producing Jackson's next album, 1982's *Thriller*, which sold fifty million albums and became the biggest-selling album of all time. Jackson and Jones remained a team for years, working on *Bad* (1987) and other projects.

Apart from his work with Michael Jackson, Jones's greatest commercial triumph came in 1985, with the slick all-star album *USA for Africa*, which featured the song "We Are the World." Written by Jackson and Lionel Ritchie and performed by forty-six music stars, including Bruce Springsteen and DIANA ROSS, the single sold seven and a half million copies, raised fifty million dollars for famine relief in Africa, and won Grammy Awards for Song of the Year and Record of the Year.

Jones showed his ingenuity for mixing pop with traditional genres with *The Dude* (1980), a pop-soul extravaganza with Jackson, STEVIE WONDER, Herbie Hancock, the jazz harmonica and guitar player Toots Thielemans, and two of Jones's protégés, the singers Patti Austin and James Ingram. He continued this pattern in 1989 with *Back on the Block*, an album that mingled Miles Davis, Dizzy Gillespie, ELLA FITZGERALD, and Sarah Vaughan with the rappers Kool Moe Dee and Big Daddy Kane. "I'll Be Good to You," a top-twenty single from that album, paired Ray Charles with the pop-soul belter Chaka Khan.

After his successful turn in 1985 as coproducer of the Steven Spielberg film adaptation of ALICE WALKER's *The Color Purple*, Jones expanded his empire into film and television production. Through Quincy Jones Entertainment, Inc. (QJE), a joint enterprise with Time Warner formed in 1990, Jones created *The Fresh Prince of Bel Air* (1990–1996), the TV series that launched actor Will Smith, and the long-running comedy show *Mad TV*. Jones's other producing projects include the multipart *History of Rock and Roll* (1995) and the 2002 documentary *TUPAC SHAKUR: Thug Angel*. The founder of Quincy Jones Music Publishing, Jones also owns Qwest Broadcasting, which, with the Tribune Company, owns television stations in Atlanta and New Orleans. In 1990 Jones established a magazine, *Vibe*, which focused on black pop music. The next year he persuaded the ailing Miles Davis to revisit classic work of the 1950s in a concert at the Montreux Jazz Festival in Switzerland. Davis hated looking back; only Jones could persuade him to do so. Davis died two months later.

The recipient of countless awards, Jones has earned seventy-seven Grammy nominations and won twenty-six times. He is a six-time Oscar nominee, and at the 1995 Academy Awards he won the Jean Hersholt Humanitarian Award. In 1990 Warner Bros. released a documentary based on his life, *Listen Up: The Lives of Quincy Jones*. Eleven years later he received a Kennedy Center Honor for lifetime achievement. As awards showered down on him in the 1980s and 1990s, some critics thought Jones outrageously overhyped. There is little disagreement, however, about his abilities in combining talent in the studio to dazzling effect. Throughout his career he showed a shrewd business sense, earning millions of dollars, riding almost every new musical trend, including fusion and rap. While he will not be remembered as an exceptional trumpeter, Jones remains one of the most celebrated and charismatic figures in the pop music business. He has also allied himself with the biggest names in jazz, pop, and film to a point where he has been absorbed into their ranks.

FURTHER READING

Jones, Quincy. *Q: The Autobiography of Quincy Jones* (2001).

Ross, Courtney, and Nelson George. *Listen Up: The Lives of Quincy Jones* (1990).

—JAMES GAVIN

 JONES, SCIPIO AFRICANUS (1863– 28 Mar. 1943), lawyer, was born in Dallas County, Arkansas, the son of a white father, whose identity remains uncertain, and Jemmima, a slave who belonged to Dr. Sanford Reamey, a physician and landowner. After emancipation, Jemmima and her freedman husband, Horace, became farmers and adopted the surname of Jones, in memory of Dr. Adolphus Jones, a previous owner. Scipio Jones attended rural black schools in Tulip, Arkansas, and moved to Little Rock in 1881 to pursue a college preparatory course at Bethel University. He then entered Shorter College, from which he graduated in 1885 with a bachelor's degree in Education. When the University of Arkansas Law School denied him admission because of his race, he read law with several white attorneys in Little Rock and was admitted to the bar in 1889. His marriage to Carrie Edwards in 1896 ended in his wife's early death and left him with a daughter to raise. In 1917 he married Lillie M. Jackson of Pine Bluff, Arkansas.

By the turn of the century Jones had become the leading black practitioner in Little Rock. His clients, who were drawn exclusively from the African American community, included several large, fraternal organizations, such as the Mosaic Templars of America. He also played an active role in Republican politics, supporting the efforts of the "Black and Tan" faction to wrest control of the state party from the "Lily Whites." In 1902 he promoted a slate of black Republicans to challenge the party regulars and the Democrats in a local election, and in 1920 he made an unsuccessful bid for the post of Republican national committeeman. The struggle to secure equal treatment for African Americans within the party lasted from the late 1880s to the 1930s and resulted in a compromise that guaranteed black representation on the Republican state central committee. As a sign of changing times, Jones was elected as a delegate to the Republican National Conventions of 1928 and 1940. Despite the existence of poll taxes that disfranchised most black voters, he also won election as a special judge of the Little Rock municipal court in 1915, at a time when few African Americans held judicial office anywhere in the country.

Jones's lifelong commitment to protecting the civil rights of blacks led to his involvement in the greatest legal battle of his career: the defense of twelve tenant farmers who were sentenced to death for alleged murders committed during the bloody Elaine, Arkansas, race riot of October 1919. The violence grew out of black efforts to establish a farmers' union and white fears that a dangerous conspiracy was being plotted at their secret meetings. When two white men were reportedly shot near a black church, the white community engaged in murderous reprisals that left more than two hundred blacks and five whites dead. An all-white grand jury quickly indicted 122 blacks, and because most of the defendants were indigent, the court appointed defense counsel for them. These white lawyers did not interview their clients, request a change of venue, or object to all-white trial juries. The trials themselves lasted less than an hour, and it took juries only five or six minutes to return guilty verdicts. Several defendants and witnesses later claimed that they had been tortured, and an angry white mob surrounded the courthouse during the trials. Besides the twelve men who were sentenced to death, sixty-seven others received long prison terms.

The National Association for the Advancement of Colored People retained Jones and George W. Murphy, a white Little Rock attorney, to appeal the convictions. Jones became the senior defense counsel after Murphy died in October 1920, and he tirelessly pursued every avenue of relief under state law, risking his life on several occasions by his courtroom appearances in the hostile community of Helena. Jones's arguments impressed the Arkansas Supreme Court, which twice ordered new trials for six defendants. In the first instance Jones pointed to technical defects in the form of the verdicts. On the second appeal he contended that the trial judge's rejection of evidence pointing to racial discrimination in the selection of jurors had deprived his clients of their equal protection rights under the Fourteenth Amendment. To prevent the impending executions of the remaining six defendants, Jones turned to the federal courts. Arguing that the prisoners had been deprived

of their constitutional right to a fair trial, he sought their release through a habeas corpus proceeding. Eventually the case reached the U.S. Supreme Court, where it resulted in a landmark decision, *Moore v. Dempsey* (1923). By looking behind the formal state record for the first time, the Court overturned the convictions and held that the defendants had been denied due process, since their original trial had been little more than a legalized lynching bee. Although Jones did not participate in the final argument of the case, his strategy had guided the litigation process from the beginning. In the aftermath of *Moore v. Dempsey*, he secured an order from the Arkansas Supreme Court for the discharge of six prisoners in June 1923. He then negotiated with state authorities to secure commutation of sentences and parole for all of the remaining Elaine "rioters" by January 1925.

In his later years Jones continued to attack racially discriminatory laws and practices in Arkansas. He was instrumental in obtaining legislation that granted out-of-state tuition payments to black students who could not enter the state's all-white professional schools. He died in Little Rock. To commemorate his community leadership, the all-white school board of North Little Rock named the black high school in his memory.

FURTHER READING

Letters from Jones are in the NAACP Papers in the Library of Congress and in the Republican Party State Central Committee Records in the University of Arkansas Library.

Cortner, Richard C. *A Mob Intent on Death* (1988).
Dillard, Tom. "Scipio A. Jones." *Arkansas Historical Quarterly* 31 (Autumn 1972): 201–219.
Ovington, Mary White. *Portraits in Color* (1927).
Waskow, Arthur I. *From Race Riot to Sit-In, 1919 and the 1960s* (1966).

—MAXWELL BLOOMFIELD

JOPLIN, SCOTT

(24 Nov. 1868?–1 Apr. 1917), ragtime composer and pianist, was born in

or near Texarkana, Texas, one of six children of Giles Joplin, reportedly a former slave from North Carolina, and Florence Givens, a free woman from Kentucky. Many aspects of Joplin's early life are shrouded in mystery. At a crucial time in his youth, Scott's father left the family, and Florence was forced to raise him as a single parent. She made arrangements for her son to receive piano lessons in exchange for her domestic services, and he was allowed to practice piano where she worked. A precocious child whose talent was noticed by the time he was seven years old, Scott had undoubtedly inherited talent from his parents, as Giles had played violin and Florence sang and played the banjo. His own experimentations at the piano and his basic music training with local teachers contributed to his advancement. Scott attended Orr Elementary School in Texarkana and then traveled to Sedalia, Missouri, perhaps residing with relatives while studying at Lincoln High School.

Joplin built an early reputation as a pianist and gained fame as a composer of piano ragtime during the Gay Nineties, plying his trade concurrently with composers such as WILL MARION COOK and HARRY BURLEIGH. Joplin was essential in the articulation of a distinctly American style of music. Minstrelsy was still in vogue when Joplin was a teenager performing in vaudeville shows with the Texas Medley Quartette, a group he founded with his brothers. Joplin reportedly arrived in St. Louis by 1885, landing a job as a pianist

Scott Joplin, "The King of Ragtime," c. 1911. Schomburg Center

at John Turpin's Silver Dollar Saloon. In 1894 he was hired at Tom Turpin's Rosebud Cafe. As musicians flocked to the Chicago Columbian Exposition in 1893, Joplin was among them, playing at nightspots close to the fair. Afterward, he returned to Sedalia, the "Cradle of Ragtime," accompanied by the pianist Otis Saunders.

Although he was playing piano in various cities, Joplin still found time to blow the cornet in Sedalia's Queen City Band. In 1895 he continued playing with the Quartette and toured as far as Syracuse, New York, where some businessmen were sufficiently impressed with his talents to publish his first vocal songs. Additionally, Joplin was hired as a pianist at Sedalia's famous Maple Leaf Club. He also taught piano, banjo, and mandolin, claiming among his students the pianists Arthur Marshall, Scott Hayden, and Sanford B. Campbell. By 1896 Joplin had settled in Sedalia and matriculated at the George Smith College for Negroes. With the confidence and ambition fostered by this formal training, he approached the Fuller-Smith and Carl Hoffman Companies, which published some of his piano rags. It was also in Sedalia that he met John Stark, who became his friend and the publisher of Joplin's celebrated "Maple Leaf Rag" (1899).

In 1900 Joplin began a three year relationship with Belle Hayden, which produced a child who soon died. He then married Freddie Alexander in 1904, but her death that same year sent him wandering about for at least a year, returning at times to Sedalia and St. Louis. In 1905 he went to Chicago, and by 1907 he had followed John Stark to New York and married Lottie Stokes, who remained with him until his death. In the years after the turn of the century, the piano replaced the violin in popularity. Playing ragtime on the parlor piano became "all the rage" in both the United States and Europe. Although there were ragtime bands and ragtime songs, classic rag soon became defined as an instrumental form, especially for the piano. Many Joplin rags consist of a left-hand part that jumps registers in eighth-note rhythms set against tricky syncopated sixteenths in the right hand. Joplin was both prolific and successful in writing rags for the piano, and he

came to be billed as "the King of Ragtime."

Ragtime or Rag—from "ragged time"—is a genre that blends elements from marches, jigs, quadrilles, and bamboulas with blues, spirituals, minstrel ballads, and "coon songs." ("Coon songs" were highly stereotyped comic songs, popular from the 1880s to the 1920s, written in a pseudo-dialect purporting to record African-American vernacular speech.) Ragtime is an infectious and stimulating music, usually in 2/4 meter, with a marchlike sway and a proud, sharp, in-your-face joviality. Its defining rhythm, based on the African bamboula dance pattern, renamed "cakewalk" in America, is a three-note figuration of sixteenth-eighth-sixteenth notes, which is also heard in earlier spirituals, such as "I Got a Home in-a That Kingdom" and "Ain-a That Good News!"

A predecessor of jazz, ragtime was correlated with the "African jig" because of its foot stamps, shuffles, and shouts, "where hands clap out intricate and varying rhythmic patterns...and the foot is not marking straight time, but what Negroes call 'stop time,' or what the books call 'syncopation'" (JAMES WELDON JOHNSON, *The Book of American Spirituals* [1925], 31). Joplin alludes to these influences in his "Stoptime Rag," where the word "stamp" is marked on every quarter beat. Joplin admonished pianists to play ragtime slowly, even though his tempo for "Stoptime" is marked "Fast or slow." Campbell most revealingly wrote that rag was played variously in "march time, fast ragtime, slow, and the ragtime blues style" (Fisk University, Special Collections).

Vera Brodsky Lawrence's *Complete Works of Scott Joplin* lists forty five rags, waltzes, marches, and other piano pieces that Joplin composed himself. In addition, he collaborated on a number of rags, including "Swipesy" with Arthur Marshall, "Sunflower Slow Drag," "Something Doing," "Felicity Rag," "Kismet Rag" with Scott Hayden, and "Heliotrope Bouquet" with Louis Chauvin. There are also various unpublished pieces and some that were stolen, lost, sold, or destroyed.

The most popular of Joplin's works, and one that brought continuous acclaim, is undoubtedly the "Maple

Leaf Rag." No matter the studied care of "Gladiolus Rag" or the majesty of "Magnetic Rag," with its blue-note features, and no matter the catchiness of "The Entertainer," "Maple Leaf" beckons more. Over and above its engaging melodies and syncopations, the technical challenges alone are more than enough to induce an ambitious pianist to tackle "Maple Leaf." Whatever its ingredients, "Maple Leaf Rag" garnered a respect for ragtime that has lasted for decades. Numerous musicians have recorded it, and it has been arranged for instruments from guitar to oboe and for band and orchestra.

Joplin also composed small and large vocal forms, both original and arranged. A few of his nonsyncopated songs are related to the Tin Pan Alley types of the day, and at least two are influenced by "coon songs." He choreographed dance steps and wrote words for the "Ragtime Dance Song," and in a few cases he either wrote lyrics or arranged music for others. Joplin composed two operas, the first of which is lost. The second, *Treemonisha*, whose libretto Joplin also wrote, is an ambitious work containing twenty-seven numbers, and requiring three sopranos, three tenors, one high baritone, four basses, and a chorus. Set "on a plantation somewhere in the State of Arkansas, Northeast of the Town of Texarkana and three or four miles from the Red River," the opera presents education as the key to success.

Throughout Joplin's preface to *Treemonisha*, one cannot help but note the parallelism of dates and geographic locations in the opera to those of his own past. The preface tells the tale of a young baby who was found under a tree, adopted, and named "Treemonisha" by Ned and Monisha. At age seven, she is educated by a white family in return for Monisha's domestic services. The opera opens with eighteen-year-old Treemonisha touting the value of education and campaigning against two conjurers who earn their livelihoods promoting superstition. After various episodes with kidnappers, wasps, bears, and cotton pickers, who sing the brilliant "Aunt Dinah Has Blowed de Horn," Treemonisha is successful and joins the finale, singing "Marching Onward" to the tune of the "Real Slow Drag."

Compositionally, syncopated music is used in *Treemonisha* only when the plot calls for it, with the musical themes and harmonies employing "crossover" alternations between classical and popular styles. However, Joplin's intentions seem to have leaned more toward the classical. The basic harmonies are decorated with his favored diminished seventh chords and secondary dominants. Altered chords, chromatics, modulations, themes with mode changes, special effects to depict confusion, and even an example of seven key changes in "The Bag of Luck" all point toward Joplin's training and musical aspirations.

Joplin accompanied the first performance of *Treemonisha* on the piano. When he sought sponsors, and when he asked Stark to publish the opera, he was refused. Tackling these jobs himself proved to be his undoing. As a result of stress and illness, Joplin lost his mental balance in early 1917 and was admitted to the New York State Hospital. A diagnosis signed by Dr. Philip Smith states that Joplin succumbed to "dementia paralytica—cerebral form about 9:10 o'clock p.m.," that the duration of the mental illness was one year and six months, and that the "contributory causes were Syphilis [of an] unknown duration" (Bureau of Records, New York City).

Campbell wrote that Joplin's funeral carriage bore names of his rag hits. Sadly, only the *New York Age* and a notice by John Stark carried his obituary. High society from New York to Paris had strutted the cakewalk accompanied by his rags since the late 1890s, but now he was forgotten. Perhaps World War I diverted people's attention away from the exuberance of raggedy rags and thus from Joplin. He received accolades for his piano rags, but his most difficult vocal music was not appreciated in his lifetime. Sixty years after his death he began to receive numerous honors, including the National Music Award, a Pulitzer Prize in 1976, and a U.S. postage stamp in 1983.

Several articles in the *Washington Post* and the *New York Times* inspired a revival of Joplin's music in the 1970s. Various films, especially *The Sting* (1973), and television productions have highlighted his work, and concerts and recordings by the finest of musicians have taken the music to new heights. Additionally, there have been several productions of *Treemonisha*. To be sure, rags were written before Joplin's *Original Rags* was published in 1899, but he must be credited with defining the classic concept and construction of ragtime and with rendering dignity and respectability to the style.

FURTHER READING

Selected repositories of music and other materials are at the New York Public Library; the Library of Congress, Washington, D.C.; the Fisk University Library, Nashville, Tennessee; the Center for Black Music Research, Chicago, Illinois; Indiana University Library, Terre Haute; and the Scott Joplin International Ragtime Foundation, Sedalia, Missouri.

Berlin, Edward A. *King of Ragtime: Scott Joplin and His Era* (1994).
Jasen, David, and Trebor J. Tichenor. *Rags and Ragtime: A Musical History* (1989).
Lawrence, Vera Brodsky. *The Complete Works of Scott Joplin* (1981).
Preston, Katherine. *Scott Joplin: Composer* (1988).

Obituary: *New York Age*, 5 Apr. 1917.

Discography
Joplin, Scott. *Classic Ragtime from Rare Piano Rolls* (1989).
Rifkin, Joshua. *Scott Joplin: Piano Rags* (1987).
Zimmerman, Richard. *Complete Works of Scott Joplin* (1993).

—HILDRED ROACH

JORDAN, BARBARA
(21 Feb. 1936–17 Jan. 1996), lawyer, politician, and professor, was born Barbara Charline Jordan in Houston, Texas, the daughter of Benjamin M. Jordan and Arlyne Patten Jordan. Her father, a graduate of the Tuskegee Institute, was a warehouse employee until 1949 when he became a minister at Houston's Good Hope Missionary Baptist Church, in which his father's family had long been active. Arlyne Jordan also became a frequent speaker at the church. The Jordans were

Representative Barbara Jordan addressing the Democratic National Convention, 1976. Library of Congress

always poor, and for many years Barbara and her two older sisters shared a bed, but their lives improved somewhat after their father became a minister. Barbara attended local segregated public schools and received good grades with little effort. She gave scant thought to her future, beyond forming a vague desire to become a pharmacist, until her senior year at Phillis Wheatley High School, when a black female lawyer spoke at the school's career day assembly. Already a proficient orator who had won several competitions, she decided to put that skill to use as an attorney.

Restricted in her choice of colleges by her poverty as well as segregation, Jordan entered Texas Southern University, an all-black institution in Houston, on a small scholarship in the fall of 1952. Majoring in political science and history, she also became a champion debater, leading the college team to several championships. She graduated magna cum laude in 1956 and went on to Boston University Law School, where she managed to excel despite rampant gender discrimination. Upon graduation she took the Massachusetts bar exam, intending to practice law in Boston, but ultimately decided to return to her parents' home in Houston. She used the dining room as her office for several years before setting up a downtown office, and she also worked as an administrative assistant to a county judge until 1966.

Jordan's first wholesale encounter with politics came during the 1960 national election campaign, when she became a volunteer for Democratic presidential candidate John F. Kennedy and his running mate, Texas senator Lyndon B. Johnson. She began at the Houston party headquarters by performing menial jobs but soon emerged as the head of a voting drive covering Houston's predominantly black precincts. The Democratic victory that fall changed Jordan's life in several ways: not only did it persuade her to enter politics; it also overturned her long-held sense that segregation was a way of life that had to be endured, and it convinced her that the lives of black people might be improved by political action.

Jordan began her political career by running for a seat in the Texas House of Representatives in 1962 and again two years later. She lost both elections but received an impressive number of votes. In 1966, following a Supreme Court–mandated electoral redistricting to allow fair representation for blacks and other minorities, Jordan won election to the Texas Senate from the newly created Eleventh District in Houston, becoming the first black state senator in Texas since 1883. Concerned that she might be branded a rabble-rousing liberal agitator, she determined to establish herself as a legislator working seriously for social change. She began by being an advocate for the ultimately successful passage of a bill establishing the state's first Fair Employment Practices Commission, to fight discrimination in the workplace. She also fought for passage of the state's first minimum wage law, for raises in workmen's compensation payments, and for the creation of a department of community affairs to deal with the problems of the state's rapidly growing urban areas. In addition, she blocked proposed legislation that

would have made voter registration more difficult.

Named outstanding freshman senator during her first year in office, Jordan went on to reelection for two more terms, serving a total of six years and bringing to passage half of the bills she introduced. In March 1972 she became the first black woman in American history to preside over a legislative body when she was elected president pro tem of the Texas legislature. By that time she had decided to try for a seat in the U.S. House of Representatives from the state's new Eighteenth District, which was 50 percent black and 15 percent Mexican American. After winning a hard-fought primary against a black male state legislator, she ran for election that fall as the Democratic candidate and easily defeated her Republican opponent. Upon taking the oath of office in January 1973, she and another new representative, ANDREW YOUNG of Georgia, became the first two African Americans in modern times to sit as elected members of the U.S. House. Thanks to the assistance of former president Lyndon Johnson, who had become a friend during Jordan's years in the Texas legislature, she was appointed to a coveted seat on the House Judiciary Committee.

Jordan served three terms in the Congress, easily winning reelection in 1974 and 1976. She was a forceful presence, voting consistently for such liberal measures as increased federal aid to public schools and an extension of the guaranteed student loan program, legal aid for the poor, an increase in the minimum wage, and the continuation of the school lunch program. During her first term she also voted for several bills designed to limit U.S. involvement in the Vietnam War, and she voted against the construction of the Alaska oil pipeline because of concerns for the environment. But she first achieved a national presence in July 1974 as a member of the House Judiciary Committee.

On the opening day of the televised hearings held by the committee to consider articles of impeachment against President Richard M. Nixon, Jordan delivered a preliminary statement that moved to their very bones almost all

who heard it. Speaking slowly and deliberately in a powerful deep and solemn voice, Jordan declared that despite not having been considered among "We, the people" when the Constitution was adopted, "the process of amendment, interpretation, and court decisions" had now guaranteed her inclusion. "Today, I am an inquisitor," she continued. "I believe hyperbole would not be fictional and would not overstate the solemnness that I feel right now. My faith in the Constitution is whole, it is complete, it is total. I am not going to sit here and be an idle spectator to the diminution, the subversion, the destruction of the Constitution." Speaking with authority, Jordan then set forth her reasons for believing that Nixon should be impeached, concluding that if the committee did not vote to do so, then the Constitution was worthless and should be sent through a paper shredder. Although she projected great control, Jordan later revealed that she was shaking with nervousness throughout the proceedings, and after casting her vote she wept.

Following Nixon's resignation not long afterward, Jordan's opening remarks, as well as her penetrating questioning during the committee hearings, remained in the public mind, and she was talked about as a candidate for higher office. In 1976 she was called upon to be a keynote speaker at the Democratic National Convention, along with Senator John H. Glenn Jr. of Ohio. Following Glenn's unremarkable address, she electrified the convention with a speech delivered in a style part–William Jennings Bryan and part–hellfire Baptist preacher. Appealing for national unity, she declared that its achievement and the full realization of America's destiny lay only through the Democratic Party.

In the 1976 fall presidential campaign, Jordan traveled the country, making speeches in support of the Democratic candidate, Jimmy Carter. Upon his victory in November, Carter discussed appointing her to the cabinet, but she was only interested in becoming attorney general, a post Carter was not willing to offer her. A year later, in December 1977, she surprised supporters by announcing that she would not seek a fourth term in Congress the following year. Although she was rumored to have health problems, she denied this, saying only that she wanted to devote herself to other concerns back in Texas. After leaving the House in early 1979, she was appointed to the Lyndon B. Johnson Chair in National Policy at the Johnson School of Public Affairs, a part of the University of Texas in Austin. Teaching courses in policy development as well as political values and ethics, she became one of the university's most popular professors, and students had to participate in a lottery to gain admission to her classes.

Jordan returned to the national political stage in 1988, when she delivered a rousing speech at the Democratic National Convention seconding the nomination of Lloyd Bentsen as the vice-presidential candidate. By this time, however, her physical ailment could not be denied: she was now confined to a wheelchair, the consequence, she said, of a "neuromuscular disorder." Later that summer she made national headlines again when she was found floating unconscious in the swimming pool at her home; she had gone into cardiac arrest while doing therapeutic exercises. She recovered, however, and by that fall was well enough to campaign for the national Democratic presidential ticket, headed by Michael Dukakis.

Jordan returned to the Democratic National Convention in 1992 as one of its keynote speakers, and again she riveted the audience with her call for support of presidential candidate Bill Clinton and his mandate for change. Although her health grew worse, she continued to teach at the university. She also served as chair of the Commission on Immigration Reform and in that capacity testified before Congress in 1995 on behalf of citizenship rights for children born in the United States to illegal immigrants.

Jordan, who never married, fiercely guarded her private life. Known to enjoy singing and playing the guitar, she was also a fan of the Lady Longhorns, the University of Texas women's basketball team, whose games she frequently attended. Following her death from viral pneumonia, which occurred at her home in Austin, it was disclosed that she had suffered from both multiple sclerosis and leukemia.

FURTHER READING

Jordan, Barbara, and Shelby Hearon. *Barbara Jordan: A Self-Portrait* (1978).

Haskins, James. *Barbara Jordan* (1977).
Rogers, Mary Beth. *Barbara Jordan: American Hero* (1998).

Obituary: *New York Times*, 18 Jan. 1996.
—ANN T. KEENE

JORDAN, JUNE

(9 July 1936–14 June 2002), poet, essayist, teacher, and activist, was born in Harlem, New York, the daughter of Jamaican-born parents, Mildred Maud Fisher, a nurse, and Granville Ivanhoe Jordan, a postal clerk. Mildred, who was half East Indian, was a quiet and religious woman who had given up a career as an artist to marry; she struggled with depression and eventually committed suicide in 1966. June's father, who was half Chinese and a follower of the black nationalist MARCUS GARVEY, made no apologies for his dissatisfaction with his only child's gender. He had wanted a boy and treated June as such. Referring to her as "he" and "the boy," Granville subjected his young daughter to rigorous mental and physical training regimens that included camping, fishing, and boxing instruction; aggressive mathematical and literary testing; and often brutal physical beatings. Jordan describes her father's abuse in her memoir: "Like a growling beast, the roll-away mahogany doors rumble open, and the light snaps on and a fist smashes into the side of my head and I am screaming awake: 'Daddy! What did I do?!'" By her fifth birthday June had endured, and excelled at, memorizing and reciting selections from the Bible and the works of PAUL LAURENCE DUNBAR, Edgar Allan Poe, Zane Grey, Sinclair Lewis, and Shakespeare. Jordan began writing poetry at age seven. When schoolmates started to buy her verses, she realized that poetry could be both powerful and useful in connecting people.

The Jordans moved to the Bedford-Stuyvesant neighborhood of Brooklyn when June was five years old. She was generally the only black student throughout her secondary school and college years. After one year at Midwood High School, she won a scholarship and transferred to the Northfield School for Girls, a private prep school in Massachusetts. Following graduation in 1953, she enrolled in Barnard College, where she met Michael Meyer, a white Columbia College student. The two married in 1955, and their son, Christopher, was born in 1958. Although she spent a year at the University of Chicago while her husband was in school there and another semester back at Barnard, she never received a college degree. Jordan later described her marriage, which at the time was illegal in forty-three states, as a "state criminalized relationship." In her "Letter to Michael," an essay in *Civil Wars: Selected Essays 1963–1980* (1982), Jordan illuminates the difficulties of interracial marriage, factors that contributed to the dissolution of her own marriage. The couple divorced in 1965.

Considering a career in urban planning, Jordan studied urban design and architecture with Buckminster Fuller in the early 1960s. Her architectural redesign plan for Harlem was published in *Esquire* in 1965 and won the Prix de Rome in Environmental Design in 1970. Even though she ultimately decided against pursuing a career as an architect, space—literal and figurative—remained a significant theme in Jordan's work.

After her divorce, Jordan struggled to support herself and her son as a teacher and freelance writer. She published short stories and poems under the name of June Meyer in a number of top magazines and journals. While Jordan's artistic voice emerged as part of the civil rights, women's rights, and antiwar movements of the 1960s and early 1970s, they did not define her. Her political consciousness developed according to her own rules.

A dedicated and engaged teacher, Jordan began her professorial career in 1967 as an English instructor at City College and poet in residence at the Teachers and Writers Collaborative, both in New York City. She taught English and literature at Connecticut College, Sarah Lawrence College, Yale University, and SUNY Stony Brook, where she was awarded tenure in 1982. In 1989 she took a position at the University of

California at Berkeley, teaching English, African American studies, and women's studies. An extremely popular teacher, Jordan exhibited the same passion for teaching as she did for writing, challenging her students to be honest in their work and with themselves. While at Berkeley, Jordan founded Poetry for the People, a program that employs poetry as a tool of empowerment through workshops at high schools and prisons, marathon poetry readings, and the study of work by African Americans and Arabs that is generally overlooked in the classroom.

One of the nation's most published African American authors, Jordan's catalogue of work includes ten books of poetry, eight volumes of essays, children's books, four plays, two librettos, a spoken-word album, several edited anthologies, and a memoir. Jordan's writing career began in earnest with the 1969 publication of her first book of poetry, *Who Look at Me*, which ends with the plea "Who see the roof and corners of my pride / to be (as you are) free? / WHO LOOK AT ME?" After the publication of *Some Changes* (1971), which, like *Who Look at Me*, focused on issues relating to African American identity, Jordan's poetry collections, including *Things I Do in the Dark: Selected Poems* (1977), *Passion: New Poems 1977–1980* (1980), *Living Room: New Poems 1980–1984* (1985), *Naming Our Destiny: New and Selected Poems* (1989), and *Haruko Love Poems* (1994), increasingly emphasized overtly political and international issues.

An early advocate of the use of black English, Jordan wrote a novel for young adults, *His Own Where* (1971), entirely in black vernacular. The book was nominated for a National Book Award. Jordan's celebrated works for children and young adults began with *The Voice of the Children* (1970), an edited volume that grew out of a workshop for black and Hispanic readers, and continued with *New Life: New Room* (1975), *Kimako's Story* (1981), and the 1972 biography of FANNIE LOU HAMER. Jordan maintained a presence on the national stage as a regular columnist for *The Progressive* and a contributor to a host of specialized and mainstream publications. Seeking a collaborative medium and an alternate venue for her work, Jordan wrote and produced several plays, including *In the Spirit of Sojourner Truth* (1979) and *For the Arrow That Flies by Day* (1981), and a guide to writing and teaching poetry entitled *June Jordan's Poetry for the People: A Revolutionary Blueprint* (1995).

At the core of these works Jordan battles injustice, repression, and oppression. "She is the bravest of us, the most outraged," ALICE WALKER contends. "She feels for all. She is the universal poet." From Oakland, California, to the Middle East and from Nicaragua to South Africa, Jordan's work advocates for women, the poor, and the disenfranchised. According to TONI MORRISON, Jordan's career was shaped by "forty years of tireless activism coupled with and fuelled by flawless art" (*Guardian*, 20 June 2002). Affirmative action, war crimes in the Balkans, the situation of women in Afghanistan, black women's health, Palestinian rights—each of these topics and hundreds more made their way into Jordan's work and classroom. ISHMAEL REED characterizes Jordan's poetry as "straightforward, unadorned, in-your-face" (*San Francisco Chronicle*, 27 June 2002). This unflinching directness, always brave and sometimes heavy-handed, is exemplified by "Poem about Police Brutality":

Tell me something
what you think would happen if
everytime they kill a black boy
then we kill a cop
everytime they kill a black man
Then we kill a cop
you think the accident rate would lower
subsequently?

Autobiographical and interdisciplinary, Jordan's work chronicles a life intent on breaking down the barriers between poetry and prose, between politics and art, and between the personal and the political. Jordan resisted being labeled and pigeonholed with regard to her writing, her politics, or her sexuality. For Jordan, who was openly bisexual, each element of life and work was part of a larger commitment to the principles of freedom and equality. "If you are free, you are not predictable and you are not controllable," she wrote in the *Progressive*.

Petite, warm, and elegant, yet tough, tenacious, and controversial, Jordan had a distinctive laugh and a sardonic sense of humor. She was a dramatic and charismatic reader who presented her work at the United Nations and the U.S. Congress, at innumerable colleges and universities, and on radio, television, and film. A resolute political activist, she served on the executive board of the Center for Constitutional Rights and the Nicaraguan Culture Alliance. Jordan was the recipient of many fellowships, honors, and awards, including a Rockefeller grant in 1969; a PEN Center USA West Freedom to Write Award in 1991; and two journalism awards, one for international reporting from the National Association of Black Journalists in 1984 and a lifetime achievement award from the National Black Writers' Conference in 1988. A three-year award from the Lila Wallace–Reader's Digest Fund facilitated the expansion of the Poetry for the People program and the completion of several writing projects, among them, Jordan's 1995 libretto for the Opera director Peter Sellers, "I Was Looking at the Ceiling and Then I Saw the Sky," and her poetry collection, *Kissing God Goodbye: Poems 1991–1997* (1997).

Jordan's last book, *Some of Us Did Not Die: New and Selected Essays of June Jordan* (2002), was published posthumously and includes pieces from two earlier volumes, *Affirmative Acts: Political Essays* (1998) and *Technical Difficulties: African American Notes on the State of the Union* (1992), along with new essays on Islam, the terrorist events of 11 September 2001, and her experience of having been raped twice. June Jordan died of breast cancer at her home in Berkeley, California, in June 2002.

FURTHER READING

The June Jordan Papers are located at the Schlesinger Library, Radcliffe College, Harvard University, Cambridge, Massachusetts.

Jordan, June. *Soldier: A Poet's Childhood* (2001).

Quiroz, Julie. "Poetry Is a Political Act: An Interview with June Jordan." *Colorlines*, Winter 1999.

Obituaries: *New York Times*, 18 June 2002; *Los Angeles Times*, 20 June 2002.

—LISA E. RIVO

JORDAN, MICHAEL

(17 Feb. 1963–), basketball player, was born Michael Jeffrey Jordan in Brooklyn, New York, the fourth of five children of James Jordan and Deloris Peoples. The family soon relocated to Wilmington in the parents' home state, North Carolina, where Jordan's father rose to supervisor in a General Electric plant and his mother worked as a bank teller. James Jordan's Air Force pension boosted the family into the middle class, and they instilled in their children a solid work ethic with an emphasis on loyalty and commitment.

Like his brothers and sisters, Jordan was a relatively short child—but exceptionally quick. He preferred baseball to basketball and pitched several no-hitters in Little League. Although he was initially a lazy child who bribed his siblings to do his chores, Jordan was invigorated by athletic competition. Regular one-on-one basketball games against his older brother Larry fueled a fiery competitiveness in him, since Larry was acknowledged to be more talented. When Michael entered Laney Wilmington High School in 1979 he was five feet, eight inches tall and determined to play varsity basketball. Following a year on the freshman team, the varsity coaches encouraged him to try out as a sophomore and then cut him. He was devastated, cried in his bedroom that afternoon, and then averaged twenty-five points per game on the junior varsity team. He made varsity the next year; grew to six feet, two inches tall and during his senior season at Laney, Jordan led the Buccaneers to a 19–4 record before matriculating at Chapel Hill in the fall of 1981. He had previously earned an invitation to summer camps at the University of North Carolina–Chapel Hill and the prestigious Five-Star Camp in Pittsburgh. At Chapel Hill he got his first exposure to "the system," Coach Dean Smith's storied method of running a high-caliber basketball program; Smith and his assistants were immediately impressed not only with Jordan's athleticism but also with his determination to sneak into scrimmages when it was not his turn.

Much of Smith's system involved teaching teamwork and humility.

Michael Jordan walks on air at the NBA All-Star Game, 1988.
© Bettmann/CORBIS

Although Jordan became increasingly cocky about his abilities, the system was the perfect antidote for his good-natured, though occasionally abrasive attitude. The Tar Heel upperclassmen did not appreciate the fast-talking, bright-eyed freshman who detailed how he would dunk on them in practice—and they harbored no small amount of spite when he quickly made good on his word. But they could take some solace in seeing Jordan fetch loose balls during practice and lug the film projector on road trips—and in winning more games. The Tar Heels went 32–2 and won the Atlantic Coast Conference tournament; a few weeks later, Jordan hit a seventeen-foot jumper to clinch the National Collegiate Athletic Association championship. At his full height of six feet, six inches, Jordan won Player of the Year honors for the next two seasons; after consulting his parents and Smith, he bypassed his senior year to enter the National Basketball Association (NBA) draft. In the interim, Jordan led the U.S. basketball team to the 1984 Olympic gold medal.

The ailing Chicago Bulls signed Jordan for five years at $800,000 per year. During his first two seasons Jordan became a phenomenon, boosting the Bulls' ticket sales by almost 90 percent and triggering a similar spike in attendance at road games. He played all eighty-two games and averaged 28.2 points, almost six assists, and more than six rebounds per contest, securing Rookie of the Year honors. During All-Star weekend, Jordan competed for the first time in the popular Slam Dunk Contest. Donning a gold chain and his trademark baggy shorts (which allowed him to wear his North Carolina shorts underneath), Jordan electrified the crowd with a combination of tremendous leaping ability and graceful aerial control.

Early in the 1985–1986 campaign, Jordan broke his foot. Doctors advised him to sacrifice the rest of the season for treatment, but he returned with more than a dozen games remaining and drove the Bulls into the play-offs against the powerful Boston Celtics. Although the Celtics swept the Bulls, Jordan averaged 43.7 points for the series, scoring a record sixty-three in the second game, and prompted the Celtic star Larry Bird to quip that he had played against "God disguised as Michael Jordan."

Jordan's dramatic performances— such as scoring more than fifty points in eight separate games during the 1986–1987 season—catapulted him into the NBA's highest echelon, and he signed lucrative endorsement deals for Wheaties cereal; McDonald's restaurants; and, most important, Nike sportswear. These companies quickly realized that Jordan's gracious public persona and clean-cut looks transcended the potential obstacle of his skin color; teenagers and children of all classes and races idolized him. Jordan hence became a crucial figure in the escalation of sports marketing into a multibillion-dollar industry. The only compensation he wanted when he originally signed with Nike was a car; in 1987 his contract guaranteed him eighteen million dollars over seven years, plus royalties from such products as the Air Jordan basketball shoe, thought to be more than twenty million dollars per year by the mid-1990s. In 1998 Forbes magazine estimated that Jordan had generated more than ten billion dollars in overall revenue for the NBA during his career.

The quintessential slow-motion image of Jordan came from the clinching dunk in the 1987 Slam Dunk Contest. Jordan ran from beyond half-court, leaped from the free-throw line, and glided through the air in a seemingly effortless manner—lifting the ball and then lowering it, contracting his legs and then spreading and extending them—finally dunking the ball fifteen

feet later. His rumored forty-four-inch vertical leap was impressive, though by no means unprecedented; the mythical quality of his dunks derived more from the way he seemed to hang in midair as if through sheer will. Primarily known for his offensive abilities, Jordan relied on his defense to catalyze the rest of his game; crowds would anxiously anticipate the inevitable moment when he would intercept a pass, streak downcourt, and take flight for a beautifully thunderous dunk.

Despite regular appearances in television and print advertisements, as well as his 1989 marriage to Juanita Vanoy (with whom he has three children), Jordan did not allow any distractions to hinder his and the Bulls' steady progress. For half a dozen seasons, Jordan had systematically improved every area of his game, becoming one of the most versatile players in the history of basketball. In 1988 Jordan won the first of five Most Valuable Player awards, as well as Defensive Player of the Year, becoming the first to win both in a single season. He would lead the NBA in scoring for ten seasons and was selected for the All-Defensive Team a record nine times. Originally considered a player who slashed toward the hoop and fired the occasional midrange jump shot, Jordan developed a deadly post game and extended his shooting range, increasing his three-point percentage by .100 to .376 in 1990. The determination reflected in these accomplishments appeared finally to inspire his teammates, and the Bulls defeated Magic Johnson's Los Angeles Lakers for the 1991 NBA championship.

Later that year a Chicago sportswriter published The Jordan Rules, an exposé of the Bulls' championship season, which portrayed Jordan as being mean-spirited toward his teammates in order to elicit better play. Nevertheless, the Bulls won their second championship in 1992, and Jordan and his teammate Scottie Pippen traveled to Barcelona, Spain, to play on the first U.S. Olympic basketball team to include professional players. This Dream Team won the gold medal with unprecedented ease.

As the Bulls hurtled toward their third consecutive championship in 1993, hints surfaced that Jordan routinely gambled enormous sums of money. A

year earlier Jordan had weathered the first of such murmurings when a murdered man was found in possession of three checks, all written by Jordan and totaling $108,000, one of them made out to a convicted cocaine dealer. Jordan claimed the checks were gambling debts from golfing, a longtime hobby. When another purported gambling golfer asserted that Jordan owed him more than a million dollars, an NBA investigation ensued. Jordan was absolved of any violation, and on the heels of winning a third consecutive NBA title that spring, he decided to retire.

He was not, however, retiring from sports altogether; in 1994 he signed a free-agency baseball contract with the Chicago White Sox. The previous August, James Jordan had been found murdered in his car, and many reporters interpreted Jordan's actions as a means of realizing the childhood dreams he had shared with his father of someday playing major league baseball. After one lackluster season in Chicago's farm system with the AA Birmingham Barons (Jordan batted .202), and with a strike imminent for the 1995 baseball season, Jordan decided to rejoin the Bulls. He played a handful of games in the regular season and averaged more than thirty points in the play-offs before the Bulls lost in the second round. Again motivated by the sour taste of losing, he embarked upon a strict training regimen and bolstered his offensive arsenal with a fade-away jumper that he fired with amazing precision and that was nearly impossible to block.

The Bulls marched to three more consecutive NBA championships from 1996 to 1998, and Jordan never missed a game. His play-off performances were particularly memorable, as he continued to exhibit an uncanny ability to elevate his play during especially tense situations. He started every play-off game of his career, played more minutes in each game than in the regular season, grabbed more rebounds, gave more assists, and averaged 33.4 points per game—three points above his career regular season average. In the 1997 finals against the Utah Jazz, Jordan had a fever of 100 degrees and severe nausea before the fifth game. But he scored thirty-eight points—fifteen in the final period—and the Bulls came from behind to win. The next year Jordan sparked another comeback and made the series-clinching shot from twenty feet away to win his final championship.

The next season, after an NBA labor dispute was settled in January 1999, Jordan again retired, cagily asserting that he was "99.9 percent certain" he was retiring permanently. He assumed an executive position with the Washington Wizards a year later. In November 2001 Jordan once again took to the court, playing for the Wizards against the New York Knicks. Jordan had a chance to tie the game with a three-point shot in the waning seconds, but he missed. Although he averaged more than twenty points with Washington and was twice voted to the All-Star team, the Wizards failed to make the play-offs both seasons.

In April 2003 Jordan was summarily dismissed from the Wizards' front office. Nevertheless, with his nearly obsessive drive for personal success, Michael Jordan established himself as the most influential African American in athletics since MUHAMMAD ALI. Both men were unparalleled masters of their respective crafts; where Ali's career brought energy and a sense of pride to blacks during the civil rights era, Jordan's avoided politics but brought the world of sports to Wall Street.

FURTHER READING

Jordan, Michael. *For Love of the Game: My Story* (1998).

Greene, Bob. *Rebound: The Odyssey of Michael Jordan* (1995).
Halberstam, David. *Playing for Keeps: Michael Jordan and the World He Made* (1999).
Krugel, Mitchell. *One Last Shot: The Story of Michael Jordan's Comeback* (2002).
LaFeber, Walter. *Michael Jordan and the New Global Capitalism* (1999).
Patton, Jim. *Rookie: When Michael Jordan Came to the Minor Leagues* (1995).

—DAVID F. SMYDRA JR.

JORDAN, VERNON

(8 Aug. 1935–), lawyer, civil rights leader, and corporate executive, was born Vernon Eulion Jordan Jr. in Atlanta, the eldest of two sons of Vernon Jordan Sr., a postal clerk at Fort McPherson, Georgia, and Mary Belle Griggs, proprietor of a catering business, who had a child from a previous union. Jordan was descended from Georgia sharecroppers who had their roots in slavery. His maternal grandfather told young Vernon, "If I could have anything in the world, I'd want to be able to go to the bathroom indoors, in a warm place, one time before I die" (Jordan, 23).

Until the age of thirteen Jordan lived in Atlanta's University Homes, the first public housing for black people built in the United States. His "project," as such low-income structures would come to be known, derived its name from the black college campuses that surrounded it and provided an abundance of positive role models for the residents. Jordan's success in school was strongly encouraged by his mother, who became president of the PTA at every school Vernon attended from elementary to high school. As an adult, his tall, athletic build greatly contributed to his distinguished presence, but as a young boy, his dark complexion was not viewed so favorably; even his diligence was mockingly seen as "acting white," rather than as being black and highly motivated.

Jordan graduated from high school with honors in 1953 and opted to attend DePauw University in Greencastle, Indiana, where there were only four other black students and no black women. In retrospect he wrote that "never once in my youth did I go to a school with enough resources to help its students compete on an equal basis with the average white student" (Jordan, 47). Yet Jordan persevered in his studies at DePauw and won several public-speaking contests.

Given his deep faith and exceptional oratorical skills, Jordan seriously considered entering the ministry, but his mother, a devout member of the African Methodist Episcopal Church, would not hear of it. Instead, Jordan entered Howard University Law School in 1957 and spent his summers driving a bus for the Chicago Transit Authority to augment his finances. After his parents' divorce in 1958, Jordan decided to secure his relationship with Shirley Yarbrough, who had graduated from Howard the year before and returned to Atlanta, where she worked as a caseworker. The two were married during Jordan's second year in law school but continued to live in separate cities until Jordan received his JD degree in 1960 and relocated to Atlanta to be with his wife and infant daughter, Vickee.

Back in Atlanta, Jordan became a law clerk for the civil rights attorney Donald Hollowell and was paid the lowly sum of thirty-five dollars a week. Together they fought discrimination cases, defended death-row prisoners, and won a landmark decision in *Holmes v. Danner* that allowed Charlayne Hunter-Gault and Hamilton Holmes to become the first black students to attend the University of Georgia in 1961. Within a few months of this victory, Jordan came to the attention of the leadership of the National Association for the Advancement of Colored People (NAACP), who appointed him field director for the state of Georgia. In this position he set a new recruitment record; led a seven-month boycott in Augusta, Georgia, against discriminatory businesses; and became a colleague of A. LEON HIGGINBOTHAM, THURGOOD MARSHALL, ROY WILKINS, and MEDGAR EVERS, his counterpart in Mississippi.

In 1964 Jordan was recruited by the Southern Regional Council, the oldest interracial organization in the South, where he became the executive assistant and the director of the Voter Education Project. In these positions Jordan began to cultivate his legendary skills as a behind-the-scenes negotiator as he distributed funds to organizations such as the Southern Christian Leadership Conference, Congress of Racial Equality, Student Nonviolent Coordinating Committee, and the NAACP. As his reputation grew, invitations and opportunities multiplied. In 1965 he attended his first meeting at the White House when President Lyndon Johnson named him to serve along with MARTIN LUTHER KING JR., DOROTHY HEIGHT, and JOHN LEWIS on the White House Council to Fulfill These Rights. He also served on the Presidential Advisory Commission on Selective Service during the Vietnam War and became the first African American to hold a teaching fellowship at Harvard University's John F. Kennedy School of Government, during the 1969–1970 academic year. Jordan acquired foreign-policy experience during his visit to Israel shortly before the Six-Day War, and he was part of an American delegation sent to discuss economic and cold war issues at the Bilderberg conference in Denmark in 1969. He later served on the Council on Foreign Relations and the Trilateral Commission.

Jordan planned to run for Congress in 1970 from the Fifth District of Georgia, but shortly after making his announcement he was offered the directorship of the United Negro College Fund. In his first year at the helm of that organization, previous fund-raising levels were surpassed by more than ten million dollars. Then, on 9 March 1971, WHITNEY YOUNG, the leader of the National Urban League, tragically drowned while in Lagos, Nigeria. Although he was only thirty-six years old, Jordan became Young's successor. As president he restructured the organization; promoted a young staffer, RON BROWN, who would later head the Democratic National Committee and become secretary of commerce, to the newly created office of general counsel; and began issuing an annual report called *The State of Black America.*

During Jimmy Carter's administration, Jordan attempted to mend the rift between African Americans and American Jews caused when ANDREW YOUNG, U.S. ambassador to the United Nations, and JESSE JACKSON met with representatives of the Palestinian Liberation Organization. Some black leaders welcomed the schism as representing the independence of black leadership; Jordan countered by saying that rather than moving apart, both groups needed to affirm a "Declaration of Interdependence" (Jordan, 265). On 29 May 1980, in Fort Wayne, Indiana, Jordan was shot in the back by an assailant using a hunting rifle. He recovered after a long convalescence, and Joseph Paul Franklin, a white supremacist and serial killer, later confessed to the shooting. In 1982 Robert Strauss invited Jordan to become a partner in the law firm of Akin, Gump, Strauss, Hauer, and Feld. Jordan, who had been one of the first African Americans to serve on the boards of such corporations as Xerox, American Express, and the Rockefeller Foundation, left the Urban League to accept this position because he believed that he had reached a point in his career

where he could open more doors by working in the private sector.

In 1986 Jordan's wife, Shirley, died after a twenty-year battle with multiple sclerosis. The following year he married Ann Dibble Cook, a professor at the University of Chicago. In 1992 Jordan, who had known Bill and Hillary Clinton for two decades, became chairman of the transition team for President-elect Clinton. Jordan declined to be considered for the position of attorney general, but he actively coaxed COLIN POWELL and others into the administration. His role in securing employment for Webster Hubbell and Monica Lewinsky with Revlon Consumer Products Corporation, a company on whose board he served, brought his actions under harsh scrutiny during the wide-ranging Whitewater investigations of President Clinton's financial and personal affairs; however, Jordan's accomplishments in the public sector, in the corporate world, and as a Washington powerbroker firmly established him as a major player in the high-stakes game of power and politics.

FURTHER READING

Jordan, Vernon E. *Vernon Can Read!* (2001).

Current Biography (1993).

Gerth, Jeff. "Being Intimate with Power, Vernon Jordan Can Wield It." *New York Times,* 14 July 1996, sec. 1.

—SHOLOMO B. LEVY

JULIAN, PERCY LAVON (11 Apr. 1899–19 Apr. 1975), chemist, was born in Montgomery, Alabama, the son of James Sumner Julian, a railway mail clerk, and Elizabeth Lena Adams, a teacher. He received his AB from DePauw University in 1920, and for the next two years he taught chemistry at Fisk University. In 1922 he was awarded Harvard University's Austin Fellowship in chemistry; he received his MA from that school in 1923. He remained at Harvard for three more years as a research assistant in biophysics and organic chemistry. In 1926 he joined the faculty at West Virginia State College, and in 1928 he became associate professor and head of the chemistry department at

Howard University. The following year he was awarded a fellowship from the Rockefeller Foundation's General Education Board to pursue his doctorate at the University of Vienna in Austria, where he earned that degree in organic chemistry in 1931. After graduating he returned to Howard, but he left in 1932 to accept a position as chemistry professor and research fellow at DePauw.

Julian's first major discovery involved physostigmine, a drug made from Calabar beans that is used to treat glaucoma and myasthenia gravis. In 1934, while he was preparing to publish his findings concerning d, 1-eserethole, the penultimate step in synthesizing physostigmine, Sir Robert Robinson, the eminent Oxford chemist, made public the results of his work on the synthesis of eserethole. Much to Julian's surprise, the eserethole described in Robinson's paper bore no resemblance to the compound he had developed. Despite the professional stature of Robinson, Julian published his own findings and detailed the differences between his results and Robinson's. The next year, when Julian successfully synthesized physostigmine from his version of d, 1-eserethole, he clearly demonstrated that he, not Robinson, had been correct.

Julian's next project involved the extraction from soybean oil of stigmasterol, a sterol used in the production of sex hormones, which in turn were used to treat a variety of medical conditions. However, he abandoned this line of research in 1936 when he was invited to join the Glidden Company of Chicago, Illinois, as director of research of the soya products division. His first task was to oversee the completion of a modern plant for extracting oil from soybeans; his second was to develop uses for the oil that the plant would produce. He soon devised a method for extracting from the oil vegetable protein, which he then developed into an inexpensive coating for paper. After he learned how to adjust the size of the soya protein molecule, Julian was able to create soya derivatives for use in textiles, paints, livestock and poultry feed, candy, ink, cosmetics, food additives, and "Aero Foam," used by the U.S. Navy during World War II to put out oil and gasoline fires and known throughout the fleet as "bean

The holder of ninety-four patents, chemist Percy Julian made important discoveries in the extraction and production of progesterone, testosterone, and cortisone. Schomburg Center

membership in the American Association for the Advancement of Science, the National Academy of Sciences, and the National Inventors Hall of Fame. Classroom buildings at MacMurray College, Coppin State College, and Illinois State University bear his name, as do elementary schools in Arizona and Louisiana and a high school in Chicago. He held ninety-four U.S. patents for methods of producing vegetable protein, sterols, and steroids and published his research in more than fifty scholarly articles. He died in Waukegan, Illinois.

Julian contributed to the advance of science in two ways. His pioneering research into the synthesization of hormones and other chemical substances made it possible for people of average means to obtain relief from such maladies as glaucoma and arthritis. His work with soybeans led to the development of a number of new and valuable products for industrial and agricultural applications.

FURTHER READING

Julian's papers did not survive.

Sammons, Vivian O. *Blacks in Science and Medicine* (1990).

Witkop, Bernhard. "Percy Lavon Julian," National Academy of Sciences, *Biographical Memoirs* 52 (1980): 223–66.

Obituary: *New York Times*, 21 Apr. 1975.
—CHARLES W. CAREY JR.

soup." Serendipitously, in 1940, when a large tank of soybean oil became contaminated with water and turned into an oily paste, Julian discovered that the paste was an excellent source from which to extract inexpensively sterols such as stigmasterol. Soon Glidden was producing in bulk quantity the female hormone progesterone, used to prevent miscarriages and to treat certain menstrual complications, and the male hormone testosterone, used in the therapy of certain types of breast cancer. In 1949, Julian developed a method for synthesizing cortisone—used to treat rheumatoid arthritis—from sterols.

In 1954 Julian, having become more interested in steroid research than in soybeans, left Glidden to start Julian Laboratories in Oak Park, Illinois, with a factory and farms in Mexico. The Mexican branch of the operation harvested and processed the roots of *Dioscorea*, a wild Mexican yam, which Julian had discovered was an even better source than soybeans from which to synthesize cortisone and the sex hormones. In 1961 he sold the

business to Smith, Kline and French, a pharmaceutical firm that was one of his best customers, but he remained as president until 1964, when he began the Julian Research Institute and Julian Associates, both in Franklin Park, Illinois. He continued to experiment with the production of synthetic drugs until his death.

Julian also played an active role in the civil rights movement. In 1956 he chaired the Council for Social Action of the Congregational Christian Churches, and in 1967 he became cochairman of a group of forty-seven prominent blacks recruited by the Legal Defense and Educational Fund of the National Association for the Advancement of Colored People (NAACP) to raise a million dollars for the purpose of financing lawsuits to enforce civil rights legislation.

In 1935 Julian married Anna Johnson; they had two children. Julian received a number of honors and awards, including the NAACP's Spingarn Medal (1947) and nineteen honorary doctoral degrees. He was elected to

JUST, ERNEST EVERETT (14 Aug. 1883–27 Oct. 1941), zoologist, was born in Charleston, South Carolina, the son of Charles Fraser Just, a carpenter and wharf builder, and Mary Mathews Cooper. Following his father's death in 1887, his mother moved the family to James Island, off the South Carolina coast. There she labored in phosphate mines, opened a church and a school, and mobilized farmers into a moss-curing enterprise. A dynamic community leader, she was the prime mover behind the establishment of a township—Maryville—named in her honor. Maryville served as a model for all-black town governments elsewhere.

Ernest attended his mother's school, the Frederick Deming Jr. Industrial

Zoologist and Howard University Professor Ernest Everett Just. Schomburg Center

School, until the age of twelve. Under her influence, he entered the teacher-training program of the Colored Normal, Industrial, Agricultural and Mechanical College (now South Carolina State College) in Orangeburg, South Carolina, in 1896. After graduating in 1899, he attended Kimball Union Academy in Meriden, New Hampshire (1900–1903), before proceeding to Dartmouth College. At Dartmouth he majored in biology and minored in Greek and history. Under the guidance of two eminent zoologists, William Patten and John H. Gerould, he developed a passion for scientific research. Some of his work, on oral arches in frogs, was included in Patten's classic book *The Evolution of the Vertebrates and Their Kin* (1912). Ernest graduated magna cum laude from Dartmouth in 1907.

Essentially, there were two career options available at the time to an African American with Just's academic background: teaching in a black institution or preaching in a black church. Just chose the former, beginning his career in the fall of 1907 as instructor in English and rhetoric at Howard University. In 1909 he taught English and biology and a year later assumed a permanent full-time commitment in zoology as part of a general revitalization of the science curriculum at Howard. He also taught physiology in the medical school. A devoted teacher, he served as faculty adviser to a group that was trying to establish a nationwide fraternity of black students. The Alpha chapter of Omega Psi Phi was organized at Howard in 1911, and Just became its first honorary member. In 1912 he married a fellow Howard faculty member, Ethel Highwarden, with whom he later had three children.

Meanwhile, Just laid plans to pursue scientific research. Patten had placed him in touch with Frank Rattray Lillie, head of the zoology department at the University of Chicago and director of the Marine Biological Laboratory (MBL) at Woods Hole, Massachusetts. Although both Patten and Lillie considered it impractical for a black to seek a scientific career (in the face of overwhelming odds against finding suitable employment), Just's persistence and determination won them over. Lillie invited Just to the MBL as his research assistant in 1909. Their teacher-student relationship quickly blossomed into a full and equal scientific collaboration. By the time Just earned a PhD in Zoology at the University of Chicago in 1916, he had already coauthored a paper with Lillie and written several of his own.

The two worked on fertilization in marine animals. Just's first paper, "The Relation of the First Cleavage Plane to the Entrance Point of the Sperm," appeared in *Biological Bulletin* in 1912 and was cited frequently as a classic and authoritative study. Just went on to champion a theory—the fertilizin theory—first proposed by Lillie, who postulated the existence of a substance called fertilizin as the essential biochemical catalyst in the fertilization of the egg by the sperm. In 1915 Just was awarded the NAACP's first Spingarn Medal in recognition of his scientific contributions and "foremost service to his race."

As Patten and Lillie had predicted, no scientific positions opened up for Just. Science was for him a deeply felt avocation, an activity that he looked forward to doing each summer at the MBL as a welcome respite from his heavy teaching and administrative responsibilities at Howard. Under the circumstances, his productivity was extraordinary. Within ten years (1919–1928), he published thirty-five articles, mostly relating to his studies on fertilization. Though proud of his output, he yearned for a position or environment in which he could pursue his research full time.

The MBL, while serving in some respects as a haven of opportunity for Just, generated thinly disguised, occasionally overt racial tensions. Just was excluded from certain social gatherings and subjected to verbal slurs. A few of the more liberal scientists cultivated his acquaintance, protecting him at times from confrontations and embarrassment, but to Just this behavior seemed paternalistic. Further, while many MBL scientists relied on his technical expertise, some showed little regard for the intellectual or theoretical side of Just's work. Others, citing a special duty to his race, urged him to abandon science in favor of teaching and more practical pursuits.

In 1928 Just received a substantial grant from the Julius Rosenwald Fund, which allowed him a change of environment and longer stretches of time for his research. His first excursion, in 1929, took him to Italy, where he worked for seven months at the Stazione Zoologica in Naples. He traveled to Europe ten times over the course of the next decade, staying for periods ranging from three weeks to two years. He worked primarily at the Stazione Zoologica, the Kaiser-Wilhelm Institut für Biologie in Berlin, and the Station Biologique in Roscoff, France. As the political turmoil in Europe grew, Just remained relatively unaffected and continued to be productive in his research. That he felt more comfortable there amid the rise of Nazism and Fascism suggests how dismal his outlook on life in America had become.

In Europe, Just worked on what he considered his magnum opus: a book synthesizing many of the scientific theories, philosophical ideas, and experimental results of his career. The book was published in 1939 under the title *Biology of the Cell Surface*. Its thesis, that the ectoplasm or cell surface has a fundamental role in development, did not receive much attention at the time but later became a focus of serious scientific investigation. Just was assisted in this work by a German, Maid Hedwig Schnetzler, whom he married in 1939 after divorcing his first wife. Also in 1939, he published a compendium of experimental advice under the title *Basic Methods for Experiments on Eggs of Marine Animals*. In 1940 Just was interned briefly in France following the German invasion, then was released to return to America, where he died of pancreatic cancer a year later in Washington, D.C.

FURTHER READING

A collection of Just's papers is preserved in the Manuscript Division of the Moorland-Spingarn Research Center, Howard University, Washington, D.C.

Gilbert, Scott F. "Cellular Politics: Ernest Everett Just, Richard B. Goldschmidt, and the Attempt to Reconcile Embryology and Genetics" in *The American Development of Biology*, eds. Ronald Rainger, Keith R. Benson, and Jane Maienschein (1988).

Gould, Stephen Jay. "Just in the Middle: A Solution to the Mechanist-Vitalist Controversy." *Natural History*, Jan. 1984, 24–33.

Manning, Kenneth R. *Black Apollo of Science: The Life of Ernest Everett Just* (1983).

Obituary: *Science* 95 (2 Jan. 1942).

—KENNETH R. MANNING

K

 KECKLY, ELIZABETH HOBBS (Feb. 1818–26 May 1907), slave, dressmaker, abolitionist, and White House memoirist, was born Elizabeth Hobbs in Dinwiddie County, Virginia, the daughter of Armistead Burwell, a white slaveholder, and his slave Agnes Hobbs. Agnes was the family nurse and seamstress. Her husband, George Pleasant Hobbs, the slave of another man, treated "Lizzy" as his own daughter, and it was not until some years later, after George had been forced to move west with his master, that Agnes told Lizzy the identity of her biological father. While her mother taught her sewing, the skill that would make her name and fortune, it was George Hobbs who first instilled in Lizzy a profound respect for learning. Ironically, it was Armistead Burwell, who repeatedly told Lizzy she would never be "worth her salt," who probably sparked her ambition to succeed and prove him wrong.

As a young girl, Lizzy lived in the master's house, where her earliest tasks were to mind the Burwell's infant

Elizabeth Keckly. University of North Carolina

daughter, sweep the yard, pull up weeds, and collect eggs. Lizzy benefited from the better diet and clothing and the possibilities for self-improvement that were often afforded to house slaves. Most important, she was taught to read and write. These advantages, added to the relatively stable presence of her extended slave family, contributed to Lizzy's proud bearing and strong sense of self. Nevertheless, living in the master's house was also dangerous. When she was five years old, her mistress, enraged because she had accidentally tilted the baby out of its crib, had her beaten so severely that she never forgot it.

At age fourteen, Lizzy was loaned to Armistead's eldest son, Robert, and his new bride, Margaret Anna Robertson. The young Burwells took Lizzy to Hillsborough, North Carolina, where Robert was the minister of the Presbyterian Church and Anna opened a school for girls. Years later Lizzy would speak of her years in Hillsborough as the darkest period of her early life. When she was eighteen, Anna goaded a neighbor and her husband to "break" her with repeated beatings. At twenty Lizzy became the sexual prey of Alexander Kirkland, the married son of one of the town's wealthiest slaveholders. For four years she endured a forced sexual relationship, until she gave birth to a son, George, and was sent back to the family in Virginia.

By this time Armistead Burwell had died, and Lizzy and her son rejoined her mother, becoming a slave in the household of Armistead's daughter, Anne, and her husband, Hugh A. Garland. In 1847 Garland moved his household to St. Louis, where he opened a law office. (One of Garland's clients was Irene Emerson, whose slaves, Harriet and DRED SCOTT, sued her for their freedom.) However, Garland could not make ends meet, and he decided to hire Lizzy out as a seamstress. It was a pivotal moment in Lizzy's life. Being hired out enabled her to hone her skills

as a dressmaker, and she soon earned the title of mantua maker for her ability to sew the complicated mantua, whose tight bodice was fitted with a series of tiny, vertical pleats in the back. But above all, sewing for hire gave her opportunities for autonomy that she could not have had working in the master's house. Indeed, during this period Lizzy developed the network of white female clients who, in 1855, lent her money to allow her to pay the twelve-hundred-dollar purchase price for her freedom and that of her son. By this time Lizzy had married James Keckly, whom she had known as a free black Virginian; the marriage quickly soured once she discovered that he was not, in fact, free and that he drank. (Though the conventional spelling of her married name is Keckley, she herself spelled it Keckly.)

Lizzy Keckly remained in St. Louis until 1860, when she moved east alone, leaving James in St. Louis and enrolling George in Wilberforce University in Ohio. (Her mother had died in 1854.) She arrived in Washington, D.C., in the spring and quickly found work as a seamstress. Within months she had built an impressive list of clients, consisting of the wives of congressmen and army officers. During the secession winter of 1860–1861, Varina Davis, wife of the Mississippi senator Jefferson Davis asked her to move south with her, though Keckly refused.

On the day after President Abraham Lincoln's first inauguration, in 1861, Elizabeth Keckly presented herself at the White House for an interview with Mary Todd Lincoln. One of her clients had recommended her to the new "Mrs. President" in return for a last-minute gown. Over the next few months Keckly made Mary Lincoln fifteen or sixteen new dresses, an enormous task and one that threw the women together for hours at a time for the elaborate fittings that were required. This collaboration was the beginning of a relationship that would deepen over time through the personal and public crises that beset the women. The first crisis they shared occurred in August 1861 when Keckly's son, who had enlisted in the Union army as a white man, was killed in the Battle of Wilson's Creek in Missouri.

A dignified, proud woman, Keckly also established herself as a notable figure in the middle-class black community in Washington. As one of the "colored" White House staff, Keckly was a member of an elite black society, along with the city's leading caterers, barbers, restaurateurs, and government messengers. She boarded with the family of Walker Lewis, a respected messenger and later steward, who had also bought his way out of slavery. She also joined the black Union Bethel Church, second only in stature to the exclusive Fifteenth Street Presbyterian Church (which she joined in 1865). Meanwhile, her dressmaking business grew steadily; at its peak it employed twenty seamstresses.

By 1862 Keckly had become an intimate member of the Lincoln family, looking after the Lincolns' two young sons, combing the president's hair, and advising Mary Lincoln on matters of decorum as well as fashion. After the Lincolns' twelve-year-old son, Willie, died of typhoid fever in February, the grief-stricken Mary Lincoln came to rely more heavily on the steadying presence of Lizzy Keckly.

During this period, Keckly was coming into her own not only as an entrepreneur but also as an activist. In April, after Congress emancipated slaves in the district, she was featured in a syndicated newspaper article about the success stories of recently freed slaves. That summer, she organized church members into the Contraband Relief Association to aid the "contrabands," newly freed slaves who were pouring into Washington by the thousands. In the fall she made her first trip to the North, ostensibly as companion to Mary Lincoln and her youngest son, Tad, traveling to New York and Boston. But she spent much of her time raising funds with black abolitionists, including the Reverend HENRY HIGHLAND GARNET, the Reverend J. Sella Martin, and FREDERICK DOUGLASS, who raised money for her organization in England. She even solicited a donation from the president and Mrs. Lincoln.

Over the course of the four years she was an insider in the White House,

Keckly became more comfortable wielding her influence. In 1864 she helped arrange for SOJOURNER TRUTH to meet with Abraham Lincoln in the White House. The Lincolns even visited the contraband camps, where Keckly worked. She was one of the Lincolns' party when they entered Richmond after the Civil War ended.

In 1865, after Lincoln's assassination, Keckly accompanied Mary Lincoln to Chicago and then returned to her business in Washington. In 1867, at Lincoln's request, the two women met in New York City, where Keckly helped Lincoln arrange for a brokerage firm to auction off her old clothes to pay off her debts. Lincoln, who returned to Chicago while Keckly stayed in New York to manage Lincoln's affairs, promised to pay her out of the proceeds of the sale. But the scheme was a disaster; the women lost money on the venture. During this period, with the help of the antislavery journalist James Redpath, Keckly wrote a memoir, devoting the last section to what the newspapers dubbed the "Old Clothes Scandal." The 1868 publication of Keckly's book, *Behind the Scenes; or, Thirty Years a Slave, and Four Years in the White House,* caused Mary Lincoln to break off their friendship.

Behind the Scenes is an invaluable source of information about the Lincolns' private life in the White House. Whatever her motives for writing it, the memoir is unquestionably the expression of Keckly's desire to leave her mark, yet after its publication her business gradually declined, and she turned primarily to teaching sewing. In 1890 she sold her Lincoln mementoes to a collector. For several years she headed Wilberforce University's Department of Sewing and Domestic Science Arts, until she suffered a mild stroke. She died in Washington, D.C., in the National Home for Destitute Colored Women and Children, an institution founded during the war and partly funded by Keckly's contraband association.

FURTHER READING

Keckley, Elizabeth. *Behind the Scenes; or, Thirty Years a Slave, and Four Years in the White House* (1868). Ed. Frances Smith Foster (2001).

Fleischner, Jennifer. *Mrs. Lincoln and Mrs. Keckly: The Remarkable Story of the*

Friendship between a First Lady and a Former Slave (2003).

—JENNIFER FLEISCHNER

KEITH, DAMON JEROME

KEITH, DAMON JEROME (4 July 1922–), federal judge, was the youngest of six children born to Perry Keith, an automotive worker, and Annie Louise Williams. The family has its roots in Atlanta, Georgia, but Damon was born in Detroit, when his father took a job at the River Rouge Foundry of the Ford Motor Company. Keith has described his father as "the finest man in my life...the epitome of what a human being should be. He was my motivation and my desire to make something of myself."

In 1943 Keith graduated from an historically black college, West Virginia State College. That same year he was drafted into the army and served during World War II in a segregated military, an experience that he later described as "absolutely demeaning." After discharge from the military, Keith attended Howard University Law School, at a time when THURGOOD MARSHALL would practice before his Howard students the arguments he would later make in historic desegregation cases before the U.S. Supreme Court. Keith graduated from Howard Law School in 1949 and worked as a janitor while studying for the bar. Not long after he was admitted to practice in 1950, he married Rachel Boone, a physician from Liberia; they had three daughters, Gilda, Debbie, and Cecile. In 1956 Keith obtained a master of law degree from Wayne State University in Detroit.

During the early part of his career, Keith was politically active while he was in practice. Before his appointment to the bench, he was one of the named partners in the firm of Keith, Conyers, Anderson, Brown & Wallis in Detroit. He served on a number of different commissions, including the Detroit Housing Commission, the Civil Rights Commission of the Detroit Bar Association, and the Michigan Civil Rights Commission. Keith was appointed to the federal bench by President Lyndon B. Johnson in 1967 and was elevated to the Sixth Circuit Court of Appeals by President Jimmy Carter in 1977. Although he took senior status, still hearing cases but with a reduced workload, in 1995, Keith has continued to write judicial decisions that record and make history in the United States.

In *United States v. Sinclair* (1971), Keith addressed the abuse of power endemic in the administration of President Richard M. Nixon. Judge Keith's ruling resulted from a criminal trial in which members of the radical leftist White Panther Party was accused of bombing the Ann Arbor, Michigan, offices of the CIA. During the trial it became clear that the federal government had tapped the phone lines of one of the White Panther defendants without obtaining a warrant beforehand. U. S. Attorney General John Mitchell justified the wiretapping on the basis of "national security," but Judge Keith found that Mitchell had exceeded its powers. In particular, Keith rejected the Nixon administration's argument that "a dissident domestic organization is akin to an unfriendly foreign power and must be dealt with in the same fashion." Moreover, he added, the "Executive branch . . . cannot be given the power or the opportunity to investigate and prosecute criminal violations . . . simply because an accused espouses views which are inconsistent with our present form of Government." Keith concluded that the powers over search and seizure claimed by the Nixon White House "was never contemplated by the framers of our Constitution and cannot be tolerated today." The Supreme Court unanimously upheld Keith's ruling in *United States v. Sinclair*, which came to be known in legal circles as "the Keith Decision."

In 2002 Keith returned to the problem of abuses of power in the executive branch, this time by John Ashcroft, President George W. Bush's attorney general. As in *Sinclair*, Keith argued in *Detroit Free Press v. John Ashcroft* that the executive branch had exceeded its powers. In the wake of the September 11, 2001, attacks on the United States, Attorney General Ashcroft had attempted to deport many Muslim noncitizens residing in the U.S. The Bush administration also attempted to prevent several Michigan newspapers and Congressman John Conyers from attending one of those deportation hearings, for a Muslim clergyman whose tourist visa had expired. Keith's Sixth Circuit Court of Appeals opinion held that secret deportation hearings that are closed to family, friends, and the press are unconstitutional. Keith concluded by noting that "the Executive Branch seeks to uproot people's lives, outside the public eye, and behind a closed door," and warned that "Democracies die behind closed doors."

Keith is one of a generation of black lawyers who experienced the era of de jure segregation, and used the Constitution to dismantle the systematic oppression of black people. In *Davis v. School District of City of Pontiac* (1970), a school desegregation case, he set for himself the task of deciding "what, if anything, now can be done to halt the furtherance of an abhorrent situation for which no one admits responsibility or wishes to accept the blame." He concluded that the school district of Pontiac, Michigan, "deliberately, in contradiction of their announced policy of achieving a racial mixture in the schools, prevented integration," and recommended busing as a remedy. In *Davis*, Keith then attacked the notion that what had occurred in Pontiac and all over the North was somehow different from legal segregation in the South. "Where a Board of Education has contributed and played a major role in the development and growth of a segregated situation, the Board is guilty of de jure segregation. The fact that it came slowly and surreptitiously rather than by legislative pronouncement makes the situation no less evil."

This sensibility, the awareness of the pernicious effects of discrimination and the importance of giving voice to those who are harmed or injured by discrimination, is also revealed in his dissent in *Rabidue v. Osceola Refining Company* (1986). Keith is credited with introducing the "reasonable woman" standard in sexual discrimination cases. He has, in the words of one of his former law clerks "reached beyond the subjectivity of his own male experience" and "embraced . . . the struggle for gender equality."

Keith has received innumerable awards and accolades from his colleagues on the bench and from the major civil rights organizations in the United States. He was given the NAACP Spingarn Medal in 1974, the Thurgood Marshall Award and the Spirit of Excellence Award from the American Bar Association, and the Edward J. Devitt Distinguished Service to Justice Award from the Detroit Urban League, among many others. Keith has been honored not just for the significance of his work as a judge. His dedication to the cause of promoting justice is not restricted to the written page and the decisions he has authored over the years. His appreciation of the importance of history is displayed in the Damon J. Keith Law Collection, an archive established at Wayne State University in 1993. This collection of photographs, documents, personal papers, memorabilia, and interviews documents the contributions of black lawyers and judges to the struggle for racial equality. Part of the collection is a traveling exhibit, Marching toward Justice.

When allegations of discrimination were leveled at a federal judiciary whose clerks were mostly white and predominantly male, Keith provided a model for the proponents of diversity. He employed more women and people of color than any other federal judge, and he chose as his clerks law graduates who practiced different religions and who came from different parts of the world. His former clerks include several law professors and the former attorney general and now governor of the state of Michigan, Jennifer Granholm. In Granholm's words, "All of us are bound by our commitment to issues of justice and civil rights and we all feel a very sincere sense of loyalty to this man who has created a family that is so powerfully driven to change the world."

FURTHER READING

Hale, Jeff A. "Wiretapping and National Security: Nixon, The Mitchell Doctrine, and the White Panthers," Ph.D. diss., Lousiana State University (1995).

Littlejohn, Edward J. "Damon Jerome Keith: Lawyer–Judge–Humanitarian," *Wayne Law Review* 42 (1996): 321–341.

—DEBORAH POST

KELLY, SHARON PRATT

KELLY, SHARON PRATT (30 Jan. 1944–), mayor of Washington, D.C., was born Sharon Pratt, the elder child of Carlisle Pratt, a superior court judge, and Mildred Petticord. When Sharon was four years old, her mother died of cancer. With her younger sister, Benaree, and their father, she went to live with her paternal grandmother and aunt. Some years later her father remarried, and Sharon lived with her father and stepmother. She attended Gage and Rudolph Elementary Schools and McFarland Junior High School and graduated from Roosevelt High School with honors. In 1965 she graduated from Howard University in Washington, D.C., with honors and a BA in Political Science; three years later she earned a JD from Howard's law school. While in law school, she married her first husband, onetime D.C. council member Arrington Dixon, and they had two daughters, Aimee Arrington Dixon and Drew Arrington Dixon. The couple divorced in 1982.

Kelly began her legal career in 1970 as house counsel for the Joint Center for Political Studies in Washington, D.C., before entering private law practice with the legal firm of Pratt and Queen in 1971. From 1972 to 1976 she taught business law at the Antioch School of Law in Washington, D.C., reaching the rank of full professor. After leaving Antioch School of Law, she served as a member of the general counsel's office at Potomac Electric Power Company (PEPCO) from 1976 to 1979, when the company appointed her director of consumer affairs. In 1986 PEPCO appointed her as its vice president for public policy. In that capacity she worked to develop programs to assist low- and fixed-income residents of the District of Columbia. Her early work in public service also included serving as vice chairman of the District of Columbia's Law Revision Commission.

While representing Washington, D.C., on the Democratic National Committee from 1977 to 1990, Kelly was elected treasurer of the committee, serving from 1985 to 1989. Her close ties to the national Democratic Party furthered her local ambitions, and she launched her mayoral campaign with a lavish, well-attended party during the 1988 Democratic National Convention in Atlanta, Georgia. Defying the odds, on 6 November 1990, Kelly became the first woman elected mayor of Washington, D.C., with a landside 86 percent of the vote. She was also the first African American woman to serve as

the chief executive of a major American city.

Commentators credited Kelly's mayoral victory to her demonstrated commitment to the D.C. community over more than twenty years. With her positive campaign slogan of "Yes, We Will," Kelly promised residents an "honest deal" that would restore the city to greatness by improving the quality of life for all of its people. She stunned observers when she promised to fire two thousand midlevel managers immediately, but many citizens were impressed with her eloquence and by the fact that she was an "outsider" with no apparent entanglements in local politics. Most important, she was not an ally of her predecessor as mayor, Marion S. Barry Jr.

In 1978 Barry had inherited a government that was already oversized and undermanaged. After nearly twelve years in office, having failed to tackle those problems and having been convicted of federal charges of cocaine possession, he chose not to run for reelection in 1990. Barry's downfall produced an upsurge of support for reforming the district's government, and Kelly, with her promise to "clean house" and her endorsement by the respected *Washington Post*, rode that political mood to easy victories in both the September Democratic primary and the November general election.

Solving the District of Columbia's myriad problems would not be so easy. The bureaucracy was regarded by many as indifferent to the citizens it was supposed to serve. Like other urban areas, the District of Columbia had a multitude of problems, such as underfinanced, weak public schools; urban economic decay; high unemployment; drug trafficking; and homelessness. Even more disturbing was a financial crisis that had resulted in the city's $300 million deficit at the end of the 1990 fiscal year. The U.S. Congress, as the city's managers, appropriated $100 million in congressional emergency funding for the following fiscal year. Kelly argued that a comprehensive overhaul of city government was also needed.

At first Kelly seemed determined to downsize government and inaugurated programs aimed at restructuring the bureaucracy by automation and retraining. Every category of crime in the District of Columbia declined during her

term as mayor. She developed public-private partnerships to facilitate many of her reforms. Area businesses were encouraged to use their ingenuity to help develop programs to serve all of the city's citizens. These partnerships fostered more jobs and encouraged international trade ventures.

By all accounts, however, Kelly's first year was traumatic. Her grandmother died, and a trusted friend and adviser tragically died when a city ambulance went to the wrong address. At the same time, James Kelly, a businessman from New York City whom she had married at the end of her first year, never seemed comfortable in the public spotlight or in playing the supporting role of First Spouse. Sharon Kelly was also never able to gain full control of a city still loyal to Barry and during Kelly's second year in office, Barry backed an initiative to recall her from office. While the recall was unsuccessful, it forced Kelly to retreat from the tough reforms she had promised during her campaign. Kelly blamed Congress for Washington's continuing financial problems and then further alienated Congress by providing it with inaccurate and false information about the city's finances.

Kelly's criticism of Congress for the city's financial woes and her support for D.C. statehood alienated potential Democratic allies who controlled Congress. By 1993 she had also built a palatial office for herself outside the District Building, the usual location of district offices and agencies, and had put a makeup artist on the city payroll. Political observers increasingly saw such extravagance and her lack of political experience as a major problem, prompting some disillusioned voters to encourage Marion Barry's comeback. After Barry had served six months in prison for his cocaine conviction in 1992, he was elected to the city council. In 1994 he defeated Kelly in that year's mayoral election.

Kelly has received an NAACP Presidential Award, the THURGOOD MARSHALL Award of Excellence, and the MARY MCLEOD BETHUNE–W. E. B. DU BOIS Award from the Congressional Black Caucus. She has been honored for distinguished leadership by the United Negro College Fund and was the recipient of an award for distinguished service from the Federation of Women's Clubs, whose mission is to improve communities through volunteer service. Although her time in office was not as stellar as she had hoped or predicted it would be, Sharon Kelly will be remembered as the first native of Washington, D.C., and the first African American woman to be elected mayor of a major American city.

FURTHER READING

Borger, Gloria. "People to Watch: Sharon Pratt Dixon," *U.S. News and World Report*, 31 Dec. 1990.

French, Mary Ann. "Who Is Sharon Pratt Dixon?," *Essence* (Apr. 1991).

McCraw, Vincent. "Anxious Dixon on Mission to Cure D.C.'s Ills," *Washington Times*, 17 Apr. 1990.

—DEBORAH F. ATWATER

KING, B. B. (16 Sept. 1925–), blues singer and guitarist, was born Riley B. King near Itta Bena, Mississippi, to Albert King and Nora Ella Pully, sharecroppers who worked farms near Indianola. Riley was named after a white planter, O'Reilly, who helped his family when his mother was in labor. The "O" was dropped, his father said, "'cause you don't look Irish" (King, 7). Later, King wanted to be called the Beale Street Blues Boy, but the world came to know him simply as B. B. King.

In 1930 Nora left Albert and the delta region of Mississippi, taking her five-year-old son to live near Kilmichael in the hill country. There she introduced him to the soulful spirituals of the Elkhorn Baptist Church and the moving testimonials of the Church of God in Christ, a Sanctified congregation where his uncle played the guitar as he preached. Uncle Archie Fair taught his nephew to play a few chords, but it was during visits to his Aunt Mima that King first heard the sounds of his greatest musical influences, BLIND LEMON JEFFERSON and Lonnie Johnson, wailing from a windup Victrola. He was only ten when his mother died, and he lived alone in their cabin until the plantation owner for whom he worked, Mr. Flake Cartledge, lent him fifteen dollars to buy a guitar and instruction manual from the Sears Roebuck catalog. From then on, King was never really alone again; music became his family and his life.

King lived briefly with his father's new family in Lexington, but he soon ran away to Indianola, where he worked in the fields and sang with a group called the Famous St. John Gospel Singers. He was torn between two related musical traditions that had very different career paths. On the one hand, he dreamed his group could emulate the success of the gospel-singing Dixie Hummingbirds, and he thought of becoming a minister, despite the stuttering problem he then had. On the other hand, he found that he could make more money on weekends playing the blues for pedestrians than he made all week driving a tractor. When King heard the electric blues guitar of T-Bone Walker, his fate was sealed. He dropped out of school in the tenth grade—one of his biggest regrets—and studied the styles of the bluesmen (and blueswomen, such as BESSIE SMITH and MA RAINEY) who performed at local juke joints.

In 1944 King married Martha Denton shortly before being drafted into the army during World War II. However, after completing basic training, he was designated as a vital farmworker and released from service. On the train back to the plantation, he and other African Americans were forced to sit behind white German prisoners of war. Of white society at that time he wrote, "You can look at enemy soldiers who were ready to cut your throat, but you can't look at the black American soldiers willing to die for you.... We were seen as beasts of burden, dumb animals, a level below the Germans" (King, 91).

In May 1946 Riley fled to Memphis, Tennessee, after accidentally damaging the tractor he drove. There he found his cousin, the guitarist Bukka White, who introduced him to the harsh realities of life as a bluesman. After ten months of drudgery, he was dissuaded and went back to his wife and the plantation. Nevertheless, he returned to Memphis in 1948, determined to make it as a bluesman at any cost. His big break came later that year when Sonny Boy Williams allowed him to sing on his radio program on KWEM. The enthusiastic response led to offers for local performances, and soon King found himself promoting a tonic called Pepticon; his first jingle was "Pepticon sure is good . . . and you can get it anywhere

in your neighborhood." This led to his own radio show on WDIA, called the "Sepia Swing Club." The name he chose as a disc jockey for this program, B. B. King, stayed with him for the rest of his career.

King recorded his first song, "Take a Swing with Me," at WDIA for Bullet Records in 1949. The company went bankrupt soon after releasing it, and King signed a contract with Modern Records, recording under their Crown and RPM labels for the next decade. He was usually paid about one hundred dollars per song and received no royalties or songwriting credits for these early productions. In 1951 he recorded a version of Lowell Fulson's "Three O'Clock Blues" that spent three months at the top of *Billboard*'s rhythm-and-blues chart. With this success, King engaged the promoters Robert Henry and then Maurice Merrit, who arranged bookings on the "Chitlin Circuit," an informal network of clubs and theaters that hired black performers. By 1952 King was spending so much time on the road that his marriage, which had suffered from distance and infidelity, ended in divorce. In 1958 he married Sue Carol Hall, though in 1966 that marriage also ended in divorce. King acknowledges having fifteen children, none with either of his wives.

King's most enduring and perhaps most passionate relationship was with Lucille, the name he gave to his trademark guitars. He once had to rescue his guitar from a nightclub that had been accidentally set ablaze by two men fighting over a woman named Lucille. King decided that from then on every guitar he owned would be his Lucille. She was personified in song and became the medium through which he could express a range of emotion, from deep pathos to liberating triumph. Drawing on the traditional twelve-bar blues style in which the singer and his guitar converse in a call-and-response counterpoint, King and Lucille became a duet recognized and loved by fans.

King worked throughout his career to overcome the perception of many scholars, critics, and casual listeners that the blues is a simple, unsophisticated art form—one that was even embarrassing to black folks of a certain age and class. He recalled appearing on a bill with some great jazz musicians, and, when his turn to perform came, the announcer told the audience, "Okay, folks, time to pull out your chitlins and collard greens, your pig feet and your watermelons, 'cause here's B. B. King." King's response to this common attitude is characteristically witty: "Being a blues singer is like being black twice" (King, 216–217).

Rock and roll came and went without King, who did not cross over, as did BO DIDDLEY and CHUCK BERRY. Soul music became popular with the Motown sound, but though he often tried new things, King remained a true bluesman. He produced dozens of moderately selling songs like "Sweet Sixteen," and he averaged more than three hundred engagements a year; thus, despite his gambling and problems with the IRS, he was, by the late 1960s, successful. Yet, rather than winding down, King's career was about to take off. In 1961 he signed with ABC Paramount. Following his second divorce in 1966, King recorded "Paying the Cost to Be the Boss" and a cathartic rendition of "The Thrill Is Gone" that connected with his widest audience ever. The song reached fifteen on the pop charts and won him the first of thirteen Grammy Awards between 1970 and 2002.

His new manager, Sidney Seidenberg, began to book King at what seemed like unlikely venues, but to King's surprise, young white audiences loved him; so did fans in Europe, Asia, and Africa. He welcomed the fame but admitted that he was "disappointed that my people don't appreciate me like the whites" (*Current Biography*, 1970). He became a frequent guest on the *Tonight Show*; had cameos on *Sanford & Son*, *The Cosby Show*, *Sesame Street*, and *General Hospital*; and appeared in numerous commercials. He was inducted into the Blues Foundation Hall of Fame in 1984 and into the Rock and Roll Hall of Fame in 1987. Although he was diagnosed with diabetes in 1990, King did not cut back on his full calendar of club dates. When asked at the age of seventy-seven why he continued to work so hard he said, "If I don't keep doing it, keep going, they'll forget" (Bernard Weinraub, *New York Times*, 12 March 2003, 1). King exemplifies the best of a long blues tradition that has many admirers but few authentic disciples.

FURTHER READING

King, B. B. *Blues All around Me: The Autobiography of B. B. King* (1996).

Current Biography (1970).

Sawyer, Charles. *The Arrival of B. B. King* (1980).

"Spinning Blues into Gold, the Rough Way." *New York Times*, 12 Mar. 2003.

—SHOLOMO B. LEVY

KING, BOSTON

(1760?–1802), slave, Loyalist during the American Revolution, carpenter, Methodist preacher, and memoirist, was born on a plantation near Charleston, South Carolina, the son of a literate African slave who worked as a driver and a mill cutter and an enslaved mother who made clothes and tended the sick, using herbal knowledge she gained from American Indians. At the age of six Boston King began waiting on his master, Richard Waring, in the plantation house. From age nine to sixteen, he was assigned to tend the cattle and horses, and he traveled with his master's racehorses to many places in America.

At sixteen King was apprenticed to a master carpenter. Two years later he was placed in charge of the master's tools; on two occasions when valuable items were stolen, the master beat and tortured King so severely that he was unable to work for weeks. After the second incident, King's owner threatened to take him away from the carpenter if the abuse was repeated. Over the next two years, King received better treatment and was able to acquire significant knowledge of carpentry. One day during the Revolutionary War, shortly after the British occupied Charleston, King obtained leave to visit his parents, who lived twelve miles away. When a servant absconded with the horse that King had borrowed for the journey, King decided to escape from what would have undoubtedly been cruel punishment by seeking refuge with the British.

Since 1775 the British had promised to free all able-bodied indentured servants and Negroes who joined the Loyalist forces. In 1779 Sir Henry Clinton, the British commander in chief, attempted to further deplete the rebel army's resources by issuing the Philipsburg Proclamation, which promised freedom of employment to any slave who deserted from a rebel master and worked within British lines. King felt well received by the British, but after a short taste of freedom he contracted smallpox. Attempting to control the epidemic, the British segregated infected black people from the rest of the camp and left them to languish without food or drink, sometimes for a day at a time. A kindly New York volunteer came to King's rescue and helped nurse him back to health, a favor that King returned a few weeks later when this man was wounded in battle. King nursed him for six weeks until he recovered. King stayed with the British in areas surrounding Charleston for several months, performing a range of personal and military services.

In December 1782 the British left Charleston, taking with them 5,327 African Americans, who relocated to various sites within the British Empire. King sailed to New York, the British military headquarters. He wanted to work as a carpenter, but lack of tools forced him to accept employment in domestic service, where "the wages were so low that I was not able to keep myself in clothes, so that I was under the necessity of leaving my master and going to another. I stayed with him four months, but he never paid me" (King, 355). In these desperate economic straits King met and married a woman named Violet who had been enslaved in Wilmington, North Carolina. A year later he went to work on a pilot boat that was captured by an American whaler; he was transported to New Brunswick, New Jersey, and once again enslaved. Although he was well fed and pleased to find that many local slaves were allowed to go to school at night, he yearned for liberty and grabbed the first chance to escape across the river and find his way back to New York.

Reunited with Violet, King remained in New York until the end of the war. Although he was glad to see the horrors of war come to an end, King and the other former slaves were terrified that they would be sent back to their old masters, as the Americans demanded. However, the British commander in chief, Sir Guy Carleton, insisted that those blacks who had been with the British before the provisional treaty was signed by both sides in Paris on 30 November 1782 would remain free, while those who had sought refuge with the British after that date were to be returned to their American masters. The British compiled a "Book of Negroes," listing the black people whom they were taking with them out of New York. Boston King, a "Stout fellow" aged twenty-three, and Violet King, a "Stout wench" aged thirty-five, "were among the 409 passengers who sailed on 31 July 1783 from New York to Shelburne" in Nova Scotia (King, 367). They settled in a black community called Birchtown, which was built on one side of the Port Roseway Harbour while Shelburne, a white Loyalist town, was built on the opposite side. The British promised land and provisions to the loyalist settlers, but while "the Whites received farm lands . . . averaging 74 acres by November 1786, of the 649 Black men at Birchtown only 184 received farms averaging 34 acres by the year 1788" (Blakeley, 277). Nonetheless, as a skilled carpenter at a time when every family needed to build a house, King appears to have found work plentiful for a time.

During the cold Canadian winter, a religious revival spread throughout Birchtown. Violet King experienced an "awakening" when listening to the preaching of Moses Wilkinson, a blind and lame former slave from Virginia. Boston King soon followed her lead. Taught by Methodist missionaries, such as Freeborn Garretson of Baltimore, "who had manumitted his own slaves immediately upon his conversion in 1775" (Carretta, 368), King in 1785 began to preach to both black and white people. Meanwhile, the black people in Birchtown were in desperate straits. The little land that they were given was so barren that they were forced to work for white farmers, when they could find work at all. A terrible famine set in, and the Kings scrambled to survive. In 1791 King moved to Preston, near Halifax, where he continued preaching and supported himself in domestic service.

Meanwhile, Lieutenant John Clarkson, the brother of the prominent British abolitionist Thomas Clarkson, arrived in Halifax as the agent for the Sierra Leone Company, which intended to resettle former slaves in Africa and to promote trade with Africa. The company promised free passage, thirty acres of land for every married man, and sufficient provisions to sustain the settlers until they were established in Sierra Leone. Although King's preaching in Preston was proceeding to his "great satisfaction, and the Society increased both in number and love" (King, 363), he had long desired to preach to Africans. On 15 January 1792 Boston and Violet King joined 1,188 other blacks who set sail from Halifax in a fleet of fifteen ships. The journey was troubled by terrible storms and disease, and when they arrived in Sierra Leone they found that once again the British had broken their promises. An outbreak of malaria killed people so fast that it was hard to bury them. Violet King died from malaria in April 1792. Boston King grew ill but recovered and found work as a carpenter and preacher.

On 3 August 1793 Governor Richard Dawes appointed King a missionary and schoolteacher at sixty pounds a year and promised to send him to England to obtain the education that he greatly desired (Blakeley, 286). After remarrying, King embarked for England in March 1794 and spent two years at the Kingswood School, a Methodist secondary school near Bristol, where he wrote his memoirs in 1796. A few months later he returned to Sierra Leone, where he worked as a teacher and preacher until his death.

FURTHER READING

King, Boston. "Memoirs of the Life of Boston King, a Black Preacher. Written by Himself, during His Residence at Kingswood-School." *Arminian* [or *Methodist*] *Magazine* 21 (March, April, May, and June 1798). Reprinted in *Unchained Voices: An Anthology of Black Authors in the English-Speaking World of the Eighteenth-Century*, ed. Vincent Carretta (1996).

Blakeley, Phyllis R. "Boston King: A Black Loyalist" in *Eleven Exiles: Accounts of Loyalists of the American Revolution*, eds. Phyllis R. Blakely and John N. Grant (1982).

—KARI J. WINTER

KING, CORETTA SCOTT (27 Apr. 1927–), was born in Heiberger, near Marion, Alabama, the second of three children of Obadiah Scott and Bernice McMurry, who farmed their own land. Although Coretta and her siblings worked in the garden and fields, hoeing and picking cotton, the Scotts were relatively well off. Her father was the first African American in the community to own a truck, which he used to transport pulpwood, and he also purchased his own sawmill, which was mysteriously burned to the ground a few days later. The family blamed the fire on whites jealous of their success.

Wanting a better life for their children, the Scotts sent all three to college. The eldest, Edythe, graduated at the top of her class at Marion's Lincoln High School in 1943 and earned a scholarship to Antioch College in Yellow Springs, Ohio; her brother, Obie, attended Central State University in nearby Wilberforce, Ohio. Coretta, who also graduated at the top of her high school class in 1945, won a scholarship to study elementary education and music at Antioch. She matriculated in 1945 and was one of only three African Americans in her class; the future jurist A. LEON HIGGINBOTHAM was one of the others. Scott was active in extracurricular activities, especially in projects designed to improve race relations. She joined the college chapter of the NAACP and performed onstage at Antioch with PAUL ROBESON, the actor, singer, and activist, who encouraged her to pursue a musical career.

Although Antioch enjoyed a liberal reputation, Coretta found that it was not immune to racial discrimination. When she applied to practice as a student teacher, the music department required that she do so at an all-black school system near the campus. The school district in which all other Antioch students did their practice work had no black teachers, and the college administration did not wish to upset the racial status quo in conservative southern Ohio by sending an African American student to teach there. Coretta Scott protested this Jim Crow policy to the office of the college president, but the president refused to support her request. She subsequently agreed to do her internship at the demonstration school on campus.

Scott studied piano and the violin, but focused on singing. She gave her first solo concert in 1948 and graduated with a BA from Antioch in Music Education three years later, in 1951. That

Coretta Scott King shaking hands with A. PHILIP RANDOLPH about 1969 as (left to right) BAYARD RUSTIN, *George Meany, Nelson Rockefeller, and others look on.* Library of Congress

year she enrolled at the New England Conservatory of Music in Boston, Massachusetts, on a full-tuition fellowship. With assistance from the Urban League, she found part-time work as a clerical assistant and also received out-of-state aid from Alabama, since her home state provided no opportunities for graduate study in music.

Moving to Boston changed the course of Coretta Scott's life in more ways than one, for in 1952 a friend there introduced her to MARTIN LUTHER KING JR., an ordained Baptist minister who was attending Boston University's School of Theology. Although she has said that she never wanted to be the wife of a pastor, Scott warmed to the theology student's sincere passion for social justice and also fell for his distinctive line of flattery. She later recalled that King "was a typical man. Smoothness. Jive. Some of it I had never heard of in my life. It was what I call intellectual jive" (Garrow, 45). King, for his part, admired Scott for standing up to his father, who wanted him to marry into one of Atlanta's leading black families. Scott bluntly told the imposing Daddy King that she, too, was from one of the finest families. Soon thereafter King Sr. accepted his son's choice and

performed the couple's wedding ceremony in June 1953. Coretta asserted her independence, however, by excluding a promise to obey her husband in her wedding vows. In 1954, the year Coretta Scott King graduated from the New England Conservatory of Music, her husband accepted the pastorate of Dexter Avenue Baptist Church in Montgomery, Alabama.

The young couple could not have known that the direction of their lives again would be dramatically altered the following year. On 1 December 1955, ROSA PARKS, a local NAACP official, was arrested for refusing to give up her seat on a city bus in Montgomery. Her arrest changed the course of southern history, for it united and mobilized Montgomery's black community under Martin Luther King's leadership in a mass boycott of the city's segregated bus system. The subsequent national and international press coverage made the young minister and his wife household names, but the limelight brought with it new dangers. During the bus boycott, angry whites made abusive and life-threatening telephone calls at all hours and shot at and bombed the King family home. In 1958 a mentally disturbed black woman attempted to assassinate

Martin by stabbing him in a New York department store.

Like any other couple's, the Kings' married life was not untroubled. Money was a constant source of friction, since Martin paid little heed to financial matters and left his wife to deal with the day-to-day problems of looking after four children. Rumors of her husband's infidelities were also widespread during his lifetime, often encouraged by FBI mischief making. Coretta has always claimed, however, that she and Martin "never had one single serious discussion about either of us being involved with another person" (Garrow, 374).

Under such trying circumstances Coretta King developed an iron will and a steely resolve to support her husband's commitment to civil rights. She also supported him by handling mail, telephone calls, and other administrative work, sometimes speaking at engagements that he was unable to attend and participating in musical programs to raise funds for the Southern Christian Leadership Conference (SCLC). Coretta's primary focus in the early years of the civil rights movement, however, was her family. She gave birth to four children: Yolande in 1955, Martin III in 1957, Dexter in 1961, and Bernice in 1963. There were occasions, however, when she resented her husband's full immersion in the civil rights movement. In 1963 she told a reporter that she regretted being absent from many of the era's most important civil rights demonstrations. "I'm usually at home," she remarked, "because my husband says, 'You have to take care of the children'" (Garrow, 308). Other women in the civil rights movement, notably ELLA BAKER, often remarked on the traditionalist—indeed, sexist—view of gender roles held by Martin Luther King and other prominent clergymen.

Coretta King was less content to take a back seat when it came to matters of war and peace, as she had been a committed pacifist since her time at Antioch, where visiting speakers like BAYARD RUSTIN had encouraged her nonviolent philosophy. Coretta strongly influenced her husband's evolving opposition to the Vietnam War. In 1961 she attended a disarmament conference in Geneva, Switzerland, as a member of the group Women Strike for Peace. While her husband refrained from publicly challenging the Kennedy and Johnson administrations' foreign policy in the early 1960s, Coretta King attended several peace rallies and picketed the White House in 1965.

Tragically, Coretta Scott King would take center stage in the civil rights movement only after her husband's assassination in Memphis, Tennessee, on 4 April 1968. Four days later she led a memorial march in Memphis, estimated at fifty thousand people. The international media spotlight continued to focus on the slain civil rights leader's family during King's funeral in Atlanta, which was attended by thousands of mourners and watched by millions on television. Coretta Scott King supported several SCLC projects in the wake of her husband's death. In the summer of 1968 she was one of the speakers at the Poor People's Campaign in Washington, D.C., and received national media attention when she, along with others in SCLC, led a protest march by striking hospital workers in Charleston, South Carolina, in 1969.

In the 1970s Coretta King established and chaired the Martin L. King Jr. Memorial Center for Nonviolent Social Change in Atlanta. This project took her around the world in search of financial support, lecturing to audiences numbering in the hundreds. The King Center, which was dedicated on Auburn Avenue in Atlanta in 1981, contains more than one million documents related to the King family's civil rights activities. Several thousand scholars have used its library resources since it was established, but in the 1990s Coretta King and her family came under fire for the way she tightly controlled her husband's legacy, including his image and papers. She was also involved in a feud with the National Park Service over their handling of the King property on Auburn Avenue.

Coretta King's most enduring contribution to American culture has been as chair of the Martin L. King Jr. Federal Holiday Commission. In the late 1970s the King Center collected six million signatures on a petition urging the creation of a Martin Luther King Jr. memorial holiday, and in November 1983 President Ronald Reagan signed the bill designating the national holiday. The center also sponsors an annual celebratory memorial program on his birth date. King's involvement in the civil rights cause continued in the 1980s and 1990s. She was prominent in demonstrations against South Africa's apartheid system and has appeared at anniversary celebrations of her husband's most memorable speech at the 1963 March on Washington. In 1997 she supported a move granting a new trial for her husband's convicted assassin, James Earl Ray, but Ray died before a new trial was scheduled. Her most recent cause has been a project to build a memorial for her husband on the National Mall in Washington, D.C. The Alpha Phi Alpha fraternity, of which he was a member, is also associated with this project.

Throughout her lifetime, Coretta Scott King has supported many progressive measures and received many awards and numerous honorary degrees. Perhaps the most prestigious and enduring was not given to her but rather is awarded in her name. The American Library Association's Coretta Scott King Award, established in the early 1970s, is given to highly distinguished African American writers and illustrators of children's literature.

FURTHER READING

King, Coretta Scott. *My Life with Martin Luther King, Jr.* (1969; rev. 1993).

Baldwin, Lewis V. *There Is a Balm in Gilead: The Cultural Roots of Martin Luther King, Jr.* (1991).
Branch, Taylor. *Parting the Waters: America in the King Years, 1954–1963* (1988).
Garrow, David. *Bearing the Cross: Martin Luther King, Jr., and the Southern Christian Leadership Conference* (1988).
Vivian, Octavia. *Coretta: The Story of Mrs. Martin Luther King, Jr.* (1970).
—BARBARA WOODS

KING, MARTIN LUTHER, JR. (15 Jan. 1929– 4 Apr. 1968), Baptist minister and civil rights leader, was born Michael King Jr., in Atlanta, Georgia, the son of the Reverend Michael King and Alberta Williams. Born to a family with deep roots in the African American Baptist church and in the Atlanta black community, the younger King spent his first twelve years in the home on Auburn Avenue that his parents shared with his maternal grandparents. A block away, also on Auburn, was Ebenezer Baptist Church, where his grandfather, the Reverend Adam Daniel Williams, had served as pastor since 1894. Under Williams's leadership, Ebenezer had grown from a small congregation without a building to become one of Atlanta's prominent African American churches. After Williams's death in 1931, his son-in-law became Ebenezer's new pastor and gradually established himself as a major figure in state and national Baptist groups. In 1934 the elder King, following the request of his own dying father, changed his name and that of his son to Martin Luther King.

King's formative experiences not only immersed him in the affairs of Ebenezer but also introduced him to the African American social gospel tradition exemplified by his father and grandfather, both of whom were leaders of the Atlanta branch of the National Association for the Advancement of Colored People. Depression-era breadlines heightened his awareness of economic inequities, and his father's leadership of campaigns against racial discrimination in voting and teachers' salaries provided a model for the younger King's own politically engaged ministry. He resisted religious emotionalism and as a teenager questioned some facets of Baptist doctrine, such as the bodily resurrection of Jesus.

During his undergraduate years at Atlanta's Morehouse College from 1944 to 1948, King gradually overcame his initial reluctance to accept his inherited calling. Morehouse president BENJAMIN MAYS influenced King's spiritual development, encouraging him to view Christianity as a potential force for progressive social change. Religion professor George Kelsey exposed him to biblical criticism and, according to King's autobiographical sketch, taught him "that behind the legends and myths of the Book were many profound truths which one could not escape." King admired both educators as deeply religious yet also learned men. By the end of his junior year, such academic role models and the example of his father led King to enter the ministry. He described his decision as a response to an "inner urge" calling him to "serve God and humanity." He was ordained during his final semester at Morehouse. By this time King had also taken his

Martin Luther King addresses a gathering after postponing the Selma-to-Montgomery March. Library of Congress

first steps toward political activism. He had responded to the postwar wave of antiblack violence by proclaiming in a letter to the editor of the *Atlanta Constitution* that African Americans were "entitled to the basic rights and opportunities of American citizens." During his senior year King joined the Intercollegiate Council, an interracial student discussion group that met monthly at Atlanta's Emory University.

After leaving Morehouse, King increased his understanding of liberal Christian thought while attending Crozer Theological Seminary in Pennsylvania from 1948 to 1951. Initially uncritical of liberal theology, he gradually moved toward Reinhold Niebuhr's neoorthodoxy, which emphasized the intractability of social evil. He reacted skeptically to a presentation on pacifism by Fellowship of Reconciliation leader A. J. Muste. Moreover, by the end of his seminary studies King had become increasingly dissatisfied with the abstract conceptions of God held by some modern theologians and identified himself instead with theologians who affirmed the personality of God. Even as he continued to question and modify his own religious beliefs, he compiled an outstanding academic record and graduated at the top of his class.

In 1951 King began doctoral studies in systematic theology at Boston University's School of Theology, which was dominated by personalist theologians. The papers (including his dissertation) that King wrote during his years at Boston displayed little originality, and some contained extensive plagiarism, but his readings enabled him to formulate an eclectic yet coherent theological perspective. By the time he completed his doctoral studies in 1955, King had refined his exceptional ability to draw upon a wide range of theological and philosophical texts to express his views with force and precision. His ability to infuse his oratory with borrowed theological insights became evident in his expanding preaching activities in Boston-area churches and at Ebenezer, where he assisted his father during school vacations.

During his stay at Boston, King also met and courted Coretta Scott (CORETTA SCOTT KING), an Alabama-born Antioch College graduate who was then a student at the New England Conservatory of Music. On 18 June 1953 the two students were married in Marion, Alabama, where Scott's family lived. During the following academic year King began work on his dissertation, which he completed during the spring of 1955.

Although he considered pursuing an academic career, King decided in 1954 to accept an offer to become the pastor of Dexter Avenue Baptist Church in Montgomery, Alabama. In December 1955, when Montgomery black leaders formed the Montgomery Improvement Association to protest the arrest of NAACP official ROSA PARKS for refusing to give up her bus seat to a white man, they selected King to head the new group. With King as the primary spokesman and with grassroots organizers such as DAISY BATES, the association led a yearlong bus boycott. King utilized the leadership abilities he had gained from his religious background and academic training and gradually forged a distinctive protest strategy that involved the mobilization of black churches and skillful appeals for white support. As King encountered increasingly fierce white opposition, he continued his movement away from theological abstractions toward more reassuring conceptions, rooted in African American religious culture, of God as a constant source of support. He later wrote in his book of sermons, *Strength to Love* (1963), that the travails of movement leadership caused him to abandon the notion of God as a "theological and philosophically satisfying metaphysical category" and caused him to view God as "a living reality that has been validated in the experiences of everyday life." With the encouragement of BAYARD RUSTIN and other veteran pacifists, King also became a firm advocate of Mohandas Gandhi's precepts of nonviolence, which he combined with Christian principles.

After the Supreme Court outlawed Alabama bus segregation laws in late 1956, King sought to expand the nonviolent civil rights movement throughout the South. In 1957 he became the founding president of the Southern Christian Leadership Conference (SCLC), formed to coordinate civil rights activities throughout the region. Publication of *Stride toward Freedom: The Montgomery Story* (1958) further contributed to King's rapid emergence as a national civil rights leader. Even as he expanded his influence, however, King acted cautiously. Rather than immediately seeking to stimulate mass desegregation protests in the South, King stressed the goal of achieving black

KING, MARTIN LUTHER, JR.

voting rights when he addressed an audience at the 1957 Prayer Pilgrimage for Freedom. During 1959 he increased his understanding of Gandhian ideas during a month-long visit to India as the guest of Prime Minister Jawaharlal Nehru. Early the following year he moved his family, which now included two children, to Atlanta in order to be nearer SCLC headquarters in that city and to become co-pastor, with his father, of Ebenezer Baptist Church. (The Kings' third child was born in 1961; their fourth was born in 1963.)

Soon after King's arrival in Atlanta, the southern civil rights movement gained new impetus from the student-led lunch counter sit-in movement that spread throughout the region during 1960. King dispatched ELLA BAKER to North Carolina to organize students who had staged a protest there. The sit-ins brought into existence a new protest group, the Student Nonviolent Coordinating Committee (SNCC). Its early leaders, such as JOHN LEWIS, worked closely with King, but by the late 1960s STOKELY CARMICHAEL and H. RAP BROWN attempted to push King toward greater militancy. In October 1960 King's arrest during a student-initiated protest in Atlanta became an issue in the national presidential campaign when Democratic candidate John F. Kennedy called Coretta King to express his concern. The successful efforts of Kennedy supporters to secure King's release contributed to the Democratic candidate's narrow victory.

As the southern protest movement expanded during the early 1960s, King was often torn between the increasingly militant student activists and more cautious national civil rights leaders. During 1961 and 1962 his tactical differences with SNCC activists surfaced during a sustained protest movement in Albany, Georgia. King was arrested twice during demonstrations organized by the Albany Movement, but when he left jail and ultimately left Albany without achieving a victory, some movement activists began to question his militancy and his dominant role within the southern protest movement.

During 1963, however, King reasserted his preeminence within the African American freedom struggle through his leadership of the Birmingham campaign. Initiated by SCLC in

January, the Birmingham demonstrations were the most massive civil rights protest that had yet occurred. With the assistance of Fred Shuttlesworth and other local black leaders and with little competition from SNCC and other civil rights groups, SCLC officials were able to orchestrate the Birmingham protests to achieve maximum national impact. King's decision to intentionally allow himself to be arrested for leading a demonstration on 12 April prodded the Kennedy administration to intervene in the escalating protests. A widely quoted letter that King wrote while jailed displayed his distinctive ability to influence public opinion by appropriating ideas from the Bible, the Constitution, and other canonical texts. During May, televised pictures of police using dogs and fire hoses against demonstrators generated a national outcry against white segregationist officials in Birmingham. The brutality of Birmingham officials and the refusal of Alabama governor George C. Wallace to allow the admission of black students at the University of Alabama prompted President Kennedy to introduce major civil rights legislation.

King's speech at the 28 August 1963 March on Washington, attended by more than 200,000 people, was the culmination of a wave of civil rights protest activity that extended even to northern cities. In King's prepared remarks he announced that African Americans wished to cash the "promissory note" signified in the egalitarian rhetoric of the Constitution and the Declaration of Independence. Closing his address with extemporaneous remarks, he insisted that he had not lost hope: "So I say to you, my friends, that even though we must face the difficulties of today and tomorrow, I still have a dream. It is a dream deeply rooted in the American dream that one day this nation will rise up and live out the true meaning of its creed—we hold these truths to be self-evident, that all men are created equal." He appropriated the familiar words of "My Country 'Tis of Thee" before concluding, "And when we allow freedom to ring, when we let it ring from every village and hamlet, from every state and city, we will be able to speed up that day when all of God's children—black men and white men, Jews and Gentiles, Catholics and Protestants—will be able to join hands and to sing in the words

of the old Negro spiritual, 'Free at last, free at last, thank God Almighty, we are free at last.'"

King's ability to focus national attention on orchestrated confrontations with racist authorities, combined with his oration at the 1963 March on Washington, made him the most influential African American spokesperson of the first half of the 1960s. Named *Time* magazine's man of the year at the end of 1963, he was awarded the Nobel Peace Prize in December 1964. The acclaim King received strengthened his stature among civil rights leaders but also prompted Federal Bureau of Investigation director J. Edgar Hoover to step up his effort to damage King's reputation. Hoover, with the approval of President Kennedy and Attorney General Robert Kennedy, established phone taps and bugs. Hoover and many other observers of the southern struggle saw King as controlling events, but he was actually a moderating force within an increasingly diverse black militancy of the mid-1960s. As the African American struggle expanded from desegregation protests to mass movements seeking economic and political gains in the North as well as the South, King's active involvement was limited to a few highly publicized civil rights campaigns, particularly the major series of voting rights protests that began in Selma, Alabama, early in 1965, which secured popular support for the passage of national civil rights legislation, particularly the Civil Rights Act of 1964.

The Alabama protests reached a turning point on 7 March when state police attacked a group of SCLC demonstrators led by Hosea Williams at the start of a march from Selma to the state capitol in Montgomery. Carrying out Governor Wallace's orders, the police used tear gas and clubs to turn back the marchers soon after they crossed the Edmund Pettus Bridge on the outskirts of Selma. Unprepared for the violent confrontation, King was in Atlanta to deliver a sermon when the incident occurred but returned to Selma to mobilize nationwide support for the voting rights campaign. King alienated some activists when he decided to postpone the continuation of the Selma-to-Montgomery march until he had received court approval, but the march, which finally secured federal court approval, attracted several thousand civil rights sympathizers, black and white, from all regions of the nation. On 25 March, King addressed the arriving marchers from the steps of the capitol in Montgomery. The march and the subsequent killing of a white participant, Viola Liuzzo, dramatized the denial of black voting rights and spurred passage during the following summer of the Voting Rights Act of 1965.

After the successful voting rights march in Alabama, King was unable to garner similar support for his effort to confront the problems of northern urban blacks. Early in 1966 he launched a major campaign against poverty and other urban problems, moving into an apartment in the black ghetto of Chicago. As King shifted the focus of his activities to the North, however, he discovered that the tactics used in the South were not as effective elsewhere. He encountered formidable opposition from Mayor Richard Daley and was unable to mobilize Chicago's economically and ideologically diverse black community. King was stoned by angry whites in the Chicago suburb of Cicero when he led a march against racial discrimination in housing. Despite numerous mass protests, the Chicago campaign resulted in no significant gains and undermined King's reputation as an effective civil rights leader.

King's influence was further undermined by the increasingly caustic tone of black militancy of the period after 1965. Black militants increasingly turned away from the Gandhian precepts of King toward the black nationalism of MALCOLM X, whose posthumously published autobiography and speeches reached large audiences after his assassination in February 1965. Unable to influence the black insurgencies that occurred in many urban areas, King refused to abandon his firmly rooted beliefs about racial integration and nonviolence. He was nevertheless unpersuaded by black nationalist calls for racial uplift and institutional development in black communities. In his last book, *Where Do We Go from Here: Chaos or Community?* (1967), King dismissed the claim of Black Power advocates "to be the most revolutionary wing of the social revolution taking place in the United States," but he acknowledged that they responded to a psychological

need among African Americans he had not previously addressed. "Psychological freedom, a firm sense of self-esteem, is the most powerful weapon against the long night of physical slavery," King wrote. "The Negro will only be truly free when he reaches down to the inner depths of his own being and signs with the pen and ink of assertive selfhood his own emancipation proclamation."

Indeed, even as his popularity declined, King spoke out strongly against American involvement in the Vietnam War, making his position public in an address on 4 April 1967 at New York's Riverside Church. King's involvement in the antiwar movement reduced his ability to influence national racial policies and made him a target of further FBI investigations. Nevertheless, he became ever more insistent that his version of Gandhian nonviolence and social gospel Christianity was the most appropriate response to the problems of black Americans.

In November 1967 King announced the formation of the Poor People's Campaign, designed to prod the federal government to strengthen its antipoverty efforts. King, ANDREW YOUNG, JESSE JACKSON, and other SCLC workers began to recruit poor people and antipoverty activists to come to Washington, D.C., to lobby on behalf of improved antipoverty programs. This effort was in its early stages when King became involved in a sanitation workers' strike in Memphis, Tennessee. On 28 March 1968, as King led thousands of sanitation workers and sympathizers on a march through downtown Memphis, black youngsters began throwing rocks and looting stores. This outbreak of violence led to extensive press criticisms of King's entire antipoverty strategy. King returned to Memphis for the last time in early April. Addressing an audience at Bishop Charles J. Mason Temple on 3 April, King affirmed his optimism despite the "difficult days" that lay ahead. "But it doesn't matter with me now," he declared, "because I've been to the mountaintop [and] I've seen the promised land." He continued, "I may not get there with you. But I want you to know tonight, that we, as a people, will get to the promised land." The following evening King was assassinated as he stood on a balcony of the Lorraine Motel in Memphis. A

white segregationist, James Earl Ray, was later convicted of the crime. The Poor People's Campaign continued for a few months after his death but did not achieve its objectives.

Until his death King remained steadfast in his commitment to the radical transformation of American society through nonviolent activism. In his posthumously published essay, "A Testament of Hope" (1986), he urged African Americans to refrain from violence but also warned, "White America must recognize that justice for black people cannot be achieved without radical changes in the structure of our society." The "black revolution" was more than a civil rights movement, he insisted. "It is forcing America to face all its interrelated flaws—racism, poverty, militarism and materialism."

After king's death, RALPH ABERNATHY assumed leadership of SCLC, and Coretta Scott King established the Atlanta-based Martin Luther King Jr. Center for Nonviolent Social Change to promote Gandhian-Kingian concepts of nonviolent struggle. She led the successful effort to honor King with a federal holiday on the anniversary of his birthday, which was first celebrated in 1986.

FURTHER READING

Collections of King's papers are at the Martin Luther King Jr. Center for Nonviolent Social Change in Atlanta and the Mugar Memorial Library at Boston University.

Branch, Taylor. *Parting the Waters: America in the King Years, 1954–63* (1988).
———. *Pillar of Fire: America in the King Years, 1963–65* (1998).
Garrow, David J. *Bearing the Cross: Martin Luther King Jr. and the Southern Christian Leadership Conference, 1955–1968* (1986).
Lewis, David Levering. *King: A Biography*, 2d ed. (1978).
Oates, Stephen B. *Let the Trumpet Sound: The Life of Martin Luther King Jr.* (1982).
Washington, James Melvin, ed. *A Testament of Hope: The Essential Writings of Martin Luther King Jr.* (1986).

Obituary: *New York Times*, 5 Apr. 1968.
—CLAYBORNE CARSON

KIRK, GABRIELLE. *See* McDonald, Gabrielle Kirk.

KITT, EARTHA MAE

(26 Jan. 1928–) singer and actor, was born to William Kitt and Anna Mae Riley, sharecroppers, in North, South Carolina. As young children, Eartha and her younger half-sister, Anna Pearl, were abandoned by their father and later by their mother. The sisters lived on a farm with a foster family until 1936, when they moved to New York City to live with their aunt, Mamie Lue Riley, a domestic. As an adolescent, Eartha attended Metropolitan High School (later called the High School of Performing Arts). She relished her unusual voice and facility with language, sang, danced, played baseball, and became a pole-vaulting champion. Eartha left school at age fourteen, and two years later she met KATHERINE DUNHAM, who offered her a dance scholarship and then a spot as a singer and dancer with her troupe. Kitt toured Mexico, South America, and Europe with Dunham and quickly emerged as a soloist. When the tour ended, she remained in Paris, launching a career as a nightclub entertainer. Her provocative and sensual dancing style and her throaty singing voice enthralled audiences from France to Egypt and from Los Angeles to Stockholm.

In 1951 Orson Welles gave Kitt her first role in the legitimate theater when he cast her as Helen of Troy in his stage production *Faust*. Kitt won critical reviews for her performance and toured with the play through Germany and Turkey, after which she returned to New York and audiences at the Village Vanguard and La Vie en Rose. When the producer Leonard Stillman saw her in *Faust*, he was inspired to revive his *New Faces* Broadway revue, and Kitt's debut in *New Faces of 1952* was an instant sensation. Brook Atkinson of the *New York Times* encapsulated audience reaction to her breakout performance in his stage review: "Eartha Kitt panics the customers with some very combustible singing and performing.... Now we know why the city is so strict about its fire laws in the theater." Stillman's hit show was followed by a 1954 film version, in which Kitt starred, and a best-selling Broadway album featuring Kitt's fiery version of "Monotonous," which began her record career. Her first

Eartha Kitt, a sophisticated performer whose public persona ranged from sex kitten to Catwoman to Cinderella's fairy godmother. © Arthur Rothstein/CORBIS

solo album, a self-titled record released in 1953, includes a range of songs from "African Lullaby" to "C'est Si Bon" and "I Wanna Be Evil."

Throughout the 1950s and 1960s Kitt flourished in a succession of entertainment media. Smitten by her combination of husky sexiness, talent, and elegant titillation, journalists published a swell of articles and interviews. She performed for sold-out crowds in cabarets and nightclubs throughout the United States and abroad, and she regularly released studio and live albums. Her starring role in the 1955 Broadway play *Mrs. Patterson*, which ran for one hundred and one performances, earned her a Tony nomination. She continued working on Broadway in the musicals *Shinbone Alley* (1957) and *Jolly's Progress* (1959). Hollywood took notice of Kitt's popularity and dynamic presence, casting her in *The Accused* (1957); the W. C. HANDY biographical film *St. Louis Blues* (1958); and the title role, opposite SAMMY DAVIS JR. and NAT KING COLE, in an all-black version of *Anna Lucasta* (1959), for which she earned an Oscar nomination. Kitt's versatility and playful style were perfect for the developing medium of television, and her increasing

visibility was due in part to frequent appearances on 1950s variety shows like *The Ed Sullivan Show, Your Show of Shows, Colgate Comedy Hour*, and *Toast of the Town*. A favorite guest of television show hosts, she was equally hospitable to television audiences, even touring her Riverside Drive penthouse for Edward R. Murrow's viewers on *Person to Person*. She made guest appearances on many of the 1960s hit shows, including *I Spy, What's My Line?*, and *Mission Impossible*.

During this period, Kitt enjoyed a glamorous and opulent lifestyle. Although she was romantically linked with the Continental playboy Porfirio Rubirosa, the movie theater chain heir Arthur Loew Jr., the cosmetics mogul Charles Revson, and Sammy Davis Jr., Kitt married William McDonald in 1960. The couple had one daughter, Kitt, and divorced in 1965.

In 1968 Kitt was invited to the White House for the "Women Doers' Luncheon," hosted by Lady Bird Johnson and publicized as a discussion on juvenile delinquency. When Kitt's speech linked America's racial and social problems to the war in Vietnam, goodwill toward the star evaporated. Beginning with news reports that claimed her comments had made the First Lady cry, Kitt was excoriated in the press. While MARTIN LUTHER KING JR. and other antiwar activists lauded her remarks (some even wore "Eartha Kitt for President" buttons), general attitudes toward the star were critical. Contrary to conventional wisdom, Kitt did continue to work after the incident, primarily overseas, although she was forced to contend with invasive FBI and CIA investigations, press ridicule, loss of popularity, and limited career options. She drew criticism again in 1972, this time from African Americans, when she performed in South Africa after receiving temporary "white status."

In the 1970s and 1980s Kitt worked primarily as a cabaret entertainer and occasionally as an actor. She resumed recording in the 1980s, releasing more than a dozen albums in less than a decade, and returned to Broadway in 1978 in an all-black version of Geoffrey Holder's *Kismet, Timbukto*, for which she earned her second Tony nomination. *I Love Men*, Kitt's 1984 album, found an audience with the gay disco crowd and enhanced her reputation as a gay icon. In the 1990s Kitt performed her one-woman show in London and New York, released a five-CD retrospective, *Eartha Quake*, and appeared in cameo roles in several Hollywood films.

Kitt's star rose during a pivotal period for black Americans. That she represented fundamental freedoms—of expression, of movement, of sexuality—at a time when American blacks struggled under legal and de facto segregation, exposes America's complex attitudes toward African Americans in general and African American women in particular. Kitt cultivated a style and persona that simultaneously challenged and tapped into existing stereotypes of black women, specifically historical representations of the "mulatto" and "jezebel" as racially ambiguous, sexual predators, manipulators, and seducers of white men.

Applauded as sophisticated, urbane, and sexually powerful, she was also depicted as a potentially dangerous sex kitten with contempt for her rural and racial past and with a preference for white men. Characterizations of Kitt's "feline" sex appeal began when Kitt played the sexy and independent alley cat Mehitabel in *Shinbone Alley* in 1957. The description stuck, and Kitt's embrace of her sex kitten image can be seen most clearly in her acceptance of the role of Catwoman in the 1960's television show *Batman* and in the naming of her 1991 memoir, *Confessions of a Sex Kitten*, and her 1999 greatest-hits album, *Purr-fect*.

Nowhere is Kitt's unique persona more apparent than in her speech. As with many performers, she sought to lose her accent and to perfect standard stage speech. The resulting speech pattern, much like that of SIDNEY POITIER, subverts people's expectations and makes it difficult to locate Kitt's origin. On the subject of her speech, Orson Welles told Kitt, "It's too clear. You don't sound as though you came from anywhere. Everyone sounds as though he's from somewhere, but you—? NO" (Kitt, *Thursday's Child*). Kitt's use of voice control and language—on her first album she sang in English, French, Spanish, Turkish, and Swahili—has allowed her the opportunity, on occasion, to suspend being labeled.

In the late 1990s Kitt charmed New York City taxi riders when she purred seatbelt warnings as one of the original Celebrity Talking Taxi voices. In 2001 Kitt's fairy tale story continued, when she was cast as the Fairy Godmother in the touring production of *Cinderella*.

FURTHER READING

Kitt, Eartha. *Alone with Me* (1976).
_____. *Confessions of a Sex Kitten* (1991).
_____. *I'm Still Here* (1989).
_____. *Thursday's Child* (1956).

—LISA E. RIVO

L

LACY, SAM (23 Oct. 1903?–8 May 2003), sports columnist and editor, was born Samuel Harold Lacy, one of five children of Rose and Samuel Erskine Lacy. Many publications (including his own autobiography) state that Lacy was born in Mystic, Connecticut, but recent research suggests that he may have been born in 1905 in Washington, D.C. His mother, a Shinnecock Indian, was a hairdresser and the family disciplinarian; his father was a notary and legal researcher as well as an avid baseball fan. Lacy was raised in Washington, D.C., moving often within the city during his youth. Although the Lacys were not members of Washington's professionally accomplished African American middle class, they strove to improve their social standing through hard work and education.

To that end, Lacy began working when he was about eight years old, shining shoes, selling newspapers, and setting pins at a bowling alley. Later, he shagged fly balls during batting practice for the Washington Nationals (later known as the Senators) baseball team. Popular with many of the ballplayers, Lacy often ran errands for them and eventually worked as a vendor at Griffith Stadium, where he saw major league stars like Ty Cobb and Babe Ruth play, as well as such Negro league stars as Oscar Charleston and John Henry Lloyd. Like the rest of America, baseball was rigidly segregated. "I was in a position to make some comparisons," Lacy reminisced in 1990, "and it seemed to me that those black players were good enough to play in the big leagues. There was, of course, no talk then of that ever happening. When I was growing up, there was no real opportunity for blacks in any sport" (Fimrite, 90).

At Armstrong Technical High School, the small, lithe Lacy played baseball, basketball, and football. After graduating in 1924, Lacy played semipro baseball, coached and promoted basketball, briefly attended Howard University, and worked as a part-time journalist and radio announcer. In October 1926 he joined the *Washington Tribune* full time, soon thereafter becoming its sports editor. In 1927 Lacy married Alberta Robinson—they had one son, Samuel Howe. They were divorced in 1952 and a year later he married Barbara Robinson, a government worker.

During the summer of 1929 Lacy left the *Tribune* to play baseball in Connecticut but returned to the newspaper in 1930, regaining his position as sports editor in July 1933. "By the mid-1930s, married for several years and with the dream of a baseball career no longer a realistic option, I finally was ready to make the move into full-time journalism with the *Washington Tribune*, where I worked from 1934 to 1938" (Lacy, 27).

It was in the mid-1930s that Lacy began agitating for social change, joining contemporaries like the labor leader A. PHILIP RANDOLPH, the law dean CHARLES HAMILTON HOUSTON, and his fellow sportswriter Wendell Smith. Indeed, for the rest of his life, having found his voice as a "race man," Lacy criticized a wide variety of racial injustices in the sports world. The list is long, but one of his first big stories came in October 1937, when he reported that Syracuse University's star player, Wilmeth Sidat-Singh, was not in fact a "Hindu," as was widely reported, but was an American-born black man. Lacy printed the truth, and Syracuse bowed to the University of Maryland's refusal to compete if the player stayed in the lineup. It was a story that elicited criticism, even among African Americans. Lacy stood behind his story, arguing that racial progress demanded honesty. Years later Lacy wrote, "Call 'em as you see 'em and accept the comebacks. Take it in stride, the same as other distractions. That's the way it was. Push forward or get pushed aside" (Lacy, 7).

Baseball, the national pastime and an important cultural institution, was at the forefront of Lacy's agenda. The injustice of the game's racial bigotry and exclusion motivated him. Perhaps encouraged by the response to the Sidat-Singh incident, Lacy met with the Senators owner, Clark Griffith, in December 1937 to discuss the hiring of black ballplayers. Lacy suggested that Griffith sign the Negro league greats JOSH GIBSON and Buck Leonard of the Homestead Grays. Griffith objected, saying that integration would devastate the Negro leagues "and put about 400 colored guys out of work." Lacy reportedly responded: "When Abraham Lincoln signed the Emancipation Proclamation, he put 400,000 black people out of jobs" (Klingaman, 6A).

A traditionalist, Griffith was not persuaded, partly owing to the profitability of renting his stadium to Negro league teams. Nevertheless, the historian Brad Snyder observes that the meeting with Griffith "marked the beginning of Lacy's campaign to integrate baseball in Washington," and Lacy began to publish a column in the weekly *Washington Tribune* titled "Pro and Con on the Negro in Organized Baseball" (Snyder, 77). Lacy also argued, sometimes didactically, that black ballplayers and those who ran the Negro leagues needed to be more professional if they were to compete in the major leagues.

In 1940, after a series of disputes with the management of the *Washington Afro-American*, which had bought and absorbed the *Tribune*, Lacy left his wife and young son in Washington and moved to Chicago, where he soon became assistant national editor for the *Chicago Defender*, one of the nation's largest and most influential black papers. While he did not cover sports for the *Defender*, Lacy continued to fight for the integration of professional baseball by intensifying "an already aggressive and voluminous letter campaign directed at major league owners and particularly Commissioner [Kenesaw Mountain] Landis" (*Dictionary of Literary Biography*, vol. 171, 1996, 176). Late in 1943 Landis relented and allowed Lacy to bring a small delegation to speak to the owners at their annual winter meeting. Unfortunately, Lacy was upstaged by the publisher of the *Chicago Defender* and by the famous actor-singer PAUL ROBESON and never got to make his case.

Shortly thereafter, a disappointed Lacy became columnist and sports editor for the weekly *Baltimore Afro-American*, a position he held for almost sixty years. Indefatigable, Lacy continued to crusade for the integration of professional baseball in his column and behind the scenes. In March 1945, after Landis died, Lacy wrote to every major league owner suggesting the creation of a committee to reconsider the integration of baseball. Lacy presented his proposal, and the executives agreed to his plan. The Major League Committee on Baseball Integration was established, including Lacy, Branch Rickey of the Brooklyn Dodgers, and Larry MacPhail of the New York Yankees. The committee never met, however, largely because of MacPhail's foot-dragging. Nonetheless, Rickey and JACKIE ROBINSON made history in August 1945, when the latter signed with the Dodgers.

After Robinson made the majors in 1947, Lacy was his close companion for three years. Lacy "chronicled Robinson's first day in the majors, naming those who sat beside him on the Dodgers bench—and how close they sat. He cataloged the insults and debris hurled Robinson's way. He counted brushback pitches. He timed applause. He reported every pulled muscle, broken nail and silver hair on Robinson's prematurely gray head" (Klingaman, 6A). Traveling all over the country with Robinson and other black sportswriters, Lacy suffered numerous racist indignities, yet kept them to himself.

In addition to crusading for the integration of baseball, Lacy wrote about auto and horse racing, boxing, college and professional basketball and football, golf, the Olympics, tennis, and track and field, amounting to roughly three thousand columns in all. A man with an acute sense of fairness, he wrote about racism in accommodations and employment practices, the exploitation of African American student athletes, and numerous other examples of discrimination and injustice.

More than a reporter, Lacy used his sports column to reflect on and to improve the world in which he lived and tried to do something about improving it. He was "a drum major for change—the broad, sweeping sort of social change that helps legitimize this nation's claim to greatness long before the best-recognized civil-rights activists came on the scene. Given baseball's popularity in the '40s, the opening [Lacy helped forge] shattered the myth of white superiority and made it possible for other race-based barriers to crumble" (Wickham, 13A). Lacy won many awards and accolades, including the prestigious 1997 J. G. Taylor Spink Award for meritorious contributions to baseball writing, which earned him a place in the writers' wing of the Baseball Hall of Fame in 1998. Lacy was only the second African American so honored. At a gathering in his honor in 2002, Lacy was lauded by Baltimore's mayor, Martin O'Malley, "for challenging the American conscience and demanding that we live up to our promise as a people" (Kane 3B).

Though some said he became something of a curmudgeon in his later years, Lacy was a soft-spoken, humble man. "In the case of baseball integration, I just happened to be in the right place at the right time," Lacy observed. "I think that anyone else situated as I was and possessing a bit of curiosity and concern about progress would have done the same thing" (Lacy, 209). Be that as it may, the sports columnist Michael Wilbon convincingly argues, "You can't write the history of sports and race in America without devoting a chapter to Sam Lacy" ("Lacy's Towering Legacy," *Washington Post*, 11 May 2003).

FURTHER READING

Lacy, Sam, with Moses J. Newson. *Fighting for Fairness: The Life Story of Hall of Fame Sportswriter Sam Lacy* (1998).

Fimrite, Ron. "Sam Lacy: Black Crusader," *Sports Illustrated*, 29 Oct. 1990.
Kane, Gregory. "A Group of Sports Legends Gathers to Honor the Greatest of Them All," *Baltimore Sun*, 6 Oct. 2002.
Klingaman, Mike. "Hall of Fame Opens Door for Writer," *Baltimore Sun*, 26 July 1998.
Snyder, Brad. *Beyond the Shadows of the Senators: The Untold Story of the Homestead Grays and the Integration of Baseball* (2003).
Wickham, DeWayne. "Journalist's Induction into Hall Long Overdue." *USA Today*, 30 July 1998, 13A.

Obituaries: *Baltimore Afro-American*, 17–23, May 2003; *Baltimore Sun* and *Washington Post*, 10 May 2003; *New York Times*, 12 May 2003; *Sports Illustrated*, 19 May 2003.

—DANIEL A. NATHAN

 LAMPKIN, DAISY
(1880s–Mar. 10 1965), civil rights and women's suffrage advocate and NAACP leader, was born Daisy Elizabeth Adams, the only child of George S. Adams and Rosa Ann Proctor. Sources differ as to the exact date and place of her birth. Lampkin's obituary in the *New York Times* states that she was 83 years of age at the time of her death in 1965, which places her birth in either 1881 or 1882. Other sources claim that Daisy was born on 9 August 1888. It is also uncertain whether she was born in Washington, D.C., or Reading, Pennsylvania, but she completed high school in the latter city before moving to Pittsburgh in 1909. In 1912 she helped organize a gathering for the woman's suffrage movement and joined the Lucy Stone League, an organization connected with the suffrage movement. She became president of the league in 1925 and headed the organization for the next forty years.

In 1912 Daisy Adams married William Lampkin, originally from Rome, Georgia, who ran a restaurant in one of Pittsburgh's wealthy suburbs. During the first years of her marriage, Lampkin worked with her husband in the restaurant business and expanded her activities as a community activist. She made street-corner speeches to mobilize African American women into political clubs, organized black housewives around consumer issues, and was a leading participant in a Liberty Bond drive during World War I, when, as the scholar Edna Chappell McKenzie notes, the black community of Allegheny County, where Pittsburgh is located, raised more than two million dollars. She also served on the staff of the Pittsburgh Urban League.

Impressed with Lampkin's talents as a fund-raiser, Robert L. Vann, editor and publisher of the *Pittsburgh Courier*, solicited Lampkin's help when he was trying to raise money during the early days of the *Courier*. She continued to work for the newspaper in the 1920s and was made vice president in 1929, a position she held for thirty-six years, until her death in 1965.

During and after World War I, Lampkin's activism among black women shaped the black freedom struggle at both local and national levels. She was chair of the Allegheny County Negro Women's Republican League and vice-chair of the Negro Voters League. At the national level, she was elected president of the Negro Women's Equal Franchise Federation, founded in 1911; she served as a national organizer and chair of the executive board of the National Association of Colored Women (NACW) and helped organize, with MARY MCLEOD BETHUNE, the National Council of Negro Women.

By the early 1920s, Lampkin was a prominent figure in black politics and served as president of the National Colored Republican Conference. In 1924 she was the only woman selected by NAACP national secretary JAMES WELDON JOHNSON to attend a meeting of black leaders with President Calvin Coolidge at the White House; the meeting was to protest the injustice meted out to African American soldiers allegedly involved in the 1917 Houston riot. She was also elected an alternate delegate at large to the national Republican Party convention in 1926, a remarkable achievement for any black person or any woman at that time, as historian Edna McKenzie notes.

When Lampkin joined the staff of the NAACP in 1927, she linked her championing of black women with that of the NAACP's agenda, focusing on breaking down barriers to full participation in American society. She served as regional field secretary in the early 1930s; became known as an unflappable, intrepid fund-raiser for the association; and was appointed national field secretary by the NAACP's board of directors in 1935. Using her skills as an organizer and superb speaker, Lampkin worked with black workers during the economic hard times of the 1930s, increasing the NAACP's membership in key cities, such as Chicago and Detroit. She not only revitalized the organization's sagging enrollment but also used her national position and prestige to push the NAACP toward a new approach for attaining civil rights in America.

Lampkin increased NAACP membership at a moment when the association faced perhaps its most severe challenges from both within and without. Within the organization, dissent centered on the fact that the NAACP was not reaching the mass of African Americans. As the Depression deepened in the early 1930s, thousands of African Americans organized themselves through unemployed councils, participated in rent strikes, and joined the CIO's rank-and-file industrial unions that were encouraged by President Franklin Roosevelt's New Deal. Some of their actions were encouraged and led by Communist Party organizers, others by groups such as A. PHILIP RANDOLPH'S Brotherhood of Sleeping Car Porters. Missing from efforts to mobilize the grass roots was the NAACP, which committed its resources to making appeals in courts on a case-by-case basis and agitated by compiling facts and deluging government officials with information.

Since its founding in 1909, the NAACP had pursued a gradual, legalistic approach to securing African Americans their full citizenship rights. The NAACP's leadership expressed little interest in mass organization of black workers. In 1931, the American Communist Party (CPUSA) challenged the NAACP's narrow agenda by taking on the legal defense of the SCOTTSBORO BOYS, nine working-class African

American males who were charged in Scottsboro, Alabama, with the alleged rape of two white women. Because the NAACP had initially refused to take on the Scottsboro Boys case, the Communists convinced at least some African Americans that their Party was more in touch with the mood and interests of working-class blacks than the NAACP. Although the CPUSA did not win massive numbers of black converts, their militant approach forced black organizations, and the NAACP, in particular, to rethink their strategy in challenging racial inequality. The competition between the Communists and the NAACP, historian Mark Naison has argued, was not just for control over the Scottsboro case but also for the "hearts and minds of the black public" (*Communists in Harlem during the Depression* [1985], 62).

As funding from white philanthropists dried up, the NAACP needed to increase its membership within the black community. Daisy Lampkin understood well the threat that Scottsboro posed for the NAACP, and she also had a solution. "The NAACP is being openly criticized by its own members," Lampkin wrote to WALTER WHITE, executive secretary of the NAACP, in 1933. "Some frankly say," she continued, "that the NAACP is less militant" than it used to be. Moreover, Lampkin told White, friends of the NAACP asked her whether she thought the NAACP had outlived its usefulness and whether the time had come for it to give way to another organization with a more "militant program." She advised both Walter White and his assistant, ROY WILKINS, to initiate a more aggressive program in order to meet the "onslaught of the Communists" (Letter from Roy Wilkins to Daisy E. Lampkin, 23 Mar. 1935, I-C-80, NAACP Papers, Library of Congress).

Lampkin demonstrated her independence as a leader within the NAACP on another occasion in 1933. A planned boycott of discriminatory practices by the Sears Roebuck shoe department by "prominent women" in the Chicago branch of the NAACP was aborted by from the national office. Walter White was concerned lest the proposed boycott sully the reputation of the NAACP in the eyes of William Rosenwald, chairman of the board of Sears, whose stock funded the Rosenwald Fund, a major contributor to projects benefiting black Americans. Such concerns did not faze the NACW. When the association met in Chicago in July 1933 for its annual convention, it condemned Sears for its discriminatory policies. Lampkin, running for vice president of the NACW at the time, strongly endorsed the resolution against Sears, which also urged "widespread publicity on the matter" (letter from A. C. MacNeal to Walter White, 29 July 29 1933, I-G-51, NAACP Papers, Library of Congress).

Perhaps to underscore her concern with the passive approach of the NAACP on this matter, Lampkin, regional field secretary at the time, did not visit the Chicago branch while attending the NACW convention, a slight that led the branch president to complain to White. As Lampkin reminded White in a letter of 22 October 1936, it was because of her influence in the "largest organization of colored women in America" that she was important to the staff of the NAACP. The public was well aware, she said, of her "many other interests," which "account to a very large degree for the success I have in getting people to work with me in campaigns for the NAACP" (NAACP papers, Library of Congress, I-C-68).

By the end of the 1930s, the NAACP had expanded its program to reach the masses of the people, following advice that Lampkin had offered to Walter White and Roy Wilkins, in the early 1930s. Lampkin continued to work tirelessly for the NAACP until October 1964, when she collapsed from exhaustion after making yet another strenuous fund-raising appeal for the NAACP. She died a few months later, in March 1965, and was survived by her husband.

The life of Daisy Lampkin exemplifies the important role black women played in twentieth century campaigns for civil rights. Although Lampkin was best known nationally for her role as a prominent NAACP leader, her contribution to the larger freedom struggles for racial and gender equality extended far beyond that organization. Whatever the venue, the impulse that drove Lampkin's life was to remove barriers that kept African Americans from the full enjoyment of their citizenship rights.

FURTHER READING

Bates, Beth Tompkins. "A New Crowd Challenges the Agenda of the Old Guard in the NAACP, 1933–1941," *American Historical Review* 102.2 (Apr. 1997).

———. *Pullman Porters and the Rise of Protest Politics in Black America, 1925–1945* (2001).

McKenzie, Edna B. "Daisy Lampkin: A Life of Love and Service." *Pennsylvania Heritage* (Summer 1983).

Trotter, Joe William, Jr. *River Jordan: African American Urban Life in the Ohio Valley* (1988).

Obituary: *New York Times*, Mar. 12, 1965: 33.

—BETH TOMPKINS BATES

LANE, WILLIAM HENRY

LANE, WILLIAM HENRY (1825?–1852), dancer, also known as "Master Juba," is believed to have been born a free man, although neither his place of birth nor the names of his parents are known. He grew up in lower Manhattan in New York City, where he learned to dance from "Uncle" Jim Lowe, an African American jig-and-reel dancer of exceptional skill.

By the age of fifteen, Lane was performing in notorious "dance houses" and dance establishments in the Five-Points district of lower Manhattan. Located at the intersection of Cross, Anthony, Little Water, Orange, and Mulberry streets, its thoroughfare was lined with brothels and saloons occupied largely by free blacks and indigent Irish immigrants. Lane lived and worked in the Five-Points district in the early 1840s. In such surroundings, the blending of African American vernacular dance with the Irish jig was inevitable. Marshall Stearns in *Jazz Dance* (1968) confirms that "Lane was a dancer of 'jigs' at a time when the word was adding to its original meaning, an Irish folk dance, and being used to describe the general style of Negro dancing." Charles Dickens, in his *American Notes* (1842), describes a visit to the Five-Points district in which he witnessed a performance by a dancer who was probably Lane: "Single shuffle, double shuffle, cut and cross cut; snapping his fingers, rolling his eyes, turning in his knees, presenting the backs of his legs in front, spinning about on his toes and heels like nothing but the man's fingers on the tambourine; dancing with two left legs, two right legs, two wooden legs, two wire legs, two spring legs."

In 1844, after beating the reigning white minstrel dancer, John Diamond, in a series of challenge dances, Lane was hailed as the "King of All Dancers" and named "Master Juba," after the African juba or *gioube*, a step-dance resembling a jig with elaborate variations. The name was often given to slaves who were dancers and musicians. Lane was thereafter adopted by an entire corps of white minstrel players who unreservedly acknowledged his talents. On a tour in New England with the Georgia Champion Minstrels, Lane was billed as "The Wonder of the World Juba, Acknowledged to be the Greatest Dancer in the World!" He was praised for his execution of steps, unsurpassed in grace and endurance, and popular for his skillful imitations of well-known minstrel dancers and their specialty steps. He also performed his own specialty steps, which no one could copy, and he was a first-rate singer and a tambourine virtuoso. In 1845 Lane had the unprecedented distinction of touring with the four-member, all-white Ethiopian Minstrels, with whom he received top billing. At the same time, he prospered as a solo variety performer and from 1846 to 1848 was a regular attraction at White's Melodeon in New York.

Lane traveled to London with Pell's Ethiopian Serenaders in 1848, enthralling the English, who were discerning judges of traditional jigs and clogs, with "the manner in which he beat time with his feet, and the extraordinary command he possessed over them." London's *Theatrical Times* wrote that Master Juba was "far above the common [performers] who give imitations of American and Negro character; there is an *ideality* in what he does that makes his efforts at once *grotesque* and *poetical, without losing sight of the reality of representation.*" Working day and night and living on a poor diet and no rest, Lane died of exhaustion in London.

In England, Lane popularized American minstrel dancing, influencing English clowns who added jumps, splits, and cabrioles to their entrées and began using blackface makeup. Between 1860 and 1865, the Juba character was taken to France by touring British circuses and later became a fixture in French and Belgian *cirques et carrousels*. The image of the blackface clown that persisted in European circuses and fairs continued to be represented in turn-of-the-century popular entertainments as well as on concert stages during the 1920s, in ballets such as Léonide Massine's *Crescendo*, Bronislawa Nijinska's *Jazz*, and George Balanchine's "Snowball" in *The Triumph of Neptune* (1926).

In the United States, Lane is considered by scholars of dance and historians of the minstrel as the most influential single performer in nineteenth-century American dance. He kept the minstrel show in touch with its African American source material at a time when the stage was dominated by white performers offering theatrical derivatives and grotesque exaggerations of the African American performer. He established a performing style and developed a technique of tap dancing that would be widely imitated. For example, the white dancer Richard M. Carroll was noted for dancing in the style of Lane and earned a reputation for being a great all-around performer; other dancers, like Ralph Keeler, who starred in a riverboat company before the Civil War, learned to dance by practicing the complicated shuffle of Juba. Toward the end of the twentieth century, Lane's legacy continued to be present in elements of the tap dance repertory. Lane's grafting of African rhythms and loose body styling onto the exacting techniques of British jig and clog dancing created a new rhythmic blend of percussive dance that was the earliest form of American tap dance.

FURTHER READING

Stearns, Marshall, and Jean Stearns. *Jazz Dance: The Story of American Vernacular Dance* (1968).
Winter, Marian Hannah. "Juba and American Minstrelsy" in *Chronicles of the American Dance*, ed. Paul Magriel (1948).
—CONSTANCE VALIS HILL

LANEY, LUCY CRAFT

(13 Apr. 1854–23 Oct. 1933), educator, was born in Macon, Georgia, the daughter of David Laney and Louisa (maiden name unknown). Both parents

were slaves: they belonged to different masters, but following their marriage they were permitted to live together in a home of their own. David Laney was a carpenter and often hired out by his owner, Mr. Cobbs. Louisa, purchased from a group of nomadic Indians while a small child, was a maid in the Campbell household. One of Lucy Laney's most cherished memories was "how her father would, after a week of hard slave work, walk for over twenty miles... to be at home with his wife and children on the Sabbath" (*Crisis*, June 1934). After the Civil War and emancipation, David Laney, who had served as a slave lay preacher, was ordained as a Presbyterian minister and became pastor of the Washington Avenue Church in Macon, Georgia. Louisa remained in the Campbell's house as a wage earner. The Laneys' newfound income provided the family some comforts that they shared with numerous cousins, orphaned children, and others in need of shelter.

When missionary teachers opened a school in Macon in 1865 Lucy Laney, together with her mother and her siblings, was among the first to enroll. She graduated from the Lewis High School in 1869 and entered Atlanta University where she received a certificate of graduation from the Higher Normal Department in 1873. In keeping with her strong conviction that "becoming educated [was] a perpetual motion affair" (*Abbott's Monthly*, June 1931), over the course of her career she enrolled in summer programs at the University of Chicago, Hampton Institute, Columbia University, and Tuskegee Institute.

Laney was keenly aware of all the advantages life had afforded her, and she believed that of those to whom much is given much is expected. Emancipation had ushered in new opportunities and responsibilities, and early in life she dedicated herself to her race's advancement. Based on her study of American history, she concluded that the four major components of a realistic program for the "uplift" of blacks were political power, Christian training, "cash," and education. She viewed education as the key to achieving the first three objectives. Her decision to become a teacher was also dictated by the limited employment opportunities available to black women. Following graduation from Atlanta University she accepted a teaching position

in Milledgeville, Georgia, and between 1873 and 1883 also taught at schools in Macon, Augusta, and Savannah.

While a student Laney had serious misgivings about the pedagogical practices at the various schools she attended. She had advised her teachers then that "some day I will have a school of my own." Her experience as a teacher in the public school system intensified her desire to establish a school. She had little patience with "dull teachers... [who] failed to know their pupils—to find out their real needs—and hence had no cause to study methods of better and best development of the boys and girls under their care." She deplored instructors who underestimated "the capabilities and possibilities" of black students and who did not know and/or teach African American history ("The Burden of the Educated Colored Woman," 1899). Moreover, she was convinced that black children needed a thorough Christian education and was disturbed by the public school's failure to address moral and religious concerns.

Laney was one of the first educators to recognize the special and urgent needs of black women in light of their central role in the education of their children. She was convinced that ignorance, immorality, and crime among blacks and perhaps some of the prejudice against them were their "inheritance from slavery." In her opinion, "the basic rock of true culture" was the home, but during slavery "the home was... utterly disregarded... [the] father had neither responsibility, nor authority; mother, neither cares nor duties" ("Educated Colored Woman," 1899). The disregard for homemaking and the home environment resulted in untidy and filthy homes that produced children of dubious character. Moreover, the absence of the sanctity of the marriage vow encouraged immorality and disrespect for black women.

While "no person [was] responsible for [their] ancestor's... sins and shortcomings," Laney argued that "every woman can see to it that she give to her progeny a good mother and an honorable ancestry." Strengthening the black family and improving its home life was therefore "the place to take the proverbial stitch in time." In addition to their role as wives and mothers, she believed that women were "by nature fitted for teaching the...young" and thus were best suited as teachers in the public school system. She was equally convinced that the teacher "who would mould character must herself possess it" and that those who would be mothers, teachers, and leaders needed to be capable in both "mind and character" ("Address before the Women's Meeting," 1897).

Laney's conviction that educated women were a prerequisite for advancement of her race was the major impetus for the founding of the Haines Normal and Industrial Institute. She began her school with six students in the basement of Christ Presbyterian Church in Augusta, Georgia, on 6 January 1886. During the following three years the school, due to increasing enrollment, was moved to various rented buildings around the city. Haines Institute was chartered by the state of Georgia as a normal and industrial school on 5 May 1888. Although the school was sanctioned by the Presbyterian board, the general assembly provided only moral support, which Laney noted "was not much to go on." In 1889, however, the board purchased a permanent site for the school and erected the institution's first building. Despite numerous problems, by 1887 primary, grammar, and normal divisions had been established, and by 1889 she was able to develop a strong literary department as well as a scientifically based normal program and industrial course. By 1892 Haines Normal and Industrial Institute was recognized as one of the best schools of its type in the nation. John William Gibson and William H. Crogman said of Laney in their classic study, *The Progress of a Race* (1897), "There is probably no one of all the educators of the colored race who stands higher, or who has done more work in pushing forward the education of the Negro woman."

Laney was the foremost female member of the generation born into slavery and educated during Reconstruction who rose to leadership and prominence in the 1880s and 1890s. In addition to being a national race leader, she was a pioneer in the struggles for Prohibition and women's rights as well as in the black women's club movement. She was instrumental in establishing the first public high school for blacks in Georgia, organizing the Augusta Colored Hospital

and Nurses Training School, and founding the first kindergarten in the city of Augusta. She was also a leader in the battle to secure improved public schools, sanitation, and other municipal services in Augusta's black community. She was a founding member of the Georgia State Teacher Association and a leader within the regional and national politics of the Young Women's Christian Association. She chaired the Colored Section of the Interracial Commission of Augusta and served on the National Interracial Commission of the Presbyterian Church. An eloquent speaker, she was a distinguished member of the lecture circuit between 1879 and 1930. A number of articles by and about Laney and her school appeared in Presbyterian church publications such as the *Home Mission Monthly*, the *Church Home and Abroad*, *Women and Mission*, the *Presbyterian Monthly Record*, and the *Presbyterian Magazine* during the years 1886–1933.

Laney, who often stated that she wanted to "wear out, not rust out," died in Augusta, Georgia, and was buried on the campus of the school that she built and to which she had devoted most of her life. The most enduring epithet for Laney, who never married or had children, was "mother of the children of the people," and her most profound contributions were the men and women she educated. Writing in the April 1907 issue of the *Home Mission Monthly* she argued that "the measure of an institution is the men and women it sends into the world. The measure of a man is the service he renders his fellows." Judging by this standard Lucy Craft Laney and the school she established were eminently successful.

FURTHER READING

Materials regarding Laney are in the Presbyterian Historical Society in Philadelphia and the William E. Harman Collection, Library of Congress.

Brawley, Benjamin. *Negro Builders and Heroes* (1937).
Daniel, Sadie Iola. *Women Builders* (1931).
Griggs, A. C. "Lucy Craft Laney," *Journal of Negro History* (Jan. 1934): 97–102.
Notestein, Lucy Lilian. *Nobody Knows the Trouble I See* (n.d.).
Ovington, Mary White. *Portraits in Color* (1927).
Patton, June O. "Augusta's Black Community and the Struggle for Ware High School," in *New Perspectives on Black Educational History*, Vincent P. Franklin and James D. Anderson, eds. (1978).

Obituary: *Augusta* (Ga.) *Chronicle*, 23 Oct. 1933.

—JUNE O. PATTON

LANGSTON, JOHN MERCER (14 Dec. 1829– 15 Nov. 1897), political leader and intellectual, was born free in Louisa County, Virginia, the son of Ralph Quarles, a wealthy white slaveholding planter, and Lucy Jane Langston, a part Native American, part black slave emancipated by Quarles in 1806. After the deaths of both of their parents in 1834, Langston and his two brothers, well provided for by Quarles's will but unprotected by Virginia law, moved to Ohio. There Langston lived on a farm near Chillicothe with a cultured white southern family who had been friends of his father and who treated him as a son. He was in effect orphaned again in 1839, when a court hearing, concluding that his guardian's impending move to slave-state Missouri would imperil the boy's freedom and inheritance, forced him to leave the family. Subsequently, he boarded in four different homes, white and black, in Chillicothe and Cincinnati, worked as a farmhand and bootblack, intermittently attended privately funded black schools since blacks were barred from public schools for whites, and in August 1841 was caught up in the violent white rioting against blacks and white abolitionists in Cincinnati.

Learning from his brothers and other black community leaders a sense of commitment, Langston also developed a self-confidence that helped him cope with his personal losses and with pervasive, legally sanctioned racism. In 1844 he entered the preparatory department at Oberlin College, where his brothers had been the first black students in 1835. Oberlin's egalitarianism encouraged him, and its rigorous rhetorical training enhanced his speaking skills. As early as 1848 and continuing into the 1860s, Langston joined in the black civil rights movement in Ohio and across the North, working as an orator and organizer to promote black advancement and enfranchisement and to combat slavery. At one Ohio state black convention, the nineteen-year-old Langston, quoting the Roman slave Terence, declared: " 'I am a man, and there is nothing of humanity, as I think, estranged to me.'... The spirit of our people must be aroused. They must feel and act as men." After receiving his BA degree in 1849, Langston decided to study law. Discovering that law schools were unwilling to accept a black student, however, he returned to Oberlin and in 1853 became the first black graduate of its prestigious theological program. Despite evangelist and Oberlin president Charles Grandison Finney's public urging, Langston, skeptical of organized religion, and especially its widespread failure to oppose slavery, refused to enter the ministry.

Finding white allies in radical anti-slavery politics, Langston engaged in local politics beginning in 1852, demonstrating that an articulate black campaigner might effectively counter opposition race-baiting; in mid-decade he helped form the Republican Party on the Western Reserve. Philemon E. Bliss of nearby Elyria, soon to be a Republican congressman, became Langston's mentor for legal study, and in 1854 he was accepted to the Ohio bar, becoming the first black lawyer in the West. That year he married Caroline Matilda Wall, a senior at Oberlin; they had five children. In the spring of 1855 voters in Brownhelm, an otherwise all-white area near Oberlin where Langston had a farm, elected him township clerk on the Free Democratic (Free Soil) ticket, gaining him recognition as the first black elected official in the nation. Langston announced his conviction that political influence was "the bridle by which we can check and guide, to our advantage, the selfishness of American demagogues."

In 1856 the Langstons began a fifteen-year residency in Oberlin. Elected repeatedly to posts on the town council and the board of education, he solidified his reputation as a competent public executive and adroit attorney. In his best-known case, Langston successfully defended EDMONIA LEWIS, a student accused of poisoning two of her Oberlin classmates (who recovered); Lewis would become the first noted African American sculptor. In promoting militant resistance to slavery, Langston helped stoke outrage over the federal prosecution under the Fugitive Slave Law of thirty-seven of his white and black townsmen and others involved in the 1858 Oberlin-Wellington rescue of fugitive slave John Price. Immediately, Langston organized the new black Ohio State Anti-Slavery Society, which he headed, to channel black indignation over the case. While his brother Charles Henry Langston, one of the two rescuers convicted, repudiated the law in a notable courtroom plea, Langston urged defiance of it in dozens of speeches throughout the state. Langston supported the plan by John Brown (1800–1859) to foment a slave uprising, although he did not participate in the 1859 raid on Harpers Ferry. Following the outbreak of the Civil War, once recruitment of northern black troops began in early 1863, he raised hundreds of black volunteers for the Massachusetts Fifty-fourth and Fifty-fifth regiments and for Ohio's first black regiment.

After the war, Langston's pursuit of a Reconstruction based on "impartial justice" and a redistribution of political and economic power elevated him to national prominence. In contrast to FREDERICK DOUGLASS, the quintessential self-made man, to whom his leadership was most often compared, Langston represented the importance of education and professionalism, joined to activism, for a people emerging from slavery. In 1864 the black national convention in Syracuse, New York, elected him the first president of the National Equal Rights League, a position he held until 1868. Despite rivalries within the league, Langston shaped it into the first viable national black organization. In 1865 and 1866 he lectured in the Upper South, the Midwest, and the Northeast and fought for full enfranchisement not only of the freed people, but also of African Americans denied suffrage in the North. In January 1867, on the eve of congressional Reconstruction, he presided over a league-sponsored convention of more than a hundred black delegates from seventeen states to Washington, D.C., to dramatize African American demands for full freedom and citizenship. That spring Langston assumed a signal role in the South as a Republican party organizer of black voters and the educational inspector-general for the Freedmen's Bureau, traveling from Maryland to Texas. In Virginia, Mississippi, and North Carolina, he helped set up Republican Union Leagues, which instructed freed people on registration and voting; in Georgia and Louisiana he advised blacks elected to state constitutional conventions on strategy. In almost every southern state, Langston defended Reconstruction policy in addresses before audiences of both races. Insistent on guaranteeing the citizenship and human rights of freed people, he appealed to black self-reliance, self-respect, and self-assertion and to white enlightened self-interest, predicting that interracial cooperation would lead to an "unexampled prosperity and a superior civilization." His charisma, refined rhetorical style, and ability to articulate radical principles in a reasonable tone drew plaudits across ideological and racial lines. Twice, in 1868 and 1872, fellow Republicans, one of whom was white, proposed that Langston run for vice president on the Republican ticket.

In the fall of 1869 Langston founded the Law Department at Howard University and took up his duties as law professor and first law dean. From December 1873 to July 1875 he was vice president and acting president of the university. He characteristically gained a warm following among students, who were particularly attracted by his manner, which was neither obsequious nor condescending. Despite Langston's accomplishments at Howard, however, the trustees rejected his bid to assume the presidency for reasons that they refused to disclose but that clearly involved his race, his egalitarian and biracial vision, and the fact that he was not a member of an evangelical church. Embittered, he resigned.

Meanwhile Langston continued to function as one of the Republican Party's top black spokesmen. In return, President Ulysses S. Grant appointed him to the Board of Health of the District of Columbia in 1871, and he moved his home from Oberlin to Washington, D.C. He served as the board's legal officer for nearly seven years, during which time he helped devise a model sanitation code for the capital. On another front, at the behest of Massachusetts senator Charles Sumner, he contributed to the drafting of the Supplementary Civil Rights

Act of 1875, which was invalidated by the U.S. Supreme Court in 1883. As radical Reconstruction crumbled, practicality and personal ambition led Langston in 1877 to endorse President Rutherford B. Hayes's conciliatory policy toward the white South. Two years later, however, he condemned the condition of the freedpeople in the South as "practical enslavement" and called for black migration, the "Exodus" movement, to the North and the West. Langston served with typical efficiency as U.S. minister and consul general to Haiti from 1877 to 1885, winning settlement of claims against the Haitian government, especially by Americans injured during civil unrest, and some improvement in trade relations between the two countries. During his final sixteen months of duty, he was concurrently chargé d'affaires to Santo Domingo.

In 1885 Langston returned to Petersburg, Virginia, to head the state college for African Americans, the Virginia Normal and Collegiate Institute. After his forced resignation less than two years later under heavy pressure from the Democrats who then controlled the state, he announced his intention to run for the U.S. House of Representatives in the mostly black Fourth District, of which Petersburg was the urban center. Running against a white Democrat and a white Republican, Langston waged a ten-month campaign "to establish the manhood, honor, and fidelity of the Negro race." Although the Democratic candidate was initially declared the victor, Langston challenged the election results as fraudulent, and Congress voted in September 1890 to seat him. Within days he was back in Virginia campaigning for reelection to a second term. Again the official count went to the Democrat, a result Langston accepted because he could expect no redress from the new Democratic Congress. The first African American elected to Congress from Virginia, Langston used his three months in the House to put his ideas on education and fair elections into the national record. His most controversial proposal, one intended to head off black disfranchisement, was a constitutional amendment imposing a literacy requirement on all voters in federal elections and a

corresponding adjustment in the size of state congressional delegations.

During the remainder of his life, Langston practiced law in the District of Columbia and continued to be active in politics, education, and promoting black rights. He published his autobiography, *From the Virginia Plantation to the National Capitol* (1894), and carried on an active speaking schedule in both the North and the South. He remained hopeful despite legal disfranchisement, segregation, and his own failure to obtain a federal judgeship. In 1896, while raising money to support the filing of civil rights cases, he predicted: "It is in the courts, by the law, that we shall, finally, settle all questions connected with the recognition of the rights, the equality, the full citizenship of colored Americans." He died in Washington, D.C.

FURTHER READING

Langston's papers, together with those of his wife, Caroline W. Langston, and son-in-law James Carroll Napier, are in the Fisk University Library. Valuable scrapbooks of newsclippings are in the Moorland-Spingarn Research Center at Howard University.

Langston, John Mercer. *Freedom and Citizenship* (1883; repr. 1969).
———. *From the Virginia Plantation to the National Capitol* (1894).

Cheek, William, and Aimee Lee Cheek. *John Mercer Langston and the Fight for Black Freedom, 1829–65* (1989).
———. "John Mercer Langston: Principle and Politics," in *Black Leaders of the Nineteenth Century*, eds. Leon Litwack and August Meier (1988).

—WILLIAM CHEEK
—AIMEE LEE CHEEK

LARSEN, NELLA

(13 Apr. 1891–30 Mar. 1964), novelist, was born Nellie Walker in Chicago, Illinois, the daughter of Peter Walker, a cook, and Mary Hanson. She was born to a Danish immigrant mother and a "colored" father, according to her birth certificate. On 14 July 1890 Peter Walker and Mary Hanson applied for a marriage license in Chicago, but there is no record that the marriage ever took place. Larsen told her publisher,

Alfred A. Knopf, that her father was "a Negro from the Virgin Islands, formerly the Danish West Indies" and that he died when she was two, but none of this has been proven conclusively.

Larsen was prone to invent and embellish her past. Mary Hanson Walker married a Danish man, Peter Larson, on 7 February 1894, after the couple had had a daughter. Peter Larson eventually moved the family from the multiracial world of State Street to a white Chicago suburb, changed the spelling of his name to Larsen, and sent Nellie away to the South. In the 1910 census Mary Larsen denied the existence of Nellie, stating that she had given birth to only one child. The family rejection and the resulting cultural dualism over her racial heritage that Larsen experienced in her youth were to be reflected in her later fiction.

Nellie Larson entered the Coleman School in Chicago at age nine, then the Wendell Phillips Junior High School in 1905, where her name was recorded as Nellye Larson. In 1907 she was sent by Peter Larsen to complete high school at the Normal School of Fisk University in Nashville, Tennessee, where she took the spelling "Larsen" and began to use "Nella" as her given name. Larsen claimed to have spent the years 1909 to 1912 in Denmark with her mother's relatives and to have audited courses at the University of Copenhagen, but there is no record of her ever having done so. Her biographer, Thadious M. Davis, says, "The next four years (1908–1912) are a mystery . . . , and no conclusive traces of her for these years have surfaced" (67).

In 1912 Larsen enrolled in a three-year nurse's training course at New York City's Lincoln Hospital, one of few nursing programs for African Americans in the country. After graduating in 1915, she worked a year at the John A. Andrew Hospital and Nurse Training School in Tuskegee, Alabama. Unhappy at Tuskegee, Larsen returned to New York and worked briefly as a staff member of the city Department of Health. In May 1919 she married Dr. ELMER IMES, a prominent black physicist; the marriage ended in divorce in 1933.

Larsen left nursing in 1921 to become a librarian, beginning work with the New York Public Library in January

Nella Larsen, whose novels address the complexity of being of mixed race in America. Library of Congress

1922. Because of her husband's social position, Larsen was able to move in the heights of the Harlem social circle, and it is there she met WALTER WHITE, the NAACP leader and novelist, and Carl Van Vechten, the photographer and author of *Nigger Heaven* (1926). White and Van Vechten encouraged her to write, and in January 1926 Larsen quit her job in order to write full-time. She had already begun working on her first novel, *Quicksand*, perhaps during a period of convalescence, and it was published in 1928. Earlier in the 1920s she had published two children's stories in *The Brownies' Book* as Nella Larsen Imes and then two pulp-fiction stories for *Young's Magazine* under the pseudonym Allen Semi. *Quicksand* won the Harmon Foundation's Bronze Medal for literature and established Larsen as one of the prominent writers of the Harlem Renaissance. After her second novel, *Passing*, was published in 1929, she applied for and became the first black woman to receive a Guggenheim Foundation Fellowship. Larsen used the award to travel to Spain in 1930 and to work on her third book, which was never published. After a year and a half in Spain and France, Larsen returned to New York.

Two shocks appear to have ended Larsen's literary career. In 1930 she was accused of plagiarizing her short story "Sanctuary," published that year in *Forum*, when a reader pointed out its likeness to Sheila Kaye-Smith's "Mrs. Adis," a story that had appeared in *Century* magazine in 1922. The editors of *Forum* pursued the charge and exonerated Larsen, but biographers and scholars have concluded that Larsen never recovered from the attack, however unfounded. The second shock was Larsen's discovery of her husband's infidelity early in 1930, although she refrained from seeking a divorce until 1933. Imes supported Larsen with alimony payments until his death in 1941, at which time Larsen returned to her first career, nursing, in New York City. She was a supervisor at Gouverneur Hospital from 1944 to 1961, and then worked at Metropolitan Hospital from 1961 to 1964 to avoid retirement. Since her death in New York City, Larsen's novels, considered "lost" until the 1970s, have been reprinted and reexamined. While she had always been included in the few histories of black American literature, her reputation was eclipsed in the era of naturalism and protest-writing (1930–1970), to be recovered along with the reputations of ZORA NEALE HURSTON and other African American women writers during the rise of the feminist movement in the 1970s.

Larsen's literary reputation rests on the achievement of her two novels of the late 1920s. In *Quicksand* she created an autobiographical protagonist, Helga Crane, the illegitimate daughter of a Danish immigrant mother and a black father who was a gambler and deserted the mother. Crane hates white society, from which she feels excluded by her black skin; she also despises the black bourgeoisie, partly because she is not from one of its families and partly for its racial hypocrisy about the color line and its puritanical moral and aesthetic code. After two years of living in Denmark, Helga returns to America to fall into "quicksand" by marrying an uneducated, animalistic black preacher who takes her to a rural southern town and keeps her pregnant until she is on the edge of death from exhaustion.

In *Passing* Larsen wrote a complicated psychological version of a favorite theme in African American literature. Clare Kendry has hidden her black blood from the white racist she has married. The novel ends with Clare's sudden death as she either plunges or is pushed out of a window by Irene, her best friend, just at the husband's surprise entrance. "What happened next, Irene Redfield never afterwards allowed herself to remember. Never clearly. One moment Clare had been there, a vital glowing thing, like a flame of red and gold. The next she was gone" (271).

Larsen's stature as a novelist continues to grow. She portrays black women convincingly and without the simplification of stereotype. Larsen fully realized the complexity of being of mixed race in America and was able to render her cultural dualism artistically.

FURTHER READING

Larsen's personal papers and books vanished from her apartment at her death, so neither a manuscript archive nor a collection of her private papers exists.

Carby, Hazel. *Reconstructing Womanhood: The Emergence of the Afro-American Woman Novelist* (1987).

Davis, M. Thadious. *Nella Larsen, Novelist of the Harlem Renaissance: A Woman's Life Unveiled* (1994).

Larson, Charles. *Invisible Darkness: Jean Toomer and Nella Larsen* (1993).

Tucker, Adia C. *Tragic Mulattoes, Tragic Myths* (2001).

—ANN RAYSON

LATIMER, LEWIS HOWARD

(4 Sept. 1848– 11 Dec. 1928), engineer and inventor, was born in Chelsea, Massachusetts, the son of George W. Latimer, a barber, and Rebecca Smith, both former slaves who escaped from Norfolk, Virginia, on 4 October 1842. When not attending Phillips Grammar School in Boston, Lewis spent much of his youth working in his father's barber shop, as a paperhanger, and selling the abolitionist newspaper *The Liberator*. Lewis's life changed drastically when his father mysteriously disappeared in 1858. His family, placed in dire financial straits, bound out Lewis and his brothers George and William as apprentices through the Farm School, a state institution in which children worked as unpaid laborers. Upon escaping from the exploitation of the Farm School system, Lewis and his brothers returned to Boston to reunite the family. During the next few years, Latimer was able to help support his family through various odd jobs and by working as an office boy for a Boston attorney, Isaac Wright.

Late in the Civil War, Latimer enlisted in the U.S. Navy. He was assigned to the *Ohio* as a landsman (low level seaman) on 13 September 1864. He served until 3 July 1865, at which time he was honorably discharged from the *Massasoit*.

After returning from sea, Latimer began his technical career in Boston as an office boy for Crosby and Gould, patent solicitors. Through his assiduous efforts to teach himself the art of drafting, he rose to assistant draftsman and eventually to the position of chief draftsman in the mid-1870s. During this time, he met Mary Wilson Lewis, a young woman from Fall River, Massachusetts. They were married in 1873 and had two children.

During his tenure at Crosby and Gould, Latimer began to invent. His first creation, a water closet for railway cars, co-invented with W. C. Brown, was granted Letters Patent No. 147,363 on 10 February 1874. However, drafting remained his primary vocation. One of the most noteworthy projects he undertook was drafting the diagrams for Alexander Graham Bell's telephone patent application, which was approved on 14 February 1876. In 1879 after managerial changes at Crosby and Gould, Latimer left their employment and Boston.

Latimer relocated to Bridgeport, Connecticut, initially working as a paperhanger. He eventually found part-time work making mechanical drawings at the Follandsbee Machine Shop. While drafting at the shop, he met Hiram Stevens Maxim, the chief engineer of the U.S. Electric Lighting Company. In February 1880, shortly after their first meeting, Maxim hired Latimer as his draftsman and private secretary. Latimer quickly moved up within the enterprise, and when the U.S. Electric Lighting Company moved to New York City, it placed him in charge of the production of carbon lamp filaments. Latimer was an integral member of the team that installed the company's first commercial incandescent lighting system, in the Equitable Building in New York City in the fall of 1880. He was on hand at most of the lighting installations that were undertaken by the company, and in 1881 he began to supervise many of their incandescent and arc lighting installations.

Latimer also invented products that were fundamental to the development of the company while directing new installations for the U.S. Electric Lighting Company. In October 1880 Maxim was granted a patent for a filament that was treated with hydrocarbon vapor to equalize and standardize its resistance, a process that allowed it to burn longer than the Edison lamp filament. Latimer began working on a process to manufacture this new carbon filament, and on 17 January 1882 he was granted a patent for a new process of manufacturing carbons. This invention produced a highly resistant filament and diminished the occurrence of broken and distorted filaments that had been commonplace with prior procedures. The filament was shaped into an *M*, which became a noted characteristic of the Maxim lamp. Latimer patented other inventions, including two for an electric lamp and a globe support for electric lamps. These further enhanced the Maxim lamp during 1881 and 1882.

In 1881 Latimer was dispatched to London and successfully established an incandescent lamp factory for the newly founded Maxim-Weston Electric Light Company. In 1882 Latimer left this company and began working for the Olmstead Electric Lighting Company of Brooklyn as superintendent of lamp construction; at this time he created the Latimer Lamp. He later continued his work at the Acme Electric Company of New York.

In 1883 Latimer began working at the Edison Electric Light Company. He became affiliated with the engineering department in 1885, and when the legal department was formed in 1889, Latimer's record of expert legal advice made him a requisite member of the new division. According to Latimer's biographical sketch of himself for the Edison Pioneers, he was transferred to the department "as [a] draughtsman inspector and expert witness as to facts in the early stages of the electric lighting business.... [He] traveled extensively, securing witnesses' affidavits, and early apparatus, and also testifying in a number of the basic patent cases to the advantage of his employers." His complete knowledge of electrical technology was exemplified in his work *Incandescent Electric Lighting, a Practical Description of the Edison System* (1890).

Latimer continued in the legal department when the Edison General Electric Company merged with the Thomson-Houston Company to form General Electric Company in 1892. His knowledge of the electric industry became invaluable when the General Electric Company and the Westinghouse Electric Company formed the Board of Patent Control in 1896. This board was responsible for managing the cross-licensing of patents between the two companies and prosecuting infringers. Latimer was appointed to the position of chief draftsman, however his duties went far beyond drafting. He assisted inventors and others in developing their ideas. He used the vast body of knowledge he had acquired over the years in their efforts to eliminate outside competition. He remained at this position until the board was dissolved in 1911, after which Latimer put his talents to use for the law firm of Hammer and Schwartz as a patent consultant.

In 1918, when the Edison Pioneers, an organization founded to bring together for social and intellectual interaction men associated with Thomas Edison prior to 1885, was formed, Latimer was one of the twenty-nine original members. A stroke in 1924 forced him to retire from his formal position, and he spent much of his last four years engaged in two other activities that were most important in his life, art and poetry. He died at his home in Flushing, New York, which in 1995 was made a New York City landmark. Latimer was one of very few African Americans who contributed significantly to the development of American electrical technology.

FURTHER READING

Latimer's papers are in the Lewis Howard Latimer Collection at the Queens Borough Public Library in Queens, N.Y. Copies of many of his papers are located at the Schomburg Center for Research in Black Culture of the New York Public Library.

Norman, Winifred Latimer, and Lily Patterson. *Lewis Latimer: Scientist* (1994).
Schneider, Janet M., and Bayla Singer, eds. *Blueprint for Change: The Life and Times of Lewis H. Latimer* (1995).
Turner, Glennette Tilley. *Lewis Howard Latimer* (1991).

Obituary: *Electrical World*, 22 Dec. 1928.

—RAYVON DAVID FOUCHÉ

LAVEAUX, MARIE

(10 Sept. 1801–16 June 1881), voodoo queen, was born in New Orleans, Louisiana, the daughter of Charles Laveaux, a free man of color who owned a grocery store in that city, and Marguerite D'Arcantel, a free woman of color about whom very little is known, although it is rumored that she was a spiritualist or root doctor. Certain sources erroneously claim that Charles Laveaux was a prominent white planter and politician. He was not, but he was probably the illegitimate son of Don Carlos (or Charles) Trudeau, a high-ranking official in Spanish-controlled Louisiana and the first president of the New Orleans city council when the United States purchased Louisiana in 1803. The historical record, which in Marie Laveaux's case is exceptionally imprecise, provides several spellings of her surname, often leaving out the "x," but most archival records suggest that Charles Laveaux used that version of his name and that this spelling was also used in records related to his illiterate daughter.

There is considerable doubt, too, about Laveaux's date of birth. Her 1881 death certificate claims that she died at the age of ninety-eight, suggesting that she was born in 1783, although most accounts give her birth date as 1794. In the late 1990s, however, a researcher found birth and baptismal records of a "mulatto girl child" named Marie Laveaux dated September 1801. This date coincides with information on her marriage certificate, which states that Laveaux was a minor, a month shy of eighteen, when she wed Jacques Paris, a Haitian-born carpenter, in August 1819.

Laveaux's marriage to Paris was short-lived. After her husband's death in the early 1820s, she became known as "the widow Paris" and began a thirty-year relationship with Captain Jean Louis Christophe Duminy de Glapion, a veteran of the War of 1812 usually referred to as a "quadroon" from Santo Domingo. It has often been claimed that the couple had fifteen children, but New Orleans church records suggest that they had only two sons, François and Archange, who died in childhood, and three daughters, Marie Héloïse, Marie Louise, and Marie Phélomise. In addition, Marie Laveaux had a half-sister,

also named Marie Laveaux, born to Charles Laveaux and his wife, a wealthy member of Louisiana's free colored Creole elite. Many of the legends about the power, wealth, and infamy of Marie Laveaux have arisen because of confusion in oral and literary sources about the women who shared her name, particularly her daughter Marie Héloïse, who was also a voodoo priestess.

In the 1830s Marie Laveaux emerged as a prominent spiritualist and healer at her home; at African American ritual dances on Sundays in New Orleans' Congo Square; and at major religious festivals, such as the midsummer St. John's Eve celebrations on the banks of Lake Pontchartrain, which attracted people of all colors. Laveaux presided over ceremonies that blended elements of Roman Catholicism, such as the invocation of saints and the use of incense and holy water, and traditional African religious dances and rituals involving drumming, chanting, animal sacrifices, and worship of Damballa or Zombi, a snake god. The scanty record of these rituals suggests that Laveaux would blow alcohol on the faces of participants as a blessing and would also wrap a snake around their (usually naked) bodies as a symbol of her control over them. Later accounts of these ceremonies, both in oral tradition and in Robert Tallant's *Voodoo in New Orleans* (1946), highlight the sexual abandon of the participants.

Laveaux's legendary power came less from these infrequent ceremonies, however, than from her skills as an everyday spiritualist who used her charms to bewitch a highly superstitious public. Not unlike J. Edgar Hoover a century later, Laveaux understood that knowledge, particularly knowledge of private indiscretions, equals power. As a hairdresser to prominent women in New Orleans, she had access to gossip about the city's wealthiest and most powerful citizens. She also gained information about the New Orleans elite from African American servants and slaves who, in return for Mamzelle Marie's spiritual protection, brought Laveaux news about their masters' and mistresses' financial, political, and sexual affairs. Laveaux used that intelligence to make herself indispensable to women seeking information on their husbands' philandering, to politicians keen to learn

of their opponents' foibles, and to businessmen who relied on her charms and amulets when the hidden hand of the market failed to work its own particular *gris-gris*. Such information—and the spells and potions to rid her clients of what ailed them—provided Laveaux with a steady income, though not the great riches that many of her followers and detractors claimed. It also ensured friends for her in the highest places in Louisiana society, which may explain why, unlike other *voodooiennes*, she was never arrested. Her seeming influence over whites strengthened her influence over black Louisianans and entrenched her position in African American folklore as one of the most powerful women of her time.

Depending on the source, white accounts of Laveaux's mid-nineteenth century heyday depict her as either saint or whore. After her death in 1881, white Catholics in New Orleans eulogized her saintly role in helping victims of yellow fever and cholera in the 1850s and her tireless work to give comfort to the city's death-row convicts. White Catholics downplayed any African elements in Laveaux's religion and also praised her alleged devotion to the Confederate cause. On the other hand, an obituary in the white Protestant-controlled *New Orleans Democrat* dismissed these claims for Laveaux's piety, describing her as "the prime mover and soul of the indecent orgies of the ignoble Voudous" (Fandrich, 267). Other newspaper accounts and later folklore suggested that Laveaux had used her Lake Pontchartrain home, the Maison Blanche, as a brothel that served wealthy white men seeking glamorous "high yellow" prostitutes, although it is possible that these accounts confused the elder Marie with her daughter, Marie Héloïse, who reputedly kept a bawdy house.

In death Laveaux remained almost as influential as in life, at least to the thousands who seek out her tomb every year in New Orleans, which, some claim, is the second most visited grave in the United States after Elvis Presley's. Like Presley's followers, Laveaux's pilgrims leave candles, money, and other objects in hope that her spirit will grant their wishes. After the September 11, 2001, terrorist attacks on New York City and Washington, D.C., and in Pennsylvania, some disciples even left notes asking that

Laveaux administer punishment to the alleged perpetrator, Osama Bin Laden.

FURTHER READING

Fandrich, Ina. "The Mysterious Voodoo Queen Marie Laveaux: A Study of Power and Female Leadership in Nineteenth-Century New Orleans." Ph.D. diss., Temple University (1994).

Raboteau, Albert. *Slave Religion* (1978).

Tallant, Robert. *Voodoo in New Orleans* (1946).

Obituary: *New Orleans Daily Picayune*, 17 June 1881.

—STEVEN J. NIVEN

LAWRENCE, JACOB ARMSTEAD (7 Sept. 1917–9 June 2000), artist and teacher, was born in Atlantic City, New Jersey, to migrant parents. His father, Jacob Lawrence, a railroad cook, was from South Carolina and his mother, Rose Lee Armstead, hailed from Virginia. In 1919 the family moved to Pennsylvania, where Jacob's sister, Geraldine, was born. Five years later, Jacob's brother, William, was born, and his parents separated.

Jacob Lawrence moved with his mother, sister, and brother to a Manhattan apartment on West 143rd Street in 1930. Upon his arrival in Harlem, the teenage Lawrence began taking neighborhood art classes. His favorite teacher was the painter Charles Alston, who taught at the Harlem Art Workshop. This workshop, sponsored by the Works Progress Administration, was first housed in the Central Harlem branch of the New York Public Library before relocating to Alston's studio at 306 West 141st Street. Many community cultural workers had studios in this spacious building. Affectionately called "306," Alston's studio in particular was a vital gathering place for creative people. Lawrence met ALAIN LOCKE, AARON DOUGLAS, LANGSTON HUGHES, CLAUDE MCKAY, RICHARD WRIGHT, and RALPH ELLISON at his mentor's lively studio.

In 1935, at age eighteen, Lawrence started painting scenes of Harlem using poster paint and brown paper. Initially chosen for their accessibility and low cost, these humble materials would remain central to the artist's work. The

Jacob Lawrence against the backdrop of one of his paintings, at the Harlem Arts Center, 1938, in a WPA photograph. Schomburg Center

next year Lawrence began what would become his ritual of doing background research for his art projects at the 135th Street branch of the New York Public Library (now the Schomburg Center for Research in Black Culture). Inspired after seeing W. E. B. DU BOIS's play *Haiti* at Harlem's Lafayette Theatre in 1936, he began researching the Haitian Revolution (1791–1804). This eye-opening research culminated in a powerful series of forty-one paintings titled *The Life of Toussaint L'Ouverture*. Completed in 1938, this series dramatically visualized the life of the formerly enslaved man who led the Haitian struggle for independence from France and the creation of the world's first black republic. These paintings also signaled paths the artist would continue

to explore in his work, namely, figurative expressionism, history painting, sequential narration, and prose captions. Moreover, the ambitious cycle revealed Lawrence's deep interest in heroism and struggles for freedom.

In September 1938 AUGUSTA SAVAGE, the sculptor and influential director of the Harlem Community Art Center, helped Lawrence gain work as an easel painter on the Works Progress Administration's Federal Art Project. During his eighteen months as a government-employed artist, Lawrence probably produced about thirty-six paintings. In addition, he worked on two more dramatic biographies of freedom fighters. In 1939 he completed *The Life of FREDERICK DOUGLASS* series. Based on the famous abolitionist's autobiography, the thirty-two painted panels—each accompanied by text—chart the heroic transformation of an escaped slave into a fiery orator and an uncompromising activist. The following year Lawrence completed *The Life of HARRIET TUBMAN* series. Composed of thirty-one panels, this epic visual and textual narrative features the courageous female conductor of the Underground Railroad. Both series were exhibited at the Library of Congress in 1940 in commemoration of the seventy-fifth anniversary of the Thirteenth Amendment to the U.S. Constitution.

In 1941, at age twenty-four, Lawrence completed his signature narrative series, *The Migration of the Negro,* a group of sixty tempera paintings illustrating the mass movement of African Americans from the rural South to the urban North. This historical cycle was done in a modern visual style with its emphasis on strong lines, simplified forms, geometric shapes, flat planes, bold colors, and recurrent motifs. Gwendolyn Knight, a Barbados-born and Harlem-based artist, helped Lawrence complete the project by assisting with the preparation of the sixty hardboard panels and the accompanying prose captions. The creative couple married in New York on 24 July 1941, shortly after completing this pivotal work. Lawrence's *Migration* series brought him wide public recognition and critical acclaim. Twenty-six of the panels were reproduced in *Fortune* magazine in November 1941. Simultaneously, New York's prestigious Downtown Gallery exhibited the cycle, and, soon after the show opened, Edith Halpert, the gallery's owner, asked Lawrence to join her roster of prominent American artists, which included Ben Shahn, Stuart Davis, and Charles Sheeler. Lawrence accepted Halpert's offer, making him the first artist of African descent to be represented by a downtown gallery. A few months later the Museum of Modern Art (MOMA) purchased half the *Migration* series and the Phillips Collection in Washington, D.C., bought the other half, marking the first acquisition of works by an African American artist at either institution. In October 1942 MOMA organized a two-year, fifteen-venue national tour of the acclaimed series.

During World War II, Lawrence served in the U.S. Coast Guard, where he continued to paint. In 1944 a group of his paintings based on life at sea was exhibited at MOMA. The following year, while he was still on active duty, Lawrence successfully applied for a Guggenheim Fellowship to begin work on a series devoted to the crisis of war. The fourteen somber panels that make up his *War* series were first shown at the New Jersey State Museum in 1947, and *Time* magazine touted the series as "by far his best work yet" (*Time* 50 [22 Dec. 1947], 61).

Lawrence began his distinguished career as a teacher in 1946 when the former Bauhaus artist Josef Albers invited him to teach summer session at Black Mountain College in North Carolina. Until his retirement in 1983 Lawrence was a highly sought-after teacher. He taught at numerous schools, including the Skowhegan School of Painting and Sculpture in Maine, Brandeis University in Massachusetts, Pratt Institute, the Art Students League, and the New School for Social Research in New York City. From 1970 to 1983 Lawrence was a full professor of art at the University of Washington in Seattle.

Lawrence's first retrospective began in 1960. Organized by the Brooklyn Museum of Art, the show traveled to sixteen sites across the country. The artist had two other traveling career retrospectives during his lifetime: one organized by the Whitney Museum of American Art in 1974, and another organized by the Seattle Art Museum in 1986.

During the civil rights movement, Lawrence visually captured the challenges of the freedom struggle of blacks in works such as *Two Rebels* (1963). His first venture into limited-edition printmaking, *Two Rebels* dramatized the struggle between black protestors and white policemen through lithography. Over the next three decades the artist would also experiment with other printmaking techniques, such as drypoint, etching, and silkscreen.

In 1962, Lawrence traveled to Nigeria, where he lectured on the influence of traditional West African sculpture on modernist art and exhibited his work in Lagos and Ibadan. Two years later the artist and his wife returned to Nigeria for eight months, to experience life in West Africa and to create work based on their stay.

After working primarily as a painter and a printmaker, Lawrence expanded his range in the late 1970s by also making murals. He received his first mural commission in 1979 when he was hired to create a work for Seattle's Kingdome Stadium. He created a ten-panel work titled *Games*. Made of porcelain enamel on steel, the $9\frac{1}{2} \times 7\frac{1}{2}$ foot mural features powerful athletes surrounded by adoring fans. This mural, which was relocated to the Washington State Convention Center in 2000, was followed by others at Howard University (1980, 1984), the University of Washington (1984), the Orlando International Airport (1988), the Joseph Addabbo Federal Building in Queens (1988), and the Harold Washington Library Center in Chicago (1991). The artist's final mural, a 72-foot-long mosaic commissioned by New York City's Metropolitan Transit Authority, was posthumously unveiled in the Times Square subway station in 2001.

When Jacob Lawrence died at home in Seattle at age eighty-two, he was exploring a theme that had captured his imagination at the beginning of his sixty-five-year artistic career. Lawrence was still painting pictures of laborers, their movements and constructions, and their tools. A collection of hand tools—hammers, chisels, planes, rulers, brushes, and a Pullman porter's bed wrench—graced his studio and inspired his work. Concerning his prized collection, the artist explained: "For me, tools became extensions of hands, and movement. Tools are like sculptures. You look at old paintings and you see in them the same tools we use today. Tools are eternal. And I also enjoy the illusion when I paint them: you know, making something that is about making something" (Kimmelman, 210–211).

Jacob Lawrence's lifelong interest in representing work and workers befits a man who left behind a monumental body of work—approximately seven hundred paintings, one hundred prints, eight murals, and hundreds of drawings, studies, and sketches. One of the most widely admired African American artists, he was passionately committed to employing his own expressive tools to creatively visualize historical struggles and modern American life.

FURTHER READING

Jacob Lawrence's papers are housed in the Archives of American Art, Smithsonian Institution, Washington, D.C.

Kimmelman, Michael. *Portraits: Talking With Artists at the Met, the Modern, the Louvre, and Elsewhere* (1998).

Nesbett, Peter T., with an essay by Patricia Hills. *Jacob Lawrence: The Complete Prints (1963–2000): A Catalogue Raisonné* (2001).

Nesbett, Peter T., and Michelle DuBois. *Jacob Lawrence: Paintings, Drawings, and Murals (1935–1999): A Catalogue Raisonné* (2000).

———, eds. *Over the Line: The Art and Life of Jacob Lawrence* (2001).

Turner, Elizabeth Hutton, ed. *Jacob Lawrence: The Migration Series* (1993).

Wheat, Ellen Harkins. *Jacob Lawrence: American Painter* (1986).

———. *Jacob Lawrence: The Frederick Douglass and Harriet Tubman Series of 1938–40* (1991).

Obituary: *New York Times*, 10 June 2000.

—LISA GAIL COLLINS

LAWRENCE, MARGARET MORGAN

(19 Aug. 1914–), pediatric psychiatrist, was born Margaret Morgan in New York City, the daughter of the Reverend Sandy Alonzo Morgan, an Episcopal priest, and Mary E. Smith, a schoolteacher. Mistrusting segregated southern hospitals, the Morgans temporarily moved from Virginia to Harlem in 1914, living with Margaret's aunt, so that their child could be born in New York. Margaret's childhood, however, was spent primarily in Vicksburg, Mississippi, where her father's next congregation was located. She grew up a precocious child, reading at three, and lived in a middle-class black neighborhood with her educated parents.

Every summer Morgan visited her aunts in Harlem, and at the age of fourteen she decided she wanted to live with them so that she could go to a better high school. She had decided to be a doctor, she told people, because her older brother had died in infancy before she was born and she wanted to save babies from dying. With her parents blessing, she moved to Harlem and attended the Wadleigh School, one of the two classical high schools for girls in New York City that required passing entrance exams. In this predominantly white high school, Margaret excelled, and on graduation day the top prize in Greek and Latin was awarded, as the principal put it, to "the Negro girl from Mississippi." She received scholarships from Cornell University, Hunter College, and Smith College and chose Cornell partly because of her state regents scholarship but also for its strong reputation in the biological sciences and, as she told friends, because it had men.

At Cornell in the fall of 1932 Morgan was the only black student in the College of Arts and Sciences. She was not allowed to live in the women's dormitory, but the dean of students found her a room with a business family, where she lived for two years. There, to pay for her room and board, she worked as a servant, wearing a uniform and waiting on the dinner table while she herself ate separately in the kitchen and slept in an uninsulated attic. She was also responsible for the housecleaning, washing, and ironing.

In her junior year Morgan moved in with a faculty family, where she had a large, comfortable room but where, once again, she earned her keep serving as household maid. In her senior year, however, she was taken in by Hattie Jones, a legendary figure in Ithaca's tiny black community. Married to a big-time gambler and driven around town in her flashy car by a good-looking young chauffeur, Hattie rented rooms in her big house and cooked huge dinners for students she called "young Negroes coming up" (Lightfoot, 98).

Determined to be a doctor, Morgan preferred courses in organic chemistry and comparative astronomy to ancient history or sociology. In her senior year she worked as a technologist for a researcher in the Agricultural College, which paid the rent and taught her how to prepare tissue specimens for microscopic study. She received excellent grades and was told by the dean of the medical school that she had done "very well" in the Medical Aptitude Test. Medical school seemed certain, and again she chose Cornell.

Cornell Medical School rejected her application. The very same dean stunned her by saying that several meetings of the admissions committee had been devoted to her application, adding that she was a very good student and a promising physician, but still they were turning her down. The dean told her, in words she would always remember, that twenty-five years earlier the medical school had conducted "an experiment," admitting a Negro, "and it didn't work out. He got tuberculosis" (Lightfoot, 175).

Morgan was accepted at Columbia, however, and in 1936 she became the third black medical student in that school's history; during her four years there she was the only African American in the school. She did well in her courses and won the respect of her teachers and classmates. Meanwhile, to pay for her meals at the residence hall, she worked in the kitchen drying silverware.

In 1938 Morgan married Charles Lawrence, but her life's goal was still to save babies, so after medical school she sought a residency in pediatrics at New York's Babies Hospital, affiliated with Columbia Medical School. Her application was rejected, because—as she was told and never believed—married interns could not live in the hospital's quarters, even though her husband was then living in Georgia and attending Atlanta University. Instead, she did her pediatric internship at Harlem Hospital and then took a master's degree in public health from Columbia in 1943.

In 1944 Lawrence left New York City and returned to the South for four years, teaching pediatrics and public health at Meharry Medical College in Nashville, Tennessee, then the premier medical school for black Americans, while her husband taught sociology at nearby Fisk University. Lawrence and her husband moved back to New York City in 1948. After psychoanalytic training at the Columbia Psychoanalytic Institute (as the first black person to go through the institute), she settled into a distinguished career of research, teaching, and clinical work at Harlem Hospital and Columbia Medical School, while her husband became an eminent sociologist at Brooklyn College.

The lucky break that put her on the path to professional distinction was her association at Columbia with a young pediatrician, Dr. Benjamin Spock, during the year she worked for her master's degree in public health. Spock opened Lawrence's eyes to the link between physical health and psychological well-being. From Spock, who was also trained in psychoanalysis, she learned to look at the social and family context of childhood disease. She put these insights to work at Harlem Hospital, where she worked to reconstruct the shattered lives of young black children through treatment and therapy in the Developmental Psychiatry Clinic, which she founded and ran for many years.

Lawrence's most important contribution to child psychiatry was her pioneering advocacy of placing in schools therapeutic teams composed of psychiatrists, neuropsychologists, social workers, and nurses. Her first book, *The Mental Health Team in the School* (1971), describing how visiting teams of mental health specialists could serve children in school, is recognized as a milestone in pediatric psychiatry, as are the programs in child psychiatry she developed in day-care centers and hospital clinics.

Throughout her career Lawrence was passionately involved in politics and a lifelong activist in the anti-poverty and civil rights movements, always seeking to improve, as she never tired of putting it, "the impoverished lives of black babies." She was particularly interested in how poor urban black families coped with adversity and how some black children were able to develop ego strength under stress, themes she explored in her second book *Young Inner City Families* (1975).

Margaret and Charles Lawrence had three children, one of whom, Sara Lawrence Lightfoot, has written a moving biography of her mother, *Balm in Gilead: Journal of a Healer* (1988). After her retirement at age seventy in 1984 from Harlem Hospital and Columbia University Medical School, Lawrence continued her private child psychiatry practice in Rockland County, New York, while remaining an active crusader to improve mental health for economically disadvantaged children. She has received many honorary degrees, the Joseph Bernstein Mental Health Award (1975), the Outstanding Women Practitioners in Medicine Award (1984), and the Cornell Black Alumni Award (1992).

In the spring of 2002, at the age of eighty-seven, Lawrence returned to Ithaca to give a talk to the Cornell community. She told the rapt audience that she had made it despite her difficulties as a student because "I knew who I was, and I knew my own gifts."

FURTHER READING

Lightfoot, Sara Lawrence. *Balm in Gilead: Journal of a Healer* (1988).

—ISAAC KRAMNICK

LEAD BELLY (15 Jan. 1888–6 Dec. 1949), folk singer and composer, was born Huddie Ledbetter on the Jeter plantation near Caddo Lake, north of Shreveport, Louisiana, the only surviving son of John Wesley Ledbetter and Sally Pugh, farmers who were reasonably well-to-do. Young Huddie (or "Hudy" as the 1910 census records list him) grew up in a large rural black community centered around the Louisiana-Texas-Arkansas junction, and he would later play at rural dances where, in his own words, "there would be no white man around for twenty miles." Though he was exposed to the newer African American music forms like the blues, he also absorbed many of the older fiddle tunes, play-party tunes, church songs, field hollers, badman ballads, and even old vaudeville songs of the culture. His uncle taught him a song that later became his signature tune, "Goodnight, Irene." Though Huddie's first instrument was a "windjammer" (a small accordion), by 1903 he had acquired a guitar and was plying his trade at local dances.

In 1904, when he turned sixteen, Huddie made his way to the notorious red-light district of nearby Shreveport; there he was exposed to early jazz and ragtime, as well as blues, and learned how to adapt the left-hand rhythm of the piano players to his own guitar style. He also acquired a venereal disease that eventually drove him back home for treatment. In 1908 he married Aletha Henderson, with whom he had no children, and the pair moved just east of Dallas, where they worked in the fields and prowled the streets of Dallas. Two important things happened to Huddie here: he heard and bought his first twelve-string guitar (the instrument that he would make famous), and he met

Lead Belly captivated audiences with his powerful voice, his twelve-string guitar, and a mixture of blues, traditional songs, and songs of protest. Library of Congress

the man who later became one of the best-known exponents of the "country blues," BLIND LEMON JEFFERSON. Though Jefferson was actually Huddie's junior by some five years, he had gained considerable experience as a musician, and he taught Huddie much about the blues and about how an itinerant musician in these early days could make a living. The pair were fixtures around Dallas's rough-and-tumble Deep Ellum district until about 1915.

Returning to Harrison County, Texas, Huddie then began a series of altercations with the law that would change his life and almost destroy his performing career. It started in 1915, when he was convicted on an assault charge and sent to the local chain gang. He soon escaped, however, and fled to Bowie County under the alias of Walter Boyd. There he lived peacefully until 1917, when he was accused of killing a cousin and wound up at the Sugarland Prison farm in south Texas. There he gained a reputation as a singer and a hard worker, and it was there that a prison chaplain gave him the nickname "Lead Belly." (Though subsequent sources have listed the singer's nickname as one word, "Leadbelly," all original documents give "Lead Belly.") At Sugarland he also learned songs like "The Midnight Special" and began to create his own songs about local characters and events. When Texas governor Pat Neff visited the prison on an inspection tour, Lead Belly composed a song to the governor pleading for his release; impressed by the singer's skill, Neff did indeed give him a pardon, signing the papers on 16 January 1925. For the next five years Lead Belly lived and worked around Shreveport, until 1930, when he was again convicted for assault—this time for knifing a "prominent" white citizen. The result was a six- to ten-year term in Angola, then arguably the worst prison in America.

In 1933, while in Angola, Lead Belly encountered folk-song collector John Lomax, who had been traveling throughout southern prisons collecting folk songs from inmates for the Library of Congress. Lead Belly sang several of his choice songs for the recording machine, including "The Western Cowboy" and "Goodnight, Irene." Lomax was impressed and a year later returned to gather more songs; this time Lead Belly

decided to try his pardon-song technique again and recorded a plea to the Louisiana governor, O. K. Allen. The following year Lead Belly was in fact released, and though he always assumed the song had done the trick, prison records show Lead Belly was scheduled for release anyway because of overcrowding.

Lead Belly immediately sought out Lomax and took a job as his driver and bodyguard. For the last months of 1934, he traveled with Lomax as he made the rounds of southern prisons. During this time he learned a lot about folk music and added dozens of new songs to his own considerable repertoire.

In December 1934 Lomax presented his singer to the national meeting of the Modern Language Association in Philadelphia—Lead Belly's first real public appearance—and then took him to New York City in January 1935. His first appearances there generated a sensational round of stories in the press and on newsreels and set the stage for a series of concerts and interviews. One of these was a well-publicized marriage to a childhood sweetheart, Martha Promise (it is not known how or when his first marriage ended); another was a record contract with the American Record Company. Lomax himself continued to make records at a house in Westport, Connecticut, a series of recordings that was donated to the Library of Congress and that formed the foundation for the book by John Lomax and Alan Lomax, *Negro Folk Songs as Sung by Lead Belly* (1936). For three months money and offers poured in, but complex tensions stemming in part from Lomax's attempts to mold Lead Belly's repertoire in a way that fit the classic folk music image of the day led to an estrangement between Lomax and Lead Belly, and before long the singer returned to Shreveport.

A year later Lead Belly and his wife returned to New York City to try to make it on their own. He found his audience not in the young African American fans of CAB CALLOWAY and DUKE ELLINGTON (who considered his music old fashioned), but in the young white social activists of various political and labor movements. He felt strongly about issues concerning civil rights and produced songs on a number of topics, the best of which were "The Bourgeois

Blues" and "We're in the Same Boat, Brother." Lead Belly soon had his own radio show in New York, which led to an invitation to Hollywood to try his hand at films. He tried out for a role in *Green Pastures* and was considered for a planned film with Bing Crosby about Lomax. The late 1940s saw a series of excellent commercial recordings for Capitol, as well as for the independent Folkways label in New York. His apartment became a headquarters for young aspiring folk singers coming to New York, including a young Woody Guthrie. Martha Promise's niece Tiny began managing Lead Belly's affairs, and his career was on the upswing when, in 1949, he became ill with amyotrophic lateral sclerosis (Lou Gehrig's disease). It progressed rapidly, and in December Lead Belly died in Bellevue Hospital in New York City. His body was returned to Mooringsport, Louisiana, for burial. Ironically, a few months later, his song "Goodnight, Irene" was recorded by the Weavers, a group of his folk-singing friends, and became one of the biggest record hits of the decade.

Lead Belly was one of the first performers to introduce African American traditional music to mainstream American culture in the 1930s and 1940s and was responsible for the popularity and survival of many of the nation's best-loved songs.

FURTHER READING

Numerous CDs feature reissues of both the singer's commercial and Library of Congress recordings, notably *Lead Belly: The Library of Congress Recordings* (Rounder 1044–46).

Lomax, John, and Alan Lomax. *Negro Folk Songs as Sung by Lead Belly* (1936).
Wolfe, Charles K., and Kip Lornell. *The Life and Legend of Leadbelly* (1992).

—CHARLES K. WOLFE

LEDBETTER, HUDDIE. *See* Lead Belly.

LEE, JARENA
(11 Feb. 1783–?), preacher and evangelist, was born in Cape May, New Jersey.

Jarena Lee, evangelizing preacher who fought for the ordination of women. Schomburg Center

She was not born a slave, but we know little about her family. They were obviously poor enough that at the age of seven Jarena was hired out as a live-in maid to a family that lived some sixty miles from her home. She had a religious awakening in 1804, and several years later she recounts achieving rebirth to a life free of sin and focused on spiritual perfection. Each of these spiritual transformations occurred after Jarena had experienced physical hardships. Her autobiography describes a long and laborious struggle that led her to the conviction that she should preach. In 1836 she published an autobiographical narrative, *The Life and Religious Experiences of Jarena Lee.* The narrative was reprinted in 1839, and in 1849 she produced an expanded version under the title *Religious Experiences and Journal of Mrs. Jarena Lee: Giving an Account of Her Call to Preach the Gospel.*

In the nineteenth century the social order of the United States and Great Britain did not condone women's speaking in public about their spiritual experiences. Few women of any race dreamed or dared to preach publicly. However, Jarena felt that she had received from God the command to preach the Christian gospel, and eventually she began

to do so. In search of a community of Christians, Jarena had sought to unite with the "English Church," but she felt "there was a wall between me and a communion with that people" (Lee, 4). In 1809, at the age of twenty-six, Jarena found in the Bethel African Methodist congregation of Philadelphia a community of people who identified with issues close to her heart. It was in this company of African American Christians that she felt at ease and clear about her mission. She decided that "this is the people to which my heart unites" (5).

Jarena approached RICHARD ALLEN, the pastor of Bethel, about her desire and call to preach. But he did not grant her a license to preach under the authority of his congregation, because, he said, the congregation still operated under the authority of the white Methodist Episcopal Church, which did not authorize female ministers. But Jarena was not deterred and even expressed some defiance at Allen's refusal to recognize her divine charge. She wrote of the incident, "O how careful ought we to be lest through our by-laws of church government and discipline, we bring into disrepute even the work of life. It should be remembered that nothing is impossible with God" (11).

Jarena married the Reverend Joseph Lee in 1811, and they would have two children before Joseph died six years into their marriage. Joseph had not supported Jarena's desire to obey her call to preach, and he refused to relocate from the "Coloured Society" in Snow Hill, Pennsylvania, where he had been assigned to serve as pastor. Although she was alone and a single mother after Joseph's death, Jarena Lee was now free to pursue her ministry.

Lee began preaching and met with enough success that in 1817 she renewed her request to Richard Allen for a license to preach under the authority of the newly formed African Methodist Episcopal Church. There still was no precedent for authorizing women preachers, but by then Allen had seen and heard her preach and was convinced that she was a woman of God. More important, he was now a bishop and was eager to have enthusiastic people who could help the new denomination expand its missionary work. Allen

directed Lee to hold prayer meetings and to preach.

Lee undertook her evangelical activity with seriousness and reported that she held many prayer meetings to exhort women and men to Jesus. She felt a bond with the AME Church, even though she never received an official license for her work. However, because Bishop Allen gave her speaking appointments in several Pennsylvania congregations, Lee proceeded with a sense of authority. She traveled with Allen and other AME ministers to denominational meetings in New York and New Jersey. She also traveled alone and with other women to large and small evangelical meetings throughout the Northeast. Lee's steadfast commitment to her divine call, coupled with her preaching success, challenged the male religious hierarchy and set forth new possibilities for the preaching ministry of African American women.

Jarena Lee did not set out to become a revolutionary; she merely wanted to preach the gospel, but doing that inevitably became a revolutionary act because it challenged the ecclesiastical beliefs and gender roles of her day. Richard Allen was Lee's most powerful friend and ally, even caring for her son for several years while she spread the word. After Allen died in 1831, Lee continued to preach at various Methodist churches and locations, but found herself ostracized from an increasing number of AME churches in Philadelphia. As she wrote, "I seemed much troubled, as being measurably debarred from my own Church as regards this privilege I had been so much used to" (77).

Not much is known of Lee's final years, except that she worked for a time with the New York Anti-Slavery Society. Later in the nineteenth century many African American women within the AME Church and in other denominations followed her lead and realized their call to preach, but it was not until 1948 that Rebecca M. Glover became the first woman ordained by the AME Church. In 2000, with the way paved in part by the consecration in 1989 of BARBARA HARRIS in the Episcopal Church, Vashti McKenzie became the first female AME bishop.

A pathfinder for African American women and a trailblazer among

Methodist women, Jarena Lee was the first known black woman to forcefully advocate for the right of women to preach in Methodist denominations. For this feat she must be considered among the vanguard of churchwomen in the United States.

FURTHER READING

Lee, Jarena. *Religious Experiences and Journal of Mrs. Jarena Lee: Giving an Account of Her Call to Preach the Gospel* (1849).

Andrews, William L., ed. *Sisters of the Spirit: Three Black Women's Autobiographies of the Nineteenth Century* (1986).
Peterson, Carla L. "Secular and Sacred Space in the Spiritual Autobiographies of Jarena Lee" in *Reconfigured Spheres: Feminist Explorations of Literary Space*, eds. Margaret R. Higonnet and Joan Templeton (1994).
—JUALYNNE E. DODSON

 LEE, RAPHAEL CARL (29 Oct. 1949–), plastic surgeon, biomedical engineer, and educator, was born in Sumter, South Carolina, the son of Leonard Powell Lee, a physician, and Jean Maurice Langston Lee, a visual artist. His father had grown up in rural coastal South Carolina, part of a large family in which he and all his siblings, despite the limited opportunities available, earned higher degrees and went into either teaching or medicine. His mother came from a line of successful entrepreneurs with real estate interests in and near Philadelphia and Washington, D.C.

As South Carolina's public schools remained racially segregated until 1963, Lee's parents enrolled him in a private Roman Catholic "mission" elementary and middle school for blacks. In the fall of 1963 he was among the first group of blacks to enter St. Jude High School in Sumter; he remained there for two years before attending Bishop England High School, also a Catholic institution, in Charleston (1965–1967). The environment at these two schools was hostile at times, he recalls, because of a vocal minority of local whites opposed to racial integration. Undeterred, he went on to earn a bachelor's degree in Electrical Engineering at the University of South Carolina (1971). Lee then moved north to Philadelphia, where he earned a master's degree in Biomedical Engineering at Drexel University (1975) and an MD at Temple University (1975); in 1979 he received an ScD in Biomedical Engineering at the Massachusetts Institute of Technology.

Lee's professional interests began to take shape while he was a junior at the University of South Carolina. He took a wide range of courses—biology and other premedical units, in addition to electrical engineering—and discovered the excitement and rewards of inter-disciplinary study. The potential medical applications of laser beams, for example, piqued his interest. As a result, Lee entered one of the nation's first combined engineering and medicine programs at Drexel and Temple. This experience motivated him to pursue a career in academic surgery, and he went on to serve as an assistant resident in surgery at the University of Chicago Hospitals between 1975 and 1977. While at Chicago, he developed a special interest in wound healing and plastic surgery—particularly the relationship between electromagnetic fields, fluid mechanics, and human connective tissues—which led him to interrupt his clinical training for a period of research at the Massachusetts Institute of Technology (MIT). He earned his doctorate at MIT in two years with a thesis entitled "Cartilage Electromechanics: The Relationship of Physicochemical to Mechanical Properties." He then completed his surgical training at the University of Chicago Hospitals, as resident in surgery (1979–1980) and chief resident in general surgery (1980–1981).

Lee returned to the Boston area in 1981 for further specialized training. He was senior assistant resident in plastic surgery at Massachusetts General Hospital (1981–1982), after which he held three academic appointments simultaneously: assistant professor of electrical and bioengineering at MIT, assistant professor of bioengineering and surgery at Harvard–MIT Division of Health Sciences and Technology, and assistant professor of surgery (plastic) at Harvard Medical School. These multiple appointments reflected the interdisciplinary emphasis of his work but also stretched him thin at times—requiring a determined balancing act that was "barely possible," he felt, in the competitive environments of Harvard and MIT. In 1989 he returned to the University of Chicago as associate professor of surgery, anatomy, and organismal biology (biomechanics). He was promoted to full professor in 1992. Since 1991 he has also served as director of the Electrical Trauma Program and medical director of the Burn Unit at the University of Chicago Hospitals.

Lee's research has resulted in several important developments in the surgical management of severe trauma, particularly electrical shock, thermal burns, and wounds (see Lee et al., *Electrical Trauma: The Pathophysiology, Manifestations, and Clinical Management* [1992]). He also established the usefulness of copolymer surfactants in repairing damaged cells after trauma (see Lee et al., "Surfactant-Induced Sealing of Electropermeabilized Skeletal Muscle Membranes *In Vivo*," *Proceedings of the National Academy of Sciences* 89 [1992]: 4524–4528). The mechanism involves sealing damaged cell membranes—a powerful illustration of how Lee's engineering and surgical background and interests came together in deeply practical ways in the medical field.

Other important outgrowths of his research include pharmaceutical strategies to reduce scarring, the use of mechanical stress to control engineering of tissues, and surgical procedures for gynecological reconstruction. (On the second of these topics, see, for example, Lee et al., "A Review of the Biophysical Basis for the Clinical Application of Electric Fields in Soft Tissue Repair," *Journal of Burn Care and Rehabilitation* 14 [1993]: 319–335.) Lee has founded two companies—Avocet Polymer Technologies, Inc. (1996), and Maroon Biotech, Inc. (2000)—to develop and market the scarring and surfactant discoveries, respectively, and he holds about a dozen related patents. Also important is a software package that he and a group of his students created to measure body surface area injury. This was the first technique to use three-dimensional simulation of individual patients to calculate burn involvement, complication, and survival rates in a vastly more accurate way than had been possible with traditional methods of visual estimation or with two-dimensional models.

Lee married Kathleen M. Kelley, MD, in 1983. Dr. Kelley holds joint appointments in the departments of psychiatry and pediatrics at the University of Chicago and is a sometime research collaborator with her husband. They have two children—Rachel Kelley Lee and Catherine Marie Lee.

A Fellow of the American College of Surgeons and diplomate of the American Board of Surgery and American Board of Plastic Surgery, Lee has held office in a number of professional associations. He was a charter member, membership chairman (1986–1988), and scientific council member (1991–1993) of the Bioelectric Repair and Growth Society; scientific council member (1994) of the Bioelectromagnetics Society; chairman of the plastic surgery section (1989–1991) of the National Medical Association; president (1996) of the Society for Physical Regulation in Biology and Medicine; and member of the research and education committee (1998) of the American Association of Plastic Surgeons. Among his numerous awards, he received a grant from the MacArthur Foundation in 1981, the first year of the prestigious MacArthur Fellows Program. Lee was selected for his original, creative research combining techniques and knowledge in surgery, electrical engineering, biophysics, and electrochemistry. *Science Digest* included him in its 1984 list of America's Top 100 Young Scientists. He was also one of four engineers featured in a 1988 exhibit—Black Achievers in Science—designed by the Museum of Science and Industry in Chicago. In 1991 he received an honorary doctorate from his alma mater, University of South Carolina, in recognition of his distinguished career.

FURTHER READING

The MIT Museum has a small biographical file, mostly clippings, photographs, and news releases, relating to Lee's early career as a faculty member at MIT.

Williams, Clarence G., ed. *Technology and the Dream: Reflections on the Black Experience at MIT, 1941–1999* (2001).
—CLARENCE G. WILLIAMS

LEE, SPIKE (27 Mar. 1957–), filmmaker and screenwriter, was born

Shelton Jackson Lee in Atlanta, Georgia, the eldest of four children of Bill Lee, a jazz composer and musician, and Jacquelyn Shelton, a schoolteacher. During Spike's youth, his family moved to Brooklyn, New York, where they lived in the neighborhoods of Crown Heights, Cobble Hill, and Fort Greene. Lee later used his intimate knowledge of these racially integrated Brooklyn neighborhoods to dramatize in his films the relations between African Americans and their non-black neighbors. Movies and television, such as the Anglo American *The Partridge Family* and the African American *Good Times*, informed Spike's understanding of popular culture. "I can remember my mother, Jacquelyn, taking me to see James Bond movies," he reminisced. "She liked them. I used to like 007 myself. I remember seeing *Help!* with the Beatles and *A Hard Day's Night*" (*By Any Means*, 2). Lee's fiction film *Crooklyn*, which he co-wrote with his siblings, documents the influence television had on them.

In 1975 Lee enrolled at his father's alma mater, Morehouse College in Atlanta, Georgia. He graduated in 1979 with a BA in Mass Communications. That summer Lee interned with Columbia Pictures, and the following fall he entered the Tisch School of the Arts at New York University, where he cultivated a working friendship with cinematographer Ernest Dickerson. "We came in together," Lee later recalled. "He was from Howard. I was from Morehouse.... We were the only blacks at NYU" (*Gotta Have It*, 32).

Lee produced his first student film, *The Answer* (1980), in response to D. W. Griffith's 1915 film *Birth of a Nation*. The following year his MFA thesis project, the forty-five-minute film *Joe's Bed-Stuy Barbershop: We Cut Heads*, which Dickerson shot, won the Academy of Motion Pictures Arts and Sciences' Best Student Film Award and became the first student film ever included in the Lincoln Center New Directors, New Films series.

In 1980 Lee and Monty Ross, a friend from Morehouse, established the production company, Forty Acres and a Mule Filmworks. Named after the historically inaccurate, but often cited, "promise" made by the U.S. government to newly emancipated slaves, Lee's company name expresses the consternation of African Americans

at America's broken promises and racist policies. The company's first production, Lee's first feature-length film, *She's Gotta Have It* (1986), with its mixture of humor and intensity, its bold exploration of sexuality and race, and its strong visual style, won the Cannes Film Festival's Best New Director Prize. Shot in ten days for $175,000, the film made over seven million dollars at the box office. Lee himself played one of the film's key roles, the fast-talking, big glasses–wearing bicycle messenger Mars Blackmon. Blackmon reappeared in a series of Lee-directed Nike commercials aired from 1988 to 1993 and reprised in 2003 upon the retirement of MICHAEL JORDAN.

In 1988 Lee reflected on his Morehouse College experiences with *School Daze*, a musical set in an historically black college. Controversial in its treatment of color and class divisions within the black community, the film pits wealthy, light-skinned "gammas" against working-class, dark-skinned "jigaboos." *School Daze* was Lee's first studio film and after the production costs reached four million dollars, Island Pictures pulled out, but Lee managed to secure additional financing from Columbia Pictures. The film eventually grossed fifteen million dollars.

With *Do The Right Thing* (1989), Lee won an Oscar for best screenplay and established himself as a filmmaker of unique vision and distinctive voice. The film, which Lee wrote and starred in, explores African American cultural life in the flashy and confident visual style that came to distinguish Lee's work. Featuring OSSIE DAVIS, RUBY DEE, Danny Aiello, and John Turturro, *Do The Right Thing*, like *School Daze*, mines divisions and differences within the African American community and beyond. In the film, a Brooklyn pizza shop becomes the nexus of escalating racial tension between Italian Americans and African Americans. The action takes place on the hottest day of the summer and climaxes with a street riot and the killing of a black youth by white policemen. Unlike most American films, *Do The Right Thing* refuses to resolve its plot or its political conflicts. Instead, it ends with contradictory on-screen quotations from Martin Luther King and Malcolm X.

Lee's next film, *Mo' Better Blues* (1990), about a jazz musician inspired by Lee's father, marks the beginning of his collaboration with leading man Denzel Washington, who later starred in *Malcolm X* and *He Got Game*. In Jungle Fever (1991), about the romance between a married, black architect and his Italian American secretary, Lee presents another bold treatment of race and class.

Malcolm X (1992), based on ALEX HALEY's biography and a script begun by JAMES BALDWIN, engendered controversy even before production began, most notably through attacks from AMIRI BARAKA. When it went over budget, Lee turned to black celebrities, including OPRAH WINFREY, MICHAEL JORDAN, and BILL COSBY, for funds. The film reputedly cost thirty-five million dollars, but it became Lee's highest grossing film, earning forty-eight million dollars at the box office. The finished film drew praise from critics and audiences, but controversies remained, including concern over Lee's refusal to implicate LOUIS FARRAKHAN and the Nation of Islam explicitly in Malcolm X's death. Although Denzel Washington earned an Oscar nomination for his performance in the title role, the film received no other recognition from the Academy. However, the film's influence on the public's perception of the leader is unequivocal, as was its effect on the marketplace. Promotional merchandise and tie-ins for the film, including clothing, toys, posters, and books, were marketed by Lee himself.

Lee followed *Malcolm X* with the smaller coming-of-age drama, *Crooklyn* (1994), and the darker *Clockers* (1995). In 1996 Lee released both *Girl 6*, written by SUZAN LORI PARKS, about an unemployed actress who takes a job as a phone sex worker, and *Get on the Bus*, about a busload of black men heading to Washington, D.C., for the 1995 Million Man March. Lee again tapped Denzel Washington for a leading role in his next film, the father-son drama *He Got Game* (1998). *Summer of Sam* (1999), set in the Bronx in the summer of 1977, has a predominantly white cast led by John Leguizamo.

Lee confronts the history of the representation of African Americans head on with the satire *Bamboozled* (2000). The film stars Damon Wayans as an Ivy League-educated black network television writer who unintentionally creates a popular hit with a purposely

offensive modern-day minstrel show featuring black actors wearing blackface. While many viewers and critics complained about the film's descent into melodrama, *Bamboozled* was praised for its fierce exposé of racism in the media. "On a deeper level," wrote Steven Holden in the *New York Times*, "*Bamboozled* addresses the broader issue of minstrelsy and American culture and poses unanswerable questions about black identity, assimilation and the give and take between white and black cultures" (6 Oct. 2000).

In addition to his fiction projects, Lee has directed a number of documentary films. He won an academy award for best documentary with *4 Little Girls* (1997), about the events surrounding the September 1963 bombing of the 16th Street Church in Birmingham, Alabama, that killed four African American girls. In 2000 Lee captured the stand-up work of comedians Steve Harvey, D.L. Hughley, Cedric the Entertainer, and Bernie Mac in the box office hit *The Original Kings of Comedy*, and in 2002 he produced and directed *JIM BROWN All American*. For HBO, Lee directed a television adaptation of John Leguizamo's one-person Broadway show, *Freak*, in 1998. Three years later, he directed a television adaptation of Roger Guenveur Smith's Obie Award–winning off-Broadway solo performance in *The HUEY P. NEWTON Story*. Lee's other television projects include filming the 1998 and 1999 *Pavarotti & Friends* concerts, organized to raise funds for children in Liberia, Guatemala, and Kosovo.

Family loyalty helped launch the acting career of Lee's sister, Joie, and the careers in the technical areas of filmmaking of his brothers, Cinqué and David. Lee commissioned his father to write the original scores for many of his films, including *She's Gotta Have It*, *School Daze*, *Do the Right Thing*, *Mo' Better Blues*, and *Jungle Fever*. Most of Lee's films dramatize family and neighborhood issues. One also finds these themes in *25th Hour* (2002), which explores a young Irish American working-class man's ties to his father and two male friends.

In 1993 Lee married Tanya Lynette Lewis. The couple has two sons, Satchel and Jackson. For over twenty years Spike Lee has maintained his status as one of only a few American filmmakers whose work articulates a personal visual

style and moral vision. He is one of a small number of African American filmmakers from the East Coast who received their film-school training in the 1980s and who produce interesting films about ordinary people, showing us that those lives are not so banal as many Hollywood films would have us believe.

FURTHER READING

Lee, Spike. *By Any Means Necessary: The Trials and Tribulations of the Making of Malcolm X* (1992).
———. *Five for Five: The Films of Spike Lee* (1991).
Lee, Spike, and Lisa Jones. *Spike Lee's Gotta Have It: Inside Guerrilla Filmmaking* (1987).
—MARK A. REID

 LEWIS, CARL
(1 July 1961–), track and field athlete, was born Frederick Carlton Lewis in Birmingham, Alabama, the third of four children of William Lewis and Evelyn Lawler, both of them teachers and coaches who had been outstanding athletes themselves at Tuskegee Institute. Lewis's father was an excellent pass receiver in football and sprinter in track and field, while his mother was a nationally ranked hurdler who was expected to compete in the 1952 Olympic Games in Helsinki before an injury cut short her career.

In 1963 Lewis's parents, after brief stints as teachers in Montgomery, Alabama, following their graduation from Tuskegee Institute, moved the family to Willingboro, New Jersey, to further their professional careers and improve their social and economic positions. It was in Willingboro that Lewis honed his enormous physical talents and first garnered national attention for his exploits in track and field. Training alongside his sister Carol, who became a nationally ranked long jumper, and coached by his parents at their Willingboro Track Club, Lewis evolved into the top-ranked long jumper and one of the best interscholastic sprinters in the country. In 1979 he established a national high school record in the long jump with a leap of 26 feet, 6 inches and captured a bronze medal in the same event at the Pan American Games.

His accomplishments on the track were so extraordinary that Lewis was

Carl Lewis jumping at the 1992 Olympic Games in Barcelona, Spain.
© AFP/CORBIS

offered dozens of athletic scholarships by several prestigious colleges and universities. He ultimately decided to attend the University of Houston so that he could train under the highly respected coach Tom Tellez. Lewis blossomed athletically at Houston, capturing many championships and establishing numerous records in the sprints and long jump using the hitch-kick technique introduced to him by Tellez. In 1980 Lewis won the first of two consecutive indoor and outdoor National Collegiate Athletic Association (NCAA) long-jump championships and was chosen to compete on the 4 × 100 United States Olympic relay team. Unfortunately, Lewis, along with FLO HYMAN and other American athletes, was denied the opportunity to compete in the Moscow Olympics because of President Jimmy Carter's decision to boycott the games as a result of the Soviet Union's invasion of Afghanistan. The following year Lewis broke the world record in the long jump with a leap of 27 feet, 10.5 inches at the Southwest Conference championships, captured NCAA titles in the 100 meters and long jump, and garnered the first of many of his titles in the 100 meters and long jump at the Track Athletic Congress (TAC) championships.

In 1982 Lewis left the University of Houston and joined the famed Santa Monica Track Club. The change in venue only seemed to fuel Lewis's competitive spirit and enhance his talents on the track. He won titles in the 100 meters, long jump, and 4 × 100 meter relay at the 1983 World Championships in Helsinki and in the same year captured the 200 meters in a time of 19.75 seconds and the long jump with a distance of 28 feet, 10.25 inches at the TAC championships. In 1984 Lewis realized lasting fame by winning gold medals in the 100 meters, 200 meters, long jump, and 4 × 100 meter relay at the Los Angeles Olympic Games. His four-gold-medal-winning performance in Los Angeles was particularly significant since it matched the victories of JESSE OWENS in the 1936 Berlin Games and thus helped revitalize interest in the track legend and the political controversy surrounding Adolf Hitler and the Berlin Olympics. Lewis's triumphs recalled the memory of Owens and the symbolic importance of his victories in a country espousing beliefs in Aryan racial superiority.

Lewis spent some time away from the track honing his artistic talents following his great performance in the Los Angeles Olympic Games. In 1986 he studied voice, dance, and acting at Warren Robertson's Theater Workshop in New York. Always interested in the entertainment business, Lewis formed his own band and produced several records that sold particularly well in Sweden and Japan. In 1988, however, Lewis was once again devoting himself full time to track and field. At the Seoul Olympics in 1988, he captured a gold medal in the long jump, a silver medal in the 200 meters, and won the gold medal in the 100 meters after Canadian Ben Johnson was disqualified for drug use. In a sub-par Olympic performance by his standards, Lewis was denied an opportunity to win another medal at Seoul when the United States 4 × 100 meter relay team failed to get to the finals because of a mishandled baton pass in the first qualifying round.

Lewis continued his Olympic success in the 1992 Barcelona Games by winning the gold medal in the long jump with a leap of 28 feet, 5.5 inches and by anchoring the gold-medal-winning 4 × 100 meter relay team. Lewis closed out his Olympic career in grand style at the 1996 Games in Atlanta by winning the gold medal in the long jump. At the athletically old age of thirty-five, he overcame the challenges of arch-rival Mike Powell and a host of much younger jumpers. Lewis thrilled the Atlanta crowd by leaping 27 feet, 10.75 inches to become the only track and field performer in Olympic history besides discuss thrower Al Oerter to garner four gold medals in a single event. This victory also made him only the fourth man in history to win nine gold medals in the Summer Games, the others being the Finnish runner Paavo Nurmi, the American swimmer Mark Spitz, and Ray Ewry, an American who competed in the long jump, the high jump, and the triple jump.

Lewis finally ended his competitive track and field career in 1997. He retired with ten Olympic medals (nine gold, one silver), ten world records, and eight titles in major championships. He also retired as the most decorated man in the history of track and field. He was the recipient of the 1981 Sullivan Award, 1982 Jesse Owens Award, 1982 and 1984 Track and Field News World Athlete of the Year award, 1983 and 1984 Associated Press Male Athlete of the Year awards, and 1999 World Sports Award of the Century for track and field. He was, moreover, a 1985 inductee into the United States Olympic Hall of Fame.

Lewis has enjoyed a busy and largely successful post-athletic career. Although he was arrested for a second time in 2003 for driving drunk and was never able to endear himself to the American public because of his perceived aloofness and arrogance, Lewis has found success in business and devoted a great deal of time to charitable organizations

527

and causes. He is a National Court Appointed Special Advocate Association spokesperson for abused and neglected children. He founded the Carl Lewis Foundation, which supports a number of charities, including the College Fund (formerly the United Negro College Fund), the Wendy Marx Foundation (organ donor awareness), and the Walkathon in Houston. He is also a board member of the "Best Buddies" program, which integrates people with special needs into society.

FURTHER READING

Lewis, Carl, with Jeffrey Marx. *Inside Track: My Professional Life in Amateur Track and Field* (1990).
──────. *One More Victory Lap* (1996).
—DAVID K. WIGGINS

LEWIS, DAVID LEVERING (25 May 1936–),
historian and biographer, was born in Little Rock, Arkansas, to John Henry Lewis and Alice Ernestine Bell, both originally from Atlanta. When John Henry Lewis sacrificed his job as principal of Little Rock's black high school to protest inequities in teachers' salaries based on race, the family moved to Wilberforce, Ohio. Lewis spent ages seven to nine in the community of Wilberforce University, where his father was the dean of theology. Named after the British abolitionist William Wilberforce, the university is the oldest African American institution of higher education. At the age of twelve, David Levering Lewis met W. E. B. DU BOIS, a fraternity brother of his father's and one of his mother's teachers at Atlanta University. The famous scholar and activist asked the young Lewis what he intended to do with his life. In a historical twist, this young boy left speechless by the question would go on to dedicate over fifteen years of his life to writing the biography of the man who asked it.

The Lewis family returned to the South in the late 1940s as John Henry Lewis assumed the presidency of Morris Brown College in Atlanta, one of the five schools of Atlanta University. David Levering Lewis attended Booker T. Washington High School, following the path set by MARTIN LUTHER KING JR. only a few years before. Also

like King, Lewis left the high school early to attend Fisk University's Early Entrants Program. If it seems odd that the biographer of W. E. B. Du Bois attended a high school named for the man's great nemesis, BOOKER T. WASHINGTON, it then seems fitting that Lewis went on to Du Bois's alma mater of Fisk University in Nashville, Tennessee. Named to honor General Clinton B. Fisk of the Tennessee Freedmen's Bureau, Fisk was founded in 1866 with the help of the American Missionary Association to educate newly emancipated African Americans.

After arriving at Fisk in 1952, Lewis quickly became interested in international issues and student leadership. Lewis's time there coincided with that of such prominent faculty members as August Meier and the thriving presidency of CHARLES S. JOHNSON. Lewis graduated Phi Beta Kappa with a bachelor's degree in History and Philosophy in 1956. He briefly attended the University of Michigan Law School but quickly realized that the law was not a good fit for him. He then entered the graduate program in History at Columbia University, where he wrote his master's thesis on John Fiske, the American philosopher and historian, and graduated with a master's degree in History in 1958. He spent the following summer working with Meier researching the history of the African American elite in Atlanta. Their work resulted in an essay that appeared in *The Journal of Negro Education* (Spring 1959). That fall Lewis entered a doctoral program at the London School of Economics to study European history with a specialization in modern France. He wrote his dissertation on French liberal Roman Catholicism and was awarded the doctorate in 1962. In the fall of that same year Lewis reported to Fort Benning, Georgia, for service in the United States Army. He spent the next year in Germany as a psychiatric technician for the military before returning to a career in academia.

Lewis held positions at the University of Ghana, Howard University, and the University of Notre Dame teaching European history. He then accepted a tenured position at Morgan State University in Baltimore and was asked by an editor at Penguin Books to write a biography of MARTIN LUTHER KING JR. Lewis was initially skeptical, given that his area

of academic specialty was European history, but he agreed to the project, and *King: A Critical Biography* was published in 1970. In the same year he accepted an associate professorship at the University of the District of Columbia (UDC) and added courses on the civil rights movement to his repertoire. After ten years at the UDC, he moved on to the University of California, San Diego (UCSD), and taught there for the next five years. While on the faculty at UCSD, Lewis completed *When Harlem Was in Vogue* (1981), a well-received account of the Harlem Renaissance that traces the explosion of black cultural production during this period. In 1968 Rutgers University had created an endowed professorship in memory of Martin Luther King Jr., and Lewis accepted the chair in 1985. Two years later he published *The Race to Fashoda: European Colonialism and African Resistance in the Scramble for Africa*.

In the late 1980s, Lewis continued to work on the biography of Du Bois he had begun a decade earlier with the help of Guggenheim and Woodrow Wilson International Center fellowships. In addition to interviewing hundreds of people, Lewis traveled to three continents and over twenty archives conducting research on Du Bois. Lewis also drew on over 115,000 pieces of correspondence that the University of Massachusetts at Amherst had acquired from Shirley Graham-Du Bois, W. E. B. Du Bois's wife, to which previous biographers had not had access. In 1993 Lewis completed the first volume of the biography, entitled *W. E. B. Du Bois: Biography of a Race, 1868–1919*, which won him the Pulitzer Prize, the Parkman Prize in History, and the Bancroft Prize in American History and Diplomacy. The book traces the life of Du Bois from his childhood in Great Barrington, Massachusetts, to his experiences at Fisk and Harvard; his seminal work, *The Souls of Black Folk*; and his leadership of the National Association for the Advancement of Colored People and the organization's publication, *The Crisis*. When the second volume, *W. E. B. Du Bois: The Fight for Equality and the American Century, 1919–1963*, was published in 2000, Lewis became the first author to win two Pulitzer Prizes in Biography for back-to-back volumes. The second installment of the biography considers Du Bois's conflict-laden relationships with other leaders of the time, most notably Booker T. Washington and MARCUS GARVEY, work with the Pan-African movement, Du Bois's time in Nazi Germany, and his death in Ghana. As Lewis has noted in interviews, he "didn't want to defend Du Bois," but to "present a conflicted figure whose attempt to achieve his ideals caused him to contradict many of them" (*Rutgers Focus*, Feb. 2001). Lewis has also edited Du Bois's study, *Black Reconstruction*, an anthology entitled *The W. E. B. Du Bois Reader*, and a collection of Du Bois's correspondence. He also wrote the introduction to the one hundredth anniversary edition of Du Bois's classic, *The Souls of Black Folk*.

A recipient of the coveted MacArthur Fellowship in 1999, Lewis has written on such diverse topics as the history of the District of Columbia (*District of Columbia: A Bicentennial History*, 1976), housing in Great Britain (*New Housing in Great Britain*, 1960, coauthored with Hansmartin Bruckmann), a cache of photographs selected by Du Bois at the turn of the twentieth century (*A Small Nation of People: W. E. B. Du Bois and African American Portraits of Progress*, 2003, coauthored with Deborah Willis), and the Dreyfus affair (*Prisoners of Honor: The Dreyfus Affair*, 1994). He has also edited anthologies regarding the civil rights movement (*The Civil Rights Movement in America: Essays*, 1986) and the Harlem Renaissance (*Portable Harlem Renaissance Reader*, 1994, and *Harlem Renaissance: Art of Black America*, 1994, coedited with David Driskell). He appears in "America 1900," part of the Public Broadcasting Service's documentary film series *American Experience*, in which he discusses African American life at the turn of the century. He was a scholar in residence at New York University in 2000, and he was a visiting scholar at Harvard University in 2001. In 2003 he joined the faculty at New York University as a university professor and professor of history. He is also a commissioner of the National Portrait Gallery.

David Levering Lewis has set the bar for highly readable, accessible, thorough, and layered renderings of periods in American history such as the civil rights movement and the Harlem Renaissance,

while his ability to create biographies capturing the complexities of black leaders' lives has earned him deserved acclaim. The recipient of numerous awards and honorary degrees, Lewis has worked for decades to preserve the history of African Americans and their leaders, particularly civil rights icons W. E. B. Du Bois and Martin Luther King Jr.

FURTHER READING

Lewis, David Levering. "Ghana, 1963: A Memoir," *The American Scholar* (Winter 1999).
———. "From Eurocentrism to Polycentrism" in *Historians and Race: Autobiography and the Writing of History*, ed. Paul Cimbala and Robert F. Himmelberg (1996).
—JENNIFER WOOD

 LEWIS, EDMONIA
(c. 1844–after 1909), sculptor, was born to an African American father and a mother of African American and Mississauga descent, whose names are not known. The Mississauga, a Chippewa (Ojibway in Canada) band, lived in southern Ontario. Information about Lewis's early life remains inconsistent and unverified. She was probably born in 1844 or 1845, most likely near Albany, New York. Orphaned by age nine, Lewis and her older brother, Samuel, were taken in by their maternal aunts, Mississaugas living near Niagara Falls. Lewis joined the tribe in hunting and fishing along Lake Ontario and the Niagara River and in making and selling moccasins, baskets, and other souvenirs. Although she later gave her Mississauga name as "Wildfire," Lewis's translation from the Chippewa may have been intended to authenticate her Indian background and appeal to whites. She remained with the Mississauga until age twelve, when Samuel, using earnings amassed during the gold rush in California, arranged for her schooling at New York Central College, an abolitionist school in McGrawville, New York.

In 1859 Lewis entered the Ladies Preparatory program at Oberlin College. There she adopted the name Mary Edmonia, using Mary with friends and faculty and Edmonia on her drawings.

Forever Free (1867). Howard University Gallery of Art

Lewis proceeded amiably until the winter of 1862, when two of her white housemates accused her of poisoning them with cantharides, or "Spanish fly." Years of antiblack and anti-Oberlin feelings came to a head, and Lewis was badly beaten by a mob and left for dead. JOHN MERCER LANGSTON defended her at a two-day trial, securing a dismissal on the basis of insufficient evidence. The following year, when she was again falsely accused—this time of stealing art supplies—she was unofficially but summarily expelled.

Undeterred by her lack of training, Lewis moved to Boston in 1863 with the intention of becoming an artist. Through supporters at Oberlin, she met William Lloyd Garrison and the portrait sculptor Edward Brackett. With the encouragement of Brackett, Lydia Maria Child, and other abolitionists, she learned the basics of clay sculpting. Her first sculptures were clay and plaster portrait medallions and portrait busts of antislavery leaders and Civil War heroes. In 1864 she sold over one hundred reproductions of her bust of Robert Gould Shaw, the Boston Brahmin who led and died with the black soldiers of the Fifty-fourth Massachusetts Volunteer Regiment, which included twenty-one men from Oberlin, some of whom Lewis knew. With enough money to travel abroad, in 1865 she sailed for Florence, Italy, where she was assisted by the world-renowned sculptor Hiram Powers. Six months later she settled in Rome, renting a studio once occupied by the neoclassicist Antonio Canova, arguably the greatest sculptor of his time.

Rome in 1866 was home to a vibrant community of American expatriate artists that included Nathaniel Hawthorne, Henry James, and the sculptor William Wetmore Story. Lewis was immediately taken under the wing of the sculptor Harriet Hosmer and her friend the actress Charlotte Cushman, principal members of the social set that Henry James called "that strange sisterhood of American 'lady sculptors'" (James, *William Wetmore Story and His Friends*, 1903, 257). In this group, which included Cushman's companion, Emma Stebbins; Anne Whitney; Louisa Lander; and Margaret Foley, Lewis saw rare examples of financially, sexually, and artistically independent women. Although she caused quite a sensation at Cushman's trendy soirees and benefited from her new friends' generosity, Lewis always remained on the perimeter, considered a bit of a novelty.

Resourceful and fiercely independent, Lewis taught herself to carve marble and established herself as a neoclassical sculptor. She eschewed the custom of employing assistants, fearing that the veracity of her work would be attacked, as had been the case with other black and women artists, including Hosmer and Whitney. Instead, Lewis, who was only four feet tall, undertook by herself what was often very physical work. In the 1860s and 1870s her studio, listed in all the fashionable guidebooks, was a frequent stop for American tourists. She supported herself primarily through commissions for small terra-cotta or marble portrait busts and marble copies of Classical and Renaissance masterworks. Over the years her busts of Abraham Lincoln, Ulysses S. Grant, Henry Wadsworth Longfellow, Senator Charles Sumner, the poet Anna Quincy Waterston, and the abolitionist Maria Weston Chapman were purchased by American collectors.

Catering to collectors' tastes, she also produced "conceits" or "fancy pieces" (sculptures using children to convey sentimental themes), of which three survive: *Poor Cupid* (1873, National Museum of American Art [NMAA]), *Asleep* (1871), and *Awake* (1872) (both in the San Jose Public Library). After her 1868 conversion to Catholicism, Lewis received several major commissions for religious works, none of which survive.

Despite her faithfulness to the formal and thematic conventions of neoclassicism, Lewis rendered unique treatments of African American and American Indian themes and figures. Her first large-scale marble sculpture, *The Freed Woman and Her Child* (1866, location unknown), was the first by an African American sculptor to depict this subject. *Forever Free* (1867, Howard University), showing a man and woman casting off the shackles of enslavement, takes its name from a line in the Emancipation Proclamation: "All persons held as slaves shall be then, thenceforward, and forever free." Like *The Freed Woman*, the female figure in *Forever Free* strongly evokes the well-known abolitionist emblem engraved by PATRICK HENRY REASON in 1835, *Am I Not a Woman and a Sister?*, which shows an African American woman on bended knee, stripped to the waist, her head tilted toward the sky, and her clasped hands raised, revealing heavy chains attached at her wrists. While Lewis's figure adopts the pose and gesture of the emblem, her freed slave, unchained and fully clothed, is no longer identifiable as African American by color or physiognomy. Lewis's alterations, made according to the stylistic dictates of the period, simultaneously elide the issue of race and restore the dignity and humanity denied African Americans by slavery.

Lewis made several versions of the biblical figure Hagar, only one of which survives, *Hagar* (1868, NMAA). The Egyptian outcast, though used by other nineteenth-century artists as a symbol of slavery, had particular meaning for Lewis, herself the victim of racial violence and banishment. Reflecting on her sculpture in 1871, she told a journalist, "I have a strong sympathy for all women who have struggled and suffered." Inspired by Longfellow's popular poem "Song of Hiawatha," Lewis produced a number of marble

works featuring American Indians. These works include busts of *Minnehaha* and *Hiawatha* (both 1868, Newark Museum), *The Marriage of Hiawatha* (1867, Walter Evans Collection), and *Old Arrow Maker*, also known as *The Wooing of Hiawatha* (three versions survive, made between 1866 and 1872). Lewis broke from strict neoclassical aesthetics by giving the arrow maker idealized but recognizable American Indian features. His daughter, however, appears white, her ethnicity represented only by posture, gesture, and costume. Lewis's depictions of American Indians as proud, dignified, and peaceful countered prevailing images of Indians (and blacks) as half-naked, eroticized savages.

Lewis returned to the United States on several occasions to exhibit and sell her work. Her 1873 cross-country trip terminating in San Francisco, certainly an unusual journey for an unaccompanied black woman, made her one of the first sculptors to exhibit in California. She reached the pinnacle of her career three years later at the 1876 Philadelphia Centennial Exposition with the exhibition of *Death of Cleopatra*, a subject popular with nineteenth-century artists and abolitionists. Lewis's enthroned life-size Egyptian queen in the throes of death directly challenged William Wetmore Story's more traditional representation of the same subject also on view at the exposition. *Cleopatra* caused a commotion, provoking strong responses from audiences and critics, including William J. Clark Jr., who wrote in 1878, "The effects of death are represented with such skill as to be absolutely repellant. Apart from all questions of taste, however, the striking qualities of the work are undeniable, and it could only have been produced by a sculptor of genuine endowments" (*Great American Sculptures*). *Death of Cleopatra*, assumed lost until it was rediscovered in 1985, is now on view at the National Museum of American Art.

Ironically, the Centennial Exposition marked the beginning of the end for neoclassical sculpture and, with it, the demand for Lewis's work. By the 1880s romanticism, exemplified by the work of Auguste Rodin, had challenged the stiffness of neoclassical sculpture, bronze had overtaken marble as the fashionable medium, and Paris had become the center of the art world. Lewis, however, remained in Rome, and by 1900 she was all but forgotten. FREDERICK DOUGLASS provided the last substantive account of Lewis's activities, which included, according to his diary, hosting Douglass and his new wife in January 1887. Except for a brief mention in an American Catholic magazine in 1909, no further record of Lewis survives. The date and place of her death remain unknown.

A generation older than the sculptors META WARRICK FULLER and May Howard Jackson and two generations older than Nancy Prophet, AUGUSTA SAVAGE, and RICHMOND BARTHÉ, Lewis was the first African American sculptor to gain an international reputation. Lewis, who never married, was an independent woman and a skilled survivor, succeeding against unprecedented odds. In all, she created about sixty unique pieces, less than half of which have been located. Remarkably, Lewis succeeded amidst a social milieu deeply stratified according to race, gender, and class and within an artistic style exclusively devoted to ideas of Western beauty and history, even while she herself did not conform to any of these standards.

FURTHER READING

BEARDEN, ROMARE, and Harry Henderson. *A History of African American Artists: From 1792 to the Present* (1993).

Hartigan, Lynda Roscoe, and the National Museum of American Art. *Sharing Traditions: Five Black Artists in Nineteenth-Century America* (1985).

Wolfe, Rinna. *Edmonia Lewis: Wildfire in Marble* (1998).

—LISA E. RIVO

LEWIS, JOHN

(21 February 1940–), civil rights leader and member of Congress, was born John Robert Lewis near Troy, Alabama, the third of seven children. Lewis's father, Eddie, was a sharecropper and small farmer, and his mother, Willie Mae, occasionally did laundry. Both of his parents were deeply religious, which may have helped shape Lewis's lifelong commitment to Christianity. As a young man, Lewis recalls, he heard MARTIN LUTHER KING JR. preach on the radio and was inspired to make the ministry his vocation. Starting by preaching in

John Lewis, with James Zwerg, after they were beaten in Montgomery, Alabama, on one of the first Freedom Rides, 1961. © Bettmann/CORBIS

the woods near his home, eventually he was allowed to preach at local churches. In 1957 he became the first of his family to graduate from high school. After graduating, Lewis enrolled in the American Baptist Theological Seminary in Nashville, Tennessee.

In 1958, at the age of eighteen, he met Dr. King, and his life was changed forever: he decided to devote it to the struggle for civil rights. Two months before the famous 1960 sit-ins in Greensboro, North Carolina, Lewis led sit-ins in Nashville. Although he was doused with cleansing powder and abused in other ways, the sit-ins eventually resulted in the desegregation of Nashville lunch counters. After graduating from seminary in 1961, Lewis enrolled at Fisk University, planning to study religion and philosophy. In 1963, however, he dropped out of college to devote his time to work in the civil rights movement. (In 1967 he returned to Fisk to earn a BA.) In 1968 Lewis married Lillian Miles; they adopted a son, John Miles.

In the spring of 1960 the Student Nonviolent Coordinating Committee (SNCC) was formed, with several Nashville students in leadership positions, notably Marion Barry, Diane Nash, and James Lawson. By 1961, two northerners, BOB MOSES and JAMES FORMAN, had also emerged as prominent SNCC activists. This interracial organization of black and

white college students was created to coordinate student participation in the civil rights movement. Between 1961 and 1965 SNCC played a pivotal role in that movement, working on voter registration campaigns in the most dangerous areas of the rural south. In a sense, SNCC made up the movement's frontline troops, and the young women and men in the organization exhibited extraordinary courage in facing danger and death. But of all the brave people in SNCC, perhaps none exhibited greater courage than Lewis. As Worth Long, a colleague in SNCC, said, "John was the most courageous person that I ever worked with in the movement.... John would not just follow you into the lion's den, he would lead you into it" (Carson, 203). In 1961 Lewis was beaten unconscious in Montgomery, Alabama, in one of the first Freedom Rides to challenge segregated interstate bus travel, and in 1965 he suffered a similar fate as he helped lead a march from Selma to Montgomery in the movement's last great protest. Arrested more then forty times, Lewis invariably responded peacefully and with expressions of Christian faith and love. Many years later, reflecting on Lewis's work in the movement, *Time* referred to him as a "living saint" (Barone, 299).

In 1963 Lewis was selected SNCC's second chair, succeeding Marion Barry. (Barry later became mayor of

Washington, D.C.) As head of SNCC, Lewis was part of the so-called Big Six civil rights leadership group. This informal group attempted to develop and coordinate movement strategy. In addition to Lewis, the group comprised Martin Luther King of the Southern Christian Leadership Conference, ROY WILKINS of the NAACP, WHITNEY YOUNG of the Urban League, JAMES FARMER of the Congress of Racial Equality, and DOROTHY HEIGHT of the National Council of Negro Women. At the 1963 March on Washington, Lewis, in his capacity as SNCC chair, was among the persons designated to give one of the major speeches. The other leaders thought his prepared text too radical, and he was asked to tone it down. Lewis initially refused, but after much cajoling he agreed to the rewriting of the speech (removing some of the language considered too radical or revolutionary). Nevertheless, the speech as delivered was the most militant of the day, reflecting the fact that SNCC was the most self-consciously radical of the major civil rights organizations.

Ironically, SNCC's evolving militancy and radicalism would lead to Lewis's ouster as SNCC chairman. In 1966 SNCC embraced the philosophy of black power. This philosophy, influenced by the ideas of MALCOLM X, called on blacks to form racially separate or independent organizations (which for SNCC meant the ouster of its white members) and to abandon the philosophy of nonviolence. Having embraced this black power philosophy, many in SNCC thought that Lewis was unsuited to lead the group in this new direction. In the initial balloting Lewis was easily reelected, but then, in a move that probably violated SNCC rules, the balloting was reopened, and STOKELY CARMICHAEL defeated Lewis. Because of his unwavering commitment to interracialism and nonviolence, Lewis was unsuited to lead SNCC in its new direction, but he was disappointed and angry about the manner in which his colleagues removed him.

After leaving SNCC, Lewis worked with several organizations involved with community organizing and civil rights. From 1970 to 1976 he was executive director of the Atlanta-based Voter Education Project (VEP). The VEP engaged in voter registration and education, a task that represented a blending of Lewis's past civil rights activism with his future political activism. In 1976, when President Jimmy Carter appointed Congressman ANDREW YOUNG of Atlanta as ambassador to the United Nations, Lewis sought to succeed him in the House of Representatives. However, he was defeated rather easily by Wyche Fowler, the white president of Atlanta's city council, although the district had a 65 percent black majority. President Carter then appointed Lewis associate director of ACTION, the umbrella agency with responsibilities for the Peace Corps and domestic volunteer service agencies. When Carter was defeated for reelection, Lewis returned to Atlanta, where in 1981 he was elected to the city council. In 1986 he was elected to the U.S. Congress.

Fowler retired from the House of Representatives in 1986 in order to run, successfully, for the U.S. Senate. Seven candidates sought to succeed him, including Lewis and JULIAN BOND, a state senator, a former SNCC worker, and a historically important figure in the civil rights movement. In the initial primary election Bond led Lewis 47 to 35 percent. But in the runoff Lewis defeated Bond 52 to 48 percent. Lewis won largely on the basis of the 90 percent support he received from the district's white voters, while Bond carried the black vote 60 to 40 percent. Since his election, Lewis, like most incumbents, has faced little or no opposition and has easily been reelected.

In some ways, it was fitting that Lewis won through the support of a multiracial coalition, given his longtime commitment to forming interracial alliances. Because of his status as a genuine American hero, Lewis quickly earned the respect and admiration of his colleagues in the House of Representatives, black and white, liberal and conservative, and Democrats and Republicans. This support facilitated his efforts to build multiracial coalitions.

Lewis was initially assigned to two relatively minor committees, but in 1993 he was appointed to the Committee on Ways and Means. The Ways and Means Committee is the oldest and most prestigious and powerful in the House.

Lewis's appointment to this powerful committee (with jurisdiction over taxes, international trade, Social Security, Medicare and Medicaid, and welfare programs) after a relatively short tenure is indicative of the esteem in which he is held by his Democratic Party colleagues in the House. Further evidence of his stature among his colleagues is his selection as one of four Democratic chief deputy whips. While Lewis has not authored major legislation, he is a frequent and passionate participant in House debates on foreign and domestic issues. He has devoted much of his time to persuading Congress to recognize the contributions of African Americans and the civil rights movement to U.S. history. His efforts include working toward the establishment of a memorial to Dr. King and a national museum of African American history on the Washington Mall and plans to make the route of the 1965 march from Selma to Montgomery a national trail. In 1999 he authored, with Michael D'Orso, *Walking with the Wind: A Memoir of the Movement.*

FURTHER READING

Barone, Michael, and Grant Ujifusa. *The Almanac of American Politics, 1988* (1988).

Carson, Clayborne. *In Struggle: SNCC and the Black Awakening of the 1960s* (1981).

Clay, Bill. *Just Permanent Interests: Black Americans in Congress, 1870–1991* (1992).

Swain, Carol. *Black Faces, Black Interests: The Representation of African Americans in Congress* (1993).

—ROBERT C. SMITH

LEWIS, OLIVER

(c. 1863–?), jockey, was born the son of a slave woman some time during the period shortly before the Emancipation Proclamation. There is little known today about the early years of Lewis, who grew up to become one of the most renowned African American jockeys in horse racing history. Using other accounts and histories from the period, however, speculation about how Lewis came to be such an adept horseman is possible.

After the Civil War, sharecropping replaced slavery as a means for plantation owners to maintain control over their newly liberated charges. Some of these sharecroppers were used as stable hands and exercise boys for the plantation owners' racehorses. The most proficient of these boys (for most of them were barely fourteen or fifteen) were chosen as jockeys, a highly desirable position. Even during slavery times, the title of "jockey" allowed an African American many freedoms that were refused his fellows. African American jockeys both during and after the Civil War were allowed free will of travel, as well as a sense of dignity and aristocracy that was denied most other blacks of the time.

Therefore, it is not difficult to imagine that a woman with a young male child would have attempted to make her son as appealing and available as possible to the wealthy racehorse owners. Oftentimes, a woman employed by one of these men would bring her son along with her to work. During the course of the mother's workday, the boy would occupy himself, playing in the vicinity of the manor house where his mother performed her duties. The plantation owner might take notice of a particularly agile or strong individual. From there, the boy went to live in the owner's stable, sleeping with the horses, caring for them, and developing instincts about the animals that most people today can barely comprehend. By the age of ten or eleven years old, these boys were expert horsemen and spent their days exercising and training the powerful, high-strung racehorses.

Given such circumstances, it is not difficult to understand why these young men were natural choices as jockeys. However, even among these competent horsemen, there were standouts. One such standout was Oliver Lewis. Lewis rode for the McGrathiana stud farm, which was owned by H. Price McGrath. Also employed by McGrath was a trainer named Ansel Williamson. Williamson, born into slavery in Virginia in 1806, was eventually bought and freed by a prominent horse breeder, Robert A. Alexander. Williamson worked for Alexander, buying and training racehorses until Alexander's death in 1867. He then went on to work at McGrathiana, training many famous racehorses as well as developing the young exercise boys into skilled jockeys.

Lewis flourished under Williamson's tutelage.

In addition to working for McGrath, Lewis was also employed as a utility rider at inaugural events for the Louisville Jockey Club. On 17 May 1875 Lewis won three races. One of these was the most significant race of his life. Ironically, it was also the race that he was not supposed to win.

H. Price McGrath had two horses entered in the inaugural running of the Kentucky Derby. The horse upon which his optimism rested was a large bay named Chesapeake. His other horse was a smaller chestnut named Aristides. McGrath made the decision that Aristides would be his "rabbit." He would use the speedy horse to tire the others early in the race, leaving room for the late-closing Chesapeake to take the lead near the end. Trainer Ansel Williamson suggested that Lewis should ride Aristides, since he was one of the few jockeys able to hold back the fiery red horse.

The parade to the post, which began the race, found Lewis as one of thirteen African American jockeys in a field of fifteen horses. When the gates opened, beginning the race, McGrath's favorite, Chesapeake, got off to a slow start. As the race progressed, Lewis had all that he could handle trying to hold back the determined Aristides. Meanwhile, Chesapeake never seemed to recover from his poor start. Owner McGrath, seeing the prospect of Chesapeake's victory fading, ordered wildly from the sidelines for Lewis and Aristides to "Go on!" (Saunders and Saunders, 14). This command was all the impetus that horse and rider needed. Lewis gave Aristides free rein, and the pair won the derby, traveling the mile-and-a-half distance in a record time of two minutes, thirty-seven-and-three-quarters seconds.

Although McGrath was given the credit for the horse's win, Lewis was undaunted by this lack of recognition and continued racing. Just a month after his derby win, Lewis was again set up on Aristides as the "rabbit." (It appears that, in most of his races for McGrath, Lewis was used as the "rabbit" rider). This time, Lewis and Aristides were to race in the famed Belmont Stakes, one of the jewels in racing's celebrated Triple Crown. As the race commenced,

Lewis held his mount back, obeying the explicit orders of the horse's owner. The horse strained to have his head, and the crowd shouted their disapproval, but Lewis kept the horse from taking the lead. Later, when Aristides won the Jerome Stakes and the Withers Stakes in New York, a white jockey, Bobby Swim, not Lewis, rode the tenacious little horse to victory. McGrath, it is reported, favored Swim because of his greater experience.

The remainder of Lewis's career as a jockey is largely unknown. Records indicate, however, that after his racing career, he went on to work as a bookkeeper and later as a racehorse trainer in Lexington, Kentucky. In 1907 a newspaper reporter spotted Lewis at Churchill Downs, the site of the Kentucky Derby. An article in the following day's newspaper related Lewis's appearance as something quite unusual. Interestingly, no one is sure how often Lewis returned to the derby. Perhaps he was a regular attendant, making his visits clandestinely, or maybe he intentionally avoided the site of his most famous race.

After Lewis's derby, fifteen of the twenty-eight following derbies were won by African American jockeys, with some of them, such as James Winkfield and ISAAC MURPHY, winning more than once. However, African Americans were slowly being pushed out of the sport. Other jockeys, resentful of their success, frequently resorted to dangerous and illegal practices to ensure that black jockeys no longer won races. African American jockeys were cut off, blocked in, jostled, and knocked off their horses to ensure their defeat. Consequently, these actions made horse owners reluctant to hire black jockeys. Eventually, black jockeys all but disappeared from the horseracing world. However, their legacy still remains.

FURTHER READING

Hotaling, Edward. *The Great Black Jockeys: The Lives and Times of the Men Who Dominated America's First National Sport* (1999).

Saunders, James Robert, and Monica Renae Saunders. *Black Winning Jockeys in the Kentucky Derby* (2003).

—MONICA R. SAUNDERS

LIELE, GEORGE (c. 1751–1828), pioneering Baptist clergyman and African American émigré to Jamaica, said of his slave origins, "I was born in Virginia, my father's name was Liele, and my mother's name Nancy; I cannot ascertain much of them, as I went to several parts of America when young, and at length resided in New Georgia" (*Baptist Annual Register*, ed. John Rippon [1793], 332). Liele's master Henry Sharp took him to Burke County, Georgia, as a young man. Liele wrote that he "had a natural fear of God" from his youth. He attended a local Baptist church, was baptized by Matthew Moore, a deacon in the Buckhead Creek Baptist Church about 1772, and was given the opportunity to travel, preaching to both whites and blacks. Liele preached as a probationer for about three years at Bruton Land, Georgia, and at Yamacraw, about a half mile from Savannah. The favorable response to Liele's "ministerial gifts" caused Sharp, who was a Baptist deacon, to free him. Liele remained with Sharp's family until Sharp's death as a Tory officer during the revolutionary war when the British occupied Savannah.

Upset over his status as a free man, some of Sharp's heirs had Liele imprisoned. Liele produced his manumission papers and with the aid of a British colonel named Kirkland resumed his public activities. He gathered a small congregation that included African Americans who had come to Savannah on the promise by the British of their freedom. One of Liele's converts was ANDREW BRYAN, who was later responsible for the development of African American Baptist congregations in Savannah. DAVID GEORGE, the pioneering organizer of black Baptist congregations in Nova Scotia and Sierra Leone, also was one of Liele's converts. Despite increasing anxiety over escalating American-British hostilities, Liele continued to hold worship services.

When the British evacuated Savannah in 1782, Liele went as an indentured servant with Kirkland to Kingston, Jamaica. After working two years to satisfy his indebtedness to Kirkland, Liele received a certificate of freedom, and about 1784 he began to preach in a small house in Kingston to what he called a "good smart congregation." It was organized with four other blacks who had come from America. The congregation eventually purchased property in the east end of Kingston and constructed a brick meetinghouse. Liele reported that raising money to pay for the new building was difficult because his congregation was composed mostly of slaves whose masters allowed "but three or four bits per week" out of which to pay for their food. The free people who belonged to Liele's church were generally poor.

Despite initial opposition from some whites, Liele's congregation grew to about 350 members by 1790. It included a few whites. Liele accepted Methodists after they had been baptized by immersion, but in a pragmatic move he did not receive slaves as members without, as he wrote, "a few lines from their owners of their good behavior toward them and religion." Liele assisted in the organization of other congregations on the island and promoted free schools for slaves as well as free black Jamaicans. On his ministerial activities Liele wrote in the early 1790s, "I have deacons and elders, a few; and teachers of small congregations in the town and country, where convenience suits them to come together; and I am pastor. I preach twice on the Lord's Day, in the forenoon and afternoon, and twice in the week, and have not been absent six Sabbath days since I formed the church in this country. I receive nothing for my services; I preach, baptize, administer the Lord's Supper, and travel from one place to another to publish the gospel and settle church affairs, all freely." By 1797 Liele had reason to be more pessimistic. Originally charged with "seditious preaching" because he was the leader of so many slaves, he was thrown into prison where he remained for three years, five months, and ten days. The charge of seditious preaching was dismissed, but his inability to satisfy debts incurred in the building of his church kept him in prison. During Liele's imprisonment his eldest son conducted preaching services.

When Liele was about forty years old he reported that he had three sons and one daughter. His four children ranged in age from nineteen to eleven. His wife, whose name is unknown, had been baptized with him in Savannah. Liele worked as a farmer and teamster besides conducting regular worship services and conducting church business. George Liele has the distinction of being the first regularly ordained African American Baptist minister in America. He is also noteworthy as the founder of the first Baptist church in Jamaica. Liele reported in 1790, "There is no Baptist church in this country but ours." An article sent to British Baptists in 1796 said of Jamaican Baptists whom Liele led: "They preach every Lord's day from 10 to 12 o'clock in the morning, and from 4 to 6 in the evening; and on Tuesday and Thursday evening, from seven to eight. They administer the Lord's supper every month, and baptism once in three months. The members are divided into smaller classes which meet separately every Monday evening, to be examined respecting their daily walk and conversation." Details regarding the last few decades prior to Liele's death in Jamaica are not known.

Liele's pioneering work in establishing the Baptist church in Jamaica set the foundation for a denominational tradition that continued until the late twentieth century. Apart from being the spiritual father of the Jamaican black Baptist churches, he was the first missionary from any African American church body to the island and may well have been the first African American to be ordained a Baptist preacher. Although nothing is known of his political and social views, he seems to have considered his primary work that of preaching the Christian Gospel and caring for the spiritual welfare of his members.

FURTHER READING

Davis, John W. "George Liele and Andrew Bryan, Pioneer Negro Baptist Preachers," *Journal of Negro History* 3 (Apr. 1918): 119–27.
"Letters Showing the Rise and Progress of the Early Negro Churches of Georgia and the West Indies," *Journal of Negro History* 1 (Jan. 1916): 69–92.
Rusling, G. W. "A Note on Early Negro Baptist History," *Foundations* 11 (Oct.–Dec. 1968): 362–68.

—MILTON C. SERNETT

LISTON, SONNY

(8 May 1932–30 Dec. 1970), world champion boxer, was born Charles Liston in rural St. Francis County, Arkansas, to the tenant farmers Helen Baskin and Tobe Liston. Like much in Liston's story, the precise date of his birth and the exact number of his siblings are unknown. He was most likely born between 1927 and 1932, and was probably the tenth of eleven children born to Helen Baskin, and the twenty-fourth of twenty-five children born to Tobe Liston. His nickname, "Sonny," may have been granted in childhood, though most people claimed that it was given to him in prison. Charles received no formal schooling. From an early age, he labored on the tenant farm with his father, who believed that if a child was big enough to sit at the dinner table, he was big enough to chop cotton. Sonny rarely spoke of his childhood, except to say, "The only thing my old man ever gave me was a beating" (Tosches, 34). Liston's autopsy would later reveal many whipping welts and the truth of that statement.

In 1946 he moved to St. Louis, Missouri, where his mother had found employment a year earlier. Broad-shouldered, strong, and powerful, Liston occasionally found work as a laborer but more often found himself in trouble for a series of thefts and muggings. In 1950 he was sentenced to five years in the Missouri State Penitentiary on charges of first-degree robbery and larceny. In prison the Catholic chaplain encouraged Liston to box. Sonny weighed two hundred pounds, stood six feet, one inch tall, and already had a reputation for brawling. Within his first month of training, no other prisoner would step into the ring with him—at least not alone. What Liston lacked in finesse, he more than made up for with a powerful left hand; at first he barely used his right, since he did not need it. His only problem was that his fists—fifteen inches in girth—were too large for standard boxing gloves. Most of Sonny's contemporaries in prison recalled that he was amiable and quiet; Liston, who had experienced far harsher treatment in the Arkansas cotton fields and on the

A ticket for the 1964 bout between Liston and Cassius Clay (MUHAMMAD ALI). Library of Congress

streets of St. Louis, later said that he did not mind his time in jail.

Liston's potential as a heavyweight contender ensured his early release and the keen attention of underworld crime figures. In 1952 he was paroled, thanks to the efforts of a Catholic priest and Frank Mitchell, the publisher of the *St. Louis Argus*, a black newspaper. Mitchell had close ties to John Vitale, the leading mobster in St. Louis, who hired Liston to work at the Union Electric plant as a "head breaker," beating or intimidating workers who, in the view of Vitale and the Teamster leadership, had stepped out of line. Mitchell also hired a former sparring partner of the heavyweight champion JOE LOUIS to work on Liston's technical deficiencies as a boxer. Over the next year Liston defeated a string of amateur opponents, among them Ed Sanders, the 1952 Olympic heavyweight champion. He turned professional in 1953 and won fourteen of his first fifteen fights, seven of them by knockouts.

Liston's personal life enjoyed an all too rare period of happiness in 1956, when he met Geraldine Chambers, who had been standing in a downpour waiting for a bus. On seeing her, he immediately reversed his car, jumped out, picked her up, and placed her on the front seat. Chambers did not appear to mind the boxer's presumptuous chivalry, and she married him several months later, shortly before he was sentenced to nine months in the St. Louis workhouse for assaulting a police officer.

In 1958 Liston moved to Philadelphia, where he was managed by Frankie Carbo, the most powerful underworld figure in boxing. Four years later, having won twenty consecutive fights, Sonny earned the right to challenge the world heavyweight champion Floyd Patterson.

Many in the African American community were wary of Liston replacing Patterson as heavyweight champion. Civil rights leaders viewed the graceful, contemplative Patterson as an ideal spokesman for the race, a man who, like Liston, had grown up in poverty, but one who used his fists only in the ring. Even President John F. Kennedy urged Patterson to fight Liston, telling the champion in the Oval Office, "You've *got* to beat this guy" (Remnick, 14). Yet for all of the media efforts to portray the fight as a battle between good and evil, it was, in fact, a fight between two boxers. Liston was hungrier and knocked Patterson out in the first round with a savage left hook that caught the champion squarely on the jaw. Liston defeated Patterson, again with a first-round knockout, in a July 1963 rematch in Las Vegas.

Although he was the undisputed world champion, Liston did not receive the adulation that other heavyweights had enjoyed. There was no victory parade in Philadelphia, though he did win an audience with Vice President Lyndon Johnson, himself a rough-hewn outsider in Kennedy's Camelot. Foreign boxing fans were more appreciative of Liston and he of them. On a tour of Britain he won standing ovations in several cities and strode through the streets of Glasgow wearing a kilt and playing the bagpipes. Told by Scots reporters that he was a warmer man than they had expected, Liston replied, "I am warm here because I am among warm people.... When I return to the United States, I will be cold again, for the people there...have treated me badly" (Tosches, 195).

Few expected Liston to lose the heavyweight crown to his young challenger, Cassius Clay, in 1964. Most experts viewed Clay's promise to deliver a "total eclipse of the Sonny" as entertaining bombast at best, but the young fighter proved much fitter and faster than they expected. Clay danced and ducked Liston's lethal jabs, frustrating the champion, cutting his eye, and then landing punch after punch of his own. At the start of the seventh round, Liston refused to leave his stool, claiming that he had an injured left shoulder. Many, including the U.S. Senate, suspected a fix, because victory for Clay would bring a profitable rematch for Liston's underworld backers. The Senate's investigation did not find evidence of collusion, though, and the rematch, in Lewiston, Maine, in May 1965 also resulted in a victory—a first-round knockout—for Clay, who had by then converted to Islam and adopted the name MUHAMMAD ALI. Again, commentators were incredulous that a single blow could knock out Liston. Slow-motion replays revealed, however, that Ali had caught Liston off balance and blindsided, with a corkscrew punch to his left temple.

Liston continued to box after that defeat, and he continued to win, though mainly against second-rate fighters. Rumors circulated about his friendship with gangsters and his involvement in narcotics. On 5 January 1971 his wife returned from a trip to St. Louis to find him dead in their Las Vegas home. He had been dead for a week, and though the coroner's report found evidence of heroin use, medical officials cited heart failure as the cause of death. At his funeral in Las Vegas, the Ink Spots sang "Sunny" in his honor, though Liston would almost certainly have preferred JAMES BROWN's "Night Train," the song that he always listened to while training. Liston's closest friends saw in him a quick, intuitive intelligence and noted his kindness, especially to children. In 1967 the Listons had adopted a three-year-old boy, Daniell. Others saw only Sonny's boorishness, his criminal record, and his connection to mobsters. By inducting him into its International Hall of Fame in 1991, the boxing world recognized that Sonny Liston's singular contribution came in the ring, as arguably the hardest-hitting fighter of his generation.

FURTHER READING

Remnick, David. *King of the World: Muhammad Ali and the Rise of an American Hero* (1998).
Tosches, Nick. *The Devil and Sonny Liston* (2000).
Young, A. S. *Sonny Liston: The Champ Nobody Wanted* (1963).

Obituary: *New York Times*, 7 Jan. 1971.
—STEVEN J. NIVEN

 LITTLE, MALCOLM. *See* Malcolm X.

LITTLE RICHARD

(5 Dec. 1932–), pioneering rock-and-roll singer, songwriter, and pianist, was born Richard Wayne Penniman in Macon, Georgia, the third of twelve children born to Charles "Bud" Penniman, a brick mason, and Leva Mae (maiden name unknown). It was a family of Seventh-Day Adventist preachers and bootleggers—not the last time that sin and salvation would mix in this performer's life story. As a child, Richard suffered abuse from his peers because his right leg was shorter than his left. "The kids didn't realize I was crippled," he told his biographer. "They thought I was trying to twist and walk feminine. The kids would call me faggot, sissy, freak" (*Rolling Stone*, 19 July–2 Aug. 1984).

Although he learned to play piano and grew up singing in church with his family (as the Penniman Singers and Tiny Tots Quartet), Penniman was kicked out of the house at age thirteen for homosexual behavior his father thought sinful. Entering the world of carnivals and vaudeville, he was adopted by a white couple, Ann and Johnny Johnson, who ran the Tick Tock Club in Macon, and spent the late 1940s performing in a red evening gown as Princess Lavonne in Sugarfoot Sam's Minstrel Show. Traveling the South, he visited clubs like New Orleans's Dew Drop Inn, where the emcee, Patsy Vidalia, was a female impersonator.

By the early 1950s rhythm-and-blues music was spreading across the country. Now known as Little Richard, the performer won an RCA recording contract in 1951 at an audition sponsored by Daddy Zenas Spears of Atlanta's WGST, but these early sessions showed little of the outrageousness to come. Subsequent sessions in 1953 and 1955 with Peacock were equally unsuccessful. Finally, Art Rupe of Specialty Records arranged for Richard to record with a New Orleans band that included such greats as the drummer Earl Palmer and the saxophonist Lee Allen. On 14 September 1955 they recorded "Tutti Frutti" and made history.

The original verses of the song were the kind of material Richard was used to performing in Southern drag queen bars: "Tutti-frutti, good booty / If it don't fit, don't force it / You can grease it, make it easy." Richard was asked to sing it for a white female songwriter, Dorothy LaBostrie, so she could sanitize the lyrics, and the story goes that he was so embarrassed that he sang facing a wall. But the cleaned-up version was revelation enough: over pounding boogie-woogie piano and an ecstatic, gospel-charged, falsetto "whoo," Richard brought matters to a head with the ecstatic yawp "A wop bop a loo bop a lop bam boom!" It might be the quintessential 1950s rock-and-roll moment.

"Tutti Frutti" sold half a million copies, the bulk of them to white teenagers fascinated by a southern black man wearing mascara and a six-inch pompadour and raving like an out-of-control preacher. There had never been anything remotely like Little Richard in mainstream pop culture. A bland cover version of "Tutti Frutti" by the white singer Pat Boone went to number twelve on the pop charts, higher than the number seventeen showing of Richard's original. Either way, the result was integrationist: a merger of black and white pop that was felt on radio and in clubs, where kids of all races began partying together.

Others picked up on Richard's barely coded signals. Writing in the 1 April 1997 *Advocate*, Bruce Vilanch argued: "Little Richard was our starter queen, the first flamboyant gay figure of our lives. He may not have been open, but he was open all night. Richard was my hero because he didn't seem to give a damn and I felt he was of

Little Richard fascinated teenage audiences with his pompadour, makeup, and the excitement of "Tutti Frutti," 1956. © Bettmann/CORBIS

my generation." Richard himself has speculated on his explicitly high-camp image: "The people in power maybe felt I wouldn't bother the white girls. Other guys looked more macho, you know, thick and built. JAMES BROWN had a much harder time—by him not having the 'tender look' like me" (*Life*, 1 Dec. 1992).

It is worth remembering Richard's musical innovations as well. Earl Palmer, who drummed on these early sessions, recalled: "I'll tell you, the only reason I started playing what they come to call a rock-and-roll beat came from trying to match Richard's right hand. Ding-ding-ding-ding!... Little Richard moved from a shuffle to that straight eighth-note

feeling... pounding on the piano with all 10 fingers" (*New York Times*, 25 Apr. 1999). Richard's touring band, the Upsetters, were Macon players with links to James Brown and the subsequent rhythmic upheaval that turned rock and roll into 1960s funk.

Richard had a string of subsequent hits in the late 1950s: "Long Tall Sally," "Slippin' and Slidin'," "Rip It Up," "Reddy Teddy," "She's Got it," "The Girl Can't Help It," "Lucille," "Send Me Some Lovin'," "Jenny, Jenny," "Miss Ann," "Keep a Knockin'," and "Good Golly, Miss Molly" sold an estimated eighteen million singles. He was featured in several of the early rock-and-roll movies, most notably, *The Girl Can't*

Help It and *Don't Knock the Rock*, both in 1956. Richard has talked about living wild in this period: for example, being handed ten thousand dollars in hundred dollar bills by D. J. Alan Freed and putting it all in the trunk of his Cadillac to draw upon as needed; and masturbating while watching his female companion, Angel, have sex with men like the white rock and roller Buddy Holly. Richard's religious beliefs, long buried, started to nag at him, however, and he says that when he saw what turned out to be the *Sputnik* satellite flying across the sky after a show in Australia in 1957, he took it as a sign from God to stop performing rock and roll. He handed his mother the keys to the Cadillac and went back to church.

The rest is anticlimactic. Richard worked in a gospel vein for portions of the 1960s, recording with the great singer Sister Rosetta Tharpe, the arranger QUINCY JONES, and the Atlantic producer Jerry Wexler. One song from this collaboration, "He Got What He Wanted (But He Lost What He Had)," became something of a trademark for him. He enrolled in Oakwood College, a bible school in Huntsville, Alabama, in 1958.

Yet Richard could never remain out of the spotlight for long, and when the Beatles hit big in 1963, citing him as an influence (now it was Paul McCartney instead of Pat Boone making those "whoo's"), he returned to rock and roll. JIMI HENDRIX played in Richard's 1960s touring band for a while, telling him, "I want to make my guitar sound just like your voice" (*Rolling Stone*, 19 July 1984), and perhaps getting a lesson in onstage flamboyance before being fired for upstaging Richard one time too many. Success was more limited for Richard now; his repertoire had barely changed, as he was hauled out to provide nostalgia for the counterculture generation. "I'm the bronze Liberace," he said at a 1970 concert. "Everything we do is '56. We don't do nothing that happened in '66" (Felton, 430).

He had been using drugs since the 1950s, and this began to spiral out of control. Richard continued to put out failed pop material into the 1970s and then returned to Christianity again, after the death of his brother Tony. *People* magazine noted in 1984 that while MICHAEL JACKSON was playing Knoxville,

Tennessee, to forty-five thousand people, his musical forefather, Little Richard, was appearing in town on the local *Praise the Lord* TV talk show, telling the host, "I was into homosexuality, and He changed me.... I was into rock 'n' roll, and He changed me."

Then he came back into the limelight once more. In 1986 he was inducted into the inaugural Rock and Roll Hall of Fame and was featured in a cameo performance in the film *Down and Out in Beverly Hills*. Ever since, he's been a kind of rock-and-roll cartoon, brought in to emote campily in commercials for Revlon, Taco Bell, and Tostitos; playing Giants of Rock package tours; and performing for the first rock president, Bill Clinton, at his inauguration and at a 1994 presidential gala. "I'm the innovator. I'm the emancipator. I'm the originator. I'm the architect of rock 'n' roll," Little Richard likes to say about himself (Dafydd Rees and Luke Crampton, *Q Rock Stars Encyclopedia* [1999], 601). But he never seems to have figured out what his accomplishment meant or reconciled his values, desires, and aspirations.

FURTHER READING

Felton, David. "Little Richard and the Silent Majority" in *The Rolling Stone Rock 'n' Roll Reader*, ed. Ben Fong-Torres (1974).

Lhamon, W. T., Jr. *Deliberate Speed: The Origins of a Cultural Style in the American 1950s.* (1990).

Palmer, Robert. *Rock & Roll: An Unruly History* (1995).

White, Charles. *The Life and Times of Little Richard: The Quasar of Rock* (1984).

Discography:
The Georgia Peach (Specialty 7012-2).
Grooviest 17 Original Hits (Specialty 2113).
The Specialty Sessions (Specialty 8508).

—ERIC WEISBARD

 **LOCKE, ALAIN LEROY**
(13 Sept. 1885–9 June 1954), philosopher and literary critic, was born in Philadelphia, Pennsylvania, the son of Pliny Ishmael Locke, a lawyer, and Mary Hawkins, a teacher and member of the Felix Adler Ethical Society. Locke graduated from Central High School and the Philadelphia School of Pedagogy in

Alain Leroy Locke, portrayed here by German artist Winold Reiss, produced influential writings in the areas of philosophy, art and aesthetics, and education between the 1920s and the 1950s. National Portrait Gallery, Smithsonian Institution/Art Resource, NY

Philadelphia in 1904. That same year he published his first editorial, "Moral Training in Elementary Schools," in *The Teacher*, and entered undergraduate school at Harvard University. He studied at Harvard under such scholars as Josiah Royce, George H. Palmer, Ralph B. Perry, and Hugo Münsterberg before graduating in 1907 and becoming the first African American Rhodes scholar, at Hertford College, Oxford. While in Europe, he also attended lectures at the University of Berlin (1910–1911) and studied the works of Franz Brentano, Alexius Meinong, and C. F. von Ehrenfels. Locke associated with other Rhodes scholars, including Horace M. Kallen, author of the concept of cultural pluralism; H. E. Alaily, president of the Egyptian Society of England; Pa Ka Isaka Seme, a black South African law student and eventual founder of the African National Congress of South Africa; and Har Dayal from India—each concerned with national liberation in their respective homelands. The formative years of Locke's education and early career were the years

just proceeding and during World War I—years of nationalist uprising and wars between the world's major nation-states. Locke joined the Howard University faculty in 1912, to eventually form the most prestigious department of philosophy at a historically African American university.

In the summer of 1915 Locke began a lecture series sponsored by the Social Science Club of the National Association for the Advancement of Colored People, titled "Race Contacts and Interracial Relations: A Study of the Theory and Practice of Race." Locke argued against social Darwinism, which held that distinct races exist and are biologically determined to express peculiar cultural traits. Locke believed that races were socially constructed and that cultures are the manifestation of stressed values, values always subject to transvaluation and revaluation. Locke introduced a new way of thinking about social entities by conceiving of race as a socially formed category, which, despite its foundation in social history, substantively affected material reality.

Locke received his doctorate in philosophy from Harvard in 1918 and shortly thereafter wrote "The Role of the Talented Tenth," which supported W. E. B. Du Bois's idea that the upward mobility of approximately one-tenth of a population is crucial for the improvement of the whole population. Locke also became interested in the Baha'i faith, finding particularly attractive its emphasis on racial harmony and the interrelatedness of all religious faiths. Locke attended the 1921 Inter-Racial Amity conference on 19–21 May in Washington, D.C., and as late as 1932 published short editorials in the *Baha'i World*. Although he did not formally join the Baha'i faith, he remained respectful of its practices.

Locke went on to help initiate the Harlem Renaissance, 1925–1939, a period of significant cultural contributions by African Americans. The years 1924–1925 were a major turning point in Locke's life. He edited a special edition of the magazine *Survey* titled the *Survey Graphic*, on the district of Harlem in Manhattan, New York. The editor of *Survey* was Paul U. Kellogg, and the associate editor was Jane Addams. That edition became the source for his seminal work reflecting the nature of valuation and the classicism of African American culture, *The New Negro: An Interpretation of Negro Life*, published in 1925. *The New Negro* was a collage of art by Winold Reiss and AARON DOUGLAS and representations of African artifacts; articles by J. A. Rogers, E. FRANKLIN FRAZIER, CHARLES S. JOHNSON, Melville J. Herskovits, and Du Bois; poetry by COUNTÉE CULLEN, LANGSTON HUGHES, Arna Bontemps, and ANGELINA WELD GRIMKÉ; spirituals; and bibliographies. *The New Negro* was intended as a work "by" rather than "about" African Americans, a text exuding pride, historical continuity, and a new spirit of self-respect not because a metamorphosis had occurred in the psychology of African Americans, "but because the Old Negro had long become more of a myth than a man." *The New Negro* embodied Locke's definition of essential features of African American culture, themes such as the importance of self-respect in the face of social denigration, ethnic pride; overcoming racial stereotypes and idioms, such as call-and-response in the spirituals or discord and beats in

jazz; and the importance that cultural hybridity, traditions, and revaluations play in shaping cross-cultural relationships. Locke promoted those features of African American folk culture that he believed could be universalized and thus become classical idioms, functioning, for Locke, as cultural ambassadors encouraging cross-cultural and racial respect. As debates over how to characterize American and African American cultural traits in literature became less a source of intellectual conflict, Locke's interests moved on to issues in education.

In 1936 Locke began work on a book series, the Bronze Booklets on the History, Problems, and Cultural Contributions of the Negro, under the auspices of the Associates in Negro Folk Education. Eight booklets were published in the series, which became a standard reference for the teaching of African American history. In one of his frequent book reviews of African American literature for *Opportunity: A Journal of Negro Life*, Locke supported the controversial novel by RICHARD WRIGHT, *Native Son*, in 1941. The novel was controversial because Wright did not portray the lead character, Bigger Thomas, as a peace-loving, passive, and victimized African American, but as a critic of liberals and radicals. Locke's support for Wright's novel represented his belief that race divided America.

Locke published his first extensive article on his philosophy in 1935, "Values and Imperatives," in *American Philosophy: Today and Tomorrow*, edited by Horace M. Kallen and Sidney Hook. Locke argued that values are inherently unstable, always subject to transvaluation and transposition. Locke contended that "All philosophies, it seems to me, are in ultimate derivation philosophies of life and not of abstract, disembodied 'objective' reality; products of time, place, and situation, and thus systems of timed history rather than timeless eternity" (313). Rather than believe that science is an adequate model for reasoning about social reality, Locke presented the view that knowledge is a function of experience and the categories of logic, science, math, and social science are heuristic value fields or distinctions.

Locke published his landmark work on education, "The Need for a New Organon in Education," in *Findings of the First Annual Conference on Adult*

Education and the Negro (1938), based on a lecture before the American Association for Adult Education, the Extension Department of Hampton Institute, and the Associates in Negro Folk Education, in Hampton, Virginia, on 20–22 October 1938. Locke proposed the concept of critical relativism (the view that there are no absolutely true propositions, but that we can have standards and criteria for critical evaluations). Locke warned against believing that all relevant knowledge can be acquired through application of formal logic and argued for the need to apply functional methods of reasoning and the importance of value judgments in considering defensible beliefs. Locke actively promoted adult education, working with the American Association of Adult Education in Washington, D.C., from 1948 to 1952.

In 1942 Locke edited, along with Bernard J. Stern, *When Peoples Meet: A Study of Race and Culture*. This anthology used a concept of ethnicity to account for both ethnic and racial contacts. Locke's approach continued his view that racial identities were socially created and were not based on substantive biological categories.

In 1944 Locke became a founding conference member of the Conference on Science, Philosophy and Religion, which published its annual proceedings of debates on the relationship of these areas of thought. He promoted the idea that cultural pluralism was an analog for why one knowledge field was an insufficient reasoning model for sure knowledge, i.e., different cultures and civilizations supported laudable values just as different disciplines could sustain different spheres of knowledge. For Locke, there was no reason to believe in a unified theory of knowledge, i.e., a theory that would tell us about the nature of all forms of knowledge. Rather, a plurality of fields of knowledge and cultural values was a preferable perspective on Locke's account.

Locke was a controversial figure. His aesthetic views contrasted with those of the Black Aesthetic Movement of the 1970s. He was satirized in novels, criticized by ZORA NEALE HURSTON as an elitist interested in controlling the definition of African American culture, reproached for failing to acknowledge the largest Pan-African movement of the

1920s, the MARCUS GARVEY–led United Negro Improvement Association, and denounced for placing too great a value on African American literature as a text representing a unique cultural texture.

Locke died in New York City. He lived a controversial life because his ideas of values, race, and culture often went against popular ideas. His concept of pragmatism was critical of, and different from, the dominant forms represented by William James and John Dewey. Locke's effort to shape the Harlem Renaissance and define the "New Negro" went against those that believed folk culture should not be changed, and his advocacy of value-oriented education within the adult education movement was viewed as a new orientation. Locke's philosophy, promoted by the Alain L. Locke Society, remains a source of controversy and debate.

FURTHER READING

Locke's papers are in the Alain L. Locke Archives, Howard University, Washington, D.C.

Harris, Leonard. *The Philosophy of Alain Locke: Harlem Renaissance and Beyond* (1989).
Harris, Leonard, ed. *The Critical Pragmatism of Alain Locke* (1999).
Holmes, Eugene C. "Alain L. Locke—Philosopher, Critic, Spokesman," *Journal of Philosophy* 54 (Feb. 1957): 113–118.
Linneman, Russell J. *Alain Locke: Reflections on a Modern Renaissance Man* (1982).
Stafford, Douglas K. "Alain Locke: The Child, the Man, and the People," *June* (Winter 1961): 25–34.
Stewart, Jeffrey C., ed., *The Critical Temper of Alain Locke: A Selection of His Essays on Art and Culture* (1983).
Washington, Johnny. *Alain Locke and His Philosophy: A Quest for Cultural Pluralism* (1986).

—LEONARD HARRIS

LOGAN, RAYFORD WHITTINGHAM

(7 Jan. 1897–4 Nov. 1981), historian of the African diaspora, professor, and civil rights and Pan-Africanist activist, was born in Washington, D.C., the son of Arthur Logan and Martha Whittingham, domestic workers. Two circumstances of Logan's parents are germane to his later life and work. Although he grew up in modest circumstances, his parents enjoyed a measure of status in the Washington black community owing to his father's employment as a butler in the household of Frederic Walcott, Republican senator from Connecticut. And the Walcotts took an interest in the Logan family, providing them with occasional gifts, including money to purchase a house. The Walcotts also took an interest in Rayford Logan's education, presenting him with books and later, in the 1920s and 1930s, introducing him to influential whites in government. Logan grew up on family lore about the antebellum free Negro heritage of the Whittinghams. It is open to question how much of what he heard was factual; nevertheless, he learned early to make class distinctions among African Americans and to believe that his elite heritage also imposed on him an obligation to help lead his people to freedom and equality.

Both lessons were reinforced by his secondary education at the prestigious M Street (later Dunbar) High School, a public but segregated institution in the District of Columbia. Jim Crow had narrowed the professional options of African American educators, and the faculty included such first-rate intellectuals as CARTER G. WOODSON, JESSIE FAUSET, and ANNA JULIA COOPER; its goal was education for leadership, and among its distinguished alumni were CHARLES HAMILTON HOUSTON, WILLIAM HENRY HASTIE, CHARLES R. DREW, and BENJAMIN O. DAVIS SR. Logan was the valedictorian of the class of 1913. He continued his academic career at Williams College, from which he was graduated Phi Beta Kappa in 1917. After he delivered one of three commencement speeches, he returned to Washington, where he enlisted in the military to fight in World War I.

The First World War was a turning point in Logan's life. Like most African Americans, he followed the lead of W. E. B. DU BOIS and the NAACP in supporting the war effort with the expectation that blacks' discharging a patriotic duty would bring them full citizenship rights. Logan rose from private to the rank of lieutenant in the segregated 372d Infantry Regiment, one of only four combat units open to black American soldiers; most blacks were restricted to militarized labor units.

Logan saw combat in the Argonne campaign of June 1918 and was wounded; the "war neurosis" that accompanied the injury triggered a series of outbursts by Logan directed at white American officers in retaliation for the accumulated racial humiliation and harassment they visited on him and all black military personnel. He spent the next year fighting the racism of the U.S. military. There were two wars going on—Mr. Wilson [Woodrow Wilson]'s and Mr. Logan's—he asserted in his unpublished autobiography. When he was demobilized in August 1919, Logan chose to remain in France. "My experiences in the army left me so bitter…that I remained an expatriate in Europe," he later wrote. "I *hated* white Americans."

Between 1919 and 1924 Logan lived in Paris and became a leading member of the Pan-African Congress movement based there. Logan worked closely with W. E. B. Du Bois, the movement's principal architect (it was the beginning of a collaboration that would last into the 1950s), as well as a number of prominent francophone blacks also resident in Paris. The Pan-African Congress, which met four times between 1919 and 1927, espoused the equality of the black race, an end to colonial abuses in Africa, eventual self-government for Europe's African possessions, and full civil rights for African Americans.

In many respects Pan-Africanism between the two world wars was a precursor to America's civil rights movement, as it was supported by the leading black Americans of the day. His five-year European expatriation introduced Logan to the international dimensions of the "race problem," and his interactions with Haitian diplomat Dantes Bellegarde laid the basis for a lifelong scholarly and political interest in the first independent black republic in the Western Hemisphere.

Having exorcised white Americans from his spirit—largely by avoiding them in Paris—Logan returned to the United States in 1924 determined to pursue the fight for civil rights as both a scholar and an activist. Between 1925 and 1938 he taught at two elite, historically black colleges: Virginia Union University in Richmond (1925–1931) and Atlanta University

(1933–1938). In the interim he served for two years as Carter Woodson's assistant at the Association for the Study of Negro Life and History. At Virginia Union, Logan taught French and history, and introduced the college's first courses on black history and on imperialism; he earned a reputation as a serious scholar and an engaging teacher.

While on the Union faculty, Logan married Ruth Robinson in 1927; they had no children. He pursued advanced degrees in History, earning his MA from Williams College in 1929, and beginning in 1930 the residency and course requirements for his PhD from Harvard University. (He completed them in 1932.) While at Atlanta he researched and wrote his doctoral dissertation, completed in 1936, on the diplomatic relations between the United States and Haiti, a groundbreaking work on race and diplomacy that was published in 1941 as *The Diplomatic Relations of the United States with Haiti, 1776–1891*. He visited Haiti twice, and was a firsthand witness to the 1934 end of the American occupation. In the 1920s and 1930s his scholarship on Haiti and colonial Africa earned him national recognition not only in the black diaspora—he was awarded Haiti's Order of Honor and Merit in 1941 for his scholarship and advocacy—but also from influential, predominantly white organizations such as the Foreign Policy Association.

In Richmond and Atlanta—and in Washington, where between 1938 and 1968 he taught at Howard University—Logan engaged in innovative civil rights activity. In the 1920s and 1930s in the first two cities he organized, in conjunction with other outspoken African Americans like Lugenia Hope, voter registration drives; the citizenship schools, which taught African Americans how to register to vote and anchored the campaigns, became models for similar activities in the 1960s. On the eve of World War II, he spearheaded a drive of mass rallies and organizing local African American coalitions against the exclusion of African Americans from the U.S. military; the force of the campaign was such that in 1940 he was invited to meet with President Franklin D. Roosevelt on the matter and drafted for the president an order prohibiting the exclusion of blacks from the service.

In 1941 Logan was a leader of A. PHILIP RANDOLPH's March on Washington Movement, which pressured Roosevelt into issuing Executive Order 8802 banning racial discrimination in defense industries; Logan participated in the final negotiations over the order. The March on Washington Movement declared victory, and the march was canceled. Logan edited *What the Negro Wants* (1944), a collection of essays by fourteen prominent African Americans that helped to bring before the entire American public the demand for a total elimination of segregation. Turning his attention once again to international affairs in the postwar era, Logan, in close alliance with Du Bois, fought to orient the United Nations, the United States, and the European powers toward justice and decolonization in Africa. He spent the last decade of his life organizing and editing with Michael R. Winston the *Dictionary of American Negro Biography* (1982).

The central point of Logan's scholarship and activism was the promotion of the dignity and equality of black people throughout the world and the critical examination of American racial hypocrisy. But in an era dominated by the incipient cold war, his scholarship and activism were too strident for the U.S. political establishment, and he often found it difficult to attain a hearing in the white mainstream. *What the Negro Wants* saw life only after he threatened to sue the publisher for breach of contract; two of his other important works, *The Negro and the Post-War World* (1945) and *The African Mandates and World Politics* (1948), were issued privately by Logan because no publisher would bring them out. His best-known work, *The Negro in American Life and Thought: The Nadir, 1877–1901* (1954; revised and republished as *The Betrayal of the Negro* [1965]), which established a useful framework for historians to analyze that period of African American history, was turned down by one publisher, and Macmillan agreed to publish it only after Logan posted a five-thousand-dollar subvention.

Rayford Logan was a distinguished and talented intellectual. While he insisted on strict adherence to the historical record and was perhaps conservative in what he considered

historical evidence, he knitted his scholarship together with a lifetime of activism. Just as he had hoped that his scholarship would reach a wide audience, he also wanted to be a major civil rights figure. He never reached this position, partly because he was often more strident than the mainstream race advancement organizations of the 1930s, 1940s, and 1950s. He was overlooked by the activists of the 1960s and 1970s in part, he believed, because that generation's impetuousness prevented it from learning from and about the sacrifices and efforts of earlier activists. (In fact, such staples of the 1960s as voter registration drives had been pioneered by Logan three decades earlier.) But there were other reasons, notably his abrasive personality and his chafing at organizational discipline. As a result, he often was on the sidelines, an incisive but little-recognized critic. He perhaps was comfortable in this marginal role because he did not have to implement his visionary, but neglected, plans, but marginality also prevented him from achieving the stature he believed he deserved in both white and black America. He died in Washington, D.C.

FURTHER READING

The major part of Logan's papers are deposited at the Moorland-Spingarn Research Center at Howard University in Washington, D.C. His diaries are deposited in the Manuscript Division of the Library of Congress.

Janken, Kenneth Robert. *Rayford W. Logan and the Dilemma of the African American Intellectual* (1993).
—KENNETH ROBERT JANKEN

LOGUEN, JERMAIN WESLEY (c. 1813– 30 Sept. 1872), bishop of the African Methodist Episcopal Zion Church and abolitionist, was born Jarm Logue in Davidson County, Tennessee, the son of a slave mother, Cherry, and white slaveholder, David Logue. After David Logue sold his sister and mother to a brutal master, Jarm escaped through Kentucky and southern Indiana, aided by Quakers, and reached Hamilton, Upper Canada, about 1835. He tried his hand at farming, learned to read at the age of twenty-three, and worked as a hotel porter and lumberjack. It was in Canada that he added an *n* to the spelling of his name to distinguish it from that of his slave master. When creditors seized his farm in 1837, Loguen moved to Rochester, New York, and found employment as a hotel porter.

The black clergyman Elymas P. Rogers urged him to attend Beriah Green's abolitionist school, Oneida Institute, at Whitesboro, New York. Loguen enrolled there in 1839, despite his lack of formal education. He started a school in nearby Utica for African American children and made a public profession of faith. He settled in Syracuse in 1841, opened another school, and married Caroline Storum of Busti, New York. They would have five children. One daughter, Amelia, married Lewis E. Douglass, the son of FREDERICK DOUGLASS; Gerrit Smith Loguen became an accomplished artist; and Sarah Marinda Loguen graduated from the medical school of Syracuse University in 1876.

After being ordained by the AMEZ Church in 1842, Loguen served congregations in Syracuse, Bath, Ithaca, and Troy. He gave his first speech against slavery at Plattsburgh, New York, in 1844 and was enlisted as an itinerant lecturer promoting the Liberty Party. Loguen's sacred vocation now focused on abolitionism, and he devoted less and less time to the local ministry. Working in cooperation with Frederick Douglass of Rochester, Unitarian minister Samuel May of Syracuse, and abolitionist and reformer Gerrit Smith of Peterboro in Madison County, Loguen actively aided fugitive slaves passing through upstate New York on their way to Canada. His home became the center of Underground Railroad activity in Syracuse, and in his autobiography, *A Stop on the Underground Railroad* (1859), he claimed to have assisted more than 1,500 runaway slaves.

Loguen was presiding elder of the AMEZ's Troy district when the Fugitive Slave Law of 1850 was passed. Loguen returned to Syracuse, where he publicly defied the law and vowed resistance. "I don't respect this law," he said, "I don't fear it, I won't obey it! It outlaws me, and I outlaw it, and the men who attempt to enforce it on me. I place the governmental officials on the ground that they place me. I will not live a slave,

and if force is employed to re-enslave me, I shall make preparations to meet the crisis as becomes a man." With other members of the Fugitive Aid Society, Loguen participated in the famous rescue of William "Jerry" McHenry at Syracuse in October 1851; fearing arrest for his actions, he fled to St. Catharines, Canada West, where he conducted missionary work and spoke on behalf of the temperance cause among other fugitives. Despite the failure of his appeal of 2 December 1851 for safe passage to Governor Washington Hunt of New York, Loguen returned to Syracuse in late 1852 and renewed his labors on behalf of the Underground Railroad and the local Fugitive Aid Society. Loguen was indicted by a grand jury at Buffalo, New York, but was never tried.

By the 1840s Loguen had moved away from the moral suasion philosophy of William Lloyd Garrison and into the circle of central New York abolitionists who endorsed political means. After the demise of the Liberty Party, Loguen supported a remnant known as the Liberty League. By 1854 Loguen had abandoned the nonviolent philosophy of many of his abolitionist colleagues and joined the Radical Abolition Society. After 1857 he devoted all of his time to the Fugitive Aid Society. He returned to Canada West to attend a convention led by John Brown (1800–1859) prior to the 1859 raid at Harpers Ferry but apparently did not know the details of Brown's plan.

In the early 1860s Loguen served as pastor of Zion Church in Binghamton, New York. He also recruited black troops for the Union army. After the Civil War, Loguen was active in establishing AMEZ congregations among the southern freedmen. He had a special interest in Tennessee, where he believed his mother and sister lived. (Earlier he had refused to purchase the freedom of his mother because her master, Manasseth Logue, his father's brother, demanded that Loguen also purchase his own freedom.) Loguen became bishop of the Fifth District of the AMEZ Church in 1868, with responsibilities for the Allegheny and Kentucky conferences. He supported the work of the Freedmen's Bureau and the American Missionary Association in the South. On the eve of leaving for a new post as organizer of AMEZ

missions on the Pacific coast, he died in Saratoga Springs, New York.

FURTHER READING

Loguen's letters are held in the Gerrit Smith Papers, George Arents Research Library, Syracuse University, and are available on microfilm in the *Black Abolitionist Papers*, C. Peter Ripley, ed.

Loguen, J. W. *A Stop on the Underground Railroad: Rev. J. W. Loguen & Syracuse* (1859, 2001).

Hunter, Carol M. *To Set the Captives Free: Reverend Jermain Wesley Loguen and the Struggle for Freedom in Central New York, 1835–1872* (1993).

Sernett, Milton C. "A Citizen of 'No Mean City': Jermain W. Loguen and the Antislavery Reputation of Syracuse," *Syracuse University Library Associates Courier* 22 (Fall 1987): 33–55.

Obituary: *Syracuse Journal*, 1 Oct. 1872.
—MILTON C. SERNETT

LORDE, AUDRE

(18 Feb. 1934–17 Nov. 1992), poet, writer, and activist, was born Audrey Geraldine Lorde in Harlem, New York City, the youngest of three daughters of Frederic Byron Lorde, a laborer and real estate broker from Barbados, and Linda Bellmar, from Grenada, who sometimes found work as a maid. Lorde's parents came to the United States from the Caribbean with hopes of earning enough money to return to the West Indies and start a small business. During the Depression the realization that the family was going to remain exiled in America slowly set in. Growing up in this atmosphere of disappointment had a profound impact on Lorde's development, as questions of identity, nationality, and community membership occupied her mind.

Ironically, this woman whose living and reputation derived from her skillful use of words had to struggle as a child to acquire speech and literacy. She was so nearsighted that she was considered legally blind. Moreover, her mother feared that she might be retarded, and her first memories of school were of being disparaged for being mentally slow. Either out of fear of her mother, a severe disciplinarian, or because of an undiagnosed speech impediment, Lorde did not begin to talk until she was four years old and was uncommunicative for many years thereafter.

Lorde received her early education at two Catholic institutions in Harlem, St. Mark's and St. Catherine's. In her fictionalized biomythography, *Zami: A New Spelling of My Name* (1982), she recalls the patronizing racism of low expectations, the overt racism of bigotry, and the oppressive learning environment that stifled her creativity. The West Indian dialect and the unusual idioms that she heard at home taught her that words could be used in different and creative ways. Freedom to construct words and sentences as she chose, however, was a right that she would have to fight for. Alternate spellings of her name and the adoption of new names were merely the most visible symbols of her struggle for self-definition. If Lorde was to be a rebel and a contrarian, words would become her weapons of choice.

Lorde began writing poetry in the seventh or eighth grade. At Hunter College High School she met another aspiring poet, Diane de Prima, and they worked together on the school literary journal, *Scribimus*. However, when the school refused to print a love sonnet Lorde had written about her affection for a boy, she sent the poem to *Seventeen* magazine, where it was published. After graduating from high school in 1951, Lord worked and studied intermittently until 1959, when she received a BA degree from Hunter College. During much of the 1950s Lorde supported herself as a factory worker and an X-ray technician and in a number of other unsatisfying positions.

A pivotal experience occurred in 1954, when Lorde spent a year at the National University of Mexico. Although she had had a brief lesbian encounter while working at a factory in Connecticut, it was in Mexico that she began to free herself of the feelings of deviance that had inhibited her sexuality. When she returned to New York the next year, she immersed herself in the "gay girl" culture of Greenwich Village, and she continued to develop her craft as a member of the Harlem Writers Guild, which brought her into contact with such poets as LANGSTON HUGHES.

It was also during this period that she became involved with the Beat poets Allen Ginsberg, Jack Kerouac, and LeRoi Jones (AMIRI BARAKA).

In 1961 Lorde received an MLS degree from Columbia University's School of Library Service, and in March 1962 she married Edward Ashley Rollins, a white attorney from Brooklyn. They were married for eight years and had two children, Elizabeth and Jonathan, before divorcing in 1970. She held a number of posts at different libraries before becoming the head librarian at Town School Library in New York City, where she served from 1966 to 1968.

Lorde's life took a dramatic turn in 1968 when she received a National Endowment for the Arts grant, resigned her position as a librarian, and accepted a post at Tougaloo College in Mississippi as poet in residence. While she was working at this historically black college, Lorde's first book of poetry, *The First Cities* (1968), received critical acclaim for its effective understatement and subtlety. It was at Tougaloo College that Lorde met Frances Clayton, who would become her companion for nineteen years. Lorde's second book, *Cables to Rage* (1970), captures the anger of the emerging Black Power movement and contains the poem "Martha," in which Lorde first confirms her homosexuality in print. From this point on, Lorde observed that different groups (blacks, feminists, lesbians, and others) wanted to claim aspects of her life to aid their cause while rejecting those elements that challenged their prejudices. Of this tendency, Lorde said in an interview, "There's always someone asking you to underline one piece of yourself—whether it's Black, woman, mother, dyke, teacher, etc.—because that's the piece that they need to key in to. They want to dismiss everything else. But once you do that, then you've lost" (Hammond, Carla M. *Denver Quarterly* 16, no. 1 [1981], 10–27).

During the 1970s Lorde returned to New York, where she entered a productive period of writing, teaching, and giving readings. Her third book, *From a Land Where Other People Live* (1973), was nominated for the National Book Award for poetry. It was followed in rapid succession by *New York Head Shop and Museum* (1974), *Coal* (1976), *Between Ourselves* (1976), and *The Black Unicorn* (1978). In these works, Lorde develops her central themes: bearing witness to the truth, transforming pain into freedom, and seizing the power to define love and beauty for oneself. Never does her work trade in clichés, employ hackneyed metaphors, or evoke saccharine sentiment. Lorde found a new voice in poetry that struck like a hammer but sounded like a bell on issues of race, gender, sexuality, and humanity.

Late in 1978, at the age of forty-four, Lorde was stricken with breast cancer. She had a mastectomy but refused to wear a prosthesis to hide the effects of the surgery. Instead, she chose to face her ordeal openly and honestly by incorporating it into her writing. In many ways *The Cancer Journal* (1980) helped women "come out of the closet" about this disease. Confronted with her own mortality, she published the autobiographical *Zami: A New Spelling of My Name* (1982), which is essentially the story of her early life, and *Sister Outsider* (1984), a collection of speeches and essays. In *Burst of Light* (1988), which won the American Book Award for nonfiction, Lorde explains that "the struggle with cancer now informs all my days, but it is only another face of that continuing battle for self-determination and survival that black women fight daily, often in triumph." Her final book of poems, *The Marvelous Arithmetics of Distance*, was published posthumously in 1993.

In an effort to help other women writers, Lorde cofounded Kitchen Table: Women of Color Press in 1980. She taught courses on race and literature at Lehman College and John Jay College of Criminal Justice, and she was the Thomas Hunter Professor of English at her alma mater, Hunter College, until 1988. Lorde's highest accolade was bestowed in 1991, when she received New York's Walt Whitman Citation of Merit, an award given to the poet laureate of New York State.

Six years after her mastectomy Lorde was diagnosed with liver cancer. She sought treatment in America, Europe, and Africa before moving to St. Croix in the Virgin Islands with her companion, Gloria I. Joseph. Shortly before her death in November 1992 Lorde underwent an African ritual in which she was renamed Gambda Adisa, which loosely translated means,

"Warrior: She Who Makes Her Meaning Known."

FURTHER READING

Lorde, Audre. *Zami: A New Spelling of My Name* (1983).

Anderson, Linda R. *Women and Autobiography in the Twentieth Century: Remembered Futures* (1997).

Keating, AnaLouise. *Women Reading Women Writing: Self-Invention in Paula Gunn Allen, Gloria Anzaldúa, and Audre Lorde* (1996).

Steele, Cassie Premo. *We Heal from Memory: Sexton, Lorde, Anzaldúa, and the Poetry of Witness* (2000).

Obituary: *New York Times*, 20 Nov. 1992.
—SHOLOMO B. LEVY

LOUIS, JOE (13 May 1914–12 Apr. 1981), world champion boxer, was born Joseph Louis Barrow, the seventh of eight children of Munroe Barrow and Lillie Reese Barrow, sharecroppers, in a shack in Chambers County, Alabama. In 1916 his father was committed to the Searcy State Hospital for the Colored Insane, where he would live for the next twenty years. Believing that her husband had died, Lillie later married Pat Brooks and moved with their children in 1926 to Detroit, Michigan, where Brooks found a job at the Ford Motor Plant.

Like many rural southerners during the Great Migration, Joe Barrow struggled in the new urban environment. Although Alabama had been no racial paradise, Michigan seemed little better. "Nobody ever called me a nigger until I got to Detroit," he later recalled (Ashe, 11). A rural Jim Crow education did not prepare him for the northern public schools, and the decision to place the quickly growing twelve-year-old boy in the fifth grade did not help matters. Shy and with a stutter, he paid little attention to his studies, although one teacher at his vocational school predicted that the boy "some day should be able to do something with his hands" (Ashe, 11). Detroit in the Depression provided few outlets for those hands, but Joe did find work in an automobile factory and as a laborer hauling ice. After a brief flirtation with the violin in his early teens, he took up boxing, and by failing to add his surname to his application to fight as an amateur, he was given a fighting name that stuck, "Joe Louis." Louis lost his first amateur fight but won fifty of his next fifty-four bouts, forty-three of them by knockouts. In 1934, on his twentieth birthday, he won the National Amateur Athletic Union light-heavyweight championship and turned professional.

Louis's amateur victories hinted at his promise, but few in the summer of 1934 expected that the gangling, 175-pound boxer would win the world heavyweight championship after only three years as a professional. That he did so was partly because of his trainer, Jack Blackburn, and his managers, Julian Black and John Roxborough, respectable black businessmen by day and numbers kingpins by night. While Blackburn worked on Louis's conditioning and balance, Black, Roxborough, and the white promoter Mike Jacobs crafted a public image for Louis that would enhance his title prospects. Before World War I the heavyweight JACK JOHNSON had so angered whites by gloating over defeated opponents and flaunting white mistresses that no African American since had been allowed to fight for the championship. Black and Roxborough therefore urged Louis never to appear in public with white women and fed the press stories of his deep religiosity and love of family and country. Combined with a remarkable record of thirty victories in thirty-one fights, that clean-living, nonthreatening image won him a crack at the title. In June 1937 the "Brown Bomber," as the white press had dubbed him, defeated Jim Braddock in an eighth-round knockout to win the world heavyweight championship.

At twenty-three Louis had become a hero to Depression-era blacks. While thousands of northern African Americans took to the streets to celebrate his victory, the southern black response was muted, though no less joyous. President Jimmy Carter recalled that African American neighbors came to his home to listen to the Braddock fight on one of the few radios in Plains, Georgia. Quietly obeying the racial propriety required of them, they showed no emotion at the end of the fight. But on returning to their own homes, as Carter remembers it, "pandemonium broke loose...as our black neighbors shouted and yelled in celebration of the Louis victory" (Sammons, 113).

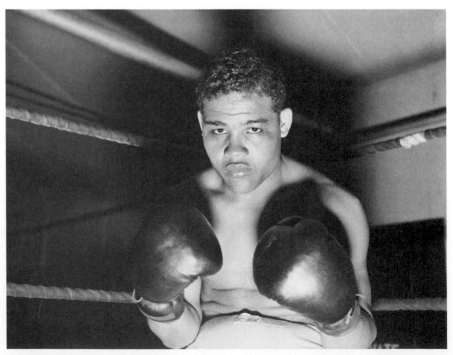

Joe Louis, in training for his 1938 match with Max Schmeling, displays the fists that earned him the nickname "Brown Bomber." © Bettmann/CORBIS

When Louis defended his title against Max Schmeling in Yankee Stadium in June 1938, the changed international climate encouraged white Americans not only to tolerate Joe Louis but also to embrace him. The 1936 Berlin Olympics had signaled both a resurgent Germany and the willingness of white Americans to appreciate a black athlete, JESSE OWENS. In that light, the media depicted Schmeling against Louis as a battle between fascism and democracy, even though there was precious little democracy for blacks in many American states, including the boxer's native Alabama.

Louis was goaded by racial taunts from the Schmeling camp and was particularly incensed that his only professional loss had been to the German in 1936. Asked if he was scared, he replied, "Yeah, I'm scared. I'm scared I might kill Schmeling" (Ashe, 15). Jack Blackburn often worried that Louis, for all of his finesse and strength, lacked a killer instinct, but when he knocked out Schmeling after only two minutes at Yankee Stadium, it became clear that such fears were unfounded. The Brown Bomber let loose a barrage of quick, savage left jabs and followed up with some stunning right punches to the German's head and body, which, Louis recalled, left Schmeling squealing "like a stuck pig" (Ashe, 16). A left hook backed up by a right to the jaw knocked Schmeling to the canvas.

After that victory Louis defeated fifteen challengers between 1938 and 1941. With the exception of the quick-fisted Irish-American Billy Conn, who led on points until Louis knocked him out in the thirteenth round, most of his opponents deserved the sobriquet "bum of the month," but no heavyweight champion had ever been so confident in his abilities as to defend his title so often. Because of the huge cut taken by his managers, however, Louis received only a fraction of the more than two million dollars that he "won" before 1942. By then he was more than $200,000 in debt to the federal government and to his promoters. The fighter's personal life was also troubled. He had married Marva Trotter in 1935, a few hours before defeating Max Baer, and the couple would have a daughter, Jacqueline, in 1943. Louis's frequent absences and extramarital affairs led to divorce in 1945. Although the couple remarried in 1946 and had a son, Joe Jr., in 1947, they divorced again in 1949.

In the 1940s Louis emerged as the most prominent—and, in the popular consciousness, the most significant—black figure in the American war effort. Within weeks of the Japanese attack on Pearl Harbor, he contributed the entire winnings from his defeat of Buddy Baer to the Navy Relief Fund. In March 1942 he earned nationwide praise for a speech in which he urged all Americans to join the war effort because "we're on God's side." Although he had misspoken—his text had read "God's on our side"—the phrase instantly became one of the most popular slogans of the war effort. In addition to fighting (without payment) in several exhibition bouts, Sergeant Joe Louis appeared in Frank Capra's The Negro Soldier, a morale-boosting documentary feature that proved as popular among whites as blacks. Louis was not, however, immune to racism within the American military. At an army camp in Alabama military police ordered Louis and the young boxer SUGAR RAY ROBINSON to sit in the assigned "colored" waiting area for a bus; they refused, were arrested, and were released only when Louis threatened to call contacts in the U.S. War Department. Louis also used his relative influence in Washington, D.C., to highlight the continued discrimination against blacks in the military.

Louis's physical prowess diminished considerably after the war, and in March 1949 he retired after an unprecedented twelve years as heavyweight champion. In the decades that followed, he focused on ways to meet his massive debts, including considerable back taxes. Sadly, but inevitably, this involved a return to the ring in 1950, where he lost to the reigning champion Ezzard Charles in 1950. Knocked out by Rocky Marciano in 1951, Louis retired for good. His latter years were spent fighting the IRS, a battle won only after his fourth wife, Martha Malone Jefferson, an attorney, convinced the government that he simply did not have any money. In 1966 Louis moved to Las Vegas, where he worked variously as a greeter in a casino and, ironically, as a debt collector. In his final decade he struggled with cocaine addiction, heart disease, and depression.

On 12 April 1981, one day after attending a world heavyweight championship match, Louis died of a massive heart attack. He was survived by Jacqueline and Joe Jr., children from his first marriage, by his fourth wife, Martha Jefferson, and by four children whom he and Jefferson had adopted. Thousands attended his lying in state at Caesars Palace in Las Vegas, and President Ronald Reagan, who had starred with Louis in the 1943 movie This Is the Army, eased military protocol to make possible a burial at Arlington National Cemetery.

In his heyday Joe Louis enjoyed fame and assumed a symbolic significance greater than any other African American. His reign as world champion marked the end of African Americans' exclusion from professional sports and also convinced whites that black achievements need not come at their expense. Most important, his victories in the ring served to inspire even the most powerless Americans, as the Swedish sociologist Gunnar Myrdal discovered when he visited a remote Georgia school in the 1930s. Myrdal interviewed the children and found that none of them had heard of President Franklin Roosevelt, W. E. B. DU BOIS, or WALTER WHITE. They had all heard of Joe Louis.

FURTHER READING

Louis, Joe, with Edna and Art Rust. My Life (1978).

ASHE, ARTHUR. A Hard Road to Glory: A History of the African American Athlete, 1919–1945 (1988).
Mead, Chris. Champion Joe Louis: Black Hero in White America (1985).
Sammons, Jeffrey T. Beyond the Ring: The Role of Boxing in American Society (1988).

Obituary: New York Times, 13 Apr. 1981.
—STEVEN J. NIVEN

LOVE, NAT (June 1854–1921), cowboy and author, was born in Davidson County, Tennessee, the son of Sampson Love and a mother whose name is unknown. Both were slaves owned by Robert Love, whom Nat described as a "kind and indulgent

Nat Love, the cowboy who claimed to be the original "Deadwood Dick" of dime novel fame. Library of Congress

Master." Nat Love's father was a foreman over other slaves; his mother, a cook. The family remained with Robert Love after the end of the Civil War.

In February 1869 Nat struck out on his own. He left because Robert Love's plantation was in desperate economic straits after the war, and he sensed that there were few opportunities other than agricultural work for young former slaves in the defeated South. Although his father had died the year before, leaving him the head of the family, Nat nevertheless left because, as he admitted, "I wanted to see more of the world."

After a short stay in Kansas, Love worked for three years on the ranch of Sam Duval in the Texas panhandle. For the next eighteen years (1872–1890) Love was a cowboy on the giant Gallinger Ranch in southern Arizona. He traveled all the western trails between south Texas and Montana

herding cattle to market and, as his autobiography reveals, engaged in the drinking, gambling, and violence typical of western cow towns. He became an expert in identifying cattle brands and learned to speak fluent Spanish on trips to Mexico. In 1889 he married a woman named Alice (maiden name unknown), with whom he had one child.

The cowboy business was doomed by the westward movement of the railroads. Love recognized this situation and in 1890 secured employment with the Denver and Rio Grande Railroad as a Pullman car porter, one of the few occupations open to black men in the West. For fifteen years Love held this position on various western railroads. His last job, beginning in 1907, was as a bank guard with the General Securities Company in Los Angeles, where he died.

Most of what is known of Love's life is from his 1907 autobiography,

The Life and Adventures of Nat Love, Better Known in the Cattle Country as "Deadwood Dick," by Himself. The one-hundred-page work seems to have been inspired by the popular and melodramatic dime novels of the day and likely contains more than a bit of fiction itself. Love certainly portrayed himself as a larger-than-life figure. He claimed he could outdrink any man in the West without it affecting him in any way. He depicted himself as one of the most expert cowboys, who could outrope, outshoot, and outride the best of them. He reported that he single-handedly broke up a robbery at an isolated Union Pacific railroad station. "I carry the marks of fourteen bullet wounds on different part [sic] of my body, most any one of which would be sufficient to kill an ordinary man," he boasted," "but I am not even crippled.... I have had five horses shot from under me.... Yet I have always managed to escape with only the mark of a bullet or knife as a reminder." Shot and captured by Indians in 1876, he said he was nursed back to health by them and adopted into the tribe; he was offered the chief's daughter in marriage. But Love had other plans and made his escape one night. He claimed as close acquaintances many western notables such as William F. "Buffalo Bill" Cody, Frank and Jesse James, Kit Carson, and "Billy the Kid" (William H. Bonney). Even as a railroad porter Love made himself out to be one of the best.

The legendary "Deadwood Dick" was created by the western dime novelist Edward L. Wheeler in the 1870s. Several men claimed to be the prototype for the character, including Love, whose autobiography places him in Deadwood in the Dakota Territory on the Fourth of July 1876. In a roping contest, he "roped, threw, tied, bridled, saddled and mounted my mustang in exactly nine minutes," a championship record he said he held until his retirement as a cowboy fourteen years later and a feat, so he claimed, that instantly won him the title of "Deadwood Dick."

The autobiography is consistently upbeat, with the author invariably winning out over those skeptical of his abilities. He mentions no incidents of racial discrimination, although they are known to have occurred in the West. While his accounts of heroic achievements and derring-do are certainly possible, he seems to have stretched the truth, not unlike other western reminiscences. And some of his claims are not verified in other sources. As one student of the West, William Loren Katz, commented, Love's autobiography is "easy to read but hard to believe" (Katz, 323). Yet his life and work do illustrate how a black man of the late nineteenth century could rise from slavery to a satisfying life in the cowboy world, where ability and fortitude did serve to mitigate race prejudice.

FURTHER READING

Love, Nat. *The Life and Adventures of Nat Love, Better Known in the Cattle Country as "Deadwood Dick," by Himself* (1907; repr. 1968).

Durham, Philip, and Everett L. Jones. *The Negro Cowboys* (1965).

Felton, Harold W. *Nat Love: Negro Cowboy* (1969).

Katz, William Loren. *The Black West* (1971).

—WILLIAM F. MUGLESTON

LYNCH, JOHN ROY

(10 Sept. 1847–2 Nov. 1939), U.S. congressman, historian, and attorney, was born on "Tacony" plantation near Vidalia, Louisiana, the son of Patrick Lynch, the manager of the plantation, and Catherine White, a slave. Patrick Lynch, an Irish immigrant, purchased his wife and two children, but in order to free them, existing state law required they leave Louisiana. Before Patrick Lynch died, he transferred the titles to his wife and children to a friend, William Deal, who promised to treat them as free persons. However, when Patrick Lynch died, Deal sold the family to a planter, Alfred W. Davis, in Natchez, Mississippi. When Davis learned of the conditions of the transfer to Deal, he agreed to allow Catherine Lynch to hire her own time while he honeymooned with his new wife in Europe. Under this arrangement, Catherine Lynch lived in Natchez, worked for various employers, and paid $3.50 a week to an agent of Davis, keeping whatever else she earned.

On Davis's return, he and Catherine Lynch reached an agreement that her elder son would work as a dining-room servant and the younger, John Roy, would be Davis's valet. Catherine accepted these conditions, recognizing that she had no alternative. Under this arrangement, John Roy Lynch studied for confirmation and baptism in the Episcopal Church, but the Civil War intervened. Lynch attended black Baptist and Methodist churches during and after the war. Because of a falling out with Davis's wife, Lynch briefly worked on a plantation until he became ill.

When Union forces reached Natchez in 1863, they freed Lynch, who was sixteen years old. He was visiting relatives at Tacony when Confederate troops overran the plantation and began seizing the ex-slaves as captives. Lynch convinced the troops that the workers had smallpox, which was a ruse, and the military released them.

Lynch worked at several jobs from 1865 to 1866, including dining-room waiter at a boardinghouse, cook with the Forty-ninth Illinois Volunteers Regiment, and pantryman aboard a troop transport ship moored at Natchez. Eventually he became a messenger in a photography shop, where he learned the photographic developing process as a "printer." He continued that line of work with another shop, and in 1866 he took over the full management of a photography shop in Natchez. Briefly attending a grammar school operated by northern teachers, he learned to read by studying newspapers, reading books, and listening to classes given in a white school near his shop. One of the books he studied was on parliamentary law, which fascinated him.

In 1868 Lynch gave a number of speeches in Natchez before the local Republican club in support of the new Mississippi state constitution. The constitution legitimized all slave marriages, including that of his mother and father. In his autobiography Lynch noted that the later constitution, passed by Democrats in 1890, did away with the feature that had legitimized marriages between whites and African Americans but not retroactively.

In 1869 the Natchez Republican club sent Lynch to discuss local political appointments with the state's military governor, Adelbert Ames. Impressed with Lynch's presentation, Ames appointed him justice of the peace,

a position Lynch had not sought. Later that year Lynch was elected to the Mississippi House of Representatives, where he served through 1873. In his first term he sat on the Judiciary Committee and the Committee on Elections and Education. In his last term he served as Speaker of the house and earned recognition and praise from Republican and Democratic legislators and the local press. During this period he formed an alliance with Governor James L. Alcorn, a white Republican who urged his party to make common cause with black voters. Lynch worked closely with other African Americans in the Mississippi Republican Party, especially BLANCHE K. BRUCE and James Hill. Later he fell into disagreement with Hill, who opposed Lynch's influence in the party.

Lynch was elected to Congress in 1872 and was reelected in 1874. In Congress, he impressed his colleagues with his knowledge of parliamentary procedure, unusual among the small contingent of southern African American Republican members of Congress. Arguing forcefully for the Civil Rights Act of 1875, he called it "an act of simple justice" that "will be instrumental in placing the colored people in a more independent position." He anticipated that, given more civil rights, blacks would vote in both parties and not depend entirely on the Republican Party.

Defeated in the 1876 congressional election, Lynch charged his opponent with fraud. In the election in 1880, through a series of dishonest practices, including lost ballot boxes, miscounts, and stuffed boxes, at least five thousand votes for Lynch were wrongfully thrown out. General James R. Chalmers, a Democrat, claimed victory, but Lynch contested the election. Finally seated late in the term, Lynch served in 1882–1883. Although he was defeated for reelection in 1882 by Henry S. Van Eaton, Lynch was regarded as a political hero by the Republican Party. He was the keynote speaker and temporary chairman of the 1884 national convention. Lynch was the last black keynote speaker at a national political convention until 1968.

In 1884 Lynch married Ella W. Somerville. They had one child before divorcing in 1900. From 1869 through 1905 he was successful in buying and selling real estate, including plantations, in the Natchez region. In 1889 President

Benjamin Harrison appointed Lynch fourth auditor of the Treasury for the Navy Department, and he served to 1893.

In 1890 Lynch protested strongly against the "George" scheme, which, under the new Mississippi state constitution, required a literacy test for voting. An "understanding" clause also allowed registrars to pass whites and deny registration to African Americans who could not satisfactorily demonstrate an understanding of the state constitution.

In 1896 Lynch and Hill led competing delegations to the Republican National Convention. Both factions were committed to William McKinley, and through a compromise, delegates from both groups were seated at the convention. One of Hill's delegates bolted the McKinley slate, reducing the influence of the Hill "machine." After the election, McKinley gave Lynch partial control over the distribution of political patronage in the state.

Lynch began to study law in the 1890s and was admitted to the Mississippi bar in 1896. He subsequently obtained a license to practice law in Washington, D.C., where he opened an office with Robert H. Terrell, who had worked with him in the Treasury Department. He continued with this practice into 1898.

With the outbreak of the Spanish-American War, McKinley selected Lynch as an additional paymaster of volunteers with the rank of major in the army. In 1900 Lynch was again a delegate to the Republican National Convention, serving on the Committee on Platform and Resolutions and as chair of the subcommittee that drafted the national platform.

After the war Lynch remained with the army and received a regular commission in 1901. For three years he was assigned to Cuba, where he learned Spanish, then he was stationed for three and a half years in Omaha, Nebraska, and for sixteen months in San Francisco. In 1907 he sailed for Hawaii and the Philippines. In the Philippines a medical examiner claimed that Lynch had a serious heart condition and was therefore unfit for service with only a few months to live. Suspecting racial discrimination, Lynch protested directly to Washington and was reassigned to California.

Lynch retired from the army in 1911 and moved to Chicago. In 1912 he married Cora Williamson, who was twenty-seven years younger than he. They had no children. Admitted to the Chicago bar by reciprocity in 1915, he practiced law for over twenty-five years. During these years he began writing about the Reconstruction period. An early revisionist, he anticipated the later writings of W. E. B. Du Bois and the post–World War II historians, who looked at the achievements of African American politicians in the 1860s and 1870s with more objectivity than prior historians. Lynch published several well-documented works, beginning with *The Facts of Reconstruction* (1914). Initially rejected by several presses, his critique of James Ford Rhodes's history was published in 1917 and 1918 as two articles in the *Journal of Negro History* and was republished in 1922 entitled *Some Historical Errors of James Ford Rhodes*. He also criticized as full of errors Claude G. Bowers's work *The Tragic Era* (1920). He later incorporated a large section of his 1913 history of Reconstruction in his autobiography, *Reminiscences of an Active Life*, completed shortly before his death in Chicago but not published until 1970, edited by JOHN HOPE FRANKLIN.

An accomplished African American author and politician, Lynch was representative of a small group who worked with some success within the existing political and patronage structure to create opportunities for themselves and to fight for civil rights. Considering his childhood as a slave and his lack of formal education, his achievements as a politician, statesman, and historian are notable.

FURTHER READING

Some Lynch correspondence is in the papers of CARTER G. WOODSON in the Manuscripts Division of the Library of Congress.

Bell, Frank C. "The Life and Times of James R. Lynch: A Case Study 1847–1939," *Journal of Mississippi History* 38 (Feb. 1976): 53–67.

Mann, Kenneth E. "John Roy Lynch, U.S. Congressman from Mississippi," *Negro History Bulletin* 37 (Apr. 1974): 239–241.

Obituary: *New York Times*, 3 Nov. 1939.

—RODNEY P. CARLISLE

LYNK, MILES VANDAHURST

(3 June 1871–29 Dec. 1956), physician, educator, and advocate for African American physicians, was born near Brownsville, Tennessee, the son of John Henry Lynk, a farmer, and Mary Louise Yancy, both former slaves. Miles's parents, members of the Colored (now Christian) Methodist Episcopal (CME) church, founded in nearby Jackson, Tennessee, named their son after the CME's first two bishops, William Henry Miles and Richard H. Vanderhorst. Miles received basic education from his mother, a country school near Brownsville, a tutor he hired with money he had earned, and a course of self-teaching, which he called attending "Pine Knot College." At age seventeen Miles taught at a Negro summer school in a neighboring county and used the money to apprentice himself to Jacob C. Hairston, a local physician and graduate of Meharry Medical College in Nashville. Robert Fulton Boyd, a Meharry professor, was sufficiently impressed with Lynk's entrance examination to admit him to Meharry Medical College in 1889. Lynk finished in two years while the normal course was three years, and, by his own account, graduated second in a class of thirteen.

His own man throughout his life, Lynk ignored the advice of friends, and opened a practice in Jackson, Tennessee, the site of recent racial unrest. In the racially tense and increasingly segregated late-nineteenth-century South, Lynk personally introduced himself to local white physicians and druggists as a way of defusing their concerns. To forestall adverse reaction to a black physician's presence in Jackson's previously all-white medical profession, Lynk used the tactic other African American physicians of the time employed and, according to his autobiography, "gave each [physician and druggist] my card with the statement that I shall endeavor to practice scientific and ethical medicine" (Lynk, 27–28).

Medicine was becoming a crowded profession, and black physicians were not always given a warm reception by white doctors worried about losing paying patients, black or white. Black physicians often charged lower fees because their predominantly African American clientele usually had low incomes. They thus attracted some white patients more interested in low cost than in their physician's race. In addition to gaining fellow physicians' acceptance, Lynk had to win over the African American population as well. Many African Americans—as a result of biases learned from whites since slavery times, bad experiences with African American healers, or superstitious belief—were reluctant to use black physicians. To overcome such prejudice, Lynk worked diligently in his practice, took the time to educate people about good hygiene and sanitation, gave lectures about health and disease to black teachers and church groups, and generally followed his motto "Do all the good you can to all the people you can in all the ways you can." These approaches seemed to work and Lynk reported in the Jackson Daily Sun that he "soon overcame their [African Americans'] scruples and built up a large and lucrative practice" (12 Dec. 1900). A brief notice in the 26 September 1891 issue of the Christian Index, a CME newspaper published in Jackson, attests to his success:

Dr. M.V. Lynk, our Colored physician in this city, has built up such a large practice that it became very necessary that he have a horse and buggy to meet his calls. He now has a splendid outfit and is doing well. Our prediction last winter that a colored doctor would do well here has proven to be true. We are quite glad to see our people giving him their patronage. This is nothing more than right.

From the start of his career Lynk worked not only for his own success but also for the betterment of African Americans, both locally and nationally. At age twenty-one, he established a monthly medical journal for African American physicians, which one black physician from Texas proudly called "a journal of our own" (Lynk, 38). Medical journals of the time ignored the publications and activities of black physicians, medical schools, medical societies, and hospitals. To give African American physicians a voice, Lynk began publishing the Medical and Surgical Observer (MSO) in December 1892. In addition to publishing medical articles and reports on black physicians' experiences, it provided Lynk the

opportunity to promote his own ideas while bringing a sense of community to often isolated African American physicians around the country. The MSO survived for only fourteen issues, until January 1894. Lynk gave no official reason for ceasing publication, though he hinted in editorials at low subscription numbers, lack of article submissions by black physicians, and decreased advertising.

One idea Lynk promoted in the MSO that came to fruition was the formation of a national association of black medical professionals. Such an association was needed, Lynk had explained in an editorial in the first issue of the MSO, because black physicians were excluded from the national American Medical Association as well as from southern (and many northern) local and regional medical societies. Black health professionals in Texas and North Carolina, he reported, had established their own societies and were trying to link up with other physicians elsewhere. On 18 November 1895 at the Cotton States and International Exposition in Atlanta where BOOKER T. WASHINGTON delivered his famous Atlanta Compromise speech, Lynk, along with a few other black physicians, and his Meharry professor Robert F. Boyd, held an organizational meeting of what became the National Medical Association.

In 1900, unable to obtain law training in Jackson, Lynk arranged with Lane College, a local CME-sponsored school, for H. R. Sadler, an African American lawyer in Memphis, to offer a law course. Lynk recruited the students, purchased a law library, and allowed his medical office to be used as a classroom. In February 1901, after earning his law degree and passing the Tennessee bar, Lynk founded the University of West Tennessee (UWT), a "college for the professional training of ambitious Negroes." One of the last of fourteen predominantly black medical schools established between Reconstruction and the start of the twentieth century (only Howard and Meharry medical schools survive today), UWT opened in a newly renovated and appropriately equipped house, with newly hired teachers, and offered its African American students medical, dental, pharmaceutical, nursing, and law training. Lynk established his school despite the rising cost of medical

education due to the rapid growth of scientific medicine, and found UWT's facilities and faculty quickly outdated. The school eventually lost its accreditation—despite a move to Memphis in 1907—and was forced to close in 1923, having graduated one hundred and fifty-five physicians and a number of lawyers, nurses, dentists, and pharmacists.

During the 1890s Lynk wrote books and edited a magazine for African Americans. Lynk Publishing House, which he established to print and sell his work, provided employment to about a dozen African American workers. By 1900 he had published The Afro-American School Speaker and Gems of Literature, for School Commencements, Literary Circles, Debating Clubs, and Rhetoricals Generally (1896), a collection of black literature, and The Black Troopers; or, The Daring Heroism of the Negro Soldiers in the Spanish-American War (1899), which sold more than fifteen thousand copies. He also edited and published several issues of an illustrated monthly literary magazine Lynk's Magazine (1898–1899), which was followed some twenty years later by another magazine The Negro Outlook (1919).

Lynk, who was married twice, in 1893 to chemist Beebe Steven, and in 1949 to Ola Herin Moore, remained active in medicine throughout his life. He combated racism and segregation by his own medical, law, and publishing work and by helping establish black institutions parallel to those in the white medical world (a journal, medical school, and medical society). The National Medical Association, which he helped found in 1895, awarded him its Distinguished Service Medal in 1952. Lynk died in Memphis.

FURTHER READING

Lynk, Miles V. Sixty Years of Medicine; or, The Life and Times of Dr. Miles V. Lynk: An Autobiography (1951).

Savitt, Todd L. "'A Journal of Our Own': The Medical and Surgical Observer at the Beginnings of an African American Medical Profession in Late Nineteenth-Century America," Journal of the National Medical Association (88, 1996).
——. Savitt, Todd L. "Four African-American Proprietary Medical Colleges: 1888–1923," Journal of the History of Medicine & Allied Sciences (55, 2000).
—TODD L. SAVITT

MABLEY, MOMS

(19 Mar. 1894?–23 May 1975), comedian, was born Loretta Mary Aiken in Brevard, North Carolina, the daughter of Jim Aiken, a businessman and grocer. Her mother's name is not known. Details of her early life are sketchy at best, but she maintained in interviews she had black, Irish, and Cherokee ancestry. Her birth date is often given as sometime in 1897. Her grandmother, a former slave, advised her at age thirteen "to leave home if I wanted to make something of myself." However, she may have been unhappy over an arranged marriage with an older man. Mabley stated in a 4 October 1974 *Washington Post* interview, "I did get engaged two or three times, but they always wanted a free sample." Her formative years were spent in the Anacostia section of Washington, D.C., and in Cleveland, Ohio, where she later maintained a home. She had a child out of wedlock when she was sixteen. In an interview she explained she came from a religious family and had the baby because "I didn't believe in destroying children." Mabley recalled that the idea to go on the stage came to her when she prayed and had a vision. But in a 1974 interview she said she went into show business "because I was very pretty and didn't want to become a prostitute." Another time she explained, "I didn't know I was a comic till I got on the stage."

In 1908 she joined a Pittsburgh-based minstrel show by claiming to be sixteen; she earned $12.50 a week and sometimes performed in blackface. By 1910 she was working in black theatrical revues, such as *Look Who's Here* (1920), which briefly played on Broadway. She became engaged to a Canadian named Jack Mabley. Though they never married, she explained she took his name because "he took a lot off me and that was the least I could do."

Moms Mabley, "The Funniest Woman in the World," shown here in character on a television appearance. © Bettmann/CORBIS

In 1921 Mabley was working the "chitlin circuit," as black entertainers referred to black-owned and -managed clubs and theaters in the segregated South. There, she recalled, she introduced a version of the persona that made her famous, the weary older woman on the make for a younger man. The dance duo Butterbeans and Suzie (Jody and Susan Edwards) caught her act and hired her, polishing her routines and introducing her to the Theater Owners Booking Association, or TOBA—black artists said the initials

stood for Tough on Blacks. She shared bills with Pigmeat Markham, Tim "Kingfish" Moore, and BILL "BOJANGLES" ROBINSON.

In the late 1920s when Mabley struggled to find work in New York, black comedian Bonnie Bell Drew (Mabley named her daughter in her honor) became mentor to Mabley, teaching her comedy monologues. Soon Mabley was working Harlem clubs such as the Savoy Ballroom and the Cotton Club and Atlantic City's Club Harlem. She appeared on shows with BESSIE SMITH and CAB CALLOWAY (with whom she had an affair), LOUIS ARMSTRONG, and the COUNT BASIE, DUKE ELLINGTON, and Benny Goodman orchestras. During the Depression, when many clubs closed, she worked church socials and urban movie houses, such as Washington's Howard and Chicago's Monogram and Regal Theatres, where she later returned as a headliner.

Mabley had bit parts in early talkies made in the late 1920s in New York. She played a madam in *The Emperor Jones* (1931), based on the Eugene O'Neill play and starring PAUL ROBESON. In 1931 Mabley collaborated on and appeared in the short-lived Broadway production *Fast and Furious: A Colored Revue in 37 Scenes* with flamboyant Harlem Renaissance writer ZORA NEALE HURSTON. In the late 1920s she appeared in a featured role on Broadway in *Blackbirds*. She played Quince in *Swinging the Dream* (also featuring Butterfly McQueen) in 1939, a jazz adaptation of *A Midsummer Night's Dream*. Other films include *Killer Diller* (1947), opposite NAT KING COLE and Butterfly McQueen; *Boardinghouse Blues* (1948), in which she played a role much like her stage character; and *Amazing Grace* (1974), in which McQueen and STEPIN FETCHIT had cameos. It was drubbed by critics but did well at the box office.

The most popular Mabley character was the cantankerous but lovable toothless woman with bulging eyes and raspy voice who wore a garish smock or rumpled clothes, argyle socks, and slippers. Though she maintained, "I do the double entendre … and never did anything you haven't heard on the streets," the nature of her material, more often than not off-color, was such that, in spite of the brilliance of her comic timing and gift of ad-libbing, she was denied the route comics such as Flip Wilson, DICK GREGORY, and BILL COSBY took into fine supper clubs and Las Vegas. A younger brother, Eddie Parton, wrote comedy situations for her, but most of her material was absorbed from listening to her world. Offstage Mabley was an avid reader and an attractive woman who wore furs, chic clothes, and owned a Rolls-Royce, albeit an inveterate smoker, a card shark, and a whiz at checkers.

In 1940 she broke the gender barrier and became the first female comic to appear at Harlem's Apollo Theatre,

where her act, which included song and dance, played fifteen sold-out weeks. Mabley was mentor to young PEARL BAILEY and befriended by LANGSTON HUGHES, who wrote a friend that he occasionally helped Mabley financially. Legend has her acquiring the nickname "Moms" because of her mothering instincts toward performers.

Her first album, *Moms Mabley, the Funniest Woman in the World* (1960), sold in excess of a million copies. In 1966 she was signed by Mercury Records. She made over twenty-five comedy records, many capturing her live performances; others, called "party records," had laugh tracks. She said black and white comics stole her material, then forgot her when they became famous.

Television was late to discover Mabley. Thanks to fan HARRY BELAFONTE, she made her TV debut in a breakthrough comedy he produced with an integrated cast, *A Time for Laughter* (1967), as the maid to a pretentious black suburban couple. Merv Griffin invited her on his show, and appearances followed with Mike Douglas and variety programs starring Flip Wilson, Bill Cosby, and the Smothers Brothers. Mabley had been known mainly to black audiences. Of this late acceptance, she mused, "It's too bad it took so long. Now that I've got some money, I have to use it all for doctor bills." Mabley was not always career savvy. She passed up an appearance on CBS's top-rated *Ed Sullivan Show*, saying, "Mr. Sullivan didn't want to give me but four minutes. Honey, it takes Moms four minutes just to get on the stage."

Because of her influence with African Americans, Mabley was seriously courted by politicians such as ADAM CLAYTON POWELL JR., whom she called "my minister." She did not aggressively support the 1960s civil rights movement, and she expressed outrage at the riots in Harlem. She was invited to the White House by Presidents John F. Kennedy and Lyndon Johnson. Of the latter event, she told a (fictional) joke about admonishing Johnson to "get something colored up in the air quick" (a black astronaut). She said, "I happen to spy him [and] said, 'Hey, Lyndon! Lyndon, son! Lyndon. Come here, boy!' " She brought the house down merely by the gall in her delivery. Mabley maintained she

corresponded with and met Eleanor Roosevelt to "talk about young men."

Various articles, which say nothing of a first husband—if there was one—note that Mabley had been separated from her second husband, Ernest Scherer, for twenty years when he died in 1974. The comedian had three daughters and adopted a son, who became a psychiatrist.

Late in her career, Mabley played Carnegie Hall on a bill with singer Nancy Wilson and jazz great Cannonball Adderley, the famed Copacabana, and even Washington's Kennedy Center (Aug. 1972).

During the filming of her last movie, Mabley suffered a heart attack, and production was delayed for her to undergo surgery for a pacemaker. Her condition weakened on tours to publicize the film, and for six months she was confined to her home in Hartsdale, in New York's Westchester County. She died at White Plains Hospital. Her funeral at Harlem's Abyssinian Baptist Church drew thousands of fans.

FURTHER READING

The Schomburg Center for Research in Black Culture of the New York Public Library and the New York Public Library for the Performing Arts maintain research files.

Bogle, Donald. *Brown Sugar: Eighty Years of America's Black Female Superstars* (1980).
Sochen, June. *Women's Comic Visions* (1991).
Watkins, Mel. *On the Real Side, Laughing, Lying, and Signifying: The Underground Tradition of African American Humor That Transformed American Culture, from Slavery to* RICHARD PRYOR (1994).
Williams, Elsie A. *The Humor of Jackie "Moms" Mabley: An African American Comedic Tradition* (1995).

Obituary: *New York Times*, 25 May 1975.
—ELLIS NASSOUR

MALCOLM X

(19 May 1925–21 Feb. 1965), Islamic minister and political leader, also known as el-Hajj Malik el-Shabazz, was born Malcolm Little in Omaha, Nebraska, the fourth of five children of Earl Little and Louise (also Louisa) Norton, both activists in the Universal Negro Improvement Association established by

Malcolm X, national spokesman for the Nation of Islam, delivers a fiery address in Harlem, 1963. Corbis

MARCUS GARVEY. Earl Little, a Georgia-born itinerant Baptist preacher, encountered considerable racial harassment because of his black nationalist views. He moved his family several times before settling in Michigan, purchasing a home in 1929 on the outskirts of East Lansing, where Malcolm spent his childhood. Their previous home had been destroyed in a mysterious fire. In 1931 Earl Little's body was discovered on a train track. Although police concluded that the death was accidental, the victim's friends and relatives suspected that he had been murdered by a local white supremacist group. Earl's death left the family in poverty and undoubtedly contributed to Louise Little's mental deterioration. In January 1939 she was declared legally insane and committed to a Michigan mental asylum, where she remained until 1963.

Although Malcolm Little excelled academically in grammar school and was popular among classmates at these predominantly white schools, he also became embittered toward white authority figures. In his autobiography he recalls quitting school in the eighth grade after a teacher warned that his desire to become a lawyer was not a "realistic goal for a nigger." As his mother's mental health deteriorated and he became increasingly incorrigible, welfare officials intervened, placing him in several reform schools and foster homes. In 1941 he left Michigan to live in Boston with his half sister, Ella Collins.

In Boston and New York during the early 1940s, Malcolm held a variety of railroad jobs while also becoming increasingly involved in criminal activities, such as peddling illegal drugs and numbers running. At this time he was often called Detroit Red because of his reddish hair. First arrested in 1944 for larceny and given a three-month suspended sentence and a year's probation, Malcolm was arrested again in 1946 for larceny as well as breaking and entering. When the judge learned that Malcolm was involved in a romantic relationship

with a white woman, he imposed a particularly severe sentence of from eight to ten years in prison. While in Concord Reformatory in Massachusetts, Malcolm responded to the urgings of his brother Reginald and became a follower of ELIJAH MUHAMMAD (formerly Robert Poole), leader of the Temple of Islam (later Nation of Islam—often called the Black Muslims), a small black nationalist Islamic sect. Attracted to the religious group's racial doctrines, which categorized whites as "devils," he began reading extensively about world history and politics, particularly concerning African slavery and the oppression of black people in America. After he was paroled from prison in August 1952, he became Malcolm X, using the surname assigned to him in place of the African name that had been taken from his slave ancestors.

By 1953 Malcolm X had become Elijah Muhammad's most effective minister, bringing large numbers of new recruits into the group during the 1950s and early 1960s. By 1954 he had become minister of New York Temple No. 7, and he later helped establish Islamic temples in other cities. In 1957 he became the Nation of Islam's national representative, a position of influence second only to that of Elijah Muhammad. In January 1958 he married Betty X (Sanders), who later became known as Betty Shabazz; together they had six daughters.

Malcolm's cogent and electrifying oratory attracted considerable publicity and a large personal following among discontented African Americans. In his speeches he urged black people to separate from whites and win their freedom "by any means necessary." In 1957, after New York police beat and jailed Nation of Islam member Hinton Johnson, Malcolm X mobilized supporters to confront police officials and secure medical treatment. A 1959 television documentary on the Nation of Islam, called *The Hate That Hate Produced*, further increased Malcolm's notoriety among whites. In 1959 he traveled to Europe and the Middle East on behalf of Elijah Muhammad, and in 1961 he served as Muhammad's emissary at a secret Atlanta meeting seeking an accommodation with the Ku Klux Klan. The following year he participated in protest meetings prompted by the killing of a Black Muslim during a police raid on a Los Angeles mosque. By 1963 he had become a frequent guest on radio and television programs and was the most well known figure in the Nation of Islam.

Malcolm X was particularly harsh in his criticisms of the nonviolent strategy to achieve civil rights reforms advocated by MARTIN LUTHER KING JR. His letters seeking King's participation in public forums were generally ignored by King. During a November 1963 address at the Northern Negro Grass Roots Leadership Conference in Detroit, Michigan, Malcolm derided the notion that African Americans could achieve freedom nonviolently. "The only revolution in which the goal is loving your enemy is the Negro revolution," he announced. "Revolution is bloody, revolution is hostile, revolution knows no compromise, revolution overturns and destroys everything that gets in its way." Malcolm also charged that King and other leaders of the recently held March on Washington had taken over the event, with the help of white liberals, in order to subvert its militancy. "And as they took it over, it lost its militancy. It ceased to be angry, it ceased to be hot, it ceased to be uncompromising," he insisted. Despite his caustic criticisms of King, Malcolm nevertheless identified himself with the grass-roots leaders of the southern civil rights protest movement. His desire to move from rhetorical to political militancy led him to become increasingly dissatisfied with Elijah Muhammad's apolitical stance. As he later explained in his autobiography, "It could be heard increasingly in the Negro communities: 'Those Muslims *talk* tough, but they never *do* anything, unless somebody bothers Muslims.'"

Malcolm's disillusionment with Elijah Muhammad resulted not only from political differences but also from his personal dismay when he discovered that the religious leader had fathered illegitimate children. Other members of the Nation of Islam began to resent Malcolm's growing prominence and to suspect that he intended to lay claim to leadership of the group. When Malcolm X remarked that President John Kennedy's assassination in November 1963 was a case of the "chickens coming home to roost," Elijah Muhammad used the opportunity to ban his increasingly popular minister from speaking in public.

Despite this effort to silence him, Malcolm X continued to attract public attention during 1964. He counseled the boxer Cassius Clay, who publicly announced, shortly after winning the heavyweight boxing title, that he had become a member of the Nation of Islam and adopted the name MUHAMMAD ALI. In March 1964 Malcolm announced that he was breaking with the Nation of Islam to form his own group, Muslim Mosque, Inc. The theological and ideological gulf between Malcolm and Elijah Muhammad widened during a month-long trip to Africa and the Middle East. During a pilgrimage to Mecca on 20 April 1964 Malcolm reported that seeing Muslims of all colors worshiping together caused him to reject the view that all whites were devils. Repudiating the racial theology of the Nation of Islam, he moved toward orthodox Islam as practiced outside the group. He also traveled to Egypt, Lebanon, Nigeria, Ghana, Senegal, and Morocco, meeting with political activists and national leaders, including the Ghanaian president Kwame Nkrumah. After returning to the United States on 21 May, Malcolm announced that he had adopted a Muslim name, el-Hajj Malik el-Shabazz, and that he was forming a new political group, the Organization of Afro-American Unity (OAAU), to bring together all elements of the African American freedom struggle.

Determined to unify African Americans, Malcolm sought to strengthen his ties with the more militant factions of the civil rights movement. Although he continued to reject King's nonviolent, integrationist approach, he had a brief, cordial encounter with King on 26 March 1964 as the latter left a press conference at the U.S. Capitol. The following month, at a symposium in Cleveland, Ohio, sponsored by the Congress of Racial Equality, Malcolm X delivered one of his most notable speeches, "The Ballot or the Bullet," in which he urged black people to submerge their differences "and realize that it is best for us to first see that we have the same problem, a common problem—a problem that will make you catch hell whether you're a Baptist, or a Methodist, or a Muslim, or a nationalist."

When he traveled again to Africa during the summer of 1964 to attend the Organization of African Unity

Summit Conference, he was able to discuss his unity plans at an impromptu meeting in Nairobi with leaders of the Student Nonviolent Coordinating Committee. After returning to the United States in November, he invited FANNIE LOU HAMER and other members of the Mississippi Freedom Democratic Party to be guests of honor at an OAAU meeting held the following month in Harlem, New York. Early in February 1965 he traveled to Alabama to address gatherings of young activists involved in a voting rights campaign. He tried to meet with King during this trip, but the civil rights leader was in jail; instead, Malcolm met with CORETTA SCOTT KING, telling her that he did not intend to make life more difficult for her husband. "If white people realize what the alternative is, perhaps they will be more willing to hear Dr. King," he explained.

Malcolm's political enemies multiplied within the U.S. government as he attempted to strengthen his ties with civil rights activists and deepen his relationship with ADAM CLAYTON POWELL JR., JAMES BALDWIN, Dick Gregory, and black leaders around the world. The Federal Bureau of Investigation saw Malcolm as a subversive and initiated efforts to undermine his influence. In addition, some of his former Nation of Islam colleagues, including Louis X (later LOUIS FARRAKHAN), condemned him as a traitor for publicly criticizing Elijah Muhammad. The Nation of Islam attempted to evict Malcolm from the home he occupied in Queens, New York. On 14 February 1965 Malcolm's home was firebombed; although he and his family escaped unharmed, the perpetrators were never apprehended.

On 21 February 1965 members of the Nation of Islam shot and killed Malcolm as he was beginning a speech at the Audubon Ballroom in New York City. On 27 February more than fifteen hundred people attended his funeral service held in Harlem and OSSIE DAVIS gave a moving eulogy that contrasted the public's perception of an angry Malcolm with the loving and gentle man he knew, a person who gave voice to the pain of his people and gave courage to those who were afraid to speak the truth. Although three men were convicted in 1966 and sentenced to life terms, one of those involved, Thomas Hagan, filed an affidavit in 1977 insisting that his actual accomplices were never apprehended.

After his death, Malcolm's views reached an even larger audience than during his life. *The Autobiography of Malcolm X*, written with the assistance of ALEX HALEY, became a best-selling book following its publication in 1965. During subsequent years other books appeared, containing texts of many of his speeches, including *Malcolm X Speaks* (1965), *The End of White World Supremacy: Four Speeches* (1971), and *February 1965: The Final Speeches* (1992). In 1994 Orlando Bagwell and Judy Richardson produced a major documentary, *Malcolm X: Make It Plain.* His words and image also exerted a lasting influence on African American popular culture, as evidenced in the hip-hop or rap music of the late twentieth century and in the director SPIKE LEE's film biography, *Malcolm X* (1992).

FURTHER READING

Malcolm X and Alex Haley. *The Autobiography of Malcolm X* (1999).
———. *Malcolm Speaks* (1989).

Carson, Clayborne. *Malcolm X: The FBI File* (1991).
Dyson, Michael Eric. *Making Malcolm* (1996).
Myers, Walter Dean. *Malcolm X: By Any Means Necessary* (1994).
Perry, Bruce. *Malcolm: The Life of a Man Who Changed Black America* (1991).
Strickland, William. *Malcolm X: Make It Plain* (1995).

Obituary: *New York Times*, 22 Feb. 1965.
—CLAYBORNE CARSON

 MALONE, ANNIE TURNBO (9 Aug. 1869– 10 May 1957), entrepreneur and philanthropist, was born Annie Minerva Turnbo on a farm in Metropolis, Illinois, the tenth of eleven children of Robert Turnbo and Isabella Cook, both farmers. Robert and Isabella owned the land they farmed and were able to provide comfortably for themselves and their children. After her parents died of yellow fever in 1877, Annie went to live with an older sister in Peoria, Illinois. As a young woman, Annie grew dissatisfied with the hair-grooming methods then in use by African American

women which often involved the use of goose fat, soap, and harsh chemicals for straightening purposes. Stronger products to straighten naturally curly hair generally damaged the hair follicles or scalp. One of the methods recommended by such products advised users to wash their hair and lay it out flat while using a hot flatiron to apply the solutions. Even washed and laid out, the hair of many women was not long enough to iron, and one of the most common beauty complaints among African American women was burned scalps; indeed, many black women suffered from baldness at an early age. In response, by 1900 Turnbo formulated and perfected a product line she named "Wonderful Hair Grower" which she sold through local stores near her home in Lovejoy, Illinois. Turbo also invented and patented both a pressing iron and a pressing comb, devices that, when used in conjunction with her products, aided in straightening African American hair.

In 1902, in an effort to expand her business opportunities, Turnbo relocated from Lovejoy to St. Louis, Missouri, where she and three assistants began selling her products door-to-door, offering women free, on-the-spot hair treatments. The approach was successful, and Turnbo undertook a highly profitable sales tour of the South in 1903. That same year she married a Mr. Pope but soon divorced him after her new husband attempted to exert control over her thriving door-to-door business. After the divorce, Turnbo opened her own salon, and a year later her products, which she called "Poro," were being sold throughout the Midwest.

In 1906 Malone copyrighted the name "Poro," a West African term that denotes an organization whose aim is to discipline and enhance the body both physically and spiritually. The company name might have another source, however: in advertisements for the company in 1908 and 1909, Annie Turnbo Pope is pictured with a woman named L. L. Roberts. Though there are no records indicating Roberts's relationship to the company, it is possible that "Poro" is a contraction composed of *Pope* and *Roberts*.

The company's sales growth was spurred by Malone's understanding and use of modern business practices, including holding press conferences,

advertising in African American newspapers, and using female salespeople. By the first decades of the twentieth century, Malone's business was thriving, and by 1910 she had opened larger offices in St. Louis. In 1917 she opened Poro College, the first cosmetology school founded to train hairdressers to care for African American hair. The large, lavish facility included well-equipped classrooms, an auditorium, ice cream parlor, bakery, and theater, as well as the manufacturing facilities for Poro products. The college was soon a center of activity and influence in St. Louis's black community, with several prominent local and national African American organizations housed on site. The college offered training courses that included etiquette classes for women interested in joining the Poro System's agent-operator network. By the 1920s the Poro business employed 175 people in St. Louis and boasted of seventy-five thousand agents working throughout the United States and the Caribbean. In 1930 Turnbo opened new headquarters in Chicago that became known as the Poro Block. At the peak of her career, in the 1920s, Turnbo's personal worth reached fourteen million dollars.

Turnbo's business success has often been overshadowed by that of her contemporary, MADAME C. J. WALKER. In fact, Walker's successful use of door-to-door sales agents was a business strategy she learned from Turnbo while employed as a Poro sales agent for several months in 1905. That same year, Walker informed friends that she had learned how to make a hair product that really worked. Perhaps in an effort to avoid direct competition with Turnbo, she moved to Denver early in 1906 to begin her own company.

In 1921 Turnbo married Aaron Malone, a decision that proved disastrous for the company. During much of the 1920s the Malones were engaged in a debilitating, behind-the-scenes power struggle that was kept hidden from all but a few Poro System executives. Before the couple's divorce in 1927 and his subsequent termination from his position as chief manager and president, Aaron Malone sought support in a bid to take over the company. In asking the courts to award him half of the company, Malone claimed the success of his wife's business was due to connections he had brought to the marriage. While Aaron managed to get support from key members of the black community, Annie Malone, with the help of influential black women leaders, including MARY MCLEOD BETHUNE, succeeded in keeping control of Poro after paying her ex-husband a settlement of around one hundred thousand dollars.

Malone's largesse had certainly helped sway public opinion in her favor. She had become a generous contributor to African American organizations. She supported a pair of black students at every African American land-grant college in the country; orphanages for African American children regularly received donations of five thousand dollars; and during the 1920s alone, she gave sixty thousand dollars each to the St. Louis Colored Young Women's Christian Association, the Tuskegee Institute, and the Howard University Medical School. Within her company Malone was equally magnanimous. Five-year employees received diamond rings, and punctuality and attendance were rewarded as well.

Soon after her divorce, Malone was back in court, when Edgar Brown filed suit against her for one hundred thousand dollars. The case was dismissed for lack of evidence. Ten years later, a former employee successfully brought suit against Malone. These legal and financial troubles exacerbated longstanding management problems at Poro. Poor oversight by Malone, bad hiring choices, rapid expansion, and the prolonged, behind the scenes power struggle with Aaron Malone had dire consequences for the company. These battles, both public and private, and her unmatched—and unchecked—generosity spelled the beginning of the end for Malone's Poro empire. Malone was forced to sell her St. Louis property in order to pay for debts incurred, in part, by her divorce and court settlements. Due to her failure to pay excise and real estate taxes, the federal government seized control of the company in 1951. Malone died of a stroke in a Chicago hospital six years later, in 1957, at age eighty-seven. Upon her death, her estate was worth only one hundred thousand dollars.

FURTHER READING

Malone's papers are available at the DuSable Museum of African American History in Chicago, Illinois.

Kathy Peiss, *Hope in a Jar: The Making of America's Beauty Culture* (1998).

Obituary: *The Chicago Defender*, 10 May 1957.
—NOLIWE ROOKS

 MARRANT, JOHN
(15 June 1755–Apr. 1791), minister and author, was born in the New York Colony to a family of free blacks. The names and occupations of his parents are not known. When he was four years old, his father died. Marrant and his mother moved to Florida and Georgia; subsequently Marrant moved to Charleston, South Carolina, to live with his sister and brother-in-law. He stayed in school until he was eleven years old, becoming an apprentice to a music master for two additional years. During this time he also learned carpentry. His careers in music and carpentry ended in late 1769 or early 1770, when he was converted to Christianity by the famous evangelical minister George Whitefield.

Over the next few years, Marrant converted many Native Americans, including members of the Cherokee, Creek, Choctaw, and Chickasaw nations. In 1772 he returned to his family for a short time. For the next three years Marrant worked as a minister in the Charleston area. There he saw a plantation owner and other white males whip thirty slaves for attending his church school.

With the onslaught of the revolutionary war, Marrant was impressed as a musician into the British navy in October or November of 1776. Not much is known of his exploits during this period besides the fact that he fought in the Dutch-Anglo War (1780–1784). As a result of his injuries, he was discharged in 1782.

Marrant eventually married. A listing in the New York City Inspection Roll of Negroes in 1783 cited a Mellia Marrant as "formerly the property of John Marrant near Santee Carolina"; this document also states that she "left him at the Siege of Georgetown." Apparently, his wife had been a slave; he bought and freed her in order to marry her. The same listing claimed that Mellia was aboard the *William and Mary* with her children Amelia and Ben, heading for Annapolis Royal, Nova Scotia. There is no evidence to support or

deny that they were Marrant's children. The information in this record is all that is known of his marriage and offspring.

To further his opportunities, Marrant moved to London, England, living there between 1782 and 1785. In Bath on 15 May 1785, he was ordained a minister in the chapel of Selina Hastings, countess of Huntingdon and a supporter of the African American poet PHILLIS WHEATLEY. During this time, despite being literate, Marrant told his story to Methodist minister William Aldridge, who later published it as *A Narrative of the Lord's Wonderful Dealings with John Marrant, a Black (Now Going to Preach the Gospel in Nova-Scotia) Born in New-York, in North-America* (1785). The narrative, in which Marrant describes his conversion and his life as a traveling minister, was so popular that it went through twenty editions by 1835. In 1785 S. Whitchurch and S. Hazard both published *The Negro Convert: A Poem; Being the Substance of the Experience of Mr. John Marrant, a Negro.*

In November 1785 Marrant moved to Birchtown, Nova Scotia, to minister to the black Loyalists who had immigrated there after the American Revolution. For the next two years he was persecuted and harassed by fellow ministers because he preached Calvinistic Methodism to whites, blacks, and Native Americans in Nova Scotia. Despite his persecution, he built a chapel in Birchtown, taught at the Birchtown school, preached to the congregation, and ministered in other towns. In late November 1786 Marrant gave up control of his school because of his exhaustion and decided to concentrate on being a traveling minister. He contracted smallpox in an epidemic in February 1787 and was ill for six months.

In Nova Scotia, Marrant lived a life of poverty and illness. In late January 1788 he moved to Boston, where he preached and apparently taught school. However, Marrant could not escape persecution. On 27 February 1789 he eluded a mob of forty armed men who were attempting to kill him because their girlfriends went to his Friday sermon. In March of that year he became a Freemason in the African Lodge. As a Freemason, Marrant gave a sermon at the Festival of John the Baptist; the sermon was published in 1789. On his way back to England, Marrant wrote his last journal entry on 7 March 1790. The journal was later published as *A Journal of the Rev. John Marrant* (1790), along with Marrant's sermon of a funeral service in Nova Scotia. The preface of the journal gave the publication date of 29 June 1790. Marrant died somewhere in England and is buried at Islington.

In his sermons, Marrant tried to teach people to love God through a comparison of biblical allegories and everyday life. For example, in his *Narrative*, Marrant's travels after his conversion are reminiscent of John the Baptist's sojourn in the wilderness. His theme is clear: let Jesus and God be your guides. This message is stressed when faith saves him from being executed by a Native-American nation: "I fell down upon my knees, and mentioned to the Lord his delivering of the three children in the fiery furnace, and of Daniel in the Lion's den, and had close communion with God.... And about the middle of my prayer, the Lord impressed a strong desire upon my mind to turn into their language, and pray in their tongue... which wonderfully affected the people" (Porter, 437).

In his short life, Marrant dedicated himself to helping others reach their religious potential. Through his published sermons and conversions, Marrant wanted to help humankind the best way he knew how: by giving them God's lessons. Even though he never reaped an earthly reward in his lifetime, his works stand as a model for religious colonial life.

FURTHER READING

Andrews, William L. *To Tell a Free Story: The First Century of Afro-American Autobiography, 1760–1865* (1988).

Gates, Henry Louis, Jr. *The Signifying Monkey: A Theory of Afro-American Literary Criticism* (1988).

Porter, Dorothy. *Early Negro Writing, 1760–1837* (1971).

Potkay, Adam, and Sandra Burr, eds. *Black Atlantic Writers of the Eighteenth Century: Living the New Exodus in England and the Americas* (1995).

—DEVONA A. MALLORY

MARS, JAMES (3 Mar. 1790–?), slave narrative author, was born in Canaan, Connecticut, the child of slaves. James's father, Jupiter Mars, was born in New York State. He had a succession of owners, including General Henry Kiliaen Van Rensselaer, with whom Jupiter served in the Revolutionary War. He was subsequently owned in Salisbury, Connecticut, and later by the Reverend Mr. Thompson, a minister in North Canaan, Connecticut. James's mother, whose name remains unknown, was born in Virginia and was owned there by the woman who became Thompson's wife. His mother, who had one child while living in Virginia, was relocated to Connecticut when Mrs. Thompson moved to Canaan to join her husband. Reverend Thompson married Mars's parents, and they had James and four other children, three of whom died in infancy.

Of Mrs. Thompson, James Mars told his father that "if she only had him South, where she could have at her call a half dozen men, she would have him stripped and flogged until he was cut in strings" (Mars, 5). The Thompsons eventually did move south, leaving the farm to be tended by Mars's parents. In 1798, when James was eight years old, Thompson, who had always preached that slavery was divinely sanctioned, returned to Connecticut, intending to sell the farm and bring his slaves to the South for sale on the southern slave market. The Mars family—James's mother, father, fourteen-year-old older brother Joseph, and younger sister—resisted by escaping to Norfolk, Connecticut. They went deeper into hiding when news arrived that Thompson had hired slave catchers to locate them and transport them to Virginia. After several days, during which the family successfully evaded recapture, Thompson decided to focus his attentions on Joseph and James, since they would bring the highest prices on the slave market.

Thompson, who originally refused to go to Virginia without the boys, eventually proposed a compromise by which Mars's father would agree to sell his sons to owners in Connecticut in exchange for his freedom and that of his wife and daughter. Jupiter Mars was permitted to approve the men to whom his sons would be sold. On 12 September 1798, Joseph was sold to a farmer named Bingham (who had once owned Jupiter) and James was sold to a man named Munger from Norfolk.

Thompson received one hundred dollars for each. Under the terms of the sale, the boys would be slaves until the age of twenty-five, the limit to which Connecticut law allowed slaves to be held. James's parents and sister remained in Norfolk, and he was permitted to see them once every two weeks.

By the age of thirteen or fourteen, James had grown dissatisfied with his lack of education, his owner's cruelty, and the terms of his servitude in comparison with the terms of indentured white boys, who were bound in service until they were twenty-one and who received one hundred dollars at the conclusion of their terms. On one occasion, when Mars was sixteen, Munger threatened to whip him, and Mars responded saying, "You had better not." Munger backed down, and as Mars tells it, "From that time until I was twenty-one, I do not remember that he ever gave me an unpleasant word or look" (Mars, 25). Mars was generally able to live as freely as any of the other boys who lived in the neighborhood.

For the next few years, Mars worked in relative contentment. "I was willing to work, and thought much of the family, and they thought something of me," he later wrote (26). Munger seems not to have been aware that under Connecticut law he could hold Mars in his service after he turned twenty-one, and he made an offer to Mars on the condition that he would stay longer. Mars thought "the offer was tolerably fair. I had now become attached to the family" (27), but Munger withdrew the verbal offer after learning that he had the legal right to keep Mars as a slave until his twenty-fifth birthday, especially since no written agreement could be produced proving otherwise.

Mars was further disappointed when Munger reneged on an agreement to give him some livestock, and he threatened to leave unless Munger would put the agreement in writing. When Munger declined, Mars left the farm for his parents' home. Munger asked Mars to return voluntarily. Instead, Mars and Munger agreed to abide by the decision of three mutually acceptable arbiters. The arbiters ruled that Mars should pay Munger ninety dollars for his freedom. After paying Munger, Mars hired himself out to another family, but after a four-year break he returned to work for the Munger family. After a trip west, he returned to find that Munger had suffered a decline in his fortunes and that his daughter was in poor health. Mars, "accustomed to take care of the sick" (31), remained with Munger's daughter until she died peacefully soon after. "That was a scene that I love to think of. It makes me almost forget that I ever was a slave to her father; but so it was" (32). Although Mars worked where he chose for the next several years, he was frequently at the Munger home and remained in close contact with his former owner until he, like his daughter, died with Mars at his side.

Mars married after Munger's death and fathered eight children. He lived in Norfolk and Hartford, Connecticut, and Pittsfield, Massachusetts. In the appendix to his narrative, Mars notes that his children followed a variety of vocations: one son enlisted in the U.S. Navy, another went to sea and fell out of touch with the family, a third enlisted in the navy at the beginning of the Civil War, and a fourth son enlisted as an artillery man and was most likely killed in the Civil War. One of Mars's daughters went to Africa and became a teacher, and another moved to Massachusetts with her family.

What we know about James Mars comes entirely from his narrative *Life of James Mars, a Slave Born and Sold in Connecticut. Written by Himself*, published in 1864. Mars indicates in his introduction that publication was not his intention when he began writing at his sister's request during the Civil War. His sister, who had lived in Africa for more than thirty years, had been born in freedom and knew little of her parents and siblings' experiences under slavery. Unlike the narratives published by escaped slaves who wrote, often with abolitionist sponsorship, with the intention of educating readers about the atrocities of the slave system and in the hopes of bringing about its end, Mars's original intentions were entirely personal: "When I had got it written, as it made more writing than I was willing to undertake to give each of them [the members of his family] one, I thought I would have it printed, and perhaps I might sell enough to pay the expenses, as many of the people now on the stage of life do not know that slavery ever existed in Connecticut" (3).

In addition to revealing the facts of his own life, Mars's narrative contributes to our understanding of the lives of slaves in the North as well as the peculiarities of slavery in the North. It provides a rare illustration of the economic and social disparities and the grave distinction between the freedom promised by the North and the actual social and economic limitations imposed upon blacks in northern states.

Mars reports that at the age of seventy-nine, he was living on meager savings and unable to work because of a fall he experienced in 1866. He intended his narrative as a testament to the experiences of other slaves who labored in Connecticut, a place that many readers were unaware ever countenanced slavery. Despite the restrictions imposed by the state of Connecticut, Mars tells his readers, he had voted in five presidential elections and twice voted for Abraham Lincoln. Mars concludes his narrative with a condemnation of his home state: "If my life is spared I intend to be where I can show that I have the principles of a man, and act like a man, and vote like a man, but not in my native State; I cannot do it there, I must remove to the old Bay State for the right to be a man. Connecticut, I love thy name, but not thy restrictions" (38). How long Mars lived after his memoir was reprinted in 1868 and the circumstances of his death remain unknown.

FURTHER READING

Mars, James. *Life of James Mars, a Slave Born and Sold in Connecticut. Written by Himself* (1864, reprinted in 1868); also published in *African American Slave Narratives: An Anthology*, ed. Sterling Lecater Bland Jr., vol. 3 (2001).

—STERLING LECATER BLAND JR.

MARSALIS, WYNTON (18 Oct. 1961–), trumpeter, was born in Kenner, Louisiana, the second of six sons of Ellis Marsalis, a jazz pianist and teacher, and Dolores Ferdinand. He was named after the jazz pianist Wynton Kelly. Wynton Marsalis was raised in a musical family with his brothers, Branford (tenor and soprano saxophones), Delfeayo (trombone), and Jason (drums).

Marsalis began playing the trumpet at the age of six, starting on an instrument given to him by the bandleader and trumpeter Al Hirt, with whom his father was then playing. At age eight, he was playing in a children's marching band and performing at the New Orleans Jazz and Heritage Festival. A prodigiously talented instrumentalist, Marsalis studied both jazz and classical music from an early age and at age twelve began classical training on the trumpet. His early musical experience was diverse and included playing in local marching bands, jazz groups, and classical youth orchestras. At high school he played first trumpet with the New Orleans Civic Orchestra. He made his professional debut at age fourteen in a performance of Haydn's Trumpet Concerto with the New Orleans Philharmonic Orchestra.

In 1977 Marsalis's performance at the Eastern Music Festival in North Carolina led to him being awarded the festival's Most Outstanding Musician Award. In 1978, at age seventeen, he performed Bach's Brandenburg Concerto no. 2 (on piccolo trumpet) with the New Orleans Symphony Orchestra. In the same year, Gunther Schuller admitted him to the summer-school program at the Berkshire Music Center at Tanglewood, in Lenox, Massachusetts, after he had auditioned with the same Bach concerto. Schuller recounted how Marsalis "soared right through it and didn't miss a note" (Giddins, 158), afterward receiving the school's Harry Shapiro Award for Outstanding Brass Player. In 1979 Marsalis was awarded a scholarship to the Juilliard School of Music in New York City. At that time he also performed with the Brooklyn Philharmonic and the Mexico City Symphony orchestras as well as playing in the pit band for Stephen Sondheim's Broadway musical *Sweeney Todd*.

In 1980, with a leave of absence from Juilliard, Marsalis joined ART BLAKEY's Jazz Messengers. He then toured in a quartet led by Herbie Hancock, performing at the Newport Jazz Festival and on the album *Herbie Hancock Quartet* (1981). In 1983 Marsalis appeared again with Hancock in a quintet that included his brother Branford. By 1982 Marsalis was touring extensively with his own quintet and appearing at such venues as the Kool Jazz Festival at Newport and with the Young

Trumpeter Wynton Marsalis, himself a jazz traditionalist, has spurred debate on "what jazz is—and isn't." Corbis

Lions of Jazz in New York. In London at the end of the year he appeared at Ronnie Scott's club and made his first classical recordings: trumpet concertos by Haydn, Hummel, and Leopold Mozart, with Raymond Leppard and the National Philharmonic Orchestra. Also in 1982 he recorded his debut album as leader, *Wynton Marsalis*. In the same year, he won the Jazz Musician of the Year Award in *Down Beat*'s readers' poll. In 1984 Marsalis undertook a classical tour, playing with orchestras across the United States and Canada. Also in 1984 he became the first (and only) musician to win Grammy Awards in both jazz and classical categories, taking Best Soloist for his jazz album *Think of One*, and Best Soloist with Orchestra for the concerto set with Leppard. He won both awards again the following year.

By the middle of the decade Marsalis was recording prolifically and accumulating significant awards and prizes. This period saw the release of *Hot House Flowers* (1984), *Black Codes (from the Underground)* (1985), and *J Mood* (1986). Subsequent recordings included the first volume of the *Standard Time* series (1987), *Live at Blue Alley* (1988), *The Majesty of the Blues* (1989), the three-volume *Soul Gestures in Southern Blue* (1991), and *Blue Interlude* (1992). In 1992 Marsalis became artistic director of jazz at New York's Lincoln Center and leader of its Jazz Orchestra (LCJO).

In 1997 he was awarded the Pulitzer Prize for Music for his "oratorio," *Blood on the Fields*, which was commissioned by Lincoln Center and premiered there with the LCJO in 1994. Jazz musicians had hitherto been ineligible for the award—it was denied to DUKE ELLINGTON in 1965—and it was a measure of Marsalis's distinction, and the enhanced prestige of jazz, that he should be the first to receive the award. The oratorio, about American slavery, was self-consciously Ellingtonian in style, theme, and scope, recalling Ellington's 1943 suite, *Black, Brown and Beige*.

In addition to his jazz albums, Marsalis has made several classical recordings: *Baroque Music for Trumpets* (1988), a collection of orchestral works by Vivaldi, Telemann, and Biber, with Raymond Leppard and the English Chamber Orchestra (ECO); *On the Twentieth Century . . .* (1993), with Judith Lynn Stillman (piano), including works by Ravel, Honegger, Bernstein, and Hindemith; and *In Gabriel's Garden* (1996), with Anthony Newman and the ECO, featuring orchestral works by Mouret, Torelli, Charpentier, and Jeremiah Clarke. Marsalis also composed for dance: in collaboration with Garth Fagan for *Citi Movement* (1993); with Peter Martins and Twyla Tharp for the ballet works on *Jump, Start and Jazz* (1997); and with JUDITH JAMISON of the ALVIN AILEY American Dance Theater

(*Sweet Release*), and the Zhong Mei Dance Company (*Ghost Story*), issued together as *Sweet Release & Ghost Story* (1999). His first composition for string quartet, *At the Octoroon Balls* (1999), was performed by the Orion String Quartet conducted by Marsalis.

Although Marsalis has enjoyed phenomenal success as a practicing musician, it is his concomitant "ambassadorial" role that has made him such a crucially significant figure in jazz. An indefatigable writer, broadcaster, educator, and administrator, he has assumed a position of unprecedented authority in shaping the meaning and value of jazz, particularly through his influential position at Lincoln Center. No one has done more than Marsalis to validate the artistic status of jazz and popularize its cultural standing. An unstinting proselytizer for jazz, he has embraced a pedagogical role through school programs, lectures, workshops, and master classes in addition to the Lincoln Center's education and performance programs and through his involvement with television and radio series, such as PBS's *Marsalis on Music* (1995), NPR's *Making the Music* (1995), and Ken Burns's PBS series *Jazz* (2001). In these endeavors, he found a firm ally and mentor in ALBERT MURRAY, the critic and author, who is also on the board of Jazz at Lincoln Center.

Marsalis's ascendancy as jazz's quasi-official spokesperson occurred during a period in which the condition of jazz appeared in disarray; his star was rising when jazz criticism was increasingly concerned with the compromised integrity of contemporary jazz. Critics complained that jazz had fragmented into hybridized, bastardized subcategories (like fusion), forms corrupted by ersatz electronic instrumentation and produced by MILES DAVIS and other musicians, who were seen to have "sold out" their jazz credentials. Marsalis sought to "reclaim" jazz from what he saw as the depredations of a commercialized popular culture (pop, rap, hip-hop) that had led to its marginalization. Hence, he has advocated a "neoclassical" agenda and subsequently has been both praised and criticized for playing the predominant role in what was often described as a "jazz renaissance" (Sancton, 66). Impeccably attired in retro-tailoring, he is, in himself, reminiscent of swing-era iconography.

Drawing on critical perspectives from his mentor and champion, Stanley Crouch, Marsalis's polemical writing has insistently repudiated the white romantic conception of jazz's "*down*" status as the imputed cultural expression of black lowlife. Marsalis also rejects the spurious stereotype of black musicians' intuitive primitivism, which he calls "the noble savage cliché" (Marsalis, 21, 24). For Marsalis, jazz is—*was*—a cultural form of the highest order, and he has worked assiduously to safeguard its "purism" through his emphasis on the centrality of a highly selective canonical jazz tradition. With an emphasis on jazz purism, rather than its pluralism, Wynton Marsalis has marked out the parameters of "what jazz is—and isn't."

FURTHER READING

Marsalis, Wynton. "What Jazz Is—and Isn't." *New York Times* (31 July 1988): 21, 24.

———, and Frank Stewart. *Sweet Swing Blues on the Road* (1994).

———, and Carl Vigeland. *Jazz in the Bittersweet Blues of Life* (2000).

Giddins, Gary. "Wynton Marsalis and Other Neoclassical Lions." *Rhythm-a-ning: Jazz Tradition and Innovation* (2000), 156–161.

Gourse, Leslie. *Wynton Marsalis: Skain's Domain: A Biography* (1999).

Sancton, Thomas. "Horns of Plenty." *Time* (22 Oct. 1990): 64–71.

Seidel, Mitchell. "Profile: Wynton Marsalis." *Down Beat* 49, no. 1 (Jan. 1982): 52–53.

Discography

Wynton Marsalis (1982, Columbia 37574).

Black Codes (From the Underground) (1985, Columbia 40009).

Blood on the Fields (1977, Columbia 57694).

—IAN BROOKES

 MARSHALL, KERRY JAMES (17 Oct. 1955–), painter, photographer, printmaker, and installation artist, was born in Birmingham, Alabama, the second son of James Marshall, a Postal Service worker, and Ora Dee Prentice Marshall, a songwriter and entrepreneur, both of Birmingham. Marshall's family moved to Los Angeles in 1963, living in the Nickerson Gardens

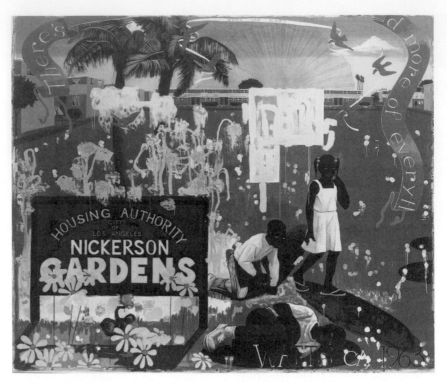

Winner of a MacArthur Foundation Award, Kerry James Marshall created Watts 1963 *as part of his 1995 Garden Series.* Watts *comments on the hopes associated with the "gardens" of housing projects built after the Korean War and the disappointment brought on by their decay.* St. Louis Art Museum

public housing project in Watts before settling in South Central Los Angeles.

Marshall's artistic inclinations were kindled by a kindergarten teacher at Birmingham's Holy Family Catholic School, who kept a picture-filled scrapbook for her young charges. This image compendium fed Marshall's obsession with making art. Impressed by his creativity and drive, his elementary, junior high, and high school teachers encouraged him with special opportunities. Marshall learned his first painting techniques from his third grade teacher. Later, an art instructor at George Washington Carver Junior High introduced Marshall to the Los Angeles County Museum of Art and a special summer drawing class taught by George De Groat at Otis Art Institute. There Marshall saw the book *Images of Dignity: The Drawings of Charles White*. White's drawings depicting realistic African American subjects with aesthetic richness and highly charged emotion inspired Marshall to reflect his own experiences in art. De Groat took his class to visit White's studio, where Marshall had his first encounter with a living artist. After meeting White, who was on

the faculty at Otis, Marshall determined to attend college there.

Marshall embarked on a self-tutorial to develop his figure-drawing skills. Drawings made when he was about fifteen years old show his emerging technical proficiency. He created his own workspace in the family garage, complete with easel and still-life set-ups. In this "studio" he experimented with egg tempera and made his own charcoal and ink. In the summer of 1972, just before his final year of high school, Marshall enrolled in a Saturday adult painting class at Otis. His instructor, the painter and animator Sam Clayberger, showed Marshall how to analyze pictorial structure. During his final year in high school, Marshall also attended Charles White's life-drawing class at Otis. These artists remained a significant mentoring influence on Marshall, who spent two years after high school graduation in 1973 working as a dishwasher and then for a flooring company. In his spare time he painted in his garage studio and audited White's and Clayberger's classes.

College was not a foregone conclusion in Marshall's family; on reaching majority children were expected to earn a living. In fact, with the exception of his

Otis experiences, Marshall was not immediately aware of higher education opportunities. Laid off from the flooring company in 1975, he approached Otis about enrollment and discovered that he needed two years of liberal arts education to enroll. He registered at Los Angeles City College, planning to transfer to Otis as a third-year student, which he did in 1977. Clayberger had given Marshall a glimpse of the kind of education he dreamed of—one based on inquiry, skills, knowledge, and standards. While attending Otis, though, Marshall began to realize that traditional practices and techniques had been subsumed by conceptual and theoretical approaches—notions that were in conflict with Marshall's ideals about formal art education. His discontent with Otis was instrumental in his subsequent formulation of a pedagogical approach emphasizing definition and clarification of skills through the acquisition of knowledge, standards, judgments, and values.

The painter and draftsman Arnold Mesches was Marshall's most challenging influence at Otis, urging Marshall to expand his artistic horizons. His entire senior year was occupied with creating a collage series loosely based on the work of ROMARE BEARDEN. The first, entitled *Thirty Pieces of Silver*, symbolically portrayed the artist as Judas with a wide grin. This grin quickly became a signature element in his paintings. After graduation in 1978, Marshall applied to the government-sponsored Comprehensive Employment Training Act program for cultural employment and training opportunities through Brockman Art Gallery and was assigned to Mesches as a paid studio assistant.

In 1980 Marshall created *Portrait of the Artist as a Shadow of His Former Self*, a painting he feels was his first to unify completely process and meaning. *Portrait* signals the beginning of his signature style of the highly stylized, streamlined iconic black persona, rendered in pure black paint, with barely discernible features, except for gleaming white eyes and teeth. A series of paintings featuring stylized black figures followed. These works were exhibited at the art gallery at Los Angeles Southwest College, and on the strength of this show Marshall secured a part-time teaching job there. Additional works from this series were featured in his first commercial gallery exhibition, at James Turcotte Gallery in Los Angeles; the show was reviewed positively by the *L.A. Times* critic William Wilson. Marshall's professional career developed quickly: in 1985 he had his first solo exhibition, at Koplin Gallery in Los Angeles; that same year he was awarded a resident fellowship at the Studio Museum in Harlem. Packing his possessions in a Volkswagen van, he set off with the intention of moving to New York permanently. However, in New York he met his future wife, the Chicago native and actress Cheryl Lynn Bruce. After completing the residency and working for a few months at the print publishers Chalk & Vermillion, he followed Bruce to Chicago in 1987. They married in April 1989.

Also in 1987 Marshall began working with the cinematographer Arthur Jaffa and his wife, the director Julie Dash, as production designer for Dash's film *Daughters in the Dust* (1989). Marshall collaborated with Dash and Jaffa on several additional film projects (*Hendrix Project* and *Praise House*, both from 1991); he also worked with Haile Gerima on *Sankofa* (1990). Meanwhile, his work as a visual artist progressed. From his first Chicago residence, a 6 × 9 foot room at the Chicago YMCA, he moved with Bruce into an apartment in Hyde Park. Marshall's larger space allowed him to increase the scale of his work dramatically. Large-scale narrative paintings were the focus of a second show at Koplin (1991) and the basis for his successful National Endowment for the Arts (NEA) Visual Art Fellowship grant application. Receiving NEA support was a major career milestone, allowing him to establish his first professional studio outside his home.

The painting *The Lost Boys* (1993) epitomized his next period of artistic growth. Marshall believes that it was in this artwork that he achieved the surface beauty and compositional sophistication he had been striving for. With this work, he began to think in terms of larger narrative series, or installations, rather than individual pictures. The year 1993 marked his first participation in museum exhibitions (Corcoran Gallery of Art in Washington, D.C., and the Museum of Modern Art in New York). He also had his first New York gallery show, at the Jack Shainman Gallery, and received the prestigious Louis Comfort Tiffany Foundation award in painting. He began teaching at the School of Art and Design at the University of Illinois at Chicago, gaining full professorship and tenure in 1998. His first solo museum show, organized by the Cleveland Center for Contemporary Art in 1994, included a catalogue and a four-city tour.

For Marshall, 1997 was a banner year. He received the Alpert Award in the Arts and was given the prestigious MacArthur Foundation's Fellows Program grant. He also was included in Documenta 10, that year's edition of the important international art exhibition held every five years in Kassel, Germany. Marshall's idea for a multifaceted project came to fruition in 1998 with Mementos, organized by the Renaissance Society, University of Chicago. His subject was broad: the tumultuous 1960s, loss, remembrance, and commemoration. Four mural-sized paintings entitled *Souvenir* formed the installation's core. Additional components, including paintings portraying MARTIN LUTHER KING JR., John F. Kennedy, and Robert F. Kennedy; a video installation; free-standing sculptures in the shape of giant rubber stamps; and relief prints of popular slogans from the 1960s, such as "Black Is Beautiful" and "We Shall Overcome," conveyed an overall sense of gravity and reverence.

Marshall explored social and political issues further in the show Carnegie International 1999/2000, at the Carnegie Museum of Art in Pittsburgh. His work *Rythm Mastr* consisted of hand-drawn and commercially printed comic-book-style narratives that were displayed in a site-specific installation incorporating exhibition cases normally used to show fragile artifacts. These cartoons were later published as a supplement to the Sunday Pittsburgh *Post-Gazette*. As a professional artist, Marshall has always sought to create works that commingle the aesthetics and sociology of African American popular culture. With *Rythm Mastr* he deftly conjoined the worlds of popular culture and fine art. In 1999, twenty-one years after he entered the program, Otis conferred an honorary doctorate on Marshall in recognition of his creativity, dedication, and career achievements.

Marshall's work is indicative of a significant development in twenty-first-century artistic discourse being practiced by a new generation of art makers: a concern with modern and postmodern art idioms combined with social and political content and a profound dedication to classical art traditions. His work is deeply rooted in the great tradition of representation and historical narrative painting, yet is imbued with personal expression and social awareness. Like other artists of his generation, such as Lorna Simpson, Glen Ligon, and Carrie Mae Weems, he has charted a new course based on the solid foundations of the past.

FURTHER READING

Holg, Garrett. "Stuff Your Eyes with Wonder." *ARTnews* (March 1998).

Marshall, Kerry James, Terrie Sultan, and Arthur Jaffa. *Kerry James Marshall* (2000).

Reid, Calvin. "Kerry James Marshall." *Bomb* (Winter 1998).

Sultan, Terrie. *Kerry James Marshall: Telling Stories* (1994).

—TERRIE SULTAN

MARSHALL, PAULE

(9 Apr. 1929–), writer, was born Valenza Pauline Burke in Brooklyn, New York, the second of three children of Barbadian immigrants Samuel Burke, a factory worker, and Ada (maiden name unknown), a domestic. As a child Marshall read the great British novelists Charles Dickens, William Makepeace Thackeray, and Henry Fielding. Their influence is especially apparent in her sense of setting and characterization.

Later, she discovered African American writers such as RICHARD WRIGHT and PAUL LAURENCE DUNBAR. The latter's use of dialect helped to legitimate her use of the cadences and grammatical structures of the vernacular used by the Bajan women of her community. Marshall writes beautifully about these women and their language in her *New York Review of Books* essay "The Making of a Writer: From the Poets in the Kitchen" (1983).

As a young adult Marshall was greatly influenced by RALPH ELLISON's *Shadow and Act*, which she has called her "literary bible," and by GWENDOLYN BROOKS's lone novel, *Maud Martha*. In addition, she claims JAMES BALDWIN as crucial to her formation as a writer and thinker. These three writers emerged as significant literary figures who received mainstream acclaim in the early 1950s. By the end of that decade, Marshall joined them as the newest and one of the most original voices of the time.

In 1948 Marshall entered Hunter College in New York City, but illness forced her to take time off from her studies. During her recuperation she began writing short stories. Marshall married her first husband, Kenneth Marshall, in 1950; nine years later she gave birth to her only child, a son, Evan Keith. Before long her artistic aspirations began to challenge her domestic life. In 1953 she graduated cum laude with a degree in English from Brooklyn College and was inducted into Phi Beta Kappa. Following graduation Marshall worked as a librarian at the New York Public Library while seeking work in journalism. As is the case with her fictional character Reena, in the novella of the same name, Marshall found that the sophisticated world of Manhattan magazine publishing was still closed to black writers unless they were already well known. Eventually, she joined the staff of *Our World* magazine, a black publication, as its only female correspondent. At *Our World* she encountered sexism in both her superiors and her colleagues, who voiced expectations that she would fail. Nonetheless, while at *Our World*, Marshall traveled extensively throughout the Caribbean and South America.

In 1954 Marshall published her first short story, "The Valley Between," the story of a young white wife and mother who, in defiance of her husband, wants to continue her education and eventually pursue a career. The story chronicles the character's ambition as well as her guilt. Marshall later said that she might have made her characters white in order to avoid having to confront the similarities between herself and her protagonist. Against her own husband's wishes, Marshall enlisted the services of a babysitter so that she would have time to work on her writing. In 1959 she published her first and best-known novel, *Brown Girl, Brownstones*. In 1963 her marriage ended in divorce.

In *Brown Girl, Brownstones* Marshall renders the speech of a Brooklyn community of Bajan immigrants, as well as African American migrants from the South, with extraordinary beauty and poetry. Along with Gwendolyn Brooks's *Annie Allen* and *Maud Martha*, *Brown Girl, Brownstones*—a portrait of Selina Boyce, a young, strong-willed girl—is one of the first books in American literature to concern itself with the interior life of a young black girl. In addition, *Brown Girl, Brownstones* is also the earliest novel to explore the intricacy of black mother-daughter relationships and one of the first to give such a complex portrait of a community of Caribbean immigrants.

In 1960 Marshall received a Guggenheim Fellowship, which she used to write a collection of four novellas titled *Soul Clap Hands and Sing* (1961). Each novella—"Barbados," "Brooklyn," "British Guiana," and "Brazil"—presents an elderly man who has to come to terms with his meaningless life. The settings range from sites in the United States to Central America, the Caribbean, and South America. Marshall received an American Academy Arts and Letters Award for *Soul Clap Hands and Sing*.

Her next work, the exquisite, complex novel *The Chosen Place, the Timeless People*, is one of Marshall's greatest accomplishments. Set in a fictional Caribbean nation, the novel explores a number of characters, black and white, male and female, North American, West Indian, and European. Through them, Marshall explores larger issues of power and dominance, colonialism, slavery, and neocolonialism. Perhaps most importantly, the novel introduces Merle Kinbona, an eccentric, educated, middle-aged, sensual, radical, intellectual black woman, and one of the most original and complex characters in contemporary fiction.

Fourteen years passed before the publication of Marshall's next novel, *Praisesong for the Widow* (1983). During this creative hiatus she married Nourry Menard, a Haitian businessman. *Praisesong* continues Marshall's portrayal of older women, her concern for characters who have lost their spiritual centers, and her exploration of the relationship between African American and Afro-Caribbean history. If her earlier work focused on specific locations, in *Praisesong for the Widow* she begins to include the Caribbean and Central and

South America in her conception of the black South.

Marshall's next novels turn to the children of diaspora. *Daughters* (1991), which received the Columbus Foundation American Book Award, is the story of Ursa MacKenzie, the buppie daughter of a West Indian politician father and a middle-class black woman from the United States. While these are her biological parents, her father's mistress, a childless businesswoman, and his own nursemaid also mother her. But most significantly she is the daughter of Afro-diasporic history; in documenting that history, she gives birth to herself.

Marshall's most recent novel, *The Fisher King* (2000), centers on a little boy, Sonny, who is a true child of the African Diaspora. His mother was raised in Paris and his father is a Senegalese street vendor in Paris. His maternal grandparents are two American expatriates, Sonny Rhett-Payne and a character modeled after LENA HORNE. One of his great-grandmothers is an aristocratic African American woman with roots in the deep South, and another is a stern West Indian woman; both of them live in brownstones on the same Brooklyn block. Thus, Sonny has roots throughout the African Diaspora, and as he is brought to live with his great-grandmothers in Brooklyn it is tempting to see that Marshall's work has come full circle.

Since 1995 Marshall has divided her time between Richmond, Virginia, and New York City. She teaches creative writing at New York University, where she also introduced the Paule Marshall and the New Generation Reading Series. The series has featured a number of young writers before they achieved public acclaim. Among these are Edwidge Danticat, Colson Whitehead, Denzy Senna, and A. J. Verdelle. In 1993 she was awarded a MacArthur Foundation Fellowship.

Marshall is a cosmopolitan intellectual whose work traces the complex connections and conflicts among black people throughout the Americas. Long before academics turned their attention to the African diaspora or the "Black Atlantic," Marshall mapped this terrain in novels, novellas, and short stories. Her experience as the child of immigrants, her childhood in a Brooklyn populated by blacks from the Caribbean and the American South, and her travels as an adult throughout the Americas all inform her artistic vision. Her literature underscores the relationship between slavery, colonialism, racism, and neo-colonialism and the formation of the modern black subject.

FURTHER READING

Marshall, Paule. "From the Poets of the Kitchen," *New York Times Book Review* (9 Jan. 1983), 3, 34–35.

DeLamotte, Eugenia C. *Places of Silence, Journeys of Freedom* (1998).

Denniston, Dorothy Hamer. *The Fiction of Paule Marshall: Reconstructions of History, Culture, and Gender* (1995).

Hathaway, Heather. *Caribbean Waves: Relocating* CLAUDE MCKAY *and Paule Marshall* (1999).

Pettis, Joyce. *Toward Wholeness in Paule Marshall's Fiction* (1995).

—FARAH JASMINE GRIFFIN

 MARSHALL, THURGOOD (2 July 1908–24 Jan. 1993), civil rights lawyer and U.S. Supreme Court justice, was born Thoroughgood Marshall in Baltimore, Maryland, the son of William Canfield Marshall, a dining-car waiter and club steward, and Norma Arica Williams, an elementary school teacher. Growing up in a solid middle-class environment, Marshall was an outgoing and sometimes rebellious student who first encountered the Constitution when he was required to read it as punishment for classroom misbehavior. Marshall's parents wanted him to become a dentist, as his brother did, but Marshall was not interested in the science courses he took at Lincoln University in Pennsylvania, from which he was graduated with honors in 1930. He married Vivian "Buster" Burey in 1929; they had no children.

Unable to attend the segregated University of Maryland Law School, Marshall enrolled in and commuted to Howard University Law School, where he became a protégé of the dean, CHARLES HAMILTON HOUSTON, who inspired a cadre of law students to see the law as a form of social engineering to be used to advance the interests of African Americans. After graduating first in his class from Howard in 1933, Marshall remained in Baltimore, where he opened a private law practice and struggled to make a living during the Depression. Marshall was active in the Baltimore branch of the National Association for the Advancement of Colored People (NAACP), and in 1936 Houston persuaded both the NAACP board and Marshall that Marshall ought to join him in New York as a staff lawyer for the NAACP. After Houston returned to Washington in 1938, Marshall remained and became the chief staff lawyer, a position he held until 1961.

Early in his Baltimore practice Marshall had decided to attack the policies that had barred him from attending the state-supported law school. Acting under Houston's direction, Marshall sued the University of Maryland on behalf of Donald Murray. The Maryland state court's 1936 decision ordering the school to admit Murray because the state did not maintain a "separate but equal" law school for African Americans was the first step in a two-decade effort to undermine the constitutional basis of racial segregation. Over the next fourteen years, Marshall pursued his challenge to segregated higher education through two main areas. In *Missouri ex rel Gaines v. Canada* (1938), a case Houston developed and argued, the U.S. Supreme Court directed the University of Missouri to either admit Lloyd Gaines to its law school or open one for African Americans. The attack culminated in Marshall's case of *Sweatt v. Painter* (1950), in which the Supreme Court held that the law school Texas had opened for African Americans was not "equal" to the well-established law school for whites.

The cases that the Supreme Court decided under the name *Brown v. Board of Education* constituted Marshall's main efforts from 1950 to 1955. Assembling a team of lawyers to develop legal and historical theories against segregation, Marshall had his greatest triumph as a lawyer in *Brown* (1954), in which the Supreme Court held that segregation of public schools by race was unconstitutional. In the 1896 case of *Plessy v. Ferguson*, the Supreme Court had upheld segregation, saying that segregation was a reasonable way for states to regulate race relations and that it did not "stamp the colored race with a badge of inferiority." Examining the background of the Fourteenth Amendment, Marshall's

The Supreme Court Justices of 1967. Left to right, seated: Associate Justices John M. Harlan and Hugo L. Black, Chief Justice Earl Warren, William O. Douglas, and William J. Brennan Jr. Standing: Abe Fortas, Potter Stewart, Byron R. White, and Thurgood Marshall. Corbis

team concluded that the amendment's framers did not intend either to authorize or to outlaw segregation. From this research Marshall came to the conclusion that under modern conditions, given the place of education in twentieth-century life, segregated public education was no longer reasonable. Marshall also relied, though less heavily, on arguments based on the psychological research of KENNETH B. CLARK showing that, *Plessy* notwithstanding, segregation did in fact damage the self-images of African American school children. During oral arguments Marshall occasionally stumbled over technical and historical details, but his straightforward appeal to common sense captured the essence of the constitutional challenge: "In the South where I spend most of my time," he said, "you will see white and colored kids going down the road together to school. They separate and go to different schools, and they come out and they play together. I do not see why

there would necessarily be any trouble if they went to school together."

There was trouble, however, as officials in the deep South engaged in massive resistance to desegregation. Marshall argued the case of *Cooper v. Aaron* (1958), which arose after Arkansas governor Orval Faubus sought to circumvent desegregation by closing four Little Rock schools on the first day of class. Marshall pointed out that Faubus's attempts to thwart the Supreme Court directive in *Brown* threatened fundamental American ideas about the rule of law, and he asked the Court to assert its constitutional authority by directing Little Rock officials to reopen and racially integrate the schools. Marshall told the justices that a ruling in favor of Faubus would be tantamount to telling the nine black boys and girls who had endured harassment and intimidation at Little Rock's Central High School throughout the 1957–1958 school year, "You fought for what you considered democracy and you lost. . . . go

back to the segregated school from which you came." Again the Supreme Court agreed with Marshall, and in August 1959 the schools reopened in line with federal desegregation orders.

A gregarious person who was always ready to use an apt, humorous story to make a point, Marshall traveled throughout the segregated South to speak to teachers and NAACP members, and in the 1940s and 1950s he became a major civil rights leader. By the mid-1950s his role as a civil rights leader had superseded his work as an attorney and he had become a widely sought-after speaker and fund-raiser. He also was active in the Episcopal Church and the Prince Hall Masons. His wife died of lung cancer in February 1955, and the following December he married Cecilia Suyatt, a secretary in the NAACP's national office; they would have two children, both boys.

Fending off attacks on the NAACP, its lawyers, and its members as well as attempting to push desegregation forward took a toll on Marshall. His travels kept him away from his family, and his NAACP salary, even when supplemented by gifts from wealthy white members, was inadequate to provide a college education for his sons. Moreover, the emergence of MARTIN LUTHER KING JR., the Southern Christian Leadership Conference, and the Student Nonviolent Coordinating Committee shifted the civil rights movement away from the legal strategies Marshall favored toward more direct-action tactics. Because of this, and to ease his financial burden and make more time for his family, in 1961 Marshall accepted an appointment to the U.S. Court of Appeals for the Second Circuit (in New York). Political maneuvering delayed his confirmation for nearly a year, after which he served on the Second Circuit for five years. His opinions were solid but hardly path-breaking. Aware of his lack of experience in business and tax law, which constituted an important portion of the Second Circuit's business, Marshall took guidance from Judge Henry Friendly in those areas.

In 1965 President Lyndon Johnson named Marshall U.S. solicitor general, the government's chief lawyer before the Supreme Court. Although neither said so explicitly, both Johnson and Marshall expected that Johnson would name Marshall to the U.S. Supreme Court as soon as possible. In 1967 Johnson manipulated Justice Tom Clark into resigning from the Court by naming his son Ramsey Clark attorney general, and that same year, saying it was "the right thing to do, the right time to do it, the right man and the right place," Johnson named Marshall to be the first African American Supreme Court justice.

Marshall joined a Court that was dominated by liberals, but within five years the Court's composition had changed dramatically following the retirement of Chief Justice Earl Warren and the deaths of Justice Hugo Black and Justice John Marshall Harlan. Instead of being active in the coalition that determined the Court's positions, Marshall found himself in a beleaguered minority that opposed the more conservative justices appointed by Richard Nixon and Ronald Reagan. Marshall rarely got the opportunity to write important majority opinions, even when his liberal colleagues led by William J. Brennan were able to cobble together a majority, because such opinions had to appeal to one or two of the justices who were significantly more conservative than Marshall, and Marshall was relatively uncompromising on matters he cared about.

Marshall's repertoire of stories endeared him to nearly every one of his colleagues, although initially some conservatives, including Lewis F. Powell, were put off by what they saw as Marshall's failure to approach the job with appropriate seriousness. Marshall did delight in puncturing what he took to be Chief Justice Warren Burger's pomposity, occasionally greeting Burger with, "What's shakin', Chiefy baby?" Yet most of Marshall's colleagues came to understand that he used his stories, often about the experiences of black Americans in the nation's court system, to make points about the cases the justices were considering. At the time of his retirement in 1991, Marshall brought more experience as a practicing lawyer to the Court than did any of his colleagues, and he often urged them to take more account of courtroom realities than of abstract deliberations about the Constitution.

Court watchers, particularly those who were unsympathetic to Marshall's positions on constitutional issues, criticized him for delegating too much of his work to his law clerks. Familiar with numerous aspects of the law from his experiences on the court of appeals and as solicitor general, Marshall had a facility for quickly determining the main thrust of each party's contentions and for deciding what result to reach. He would provide a sketchy outline of what an opinion should say; after that, the law clerks did substantially all of the opinion drafting in his chambers, as was the case in other chambers as well. Marshall did not edit his clerks' drafts as closely as other justices did, but he rejected drafts that did not capture the substance or the intensity of his views, and thus the guidance he gave made the opinions his own.

Marshall's most important contribution to constitutional doctrine was his "sliding-scale" theory of the Fourteenth Amendment's guarantee of equal protection of the laws, which he stated in most detail in dissenting opinions in *Dandridge v. Williams* (1970) and *San Antonio Independent School District v. Rodriguez* (1973). The Court's stated doctrine distinguished between two "tiers" of judicial scrutiny. One tier involved "suspect" classifications, such as race or "fundamental" interests; statutes using those classifications received strict scrutiny and rarely were upheld. The other tier contained all other statutes; statutes in this category simply had to have a "rational basis" and rarely were struck down. As the Court grappled with more and more cases involving discrimination against women, aliens, and nonmarital children, and cases dealing with the provision of public assistance, Marshall pointed out that the rigid two-tiered approach was inadequate, because for one thing, it failed to take account of variations in the importance of different interests; perhaps even more important, it failed to describe the outcomes of the Court's cases. Marshall proposed that the Court adopt an approach that openly balanced the importance of the goals the government was trying to achieve, the nature of the interest(s) affected, and the character of the group adversely affected by the classifications of a given statute. Although the Court did not expressly adopt Marshall's suggestion, some of its decisions seemed implicitly to do so, and many scholars believe that his analysis was more representative of the Court's decision making than was the doctrine that the Court claimed to be applying.

Beyond his specific doctrinal contributions, Marshall provided a voice on the Court, and in the Court's internal deliberations, for black Americans and others with few champions. After he retired, several of his colleagues said that Marshall's opinions had brought the real world into the Court's deliberations. When the Court, in upholding a federal filing fee for bankruptcy (*United States v. Kras* [1973]), suggested that it should not be difficult for a poor person to set aside about $2 a week to pay the fee, Marshall became indignant, writing in his published opinion, "No one who has had close contact with poor people can fail to understand how close to the margin of survival many of them are."

Marshall drew on his experience as a criminal defense lawyer when he argued that in all cases capital punishment is a form of cruel and unusual punishment barred by the Constitution. After the Court rejected that proposition in *Gregg v. Georgia* (1976), Marshall continued to express his disagreement; his dissents often asserted that the fair administration of justice was compromised in death penalty cases, particularly when defendants facing death sentences had received inadequate legal assistance.

Marshall's overall approach to constitutional law combined Charles Hamilton Houston's view that it is a form of social engineering with a pragmatic grasp of courtroom and practical realities. For example, he refused to deem that the police practice of arresting drunks was unconstitutional, in part because he believed that society had not instituted a better method of dealing with the problem than to lock up drunks until they were sober. He was willing to endorse large-scale reforms through constitutional law, as in attempts to effect desegregation and to rid the law of the death penalty, because *Brown* had taught him that a bold Supreme Court pronouncement often had an indirect but lasting impact on social practices.

Feeling the effects of age, and having lost his closest ally on the Court when Brennan retired in 1990, Marshall announced his retirement on 27 June 1991. The Court was substantially more conservative when Marshall left than when he arrived. During his tenure the nation's political system had drifted to the right; so had the Court, a trend that would continue with the appointment of his successor, CLARENCE THOMAS. Marshall never was able to act as a social engineer on behalf of African Americans and others who had made up the New Deal and Great Society political coalition; instead he came to occupy a different role on the Court, that of the great dissenter.

Earlier on the day of his retirement Marshall filed his final dissent. In *Payne v. Tennessee* a majority of the Court overruled the controversial decision in *Booth v. Maryland* (1987) and allowed prosecutors to introduce statements about the personal impact that a murder had had on the victim's family and friends. Beginning with the statement "Power, not reason, is the new currency of this Court's decision making," Marshall's dissent bitterly criticized the majority opinion. Although the Warren Court, whose work Marshall had endorsed and contributed to during the 1960s, was not averse to overruling precedents, Marshall believed that those cases were different: old rules that either did not work or were inconsistent with later developments had been displaced. In *Payne*, by contrast, Marshall believed that the only change that had taken place between 1987 and 1991 was the makeup of the Court. To have constitutional law turn on the personalities of the judges was, in Marshall's view, inconsistent with the ideal of the rule of law.

Marshall died at Bethesda Naval Hospital in Maryland. Many tributes noted that he would have deserved a major place in histories of constitutional law even had he not served on the Supreme Court, because his efforts as chief lawyer for the NAACP in leading the Court to restructure constitutional law with regard to race was as important a contribution as any in modern history. Marshall made fewer contributions to constitutional law as a justice, largely because he was not part of the Court's more conservative majority, but his passionate voice for the poor and for African Americans resonated in his dissenting opinions, and he remained an inspiration to those who believed in the possibility of achieving justice through the Constitution.

FURTHER READING

Marshall's professional papers, along with a small number of personal papers, are collected in the NAACP Papers and the Thurgood Marshall Papers, both in the Manuscript Division of the Library of Congress.

Davis, Michael, and Hunter Clark. *Thurgood Marshall: Warrior at the Bar, Rebel on the Bench*, rev. ed. (1994).

Kluger, Richard. *Simple Justice* (1975).

ROWAN, CARL. *Dream Makers, Dream Breakers: The World of Justice Thurgood Marshall* (1993).

Thurgood Marshall Commemorative Issue. *Howard Law Journal* vol. 35, 1991: 1–114.

"A Tribute to Justice Thurgood Marshall." *Harvard Law Review* 105 (Nov. 1991): 23–76.

"Tribute to Justice Thurgood Marshall." *Stanford Law Review* 44 (Summer 1992): 1213–1299.

Tushnet, Mark. *Making Civil Rights Law: Thurgood Marshall and the Supreme Court, 1936–1961* (1994).

———. *Making Constitutional Law: Thurgood Marshall and the Supreme Court, 1961–1991* (1997).

Obituaries: *New York Times* and *Washington Post*, 25 Jan. 1993.

—MARK TUSHNET

MASSEY, WALTER EUGENE (5 Apr. 1938–),

physicist, science and engineering administrator, and college president, was born in Hattiesburg, Mississippi, the first of two sons born to Almar C. Massey, a manual laborer for the Hercules Chemical Company, and Essie Nelson, an elementary school teacher and principal. Massey received support and encouragement not only from his parents, but also from a cadre of excellent African American teachers, who, due to restricted employment opportunities in rigidly segregated Mississippi, pursued teaching with passion and dedication. Massey attended the Sixteenth Section Elementary School in Hattiesburg, where his mother taught, and the Royal Street High School in the same city. He excelled in school and entered Atlanta's Morehouse College on a Ford Foundation scholarship after completing the tenth grade. As a student at Morehouse, Massey, like MARTIN LUTHER KING JR. and other African American men who attended the college between 1940 and 1967, came under the influence of the president, the renowned Dr. BENJAMIN MAYS.

Buttressed by the high standards of excellence advocated by Mays and by the mentoring he had received from a cast of outstanding teachers from the Sixteenth Section to Morehouse College, Massey embarked on a journey that led him to an international reputation as an educator and science and engineering administrator. After spending one year in graduate school at Howard University, Massey entered Washington University in St. Louis, Missouri. At Washington University he began work on understanding the behavior of liquid helium with Dr. Eugene Feenberg as his adviser. Massey's interest in liquid helium led later in his career to work for which he is best known as a physicist. This work, in which he collaborated with Humphrey Maris, provided a theoretical explanation for the anomalous dispersion of sound in superfluid helium. He received both a master's degree and a doctorate from Washington University in 1966.

Subsequently he became a staff physicist at the Argonne National Laboratory in Chicago, an institution to which he returned in 1979 as director. Massey joined the faculty at the University of Illinois as an assistant professor of physics in 1968. In 1969 he married Shirley A. Streeter of Chicago, Illinois. The couple had two sons, Keith and Eric. After two years at Illinois, Massey became associate professor of physics at Brown University in Providence, Rhode Island, where he remained for nine years. While at Brown, Massey became Professor of Physics and served as Dean of the College from 1975 until 1979. After leaving Brown he served for five years as director of the Argonne National Laboratory; he also accepted the position of vice president for research at the University of Chicago, where he remained for seven years. In 1991 he became the director of the foremost federal agency for the support of basic research in the physical sciences, mathematics, and engineering, the National Science Foundation (NSF). At the NSF he advocated a stronger coupling between academe and industry in the pursuit of research in science and engineering. In 1993 he joined the University of California system as provost and senior vice president for academic affairs. In 1995 he returned to Morehouse as its ninth president. In this leadership position he has advocated the development of leaders and high academic standards; he has also sought to enhance the stature of the college both nationally and internationally.

Massey's career has been characterized by a number of firsts. He was the first African American to receive a doctorate in physics at Washington University, the first African American dean at Brown University, the first African American director at the Argonne National Laboratory and at the National Science Foundation, the first African American vice president at the University of Chicago, and the first African American provost of the University of California system. As an educator, Massey has taught physics at several universities; however, the leadership he has provided in the development of policy and direction in educational organizations has been more significant. In 1971 and 1972 he served on the executive committee on "Physics in the Predominantly Black Colleges" for the American Institute of Physics. During the same period he implemented a program at Brown University to prepare teachers to teach science and mathematics in urban school systems. Later in the same decade he served on the board of advisers for the Fund for the Improvement of Post-Secondary Education, the Energy Advisory Committee of the Association of American Universities, and the Commission on Institutional Development and National Affairs of the American Association of Colleges. He has served on the boards of trustees of Washington University, Brown University, and Rockefeller University. In 1996 he became a member of the Annenberg Institute of School Reform and the advisory board of the Georgia Institute of Technology. He joined the board of directors of the Morehouse School of Medicine in 1997. In 1999 he became a member of the National Commission on Mathematics and Science Teaching for the 21st Century and the Gates Millennium Scholars Advisory Council.

Walter Massey's career has been characterized by his willingness to serve in leadership roles in varied organizations. He has not just remained active in professional and civic organizations but has often assumed the mantle of leadership. Notably, he served as chairman (1989–1990) and president (1988–1989) of the American Association for the Advancement of Science and as vice president (1990) of the American Physical Society. He served on the National Science Board from 1978 through 1984 and the President's Council of Advisers on Science and Technology from 1990 until 1992. He rejoined the president's council in 2001. Also in 2001 he became a member of the board of directors of the Rotary Club of Atlanta. Since 1998 he has served as chairman of the Atlanta Committee for Public Education.

At Morehouse, Massey has been actively involved in the college's Minority Research Institute, which has focused on research to strengthen and improve prospects for African American male youth, who at the end of the twentieth century were disproportionately affected by numerous American societal maladies and pathologies. At Morehouse he fostered the development of a formal leadership program and established the goal of being the best liberal arts college as an aim commensurate with the Morehouse legacy. As president of Morehouse, Massey found the ideal arena in which to meet the challenges of Benjamin Mays and that cast of outstanding African American educators who mentored and nurtured him.

FURTHER READING

"Former NSF Director Massey Returns to Alma Mater, Morehouse College, As Institution's New President," *The Scientist* 9 (21 Aug. 1995), 15.
Manning, Kenneth. "Race, Gender and Science" *History of Science Society Online Newsletter* [http://www.hssonline.org/society/about/newsletter/] (1995).
Sammons, Vivian O. *Blacks in Science and Education* (1989).

—ROBERT M. DIXON

MATTHEW, WENTWORTH ARTHUR

(23 June 1892–3 Dec. 1973), rabbi and educator, is believed to have been born in St. Marys, St. Kitts, in the British West Indies, the son of Joseph Matthew and Frances M. Cornelius. Matthew gave seemingly contradictory accounts of his ancestry that put his place of birth in such places as Ethiopia, Ghana, and Lagos, Nigeria. Some of those lingering discrepancies were partially clarified when Matthew explained that his father, a cobbler from Lagos, was the son of an Ethiopian Jew, a cantor who sang traditional Jewish liturgies near the ancient Ethiopian capital of Gondar. Matthew's father then married a Christian woman in Lagos, and they gave their son, Wentworth, the Hebrew name Yoseh ben Moshe ben Yehuda, also given as Moshe Ben David. His father died when he was a small boy, and his mother took him to live in St. Kitts, where she had relatives.

In 1913 Matthew immigrated to New York City, where he worked as a carpenter and engaged in prize fighting, though he was just a scrappy five feet, four inches tall. He reportedly studied at Christian and Jewish schools, including the Hayden Theological Seminary and the Rose of Sharon Theological Seminary (both now defunct), Hebrew Union College in Cincinnati, and even the University of Berlin, but there is no independent evidence to corroborate his attendance at these institutions. In 1916 Matthew married Florence Docher Liburd, a native of Fountaine, Nevis, with whom he had four children. During World War I Matthew was one of many street exhorters who used a ladder for a pulpit and Harlem's bustling sidewalks as temporary pews for interested pedestrians. By 1919 enough people were drawn to his evolving theology of Judaism and black nationalism that he was able to found "The Commandments Keepers Church of the living God The pillar and ground of the truth And the faith of Jesus Christ." He attempted to appeal to a largely Christian audience by pointing out that observance of the Old Testament commandments was the faith of Jesus; however, it became apparent that visitors often missed this point and assumed that any reference to Jesus implied a belief in Jesus. To avoid this confusion with Christianity, Matthew ceased to use the title "Bishop" and removed all references to Jesus from the organization's literature and papers of incorporation.

The transition from a church-based organization holding Jewish beliefs to a functioning synagogue that embraced most of the tenets of mainstream Orthodox Judaism was accomplished by Matthew's association with Rabbi ARNOLD FORD. Ford was a luminary in the Universal Negro Improvement Association, the black nationalist organization led by MARCUS GARVEY. Ford offered Hebrew lessons and religious instruction to a number of laypeople and clergy in the Harlem area. He worked with both Matthew's Commandments Keepers Congregation and the Moorish Zionist Congregation led by Mordecai Herman in the 1920s before starting his own congregation, Beth B'nai Abraham. In 1931, after Ford immigrated to Ethiopia, he sent a letter to Matthew granting him "full authority to represent Us in America" and furnishing him with a *Shmecah*, a certificate of rabbinic ordination (Ford to Matthew, 5 June 1931). Throughout the rest of his career, Matthew would claim that he and his followers were Ethiopian Hebrews, because in their lexicon "Ethiopian" was preferred over the term "Negro," which they abhorred, and because his authority derived from their chief rabbi in Ethiopia.

As an adjunct to his congregation, Matthew created a Masonic lodge called the Royal Order of Aethiopian Hebrews the Sons and Daughters of Culture. He became a U.S. citizen in 1924 and the following year created the Ethiopian Hebrew Rabbinical College for the training of other black rabbis. Women often served as officers and board members of the congregation, though they could not become rabbis. In the lodge there were no gender restrictions, and women took courses and even taught in the school. Religion, history, and cultural anthropology, presented from an Afrocentric perspective, were of immense interest to Matthew's followers and pervaded all of his teaching. The lodge functioned as a secret society where the initiated explored a branch of Jewish mysticism called kabbalah, and the school sought to present a systematic understanding of the practice of Judaism to those who initially adopted the religion solely as an ethnic identity. While the black press accepted the validity of the black Jews, the white Jewish press was divided; some reporters accepted them as odd and considered their soulful expressions exotic, most challenged Matthew's identification with Judaism, and a few ridiculed "King Solomon's black children" and mocked Matthew's efforts to "teach young pickaninnies Hebrew" (*Newsweek*, 13 Sept. 1934).

Matthew traveled frequently around the country, establishing tenuous ties with black congregations interested in his doctrine. He insisted that the original Jews were black and that white Jews were either the product of centuries of intermarriage with Europeans or the descendents of Jacob's brother Esau, whom the Bible describes as having a "red" countenance. Matthew argued that the suffering of black people was in large measure God's punishment for having violated the commandments. When black people "returned" to Judaism, he believed, their curse would be lifted and the biblical prophecies of redemption would be fulfilled. Most of the black Jewish congregations that sprung up in the post-Depression era trace their origin to Matthew or to William Crowdy, a nineteenth century minister whose followers also embraced some aspects of Judaism but who, unlike Matthew's followers, never abandoned New Testament theology. Matthew often inflated the size of his community by counting those with only a loose affiliation and who exhibited any affinity to Judaism along with the members who adhered more strictly to his doctrine of Sabbath worship, kosher food, bar mitzvahs, circumcision, and observance of all Jewish holidays. His core supporters probably never exceeded ten thousand followers from a few small congregations in New York, Chicago, Ohio, and Philadelphia. Many of his students established synagogues in other parts of New York City; often these were short-lived, and those that thrived tended to become rivals rather than true extensions of Matthew's organization.

Two of Matthew's sons served in the military during World War II, and the congregation watched with horror as atrocities against Jews were reported. In 1942 Matthew published the *Minute Book*, a short history of his life's work, which he described as the "most gigantic struggle of any people for a place under the sun." Matthew would later create *Malach* (Messenger), a sporadically published newsletter. Having supported the Zionist cause, the congregation celebrated the creation of the state of Israel in 1948, but by the 1950s their dreams of settling in Africa or Israel had been replaced by a more modest vision of establishing a farming collective on Long Island. The congregation purchased a few parcels of land in North Babylon in Suffolk County, New York, and began building a community that was to consist of a retirement home for the aged, residential dwellings, and small commercial and agricultural industry. Opposition from local residents and insufficient funding prevented the property from being developed into anything more than a summer camp and weekend retreat for members, and the land was lost in the 1960s.

When a new wave of black nationalism swept the country during the civil rights movement, there were periods of solidarity between blacks and Jews, but also painful moments of tension in major cities. Matthew maintained a supportive relationship with ADAM CLAYTON POWELL JR. in Harlem, with Percy Sutton, who as borough president of Manhattan proclaimed a day in Matthew's honor, and with congressman CHARLES RANGEL, who was a frequent guest at Commandments Keepers. Matthew also became affiliated with Rabbi Irving Block, a young white idealist who had recently graduated from Jewish Theological Seminary and started the Brotherhood Synagogue. Block encouraged Matthew to seek closer ties with the white Jewish community, and he urged white Jewish institutions to accept black Jews. Matthew applied for membership in the New York Board of Rabbis and in B'nai B'rith but was rejected. Publicly, leaders of the two organizations said that Matthew was turned down because he was not ordained by one of their seminaries; privately, they questioned whether Matthew and his community were Jewish at all. After reflecting on this incident and its aftermath, Matthew said, "The sad thing about this whole matter is, that after forty or fifty years...they are planning ways of discrediting all that it took us almost two generations to accomplish" (Howard Waitzkin, "Black Judaism in New York," *Harvard Journal of Negro Affairs* 1, no. 3 [1967], 31).

In an effort to circumvent Matthew's leadership of the black Jewish community, the Committee on Black Jews was created by the Commission on Synagogue Relations. The committee in turn sponsored an organization called Hatza'ad Harishon (The First Step), which attempted to bring black people into the Jewish mainstream. Despite the organizers' liberal intentions, the project failed because it was unable to navigate the same racial and ritual land mines that Matthew had encountered. Matthew had written that "a majority of the [white] Jews have always been in brotherly sympathy with us and without reservation" (*New York Age*, 31 May 1958), but because he refused to assimilate completely he met fierce resistance from white Jewish leadership. As he explained,

We're not trying to lose our identity among the white Jews. When the white Jew comes among us, he's really at home, we have no prejudice. But when we're among them they'll say you're a good man, you have a white heart. Or they'll be overly nice. Deep down that sense of superiority-inferiority is still there and no black man can avoid it.

(Shapiro, 183)

Before Matthew's death at the age of eighty-one, he turned the reins of leadership over to a younger generation of his students. Rabbi Levi Ben Levy, who founded Beth Shalom E. H. Congregation and Beth Elohim Hebrew Congregation, engineered the formation of the Israelite Board of Rabbis in 1970 as a representative body for black rabbis, and he transformed Matthew's Ethiopian Rabbinical College into the Israelite Rabbinical Academy. Rabbi Yehoshua Yahonatan and his wife, Leah, formed the Israelite Counsel, a civic organization for black Jews. Matthew expected that his grandson, Rabbi David Dore, a graduate of Yeshiva University, would assume leadership of Commandments Keepers Congregation, but as a result of internecine conflict and a painful legal battle, Rabbi Chaim White emerged as the leader of the congregation and continued Matthew's legacy.

Matthew and his cohorts were autodidacts and organic intellectuals who believed that history and theology held the answers to their racial predicament. In their Darwinian view of politics, people who do not know their cultural heritage are inevitably exploited by those who do. Hence, discovery of their true identities was essential to achieving self-respect and political freedom. In this regard, Matthew, NOBLE DREW ALI, and ELIJAH MUHAMMAD agreed in their cultural assessment of the overriding problem facing black people, though they chose different religious paths.

FURTHER READING

The largest collection of papers and documents from Matthew and about black Jews is to be found at the Schomburg Center for Research in Black Culture of the New York Public Library. Smaller collections are at the American Jewish Archives in Cincinnati.

Brotz, Howard. *The Black Jews of Harlem: Negro Nationalism and the Dilemmas of Negro Leadership* (1970).
Landing, James E. *Black Judaism: Story of an American Movement* (2002).
Ottley, Roi. *New World A-Coming: Inside Black America* (1943).
Shapiro, Deanne Ruth. *Double Damnation, Double Salvation: The Source and Varieties of Black Judaism in the United States*, M.A. Thesis, Columbia University (1970).
—SHOLOMO B. LEVY

MATTHEWS, VICTORIA EARLE

(27 May 1861–10 Mar. 1907), writer, educator, and activist, was the youngest of nine children born to Caroline Smith, a former slave, in Fort Valley, Georgia. Oral family history has it that Victoria's father was her mother's owner. Her mother migrated to New York with her daughters Victoria and Anna around 1873. Victoria attended Grammar School 48 in New York City until she was compelled to leave because of poverty; she took work as a domestic servant, the only employment available to many African American women at that time. HALLIE QUINN BROWN's *Homespun Heroines and Other Women of Distinction* (1926) notes of Matthews, however, that she "never lost an opportunity to improve her mind" (209). Matthews developed her own literacy program, acquiring knowledge from independent study, lectures, and contact with educated people. Marriage at the age of eighteen to William Matthews, a carriage driver, enabled her to escape her home life, but it led to an unhappy and perhaps lonely domestic situation.

During the early years of her marriage, Matthews contributed articles about her childhood to *Waverly Magazine*, the *New York Weekly*, and *Family Story Paper*. She was also a news correspondent for the *New York Times*, the *New York Age*, the *Brooklyn Eagle*, the *Boston Advocate*, the *Washington Bee*, and the *Richmond Planet*. In 1893, under the pen name "Victoria Earle," she published her most ambitious work, the short story *Aunt Lindy*. Five years later, with encouragement from the *New York*

Age editor T. THOMAS FORTUNE, she edited *Black Diamonds: The Wisdom of BOOKER T. WASHINGTON*, a selection of his speeches and talks to students.

Matthews's writing brought her into contact with prominent white and black women and led to membership in the Women's National Press Association. Linking the written word and action, she organized a dinner to honor the achievements of the anti-lynching crusader and *New York Age* journalist IDA B. WELLS-BARNETT. This event inspired Matthews and Maritcha Remond Lyons, a Brooklyn schoolteacher, to organize the Woman's Loyal Union, which became involved in racial protest and women's issues. As a delegate of the union, Matthews attended the 1895 Congress of Colored Women in Atlanta and presented a stunning address, "The Value of Race Literature," emphasizing the importance of preserving the cultural contributions of African Americans. An outgrowth of the Congress was the founding of the National Federation of Afro-American Women (NFAAW). Matthews was appointed to the editorial board of the *Woman's Era*, the NFAAW's official journal, and chair of its executive committee. Her resourcefulness was invaluable in planning the 1896 convention in Washington, D.C., which merged the NFAAW and the National Colored Women's League of Washington into the National Association of Colored Women.

Matthews felt compelled to raise her voice and pen in defense of black womanhood. Addressing the San Francisco Society of Christian Endeavor in 1897, she expressed her indignation over the attacks on black females as immoral women. In her lecture, "The Awakening of the Afro-American Woman," she also challenged black and white women to assume some responsibility for the less fortunate. Matthews believed that all women's educational, religious, and temperance organizations should cooperate to combat both negative public attitudes and discriminatory laws that degraded black womanhood.

After the death of her only child, Matthews dedicated her life to social welfare work among the black poor. On 11 February 1897 she established the White Rose Mission "as a Christian nonsectarian Home for Colored Girls and Women and to train them in the principles of practical self-help and right living" (Meier, *Negro Thought in America, 1880–1915* [1978], 134). Incorporated in 1898 with a biracial board of directors, the White Rose Home and Industrial Association for Working Girls provided a space where black women newly arrived from the South were befriended, counseled, and prepared for jobs through courses in cooking, sewing, and housekeeping. The women were then found jobs, usually in domestic service. Seeking to protect rural women from the dangers of urban life, the White Rose Home rigorously enforced its rules and curfews.

To further race consciousness, Matthews established a library of African American history books and taught a course in black history. Ruth Alice Moore (later ALICE DUNBAR-NELSON) ran a kindergarten at the home, while other volunteers provided a range of programs, lectures, and clubs. Matthews's leadership of the White Rose Home allowed her to exchange ideas with like-minded white reformers and social workers, among them Mary Stone, Mary White Ovington, Grace Hoadley Dodge, and Frances Kellor.

Prior to Matthews, only a few reformers addressed the influence of the urban environment on the behavioral patterns of black women in both the North and the South. She toured the South in 1895 and, appalled by the red-light districts in New Orleans and other southern cities, warned the Hampton Negro Conference of the dangers faced by young black female migrants to the cities. Matthews's Hampton address inspired the organization of volunteers at the nearby Norfolk, Virginia, docks to counsel arriving migrants. White Rose agents in New York likewise watched the docks to prevent the women from becoming victims of a "white slave" traffic that existed from New Orleans to New York. These developments led Matthews to establish the White Rose Travelers' Aid Society in 1905.

When Matthews discovered that several New York employment agencies sent black women seeking work as domestic servants to houses of ill repute, she decided to "check the evil" of these "unprincipled men who haunted the wharves" (Osofsky, *Harlem: The Making of a Ghetto: Negro New York, 1890–1930* [1971], 56). Afraid that this practice would prevent these migrants from acquiring respectable employment, Matthews expertly gathered evidence and reported similar conditions for black women in New York, Chicago, Boston, and San Francisco.

Matthews's death from tuberculosis at the age of forty-five left the White Rose Home without a public figure immersed in social work. She is recognized in connection with the organization not only of women's clubs but also of a movement in New York City to aid African American women. Her name is inextricably linked to the White Rose Home and its mission of providing social services for thousands of African American women.

FURTHER READING

The Empire State Federation of Women's Clubs Papers, SUNY, Albany, New York, contains information relating to the White Rose Mission and Industrial Association founded by Victoria Earle Matthews in 1897 and supported by the clubs of the Empire State Federation. Records of the National Association of Colored Women's Clubs, 1895–1992, contains the minutes of its national conventions, which Victoria Earle Matthews attended in both 1895 and 1896, and its publication, the *National Association Notes*.

Brown, Hallie Q. *Homespun Heroines and Other Women of Distinction*, 1926 (1988).

Davis, Elizabeth. *Lifting as They Climb* (1933).
Wesley, Charles. *The History of the National Association of Colored Women's Clubs: A Legacy of Service* (1984).

Obituary: *New York Age*, 14 Mar. 1907.
—FLORIS BARNETT CASH

 MATZELIGER, JAN EARNST (15 Sept. 1852– 24 Aug. 1889), inventor, was born in Paramaribo, Surinam (Dutch Guiana), the son of Carl Matzeliger, a Dutch engineer in charge of government machine works for the colony, and a native Surinamese mother. At the age of ten, Matzeliger began serving an apprenticeship in the machine works. In 1871 he signed on to the crew of an East Indian merchant ship and set out to seek his fortune overseas. After a two-year voyage, he landed at Philadelphia, where he probably worked as a cobbler. In 1877 he settled in the town of Lynn, Massachusetts, the largest shoe-manufacturing center in the United States. His first job there was with the M. H. Harney Company, where he operated a McKay sole-stitching machine. He also gained experience in heel-burnishing, buttonholing, machine repair, and other aspects of shoe manufacture. Later, he was employed in the shoe factory of Beal Brothers. In his spare time Matzeliger drove a coach, studied to increase his proficiency in the English language, and painted oils and watercolors (mostly landscape scenes). After covering rent and other essentials, his small earnings went into the purchase of books, including such useful reference tools as *Popular Educator* and *Science for All*.

At the time, a major challenge facing the shoe industry was how to improve the technique of "lasting"—or connecting the upper flaps to the soles of the shoe. Lasting was still done entirely by hand, an arduous process that slowed production. Several lasting machines had been tried without success. With characteristic zeal, Matzeliger took up this challenge, which had eluded the best mechanical minds. He spent long evening hours in his garret room experimenting and building models. In March 1883 he finally received Patent No. 274,207 for his "Lasting Machine." With sole and upper positioned on a lathe, the machine alternately drove tacks, rotated the shoe, and pleated the leather—an automated replication of the manual technique. Two years later he ran a successful factory test in which, over the course of a day, his machine lasted a record seventy-five pairs of shoes (a hand laster could produce no more than fifty in a ten-hour period). With further improvements, it lasted up to 700 pairs a day. This invention, dubbed the "niggerhead," came into universal use in the shoe industry. (It is unclear how the machine acquired its name. The term "niggerhead," applied in several contexts at the time was used in the apparel industry to designate a type of fabric.)

Matzeliger's "dark complexion" made him stand out among his mostly white fellow workers, and his reception by the community varied. A religious man, he tried without success to join the local Unitarian, Episcopal, and Catholic churches. In 1884 he was accepted into the Christian Endeavor Society, the youth wing of the North Congregational Church. He was active in the society's Sunday school and fund-raising work. His diligence, polite bearing, and easygoing personality endeared him to those whose minds had not been completely closed by racial prejudice. Among his circle of friends were the younger group of factory workers and members of the Christian Endeavor Society. He never married.

Although he remained active in the developing shoe machinery technology, and was awarded four related patents between 1888 and 1891, Matzeliger's financial benefit from the work was relatively modest. He sold the patents to his backers for fifteen thousand dollars worth of stock in their company. By the end of the century, this company had become part of the United Shoe Machinery Corporation. Matzeliger's patents provided a nucleus of economic strength for the corporation in its early years. Matzeliger was long since gone, however, having died of tuberculosis. At the time of his death he was being cared for by friends at his home in Lynn. Three of his five patents were granted posthumously.

FURTHER READING

A small collection of correspondence, photographs, and other materials is preserved in the Manuscript Division of the Moorland-Spingarn Research Center, Howard University.

Haber, Louis. "Jan Earnst Matzeliger," in *Black Pioneers of Science and Invention* (1970), 25–33.
Kaplan, Sidney. "Jan Earnst Matzeliger and the Making of the Shoe." *Journal of Negro History* 40 (Jan. 1955): 8–33.
Mitchell, Barbara. *Shoes for Everyone: A Story about Jan Matzeliger* (1986).
—KENNETH R. MANNING

MAYS, BENJAMIN E.

(1 Aug. 1894–28 Mar. 1984), educator and clergyman, was born Benjamin Elijah Mays in Greenwood County, South Carolina, the youngest of eight children of Hezekiah Mays and Louvenia Carter, both tenant farmers who had been born in slavery. Mays's earliest memory was of the 1898 Phoenix Riot in Greenwood County, which was sparked by internecine battles for control of the Democratic Party and white efforts to disfranchise African Americans. Mays, who was only four at the time, recalled a mob riding with guns and making his father kowtow to save his life. He also remembered the problems his parents had faced living as tenant farmers in the cotton economy of South Carolina.

Three things about his formative years were significant to Mays. The first was his father's abuse of alcohol. He recalled that his father drank even near the church, and he remembered the fights between his parents when his father was drunk. As a result of his father's behavior, Mays abstained from alcohol. The second formative influence on Mays was the religious life of his mother. She would lead the family in nightly ritual prayer, and her abiding faith instilled a disciplined spirituality into Mays's life. Her piety strongly influenced his religious sensibilities and her belief in the power of education helped to shape his emerging worldview. Third, Mays benefited from support at church and school, and from his oldest sister, Susie, who taught him rudimentary reading and math. Throughout his adolescent years, such encouragement at home, church, and school persuaded Mays to seek an education as a means of overcoming rural poverty. Later in life, he would remember his prayers in the cotton fields to God to grant him the opportunity to get an education.

Mays left home after his father objected to his being a full-time student. He completed high school at South Carolina State College in Orangeburg, graduating as the valedictorian of his class in 1914. From there he would follow the abolitionist nexus, attending Virginia Union University in Richmond, a Baptist-affiliated historically black college founded by the American Home Mission Society in 1865. While a student at Virginia Union, Mays met two alumni of Bates College, who had joined Union's faculty; they encouraged him to transfer to Bates College, a predominantly white Baptist-affiliated institution, in Lewiston, Maine. Bates was liberating for Mays. He attended the college so that he could compete academically with northern whites. The experience satisfied his need to gain respect and overcome the culture of inferiority with which segregated society had marked all African Americans. Mays became a member of Phi Beta Kappa Society, and, at the age of twenty-six, graduated from Bates with honors.

After completing his degree at Bates, Mays decided upon a career in the ministry. Although numerous black Baptist congregations would have accepted him as pastor with only a bachelor's degree, he declined to take any such post and instead chose to enroll in the University of Chicago Divinity School in 1920. He initially wanted to attend Andover-Newton Seminary in Massachusetts, but he was not accepted because of his race. Chicago proved to be stimulating and on the cutting edge of theology and sociology. Unfortunately, the university offered him very little money to complete his master's work without interruption.

After having finished the first year of his program, Mays delayed his education for three years to teach at Morehouse College, in Atlanta, Georgia. Morehouse's president, JOHN HOPE, recruited Mays to teach math and psychology. Though the original contract was for one year, Mays remained at Morehouse for three years, during which he taught and influenced many students and colleagues who would go on to notable achievements, among them the sociologist E. FRANKLIN FRAZIER, the theologian HOWARD THURMAN, and the civil rights lawyer James Nabrit. The high standards set at Morehouse under Hope's leadership was an inspiration to Mays. It was a model of how dedicated leadership could bring about racial uplift and inspire African Americans to even greater accomplishments.

Although Mays loved Morehouse, he still wanted to be an active church pastor. While at Morehouse, he served as pastor of a small congregation—Shiloh Baptist Church. Tragically for Mays, his first wife, Ellen Harvin, who had encouraged him in his pursuit of the ministry, died in Atlanta in childbirth in 1923. Although the tragic loss of his wife grieved him, Mays pursued his calling and returned to the University of Chicago in the academic year 1924–1925 to complete his master's thesis, entitled "Pagan Survivals in

Christianity," under the New Testament historian Shirley Jackson Case.

In the spring of 1925, Robert Shaw Wilkinson, the president of South Carolina State College, recruited Mays to teach at his alma mater. During his brief tenure in Orangeburg, Mays met Sadie Gray, a teacher and social worker, and married her in 1926. Their marriage broke the college's rule that married women could not be members of the faculty, which sent Mays and his wife in search of employment. The National Urban League soon employed them both as social workers in Tampa, Florida, where they stayed for two years, with Mays serving as director of the league. Although Mays did not find the job fulfilling, with characteristic dutifulness he completed a study of Tampa in 1928 with the white liberal sociologist Arthur Raper. In 1928 Mays and his wife returned to Atlanta, where he worked for the national YMCA while continuing to seek the pastorship of a church. At the end of his term with the YMCA in 1930, Mays received a stipend from a Rockefeller Foundation–funded organization, the Institute for Social Religious Research, to study African American churches.

After the publication in 1933 of *The Negro's Church*, co-authored with Joseph Nicholson, Mays was able to return to the University of Chicago to complete a PhD in Theology. His dissertation, *The Negro's God as Reflected in His Literature*, was published as a book in 1938. Upon completion of his degree, Mays once more sought a pulpit. Once again, however, the academy, not the church, called him. In 1934 MORDECAI JOHNSON, the president of Howard University, recruited Mays to be the dean of the university's School of Religion. Mays thought that if he could not actively lead a church, the next-best calling was to the train the clergy. During his six-year tenure at Howard, he recruited faculty and students, built the library, and secured accreditation for the School of Religion. As a result of his work at Howard and the internal struggle that took place after the death of John Hope, Mays was voted by the trustees to the post of president of Morehouse College in 1940.

From 1940 to 1967 Mays served as president of Morehouse College. While working in this capacity, he continued

to build on the legacy of John Hope. Like Hope, he was active in the Federal Council of Churches, serving as the first African American vice president and on the central committee of the World Council of Churches as well as pursuing civil rights causes. In addition, he was widely sought after as a public speaker and weekly columnist for the *Pittsburgh Courier*. As president of the college, he mentored a generation of students engaged in the struggle for human rights. Mays's most famous student, MARTIN LUTHER KING JR., called him "his spiritual and intellectual mentor" (*New York Times*, March 29, 1984, D23). For Mays, it was tragic that he was called upon to give the eulogies for King and, later, for WHITNEY YOUNG JR., the director of the National Urban League.

Upon his retirement, Mays nursed Sadie Gray Mays through her last illness; she died in 1969. He also wrote his autobiography, *Born to Rebel*, took speaking engagements, and served as the president of the Atlanta Board of Education. In 1982 the NAACP awarded him its highest honor, the Spingarn Medal. In 1984, just short of his ninetieth birthday, Mays died in Atlanta. He is buried on the campus of Morehouse College.

FURTHER READING

The Benjamin E. Mays Papers are held at Howard University's Moorland-Spingarn Research Center in Washington, D.C.

Mays, Benjamin. *Born to Rebel: An Autobiography* (1987).
———. *The People Have Driven Me On* (1981).

Burton, Vernon. "Foreword," in *Born to Rebel* (1987).
Jelks, Randal M. "The Academic Formation of Benjamin E. Mays, 1917–1936," in *Walking Integrity: Benjamin Elijah Mays, Mentor to Generations*, ed. Lawrence Edward Carter (1996).
Wills, David W. "An Enduring Distance: Black Americans and the Establishment," in *Between the Times: The Travail of the Protestant Establishment in America, 1900–1960*, ed. William R. Hutchinson (1989).

Obituary: *New York Times*, March 29, 1984.
—RANDAL MAURICE JELKS

MAYS, WILLIE

(6 May 1931–), baseball player, was born Willie Howard Mays Jr. in Westfield, Alabama. His paternal grandfather, Walter Mays, and his father, William Howard Mays Sr., were semiprofessional baseball players, and his mother was a high school track star. After his parents divorced when he was three years old, Mays was raised by his father and two adopted sisters in Fairfield, Alabama.

Mays starred in football and basketball at Fairfield Industrial High School. As the school had no baseball team, Mays began playing semiprofessional baseball as a young teenager. By age fourteen he was playing right field with his father's semiprofessional steel mill team. In 1947 his father introduced him to Piper Davis, the manager of the Birmingham Black Barons, a professional baseball team in the Negro American League. He got two hits in his first game for the Black Barons and was signed for $250 per month, even though he could play only home games because he was still in high school. In a sign of things to come, Mays hit a double in his first at bat against the great pitcher SATCHEL PAIGE of the Kansas City Monarchs. He played for the Black Barons from 1947 through 1949.

The Boston Braves scouted Mays in 1949 and 1950 but did not sign him. However Eddie Montague, a scout for the New York Giants, reported that Mays was the greatest ballplayer he had ever seen, and the Giants signed him at a salary of five thousand dollars on the day Willie graduated from high school. They paid the Black Barons ten thousand dollars for Mays's contract. In 1950 Mays was assigned to a minor league team in Sioux City, Iowa, but because the team would not accept black players, he was subsequently sent to the Trenton, New Jersey, minor league team. In 1951 he was promoted to the New York Giants top farm team, the Minneapolis Millers. He batted .477 during the first two months of the season and was promoted to the New York Giants on 25 May 1951. Despite his short stay in Minneapolis, he became such a fan favorite that the Giants placed an advertisement in the local newspaper to apologize to the community for promoting him.

Willie Mays, the first African American to captain a major league baseball team, drives in a run for the Giants, 1965. © Bettmann/CORBIS

Mays's impact on the Giants was immediate and profound. Although he did not hit well in his first games, his fielding prowess was so extraordinary that the Giants' manager, Leo Durocher, affirmed that Mays was to be his regular center fielder no matter how poorly he batted. His hitting improved as he helped the Giants win the National League pennant in his first season. Mays's performance earned him the Rookie of the Year award. His enthusiastic "Say Hey" greeting and impassioned play led to his nickname, the "Say Hey Kid."

In 1952 Mays was drafted into the U.S. Army and assigned to Fort Eustis, Virginia. During this time he played baseball and created his distinctive technique of catching fly balls at the level of his belt buckle, his famous "basket catch." He finally returned to a languishing New York Giants team in 1954. When a fan noticed Durocher greeting Mays, he remarked, "Leo is shaking hands with the pennant." Mays won the batting title, hit forty-one home runs, and was awarded the National League Most Valuable Player award. That year he led the Giants to the pennant and the World Series championship against the favored Cleveland Indians.

The 1954 World Series was marked by one of the most remarkable fielding plays in baseball history, known as "the Catch." In the eighth inning of the first game, with the score tied and two runners on base, Vic Wertz of the Indians hit a fly ball over Mays's head in center field. Mays turned around, ran straight back, and caught the ball over his shoulder 450 feet from home plate. He twirled around in one motion and threw to the infield, which kept any runners from scoring. "The Catch" epitomizes Mays's place as the greatest fielding center fielder in baseball history.

Mays married Margueritte Wendell in 1956 and they adopted a son, Michael, in 1959. Their marriage ended in divorce in 1961. The breakdown in his marriage coincided with the Giants's move to San Francisco in 1958. Although he was the star of the team, Mays was not immediately accepted into the community and was kept from buying a house in a white neighborhood when homeowners protested. On the diamond he was often unfavorably compared to San Francisco's local hero, Joe DiMaggio, who, ironically, had been Mays's boyhood idol. Mays let his play overcome the critics. He led the Giants to a pennant in 1962, and in 1964 he became the first African American ever to captain a major league baseball team. Two years later, Mays signed a contract with the Giants that made him the highest-paid player in baseball history. *Sporting News* voted him the player of the decade for the 1960s. Mays married Mae Louise Allen in 1971, a year before

the Giants traded him to the New York Mets, and two years before he completed his career as the Mets' player-coach. In 1979, he became the ninth player to be elected to the Baseball Hall of Fame in his first year of eligibility.

Mays's greatness lies in his superiority in all areas of the game: running, fielding, throwing, power hitting, and hitting for average. The adulation of his fans for one of baseball's greatest all-around players rests on Mays's twenty-two-year career of consistently phenomenal statistics and defensive plays. From 1954 through 1962 he led the National League in at least one offensive category every year. He holds the records of 7,290 outfield chances and 7,095 putouts and led the league in outfield double plays from 1954 to 1956 and, remarkably, ten years later, in 1965. He also holds seven club records for the New York Giants (for which he played only five full seasons) and fifteen club records for the San Francisco Giants.

Mays's career totals put him in the top ten in nine offensive categories, including 2,992 games played, 660 home runs, 63 multiple-home-run games, 1,903 runs batted in, and 2,062 runs scored. He won the Most Valuable Player award in 1954 and 1965 and led the league in batting in 1954. He also led the National League four seasons in home runs and four consecutive seasons in stolen bases. He had ten seasons batting over .300, ten seasons batting in at least a hundred runs, and twelve consecutive seasons scoring at least a hundred runs. He hit at least thirty home runs in eleven seasons, twenty doubles in sixteen seasons, and five triples in twelve seasons. In 1971, he hit five triples at the age of forty.

Mays is one of only three players to have five hundred home runs and three thousand hits and one of only six players to hit four home runs in a single game. He was the first player to have twenty doubles, triples, home runs, and stolen bases in a season (1957), thirty home runs and thirty stolen bases in a season (1956 and 1957), and fifty home runs and twenty stolen bases in a season (1955). He also was the first player to reach three hundred home runs and three hundred stolen bases. In recognition of all these accomplishments, Mays was selected for the National League All-Star team twenty-four consecutive times.

Despite all Mays gave to the game, Baseball Commissioner Bowie Kuhn banished him from baseball in 1979 because he was hired to work in public relations by Bally's Casino; Major League Baseball had long prohibited players and coaches from having any association with gambling entities. He was finally welcomed back into baseball in 1985 by Commissioner Peter Ueberroth. The San Francisco Giants then hired him in 1986 as a special assistant to the president and made this a lifetime appointment in 1993.

Mays's impact in baseball, sports, and society goes well beyond his statistics and awards. Remembering his humble beginnings, he has continuously promoted activities to help underprivileged children. During his adolescence he watched Saturday football games at Miles College, a black school in Birmingham. In 1968 he returned to Miles College as national chair of their fund-raising campaign to build the Willie Mays Health and Physical Education Center. During his years as a New York Giant, he was famous for playing stickball with neighborhood children in Harlem; in San Francisco in the 1960s he became a mentor to O. J. SIMPSON, who was at that time a wayward teenager from the city's Potrero Hill housing projects. When Mays returned to New York with the Mets, he supported New York's Fresh Air Fund to allow inner-city children to spend time in summer camps outside the city. Mays's Say Hey Foundation, formed in 1980, is dedicated to providing higher education for underprivileged children.

Mays has actively promoted the inclusion of Negro League players into the Hall of Fame. When the Hall of Fame proposed setting up a separate exhibit for Negro League players and accomplishments, he forcefully argued that Negro League baseball should be recognized as part of the highest level of baseball and that its players should be integrated into exhibits of baseball's greatest athletes. Although blacks and whites played separately, he believed they should be remembered together. In 2000 the San Francisco Giants honored Mays by addressing their new ballpark "24 Willie Mays Plaza" and adorning it with a nine-foot-tall statue of the "Say Hey Kid."

FURTHER READING

Mays, Willie, with Lou Sahadi. *Say Hey: The Autobiography of Willie Mays* (1988).

Einstein, Charles. *Willie Mays: My Life and Times in and out of Baseball* (1972).
———. *Willie's Time: A Memoir of Another America* (1979).

—STANTON W. GREEN

McCLENDON, ROSE

(27 Aug. 1884–12 July 1936), actress, was born Rosalie Virginia Scott in Greenville, South Carolina, the daughter of Sandy Scott and Tena Jenkins. Around 1890 the family moved to New York City, where her parents worked for a wealthy family as a coachman and a housekeeper, respectively. An avid reader, McClendon and her brother and sister were educated at Public School No. 40 in Manhattan. Although she admitted to having no inclinations for the stage at this time, as a child she participated in plays at Sunday school and later performed in and directed plays at St. Mark's African Methodist Episcopal Church. In 1904 she married Henry Pruden McClendon, a licensed chiropractor and Pullman porter for the Pennsylvania Railroad. The couple had no children and McClendon was content as a housewife for a number of years while also active in the community and at St. Mark's.

In 1916 McClendon received a scholarship to attend the American Academy of Dramatic Art at Carnegie Hall, studying acting under Frank Sargent and others. Three years later McClendon made her professional theatrical debut at the Davenport Theatre in New York during the 1919–1920 season, appearing in John Galsworthy's *Justice* with the Bramhall Players. For the next fifteen years McClendon appeared in almost every important drama about black life that was produced in New York, which earned her the title of the "Negro race's first lady."

McClendon gained some critical attention in a touring production of *Roseanne* (1924), which starred Charles Gilpin, but it was the small role of Octavie in Laurence Stallings and Frank Harling's *Deep River* that first brought McClendon critical success and the acknowledgment of her peers. The play opened on 21 September 1926 in Philadelphia and on 4 October moved to New York City. As Octavie, McClendon

Rose McClendon, photographed in 1935 by Carl Van Vechten. Library of Congress

entered and walked slowly down a grand staircase and exited through a garden—all without saying a word. Of her performance, critic John Anderson of the *New York Evening Post* said McClendon created "out of a few wisps of material an unforgettable picture" (5 Oct. 1926). In Philadelphia, director Arthur Hopkins convinced Ethel Barrymore to "watch Rose McClendon come down those stairs," and Barrymore later referred to McClendon's performance as "one of the memorable, immortal moments in the theatre" (*Journal of Negro History*, Jan. 1937).

On 30 December 1926 McClendon appeared as Goldie McAllister in Paul Green's Pulitzer Prize–winning play *In Abraham's Bosom* for the Provincetown Players at the Provincetown Theatre, which also starred Abbie Mitchell and Julius Bledsoe. The play was a success and ran for 277 performances. A revival was staged after the Pulitzer was awarded. In 1928 McClendon played Serena in Dorothy and Du Bose Heyward's *Porgy*. The play had an extended run of 217 performances in New York, after which McClendon toured with the show across the country and abroad. McClendon was called "the perfect Aristocrat of Catfish Row" and won critical acclaim for her role. In 1931 she played Big Sue in Paul Green's *House of Connelly*, the first production of the Group Theatre. The production, which opened

23 February 1931, starred Franchot Tone and Morris Carnovsky and was sponsored in part by the Theatre Guild. *House of Connelly* was an immediate success and became an important part of the Group Theatre's contribution to American theater. In 1932 McClendon took the role of Mammy in *Never No More*, and for the 1933 season she played various roles in the radio series *John Henry, Black River Giant*.

In 1935 McClendon played Cora in LANGSTON HUGHES's *Mulatto*, which premiered at the Vanderbilt Theatre in New York on 24 October. *The Oxford Companion to American Theatre* asserts that the play itself was inferior but succeeded on the strength of McClendon's performance. Doris Abramson expressed a similar sentiment and praised McClendon, saying, "This great Negro actress brought power and dignity to the role" (Abramson, 79). The New York critics agreed. Brooks Atkinson called her "an artist with a sensitive personality and a bell-like voice. It is always a privilege to see her adding fineness of perception to the parts she takes" (*New York Times*, 25 Oct. 1935). The show ran 373 performances, a record for a play by a black author. However, ill health forced McClendon to leave the cast a few months after the opening. She died of pneumonia a year later in New York City.

Beyond her own acting, McClendon was deeply concerned with the state of the black theater art, and she used her influence to promote it during what became known as the Harlem Renaissance. She directed productions for the Harlem Experimental Theatre, founded in 1928, and helped found in 1935 the Negro People's Theatre, which through McClendon's guidance became incorporated into the Federal Theatre Project's Black Unit in Harlem. McClendon also served on the advisory board of the Theatre Union, a nonprofit producing company founded in 1932 to produce socially significant plays at popular prices. She saw the theater as an important medium for depicting a true picture of African American life. She hoped the Federal Theatre Project support would produce quality black actors and writers.

As one of the great actresses of her time, McClendon became a strong symbol for black theater at a time when African Americans were just gaining their theatrical voice; indeed, when

McClendon first appeared on the stage, blacks were not yet allowed into theater audiences. In the year after her death, the Rose McClendon Players were organized by Dick Campbell in memory of her vision for the black theater. While the company faltered after the Second World War, it launched the careers of numerous artists who would make their mark in the postwar American theater—her vision fulfilled.

FURTHER READING

McClendon's scrapbook and clippings are in the Schomburg Center for Research in Black Culture of the New York Public Library.

Abramson, Doris. *Negro Playwrights* (1969).
Bond, Frederick. *The Negro and the Drama* (1940).
Isaacs, Edith J. R. *The Negro in the American Theatre* (1947).

Obituaries: *New York Times*, 14 July 1936; *Afro-American* and *New York Amsterdam News*, 18 July 1936; *Journal of Negro History* (Jan. 1937).

—MELISSA VICKERY-BAREFORD

 McCOY, BILL. *See* Railroad Bill.

 McCOY, ELIJAH

(27 Mar. 1843–1929), inventor, was born in Colchester, Canada West (now Ontario), the son of George McCoy and Mildred Goins, former slaves who had escaped from Kentucky. In 1849 his parents moved the family to Ypsilanti, Michigan, where Elijah began attending school. In 1859 he went to Edinburgh, Scotland, to undertake an apprenticeship as a mechanical engineer; he stayed there five years.

Unable to obtain a position as an engineer after he returned to the United States, McCoy began working as a railroad fireman for the Michigan Central Railroad. This position exposed him to the problems of steam engine lubrication and overheating. Locomotive engines had to be periodically oiled by hand, a time-consuming task that caused significant delays in railroad transport

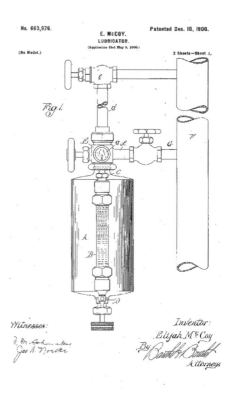

The patent illustration for Elijah McCoy's displacement lubricator, 1900. U.S. Patent and Trademark Office

of commercial goods and passengers. Poorly lubricated locomotives also used more fuel than those that were efficiently lubricated.

McCoy began his career as an inventor by first examining and improving the lubrication of stationary machines. On 23 June 1872 he patented "an improvement in lubricators for steam engines," the first of his automatic lubrication devices for use on stationary engines. The rights for this patent were assigned to S. C. Hamlin of Ypsilanti. McCoy received several additional patents for improvements in lubricators that were all for use on stationary engines and on steam engines for ships.

In 1882 McCoy began receiving patents for lubricators specifically designed for railroad locomotive engines. His hydrostatic lubricator for locomotives made quite an impact. Largely constructed of brass, the lubricators, approximately twelve inches in height, had valves that fed the oil to the engine and that regulated the steam pressure. These lubricators were assigned to Charles and Henry Hodges and were manufactured by the Detroit Railway

Supply Company. The money McCoy received from these patent assignments he used for further studies of the problems of lubrication.

McCoy continued to receive patents for improvements to his hydrostatic lubricator, and railroad officials soon took note. Even though other locomotive lubricators were on the market, McCoy's lubricators sold well. He became an instructor in the correct installation and maintenance of his lubricators and also served as a consultant for several lubricator manufacturing companies, such as the Detroit Lubricator Company.

In 1915 McCoy patented a graphite lubricator, specifically designed for use on the newly introduced "superheater" locomotive engines. Because of the extreme temperatures of the steam, it was difficult to control and regulate the supply of oil with which the superheater engines were lubricated. McCoy's new lubricator relied on the use of a solid lubricant, graphite, combined with oil that solved this problem. The basic design was economical and simple with few moving parts. The amount of lubricant was controlled by an equalizing valve that regulated the flow of oil and graphite over the engine cylinder. One enthusiastic customer reported that his locomotive made thirteen round trips between Chicago and the Mississippi River, and when the engine was examined it was in "perfect condition." On these trips the amount of oil used for lubrication was reduced by one-third to one-half, and the amount of coal was reduced by four to six tons. McCoy considered the graphite lubricator to be his greatest invention.

The Elijah McCoy Manufacturing Company, located in Detroit, was established in 1916 to sell the graphite lubricator. But apparently McCoy was only a minor stockholder; the company went out of business a few years after it began. Many questions remain about the extent to which McCoy himself profited from his own inventions. McCoy could have become a very wealthy man given the commercial success of his lubricator design. But many of his patents were quickly assigned to others, and he merely served as a figurehead for the company bearing his name.

McCoy married Mary E. Delaney, his second wife, in 1873. They later moved to Detroit, where she became a well-known civil rights and women's rights activist and clubwoman. The McCoys were very close, and after her death in 1923 Elijah McCoy's health began to deteriorate. Never a very sociable man, he began to withdraw from the world around him. In 1928 he was committed to Eloise Infirmary, suffering from senile dementia, and he died there. By the time of his death he had received at least fifty patents, many held in foreign countries and virtually all of them in the area of engine lubrication.

The theory is often propounded that one of McCoy's enduring legacies is the phrase "the real McCoy." The proposed explanation is that the quality of his lubricators was so outstanding in comparison to others on the market that railroad inspectors and engineers are said to have challenged their crews as to whether they had installed "the real McCoy." Actual evidence of such use has yet to be discovered. However, the phrase, in the form "the real Mackay" (pronounced *muh-KYE* in Scotland), may have been used as an advertising slogan by the G. Mackay and Co. distillery in Edinburgh, Scotland, as early as 1870, and it appears in a letter by the Scottish author Robert Louis Stevenson in 1883, only a year after McCoy patented his locomotive lubricator. In 1899 a San Francisco newspaper applied the idiom to a flamboyant white boxer known as "Kid McCoy." This and other evidence suggests that "the real McCoy" could easily be applied to anyone of note named McCoy. Its application to Elijah McCoy has certainly helped in recent years to keep his memory alive.

FURTHER READING

Hayden, Robert C. *Eight Black American Inventors* (1972).
Klein, Aaron. *Hidden Contributors: Black Scientists and Inventors in America* (1971).
Marshall, Albert P. *The "Real McCoy" of Ypsilanti* (1989).

—PORTIA P. JAMES

McDANIEL, HATTIE

(10 June 1895–26 Oct. 1952), film actress and singer, was born in Wichita, Kansas, the youngest daughter of Henry McDaniel, an itinerant preacher, carpenter, and entertainer, and Susan Holbert. The McDaniels moved to Denver, Colorado, in 1901, where Hattie enjoyed a more settled childhood than her seven older siblings had. Five other children had died in infancy. At home, at school, and at church, Hattie sang spirituals and recited passages from the Bible. Usually she enchanted, though not always. She later recalled: "My mother would say, 'Hattie, I'll pay you to hush,' and she'd give me a dime. But in a few minutes I'd be singing and shouting again" (Jackson, 9). By 1910 Hattie was already an accomplished singer and dancer, appearing in several minstrel shows in Denver. She later toured with her father and her brothers Sam and Otis in the Henry McDaniel Minstrel Show, a troupe popular throughout Colorado.

Around 1920 Henry's poor health and Otis's death forced Hattie to find work as a cook, a clerk, and a laundress, though she longed to return to the stage. Her break came later that year, when she joined Professor George Morrison and his Melody Hounds on a tour throughout the West and Mexico. McDaniel's well-received performances on that tour led to steady employment in the vaudeville circuits of the West and South for most of the 1920s. In 1925 she sang on the Denver radio station KOA, an appearance often credited as the first on radio by an African American. Although she could dance and displayed a keen talent for comedy, McDaniel rose to prominence as a blues singer, performing standards and recording some of her own compositions, including "Brown-Skin Baby Doll" and "Just One Sorrowing Heart."

McDaniel's singing career prospered until the Great Depression, when she was forced to find work as an attendant in the ladies room of Club Madrid, a nightclub and casino near Milwaukee. Some of the customers, unaware of McDaniel's two decades in show business, urged the manager to let the singing washroom attendant perform with the house band; a rousing rendition of the "St. Louis Blues" earned her a standing ovation and more than ninety dollars in tips that night. McDaniel quickly became one of the hottest acts in Milwaukee, and the regulars at Club Madrid urged her to leave for

Hattie McDaniel (left) receives her Academy Award for her supporting role as the feisty Mammy in Gone with the Wind *(1939).* © Bettmann/CORBIS

Los Angeles and take her chances in the movies. The rags-to-riches scenario could have made a great Hollywood script, if only Hollywood wrote such scripts for blacks.

The "riches" part took a few years. McDaniel arrived in Los Angeles in 1931, not exactly an ingénue but still a relative unknown. With characteristic optimism, she made the most of her only connection, her brother Sam, who played the Doleful Deacon on the weekly KNX radio show "The Optimistic Do-Nut Hour." Within a few weeks she was the star of the show and also wrote her own songs and gags. Despite her popularity, McDaniel received only five dollars per show. She earned the same amount for each movie in which she appeared as an extra or sang in the chorus. To augment her meager wages, she worked as a domestic, later joking that she had washed three million dishes on her way to stardom. By the mid 1930s McDaniel no longer needed to wash those dishes, as she had become that rarity in Hollywood: an actress with steady employment, and would ultimately appear in more than three hundred movies, most often as a maid. Her most notable performances came in John Ford's *Judge Priest* (1934) with Will Rogers and in James Whale's *Show Boat* (1936), where she played Queenie alongside PAUL ROBESON.

McDaniel's most acclaimed role, as Mammy in David O. Selznick's *Gone with the Wind* (1939), also proved to be the most controversial. To be sure, the NAACP and the black press criticized the film's romanticized depiction of the antebellum South. Yet most commentators—black and white—credited McDaniel's performance as the feisty but loyal Mammy to Scarlett O'Hara as worthy of the Academy Award for Best Supporting Actress. McDaniel displayed her trademark flair for biting asides and broad comedy, but it was the melodramatic scene in which she mourned the death of Scarlett's child that clinched the Oscar. Accepting the award—the first ever won by an African American—a tearful McDaniel expressed the hope that she would always be a credit to the motion picture industry and to her race.

During World War II, however, McDaniel found herself under fire from the NAACP's executive secretary, WALTER WHITE, for allegedly failing in that latter goal. At a time when the NAACP was spearheading a "Double V" campaign for victory against fascism abroad and racism at home, White criticized black actors for portraying the servile stereotypes of eye-rolling Mammies and cringing Uncle Toms. As the most prominent black actress at that time, McDaniel became a lightning rod for these attacks, and she deeply resented what she saw as White's interference in her livelihood. She passionately believed that her skills as an actor glorified African American womanhood, and indeed, at her best, she portrayed servant characters with greater depth and complexity than White charged. Moreover, sexism as much as racism restricted her roles. The slim, glamorous LENA HORNE—the black role model favored by Walter White—could insert a clause in her contract refusing to play maids; McDaniel had a clause in her contract forbidding her to lose weight.

The final years of McDaniel's life were not particularly happy. Although she appeared in several more movies, none brought her the acclaim of *Gone with the Wind*. She remained in the public eye, notably as the star of *Beulah*, a highly popular CBS radio show that ran from 1947 to 1951, in which she played a maid who did not speak in dialect. In 1951 a heart attack forced her to stop working on a television version of the show. McDaniel had suffered from diabetes and heart disease, and also from depression, for several years. An unsettled family life did not help. All four of her marriages were brief and often stormy, and her fervent desire for a child was never fulfilled; a well-publicized false pregnancy at the age of forty-nine made matters worse. At her lavish parties she remained the gregarious "Hi-Hat Hattie," but her friends noticed that she drank a little more, swore a little more, and on one occasion attempted suicide. Criticism from the NAACP still rankled, particularly because she had worked with the organization in 1945 to challenge successfully a restrictive covenant in her Los Angeles neighborhood. That court ruling helped the NAACP build its national campaign against restrictive covenants, which was finally endorsed by the U.S. Supreme Court in its 1948 *Shelley v. Kraemer* decision. In 1952 McDaniel was diagnosed with breast cancer; she died in the Motion Picture Country Home and Hospital in Woodland Hills, California.

It is not surprising that McDaniel's favorite poem was "We Wear the Mask," by PAUL LAURENCE DUNBAR. It stands as an appropriate tribute to a woman whose image received so much attention that the person behind the mask was often lost:

We wear the mask that grins and lies,
It hides our cheeks and shades our eyes,—
This debt we pay to human guile;
With torn and bleeding hearts we smile,
And mouth with myriad subtleties.

FURTHER READING

McDaniel's most important papers are in the Margaret Herrick Library of the Academy of Motion Picture Arts and Sciences, Beverly Hills, California.

Bogle, Donald. *Toms, Coons, Mulattoes, Mammies and Bucks: An Interpretive History of Blacks in American Films* (1973).

Cripps, Thomas. *Slow Fade to Black: The Negro in American Film, 1900–1942* (1993).

Jackson, Carlton. *Hattie: The Life of Hattie McDaniel* (1990).

Watts, Jill. *"We Wear the Mask": The Life of Hattie McDaniel* (2004).

Obituaries: *New York Times*, 27 Oct. 1952; *Los Angeles Examiner*, 2 Nov. 1952.

—STEVEN J. NIVEN

McDONALD, GABRIELLE KIRK

(12 Apr. 1942–), federal judge and international war crimes jurist, was born to James G. Kirk, a railroad dining car waiter, and Frances Retta English in St. Paul, Minnesota. Her father, who was later the director of the Community Development Corporation in St. Paul, and her mother divorced when Gabrielle was a young child, and she moved with her mother and brother, James, to New York City and later to Teaneck, New Jersey. Kirk's mother, an editor at Prentice-Hall, was a forceful presence who resisted a New York landlord's attempt to evict the Kirk family from their home when he discovered that they were black; he had rented to the light-skinned Frances English believing that she was white. Determined from an early age to become a civil rights attorney, Kirk briefly attended Boston University and Hunter College in New York City before enrolling in Howard Law School in Washington, D.C., in the early 1960s.

In 1966 Kirk received the Kappa Beta Pi Legal Sorority Award for Academic Excellence and an award for best oral argument and graduated first in her class at Howard Law School, a distinction that she shares with THURGOOD MARSHALL, who was at that time solicitor general of the United States. In a tribute to Marshall in 1993 Kirk wrote that she had been driven by his vision of using the law as an instrument of liberation. She began her legal career as a staff attorney for the NAACP Legal Defense Fund (LDF), an organization shaped by Marshall's leadership in the 1940s and 1950s. By 1966, however, the passage of the 1964 Civil Rights Act had transformed the legal terrain upon which the LDF operated. It now focused on using Title VII of that act, which deals with employment discrimination, to assist African Americans seeking workplace fairness in large, unionized companies. Kirk led the LDF attorneys on several of these cases, notably a successful suit against Philip Morris, which, like other tobacco companies, had hired blacks for only the lowest-paying, most menial tasks. Kirk's victory in that 1967 case marked the first successful use of Title VII to improve equal employment opportunities.

After three years of working for the LDF, Kirk married the attorney Mark McDonald and with him founded McDonald and McDonald, a law firm in Houston, Texas, specializing in discrimination lawsuits against major Texas corporations. The couple had two children, Michael and Stacy, and later divorced. Even opposing corporate attorneys admitted that Kirk McDonald was one of the best trial lawyers in the South, particularly in 1976, when her firm won a settlement of $1.2 billion for four hundred black workers at the Lone Star Steel Company. In addition to her work in private practice, Kirk McDonald also taught at the Thurgood Marshall School of Law at Texas Southern University in 1970 and from 1975 to 1977, and at the University of Texas at Austin in 1978. Recognizing her broad legal expertise, President Jimmy Carter appointed Gabrielle McDonald in 1979 to the U.S. District Court for the Southern District of Texas, the first federal judgeship awarded to an African American in that state.

As a federal judge, McDonald faced a vast caseload—nearly one thousand a year—focusing on a broad spectrum of constitutional matters. Her earliest rulings were broadly liberal, notably, *Andrews v. Ballard* (1980), which overturned provisions of Texas law that had virtually outlawed acupuncture and other alternative medical practices in the state. McDonald's highest-profile case came in a 1981 dispute between white and Vietnamese shrimpers in the Gulf of Mexico. The Ku Klux Klan, supporting the white shrimpers, asked McDonald to recuse herself from the case, claiming that they could not receive a fair trial from a "Negress." Her family was also sent hate mail, including four one-way tickets to Africa. McDonald refused to remove herself from the case, however, and ultimately enjoined the Klan from intimidating the Vietnamese shrimpers. Commentators noted that her carefully worded injunction did not infringe upon the Klan's constitutional right to assemble.

Indeed, in her nine years on the federal bench, McDonald earned a reputation for fairness across the political spectrum. Conservatives praised her in 1986 when she upheld as constitutional a Houston ordinance that restricted the location of and signage used by topless bars. MacDonald ruled that topless dancing "is not without its First Amendment right to freedom of expression" but also that the ordinance, which prohibited such bars from operating within 750 feet of a church, school, or day-care center, did not restrict free speech, since it did not prevent them from operating elsewhere in the city. Such rulings did not endear her to some civil rights lawyers who viewed her jurisprudence as too cautious.

By 1988 McDonald had begun to chafe at her ever-increasing caseload, and she stepped down from her lifetime judicial appointment. She worked for law firms in San Antonio and Austin until 1993, when a former LDF colleague at the U.S. State Department asked her to serve on the International Criminal Tribunal for the Former Yugoslavia (ICTY). Although she was surprised by the request, given her lack of experience in international law, she accepted, and the administration of President Bill Clinton submitted her name to the United Nations. In September 1993, after receiving the highest number of votes cast by the U.N. General Assembly for the tribunal's members, McDonald began to divide her time between Houston and the ICTY headquarters at The Hague in the Netherlands.

In May 1996 McDonald sat as one of three judges at the first war crimes proceedings since the Nuremberg trials after World War II. Exactly one year later, the panel sentenced Duško Tadić, a Bosnian Serb, to twenty years in prison for systematically raping, torturing, and murdering Muslims in a Serb-run prison camp in 1992. International commentators noted that, as the presiding judge, McDonald skillfully balanced her concern for the victims of the war crimes, especially rape victims, with scrupulous fairness and respect for the rights of the defendants.

The ICTY's findings in the Tadić case were significant in that they proved under international law the Serb policy of "ethnic cleansing" and set a precedent for further prosecutions. At the end of her tenure as president of the ICTY, McDonald praised the tribunal for melding different legal systems and traditions and for establishing clear international procedures for indictments and rules of evidence. She also argued that a permanent court with stronger backing from the United Nations would have brought war criminals to trial more quickly than had been the case in Serbia and in the similar tribunal dealing with atrocities in Rwanda. The establishment by the United Nations of an International Criminal Court (ICC) in 2002 appeared to have furthered McDonald's ideals, but the U.S. government declared its implacable opposition to such a court. Fearing, as President George W. Bush stated, that "our diplomats and our soldiers could be drug into this court," his administration joined Iraq, Israel, and North Korea in opposing a permanent organization to adjudicate war crimes.

After stepping down from the ICTY in 1999, McDonald accepted a position as a human rights adviser to Freeport-McMoRan Copper and Gold, Inc. This New Orleans–based company had come under attack from human rights organizations for dumping toxic waste from its copper and gold mines, the world's largest, in West Papua, Indonesia. By 2002 Freeport-McMoRan's

more enlightened corporate policies had facilitated the passage of new legislation that ensured the indigenous population of West Papua a greater share of natural resource revenues. McDonald also participated in 2001 in an international mock tribunal that found the Japanese government guilty of creating, regulating, and maintaining a policy of sexual enslavement of "comfort women" for its troops in several Asian countries during World War II.

Several organizations have recognized McDonald's contributions to civil rights and human rights, among them, the National Bar Association, an African American organization that gave her its RONALD BROWN International Law Award, and the American Bar Association Commission on Women in the Profession, which chose her as its "Woman Lawyer of Achievement" in 2001. Perhaps the greatest testament to Gabrielle McDonald's commitment to human rights was given by Kofi Annan, secretary general of the United Nations, who wrote:

Perhaps more than any other single person, Judge McDonald helped bring us closer to a world which once seemed beyond attainment—a world in which those whose deeds offend the conscience of humankind will no longer go unpunished, in which human rights will be truly universal and in which the rule of law will finally prevail.

FURTHER READING

Felde, Kitty. "Profile of Gabrielle Kirk McDonald." *Human Rights Brief* 7, no. 3 (Spring 2000).

Horne, William. "Judging Tadić." *American Lawyer* (Sept. 1995).

May, Richard, David Tolbert, John Hocking, et al. *Essays on ICTY Procedure and Evidence in Honour of Gabrielle Kirk McDonald* (2000).

—STEVEN J. NIVEN

 McGUIRE, GEORGE ALEXANDER
(26 Mar. 1866–10 Nov. 1934), bishop and founder of the African Orthodox Church, was born in Sweets, Antigua, British West Indies, the son of Edward Henry McGuire and Mary Elizabeth (maiden name unknown). He graduated from the Antigua branch of Mico

College for Teachers in 1886. Baptized in his father's Anglican Church, he was educated in the Moravian tradition of his mother, graduating in 1888 from the Moravian seminary at Nisky, St. Thomas, in the Danish West Indies. Thereafter he pastored a Moravian congregation at Frederiksted, St. Croix. He married Ada Roberts in 1892; they had one daughter.

McGuire immigrated to the United States in 1894. The following year he was confirmed in the Protestant Episcopal Church. He studied for the Episcopal ministry under a fellow West Indian, Henry L. Phillips of Philadelphia. McGuire found himself in a church that desired to minister to African Americans but was generally unwilling to accept any blacks as equal to whites. McGuire's talent and Phillips's mentorship allowed him to advance swiftly through the offices open to him. Ordained deacon in 1896 and priest the next year, he pastored a succession of black congregations, including St. Andrew's, Cincinnati (1897–1899); St. Philip's, Richmond (1899–1901); and St. Thomas's, Philadelphia (1901–1904).

In 1905 McGuire accepted the appointment of Bishop William Montgomery Brown as archdeacon for colored work in the diocese of Arkansas. This was the highest position open to a black man serving the church within the United States. The denomination's national General Convention, however, was considering two proposals for allowing blacks to serve as domestic bishops: the first would place black bishops in charge of all-black missionary districts independent of local dioceses; and the second would allow dioceses to elect suffragan bishops who would work under the supervision of the diocesan bishop. Soon after McGuire's arrival, Brown proposed a third plan: black Episcopalians should be separated into an independent denomination. In 1906 McGuire seems to have preferred the missionary plan; later, under his own initiative, he attempted to enact Brown's plan.

Racial conflicts in the Arkansas diocese led McGuire to accept an invitation to return to the North in 1909 to pastor St. Bartholomew's, a young congregation of West Indians in Cambridge, Massachusetts. Under McGuire's leadership the church grew dramatically, but again he was frustrated by the racism of the Episcopal Church, evident in the diocese's refusal to grant the congregation voting rights. In 1911 he moved to New York to become field secretary of the American Church Institute for Negroes. Two years later he accepted a call to serve as rector of St. Paul's Church, Falmouth, in his native Antigua.

While in the Islands McGuire encountered the ideas of racial independence and nationalism advocated by MARCUS GARVEY. These resonated with McGuire's experience of whites' inability to treat blacks as equals within the church. He returned to New York in 1919 to support Garvey's newly formed Universal Negro Improvement Association (UNIA) and African Communities League. McGuire soon established his own congregation, the Church of the Good Shepherd, which affiliated briefly with the Reformed Episcopal Church but soon united with a few other congregations to form the Independent Episcopal Church.

In August 1920 the first International Convention of the Negro Peoples of the World elected McGuire chaplain-general of the UNIA and "titular Archbishop of Ethiopia." McGuire strengthened the work of local UNIA chaplains and, according to the UNIA's *Negro World*, sought to create a church "big enough for all Negroes to enter, retaining their own worship" (2 Apr. 1921). McGuire linked Christianity and racial independence in *The Universal Negro Catechism* (1921) and *The Universal Negro Ritual* (1921), which he composed for the UNIA. The catechism taught that if one "had to think or speak of the color of God" it should be described "as black since we are created in His image and likeness." The infant baptism rite charged the baptized to "fight manfully . . . for the freedom of his race, and the redemption of Africa unto his life's end."

The formality of the rituals did not appeal to many Protestant supporters of the UNIA, nor did McGuire's ordination of a UNIA leader as a presbyter of the church. Within a year the *Negro World* was at pains to stress, "We favor all churches, but adopt none as a UNIA Church" (16 July 1921). Although Garvey desired to unite blacks into "a great Christian confraternity," he did not want the church and hierarchy

that McGuire sought to create. After a brief period of estrangement McGuire resumed a prominent role in the UNIA, presiding over the movement's "canonization" of Jesus as the "Black Man of Sorrows" in 1924.

Unable to establish a church linked to the UNIA, McGuire sought to provide an independent black church for Anglo-Catholics. Elected bishop of the Independent Episcopal Church in September 1921, he insisted that the church be renamed the African Orthodox Church (AOC) to emphasize its racial leadership. He maintained that his new church was "neither schismatic nor heretical," but a legitimate national or racial "branch" of the one Holy Catholic Church.

When trying to form a church linked to the UNIA, McGuire had been willing to forgo apostolic succession, but he believed this was essential to authenticate the claims of the AOC. Refused consecration by Episcopal, Catholic, and Russian Orthodox bishops, he finally received it from Joseph René Vilatte of the Old Catholic Church of America. Having an autonomous church headed by a black bishop in apostolic succession was a great source of pride for McGuire and his followers, but the questionable authenticity of Vilatte's consecrations haunted their relations with other churches.

McGuire crafted a liturgy for his church based largely on the Book of Common Prayer and Anglo-Catholic practices, but also incorporating a few elements from Eastern Orthodoxy. The liturgy included prayers for the race and the redemption of Africa, though less pronounced than those in the *Universal Negro Ritual*. McGuire also founded Endich Theological Seminary in 1923 and edited the church's monthly *Negro Churchman* from 1923 to 1931. By the mid-1920s church membership numbered twelve thousand, with congregations in the northeastern United States, Nova Scotia, and the Caribbean. In 1927 McGuire was raised to the rank of patriarch and expanded the church to South Africa by receiving a few congregations and consecrating their leader, Daniel William Alexander, as bishop. McGuire died in New York City as head of a slowly expanding church.

McGuire broke new ground in extending the autonomy enjoyed by many black Protestants to black

Anglo-Catholics. He was among the most important religious leaders in Garvey's movement and a talented member of the corps of West Indian clergy serving the Episcopal Church in the United States. The churches led by Alexander in Africa proved to be an enduring and significant presence on that continent. Yet in the U.S. the AOC became a small, though enduring, community of less than 6,000 people. As a black church leader who boasted of a claim to apostolic succession that few recognized, McGuire remained a marginal figure in both the church and predominantly Protestant black America.

FURTHER READING

Burkett, Randall K. *Black Redemption: Churchmen Speak for the Garvey Movement* (1978).
———. *Garveyism as a Religious Movement: The Institutionalization of Black Civil Religion* (1978).
Farajajé-Jones, Elias. *In Search of Zion: The Spiritual Significance of Africa in Black Religious Movements* (1990).
Lewis, Harold T. *Yet with a Steady Beat: The African American Struggle for Recognition in the Episcopal Church* (1996).
McGuire, George Alexander. *The Universal Negro Catechism* (1921).
———. *The Universal Negro Ritual* (1921).
—DAVID R. BAINS

 McKAY, CLAUDE
(15 Sept. 1890–22 May 1948), poet, novelist, and journalist, was born Festus Claudius McKay in Sunny Ville, Clarendon Parish, Jamaica, the son of Thomas Francis McKay and Hannah Ann Elizabeth Edwards, farmers. The youngest of eleven children, McKay was sent at an early age to live with his oldest brother, a schoolteacher, so that he could be given the best education available. An avid reader, McKay began to write poetry at the age of ten. In 1906 he decided to enter a trade school, but when the school was destroyed by an earthquake he became apprenticed to a carriage- and cabinet-maker; a brief period in the constabulary followed. In 1907 McKay came to the attention of Walter Jekyll, an English gentleman residing in Jamaica who became his mentor, encouraging him to write dialect verse. Jekyll later set some of

Socialist novelist, poet, and journalist Claude McKay. © CORBIS

McKay's verse to music. By the time he immigrated to the United States in 1912, McKay had established himself as a poet, publishing two volumes of dialect verse, *Songs of Jamaica* (1912) and *Constab Ballads* (1912).

Having heard favorable reports of the work of BOOKER T. WASHINGTON, McKay enrolled at Tuskegee Institute in Alabama with the intention of studying agronomy; it was here that he first encountered the harsh realities of American racism, which would form the basis for much of his subsequent writing. He soon left Tuskegee for Kansas State College in Manhattan, Kansas. In 1914 a financial gift from Jekyll enabled him to move to New York, where he invested in a restaurant and married his childhood sweetheart, Eulalie Imelda Lewars. Neither venture lasted a year, and Lewars returned to Jamaica to give birth to their daughter. McKay was forced to take a series of menial jobs. He was finally able to publish two poems, "Invocation" and "The Harlem Dancer," under a pseudonym in 1917. McKay's talent as a lyric poet earned him recognition, particularly from Frank Harris, editor of *Pearson's* magazine, and Max Eastman, editor of *The Liberator,* a socialist journal; both became instrumental in McKay's early career.

As a socialist, McKay eventually became an editor at *The Liberator,* in addition to writing various articles for a number of left-wing publications. During the period of racial violence against blacks known as the Red Summer of 1919, McKay wrote one of his best-known poems, the sonnet, "If We Must Die," an anthem of resistance later quoted by Winston Churchill during World War II. "Baptism," "The White House," and "The Lynching," all sonnets, also exemplify some of McKay's finest protest poetry. The generation of poets who formed the core of the Harlem Renaissance, including LANGSTON HUGHES and COUNTÉE CULLEN, identified McKay as a leading inspirational force, even though he did not write modern verse. His innovation lay in the directness with which he spoke of racial issues and his choice of the working class, rather than the middle class, as his focus.

McKay resided in England from 1919 through 1921, then returned to the United States. While in England, he was employed by the British socialist journal, *Workers' Dreadnought,* and published a book of verse, *Spring in New Hampshire,* which was released in an expanded version in the United States in 1922. The same year, *Harlem Shadows,* perhaps his most significant poetry collection, appeared. McKay then began a twelve-year sojourn through Europe, the Soviet Union, and Africa, a period marked by poverty and illness. While in the Soviet Union he compiled his journalistic essays into a book, *The Negroes in America,* which was not published in the United States until 1979. For a time he was buoyed by the success of his first published novel, *Home to Harlem* (1928), which was critically acclaimed but engendered controversy for its frank portrayal of the underside of Harlem life.

His next novel, *Banjo: A Story without a Plot* (1929), followed the exploits of an expatriate African American musician in Marseilles, a locale McKay knew well. This novel and McKay's presence in France influenced Léopold Sédar Senghor, Aimé Césaire, and other pioneers of the Negritude literary movement that took hold in French West Africa and the West Indies. *Banjo* did not sell well. Neither did *Gingertown* (1932), a short story collection, or *Banana Bottom* (1933). Often identified as McKay's finest novel, *Banana Bottom* tells the story of Bita Plant, who returns to Jamaica after being educated in England and struggles to form an identity that reconciles the aesthetic values imposed upon her with her appreciation for her native roots.

McKay had moved to Morocco in 1930, but his financial situation forced him to return to the United States in 1934. He gained acceptance to the Federal Writers Project in 1936 and completed his autobiography, *A Long Way from Home,* in 1937. Although no longer sympathetic toward communism, he remained a socialist, publishing essays and articles in *The Nation,* the *New Leader,* and the *New York Amsterdam News.* In 1940 McKay produced a nonfiction work, *Harlem: Negro Metropolis,* which gained little attention but has remained an important historical source. Never able to regain the stature he had achieved during the 1920s, McKay blamed his chronic financial difficulties on his race and his failure to obtain academic credentials and associations.

McKay never returned to the homeland he left in 1912. He became a U.S. citizen in 1940. High blood pressure and heart disease led to a steady physical decline, and in a move that surprised his friends, McKay abandoned his lifelong agnosticism and embraced Catholicism. In 1944 he left New York for Chicago, where he worked for the Catholic Youth Organization. He eventually succumbed to congestive heart failure in Chicago. His second autobiography, *My Green Hills of Jamaica,* was published posthumously in 1979.

Assessments of McKay's lasting influence vary. To McKay's contemporaries, such as JAMES WELDON JOHNSON, "Claude McKay's poetry was one of the great forces in bringing about what is often called the 'Negro Literary Renaissance.' " While his novels and autobiographies have found an increasing audience in recent years, modern critics appear to concur with Arthur P. Davis that McKay's greatest literary contributions are found among his early sonnets and lyrics. McKay ended *A Long Way from Home* with this assessment of himself: "I have nothing to give but my singing. All my life I have been a troubadour wanderer, nourishing myself mainly on the poetry of existence. And all I offer here is the distilled poetry of my experience."

FURTHER READING

The bulk of McKay's papers is located in the James Weldon Johnson Collection at Yale University.

Bronz, Stephen H. *Roots of Negro Racial Consciousness: The 1920s, Three Harlem Renaissance Authors* (1964).

Cooper, Wayne F. *Claude McKay: Rebel Sojourner in the Harlem Renaissance, a Biography* (1987).

Cooper, Wayne F., ed. *The Passion of Claude McKay* (1973).

Gayle, Addison. *Claude McKay: The Black Poet at War* (1972).

Giles, James R. *Claude McKay* (1976).

Tillary, Tyrone. *Claude McKay: A Black Poet's Struggle for Identity* (1992).

Obituary: *New York Times*, 24 May 1948.

—FREDA SCOTT GILES

McKISSICK, FLOYD BIXLER (3 Mar. 1922–28 Apr. 1991), civil rights lawyer and activist, was born in Asheville, North Carolina, the son of Ernest McKissick, a hotel bellman, and Magnolia Esther Thompson, a seamstress. When Floyd was four years old, an angry bus driver ordered him to the rear of the bus after he had wandered into the white section to join some white children who were watching the driver. That incident revealed to him that black children did not have the same freedom and opportunity in North Carolina as white children did. Black children attended segregated schools with inferior facilities, sat in the back of the bus, and could not sit down and eat at lunch counters. They received harsh treatment from city employees like bus drivers and police officers. They did not have public skating rinks or swimming pools, and they could not use the public library. As a result of his awareness, McKissick decided early in life that he would study law to fight for equal rights for black Americans. In fall 1939 he began a prelaw course at Morehouse College in Atlanta, Georgia, working his way through the year as a dining hall waiter. At Morehouse he became the personal waiter for black political activist, sociologist, and historian W. E. B. DU BOIS. Du Bois's belief that blacks must demand absolute equality without compromise, and his opinion that educated black people had an obligation to improve the condition of the race, had an influence on the young college student.

McKissick left Morehouse in February 1942, after the United States entered World War II. In that same year he married his childhood sweetheart, Evelyn Williams; they would have three daughters and one son. McKissick joined the U.S. Army and was eventually assigned to a field artillery unit. He taught in army literacy programs in the United States for two years before he was shipped overseas. Eventually, he served in battle in Europe, where he earned a Purple Heart.

Eager to continue his education, McKissick applied to the segregated University of North Carolina after his discharge from the army in 1945. His application was not even acknowledged. Unwilling to concede defeat, he got a job as a waiter to earn enough money to reenter college. He began his long career as a civil rights activist in 1947 when he joined BAYARD RUSTIN on the Journey of Reconciliation. The journey, a bus trip, was organized by the Congress of Racial Equality (CORE) to test a recent Supreme Court decision requiring the integration of interstate travel. The objectives of CORE, an interracial organization founded in Chicago, Illinois, in 1942, were to draw attention to and take direct action against racial discrimination in public facilities.

In the late 1940s McKissick returned to Morehouse and again applied to the all-white law school at the University of North Carolina. When he was rejected, THURGOOD MARSHALL and the National Association for the Advancement of Colored People (NAACP) filed a suit on his behalf. While he waited for the case to be decided, McKissick attended the all-black law school at North Carolina College. In 1951 he won his suit and became the first African American to earn the LLB degree at the University of North Carolina, although all of his course work already had been completed at North Carolina College.

McKissick passed the North Carolina bar exam in 1952 and began a general law practice in Durham, North Carolina. In 1958 he filed his first civil rights case, a suit on behalf of his eldest daughter to integrate a public school in Durham. Active in Durham's black community, he joined the Durham Business and Professional Chain (a black businessmen's organization), became an adviser to the state's NAACP youth groups, and became the director of Durham's CORE chapter.

Because of his role as adviser to the NAACP youth groups in North Carolina, McKissick was contacted by the students who began the sit-in at the Woolworth's lunch counter in Greensboro, North Carolina, in February 1960. That sit-in marked the beginning of a great increase in the demand by blacks for equal rights. McKissick helped the students expand the sit-ins to other towns, and he led workshops on nonviolence for sit-in participants. During the first half of the 1960s McKissick represented many of the demonstrators who were arrested in direct action campaigns against segregated facilities in the South. He often served as a negotiator between the demonstrators and the local authorities, seeking to secure integrated facilities and fair employment policies.

From 1963 to 1966 McKissick served as the national chairman of CORE's board, the group responsible for determining policy at the national level. In 1966 he replaced JAMES FARMER as the director of the national office, assuming responsibility for implementing CORE's policies. After JAMES MEREDITH, the first black man admitted to the University of Mississippi, was shot, McKissick joined the Reverend MARTIN LUTHER KING JR. and STOKELY CARMICHAEL, president of the Student Nonviolent Coordinating Committee (SNCC), to complete Meredith's March Against Fear in 1966. McKissick supported Carmichael's effort to change the emphasis of the march to voter registration and the achievement of black power. During the period that McKissick led CORE, it became an all-black organization that was more militant in its demands for black political and economic power. As the decade became more violent, McKissick and CORE moved away from nonviolence as a philosophy and advocated self-defense.

In 1968 McKissick resigned as national director of CORE to pursue his dream of building a black community that would ultimately become economically and politically self-sufficient. Soul City, North Carolina, located about fifty miles from Durham, began with a grant from the U.S. Department of Housing and Urban Development. McKissick hoped that black-owned businesses would be attracted to the area once housing and a community infrastructure were in place. However, his plans for Soul City never materialized, partly because federal money for the project ceased. In 1979 the Department of Housing and Urban Development foreclosed on Soul City although McKissick and others continued to live there.

In 1969 McKissick published *Three Fifths of a Man*, his analysis of the race problem in the United States. McKissick believed the problem was primarily economic and that a redistribution of the nation's wealth was needed to enable black people to share in the nation's prosperity. In the book, McKissick expressed his belief that the Declaration of Independence and the U.S. Constitution already contained all the tools necessary to solve the nation's racial problems; they only had to be enforced. McKissick continued to practice law in Durham until June 1990, when he was appointed by North Carolina governor James G. Martin as a judge in the state's Ninth Judicial District. McKissick died in Soul City.

As the national leader of CORE from 1963 to 1968, McKissick helped determine the direction of the 1960s civil rights movement. As a result of this movement, Congress passed extensive civil rights legislation in 1964 and 1965. These laws instituted profound changes in American society.

FURTHER READING

McKissick's papers are located at the Hayti Heritage Center in Durham, North Carolina.

Farmer, James. *Lay Bare the Heart: An Autobiography of the Civil Rights Movement* (1985).
Meier, August, and Elliott Rudwick. *CORE: A Study in the Civil Rights Movement, 1942–1968* (1973).

Obituaries: *New York Times, Raleigh News and Observer,* and *Washington Post,* 30 Apr. 1991.

—JENIFER W. GILBERT

McLENDON, JOHNNY

(5 Apr. 1915–8 Oct. 1999), basketball coach, was born John B. McLendon Jr. in Hiawatha, Kansas. McLendon obtained a piecemeal education, steadily taking advantage of each opportunity that he was offered. He graduated from Sumner High School in Kansas City, Kansas, in 1932 and entered Kansas City Junior College. He finished his BS in Physical Education at the University of Kansas in 1936 and earned a master's degree from the University of Iowa in 1937. One of McLendon's professors in the physical education program at Kansas was Dr. James Naismith, who had invented the game of basketball in 1891, while he was a student at the International YMCA Training School (now Springfield College), in Springfield, Massachusetts.

In his undergraduate years, McLendon took a couple of high school coaching jobs in Lawrence and Topeka. Following his graduate studies, he was hired as an assistant basketball coach at the North Carolina College for Negroes (NCCN) in Durham (now North Carolina Central University). He ascended to head coach in 1940 and immediately began churning out successful teams that played a revolutionary style of basketball.

Since basketball was mostly played in a slow, painstaking manner, it had traditionally been considered a game destined to be dominated by taller, bigger teams. Players moved among one another in proximity, attempting to displace opponents physically through a process called "screening." This style emphasized patience on offense and rigid defensive fundamentals, both of which capitalized on the assets of bigger players while virtually eliminating their primary liabilities, slowness, and premature fatigue.

McLendon saw a way to physically and mentally exhaust his opponents, no matter their size. To accomplish this, he did more than any coach in history to hone the fundamentals of the "fast break," a single type of play that became synonymous with his overall basketball philosophy. In the older style of basketball, a fast break was an unplanned, opportunistic play that occurred when a player exploited a brief advantage by stealing the ball and running faster than everyone else. McLendon's genius was to see the potential of the fast break in the routine and inevitable moments of a game—a loose ball, a rebound, a blocked shot—and to give each player a specific role in the action of the play. His fast breaks required that players maintain maximum spacing over the entire court, which allowed for greater creativity and adaptation than did traditional offensive plays designed for the half court. McLendon's fast break demanded a frantic defensive intensity and superior physical conditioning and often resulted in victories of forty points or more. This new style collided with traditional basketball as the jazz of MILES DAVIS did with the more formal ragtime of SCOTT JOPLIN: whereas the older school was fixed in its precision, the newer one was thrilling and unpredictable in its improvisational creativity.

McLendon also devised a way to apply fast-break principles to a half-court offense, namely, by putting one player in each corner of the court and allowing the fifth to roam in the middle. This extremely effective offense came to be known as "Four Corners"; when the University of North Carolina's coach Dean Smith adopted it at Chapel Hill in the mid-1960s, he was popularly credited as its inventor. Using the fast break and Four Corners to near perfection, NCCN compiled a record of 239–68 between 1940 and 1952. With two other coaches from the Central Intercollegiate Athletic Association for historically black colleges and universities, McLendon founded the CIAA tournament in 1946 and, in 1950, the Tournament of the Carolinas. McLendon's teams proceeded to win eight titles between the two tournaments.

McLendon's tenure at NCCN, and later at Hampton Institute and the Tennessee Agricultural and Industrial State Normal School (now Tennessee State University), resulted in a catalog of "firsts." In 1943 he coached the first black player to be signed by an NBA team, NCCN's Harold Hunter, who played for the Washington Caps. He also cofounded the National Athletic Steering Committee, a precursor to the Black Coaches Association, which worked toward desegregating college basketball. McLendon's efforts paid dividends in the late 1950s, when black colleges were allowed to compete for a single spot in the National Association of Intercollegiate Athletics Tournament. From 1957 to 1959 McLendon led Tennessee A & I through both tournaments for three straight years, becoming the first black basketball coach to win a national title and the first college coach to win three consecutively. Their first national title came almost a full decade before Texas Western's all-black team defeated Adolph Rupp's all-white Kentucky squad in the 1966 NCAA championship, the game commonly cited as the first national championship for an African American team.

McLendon's success in the college ranks led to his appointment as head coach of the National Industrial Basketball League's (NIBL) Cleveland Pipers in 1959. In an exhibition game the following year, he directed his amateur Pipers to an unprecedented victory over a U.S. Olympic team that included the future NBA stars Jerry West and Oscar Robertson. When the NIBL became the professional American Basketball League (ABL) in 1961, McLendon consequently became the first black coach of a team in a professional basketball league. The Pipers won the ABL championship that season, but in 1962 their owner, George Steinbrenner (later the owner of the New York Yankees), withheld players' paychecks because of their supposedly lackadaisical play. McLendon resigned, protesting that he could not "stand by and see a good group of young athletes intimidated" (Ashe, 56).

McLendon returned to college ball at Kentucky State, where he coached from 1963 to 1966, and he wrote two books on fast-break basketball. His final college coaching position marked a long-awaited breakthrough, when he became the first black coach at a predominantly white institution, Cleveland State University. He held the post until 1969, when he returned to the professional ranks for one season as head coach of the fledgling American Basketball Association's Denver Rockets (now the NBA's Denver Nuggets).

One of the most telling moments in McLendon's career remained secret for over fifty years. While he was at North Carolina College in 1944, McLendon coached his team in the first integrated college basketball game

in the country, against an all-white intramural team from the neighboring Duke University Medical School. The game did not achieve public notice until the historian Scott Ellsworth interviewed Coach McLendon in 1995 and published his findings in a *New York Times Magazine* article the following year. According to Ellsworth, "The Secret Game" was held on a Sunday morning, 12 March 1944, in the NCCN gymnasium. They played on Sunday morning, knowing that many Durham residents, both black and white, would be in church, and they played at NCCN because it was less difficult, logistically, than sneaking the NCCN players onto Duke's campus.

The medical school team boasted at least five players who had experience in some of the most competitive undergraduate programs around the country; it was rumored to be the best team at Duke—indeed, possibly in Durham. But McLendon's 1944 Eagles, despite having only seven players, had posted a 19–1 record. Somehow a hypothetical question arose among Durham's students and in some of the town's barbershops: If the two teams ever played each other, who would win? The teams eventually became intrigued with the question themselves, but when they finally took the court together—with one referee and a scorekeeper, to make it official—they realized how dangerous their participation in such a game in the segregated South could potentially be.

Both teams struggled to find their rhythm early, but when NCCN's furious defense and explosive fast break finally erupted, they ran away with the game. The NCCN guard Aubrey Stanley, just sixteen years old, remembered that it suddenly occurred to him that Duke's players "weren't supermen. They were just men. And we could beat them" (Ellsworth). By halftime word had leaked on the NCCN campus, and students were climbing outside the gymnasium to peer through the windows. They witnessed seven of their classmates soundly defeat Duke, 88–44.

As Ellsworth writes, the next thing they saw was even more shocking: the two teams traded players and played a second game—with two integrated teams. The score was not recorded, but McLendon later described the experience

of watching two communities and two distinctive basketball styles coalesce for the first time: "That was the way basketball's supposed to be" (Ellsworth).

McLendon and his wife, Joanna, had four children. He was inducted into the James Naismith Basketball Hall of Fame in 1978. His career college coaching record was 523–165; his professional record was 108–71. Before his death in 1999 in Cleveland, Ohio, the National Association of Collegiate Directors of Athletics endowed a scholarship in his name for minority students who intended to pursue graduate studies in athletic administration. McLendon regarded this scholarship among his highest achievements.

FURTHER READING

McLendon, John B., Jr. *Fast Break Basketball: Fundamentals and Fine Points* (1965).

ASHE, ARTHUR. *A Hard Road to Glory: A History of the African American Athlete Since 1946* (1988).
Ellsworth, Scott. "Jim Crow Loses: The Secret Game." *New York Times Magazine* (31 Mar. 1996). Available at http://www.nccu.edu/campus/athletics/jmsecret.html.
—DAVID F. SMYDRA JR.

MEREDITH, JAMES HOWARD (25 June 1933–),

civil rights activist, was born J. H. Meredith near Kosciusko, Mississippi, the son of Moses "Cap" Meredith, a farmer, and Roxie Smith Meredith, a school cafeteria worker. J.H. adopted the names James Howard when he entered the U.S. Air Force in 1951; until then he went by the initials given to him by a father who did not want neighboring whites to call his son by his first name only. Indeed, the stubborn—some might say, reckless—courage that James Meredith displayed in integrating the University of Mississippi owed much to the example of his father, who refused to display the deference expected of blacks in Jim Crow Mississippi. Cap Meredith viewed his eighty-five-acre homestead as a sovereign state and ruled it like a patriarch. He restricted his children's contacts with outsiders, black or white, and prohibited them from ever entering a white family's home by the back door or from working in service to

James Meredith became the first black person to enroll at the University of Mississippi in 1962, in spite of violent riots and opposition from Governor Ross Barnett. © Bettmann/CORBIS

whites. The Merediths also instilled in their children a passionate belief in the power of education; all ten completed high school, and seven attended college, a remarkable feat in the segregated, desperately poor Mississippi hill country of the 1940s.

On graduating from high school in 1951, Meredith joined the air force, serving first in Kansas and then Japan as a clerk-typist, rising in rank to staff sergeant. After his military service, he hoped to return to Mississippi to study law and to carry out what he described in his autobiography as a "divine responsibility" to end white supremacy in his home state (21). In the meantime, he took classes at the University of Kansas, Washburn University in Topeka, Kansas, the U.S. Armed Forces Institute, and the University of Maryland's Far Eastern Division in Japan. He also maintained a keen interest in the emerging civil rights movement, though he drew greater inspiration from DAISY BATES's efforts to integrate the schools in Little Rock, Arkansas, than from the nonviolent philosophy espoused by MARTIN LUTHER KING JR. during the 1955 bus boycott in Montgomery, Alabama.

Meredith later recalled that he found the concept of nonviolence "crazy," at least when applied to Mississippi (Doyle, 20). He believed that blacks could secure full citizenship rights only if they were supported by the full force of the U.S. military, as had been the case at Little Rock when President Dwight D. Eisenhower sent in the 101st Airborne Division to escort nine black students into Central High School. Meredith viewed his goal of ending white supremacy as a "war," but after receiving an honorable discharge from the air force in 1960, he kept his powder dry for a time, returning home to study history and political science at Jackson State College, a black institution.

The student sit-in movement that began in Greensboro, North Carolina, in early 1960 had not yet spread to Mississippi, but Meredith joined a secret society on the Jackson State campus that distributed antisegregation pamphlets and debated the possibility of active opposition to Jim Crow. In January 1961, however, having decided that it was time to move beyond debate, he applied for admission to the all-white University of Mississippi. MEDGAR

EVERS, the field secretary of the Mississippi NAACP, offered his assistance and persuaded the national NAACP Legal Defense Fund (LDF) to provide Meredith with the legal expertise needed to overcome the university's inevitable opposition. Meredith proved to be exactly the kind of determined plaintiff needed to win such a case, although his "Messiah complex" and self-righteousness often exasperated the LDF's CONSTANCE BAKER MOTLEY (Doyle, 32). Such tenacity paid off, however, in June 1962, when Judge John Minor Wisdom of the Fifth Circuit Court of Appeals condemned the University of Mississippi's "carefully calculated campaign of delay, harassment, and masterly inactivity" and ordered Meredith's immediate admission. Only a "man with a mission and a nervous stomach," Wisdom concluded, could have broken the color line at Ole Miss (Doyle, 33).

Yet Wisdom's ruling neither completed Meredith's mission nor settled the applicant's stomach, because Mississippi's governor, Ross Barnett, vowed to defy what he called the "unlawful dictates" of the federal government and even traveled to the Oxford campus to personally—and theatrically—block Meredith's admission. Barnett's flagrant defiance of federal authority climaxed in his inflammatory speech before an Ole Miss football game on 29 September 1962, one day before Meredith's scheduled arrival on campus. One spectator later recalled that the students "were being whipped into a fever-pitch of emotion by their own leaders . . . it was just like the Nazis had done" (Dittmer, 140).

What the crowd did not know was that Barnett, for all of his outward bravado, was secretly negotiating with Attorney General Robert Kennedy to allow Meredith's admission. The next day, one hour after marshals escorted Meredith into his dormitory, thousands of white students, townspeople, and segregationists from out of town began an armed riot that left two men dead, injured 168 marshals, and left the bucolic, magnolia-lined campus looking more like a war zone. Federal authorities later confiscated scores of guns and other weapons from fraternity houses such as Sigma Nu, although that fraternity's president, Trent Lott—who was later the majority reader of the U.S.

Senate—reportedly ordered his brothers away from the riot for their safety. Although President John F. Kennedy made a nationally televised appeal for calm, peace was restored only when he ordered in twenty-three thousand combat troops. One day later, under heavy military escort, James Meredith became the first African American to register at Ole Miss.

After graduating nine months later, Meredith studied at Ibadan University in Nigeria and began work toward a law degree at Columbia University in New York. In 1966, however, he set out on what appeared to be another iconoclastic mission: a "walk against fear" from Memphis, Tennessee, to Jackson, Mississippi, aimed at persuading blacks in his home state that, following the passage of the 1965 federal Voting Rights Act, it was now safe to register to vote. Meredith's march attracted the attention of only a few reporters until he was shot three times as he crossed the Mississippi border; fortunately, his assailant had been armed only with buckshot, but Meredith was hospitalized with some eighty pellets imbedded in his body.

Images of the shooting brought the leading lights of the civil rights movement to Mississippi to continue Meredith's march. They succeeded in adding thousands of new black voters to the electoral register. Meredith rejoined the final leg of the march from Tougaloo College to Jackson, where fifteen thousand people gathered to hear King declare Meredith's walk against fear "the greatest demonstration for freedom ever held in Mississippi" (Dittmer, 402). The march also exposed fissures in the civil rights movement as younger activists, such as the Student Nonviolent Coordinating Committee's STOKELY CARMICHAEL, responded to violent intimidation by state troopers by advocating a more aggressive philosophy of "black power," much to the consternation of King and others still committed to nonviolence.

After publishing a well-received autobiography, *Three Years in Mississippi* (1966), and receiving a law degree from Columbia in 1968, Meredith faded from public view. He taught briefly at the University of Cincinnati, in Ohio; ran several unsuccessful campaigns for Congress; and managed a nightclub

and a car rental business. Many who had lauded his courage at Ole Miss were incredulous, however, in 1989, when he took a position as a special assistant to Jesse Helms, the far-right-wing senator from North Carolina. They were horrified, too, two years later, when Meredith advocated support for David Duke, a former—though unrepentant—Louisiana Klansman running for the U.S. Senate. Following the death in 1979 of June Wiggins, his first wife and the mother of his three sons, Meredith married Judy Allsobrook, a journalist, and adopted her son and daughter.

Defeating white supremacy in Mississippi was no easy task. It would take men and women as obdurately defiant as James Meredith, Medgar Evers, and FANNIE LOU HAMER to overcome the will of a white majority determined to keep blacks as second-class citizens. Though many commentators viewed Meredith's rightward shift in the 1980s as strange—or even heretical—his seemingly erratic career makes more sense if he is viewed, rather, as an iconoclast. Neither consistency nor propriety mattered much to Meredith, but nobody could accuse him of lacking determination. As Medgar Evers once noted, James Meredith had "more guts than any man I know," but he also found him to be "the hardest headed son-of-a-gun I ever met" (Doyle, 32).

FURTHER READING

James Meredith's papers are housed in the Department of Archives and Special Collections, J. D. Williams Library, University of Mississippi, Oxford, Mississippi.

Meredith, James. *Three Years in Mississippi* (1966).

Dittmer, John. *Local People: The Struggle for Civil Rights in Mississippi* (1994).
Doyle, William. *An American Insurrection: The Battle of Oxford, Mississippi, 1962* (2001).
—STEVEN J. NIVEN

MERRICK, JOHN
(7 Sept. 1859–6 Aug. 1919), insurance company founder and entrepreneur, was born a slave in Sampson County, North

Carolina. Merrick never knew his father, but his mother, Martha, was a strong presence in his life. Little is known of Merrick's early years, except that, to help support his mother and brother, he began working in a brickyard in Chapel Hill when he was twelve. In 1877 he moved with his family to Raleigh, where he worked as a helper on the crew that constructed the original buildings on the campus of Shaw University. Merrick could have remained in the construction trade—he advanced to brick mason, a highly skilled and relatively well paid occupation—but he had far greater aspirations. Merrick's first goal was to open his own barber shop, one of the few business opportunities open to black southerners at that time. So he soon quit being a brick mason and took a menial job as a bootblack in a barber shop, in the process learning the barbering trade. After becoming a barber in Raleigh, Merrick began to attract as his customers several of the area's most prestigious men, among them tobacco magnates Washington Duke and Julian S. Carr, who convinced him and another barber in the shop, John Wright, to move to the nearby tobacco town of Durham and open a decent barber shop there.

Durham was a quintessential "New South" city. Created in the wake of burgeoning industrialization in the region, Durham was a frontier of sorts, undeveloped and open, one of the few places in the South where African Americans had a chance of achieving success on their own terms. Merrick and Wright opened a shop in Durham in 1880 and ran it together until 1892, when Wright sold out to Merrick. Soon after arriving, Merrick began to branch out, purchasing in 1881 the first of many lots in Hayti, the developing African American section of town, where he himself lived. Merrick constructed small rental houses on these lots, eventually becoming one of Hayti's largest landholders. In the late 1890s he expanded his barbering business—at one time owning as many as nine shops—and also developed a broadly advertised cure for dandruff.

Merrick's most significant involvement during his early years in Durham was his purchase, along with several others, of the Royal Knights of King David, a black fraternal order, in 1883. An important feature of the Royal Knights, as with other fraternal orders of the era, was the provision of insurance plans to its members. Merrick came to realize, however, that the meager death benefits offered by the Royal Knights were not enough to provide adequate coverage for African Americans. As a result, in conjunction with several other prominent blacks in Durham and Raleigh, Merrick founded the North Carolina Mutual and Provident Insurance Company in Durham in 1898. The firm began operations in April 1899 but almost failed after six months, primarily from lack of adequate attention by the founders. At that point Merrick and Aaron McDuffie Moore, Durham's first black physician, bought out the other investors and reorganized the firm as the North Carolina Mutual Insurance Company. They also hired Charles Clinton Spaulding, a relative of Moore's, to take over full-time management of the concern. Although Merrick was not the firm's operating manager, he was the primary figurehead during its first two decades. Initially, North Carolina Mutual only underwrote industrial insurance, but the firm soon expanded into industrial straight life and, later, into other policies. Income, which was just $840 in the company's first year, had surged to about $1.7 million by 1919, the year of Merrick's death.

North Carolina Mutual was only one of Merrick's many business enterprises in Durham. He was vice president of the Mechanics and Farmers Bank, organized in 1907. A vitally important element in the development of local capitalist ventures by African Americans, Mechanics and Farmers Bank helped Durham become what sociologist E. FRANKLIN FRAZIER called the "capital of the black middle class." By the early 1920s, when the bank had more than $600,000 in deposits and assets of $800,000, it had become a crucial source of capital for blacks who wanted to purchase homes and start small businesses. In 1910, when BOOKER T. WASHINGTON visited Durham, he described it as the most progressive city in the South and praised Merrick for his incomparable leadership in the black business community.

Merrick's real estate purchases led him to join with Moore and Spaulding

in organizing the Merrick-Moore-Spaulding Land Company to own and manage properties owned by Merrick and by North Carolina Mutual. In 1906 North Carolina Mutual established its own newspaper, the *Durham Negro Observer*. Its more successful successor, the *North Carolina Mutual*, was for decades the city's only African American newspaper. In 1908 Merrick and several others started Bull City Drug Company to operate drugstores in Hayti. One of Merrick's most important, though short-lived, ventures was the Durham Textile Mill, established in 1914 to manufacture socks. The mill was historically significant because it attempted to show, contrary to white southern myth, that African Americans could profitably be employed as textile workers.

At Merrick's death, from cancer, he was survived by his wife, Martha Hunter, and four of their five children. His son Edward later served for many years as treasurer of North Carolina Mutual, which eventually became the largest black business enterprise in America (until after World War II) and which still operates in virtually every state. It was John Merrick's organizational ability, his contacts with the white community, and his status in the broader African American community that did much to make the venture the success it became. His influence with wealthy whites was well known. It was Merrick who persuaded the Duke family to provide funds for the establishment of private Lincoln Hospital in 1901. Indeed, Merrick's greatest talent was perhaps his ability to push for greater economic and social opportunities for blacks while adapting those efforts to the realities of the time. In seeking white investment for various black business concerns, he never put the independence of those ventures in jeopardy.

FURTHER READING

Andrews, Robert McCants. *John Merrick: A Biographical Sketch* (1920).
Kennedy, William J. *The North Carolina Mutual Story* (1970).
Weare, Walter B. *Black Business in the New South: A Social History of the North Carolina Mutual Insurance Company* (1973).
—JOHN N. INGHAM

MFUME, KWEISI

(24 Oct. 1948–) television and radio host, U.S. congressman, and president and chief executive officer of the NAACP, was born Frizzell Gray, the first of four children of Mary Elizabeth Willis in Turners Station, Maryland. His mother worked at several occupations, including as an elevator operator and as a domestic, while Clifton Gray, his stepfather, was employed as a truck driver. Frizzell was raised believing that he shared the father of his three sisters; only later did he learn that he was not Gray's biological son. Frizzell spent his early childhood in Turners Station, a small rural black community thirteen miles south of Baltimore City, wedged between predominately white Dundalk and Sparrows Point, home to Bethlehem Steel, the largest employer in the area. Founded in the late 1880s by an African American doctor, Turners Station was isolated on the western shore of the Chesapeake Bay. In the early 1940s the town had one doctor and one elementary school; older students had to commute to continue their education.

While Gray's youth was filled with typical rural pursuits, such as baseball, fishing, and crabbing, he also had to contend with an abusive stepfather and the limitations of segregation. As it did for many young African Americans of his generation, the civil rights movement politicized him, fostering the sense that he was a representative of his

Kweisi Mfume addresses the Democratic National Convention, 2000.
© Reuters/CORBIS

race and that his victories, whether on the baseball field or in the classroom, reflected back on his community. A distant descendant of Maryland slaves, Gray was aware of not only his family's experiences but also the history of the larger African American community. The contributions of leaders such as WILLIAM MONROE TROTTER and W. E. B. DU BOIS were well known in the Gray household and provided a foundation for his sense of history, racial consciousness, and community responsibility.

Gray's parents separated in late 1959, and by March 1960 his mother had moved the children to Baltimore's West Side, an urban center rich in politics and culture. Nationally recognized African American leaders, such as the civil rights attorney THURGOOD MARSHALL, and political families like the Mitchells of the NAACP and the Murphys of the Baltimore *Afro American*, had started their careers there. West Baltimore was also made famous by Pennsylvania Avenue, home of the Royal Theater and the New Albert Hall, which featured the best-known African American entertainers, including ELLA FITZGERALD, DUKE ELLINGTON, and BILLIE HOLIDAY, who spent her formative years in Baltimore.

Frizzell's adolescent experiences were shaped by the two worlds of west Baltimore. He attended school, sold copies of the Baltimore *Afro American* newspaper, owned by the Murphy family and led by Carl, a longtime civil rights activist, who served as president and editor. Gray also played the French horn in the Falcon Drum and Bugle Corps. At the same time the world of the streets drew him away from respectable pursuits and introduced him to a *demimonde* of prostitution, gambling, and crime. By his own accounts he had thirteen brushes with the law but most were not serious enough to land him in jail.

Gray's childhood ended abruptly with the death of his mother in April 1964. He discovered then that his biological father was Rufus "Rip" Tate, and not Clifton Gray, as he had always believed. Gray promised his mother on her deathbed that he would care for his younger sisters. In 1965, he left school, armed with only a tenth grade education, working three poorly paying jobs, eventually moving into the more lucrative world of numbers running. It was on the streets in 1968

that he had his first brush with local politics, volunteering in the campaign of Parren Mitchell during his first run for Congress. Mitchell, the brother of Clarence Mitchell Jr., the head of the Washington, D.C., branch of the NAACP, would be one of the founding members of the Congressional Black Caucus, pioneering the road that Gray would follow.

In the early 1970s Gray began to abandon the world of the streets. He completed his GED, and met Linda Shields, whom he married in 1972. He enrolled in the Community College of Baltimore, where he quickly developed into a skillful activist and organizer in the emerging black student movement. Gray cofounded the Black Student Union, served as the editor of the school newspaper, and led the protest and sit-in movement for a black studies program. He also led a student boycott of Gulf Oil because of its investments in South Africa. Gray merged his political activism with a budding career in radio broadcasting. For a short time he worked as an on-air host at WEBB, a radio station owned by the legendary entertainer JAMES BROWN. Gray's Sunday show featured music inspired by the civil rights and Black Power movements, speeches by MALCOLM X, and an open dialogue with his African American audience on racial justice. In many ways, Gray's programming choices were emblematic of the new generation of civil rights activists' merging of political and cultural traditions to promote a new and more radical political action. Gray changed his name to Kweisi Mfume, which he interprets as "conquering son of kings," a reflection of his new consciousness. His career as a student activist laid the foundation for his continuing crusade for racial justice, both nationally and internationally.

After graduating from the Community College of Baltimore, Mfume continued his education and political development at Morgan State University, a historically black institution, combining his interest in communications and politics. He was one of the founding members of Morgan's radio station, WEAA, and, after graduating magna cum laude from the university in 1976, he worked as its program director, using his own show as a format to discuss issues affecting the African American

community. His marriage ended in part because of his political activities while in college, but Mfume's passion for activism was undiminished.

In 1979 Mfume ran as a Democrat for a seat on the Baltimore city council, challenging politicians who ignored problems in the African American community and the ironfisted governing style of Mayor William Donald Schaffer. In his grassroots campaign, he drew support from childhood and college friends and sought advice from well-known black business people and politicians, including Verda F. Welcome, the first African American woman elected to the state legislature in Maryland's history. Mfume displayed his trademark tenacity during this hard-fought campaign. Initially declared the loser by fewer than fifty votes, Mfume demanded a recount and was declared the winner by three votes. He served for seven years on the council, while continuing to host a talk show on WEAA. In 1984 he completed an MA degree in Liberal Arts at Johns Hopkins University, with a concentration in international studies. As a member of the city council, Mfume promoted diversity in municipal agencies, increased opportunities for minority-owned businesses, fostered improvements in public safety, and cosponsored legislation that led to the divestment of city investments in South Africa.

Mfume's desire to effect change on both national and international levels inspired him to run for U.S. Congress in 1986, when Parren Mitchell announced his retirement. Although he faced vigorous opposition, Mfume was elected to the 100th Congress by an overwhelming majority. Mfume joined a new generation of African American political officials who came of age during the civil rights movement, including Floyd Flake of New York, JOHN LEWIS of Georgia, and Albert Michael (Mike) Espy of Mississippi, each in their first term in the House of Representatives.

Mfume served Maryland's Seventh Congressional District for ten years. He was instrumental in passing legislation for civil rights, fair housing, and the Americans with Disabilities Act. He continued working in broadcasting, hosting an award-winning Baltimore television talk show, *The Bottom Line*, for seven years. In 1993 he was elected chairman of the twenty-two-year-old Congressional Black Caucus (CBC), where he called attention to discrimination in corporate America, established a dialogue with the NAACP and the Urban League, and created a strong working relationship between the CBC and the Congressional Hispanic Caucus. In addition, Mfume was seated on the Banking and Financial Services, Ethics, and Small Business committees. During his third term he served on the Joint Economic Committee of the House and Senate, which he later chaired.

As part of a U.S. delegation, Mfume traveled to South Africa in 1994 to witness Nelson Mandela's inauguration. His numerous appearances on political programs hosted by the major television networks increased his national prominence. Respected as a politician who excelled at building interracial and intraracial bridges, and for representing all Americans, he also challenged the nation's leaders when he believed that they had failed the country. Mfume criticized President Ronald Reagan's unwillingness to impose sanctions on apartheid South Africa, opposed President George H. W. Bush's 1991 war in Kuwait and Iraq, and chided President Bill Clinton for his tardiness in addressing human rights violations in Haiti in the 1990s.

In February 1996 Mfume formally announced that he would leave Congress to serve as the president and CEO of the NAACP. The nation's oldest civil rights organization was at that time still reeling from financial problems, including a $3.2 million debt, and the stormy two-year tenure of Benjamin Chavis as president. Mfume's skills as a legislator, his status as an elected official, and his ability to cross both race and class lines propelled the civil rights organization in a new direction. Along with civil rights, his vision for a revitalized NAACP addressed issues such as health care, economic and educational growth, political mobilization, and youth programs. As the head of the NAACP, Mfume launched a variety of campaigns, from increasing the numbers of people of color on television to increasing the participation of African Americans in local and national elections.

FURTHER READING

Mfume, Kweisi. *No Free Ride: From the Mean Streets to the Mainstream* (1996).

Holmes, Steven. "The N.A.A.C.P.'s New Hope: Kweisi Mfume," *New York Times*, 11 Dec. 1995: B8.

McConnell, Roland C., ed. *Three Hundred and Fifty Years: A Chronology of the Afro-American in Maryland 1634–1984* (1985).

Snipe, Tracy D. "The Role of African American Males in Politics and Government." *Annals of the American Academy of Political and Social Science* (2000) 569: 10–28.

Swain, Carol. *Black Fences, Black Interests: The Representation of African Americans in Congress* (1995).

—PRUDENCE D. CUMBERBATCH

MICHAUX, LIGHTFOOT SOLOMON

(7 Nov. 1884–20 Oct. 1968), radio evangelist, was born in Newport News, Virginia, the son of John Michaux, a fish peddler and grocer, and May Blanche. Lightfoot, whose ancestry was African, Indian, and French Jewish, spent his formative years in Newport News among Jewish and white gentile merchants on Jefferson Avenue, the main commercial street where the Michauxs lived in quarters above the family's store. He attended the Twenty-second Street School, quitting after the fourth grade to become a seafood peddler. Impressed with the town's commercial atmosphere, he aspired to be a successful businessman. While engaged in one business venture, he met Mary Eliza Pauline, a mulatto orphan. They married in 1906; the couple had no children of their own but helped raise Michaux's two young sisters.

During World War I, Michaux obtained government contracts to furnish food to defense establishments. With the profits from his enterprises he moved his business to Hopewell, Virginia, in 1917. Finding no churches in that wartime boom town, he and his wife joined with a Filipino evangelist to found a church there. Michaux's wife subsequently convinced him to accept the call to preach, and in 1918 he was licensed and ordained in the Church of Christ (Holiness) U.S.A. He returned to Newport News in 1919, went into business with his father, and launched a tent revival. The first 150 of Michaux's converts formed a congregation within the Church of Christ denomination. In 1921 the Michaux congregation seceded from the Church of Christ to establish an independent church, calling it the Church of God. This church, along with its other related operations, was incorporated under an umbrella grouping known as the Gospel Spreading Tabernacle Association. In 1922 Michaux and several of his members were arrested for singing on the streets of Newport News during early morning hours while inviting townsfolk to join the church. When Michaux was fined, he unsuccessfully appealed to the Virginia Supreme Court, contending that

Radio evangelist Elder Lightfoot Michaux had the longest continuous broadcast in radio annals, from 1929 to 1968. Corbis

his actions were based on a directive from God. In 1924 he began to establish branch churches in cities along the East Coast as he followed members who had migrated north to find jobs during the postwar recession.

Michaux began his radio ministry in 1929 at station WJSV in Washington, D.C., and became famous as a radio evangelist. The broadcast moved to the Columbia Broadcasting System (CBS) in 1932, the eve of radio's golden era. As a result of the radio program's syncopated signature song, "Happy Am I," Michaux became known from coast to coast and overseas as the "'Happy Am I' Preacher." His aphorisms and fundamentalist-like sermons of hope and good neighborliness caught the attention of millions. His wife, an exhorter and the premiere broadcast soloist, was a regular on the radio program. Michaux's radio program was so popular that American and foreign dignitaries flocked to his live, theatrically staged radio broadcasts. The British Broadcasting Corporation contracted with him for two broadcasts in the British Empire, in 1936 and 1938. Booking agents and moviemakers offered him contracts. In 1942 he collaborated with Jack Goldberg to make one commercial film, *We've Come a Long, Long Way*.

During the Great Depression, Michaux used his radio pulpit to offer free housing and employment services to the black and white indigent, and he invited the hungry to sell copies of the church's *Happy News* paper in exchange for meals in the Happy News Cafe. After President Herbert Hoover evicted the Bonus Army (fifteen thousand unemployed World War I veterans and their families who converged on the capital in 1932 to demand immediate payment of bonuses that were not due until 1945) for which Michaux had been holding worship services, Michaux used his radio pulpit to campaign for Franklin Delano Roosevelt in 1932, 1936, and 1940. For this reason, observers credit Michaux with influencing the first African Americans to leave the Republican Party and enter the Democratic fold in 1932. Political observers were baffled therefore when, in 1952, Michaux campaigned as vigorously for Republican candidate Dwight Eisenhower as he had for Roosevelt and Harry Truman.

Crowds attended Michaux's annual baptisms, which he moved from the Potomac River bank in 1938 and held in Griffith Stadium until 1961. These patriotically festooned stadium services were full of pageantry, fireworks, and enthralling precision drills and choral singing from the 156-voice Cross Choir. Vocal renditions were supported by the syncopated instrumentation of the church band, while hundreds were baptized annually in a canvas-covered tank at center field. About Michaux and his baptismal services, Bill Sunday quipped that "any man who had to hire a national baseball park, seating 35,000 to hold ... meetings is the man to preach the gospel."

One reporter observed that Michaux should "not be passed off as just another gospel spreader ... but should be regarded as a shrewd businessman." He had made lucrative deals in real estate, such as the 1934 purchase of 1,800 acres of land along the beachfront in Jamestown, Virginia, where he intended to develop a National Memorial to the Progress of the Colored Race of America. His plans for selling investment shares fell through when lawsuits that alleged mismanagement of monies were filed against him. Around 1940 he purchased the old Benning Race Track in Washington and received $3.5 million from the Reconstruction Finance Corporation to construct Mayfair Mansions, a 594-unit housing development, which was completed in 1946. Despite allegations on Capitol Hill in the 1950s of favoritism from federal lending agencies, in 1964 he acquired six million dollars in FHA loans to build Paradise Manor, a 617-apartment complex adjacent to Mayfair Mansions. These successes were due in part to his friendship with prominent Washingtonians, some of whom were honorary members of the "Radio Church."

While Michaux initially espoused race consciousness and proclaimed the brotherhood of all races, he became increasingly conservative in his later years. In the 1960s he criticized the civil rights and black nationalist movements and alleged that the activities of ELIJAH MUHAMMAD and MARTIN LUTHER KING JR. were contributing to racial polarization.

Because of his successful radio ministry in the nation's capital, Michaux had moved the church's headquarters there in 1929 and had renamed and reincorporated it several times. During the forty-nine years of his career he established seven churches and several branches and attracted a membership that numbered in the thousands. He amassed and bequeathed to the church an estate, consisting of temples, apartment dwellings, cafes, tracts of land, and private residences in several cities, that was estimated to be in excess of twenty million dollars in 1968. When Michaux died in Washington, D.C., his radio program was estimated to be the longest continuous broadcast in radio annals.

Continuing to operate under the name Church of God, the institution founded by Michaux had 3,000 members and eleven churches by the mid-1990s. Michaux's most significant contribution was in religious broadcasting, where he pioneered in the use of electronic and print media for worldwide evangelism.

FURTHER READING

The bulk of material on Michaux is located in the Church of God's headquarters in Washington, D.C. Additional correspondence is located in the Franklin D. Roosevelt, Harry Truman, and Dwight D. Eisenhower papers and in Department of Interior Correspondence in the National Archives. Sound recordings from Michaux's radio ministry are at the Library of Congress.

Lark, Pauline, ed. *Sparks from the Anvil of Elder Michaux* (1950).
Webb, Lillian Ashcraft. *About My Father's Business: The Life of Elder Michaux* (1981).

Obituaries: *New York Times* and *Washington Post*, 21 Oct. 1968.
—LILLIAN ASHCRAFT-EASON

 MICHEAUX, OSCAR (2 Jan. 1884–1 Apr. 1951), filmmaker, writer, and entrepreneur, was born on a farm near Metropolis, Illinois, the fifth of eleven children of former slaves, Calvin Swan Micheaux and Belle Willingham. After leaving home at age sixteen and working in several southern Illinois towns, he moved to Chicago and opened a shoe-shine stand in a white barber shop. Contacts he made there led to a job as a Pullman porter. Train porters were assigned to passengers for the length of their travel, and Oscar took full advantage of the opportunity to mingle with wealthy whites and watch while they conducted business.

Micheaux fell in love with the Northwest and Great Plains while working the Chicago-to-Portland run, and in 1905 he used his savings to purchase land in southern South Dakota, on the newly opened Rosebud Sioux Indian Reservation. By age twenty-five he had amassed five hundred acres and began publishing articles in the *Chicago Defender* with titles like "Colored Americans Too Slow To Take Advantage Of Great Land Opportunities Given Free By The Government," urging African Americans to follow in his footsteps and take up homesteading. Micheaux's homespun "Go west, young black man" philosophy combined elements of Frederick Jackson Turner's "frontier thesis," principles of American exceptionalism and individualism, and BOOKER T. WASHINGTON's belief in racial uplift through self-reliance, "brains, property, and character." His confidence in the curative power of the western frontier and the successful pioneer formed the foundation of Micheaux's future efforts and attitudes.

In 1910 Micheaux married Orlean McCracken, the daughter of a Chicago minister who became the model for the villainous clergyman later depicted in Micheaux's films. Unhappy with pioneer life, she left the marriage within a year. Micheaux's bad luck continued with foreclosures of his land in 1912, 1913, and 1914. Looking for a new source of income, he wrote *The Conquest: The Story of a Negro Pioneer*, a thinly-veiled autobiographical novel about the experiences of "Oscar Devereaux," a lone African American homesteader in South Dakota. Micheaux, who had begun marketing the book even before its completion in 1913, sold copies door to door throughout the Great Plains and South. Sales were good, and he formed his own company, the Western Book Supply Company, through which he published and distributed two more semiautobiographical novels: *The Forged Note: A Romance of the Darker Races* (1915) and *The Homesteader* (1917).

In 1918 the Lincoln Motion Pictures Company, which had been established three years earlier by the African American brothers Nobel and George Johnson, approached Micheaux about filming *The Homesteader*. After the brothers refused to let him direct the picture, Micheaux decided to make the film himself. He renamed his business the Micheaux Book and Film Company and raised fifteen thousand dollars by convincing small investors of the market potential for black films. *The Homesteader* (1919), an eight-reel silent film melodrama of love, murder, suicide, and passing, was the longest African American feature film produced by that date. Micheaux used photos of himself and ad copy that spoke directly to issues of race, "Every Race man and woman should cast aside their skepticism regarding the Negro's ability as a motion picture star, and go." His second film, *Within Our Gates* (1920), included a graphic scene of the lynching of an African American sharecropper, prompting consternation from both blacks and whites. He followed with *The Brute* (1920), starring the black boxer Sam Langford, and the controversial film *The Symbol of the Unconquered* (1920), featuring a hero who strikes oil in the West and fights the Ku Klux Klan.

Micheaux produced an average of two pictures a year throughout the 1920s, including *The Gunsaulus Mystery* (1921), a reworking of the events surrounding the 1913 lynching of the Jewish Atlantan Leo Frank; *The Virgin of the Seminole* (1922), whose young black protagonist becomes a Canadian Mountie and successful ranchero; and *Deceit* (1923), the story of a black filmmaker, "Alfred DuBois," who clashes with censors. Micheaux gave PAUL ROBESON his first screen role in *Body and Soul* (1925) and became the first black filmmaker to use African American source material with *The House Behind the Cedars* (1924), based on CHARLES W. CHESNUTT's 1900 novel of the same name. The filmmaker also adapted several plays by the African American sailor Henry Francis Downing as well as the 1922 novel *Birthright* by the white southerner T. S. Stribling.

With more than twenty films in distribution, Micheaux filed for bankruptcy in 1928. Undeterred, he reemerged a year later as Micheaux Pictures, this time with backing from whites. By 1931, when he released *The Exile*, the first all-sound film made by an African American filmmaker, most black moviemakers were closing up shop. The advent of sound and Hollywood's foray into black-cast films were severely challenging the commercial viability of race movies. Micheaux responded by recycling material and themes and by remaking a half dozen of his silent films into "talkies." With a nod to Hollywood, he produced the musicals *The Darktown Revue* (1931) and *Swing!* (1938), and he introduced musical sequences and nightclub settings into his melodramas, suspense films, and gangster movies.

Micheaux suspended film production during World War II and returned to writing. Of the four novels he published in quick succession, *The Wind from Nowhere* (1944), proved the most successful, and he used the proceeds to make America's last race film, *The Betrayal* (1948). Although it was promoted as the "Greatest Negro photoplay of all time," audiences' apathy and poor critical reception doomed the picture and, with it, the last vestiges of race films.

While only thirteen of his films survive, Micheaux produced at least thirty-eight and perhaps as many as fifty films, making him the most prolific African American filmmaker. Working on the margins of a new medium, he told stories from a black perspective, populated by black characters. Micheaux, who entered the film business with little education and no contacts, succeeded by sheer entrepreneurial skill, creative vision, and salesmanship. He parlayed door-to-door sales into a grassroots promotional machine that both maximized the opportunities offered by established urban movie theaters catering to black audiences and introduced distribution and exhibition routes into underserved areas. Sweeping into town in a chauffeur-driven car, wearing a long fur coat and a wide-brimmed hat, Micheaux created a mystique around himself and a hunger for his films. He made extensive use of the African American press and built a following for his stars, in part through a star system modeled after white Hollywood, promoting Lorenzo Tucker as the "black Valentino," Slick Chester as the "colored Cagney," and Bee Freeman as the "sepia Mae West."

Courting controversy, Micheaux introduced into his films such explosive subjects as rape, church corruption, racial violence, and miscegenation. Protests were customary, and censor boards routinely rejected or severely edited the films. In a typical ruling, Virginia's censor board rejected *Son of Satan* (1924), claiming, "It touches unpleasantly on miscegenation. Furthermore, many of its scenes and sub-titles will prove irritating if not hurtful alike to quadroons, octoroons, half-breeds and those of pure African descent.... there is the intermingling of the two races which would prove offensive to Southern ideas... [and the riot scenes] smack far too much of realism and race hatred" (Bowser, *Oscar Micheaux and His Circle*, 252). Micheaux turned protestations into promotion, advertising "banned" films and "uncensored" versions and aggressively selling his films' racial themes, which he often tied to current events of significance to African Americans. Advertisements for *The Homesteader* called the film "a powerful drama... into which has been deftly woven the most subtle of all America's problems—THE RACE QUESTION," while ads for *The Dungeon* (1922) linked the film to the federal antilynching bill, known as the Dyer Bill. Several years later, promotion for *The House Behind the Cedars* remarked on its parallel to the 1925 Leonard "Kip" Rhinelander case, in which a man sued for annulment after discovering that his wife was black.

Limited resources necessarily compromised quality, and the production values of Micheaux's films were poor. Crews were often hired by the day, with multiple camera operators working on the same film. Mixing professionals with amateurs was common. Action was generally filmed in one take, without benefit of rehearsal, and limited to one set, filmed on borrowed locations. To meet hurried production schedules, Micheaux edited his films based on the footage available, sometimes reediting, retitling, and rereleasing existing films. As Thomas Cripps explains, "It was

as though [Paul Laurence] Dunbar or Langston Hughes published their first drafts without benefit of editing, their flair and genius muffled in casual first strikes" (183). A few contemporary scholars have disagreed, arguing instead that Micheaux was a maverick aesthetic stylist who intentionally eschewed what we now call Classic Hollywood Style.

Criticisms of Micheaux and his films from African Americans in general and the black press in particular began in the 1920s and became increasingly common by the 1930s. These voices decried what they perceived as Micheaux's preference for light-skinned actors, his "negative" depictions of African Americans, and the poor quality of his productions. Threats of protest and boycott often hung over the release of his films. A black critic voiced the concern of many when he took the filmmaker to task for his "intraracial color fetishism" where "all the noble characters are high yellow; all the ignoble ones are black" (*New York Amsterdam News*, 1930). Occasionally, censure came from outside the black community. Upon the release of *God's Stepchildren* (1938), the Young Communist League charged that the film "slandered Negroes, holding them up to ridicule" and set "light-skinned Negroes against their darker brothers" (Cripps, 342).

Micheaux died in 1951 in Charlotte, North Carolina, while on a promotional tour. He was survived by his wife of twenty-five years, Alice B. Russell, an actress who had appeared in and produced a number of his films. Despite, and perhaps owing to, the fact that audiences continue to argue about Micheaux's depictions of African Americans and African American life, his work remains powerfully relevant. An alternative to popular media images of African Americans, Micheaux's films offered unusually complex, sophisticated, and varied representations.

FURTHER READING

Bowser, Pearl, Jane Gaines, and Charles Musser, eds. *Oscar Micheaux and His Circle: African American Filmmaking and Race Cinema of the Silent Era* (2001).

Bowser, Pearl, and Louis Spence. *Writing Himself into History: Oscar Micheaux, His Silent Films, and His Audiences* (2000).

Cripps, Thomas. *Slow Fade to Black: The Negro in American Film, 1900–1942* (1977, 1993).

—Lisa E. Rivo

 MILLER, CHERYL
(3 Jan. 1964–), basketball player, coach, and sportscaster, was born Cheryl Deanne Miller in Riverside, California, the third of five children of Saul Miller, a computer technician and musician, and Carrie Miller (maiden name Turner), a registered nurse. At age seven Cheryl began to learn the game of basketball by competing against her two older brothers on the court her father had built in the family's backyard. She continued to hone her basketball skills playing one on one with her younger brother Reggie, who would go on to become a college and NBA star. Cheryl graduated from Riverside Polytechnic High School in 1982 and went on to receive a BA in Communications from the University of Southern California (USC) in 1986.

Cheryl's intense preparation as a youngster served her well as she earned varsity letters in each of her four years of competition while in high school. Her athletic achievements as a high school basketball player reflect individual greatness and the impact a single player can have on a program. At the conclusion of her high school career, Cheryl averaged nearly 33 points and 15 rebounds per game, and in her senior season she scored an astounding 105 points in a single contest. An unselfish player, she also contributed 368 assists, while leading Riverside High School to a number of team honors, including the California Interscholastic Federation statewide championship in 1982. Riverside's overall record during Miller's tenure was a remarkable 132–4. She was named a *Parade* All-American for four straight years, becoming the first male or female athlete to earn that honor. In addition, Miller was named *Street and Smith's* High School Player of the Year in 1981 and 1982.

Miller's accolades and the unprecedented public response to her high school career reflected the massive rise in the popularity of girls' and women's basketball in the late 1970s and the early 1980s. Between 1972 and 1981 the number of girls participating in high school basketball increased from 400,000 to 4.5 million. This increase can be attributed, at least in part, to congressional passage of Title IX of

Cheryl Miller and her teammates celebrate their gold medals at the 1984 Olympics in Los Angeles. © Wally McNamee/CORBIS

the Omnibus Education Act of 1972 on 23 June 1972. As an extension of the Civil Rights Act of 1964, Title IX prohibited sex discrimination in any educational program receiving federal financial assistance. As a result, resources poured into girls' and women's sports, including basketball, in an effort to create more equitable athletic opportunities based upon sex. Miller's athletic career, including her move to the college ranks, was shaped by these revolutionary changes taking place in the landscape of women's sports. Hoping to consolidate and advance those changes, Miller joined with the volleyball legend FLO HYMAN on Capitol Hill in 1985 to testify in support of strengthening Title IX.

Miller's basketball talents, along with her strong academic skills, attracted the attention of colleges as early as her junior high school days, though she ultimately chose the nearby USC from the more than 250 college basketball programs that tried to recruit her. Such frenzied interest in one of the nation's best female basketball prospects reflected the growth of the women's college game and would not have been a likely scenario just a decade earlier. In the fall of 1982 Miller, at six feet, three inches tall, joined a host of other very talented USC players, including Paula and Pam McGee, Paula Longo, and Cynthia Cooper, under the direction of Coach Linda Sharp. Expectations were high, and the USC squad did not disappoint themselves or their fans. During Miller's first year USC finished with thirty-one of thirty-three wins for the season and their first national championship. By the end of her

sophomore year the team had earned its second national title. Miller's individual athletic accomplishments while at USC are impressive. She finished her college career averaging over 23 points per game, an average of 12 rebounds per contest, and 700 steals in the 128 games in which she was a participant. During the four years Miller played for USC the team won 112 games against only 20 losses.

Miller won many national collegiate honors, including in 1985 and 1986 the Broderick Cup, given to the nation's best female player. *Sports Illustrated* named Miller the best basketball player, male or female, in the nation in 1986. Miller was also a four-time All-American and a three-time Naismith Player of the Year, and in 1986 she won the prestigious Wade Trophy, given by the National Association for Girls and Women in Sports for excellence in academics and community service as well as basketball prowess. In March 1986 USC retired her jersey number "31," the first time the institution had bestowed such an honor on an athlete. In 1995 Miller was inducted into the Naismith Memorial Basketball Hall of Fame, and in 1999 she was an inductee of the inaugural class of the Women's Basketball Hall of Fame in Knoxville, Tennessee.

Had Miller graduated from college in the mid-1990s instead of the mid-1980s, professional basketball opportunities in the United States would have awaited her, with the emergence of the American Basketball League and the Women's National Basketball League. However, the Women's Professional Basketball League collapsed in the early 1980s after only three years in existence, forcing the best American women's basketball players to travel to Europe if they desired to play professionally after college. For Miller this was not an option, as she wanted to remain close to her family in Southern California.

Miller's collegiate basketball successes did provide her with the chance to represent the United States in international competition. She played on the U.S. team in the Pan American Games in 1983 and 1986, winning the gold medal in 1983. Miller also helped the United States win the gold medals at the Los Angeles Olympics and at the 1986 Goodwill Games in Moscow, after which she said, "This is even better than the Olympics in '84.... This is beating the Russians in Russia, I've waited a long time for this." Whether playing before a national or an international audience, Miller's play embodied intense emotion and a flamboyant style, drawing critics and fans alike. While even her critics were quick to underscore Miller's great athleticism, some, including fellow basketball star Ann Meyers, believed Miller's showboating on the court detracted from her overall potential contributions to the game. Unfortunately, Miller suffered knee injuries in 1987 and 1988 that brought her competitive playing days to an end.

Capitalizing on the academic skills learned at USC, Miller became a television sportscaster, working first for ABC's *Wide World of Sports* before becoming a sideline reporter and studio analyst for TNT and TBS. In 1996 she became the first female analyst for a nationally televised basketball game. In addition to her broadcasting career, Miller has also tried her hand as a coach. In 1993 she accepted the head women's basketball coaching position at her alma mater, USC. However, her hiring was not without controversy. Miller replaced Marianne Stanley, who was not retained by USC after she demanded a salary commensurate with that of the Trojans' men's coach, George Raveling. Some USC players, including the star, Lisa Leslie, voiced their support of Stanley and opposed her dismissal. Furthermore, several college coaches turned down employment offers from USC to express their solidarity with Stanley. Despite that uneasy baptism as coach of the Women of Troy, Miller persevered, guiding her team to the NCAA women's basketball play-offs in 1993–1994 and 1994–1995 seasons. In the fall of 1995 she resigned her position at USC to move back into broadcasting, leaving the team with an impressive record of forty-four wins and fourteen losses.

The formation of the Women's National Basketball Association in 1997 enabled Miller to return to the court as head coach of the Phoenix Mercury. In four seasons with Phoenix, Miller directed her team to seventy wins against fifty-two losses, including play-off appearances in three of those years. As a player in the 1980s and a coach in the 1990s Cheryl Miller's emotion, skill, and passion has helped to transform competitive women's basketball from a slower, more deliberate passing game to a fast-paced, high-energy game enjoyed by players and spectators alike.

More than simply a role model for elite female basketball players, Cheryl Miller also has given young girls across the country a strong, confident image to emulate. Moreover, her dedication to the sport and her superior athleticism brought the game to a national stage in the 1980s. Miller's efforts secured an even brighter future for young girls whose desire is to play basketball, from backyard pickup games to professional contests, in the United States.

FURTHER READING

Freeman, Patricia. "The Magic of Cheryl Miller." *Women's Sports and Fitness* (February 1986).

Kirkpatrick, Curry. "Lights! Camera! Cheryl!" *Sports Illustrated* (20 Nov. 1985).

—RITA LIBERTI

MILLER, KELLY

(18 July 1863–29 Dec. 1939), educator and essayist, was born in Winnsboro, South Carolina, the son of Kelly Miller, a free black who served in the Confederate army, and Elizabeth Roberts, a slave. The sixth of ten children, Miller received his early education in one of the local primary schools established during Reconstruction and later attended the Fairfield Institute in Winnsboro from 1878 to 1880. Awarded a scholarship to Howard University, he completed the Preparatory Department's three-year curriculum in Latin, Greek, and mathematics in two years (1880–1882), then attended the College Department at Howard University from 1882 to 1886.

After his graduation from Howard, Miller studied advanced mathematics (1886–1887) with Captain Edgar Frisby, an English mathematician at the U.S. Naval Observatory. Frisby's chief at the observatory, Simon Newcomb, who was also a professor of mathematics at Johns Hopkins University, recommended Miller for admission. The first black student admitted to Johns Hopkins, Miller studied mathematics, physics, and astronomy there from 1887 to 1889 but did not graduate because he ran out of funds. After teaching mathematics briefly at the M Street High School in Washington, D.C. (1889–1890), he was appointed to the faculty of Howard University in 1890. Five years later Miller added sociology to Howard's curriculum because he thought that the new discipline was important for developing objective analyses of the racial system in the United States. From 1895 to 1907 Miller was professor of mathematics and sociology, but he taught sociology exclusively after that, serving from 1915 to 1925 as head of the new sociology department. In 1894 Miller had married Annie May Butler, a teacher at the Baltimore Normal School; the couple had five children.

Noted for his brilliant mind, Miller rapidly became a major figure in the life of Howard University. In 1907 he was appointed dean of the College of Arts and Sciences. During his twelve-year deanship, the college grew dramatically, as the old classical curriculum was modernized and new courses in the natural sciences and the social sciences were added. Miller's recruiting tours through the South and Mid-Atlantic states were so successful that the enrollment increased from seventy-five undergraduates in 1907 to 243 undergraduates in 1911.

Although Miller was a leader at Howard for most of his tenure there, his national importance derived from his intellectual leadership during the conflict between the "accommodationism" of BOOKER T. WASHINGTON and the "radicalism" of the nascent civil rights movement led by W. E. B. DU BOIS. Critical of Washington's famous Cotton States Exposition Address (1895) in 1896, Miller later praised Washington's emphasis on self-help and initiative. Miller remained an opponent of the exaggerated claims made on behalf of industrial education and became one of the most effective advocates of higher education for black Americans when it was attacked as inappropriate for a people whose social role was increasingly limited by statute and custom to agriculture, some skilled trades, unskilled labor, and domestic service.

In the *Educational Review, Dial, Education*, the *Journal of Social Science*, and other leading journals, Miller argued that blacks required wise leadership in the difficult political and social circumstances following the defeat of Reconstruction, and only higher education could provide such leaders. Moreover, the race required physicians, lawyers, clergymen, teachers, and other professionals whose existence was dependent on higher education. Excluded from most white colleges, black Americans would have to secure higher education in their own institutions, Miller argued, and some of them, like Howard, Fisk, and Atlanta universities, would emphasize liberal education and the professions rather than the trades and manual arts (industrial education) stressed at Hampton and Tuskegee institutes. In the debate between the advocates of collegiate and industrial education, Miller maintained that the whole matter was one of "ratio and proportion" not "fundamental controversy." Recognized as one of the most influential black educators in the nation because of his extensive writing and his leadership at Howard, Miller was sought out by both camps in the controversy but was trusted by neither because of his refusal to dogmatically support either of the rival systems.

Miller's reputation as a "philosopher of the race question" was based on his brilliant articles, published anonymously at first, on "radicals" and "conservatives" in the Boston Transcript (18 and 19 Sept. 1903). With some alterations, these articles later became the lead essay in his book Race Adjustment (1908). Miller's essays insisted on the right of black Americans to protest against the injustices that had multiplied with the rise of the white supremacy movement in the South, as the Du Bois "radicals" did, but he also advocated racial solidarity, thrift, and institution-building as emphasized by the followers of Washington. Characteristically, Miller had two reputations as a public policy analyst, first as a compromiser between black radicals and conservatives, and second as a race spokesman during the prolonged crisis of disenfranchisement and the denial of civil rights by white supremacists and their elected representatives in Congress. The Disgrace of Democracy: An Open Letter to President Woodrow Wilson, a pamphlet published in August 1917, was Miller's most popular effort. Responding to recent race riots in Memphis

and East St. Louis, Miller argued that a "democracy of race or class is no democracy at all." Writing to Wilson, he said, "It is but hollow mockery of the Negro when he is beaten and bruised in all parts of the nation and flees to the national government for asylum, to be denied relief on the basis of doubtful jurisdiction. The black man asks for protection and is given a theory of government." More than 250,000 copies of the pamphlet were sold, and military authorities banned it at army posts.

Although Miller was best known as a controversialist, he also made important but frequently overlooked contributions to the discipline of sociology. His earliest contribution was his analysis of Frederick L. Hoffman's Race Traits and Tendencies of the American Negro, published by the American Economic Association in 1896. Hoffman attempted to demonstrate that the social disorganization of black Americans (weak community institutions and family structure) was caused by an alleged genetic inferiority and that their correspondingly high mortality rate would result in their disappearance as an element of the American population. Miller's refutation of Hoffman's claims, A Review of Hoffman's "Race Traits and Tendencies of the American Negro," published by the American Negro Academy in 1897, was based on a technical analysis of census data.

Perhaps Miller's most lasting contribution to scholarship was his pioneering advocacy of the systematic study of black people. In 1901 he proposed to the Howard board of trustees that the university financially support the publications of the American Negro Academy, whose goals were to promote literature, science, art, higher education, and scholarly works by blacks, and to defend them against "vicious assaults." Although the board declined, it permitted the academy to meet on the campus. Convinced that Howard should use its prestige and location in Washington to become a national center for black studies, Miller planned a "Negro-Americana Museum and Library." In 1914 he persuaded Jesse E. Moorland, a Howard alumnus and Young Men's Christian Association official, to donate to Howard his large private library on blacks in Africa and in

the United States as the foundation for the proposed center. This became the Moorland Foundation (reorganized in 1973 as the Moorland-Spingarn Research Center), a research library, archives, and museum that has been vital to the emergence of sound scholarship in this field.

The years after World War I were difficult ones for Miller. J. Stanley Durkee, the last of Howard's white presidents, was appointed in 1918 and set out to curtail the baronial power of the deans by building a new central administration. Miller, a conspicuously powerful dean, was demoted in 1919 to dean of a new junior college, which was later abolished in 1925. A leader in the movement to have a black president of Howard, Miller was a perennial favorite of the alumni but was never selected. Although Miller's influence at Howard declined significantly by the late 1920s through his retirement in 1934, his stature as a commentator on race relations and politics remained high. He had become alarmed by the vast social changes stimulated by World War I and was seen as increasingly conservative. He opposed the widespread abandonment of farming by black Americans and warned that the mass migration to cities would be socially and culturally destructive. At a time when many younger blacks regarded labor unions as progressive forces, Miller was skeptical of them, citing their history of persistent racial discrimination. He remained an old-fashioned American patriot despite the nation's many disappointing failures to extend democracy to black Americans. As a weekly columnist in the black press, Miller published his views in more than one hundred newspapers. By 1923 it was estimated that his columns reached half a million readers. Miller died at his home on the campus of Howard University.

FURTHER READING

A limited collection of Miller's papers, including an incomplete autobiography and a scrapbook, is at the Moorland-Spingarn Research Center at Howard University.

Eisenberg, Bernard. "The Negro Leader as a Marginal Man." Journal of Negro History 45 (July 1960).
Holmes, D. O. W. "Kelly Miller." Phylon (Second Quarter 1945).

Meier, August. "The Racial and Educational Philosophy of Kelly Miller, 1895–1915." *Journal of Negro Education* (July 1960).

Obituary: CARTER G. WOODSON, *Journal of Negro History* (Jan. 1940).
                                        —MICHAEL R. WINSTON

MILLS, FLORENCE

(25 Jan. 1895–1 Nov. 1927), entertainer, was born Florence Winfree in Washington, D.C., the daughter of John Winfree, a carpenter, and Nellie Simons, who did laundry. Educated locally, by age five Mills was winning contests in cakewalking and buck dancing. Her first professional engagement came as Baby Florence Mills in the second company (1902) of the BERT WILLIAMS–GEORGE WILLIAM WALKER *Sons of Ham*, singing a song she had learned from its originator, Aida Overton Walker, entitled "Miss Hannah from Savannah," the tale of a high-class African American who had come north.

Mills served a lengthy apprenticeship before becoming an "overnight" sensation in *The Plantation Revue* in 1922. After several years in vaudeville with the Bonita Company as a "pick" (i.e., a pickaninny), she and her sisters,

Singer, dancer, and persistent voice for social justice, Florence Mills was photographed by JAMES VANDERZEE in 1927, shortly before her death.
© Donna Mussenden VanDerZee

Olivia and Maude, became the vaudeville Mills Sisters. When this act broke up, Mills joined others until 1914, when she began to sing in Chicago nightclubs. Jazzman Mezz Mezzrow recalled her "grace and...dignified, relaxed attitude. Florence, petite and demure, just stood at ease and sang like a humming bird" (*Really the Blues*, 22).

At the Panama Club Mills formed the singing Panama Trio with Ada Smith—later known as BRICKTOP, a favorite of American expatriates in Paris—and Cora Green; the trio toured the Pantages vaudeville circuit, where in 1916 Mills joined the Tennessee Ten. After four seasons with the group as the female singer/dancer in a trio with U. S. "Slow Kid" Thompson and Fredi Johnson, Mills married Thompson. The year of their marriage is not firmly established, and they had no children. (She may have had an earlier marriage, in 1912, to James Randolph.)

Mills and Thompson were recruited into *Shuffle Along*, the 1921 black musical comedy by NOBLE SISSLE and EUBIE BLAKE that began a decade-long Broadway vogue for shows featuring African American performers. *Shuffle Along* lured predominantly white audiences farther "uptown" than before to the Sixty-third Street Theater and ran for a year and a half before enjoying a two-year road tour.

Shuffle Along coincided with the general post–World War I upsurge in theatrical, musical, and literary achievement by African Americans that became known as the Harlem Renaissance. Even the poet CLAUDE MCKAY, who characterized Harlem as "the glorified servant quarters of a vast estate" in *Harlem: Negro Metropolis*, expressed the hope that *Shuffle Along* might help black performers break through the "screen of sneering bigotry" to express their authentic "warmth, color and laughter."

Replacing *Shuffle Along*'s original female star, Gertrude Saunders, Mills soon stopped the show singing "I'm Craving for That Kind of Love" with her particular blend of ethereality and sensuality. Shortly her picture appeared on the sheet music of the show's hit, "I'm Just Wild about Harry." White entrepreneur Lew Leslie hired Mills to star in his 1922 black revue at the Plantation Club at Fiftieth and Broadway. Adding a few acts, he then

moved the entire show into the Forty-eighth Street Theatre.

Sometimes dressed in feathers and sometimes in male evening clothes, Mills created a sensation, particularly by her spontaneous dancing. She said, "I just go crazy when the music starts, and I like to give the audience all it craves. I make up the dances to the songs beforehand, but then something happens like one of the orchestra talking to me and I answer back and watch the audience." Musical historian Allen Woll quoted an uncredited critic: "In that season not to have seen and heard Florence Mills was to be quite out of the know on Broadway" (*Black Musical Theatre from Coontown to Dreamgirls*, 96).

Leslie took the Plantation Revue to London in 1923 as the second (and most effective) half of an Anglo-American revue, *From Dover Street to Dixie*; Mills sang "I'm a Little Blackbird Looking for a Blue Bird," a poignant piece that wrung audiences dry. Impresario Charles B. Cochran wrote of the tension on its opening night, partly due to the recent failure of another black American revue. Upon Mills's appearance, he told his companion, "She owns the house—no audience in the world can resist that.... [She] controlled the emotions of the audience as only a true artist can...there was a heart-throb in her bird-like voice...her thin, lithe arms and legs were animated with a dancing delirium. It was all natural art" (*Secrets of a Showman*, 97–98).

After further European touring with *Dixie*, Leslie brought an enhanced version, built around Mills, to the Shuberts' Broadhurst Theatre in the heart of Times Square as *Dixie to Broadway*, and Mills was also added to the *Greenwich Village Follies of 1923*. JAMES WELDON JOHNSON wrote in *Black Manhattan* that *Dixie to Broadway* "broke away entirely from the established tradition of Negro musical comedies" in starring one woman. Writing in the *New York World* (23 Nov. 1924), Lester Walton said that "the long cherished dream...to see a colored musical comedy successfully playing in the very heart of Broadway" had become a reality. *Dixie to Broadway*, like other African American shows of the era, however, was produced by whites, who made most of the money. Still, Mills was quoted as saying that attitudes toward "colored people" were gradually changing; she saw a great future for "high browns."

After *Dixie to Broadway*, Mills settled in Harlem amidst leaders of the Renaissance such as Johnson, LANGSTON HUGHES, COUNTÉE CULLEN, ZORA NEALE HURSTON, JEAN TOOMER, WALTER WHITE, and actor Charles Gilpin. In 1925 Mills turned down an offer to star in a revue at the Folies Bergère in Paris; after ETHEL WATERS also declined, JOSEPHINE BAKER took the job and became famous. Artist Miguel Covarrubias caricatured Mills, and in 1926 the classical composer WILLIAM GRANT STILL wrote a jazz piece for her. Likewise, the choreographer Buddy Bradley wrote that prima ballerina Alicia Markova reminded him of Mills. Theater historian Loften Mitchell wrote that in the Harlem of the 1920s her name "was on the lips of everyone in the community. People sat in parlors, on stoops, or stood in hallways, trying to find words that might describe her" (*Black Drama*, 78).

Leslie's next show *Blackbirds*, named for Mills's trademark song, was built around Mills. After six weeks early in 1926 at the Alhambra Theater in Harlem, it opened in Paris, where it ran for six months, moved to London, and continued until August 1927. With slick bobbed hair and soft eyes, she was, Cochran wrote, the only performer he had ever seen who could count on an ovation upon entry and before doing a number. The Prince of Wales confessed to seeing *Blackbirds* twenty-two times. In London there were Florence Mills dolls, and the most fashionable shade for clothing was the "Florence Mills shade." The black British jazz musician Spike Hughes, however, questioned her authenticity: whites who thought she epitomized "Negroes" also thought the for-whites-only shows at the Cotton Club in Harlem were authentic. Comparing her unfavorably with BESSIE SMITH, who sang mainly for black audiences, Hughes said he could not tell from her singing whether she was black or white, British or American.

Mills returned to New York in late September 1927, and huge crowds turned out in Harlem to greet her. The 14 October 1927 edition of the *Inter State Tatler* called on her "to give the people the one great gift within her

power...a national, or if you please, a race drama.... Miss Mills can do more than anyone else to satisfy the latent, unexpressed hunger for race drama."

Mills was twice operated on for appendicitis in late October 1927 and died in New York City of peritonitis and paralyticileus resulting from the appendicitis. Tributes came from London, where composer Constant Lambert wrote an "Elegiac Blues" for her, and Paris, where, according to the *New York Times* correspondent, she was lauded as greatest of all. More than 75,000 mourners viewed her body before her funeral, which was attended by 5,000 people in a church meant for 2,000, while thousands waited outside. Jazz composer Andy Razaf contributed a poem beginning "All the World is Lonely / For a Little Blackbird" and ending "Sadness rules the hour / Left us only in tears." A chorus of 500 sang to the accompaniment of a 200-piece orchestra. An estimated 150,000 watched the funeral procession. Johnson wrote, "An airplane...released a flock of blackbirds.... They fluttered overhead a few seconds and then flew away" (*Black Manhattan*, 201).

FURTHER READING

Materials concerning Florence Mills are at the Billy Rose Theatre Collection of the New York Public Library for the Performing Arts, Lincoln Center.

Clarke, John Henrik, ed. *Harlem USA* (1964).
Lewis, David Levering. *When Harlem Was in Vogue* (1997).
Sampson, Henry T. *Black in Blackface: A Source Book on Early Black Musical Shows* (1980).
Shapiro, Nat, and Nat Hentoff. *Hear Me Talkin' to Ya* (1955).

Obituary: *New York Times*, 2 Nov. 1927.
—JAMES ROSS MOORE

MINGUS, CHARLES, JR. (22 Apr. 1922–5 Jan. 1979), bassist and composer, was born in Nogales, Arizona, the youngest of three children and the only son of Charles Mingus Sr., a retired U.S. Army staff sergeant and postal worker from North Carolina, and Harriett Sophia Phillips, from Texas. Seeking medical treatment for

Harriett, the family moved to the Watts community of Los Angeles in October 1922. Shortly after the move, Harriett Mingus died from chronic myocarditis, an inflammation of the heart muscles associated with alcohol consumption. Mingus Sr. married again, to Mamie Carson, whose son, Odell Carson, took Mingus as his surname. All the children were encouraged to take music lessons. Mingus's sisters Grace and Vivian learned the violin and piano; Odell took up the guitar; and Mingus began on the trombone, then moved to cello, piano, and bass. Mingus studied bass with the former New York Philharmonic bassist H. Rheinschagen and the jazz bassist Red Callender, and their influences led Mingus to take pride in technical perfection and improvisation in his bass playing and composing. He was further influenced by the music he heard with his stepmother in her Pentecostal church.

After high school Mingus directed all his energies toward becoming a professional musician, although he made ends meet by working at the post office. At the onset of World War II, several of Mingus's friends enlisted, but Mingus himself failed a preliminary medical examination, disqualifying him from service. During the 1940s Mingus worked as a sideman for a number of jazz luminaries, including LOUIS ARMSTRONG, Kid Ory, Dinah Washington, BILLIE HOLIDAY, and LIONEL HAMPTON. While with Hampton, he recorded his first composition, *Mingus Fingers*. In 1944 Mingus married Canilla Jeanne Gross; they had two children before divorcing in 1947.

The 1950s were a decade of change and transition for Mingus. He had grown up in Los Angeles, playing in the black district of Central Avenue with visiting musicians and musicians who had been childhood friends, including Britt Woodman and Buddy Collette, who were actively involved in the 1953 amalgamation of the Los Angeles segregated locals of the American Federation of Musicians. The popularity of jazz in the 1950s provided Mingus with ample opportunities for work both as a sideman and as a bandleader. He seized these opportunities, moving from Los Angeles to New York City, the recording center of the music business. His bands played in New York nightclubs and also traveled across the United States and in Europe. In 1950, just before moving to New York, Mingus married his second wife, Celia Nielson, with whom he had a son, Dorian.

Mingus's skill as a bassist combined virtuosity with improvisation. Unlike the earlier generation of bassists, whose role was simply to keep the rhythm section in time, Mingus, and others of his cohort, like Oscar Pettiford, envisaged the bass as a solo instrument. Jimmy Blanton, who played with DUKE ELLINGTON in the early 1940s, was widely regarded as pioneering this new direction. One of Mingus's most famous solos is the introduction to his composition "Haitian Fight Song," on *The Clown* album (1957). As well as a soloist, Mingus also defined himself as a composer and found Ellington a major influence. He experimented stylistically with his compositions to challenge prevailing ideas that jazz was primarily an improvised music. As with his performance style, Mingus's compositions were an attempt to integrate collective improvisation techniques with a written score. His compositions were also marked by blues chords, gospel influences, an attention to individual musician's styles, polyrhythms, and modal sections. Mingus usually recorded his own compositions. He also wrote extended-form pieces such as *Cumbia and Jazz Fusion* (1977) and *The Black Saint and the Sinner Lady* (1963).

Mingus struggled with a question that many other artists have attempted to resolve—how to control their music both artistically and financially. With his wife, Celia, and drummer Max Roach, in 1952 Charles Mingus established an independent record label called Debut (now distributed through Fantasy Records). Over the course of its five-year life, the company released at least twenty-seven albums by musicians (including Mingus) as diverse as the pianists Hazel Scott, Bill Evans, Paul Bley, and John Dennis; the drummers ART BLAKEY, Arthur Taylor, and Max Roach; the bassists Oscar Pettiford and Percy Heath; the trumpeters MILES DAVIS, Kenny Dorham, and Thad Jones; the trombonists Kai Winding, J. J. Johnson, and Jimmy Knepper; and the saxophonists John La Porta and Jimmy Heath. Running

an independent label was a tricky and exhausting enterprise, and Mingus, Roach, and Celia were responsible for the artistic and creative aspects of the business as well as its management, production, and distribution. As a consequence, Debut, like other independents, suffered from a financial instability that resulted in its eventual demise. After a brief attempt at reconciliation, Mingus and Celia divorced in 1958, shortly after the dissolution of Debut.

The social and political climate of the civil rights movement and the cold war encouraged Mingus to express an explicitly political voice in his compositions, indicating his belief that music should speak to the times and that it could be a protest against social injustice. Among these compositions are *Fables of Faubus* (1958), an indictment of Arkansas Governor Orval Faubus's stance on school integration; *Oh Lord, Don't Drop that Atomic Bomb on Me* (1961); *Prayer for Passive Resistance* (1958); and *Remember Rockefeller at Attica* (1974), a response to New York Governor Nelson Rockefeller's treatment of prisoners during the 1971 Attica uprising.

In 1960 Mingus married for the third time, to Judy Starkey, with whom he had two children. The couple divorced in 1970. Mingus recorded with a variety of artists in the 1960s, including Ellington, Eric Dolphy, Toshiko Akiyoshi, and LANGSTON HUGHES, and for labels such as Impulse!, Atlantic, Candid, and Columbia. Still trying to make his music a profitable enterprise, in 1964 Mingus established the Jazz Workshop Inc., publishing and mail order companies from which fans could purchase copies of his live albums, *Mingus at Monterey* (1964), *Town Hall Concert* (1962), *My Favorite Quintet* (1965), and *Music Written for Monterey, Not Heard, Played in its Entirety at UCLA* (1965). In the late 1960s Mingus experienced a fallow creative period and disappeared from the jazz scene. Although sometimes performing in local New York nightclubs, he did not record, and it is unclear whether he attempted much composition.

In the 1970s Mingus experienced a creative rebirth, releasing some of his most exciting music, including the widely acclaimed double album

Changes (1974). ALVIN AILEY used Mingus's compositions for a ballet, *The Mingus Dances*, performed by New York's City Center Joffrey Ballet in 1971. His autobiography, *Beneath the Underdog* (1971), on which Mingus had been working sporadically for over a decade, was at last published. The reviews were mixed, many critics seeking a more straightforward autobiography than the fictionalized self-analysis that was *Beneath the Underdog*. The work explored Mingus's childhood, his romances, and his music, but in a way that challenged deeply set ideas about what to expect in a musician's memoir. Rather than report the facts of his career, Mingus took a more courageous step and tried to "reveal the truth" of himself in words as he had long done in music. Now considered a classic of jazz autobiography, *Beneath the Underdog* continues to challenge ideas about how musicians create and think about the world in which they live.

Mingus and his longtime companion and business partner, Sue Graham Ungaro, married in 1975. In her memoir, *Tonight at Noon*, Sue Mingus recounts the story of their relationship and the impact the physical paralysis of amyotrophic lateral sclerosis (ALS) had on Mingus during the last several years of his life. As Mingus struggled with the debilitating paralysis, he continued to compose by singing into a tape recorder. He and Joni Mitchell collaborated on her *Mingus* (1979) album, for which she wrote lyrics to his compositions.

Charles Mingus died in Cuernavaca, Mexico, where he and his wife had gone in search of treatment for his ALS. Mingus's ashes were scattered over the Ganges River in India by his wife.

On 3 June 1989 Mingus's two-hour magnum opus, *Epitaph*, premiered at Lincoln Center in New York under the baton of conductor Gunther Schuller. Throughout his life, Mingus hinted that he was working on such a project. Although he had recorded portions of the score on earlier albums, it was not until his death that the various parts of the piece were put together and performed.

FURTHER READING

Charles Mingus's papers are housed in the Music Division at the Library of Congress in Washington, D.C.

Mingus, Charles. *Beneath the Underdog* (1971).

Coleman, Janet, and Al Young. *Mingus/ Mingus* (1989).

Collette, Buddy, with Steven Isoardi. *Jazz Generations* (2000).

Mingus, Sue Graham. *Tonight at Noon* (2002).

Priestley, Brian. *Charles Mingus: A Critical Biography* (1982).

Santoro, Gene. *Myself When I Am Real: The Life and Music of Charles Mingus* (2000).

Discography

Charles Mingus: The Complete Debut Recordings (Debut 12-DCD-4402-2).

Charles Mingus: Passions of a Man, the Complete Atlantic Recordings 1956–1961 (Atlantic R2 72871).

—NICHOLE T. RUSTIN

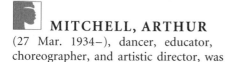

MITCHELL, ARTHUR

(27 Mar. 1934–), dancer, educator, choreographer, and artistic director, was

The first African American to dance with the New York City Ballet, Arthur Mitchell founded the Dance Theatre of Harlem in 1969. Library of Congress

born Arthur Adams Mitchell Jr. in Harlem, New York, the second of six children of Arthur Adams Mitchell and Willie Mae Hearns, who were both from Savannah, Georgia. Mitchell's father, a riveter by trade, also worked as a building superintendent to secure a rent-free apartment for his family. The Mitchells moved several times before Arthur Sr. found a suitable situation where he could earn extra money by working at carpentry, plumbing, and automobile repair.

Aware of his family's financial difficulties, the younger Mitchell worked delivering newspapers and shining shoes to supplement the family income. By the age of twelve he was working in a butcher shop, and was employed there until he became a dance instructor. Mitchell's early creative outlets were varied. He sang in the neighborhood Police Athletic League's Glee Club and the Convent Avenue Baptist Church Choir. At the age of ten he began studying tap dance at the Police Athletic League. Mitchell notes that he later auditioned for the New York City School for the Performing Arts "using a routine an old vaudeville man, Tom Nip, taught me: Steppin' Out With My Baby." Despite his lack of formal dance training, Mitchell was accepted into the dance program in 1949. Although in his first year a teacher suggested he give up dance, Mitchell's resolve was so strong that he redoubled his efforts to prepare his body, overextending himself and tearing his stomach muscles in the process.

Mitchell was encouraged to specialize in modern dance, since there were professional opportunities for black dancers in that style. His professional career as a dancer and choreographer began during his junior and senior years when he was one of two current students to join the alumni in the Repertory Dance Company of the High School of Performing Arts. His first choreographed piece, *Primitive Study*, presented in Altoona, Pennsylvania, was well received. He was cast in several works, performing with the modern dancers Sophie Maslow, Anna Sokolow and the New Dance Group, Donald McKayle, John Butler, and Louis Johnson. In 1952, his senior year, Mitchell performed in Gertrude Stein's *Four Saints in Three Acts* in Paris and later on Broadway. He became the first male dancer ever to receive the coveted Dance Award at graduation.

Throughout his dance training, Mitchell continued to provide financial support to his family. When he was only fifteen, his father became ill and was unable to work, so Mitchell stayed on at the butcher shop and worked at other odd jobs, even as he maintained a demanding training and performance schedule. Upon graduation from high school, Mitchell turned down a scholarship to Bennington College, where he would have continued to study modern dance, and accepted a scholarship to the School of American Ballet (SAB), the official school of the New York City Ballet (NYCB). Mitchell also received a scholarship to study ballet at the KATHERINE DUNHAM School of Cultural Arts. Here he was introduced to the ballet master Karel Shook as well as many of the most accomplished black dancers of the time including ALVIN AILEY, Katherine Dunham, Donald McKayle, and Talley Beatty. Both Mitchell and Ailey were taking classes with Shook while they were dancing in the Broadway production of *House of Flowers*. Beatty not only danced with Dunham at this time, but had also studied at the SAB a few years before Mitchell.

In the 1950s there were few black ballet dancers, and most were in all-black dance companies. The scholarship to SAB represented both an opportunity and a challenge to Mitchell, an already accomplished modern dancer. He now had the opportunity to broaden his professional repertoire and the chance to enter the professional ballet arena, still largely closed to black dancers. Studying under George Balanchine and Karel Shook, Mitchell quickly transformed himself from a modern dancer to a ballet dancer. He progressed through the School of American Ballet curriculum in the requisite three years, although he did not initially train as a ballet dancer. A large part of this success was due to Mitchell's rigorous training schedule and his determination to succeed in an arena where very few black dancers were allowed. Shook, who became both teacher and mentor, gave Mitchell private lessons in addition to his regular classes at both schools. These lessons not only deepened Mitchell's ballet training, but also served as the basis for a lasting collaboration between the two. When the Dunham School closed in 1954,

Shook opened the Studio of Dance Arts and hired Mitchell as a dance instructor. Mitchell could finally use dance to support his vision as a performing artist and to support his family.

Mitchell continued his ballet training and performed with a variety of choreographers and Broadway producers—both black and white—during the early 1950s, including McKayle, Johnson, William Dollar, Guy Lombardo, Truman Capote, and Harold Arlen, to gain exposure and stage experience. In 1955, after finishing his three years at the School of American Ballet, Mitchell joined the John Butler Dance Theatre. In August 1955 he was invited to become a permanent member of the NYCB, becoming the first black dancer to serve as a permanent member of a major ballet company in the United States.

Mitchell's passion and dedication to ballet, combined with the focus on talent of NYCB cofounder and choreographer George Balanchine, earned him a place in the company. Although hired as a member of the corps de ballet, in his first week with the company he debuted in *Western Symphony,* substituting for Jacques D'Amboise. This performance, and the critical acclaim it garnered, led to more opportunities for featured performances and to roles that were created especially for him. Balanchine's first modern ballet, *Agon,* included a pas de deux, danced with Diana Adams, created for Mitchell, and in 1962 Balanchine created the role of Puck in *A Midsummer Night's Dream* for him. Mitchell danced in almost all the ballets of the company during his long and distinguished fifteen-year career. He also taught at the School for American Ballet.

Although his principal activity was with the NYCB, Mitchell organized other dance projects, resulting in two appearances at the Festival of Two Worlds held in Spoleto, Italy, in 1960 and 1961. In 1966 Mitchell participated in a cultural exchange program with the Brazilian government, where he established the National Ballet of Brazil, serving as choreographer and director. He also appeared on Broadway in *House of Flowers* (along with Alvin Ailey and Donald McKayle), *Carmen Jones, Kiss Me Kate, Shinbone Alley, Noël Coward's Sweet Potato,* and *Arabian Nights.*

The assassination of MARTIN LUTHER KING JR. in 1968 was a turning point

in Mitchell's career. He learned of this tragedy on his way to Brazil to work with the National Ballet, and resolved to put his energies into a project in the United States rather than continue to work overseas. Upon his return from Brazil, Mitchell began to teach ballet to black children in a converted garage. In 1968 Mitchell organized the Dance Department of the Harlem School of the Arts, founded by Dorothy Maynor, and invited Shook to join him. The relationship between Mitchell and Maynor became strained, and the collaboration ended in 1969.

Mitchell and Shook, with funding from Mrs. Alva B. Gimbel and the Ford Foundation, founded the Dance Theatre of Harlem (DTH) to provide classical ballet training to black students in that same year. In its first year, the school went from thirty pupils to four hundred, and soon developed a company to showcase the students' talents. Two years after its founding, DTH was invited to perform *Concerto for Jazz Band and Orchestra* with the New York City Ballet (NYCB), with DTH dancing the jazz portion and NYCB dancing the classical portion. Both companies closed the piece with classical ballet, a temporarily integrated ballet collaboration that was the first of its kind. Mitchell developed DTH into a world-renowned institution, beginning with its first New York City season in 1974 and a season at Covent Garden in London in 1981. In 1992 DTH became the first American company to dance in South Africa in thirty years.

Arthur Mitchell has earned numerous awards and honors, including Living Landmark status by the New York Landmark Conservancy, the MacArthur Foundation Genius Fellowship, the School of American Ballet Lifetime Achievement Award, the Award for Distinguished Service to the Arts from the American Academy of Arts and Letters, the NAACP Hall of Fame Image Award, and the PAUL ROBESON Leadership Award. Other awards of distinction include the induction of DTH into the Kirov Ballet Museum, the John F. Kennedy Center for the Performing Arts Award for Excellence, and the Barnard College Medal of Distinction. He also received honorary doctorates from the North Carolina School of the Arts, Harvard, Yale,

Princeton, the Juilliard School, and Williams College.

FURTHER READING

Long, Richard A. *The Black Tradition in American Dance* (1989).
Thorpe, Edward. *Black Dance* (1990).
—C. DALE GADSDEN

 MOLYNEAUX, TOM
(c. 1784–4 Aug. 1818), pugilist, first appeared on the London boxing scene in 1809. All that is known of his earlier life is that he was a freed slave, probably from Baltimore. He had come to Great Britain by way of working on the New York docks. No evidence supports the fanciful claims of the journalist Pierce Egan that he was descended from a warlike hero who had been the all-conquering pugilist of America.

Molyneaux appeared at Bill Richmond's "Horse and Dolphin" tavern in St. Martin's Lane. The tavern, next door to the Fives Court where sparring exhibitions took place, was a natural magnet for a big, tough, aspiring fighter. Richmond, himself an African American, was well established in the ring and had a high reputation among wealthy backers. He was so impressed by the newcomer that he set about promoting him with such success that after only two easily won fights—one a pickup match following a bullbait, and another against a hardy old London fighter, Tom Blake—Molyneaux was matched against Tom Cribb, the champion.

Richmond's training added some science to Molyneaux's original wild, rushing methods, while Cribb prepared little for the fight. When it took place, at Cropthorne, near East Grinstead in Sussex, on 18 December 1810, the champion was overweight and out of shape. The fight was the highlight of Molyneaux's career and was eventually to be the subject of some twentieth-century controversy over its fairness. The crowd, apart from Molyneaux's backers, were certainly on Cribb's side and showed it, but the contest's questionable events were not unusual by the undemanding standards of the day—the breaking of the ring by spectators when Molyneaux was gaining the upper hand and the delays by

Cribb's seconds when their man needed a longer break to recover. In the end, Cribb did win, possibly after Molyneaux had fallen against one of the ring posts or had banged his head on the ground in a wrestling fall. The few eyewitness accounts vary, but none at the time alleged any unfairness. It was nearly twenty years later, when moral expectations about sport were beginning to be raised, that a reminiscing Pierce Egan, who almost certainly saw the fight, referred to a possible injustice toward Molyneaux. Molyneaux himself made no such accusations in his letter to Cribb (doubtless the literate Richmond's work) challenging him to a return match.

Cribb at once began preparing for this contest under the strict training regime of Captain Allardyce Barclay, who had just won national fame by covering one thousand miles in one thousand hours on foot. By contrast, Molyneaux went on a lucrative provincial tour with Richmond, intermittently exhibiting and sparring; took on a relatively meaningless fight with Rimmer, a rough and ready Lancastrian, in May 1811; and relished his fame and the chance to live the good life as he saw it. The outcome was defeat in the rematch, in September 1811, at Thistleton Gap, near Leicester, where Cribb was the fit man and Molyneaux the jaded fighter.

Molyneaux's career was now all anticlimax. An attempt by Richmond to rehabilitate his man in a match against Jack Carter ended with Carter's dubious surrender after he appeared to be winning throughout the fight. Carter and Molyneaux went on tour together, and Richmond broke with his now unmanageable countryman who was giving full rein to all his passions—for fine clothes, food, drink, and the indiscriminate company of women. There was one more fight in Scotland in 1813, against the young William Fuller who, by a fine irony, was in his turn to move to the United States and do much to promote the cause of boxing in North America. Molyneaux moved on to Ireland, where his damaging lifestyle took its final toll. He died in the arms of two other African Americans serving in the Seventy-seventh Regiment in the guardhouse of Galway Barracks, where he was taking refuge. It was a

mere seven and a half years after his first famous battle with Tom Cribb.

The impact made by Molyneaux's achievements in his own country was minimal and scarcely noted in the press. However, his importance in the history of prizefighting was considerable. While he was by no means the first black fighter in the British ring, he made the path somewhat easier for the dozen or more black boxers who appeared during the next twenty years. His challenge, too, raised the issue of the nature of the "Championship," and the question, scarcely asked at the time, as to whether it was a solely British preserve. Finally, the sight of a white and a black fighter struggling against each other at the highest levels of sport had a significance that went beyond boxing and sport itself.

FURTHER READING

Anonymous. *Pancratia, or a History of Pugilism*, 2nd ed. (1815).
Brailsford, Dennis. *Bareknuckles: A Social History of Prize-Fighting* (1988).
Egan, Pierce. *Boxiana* (5 vols., 1812–1829).
Gorn, Eliot J. *The Manly Art: Bare Knuckle Prize Fighting in America* (1986).
—DENNIS BRAILSFORD

MONK, THELONIOUS (10 Oct. 1917–5 Feb. 1982), pianist, composer, and bandleader, was born Thelonious Sphere Monk (though his birth certificate reads "Thelious Junior Monk") in Rocky Mount, North Carolina, the son of Thelonious Monk Sr., a laborer, and Barbara Batts, a maid. When Thelonious was three, the family moved to New York City, settling on the Upper West Side's San Juan Hill. He was surrounded by music as a youth. His father played music in the home, probably even the blues. Thelonious came to love the "Harlem stride" piano style, and it is likely, growing up in a West Indian neighborhood, that he heard Caribbean music and light opera. Scholars have heard echoes of all of these styles of music, especially blues and stride, in his playing. The Monk family did not initially provide for Thelonious's musical education, though his sister, Marion, took piano lessons as part of the standard education of

an upwardly mobile young woman. Her younger brother enjoyed watching these lessons and took in much of what she was taught. By the age of twelve, he had developed some piano technique, and Marion's teacher suggested that his talent should be cultivated.

Thelonious distinguished himself early on as a scholar as well, excelling particularly in mathematics and earning admission to the prestigious Stuyvesant High School. But because of an invisible race barrier at the school, he was not allowed to play in the band, and in his sophomore year he left school in order to play music full time. Like many jazz musicians, Monk came of age musically in both the sacred and secular worlds of black vernacular music making. By his early teens he had played for "rent parties" and served as an organist at Union Baptist Church, but he became truly acquainted with the rigors of life as a professional musician working as an accompanist for a barnstorming evangelist from 1935 to 1937. There is no documentation of what Monk played for the preacher, but some things can be reasonably surmised. Playing for a preacher on a circuit of diverse African American audiences around the country would have required considerable flexibility in musical interaction and would certainly have been good training for the modern jazz performances Monk engaged in soon after.

Upon returning to New York, Monk played sporadically in a number of clubs around the city, with his own quartet and as a sideman, until 1947, when he was hired for the house band at Minton's Playhouse. DIZZY GILLESPIE singled out Monk's role in the development of bebop's complex harmonic language in jam sessions at Minton's. Monk was already a prolific composer, and his songs "'Round Midnight," "Epistrophy," and "I Mean You" quickly became jazz standards. Monk's dramatic sense of style and self-presentation at the time may well also have had an impact on early boppers, who were becoming famous as much for their sartorial and linguistic style as for their music.

Monk's career appeared to be gaining steam, but it was surprisingly derailed in the mid-1940s, leaving him a marginal figure as other jazz modernists gained fame. Many explanations have been suggested, the most plausible being that although his musical ideas had contributed significantly to the bop style, he really did not play bebop himself. The few recordings made in situ at Minton's in the mid-1940s give the impression that Monk's playing at the time owed a great deal to pianists from an earlier generation and that while he was a very capable accompanist, he was not a virtuoso soloist, as were his contemporaries Gillespie, CHARLIE PARKER, and Bud Powell.

In 1947 Monk married Nellie Smith. She was important to Monk in numerous ways, often earning the family living when Monk was unable to, but perhaps most significantly supporting him emotionally and physically during periods when he was under psychological strain. The home life that Thelonious and Nellie nurtured was remarkable in that it contradicts cherished stereotypes about jazz musicians. The two were devoted to each other and their two children, Thelonious Sphere III and Barbara. Both Thelonious and Nellie were essentially homebodies, more interested in cultivating family life than being "on the scene." Leaving aside the irregularities of a musician's life and Monk's nonconformist style, their lives looked little like anything out of bohemian idylls of the jazz life.

Monk made his first recordings as a leader for the Blue Note label in 1947. These remain striking for the extent to which they present his musical conception in all its stark and complex beauty. They are remarkable especially for their distance from other jazz recordings from the time, for their sparse textures, for an idiosyncratic use of dissonance, and for the freshness of the musical signatures that would later become familiar. In 1951 Monk had a substantial setback both personally and professionally when he was convicted of possession of narcotics. Worse than his imprisonment was the loss of his cabaret card, a license to perform in New York City taverns and nightclubs. Whether Monk was framed on the narcotics charges, as has been suggested, the punitive withdrawal of his livelihood was clearly unjust—a glaring example of the ways in which New York police used the card system to punish arbitrarily.

Even though he could not appear live in New York's high-profile jazz venues, the period from 1952 began a slow process of Monk's emergence as a major public figure. In 1952 Monk signed with Prestige records, where he was unhappy despite the opportunity to record with such jazz greats as MILES DAVIS and Sonny Rollins. Three years later Monk's contract with Prestige was bought out by the new label Riverside Records, leading to what was perhaps the most fruitful recording period in his life. Monk's recordings with Riverside are unsurpassed, whether solo, with a trio, in quartet settings with leading tenor players of the day, including JOHN COLTRANE, Johnny Griffin, and Charlie Rouse, or with larger ensembles.

With the help of his friend and sometime benefactor, the Baroness Pannonica de Koenigswarter, Monk secured the return of his cabaret card in 1957. There followed a period of intense activity, including two extended engagements at the Five Spot, a Greenwich Village tavern that soon became a central spot in "hipster" culture. In 1962 he signed with Columbia records, a major label with the ability to promote him quite broadly. Throughout the 1960s Monk appeared regularly in the United States and abroad, at nightclubs, concert halls, and jazz festivals with a fairly stable quartet, and in 1964 he became only the third jazz musician to have his portrait on the cover of *Time* magazine.

The 1960s were, nevertheless, a period of mixed fortunes for Monk. Even as audiences appeared to have caught up to his music at last, and as bookings became more regular and fees more lucrative, Monk went into a decline. The playing on his recordings for Columbia, though marked by occasional brilliance, became routine, often lacking the quality of discovery that had made his earlier work so compelling. More alarming was the deterioration in his mental health. Periods of dissociation were exacerbated by inept psychiatric care.

Monk's contract with Columbia ended in 1968, although he continued to perform regularly, albeit sporadically, until 1974 and recorded some of his finest trio and solo performances for the Black Lion label in 1971. By the end of 1972, however, he began to withdraw. He and his wife moved to the Baroness de Koenigswarter's residence in Weehawken, New Jersey, and by 1975 Monk had become almost totally reclusive. He described himself as simply being tired, and his illness was never satisfactorily diagnosed or treated.

Monk died from an aneurysm in Weehawken just as the jazz world was beginning to rediscover his music. While he had perhaps been something of a fad in the 1960s—lauded, but not quite understood—and had quickly fallen out of favor by the early 1970s, in the 1980s Monk's lasting place in the jazz canon was cemented. Starting in 1982 musicians began exploring his music in a series of tribute albums and concerts that has not abated to the present day. Along with DUKE ELLINGTON and a few others, Monk has become one of those overarching figures that jazz musicians from literally every style draw upon and learn from.

FURTHER READING

Fitterling, Thomas. *Thelonious Monk: His Life and Music* (1997).
Gourse, Leslie. *Straight, No Chaser: The Life and Genius of Thelonious Monk* (1997).
Kelly, Robin D. G. *Misterioso: In Search of Thelonious Monk* (Forthcoming).

Obituary: *New York Times,* 18 Feb. 1982.

Discography
Sheridan, Chris. *Brilliant Corners: A Bio-discography of Thelonious Monk* (2001).
—GABRIEL SOLIS

MORGAN, GARRETT AUGUSTUS (4 Mar. 1877?–27 July 1963), inventor and entrepreneur, was born in 1875 or 1877 in Paris, Kentucky, the seventh of eleven children to former slaves Elizabeth "Eliza" Reed, a woman of African and American Indian ancestry, and Sydney Morgan, a railroad worker of mixed race. Garrett left home for Cincinnati, Ohio, at age fourteen with only six years education. After six years working as a handyman for a wealthy landowner, he moved to Cleveland, Ohio, where he remained until his death. Enchanted by all things mechanical, Garrett worked as a mechanic for several sewing machine shops and in 1901 sold his first invention, a sewing machine belt fastener.

Morgan opened his own sewing machine sales and repair shop in 1907.

He soon earned enough money to buy a house and help support his mother, and in 1908 he married a seamstress, Mary Anne Hassek. The union lasted fifty-five years and produced three sons, John Pierpoint, Garrett Jr., and Cosmos Henry. (Morgan's first marriage in 1896 to Madge Nelson had ended in divorce after only two years.)

Morgan consistently improved the quality and sophistication of his company's sewing machines with innovations like his zigzag stitching attachment. In 1909 he expanded his business with the establishment of the Morgan Skirt Factory, a men's and women's clothes-manufacturing plant that eventually employed more than thirty workers. Morgan's next business enterprise resulted from a serendipitous discovery he made while experimenting with lubricants in an effort to reduce the damage done to wool fabrics by the fire-producing friction of fast-moving sewing machines. Coming across a concoction that appeared to straighten hair, he tested it on a neighbor's Airedale terrier and then on himself. In 1913 he formed the G. A. Morgan Hair Refining Company, offering hair-straightening cream and a complete line of hair products to an enthusiastic public.

In an effort to help firefighters, Morgan set out to create a reliable, portable, water-resistant protective mask that worked without impeding sight, hearing, or mobility. Through studying both the behavior of combustion and the activities of firefighters, Morgan learned that smoke and gases proved the most lethal dangers. By 1912 he had developed a "breathing device" that provided fifteen to twenty minutes of clean air and that could be put on or pulled off in a matter of seconds. Morgan patented his National Safety Hood in 1914 and established the National Safety Device Company to produce and sell it. After several months of unsuccessful attempts to enlist black investors, Morgan turned to financing from outside the African American community. To drum up business, he advertised in trade journals and with direct-mail pieces that included customer testimonials and newspaper accounts. Morgan traveled nationwide, demonstrating the mask at fairs and exhibitions. Elaborate publicity stunts included spending twenty minutes

wearing the hood inside tents filled with toxic fumes or mixtures of tar, sulfur, formaldehyde, and manure set on fire. For demonstrations in the South, Morgan employed white salesmen who pretended to be "Garrett Morgan" while he "played" an Indian assistant.

The Lake Erie crib disaster of July 1916 proved to be the defining moment for Morgan and his mask. Following an explosion in a tunnel under construction deep below Lake Erie, Morgan and his brother Frank donned his safety hoods and made four trips through smoke and toxic gases to rescue workers. Along with citations, including a gold medal from the city of Cleveland, came orders for Morgan Safety Hoods from fire and police departments and mining companies nationwide. Some orders, however, were rescinded after it was revealed that the mask's inventor was black. The dramatic tunnel rescues also led to a contract with the U.S. Navy to develop the hood for combat use. By World War I, Morgan had modified the mask to carry its own air supply, creating the first gas mask, which by 1917 was standard equipment for the U.S. Army.

Morgan began work on what would become his second major invention after witnessing a traffic accident between a horse carriage and a car. While the automobile had gained popularity after World War I, traffic rules and road behavior were evolving more slowly. After analyzing traffic patterns, Morgan invented the G. A. Morgan Safety System, the precursor of today's electric traffic signal. Advertised as "better protection for the pedestrian, school children, and R.R. crossings," Morgan's device—a tall pole with "stop" and "go" flaps raised and lowered by a crank at the base—established a new system of traffic control. The mechanism also introduced a neutral position, the forerunner of the "caution" or "yellow light." Morgan's invention was granted a patent in 1923, and patents in Canada and England followed. Concerned that the racism he would inevitably face in producing and marketing the device himself would limit the traffic signal's adoption, he sold the invention to the General Electric Company for forty thousand dollars.

Morgan was an active community and civic leader, serving as treasurer of

the Cleveland Association of Colored Men and on the board of the Home for Aged Colored People. In 1920 he established, and through 1923 published, the *Cleveland Call*, a weekly African American newspaper today called the *Cleveland Call and Post*. In 1931 Morgan ran unsuccessfully for city council as an independent candidate, promising relief for the unemployed, better housing conditions, and improved policing and hospital access.

Early gas-mask testing had compromised Morgan's health, and in 1943 he was diagnosed with glaucoma. By the 1950s he was nearly blind. An inveterate innovator—smaller inventions include a women's hat fastener, a round belt sewing machine fastener, a friction drive clutch, and a curling comb—Morgan continued inventing even after he lost his sight. Several years before his death in 1963, he developed a pellet designed to extinguish a cigarette if the smoker fell asleep while smoking. Morgan received several awards, including a citation from the United States government for inventing the traffic signal, and an honorary membership in the International Association of Fire Engineers. In 1976 a public school in Harlem was named for him and in 1997 the U.S. Department of Transportation launched the Garrett A. Morgan Technology and Transportation Futures Program, which encourages students to pursue careers in engineering and transportation.

FURTHER READING

Morgan's papers are at the Western Reserve Historical Society in Cleveland, Ohio.

Brodie, James Michael. *Created Equal: The Lives and Ideas of Black American Innovators* (1993).
Jenkins, Edward Sidney. *To Fathom More: African American Scientists and Inventors* (1996).

—LISA E. RIVO

 MORRISON, TONI (18 Feb. 1931–), novelist and Nobel laureate, was born Chloe Ardelia Wofford in Lorain, Ohio, a poor, ethnically diverse steel town. She was the second of four children of George Wofford, who worked, variously, as a

Toni Morrison, winner of the 1993 Nobel Prize for Literature, in 1977. © Helen Marcus 1978

welder in a steel mill, and as a road construction and shipyard worker, and Ella Ramah Willis. Both of Morrison's parents had migrated north, seeking better opportunities and to escape racial and economic oppression in the South. Her maternal grandparents had come to Ohio from Alabama and Kentucky; her father was originally from Georgia. Like many African American migrants, her family eventually realized that the North was not free of racism and poverty. Yet Morrison's childhood in Lorain taught her to value a community in which people shared the limited resources available to them. She also learned to appreciate the value of storytelling at an early age.

Morrison converted to Catholicism when she was twelve years old. In honor of St. Anthony, she took Anthony as her baptismal name, which her friends shortened to Toni. A 1949 honors graduate of Lorain High School, she earned her BA in English at Howard University, in Washington, D.C., in 1953, where she joined the Howard University Players, a repertory troupe that performed for African American audiences in the South. After completing her thesis on William Faulkner and Virginia Woolf, in 1955 she received an MA in English from Cornell University. Early in her career she taught as an instructor of English, first at Texas Southern University, in Houston (1955–1957), and then at Howard (1957–1964). She married Harold Morrison, a Jamaican-born architect, in 1958, with whom she had two sons, Harold Ford and Slade Kevin. The couple divorced in 1964, and, pregnant with her younger son, Morrison took Ford and returned to Lorain.

Morrison has said that during the early years of the civil rights struggle, she was not especially interested in the movement to integrate institutions and public facilities. She had certainly seen firsthand the injustices of Jim Crow segregation, but she had been sustained by the power, wisdom, and imagination nurtured within black communities, and was concerned that integration would diminish the richness of African American culture. She doubted that integration alone would resolve the fundamental issues of racism and economic deprivation. Instead, like ZORA NEALE HURSTON, as well as many black teachers in southern schools, Morrison believed that African American children could thrive if schools in black communities received significant financial investment in faculty, buildings, and materials.

In 1965 Morrison was hired as a senior editor at Random House in its textbook subsidiary, L. W. Singer Publishing, in Syracuse, New York. She was promoted in 1967 to a senior editorship at Random House's New York City headquarters, where she worked for the next seventeen years. While at Random House Morrison built up an impressive client list of more than twenty authors, publishing thirty-five books. Projects for which she was responsible include Leon Forrest's *There Is a Tree More Ancient Than Eden* (1973) and *The Bloodworth Orphans* (1977); George Jackson's *Blood in My Eye* (1972); Ivan van Sertima's *They Came before Columbus* (1976); fiction and essays of Toni Cade Bambara; Gayl Jones's first three novels; JUNE JORDAN's *Things That I Do in the Dark* (1977); Chinweizu's *The West and the Rest of Us* (1975); and ANGELA DAVIS's *An Autobiography* (1974).

During this period Morrison continued to teach at the university level. Appointed an associate professor of English at the State University of New York at Purchase in 1971–1972, she was also a visiting lecturer at Yale University in 1976–1977. From 1984 until 1989 she held the Albert Schweitzer Professorship of Humanities at the State University of New York, Albany, and was a visiting professor at Bard College from 1986 to 1988. In 1998 she was named the A. D. White Professor at Large at Cornell University.

She was appointed the Robert F. Goheen Professor of Humanities at Princeton University. Notwithstanding the considerable demands of her teaching and editorial work, she found time during these years to launch her own distinguished career as a writer.

Morrison produced *The Bluest Eye* (1970) during a period that saw the emergence of a new black aesthetic, and in the novel she explores the destructive impact of racist and elitist standards of beauty and value upon young black girls in particular and upon African American communities generally. *Sula* (1973), which was nominated for the National Book Award and received the Ohioana Book Award, appeared in the midst of the reinvigorated feminist movement and examines how the friendship between two women, as well as their relationships with men, are affected by the politics of labor, social mobility, and migration. *Song of Solomon* (1977) addresses the impact of post-Reconstruction migration and class politics on several generations of a wounded and haunted family; it was chosen as a main selection of the Book of the Month Club and received the National Book Critics Circle Award and the American Academy and Institute of Arts and Letters Award. With the publication of this book, Morrison began to see herself as a writer, rather than as an editor who also wrote.

Tar Baby (1981) is concerned with the impact of colonialism upon the relationships and conflicting cultures in a multiracial household. After it appeared, Morrison was appointed to the American Academy and Institute of the Arts and was featured on the cover of *Newsweek. Beloved* (1987) is a powerful novel that set a new standard for African American literature, and, indeed, a new benchmark in the history of American letters. Set during the era of Reconstruction, *Beloved* is based loosely on the true story of Margaret Garner, a fugitive slave who killed her own child rather than allow her to be sold into slavery. By means of powerfully lyrical, deeply suggestive language, the novel resurrects the dead baby and presents her insatiable desire for maternal love as well as the unfathomable depths of the mother's sense of loss. Moreover,

it explores the profound impact of the traumatic memory of slavery upon black bodies, black communities, and, by extension, American culture. *Beloved* won Morrison numerous awards, most notably the Pulitzer Prize. It did not, however, win the National Book Award, for which it was nominated. In response to this perceived oversight, forty-eight African American writers and critics published a letter in the *New York Times* to express their outrage; in 1996 she received the National Book Award for Distinguished Contribution to American Letters.

Jazz, published in 1992, explores from an improvisational, captivating narrative perspective a set of passionate relationships in 1920s Harlem shaped by the experience of migration and the uncertainties of the urban context. The following year Morrison became the first African American to receive the Nobel Prize in Literature, and the Swedish Academy issued a stamp in her honor. Her most recent novels are *Paradise* (1998), a powerful story of intimacy and violence set in an all-black community in Ruby, Oklahoma, and *Love* (2003), which explores both the passions several women feel for and project upon one man and that man's own complex emotional life.

Morrison is no doubt best known for her novels, which have earned her an extraordinary range of prizes and a wide readership. *Song of Solomon, Paradise, The Bluest Eye*, and *Sula* were all discussed on the *Oprah Winfrey Show*, and in 1998 a screen adaptation of *Beloved*, directed by Jonathan Demme and starring OPRAH WINFREY, Danny Glover, and Thandie Newton, was released. Morrison has, however, produced important work in a variety of other genres as well. Her name does not appear on it, but in 1974 she edited *The Black Book*, a collection of print artifacts that represent black lives as well as black cultural expression. The text, which contains newspaper clippings, photographs, songs, advertisements, slave bills of sale, Patent Office records, receipts, rent-party jingles, and other memorabilia, was the first of Morrison's critical forays into the production of historical memory. This concern has continued with two edited collections of

essays on topical issues: *Race-ing Justice, Engendering Power: Essays on Anita Hill, Clarence Thomas, and the Construction of Social Reality* (1992) and, with Claudia Brodsky Lacour, *Birth of a Nation'hood: Gaze, Script, and Spectacle in the O. J. Simpson Case* (1997). In each collection, Morrison and other prominent literary and cultural critics and legal theorists tease out and rigorously analyze the implicit, repressed, and interlocking narratives of race, gender, and sexuality that underlie two pivotal events in late twentieth century American life: the CLARENCE THOMAS Senate confirmation hearings and the O. J. SIMPSON criminal trial.

Her unpublished play, "Dreaming Emmett," concerned with the meanings of what is perhaps the most publicized lynching in U.S. history, that of EMMETT TILL in Mississippi in 1955, was produced in Albany, New York, in 1986. Her critical book, *Playing in the Dark: Whiteness and the Literary Imagination* (1992), is an influential and oft-cited analysis of ways in which preoccupations associated with writing by major authors such as Edgar Allan Poe, Herman Melville, and Willa Cather depend upon the construction of black figures who embody repressed fears and anxieties.

Morrison has participated in collaborative projects with other artists. For example, she wrote the lyrics to *Honey and Rue*, a song cycle set to music by the pianist, composer, and conductor Andre Previn and performed by Kathleen Battle, which premiered in Chicago in 1992. With Max Roach, the jazz percussionist and composer, and the dancer and choreographer BILL T. JONES, she wrote "Degga," a dance, musical, and narrative piece that was performed at the Lincoln Center for the Performing Arts in New York City in 1995. In recent years she has written four children's books with her son Slade: *The Big Box* (1999), illustrated by Giselle Porter; *The Book of Mean People* (2002); and, in 2003, *Who's Got Game?: The Ant or the Grasshopper?* and *Who's Got Game?: The Lion or the Mouse?*, both illustrated by Pascal Lemaitre.

Toni Morrison has produced some of the most artistically, historically, and politically important work of the late twentieth and early twenty-first centuries, as well as some of the most formally precise and challenging prose of literature written in English. Her experiments with narrative perspective and chronology require readers to enter the worlds she creates on her terms, to relinquish the desire for certainty and closure, to accept the partial, competing truths of multiple points of view, and to acknowledge the mutually constitutive relationship between myriad ostensible polarities such as past and present, body and spirit, life and death. She ranks among the most highly regarded and widely read fiction writers and cultural critics in the history of U.S. literature. Her prose makes visible and articulate what is often unseen and unheard in African American culture as well as in American culture more broadly. From one perspective, her work would seem to have a timeless quality, since it appeals to such a broad audience, but it is always steeped in the realities of the political, social, economic, and historical constraints of African American culture.

Morrison has achieved an extraordinary visibility internationally as well as nationally—her novels have been translated into many languages, and her work has received attention from scholars, critics, and general readers all over the world. As a result, she has become a figure who challenges preexisting notions of what it means to be an American writer, a black writer, a woman writer, and a black intellectual. A novelist of the first rank, she is also a critic of her own work, a theorist of the presence of African Americans and their writings in U.S. literature more broadly, and a trenchant interpreter of the contemporary cultural and political scene.

FURTHER READING

Als, Hilton, "Ghosts in the House." *The New Yorker* (27 Oct. 2003): 64–75.

Matus, Jill. *Toni Morrison* (1998).

Peach, Linden. *Toni Morrison* (2000).

Samuels, Wilfred D., and Clenora Hudson-Weems. *Toni Morrison* (1990).

Taylor-Guthrie, Danille. *Conversations with Toni Morrison* (1994).

—VALERIE SMITH

MORROW, E. FREDERIC (20 Apr. 1909– 19 July 1994), public servant and business executive, was born Everett Frederic Morrow in Hackensack, New Jersey, the son of John Eugene Morrow, a library custodian who was ordained as a Methodist minister in 1912, and Mary Anne Hayes, a former farmworker and maid. He was educated in public schools in Hackensack, where, he would later write in his second work of memoir, *Way Down South Up North* (1973), race relations were as treacherous as the situation in the deep South. Morrow then attended Bowdoin College, to which he believed he won admission only because administrators assumed that he was a relative of Dwight Morrow, a leading politician, lawyer, and banker of the day. Having gained a BA degree during the depths of the Depression, Morrow secured a social-work job sponsored by a New Deal agency and later worked as a bank messenger on Wall Street.

In 1935 Morrow joined the National Urban League as business manager of *Opportunity* magazine, and two years later he moved to the NAACP as a field secretary. At the NAACP, Morrow promoted the organization's grassroots development, traveling across the nation to foster the growth of membership and fund-raising. His military service during World War II was with the U.S. Army Field Artillery, which he entered in 1942. Although at first he found access to officer training blocked on racial grounds, he eventually rose to the rank of major. On leaving the army in 1946, he attended the Rutgers University School of Law, from which he graduated with a JD degree in 1948. After a law clerkship in Englewood, New Jersey, Morrow returned briefly to active duty in the armed forces during the Korean War. In 1950 he joined the Columbia Broadcasting System (CBS) as a writer in its public affairs division.

A longtime Republican, Morrow began his full-time participation in politics when he joined Dwight Eisenhower's campaign train during the fall of 1952. At the end of the campaign, Morrow resigned from CBS after receiving an offer from Sherman Adams, Eisenhower's chief of staff, of a job in the administration. But Morrow did not then secure an appointment, and he later discovered that members of the White House staff had threatened to leave if Morrow joined them. In July 1953 he gained an assignment as adviser on business affairs in the Department of Commerce.

Morrow finally won appointment to the White House in July 1955, when he was named administrative officer for special projects. His duties in this capacity included support services for the work of two special assistants to Eisenhower, Harold E. Stassen on nuclear disarmament, and Nelson A. Rockefeller on psychological warfare. At the end of 1957 Morrow joined the staff of White House speechwriter Arthur Larson, but within a few months he had returned to his former position. Although Morrow resisted special responsibility for African American affairs, preferring to be recognized as a member of the general staff, Adams assigned these duties to him in April 1958 when Maxwell Rabb, previously charged with liaison with minority groups, left the administration. In 1957 Morrow married Catherine Gordon.

The first African American member of a president's executive staff, Morrow was important to the White House as a symbol of racial progress. He accompanied Richard Nixon, the vice president, on a tour of African nations in 1957, and he gave speeches in support of the administration's record on civil rights. Yet Morrow's experiences tended to suggest that change was symbolic rather than substantive. He encountered both personal and professional humiliations in the White House. He was not, for example, officially sworn in as a member of the presidential staff until January 1959, and Eisenhower was unusually absent from the ceremony in order to avoid press attention to the delay. As the struggle for civil rights unfolded during the 1950s, senior figures rarely sought and even more rarely heeded the advice of Morrow, who occupied a marginal role in the administration, often being assigned duties of a mundane nature. Morrow felt "ridiculous standing on platforms all over the country, trying to defend the Administration's record on civil rights" (*Black Man in the*

MORTON, FERDINAND QUINTIN

White House, 179). The work exposed him to criticism among some African Americans, and Morrow observed that he was perceived "as a symbol of disloyalty and a kind of benevolent traitor" (266). Among the initiatives on which Morrow disagreed with the administration's action was the civil rights act of 1957; when Congress weakened the bill, he believed that Eisenhower should have vetoed it. During the Little Rock crisis of the same year, Morrow found himself excluded from decision-making circles, and he supported swifter and stronger action against Governor Orval Faubus's challenge to desegregation there.

Despite the gains made by Eisenhower among African Americans in 1956, especially in southern cities, Morrow believed that the Republican Party neglected an opportunity to boost its popularity among this group, preferring instead to seek votes in the white South. Leading Republicans, he discovered, were surprised that the gradualist progress under Eisenhower toward strengthening civil rights was not enough to challenge Democratic strength among African Americans. Morrow emphasized that economic factors ensured that many African Americans were wary about support for the Republican Party, but he told leading Republicans that expressions of concern about racial inequality and affirmative measures to include African Americans in party activities could transform this gloomy picture. "In most of the areas where I had been," he wrote of his travels during the 1958 midterm campaigns, "the Republican leadership was aloof, still looked upon Negroes as a lower class, and talked down to them rather than giving them any chance of equality" (*Black Man in the White House*, 261–262). Most Republicans did not respond positively to these suggestions, and Morrow discovered that the party overall was already viewing the African American community as a lost constituency. Morrow nevertheless joined the Nixon campaign during the fall of 1960, having developed a respect for the vice president as a politician with a commitment to equality. His hopes were disappointed, however, when he found himself excluded from the inner circle of a campaign that targeted gains in the white South

rather than among African American voters.

In contrast to his white colleagues, Morrow found few opportunities in the private sector open to him at the end of the Eisenhower administration. In a *New York Times* interview, he spoke of "the jungle of racial barriers" that still affected his career, despite his position in the White House (23 Dec. 1960). Morrow wrote an account of his time in the Eisenhower administration, published as *Black Man in the White House* (1963). A significant text that testified to the difficulties and indignities suffered by Morrow and provided an insider account of the administration's approach to civil rights, the book sparked some controversy for its revelations of prejudice and discrimination within the White House. Although Morrow insisted that the president's intentions were good, his conclusion about Eisenhower's achievements in civil rights was ultimately a negative one. As he put it, "At no time had [Eisenhower] made any overt gestures that would encourage Negroes to believe that he sympathized with, or believed in, their crusade for complete and immediate citizenship" (300).

Morrow again broke racial barriers in 1964, when he joined the senior management of the Bank of America as an assistant vice president, becoming a vice president within three years and a division head within five. He encountered many frustrations similar to those that had blighted his earlier career, however, and concluded in his third work of autobiography, *Forty Years a Guinea Pig*, that "in the big corporations of America, Black executives, even senior ones, *can be in it but not of it*" (4). Morrow did not return to public life, turning down an invitation to join Nixon's 1968 presidential campaign. Retiring from the Bank of America as a senior vice president in 1975, he joined the Educational Testing Service in Princeton, New Jersey, as an executive associate.

Morrow died in New York City from complications following a stroke. Morrow's work in the White House made him significant during the 1950s as an African American pioneer at the highest levels of American government. That his work for the

Eisenhower White House remained symbolic rather than substantial was a frustration to Morrow and a reminder of the limited nature of racial progress at this time.

FURTHER READING

There are collections of E. Frederic Morrow's papers at the Dwight D. Eisenhower Library, Abilene, Kansas, and at the Department of Special Collections, Mugar Memorial Library, Boston University.

Morrow, E. Frederic. *Black Man in the White House: A Diary of the Eisenhower Years by the Administrative Officer for Special Projects, the White House, 1955–1961* (1963).
———. *Forty Years a Guinea Pig* (1980).
———. *Way Down South Up North* (1973).

Burk, Robert Frederick. *The Eisenhower Administration and Black Civil Rights* (1984).
Katz, Milton S. "E. Frederick [sic] Morrow and Civil Rights in the Eisenhower Administration." *Phylon* 42.2 (1981).

Obituary: *New York Times*, 21 July 1994.
—ROBERT MASON

MORTON, FERDINAND QUINTIN (9 Sept. 1881– 8 Nov. 1949), attorney and political leader, was born in Macon, Mississippi, the son of Edward James Morton, a clerk in the U.S. Treasury Department, and Willie Mattie Shelton. Morton's parents were former slaves. His father accepted the position with the Treasury Department in 1890, when the family moved north to Washington, D.C. Morton attended school in Washington, then enrolled at Phillips Exeter Academy in New Hampshire. He graduated in 1902 and entered Harvard. He left Harvard after his junior year, in 1905, seemingly for financial reasons. Despite the fact that he was not a college graduate, he began studying at Boston University Law School that fall. He remained there for only a year and a half, again leaving without a degree, probably because of monetary problems.

Morton next became involved in politics. In 1908 he moved to New York City and began working on the campaign of Democratic presidential candidate William Jennings Bryan, giving speeches on his behalf. Bryan lost the presidency to Republican William Howard Taft, but Morton retained his taste for Democratic Party politics. Still possessed with the desire to practice law, he worked as a law clerk for two years, then passed the New York State Bar examination in 1910.

In addition to his work as a lawyer, Morton kept busy in the political arena. Shortly after his experiences with the Bryan campaign, he became a member of the United Colored Democracy, a political group established for the purpose of convincing New York's black population, made up traditionally of Republicans, to switch to the Democratic Party. The New York Democratic machine, known as Tammany Hall, was led by Charles F. Murphy, a man who admired Morton's speaking abilities and his intelligence. In 1915 Murphy secured Morton's nomination as leader of the United Colored Democracy in hopes of winning political backing from Harlem.

Balancing politics with his legal career, Morton practiced law for six years. In 1916 he was appointed assistant district attorney for New York County, and in 1921 he was placed in charge of the office's Indictment Bureau. Morton's tenure at that post was short-lived, however, because on 1 January 1922 he was appointed by Mayor John F. Hylan as the first black member of the New York Municipal Civil Service Commission. Morton's position on the commission helped guarantee an increase in the number of blacks employed by the city.

Blacks, however, were facing increased obstacles in other areas. In the 1920s white Democratic leaders tried to bring about the dissolution of the United Colored Democracy and instead incorporate its members into the more traditional Democratic political organizations. Morton refused to allow this to happen, believing that such a measure would do considerable damage to the political power of blacks as a whole, not to mention the harm it would inflict upon his own political clout. Morton eventually left his position with the United Colored Democracy in 1933, when newly elected New York City mayor Fiorello La Guardia threatened to remove him from the Civil Service Commission if he did not. Morton chose to remain on the commission, where his salary exceeded ten thousand dollars per year, placing him among the highest paid blacks employed by the city.

To fill the void left by his departure from politics, Morton in 1935 accepted the job of baseball commissioner of the Negro National League. He served as commissioner for four years, spanning the final two years that the National League was the sole black league and the first two years after the foundation of the rival Negro American League. In his role as commissioner, Morton was rarely called upon to do anything of consequence. His function was limited to appearances at league meetings. When in 1938 he attempted to call a league meeting on his own authority, Gus Greenlee, the powerful owner of the Pittsburgh Crawfords, told the other owners not to bother to attend. The owners complied with Greenlee. Later that year the league abolished the office of commissioner.

On 16 July 1946 Morton was elected president of the Civil Service Commission. He continued as president until 10 January 1948, when the effects of Parkinson's disease forced him to retire. Morton, who never married, died in Washington, D.C., when the hospital bed in which he was receiving treatment caught fire from a lit cigarette.

FURTHER READING

Two brief studies of Morton in the Schomburg Center for Research in Black Culture of the New York Public Library provide details of his life, James Gardner, "Brief History of Ferdinand Q. Morton of N.Y," and Samuel Michelson, "History of the Democratic Party in Harlem."

Peterson, Robert. *Only the Ball Was White* (1970).

Obituaries: *New York Times* and *New York Herald Tribune*, 9 Nov. 1949.

—FRANCESCO L. NEPA

MORTON, JELLY ROLL (20 Oct. 1890–10 July 1941), was born Ferdinand Lamothe (sometimes mistakenly given as Le Menthe) in New Orleans, the son of Edward Lamothe, who disappeared soon after his son was born, and Louise Monette, who was not legally married to his father. Monette then married William Mouton, who changed his name to Morton, and they had two daughters. There is some confusion over Ferdinand's birth date, because he claimed that he was born in 1885. However, scholars have discovered church records that reveal the 1890 date. Gary Giddins, a jazz scholar and historian, speculates that one reason Morton gave 1885 as his birth date was that had he been born in 1890, he would have been only twelve years old in 1902, the year he claimed to have invented jazz.

Morton was a Creole of color, a member of the New Orleans black community rooted in French, Caribbean, and African culture that flourished when Louisiana was a French colony in the eighteenth century. Creoles of color were generally Catholic, spoke French, and often considered themselves the elite of the black community. Many were well educated, and music was an essential part of their recreational life. When Morton was born, New Orleans was a musical bouillabaisse, filled with the sounds and rhythms of street bands, Italian opera, French quadrilles, Latin tangos, military music, ragtime, popular music, the blues, and the "hot" music from the night spots. Morton recalled that as a child he set out to "whip the word and conquer all [musical] instruments" (Lomax, 4). Even in his childhood his musical abilities were evident. By the time he was fifteen, Morton said he was considered "one of the best junior pianists in the city."

While still a teenager, Morton was offered a job playing the piano in the red-light district of New Orleans. When he told his grandmother what he was doing, Morton said she banished him from the family, telling him, "A musician is nothing but a bum and a scalawag. I don't want you around your sisters. I reckon you better move." Morton began to play in the "high class" bordellos in the tenderloin district. He became one of the kings of the piano, second only to Tony Jackson, who was considered the greatest piano player of his time. Morton claimed that before he invented jazz, most musicians played the blues or ragtime. "Ragtime," he said, "is a certain kind of syncopation...but jazz is a style that can be applied to any kind of tune. Jazz music came from New Orleans" (Lomax, 67).

Morton's music was shaped, in part, by the world of racial segregation. Segregation and disfranchisement had been relatively fluid and flexible in New Orleans in the decades following Reconstruction. By the 1890s, however, Louisiana—like the rest of the South—legalized segregation. In June 1892 HOMER PLESSY, a Creole of color from New Orleans, challenged Louisiana's law segregating public transportation. In 1896 the U.S. Supreme Court established the doctrine of "separate but equal," sanctioning segregation. Two years later the court unanimously approved laws designed to reduce black voting. In New Orleans, as in the rest of the South, blacks were not even allowed in the same houses with white prostitutes. Thus, Morton was required to sit behind a screen in the bordello where he worked to prevent him from looking at the white prostitutes when they danced for their customers. Morton said he got around the restriction by cutting a slit in the screen.

For Morton, music provided an escape from the world of Jim Crow, and it allowed him both creative freedom and the freedom to travel. By the end of the first decade of the twentieth century, he was touring the South. During this period he wrote some of his classic songs, including "Alabama Bound" and "King Porter Stomp." He performed with various vaudeville companies and minstrel shows as musician, actor, and comic entertainer, and he worked as a gambler, pimp, and pool hustler when things were slow. Because of his association with prostitutes, he got a reputation as a lady's man and was given the nickname "Jelly Roll," a slang term for the female or male genitalia and for sexual intercourse.

Morton moved about from St. Louis and Chicago to New York and Kansas City, until he landed on the West Coast in 1917. After World War I, Chicago became the capital of "hot music." Many of New Orleans's greatest jazz musicians performed there, including LOUIS ARMSTRONG, KING OLIVER, and Johnny St. Cyr. Southern musicians had joined the massive migration of hundreds of thousands of blacks fleeing the Jim Crow South in search of a better way of life in the North. Jazz quickly crossed the northern color line as young whites flocked to listen, dance, and play the new music.

Jelly Roll Morton arrived in Chicago in 1923, at the height of his musical powers. He quickly became one of the biggest names in jazz, playing dance halls and clubs throughout the Midwest for both black and white audiences. He teamed up with the Melrose brothers, white music entrepreneurs who negotiated his record and sheet music contracts (and who allegedly skimmed much of the profits for themselves, as did many other white producers of black music). Morton put together the Red Hot Peppers, a recording band composed of top New Orleans musicians, including Kid Ory, Barney Bigard, Johnny Dodds, Johnny St. Cyr, and Baby Dodds, to record songs like "Black Bottom Stomp," "Sidewalk Blues," and "Turtle Twist." Alan Lomax, a music and folk historian, considered Morton's sessions with the Peppers, "the best recorded performances in jazz" of the period.

By the end of the 1920s Morton's career was booming. Money was rolling in, and everybody loved his music. He flashed diamonds wherever he went—on his watch, belt buckle, and tie clip—and he even sported a diamond tooth. Morton owned over a hundred suits and dozens of pairs of shoes. His business cards read "Jelly Roll Morton—Inventor of Jazz." His critics called him a braggart and a fabricator, but Morton may not have been too far off the mark. For if he did not invent jazz, he was certainly one of its founding fathers and one of its greatest piano players, composers, and arrangers. As Giddins notes, Morton "did prove to be... the catalyst who transfigured ragtime and minstrelsy into a new music that adroitly weighed the respective claims of the composer and the improviser—in a word—jazz" (Giddins, 70). Morton's style suitably impressed his fellow performer Mabel Bertrand, whom he met in 1927 and married the following year.

Morton's bragging earned him enemies among his fellow musicians as well as among whites who controlled his bookings and money. In the 1930s Morton's career all but disappeared. A new generation of musicians had emerged, and swing developed as a new form of jazz. Big bands like those led by DUKE ELLINGTON, FATS WALLER, Fletcher Henderson, and Benny Goodman were all the rage. Younger musicians considered Morton a dinosaur, even while others continued to play his music with great success. For a while Morton played at the Red Apple in New York, a second-rate club in Harlem.

Morton left New York in 1935 and wound up at the Jungle Inn, an obscure club in Washington, D.C., tending bar and playing the piano. Down and out and in poor health, Morton seemed at the end of the line. But his glory days were not over. Young people started to come to hear him play music and talk about the glamorous days of New Orleans jazz. When he heard that W. C. HANDY had been introduced as the creator of jazz on a radio show, Morton exploded. He wrote an angry public letter stating that it was he, not Handy, who created jazz. The article made headlines and put Morton back in the limelight.

In 1938 Alan Lomax, a musicologist at the Archive of Folk Song at the Library of Congress, invited Morton to record his music for the Library of Congress. The session became not only a classic recording of Morton's jazz but also a unique historical portrait of the era. Mixing fact and legend, myth and reality, Morton narrated the musical life of New Orleans at the turn of the century. He played many of the songs he had written, some with ribald or frankly sexual lyrics. He brought the golden age of New Orleans to life again, resurrecting many of its legendary figures, from the trumpeter BUDDY BOLDEN and the pianist Tony Jackson to the blues singer Mamie Desdoumes and the rebel Robert Charles, whose legendary shoot-out with the police had made him a hero in the black community.

If the Library of Congress sessions secured Morton's fame for posterity, his financial condition was still anything but secure. In straitened circumstances and seriously ill, he tried desperately to collect back royalties from his publishers. Morton had attempted to join ASCAP, the musicians union, in 1934, because the union had the authority to collect some of the royalties due Morton. But ASCAP was slow to admit blacks as members, and it was not until 1939 that Morton was accepted.

The union, however, did little to secure him his royalties.

In 1939 Morton's career had a brief resurgence. He recorded with SIDNEY BECHET for Victor records and played many of his old songs. He continued to write music, most of which was not discovered until after his death. Ill and dying, his playing days over, Morton moved to Los Angeles in 1940. Too sick to perform or record, he remained confined to his bed until his death.

FURTHER READING

Giddins, Gary. *Visions of Jazz: The First Century* (1998).

Lomax, Alan. *Mr. Jelly Roll: The Fortunes of Jelly Roll Morton, New Orleans Creole and "Inventor of Jazz,"* with a new afterword by Lawrence Gushee (2001).

Reich, Howard, and William Gaines. *Jelly's Blues: The Life, Music, and Redemption of Jelly Roll Morton* (2003).

Obituary: *Downbeat* (Los Angeles), 1 Aug. 1941.

Discography

Jelly Roll Morton: Pioneer of Jazz 1923–1939 (Jazz Records 2003).

Jelly Roll Morton: Jazz King of New Orleans (RCA/Bluebird 2002).

Jelly Roll Morton: The Library of Congress Recordings (Charly 1990).

—RICHARD WORMSER

 MOSES, ROBERT P.
(23 Jan. 1935–), civil rights activist and math literacy advocate, was born Robert Parris Moses in New York City to Gregory Moses, a janitor, and Louise Parris. Bob Moses would later recall that his father's job was a good one during the Depression but that Gregory Moses, a hard-working, intelligent man, resented the lack of opportunities for African Americans in the 1930s. Determined that his sons would not face the same frustrations, Gregory Moses pushed them hard academically. Robert, a quiet and bookish child, won admission to the Stuyvesant High School for gifted students, where teachers encouraged his precocious interest in Chinese philosophy. He also captained the school baseball team and was elected senior class president. In 1952 Moses sought and won a scholarship

Robert Moses was a driving force behind the SNCC voter registration campaigns in Mississippi from 1961 to 1964. © Steve Schapiro

to Hamilton College, a small, highly selective, and conservative school in Clinton, New York.

One of only a handful of black students at Hamilton, Moses found upstate New York to be a sharp contrast to Harlem, but he soon immersed himself in a range of college activities. At first he participated in a fundamentalist Christian study group and considered entering the ministry, but he was gradually drawn to the pacifist beliefs of several of his professors. They encouraged Moses to attend Quaker workshops and summer camps in Europe, where he helped to build low-income housing for the homeless, picked potatoes, and came to share his fellow volunteers' commitment to social justice. Following graduation in 1956, Moses traveled to Japan to explore his interest in Zen Buddhism. He had also become fascinated by the existential philosophy of Albert Camus, who argued that people should be driven by their individual consciences in confronting evil.

When Moses entered Harvard University's philosophy department in 1957, however, he focused not on Camus but on analytical philosophy, for which his interest in mathematics and questions of logic served him well. Soon after completing his MA, he returned to New York City in 1958 to be near his father, who had suffered a nervous breakdown following his wife's death from cancer. Moses found a job teaching math at the city's elite Horace Mann

High School and became involved in civil rights activism with the veteran New York pacifist BAYARD RUSTIN.

Inspired by the wave of student sit-ins in early 1960, Moses traveled to Atlanta, Georgia, on Rustin's recommendation, to meet with ELLA BAKER. Baker, a veteran NAACP organizer in the South, was at that time executive secretary of the Southern Christian Leadership Conference (SCLC), founded by MARTIN LUTHER KING JR. in 1957. She was instrumental in promoting a new, youth-led organization, the Student Nonviolent Coordinating Committee (SNCC), that shared SCLC's goals of ending segregation through nonviolent protest, but which she hoped would be less reliant on charismatic leaders like King. Her philosophy of civil rights organizing appealed to Moses, since it was to all intents and purposes a practical expression of Camus's existentialism.

Baker and Moses believed that a racist society could be transformed only if those who suffered under it came to understand their oppression and then took a personal stand against their oppressors. Believing that SNCC had much to learn from local black leaders, Baker sent Moses to Cleveland, Mississippi, where the NAACP leader Amzie Moore persuaded him to focus his efforts on voter registration, rather than try to replicate a sit-in of the type that had been effective in lunch counter demonstrations in Greensboro, North Carolina. In 1960 a mere 5 percent of black adults in Mississippi were registered to vote. Only with the power of the ballot, Moore argued, could African Americans overcome their own fear, and only then could they overcome segregation. Moses recognized that white resistance would be intense, but the Harvard philosophy student, known for his soft-spoken, sensitive demeanor, could barely conceal his euphoria about the prospect of battle. "Nobody starry-eyed," he wrote a fellow SNCC staffer, "these are nasty jobs but we're going to find some nasty people to do them, so put me down 'cause I'm not only getting mean I'm getting downright nasty" (quoted in Branch, 331).

Moses returned to Mississippi in the summer of 1961 to serve as SNCC's full-time field secretary. He began by opening a voter-registration school in McComb, in the southwestern part of the state, to help would-be voters pass Mississippi's notorious literacy tests, which had been designed to keep blacks off the register. Working door to door, Moses and other SNCC volunteers persuaded forty locals to register, though by the end of the year only six black voters had been added to the electoral rolls. Such minimal gains came at a considerable cost. Practically every activist was intimidated, beaten, and jailed. Moses was arrested several times, and on one occasion a cousin of the local sheriff attacked him with the butt of a knife near the local courthouse. To the amazement of his colleagues, Moses continued, head bloodied, towards the courthouse, where he attempted to help a handful of residents register. Some who tried to register faced economic reprisals from white landlords and employers, and Herbert Lee, a farmer who had assisted SNCC, was shot and killed by E. H. Hurst, the county's representative in the Mississippi legislature. The McComb movement nonetheless emboldened Moses and others in SNCC, who came to understand the radical, indeed revolutionary, nature of their task. They also learned that revolutions do not happen overnight.

Throughout 1962 and 1963 Moses immersed himself in SNCC's day-to-day efforts to increase voter registration in Mississippi, and he also directed voter registration for the Council of Federated Organizations (COFO), an alliance of the state's civil rights

groups. COFO targeted counties in the Mississippi Delta that had potential black electoral majorities but which were dominated by a tight oligarchy of white planters and businessmen. In May 1963 Moses testified before Congress about the failure of President Kennedy's administration to protect civil rights workers and Delta blacks who faced beatings and economic reprisals for attempting to vote.

Believing that the federal government would intervene only if SNCC and COFO provoked a direct confrontation with the white power structure in Mississippi, Moses encouraged more than a thousand student volunteers to come to the state in the summer of 1964 to aid in voter registration and literacy projects. Almost immediately, three of the "Freedom Summer" volunteers, James Chaney, who was black, and Andrew Goodman and Michael Schwerner, both white, went missing near Philadelphia, Mississippi, and were later found shot and beaten to death. The evidence was strong that members of the Ku Klux Klan had killed the three men, but the FBI's far-from-rigorous investigation of the murders did little to inspire Moses's faith in federal protection. The murders and the media coverage of Freedom Summer did, however, raise public awareness of the depth of white resistance to the rule of law in Mississippi.

The volunteers also helped Moses and local activists establish a new political organization, the Mississippi Freedom Democratic Party (MFDP), which drew eighty thousand members, almost all of them black, to rival the established state Democratic organization led by white supremacists like U.S. Senator James Eastland. Despite the efforts of Moses and FANNIE LOU HAMER, the MFDP failed to be seated at the 1964 Democratic National Convention in Atlantic City, New Jersey. Nonetheless, Hamer's televised testimony about the brutal beatings that she and other black registrants suffered in exercising their constitutional rights electrified the convention hall and convinced many Americans of the justice of the MFDP cause. Within a year Congress passed the Voting Rights Act, finally ensuring black voters the same constitutional protections enjoyed by all other citizens.

By 1965 Moses was becoming increasingly uneasy about his reputation

as an inspirational, almost mystical, figure within SNCC. To many of his colleagues, especially whites, his name was no coincidence; they believed that the humble, soft-spoken Bob Moses would lead the civil rights movement to the promised land of equal justice and civil rights. Such thinking was at odds with Moses's enduring belief that the needs and desires of local leaders like Hamer should drive the movement. He changed his surname briefly to Parris and took a leave of absence from SNCC.

In 1966 Moses divorced Dona Richards, a fellow SNCC activist, after a brief marriage, and fled to Montreal, Canada, to avoid being drafted. At thirty-one years of age Moses was much older than the average soldier, and he believed that his vocal opposition to the Vietnam War had led the FBI to manipulate his induction. Physically and psychologically exhausted by the previous five years of struggle, he chose the anonymity of a series of laboring jobs in Canada before traveling to Tanzania in 1968 with his new wife, Janet Jemmott. Moses taught mathematics in a Tanzanian high school for eight years and returned to the United States in 1977, following President Jimmy Carter's amnesty for draft resisters. He settled in Cambridge, Massachusetts, with Jemmott and their four children, and planned to complete the Harvard philosophy doctorate he had begun two decades earlier.

Moses set aside his PhD in 1982, however, when he received a MacArthur Foundation award to establish the Algebra Project, a campaign to increase mathematical knowledge among blacks and other racial minorities. Just as African Americans in the twentieth century had needed access to literacy and voting rights to ensure their full participation in society, Moses argued, so would blacks need access to the math and science skills essential to full participation in the technologically driven twenty-first century. By drawing on the lessons of the civil rights movement, particularly in trusting local people and communities to empower themselves, the Algebra Project has expanded to New York, Baltimore, the San Francisco Bay Area, and the Midwest and, most significantly, to many of the same counties in the Mississippi Delta where Moses and others campaigned for voting rights in the 1960s.

FURTHER READING

Moses, Bob. *Radical Equations: Math Literacy and Civil Rights* (2001).

Burner, Eric. *And Gently Shall He Lead Them: Robert Parris Moses and Civil Rights in Mississippi* (1994).

Branch, Taylor. *Parting the Waters: America in the King Years, 1954–63* (1988).

Carson, Clayborne. *In Struggle: SNCC and the Black Awakening of the 1960s* (1981).

—STEVEN J. NIVEN

MOTLEY, CONSTANCE BAKER (14 Sept. 1921–),

lawyer, jurist, New York state senator, and prominent civil rights advocate, was born Constance Baker in New Haven, Connecticut, the ninth of twelve children born to Willoughby Alva Baker and Rachel Keziah Huggins, immigrants from the West Indian island of Nevis. Her father worked as a chef for Skull and Bones, a secret society at Yale, and owned a restaurant briefly in the 1930s, but the Depression caused the endeavor to fail. Her mother was a leader in the black community, particularly as a member of St. Luke's Church. One of the oldest African American Episcopal churches in the nation, the church served predominantly West Indian families.

Constance Baker was an excellent student and had published both a poem and a prize-winning essay on tuberculosis by the time she graduated from high school. At fifteen, Baker decided that she wanted to pursue a legal career. In her autobiography, *Equal Justice under Law* (1998), she writes, "My mother thought I should be a hairdresser; my father had no thoughts on the subject" (41). In spite of receiving little encouragement, Baker was determined to become an attorney. Her parents could not afford to send her to college, so after graduation Baker got a job with the New Deal's National Youth Administration, which entailed sewing hospital garments and refinishing old chairs for fifty dollars a month (the same salary, Baker once noted, that prisoners were receiving for the work).

In December 1940 Baker attended a meeting organized by Clarence Blakeslee, a local businessman and philanthropist, regarding the Dixwell Community House. Blakeslee had provided much of the money to create this youth center, which was designed to provide a space for community activities. It had not succeeded as he had hoped, however, so he organized a meeting to discuss possible solutions. As president of the New Haven Negro Youth Council, Baker caused a stir at the meeting by pointing out that the members of the community center's board of directors were all from Yale, and therefore the community itself had no real input or sense of ownership.

Blakeslee was so impressed by Baker's independent nature and strong academic record that he volunteered to finance her education. Baker quickly applied to Fisk University in Nashville, Tennessee, and was off to college in February 1941.

As she made her way to Fisk, Baker experienced the Jim Crow South for the first time, and it made a deep impact on her. Indeed, she would dedicate much of her life to striking down discriminatory segregation laws. While attending Fisk, she was disappointed by how many of her fellow students cared more about their social lives than civil rights. When World War II began, many of the best faculty members at Fisk went on to government jobs. Worried that Fisk might lose its accreditation and therefore hurt her chances to be accepted to Columbia Law School, Baker transferred to New York University (NYU) and lived at the YWCA in Harlem. By attending Harlem community meetings and engaging in spirited conversations with her classmates, Baker broadened her political perspectives and actively began to debate civil rights, economics, and the war. She earned a BA in Economics from NYU in October 1943 and went on to Columbia Law School in February 1944. She was surprised to find many other women also pursuing legal careers, given the sexism present in the legal profession at the time.

In October 1945 Baker started working for the NAACP Legal and Educational Defense Fund (LDF), before completing law school. As a law clerk for her mentor THURGOOD MARSHALL, Baker worked on several cases involving segregation in public education. An example of such is *Sweatt v. Painter* (1950), in which Heman Marion Sweatt challenged the University of Texas Law School's interpretation of the "separate but equal" ruling of *Plessy v. Ferguson*. The school had created a separate school for Sweatt, a black student, in an Austin basement. The result of this case was the admission of a black student to a white institution.

Baker passed the New York State bar examination in 1948, and the following year was appointed assistant counsel at the LDF. In her first solo effort, she argued against legal segregation in the public schools of Hempstead, New York, and emerged victorious. Also in 1949 she married Joel Motley, a real estate and insurance broker whom she had

As counsel for the NAACP Legal Defense Fund, Constance Baker Motley won nine of the ten cases she argued before the Supreme Court, including JAMES MEREDITH's suit to attend the University of Mississippi in 1962. © Bettmann/CORBIS

met in 1945 at the YMCA in Harlem when he was a student at NYU's Law School. The couple had one son.

As associate counsel, and later chief counsel, of the NAACP Legal Defense Fund, Constance Baker Motley wrote briefs for *Brown v. Board of Education* (1954) and would go on to argue many cases based on the egalitarian principles put forth in this landmark decision. She worked to desegregate not only public education, but also the areas of housing, transportation, recreation, and public facilities. She argued the cases of Charlayne Hunter Gault and Hamilton Holmes to attend the University of Georgia (1959–1961), Vivian Malone and James Hood to attend the University of Alabama (1963), and Harvey Gantt to attend Clemson College (1963). Motley won nine of the ten cases she argued before the U.S. Supreme Court and represented such civil rights leaders as MARTIN LUTHER KING JR. and RALPH ABERNATHY. One of her most notable cases centered on JAMES MEREDITH's 1962 suit to attend the University of Mississippi. Although the suit was ultimately successful, it would take more than 20,000 federal troops to restore order on the Ole Miss campus and to quell protests against Meredith's admission. The violent reaction to the Meredith case was extreme, but not unusual; during her twenty years with the NAACP Legal Defense Fund, Motley participated in almost every legal case related to the civil rights movement and often faced great personal danger while doing so.

While working for the NAACP, Motley also served on the New York State Advisory Council on Employment and Unemployment Insurance from 1958 to 1965. In 1963 she served out the remainder of James Watson's term as a New York state senator, and was then elected to the office in the following year, making her the first African American woman to serve in this capacity. While in this office, Motley lobbied to create low-income housing in New York's urban sectors. In 1965 Motley was elected as president of the borough of Manhattan, the first woman to be given this distinction, and she worked to revitalize Harlem. On 25 January 1966 President Lyndon B. Johnson nominated Motley to the Southern District Court of New York, the largest federal trial bench in the nation, making Motley

the first African American woman to be named to a federal bench. After serving the court for sixteen years, Motley was named chief judge of the U.S. District Court for the Southern District of New York; she assumed senior status in 1986.

Motley has received many accolades for her work, such as the New York State Bar Association's Gold Medal award, Columbia University Law School's Medal of Excellence, the New York Women's Bar Association's Florence E. Allen Award, the Twentieth Anniversary Award from the Association of Black Women Attorneys, the NAACP Legal Defense and Educational Fund's Equal Justice Award, and, in 2003, the NAACP's Spingarn Medal for outstanding achievement by a black American. She was inducted into the National Women's Hall of Fame in 1993 and has received honorary degrees from over thirty colleges, universities, and law schools. In 1998 Motley published her autobiography, *Equal Justice under Law,* a memoir of the legal battles Motley and the NAACP waged for civil rights.

Constance Baker Motley once said, "Something which we think is impossible now, is not impossible in another decade." In a distinguished legal career spanning fifty years, Motley was instrumental in the struggle for civil rights. Her optimism for social change was founded not only in her own accomplishments, but also in the many lives those accomplishments changed for the better.

FURTHER READING

Constance Baker Motley's papers are held in the Sophia Smith Collection at Smith College in Northampton, Massachusetts.

Motley, Constance Baker. *Equal Justice under Law: An Autobiography* (1989).

Greenberg, Jack. *Crusaders in the Courts* (1994).
Taylor, Telford. *Perspectives on Justice: Telford Taylor, Constance Baker Motley, James K. Feibleman* (1975).

—JENNIFER WOOD

 ## MOTON, ROBERT RUSSA (26 Aug. 1867– 31 May 1940), educator and race leader, was born in Amelia County, Virginia, to Booker Moton, a field-hand supervisor,

and Emily Brown, a domestic servant. Robert enjoyed a relatively pleasant childhood on the Samuel Vaughn plantation in Prince Edward County, where his parents moved to obtain work. At the age of thirteen, Robert went to Surry County, Virginia, where he worked as a laborer in a lumber camp. Seeking a formal education, Moton enrolled at Hampton Institute in 1885, where he remained until his junior year, when he withdrew to work and study law. After earning a license to practice law in Virginia, Moton resumed his education at Hampton in 1889, completed his senior year, and was appointed assistant commandant for the cadet corps of male students in 1890, becoming commandant in 1891 with the rank of major. Over the next twenty-five years Moton remained an ardent proponent of the institute's pedagogy, which stressed the acquisition of industrial skills and the cultivation of values centered on hygiene, grooming, and proper deportment, a combination thought by some to be the key to African American success in the years following Reconstruction.

Moton steeped himself in this educational ideology and emerged as a campus leader at Hampton Institute during the same period that his fellow Hampton alumnus BOOKER T. WASHINGTON stepped into the national spotlight as the principal of Tuskegee Institute and the heir apparent to FREDERICK DOUGLASS. As Washington continued to expand his political role and extend his influence, he increasingly sought out bright representatives and promising leaders in the black community to join his movement, establishing a network that some derisively described as "the Tuskegee Machine." The unassuming and genteel Moton was soon pulled into Washington's orbit.

Beginning in 1908 Moton traveled with Washington on major speaking tours, during which Washington would often use Moton as an example of the potential of the "full-blooded" black man of "pure African stock," and he encouraged Moton to lead choirs or audiences in the singing of African American spirituals. The musical role aside, Moton's dark skin and statuesque presence enabled Washington to make the point that excellence resides in every segment of the African American population, not only among those of mixed parentage. Because of his frequent appearances with Washington, Moton soon became recognized as a close associate and confidant. Moton's first wife, Elizabeth Hunt Harris, had died within a year of their marriage in 1905, and he and Jennie Dee Booth were married in 1908; they had five children.

Moton worked diligently in 1910 to effect a rapprochement between the Washington camp and the more strident leaders, white and black, of the newly founded National Association for the Advancement of Colored People. He had tried, unsuccessfully, as early as 1905 in the New York Conference to reconcile with Washington the so-called radicals led by the scholar W. E. B. Du BOIS, whom Washington himself had tried to draw to his side years before. With Washington's death in 1915, Moton led the field of his most likely successors, and aided by Theodore Roosevelt, a Tuskegee trustee, he became the second principal of Tuskegee Institute.

As the principal of Tuskegee, Moton continued the policies of his mentor and amassed an impressive record of achievement. Having previously served as an adviser to Presidents William Howard Taft and Woodrow Wilson, Moton maintained amicable relations with the White House under subsequent administrations, from Warren G. Harding to Franklin D. Roosevelt. During World War I, Moton was a leader in the campaign to have an all-black officers training camp established at Des Moines, Iowa. He persuaded the Wilson administration to appoint EMMETT JAY SCOTT as "special adviser on Negro Affairs" to Secretary of War Newton D. Baker, and after the war Moton traveled to France in 1919 as an emissary to black troops. He boosted their morale, but in the eyes of some, his pleas for patience and his aversion to agitation lowered the expectation that African American military participation in the war would translate into an abatement of racism on the home front.

In the early years of his tenure at Tuskegee, Moton experienced acute criticism from his rivals for failing to be more assertive in the fight for African American civil rights. It is likely that Moton's choice of tactics was not motivated by a lack of courage, but rather stemmed from his belief that, given the racial climate of

the early twentieth century, economic development and self-help would produce more tangible results for his constituents than any amount of protest. To that end, in 1919 he assumed the chairmanship of the National League on Urban Conditions among Negroes, a predecessor to the National Urban League. In 1921, Moton was elected president of the National Negro Business League, a powerful organization of black entrepreneurs loyal to Washington.

In 1922 Moton was invited to speak for his race at the unveiling of the Lincoln Memorial. The speech he submitted was uncharacteristically bold and forthright, paraphrasing Lincoln and offering a rare indictment of American racism: "No more can the nation endure half privileged and half repressed; half educated and half uneducated; half protected and half unprotected;... half free and half yet in bondage" (Fairclough, 411). Taft ordered all such critical statements excised from Moton's speech. Those sentiments would not find expression at the Lincoln Memorial until MARTIN LUTHER KING JR. gave voice to them on that very spot forty-one years later.

Moton is credited with making Tuskegee Institute a college when, in 1925, the catalog announced a course of study leading to a BS in both Agriculture and Education. In his twenty years as principal of Tuskegee, Moton increased the institute's endowment from $2.3 million to $7.7 million. Drawing on his experiences as an educator in the deep South, Moton attempted to provide insightful leadership as chairman of President Herbert Hoover's commission on educational problems in Haiti; had his recommendations been heeded more often, Haiti's schools would have been greatly improved. Moton went on to found the Negro Organization Society of Virginia, and dedicate himself to the improvement of the health of African Americans by, among their things, helping Booker T. Washington establish a national Negro Health Day.

In 1923 he secured the building of a Veterans Administration Hospital in Tuskegee, in part by donating three hundred acres of Tuskegee's campus to guarantee the project. Eventually, the facility came to comprise some forty-five buildings, making it one of the largest hospitals in the state and an important

training ground for black doctors and nurses. Tragically, in 1931, shortly before Moton's retirement in 1935, the U.S. Public Health Service began a clandestine medical experiment at the hospital on 399 black men in the late stages of syphilis. Most of these men were illiterate sharecroppers from the poorest parts of Alabama, and neither they nor their wives were told what they were suffering from; rather they were told they were being treated for "bad blood," a folk term for a variety of ailments. In fact, the course of the disease in these men was merely being observed; effective treatment was withheld, even after penicillin became available in the 1940s.

This "experiment" continued until it was exposed in the Washington Evening Star in 1972, and though the survivors and their families were awarded nine million dollars in a class action suit, it was not until May 1997 that a formal apology came from the government, when President Bill Clinton acknowledged, "What was done cannot be undone. But we can end the silence. We can stop turning our heads away. We can look you in the eye and finally say on behalf of the American people, what the United States government did was shameful, and I am sorry" (Jet 2 June 1997, 6). Although it is unlikely that Moton had any knowledge of this experiment, and while Tuskegee was not directly involved, the reputation of the institute and those affiliated with it during those years was markedly damaged; in partial reparation President Clinton announced a grant for establishing the Tuskegee University National Center for Bioethics in Research and Health Care.

In 1920 Moton published his autobiography, Finding a Way Out, followed in 1928 by a political treatise, What the Negro Thinks, which was intended to bring attention to the ideas, issues, and problems affecting African Americans. He broadened his leadership activities in both white and black communities, serving as the chair of the Colored Advisory Commission to the American National Red Cross on the Mississippi Floods Disaster and as chair of the Campaign Committee Commission on Interracial Cooperation (1930), which was led by JOHN HOPE, president of Morehouse College and Atlanta University. Moton also became the president of Tuskegee Institute Savings Bank.

Among the many accolades he received were honorary degrees from Harvard University and Howard University, as well as the prestigious Harmon Award and Spingarn Medal from the NAACP. In 1935 Moton's son-in-law, Frederick D. Patterson, succeeded him as the third president of the institute and largely continued the traditions that Washington and Moton had so firmly established. Moton's legacy is best appreciated for the role he played in establishing a strong foundation for historically black colleges during a time when Tuskegee was the flagship of black educational institutions. Although his politics may seem tepid compared with the stance of later generations of black leaders, many of those firebrands received their education from institutions like Tuskegee.

FURTHER READING

The main body of Moton's papers can be found at the Hampton University Archives, Collis P. Huntington Memorial Library; the Robert Russa Moton Papers, Hollis Burke Frissell Library, Tuskegee University; and the Moton Family Papers, Library of Congress, Washington, D.C.

Moton, Robert Russa. *Finding a Way Out* (1920).

Fairclough, Adam. "Civil Rights and the Lincoln Memorial: The Censored Speeches of Robert R. Moton (1922) and John Lewis (1963)." *Journal of Negro History* 82.4 (Autumn 1997).

Hughes, William Hardin, ed. *Robert Russa Moton of Hampton and Tuskegee* (1956).

Jones, James H. *Bad Blood: The Tuskegee Syphilis Experiment* (1993).

Obituary: *New York Times*, 1 June 1940.
—MACEO CRENSHAW DAILEY JR.

MUDDY WATERS. *See* Waters, Muddy.

MUHAMMAD, ELIJAH (10 Oct. 1897–25 Feb. 1975), leader of the Nation of Islam, was born Robert Poole in Sandersville, Georgia, the son of William Poole, an itinerant Baptist preacher and sharecropper, and Mariah Hall, a domestic for local white families. In 1900 the family moved to Cordele, Georgia, where Muhammad went to public school until the fourth grade when he dropped out to supplement his family's income as a laborer in sawmills and with the Cherokee Brick Company. In 1919 he married Clara Evans of Cordele, and they had two daughters and six sons.

With thousands of other African Americans from the rural South, Muhammad migrated to Detroit, Michigan, in the early 1920s. A depressed southern agricultural economy, hampered by boll weevil infestation of cotton crops and increasing mechanization of farm labor, forced many small farmers to join the Great Migration to the booming industrial cities of the North. Muhammad and some of his brothers found work in the automobile plants of Detroit. In 1931 he met Master Wallace Fard (or Wali Farad), a peddler of sundry goods in Detroit's ghettos, who claimed that he had a message of redemption for the "Asiatic black man." Using the Bible and the Qur'ān, the Muslim scripture, Fard began proselytizing among poor people in July 1930, starting with meetings in houses until he had enough members to rent a storefront, which he called Temple of Islam No. 1. Through his hard work, disciplined devotion, and intelligence, Robert Poole was chosen by Fard to be his chief aide. Fard made him a "minister of Islam" and changed his name to Elijah Muhammad.

Fard mysteriously disappeared in 1934, claiming that he was going back to Mecca. With no traces of their leader, the Nation of Islam split into several contending factions, and violent squabbles erupted. Fearing for their lives, Muhammad led his followers to several midwestern cities before finally settling in Chicago in 1936. Temple of Islam No. 2 was established in Chicago as the main headquarters for the fledgling Nation of Islam. With only thirteen members at the beginning, the Nation of Islam experienced its growth spurt only after Muhammad's incarceration from 1943 to 1946 for refusing the draft during World War II. His imprisonment demonstrated his faith and contributed to his emergence as a confident leader. In 1950 at a

Elijah Muhammad, leader of the Nation of Islam, speaking at a rally in 1964. Library of Congress

Savior's Day rally, several hundred members attended. Muhammad also instituted the worship of Master Fard as Allah, a black man as god, and stated that he himself was Allah's messenger or prophet. As the main leader of the Nation of Islam, he was always addressed with the honorific "the Honorable." Muhammad built on the teachings of Fard and combined aspects of Islam and Christianity with the black nationalism of MARCUS GARVEY into a "proto-Islam," where aspects of Islamic teachings and practices were used to coat a message of black nationalism that had a strong racial slant. Muhammad also installed the ritual of celebrating Master Fard's birthdate, 26 February, as Savior's Day, a special time for gathering the members of the Nation in Chicago.

In the racial mythology of the Nation of Islam, the black man was the "original man." Whites were created as a hybrid race by a black mad scientist named Yacub, and they were to rule for a period of six thousand years through deceit and "tricknology." At the end of that period, a battle of Armageddon will occur, and black people will emerge victorious and resume their rightful place as rulers of the earth. In this mythology the usual color valences of the English language are reversed: white is associated with evil and death, and black with goodness and life. Whites are also viewed as "devils." In the lives of many poor black people, this mythology functioned as a theodicy, an explanation of the injustices, pain, and suffering that they were experiencing in a deeply segregated American society.

Muhammad's message of racial separation focused on the recognition of the true black identity and stressed economic independence. "Knowledge of Self" and "Do for Self" became the rallying cries in Muhammad's sermons and writings, *The Supreme Wisdom: The Solutions to the So-Called Negroes' Problems* (1957) and *Message to the Black Man* (1965). Muhammad stressed that black people had lost the knowledge of their true selves, so that they were viewed by the wider society as "Negroes" or as "coloreds" and not as the "original black man." Moreover, he understood the vulnerability of the black psyche, and he hammered away at the slave mentality that had encumbered the demeanor and lifestyle of African Americans. As a means of getting black people to find a new identity, he had them drop their surnames, which most of them had inherited from their slave masters, and replace them with an X. X meant an unknown quantity; it also meant ex-slave, ex-Christian, ex-smoker, and ex-alcoholic. By reforming the mental attitudes and the behavior of his followers, he set about creating a new nation of black people.

In a similar manner, Muhammad placed priority on economic independence for members of the Nation of Islam. They could not be on welfare and had to work. It was best if they owned their own businesses. So members of the Nation set up hundreds of small businesses, such as bakeries, grocery stores, restaurants, and outlets for fish and bean pies. The men of the movement were required to sell a weekly quota of the Nation's newspaper, *Muhammad Speaks*, which became the main financial support for the movement. The Nation had also established its own educational system in 1932; although it was called the University of Islam, the focus was on the years from elementary to high school. Members of the Nation also followed

Muhammad's strict dietary rules outlined in his book *How to Eat to Live* (1972), which enjoined one meal per day and complete abstention from pork, drugs, tobacco, and alcohol. He also instituted a Ramadan fast of one week during the month of December, mainly to counter the pervasive influence of the Christmas celebration of Christians in African American communities.

In *Message to the Black Man* Muhammad taught that black people were not Americans, that they owed no allegiance to the American flag, and that they should not join the military. Muhammad spent four years in a federal prison for encouraging draft refusal during World War II and for refusing the draft himself. Several of his sons also spent time in prison for refusing the draft during the Korean War. The eventual goal of the movement was to create a separate black nation, a homeland for black people. The actual place or territory of this black nation—whether it would be in the United States, Africa, or elsewhere—was never specified.

Two internal organizations within the Nation of Islam were created for men and women. The Muslim Girls Training (MGT) provided classes for training young women in the domestic arts, housekeeping, cooking, and raising children. The private sphere of the home was the realm for women. Women could not go out alone at night; they had to be escorted by a Muslim male. The Fruit of Islam was set up as the security arm of the Nation. Trained in the martial arts, security techniques, and military drill, they guarded the ministers and leaders of the Nation. Everyone entering a Muslim temple or attending a national meeting was subject to body searches by the Fruit or the MGT. At national meetings, drill competitions were held for Fruit of Islam groups from different cities. Muhammad's brother-in-law, Raymond Sharieff, was the chief commander of the national Fruit of Islam.

The Nation of Islam reached its peak years through the efforts of Minister MALCOLM X, with whom Elijah Muhammad had corresponded when Malcolm was in prison. After his release in 1952, Malcolm became an indefatigable organizer and proselytizer for the Nation. He founded many

temples of Islam on the East Coast, throughout the South, and on the West Coast. Malcolm was a favorite visitor in Muhammad's home, and he was regarded as their seventh son. As a charismatic speaker, Malcolm encouraged the rapid spread of the Nation of Islam in the 1950s and early 1960s. He also started *Muhammad Speaks* in May 1960 in the basement of his home. Muhammad appointed Malcolm as the minister of Temple No. 7 in Harlem, the most important temple outside Chicago, and in 1962 he named Malcolm his national representative. However, in December 1963, after President John F. Kennedy was assassinated in Dallas, Muhammad ordered a three-month period of public silence for Malcolm as a result of Malcolm's comment that the assassination was an expression of the violence inherent in the culture of white America. His ill-spoken words inflamed the American public. As the period of silence was extended beyond three months, Malcolm eventually resigned from the Nation of Islam and began his own organizations. He also publicly accused Muhammad of fathering a number of illegitimate children with several of his secretaries. Malcolm was assassinated on 22 February 1965 at the Audubon Ballroom in Harlem. Muhammad and the leadership of the Nation denied any involvement in Malcolm's death.

Muhammad appointed one of Malcolm's protégés, Minister LOUIS FARRAKHAN from Boston, to become the national representative and minister of Temple No. 7 in Harlem. During its peak years in the 1960s, the Nation of Islam had close to 500,000 devoted followers, influencing millions more particularly during the period of increased cultural awareness among blacks from 1967 to 1975. It also accumulated an economic empire worth more than eighty million dollars, which included farms in Georgia and Alabama, a modern printing press operation for its newspaper, a bank, and plans for establishing a Muslim hospital and university. As a person suffering from respiratory illnesses, Muhammad also had a large house in Phoenix, Arizona, where he often spent the winters.

Although he had only a third-grade education, Muhammad became the leader of the most enduring black militant movement in the United States. He was a shrewd judge of character and was able to control and contain a number of fiery, charismatic personalities in his movement. He died in Chicago and was succeeded by the fifth of his six sons, Wallace Deen Muhammad. After Wallace disbanded the Nation of Islam and led many of its members into the fold of Sunni Islam, or orthodox Islam, Farrakhan resurrected the Nation of Islam in 1978, using the teachings of Elijah Muhammad as its primary vehicle. Farrakhan also instituted a second Savior's Day celebration in his Nation, honoring the birthdate of Elijah Muhammad.

FURTHER READING

Clegg, Claude Andrew, III. *An Original Man: The Life and Times of Elijah Muhammad* (1997).

Essien-Udom, E. U. *Black Nationalism* (1962).

Evanzz, Karl. *Messenger: The Rise & Fall of Elijah Muhammad* (1999).

Lincoln, C. Eric. *The Black Muslims in America* (1961).

—LAWRENCE H. MAMIYA

MURPHY, ISAAC

(16 Apr. 1861–12 Feb. 1896), jockey, was born Isaac Burns on a farm near Frankfort, Kentucky, the son of James Burns, a bricklayer, and a mother (name unknown) who worked as a laundrywoman. During the Civil War his father, a free black, joined the Union army and died in a Confederate prisoner-of-war camp. Upon the death of his father, his widowed mother moved with her family to Lexington, Kentucky, to live with her father, Green Murphy, a bell ringer and auction crier. Accompanying his mother to work at the Richard and Owings Racing Stable, the diminutive Isaac was noticed by the black trainer Eli Jordan, who had him suited up for his first race at age fourteen. His first winning race was aboard the two-year-old filly Glentina on 15 September 1875 at the Lexington Crab Orchard. Standing five feet tall and weighing only seventy-four pounds, Murphy had by the end of 1876 ridden eleven horses to victory at Lexington's Kentucky Association track.

Since colonial times, African Americans had been involved in the care and training of horses, particularly on antebellum and post–Civil War farms and plantations in the South. They had also ridden them as jockeys, an occupation once considered beneath the dignity of white men. At the inaugural Kentucky Derby in 1875, fourteen of the fifteen jockeys were black. Blacks triumphed in fifteen of the first twenty-eight derbies. In his first Kentucky Derby in 1877, Murphy (who had adopted his grandfather's surname as a tribute) placed fourth aboard Vera Cruz. He later rode the same horse to victory in another major stakes race and tallied nineteen first-place finishes that year. Two years later, Murphy signed with J. W. Hunt Reynolds and came in second in the Kentucky Derby with the moneymaker Falsetto. Among Murphy's numerous victories between 1879 and 1884 (the year he signed with Ed Corrigan of New York) were the Clark Handicap in Louisville, Kentucky; the Distillers Stakes in Lexington, Kentucky; the Saratoga Cup in New York; the Brewers Cup in St. Louis, Missouri; and the first American Derby in Chicago, Illinois. Incredibly, he posted wins in forty-nine of the fifty-one races he entered at Saratoga in 1882. His first Kentucky Derby win at Churchill Downs, on 27 May 1884 aboard Modesty, was clocked at 2 minutes, 40.25 seconds, two lengths ahead of his nearest rival. It was the first of three such conquests there; the other two occurred successively in 1890 and 1891, with the mounts Riley and Kingman, respectively.

Renowned for his adept manipulation of his mounts via intuitive, precise pacing, Murphy rarely employed stirrups or the whip except to please the crowd, and his trademark come-from-behind finishes became known as "Murfinshes." It was his habit to lay on the horse's neck to coax it to the finish line. At a time when jockeys customarily wagered on the outcome of races, Murphy, a devout Baptist, enjoyed a reputation for scrupulous honesty and integrity. A mild-mannered, gracious man who never swore, he married Lucy Osborn in 1882; they had no children. Murphy and his wife resided in a mansion at 143 North Eastern Avenue in Lexington, overlooking the backstretch

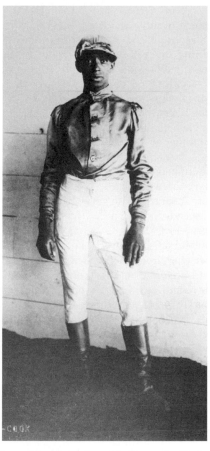

Isaac Murphy, who rode Kentucky Derby winners in 1884, 1890, and 1891. Corbis

of a nearby racetrack. At the peak of his career, his yearly salary ranged from ten thousand to twenty thousand dollars excluding bonuses, making him the highest-paid jockey in the nation. His income befitted a man who rode nearly every premier horse of the era to victory at all the major racing events except the Futurity. It is believed that Murphy was the first black American to own a racehorse—he owned several, in fact—and he invested his winnings in racehorses and real estate. He spent extravagantly on clothes and soirees at his home and was attended at the track by his personal valet.

Several writers have asserted that Murphy's most memorable and exciting race was that which occurred at Sheepshead Bay in New York on 25 June 1890. It matched him against the heralded white jockey Ed "Snapper" Garrison and attempted to settle the long-standing debate as to who was the better professional. The event had pronounced racial overtones that in certain respects prefigured the JACK

JOHNSON versus Jim Jeffries boxing match twenty years later. Murphy, riding Salvador, edged out Garrison, aboard Tenny, by half a head in one of the most publicized races of the century.

Ironically, just two months later Murphy's popularity was tarnished and his career began to unravel when he fell off of his mount at the end of the running of the Monmouth Handicap. He maintained that he suffered from chronic dieting and that he may even have been drugged. Nonetheless, he was charged with drunkenness and suspended. The press, including the *New York Times* (27 Aug. 1890), was quite baffled by such uncharacteristic behavior from the gentlemanly Murphy and roundly chastised him. Although he continued to rack up victories at the track the following year (1891), his penchant for champagne and the struggle to hold down his weight, which had risen to 140 pounds, eventually took their toll. In 1892 he won six races, the next year four races, and in 1894, the year he was suspended for a second time for being drunk at the track, he failed to win a race. Retirement was forced upon him in November 1895. Within three months Murphy died in Lexington, the ravages of alcohol and dieting having weakened his resistance to pneumonia. He left thirty thousand dollars to his wife, but this sum was hardly enough to satisfy his creditors and she died a pauper.

Murphy, arguably the most influential and widely respected African American athlete of the nineteenth century, was curiously ignored for many years by historians and journalists. Half a century after his death, an article filled with anecdotes and quotations pertaining to his career appeared in the *Negro Digest* (Nov. 1950). Its title bemoaned, "No Memorial for Isaac Murphy." In 1967, through the efforts of Lexington sportswriter Frank Borries Jr., Murphy's remains were transported from their ignominious location in the city's decrepit No. 2 Cemetery and reinterred in Man o' War Park. In 1977 the remains of both the jockey and the famed thoroughbred (whom Murphy never rode) were moved to hallowed ground near one another at the Kentucky Horse Park outside of Lexington. In 1955 he was the first jockey inducted into the National Museum of Racing

Hall of Fame, and in 1956 he was also enshrined in the National Jockey's Hall of Fame at Pimlico, Maryland.

Murphy's three Kentucky Derby wins were later exceeded by Eddie Arcaro (five), Bill Hartack (five), and Bill Shoemaker (four); his back-to-back Kentucky Derby wins were later equaled by African American Jimmy Winkfield (1901 and 1902), Ron Tucotte (1972 and 1973), and Eddie Delahoussaye (1982 and 1983). To his recollection, he was victorious in 44 percent of his contests, winning 628 of 1,412 mounts; but according to other sources, Murphy's winning percentage was closer to 33 percent. In any event, 33 percent represented the best winning record of any jockey in American turf history. The annual Isaac Murphy Award was established in 1993 by the National Turf Writers' Association to honor the jockey with the best win-loss record. The Isaac Murphy Stakes (formerly the American Derby, which Murphy won on four occasions) was initiated in 1997 at Chicago's Arlington International Racecourse.

FURTHER READING

ASHE, ARTHUR R. *A Hard Road to Glory: A History of the African American Athlete, 1619–1918* (1988).

Bolus, Jim. "Honest Isaac's Legacy," *Sports Illustrated* (29 Apr. 1996).

Borries, Betty. *Isaac Murphy: Kentucky's Record Jockey* (1988).

Cushing, Rick. "Isaac Murphy: A Pioneer Who's Had Few Followers." *Louisville Courier-Journal* (30 Apr. 1990).

Phelps, Frank T. "The Nearest Perfect Jockey." *Thoroughbred Record*, 13 May 1967, 1245–1248.

Savage, Stephen P. "Isaac Murphy: Black Hero in Nineteenth Century American Sport, 1861–1896." *Canadian Journal of History and Physical Education* 10 (1979): 15–32.

Tarelton, L. P. "A Memorial." *Thoroughbred Record* (21 Mar. 1896) 136.

—ROBERT FIKES

MURRAY, ALBERT

(12 May 1916–), writer and critic, was born in Nokomis, Alabama, the son of Sudie Graham, a Tuskegee Institute student, and John Young, a businessman. Soon after his birth Mattie Murray, a housewife, and her

husband, Hugh, a laborer and timber worker, adopted him. Murray, who later enjoyed a close relationship with Graham and Young, joked of his adoption by less-wealthy parents, "It's just like the prince left among the paupers" (Gates, 30). He learned about the folkways of segregation in Magazine Point, a community on the outskirts of Mobile, Alabama, where his family had moved during World War I. "We didn't dislike white people," he recalled. "We saw too many bony-butt poor white crackers. We were going to feel inferior to them?" (Maguire, 139). Murray's rejection of any notion of black inferiority was further strengthened by exposure to Mobile's baseball legend SATCHEL PAIGE and to teachers at the intellectually rigorous Mobile County Training School. A studious youth, interested in drama, Murray was also quarterback on the school football team and captain of the basketball squad. Voted the school's best all-round student in 1935, he received a scholarship to Tuskegee Institute.

Tuskegee's well-stocked libraries suited Murray's voracious appetite for literature. Although he was aware of the black writers associated with the Harlem Renaissance, he was drawn instead to the white Southern Renascence novelists Robert Penn Warren and William Faulkner and to the modernist fiction writers Ernest Hemingway and Thomas Mann. This passion, along with jazz, he shared with his older Tuskegee contemporary, RALPH ELLISON. But unlike Ellison, who left for New York in 1936, Murray followed an intellectual and critical development that was rooted in his native South. He graduated from Tuskegee in 1939 and, after briefly studying at the University of Michigan, returned to his alma mater to teach literature and composition a year later. In 1941 he married Mozelle Menefee, a Tuskegee student, and two years later enlisted in the Army Air Forces, serving until 1946.

During World War II, easy access to air travel gave Murray the opportunity to fly to New York City and scavenge the Gotham Book Mart, and he returned to Manhattan in 1947 to study for a master's degree at New York University. He also reacquainted himself with Ellison, who was then on the verge of literary stardom with the publication of *Invisible Man* (1952), and spent as much time as possible in the city's jazz clubs. There he developed friendships with DUKE ELLINGTON and COUNT BASIE and began to conceptualize jazz not only as a metaphor for African American and American society but also, with its riffs and breaks, its sudden changes and bursts of creativity, as a means of understanding life itself. After returning to Tuskegee to teach in 1948, Murray was called back to the air force in 1951 and remained there for the next eleven years.

Murray later recalled that long periods of inactivity in the armed forces gave him plenty of time to read, think, and travel to Morocco, Greece, and Italy. However, military service also delayed his grand ambition to be "the JOE LOUIS of literature" (Maguire, 107). His career as a published writer began to take shape in the early 1960s, however, when he retired from the air force with the rank of major and settled in Harlem with his wife and their only child, Michelle. Murray quickly immersed himself in the New York literary scene and found common intellectual spirits in Ellison, the writer JAMES BALDWIN, and the artist ROMARE BEARDEN. Although he taught at Columbia University's School of Journalism in 1968, Murray devoted most of his time to writing essays for small but influential journals like the *New Leader*.

Several of these essays later appeared in his first full-length work, *The Omni-Americans* (1970), an iconoclastic manifesto that celebrated the "incontestably mulatto" culture of America at a time when the nationalistic Black Arts Movement of Larry Neal and AMIRI BARAKA was in vogue. In this volume Murray dismissed what he saw as the posturing of the Black Power movement and lambasted its guru, ELDRIDGE CLEAVER, for adopting the "pseudo-existential *esthetique du nastiness* of Norman Mailer" (178).

Murray also criticized social theorists like KENNETH B. CLARK and Daniel Patrick Moynihan, whose studies depicted the cultural deprivation of inner-city blacks. A culture that had produced Ellington, MA RAINEY, and JACK JOHNSON, Murray argued, could in no way be seen as deprived or inferior. Although White Anglo-Saxon Protestants might dominate America's

economic and legal power structure, he contended that the nation's culture "even in its most rigidly segregated precincts is patently and irrevocably composite." Black nationalists and white liberals alike, in Murray's view, were misguided in suggesting that African Americans lived outside the mainstream. Blacks—or, as he insisted, Negroes—*were* the mainstream, and their "blues idiom," the African American cultural forms of spirituals, jazz, and the blues, defined what was truly distinctive about the United States. Moreover, he concluded, "When the Negro musician or dancer swings the blues, he is fulfilling the same fundamental existential requirement that determines the mission of the poet, the priest and the medicine man" (*The Omni-Americans*, 58).

Although the *Omni-Americans* did not enjoy popular success, it received mainly favorable reviews and established the broad contours of Murray's later work: his disparagement of "social workers, liberals, and other do-gooders" who contributed to the "fakelore of black pathology"; his use of a rich southern black vernacular; and his concept of a blues idiom that spoke to the beauty, pain, and complexity of the human condition. Over the next three decades he employed a variety of literary genres to elaborate on these themes: travelogue in *South to a Very Old Place* (1971), published lecture in *The Hero and the Blues* (1973), semiautobiographical fiction in *Train Whistle Guitar* (1974) and *The Spyglass Tree* (1991), biography in *Good Morning Blues: The Autobiography of Count Basie as Told to Albert Murray*, literary correspondence in *Trading Twelves: The Selected Letters of Ralph Ellison and Albert Murray* (2001), and poetry in *Conjugations and Reiteration* (2001).

Most critics, however, regard *Stomping the Blues* (1976) as Murray's finest work, a labor of love that capitalizes on his encyclopedic knowledge of the jazz world and showcases his talent for making words swing as ebulliently as a LOUIS ARMSTRONG solo. The blues, Murray argued, speaks to our fundamental ability to improvise and persevere in the face of adversity and to transcend that hardship with creativity, not to give in to the blues, but to shake them off. As

he stated on PBS's *McNeill-Lehrer News Hour* in March 1996, "Life is rough. So are you going to cut your throat, or are you gonna get yourself together and stomp at the Savoy by 9:30 that night?" That philosophy proved highly influential not only to cultural critics such as Stanley Crouch but also to jazz musicians, notably the trumpeter and composer WYNTON MARSALIS. In the 1990s both Marsalis and Murray served on the board of New York City's prestigious "Jazz at Lincoln Center" program and influenced the center's preference for revivals of stomping "old masters," such as Basie and Ellington, over newer or more experimental jazz artists.

Three decades after the publication of *The Omni-Americans*, Albert Murray's view of the nation as a cultural hybrid seemed far less dissonant than it had in 1970. If Bill Clinton, a saxophone-playing white southerner, can be praised as America's "first black President" and inducted into the Arkansas Black Hall of Fame, then Murray's description of the "incontestably mulatto" culture of the United States seems particularly apt. Indeed, if Murray has a failing as a cultural critic, it may be that his vision has been too narrow. By focusing so exclusively on early-twentieth-century African American culture, he ignores the even greater global resonance of later black musical forms, notably soul—which he dismisses in *Stomping the Blues* as "sentimental"—and hip hop, which has developed its own idiomatic style in communities as diverse as Toledo, Tangiers, and Tokyo.

FURTHER READING

The Albert Murray papers are housed at the Houghton Library, Harvard University, Cambridge, Massachusetts.

Gates, Henry Louis, Jr. *Thirteen Ways of Looking at a Black Man* (1997).
Maguire, Roberta S., ed. *Conversations with Albert Murray* (1997).

—STEVEN J. NIVEN

MURRAY, PAULI
(20 Nov. 1910–1 July 1985), lawyer, writer, and minister, was born Anna Pauline Murray in Baltimore, Maryland, the daughter of William Henry

Pauli Murray was at the forefront of social change in the United States from the 1940s to the 1980s.
© Bettmann/CORBIS

Murray, a public school teacher, and Agnes Fitzgerald, a nurse. She had African, European, and Native American ancestry. Her parents both died when she was a child (her mother had a cerebral hemorrhage in March 1914; her father was murdered in a state hospital in June 1923), and she grew up from age three in North Carolina with her maternal grandparents and her mother's oldest sister, Pauline Fitzgerald Dame, a public school teacher who adopted her.

Murray graduated in 1926 from Hillside High School (which went only through grade eleven) in Durham, North Carolina, and then lived with relatives in New York City and graduated in 1927 from Richmond Hill High School. After working for a year in Durham for a black newspaper and a black insurance company, she returned to New York and entered Hunter College in 1928. She changed her name to Pauli, and, after time out for work and for what proved only a brief marriage (1930; later annulled), earned a BA in English in 1933. She spent a year as field representative for *Opportunity* magazine, the voice of the National Urban League. She worked for four years (1935–1939) with the Works Progress Administration as a remedial reading teacher and then with the Workers' Education Project. Wishing to return home, she applied

in 1938 for graduate study at the University of North Carolina, where her white great-grandfather had studied and his father had been a trustee, but that school rejected her because of her race.

Murray was active in civil rights in the 1940s. The first time was unintended, when she found herself arrested for "disorderly conduct" in March 1940 in Petersburg, Virginia, while taking a bus south to visit her family in North Carolina. Determined to implement what she understood of Gandhi's *Satyagraha* (nonviolent direct action)—despite what she later termed her "urge toward kamikaze defiance of Jim Crow"—she challenged the constitutionality of segregating interstate bus passengers. She courteously demanded fair treatment in jail while awaiting trial; returning to jail rather than paying the fine when she was convicted. As a result of this experience, she learned that "creative nonviolent resistance could be a powerful weapon in the struggle for human dignity." From 1940 to 1942 she worked with the Workers Defense League in a coast-to-coast campaign for a new trial for Odell Waller, a black sharecropper who, convicted by an all-white jury of men who had paid their poll taxes, was eventually executed for the murder of his landlord in Pittsylvania County in Virginia.

Murray's involvement in the Waller case led to her decision to attend law school, and she entered Howard University in 1941 "with the single-minded intention of destroying Jim Crow." During her time at Howard, she planned and participated in student sit-ins from 1943 to 1944 designed to achieve the desegregation of drugstores and cafeterias in the nation's capital. She earned a law degree at Howard University in 1944, graduating cum laude and first in her class.

Deciding to obtain a graduate degree so that she could return to teach law at Howard, she applied to Harvard Law School, but that school rejected her because of her gender. She went instead to Boalt Hall Law School at the University of California at Berkeley, where she earned an LLM in 1945 with a thesis titled "The Right to Equal Opportunity in Employment." Years later, she attended Yale University Law

School, where she earned a JDS in 1965 with a dissertation titled "Roots of the Racial Crisis: Prologue to Policy." She abandoned her plans to teach at Howard when her mentor there, Leon A. Ransom, was bypassed in 1946 for the deanship. Between her studies at Berkeley and Yale, she worked briefly as deputy attorney general in California and for the American Jewish Congress's Commission on Law and Social Action in New York, passed the bar exams in California and New York, ran as a Liberal Party candidate for a seat on the City Council from Brooklyn in 1949, and from 1946 to 1960 spent much of her time in private practice in New York, eventually (1956–1960) in the law firm of Paul, Weiss, Rifkind, Wharton, and Garrison.

Race, Murray had learned, was not the only major obstacle to a black woman's educational and professional advancement. She contributed to the constitutional theory of litigation against racial and sexual discrimination, and later put that theory into practice when she served on President John F. Kennedy's Commission on the Status of Women (1962–1963). That Commission helped to ensure that the 1964 Civil Rights Act included a ban on sex, as well as race, discrimination in employment. In 1966 she was a founding member of the National Organization for Women, established as a feminist counterpart to the NAACP. And she conceived her last major work, *Song in a Weary Throat: An American Pilgrimage* (1987), as "an autobiographical book on Jim Crow and Jane Crow" alike, on the costs of and struggles against segregation and discrimination by gender as well as by race.

Recent scholarship by the historian Doreen Drury suggests that Murray also struggled mightily in her personal life to come to terms with her transgendered sexuality. Drury argues that Murray was sexually attracted to women, but did not view herself as a lesbian. Instead, Drury posits, Murray viewed herself as a latent heterosexual male. In 1957 Murray met Irene Barlow and maintained a loving, spiritual and emotional relationship with her until Barlow's death in 1973.

As she made her political and spiritual pilgrimage through the twentieth century, Murray changed professions from time to time. Leaving her position with the New York law firm, she taught in West Africa at the Ghana Law School in Accra (1960–1961) and coauthored *The Constitution and Government of Ghana* (1961). After her studies at Yale, she served as vice president at Benedict College, a black school in South Carolina (1967–1968). In 1968 she accepted a temporary position at Brandeis University. Five years later she relinquished a tenured position there as the Louis Stulberg Professor of Law and Politics in the American Studies department, for she felt called to the Episcopal ministry, and in 1976 she earned an MDiv from the General Theological Seminary in New York City. That year the Episcopal Church changed its policy to permit the ordination of women priests, and in January 1977 at the National Cathedral in Washington, D.C., she was ordained and consecrated one of the church's first female priests and the first who was black. From 1977 to 1984 she served churches in Washington, D.C., and Baltimore, Maryland.

An accomplished writer as well as lawyer, educator, and minister, Murray also attempted to achieve social change by writing letters to newspapers and public officials, an activity she called "confrontation by typewriter." She published essays and articles in progressive magazines and in law and theology journals, and authored *States' Laws on Race and Color* (1951). That volume, the first to comprehensively catalogue the pervasiveness of racial segregation laws in almost every state in the nation, proved invaluable to the NAACP's Legal Defense Fund and others seeking to overcome Jim Crow. She wrote an account of her North Carolina family and childhood, *Proud Shoes: The Story of an American Family* (1956), a volume of poetry, *Dark Testament and Other Poems* (1970), and her posthumously published, award-winning *Song in a Weary Throat*, which was republished as *Pauli Murray: The Autobiography of a Black Activist, Feminist, Lawyer, Priest, and Poet* (1989).

At the forefront of social change in the United States from the 1940s to the 1980s, Murray achieved prominence as a lawyer, poet, educator, and minister.

She worked to promote the rights of workers during the New Deal, of African Americans, notably in the 1940s, and of women, especially in the 1960s, as she demonstrated her commitment to "consciousness combined with action" and "reconciliation as well as liberation." By the 1970s she could note with some pleasure that, though she routinely lost her legal challenges in the 1930s and 1940s, the Supreme Court eventually decided cases the way she had hoped, and she had "lived to see my lost causes found." And yet she looked in vain for "a truly integrated society," and she entered the ministry in part because, she realized, "we had reached a point where law could not give us the answers." In an afterword to her autobiography, a friend, historian Caroline F. Ware, wrote of "the tremendous energy that drove her to achieve excellence in everything she undertook." The recipient of honorary degrees and other awards, Murray retired in 1984 and died in Pittsburgh, Pennsylvania.

FURTHER READING

The Pauli Murray Papers are in the Schlesinger Library, Radcliffe College, Cambridge, Massachusetts.

Murray, Pauli. *Pauli Murray: The Autobiography of a Black Activist, Feminist, Lawyer, Priest, and Poet* (1989).

Diamonstein, Barbaralee, ed. *Open Secrets: Ninety-four Women in Touch with Our Time* (1972).

Obituaries: *Washington Post* and *New York Times*, 4 July 1985; *Jet*, 22 July 1985.

—PETER WALLENSTEIN

MURRAY, PETER MARSHALL (9 June 1888–19 Dec. 1969),

physician, was born in Houma, Louisiana, the son of John L. Murray, a longshoreman, and Louvinia Smith, a laundress and practical nurse. Murray received his BA from Dillard University in 1910. His medical degree, awarded by Howard University in 1914, was one early sign of his drive and talent, bolstered by solid preparation. Like many Howard students, he financed his medical

education by working a full-time government job, in his case a clerical post in the census bureau. But his responsibilities went beyond his own wants. His ailing mother in Louisiana also needed help, so he took a second job, a night watchman position; its sole advantage was that it gave him some time for study. After receiving his degree he remained in Washington, first as an intern at Freedmen's Hospital and then as a Howard instructor in surgery. In 1917 he married Charlotte Wallace, the daughter of a Colored Methodist Episcopal minister; the couple had one child.

By 1920, his preparation over, Murray was ready to make his own way. The path he took was that of hundreds of talented young blacks. Their destination was New York City and Harlem, and the influence Murray would exert—in the 1920s and until his death there a half-century later—in opening medicine and surgery to blacks made him as much a part of the Harlem Renaissance as JEAN TOOMER or LANGSTON HUGHES. By the mid-1920s he had performed surgery and won staff privileges in a number of New York and New Jersey hospitals, whose staffs were previously all white, including in 1928 the prestigious Harlem Hospital (where Murray was the second black physician admitted to practice and where he served until his retirement in 1953). In 1930 he was the first black physician to be board-certified in gynecology. In 1949, as a member of the Medical Society of the County of New York, the nation's largest affiliate of the American Medical Association, Murray became the first black to gain a seat in the AMA House of Delegates. From that position he pushed the AMA to officially repudiate the segregation practices of southern medical societies. Though the AMA took no action that year, Murray sensed a growing readiness, and in 1950, aided by pressure from the NAACP and from National Medical Association editor WILLIAM MONTAGUE COBB (who like Murray had been battling AMA exclusion for years), Murray won the passage of an AMA resolution urging segregated affiliates to eliminate racial restrictions. Leaving the pace of change up to the southern societies, the AMA appeal brought no immediate change, but it did put segregation under a cloud. By the mid-1950s, owing to pushing by black doctors at the local level, every southern state organization but two had integrated. Now, the way lay open for black doctors not just to mingle professionally with white physicians but also—and more important—to gain staff privileges at southern hospitals. In addition they were able to become part of the medical referral system and win appointment to state and local boards of health—all relevant to professional success and all contingent on membership in local AMA affiliates. In 1954, in recognition of Murray's achievements, his New York medical society elected him its first black president.

Murray's success in breaching white barriers was draped in irony, however. He built it not by militantly challenging white discrimination but by going along with medical segregation, to the extent of publicly acknowledging white medical superiority and black professional dependence. Had BOOKER T. WASHINGTON been alive in the pre–World War II era, he surely would have applauded Murray's strategy, for it seemed to bear out his own faith that the route to black inclusion in white society lay in hard work and accommodation to segregation.

One memorial to Murray's racial conservatism was his long campaign as leader of the all-black National Medical Association (which he served as president-elect in 1931, president in 1932, and chairman of its publications committee from 1943 to 1957) to improve black hospitals—a crusade that aimed to improve opportunities for black physicians and patients alike. That campaign also exposed the sharp division within the black medical community between those who, like Murray, supported accommodation and a minority that insisted on integration as the only moral course.

In 1932, for example, spokesmen for the latter strategy—a group led by a combative New York doctor, LOUIS TOMPKINS WRIGHT—strongly opposed the creation of a new, all-black Veterans Administration hospital in the city on the ground that it would transplant segregation to a region where it had not yet taken root. To Murray, who favored the VA facility, Wright's position was not only misguided but also demagogic. Admittedly, he told the National Medical Association (in his 1932 presidential address), demanding "our full rights" instead of half a loaf "might send a thrill down your spines." But when the issues were the welfare of thousands of black veterans and the professional needs of hundreds of black doctors, Murray felt, as did one professional correspondent, that "we must look to practical results rather than resort to cowardly cant." Discrimination was objectionable, but "we must not be so everlastingly afraid of so-called segregation that we rule ourselves out of ... opportunities. It is not the ideal America that we are dealing with.... It is a prejudiced America."

Although the VA hospital project collapsed, Murray persevered in what he saw as the more realistic approach to "prejudiced America." One critical need of black Americans was better hospital care. Not only were available facilities shockingly deficient, but also their physicians were poorly prepared and professionally torpid. To Murray the surest way to address those problems was by improving black hospitals. Usually that meant providing white directors; blacks, he lamented in 1932, simply were not capable of running their own facilities.

But black physicians would ultimately benefit. One defect of black medical education was a lack of accredited internships (a shortfall of about twenty per year). Although 1,400 approved posts went unfilled in white hospitals each year, Murray's preferred solution was not to try to open any of them to blacks but to create accredited internships by making black hospitals better. Although his foes protested, Murray's segregationist strategy usually prevailed in the councils of white foundations (such as the Duke Endowment and the Rosenwald Fund) because they found it philosophically preferable to integration. Probably Murray owed his own rise in establishment medicine to the same cause: whites liked him because he was safe, a man unlikely to make an issue of segregation.

To his credit, however, once he was inside white gates, Murray tried to push them open to other blacks—witness his effort against AMA segregation. Moreover, where black professional gains clearly depended on forcing open the doors of white institutions, Murray did not hang back. Thus, early on he lined up the NMA behind the desegregation of health department staffs, medical schools, and internships in tax-supported hospitals. Integrationists like Louis Tompkins Wright might have finally won the day, but until desegregation occurred, conservative realists like Murray pushed black medicine steadily ahead via the segregated road.

In the annals of African American history, the career of Peter Marshall Murray is in a way comparable to those of PHILLIS WHEATLEY, MATTHEW HENSON, JULIAN BOND, and EDWARD BROOKE. Just as those individuals registered important "firsts"—the first black published poet, polar explorer, major party vice presidential nominee, and modern U.S. senator—Murray, too, was a breaker of color bars, in medicine and public health. He died in New York City.

FURTHER READING

Murray's papers are in the Moorland-Spingarn Research Collection at Howard University.

Beardsley, E. H. *A History of Neglect: Health Care for Blacks and Mill Workers in the Twentieth Century South* (1987).
LOGAN, RAYFORD W. *Howard University: The First 100 Years, 1867–1967* (1969).
Murray, Peter, "Presidential Address." *Journal of the National Medical Association* 24 (Nov. 1932): 1–8.

Obituary: *New York Times*, 21 Dec. 1969.

—E. H. BEARDSLEY

N

NABRIT, SAMUEL MILTON (21 Feb. 1905–), biologist, university administrator, and public-policy maker, was born in Macon, Georgia, the son of James Madison Nabrit, a Baptist minister and educator, and Augusta Gertrude West. The elder Nabrit, who taught at Central City College and later at Walker Baptist Institute, encouraged his son to prepare for a career in higher education by studying Latin, Greek, and physics. Samuel rounded out his education by playing football and baseball, and honed his managerial and journalistic skills working on his high school (and later college) student newspaper. He entered Morehouse College in Atlanta in 1921, and after receiving a traditional liberal arts education, was awarded a BS in 1925. Samuel's brother, James Madison Nabrit Jr., was an important aide in the NAACP's legal team during the 1950s. Working closely with THURGOOD MARSHALL in his unsuccessful attempts to begin the desegregation of graduate and professional schools in Texas and Oklahoma, James later served as president of Howard University.

The precocious Nabrit's college career was so successful that he gained the attention of Morehouse president JOHN HOPE, who recruited Nabrit to teach zoology. Beginning in 1925 Nabrit taught biology while he also worked on and earned an MS at the University of Chicago. He then pursued a doctorate at Brown University in Rhode Island under the tutelage of the distinguished zoologist J. W. Wilson, and during the summers between 1927 and 1932 he conducted research on the regeneration of fish embryos at the famed Marine Biological Laboratory at Woods Hole, Massachusetts. Despite his academic achievements, Nabrit was snubbed by the renowned African American zoologist ERNEST EVERETT JUST at Woods Hole, who believed that African Americans in the sciences had to prove themselves superior to their white peers in order to deserve recognition.

Nabrit was awarded his doctorate from Brown in 1932, making him the first African American to receive a PhD from that prestigious Ivy League institution. Furthermore, his research on regeneration was published in the renowned *Biological Bulletin*, and citations of his work appeared in such important scientific publications as the *Anatomical Record*, the *Journal of Experimental Zoology*, and the *Journal of Parasitology*. Indicative of the significance of his research, his groundbreaking contributions were still being cited as late as 1980.

After receiving his doctorate, Nabrit served in two administrative posts at Atlanta University for the next twenty-three years, first as chair of the department of biology, and then after 1947 as dean of the graduate school of arts and sciences. Nabrit's most significant administrative contribution during his years as dean was his nurturing of the National Institute of Science, an organization founded in 1943 for the purpose of resolving research and teaching problems peculiar to African American scientists, most of whom were teaching at historically black colleges and universities. Nabrit also wrote articles and book reviews for journals, including *Phylon, Science Education*, and the *Negro History Bulletin*, in order to broaden the perspectives, opportunities, and expectations of African American scientists and mathematicians.

The capstone of Nabrit's administrative career came in 1955, when he was appointed president of the fledgling, all-black Texas Southern University in Houston. Serving for more than a decade, Nabrit was also appointed to key national educational association committees. Moreover, his services were welcomed by federal officials in the U.S. Department of State and the U.S. Department of Health and Human Services. Nabrit was appointed to the National Science Board by President Dwight D. Eisenhower in 1956. A decade later, President Lyndon B. Johnson appointed Nabrit to the highly controversial Atomic Energy Commission. Nabrit's long and illustrious career ended in 1981, after a fifteen-year tenure as the director of the Southern Fellowship Fund.

Despite his numerous achievements, Nabrit experienced some disappointing moments. When Allan Shivers, the arch-segregationist governor of Texas, spoke at Texas Southern University in 1956, the integrationist NAACP protested during the ceremony. As the president of a state-supported all-black college dependent on people like Shivers for funding, Nabrit was inhibited from challenging the system of segregation or offering support to such demonstrations. Although Nabrit had supported Texas Southern students in their protest against the kidnapping and torture of Felton Turner in March 1960, he created a stir among African American activists when he warned Eldrewey Stearns, a prominent Houston reformer, about the use of college students as picketers at the Loew's Theater in downtown Houston in 1961.

Nabrit, with his gradualist style of reform (an orientation similar to that of JAMES E. SHEPARD, president of the North Carolina College for Negroes), will be remembered for his concrete efforts to bring African Americans into the mainstream of American scientific and technical education.

FURTHER READING

Cole, Thomas R. *No Color Is My Kind: The Life of Eldrewey Stearns and the Integration of Houston* (1997).

Manning, Kenneth R. *Black Apollo of Science: The Life of Ernest Everett Just* (1983).

—VERNON J. WILLIAMS JR.

NELL, WILLIAM COOPER (20 Dec. 1816–25 May 1874), abolitionist and historian, was born in Boston, Massachusetts, the son of William Guion Nell, a tailor, and Louisa (maiden name unknown). His father, a prominent figure in the small but influential African American community in Boston's West End during the 1820s, was a next-door neighbor and close associate of the controversial black abolitionist DAVID WALKER. Nell studied at the all-black Smith School, which met in the basement of Boston's African Meeting House. Although he was an excellent student, in 1829 he was denied honors given to outstanding pupils by the local school board because of his race. This and similar humiliations prompted him to dedicate his life to eliminating racial barriers. To better accomplish that task, Nell read law in the office of local abolitionist William I. Bowditch in the early 1830s. Although he never practiced, his legal skills and knowledge proved valuable in the antislavery and civil rights struggles of his era.

Nell naturally gravitated toward the emerging abolitionist crusade. In 1831 he became an errand boy for the *Liberator*, the leading antislavery journal, beginning a long and close relationship with its editor, William Lloyd Garrison. His talents were quickly recognized, and he was soon made a printer's apprentice, then a clerk in the paper's operations. In the latter position, which he assumed in 1840, he wrote articles, supervised the paper's Negro Employment Office, arranged meetings, corresponded with other abolitionists, and represented Garrison at various antislavery functions. The pay was low, so he was forced to supplement his income by advertising his services as a bookkeeper and copyist. But he remained one of Garrison's most ardent supporters, even as the Boston abolitionist grew increasingly controversial because of his singular devotion to moral rather than political means and his embrace of a wide variety of reforms.

After the antislavery movement divided into two hostile camps in 1840 over questions of appropriate tactics and women's role, Nell vehemently criticized those black abolitionists who parted company with Garrison. He moved to Rochester, New York, in 1848 and helped FREDERICK DOUGLASS publish the *North Star*. But when growing conflict between Garrison and Douglass forced him to choose sides, he returned to Boston and the *Liberator*. In 1856 Nell traveled through lower Canada West (now Ontario) and the Midwest, visiting black communities, attending antislavery meetings, and submitting regular reports to the *Liberator*. His accounts of this journey are a useful record of African American life in those areas at the time.

Nell was perhaps the most outspoken and consistent advocate of racial integration in the antebellum United States. He worked closely with white reformers and regularly pressed other blacks to abandon "all separate action, and becom[e] part and parcel of the general community" (Smith, 184). Nell participated in a statewide campaign to end segregated "Jim Crow" cars on Massachusetts railroads in the early 1840s. He used the antislavery press as a vehicle to attack black exclusion from or segregation in churches, schools and colleges, restaurants, hotels, militia units, theaters, and other places of entertainment.

From 1840 to 1855 Nell led a successful petition campaign to integrate the public schools of Boston, which ended when the Massachusetts legislature outlawed racially separate education in the state. He even opposed the existence of voluntary separatism among African Americans. In 1843 he represented Boston at the National Convention of Colored Citizens in Buffalo and used that forum as a vehicle to speak out against exclusive black gatherings and activism. An outspoken critic of the black churches, he often attended the predominantly white Memorial Meeting House in West Roxbury.

But Nell supported separate black organizations when they met needs not performed by integrated ones. For example, in 1842 he helped establish the Freedom Association, a local black group founded to aid and protect fugitive slaves. He remained active in this group for four years until the interracial Boston Vigilance Committee was founded for the same purpose. Although he established numerous cultural and literary societies—most notably the Adelphic Union and the Boston Young Men's Literary Society—among Boston blacks after 1830, these were always open to individuals of every race and class.

Nell tempered his opposition to politics and exclusive black activism in the early 1850s. He was nominated by the Free-Soil party for the Massachusetts legislature in 1850. After the Fugitive Slave Act of 1850 was passed, he stepped up his role in local Underground Railroad activities until illness forced his temporary retirement from the antislavery stage.

About this time Nell began extensive research on the African American experience in the United States. He perceived that black history and memory would help shape the identity of his race and advance the struggle against slavery and racial prejudice. His research resulted in the publication of *Services of Colored Americans in the Wars of 1776 and 1812* (1851), *Colored Patriots of the American Revolution* (1855), and dozens of articles and pamphlets. The careful scholarship and innovative use of oral sources in Nell's works, which were far broader than their titles suggest, made them the most useful and important histories of African Americans written in the Civil War era.

Nell's historical activism also took a more popular turn. In 1858 he organized the first of seven annual CRISPUS ATTUCKS Day celebrations in Boston to honor African American heroes of the American Revolution. Held the fifth day of every March in Faneuil Hall, the festivities consisted of speeches, martial music, displays of revolutionary war relics, and the recollections of aged black veterans. These gatherings symbolically rejected the decision of the U.S. Supreme Court in *Dred Scott v. Sandford* (1857), which unequivocally denied black claims to American citizenship. Nell also petitioned the Massachusetts state legislature on numerous occasions for an Attucks monument in Boston.

When the Civil War came, Nell embraced the Union cause, anticipating the end of slavery and racial inequality in American life. His hopes were buoyed in 1861, when he was employed as a postal clerk in the Boston post office. This made him the first African American appointed to a position in the U.S. government, and he held the job until his death. He was further encouraged by the Emancipation Proclamation and the decision to enlist black troops in the Union army.

The end of the war brought a series of personal changes for Nell. When the *Liberator* ceased operations in December 1865, it marked the denouement of Nell's lengthy career in reform journalism. But it did not mean the abandonment of activism; during the late 1860s he waged a successful campaign to end racial discrimination in theaters and other public places in Boston. Nell married Frances A. Amers of New Hampshire in 1869; they had two sons. He spent the remainder of his life completing a study of African American troops in the Civil War. It was apparently unfinished when he died in Boston of "paralysis of the brain."

FURTHER READING

Nell's published letters and editorials are available in the microfilm edition of *The Black Abolitionist Papers*, C. Peter Ripley, ed.

Horton, James O. "Generations of Protest: Black Families and Social Reform in Ante-Bellum Boston." *New England Quarterly* 94 (1976): 242–256.

Horton, James O., and Lois E. Horton. *Black Bostonians: Family Life and Community Struggle in the Antebellum North* (1979).

Smith, Robert P. "William Cooper Nell: Crusading Black Abolitionist." *Journal of Negro History* 55 (1970): 182–199.

Wesley, Dorothy Porter. "Integration versus Separatism: William Cooper Nell's Role in the Struggle for Equality" in *Courage and Conscience: Black and White Abolitionists in Boston*, ed. Donald M. Jacobs (1993).

Obituary: *Pacific Appeal* (San Francisco), 18 July 1874.

—ROY E. FINKENBINE

 NEWTON, HUEY P.
(17 Feb. 1942–22 Aug. 1989), leader of the Black Panther Party, was born Huey Percy Newton in Monroe, Louisiana, the son of Amelia Johnson Newton and Walter Newton, a sharecropper and Baptist preacher. Walter Newton so admired Louisiana's populist governor Huey P. Long that he named his seventh and youngest son after him. A proud, powerful man, Newton defied the regional convention that forced most black women into domestic service and never allowed his wife to work outside the home. He always juggled several jobs to support his large family. Like thousands of black southerners drawn to employment in the war industries, the Newtons migrated to California during the 1940s. Settling in Oakland, the close-knit family struggled to shelter young Huey but could not stop the mores of the ghetto from shaping his life. Years later, those same ghetto neighborhoods became the springboard of the Black Panther Party that thrust Newton into national prominence.

While attending Oakland's Merritt College, Newton met BOBBY SEALE, a married student recently discharged

Huey Newton, shown here in 1967 at the headquarters of the Black Panther Party, which he founded with BOBBY SEALE in 1966. © Ted Streshinsky/CORBIS

from the army, when they became involved in developing a black studies curriculum. Discovering that they both felt impatient with student activism in the face of blatant discrimination and police violence, the two formed a new organization in October 1966. Adopting the symbol of the all-black political party in Lowndes County, Alabama, that Black Power spokesman STOKELY CARMICHAEL had helped organize, they named their organization the Black Panther Party for Self-Defense.

Seale and Newton wrote out a ten-point platform and program for the group, demanding as its first point "power to determine the destiny of our black community." The program outlined aspirations for better housing, education, and employment opportunities and called for an end to police brutality. It insisted that blacks be tried by juries of their peers, that all black prisoners be released because none had received fair trials, and that blacks be exempted from military service. It concluded with a quotation from the Declaration of Independence asserting the right to revolution.

Initiating patrols to prevent abusive behavior by local police, the disciplined, uniformly dressed young Panthers immediately attracted attention. Wearing black leather jackets and black berets, the men and women openly carried weapons on their patrols. These acts were legal under the gun laws then in force, but the California legislature swiftly acted to prohibit the patrols in July 1967.

The Black Panthers were buoyed along by the current of dissent and protest surging through black communities. As in other urban areas, Oakland's black families felt a deep sense of injustice at the treatment meted out by the police, and the Black Panther Party continued to attract members. In October 1967 Newton was wounded following a late-night traffic stop in which Oakland police officer John Frey was killed. Upon his arrest, the startling news that the minister of defense of the Black Panther Party was accused of killing a white policeman was broadcast nationally. Police killings of black youths had triggered numerous riots and urban uprisings, but in all the previous incidents no policemen had been killed. Newton's indictment for murdering Frey threw

a spotlight over Oakland's Black Panther Party. Soon, Charles R. Garry, a prominent San Francisco trial attorney, took up Newton's legal defense, and the Black Panther's minister of information, ELDRIDGE CLEAVER, initiated the "Free Huey" movement that made Newton internationally famous.

Newton's case became the centerpiece of a massive mobilization campaign advocating the Black Panther Party program. Membership soared. During the murder trial in the summer of 1968, a fateful year marked by the assassinations of the Reverend MARTIN LUTHER KING JR. and U.S. senator and presidential candidate Robert Kennedy, thousands of supporters flocked to rallies outside the Oakland courthouse. The international effort in defense of Newton succeeded in blocking his conviction (and execution) for murder, but the jury found him guilty of manslaughter.

Newton openly advocated revolutionary changes in the relationship between poor blacks and the larger white society and concentrated on the untapped potential of what he called the urban "lumpen proletariat" to forge a vanguard party. The "Free Huey" movement galvanized blacks, resulting in phenomenal growth and the development of a national Black Panther Party buoyed by the rallying cry "All Power to the People!" The Panthers advocated self-determination to replace the racist, economic subjugation of blacks they viewed as "colonialism." By the time Newton was released following a successful appeal in 1970, the Black Panther Party had offices in more than thirty cities, including New York, Philadelphia, Chicago, and Los Angeles. It had established an international section in Algeria and inspired the creation of similar organizations in Israel, the West Indies, and India.

As were numerous leaders and members of the Black Panther Party, Newton was subjected to nearly constant surveillance, police harassment, frequent arrests, and a barrage of politically inspired invasions of privacy. He faced two retrials on the manslaughter charge but was never again convicted of killing Frey (both trials ended in hung juries). In the meantime, Panther leaders in Los Angeles and Chicago were shot to death in 1969 under circumstances in which special police units

worked secretly with federal intelligence agents—many of the criminal charges brought against Panthers resulted from clandestine police-FBI collaborations engineered by COINTELPRO (the U.S. government's counterintelligence program). Between 1968 and 1973, thousands of Panthers were arrested, hundreds were tried and imprisoned, while thirty-four were killed in police raids, shoot-outs, or internal conflicts.

Newton's symbolic appeal to young blacks was powerful, especially because of the defiant resistance to police authority he represented. Such conduct had never been so central to any previous black leader, and it shocked many who were accustomed to a more restrained demeanor. Newton, who often expressed the belief that it was crucial "to capture the peoples' imagination" in order to build a successful revolutionary movement, was more effective as a catalyst than as a traditional leader. Newton was not an especially captivating speaker or skilled political organizer; rather his talent lay in inspiring a small group of exceptionally talented individuals, directing their energies, and eliciting a loyalty so profound that they were willing to risk their lives building the revolutionary organization he founded.

The unique way the Black Panther Party fused conflicting elements within one organization paid tribute to Newton's vision. Free breakfasts for schoolchildren and other programs provided community service, but unlike other reformers, the Panthers also simultaneously engaged in electoral politics and challenged the imperialist domination of blacks—all with a flamboyant bravado. While the traditional civil rights organizations sought "first-class citizenship," the Panthers viewed the legacy of slavery, segregation, and racism as a form of colonialism in which blacks were subjects, not citizens of the United States; instead of seeking integration, the Panthers identified with the struggles of other colonized Africans and Asians, and sought black liberation.

The Black Panthers were not ideologically consistent over time; the party moved from a nationalism inspired by MALCOLM X to a Marxist anti-imperialism influenced by Frantz Fanon, Che Guevara, and Mao Tse Tung and finally into a synthesis that Newton called "intercommunalism," which he claimed was required by the collapse of the nation state within the global economy. Although the Black Panthers remained an all-black organization, it forged coalitions with other radical groups involving whites, Asians, and Latinos. The volatile mixture of external repression, internal dissension, and an escalating use of purges led to several highly publicized expulsions that divided the governing central committee.

Precipitated by Newton's denunciation and expulsion of Eldridge Cleaver and the entire International Section in February 1971, the Black Panther Party broke into rival factions, a division the press named the "Newton-Cleaver split." The factions were loosely defined by ideological differences. Whereas the Newton-controlled portion of the party abruptly backtracked and began to advocate moderate solutions to black oppression—and ceased to attract new members—those opposing Newton escalated their devotion to revolutionary tactics and coalesced around a network of freedom fighters who eventually formed the underground Black Liberation Army.

An increasingly paranoid Newton took bold steps to consolidate his personal supremacy over the volatile organization, and as chapters dwindled or were closed, he introduced the "survival pending revolution" program. While the Panthers publicly engaged in conventional political and economic activities, Newton, who had become heavily addicted to cocaine, led the organization into subterranean criminal activities. Following indictments brought against him for assaulting several Oakland residents, including a prostitute who later died, Newton fled to Cuba in 1974. He left behind an organization virtually in shambles, saddled with an Internal Revenue Service investigation into its finances, and dwindling numbers of supporters. Even party chairman Bobby Seale repudiated the unsavory developments and left the organization.

En route to Cuba, Newton married his secretary, Gwen Fontaine. Following his return in 1976, Newton was tried on assault and murder charges but was not convicted. He then enrolled in the History of Consciousness program on the Santa Cruz campus of the University of California. He received his PhD from that program in 1980, by which time the Black Panther Party had virtually

disbanded. Although a small retinue of supporters continued to be drawn to Newton's strong personal magnetism, he ceased to function as the leader of a revolutionary movement. By 1982 his marriage had ended in divorce and the last vestige of the Black Panther Party, its Youth Institute, had closed for lack of funds.

Newton married Frederika Slaughter of Oakland in 1984. His repeated efforts to overcome alcohol and cocaine addiction were not successful, and he briefly spent time in prison in 1987 for a probation violation. Early on the morning of 22 August 1989 Newton was shot and killed in Oakland by a twenty-five-year-old crack dealer whom he had insisted give him drugs free because of who he was. Newton's flamboyance, vision, and passion came to symbolize an entire era, yet in the end, the same demons that ravaged the community he had sought to transform destroyed him as well.

FURTHER READING

Huey P. Newton's papers, which include a significant amount of legal material, are housed at the Department of Special Collections, Stanford University Library.

Newton, Huey P. *Revolutionary Suicide* (1973; repr. 1995).

Hilliard, David, and Don Weise, eds. *The Huey P. Newton Reader* (2002).
Jeffries, Judson L. *Huey P. Newton: The Radical Theorist* (2002)
Keating, Edward M. *Free Huey* (1970).
Van Peebles, Mario, with Ula Y. Taylor and J. Tarika Lewis. *Panther* (1995).

Obituary: *New York Times*, 23 Aug. 1989.
—KATHLEEN N. CLEAVER

NIGGER ADD (1845?– 24 Mar. 1926), cowboy, roper, and bronc rider, also known as Negro Add or Old Add, was born Addison Jones, reportedly in Gonzales County, Texas; his father and mother are unknown. The early life of Add is clouded in conjecture. He may have been a slave on the George W. Littlefield plantation in Panola County, Mississippi, and relocated with the Littlefields when they settled in Gonzales County, Texas, in 1850. It is also possible that he was born in

Gonzales County and was purchased by the Littlefields after they arrived. There is no record of his youth and early adulthood.

There are many stories about Add in cowboy memoirs and biographies, but the only name given is Nigger Add or Old Negro Add. It apparently seemed of little consequence in cowboy country that Add had a last name. (Addison Jones's full name was revealed in print for the first time by Connie Brooks in 1993.) Contemporaries who spoke or wrote about Add agreed, however, that he was an outstanding cowboy and bronc buster. Vivian H. Whitlock, who cowboyed with Add for several years on the LFD ranch in Texas and eastern New Mexico, called him "the most famous Negro cowpuncher of the Old West." J. Evetts Haley, biographer of George W. Littlefield, called him "the most noted Negro cowboy that ever 'topped off' a horse."

Add's reputation with horses was due to his ability, as he used to say, "to look a horse square in the eye and almost tell what it was thinking" and to ride every horse he saddled, with one exception. Add is reported to have been thrown only by a bronc named Whistling Bullet. In typical cowboy fashion Add tried Whistling Bullet again, and according to Pat Boone, a district judge in Littlefield, Texas, he was the only man to ride him.

While the work of "taking the first pitch out of a bronc" often fell to black cowboys, Add performed this task with a special skill, daring, and raw nerve. Several cowboys commented that they saw Add perform this feat on various occasions. According to Haley,

He would tie a rope hard and fast around his hips, hem a horse up in the corner of a corral or in the open pasture, rope him around the neck as he went past at full speed, and where another man would have been dragged to death, Add would, by sheer skill and power on the end of a rope, invariably flatten the horse out on the ground.

(184)

Cowboys from neighboring ranches often worked round-ups together, and Add, who was known and respected by ranchers and cowboys of eastern New Mexico and West Texas, was a familiar sight. N. Howard "Jack" Thorp, noted cowboy song collector and songwriter, spoke of camping with Add and a group of black cowhands from South Texas in March 1889 at the beginning of his first song-hunting trek. Later Thorp helped to ensure Add's place in history by writing a cowboy song titled "Whose Old Cow?" that in a humorous fashion recognized Add's ability to identify earmarks and brands.

As cowboys gained experience in the cattle business, they rose from the rank of tenderfoot to top hand or even range boss or foreman. Thorp, in fact, referred to Add as the LFD outfit's range boss. West Texas black cowboys, however, had little chance to pass cowboy status, as was suggested by Whitlock: "He [Add] was a good cowhand, but because of the custom in those days, never became what was known as a 'top' hand." There also was a certain unwritten yet generally understood deference black cowboys were expected to extend to their white counterparts. This situation was the legacy of slavery, which crossed the frontier with the settlers, ranchers, and cowboys. A black cowboy who challenged those traditions did so at his peril.

Add at various times came up to that line and sometimes crossed it. One white cowboy, Mat Jones, said that Add was "a privileged character" (*Fiddle-footed* [1966]). This may have referred to the fact that he was well liked or even protected by LFD officials. Jones told a story that became legend on the LFD about Cliff Robertson, a white cowboy who came from a neighboring ranch as a "rep," or representative. Ranches often sent reps who were seasoned cowboys to other ranches during round-ups to make sure that their stock was identified, properly branded, and returned to their home ranch. Add rode up to change his horse and said to Robertson, "What horse do you want, lint?" The term "lint" was a derisive one that referred to a young, inexperienced cowboy from East Texas with cotton lint still in his hair. Robertson tried to catch his own horse and threw a lasso and missed. Add then threw his rope and caught the horse and began to drag it out. Robertson, feeling insulted and embarrassed, came after Add with his rope doubled, or, as some cowboys said, with a knife to cut the rope. At this point Bud Wilkerson, the LFD's range wagon boss, rode between them and said to Add, "Drag

the horse out, and I will tend to the lint." Robertson was so angered by the experience that he cut out his horses and went back to his home ranch.

Add, like many cowboys, traveled to other ranches where he could not depend on the protection and goodwill of the LFD. Jones related another story when Add was the LFD rep at the Hat ranch and breached the proper etiquette for a black cowboy. Add went to drink from a water bucket and, finding it empty, followed a standard cowboy procedure that he apparently used on the LFD without thought. He began to siphon water through a hose attached to a large water tank. To get the water started, Add used a method referred to as "sucking the gut." As Add was in the process of starting the water, a white cowboy named Tom Ogles picked up a neck yoke and hit him on the back of the neck, knocking him out. When he regained consciousness, Add, who was reported to have knocked out a black man from a neighboring town with one punch and was described by everyone as stocky, short, and very powerfully built, did nothing. He waited for the remuda to arrive, got his horse, and rode home. This incident provided ample evidence that Add recognized the limitations that society had placed on him.

Add's reputation as a roper also gained him respect and renown. He was able, according to some of his fellow cowboys, to go into a corral and rope any horse with uncanny accuracy. One roping story told by Whitlock attests to Add's roping talents as well as his sense of cowboy humor. One day Add was sitting on his horse in front of the Grand Central Hotel in Roswell, New Mexico, when a runaway team of horses pulling a milk wagon came racing down the street. He made a big loop in his lariat, rode alongside the team, threw it around the horses' heads, and allowed the slack to drape over the wagon. He then turned his horse off in a steer-roping style and caused the wagon, horses, and milk bottles to crash and scatter all over the street. After Add retrieved his rope, he was reported to have said, "Them hosses sure would've torn things up if I hadn't caught them."

Addison Jones was more fortunate than many black cowboys west of the Pecos in that he found someone locally to marry. It was not uncommon for

black men in West Texas either to travel back to East Texas to find a wife or to remain single. In 1899 Add and Rosa Haskins were married by Rev. George W. Read. Add gave his age as fifty-four, while his bride was listed as thirty-six. Haskins, who was a cook and domestic for a number of prominent Roswell families, came to New Mexico from Texas sixteen years before she married Add. There is very little to indicate whether the couple enjoyed marital bliss, but according to Thorp, the announcement of the wedding to a few friends prompted ranchers throughout the Pecos valley to send wedding gifts to Old Add. The lack of a wedding registry and communications may have been the reason that Add and Rosa found nineteen cookstoves at the freight office in Roswell when they came to pick up their wedding presents.

Add's life was lived and ended, according to former Texas and New Mexico sheriff Bob Beverly, the way an old cowboy's life should be:

Add...realized his work was over. He had ridden the most dangerous trails and had conquered the wildest horses. He had always been thoroughly loyal to the Littlefields and the Whites. He was at the end of his road and he laid down and died knowing full well that his efforts had been recognized and appreciated by the really great cowmen of Texas and New Mexico.

(Bonney, 141)

Addison Jones died in Roswell and, according to Elvis Fleming, suffered a final double indignity of having his name misspelled and the improper birth data carved into his tombstone. The name on Add's grave is Allison Jones, with a birth date of 24 March 1856, rather than 1845. Old Add lived an ordinary yet extraordinary life as a black cowboy in West Texas and New Mexico. He succeeded in living a life worth remembering, which was something few cowboys, black or white, were able to achieve.

FURTHER READING

Bonney, Cecil. *Looking over My Shoulder: Seventy-five Years in the Pecos Valley* (1971).
Brooks, Connie. *The Last Cowboys: Closing the Open Range in Southeastern New Mexico, 1890s-1920s* (1993).
Fleming, Elvis E. "Addison Jones, Famous Black Cowboy of the Old West" in *Treasures of History III*, Historical Society for Southeast New Mexico (1995): 34–46.

Haley, J. Evetts. *George W. Littlefield, Texan* (1943).

Whitlock, Vivian H. *Cowboy Life on the Llano Estacado* (1970).

—MICHAEL N. SEARLES

NIXON, EDGAR DANIEL

(12 July 1899–25 Feb. 1987), Alabama civil rights leader, was born in Robinson Springs, Alabama, near Montgomery, the son of Wesley Nixon, a tenant farmer and, in later years, a Primitive Baptist preacher, and Susan Chappell. Nixon's mother died when he was nine, and thereafter he was reared in Montgomery by a paternal aunt, Winnie Bates, a laundress. Nixon attained only an elementary education, and at thirteen began full-time work, first in a meat-packing plant, then on construction crews, and in 1918 as a baggage handler at the Montgomery railway station. As a result of friendships that he made in this last job, he managed in 1923 to become a Pullman car porter, a position he would hold until his retirement in 1964. In 1927 he was married to Alleas Curry, a schoolteacher. The couple soon separated, but they had Nixon's only child. In 1934 he married Arlet Campbell.

Exposed by his railroad travels to the world beyond Montgomery, Nixon grew increasingly to hate racial segregation. He became a devoted follower of A. PHILIP RANDOLPH, who was attempting in the late 1920s and early 1930s to unionize the all-black Pullman porters. In 1938 Nixon was chosen as president of the new union's Montgomery local. In 1943 he organized the Alabama Voters League to support a campaign to obtain voter registration for Montgomery's blacks. The effort produced a vigorous white counterattack, but Nixon himself was registered in 1945.

Montgomery's blacks were sharply divided between a middle-class professional community centered around the campus of Alabama State College for Negroes and the working-class blacks who lived on the city's west side. The Montgomery branch of the National Association for the Advancement of Colored People (NAACP) was dominated by college-area professionals and failed to support Nixon's voter registration drive actively. Nixon therefore began organizing the poorer blacks of west Montgomery, where he resided, to attempt a takeover of the branch. He was defeated for branch president in 1944 but was elected in 1945 and reelected in 1946 in bitterly contentious races. In 1947 he was elected president of the Alabama Conference of NAACP Branches, ousting the incumbent, Birmingham newspaper editor Emory O. Jackson. But national NAACP officials, who were hostile to his lack of education, quietly arranged for Nixon's defeat for reelection to the state post in 1949. And in 1950 he also lost the presidency of the Montgomery branch to the same man he had beaten in 1945. Nevertheless, in 1952 he won election as president of the Montgomery chapter of the Progressive Democratic Association, an organization of Alabama's black Democrats. And in 1954 he created consternation among Montgomery's whites by becoming a candidate to represent his precinct on the county Democratic Executive Committee. Though he was unsuccessful, he thus became the first black to seek public office in the city in the twentieth century.

During his years with the NAACP, Nixon had become a friend of ROSA PARKS, the branch secretary during much of this period. When Parks was arrested on the afternoon of 1 December 1955 for violating Montgomery's ordinance requiring racially segregated seating on buses, she called Nixon for help. After he bailed her out of jail, he began telephoning other black leaders to suggest a boycott of the buses on the day of Parks's trial, 5 December, to demonstrate support for her. The proposal was one that black leaders had frequently discussed in the past, and it was greeted enthusiastically by many of them. The black Women's Political Council circulated leaflets urging the action, and a meeting of black ministers gave it their approval. The boycott on 5 December was so complete that black leaders decided to continue it until the city and the bus company agreed to adopt the plan of seating segregation in use in Mobile, under which passengers already seated could not be unseated. The Montgomery Improvement Association was formed to run this extended boycott, and Nixon became its treasurer.

Nixon, however, became increasingly antagonistic toward the association's president, the Reverend MARTIN LUTHER KING JR. Nixon viewed King as an ally of the Alabama State College professionals, and he believed that King's growing fame was depriving him, and the poorer blacks whom he represented, of due credit for the boycott's success. After King moved to Atlanta in 1960, Nixon engaged in a protracted struggle for leadership of Montgomery's blacks with funeral director Rufus A. Lewis, the most prominent figure among his rivals in the middle-class Alabama State community. The contest culminated in the 1968 presidential election, when Nixon and Lewis served on alternative slates of electors, each of which was pledged to Hubert H. Humphrey. The Lewis slate defeated the Nixon slate handily in Montgomery. Nixon thereafter slipped into a deeply embittered obscurity. He accepted a job organizing recreational activities for young people in one of Montgomery's poorest public housing projects, a position he held until just before his death in Montgomery.

FURTHER READING

The Library of Alabama State University, Montgomery, holds several scrapbooks of clippings and other material related to Nixon. Transcripts of oral history interviews with Nixon are held at Alabama State University; the Martin Luther King Center, Atlanta; and Howard University, Washington, D.C. See also the Montgomery NAACP Branch Correspondence, NAACP Papers, Library of Congress.

Baldwin, Lewis V., and Aprille V. Woodson. *Freedom Is Never Free: A Biographical Portrait of Edgar Daniel Nixon, Sr.* (1992).

Garrow, David J. *Bearing the Cross: Martin Luther King Jr. and the Southern Christian Leadership Conference* (1986).

Mills Thornton, J., III. *Dividing Lines: Municipal Politics and the Struggle for Civil Rights in Montgomery, Birmingham, and Selma* (2002).

Obituary: *New York Times*, 27 Feb. 1987.

—J. MILLS THORNTON

NORMAN, JESSYE

(15 Sept. 1945–), opera singer, was born in Augusta, Georgia, to Silas Norman, an insurance salesman who also sang in the church choir, and Janie

King, a secretary and accomplished amateur pianist. The Normans made certain that their five children studied piano and they encouraged Jessye to sing in church and community programs at a very early age. A 78 rpm recording of Brahms's *Alto Rhapsody*, sung by MARIAN ANDERSON, was one of Norman's most powerful inspirations. At age ten, she recounts, "I heard her voice and I listened.... And I wept, not knowing anything about what it meant" (Gurewitsch, 96).

After graduating with honors from Augusta's Lucy Craft Laney High School in 1963, Norman went on to study voice with Carolyn Grant at Howard University in Washington, D.C. During the summer after her graduation in 1967, she attended the Peabody Conservatory in Baltimore, Maryland, after which she studied voice with Pierre Bernac and Elizabeth Mannion at the University of Michigan, receiving a Master of Music degree in 1968.

Norman's professional career began overseas in 1968 after she won first

Jessye Norman, in dress rehearsal for her debut at the New York Metropolitan Opera in the role of Cassandra in Berlioz's Les Troyens, *1983.*
© Bettmann/CORBIS

prize in an International Music Competition sponsored by Bavarian Radio in Munich, Germany. The following year she signed a three-year contract with Deutsche Oper Berlin, and made her triumphant operatic debut on 12 December 1969 as Elisabeth in Richard Wagner's *Tannhäuser*—a demanding role for a twenty-four-year-old. In 1972 she made her professional American debut in Verdi's *Aïda* at the Hollywood Bowl in Los Angeles, with James Levine conducting. Throughout the 1970s Norman's opulent voice and extraordinary intelligence continued to draw rave reviews and she was booked in concerts and festivals worldwide.

Norman's debut with the Metropolitan Opera in New York City in September 1983 propelled her to new heights of popularity, especially with American audiences. The Met featured Norman as the tormented prophetess Cassandra, in Berlioz's epic *Les Troyens*, a role she had sung in 1972 at Covent Garden in London. At subsequent performances, Norman changed roles from the dark-hued mezzo-soprano of Cassandra to the rich, searing soprano of Dido. Because of her gifts in character portrayal, she was able to interpret and delineate each role with authority and a profound sense of tragedy.

Norman's other performances with the Met include twenty-two performances as the Prima Donna/Ariadne in Richard Strauss's *Ariadne auf Naxos* and the Wagner roles of Elisabeth in *Tannhäuser*, Kundry in *Parsifal*, and Sieglinde in *Die Walküre*. Norman has lent her hypnotic, expressive, and robust voice to modern work as well. Critics called her richly dramatic interpretation of Schoenberg's *Erwartung* a tour de force, and praised her performances in Bartok's *Bluebeard's Castle*, Poulenc's *Dialogues of the Carmelites*, and Stravinsky's *Oedipus Rex*.

Primary among Norman's unique talents is her wide vocal range. She can move with grace and sensitivity from a sparkling high C-sharp to a voluptuous middle range to a rich low G. Her ability to draw expressive power and color from her roles has encouraged diversity within her repertoire as well. She maintains, "I don't allow myself to be cast in a particular repertoire—or *only* in a particular repertoire—because

I like to sing what I'm able to sing" (Gurewitsch, 99). Her curiosity has also drawn her to the less standard works, such as those of Monteverdi, Rameau, Purcell, Stravinsky, Schoenberg, and Philip Glass, which challenge her passions as well as her intellect. She opened Lyric Opera of Chicago's 1990–1991 season in Robert Wilson's innovative production of Gluck's *Alceste*. To understand the intense emotions of Phèdre in Rameau's opera, *Hipployte et Aricie*, she read Racine. Norman strives to know her characters completely, visualizing the minutest details of every scene.

Performing under such distinguished conductors as Claudio Abbado, Riccardo Muti, Colin Davis, Daniel Barenboim, and Seiji Ozawa in orchestras around the world, Norman has honed a signature style and repertoire, which includes Isolde's impassioned "Liebestod" from Wagner's *Tristan und Isolde*, which she sang with the New York Philharmonic in 1989. Norman is also famous for her stunning interpretations of Mahler's *Das Lied von der Erde* and Richard Strauss's *Four Last Songs*, about which music critic Robert C. Marsh wrote, "If we must die, let us go with Jessye Norman singing" (*Chicago Sun-Times*, 21 Oct. 1986). In August 2002 she sang Alban Berg's romantic *Seven Early Songs* with the Metropolitan Opera Orchestra in Baden Baden, Germany.

Recitals with piano, which allow her to explore the art song repertoire, as well as spirituals and popular music, have especially appealed to the singer. In any language she always knows the meaning behind every word, each of which is lovingly caressed through her singing. "Time and again she found just the right inflection or color to illuminate the text," explains Derrick Henry (*Atlanta Journal-Constitution*, 11 Mar. 1989).

In 2000 Norman premiered Judith Wier's song cycle, *woman.life.song*. Based on texts by TONI MORRISON, MAYA ANGELOU, and Clarissa Pinkola Estes, the work was commissioned for Norman by Carnegie Hall. Norman's collaborations with other African American artists include performing the sacred music of DUKE ELLINGTON, and theatrical partnerships with the ALVIN AILEY Repertory Dance Ensemble, and the choreographer BILL T. JONES.

Jessye Norman's brilliant career is reflected in the numerous awards and honors she has received. A prolific recording artist, Norman has recorded more than seventy albums her recordings—from Purcell and Beethoven to Cole Porter and jazz—number more than seventy, among them her 2003 recording of Mahler's *Kindertotenlieder* commemorating the 150th anniversary of the Vienna Philharmonic. She is the recipient of four Grammy Awards, a *Grand Prix National du Disque*, a Gramophone Award, and an Edison Prize. A special favorite in France, she received the title *Commandeur de l'Ordre des Arts et des Lettres* in 1984 and the *Legion d'Honneur* from President François Mitterrand in 1989. She holds over thirty honorary doctoral degrees from universities, including Brandeis, Harvard, the University of Michigan, and Howard. In 1997 she became the youngest recipient of a Kennedy Center Honors award, and in 1999 President Clinton invited her to sing at the White House for the fiftieth anniversary celebration of the North Atlantic Treaty Organization.

In 1990 Jessye Norman was appointed an honorary U.N. ambassador. She has also served on the board of directors of numerous organizations, including the Lupus Foundation, the New York Public Library, the New York Botanical Garden, the Dance Theatre of Harlem, the National Music Foundation, and the Elton John AIDS foundation. The Amphitheater and Plaza overlooking the Savannah River in Norman's hometown of Augusta have been named for her.

With all her glories, however, Norman has managed to retain her unpretentious demeanor. She has a quick wit and a smile that "hits the eyes like the sudden opening of Venetian blinds on a sunny day" (*Current Biography Yearbook* [1976], 295). A tall woman (five feet, ten inches) with a large, imposing frame, she had a ready answer to a friend who asked how she managed to get up after falling in Dido's suicide scene. With a wink, she said, "I choreographed every muscle beforehand." Norman is active in community affairs, especially in helping to promote historically black educational institutions. A dignified artist with elegance, poise, and grace, Jessye Norman has brought joy and wisdom to both her art and her audiences.

FURTHER READING

The Metropolitan Opera Archives, New York, contains press clippings, reviews, cast lists, and other production information relating to Norman's career.

Gurewitsch, Matthew. "The Norman Conquests." *Connoisseur*, Jan. 1987, 96–101.
Mayer, Martin. "Double Header." *Opera News*, 18 Feb. 1984, 9–11.
Story, Rosalyn M. *And So I Sing: African-American Divas of Opera and Concert* (1990).

—ELISE K. KIRK

NORTHUP, SOLOMON

(July 1808–1863?), author, was born in Minerva, New York, the son of Mintus Northup, a former slave from Rhode Island who had moved to New York with his master early in the 1800s and subsequently been manumitted. Though Solomon lived with both his parents and wrote fondly of both, he does not mention his mother's name or provide any details regarding her background, except to comment that she was a quadroon. She died during Solomon's captivity (1841–1853), whereas Mintus died on 22 November 1829, just as Solomon reached manhood. Mintus was manumitted upon the death of his master, and shortly thereafter he moved from Minerva to Granville in Washington County. There he and his wife raised Solomon and his brother Joseph, and for the rest of his life Mintus remained in that vicinity, working as an agricultural laborer in Sandy Hill and other villages. He acquired sufficient property to be registered as a voter—a notable accomplishment in those days for a former slave.

As a youth Solomon did farm labor alongside his father. Only a month after the death of Mintus, Solomon was married to Anne Hampton, and he soon began to do other kinds of work as well. He worked on repairing the Champlain Canal and was employed for several years as a raftsman on the waterways of upstate New York. During these years, 1830–1834, Anne and Solomon lived in Fort Edward and Kingsbury. In addition to his previous labors, Solomon began

farming, and he also developed a substantial reputation as a fiddler, much in demand for dances. Anne, meanwhile, became well known as a cook in local taverns. They moved to Saratoga Springs in 1834, continuing in the same professions. They maintained their household there, which soon included three children, until 1841, when what had been a quite normal life took a dramatic turn for the worse.

In March of that year Solomon Northup met a pair of strangers in Saratoga who called themselves Merrill Brown and Abram Hamilton. Claiming to be members of a circus company, they persuaded him to accompany them for a series of performances until they rejoined their circus. As their terms seemed lucrative and Northup needed money, he agreed to join them as a fiddler. These con men, to secure Northup's trust, told him that he should obtain free papers before leaving New York, since they would be entering the slave territories of Maryland and Washington, D.C. They further lulled him by paying him a large sum of money. In Washington, however, Northup was drugged, chained, robbed, and sold to a notorious slave trader named James H. Burch.

Thus began Northup's twelve years as a slave. His narrative, *Twelve Years a Slave: Narrative of Solomon Northup*, far more than just a personal memoir, provides a detailed and fascinating portrait of the people, circumstances, and social practices he encountered. His account of the slave market, his fellow captives, and how they were all treated is especially vivid. Burch's confederate, Theophilus Freeman, transported Northup and the others by ship to New Orleans, where they were sold in a slave market. Northup was purchased by William Ford, a planter in the Red River region, and though Ford was only his first of several masters, Northup spent his entire period of captivity in this section of Louisiana.

Despite the heinous injustice of Northup's kidnapping and enslavement, he speaks quite favorably of the man who becomes his master: "In my opinion, there never was a more kind, noble, candid, Christian man than William Ford. The influences and associations that had always surrounded him, blinded him to the inherent wrong at the bottom of the system of Slavery" (*Puttin' on Old Massa*, ed. Osofsky, 270). This passage, distinguishing between Ford's personal character and environmental influences, reflects Northup's extraordinary fair-mindedness, a trait that makes his text especially compelling and persuasive. Nonetheless, Northup's respect for Ford did not reconcile him to accept his plight as a slave. Northup, called "Platt" while enslaved, made attempts as opportunities arose to escape and to notify his friends and family in New York of his situation. As his narrative shows, however, the constant surveillance and severe punishments of the slave system stifled such efforts. Even to obtain a few sheets of writing paper required waiting nine years. He feared to reveal his identity as a free man, lest he suffer extreme reprisals.

Northup's skills as a rafter brought him distinction along the Red River, but financial difficulties forced Ford to sell him in the winter of 1842 to John M. Tibeats, a crude, brutal, and violent neighbor. The choleric Tibeats compulsively worked, whipped, and abused his slaves. Eventually he attacked Northup with an ax, and in self-defense Northup drubbed him mercilessly, then fled to the swamps. Luckily, by a legal technicality, Ford retained partial ownership of Northup, and when the fugitive arrived back on Ford's plantation after several days of struggling through the swamps, Ford was able to shield him from Tibeats's wrath. New arrangements were made, which contracted Northup out to work for Edwin Epps, an alcoholic plantation owner in Bayou Boef, who remained Northup's master for the next decade. Northup's skills as a carpenter, a sugarcane cutter, and especially as a fiddler kept his services in demand, making him perhaps the most famous slave in the region—but, ironically, known by the false name Platt.

Northup's fortunes took a turn for the better in 1852 when a Canadian carpenter named Bass came to work on Epps's new house. A genial but passionate man, Bass was regarded as an eccentric in the community because of his outspoken antislavery views. Hearing him debate Epps on the topic, Northup decided that Bass was a white man worth trusting. The two became friends,

and Bass promised to mail a letter for Northup. At Northup's direction, Bass composed a letter to William Perry and Cephas Parker of Saratoga, New York, informing them of Northup's situation. When these men received the letter, they consulted Henry B. Northup, the son of Mintus Northup's former master. He, in turn, initiated a complicated series of arrangements that led to his being appointed by the governor of New York as a special agent charged to secure the rescue of Solomon Northup from slavery in Louisiana. Fortunately New York had enacted in 1840 a law designed to address cases like Solomon's, where New York citizens were kidnapped into slavery. The process, however, required obtaining proofs of citizenship and residence and various affidavits. Consequently it was the end of November before Henry Northup was empowered to act on behalf of the governor. Solomon, meanwhile, grew deeply depressed, having no way of knowing whether the letter had been delivered.

Nevertheless, Henry Northup acted with dispatch and arrived in Marksville on 1 January 1853 to seek out and liberate Solomon Northup. Unfortunately, though the local officials cooperated with his mission, no one knew a slave named Solomon Northup. A lucky inference by the local judge produced an encounter between Henry Northup and Bass, who revealed his authorship, the slave name, and the location of Solomon. Henry and the sheriff journeyed to the Epps plantation and laid claim to Solomon before the furious Epps could avoid a large financial loss by sending him away. After a brief formal proceeding, Solomon regained his freedom and returned northward with Henry.

They decided to stop in Washington and bring kidnapping charges against James Burch, which they filed on 17 January 1853. Due to various technicalities, Burch evaded conviction, but the case did serve the important purpose of bringing many facts into the public record, thereby confirming Solomon's own account. He arrived in Sandy Hill, New York, on 20 January and proceeded to Glens Falls, where he was reunited with his wife and children, who had grown to adulthood in his absence. The narrative ends at this point, and little is known of Northup's subsequent life,

except that he contracted with David Wilson, a local lawyer and legislator, to write this memoir, which was published later in 1853. It sold quite well and resulted in the identification and arrest of Northup's kidnappers, whose real names were Alexander Merrill and Joseph Russell. Their trial opened 4 October 1854 and dragged on for nearly two years, snarled by technicalities over jurisdiction, which finally received a ruling by the state supreme court that returned the case to the lower courts, who in turn simply dropped it. Northup never received legal recompense for the crimes committed against him. The sale of his book earned him three thousand dollars, which he used to purchase some property, and he returned to work as a carpenter. Nothing is known of his ensuing years. He apparently died in 1863, but scholars have not been able to confirm this. His narrative remains, however, one of the most detailed and realistic portraits of slave life.

FURTHER READING

Northup, Solomon. *Twelve Years a Slave*, Sue L. Eakins and Joseph Logsdon, eds. (1853; repr. 1968).

Blassingame, John. *The Slave Community* (1972).
Phillips, Ulrich Bonnell. *American Negro Slavery* (1918, 1966).
Stampp, Kenneth. *The Peculiar Institution* (1956).

—DAVID LIONEL SMITH

NORTON, ELEANOR HOLMES (13 June 1937–), women's and civil rights activist and congresswoman, was born Eleanor Katherine Holmes, the oldest of three daughters of Coleman Sterling Holmes, a public health and housing inspector, and Vela Lynch Holmes, a teacher, in segregated Washington, D.C. Oral history dates the family's residence in Washington to the early 1850s, when her paternal great-grandfather walked off a Virginia plantation to freedom in the District of Columbia. Holmes's father attended Syracuse University in upstate New York and worked his way through law school, though he never took the bar exam and never practiced law. Holmes's mother, born on a family farm in North Carolina, completed normal school in New York, where she earned a teaching certificate. After she married and moved to Washington, she earned a bachelor's degree from Howard University and passed the district's teacher certification exam, becoming the financial stronghold of her family.

As a child, Holmes grew up admiring the educator and social activist MARY CHURCH TERRELL and was influenced deeply by her paternal grandmother, Nellie Holmes, who taught her "the assertiveness she was expected to show in public" (Steinham, 33). Her father reinforced the prospect of command and responsibility especially expected of the eldest daughter. Throughout her childhood her father taught Holmes to strive for the best and to insist on respect. At home and at school she consistently received messages advocating equality among the races. Holmes's leadership began early in school and community activities. Quite popular among her age group, she was junior high school class president, leader of a community service club for teens, a debater, and a debutante during her senior year. She also excelled in her work from elementary through secondary school. In 1955, a year after the U.S. Supreme Court's *Brown v. Board of Education* school desegregation decision, Holmes graduated as one of the top students from Washington's prestigious Paul Laurence Dunbar High School in its last segregated class.

During the fall of 1955, as the civil rights movement was gathering momentum, Holmes entered Antioch College, in Ohio. Although she selected Antioch in large measure because of the work-study plan that would enable her to earn money for tuition, the very liberal atmosphere at the college shaped her emerging progressive political views. At Antioch, Holmes's concern for racial justice matured and expanded to include broader questions of equality and social action. Ever a leader among her peers, Holmes eventually chaired both the campus Socialist Discussion Club and the campus NAACP chapter, the latter of which sent a "sizeable contribution" (Steinham, 65) to support the Montgomery bus boycott. In early 1960, during her last semester, when a wave of student-led sit-ins against segregated facilities spread across the South,

Holmes organized similar protests in towns near the Antioch campus. She graduated from Antioch in June 1960, ranked twentieth among 165 graduates.

That fall, in a class with few women of any race and not many African Americans, she entered Yale Law School, along with MARIAN WRIGHT EDELMAN. In New Haven, Holmes continued her civil rights activism. She helped found and coordinate a chapter of the Congress on Racial Equality (CORE), and during the summer of 1963 she worked with the Student Nonviolent Coordinating Committee (SNCC) in Mississippi. Her presence in Mississippi proved to be pivotal, since she was able to initiate crucial outside contact with FANNIE LOU HAMER, Lawrence Guyot, and several others who had been arrested and beaten and were being held in Winona, Mississippi. Guyot, also a SNCC worker, had received the same treatment as Hamer and others when he went to investigate their disappearance. Later that summer Holmes represented U.S. students on a European tour and worked at the New York headquarters of the March on Washington. In the fall she returned for her final year at Yale. She completed a four-year dual program in the spring, taking degrees in Law and American Studies and earning honors in the latter subject.

Having anticipated a career in civil rights law, Holmes headed for work with SNCC in Mississippi in 1964, immediately upon completion of her degree at Yale. That was the summer of the historic Mississippi Freedom Democratic Party (MFDP) challenge at the Democratic Party's Atlantic City convention. Holmes was assigned to her hometown delegation, Washington, D.C., where she joined the civil rights and labor attorney Joseph L. Rauh Jr. in writing a brief arguing the MFDP's case to the Democratic Party credentials committee. In Atlantic City, Holmes directed MFDP lobbying, including activities as varied as preparing and placing MFDP representatives to speak with credentials committee members and coordinating demonstrations outside the convention center. Yet despite the efforts of Rauh, Norton, BOB MOSES, and Fannie Lou Hamer, the MFDP failed to achieve its goal of supplanting the regular, whites only, Mississippi delegation at

the convention with an integrated slate of delegates.

Continuing her preparation for civil rights work, she took a post in the fall as clerk for the newly appointed U.S. District Court judge, A. LEON HIGGINBOTHAM (a fellow graduate of Antioch), in Philadelphia. A year later, on 9 October 1965, Eleanor Holmes married Edward Norton, whom she had met four months earlier at the home of a longtime friend. The couple moved to Manhattan, where Edward Norton was finishing law school at Columbia University, and where Eleanor Holmes Norton took a position with the American Civil Liberties Union (ACLU). The Nortons, who separated after twenty-five years of marriage, had two children, Katherine and John.

At the ACLU, Norton's reputation as a First Amendment expert emerged through the notoriety of her *amicus curiae* brief supporting JULIAN BOND's efforts to be seated in the Georgia State legislature, and her successful defense of George Wallace, the segregationist governor of Alabama, and of the National States Rights Party, a white supremacy group. Norton also filed and won what was likely the first class action suit involving gender when she challenged *Newsweek* magazine's practice of barring women from jobs as reporters. In 1970 Norton was named head of New York City's Human Rights Commission, where she implemented new civil rights laws and pioneered antidiscrimination policies and programs. Her significant accomplishments at this time included diversifying the city's definition of civil rights constituencies and conducting a complete review and reordering of the city's public school staffing that made way for a more diverse workforce in school classrooms and administration. Within a year the Human Rights Commission post expanded to include a role as the mayor's executive assistant. During this time Norton taught a course in women and the law at New York University Law School and coauthored the groundbreaking book *Sex Discrimination and the Law: Causes and Remedies* (1975). Norton continued to work as New York's human rights commissioner for seven years until, in 1977, President Jimmy Carter appointed her the first woman to chair the Federal

Equal Employment Opportunity Commission (EEOC).

When Norton took over as EEOC director, the agency had a massive backlog of complaints and a slow-moving bureaucracy. She engineered the agency's reorganization, which resulted in streamlined and speedy claims processing and near complete handling of backlogged cases. She also led the EEOC's broad-scale approach to employment discrimination by going after corporate and industrial "patterns and practices" instead of focusing solely on single cases. This resulted in closing prominent agreements with major corporations, including AT&T and the Ford Motor Company. Norton also initiated new EEOC procedures on fair employment and established pioneering guidelines to deal with the problem of sexual harassment in the workplace. Both of these initiatives continue to influence fair employment and sexual harassment policy today. In January 1981 Norton resigned the post as the administration of Ronald Reagan took office. One of Norton's predecessors at the EEOC was CLARENCE THOMAS.

After a brief time recuperating from the grueling schedule of the EEOC, Norton took a post as professor at the Georgetown University Law Center. She taught constitutional law and cofounded the Women's Law and Policy Fellowship Program. She also kept a busy speaking schedule, continuing to advocate civil rights improvements despite the country's turn away from advances of the era. While a professor at Georgetown, Norton joined RANDALL ROBINSON, Walter Fauntroy, and Mary Frances Berry in a 1984 protest at the South African Embassy in Washington, D.C., that highlighted growing American opposition to the South Africa's apartheid regime. In 1990 she was elected to the 102nd Congress, succeeding Walter Fauntroy as the district's nonvoting representative. Taking office at a difficult time in D.C.'s history, Norton was successful in helping to restore credibility and resources to the beleaguered District of Columbia. She also attempted to make the issue of voting representation in Congress for District of Columbia residents a national civil rights issue.

Known as tenacious, sharp, and focused in all her work, Norton's career of public service reflects her ongoing evolution as an advocate of equal rights for all Americans. Norton has received numerous honorary degrees and in 1982 was elected to the Yale University Corporation. She later was selected to serve on boards of several Fortune 500 corporations, including Pitney Bowes, Metropolitan Life Insurance, and Stanley Works.

FURTHER READING

Lester, Joan Steinau. *Fire in My Soul* (2003).
—ROSETTA E. ROSS

O'LEARY, HAZEL R.

(17 May 1937–), U.S. secretary of energy, was born Hazel Reid in Newport News, Virginia, the youngest of two daughters of Dr. Russell E. Reid, and a mother about whom little is known, except that she was also a physician. Hazel and her sister, Edna, were raised in Newport News by their father and stepmother, Hazel Palleman Reid, in a loving and supportive environment that encouraged a solid education, independence, and compassion for others. Hazel's grandmother, founder of Newport News's only black public library, kept a box of clean and neatly packed clothes on her back porch for neighbors to take as needed.

Hazel's life lessons began in the Reid household and continued with her elementary and middle school teachers at the segregated public schools in Newport News, where she was a star pupil. Although the Reid sisters led sheltered childhoods, their parents also encouraged their independence and intellect. Hazel was an exceedingly bright and competitive child with an abundance of self-confidence. Visionary when it came to their children's futures, the Reids sacrificed both emotionally and financially to send their daughters "up north" to complete their education. From eighth grade through high school, Hazel and Edna lived under the care of an aunt, who resided in Essex County, New Jersey. Hazel studied voice and alto horn at the Arts High School for artistically talented youth and graduated with honors from that high school in 1956. She moved to Nashville, Tennessee, that year to attend Fisk University and received a BA degree cum laude from Fisk in 1959.

In 1960, just a year after graduating from Fisk, Hazel Reid married Dr. Carl Rollins. During her early years of marriage, she put her education on hold while she perfected

Hazel O'Leary, U. S. secretary of energy, was one of four African American cabinet members appointed by President Clinton in 1992. Corbis

her role as housewife. After the birth of a child, Carl G. Rollins, in 1963, however, she resumed her education, enrolling in Rutgers University School of Law. She graduated in 1966 with a JD degree. Over the next twenty-five years, Hazel Reid Rollins's intellect, ambition, and self-confidence would serve her well, propelling her into increasingly prominent roles in state and federal government. In 1967 she was appointed assistant prosecutor in Essex County, New Jersey, and was subsequently appointed assistant attorney general in that state. Carl and Hazel Rollins's marriage dissolved shortly before her next career move—to Washington, D.C. Upon moving there with her son, she

joined the prominent accounting firm of Coopers and Lybrand as one of the first African American partners and one of a few female partners at that time.

In 1974 Hazel Rollins left the accounting firm and resumed her career in public service. Over the next twenty-five years she served under three presidents, Gerald Ford, Jimmy Carter, and Bill Clinton. In all three administrations her keen understanding of energy and energy conservation policy would be tapped. In 1974, during Ford's tenure, Rollins joined the Federal Energy Administration (FEA) as director of the Office of Consumer Affairs/Special Impact—managing a number of the antipoverty programs initiated during the Great Society years of the 1960s. Despite Rollins's appearance of privilege, she was known in some Washington circles as an advocate for the poor. In the Carter administration she served, from 1976 to 1977, as general counsel for the Community Services Administration; as assistant administrator for conservation and environment with the FEA; and, in 1978, as chief of the Department of Energy's (DOE) Economic Regulatory Administration.

Rollins has been described as a lightning rod—attracting controversy wherever she happened to work and garnering either hot or cold reactions from friends and foes. As a regulator and an administrator, she has received both praise and criticism over the years. Described as a fair administrator, however, she gained respect even from environmentalists and energy executives, who lauded her conservation initiatives—including underwriting the cost of insulating homes for low-income families.

During her tenure with the Carter administration, Rollins met and worked with John F. O'Leary, deputy secretary for the DOE. Their friendship probably was ignited by a shared interest in and passion for the world of energy and conservation. In 1980 they married and, shortly thereafter, founded an international energy, economics, and strategic planning firm. Hazel O'Leary resigned her post at DOE to run the firm. John O'Leary passed away in 1987, leaving the responsibility of running O'Leary and Associates to his wife. In 1989 O'Leary closed the doors of the firm and, over the next three years, reestablished working relationships with other energy entities. These companies included Applied Energy Services, an independent power producer; NRG Energy, the major unregulated subsidiary of Northern States Power Company; and, later, its parent company, Minneapolis-based Northern States Power Company—an energy supplier to five contiguous states in the northern Midwest.

In November 1992 president-elect Bill Clinton made history when he appointed four African Americans to his cabinet. Hazel Rollins O'Leary was one of the earliest selections. Despite her past controversy among environmentalists, she

was confirmed unanimously as secretary of energy just one day after Bill Clinton's inauguration, and she was sworn into office in a White House ceremony one day later. O'Leary, only the seventh secretary of energy, was the first racial minority and first the woman to control one of the most unwieldy departments in the federal government. Early in her tenure O'Leary was dubbed one of the bright stars of the Clinton cabinet, bringing what one reporter described as a savvy respect for the consumer market, grassroots politics, and environmental concerns. Over time, however, it was these very attributes that would be used against her.

O'Leary viewed her mission at the department as that of shepherding the organization into the twenty-first century—and, to a large extent, she accomplished that mission. She boldly undertook initiatives that greatly influenced the lives of the American people and opened public debate within the DOE, the national laboratory system, and the national security community on nuclear weapons and their associated cleanup program and on nuclear testing. She is also credited with influencing President Clinton's decision to end nuclear testing in the United States and with spearheading a more accessible DOE.

Yet it was her "outside the box" approach to government and her non-traditional leadership style that can be credited with her rocky tenure in the Clinton administration. Her last year was fraught with public and legal crises, including congressional criticism and investigations into her trade missions to foreign countries and her trip expense reports. In an exit interview with the *New York Times* in January 1997, an obviously weary O'Leary described her four years in office as "exhausting" and despaired that probably no secretary of energy taking office after her would undertake the important trade missions she had, given the scrutiny she had undergone.

DOE Secretary O'Leary submitted her resignation to President Clinton in December 1996. Upon leaving the Clinton administration in January 1997, she gravitated again to the private sector. She signed on as CEO for Blaylock &

Partners LP, a New York–based full-service investment firm whose major client focus is on energy, transportation, telecommunications and technology, and consumer products. O'Leary's role includes support of the firm's expanding mergers and acquisitions interests, particularly in energy-related businesses.

Hazel O'Leary's uncharacteristic courage and sense of fair play in a bureaucratic environment is part of her legacy. At the DOE she was a leader who took bold steps to reform an out-of-control bureaucracy and make government a place that worked for all people. In doing so, she raised the bar for those coming after her. As a business leader and world-renowned public figure, O'Leary remains a role model for young people, women, and minorities, who understand the difficulties of success against the odds. As she travels the world, this strikingly attractive and warm woman remains a sterling example of her parents' teachings: reverence, honor, and a good education transcend any obstacle.

FURTHER READING

Healey, Jan. "Hazel R. O'Leary: A Profile." *Congressional Quarterly* 177 (23 Jan. 1993).

Lippman, Thomas W. "An Energetic Networker to Take Over Energy," *Washington Post*, 19 Jan. 1993.

Thompson, Garland L. "Four Black Cabinet Secretaries—Will It Make the Difference?," *Washington Times*, 4 Feb. 1993.

Wald, Matthew. "Interview with Secretary Hazel O'Leary," *New York Times*, 20 Jan. 1997.

—JANIS F. KEARNEY

 OLIVER, KING
(11 May 1885–8 Apr. 1938), cornetist and bandleader, was born Joseph Oliver in or near New Orleans, Louisiana, the son of Jessie Jones, a cook; his father's identity is unknown. After completing elementary school, Oliver probably had a variety of menial jobs, and he worked as a yardman for a well-to-do clothing merchant. He appears to have begun playing cornet relatively late, perhaps around 1905. For the next ten years he played in a variety of brass

King Oliver (standing in center with cornet) led his Dixie Syncopators at the Plantation Café on Chicago's South Side from 1925 to 1927. © Bettmann/CORBIS

bands and large and small dance bands, coming to prominence about 1915. Between 1916 and 1918 Oliver was the cornetist of trombonist Edward "Kid" Ory's orchestra, which was one of the most highly regarded African American dance orchestras in New Orleans. Early in 1919 Oliver moved to Chicago and soon became one of the most sought-after bandleaders in the cabarets of the South Side black entertainment district.

In early 1921 Oliver accepted an engagement in a taxi-dance hall on Market Street in San Francisco, and he also played in Oakland with his old friend Ory and perhaps in local vaudeville as well. After a stop in Los Angeles, he returned to Chicago in June

1922, beginning a two-year engagement at the Lincoln Gardens. After a few weeks, Oliver sent to New Orleans for his young protégé LOUIS ARMSTRONG, who had been Oliver's regular substitute in the Ory band some five years earlier. With two cornets (Oliver and Armstrong), trombonist Honore Dutrey, clarinetist Johnny Dodds, string bassist William Manuel Johnson, drummer Warren "Baby" Dodds, and pianist Lillian Hardin (LIL ARMSTRONG), King Oliver's Creole Jazz Band made a series of recordings for the Gennett, OKeh, Columbia, and Paramount labels (some thirty-seven issued titles), which are regarded as supreme achievements of early recorded jazz. (Other musicians substitute for the regulars on a few of

these recordings.) There is ample evidence that a great many musicians, black and white, made special and repeated efforts to hear the band perform live.

By early 1925 Oliver was leading a larger and more up-to-date orchestra with entirely new personnel. This group was the house band at the flashy Plantation Cafe (also on the South Side) and as the Dixie Syncopators made a series of successful recordings for the Vocalion label. Oliver took his band to the East Coast in May 1927, but after little more than a month, it dispersed. For the next four years Oliver lived in New York City, touring occasionally and making records for the Victor Company at the head of a variety of ad hoc orchestras;

these are widely considered inferior to his earlier work.

His popularity waning and his playing suffering because of his chronic gum disease, Oliver spent an unprosperous six years between 1931 and 1937 incessantly touring the Midwest and the Upper South. Savannah, Georgia, became his headquarters for the last year of his life; he stopped playing in September 1937 and supported himself subsequently by a variety of odd jobs. He died in Savannah of a cerebral hemorrhage; he was buried in Woodlawn Cemetery in New York City. The Reverend ADAM CLAYTON POWELL officiated, and Louis Armstrong performed at the funeral service. He was survived by his wife, Stella (maiden name unknown), and two daughters.

Oliver is the most widely and favorably recorded of the earliest generation of New Orleans ragtime/jazz cornetists, most influential perhaps in his use of straight and plunger mutes; aspects of Louis Armstrong's style clearly derive from Oliver. Oliver's best-known contributions as a soloist are his three choruses on "Dipper Mouth Blues," copied hundreds of times by a wide variety of instrumentalists on recordings made during the next twenty years. His major achievement, however, remains the highly expressive and rhythmically driving style of his band as recorded in 1923–1924. While the band owed its distinctiveness and energy, like all early New Orleans jazz, to the idiosyncratic musical talents of the individual musicians, its greatness was undoubtedly the result of Oliver's painstaking rehearsals and tonal concept.

FURTHER READING

Gushee, Lawrence. "Oliver, 'King'" in *New Grove Dictionary of Jazz*, ed. Barry Kernfeld (1988).
Wright, Laurie. *"King" Oliver* (1987).

Obituary: *Chicago Defender*, 16 Apr. 1938.

—LAWRENCE GUSHEE

 O'NEAL, FREDERICK DOUGLASS (27 Aug. 1905–25 Aug. 1992), actor, activist, arts leader, and union organizer, was born in Brooksville, Mississippi, to Minnie Bell Thompson, a former teacher, and Ransome James O'Neal Jr., a teacher who later joined the family business, RJ O'Neal and Son, a general store started by his father, Ransome Sr. Named after the famed abolitionist FREDERICK DOUGLASS, O'Neal was the sixth of eight children. He developed an interest in the theater at an early age and at age eight gave a recitation in grade school that proved to be a formative moment in his decision to pursue acting as a career. His father constructed a little hall next to the family store, where Frederick, at age ten and eleven, put on small shows. After his father died unexpectedly when Frederick was fourteen, his mother sold the store and moved her family to St. Louis, Missouri, in 1920. Frederick, who had attended public school in Brooksville, finished elementary school at Waring School in St. Louis. In 1922 he entered Sumner High School. Soon after, he began work as a file clerk at the Meyer Brothers Drug Company, a job that necessitated his move to night school. Frederick also worked the graveyard shift as a post office clerk, further interfering with his desire to become an actor.

During the 1920s and 1930s O'Neal grew even more determined to become an actor. He joined the St. Louis branch of the Urban League in 1920 in order to perform in their annual plays, which included the 1926 production of Shakespeare's *As You Like It*, in which he starred. In 1927, with assistance from the Urban League's director, John Clark, and the entrepreneur ANNIE TURNBO MALONE, O'Neal founded the St. Louis Aldridge Players. Named after the actor IRA ALDRIDGE (and later renamed the Negro Little Theatre of St. Louis), the troupe produced three plays per year and remained in operation until 1940. Dedicated to community service and to the encouragement of black playwrights, the Aldridge Players performed at the St. Louis YMCA, at local high schools, and at Annie Turnbo Malone's Poro Beauty College.

In 1936, on the advice of ZORA NEALE HURSTON, O'Neal left St. Louis for New York to further his acting career. With his previous experience at Meyer Drug Store, he landed a day job working as a laboratory assistant. At night he studied voice, movement, and acting at the New Theatre School and the American Theatre Wing. He also received a scholarship for private lessons. This training provided a solid foundation for his future work in theater and film. And while he had hoped to work with the New York Negro Unit of the Federal Theatre Project before it was disbanded in 1939, he joined the Rose McClendon Players in 1938, remaining with the company until it folded a year later.

Following the dissolution of the Rose McClendon Players, O'Neal and the playwright Abram Hill founded the American Negro Theater (ANT) to provide opportunities for black theater artists, writers, and designers. O'Neal served as company manager. Modeled after its insect namesake, the "ant," the American Negro Theatre proclaimed itself to be a communal effort eschewing the conventional star system in favor of working diligently and collectively for the good of the whole. ANT's first production, *On Strivers Row*, a satire of the black middle class written by Hill, ran for five months on weekends in the basement theater of the Harlem branch of the public library. *Row* was followed by the folk opera *Natural Man*, a play by Theodore Browne that featured O'Neal in the role of the preacher. In 1944 ANT mounted its most successful production, an adaptation of Yordan's play about a Polish working-class family in a Pennsylvania industrial town, *Anna Lucasta*. The play, costarring O'Neal as Frank, garnered critical acclaim and soon moved to Broadway, where it ran for 956 performances and won O'Neal both the Clarence Derwent Award and the New York Critics Award.

While working with the ANT in 1941, O'Neal met Charlotte Talbot Hainey at a YMCA dance. The couple married on 18 April 1942; they had no children. In October, O'Neal was drafted into the army and stationed at Fort Dix, New Jersey, after which he was transferred to Fort Huachuca, Arizona, where he served until his honorable discharge in 1943. Free from the service, O'Neal returned to his wife and to his career in the theater in New York City.

From the 1940s through the 1960s O'Neal enjoyed a successful movie and stage career. His first film appearance was in the 1949 feature *Pinky*, the Elia

Kazan drama about passing, starring Jeanne Crain, ETHEL WATERS, and Ethel Barrymore. O'Neal was cast in a number of lesser film productions, playing a variety of "jungle roles," including King Burlam in *Tarzan's Peril* (1951), a Mau-Mau leader in *Something of Value* (1957), and Buderga in *The Sins of Rachel Cade* (1961). On Broadway, O'Neal costarred as Lem Scott in the 1953 play *Take a Giant Step*. Six years later he recreated the role in the film version, which starred RUBY DEE and the singer Johnny Nash. O'Neal also reprieved the role of Frank in the 1958 film version of *Anna Lucasta* co-starring EARTHA KITT and SAMMY DAVIS JR. In 1959 he portrayed Moses in the Hall of Fame production of *The Green Pastures*. In the theater, he appeared in *The Winner* in 1954, as Houngan in *House of Flowers* in 1954, and as the preacher in *God's Trombone* in 1960.

As O'Neal furthered his leadership and activism in the arts, he also performed on television. He was a regular on the television sitcom *Car 54, Where Are You?* in the 1960s. He played in Jack Smight's *Strategy of Terror* (1959); *Free, White and 21* (1963); and OSSIE DAVIS's *Cotton Comes to Harlem* (1970).

At the same time as he found success in his own career, O'Neal fought passionately for the rights of all black actors. Recognizing the unequal treatment of black performers, O'Neal in the 1950s published articles in *Crisis* and *Equity News*, the newsletter of the professional actors' union, Actor's Equity Association (AEA), calling for producers to cast black actors in roles that were not racially specific. He also gave speeches on the need for "nontraditional casting" before groups such as the Catholic Interracial Council. The council, along with the NAACP, organized protests in 1953 against racial representation on network television. As a result of his activism, O'Neal found himself blacklisted by several television networks. This experience led him to become increasingly active in the struggle for the rights of actors and ultimately resulted in his being elected as the first black president of AEA in 1964.

O'Neal's service as president of AEA marked a continuation of his institutional agitation for the equal treatment of black actors. In 1944, as

chair of AEA's Hotel Accommodations Committee, he had worked to change the discriminatory housing practices faced by black traveling performers. In 1961, at time when he also functioned as first vice president of the AEA, O'Neal had served as president of the Negro Actors Guild, a branch of AEA dedicated to advocating for the rights of black performers. As AEA president from 1964 through 1973, O'Neal forthrightly advanced the concerns of minority actors. He also lobbied for the establishment of the National Foundation for the Arts and Humanities, which was signed into law by President Lyndon B. Johnson in September 1965. One of the final acts of O'Neal's terms as president was the establishment of the AEA Paul Robeson Citation Award. PAUL ROBESON himself was the first recipient in 1974. That same year, O'Neal assumed the presidency of Associate Actors and Artists of America, the international governing union of actors, and he held this post for eighteen years.

Later in life O'Neal received many accolades. He won the Negro Trade Union Leadership Council Humanitarian Award in 1974, the Frederick Douglass Award in 1975, and the NAACP Man of the Year Award in 1979. The AEA presented him with the 1985 Paul Robeson Citation Award, the award he had helped found. In 1990 he received the Black Filmmakers Hall of Fame Award and was also named an American Theatre Fellow by the John F. Kennedy Center. After a prolonged battle with cancer, he died in his Manhattan home, only four months after he and his wife had celebrated their fiftieth wedding anniversary and two days before his eighty-sixth birthday. On 15 September 1992 friends and family gathered at the Schubert Theater in New York City for a final tribute to Fredrick Douglass O'Neal, a pioneer and leader in the American theater.

FURTHER READING

"Actors' New Boss: Frederick O'Neal Heads Actors' Equity Assn," *Ebony* 19 (June 1964).

Simmons, Renee. *Frederick Douglass O'Neal: Pioneer of the Actor's Equity Association* (1996).

Obituary: *Jet*, 14 Sept. 1992.

—HARRY ELAM

 O'NEAL, STANLEY
(7 Oct. 1951–), corporate executive, was born Earnest Stanley O'Neal in Roanoke, Alabama, the oldest of four children of Earnest O'Neal, a farmer, and Ann Scales, a domestic. The family lived in a small farming town called Wedowee, but because its hospital would not admit African Americans, he was born in the neighboring town of Roanoke. The grandson of a former slave, O'Neal lived with his family in poverty. Although his house had no indoor plumbing, it was inhabited by a loving extended family of aunts, uncles, and cousins. With a population less than eight hundred, Wedowee offered scarce resources. O'Neal was educated in a one-room schoolhouse heated with a wooden stove and with one teacher to instruct all the grades. Outside the classroom, he and his siblings spent hours picking cotton on their grandfather's fields. Very early on, O'Neal's father told him that he was not the farming type and advised him to explore other options for his future.

These options increased when the family moved to Atlanta, Georgia, in the 1960s. When they arrived, the O'Neals moved into a federal housing project, which Stanley welcomed because "it was 'ten stories higher' than anything he had ever known" (*Fortune*, 28 Apr. 1997). O'Neal attended West Fulton High School, where he was one of the first black students. In addition to his schoolwork, he took on various odd jobs to help his family. His father got a job on the General Motors (GM) assembly line in Doraville, Georgia, just as the factory was being integrated. After high school graduation, O'Neal reached a turning point in his life when GM offered him the chance to study at the General Motors Institute (now Kettering University). He studied in six-week stints, alternating between work in a factory and his education in the classroom. He graduated with a BS in Industrial Administration in 1974, the first in his family to graduate from college. He was ranked in the top 20 percent of his class and accepted an offer to become a supervisor at the very factory where his father worked. After some time working there, GM gave him a scholarship to study at Harvard

Business School. He graduated in 1978 and set off for New York City to work in one of the most dynamic business environments in the world.

Awaiting him in New York City was a job as an analyst for GM. O'Neal moved up the corporate ladder quickly, his rise fueled by his strong command of numbers and a work ethic that had him sitting in his office till 10:00 PM on a regular basis. After two years he became a director, and in 1982 he moved to Spain to become treasurer of the company's Spanish division. In 1984 he returned to New York as GM's assistant treasurer. In the treasury office he worked with his future wife, Nancy Garvey, an economist. The two married in 1983 and had twins, a son and a daughter.

Another turning point in O'Neal's life came in 1986, when he decided that he was ready for new challenges and a new industry. Having clearly demonstrated that he understood the language of numbers at GM, he decided to go to Wall Street to join the financial services firm Merrill Lynch. O'Neal first made a name for himself in the company's corporate finance division, a lucrative area that he understood, because he had had to deal with many investment bankers at GM. Within five years he was chosen to head Merrill Lynch's high-yield department.

O'Neal came to this position at a time when high-yield bonds, more commonly known as "junk bonds," were distrusted because of a scandal involving Drexel Burnham Lambert, another Wall Street firm. Despite the tough market, Merrill Lynch rose to the top of this field, acting as lead manager of deals worth $3.9 billion dollars. For the rest of O'Neal's tenure as head of the group, the firm remained at or near the top of the industry, resulting in O'Neal's selection as head of Merrill's entire capital markets division in 1996. After he left, the high-yield department dropped to eighth place in industry rankings.

In 1998 O'Neal moved to the top management level at Merrill Lynch when he was named chief financial officer, his first administrative job. This signaled to Wall Street insiders that he was in the running to be the firm's chief executive officer. It provided another chance for O'Neal to prove his leadership qualities, because in the fall of that year a Russian

financial crisis and the collapse of a powerful hedge fund named Long Term Capital Management sent the bond markets into a free fall. Merrill Lynch found itself stuck with bonds dropping in value, and O'Neal took charge of navigating the firm through the tough time.

From there, O'Neal's ascent was meteoric. In February 2000 he was named the head of the firm's private client group, a significant position, because Merrill Lynch has the largest brokerage on Wall Street. He was the first person to run the fifteen thousand brokers who himself had never been a broker. In the summer of 2001 O'Neal was named president and chief operating officer, and in December 2002 he took over as chief executive officer. He was the first African American to head a major firm on Wall Street.

As O'Neal stepped into his new historic position, he also inherited a number of challenges. One problem came from the moribund economic climate that had emerged after the boom years of the 1990s. Fewer companies were going public, stock prices had declined dramatically, and the drop in activity had shrunk profits on Wall Street. In addition to these inauspicious market conditions, Merrill Lynch was trying to escape scandal. Months before O'Neal took over as CEO, the firm agreed to a $100-million-dollar fine to settle a probe issued by the New York State's attorney general's office that charged Merrill research analysts with issuing false praise of corporations to win investment-banking business.

Now that O'Neal has taken the helm, it is his primary responsibility to steer the firm out of the haze of these problems. So far, he has attacked these problems by drastically cutting costs and putting a greater emphasis on the most profitable areas of Merrill's business. His vision is to "build a 'new kind of financial-services firm' that redefines Wall Street by offering a far greater range of services" (*Business Week*, 5 May 2003). O'Neal may well be the right person to do it. He is often described as cool and calm, and his track record has shown an ability to help get his team out of complicated financial situations.

O'Neal has a unique background among major Wall Street executives. His rapid rise drew such great attention that

in 2002 *Fortune* named him the "Most Powerful Black Executive in America." Although he is quick to emphasize his work and talents, O'Neal also knows that he is a symbol. He once said, "Somebody has to be first, so it may as well be me. One of the things that has become clear to me as I have got more publicity is, like it or not, I am a role model. That's an aspect of who I am and I embrace it" (*Financial Times*, 25 July 2001).

FURTHER READING

Bell, Gregory S. *In the Black: A History of African Americans on Wall Street* (2001).
Clarke, Robin D. "Running with the Bulls," *Black Enterprise*, Sept. 2000.
Thornton, Emily. "The New Merrill Lynch," *Business Week*, 5 May 2003.

—GREGORY S. BELL

ONESIMUS (fl. 1706–1717), slave and medical pioneer, was born in the late seventeenth century, probably in Africa, although the precise date and place of his birth are unknown. He first appears in the historical record in the diary of Cotton Mather, a prominent New England theologian and minister of Boston's Old North Church. Reverend Mather notes in a diary entry for 13 December 1706 that members of his congregation purchased for him "a very likely *Slave*; a young Man who is a *Negro* of a promising aspect of temper" (Mather, vol. 1, 579). Mather named him Onesimus, after a biblical slave who escaped from his master, an early Christian named Philemon.

This Onesimus fled from his home in Colossae (in present-day Turkey) to the apostle Paul, who was imprisoned in nearby Ephesus. Paul converted Onesimus to Christianity and sent him back to Philemon with a letter, which appears in the New Testament as Paul's Epistle to Philemon. In that letter Paul asks Philemon to accept Onesimus "not now as a servant, but above a servant, a brother beloved" (Philemon 1.16 [AV]). Mather similarly hoped to make his new slave "a Servant of Christ," and in a tract, *The Negro Christianized* (1706), encouraged other slaveowners to do likewise, believing that Christianity "wonderfully Dulcifies, and

Mollifies, and moderates the Circumstances" of bondage (Silverman, 264).

Onesimus was one of about a thousand persons of African descent living in the Massachusetts colony in the early 1700s, one-third of them in Boston. Many were indentured servants with rights comparable to those of white servants, though an increasing number of blacks—and blacks only—were classified as chattel and bound as slaves for life. Moreover, after 1700, white fears of burglary and insurrection by blacks and Indians prompted the Massachusetts assembly to impose tighter restrictions on the movements of people of color, whether slave, servant, or free. Cotton Mather was similarly concerned in 1711 about keeping a "strict Eye" on Onesimus, "especially with regard unto his Company," and he also hoped that his slave would repent for "some Actions of a thievish aspect" (Mather, vol. 2, 139). Mather believed, moreover, that he could improve Onesimus's behavior by employing the "Principles of Reason, agreeably offered unto him" and by teaching him to read, write, and learn the Christian catechism (Mather, vol. 2, 222).

What Onesimus thought of Mather's opinions the historical record does not say, nor do we know much about his family life other than that he was married and had a son, Onesimulus, who died in 1714. Two years later Onesimus gave the clearest indication of his attitude toward his bondage by attempting to purchase his release from Mather. To do so, he gave his master money toward the purchase of another black youth, Obadiah, to serve in his place. Mather probably welcomed the suggestion, since he reports in his diary for 31 August 1716 that Onesimus "proves wicked, and grows useless, Froward [ungovernable] and Immorigerous [rebellious]." Around that time Mather signed a document releasing Onesimus from his service "that he may Enjoy and Employ his whole Time for his own purposes and as he pleases" (Mather, vol. 2, 363). However, the document makes clear that Onesimus's freedom was conditional on performing chores for the Mather family when needed, including shoveling snow, piling firewood, fetching water, and carrying corn to the mill. This contingent freedom was also dependent upon his returning a sum of five pounds allegedly stolen from Mather.

Little is known of Onesimus after he purchased his freedom, but in 1721 Cotton Mather used information he had learned five years earlier from his former slave to combat a devastating smallpox epidemic that was then sweeping Boston. In a 1716 letter to the Royal Society of London, Mather proposed "ye Method of Inoculation" as the best means of curing smallpox and noted that he had learned of this process from "my Negro-Man Onesimus, who is a pretty Intelligent Fellow" (Winslow, 33). Onesimus explained that he had

undergone an Operation, which had given him something of ye Small-Pox, and would forever preserve him from it, adding, That it was often used among [Africans] and whoever had ye Courage to use it, was forever free from the Fear of ye Contagion. He described ye Operation to me, and showed me in his Arm ye Scar.

(Winslow, 33)

Reports of similar practices in Turkey further persuaded Mather to mount a public inoculation campaign. Most white doctors rejected this process of deliberately infecting a person with smallpox—now called variolation—in part because of their misgivings about African medical knowledge. Public and medical opinion in Boston was strongly against both Mather and Dr. Zabdiel Boylston, the only doctor in town willing to perform inoculations; one opponent even threw a grenade into Mather's home. A survey of the nearly six thousand people who contracted smallpox between 1721 and 1723 found, however, that Onesimus, Mather, and Boylston had been right. Only 2 percent of the six hundred Bostonians inoculated against smallpox died, while 14 percent of those who caught the disease but were not inoculated succumbed to the illness.

It is unclear when or how Onesimus died, but his legacy is unambiguous. His knowledge of variolation gives the lie to one justification for enslaving Africans, namely, white Europeans' alleged superiority in medicine, science, and technology. This bias made the smallpox epidemic of 1721 more deadly than it need have been. Bostonians and other Americans nonetheless adopted the African practice of inoculation in future smallpox outbreaks, and variolation remained the most effective means of treating the disease until the development of vaccination by Edward Jenner in 1796.

FURTHER READING

Herbert, Eugenia W. "Smallpox Inoculation in Africa." *Journal of African History* 16 (1975).

Mather, Cotton. *Diary* (1912).

Silverman, Kenneth. *The Life and Times of Cotton Mather* (1984).

Winslow, Ola. *A Destroying Angel: The Conquest of Smallpox in Colonial Boston* (1974).
—STEVEN J. NIVEN

 **OTABENGA** (1883?–20 Mar. 1916), elephant hunter, Bronx Zoo exhibit, and tobacco worker, was born in the rain forest near the Kasai River in what is now the Democratic Republic of Congo. The historical record is mute on the precise name of his tribe, but they were a band of forest-dwelling pygmies—averaging less than fifty-nine inches in height—who had a reciprocal relationship with villagers of the Congolese Luba tribe. Otabenga and his fellow pygmies hunted elephants by playing a long horn known as a *molimo* to replicate the sound of an elephant bleat. Once they had roused the animal from the forest, they killed it with poisoned spears and traded the elephant hide and flesh to the Luba villagers in exchange for fruits, vegetables, and grains. Very little is known about Otabenga's family life, other than that he was married with two children by the age of twenty.

Around that time, while Otabenga was on an elephant hunt, his wife, children, and fellow members of his band were killed by Congolese agents of the Belgian colonial Force Publique, who had raided their community in search of ivory. When he returned, the Force Publique whipped him and forced him to march for several days, leaving him as a slave in a village inhabited by the warlike Baschilele. It was there, in March 1904, that the Reverend Samuel Phillips Verner, a white South Carolinian missionary, anthropologist, and pursuer of get-rich-quick schemes,

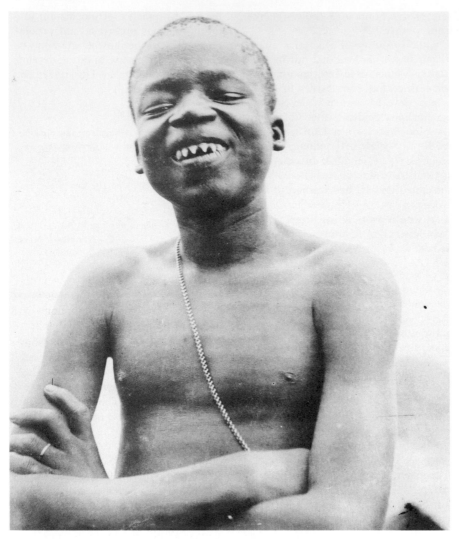

Otabenga displayed his filed teeth for nickels and dimes at the 1904 St. Louis World's Fair. American Museum of Natural History

secured Otabenga's release from the Baschilele for the sum of a pound of salt and a bolt of cloth.

Verner had first traveled to the Congo in the 1890s, and his stay with the missionary WILLIAM H. SHEPPARD enabled him to learn the topography and many languages of the Congo. In 1904 he returned to find pygmies for an exhibit of native peoples to be held at the St. Louis World's Fair. In doing so, Verner and the fair organizers were guided by the scientific racism that pervaded American and European thought at that time. Eminent scholars at Harvard and other leading colleges believed that a racial hierarchy existed among the different peoples of the world and that northern European humans represented the highest stage

of evolutionary development. Display and rigorous scientific study of allegedly "primitive" groups like the Congolese pygmies and North American Apaches, the fair's organizers believed, would educate the eighteen million visitors to St. Louis about the evolutionary process.

Few of the fair's visitors were interested in such science—or pseudoscience. Most gawked at Otabenga and the Batwa pygmies whom Verner had also found in the Congo. Others took intrusive photographs and, on occasion, poked and prodded them. One newspaper described him as a "dwarfy black specimen of sad-eyed humanity" (Bradford and Blume, 256). The inhumanity of his hosts, on the other hand, was little commented upon. Press reports did, however, note the public's fascination

with Otabenga's teeth, which he had filed into sharp triangles, a practice erroneously cited as evidence of his cannibalism. Displaying a keener understanding of his hosts' values and culture than those hosts showed for his own, Otabenga charged fairgoers a fee of a nickel or a dime before he would display his two rows of sharpened incisors.

When the fair ended in December 1905, Verner returned with the pygmies to Africa. There Otabenga married his second wife, a Batwa woman who died from a snakebite soon afterward. The Batwa blamed Otabenga for her death and shunned him. That decision appears to have strengthened his relationship with Verner, also an outsider, who had remained in the Congo to collect artifacts and native animals for sale to American museums and zoos. To that end, the two traveled throughout the Congo for several months, and, according to a biography of Otabenga drawn chiefly from Verner's reminiscences, their relationship evolved into one of great mutual regard. In August 1906 they returned to America, where Verner left Otabenga in the care of the Museum of Natural History in New York City and then in the hands of William Hornaday, president of the Bronx Zoological Gardens.

Otabenga initially had free rein to wander the zoo, occasionally assisting the keepers and observing both animals and New Yorkers at close quarters. Hornaday then encouraged Otabenga to sleep in the monkey house and placed a sign on his cage informing spectators that it contained "The African Pygmy" and listing his name, age, height, and weight. Otabenga's biographers write that, inspired by a combination of "Barnumism, Darwinism, and racism," Hornaday scattered bones around the cage to highlight the pygmy's alleged savagery and introduced into his enclosure an orangutan. Otabenga would play with the orangutan to the fascination of the thousands of spectators who flocked to the zoo. The spectacle prompted a flurry of articles in the *New York Times*, but only a few criticized the pygmy's treatment. The Reverend James Gordon, the head of an African American orphanage, did, however, protest Hornaday's presumption that Africans provided an evolutionary "missing link" to apes. Gordon did this mainly out of respect for Otabenga's humanity but also because he opposed Darwinism. Hornaday ignored such protests, but he did respond when Otabenga brandished a knife at a zookeeper who had provoked and forcibly restrained him. With Verner's permission, and with Otabenga's own seeming approval, the African was then placed in Reverend Gordon's care.

Thereafter the press and the public showed little interest in Otabenga, though his later years serve in some ways as a rebuke to those who had placed him in a cage and doubted his humanity. He learned to read and write at the orphanage and later studied for a semester at a Baptist school in Lynchburg, Virginia, where he converted to Christianity. After working for several years as a farm laborer on property owned by the Reverend Gordon on Long Island, New York, Otabenga returned to Lynchburg. He found the climate of the Blue Ridge foothills more amenable than New York's and also better for hunting, although wild turkey had replaced elephants as his game. Much to his delight, he discovered marijuana plants in the woods near Lynchburg, enabling him to smoke the seeds that he had known as *bangi* in his homeland. Although he was able, like most immigrants, to replicate some aspects of his native culture, Otabenga also adapted to American ways. He changed his name to Otto Bingo, wore overalls like those of his fellow tobacco factory workers during the week, and at week's end put on his Sunday best, in the manner of his fellow Baptists. He even capped his sharpened teeth. As a friend of the noted Lynchburg poet Anne Spencer, Otabenga also met African American leaders, including W. E. B. Du Bois and Booker T. Washington.

Such a life of relative normality may have failed to compensate for the personal tragedies Otabenga endured: the death of two wives and two children, the slaughter of his band of pygmies, his capture and near execution by the Force Publique, his exile in the United States, and his humiliations in St. Louis and the Bronx. Such explanations offer clues, but, of course, they can never fully explain the reasons for his suicide on 20 March 1916.

Otabenga lived in the era described by the historian Rayford W. Logan as the nadir of American race relations. During the thirty or so years of Otabenga's life, four thousand Americans were lynched, the vast majority of them black southerners. Hundreds of black Americans also died in white-instigated race riots in those years—in Wilmington, North Carolina, in 1898; in New Orleans in 1900; and in Atlanta, Georgia, and Bronzeville, Texas, both in 1906. In addition to this wave of physical violence, southern Democrats led white supremacy campaigns in those same decades that systematically disfranchised black voters and institutionalized the concept of separate and unequal facilities. The federal government either ignored or, as in the case of *Plessy v. Ferguson* (1896), endorsed these efforts to erode the Constitution's promise of equal protection under the law. That historical context suggests, tragically, that Otabenga's life story is much less extraordinary, and perhaps much more representative, than at first appears.

FURTHER READING

Bradford, Phillips Verner, and Harvey Blume. *Ota Benga: The Pygmy in the Zoo* (1992).
Kennedy, Pagan. *Black Livingstone: A True Tale of Adventure in the Nineteenth-Century Congo* (2002).
Turnbull, Colin. *The Forest People* (1961).

—Steven J. Niven

OWENS, JESSE

(12 Sept. 1913–31 Mar. 1980), Olympic track champion, was born James Cleveland Owens in Oakville, Alabama, the son of Henry Owens and Mary Emma Fitzgerald, sharecroppers. Around 1920 the family moved to Cleveland, Ohio, where the nickname "Jesse" originated when a schoolteacher mispronounced his drawled "J. C." A junior high school teacher of physical education, Charles Riley, trained Owens in manners as well as athletics, preparing him to set several interscholastic track records in high school. In 1932 the eighteen-year-old Owens narrowly missed winning a place on the U.S. Olympic team. Enrolling in 1933 at Ohio State University, Owens soared to national prominence under the tutelage of coach Larry

Snyder. As a sophomore at the Big Ten championships, held on the Ann Arbor campus of the University of Michigan, on 25 May 1935 he broke world records in the 220-yard sprint, the 220-yard hurdles, and the long jump, and equaled the world record in the 100-yard dash.

Scarcely did the success come easily. As one of a handful of black college students at white institutions in the 1930s, Owens suffered slurs on campus, in the town of Columbus, and on the athletic circuit. Personal problems also intruded. Just over a month after his astounding athletic success at Ann Arbor, Owens was pressured to marry his high school sweetheart, Minnie Ruth Solomon, with whom he had fathered a child three years earlier. Academic difficulties added to his ordeal. Coming from a home and high school bare of intellectual aspirations, Owens found it impossible to perform well academically while striving for athletic stardom. For two years at Ohio State he stayed on academic probation; low grades made him ineligible for the indoor track season during the winter quarter of 1936.

Allowed again to compete during the spring quarter outdoor track season, Owens set his sights on winning a place on the 1936 Olympic team. His great obstacle was a less-heralded but strong Temple University athlete, Eulace Peacock. A varsity football running back, Peacock had already beaten Owens in five of their previous six head-to-head sprints and long jumps. At the Penn Relays in late April, however, the heavily muscled Peacock snapped a hamstring that kept him limping through the Olympic trials.

Eighteen African American athletes represented the United States in the 1936 Olympics in Berlin, dominating the popular track and field events and winning fourteen medals, nearly one-fourth of the fifty-six medals awarded the U.S. team in all events. Owens tied the world record in the 100-meter sprint and broke world records in the 200-meter sprint, the long jump, and the 4-by-100-meter relay to win four gold medals. On the streets, in the Olympic village, and at the stadium, his humble demeanor and ready smile mesmerized foes and friends alike. As part of its concerted propaganda efforts, the Nazi regime commissioned German filmmaker Leni

Jesse Owens bursts into action at the 1936 Olympics in Berlin, Germany, where he tied one and set three new world records. Bettmann/Corbis

Riefenstahl to make a film of the games. The resulting film, *Olympia*, released in 1938, featured Owens prominently. German chancellor Adolf Hitler ceremoniously attended the games to cheer for German athletes. In the most enduring of all sports myths, Hitler supposedly "snubbed" Owens, refusing to shake his hand after his victories; Hitler allegedly stormed out of the stadium enraged that Owens's athleticism refuted the Nazi dogma of Aryan superiority. This morally satisfying, endearingly simple yarn has no basis in fact. Spread by the *Baltimore Afro-American* (8 Aug. 1936) and other American newspapers, the story quickly became enshrined as one of the great moral minidramas of our time.

After the Berlin Games, Owens incurred the wrath of Olympic and Amateur Athletic Union (AAU) officials when he returned home to capitalize on various commercial offers rather than complete an exhibition tour of several European cities; the tour had been arranged to help pay the expenses of the U.S. team. He left the tour in London, provoking the AAU to ban him from future amateur athletic competition. Supported in his decision by Snyder, Owens returned to the United States to cash in on numerous endorsement offers. Most of the offers proved bogus, however, but from Republican presidential candidate Alf Landon he received a goodly sum to campaign for black votes. Shortly after Landon's defeat, Owens was selected as the Associated Press Athlete of the Year, and on Christmas Day 1936 he won a well-paid, highly publicized race against a horse in Havana, Cuba. Various other fees for appearances and endorsements brought his earnings during the four months following the Berlin Olympics to about twenty thousand dollars.

For the next two years he barnstormed with several athletic groups, supervised playground activities in Cleveland, and ran exhibition races at baseball games. In 1938 he opened a dry-cleaning business in Cleveland, but within the year it went bankrupt. Now with three daughters and a wife to support, he nevertheless returned to Ohio State hoping to finish his baccalaureate degree. He gave up that dream just a few days after Pearl Harbor, and during World War II he held several short-term government assignments before landing a job supervising black workers in the Ford Motor Company in Detroit.

With the onset of the cold war, in the late 1940s Owens enjoyed a rebirth of fame. In 1950 he was honored by the Associated Press as the greatest track athlete of the past half century. Moving to Chicago, he served briefly as director of the South Side Boys' Club, the Illinois State Athletic Commission, and the Illinois Youth Commission, and emerged as an effective public speaker extolling patriotism and athleticism to youth groups, churches, and civic clubs. In 1955 the U.S. State Department tapped him for a junket to India, Malaya, and the Philippines to conduct athletic clinics and make speeches in praise of the American way of life. At government expense, in 1956 he went as a goodwill ambassador to the Melbourne Olympics, then served for a time in President Dwight D. Eisenhower's People-to-People Program. Republican to the marrow, Owens largely ignored the civil rights movement.

Deprived of White House patronage when the Democrats returned to power in 1960, he linked his name to a new public relations firm, Owens-West & Associates, in Chicago. While his partner managed the business, Owens stayed constantly on the road addressing business and athletic groups. For several years he carelessly neglected to report his extra income and in 1965 was indicted for tax evasion. He pleaded no contest and was found guilty as charged by a Chicago federal judge. At the sentencing, however, the judge lauded Owens for supporting the American flag and "our way of life" while others were "aiding and abetting the enemy openly" by protesting the Vietnam War. To his great relief, Owens was required merely to pay his back taxes and a nominal fine.

At the Mexico City Olympics in 1968, the politically conservative Owens reacted in horror to the demonstrative Black Power salutes of track medalists TOMMIE SMITH and John Carlos. He demanded of them an apology; they dismissed him as an Uncle Tom. Two years later, in a book ghostwritten by Paul Neimark, *Blackthink: My Life as Black Man and White Man* (1970), Owens savagely attacked Smith, Carlos, and others of their ilk as bigots in reverse. Laziness, not racial prejudice, condemned American blacks to failure, Owens insisted. "If the Negro doesn't succeed in today's America, it is because he has chosen to fail" (84). In response to hostile reactions from black readers and reviewers, Owens again collaborated with Neimark to rephrase his principles in more moderate terms published in *I Have Changed* (1972). Two more Neimark-Owens potboilers, *The Jesse Owens Story* (1970) and *Jesse: A Spiritual Autobiography* (1978), blended reminiscences with prescriptions of the work ethic, patriotism, and religious piety as means to success.

Owens's own success in the 1970s came largely from contracts with major corporations. Atlantic Richfield Company (ARCO) owned his name for exclusive commercial use and sponsored annual ARCO Jesse Owens games for boys and girls. At business conventions and in advertisements, Owens also regularly represented Sears, United Fruit, United States Rubber, Johnson & Johnson, Schieffelin, Ford Motor Company, and American Express. His name was made all the more useful by a bevy of public awards. In 1972 he finally received a degree from Ohio State, an honorary doctorate of athletic arts. In 1974 he was enshrined in the Track and Field Hall of Fame and honored with a Theodore Roosevelt Award from the National Collegiate Athletic Association for distinguished achievement since retirement from athletic competition.

To his black critics, the aging Owens was an embarrassment, a throwback to the servile posture of BOOKER T. WASHINGTON; to his admirers, his youthful athleticism and enduring fame made him an inspiration. On balance, his inspirational achievements transcended race and even politics. In 1976 he received the Medal of Freedom from Republican president Gerald Ford for serving as "a source of inspiration" for all Americans; in 1979 Democratic president Jimmy Carter presented Owens a Living Legends award for inspiring others "to reach for greatness." Within the next year, Owens died in Tucson, Arizona.

FURTHER READING

Barbara Moro's transcript of interviews with Jesse Owens and Ruth Owens in 1961 is in the Illinois State Historical Library, Springfield.

Bachrach, Susan D. *The Nazi Olympics: Berlin 1936* (2000).
Baker, William J. *Jesse Owens: An American Life* (1986).
Hart-Davis, Duff. *Hitler's Games: The 1936 Olympics* (1986).
Johnson, William O., Jr. *All That Glitters Is Not Gold: The Olympic Game* (1972).
Mandell, Richard D. *The Nazi Olympics* (1971).

Obituary: *New York Times*, 1 Apr. 1980.

—WILLIAM J. BAKER

P–Q

PAIGE, SATCHEL

(7 July 1906–8 June 1982), Negro League baseball pitcher and Hall of Famer, was born Leroy Robert Paige in Mobile, Alabama, the son of John Paige, a gardener, and Lulu (maiden name unknown), a washerwoman. Paige acquired his nickname as a youth after rigging a sling for toting satchels for travelers from the Mobile train station. He joined his first organized team, at the W. H. Council School, at age ten and soon developed a reputation as one of Mobile's best schoolboy players. But he also gained notoriety with the truant officer for frequently playing hooky and getting into gang fights. When he was twelve, Paige was committed to the Industrial School for Negro Children at Mount Meigs, Alabama, after he stole a handful of toy rings from a store. Paige later reflected that the five and a half years he spent at Mount Meigs "did something for me—they made a man out of me . . . and gave me a chance to polish up my baseball game."

The slender, six-foot, three-and-one-half inch Paige joined the semipro Mobile Tigers for the 1924 season. By his own account, he won thirty games and lost only one that year. Two years later, the peripatetic Paige jumped to the Chattanooga Black Lookouts of the Negro Southern League. Sold to the Birmingham Black Barons of the Negro National League in 1927, he moved on to the Nashville Elite Giants of the Negro Southern League in 1931. The team left Nashville for Cleveland that year, but the Depression hurt attendance, and the club folded before season's end.

That left Paige a free agent, of which he took advantage by selling his services to Gus Greenlee's Pittsburgh Crawfords. Greenlee, who ran the numbers in Pittsburgh's Hill District from his Crawford Grill, had taken on a black sandlot

Satchel Paige, pictured in 1942 in Kansas City Monarchs uniform, standing in the dugout with baseball in hand. Corbis

club the year before and was intent on remaking them into the top black club in the country.

Greenlee recruited some of the best players in the nation, including future Hall of Famers JOSH GIBSON, COOL PAPA BELL, JUDY JOHNSON, and Oscar Charleston. He built Greenlee Field, the finest black-owned stadium in the country, for the Crawfords to play in, and he resurrected the Negro National League, which had collapsed in 1931. With Gibson and Paige, the Crawfords had not only black baseball's best battery, but its two most marketable and highly paid players. Paige, who had filled out to 180 pounds, pitched for the Crawfords and also hired himself out on a freelance

basis to semipro teams through the 1933 season. (It was not uncommon for a black pro club to add a semipro player, usually a pitcher, when playing an unusually heavy schedule of games. Negro League players also sold their services on an ad hoc basis.) After a contract dispute with Greenlee, Paige left the Crawfords for a white semipro club in Bismarck, North Dakota, in 1935, returning for the 1936 season.

He did not stay for long. During spring training in New Orleans the following year, he was seduced by a lucrative offer to pitch for Ciudad Trujillo, a club in Santo Domingo associated with Dominican Republic dictator Rafael Trujillo. Paige said in his autobiography that he was offered thirty thousand dollars for his services and for recruiting eight other players, with the division of the money up to him. Gibson, Bell, and a half-dozen other Crawfords joined him, decimating the Crawfords but winning the island championship for Ciudad Trujillo.

Branded an outlaw by the Negro National League, Paige barnstormed with the Trujillo All-Stars on his return to the United States. Barnstorming meant traveling from town to town, usually living on buses, playing against teams of white major leaguers or local semipros, and splitting the proceeds at the gate. Greenlee then sold Paige's contract to the Newark Eagles, but he refused to report. Instead, he pitched in the Mexican League during the 1938 season, until a sore arm caused him to return to the United States.

Paige's career seemed over, and most black teams declined to bid for his services. Finally, Kansas City Monarchs' owner J. L. Wilkinson signed him to play for the Monarchs' second team, which barnstormed through the Northwest and Canada. Still a draw at the gate, Paige was advertised to pitch every game. Relying more on guile than his once-famous fastball, he would pitch for three innings before retiring to the bench. But as the summer wore on, his arm came back, and he reported to spring training with the Monarchs' regular club for the 1940 season.

For the next nine seasons, with Paige as their ace, the Monarchs challenged the Homestead Grays as black baseball's best team. A regular at the Negro League East-West All-Star game, Paige was known for his "bee ball" (you could hear it but not see it), pinpoint accuracy, and hesitation pitch. During the 1942 Negro League world series, he won three of the Monarchs' four victories over the Grays.

In 1948, Paige made his long-awaited debut in the major leagues. Cleveland Indians' owner Bill Veeck signed him during the 1948 pennant drive, and the forty-two-year-old "rookie" responded with six victories and only one defeat. Some 201,000 fans attended his first three starts, as the Indians set night game attendance records at home and in Chicago. Paige pitched for the Indians through the 1949 season, but he lost his spot on the roster after Veeck sold the team. His record that year was 4–7, with

a 3.04 ERA and five saves. Paige returned to the long bus rides through the night that characterized independent baseball, pitching for the Philadelphia Stars and for remnants of the Kansas City Monarchs.

He returned to the majors in 1951, reunited with Veeck, by then the owner of the St. Louis Browns. Paige won twelve games in 1952 for the hapless Browns and was selected to the American League All-Star team. After the 1953 season, Paige once again returned to barnstorming, but he was soon back in the minors, with stays at Miami in the International League (1956–1958) and Portland of the Pacific Coast League (1961). His last major league appearance came with the Kansas City Athletics in 1965. The Athletics' owner, Charles O. Finley, who signed Paige to help him qualify for a major league pension, put a rocking chair in the bullpen for the fifty-nine-year-old pitcher, who hurled three shutout innings against the Boston Red Sox. He is thought to be the oldest player to appear in a major league game.

Paige ended his career in 1967, riding the bus with black baseball's last team, the Indianapolis Clowns. He coached for the Atlanta Braves the following season. His major league statistics of 28 wins, 31 losses, 476 innings pitched, and a 3.29 ERA were only a belated addition to the numbers he put up during five decades on the mound.

Negro League and independent baseball records are incomplete, but, by his own account, Paige threw an estimated 55 no-hitters and won more than 2,000 of the 2,500 games in which he pitched. Many of the games were against semipro opposition. "I had that suit on every day, pretty near 365 days out of the year," he said. Paige told his biographer that he reckoned he had pitched before about ten million fans. Given his constant travels and ability to pitch virtually every day, it is likely that more fans personally witnessed Paige play than any other ballplayer.

Paige is perhaps most popularly remembered for the all-star aggregations of Negro Leaguers he led in exhibition games against teams of major league stars during the 1930s and 1940s. In these encounters, which sometimes matched Paige versus Dizzy Dean or another Hall of Fame pitching opponent, the Negro Leaguers more than held their own. His feats in such games

became part of baseball mythology. Many a fan recounts a story about a game in which Paige intentionally walked the bases loaded with major leaguers, told his fielders to sit down, and then struck out the side.

Paige married Janet Howard in 1934, but they divorced in 1943. He later married Lahoma Brown in 1974 and had six children with her.

Paige, who toured with the Harlem Globetrotters and appeared in a motion picture, *The Wonderful Country*, which starred Robert Mitchum, offered six rules as his guide to longevity:

1. Avoid fried meals, which angry up the blood.
2. If your stomach disputes you, lie down and pacify it with cool thoughts.
3. Keep the juices flowing by jangling around gently as you move.
4. Go very light on the vices, such as carrying on in society. The social rumble ain't restful.
5. Avoid running at all times.
6. Don't look back. Something might be gaining on you.

Satchel Paige embodied life in baseball's Negro Leagues. Black baseball's best-known performer, the lanky right-hander barnstormed his way across the United States, Canada, and into the Caribbean basin in a career that spanned half a century. By combining showmanship and incredible durability with magnificent talent, Paige became one of baseball's most enduring legends. In 1971, he was the first Negro League player elected to baseball's Hall of Fame. "To tell you the truth," Paige said in 1981, "all over Cuba, Santo Domingo, Puerto Rico, South America, everywhere I played, I had bouquets on my shoulder...I just could pitch. The Master just give me an arm.... You couldn't hardly beat me." He died in Kansas City, Missouri.

FURTHER READING

Paige, Leroy Satchel, with David Lipman. *Maybe I'll Pitch Forever* (1962).

Holway, John B. *Josh and Satch: The Life and Times of Josh Gibson and Satchel Paige* (1991).
Ribowsky, Mark. *Don't Look Back: Satchel Paige in the Shadows of Baseball* (1994).

—ROB RUCK

PARKER, CHARLIE

(29 Aug. 1920–12 Mar. 1955), jazz alto saxophonist, known as "Bird," "Yardbird," or "Yard," was born Charles Parker Jr. in Kansas City, Kansas. He was the only child of Charles Parker Sr., a chef on the Pullman Line who was a former dancer and singer, and Addie Boxley, a charwoman for Western Union who also cleaned houses, did laundry, and rented to boarders. Parker had an older half-brother, John "Ikey," who was his father's son from a previous relationship. The Parkers, without the often absent Charles Sr., moved to Kansas City, Missouri, in 1927. Charlie attended Penn School in Westport and during that time began to play the alto saxophone. He enrolled at Lincoln High School in 1932 and joined the school marching band, where he played the alto horn and later the baritone horn. During this time Charlie started playing alto saxophone with the pianist Lawrence Keyes and spent his nights on Twelfth Street listening to professional musicians, including the orchestra of COUNT BASIE and the tenor saxophonist Lester Young. Parker was able to experience the Kansas City nightlife because his mother worked at night, and this lifestyle probably contributed to his dropping out of high school.

During these years Parker participated in after-hours jam sessions to test himself against more experienced musicians. Two well-known jam sessions were failures—his performances were considered unacceptable. The first took place at the High Hat Club; after that he "did not play again for three months" (Russell, 64–65). After Parker's second failure in 1936 at the Reno Club, he left the club humiliated. He did not give up easily, however, and continued to seek instruction from more advanced musicians.

On 10 April 1934 the Ruffin family, including their daughter, Rebecca Ellen, moved into the Parkers' house as boarders. On 25 July 1936 Charlie and Rebecca were married. Addie Parker had to give her consent, because both of them were underage. Parker and Rebecca had a son, Francis Leon, born 10 January 1938. After his wedding Parker began working with Ernest Daniels in the Ozarks. On route to an

Charlie "Bird" Parker, legendary alto saxophonist. Library of Congress

engagement, he was in a serious car accident; during his recuperation he began using drugs. After his recovery, Parker started working with Tommy Douglas, a well-educated musician who taught Parker the fundamentals of his art, instructing him about reeds and proper embouchure (the formation of the mouth and lips while playing). Douglas may also have been the first to teach Parker about the use of "passing chords," whereby a musician superimposes additional chords over a given chord progression while improvising.

In the summer of 1937 Parker took a job with George E. Lee in the Ozarks. When the band was not performing, Parker received instruction in the cycle of fifths and passing chords from fellow band members, the guitarist Efferge Ware and the pianist Carrie Powell. Parker also transcribed and memorized several improvised solos of the tenor saxophonist Lester Young from recordings of Count Basie. When Parker returned to Kansas City in the fall of 1937, he participated in another jam session at the Reno Club, this time to

the approval of the other musicians. Later that fall, Buster "Prof" Smith hired Parker to play in his band, which included Jesse Price and Jay McShann. Smith taught Parker how to adjust reeds and became Parker's musical mentor. In 1938 Smith moved to New York, and the band broke up.

During this time the Kansas City Pendergast political machine was overturned, and, as a result, many nightclubs were closed. Parker left Kansas City for Chicago in the fall of 1938. In Chicago, he sat in with the King Kolax band, and the musicians in attendance were astounded at his virtuosity. In a few weeks Parker was on a bus to New York to locate his teacher and mentor Buster Smith. Smith and his wife took Parker into their home for a short time. To support himself, Parker took a dishwashing job at Jimmy's Chicken Shack, where he heard and was probably influenced by the pianist Art Tatum. In New York, too, Parker befriended the guitarist Bill "Biddy" Fleet, who gave him advice about harmony. Parker was soon performing around the city and in jam sessions at Clark Monroe's Uptown House and Dan Wall's Chili House.

In 1940 Parker received a telegram telling him that his father had died, and he returned to Kansas City for the funeral. He remained in Kansas City, where he befriended the pianist and arranger Tadd Dameron, who taught him the practical applications of music theory. Later in 1940 Parker joined the Jay McShann Orchestra, where he "rehearsed the reed section, played many solos, and kept everyone in good spirits" (Giddins, 58). Parker can be heard playing as a soloist on several recordings of the McShann band on Decca Records and on several bootleg recordings dating to this time. His first recorded solos were innovative improvisations that were studied and memorized by many jazz musicians. After numerous tours and recordings, Parker left McShann in December of 1942.

Parker returned to New York City and joined the Earl Hines band on the recommendation of George "Scoops" Carey, who had heard Parker in Chicago a few years earlier. Parker played tenor saxophone in the Hines band, which included DIZZY GILLESPIE, with whom Parker would establish a strong musical friendship. Hines did not record during Parker's tenure with the band, because of the American Federation of Musicians' ban on recording during this period. However, several jam session recordings that feature Parker from that time are now available.

On 10 April 1943 Parker married Geraldine Scott in Washington, D.C., but the marriage was not considered legal, because he was still married to Rebecca at the time. The relationship with Geraldine probably ended sometime in 1944. Parker left the Hines band after May 1943 and returned to Kansas City, his drug problem worsening. He worked for a short time around Kansas City before he was hired by Billy Eckstine to join his new big band, which included Dizzy Gillespie. Parker left Eckstine's band in 1944, and there are no extant recordings of that particular group. At about that time, Rebecca officially divorced Parker, and she retained custody of their son.

Parker returned to New York City, where he performed and recorded with Lloyd "Tiny" Grimes and Dizzy Gillespie and with his own groups. The re-

cordings with Gillespie from 1945 are considered to be prototypical of the new bebop style. During this time Parker was living with Doris Sydnor. In December 1945 Parker went to Los Angeles with Dizzy Gillespie and his group. When the L.A. engagement ended the following February, Parker stayed on, and his drug addiction reached extreme levels. His drug problem and declining health finally led to a physical breakdown and his arrest. He was hospitalized at Camarillo State Hospital, where Doris Sydnor visited him often. In January of 1947 he was released from Camarillo and continued performing in the Los Angeles area and recording for Ross Russell's Dial Records. Parker and Doris Sydnor returned to New York in April 1947 and were married on 20 November 1948.

In 1947 Parker formed his own band, including MILES DAVIS, Duke Jordan, Tommy Potter, and Max Roach. The group recorded for Dial, Savoy, and Clef, and they performed extensively. In 1948 Parker began an almost exclusive recording relationship with Norman Granz that included recordings with "conventional and Latin big bands, a string section, a big band and string combination, a vocal and wind ensemble, an all-star jam session, a reunion with Dizzy Gillespie and THELONIOUS MONK, and several one-time small groups" (Woideck, 46). Granz was able to get wide distribution for Parker's records, and it was not long before Parker was regularly winning magazine polls. In 1949 Parker's new quintet, including Kenny Dorham, Al Haig, Tommy Potter, and Roy Haynes, traveled to Paris, where they were well received. Upon returning to the United States, Parker replaced Kenny Dorham with the trumpeter Red Rodney. Also in 1949 the nightclub Birdland, a celebration of Parker's nickname "Bird," opened in New York.

When Parker's marriage with Sydnor ended in 1950, he began living with Chan Richardson. Although Parker and Richardson were never legally married, she took his name, and Parker adopted Richardson's daughter Kim. Parker and Richardson also had a daughter, Pree, born 17 July 1951 and a son, Baird, born 10 August 1952. In 1950 Parker's regular quintet gradually broke up as

agents found it easier and more profitable to book Parker as a solo act. During the same year Parker was hospitalized for a stomach ulcer caused by his heavy drinking. In July 1951 his cabaret card was revoked because of his drug arrest, and his ability to earn a living was severely limited. He had to travel outside New York, usually as a solo performer, to gain employment. He performed with Granz's "Jazz at the Philharmonic" tours and continued to record for Granz, even though he was apparently unhappy with the situation. In 1953 Parker's cabaret card was reinstated after the authorities heard his plea to work because of his daughter's health problems.

Pree Parker died on 6 March 1954 while Parker was performing in Los Angeles. This emotional blow contributed to Parker's increased drinking and drug abuse. When he returned to New York, he was hospitalized twice at Bellevue after apparent suicide attempts. In December 1954 Parker and Richardson separated, and Parker recorded for Granz for the last time. Parker died on 12 March 1955, probably in the apartment of the jazz patron Pannonica de Koenigswarter in the Stanhope Hotel in Manhattan. His death was attributed to "stomach ulcers and pneumonia, with a contributing condition of advanced cirrhosis and the possibility of a heart attack" (Russell, 358). Parker's funeral took place in New York, and he was buried in Lincoln Cemetery in Kansas City, Missouri.

Parker, who acquired his musical education through the African American oral and aural traditions, made numerous important contributions to jazz and remains one of the most important jazz musicians in history. He was a major innovator of the bebop style, influencing jazz performers on every instrument during his life and since. Parker was a primary influence on such jazz innovators as Dizzy Gillespie, Bud Powell, Miles Davis, JOHN COLTRANE, Paul Chambers, and Cannonball Adderley. Parker's improvisations were innovative in their use of syncopation, accents, asymmetric phrasing, melodic invention, ornamentation, and harmonic substitution. He was also adept at musical quotations of jazz musicians who inspired him, including Lester Young, Coleman Hawkins, and Roy Eldridge, as well as musical quotations of classical themes and popular songs of the day. His improvisations revolutionized jazz to the extent that nearly every jazz musician since has absorbed his musical vocabulary.

Parker contributed numerous compositions to the jazz repertoire, most of which were based on the chord progressions of the twelve-bar blues or standard repertoire of the day. Some of his best-known compositions include "Billie's Bounce," based on the twelve-bar blues; "Anthropology," based on "I Got Rhythm" by George and Ira Gershwin; "Ornithology," based on "How High the Moon" by Nancy Hamilton and Morgan Lewis; and "Donna Lee," based on "Back Home Again in Indiana" by Ballard McDonald and James F. Hanley. Parker's practice of composing new melodies on existing chord progressions crystallized his melodic vocabulary, and many of his compositions have become standards of the jazz repertoire.

FURTHER READING

Giddins, Gary. *Celebrating Bird: The Triumph of Charlie Parker* (1987).

Reisner, Robert G. *Bird: The Legend of Charlie Parker* (1962).

Russell, Ross. *Bird Lives! The High Life and Hard Times of Charlie (Yardbird) Parker* (1973).

Woideck, Carl. *Charlie Parker: His Music and Life* (1996).

Obituary: *New York Times*, 15 Mar. 1955.

Discography

Bregman, Robert M., Leonard Bukowski, and Norman Saks. *The Charlie Parker Discography* (1993).

—KENT J. ENGELHARDT

PARKER, WILLIAM

(1822?–?), slave narrative author and resistance leader, was born a slave to Louisa Simms in Anne Arundel County, Maryland, at Rowdown, a plantation with approximately seventy slaves, mostly field hands. What we know about William Parker is drawn from his own account published in 1866. His mother died early in his life, and William was raised by his grandmother, who was a cook in the plantation's main house.

Upon the death of Rowdown's owner, Major William Brogdon, the plantation was divided between his sons, William and David. William, along with many other slaves, including his brother and his uncle, was sent to live with David, who had built a house called Nearo on the southwestern portion of the farm. According to Parker's narrative, neither of the young masters abused his slaves, and William and the other slaves "were as contented as it is possible for slaves to be" (154). Slave sales, however, were another matter altogether. "No punishment was so much dreaded by the refractory slave as selling," Parker wrote (155). After William's friend Levi was deceived and sent by his owner to deliver a letter to a family acquaintance, a man to whom he had secretly been sold, Parker began to consider escape seriously. He estimates that he was sixteen or seventeen at the time.

After a confrontation with his owner, William and his brother, Charles, escaped via Baltimore, Maryland, and York, Pennsylvania, to a farm area about five miles east of Lancaster, Pennsylvania. After working there for three months, William visited his brother, who had settled in Bart Township, near Smyrna, fifteen miles to the east. William remained with him for thirteen months before getting work with a physician named Dr. Dengy.

Through Quaker influence, the region, located in the southeastern portion of Pennsylvania, had long been a focal point of antislavery activity and an important stop on the Underground Railroad. The tensions between slave catchers and abolitionists were intensified by the 1850 Fugitive Slave Law, which required free states to return escaped slaves to their southern owners or face federal penalties. Lancaster County was particularly dangerous for black Americans because of the Gap Gang, a roving group that patrolled the region looking for escaped slaves, who could be returned for bounty, and for free blacks, who could be captured and sold into slavery. The violence of these patrols increased after a series of altercations, including one clash that left three slave catchers dead following their attempt to return an escaped slave girl to Maryland.

While living with Dr. Dengy, Parker attended an antislavery meeting at which FREDERICK DOUGLASS—with whom he had been acquainted when they were both slaves in Maryland—and William Lloyd Garrison spoke. Parker joined with Douglass and other African Americans in opposing the Fugitive Slave Law by forming a self-protection society to defend African Americans against slave catchers and northern white vigilantes. By then Parker had married a woman named Eliza Ann Elizabeth Howard, who was also an escaped slave from Maryland. Eliza's mother, brother, and sisters had also escaped and were living in the Lancaster area. Eliza, who married Parker when she was about sixteen years old, was twenty-one and the mother of their three children when Parker began his abolitionist work.

Parker reports in his narrative that on 9 September 1851 Edward Gorsuch, accompanied by a small group of men, arrived in Philadelphia, Pennsylvania, from rural Baltimore County, Maryland, with the intention of traveling to Christiana, Pennsylvania, to capture four former slaves who in November 1849 had stolen five bushels of Gorsuch's wheat. The four escaped slaves had been directed to Parker, who had developed a reputation in his community for assisting fugitive slaves. Gorsuch had learned that the men he sought resided with Parker, and he intended to reclaim them. Gorsuch and his six men, however, encountered more than Parker and the fugitives. Seventy-five to one hundred armed neighbors—both black and white—had responded to a horn blown by Parker's wife. The armed confrontation quickly escalated, leaving Gorsuch dead and his son, his nephew, and others wounded. The incident came to be known as the Christiana Resistance.

Newspapers widely circulated accounts of the resistance, and Parker quickly became a marked man. To avoid arrest, Parker, sending his wife separately, journeyed to Canada via the Underground Railroad. He traveled north through Rochester, New York, where he briefly stopped at Frederick Douglass's home before departing for Toronto, Ontario, arriving in Canada in September 1851. There, Parker learned that Pennsylvania's governor, William Johnston, was seeking his return to the state under the terms of the Extradition Treaty. Parker's wife arrived two months after Parker's arrival in Toronto, having narrowly escaped capture on several occasions. With the help of supporters, Parker was eventually able to purchase land and build a house. Little is known of his life in Canada, and the date and circumstances of his death are unknown.

Parker's narrative, "The Freedman's Story. In Two Parts," first published in 1866 in the *Atlantic Monthly*, illuminates a number of aspects of slavery, including, to some extent, the workings of the Underground Railroad. The account chronicles the experiences of African Americans in antebellum Lancaster County, Pennsylvania, and makes clear that African American resistance was organized around an intricate network of warnings, plans, and armed defense. The narrative is significant as well for its first-person account of the Christiana Resistance. The veracity of Parker's narrative, however, remains in doubt. Because Parker was most likely illiterate, his narrative was edited by someone identified only as "E.K.," who writes in the introduction, "The manuscript of the following pages has been handed to me with the request that I would revise it for publication, or weave its facts into a story which should show the fitness of the Southern black for the exercise of the right of suffrage." The narrative, published fifteen years after the Christiana Resistance, clearly has an agenda that reaches beyond the particulars of Parker's life. According to Parker's account, for example, he was a primary participant during the resistance. Contemporaneous accounts, however, indicate that he was only one of many resistance leaders.

Although potentially compromised, Parker's narrative provides the only account of the incident from a combatant who was inside the house. And even though the centrality and extent of Parker's involvement may be questioned, the strength of his beliefs should not. Parker's involvement in the Christiana Resistance represents the larger dissatisfaction that many felt with the Compromise of 1850 and the Fugitive Slave Law.

FURTHER READING

Parker, William. "The Freedman's Story. In Two Parts." *Atlantic Monthly: A Magazine of Literature, Science, Art and Politics* 17 (Feb. and Mar. 1866).
—STERLING LECATER BLAND JR.

PARKS, GORDON, JR.

(7 Dec. 1934–3 Apr. 1979), filmmaker, was born in Minneapolis, Minnesota, the eldest son of Sally Alvis and GORDON PARKS SR., the latter an award-winning photojournalist, author, composer, and filmmaker. Born less than a year into his parents' marriage, Gordon Jr. was nicknamed Butch as a newborn by his maternal grandfather, Joe Alvis. "There was not too much I could give my first three children being a waiter on a railway," recalled Gordon Parks Sr. in the 2001 film documentary *Half Past Autumn*. In 1940 the Parks family moved to Chicago. There Gordon Jr. spent much of his childhood while his father forged his career. Parks developed a passion for riding horses, which became a lifelong interest.

When he was sixteen Parks moved to Paris, where his father had been assigned for two years by *Life* magazine. In Europe, he developed a keen interest in the fine arts, also cultivating a desire to travel that greatly influenced his later career as a filmmaker. He attended the American School in Paris, where he learned French as a second language, and accompanied his father to concerts, museums, and weekend and summer jaunts to St. Tropez and Cannes. While in school he took up painting and began to direct student plays.

After moving back to New York, Parks watched as his parents' marriage crumbled. Estranged from his mother, Parks and his siblings, Toni and David, went to live with his father. In 1952 he graduated from high school in White Plains, New York. In an attempt to distance himself from the career path of his famous father, Parks worked for a time in the garment district of New York City, moving clothing racks. When he was photographing a story for *Life* magazine, however, Gordon Sr. offered his son the opportunity to spend a weekend hanging out with the infamous gang leader Red Jackson. The opportunity presumably had an effect on the inner-city realism that Parks later brought to his first feature film, *Superfly*.

In 1957 Parks was drafted into the U.S. Army. While stationed in Desert Rock, Nevada, his convoy truck broke down and he narrowly missed radiation

exposure from a nearby atomic test. After six months of close observation, he was discharged from the army and returned to New York City. During the early 1960s Parks played guitar and sang folk music in bars and coffeehouses in New York City's Greenwich Village.

Much of Parks's professional life, however, was spent in the shadow of his father. Because their names are so much alike, many of Parks's accomplishments have been mistakenly credited to his father. Commenting on their father-son relationship, Parks's stepmother, Genevieve, noted in the film documentary *Half Past Autumn* that there was always a "certain air of competitiveness between the two." Like his father, Parks developed a professional interest in photography, using the name Gordon Rogers for several years to distance himself from his birth name. In 1969 he was hired as a still photographer for the Marlon Brando film *Burn!* and performed the same role on a more famous Brando film in 1972—*The Godfather*. Parks also worked as a cameraman on his father's 1969 debut film, *The Learning Tree*. From these experiences, Parks learned much about making films. "I love movies, I've spent hours at movies, our generation is all movies," he said in an interview. "I've lived with film all my life" (*Oakland Post*, 3 Aug. 1972).

In 1972 Parks capitalized on his passion for movies by directing the action-thriller *Superfly*. The story of Priest, a drug pusher attempting to better his life, *Superfly* became noted for its gritty realism and its ability to elicit audience sympathy for its criminal antihero. Released on the heels of his father's landmark 1971 detective drama, *Shaft*, the film was largely produced by black businessmen, using a black crew, on a shoestring budget of $500,000. Widely considered the zenith of the so-called blaxploitation films of the early 1970s, *Superfly* went on to gross tens of millions of dollars. The film sparked a huge commercial boom in black-themed films and catapulted the careers of a number of black directors. Critics have credited Parks with some of the film's more interesting touches, including its steamy, risqué sex scene, the photographic black-and-white stills that appear toward the middle of the narrative, and the decision to foreground the film's now-classic musical score composed by Curtis Mayfield. *Superfly*, however, unleashed a maelstrom of controversy about the moral direction of black films in Hollywood. While some critics saw it as a harsh and invigorating depiction of black urban life, others criticized the film for its romanticization of machismo, drug use, and crime.

Having moved to his horse ranch in the California Valley, Parks continued to direct films. In 1974 he helmed the lumbering *Thomasine and Bushrod*, starring Max Julien and Vonetta McGee. A black "Bonnie and Clyde" set at the turn of the twentieth century, the film recounts the story of Oklahoma thieves who steal from rich whites to give to poor people of color. His next film, *Three the Hard Way* (1974), starred the action heroes JIM BROWN, Fred Williamson, and Jim Kelly as a trio out to save the United States from a white-supremacist plot to taint the national water supply. In 1975 he directed *Aaron Loves Angela*, an inner-city update of the *Romeo and Juliet* story transformed into a black and Puerto Rican conflict, which was released just months before his father's *Leadbelly*. Each of Parks's releases faded into obscurity, either due to studio neglect or audience disinterest, and many critics felt that Parks had lost his artistic footing since *Superfly*.

In 1979 tragedy struck. Parks had just started an independent production company, African International Productions/Panther Film Company, and planned to make the first of three films on the African continent. On 3 April 1979 he died in Kenya when his plane crashed in an aborted takeoff on the runway of the Nairobi airport. After his cremation, some of his ashes were left in Africa and the rest brought back to New York City, where services were held at the United Nations' Chapel. At the time of Parks's death, his wife, Leslie, was pregnant with his first child, Gordon III.

Even in death, newspaper and radio reports mistakenly announced that Gordon Parks Sr. had been killed, and bibliographical accounts still often confuse the two men.

FURTHER READING

Bogle, Donald. *Toms, Coons, Mulattoes, Mammies, and Bucks: An Interpretive History of Blacks in American Films* (1989).

Kovel, Mikel J. *Blaxploitation Films* (2001).

Parks, Gordon, Sr. *Half Past Autumn: A Retrospective* (1997).

——. *Voices in the Mirror: An Autobiography* (1990).

Obituary: *Jet*, 19 Apr. 1979.

—JASON KING

PARKS, GORDON, SR.

(20 Nov. 1912–), photographer, filmmaker, author, and composer, was born Gordon Roger Alexander Buchanan Parks in the small prairie town of Fort Scott, Kansas, to Andrew Jackson Parks, a dirt farmer, and Sarah Ross, a maid. Gordon was the youngest of fifteen children, the first five of which, he later discovered, were really half-siblings, born to his father and a woman other than his mother. Gordon's poor Kansas childhood, and his memories of its unbridled racism, feature prominently in his later work, especially his books "thick

This evocative photograph of Ella Watson, a federal government cleaning woman, taken by Gordon Parks Sr. in 1942, has been dubbed "American Gothic" in reference to Grant Wood's famous painting of the same name. © CORBIS

with those memories." The first phase of Gordon's life ended with the death of his mother in 1928. "Before the flowers on my mother's grave had wilted," Parks remembered, "my father had me on a train to my sister in Minnesota. I ran into some hell there" (Russell, 145). Within a month of his arrival in Minneapolis–St. Paul, Gordon's brother-in-law kicked him out of the house, forcing him to survive the winter by riding the subway trains at night and hanging out in pool halls during the day. High school was merely a place to stay out of the cold, and Gordon soon dropped out. Years later Parks dedicated one of his forty-six honorary degrees to his high school teacher who counseled her black students, "Don't bother to go to college and spend your mother's and father's money, because you're gonna be porters and maids" (Russell, 145).

For a while, at least, that teacher was right. Parks worked as a waiter and busboy, first at the Minnesota Club and later at the Hotel Lowry, where he catered to white patrons and met musicians in the big bands. Having taught himself to play by ear, Parks began composing songs and landed a job playing piano in a St. Paul brothel. Invited to join a touring orchestra, Parks arrived in Harlem in March 1933. The group, however, disbanded almost immediately, and he was stranded without a job. After making a few deliveries for a dope dealer, he joined the newly established Civilian Conservation Corps (CCC), planting trees and clearing camping grounds and beaches until July 1934.

While in the CCC, Parks met and married Sally Alvis. The couple moved back to Minneapolis and had three children, GORDON PARKS JR., Toni, and David. Parks returned to playing piano and waiting tables until 1935, when he was hired by the North Coast Limited railroad. A discarded magazine featuring the work of Farm Security Administration (FSA) photographers, such as Walker Evans, Dorthea Lange, Ben Shahn, and Arthur Rothstein, captured Parks's attention. After visiting the Art Institute of Chicago on a layover and watching a newsreel of the 1937 sinking of the USS *Panay* taken by photojournalist Norman Alley, who was present at the screening, Parks bought his first camera, a Voightlander Brilliant, at a Seattle pawnshop.

After Parks was fired following a racial incident provoked by a white steward, he played for a season as a semiprofessional basketball player with the House of David team before being hired by the Chicago and Northwestern Railway. Parks photographed while on the road and regularly contributed to the *Minneapolis Spokesman* and the *St. Paul Recorder*, and in February 1938 he had his first exhibition in the window of a Minneapolis Eastman Kodak store. Parks's personal charisma and his eye for beauty—in women and line—led him to fashion photography. At the urging of Marva Louis, JOE LOUIS's wife, Parks moved his family to Chicago, where he photographed fashions and did portrait work for both black and white clients. In what would become a lifelong pattern, he divided his time between these glamorous subjects and photojournalism. In Chicago he documented the devastating effects of poverty, accompanied FSA photographer Jack Delano on several assignments, and shadowed

Edwin Rosskam during preparation for the book *12 Million Black Voices*, for which RICHARD WRIGHT wrote the text. The book proved a powerful influence on Parks's work, especially in shaping his approach to the relationship of word and image and the sequencing and juxtaposing of images.

When Parks won a Julius Rosenwald Fellowship in 1941, the first ever awarded in photography, he arranged for an apprenticeship at the FSA in Washington, D.C., under Roy Emerson Stryker. Parks and his family were not prepared for the racism they encountered upon their arrival in the nation's capital. "You have to get at the source of their bigotry, and that's not easy," Stryker counseled Parks. "The camera becomes a powerful weapon" (Parks, 1997, 32). Stryker sent Parks to research the FSA photo files and suggested that he talk with Ella Watson, an African American cleaning woman who worked in the building. Among the series of photos Parks took of Watson and her family was a posed image of Watson standing in front of an American flag with a mop in one hand and a broom in the other. The photo, later dubbed "American Gothic," referencing Grant Wood's 1930 painting of the same name, was Parks's first official FSA photo, and it became one of photography's iconic images.

Stryker sent Parks on assignment in New England, upstate New York, and Washington, D.C and, in August 1943, to photograph Richard Wright in Harlem. When the FSA was disbanded in 1943, Parks went with Stryker to the Office of War Information (OWI), for which he photographed the military's first black fighter pilots under the command of lieutenant colonel BENJAMIN O. DAVIS JR. In 1944 Parks resigned and moved to Harlem, looking for work in fashion photography. Through Edward Steichen, he was hired by *Glamour* and then *Vogue*. From 1944 to 1948 he also worked for Stryker at Standard Oil of New Jersey, which had launched a photography project established to document American life.

Parks's photographic style—unsentimental, confident, and graphically strong—was already established, and in 1947 he published his first book, a how-to volume entitled *Flash Photography*. The next year he followed with

Camera Portraits: Techniques and Principles of Documentary Portraiture, which included, among others, portraits of ADAM CLAYTON POWELL JR. and RALPH ELLISON.

In 1948 Parks talked his way into a job at *Life* magazine, the nation's most popular and influential general interest magazine. *Life*'s first black staff photographer, Parks remained with the magazine for over twenty years, completing more than three hundred assignments and fifteen magazine covers. His first assignments, balancing the disparate worlds of fashion and a photo essay centering on sixteen-year-old Harlem gang leader Red Jackson, were illustrative of the range of his *Life* career. After eighteen months Parks was assigned to *Life*'s Paris bureau for two years. Over the years, Parks photographed cowboys and priests, movie stars and royalty, Broadway shows and the emerging world of television, international events and political campaigns, fashion shows and the daily lives of Americans. "Tyrants, dictators, dethroned kings, beggars, queens, harlots, priests, the uplifting and the despoilers," recalled Parks, "all stared into my camera with eyes that were unveiled. The camera revealed them as they were—human beings imprisoned inside themselves" (Parks, 1997, 13). Lauded for his portraits, Parks photographed such leading personalities as ALTHEA GIBSON, SUGAR RAY ROBINSON, SIDNEY BECHET, EARTHA KITT, LOUIS ARMSTRONG, DUKE ELLINGTON, Leonard Bernstein, Barbra Streisand, Marcel Duchamp, Alberto Giacometti, Alexander Calder, and Dwight D. Eisenhower.

Meanwhile, Parks was producing photo essays on social issues, and by the 1960s he had become one of the country's most respected and influential photojournalists. In 1956 Parks documented the effects of segregation on one family in the photo essay "Segregation in the Deep South, Choctaw County, Alabama." Over the next few years, he continued to tackle America's underbelly with "Segregation in the North," "Crime Across America," and "Unemployment in Philadelphia." "Freedom's Fearful Foe: Poverty," published in the 16 June 1961 issue of *Life* and arguably Parks's most influential photo essay, was originally slated for only one photo. The stark photos of an ailing and malnourished Brazilian boy, Flavio de Silva of Rio de Janeiro, prompted a spontaneous response from American readers, who sent in thirty thousand dollars. Several years later when *Life* editor Phil Kunhardt asked, "Why are black people rioting in the middle of America," Parks responded by moving in with the Fontenelle family in Harlem for one week. The result was "Poverty in Harlem," a groundbreaking photo essay published in 1968.

"*Life* magazine was very good about not assigning me 'black stories,' " Parks always maintained. He did, however, cover—in word and image—the significant figures and events of the civil rights and Black Power movements, joining Charlie Moore, MONETA SLEET, Robert Haggins, Jonathan Eubanks, Jack T. Franklin, and Ernest Withers as one of the most significant documentarians of the period. In 1963 he published major stories on the March on Washington and on black Muslims. Following MALCOLM X's assassination two year later, Parks published the photo essay "Death of Malcolm X," after which, on the recommendation of the FBI, who took seriously threats from the Nation of Islam, the Parks family was sent overseas for a short time. As the decade progressed, Parks photographed STOKELY CARMICHAEL, Kathleen and ELDRIDGE CLEAVER, and MUHAMMAD ALI, covered the funeral of MARTIN LUTHER KING JR., and spent three weeks with the Black Panthers in Berkeley, California.

Unpretentious, spare, and straightforward, Parks's photographs belie the formal rigor of their construction. Parks's careful attention to the strategic possibilities of space and light, and his decisive use of objects and signs, both literal and poetic, produced a lifetime of rich images. As his photographic career progressed, Parks became increasingly interested in color and abstraction, and by the 1980s he was exhibiting paintings and works in other media as well as color photographs.

In 1963, encouraged by his friend and *Life* photographer Carl Mydans, who chided, "Man you've got a novel in you," Parks published *The Learning Tree*, a novel based on his Kansas childhood. The book became a best seller, and *Life* commissioned a series of photographs that it published alongside Parks's essay "How It Feels to Be

Black." With help from filmmaker John Cassavetes, Parks wrote, directed, and scored a Hollywood film based on the book in 1969. Thirty years later the film was among the twenty-five films placed on the National Film Registry of the Library of Congress. Parks's first films, documentaries made in the mid- to late 1960s, had grown out of *Life* stories: *Flavio* (1964), *Diary of a Harlem Family* (1968), and *The World of Piri Thomas* (1968). After the success of *The Learning Tree*, he entered the arena of popular fiction film with *Shaft* (1971), starring Richard Roundtree. *Shaft's Big Score!* (1972) and *The Super Cops* (1974) followed. Parks returned to documentary filmmaking with LEAD BELLY (1976) and SOLOMON NORTHUP's *Odyssey* (1984).

Parks published three full-length autobiographies, in 1966, 1979, and 1990. He was one of the founders of *Essence* magazine, serving as editorial director from 1970 to 1973, during which time he published *Born Black* (1971), a collection of essays. *The Weapons of Gordon Parks*, a television adaptation of his earliest memoir, was presented on network television in 1969. Parks combined photographs and poetry in *A Poet and His Camera* (1968), *Whispers of Intimate Things* (1971), *In Love* (1971), *Moments Without Proper Names* (1975), *Aries in Silence* (1994), and *Glimpses Toward Infinity* (1996). Other publications included two historical novels, *Shannon* (1981), set in New York during World War I, and *The Sun Stalkers* (2003), based on the life of the painter Joseph M. W. Turner. Parks also produced an autobiographical film, *Gordon Parks: Moments Without Proper Names*, which aired in 1988.

In addition to his photographic, film, and literary work, Parks continued playing and composing music, including several classical compositions. Beginning with *The Learning Tree*, he wrote several film scores, some of which were released as independent albums. In 1989 he wrote the libretto and music for *Martin*, a ballet based on the life of Martin Luther King Jr., which he later put on film.

In 1961 Parks and Sally Alvis divorced. Two years later he married Elizabeth Campbell, daughter of pioneering black cartoonist Elmer "E. Simms" Campbell. The couple had a daughter, Leslie, and divorced in 1973. The same

year he married Genevieve Young, his editor at Harper and Row. The couple divorced in 1979, the same year that his son, Gordon Parks Jr., director of the film *Superfly*, was killed in a plane crash at the age of forty-four.

Parks was awarded the NAACP's highest honor, the Spingarn Medal, in 1972, and a National Medal of Arts in 1988. In 1997 the Corcoran Gallery of Art in Washington, D.C., organized *Half Past Autumn*, the first major museum retrospective of Parks's work. Described by Parks as a "a tone-poem," the exhibition, which traveled through 2003 to ten major cities, included over two hundred photographs, as well as films, novels, poetry, and music. A companion documentary of the same name, coproduced by DENZEL WASHINGTON, aired on HBO in 2000. Parks wrote the exhibition's accompanying book, dedicating it "For Momma and Poppa I stay drenched in the showers of their love."

FURTHER READING

Parks's papers, photographs, films, and music are held by the Library of Congress.

Parks, Gordon. *A Choice of Weapons* (1966).
———. *Half Past Autumn: A Retrospective* (1997).
———. *To Smile in Autumn* (1979).
———. *Voices in the Mirror: An Autobiography* (1990).

Bush, Martin. *The Photographs of Gordon Parks* (1983).
Russell, Dick. *Black Genius* (1998).

—LISA E. RIVO

PARKS, ROSA

(14 Feb. 1913–), was born Rosa Louise McCauley in Tuskegee, Alabama, the daughter of James McCauley, a carpenter, and Leona Edwards, a teacher. Her father migrated north when Rosa was two years old, and her mother schooled her at home until, at age eleven, she enrolled in the Montgomery Industrial School for Girls. She attended Alabama State Teacher's High School, but left before graduation to care for her mother. On 18 December 1932 Rosa Louise McCauley married Raymond Parks, a barber from Wedowee in Randolph County, Alabama. With her husband's encouragement, Parks completed

Rosa Parks is fingerprinted after being arrested for refusing to give up her seat, 1955. Library of Congress

her high school education in 1934. A member of the St. Paul AME Church, she was responsible for preparing Holy Communion.

From the beginning of their marriage Raymond and Rosa Parks embraced social activism, working, for example, to secure the release of the SCOTTSBORO BOYS, nine black youths accused of raping two white girls. During the 1940s Rosa Parks joined the Montgomery chapter of the NAACP, and as secretary of the branch from 1943 until 1956 she often hosted the organization's dynamic field secretary, ELLA BAKER, when she visited Montgomery. E. D. NIXON, organizer of the Black Brotherhood of Sleeping Car Porters Union in Montgomery and head of the Progressive Democrats, was president of the local NAACP chapter.

Rosa Parks proved adept at working with young people. She helped train a group of NAACP youths to protest segregation in the Montgomery Public Library, and she participated in voter-registration drives. Indeed, in 1945 Parks became one of just a few African Americans who were registered to vote in Montgomery. The registrar had failed her the first two times she took the literacy text. The same determination displayed in her pursuit of the vote surfaced when Parks chose to be arrested

rather than to abide segregation on Montgomery's buses. It is important to underscore the extent to which Parks was anchored to the organizational and institutional infrastructure of the Montgomery black community. This is essential to understanding why she was able to inspire the modern civil rights movement.

Weary of the daily humiliations of second-class citizenship and the indignity of Jim Crow racial subordination, on 1 December 1955, the bespectacled and composed Rosa Parks refused to comply with the bus driver James F. Blake's order that she give the bus seat she occupied in the first row of the black section to a white male passenger. Three other African Americans vacated their seats, but Parks refused to move. The city's complex segregation laws dictated that African Americans pay their fares, exit the bus, and reenter through the rear door. Whites enjoyed the privilege of sitting in the front of the bus, and blacks occupied reserved seats in the rear. If the white section filled up and more white passengers boarded the bus, the black passengers were required to move.

Parks had not planned to disobey the law on that fateful day, but her thirty-year commitment to social justice prepared her to do so. Indeed, in June 1955

Parks had attended a summer workshop at the Highlander Folk School founded by Myles Horton in Monteagle, Tennessee, which had long been a training ground for labor organizers and social activists. In 1959 the state of Tennessee would label the Highlander Folk School a subversive organization. Still, at Highlander, Parks, like her fellow activists Ella Baker and SEPTIMA CLARK, acquired a deeper appreciation of and skills for community organizing, use of direct-action tactics, and administration of citizenship schools. Their preparation and long involvement in community affairs placed black women at the center of the civil rights movement.

For her defiance of the segregation ordinance, the Montgomery police hauled Parks off to jail. Montgomery's police lieutenant, Drue Lackey (who served as police chief from 1965 to 1970), took her fingerprints. Responding to a call from Nixon, the white attorney Clifford Durr took her case, but Nixon posted her bail. The court found Parks guilty of disorderly conduct and fined her ten dollars and another four dollars in court costs. Rosa Parks was not the first black woman to have suffered arrest for refusal to countenance bus segregation. In 1941 an angry mob beat Hannah Cofield before she was arrested for refusing to yield her seat to a white passenger. In 1944 Viola White met a similar fate. In March 1955, a few months before Parks's arrest, Claudette Colvin, an unmarried, pregnant fifteen-year-old girl, had objected to vacating her seat and was jailed.

The local black leadership had long debated challenging bus segregation, but decided to wait for an incident involving someone who embodied the politics of respectability and whose private life could withstand relentless scrutiny. Thus, although Cofield, White, Colvin, and later, Mary Louise Smith, protested bus segregation, their resistance failed to ignite a larger social protest movement. Propitiously, in July 1955, the U.S. Court of Appeals in Richmond, Virginia, declared in *Flemming v. South Carolina Electric and Gas Company* that bus segregation, even on buses that operated within one state, was unconstitutional.

When the police arrested Rosa Parks, diverse factions within the Montgomery black community swung into nonviolent direct action. On 2 December 1955 the Women's Political Council (WPC), under the leadership of Jo Ann Robinson, an English professor at Alabama State College, mimeographed and, with two hundred volunteers, distributed more than thirty thousand handbills imploring black citizens to stay off the buses. The flyer declared, "Another Negro woman has been arrested and thrown into jail, because she refused to get up out of her seat on the bus for a white person to sit down.... Negroes have rights, too, for if Negroes did not ride the buses, they could not operate.... The next time it may be you, or your daughter, or mother (Robinson, 45–46).

Actually, the WPC had long prepared to declare a boycott. Black leaders called a mass meeting at Holt Street Baptist Church and voted to continue the boycott under the aegis of the newly formed Montgomery Improvement Association (MIA). A number of women served on the MIA executive committee, including Robinson and Parks and Erna Dungee Allen, who served as financial secretary. A young minister of Dexter Avenue Baptist Church, the Reverend Martin Luther King Jr. accepted the presidency of the MIA and led the discussions and negotiations with white authorities. Parks's arrest sparked the bus boycott movement that began on 5 December 1955 and lasted 381 days, ending on 20 December 1956. The black attorney Fred D. Gray, on behalf of the MIA, filed a lawsuit against segregation in federal court on 1 February 1956. On 2 June 1956 in a 2–1 decision, the federal court found the Montgomery bus-segregation ordinances to be unconstitutional. On appeal, on 13 November 1956, the U.S. Supreme Court concurred with the federal court, ruling that racial segregation on public transportation in Montgomery and throughout the South was unconstitutional.

Parks's successful challenge to racial segregation attracted threats of violence and harassment and resulted in the loss of her job as a seamstress at Montgomery Fair Department Store. In 1957 Raymond and Rosa Parks and Rosa's mother joined her younger brother, Sylvester, in Detroit to seek jobs and personal security. For several years Rosa Parks worked as a seamstress. In 1965 she accepted a special assistant position on the staff in the Detroit office of Representative John Conyers Jr. She remained in his employ for nearly twenty years, during which time she assisted Conyers in his efforts to make Martin Luther King Jr.'s birthday a national holiday. In 1977 Parks's husband and brother died. Ten years later she and a friend, Elaine Eason Steele, founded a nonprofit organization, the Raymond and Rosa Parks Institute for Self-Development, to honor her husband's memory and commitment to the struggle for social justice and human rights.

In the last decades of the century Parks received national recognition for her role in the civil rights movement. The NAACP gave her its highest honor, the Spingarn Award, in 1977. She also received the Presidential Medal of Freedom, the nation's highest civilian honor. On 15 June 1999, Parks was awarded the Congressional Gold Medal. In introducing the bill authorizing the award, Representative Julia Carson of Indiana declared, "Rosa Parks is the Mother of America's Civil Rights Movement. Her quiet courage that day in Montgomery, Alabama launched a new American revolution that opened new doors of opportunity and brought equality for all Americans close to a reality" ("Carson Calls for Cosponsors for Bill to Award Congressional Gold Medal to Rosa Park," 24 Feb. 1999).

FURTHER READING

Parks, Rosa. "Rosa Louise Parks Biographical Sketch" from the Rosa and Raymond Parks Institute for Self Development, Detroit, Michigan (2003).

Parks, Rosa, with Jim Haskins. *My Story* (1999).

Brinkley, Douglas. *Rosa Parks* (2000).

King, Martin Luther, Jr. *Stride toward Freedom: The Montgomery Story* (1958).

Robinson, Jo Ann Gibson. *The Montgomery Bus Boycott and the Women Who Started It: The Memoir of Jo Ann Gibson Robinson* (1984).

Thornton, J. Mills, III. *Dividing Lines: Municipal Politics and the Struggle for Civil Rights in Montgomery, Birmingham, and Selma* (2002).

United States House of Representatives Press Release, "Carson Calls for Cosponsors for Bill to Award Congressional Gold Medal to Rosa Parks," February 24, 1999.

—Darlene Clark Hine

PARKS, SUZAN-LORI

(10 May 1964–) playwright, was born at Fort Knox, Kentucky, to Francis McMillan, an educator, and Donald Parks, an army officer and, later, professor. From her parents Suzan-Lori gained cultural exposure, a love for literature, and an understanding of the value in education. Her ability as a writer surfaced early on, and she began writing stories at age five. With her father in the army, Suzan-Lori spent her childhood years in a variety of different locales, including six American states and West Germany. Rather than the traditional American schools attended by the children of most servicemen, Suzan-Lori attended a German high school.

Parks then entered Mount Holyoke College in South Hadley, Massachusetts, graduating cum laude and Phi Beta Kappa in 1985 with a BA in English and German. While at Mount Holyoke, she studied creative writing with the celebrated writer James Baldwin. Impressed with her ability as well as her dexterity with dialogue, Baldwin recommended that she try her skills at playwriting. After graduating from college, Parks studied acting at the Drama Studio in London in 1986.

Parks exploded onto the American theater scene on her return to the United States from London. Beginning in 1986 sections of her play *Imperceptible Mutabilities in the Third Kingdom* premiered at the Brooklyn Arts Council Association Downtown (BACA) and the Brooklyn Fringe Festival, both in New York. Parks's work attracted so much attention that in 1989 the BACA mounted the entire four parts of the play. Directed by Parks's longtime associate Liz Diamond, the play won the 1990 Obie Award for Best Off-Broadway Play. *Imperceptible Mutabilities*, abstract in both form and language, explores in five playlets the legacy of African American experiences under the hegemony of a racist white world. Parks uses symbolism, metaphor, humor, and irony to probe the relationship between the African American historical past and the construction of contemporary African American identity. In one particularly striking section, entitled "Emancipation Day," black actors performed in whiteface at the BACA.

Her next work, *Betting on the Dust Commander*, premiered at the Gas Station in New York in 1987. The following year, her play *Pickling* was produced at the BACA Downtown and broadcast on New American Radio in 1990. Parks's critically acclaimed *Death of the Last Black Man in the Whole Entire World* was first produced in New York at the St. Marks Poet's Theatre in 1988 and then at the BACA Downtown in 1990. Two years later it was reproduced under the direction of Liz Diamond at Yale Repertory Theatre in New Haven. In the play Parks confronts historical events, questions stereotypes, and debunks cultural myths through the story of a husband and wife in crisis. The wife, Black Woman with Fried Drumstick, struggles with the return of her husband, Black Man with Watermelon, whom she believed to be dead.

Parks's plays were extremely experimental. She crafted both hyperrealistic dramas and nonrepresentational expressionistic plays. Even as her style changed, Parks has remained profoundly interested in questions of African American identity and history. American history, she argues, has too often excluded African American experiences, and so she seeks to "make some history up" (Pearce, 26). She is particularly interested in language and celebrates the elasticity, power, and poetry of black dialect.

The America Play, one of Parks's most intellectually provocative and stylistically challenging works, premiered at the Public Theater in New York City in 1994, under the direction of Liz Diamond. Parks set the first act of the play, a monologue delivered by an African American character called the Foundling Father—who resembles Abraham Lincoln—in what she calls "A great hole. In the middle of nowhere. The hole is an exact replica of the Great Hole of History" (*The America Play*, 159). In

the second act wife Lucy and son Brazil search for the now deceased father, the Lincoln character. The play interrogates the relationship of African American history to the myth of Lincoln's freeing the slaves, the perpetuation of which has created real scars for African Americans.

Parks won her second Obie Award for Best Off-Broadway Play in 1996 for *Venus*. Written with the assistance of grants from the Kennedy Center Fund for New American Plays and the W. Alton Jones Foundation, *Venus* was first staged at the Yale Repertory Theatre under the direction of Liz Diamond in 1996 and remounted at the Public Theater under the direction of the famed avant-garde theater artist Richard Foreman. With *Venus* Parks revisits the story of Saartjie Baartman, the South African !Kung, or Khoi-Khoi, tribeswoman who was brought to London in 1810 by the British trader Hendrik Ceza-Boer for display as the "Venus Hottentot" in a sideshow. In thirty-one scenes, the play chronicles the path of Baartman's life in reverse, beginning with her death in Paris and moving back to her capture from South Africa. The play ends as it began, with Baartman's death.

Venus marked a turning point in Parks's theatrical career. *In the Blood*, which opened in 1999 at the Public Theater under the direction of David Esbjornson, was the first of two plays—"The Red Letter Plays"—which adapt and explore the story of Hester Prynne, the doomed sinner in Nathaniel Hawthorne's book *The Scarlet Letter*. Like her namesake Hester Prynne, Parks's Hester La Negrita, a homeless woman with a brood of illegitimate children living beneath a bridge, has been ostracized from society because of her sexual transgression. The play was nominated for the Pulitzer Prize.

Parks directed the first production of her second "Red Letter Play," *Fucking A*, for Infernal Bridegroom Productions in Houston, Texas, in February 2000. The play opened at the Public Theater in New York under the direction of Michael Greif in 2003. Different in style from *In the Blood* and her earlier works, *Fucking A* employs an invented language, or "Talk," that the characters occasionally speak. The play's central figure, Hester, who performs illegal

abortions, wears an "A" on her chest as a symbol of her profession.

In 2002 Parks became the first African American woman to win the Pulitzer Prize for Drama with *Topdog/Underdog*. The play, which opened at the Public Theater under the direction of George C. Wolfe, moved to Broadway soon after. It continued earlier themes of legacy, identity, and history through its two characters, brothers whose conflict uncovers painful family secrets and long-festering fraternal jealousies. Their names—Lincoln and Booth—represent the source of their conflict and evidence of their destinies.

Parks received a Ford Foundation Grant, a Whiting Foundation Writers Award, a Lila Wallace Reader's Digest Award, and a CalArts/Alpert Award in the Arts. In 2001 she was awarded a Guggenheim Foundation Fellowship and, the following year, a MacArthur Foundation Award. Parks produced a film, *Anemone Me* (1990), and wrote the screenplay for SPIKE LEE's film *Girl 6* (1996). Parks's first novel, *Getting Mother's Body*, was published in 2003. She is currently writing a musical about the Harlem Globetrotters, *Hoops*, for Disney Productions and adapting TONI MORRISON's novel *Paradise* for Oprah Winfrey Productions. She lives in Venice Beach with her husband, the blues musician Paul Scher, whom she married in 2001, and directs the A.S.K. Theater Projects Writing for Performance Program (MFA) at Cal Arts in Valencia California.

FURTHER READING

Bryant, Aaron. "Broadway, Her Way: African American Playwright Suzan-Lori Parks." *New Crisis* 109.2 (Mar.–Apr. 2002).

Garrett, Shawn Marie. "The Possession of Suzan-Lori Parks." *American Theatre* 17.8 (2000).

Jiggetts, Shelby. "Interview with Suzan-Lori Parks." *Callaloo* 19.2 (1996).

Pearce, Michele. "Alien Nation: An Interview with the Playwright." *American Theatre* 11.3 (Mar. 1994).

Solomon, Alisa. "Signifying on the Signifyin': The Plays of Suzan-Lori Parks." *Theater* 21.3 (1990).

Zoglin, Richard. "Moving Marginal Characters to Center Stage," *Time*, 19 Feb. 2001.

—HARRY ELAM

PARSONS, LUCY (1853?– 7 Mar. 1942), labor activist and writer, was born in north central Texas. Information about her parentage is inconclusive, though she may have been the daughter of Pedro Diáz González and Marie (maiden name unknown); her ancestry was in part African American. At the time she met her future husband in the early 1870s she was living with Oliver Gathings, a former slave. After using many maiden names, Lucy finally settled on González when she married in an attempt to establish a Mexican ancestry that would appear more acceptable to dominant whites in that part of Texas.

In the late nineteenth century the Ku Klux Klan rose to power in several southern states and successfully ended Reconstruction's all-too-brief experiment in biracial democracy. During the period in which the Klan and others violently reasserted "white supremacy," Lucy witnessed atrocities that affected her deeply. Around 1870 she met Albert Parsons and reportedly they wed on 10 June 1871, although it is uncertain whether Lucy and Albert Parsons ever officially married. Laws against miscegenation may have prevented their marriage in Texas. The couple had two children. Lucy's husband was hired as a journalist in Philadelphia, and after Lucy joined him they traveled in 1873 to Chicago, where there is no record that they wed in that city.

Settling in a poor working-class German neighborhood that housed basement sweatshops, Lucy Parsons was exposed to unemployment, poor working conditions, and workers' protests. After Albert joined the Social Democratic Party of North America, members often met in the Parsonses' home and through them Lucy came in contact with the works of Karl Marx and other socialist thinkers. She also found acceptance among her socialist friends who never questioned her racial background.

At that time in industrializing America tensions between workers and owners ran at a fever pitch, and rumors of revolution escalated the fears of industrialists while giving hope to the poor. In 1877 a strike by railroad workers erupted on the eastern seaboard and gathered strength as it moved across the country to Chicago. After Albert spoke before striking railroad workers, he was fired from his job as a typesetter, and Lucy took over the support of the family, working as a seamstress and opening her own dress and suit shop.

Parsons, no less radical than her husband, opposed the capitalist system and the way that American workers were treated. Following the 1877 strikes, which ended in failure and the death of many workers, both Parsons and her husband realized that they needed to move to the forefront of the labor movement. Joining the Chicago Working Women's Union in 1879 and hoping to add fuel to the fight for equal pay for equal work, Parsons supported the call for a woman's suffrage plank in the Socialist Labor platform. She believed that the conflict between workers and owners had come to an impasse and saw revolution as the only solution.

Parsons expressed her opinions in *The Alarm*, the weekly newspaper of the International Working People's Association (IWPA), as well as in *The Socialist*, the *Denver Labor Enquirer*, and the *Labor Defender*. Her well-known article, "To Tramps," published in the first issue of *The Alarm* in 1884, was reprinted and widely distributed by the IWPA. In the article Parsons advised tramps who were thinking of committing suicide because of their suffering in the economic depression of 1883–1884 not to die alone but to take with them a few rich people and to "learn the use of explosives."

In 1885–1886 Parsons joined in organizing seamstresses to demand an eight-hour day. Strikes and protests heightened in May 1886 when during a meeting at Haymarket Square in Chicago, an unknown person threw a bomb, which, when followed by police gunfire, resulted in the death of seven policemen and injured at least sixty bystanders. Although at the time she and her husband were walking away from the crowds, Albert was arrested with seven other men, convicted, and sentenced to hang. Arrested and released herself, Parsons was placed under surveillance by the authorities and was assailed by rumors about her past and racial origins. At her husband's trial Lucy wore black to proclaim the death of free speech and spent the next year and a half fighting to have the death sentences commuted for Albert and the others. Parsons took her message to the American people in Ohio, New Jersey, and Connecticut, hoping they might secure her husband's release. She did not soften her message, however, but explained why she believed that anarchism would rectify the evils of the country's capitalist system.

After her husband was hanged in November 1887, Parsons spent more than fifty years speaking to audiences about freedom, equality, and justice for the downtrodden. Two years after her husband's execution she published *The Life of Albert R. Parsons, with Brief History of the Labor Movement in America* and in 1891 coedited *Freedom, A Revolutionary Anarchist–Communist Monthly*. In 1905 and 1906, the years she edited *The Liberator*, she helped unionist Big Bill Haywood found the Industrial Workers of the World (IWW) also known as the Wobblies. The IWW a coalition of socialist, anarchist, and labor union activists sought to challenge untrammeled corporate power, most notably in the mining regions of the far west. Parsons joined with the IWW in a series of strikes in 1913 in San Francisco, and was arrested the following year in Chicago, where she was campaigning against hunger and led a group of striking workers. Perhaps her most significant contribution to the African American working-class cause lay in helping to found the International Labor Defense in 1925, a radical organization that aided workers and political dissidents, including the Atlanta Communist ANGELO HERNDON and the wrongly convicted SCOTTSBORO BOYS in the 1930s. Parsons finally broke with her anarchist past in the 1930s and joined the Communist Party, which she saw as the only solution to the problems of the working-class, in 1939. She remained active until 1942, when a fire engulfed her home in Chicago, taking her life.

Police removed the personal writings of Lucy Parsons from her home, but her words echoed in the memory of many. A woman of warmth and conviction, she held to no middle ground but loved and hated with intensity. Many remembered her only as the defender of her husband's name, but her concerns were far reaching. She argued that working women were "slaves of slaves" and that they were "exploited more ruthlessly than men." Her stand extended beyond women's rights to equal pay. She also advocated their right to divorce, to practice birth control, and to be free from rape. Her radical spirit gave her the voice to continually keep the issues of human rights alive.

FURTHER READING

Ashbaugh, Carolyn. *Lucy Parsons: American Revolutionary* (1976).
Foner, Philip S. *History of the Labor Movement in the United States*, vol. 2 (1947).
Women and the American Labor Movement: From Colonial Times to the Eve of World War I (1979).

Obituaries: *Chicago Tribune*, 8 and 9 March 1942.

—MARILYN ELIZABETH PERRY

PARSONS, RICHARD DEAN (4 Apr. 1948–), corporate executive and lawyer, was born in Brooklyn, New York, the second of the five children of Lorenzo Parsons, a technician, and Isabelle Judd. When Richard was five years old, the family moved to a middle-class neighborhood in Queens. He later recalled his father as "intellectual and gentle" and his mother as "full of steely determination and grit" (Clarke, 153). In his childhood, academic excellence was far from Richard's top priority, and at John Adams High School he did well but always with as little effort as possible. Still, his talents propelled him to graduate early, at the age of sixteen. In 1964 he applied to the University of Hawaii primarily because he had been attracted to his Hawaiian-born high school physics lab partner, who had constantly told him stories about the exotic state.

Parsons worked at various odd jobs, including at a parking garage and gas company, to support himself while at the University of Hawaii. He became social chairman of his fraternity and made the varsity basketball team but remained unenthusiastic about academics. On occasion, he showed up for final exams after skipping a class for an entire semester. He later described his college experience as "fun filled but academically disastrous" (*Los Angeles Times*, 4 Dec. 1994).

The real turning point in his life came when Parsons married his college sweetheart, Laura Ann Bush, a child psychologist, after graduation in 1968. After earning a scholarship to Union

University's Albany Law School, Parsons graduated as class valedictorian in 1971 and earned the highest score among the 3,600 people taking the New York State bar exam. Upon the recommendation of his law professor, Parsons interviewed for a position in the office of New York's governor, Nelson Rockefeller. In 1971, at the age of twenty-three, Parsons became an assistant counsel to the governor.

Although he was much younger than the other lawyers on staff, Parsons quickly became an important part of the office. Rockefeller, in turn, became an important mentor to the young lawyer, and Parsons later described himself as a "Rockefeller Republican," socially liberal and fiscally conservative. Within two years, Parsons was promoted to first assistant counsel, a job that necessitated representing the governor in Albany and at sundry gatherings. Because it was rare to find an African American in these circles, Parsons often disrupted people's expectations. On one occasion, after sitting down for a meeting at the Metropolitan Museum of Art, he was met with silence. "We are waiting for Governor Rockefeller's counsel" one of the other men said. "I hate to tell you," Parsons replied, "but I am already here" (*New York Times*, 10 June 1988).

When Rockefeller became vice president under Gerald Ford in 1974, Parsons followed him to Washington, D.C., and became a White House deputy counsel and, soon after, associate director of domestic counsel. The following year, when Ford lost to Jimmy Carter, Parsons moved back to New York. Upon his return, Judge Harold Tyler Jr., a colleague from the Washington deputy attorney general's office, invited him to join his law office, the powerful firm of Patterson, Belknap, Webb, and Tyler. Parsons worked there for more than a decade and eventually became one of two black partners. In 1988 Harry Albright, chief executive officer of one of the firm's clients, Dime Savings Bank of New York, was looking for someone to groom as his successor. In July of that year he chose Parsons, who joined Dime Savings as president.

Parsons immersed himself in this new challenge, which enabled him to work in the growing and increasingly important financial services sector. By 1990 he was promoted to chief executive officer, becoming the first African American to head a major banking institution. After

the New York real estate crash in the early 1990s left Dime stuck with nonperforming loans, Parsons won universal praise for leading the company away from the brink of bankruptcy. He demonstrated his leadership by ridding the bank of one billion dollars of bad debt, cutting costs, and negotiating with regulators. In 1994, after restoring Dime's fiscal health, Parsons oversaw its merger with Anchor Savings Bank, a move that created the fourth-largest thrift in the nation.

Parsons ruffled some feathers when he supported the Italian American Rudolph Giuliani's mayoral bid over DAVID DINKINS in 1993. Giuliani, who had befriended Parsons when they were both young attorneys at Patterson, Belknap, Webb, and Tyler, rewarded Parsons's support by naming him head of his transition team and offering him the job of deputy mayor for economic development. Parsons turned down the offer but agreed to serve as chair of New York's Economic Development Commission. With Dime's turnaround complete, Parsons decided to move on to another challenge, and in February 1995, after three years on the board of directors, he became president of Time Warner Inc. Parsons, who quickly won over many in top management with his warm demeanor, became the company's problem solver by bringing opposing parties to common ground and making them feel good about their compromises. As president, he oversaw the company's filmed entertainment and music businesses and all corporate staff functions, including financial activities, legal affairs, public affairs, and administration.

Arguably his greatest challenge came after Time Warner merged with the Internet company America Online (AOL) in January 2000. At the time of the merger, the combined company was valued at $284 billion. More than two years later, after the Internet bubble burst, it was valued at approximately $60 billion. Eventually, the two architects behind the deal—Time Warner's Gerald Levin and AOL's Steve Case—both stepped down from their leadership positions. By 1999 Parsons had been elevated to co-chief operating officer, overseeing the company's content businesses, Warner Brothers, New Line Cinema, Warner Music Group, and AOL Time Warner Book Group, in addition to its human resources and legal departments. Parsons took over as CEO in May 2002 and chairman of the board in May 2003, becoming, along with KENNETH CHENAULT at American Express and FRANKLIN DELANO RAINES at Fannie Mae, one of a handful of black executives to lead a Fortune 500 company. Some business observers have suggested that Parsons is ideally suited to the job of restoring Time-Warner's reputation and profits. His famously congenial manner may also calm the reported culture clashes between the two companies. *Business Week* reported on 19 May 2003, for example, that "Parsons inspires extravagant admiration among close colleagues past and present".

Parsons has been active in other initiatives. From 1995 to 2001 he was chair of Upper Manhattan Zone, an organization that aims to bring economic development to Harlem, and his revitalization efforts earned praise from veteran Democratic congressman CHARLES RANGEL, among others. In 2001 Parsons served as cochair of President George W. Bush's commission on Social Security reform. Parsons, who sat on the board of directors of Citigroup, Fannie Mae, and Estée Lauder, is chair of the Apollo Theater Foundation and serves on the boards of the Colonial Williamsburg Foundation, the Museum of Modern Art, Lincoln Center, and Howard University. Since its inception in 1986, Parsons has been a consultant to the Executive Leadership Council, a nonprofit organization for African American senior executives. In 2002 Fortune ranked him the third most powerful black executive in the country behind STANLEY O'NEAL and Kenneth Chenault. In an age when the power of media lies in the hands of only a few individuals, Richard Dean Parsons has become one of the most important executives in the world.

FURTHER READING

Bianco, Anthony, and Tom Lowry. "Can Dick Parsons Rescue AOL Time Warner?," *Business Week* (19 May 2003).

Clarke, Caroline V. *Take a Lesson: Today's Black Achievers on How They Made It and What They Learned along the Way* (2001).

Margolick, David. "At the Bar," *New York Times*, 10 June 1988: B9.

Wollenberg, Skip. "New Time Warner President Taking On His Biggest Job Yet," *Los Angeles Times*, 4 Dec. 1994: 11.

—GREGORY S. BELL

PATTON, CHARLEY

(Apr. 1891–28 Apr. 1934), blues singer and guitarist, was born on Heron's Place between Bolton and Edwards, Mississippi, the oldest son of William Patton and Annie Martin, farmers. Patton was of mixed descent, with white, black, and Native American forebears. His name is sometimes spelled "Charlie." The nature of his formal schooling is uncertain but may have included some elementary school education. During Patton's early teen years, his family moved to the Will Dockery plantation between Cleveland and Ruleville, which in time became the base of his musical activities.

There Patton began acquiring the necessary musical skills that would enable him to perform alone or with bands. It is believed that Patton started with basic guitar chords shown to him by Henry Sloan. By 1908 Patton was an itinerant blues musician, performing mostly in the Mississippi Delta region between Vicksburg, Mississippi, and Memphis, Tennessee, in juke joints and stores, or at picnics and house parties.

Certainly before World War I Patton codified his musical art with three songs: "Pony Blues," "Banty Rooster Blues," and "Maggie." Patton would affix new lyrics to these songs for a new subject or occasion and also developed secondary themes for musical variety. A substantial portion of the repertoire recorded by Patton later in his career can be traced to these three songs. Other early pieces from this time were "Mississippi Boweevil Blues" and "Green River Blues."

With this early repertoire Patton made an impact on regional musicians from 1910 to 1915. Among those who traded melodies and lyrics with Patton were Willie Lee Brown, Tommy Johnson, Dick Bankston, and Jake Martin, who met often in Drew, Mississippi, a central location in the upper Delta. After 1915 they separated to develop their respective styles. However, some fifteen years later, Patton, Brown, and Johnson recorded their respective variants of "Pony Blues" and "Maggie," revealing their close musical ties.

During World War I Patton was called for the army but failed to pass the physical, probably because of a heart disorder that would eventually end his life. He played on, however, making his musical rounds in the Mississippi Delta. With his distinctive

Charley Patton, "the King of the Delta Blues," played a central role in the development of the Mississippi Delta blues style. Painting by Neil Harpe

hoarse voice and flashy performing antics, such as throwing his guitar and playing it behind his head, Patton came to be a leading draw for black sharecroppers and white landowners alike. Sometimes he would perform on Sundays, even preaching a little, a sample of which he recorded in late 1929 as "You're Gonna Need Somebody When You Die."

Throughout the 1920s Patton continued to return to the Dockery plantation from time to time, but he often stayed with friends and lovers in other Mississippi Delta towns and hamlets, including Cottondale, the Osa Pepper plantation, Mound Bayou, and Merigold. Sometimes his playing dates would take him to Lula, Lake Cormorant, and across the state border to Memphis. In 1927 the Mississippi River overflowed its banks and inundated many Delta communities; Patton chronicled the disaster in his song "High Water Everywhere," sprinkling his narrative with many Mississippi place names. His contact with and influence on younger musicians continued with the likes of Booker Washington "Bukka" White, Howlin' Wolf, Booker Miller, and Willie Moore.

Meanwhile, record companies began producing "race records" by black artists for black listeners. Although urban singers established the "race" market, the first hit records by the rural Texas musician BLIND LEMON JEFFERSON in 1926 made it possible for other country blues performers to record. On the recommendation of Jackson, Mississippi, talent scout H. C. Speir, Paramount Records engaged Patton for a session on 14 June 1929. Performing in the Gennett Records studio in Richmond, Indiana, Patton made fourteen three-minute 78-rpm sides, among them his signature tunes "Pony Blues" and "Banty Rooster Blues," whose back-to-back release on one record enjoyed high sales. Recognizing a new record star, Paramount quickly brought him north in late 1929 for a second session, this time in its newly completed studios in Grafton, Wisconsin. Bringing along Henry "Son" Sims, a fiddler from Farrell, Mississippi, Patton laid down twenty-six performances acceptable for commercial release. "High Water Everywhere" was the big hit of the session, retaining the label's interest in him.

Throughout his life Patton took a number of wives, many of whom were common-law, but a few he legally married. Researchers agree that Patton had eight or nine wives, and four spouses should be noted. In 1908 Patton married Mille Barnes (or Bonds), and they had a daughter known either as Willie Mae or China Lou. Ten years later he took Roxie Morrow as a wife; they did not have children. In 1922 Patton formally married Mandy France on the Pepper plantation. The best known of Patton's wives, however, was Bertha Lee Pate, who met Patton in Lula around 1930 and stayed with him through much of his remaining life, moving with him to the Heathman-Dedham plantation near Holly Ridge and Indianola, Mississippi.

With the commercial success of "High Water Everywhere," Patton was contacted in May 1930 for a third Paramount Records session, and like his second session, he was allowed to bring any musicians he felt talented enough to record. This time he asked Willie Brown, singer and guitarist Eddie "Son" House Jr., and pianist Louise Johnson to join him. In the studio the four musicians took their respective turns at the microphone; Patton waited until the others were finished before recording four songs, one of which was "Dry Well Blues," about a drought then ravaging the South.

During the worst years of the Depression, Patton stayed near Indianola, but he still traveled throughout the Delta to play for black and white audiences. Occasionally he would perform with Brown and House, and in 1933 the three musicians approached Speir in Jackson, hoping for a formal session to record some spirituals. Vocalion Records heard the test disc that resulted and invited Patton to a session in New York City on 30 and 31 January and 1 February 1934. His wife Bertha Lee traveled with Patton to the session and even sang on several sides. Although in poor health by this time, Patton successfully played through his latest blues "34 Blues" and "High Sheriff Blues," but he also recorded "Oh Death" and "Troubled 'bout My Mother," songs that reflect his premonitions of his approaching death.

After returning to the Indianola area, Patton continued to perform despite his weakening physical condition. He succumbed in Indianola to the mitral heart valve disorder that he had had since his youth. Over the years, memories of Patton were kept alive by Bertha Lee Patton, House, Moore, Howlin' Wolf, and other musicians and relatives. In 2003 the Revenant Records reissue of Patton's complete recordings won three Grammy Awards, including Best Historical Album and Best Liner Notes.

FURTHER READING

Calt, Stephen, and Gayle Wardlow. *King of the Delta Blues: The Life and Music of Charlie Patton* (1988).

Evans, David. Liner notes to *Screamin' and Hollerin' the Blues: The Worlds of Charley Patton* (Revenant Records 212, 2001).

Fahey, John. *Charley Patton* (1970).

Discography

Screamin' and Hollerin' the Blues: The Worlds of Charley Patton (Revenant Records 212).

Charlie Patton: Complete Recorded Works in Chronological Order (vols. 1–3, Document Records 5009, 5010, 5011).

Charlie Patton: Founder of the Delta Blues 1929–34 (Yazoo Records 1020).

—EDWARD KOMARA

PAUL, NATHANIEL

(?–18 Sept. 1839), abolitionist and minister, was born in New Hampshire, probably in Exeter, Rockingham County, to unidentified parents. His brother, Thomas Paul, became a minister and community leader in Boston, Massachusetts. The Free Will Baptist Church educated both black and white youths, and Paul may have been a student with his brother at its academy in Hollis, New Hampshire. In 1820 he became pastor of the First African Baptist Church in Albany, New York. Influenced by evangelicals and reformers, northern New York was a hotbed of abolitionist activity on the part of both blacks and whites. New York had extirpated slavery gradually, first, in 1799, legislating that all blacks born to slave mothers on or after 4 July 1799 would be indentured servants and then, in 1817, declaring that all slaves born before 4 July 1799 would be freed on 4 July 1827.

In an 1827 address Paul criticized the slave trade and slavery, celebrated the 1817 law, and named all ninety-five elected New York State officials who had voted for the emancipation act. Like many African Americans in the 1820s, he supported the resettlement of free blacks when it seemed likely to foster social and economic progress, but he opposed the American Colonization Society (ACS), which promoted the expatriation of manumitted slaves to Liberia—an action that most abolitionists believed fortified American slavery. In 1824 Thomas Paul visited Haiti, which was then being touted as a place African Americans might relocate, but he returned to Boston. In 1830 Nathaniel Paul, with his brother Benjamin, resettled in a free black community, Wilberforce, being constructed in Lucan, Ontario, Canada. In 1832 he commenced a speaking tour of England, Ireland, and Scotland, seeking funds for a manual labor academy at Wilberforce and countering propaganda spread by an ACS agent, Elliott Cresson. Cresson was exaggerating the antislavery thrust of the ACS as he sought to gain support for colonization in British abolitionist and political circles.

Paul cooperated with the noted abolitionist William Lloyd Garrison, another opponent of the ACS, in touring Britain, but a rift between the two men occurred when Paul provided funds for Garrison's journey home to the United States. Paul considered the money a personal loan, while Garrison insisted that it was an expense of their joint abolitionist activities. Paul remained in Britain until 1836, marrying an Englishwoman in 1833 and meeting the most prominent figures in British abolitionism. Upon returning to Wilberforce, at the request of its leader, AUSTIN STEWARD, Paul revealed that although he had collected more than eight thousand dollars in British donations, he had nothing to remit, since his expenses of seven thousand dollars and his fifty-dollar monthly salary totaled over nine thousand dollars. In 1836 Paul returned to Albany, where he became pastor of the Hamilton Street Baptist Church. Poverty marked the last three years of his life.

Several addresses and letters written by Paul survive. His *Address, Delivered on the Celebration of the Abolition of Slavery, in the State of New-York* (1827) noted the oppression and the pernicious influence on society of slaveholding. Paul denounced the persistence of slavery in a republican nation that had been forged in revolution. He praised the American revolutionaries, arguing that slavery was a legacy of colonialism that had improperly survived in the new nation. Addresses, letters, and reports recounting his experience in Britain suggest that he was a gifted author and dynamic orator who effectively countered ACS propaganda as well as soliciting donations for what seemed to be the benefit of African Americans. He proved to be a popular lecturer, and he claimed to prefer English to American life. In this he was not alone, for Henry Nell, the African Canadian sent from Wilberforce by Steward to demand Paul's return, did not himself leave England after accomplishing his errand. Moreover, Paul was in England during parliamentary discussion of West Indian emancipation and the enactment of the Emancipation Act of 1833; his letters to American abolitionists provided information about these momentous events.

Although he was a celebrated figure in the transatlantic abolitionist movement, Paul was also a citizen of Wilberforce and should be viewed in its context. In 1829 black residents of Cincinnati, Ohio, began plans for a mass exodus to Canada. Discriminatory state laws and antiblack riots in 1829 had made many of them pessimistic about their future in the United States. Ohio and Indiana Quakers donated funds for

the purchase of land, and the first settlers arrived in Wilberforce in October 1829, followed by members of the Paul family in 1830. Although the settlement was praised at a distance by leading abolitionists, it probably never held more than two hundred inhabitants (one thousand blacks left Cincinnati in 1829–1830, but many settled instead in nearby towns), and it seemed a failure to most sympathetic people who visited it.

Expectations of settlers and abolitionists alike were high, but Wilberforce itself faltered. Schools were open only irregularly. Emigrants from the city of Cincinnati proved unable to farm productively. The officials of the settlement continually bickered over allegations of misuse of funds, questions of representation of the settlers for the purpose of fund-raising, and accusations of moral improprieties. By the 1850s Wilberforce was home to only about fifty people. The lack of a monetary return from Paul's tour and his retreat to Albany in 1836 were symptomatic of the larger problems of resettling people who had been harassed from their homes and of securing competent leadership for a community attempting to reconstitute itself as it fled from racism, inequality, and violence. Paul was a gifted man who fought racism and slavery but who was unable to square his self-interest and the needs of the black community that employed him.

FURTHER READING

Transcriptions of Nathaniel Paul's speeches and his letters from Britain, in which he relayed information about his speaking tour, appeared in the *Liberator* (1831–1865), William Lloyd Garrison's abolitionist newspaper, published in Boston. His speeches and letters have been reprinted in *The Black Abolitionist Papers, Volume 1: The British Isles, 1830–1865*, ed. C. Peter Ripley et al. (1985): 42–59.

Mitchell, J. Marcus. "The Paul Family" in *Old-Time New England* (1973), 73–77.
Pease, William H., and Jane H. Pease. *Black Utopia: Negro Communal Experiments in America* (1963), 46–62.
Taylor, Nikki. "Reconsidering the 'Forced' Exodus of 1829: Free Black Emigration from Cincinnati, Ohio, to Wilberforce, Canada." *Journal of African American History* 87 (Summer 2002): 283–302.

—JOHN SAILLANT

PAYNE, DANIEL ALEXANDER

(24 Feb. 1811–2 Nov. 1893), minister and educator, was born in Charleston, South Carolina, the son of London Payne, a free African American, and Martha (maiden name unknown), a Catawba Indian, both of whom died in the early 1820s. For two years he attended the Minor's Moralist Society School; he then continued his education with a tutor and through extensive independent reading. He joined the Methodist Episcopal Church in 1826.

Payne established a school for blacks in 1828 but closed it in 1834 when South Carolina outlawed education for slaves. Moving to Gettysburg, Pennsylvania, in 1835, Payne studied on a scholarship at the Lutheran Theological Seminary, but failing eyesight forced him to leave before graduation. He was licensed to preach in 1837 and ordained in 1839, thus becoming the first African American minister in the Franckean Evangelical Lutheran Synod. In 1840 he opened a second school for African Americans, through which he was introduced to the African Methodist Episcopal (AME) Church. He left the Franckean Church in 1841—partly because of its reluctance to give an African American minister the responsibility for a parish—and joined the AME Church.

Serious ideological differences quickly became evident between Payne and the AME Church; he favored a formal service conducted by educated ministers, while many of the AME's members opposed an educated clergy and preferred an emotional, evangelical style of worship. Payne was assigned first to the Israel Bethel Church in Washington, D.C., then to the Bethel Church and later the Ebenezer Church in Baltimore. In addition to the usual duties of a pastor, he worked to standardize the AME service, to keep records of church history, and to improve religious education. Although initial resistance to his attempts to educate the clergy was strong, by 1844 the General Conference had accepted his recommendation to standardize a course of study for all ministers.

In 1850 Payne published *Pleasures and Other Miscellaneous Poems*. Elected a bishop in 1852, Payne worked to expand the church's home and overseas mission programs, especially those involving newly freed slaves. This later led to rapid growth in the church's membership in the postwar South. Payne had married Julia A. Ferris in 1847. After her death, he married Eliza J. Clark in 1853.

In 1863 Payne purchased and became president of Wilberforce University in Ohio, the first African American–controlled college in the United States. He facilitated the growth of the university by raising standards for both students and faculty and by improving its financial stability. While visiting South Carolina in 1865, Payne founded the South Carolina Conference of the AME Church, which was to play an important role in the denomination's expansion in the South. In 1866 he published his church history, *Semi-Centenary and the Retrospection of the African Methodist Episcopal Church in the United States of America*. He resigned the presidency of Wilberforce in 1876 and became chancellor and dean of the theological school, positions he held until his death.

A prolific author, Payne wrote numerous poems, essays, speeches, and sermons. In later life he published his autobiography, *Recollections of Seventy Years* (1888), as well as *Treatise on Domestic Education* (1885) and *History of the African Methodist Episcopal Church* (1891). His last public appearance was at the World Parliament of Religions at the World's Columbian Exposition in Chicago in 1893. He died in Xenia, Ohio, a few weeks later.

Payne's importance lies in his contributions to the history of African Americans in the nineteenth century and the history of the African Methodist Episcopal Church. He also played a significant role in the expansion of educational opportunities for African Americans, both before and after emancipation.

FURTHER READING

Payne, Daniel Alexander. *Recollections of Seventy Years* (1888).

Coan, Josephus R. *Daniel Alexander Payne: Christian Educator* (1935).
Smith, C. S. *The Life of Daniel Alexander Payne* (1891).

—ELIZABETH ZOE VICARY

 PAYTON, PHILIP A., JR. (27 Feb. 1876–29 Aug. 1917), Harlem real estate agent, was born in Westfield, Massachusetts, the son of Philip Payton Sr., a barber and tea merchant, and Anna Marie Rynes. Payton's father was a graduate of Weyland Seminary in Washington, D.C., and his shop was an important gathering place for Westfield's small black community. The younger Payton went to public schools in Westfield and in 1899 obtained a degree from Livingston College in Salisbury, North Carolina. Payton married Maggie (maiden name unknown) that same year and relocated to New York City, where he held odd jobs, including department store attendant and barber. As a janitor to a real estate firm, Payton became intrigued with real estate and decided to go into business for himself.

Payton's entrance into the real estate field was well timed. In 1900 New York was a mecca for black migrants from the South. Decent-paying jobs were more plentiful, and the racial climate was more tolerant. Migrants, however, found that the housing market in Harlem was closed to them, as it was in most of the city. Many middle-class blacks felt intense frustration about their lack of access to decent housing. White real estate agents and landlords refused to sell or rent to blacks and confined them to a dilapidated stretch of Manhattan between Thirty-seventh and Fifty-eighth streets and other rundown areas.

Overspeculation in Harlem in the 1890s and early 1900s created an unusual opportunity for blacks to gain access to decent housing in other sections of the city. In the late nineteenth century Harlem became a fashionable neighborhood for successful New Yorkers. White landowners bought up property and built high-grade apartments with the expectation that the area would prosper. However, real estate developers were overconfident about the area's future and drove up land prices out of proportion to their actual value. When the housing market collapsed in 1904–1905, many owners had difficulty locating white tenants willing to pay the high rents the owners had to charge to meet their financial obligations. Payton, along with other black and white real estate agents, exploited this collapse in

values and opened large areas of Harlem to black tenants.

Earlier, in 1900, Payton and a partner had opened an office on West Thirty-second Street specializing in managing "colored" tenements. For a while Payton struggled; his partner quit, and he was evicted from his offices more than once. Payton received his first break when owners of an apartment building on 134th Street could not find new tenants. They turned the building over to Payton to rent to blacks. He was successful and between 1900 and 1907 expanded his operation to become a wealthy, nationally recognized black business leader.

Payton's success was based on his audacity as a businessman, his skill as a promoter, and his reputation as an advocate of black-owned business in New York and elsewhere. He formed a limited partnership with a group of ten black businessmen and specialized in five-year leases on white-owned property rented to blacks. After 1904 Payton's creation, the Afro-American Realty Company, proceeded to attract new investors and tenants through extensive advertising in local and national black newspapers and on billboards, trains, and in subway stations. Payton also attracted attention by successfully confronting white realty companies that opposed his business strategy. He was aided by strong relationships with a small group of white real estate agents and bankers, who tacitly supported his efforts.

Payton's activities in promoting black-owned enterprises in New York and in other urban centers included becoming a manager of the National Negro Business League, and in 1905 he organized a local black defense society to protest police brutality. Payton was also closely allied with prominent black leaders such as Frederick R. Moore, the editor of the *New York Age*, and associates of BOOKER T. WASHINGTON such as Charles W. Anderson and EMMETT JAY SCOTT. While Payton counted Washington himself among his network of associates, their relationship was often troubled by philosophical differences and Payton's reluctance to fully endorse Washington's efforts to expand his influence in New York City. Payton drew together a group of black real estate agents and other businessmen, including John M. Royall, John E. Nail, and

Henry C. Parker, who adopted Payton's methods to advance black expansion in Harlem even after Payton's own fortunes began to decline in 1907–1908.

After a series of organizational shake-ups, Afro-American Realty Company stockholders began to question Payton's high-risk speculating policies as well as his autocratic management style. In 1906 the stockholders sued Payton on the grounds that he ran the company without any input from the board of directors and was therefore responsible for any losses the company might accrue. Because the company claimed that it owned property free and clear when actually all of it was heavily mortgaged, the courts found the company guilty of misrepresentation (although Payton himself was cleared). Banking on his friends and his reputation, Payton kept the company afloat for another two years. However, the bad press created by the lawsuit and Payton's own speculations made obtaining credit increasingly difficult, and by 1908 the company had failed. Payton remained personally active in Harlem properties. In the summer of 1917 he obtained six apartment buildings on West 141st Street valued at $1.5 million, the biggest deal of his career. In late August, however, he became ill and died at his summer home in Allenhurst, New Jersey.

Philip A. Payton Jr. was a prominent black real estate entrepreneur who helped open the housing market in the Harlem section of New York City to blacks in the early twentieth century. He provided quality housing to black New Yorkers of all classes, became an influential business leader, an associate of national black leaders, and a symbol to black entrepreneurs and home-seekers who referred to him as the "Father of Colored Harlem."

FURTHER READING

Many important documents relating to Payton can be found in the Booker T. Washington Papers at the Library of Congress and at the New York City Hall of Records.

Dailey, Maceo. "Booker T. Washington and the Afro-American Realty Company." *Review of Black Political Economy*, Winter 1978: 184–201.

Ingham, John, and Lynne B. Feldman. *African American Business Leaders* (1994).

JOHNSON, JAMES WELDON. *Black Manhattan* (1930).

Osofsky, Gilbert. *Harlem: The Making of a Ghetto* (1971, 1996).

Richardson, Clement. *National Cyclopedia of the Colored Race* (1919).

—JARED N. DAY

 PAYTON, WALTER
(25 July 1954–1 Nov. 1999), Hall-of-Fame football running back, was born in Columbia, Mississippi, the youngest of three children of Edward, a laborer, and Alyne Payton. Payton did not begin his football career until his junior year in high school. Before joining his brother, Eddie, in the backfield at segregated John J. Jefferson High School, Payton played drums in the marching band. He graduated from Columbia High School in 1970, following the integration of the Columbia public school system. Payton's two long touchdown runs in Columbia's 14–7 season-opening victory over rival Prentis High School are said to have silenced critics of school desegregation in his hometown.

Payton played college football at Jackson State University, from which he graduated with a degree in Special Education. At Jackson, Walter was reunited with his sister, Pam, and his brother, Eddie, and he lined up with Eddie in a backfield that came to be known as "Payton's place." Rushing for 3,563 yards and scoring sixty-six touchdowns, Payton helped lead the Tigers to two Southwestern Athletic Conference (SWAC) championships. Shredding defenses throughout the SWAC, Payton finished his college career with 464 points, a record in the National Collegiate Athletic Association. This total included a 46-point game and a 160-point season, which led the nation in 1973. Despite playing for a small, historically black college that received little press attention and no television coverage, Payton finished fourth in the balloting for the 1974 Heisman Trophy, awarded annually to the nation's

Walter Payton in 1974 at Jackson State College. © Bettmann/CORBIS

outstanding college football player. His dazzling collegiate scores are especially impressive considering the high level of competition he faced in the SWAC. Well into the 1970s historically white southern universities did not recruit black athletes in great numbers, making black colleges and universities a vast source of draftable football talent.

The Chicago Bears made Payton their first-round pick in the 1975 National Football League (NFL) draft. A powerfully effective combination of balance, speed, and strength defined Payton's physical style of running. Small compared with other running backs of his era, at just five feet, ten inches tall and 195 pounds, he was as likely to bounce off would-be tacklers as to go down. Payton rushed for 16,726 yards in the course of a 13-year professional career, making him the NFL's all-time leading rusher at the time of his retirement. A dynamic offensive force, he was also a punishing blocker and dependable receiver as well as a fearless runner. He led the league in rushing five consecutive times from 1976 to 1980 while posting ten seasons in which he gained more than a thousand yards. Known as "Sweetness," he was named All-Pro seven times and played in nine Pro Bowls. In 1977 he became the youngest NFL Most Valuable Player (MVP) while leading the Bears to their first trip to the play-offs in fourteen years. During that season Payton set a league record for single-game rushing, gaining 275 yards against the Minnesota Vikings. This performance was one of the record seventy-seven games in which Payton gained a hundred or more yards.

A dedicated and disciplined athlete, Payton did not possess the blazing speed of Gale Sayers or JIM BROWN's raw power. As a result, much of his success in the NFL can be attributed to a grueling off-season regimen he conducted on his legendary Mississippi training course, which featured a steep vertical incline known as "the Hill." Payton's conditioning program helped him play in 188 consecutive games, missing only one contest—during his rookie season—in the course of his long career. Combining his desire to excel with a tenacious work ethic, Payton established his reputation as a consummate teammate. This made him

one of Chicago's most beloved sports figures long before the Bears brought the city its first major professional sports championship in over two decades. Payton was named the NFL's MVP for the second time during the 1985 season, as the Bears posted a 15–1 regular-season record and went on to win Super Bowl XX with a lopsided 42–6 victory over the New England Patriots.

Payton's NFL career concluded at the end of the 1987 season. His uniform number 34 was retired in a ceremony at Chicago's Soldier Field during the Bears' final regular-season home game of that year. Following his retirement Payton maintained contact with the game by serving as a member of the Bears' board of directors. However, he was not content to serve in this largely symbolic capacity. Always one to aim high, he aspired to become the first African American owner of an NFL franchise. Lacking the capital necessary to become a majority owner, Payton entered into a partnership with an investment group bidding for a proposed expansion franchise based in St. Louis. He waged a four-year campaign to make this dream a reality. When league officials awarded new teams to Jacksonville and Charlotte instead of St. Louis, Payton was deeply disappointed. In the wake of this decision, he cut many of his ties with the league. In 1993, the same year that the expansion decision was made, Payton was elected to the Pro Football Hall of Fame. His twelve-year-old son, Jarrett, deliver his induction speech.

The transition to life after football was not easy for Payton. In his memoir he describes it as a process of "withdrawal" (Payton, 2000, 138–139). Seeking to fill the void left by the game, Payton shifted his focus to auto racing. Payton raced cars on a number of levels, including the Sports 2000, GT-3, and Trans-Am circuits. Payton's days as a driver ended following a wreck in Elkhart, Wisconsin. His lifelong passion for speed and competition continued when he became the owner of an Indycar and CART racing team. During the mid-1990s Payton also began taking an active interest in the business ventures undertaken by Walter Payton Incorporated. The good fortune that he enjoyed in the business world

helped underwrite the numerous charitable activities that Payton and his wife, Connie, undertook through the Walter Payton Foundation, assisting needy children and improving education in Chicago.

In January 1999 Payton was told he had primary sclerosing cholangitis, a rare form of liver disease. Amid wild speculation about his health, Payton held a press conference on 2 February 1999. He revealed his need for a liver transplant and that he had been given less than two years to live. This emotional event sent shock waves through Chicago and the sports world at large. Soon after, it was also discovered that Payton had cancer of the bile duct, which quickly spread to his lymph nodes. These conditions forced him to withdraw his name from the organ transplant list. A man of deep faith, Payton battled his illnesses valiantly, choosing to let his health struggle become a focal point in the campaign to increase awareness about organ donation.

On 6 November 1999 two thousand people gathered at Soldier Field for a public celebration of Payton's life and legacy. An array of speakers, including the Reverend JESSE JACKSON and Payton's Hall-of-Fame teammate the linebacker Mike Singletary recalled his greatness on and off the field. In 2000 the city of Chicago honored Payton's commitment to excellence and the work of the Walter and Connie Payton Foundation by naming its state-of-the-art, selective-enrollment Math, Science, and World Language High School the Walter Payton College Preparatory High School.

FURTHER READING

Payton, Walter, with Jerry B. Jenkins. *Sweetness* (1978).
Payton, Walter, with Don Yaeger. *Never Die Easy* (2000).

LeGere, Bob, et al. *Sweetness: The Courage and Heart of Walter Payton* (1999).

Obituary: *Chicago Tribune*, 2 Nov. 1999.
—MICHAEL A. ANTONUCCI

PENNIMAN, RICHARD.
See Little Richard.

PENNINGTON, JAMES WILLIAM CHARLES

(15 Jan. 1809–20 Oct. 1870), escaped slave, minister, and abolitionist, was born James Pembroke in Hagerstown, Maryland, to Bazil, a handyman and shepherd, and a woman named Nelly. Both his parents were slaves. James Tighlman, their owner, gave James's mother and an older brother to his son, Frisbie Tighlman. The family was reunited when Frisbie Tighlman purchased Bazil, though they were relocated to an area some two hundred miles from Maryland's Eastern Shore.

Even though the family had been reunited, as slaves James's parents were still unable to provide the nurturing attention he required. On one occasion Tighlman beat Bazil in James's presence, and his remarks to Bazil had a lasting impact on the young boy: "I will make you know that I am master of your tongue as well as of your time" (Pennington, 7). While he did not immediately escape, James was committed to striking for freedom; in his mind he was never a "slave" after this incident. Although he, too, would experience the "tyranny and abuse of the overseers" (3), he managed to equip himself with skills requisite for life as a free man. At age eleven, he became a trained stonemason, and he worked as a certified blacksmith for more than nine years. But the expert blacksmith yearned for freedom and would become a fugitive. "The hour was come," and he determined that he had to act "or remain a slave for ever" (7).

One afternoon in November 1827, he struck for freedom and, several days later, arrived in Pennsylvania, where the first person he met was a Quaker woman. He lived and worked for a while with a Quaker couple, Phebe and William Wright, who taught him to read. To protect himself, he adopted the name James William Charles Pennington. (Pennington was a common name among Pennsylvania Quakers.) After living with and working for Quaker families, he settled in Newtown, Long Island, New York. He became a Christian, and this intensified his concern for his parents and eleven siblings, as well as others in slavery.

Pennington decided to fight against the institution of slavery from northern soil. With the guidance of the Presbyterian family with whom he resided in Newtown, Pennington began formal preparation for the ministry in 1835. He moved to New Haven, Connecticut, where he taught in a black school, and assisted the pastor of Temple Street Congregational Church. Although Pennington could not formally register at Yale Divinity School, he was allowed to sit in the hallway and listen to lectures. Three years later he returned to Newtown, was ordained as a Presbyterian minister, and served as pastor of the black Presbyterian Church from 1838 to 1840. During the next thirty-two years Pennington served seven churches in three denominations (Presbyterian, Congregational, and African Methodist Episcopal Zion) and five states.

On 16 July 1840 Pennington was called to serve at the Talcott Street (Fifth) Congregational Church in Hartford, Connecticut, and he came to play a role in the celebrated *Amistad* case, examining whether captured Africans who had rebelled and taken over the ship (the *Amistad*) they were being transported in were legally slaves. Most of the captives were from the Mende region of West Africa, in present-day Nigeria, and in April 1840 Judge Andrew T. Judson ruled that their leader CINQUÉ and the others be freed, delivered to the president of the United States, and returned to Africa.

In July 1840 Pennington helped raise money for the captives, whose case had been appealed to the U.S. Supreme Court, where former President John Quincy Adams argued the captives' case. While the U.S. Supreme Court reaffirmed that they be freed, it did not require that the president return them to Africa. Along with his wealthy friend, the New York merchant Lewis Tappan, Pennington raised enough funds for the return of the *Amistad* victims. In September 1841 Pennington organized and was elected president of the Union Missionary Society. Hosted by Pennington's church, the society sent the first two missionaries from an African American mission society to the interior of Africa.

Pennington's role in helping the *Amistad* captives and in sending African American missionaries to Africa enhanced his popularity in Connecticut. In 1843 he was selected to represent the Connecticut Anti-Slavery Society at the World Anti-Slavery Society Convention in London. He also represented the American Peace Society and his own Union Missionary Society at the World Peace Convention meeting in London that year. He then returned to Hartford, where he was twice elected president of the Hartford Central Association of Congregational ministers.

Still legally a fugitive slave, Pennington tried to secure his freedom. As of 1844 he had not even told his wife, Harriet, that he had escaped from slavery. (It is not known when Pennington married Harriet—who died in 1846—and there is no record that the couple had children.) He did not reveal his status to his congregation until 1846, when he traveled to Jamaica, in part to raise funds to purchase his freedom. After his return later that year, Pennington played a major role in the creation of the American Missionary Association, which absorbed his Union Missionary Society. Pennington was appointed to the executive committee of the new organization.

Following the death of Theodore S. Wright, in 1847, Pennington was invited to become the new pastor of Shiloh Presbyterian Church in New York City, the most influential African American Presbyterian congregation in the nation. After concluding a promised return to Talcott and becoming vice president of the National Negro Convention Movement, a northern association of blacks committed to improving the condition of freemen and working for the abolition of slavery in the South, Pennington began his duties as pastor at Shiloh. While settling in as the pastor of his new congregation, Pennington married Almira Way at the home of a Mr. Goodwin, the former editor of the *Hartford Courant* newspaper. It is not known whether the couple had children.

In 1849 Pennington made a second European tour to promote the cause of peace and abolitionism. On this visit the University of Heidelberg in Germany awarded him the doctor of divinity degree. He was the first African American to receive this honor. Conferred on 19 December 1849, it acknowledged Pennington foremost as a leader of his people as well as one who had published distinguished literary works while still legally a slave. Passage of the Fugitive Slave Law in 1850 prompted Pennington to more assiduously pursue the legal purchase of his freedom. From Scotland, where he was lecturing as a guest of the Glasgow Female Anti-Slavery Society, Pennington inquired whether he should return. His friend John Hooker of Farmington, Connecticut, advised Pennington to stay abroad while Hooker negotiated his purchase. On 3 June 1851 Hooker paid the Tighlman estate $150, making Pennington the property of Hooker. After contemplating the irony of "owning" a man with a doctor of divinity degree, Hooker executed the documents making Pennington a free man. James Pembroke had been transformed into James Pennington.

Now free, Pennington later purchased the freedom of his brother Stephen. Both of his parents had died in slavery, as had a sister. Several of his other siblings tasted freedom, though some were sold south. Legally free and armed with a doctorate in divinity, Pennington became even bolder. In June 1855 he defied the New York City law that prohibited African Americans from riding on the inside of a horse-drawn car. He was arrested and charged with violent resistance, but the New York Supreme Court, on appeal, ruled in Pennington's favor; segregation was subsequently made illegal on public transportation in New York City, one hundred years before ROSA PARKS initiated the Montgomery bus boycott in Alabama.

In addition to his activism, Pennington also contributed to African American scholarship, publishing twenty-four articles and sermons, including *An Address Delivered at Newark, New Jersey, at the First Anniversary of West Indian Emancipation, August 1, 1839*, and "The Self-Redeeming Power of the Colored Races of the World" in the *Anglo-African Magazine* (1859). He also published two books: his autobiography, *The Fugitive Blacksmith* (1850), and *A Textbook History of the Origin and History of the Colored People* (1841), which was one of the earliest works of African American historical scholarship.

Yet despite his many achievements, Pennington appears to have succumbed to alcohol addiction in the 1850s, perhaps brought on by the pressures of service. After 1865 he was no longer the spiritual leader of Shiloh. While he recovered from alcoholism, Pennington wrote several significant articles on the future of the black race, though he would never recapture the fame he had once known. He served as an ordained AME African Methodist Episcopal minister in Natchez, Mississippi, in 1865 and was pastor of a Congregational church in Portland, Maine, in 1868 before going to a Presbyterian church in Jacksonville, Florida, where he died in October 1870.

FURTHER READING

Nineteen unpublished letters, written by James W. C. Pennington between 1840 and 1870, are held at the American Missionary Association Archives, Amistad Research Center, Tulane University, New Orleans, Louisiana.

Pennington, James W. C. *The Fugitive Blacksmith; or, Events in the History of James W. C. Pennington, Pastor of a Presbyterian Church, New York, Formerly a Slave in the State of Maryland, United States* (1849), reprinted in *Five Slave Narratives*, ed. William L. Katz (1969).

Thomas, Herman E. *James W. C. Pennington: African American Churchman and Abolitionist* (1995).
Washington, Joseph R. *The First Fugitive and Foreign and Domestic Doctor of Divinity* (1990).

—HERMAN E. THOMAS

PERRY, LINCOLN. *See* Fetchit, Stepin.

PETRY, ANN (12 Oct. 1908–30 Apr. 1997), author and pharmacist, was born Ann Lane in Old Saybrook, Connecticut. The youngest daughter of Peter C. Lane, a pharmacist and proprietor of two drugstores, and Bertha James, a licensed podiatrist, Ann Lane grew up in a financially secure and intellectually stimulating family environment. After graduating from Old Saybrook High School, she studied at the Connecticut College of Pharmacy (now the University of Connecticut School of Pharmacy) and earned her Graduate in Pharmacy degree in 1931. For the next seven years Lane worked as a pharmacist in the family business. Her family's long history of personal and professional success served as the foundation for her own professional accomplishments. She cherished the family's stories of triumph over racism and credited them with having "a message that would help a young black child survive, help convince a young black child that black is truly beautiful" (Petry, 257). These family narratives and their message of empowerment enabled her to persevere in the sometimes-hostile racial environment of New England.

After Lane's marriage on 22 February 1938 to George D. Petry, of New Iberia, Louisiana, she and her husband relocated to Harlem, New York City. Harlem provided her with the environment in which to expand her creative talents and source material for her future fiction. From 1938 to 1944 Petry explored a variety of creative outlets: performing as Tillie Petunia in Abram Hill's play *On Striver's Row* at the American Negro Theater, taking painting and drawing classes at the Harlem Art Center, and studying creative writing at Columbia University. She also served as an editor and reporter for *People's Voice* from 1941 to 1944. Equally important for her creative work, however, was the time Petry spent organizing the women in her community for Negro Women Inc., a consumer advocacy group, and running an after-school program at a grade school in Harlem. These experiences gave Petry insight into the harsh realities facing working-class black Americans and offered her a distinct

Ann Petry's novel The Street, *about a single mother in Harlem and her efforts to protect her child from the street's dangers, sold 1.5 million copies in 1946.* Schomburg Center

contrast to the financially comfortable world in which she was raised. Witnessing the struggles of impoverished black families in Harlem and observing the social codes of more affluent communities, such as Old Saybrook, enriched Petry's fiction, which explores the ways in which social expectations, along with the forces of racism and sexism, can constrain individual lives.

Petry published her first short story shortly after moving to Harlem. "Marie of the Cabin Club" (1939) appeared in an issue of *Afro-American*, a Baltimore newspaper, under the pseudonym Arnold Petri. In 1943, under her own name, Petry published "On Saturday the Siren Sounds at Noon" in the *Crisis*. An important turning point in her career came when this publication caught the attention of an editor who suggested that she apply for the Houghton-Mifflin Literary Fellowship Award. She submitted the first chapters and an outline of what would become her most famous novel, *The Street*, and won the fellowship in 1945. Funded by a $2,400 stipend, Petry finished the novel in 1946.

The Street garnered immediate critical and popular acclaim. Twenty thousand copies sold in advance of its release, and the novel's sales surpassed 1.5 million copies, making it the first novel by a black woman to sell over a million copies. The story of Lutie Johnson, an ambitious black woman trying to work toward financial security, *The Street* uses the bleak landscape of an impoverished Harlem street to personify the relentlessness of racism. In its use of some elements of urban realism, *The Street* evokes comparison to RICHARD WRIGHT's *Native Son*, in which Bigger Thomas's social position—poor, black, and uneducated—inevitably leads to violence and tragedy. But Petry's novel offers what some critics consider a more nuanced examination of the way in which racism shapes black experience. Lutie Johnson not only contends with racism but also confronts sexism from white and black communities alike on an almost daily basis. Furthermore, unlike Bigger Thomas, she is a reasonably well-educated and ambitious woman, driven by the mythology of the American Dream and convinced that her hard work will ultimately be rewarded. Lutie's tragic failure to achieve her goals indicts not only the racism of

American society but also the deceptive mythologies that encourage people like Lutie to believe that they have an equal chance at success.

The Street's enthusiastic reception made Petry a public figure. Seeking privacy, she and her husband returned in 1947 to Old Saybrook, where they lived for the rest of Petry's life. In the same year, Petry published *Country Place*, a novel that also explores the role of environment and community on individuals, though it does not deal explicitly with black characters or experiences. In 1949 Petry gave birth to the couple's only child, Elisabeth Ann Petry, and published the first of what would be several books for children and young adults, *The Drugstore Cat*.

While it is not as well known as *The Street*, *The Narrows*, published in 1953, further complicates the issues Petry raises in her first novel. Set in a fictional New England city, *The Narrows* explores the repercussions of a love affair between a black man and a white woman. The nearly inevitable downfall of Link Williams in *The Narrows* revisits Lutie Johnson's situation in *The Street*. Both characters are ambitious and intelligent, yet constrained by the mechanisms of racism, which prevent them from ever really succeeding. *The Narrows* offers a pointed commentary on social behavior, not only interracial romance but also excessive class consciousness. Within this frame, Petry suggests that social codes and behavioral expectations are damaging to black and white communities alike.

Petry's themes of community relationships and the complexity of black experience in the United States continued in her later publications, including the nonfiction children's books *Harriet Tubman, Conductor on the Underground Railroad* (1955), *Tituba of Salem Village* (1964), and *Legends of the Saints* (1970). In 1971 Petry published *Miss Muriel and Other Stories*. A compilation of stories from the 1940s through 1971, the collection draws on Petry's experiences in Harlem as well as in small-town America. In addition to writing, Petry undertook several visiting lectureships, earned a National Endowment of the Arts creative writing grant in 1978, and was awarded several honorary degrees, including an honorary DLitt from Suffolk University

in 1983 and honorary degrees from the University of Connecticut in 1988 and Mount Holyoke College in 1989. Petry died in Old Saybrook on 30 April 1997.

As the first best-selling African American woman writer, Ann Petry holds a firm place in American literary history as both a groundbreaker and a literary predecessor to some of the twentieth century's most significant black women novelists. The works of Gloria Naylor, ALICE WALKER, and TONI MORRISON continue to explore the complicated interplay of race, gender, and socioeconomic status that Petry illuminated so well in her fiction.

FURTHER READING

First editions of Petry's work, correspondence, and critical reviews are housed in the Ann Petry Collection at the African American Research Center, Shaw University, Raleigh, North Carolina. Additional manuscript materials may be found at the Mugar Memorial Library at Boston University; the Beinecke Rare Book and Manuscript Library at Yale University, New Haven, Connecticut; the Woodruff Library at Atlanta University; and the Moorland-Springarn Research Center at Howard University, Washington, D.C.

Petry, Ann. "Ann Petry." *Contemporary Authors Autobiography Series* (1988).

Ervin, Hazel Arnett. *Ann Petry: A Bio-Bibliography* (1993).
Holladay, Hilary. *Ann Petry* (1996).

Obituary: *New York Times*, 30 Apr. 1997.
—CYNTHIA A. CALLAHAN

PICKENS, WILLIAM

(15 Jan. 1881–6 Apr. 1954), was born in Anderson County, South Carolina, the sixth of ten children of Jacob and Fannie Pickens, both of whom were former slaves. The family of sharecroppers moved frequently—some twenty times by Pickens's estimate—and relocated to Arkansas in 1887. William was raised in a household in which learning was revered, and he became valedictorian of his graduating class at Union High School in Little Rock in 1899. Following a summer working with his father in railroad construction in Arkansas, Pickens entered Talledega College, a missionary institution in Alabama, where

he majored in foreign languages, and earned a BA in 1902. Pickens earned a second bachelor's degree, in linguistics, from Yale University, in New Haven, Connecticut, where he received the Phi Beta Kappa key in 1904. He later earned an MA degree from Fisk University, in Nashville, Tennessee; a doctorate in Literature from Selma University (Alabama); and an LLD from Wiley University (now Wiley College) in Marshall, Texas.

In 1905 Pickens married Minnie Cooper McAlpine, a graduate of Tougaloo College, with whom he had three children: William, Harriet, and Ruby. Pickens possessed diverse talents and authored two autobiographies, *Heir of Slaves* (1911) and *Bursting Bonds* (1923), as well as a short-story collection, *Vengeance of the Gods* (1922), and a collection of essays, *The New Negro* (1916). Between 1904 and 1914 Pickens taught foreign languages at his alma mater, Talladega, before moving to Wiley University to head their Greek and sociology departments. The following year he accepted a position as dean of Morgan College (now Morgan State University) in Baltimore, Maryland. Although he initially supported BOOKER T. WASHINGTON's more pragmatic approach to race relations, Pickens evolved into a civil rights militant fairly early in his intellectual career. He supported W. E. B. DU BOIS's radical Niagara Movement and was a charter member of the National Association for the Advancement of Colored People (NAACP) and the American Civil Liberties Union. He was also ecumenical in his organization affiliations, working to some degree with the League for Industrial Democracy, the YMCA, and the Council for Pan-American Democracy. Given his broad education and training, Pickens was something of a maverick. He proposed to the businesswoman MADAME C. J. WALKER that he accompany her on a trip around the world and write a book about her travels, and in the early 1920s he flirted briefly with MARCUS GARVEY's United Negro Improvement Association (UNIA) while he was still an NAACP employee. Pickens was later a fierce critic of the UNIA, however, and even demanded that Garvey be imprisoned.

In 1919 Pickens left Morgan College—where he had risen to the vice presidency—to take a position as assistant to JAMES WELDON JOHNSON of the NAACP. As a founding member of the association, Pickens was well connected with its leadership and had also tirelessly recruited members at Talladega, Wiley, and Morgan College. In 1915 he had accompanied the NAACP chairman Joel E. Spingarn on a dangerous fact-finding mission to Oklahoma, to gather information for a test case challenging Jim Crow on the railroads. In 1920 Johnson was appointed the first black executive secretary of the NAACP, and Pickens was subsequently appointed to the post of field secretary.

During his tenure as field secretary, Pickens shepherded the NAACP through a period of fluctuating membership during the 1920s and the Depression, and he helped lay the groundwork for the association's massive increase in resources and membership in the 1940s. His relations within the NAACP, however, were often rocky, especially with WALTER WHITE, who succeeded Johnson as executive secretary in 1930. Mary White Ovington, chair of the NAACP board, also reprimanded Pickens in 1931 for praising the Communist Party's work in support of the SCOTTSBORO BOYS in the midst of open hostility between the Communists and the NAACP. Pickens subsequently adopted the NAACP party line and even traveled to Scottsboro, where he tried, unsuccessfully, to persuade the nine imprisoned youths to abandon their Communist backers. Pickens's decision to accept a position with the U.S. Department of the Treasury in 1942 probably was motivated, at least in part, by his deteriorating relations with White. He was succeeded as field secretary by the radical grassroots organizer ELLA BAKER.

In 1942 Pickens was cited as a subversive by the House Un-American Activities Committee (HUAC) and its conservative chairman, Martin Dies. In a gesture that eerily presaged Senator Joseph McCarthy's allegations in Wheeling, West Virginia, almost a decade later, Dies, a conservative Texas Democrat, presented the House of Representatives with a list of thirty-nine "subversives" who should be removed from the federal payroll. Of those people, William Pickens was the only one in federal employ at the time. As a director of the War Savings Staff, Pickens was charged with increasing the number of African Americans purchasing war bonds. In short order, a measure was introduced that held up the federal budget until such time as Pickens's allegiances could be ascertained. Wary of provoking conservative southern Democrats who had perpetually threatened to hobble Franklin Roosevelt's presidency, Pickens gave a politic response to the charges. "I do not know Mr. Dies," he remarked, "but feel sure from the position he holds that he would not want to speak anything but the truth. Therefore, I conclude that somebody has misled Mr. Dies" (press release, 18 Sept. 1942, Associated Negro Press Papers, Library of Congress).

With the budget hanging in the balance, some members of the HUAC were surprised at Pickens's appearance—not knowing that he was African American. Pickens's appearance thus gave the arch-segregationist Dies an opportunity to link subversion and civil rights. Northern Democrats, mindful of the Great Migration and the swelling numbers of black Democratic voters, however, were less than thrilled with the prospect of questioning Pickens. William Dawson, the black freshman congressman from Chicago, devoted his maiden speech to Pickens's defense, and Walter White sent a series of letters to members of the House of Representatives protesting the charges against Pickens. Those charges were ultimately dismissed, and Pickens remained in his position at the Treasury Department.

After World War II, Pickens attempted to return to the NAACP but was blocked by Walter White. Shut out of the organization where he had worked for twenty-three years, Pickens remained with the Treasury Department until 1951, when he retired. Pickens's political radicalism diminished somewhat during this period, and strains of his youthful admiration for Booker T. Washington might be seen in his Treasury Department campaigns to educate blacks on economic matters, savings bonds, and thrift. Pickens traveled extensively after his retirement and died during a cruise aboard the SS *Mauritania*, on 6 April 1954, just one month before the U.S. Supreme Court issued its landmark school desegregation ruling in *Brown v. Board of Education*.

Pickens played a significant role in the development of the NAACP.

Between 1920 and 1940 he recruited more members and organized more branches than any other officer in the association, and his efforts helped transform the organization from a small civil rights lobby to a mass organization with nationwide influence.

FURTHER READING

The primary archival collection of William Pickens's papers is housed at the Schomburg Center for Research in Black Culture of New York City. Substantial information regarding his public career, however, can be found in the NAACP collection at the Library of Congress.

Pickens, William. *Bursting Bonds* (1923, 1991).
———. *Heir of Slaves* (1911).

Avery, Sheldon. *Up from Washington: William Pickens and the Negro Struggle for Equality, 1900–1954* (1989).

Obituary: *New York Times*, 7 Apr. 1954.
—WILLIAM J. COBB

PICKETT, BILL

(5 Dec. 1871–2 Apr. 1932), African American rodeo entertainer, was born in Jenks-Branch community in Travis County, Texas, the son of Thomas Jefferson Pickett, a former slave, and Mary "Janie" Virginia Elizabeth Gilbert. The second of thirteen children, Pickett reportedly grew to be five feet, seven inches tall and approximately 145 pounds. Little is known about his early childhood, except that he attended school through the fifth grade. Afterward he took up ranch work and soon developed the skills, such as roping and riding, that would serve him well in rodeo. On 2 December 1890 Pickett married Maggie Turner of Palestine, Texas, the daughter of a white southern plantation owner and his former slave. They had nine children. The Picketts joined the Taylor Baptist Church, where Pickett served as deacon for many years.

Sometime prior to 1900 Pickett and his brothers organized the Pickett Brothers Bronco Busters and Rough Riders Association, operating out of Taylor, Texas. Benny was president, Bill was vice-president, Jessie was treasurer, Berry was secretary, and Charles was general manager. They proudly advertised in their handbills: "We ride and break all wild horses with much care. Good treatment to all animals. Perfect satisfaction guaranteed. Catching and taming wild cattle a specialty." The association operated for several years and boasted of an excellent reputation among the residents of Taylor.

By this time Pickett had originated the tactic of "bulldogging," for which he would become internationally known. A skilled steer wrestling maneuver, bulldogging involved the performer's riding alongside a steer, throwing himself on its back, gripping the horns, and twisting the animal's neck and head upward, causing the beast to fall over. The rider and the steer would skid to a stop in a cloud of dust. Pickett would then sink his teeth into the steer's upper lip or nose and release both his hands. It is believed that Pickett developed his technique as a result of having witnessed a cattle dog holding a "cow critter" with its teeth. According to author Col. Bailey C. Hanes, Pickett perfected the maneuver when working with cattle in the brush country of Texas, where direct interaction with the steer was required to bring the animal under control. Pickett soon began displaying his bulldogging technique before audiences, first at stockyards and later at county fairs. These audiences would watch in amazement as Pickett restrained a steer only by his vise-like teething grip on the animal's lip or nose. This unique approach to steer wrestling immortalized Pickett, as it became the first original rodeo technique that can be traced to one individual.

In 1904 Pickett became an instant celebrity at the Cheyenne Frontier Days in Wyoming. The *Wyoming Tribune* reported in part,

The event par excellence of the celebration this year is the great feat of Will Pickett, a Negro who hails from Taylor, Texas.... Pickett is not a big man but is built like an athlete and his feat will undoubtedly be one of the great features of this year's celebration. It is difficult to conceive how a man could throw a powerful steer with his hands unaided by rope or a contrivance of some kind and yet Pickett accomplishes this seemingly impossible task with only his teeth.

New York's *Harper's Weekly* had sent John Dicks Howe, a special reporter, to cover the event. He reported,

20,000 people watched with wonder and admiration a mere man, unarmed and without a device or appliance of any kind, attack a fiery, wild-eyed and powerful steer and throw it by his teeth.... The crowd was speechless with horror, many believing that the Negro had been crushed...Pickett arose uninjured, bowing and smiling. So great was the applause that the darkey again attacked the steer...and again threw it after a desperate struggle.

On 10 August 1905 Pickett was honored with national attention in *Leslie's Illustrated Weekly* tabloid as "a man who outdoes the fiercest dog in utter brutality." Capitalizing on his popularity, he signed a contract in 1907 with the Miller Brothers, owner of the famous 101 Ranch Wild West Show based along Oklahoma's Cherokee Strip. Becoming the show's headline performer, Pickett made appearances across the United States as well as in Canada, Mexico, Argentina, and England. Colonel Zack T. Miller described Pickett as "the greatest sweat and dirt cowhand that ever lived—bar none." His style of bulldogging gave him many nicknames, including the "Dusky Demon," "The Modern Ursus," and the "Wonderful Colored Cowboy." The wiry performer was also acclaimed for his bronco riding and steer and calf roping talents. Around 1914 he starred in a silent film called *The Bull-Dogger*, produced by the Norman Film Manufacturing Company. The film advertised the techniques of his steer-wrestling artistry, but no copies of the film have ever been located.

Pickett retired as a rodeo performer in 1916 and worked on the 101 Ranch until 1920, before settling on a 160-acre homestead near Chandler, Oklahoma. After Maggie's death in 1929, he returned to the 101 Ranch as a ranch hand to overcome personal financial difficulties brought on by the Great Depression. While attempting to cut horses out of a herd, Pickett was roping a chestnut stallion on foot when the horse suddenly turned on him and fractured his skull. Never regaining consciousness, Pickett died eleven days later at a hospital in Ponca City, Oklahoma. The Cherokee Strip Cowpunchers Association erected a marker in honor of him, with a hand inscription of "Bill Pickett, C.S.C.P.A.," on the 101 Ranch that he made famous, near the monument to Ponca Indian Chief White Eagle.

FURTHER READING

Hanes, Colonel Bailey C. *Bill Pickett, Bulldogger* (1977).
Katz, William Loren. *Black Indians: A Hidden Heritage* (1986).

—LARRY LESTER

PINCHBACK, P. B. S.

(10 May 1837–21 Dec. 1921), politician, editor, and entrepreneur, was born Pinckney Benton Stewart Pinchback in Macon, Georgia, the son of William Pinchback, a Mississippi plantation owner, and Eliza Stewart, a former slave of mixed ancestry. Because William Pinchback had taken Eliza to Philadelphia to obtain her emancipation, Pinckney was free upon birth.

In 1847 young Pinckney and his older brother Napoleon Pinchback were sent to Cincinnati to be educated. When his father died the following year, Eliza and the rest of the children fled Georgia to escape the possibility of re-enslavement and joined Pinckney and Napoleon in Cincinnati. Because the family was denied any share of William Pinchback's estate, they soon found themselves in financial straits. To help support his family, Pinckney worked as a cabin boy on canal boats in Ohio and later as a steward on several Mississippi riverboats. In 1860 he married Nina Emily Hawthorne. Four of their six children survived infancy.

When the Civil War started, Pinchback made his way back to the South. In May 1862 he jumped ship at Yazoo City, Mississippi, and managed to reach New Orleans, already in Union hands. There he enlisted in a white Union regiment as a private, but within a few months he was assigned to recruit black soldiers. He rose in rank to captain in the Second Louisiana Native Guards, later renamed the Seventy-fourth U.S. Colored Infantry. In September 1863 Pinchback resigned from the army, citing discriminatory treatment by white officers and voicing opposition to the army's practice of better compensating white soldiers. He reentered the army as a recruiter when General Nathaniel P. Banks, commander of the New Orleans Union forces, decided to expand the participation of African American troops in the defense of New Orleans. When Banks refused Pinchback a commission as captain, he resigned again.

Pinchback's advocacy of African American rights started during the Civil War. As early as November 1863 he spoke in New Orleans at a rally for political rights, asserting that if black Americans were not allowed to vote, they should not be drafted into the Union army. He then spent two years in Alabama speaking out publicly in support of African American education. On his return to Louisiana in 1867, he became involved in state politics. He was elected to the constitutional convention of 1868, where he worked to create a state-supported public school system and wrote the provision guaranteeing racial equality in public transportation and licensed businesses.

In 1868 Pinchback was elected to the Louisiana State Senate and, as a delegate, attended the Republican National Convention in Chicago. In 1871 he became president pro tempore of the senate and, because of this position, advanced to lieutenant governor upon the death of the incumbent Oscar J. Dunn late that year. Pinchback clashed politically with Governor Henry C. Warmoth, a carpetbagger who had previously vetoed a civil rights bill that Pinchback sponsored. When Warmoth was impeached in 1872, Pinchback served briefly as acting governor, from 9 December 1872 to 13 January 1873. He was the only African American to hold a governorship during Reconstruction.

Although Pinchback, a Republican, was an important figure in state politics, he was unable to hold any other major political office. Earlier in 1872 radicals in the state's Republican Party had sought to nominate him for governor, but he declined the nomination in the interest of preserving party unity. As a reward for his withdrawal, he was nominated for the position of U.S. congressman at large, and he apparently won the election. While the outcome was being contested by the Democrats, during Pinchback's tenure as acting governor, he was also elected by the state legislature to the U.S. Senate, again drawing protests from the Democrats. Eventually their allegations that Pinchback was guilty of bribery and election irregularities led to his being denied both the seat in the U.S. House of Representatives and the one in the Senate. This was not Pinchback's first brush with corruption. In 1870, when he was serving as a state senator, he acted on inside information to purchase a tract of land that he quickly sold to the city of New Orleans for a tidy profit.

In 1877 Pinchback left the Republican Party to support the newly elected Democratic governor, F. T. Nicholls. In return, Governor Nicholls appointed him to the state board of education. In 1879 Pinchback served as a delegate to the state constitutional convention, where he drafted a plan to create Southern University. He was a trustee of that school in the 1880s.

Pinchback was active in the New Orleans business community while he was engaged in politics. He was a co-owner of the city's *Louisianian* newspaper, which not only gave Pinchback a forum to articulate his political views but also helped shape the political and social opinions of the local African American community. In addition, he operated a brokerage and commission house and from 1882 to 1886 was surveyor of customs for the port of New Orleans.

In 1887 Pinchback entered Straight University Law School and passed the state bar exam. After working as a U.S. marshal in New York City in the early to mid-1890s, he practiced law in Washington, D.C., and became part of the city's black elite, entertaining often. He continued to profit from worthwhile business ventures as part owner of a cotton mill and sole owner of the Mississippi River Packet Company. His political activities shifted to support of BOOKER T. WASHINGTON, after whose death, however, Pinchback's clout was sapped. Pinchback died in Washington, D.C.

FURTHER READING

Collections of Pinchback's papers are in the Moorland-Spingarn Research Center at Howard University and the Howard-Tilton Memorial Library at Tulane University. Also worth consulting is the correspondence between Pinchback and Booker T. Washington in the Booker T. Washington Papers at the Library of Congress.

Haskins, James. *Pinckney Benton Stewart Pinchback* (1973).

Ingham, John N., and Lynne B. Feldman. *African American Business Leaders* (1994).

Simmon, W. J. *Men of Mark: Eminent, Progressive and Rising* (1887).

Obituaries: *Baltimore Afro-American*, 30 Dec. 1921; New Orleans *Times Picayune* and *Washington Post*, 22 Dec. 1921.

—ERIC R. JACKSON

PIPPIN, HORACE

(22 Feb. 1888–6 July 1946), painter, was born in West Chester, Pennsylvania, the son of Horace Pippin. On a biographical questionnaire Pippin listed his mother as Harriet Johnson Pippin, but Harriet may actually have been his grandmother; she was the mother of Christine, a domestic servant, who may have been Pippin's birth mother. When Pippin was quite young the family moved to Goshen, New York, so that his mother could find work, and it was there that Pippin attended a one-room school through the eighth grade. He showed an ability for and love of drawing while in school, but because he had to help support his family, he began a series of menial jobs at the age of fourteen. In 1905 he took a job as a porter in a hotel, and he worked there until his mother's death in 1911. He then moved to New Jersey, where he worked at a number of manual labor jobs in industry until April 1917, when the United States declared war on Germany. Pippin enlisted in the army in July 1917 and was trained at Camp Dix, New Jersey, achieving the rank of corporal before leaving basic training.

Pippin continued to sketch, but soon he was sent abroad to France, where he became a part of the famous 369th Infantry, an all-volunteer black regiment (except for the white officers) whose bravery was so extraordinary that the entire regiment was awarded the Croix de Guerre by the French government. In the fall of 1918 Pippin was shot in the right shoulder, and the bullet destroyed muscle, nerves, and bone. His arm hung uselessly from his side, and after five months in army hospitals he was discharged, returning emotionally and physically exhausted to his mother's relatives in West Chester.

This self-portrait of artist Horace Pippin painted in 1944 is oil on canvas adhered to cardboard. Metropolitan Museum of Art

Pippin was unable to make a living through physical labor and attempted to survive simply on his small soldier's pension. He met Jennie Ora Featherstone, a widow with a young son, and they were married in 1920. She took in laundry to help support him, but Pippin was psychologically devastated by his disability, and his memories of the war lingered. He found some relief in local American Legion meetings, and ultimately he began to make art again. He began with some decorated cigar boxes and then turned to burning his drawings into wooden panels. He strengthened his arm enough to draw and paint, and he began to create powerful images based on his memories of the war. Making art helped to heal him and gave him a sense of purpose. He soon expanded to oil paints, but because of his injury he rarely painted anything larger than 25 × 30 inches.

Pippin was an unschooled artist, called a "primitive" in the 1930s.

However, he had a tremendous ability to relay a narrative using simple, flat forms that moved rhythmically and dramatically across the composition. His works are quite sophisticated in their constructions, even though Pippin stated quite emphatically that he simply painted what he saw. In spite of his talent, viewers of that time often connected his purity of vision with a certain naiveté and believed him to be only an instinctual artist, even linking that quality to the primitivism of Africa.

One of the most powerful images among his early works is *The End of the War: Starting Home* (1931), which depicts the grim reality of trench warfare. During this time painting was still an extremely slow process for Pippin, and his production was limited. As time went on he became more prolific, moving to images based on calendar art and then to portraits. He also turned to religious themes, images of African American life, interiors, and still life paintings.

In 1937 Pippin began to sell his paintings in local shops, and it was quite possibly in this way that the famous American illustrator N. C. Wyeth and the art critic Christian Brinton saw one of his important works, *Cabin in the Cotton I* (1935). Pippin's paintings may also have come to Brinton's attention through friends of the artist who alerted this connoisseur of new talent. *Cabin in the Cotton I* was the first of a series of paintings based on what the artist imagined was the African American's life in the South, and it was the first work to deal with the life of his people, a subject that would soon make up a large part of Pippin's oeuvre.

Brinton soon championed his new discovery and decided to hang two works by Pippin in the Chester County Art Association's Sixth Annual Exhibition, which attracted 2,550 people. Pippin's *Cabin in the Cotton I* captivated the public, encouraging Brinton to give his full support to his new "discovery," thus helping connect Pippin to several important figures in the New York art scene, including Holger Cahill, then acting director of the Museum of Modern Art and a tremendous supporter of American folk art. Cahill included Pippin's work in an important exhibition, Masters of Popular Painting—Artists of the People, at the Museum of Modern Art; Pippin was the only black artist to be included.

During this period ten of Pippin's paintings and seven burnt-wood panels were also exhibited at the West Chester Community Center, a focus of black cultural activity. Pippin's work also came to the attention of a Philadelphia dealer, Robert Carlen, and it was while the work was at Carlen's gallery that Dr. Albert C. Barnes saw it. Barnes, an important collector, was very early interested in art by African Americans, and he immediately purchased several works, as did his assistant, Violet de Mazia. Barnes wrote a new essay for Pippin's show with Carlen in which he commented on the artist's ability to tell a story simply and directly with his own language. Both Brinton and Barnes tried on several occasions to "educate" Pippin about modern art and painting, but, fortunately, Pippin ignored them both and continued on his own individual path. However, Carlen and Pippin formed an enduring business relationship. Pippin later exhibited with the New York gallery of Edith Halpert, while still exhibiting with Carlen in Philadelphia.

Pippin's African American heritage continued to offer subjects for the artist, ranging from images of Abraham Lincoln to portraits of the famous soprano MARIAN ANDERSON to scenes of everyday life. He created a series on the abolitionist John Brown, in addition to painting a number of images with religious themes, which reflected both his own devout nature and the importance of the church in black American life. Pippin was opposed to war and depicted the "peaceable kingdom" in a number of works titled *Holy Mountain*. He loved nature and continued to paint floral images as well as interiors remembered from his childhood. His originality attracted a wide audience, and his work became increasingly sophisticated over time, drawing admiration from a number of critics of modern art.

Unfortunately his last years, while financially secure, were personally unhappy. His stepson left to join the armed forces, and his wife was institutionalized because she suffered from emotional problems. Having grown more and more lonely, Pippin died in West Chester from a stroke in his sleep; his wife, who was confined to a state mental hospital, died two weeks later, never learning of her husband's death.

FURTHER READING

BEARDEN, ROMARE, and Harry Henderson. *A History of African American Artists* (1993).
Stein, Judith E. *I Tell My Heart: The Art of Horace Pippin* (1993).

—J. SUSAN ISAACS

PLEASANT, MARY ELLEN

(1812?–1904), legendary woman of influence and political power in Gold Rush and Gilded Age San Francisco, was born, according to some sources, a slave in Georgia; other sources claim that her mother was a Louisiana slave and her father Asian or Native American. Many sources agree that she lived in Boston, as a free woman, the wife of James W. Smith, a Cuban abolitionist. When he died in 1844 he left her his estate, valued at approximately forty-five thousand dollars.

Mary Ellen next married a man whose last name was Pleasant or Pleasants and made her way to California, arriving in San Francisco in 1849. Her husband's whereabouts after this time have never been made clear. She started life in San Francisco as a cook for wealthy clients, then opened her own boardinghouse. Her guests were said to be men of influence, and it was rumored that her places were also houses of prostitution.

Many sources state that Pleasant was a very active abolitionist, helping escaped slaves find jobs around the city. When she heard of John Brown's desire to incite slave rebellions, she supposedly met with him in Canada in 1858, handing him thirty thousand dollars of her own money to further his cause. When Brown's attempt to seize the arsenal at Harpers Ferry failed, authorities began searching for her, though she was able to disguise herself and find her way back to San Francisco under the name of Mrs. Ellen Smith. When Brown was captured, he supposedly had a note in his pocket that said, "The ax is laid at the root of the tree. When the first blow is struck, there will be more money to help." It

Mary Ellen Pleasant. William Loren Katz Collection

was signed with the initials W. E. P., though some conjecture that Pleasant signed the note and deliberately made her "M" look like a "W."

Back in San Francisco, Pleasant fought racism by suing a streetcar company for not allowing her to ride. She sued twice, once in 1866 and again in 1868. She finally received damages in the latter suit, but she had to have a white man witness the streetcar conductor refusing her a seat in order to win her case. During the 1860s she supposedly found wives for wealthy men as well as homes for their illegitimate children. She placed former slaves as servants in homes all over the city, creating a communication network for the receipt of gossip and information, in the much the same way that her contemporary, the voodoo priestess MARIE LAVEAUX, built a power base in New Orleans.

Pleasant is best known for being the housekeeper of banker Thomas Bell, who married Teresa Percy, one of Pleasant's protégés. By this time Pleasant was known to white San Franciscans as "Mammy," and was said to have some sort of power over the Bells. It was even rumored that voodoo rituals were held in the Bell home on Octavia Street, and the mansion soon became known as the "House of Mystery." Pleasant was considered a woman of mystery herself, and was described in newspaper articles and in the memoirs of native San Franciscans as "strange" "mesmeric" and "picturesque."

In 1883 and 1884 Pleasant's name was again in local newspapers because of her involvement in the court case of *Sarah Althea Hill v. William Sharon*. Sharon, a millionaire, former Nevada senator, and owner of the opulent Palace Hotel, was being sued by Hill for support under the terms of a secret marriage contract. The contract later proved to be a forgery and supposedly had been arranged by Pleasant. Pleasant's access to and seeming power over the rich men of San Francisco made this a believable story to most of the city's citizens. During the trial, Hill claimed to be "controlled" by Pleasant, and Pleasant's appearance in court always caused a stir, as recorded on 6 May 1884 in the *San Francisco Call*: "Mammy Pleasant, as the plaintiff calls her colored companion, shows herself in court only as a bird of passage, so to say. She bustles in, converses pleasantly with the young men attached to the defendant's counsel...and like a wind from the south astray in northern climes departs and leaves but chill behind."

One of the few established facts in the life of Mary Ellen Pleasant is that Thomas Bell died in 1892, after a fall from the second story landing of the House of Mystery. Many thought Pleasant had murdered him; if so, and if the murder was for gain, it was fruitless, for when his wife inherited Bell's money, she eventually forced Pleasant out of the house and into a small flat in the city's African American district. Living in poverty, Pleasant was taken in by the Sherwood family, to whom she had rendered assistance at one time. When Pleasant died in San Francisco, she was placed in the Sherwood family plot in the Tucolay Cemetery in Napa, California. At her request, her gravestone contained the words: "She Was a Friend of John Brown." After her death the *San Francisco Call* (12 Jan. 1904) reported a mysterious matter that pertained to her association with John Brown: "Among her effects are letters and documents bearing upon the historical event in which she played an important part. The Brown family raided her flat when Mrs. Sherwood took her home. After her death, the Sherwoods found Mrs. Pleasant's trunks in her Webster Street flat to be all but empty."

Pleasant seems to have wielded power over influential people, yet because she was African American and female, her activities did not reflect her racial and social status, which possibly led to the rumors that she engaged in voodoo and even murder. She moved freely through the highest levels of society, yet she dressed always like a servant. She left nothing in writing, and surviving diaries and newspaper articles paint her as a mysterious and sinister figure. At the same time, some recalled Pleasant as "generous," claiming that she used her own money to aid African American railroad strikers and assisted with other black causes. A few San Franciscans who were children during Pleasant's lifetime remembered her as a churchgoing "lovely old lady" and said that they never believed the voodoo stories.

Historians have rediscovered Mary Ellen Pleasant, and perhaps new materials will come to light to reveal more about this woman whose presence haunts the annals of nineteenth-century San Francisco.

FURTHER READING

Few primary materials on Mary Ellen Pleasant have survived or been discovered. A photograph, generally agreed to be that of Pleasant, is in the Schomburg Center for Research in Black Culture of the New York Public Library. Pleasant's biographer, Helen Holdredge, has placed notes and transcripts of interviews in the San Francisco Public Library.

Holdredge, Helen. *Mammy Pleasant* (1953).
Hudson, Lynn. *The Making of "Mammy" Pleasant: A Black Entrepreneur in Nineteenth Century San Francisco* (2003).
Wheeler, B. Gordon. *Black California: The History of African Americans in the Golden State* (1993).

—LYNN DOWNEY

PLESSY, HOMER ADOLPH (1858?–1925), plaintiff in the 1896 landmark U.S. Supreme Court case *Plessy v. Ferguson*, was born probably in New Orleans. Beyond the case, very little is known about Plessy. He was said to be thirty-four years old at the time of his arrest in 1892, which places his birth around 1858; yet his tombstone lists his age as sixty-three years old when he died in 1925, which places his birth around 1862. Described as a "Creole of Color," Plessy was white in appearance but known to have had a black great-grandmother. He worked as a carpenter.

On 7 June 1892, on a sixty-mile train trip from New Orleans to Covington, Louisiana, Plessy, defined as black by Louisiana law because of his mixed-race heritage, sat in the coach designated for white passengers. Railroad officials were aware that he had boarded the train in order to test the 1890 Louisiana statute requiring all railroad companies to provide and enforce separate-but-equal accommodations for black and white passengers. Thus, although Plessy had no discernible black features, he was asked to move to the car reserved for black passengers. When Plessy refused, he was arrested.

Through his attorneys, Albion Tourgée and S. F. Phillips, and with the aid of the Citizens Committee to Test the Constitutionality of the Separate Car Law (Comité des Citoyens), an organization of blacks in New Orleans, Plessy filed a suit questioning the constitutionality of the state statute. After the suit was overruled by the lower court, Plessy petitioned the Louisiana Supreme Court for writs of prohibition and certiorari against the lower court judge, John Ferguson, prohibiting him from holding Plessy's trial. The request was denied, but the court allowed his case to go before the U.S. Supreme Court on a writ of error.

The argument in *Plessy v. Ferguson* revolved around the constitutionality of the Louisiana statute and whether it violated the Fourteenth Amendment's equal protection clause. The question of equal accommodation was not discussed. As for race, Plessy did not admit to any court that he had African blood. Tourgée argued that because Plessy had no distinguishable black features he was entitled to all the privileges and immunities of white people. And, further, that the Louisiana law gave railroad officials the power to determine racial identity arbitrarily and assign coaches accordingly.

The Supreme Court rejected Tourgée's arguments. With Justice Henry Billings Brown delivering the majority opinion, the Court ruled against Plessy. A compelling aspect of the decision was the opinion of Justice John Marshall Harlan, the lone dissenter. Whereas Brown, employing nineteenth-century Darwinian reasoning, argued that blacks *perceived* "a badge of inferiority" because of the law enforcing segregation, Harlan argued that "our constitution is color blind, and neither knows nor tolerates classes among citizens. In respect to civil rights, all citizens are equal before the law." However, the Court established the doctrine of separate but equal, which would not be revisited until well into the twentieth century when it was unanimously overturned in another landmark case, *Brown v. Board of Education* (1954).

Homer Plessy's trial was held on 11 January 1897, four and a half years after his arrest. He pleaded guilty and paid a twenty-five-dollar fine. Plessy died in New Orleans.

FURTHER READING

HIGGINBOTHAM, A. LEON. *Shades of Freedom* (1996), Chapter 9.
Lofgren, Charles A. *The Plessy Case: A Legal-Historical Interpretation* (1987).
Thomas, Brook, ed. *Plessy v. Ferguson: A Brief History with Documents* (1998).
Woodward, C. Vann. "The Case of the Louisiana Traveler" in *Quarrels That Have Shaped the Constitution*, ed. John A. Garraty (1964).
—MAMIE E. LOCKE

POINDEXTER, HILDRUS AUGUSTUS

(10 May 1901–20 Apr. 1987), physician, microbiologist, and public health specialist, was born on a farm near Memphis, Tennessee, the son of Fred Poindexter and Luvenia Gilberta Clarke, tenant farmers. After attending the normal (teacher training) department of Swift Memorial College, a Presbyterian school for blacks in Rogersville, Tennessee (1916–1920), he entered Lincoln University (Pa.) and graduated with an AB cum laude in 1924. Also in 1924 he married Ruth Viola Grier, with whom he would have one child, a daughter. He attended Dartmouth Medical School for two years before earning an MD at Harvard University in 1929, an AM in Bacteriology at Columbia University in 1930, a PhD in Bacteriology and Parasitology at Columbia in 1932, and an MPH from Columbia in 1937.

Poindexter had hoped to proceed directly into public health fieldwork in 1929, following his graduation from Harvard, but his application for a laboratory post in a U.S. government laboratory in Manila was declined because of his race. Instead, he served an internship at the John A. Andrew Hospital at Tuskegee Institute in Alabama, one of the few facilities open to African Americans seeking postgraduate training. In addition to his regular duties at the hospital, he began an epidemiological survey and implemented a health education program in Union Springs, Bullock County, a poor, predominantly black settlement. He left after ten weeks to accept a two-year fellowship offered by the General Education Board. This Rockefeller-funded fellowship, for graduate study at Columbia University,

was part of a larger plan of the administration at Howard University to provide advanced training for several promising young black medical scientists, who, after earning their PhDs, would assume faculty positions at the medical school and help to upgrade the curriculum and research program.

Poindexter served at Howard University as assistant professor of bacteriology, preventive medicine, and public health (1931–1934), associate professor (1934–1936), and professor and department head (1936–1943). He also held posts at Freedmen's Hospital as bacteriologist, immunologist, and assistant director of the allergy clinic. Despite the pressure of administrative, teaching, and clinical duties, he resumed the research he had begun as an intern in Alabama. For three years (1934–1937), he returned periodically to the South and worked, with Rockefeller support, as an epidemiologist for the states of Alabama and Mississippi. The information he had gathered earlier, along with new data, provided him with an opportunity to draw some general conclusions about the state of African American health in the rural South. Poindexter identified malnutrition, syphilis, insect-borne diseases such as malaria, and hookworm infestation as the four most important health problems confronting rural southern blacks. He distributed blame for these conditions almost equally among blacks and whites. Blacks, he felt, were overly swayed by an "illiterate religious leadership" and a "mania for cotton and corn crops," while he believed whites tolerated an "apathetic county health service" and an "inequitable system of education." His solution called for joint "practical education" efforts by state boards of health, black churches, and the schools.

In 1943 Poindexter was appointed a tropical medicine specialist in the U.S. Army, serving in the racially segregated hospital at Fort Huachuca, Arizona, and later as a malariologist, parasitologist, and epidemiologist (with rank of major) at Guadalcanal and elsewhere in the Pacific. In recognition of his military service, he was awarded the Bronze Star and four combat stars. He retired from the army (with the rank of lieutenant-colonel) effective 26 March 1947.

Poindexter's role during World War II laid the groundwork for nearly two decades of federal public health service. On 13 January 1947 he received a commission as senior surgeon with the United States Public Health Service (USPHS). His first post was with the USPHS Mission in Liberia (MIL) as chief of laboratory and medical research in West Africa. This post he held until his appointment a year later as medical director and chief of mission for MIL and as medical and health attaché to the American embassy in Monrovia. In 1953 he was transferred to Indochina and served (1955–1956) as chief of health and sanitation, U.S. Operation Missions (OM) in Vietnam, Cambodia, and Laos. Other OM appointments followed in Surinam (1956–1958), Iraq (1958–1959), Libya (1959–1961), and Sierra Leone (1962–1964). While in Iraq he also served as professor of preventive medicine at the Royal Baghdad Medical College. Poindexter was a consulting malariologist in Jamaica (1961–1962) and undertook several assignments under USPHS's international section during the early 1960s. He retired from USPHS in 1965.

Poindexter's work in Liberia included the training of indigenous health care personnel, conducting epidemiological surveys and other research projects, antibiotics assay and evaluation, implementing preventive programs, initiating immunization and epidemic control, improving nutrition, and orchestrating demonstration projects in health education. MIL was one of the programs that had emerged from a 1943 agreement between the U.S. and Liberian presidents for increased U.S. assistance in health, economics, agriculture, and other fields. Poindexter's predecessor, John B. West, had begun the program in 1946. While their work focused on technical assistance, the doctors were interested in larger cultural factors as well. Poindexter, for example, wrote about the need not just to correct "social and economic handicaps" but also to develop—for the mutual benefit of Africans and non-Africans alike—"a clearer picture of the people as they live and breathe." His approach to subsequent assignments in Indochina, South America, the Caribbean, and elsewhere in Africa was similar.

Poindexter was a certified specialist of both the American Board of Preventive Medicine and Public Health and the American Board of Microbiology. In 1949 he became the first black member of the American Society of Tropical Medicine and subsequently served as a vice president of the Washington, D.C., chapter and as a trustee of the national body. He had been denied admission to the society in 1934 because of his race.

Following his retirement from USPHS, Poindexter returned briefly to Howard University as professor of community health practice. He remained active in teaching and research for the next fifteen years. He trained Peace Corps workers; served as a special consultant to the U.S. Department of State and the Agency for International Development, including a six-month tour of duty in 1965 with the relief and rehabilitation unit in Nigeria; and published several articles on public health issues, notably on malaria, sexually transmitted diseases, and medical problems of the elderly. He died at his home in Clinton, Maryland.

FURTHER READING

Correspondence, manuscripts, and other papers of Hildrus Augustus Poindexter are preserved in the Moorland-Spingarn Research Center, Howard University.

Poindexter, Hildrus Augustus. *My World of Reality* (1973).

Cobb, W. Montague. "Hildrus Augustus Poindexter, M.D., M.P.H., Ph.D., D.Sc., 1901–." *Journal of the National Medical Association* 65 (May 1973): 243–47.
Miller, Carroll L. "Hildrus Augustus Poindexter (1901–)." Howard University *Profiles*, Feb. 1980: 1–15.

Obituary: *Washington Post*, 25 Apr. 1987.
—KENNETH R. MANNING

 POITIER, SIDNEY
(20 Feb. 1927–), actor, director, and producer, was born the son of Reginald Poitier, a tomato farmer, and Evelyn in Miami, Florida, where his parents were visiting. The family of ten lived on Cat Island in the Bahamas, but when the tomato business no longer proved

lucrative, they moved to Nassau, where Sidney attended Western Senior High School and Governor's High School. But even in the more prosperous urban center of Nassau, the Poitier family remained impoverished, and Sidney was forced to leave school during the Depression in order to help his father.

Despite their financial difficulties, Reginald instilled a sense of pride in his family, and Sidney learned never to indulge in self-pity but rather to make the best out of every situation. With the urban landscape arrived the difficulties of adolescence and the influence of wayward youth, and when Sidney fell into some trouble his parents sent him to Miami to live with relatives. Working as a delivery boy, Sidney encountered racism in the form of police hostility and the Ku Klux Klan. Such experiences were jarring for a young teenager accustomed to the all-black environment of his native Bahamas, and, stifled by the oppressive racism, Sidney headed for New York. He quickly found a job as a dishwasher and struggled to make a reasonable living. In 1943 he joined the army, and after serving two years in a medical unit during World War II, he returned to Harlem in 1945.

While scouring local newspapers in search of a job, Poitier stumbled upon an advertisement for "actors wanted" and decided to audition at the American Negro Theater. But his first audition would end rather dismally; he was interrupted and told to stop wasting the director's time. That director, FREDERICK DOUGLASS O'NEAL, was not impressed with Poitier's halting, accented English as he struggled through the dialogue. Poitier was undaunted and left the theater even more determined to act. During the next six months he used the radio to help him learn American English, and by imitating the voices he heard, he managed to strip himself of his Bahamian accent. In addition, he devoured any available written text, knowing that reading extensively would help him accomplish his goal. Initially driven simply by a desire to show O'Neal that he could indeed act, Poitier soon began to take the theater seriously. His efforts paid off, and at his next audition O'Neal agreed to give him acting lessons in exchange for janitorial work.

Poitier was given his first break when he was designated to replace a

In 1964 Sidney Poitier became the first African American to win an Academy Award for best actor for his performance in Lilies of the Field. *Corbis*

then little known actor named HARRY BELAFONTE for a major run-through at which an important casting director would be present. The director was impressed by his performance and offered him a role in the Broadway production of *Lysistrata*. Unfortunately, what should have been a promising debut performance was tarnished by an attack of nervousness that caused Poitier to flub most of his lines. But the critics were gentle, noting particularly Poitier's gift for comedy. Following this production, Poitier appeared in *Anna Lucasta* (1947) and in *You Can't Take It with You* and *On Striver's Row*. In 1959 he originated the role of Walter Lee Younger in Lloyd Richards's production of LORRAINE HANSBERRY's *A Raisin in the Sun*. Upon auditioning for an upcoming film, *No Way Out* (1949), he was cast in the leading role as a doctor struggling to do his job well during the tense racial climate after World War II. This "racial problem" film—in which the star struggles to negotiate his black identity under difficult circumstances caused by racism—was the first of many during his career. Also in 1950 Poitier married the dancer Juanita Hardy, with whom he would have four children before the couple's divorce in 1965.

The success of *No Way Out* led to roles in *Cry, the Beloved Country* (1952) and *The Blackboard Jungle* (1955). With these films under his belt, Poitier gained access to more of what Hollywood had to offer, and he worked consistently during the 1950s and 1960s, appearing in *Edge of the City* (1957), *Something of Value* (1957), *The Defiant Ones* (1958), and *Porgy and Bess* (1959). In each case he portrayed polite, well-spoken African Americans, defying the stereotype of the singing, dancing, and joking black man that had prevailed in American film. With his performance in *The Defiant Ones* he became the first African American to be nominated for an Academy Award as Best Actor.

With his reputation established as an African American force to be reckoned with, Poitier delivered moving performances in *All the Young Men* (1960) and again as Younger in the film version of *A Raisin in the Sun* (1961). These two roles led up to his part in *Lilies of the Field* (1963), the story of a construction worker who comes to the aid of a group of German-speaking nuns. With this performance Poitier became the first African American to win the Academy Award for Best Actor in 1964. Thereafter Poitier was even

more sought after as an actor, and in 1967 alone he appeared in three films for which he earned enormous success. He starred in *To Sir with Love* (1967) and *In the Heat of the Night* (1967), and then, in the role that he may be best known for, he was cast as a successful young doctor who is engaged to a young white woman and who meets her parents for the first time in *Guess Who's Coming to Dinner?* (1967).

With each role, Poitier was highly conscious of representing his family and his race, and he accepted only those roles that he believed portrayed African Americans in a positive light. For all of his efforts, he still received ample criticism from other black actors who believed Poitier was doing a disservice to his race by embodying the "good Negro" stereotype—the noble and magnanimous black man who never steps out of the mainstream perception of what a "proper" black man ought to be and do.

During the 1970s, however, Poitier starred in *They Call Me Mr. Tibbs* (1970) and *Buck and the Preacher* (1972), both roles that symbolized a departure from the distinguished characters he had previously portrayed. The latter was also his directorial debut. Two years later he collaborated with BILL COSBY in *Uptown Saturday Night* (1974). In 1974 he also married the actress Joanna Shimkus; they have two children. He also worked with Paul Newman and Barbra Streisand, among others, to form First Artists, an independent production company. He subsequently filmed two sequels to *Uptown Saturday Night*: *Let's Do It Again* (1975) and *A Piece of the Action* (1977).

In 1980 Poitier published an autobiography, *This Life*, and gave up acting in favor of directing such movies as *Stir Crazy* (1980), *Hanky Panky* (1982), and *Fast Forward* (1985). He collaborated with Bill Cosby once again in 1990 and directed *Ghost Dad*. When Poitier returned to acting, it was to make a few television films, such as *Separate but Equal* (1991), *Children of the Dust* (1995), *To Sir with Love II* (1996), and *Mandela and de Klerk* (1997); he ended the decade in the title role of the television film *The Simple Life of Noah Dearborn* (1999).

Poitier began the twenty-first century with the publication of a second autobiography, *The Measure of a Man: A Spiritual Autobiography* (2000). He also served briefly as the Bahamian ambassador to Japan. Poitier lives in Beverly Hills, California, with his family. He has received numerous honors and awards, including the Lifetime Achievement Award from the American Film Institute and a knighthood from England's Queen Elizabeth. At the seventy-fourth Academy Awards in 2001, Poitier was presented with a prestigious Honorary Oscar. During the presentation the academy president Frank Pierson declared, "When the academy honors Sidney Poitier, it honors itself even more," thus indicating Poitier's place as a Hollywood icon.

FURTHER READING

Poitier, Sidney. *The Measure of a Man: A Spiritual Autobiography* (2000).
———. *This Life* (1980).

Ewers, Carolyn H. *Sidney Poitier: The Long Journey, a Biography* (1969).
Keyser, Lester J., and André H. Ruszkowski. *The Cinema of Sidney Poitier: The Black Man's Changing Role on the American Screen* (1980).

—RÉGINE MICHELLE JEAN-CHARLES

POOLE, ROBERT. *See* Muhammad, Elijah.

PORTER, JAMES AMOS (22 Dec. 1905–28 Feb. 1970), painter, art historian, and writer, was born in Baltimore, Maryland, the son of John Porter, a Methodist minister, and Lydia Peck, a schoolteacher. The youngest of seven siblings, he attended the public schools in Baltimore and Washington, D.C., and graduated cum laude from Howard University in 1927 with a bachelor of science in Art. That same year Howard appointed him instructor in art in the School of Applied Sciences. In December 1929 he married Dorothy Louise Burnett of Montclair, New Jersey; they had one daughter.

In 1929 Porter studied at the Art Students League of New York under Dimitri Romanovsky and George Bridgeman. In August 1935 he received the certificat de présence from the Institut d'Art et Archéologie, University of Paris, and in 1937 he received a master of arts in Art History from New York University, Fine Arts Graduate Center.

Porter first exhibited with the Harmon Foundation in 1928 and in 1933 was awarded the ARTHUR SCHOMBURG Portrait Prize during the Harmon Foundation Exhibition of Negro Artists for his painting *Woman Holding a Jug* (Fisk University, Carl Van Vechten Collection). Other early exhibitions in which he participated include the Thirty-second Annual Exhibition of the Washington Water Color Club (Gallery Room, National Gallery of Art, Smithsonian Institution, Washington, D.C., 1928), Exhibition of Paintings and Sculpture of American Negro Artists at the National Gallery of Art (Smithsonian Institution, 1929), Exhibition of Paintings and Drawings by James A. Porter and Block Prints by James Lesesne Wells (Young Women's Christian Association, Montclair, N.J., 1930), and Exhibition of Paintings by American Negro Artists at the United States National Museum (Smithsonian Institution, 1930); his first one-man show was Exhibition of Paintings and Drawings by James A. Porter (Howard University Gallery of Art, 1930).

Porter began writing about art in the late 1920s. One of his earliest articles, "Versatile Interests of the Early Negro Artist," appeared in *Art in America* in 1931. One of his most important and still-discussed articles, "Four Problems in the History of Negro Art," published in the *Journal of Negro History* in 1942, mentions numerous artists and analyzes the following four problems: documenting and locating the earliest art by blacks—or the reality of handicrafts and fine arts by Negroes before 1820; discovering when racial subject matter takes vital hold on the black artist—or the Negro artist's relation to the mainstream of American society; investigating the decline of productivity among black artists between 1870 and 1890 (a process that coincided with the end of an era, especially of neoclassicism and

portraiture), concentrating on the period of Reconstruction; and determining the role of visual artists in the New Negro Movement of 1900–1920, the period of self-expression for the Negro.

Porter's classic book, *Modern Negro Art* (1943), has proved to be one of the most informative sources on the productivity of the African American artist in the United States since the eighteenth century. Its placement of African American artists in the context of modern art history

was both novel and profound. For some, *Modern Negro Art* was considered presumptuous and certainly premature. But Porter's bold and perceptive scholarship helped those who subsequently focused their attention on African American expression in the visual arts to see the wealth of work that had been produced in the United States for over two centuries" (*James A. Porter Inaugural Colloquium on African American Art*, brochure, 31 Mar. 1990, Howard Univ.).

First reprinted in 1963 for use as a standard reference work on black art in America, it was reprinted again in 1992 and is considered by many to be the fundamental book on black art history. As Lowery S. Sims of the Metropolitan Museum of Art has noted in the 1992 edition, *Modern Negro Art* "is still an indispensable reference work fifty years after its initial publication"; and, in the view of art historian Richard J. Powell, it "continues to provide today's scholars with early source information, core bibliographic material, and other essential research tools for African American art history" (*Modern Negro Art* [1992]).

Porter also wrote about many artists, including HENRY OSSAWA TANNER, ROBERT S. DUNCANSON, Malvin Gray Johnson, and Laura Wheeler Waring. His other writings include monographs, book reviews, introductions to books, including Charles White's *Dignity of Images* and LOÏS MAILOU JONES's *Peintures, 1937–1951*, introductions and forewords to exhibition catalogs, and newspaper and periodical articles.

In 1953 Porter was appointed head of the Department of Art and director of the Gallery of Art at Howard University. This dual position enabled him to organize exhibitions featuring artists of many races from many countries who previously had not been recognized. He is credited with enlarging the permanent art collection of Howard University and strengthening the art department's collection of works by black artists as well as its art curriculum. Porter's leadership led the Kress Foundation to include Howard among the roughly two dozen American universities selected in 1961 to receive the Kress Study Collection of Renaissance paintings and sculpture as a stimulus to the study of art history.

In 1955 Porter received the Achievement in Art Award from the Pyramid Club of Philadelphia and also was appointed a fellow of the Belgium-American Art Seminar studying Flemish and Dutch art of the sixteenth to eighteenth centuries. In 1961 he was a delegate at the UNESCO Conference on Africa, held in Boston, and he served as a member of the Arts Council of Washington, D.C. (1961–1963), and as a member of the conference Symposium on Art and Public Education (1962). In August 1962 he was a delegate-member of the International Congress on African Art and Culture, sponsored by the Rhodes National Gallery, in Salisbury, Southern Rhodesia.

In 1963–1964, having been awarded a Washington *Evening Star* faculty-research grant to gather materials for a projected book on West African art and architecture, Porter took a sabbatical leave to West Africa, including Nigeria and Egypt. From September 1963 to July 1964 he collected various pieces of African art throughout West Africa and Egypt and participated in a USIA exhibition. Also in this period he lectured on African and Afro-American art for the radio broadcast *Voice of America*. In August 1964 he traveled to Brazil in search of documentation of the African influence on and contribution to Brazilian colonial and modern art and to Latin American art and culture. Porter thought a worldview was needed to explore the transcontinental, historical, and cultural perspectives of the Negro, and he wanted the quantitative and qualitative factors examined that affected the African's experience outside Africa. Only through comparative research of this kind, Porter argued, would it become possible to relate and reconstruct the dissimilar experiences and cultural expression of the transplanted Negro. Upon returning

to the United States in the fall with twenty-five of his own paintings that he had completed while in Lagos, Nigeria, Porter said that he hoped "my paintings reflect the enthusiasm and the understanding [and] admiration which I have felt for Africa and the Africans, even though, admittedly the most skillful expatriate artist may utterly fail to capture those ineffable traits in the African people which we believe are made visible to us in their arts" ("Professor Porter Paints in Nigeria," *Howard University Magazine* 7, no. 4 [July 1965]: 12–16).

In March 1965 Porter and twenty-six other teachers in the United States were named "America's most outstanding men of the arts." They received the first National Gallery of Art Medals and Honoraria for Distinguished Achievement in Art Education, which were presented at a White House ceremony by First Lady Lady Bird Johnson. These medals were specially designed as part of a daylong celebration commemorating the twenty-fifth anniversary of the founding of the National Gallery of Art.

Since Porter's death in Washington, D.C., his legacy has been honored in various ways. The James A. Porter Gallery of African American Art was dedicated at the Howard University Gallery of Art on 4 December 1970. Aesthetic Dynamics organized in Wilmington, Delaware, Afro-American Images (1971), an exhibition dedicated, according to the catalog, to "a man ahead of his time. Unique in the sense that he was totally involved in the creative expression which characterizes the Black life-style in African, Latin American and African American art as an historian and was an accomplished practicing artist as well." In March 1990 the Department of Art at Howard University organized the James A. Porter Inaugural Colloquium on African American Art. This annual event seeks to continue Porter's efforts to bring previously invisible artists to the attention of the American mainstream and to define and assess the enduring artistic values that are meaningful for African Americans. In *James A. Porter, Artist and Art Historian: The Memory of the Legacy*, the catalog for a retrospective exhibition held at the Howard University Gallery of Art

in 1992–1993, ROMARE BEARDEN wrote that, because of Porter's efforts, college art programs, in particular, art programs in traditionally black colleges, are no longer considered secondary to the other disciplines.

FURTHER READING

Porter's papers are in the Dorothy Porter Wesley Archives, Wesport Foundation and Gallery, Washington, D.C.

BEARDEN, ROMARE. *A History of African American Artists from 1792 to the Present* (1993).

Davis, Donald F. "James Porter of Howard: Artist, Writer." *Journal of Negro History* 70 (1985): 89–91.

Powell, Richard. *Black Art: A Cultural History* (2003)

Obituaries: *Evening Star* (Washington, D.C.), 3–4 Mar. 1970; *International Herald Tribune*, 5 Mar. 1970; *Washington Post*, 14 Mar. 1970; *Jet*, 19 Mar. 1970; *Art Journal* 29 (1970).
—CONSTANCE PORTER UZELAC

 POWELL, ADAM CLAYTON, JR.
(29 Nov. 1908–4 Apr. 1972), minister and congressman, was born in New Haven, Connecticut, the son of the Reverend Adam Clayton Powell Sr. and Mattie Fletcher Shaffer. The family moved to New York City in 1909 after the senior Powell became minister of the Abyssinian Baptist Church, then located at Fortieth Street between Seventh and Eighth avenues. In 1923, at the elder Powell's urging, the church and the family joined the surge of black migration uptown to Harlem, with the church moving to 138th Street between Seventh and Lenox avenues.

Adam Powell Jr. earned an AB at Colgate University in 1930 and an AM in Religious Education at Columbia University in 1932. So light-skinned that he could pass for white, and did so for a time at Colgate, he came to identify himself as black, and, although from a comfortable background, he advocated the rights of workers.

Powell's rise to power, and his adoption of various leadership roles in civil rights, dated from the 1930s. His power base throughout his career was the Abyssinian Baptist Church, where

Adam Clayton Powell Jr., congressman from Harlem, minister, and lifelong warrior for civil rights. Library of Congress

his father ministered to his flock's social and economic as well as spiritual needs. There, during the Great Depression, young Powell directed a soup kitchen and relief operation that supplied thousands of destitute Harlemites with food and clothing. In 1930 he became the church's business manager and director of its community center. In 1937 he succeeded his father as pastor. He married Cotton Club dancer Isabel Washington in 1933 and adopted her son from a previous marriage.

Beginning in 1936 Powell published a column, "The Soap Box," in the black weekly *Amsterdam News*. Active in a campaign for equal employment opportunities for black residents of Harlem, his first major social campaign involved efforts to improve blacks' employment opportunities and working conditions at Harlem Hospital. By the mid-1930s "Don't buy where you can't work" became a slogan in Harlem, as it already had become in Chicago and some other cities. Powell became

a leader of organized picketing of offending stores. By 1938 he led the Greater New York Coordinating Committee for Employment, which pushed successfully in the next few years for jobs for blacks not only in stores but also with the electric and telephone companies, as workers at the 1939 New York World's Fair, as drivers and mechanics on city buses, and as faculty at the city's colleges.

During World War II Powell continued proselytizing from old platforms, and he found new ones. He preached at Abyssinian Baptist, which had the largest Protestant congregation in the United States; led the militant Harlem People's Committee; published the *People's Voice*, a Harlem weekly; and wrote *Marching Blacks: An Interpretive History of the Rise of the Black Common Man* (1945). Divorcing his first wife, he married pianist and singer Hazel Scott in 1945, and they had a son. Powell's prominence in Harlem resulted in his election in 1941 to the New York

City Council, where he continued to hone his combination of political and protest skills. And from this political base he ran for Congress in 1944 when a new congressional district was formed for Harlem. Winning, he became New York City's first black congressman; William L. Dawson of Chicago was the only other African American then in Congress.

For many years an often lonely voice in Congress, Powell called for a permanent Fair Employment Practices Commission, an end to the poll tax in federal elections, and an end to racial segregation in the military. Finding that House rules banned him because of his race from such facilities as dining rooms, steam baths, and barbershops, he nonetheless proceeded to make use of all such facilities, and he insisted that his staff follow his lead. He brought an end to the exclusion of black journalists from the press gallery in the House of Representatives. As early as the 1940s he was characteristically offering what became known as the "Powell Amendment" to spending legislation. The proviso, supported by the National Association for the Advancement of Colored People, would have banned federal funds from any project that supported racial segregation, and though it failed to pass it made him known as "Mr. Civil Rights."

A New Deal Democrat, Powell nonetheless maintained political independence, whether from his father or from the Democratic Party's leadership. Charting his own way, though his father remained a Republican, Powell campaigned in 1932 for the Democratic presidential nominee Franklin D. Roosevelt. In 1944 he ran for Congress as the nominee of the Republican and American Labor parties as well as the Democratic Party. In 1956 he broke with the Democrats over the party's temporizing stance on civil rights issues to support Dwight Eisenhower's reelection campaign. Throughout his years in Congress he saw his main mission as thwarting the southern wing of his own party in Congress. He demonstrated no patience with liberal Democrats who trimmed sails or pulled punches when civil rights legislation was at stake.

One of Powell's chief roles, often behind the scenes, was to monitor the behavior of organized labor and the federal government on the racial front. He believed apprenticeship programs in the labor market should be open to blacks, progressive legislation should be enacted, and no federal agency should practice or foster racial segregation or discrimination. During the 1960s he tried to ensure that blacks would hold leadership positions in the Peace Corps, the Poverty Corps, and federal regulatory agencies. Ambassadorships, cabinet positions, and the Supreme Court, he urged, should have black representation. His relations with the Eisenhower administration enabled him to arrange in 1954 for Ethiopian emperor Haile Selassie, while on a visit to the United States, to visit Abyssinian Baptist Church. There the emperor presented Powell with a large gold medallion, which he proudly wore on a chain around his neck for the rest of his life.

Powell divorced his second wife and married Yvette Flores in 1960, and they had a son. As a result of the seniority system in Congress, Powell's peak in power came in the 1960s, the years of the New Frontier and the Great Society. For three terms, from 1961 to 1967, he chaired the House Committee on Education and Labor. From his committee came such landmark legislation as the 1961 Minimum Wage Bill, the Vocational Education Act, the Manpower Development and Training Act, various antipoverty bills, and the Elementary and Secondary Education Act. When the National Defense Education Act of 1958, with its promotion of education in science, mathematics, and foreign languages, came up for renewal in 1964, Powell steered through an expansion of coverage to the humanities and social sciences. And when the Civil Rights Act of 1964 became law, Title VI, which authorized all federal agencies to withhold aid from institutions that practiced racial segregation or discrimination, embodied the "Powell Amendment." His time had come; he pushed ahead to challenge school segregation in the North.

Powell's fall from power came at the height of his national prominence. Always flamboyant and controversial, he displayed moral behavior anything but ascetic, spent tax dollars merrily on pleasure trips, and often missed important votes in Congress. In a television interview in March 1960 Powell referred to a Harlem widow, Esther James, as a "bag woman," someone who collected graft for corrupt police. She sued and won. Powell refused to apologize, or pay, or even respond to subpoenas to appear in court to explain his failure to comply. After he was cited for contempt of court in November 1966, a Select Committee of the House investigated Powell's affairs, partly because of the James case and partly because of an alleged misuse of public funds. Powell remained convinced that the real purpose was a racist attempt to silence a key proponent of civil rights. In March 1967 the Select Committee recommended Powell's public censure and his loss of seniority. The full House went farther and voted to exclude Powell from the Ninetieth Congress. In a special election to fill the vacant seat, Powell trounced his opponents. Then after a successful fund-raising effort he paid James her award. An agreement was worked out that ended the threat of jail for contempt of court so—after spending much of 1967 in an idyllic exile on Bimini—he could return to New York whenever he wished. In January 1969 the House voted to seat him in the Ninety-first Congress, though it stripped him of his seniority and fined him for misuse of payroll and travel funds. Later that year, in *Powell v. McCormack*, the Supreme Court ruled against the House's exclusion of him in 1967.

After being out of Congress in 1967–1969, Powell retrieved his seat. But he was no longer committee chairman, and his power had evaporated. Worse, in 1969 Powell was hospitalized with cancer. Weakened physically and politically he nonetheless entered the Democratic primary in 1970 but was narrowly defeated by state assemblyman CHARLES RANGEL. Powell's time in Congress was over. He wrote an autobiography and retired in 1971 from Abyssinian Baptist.

Powell liked one characterization of him as "arrogant, but with style." His legacy is a mixed one, for his personal presumptions clouded his political accomplishments. Yet during the 1940s and 1950s he ranked with A. PHILIP RANDOLPH among the great leaders of African Americans. He proved a resourceful and effective leader in America's largest city from the 1930s through World War II. From the mid-1940s through the mid-1960s he combined his political position as a congressman with a commitment to progressive politics that far outstripped his few black congressional predecessors of the 1930s or his few black colleagues of the 1940s and 1950s. In the 1960s he had greater power to get things done, but he was also less irreplaceable, for American politics had begun to catch up with his positions on matters of race and class. He died in Miami, Florida.

FURTHER READING

No large collection of Powell papers exists, but scattered materials by or about him are at the Schomburg Center for Research in Black Culture of the New York Public Library and the Lyndon B. Johnson Presidential Library in Austin, Tex.

Powell, Adam Clayton, Jr. *Adam by Adam: The Autobiography of Adam Clayton Powell Jr.* (1971).

Hamilton, Charles V. *Adam Clayton Powell Jr.: The Political Biography of an American Dilemma* (1991).

Haygood, Wil. *King of the Cats: The Life and Times of Adam Clayton Powell Jr.* (1993).

Reeves, Andree E. *Congressional Committee Chairmen: Three Who Made an Evolution* (1993).

Obituaries: *New York Times* and *Washington Post*, 5 Apr. 1972.
—PETER WALLENSTEIN

 POWELL, COLIN
(5 Apr. 1937–), U.S. Army general and secretary of state, was born in Harlem in New York City to the Jamaican immigrants Luther Powell, a shipping clerk, and Maud Ariel McKoy, a seamstress, both of whom worked in New York City's garment district. When he was six years old, Powell moved with his family to Hunts Point, an ethnically diverse neighborhood in the South Bronx. Powell's autobiography portrays Hunts Point as a community of stable families and a certain rough-hewn racial tolerance, but it does not ignore the neighborhood's upsurge in drug- and gang-related crime, particularly after World War II. The Powells escaped the

General Colin Powell became secretary of state in George W. Bush's administration. Library of Congress

crumbling South Bronx tenements in the mid-1950s, however, a testament to his parents' unstinting work ethic and shrewd housekeeping. But luck also played a part. Luther Powell, a regular numbers player, placed a twenty-five-dollar bet on a number that he had dreamed about and then saw again on a hymn board in church. That number hit and netted the Powells ten thousand dollars, a sum three times Luther's annual salary and more than enough for a down payment on a three-bedroom home in the borough of Queens.

By the time his family moved to Queens, Powell had already enrolled in the City College of New York (CCNY). He was a competent, though not stellar, student, and his parents worried about their son's apparent aimlessness. But in his first semester at CCNY, Powell found the structure and order that he had previously known only as an acolyte in the Episcopal Church. "Something had caught my eye," Powell recalls in his autobiography, "young guys on campus in uniform" (Powell, 25). On joining the college ROTC and receiving his own uniform, he began, for the first time in his life, to feel a sense of purpose. Thereafter, Powell's college career revolved around the Pershing Rifles, an ROTC fraternity, in which he enjoyed the camaraderie of his fellow cadets and

excelled as a drill leader. Such drills proved invaluable in strengthening his self-confidence, particularly in teaching him that "being responsible sometimes means pissing people off" (Powell, 35). Powell earned his degree from CCNY in June 1958 but found the ceremony anticlimactic after graduating first in his ROTC class with the rank of cadet colonel. He also received a commission as a second lieutenant in the army.

Powell's first military assignment was in Fort Benning, Georgia. He resented the racism and indignities that he encountered, particularly in the seg-regated communities surrounding the camp, but he refused to let his anger dictate his actions. He vowed then to answer racist critics of blacks in the military by striving to be the consum-mate professional soldier. This he did at Fort Benning and on later assignments in West Germany; at Fort Owens, Mas-sachusetts; and at the Unconventional Warfare Center at Fort Bragg, North Carolina, where he trained as one of sixteen thousand military advisers who were to be sent by President John F. Kennedy to assist the anti-communist South Vietnamese government of Ngo Dinh Diem. Powell arrived in Saigon on Christmas Day 1962, leaving behind his wife of just four months, Alma Johnson, a speech pathologist from Birmingham, Alabama, whom he had met in Boston while he was serving at Fort Owens. The Powells had three children: Annemarie, Linda, and Michael.

Powell's first tour of duty in Vietnam was relatively uneventful, though he returned to Fort Benning in November 1963 with a Purple Heart, after being wounded by a Vietcong booby trap. In 1967 he attended the highly selective U.S. Army Command and General Staff College at Fort Leavenworth, Kansas, and graduated second in a class of 1,244. Powell's military reputation was further enhanced when he returned to Vietnam in 1968 and received a second Purple Heart, the Legion of Merit, and the Soldier's Medal for rescuing two crewmen from the burning wreckage of a helicopter.

On his first Vietnam tour, Powell had believed that the American presence in Indochina was justified by the goal of defeating communism, but by 1969 he had begun to question—in private, at least—the course of that war. He

later came to believe that the expansion of the U.S. military draft after 1965 resulted in a breakdown in morale and in the deployment of too many poorly trained officers and noncommissioned personnel. The inexperience of these soldiers, he argues in his 1995 autobiography, led to atrocities such as that at My Lai in the Batangan peninsula in March 1968, in which 347 unarmed Vietnamese civilians, mostly old men, women, and children, were tortured and killed by troops of the Americal Division. Powell, a major in the same division, arrived in Vietnam after that incident, but has been criticized for not thoroughly investigating subsequent reports of a massacre at My Lai.

Powell left Vietnam in July 1969 to study for an MBA at George Wash-ington University in Washington, D.C. He graduated in 1971, was promoted to the rank of lieutenant colonel, and began working in the Pentagon as an operations research analyst. While that position marked Powell's ascent on the military career ladder, his selection for a White House Fellowship in 1972–1973 brought him into the quite different milieu of Washington politics. Powell chose to work in the Office of Manage-ment and Budget (OMB), an unglam-orous but powerful department, where he worked with Frank Carlucci, the deputy to the OMB's director, Caspar Weinberger. On completing his fellow-ship, Powell served for a year as a battal-ion commander in South Korea before returning to Washington to attend the National War College. He graduated in 1976; was given a brigade command with the 101st Airborne Division at Fort Campbell, Kentucky; and then served as a Pentagon aide in the administration of President Jimmy Carter, an appointment that resulted in Powell's promotion to brigadier general at the age of only forty-two. Powell did not, however, support his commander in chief's reelection and voted for Carter's Republican challenger Ronald Reagan, in 1980.

Reagan's victory enabled Powell to work again with his former bosses Weinberger and Carlucci, who became secretary and deputy secretary, respectively, at the Defense Department. Both men valued Powell highly and did much to further his career, alternatively recommending him for military promotions and recalling him to Washington to serve in various political posts. In 1981 they encouraged his return to a military posting by appointing him assistant division commander in Fort Carson, Colorado. Powell's next assignment, at Fort Leavenworth, Kansas, further broadened his résumé, acquainted him with the army's newest weaponry and technology, and gained him a second star and promotion to the rank of major general.

Powell was reluctant to leave the Kansas base, where he had helped establish a memorial honoring the Buffalo Soldiers, black cavalry and infantrymen who had served on America's western frontier after the Civil War. In 1983, however, he returned to Washington to serve as Weinberger's military assistant, a post that made him the chief gatekeeper of information to and from the defense secretary. By all accounts, Powell excelled at this role. His direct, even blunt approach ruffled some feathers, but most Pentagon insiders found his honesty, humor, and apparent lack of political guile refreshing. Above all, he earned high marks in Washington for his consummate people-handling skills. One Pentagon veteran remarked of Powell that he had "never seen anyone who could run a meeting more effectively with senior people and cut through the crap and get a decision" (Means, 206).

Although he was Weinberger's chief aide from 1983 to 1986, Powell was not tainted by the Iran-Contra affair that resulted in Weinberger's indictments in 1992 for perjury and for misleading Congress. A full accounting of Powell's role in the scandal may never be known, however, since President George H. W. Bush pardoned Weinberger in 1992, just weeks before his trial for perjury. Powell, for his part, denies any complicity in Iran-Contra and notes in his autobiography that he and Weinberger opposed the arms-for-hostages deal hatched by the national security adviser Admiral John Poindexter. Independent Counsel Lawrence Walsh's investigation into the affair found, though, that Weinberger and his closest aides had greater knowledge of the illegal arms sales than they had admitted. Nonetheless, Iran-Contra advanced Powell's career. At the time the scandal broke, he was in command of the Fifth U.S. Corps in Frankfurt, West

Germany, but returned to Washington in January 1987 as deputy to Frank Carlucci, whom Reagan had appointed to replace the disgraced Poindexter as national security adviser. Ten months later, when Carlucci replaced Weinberger as secretary of defense, the president appointed Powell, by then a lieutenant general, as America's first African American national security adviser.

Powell took that post at a time of rapid change in global affairs. By the late 1980s the radical reforms instituted by the Soviet leader Mikhail Gorbachev had set in motion the breakup of the Eastern Bloc, although at that time neither the Soviets nor the Americans predicted that it would happen so rapidly. At the same time, the Reagan administration came to portray Islamic fundamentalism as an even greater threat to the American national interest than the Soviets. On most matters, Powell shared the basic foreign policy philosophy of the Reaganites—increased military spending, support for anti-communist regimes, and unswerving loyalty to Israel. Powell's genius lay, however, in quickly summarizing and analyzing a complex and rapidly changing world to President Reagan, a man he viewed as a "visionary" but who, as Iran-Contra made abundantly clear, had only a vague grasp of the details and constitutionality of foreign policy. Capitol Hill veterans, military professionals, and television pundits were likewise impressed by the professionalism and clarity of Powell's briefings on national security affairs.

Although Reagan's successor, George H. W. Bush, offered Powell a number of high-ranking cabinet posts, he chose to return to the military. Powell's time as commander in chief of Forces Command at Fort McPherson, Georgia, lasted only four months, long enough to earn him a fourth star and the service record required for the military's top post, chairman of the joint chiefs of staff. In August 1989 Bush duly nominated Powell to that post, making him the youngest soldier and the first African American to lead the nation's military. The implosion of the Soviet empire in that year left the United States as the world's largest superpower and set the stage for an era of unprecedented American military engagement across the globe. As chairman, Powell oversaw

the most significant deployments of American military force since Vietnam.

Powell initially advised Bush against the use of force in Panama in 1989, but he earned plaudits for his deft handling of both the military and media campaigns once the president decided to remove from power the Panamanian dictator Manuel Noriega. Many in the international community condemned the death of nearly one thousand Panamanian civilians, but the war proved highly popular in the United States, primarily because the military had used a strategy that became known as the "Powell doctrine." According to this doctrine, the United States in Vietnam had fought a half-hearted war "for half-hearted reasons that the American people could not understand or support" (Powell, 144–145). Powell's strategy for future American wars, therefore, was to "have a clear political objective and stick to it." He advocated that the United States "use all the force necessary," and that it should not "apologize for going in big if that is what it takes. Decisive force ends wars quickly and in the long run saves lives" (Powell, 420–421).

As with Panama, Powell initially advised President Bush to act cautiously in August 1990, when Iraq invaded Kuwait. Once Bush had decided on a military campaign to remove Iraqi forces, however, Powell again proved highly effective. He oversaw the logistics of a massive American military buildup in Saudi Arabia and proved adept at handling the unprecedented demands of the emerging twenty-four-hour global news media. Most famously, Powell informed the watching billions of his "very, very simple" strategy for defeating Iraq: "First we are going to cut it off, and then we are going to kill it" (Means, 278). With strong international support, the Allied forces did just that in 1991, suffering only 246 combat deaths—60 percent of them American—in the 45-day air- and ground-war campaign.

By contrast, Iraqi losses were devastating. According to U.S. Census Bureau estimates, 158,000 Iraqis died as a result of the war and its immediate aftermath, three-quarters of them civilians. Such figures make it all the more remarkable that Powell was subsequently attacked in some quarters for advocating a ceasefire once

Kuwait was liberated and Iraqi forces crushed. He answered those critics in his 1995 autobiography by arguing that occupying Iraq would have eroded the powerful international coalition that had made victory possible. Assassinating the Iraqi president, Saddam Hussein, Powell added, would have destabilized the entire Middle East by fragmenting Iraq into separate Sunni, Shia, and Kurdish enclaves. Shortly after the end of the conflict, the NAACP honored Powell with the Springarn Medal, its annual award for achievement by an African American.

Powell emerged from the Gulf War as the most popular American soldier since Dwight Eisenhower, and commentators speculated that President Bush might replace his widely ridiculed vice president, Dan Quayle, with the charismatic Powell for the 1992 presidential race. Bush, perhaps fatally for his re-election chances, remained loyal to Quayle. Powell likewise remained loyal to Bush, spurning the advances of Bill Clinton, who approached him regarding the Democratic vice-presidential nomination through their mutual friend VERNON JORDAN. Powell's retirement as chairman of the joint chiefs of staff in 1993 prompted further rumors about his presidential ambitions, speculation that was fueled by the enthusiastic reception that met Powell's 1995 autobiography, *My American Journey*, and the vastly popular book tour that followed. Powell ultimately resisted strong pressure to challenge Clinton as either an independent or a Republican candidate, even though opinion polls suggested that he would have received support from Americans of both parties and all races. Republicans, mostly white, identified with Powell's military record, while Democrats, who were disproportionately African American, applauded the general's support for affirmative action and abortion rights. Powell chose instead to establish American Promise, an organization that advocates volunteerism and mentoring to help disadvantaged children. He did not entirely abandon politics, however, and campaigned for the Republican Party in both 1996 and 2000.

Powell returned to Washington in 2001, when President George W. Bush appointed him secretary of state in a foreign policy team that included CONDOLEEZZA RICE as national security adviser. Early reviews of the Bush presidency highlighted tensions between Powell, who believed that the United States should seek international cooperation in solving global crises, and others, such as Rice and Defense Secretary Donald Rumsfeld, who argued for a more unilateralist approach. Those distinctions blurred significantly in the aftermath of the 11 September 2001 terrorist attacks on the World Trade Center and the Pentagon. Powell joined with a united Bush cabinet to advocate the removal from power in Afghanistan of the Taliban, a fundamentalist Muslim sect suspected of financing the al-Qaeda terrorist network that had carried out the terrorist attacks.

In 2002 Rumsfeld, Rice, and others advised President Bush to launch a preemptive strike on Iraq to destroy an alleged, though as yet unproven, link between that nation and al-Qaeda. Others in the Bush administration advocated a military invasion of Iraq to remove weapons of mass destruction, allegedly held by Iraq in defiance of UN Security Council resolutions. Powell initially urged Bush to work toward those goals in association with the UN, but he apparently abandoned that strategy in early 2003, when France, Russia, and China made clear that they would use their Security Council veto powers against any preemptive strike by the United States. As a consequence, the United States launched a military invasion of Iraq in March 2003 without UN sanction, but with the support of about thirty allies described by Powell as a "coalition of the willing." Since only Britain and Australia provided significant support to the American cause, some war critics contrasted Powell's diplomatic efforts unfavorably with his predecessor during the first Gulf War, James Baker, who had enlisted financial and military support from France, Japan, Germany, and even some of Iraq's Arab neighbors.

American military success in both Iraq conflicts owed much to Colin Powell. For three decades as a career soldier and Washington insider, he lobbied vigorously for the technologically advanced, state-of-the-art weaponry that devastated the Iraqi army and left minimal American casualties. Both military victories secured another of Powell's career goals: restoring public support for and trust of the U.S. military that had eroded after Vietnam. Powell's diplomatic legacy is less clear, however. In 2002–2003, he could not bridge the divide between an increasingly nationalistic Bush administration and members of the United Nations fearful of American military and economic supremacy. In the uncertain new world order that emerged after the second Iraq war, Secretary of State Powell would have to draw upon his much vaunted charisma and powers of persuasion to reconcile two potentially antagonistic objectives: maintaining American military hegemony while ensuring international cooperation and stability.

FURTHER READING

Powell, Colin. *My American Journey* (1995).

Means, Howard. *Colin Powell* (1992).
Woodward, Bob. *The Commanders* (1991).
—STEVEN J. NIVEN

PRICE, LEONTYNE
(10 Feb. 1927–), opera singer, was born Mary Violet Leontine Price in Laurel, Mississippi, one of two children of James Anthony Price, who worked in the local sawmills, and Katherine Baker, a popular Laurel midwife. Katherine nurtured her daughter's talent by enrolling her in piano lessons at age three, and by encouraging her to sing in church and community events. Listening to recordings at home and attending concerts, including a memorable performance by MARIAN ANDERSON, enlarged Leontyne's passion for music. In 1944 she graduated from Oak Park Vocational High School and received a scholarship to Wilberforce College in Ohio. Although she planned a career in music education, Leontyne's vocal gifts attracted such attention that she changed her major to voice, graduating with a BA in 1948.

After graduating, Price enrolled at the Juilliard School of Music in New York City, which she attended on a four-year scholarship. While in her senior year at Wilberforce, she had performed on the same program as PAUL ROBESON. Wanting to help the young singer, Robeson helped her pay for Julliard

Leontyne Price in costume for her leading role in Louis Mélançon's Antony and Cleopatra *at the Metropolitan Opera in New York in 1966.* Library of Congress

by giving a fundraising concert for the Leontyne Price Fund, established by her professors. Living in New York enabled the young singer to attend the Metropolitan Opera, exposing her to the world's finest operatic productions. When she sang the part of Mistress Ford in Verdi's *Falstaff* in a Juilliard opera workshop, her talent so impressed composer Virgil Thomson that he cast her in the revival of his all-black American classic, *Four Saints in Three Acts* (1934), which was staged in New York and Paris in 1952.

Price made her triumphant international debut as Bess in Robert Breen's revival of George Gershwin's dramatic masterpiece *Porgy and Bess*. Abandoning plans to study in Europe on a Fulbright Fellowship, Price accepted the starring role in the touring production which opened in Dallas in June 1952 and continued in Chicago, Pittsburgh, and Washington, D.C., where President Truman attended the performance, and on to several major European cities. In March 1953 the show opened at New York's Ziegfeld Theater, where it continued for 304 performances. For a young singer in her mid-twenties, the applause and accolades were stunning. She was "a Bess of vocal glory" (Hollis Alpert, *The Life and Times of Porgy and Bess* [1990], 155), and critics praised her imaginative interpretation and her focused soprano voice. As her repertoire expanded to include the operas of Mozart, Orff, Massenet, Verdi,

and others, Price's glamorous demeanor came to the fore. As one observer noted, she "literally spilled charm over the footlight" (Harrison).

Price made history when in 1955 she became the first black prima donna to appear in a major production of opera on television. Despite some strenuous objections and cancellations by several local affiliates, Price sang the lead in Puccini's *Tosca* on NBC. The following year, she appeared on the air as Pamina in Mozart's *Die Zauberflöte*. In September 1957 she thoroughly enchanted audiences at the San Francisco Opera and won high acclaim for her first appearance in a staged opera with a major company when she performed as the devout Madame Lidoine in Poulenc's *Dialogues of the Carmelites*. When she sang Verdi's *Aida* under Herbert von Karajan at the Vienna State Opera in 1958, a felicitous association with the noted conductor brought her engagements in such important European venues as the Verona Arena, the Salzburg Festival, and London's Covent Garden.

The Ethiopian princess in *Aida* has long been a signature role for Price. When she sang *Aida* at La Scala in 1960, she was hailed as the quintessential Verdi soprano: "Our great Verdi would have found her the ideal" (Walsh, 67). Indeed, the monumental *Requiem* and other works by Verdi that Price has sung with the Metropolitan Opera, such as *Aida, La Forza del Destino, Ernani*, and

Un Ballo in Maschera, are among the soprano's most compelling showpieces. As Amelia in *Un Ballo in Maschera*, her lush *lyrico spinto* (a lyric soprano with dramatic power) dazzled audiences in the standing-room-only house. By the time Price left the Metropolitan Opera in *Aida* in 1985, she had sung the role at the Met more than forty-two times.

Price made her debut with the Metropolitan Opera in Verdi's *Il Trovatore* on 27 January 1961, receiving a forty-five-minute standing ovation. "As Leonora," wrote Ronald Eyer, "Leontyne Price was a sensational success.... The lovely fast vibrato which is characteristic of her voice gave liquidity and warmth to the soaring line; her coloratura was of extraordinary flexibility and lightness of touch for so large a voice" (*New York Herald Tribune*, 28 Jan. 1961). Price's other Metropolitan Opera roles have included Anna in Mozart's *Don Giovanni*, Cio-Cio-San in Puccini's *Madama Butterfly*, and the Prima Donna/Ariadne in Strauss's *Ariadne auf Naxos*. Few, however, will forget her luminous tones and beautifully shaped phrases when she sang her last *Il Trovatore* at the Met in 1982, at age fifty-five.

Perhaps the strongest character Price ever played was that of Cleopatra in Samuel Barber's *Antony and Cleopatra*. The opera, commissioned by the Metropolitan Opera for the opening of its new fifty-million-dollar house at Lincoln Center, was given its premiere on 16 September 1966 with Thomas Schippers conducting. Although her interpretation of the character was spellbinding and her vocal powers in finest form, Price had to rise to the challenges of Franco Zeffirelli's over-effulgent staging and an electrical upset that forced Cleopatra to make her entrance in total darkness. "I was locked in the pyramid at the first aria," Price recounted. "There was no way in the world I could make that cue. I was to be dressed in the pyramid for the next scene, and I simply said 'Zip this one back up, whether it fits or not. I'll keep singing and just go out'" (Leontyne Price in an interview with Peter Dickinson, BBC broadcast, "Samuel Barber Retrospective," 23 Jan. 1982). And so she did.

Few artists have received so many distinguished honors from U.S. presidents as Price. On 4 July 1964 Lyndon Johnson awarded the Presidential Medal of Freedom to both Price and the American composer Aaron Copland. They became the first musicians to receive the distinguished award, created by John F. Kennedy shortly before he died. Price also made history when she performed in the first nationally televised concert series from the White House, initiated by President Carter in 1978. On 26 March 1979 the soprano's majestic interpretation of "Pace, pace, mio Dio," from *La Forza del Destino*, for the signing of the Israeli-Egyptian peace treaty at the White House moved all who heard her. She also sang for the White House ceremonies welcoming Pope John Paul II, and in 1980 she was a recipient of the Kennedy Center Honors for a lifetime achievement in the arts. Price received the NAACP's Spingarn Medal in 1965.

Price was one of the first African American prima donnas to appear regularly on the world's great opera stages. In her later years she sang less in opera and more in recitals, focusing on spirituals, Broadway tunes, hymns, and art songs. For her many fine recordings she received at least eighteen Grammy Awards. Married on 31 August 1952 to the baritone William Warfield (her co-star in *Porgy and Bess*), Price was divorced in 1973. She continues to live in Greenwich Village in Manhattan, giving master classes and enjoying the picturesque charm of her federal-style home. With her vocal powers and distinguished presence, Leontyne Price has drawn international acclaim. Her fortitude and achievements have become models not only for young black singers but also for aspiring artists everywhere.

FURTHER READING

Lyon, Hugh Lee. *Leontyne Price: Highlights of a Prima Donna* (1973).
Steane, J. B. *Divas of the Century, Vol III* (2000).
Story, Rosalyn M. *And So I Sing: African American Divas of Opera and Concert* (1990).

Discography: *The essential Leontyne Price* (BMG Classics).

—ELISE K. KIRK

PRINCE, NANCY

(15 Sept. 1799–?), abolitionist, writer, lecturer, women's rights activist, and social critic, was born Nancy Gardner in Newburyport, Massachusetts, the daughter of an African American and Indian mother and an African father, Thomas Gardner, who was born in Nantucket, Massachusetts, and died within three months of Nancy's birth. What is known about her is drawn primarily from her 1850 memoir, *A Narrative of the Life and Travels of Mrs. Nancy Prince*. While Prince does not name her mother in her narrative, she provides descriptions of both parents that highlight their African descent, and she recounts her grandfather's violent removal to America, along with his memories of a proud life in Africa. She briefly notes the capture of her Indian grandmother by local English colonials. Her narrative speaks clearly to issues of race, gender, slavery, and morality in the United States and the Caribbean.

Nancy's childhood in Gloucester, Massachusetts, was marked by poverty, homelessness, hard labor, and profound concern for her own survival and that of her more than seven siblings still living at home. Her mother married three times; each of her husbands died from illness or overwork, and her second and third husbands were hostile toward Nancy and the other children they did not father. By the time they reached adolescence, Nancy; her brother George; and her oldest sister, Silvia, had become responsible for their younger siblings and their mother. They collected fruits and fish to sell and ran errands in order to provide food and resources to support the struggling family. George, overwhelmed by the enduring poverty, soon signed on to a ship sailing from the local harbor, and Silvia hired out as a domestic with a family that lived seventy miles from their family home in Gloucester. Nancy took a service position in a home in Salem, Massachusetts, where she worked until she became ill from hard labor and poor treatment. Her employers were pious, and she had hoped to receive religious instruction while among them. But although they observed family prayers twice daily, their cruelty to fourteen-year-old Nancy provided her

with an early opportunity to question the morality of white Christians.

The experiences of her sister and mother undoubtedly shaped Nancy's adult choices. Silvia, who by 1815 had moved to Boston to secure better wages, became a prostitute. In the winter of 1816, with the help of friends, Nancy rescued her sister from a brothel. Never stable or comfortable among her family again, Silvia died in 1827. In her narrative, Nancy briefly eulogizes her sister, calling her "precious" and "very dear" and revealing that she had often protected Silvia from their stepfather's abuse. Silvia's fall and death were not the result of a flawed character, Prince argues, but rather a consequence of the limited choices available to poor women, especially poor African American women.

Thrice widowed and the mother of at least ten children who had been either hired out or placed for care with local families, Nancy's mother became financially and emotionally dependent on her father, Tobias Wornton, called Backus, the only constant male presence in her life. When he died, about the same time as her third husband, she lost all reliable means of support. Unable to work because of her poor health, she eventually suffered a mental collapse and took to wandering miles from home until she died without ceremony in 1827, the same year as her daughter Silvia died. "My mother wandered about like a Jew," Nancy wrote about her mother (17).

In her narrative, Nancy casts her childhood and adolescence as determined by her race, gender, and class. If her mother's life was to be any model, Nancy saw her own life as proceeding toward misfortune and disease of the body, mind, and spirit. The chain of predetermination was broken for Nancy on 6 May 1819, however, when she was baptized by the Reverend Thomas Paul of Cambridge, Massachusetts, a religious and political leader known for his abolition work. Within three years, Nancy left employment as a domestic, learned a trade, and developed a "determination to do something for myself" (20). By 1822 she decided to leave the country. In September 1823 Nancy met Nero Prince, who had recently arrived from Russia, where he served as one of twenty "colored" men in the court of the emperor

Alexander. They married on 15 February 1824 and sailed for Russia on 14 April.

The Russian experience is at the heart of Prince's narrative and at the core of her development as a political advocate, activist, and social critic. She was accepted as a member of her local St. Petersburg community quite easily, and during the flood of 1824 her home became a place of refuge for flood victims. In her narrative, Prince comments in travelogue style on the Russian folk, community life, holiday and funeral celebrations, religious and family life, the flood of 1824, high court culture, and the life and pastimes of the empress Elizabeth, and she details political assassination, violent regime change, and war between Russia and Turkey. She comments as well on the lack of race prejudice in the empire and the fact that serfs are treated better in Russia than slaves are treated in America. The contrast she draws between American and Russian laboring classes, although assailable today, formed the basis of her antislavery activism upon her return to the United States.

By late 1833, troubled by the harsh winter climate, Prince returned to the United States, while her husband remained in Russia, apparently in the court's service under the new emperor. Nero Prince, intending to return to his wife in New England after two years of accumulating property, died before reaching home. Taking up the cause of children, Nancy Prince continued the work she had begun during the 1824 Russian flood, establishing an asylum for orphaned children. When the project failed financially after three months, Prince deepened her interest in antislavery causes, aligning her philosophy with that of William Lloyd Garrison's. Impassioned statements in her narrative indict American immorality and sin and warn that the sins are not hidden from God's notice.

After attending a lecture about the lives of former slaves in Jamaica and their need for spiritual, social, and financial support, Prince was persuaded to volunteer with a missionary contingent, and on 16 November 1840 she sailed from Charlestown, Massachusetts, to St. Ann Harbor, Jamaica. Her goal in Jamaica was to "raise up and encourage the emancipated inhabitants, and

teach the young children to read and work, to fear God, and put their trust in the Saviour" (45). Her good intentions notwithstanding, Prince had considerable difficulty accepting the cultural and religious habits of local Jamaicans. In her narrative she complains of lax standards among religious leaders and the women's societies within the church, and she opines that "the meeting house is more like a play house than a place of worship" (47).

In 1841 she published *The West Indies: Being a Description of the Islands*, a pamphlet in which she exposes and explains the destructive effects of slavery on the culture and character of the Jamaican people, and she reveals and derides corruption among black and white church-sponsored missionaries, who were colluding to take advantage of the recently emancipated population. In addition, *The West Indies* provided American readers with a thorough topographical description of the island and information about the island's black, white, and "mulatto" inhabitants. Prince reports on the British colony's violent internal civil conflict, turmoil in the church in the period immediately after emancipation, and extra-colonial efforts to aid the newly freed, industrious, often illiterate, and proud former slaves. The pamphlet, which is difficult to find in libraries today, is reprinted for the most part, though in slightly different order, in Prince's narrative.

A life of labor on behalf of others placed Nancy Prince in the company of prostitutes, in the czarist court in St. Petersburg, and among missionaries selling Bibles in Jamaica. Through all these experiences, Prince remained self-sufficient, committed to her labors and her faith, and humble. Hard labor, extreme weather, and limited medical attention over her lifetime eventually left her infirm. In 1850 Prince published *A Narrative of the Life and Travels of Mrs. Nancy Prince*. "My object is not a vain desire to appear before the public," Prince wrote in her introduction, "but, by the sale, I hope to obtain the means to supply my necessities" (3). A second edition of Prince's eighty-nine-page book was published in 1853. Although it is seldom anthologized, Prince's narrative is a rare combination of faith story, travelogue, and narrative of political development. The date

and place of Prince's death remain unknown.

FURTHER READING

Prince, Nancy. *A Narrative of the Life and Travels of Mrs. Nancy Prince* (1850; 1853).

Peterson, Carla L. *"Doers of the Word": African American Women Speakers and Writers in the North, 1830–1880* (1995).
—MARTHA L. WHARTON

 PROSSER, GABRIEL. *See* Gabriel.

PRYOR, RICHARD
(1 Dec. 1940–), comedian and actor, was born Richard Franklin Lenox Thomas Pryor in Peoria, Illinois, the son of LeRoy "Buck Carter" Pryor Jr. and Gertrude Thomas. Carter managed the family bar, the Famous Door, while Thomas and her mother-in-law—whom Pryor called Mama—managed a handful of mixed clientele brothels in Peoria's black neighborhood. Between spying on the couples (which occasionally included his mother) and frequenting the Famous Door, Pryor lived a childhood of inconsistency and emotional turbulence; he did, however, credit Mama and his parents for the relative affluence that accompanied their professions. Prompted by Thomas's severe alcoholism and subsequent disappearances, sometimes for as long as six months, Carter divorced her in 1950. Thomas moved to her family farm in Springfield, Missouri, and Pryor would later identify his visits there as the most peaceful moments of his life.

When Pryor was six years old, a local teenager sexually molested him; at about the same age he also discovered he could make his family laugh with pratfalls off the front porch or by slipping on dog feces. He earned high marks at a Catholic grade school but was expelled at the age of ten when the school's administration learned of his family's businesses. In junior high his teacher bribed him to do homework by promising him a few minutes every week to tell jokes at the front of the classroom. Gaining confidence and enjoying the attention, Pryor continued his class shenanigans until a couple of years later, when another teacher requested that he stop. Pryor responded by jokingly—so he claimed—swinging at the teacher. He was expelled instantly and left to work odd jobs in Peoria for four years until he joined the army at age eighteen. Pryor was stationed in Idar-Oberstein in West Germany, but his tour ended in 1960 when he aided a fellow black soldier in a bar fight by stabbing the white opponent.

Narrowly escaping jail, Pryor was discharged and allowed to return home, where he flitted about for a couple of months before conning the manager of a local "black and tan" nightclub (that is, one catering to blacks and whites) into letting him play the piano and sing. Pryor could do neither. But his onstage charisma and likability rescued him, and he became the regular emcee. He began working other such clubs and was soon introduced to marijuana and amphetamines. Also in 1960 Pryor married his girlfriend, who was pregnant with his first son, but he left Peoria almost immediately after Richard Jr.'s birth, accompanying some local comedians and singers on a tour of the Midwest and Canada.

After a year of touring, Pryor, along with many black comedians of the time, was particularly affected in 1963 by seeing BILL COSBY on the cover of *Newsweek*, and he thought, "Goddamn it, this nigger's doing what I'm fixing to do. I want to be the only nigger. Ain't no room for two niggers" (Pryor, 68). He left immediately for New York, and although he "only had $10" in his pocket, he swore he looked at least "like $50" (Pryor, 69).

Pryor's contemporaries in the Greenwich Village comedy scene included Cosby, Woody Allen, George Carlin, Dick Gregory, Flip Wilson, and Joan Rivers. Under pressure to avoid a resemblance to every club owner's bête noire, the raunchy and unpredictable Lenny Bruce, Pryor emulated Cosby as closely as possible. Moving quickly from small jazz clubs to larger venues, such as the Apollo Theater in Harlem, Pryor made his first television appearance on 31 August 1964 on Rudy Vallee's *On Broadway Tonight*; appearances on *The*

Merv Griffin Show and *The Ed Sullivan Show* soon followed. By this time Pryor, at the urgings of a prostitute he was dating, had also begun using cocaine. Except for a purported seven-month period of sobriety more than a decade later, Pryor fought cocaine addiction until he reached a degenerative state of illness in the early 1990s.

The increasing turmoil of Pryor's personal life provided a body of subject matter that he expertly wove into his performances, but the success that accompanied his newly emerging comedic style only worsened his addictions and increased his philandering. The late 1960s sped by in a whirlwind that included his first movie appearance—a bit role in Sid Caesar's film *The Busy Body* (1967)—the birth of two more children, another failed marriage, and his father's death. Finally, Pryor had a nervous breakdown in Las Vegas, when he walked onstage, froze, and spoke only one sentence before walking off: "What the fuck am I doing here?"

In 1969, with the help of friends, Pryor attempted to write, produce, and star in an innovative, yet poorly executed racial satire entitled *The Trial*, in which one white man is tried for every racial crime in American history. But Pryor destroyed the only copy of the script in a domestic dispute. His career brought to a standstill by unarticulated frustrations, Pryor moved to Berkeley, California, in 1970 and lived eccentrically, walking the streets in a kimono and getting high for days at a time. Still, he managed to stumble upon a sympathetic and like-minded emerging set of African American intellectuals and activists, namely ISHMAEL REED, ANGELA DAVIS, and Claude Brown. Pryor shut himself in and compulsively read a collection of MALCOLM X's speeches and listened to MARVIN GAYE's song "What's Goin' On?" Determined to find his voice, he began delivering increasingly experimental performances in small clubs. He would typically speak a curse word, such as "bitch" or "motherfucker," dozens of times, attempting to hit a different inflection for every one. Eventually he tried "nigger." Speaking the one word that every club owner had hitherto prohibited provided the breakthrough he needed.

In 1971 Pryor returned to the Improv in New York City to record new material for his first concert film, *Smokin'*, and his second stand-up album, *Craps after Hours*. Mel Brooks then solicited him to help pen the ribald comedy *Blazing Saddles*, for which it was understood that Pryor would play the lead, a black sheriff in the Old West. The studio, however, apparently feared Pryor's controversial edge and cast Cleavon Little instead. But Pryor demonstrated his commitment to acting by playing Piano Man in Diana Ross's vehicle *Lady Sings the Blues* (1972), for which he earned an Academy Award nomination.

Television opportunities soon presented themselves: Pryor most enjoyed collaborating on Lily Tomlin's variety show, but he also hosted NBC's new skit series, *Saturday Night Live*, and the network quickly offered him his own show. He locked horns with the censors, however, and *The Richard Pryor Show* ran for only four episodes. Otherwise, Pryor continued to experience a creative boon in comedy and film. Three consecutive albums won Grammys: *That Nigger's Crazy* (1974), *Is It Something I Said?* (1975), and *Bicentennial Nigger* (1976). He played his first dramatic film lead in *Greased Lightning* (1976), in which he portrayed race car legend WENDELL SCOTT. Pryor teamed with Gene Wilder in *Silver Streak* that same year, and delivered in *Blue Collar* (1978) what some critics consider his most accomplished performance. His cocaine use dangerously increased as well, and he suffered the first of two heart attacks. A recovered Pryor then divorced his third wife, Deboragh McGuire, and began dating Jennifer Lee, with whom he traveled to Africa at decade's end and later married.

In perhaps his most rounded concert film, *Live on the Sunset Strip* (1982), Pryor explains the revelatory experience of waiting in a Kenyan hotel lobby after a three-week sojourn: "A voice said, 'What do you see? Look around.' And I looked around, and I looked around, and I saw people of all colors and shapes, and the voice said, 'You see any niggers?' I said, 'No.' It said, 'You know why? 'Cause there aren't any'" (Pryor, 175). In three weeks Pryor had not used the word once; he vowed never to use it again, a vow he faithfully kept for some time. Many black entertainers, however, chastised him for "selling out" and rejecting what they believed was a reclaimed term of black empowerment. More important than such shifting semantics, however, was Pryor's unique take on American racial dynamics, prompting one critic to observe that if Pryor "played the race card, it was only to show how funny he looked when he tried to shuffle the deck" (Als, 385).

In *Sunset Strip*, Pryor also speaks of the notorious self-immolation he had suffered a year earlier while freebasing cocaine, a tremendously dangerous method of using the drug that involves inhaling the fumes of a melted clump of cocaine laced with ether. Although accounts differ, a strung-out Pryor apparently poured cognac or rum over his body and flicked a lighter, then ran out of his Los Angeles house and down the street, where the fire extinguished itself by burning his clothes into his skin. In shock, Pryor continued walking alongside police officers who were asking him to stop for an ambulance. Pryor responded, "If I stop, I'll die."

Pryor's work in subsequent years became uneven. Lee divorced him after six months, and his directorial debut, the autobiographical *Jo Jo Dancer, Your Life Is Calling* (1986) teetered indecisively between comedy and drama. He fired his confidant and business partner, the former football star JIM BROWN, from his film production company, a decision that further strained his relationship with the black entertainment community, and he repeatedly agreed to appear in lifeless but high-paying movies like *The Toy* (1982), *Superman III* (1983), and *Brewster's Millions* (1985). It was on the set of *Critical Condition* in 1986, however, that Pryor first felt the symptoms of multiple sclerosis; he was officially diagnosed at the Mayo Clinic later that year. Keeping the affliction secret, Pryor made another movie with Gene Wilder in 1986 and teamed with REDD FOXX and Eddie Murphy in 1989's *Harlem Nights*. The multiple sclerosis, compounded with decades of heavy drug use, contributed to another heart attack and subsequent quadruple bypass surgery in 1991.

Pryor logged one final "stand-up" performance in 1992 at the Circle House Theater in San Francisco, sitting in a leather chair onstage with a cane by his side. Buoyed by positive reviews, he briefly attempted a tour, which exhaustion brought to a close in early 1993. He reunited with Jennifer Lee in 1994, who assumed caretaking duties. In 1998 Pryor was awarded the Kennedy Center's inaugural Mark Twain Prize, a significant tribute for which he was feted by lifelong friends and fellow comedians.

FURTHER READING

Pryor, Richard, with Todd Gold. *Pryor Convictions and Other Life Sentences* (1995).

Als, Hilton. "A Pryor Love" in *Life Stories: Profiles from The New Yorker*, ed. David Remnick (2001).
Haskins, Jim. *Richard Pryor: A Man and His Madness* (1984).
Robbins, Fred, and David Ragan. *Richard Pryor: This Cat's Got Nine Lives!* (1982).
Williams, John A., and Dennis A. Williams. *If I Stop I'll Die: The Comedy and Tragedy of Richard Pryor* (1991).

—DAVID F. SMYDRA JR.

PURYEAR, MARTIN

(23 May 1941–), sculptor, was born in Washington, D.C., the oldest of seven children of Reginald Puryear, a postal worker, and Martina Morse, a schoolteacher. Martin was an avid reader and an illustrator of detailed drawings of insects and birds. After graduating from Archbishop Carroll High School in 1959, he entered The Catholic University of America, switching his major from biology to art in his junior year. He also began working in wood, designing and building furniture, canoes, and a collapsible guitar. After receiving a BA in Art in 1963, Puryear joined the Peace Corps, serving from 1964 to 1966 in Sierra Leone, West Africa. He taught French, English, and biology and studied the work of local carpenters and artisans, whose work he discovered, combined beauty with utility. The vernacular architecture of the area and the centrality of simple man-made objects in West African daily life would serve as contributing forces in his later work.

An admiration for Scandinavian design and woodworking brought Puryear to Sweden after his service in Africa ended. While studying printmaking and wood sculpture at the Swedish Royal Academy of Art in Stockholm, he fell further in love with objects and their construction. As he had been in Sierra Leone, he was drawn to sculptural work born of wood construction rather than wood carving, and he augmented his formal studies with a brief apprenticeship under the renowned furniture maker James Krenov. Puryear's return to the United States in 1969 coincided with seismic and fast-moving developments in the history of modern sculpture, including minimalism, postminimalism, and earthworks—all profound influences on his work. Puryear began graduate training at Yale University in 1969, and, under the tutelage of Al Held, Richard Serra, Robert Morris, and Salvatore Scarpitta, he earned an M.F.A. in Sculpture in 1971. From 1971 to 1973 he taught at Fisk University in Nashville, Tennessee, after which he moved to Brooklyn, New York, where he produced his first mature pieces, including *Rawhide Cone* (1974, artist's collection), *Bask* (1976, Guggenheim Museum), and *Circumbent* (1976, artist's collection). He also continued teaching, commuting to the University of Maryland from 1974 to 1978.

In February 1977 a fire destroyed Puryear's studio. "The fire," he later reflected, "was followed by a period of grieving and then by an incredible lightness, freedom, and mobility" (Benezra, 24). Having lost most of his work and possessions, Puryear responded with *Cedar Lodge* (1977) and *Where the Heart Is (Sleeping Mews)* (1977), two temporary installations inspired, respectively, by a teepee and a yurt (a portable hut used by Mongol and Afghan nomads), and several pieces were dedicated to the mountain man JIM BECKWOURTH. In 1978 Puryear accepted a teaching position at the University of Illinois and relocated to Chicago, where he remained until 1990.

By the late 1970s Puryear's work began attracting critical attention. In 1977 he received both a National Endowment for the Arts Individual Artist Fellowship and a Robert Rauschenberg Foundation Grant, as well as his first solo museum exhibition, held at the Corcoran Gallery of Art

Martin Puryear's sculpture Old Mole *(1985) is just over five feet tall and made of red cedar.* Philadelphia Museum of Art

in Washington, D.C. His sculptures appeared in exhibitions across the country, including the 1979 and 1981 Whitney Museum Biennials. One-person shows followed, culminating in a large traveling exhibition organized by the University of Massachusetts. Puryear's studio works of the late 1970s and early 1980s, dominated by a series of wall-mounted, circle-like wood sculptures, mostly untitled, gave way to larger, freestanding wood sculptures, such as *Old Mole* (1985, Philadelphia Museum of Art) and *Cask Cascade* (1985, private collection). He introduced wire in works like *Keeper* (1984, private collection) and wire mesh combined with tar in such pieces as *Sanctum* (1985, Whitney Museum) and *Maroon* (1987–1988, Milwaukee Art Museum). In the late 1980s and 1990s Puryear experimented further with new materials and delivered a variety of intriguing new compositions with the unique *Lever Series* (1988–1989) and such beguiling pieces as *Horsefly* (1996–2000, private collection)

After receiving a MacArthur Foundation Fellowship in 1989, Puryear represented the United States at the Twentieth São Paulo Biennial in Brazil with a suite of eight large sculptures

that won the grand prize. The following year he moved to upstate New York with his wife of four years, Jeanne Gordon, a classical pianist and artist. By then he was the father of a young daughter and no longer teaching full time, and his production and visibility increased. Puryear was the subject of a number of exhibitions, including a major traveling retrospective organized by the Art Institute of Chicago in 1991. In 1992, at the invitation of the French government, he served as artist in residence at the Calder Atelier in Sache, and from 1997 to 1998 he was an artist in residence at the American Academy in Rome.

A self-described outsider who "never felt like signing up and joining and being part of a coherent cadre of anything, ideologically, or esthetically, or attitudinally" (*New York Times*, 1 Nov. 1987), Puryear remained somewhat outside the shifting fashions and politics of the art world. Drawing from a diverse range of artists and styles, including Constantin Brancusi, Isamu Noguchi, Jan Arp, Louise Bourgeois, dadaism, modernism, and Russian constructivism, Puryear's work rejects pigeonholing. Inspired by the landscapes and artistic production of other cultures, he traveled

worldwide, including to Japan, where he studied landscape design and architecture in 1983 on a Guggenheim Fellowship. Perhaps his outsider status and journeyman's spirit account for Puryear's admiration for MATTHEW HENSON, JEAN BAPTISTE POINTE DU SABLE, and Jim Beckwourth, historic black men who transcended racial and social as well as spatial boundaries.

The surfaces and construction of Puryear's wood and mixed-media sculptures are labor intensive, and they look it, revealing forms and methods borrowed from the folk technology, art, and architecture of nonindustrial cultures. Employing accumulative building processes such as wrapping, weaving, tying, and joinery associated with furniture making and shipbuilding, Puryear bridges the divide between art and craft. He celebrates traditional wood-bending techniques with *Alien Huddle* (1993–1995, private collection) and *Plenty's Boast* (1994–1995, Nelson-Atkins Museum of Art), basket weaving with *The Spell* (1985, artist's collection) and *Charm of Substance* (1989, St. Louis Art Museum), and architectural construction with *Thicket* (1990, Seattle Art Museum). "At bottom it's a class issue really," he argues. "'Art' means thought; 'craft' means manual work. In Japan you'll never see that kind of snobbery; potters and carpenters are honored there as living national treasures" (*Time*, 9 July 2001).

In their geometric abstraction, economy of form, and clarity of shape, Puryear's sculptures draw upon a minimalist sensibility, but he never considered himself a minimalist: "I tasted Minimalism. It had no taste. So I spat it out" (*Washington Post*, 25 Mar. 1988). Minimalism's rejection of craft, its insistence on industrial materials and fabrication, and its denial of metaphor did not appeal to Puryear, whose work succeeds by its subjectivity, reverence for materials, and evocation of narrative through form. "I value the referential quality of work, the fact that it has the capacity to allude to things" (*Chicago Tribune*, 3 Nov. 1991). Enigmatic and mysterious, Puryear's sculptures encourage interpretation. "I do not start with a particular thing and abstract from it. I have more a recombinant strategy. It's like combining from many sources into something that has clarity and unity. I like a flickering quality, when you can't say exactly what the reference is" (*Chicago Tribune*, 3 Nov. 1991). The results are complex and elegant abstractions—distilled essential forms—suggesting humans, animals, and objects, often in states of metamorphosis and transformation.

Evoking containers, boats, shelters, birds, tools, heads and profiles, cocoons, and amoebas, his sculptures suggest man-made and biomorphic elements without mimicking them. Some might see a bird's beak, falcon's talon, shark's tooth, or birdcage in *Seer* (1984, Guggenheim Museum). At twelve feet high, *Untitled* (1997–2001, Donald Young Gallery) is simultaneously a children's game, dinosaur, construction crane, and sea monster. "If you believe strongly," Puryear contends, "you can pump life into materials" (*Washington Post*, 25 Mar. 1988).

Puryear plays with notions of inside and outside, size, volume, and perspective, challenging our sensual, emotional, and intellectual expectations. The basketlike *Brunhilde* (1998–2000, artist's collection), for example, was laboriously constructed to look like weaving, though its pieces are not interlaced. *Self* (1978, Joslyn Art Museum), *Confessional* (1996–2000, artist's collection), and *Untitled* (1997, Museum of Modern Art) appear solid but are actually hollow. Narrowing from two feet to one inch, *Ladder for Booker T. Washington* (1996, artist's collection) teases the eye while meting out social commentary. Another poignant experimentation with perspective and transformation, *This Mortal Coil* (1998–1999) features an eighty-five-foot-high spiral staircase, its massive red cedar steps becoming lighter with its ascension, eventually turning into muslin. Aided by materials like wire mesh and tinted glass, Puryear achieves both solidity and transparency with massive pieces that are, in fact, quite fragile.

In addition to his studio work, Puryear created a number of significant outdoor sculptures, beginning with *Box and Pole* (1977, Artpark, Lewiston, New York), a dramatic juxtaposition of a one-hundred-foot-tall pole and a four-and-one-half-foot wooden cube. Other major outdoor installations include *Bodark Arc* (1982, Nathan

Manilow Sculpture Park, Governor's State University, Illinois), *Knoll* (1983, National Oceanographic and Atmospheric Administration, Seattle, Washington), *Ampersand* (1987–1988, Walker Art Center, Minneapolis, Minnesota), *North Cove Pylons* (1994, Battery Park, New York City), *Bearing Witness* (1995, Ronald Reagan Building Plaza, Washington, D.C.), and *That Profile* (1999, Getty Museum, Los Angeles), which Puryear conceived as "a drawing in space that would change as you walk around it."

"This isn't showoff sculpture," explained critic Peter Plagens. "It's just old-fashioned lyricism whose tires you can kick" (*Newsweek* 11 Nov. 1991). Encountering a Puryear sculpture is like discovering a vestigial artifact or relic, mysterious in its anachronism but rich in history.

FURTHER READING

Benezra, Neal, and the Art Institute of Chicago. *Martin Puryear* (1991).

Crutchfield, Margo A., and the Virginia Museum of Fine Arts. *Martin Puryear* (2001).

Davies, Hugh Marlais, Helaine Posner, and the University of Massachusetts. *Martin Puryear* (1984).

—LISA E. RIVO

 QUARLES, BENJAMIN ARTHUR (23 Jan. 1904– 16 Nov. 1996), historian, was the eldest of five children born in Boston, Massachusetts, to Arthur Quarles, a subway porter, and Margaret O'Brien. Although he grew up in a poor neighborhood and, like his siblings, had to work menial jobs, Quarles graduated from English High School in 1922. Later, he and his brothers worked as waiters in Florida and as seamen on ships sailing from Boston to Bar Harbor, Maine. Both of these jobs were typical of the forms of employment available to African American men in New England from the late eighteenth century into the twentieth century.

In 1927 Benjamin Quarles enrolled at Shaw University in Raleigh, North Carolina, where he became a debater and a student leader, graduating in 1931 as valedictorian of his class. Following commencement he enrolled at the

University of Wisconsin, Madison, after being awarded a Social Science Research Council Fellowship for graduate study in history. After studying there for four years and earning his master's degree, Quarles returned to Shaw University to teach history. Two years later he married Vera Bullock of Greensboro, North Carolina. Their daughter, Roberta, was born in 1938. Still writing his dissertation in 1939, Quarles moved with his family to another black institution, Dillard University in New Orleans. After teaching at Dillard for two years, he became head of the social sciences division and, later, dean of the college.

While still a graduate student, Quarles began publishing in the *Journal of Negro History*. His 1940 article, "Frederick Douglass and the Woman's Rights Movement," became a classic, marking the beginning of his focus on gender in his discussions of black life in U.S. history. In the meantime, he completed his dissertation on FREDERICK DOUGLASS, earning his PhD in History from the University of Wisconsin in 1940. Quarles's reputation as a young scholar began to grow, enabling him to earn five fellowships between 1931 and 1945, including one from the Rosenwald Fund.

By 1948 Quarles had expanded his dissertation into a full-length scholarly biography of Frederick Douglass, published by the Associated Publishers, Inc., an affiliate of the Association for the Study of Negro Life and History, which CARTER G. WOODSON had cofounded in 1915. *Frederick Douglass*, the first definitive study of the nineteenth-century civil rights giant, was reprinted several times over the next five decades. According to the recollections of colleagues and family members, no white publishers had been interested in the manuscript, but the book was well received among black academics and intellectuals. Members of the Frederick Douglass Cultural Society, for example, held a book party, sponsored by the Frederick Douglass Book Center in Harlem, New York, to honor the publication. More than fifty years later Douglass's biographer William S. McFeely described Quarles's biography as an excellent study, still relevant to twenty-first-century readers interested in Douglass.

Although he was committed to academic publishing and research, Quarles, like many of his black cohorts in higher education, also served his community. While teaching and living in New Orleans during the 1940s, Quarles was secretary of the New Orleans Urban League and served on the New Orleans Council of Social Services. Always the scholar, during the 1950–1951 academic year Quarles went on sabbatical leave from Dillard to research his second book, *The Negro in the Civil War* (1953), a work that highlighted his expertise in black military history.

While he was away, his wife, Vera, died suddenly, leaving Quarles and their daughter, Roberta, alone and devastated. In December 1952, however, he married Dr. Ruth Brett, dean of students at Fisk University. The following academic year they left for Morgan State College in Baltimore, Maryland, an historically black institution, where Quarles became chair of the history department; he remained in that position until the mid-1960s. Their daughter, Pamela, was born in 1954. By 1956 Ruth Brett Quarles was developing the Counseling Center at Morgan, of which she became coordinator; both she and her husband continued to work at the college (which became a university in 1974) until their retirement. While teaching and writing at Morgan, Quarles earned more fellowships, including a prestigious Guggenheim in 1959.

In his professional prime as a renowned historian, Quarles thrived at Morgan, where he became known as an outstanding mentor and popular professor and, in 1963, was selected as the college's first Teacher of the Year. During the 1950s and 1960s he continued to serve the community and his profession as vice president of the Urban League and as vice president of the Association for the Study of Negro Life and History. As a mentor and scholar during this period, the self-effacing Quarles never acknowledged that he was special. Others, however, always praised his willingness to help and promote them. Despite his claims of being unworthy of special awards, several were forthcoming. In 1967 Maryland's U.S. Senator Daniel Brewster attended the Morgan State College

celebration of Frederick Douglass's birth and introduced Benjamin Quarles as the speaker. The senator was so impressed with Quarles's lecture that he entered it into the *Congressional Record* (23 February 1967).

When Morgan's president, Martin D. Jenkins, recommended Quarles to the governor of Maryland for a newly established honor, Distinguished Professor, Quarles became the first to receive such an award. Outside the state of Maryland, he continued to be honored for scholarship and mentoring. Between 1966 and 1996 Quarles received twelve honorary doctorate degrees. In addition, he received the American Historical Association's Senior Historian Scholarly Distinction Award and the Smithsonian Institution's National Museum of American History Lifetime Achievement Award (1996).

Retiring from active teaching in 1974 did not slow down Quarles's scholarly work. He continued serving on the editorial boards of the *Journal of Negro History* and the *Maryland Historical Magazine*. Throughout the 1970s Quarles served on several community committees and boards, including the Joint Center for Political Studies' Project Advisory Committee on Black Congress Members. He was also a member of the Committee of Advisers of the National Humanities Center Fellowships and the Department of Army Historical Advisory Committee. A prolific writer, Quarles continued to research and write into his mid-eighties, at which time he published the revised and expanded edition of his popular textbook *The Negro in the Making of America* (1987).

Although Quarles is best known for his biography of Frederick Douglass and his textbooks, scholars have also praised his influential and pathbreaking volume *The Negro in the American Revolution* (1961) and *Black Abolitionists* (1969). He has been revered as a major pioneer in writing about the African American experience before the Civil War, publishing a total of fourteen books from 1948 to 1988. In 1996 the historian V. P. Franklin wrote that Quarles was successful not only in writing about black troops in U.S. wars but also in examining the broad cultural

contributions of African Americans to American society. Franklin described Quarles as one of the most distinguished scholars of African American history.

Quarles's reputation as a mentor to the younger generation of African American scholars included his support in 1979 for black women historians seeking to organize their own professional association. As an adviser to the Association of Black Women Historians, he helped secure a National Endowment for the Humanities grant for a research conference funded in 1983.

When Ruth Brett Quarles retired in 1980, the couple continued to reside in Baltimore. By 1988 they decided to donate Quarles's papers and awards to the Morgan State University Soper Library and moved to the Collington Episcopal Life Care Community in Mitchellville, Maryland. They were living in this community when Quarles began to experience poor health. He died in Mitchellville of heart failure at the age of ninety-two.

The views of colleagues in his field may best speak to the impact that Benjamin Quarles had on his profession for over fifty years. In assessing his scholarship and historiographical development, the historian August Meier found that, in his work, Quarles, like his contemporary JOHN HOPE FRANKLIN, brought attention to the diversity of black life in U.S. history.

FURTHER READING

Franklin, V. P. "Introduction," Benjamin Quarles, *The Negro in the Making of America* (3rd ed., 1996).

McConnell, Roland C., and Daniel B. Brewster. "Introduction," Benjamin Quarles, *Frederick Douglass: Challenge and Response* (1987).

McFeely, William S. "Introduction," Benjamin Quarles, *Allies for Freedom and Blacks on John Brown* (repr., 2001).

Meier, August. "Introduction," Benjamin Quarles, *Black Mosaic: Essays in Afro-American History and Historiography* (1988).

Quarles: Memorial Convocation; Celebrating the Life and Legacy of Dr. Benjamin Quarles (1996).

Turner, W. Burghardt, and Joyce Moore Turner, eds. *Richard B. Moore: Caribbean Militant in Harlem* (1988).

Obituary: *Baltimore Sun*, 19 Nov. 1996.

—ROSALYN TERBORG-PENN

R

RAILROAD BILL

(?–7 Mar. 1896), thief and folk hero, was the nickname of a man of such obscure origins that his real name is in question. Most writers have believed him to be Morris Slater, but a rival candidate for the honor is an equally obscure man named Bill McCoy. But in song and story, where he has long had a place, the question is of small interest and Railroad Bill is name enough. A ballad regaling his exploits began circulating among field hands, turpentine camp workers, prisoners, and other groups from the black underclass of the deep South, several years before it first found its way into print in 1911. A version of this blues ballad was first recorded in 1924 by Gid Tanner and Riley Puckett, and THOMAS A. DORSEY, who sang blues under the name Railroad Bill. The ballad got a second wind during the folk music vogue of the 1950s and 1960s, and in 1981 the musical play *Railroad Bill* by C. R. Portz was produced for the Labor Theater in New York City. It subsequently toured thirty-five cities.

The name Railroad Bill, or often simply "Railroad," was given to him by trainmen and derived from his penchant for riding the cars as an anonymous nonpaying passenger of the Louisville and Nashville Railroad (L&N). Thus he might appear to be no more than a common tramp or hobo, as the large floating population of migratory workers who more or less surreptitiously rode the cars of all the nation's railroads were labeled. But Railroad Bill limited his riding to two adjoining South Alabama counties, Escambia and Baldwin. Sometime in the winter of 1895 he began to be noticed by trainmen often enough that he soon acquired some notoriety and a nickname. It did not make him less worthy of remark that he was always armed, with a rifle and one or more pistols. He was, as it turned out, quite prepared to offer resistance to the rough treatment normally meted out to tramps.

An attitude of armed resistance from a black man was bound inevitably to bring him into conflict with the civil authorities, who were in any case inclined to be solicitous of the L&N, the dominant economic power in South Alabama. The conflict began on 6 March 1895, only a month or two after trainmen first became aware of Railroad Bill. L&N employees discovered him asleep on the platform of a water tank in Baldwin County, on the Flomaton to Mobile run, and tried to take him into custody. He drove them off with gunfire and forced them to take shelter in a nearby shack. When a freight train pulled up to take on water he hijacked it and, after firing additional rounds into the shack, forced the engineer to take him farther up the road, whereupon he left the train and disappeared into the woods. After that, pursuit of Railroad Bill was relentless. A month to the day later he was cornered at Bay Minette by a posse led by a railroad detective. A deputy, James H. Stewart, was killed in the ensuing gunfight, but once again the fugitive slipped away. The railroad provided a "special" to transport Sheriff E. S. McMillan from Brewton, the county seat of Escambia, to the scene with a pack of bloodhounds, but a heavy rainfall washed away the scent.

In mid-April a reward was posted by the L&N and the state of Alabama totaling five hundred dollars. The lure of this reward and a rumored sighting of the fugitive led Sheriff McMillan out of his jurisdiction to Bluff Springs, Florida, where he found Railroad Bill and met with death at his hands. The reward climbed to $1,250, and the manhunt intensified. A small army with packs of dogs picked up his scent near Brewton in August, but he dove into Murder Swamp near Castelberry and disappeared. During this period, from March to August, the legend of Railroad Bill took shape among poor blacks in the region. He was viewed as a "conjure man," one who could change his shape and slip away from pursuers. He was clever and outwitted his enemies; he was a trickster who laid traps for the trapper and a fighter who refused to bend his neck and submit to the oppressor. He demanded respect, and in time some whites grudgingly gave it: Brewton's *Pine Belt News* reported after Railroad Bill's escape into Murder Swamp that he had "outwitted and outgeneraled at least one hundred men armed to the teeth." During this period a Robin Hood–style Railroad Bill emerged, who, it was said, stole canned goods from boxcars and distributed them to poor illiterate blacks like himself. Carl Carmer, a white writer in the 1930s, claimed that Railroad Bill forced poor blacks at gunpoint to buy the goods from him, but Carmer never explained how it was possible to get money out of people who rarely if ever saw any. Railroad Bill staved off death and capture for an entire year, a virtual impossibility had he not had supporters among the poor black population of the region.

Sightings became infrequent after Murder Swamp, and some concluded Railroad Bill had left the area. The "wanted" poster with its reward was more widely circulated. The result was something like open season on vagrant blacks in the lower South. The *Montgomery Advertiser* reported that "several were shot in Florida, Georgia, Mississippi and even in Texas," adding with unconscious grisly humor, "only one was brought here to be identified." That one arrived at Union Station in a pine box in August, escorted by the two men from Chipley, Florida, who had shot him in hopes of collecting the reward. Doubts about whether he remained in the area were answered on 7 March 1896, exactly a year and a day after the affair at the water tower when determined pursuit began. Railroad Bill was shot without warning, from ambush, by a private citizen seeking the reward, which by now included a lifetime pass on the L&N Railroad. Bill had been sitting on a barrel eating cheese and crackers in a small Atmore, Alabama, grocery. Perhaps he was tired as well as hungry.

Railroad Bill's real name probably will never be known. At the time of the water tower incident and up to the killing of Deputy Stewart he had only the nickname, but in mid-April the first "wanted" posters went up in Mobile identifying Railroad Bill as Morris Slater, who, though the notice did not state it, had been a worker in a turpentine camp near Bluff Springs, Florida. These camps were often little more than penal colonies. They employed convict labor and were heavily into debt peonage. People were not supposed to leave, but Slater did, after killing the marshal of Bluff Springs. When railroad detectives stumbled on this story their interest was primarily in Slater's nickname. He had been called "Railroad Time," and "Railroad" for short, because of his quick efficient work. The detectives quickly concluded, because of the similarities in nicknames, that Slater was their man. The problem, of course, is that the trainmen called their rider Railroad Bill precisely because they had no idea who he was and well before railroad authorities heard about Slater. If the detectives were right, then it follows that the same man independently won strangely similar nicknames in two different settings, once because he was a good worker, and again because he was a freeloader.

No one from the turpentine camp who had known Slater identified the body, but neither the railroad detectives nor the civil authorities involved questioned the identification. The body was taken to Brewton, on its way to Montgomery, where it would go on display for the public's gratification, but it was also displayed for a time in Brewton and recognized. The *Pine Belt News* reported that residents recognized the body as that of Bill McCoy, a man who would have been about forty, the approximate age of the corpse, since he had been brought to the area from Coldwater, Florida, as a young man eighteen years earlier. McCoy was remembered as a town troublemaker who two years earlier had threatened T. R. Miller, the richest man in town, when he worked in Miller's sawmill and lumberyard. He had fled the scene hastily, not to be seen again until his corpse went on display as Railroad Bill. But, apart from the local

newspaper stories, no one disputed the Slater identification, and the local Brewton people seem to have concluded that Morris Slater must have been a name used by Bill McCoy after he fled the town. The problem with that conclusion is that when the incident at Miller's sawmill occurred Morris Slater had already earned the nickname "Railroad Time" in a Florida turpentine camp.

FURTHER READING

The Brewton newspapers *Pine Belt News* and *Standard Gauge* are the best places to follow the story of Railroad Bill.

Penick, James L. "Railroad Bill." *Gulf Coast Historical Review* 10 (1994): 85–92.
Wright, A. J., comp. *Criminal Activity in the Deep South, 1700–1933* (1989).
—JAMES L. PENICK

RAINES, FRANKLIN DELANO (14 Jan. 1949–), corporate executive and government official, was born Franklin Delano Raines in Seattle, Washington, the fourth of seven children of Delno Thomas Raines, a custodian, and Ida Mae Raines, a cleaning woman. He was named after his uncle Frank and his father, but the hospital misspelled his middle name as "Delano."

The Raines family eventually moved into a house that Delno Raines had built himself over the course of five years. The household was constantly fighting economic challenges. When Raines was a young boy, his father was hospitalized for an illness and lost his job. As a result, the family received welfare for two years. Eventually, Delno Raines got full-time work as a custodian for the city of Seattle. Ida Raines added to their income by working as a cleaning woman for the aircraft company Boeing. But Raines would always remember the lessons of being on the brink of financial ruin. He later recalled that the experience of living with nothing to fall back on made him "quite sensitive to issues of personal and financial security. That probably made me very conservative in my own financial dealings and also made me worry a lot about people" (Stevenson, *New York Times*, 17 May 1998).

Very early in his life it was clear that Raines was an achiever and destined for great things. When he was in high school, the *Seattle Times* called him "Mr. Everything" (Karen Tumulty, *Time*, 10 Feb. 1997). He was state debate champion, captain of the high school football team, and student president of his high school. His academic excellence (reflected in his 4.0 average) earned Raines a four-year scholarship to Harvard University, which he entered in 1967. He worked toward a BA in Government and impressed many, including Professor Daniel Patrick Moynihan, the future U.S. senator. In 1969 Raines was asked to intern at the White House in the Urban Affairs Department headed by Moynihan. At age twenty Raines was making a presentation to President Nixon.

After graduating in 1971 Raines went to Magdalen College at the University of Oxford as a Rhodes Scholar. After that, in 1974, he entered Harvard Law School, from which he graduated cum laude in 1976. After a seven-month stint at the law firm Preston, Gates, and Ellis, Raines's impressive résumé earned him a position as assistant director for economics and government in the Office of Management and Budget in President Jimmy Carter's administration. This was the beginning of a career that would marry his political savvy and his financial acumen. In 1979 he moved to Wall Street and became an investment banker for the prestigious firm Lazard Frères.

Raines worked in the municipal finance department and advised cities and states about their finances and ability to raise money for government projects, such as bridges and buildings. The political skills that he had developed over his career continued to help him in his new position. Raines landed accounts with major cities like Washington, D.C., Chicago, and Detroit. He also worked on statewide accounts for Texas and Iowa, among others. With his help these municipalities, many of which were in dire financial trouble, were able to strengthen their finances. The most dramatic example of his work came in Washington, D.C. He helped reorganize the city's finances with such success that Wall Street allowed Washington to borrow money for the first time in a century.

Raines's success was rewarded in 1985 when he was named a partner at Lazard Frères. This appointment had broader implications. He had already been one of a handful of African Americans investment bankers in the clubby world of Wall Street. Now he was the first African American partner at a major investment bank. Raines once reflected about the importance of his achievement in the securities industry by saying, "I felt it was significant because for years, people would be wowed by the fact that you were black and a vice president. Now partner or managing director became the new standard" (Bell, 143).

During this period things were also blossoming in Raines' personal life. He married Wendy Farrow in 1982, and the couple went on to have three daughters. His commitment to his family persuaded Raines to make a career-altering decision. In 1991, after twelve years of working in municipal finance, he decided to leave Lazard. Tired of the extensive traveling that was necessary in his work with municipalities around the country, a workload that had him on a plane as many as five days a week, he decided that he would quit his lucrative career on Wall Street to spend more time with his family.

Raines, with his impeccable reputation, was not out of work for long. Later that year he was asked to join

Franklin Raines on Fox TV in April 1998. Getty Images

Fannie Mae, a huge mortgage corporation located only minutes from his house. Fannie Mae, formerly known as the Federal National Mortgage Association, was created in 1938 as a government agency. In the 1960s it was turned into a corporation owned by shareholders. It purchases mortgages from lending institutions and resells them to the secondary market. As vice chairman, Raines had the main responsibility to improve Fannie Mae's technology. He was also in charge of the firm's credit policy and legal issues, along with sundry other functions.

Raines continued in this position until 1996, when President Bill Clinton called to ask him to head the Office of Management and Budget. He reentered public service and led the country to its first balanced budget since 1969. After years of success in this position, Fannie Mae came calling again, and in January 1999 Raines made history. He became the first African American to lead a Fortune 500 company, and soon other black executives like STANLEY O'NEAL, RICHARD DEAN PARSONS, and KENNETH CHENAULT would also head major corporations.

Fannie Mae is the largest source of private financing for home mortgages. One of Raines's primary objectives was to increase his company's business by spurring more home ownership in the minority community. It is an issue close to his heart, because his father could not get a mortgage loan until the house he was building was almost finished. The company itself also is concentrating on creating a talented and diverse workforce. In 2002 *Fortune* ranked Fannie Mae number one on their "50 Best Companies for Minorities" list (Jonathan Hickman, *Fortune*, 8 July 2002).

Frank Raines has come a long way from his old neighborhood in Seattle. He has conquered prestigious universities, Wall Street, and government and now heads one of the biggest corporations in the world. In addition to his responsibilities to his shareholders and employees, he also recognizes the responsibility of being a "first." As he once said, "It's part of my job to insure that the path I've been able to follow can be followed by other black kids. There are a lot of shoulders I get to stand on. I need to provide a

hand and shoulders for others to follow" (Stevenson, *New York Times*, 17 May 1998).

FURTHER READING

Bell, Gregory S. *In the Black: A History of African Americans on Wall Street* (2001).
Cose, Ellis. *The Envy of the World: On Being a Black Man in America* (2002).
Stevenson, Richard W. "A Homecoming at Fannie Mae." *New York Times*, 17 May 1998, BU1.

—GREGORY S. BELL

RAINEY, MA (26 Apr. 1886–22 Dec. 1939), vaudeville artiste and "Mother of the Blues," was born Gertrude Pridgett in Columbus, Georgia, the daughter of Ella Allen, an employee of the Georgia Central Railroad, and Thomas Pridgett, whose occupation is unknown. Around 1900, at the age of fourteen, Pridgett made her debut in the Bunch of Blackberries revue at the Springer Opera House in Columbus, one of the biggest theaters in Georgia and a venue that had been graced by, among others, Lillie Langtry and Oscar Wilde. Within two years she was a regular in minstrel tent shows—troupes of singers, acrobats, dancers, and novelty acts—which traveled throughout the South. At one show in Missouri in 1902 she heard a new musical form, "the blues," and incorporated it into her act. Although she did not discover or name the blues, as legend would later have it, Gertrude Pridgett was undeniably one of the pioneers of the three-line stanza, twelve-bar style now known as the "classic blues."

In 1904 the seventeen-year-old Gertrude married William Rainey, a comedian, dancer, and minstrel-show veteran. "Ma" and "Pa" Rainey soon became a fixture on the southern tent-show circuit, and they achieved their greatest success in 1914–1916 as Rainey and Rainey, Assassinators of the Blues, part of the touring Tolliver's Circus and Musical Extravaganza. Their adopted son, Danny, "the world's greatest juvenile stepper," also worked with the show.

The summer tent shows took the Raineys throughout the South, where Ma was popular among both white and black audiences. Winters brought Ma, billed as Madame Gertrude Rainey, to New Orleans, where she performed with several pioneering jazz and blues musicians, including SIDNEY BECHET and KING OLIVER. Around 1914 Ma took a young blues singer from Chattanooga, Tennessee, BESSIE SMITH, under her wing—legend erroneously had it that she kidnapped her—and the two collaborated and remained friends over the next two decades. During these tent-show years, Ma honed a flamboyant stage persona, making her entrance in a bejeweled, floor-length gown and a necklace made of twenty-dollar gold pieces. The blues composer THOMAS A. DORSEY recalled that Ma had the audience in the palm of her hand even before she began to sing, while LANGSTON HUGHES noted that only a testifying Holiness church could match the enthusiasm of a Ma Rainey concert.

Rainey's voice was earthy and powerful, a rural Georgian contralto with a distinctive moan and lisp. One blues singer also suggested that Ma held a dime under her tongue to prevent a stutter. Far from hindering her performance, these imperfections made Rainey's vocal style even more appealing to an audience that shared her down-to-earth philosophy, captured in "Down in the Basement":

Grand Opera and parlor junk
I'll tell the world it's all bunk
That's the kind of stuff I shun
Let's get dirty and have some fun.

Rainey often sang of pain and love lost or betrayed, but her songs—and her life—also celebrated the bawdy and unabashed pleasures of the flesh. Ma joked with her audiences that she preferred her men "young and tender" (Barlow, 159), but in songs such as "Lawd Send Me a Man Blues," the preference matters less than the pleasure: "Send me a Zulu, a voodoo, any old man,/I'm not that particular, boys, I'll take what I can."

By World War I, Ma Rainey's star had eclipsed that of Pa's. (They separated in the late teens, and Pa died soon after.) In 1923 Rainey began a recording career with Chicago's Paramount Records, which brought her down-home country blues to a national audience. Over the next five years, she recorded more than a hundred songs with many of the leading instrumentalists of the day, including Lovie Austin, Coleman Hawkins, and Thomas A. Dorsey, who also led Ma's touring band. In 1924 a young LOUIS ARMSTRONG played cornet on her most famous release, "See See Rider." Though already a blues standard, Ma's rendition was the first and, bluesologists contend, the definitive recording of the song.

Her success as a recording artist and the general popularity of the "race records" industry led to a string of headlining tours with the Theater Owners Booking Association (TOBA). Black performers often called the organization "Tough on Black Asses," because of its low wages and grueling schedule, but Rainey's sense of fairness may have assuaged any complaints from the touring entourage of singers, dancers, and comedians. Unlike many TOBA headliners, Ma never skipped town without paying her fellow performers. As a teenager, Lionel Hampton, who knew Ma through his bootlegger uncle in Chicago, "used to dream of joining Ma Rainey's band because she treated her musicians so wonderfully and always bought them an instrument" (Lieb, 26). Rainey's TOBA shows were even more popular than her tent shows had been, and her audience spread to midwestern cities, whose black populations had swelled during the Great Migration. The shift from tents to theaters also provided new outlets for Ma's showmanship. She now made an even grander entrance, stepping out of the doors of a huge Victrola onto the stage, wearing her trademark spangles and sequins.

Contemporaries often contrasted Ma's evenhanded temperament with Bessie Smith's hard-drinking, fiery temper, but Rainey was not unacquainted with the wrong side of the law. Ma's love of jewelry once led to an arrest onstage in Cleveland, Ohio, when police from Nashville, Tennessee, arrested her for possession of stolen goods. Ma denied knowing that the items were hot, but was detained in Nashville for a week and forced to return the jewelry. More notoriously, Rainey spent a night in jail in Chicago in 1925, when neighbors called the police to complain about a loud and drunken party that she was holding with a group of women. When the police discovered the women in various states of undress, they arrested Ma for "running an indecent party." Her friend Bessie Smith bailed her out the next day.

That incident and several biographies of Smith have highlighted Rainey's open bisexuality and the possibility of a lesbian relationship between the two women. To be sure, Ma Rainey's life and songs rejected the prevailing puritan orthodoxy when it came to sexuality. In "Sissy Blues," written by Tom Dorsey, she bemoans the loss of her man to his male lover: "My man's got a sissy, his name is Miss Kate,/ He shook that thing like jelly on a plate." Most famously, in "Prove It on Me Blues," Rainey declares, "Went out last night with a crowd of my friends,/ They must've been women, 'cause I don't like no men." Ma's bold assertion of her preference for women alternated with a coy, but knowing wink to the taboo of that choice: "'Cause they say I do it, ain't nobody caught me,/ Sure got to prove it on me." Paramount's advertisement for the record was somewhat less coy, depicting a hefty Ma Rainey in waistcoat, men's jacket, shirt, tie, and fedora—though still wearing a skirt—towering over two slim, femininely dressed young women while a policeman looks on.

The sexual politics of the lyrics were just one aspect of the song, however. Paramount appeared just as keen to highlight that it was "recorded by the latest electric method," all the better to hear Ma's vocals and the "bang-up accompaniment by the Tub Jug Washboard Band." Indeed, the company saw no problem in promoting some of its most popular gospel spirituals on the same advertisement. Like Ma Rainey herself, the race records industry of the 1920s may have been less squeamish about open declarations of homosexuality than many media giants in the late twentieth century.

Paramount ended Rainey's recording contract in 1928, shortly after the release of "Prove It on Me Blues," but not because of any controversy regarding the record itself. The company argued that Ma's "down home material had gone out of fashion," though that did not deter the label from signing male country blues performers who accepted lower fees. Ma returned to the southern tent-show circuit with TOBA, but by the early 1930s the Great Depression and the rival attractions of radio and the movies had destroyed the mass audience for the old-time country blues and black vaudeville at which Rainey excelled. Undeterred, though as much through necessity as choice, Ma returned to her southern roots, touring the oil-field towns of East Texas with the Donald MacGregor Carnival. Gone were the gold necklaces, the touring bus, and the grand entrance out of a huge Victrola. Now MacGregor, formerly the "Scottish Giant" in the Ringling Brothers' circus, stood outside Ma's tent and barked his introduction of the "Black Nightingale" inside. Rainey's performances were as entertaining as ever, but the uncertainty and poor wages of the tent-show circuit may have somewhat diminished her trademark good humor and generosity. A young guitarist who toured with her in those years, Aaron "T-Bone" Walker, described Rainey as "mean as hell, but she sang nice blues and never cursed *me* out" (Lieb, 46–47).

The death of her sister Malissa in 1935 brought Ma Rainey back to Columbus to look after her mother. At some time before that Ma had separated from her second husband, whose name is not known. Although she no longer performed, Rainey opened two theaters in Rome, Georgia, where she died of heart disease in December 1939, aged fifty-three. The obituary in Ma's local newspaper noted that she was a housekeeper but failed to mention her musical career. In the 1980s, however, both the Blues Foundation Hall of Fame and the Rock and Roll Hall of Fame recognized Ma Rainey's significance as a consummate performer and as a pioneer of the classic blues.

FURTHER READING

Barlow, William. "*Looking Up at Down*": The *Emergence of Blues Culture* (1989).

Carby, Hazel. "It Jus' Be's Dat Way Sometime: The Sexual Politics of Women's Blues" in *The Jazz Cadence of American Culture*, ed. Robert G. O'Meally (1998).

Davis, Angela Y. *Blues Legacies and Black Feminism: Gertrude "Ma" Rainey, Bessie Smith, and Billie Holiday* (1998).

Lieb, Sandra. *Mother of the Blues: A Study of Ma Rainey* (1981).

Discography

Complete Recorded Works in Chronological Order, 1923–1927 (vols. 1–4, Document Records DOCD 5581–5584).

Complete Recorded Works: 1928 Sessions (Document Records DOCD 5156).

—STEVEN J. NIVEN

RANDOLPH, A. PHILIP (15 Apr. 1889–16 May 1979), labor organizer, editor, and activist, was born Asa Philip Randolph in Crescent City, Florida, to Elizabeth Robinson and James Randolph, an African Methodist Episcopal Church preacher. In 1891 the Randolphs moved to Jacksonville, where James had been offered the pastorship of a small church. Both Asa Philip and his older brother, James Jr., were talented students who graduated from Cookman Institute (later Bethune-Cookman College), the first high school for African Americans in Florida.

Randolph left Florida in 1911, moving to New York to pursue a career as an actor. Between 1912 and 1917 he attended City College, where he was first exposed to the ideas of Karl Marx and political radicalism. He joined the Socialist Party in 1916, attracted to the party's economic analysis of black exploitation in America. Randolph, along with W. E. B. DU BOIS, HUBERT HENRY HARRISON, and Chandler Owen, was one of the pioneer black members of the Socialist Party—then led by Eugene Debs. Like a number of his peers, Randolph did not subscribe to a belief in a "special" racialized oppression of blacks that existed independent of class. Rather, he argued at this point that socialism would essentially "answer" the "Negro question." His faith in the socialist solution can be seen in the title of an essay he wrote on racial violence, "Lynching: Capitalism Its Cause; Socialism Its Cure" (*Messenger*, September 1921).

In 1916 Randolph and Owen began working to organize the black labor force, founding the short-lived United Brotherhood of Elevator and Switchboard Operators union. Shortly thereafter, they co-edited the *Hotel Messenger*, the journal of the Headwaiters and Sidewaiters Society. After being fired by the organization, they created *The Messenger* in 1917—with crucial financial support from Lucille Randolph, a beauty salon owner whom Randolph had married in 1914. The couple had no children. Lucille Randolph's success as an entrepreneur was a consistent source of stability—despite the fact that her husband's reputation as a radical scared away some of her clientele. Billing itself

Civil rights leader and editor A. Philip Randolph in 1964. Library of Congress

as "The Only Radical Negro Magazine," the boldly iconoclastic *Messenger* quickly became one of the benchmark publications of the incipient "New Negro" movement. A single issue contained the views of Abram Harris, KELLY MILLER, GEORGE SCHUYLER, ALICE DUNBAR-NELSON, COUNTÉE CULLEN, EMMETT JAY SCOTT, and CHARLES S. JOHNSON.

In the context of the postwar red scare, however, Randolph's leftist politics brought him to the attention of federal authorities determined to root out radicals, anarchists, and communists but who showed little regard for civil liberties. With the *Messenger* dubbed "the most dangerous of all Negro publications" by the Bureau of Investigation (later the FBI), Randolph and Owen were arrested under the Espionage Act in 1918 but were eventually acquitted of all charges.

When the Socialist Party split in 1919 over the issue of affiliation with the newly created socialist state in Russia, Randolph and Owen remained in the Socialist Party faction. The left wing of the party broke away, eventually coalescing into the Communist Party, USA (CPUSA). Randolph's ties to the Socialist Party remained firm, and he ran as the party's candidate for New York State comptroller in 1920 and as its candidate for secretary of state in 1921. Initial relations with the black CPUSA members were warm, with the communists Lovett Fort-Whiteman and W. A. Domingo writing for the *Messenger*. By the late 1920s, however,

Randolph had become involved in the sometime fractious politics of the black left in the New Negro era.

In the early 1920s Randolph worked for the "Garvey Must Go" campaigns directed by an ad-hoc collection of black leaders opposed to the charismatic—and often belligerent—black nationalist MARCUS GARVEY. Randolph and Garvey had shared a common mentor in the socialist intellectual Hubert Harrison. Randolph claimed, in fact, to have introduced Garvey to the tradition of Harlem street corner oratory. Randolph's opposition to Garvey appears to have been rooted in his perspective that Garvey's Universal Negro Improvement Association ignored the "class struggle nature of the Negro problem," as well as in his belief that Garvey was untrustworthy.

At the same time that W. A. Domingo charged that the *Messenger*'s attacks on Marcus Garvey had metastasized into a general anti-Caribbean bias, the magazine began devoting much less attention to radical politics in general and Russia specifically. Randolph's embryonic anticommunism was partially responsible for this shift, but the *Messenger* had also attempted to broaden its base by appealing to more upwardly mobile black strivers.

With the *Messenger* in editorial and financial decline, Randolph accepted a position as the head of the newly established Brotherhood of Sleeping Car Porters (BSCP) and spearheaded a joint drive for recognition of the union by the American Federation of Labor (AFL) and the Pullman Company. Randolph led the organization to affiliation with the AFL in 1928—a significant accomplishment in the face of the racial discrimination practiced by many of their sibling unions in the AFL. Randolph's decision to cancel a planned BSCP strike in 1928, however, resulted in a significant loss of confidence in the union and opened him up to criticism from the Communist Party, among others.

The Communist Party–affiliated American Negro Labor Congress, created in 1925, became increasingly critical of Randolph and the BSCP by the end of the decade. At the same time, Randolph's thinking and writing took a strong and persistent anticommunist turn. In the 1930s the economic

upheaval of the Great Depression and the controversial treatment of the wrongfully imprisoned SCOTTSBORO BOYS brought Communists an unprecedented degree of recognition and status within black America. The era's radicalism found expression in 1935 in the creation of the National Negro Congress (NNC)—an umbrella organization with liberal, radical, and moderate black elements. Randolph was selected as the organization's first president in 1936. Given his standing as a radical socialist, labor organizer, and civil rights advocate, Randolph was one of the few prominent African Americans with ties to many of the diverse constituencies that made up the NNC.

Global politics shaped the organization from the outset. The NNC had been founded in the midst of the "Popular Front" era and, in many ways, had been facilitated by the shared concern of communists, liberals, socialists, and moderates about the spread of fascism across Europe and the lack of civil rights for blacks in America. However, the Hitler-Stalin Pact of 1939 effectively ended the Popular Front, and tensions within the NNC increased. Randolph resigned in 1940, charging that Communist influence had undercut the NNC's autonomy and saying famously that "it was hard enough being black without also being red" (press release, 4 May 1940, in NAACP papers, A-444).

World War II brought Randolph a new set of challenges. With America on the verge of the war in 1941, he organized the March on Washington movement, an attempt to bring ten thousand African Americans to Washington to protest discrimination in defense industries. President Franklin Roosevelt, recognizing the possible impact upon morale and public relations and the significance of the black vote in the 1932 and 1936 presidential elections, issued Executive Order 8806, which forbade discrimination in defense industries and created the Fair Employment Practices Commission. In response, the proposed march was cancelled. Randolph, however, remained at the head of the organization until 1946.

In 1948 Randolph, along with BAYARD RUSTIN, with whom he would work closely in later years, organized the League for Nonviolent Civil Disobedience against Military

Segregation. The organization's efforts led to a meeting with President Harry S. Truman in which Randolph predicted that black Americans would not fight any more wars in a Jim Crow army. As with the planned march on Washington, the 1948 efforts influenced Truman's decision to desegregate the military with Executive Order 9981.

During the 1950s Randolph became more closely aligned with mainstream civil rights organizations like the NAACP—organizations that he had fiercely criticized earlier in his career. He also became more outspokenly anticommunist, traveling internationally with the Socialist Norman Thomas to point out the shortcomings of Soviet Communism. He was elected to the executive council of the newly united AFL-CIO in 1955. The high-water mark of his influence, however, had passed. Randolph did not exert as much influence with the union president George Meany as he had with the AFL president William Green, whom he had known since the BSCP's affiliation in 1928. In 1959 Randolph assumed the presidency of the Negro American Labor Council (NALC). That same year, Randolph's address on the subject of racism within the AFL-CIO elicited a stern rebuke from Meany. Wedged between the radical younger members of the NALC and his contentious relationship with Meany, Randolph resigned his position in 1964.

Randolph reemerged in the 1960s in connection with the modern civil rights movement; in 1962 Rustin and the seventy-two-year-old Randolph proposed a march on Washington to MARTIN LUTHER KING JR. and the NAACP's ROY WILKINS. Randolph was the first speaker to address the 200,000 marchers at the Lincoln Memorial on 28 August 1963, stating that "we are not a pressure group, an organization or a group of organizations, we are the advance guard for a massive moral revolution for jobs and freedom." The march was a decisive factor in the passage of the Civil Rights Act of 1964.

Randolph presided over the creation of the A. Philip Randolph Institute in 1964 and spearheaded the organization's efforts to extend a guaranteed income to all citizens of the United States. His anticommunist views led him to support the war in Vietnam—a stance that put him at odds with his onetime ally Martin Luther King, among others. He distrusted the evolving radicalism that characterized the decade, stating that Black Power had overtones of black racism. His public support for the United Federation of Teachers in the Ocean Hill–Brownsville conflict of 1968, in which black community organizations attempted to minimize the authority of the largely white teachers union, further alienated Randolph from the younger generation of Black Power advocates.

By the time of his death in Manhattan in 1979 Randolph had become an icon in the struggle for black equality in the twentieth century. More than any other figure, A. Philip Randolph was responsible for articulating the concerns of black labor—particularly in the context of the civil rights movement. His organizing abilities and strategic acumen were key to the desegregation of defense contracting and the signal legislative achievement of the civil rights era: passage of the Civil Rights Act of 1964.

FURTHER READING

A. Philip Randolph's papers are housed in the Library of Congress. Microfilm versions are available at other institutions, including the Schomburg Center for Research in Black Culture of the New York Public Library.

Anderson, Jervis. *A. Philip Randolph* (1972).
Kornweibel, Theodore. *No Crystal Stair: Black Life and the* Messenger, *1917–1928* (1975).
Marable, Manning. "A. Philip Randolph, An Assessment" in *From the Grassroots* (1980).
Pfeffer, Paula. *A. Philip Randolph: Pioneer of the Civil Rights Movement* (1990).

Obituary: *New York Times*, 17 May 1979, A1, B12.

—WILLIAM J. COBB

RANGEL, CHARLES

(11 June 1930–), member of the U.S. Congress, was born in Harlem, New York City, the second of three children of Ralph Rangel and Blanche Wharton. When Rangel was still young, his father abandoned them; his mother worked in New York's garment industry and occasionally did house cleaning to support them. She was active in the International Ladies Garment Workers Union and in Harlem's civic life. In 1948 Rangel joined the army, serving until 1952; he earned a Purple Heart and a Bronze Star for his service during the Korean War. Discharged as a staff sergeant, Rangel attended New York University on the G.I. Bill and in 1957 earned a BA in Business Administration. In 1960 he earned a law degree from St. John's University Law School, Brooklyn, and began the practice of law in Harlem, where he also joined the local Democratic Party club. Rangel subsequently worked in a variety of legal positions, including legal assistant to the New York district attorney, counsel to the New York City Housing and Redevelopment Board, and assistant U.S. attorney. In 1964 he married Alma Carter, a social worker, and together they had two children.

In 1966 Rangel's involvement in Harlem Democratic Party politics paid off, when he was elected to the New York State General Assembly. Rangel's rise in Harlem politics was promoted by the legendary J. Raymond Jones, the first African American chair of the New York County (Manhattan) Democratic Party Committee. Four years later Rangel defeated another legend in Harlem politics—ADAM CLAYTON POWELL JR.—and was elected to the House of Representatives. Powell, the pastor of one of Harlem's most influential churches and the first African American elected to the U.S. Congress from New York, for years had been the best-known and most influential black politician in the United States. However, despite his iconic status in Harlem and among African Americans in general, by 1970 he was vulnerable—in 1967 he had been expelled from Congress, and though he was reelected in 1968, his power was greatly diminished. In addition, because of an outstanding civil warrant, Powell could visit Harlem only on Sundays. Rangel seized the opportunity to challenge him, narrowly defeating him in the four-person Democratic primary election. Winning by a mere 150 votes and one percentage point, Rangel was successful mainly as a result of white votes. In a development unrelated to the election, a largely white section of the Upper West Side of Manhattan had been added to Powell's district. Rangel won in these white areas by fifteen hundred votes. However, like most incumbent members of the House, once elected Rangel was easily returned to office, often running unopposed or winning by margins of victory of 80 percent or more against little-known opponents. The only serious challenge to his reelection occurred in 1994, when Adam Clayton Powell IV, a city councilman and the son of the former congressman, ran against him. Fearing the allure of the Powell name, Rangel raised nearly a million and a half dollars and easily defeated the young Powell.

Rangel came to the House the year several new black members were elected, including Bill Clay of Missouri, Louis Stokes of Ohio, and SHIRLEY CHISHOLM of New York, increasing the size of the black congressional delegation from six to thirteen. Younger and more activist than their senior colleagues, Rangel and these new members decided to form the Congressional Black Caucus. Many white and several of the senior black members of the House, including Robert C. Nix of Pennsylvania and Augustus Hawkins of California, opposed the formation of the caucus, arguing that it was inappropriate for members of Congress to organize on the basis of race. But influenced by the ascendant Black Power philosophy, which called on blacks to establish racially separate organizations, Rangel and his colleagues argued that a caucus of blacks was necessary to advance the interest of blacks in the House, getting good committee assignments, for example, and nationally, through the development and articulation of a black legislative agenda. In 1974 Rangel was elected chair of the caucus, becoming its third chair after Congressmen Charles Diggs and Louis Stokes.

In his first term Rangel was assigned to two relatively minor committees—Public Works and Science and Aeronautics—whose jurisdictions had little to do with issues of concern to Harlem or blacks. However, in his second term he was assigned to the Judiciary Committee, which has jurisdiction over civil rights legislation, and to the Committee on the District of Columbia, which oversees the largely black city of Washington, D.C. Rangel was on the Judiciary Committee in 1974 when, in nationally televised proceedings, it considered articles of impeachment against President Richard Nixon. He spoke and voted in favor of each of the three articles charging Nixon with "high crimes and misdemeanors" that merited impeachment. Nixon resigned shortly after the committee approved the articles. In 1986 Rangel was appointed to the Ways and Means Committee, the oldest, most prestigious, and most powerful House committee, with jurisdiction over taxes, international trade, Social Security, Medicare and Medicaid, and welfare. In 1995 Rangel, the first African American to serve on the committee, became the committee's ranking Democrat, meaning that he will become its first African American chair if the Democrats win a majority of House seats.

Reflecting the concerns of his district specifically and, to some extent, the concerns of blacks nationwide, Rangel also served on the Select Committee on Crime and the Select Committee on Narcotics Abuse, chairing the latter from 1983 until it was abolished in 1993. More so than many big-city ghettos, Harlem has been plagued by problems of crime and drug trafficking. Rangel used his position of leadership on the Narcotics Committee to press for policies to interdict the flow of drugs into the country and to spend money on rehabilitation as well as incarceration. However, Rangel's position on narcotics generally has been relatively conservative. For example, he opposed the legalization of marijuana and other drugs and the provision of free needles to addicts to combat AIDS.

Rangel has several important legislative accomplishments to his credit. He was a principal author of federal empowerment zone legislation (1993) and the Targeted Jobs Tax Credit (1978), both designed to attract jobs to low-income areas like Harlem. He also sponsored the Low Income Housing Tax Credit (1986) to encourage home ownership among the poor. And he was a principal author of the Africa Growth and Opportunity Act, legislation designed to encourage trade between the United States and African nations.

At the beginning of the twenty-first century, after more than thirty years in the House, Rangel was one of its most influential and widely respected members. He was also a leading player in national Democratic Party politics and a broker in New York City and New York State politics, successfully maneuvering in 2002 to obtain the Democratic Party nomination for governor for Carl McCall, an African American. He encouraged and helped Hillary Clinton, the wife of the former president, win a seat in the U.S. Senate, representing New York. He was also instrumental in persuading President Bill Clinton to locate his post-presidential office in Harlem. In 2003, as the United States approached war with Iraq, Rangel introduced legislation to reinstate the military draft, arguing that all social classes, rather than mainly the lower-middle class and the poor, should be represented in the military. Like his predecessor, Rangel managed to project his representation of Harlem onto a national platform, where he is recognized as one of the highest ranking and most influential black elected officials in the United States.

FURTHER READING

Clay, Bill. *Just Permanent Interests: Black Americans in Congress, 1870–1991* (1992).

Swain, Carol. *Black Faces, Black Interests: The Representation of African Americans in Congress* (1993).

—ROBERT C. SMITH

 REASON, PATRICK HENRY (April? 1816– 12 Aug. 1898), printmaker and abolitionist, was born in New York City, the son of Michel Reason, of St. Anne, Guadeloupe, and Elizabeth Melville, of Saint-Dominique. Patrick was baptized as Patrick Rison in the Church of St. Peter on 17 April 1816. While it is not known why the spelling of his name changed, it may have been a homage to the political leader Patrick Henry. While he was still a student at the African Free School in New York, his first engraving was published, the frontispiece to Charles C. Andrews's *The History of the New York African Free-Schools* (1830). It carried the byline "Engraved from a drawing by P. Reason, aged thirteen years." Shortly thereafter, Reason became apprenticed to a white printmaker, Stephen Henry Gimber, and then maintained his own studio at 148 Church Street in New York, where he offered a wide variety of engraving services. Reason was among the earliest and most successful of African American printmakers.

A skilled orator, Reason delivered a speech, "Philosophy of the Fine Arts," to the Phoenixonian Literary Society in New York on 4 July 1837. (It is unclear whether this association was the same as the Phoenix Society, a benevolent organization that had been founded by the Reverend Peter Williams in 1833.) The *Colored American* newspaper reported this speech to be "ably written, well delivered, and indicative of talent and research." In 1838 Reason won first premium (prize) for his India ink drawing exhibited at the Mechanics Institute Fair, and he advertised himself in the *Colored American* as a "Historical, Portrait and Landscape Engraver, Draughtsman & Lithographer" who could produce "Address, Visiting and Business Cards, Certificates, Jewelry &c., neatly engraved." He also gave evening instruction in "scientific methods of drawing," worked for Harpers Publishers preparing map plates, and did government engraving. Reason appeared as a "col'd" ("colored") engraver in New York City directories from 1846 to 1866.

Perhaps Reason's best-known works are his copper engravings of chained slaves. The first, featuring a female figure and the caption "Am I Not a Woman and a Sister?" (1835), was a common letterhead of abolitionists from the mid-1830s onward and was reproduced on both British and American antislavery plaques, publications, coins, and medals. (However, while he was a staunch abolitionist, Reason did not initially support women's rights; he attended the annual meeting of the American Anti-Slavery Society in 1839 and signed a protest against extending the vote to women in the society and against their serving as officers.) A later similar engraving (1839?) depicts a kneeling young male slave wearing tattered clothing, his wrists bound by long, thick manacles. With his head cocked to the side in a forlorn expression, he clasps his hands in prayer. This version, entitled *Am I Not a Man and a Brother?*, embellished membership certificates of Philadelphia's Vigilant Committee, a group of young African American activists who aided escaped slaves. The committee's secretary, Jacob C. White Sr., or its president, Robert Purvis, whose names are on the certificate, may have commissioned the piece. Reason's source for the imagery may have been Wedgwood relief designs or a seal (1787) bearing the same motto along with a chained kneeling slave in a similar position and attitude, used by the English Committee for the Abolition of the Slave Trade.

As a freelance engraver and lithographer, Reason produced portraits and designs for periodicals and frontispieces in slave narratives in the mid-nineteenth century. Typically, his portraits were profile or three-quarters, bust-length images of men with stoic expressions and dressed in coats and ties, set against black backgrounds. Examples appear in Lydia Maria Child's *The Fountain for Every Day in the Year* (1836), *A Memoir of Granville Sharp* (1836) for which Reason based his work on an earlier engraving of the British abolitionist and reformer by T. B. Lord, *Narrative of James Williams, an American Slave: Who Was Several Years a Driver on a Cotton Plantation in Alabama* (1838), John Wesley's *Thoughts on Slavery Written in 1774* (reprinted in 1839), *Liberty Bell* (1839, "The Church Shall Make You Free"), and *Baptist Memorial* (members of the London Emancipation Society, the Reverend Baptist Noel and the Reverend Thomas Baldwin). Three works by Reason appeared in the *U.S. Magazine and Democratic Review*: portraits of the Ohio antislavery senator Benjamin Tappan, after a painting by Washington Blanchard (June 1840 which later appeared in the *Annual Obituary Notices* in 1857 and 1858); the lawyer and diplomat George Mifflin Dallas (Feb. 1842); and the mathematician Robert Adrain, after a painting by Ingraham (June 1844).

Reason also completed two portraits of the antislavery lecturer HENRY BIBB, a lithograph (1840) and a copper engraving featured in *Narrative of the Life and Adventures of Henry Bibb, an American Slave* (1849). While the lithograph depicts Bibb standing rigidly before a draped window, the engraving portrays him casually holding a book in his right hand, posed against a dark background. Among Reason's other works were an engraving of a mountainous landscape after a drawing by W. H. Bartlett and a copper

nameplate for Daniel Webster's coffin. Additional subjects included the slave James Williams (1838), the abolitionist PETER WILLIAMS JR., New York governor De Witt Clinton, and the physician JAMES McCUNE SMITH. In 1838 Reason arranged a public meeting to honor Smith on his return from a European trip. In 1840 he worked with Smith at the Albany Convention of Colored Citizens in drafting a letter to the U.S. Senate protesting racist remarks made by Secretary of State John C. Calhoun to the British minister to the United States regarding a slave revolt onboard the *Creole*.

In the 1840s and 1850s Reason was active in a number of civic groups and fraternal orders. He served as secretary of the New York Society for the Promotion of Education among Colored Children, founded in 1847. As a member of the New York Philomathean Society, organized in 1830 for literary improvement and social pleasure, he petitioned the International Order of Odd Fellows for the society to become a lodge of the association. Although the application was refused, the society received a dispensation from Victoria Lodge No. 448 in Liverpool and became Hamilton Lodge No. 710 in 1844. Reason served as grand master and permanent secretary of the group in the 1850s. His speech at the annual meeting in 1856 was declared the finest given up to that time. Reason not only developed the secret ritual of the order but also composed the Ruth degree, the first "degree to be conferred under certain conditions on Females," and in 1858 he was the first person to receive the honor.

Reason also served as grand secretary of the New York Masons from 1859 to 1860 and as grand master from 1862 to 1868, receiving the Thirty-third Degree of Masonry in 1862. Simultaneously, he was grand master of the Supreme Council for the States, Territories, and Dependencies. The printmaker created original certificates of membership for both the Grand United Order of Odd Fellows and the Masonic Fraternity.

Reason may have taught in the New York schools after 1850. Public School No. 1 was associated with the American and Foreign Anti-Slavery Society, an organization with which Reason had

close ties. In 1852 MARTIN R. DELANY described Reason in *The Condition, Elevation, Emigration, and Destiny of the Colored People of the United States* as "a gentleman of ability and a fine artist" who "stands high as an engraver in the city of New York. Mr. Reason has been in business for years...and has sent out to the world, many beautiful specimens of his skilled hand." Reason also produced other artistic work. During the New York draft riots of 1863, merchants formed a committee for the relief of African American victims. The Reverend HENRY HIGHLAND GARNET wrote an address to the group that was "elaborately engrossed on parchment and tastefully framed by Patrick Reason, one of their own people."

In 1862 Reason married Esther Cunningham of Leeds, England; the couple had one son. Invited to work as an engraver with several firms in Cleveland, Reason moved to Ohio in 1869 and for the next fifteen years worked for the Sylvester Hogan jewelry firm. When Reason died in Cleveland, he left behind a large body of work that established him as one of the finest printmakers of the nineteenth century.

FURTHER READING

Brooks, Charles. *The Official History and Manual of the Grand United Order of Odd Fellows in America* (1871).
Jones, Steven Loring. "A Keen Sense of the Artistic: African American Material Culture in 19th Century Philadelphia." *International Review of African American Art* 12.2 (1995).
Porter, James A. *Modern Negro Art* (1943).

Obituary: *Cleveland Gazette*, 20 Aug. 1898.
—THERESA LEININGER-MILLER

 REED, ISHMAEL
(22 Feb. 1938–), writer, was born Ishmael Scott Reed in Chattanooga, Tennessee, to Thelma Coleman, a saleslady. Coleman never married Reed's natural father, Henry Lenoir, a fund-raiser for the YMCA, but before 1940 she married an autoworker, Bennie Reed, whose surname Ishmael received. (Ishmael has seven siblings and half-siblings.) Coleman moved with her children to Buffalo, New York, in 1942, where Ishmael attended two different high schools

before graduating in 1956; he also made his initial forays into journalism by writing a jazz column in a local black newspaper the *Empire Star*, while still a teenager.

Reed began his college studies in evening courses at the University of Buffalo but ascended to the more rigorous daytime curriculum when an instructor read one of his short stories, in which Reed satirized the Second Coming of Christ by making him an advertising agent who is scorned by the industry because of his unique sales approach. "Something Pure," as the story was titled, gave an early indication of what would become Reed's inimitable style. Reed had read Nathanael West in high school, and West's biting social fiction and floating narrative voice were critical influences. In classes at Buffalo, Reed also absorbed the poetry of William Blake and William Butler Yeats, both of whom developed personal mythologies as an integral part of their work.

Reed's soaring intellectual life at the university was grounded by the meager prospects of a young, black, male adult of the time. Low on money and discontented with academe's aloofness to social realities, he abandoned school to return as a correspondent with the *Empire Star*, moved into a Buffalo housing project in order to better assimilate the concerns of the city's underprivileged black population, and embarked on what turned out to be a discouraging attempt at activism. In one instance, he knocked on doors and registered voters on behalf of a black councilman who covertly threw the election to win favor for another job. In 1961 Reed tried his hand at moderating a radio program that was subsequently cancelled when he and another *Star* editor interviewed MALCOLM X, who was at the time the controversial spokesman for the Nation of Islam.

Compounding Reed's professional frustrations were his new responsibilities as a husband and father. In September 1960 he married Priscilla Rose, with whom he had a daughter, Timothy Brett, in 1962. Shortly after his daughter was born, however, Reed left for New York City and officially separated from his wife in 1963.

Determined to become a full-time writer, Reed immersed himself in the literary and creative cityscape of 1960s New York. He extended his literary talents to poetry through his association with the Umbra Workshop, a collective for black poets, and bolstered his journalistic expertise by working for a New Jersey weekly called the *Newark Advance*, assuming the editorship in 1965. Revamping the *Advance* inspired Reed to start his own paper, which he accomplished later that year by cofounding the *East Village Other*, taking the name from Carl Jung's theory of "Otherness." Increasingly enamored of the possibilities of cultural collision, Reed was finally beginning to enjoy an artistic career that had expanded sufficiently to satisfy his interests. This creative growth was especially marked by the release of his first novel, *The Freelance Pallbearers* (1967), a critically successful debut.

The Freelance Pallbearers grew out of Reed's attempt to parody Newark politics, but it eventually developed into a satire of the United States as a whole—in particular, the volatile social failures of the 1960s and the country's problematic participation in the Vietnam War. The novel's stand-in country for the United States is "HARRY SAM," which, as one critic points out, is a virtual homonym for "harass 'em," an attitude that Reed asserts the country takes toward its ideological opponents (Fox, 42). Reed directs his satire toward blacks as well, by drawing as his novel's protagonist Bukka Doopyduk, a black hospital worker representing African Americans who prefer assimilation over social protest. The title refers to the liberals who, in Reed's story, permit their leaders to be murdered, yet tardily appear over their corpses to praise their work and carry them away. As Henry Louis Gates Jr. asserts, the novel adopts the self-discovering confessional prose that is the most identifiable convention of African American literature, seen most notably for Reed in RALPH ELLISON's *Invisible Man*. Through this voice, *The Freelance Pallbearers* establishes a fundamental element of Reed's writing; namely, the interrogation of artistic conventions in western culture, both white and black and everything in between.

Roused by the acclaim he received from *The Freelance Pallbearers*, Reed soon realized he needed to leave New York. His conscientious lower-class background made him suspicious of fame and the damage it would inflict upon his art. "If I had remained," he later wrote, "I would have been loved and admired to death" (*Reader*, xiv). So he left for California and eventually settled in Oakland, accepting a guest lecturing position at the University of California at Berkeley. He has held the post ever since, though not without some friction; after a few years he was encouraged to apply for tenure and was then refused, though he was allowed to continue teaching. Oakland proved to be an even more fertile environment for Reed's creativity than New York, as it cast him among a community of grassroots activist-intellectuals and cultural personalities, such as Cecil Brown, ANGELA DAVIS, and, for a short while in the 1970s, RICHARD PRYOR. He finally divorced Rose in 1940 and married Carla Bank, a dancer, with whom he had his second daughter, Tennessee.

In 1969 Reed released his second novel, *Yellow Back Radio Broke-Down*, which he has described as an effort to deconstruct ("break down") the yellow-back serial novels of the Old West and, by inference, the history of America. *Yellow Back* also expands upon Reed's increasing fascination with aspects of voodoo as a means of restructuring our perspective of American culture. Most telling, however, are Reed's emerging ideas concerning the novel and art generally, specifically in regard to its potential utilization by underrepresented communities. One character rages, "'No one says a novel has to be one thing. It can be anything it wants to be, a vaudeville show, the six o'clock news, the mumblings of wild men saddled by demons. All art must be for the end of liberating the masses.'"

It logically followed that Reed's next novel, *Mumbo Jumbo* (1972), would serve as a manic exploration for an authoritative African American text, an entity that, as Reed's novel powerfully points out, simply does not exist—but this nonexistence only emphasizes that the monolithic text of whiteness and homogeneous western culture holds no true ballast either. Put differently, *Mumbo Jumbo* is an articulate defense of the dynamism of American race and culture, with particular attention to the instability of the form of the novel. Calling on his own idiosyncratic background in various media—music,

REID, IRA DE AUGUSTINE

radio, newspapers, magazines, and fiction—Reed infuses his novel with photographs, illustrations, charts, footnotes, copies of handbills, door signs, a bibliography, and more. The term Reed chooses for African American culture is "Jes Grew"—a rubric that lays bare the fallacy that African American traditions simply sprang out of nowhere—and in the novel it assumes the form of an epidemic whose victims uncontrollably execute a ragtime dance step, thereby preventing their assimilation in American society.

Mumbo Jumbo was nominated for a National Book Award, the second such honor of Reed's career; he had been likewise nominated for his first extensive collection of poetry, *Conjure*, the year before. Both *Conjure* and *Mumbo Jumbo* provide a name for Reed's engagement with African American religion: "Neo-Hoodoo." An integral figure in Neo-hoodoo is the trickster figure, whom Reed effectively emulates in his writing. Albeit any summation of Neo-hoodoo risks oversimplification, it can best be understood as a politicized and religious response to Judeo-Christian and Islamic ideologies. Reed's art attempts to reconfigure the motley aggregate of beliefs that Westerners mistakenly hold as unshakable.

By the mid-1970s Reed was accepting awards from the Guggenheim Foundation (1974) and the National Institute of Arts and Letters (1975), among others. Yet with his fourth and fifth novels, as well as a growing corpus of essays that express his vitriol in a more direct manner, the controversy surrounding his work steadily increased. Reviewing Reed's fourth novel, *The Last Days of Louisiana Red* (1974), Barbara Smith wrote in the *New Republic* that Reed was showing a disturbing reliance on "the tired stereotypes of feminists as man-hating dykes" (23 Nov. 1974). And Reed reports that when he accepted an award for the novel, an "inebriated" Ralph Ellison—a longtime opponent of his work—shouted, "Ishmael Reed, you ain't nothin' but a gangster and a con artist" (*Reader*, xviii). With his fifth novel, *Flight to Canada*, a satirical rewriting of the slave narrative that is generally considered his most accessible work, Reed enjoyed a more positive response.

While Reed would publish four more novels by 1993—*The Terrible Twos* (1982), *Reckless Eyeballing* (1986), *The Terrible Threes* (1989), and *Japanese by Spring* (1993)—the emphasis of his writing clearly shifted to essays, poetry, and drama. While all of these writings demonstrate a consummate artistry, they rarely achieved for him the notoriety of his early novels. In a way, Reed suffered the mishap of publishing utterly original work in the first half of his career and then being forced to explain himself in the second half—a task he has undertaken grudgingly.

Nonetheless, perhaps the most consistently positive aspect of his career in letters has been his stewardship for culturally underrepresented writers, as an editor of both magazines and anthologies. Toward this end, Reed cofounded the Yardbird Publishing Company in 1971 and the Before Columbus Foundation in 1976, both of which endeavored to gain notice, if not notoriety, for American writers of all ethnic backgrounds. Recently, Reed has edited collections of Native American literature, Asian American literature, and multicultural poetry. With the emergence of the Internet in western literary discourse, Reed also launched, in the late 1990s, a variety of online magazines, most notably *KONCH*, a forum for current events, and *VINES*, a serial collection of student writing. In 2000 Reed culled his best work from fiction, poetry, drama, and nonfiction which he collected in *The Reed Reader*.

By creating an uninhibited space in his work for play and creativity, a space that invokes seemingly every facet of American life, from religion to pop culture, Reed ranks among the country's preeminent postmodern writers. But unlike the works of Thomas Pynchon and William Gaddis, to name just two other highly esteemed postmodernists, Reed's writing is infused with a profound social concern that motivates a relentless indictment of the transgressions of modern America against minorities and the lower classes.

FURTHER READING

Reed, Ishmael. *Conversations with Ishmael Reed*, eds. Bruce Dick and Amritjit Singh (1995).
———. *The Reed Reader* (2000).

Boyer, Jay. *Ishmael Reed* (1993).

Fox, Robert Elliot. *Conscientious Sorcerers* (1987).
Gates, Henry Louis, Jr. "The Blackness of Blackness: A Critique on the Sign and the Signifying Monkey" in *The Signifying Monkey* (1988).
———. "Ishmael Reed" in *Dictionary of Literary Biography* (1984).
McGee, Patrick. *Ishmael Reed and the Ends of Race* (1997).

—DAVID F. SMYDRA JR.

REID, IRA DE AUGUSTINE

(2 July 1901–15 Aug. 1968), African American sociologist and educator, was born in Clifton Forge, Virginia, the son of Daniel Augustine Reid, a Baptist minister, and Willie Robertha James. He was raised in comfortable surroundings and was educated in integrated public schools in Harrisburg, Pennsylvania, and Germantown, a Philadelphia suburb. Reid's academic promise was as apparent as his family connections were useful. Recruited by President JOHN HOPE of Morehouse College in Atlanta, Georgia, in 1918 Reid completed the college preparatory course at Morehouse Academy and in 1922 received his BA from Morehouse College.

Reid taught sociology and history and directed the high school at Texas College in Tyler from 1922 to 1923. He took graduate courses in sociology at the University of Chicago the next summer. From 1923 to 1924 he taught social science at Douglas High School, Huntington, West Virginia. Reid then embarked on a model apprenticeship that George Edmund Haynes, cofounder of the National Urban League, had established for social welfare workers and young social scientists as part of the Urban League program. Selected as a National Urban League fellow for the year 1924–1925, Reid earned an MA in Social Economics at the University of Pittsburgh in 1925, and that same year he married Gladys Russell Scott. They adopted one child.

Also in 1925 Reid was appointed industrial secretary of the New York Urban League, a position he held until 1928. In this role he worked with CHARLES S. JOHNSON, director of research and investigations of the National Urban League, helping the

705

league position itself as a source of information about the economic conditions of African Americans as well as an agency for social reform. Reid surveyed the living conditions of low-income Harlem African American families, conducted a study that was published as *The Negro Population of Albany, New York* (1928), and served as Johnson's research assistant in a National Urban League survey of blacks in the trade unions.

Reid also served as Johnson's assistant in collecting data for the National Interracial Conference of 1928 held in Washington, D.C. This conference represented a popular front of "new middle-class" social welfare activists and social scientists, white and black, who were professionally concerned with the race problem in the United States. The conference produced the landmark *Negro in American Civilization: A Study of Negro Life and Race Relations in the Light of Social Research* (1930). It was a volume that witnessed the emergence of a liberal consensus on race that would be reaffirmed by Gunnar Myrdal in 1944 in *An American Dilemma* and certified by the U.S. Supreme Court a decade later.

Reid's three-year tenure as industrial secretary completed another phase of his apprenticeship. In 1928 he succeeded Johnson as director of research for the national body, a position he held until 1934. As part of the league's procedure for establishing local branches, Reid's work included surveying seven black communities, which resulted in two important reports, *Social Conditions of the Negro in the Hill District of Pittsburgh* (1930) and *The Negro Community of Baltimore—Its Social and Economic Conditions* (1935). Drawing on earlier Urban League research, Reid also published one of the first reliable studies of blacks in the workforce, *Negro Membership in American Labor Unions* (1930).

Reid was enrolled as a graduate student in sociology at Columbia University throughout the period 1928–1934. While employed by the Urban League he began the research on West Indian immigration on which his PhD dissertation would be based.

In 1934 Hope, then president of Atlanta University, encouraged W. E. B. DU BOIS, chair of the Department of Sociology, to hire Reid. Du Bois complied happily. Reid, he remarked in 1937, "is the best trained young Negro in sociology today." Six feet four inches tall, confident, well dressed, and witty, Reid was an impressive figure. His biting intelligence was acknowledged—if not always appreciated—and his urbane manner made him an effective interracial diplomat in an era when black equality was an implausible hypothesis for most white Americans.

Reid worked closely with Du Bois at Atlanta University until the latter's forced retirement in June 1944, at which time he ascended to chair of the Department of Sociology, serving from 1944 to 1946. Having served under Du Bois as managing editor of *Phylon: The Atlanta University Review of Race and Culture* since 1940, the year of its founding, Reid also succeeded his senior colleague as editor in chief of the journal (1944–1948).

From 1934 until his departure from Atlanta University in 1946, Reid's work as a social scientist also had important policy implications. Under the auspices of the Office of the Adviser on Negro Affairs, Department of the Interior, Reid directed a 1936 survey of *The Urban Negro Worker in the United States, 1925–1936* (vol. 1, 1938), an undertaking financed by the Works Progress Administration. Three years later *The Negro Immigrant: His Background, Characteristics and Social Adjustment, 1899–1937* (1939) was published; it was based on the dissertation that had earned him a PhD in Sociology from Columbia University that same year. In 1940 Reid published *In a Minor Key: Negro Youth in Story and Fact*, the first volume of the American Youth Commission's study of black youths. This was a cooperative endeavor of anthropologists, psychiatrists, and sociologists to study the impact of economic crisis and minority-group status on the development of youngsters in black communities. From the standpoint of the history and politics of the social sciences, the project—funded by the Laura Spelman Rockefeller Memorial—reflected the Social Science Research Council's endorsement of a "culture and personality" paradigm that would support liberal policy initiatives.

While at Atlanta Reid also drafted "The Negro in the American Economic System" (1940), a research memorandum used by Myrdal in *An American Dilemma* four years later. In 1941, in collaboration with sociologist Arthur Raper of the Commission on Interracial Cooperation, Reid published *Sharecroppers All*, a pioneering study of the political economy of the South. The text reflects the emerging characterization of the depression South by social scientists and New Dealers as the country's number one economic problem; it signaled their growing impatience at the public costs of the region's class and race relations and dysfunctional labor market.

After Du Bois's retirement from Atlanta University, Reid grew restless there. As a result of his desire for more congenial academic surroundings, on the one hand, and the cracks emerging in the walls of segregation, on the other, Reid became one of the first black scholars to obtain a full-time position at a northern white university (New York University, 1945).

This was again an exemplary chapter in his life. Under the racial regime of "separate-but-equal," job opportunities for black scholars, however well trained and qualified, were restricted to historically black institutions in the South. However, in the early 1940s, as tactical Trojan horses in a foundation-sponsored campaign to desegregate the ranks of the professoriat, a handful of accomplished black academics—among them anthropologist Allison Davis and historian JOHN HOPE FRANKLIN—were installed at northern institutions. Reid became visiting professor of sociology at the New York University School of Education (1945–1947) and, sponsored by the American Friends Service Committee, was visiting professor of sociology at Haverford College, Haverford, Pennsylvania (1946–1947). In 1948 Reid became professor of sociology and chair of the Haverford Department of Sociology and Anthropology, a position he held until his retirement in 1966.

Reid and his wife joined the Society of Friends in 1950, and over the next fifteen years he was involved increasingly in the educational activities of the American Friends Service Committee. Though Reid's scholarly output decreased during this period, his important earlier contributions were gradually acknowledged. He was named assistant editor of the *American Sociological Review* (1947–1950). Ironically, with the coming of the McCarthy era, Reid was honored for professional contributions that now earned him public suspicion. His passport was suspended from 1952 to 1953 by State Department functionaries for suspected communist sympathies. When he firmly challenged this action, the passport was soon returned. Reid served as vice president and president of the Eastern Sociological Society from 1953 to 1954 and from 1954 to 1955, respectively. He was elected second vice president of the American Sociological Association itself from 1954 to 1955.

After the milestone 1954 Supreme Court decision in *Brown v. Board of Education*, Reid was invited to edit "Racial Desegregation and Integration," a special issue of the *Annals of the American Academy of Political and Social Science* (304 [Mar. 1956]). This was another indication of his new visibility within the social science fraternity.

Reid's wife died in 1956. Two years later he married Anna "Anne" Margaret Cooke of Gary, Indiana.

Late in his career Reid enjoyed a wider public. Among other activities, he served on the Pennsylvania Governor's Commission on Higher Education and was a participant in the 1960 White House Conference on Children and Youth. In 1962 Reid was visiting director, Department of Extra-mural Studies, University College, Ibadan, Nigeria. From 1962 to 1963 he was Danforth Foundation Distinguished Visiting Professor, International Christian University, Tokyo, Japan. Reid retired as professor of sociology at Haverford College on 30 June 1966. He died in Bryn Mawr, Pennsylvania.

In addition to his personal achievements, Ira Reid is an important representative of the first numerically significant cohort of professional black social scientists in the United States.

FURTHER READING

No comprehensive collection of Reid manuscript materials exists. However, information about Reid, the various projects and organizations with which he was associated, as well as relevant memoranda and correspondence may be found in the John Hope Presidential Papers and the *Phylon* Records, Editorial Correspondence (1940–1948), Special Collections/Archives, Robert W. Woodruff Library, Atlanta University; and in the Charles S. Johnson Papers and the Julius Rosenwald Fund Archives (1917–1948), Special Collections, Fisk University Library, Nashville, Tenn. See also

the Ira De A. Reid File, Office of College Relations, Haverford College, and Ira De A. Reid File, Quaker Collection, Haverford College Library, Haverford, PA; Ira De Augustine Reid Papers, Schomburg Center for Research in Black Culture, Rare Books, Manuscripts, and Archives Section, of the New York Public Library.

"Ira De A. Reid" in *Black Sociologists: Historical and Contemporary Perspectives*, eds. James E. Blackwell and Morris Janowitz (1974), 154–155.

Ives, Kenneth, et al. *Black Quakers: Brief Biographies* (1986).

Obituaries: *New York Times*, 17 Aug. 1968; *Philadelphia Evening Bulletin*, 19 Sept. 1968.
　　　　　　　　　　　　　—PAUL JEFFERSON

REMOND, CHARLES LENOX (1 Feb. 1810– 22 Dec. 1873), abolitionist and civil rights orator, was born in Salem, Massachusetts, the son of John Remond and Nancy Lenox, prominent members of the African American community of that town. His father, a native of Curaçao, was a successful hairdresser, caterer, and merchant. Charles attended Salem's free African school for a time and was instructed by a private tutor in the Remond household. His parents exposed him to antislavery ideas, and abolitionists were frequent guests in their home. He crossed the paths of a number of fugitive slaves while growing up and by the age of seventeen considered himself an abolitionist. He had also developed considerable oratorical talent.

Remond was impressed by William Lloyd Garrison's antislavery views, particularly the notion of slaveholding as a sin. He heard Garrison speak in 1831 in Salem, and the two became long-time associates when in 1832 Remond became a subscription agent for Garrison's abolitionist newspaper, the *Liberator*. This move helped launch his career as a professional speaker and organizer at a time when the antislavery movement was gaining large numbers of new adherents. Remond traveled in Rhode Island, Massachusetts, and Maine in 1837, soliciting subscriptions and encouraging abolitionists to form local antislavery societies. The *Weekly Anglo-African* depicted Remond's early abolitionism: "He labored in its early

movements most faithfully: he bore the brunt of the calumnies and oppression, the mobbings, the hootings, the assaults which were heaped upon that noble band in the times of 1834–7" (1 Feb. 1862).

The American Anti-Slavery Society hired Remond as its first black lecturing agent in 1838. He brought a new authenticity to the speakers' platform; his charm and eloquence aroused and impressed the predominantly white audiences. In 1842 he was joined by his younger sister, SARAH PARKER REMOND. An associate of Garrison's wing of the antislavery movement, Remond recommended immediate emancipation through moral suasion rather than political action or colonization, positions that isolated him from a growing group of black abolitionists. He opposed HENRY HIGHLAND GARNET's call for slave insurrection at the 1843 National Convention of Colored Citizens. Citing a flawed U.S. Constitution that sanctioned slavery, Remond advocated the dissolution of the Union, a view unpopular with former slaves. While Remond claimed that none of his ancestors had been slaves, he consistently declared southern slavery and northern discrimination dual violations of the Bill of Rights. He urged blacks to protest the discrimination they experienced daily. "We need more radicalism among us," he wrote to the *Liberator*. "We have been altogether too fearful of martyrdom—quite too indifferent in our views and sentiments—too slow in our movements" (21 May 1841).

The highlight of Remond's career came in 1840, when the American Anti-Slavery Society selected him as a delegate to the World's Anti-Slavery Convention in London. Financed by female antislavery groups, Remond welcomed women's involvement in the movement and refused to take his seat at the convention when it voted to bar women's participation. In the eighteen months following the convention, he lectured to great acclaim throughout the British Isles on such topics as slavery, racial prejudice, and temperance. The antislavery press commented widely on Remond's gracious reception in England, in contrast to the discriminatory treatment he endured on his passage abroad and upon his return to Boston. His comparison between travel in the United States and Britain formed the basis of his noted 1842 address to the Massachusetts legislature, "The Rights of Colored Persons in Travelling," with which he became the first African American to speak before that body. His address is an important document of the widespread campaign to end segregated seating in railway cars in the 1840s. Throughout his career he reminded whites of the proscriptive laws and practices against blacks in northern states.

Remond was the most renowned African American orator until 1842, when FREDERICK DOUGLASS began speaking to American audiences. The two men often toured together in the 1840s, and in the fall of 1843 they sustained a heavy lecturing schedule in the Midwest, amid fears of antiabolitionist riots. On 28 October 1845 Douglass wrote Garrison of Remond's effective antislavery oratory: "His name is held in affectionate remembrance by many whose hearts were warmed into life on this question by his soul-stirring eloquence" (CARTER G. WOODSON, *The Mind of the Negro as Reflected in Letters Written during the Crisis 1800–1860* [1926]). Remond's and Douglass's friendship deteriorated when Douglass publicly broke with Garrison in 1852. Contemporaries remarked that Remond felt shunned when Douglass swiftly rose to eminence in antislavery circles. Remond's corresponding decline in stature may be due to the fact that he suffered from tuberculosis, which forced him to abandon the lecture field for long periods of time.

Remond became increasingly impatient with the progress of antislavery, prompting him to reevaluate the utility of moral suasion in the antislavery struggle. The Fugitive Slave Act of 1850, which strengthened slaveholders' ability to reclaim their human property, prompted Remond to defend forcible resistance, to relax his opposition to slave insurrection, and to endorse political action. He became increasingly critical of white abolitionists for not attacking racial prejudice as vehemently as they did slavery. Though he remained ambivalent about the Republican Party, Remond welcomed the outbreak of the Civil War. When Massachusetts opened enlistment to African Americans in January 1863, Remond, Douglass, Garnet, WILLIAM WELLS BROWN, and other black leaders traveled through the northern states and Canada to recruit

African Americans to the ranks of the Fifty-fourth Massachusetts Infantry Regiment. With the war's end Remond supported the continuation of antislavery societies to secure civil and political rights for blacks, a position that divided him from Garrison. He rejected the inclusion of women's rights issues in the campaign for black suffrage, arguing that their inclusion would hinder the achievement of black male enfranchisement, on which the eventual success of woman suffrage depended. Remond made his final lecture tour for a New York State Negro suffrage campaign in 1867. His poor health permitted him to appear only sporadically at civil rights meetings thereafter.

Remond spent most of his time lecturing rather than writing on behalf of antislavery. As one of the earliest black orators, he served as a role model, yet his ideological proximity to the predominantly white Garrisonians isolated him from other black abolitionists. Contemporaries extolled his oratory and compared his style to that of Wendell Phillips. However, as a black man who had never been a slave, his appeal and value to the antislavery movement were limited. Fellow abolitionists remarked upon his increasingly querulous demeanor, bitterness, and irascibility.

Beginning in 1865 Remond worked as a streetlight inspector and was appointed as a stamp clerk in the Boston Custom House in 1871. He died of tuberculosis at his home in Wakefield, Massachusetts. He was married twice, first to Amy Matilda Williams, who died on 15 August 1856, and then to Elizabeth Thayer Magee, who died on 3 February 1872. He and his second wife had four children.

FURTHER READING

No substantial collection of Remond's personal papers exists. Many speeches and letters can be found in the microfilm edition of C. Peter Ripley and George Carter, eds., *The Black Abolitionist Papers, 1830–1865* (1981).

Porter, Dorothy B. "The Remonds of Massachusetts: A Nineteenth Century Family Revisited." *Proceedings of the American Antiquarian Society* 95 (Oct. 1985): 259–295.
Usrey, Miriam L. "Charles Lenox Remond: Garrison's Ebony Echo." *Essex Institute Historical Collections* 56 (Apr. 1970): 112–125.
—STACY KINLOCK SEWELL

 REMOND, SARAH PARKER (6 June 1826– 13 Dec. 1894), abolitionist, physician, and feminist, was born in Salem, Massachusetts, the daughter of John Remond and Nancy Lenox. Her father, a native of Curaçao, immigrated to the United States at age ten and became a successful merchant. Her mother was the daughter of African American revolutionary war veteran Cornelius Lenox. Sarah grew up in an antislavery household. Her father became a life member of the Massachusetts Anti-Slavery Society in 1835, and her mother was founding member of the Salem Female Anti-Slavery Society, which began as a black female organization in 1832. Sarah's brother, CHARLES LENOX REMOND, was a well-known antislavery lecturer in the United States and Great Britain.

Sarah Parker Remond attended local public schools in Salem until black students were forced out by committee vote in 1835. Determined to educate their children in a less racist environment, the Remond family moved to Newport, Rhode Island, in 1835. After the family returned to Salem in 1841, Remond's education was further developed at home with English literature and antislavery writings. She was an active member of the Salem Female Anti-Slavery Society, the Essex County Anti-Slavery Society, and the Massachusetts Anti-Slavery Society. Her experience with the Salem school committee led to early activism against racial segregation. She was awarded five hundred dollars by the First District Court of Essex after being forcibly ejected from her seat at a public place of entertainment in 1853.

In 1842 Remond began touring on the antislavery circuit with her brother Charles, who was the first black lecturing agent of the Massachusetts Anti-Slavery Society. Sarah and Charles toured New York State with Wendell Phillips, Abigail Kelley Foster, Stephen Foster, and Susan B. Anthony in 1856. Remond accepted an appointment as a lecturing agent of the American Anti-Slavery Society in 1858. On 28 December 1858 she sailed to Great Britain with three goals: to work for the antislavery cause, to pursue an education, and to live for a time away from American racism. She attended the Bedford College for Ladies in London while traveling

Sarah Parker Remond became a popular lecturer on abolition and women's rights, especially in England in the 1850s. Peabody and Essex Museum

as an antislavery lecturer to more than forty-five cities in England, Scotland, and Ireland between 1859 and 1861. Her approach on the antislavery circuit was different from black male American abolitionists. She won over the British public by drawing on her demeanor as a "lady," while recounting stories of sordid sexual exploitation forced on female slaves. She was popular in Great Britain, where lectures by women were rare. She was one of the first women to lecture in Great Britain to "mixed-sex" audiences. Because she was removed by both her race and nationality from British class politics and gender conventions, she was able to appeal to both the working class and the social elite.

Perhaps her popularity as an abolitionist in London caused the American legation in London to deny her request for a visa to travel to France in November 1859. The legation claimed that because of her race she was not a citizen of the United States. Support

for her included editorials in most of the major London papers. The *Morning Star* compared the "visé affair" to the DRED SCOTT decision, which had been used by the United States as a basis for its actions. Benjamin Moran, the American assistant secretary of legation, wrote on 10 December 1859 that George Dallas, the American minister to Great Britain, threatened to go home should any more attacks of the kind appear, and if he went, he would be the last American minister in England for some time. Moran believed that public opinion on this matter reached Buckingham Palace. On 25 February 1860 he wrote, "on the subject of darkies, I am reminded that the queen looked at me very [oddly] on Thursday, & I now suspect the Remond affair was dancing about in her mind, and that she wished to know what kind of person (if she thought of the matter at all) the Secretary was that refused that lady of color a visé."

Remond's manner and standing in American antislavery circles made her a great many friends in the "upper circle" of British abolitionists. She lived for a time at the home of Peter Alfred Taylor, a member of Parliament and treasurer of the London Emancipation Committee. A center for London radicals, the Taylor home was also the meeting place for many of London's early female reformers because Taylor's wife, Mentia, was active in the woman suffrage movement. Remond worked with the Taylors in establishing the first two emancipation groups in London. In June 1859 concerned individuals, including famed runaway slaves WILLIAM AND ELLEN CRAFT, formed the London Emancipation Committee. Remond was active in this group until 1 August 1859. After the committee failed to invite her to address a public meeting held in London to celebrate the twenty-fifth anniversary of the abolition of British colonial slavery, Remond stopped attending its meetings. The London Emancipation Committee concluded operations in February 1860 at a meeting attended by men only.

Four years later Remond and Mentia Taylor were founding members of the London Ladies Emancipation Society, which claimed that slavery was a question especially and deeply interesting to women. In 1864 the society put into circulation more than twelve thousand pamphlets printed by the feminist publisher Emily Faithful. Remond's contribution was entitled *The Negroes and Anglo-Africans as Freed Men and Soldiers*. After the end of the Civil War, Remond was a member of the Freedman's Aid Association along with Ellen Craft. In 1865 she wrote a letter of protest to the *London Daily News* when the London press began attacking blacks after an insurrection in Jamaica.

Remond returned to the United States later in 1865 and worked for a short time with the American Equal Rights Association. She had served as a delegate to the National Woman's Rights Convention in 1858. In 1866 she moved to Florence, Italy, to attend a medical training program at Santa Maria Nuovo Hospital. After receiving a diploma for "professional medical practice" in 1871, she started a medical practice in Florence. On 25 April 1877 she married an Italian named Lazzaro Pintor. Sarah

Parker Remond is buried in the Protestant Cemetery in Rome, Italy.

FURTHER READING

Remond, Sarah Parker. "Sarah Parker Remond" in *Our Exemplars, Poor and Rich; or, Biographical Sketches of Men and Women Who Have, by an Extraordinary Use of Their Opportunities, Benefited Their Fellow-Creatures*, ed. Matthew Davenport Hill (1861).

Midgley, Clare. *Women against Slavery: The British Campaigns, 1780–1870* (1992).

Porter, Dorothy B. "The Remonds of Salem, Massachusetts: A Nineteenth-Century Family Revisited." *Proceedings of the American Antiquarian Society* 95 (1985): 259–295.

Ripley, C. Peter, ed. *The Black Abolitionist Papers*, vol. 1, *The British Isles, 1830–1865* (1985).

—KAREN JEAN HUNT

REVELS, HIRAM RHOADES

(27 Sept. 1827?– 16 Jan. 1901), clergyman, educator, and first African American senator, was born in Fayetteville, North Carolina, the son of free parents of mixed blood. Little is known of his family or early years. At eight or nine he enrolled in a private school for black children, where he was "fully and successfully instructed by our able teacher in all branches of learning." About 1842 his family moved to Lincolnton, North Carolina, where Revels became a barber.

Hiram Rhoades Revels, in 1869 the first African American elected to the U. S. Senate. Library of Congress

Two years later he entered Beech Grove Seminary, a Quaker institution two miles south of Liberty, Indiana. In 1845 he enrolled at another seminary in Darke County, Ohio, and during this period may also have studied theology at Miami University in Oxford, Ohio.

Revels's preaching career with the African Methodist Episcopal (AME) Church began at this time. He was ordained as a minister in the Indiana Conference at some point between 1845 and 1847 and was confirmed as an elder by the same organization in 1849. His first pastorate may have been in Richmond, Indiana, and he is known to have served the Allen Chapel Church in Terre Haute during the 1840s. In the early 1850s he married Phoeba A. Bass, with whom he had six children.

Revels traveled extensively, becoming a noted preacher in the Indiana-Ohio-Illinois area before the end of the 1840s. An urge to carry the gospel to slaves led him to expand his circles, and in the 1850s he journeyed to lecture and teach in Missouri, Kansas, Kentucky, and Tennessee. His freedom of movement suggests that Revels was not a known abolitionist, but he later recounted that he "always assisted the fugitive to make his escape" when in a free state (Thompson, 31).

In late 1853 Revels moved his ministry to an AME church in St. Louis, but because of a dispute with the bishop during the following year, he left both the congregation and the AME denomination, accepting the pastorate of Madison Street Presbyterian Church in Baltimore, Maryland. He stayed in that position for two years before entering Knox College in Galesburg, Illinois. In 1857 he returned to Baltimore and to his former denomination, becoming the pastor of an AME church in the city. He also was named principal of a high school for blacks, beginning his career as an educational administrator.

With the outbreak of the Civil War, Revels helped organize black work battalions for the Union army. In 1863 he moved back to St. Louis to teach at a high school for blacks and there continued his efforts to aid the North, participating in the organization of the first black regiment from Missouri. Again he did not stay long, moving to Mississippi in 1864 to work with the freedmen. Based primarily in Jackson, he was instrumental in the establishment of several schools and churches in the Jackson-Vicksburg area. Some sources claim that he was also a regimental chaplain and worked with the Vicksburg provost marshal's office.

In late 1865 Revels aligned himself with the AME Church North, the denomination with which he would be associated for the rest of his career. He held pastorates in Leavenworth, Kansas, Louisville, Kentucky, and New Orleans, Louisiana, before becoming the presiding elder at a church in Natchez, Mississippi, in June 1868. That summer Adelbert Ames, military governor of Mississippi, appointed Revels to the city board of aldermen. Although little is known about his term of service, his primary focus was apparently on improving the city educational system.

As his prominence in the community grew, Revels, who was one of the most highly educated African Americans in the state, was encouraged to seek higher office, and in late 1869 he agreed to run as a Republican for the Adams County seat in the state senate. With the military Reconstruction government assuring black voting privileges, Revels won easily, as three-fourths of the people in the county were African Americans. He was one of thirty-six blacks chosen for the legislature from across the state.

Revels was invited to offer the invocation at the opening of the legislative session. One participant later recalled that the prayer "made [him] a United States Senator, because he made a deep, profound and favorable impression upon everyone who was fortunate enough to be within the sound of his voice" (*Journal of Negro History* 16: 107). Two unexpired Senate terms, dating from before the Civil War, did have to be filled, and the black legislators were insistent that at least one seat be given to an African American. Their preferred candidate, James Lynch, had been appointed secretary of state, so they turned to Revels. After three days and seven ballots, Revels was elected on 20 January to fill the seat vacated by Jefferson Davis in 1861.

The nation's first African American senator arrived in Washington ten days after his election. He could not present his credentials until Mississippi was formally readmitted to the Union, which finally took place on 23 February. Three days of contentious debate over whether to seat Revels followed, with the Senate voting forty-eight to eight in favor of accepting his credentials on 25 February. Revels was then sworn in and seated.

Although his brief Senate term was relatively undistinguished, Revels's skill as an orator, honed through decades in the pulpit, earned favorable attention from the national press. He introduced three bills, but only one passed—a petition for the removal of civil and political disabilities from an ex-Confederate. He favored amnesty for white southerners "just as fast as they give evidence of having become loyal men and of being loyal," a stance that drew criticism from some in the black community. Revels served briefly on the District of Columbia Committee and nominated the first African American for enrollment at West Point (the candidate failed the entrance examination).

Revels returned to Mississippi upon the completion of his term in March 1871, and Governor James L. Alcorn asked him to oversee the establishment of a college for black males. The legislature suggested that the school be named Revels University, but the former senator declined the honor, recommending that the governor's name be used. In 1872 Alcorn University opened in Claiborne County, Mississippi, with Revels as the first president. His duties were interrupted briefly in 1873, when he was named secretary of state ad interim.

The new governor, Ames, who had given Revels his start in politics, pressured Revels into resigning the Alcorn presidency in July 1874, apparently because of Revels's political ties with ex-governor Alcorn. A third of the student body and a number of faculty members left in protest against the action. Revels was reappointed as president two years later, when John M. Stone became governor. In the interim he served churches in Holly Springs and New Orleans and briefly edited the *Southwestern Christian Advocate*.

Health problems and Alcorn's financial woes led Revels to resign again in 1882. He moved back to Holly Springs, where he taught theology at Rust College for a few years and assisted the pastor of the local AME North church. He died while attending a religious conference in Aberdeen, Mississippi.

FURTHER READING
Revels's papers are at the Schomburg Center for Research in Black Culture of the New York Public Library, and at Alcorn State University. Revels's unpublished autobiography is in the CARTER G. WOODSON Collection, Library of Congress.

Gravely, William B. "Hiram Revels Protests Racial Separation in the Methodist Episcopal Church (1876)." *Methodist History* 8 (1970): 13–20.
Lawson, Elizabeth. *The Gentleman from Mississippi, Our First Negro Senator* (1960).
Thompson, Julius E. *Hiram R. Revels, 1827–1901: A Biography* (1982).

Obituaries: *Natchez* (Miss.) *Daily Democrat*, 18 Jan. 1901; *Southwestern Christian Advocate*, 31 Jan. 1901.

—KENNETH H. WILLIAMS

 REVEREND IKE
(1 June 1935–), religious leader, was born Frederick Joseph Eikerenkoetter II in Ridgeland, South Carolina, to Frederick Joseph Eikerenkoetter Sr., a Baptist minister and architect, and Rema Estelle Matthews, a teacher. As a boy, he was exposed to the fundamentalist theology of the Bible Way Church in Ridgeland, where his father was the pastor, and he became an assistant minister at the age of fourteen. After graduating from high school in 1952, Frederick won a scholarship to the American Bible College in New York and earned a Bachelor of Theology degree in 1956. He then became a chaplain in the U.S. Air Force and started what might have become a traditional and uneventful ministerial career. However, after only two years, Eikerenkoetter left the security of the chaplaincy to embark on a new vocation as an evangelist.

Back in South Carolina, he veered from his Baptist roots and began to develop an eclectic ministry, akin to Pentecostalism, that relied heavily on faith healing, the excitement of revival meetings, and the appeal of a charismatic preacher. By 1962 the United Church of Jesus Christ, which he had founded a few years earlier, had only a few members and met in a converted storefront, yet even then he anticipated building a great church empire, and, for this reason, he established the United Christian Evangelist Association, which

would become the organizational and business umbrella for his future endeavors. In 1964 he married Eula Mae Dent; together they had one son, Xavier. Ultimately, his wife would become the co-pastor of his ministries, and his son would be given the title Bishop Coadjutor. They moved to Boston in 1965, where he founded the Miracle Temple and acquired his first radio audience.

Until Eikerenkoetter's ascendance, the Reverend C. L. FRANKLIN, with his syndicated radio programs and recording contracts, was the most popular black preacher in America. Historically, the success of most black ministers relied on how well they delivered a standard Protestant message that emphasized faith in God and hard work and that generally deprecated the desire for material pleasures. Indeed, many ministers became quite wealthy by advocating this austere doctrine. Eikerenkoetter offered a radically different theology that contrasted sharply with the old-time religion in both form and substance.

Like FATHER DIVINE at the turn of the century, who was influenced by Charles Fillmore and Robert Collier, the pioneers of New Thought philosophy, Eikerenkoetter was also drawn to ideas that originated with New Thought because they placed greater power and responsibility upon the individual to affect the course of his or her life in this world, rather than praying for a better life in the hereafter. Eikerenkoetter, however, never proclaimed himself to be God or a messiah, as Father Divine and DADDY GRACE had strongly intimated. It is likely that Eikerenkoetter was exposed to New Thought philosophy through white ministers, such as Norman Vincent Peale, and motivational speakers, such as Dale Carnegie, who had popularized a new gospel of positive thinking. Eikerenkoetter was the first to package this concept within an African American religious ethos and successfully market it to black consumers.

In 1966 two decisions contributed greatly to Eikerenkoetter's success: he established his flagship congregation on 125th Street in Harlem, New York, and he began to use the name Reverend Ike instead of the difficult-to-pronounce Dutch name Eikerenkoetter. Not even the flamboyant Harlem minister ADAM CLAYTON POWELL JR. was as flashy or as ostentatious as Reverend Ike, who flaunted his diamond rings, fur coats, and mink-upholstered Rolls-Royce. While the mainstream press ridiculed his extravagance and considered it proof that he was a charlatan, Reverend Ike argued to his critics and to the thousands who were drawn to him that his very wealth was proof that his program worked. In contrast to a long tradition of pie-in-the-sky preaching, Ike repeatedly said, "I want my pie now, with ice cream on top" (Morris, 180). He taught that "the LACK of money is the root of all evil" (Morris, 184) and to overcome the guilt that many religious people had about desiring money, he developed the mantra "I like money. I need money. I want money.... Money is not sinful in its right place. Money is good" (Morris, 176).

The response to this theology of prosperity was so overwhelming that in 1969 the congregation purchased the historic Palace Auditorium, which occupied a full block on Broadway and 175th Street. Five thousand people attended services there each week, and the building also contained his school, the United Church and Science of Living Institute. Reverend Ike claimed that millions of people subscribed to his magazine, *Action!*, or listened to him on more than eighty-nine radio stations. In 1971 he became the first black leader since MARCUS GARVEY to pack Madison Square Garden, and in 1973 he became the first black preacher to acquire a television program, *Joy of Living*. Through all of these outlets he sold literature extolling his "Blessing Plan," as well as products promising to heal or enrich the purchaser—if the person had faith and contributed to his church.

At the height of his popularity in the late 1970s, Ike was prominent among a new generation of televangelists. He received offers to speak to diverse audiences and once even lectured on psychiatry at Harvard Medical School. In an effort to deflect criticism that his ministry was completely self-serving, his church sponsored programs to help drug addicts, and he purchased a lifetime membership with the NAACP. During the 1980s, however, his star began to fade, and the former religious icon quickly became a parody of black preachers who prey on the poor and desperate. His public image also suffered from a number of unsuccessful criminal investigations by the Internal

Revenue Service and the Postal Service and by a sexual harassment suit brought by a male employee against him in 1995. Reverend Ike's ministry survived these accusations, but it never regained its former stature.

Lingering questions about Reverend Ike's motives and character obscured the theological innovations that he pioneered, and excessive attention to Ike's showmanship prevented many observers from recognizing that at its core his message appealed to African Americans who legitimately wanted a greater share of American prosperity.

FURTHER READING

The records and papers of Reverend Ike are not publicly available. The most scholarly study of his ministry is an unpublished dissertation by Martin V. Gallatin, "Rev. Ike's Ministry: A Sociological Investigation of Religious Innovation," New York University, 1979.

Baer, Hans A., and Merrill Singer. *African American Religion* (2002).
Morris, James. *The Preachers* (1973).
Riley, Clayton. "The Golden Gospel of Reverend Ike." *New York Magazine*, 19 Mar. 1975.
Sanders, Charles L. "The Gospel According to Rev. Ike." *Ebony*, Dec. 1976.
—SHOLOMO B. LEVY

RICE, CONDOLEEZZA

(14 Nov. 1954–), national security adviser and educator, was born in Birmingham, Alabama, the only child of John Wesley Rice Jr., an educator and minister, and Angelena Ray, a teacher. Her mother, an accomplished pianist, named her after the Italian musical direction *con dolcezza*, meaning to play "with sweetness." The Rices viewed the restrictions of Jim Crow Alabama as obstacles for their daughter to overcome. She did so effortlessly, taking early lessons in ballet, French, flute, and piano. Extra tutoring from her father enabled her to skip the first and seventh grades.

Though she enjoyed a comfortable, if by no means wealthy, childhood, Rice was not immune to the harsh realities of Birmingham under Bull Connor, the city's notoriously racist commissioner of public safety. Like everyone else in the city, she attended segregated

schools, and one of her classmates was killed in the 1963 bombing of the Sixteenth Street Baptist Church by white supremacists. While her mother fostered Condi's interest in music, her father inspired a love of politics. He was an avid Republican—as were many middle-class blacks at a time when Governor George Wallace dominated the Alabama Democratic Party—and he sat with his five-year-old daughter to watch the televised Nixon-Kennedy presidential debates in 1960. Family lore has it that on a childhood trip to Washington, D.C., Condoleezza stood in front of the White House and declared that she would one day live there.

When her family moved to Denver, Colorado, in 1968, however, Rice appeared more likely to follow a career in music than politics. At the age of fifteen, she entered the University of Denver, where her father served as an administrator, to study piano. Midway through college, she left the music program, believing that she could not succeed as a concert pianist. Rice focused her energies on a new love, studying the politics and policy of the Soviet Union. Her mentor, Joseph Korbel, a Czech refugee from both Nazism and Stalinism, headed the university's School of International Studies and was influential in shaping Rice's belief that the United States should adopt hard-line policies against the Soviet Union. After receiving her BA in 1974, Rice spent a year in Indiana at Notre Dame earning a master's degree in International Studies. By then, she had developed a passion for the Russian language and for the arcana of Soviet military strategy, and she returned to the University of Denver to complete a doctoral dissertation in 1981, later published as *Uncertain Allegiance: The Soviet Union and the Czechoslovak Army* (1984).

A postdoctoral fellowship at Stanford University in 1981 helped Rice shift her interests from the more purely academic to public policy. Stanford was home to several conservative think tanks, notably the Hoover Institution, where she found much in common with a new mentor, Brent Scowcroft, a military affairs specialist who had advised presidents from Richard Nixon to Ronald Reagan, and who became national security adviser to President George H. W. Bush in 1989. Scowcroft appointed Rice, by then a

Those brusque, no-nonsense qualities proved invaluable, however, when President George Bush's son, George W. Bush, was seeking a national security expert to advise him for the 2000 presidential campaign. The younger Bush, a man with little knowledge of foreign affairs, needed a clear-thinking, direct mentor to guide him through the thickets of global policy. In Rice, famed for her lucid and entertaining lectures at Stanford, he found the ideal teacher and a common spirit, as well as someone who shared his love of professional sports and physical exercise. She was also an intimate of his father's, a family connection that mattered greatly to "Team Bush." After his controversial victory in the 2000 election, George W. Bush appointed Rice as his national security adviser.

Rice's actions in the first Bush White House had placed her in the camp of COLIN POWELL and others who advocated a pragmatic foreign policy based on cooperation with America's allies and the United Nations. But she now gravitated toward the "moralist" camp of Vice President Dick Cheney, who believed that America should stand alone in foreign affairs. The terrorist attacks of September 11, 2001, appear to have cemented Rice's commitment to a more unilateral foreign policy.

In 2002 Rice received the NAACP's President's Award for her expertise and influence in foreign affairs. That tribute recognizes Rice's role as one of President Bush's closest advisers in foreign affairs. It also reflects her achievement as the nation's first female national security adviser and as perhaps the most influential black woman in global politics since Cleopatra.

Condoleezza Rice at the announcement of her appointment by President-elect George W. Bush as National Security Advisor, 2000. Corbis

tenured professor at Stanford, to the National Security Council staff that same year. Rice's time in the first Bush White House coincided with the collapse of the Soviet Union, and her expertise in that policy area greatly enhanced her personal and political standing with the president. Unlike Defense Secretary Dick Cheney and other hard-liners, Rice urged Bush to work pragmatically with the Soviet President Mikhail Gorbachev in his efforts to reform the Soviet Union and the Eastern Bloc. That stance, and her moderate views on abortion and affirmative action, earned Rice the enmity of the conservative hawks who came to dominate the Republican Party after Bush's defeat by Bill Clinton in 1992.

During the Clinton years, Rice returned to academia and, with Philip Zelikow, published an award-winning examination of the end of the cold war, *Germany Unified and Europe Transformed: A Study in Statecraft* (1999). She also served from 1993 to 1999 as the provost of Stanford, and was the first woman and the first African American to hold that post. She succeeded in reversing Stanford's financial problems by slashing the university budget, a move that won her the admiration of the board of trustees but also the ire of many faculty, staff, and students. The U.S. Department of Labor even began an investigation into racial and gender discrimination at the university after several women complained that Rice's budget cuts had disproportionately harmed minorities. Rice later admitted that her tenure as provost had been her toughest ever job and that she may have been too much of a "hard-ass" (Lemann, 171).

FURTHER READING

Rice's role in the 1989–1993 Bush administration may be gleaned from sources at the George H. W. Bush Presidential Library and Museum in College Station, Texas, though many of those records remain classified. The Stanford University Archives, Palo Alto, California, contain materials relevant to her tenure as provost of Stanford.

Felix, Antonia. *Condi: The Condoleezza Rice Story* (2002).
Lemann, Nicholas. "Without a Doubt." *New Yorker*, 14 & 21 Oct. 2002.

—STEVEN J. NIVEN

RILLIEUX, NORBERT

(17 Mar. 1806–8 Oct. 1894), inventor, chemical engineer, was born in New Orleans, Louisiana, the son of Vincent Rillieux Jr., an engineer, and Constance Vivant, who belonged to a wealthy free black family of landowners and landlords. Vincent Rillieux Jr., a businessman and inventor of a steam-operated press for baling cotton, was white, but Norbert and his mother belonged to the mainly Francophone and Catholic ethnic group of "free people of color" (often referred to as "Black Creoles" after the Civil War). Little is known of Norbert Rillieux's childhood from the time of his baptism in the St. Louis Cathedral of New Orleans to the time he and his brother Edmond were sent, like many other young free men of color, to France to be educated. By 1830 Norbert was an instructor in applied mechanics at the École Centrale in Paris and is reported to have published several papers on steam power.

The following year, in 1831, Norbert Rillieux made an extraordinary discovery that prompted his return to New Orleans and would eventually transform the sugar-refining process in Louisiana and throughout the world. The traditional manner of reducing sugarcane juice for sugar production, called the "Jamaica Train," required the tedious and backbreaking labor of numerous slaves who, armed with long ladles, skimmed the boiling sugar juice from one open kettle to the next. Rillieux developed an ingenious apparatus, employing condensing coils that used the vapor from one vacuum chamber to evaporate the juice from a second chamber. The new invention—safer, more efficient, and less expensive than the open-kettle system—has been described as having been as significant for the sugar industry as Eli Whitney's cotton gin was for the processing of cotton.

Rillieux failed to interest French planters in his invention, but in 1833 he was invited back to New Orleans by the planter and banker Edmund Forstall to be chief engineer of a new sugar refinery. The appointment did not materialize, but Rillieux continued to perfect his apparatus and also made a fortune in land speculation, which he lost in the nationwide financial collapse of 1837.

Some elegant architectural drawings that he produced with his brother Edmond during this period survive in the Notarial Archives in New Orleans. In 1843 two prominent planters hired Rillieux to install evaporators, Theodore Packwood at his plantation later known as Myrtle Grove, and Judah P. Benjamin at his Bellechasse plantation. Within three years Packwood won first prize and Benjamin and Packwood second prize for best sugar, the awards mentioning use of Rillieux's patent sugar boiling apparatus. On 26 August 1843 Norbert Rillieux was awarded his first patent from the U.S. Patent Office for a double effect evaporator in vacuum, followed by a patent in 1846 for a triple effect evaporator with horizontal tubular heating surface. Approval for a later patent (1857) was at first denied on the erroneous assumption that Rillieux was a slave and therefore not a U.S. citizen. "Now, I was the applicant for the patent and not the slave. I am a Citizen of the United States and made oath of the fact in my affidavit," Rillieux wrote.

Judah Benjamin, the brilliant Jewish jurist who later served as Jefferson Davis's secretary of state for the Confederacy, became Rillieux's major supporter in Louisiana sugar circles. He publicized Rillieux's apparatus in a series of articles in J. D. B. De Bow's popular commercial magazine (which came to be known as De Bow's Review). In 1846 Benjamin described the sugar produced by Rillieux's method as the best in Louisiana, its "crystalline grain and snowy whiteness... equal to those of the best double-refined sugar of our northern refineries." For ten years at least, Rillieux was a conspicuous figure in New Orleans manufacturing. Benjamin's earliest biographer, Pierce Butler, reported that "frequently, for quite long visits, came the dried-up little chemist Rillieux, always the centre of an admiring and interested group of planters from the neighborhood as he explained this or that point in the chemistry of sugar or the working of his apparatus." Rillieux was described by one contemporary as "the most sought-after engineer in Louisiana," but he was still, by Louisiana law, a "person of color," suffering under increasing legal and social restrictions as North-South tensions escalated.

It is not known exactly when Rillieux returned to France. He had many reasons, including the new restrictions imposed in 1855 on free people of color in New Orleans. Apparently Rillieux returned to France just before or during the Civil War and remained there until his death. There is no evidence that he knew his most famous relative, the Impressionist Parisian painter Edgar Degas, whose mother was Rillieux's first cousin. (This family connection was recently announced by Christopher Benfey in "Degas and the 'Black World': Art and Miscegenation in New Orleans," New Republic, 21 [Oct. 1996].) Late in life Rillieux became interested in Egypt, and in 1880 he was found deciphering hieroglyphics in the Bibliothèque Nationale by the Louisiana planter Duncan Kenner. During his seventies he was still working on refinements to various devices for beet and cane sugar production. Norbert Rillieux was buried in Paris's Père Lachaise cemetery, survived by his wife, Emily Cuckow Rillieux, who lived in comfortable circumstances for another eighteen years.

FURTHER READING

Heitmann, John A. *The Modernization of the Louisiana Sugar Industry 1830–1910* (1987).

Meade, George P. "A Negro Scientist of Slavery Days." *Scientific Monthly* 62 (1946): 317–326, reprinted, *Negro History Bulletin* 20, no. 7 (Apr. 1957): 159–163.

Obituary: *Louisiana Planter and Sugar Manufacturer*, 24 Nov. 1894.

—CHRISTOPHER BENFEY

ROBESON, PAUL

(9 Apr. 1898–23 Jan. 1976), actor, singer, and civil rights activist, was born Paul Leroy Robeson in Princeton, New Jersey, the son of William Drew Robeson, a Protestant minister, and Maria Louisa Bustill, a schoolteacher. Robeson's mother died when he was six years old, and he grew up under the influence of a perfectionist father, a former runaway slave who fought in the Union army. During his senior year at the Somerville, New Jersey, high school, he achieved the highest score in a statewide scholarship examination to attend Rutgers College (later Rutgers University). The lone black at Rutgers as a freshman in 1915 and only

Paul Robeson, an individual of extraordinary talents, as photographed by Carl Van Vechten in 1933. Library of Congress

the third African American to attend the institution, Robeson was an outstanding student and athlete. A varsity debater, he won class prizes for oratory all four years, was elected to Phi Beta Kappa as a junior, was one of four seniors chosen for membership in the Cap and Skull honorary society, and was named class valedictorian. The six-foot, three-inch, 215-pound Robeson earned twelve varsity letters in four sports (baseball, basketball, football, and track) and was twice named football All-America (1917 and 1918). According to former Yale coach Walter Camp, "There never has been a more serviceable end, both in attack and defense, than Robeson." Despite his popularity with fellow students, a series of social slights and racial incidents in football brought to the fore long-standing concerns about race. Robeson's senior thesis predicted the eventual use of the Fourteenth Amendment to advance civil rights, and his commencement address boldly combined the accommodationist philosophy of BOOKER T. WASHINGTON with the more militant views of W. E. B. DU BOIS.

Robeson received the BA degree in 1919 and moved to Harlem preparatory to entering the Columbia University Law School in 1920. He helped finance his legal education by playing professional football for three seasons (1920–1922) with the Akron Pros and the Milwaukee Badgers. In 1921 he married Eslanda "Essie" Cardozo Goode, a member of a prominent Washington, D.C., black family, who worked as a laboratory pathologist at Columbia's medical school; they had one child. Recognizing Robeson's lack of enthusiasm for the law and football, his wife urged him to take up acting. After playing the lead in a Harlem YMCA production of *Simon the Cyrenian* in 1920, he appeared in several other local productions and became acquainted with the Provincetown Players, a Greenwich Village theatrical group that included Eugene O'Neill. He debuted professionally in a short-run Broadway play, *Taboo*, in 1922. Robeson, meanwhile, finished his legal studies, received the LLB degree in February 1923, and joined a New York City law firm headed by a Rutgers alumnus. But discouraged by discrimination within the firm and the legal profession generally, he quit a few months later, before taking the bar exam, to pursue an acting career.

Robeson launched his stage career in 1924 in the lead roles in two O'Neill plays, *The Emperor Jones* and *All God's Chillun Got Wings*, the latter a daring drama about interracial marriage. He achieved a spectacular triumph in London in 1930 when he not only became one of the first black actors to play Othello but also rendered the finest portrayal of the character yet seen. Robeson was also an accomplished singer, and at Essie's urging he performed at Carnegie Hall in 1925. The first soloist to devote an entire concert to Negro spirituals, Robeson both enthralled the sold-out audience and boosted the popularity of the musical genre. Robeson steadfastly refused to sing operatic and classical music, preferring to emphasize Negro spirituals and international folk songs. In time his rich basso-baritone voice was familiar to millions through national and international concert tours, radio performances, and more than three hundred recordings. He combined singing and acting in several musicals and was best known for his rendition of "Ol' Man River" in *Show Boat* (London, 1928; New York, 1932; Los Angeles, 1940). Robeson also appeared in eleven motion pictures, including film versions of *The Emperor Jones* (1933) and *Show Boat* (1936) and Hollywood extravaganzas such as *King Solomon's Mines* (1937).

Robeson chafed at the stereotyping and racial slights suffered by blacks in the movie industry and demanded positive leading roles; he was most proud of his work in *Song of Freedom* (1936) and *The Proud Valley* (1940). Robeson's legacy, as actor/director SIDNEY POITIER noted, was profound: "Before him, no black man or woman had been portrayed in American movies as anything but a racist stereotype" (quoted in *Current Biography* [1976], 345–46).

Robeson's political ideas took shape after George Bernard Shaw introduced him to socialism in 1928. To escape American racism, he lived during most of the 1930s in Europe, returning to the United States only for movie and concert appearances. Impressed by the absence of racial and class discrimination in the Soviet Union during a concert tour in 1934, Robeson subsequently spent extended periods in Moscow, learned Russian, and enrolled his son in Soviet schools. He became politically active in opposing fascism, imperialism, and racism. He gave benefit performances in England for refugees from fascist countries, associated with British left-wing political groups, became acquainted with key figures in the West African Political Union, including Jomo Kenyatta and Kwame Nkrumah, and in 1938 traveled to Spain to support the republican troops engaged in the civil war against Francisco Franco's fascists.

When forced by the outbreak of World War II to return to the United States in 1939, Robeson was as well known as a critic of American racism and champion of the Soviet Union as an entertainer. He protested the segregation of organized baseball, appeared frequently at union and labor meetings, delivered antiracist lectures during concerts, joined the Pan-Africanist Council on African Affairs, and quit Hollywood because "the industry is not prepared to permit me to portray the life or express the living interests, hopes, and aspirations of the struggling people from whom I come." Robeson's political activism drew criticism but did not hurt his career, primarily because of the U.S.-Soviet military alliance. Indeed, he enjoyed his greatest hour as a performer in October 1943 when he became the first black actor to play Othello in the United States. Following a then record-setting 296 performances for a Shakespearean drama on Broadway, the company undertook a nationwide tour and Robeson received the Donaldson Award as the best actor of the year. In 1945 the National Association for the Advancement of Colored People (NAACP) awarded him the prestigious Spingarn Medal.

However, when Robeson continued to use the Soviet Union as a hammer to pound against racism in the United States, he suffered the fate of other political leftists during the anti-Communist hysteria of the cold war. In 1946 he denied under oath to a California State Legislative committee that he was a member of the Communist Party but thereafter refused as a matter of conscience and constitutional right to comment on his political beliefs or affiliation. Instead, he continued to speak out against American racism and to praise the Soviet "experiment in socialism," associated openly with Marxist organizations, and, as a founder and chairman of the Progressive Party, campaigned for Henry Wallace in the 1948 presidential election. While addressing the World Peace Congress in Paris in 1949, he said: "It is unthinkable that American Negroes could go to war on behalf of those who have oppressed us for generations against a country [the Soviet Union] which in one generation has raised our people to the full dignity of mankind." He was immediately denounced by the black and white press, repudiated by most black civil rights organizations, and attacked by government agencies and congressional committees. The U.S. House of Representatives Committee on Un-American Activities labeled him a "Communist" and a "Communist sympathizer" and enlisted JACKIE ROBINSON, who in 1947 had integrated organized baseball, to "give the lie" to Robeson's statement. He was hounded by the Federal Bureau of Investigation, and in 1950 the State Department took away his passport, refusing to issue a new one until he signed a non-Communist oath and pledged not to give political speeches abroad. He refused, and his persistent use of the Fifth Amendment during House and Senate hearings and the Soviet Union's awarding him the International Stalin Peace Prize in 1952 only exacerbated the public's perception of him as a subversive. Outraged

Rutgers alumni demanded that his name be excised from the school's athletic records and that the honorary master of arts degree awarded to him in 1930 be rescinded. He was blacklisted as an entertainer, and his recordings were removed from stores. His income fell from over $100,000 in 1947 to $6,000 in 1952. Unable to travel abroad to earn money, Robeson was forced to sell his estate, The Beeches, in Enfield, Connecticut.

By the late 1950s the burgeoning civil rights movement along with the lessening of cold war paranoia and the demise of McCarthyism led to a rehabilitation of Robeson's reputation, particularly among African Americans. Critical was Here I Stand (1958), a brief autobiography as manifesto in which Robeson reaffirmed his admiration for the Soviet Union and in which he stated, "I am not and never have been involved in any international conspiracy." He also declared his "belief in the principles of scientific Socialism" as the basis for a society "economically, socially, culturally, and ethically superior to a system based upon production for private profit." Although essentially a recitation of the stands he had taken all along, as the first sentence of the foreword—"I am a Negro"—made clear, the book was primarily a declaration of allegiance to the black community. Here Robeson presaged the Black Power politics of the 1960s by rejecting gradualism in civil rights, insisting that "the Negro people's movement must be led by Negroes," and advocating change through the "mass action" of "aroused and militant" black masses. He performed several concerts, recorded an album, and after being reissued a passport in 1958 (following a Supreme Court decision in a related case that confirmed his contention that the right to travel was independent of political views), left for Europe to revitalize his career.

But fifteen years of persistent harassment and political attacks had taken its toll, destroying not only his career but also his health and, ultimately, his sanity. Despite a tumultuous welcome, his sojourn in the Soviet Union was bleak. He was frequently hospitalized for exhaustion and a circulatory ailment as well as emotional instability. He attempted suicide; excessive drug and electric shock therapy likely

caused permanent brain damage. He returned to the United States in 1963 and went into seclusion. His wife's death in 1965 ended their long marriage of convenience. Robeson's numerous infidelities had led to several separations, but Essie, who obtained a PhD in Anthropology and wrote African Journey (1945), resignedly managed his career in exchange for economic and social status. Robeson then moved to Philadelphia, where he lived with a sister. Virtually an invalid and suffering from acute depression, he refused interviews and was seen only by family and close friends. Too ill to attend the "75th Birthday Salute to Paul Robeson" staged at Carnegie Hall in April 1973 by leaders in the entertainment and civil rights fields, he sent a recorded message: "I want you to know that I am still the same Paul, dedicated as ever to the worldwide cause of humanity for freedom, peace and brotherhood." Three years later he died in Philadelphia.

Paul Robeson is an American tragedy. He was an enormously talented black man whose imposing personality and uncompromising political ideals were more than a racist and anti-communist United States could appreciate or tolerate. One of the major performing artists of the twentieth century, his achievements as a stage actor, movie star, and singer are individually outstanding but collectively astounding. He was easily the most influential black entertainer of his day. Because he spent so much time abroad, Robeson never established close political associations in black America and thus served the African American community more as a symbol of black consciousness and pride than as a spokesperson. A victim of character assassination during the cold war, Robeson—unlike many black (and white) entertainers who maintained silence to protect or advance their careers—courageously combined art and politics. If he was politically naive and oblivious to the realities of Stalinist Russia, he astutely connected American racism and the international oppression of colored peoples. And Robeson proved to be ahead of his time in rejecting both the black nationalism of separation and repatriation as well as the assimilationism of the NAACP in favor of a cultural pluralism in which ethnic integrity was maintained amid international solidarity.

For all his achievements, Robeson's pro-Soviet stance continues to preclude just recognition. He remains the only two-time All-American not in the College Football Hall of Fame.

FURTHER READING

By far the largest and most important collection of manuscript materials pertaining to Paul Robeson's life and career is the Robeson Family Archives, featuring the writings of his wife, in the Moorland-Spingarn Research Center, Howard University, Washington, D.C.

Robeson, Paul. *Here I Stand* (1958).

Davis, Lenwood G., comp. *A Paul Robeson Research Guide: A Selected Annotated Bibliography* (1982).

Duberman, Martin Bauml. *Paul Robeson* (1988).

Foner, Philip S., ed. *Paul Robeson Speaks: Writings, Speeches, Interviews, 1918–1974* (1978).

Gilliam, Dorothy Butler. *Paul Robeson: All-American* (1976).

Robeson, Eslanda Cardozo. *Paul Robeson, Negro* (1930).

Robeson, Paul, Jr. *The Undiscovered Paul Robeson: An Artist's Journey, 1898–1939* (2001).

Seton, Marie. *Paul Robeson* (1958).

Obituaries: *New York Times*, 24 Jan. 1976; *Amsterdam News* (New York City), 31 Jan. 1976.

—LARRY R. GERLACH

ROBINSON, BILL

(25 May 1878–25 Nov. 1949), tap dancer, known as "Bojangles," was born Luther Robinson in Richmond, Virginia, the son of Maxwell Robinson, a machinist, and Maria (maiden name unknown), a choir director. After both parents died in an accident around 1885, Luther and his brother William lived with their grandmother, Bedilia Robinson, a former slave who sought salvation through faith and disavowed dancing of any kind in her house. Too old and infirm to care for the boys, she entrusted them to a local judge, John Crutchfield.

Robinson appropriated his brother's name, calling himself Bill, and took to the streets to earn nickels and dimes by dancing and scat-singing. In Richmond, he got the nickname "Bojangles," from "jangler," meaning contentious, and he

invented the famous phrase "everything's copasetic," meaning everything's tip-top or first-rate. Robinson ran away to Washington, D.C., picking up odd jobs dancing in beer gardens around town. He got his first professional break in 1892 as a pickaninny in the chorus line of Whallen and Martel's *South Before the War*, a touring show that featured Mayme Remington, a former French burlesque dancer who became a top headliner in the 1890s. Shortly after arriving in New York in 1900, Robinson challenged *In Old Kentucky* star dancer Harry Swinton to a Friday night buck-and-wing dance contest and won. With a gold medal and the valuable publicity attendant on winning, he was quickly targeted as the man to challenge.

Robinson worked wherever and whenever he could, and with a variety of partners, including Theodore Miller, Lula Brown, and Johnny Juniper. Bound by the "two-colored" rule in vaudeville, which restricted blacks to performing in pairs, he teamed with George W. Cooper from 1902 to 1914. They played the classiest tours in white vaudeville, the Keith and Orpheum circuits, without the blackface makeup expected of African American performers at the time. They also toured London with great success. Robinson married Lena Chase in 1907, although touring and professional activities kept

them apart and forced them to separate around 1915 and divorce in 1922.

Robinson was a staunch professional, adamant about punctuality and a perfectionist with his routines. He was also known to anger quickly, gamble, and carry a gold-plated revolver. After an assault charge in 1908 that split up his act with Cooper, Robinson decided to launch his solo career and became one of the few blacks to perform as a soloist on the Keith circuit. He was a headliner at New York's Palace Theatre, the undisputed crown jewel of vaudeville theaters. At one point in his career, he made $6,500 a week in vaudeville and was billed as the "World's Greatest Tap Dancer." Being billed as a champion dancer meant winning dance competitions of the toughest kind to stay on top. Contests were audited by a panel of judges who sat under the stage, in the wings, and in the house, judging the dancer on the tempo and execution of steps. Robinson was challenged to dozens of contests and won, and according to tap dance lore competed against dancers such as James Barton, Will Mahoney, Jack Donahue, Fred Astaire, and Ray Bolger. Robinson's stair dance, first performed in 1918, was distinguished by its showmanship and sound, each step emitting a different pitch and rhythm. Onstage his open face, twinkling eyes, and infectious smile were

Considered by many the greatest tap dancer of all time, Bill "Bojangles" Robinson (left) appears with LENA HORNE and CAB CALLOWAY in a 1943 publicity still from the Hollywood movie Stormy Weather. *© Bettmann/CORBIS*

irresistible, as was his tapping, which was delicate and clear. Buck or time steps were inserted with skating steps or crossover steps on the balls of the feet that looked like a jig, all while he chatted and joked with the audience. Robinson danced in split clog shoes, ordinary shoes with a wooden half-sole and raised wooden heel. The wooden sole was attached from the toe to the ball of the foot and left loose, which allowed for greater flexibility and tonality.

In 1922, Robinson married Fannie Clay, who became his business manager, secretary, and partner in efforts to fight the barriers of racial prejudice. He was a founding member of the Negro Actors Guild of America. Hailed as the "Dark Cloud of Joy" on the Orpheum circuit, Robinson performed in vaudeville from 1914 to 1927 without a single season's layoff. Yet Broadway fame did not come until he was fifty years old, with the all-black revue *Blackbirds of 1928*, in which he sang and danced "Doin' the New Low Down." Success was instantaneous and he was saluted as the greatest of all dancers by at least seven New York newspapers. Broadway shows that followed included *Brown Buddies* (1930), *Blackbirds of 1933*, *All in Fun* (1940), and *Memphis Bound* (1945). The opening of *The Hot Mikado* (1939) marked Robinson's sixty-first birthday and he celebrated by dancing down Broadway, from 61st Street to the Broadhurst Theatre at 44th Street.

In the 1930s Robinson also performed in Hollywood films, a venue that had hitherto restricted African American performers. His first film, *Dixiana* (1930), had a predominantly white cast, but *Harlem Is Heaven* (1933) was one of the first all-black films ever made. Other films include *Hooray for Love* (1935), *In Old Kentucky* (1935), *The Big Broadcast of 1937* (1935), *One Mile from Heaven* (1937), *By an Old Southern River* (1941), and *Let's Shuffle* (1941). The well-known all-black film *Stormy Weather* (1943) featured Robinson, LENA HORNE, CAB CALLOWAY, and KATHERINE DUNHAM and her dance troupe. Robinson and Shirley Temple teamed up in *The Little Colonel* (1935), *The Littlest Rebel* (1935), *Just Around the Corner* (1938), and *Rebecca of Sunnybrook Farm* (1938), in which he taught the child superstar to tap dance.

In 1936, Robinson opened the downtown Cotton Club in New York (south of the more famous uptown Harlem Cotton Club) and introduced a new dance, the "Suzi-Q"; he was later featured in several Cotton Club shows. Claiming to have taught tap dancing to Eleanor Powell, FLORENCE MILLS, Fayard and Harold Nicholas, and Astaire, Robinson profoundly influenced the next generation of dancers at the Hoofers Club in Harlem, where he also gambled and shot pool. Throughout his lifetime, he was a member of many clubs and civic organizations and an honorary member of police departments in cities across the United States. Robinson was named "Mayor of Harlem" in 1933. His participation in benefits is legendary and it is estimated that he gave away well over one million dollars in loans and charities. During his long career, he never refused to play a benefit, regardless of race, creed, or color of those who were to profit by his performance. In 1943 he divorced Fannie Clay and married the young dancer Elaine Plaines.

"To his own people," Marshall Stearns wrote in *Jazz Dance*, "Robinson became a modern John Henry, who instead of driving steel, laid down iron taps." Although he was uneducated, Robinson was accepted in high places that were previously beyond the reach of most African Americans. He commanded the respect due to a gifted artist and became the most famous tap dancer of the twentieth century. Robinson's exacting yet light footwork was said to have brought tap "up on its toes" from an earlier flat-footed shuffling style. Although he invented few new steps, he presented those he used with technical ease and a sparkling personality, turning relatively simple tap dancing into an exciting art.

When Robinson died in New York City, newspapers claimed that almost 100,000 people witnessed the passing of the funeral procession, a testament to the esteem in which he was held by members of his community. The founding of the Copasetics, a fraternity of male tap dancers formed the year Robinson died, ensured that his excellence would not be forgotten.

FURTHER READING

Fletcher, Tom. *One Hundred Years of the Negro in Show Business* (1954).
Frank, Rusty. *Tap! The Greatest Tap Dance Stars and their Stories, 1900–1955* (1990).
Haskins, Jim, and N. R. Mitgang. *Mr. Bojangles: The Biography of Bill Robinson* (1999).
Stearns, Marshall, and Jean Stearns. *Jazz Dance: The Story of American Vernacular Dance* (1968).

—CONSTANCE VALIS HILL

 ROBINSON, EDDIE (13 Feb. 1919–), college football coach, was born Edward Gay Robinson in Jackson, Louisiana, the son of Frank Robinson, then a sharecropper, and Lydia Stewart, a domestic worker. His parents separated when he was six years old and he lived in a two-room house with his grandparents. Both parents and grandparents were hard-working, industrious people and strict disciplinarians. Looking to break the cycle of sharecropping, Frank Robinson moved in 1925 to Baton Rouge, Louisiana, to work for Standard Oil and later separated from Lydia Stewart and married Ann Floyd, a schoolteacher. Young Eddie marveled at the respect and special status that Floyd enjoyed in the community, reflecting the high esteem that African Americans conferred on education and teachers.

While Eddie was attending Scott Street Elementary School in Baton Rouge, one of his teachers invited football players dressed in full uniform to class for a project. Eddie was quite taken with the coach, Julius Kraft, and was greatly impressed by the respect his players gave him. Although he was only ten years old, he knew then that he wanted to be a football coach. Football became an obsession for him. Eddie was the first in his family to finish elementary school, and he later graduated from McKinley High School. Although he initially wanted to attend Southern University in Baton Rouge, he was not offered a scholarship, so he chose to attend Leland College in nearby Baker, Louisiana.

Robinson was raised in a segregated community with little contact with whites. He worked at several jobs to make ends meet, including one at an icehouse, where he loaded fifty-pound blocks. He also worked at a fish market after school and during the summers, making only four dollars per week. Upon graduation from Leland College, he married Doris Mott, his childhood sweetheart, in June 1941. They had two children, Lillian Rose and Eddie Jr. That same year Robinson was hired to coach football at the Louisiana Negro Normal and Industrial Institute, a two-year college with fewer than one hundred male students. The school, later renamed Grambling State University, offered Robinson a starting salary of $63.75 a month.

Robinson coached at Grambling State University for fifty-six years (1941–1997). His tenure lasted through eleven presidents and four major American wars, and he retired as the winningest coach in the history of college football, with a record of 408 wins, 165 losses, and 15 ties. That mark bettered the winning records of such coaching greats as Amos Alonzo Stagg, Pop Warner, and even Alabama's legendary Paul "Bear" Bryant. During Robinson's tenure, the Grambling Tigers won eight national black college titles and seventeen conference championships. In 1942, his second season, Robinson fielded a team that went undefeated and was not scored against, a feat that has been repeated only once in the history of college football.

Under Robinson's leadership, Grambling also became one of professional football's most productive training grounds. All told, he sent more than two hundred Grambling players to the National Football League, including the Pro Football Hall of Fame inductees Willie Davis, Junius "Buck" Buchanan, and Willie Brown. The first African American drafted (in 1949) from a historically black college, Tank Younger, was from Grambling, while the Tiger defensive standout Junius "Buck" Buchanan was the first African American to be selected in the first round of the NFL's draft (1963). Another Grambling favorite, James Harris, signed for the Los Angeles Rams, and in 1969 became the first black quarterback to start an NFL play-off game in 1969. Perhaps the most successful of Eddie Robinson's protégés, however, was Doug Williams, who starred for Grambling in the late 1970s and in 1988 became the first African American quarterback to start in a Super

Bowl. Williams, who led the Washington Redskins to victory, was selected the Most Valuable Player of Super Bowl XXII.

Although desegregation sapped much of the talent from historically black colleges like Grambling, Robinson continued to recruit talented student-athletes. Recognizing that historically white schools were now competing for the best and brightest black student-athletes, Robinson formed a strategy to ensure that Grambling remained attractive to African American athletes. He created and promoted a series of national games for Grambling against other Historically Black Colleges and Universities (HBCU's) that drew network coverage and large audiences. The most significant of them, the annual Bayou Classic between Grambling and Southern, attracts an annual attendance of over sixty-five thousand spectators. Following the assassination of MARTIN LUTHER KING JR. in 1968, Robinson also established the Urban League Classic at New York's Yankee Stadium. The game was later renamed the Whitney Young Classic, after the death of the National Urban League's former executive director WHITNEY YOUNG. The success of the first of these "classics" led to three other national games that embodied Robinson's philosophy of linking sport and the civil rights movement.

Coach Eddie Robinson has won more games than any coach in the history of college football. His fifty-six-year tenure at the same institution may never be repeated, and he has observed the social transformation of America through sports for over six decades. Penn State's coach, Joe Paterno, summed up the Grambling legend's legacy: "Nobody has ever done or will do what Eddie Robinson has done for this game. Our profession will never be able to repay Eddie Robinson for what he has done for the country and the profession of football" (Lapchick).

FURTHER READING

Davis, O. K. *Grambling's Gridiron Glory* (1985).
Lapchick, Richard E. *Never Before, Never Again: The Autobiography of Eddie Robinson* (1999).
Lee, Aaron. *Quotable Eddie Robinson: 408 Memorable Quotes about Football, Life and Success by and about College Football's All-Time Winningest Coach* (2003).

Wash, A., and P. Webb, eds. *Reflections of a Legend: Coach Eddie G. Robinson* (1997)
—FRITZ G. POLITE

 ROBINSON, JACKIE
(31 Jan. 1919–24 Oct. 1972), baseball player, was born Jack Roosevelt Robinson in Cairo, Georgia, the son of Jerry Robinson, a farmworker and sharecropper, and Mallie McGriff, a domestic worker. Six months after Robinson's birth, his father deserted the family. Faced with severe financial difficulties, Robinson's mother moved her family to Pasadena, California, in pursuit of a better life. The Robinsons settled in a white Pasadena neighborhood—where they received a chilly reception—and Robinson's mother supported her family in modest fashion as a domestic worker.

Robinson demonstrated his athletic prowess from an early age. After graduating from high school in Pasadena in 1937 as one of the city's most celebrated athletes, he entered Pasadena Junior College. He established himself as an exceptional multi-sport athlete at Pasadena and won junior college All-American honors in football. By the time of his graduation from Pasadena in 1939, he was one of the most widely recruited athletes on the West Coast. Robinson eventually decided to enter the University of California at Los Angeles (UCLA), which he attended from 1939 to 1941. Playing four sports at UCLA, Robinson continued to display extraordinary athletic ability, causing one sportswriter to label him "the Jim Thorpe of his race" (Tygiel, 60). He twice led the Southern Division of the Pacific Coast Conference in basketball scoring, averaged 11 yards per carry as an All-American running back during his junior year on the football team, and won the National Collegiate Athletic Association (NCAA) broad jump championship in track and field. Ironically, Robinson's weakest performance came in baseball; he played only one season at UCLA and had minimal success, batting only .097. Robinson was not the only athlete in his family; his older brother Mack finished second to JESSE OWENS in the 200-meter sprint at the 1936 Berlin Olympics.

Jackie Robinson at bat for the Brooklyn Dodgers in 1954, seven years after he broke the color line in major league baseball for the first time since 1885. Library of Congress

Robinson dropped out of college during his senior year at UCLA to help support his family. After brief stints as an assistant athletic director at a National Youth Administration camp in California and as a player with two semiprofessional football teams—the Los Angeles Bulldogs and the Honolulu Bears—Robinson was drafted into the U.S. Army in the spring of 1942.

The U.S. Army of the 1940s was a thoroughly segregated institution. Although initially denied entry into the army's Officers Candidate School because of his race, Robinson, with the assistance of boxer JOE LOUIS, successfully challenged his exclusion and was eventually commissioned a second lieutenant. Robinson spent two years in the service at army bases in Kansas, Texas, and Kentucky. During this time Robinson confronted the army's discriminatory racial practices; on one occasion he faced court-martial charges for insubordination arising from an incident in which he refused to move to the back of a segregated military bus in Texas. A military jury acquitted Robinson, and

shortly thereafter, in November 1944, he received his honorable discharge from the army.

Following his discharge, Robinson—who continued to enjoy a reputation as an extraordinarily gifted athlete—spent the spring and summer of 1945 playing shortstop with the Kansas City Monarchs in the Negro Leagues. Robinson proved to be a highly effective player, batting about .345 for the year. At this time major league baseball did not permit black players to play on either minor league or major league teams, pursuant to an unwritten agreement among the owners that dated back to the nineteenth century. Pressure to integrate baseball, however, had steadily increased. Many critics complained of the hypocrisy of requiring black men to fight and die in a war against European racism but denying them the opportunity to play "the national pastime." During the early 1940s a few major league teams offered tryouts to black players—Robinson had received a tryout with the Boston Red Sox in 1945—but no team actually signed a black player.

In the meantime, however, Branch Rickey, president of the Brooklyn Dodgers baseball team, had secretly decided to use African Americans on his team. Rickey was convinced of the ability of black ballplayers, their potential gate attraction, and the injustice of their exclusion from major league baseball. Using the ruse that he wanted to develop a new league for black players, Rickey deployed his scouts to scour the Negro Leagues and the Caribbean for the most talented black ballplayers during the spring and summer of 1945. In particular Rickey sought one player who would break the color line and establish a path for several others to follow; he eventually settled on Robinson. Although Robinson was not the best black baseball player, his college education, experience competing in interracial settings at UCLA, and competitive fire attracted Rickey. In August 1945 Rickey offered Robinson a chance to play in the Dodgers organization but cautioned him that he would experience tremendous pressure and abuse. Rickey extracted from Robinson a promise not to respond to the abuse for his first three years.

Robinson spent the 1946 baseball season with the top Dodgers minor league club located in Montreal. After leading the Montreal Royals to the International League championship and winning the league batting championship with a .349 average, he joined the Dodgers the following spring. Several of the Dodgers players objected to Robinson's presence and circulated a petition in which they threatened not to play with him. Rickey thwarted the boycott efforts by making clear that such players would be traded or released if they refused to play.

Robinson opened the 1947 season as the Dodgers' starting first baseman, thereby breaking the long-standing ban on black players in the major leagues. During his first year he was subjected to extraordinary verbal and physical abuse from opposing teams and spectators. Pitchers threw the ball at his head, opposing base runners cut him with their spikes, and disgruntled fans sent death threats that triggered an FBI investigation on at least one occasion. Although Robinson possessed a fiery temper and enormous pride, he honored his agreement with Rickey not to retaliate to the constant stream of abuse. At the same time he suffered the indignities of substandard segregated accommodations while traveling with the Dodgers.

Robinson's aggressive style of play won games for the Dodgers, earning him the loyalty of his teammates and the Brooklyn fans. Despite the enormous pressure that year, he led the Dodgers to their first National League championship in six years and a berth in the World Series. Robinson, who led the league in stolen bases and batted .297, was named rookie of the year. Overnight, he captured the hearts of black America. In time he became one of the biggest gate attractions in baseball since Babe Ruth, bringing thousands of African American spectators to major league games. Five major league teams set new attendance records in 1947. By the end of the season, two other major league teams—the Cleveland Indians and the St. Louis Browns—had added black players to their rosters for brief appearances. By the early 1950s most other major league teams had hired black ballplayers.

In the spring of 1949, having fulfilled his three-year pledge of silence, Robinson began to speak his mind and angrily confronted opposing players who taunted him. He also enjoyed his finest year, leading the Dodgers to another National League pennant and capturing the league batting championship, with a .342 mark, and the most valuable player award. Off the field, Robinson received considerable attention for his testimony in July 1949 before the House Committee on Un-American Activities in opposition to PAUL ROBESON's statement that African Americans would not fight in a war against the Soviet Union. During the next few years Robinson, unlike many other black ballplayers, became outspoken in his criticism of segregation both inside and outside of baseball.

Robinson ultimately played ten years for the Dodgers, primarily as a second baseman. During this time his team won six National League pennants and the 1955 World Series. Robinson possessed an array of skills, but he was known particularly as an aggressive and daring base runner, stealing home nineteen times in his career and five times in one season. In one of the more memorable moments in World Series history, Robinson stole home against the New York Yankees in the first game of the 1955 series. Robinson's baserunning exploits helped to revolutionize the game and to pave the way for a new generation of successful base stealers, particularly Maury Wills and Lou Brock. Robinson batted .311 for his career and in 1962 became the first black player to win election to the National Baseball Hall of Fame. On 15 April 1997, the fiftieth anniversary of Robinson's first major league game, Major League Baseball, in an unprecedented action, retired Robinson's number 42 in perpetuity.

After the 1956 season, the Dodgers traded Robinson to the New York Giants, their crosstown rivals. Robinson declined to accept the trade and instead announced his retirement from baseball. Thereafter, Robinson worked for seven years as a vice president of the Chock Full O'Nuts food company, handling personnel matters. An important advocate of black-owned businesses in America, Robinson helped establish several of them, including the Freedom National Bank in Harlem. He also used his celebrity status as a spokesman for civil rights issues for the remainder of his life. Robinson served as an active and highly successful fund-raiser for the National Association for the Advancement of Colored People and conducted frequent fund-raising events of his own to support civil rights causes and organizations. He wrote a regular newspaper column throughout the 1960s in which he criticized the persistence of racial injustice in American society, including the refusal of baseball owners to employ blacks in management. Shortly before his death, Robinson wrote in his autobiography *I Never Had It Made* that he remained "a black man in a white world." Although a supporter of Richard Nixon in the 1960 presidential campaign, Robinson eventually became involved with the liberal wing of the Republican Party, primarily as a close adviser of New York governor Nelson Rockefeller.

Robinson had married Rachel Isum in 1946, and the couple had three children. Robinson suffered from diabetes and heart disease in his later years and died of a heart attack in Stamford, Connecticut.

Probably no other athlete has had a greater sociological impact on American sport than did Robinson. His success on the baseball field opened the door to black baseball players and thereby transformed the game. He also helped to facilitate the acceptance of black athletes in other professional sports, particularly basketball and football. His influence spread beyond the realm of sport, as he emerged in the late 1940s and 1950s as an important national symbol of the virtue of racial integration in all aspects of American life.

FURTHER READING

The National Baseball Library and Archive in Cooperstown, N.Y., contains extensive material on Robinson. The Arthur Mann and Branch Rickey papers, both located in the Library of Congress, also contain documentary material on Robinson.

Robinson, Jackie. *Baseball Has Done It* (1964).
——, with Alfred Duckett. *I Never Had It Made* (1972).
——, with Wendell Smith. *Jackie Robinson: My Own Story* (1948).
——, with CARL ROWAN. *Wait Till Next Year* (1960).

Falkner, David. *Great Time Coming: The Life of Jackie Robinson, from Baseball to Birmingham* (1995).
Frommer, Harvey. *Rickey and Robinson: The Men Who Broke Baseball's Color Barrier* (1982).
Robinson, Rachel. *Jackie Robinson: An Intimate Portrait* (1996).
Tygiel, Jules. *Baseball's Great Experiment: Jackie Robinson and His Legacy* (1983).

Obituary: *New York Times*, 25 Oct. 1972.
—DAVISON M. DOUGLAS

 ROBINSON, JAMES HERMAN (24 Jan. 1907– 6 Nov. 1972), minister and founder of Operation Crossroads Africa, was born in Knoxville, Tennessee, one of six children of Henry John Robinson, a slaughterhouse laborer, and Willie Bell Banks, a washerwoman. Robinson grew up in abject poverty in a section of town called the Bottoms, where poor blacks and whites lived. Because of his father's frequent periods of unemployment and his mother's failing health, the Robinson family could not escape the reality of poverty and segregation in the Jim Crow South. Those already at the bottom of the economic pile were also denied access to the educational opportunities that might otherwise have helped them to escape poverty. Given the dire circumstances in which the family lived,

James had a difficult time accepting the strong religious convictions of his father, who was a member of a sanctified church and spent much of his free time there. As his family's economic conditions remained unchanged, James began to view religion as a waste of time, and questioned his father's and his own faith in God.

In 1917 the Robinson family moved to Cleveland, Ohio, to escape poverty and segregation, but the greater opportunities they had anticipated remained elusive. Robinson attended an integrated school for the first time and found the experience unsettling because of the discrimination he faced from white teachers and students. His father did find work, in another slaughterhouse, but the family continued to live in poverty and in overcrowded housing. Because of these economic hardships, Robinson was not encouraged to remain in school. After his mother died, he moved to Youngstown, Ohio, to live with his grandparents, but was forced to return to Cleveland after the death of his grandmother. Henry Robinson, who had since remarried, had little interest in furthering his son's desire to get an education. James, nevertheless, found various jobs to support himself and, without his father's knowledge, attended Fairmont Junior High School and East Technical High School.

Even as a child, Robinson understood that racism was nefarious and contradictory to Christian teaching. His thoughts and feelings on this issue intensified after he moved north to the "Promised Land," because, although there were no "white" and "colored" signs to dictate where and how one lived, invisible racial boundaries continued to restrict his mobility and opportunities. Robinson's early life had been marked by many negative experiences, but there were also positive ones, most notably at the Cedar Branch Hi-Y Club, a high school chapter of the YMCA. Before coming to Hi-Y, Robinson was discouraged and distraught, but his experiences at the club expanded his worldview through interaction with middle- and upper-middle-class African Americans. He joined the debate club and through its outings he learned more of himself, the state of race relations, and the role and importance of religion. Ernest Escoe, the debate club's adviser, and Escoe's wife, Sally, supported Robinson and encouraged him to attend St. James African Methodist Church. It was there that he found his calling in life: "to be a servant of the people" (*Road without Turning*, 132). Robinson graduated from East Technical High School in 1929 at the age of twenty-two, but money problems continued to hinder him. He would have been homeless if it were not for Percy and Daisy Kelley. Percy, a waiter in a coffee shop, befriended Robinson, and the Kelleys allowed him to share their home.

Robinson continued his education at Western Reserve University in Cleveland, but dropped out due to financial problems. He then approached the minister of Mount Zion Congregational Church with a plan for a sports program to keep young men out of trouble; after Robinson had established several more clubs, a Presbyterian minister noticed his hard work and informed him that the church would fund his education. He enrolled at Lincoln University in Pennsylvania, but because the church did not provide enough funding to support him completely, Robinson spent his summers serving as pastor of a church in Beardon, Tennessee, near Knoxville. He described the social and economic conditions in Beardon as worse than the Bottoms, and used the pulpit to speak out against racial injustice and for civil rights. Robinson's experiences at Beardon, along with those at Lincoln, further expanded his understanding of race relations and the plight of the less fortunate. Because he was older than most of his classmates, Robinson found the practice of freshmen and fraternity hazing immature and self-defeating. Even more perplexing to him was the fact that, although Lincoln was a historically black college, most of the faculty and administration were white. Robinson spoke out against this glaring inequality throughout his time at Lincoln, where he graduated in 1935 at the top of his class.

After graduating from Lincoln, Robinson attended New York City's Union Theological Seminary (1935–1938), where he was president of his senior class, and director of the Morningside Community Center (1938–1961). In spite of those successes, his time at Union Seminary was troubled. He tried to uphold Christian values while enduring discrimination from his white classmates. But he also found it difficult to befriend other African American students, as he found them aloof and indifferent to the racism and discrimination they faced. Robinson's seminary experiences encouraged him to propose greater multiracial cooperation within the ministry.

The year 1938 proved to be a turning point in Robinson's life: he graduated from Union, was ordained as a minister, became head of Church of the Master Presbyterian Church in Harlem, and married Helen Brodie. They had no children. He also worked as a youth director for the NAACP from 1938 to 1940.

For the rest of his career and life, Robinson saw his mission as being a servant of the people. He believed that his ministry and church could improve communities by providing people with the economic and social resources that they need to empower themselves. Believing that interracial cooperation was central to this goal, he recruited mainly white students from colleges in New York City to work on projects near his church in Harlem. These projects were very successful, and in 1948 land was donated in New Hampshire to establish Camp Rabbit Hollow, a rural setting in which black children from Harlem and white college students could interact and work together, fostering mutual understanding, cooperation, and respect.

The success of these interracial programs, and his experiences touring Africa, Asia, and Europe in the 1950s, encouraged Robinson to found Operation Crossroads Africa in 1958. Believing that "men will lose consciousness of their differences and divisions when they interest themselves in the common problems of one another" (*Jet* obituary, 48), Robinson encouraged American students and other volunteers to work on community development projects in Africa. In its first twenty years, over 5,000 American volunteers of all races traveled to Africa and the Caribbean to help build and repair housing, roads, health clinics, and schools. Civil rights activists figure prominently among Operation Crossroads alumni, including ELEANOR HOLMES NORTON, later chair of the EEOC and a U.S. congresswoman, who helped build a school in Gabon in the early 1960s. That experience, Norton recalled in 1977, "made me think

ROBINSON,JO ANN

about myself as a black person and as an American more profoundly than at any point since" (Rule, 58).

Robinson continued to focus on African affairs throughout the 1960s. His development efforts gained worldwide admiration and spurred other transnational volunteer programs, including Canadian Crossroads International and the U.S. Peace Corps, which John F. Kennedy founded in 1961. President Kennedy recognized his debt to Robinson by calling Operation Crossroads Africa "the progenitor of the Peace Corps" (Rule, 58). During the 1950s Robinson published four books, *Tomorrow Is Today* (1954), *Adventurous Preaching, Love of This Land,* and *Christianity and Revolution in Africa* (all 1956). Following his divorce from Helen Brodie in 1954, he married Gertrude Cotter in 1958. The couple had no children. In 1962, he resigned from Church of the Master to be a minister-at-large and to direct Operation Crossroads Africa on a full-time basis. That same year, he published *Africa at the Crossroads.*

James Robinson died in New York City in 1972, having dedicated his life to fostering a better understanding among people throughout the world. His greatest achievement lay in forging links between Africans and African Americans and between Africa and the United States. "The darkest thing about Africa," Robinson once remarked, "is America's ignorance of it" (Rule, 58). Since 1958 Operation Crossroads Africa has worked diligently to remove that veil of ignorance.

FURTHER READING

James Robinson's papers are housed in the Amistad Research Center at Tulane University in New Orleans.

Robinson, James Herman. *Road without Turning: The Story of Reverend James H. Robinson* (1950).
———. *Tomorrow Is Today* (1954).
Lee, Amy. *Throbbing Drums: The Story of James H. Robinson* (1968).
Plimpton, Ruth. *Operation Crossroads Africa* (1962).
Rule, Sheila. "A Peace Corps Precursor Observes 20th Anniversary of its Founding." *New York Times,* 4 Dec. 1977, 58.

Obituary: *Jet,* 30 Nov. 1972.
—CASSANDRA VENEY

ROBINSON, JO ANN (17 Apr. 1912–29 Aug. 1992), civil rights activist, was born Jo Ann Gibson on a farm in Crawford County, Georgia, the youngest of twelve children of Owen B. Gibson and Dollie Webb. After the death of her father in 1918, her mother struggled to operate the farm. In 1926, however, her mother sold out and moved the family to the nearby city of Macon, to live with a son who was a postman. Jo Ann attended high school in Macon, graduating in 1929 as the valedictorian of her class. She then began teaching in the Macon public schools, continuing to do so while also attending Fort Valley State College. She received a BS degree from Fort Valley in 1936. In 1943 she married Wilbur Robinson, a soldier in the U.S. Army, and in 1944 they had a child. But the child died in infancy, and in 1946 the Robinsons divorced. Robinson then resigned her position with the Macon school system and entered graduate school at Atlanta University, from which she received an MA in 1948. In the school year 1948–1949 she taught English at Mary Allen College in Crockett, Texas, and in the fall of 1949 she joined the faculty of Alabama State College for Negroes in Montgomery.

Almost as soon as she arrived in Montgomery, she became an active member of the Women's Political Council, which had been formed the preceding spring by female Alabama State College faculty as a black analogue of the all-white League of Women Voters. Robinson became the council's president in 1952 and registered to vote for the first time on 6 January 1953. As early as October 1952 the council had begun pressing the Montgomery bus company and the Montgomery City Commission to adopt the pattern of bus segregation in use in the Alabama city of Mobile, under which drivers could not unseat black passengers to make room for boarding whites. Robinson became the principal black spokesperson in meetings with city authorities during 1953 and 1954 about racial problems on the city buses. These meetings rectified one significant black complaint, that buses would stop at every corner in white neighborhoods but only at every other corner in black areas. But no progress was made on the problem of the unseating of black passengers.

On 21 May 1954, just after the U.S. Supreme Court's Brown v. Board of Education decision forbidding racial segregation in public schools, Robinson sent Mayor William A. Gayle a letter warning him that unless concessions on the bus-seating question were made, Montgomery's blacks might undertake a boycott of the busses. The arrest and conviction of a black high school student, Claudette Colvin, in March 1955 for failing to obey a driver's order to yield her seat, further exacerbated the tensions surrounding this issue. Thus, when the black attorney Fred D. Gray called Robinson on the evening of 1 December 1955 to tell her of the arrest of ROSA PARKS under exactly the same circumstances, Robinson was primed for action. Early the next morning she went to her office at Alabama State College and mimeographed a leaflet calling for a one-day boycott of the buses on the day Parks's trial was to be held, 5 December. She and her council associates spent the rest of the day distributing the leaflets throughout the black sections of the city. The result was that when Montgomery's black leaders met that evening at the Dexter Avenue Baptist Church, at the call of EDGAR D. NIXON, president of the local of the Pullman porters' union, to discuss the possibility of a boycott, they found themselves faced with a fait accompli because of Robinson's actions, and so they voted to support the boycott proposal.

The boycott on 5 December proved to be a complete success. When Parks was convicted and fined ten dollars and costs, black leaders at a meeting that afternoon decided to continue the boycott until the bus company adopted the Mobile pattern of segregation. They formed an organization to run the protest, the Montgomery Improvement Association (MIA), and chose Robinson's pastor, the Reverend MARTIN LUTHER KING JR., to head it. During the boycott, which lasted for more than a year, Robinson continued to play a crucial role. She was one of the black negotiators who met with a white mediation committee appointed by the mayor, and she insisted that the two racial delegations be equal in numbers. She was also a member of the Improvement Association's executive board and its strategy committee. In this role, she was a central figure in persuading these bodies in January 1956 to agree to file suit in federal court challenging the constitutionality of bus segregation, even though doing so meant abandoning the demand for the adoption of the Mobile pattern of seating. Both during and after the boycott, she edited the MIA's newsletter, which assisted in raising contributions for the organization from throughout the country.

She had promised the president of Alabama State College, H. Councill Trenholm, that she would keep secret her part in initiating the boycott, to protect the college from state legislative reprisal, and her contributions did not become publicly known until 1980, when historical investigation finally revealed them. Nevertheless, she found herself caught up in Governor John M. Patterson's furious attacks on the college when its students organized sit-ins at segregated Montgomery facilities in the spring of 1960, and she was compelled to resign from the faculty in May of that year. She taught at Grambling College in Louisiana during the academic year 1960–1961 and then became a public school teacher in Los Angeles, California. She taught in Los Angeles until her retirement in 1976. In 1987 the University of Tennessee Press published her memoir, *The Montgomery Bus Boycott and the Women Who Started It*.

FURTHER READING

Robinson, Jo Ann Gibson. *The Montgomery Bus Boycott and the Women Who Started It: The Memoir of Jo Ann Gibson Robinson* (1987).

King, Martin Luther, Jr. *Stride toward Freedom: The Montgomery Story* (1958).
Thornton, J. Mills, III. *Dividing Lines: Municipal Politics and the Struggle for Civil Rights in Montgomery, Birmingham, and Selma* (2002).

—J. MILLS THORNTON III

ROBINSON, JOHN C.

(26 Nov. 1903–27 Mar. 1954), aviator who promoted flight training for African Americans but gained his greatest fame as a pilot for Ethiopian emperor Haile Selassie, was born in Carabelle, Florida. His father's name is unknown; his mother, Celest Robinson, may have been born in Ethiopia. Raised by his mother and stepfather in Gulfport, Mississippi, Robinson graduated from Tuskegee Institute in Alabama in 1924. For the following six years, he was a truck driver in Gulfport. Then he moved to Chicago, where he and his wife, Earnize Robinson, operated a garage. In 1931 he graduated from the Curtiss-Wright Aeronautical Institute in Chicago. He taught at Curtiss-Wright Institute and organized African American men and women pilots in the Chicago area into the Challenger Air Pilots Association.

Early in 1935 the Tuskegee Institute invited Robinson to organize the first course in aviation entirely for African Americans. By that time, he held a transport flying license and had piled up 1,200 hours of flight time, much of it as an instructor at South Side Chicago airports. At about the same time as the Tuskegee offer, a nephew of Emperor Haile Selassie invited Robinson to come to Ethiopia. Benito Mussolini's Italian legions were threatening, and Ethiopia needed experienced aviators, even though some press reports at the time said that none of the emperor's twenty-five airplanes was flyable. Robinson appeared to have selfless motives, in contrast with the many intriguers and opportunists who flocked into Addis Ababa during Ethiopia's futile attempts to repel the Italians. He "had come to Ethiopia to testify to the solidarity of the colored peoples" (Del Boca, 86).

Soon after arriving, Robinson displayed what would become a familiar penchant for prickly behavior toward others. He clashed with the only other African American pilot on the scene, Col. Hubert Julian, a Harlem native who had renounced his U.S. citizenship to serve in the Ethiopian air force. Julian, known as the "Black Eagle," apparently lost the contest, because he was banished to a far-off province to drill infantry recruits. That left Robinson, the "Brown Condor," in charge of the ragtag air force. Now a colonel, he had to deal with an Italian air force that controlled the skies over Ethiopia during the invasion in 1935 and 1936. In an unarmed monoplane, he repeatedly flew courier missions between the front lines and Addis Ababa. Robinson escaped from Ethiopia on 4 May 1936, the day before the country capitulated. Returning to the United States, he toured the country on behalf of United Aid for Ethiopia. That fall, he returned to Tuskegee Institute to teach the aviation course he had given up before he left for Ethiopia.

When World War II ended, Robinson returned to Ethiopia, where Selassie granted him his old rank of colonel. Within a year, however, he was at odds with a group of Swedish technicians who were in Ethiopia to work with equipment sent by Swedish munitions makers. In August 1947 the conflict exploded into violence. Robinson was arrested and jailed for an assault on Swedish Count Carl Gustav von Rosen, who was then commander in chief of the Ethiopian air force. Robinson was found guilty by a jury, lost his appeal, and spent an undetermined amount of time in prison.

In 1951 *Ebony* magazine reported that Robinson—still the best-known African American in Ethiopia—had become disillusioned by his conviction and was thinking of returning to the United States. "But," said *Ebony*'s reporter, "despite Selassie's apparent indifference to him, he remains something of a national hero to the Ethiopian people."

Robinson died as a result of severe burns sustained on 13 March 1954, when the training plane he was flying crashed and burned at the Addis Ababa airport, after narrowly missing a nurses' home. The apparent cause of the accident was engine failure. Also killed in the accident was Bruno Bianci, an Italian engineer.

Although Robinson was a glamorous figure in Ethiopia's highly publicized resistance to Mussolini, his greatest legacy may have been his attempt to increase African American interest in aviation in the United States. Had he remained in his native country after World War II, he would have witnessed the integration of the armed forces—perhaps by some of the pilots he helped train.

FURTHER READING

Del Boca, Angelo. *The Ethiopian War, 1935–1941* (1965; Eng. trans. 1969).
Gubert, Betty Kaplan. *Invisible Wings: An Annotated Bibliography on Blacks in Aviation, 1916–1993* (1994).
Scott, William R. *The Sons of Sheba's Race: African Americans and the Italo-Ethiopian War, 1935–1941* (1993), 69–80.

Obituaries: *Chicago Tribune* and *New York Times*, 28 Mar. 1954.

—DAVID R. GRIFFITHS

ROBINSON, RANDALL

(6 July 1941–), lawyer, human rights activist, and founder and president of TransAfrica and TransAfrica Forum, was born in Richmond, Virginia, one of four children of Maxie Cleveland Robinson Sr., a high school history teacher, and Doris Alma Jones, an elementary school teacher. His sister Jewell was the first African American admitted to Goucher College in Maryland, and his brother Max was the first African American to anchor a national news program. Although both his parents attended college, the family experienced poverty early on, like most African American families living in Richmond at the time. Robinson attended public schools and felt the effects of racism and discrimination as he negotiated his way within the confines of a segregated society.

Following graduation from high school in 1959, Robinson attended Norfolk State College in Virginia on a basketball scholarship, but he left the university during his junior year. He married Brenda Randolph, a librarian, in 1965. They had two children, Anike and Jabari, before divorcing in 1982. Robinson served in the army, and, following his discharge, attended Virginia Union University, graduating in 1967. Robinson then entered Harvard University Law School but soon discovered that his life's work would not include practicing law.

After my first year of law school, I all but knew that I would never practice law.... I knew early that I simply couldn't endure the tedium of practice. I couldn't make myself enjoy the numbing task of drafting coma-inducing legal briefs and then plodding through the even more deadly labyrinthine and dreary passageways of legal procedure

(Robinson, 1998:68)

Nonetheless, he graduated in 1970. His experiences at Harvard and living in the predominantly African American community of Roxbury had a profound effect on him. As a southerner, he had endured segregation, and knew what to expect from the whites he encountered, but Boston was in the North, and he had anticipated an integrated city. The racial strife that polarized the city in the sixties and seventies and its accompanying violence surprised and perplexed him.

Robinson became increasingly fascinated by Africa as he began to read more about the continent. He became interested in the liberation struggles of Angola, Mozambique, and Guinea-Bissau, and in 1970 he established the Southern Africa Relief Fund to provide military assistance to those who were struggling to end colonial and white minority rule, raising four thousand dollars. In addition, he became interested in U.S. foreign policy in Africa and its relationship to American multinational corporations. Robinson recalls in his autobiography that, "at the age of twenty-nine, I knew only that I wanted to apply my career energies to the empowerment and liberation of the African world" (Robinson, 69). He realized that black people throughout the world were in a similar situation; they suffered from the same legacies of slavery, colonialism, and racism. In Robinson's view it was essential that the peoples of the black diaspora had a voice in the decisions that affected their daily lives.

Robinson's sense of mission about the African continent was fulfilled in 1970 when he was given a Ford Foundation grant that allowed him to spend six months in Tanzania. Again he could not escape racism and discrimination, and he achieved a broader understanding of the effects of colonialism. When he attempted to rent a car he was informed by an East Indian clerk that he would have to pay a deposit and that no cars were available. He returned to his hotel room and telephoned the same business. This time, when the clerk heard an American accent, but did not see Robinson's skin color, he was told that a car was available and that the deposit was much lower. Even in Tanzania, he could not escape his skin color, and he realized the economic impact of the East Indian community brought to that nation by the British, who dominated the private retail sector.

Upon his return to the United States in 1971, he practiced law for the Boston Legal Assistance Project and then worked as community organizer for the Roxbury Multi-Service Center. Robinson's interest in Africa continued, and he organized the Pan African Liberation Committee to bring attention to American investment on the continent and its role in colonial liberation struggles. He devoted particular attention to

the roles of his alma mater, Harvard University, and Gulf Oil in sustaining corrupt regimes in Africa and other parts of the third world. In 1975 Robinson moved to Washington, D.C., serving first as a staff assistant for Congressman William Clay and then as an administrative assistant for Congressman Charles Diggs. While working on Diggs's staff, he visited South Africa in 1976 and gained a deeper understanding of the pernicious nature of that country's apartheid system.

Two years later TransAfrica was established under Robinson's leadership. The organization soon emerged as the leading African American advocacy group on issues affecting people of African descent: white minority rule in southern Africa, ethnic strife and war throughout the African continent, human rights violations, the plight of Haitian refugees, and the lack of economic, social, and political resources available to black people throughout the diaspora. Through Robinson's leadership, people from various religious, ethnic, social, and economic backgrounds attempted to shape American foreign policy in Africa through a series of protests, marches, and demonstrations. Robinson believed that civil disobedience was important to draw national attention to the conditions of blacks living under apartheid. It was a mechanism to galvanize students, workers, intellectuals, politicians, celebrities, the young and old, blacks, whites, and others around a common issue. His ultimate goal was to convince Congress to pass economic sanctions against South Africa's apartheid government. Others inspired by TransaAfrica constructed shantytowns on college campuses to protest their universities' investment in apartheid South Africa. Though TransAfrica's methods were much more confrontational, Robinson's anti-apartheid efforts paralleled those of Leon Sullivan, who worked closely with American corporations to end investment in South Africa.

Robinson thought that it was important for college students to understand the role that university investments played in maintaining apartheid. He also believed that people should be conscious of how their governments and companies invested their money in South Africa, and he encouraged them to push for divestment. Robinson appeared on national television, before congressional committees, and wherever else he could, to encourage the U.S. government to change its policy toward South Africa by enforcing economic sanctions against the apartheid regime and to call for the end of white minority rule in Namibia. To further debate on such matters, he established the TransAfrica Forum in 1981, an organization that engages in outreach work for the African American community and the broader public by providing seminars and conferences to inform people about the impact of US foreign policy on Africa and its diaspora.

In 1986 Robinson's hard work with the Congressional Black Caucus and other members of Congress resulted in the passage—over President Ronald Reagan's veto—of the Comprehensive Anti-Apartheid Act, which served to strengthen existing sanctions and urged a transition to democratic rule in South Africa. (Some Reagan administration officials felt a closer affinity to the anti-communist regime in Pretoria than to Nelson Mandela's African National Congress, which included communists like Joe Slovo in leadership positions).

Robinson married Hazel Ross, who worked with him at TransAfrica, in 1987. They have one daughter, Khalea.

Although ending white minority rule in southern Africa was at the forefront of Robinson's work, he continued to push for improved economic conditions in the Caribbean, better treatment of Haitian refugees by the U.S. government, and the removal of dictators in Africa. In addition, he spoke out against the human rights violations committed by Sani Abacha's dictatorship in Nigeria and democratic failures in other African countries. He also called for reparations for blacks in the United States and was a vocal critic of the African Growth and Opportunity Act, passed by Congress in 2000 in an effort to move Africa-U.S. policy from aid to trade. His books include *Defending the Spirit: A Black Life in America* (1998), *The Debt: What America Owes Blacks* (2001), and *The Reckoning: What Blacks Owe to Each Other* (2002). These works, like Robinson's life and career in general, have been dedicated to ensuring that American foreign policy makers address the issues, concerns, and needs of the African diaspora.

FURTHER READING

Robinson, Randall. *Defending the Spirit: A Black Life in America* (1998).
—CASSANDRA VENEY

 ROBINSON, SUGAR RAY (3 May 1920?–12 Apr. 1988), world boxing champion, was born Walker Smith Jr. in Detroit, Michigan, the third child of Walker Smith, a laborer, and Leila Hurst, a seamstress. Robinson divided his youth between Detroit and Georgia and later moved to New York City. It was in Detroit that he was first exposed to boxing. As he recalls in his biography, *Sugar Ray*, he carried the bag of the future heavyweight champion of the world, Joe Louis Barrow, soon to be JOE LOUIS, to the local Brewster Street Gymnasium.

Smith adopted the name Ray Robinson quite unintentionally. When his manager, George Gainford, needed a flyweight to fill a slot in a boxing tournament in Kingston, New York, young Walker Smith was available. In order to box, however, he needed an Amateur Athletic Union identity card. The AAU card verified that participating boxers were not professionals. Gainford had a stack of cards and pulled one out with the name "Ray Robinson" on it. The real Ray Robinson no longer boxed for Gainford's team, but the name stuck. The "Sugar" moniker was added later after Gainford, or perhaps a reporter or

bystander (reports vary), declared that Ray was "as sweet as sugar."

Robinson turned professional on 4 October 1940, after great success as an amateur, including winning the Golden Gloves featherweight title. He was also briefly married at this time to a woman named Marjorie. That marriage was annulled after a short period, though they had a son together named Ronnie. Robinson had two other marriages. The second, in 1943, was to Edna Mae Holly. They had a son named Ray Robinson Jr., born on 13 November 1949. Ray Sr.'s final marriage was to Millie Bruce.

In 1943 Robinson joined the U.S. Army, where he spent most of his time fighting in boxing exhibitions and renewed his relationship with Joe Louis. The two men were arrested on one occasion at a military camp in Alabama for refusing to use a segregated waiting area, but were later released.

Robinson held the world welterweight title from 1946 to 1951 and was then middleweight champion five times between 1951 and 1960. At his peak his record was 128–1–2 with 84 knockouts. He never took a ten-count in his 202 fights, though he once suffered a TKO. In Robinson's day a boxer typically fought only eighty to one hundred bouts; today's boxers fight far fewer contests. Such a punishing schedule and his advancing years finally took their toll; thirteen of his nineteen defeats occurred between 1960 and 1965, when he was in his forties and well past his prime.

Sugar Ray Robinson boxing Bobo Olson in 1956 and regaining the middleweight championship of the world. Corbis

One of the most poignant bouts in Robinson's career was his June 24, 1947, fight with Jimmy Doyle in Cleveland, Ohio. A week before the fight Robinson dreamed that he had killed Doyle in the ring. He told his manager, "the kid dropped dead at my feet, George." Robinson informed all who listened that he did not want to fight, fearing that the premonition would come true. In the end it did. Robinson knocked Doyle out in the eighth round of this fight, and Doyle never awakened.

Robinson's most notable bouts were those against Jake LaMotta in the mid 1940s and early 1950s, when they battled each other a total of six times. Those fights and LaMotta's life were intertwined with Robinson's. With the exception of their first encounter, Robinson won all of these bouts, including his first world middleweight title on February 14, 1951. LaMotta's life was memorialized in the Academy Award–winning motion picture *Raging Bull*.

Perhaps Robinson's greatest boxing accomplishment was his success at a wide range of fighting weights. As an amateur he had been a featherweight, a division restricted to those weighing between 122 and 130 pounds, and began his professional career as a lightweight, where the fighting limit was 140 pounds. His first world championship victory came at the welterweight division (140–147 pounds) in December 1946, when he defeated Tommy Bell after fifteen bruising rounds in New York. In 1950 Robinson moved up to the middleweight division, where a fighter can weigh up to 160 pounds. It was at that weight that he defeated Jake LaMotta to win the world championship in 1951. In the late 1950s he even contemplated a bout with the then heavyweight champion of the world, Floyd Patterson. Though that bout never took place, press reports claimed that Robinson was offered one million dollars to take on a boxer who outweighed him by dozens of pounds.

Robinson did, however, challenge light heavyweight champion Joey Maxim. That bout was held in Madison Square Garden on 25 June 1952, which turned out to be one the hottest nights in fifty-three years. The temperature at ringside was 104 degrees. Although most of the scorers had Robinson ahead on points at the end of the bout, he lost when he passed out from exhaustion in the thirteenth round. In the tenth round the referee had to be relieved of

his duties, as he was also on the verge of passing out from the heat.

Six months after the Maxim fight, Robinson announced his retirement and his intention of becoming a full-time entertainer. He developed a stage show that included tap dancing, singing, and telling jokes. He performed at venues including the French Casino in New York City as well as clubs on the French Riviera. For a variety of reasons, including the need for cash, Robinson reentered the ring three years later.

Beyond the ring and his boxing records, Robinson was responsible for a number of firsts. One of his little-mentioned contributions to sports is that Robinson was the first to have an official "entourage," the precursor of the modern athlete's posse. He first heard the word as he was disembarking from the cruise ship *Liberté* on a trip to France. When one of the porters asked whose trunks and suitcases were being unloaded, he was told that it was for Robinson's "entourage." Robinson used that term from then on. Perhaps because so many other boxers, notably Joe Louis, suffered financially at the hands of unscrupulous managers and agents, Robinson was deeply involved in the management of his boxing career, as well as his investments outside of the ring. Those outside investments included the ownership of a bar, a dry cleaning store, a barbershop, and a lingerie store in Harlem. He often negotiated his own boxing deals and was known for pulling out of agreements when he did not feel that promoters were adhering to the negotiated terms.

Robinson's final moment of glory in the ring came on 10 December 1965. That night he formally retired from boxing before a crowd of 12,146 fans at Madison Square Garden. Four of his key lifetime opponents entered the ring before him. As Robinson entered to a standing ovation, he was lifted by his competitors and former challengers, Carmen Basilio, Gene Fullmer, Randy Turpin, and Carl "Bobo" Olson. Jake LaMotta, Robinson's best-known opponent, was not invited, as he had thrown a fight in that very venue in 1957. Robinson closed out that evening with a speech where he said, "I'm not going to say goodbye. As they say in France, it's *a tout à l'heure*—I'll see you later."

Following his second retirement from the ring, Robinson focused again on his

entertainment career. He appeared in a number of motion pictures, notably *The Detective* (1968), starring Frank Sinatra, and *Candy* (1968), with Richard Burton and Marlon Brando. He was a regular on television, appearing on *The Flip Wilson Show*, among other variety programs, and on *Mission Impossible*, *The Mod Squad*, and *Fantasy Island*. He also focused much of his time and efforts on his Sugar Ray Youth Foundation, founded in 1969 and based in Los Angeles, California, and which provided the means for tens of thousands of children to participate in sports and other programs. One of its most distinguished alums was the Olympian and 100 meter dash world record holder FLORENCE GRIFFITH-JOYNER.

In his final years Robinson suffered from Alzheimer's disease and curtailed almost all of his public appearances. His third wife, Millie, was constantly by his side at this stage. He died as a consequence of diabetes and Alzheimer's in Culver City, California. The mourners at his funeral included boxers Archie Moore and Mike Tyson, as well as Elizabeth Taylor and Red Buttons. The Reverend JESSE JACKSON delivered the eulogy. Robinson is buried, in the company of numerous other celebrities, at Inglewood Cemetery in Inglewood, California.

Sugar Ray Robinson is best known as the greatest boxer, pound for pound, of all time, according to *Ring* magazine. During his life his presence extended beyond his boxing skills to showmanship, class, and grace. In 1999 the Associated Press named him both the greatest welterweight and greatest middleweight boxer of all time and ultimately named him the fighter of the century, just ahead of MUHAMMAD ALI.

FURTHER READING

Robinson, Sugar Ray, with Dave Anderson. *Sugar Ray* (1970).

Mylar, Thomas. *Sugar Ray Robinson* (1996).
Schoor, Gene. *Sugar Ray Robinson* (1951).

Obituary: *New York Times*, 13. Apr. 1989.
—KENNETH L. SHROPSHIRE

ROPER, MOSES (1815–?), fugitive slave, antislavery agitator, memoirist, and farmer, was born in Caswell

County, North Carolina, the son of a white planter, Henry H. Roper, and his mixed-race (African and Indian) house slave, Nancy. Moses Roper's light complexion and striking resemblance to his father proved embarrassing to the family. The animosity of the wife of his father, coupled with the death of Moses's legal owner, probably a man named John Farley, led to Henry Roper's decision to trade mother and son to a nearby plantation when Moses was six years of age. Soon after, he was sold to a "Negro Trader" and shipped south. He never saw his mother again. Over the next twelve years he was sold repeatedly in North and South Carolina, Georgia, and Florida.

Moses Roper's white skin had an impact on his value on the slave market. Unable to secure a buyer, various slave traders found it necessary to hire the young boy out. Before the age of eleven, he worked first as a waiter and then as a tailor's apprentice. When he was eleven, Roper was sold to a Dr. Jones, a planter from Georgia, beginning a remarkable period during which, by his own accounting, he was sold at least thirteen times. It was his last owner, John Gooch, a cotton planter from Kershaw ("Cashaw" in Roper's narrative) County, South Carolina, who proved the worst. Gooch was a brutal man who flogged Roper unmercifully for minor offenses. Roper claimed that when Gooch was away on business, his wife stood in, whipping him with impunity. After repeated torture, the fourteen-year-old Roper could take no more and attempted to escape. He was soon captured near the Gooch plantation and harshly flogged. But this began a period during which Roper ran away whenever the opportunity presented itself. Once he made it as far as Charlotte, North Carolina, before being captured and returned to Gooch, who always stood ready to make his slave pay for the transgression.

In 1833 Roper's life changed for the better when Gooch sold him to a northern Florida slave trader whose economic travails soon led to bankruptcy. To pay his debts, the trader sold Roper to a local planter with a reputation for extreme brutality. Rather than endure that abuse, Roper once again took to the roads and swamps, eventually making his way to Savannah, Georgia, where he convinced a sea captain to take him on as a steward. After a period of extreme anxiety for Roper, the ship set sail for New York.

Roper took advantage of an escape network along the eastern seaboard that historian David Cecelski has characterized as the "maritime underground railroad." Coastal geography as well as demography made this region of the slaveholding South more porous than most. In North Carolina alone, blacks composed 45 percent of the population of the tidewater counties. Black watermen worked as stevedores, stewards, and pilots. Many lived and worked as squatters and swampers. Their world was the "underside of slavery," where the institution was anything but stable. Their actions betrayed the "complex, tumultuous, and dissident undercurrent to coastal life in the slavery era" (Cecelski, "Shores of Freedom," 176). Runaway slaves like Roper found a ready-made network of allies willing to assist them on their way northward. Roper estimated that he had traveled nearly five hundred miles to get to Savannah from Florida along the tangle of rivers and creeks that crisscross the region.

In August 1834 Roper arrived in New York City. His euphoria was short-lived, however, when he was informed that he could easily be recaptured. He continued up the Hudson River towards Poughkeepsie, New York, battling both a racist crew who claimed to know his true identity and a cholera outbreak that nearly killed him. Roper eventually journeyed into Vermont, securing work as a farmhand. Soon after his arrival, he was informed that he was being "advertised" in area newspapers. He fled Vermont for New Hampshire and after a short while went to that hotbed of abolitionist agitation, Boston, Massachusetts, where he made contact with local abolitionists, including William Lloyd Garrison. Roper's name appears as one of the signatories of the constitution of the American Anti-Slavery Society. But even in Boston, life for a fugitive slave was precarious. After several weeks of working for a Brookline shopkeeper, Roper was told by two of his black neighbors that a "gentleman" had been inquiring for a person matching his description. He left Boston, hiding first in the Green Mountains and then making his way to New York City, where he was able to secure passage on a ship, the *Napoleon*, bound for England.

Roper arrived in Liverpool, England, in November 1835, armed with letters of recommendation to noted British abolitionists John Morrison, John Scoble,

and George Thompson, who quickly embraced the young fugitive and pressed him into service as an antislavery lecturer. When Roper expressed an interest in getting an education, his patrons convinced Dr. Francis Cox to assume the financial burden for sending him to boarding school, first at Hackney and then at Wallingford. Roper also attended University College in London for a short while in 1836. All the while he continued lecturing to reform audiences across the country, becoming one of the first former slaves to play such a role.

In 1837 Roper published in London a narrative of his life as a slave, *A Narrative of the Adventures and Escape of Moses Roper from American Slavery*; it was published in the United States one year later. The publication was accompanied by an extensive lecture tour. In 1839 he married Ann Stephen Price, an Englishwoman from Bristol who assisted him in carrying on the antislavery work. In 1844, after nine years of lecturing, Roper estimated that he had given two thousand lectures. He informed the British Anti-Slavery Society that he was going to retire and asked that they assist him in putting together the funds to purchase a farm in the British colony on the Cape of Good Hope in southern Africa. There he hoped to put the agricultural knowledge that he had gleaned during his labors as a slave to better use. Roper never made it to Africa, but he did secure the capital to purchase a farm in western Canada. He returned to England twice, in 1846 to supervise another edition of his narrative, and in 1854 to lecture. Unfortunately, historians have been unable to determine how Roper spent the remainder of his life.

Given the intense suffering of Roper's early years, his is a remarkable tale of resilience that ultimately illuminates the network that was the "maritime underground railroad." If Roper is a minor character in the history of American slavery and abolitionism, it is important to note that he was also a key transatlantic connection in the early stages of an international movement to abolish slavery.

FURTHER READING

Roper, Moses. *A Narrative of the Adventures and Escape of Moses Roper from American Slavery* (1838; repr. in William L. Andrews, ed. North Carolina Slave Narratives [2003], 21–76).

ROSE, EDWARD

Cecelski, David S. "The Shores of Freedom: The Maritime Underground Railroad in North Carolina, 1800–1861." *North Carolina Historical Review* 71 (Apr. 1994).

———. *The Waterman's Song: Slavery and Freedom in Maritime North Carolina* (2001).

Ripley, C. Peter, et al., eds. *The Black Abolitionist Papers.* Vol. 1, *The British Isles, 1830–1865* (1985).

—MARK ANDREW HUDDLE

ROSE, EDWARD (?–1833?), mountain man and Indian interpreter, may have been born in Kentucky, near Louisville, most likely of African, Indian, and white ancestry. The year and date of his birth remain unknown, as do the names and occupations of his parents. It is possible that Rose was born a slave. The details of Rose's life have been gleaned from the narratives and records of others, including Washington Irving, who claimed that after leaving home as a teenager, Rose became a kind of roving bandit, "one of the gangs of pirates who infested the islands of the Mississippi, plundering boats as they went up and down the river ... waylaying travelers as they returned by land from New Orleans ... plundering them of their money and effects, and often perpetuating the most atrocious murders" (*Astoria*, ch. 24). It appears that Rose left New Orleans after the police broke up his gang, eventually settling in St. Louis, where, in the spring of 1806, the local newspaper described him as big, strong, and hot-tempered, with a swarthy, fierce-looking face.

That same year Rose traveled up the Osage River with a group of hunters, after which he must have returned to St. Louis, because in the spring of 1807 he left from there with Manuel Lisa's fur-trading expedition up the Missouri River, the first major expedition organized after Lewis and Clark's return to St. Louis. Led by Lisa, a St. Louis businessman, the party traveled north, up the Missouri River through present-day North and South Dakota, and then southwest, along the Yellowstone River to the mouth of the Bighorn River, where they established the first trading post on the upper river, Fort Manuel (also called Fort Lisa), in what became Montana. After trading jewelry, tobacco,

liquor, weapons, and blankets for pelts with the local Crow Indians (Absaroke or Sparrowhawk people), Lisa and his men returned to St. Louis. Rose, however, chose to remain behind. Living with the Crow in what is now southern Montana and northern Wyoming, Rose learned their culture and language. Because of his appearance, Rose was known as Nez Coupe ("Scarred Nose") and later, after a particularly fierce battle, as Five Scalps.

It has been suggested that during this time Rose partnered with the French frontiersman and husband of Sacagawea, Toussaint Charbonneau, in escorting Arapaho women captured by Snake Indians to European trappers willing to pay for Indian women. In any event, in the spring of 1809 Rose joined an expedition organized for the purpose of escorting Sheheke (also known, by whites, as Big White), the principal chief of Matootonha, a lower Mandan village, through hostile territory back to his tribe. In 1806 Sheheke, along with his wife and children, had accompanied Lewis and Clark to St. Louis and Washington, D.C., via Monticello, where they met Thomas Jefferson. The first attempt to return Sheheke in 1807, led by Nathaniel Pryor, had failed because of resistance from the Sioux and Arikara. Two years later, with a contract for seven thousand dollars paid to the Missouri Fur Company by the U.S. government, twenty men, including Rose, spent three months traveling with the chief and his family northwest, up the Missouri River to Matootonch, in present-day North Dakota. On the way back to St. Louis, Rose elected to rejoin the Crow.

In 1811 Rose was hired by the "Astorians"—John Jacob Astor's Pacific Fur Company—as a guide for the first expedition to the Pacific Ocean since Lewis and Clark had returned six years earlier. Led by Wilson Price Hunt, a merchant from New Jersey with no experience as a hunter or trapper, the party included sixty-four men and eighty-four horses. Rose joined the party on the plains near the Arikara villages just north of the present-day border between North and South Dakota and guided the expedition through Crow territory. Suspicious of his loyalty to the Crow, Hunt never trusted Rose. Predisposed to believe reports that Rose was organizing a mutiny, Hunt fired him as soon as the party reached the Black Hills of South Dakota, an error in judgment that contributed to many of the expedition's

failures. Immediately after dispatching Rose, in an indication of what lay ahead, Hunt and his group became lost as they tried to pass through mountains. A few days later Rose returned with several Crow and helped the party find a pass.

Washington Irving's description of Rose in his 1836 book *Astoria; or, Anecdotes of an Enterprise Beyond the Rocky Mountains* must have been typical of attitudes toward Rose, whom Washington describes as "one of those anomalous beings found on the frontier, who seem to have neither kin nor country ... and was, withal, a dogged, sullen, silent fellow, with a sinister aspect, and more of the savage than the civilized man in his appearance" (*Astoria*, ch. 22) "This fellow it appears," Washington continues, "was one of those desperadoes of the frontiers, outlawed by their crimes, who combine the vices of civilized and savage life, and are ten times more barbarous than the Indians with whom they consort" (*Astoria*, ch. 24).

A year later, in 1812, Manuel Lisa found Rose living with the Arikaras and hired him as a scout. Rose, however, never it made it to their meeting place in New Orleans, having attached himself to an Omaha Indian woman, with whom he remained in her tribe until he was arrested for drinking and fighting and taken to St. Louis. Records show that Rose was released in 1813 by Superintendent of Indian Affairs William Clark, in exchange for Rose's promise to stay out of Indian territory.

Historians are unsure of Rose's activities in the following decade, until 10 March 1823, when he left St. Louis with one hundred men on the ill-fated trapping expedition of William Henry Ashley and Andrew Henry, owners of the Rocky Mountain Fur Company. From the outset Ashley dismissed Rose's counsel against bartering for horses with the Arikara and against mooring company boats on the same side of the river as the tribe. More disastrously, Ashley ignored Rose's warning of an impeding Arikara attack, and when the ambush came, the company's losses were heavy. Attacks on the traders continued until Colonel Henry Leavenworth arrived from Fort Atkinson with two hundred fur traders, frontiersmen, and Lakota and Tankton warriors organized into a frontier militia known as the Missouri Legion. Rose was made an ensign, and the militia attacked the Arikara villages in August 1823. In his official report

729

submitted to General Henry Atkinson and dated 20 October 1823, Leavenworth singled out Rose: "I had not found anyone willing to go into those villages, except a man by the name of Rose.... He appeared to be a brave and enterprising man, and was well acquainted with those Indians.... He was with General Ashley when he was attacked. The Indians at that time called to him to take care of himself, before they fired upon General Ashley's party" (quoted in Burton, 11).

Trying to salvage the expedition, Ashley assembled a small party of men, described by Harrison Clifford Dale in the *Ashley-Smith Explorations* (1941) as "the most significant group of continental explorers ever brought together." This group included Rose and other such noted frontiersmen as James Clyman, David Jackson, William Sublette, Jim Bridger, Hugh Glass, and Thomas Fitzpatrick. Led by Jedediah Smith, the party traveled up the Grand River and through the Black Hills to the Rockies. From Clyman's diary we learn that Rose's familiarity with the Indian language and customs saved the party from disaster.

Rose served with Smith for the next two years, leaving in May 1825 to join a large treaty-making expedition up the Missouri under the command of General Atkinson and Major Benjamin O'Fallon. Forty men on horseback, under the command of a Lieutenant Armstrong, went with Rose by land; the rest traveled up the river in nine boats. The Yellowstone expedition, as it came to be known, succeeded in signing peace treaties with all the tribes of the river except the Blackfoot. Reports of the expedition by several authors delight in recounting Rose's mythmaking adventures. A clerk whose expedition journal was published in 1929 in the *North Dakota Historical Society Quarterly* documented one oft-repeated tale of Rose's heroics and skill: "Thursday 30 June. Rose, an interpreter, one of the party, we understand, covered himself with bushes and crawled into the gang of 11 Bulls [buffalo] and shot down 6 on the same ground before the others ran off."

Much of the information we know about Rose comes from a biographical sketch of him that Captain Ruben Holmes, a member of the Atkinson-O'Fallon expedition, published in the *St. Louis Beacon* in 1828 (reprinted in the *St. Louis Reveille* in 1848). In "The Five Scalps" (1848), Holmes describes Rose's confrontation with a band of six hundred hostile Crow warriors: "One foot was on the pile of muskets, to prevent the Indians from taking any from it...his eye gleamed with triumphant satisfaction. There was an expression about his mouth, slightly curved and compressed, and a little smiling at the curves, indicative of a delirium of delight—his eye, his mouth, the position of his head, and scars on his forehead and nose all united in forming a general expression, that, of itself, seemed to paralyze the nerves of every Indian before him."

Rose apparently rejoined the Crow after the 1825 expedition, and nine years later he rode alongside them in their battles with the Blackfoot. "The old Negro," Zenas Leonard wrote in his autobiography, *Adventures of Zenas Leonard, Fur Trader* (1839), "told them that if the red man was afraid to go among his enemy, he would show them that a black man was not." Rose was one of first black frontiersmen to earn a wide reputation, preceding JIM BECKWOURTH, who was born around 1800, by a generation. Indeed, Beckwourth, who in his autobiography, *The Life and Times of James P. Beckwourth* (1856), called Rose "one of the best interpreters ever known in the whole Indian country," may have claimed some of the older man's exploits for himself.

When and how Rose—whom Harold Felton describes as "a mountain man's mountain man, a trail blazer's trail blazer" (vii)—died remains unknown. Legend has it that Rose, Hugh Glass, and a third mountain man named Menard were killed and scalped on the frozen Yellowstone River in the winter of 1832–1833 by a band of Arikaras hostile to the Crow. A site called Rose's Grave is located at the junction of the Milk and Missouri rivers, on the Milk River near the Yellowstone River.

FURTHER READING

Burton, Art T. *Black, Buckskin, and Blue: African American Scouts and Soldiers on the Western Frontier* (1999).
Felton, Harold W. *Edward Rose: Negro Trail Blazer* (1967).
Irving, Washington. *Astoria; or, Anecdotes of an Enterprise Beyond the Rocky Mountains* (1836).

—LISA E. RIVO

ROSS, DIANA

(26 Mar. 1944–), singer and actress, was born in Detroit, Michigan, the second of six children of Fred Ross, a college-educated factory worker, and Ernestine Moten. Although Fred and Ernestine had intended to name their daughter Diane, a clerical oversight at the hospital altered the name to Diana. She was known as Diane to family and close friends, and the use of this familiar name has remained an indicator throughout her life of those among her inner circle. The family lived in a black middle-class neighborhood where, as she ironed her family's laundry, she could see from her window fifteen-year-old Smokey Robinson singing with his friends on his front porch (Taraborrelli, 36). When Ross turned fourteen the family moved to the Brewster projects, a low-income development that had not yet warranted the stigmatizing nomenclature of "ghetto" or "slum." The Rosses had an affordable three-bedroom home and attended Olivet Baptist Church, where Ross sang in the junior choir with her siblings, while her parents sang in the adult choir.

Ross attended Cass Technical High School, an esteemed public school, where she registered high marks in cosmetology and dress design; upon graduating in 1962 she was voted the best dressed in her class. In high school many of Ross's peers had begun singing at parties and on street corners. One of these groups, the Primes, would eventually become the Temptations—but in the meantime their manager wanted a sister group to complement their local performances. The manager began with his girlfriend's husky-voiced sister, Florence Ballard, as the centerpiece; recruited two of her friends, Mary Wilson and Betty McGlown; and searched exhaustively for the final voice. Primes singer Paul Williams finally suggested Ross, and the Primettes—undaunted by McGlown's leaving the group to get married—quickly established themselves on the Detroit scene, earning fifteen dollars a week in local clubs and signing a deal with LuPine records, with whom they recorded two singles that were never released. But BERRY GORDY JR. at Motown Records, heeding the advice of his young star in the making, Smokey Robinson, was ready on

15 January 1961 to sign the four women. (They had recruited Barbara Martin to replace McGlown.) Gordy renamed the group the Supremes and began processing them through the Motown Artists Development Department, where they were schooled in style, public speaking, and overall deportment.

Hardly an immediate success, the Supremes floundered for three years, one album, and eight mediocre singles, in addition to weathering the first of many personnel changes. Ballard briefly departed in 1962 to tour with the Marvelettes, and Martin quit in order to have a baby. Ross sang lead only about half the time, and, at that point, the Supremes were attempting to succeed as a trio that sang songs with four-part harmonies. They toured briefly in 1962 under the auspices of a Motown revue, but it was not until another tour in June 1964, when Motown released "Where Did Our Love Go?," that the Supremes had their first number-one hit. Written by Lamont Dozier and Brian and Eddie Holland—three of Motown's premier writers and producers—the single was the first of a string of hits that helped define the Motown sound as a successful crossover hybrid of gospel, rock and roll, rhythm and blues, and pop.

The Supremes made numerous television appearances, most often on the *Ed Sullivan Show*, where their glamorous evening gowns and dashing wigs projected an image of black womanhood rarely seen by white Americans. During the mid-1960s the Supremes could boast a yearly income of $250,000 each. Ross literally took center stage by this point, singing lead and prompting Gordy to change the group's name to "Diana Ross and the Supremes." By 1969 they had hit number one with eleven singles, registering about half a dozen in the pop music canon: "Baby Love" (1964), "Come See about Me" (1964), "Stop! In the Name of Love" (1965), "I Hear a Symphony" (1965), and "You Can't Hurry Love" (1966). They finished the decade with their twelfth hit, the ironically titled "Someday We'll Be Together"—almost nine years to the day after signing with Motown, on 14 January 1970. Ross left to pursue a solo career. The Supremes continued shuffling personnel for another seven years before disbanding in 1977, never again hitting number one.

Ross continued manufacturing hit after hit for Motown, starting with 1970's "Ain't No Mountain High Enough." She would eventually score seven more number-one hits as a solo artist, first with Motown and then with RCA, with whom she signed in 1981 for twenty million dollars. But the most dynamic element of her career to develop in the 1970s was her acting. She landed the lead in the BILLIE HOLIDAY biopic *Lady Sings the Blues* (1972) and was nominated for an Academy Award for Best Actress. Her next project, the Motown-backed vehicle *Mahogany* (1975), attempted to capitalize on her superstar status. The film's production was notoriously troubled, as rumors surfaced about Ross's demanding personality and Gordy's curious decision to direct the film himself. *Mahogany* garnered hardly any positive reviews, but Ross did gain another number-one hit from the soundtrack, "The Theme from *Mahogany* (Do You Know Where You're Going To?)."

In 1978 she again compelled her critics to claim that she was overbearing—and her supporters to praise her business acumen—by purchasing the movie rights to the Broadway smash *The Wiz* and reworking the story so that she could play the lead of Dorothy. The ensemble cast of MICHAEL JACKSON, RICHARD PRYOR, and LENA HORNE was not nearly enough to salvage this African American retelling of *The Wizard of Oz* from more sternly negative reviews.

The 1970s were also tumultuous personally for Ross. In 1970 she married Robert Silberstein, a music manager, with whom she had three children (though the first, she later admitted, was fathered by Gordy). They divorced in 1975; two years later, Ross married an international businessman named Arne Naess Jr., with whom she had two more children, but they divorced in 2000. Musically, she seemed to fall into a rut, always staying even with the latest trend, as with her tepid disco tracks, rather than innovating, as she had with the Supremes earlier in her career. In 1989 she returned to Motown as both a performer and a director of the company. She continued releasing albums but seemed to drift further and further from mainstream pop success. Ross wrote her autobiography, *Secrets of a Sparrow*, in 1993.

FURTHER READING

Ross, Diana. *Secrets of a Sparrow* (1993).

Haskins, James. *Diana Ross* (1985).

Itkowitz, Leonore K. *Diana Ross* (1974).
Taraborrelli, J. Randy. *Call Her Miss Ross* (1989).

—DAVID F. SMYDRA JR.

ROWAN, CARL THOMAS (11 Aug. 1925–23 Sept. 2000), journalist, diplomat, and United States Information Agency director, was born in Ravenscroft, Tennessee. He was one of three children of Thomas David Rowan, a lumberyard worker with a fifth-grade education who had served in World War I, and Johnnie Bradford, a domestic worker with an eleventh grade education. When Rowan was an infant, his family left the dying coal-mining town of his birth to go to McMinnville, Tennessee, lured by its lumberyards, nurseries, and livery stables. But there, in the midst of the Great Depression, they remained mired in poverty. The elder Rowan sometimes found jobs stacking lumber at twenty-five cents an hour and, according to his son, probably never made more than three hundred dollars in a single year. Meanwhile his mother worked as a domestic, cleaning houses and doing the laundry of local white families.

The family lived in an old frame house along the Louisville and Nashville Railroad tracks; Carl and his siblings slept on a pallet on a wooden floor. In his 1991 autobiography, *Breaking Barriers*, Rowan recalled a traumatic incident in 1933 when he, at age eight, awakened to his sister's screams after she had been bitten on the ear by a rat. "We had no electricity, no running water, and, for most of the time, no toothbrushes," Rowan wrote in *Breaking Barriers*. "Toilet paper was a luxury we did not know when second-hand newspapers were good enough for our outhouse" (*Breaking Barriers*, 10). He also recalled staving off hunger by hunting for rabbit. "I survived the Depression eating fried rabbit, rabbits and dumplings, broiled rabbit, rabbit stew and a host of similar dishes made possible because Two-Shot Rowan so often came home with a rabbit or two draining blood down his pants leg," he said, referring to his father (*Breaking Barriers*, 11).

Rowan credited his mother, who often praised his abilities, and Bessie Taylor Gwynn, a teacher in his segregated high school, for rescuing him

Carl Rowan with President Johnson in 1964, after Rowan's appointment as director of the United States Information Agency. © Bettmann/CORBIS

from a life of poverty. They instilled in him a love of academics, and because blacks were not allowed to use the local library, Gwynn smuggled books out of the white library for Carl. "This frail looking woman, who could make sense of the writings of Shakespeare, Milton, Voltaire, and bring to life BOOKER T. WASHINGTON and W. E. B. DU BOIS, was a towering presence in our classrooms," he once wrote. During forty-seven years of teaching, Gwynn also taught Rowan's mother and siblings. Rowan praised her for immersing him in a "wonderful world of similes, metaphors, alliteration, hyperbole, and even onomatopoeia. She acquainted me with dactylic verse, with the meter and scan of ballads, and set me to believing that I could write sonnets as good as any ever penned by Shakespeare, or iambic pentameter that would put Alexander Pope to shame (*Breaking Barriers*, 31–32). Gwynn insisted that Rowan keep up with world affairs, so he became a delivery boy for the *Chattanooga Times*, which afforded him the opportunity to read the newspaper each day. "'If you don't read, you can't write, and if you can't write, you can stop dreaming,' Miss Bessie told me. So I read whatever she told me to read and tried to remember what she insisted that I store away."

While a student at Tennessee State University, an historically black college in Nashville, Rowan, at age nineteen, became one of the first twenty African Americans commissioned as officers in the United States Navy during World War II. Rowan was the only African American in a unit of 335 sailors. With the assistance of the GI Bill, he went on to earn a college degree in Mathematics from Oberlin College in Ohio and a master's degree in Journalism from the University of Minnesota. In 1950 he married Vivien Murphy, the college-educated daughter of a Norfolk Navy Yard worker. The couple had three children: Carl Jr., Jeffrey, and Barbara.

Rowan began his journalism career in 1948 as a copy editor at the *Minneapolis Tribune*, and in 1950 the paper hired him as one of only a handful of black, general assignment reporters in the country. While African Americans had worked on mainstream newspapers as far back as the Civil War, black reporters were still a rarity in the early 1950s. His first major assignment was a series of articles on African American life in the Deep South, for which he traveled six thousand miles in six weeks. Flying out of Nashville, he said, "I was shocked in 1951 to see signs on two airport chairs proclaiming: FOR COLORED PASSENGERS ONLY. I was even more shocked to see four airport toilets marked WHITE MEN, COLORED MEN, then WHITE LADIES, and the last inviting COLORED WOMEN." For his series he garnered an award for best newspaper reporting by the Sidney Hillman Foundation, and the Minneapolis Junior Chamber of Commerce named him Outstanding Young Man of 1951. He also secured a book contract for his first book, *South of Freedom* (1953). He went on to cover the Supreme Court's historic school desegregation ruling, *Brown v. Board of Education* (1954) and some of the other major civil rights battles of the fifties, including the Montgomery bus boycott, which formed the basis for his third book, *Go South to Sorrow*.

In 1961 President John F. Kennedy appointed Rowan assistant secretary of state for public affairs, which at the time was the highest position held by an African American in the State Department. He later became a delegate to the United Nations during the Cuban missile crisis and served as the U.S. ambassador to Finland from 1963 to 1964. In 1964 President Lyndon Johnson chose Rowan to replace Edward R. Murrow as director of the U.S. Information Agency, which, through its Voice of America radio broadcasts, provided information about the policies and culture of the United States. Though Rowan was picked for the job on his merits, his selection was also a major cold war propaganda coup for the U.S.; the Soviets, in their efforts to woo decolonizing nations in Africa and elsewhere, had long highlighted racial discrimination in the United States. In appointing Rowan and other African Americans like ROBERT C. WEAVER (Secretary of Housing and Urban Development) and THURGOOD MARSHALL (U.S. Solictor-General and later Supreme Court justice), to prominent positions in government, President Johnson was seeking to counter such Soviet claims. As a result of these two appointments, Rowan became the first African American to sit in on Cabinet and National Security Council meetings.

Rowan returned to journalism after more than four years in government and became one of the most widely known journalists, black or white, in the nation when he signed with Westinghouse Broadcasting to deliver three commentaries a week. He simultaneously signed with the *Chicago Daily News* and Publishers Newspaper Syndicate to write three columns a week, which would appear in more than one hundred newspapers. That made him the first syndicated black columnist, a position he used to highlight racial injustice and policies injurious to the poor. Rowan broke another racial barrier in 1972 when he became the first African American elected to membership in the Gridiron Club, a prestigious organization of Washington journalists established in 1885. Inclusion in elite circles, however, did not cause him to temper his outspoken views on racial injustice. In 1974, as the nation marked the twentieth anniversary of *Brown v. Board of Education*, Rowan noted that "we are still a racist society," and added that some of the litigants in the decision never enjoyed ever one day of integrated education. Instead Rowan notes, "they saw evasion, circumvention, massive resistance and a generation of litigation."

Rowan also was, for three decades, a regular panelist on the PBS talk show *Inside Washington* until he retired in 1996. During three decades he earned many awards and wrote eight books, including *Dream Makers, Dream Breakers: The World of Justice Thurgood Marshall* and *The Coming Race War in America*, which took aim at the state of race relations in America.

In 1987 Rowan founded Project Excellence, a nonprofit group that by the time of his death in April 2000 had provided millions of dollars in scholarships to some three thousand black teenagers in Washington, D.C.

FURTHER READING

The Carl T. Rowan papers are housed at the Oberlin College Archives in Oberlin, Ohio.

Rowan, Carl T. *Breaking Barriers* (1991).

Matusow, Barbara. "Visible Man," *Washingtonian* 30 (Fall 1995): 44–49.

Zehnpfennig, Gladys. *Carl T. Rowan: Spokesman for Sanity* (1971).

Obituary: *New York Times*, 24 Sept. 2000.
—PAMELA NEWKIRK

RUDD, DANIEL

(7 Aug. 1854–4 Dec. 1933), newspaper editor and Catholic lay leader, was born in Bardstown, Kentucky, the son of Robert Rudd, a slave on the Rudd estate, and Elizabeth "Eliza" Hayden, a slave of the Hayden family in Bardstown. He was baptized a Catholic when an infant. Although little information exists about his early life, it may be conjectured that his Catholic upbringing was due chiefly to his mother who acted as sexton in the local church for more than sixty years. After the Civil War, he went to Springfield, Ohio, where an older brother had already established himself, to get a secondary school education.

There is little information about Rudd until 1884 when he began a black newspaper, the *Ohio State Tribune*. In 1886 Rudd changed the name of the weekly newspaper to the *American Catholic Tribune*, proudly displaying on the editorial page the words "The only Catholic Journal owned and published by Colored men." The newspaper's focus was the Catholic Church and the African American. Rudd's purpose was to demonstrate to African Americans that the Catholic Church was truly the best hope of black Americans. He was convinced that Catholicism would elevate the cultural level of the black race and thus attract an enormous influx of black converts to the Catholic Church. Believing that the authority structure of the church could change racist behavior and influence racist thought, he asserted, "The Catholic Church alone can break the color line. Our people should help her to do it." Although black Catholics could point to the Catholic Church's teaching on the dignity of the person as inherently antiracist, Rudd made the case more directly for the usefulness of Roman Catholicism in changing the moral and religious status of African Americans. He published the following on the front page of his paper: "The Holy Roman Catholic Church offers to the oppressed Negro a material as well as spiritual refuge, superior to all the inducements of other organizations combined.... The distinctions and differences among men are unrecognized within the pale of the Church.... The Negro and the Caucasian are equally the children of one Father and as such, are equally welcomed, with equal rights, equal privileges."

On the other hand, Rudd used the newspaper to speak out forcefully against racial discrimination. He editorialized in favor of an integrated school system in Cincinnati, Ohio, and against segregated schools and institutions. Race pride was important to him, so he used his newspaper to highlight the achievements of leading African Americans of his day.

By 1887 Rudd had moved his weekly newspaper to Cincinnati, where he had a small staff of assistant editors and traveling correspondents who doubled as sales representatives. The paper in most editions ran to four pages. Front-page articles carried religious news from various black Catholic communities along with other items related to African Americans. A column or two was often dedicated to an exposition of Catholic belief or practice. Many articles were reprints from other newspapers, including items from the Catholic press and the African American press. According to some estimates, the newspaper had as many as ten thousand subscribers in the period prior to the move to Detroit, Michigan. Rudd received the approbation of some members of the church hierarchy and some small contributions, but there is no indication of any long-term subsidy from Catholic leaders or laypeople.

Rudd also traveled across the country as a tireless lecturer. The message was usually the same: "The Catholic Church is not only a warm and true friend to the Colored people but is absolutely impartial in recognizing them as the equals of all." He spoke to varied audiences in places like Lexington, Kentucky, and Fort Wayne, Indiana (1887); Natchez, Mississippi, and Nashville, Tennessee (1891); Syracuse, New York (1895); and Lewiston, Maine (1896). Fluent in German, he spoke to German organizations such as the *Central Verein* in Toledo, Ohio, in 1886 and to students at a German orphanage in Linwood, Ohio, in 1890.

In the summer of 1889 Rudd was sent to Europe to participate in the Anti-Slavery Conference organized by Cardinal Charles-Martial Lavigerie, the primate of Africa. The trip was made possible, it seems, by a subvention from William Henry Elder, the archbishop of Cincinnati. Rudd was already in Germany when the conference which was to be held in Lucerne, Switzerland, was postponed; he nevertheless continued his trip to Lucerne, where he met with Cardinal Lavigerie, and to London, where he visited Cardinal Henry Edward Manning before returning to America.

Rudd was responsible for the five black Catholic lay congresses that were held between the years 1889 and 1894. He first called for a congress of black Catholics in the columns of his newspaper as early as 1888, writing, "Colored Catholics ought to unite.... Let leading Colored Catholics gather together from every city in the Union [where] they may get to know one another and take up the cause of the race." The first nationwide assembly of black Catholics, meeting in Washington, D.C., in early January 1889, was well attended and widely acclaimed. The second congress was held in Cincinnati in 1890 and the third in Philadelphia, Pennsylvania, in 1892. Rudd published the proceedings of these congresses on his own press. His influence in the last two congresses, held in Chicago, Illinois, in 1893 and in Baltimore, Maryland, in 1894, is less evident.

Rudd played other significant roles in American Catholicism and black journalism. He was on the steering committee for the first national Lay Catholic Congress held in Baltimore in November 1889 and was a founding member of the Catholic Press Association (1890) and the Afro-American Press Association and was actively involved in both. By 1894 he had moved the publication of the *American Catholic Tribune* to Detroit for unknown reasons. There are no extant copies of the newspaper dating after 1894, but only after 1897 did Rudd's name cease to appear as a publisher in the Detroit City Directory.

Under circumstances that are not clear Rudd had, according to census records, moved to Bolivar County in Mississippi by 1910. He later moved to eastern Arkansas where he acted as accountant and business manager for two well-to-do black farmers. He seemingly had little contact with the small black Catholic community in Arkansas centered around Pine Bluff. The black Catholic congresses had ceased to meet after 1894 for reasons that remain unclear, and Rudd thereafter was no longer an influential leader in the black Catholic movement. In his correspondence with John B. Morris, the bishop of Little Rock, he alluded to his former role and indicated his continued interest in the cause of black Catholics, even expressing a desire to represent the diocese at a meeting of the National Association for the Advancement of Colored People. In 1917 Rudd was the coauthor of a biography of Scott Bond, one of the successful black farmers of the region for whom he worked as an accountant (*From Slavery to Wealth, the Life of Scott Bond: The Rewards of Honesty, Industry, Economy, and Perseverance*, 1917, 1971). Rudd's attention in his later years seemingly centered on the furtherance of black business. After suffering a stroke, he returned to Bardstown in 1932, where he died.

A member of the first generation of postslavery African Americans, Rudd was one of the more significant figures in the history of black Catholics in the United States. Here was a former slave welcomed by two cardinals, a black man lecturing to white audiences both in

the North and in the South. He began the longest running African American Catholic newspaper in the country and single-handedly launched a black Catholic lay movement when he began the black lay congresses. From this effort emerged other black Catholic lay leaders from whom came the first articulation of a black Catholic theological position. As the first African American Catholic layman to call publicly for the Catholic Church to live up to its teachings on social justice and social equality, Rudd opened the way for later black Catholic activists in the civil rights movement.

Rudd never married. He could be difficult; many ecclesiastics and white lay leaders saw him as "pushy" because he would not accept circumstances that he deemed disrespectful to the black race. Among Catholic laymen of his time, he was unique; among black leaders of his generation, he was extraordinary; in the light of recent American Catholic history, he was prophetic.

FURTHER READING

Copies of Rudd's newspaper are in the Archdiocese of Philadelphia Archives in Overbrook, Pa. His correspondence is in the Archdiocese of Cincinnati Archives, the Little Rock Diocesan Archives, and the Josephite Archives in Baltimore.

Davis, Cyprian. *The History of Black Catholics in the United States* (1990).
Lackner, Joseph H. "Daniel Rudd, Editor of the American Catholic Tribune, from Bardstown to Cincinnati." *Catholic Historical Review* 80 (1994): 258–281.
Spalding, Thomas. "The Negro Catholic Congresses, 1889–1894." *Catholic Historical Review* 55 (1969): 337–357.

—CYPRIAN DAVIS

RUDOLPH, WILMA

(23 June 1940–12 Nov. 1994), track and field athlete, was born Wilma Glodean Rudolph in St. Bethlehem, Tennessee, the daughter of Edward Rudolph, a railroad porter, and Blanche (maiden name unknown), a domestic. Born nearly two months premature and weighing only four-and-a-half pounds, Wilma was a sickly child who contracted both double pneumonia and scarlet fever, which resulted in her left leg being partially paralyzed. Her doctors doubted that she

would ever regain the use of her leg. Undaunted, Wilma's mother made a ninety-mile bus trip once a week with her to Nashville, Tennessee, so she could receive heat, water, and massage treatments. At age five she began wearing a heavy steel brace and corrective shoes to help straighten her leg. After years of physical therapy, at age twelve she was finally able to move about without her leg brace.

When she entered a racially segregated high school in Clarksville, Tennessee, Rudolph tried out for the basketball team and, in recognition of her abilities, made the all-state team four times. As an outstanding athlete she came to the attention of Ed Temple, the premier women's track coach at Tennessee State University. Though Rudolph was still in high school, Temple invited her to spend the summer with other track athletes at the university training camp. In 1956 she participated in the national Amateur Athletic Union track and field competition, winning the 75-yard and 100-yard events as well as anchoring the winning relay team. Encouraged by her coach, she traveled with the Tennessee State team to the tryouts for the 1956 Olympic Games in Melbourne, Australia. At sixteen Rudolph became the youngest member of the U.S. women's track and field team. Though she did not make the Olympic finals in the 200-meter event,

Wilma Rudolph in 1960, when she became the first American woman to win three Olympic golds. Library of Congress

she and her team won a bronze medal in the 400-meter relay event.

Rudolph returned home to complete her last two years of high school and looked forward to going to college. However, in her senior year of high school she became pregnant and gave birth to a daughter. Her boyfriend wanted to marry her, but Rudolph was unwilling to give up her fledgling track career. Her daughter was sent to live with a married older sister in St. Louis. In 1957 Rudolph enrolled at Tennessee State on a track scholarship and continued to train for the 1960 Olympic Games in Rome, Italy.

During the 1960 Olympics, temperatures in Rome hovered around 100 degrees. Rudolph contended not only with the weather, but with an ankle injury she suffered the day before the first race. Despite her impairment she won three gold medals: one in the 100-meter event, setting a world record with a finishing time of 11.0 seconds; another in the 200-meter dash with a time of 23.2 seconds; and her third as anchor of the women's 400-meter relay team. She thus became the first American woman to win three gold medals in a single Olympics.

In 1961 Rudolph competed in the previously all-male Millrose Games, tying her own world record in the 60-yard dash with a time of 6.9 seconds. She also became the first woman to compete in the heralded New York Athletic Club meet, the Los Angeles Times Games, and the Penn Relays. That year she received the Sullivan Award as the nation's top amateur athlete.

In 1962 Rudolph was awarded the coveted Babe Didrikson Zaharias Award as the most outstanding female athlete in the world. That same year she competed in a meet against the Soviet Union held at Stanford University. She won the 100-meter dash and overcame a 40-yard deficit to win the women's 400-meter relay. When Rudolph recalled the race she said: "That was it. I knew it. The crowd in the stadium was on its feet, giving me a standing ovation, and I knew what time it was. Time to retire, with a sweet taste."

After retiring from competition, Rudolph returned to college and graduated from Tennessee State University in 1963 with a degree in education. She first took a job teaching second grade

and coaching basketball. She coached track for a brief time at DePauw University in Greencastle, Indiana. Over the next several years she worked in a variety of positions as a goodwill ambassador to French West Africa, a radio show co-host, an administrative assistant at the University of California at Los Angeles, and an executive for a hospital in Nashville. In 1982 Rudolph established the Wilma Rudolph Foundation, a nonprofit organization dedicated to educating and inspiring underprivileged children. In so doing she said, "If I have anything to leave, the foundation is my legacy."

In 1961 Rudolph had married William Ward, but the marriage dissolved the next year. In 1963 she married Robert Eldridge, who was the father of her first child. They would have one more daughter and two sons before they divorced in 1976.

In July 1994, while giving a speech, Rudolph fainted. Diagnosed with brain cancer, she died at her home in Brentwood, Tennessee. Overcoming physical challenges and racial barriers, Rudolph became a world-class athlete whose legacy inspired successive generations. In an earlier interview she remarked, "I just want to be remembered as a hardworking lady with certain beliefs."

FURTHER READING

Rudolph, Wilma. *Wilma* (1977).

Bernstein, Margaret. "That Championship Season." *Essence*, July 1984.
Davis, Michael D. *Black American Women in Olympic Track and Field* (1992).
Jackson, Tenley-Ann. "Olympic Mind Power." *Essence*, July 1984.
Rhoden, William C. "The End of a Winding Road." *New York Times*, 19 Nov. 1994.

Obituary: *New York Times*, 13 Nov. 1994.
—GAYNOL LANGS

RUFFIN, JOSEPHINE ST. PIERRE (31 Aug. 1842–13 Mar. 1924), editor and woman's club organizer, was born in Boston, Massachusetts, the daughter of Eliza Matilda Menhenick of Cornwall, England, and John St. Pierre, a clothing seller whose father was a French immigrant from Martinique. Though Josephine's

complexion was very light, public schools in Boston were closed to people of color until 1855, so she received her early education at nearby Salem and Charlestown. Later she attended Boston's Bowdoin School and took two years of private tutoring in New York. In 1858 she married George Lewis Ruffin, who made his living as a barber but later became a prominent Boston legislator and judge. The marriage produced five children.

Because of the slavery issue in the United States, Ruffin and her family moved briefly to Liverpool, England, in 1858 but soon returned to Boston to fight for civil rights when the Civil War began. Even at her young age, Ruffin was beginning to demonstrate her organizational and leadership skills. Despite the demands of raising a family, she was soon busy recruiting soldiers for the war effort and working for the U.S. Sanitary Commission. She also worked with other charitable groups, such as the Boston Kansas Relief Association, which helped freed slaves who migrated west, and the Massachusetts School Suffrage Association.

In 1890 Ruffin used what little was left of her husband's resources (he died in 1886 nearly destitute because he gave much of his money to charitable and civil rights work) to embark on a new adventure. With her family's help, she founded the *Woman's Era*, a monthly magazine devoted almost exclusively to issues affecting African American women. The publication covered society news but also dealt with more serious social issues like abolition, suffrage, and living conditions in the cities. Though the articles were written by a staff, Ruffin acted as editor, layout person, and editorial writer—she even became her own advertising executive. Besides editing and publishing her own magazine, she supplemented her income in 1891 by acting as editor in chief of the *Boston Courant*, a black weekly newspaper. She gave up this work, though, in 1893 to devote more time to the *Era*, and she also joined the New England Women's Press Association in 1893. Though the *Woman's Era* gave Ruffin a decent living for several years, it suffered from insufficient advertising revenue, as did most of the African American periodical press of the time. Also the *Woman's Era* catered to the elite

African American society of Boston, and its one-dollar-per-year subscription price was more than most ordinary African American women could afford. The last issue was dated January 1897.

Ruffin's work as an editor and her friendship with many influential people aroused in her an interest in the field for which she is best remembered. In 1894, influenced by Julia Ward Howe and others, she organized with her friend, Maria Baldwin, and her daughter, Florida Ruffin Ridley, the Woman's Era Club. Using the *Woman's Era* as its official publication, the club devoted itself to the education of young African American women and to charitable causes. The Woman's Era Club became so successful under Ruffin's leadership that it grew in 1896 from a sixty-member Boston club into the National Association of Colored Women, with thousands of members. Ruffin tried to gain more support from the white women's clubs by joining the Massachusetts State Federation of Women's Clubs, and she also joined the all-white General Federation of Women's Clubs and was asked to serve on its executive committee. Not realizing that she was president of a black club, the federation had accepted her membership. When she arrived at the biennial convention in Milwaukee in 1900, however, the situation was quite different. What happened there was one of the defining moments of Josephine Ruffin's career and one of the most unfortunate incidents in the history of the women's club movement. Southern delegates were outraged that an "octoroon" wanted to become a member of the General Federation, and they insisted that the membership remain white. The executive board of the federation claimed that she had violated the rules by not revealing that the Woman's Era Club was a black club. The federation was fearful of losing southern members, and despite protests from Ruffin's supporters, it refused to recognize her organization or seat her as a delegate to a black club, although it was willing to seat her as a member of the two white clubs to which she already belonged, the New England Women's Press Association and the Massachusetts State Federation of Women's Clubs. Never one to compromise her principles, however, Ruffin refused its offer.

Ruffin remained president of the Woman's Era Club until 1903, but her activities in it gradually began to dwindle, although her involvement in the community remained strong. Among other organizations to which she gave her time were the Association for the Promotion of Child Training in the South and the American Mount Coffee School Association, which helped raise funds for a school in Liberia. She was also instrumental in establishing the Boston chapter of the National Association for the Advancement of Colored People, of which she remained a member for many years.

Advanced age did not stop Josephine Ruffin from giving her time and energy to worthy causes. Her daughter, Florida Ridley, recalled that Ruffin attended the "Women's Day" celebration in Boston when she was seventy-nine, and, at the age of eighty-two, she took a taxi on a stormy night to attend a meeting of the League of Women for Community Service. Less than a month later she died of nephritis at her home in Boston.

FURTHER READING

The Ruffin family papers are at the Amistad Research Center, Tulane University. Incomplete files of the *Woman's Era* are in the Moorland-Spingarn Research Center at Howard University and at the Boston Public Library.

Brown, Hallie Quinn. *Homespun Heroines and Other Women of Distinction* (1926).
Bullock, Penelope. *The Afro-American Periodical Press, 1838–1909* (1981).
Logan, Rayford W. *The Betrayal of the Negro from Rutherford B. Hayes to Woodrow Wilson* (1965).
Wesley, Charles H. *The History of the National Association of Colored Women's Clubs* (1984).

—Roger A. Schuppert

RUGGLES, DAVID

(15 Mar. 1810–26 Dec. 1849), abolitionist and journalist, was born in Norwich, Connecticut, the son of David Ruggles and Nancy (maiden name unknown), both free blacks. Educated at the Sabbath School for the Poor, he moved to New York City at the age of seventeen. In 1829 he opened a grocery, selling goods of "excellent quality" but no "spirituous liquors." He later served as an officer in the New York City Temperance Union.

In 1833 Ruggles sharpened his speaking skills as an agent for the *Emancipator and Journal of Public Morals*, the organ of the American Anti-Slavery Society. He attacked colonization and spoke in support of the black national convention movement and the newly established Phoenix Society, organized to nurture black education. The society sponsored the Phoenix High School for Colored Youth, which by 1837 employed thirteen teachers.

With Henry Highland Garnet, Ruggles organized the Garrison Literary and Benevolent Association, named after famed abolitionist William Lloyd Garrison, which sponsored a reading room. In 1834 he opened the first known African American–owned bookshop, which served the abolitionist and black community. An antiabolitionist mob destroyed the store, however, in 1835.

Ruggles became well known to white abolitionists through his numerous articles in the *Emancipator*. In 1834 he published his first pamphlet, the anticolonization satire, *Extinguisher, Extinguished . . . or David M. Reese, M.D. "Used Up."* He expanded his abolitionist arguments in 1835 in *The Abrogation of the Seventh Commandment by the American Churches*. Published by Ruggles's own press, another African American first, the pamphlet stood proslavery arguments that the abolition of slavery would lead to interracial sex on their heads. He charged slaveowners with violating the Seventh Commandment by forcing slave women to surrender "to their unbridled lusts," thus offending "every principle of feminine sensibility and Christian morals." In this appeal to the emerging northern feminist movement, Ruggles beseeched northern women to shun their southern white sisters who brought their slaves north "while on a summer tour." Those same women, he thundered, passively allowed their husbands to father children in the slave quarter or used as domestics "the spurious offspring of their own husbands, brothers, and sons." He found these actions of southern white women "inexcusably criminal" and demanded that northern women close their churches to them. Angelina Weld Grimké used Ruggles's arguments in a speech before the Anti-Slavery

Convention of American Women held in New York City in 1837.

In 1835 Ruggles founded and headed the New York Committee of Vigilance, which sought to shield the growing number of fugitive slaves from recapture and protect free blacks from kidnapping. Cooperating with white abolitionists Lewis Tappan and Isaac T. Hopper, Ruggles and other black leaders were daring conductors on the Underground Railroad and harbored nearly one thousand blacks, including FREDERICK DOUGLASS, before transferring them farther north to safety. A fearless activist, he raised funds for the committee, served writs against slave catchers, and directly confronted suspected kidnappers. In frequent columns for the *Colored American*, he exposed kidnapping incidents on railroads. In 1839 he published the *Slaveholders Directory*, which identified the names and addresses of politicians, lawyers, and police in New York City who "lend themselves to kidnapping." His bold efforts often led to his arrest and imprisonment, which contributed to his failing health and eyesight.

Between 1838 and 1841 Ruggles published five issues of the *Mirror of Liberty*, the first African American magazine. Circulated widely throughout the East, Midwest, and the South, the magazine reported on the activities of the Committee of Vigilance, kidnappings and related court cases, antislavery speeches, and the activities of black organizations. Despite its irregular appearances, its publication was a significant achievement. In 1844 Ruggles attempted unsuccessfully to establish a second magazine, entitled the *Genius of Freedom*. In 1838 he attacked colonization once more in *An Antidote for a Poisonous Combination*.

Ruggles's antislavery zeal caused a fractious dispute with SAMUEL CORNISH in 1838. Without the permission of editor Cornish, Ruggles published the accusation in the *Colored American* that John Russell, a local black and landlord of a home for African American seamen, trafficked in slaves. Russell successfully sued Ruggles and the newspaper for libel, and Cornish blamed Ruggles for the subsequent upheaval that split the black community. By 1839, stung by the divisive battle with Cornish, accused of mishandling funds

by the Committee of Vigilance, and suffering from poor health and near blindness, Ruggles moved to Northampton, Massachusetts. There Lydia Maria Child and the Northampton Association of Education and Industry gave him succor in the 1840s while he continued his activities on the Underground Railroad. In 1841 he showed his old grit when he pioneered protest against segregation on public transit by refusing to leave his seat in a New Bedford, Massachusetts, railroad car.

Beset by illness and weary of failed cures, Ruggles in the 1840s tried successfully the water-cure treatments made famous by Vincent Priessnitz of Austrian Silesia. In Northampton, Ruggles overcame his poor health and built a prosperous practice as a doctor of hydropathy. In 1846, with the help of the Northampton Association, he refurbished an old watermill and opened the first establishment devoted to water cures in the United States. Using "cutaneous electricity" treatments, Ruggles became nationally known. He assisted a variety of patients, from the wife of a southern slave owner to William Lloyd Garrison and SOJOURNER TRUTH. He died in Northampton from a severe bowel inflammation. As an abolitionist, journalist, and physician, Ruggles gave selflessly to help others.

FURTHER READING

The most complete collection of Ruggles's writings is in Ripley et al., eds., *The Black Abolitionist Papers* (1981–1983), microfilm.

Porter, Dorothy B., ed. *Early Negro Writing, 1760–1837* (1971).
Ripley, C. Peter. *Black Abolitionist Papers*, vol. 3 (1991).

—GRAHAM RUSSELL HODGES

RUSSELL, BILL

(12 Feb. 1934–), basketball player and coach, was born William Fenton Russell in Monroe, Louisiana, the son of Charles and Katie Russell, both laborers. Mister Charlie, as his two sons called him, worked in a paper bag factory, while his wife worked odd jobs on a stopgap basis. She took jobs as a maid in white households only when money was especially scarce or when she

particularly wished to spoil Bill, whom she openly considered her favorite child. Both Mister Charlie and Russell's paternal grandfather, usually called simply "the Old Man," set a high bar for their male progeny in Monroe. Before his ninth birthday, Russell had witnessed his father ward off an armed white man with only a tire iron and his grandfather punch a mule to its knees with just one blow.

In 1943, unable to tolerate the pressures of Jim Crow any longer, Mister Charlie left for Detroit, Michigan, and then for Oakland, California, to work as a laborer and save up enough money to send for his family. Bill, his brother Charlie, and Katie joined him in California later that same year. Oakland afforded the Russells slightly better opportunities; Mister Charlie launched a successful trucking business, and the family began saving money. But when Russell was twelve his mother died, and Mister Charlie had to abandon his business to take a foundry job closer to his sons.

Frustrated by their teachers' skeptical opinions of their intellectual capacities, the Russell boys immersed themselves in athletics—Charlie, two years older than Bill, was much more successful early on. While Charlie's basketball prowess got him into Oakland Tech high school, Bill drifted through Hoover Junior High, where he was cut from football and basketball teams, and finally landed at nearby McClymonds High. Discouraged after being cut from the varsity basketball team as a sophomore, Russell was accepted by the jayvee coach George Powles for his squad. With only fifteen jerseys for sixteen youths, Russell and a teammate alternated games as the fifteenth player.

By his senior year Russell had grown to six feet, nine inches but did not distinguish himself until his final game, scoring a career high of fourteen points. A University of San Francisco (USF) alumnus was informally scouting Russell's opponent but signed Russell instead. It was the young center's only scholarship offer. Before attending USF, Russell played for a few months on a California high school all-star team that toured the Pacific Northwest and British Columbia. Russell's skills grew significantly, as did his body, and he entered his freshman year at his full height of six feet, ten inches.

Bill Russell, in a contest with the New York Knicks in 1960, led the Boston Celtics to eleven National Basketball Association championships between 1957 and 1969. Library of Congress

Led by Russell at center and K. C. Jones (also a future Celtic) at guard, the San Francisco Dons won fifty-five straight games, including national championships in 1955 and 1956. Russell was also a world-class high jumper for the track-and-field team but characteristically credited his success in that event more to what he called "the psych" than to any exceptional athletic ability. As he put it, "There wasn't a guy I jumped against I couldn't beat if I had the chance to talk to him beforehand" (Wolff, 138). Between his junior and senior years Russell was delighted to witness an NCAA rule change that sportswriters dubbed the "Russell rule." Since an offensive player can stand in the foul lane for no longer than three seconds, officials widened the lane from six feet to twelve feet, hoping to push Russell, who by this time could redirect his teammates' shots at will, farther from the basket. But since Russell himself placed more emphasis on defense, he relished the advantage he gained from defending a more spread out offense; he could now roam the less-crowded paint with ease and block a greater number of shots, each block a potential two-point advantage for the Dons.

After graduation, Russell played on the U.S. Olympic team in the 1956 Melbourne Games. By no means naive, he was still tremendously affected by the political and economic corruption that permeated the event. Russell later wrote in *Go Up for Glory* that the Olympics "has to be the greatest bit of sugar-'n-spice-in-the-mouth-and-bourbon-in-the-belly-carney-type-conning since Barnum and Bailey" (56). After beating the Russians in the gold medal game 89–55, Russell flew back to Oakland, married his college sweetheart, Rose Swisher, and joined the Boston Celtics in midseason.

The Celtics coach, Red Auerbach, had orchestrated a dramatic trade with their strongest rival, St. Louis, in order to sign Russell—which they did for $19,500, making him the highest-paid NBA rookie. Averaging 14.7 points and 19.6 rebounds per game, Russell infused the Celtics with a newfound defensive rigor, helping them beat St. Louis

in 1957 for their first world championship. The next year Russell sprained his ankle early in the finals, and the Celtics lost to St. Louis. Then, from 1959 to 1966, the Celtics won eight consecutive NBA championships, a feat that has never even been approached by a professional team in any other American sport. Russell earned league MVP honors in 1958, 1961, 1962, 1963, and 1965 as well as an All-Star game MVP award in 1963. Besides his formidable scoring threat and Herculean rebounding—rivaled only by his legendary foe, WILT CHAMBERLAIN—Russell's forte was the blocked shot, for which he routinely deployed the same "psych" he had developed as a college high jumper and player. (Unfortunately, statistics were not kept for the blocked shot during Russell's career.)

Russell also distinguished himself as an outspoken human rights figure. (Like MALCOLM X, he vehemently preferred the phrase "human rights" over "civil rights.") Already a notorious opponent of unwritten NBA quotas, he held integrated basketball camps in the South after the assassination of MEDGAR EVERS, and he visited Africa in 1959 as a liaison of the U.S. Department of State, to teach children basketball. He was so impressed with the ongoing project of Liberia that he invested in a rubber plantation that significantly bolstered their economy. Back home a few years later, he met with MUHAMMAD ALI to discuss Ali's refusal to answer the U.S. draft, and he proclaimed afterward his belief in the boxer's sincerity: "I'm not worried about Muhammad Ali. What I'm worried about is the rest of us" (*Sports Illustrated*, 19 June 1967). In 1964 Russell declared in the *Saturday Evening Post* that celebrity black athletes, no matter their fame or wealth, have a responsibility to "the total condition of the Negro." In 1966 he demonstrated his commitment to that philosophy by writing a blistering autobiography, *Go Up for Glory*, in which he interprets his life primarily through challenges related to race, rather than sports.

Early in his career Russell became known for vomiting before every game; privately, during the last couple of seasons of the Celtics' championship run, he came to depend on high doses of sleeping pills to calm his nerves. The vomiting embodied the tension in his life between an intense competitiveness and a high-strung vulnerability, all of which contributed to a nervous breakdown in 1965. Nonetheless, upon Auerbach's retirement the next year, Russell was named player-coach for the 1967 campaign, thereby becoming the first African American coach of an integrated team in a major professional sports league. The next season the Celtics lost to Chamberlain's Philadelphia 76ers, but before retiring in 1969 Russell would lead the Celtics to two more consecutive championships, quipping late in his career, "Now I just throw up for the playoffs" (Wolff, 138).

His last year as a player-coach was also the last year of his marriage to Rose, with whom he had three children, William "Buddha" Felton Jr., Jacob, and Karen Kenyatta. In 1974 Russell was elected to the Basketball Hall of Fame despite his personal objections to the hall's treatment of minority players as well as his aversion to the vacuity of celebrity honors. At this time Russell was still an NBA coach for the fledgling Seattle Supersonics; following a four-year record of 162–166, he backed away from the game and married Didi Anstett in 1977. A decade later Russell gave coaching another try, this time with the Sacramento Kings—but after a 17–41 start he stepped down before season's end.

Russell wrote two more books: a supplemental autobiography in 1979, *Second Wind: The Memoirs of an Opinionated Man* (with Taylor Branch), and *Russell Rules: Eleven Lessons on Leadership from the Twentieth Century's Greatest Winner* (2002). Whatever the mixed results of his latter-day coaching efforts, Russell holds the distinction of being the "winningest" competitor in any major U.S. sport in any era. Between 1955 and 1969 Russell tallied two NCAA championships, an Olympic gold medal, and eleven NBA world championships. Popularly regarded as a consummate team player, Russell still totaled seven MVP awards during that run.

FURTHER READING

Russell, Bill. *Russell Rules: Eleven Lessons on Leadership from the Twentieth Century's Greatest Winner* (2002).

———, with Taylor Branch. *Second Wind: The Memoirs of an Opinionated Man* (1979).

———, with William McSweeny. *Go Up for Glory* (1966).

Shapiro, Miles. *Bill Russell* (1991).
Wolff, Alexander. *100 Years of Hoops* (1991).
—DAVID F. SMYDRA JR.

 RUSSWURM, JOHN BROWN (1 Oct. 1799– 9 June 1851), journalist and first nonwhite governor of Maryland in Liberia Colony, West Africa, was born in Port Antonio, Jamaica, the son of John Russwurm, a white American merchant, and an unidentified Jamaican black woman. As a boy known only as John Brown, Russwurm was sent to Canada for an education by his father. After his father's settlement in Maine and marriage in 1813 to a white New England widow with children, he entered the new family at his stepmother's insistence. John Brown thereupon assumed his father's surname and remained with his stepmother even after the senior Russwurm's death in 1815. His schooling continued at home and, later, at preparatory institutes such as the North Yarmouth Academy in Maine. He made a short, unhappy visit to Jamaica and returned to Portland, Maine, to begin collegiate study. Thrown on his own after just one year because of his sponsor's inability to continue support, young Russwurm took a succession of brief teaching jobs at African free schools in Philadelphia, New York, and Boston.

Russwurm entered Bowdoin College in Brunswick, Maine, in September 1824 and soon evinced an interest in books by joining the Athenean Society, a campus literary group. He graduated two years later with a BA. Asked to give a commencement oration, he titled his speech, "The Condition and Prospects of Hayti." He claimed that Haitians, having overthrown French rule, exemplified the truth that "it is the irresistible course of events that all men, who have been deprived of their liberty, shall recover this previous portion of their indefeasible inheritance." That a young man partially of African descent had graduated from college, the second or third nonwhite to do so in the United States, and had spoken so eloquently of freedom garnered attention from several newspapers and journals, which published extracts of his remarks. Bowdoin College awarded Russwurm an honorary master of arts degree in 1829.

John Brown Russwurm, founder of the first African American newspaper, Freedom's Journal, *in New York in 1827.* Schomburg Center

As a college student Russwurm entertained the idea of emigrating to Haiti, but, diploma in hand, he went to New York City and, with SAMUEL CORNISH, a Presbyterian minister, began publishing *Freedom's Journal*, the first black newspaper in the United States. The editors declared in the inaugural issue, on 16 March 1827, that they wanted to disseminate useful knowledge of every kind among an estimated 500,000 free persons of color, to bring about their moral, religious, civil, and literary improvement, and, most important of all, to plead their cause, including their civil rights, to the public. They emphasized the value of education and self-help. Although they vowed that the journal would not become the advocate of any partial views either in politics or in religion, it spoke clearly for the abolition of slavery in the United States and opposed the budding movement to colonize freed blacks in Africa. Weekly issues carried a variety of material: poetry, letters of explorers and others in Africa, information on the status of slaves in slaveholding states, legislation pending or passed in states that affected blacks, notices of job openings, and personal news such as marriages and obituaries. Advertisements for adult education classes appeared frequently and Russwurm even appealed for subscribers to attend an evening school in lower New York where he taught reading, writing, arithmetic, English grammar, and geography. Agents in twelve states as well as in Canada, Haiti, and England sold subscriptions, but total circulation figures can only be guessed as several hundred copies. Six months after the newspaper's beginning Cornish resigned as an editor, ostensibly in order to return to the ministry and to promote free black schools, but more likely because he disagreed with Russwurm's new views on African colonization.

Russwurm was becoming convinced that blacks could not achieve equality with whites in the United States and that emigration to Africa was their best hope. In one of his last editorials, he wrote that "the universal emancipation so ardently desired by us & by all our friends, can never take place, unless some door is opened whereby the emancipated may be removed as fast as they drop their galling chains, to some other land besides the free states." The final issue of the journal appeared on 28 March 1829, whereupon, two months later, Cornish resumed its editorship under a new title, *The Rights of All*. His vigorous denunciation of the colonization movement in fact represented the majority view among slaves and free blacks.

That fall Russwurm sailed for Monrovia, capital of the colony of Liberia, which had been established in 1822 by the American Colonization Society, a national group that favored the voluntary repatriation of blacks to Africa as a solution to accelerating racial problems. He assumed editorship of the foundering, government-controlled *Liberia Herald* in 1830, became the official government printer by virtue of his appointment as colonial secretary, undertook the supervision of public education, and engaged in trade. In 1833 he married Sarah E. McGill, daughter of George R. McGill, a Baltimorean who had emigrated to Liberia six years earlier and was then acting colonial agent for the society. The couple had five children, including an adopted son. Russwurm's tenure in the public affairs of Liberia was characterized by controversy over freedom of the press and his close links with unpopular colonial officials. The colonists wanted the *Herald* to be

independently run, which it could not be, they believed, if the editor were a government employee. Russwurm was removed from his editorship and from other posts in 1835.

Of equal importance historically to his role in pioneering the American black press is Russwurm's fifteen-year career as the governor of Maryland in Liberia, a colony founded in 1834 at Cape Palmas, two hundred miles south of Monrovia, by the Maryland State Colonization Society. This organization was originally a state auxiliary of the American Colonization Society, but its leaders, disappointed by the disparate views among supporters from northern and southern states, by the slow pace of emigration, and by poor management in Monrovia, created a settlement of their own to which primarily freed Maryland blacks would emigrate. It was heavily subsidized by annual grants from the Maryland legislature. The first two governors of the colony, both whites, were overcome by ill health during their brief stays on the West African coast. The society's board of managers in Baltimore therefore concluded that it must appoint a nonwhite who was already acclimated to Africa and familiar with the governance of a settlement and who not only could survive but also develop in the colonists a sense of autonomy and an expectation of self-government.

Russwurm received his appointment in September 1836 and, proceeding immediately to Cape Palmas, found a small town called Harper, a few outlying farms, a mission of the American Board of Commissioners for Foreign Missions, and a population of about two hundred immigrants. Over the next ten years, the governor created a currency system, improved business procedures, and adopted a legal code. He attempted to smooth relations with neighboring African groups but, having mixed success, enlarged the militia and encouraged the American African Squadron, whose goal was the suppression of the slave trade, to visit along the coast as a display of support. He worked to stimulate agriculture, both by encouraging the colonists on their own farms and by the enlargement of the public farm on which he planted a nursery and experimented with various crops. He oversaw numerous public improvements and the addition of territory to the colony.

Russwurm's judicious application of the colony's constitution and ordinances, political preeminence over the often fractious settlers, and ability to govern well with decreasing supervision of the board in Baltimore coincided with a mounting demand among the colonists in the late 1840s that Maryland in Liberia either be granted independence or that it seek annexation to the newly created Republic of Liberia. The governor himself seems not to have taken a stand, possibly because of his disappointment with the current generation of colonists, whom he characterized as still too unenlightened to accomplish much. Furthermore he was in poor health and suffered from ulcerations on his foot, which may have been related to gout. In spite of these factors and the sudden death of his adopted son, Russwurm continued to direct the colony, and even on the day of his own death, he attended to a portion of his official duties before succumbing to multiple ailments at the government house in Cape Palmas.

The citizens lauded Russwurm as statesman, philanthropist, and Christian. They named an island off Cape Palmas and a township after him. Back in Baltimore, members of the board recalled his visit to the United States in 1848, when he not only exhibited an excellent and courteous bearing but confirmed that he was an educated and accomplished gentleman. They spoke of his faithful service and how he had vindicated their belief in "the perfect fitness of his race for the most important political positions in Africa." They ordered the construction of a marble obelisk with suitable inscriptions over his grave at Cape Palmas. The board's high estimate was reinforced by his stepmother in a laudatory letter in which she characterized him as a literary man whose family and library were to him the world. By the time of Russwurm's death, the settlement numbered nearly a thousand inhabitants and owned a strip of coastline stretching northward more than a hundred miles.

Russwurm sometimes likened himself to Moses, leader of the Israelites, in trying to push his people ahead; indeed, under his administration a colony of former American slaves achieved a large degree of self-government. He proved capable of handling difficulties with settlers, with adjacent Africans, and with white missionaries. His physical and executive perseverance gave the settlement the benefit of stability until it could consider viable alternatives to its dependent relationship with the Maryland State Colonization Society. The survival of the colony, now known as Maryland County in the Republic of Liberia, is attributable principally to the success of Russwurm's governorship.

FURTHER READING

Bowdoin College in Brunswick, Maine, holds about nine hundred items, many of them of a secondary nature, in its special collections and also has copies of Russwurm material from the Tennessee State Library and Archives, Nashville. Smaller collections can be found at the Maryland Historical Society, in the American Colonization Society Papers at the Library of Congress, in the African Squadron Papers at the National Archives, and in the American Board of Commissioners for Foreign Missions Papers at Houghton Library, Harvard College.

Campbell, Penelope. *Maryland in Africa, the Maryland State Colonization Society 1831–1857* (1971).

Hutton, Frankie. *The Early Black Press in America, 1827 to 1860* (1993).

—PENELOPE CAMPBELL

RUSTIN, BAYARD TAYLOR (17 Mar. 1912–24 Aug. 1987), civil rights organizer

and political activist, was born in West Chester, Pennsylvania, the son of Archie Hopkins and Florence "Cissy" Rustin. Hopkins abandoned his sixteen-year-old lover before their child was born, and it was not until Bayard was eleven that he discovered that Cissy was his mother, not his sister, and that his "parents" Janifer Rustin, a caterer, and Julia Rustin, a nurse, were, in fact, his grandparents. Throughout his life, Bayard Rustin referred to Janifer as "papa" and Julia as "mama" and enjoyed a more comfortable family life than his complicated origins might suggest.

Rustin attended the public schools of West Chester and displayed a precocious talent for dissent. In grade school he resisted teachers who tried to make him write with his right hand, and in high school he refused to compete in a state track meet unless he and a fellow black student could stay in the same hotel as their white teammates. In both cases he won. The teenaged Rustin was less successful in his attempts to desegregate West Chester's movie theater, however, resulting in the first of nearly thirty arrests for civil disobedience. On graduating from high school in 1932, Rustin attended Wilberforce University in Ohio, though he spent barely a year there before being dismissed, either for refusing to join the ROTC or for falling in love with the son of the university's president. He then returned to West Chester to study at Cheyney State Teachers College and appeared as a tenor soloist on several radio shows in Philadelphia. He also became active in the Society of Friends, a move that pleased his grandmother, who had been raised in the Society and remained a Quaker in spirit, even though she had joined the African Methodist Episcopal Church.

After Cheyney State dismissed him in 1937 for an indiscretion that he later alluded to as "naughty," Rustin left for Manhattan (Anderson, 38). There he attended a few classes at the City College of New York but divided most of his time between social activism—serving as an organizer for the Young Communist League (YCL) in Harlem—and music. In 1939 he sang in the chorus of *John Henry*, an all-black musical starring PAUL ROBESON, and performed with the blues singer LEAD BELLY and the folk-song revivalist Josh White at the Café Society Downtown, an integrated nightclub in Greenwich Village. Although he sang at demonstrations—and in jails—throughout his career, Rustin increasingly focused on social and political organizing.

In 1941 he began working with the labor leader A. PHILIP RANDOLPH, who mentored Rustin on the tactics and strategies required of mass political organizing and persuaded him to abandon communism in favor of democratic socialism. Randolph also introduced Rustin to the writings of Mohandas K. Gandhi, the pacifist leader of the Indian resistance to British rule, and to A. J. Muste, who adhered to the Gandhian principle of achieving social change through nonviolent direct action and who led the Fellowship of Reconciliation (FOR), a pacifist organization. In 1942, after Muste appointed him the FOR's youth secretary,

Rustin traveled throughout the nation in the hope of recruiting a cadre of pacifists and raising awareness of the plight of Japanese Americans placed in internment camps. Given the vast public sympathy for the war effort once Japan attacked Pearl Harbor in December 1941, that proved to be no mean task and often a dangerous one. In 1944 federal authorities imprisoned Rustin for refusing to appear before his military draft board.

On release from prison in 1947 Rustin joined the Congress on Racial Equality (CORE) in its Journey of Reconciliation, an attempt to end segregation in interstate travel by sitting in the front seats of buses designated by law and custom for whites only. The unwillingness of southern whites to countenance such a change became clear in Chapel Hill, North Carolina, when Rustin was dragged from the front of a Trailways bus by police and sentenced to thirty days on a chain gang. The failure of CORE's campaign did not shake Rustin's belief that nonviolent direct action could help destroy Jim Crow, however, and in the early 1950s he embarked on a series of lectures and workshops promoting civil disobedience in the United States, Europe, South Africa, and Ghana. Many in the international peace movement viewed Rustin as an inspirational speaker and expert tactician and expected that he might replace the aging Muste as head of the FOR.

Bayard Rustin in August 1963. Library of Congress

Instead, in 1953, the FOR board demanded Rustin's resignation after his arrest in Los Angeles on a morals charge, the euphemism of the day for performing homosexual acts in public. Rustin agreed to leave the organization immediately, reflecting both his inner conflict about his sexual orientation at that time and the prevailing homophobic mood of 1950s America. Even though he was unwilling to abandon his sexual preference, he agreed with Muste that his homosexuality was wrong and that his actions had diminished the FOR's moral standing.

Although the arrest chilled his friendship with Muste, Rustin's other mentor, A. Philip Randolph, stood by him, sending Rustin to Alabama in December 1955 to advise MARTIN LUTHER KING JR., the leader of the Montgomery bus boycott. Rustin counseled King on the theories and practicalities of nonviolent direct action and helped transform the young minister's narrowly defined boycott into a fully formed Gandhian mass movement. King later wrote of the Montgomery protest that "Christ furnished the spirit while Gandhi furnished the method" (quoted in Anderson, 188). He might have added that Rustin furnished the essential tactical knowledge, based on a lifetime of practicing nonviolent resistance. Along with ELLA BAKER, Rustin also founded In Friendship, a New York–based group, to raise northern awareness of, and money for, the Southern Christian Leadership Conference (SCLC), a regional civil rights body led by King, which Rustin had helped organize in 1957.

In March 1960 Rustin headed the Committee to Defend Martin Luther King, after the state of Alabama indicted the SCLC leader on trumped-up charges of tax evasion and perjury. Three months later, however, the congressman ADAM CLAYTON POWELL JR. threatened to announce publicly—and mendaciously—that King and Rustin were lovers; Powell was furious that Rustin had planned a demonstration at that summer's Democratic National Convention without consulting him. Even though he knew the charges were false, Rustin resigned as King's special assistant, to prevent a scandal he feared would jeopardize the movement at a critical juncture. Rustin later commented that King's refusal to support him or even to ask him personally to resign was "the only time Martin really pissed me off" (quoted in Levine, 121).

Exiled from the main leadership of the civil rights struggle, Rustin worked in 1961–1962 with the World Peace Brigade, an organization dedicated to the nonviolent overthrow of colonial rule in Africa. He returned a year later to an American civil rights struggle in which the Student Nonviolent Coordinating Committee (SNCC) had joined the SCLC and CORE in supporting nonviolent direct action to challenge segregation. Randolph, King, and Rustin believed that only a mass demonstration could build on those protests and persuade Congress to pass meaningful civil rights legislation, and Randolph insisted that his deputy should organize that mass protest. Building on a lifetime of working with civil rights, labor, and peace activists across the nation, Rustin orchestrated a broad, multicultural coalition of support for the March on Washington in August 1963. Most of the 250,000 marchers and the millions watching on television that day would remember King's "I Have a Dream" speech, but the overall success of the demonstration owed as much to Rustin's meticulous attention to detail as to King's stirring rhetoric.

The March on Washington served as a springboard for the 1964 Civil Rights Act and the 1965 Voting Rights Act, but it also marked the high point of unity in the civil rights movement. While younger members of SNCC and CORE began to embrace "Black Power," Rustin argued that blacks, poor whites, and other disenfranchised Americans could win social justice only through the same broad-based coalitions that had ended segregation. His equivocal stance on the Vietnam War provoked even more fury from former allies like JULIAN BOND of SNCC, who believed that Rustin had sold his soul to President Lyndon Johnson and the Democratic Party. The reality was somewhat more complex. Rustin certainly wanted influence in the Democratic Party, and he feared that opposing Johnson's policies in Vietnam would jeopardize the president's domestic War on Poverty. But Rustin's support for a gradual, negotiated withdrawal of U.S. troops also reflected an evolution in his thinking about war and peace. He had begun to question his absolute pacifism after World War II, in part because of guilt about being a conscientious objector in a war that had included the Holocaust. Like many former communists, he also despised the Soviet Union's repressive domestic and foreign policies and feared that a victory for the Vietcong would destroy any vestiges of democracy in South Vietnam.

Rustin's influence on international politics and the civil rights agenda waned in the 1970s and 1980s. He earned praise for his work to aid Haitian and Southeast Asian refugees, but was criticized for supporting increased U.S. economic and military aid to Israel, and for comparing the Palestine Liberation Organization to the Ku Klux Klan. On domestic matters Rustin gave qualified support to the affirmative action programs favored by most African Americans, but he continued to favor policies that would radically redistribute wealth to the poor of all races.

In his final decade Rustin became more open about his homosexuality, but he did not take an active role in the growing gay rights movement. He died in New York City in August 1987 after being hospitalized for a burst appendix and then suffering a heart attack in the hospital. He was survived by his partner of twelve years, Walter Naegle. Rustin's most enduring legacy is his stewardship of the 1963 March on Washington, a demonstration that reflected his own dream of a grand multiracial coalition working peacefully for social and economic justice.

FURTHER READING

Bayard Rustin's papers are housed at the A. Philip Randolph Institute in New York City and are also available on microfilm from the University Publications of America.

Rustin, Bayard. *Down the Line: The Collected Writings of Bayard Rustin* (1971).
———. *Strategies for Freedom: The Changing Patterns of Black Protest* (1976).

Anderson, Jervis. *Bayard Rustin: Troubles I've Seen* (1997).
D'Emilio, John. *Lost Prophet: The Life and Times of Bayard Rustin* (2003).
Levine, Daniel. *Bayard Rustin and the Civil Rights Movement* (2000).

Obituaries: *New York Times*, 25 Aug. 1987; *Jet*, 7 Sept. 1987; *New Republic*, 28 Sept. 1987.

—STEVEN J. NIVEN

S

 ## SAAR, BETYE

(30 July 1926–), artist and educator, was born Betye Irene Brown in Pasadena, California, to Beatrice (maiden name unknown), a seamstress who enjoyed quilting, and Jefferson Brown, a salesman who liked to sketch and write. Jefferson Brown died from kidney problems when she was six years old, and Betye and her brother and sister lived with her mother's great-aunt and great-uncle until her mother remarried a man named Emmett six years later. After the second marriage, Beatrice had two more children, a boy and a girl. Betye spent summers with her grandmother in Watts, where she saw Simon Rodia's *Watts Towers*, a vernacular example of assemblage consisting of eight tall conical spirals. Built from steel rods, covered in concrete, and encrusted with found objects like bottle caps, glass, broken tiles, and shells, the *Watts Towers* seemed like "fairy-tale castles" (Isenberg, *State of the Arts*, 23) to Saar and became an important early influence on the artist. As a child, Betye enjoyed drawing and working with crafts, puppetry, and clay, and she often played in her grandmother's garden and at the beach, digging up small beads, shells, and stones that she saved in her collection.

Betye received her BA in Design from the University of California at Los Angeles in 1949, and in 1952 she married another artist, Richard Saar. The couple had three daughters—Lezley and Alison (who became artists) and Tracye. Like many female artists during the 1950s and 1960s, Saar worked at home while she raised her children. She turned her kitchen into a printmaking studio and also worked as a designer and jewelry maker. In 1956 she began graduate work in education and printmaking at the University of Southern California and the California State Universities at Long Branch and Northridge. In 1968 Betye

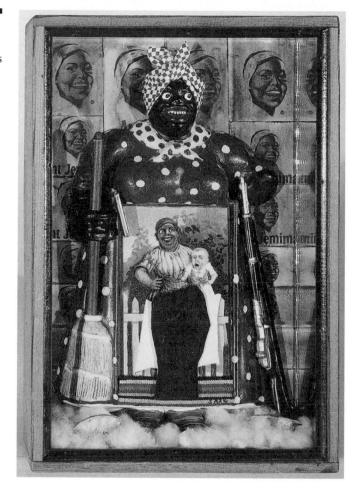

Betye Saar's mixed-media assemblage The Liberation of Aunt Jemima. University of California, Berkeley Art Museum; Photographed for the UC Berkeley Art Museum by Benjamin Blackwell

and her husband divorced. That year she saw an exhibition of the American surrealist Joseph Cornell; his boxes made of found objects appeared like intimate, mysterious worlds and gave her the idea to use boxes to create art.

By this time Saar had already used windows as the armature for numerous prints and drawings, such as *Sorcerer's Window* (1966) and *Black Girl's Window* (1969), the latter an autobiographical work depicting a young black girl peering through and pressed up against a closed window. Into the various panes

Saar incorporated objects like tarot cards, zodiac signs, and fetishes that suggest an interest in mysticism and spirituality. Like many African American artists at this time, Saar began thinking more deeply about her personal connection to African history and religion, and some of her works, such as *Nine Mojo Secrets* (1971) and *Spirit Catcher* (1976–1977), suggest this fascination. On a trip to Chicago, Saar visited the Field Museum and made sketches based on works in their collection of Oceanic, Egyptian, and African art.

In the late 1960s and early 1970s, against the backdrop of the civil rights movement, the Black Power movement, and the burgeoning Women's Art movement, Saar began collecting popular racist images that stereotyped African Americans. In her words, "I felt these images were important as documentation of how whites have historically perceived African Americans and how we have been portrayed as caricatures, as objects, as less-than-human.... I began to recycle and transform Sambos, Toms and Mammies in my assemblages" (Michael Rosenfeld Gallery, 3).

In 1972 Saar created what has become her most famous work, *The Liberation of Aunt Jemima*, which transformed a demeaning collectable Mammy figurine into a powerful, confrontational revolutionary, part feminist and part Black Power icon. The work not only suggests her allegiance to Cornell but also demonstrates her understanding of contemporary art movements like pop. Against the background of the box are serial repetitions of Aunt Jemima as she appeared on the General Mills pancake boxes. Instead of a grid of apolitical Campell's soup cans, such as the ones Andy Warhol produced, Saar appropriated an image circulated in the mass media that reinforces stereotypes about African American women. Using a deconstructive strategy, Saar adopted these racist images and deployed them in a new context as a way to critique them.

During the 1970s Saar also created a series of nostalgic assemblages using turn-of-the-century photographs and pieces of personal clothing and jewelry. Saar found photographs of unknown African Americans in second-hand stores, flea markets, and yard sales and combined them with various objects to construct stories about anonymous people overlooked by history. One work, *Record for Hattie* (1976), however, is biographical and represents her beloved great-aunt through the use of personal memorabilia, including a pearl necklace, a hand mirror, a small cross, a dried rose, a pincushion, a baby picture, and a childhood autograph book. Using objects Saar acquired after Hattie's death in 1974, at age ninety-eight, *Record for Hattie* relies on associative play that allows the viewer to move from detail

to detail to conjure a sense of who this woman once was.

During the 1970s, in addition to galleries, Saar began to exhibit in museums more frequently, garnering increasing critical acclaim. In 1973 she had a solo exhibition at the California State University, and in 1975 the Whitney Museum of American Art in New York City hosted a one-person show of Saar's work. At a time when artists in the Art Worker's Coalition and other related groups were protesting the scarcity of women and minorities in the Whitney's permanent collection and special exhibitions, this retrospective demonstrated the importance of Saar's work. Additional shows followed in 1976 in Hartford, Connecticut, at the Wadsworth Atheneum; in 1977 at the San Francisco Museum of Modern Art, and in 1980 at the Studio Museum of Harlem in New York.

Like many artists during the 1980s, Saar began to build on the environmental implications of assemblage, extending her works into large-scale installations that often filled entire rooms. In 1987 she worked as artist in residence at the Massachusetts Institute of Technology. There she exhibited her newest altar-like work, *Mojotech*, a piece that investigates the interrelationships between science and magic through a horizontal series of altars that give the impression of a miniature city rising into a mist filled with small objects, or mojos.

During the 1990s Saar returned to political art in response to what she saw as a troublesome resurgence of racism. In 1998 she received a traveling exhibition, her first solo show at the Michael Rosenfeld Gallery in New York, entitled *Workers + Warriors, the Return of Aunt Jemima*. In this new series dealing with African American women's roles as domestic workers, Saar used antique washboards, creating pieces such as *Dubl-Duty-I'se Back Wid a Vengeance* (1997) and *Call to Arms* (1997) that resuscitate the stereotypical Mammy imagery that Saar first appropriated in the early 1970s. While working on this series, Saar began to gather tin signs, postcards, advertisements, household objects, and other commercial materials containing racist imagery from flea markets in New York. Reconfiguring these objects in new ways, she created a series that was shown in

2000 at her second exhibition at the Michael Rosenfeld Gallery, *Betye Saar: In Service: A Version of Survival*. The works in this show emphasized the roles, such as butlers, cooks, shoe-shine boys, entertainers, and porters, that African Americans played in the service industry during Reconstruction and after emancipation from slavery. In 2002 Saar presented her third show at the Rosenfeld Gallery, *Betye Saar: Colored: Consider the Rainbow*. In this series she investigated the ways in which African Americans have judged one another based on the color of their skin, dating back to slave-plantation culture.

Saar has often been lauded for her work and especially for integrating into it many issues of concern to feminists and African Americans. Among her numerous awards, she has received five honorary doctorates, honors from the National Endowment for the Arts and the John Simon Guggenheim Memorial Foundation, and a fellowship from the J. Paul Getty Fund for the Visual Arts. Over the course of her career she has participated in over fifty solo exhibitions and many group exhibitions. Her work is represented in over thirty major museum collections throughout the United States.

FURTHER READING

Isenberg, Barbara. *State of the Arts: California Artists Talk about Their Work* (2000).

Michael Rosenfeld Gallery. *Betye Saar: Workers + Warriors, the Return of Aunt Jemima* (1998).

Nemser, Cindy. *Art Talk: Conversations with 15 Women Artists* (1995).

Wright Gallery, University of California at Los Angeles. *Secrets, Dialogues, Revelations: The Art of Betye and Alison Saar* (1990).

—LISA D. FREIMAN

 SATCHER, DAVID
(2 Mar. 1941–), physician, scholar, and U.S. Surgeon General, was born in Anniston, Alabama, the son of Anna and Wilmer Satcher, a foundry worker. Although neither parent had completed elementary school, they instilled in David a high regard for scholarly accomplishment and perseverance amidst segregation. A childhood bout with whooping cough and pneumonia

began his long and fruitful interest in medical research and health, particularly with regard to the health of minority and disadvantaged groups. He often recalled that his own difficulty in getting health care and gaining access to hospitals as well as his experience of "people dying at home" led him into medicine "with the view that I wanted to be like the physician who came out to the farm to see me, and I wanted to make a difference for people who didn't have access to care" (*NewsHour: A NewsHour with Jim Lehrer Transcript*, 21 Jan. 2002).

David attended segregated public schools in Alabama. Despite the use of secondhand schoolbooks in these separate and unequal facilities, the teachers and administrators took a real interest in the students, and David was pushed toward excellence in the classroom by a few of his teachers. In high school, he won an American Legion essay contest with the assistance of his English teacher. Observing his excellence in chemistry, another teacher, taking David under his wing, took him to visit the historically black Morehouse College in Atlanta, Georgia. Upon graduation from high school David entered Morehouse, where he excelled in academics, as a member of the track-and-field team, and in the school's choir.

After Satcher graduated from Morehouse in 1963 with a BA in Science, he entered Case Western Reserve University in Cleveland, Ohio, where he received his MD and also a PhD in Cytogenetics, a branch of genetic research that studies the structure of chromosomes, in 1970. It was as a student in the 1960s that Satcher began to work as an advocate for the training of black physicians and for better health care for disadvantaged and minority groups. As a student, he spearheaded efforts at Case Western to increase African American enrollment in the medical program. In 1970 he began a two-year residency at the Strong Memorial Hospital at the University of Rochester in New York, followed by a position in South Central Los Angeles at the Charles R. Drew Postgraduate Medical School and Martin Luther King Jr. Hospital, a facility opened in the Watts community after the 1965 riots.

During the 1970s Satcher directed an innovative sickle-cell-anemia treatment program at King-Drew Hospital for six years and served for two years as a faculty member at the UCLA School of Medicine and Public Health. Working between UCLA and King-Drew, he created a joint program where medical students could broaden their training and where physicians would become more involved in the care of residents in the Watts neighborhood. By 1977 Satcher had risen to the post of interim dean of the Drew Medical School. In 1979 he left California, returning to his alma mater, where he served as professor at the Morehouse School of Medicine and as chair of the Department of Community Medicine until 1982.

During this time of professional growth and advancement, Satcher and his wife, Nola Richardson, also raised four children. By this time he was widely respected for his administrative ability and for his activism and research in community health. In 1982, he became president of Meharry College in Nashville, Tennessee, where he remained until 1993, when he was asked to lead the Centers for Disease Control and Prevention (CDC). As director of national CDC programs, Satcher focused on taming the rising threat of breast cancer in the United States and on upgrading prevention and screening programs for breast and cervical cancer, which under his tenure at the CDC were extended from eighteen to fifty states. He also directed considerable attention to the issues of childhood immunization and infectious diseases.

In 1998 President Bill Clinton nominated Satcher to become the sixteenth surgeon general of the United States. Like one of his predecessors, JOYCELYN ELDERS, Satcher's appointment to the post of surgeon general was not without controversy. Conservatives attempted to block his nomination, citing his views on sex education as a means of improving health, his support of AIDS research in the developing world, his support for needle-exchange programs in the fight against AIDS in the United States, and his opposition to the U.S. Congress's efforts to enact a ban on so called partial-birth abortions. Despite this criticism, Satcher's appointment was confirmed by a Senate vote of sixty-three to thirty-five.

After his confirmation, Satcher also served as assistant secretary for health, making him only the second person in history to hold both positions simultaneously. As surgeon general, Satcher served as administrator and chief spokesperson for the Public Health Sevice Commissioned Corps and as the principal adviser to the president on public health issues affecting the nation, providing national leadership and guidance for developing public health strategies. As assistant secretary for health, Satcher conducted broad assessments designed to anticipate future public health problems and coordinated population-based, minority health, and women's health initiatives.

Preventing suicide, improving mental health, reducing cigarette smoking, stemming the tide of youth violence, preventing and treating obesity, and bettering sex education were among the many central issues defining Satcher's term as surgeon general. He also continued the community health activism that had been the backbone of his professional career. Among Satcher's major accomplishments was a report from his office on suicide and mental health, drawing public and professional attention to particular hidden aspects of these problems. Satcher placed the issue of suicide among teenagers on a national platform and led the development of prevention programs targeting youths. On the topic of sex and sexuality, Satcher insisted that the nation had condoned a kind of "conspiracy of silence," and he worked to promote public discussion on sex education and health. His June 2001 report on sex education, *Call to Action to Promote Sexual Health and Responsible Sexual Behavior*, proved to be controversial, eliciting disapproval from conservatives. Satcher, however, remained steadfast in his determination to push this agenda.

After Satcher's term as surgeon general ended in 2002, he served as visiting senior fellow at the Henry J. Kaiser Family Foundation in Washington, D.C., and then returned to the Morehouse School of Medicine to direct the newly established National Center for Primary Care. This center focused attention on the health disparities among minorities, disadvantaged groups, and vulnerable populations and their lack of access to health care, issues of critical concern for Satcher.

During his distinguished career, Satcher has received numerous awards and honorary degrees. He was a Robert Wood Johnson Clinical Scholar and Macy Faculty Fellow and has received honors from the National Medical Association, American Medical Association, American College of Physicians, American Academy of Family Physicians, American Academy for the Advancement of Science, and *Ebony* magazine. In 2000 his contributions to the study of mental health and illness earned him the Didi Hirsch Erasing Stigma Mental Health Leadership Award and the National Association of Mental Illness Distinguished Service Award. He has also received the Bennie Mays Trailblazer Award and the Jimmy and Rosalynn Carter Award for Humanitarian Contributions to the Health of Humankind from the National Foundation for Infectious Diseases. In 1997 Satcher received the New York Academy of Medicine Lifetime Achievement Award. Satcher is also a member of the Omega Psi Phi Fraternity Inc.

FURTHER READING

Edmunds, M., and C. Fulwood. "Strategic Communications in Oral Health: Influencing Public and Professional Opinions and Actions," *Ambul Pediatrics* 2, Suppl. (Mar. 2002).

Kleinman, D. V. "2001 Public Service Award: David Satcher, MD, PhD," *Journal of Public Health Dent* 61, no. 4 (Fall 2001).

Lewis, Jolie. "A New Season for David Satcher," *Case Western Reserve University Magazine* (Fall 2002).

McBeth, A. "Community Care Partnership: Planning with the Community," *Semin Nurse Management* 8, no. 2 (June 2000).

—KEITH WAILOO
—RICHARD M. MIZELLE JR.

SAVAGE, AUGUSTA

(29 Feb. 1892–26 Mar. 1962) sculptor, educator, and advocate for black artists, was born Augusta Christine Fells in Green Cove Springs, Florida, the seventh of fourteen children of Edward Fells, a laborer and Methodist minister, and Cornelia Murphy. As a child,

Augusta routinely skipped school, preferring to model small figurines at local clay pits, much to the consternation of her religious father, who, as she recalled in a 1935 interview, "almost whipped the art out of me" (Bearden, 168). At age fifteen, Augusta married John T. Moore, and a year later a daughter, Irene Connie Moore, was born; John Moore died several years later. In 1915 the Fells family moved to West Palm Beach, where Augusta taught clay modeling at her high school. She later spent a year at Tallahassee Normal School (now Florida A&M). At some point after 1915 Augusta married a carpenter named James Savage. The couple had no children and divorced in the early 1920s.

Encouraged by sales of her small sculptures at local events, Savage left her daughter in the care of her parents and moved to New York City in 1921. With the help of the sculptor Solon Borglum, she was granted admission to Cooper Union, a tuition-free art school, where she completed the four-year program

in only three years. Savage augmented her studies with self-directed reading in African art at the Harlem Branch of the New York Public Library. When the librarian Sadie Peterson (later Delaney) persuaded the library to commission a bust of W. E. B. DU BOIS, Savage's life as a working artist began. Several commissions followed, including a bust of MARCUS GARVEY, who sat for the young artist on Sunday mornings in her Harlem apartment. It was through Garvey that Savage met her third husband, Robert L. Poston. The couple married in October 1923; five months later, however, she was again widowed.

In 1922 Savage applied to a summer art school program for American women at the palace of Fontainebleau outside Paris. The seven white American artists who constituted the selection committee, however, yielded to complaints from two Alabama women who refused to travel with a "colored girl" and rejected her application. When Savage exposed the committee's racism, becoming the first

Augusta Savage, pictured here with her Realization, *received particular recognition for her portrait busts of African American heroes and leaders including W. E. B. DU BOIS and FREDERICK DOUGLASS.* Yale Collection of American Literature, Beinecke Rare Book and Manuscript Library. Courtesy of Van Vechten Trust

black artist to challenge the white art establishment openly, the story was reported in both the African American and the white press. Making her case directly to the public, Savage reasoned, "Democracy is a strange thing. My brother was good enough to be accepted in one of the regiments that saw service in France during the war, but it seems his sister is not good enough to be a guest of the country for which he fought" (*New York World*, 20 May 1923). Despite her protestations, the committee's decision was not reversed, and while Savage's outspoken position brought her respect as a civil rights leader, she also won a reputation within the art world as a troublemaker. "No one knows how many times she was excluded from exhibits, galleries, and museums because of this confrontation," speculated ROMARE BEARDEN (170).

Economic limitations denied Savage a second opportunity to study abroad when, in 1925, through the efforts of W. E. B. Du Bois, the Italian-American Society offered her a scholarship to the Royal Academy of Fine Arts in Rome. Savage, who was working at menial jobs to support herself and her parents, was forced to turn down the scholarship when she was unable to raise enough money for living expenses. Her economic and familial burden increased—by 1928 she had eight relatives living in her three-room apartment—and Savage remained in Harlem, studying when she could and exhibiting wherever possible.

A life-sized bronze bust of an adolescent boy, *Gamin* (1929), revived Savage's dream of studying abroad. The sculpture, which *Opportunity* magazine put on its first cover in June 1929, delighted audiences and helped Savage secure two consecutive Julius Rosenwald Fund fellowships for study in Paris. While in Paris, she studied at the Académie de la Grand Chaumière and with the award-winning sculptors Felix Benneteau-Desgrois and Charles Despiau. She exhibited at the key Parisian salons and enjoyed the company of an expatriate social circle that included CLAUDE MCKAY, HENRY OSSAWA TANNER, COUNTÉE CULLEN, and Elizabeth Prophet.

Upon her return to New York in 1932 Savage exhibited at the Anderson Galleries, the Argent Gallery, and the Harmon Foundation and received commissions for busts of JAMES WELDON JOHNSON, W. C. HANDY, and others. But by 1932 much had changed. The Depression was taking its toll on institutions and innovations that had flourished in Harlem in the previous decade. Private funding for the arts was drying up, and by 1933 even the Harmon Foundation had suspended giving monetary awards. Savage recognized the effect of these shifts on her own endeavors and on the artistic community more generally. Convinced that her work might not be economically viable, she focused on generating her own creative opportunities, on teaching, and on supporting other African American artists.

Savage had long been unhappy with exhibition and patronage systems that gave white bureaucrats power over opportunities extended to African American artists, and after the Fontainebleau controversy, she had the skills to confront institutional racism and garner public support. Through the establishment of a series of influential art institutions and exhibitions, Savage became an aggressive spokesperson for nurturing black talent, for bringing art into the community, and for including black artists in mainstream arenas. In 1932 she opened the Savage School of Arts, which became the largest program of free art classes in New York. A demanding and devoted teacher, Savage was a powerful influence on her students, who included JACOB LAWRENCE, Norman Lewis, William Artis, and Ernest Crichlow. Psychologist KENNETH B. CLARK, also a former Savage student, recounts her unique and open approach: "Once I was doing this nude and was having trouble with the breasts.... Augusta came along and said, 'Kenneth, you're having trouble with that breast.' I said, 'Yes I am.' And she simply opened her blouse and showed me her breast" (Bearden, 173).

Harlem's leading intellectuals often met at Savage's studio, and in 1933 she and AARON DOUGLAS cofounded the Vanguard, a salon-style group that met weekly to discuss progressive causes and cultural issues. Two years later Savage and Charles Alston established the Harlem Artists Guild, which lobbied for funding for African American artists. In 1936 Savage was appointed an assistant supervisor for the Federal Arts Project (FAP), a division of the Works Progress Administration (WPA), employing thousands of artists. Savage convinced WPA administrators of the existence of nearly two hundred active African American artists and demanded that they be given assignments and supervisory positions through WPA programs. Within a year she became the first director of the Harlem Community Art Center, the FAP's most successful community center. More than three thousand students and ten thousand visitors were drawn to the Center during its first year. Under Savage's direction, an interracial staff of artists, including Douglas, Alston, WILLIAM H. JOHNSON, Palmer Hayden, and Selma Burke, taught workshops in a variety of mediums.

Savage took a break from administration in 1938, after she received a commission to create a monumental statue reflecting "the American Negro's contribution to music, especially to song" for the 1939 New York World's Fair. One of only four women given a commission and one of only two black artists represented at the fair, she produced a harp-shaped sixteen-foot sculpture of a stylized African American choir supported by a monumental arm. Even though the sculpture, inspired by JAMES WELDON JOHNSON and JOHN ROSAMOND JOHNSON's song "Lift Every Voice and Sing," was one of the fair's most popular and most publicized attractions, it was destroyed at the close of the fair when Savage was unable to pay for the piece to be cast.

Savage had intended to return to the Harlem Community Art Center, but her opponents at the WPA effectively pushed her out, and she officially resigned in April 1939. "In the end Savage was left a famous but poor, unemployed black artist," lamented Bearden (177). At age forty-seven, never having received a one-woman show or a museum exhibition, Savage organized a retrospective of her work at Argent Galleries. Frustrated by poor reviews, she returned to arts administration and in June 1939 opened the Salon of Contemporary Negro Art in Harlem, the nation's first gallery devoted to the exhibition and sale of work by African American artists. Although more than five hundred people came to see the work of such artists as RICHMOND

BARTHÉ, BEAUFORD DELANEY, James Lesesne Wells, LOÏS MAILOU JONES, and META WARRICK FULLER, poor sales and lack of resources forced the gallery to close a few months after its opening. The next year Savage attempted to jump-start her sculptural career with a nine-city tour of her work to conclude at the American Negro Exposition in Chicago in July 1940. But while the popular response to her work was positive, she sold very few pieces, and when she could not cover the shipping costs to New York, many of her works were abandoned or destroyed.

Savage continued to teach but increasingly isolated herself from her contemporaries. In the early 1940s she moved to an old chicken farm in Saugerties, New York, where she remained until 1961, when failing health necessitated a move to her daughter's house in the Bronx. Augusta Savage died of cancer in 1962. Unfortunately, few of her sculptures remain; for a 1988 exhibition at the Schomburg Center, only nineteen small pieces could be located.

FURTHER READING

Bearden, Romare, and Harry Henderson. *A History of African American Artists: From 1792 to the Present* (1993).

King-Hammond, Leslie, Tritobia Hayes Benjamin, and the Afro-American Historical and Cultural Museum. *Three Generations of African American Women Sculptors* (1996).

Schomburg Center for Research in Black Culture. *Augusta Savage and the Art Schools of Harlem* (1988).

—LISA E. RIVO

SCHOMBURG, ARTHUR ALFONSO (24 Jan. 1874–10 June 1938), historian, bibliophile, and curator, was born Arturo Alfonso Schomburg in San Juan, Puerto Rico, the son of Mary Joseph, an unwed midwife or laundress who had been born free in 1837 on St. Croix, Virgin Islands. His father's name is unknown, though Schomburg recorded that he was born in 1839, the son of a German émigré merchant.

Details of Schomburg's education are also sparse. He may have attended the College of St. Thomas, a secondary school, but there is no documentation. Schomburg knew French, and his writings in Spanish are both grammatically correct and eloquent. His lack of formal education ate away at him all his life, and it was surely one of the spurs to his untiring search for information and his efforts to make the results widely known. As a child, he belonged to a club of young people who studied history, and also learned about Puerto Rican history and nationalism from the island's cigar makers.

Schomburg moved to New York City on 17 April 1891. He lived among tobacco workers and participated in their meetings, fund-raising, and publication activities. The Cuban and Puerto Rican independence movements of that time inspired his youthful activism and scholarly bent, and the Cuban Revolutionary Party's newspaper, *Patria*, published his first article, a description of Las Dos Antillas, a political club he had cofounded earlier that year. Still a teenager, Schomburg worked as an elevator operator, bellhop, printer, and porter, and also taught Spanish in the night school where he learned English. Schomburg, an exceptionally social and fraternal man, joined a Masonic lodge, El Sol de Cuba No. 38, founded by Cuban and Puerto Rican exiles in 1881. English-speaking blacks were encouraged to join, and Schomburg translated the proceedings into English. He began acquiring and organizing the lodge's papers, books, correspondence, and photographs, and was elected master in 1911. The lodge, by then mostly black, changed its name to PRINCE HALL, after the first black Mason in the United States.

This name change was emblematic of Schomburg's realization that his future was in America. The Spanish-American War of 1898, which put Cuba, Puerto Rico, and the Philippines under the control of the United States, effectively ended the revolutionary efforts of the exiles. Family ties also strengthened Schomburg's commitment to his adopted land. In 1895 he married Elizabeth Hatcher, an African American from Staunton, Virginia, but she died in 1900 having borne three children. His second marriage, to Elizabeth Morrow Taylor of Williamsburg, North Carolina, lasted from 1902 until 1909, when she died, leaving two children. Visits to his five children, who were being raised by maternal relatives, exposed the New Yorker to the full-blown racism of the Jim Crow South.

Arthur Alfonso Schomburg, whose library forms the core the New York Public Library's Schomburg Center for Research in Black Culture. Schomburg Center

Schomburg worked as a clerk and messenger for Pryor, Mellis and Harris, a law firm, from 1901 to 1906. On 1 February 1906 he took a job with the Bankers Trust Company on Wall Street, where he remained for twenty-three years. He rose from messenger to supervisor of the bank's foreign mailing section, where his knowledge of French and Spanish, his exceptional memory, and his attention to detail were valuable qualities.

But Schomburg's real work was not on Wall Street; it was wherever he found others equally impassioned to prove that black people did indeed have an international history of accomplishment that stretched past slavery days to Africa. In April 1911 Schomburg was one of five founders of the Negro Society for Historical Research. The society aimed "to show that the Negro race has a history that antedates that of the proud Anglo-Saxon race"; they planned "to collect useful historical data relating to the Negro race, books written by or about Negroes, rare pictures of prominent men and women...letters...African curios of native manufacture" (Sinnette, 43). It acquired members in Europe, the Americas, the Caribbean, and Africa, including the vice president of Liberia, James Dossen, EDWARD BLYDEN of Sierra Leone, and Mojola Agbebe of Nigeria—which must have gratified Schomburg, a Pan-Africanist.

Schomburg, activist and expansive in outlook, generously made available to those in his wide network his private library, acquired with a limited budget. He had already begun to carry out the society's mission of collecting historical documents. At about this time he married his third wife. By 1916 their household was filled with three young children and Schomburg's growing library.

The American Negro Academy, founded in Washington, D.C., in 1897 and limited to forty members, elected Schomburg to membership in 1914. Schomburg became the academy's fifth president (1920–1929). The group held annual conventions, encouraged publication of scholarly works, and urged members to acquire books and manuscripts by and about people of African descent. At the 1915 convention, Schomburg's paper, "The Economic Contribution by the Negro to America," brought to the academy's attention the theme that had always engaged him: that people of African origin, wherever they were in the world, had made significant but unrecognized contributions in all fields to white society. Schomburg's research, writings, and talks about Haitians and blacks of European, Central, and South American birth broadened the perspective of the academy's members.

In 1918 Schomburg was elected grand secretary of the Prince Hall Grand Lodge of the State of New York, a position that required frequent travel and attention to many organizational activities, including planning a new temple. He was still able to mount a weeklong exhibition at the Carleton Street YMCA in Brooklyn. On view were rare books, manuscripts, engravings, paintings, and sculpture, as well as African art. Only one earlier exhibition, in New York in 1909, had displayed African art as art, not as ethnographic curiosities.

By 1925 Schomburg had formed a library of nearly four thousand books and pamphlets and about one thousand manuscripts and prints, which he wished to make widely available to inspire Negro youth. With a grant of ten thousand dollars from the Carnegie Corporation in 1926, the New York Public Library purchased the collection and housed it in its 135th Street Library. Among its rarest items were BENJAMIN

BANNEKER's almanacs (1792–1796) and manuscripts by PAUL LAURENCE DUNBAR and Toussaint L'Ouverture.

The library also became a gathering place for the writers and artists of the Harlem Renaissance. Schomburg's most influential essay, "The Negro Digs Up His Past," appeared in one of the preeminent texts of that movement, ALAIN LOCKE's *The New Negro* (1925) and was often reprinted. His essay called for rigorous historical research, not "a pathetically over-corrective, ridiculously overlaudatory ... apologetics turned into biography." Though he urged that "history must restore what slavery took away," half a century passed before his collection was recognized as a treasure house and received funding for renovation and new construction.

After the sale of his collection Schomburg began to spend more time at the 135th Street Library. When he retired from Bankers Trust at the end of 1929, he planned to devote his time to research and to travel to Spain again. Even before his retirement, however, CHARLES S. JOHNSON, chairman of the social science department of Fisk University in Nashville, Tennessee, invited him to build Fisk's Negro Collection. From November 1930 until the end of 1931 Schomburg was the curator of that collection, acquiring 4,524 books out of a total of 4,630. Fisk librarian Louis Shores wrote that Schomburg's "bibliographic memory was spectacular." Schomburg returned to New York in 1932 to accept his final position as curator in charge of his own collection, serving until his death six years later.

Money was short because of the Great Depression, but Schomburg managed to add outstanding items to the New York collection, including the long-sought *Ad Catholicum* of Juan Latino (1573) and a folio of engravings by PATRICK HENRY REASON, a nineteenth-century black artist. The marble-and-bronze sculpture of IRA ALDRIDGE as Othello, which often serves as the graphic symbol of the Schomburg Center, was bought in 1934, with assistance from a fellow bibliophile, Arthur B. Spingarn. Donations from authors, artists, and Schomburg's many friends further enriched the collection, as did purchases paid for by Schomburg himself.

The acquisition of Schomburg's collection by the New York Public Library

vindicated his forty-year search for the evidence of black history. He was gratified that it would be freely available to all. A teenage immigrant without influential family, formal education, or ample funds, consigned to a segregated world, he nevertheless amassed a collection of inestimable value. Schomburg was "a man who built his own monument," said one eulogist. From his core of five thousand items, the Schomburg Center for Research in Black Culture would grow to five million items and become the world's most important repository in the field. Schomburg's name is also commemorated in a street in San Juan, Puerto Rico, an elementary school in the Bronx, and a housing complex in Harlem.

FURTHER READING

A large collection of Schomburg's papers is at the Schomburg Center for Research in Black Culture of the New York Public Library, along with extensive clipping files about him.

Gubert, Betty Kaplan, and Richard Newman. *Nine Decades of Scholarship: A Bibliography of the Writings 1892–1983 of the Staff of the Schomburg Center for Research in Black Culture* (1986).

Sinnette, Elinor Des Verney. *Arthur Alfonso Schomburg: Black Bibliophile and Collector* (1989).

Obituary: *New York Times*, 11 June 1938.
—BETTY KAPLAN GUBERT

 SCHUYLER, GEORGE SAMUEL (25 Feb. 1895–31 Aug. 1977) journalist, was born in Providence, Rhode Island, to George Francis Schuyler and Eliza Jane Fischer, both cooks. He was raised in Syracuse, New York, and often remarked that his family had never lived in the South and had never been slaves. That did not mean that they had not suffered discrimination, however, for as Schuyler wrote in his 1966 autobiography: "A black person learns very early that his color is a disadvantage in a world of white folks. This being an unalterable circumstance, one also learns to make the best of it" (Schuyler, 1).

For Schuyler, that early exposure to racism came on his first day at school, when he registered three firsts: he was called "nigger," fought the

Journalist and novelist George Samuel Schuyler as photographed by Carl Van Vechten in 1941. Library of Congress

Italian-American boy who used the slur, and received a bloody nose for his pains. After that experience, his mother told him to always fight back when called names, and she also taught him about the achievements of FREDERICK DOUGLASS, HARRIET TUBMAN, and other great African Americans. From then on, Schuyler later recalled, he never felt inferior to whites, even though he saw no person of color in any position of authority until he was fourteen and witnessed black soldiers on exercise in Syracuse.

Perhaps because of the childhood school incident and because he saw few prospects for young black men in his hometown, Schuyler left school at seventeen and joined the army. He served for seven years in the Twenty-fifth U.S. Infantry, a predominantly black regiment famed for its Buffalo Soldiers, who had been recruited for "pacification" campaigns against Indians in the post–Civil War American West. Stationed at first in Seattle, Washington, Schuyler found the Pacific Northwest to be little different from upstate New York in terms of racial discrimination. Schuyler's next posting, in Hawaii, proved much more congenial to him, in part because of the camaraderie among African American recruits and the seemingly endless opportunities in Honolulu for "rum and roistering" (Schuyler, 71). But he also loved

the breathtaking landscape of Hawaii and initially planned to stay in Honolulu at the end of his service in 1915.

Finding few opportunities in civilian life, he reenlisted in his former regiment and began his first efforts at journalism, writing satirical pieces for the *Service*, a weekly magazine for soldiers in Hawaii. When the United States entered World War I, he received a commission and, according to his autobiography, served at Camp Dix, New Jersey, and Camp Meade, Maryland. Schuyler's memoir does not mention, however, that he went AWOL for three months in 1918 after he had visited Philadelphia in uniform and was denied service by a Greek bootblack. He later surrendered to military authorities in San Diego and was sentenced to five years in prison on Governor's Island in New York; in his autobiography, he claims to have worked at that prison as a clerk.

After serving only nine months in jail, Schuyler was released for good behavior and worked a series of low-paying laboring jobs in Syracuse, where he joined the Socialist Party in 1921. He then moved to New York, where he drew upon his experiences in a Bowery flophouse in "Hobohemia," a satirical essay that he wrote in 1923 for the *Messenger*, a socialist newspaper founded by A. PHILIP RANDOLPH. That same year, Schuyler joined the *Messenger*'s editorial staff and wrote a monthly column, "Shafts and Darts: A Page of Calumny and Satire," which aimed to "slur, lampoon, damn, and occasionally praise anybody or anything in the known universe" (Peplow, 22). Although he also targeted white hypocrisy and racism, Schuyler most effectively skewered what he saw as the cant and hypocrisy of African American leaders, notably MARCUS GARVEY.

As he no doubt intended, Schuyler's satirical barbs provoked outrage among his targets, especially his fellow Negro intellectuals. In "The Negro-Art Hokum," which appeared in the *Nation* in 1926, Schuyler declared that there is no distinct, unified African American aesthetic separate from an American aesthetic. More controversially, he summarized that view by stating that "the Aframerican is merely a lamp-blacked Anglo-Saxon" (Leak, 14). The essay provoked a bitter response among Harlem Renaissance artists—notably

LANGSTON HUGHES—who were at that time exalting the unique achievements of black American culture. Schuyler's combative essays proved good copy, however, and by the late 1920s he was the most widely read black journalist in America. In addition to a regular opinion column in the *Pittsburgh Courier*, his essays appeared in national publications such as the *American Mercury*, a periodical founded by the gadfly journalist H. L. Mencken, who greatly influenced Schuyler's iconoclastic style. Schuyler's prodigious journalistic output coincided with his marriage in 1928 to Josephine Cogdell, a white Texas heiress, artist, and former model. The union produced a daughter, Philipa Duke Schuyler, a child prodigy who, at the age of thirteen, performed her own composition, "Manhattan Nocturne," with the New York Philharmonic.

The 1930s marked the peak of Schuyler's influence as a cultural critic. *Black No More* (1931), the first black science fiction novel, reversed traditional American race roles by means of a whitening agent that made Americans of African descent a shade lighter than whites of European descent. In the process, Schuyler lampoons W. E. B. DU BOIS as "Dr. Shakespeare Agamemnon Beard"—a portrayal Du Bois greatly enjoyed—and introduces a black nationalist character, "Santop Licorice," a thinly veiled Garvey, who was less forgiving of Schuyler's acerbic wit. Du Bois joined Garvey, however, in criticizing *Slaves Today* (1931). This satire was drawn from Schuyler's experiences in Liberia in the early 1930s, when he had written a series of articles—published in the *Courier* and syndicated to several other newspapers—criticizing the African republic for its corrupt government and toleration of slavery.

Despite his frequent criticisms of Garvey, Schuyler wrote two black nationalist pulp science fiction serials under the pseudonym of Samuel I. Brooks for the *Pittsburgh Courier* in the late thirties. Schuyler's adoption of a nationalist alter ego and his criticisms of "Brooks's" serials as "hokum and hack work" appear paradoxical. The literary scholar Henry Louis Gates Jr. suggests, however, that Schuyler/Brooks purposively adopted the dual role in an intellectual playing out of Du Bois's metaphor of black double-consciousness.

Around the same time, Schuyler's political philosophy also changed; George Schuyler, radical and socialist, metamorphosed into George Schuyler, reactionary and conservative. One factor may have been what Schuyler saw as the exploitation of the SCOTTSBORO BOYS' case by the Communist Party in the late 1930s, but the bulk of his writings before the McCarthy era place him firmly on the progressive left. Indeed, from 1934 to 1944 he served as business manager of the NAACP and worked closely with his protégé, ELLA BAKER, in promoting workers' and consumers' cooperatives. Both before and during World War II, Schuyler used his columns in the *Pittsburgh Courier* to attack the hypocrisy of blacks fighting against fascism abroad while suffering Jim Crow at home.

After World War II, Schuyler's conservatism became unambiguous. His anticommunism and opposition to the Soviet Union may not have been unique among black intellectuals at that time, but his strident defense of Senator Joseph McCarthy certainly was. Likewise, most African Americans would have agreed with Schuyler's contention in "The Negro Question without Propaganda" (1950) that lynching had declined since 1900, but few, especially in the South, could take seriously his claim that force was rarely used to keep blacks from the polls. Indeed, as the civil rights movement made impressive legal and political victories in the 1950s and 1960s, Schuyler moved farther and farther to the right, not only criticizing MALCOLM X as a latter-day Garvey, but also attacking MARTIN LUTHER KING JR. as a communist stooge. When black newspapers refused to publish his essay discrediting King's 1964 Nobel Prize, Schuyler published the piece in the rabidly conservative *Manchester* (N.H.) *Union Leader*. In the 1960s and 1970s Schuyler also contributed several articles to *American Opinion*, the journal of the John Birch Society, an organization so profoundly right wing that it regarded President Dwight Eisenhower as a communist sympathizer.

Schuyler died in relative obscurity in New York City. Most commentators noted his political journey from left to right, but the historian John Henrik Clark was probably more accurate in noting Schuyler's consistency as a rebel. Clark recalled that he "used to tell people that George got up in the morning, waited to see which way the world was turning, then struck out in the opposite direction" (*New York Times*, 7 Sept. 1977).

FURTHER READING

Schuyler's papers are housed at the Schomburg Center for Research in Black Culture of the New York Public Library

Schuyler, George S. *Black and Conservative* (1966).

Gates, Henry Louis, Jr. "A Fragmented Man: George Schuyler and the Claims of Race," *New York Times Book Review*, 20 Sept. 1992.

Leak, Jeffery B. *Rac[e]ing to the Right: Selected Essays of George Schuyler* (2001).

Peplow, Michael W. *George S. Schuyler* (1980).

Obituary: *New York Times*, 7 Sept. 1977.
—STEVEN J. NIVEN

SCOTT, DRED (c. 1800–17 Sept. 1858), slave and plaintiff in the 1857 landmark U.S. Supreme Court case *Dred Scott v. John F. A. Sanford*, was born of unknown parentage in Southampton County, Virginia, the property of plantation owner Peter Blow. After brief sojourns in Huntsville and Florence, Alabama, in 1830 the Blow family settled in St. Louis where, strapped for funds, Blow sold Scott to Dr. John Emerson. In 1833 Emerson's career as army surgeon took him, among other places, to Illinois and to what was then a part of Wisconsin Territory (now Minnesota). Scott accompanied him into these areas, one a free state and one a territory that had been declared free by the Northwest Ordinance of 1787 and the Missouri Compromise of 1820. In 1836 or 1837, while at Fort Snelling in Wisconsin Territory, Scott married Harriet Robinson, whose master, Major Lawrence Taliaferro, transferred her ownership to Emerson. Dred and Harriet Scott subsequently had two daughters. Posted in 1840 to the Seminole War in Florida, Emerson left his wife, Eliza Irene Sanford Emerson, and the slaves in St. Louis. Emerson returned the following year but died shortly thereafter.

The exact whereabouts of the Scotts for the next few years are uncertain, except that they were hired out to various people in St. Louis, a frequent experience for city-dwelling slaves. They seem also to have reestablished close relations with the Blow family, Dred's former owners.

On 6 April 1846 Dred and Harriet Scott sued Irene Emerson for freedom. *Dred Scott v. Irene Emerson* was filed in a Missouri state court under Missouri state law. (Two separate litigations were pursued. Since both entailed the same law and evidence, only Dred's advanced to conclusion; Harriet's suit was held in abeyance, under agreement that the determination in her husband's case would apply to hers.) Contrary to later widespread rumor, no political motivation attached to the institution of this suit; only when it reached the Missouri Supreme Court did it acquire the political overtones that made it so famous later. The suit was brought for one reason only: to secure freedom for Dred Scott and his family. Evidence suggests that Scott learned of his right to freedom from the white abolitionist lawyer Francis Butter Murdoch, recently moved to St. Louis from Alton, Illinois, where he had prosecuted criminal offenders in the Elijah P. Lovejoy riots and murders. Another possible instigator was the Reverend John R. Anderson, a former slave who was pastor of the Second African Baptist Church in St. Louis to which Harriet Scott belonged. Murdoch posted the necessary bonds and filed the legal papers that actually instituted the suit. Shortly thereafter, however, he moved to California.

Based on Missouri law and precedents, Scott's case for freedom seemed incontrovertible. Earlier Missouri Supreme Court decisions had emancipated a number of slaves whose travels had taken them to free states or territories. Indeed, one of those cases was strikingly similar to Scott's; that slave had also accompanied an army officer to the same military posts in Illinois and Wisconsin Territory as Dred Scott had done. Perhaps that explains why members of the Blow family so readily backed the slave's case when Murdoch left St. Louis. Indeed, even as the litigation dragged on beyond what had promised to be a very quick solution, they continued

This portrait of Dred Scott was painted by Louis Schultze in 1882 after the only known photograph of the sitter. Missouri Historical Society

to provide necessary legal and financial support.

Unanticipated developments converted an open-and-shut freedom suit into a cause célèbre. In the trial on 30 June 1847, the court rejected one piece of vital evidence on a legal technicality—that it was hearsay evidence and therefore not admissible—and the slave's freedom had to await a second trial when that evidence could be properly introduced. It took almost three years, until 12 January 1850, before that trial took place, a delay caused by events over which none of the litigants had any control. With the earlier legal technicality corrected, the court unhesitatingly declared Dred Scott to be free.

But during the delay, money earned by the slaves had been held custodially by the local sheriff, to turn over to either the estate of the late John Emerson (which really meant to Irene Emerson, according to her husband's will) or the freed slaves, depending upon the outcome of the suit. Though not a large sum, those accrued wages made ownership of the slaves more worthwhile in 1850 than it had been in 1847. Meanwhile, Irene Emerson had left St. Louis

to marry Dr. Calvin Clifford Chaffee, a Massachusetts abolitionist, who was unaware of the litigation involving his wife. She left her St. Louis affairs in the hands of her businessman-brother, John F. A. Sanford, who had earlier been named executor of Dr. Emerson's estate. In Irene Emerson's name, then, and hoping to secure the accumulated Scott family wages, Sanford's attorneys appealed the freedom decision to the Missouri Supreme Court. But also during the delay, slavery had become a national issue of voluble divisiveness. In a singularly partisan 2–1 decision, which overturned long-standing "once free always free" judicial precedent—that once a slave resided in free territory with the knowledge and even tacit consent of the master, he or she became free by virtue of that residence and did not lose that freedom merely upon returning to a slave state—the Missouri Supreme Court on 22 March 1852 blatantly endorsed proslavery tenets, reversed the lower court, and remanded Dred Scott to slavery (*Dred Scott v. Irene Emerson*, 15 Missouri 576).

To clarify the "once free always free" doctrine based on freedom secured under the Northwest Ordinance of

1787 and the Missouri Compromise of 1820, friends of Scott instituted a new case in the federal courts, *Dred Scott v. John F. A. Sanford*. (Court records erroneously misspelled the name as "Sandford.") Though often in St. Louis, Sanford was a legal resident of New York. Scott as a citizen of Missouri suing Sanford thereby created a "diversity" case—that is, a citizen of one state suing a citizen of another state—which could litigate in the federal courts. But it also created a new issue when Sanford's attorneys claimed that Scott was not a citizen because he was "a negro of African descent" and therefore lacked the right to sue in the federal courts. Rather than deal with the matter on those jurisdictional grounds, the court found for Sanford, and the case was appealed to the Supreme Court of the United States.

There, nationally known legal figures argued the case: Montgomery Blair and George T. Curtis for Scott, and Reverdy Johnson and Henry S. Geyer for Sanford. The suit was argued twice, in February 1856 and in December 1856. Up to then virtually unknown, the case now aroused nationwide publicity and deep partisan interest. At first the Court exercised judicial restraint and thought cautiously to avoid controversial slavery matters. Prodded by prosouthern Chief Justice Roger B. Taney and associate justices James M. Wayne and Peter V. Daniel, and by antislavery associate justices John McLean and Benjamin R. Curtis, the Court decided to deal with those explosive issues.

The famous—or infamous—decision, which remanded Dred Scott to slavery, was pronounced on 6 March 1857 by Chief Justice Taney. Each of the concurring and dissenting justices rendered a separate opinion (*Dred Scott v. John F. A. Sanford*, 19 Howard 393). Extreme proslavery and extreme antislavery views were expressed. According to Taney's "Opinion of the Court," blacks were not considered citizens of the United States. Slaves were property protected by the Constitution, and any law prohibiting slavery in the territories (e.g., the Missouri Compromise) was unconstitutional. Regardless of prior free or slave condition, the status of a person entering into a slave state depended on the law of that state.

The decision triggered violent reaction in an already tense sectional-ridden atmosphere. Fearing that it pushed American law close to legalizing slavery throughout the entire country, anti-slavery forces mounted unprecedented assaults on the decision and on the majority members of the Court. Proslavery forces responded with equal fervor to defend their cause. The tragic result was to split a divided country even more and push it closer to civil war.

As to the slaves themselves, they remained in St. Louis throughout all this litigation, working at various jobs. Legally, however, they had become the property of Dr. Chaffee, Irene Emerson's second husband. Incredibly, though, he did not become aware of that consequence until just a week or two before the decision was announced, and his attorneys informed him that he could do nothing about that ownership until the litigation was concluded. Shortly after the Supreme Court announced its decision, the embarrassed Chaffee transferred his ownership to Taylor Blow in St. Louis—since by Missouri law a slave could be emancipated there only by a citizen of that state. Accordingly, on 27 May 1857 Blow executed the necessary documents to free the slaves. Scott lived only a year and a half longer, working most of that time as a porter in Barnum's Hotel in St. Louis. There he died of tuberculosis. His remains are interred in St. Louis.

FURTHER READING

Ehrlich, Walter. *They Have No Rights: Dred Scott's Struggle for Freedom* (1979).
Fehrenbacher, Don E. *The Dred Scott Case: Its Significance in American Law and Politics* (1978).
Finkelman, Paul. *An Imperfect Union* (1981).
Hyman, Harold M., and William M. Wiecek. *Equal Justice under Law: Constitutional Development, 1835–1875* (1982).
—WALTER EHRLICH

SCOTT, EMMETT JAY

(13 Feb. 1873–12 Dec. 1957), educator and publicist, was born in Houston, Texas, the son of Horace Lacy Scott, a civil servant, and Emma Kyle. Scott attended Wiley College in Marshall, Texas, for three years but left college in 1890 for a career in journalism. Starting as a janitor and messenger for a white daily newspaper, the *Houston Post*, he worked his way up to reporter. In 1894 he became associate editor of a new black newspaper in Houston, the *Texas Freeman*. Soon he was named editor and built this newspaper into a leading voice in black journalism in its region. Initially, he tied his fortune to the state's preeminent black politician, Norris Cuney, and was his secretary for a while.

When Cuney retired, Scott turned to BOOKER T. WASHINGTON, founder of the Tuskegee Institute in Alabama. Scott greatly admired Washington, praising his 1895 "Atlanta Compromise" speech. Two years later he invited Washington to speak in Houston. Scott handled the publicity and promotion so well that Washington hired him as his private secretary. When Scott moved to Tuskegee on 10 September 1897, he brought with him his wife, Eleonora Juanita Baker, daughter of a newspaper editor. They had been married in April 1897 and eventually had five children.

From 1897 until Washington's death in November 1915, Scott was his closest adviser and friend. The two worked together so smoothly that determining which man authored a particular letter can be a challenge. As his top aide, Scott ran Tuskegee when Washington was away. Washington acknowledged that Scott made "himself invaluable not only to me personally, but to the institution" (Washington, *The Story of My Life and Work* [1901]). Scott developed and operated the "Tuskegee Machine," an elaborate apparatus by which Booker T. Washington controlled, influenced, and manipulated African American leaders, press, and institutions. He also worked closely with Washington in founding the National Negro Business League in 1900. Washington was president of the league, but Scott, as secretary from 1900 to 1922, actually ran it. The two coauthored *Tuskegee and Its People* (1905).

Scott served on the three-man American Commission to Liberia in 1909, the report of which led to an American protectorate over Liberia. In 1912 Tuskegee Institute's board made Scott the secretary of the school. When Washington died in 1915, Scott was a leading candidate to succeed him, but ROBERT RUSSA MOTON of Hampton was chosen instead. Scott remained as secretary. He and Lyman Beecher Stowe coauthored a highly laudatory biography, titled *Booker T. Washington*, published in 1916. That year, Scott and others in the Tuskegean camp reconciled with Washington's rival and National Association for the Advancement of Colored People (NAACP) founder W. E. B. DU BOIS, at the Amenia Conference on Long Island, New York.

The entrance of the United States into World War I gave Scott a chance to leave Tuskegee and end any rivalry with Moton. He became special assistant to the secretary of war and was in charge of affairs relating to African Americans. While in this post he wrote *Scott's Official History of the American Negro in the World War* (1919). He also wrote *Negro Migration during the War* (1920), under the auspices of the Carnegie Endowment for International Peace. Scott stayed in Washington after the war, becoming a top administrator at Howard University. From 1919 to 1932 he was the university's secretary-treasurer and business manager. He was the top black official until Howard's first black president, MORDECAI JOHNSON, was appointed in 1926. The two clashed, and Scott was relegated to the position of secretary of the university but remained at Howard until he retired in 1938.

Meanwhile, he was active in business and politics. Among his business ventures in the African American community were banking, insurance, and real estate. In politics he was a staunch Republican. He served on an advisory committee for the 1924 Republican National Convention, specializing in black affairs, and he was the assistant publicity director of the Republican National Committee from 1939 to 1942. In 1941 Scott went to work at the Sun Shipbuilding Company of Chester, Pennsylvania, at the request of the Republican Party. The company president, John Pew, was a major funder of the party. Pew's company was nonunion. With Scott's help the company established Yard No. 4, staffed by African Americans supervised by Scott. When the war ended in 1945, Scott's yard was dismantled, and Scott retired to Washington. From time to time, he did public relations work. He died in Washington, D.C.

FURTHER READING

Scott's personal papers are in the Morris A. Soper Library of Morgan State University, Baltimore. His letters and other materials are also found among the Booker T. Washington Papers in the Library of Congress.

Harlan, Louis. *Booker T. Washington: The Making of a Black Leader, 1856–1901* (1972).

———. *Booker T. Washington: The Wizard of Tuskegee, 1901–1915* (1983).

LOGAN, RAYFORD W. *Howard University* (1969).

Meier, August. *Negro Thought in America, 1880–1915* (1963).

Obituaries: *Atlanta Daily World* and *Washington Post*, 13 Dec. 1957; *Washington Afro-American* and *New York Times*, 14 Dec. 1957; *Afro-American* (national edition), 21 Dec. 1957.

—EDGAR ALLAN TOPPIN

 SCOTT, WENDELL

(25 Aug. 1921–23 Dec. 1990), race-car driver, was born Wendell Oliver Scott in the Crooktown section of Danville, Virginia, the first of two children of William Scott, a mechanic, and his wife, Martha, who each had one daughter from previous marriages. Before Scott entered the first grade, William took a mechanical job in Pittsburgh and moved the whole family to Pennsylvania. After a few years they relocated to Louisville, Kentucky, to live with Martha's aunt. (This side of the family was related to MUHAMMAD ALI, making Wendell a distant cousin of the famed boxer.) Meanwhile, Martha's mother, who owned Scott's Grocery back in Danville, took ill. Martha moved the family back to Virginia so that she could run the store, where Wendell worked while he went to school.

At the age of eighteen Scott began driving for a local taxicab company and, four years later, joined the army. He served as a mechanic and a paratrooper in the 101st Airborne and returned to Danville after his discharge in 1945. Scott proceeded to run moonshine from illegal rural stills to the Danville Fairgrounds Speedway with a specially outfitted truck that he later claimed could "do 95 [mph] in second gear, and 118 in high" (Wilkinson). He would then remain at the fairgrounds to watch the

NASCAR race driver Wendell Scott. © Pal Parker Archives

stock-car races held there on short-distance dirt tracks.

During one run in 1948, however, Scott swerved to avoid pedestrians and crashed. He sustained no major injuries but was cited by the police and received three years' parole. In 1950 the Danville racing promoter Martin Roberts asked the police if they knew of any fast black drivers in the county. They named Scott, who at the time had opened and was successfully managing Scott Garage. Scott bought a used race car, and though he was denied entry to many races, he eventually debuted at the Danville Fairgrounds as the first black racer in a Dixie Circuit event. The Dixie Circuit operated throughout Virginia and North Carolina but was not recognized by the National Association for Stock Car Auto Racing (NASCAR). Scott won over eighty Dixie Circuit contests in less than four years.

He then graduated to the Modified Division of NASCAR, whose entrants were permitted to alter their vehicles in ways that were generally not allowed on the top-flight Grand National Series (now called the Winston Cup Series).

This aspect of the Modified Division was crucial to Scott's success, as his skin color blocked him from securing a sponsor who could supply him with a competitive car. Thus, Scott used his own mechanical skills to outfit his number 34 car in ways that more than compensated for this handicap. His friend and competitor Earl Brooks remembered that Scott often used a set of baby scales to perform the same measurements of engine parts for which other racing teams employed highly calibrated equipment.

Scott persevered on the Dixie and Modified circuits despite numerous incidents in which racing organizers prohibited him from competing by citing specious regulations that they invented especially for him, such as the presence of too many paint chips on his car. And since stock-car races were primarily held in the segregated South, most crowds would cheer when Scott's competitors attempted to force his car off the track. But Scott's mild-mannered patience, combined with his abilities in the garage and on the track, garnered him over forty Modified racing victories as well as the 1959 Virginia State Championship.

In 1961 NASCAR finally deemed Scott's accomplishments worthy to qualify him for Grand National competition, and he debuted at the Spartanburg Fairgrounds in South Carolina. Five times that year he finished in the top ten, earning $3,240. Scott doubled his success the following year, tallying eleven top-ten finishes and $7,000 in winnings. The Grand National Series operated on a point system that considered a driver's starting positions, laps completed, average speeds, and finishing positions—and Scott's point totals increased steadily from thirty-second place in 1961 to sixth in 1966. In 1964 he set the Grand National record for a last-place starter; he began the World 600 in Charlotte in fortieth place and finished in ninth. Scott's most successful year overall came in 1969, when he won $47,451 and placed ninth in the point standings.

The only Grand National victory of Scott's career came on 1 December 1963 in Jacksonville, Florida, yet even this occasion was marked by yet another outright display of racism. On the Jacksonville Speedway's half-mile track, Scott lapped Buck Baker twice, traveling 101 miles by the time Baker, in second place, completed the requisite 100. But the race organizers awarded Baker the checkered flag, the trophy, and photo ops in the winner's circle with the white beauty queen. Once the crowd left, organizers apologized to Scott and presented him with the $1,150 winner's check and a block of wood to serve as his trophy.

With his consistent racing success Scott was eventually approached—twice—to receive sponsorship, but both deals quickly soured. In 1964 the Ford executive Lee Iacocca provided Scott with a race car, albeit a used one. And even though it was the most advanced car Scott had ever had, he still saw fit to redesign the frame more to his liking. Ford, however, supplied Scott with engine parts that, as Earl Brooks characterized them, did not fully meet NASCAR specifications. Apparently thinking that Scott would not know the difference, Ford had attempted to outfit him with a car that gave him a decided, though illegal, edge in competition. Scott insisted that the car must adhere to NASCAR rules, and the sponsorship subsequently dissolved. In 1971 a white

promoter promised Scott a top-quality race car for an event at the Charlotte Motor Speedway but reneged under pressure from other racing executives.

Scott was involved in only two multiple-car pileups during his career. The first was a thirty-seven-car accident at the Daytona Speedway in 1960, in which he was not seriously injured. In the second, an eighteen-car pileup at Talledega, Alabama, in 1973, Scott suffered fractures in his pelvis, ribs, and leg, as well as a gash in his arm that required seventy stitches. The incident forced him into retirement, though Scott occasionally raced again. He settled in Danville once again and continued managing Scott Garage.

By the end of his twelve-year NASCAR career, Scott had earned a total of $188,000, racing in 506 events. In 1977 his life and career were the inspiration for the RICHARD PRYOR movie *Greased Lightning*, for which Scott served as technical adviser. He was not impressed with the stuntmen employed for the driving scenes and received scant payment for his work.

Wendell Scott received numerous awards and has been inducted into several halls of fame, including the National Black Athletic Hall of Fame in 1977, the International Motorsports Hall of Fame in 1999, and the Black Sports and Entertainment Hall of Fame in 2003. Until the early 1970s Scott was the only black driver on the Grand National Series, and by the end of his career there were only two more. Scott died from complications resulting from spinal cancer in December of 1990. The General Assembly of Virginia officially mourned Scott's death with a resolution on 16 January 1991, and on the anniversary of his death in 1997, Danville renamed his hometown street "Wendell Scott Drive." He was survived by seven children, including four sons who often served as his pit crew.

FURTHER READING

Daniel, Pete. *Lost Revolutions: The South in the 1950s* (2000).

Golenbock, Peter. *American Zoom: Stock Car Racing—from the Dirt Tracks to Daytona* (1993).

Wilkinson, Sylvia. *Dirt Tracks to Glory: The Early Days of Stock Car Racing as Told by the Participants* (1983).

Obituary: *New York Times*, 25 Dec. 1990.

—DAVID F. SMYDRA JR.

 SCOTTSBORO BOYS

Olen Montgomery (1914–?), Clarence Norris (12 July 1912–23 Jan. 1989), Ozie Powell (1915–?), Haywood Patterson (1913–24 Aug. 1952), Willie Roberson (4 July 1916–c. 1959), Charlie Weems (1911–?), Eugene Williams (1918–?), Andrew "Andy" Wright, (1912–?), and Leroy "Roy" Wright (1918–1959), became an international cause célèbre after they were accused of raping two white women on a Southern Railroad freight train traveling on 25 March 1931 through northern Alabama en route to Memphis, Tennessee. Like many Depression-era Americans, the nine young men and the two women had been riding the rails in search of work. Shortly after their train crossed into Alabama, a white male hobo stepped on the hand of Haywood Patterson, who had been hanging on to one of the freight carriages. A scuffle ensued in which Patterson and his friends forced the white hobo and his colleagues off the train, after which the whites reported the assault to a stationmaster, who in turn informed the sheriff of Jackson County, Alabama. The sheriff deputized a posse of heavily armed white men, who stopped the train at the small town of Paint Rock and rounded up every black male on the train. The nine youths were then tied together, loaded on a truck, and driven to jail in Scottsboro, the Jackson county seat.

When the prisoners arrived at the jail, they found that the two women, Ruby Bates and Victoria Price, had told the authorities that twelve Negroes armed with pistols and knives had raped them. Price later identified six of the nine jailed teenagers as her assailants, prompting a prison guard to declare—though he provided no evidence—that the three others must have raped Bates. A presumption of the black youths' guilt led hundreds of angry whites to surround the jail in the hope of lynching the accused, but their plans were thwarted when the governor of Alabama ordered the National Guard to protect the Scottsboro jail.

However, the state of Alabama showed less interest in the defendants' broader procedural rights, assigning them two ineffective attorneys—one drunk and the other elderly—who

The Scottsboro Boys—(left to right) Norris, Montgomery, A. Wright, Roberson, Powell, Williams, Weems, R. Wright, Patterson—were arrested and accused of rape in March 1931. Corbis

defended their clients with little skill and even less enthusiasm. The lawyers failed to probe inconsistencies in the women's testimony, including a physician's report that contradicted Price's claim of a brutal gang rape. They also ignored the fact that Willie Roberson, suffering from syphilis, could barely walk and certainly could not jump from one railroad car to another as claimed; his condition—which had left him with sores on his genitals—would also have made intercourse extremely painful. The defense was also compromised when Roy Wright, Haywood Patterson, and Clarence Norris testified that they had seen some of the others rape the two women, though it later emerged that these accusations had been coerced by prison guards. Roy Wright told a *New York Times* reporter in 1933 that the guards "whipped me and it seemed like they was going to kill me. All the time they kept saying, 'Now will you tell?' and finally it seemed like I couldn't stand no more and I said yes. Then I went back into the courtroom and they put me up on the chair in front of the judge and began asking a lot of questions, and I said I had seen Charlie Weems and Clarence Norris with the white girls" (quoted in Goodman, 97).

After a trial lasting only three days, the all-white, all-male jury found the teenagers guilty and recommended that eight of them be sentenced to death in the electric chair on 10 July 1931. The prosecution had requested that Roy Wright, who was only twelve or thirteen, should receive a life sentence,

but because seven of the jurors held out for the death penalty for him, too, the judge declared a mistrial in his case.

The Scottsboro Boys were hardly the first black victims of injustice in southern courts, but their youth and the paucity of evidence against them provoked an immediate uproar. Four of the teenagers were from Chattanooga, Tennessee, and had been traveling to Memphis in search of work hauling logs on the Mississippi. Roy Wright and his nineteen-year-old brother, Andy, had been raised by their mother, Ada, after their father died when Andy was twelve. His father's death had forced Andy, who had shown promise in grade school, to find work as a truck driver, though at the time of his arrest he was unemployed. Roy worked in a grocery store. Eugene Williams, thirteen years old, had been a dishwasher in a Chattanooga cafe. Haywood Patterson was the fourth of nine surviving children born to sharecroppers in Elberton, Georgia. In March 1931 he was eighteen and had spent the previous four years riding the rails of the South and Midwest in search of work. Patterson could barely read and write, having left school after the third grade, but he "knew the train schedules, when the freights left and where they arrived [and] could light a butt in the wind on top of a moving boxcar" (quoted in Goodman, 93).

The five other Scottsboro defendants did not know the four Chattanooga teenagers before boarding the train to Memphis; they also did not all know each other. At nineteen or twenty,

Charles Weems was the oldest of the nine youths arrested. His mother had died when he was only four, and six of his seven siblings had also died. Clarence Norris was the second of eleven children born to a former slave and his wife in Warms Springs, Georgia. He had attended school up to the second grade, and at age seven he joined his sharecropping parents in the cotton fields, where he did "everything a grown man could do ... or my daddy would whup me good" (Norris, 28). By the time he was a teenager, beatings from his father had become more frequent, and Norris left home, working a series of laboring jobs before seeking his luck on the rails.

Ozie Powell had also been born in rural Georgia and, like Norris, could barely read and write. Sixteen at the time of his arrest, he had been living in Atlanta for three years, working in sawmills and lumber camps. Seventeen-year-old Olen Montgomery was from Monroe, Georgia, and had attended school through the fifth grade. His vision was extremely poor because of cataracts, and he was traveling to Memphis to buy new glasses when he was arrested. Montgomery, like Powell, had not participated in the fight on the freight train. Nor had Willie Roberson, who was born in Columbus, Georgia. His father abandoned the family a few weeks after Willie's birth, and his mother died two years later, leaving him in the care of his grandmother until she, too, died around 1930. At the time of his arrest, Roberson, who was illiterate and had a severe speech defect, was traveling to Memphis to get treatment for syphilis and gonorrhea. These diseases had left him crippled, but his cane, like Olen Montgomery's glasses, was confiscated after his arrest.

The nation's leading civil rights organization, the NAACP, might have been expected to take on the Scottsboro Boys case, but its executive secretary, WALTER WHITE, was initially reluctant to get involved in a controversial rape case in the deep South. The American Communist Party had no such qualms and quickly convinced the Scottsboro Boys and their parents that their best hope of overturning their convictions lay with its legal arm, the International Labor Defense (ILD). When the U.S. Supreme Court overturned the boys' convictions in *Powell v. Alabama* (1932) and ordered a retrial in March 1933, the ILD's

Joseph Brodsky and the famed criminal attorney Samuel Leibowitz—who was not a Communist—took up their case.

The Communist Party's involvement in the case helped dramatize the Scottsboro case throughout the nation. On May Day of 1931, demonstrations by 300,000 workers in over one hundred American cities demanded the Scottsboro Boys' release. In addition to communist and socialist agitation, a wide range of black and white church leaders; liberal politicians, including New York City's mayor, Fiorello La Guardia; and thousands of ordinary men and women voiced their criticism of the Alabama courts. Although W. E. B. Du Bois was suspicious of the ILD's and the Communists' motives in supporting the Scottsboro Boys, most African Americans agreed with the Oklahoma journalist Roscoe Dunjee, who asked: "What does it matter whether God, the devil, or Communists save those helpless black boys?" (quoted in Goodman, 69). Both Countée Cullen and Langston Hughes wrote poems demanding justice for the Scottsboro Boys.

International support for the Scottsboro Boys was perhaps even more dramatic. A series of European demonstrations, at which Roy and Andy Wright's mother, Ada, was a prominent speaker, also began that summer. More than 150,000 people attended one rally in Berlin in 1932, while other, occasionally violent, protests were staged in Geneva, Paris, and Glasgow. Thousands of Canadian, African, South American, and Chinese supporters of the Scottsboro Boys also sent petitions and letters to the governor of Alabama and to the White House, demanding the boys' release.

International pressure was one thing, but getting justice for black men accused of raping white women in Alabama was quite another. While they waited for a retrial, the Scottsboro Boys remained on death row in appalling conditions; from their cells they could hear the screams of inmates being electrocuted. In all, Clarence Norris recalled, he saw fifteen men walk through the notorious green door to the death chamber. Only one of them was white.

In the first retrial, which involved only Haywood Patterson, Leibowitz exposed the weaknesses of the prosecution's original case. He called the physician who had treated Price and Bates to testify that he had found no bleeding or vaginal damage. A white male witness also testified that he and another white man had had sexual intercourse with Price and Bates on the evening before the two women boarded the train at Huntsville, Alabama, which, Leibowitz argued, explained the nonmotile semen found inside the women's vaginas. Most dramatically, Ruby Bates now testified that there had been no rapes and that she and Price had concocted the original charges out of a fear that they would be arrested for vagrancy. Regardless of that evidence, the jury again found Patterson guilty—after deliberating for only five minutes—and again sentenced him to death. However, the presiding judge, James Horton, agreed with Leibowitz that the evidence indicated Patterson's and the other boys' innocence and ordered a retrial.

That retrial in November 1933 proved even more farcical than the first trial. The presiding judge, William Callahan, all but instructed the jury to convict Patterson. They did so. Patterson later recalled that the judge could not get him to the chair fast enough. He added, "When Callahan sentenced me to death for the third time, I noticed he left out the Lord. He didn't even want the lord to have any mercy on me" (Patterson, 50). One week later Clarence Norris was also convicted and sentenced to death.

Throughout 1934 the ILD petitioned the Alabama courts for a retrial and publicized the inhumane conditions and the physical and mental abuse the Scottsboro Boys received in jail. The Alabama authorities denied those petitions, but in January 1935 the U.S. Supreme Court allowed a review of the convictions of Norris and Patterson. That April, in what proved to be a landmark case, *Norris v. Alabama*, the Supreme Court reversed both convictions on the ground that African Americans had been excluded from the pool of jurors selected to try the case. In the long term, the ruling can be seen as one of the first steps in a series of Supreme Court decisions assuring blacks equal protection rights, leading to the 1954 *Brown v. Board of Education* decision that declared racial segregation unconstitutional. In the short term *Norris v. Alabama* required only that African Americans be included in the pool of potential jurors; it did not guarantee equal black representation on actual juries. This became readily apparent in November 1935, when an Alabama grand jury, with only one black member, issued new indictments that again charged the nine Scottsboro defendants with rape.

The indictments prompted the ILD to make common cause with other civil rights groups, including the NAACP, in a broad-based Scottsboro Defense Committee (SDC) for the next trial in January 1936. Patterson was again convicted—again by an all-white jury—and sentenced to seventy-five years in prison. The following day, however, when Norris, Roy Wright, and Powell were being driven back to Birmingham jail, they got into an argument with their escorts, Sheriff Sandlin and his deputy. The deputy struck Powell about the head; Powell responded by slashing the deputy's throat with a knife that he had concealed. Sheriff Sandlin then shot Powell in the head at close range. The doctors who removed the bullet from his brain gave him a 50 percent chance of surviving; Powell did survive, but he suffered from severe brain damage for the rest of his life.

That incident and a series of appeals by the SDC delayed the trials of the other prisoners until the summer of 1937. Clarence Norris was again found guilty and again received the death sentence, though the governor of Alabama later commuted that sentence to life imprisonment. Andy Wright and Charlie Weems were also found guilty and received prison sentences of ninety-nine and seventy-five years, respectively. Ozie Powell, the only Scottsboro Boy to plead guilty—to a lesser charge of assault—was sentenced to twenty years. The SDC reached a compromise with the Alabama authorities to drop all charges against Roy Wright and Eugene Williams, the youngest of the Scottsboro Boys, and against Olen Montgomery and Willie Roberson, who had not been in the boxcar when the alleged rape took place.

Upon their release, Wright, Williams, Montgomery, and Roberson traveled to New York, where they were mobbed by crowds and appeared briefly in a vaudeville show at Harlem's famed Apollo Theatre. Williams and Montgomery had both dreamed of music careers while in prison, and the latter had even composed a song, "Lonesome Jailhouse Blues," but neither found lasting success as musicians. Williams left to live with relatives in St. Louis, Missouri, apparently with plans to attend Western Baptist Seminary, and was not heard of again. Along with Roy Wright, Montgomery embarked on a publicity tour to raise funds for the release of the remaining Scottsboro Boys and spent the next few years traveling between New York, Atlanta, and Detroit in search of work. A heavy drinker, Montgomery was arrested several times for public disorder and probably returned to Georgia in 1960.

Roy Wright at first adapted well to his newfound freedom. Sponsored by the entertainer BILL "BOJANGLES" ROBINSON, he enrolled in a vocational school and later served in the army, married, and then joined the merchant marine. While on leave from the army in 1959, however, he shot and killed his wife, believing that she had been unfaithful, and then committed suicide. Willie Roberson remained in New York City, settling in Brooklyn, where he found regular employment, though he was arrested once—wrongfully he claimed—for disorderly conduct. He died sometime around 1959, following an asthma attack.

The release of four of the boys signaled the end of one part of the Scottsboro saga. By the late 1930s American and international opinion had begun to focus on the impending world war, and even the black press devoted less attention to the case. The SDC and the ILD persisted in their efforts to gain the release of the five others, but the Alabama authorities proved equally determined that their sentences should stand. Andy Wright, Weems, and Norris were assigned to a new prison, Kilby, where they worked twelve-hour shifts at a cotton mill and were beaten systematically by their guards. On one occasion a guard stabbed Weems, though he had intended to stab Wright. Norris had a finger severed in a work accident and received several whippings and beatings.

In August 1943 Weems was paroled and found a job in an Atlanta laundry. Little is known about him after that, other than that he married and that his eyesight continued to suffer from a tear

gas attack by prison guards, who had found him reading a communist publication in his cell. Wright and Norris were paroled in early 1944 on the condition that they labor at a lumberyard near Montgomery, Alabama. Forced to share a single bed in a tiny room, their living and working conditions were worse than at Kilby. They were nonetheless free to marry—Norris to Dora Lee of Montgomery and Wright to Ruby Belle of Mobile, Alabama. Both men left Montgomery in violation of their paroles in late 1944 but later returned to serve more time at Kilby prison.

Ozie Powell served his sentence at Atmore farm, a penitentiary that, like Parchman in Mississippi and Angola in Louisiana, was notorious for its brutal and inhumane treatment of prisoners. Little is known about Powell's experiences there, other than that he was beaten and that he continued to suffer from depression and paralysis on his right side, a consequence of the gunshot wounds he had suffered at the hands of Sheriff Sandlin. He was released from Atmore in 1946 and returned to Georgia.

Much more is known about Haywood Patterson's time at Atmore, because of his memoir, *Scottsboro Boy* (1950). In February 1941 a guard paid one of Patterson's friends a few dollars to kill him; he stabbed Patterson twenty times and punctured a lung, but the Scottsboro Boy survived. The certainty of violence and the uncertainty of when it might occur made Patterson keep faith only in himself and in the knife that was his constant companion. Like other men who survived Atmore, Patterson became a sexual predator; by giving a brutal beating to a "young wolf" who had made advances on his "gal-boy," he gave warning to his fellow prisoners that nobody would "make a girl" out of him.

After an escape attempt in 1943, the authorities sent Patterson to work at the cotton mill at Kilby prison. At first the violent reputation he had earned at Atmore served him well. The guards left him alone to run what he called his "store," selling cigarettes and other goods to fellow prisoners. He was not immune to unofficial beatings and official whippings from the guards, however, and he endured several spells in solitary confinement. In July 1948, believing that he would never be

released, Patterson decided to "parole himself" by escaping from the Kilby farm, where he was working at the time, to his sister's home in Detroit, Michigan. There, at age thirty-six, he drank his first beer, but his freedom was short-lived.

He took a series of laboring jobs and began working on his autobiography with the writer Earl Conrad. Two weeks after the release of *Scottsboro Boy* in June 1950, the FBI arrested him in Detroit for escaping from Kilby; he was released on bail, and the governor of Michigan refused to extradite him to Alabama to serve his sentence. In December 1950 Patterson was charged with murder after he stabbed and killed a man in a barroom fight. Patterson claimed that he had acted in self-defense, but he was convicted in September 1951 of manslaughter and sentenced to six to fifteen years in the Michigan State penitentiary. He died in prison of cancer less than a year later.

In June 1950, nineteen years after being arrested in Paint Rock, Andy Wright was the last of the Scottsboro Boys to be released, and he moved to Connecticut. Like Montgomery, Powell, Weems, and Williams, it is not known when—or if—Andy Wright died. The failure of historians, journalists, and documentary filmmakers since the 1960s to find them suggests that, if they lived, they probably chose obscurity rather than having to relive the trauma of their years in prison and on death row.

That Clarence Norris titled his own memoir *The Last of the Scottsboro Boys* (1979) suggests that he believed the others had died. This autobiography detailed Norris's life after breaking parole in 1946. He moved first to his sister's home in Cleveland, Ohio, where he found a job shoveling coal in a furnace room and spent some of his first wages at a brothel. There he slept with a white woman to discover why the Alabama authorities had been enraged by even the idea of interracial sex. He discovered, however, that when it came to sex, there "ain't no difference" between white and black women (Norris, 208). He married again, worked a series of laboring jobs interspersed with bouts of unemployment, and moved to New York in 1953. There he was arrested several times, once for stabbing his girlfriend.

By 1960 Norris had settled down with Melba Sanders, his third wife, with whom he had two children, Adele and Deborah. He moved to Brooklyn, found a permanent job that he liked, as a vacuum sweeper in a warehouse, and in the early 1970s began working with the NAACP to get his parole violation expunged. After a lengthy battle, the state of Alabama eventually relented, and in October 1976 Governor George Wallace granted Norris an official pardon. Norris was later diagnosed with Alzheimer's disease and died in January 1989. None of the Scottsboro Boys or their families has ever received compensation for their wrongful arrests and imprisonment.

Some historians have depicted the campaign to free the Scottsboro Boys as a harbinger of the post–World War II civil rights movement that challenged and finally ended legal segregation and second-class citizenship for African Americans. Others have viewed the case as one of the first modern global campaigns for human rights, a forerunner of efforts to win the release of political prisoners from Andrei Sakharov to Nelson Mandela. Both assessments are true, but the Scottsboro Boys knew instinctively that the *reasons* for their imprisonment and inhumane treatment were brutally simple. As Olen Montgomery told a Tuskegee psychiatrist in 1937, "I'm just being held here because I'm a Nigger. That's why I'm in jail; not nothing I've done" (Goodman, 275).

FURTHER READING

Carter, Dan T. *Scottsboro* (1969; rev. ed., 1979).
Goodman, James. *Stories of Scottsboro* (1994).
Miller, James A., et al. "Mother Ada Wright and the International Campaign to Free the Scottsboro Boys, 1931–1934," *American Historical Review* (Apr. 2001).
Norris, Clarence. *The Last of the Scottsboro Boys* (1979).
Patterson, Haywood. *Scottsboro Boy* (1950).
—STEVEN J. NIVEN

SEALE, BOBBY

(22 Oct. 1936–), cofounder of the Black Panther Party, was born Robert George Seale in Dallas, Texas. His mother, Thelma (maiden name unknown), raised Bobby, as well as his brother, sister, and cousin, while his father, George Seale, worked as a carpenter throughout Texas. Seale recalled that his father was often absent, and, when home, would often beat him. During World War II, after moving throughout Texas, the family moved to Oakland, California, where George Seale opened his own store.

Bobby enlisted in the air force as a sheet metal mechanic at age eighteen and was stationed in South Dakota. After almost four years, he was dishonorably discharged following a dispute with a colonel, in part because he owed money to a relative of the officer. After returning to Oakland, Seale worked as an aircraft mechanic, a draftsman, and as a comedian and jazz drummer. In 1960, after spending eighteen months in Los Angeles, he enrolled in Merritt College in West Oakland and supported himself by working for a government antipoverty program. Though his original interest was in engineering, Seale soon immersed himself in studying black history. He also married Artie, his nineteen-year-old girlfriend, with whom he had a son, Malik; they separated several years later as Seale became more involved in civil rights organizing. At Merritt he joined the black nationalist Afro-American Association, where he met fellow student HUEY NEWTON. They soon became dissatisfied with the organization's emphasis on "cultural nationalism" and developed an interest in establishing a more radical nationalist agenda influenced by the black Martiniquean intellectual Frantz Fanon, author of *Wretched of the Earth*. Like Fanon, Seale and Newton envisaged a nationalism that not only promoted black unity but also highlighted the struggle against racial oppression and economic inequality. With this new perspective, Newton and Seale helped found the Soul Student Advisory Council, which organized a protest on campus against the military conscription of blacks.

Both admired the uncompromising attitude and militancy of MALCOLM X, whom Seale had heard speak in Oakland, and Malcolm's assassination in 1965 spurred them to continue organizing to defend the rights of black people. In early 1966 Newton, a law student, decided to observe the police in order to publicize their violations of the rights of blacks. Seale and Newton developed a distinctive uniform of leather jackets and black berets. More significantly, inspired by the dissident North Carolina NAACP leader Robert F. Williams, the author of *Negroes with Guns* (1962), they began carrying guns for self-defense. (According to California law at the time, carrying loaded weapons was legal so long as they were not concealed.)

In the spring of 1966 police arrested Seale and Newton in Berkeley for

Bobby Seale following his arraignment at Berkeley County Courthouse in February 1968. © Bettmann/CORBIS

fighting the police at an antiwar rally; after pleading no contest, they were each sentenced to a year of probation. In October they formed the Black Panther Party in Oakland, which they named after the symbol of the Lowndes County Freedom Organization, which had been organized by civil rights activists in Alabama. The Panthers' initial ten-point program focused on the oppression of black people in the urban North, particularly problems of unemployment, poor housing, police brutality, and bad schools. The first point read, "We want freedom. We want power to determine the destiny of our black community." The tenth point began, "We want land, bread, housing, education, clothing, justice, and peace." Adapting Fanon's perspective to American conditions, the early Panthers placed a heavy emphasis on organizing poor blacks, the "lumpen proletariat" or the "brothers on the block," as they were known in Panther parlance. Within three years the Panthers grew into a national organization, with offices in the Midwest and Northeast as well as California. They soon developed an eclectic ideology, mixing black nationalism with socialism, and drawing not only from Fanon, but also from Cuban, Vietnamese, and Chinese socialist revolutionaries.

Almost as soon as the Panthers had become a national force, there was a concerted effort by local and federal authorities, led by COINTELPRO (the FBI's counterintelligence program), to infiltrate and weaken the groups. COINTELPRO's tactics were so successful that, by the end of the decade, most Panther leaders were either dead, in jail, or in exile. In May 1967 Sacramento police arrested Seale, along with thirty other Panthers, for having protested—arms in hand—a bill that would have prohibited carrying loaded weapons. In October, Newton was arrested on murder charges. Six months later, in April 1968, after a shoot-out with police left Panther Bobby Hutton dead, Panther Minister of Information ELDRIDGE CLEAVER was arrested and, by the end of the year, went into exile. In January 1969 an FBI-aggravated feud between the Panthers and a rival "cultural nationalist" organization led by Maulena Karenga resulted in the death of two Panthers in a gun battle on the UCLA campus. In December 1969

Chicago Panther leaders Fred Hampton and Mark Clark were killed by the police.

Seale did not escape this campaign of repression. In 1968 he was among eight leftists (including the white radicals Tom Hayden, Abbie Hoffman, and Jerry Rubin) who were arrested for protesting at the Democratic National Convention in Chicago. Ironically, Seale was not involved in the planning of the protests, but had merely substituted for Cleaver. After having his case separated from the other defendants, and after he had spent two years behind bars, the authorities ultimately dropped the charges against Seale. The case was most memorable, however, for the remarkable treatment of Seale during the trial. Prior to trial, Seale's attorney was hospitalized; instead of granting a delay in the case, the judge insisted that the trial go ahead, but refused Seale the right to defend himself. When Seale insisted on his right to cross-examine witnesses, the judge had him bound and chained to his chair. For many Americans, Seale's treatment illustrated the deep-rooted racism of the American justice system.

While on trial in Chicago, Seale was also indicted for the 1969 killing of a former Panther, Alex Rackley, in New Haven, Connecticut. Rackley, the prosecution argued, had been suspected of being a police informer by Panthers. Seale, along with thirteen other Panthers, was arrested. On the basis of testimony of a Panther rumored to be an informer himself, the prosecution claimed that Seale, who had been in New Haven as part of a lecture tour, had ordered local Panthers to torture and kill Rackley. Convinced that this was part of the government's campaign to destroy the Panthers, many students at nearby Yale University protested the trial by calling the university's first student strike. Even Yale's president declared that it was impossible for black militants like Seale to receive a fair trial amid the racist, antiradical hysteria created by the police and the prosecution. On 1 May 1970 some twelve thousand people protested Seale's trial and the court's refusal to grant him bail. After a six-month-long trial in 1970–1971, three of the "New Haven Nine" were convicted, but Seale and codefendant Erika Huggins, whose connections to Rackley's death were tenuous at best, were released after the jury returned a

hung verdict and the judge ruled that a fair trial was impossible.

The government's relentless repression of the Panthers aggravated tensions within the organization. Newton and Seale sought to strengthen the Panthers by launching community initiatives, such as its famous free breakfast program. They also sought allies among white, liberal intellectuals. Cleaver, in exile in Algeria, emphasized traditional, revolutionary Panther rhetoric, and the party began to split. In 1973 Seale ran for mayor of Oakland and came in second among nine candidates.

Seale soon drifted out of politics, however, and left the Black Panther Party in 1974. He married former Panther Leslie M. Johnson, with whom he had a son and a daughter, and he maintained his interest in helping the black community, though no longer as a radical activist. During the mid-1980s he worked with Youth Employment Strategies in Philadelphia, encouraging young people to work and to continue their education. In 1988 he wrote a cookbook, *Barbeque'n with Bobby Seale* and he has also marketed his own barbecue sauce. He lectured widely, both on the history of the Panthers and on his theory of social change, which he termed "polylectic reality" and "cooperational humanism."

FURTHER READING

Seale, Bobby. *A Lonely Rage: The Autobiography of Bobby Seale* (1978).

———. *Seize the Time: The Story of the Black Panther Party* (1970).

Freed, Donald. *Agony in New Haven: The Trial of Bobby Seale, Ericka Huggins, and the Black Panther Party* (1973).

—JACOB ZUMOFF

 SHABAZZ, EL-HAJJ MALIK EL-. *See* Malcolm X.

SHAKUR, TUPAC AMARU (16 June 1971– 13 Sept. 1996), rapper, was born Lesane Parish Crooks in New York City to Afeni Shakur (born Alice Faye Williams), a Black Panther, and Billy Garland, who had very little contact with his son. Tupac was named after the last Inca chief, Tupac

Amaru—Tupac meaning "he who shines" and Amaru meaning "large serpent," often translated as "shining serpent"; Shakur is Arabic for "Thankful to God." Raised by their mother, with some help from their stepfather, Jeral Wayne Williams (also known as Mutula Shakur), Tupac and his sister, Sekyiwa, had to learn to cope with their mother's drug addiction, abandonment by their father, and scrutiny from law enforcement. The family was often destitute and moved numerous times throughout Tupac's childhood.

Although Tupac's family life was often in disarray, his mother encouraged him to develop his interests in the arts, and he continued his creative arts education even as he moved from school to school. He spent much of his childhood in New York, where he joined the 127th Street Ensemble Theater group in Harlem and performed at the Apollo Theater in 1984, where he debuted as Travis in LORRAINE HANSBERRY's *A Raisin in the Sun*. His family later moved to Baltimore, Maryland, where he attended the High School for Performing Arts and focused on acting and dance. He moved to Marin County, California, in 1988 and attended the Tamalpais School for the Performing Arts. He did not graduate from high school, but earned his GED after dropping out to become a dancer and rapper.

Shakur began writing rap and poetry as a teenager. His book of poetry, later published by his mother under the title *The Rose That Grew from Concrete* (1997), provides early evidence of his skill with language, especially to represent the angst, sense of betrayal, and regrets of an adolescent black male overwhelmed by the effects of poverty, longing, and abandonment. Many of the poems, while immature, are political in content and critique the criminal justice system, the U.S. government, and the treatment of the Black Panther Party. When Shakur entered the hip-hop scene in earnest in 1991, he did so as a young black man with an artistic background, a trenchant political and social viewpoint, and a score to settle with the world.

After participating in several musical groups in the San Francisco Bay Area, Shakur joined the Digital Underground as a tour dancer and then as a rapper. In late 1991 he released his first solo album, *2pacalypse Now*, which sold more than half a million copies, and created one of the most socially critical songs and videos of the 1990s. "Brenda's Got a Baby" is critical of black culture as well as of the police and the U.S. government, and it framed Shakur's public persona for years to come. In this song he was exploring the problems of teenage pregnancy and child neglect at a time when pregnancy and birth rates were alarmingly high for African American girls. He describes the devastation in detail and challenges families and communities to act as well as to care.

2pacalypse Now became infamous when it was cited in the defense plea of Ronald Howard, a young man in Houston, Texas, who had murdered a state trooper, allegedly after listening to Shakur's recording of "Souljah's Song," which depicts a young man harassed by the police to the point that he retaliates. Howard's attorneys argued that the recording was the cause of the shooting. As a result of the publicity from this case, Shakur was denounced by Vice President Dan Quayle and by various black political leaders. The depiction of the police-hating hip-hop artist fit perfectly with popular notions of the West Coast "gangsta" style of rap that glorifies gang violence and depicts women in unabashedly sexist terms. To compound his gangsta image, Shakur starred in Ernest Dickerson's 1992 film *Juice*, in which he portrayed Bishop, who expresses his identity and manhood through violence.

The early 1990s also resulted in several disputes between Shakur and the police. In late 1991, Shakur filed a ten million dollar lawsuit against the Oakland police for alleged brutality following an arrest for jaywalking. In 1992 he was implicated in the fatal shooting of a six-year-old child in Marin City, a shooting he said haunted him for the rest of his life. By the end of that year the image of Shakur as the typical gangsta rapper was indelibly stamped on the popular imagination, although the socially conscious aspects of his work were hardly mentioned at all. The public attention paid to Shakur's troubles with the law and the lack of attention paid to his political criticism and messages of empowerment frustrated him as well as his fans. In fact, the representation of Shakur as a menace without a critical view of society or "the game" may have fueled his followers' commitment. They savored debate about his problems, beliefs, artistic ability, politics, actions, and antics. His fan base grew stronger in the face of mounting criticism of his actions.

During 1993 Shakur's success was offset by legal problems. His release *Strictly 4 My N.I.G.G.A.Z.* quickly went gold with the party anthem "I Get Around" and the tribute to black women "Keep Ya Head Up," in which he talks not only about strength and survival but about healing as well. It was perhaps at this time that the split between the public image of Shakur and his fans' notion of him as a complex analyst of social ills and truths began to emerge in earnest. For instance, while he could be misogynistic on one recording, on another he might represent a feminist and class-oriented perspective. In 1993, he costarred with Janet Jackson in the John Singleton film *Poetic Justice*. That same year, after moving to Atlanta, he was arrested on several charges, including shooting two off-duty police officers, though he was later acquitted.

During the following years, events accelerated on many fronts. Accused of sexual assault and weapons charges in November 1993, Shakur was found guilty of sexual abuse and ordered to serve four and a half years in New York's Rikers Island penitentiary. Death Row Records CEO Suge Knight posted $1.4 million bond to release Shakur, who immediately flew to Los Angeles and signed with Death Row. While out on bail before sentencing, Shakur was shot five times as he entered a recording studio in New York. This shooting fueled a long-standing feud between East Coast and West Coast artists about respect, airplay, and record promotion. Shakur publicly accused the rapper The Notorious B.I.G. (also known as Biggie Smalls or Christopher Wallace) and B.I.G.'s friend and producer Puff Daddy (Sean Combs, also known as P Diddy) of being implicated in his attempted murder. Several confrontations between Shakur and B.I.G. and their crews followed. In response Shakur released the single "Hit 'Em Up," an angry, profanity-laced, and caustically insulting rant against those whom he perceived to be his enemies. Shakur recovered from his wounds and produced *Me against the World*, which was released in 1995 while he was in prison in New York's Riker's Island Penitentiary. This album, which includes the song "Dear Momma," a tribute to black mothers and a public apology to and declaration of love for his own mother, sold over two million copies. In March 1996, paroled from jail, Shakur released the first hip-hop double CD, *All Eyez on Me*, which sold over three million copies.

On 7 September 1996, after leaving the Mike Tyson–Bruce Seldon fight in Las Vegas, Shakur was shot four times while riding in a car driven by Suge Knight. He died six days later, only twenty-six years old. In many respects, Shakur's death initiated a deeper discussion of both social and political problems among youth, many of whom consider him a hero and martyr. On 5 November 1996, two months after his death, his album *The Don Killuminati: Seven Day Theory* was released posthumously under the pseudonym Makaveli. This was followed by a major release in November 1997 of *RU Still Down? [Remember Me]*, a double CD of previously unreleased tracks on Amaru Records, a label established by Shakur's mother. A year later, *2Pac's Greatest Hits*, a double CD, was released by Death Row/Interscope/Amaru Records. These releases fueled speculation that Shakur was still alive. In 2001 *Forbes Magazine* listed him as "one of the top grossing celebrities no longer alive" with the 2001 album *Until the End of Time*, which reportedly sold 2.7 million copies and earned an estimated seven million dollars.

Many were concerned that the violence of rap, exemplified in Shakur's death, would be emulated by youth. Instead, young people heard lyrics of empowerment, responsibility, and self-love. Shakur's final video, "I Ain't Mad at Ya," was one of many songs that predicted his violent death while pointing out injustice and arguing for redemption. He claimed that his concept of the "thug life," a phrase he had tattooed on his chest and that he explained as an acronym for "The Hate U Give Little Infants Fucks Everybody," led to hundreds of ministries organized around hip-hop and what they referred to as thugology—the saving of the spiritual self and community by dealing with the realities of youth. It also became the organizing force around self-empowerment programs and after-school programs. Shakur starred in six movies,

released four albums, and earned two Grammy nominations. Since his death there have been at least four posthumous albums and numerous books, videos, and tributes. Shakur struggled through words and performance and through his outward show of love, outrage, hate, and confusion to find a moral center in his life. Despite all that he endured, his loudest message may have been that even through conflict, one should keep trying. The 2003 release of the documentary and soundtrack *Resurrection* not only implies a resolution with many of his foes, but also includes a statement of his purpose: "to reach the kid who believes it hopeless." As he assures his fans in "Keep Ya Head Up," "While the rich kids is drivin' Benz / I'm still tryin' to hold on to my survivin' friends / And it's crazy, it seems it'll never let up, but please / you got to keep your head up." Shakur's five-year solo recording career included many hits that his fans considered prophetic, insightful, socially conscious, and at times violent. By the time of his death, he was considered one of the most influential, talented, and controversial hip-hop artists and entertainers of his time. While his music, his life, and his death articulate many of the problems of race and class in the United States, it remains to be seen how his fans will translate their understanding of Shakur into action in their own lives.

FURTHER READING

Batsfield, Darren Keith. *Back in the Day: My Life and Times with Tupac Shakur* (2002).

Brooks, Darren. *Maximum 2Pac: The Unauthorised Biography of 2Pac* (2003).

Datcher, Michael, Kwame Alexander, and Mutulu Shakur. *Tough Love: The Life and Death of Tupac Shakur, Cultural Criticisms and Familial Observations* (1997).

Dyson, Michael Eric. *Holler If You Hear Me: Searching for Tupac Shakur* (2001).

Frokos, Helen. *Tupac Shakur (They Died Too Young)* (2000).

JONES, QUINCY, and the Editors of Vibe Magazine. *Tupac Amaru Shakur, 1971–1996* (1997).

—MARCYLIENA MORGAN

SHARPTON, AL
(3 Oct. 1954–), minister, activist, and U.S. presidential candidate, was born Alfred Charles Sharpton Jr. in Brooklyn, New York, the younger of two children of

Alfred Charles Sharpton Sr., a contractor, and Ada Richards Sharpton, a seamstress. His father and mother had migrated to Brooklyn from Florida and Alabama, respectively. Their son, Al, became steeped at an early age in the culture of the Pentecostal Church, gaining recognition as a "wonder boy preacher." He was ordained at the age of ten by his pastor, Bishop Frederick Douglass Washington, charismatic founder of the Sharpton family's church, the Washington Temple Church of God in Christ.

Sharpton's first residence was in the working-class neighborhood of East New York in Brooklyn, but while he was still young his family moved to the nearby black middle-class community of Hollis, Queens. His idyllic childhood was dealt a devastating blow when his father left the household and moved in with another woman; the trauma was aggravated by the fact that the other woman was Ada Sharpton's daughter from a previous marriage—Sharpton's half-sister, Tina. Ada and her two children, Al Jr. and Cheryl, fell into dire economic straits. Unable to pay the bills, they lived for a time without electricity or heat and eventually went on welfare, finding a succession of apartments in the Crown Heights and East Flatbush neighborhoods of Brooklyn.

In the coming years Sharpton would associate with a series of replacement father figures, who would set the pattern for his personal, religious, and political development. The boy preacher became increasingly enchanted by a flashy minister on the other side of the East River, in Harlem. The Reverend ADAM CLAYTON POWELL JR. was the pastor of the Abyssinian Baptist Church and a U.S. congressman. One of Powell's notable traits was that he was "particularly irritating to whites," Sharpton later noted. Young Sharpton spent hours with the brash, cigar-chomping minister, consciously trying to imitate Powell's fearless panache and his suave and savvy manner.

While he was a student at Samuel J. Tilden High School in Brooklyn, Sharpton immersed himself in student government and the debating team. Michael Klein asserted in his biography of Sharpton, *The Man behind the Sound Bite*, that when many black and white students were becoming radicals, Sharpton took debating positions against the

Activist Al Sharpton with Jacqueline Jackson in March 2000 entering the Justice Department to seek prosecution of the four New York City police officers who shot and killed immigrant Ghanaian Amadou Diallo. Corbis

Maoists and Black Panther sympathizers. In high school Sharpton was introduced to the strategy of the economic boycott when he was appointed in 1969 as youth director of the Brooklyn office of Operation Breadbasket, an organization that was led by the Reverend JESSE JACKSON, Sharpton's mentor who later became his rival. Affiliated with the Southern Christian Leadership Conference (SCLC), Operation Breadbasket targeted businesses believed to be discriminating against blacks and then boycotted those companies until they agreed to adopt procedures to promote sensitivity and increase diversity within their organizations. Some critics equated this tactic with extortion, but both Sharpton and Jackson had seen the effectiveness of boycotts during the civil rights movement and found its use (and even threatened use) to be powerful options in their overall political strategy. When Jackson left Operation Breadbasket in 1971, Sharpton also resigned to start his own organization, the Brooklyn-based National Youth Movement.

As leader of the National Youth Movement, Sharpton would become a major figure in New York City, organizing boycotts and leading protests against police brutality in the 1980s. Glib in the language of the streets, he was able to draw large numbers of young people to his demonstrations. His advance to fame, and to controversy, was also linked with the personality of JAMES BROWN, the so-called Godfather of Soul, whom Sharpton met in 1973. Brown wore his hair in the "conked" or straightened style that some blacks, as the Afro came into fashion, considered a sign of racial self-loathing. As a tribute to Brown's influence, Sharpton began wearing his own hair in the same fashion, which made him easily recognizable among black activists and also made him the butt of unkind jokes.

In 1975 Sharpton dropped out of Brooklyn College after two years of study to begin promoting Brown's concerts, which is how he met Kathy Jordan, a backup singer for Brown whom he married in 1983; they have two children. In 1974, while Sharpton was arranging a performance for Brown in Zaire, Africa—during the "Rumble in the Jungle," a boxing match between MUHAMMAD ALI and George Foreman—Sharpton began dealing with the boxing promoter Don King. Because of King's alleged connections to organized crime, FBI agents turned their attention also to Sharpton. In the early 1980s they approached him and threatened to prosecute him if he did not become an informant.

Sharpton later acknowledged turning over information about suspected drug dealers, but he denied spying on black radicals. But the New York City newspaper *Newsday* published a series of stories in 1988 showing that Sharpton helped the FBI try to locate a black revolutionary, Joanne Chesimard (also known as Assata Shakur), who was wanted in the killing of a New Jersey state trooper. Through most of the 1980s these dealings with the FBI were unknown to Sharpton's fellow activists. His notoriety as a militant civil rights leader crested after the December 1986 death of Michael Griffith, a young black man killed in the predominantly white section of Howard Beach in Queens. Teaming up with two black lawyers, Alton Maddox and C. Vernon Mason, Sharpton led protest marches and demanded the appointment of a special prosecutor. A special prosecutor was named, and in December 1987 a jury convicted three white youths from Howard Beach of manslaughter. It was considered a vindication of Sharpton's street protests. Law enforcement officials would later indict Sharpton and the National Youth Movement with a variety of tax and financial charges for which Sharpton was acquitted on all counts.

In November 1987 a black teenager named Tawana Brawley said that she had been sexually assaulted by white men in Wappingers Falls, New York. Sharpton, Maddox, and Mason began their fateful involvement in the case as advisers to the girl and her family. Sharpton and the other advisers continued to maintain that Brawley had been raped, even after the state attorney general and newspaper investigative reports had concluded the allegations were a "hoax." Witness testimony and physical evidence showed that Brawley and her mother fabricated the tale of abduction and assault because she feared punishment from her stepfather for staying out all night. In 2001 Sharpton paid sixty-five thousand dollars in damages, following a jury's determination that he had defamed Steven A. Pagones, a white attorney whom Sharpton had accused of involvement in the sexual attack and who was exonerated by a special grand jury in 1988.

Sharpton's reputation was severely damaged in January of 1988, when *Newsday* published its first articles on Sharpton's ties to the FBI. The disclosures divided the black activist community, and many radicals refused to participate in protests with Sharpton, fearing that he was spying on them. Sharpton claimed that the articles were part of a plot to have him assassinated. One of the most verbally agile figures to set foot on the public stage in New York, Sharpton rebounded from that crisis, as he did from many others.

In the early years of the 1990s Sharpton went through a personal and spiritual transformation that changed the course of his political career. During a 12 January 1991 demonstration in the Bensonhurst section of Brooklyn—where the black teenager Yusuf Hawkins had been murdered the previous year by a gang of whites—Sharpton was stabbed in the chest by a white man. While recovering in the hospital, Sharpton began to reassess and redirect his energies, and he became a more traditional politician, soon casting his eye on elective office. His shift to establishment politics was eased on 2 July 1990, when a jury acquitted him of all sixty-seven counts of fraud, which had been brought by the state attorney general Robert Abrams. Abrams had accused Sharpton of stealing about a quarter of a million dollars from the National Youth Movement.

In 1992 Sharpton ran in the Democratic primary race for U.S. Senate. While he did not win the election, he garnered two-thirds of the black vote and established himself as a credible power broker. He made a similarly strong challenge in a 1994 U.S. Senate race and set the stage for a run in 1997 for the mayoralty of New York City. All the while, Sharpton maintained his image as the city's leading voice of protest against police brutality. Yet Sharpton's growing popularity in the black community sent chills through much of the city's white population, resulting in a white political backlash that contributed to the 1993 reelection defeat of the city's first black mayor, DAVID DINKINS. Reacting to the February 1999 killing of Amadou Diallo—an unarmed African immigrant shot in a hail of forty-one bullets fired by four white policemen—Sharpton put together one of the most effective civil disobedience campaigns in modern city history. He persuaded hundreds of politicians, actors, labor leaders, and

others to join him in getting arrested at protests outside police headquarters in Manhattan.

He also increasingly began to appeal to the Latino community, traveling, for example, to the Puerto Rican island of Vieques to protest U.S. bombing exercises there. On 23 May 2001 he was sentenced to three months in jail for that act of civil disobedience. He served the time at a federal detention center in Brooklyn. In 2003 Sharpton filed papers as a candidate for the U.S. presidency. His candidacy drew the support of leading black intellectual CORNEL WEST, who agreed to serve as an adviser. Sharpton's quick wit, refreshing candor, and populist appeal distinguished him among a crowded field of Democratic contenders—even though his chances of winning the Democratic nomination were known to be slight. Sharpton was nonetheless clearly hoping to emerge as a spokesman for black America, a role that had been played during the 1980s and early 1990s by his onetime mentor, Jesse Jackson.

FURTHER READING

Sharpton, Al, and Karen Hunter. *Al on America* (2002).
Sharpton, Al, and Anthony Walton. *Go and Tell Pharaoh: The Autobiography of the Reverend Al Sharpton* (1996).

Klein, Michael. *The Man behind the Sound Bite* (1991).
Mandery, Evan J. *The Campaign: Rudy Giuliani, Ruth Messinger, Al Sharpton, and the Race to Be Mayor of New York City* (1999).
—RON HOWELL

SHELTON, LEE. *See* Stagolee.

SHEPARD, JAMES EDWARD (3 Nov. 1875– 6 Oct. 1947), educator and college founder, was born in Raleigh, North Carolina, the eldest of twelve children of Hattie Whitted and Augustus Shepard, a prominent Baptist minister. He attended local primary schools and graduated in 1894 with a pharmacy degree from

Shaw University in Raleigh. In 1895 he married Annie Day Robinson, the granddaughter of Thomas Day, a well-known antebellum cabinetmaker. The couple had two daughters, Annie Day and Marjorie Augusta.

After college Shepard practiced pharmacy for several years and quickly established himself among North Carolina's leading black entrepreneurs. In 1898 he became one of the first seven investors in the North Carolina Mutual Life Insurance Company in Durham, which eventually became the largest black-owned business in the South. He also helped incorporate another Durham institution, the Mechanics and Farmers Bank, in 1907. While making these entrepreneurial inroads, Shepard kept one foot in the world of politics. An active member of the Republican Party, he held two political appointments at the turn of the century: a clerkship in the Recorder of Deeds Office in Washington, D.C., from 1898 to 1899 and Raleigh's deputy collector for the Internal Revenue Service from 1899 to 1905.

In the wake of black disfranchisement in North Carolina in 1900, Shepard recognized that future political appointments were unlikely. When his Internal Revenue Service appointment expired, he turned his attention to matters of religious service and social uplift. From 1905 to 1909 he served as field superintendent for the International Sunday School Association and was the only African American to address the World Sunday School Convention in Rome in 1907.

During the early years of Jim Crow, Shepard urged southern blacks to focus on moral and educational development rather than political agitation. His accommodationist approach proved amenable to local Democratic elites and allowed Shepard to build a broad network of white southern patrons. At the same time, he did not abandon his interest in politics and maintained close ties with national leaders in the Republican Party.

Shepard drew upon his local and national connections in raising money for the National Religious Training School and Chautauqua for the Colored Race, which he opened in Durham in 1910. The school initially held short institutes for ministers and offered a selection of liberal arts, home economics, and commercial courses. Shepard's early promotional pamphlets for his school hewed to white-approved precepts for black education by promising to combine academic and industrial training and to instill in his students a solid work ethic. Such carefully crafted appeals won him endorsements from local and national white leaders, including Theodore Roosevelt. Shepard's growing ambitions for his school, however, soon outstripped its budget. The institution ran into such severe debt in 1915 that he was forced to put it up for auction. The school survived this crisis when the wife of the philanthropist Russell Sage purchased it for Shepard, who then reopened it as the National Training School and began training future teachers as well as preachers. In the late 1910s Shepard developed his school along collegiate lines and expanded its offerings in the liberal arts.

Again facing mounting debts in the early 1920s, Shepard engaged in talks with state officials about the possibilities for the incorporation of his school as a public institution. The state, which needed an increased supply of black teachers, agreed to assume Shepard's debt on the condition that he discontinue all college work except that required to operate a normal school. Shepard agreed to this plan; when the fall semester opened in 1923, the National Training School had become the Durham State Normal School.

Despite his agreement with state officials, Shepard never fully accepted the idea of limiting his school to a teacher-training curriculum. In 1925 he hired a lawyer to author and find legislative sponsorship for a bill allowing for the creation of a liberal arts college at Durham State Normal School. Shepard himself went before a legislative committee and offered an impassioned plea for his plan. The North Carolina General Assembly granted his request, acknowledging both Shepard's enduring political talents and the white South's growing desire to curb black migration and contain the more assertive "New Negro" of the 1920s. In February 1925 the Durham State Normal School became the North Carolina College for Negroes, the first publicly supported liberal arts college for blacks in the nation. Shepard faced

enormous challenges during the school's first decade, including a devastating fire in 1925 and the tight state budgets of the Depression years. Nonetheless, through a combination of private donations and state and federal aid, he quickly expanded North Carolina College for Negroes, which in 1938 won an "A" rating from the Southern Association of Colleges and Secondary Schools.

In addition to his college presidency, Shepard held numerous other positions of leadership in North Carolina. In the 1920s he served as president of the state's black teachers association and as Grand Master of the Prince Hall Free and Accepted Masons. By the early 1930s Shepard's civic leadership had become more explicitly political. In 1935 he became one of the founding members of the Durham Committee on Negro Affairs, a coalition that sought to increase local black political power. He took that goal on the air in the 1940s with statewide radio addresses that urged black citizens to register to vote.

In mobilizing black communities, however, Shepard consistently avoided political strategies and organizations that met with strong southern white disapproval. He disassociated himself from the growing NAACP membership in the South and frustrated that association's efforts to organize educational equalization lawsuits. In 1930 he opposed the NAACP's campaign to block the Supreme Court nomination of Judge John J. Parker, a native North Carolinian who had used race-baiting tactics in past campaigns. He also opposed—and helped derail—the NAACP's 1933 sponsorship of Thomas Raymond Hocutt, a graduate of the North Carolina College for Negroes who attempted to integrate the pharmacy school at the University of North Carolina in Chapel Hill. Throughout the early 1930s Shepard discouraged members of the black teachers association from waging a salary equalization suit against the state. And in the late 1930s he refused to support the future civil rights activist and Durham native PAULI MURRAY, when she, like Hocutt, sought admission to the state's flagship white university.

Some black critics charged that Shepard's antagonism toward the NAACP amounted to self-serving attempts at institutional preservation

and expansion. Not long after the University of North Carolina denied admission to Pauli Murray, state legislators voted to add graduate work at the North Carolina College for Negroes. The school began offering master's degrees in 1939, opened a law school in 1940, and established a school of library science in 1941. As the NAACP, nationally and locally, pushed for racial integration within higher education, Shepard called for the development of his school into a full-fledged university.

Shepard did not live to see his school attain university status or to witness the civil rights movement that fundamentally changed the course of educational development in the South. After suffering a stroke in 1947, he died in Durham at the age of seventy-one. Less than two years after his death, a group of students from North Carolina College for Negroes picketed the state capitol, protesting conditions at their unaccredited law school. Their demonstration helped pave the way for the 1951 integration of the law school at the University of North Carolina at Chapel Hill, the first major victory in the desegregation of higher education in the state.

Shortly after his death, a local white newspaper columnist commented that Shepard "was regarded by many legislators [as] the best politician ever to come before them" (*Greensboro Daily News*, 31 Dec. 1948). Toward the end of his life, Shepard's deferential style of politics earned him the admiration of white southerners, even as it distanced him from a new, more radical generation of blacks in the emerging civil rights movement. Nevertheless, his pragmatic interracial bargaining helped create a school (renamed North Carolina Central University in 1969) that stands as an enduring testament to his role in black institution building in the Jim Crow South.

FURTHER READING

There is a small collection of Shepard's speeches and related clippings at the James E. Shepard Memorial Library, North Carolina Central University, Durham, North Carolina.

Gershenhorn, Jerry. "*Hocutt v. Wilson* and Race Relations in Durham, North Carolina, during the 1930s," *North Carolina Historical Review* 78 (July 2001).

Murray, Pauli. *Song in a Weary Throat: An American Pilgrimage* (1987).

Weare, Walter B. *Black Business in the New South: A Social History of the North Carolina Mutual Life Insurance Company* (1973).

Obituaries: *New York Times* and *News & Observer* (Raleigh, N.C.), 7 Oct. 1947.
—SARAH C. THUESEN

SHEPPARD, WILLIAM HENRY (8 or 28 Mar. 1865–25 Nov. 1927), missionary, explorer, and human rights advocate, was born in Waynesboro, Virginia, the son of William H. Sheppard, a barbershop owner, and Sarah Francis "Fannie" Martin, a bath maid at a local spa, who had been born free. Because of his mother's free status, William, born just weeks before the end of the Civil War, was never classified as a slave, but his father may have been. Compared with most blacks in postbellum Virginia, the Sheppards lived in relative comfort, though William began full-time employment at eleven, first as a stable boy and then as a waiter. In 1881 Sheppard enrolled at the night school run by BOOKER T. WASHINGTON at Hampton Institute, Virginia, and financed his education by working on the institute's farm and in its bakery. He also helped found a mission school for poor blacks nearby and wrote in his autobiography, "I felt from that afternoon that my future work was to carry the gospel to the poor, destitute, and forgotten people" (Kennedy, 11).

To achieve that goal, Sheppard studied for the ministry at Tuscaloosa Theological Institute (now Stillman College) in Alabama in the mid-1880s and was assigned by the southern Presbyterian Church to congregations in Montgomery, Alabama, and Atlanta, Georgia. Disliking his urban pastorates, he lobbied the Presbyterian Foreign Mission Board for two years to send him to Africa, but the board refused to do so until 1890, when it recruited a white Alabamian minister, Samuel Lapsley, to join him in founding a mission to the Congo. Leaving his fiancée, Lucy Gantt, behind, Sheppard sailed with Lapsley from New York to London in February 1890. Before leaving for the Congo, Lapsley met with and received assistance for the mission from King Leopold II of Belgium, a man recognized by his fellow European monarchs as "Protector of the Congo." In truth, Leopold's governance of the Congo more closely resembled a protection racket, benefiting the Europeans who invested in his rubber plantations, mines, and railroads, but at a tragic cost to millions of native Congolese, driven out of their homes and beaten, tortured, and enslaved in brutal labor camps.

Sheppard and Lapsley were, however, unaware of the ongoing genocide when their ship anchored at Sharks Point on the Congo River delta in May 1890. The two men then embarked on an arduous twelve-hundred-mile journey through territory rarely traversed by outsiders, braving storms; treacherous, crocodile-filled rivers; and exposure to malaria and other diseases. Sheppard proved adept at navigating the unknown terrain and establishing an easy rapport with locals, which was greatly enhanced when he shot two hippopotami to save a village of Bateke people who were near starvation. The Bateke repaid their debt to the man they called Mundele Ndom, "the black white man," by rescuing him from attack by a crocodile. Booker T. Washington would have been proud of Sheppard's entrepreneurial skills—and frugality—as he cajoled, haggled, and bartered in several villages to find the porters and supplies needed for the final stage of the missionaries' journey, first by canoe and then by steamship, through the perilous Kasai River basin.

On 18 April 1891 Sheppard and Lapsley finally arrived at Luebo in the Kasai District, where they established the American Presbyterian Congo Mission among the Kete, a moderately prosperous farming people. After the dangers of the previous year, Sheppard marveled at the beauty of the Upper Kasai's palm tree–filled landscape and gloried at the clear night skies that "shine nowhere so brightly and beautifully as in 'Darkest Africa'" (Kennedy, 64). Even though the men established a small farm and built several huts and rudimentary roads, they failed in their primary task of converting the Kete to Christianity.

When Lapsley died from blackwater fever in 1892, Sheppard assumed sole charge at Luebo and immediately planned a new mission, this time to the Kuba people, who lived in uncharted lands deep within the Kasai interior.

After mastering the Kuba language and navigating the byzantine pathways of the Kasai outback, he arrived at a village on the edge of the Kuba kingdom, only to be apprehended by a prince, N'toinzide, who threatened to put the entire village on trial for entertaining a foreigner. Sheppard expected to be put to death, but he was instead brought to N'toinzide's father, King Kot aMweeky, who declared the missionary to be the spiritual reincarnation of Bope Mekabe, an ancient king of the Kuba. Sheppard remained at the king's palace for several months, observing the orderly, prosperous, and technologically advanced culture of the Kuba and collecting fine pottery, intricate tapestries, and ceremonial wood carvings, among other artifacts, that he would later donate to the Hampton Institute. Although Sheppard found much to admire in Kuba society, he deplored the practice of poisoning suspected witches and the ritual killing of enemy captives in funeral sacrifices. Hoping eventually to discourage such traditions, he persuaded Kot aMweeky to grant him nine acres of land upon which to build a mission. On receiving that grant, Sheppard left for London in 1893, where his exploits among the Kuba had earned him comparisons to the famed Scottish missionary and explorer David Livingstone and membership in the Royal Geographic Society.

Traveling back to America, Sheppard married Lucy Gantt in Jacksonville, Florida, in February 1894 and returned with her to the Congo three months later. There she had three daughters, Miriam and Lucille, who died as infants, and Wilhelmina, who survived the malarial Congo for five months before being taken home to Virginia to be raised by an aunt. In 1901 Lucy Sheppard had a son, William Lapsley Maxamalinge, shortened to Max, who was named after her husband's first partner at Luebo and a Kuba prince. Sheppard also had a relationship with a Kuba woman, who bore him a son, Shepete, in 1900.

From 1894 to 1896 Sheppard's mission at Luebo was staffed entirely by African Americans, until the Presbyterian leadership in America insisted on assigning a white missionary, William Morrison, to oversee them. Morrison shared Sheppard's goal of establishing a mission among the Kuba but was even more concerned about exposing the mounting evidence of atrocities perpetrated by the Belgian colonial regime. In 1899 Morrison dispatched Sheppard to report on an alleged massacre of Kuba villagers by native Zappo-Zap forces armed with European weaponry. Posing as a Belgian official, Sheppard took photographs of piles of dead bodies and dying people and persuaded the Zappo-Zap leader to admit that they had killed more than eighty villagers for refusing to pay their Belgian overlords a "tax" of rubber, food, and slaves. In addition to the charred, dismembered bodies—a scene reminiscent of a southern lynching—Sheppard made the grisly discovery of a pile of eighty-one right hands. Even though the Belgian courts assigned blame to the Zappo-Zaps alone, Sheppard's report provoked a flurry of international protests against the Congo regime and prompted Mark Twain to publish a damning satire of Belgian colonialism, "King Leopold's Soliloquy."

In the main, however, Sheppard was less vocal than Morrison or Twain in condemning Belgian atrocities, at least as long as he remained in the Congo and needed the colonial regime's support for a planned new mission. That accommodationist stance did not, however, prevent the Belgian state rubber company from attempting to sue him in 1908 for slander; Sheppard had published an article criticizing the company's forced labor practices and their destruction of Kuba traditions and culture. The Belgian authorities ultimately dismissed the charges, but the trial helped focus global attention on atrocities in the Congo and made Sheppard one of the first internationally recognized human rights advocates.

Sheppard's moment of fame was short-lived, however. He returned to the United States in 1910, after the Presbyterian Foreign Missions Board expelled him for several counts of adultery, charges that he admitted. Not wishing to tarnish the reputation of a bona fide hero—or the reputation of the church itself—the Missions Board kept the charges secret but placed Sheppard on probation, forcing the minister and his family to scrape together a living in Staunton, Virginia. In 1912 the church relented and hired Sheppard as a pastor in Louisville, Kentucky, where he died after a stroke in 1927. Although he lived his final years in relative obscurity, more than a thousand people attended his funeral, a testament to Sheppard's enduring appeal.

At the turn of the twentieth century, no other black missionary enjoyed a greater international reputation than William Sheppard. Sheppard's condemnation of Belgian atrocities and his public lectures on the treasures of the Kuba also provided a necessary antidote to prevailing Victorian notions that contrasted civilized Europe with the uncultured savagery of "darkest Africa."

FURTHER READING

There are two main collections of Sheppard materials and manuscripts: the Presbyterian Historical Society, Montreat, North Carolina, and the Hampton University Archives, Hampton, Virginia.

Sheppard, William H. *Presbyterian Pioneers in Congo* (1917).

Kennedy, Pagan. *Black Livingstone: A True Tale of Adventure in the Nineteenth-Century Congo* (2002).

—STEVEN J. NIVEN

SLATER, MORRIS. *See* Railroad Bill.

SIMMONS, RUTH J.
(3 July 1945–), educator and university president, was born Ruth Jean Stubblefield in Grapeland, Texas, the youngest of twelve children of Isaac Stubblefield and Fannie, maiden name unknown. Her parents were cotton sharecroppers who moved the family to Houston, Texas, when Ruth was seven years old. In Houston, Isaac worked in a factory and served as minister of Mount Hermon Missionary Baptist Church while Fannie worked as a domestic for white families. As a child Ruth learned from her family that though they were poor in material possessions, they were rich in spirit and potential.

Ruth's mother had a tremendous influence on her development. By watching her mother iron clothes and scrub floors for wealthy whites, she said, "I was given the privilege to observe a remarkable woman take pride in her work and carry herself with extraordinary dignity, and with extraordinary kindness" (Simmons, 23). When asked what made her capable of becoming such an important and groundbreaking leader in education, she credited her mother's example. When Ruth Simmons was fifteen her mother died, and Vernell Lillie, a drama instructor at Phillis Wheatley High School, became one of a series of teachers who helped fill the void left by the loss. Lillie became a role model for Simmons, inspired her to excel academically, and encouraged her to apply for a scholarship at Dillard University, where she could find other nurturing teachers and an outlet for her theatrical talent.

With each success Simmons gained confidence and began to realize that she could achieve anything. While at Dillard, Simmons spent a summer studying at the Universidad Internacional in Saltillo, Mexico, and during her junior year participated in a student-exchange program with Wellesley College in Massachusetts. There she discovered that she could compete with students from more privileged backgrounds. She also had her first experience with the black consciousness movement of the 1960s and, because of it, felt compelled to do her part to dismantle white supremacy in all its forms.

In 1967 Simmons received her BA in French, summa cum laude, and went on to study French in Lyons, France, on a Fulbright fellowship. When she returned in 1968, she married Norbert Simmons, a lawyer, with whom she would later have two children; the couple divorced in 1989. She briefly worked as an interpreter at the U.S. Department of State in Washington, D.C., and then entered Harvard University, where she earned an MA and, in 1973, a PhD in Romance Languages and Literature. Her first faculty appointment was as assistant professor of French at the University of New Orleans, where she also entered academic administration when she was appointed associate dean of the College of Liberal Arts in 1975.

Simmons became visiting associate professor of Pan-African studies at the University of Southern California in Los Angeles in 1978 and was quickly promoted to assistant and then to associate dean before being appointed director of Butler College at Princeton University in New Jersey in 1983. Her research on French-speaking African and Caribbean nations focused on writers such as Aime Cesaire and David Diop and led to the publication of *Haiti: A Study of the Educational System and Guide to US Placement* (1985). Even as she made professional and scholarly strides, Simmons maintains that her priority during these years was raising her two children, Khari and Maya. After seven years at Princeton, Simmons traveled to Spelman College in Atlanta, Georgia, where she served as provost for two years; she then returned to Princeton to become their vice provost.

During her tenure at Princeton she was asked by the university to prepare a study of racial problems on campus that came to be known as the "Simmons Report"; it became a model for other institutions. As the acting director of the Afro-American studies program in 1985, she was instrumental in recruiting the author TONI MORRISON and the renowned philosopher CORNEL WEST to the faculty. In 1995 Simmons assumed the presidency of the highly prestigious Smith College in Northampton, Massachusetts, the largest women's college in the United States. She was Smith's first African American president. There she established the nation's first engineering program at a women's college, founded a journal, *Meridians*, focusing on the careers of minority women, and nearly doubled the college's endowment.

In November 2000 Simmons made history again by being named president of Brown University. When she arrived on campus, she said, "I'm not a social worker. I'm here to lead a great university into even greater academic achievement" (*Providence Journal-Bulletin*, 18 July 2001). She engaged such difficult issues as a controversy over the rights and responsibilities of free speech in an academic environment, a campaign to unionize graduate teaching assistants (which she opposed), raising faculty salaries, and establishing need-blind admissions. While her decisions did not always please everyone, her thoughtful and amiable manner quickly endeared her to every segment of the university.

As her star rose with each achievement, Simmons received greater attention for being the first African American woman to reach new heights. She accepted her role as a leader in the fight for social justice for women and minorities with grace and aplomb. In the realm of civic activities, Simmons often left the ivory towers to deliver motivational speeches to students in inner cities and rural areas. She used her position on such corporate boards as Pfizer Inc. and the Goldman Sachs Group to champion her belief that true corporate responsibility does not end with producing profits for the shareholders, but extends to helping produce a safe and just world for our children, the holders of the future. Her philosophy is that ethics and civility are learned skills that sustain a civilization. In Rhode Island she became a strong advocate for educational programs that target women, because, as she said, "when you educate women, you educate families" (Davis). Simmons's life and accomplishments have themselves become the best example of the beliefs she espouses to others. As such, she has established a trajectory that points ever upward toward greater service.

FURTHER READING

Simmons, Ruth. "My Mother's Daughter: Lessons I Learned in Civility and Authenticity," *Texas Journal of History and Culture, Texas Journal for the Humanities* 20, no. 2 (Spring/Summer 1998).

Passi-Klaus, Susan. "From Inner City Roots to Ivy League President: Ruth Simmons Story," *Sharing Gods Gifts: Black College Fund* n.d. 8 July 2003.

—JOHNNETTA B. COLE

SIMPSON, O. J.

(9 July 1947–), football player, sportscaster, and actor, was born Orenthal James Simpson in San Francisco, California, to Jimmie Simpson, a cook, and Eunice Durden, a nurse's aide. The child disliked his unusual first name, which was given to him by an aunt who had heard of a French actor named Orenthal. Sometime during his childhood—accounts differ as to when—he began using his initials "O.J.," which friends later adapted to "Orange Juice" and, later, to "Juice." When O.J. was four, Jimmy Simpson abandoned his wife and family, leaving Eunice to raise four children in a two-bedroom apartment in the rundown Potrero Hill public housing projects near San Francisco's Chinatown. Eunice Simpson worked long hours to provide for her children, but it was often a hard struggle. When O.J. contracted rickets as an infant, for example, he was left bowlegged and in need of leg braces that his mother could not afford. Eunice improvised by connecting an iron bar to a pair of O.J.'s shoes and making him wear it for several hours a day until he was five.

Despite his early handicap, O.J. displayed a precocious athletic ability. He played Little League baseball and hoped one day to emulate his idol, the San Francisco Giants' centerfielder WILLIE MAYS. Like many of his contemporaries in Potrero Hill, Simpson was also drawn to local youth gangs and joined one of the project's most notorious, the Persian Warriors, in junior high school. Styling himself as the "baddest cat" in the neighborhood, he ran afoul of the law a few times, mainly for fighting or petty theft. O.J. was arrested at fifteen for stealing bottles from a liquor store, for which he had to spend a week at a juvenile detention center. Shortly afterward he received an unexpected visit from Willie Mays, who hoped to steer the gifted teenage athlete away from a life of crime. Mays made a great impression on O.J., who warmed to the ballplayer's easy manner and was even more impressed by the trappings of Mays's success, especially his large, expensively furnished home. From that point on, if not before, the prospect of great material reward and of becoming a celebrity would shape O.J.'s powerful drive to succeed as a professional athlete.

After suffering a hand injury in junior high school, however, O.J. abandoned baseball in favor of track and then football, starring for Galileo High School initially as a defensive lineman but later as a fullback. In his senior year—1965—his dominating speed and strength earned him all-city honors, but his poor academic record meant that no major college program recruited him. Instead, O.J. attended the City College of San Francisco between 1965 and 1967, where he set a junior college record by scoring fifty-four touchdowns and rushing for 2,445 yards in only two seasons. That record ensured the attentions of several major colleges, from which he selected the University of Southern California. He went on to lead

O. J. Simpson poses with his Maxwell Award for the outstanding college football player, 1968. Associated Press

the Trojans to the Rose Bowl in 1967 and 1968.

Most commentators viewed Simpson as the most exciting and explosive running back to emerge for at least a decade, and his two-season total at USC of thirty-five touchdowns and 3,295 yards gained in rushing earned him the Heisman Trophy in 1968. Shortly after he received that award, Simpson's wife, Marguerite Whitley, gave birth to a daughter, Arnelle. The couple, who married in 1967, would have two more children, Jason and Aaren, the latter of whom drowned in a swimming pool accident in 1979, the year his parents divorced.

Under the rules of the newly instituted National Football League draft, the NFL's poorest team, the Buffalo Bills, picked Simpson, the nation's top collegiate player, for the 1968–1969 season. Although he resented leaving the Sunbelt glamour of Southern California for upstate New York, and tried on several occasions to get out of his contract, Simpson remained in Buffalo until 1977. But in his first four seasons, even he could not prevent the hapless Bills from crashing to forty-two defeats and two ties, while winning only twelve games. Simpson's personal statistics were also less stellar than had been expected

of him—he averaged only five touchdowns in each of his first four seasons.

Simpson's fortunes took an upswing in 1973, however, when the former Bills coach Lou Saban returned to Buffalo and restructured the team to play to Simpson's strengths, namely, to get the football to him and let him run. With an intimidating offensive line blocking for him, "the Juice" ran for 2,003 yards in 1973, breaking JIM BROWN'S record for a season by 140 yards. Though Simpson won the bulk of the headlines and plaudits, he was the first to recognize that the "Electric Company," as the linemen were known, had been crucial in "turn[ing] on the Juice" (Wood, 43).

Simpson enjoyed exceptional seasons in 1974, when the Bills made the postseason for the only time in his career (they lost to Pittsburgh in the AFC divisional playoffs), and in 1975, when he scored a career-high twenty-three touchdowns, which was then a record. In 1976 the Bills returned to their losing ways under a new coach, but Simpson managed to be selected for the Pro Bowl, as he had been in every season since 1972. The following season, Simpson's last for Buffalo, was also his poorest by far. He played in only seven games because of injuries and

scored no touchdowns. In 1978 Simpson returned to San Francisco to play for the '49ers, though it was clear by then that he had run out of juice. Nonetheless, when he retired in 1979, Simpson trailed only Jim Brown in rushing yards and was widely regarded as the NFL's most dominating running back of the 1970s. He was inducted into the NFL Hall of Fame in 1985.

Unlike many high-achieving professional athletes with similar goals, Simpson had little difficulty adjusting to a new career in broadcasting. Indeed, he had established himself with ABC Sports as a freelance during his time at Buffalo and also worked for that network during the 1976 Olympics. Beginning in 1978 he worked as a commentator and host for NFL football on NBC, switching to ABC's *Monday Night Football* from 1983 to 1986 before returning to NBC in 1989. Simpson also had supporting roles in the television series of ALEX HALEY's *Roots* (1977) and in several high-grossing Hollywood movies, notably the *Towering Inferno* (1974) and *The Naked Gun* (1989), but he rarely earned much critical praise.

It was, however, his appearance in a series of commercials for the Hertz car rental company during the 1970s that consolidated Simpson's reputation as a household name. Even those who never watched football came to recognize the affable Simpson, dapper in a three-piece business suit, sprinting, shimmying, and vaulting his way through a busy airport to catch his Hertz rental car. Simpson was eager to please corporate America. Unlike his contemporaries MUHAMMAD ALI and KAREEM ABDUL-JABBAR, he was not politically active, nor did he appear dangerously "militant" to whites. He did, however, help craft his own Horatio Alger life story of making it from Potrero Hill to the Hollywood Hills, and he donated to charitable causes. As a result, corporate America loved Simpson too. His contracts with Hertz, General Motors, RCA, Wilson Sporting Goods, and several other companies helped make him the first African American celebrity to be marketed as "colorless," with an appeal that appeared to transcend race.

By the early 1990s Simpson's income from football, the movies, and his media career had given him the affluent, celebrity lifestyle that he had dreamed of since visiting Willie Mays as a teenager. He had remarried in 1985, to Nicole Brown, whom he had first met eight years earlier. The tabloids made some sport of the fact that Nicole was white and much younger than Marguerite, who was black, but it did little to dent Simpson's popularity. Simpson and Brown had a son and a daughter, but the breakdown of their marriage became public in January 1989, when Brown called the police to Simpson's mansion in the Brentwood section of Los Angeles and alleged that her husband had beaten her and threatened to kill her. In May of that same year Simpson was sentenced to two years' probation for spousal abuse and ordered to attend counseling sessions. Simpson's conviction did not affect his television and film career, nor did he lose any of his corporate sponsors, but his marriage ended in divorce in October 1992.

On 17 June 1994, five days after Nicole Brown and her friend Ronald Goldman were found stabbed and murdered near Brown's Brentwood apartment, the Los Angeles police charged O. J. Simpson with the crime. Simpson fled, leading the police on a bizarre, fifty-mile, slow-speed chase on the Los Angeles freeway in a white Ford Bronco driven by his boyhood friend A. C. Cowlings. A note written by Simpson before he fled suggested that he intended to commit suicide. Television networks and news channels such as CNN filmed the chase live from helicopters, capturing the scores of well-wishers urging, "Go, Juice, Go," as though they were extras in a TV movie or a Hertz commercial rather than bystanders in what was, regardless of Simpson's innocence or guilt, a brutal murder case. When the police finally caught up with Simpson, he denied responsibility for both murders.

After a trial that lasted more than nine months and dominated the nation's tabloids and talk shows, a Los Angeles jury cleared Simpson of both murders in October 1995. The racial makeup of the jury—nine blacks, two whites, and a Hispanic—and the contrasting responses of most African Americans and most whites to the verdict provoked as much controversy as the trial itself had done. Most whites were convinced by the physical and DNA evidence presented by the prosecution, and by the star's history of spousal abuse, that Simpson was guilty. Though many blacks were also convinced of Simpson's guilt, African

Americans generally were more willing to doubt that the prosecution had proved its case beyond all reasonable doubt. Many had significant reservations about the role of the Los Angeles police officers in investigating the murders, notably Detective Mark Fuhrman, who was widely regarded as a racist.

Though much was made at the time in the media, and also among prominent intellectuals, about the Simpson trial's racial symbolism and significance, public interest in all things O.J. dissipated remarkably quickly. Several of the scores of legal advisers, policemen, witnesses, and assorted Simpson trial hangers-on did, however, parlay their momentary vogue into a range of book and television deals. Simpson, for his part, continued to maintain his innocence, and in *I Want to Tell You: My Response to Your Letters, Your Messages, Your Questions* (1995), he vowed to find the killers of Ron Goldman and Nicole Brown. The Goldman and Brown families insisted that Simpson was the murderer and launched a wrongful death civil lawsuit against him in 1996. In February 1997 the mainly white jury found Simpson guilty and liable to pay $8.5 million to the victims' families. Though the verdicts in the criminal and civil trials were different, the two-and-a-half-year saga of the O.J. Simpson trials ensured that the former Heisman Trophy winner and Buffalo Bills star would be remembered by history less for what he did on the gridiron than for what he did—or did not do—near his former wife's Brentwood apartment in June 1994.

FURTHER READING

Simpson, O.J., and Pete Axthelm. *O.J.: The Education of a Rich Rookie* (1970).

MORRISON, TONI, and Claudia Brodsky Lacour, eds. *Birth of a Nation'Hood: Gaze, Script, and Spectacle in the O.J. Simpson Case* (1997).
Toobin, Jeffrey. *The Run for His Life: The People v. O.J. Simpson* (1996).
Wood, Peter. "What Makes Simpson Run," *New York Times*, 14 Dec. 1975.
—STEVEN J. NIVEN

SINGLETON, BENJAMIN (15 Aug. 1809–1892), black nationalist and land promoter known as "Pap," was born into slavery in Nashville, Tennessee.

Little is known about the first six decades of his life. In his old age Singleton reminisced that his master had sold him to buyers as far away as Alabama and Mississippi several times, but that each time he had escaped and returned to Nashville. Tiring of this treatment, he ran away to Windsor, Ontario, and shortly thereafter moved to Detroit. There he quietly opened a boardinghouse for escaped slaves and supported himself by scavenging. In 1865 he came home to Edgefield, Tennessee, across the Cumberland River from Nashville, and supported himself as a cabinetmaker and carpenter.

Although Singleton loved Tennessee, he did not see this state in the post–Civil War era as a hospitable place for African Americans. Since coffin making was part of his work, he witnessed firsthand the aftermath of the appalling murders of African Americans by white vigilantes: "Julia Haven; I made the outside box and her coffin, in Smith County, Tennessee. And another young lady I know, about my color, they committed an outrage on her and then shot her, and I helped myself to make the outside box" (Senate Report 693, vol. III, 382–383). Already Singleton dreamed that he and other African Americans would possess their own land, so that they could be independent of whites, but the high price of land in Tennessee made large-scale purchases of land impractical. He observed that "the whites had the land and the sense, and the blacks had nothing but their freedom" (Athearn, 228).

Although Singleton stated that he was a Ulysses S. Grant Republican, African Americans were never able to win a significant political role in the reconstruction of Tennessee, and he was less interested in politics than in economics. Nourishing his dream of black landownership, he increasingly focused on locations outside the state. His attention was drawn to Kansas, John Brown's former state and the locus of much land settlement since Congress had passed the Homestead Act in 1862. He envisioned the establishment of communities of African Americans who had left the South for the free soil of Kansas.

He made his first scouting expedition to Kansas in 1873 and found that "it was a good country." Along with several friends, he formed the Edgefield Real

Estate and Homestead Association to encourage African Americans' purchase and settlement of land outside the South. Singleton printed and widely distributed fliers that advertised Kansas land, mailing them to African Americans in every southern state. As a result of his promotional activities, hundreds of African Americans in Kentucky and Tennessee decided to move to Kansas in 1877 and 1878. At least four black Kansas communities founded during this time, in Cherokee, Graham, Lyons, and Morris counties, owed their origins largely to his efforts. Singleton himself lived for most of 1879–1880 in the colony of Dunlap in Morris County. In addition, some Tennessee migrants settled in Kansas cities such as Topeka, where the African American community became known as "Tennessee Town." Singleton seems to have made little money from his land promotion, but that was not his aim. He saw himself as a prophet who was fulfilling God's plans rather than as a businessman. "I have had open air interviews with the living spirit of God for my people," he stated, "and we are going to leave the South."

In 1879 approximately twenty thousand destitute African Americans left Mississippi, Louisiana, and Texas to settle in Kansas. Although Singleton's fliers had circulated in these states, the fresh wave of "Exodusters" seems not to have been occasioned by his publicity but by political repression and economic hardship in the states they left and by millenarian hopes for their destination. These new migrants suffered much hardship in Kansas, too, as they struggled to find work. A national controversy erupted over the reasons for the exodus, with Democrats accusing Republicans of encouraging the migration for political gain. Singleton excoriated black leaders such as FREDERICK DOUGLASS who spoke out in opposition to the exodus. He felt that after many years of receiving patronage from their white friends, middle-class black men like Douglass "think they must judge things from where they stand, when the fact is the possum is lower down the tree—down nigh to the roots." He appeared in 1880 as a witness before a committee of the U.S. Senate that was investigating the exodus. Unshaken by the Democrats' cross-examination,

he garnered much publicity for his claim that he was the "whole cause" of the Kansas migration. His claim was in fact greatly exaggerated, but he nevertheless won fame as "the Moses of the Colored Exodus." By late 1880, however, he no longer advocated African American migration to Kansas, arguing that the state could not absorb any more impoverished immigrants. Still, after the initial hardships of relocation, many of the migrants achieved some success and preferred their new home to the South.

Singleton lived most of the remaining years of his life in the Tennessee Town neighborhood of Topeka, where he settled in 1880. He founded and actively supported a number of short-lived political associations, including the United Colored Links, an organization that sought race unity in order to build up factories and other industries controlled by African Americans, and to fashion a coalition with white workers through the Greenbacker Party. In the mid-1880s he actively supported a proposal by Bishop HENRY MCNEAL TURNER of the AME Church that African Americans should return to Africa and build up industry and governments there. This plan, in Singleton's words, would enable "the sons and daughters of Ham [to] return to their God-given inheritance, and Ethiopia [to] regain her ancient renown." African Americans, he said, would find that their needs could only be met by a separate black nation. Unlike his successful promotion of Kansas migration, Singleton was never able to instigate migration of African Americans to Africa. After years of poor health, he died in St. Louis.

Against all odds, Singleton was able to achieve part of his dreams. A black nationalist who attempted to provide African Americans with economic independence, he was able to foster the establishment of several all-black communities in Kansas through his exceptionally strong sense of a God-given mission. He fell short of his goal of true freedom for his people, as a lack of money and the strength of racial prejudice proved to be too much to overcome.

FURTHER READING

Singleton's scrapbook and press clippings are held in the manuscript collection of the Kansas State Historical Society, Topeka.

Athearn, Robert. *In Search of Canaan: Black Migration to Kansas, 1879–1880* (1978).

Bontemps, Arna, and Jack Conroy. *They Seek a City* (1945).

Hamilton, Kenneth Marvin. "The Origins and Early Promotion of Nicodemus: A Pre-Exodus, All-Black Town," *Kansas History* 5 (1982): 220–242.

Painter, Nell Irvin. *Exodusters: Black Migration to Kansas after Reconstruction* (1977).

—STEPHEN W. ANGELL

SISSLE, NOBLE

(10 July 1889–17 Dec. 1975), vocalist, lyricist, and orchestra leader, was born in Indianapolis, Indiana. His early interest in performance was influenced by his father, George Andrew, a Methodist Episcopal minister and organist, and by his schoolteacher mother, Martha Angeline, who stressed good diction. When he was seventeen the family moved to Cleveland, Ohio, and Sissle attended the integrated Central High School. Sissle had begun his professional life by joining Edward Thomas's all-male singing quartet in 1908, which toured a Midwest evangelical Chautauqua circuit. Upon graduating from high school, Sissle toured again, this time with Hann's Jubilee Singers. After brief enrollments at DePauw University and Butler

Noble Sissle, composer and creator with EUBIE BLAKE *of such celebrated American musicals as* Shuffle Along. *Library of Congress/Carl Van Vechten*

771

University in Indiana, Sissle got his show business break when he was asked by the manager of the Severin Hotel to form a syncopated orchestra in the style of JAMES REESE EUROPE. Syncopated orchestras (also known as "society orchestras" and "symphony orchestras") played dance arrangements, restructured from the violin-based music of traditional dance orchestras, to feature mandolins, guitars, banjoes, and saxophones. As music historian Eileen Southern notes, the syncopated orchestra sound was not "genuine ragtime, but it was nevertheless a lusty, joyful music, full of zest" (347). Sissle's pioneering work with syncopated orchestras formed the basis for his important contributions to the newly developing sounds of American popular music, dance music, and musical theater.

In the spring of 1915 Sissle was offered a summer job as a vocalist and bandolin player for Joe Porter's Serenaders. He moved to Baltimore, where he met his first and most significant collaborating partner, EUBIE BLAKE, who had published his first piano rag at the age of fifteen and honed his craft by studying great ragtime pianists. When Blake met Sissle, he said, "You're a lyricist. I need a lyricist." Soon Sissle and Blake, with Eddie Nelson, wrote their first hit. "It's All Your Fault" was recorded by the singer Sophie Tucker and netted the trio two hundred dollars. In the fall and winter of 1915–1916 Sissle played with Bob Young's sextet in Baltimore, Palm Beach, and other Florida venues. After playing in E. F. Albee's Palm Beach Week show at the Palace Theatre, New York, Sissle took a letter of introduction from the white socialite Mary Brown Warburton to James Reese Europe. Europe invited Sissle to join his Clef Club Symphony Orchestra. Sissle persuaded Europe to find work for Blake, and Sissle himself had his own small orchestra gig in New Jersey.

When Sissle and Europe joined the army in 1917 upon the entry of the United States into World War I, the band they formed, the 369th U.S. Infantry Jazz Band, toured as the "Hell Fighters." Their command performance in Paris, France, in 1918 electrified the crowd of thirty thousand. During their tour of duty, Europe and Sissle wrote songs together and sent them back to Blake (who, at thirty-five, was too old to enlist), who put them to music. Such

songs as "Too Much Mustard," "To Hell with Germany," "No Man's Land Will Soon Be Ours," and "What a Great, Great Day" clearly reflected the patriotic fervor of the period. With the end of the war, Sissle, Blake, and Europe began discussing a new musical. The tragic murder of Europe at the hands of a disgruntled band member in May 1919 cut short his participation in the musical genre. Sissle and Blake went on to become true songwriting partners in New York. The words of the hit song "Syncopation Rules the Nation" became a reality as they put the roar in the "Roaring Twenties."

Encouraged by Europe's former managers, Sissle and Blake reworked their material from the Clef Club shows and became the "Dixie Duo" on the Keith Orpheum vaudeville circuit. Blake banged out songs on an onstage upright piano, instead of a more traditional minstrel instrument such as the banjo or violin. However, the Dixie Duo's performances were greatly influenced by blackface minstrelsy. Sissle and Blake, and other African American duos such as BERT WILLIAMS AND GEORGE WILLIAM WALKER (billed as "Two Real Coons"), existed on the narrow band between blackface minstrelsy and vaudeville. The racist and sexist joke material of minstrelsy was still standard, as was the glorification of plantation life "befo' de War." Progress was made beyond the stereotype through the innovations of ragtime music and by adopting sophisticated dress. By playing ragtime music but not performing in blackface, Sissle and Blake further separated black popular entertainment from its artistic dependency on minstrelsy.

In 1920, after seeing Sissle and Blake perform at an NAACP benefit performance in Philadelphia, Aubrey Lyles and Flournoy E. Miller asked them to collaborate on a new musical. Miller and Lyles, a vaudeville comedy duo who had met while students at Fisk University in Nashville, were interested in developing one of their comedic routines, "The Mayor of Dixie" (c. 1918), into a musical comedy. Miller believed blacks could and should perform in white theaters, but only in musical comedy. From 1910 to 1917 all-black musical shows had begun to define Broadway as the place for black talent. However, after 1917 black theater had experienced, in

the words of JAMES WELDON JOHNSON, a "term of exile."

By 1921 Sissle and Blake had completed their development work in black popular music and theater and were ready to introduce their sound to mixed audiences. They did so in two musical theater productions, *Shuffle Along* (1921) and *Chocolate Dandies* (1924, initially titled "In Bamville"), which moved black musical theater further from its roots in blackface minstrelsy and vaudeville.

Shuffle Along was actually a hodgepodge of material gleaned from the work of Miller and Lyles and the "Dixie Duo" of Sissle and Blake. But with the song "Love Will Find a Way," Sissle and Blake wrote the first romantic love song between two African Americans performed on Broadway. During the opening night performance in New York City, Miller, Lyles, and Sissle stood waiting by the stage door as Lottie Gee and Roger Matthews sang the song, ready to flee if the audience turned violent; they didn't, and the show was an overwhelming hit. Another landmark aspect of *Shuffle Along* is that the Sixty-third Street Theatre allowed blacks and whites to sit together in the orchestra seats. It also introduced the Broadway audience to a host of great African American performers, both during its New York run and its subsequent tour. In addition to Miller, Lyles, Sissle, and Blake, such notable performers as Gee, Gertrude Saunders, Adelaide Hall, JOSEPHINE BAKER, FLORENCE MILLS, and PAUL ROBESON were in the cast at various points. Orchestra members included WILLIAM GRANT STILL, the composer, as an oboist. But the great success of *Shuffle Along* also depended on prescribed conventions. Its creators were extremely anxious about introducing jazz music and dance to Broadway; Blake worried that "people would think it was a freak show." For example, the orchestra members had to memorize their parts, because, as Blake stated, white people were uncomfortable with seeing blacks read music. The creators of *Shuffle Along* had to strike a fine balance between the skill and professionalism integral to creating a great musical comedy, and the white audience's unease with the presentation of such a piece being written, composed, directed, and performed by blacks.

After the tremendous triumph of *Shuffle Along*, Miller, Lyles, Sissle, and Blake had difficulty deciding what to do next and opted to go their separate ways. Sissle and Blake wrote twelve songs for the musical *Elsie* (1923); they were jobbed in for the music only and had no influence on the production. They then worked on a new musical that became *Chocolate Dandies*. With a cast of 125, *Dandies* was an elaborate musical modeled on the revues of Florenz Ziegfeld and George White. Written by Sissle and Lew Payton, with music by Sissle and Blake, *Dandies* was Sissle and Blake's attempt to build a musical from the ground up. Staged in the South, *Dandies*' Bamville is a town where all life is centered on a racetrack. It recognizes the performance legacy of blackface minstrelsy and also pokes fun at it, as in Sissle's lyrics for the most overtly minstrelsy-influenced number in the show, "Sons of Old Black Joe": "Though we're a dusky hue let us say to you/We're proud of our complexion." Sissle and Blake were able to create a musical comedy that was enjoyable but also mildly critical of musical theater's racist history. And their cast reflected, again, some of the greatest performers of their day, including Johnny Hudgins, Baker, Valada Snow, Gee, and Sissle, with Blake leading the band. In the end, *Chocolate Dandies* was not more economically successful for Sissle and Blake than *Shuffle Along*, but they considered it their greatest collaborating achievement.

After *Chocolate Dandies* closed in May 1925, with a loss of sixty thousand dollars, Sissle and Blake returned to vaudeville. A European tour soon followed, and the pair toured England, Scotland, and France billed as the "American Ambassadors of Syncopation." They were commissioned to write songs for Charles B. Cochran's (the Ziegfeld of England) revues. Sissle wanted to continue living in England, but Blake was unhappy with life there, so they returned to the United States, with Sissle resentful that he could no longer work for Cochran. In 1927 Sissle returned to Europe, where he toured France and England. With the encouragement of Cole Porter, he formed an orchestra for Edmond Sayag's Paris café Les Ambassadeurs, performing as the "Ace of Syncopation." Sissle's

band included many expatriate black musicians, including SIDNEY BECHET. In 1930 the Duke of Windsor played drums with Sissle's orchestra when they played for the British royal family in London. The orchestra took its first American tour in 1931, playing at the Park Central Hotel in New York and on a CBS nationwide radio broadcast. Meanwhile, Sissle and Blake reunited with Flournoy Miller to write *Shuffle Along of 1933*. The revision proved to be unpopular in the Depression-laden times, running for only fifteen performances in New York and touring briefly. Sissle returned to his orchestra in February of the same year, touring from 1933 through the late 1940s. Sissle also wrote and helped stage a pageant in Chicago, *O, Sing a New Song*, choreographed by the young KATHERINE DUNHAM. LENA HORNE, Billy Banks, and Bechet all toured with Sissle at various points during this period. Sissle married his second wife Ethel in 1942 and became a father with the birth of Noble Jr. and Cynthia. (His first wife was Harriet Toye, whom he'd married on Christmas Day of 1919; their relationship had ended by 1926.) During World War II he toured a new version of *Shuffle Along* with the USO. After 1945 Sissle became increasingly involved in life away from the stage. He was a founder and the first president of the Negro Actors' Guild and became the honorary Mayor of Harlem in 1950. Both Sissle and Blake were involved with the Broadway production of *Shuffle Along 1952*. Developed as a star vehicle for PEARL BAILEY (who dropped out of the production), *Shuffle Along 1952* was changed through "modernization" and was an artistic and box office failure, and Sissle himself was injured when he fell into the orchestra pit during a rehearsal. His last recording, *Eighty-six Years of Eubie Blake*, was recorded with Blake in 1968.

Sissle died in Tampa, Florida. With James Reese Europe and Eubie Blake, and in his own work as an orchestra leader, Sissle created the sounds of syncopated dance music, ragtime, and musical theater that defined American music in the first third of the twentieth century.

FURTHER READING

Kimball, Robert, and Bolcom Williams. *Reminiscing with Noble Sissle and Eubie Blake* (1973).

Krasner, David. *A Beautiful Pageant: African American Theatre, Drama, and Performance in the Harlem Renaissance, 1910–1927* (2002).
Southern, Eileen. *The Music of Black Americans: A History* (1997).

Obituary: *New York Times*, 18 Dec. 1975.

Discography
The Eighty-six Years of Eubie Blake (1969).
James Reese Europe and the 369th U.S. Infantry "Hell Fighters" Band, Featuring Noble Sissle (1996).
Sissle and Blake's Shuffle Along. Selections (1976).

—ANNEMARIE BEAN

SLEET, MONETA, JR.
(14 Feb. 1926–30 Sept. 1996), photojournalist, was born in Owensboro, Kentucky, the elder of two children of Moneta Sleet Sr. and Ozetta Allensworth, both teachers. Owensboro was a segregated town, but it fostered a close-knit black community that offered a safe environment in which to raise Moneta and his sister, Emmy Lou. Moneta's parents were college educated, and they instilled in their son a high regard for education and a deep respect for their racial heritage. By the time Moneta was ten years old, he had become the family photographer, shooting with a Brownie box camera. At Western High School, he joined the camera club, learning from his chemistry teacher how to develop pictures. He graduated in 1942.

Sleet enrolled at Kentucky State College in 1942, and majored in business while working as assistant to Dean John T. Williams, who was himself an accomplished photographer and from whom Sleet "learned a great deal... especially how to deal with people and portraiture" (Sleet, 7). Sleet joined the army in 1944 and served with the all-black Ninety-third Engineers unit in India and Burma. After returning from World War II in 1946, Sleet finished his BS degree and moved to New York City, where he took a course in photography at the School of Modern Photography. Sleet earned an MA in Journalism from New York University in 1950, after a short stint teaching photography at all-black Maryland State College. That same year, he married Juanita Harris, a schoolteacher from Maryland.

The couple had three children, Gregory, Michael, and Lisa, between 1951 and 1956. Although he often photographed his children, Sleet was particularly fond of a series of photographs that featured Michael at his school for children with special needs. Michael's mental disability encouraged the Sleets' involvement with the Association for the Help of Retarded Children.

Sleet took his first journalism job with the black press, sports writing and photographing for New York's *Amsterdam News* in 1950. Later, he joined the staff of *Our World* magazine, a black-owned and -operated large-format news and feature magazine, where, under the editorial direction of John Davis, he learned the narrative possibilities of the picture essay. Davis guided Sleet by brainstorming with him and offering suggestions on possible shooting scenarios that might best communicate emotions and events through images.

By the time Sleet became a staff photographer for JOHN H. JOHNSON's *Ebony* magazine in 1955, his political, artistic, and journalistic sensibilities had been honed. His position as staff photographer suited the family-oriented Sleet, because it offered him stability. He remained with the magazine for the next forty-one years. As a photographer at a black-owned, -operated, and -focused publication, Sleet felt he had a supportive vehicle through which he could communicate his commitment to African American equality and the black freedom struggle. Although he soon realized that he had little influence over how his images were employed by *Ebony*'s editors, Sleet was content that his photographs would be used in the service of furthering the cause of civil rights. "My basic feeling," he later explained, "was, of course, I was observing... and trying to record, but I also felt a part of it because I'm black, and it was one way I could pay my dues. My contribution was to record and pass on, to whoever [sic] might see, what was happening" (interview with author, 1992).

In his first five years with *Ebony*, the civil rights movement was gaining strength in the United States. Sleet hoped his photographs would garner support from readers and mobilize them to act. His photos of ROSA PARKS and MARTIN LUTHER KING JR. during the 1956 Montgomery bus boycott and of participants in the 1963 March on Washington, D.C., and the 1965 Selma to Montgomery march humanized the civil rights struggle while documenting the events.

Sleet is perhaps best known for the photos he took at King's 1968 funeral, including the iconic image of Bernice King sitting in the lap of her mother, CORETTA SCOTT KING, for which he became, in 1969, the first African American recipient of the Pulitzer Prize in Photography. Outside the United States, Sleet covered the independence celebrations of the newly liberated African nations Ghana (1957), Nigeria (1961), Kenya (1963), and South Africa (1994). His portraits, including those of Haile Selassie, BILLIE HOLIDAY, THELONIOUS MONK, and MILES DAVIS, and his extraordinary series of landscapes in Surinam, Sudan, and Mali are admired for both their journalistic and artistic excellence.

Sleet's work first appeared in a museum exhibition at the Metropolitan Museum of Art's 1960 show *Photography in the Fine Arts, II*. Sleet has participated in a number of significant exhibitions, including *Black Photographers* (1974), *Tradition and Conflict: Images of a Turbulent Decade 1963–1973* (1985), *The Black Photographer: An American View* (1985), *A Century of Black Photographers, 1840–1940* (1989), *Black Photographers Bear Witness* (1989), and *Reflections in Black: A History of Black Photographers 1840 to the Present* (2000). Sleet's first solo show was mounted in 1970 at the St. Louis Art Museum. One-person exhibitions followed at the New York Pubic Library (1986), the St. Louis Art Museum (1993), and the Schomburg Center for Research in Black Culture (1999). His photographs are held in the collections of the St. Louis Art Museum and the Schomburg Center for Research in Black Culture of the New York Public Library.

"The type of photography I do is one of showing from my point of view," Sleet said in 1992. "I must confess that I don't think I'm very objective. The area and the type of work I do is one of advocacy, I think, particularly during the civil rights movement because I was a participant just like everybody else. I just happened to be there with my camera.... I felt and firmly believe that my mission was to photograph and to show the side of it that was the right side" (interview with author). Sleet received numerous awards over his career, including the Citation for Excellence from the Overseas Press Club of America (1957), a prize from the National Association of Black Journalists (1978), a commendation from the National Urban League (1978), and induction into the Kentucky Journalism Hall of Fame at the University of Kentucky (1989). He died in Baldwin, New York, in 1996.

FURTHER READING

Sleet, Moneta, Jr. *Special Moments in African American History 1955–1996: The Photographs of Moneta Sleet Jr.; Ebony Magazine's Pulitzer Prize Winner* (1998)

Smith, Cherise. "Moneta Sleet Jr. as Active Participant: The Selma March and the Black Arts Movement" in *New Thoughts on the Black Arts Movement* (2004).

Obituary: *New York Times*, 2 Oct. 1996.
—CHERISE SMITH

 SLOWE, LUCY DIGGS (4 July 1883–21 Oct. 1937), educator, feminist, and tennis player, was born in Berryville, Virginia, a farming community in Clark County. Following the premature deaths of her parents, Henry Slowe and Fannie Potter, the owners of the only hotel in Berryville, young Lucy joined the home of Martha Slowe Price, her paternal aunt in Lexington, Virginia. A few years later she and the Price family moved to Baltimore, Maryland, to improve their economic and educational opportunities. Looking back on her childhood, Lucy noted that her aunt had very pronounced ideas on dignity, morality, and religion, which she did not fail to impress upon Lucy and her cousin.

Always an excellent student, Lucy was salutatorian of her 1904 class at Baltimore Colored High School and the first female graduate of her high school to receive a college scholarship to Howard University. At Howard University she was active in numerous literary, social, musical, and athletic pursuits. In her senior year, she served as president of the women's tennis club and vice president of the Alpha Phi

Literary Society and was a chaperone for female undergraduates. She graduated in 1908 as class valedictorian. Her involvement with extracurricular life at Howard sparked her interest in a career in education.

In 1908, while still an undergraduate at Howard, Slowe was a charter member of Alpha Kappa Alpha Sorority, Inc. She drafted its first constitution and was the first vice president. Slowe's relationship with Howard administrators is cited as a major reason why the constitution of Alpha Kappa Alpha Sorority Inc., was approved. Slowe's values and aspirations helped shape the mission and traditions of America's first Greek letter organization for black women. New pledges of Alpha Kappa Alpha worldwide annually memorize her name as one of their sorority's founders.

At Howard, Slowe developed a love for the game of tennis. For many years she was considered one of the three top black female tennis players in America. In the summer of 1910 she, along with other male and female black tennis players, conducted one of the first recorded black traveling tours to introduce tennis to black communities across the nation. In 1917 she won the singles title at the first American Tennis Association (ATA) national tournament, an organization founded to promote black tennis. She was one of the founding members of the ATA, and by virtue of winning the first ATA national tournament, she became the first female black national champion in any sport. Slowe continued to play tennis well into her adult years and to encourage black children to play the game.

After graduation Slowe returned to Baltimore in September 1908 to teach English at her high school. During summers and extended school breaks she pursued a master's degree at Teachers College, Columbia University, in what is now known as educational administration. She completed her master's studies in 1916, developing lifetime relationships with faculty at Teachers College. She was a frequent visitor there, giving lectures and engaging her peers in the study of student personnel issues. Slowe attributed much of her success to her ongoing research in this field.

In 1916 Slowe was invited to return to Washington, D.C., to teach English

at Armstrong High School and serve as "lady principal," or dean of girls. After three years at Armstrong High School, she was selected to organize Shaw Junior High School, Washington's first junior high for blacks. In 1920 she established an extension center of Columbia University at Shaw, which trained hundreds of black teachers. Many Washingtonians questioned the need for a black junior high school, but Slowe silenced her critics by creating a model school.

Slowe was appointed dean of women and associate professor of English at Howard University in June 1922. In an era when the enrollment of black women at colleges was on the rise, she shaped a new vision of what a college education could do for African American women. She developed a progressive student-life program for women, focusing on housing, health, social life, community service, and educational and vocational guidance. Slowe emphasized the need for women to be prepared for independent life and to take advantage of any and all professional opportunities. Moreover, she used Howard as a laboratory to train black female educators across the country. When Slowe assumed her position, she was the first female dean of women at Howard and the first formally trained student personnel dean on a black college campus.

At Howard, Slowe implemented a series of programs designed to provide a more equitable campus experience. She created a Women's Student League to provide a platform for leadership and self-governance, with mandatory membership for all female students. Slowe created cultural and social events which were previously unavailable to women at Howard University. She elevated the role of female staff under her supervision by teaching them how to counsel and mentor, rather than matron and monitor. Numerous Howard traditions were launched during the Slowe era, including the Christmas vespers service, a concert-lecture series, teas, coffee hours, current-events discussions, volunteer activities in the community, and book clubs. She also established an annual fund, raising money for needy women students. Her most lasting legacy was the creation of the Fourth Street campus, designed for women.

Slowe understood the importance of organizations. She founded or was active

in many organizations dedicated to the problems of African Americans. In 1935 Slowe was one of the founders of the National Council of Negro Women and served as its first secretary. She was also the leading force behind the creation of the National Association of Deans of Women and Advisors of Girls in Negro Schools, serving as president for many years. She served on numerous boards in and around Washington, D.C., and worked with the National Young Women's Christian Association and the Women's International League for Peace and Freedom. These organizations were an integral part of her efforts to improve the treatment and condition of black women college students.

The Jim Crow society of her day did dampen her belief in the benefits of an integrated society for blacks and whites. Slowe worked for social justice and integration. Her lifelong association with educators at Columbia's Teachers College provided her with opportunities to influence predominantly white institutions. Slowe once advised Boston College not to house black students in segregated housing, reflecting her belief that a college campus ought to be a place where people of different races learned from each other. She was an adviser to the Race Relations Group of the North American Home Missions of the National Student Council and thought that communication between racial groups was very important, both on and off the campus.

Not all of Slowe's ideas were readily accepted. Her work with the National Association of College Women was largely directed toward establishing higher academic standards for women, to steer them as much toward political science and natural sciences as education and home economics. Her belief that rules governing women at Howard ought to be reduced to a minimum and personal honor and responsibility increased to a maximum conflicted with the prevailing paternalist philosophy of the day. She unnerved some in the black community by challenging them to see their daughters as professionals and leaders, not just teachers and socialites. Her little known "memorandum on the sexual harassment of black women" was considered a betrayal by some and suicidal by others. Often at odds with male leadership in the black community,

Slowe noted in a letter dated 22 May 1928, "I have had the courage of my convictions even though sometimes I have had to suffer personal discomfort for standing up for them."

Following an extended illness caused by influenza and kidney disease, Slowe died at the age of fifty-three in Washington, D.C. In recognition of her life, the District of Columbia Public Schools named an elementary school in her honor. Howard University named a dormitory for her, and a window at the university's Andrew Rankin Chapel also honors her. Beyond these tributes to a life serving others, Slowe deserves scholarly recognition from professionals in student personnel work as well as from feminists and historians of education. Her enlightened practices in student personnel work and her forward-looking attitudes about women and their place in both the university and society mark her as an activist and a thinker well ahead of her time.

In the introduction to *Ain't I a Woman: Black Women and Feminism,* Bell Hooks writes: "At a time in American history when black women in every area of the country might have joined together to demand social equality for women and a recognition of the impact of sexism on our social status, we were by and large silent." Lucy Diggs Slowe was not silent. She devoted her life to joining with other women, black and white, to advance the educational, cultural, and social opportunities for women in general and black women in particular. She practiced, published, and preached her ideas, leaving a human and ideological legacy that helped open closed doors of education for all.

FURTHER READING

The Moorland Spingarn Collection at Howard University contains the personal papers of Lucy Diggs Slowe and the majority of the available biographical materials on her.

Ransom, Joanna Houston. "Innovations Introduced into the Women's Program at Howard University by the Late Dean Lucy D. Slowe," *Journal of the National Association of College Women* 14 (1937).
Turner, Geneva C. "Slowe School," *Negro History Bulletin,* Jan. 1955.

—LEROY NESBITT JR.
—DESMOND WOLFE

SMALLS, ROBERT

(5 Apr. 1839–23 Feb. 1915), congressman, was born in Beaufort, South Carolina, the son of an unknown white man and Lydia, a slave woman who worked as a house servant for the John McKee family in Beaufort. Descendants of Smalls believed that his father was John McKee, who died when Robert was young. The McKee family sent Robert to live with their relatives in Charleston, where he worked for wages that he turned over to his master. Smalls apparently taught himself the rudiments of reading and writing during this period. Later he attended school for three months, and as an adult he hired tutors. In 1856 Smalls married Hannah Jones, a slave who worked as a hotel maid. They had three children, one of whom died of smallpox. The couple lived apart from their owners, to whom they sent most of their income.

In 1861 Smalls began working as a deckhand on the *Planter,* a steamer that operated out of Charleston Harbor. By 1862 he was the craft's pilot. He knew the locations of Confederate armaments in the channels and on shore, and he knew of the U.S. Navy fleet anchored just outside Charleston Harbor. When he learned of the Federal occupation of Beaufort, Smalls determined with several other slave sailors to guide the *Planter* to Union waters. Secretly loading their families on board, the men rushed the vessel out of Charleston Harbor under cover of darkness and surrendered it to the U.S. Navy. Congress awarded Smalls and his aides monetary compensation for liberating the *Planter* from Confederate hands. From occupied Beaufort, Smalls piloted the vessel, now outfitted as a troop transport, around the Sea Islands, carrying messages, supplies, and men for the Union army. He always maintained that eventually he was commissioned as a captain, but his papers were lost, and after the war he had difficulty proving his service when he tried to obtain a pension. He piloted other ships as well, including the ironclad *Keokuk* in an unsuccessful assault on the city of Charleston.

During the war Smalls and his family traveled to the North to elicit popular sympathy for the slaves' plight and to attest to the service ex-slaves might perform if the Federal government

would allow them the opportunity. Smalls began a store for freedpeople in Beaufort and, at the war's end, bought his former owner's house, where he resided until his death, for unpaid taxes. By 1870 Smalls had six thousand dollars in real estate and one thousand dollars in personal property.

Smalls entered politics as a delegate to South Carolina's constitutional convention of 1868 and in the same year won election as a Republican to the state's general assembly. He served in that body until 1875, first as a representative and later as a state senator. In 1874 Smalls was elected congressman from South Carolina's Fifth District, which included Beaufort. During his second congressional term in 1877, a South Carolina jury convicted him of accepting a bribe while he served in the state senate. Smalls had chaired the Printing Committee, which parceled out the state's printing. Evidence suggested that a leading printer bribed Smalls in return for state business. The judge sentenced Smalls to three years in the state penitentiary at hard labor. Smalls protested his innocence and appealed, losing before the state supreme court. He appealed to the U.S. Supreme Court, but before the case could be resolved, the Democratic governor, William D. Simpson, pardoned him in exchange for a federal agreement to drop an investigation into the Democrats' violation of election laws.

With his conviction blighting his reputation and the Democratic paramilitary group known as the Red Shirts terrorizing his constituents, Smalls lost a third bid for Congress in 1878. He ran again in 1880 but lost in an election characterized by fraud on the part of the Democrats. This time Smalls contested the result, and the House awarded him the seat. In 1882 he failed to receive his party's nomination after Democrats redistricted Beaufort into the Seventh District. When the victorious Republican died in office in 1884, however, Smalls was elected to serve the remainder of the term, and he won reelection to another term later in the year. He lost the seat permanently in 1886, as Democrats threw out ballots with impunity and extralegal violence kept black voters from the polls.

Hannah Smalls died in 1883, and Robert married Annie Wigg in 1890.

They had one son before her death in 1895. Effectively excluded from local politics by the Democrats' electoral fraud and the state's disenfranchisement of African Americans in 1895, Smalls remained active in the Republican Party at the national level. Those contacts gained him appointment as collector of customs for the Port of Beaufort in 1889, a post he lost with the Democratic national victory of 1892. He regained the office in 1898 with the return of a national Republican administration. He served until 1913, despite growing lily-white sentiment in the Republican Party and the difficulties of discharging his duties in now-segregated Beaufort. Beset by several grave illnesses, Smalls died there, disillusioned by the reversal of the African American political gains for which he had worked in Reconstruction.

FURTHER READING

No single collection of Smalls's private or public papers exists, but his letters and documents are in other collections, notably the FREDERICK DOUGLASS and CARTER G. WOODSON collections at the Library of Congress and the Governor Wade Hampton Collection at the South Carolina Department of Archives and History. His public career is documented in records of the South Carolina General Assembly, the U.S. House of Representatives, and the Veterans Administration at the National Archives.

Miller, Edward A., Jr. *Gullah Statesman: Robert Smalls from Slavery to Congress, 1839–1915* (1995).

Rabinowitz, Howard N., ed. *Southern Black Leaders of the Reconstruction Era* (1982).

Uya, Okon Edet. *From Slavery to Political Service: Robert Smalls, 1839–1915* (1971).

Williamson, Joel. *After Slavery: The Negro in South Carolina during Reconstruction, 1861–1877* (1965).

Woodson, Carter Godwin. "Robert Smalls and His Descendants," *Negro History Bulletin* 11 (Nov. 1947): 27–33.

—GLENDA E. GILMORE

SMITH, AMANDA BERRY (23 Jan. 1837–
24 Feb. 1915), evangelist, missionary, and reformer, was born in Long Green, Maryland, the daughter of Samuel Berry and Mariam Matthews, slaves on neighboring farms. By laboring day and night, Samuel Berry earned enough to buy his freedom and that of his wife and children, including Amanda. By 1850 the family had moved to a farm in York County, Pennsylvania. Their home was a station on the Underground Railroad.

Samuel and Mariam Berry stressed the value of education and hard work. Taught at home, Amanda learned to read by age eight; later she briefly attended a local school in which white students were given priority. At age thirteen she entered household service, living with a series of white employers in Maryland and Pennsylvania. She married Calvin M. Devine in 1854 but soon regretted his lack of piety and his indulgence in alcohol. After a period of fasting and earnest prayer, she experienced conversion in 1856 and envisioned a life devoted to evangelism. Devine enlisted in the Union army in 1862 and died fighting in the Civil War. The couple had two children, but only one reached adulthood.

Amanda moved to Philadelphia and by 1864 had married James Henry Smith, a coachman who was an ordained deacon in the African Methodist Episcopal (AME) Church. He later reneged on his prenuptial promise that he would undertake active ministry, and his unkindness and religious skepticism seemed to hinder her spiritual growth. She continued working as a domestic and taking in laundry. Their three children died young.

Close but not always harmonious ties with other devout women introduced Amanda Smith to the Holiness movement that swept nineteenth-century Protestantism. Advocates of Holiness urged believers, regardless of sex, race, social status, or church affiliation, to testify publicly about their spiritual experience. Irresistibly drawn to the movement's controversial tenet that entire sanctification—purification from intentional sin—was attainable by faith, she fervently sought this transformative blessing. In 1865 the Smiths moved to New York City, where James found work, but three years later Amanda declined to accompany him when he relocated again to take a well-paid position. During a Methodist church service in September 1868, she "felt the touch of God from the crown of my head to the soles of my feet." Walking home, she shouted praises and sang with joy at being sanctified, "married to Jesus" (Smith, 77, 81).

Smith expanded her religious activities after James died in 1869, supporting herself and her surviving child during midnight hours at the washtub and ironing table. By her own testimony she wrestled with fears and temptations presented by Satan; she constantly prayed to learn God's will for her by interpreting randomly chosen Bible verses, dreams, and internal voices. In 1870 she determined to trust providence and went to work full-time organizing groups for testimony and spiritual nurturance, praying with the sick, and singing and preaching at camp meetings and urban revivals. Participating in national Holiness camp meetings enlarged her network of friends. Although she periodically encountered resistance to female preachers, clergymen of various denominations invited her to address large racially mixed and all-white audiences. Her own AME Church, like most denominations, withheld ordination from women, and Smith did not press for institutional authorization or financial support. Confident that God had ordained her, she accepted individuals' donations and hospitality. She was the most widely known of the nineteenth century's black women itinerant preachers.

In 1878 Smith felt called to England, Ireland, and Scotland to participate in temperance revivals and Holiness conventions. After traveling on the European continent in 1879, she proceeded overland to India. There she worked with James M. Thoburn, Methodist Episcopal bishop of India, who had previously observed her in the United States. Thoburn affirmed, "I have never known anyone who could draw and hold so large an audience as Mrs. Smith" (Smith, vi). In 1882 she went to West Africa to help "civilize" the natives and to cultivate mainstream Protestant values among black Americans who had immigrated to Liberia. Cooperating with Baptists, Congregationalists, and Presbyterians in potentially competitive situations, she proselytized, promoted temperance and Western-style education, and started a Christian school for boys.

Returning to the United States in 1890, Smith resumed preaching and activism despite her failing health. With her own savings and supporters' contributions, she founded a home for black orphans in Harvey, Illinois. It opened in 1899 and was later named the Amanda Smith Industrial School for Girls, operating until it burned in 1918.

Exhausted by years of fundraising, Smith retired in 1912 to Sebring, Florida, where she died in a home a donor had built for her.

The careers of Amanda Smith and contemporary women evangelicals and reformers reinforced the proposition, unwelcome in some quarters, that females could function without male control. The black Methodist Episcopal clergyman Marshall W. Taylor portrayed Smith as an exemplar of their race's progress and "a Christian of the highest type," unmatched by any living person, black or white (Taylor, 57–58).

Smith's *Autobiography* is valuable to scholars of black women's writing and to historians of the Holiness, temperance, and foreign missions movements; the roles of women in the Methodist Episcopal and AME churches; and blacks' experiences and perspectives during the Reconstruction era and ensuing decades of heightened interracial tension. Smith's description and interpretation of conditions in Liberia and Sierra Leone reflect certain Anglo-American views of "heathen darkness" and "superstitions" (Smith, 346, 451), but she firmly rejected the assumption that black people were inferior. General readers will find this book a circumstantial, often engaging account of the joys and rigors of a life committed to improvement.

FURTHER READING

Smith, Amanda. *An Autobiography: The Story of the Lord's Dealings with Mrs. Amanda Smith, the Colored Evangelist* (1893; repr. 1988).

Cadbury, M. H. *The Life of Amanda Smith* (1916).

Humez Jean M. "'My Spirit Eye': Some Functions of Spiritual and Visionary Experience in the Lives of Five Black Women Preachers, 1810–1880" in *Women and the Structure of Society*, eds. Barbara J. Harris and JoAnn K. McNamara (1984).

Taylor, Marshall W. *The Life, Travels, Labors, and Helpers of Mrs. Amanda Smith, the Famous Negro Missionary Evangelist* (1886).
—MARY DE JONG

SMITH, BESSIE

(15 Apr. 1894?–26 Sept. 1937), blues recording artist and performer, was born in Chattanooga, Tennessee, the third of seven children, to William Smith and Laura (maiden name unknown). The exact date of Bessie's birth is unknown, partly because in the rural and poor place in which she was born the official records of African Americans were given little care. The abject poverty in which Bessie's family lived contributed to the death of her eldest brother, who died before Smith was born, and her father, a part-time Baptist preacher, who died shortly after her birth. By the time Bessie was eight or nine, her mother and a second brother had died. Viola, the oldest sister, raised the remaining brothers and sisters.

There are a number of gaps in the record of Smith's career, some of which have been filled by myth. There is evidence that she began singing when she was nine—performing in the streets of Chattanooga for nickels and dimes with her brother Andrew, who played the guitar. Her first professional opportunity came when her oldest surviving brother, Clarence, arranged an audition for a traveling show owned by Moses Stokes, which included, among others, MA RAINEY. Legend has it that Rainey kidnapped Smith, teaching her how to sing the blues while taking her throughout the South. Actually, Smith did not need Rainey's coaching, since she had a natural talent, with unparalleled vocal abilities and a remarkable gift for showmanship.

No one knows how long she stayed with Stokes's show, but there is evidence that Smith spent a long time performing at the 81 Theater in Atlanta, Georgia. Her shows there earned her only ten dollars a week, but her audiences were so taken by the power of her voice that they would throw money on the stage. Records show that she had begun touring with the Theater Owner's Booking Association and Pete Werley's Florida Blossoms troupe by 1918. Aside from singing, her performances for these shows included dancing in chorus lines and performing comedy routines. As Smith made her rounds in the southern circuits, she gathered increasing numbers of adoring fans and became known to producers like Frank Walker of Columbia Records, who hired her years

Bessie Smith, greatest of the classic blues singers of the 1920s. Library of Congress/Carl Van Vechten

SMITH, BESSIE

later and supervised her 1923–1931 recording sessions.

Smith met and married Earl Love, a man about whom little is known, except for the fact that he came from a prominent black southern family and that he died shortly after his 1920 marriage to Smith. After his death, Smith moved to Philadelphia, where she met Jack Gee, a night watchman, whom she married in 1923 and with whom she adopted a child, Jack Gee Jr. Smith and Gee's marriage was passionate but tumultuous and they separated in 1929.

During the early 1920s Smith's career developed rapidly. She began performing at the Standard Theater in Philadelphia and Paradise Gardens in Atlantic City, and by 1923 she had recorded her first song, "Downhearted Blues," for Columbia Records. Though another blues singer had recently recorded and popularized the song, Smith's version sold seventy-eight thousand copies in less than six months. Following this success, Smith recorded seven more songs, this time with the piano accompaniment of Fletcher Henderson. Smith then toured the South, where she was greeted as the star she was quickly becoming.

Like most blues singers of her time, Smith sang of love and sex and, in particular, of the challenges black men and women face in romantic relationships. But Smith was able to evoke the vigor of sex and the joy and sorrow of love in ways few others could match. Her slow tempos and deeply felt inflections enraptured her audiences, who remained largely African American. When she sang of love, she sang of love lost, often to infidelity and sometimes to death. But while she expressed the grief of such loss, she also projected the image of the loud-talking mama who would not take life passively. Smith drew easily on her own life to project this image. Her life with Gee was plagued by infidelity, though Gee was not the only guilty party; Smith was known for her affairs, some of them with women. No one knows when Smith began to have female lovers; some assume, without any actual evidence, that the first was MA RAINEY. By 1926 there was public knowledge of her relationship with a chorus girl from her troupe.

Smith sang her life story, and audiences and listeners felt that she was singing theirs. Her music did so well that it was said that people who did not have money to buy coal bought Bessie Smith records. By 1925 she had recorded nine more, with a young cornet player named LOUIS ARMSTRONG. By the end of her career, Smith had sold between eight and ten million records and recorded a total of 160 sides.

Yet Smith never forgot what she had left behind in the South. In her "Back Water Blues," she poetically evokes the sorrow of a people forced out of their homes by floods in the Louisiana backlands, while presenting a subtle statement of social protest. She also testified to the poverty that plagued African Americans in northern urban centers. In "Poor Man's Blues," which she wrote and which some consider her finest record, Smith eloquently exposes the "cruel irony of poverty in the land of riches" (Harrison, 70). Smith sang about the sickness and despair—often accompanied by alcoholism and drug addiction—that afflicted communities besieged by racism and inequality, and she sang of the rage that resulted from these ills. "Her blues could be funny and boisterous and gentle and angry and bleak, but underneath all of them ran the raw bitterness of being a human being who had to think twice about what toilet she could use" (Shapiro and Hentoff, 127).

Smith met the world with a bold toughness of spirit. She generally gave people—no matter their race or background—a tongue-lashing if they gave her trouble and sometimes she actually used physical force. She literally beat pianist Clarence Williams because he had been pocketing money that should have been hers. Her boldness, coupled with her immense talent, allowed Smith to earn as much as two thousand dollars per week. However, with artistic and monetary success came problems. Smith, who had always had a taste for alcohol, began to drink heavily when she became estranged from her husband. By the time she and Gee separated, her drinking had begun to make her temperamental and unreliable as an artist. She turned from a "hardworking performer who ran her shows with military discipline into a mean drunk who thought nothing of breaking a contract or leaving a troupe stranded penniless in some godforsaken town" (Albertson, 111). She also squandered the money she made. While some of her profligacy with money was due to the fact that she was generous—Smith was a renowned for giving money to friends in need—much of it was also a result of her destructive behavior.

Her problematic behavior, the impact of the Depression, changes in musical tastes, and the negative effect of the advent of radio on the record industry conspired to bring about Smith's decline. By 1931 Columbia Records was forced to drop her, as the sales of her records had decreased dramatically. Smith attempted to revise her repertoire, and in 1929 she starred in a Broadway show and acted in the motion picture *St. Louis Blues* in order to save her career. But the efforts proved fruitless—while she could still pack shows, her record sales continued to drop. Yet the power of her art was still evident. "Nobody Knows You When You're Down and Out," which she recorded that same year, captures the sorrow of her own decline as it speaks to a larger truth.

Smith died in a car crash in Clarksdale, Mississippi, in 1937, still trying to regain her professional footing. According to popular myth, she died because a whites-only hospital refused to admit her. The truth is that Smith could have been taken sooner to the African American hospital where she died, but it is unlikely that she could have survived given the seriousness of her injuries. Known as the Empress of the Blues, Smith laid the foundation for all subsequent women's jazz and blues singing, influencing hundreds of musicians and singers, among them Louis Armstrong, BILLIE HOLIDAY, and MAHALIA JACKSON. Ironically, no one from the music industry attended her funeral. In contrast, the number of adoring fans attending was seven thousand strong, and she continues to be loved today.

FURTHER READING

Albertson, Chris. *Bessie* (1972).
Davis, Angela Y. *Blues Legacies and Black Feminism* (1998).
Harrison, Daphne D. *Black Pearls: Blues Queens of the 1920s* (1988).
Shapiro, Nat, and Nat Hentoff, *The Jazz Makers* (1957).

Discography
The Bessie Smith Collection, (Columbia CK 44441).

Bessie Smith: Empress of the Blues (Charly Records CDCD 1030).
The Bessie Smith Story (vols. 1–4, Columbia CL 855–858).

—GLENDA R. CARPIO

 **SMITH, JAMES McCUNE** (18 Apr. 1813–17 Nov. 1865), abolitionist and physician, was born in New York City, the son of slaves. All that is known of his parents is that his mother was, in his words, "a self-emancipated bond-woman." His own liberty came on 4 July 1827, when the Emancipation Act of the state of New York officially freed its remaining slaves. Smith was fourteen at the time, a student at the Charles C. Andrews African Free School No. 2, and he described that day as a "real full-souled, full-voiced shouting for joy" that brought him from "the gloom of midnight" into "the joyful light of day." He graduated with honors from the African Free School but was denied admission to Columbia College and Geneva, New York, medical schools because of his race. With assistance from black minister Peter Williams Jr., he entered the University of Glasgow, Scotland, in 1832 and earned his BA (1835), MA (1836), and MD (1837) degrees. He returned to the United States in 1838 as the first professionally trained black physician in the country.

Resettled in New York City, in 1838 or 1839 Smith married Malvina Barnet, with whom he was to have five children, and successfully established himself. He set up practice in Manhattan as a surgeon and general practitioner for both blacks and whites, became the staff physician for the New York Colored Orphan Asylum, and opened a pharmacy on West Broadway, one of the first in the country owned by a black.

Smith's activities as a radical abolitionist and reformer, however, secured his reputation as one of the leading black intellectuals of the antebellum era. As soon as he returned to the United States, he became an active member of the American Anti-Slavery Society, which sought immediate abolition by convincing slaveholders through moral persuasion to renounce the sin of slavery and emancipate their slaves. By the late 1840s he had abandoned the policies of nonresistance and nonvoting set forth by William Lloyd Garrison and his followers in the society. Instead, Smith favored political abolitionism, which interpreted the U.S. Constitution as an antislavery document and advocated political and ultimately violent intervention to end slavery. In 1846 Smith championed the campaign for unrestricted black suffrage in New York State; that same year he became an associate and good friend of Gerrit Smith, a wealthy white abolitionist and philanthropist, and served as one of three black administrators for his friend's donation of roughly fifty acres apiece to some three thousand New York blacks on a vast tract of land in the Adirondacks. He became affiliated with the Liberty Party in the late 1840s, which was devoted to immediate and unconditional emancipation, unrestricted suffrage for all men and women, and land reform. In 1855 he helped found the New York City Abolition Society, which was organized, as he put it, "to Abolish Slavery by means of the Constitution; *or otherwise,*" by which he meant violent intervention in the event that peaceful efforts failed (though there is no indication that he resorted to violence). When the Radical Abolition Party, the successor to the Liberty Party, nominated him for New York secretary of state in 1857, he became the first black in the country to run for a political office.

In his writings, Smith was a central force in helping to shape and give direction to the black abolition movement. He contributed frequently to the *Weekly Anglo-African* and the *Anglo-African Magazine* and wrote a semiregular column for *Frederick Douglass' Paper* under the pseudonym "Communipaw," an Indian name that referred to a charmed and honored settlement in Jersey City, New Jersey, where blacks had played an important historic role. He also wrote the introduction to FREDERICK DOUGLASS's 1855 autobiography, *My Bondage and My Freedom,* and he often expressed his wish that Douglass relocate his paper from Rochester to New York City. Douglass considered Smith the "foremost" black leader who had influenced his reform vision.

Smith's writings focused primarily on black education and self-help, citizenship, and the fight against racism; these themes represented for him the most effective means through which to end slavery and effect full legal and civil rights. He was a lifelong opponent of attempts among whites to colonize blacks in Liberia and elsewhere and a harsh critic of black nationalists who, beginning in the 1850s, encouraged emigration to Haiti and West Africa rather than a continuation of the fight for citizenship and equal rights. Although he defended integration, he also encouraged blacks to establish their own presses, initiatives, and organizations. "It is emphatically our battle," he wrote in 1855. "Others may aid and assist if they will, but the moving power rests with us." His embrace of black self-reliance in the late 1840s paralleled his departure from the doctrines of Garrison and the American Anti-Slavery Society, which largely ignored black oppression in the North—even among abolitionists—by focusing on the evils of slavery in the South. Black education in particular, he concluded, led directly to self-reliance and moral uplift, and these values in turn provided the most powerful critique against racism. He called the schoolhouse the "great caste abolisher" and vowed to "fling whatever I have into the cause of colored children, that they may be better and more thoroughly taught than their parents are."

The racist belief in the innate inferiority of blacks was for Smith the single greatest and most insidious obstacle to equality. In 1846 he became despondent over the racial "hate deeper than I had imagined" among the vast majority of whites. Fourteen years later he continued to lament that "our white countrymen do not know us"; "they are strangers to our characters, ignorant of our capacity, oblivious to our history." He hoped his own distinguished career and writings would serve as both a role model for uneducated blacks and a powerful rebuttal against racist attacks. As a black physician, he was uniquely suited to combat the pseudoscientific theories of innate black inferiority. In two important and brilliantly argued essays—"Civilization" (1844) and "On the Fourteenth Query of Thomas Jefferson's Notes on Virginia" (1859)—he incorporated his extensive knowledge of biology and anatomy to directly refute scientific arguments of the innate inferiority of blacks.

The driving force behind Smith's reform vision and sustained hope for equality was his supreme "confidence in

God, that firm reliance in the saving power of the Redeemer's Love." Much like other radical abolitionists such as Douglass and Gerrit Smith, he viewed the abolition movement and the Civil War in millennialist terms: slavery and black oppression were the most egregious of a plethora of sins ranging from tobacco and alcohol to apathy and laziness that needed to be abolished in order to pave the way for a sacred society governed by "Bible Politics," as he envisioned God's eventual reign on earth. He strove to follow his savior's example by embracing the doctrine of "equal love to all mankind" and at the same time remaining humble before him. He likened himself to "a coral insect . . . loving to work beneath the tide in a superstructure, that some day when the labourer is long dead and forgotten, may rear itself above the waves and afford rest and habitation for the creatures of his Good, Good Father of All." Following his death in Williamsburg, New York, from heart failure, his writings and memories remained a powerful source of inspiration, a "rest and habitation" to future generations of reformers.

FURTHER READING

The Gerrit Smith Papers, housed in the George Arents Research Library at Syracuse University and widely distributed on microfilm, include thirty letters from James McCune Smith to Gerrit Smith that contain valuable information. *Frederick Douglass' Paper* contains more essays by Smith than any other contemporary publication.

Blight, David W. "In Search of Learning, Liberty, and Self Definition: James McCune Smith and the Ordeal of the Antebellum Black Intellectual," *Afro Americans in New York Life and History* 9, no. 2 (July 1985): 7–25.
Ripley, C. Peter, ed. *The Black Abolitionist Papers*, vols. 3–5 (1991).

—JOHN STAUFFER

SMITH, TOMMIE

(6 June 1944–), Olympic track-and-field gold medalist and world record holder, was born in Clarksville, Texas, to James Richard, a sharecropper, and Dora Smith. Tommie, the seventh of twelve children, grew up on a farm where his family raised hogs and cows and picked cotton. Like many black Texans

hoping to escape the misery of the Jim Crow South, the Smiths moved to the San Joaquin Valley of California and settled in Lemoore. There, Smith's athletic track career began in the fourth grade, when he raced the fastest kid at his school, his older sister, Sallie, and won. He struggled academically but nonetheless decided in the sixth grade that he wanted to be a teacher. Recognizing the lack of attention given to his own learning difficulties, he hoped that he might serve students more effectively.

Smith grew rapidly as he entered his teenage years, and he excelled at a variety of sports. In ninth grade, by which time he was already six feet, two inches tall, he ran the 100-yard dash in only 9.9 seconds; cleared the high jump at 6 feet, 5 inches; and recorded 24 feet, 6 inches in the long jump. He improved his 100-yard-dash time in 1963, when he ran the sprint in 9.5 seconds and the 220-yard dash in 21.1 seconds. Most Valuable Athlete awards in basketball,

football, and track and field during his sophomore, junior, and senior years of high school earned Smith an athletic scholarship for the three sports at San Jose State University. Smith majored in social science and teaching at San Jose State and was also enrolled in the Army Reserve Officers Training Corps.

After attempting to compete as a three-sport athlete during his freshman year of college, he opted to focus on track and field for Coach Bud Winter. As a sophomore in 1965, Smith ran the 220-yard sprint in 20.0 seconds, tying the world record. Known for his powerful acceleration and for wearing dark sunglasses in his races, Smith soon emerged as a world-class sprinter and as a critical member of "Speed City," the nickname given to San Jose's track program. In 1966 Smith cut his 220-yard-dash time to 19.5, establishing a world record. He won the AAU and the NCAA titles in the 200-meter dash in 1967 and repeated his AAU title win the next year. Smith married the heptathlete

Tommie Smith (center) and John Carlos captured the world's attention when they raised black-gloved hands and bowed their heads in protest against racism during the 1968 Olympic Games. Library of Congress

Denise Paschal in 1967; their son, Kevin, was born in 1968.

That same year, Smith captured the world's attention by raising his fist in a "black power" salute on the victory podium at the 1968 Mexico City Olympic Games. Smith's actions took place during a time of turmoil on many college campuses as students protested the Vietnam War and demanded equality for women and racial minorities. African American athletes, both college and professional, became involved in these protests, while critics denounced collegiate athletic programs for exploiting African American athletes. At Smith's college, San Jose State, the sociology instructor Harry Edwards encouraged black athletes to become politically active on campus and to fight for equality. Edwards established the Olympic Project for Human Rights and encouraged Smith and some of his teammates to consider the power of the platform that sport provided for the civil rights struggle.

In November 1967 Smith attended the Western Regional Black Youth Conference held in Los Angeles. At that conference Edwards organized a meeting of black collegiate athletes to discuss the possibility of boycotting the 1968 Olympic Games. Coming from a world-class sprinter, Smith's declaration that he would support the boycott garnered significant attention. In an interview published in *Life*, Smith spoke of the difficulties African American students faced on predominantly white college campuses. Smith also addressed the need for athletic departments to hire black coaches and trainers in a *Newsweek* cover story, "The Angry Black Athlete." He began to receive hate mail in response to his statements.

After much deliberation, Smith decided not to boycott the Olympics, but he was still the subject of great media scrutiny at the U.S. Olympic Trials hosted in Los Angeles. Smith qualified in his specialty, the 200 meters. With the threat of the boycott resolved, the International Olympic Committee's (IOC) president, Avery Brundage, informed the black athletes who made the team that he would not tolerate any trouble. In the qualifying heats of the 200 meters, Smith wore tall black socks as his means of making a statement. He felt pain in his hamstrings but was determined to compete in the finals. On 16 October 1968 Tommie Smith

won the gold medal in the 200 meters at the Olympic Games with a world-record time of 19.83 seconds. His San Jose State teammate John Carlos finished third.

Before the medal ceremony, Smith approached Carlos to discuss a non-violent protest during the award ceremony. Smith wore a black glove on his right hand, with Carlos wearing the left glove. They each wore black socks with no shoes. As the American national anthem began to play, Smith and Carlos bowed their heads and raised their gloved fists in the air. The image was seen around the world, and the response was immediate. Some teammates were very supportive, while other American athletes criticized the use of the award platform as a place of protest. Others thought that sport was not the place for politics. Smith told the media that his raised fist with the black glove represented "black power" in America, and his black scarf represented black pride. His black socks with no shoes represented black poverty in racist America.

The U.S. Olympic Committee (USOC) did not want to make Smith and Carlos into martyrs, but they were pressured by Brundage and the IOC to punish the athletes. Smith and Carlos were suspended from the team, banned from the Olympic Village, and sent home. Brundage and the USOC warned the pair's teammates that further protests would result in the same punishment. Even so, several black athletes expressed solidarity with Smith and Carlos. The 4 × 400–meter relay team wore black tams on the victory stand but did stand at attention during the national anthem. The long jumpers Bob Beamon and Ralph Boston, who won gold and bronze medals, respectively, wore black socks on the victory stand as a protest. Other teammates were less forgiving. Years later they remained critical, believing that the actions of Smith and Carlos reflected poorly on the entire team and overshadowed the accomplishments of the other members of the 1968 squad.

Following the Olympics, Smith returned to San Jose State for his final semester of college. Along with Carlos, he was both celebrated and denounced on campus for his black power protest; the ROTC even demanded that Smith return his military uniform. Smith graduated with a BA degree and later earned a master's degree in Sociology

from the Goodard-Cambridge Graduate Program for Social Change in Cambridge, Massachusetts. Upon graduation from San Jose State, Smith played football on the taxi squad of the Cincinnati Bengals, earning three hundred dollars a week. He recorded only one reception, for forty-one yards, in a professional game. Cut after the 1971 preseason, Smith played one month for the Hamilton Tiger-Cats of the Canadian Football League. Jack Scott, the radical athletic director at Oberlin College in Ohio, hired Smith in 1972 to coach track and field. Denied tenure at Oberlin in 1978, Smith relocated to California to coach the men's track-and-field team at Santa Monica College. That same year, he married his second wife, Denise Kyle. They have three children, Danielle, Timothy, and Anthony.

Smith's achievements on the track have left a lasting imprint on the record books. He is the only man to simultaneously hold eleven world records. His records of 10.1 seconds in the 100 meters, 19.83 seconds in the 200 meters, and 44.5 seconds in the 400 meters still rank high on the all-time lists. His 19.83 seconds in the 200 meters, set at the 1968 Olympic Games, stood until 1979 and was an Olympic record until 1984. He has received numerous honors for his athletic accomplishments, including induction into the National Track and Field Hall of Fame in 1978, the California Black Sports Hall of Fame in 1996, and the San Jose State University Sports Hall of Fame in 1999. Although they were once viewed as controversial and confrontational, the image of Tommie Smith and John Carlos giving the black power salute has come to be celebrated in recent years. San Jose State plans to erect a statue of the salute commemorating the two former student athletes.

FURTHER READING

Bass, Amy. *Not the Triumph, but the Struggle: The 1968 Olympics and the Making of the Black Athlete* (2002).

Edwards, Harry. *The Revolt of the Black Athlete* (1969).

Wiggins, David K. "'The Year of Awakening': Black Athletes, Racial Unrest and the Civil Rights Movement of 1968," *International Journal of the History of Sport* 9 (1992).

—MAUREEN M. SMITH

SMITH, WILLIE MAE FORD (23 June 1904–

2 Feb. 1994), gospel singer and evangelist, was born Willie Mae Ford in Rolling Fork, Mississippi, to Clarence Ford, a railroad worker, and Mary Williams, a restaurateur. The seventh of fourteen children, Willie Mae had varying experiences in her early life as the family moved frequently throughout the Midwest. Clarence Ford worked hard to give his children a stable home. He and his wife were devout Christians whose interest in gospel singing extended beyond their music making in the home to area churches in and around Memphis, Tennessee, where the family moved shortly after Willie Mae's birth.

The vibrant black community and musical environment of Memphis introduced Willie Mae to the two genres that would greatly influence both her musical development and the course of her life—blues and gospel singing. Willie Mae's experience with the blues, considered by most Protestant blacks to be the "Devil's music," came in the form of singing blues songs on the streets of Memphis for money. Not unlike the Reverend Gary Davis and other early blues singers, Willie Mae would later claim that only through salvation in the church was she rescued from this life of sin. She overcame the moral reservations associated with the secular music genre and through the blues influence she developed the robust and resonating quality of her contralto voice. Willie Mae gained further experience in church, singing the long-meter hymns and spirituals that her mother enjoyed. As a small girl she was placed upon a table in the church, from this stage she enthralled her first audiences.

In 1917 the family settled in St. Louis, Missouri. Encouraged by her father, Willie Mae became the leader of a female quartet that included her sisters Mary, Emma, and Geneva. The Ford Sisters patterned themselves after popular male quartets of the day and earned a reputation throughout Missouri and Illinois. The group presented the "new" sound in gospel music—female groups that sang both a cappella and with piano accompaniment. The Ford Sisters reached a high point in their career when they performed at the National Baptist Convention in 1922. The National Baptist Convention was the largest body of black Protestants in America, the concerts that took place at these events influenced the latest trends in black gospel across the country. The Baptist musical tradition was quite conservative compared with those of Pentecostal and Holiness churches, but by 1922 the convention was just beginning to accept the new type of singing. The Ford Sisters' reception at the convention was lukewarm, and despite efforts to keep the group functioning, domestic responsibilities proved more pressing than their desire to sing. By the mid-1920s the group had disbanded.

Willie Mae had discontinued her education after the eighth grade and was determined to become successful as a singer; therefore, she continued singing when her sisters could not, ultimately becoming a consummate soloist. In time, her reputation for soulful, spirit-filled performances earned her a place of distinction both in the St. Louis area and at the annual National Baptist Convention. There is uncertainty as to the date of her marriage; most sources cite either 1924 or 1929 as the year in which she married James Peter Smith, who owned a small moving company. The union produced two children, Willie James and Jacquelyn, who would often accompany their mother when she performed in and around St. Louis. When the Depression threatened James's business, Willie Mae began traveling more widely, conducting musical revivals to supplement the family income.

On one of these occasions she met the gospel composer and former blues pianist THOMAS A. DORSEY. Impressed by Smith's voice, Dorsey invited her to Chicago in 1932 to help organize the National Convention of Gospel Choirs and Conventions (NCGCC), which brought together directors and choirs from Baptist churches throughout the United States. Each year an annual convention was held in a different city, where new compositions were presented that directors could teach to their local choirs. Smith's participation in the NCGCC placed her at the center of a musical movement that would diversify the marketing of gospel music and expand its audience beyond the traditional venues.

By 1936 her role in Dorsey's gospel dynasty was secured when he appointed her the principal teacher of singing and the director of the soloist bureau of the convention. Smith's devotion to the Dorsey convention did not, however, prevent her from performing on her own, and she continued to travel extensively throughout the late 1930s and early 1940s. In 1937 her performance at the National Baptist Convention of an original composition, "If You Just Keep Still," gained her particular attention. From 1937 onward Smith spent a great deal of time on the road, while her husband raised their two children. She performed frequently in churches in Cincinnati, Buffalo, Detroit, Kansas City, Atlanta, and small towns around the Midwest and the South.

Her performance style changed considerably during the late 1930s and early 1940s when she joined the Church of God Apostolic, one of many Pentecostal denominations emerging during this period. She took on as accompanist a young woman named Bertha, whom she and James adopted. The combination of Smith's robust voice and Bertha's piano style was formidable and had a marked influence on the performance style of a number of gospel soloists and groups. Smith began to integrate into her performances elements of the singing styles of Sanctified churches, including rhythmic bounce, expressive timbres in the voice conveyed through melodic embellishments, slides, moans, groans, percussive attacks of words, phrases, and distinctive harmonies.

Central to Smith's performance was her inclusion of sermonettes, five- to ten-minute sermons delivered before, after, and even during a song. The emotional quality of these sermonettes was intensified by her physical enactment of the text, though this, at times, brought the criticism of ministers and deacons who objected to her movements as undignified. Nevertheless, audiences packed the churches where Smith performed, and her popularity grew.

Although her live performances were highly successful, Smith never achieved the popularity that gospel recordings had helped her counterparts Roberta Martin and MAHALIA JACKSON attain. During the 1940s she concentrated on preaching

STAGOLEE

and singing, openly acknowledging her "calling" to preach the gospel, though a woman preacher was not readily accepted in many black churches. Her career took a turn following the death of her husband in 1950. Soon afterward, Bertha grew disenchanted with traveling and eventually gave up her position as accompanist. Smith was never fully able to establish with other accompanists the musical rapport she had had with Bertha, and she began performing less frequently in order to devote more time to her domestic responsibilities.

"Mother Smith," as she came to be known in congregational and church circles, began teaching gospel singing after the 1950s and mentored a number of noteworthy vocalists, including the O'Neal Twins, Edna Gallmon Cooke, and Brother Joe May, who reportedly was the first to call her "Mother." In the 1970s she resurfaced to record several albums on the Savoy label and appear at the Newport Jazz Festival, and was featured in the 1982 film *Say Amen, Somebody* that solidified her place in gospel history. In 1988 she received the Heritage Award from the National Endowment of the Arts and a year later appeared in Brian Lanker's book *I Dream a World: Portraits of Black Women Who Changed America*. On 2 February 1994, at the age of eighty-nine, Willie Mae Ford Smith died of congestive heart failure in a St. Louis nursing home.

Ford's contribution to the gospel world was multifaceted. She defined the role of the female soloist at a time when gospel music was dominated by male quartets and groups. She effectively translated a blues-derived style into gospel singing and brought the regional traditions of St. Louis to national attention. More important to the gospel genre, perhaps, was her introduction of the sermonette and song format that became popular years later with the singers Shirley Caesar and Dorothy Norwood.

FURTHER READING

Boyer, Horace Clarence. *How Sweet the Sound: The Golden Age of Gospel* (1995).
Dargan, Thomas, and Kathy White Bullock. "Willie Mae Ford Smith of St. Louis: A Shaping Influence upon Black Gospel Singing Style," *Black Music Research Journal* 9 (Fall 1989): 249–270.
Heilbut, Anthony. *The Gospel Sound: Good News and Bad Times* (1985).

Discography
Going on with the Spirit (Nashboro 7148).

I Believe I'll Run On (Nashboro 7124).
The Legends: The O'Neal Twins, Thomas Dorsey, the Barrett Sisters, Sallie Martin, Willie Mae Ford Smith (Savoy SL-14742).
—TAMMY L. KERNODLE

STAGOLEE (16 Mar. 1865–11 Mar. 1912), the archetypal "bad man" of song, toast, and legend, was born Lee Shelton somewhere in Texas. Shortly after Shelton murdered William "Billy" Lyons in 1895, blues songs began to appear recounting the event, giving rise to the figure of Stagolee. Little is known about Shelton's origins and childhood except the name of his father, Nat Shelton. The date of his birth is known only from his prison death certificate. The elegant style of his signature in his arrest records suggests that he had some schooling. Although he became the mythical Stagolee—a "bad mother" who shot somebody just to see him die—Lee Shelton was of ordinary stature. Prison records describe him as being five feet, seven and one-half inches tall. His hair and eyes are described as black, his "complexion" as "mulatto." Under the column "marks and scars," the authorities listed the following: "L[eft] eye crossed. 2 scars [on] R[ight] cheek. 2 scars [on] back head .1 scar on L[eft] shoulder blade" (Brown, 38).

The *St. Louis Star-Sayings* of 29 December 1895 refers to Lee Shelton as "Stag" Lee; the coroner's report on Lyons calls him "Stack" Lee. The name "Stag" carries connotations of male sexual potency, but it also has associations with "Stagg Town," which was widely used to refer to a black settlement or district, especially one characterized by poverty, crime, vice, and prostitution. Alternatively, or additionally, Shelton's nickname may be related to that of the *Stack Lee*, a riverboat belonging to the Lee Line. Given the reputation of the riverboats for gambling, high living, and prostitution, this too has fitting connotations for Shelton. The trisyllabic versions of his name, spelled variously as Stagolee, Stagger Lee, Stackalee, Stackerlee, and Stack-o-lee, probably derive from the rhythmic requirements

of the ragtime and blues in which the story was first couched.

In *Gould's St. Louis Directory* for 1894, "Stack L. Shelton" is listed as a waiter living at 1314 Morgan Street. In 1897 he appears as "a driver," living in a somewhat better neighborhood on North Twelfth Street. Some years later, the *St. Louis Post-Dispatch* called him "formerly a Negro politician" and said he was the "proprietor of a lid club for his race" (17 Mar. 1911). A "lid club" was an establishment that "kept a lid" on such criminal activities as gambling, while serving as a front for other illegal activities, including prostitution. At least until 1911, Shelton ran the Modern Horseshoe Club on Morgan Street, in the city's red-light district. There is no reason to doubt that he ran the club as a gambling saloon, and its name certainly suits his profession as a driver. As a carriage driver, or "hack-driver," Lee Shelton would have been able to direct both black and white male visitors to St. Louis to their choice of bordello. The most prestigious underworld nightclubs in "Deep Morgan" were the Chauffeurs Club, the Deluxe Club, the Jazzland Club, the Cardinal's Nest, and the Modern Horseshoe. By the 1920s these were also the best blues clubs in the city. It is no wonder, then, that "Stagolee" is a blues song, since Lee Shelton was himself the owner of a famous blues café.

On Christmas night 1895, according to eyewitnesses, the extravagantly dressed Shelton entered the Bill Curtis Saloon on the corner of Morgan and Thirteenth Streets and asked, "Who's treating?" Someone pointed out Billy Lyons, and the two drank and laughed together until an argument began, during which Shelton grabbed Lyons's derby hat and broke the form. Lyons in turn grabbed Shelton's hat—identified in many of the songs as a Stetson, the very symbol of masculinity. Shelton demanded his hat back, and Lyons refused. Shelton pulled his .44 revolver and hit Lyons on the head with it. According to an eyewitness, George McFaro, Lyons then pulled out a knife and taunted Shelton, "You cockeyed son of a bitch, I'm going to *make* you kill me." Shelton backed off, took aim, and shot. He walked over to the dying Lyons, said, "Nigger, I told you to give me my

784

hat," snatched his hat, and walked out (Brown, 21–24).

The *St. Louis Star-Sayings* suggests that the killing may have been "the result of a vendetta" (29 Dec. 1895). Five years earlier a stepbrother of Lyons had killed a friend of Shelton's. Further motivation may have arisen from the rivalry of various politically motivated "social clubs" organized ostensibly for the moral uplift of young black men. Shelton was leader of the recently formed Four Hundred Club, with Democratic Party ties, and Lyons had connections with a group led by Henry Bridgewater, a prominent black Republican and saloon owner. Motive, however, is not a problematic theme of the Stagolee blues; indeed, most versions focus on the mere taking of his hat as the catalyst that provokes Stag's deadly reaction. Even the suggestion of the bluesman Mississippi John Hurt that it was a magic hat goes beyond the necessities of the mythical narration. The archetype of "badness" needs no deeper rationale.

Shelton was arrested at three o'clock on the morning of the 26th. By Friday, 27 December, he had hired a white lawyer, Nat Dryden, one of the best lawyers in St. Louis (although an alcoholic and an opium addict), and the first lawyer in Missouri to gain the conviction of a white man for murdering a black. At an inquest that day, Judge David Murphy signed a warrant against Shelton for first-degree murder. After being bound over to a grand jury on 3 January 1896, Shelton was released on a four-thousand-dollar bond, a considerable sum in 1896. The trial began on 15 July, during which Dryden argued that Shelton shot Lyons in self-defense. Three days later, after twenty-two hours of deliberation, the jury was unable to agree on a verdict. Shelton was again released on bond and apparently returned to running the Modern Horseshoe.

Nat Dryden died after a drinking binge in August 1897, before a second trial was held. There are no records of that second trial, but on 7 October 1897 Shelton began a twenty-five year sentence at the Missouri State Penitentiary. He was paroled on Thanksgiving Day 1909, but two years later he was in trouble again, "accused of robbing the home of William Akins,

another Negro, last January, beating Akins on the head with a revolver and breaking his skull" (*St. Louis Post-Dispatch*, 17 Mar. 1911). Shelton was sentenced to five years and returned to prison on 7 May 1911. When he reentered prison, he was suffering from tuberculosis and his weight dropped to 102 pounds. Under pressure from other Democrats, Governor Herbert S. Hadley granted the weakened Shelton another parole; however, the Missouri attorney general objected, and Shelton died in the prison hospital on 11 March 1912.

But well before he died, Stagolee himself may have heard the song that gave rise to his mythic status. One version was collected in Memphis in 1903, and in 1911 hoboes were singing a version in Georgia. A circus performer heard it in the Indian Territory in 1913, at about the same time a white youngster hunting with his father heard Negroes singing it in Virginia's Dismal Swamp. Indeed, the rapid spread of these songs exemplifies the workings of the oral tradition, and different details—the name of Shelton's wife or girlfriend (Lilly or Nellie), the name of the judge, even the name of a bartender who witnessed the shooting—survive in different renditions. In evidence of its widespread popularity among black and white audiences, several jazz and dance orchestras, including Fred Waring's Pennsylvanians, recorded versions in the early 1920s. In its opening stanzas, Mississippi John Hurt's 1928 classic blues rendition captures perfectly the tone of the implacable heartlessness of its hero:

Police officer, how can it be?
You can arrest everybody but cruel
    Stagolee.
That bad man! O, cruel Stagolee.

Billy de Lyons told Stagolee, "Please don't
    take my life,
I got two little babes and a darlin' lovin'
    wife."
That bad man! O, cruel Stagolee.

"What I care about your two little babes,
    your darlin' lovin' wife?
You done stole my Stetson hat, I'm bound
    to take your life."
That bad man! O, cruel Stagolee.

"Stagolee" became a staple of the blues repertoire and has been recorded

by over two hundred musicians in styles ranging from blues to jazz, R&B, and rock and roll, including versions by MA RAINEY (1925), DUKE ELLINGTON (1927), CAB CALLOWAY (1931), BIG BILL BROONZY (1946), SIDNEY BECHET (1946), Lloyd Price (1959), JAMES BROWN (1967), the Clash (1979), and Bob Dylan (1993). In the Jim Crow atmosphere of the early twentieth century, Stagolee became a trope for the resentment felt by people marginalized by the dominant white society. For over a century, Stagolee has remained a symbol of rebellion—oppositional, subversive, underground, and largely invisible—as part of the unofficial subculture of prostitutes, gamblers, criminals, and other "undesirables" (Brown, 120). The tale is variously told, but the character of Stagolee continues to exemplify what it is to be "bad," whether "bad" is meant as a compliment or an insult.

FURTHER READING

Barlow, William. *Looking Up at Down: The Emergence of Blues Culture* (1989).
Brown, Cecil. *Stagolee Shot Billy* (2003).

—CECIL BROWN
—JOHN K. BOLLARD

STAUPERS, MABEL DOYLE KEATON

(27 Feb. 1890–30 Sept. 1989), National Association of Colored Graduate Nurses executive officer, was born Mabel Doyle in Barbados, British West Indies, to Thomas and Pauline Doyle. In 1903 her family settled in Harlem, where her father became a brake inspector for the New York Central Railroad. Staupers attended public schools in New York and graduated from Freedmen's Hospital School of Nursing (now the Howard University College of Nursing) in Washington, D.C., in 1917. After graduation, she began her professional career as a private-duty nurse in New York, but she soon went to work as a nurse administrator in Philadelphia. In 1922 she returned to Harlem and began an illustrious career as a nurse and an administrator.

The Great Migration of African Americans from the rural South resulted in an increase of over 66 percent in Harlem's black population between 1910 and 1920. The attendant social problems of such rapid population change—inadequate housing, unemployment, and insufficient public health services—made Harlem a center for reform-related activism. Staupers, on behalf of the New York Tuberculosis and Health Association, undertook to survey the Harlem community to determine its public health needs. As a consequence of her final report, the Harlem Committee of the New York Tuberculosis and Health Association was created. Staupers served as its executive secretary for twelve years, during which time the Harlem Committee helped to create the city's first hospital for black tuberculosis patients and initiated a public health library and a variety of programs for children, adults, physicians, nurses, and social workers. By the late 1920s the committee had duplicated many of these programs and their publications in Spanish. Staupers's work with the Harlem Committee undoubtedly established her as an important person in the area of public health, but it was through her role as executive secretary and president of the National Association of Colored Graduate Nurses that she achieved a national reputation. The NACGN was founded in 1908 in New York City, and Staupers joined in 1916 while she was still a nursing student. During its early years the organization's leaders worked to improve and standardize nursing instruction and to raise the status of black nurses. After Staupers became executive secretary in 1934, the organization expanded, growing in membership from 175 to 821 by 1939. The NACGN was especially effective in its efforts to integrate the nursing profession, to improve black public health, and to cultivate leadership ability among black nurses while creating leadership roles for them. To reach these goals, Staupers and Estelle Massey Riddle Osborne, the NACGN's first president, gained financial support from the Rosenwald Foundation, the General Education Board, and other sympathetic people and organizations. These funds enabled nurses to conduct regional and national conferences, to publish and circulate papers and reports, and to serve as a liaison between black nurses and the agencies and institutions that trained, employed, and promoted them.

An important goal for Staupers and other black nursing leaders was the complete integration of the American Nurses Association, for without full membership in the ANA no nurse could consider herself fully credentialed. Reaching this goal was no small accomplishment. ANA membership was gained either through state associations or through alumnae associations, yet most black nurses lived and worked in states that would not allow them to join, and the only black institution that had affiliate status with the ANA was Freedmen's Hospital Nursing School.

Staupers and her colleagues undertook a variety of steps to open the ANA to black nurses. In 1938, for example, she helped create the NACGN Advisory Council, composed of representatives of the major nursing and public health organizations and a variety of private philanthropic agencies and public institutions. This council became a vehicle for pressuring the white national organizations to open their doors to black members. Estelle Osborne recommended that in the South, where state laws precluded the formal association of black and white nurses, the ANA should recognize the black organization as an ANA affiliate. In the North a different strategy was required. Large numbers of black nurses in the North had graduated from southern schools and had migrated from states that excluded them from membership in the state affiliate. At the least, an "individual membership" category was necessary. Staupers began the effort to establish this new category in New York, with the hope that if the New York State affiliate opened its membership to black nurses, other northern states would follow suit. But before the ANA was integrated, World War II began, and the campaign to integrate nursing spread to a new front.

Although the war created an increased need for nurses, neither the army nor the navy accepted black nurses. The armed forces took their nurses from among American Red Cross Nursing Service applicants, so Staupers encouraged black nurses to submit Red Cross applications. She also coordinated a campaign to pressure the military to change its policy. When the War Department decided in 1941 to accept a maximum of fifty-six black nurses at segregated military camps, Staupers coordinated a massive protest movement. By 1944 there were almost three hundred black army nurses, but the army still had a quota, and the navy still had no black nurses. Staupers wrote letters to military leaders on behalf of the NACGN, and she sent news releases to black newspapers publicizing the government's discriminatory policy. She lobbied the surgeon general of the army and worked to persuade members of Congress to pass bills explicitly prohibiting racial discrimination "in the selection, induction, voluntary recruitment, and commissioning of nurses" in the armed forces.

In the fall of 1944 Staupers met with President Franklin D. Roosevelt to detail the problems arising from the quota on black nurses in the army, the segregation of the camps in which they worked, and their work assignments, which were usually limited to caring for German prisoners of war. When the surgeon general of the army announced in early 1945 that a special draft for nurses might be necessary, Staupers was present and asked why they did not accept the black nurses who were willing to serve. She also helped coordinate a successful letter-writing and telegram campaign protesting proposed amendments to the Selective Service Act that would have allowed the drafting of nurses. Within two months Staupers's efforts had paid off. The army eliminated its quota for black nurses, and shortly thereafter the navy announced a "color-blind" recruitment policy.

During the war Staupers and members of the NACGN Advisory Council continued to put pressure on the ANA, and in 1942, following the example of the American Red Cross and the National League of Nursing Education, the ANA began to admit black nurses through their membership in the NACGN. Emboldened by the 1945 change in military policy, in January 1946 Staupers asked the ANA to directly admit black nurses from any state that denied them membership on the basis of race. The ANA agreed in September to admit qualified black nurses to the organization and its state affiliates. Although this process was not complete until 1948, Staupers considered her work done and stepped down as executive secretary of the NACGN.

The historian Darlene Clark Hine has written that it is likely that "the complete integration of black women into American nursing on all levels" would not have occurred without the work of Mabel Staupers" (Hine, 186). And, indeed, Staupers seemed indefatigable. Her work during the 1920s and early 1930s was critical to the creation of public health policies and programs in New York City. The historian Susan L. Smith notes that Staupers also was instrumental in establishing and organizing National Negro Health Week. She was a master coalition builder, linking black nurses and their organizations to other nursing groups and to philanthropic, government, civic, and social leaders throughout the country. She became the NACGN's last president in 1949 and led the process of folding the goals and objectives of the NACGN into the ANA.

Although the NACGN ceased to exist in 1951, Staupers continued to encourage black nurses to protect the gains they had made and to submit histories of black nurses to the Schomburg Collection for Research in Black Culture of the New York Public Library. Ten years later she would publish her own history of the NACGN, *No Time for Prejudice: The Story of the Integration of Negroes in Nursing in the United States* (1961). In one of her final acts as president of the NACGN, Staupers encouraged her members to participate in the profession in ways to make real the new policy of integration. On 15 March 1951 the headquarters of the NCAGN closed; the ANA was finally a fully integrated professional organization for nurses. She died in Washington, D.C.

Although the NAACP awarded Staupers its prestigious Spingarn Medal in 1951 for her work in integrating the nursing profession, she did not "retire" from the profession after finishing her work as president of the NACGN. Almost immediately, she became a member of the Board of Directors for the ANA. Staupers remained active in the national black nursing sorority, Chi Eta Phi, and she received many honors for her life's work from universities, church groups, nursing organizations, and civic associations.

FURTHER READING

Information on Staupers can be gleaned from the Mabel Keaton Staupers Papers in the Howard University–Moorland-Spingarn Research Center, Washington, D.C., and from the Mabel Keaton Staupers Papers, housed at the Schomburg Center for Research in Black Culture of the New York Public Library.

Hine, Darlene Clark. *Black Women in White: Racial Conflict and Cooperation in the Nursing Profession, 1890–1950* (1989).
Shaw, Stephanie J. *What a Woman Ought to Be and to Do: Black Professional Women Workers during the Jim Crow Era* (1996).
Smith, Susan L. *Sick and Tired of Being Sick and Tired: Black Women's Health Activism in America, 1890–1950* (1995).

Obituary: *New York Times*, 6 Oct. 1989.
—STEPHANIE J. SHAW

STEWARD, AUSTIN

(1793–1865), antislavery reformer, was born in Virginia, the son of Robert Steward and Susan (maiden name unknown), slaves. About 1800 a well-to-do planter, William Helm, purchased the family. Escaping business reverses and debts, Helm moved to Sodus Bay on New York's Lake Ontario frontier and shortly thereafter, in 1803, to Bath, New York, taking young Austin with him. Hired out for wages, Steward entered the employ of a Mr. Tower in Lyons, New York, where he worked until 1812. Escaping, he went to Canandaigua, where he worked for local farmers and attended an academy in Farmington. While thus employed, Steward learned of New York's 1785 law banning the sale of slaves brought into the state subsequent to that date. Drawing upon the state's 1799 gradual emancipation statute as well as an 1800 court decision, *Fisher v. Fisher*, which ruled that hiring out a slave constituted an intentional and fraudulent violation of the 1785 law, he openly asserted his freedom and continued to hire his labor in his own name, despite challenges from Helm.

Sometime between 1817 and 1820 Steward moved to Rochester. In 1825 he married a Miss B. of Rochester, the youngest daughter of a close friend, who bore him eight children, and, overcoming white opposition, he ran a successful grocery business. During these prosperous years, Steward became an activist on behalf of other northern blacks, both de jure and de facto free, who were subject to prejudice and treated as second-class citizens. From 1827 to 1829 he was an agent for *Freedom's Journal* and the *Rights of All*, both black newspapers. In 1830 he served as vice president of the first Annual Convention for the Improvement of Colored People, held in Philadelphia.

Steward and his family moved to Upper Canada (now western Ontario) in 1831, where they joined a group of African Americans who had fled Cincinnati after the race riots of 1829. There they had established, under the leadership of their agent Israel Lewis, an organized black community called Wilberforce. Steward invested the savings from his grocery in the project and undertook a major role in its proceedings, replacing Lewis as its principal leader until the community collapsed six years later. His career there, however, was beset with ill fortune. He soon fought with Lewis over the handling of the community's finances and other matters until in 1836 Lewis was dropped as the community's principal agent. The brothers Benjamin Paul and Nathaniel Paul, who replaced him, proved equally unsatisfactory, the latter, who was sent to England to raise funds, never rendering a satisfactory account of his mission. By 1837 Wilberforce, wracked by internal dissension, had virtually ceased to exist, and Steward, his savings gone and his reform efforts blasted, returned to Rochester with his family.

Reestablishing himself in the grocery business, Steward prospered for a season, but the aftershocks of the 1837 panic and a disastrous fire finally destroyed the enterprise. Steward moved back to Canandaigua about 1842, where he taught school and continued his antislavery work as an agent for the *National Anti-Slavery Standard*. Although he gradually faded into obscurity, he was active for a while in the emerging political antislavery movement. He served as president of the New York Convention of Colored Men in 1840, 1841, and 1845 and lobbied for black male suffrage on equal terms as white suffrage.

Steward, like most other black activists, remained on the periphery of the antislavery movement, whose inner circles kept even noted abolitionist FREDERICK DOUGLASS at a distance.

Moreover, by the 1840s Steward, tainted by his association with the failed Canadian settlement and lacking a personal following, was pushed from the black national convention limelight by younger, more aggressive black leaders such as HENRY HIGHLAND GARNET, JAMES MCCUNE SMITH, and Charles B. Ray.

Steward is best remembered for his autobiography, *Twenty-Two Years a Slave and Forty Years a Freeman*, published in 1857. It provides only a sketchy outline of his life and addresses his understanding of the evils of slavery, but it testifies primarily to the vicissitudes that African Americans experienced even in the North in its depiction of the struggle of one exceptional black man against social and economic discrimination and exclusion from the full political and legal privileges that white citizens enjoyed.

Steward pressed to achieve full citizenship for himself and others like him. For example, he attempted, unsuccessfully, to enlist in the Steuben County militia during the War of 1812, embraced the popular temperance reform of the 1830s, and served a term as clerk of Biddulph Township during his years in Canada. In the end, however, he always remained a marginal figure. His autobiography was his most effective undertaking; his strongest message was a plea to "those who have the power" to "have the magnanimity to strike off the chains from the enslaved, and bid him stand up, a Freeman and a Brother!" He died in Rochester, New York.

FURTHER READING

Steward, Austin. *Twenty-Two Years a Slave and Forty Years a Freeman* (1857), reprinted with an introduction by Graham Russell Hodges (2002); reprinted with an introduction by Jane H. Pease and William H. Pease (1969).

Pease, Jane H., and William H. Pease. *Black Utopia: Negro Communal Experiments in America* (1963).
———. *They Who Would Be Free: Blacks' Search for Freedom, 1830–1861* (1974; repr. 1990).
Ripley, C. Peter, ed. *The Black Abolitionist Papers*, vol. 3 (5 vols., 1985–1992).
Winks, Robin. *The Blacks in Canada* (1971).
—WILLIAM H. PEASE
—JANE H. PEASE

STEWARD, THEOPHILUS GOULD

(17 Apr. 1843–11 Jan. 1924), author, clergyman, and educator, was born in Gouldtown, New Jersey, the son of James Steward, a mechanic who had fled to Gouldtown as an indentured child servant, and Rebecca Gould, a descendant of the seventeenth-century proprietor of West Jersey, John Fenwick. His family's interest in history and literature supplemented his elementary school education in Bridgeton, and his mother encouraged him to challenge "established truths." He began preaching in 1862, was licensed to preach by the African Methodist Episcopal (AME) Church in 1863, and was appointed to serve a congregation in South Camden, New Jersey, in 1864.

In May 1865 Steward accompanied AME bishop DANIEL ALEXANDER PAYNE and others on a mission to South Carolina, where they reestablished the denomination, which had been banned from the state after the DENMARK VESEY slave rebellion conspiracy of 1822. From 1865 to 1868 Steward nurtured new AME congregations in South Carolina. In 1866 he married Elizabeth Gadsden; before her death in 1893, they had eight children.

From 1868 to 1871 Steward was the pastor of the AME congregation in Macon, Georgia, which was later renamed Steward Chapel AME Church in his honor. From his base in Macon, Steward actively participated in the business and politics of Reconstruction. He worked as a cashier for the Freedmen's Bank in Macon and speculated in cotton futures. He helped to write the platform of Georgia's Republican Party in 1868 and served as an election registrar in Stewart County, Georgia. He organized a successful protest by freed slaves in Americus, Georgia, against compulsory labor contracts and attacked the practice of limiting jury service to white males.

Leaving Georgia in 1871, Steward spent the next twenty years as the pastor of AME congregations in Brooklyn, New York; Philadelphia, Pennsylvania; Wilmington, Delaware; and Washington, D.C. In 1873 he undertook a mission to Haiti, establishing an AME congregation in Port-au-Prince, and in 1877 he completed his first book, *Memoirs*

of Mrs. Rebecca Steward (1877). From 1878 to 1880 he studied at Philadelphia's Protestant Episcopal Church Divinity School.

In the subsequent decade, Steward published two theological works, *Genesis Re-read* (1885) and *The End of the World* (1888). In these two books, he undertook Christian reinterpretations of the first and the last things—the doctrines of creation and of the eschaton. *Genesis Re-read* offered a liberal evangelical's assimilation of Darwinian evolutionary theory into Christian doctrine by arguing that evolution took place within a divine plan. *The End of the World* contested Anglo-Saxon triumphalism by contending that a final clash of nations would purge Christianity of its bondage to racism and give birth to "new nations," borne out of darkness to walk "in the light of the one great God, with whom there are no superior races and no inferior races."

Defeated in a bid for the presidency of the AME denomination's Wilberforce University in 1884 and at odds with its bishops because of repeated challenges to their authority, Steward won an appointment as chaplain to the Twenty-fifth U.S. Colored Infantry Regiment in 1891. His wife died in 1893, and three years later, in 1896, he married Susan Maria Smith McKinney, a widow and physician; they had no children. After service at Fort Missoula, Montana, and Chickamauga, Georgia, Steward and his regiment were sent to Cuba in 1898 at the beginning of the Spanish-American War. On his return to Brooklyn later that year, he addressed a celebration of the war's conclusion.

Steward wrote a novel, *A Charleston Love Story*, in 1899, but his main interest was military history. In addition to two pamphlets, *Active Service; or, Gospel Work among the U.S. Soldiers* (1897) and *How the Black St. Domingo Legion Saved the Patriot Army in the Siege of Savannah in 1779* (1899), he published *The Colored Regulars in the U.S. Army* (1899), a vindication of the service of African American soldiers in the Spanish-American War.

Sent to the Philippines in 1900, Steward was stationed in Manila, where he served as superintendent of schools for Luzon province. In 1902 he was transferred back to the

United States with the Twenty-fifth Infantry Regiment and stationed at Fort Niobrara, Nebraska, and Fort Brown near Brownsville, Texas. In August 1906 white residents reported that soldiers from Steward's regiment had briefly roamed through Brownsville's streets, freely shooting up its cafes and dance halls, killing a civilian and injuring a police officer. The soldiers maintained their innocence and implicated no one, but President Theodore Roosevelt dismissed them from service without honor and barred them from future government service. Steward, who had retired from the army in 1907, did not join in the African American community's outcry against Roosevelt's arbitrary action. But in his autobiography he wrote, "I have yet to find one officer who was connected with that regiment who expresses the belief that our men were guilty."

In 1907 Theophilus and Susan Steward moved to Ohio, where he became vice president, chaplain, and professor of French, history, and logic and she became the college physician at Wilberforce University. Active in fundraising efforts for Wilberforce, Theophilus Steward advocated military training for African American men as preparatory to their struggle for freedom. In 1911 the Stewards were the AME delegates to London's Universal Races Congress.

An active contributor to such newspapers as the *Cleveland Gazette* and the *Indianapolis Freeman*, Steward returned to familiar territory in his last books: family history in *Gouldtown, a Very Remarkable Settlement of Ancient Date* (1913), and military history in *The Haitian Revolution, 1791 to 1804* (1914). He published his autobiography, *From 1864 to 1914: Fifty Years in the Gospel Ministry*, in 1921.

FURTHER READING

Steward's papers are at the Schomburg Center for Research in Black Culture of the New York Public Library.

Miller, Albert George. *Elevating the Race: Theophilus G. Steward, Black Theology, and the Making of an African American Civil Religion, 1865–1924* (2003).
Seraile, William. *Voice of Dissent: Theophilus Gould Steward (1843–1924) and Black America* (1991).

—RALPH E. LUKER

STEWART, MARIA W.

(1803–Dec. 1879), political activist, lecturer, evangelical writer, and autobiographer, was born Maria Miller in Hartford, Connecticut, where she was orphaned by age five. Nothing is known about her parents. As a five-year-old girl, she was "bound out," or indentured, to a clergy family for ten years. She then moved to Boston, Massachusetts, where she supported herself as a domestic for the next ten years. Maria enjoyed no formal education but struggled through her youth and young adulthood to become literate and to gain an education. Until she was twenty years old, she attended Sabbath school classes, where she learned to read the Bible, and this served as a staple in her pursuit of learning.

Miller married James W. Stewart on 10 August 1826 in the Reverend Thomas Paul's African Baptist Church in Boston. In addition to taking his last name, Maria adopted Stewart's middle initial "W." The couple become involved in Boston's small, but growing black middle-class community, and like many of their entrepreneurial neighbors, they enjoyed financial security. James Stewart was a successful and independent shipping outfitter, whose business was situated in prime wharf space. Considerably older than Maria, he was, according to her witnessed claim for his service pension, "a tolerably stout well built man; a light, bright mulatto" (Richardson, 117). There was even a suggestion that his business peers thought him to be white until he married Maria, after which time he was listed as a black businessman.

Nevertheless, the Stewarts were not content with their own success and earnestly took up the cause of slaves and poor blacks. The political writer and activist DAVID WALKER, cofounder of the Massachusetts General Colored Association, one of the first avowedly black political organizations in the country, had a profound impact on the couple and on Maria especially. Walker's 1829 work, *Appeal to the Colored Citizens of the World*, one of the most influential black political documents of the nineteenth century, exposed the inhuman treatment of African Americans in general and slaves in particular, and responded directly to the racist sentiments espoused by Thomas Jefferson in his 1826 *Notes on the State of Virginia*, which stated in part that blacks were descended "from the tribes of Monkeys or Orang-Outanges."

As owner of a "slop shop," or used-clothing shop, Walker was able to distribute his pamphlet to every port along the Eastern Seaboard, the Caribbean, and other international ports in which the sailors docked, by planting his pamphlet in the pockets of clothing that he sold to mariners. Walker befriended James and Maria and used James's contacts, as the only black businessman in his trade, to distribute his pamphlet more widely, which he did by hiding the text in the folds of sails and in ship fittings.

Walker died in 1830, apparently of consumption, although rumors still persist that he was poisoned. James W. Stewart had died a year earlier. The two deaths were tremendously difficult for Maria Stewart and were exacerbated by the probate court's rejection of her husband's last will and testament. As a result, she lost all rights and property interest in her husband's estate and was left widowed and poor. This period of turmoil and grief pressed Stewart to reconsider her faith, and by 1831 she had publicly professed her faith in Christ.

This epiphany marked a new, active, and strident commitment to political action. She became a "warrior" and an advocate for "oppressed Africa." Her essay "Religion and the Pure Principles of Morality, the Sure Foundation on Which We Must Build" (1831) became the first political manifesto authored and published by an African American woman. While she does not advocate violence in the demand for freedom, in the manner of her political mentor, Walker, she militantly advocates that blacks improve their skills, sharpen their minds, and heighten their expectations. Issues of freedom, liberty, and civil rights are central to the text's message, as is her insistence that her vehemence is holy. Her religious conversion catalyzed her political life and propelled her into the public arena.

Appearing with most of Stewart's writings, and, in fact, integral to these texts, are religious prayers and meditations on key issues in her life—gender, gaining education, race, and political concerns. God became, in Stewart's estimation, an intercessor for the race. A biblical sense of morality, time, and prophetic resolution drives her texts. This is made especially clear in her call to women to educate themselves and their children. Stewart was not suggesting that African American women pursue literacy as a middle-class nicety but that education was a political necessity. The race would benefit from schools, libraries, and innovation offered to its women. Stewart was to speak forthrightly about women's influence over husbands and children and the attendant obligation to be moral and progressive in their politics well before Elizabeth Cady Stanton's 1848 Seneca Falls meeting where interested social reformers met, initiating the Women's Right's movement.

Nevertheless, Stewart's "holy zeal" carried her beyond the political arena with which her Boston friends were comfortable. She demanded of men and women a responsibility for the health, morality, and economic and political fortunes of the race that they could not meet. As her friends fell away, she recognized that her time in the public stream had come to an end. In her final address before friends and political acquaintances, she asked, "What if I am a woman?" (Richardson, 68), going to the heart of public disenchantment with her stridency. Stewart recognized that her zeal transgressed the norms for female, especially black female, behavior. Yet, she wrote, "brilliant wit will shine, come from whence it will; and genius and talent will not hide the brightness of its luster" (Richardson, 70). Her enthusiasm for the progress of African Americans was a call that could not be dampened by waning public opinion.

This same address, "Mrs. Stewart's Farewell Address to Her Friends in the City of Boston" (21 September 1833), served as a eulogy to her fiery public career. Stewart continued her activism in New York and Washington, D.C. In New York she attended the 1837 Women's Anti-Slavery Convention and was a member of a black women's literary society. In the District of Columbia, in the early 1870s, she served as matron of the Freedmen's Hospital and Asylum, a refuge for Civil War veterans, freed slaves, and their families. The Hospital and Asylum housed and trained the physically and mentally ill, the homeless, and those displaced by the significant cultural, economic, and social shifts brought on by the end of the war and Reconstruction.

In 1879 Stewart published *Meditations by Mrs. Maria W. Stewart*, which includes autobiographical information about her experiences during the Civil War. She died later that year while occupying the matron's position at the hospital and was buried on 17 December 1879, exactly fifty years after her husband, James, in Graceland Cemetery, Washington, D.C. Eulogized in *The People's Advocate*, a black newspaper circulated in Washington, D.C., she was remembered for her missionary work throughout Baltimore and Washington and for her generosity toward those in straitened circumstances.

Stewart was the first American woman to address a race- and sex-mixed audience publicly during an era when women's public speech was usually restricted to female audiences and African Americans generally did not address whites on political or moral issues. Her deep commitment to moral and religious purity and to the abolition of slavery led her to strident public advocacy in a manner uncommon for women of her day.

FURTHER READING

Hinks, Peter, ed. *David Walker's Appeal, to the Coloured Citizens of the World, but in Particular, and Very Expressly, to Those of the United States of America* (2000).

Logan, Shirley Wilson. *With Pen and Voice: A Critical Anthology of Nineteenth-Century African American Women* (1995).

Richardson, Marilyn, ed. *Maria W. Stewart, America's First Black Woman Political Writer* (1987).

Obituary: *The People's Advocate*, 28 Feb. 1880.
—MARTHA L. WHARTON

STILL, WILLIAM

(7 Oct. 1821–14 July 1902), abolitionist and businessman, was born near Medford in Burlington County, New Jersey, the youngest of the eighteen children of Levin Still, a farmer, and Charity (maiden name unknown). Still's father, a Maryland slave, purchased his own freedom and changed his name from Steel to Still. His mother escaped from slavery and changed her given name from Cidney to Charity. With a minimum of formal schooling, William studied on his own, reading whatever was available to him. He left home at age twenty to work at odd jobs and as a farmhand. In 1844 he moved to Philadelphia, where he found employment as a handyman, and in 1847 he married Letitia George. They had four children.

In 1847 the Pennsylvania Society for the Abolition of Slavery hired Still as a clerk, and he soon began assisting fugitives from slavery who passed through the city. After the passage of the Fugitive Slave Act of 1850, the society revived its Vigilance Committee to aid and support fugitive slaves and made Still chairman. One of the fugitives he helped was Peter Still, his own brother who had been left in slavery when his mother escaped. Finding Peter after a forty-year separation inspired Still to keep careful records of the former slaves, and those records later provided source material for his book on the Underground Railroad.

While with the Vigilance Committee, Still helped hundreds of fugitive slaves, and several times he nearly went to prison for his efforts. In 1855, when former slaves in Canada were being maligned in the press, he and his brother traveled there to investigate for themselves. His reports were much more positive and optimistic than the others and helped counteract rumors that former slaves were lazy and lawless. Five years later he cited cases of successful former slaves in Canada in a newspaper article that argued for freeing all the slaves.

Although Still had not approved of John Brown's raid on Harpers Ferry, afterward Brown's wife stayed with the Stills for a time, as did several of Brown's accomplices. Still's work in the antislavery office ended in 1861, but he remained active in the society, which turned to working for African American civil rights. He served as the society's vice president for eight years and as president from 1896 to 1901.

Still's book, *The Underground Railroad* (1872), was unique. The only work on that subject written by an African American, it was also the only day-by-day record of the workings of a vigilance committee. While he gave credit to "the grand little army of abolitionists," he put the spotlight on the fugitives themselves, saying "the race had no more eloquent advocates than its own self-emancipated champions." Besides recording their courageous deeds, Still hoped that the book would demonstrate the intellectual ability of his race. Along with the records of slave escapes he included excerpts from newspapers, legal documents, correspondence of abolitionists and former slaves, and some biographical sketches. He published the book himself and sent out agents to sell it. The book went into three editions and was exhibited at the Philadelphia Centennial Exposition in 1876.

Although he had not suffered personally under slavery, Still faced discrimination throughout his life and was determined to work for improved race relations. His concern about civil rights in the North led him in 1859 to write a letter to the press, which started a campaign to end racial discrimination on Philadelphia streetcars, where African Americans were permitted only on the unsheltered platforms. Eight years later the campaign met success when the Pennsylvania legislature enacted a law making such discrimination illegal. In 1861 he helped organize and finance the Pennsylvania Civil, Social, and Statistical Association to collect data about the freed slaves and to press for universal suffrage.

Still was a skilled businessman as well as an effective antislavery agent. He began purchasing real estate while working for the antislavery society. After leaving that position he opened a store where he sold new and used stoves and coal. In 1861 he opened a coal yard, a highly successful business that led to his being named to the Philadelphia Board of Trade. In 1864 he was appointed post sutler at Camp William Penn, where black soldiers were stationed.

Still's independent nature was illustrated in 1874 when he repudiated the Republican candidate for mayor of Philadelphia and supported instead a reform candidate. He explained his position at a public meeting and later in a pamphlet entitled *An Address on Voting and Laboring* (1874). He was also a lifelong temperance advocate,

and as a member of the Presbyterian Church he established a Mission Sabbath School. His other civic activities included membership in the Freedmen's Aid Commission, organizing around 1880 one of the first YMCAs for black youth, and helping to manage homes for the aged and for destitute black children and an orphan asylum for children of black soldiers and sailors. Poor health forced him to retire from his business affairs six years before his death at his home in Philadelphia.

FURTHER READING

Part of William Still's journal of the Philadelphia Vigilance Committee, along with some personal correspondence, is in the Historical Society of Pennsylvania in Philadelphia.

Still, William. *A Brief Narrative of the Struggle for the Rights of the Colored People of Philadelphia in the City Railway Cars* (1867).
Gara, Larry. "William Still and the Underground Railroad," *Pennsylvania History* 28 (Jan. 1961): 33–44.
Norwood, Alberta S. "Negro Welfare Work in Philadelphia Especially as Illustrated by the Career of William Still,..." M.A. thesis, Univ. of Penn., 1931.

Obituary: *Philadelphia Public Ledger*, 15 July 1902.

—LARRY GARA

 STILL, WILLIAM GRANT (11 May 1895– 3 Dec. 1978), composer, orchestrator, arranger, and musician, once called the "Dean of Afro-American Composers," was born in Woodville, Mississippi, the son of William Grant Still, a music teacher and bandmaster, and Carrie Lena Fambro, a schoolteacher. His father died during Still's infancy. Still and his mother moved to Little Rock, Arkansas, where she taught school and in 1909 or 1910 married Charles Shepperson, a railway postal clerk, who strongly supported his stepson's musical interests. Still graduated from high school at sixteen, valedictorian of his class, and went to Wilberforce University.

Still's mother had wanted him to become a doctor, but music became his primary interest. He taught himself to play the oboe and clarinet, formed a string quartet in which he played violin,

William Grant Still, trained at both Oberlin Conservatory and the New England Conservatory in Boston, composed jazz, popular music, opera, and classical works with African American themes. Library of Congress/Carl Van Vechten

arranged music for his college band, and began composing; a concert of his music was presented at the school. In 1915, just a few months shy of graduation, Still dropped out of Wilberforce in order to become a professional musician, playing in various dance bands, including one led by W. C. HANDY, "the Father of the Blues." That year he married Grace Bundy, with whom he had four children. They divorced in the late 1920s.

A small legacy from his father, which Still inherited on his twenty-first birthday, allowed him to resume his musical studies in 1917, this time at Oberlin College's conservatory. World War I interrupted Still's studies, and he spent it in the segregated U.S. Navy as a mess attendant and as a violinist in an officers' mess. After being discharged in 1919, Still returned to the world of popular music. He had a strong commitment to serious music and received further formal training during a short stay in 1922 at the New England Conservatory. From 1923 to 1925 he studied, as a private scholarship pupil, with the noted French "ultra-modernist" composer Edgard Varèse, whose influence can be heard in the dissonant passages found in Still's early serious work.

Still managed to make his way both in the world of popular entertainment and as a serious composer. He worked successfully into the 1940s in the entertainment world as a musician, arranger, orchestrator, and conductor. As an arranger and orchestrator, he worked on a variety of Broadway shows, including the fifth edition of Earl Carroll's *Vanities*. He also worked with a wide variety of entertainers, including Paul Whiteman, Sophie Tucker, and Artie Shaw. Still arranged Shaw's "Frenesi," which became one of the best-selling "singles" of all time. He also conducted on the radio for all three networks and was active in early television.

Despite his many commercial activities, Still also produced more serious efforts. Initially these works, such as *From the Land of Dreams* (written in 1924 and first performed a year later) and *Darker America* (also written in 1924 and first performed two years later), were described by critics as being "decidedly in the ultra-modern idiom." He soon moved into a simpler harmonic milieu, often drawing on jazz themes, as in *From the Black Belt* (written in 1926 and first performed in 1927), a seven movement suite for orchestra.

Still's most successful and best-known work, *Afro-American Symphony* (completed in 1930 and first performed a year later), draws heavily on the blues idiom; Still said he wanted "to demonstrate how the blues, so often considered a lowly expression, could be elevated to the highest musical level." To some extent the symphony is "programmatic," since after its completion Still added verses by black poet PAUL LAURENCE DUNBAR that precede each movement. Still believed that his symphony was probably the first to make use of the banjo. The work was well received and has continued to be played in the United States and overseas.

Still was a prodigious worker. His oeuvre includes symphonies, folk suites, tone poems, works for band, organ, piano, and violin, and operas, most of which focus on racial themes. His first opera, *Blue Steel* (completed in 1935), addresses the conflict between African voodooism and modern American values; its main protagonist is a black worker in Birmingham, Alabama. Still's first staged opera, *Troubled Island* (completed in 1938), which premiered at the New York City Opera in March 1949, centers around the character of Jean Jacques Dessalines, the first emperor of Haiti. The libretto, begun by the black poet LANGSTON HUGHES and completed by Verna Arvey, depicts the Haitian leader's stirring rise and tragic fall. Still married Arvey in 1939; the couple had two children. Arvey was to provide libretti for a number of Still's operas and choral works.

Among Still's other notable works are *And They Lynched Him on a Tree* (1940), a plea for brotherhood and tolerance presented by an orchestra, a white chorus, a black chorus, a narrator, and a soloist; *Festive Overture* (1944), a rousing piece based on "American themes"; *Lenox Avenue*, a ballet, with scenario by Arvey, commissioned by CBS and first performed on radio in 1937; *Highway 1, USA* (1962), a short opera, with libretto by Arvey, dealing with an incident in the life of an American family and set just off the highway in a gas station.

Still received many awards. Recognition had come relatively early to him—in 1928 the Harmon Foundation honored him with its second annual award, given to the person judged that year to have made the "most significant contribution to Negro culture in America." He won successive Guggenheim Fellowships in 1934 and 1935 and was awarded a Rosenwald Fellowship in 1939.

Still's early compositions were in an avant-garde idiom, but he soon turned to more conventional melodic and harmonic methods, in what he later described as "an attempt to elevate the folk idiom into symphonic form." This transition may have made his serious work more accessible, but for much of his career he sustained himself and his family by pursuing more commercially successful endeavors.

Still dismissed the black militants who criticized his serious music as "Eur-American music," insisting that his goal had been "to elevate Negro musical idioms to a position of dignity and effectiveness in the fields of symphonic and operatic music." And at a 1969 Indiana University seminar on black music he asserted, "I made this decision of my own free will.... I have stuck to this decision, and I've not been sorry."

During his lifetime Still broke many racial barriers. He was heralded as the first black man to have a major orchestral work played before an American audience, the first to conduct a major symphony orchestra (the Los Angeles Philharmonic) in an evening of his own compositions (at the Hollywood Bowl in 1936), and the first to conduct a major all-white orchestra in the deep South (the New Orleans Philharmonic in 1955 at Southern University). He is also credited with being the first black man to have an opera performed by a "significant" American company (the New York City Opera in 1949). He composed into his late seventies; the Fisk Jubilee Singers performed a piece by him at the Fisk University Centennial Celebration in 1971. He died in Los Angeles.

FURTHER READING

Arvey, Verna. *William Grant Still* (1939).

Haas, R. B., ed. *William Grant Still and the Fusion of Cultures in American Music* (1972; repr. 1995).

Smith, Catherine Parsons. *William Grant Still: A Study in Contradictions* (2000).

Still, Judith Anne, et al. *William Grant Still: A Bio-Bibliography* (1996).

—DANIEL J. LEAB

STOCKTON, BETSEY

(c. 1798–24 Oct. 1865), educator and missionary, was born in slavery of unrecorded parentage. As a child Betsey was given by her owner, Robert Stockton, as a wedding gift to his daughter when she married Reverend Ashbel Green, the president of the College of New Jersey (now Princeton University). Most of Betsey Stockton's early life was passed as a slave domestic in the Green home at Princeton, except for four years that she spent with Green's nephew Nathaniel Todd when she was an adolescent. At Todd's she underwent a period of training intended to instill more piety in her demeanor, which had not been developed in the affectionate, indulgent Green household. Stockton returned to the Green home in 1816 and was baptized in the Presbyterian church at Princeton in 1817 or 1818, having given evidence through speech and deportment of her conversion to Christian ways. At

Betsey Stockton, educator and missionary to Hawaii. Hawaiian Mission Children's Society Library

the time of her baptism Stockton was formally emancipated from slavery, since the Greens were abolitionists who believed that Christian baptism prepared her for freedom. Stockton became very well educated through their tutoring and the use of their enormous private library. So competent did Stockton become that the Greens finally placed her in charge of their entire household, and she remained as a paid domestic and family member.

Stockton often spoke to Green about her wish to journey abroad, possibly to Africa, on a Christian mission. Green introduced her to Charles S. Stewart, a young missionary, newly ordained in 1821, who was about to be sent by the American Board of Commissioners for Foreign Missions (ABCFM) to Hawaii. The ABCFM made special concessions to allow Stockton to join the mission because of her piety and interest in traveling and missionary work. Michael Osborn of the theological seminary at Princeton wrote a recommendation for Stockton, stating that she had a full and complete knowledge of all the Scriptures, the Jewish antiquities, the geography of the holy lands, and the larger catechism in addition to a keen understanding of English composition, literature, and mathematics. In short, she was well qualified for missionary endeavors. Through a special agreement between Green, the Stewarts, and the ABCFM,

she joined the mission both as a domestic in the Stewart household and as a missionary. The agreement stated that although she was to assist Harriet Stewart domestically, Stockton was not to be called upon for menial work "more than any other member of the mission, or this might manifestly render her life servile, and prevent her being employed as a teacher of a school, for which it is hoped that she will be found qualified."

Stockton arrived in Hawaii in April 1823. She was part of the second company of Congregational missionaries sent to the islands to convert Hawaiians to Christianity. Upon their arrival in Honolulu, the company was greeted by an African from Schenectady, Anthony Allen, who was living in Hawaii. Allen presented the new arrivals, possibly because of the presence of Stockton, with gifts of food, including a whole goat for their trip to Lahaina, Maui, where they were stationed.

Stockton distinguished herself in Lahaina by offering education to the common people instead of erecting schools only for the *alii* (chiefs, or nobility). In the past, the Hawaiian chiefs had not allowed the missionaries to teach the commoners. By August 1824, however, the chiefs had determined that the missionaries could teach the lower levels of Hawaiian society as well. Charles Stewart's journal reveals the chiefs' new attitude:

Indeed, till within a few weeks, they (*alii*) have themselves claimed the exclusive benefit of our instructions. But now they expressly declared their intentions to have all their subjects enlightened by the *palapala* (letters or learning), and have accordingly made applications for books to distribute among them. In consequence of this spirit, we have today been permitted to establish a large and regular school among their domestics and dependents.

Stockton's school was formed upon special request from commoners in Lahaina, as Stewart's journal entry of 20 August 1824 revealed:

Now the chiefs have expressed their determination to have instruction in reading and writing extended to the whole population and have only been waiting for books, and an increase in the number of suitably qualified native teachers, to put the resolution, as far as practical, into

effect. A knowledge of this having reached some of the *makaainana*, or farmers of *Lahaina*...including the tenants of our own plantation, application was made by them to us for books and slates, and an instructor; and the first school, consisting of about thirty individuals, ever formed among that class of people, has, within a few days, been established in our enclosure, under the superintendence of B—[Betsey], who is quite familiar with the native tongue.

The missionaries, including Stockton, believed that education among the common people would prove, as it had among the chiefs, "the most effectual means," as Stewart wrote, "of withdrawing them from their idle and vicious habits and of bringing them under the influence of our own teachings in morality and religion." Stewart praised Stockton's efforts: "B—[Betsey] is engaged in a fine school kept by her every afternoon in the chapel adjoining our yard," and she took part in all the social activities of the mission settlement.

In 1825 over 78,000 spelling books had issued from the mission presses, and by 1826, 8,000 Hawaiians had received instruction on Maui. Stockton's efforts to educate the commoners had borne fruit, and the missionary efforts combated drunkenness, adultery, infanticide, gambling, theft, deceit, treachery, death, and what Stewart called "every amusement of dissipation." The missionary and educational efforts that Stockton extended to the masses also had a democratizing effect on the Hawaiians, as, while the chiefly class taxed off most of the food the commoners produced, they could not take away promised salvation. As Stewart remarked of the commoners, "Their only birthright is slavery.... Surely to such, the message of salvation must prove indeed 'glad tidings of great joy.'"

If, after the shortest and most perfect tuition, many are capable of composing neat and intelligent letters to each other, now, almost daily passing from island to island, and from district to district; so far from judging them not susceptible of attainments in the common branches of education, we need not fear to encourage a belief, that some may yet rejoice in the more abstruse researches of philosophy and science. They can be civilized, they can be made to partake, with missions of their fellow-beings, in all the advantages of letters and the arts. Nor is there more doubt, that they can be converted to Christianity.

The Stewarts decided to return to Cooperstown, New York, after two and a half years because of Harriet Stewart's poor health. Stockton accompanied them, leaving native Hawaiian teachers she had trained to take her place. She ran the Stewart household and assisted Harriet Stewart with her children until Harriet Stewart's death in 1830. Stockton continued to care for the Stewart children, perhaps until Charles Stewart remarried in 1835. Venturing forth on her own, she taught at an infant school in Philadelphia, journeyed to Canada where she established a school for Indians along the same lines as the school she had started in Hawaii, and then returned to Princeton to set up a school, which later became the Witherspoon Street Colored School, the culmination of her life's work. She labored there, supported by northern blacks and whites and was committed to abolition in the area, until her death.

She was a strong role model for the less fortunate at every institution she established and administered. At her death, the *Freedom's Journal* of Cooperstown observed, "The superintendent and visitors of the public schools unhestitantly state that, in their inspections, they found no school better trained, better instructed, or with evidence of greater success than hers." Stockton was buried with the Stewart family at Lakewood, and her tombstone attests to that family's kinship with her: "Of African blood and born in slavery she became fitted by education and divine grace, for a life of great usefulness, for many years was a valued missionary at the Sandwich Islands in the family of Rev. C. S. Stewart, and afterwards till her death, a popular and able Principal of Public schools in Philadelphia & Princeton honored and beloved by a large circle of Christian Friends." Betsey Stockton had overcome bondage to distinguish herself as an educator of the disadvantaged and underprivileged.

FURTHER READING

The Hawaiian Mission Children's Society (HMCS) in Honolulu, Hawaii, contains the journal of Charles S. Stewart that describes Stockton's role in Lahaina, Maui. The HMCS collection also includes letters from contemporaries and diaries with references to her contributions.

French, Thomas. *The Missionary Whaleship* (1961).

—BARBARA BENNETT PETERSON

 STOKES, LOUISE (1913–25 Mar. 1978), Olympian in track and field and professional bowler, was born in Malden, Massachusetts, the eldest of six children of William Stokes, a gardener, and Mary Wesley, a domestic worker. Stokes began her running career during her time at Beebe Junior High in Malden when one of her basketball teammates suggested, because of her speed, that she join the local Onteora Track Club, sponsored by William H. Quaine, Malden's park commissioner. At the club, she soon began to excel in the sprints and jumping events.

At Malden High School, where she also played basketball, Louise repeatedly set records in track. She was awarded the James Michael Curley Cup as a junior for outstanding track performance of the year. She set the New England record in the 100 meters, and tied the world record in the standing broad jump, jumping eight feet, five and three-quarter inches. She was also competitive in the high jump. These outstanding performances brought her to the Olympic Trials a year later.

At the 1932 Olympic Trials in Evanston, Illinois, Louise's third-place finish in the 100 meters won her a spot on the women's 400-meter relay team for the Los Angeles Olympic Games, along with Tidye Pickett. Photos of the 1932 Olympic Track team include a determined-looking Stokes in the lineup along with Pickett, but coach George Vreeland selected only white women for the final relay team. Historian A. D. Emerson suggests that "the exclusion of Tidye Pickett and Louise Stokes from the 1932 Olympics remains a pivotal point in Olympic history where politics and racial tensions threatened any future possibilities for black female athletes to compete on a world stage in representing the United States in the Olympic games" (Emerson, 9). The exclusion of Stokes was a questionable call, as she had beaten Mary Carew, who was selected, in a majority of races, and

they had tied for fourth in the Olympic Trials. Furthermore, when the Olympic team stopped in Denver on the way to Los Angeles, Stokes and Pickett were given a room separate from the rest of the team near a service area on an upper floor, and were served dinner in their rooms rather than at the banquet for the team. This blatant exclusion foreshadowed what happened later.

One aspect of the treatment of Stokes and Pickett was no doubt related to the dominant culture's uneasy relationship to women in sports, particularly sports that were considered "masculine" such as track and field. Stereotypical definitions of white femininity prevailed, so that women were considered too weak to participate in track, or there was a stigma if they did. The women's 800-meter run at the 1928 Olympics, after which two untrained women lay down on the field in understandable exhaustion after their run, was the basis for a movement by the International Olympic Committee in 1929 to remove women's track and field from the 1932 Olympics. Participating in track and field was considered unseemly for middle-class white women, and the decision to exclude Stokes and Pickett from the final relay team was perhaps affected on some level by this, as officials may not have wanted to stigmatize the track team further by including women of color. Ironically, Babe Didrikson, who was the standout celebrity of the 1932 Games, but who also suffered from a stigma because of her working-class roots and masculine self-presentation, missed her opportunity for solidarity and made it clear that she did not want black women on the team.

There was enough tension surrounding the selection of the relay team that the NAACP sent a telegram to team captain Jean Shiley in Los Angeles, seeking to ensure fair treatment for Stokes and Pickett. It does seem clear that prevailing racist attitudes and practices combined with stereotypes about femininity to give Stokes and Pickett less than a fair chance. They spent the 1932 Olympics in the bleachers, watching their teammates win the gold medal in the 400-meter relay.

Stokes continued to compete after the 1932 Olympics, winning sprints at distances from 25 to 200 meters, as well as the high jump and broad jump. At the U.S. trials for the 1936 Olympics in Berlin, she placed fifth in the 100 meters but once again made the team as a member of the 400-meter relay. In what must have been devastating to Stokes, history repeated itself when at the Berlin Games, Stokes found she had been replaced by a white runner. Despite the fact that she was not selected to compete in the finals, the town of Malden treated her as a hero with a welcome home parade upon her return.

Stokes planned to try out for the 1940 Olympic Games, but World War II precipitated the cancellation of the Games. She retired from running, working as an elevator operator, and became a professional bowler. She founded the Colored Women's Bowling League in 1941 and was a preeminent bowler for the next thirty years. She married Wilfred Fraser in 1944 and had one son. The New England Amateur Athletic Union, for which she had contributed some of the pioneering performances by black women in track, honored her in 1974 by establishing Louise Fraser Day at Boston University. She continued to be an active leader in community youth sports in Malden and neighboring Medford until her death.

Louise Stokes Fraser was one of the first two African American women to earn a place on the U.S. Olympic team, clearing the way for the 1948 Olympians ALICE COACHMAN and Audrey "Mickey" Patterson Tyler to be the first black Olympic medalists. Her accomplishments mark the beginning of the long history of black female excellence in Olympic track and field.

FURTHER READING

Emerson, A. D. *Olympians against the Wind: The Black American Female Difference* (1999).

Pieroth, Doris H. *Their Day in the Sun: Women of the 1932 Olympics* (1996).

—LESLIE HEYWOOD

STONE, TONI

(21 Jan. 1921–2 Nov. 1996), professional baseball player, was born Marcenia Lyle, one of four children, in West Virginia and spent her childhood in St. Paul, Minnesota. Her father was a barber and her mother a beautician. As a child, Marcenia was attracted to playing all

kinds of sports; she abandoned softball for baseball as a teenager, because she found baseball a faster and more competitive game. She began playing with boys' teams in the St. Paul Catholic league and at one time saved Wheaties box tops so that she could play on teams that the cereal company sponsored across the country.

When the former St. Louis Cardinal manager Gabby Street came to St. Paul to head a baseball school, Marcenia asked for a tryout and kept pestering him until he gave her a chance to play. Street was impressed by her skill and her persistence and invited her to join his baseball school; he even paid for her cleats. Against her parents' wishes, Marcenia continued to pursue baseball after she graduated from St. Paul's Roosevelt High School, playing for a men's semipro team in St. Paul and then moving to San Francisco, where her sister was in the military. In San Francisco, she played for the barnstorming team the Sea Lions and gave herself the name Toni Stone, because, she reported, she thought it sounded like "Tom Boy."

In 1947 JACKIE ROBINSON became the first African American man to play baseball in the major leagues when Branch Rickey signed him to the Brooklyn Dodgers. As Major League Baseball began to integrate, the Negro Leagues deteriorated. More and more fans of the Negro Leagues turned their attention to Robinson and other African American players who followed him into the majors. The Negro Leagues faced financial problems and tried to increase box office revenues with creative marketing that included special exhibition play, comical stunts proceeding games, and raffles.

Stone took advantage of this moment when black baseball was searching for ways to bring more fans through the turnstiles. While she was a serious player with a fierce dedication to the game, others saw her as novelty act. From 1949 to 1953 she played for a string of barnstorming, semipro, and minor league teams in the Negro Leagues. She played for the New Orleans Black Pelicans, the New Orleans Creoles, and the House of David. With increased attention from both fans and front office

Toni Stone displays the form that made her the first woman player in the Negro Leagues. Negro League Baseball Museum

personnel, Stone began to believe that she might become the first woman to play professional baseball. "There was nothing else I was interested in," she told *Ebony*. "I dreamed about it every night."

In 1950 Stone married a former army officer, Aurelious Alberga, a man forty years her senior. Like her parents, Alberga opposed Stone's playing professional baseball. "He would have stopped me if he could," Stone later said. "But he couldn't" (Gregorich, 175). In 1953 Stone received a call from Syd Pollack, owner of the Indianapolis Clowns, a famous Negro Leagues team known for its comical high jinks as well as its superb play. Pollack offered Stone a contract to play second base and told reporters he was signing her not for publicity purposes but because she played a good brand of baseball. Pollack also was looking for a way to increase interest in his team, since he had lost the second baseman HANK AARON to the major leagues the year before. When Pollack asked Stone to play in a skirt, as female players did in the segregated white All-American Girls Professional Baseball League, she refused. She also would not consent to play in shorts and made it clear that she would dress in the same uniforms as her male teammates did.

During the 1953 season Stone hit .243 and played in fifty games. At five feet, seven inches tall and 148 pounds, Stone held her own physically and was noted for being fast on the base paths. She was clocked in the 100-yard dash at eleven seconds. Reporters noted that competitors treated her no differently from male players on the diamond: pitchers occasionally brushed Stone back with throws to her head, charging basemen slid spikes-up when she was covering second. Stone was proud of scars on her left wrist sustained when a runner tried to knock her down at second. "He was out," she noted (*New York Times*).

Not all players welcomed Stone. In reflecting on her career years later, she remembered that some players made it clear that women should not play professional baseball. "They'd tell me to go home and fix my husband some biscuits," she recalled (Gregorich, 174). But Stone stuck it out because she wanted to play and resented that

sexism held her back. "A woman has her dreams, too," she told those who questioned why she stayed. "When you finish high school, they tell a boy to go out and see the world. What do they tell a girl? They tell her to go next door and marry the boy that their families picked for her. It wasn't right. A woman can do many things" (Thomas, 60).

The highlight of Stone's career came during her first season with the Clowns, when she got a single off the legendary pitcher SATCHEL PAIGE during an exhibition game in Omaha, Nebraska. Stone was almost as surprised as Paige and laughed all the way to first base. The clean single over second base was "the happiest moment of my life," she said (Gregorich, 174). In 1954 Pollack sold Stone's contract to the Kansas City Monarchs. That year Pollack added two women players to the Clowns' line-up: the second baseman Connie Morgan and the pitcher Mamie "Peanut" Johnson. Stone drew little playing time in Kansas City. Frustrated with sitting on the bench, Stone wanted the Monarchs' manager, Buck O'Neil, to play her as much as the Clowns' manager, Oscar Charleston, had. "He'd let me get up there and hit," she said of Charleston (Gregorich, 174). But O'Neil did not give her much playing time. At the end of the season, Stone returned to San Francisco, where she worked as a nurse and cared for her ailing husband, who lived another three decades and died at age 103. Not playing professional baseball, she said, "hurt so damn bad I near had a heart attack" (Thomas, 60).

Stone continued to play recreational baseball until her early sixties and, after years of being forgotten by sports historians, she was delighted in 1985 to be inducted into the Women's Sports Foundation International Sports Hall of Fame. She also participated in National Baseball Hall of Fame events in 1991 that honored Negro League ball players. In 1995 a play entitled "Tomboy Stone," written by Roger Nieboer, was performed in St. Paul at the Great American History Theatre.

Toni Stone died of heart failure at age seventy-five in Alameda, California. A baseball field in her hometown of St. Paul was dedicated in her memory in 1997. Stone's lifelong commitment to baseball proved that women have always had the interest and the talent to play

the sport. "Maybe I'll be the first woman to play major league baseball. At least I may be the one who opens the door for others," Stone said hopefully in 1953. A half a century later, her dream has yet to be realized.

FURTHER READING

Berlage, Gai Ingham. *Women in Baseball: The Forgotten History* (1994).

Gregorich, Barbara. *Women at Play: The Story of Women in Baseball* (1993).

"Lady Ball Player: Toni Stone Is First of Sex to Play with Professional Team," *Ebony*, July 1953.

Thomas, Ron. "She Made It a League of Her Own," *Emerge*, May 1996.

Obituary: *New York Times*, 10 Nov. 1996.

—MARTHA ACKMANN

SUBLETT, JOHN WILLIAM. *See* Bubbles, John.

SULLIVAN, LEON HOWARD (16 Oct. 1922– 24 Apr. 2001), Baptist clergyman, civil rights leader, and human rights activist, was born in Charleston, West Virginia, the son of Charles Sullivan, a truck driver, and Helen Trueheart, a domestic. Because his parents were frequently away from home working, Sullivan was reared by his maternal grandmother, Carrie, to whose influence he credited his strong religious faith, firm determination, and lifelong philosophy of self-help.

One particular childhood experience helped inspire Sullivan's passion for social justice. At age eight, he bought a Coke at the local drugstore but was forbidden to sit down by a white clerk, who angrily informed him that blacks were always required to stand. Sullivan recounted this abuse to his grandmother, who encouraged him to help end such prejudicial treatment when he grew up.

Six feet, five inches tall and a gifted athlete, Sullivan received a basketball and football scholarship to the historically black West Virginia State College. When an injury ended his athletic career, he paid for his education by working in a steel mill.

He also became a Baptist preacher at age seventeen and served part time as pastor at two local churches. After earning a BA degree in 1943, Sullivan became assistant minister to ADAM CLAYTON POWELL JR., New York congressman and pastor of the Abyssinian Baptist Church in Harlem. Sullivan oversaw church programs addressing youth issues, crime, and drugs. He also served, at age twenty-two, under A. PHILIP RANDOLPH in the March on Washington movement, an experience that helped shape Sullivan's ideas regarding nonviolent direct action and community mobilization.

In New York, Sullivan met Grace Banks; they married in 1944 and had three children, Howard, Julie, and Hope. In 1945 Sullivan became pastor of the First Baptist Church in South Orange, New Jersey, and began experimenting with new models of church ministry, such as building homes for the poor and lobbying the city for better opportunities for blacks. He also continued his formal education at Union Theological Seminary and Columbia University.

In 1950 Sullivan moved to Zion Baptist Church in downtown Philadelphia, where he served as pastor for thirty-eight years, expanding his congregation from six hundred to more than six thousand members. He was nicknamed "the Lion of Zion" for his powerful preaching style and his intrepid manner of tackling seemingly intractable social issues. In Philadelphia, Sullivan studied the nature of corporate business in America, mainly through his participation in Americans for the Competitive Enterprise System and the Junior Chamber of Commerce. He perceived that in cities with substantial black populations, such as Philadelphia, minority purchasing power was integral to corporate profitability and that organized action by black consumers could thus redirect corporate conduct to socially responsible ends.

In 1958 Sullivan organized a network of four hundred African American preachers who exhorted their congregations to boycott businesses that declined to employ blacks in managerial and professional positions, adopting a slogan used by his mentor, Powell, in Harlem during the Depression: "Don't buy where you don't work." Within four years three hundred Delaware Valley employers adopted fair employment practices as a result of this campaign. This program became the model for the nationwide Operation Breadbasket movement, led by MARTIN LUTHER KING JR. and later by JESSE JACKSON.

Recognizing that "integration without preparation is frustration," Sullivan founded in 1964 a training initiative called Opportunities Industrialization Centers (OICs) to help the poor, including the long-term unemployed, school dropouts, and those with criminal records, develop the skills required for newly opening career possibilities. The first OIC was headquartered in one of the poorest neighborhoods in Philadelphia. Schoolchildren collected pennies to provide financing, and in the early years Sullivan re-mortgaged and then borrowed against his home to meet payroll. Sullivan developed OICs in 140 American cities, and it became the largest employment-training program in the nation.

OIC won the enthusiastic support of President Lyndon Johnson, who regarded it as a vital contribution to the War on Poverty and worthy of federal financial support. Sullivan also opened OICs abroad. Three million people thus far have been prepared by OIC for employment at some twenty thousand companies. Additional Sullivan initiatives created black-owned shopping centers, apartment complexes, assisted living centers, an aerospace manufacturing company, and other facilities, often through modest weekly contributions or investments by members of Zion Baptist Church and other supporters.

In 1971 Sullivan became the first person of color on the board of directors of a major American corporation when he joined General Motors (GM), then the largest company in the world and the largest American employer in South Africa. On his initial visit to South Africa in 1975, Sullivan witnessed first hand the dehumanizing consequences of apartheid. Further, on his return journey he was detained at the Johannesburg airport by the security police, who stripped him to his underwear and menaced him with a .45-caliber pistol. At that moment Sullivan determined to take up personally the challenge of abolishing apartheid through nonviolent, economic measures.

The GM board agreed to Sullivan's unprecedented proposal that the company take the lead in organizing American corporations against apartheid. For two years, Sullivan held private meetings with the leaders of over one hundred companies, although on 1 April 1977 only twelve of them endorsed Sullivan's initial "Principles for U.S. Firms in South Africa." These principles challenged apartheid statutes by requiring workplace racial integration, fair employment practices, training and supervisory positions for blacks and other nonwhites, and eventually improved housing, schooling, recreation, and health facilities for workers. The media dubbed these anti-apartheid measures "the Sullivan Principles," and the name permanently stuck.

Sullivan's principles were expanded five times over eleven years, bringing corporations into increasing conflict with the South African government and ultimately constituting a program of corporate civil disobedience against apartheid within the workplace and in the larger society. At the height of the campaign, 194 American companies subscribed to the principles, representing $500 billion in stocks and investments. This was perhaps the first time in history that companies organized to defy and undermine a nation's laws in order to overturn an unjust system of government.

Sullivan was criticized by some who favored corporate withdrawal from South Africa, but such detractors were generally unaware that Sullivan was continually laboring behind the scenes and conferring with corporate leaders to increase pressure on the South African government. He threatened, for example, to organize a worldwide boycott of South African diamonds. Sullivan endured such criticism in silence, and even weathered numerous death threats, believing that his approach was the best way to avoid a race and ideological war that could engulf all of southern Africa. On 7 May 1985 Sullivan issued a two-year deadline for the South African government to end apartheid or face the economic effects of the departure of American companies. Overriding President Ronald Reagan's veto, the U.S. Congress then passed the omnibus Anti-Apartheid Act of 1986, requiring American corporations to comply with the principles. Some seventy corporations left South Africa when the deadline passed. The South African government repealed the apartheid laws by 1991, and in successive years nonwhites were given the vote, and Nelson Mandela was elected president. Most of the corporations then returned. As a complement to the resistance to apartheid undertaken by South Africans themselves, Sullivan's principles made a unique contribution toward rendering apartheid financially unsustainable and provided models of integration for a new, post-apartheid society.

The dismantling of apartheid allowed Sullivan to devote additional time to other initiatives. In 1983 he had founded the International Foundation for Education and Self-Help (IFESH), a private, nongovernmental organization addressing development issues, primarily in sub-Saharan Africa but also in Latin America and Asia. He moved to Scottsdale, Arizona, the foundation's headquarters, to become more directly involved in its work of building schools, training teachers, educating bankers, promoting agricultural development, and combating HIV/AIDS. He also convened a series of "African–African American Summits" to develop intercontinental strategies regarding Africa's distinctive developmental needs and opportunities. In his last major initiative, Sullivan expanded his original antiapartheid principles into a worldwide code of conduct termed the "Global Sullivan Principles of Social Responsibility" (GSP), which he announced in November 1999 at the United Nations. Seventeen months later, at the time of his death, over three hundred corporations, civic organizations, and academic institutions had endorsed the GSP.

In 1998 Sullivan published an autobiography, *Moving Mountains: The Principles and Purposes of Leon Sullivan*. Three years later, having recovered from leukemia a decade earlier, he succumbed in Scottsdale to a recurrence of the disease. Shortly after his death, family members, friends, and supporters created the Leon H. Sullivan Foundation, headquartered in Washington, D.C., to continue his work.

Sullivan was one of the most honored Americans of his time. In 1963 *Life* magazine named him one of the "100 Outstanding Young Adults in the United States." He received numerous awards, including fifty honorary doctorates and the 1971 Spingarn Award, the NAACP's highest honor for achievement. President George H. W. Bush conferred upon him the Presidential Medal of Freedom, President Bill Clinton presented him with the Eleanor Roosevelt Human Rights Award, and he was several times nominated for the Nobel Peace Prize. In 2000 the city of Charleston dedicated "Leon Sullivan Way," honoring a man who as a child could not even walk down certain streets simply because he was black. Representatives of scores of foreign countries attended his funeral in Arizona and a memorial service at the Zion Baptist Church in Philadelphia.

Sullivan was a relentless innovator who understood that blacks and other oppressed minorities hold in their own hands the economic power to resist injustice and secure political, social, and financial equality. His work went far toward helping corporations understand that their range of responsibilities extends beyond obeying the law and producing profits for shareholders. Through Sullivan's influence, many corporations now recognize their obligations to a more diverse set of "stakeholders," appreciating that addressing the needs of the disadvantaged and actively supporting economic, educational, and social development are not only key elements of responsible corporate conduct, but are also good for business itself.

FURTHER READING

Sullivan's papers are scheduled to be housed in the Library of Congress.

Sullivan, Rev. Leon Howard. *Moving Mountains: The Principles and Purposes of Leon Sullivan* (1998).

A Principled Man: Rev. Leon Sullivan. Marshall University and MotionMasters, 2000.

Obituaries: *New York Times,* 26 Apr. 2001; *Washington Post,* 29 Apr. 2001.

—THOMAS J. WYLY

T

TANNER, BENJAMIN TUCKER (25 Dec. 1835–15 Jan. 1923), African Methodist Episcopal (AME) bishop, was born in Pittsburgh, Pennsylvania, the son of Hugh S. Tanner and Isabel (maiden name unknown). Straitened circumstances forced him to support himself as a part-time barber while studying at Avery College in Allegheny City (now Pittsburgh), Pennsylvania, from 1852 to 1857. But in 1856 his life took a new direction when he converted to Methodism and received a license to preach. He trained at Allegheny and Western Theological Seminary for three years and in 1860 was ordained both deacon and elder in the AME Church. Unable to afford travel expenses to an appointment in Sacramento, California, he served instead as a substitute minister at a Presbyterian church in Washington, D.C. In 1858 he married Sarah Elizabeth Miller; they had seven children, the most famous of whom was HENRY OSSAWA TANNER, who became a painter of international renown.

During the Civil War, Tanner ministered to freedmen in the U.S. Navy. He founded the Alexander Mission on E Street in 1862, the same year he was accepted into the AME Baltimore Conference. Thereafter he was appointed minister to churches in Georgetown (1863–1866) and Baltimore (1866–1867). In 1867 he became principal of the AME school in Frederick, Maryland, and published his first book, *An Apology for African Methodism*, a study of AME beliefs and polity. In 1868 the General Conference made him its chief secretary and editor of its journal, the *Christian Recorder*. He labored for sixteen years in Washington, D.C., in that capacity, developing a large readership and building a distinguished literary career through terse, forceful writing. In 1884 he helped found and served as first editor of the *AME Church Review* quarterly.

In 1888 Tanner was elected bishop by the General Conference. During his first quadrennial assignment as bishop, he supervised AME activities in Canada, Bermuda, and the West Indies. Thereafter he resided primarily in the Northeast, working diligently among constituents in New England, New York, New Jersey, and eastern Pennsylvania. He urged members everywhere to remain loyal to the church because of the strength that it provided. African Americans had risen out of slavery, he reminded listeners, and they still faced a thousand forms of discrimination in their own day. In such conditions only Christian truth gave AME adherents true freedom; the church was God's instrument for producing good works that would endure. He encouraged members to see that the communion and love found within the church gave people the power to overcome human suffering and social ills. In this way he was an early advocate of black unity and self-help.

Tanner took interest in other denominations and in ways of cooperating with them. In 1901 he attended the Third Ecumenical Methodist Conference in London, England, and presented a paper titled "The Elements of Pulpit Eloquence." As early as 1892 he had begun working with other bishops in attempts to unite major black churches. In 1908 he participated in the first Tri-Council of Colored Methodist Bishops, a meeting of representatives from his own denomination, the AME Zion Church, and the Colored ME Church. This black counterpart to the National Council of Churches, founded the same year, allowed for much more cooperation in providing standard hymnals, catechisms, and other liturgical aids. Turner did not succeed in persuading the three groups to merge into a single ecclesiastical body, but he did heighten their commitment to better the social conditions of black citizens while simultaneously meeting their spiritual needs. In 1908 he retired on half pay, the first in his denomination to receive an Episcopal pension. After fifteen more years of occasional preaching and writing, he died in Philadelphia. Tanner's book-length publications include *The Negro's Origin; or, Is He Cursed of God?* (1869), *An Outline of Our History and Government for African Methodist Churchmen* (1884), *Theological Lectures* (1894), and *The Dispensations in the History of the Church, and the Interregnum* (2 vols., 1898, 1899).

FURTHER READING

Seraile, William. *Fire in His Heart: Bishop Benjamin Tucker and the A.M.E. Church* (1999).

Obituaries: *New York Times* and *Philadelphia Public Leader*, 16 Jan. 1923.
—HENRY WARNER BOWDEN

TANNER, HENRY OSSAWA (21 June 1859–25 May 1937), painter and draughtsman, was born in Pittsburgh, Pennsylvania, the son of BENJAMIN TUCKER TANNER, a bishop of the African Methodist Episcopal Church and editor of the *Christian Recorder*, and Sarah Miller. Tanner's parents were strong civil rights advocates; his middle name, Ossawa, was a tribute to the abolitionist John Brown of Osawatomie.

The Tanner family moved in 1868 to Philadelphia, where Henry saw an artist at work in Fairmont Park and "decided on the spot" to become one. His mother encouraged this ambition although his father apprenticed him in the flour business after he graduated valedictorian of the Roberts Vaux Consolidated School for Colored Students in 1877. The latter work proved too strenuous for Tanner, and he became ill. After a convalescence in the Adirondacks, near John Brown's farm, in 1879 he entered the Pennsylvania Academy of Fine Arts and studied under Thomas Eakins and Thomas Hovenden, his mentor. At the academy the

Raised in Philadelphia, Henry Ossawa Tanner studied with American master Thomas Eakins and then left behind the racism of his homeland in 1891 to settle in Paris, where he pursued a long and successful career. Smithsonian Archive

illustrator Joseph Pennell and a group of his friends heaped racial abuse on Tanner, who would not be deterred from his goal, because the academy was "where I had every right to be."

Tanner's professional career began while he was still a student. He made his debut at the Pennsylvania Academy Annual Exhibition in 1880. During this period he specialized in seascape painting, such as *Hazy Morning at Narragansett* (c. 1880; Washington, D.C., private collection), while also rendering memories of his Adirondack sojourn as evinced by *Burnt Pines-Adirondacks* (c. 1880; Hampton University Museum). His tendency toward using overlapping shapes and diagonal lines to render recession into space was announced in these works and can be seen over the whole of Tanner's career. Also, the rich browns, blues, blue-greens, and mauves, with accents of bright red, in the palettes of these pictures remained constant in the artist's oeuvre.

During the mid-1880s Tanner decided to become an animal painter, because they were less numerous than marine painters. A superb example of this genre is *Lion Licking His Paw* (1886;

Allentown Art Museum). His unlocated picture of an elk attacked by wolves, shown at the World's Industrial and Cotton Centennial Exhibition at New Orleans in 1884, prompted the Reverend William J. Simmons to conclude in his book *Men of Mark* (1887): "His pictures take high rank.... [Do not] think he is patronized...through the influence of his father, or because someone takes pity on him, trying to help a colored man to rise. No! It is merit" (185). In addition to easel paintings Tanner provided illustrations for the July 1882 issue of *Our Continent* and the 10 January 1888 issue of *Harper's Young People*.

In 1889 Tanner opened a photography studio in Atlanta, Georgia. After it failed, he taught drawing at Clark College in Atlanta, where he met Bishop and Mrs. Joseph Crane Hartzell, who arranged Tanner's first solo exhibition in Cincinnati in 1890 to help him raise funds for European study. Tanner set sail on 4 January 1891 for Rome, but after arriving in Paris, he decided to remain there and enrolled in the Académie Julian, where his teachers were Jean-Paul Laurens and Jean-Joseph Benjamin-Constant. Tanner was

also influenced by the painter Arthur Fitzwilliam Tait, whose work Tanner had encountered while convalescing in the Adirondacks. He was affected by the works of the artists in the circle of Paul Gauguin at Brittany in the early 1890s and later by the art of Diego Velazquez and El Greco. Tanner did not, however, become an imitator of any of these artists' styles. Tanner made Paris and Trépied, France, his permanent homes for the remainder of his life, although he visited the United States periodically.

Tanner returned to the United States in 1893 and delivered a paper on the achievements of black painters and sculptors at the Congress on Africa held at the World's Columbian Exposition. In his own work he was motivated at this time to concentrate on sober, sympathetic depictions of African American life to offset a history of one-sided comic representations. *The Banjo Lesson* (1893; Hampton University Museum), in which an older man instructs a young lad, is the first painting that can be ascribed to Tanner's new efforts. It was inspired by the poem "A Banjo Song," which PAUL LAURENCE DUNBAR included in his 1892 *Oak and Ivy* collection. Stylistically, Tanner's like for multiple and conflicting light sources sparkle in *Banjo Lesson* and became a characteristic of his manner. He unveiled it at the Paris Salon—the prestigious French annual juried exhibition. The *Banjo Lesson*'s theme of age instructing youth recurs in *The Thankful Poor* (1894; William H. and Camille O. Cosby Collection) and *The Young Sabot Maker* (1895; Washington, D.C., private collection), which conjures up images of Jesus in the carpentry shop of Joseph.

At the turn of the twentieth century Tanner was devoting himself almost exclusively to biblical scenes as a result of both his devout family background and economic opportunities provided by the subject. Tanner's art was also informed by his extensive travels to the Holy Land in 1897 and 1898–1899 and to North Africa in 1908 and 1912. Among his famous works depicting religious scenes are *Resurrection of Lazarus* (1896; Musée d'Orsay, Paris), which was bought by the French government; *Nicodemus Visiting Jesus* (1899; Pennsylvania Academy of the Fine Arts); *Mary* (1900; LaSalle University Art Museum); *Return of the Holy Women* (1904; Cedar

Rapids Art Gallery); *Two Disciples at the Tomb* (1905–1906; Art Institute of Chicago); and *Christ at the Home of Lazarus* (c. 1912; unlocated). Almost all of Tanner's biblical themes are centered around ideas of birth and rebirth, both physically and spiritually. Devoted since childhood to equality for African Americans, Tanner chose these themes because they related to President Abraham Lincoln's Emancipation Proclamation, which promised freedom, or birth and rebirth, to black slaves. This approach was also consistent with Tanner's desire to render sympathetic depictions of African Americans.

Although Tanner made a relatively small number of portraits over his career, those he did paint were of individuals involved with equality and other humane concerns. Notable are the James Whistler–inspired *Portrait of the Artist's Mother* (1897; Riverdale, N.Y., private collection); the formal portrayal of his early supporter and secretary of the Freedman's Air and Southern Education Society, *Joseph Crane Hartzell* (1902; Hampton University Museum); the distinguished civil rights leader Rabbi Stephen Samuel Wise (c. 1909; unlocated); and the illustrious educator *BOOKER T. WASHINGTON* (1917; State Historical Society of Iowa). Stylistically, Tanner's portraits follow the patterns of his subject pictures; however, they are characterized by a very shallow recession into space or a certain flatness. On the other hand, there is a continued consistency of the rich brown, blue, blue-green, and mauve palette spiked with bright reds, while multiple light sources abound. These stylistic characteristics are particularly notable in genre scenes based on Tanner's visits to North Africa, as can be seen in *Flight into Egypt: Palais de Justice, Tangier* (c. 1908; National Museum of American Art) and *Sunlight, Tangier* (c. 1912–1914; Milwaukee Art Museum).

Tanner's mature style, which began around 1914, is characterized stylistically by experiments with the thick buildup of enamel-like surfaces, as in one of his last paintings, *Return from the Crucifixion* (1936; Howard University Gallery of Art). During the early years of World War I, Tanner was so frustrated over the military situation that he was unable to create art. While his artistic production was in abeyance, Tanner was a major figure in the American Red Cross; he worked with convalescing soldiers while serving as assistant director of Farm and Garden Services. His artistic career was resumed on 11 November 1918, Armistice Day, when the American Expeditionary Force authorized Tanner's travel to make sketches of the war front, as represented in *Canteen at the Front* (1918; Washington, D.C., American Red Cross).

Tanner garnered ample recognition in the international art literature of his time from critics for periodicals such as *Revue de l'Art, Gazette des Beaux-Arts, International Studio, Fine Arts Journal*, and *Brush and Pencil*. One contemporary critic stated in 1911, "He makes his home continuously in Paris, where many claim that he is the greatest artist that America has produced" (E. J. Campbell, "Henry O. Tanner's Biblical Pictures," *Fine Arts Journal* 25 [Mar. 1911]: 166). In the final years of his career Tanner's work depicted a preponderance of good-shepherd themes, with which he expressed a strong sense that Jesus watches over his flock and that together man and God overcome evil. Tanner exhibited frequently on both sides of the Atlantic, and several medals from the French Salon jury made him exempt from the jurying process, or *hors concours*, in 1906. He was awarded a gold medal at the 1915 Panama-Pacific Exposition and the prestigious French Cross of the Legion of Honor in 1923. Tanner was elected full academician of the National Academy of Design in 1927.

Tanner's personal life was interwoven with his professional career. In 1899 he married Jessie Macauley Olssen, a white woman from San Francisco who frequently served as his model. They had one child. His wife died in 1925.

Henry O. Tanner was extremely proud of his race but at times lamented the humiliation and sorrow that being black caused him. Moreover, he was sad that he could not live freely in America, the country he loved. It would be impossible to imagine the succeeding generation of African American artists who contributed to the Harlem Renaissance without the example of Tanner's single-minded pursuit of artistic success and his subsequent international recognition. Tanner died in Paris and was buried at Sceaux, Hauts-de-Seine. The U.S. Postal Service issued a commemorative stamp in his honor in 1973.

FURTHER READING

Tanner's papers are in the Archives of American Art, Smithsonian Institution. Valuable information is also included in the Alexander papers at the archives of the University of Pennsylvania.

Mathews, Marcia M. *Henry Ossawa Tanner: American Artist* (1969).
Mosby, Dewey F. *Across Continents and Cultures: The Art and Life of Henry Ossawa Tanner* (1995).
———. *Henry Ossawa Tanner* (1991).

Obituary: *New York Herald Tribune*, 26 May 1937.

—DEWEY FRANKLIN MOSBY

 TAYLOR, MAJOR (26 Nov. 1878–21 June 1932), bicyclist, was born Marshall Walter Taylor in Indianapolis, one of eight children of Gilbert Taylor and Saphronia Kelter, free blacks from Kentucky who moved to Indianapolis after the Civil War. Gilbert, a veteran of the Union Army, became a coachman for a well-to-do white family, the Southards, whose son became Marshall's close friend. According to Taylor's autobiography, he spent his childhood years playing with upper-class white children and was able to have his own bicycle. In his teens Taylor found work in bicycle shops, where his phenomenal trick riding skills attracted crowds and caught the attention of shop owners. They outfitted him in a flashy uniform and nicknamed him "Major," a name that became his trademark for the rest of his life. When Taylor won his first race at age thirteen, Louis D. Munger, a bicycle manufacturer, saw his potential and took the lad under his wing. He remained Taylor's employer, guide, promoter, and confidante until he died in 1929.

Taylor's prime riding years came at a propitious time, coinciding with the development of the modern chain-driven safety bicycle and the pneumatic tire. With the cumbersome high-wheelers gone at last, cycling became the most popular sport in the nation, ahead

Major Taylor, the first African American sports superstar. Indiana State Museum

of baseball, football, basketball, and boxing. The League of American Wheelmen had ten thousand members in 1890 and one hundred thousand eight years later. The winning cyclists of the day were feted and idolized by millions, but the professional side of cycling was lily-white until Taylor came along.

Indianapolis in the 1890s was segregated. Although Taylor had been spared much of the degradation of Jim Crow segregation in his early years, when he began to win racing prizes competing against white riders, he became the target of slurs and threats. In the fall of 1895 Munger and Taylor moved to Worcester, Massachusetts, where Munger established the Worcester Cycle Manufacturing Company and set about grooming Taylor for his spectacular career. Worcester had been a center of abolitionism before the Civil War, and memories of that liberal tradition remained. Taylor was permitted to join the YMCA, where he undertook an intensive bodybuilding program. Three years later, despite threats, boycotts, and prejudice, Taylor won the title of world champion in sprints. He became national champion in 1900 and the first black superstar. He may have made over seventy-five thousand dollars during his career.

Despite his brilliant statistics (seven world records in 1898 alone), Taylor lost many races because of unfair combinations. White riders used the "pocket" technique to block him from breaking away from the pack at the close of a race. His finishing kick was the most spectacular in the world, but he could not use it when he was jammed in by riders on sides and front. Without fully realizing what was happening, Taylor became a symbol of national significance. As the first black athlete to challenge whites successfully in a major professional sport, he became a celebrity, sometimes competing before paying crowds of ten thousand and more. Some whites found it unthinkable for a black man to dominate such an important and lucrative sport, and the League of American Wheelmen split on the race issue, largely because of Taylor.

Bicycle racing offered a variety of contests, ranging from the quarter-mile sprint to the 594-kilometer road race between Paris and Bordeaux. Taylor was a sprint man; in his prime he could beat anyone in the quarter-mile, half-mile, mile, and two-mile races. He once did the mile in one minute and thirty-one seconds from a standing start and in one minute and nineteen seconds from a flying start; both times were world records. Although he seldom entered the longer contests, he did win one seventy-five-mile road race.

The controversy over race that made Taylor the target of bigotry also made him the hottest item on the track. The more he was ganged up on and fouled, the more popular he became with the fans. More than one promoter had to swallow his misgivings and allow Taylor to compete, even though Taylor was not permitted to join either of the main cycling associations. Taylor's manager, William Brady, also managed the white heavyweight boxing champions Jim Corbett and Jim Jeffries.

In 1900 Taylor married Daisy Victoria Morris and purchased a nice house in the tony white neighborhood of Columbus Park. At first they encountered ugly hostility from some of the bigoted residents of the Worcestor community, but eventually most of his neighbors came to take pride in having a celebrity in their midst. He was a faithful member of John Street Baptist Church, he neither drank nor smoked, and he read his Bible every day. Unlike the flamboyant and controversial boxer JACK JOHNSON, Taylor was a model of propriety in the eyes of middle-class whites, and he became wildly popular in central Massachusetts. When the Worcester Coliseum velodrome was built in 1900, he was the main star on opening night and for months to come.

In 1901 Taylor sailed for Europe on a spectacularly successful tour of sixteen cities, during which he successively defeated the national champions of Denmark, Germany, Belgium, England, and Italy, plus other noted racers. Despite his refusal to race on Sundays, he attracted huge crowds, who, even as he was trimming their national champions, cheered for *le nègre volant* ["the flying Negro"], as Robert Coquelle, a French writer and cycling promoter, had dubbed him. Taylor returned to Europe in 1902 and won forty races against the best riders the Europeans could muster. After a third triumphant tour in 1903, Coquelle and Paul Hamelle, in a monograph on Taylor, concluded that he was "the most extraordinary, the most versatile, the most colorful, the most popular cyclist, the champion around whom more legends had gathered than any other and whose life story most resembled a fairy tale" (quoted in Ritchie, 204).

Taylor toured Australia from 1902 to 1904, competing before huge crowds, breaking records, and winning plaudits for his distinctive fluid style, with very little movement of the upper body. After returning to Worcester, he retired from competition to spend more time with his wife and their daughter, Sydney. He became a familiar figure in downtown Worcester at the wheel of his French limousine. In 1907 Taylor was enticed back to Europe. Thirty pounds overweight, he underwent a grueling training schedule that got him back into shape. Despite a slow start, he logged some spectacular wins. He went back in 1908 and 1909, but by then his career was on the wane. He retired permanently from cycling in 1910.

Taylor's life after his retirement went downhill. Although he had been prudent with his money during his racing years, he had no other skills. He invested fifteen thousand dollars in a business venture that flopped. He tried to enter Worcester Polytechnic Institute to study engineering but was turned down, ostensibly because he had no high school degree. His health began to give way, and he may have had an enlarged heart from all those years of training. In the 1920s he came down with a painful case of shingles. With no steady income, he was forced to sell his wife's jewelry and other items that he had purchased in better times. Finally, he had to sell their cherished home, and the family moved into a modest apartment. His wife, who had come from an educated family, went to work as a seamstress. Gradually, she became estranged from Taylor, as did their daughter.

In December 1926 Harry Worcester Smith, a noted sportsman and Taylor's long-time friend, organized an appeal for the old champion. "No citizen who has ever lived in Worcester has made the worldwide fame enjoyed by Major Taylor," Smith wrote to the Worcester *Evening Gazette*. "The black man, racing against white for large purses, fighting combinations of race against race all over the world, wrote his name in flaming letters high in the sky of sportsmanship. None ever shone brighter." The appeal brought in twelve hundred dollars, which surely helped, although it probably was a terrible psychological blow to an intensely proud man to have to accept even that kind of charity.

Taylor's final energies went into his autobiography, published at his own expense as *The Fastest Bicycle Rider in the World: The Story of a Colored Boy's Indomitable Courage and Success against Great Odds* (1929). It is a long, rambling book, filled with details of individual races but not enough information

about Major Taylor, the man. Ill and broke, Taylor went door to door selling his book. His wife left Worcester and went to New York; she never saw Taylor again. In 1930 he, too, left Worcester and headed for Chicago, his car filled with copies of his book. In Chicago he lived at the YMCA, from which he went forth every day to peddle his autobiography. He died in the charity ward of Cook County Hospital and was buried in the pauper's section of the Mount Glenwood Cemetery. The Chicago *Defender*, an African American newspaper, was the only one to note his death.

In 1948 a group of former bicycle racers and black athletes, with the financial help of Frank Schwinn, owner of the Schwinn Bicycle Company, had Taylor reburied in a more fitting place in the cemetery, with an appropriate plaque. But Major Taylor's best epitaph may be taken from the preface to his autobiography: "I am writing my memoirs, however, in the spirit calculated to solicit simple justice, equal rights, and a square deal for the posterity of my downtrodden but brave people, not only in athletic games and sports, but in every honorable game of human endeavor." In 2000, a century after he had become national champion, a campaign was begun in Worcester to raise $250,000 for a statue of Major Taylor, to be placed in front of the Worcester Public Library.

FURTHER READING

A collection of Major Taylor's papers, trophies, and memorabilia is housed at the Indiana State Museum in Indianapolis.

Taylor, Marshall W. *The Fastest Bicycle Rider in the World: The Story of a Colored Boy's Indomitable Courage and Success against Great Odds* (1929, repr. 1972).

Nye, Peter. *Hearts of Lions: The History of American Bicycle Racing* (1988).
Ritchie, Andrew. *Major Taylor: The Extraordinary Career of a Champion Bicycle Racer* (1988).

—ALBERT B. SOUTHWICK

TEMPLE, LEWIS (1800–18 May 1854), blacksmith, abolitionist, and inventor, was born in Richmond, Virginia. Of his parents and formal education, nothing is known; according

to one biographer, he was unable to sign his name. Sometime during the 1820s Temple migrated to the whaling town of New Bedford, Massachusetts, where in 1829 he married Mary Clark, a native of Maryland. In 1830 their first child, Lewis Jr., was born, followed by a daughter, Nancy, in 1832. Some time later, a third child, Mary, was born; she died at age six.

What little is known about Temple suggests a resourceful and principled individual. Whether he escaped Virginia as a slave or left as a freeman is uncertain, but in any case he had a better life in Massachusetts than the one he would have led in Richmond, apparently finding work in New Bedford soon after his arrival. Town records indicate that by 1836 he had established his own whalecraft shop on one of the wharves that serviced ships. An active participant in local affairs, he paid the annual poll tax and was elected vice president of an antislavery organization, the New Bedford–Union Society, established in 1833. In 1847 the middle-aged Temple was arrested and charged with "rioting," after he and three other black men were accused of disrupting a "pro-slavery lecture." New Bedford was, in fact, home to a large African American community. As a prominent resident of the town, he almost certainly aided a number of runaway slaves, including FREDERICK DOUGLASS.

In 1848 Temple invented "Temple's Toggle," which historians of maritime technology have proclaimed as the most important innovation in whaling since the twelfth century. Whalers harvested their prey by first piercing the animal's body with a fluted (barbed) harpoon that was tied to a boat or floating drag. After a period of struggle, the hunters finished off the exhausted whale with a lance. Unfortunately for whalers, however, many whales dislodged traditional harpoons, which were forged from a single piece of iron. Temple's solution was a two-piece harpoon whose external appearance resembled the older, single-piece weapon. Once the Temple harpoon entered the whale, the animal's movements caused the fluted part to pivot on an axle by ninety degrees (i.e., "toggle"), thereby making all but impossible its removal through the surface wound. This simple idea dramatically increased the efficiency of whaling, and in a few years virtually all American harpoonists used the Temple toggle, continuing to do so into the 1950s.

Temple's role in the invention of the toggle harpoon was far more complex than this story suggests, however. European whale hunters had used similar harpoons centuries earlier, although they abandoned the device during the Middle Ages. The toggle subsequently survived in various forms among the Eskimos of Greenland. Curiously, European and American whalers knew of the Eskimo harpoons as early as 1654 but continued to employ single-piece irons. Two centuries later many, if not most, of the half dozen or more blacksmiths in New Bedford probably had heard of the Greenland technology, but Temple took the initiative of translating that knowledge into American form. The Temple toggle also owes its origins to the nearly unique ethnic diversity of the whaling industry. During the early nineteenth century American owners of whaling ships, largely because of the difficulty of recruiting local sailors, began signing on men who hailed from virtually every corner of the world. Although the proportion of African American sailors went into decline after 1830, it is nevertheless possible that Temple learned of Eskimo harpoons from an Eskimo seaman.

After inventing the toggle, Temple lived and worked in New Bedford for six years. Doubtless still active in an abolitionist movement electrified by the Fugitive Slave Act of 1850, he also signed a temperance petition addressed to the town's mayor in 1853. Regrettably, he never attempted to patent his invention, although he lived long enough to witness the whaling industry begin to adopt it almost universally. Nevertheless, he began to achieve a measure of prosperity, partly because he obtained a maintenance contract with the city government. In 1854 he hired a contractor himself, to build a large whalecraft shop.

Temple died under tragic circumstances. During an autumn evening in 1853 he tripped over a plank of wood that city workers had carelessly left behind at a sewer construction site. The injuries ruined him for physical labor and weakened his health. Although Temple petitioned the city

for two thousand dollars in compensation, a favorable decision eluded him until ten days after his death, on 18 May 1854. Although the Common Council ordered the sum to be paid to his estate, for unknown reasons his heirs collected none of it.

FURTHER READING

Grover, Kathryn. *The Fugitive's Gibraltar: Escaping Slaves and Abolitionism in New Bedford, Massachusetts* (2001).

Haber, Louis. *Black Pioneers of Science and Invention* (1970).

Hayden, Robert C. *Eight Black American Inventors* (1972).

James, Portia P. *The Real McCoy: African American Invention and Innovation, 1619–1930* (1989).

Kaplan, Sidney. "Louis Temple and the Hunting of the Whale," *Negro History Bulletin*, Oct. 1953.

—GARY L. FROST

 TERRELL, MARY ELIZA CHURCH (23 Sept. 1863– 24 July 1954), educator and social activist, was born in Memphis, Tennessee, the daughter of Robert Reed Church, a businessman, and Louisa Ayres, a beautician and hair salon owner. Her father, a former slave, used his business acumen to become the first black millionaire in the South.

Mary's educational experiences reflected her privileged background. After completing her elementary education at the Antioch College laboratory school in Yellow Springs, Ohio, she attended the Oberlin Academy (1875–1880) and Oberlin College (1880–1884), earning a BA with a concentration in Classical Languages. While at Oberlin College, she received many honors, including appointment as the freshman class poet, editor of the *Oberlin Review*, and member of the Aeolian Society. It was also at Oberlin that she encountered overt racism, which strengthened her resolve to excel.

After graduation Mary wanted to teach but was persuaded by her father not to work and, instead, to return to Memphis. He considered it inappropriate for a young woman of her social and economic standing to work for wages. A

year later, however, against her father's wishes, she accepted a teaching position at Wilberforce College in Ohio. In 1887 she moved to Washington, D.C., and joined the faculty at the M Street Colored High School (later Dunbar High School). There she met her future husband, Robert Heberton Terrell, chairman of the language department, who later became a municipal judge in Washington.

In 1888 Mary reconciled with her father, who then financed her two years of study and travel in Europe. After much inner searching she decided to return to the United States, understanding that again her race, rather than her deeds, would influence her ability to achieve her goals.

Because Washington's school board would not employ married women, Mary, who had wed Robert Terrell in 1891, was forced to resign her position. Three of her children died in infancy, but one daughter survived, and in 1905 the couple adopted the daughter of Mary's half brother. Mary Terrell had already realized she could not be satisfied with performing only the domestic and social duties expected of a middle-class wife, however. In 1892, when she learned of the lynching of her childhood friend Thomas Moss, she, along with FREDERICK DOUGLASS, requested a personal appointment with President Benjamin Harrison to appeal for his public condemnation of lynching. Anticipating political repercussions, Harrison, as would many presidents succeeding him, refused to honor their appeal.

Moss's lynching in Memphis motivated Terrell to reevaluate her responsibilities as a black woman. She quickly emerged as a committed social activist. In 1892 she helped form the Colored Women's League in Washington. As a founder and the first president of a federation of such organizations, the National Association of Colored Women (NACW), 1896–1901, Terrell's influence extended throughout the nation. As leader of the NACW, an organization that encouraged the development of self-help and social service programs among black women, Terrell was recognized as a leading female spokesperson for African Americans.

Mary Eliza Church Terrell, founder and the first president of the National Association of Colored Women. Library of Congress

During her tenure as the NACW president, she addressed many interests and concerns affecting African Americans, and specifically black women, such as disenfranchisement, segregation in the public sector, economic inequities, and lynching.

Terrell incorporated data on the status of black women in many of her speeches. She earned a reputation as a dynamic speaker who over the course of thirty years addressed audiences throughout the United States and abroad. As a noted advocate for racial and gender equity, Terrell was invited to speak at the 1898 biennial session of the National American Woman Suffrage Association (NAWSA). Because her speech, "The Progress and Problems of Colored Women," was highly praised, she was asked to address a much broader topic, "The Justice of Woman Suffrage," at the 1900 NAWSA biennial session. In spite of the efforts of some white suffragists to exclude black women from the movement, Terrell remained an active suffragist. Even after the ratification of the Nineteenth Amendment, she continued her efforts to ensure that black women would also benefit from the amendment's passage. In 1904, as the only African American delegate, Terrell spoke before the International Council of Women in Berlin. Her speech, given in German, received glowing accolades.

Underlying Terrell's activism was a desire to empower black women as they worked toward inclusion and equity for all African Americans. In the introduction to her autobiography, she stated, "A white woman has only one handicap to overcome—a great one, true, her sex; a colored woman faces two—her sex and her race. A colored man has only one—that of race." Terrell consistently championed causes, programs, and organizations that sought the improvement of the quality of life for black women and, by extension, all African Americans. She was also very active in the national and international arenas of interracial cooperation. Terrell was extremely proud of her years of unpaid service on the Washington, D.C., Board of Education (1895–1901, 1906–1911). The first black woman in the United States to hold such a position, she wrote in her autobiography that she had attempted to "promote the welfare of the pupils, facilitate the work of the teachers and raise the standards."

Terrell was a member of many organizations, including the National Association for the Advancement of Colored People (NAACP), for which she was a charter member of the national branch, and was an ardent worker for the Republican Party. While Terrell was president of the Women's Republican League of Washington, D.C., her organizing skills were recognized by the national party. In 1920 Republican Party officials appointed her director of work among black women in the East. She was reappointed to the same position in 1932.

To ensure that her voice was heard, Terrell became a prolific writer. She is credited with the writing of twenty-six articles and numerous poems and short stories. Her writings appeared in such journals and newspapers as *The North American Review, The Independent, The Crisis, The Journal of Negro History, The Nineteenth Century and After,* and the *Boston Herald.* Racism and its effects upon African Americans and the United States was often the theme of her writings. Her autobiography, *A Colored Woman in a White World,* highlighting her personal struggles against racism, was published in 1940.

During the 1940s and 1950s Terrell's national recognition was enhanced by her efforts to end segregation in the public accommodations of Washington, D.C. Often described as a militant activist during the years just before her death, Terrell joined those who advocated, for the times, more aggressive acts of protest and resistance—boycotts, picket lines, and sit-ins. The organized protest against the Thompson Restaurant in Washington resulted in the 1950 case of the *District of Columbia v. John Thompson*, though it was not until 1953 that segregation in eating facilities was ruled unconstitutional in the nation's capital, upholding 1872–1873 laws prohibiting discrimination against "respectable persons" in restaurants. The Supreme Court's validation of the old laws paved the way for desegregation of restaurants, hotels, and theaters in the District of Columbia.

Throughout her life Terrell's fortitude and vision inspired many to work for the advancement of African Americans. In the black woman's club movement, she motivated middle-class women to use their skills and resources to develop child-care centers, mothers' clubs, and kindergartens for those of lesser means. Convinced that rights for black women were inextricably tied to equal rights for the race, Terrell also promoted woman suffrage, adult education, and job training opportunities. After the death of her husband in 1925, she chose not to remarry. Until her death at her home in Highland Beach, Maryland, Terrell remained a staunch advocate for reform and progress.

FURTHER READING

Mary Church Terrell's papers are housed at the Library of Congress and the Moorland-Spingarn Research Center at Howard University. Significant references to her life's works are also included in various record groups at the Bethune Archives in Washington, D.C.

Terrell, Mary Church. *A Colored Woman in a White World* (1940).
Jones, Beverly. *Quest for Equality: The Life and Writings of Mary Eliza Church Terrell, 1863–1954* (1990).

Obituaries: *New York Times* and *Washington Post*, 29 July 1954.

—CYNTHIA NEVERDON-MORTON

TERRY, LUCY (c. 1730–1821), poet, is generally recognized as the first African American woman to have written a poem, the substance of her documented literary effort. Penned in 1746 but not published until 1855, when it appeared in Josiah Gilbert Holland's *History of Western Massachusetts*, the poem is of greater historical than literary significance. It clearly belied the widely accepted perception that persons of African descent were incapable of mastering the English language or shaping it into imaginative creations.

Terry was a slave in the household of Ebenezer Wells of Deerfield, Massachusetts, where she had been taken after Wells purchased her as a child in Rhode Island. The date of her arrival in the United States and her exact date of birth cannot be determined. Scholars have estimated that she was probably sixteen when her poem, "Bars Fight," was composed. Having been kidnapped in Africa, Terry had been in the United States long enough by 1746 for sanctioned or surreptitious study in English and long enough to read, learn, and imitate forms of poetry to which she had access. Terry married Abijah Prince, who was free, in 1756, at which time he purchased her freedom; the couple had six children. Her husband became a successful landowner and was one of the founders of Sunderland, Vermont. One anecdote recounts that "she successfully argued her own case in a court land dispute"; the case, which reached the U.S. Supreme Court, involved encroachment upon land that Terry and her husband owned. Another anecdote reports her convincing "the authorities at Williams College to admit her son," and yet another refutes this by claiming that she lost her bid to get her son enrolled.

"Bars Fight" might well be the description of a war of words as an actual human battle. Depicting an Indian raid on a Massachusetts settlement in the mid-eighteenth century, the poem recounts in clichéd doggerel the clash between victimized Anglo-Americans and "barbarous" Indians. Terry names Samuel Allen, who "like a hero fout," but his bravery does not prevent the cowardice in some of his fellows ("John Sadler fled across the water") or injury to one Eunice Allen—"And had not her petticoats stopped her, / The awful creatures had not catched her, / And tommy hawked her on the head / And left her on the ground for dead." Aligning herself with the whites, Terry naturally locates the center of humanity with them, thus implying condemnation of the "savage others" who invaded the sacred village inhabited by the "civilized" whites.

In her late eighties, Terry was a familiar sight to folks along the route from Sunderland to Guilford, a thirty-six mile trip she made each year to visit the burial site of her husband, who had died in 1794. Terry died in Sunderland.

Lucy Terry allows us to extend the African American poetic tradition by several years. The next known poet would be JUPITER HAMMON, whose eighty-eight-line poem, "An Evening Thought. Salvation by Christ, with Penetential Cries," was composed in 1760 and published early in 1761. It would be 1773 before PHILLIS WHEATLEY published her first volume of poetry. That Lucy Terry, an enslaved African, wrote a poem in 1746 is one of the strongest confirmations on record that Africans were not mentally deficient, that they could master English, and that they could soar to the inspiration of the muses as effectively as their contemporaries. Her accomplishment, though it might appear minimal by standards of the early twenty-first century, makes Lucy Terry a foremother, an ancestor of the African American literary tradition.

FURTHER READING

Kaplan, Sidney. "Lucy Terry Prince: Vermont Advocate and Poet" in *The Black Presence in the Era of the American Revolution 1770–1800* ed. Sidney Kaplan (1973), 209–11.
Redmond, Eugene. *Drumvoices: The Mission of Afro-American Poetry, A Critical History* (1976).
Robinson, William H, Jr. *Early Black American Poets: Selections with Biographical and Critical Introduction* (1969).

—TRUDIER HARRIS

THOMAS, CLARENCE (23 June 1948–), U.S. Supreme Court justice, was born in Pin Point, Georgia, the son of M. C. Thomas, a maintenance worker, and Leola Anderson,

Clarence Thomas, associate justice of the U. S. Supreme Court nominated by President George Bush in 1991. © Reuters Newmedia Inc./CORBIS

a worker in a crab-and-oyster plant. Two years later M. C. Thomas moved to Philadelphia, leaving his young wife to look after Clarence, their eldest child, Emma Mae, and a son not yet born, who would be named Myers after his maternal grandfather, Myers Anderson. The family struggled. Like most of their neighbors, they lived in a one-room wooden shack with no indoor plumbing, and although Leola Thomas was renowned as the fastest crab-and-oyster packer in town, the meager wages she earned barely covered the needs of a family of four. To make ends meet, she worked extra hours as a domestic.

In 1954 Clarence Thomas entered the first grade at Pin Point's all-black Florence Public School, a few months after the U.S. Supreme Court's landmark school desegregation decision in *Brown v. Board of Education*. White resistance to change, however, ensured that the public schools of Georgia remained segregated throughout the 1950s. When the children were not in school or with their mother at work, Clarence and Myers had free rein to climb the palmettos, maples, and magnolias that towered over Pin Point and to scoop crabs from the banks of nearby marshes. Such idyllic memories may explain Thomas's later insistence that his family was not "poor" and that, unlike the inner cities of the 1980s, Pin Point offered a safe, peaceful, and "positive environment" in which to grow up (Greenya, 27).

Yet Thomas left Pin Point at the age of seven, after their house burned down, and the family moved to a crowded tenement in Savannah. One year later, when Leola Thomas could no longer cope, Myers Anderson adopted his daughter's two sons and provided them with a far more positive environment for future success than their sister would enjoy. While Emma Mae returned to hardscrabble Pin Point to live with an aunt, the boys lived in a comfortable six-room house with indoor plumbing and could depend on Anderson, a successful entrepreneur who ran a home-heating-oil business, to provide financial security. Her brothers might have argued, however, that Emma Mae did not have to endure the onerous tasks required of them by their grandfather, who worked from sunup to sundown and expected at least as much from Clarence and Myers. Though

Thomas later praised his grandfather as the epitome of a hard-driven, self-made entrepreneur, his recollection of Myers Anderson in the early seventies was not quite so fond. He told friends at Yale Law School that if he or his brother even overslept, they were beaten.

Strict discipline was also the rule at the all-black Catholic parochial schools in which Anderson enrolled his grandsons, though the nuns at these institutions provided the Thomas boys with an academically rigorous education as well. Anderson, a Baptist, converted himself and his grandsons to Catholicism and was determined that Clarence enter the priesthood. At first, Thomas shared his grandfather's goal, and in 1964 he was one of the first two African Americans to enter the St. John Vianney Seminary outside Savannah. He excelled academically there and at the Immaculate Conception Seminary in Missouri, which he attended in 1967. But like many student pioneers of desegregation, he struggled socially. By 1968 the racist attitudes of his fellow seminarians convinced Thomas that there were "too many rednecks" at Immaculate Conception, and he abandoned his dream of becoming a priest, transferring to Holy Cross, a Jesuit college in Worcester, Massachusetts, that accepted him under its new affirmative action program.

At Holy Cross, Thomas flirted with the separatist ideas of the Black Power movement, but he was also the only black student on campus to oppose a planned separate dormitory for African Americans. However, when that dorm opened, he moved in, taking with him his white roommate. Thomas also volunteered at a Black Panther–run breakfast program for underprivileged children in Worcester, but he devoted most of his time to his studies, graduating ninth in his class and with honors in English. One day after graduation he married Kathy Ambush, a student at a nearby college, with whom he had one son, Jamal. The couple divorced ten years later.

Thomas's academic progress appears to some as a textbook example of affirmative action. Access to the superior facilities at Holy Cross, along with a dedication to hard work, gave Thomas the grades that enabled him, again under an affirmative action program, to enroll at Yale Law School. By the time he graduated from Yale in 1974, however, Thomas had begun to believe that such programs stigmatized their beneficiaries as less qualified than other students. Still, his first full-time job, as a lawyer working for John C. Danforth, the attorney general of Missouri, was also the consequence of a kind of affirmative action. Danforth, a Yale Law School graduate and a moderate Republican, had gone to his alma mater specifically to recruit a black attorney for his office.

Although he had been an ardent Democrat at Holy Cross and Yale, Thomas switched his allegiance to the Republican Party in the mid-1970s, in part because of the influence of Thomas Sowell, a conservative black economist who opposed federal welfare and affirmative action programs. Thomas's friendship with Jay Parker, a black Republican activist, also furthered his political ambitions. Parker, who notoriously had links to the apartheid regime in South Africa and Central American death squads, was also a confidante of Edwin Meese III, who ran the Republican transition team after Ronald Reagan won the 1980 presidential election. Meese asked Parker to oversee the transition at the Equal Employment Opportunity Commission (EEOC), and Parker recruited Thomas, then an aide to Danforth in the U.S. Senate, to assist him.

In 1981 President Reagan appointed Thomas to serve as the assistant secretary for civil rights in the Department of Education and nine months later nominated him to chair the EEOC, the federal agency responsible for enforcing the nation's civil rights laws. Thomas's eight-year tenure, the longest in the commission's history, was credited with improving the agency's efficiency and morale, although many in the civil rights community criticized him for trying to weaken or even end affirmative action. During Senate hearings on his reappointment as EEOC chief in 1986, however, Thomas stated his personal reservations about affirmative action but

accepted that since the Supreme Court had ruled in favor of such programs, he would uphold such laws. Such pragmatism ensured that only two of the committee's fourteen senators opposed his reappointment.

Indeed, it was Thomas's increasingly outspoken speeches and law review articles, rather than his specific actions as EEOC chief, that earned him the enmity of civil rights leaders. In a well-publicized 1980 interview in the *Atlantic Monthly*, Thomas singled out his own sister to exemplify what he believed were the evils of welfare dependency, claiming that she "gets mad when the mailman is late with her welfare check." (Emma Mae Thomas has rejected this claim, arguing that she was, in fact, employed in a nursing home at the time of her brother's statement and that she had previously gone on welfare to look after their aunt, who had suffered a stroke.) Thomas also made headlines in 1984, when he complained to the *Washington Post* that civil rights leaders preferred to "bitch, bitch, bitch, moan and moan, whine and whine" to the media rather than work on the problems faced by black families. Such blunt critiques raised some hackles, from JESSE JACKSON, among others, but they did not prevent President George Bush from nominating Thomas to the U.S. Circuit Court of Appeals for the District of Columbia in 1989. Several months later the Senate Judiciary Committee voted thirteen to one to confirm his appointment.

President Bush's nomination of Thomas in 1991 to the U.S. Supreme Court proved much more controversial. Although the Bush administration made much of Thomas's personal journey from segregated Pin Point to the federal judiciary, civil rights groups highlighted the nominee's lack of judicial experience. The NAACP, which had not challenged Thomas's previous nominations, eventually opposed him, a major blow to the Bush administration, albeit one that was leavened by opinion polls suggesting that a significant minority of African Americans supported the nominee. Several prominent black businessmen, including JOHN H. JOHNSON, the publisher of *Ebony* magazine, declared their backing for Thomas, as did the

poet MAYA ANGELOU. Like many who defended the nominee, Angelou did so despite her opposition to his record at the EEOC, in the belief that Thomas was "young enough to be won over" to the cause of affirmative action and the goals of the NAACP.

On the eve of the 10 September 1991 Senate hearings on the nomination, most political analysts predicted a tight vote but anticipated that Thomas would be approved. The senators—and the nation at large—could not, however, have anticipated the controversial allegations of Anita Hill, a former aide to Thomas at the Department of Education and the EEOC, who testified to the Senate Judiciary Committee that her boss had sexually harassed her on several occasions. Thomas denied Hill's allegation that he had tormented her with sexual innuendo and had persisted in his graphic descriptions of pornographic movies and boasts about his sexual prowess, even though she had asked him to desist. Indeed, in the glare of the massed ranks of the media and with millions watching on television, the nominee condemned the allegations as part of a cynical attempt to derail his nomination. Using a metaphor that angered many of his black critics but also earned him sympathy among some African Americans, Thomas claimed to be the victim of a "high-tech lynching for uppity blacks" who refused to toe the line with the liberal civil rights establishment.

Hill's allegations and Thomas's denials transformed the hearings. Republicans rallied around the nominee, although some partisans appeared even more interested in casting aspersions on Hill's character and credibility. The judge, for his part, believed that his political opponents and the media had maliciously intruded on his private life, and he resented press coverage that he thought was critical of Virginia Lamp Thomas, whom he had married in 1987 and who was white. Opinion polls taken immediately after Hill's testimony indicated that a majority of both black and white Americans believed the judge, not Hill. Poll data suggesting that southern blacks were particularly supportive of Thomas also persuaded several previously uncommitted southern Democrats to vote for him. On 15 October enough of these Democrats voted for Thomas to secure his confirmation by fifty-two votes to forty-eight.

During the next few months, however, it became clear that the Hill-Thomas hearings had sparked a national debate on the issue of sexual harassment and that public opinion had turned in favor of believing Hill's allegations. The National Organization for Women and other feminist groups were already opposed to Thomas for his declared opposition to affirmative action and for speeches in which he opposed a woman's right to an abortion. The skeptical questioning of Hill by the all-white and all-male Judiciary Committee prompted these groups to mount a crusade against sexual harassment in the workforce and also encouraged several women to run for the U.S. Senate in 1992. One of them, Carol Moseley-Braun, became the first African American woman and the first black Democrat elected to that chamber.

The consistently conservative cast of Justice Thomas's judicial opinions and votes disappointed those who believed that he would have a liberal change of heart once he was on the bench. Even so, in 2002 he received praise from some of his detractors for his efforts to end First Amendment protection of cross burning. On the whole, however, Thomas has proved to be no less determined in his conservative beliefs than his predecessor THURGOOD MARSHALL was in his liberal views. In affirmative action cases such as *Aderand Constructors v. Pena* (1995), Thomas voted with the majority to weaken federal guarantees that minority firms receive a portion of government contracts. Significantly, his opinion noted that his own grandfather had not needed racial preferences to obtain contracts for his fuel business. He was also in the majority in voting rights cases, such as *Shaw v. Reno* (1993), which weakened the use of race in determining the composition of congressional districts. Liberal civil rights advocates have expressed particular hostility to Thomas's position in cases involving the constitutional rights of criminal defendants, notably his dissent in *Hudson v. McMillan* (1992), in which he declared that the beating of a

prisoner by his guards was neither cruel nor unusual punishment.

Justice Thomas and his fellow conservatives on the bench set aside their general disposition to favor states rights in the 2000 presidential election case of *Bush v. Gore*, overturning the Florida Supreme Court's opinion that the state should continue its recount of questionable ballot tallies. That decision gave George W. Bush the presidency and ensured an administration that, like Thomas, opposed affirmative action, favored the death penalty, and sought to limit abortion rights. During his bruising confirmation process in 1991, Thomas's views had appeared wildly radical to many commentators. A decade later those views had entered the mainstream of American politics.

FURTHER READING

Greenya, John. *Silent Justice: The Clarence Thomas Story* (2001).

Mayer, Jane, and Jill Abramson. *Strange Justice: The Selling of Clarence Thomas* (1994).

MORRISON, TONI, ed. *Race-ing Justice, Engendering Power: Essays on Anita Hill, Clarence Thomas, and the Construction of Social Reality* (1992).

Thomas, Andrew Peyton. *Clarence Thomas: A Biography* (2001).

—STEVEN J. NIVEN

THOMAS, VIVIEN THEODORE (29 Aug. 1910–26 Nov. 1985), pioneering cardiovascular surgeon, was born in Lake Providence, Louisiana. In 1912, to avoid the frequent flooding of their river town home, his parents, William Maceo Thomas and Mary Eaton, moved their family to higher ground in Nashville, Tennessee. William, a carpenter and contractor, and Mary, a seamstress, found plenty of work in the prosperous capital, and they were soon able to buy a plot of land and build a house.

Vivien, the youngest of four children, took advantage of Nashville's reputation as an educational center. There was an excellent public school system as well

as several institutions of higher education—including one of only two medical schools in the nation that admitted qualified African Americans. He graduated from high school in 1929. As important to his education as the standard curriculum of languages, mathematics, history, and the sciences was the training he received in carpentry from his father. Studying in the morning and working afternoons and weekends, Thomas earned not only his diploma and craft skills but also a decent wage. He had planned to spend the money he saved from his carpentry work on college tuition. However, the Depression forced him to delay his education plans.

Thomas found a new job at Vanderbilt University in Dr. Alfred Blalock's laboratory. Blalock was researching experimental shock, particularly how muscle injuries cause low blood pressure. Working in this lab under Dr. Joseph Beard, Thomas developed his surgical skills and a deep enthusiasm for laboratory research. In 1930 the collapse of the bank that held all his savings dashed Thomas's hopes for a college education. Blalock persuaded an angry and resentful, and now broke, Vivien Thomas to continue at the lab and work toward a career in research. Over the next decade Thomas remained at the lab, developing his surgical skills until he became an integral member of the expanding laboratory team. In 1940 Blalock accepted an offer to become surgeon in chief and chairman of the Department of Surgery at Johns Hopkins University, and he invited Thomas to go to Baltimore with him. Weighing alternative job possibilities and new family responsibilities—he had married Clara Beatrice Flanders in 1933, and they had had two daughters by 1938—Thomas decided to accept Blalock's offer.

Thomas faced quite an adjustment in moving to Baltimore, including learning how to deal with racial tensions in the hospital. As the only African American scientific researcher at Hopkins, Thomas had to negotiate the prejudices of his colleagues and the hospital complex. His advanced surgical skills, Blalock's support, and the great latitude Blalock gave Thomas in laboratory matters helped him overcome his sensitivity to this situation.

Blalock's team, with Thomas conducting the bulk of the laboratory work, continued their investigation of surgical shock and cardiovascular surgery. In particular, they addressed a World War II phenomenon known as "crush syndrome," in which people who had been crushed under fallen debris suffered high blood pressure and went into shock. Although Thomas's work on this project had attracted the attention of the U.S. government, it was the part he played in researching "blue babies" that earned him his place in the history of medicine.

In 1943 Dr. Helen B. Taussig, a pediatric cardiologist and director of the Cardiac Clinic in the Harriet Lane Home for Invalid Children, approached Blalock concerning heart disease in children. She was especially interested in the problem of blue babies, in whom anatomical abnormalities of the heart result in an insufficient amount of oxygen in the blood, giving a bluish tint to the complexion.

Drawing on Taussig's extensive clinical and autopsy observations and her large collection of defective hearts, Thomas and Blalock organized a research protocol. Applying their shock work to this new problem, Thomas successfully recreated the heart defect in dogs. Reversing the procedure, he discovered that by rerouting an artery to send the blood through the lungs a second time he could increase the amount of oxygen in the blood stream. All that remained was the daunting move to use their technique on a human patient. After training himself in Thomas's technique, Blalock preformed the first blue baby operation—with Thomas literally standing over his shoulder—on a very young girl named Eileen. It was a success, and her rapid recovery attracted the world's attention, drawing patients from around the nation and Europe. In 1950 the Blalock team administered the 1,000th blue baby treatment.

A crucial member of the laboratory, Thomas did not receive public recognition for his research until much later. Only after twenty years did he find himself listed as a collaborator on a Blalock publication. Even though Blalock eventually persuaded the hospital to increase Thomas's substandard pay, Thomas was

forced to supplement his income by selling medical supplies to Baltimore's African American physicians. Over the next three decades Thomas matured as a scientist and administrator as the laboratory expanded in size and scope. Under a series of laboratory directors and as collaborator with an even larger number of surgical research investigators and medical students, he made additional significant contributions to cardiac research.

After working in the background for nearly thirty years, Thomas finally began to receive the recognition he was due. In 1969 the physicians he had collaborated with since 1941 paid him the honor of commissioning his portrait. Still hanging in the Blalock Lobby of the Johns Hopkins Hospital next to Blalock's, it is a testament to Thomas's influence. In 1976 the University of Maryland at College Park awarded Thomas an honorary doctor of science degree. That same year the Johns Hopkins University presented him with an honorary doctor of law degree and appointed him to the faculty as Instructor of Surgery. He retired in 1979, and, after being ill for several months, died in Baltimore in 1985.

FURTHER READING

Thomas's papers are located at the Alan Mason Chesney Medical Archives of the Johns Hopkins Medical Institutions.

Thomas, Vivien. *Pioneering Research in Surgical Shock and Cardiovascular Surgery: Vivien Thomas and His Work with Alfred Blalock* (1985), republished as *Partners of the Heart: Vivien Thomas and His Work with Alfred Blalock: An Autobiography* (1997).

Harvey, A. McGehee. *Adventures in Medical Research: A Century of Discovery at Johns Hopkins* (1976).

Obituary: *News American* and *Baltimore Sun*, 27 Nov. 1985.

—LLOYD ACKERT

THOMPSON, ERA BELL (10 Aug. 1906–30 Dec. 1986), author and editor, was born in Des Moines, Iowa, the daughter of Stewart C. Thompson and Mary Logan. In 1914 she moved with her family to Driscoll,

North Dakota, where her father was a farmer and, from 1917 to 1921, a private messenger for Governor Lynn Frazier during legislative sessions. After moving to Bismarck in 1920, her father operated a secondhand store, and when he died in 1928, Era Thompson briefly operated the store to pay off his debts.

Thompson attended the University of North Dakota from 1925 until she was forced to drop out of college in 1927, owing to illness. She wrote for the campus newspaper and excelled in athletics, establishing five state and tying two national intercollegiate women's track records. In 1930, having won twenty-five dollars in a contest to name a bedspring ("King Koil"), she used the money to visit friends in Grand Forks, North Dakota. There she met the Reverend Robert E. O'Brian, a Methodist pastor, who later became president of Morningside College. Thompson moved with him and his family to Sioux City, Iowa. A recipient of a Wesleyan Service Guild Scholarship (1931), she graduated from Morningside College in 1933 with a BA in Social Science. While a student, she wrote humor and sports columns for the campus newspaper and won a sweater in athletics.

Thompson moved to Chicago in 1933 and found that the only jobs available were doing housework. "It didn't help to tell people I was a college graduate," she recalled. She moved from housework to the Illinois Occupational Survey to the Works Progress Administration, where she demonstrated her continued journalistic ambitions by publishing an in-house newspaper at a WPA job. Thompson did postgraduate study at the Northwestern University Medill School of Journalism in 1938 and 1940 while continuing to work at her WPA job. From 1942 to 1947 she was an interviewer with the U.S. and Illinois Employment Service. "After ten years' experience in Chicago, with and without jobs, it is a pleasure to be on the other side of the desk, on the giving side instead of the asking," she wrote at that time.

In 1945 she received a Newberry Library fellowship to write her autobiography. *American Daughter*, which emphasized her North Dakota childhood, was published in 1946 and reprinted in 1967 and 1986. Thompson wrote with warmth and good humor about her early life in a predominantly white state and about her eventual discovery of black history and culture. The book is positive and optimistic, characteristics the author maintained throughout her life. In the preface to the 1967 edition, Thompson wrote, "Usually an autobiography is written near the end of a long and distinguished career, but not taking any chances, I wrote mine first, then began to live."

Thompson joined the Johnson Publishing Company, in Chicago, as associate editor of *Negro Digest* in 1947; she served as co-managing editor of *Ebony* magazine from 1951 to 1964 and as international editor from 1964 until her death, although she was semiretired after 1970. While she was with *Ebony* she wrote more than forty bylined articles. Thompson traveled widely, visiting 124 countries on six continents. "I spend two or three months in a country before doing any writing about it, until I have had extensive interviews with hundreds of people and have the 'feel' of the country," she told a newspaper interviewer in 1966. *Africa, Land of My Father*, based on a tour of eighteen African countries, was published in 1954.

As an African American female journalist, Thompson was a pioneer. "I wanted to be a journalist," she told an interviewer in 1966. "There wasn't anyone to tell me there weren't any opportunities for a Negro in journalism, so I went ahead and prepared myself for that career." Herbert Nipson, with whom she worked as comanaging editor of *Ebony*, described her as "a very independent person who worked and fought for women's rights long before it became a national issue." A senior *Ebony* editor, Lerone Bennett Jr., said Thompson "opened the paths for women at the management level for journalists in this country."

Thompson also worked to foster greater understanding between the races and to break down the barriers of prejudice. She closed her autobiography optimistically, declaring, "The chasm is growing narrower. When it closes, my feet will rest on a united America." Although she saw the chasm widen at times, she remained confident for most of her life that, as she wrote in 1946, "most Americans are fair; that my people and your people can work together

and live together in peace and happiness, if they but have the opportunity to know and understand each other." Her background gave her a unique perspective that she used to promote racial understanding. Her books and articles provided insight on racial attitudes in various societies. A two-part series on racial "amalgamation" in Brazil (1965) revealed the complexities of racial barriers in that country. *White on Black: The Views of Twenty-two White Americans on the Negro* (1963), which she coedited, traced the changes in attitude witnessed in *Ebony* over the period 1950–1963.

Thompson received two honorary degrees and the Distinguished Alumni Award from Morningside College (1974). Other honors included the Society of Midland Authors Patron Saints Award (1968) and the Theodore Roosevelt Roughrider Award bestowed by the state of North Dakota (1976). She was one of fifty black women featured in Women of Courage, an exhibit at the Chicago Public Library's Cultural Center in February 1986. She died at her home in Chicago. She had never married.

FURTHER READING

Thompson's papers are in the Carter G. Woodson Library, Chicago.

Thompson, Era Bell. *American Daughter* (1945, repr. 1986).

Anderson, Kathie Ryckman. "Era Bell Thompson: A North Dakota Daughter," *North Dakota History* 49 (Fall 1982).

Obituaries: *Chicago Tribune* and *Chicago Defender*, 31 Dec. 1986; *Chicago Sun-Times*, 1 Jan. 1987

—GERALD G. NEWBORG

THOMPSON, JOHN

(1812–?), fugitive slave, memoirist, and sailor, was born into slavery on the Wagar plantation in southern Maryland, the son of two field slaves whose names remain unknown. Although there is little information about Thompson's life beyond his memoirs, his descriptions of his experiences in slavery as well as his

adventures as a black seaman are important contributions to our knowledge of both those worlds.

John Thompson's recollections of his early years are vague at best. His realization that he was a slave came at age six, when he witnessed the sale of his oldest sister. Even at that early age, as Thompson recounted in his memoirs, he was engaged in backbreaking work in the corn, wheat, and tobacco fields of the Wagar plantations. Like many slave-narrative authors, including HARRIET JACOBS, HENRY BIBB, SOLOMON NORTHUP, WILLIAM PARKER, SOLOMON BAYLEY, JAMES MARS, and WILLIAM GRIMES, Thompson stressed the arbitrary violence of daily life and the dehumanizing effects of slavery on both slave and master. His early memories are replete with acts of barbarism inflicted on the slave population by members of the Wagar family, both children and adults.

The most important event of Thompson's youth came when he was assigned to carry the lunches of two young members of the Wagar clan to school each morning. Thompson remarked to one of the children, Henry Ashton, that he wanted to learn to read. Young Ashton volunteered to give him lessons, despite Thompson's warnings that Ashton's uncle, John Wagar, would object. For the next two years Henry taught Thompson from his own reading and spelling books. They would often leave early for school and then take advantage of the cover offered by the wooded terrain in the region. By the time the lessons ended two years later, John Thompson had mastered the rudiments of reading and writing. Thompson remarked that his new skills changed his life by allowing him access to the teachings of the Holy Bible. But they also made him a subversive influence on the slave culture of the Old South. Later in his life, the skills that contributed to his religious awakening also led to his decision to flee to the North.

Central to Thompson's narrative are the role of religion in the slave quarters and the shifting attitudes of the planter class to the upsurge in slave religiosity. Planter society in southern Maryland, according to Thompson, was predominantly Catholic or Episcopalian. By the

1820s new denominations were organizing meetings and making inroads in the slave quarters. The Methodists and Baptists used their plainspoken theology, revival techniques, and democratic ecclesiastical structures to win many slave converts. Thompson was especially enamored of Methodism, about which he wrote in ecstatic terms. In those years, however, the fervor generated by the Methodist "meetings" caused great anxiety in the hearts and minds of slaveholders, though they were loath to outlaw the denominations outright. Laws and ordinances were passed to regulate the movement and gathering of slaves, especially on Sundays. To be outside the slave quarters after dark was punishable by flogging or worse. Thompson claimed that the Wagar family went so far as to purchase a slave whose main talent was playing the fiddle, believing that music and dancing were safer emotional outlets for the enthusiasm of the slaves.

Interestingly, there was a noticeable shift in the minds of those Maryland tidewater planters concerning the influence of religion among the slaves. By the middle 1830s planters financed the construction of churches and the formation of slave congregations. They also advocated the preaching of a theology of submission among slaves. Religion became yet another mechanism of social control in slave society. Thompson's writing demonstrates that those beliefs were a double-edged sword. Slaves were apt to interpret Christian teaching in ways that helped them to endure the hardships of slavery and to craft a worldview of resistance and hope. When he fled the South, Thompson was aided along the way by his own faith as well as by other people of faith who provided the informal network that facilitated his escape.

Thompson's faith was not the only aspect of his life that proved subversive to the slave system. As he grew older, his literacy became another source of trouble and the inadvertent cause of his own growing awareness of his debased station in life. He claimed that for years he secretly carried with him a newspaper article containing an 1830 speech by John Quincy Adams, which served as an inspiration to him while he was in bondage. When it was accidentally discovered that he possessed the ability to read and write, the news spread among local slaveholders like wildfire. Local constables and magistrates instructed slave patrols to pay special attention to Thompson. On two occasions he was arrested on fabricated charges of writing "passes" for escaped slaves. In fact, it was that charge to which Thompson attributed his own escape. When three of Thompson's slave acquaintances disappeared one evening, the local magistrate put a three-hundred-dollar bounty on his head, prompting Thompson to flee northward.

Thompson's narrative does not end when he gains his freedom. Within a year of crossing into Pennsylvania, he made his way first to Philadelphia, where he continued to hone his reading and writing skills in night school, and finally to New Bedford, Massachusetts. New Bedford was the center of the American whaling industry and home to an estimated seven hundred fugitive slaves and free blacks, including LEWIS TEMPLE, who established his own whalecraft shop in the 1830s. Many fugitive slaves found places on whaling crews, and Thompson, too, looked to whaling as an effective means of evading the slave catchers who had dogged his path. He persuaded a captain preparing for a long journey to take him on as a steward.

Thompson learned the basics of keeping a ship's mess from another fugitive slave in New Bedford. Even after it was discovered that he had misrepresented his skills, the captain took pity on him, loaned him a cookbook, and gave him a few cursory lessons in the preparation of breads and pastries. Thus began a two-year voyage that very nearly took the fugitive slave around the world. The *Milwood* sailed along the Outer Banks of Newfoundland, south along the coast of Africa, around the Cape of Good Hope to Madagascar, into the Indian Ocean, and as far as New Zealand before it returned to New Bedford. Thompson's memoir provides an in-depth description of nineteenth-century whaling practices. He was also a keen observer of the many peoples and cultures that he encountered along the way. He toured a mosque at prayer time and watched conflicts arising from a civil war in the Comoros islands. By the time of his return to the United States, Thompson was a tested seaman and cosmopolitan world traveler.

The scarcity of sources for Thompson's life is certainly frustrating to the historian, but the story he left behind is a treasure trove of information about both the Underground Railroad, made famous by HARRIET TUBMAN, and the "maritime underground railroad," which enabled seafaring fugitives like MOSES ROPER to escape to freedom.

FURTHER READING

Thompson, John. *The Life of John Thompson, A Fugitive Slave; Containing His History of 25 Years in Bondage, and His Providential Escape* (1856).

Cecelski, David S. "The Shores of Freedom: The Maritime Underground Railroad in North Carolina, 1800–1861," *North Carolina Historical Review* 71 (April 1994): 174–206.

Grover, Kathryn. *The Fugitive's Gibraltar: Escaping Slaves and Abolitionism in New Bedford, Massachusetts* (2001).

Mathews, Donald G. *Slavery and Methodism: A Chapter in American Morality, 1780–1845* (1965).

—MARK ANDREW HUDDLE

THURMAN, HOWARD W. (18 Nov. 1899?–10 Apr. 1981), theologian and mystic, was born Howard Washington Thurman in Daytona, Florida, the second of three children of Saul Solomon Thurman, who laid railroad track, and Alice Ambrose, a domestic worker. Most sources date his birth year as 1900; the most recent collection of his works gives 1899. Thurman was seven when his father died. Other than his mother, the most influential person upon Thurman's childhood was his grandmother, Nancy Ambrose, a former slave and midwife who helped raise Howard and his two sisters. Thurman remembered her as a devout and strong woman who bolstered the children's self-esteem by teaching them the lesson she had learned from a slave preacher years before, "Remember, you aren't slaves, you aren't niggers, you are God's children" (Thurman, 21).

Walking along the seashore as a child, Thurman had a mystical experience of the unity of all living things and of himself as bound up with nature. He regarded this experience as one of the defining moments of his life, a touchstone of integrity and stability.

Thurman began high school in 1915 at the Florida Baptist Academy in Jacksonville. He graduated as valedictorian of his class and qualified for a tuition scholarship to Morehouse College in Atlanta, which he entered in 1919. There he became friends with his debating coach, BENJAMIN MAYS, studied with E. FRANKLIN FRAZIER, and majored in economics. The intellectual breadth and self-confident leadership of Morehouse president JOHN HOPE and dean Samuel Howard Archer left a lasting impression.

In his senior year, Thurman declined an invitation to teach at Morehouse and applied to Newton Theological Seminary in Massachusetts to study religion, only to learn that Newton did not admit black students. In 1923 Thurman entered Rochester Seminary in New York, living for the first time in a totally white world. His mentor at Rochester, George Cross, recognized Thurman's intellectual and spiritual gifts and urged him to devote himself to "the timeless issues of the human spirit" instead of becoming absorbed in the struggle for civil rights (Thurman, 60).

After graduating from Rochester in 1926, Thurman married Kate Kelley, a social worker, and moved to Oberlin, Ohio, to serve as pastor of Mt. Zion Baptist Church. At Oberlin, Thurman began to feel a connection between his own inner life of prayer and the needs of his congregants. His sermons became more reflective and meditative, less informational, as he sought to communicate on a deeper level. These explorations of the inner spirit attracted a steady stream of white visitors.

Thurman came across a small book, *Finding the Trail of Life* (1926), by the Quaker mystic Rufus Jones and immediately recognized a kindred spirit. Jones's emphasis on religious experience so impressed Thurman that he began a program of independent study at Haverford College in Philadelphia, where Jones taught Philosophy of Religion. He read the classics of Christian spirituality, participated in seminars and weekly conferences with Jones, and occasionally attended Quaker meetings. Thurman's childhood intuition of the unity of all being, his sensitivity to nature, and his growing conviction that spiritual experience is the ground of wholeness and community were confirmed by his courses in mysticism and by his personal encounters with Jones.

Returning south later that year, Thurman took up a joint position teaching religion at Morehouse and the Bible as literature at Spelman College, also in Atlanta. A series of talks on the spirituals allowed him to reflect upon the sources of African American spirituality and eventually resulted in *Deep River* (1945), one of his most important books. He enjoyed teaching but found his greatest satisfaction in spiritual counseling. In 1932 his wife Kate contracted tuberculosis and died. Grieving, and exhausted by his teaching and pastoral duties, Thurman sailed for Europe, seeking restoration and direction.

In 1932 MORDECAI JOHNSON, president of Howard University, appointed Thurman as a professor in the School of Religion. That same year, Thurman remarried. His wife, Sue Bailey, a collegiate secretary for the YWCA, was a graduate of Spelman. In 1935 Thurman and his wife accepted an invitation to travel to India on a goodwill visit sponsored by the Christian Student Movement and the International Committee of the YMCA-YWCA. The trip proved to be a catalyst for the vocations of both Thurmans.

In India the Thurmans had a three-hour conversation with Mahatma Gandhi, who questioned them about racial discrimination among American Christians and asked them to sing for him the slave spiritual "Were You There when They Crucified My Lord?" which he deeply admired because "it got at the universal human experience under the healing wings of suffering" (Thurman, 134). Attacked by a Hindu lawyer for his allegiance to Christianity, a religion that historically enslaved and oppressed dark-skinned peoples, Thurman responded by distinguishing the religion of Jesus, which supported the oppressed, from Christianity, which often supported discrimination and oppression. Elaborating this theme most fully in *Jesus and the Disinherited* (1949) and *The Luminous Darkness* (1965), Thurman claimed that Jesus, as a member of an oppressed and rejected minority, identifies with the disinherited and offers to them the realization that they are of infinite value as children of God.

A daylong encounter with Kshiti Mohan Singh, a scholar of Hinduism, conversation with the poet Rabindranath Tagore, visits to Hindu temples, and a visionary experience at the Khyber Pass inspired Thurman to seek a religious fellowship that could transcend racial barriers by emphasizing the commonality of spiritual experience.

His appointment as dean of Rankin Chapel at Howard in 1936 increased Thurman's national reputation as a preacher and teacher of extraordinary talent. Experimenting with worship, he introduced dramatic tableaux and liturgical dance to the chapel's vespers service. In 1943 he received a letter from Alfred Fisk, a white Presbyterian minister and philosophy professor, seeking a black seminarian or young minister to fill a part-time position as co-pastor of an interracial congregation in San Francisco. Thurman interpreted Fisk's letter as a providential call. Risking financial security, he took leave from his position at Howard and moved to San Francisco with his wife and two daughters.

In 1944 Fisk and Thurman became cofounders and co-pastors of the Church for the Fellowship of All Peoples, a community integrated in both leadership and membership, and dedicated to the ideal that religious experience must unite rather than divide. Services at the church included meditation and reflective silence and celebrated the variety of cultures represented in the congregation. Church members pledged themselves to a statement of commitment, instead of a traditional creed. The congregation decided to forego denominational ties that might impose doctrinal limits on inclusiveness and chose not to locate in a black neighborhood to avoid becoming a black-only church. In *Footsteps of a Dream* (1959), an account of the origin of Fellowship Church, Thurman acknowledged that the logic of his position on interracial community required the eventual demise of the separate black church.

Supporters from around the nation (including Eleanor Roosevelt) joined a network of associate members to further the Fellowship ideal. In 1946 Fisk returned to full-time teaching and Thurman became the senior pastor of Fellowship Church. He traveled extensively, lecturing and preaching to support the church and to spread news of its vision of interracial and interfaith community. Books of sermons and meditations transmitted his ideas to a far larger reading public.

In 1953 Thurman left Fellowship Church to become dean of Marsh Chapel at Boston University. He continued to preach, lecture, and write on behalf of ecumenical and interracial cooperation, stressing his conviction that the search for community is embedded in the very fabric or structure of life itself. He retired in 1965. Returning to San Francisco, he continued to write and lecture, while he chaired the Howard Thurman Educational Trust, a charitable and educational foundation. Several of his most important works were published in these years, including *The Search for Common Ground* (1971) and his autobiography, *With Head and Heart* (1979). After his death in 1981, the trust continued to make available Thurman's books and taped sermons to a worldwide audience. Over one hundred Howard Thurman listening rooms located in the United States, Asia, Africa, and Europe enabled new generations to hear his voice.

Thurman's influence, although considerable, was more personal than institutional. The liberal character of his theology, which emphasized spiritual experience over church doctrine, and ecumenical fellowship over denominational tradition, limited the impact of his personal charisma upon institutional change. To those who criticized him for not leading a social movement, like a Gandhi or a MARTIN LUTHER KING JR., Thurman responded that he was not a movement man; that his gift was to articulate the truth of universal spiritual experience. He chose to lead by example and by offering counsel behind the scenes as a board member for the Fellowship of Reconciliation, the Congress of Racial Equality (CORE), and the National Association for the Advancement of Colored People (NAACP). WHITNEY YOUNG, VERNON JORDAN, Lerone Bennett, Nathan Huggins, and Martin Luther King Jr. were a few of the better-known individuals among many who said they were influenced by Thurman's life and words.

Most of Thurman's books have been reprinted, and a three-volume edition of his papers is currently in preparation. Articles, dissertations, and monographs about his thought have appeared steadily since his death. The Howard Washington Thurman National Memorial is located at Morehouse and contains the remains of Howard and Sue Bailey Thurman.

FURTHER READING

Howard Thurman's papers are housed in the Department of Special Collections at Boston University. The Howard Thurman Papers Project is at Morehouse College.

Thurman, Howard. *With Head and Heart: The Autobiography of Howard Thurman* (1979).

Makechnie, George K. *Howard Thurman: His Enduring Dream* (1988).

Yates, Elizabeth. *Howard Thurman: Portrait of a Practical Dreamer* (1964).

—ALBERT J. RABOTEAU

THURMAN, WALLACE

(16 Aug. 1902–21 Dec. 1934), Harlem Renaissance writer and editor, was born in Salt Lake City, Utah, the son of Oscar Thurman and Beulah Jackson. His father left the family while Wallace was young, and his mother remarried several times, possibly contributing to his lifelong feelings of insecurity. Thurman's lifetime struggle with ill health began as a child, and his fragile constitution and nervous disposition led him to become a voracious reader with literary aspirations. Thurman entered the University of Utah in 1919, but he quickly transferred to the University of Southern California, where he studied for entrance into medical school until 1923. After leaving college, Thurman worked in a post office to support himself while he wrote a column for a black newspaper and edited *Outlet* magazine. In the fall of 1925 Thurman journeyed to Harlem, where he worked for meals in various capacities for Theophilus Lewis, editor of *Looking Glass*, whose recommendation resulted in a position as managing editor for the *Messenger*. Thurman used his skills in the publishing industry to support his artistic endeavors, and he later moved to the white magazine *World Tomorrow* as circulation manager. Eventually he became editor in chief at the publishing firm of Macaulay Company.

Thurman's first priority, however, was always art, and his most noteworthy contribution to the Harlem Renaissance was his publication in 1926 of the short-lived magazine *Fire!!* Although *Fire!!* was shakily financed by contributions from its own editorial collective, its impact went beyond its meager circulation. Through the magazine, Thurman established himself as the galvanizing force behind the younger generation of Harlem Renaissance writers, such as ZORA NEALE HURSTON and LANGSTON HUGHES, who wished to be freed from what they perceived as the propagandistic motivations and thematic limitations advocated by older black critics such as W. E. B. DU BOIS and ALAIN LOCKE. These critics, as well as much of the black press, reacted negatively to the journal, claiming that its content was too lascivious and that the journal gloried in images of dissipated black working-class life instead of glorifying the respectable black middle classes. In the aftermath of the commercial failure of *Fire!!*, Thurman began another journal, *Harlem*, that was less controversial among critics and less confrontational with its readers. It specialized in short fiction and theater and book reviews and sought to provide its readers with a guide to Harlem's activities and attractions. This magazine also lasted one issue.

Despite his homosexual identity Thurman married Louise Thompson in 1928, shortly before his 1929 theatrical success, *Harlem*. The couple had no children. Cowritten with William Jourdan Rapp, *Harlem* dealt with the topic of southern transplants adjusting to life in the black urban metropolis. Based on Thurman's short story "Cordelia the Crude" in *Fire!!*, the play dealt with black urban realities such as male unemployment and it introduced white theatergoers to the Harlem rent parties and the numbers racket. It was to have been the first part of a trilogy, coauthored with Rapp, titled *Black Belt*. The second play in the trilogy, *Jeremiah the Magnificent*, dealt evenhandedly with the MARCUS GARVEY phenomenon, yet the play was never produced. The final play, *Black Cinderella*, explored intraracial prejudice but remained unfinished, possibly because the authors were discouraged by their inability to stage *Jeremiah the Magnificent* or to interest Hollywood in *Harlem*.

In 1929 Thurman published his first novel, *The Blacker the Berry*, to mixed reviews. The novel tells the story of Emma Lou Morgan, a dark-skinned black woman whose obsession with light skin (or internalized self-hatred) results repeatedly in personal misfortune. Thurman deftly investigated the many ironies of this situation, as middle-class Emma Lou's own prejudice against dark-skinned working-class blacks remains disconnected in her own mind from the unjust social snobbery that she encounters from the mulatto society whose social circle she covets. In 1932 Thurman published a satirical roman à clef, *The Infants of Spring*. This novel offered a somewhat grim prognosis for the lasting achievements of the Harlem Renaissance. Thurman portrayed the young black artists in the novel as hampered by the suffocating management of older black critics, the faddish attention of a white audience, and their own bloated egos. Thurman evinced concern for the fate of talented if untrained artists within a racially charged milieu that simultaneously inflated their accomplishments while circumscribing their significance. He also explored the difficulties inherent in trying to negotiate the opposite demands of art as racial propaganda and art as transcending race. In that same year, Thurman also released a muckraking novel, *The Interne*, cowritten with Abraham L. Furman, about unethical medical practices and the pressures of a medical bureaucracy on a young intern at a hospital where Thurman, ironically, died several years later.

In 1934 Thurman went to Hollywood to write scripts for an independent production company for $250 a week.

He wrote scripts for two films, one of which, *Tomorrow's Children*, a serious social problem film dealing with state-mandated sterilization, survives today. Ill health cut short his tinsel-town sojourn, and he returned to Harlem later that same year. Although warned about taxing himself, Thurman collapsed at a party and was admitted to City Hospital on Welfare Island. He was diagnosed with tuberculosis and gradually weakened until his death. The death of Thurman and fellow Harlem Renaissance writer Rudolph Fisher within days of each other marked for many the symbolic end of the Harlem Renaissance.

FURTHER READING

The majority of Thurman's papers are in the James Weldon Johnson Collection at the Beinecke Library, Yale University. Smaller collections of his letters are in the Moorland-Spingarn Research Center at Howard University and the William Jourdan Rapp Collection at the University of Oregon Library.

Bontemps, Arna. "Portrait of Wallace Thurman," in *The Harlem Renaissance Remembered*, ed. Bontemps (1972).
LEWIS, DAVID LEVERING. *When Harlem Was in Vogue* (1981).

Obituary: *New York Amsterdam News*, 29 Dec. 1934.

—MICHAEL MAIWALD

 TILL, EMMETT LOUIS
(25 July 1941–28 Aug. 1955), murder victim, was born near Chicago, the son of Louis Till, a soldier, and Mamie (maiden name unknown), a clerical worker. After completing the seventh grade in an all-black elementary school on the South Side of Chicago, "Bobo" Till was sent on vacation to the Mississippi Delta in late summer 1955. His hosts were his great-uncle, Moses Wright, a sharecropper, and Wright's wife, Elizabeth.

On the evening of 24 August, after a week of visiting, the fourteen-year-old Till joined seven other black teenagers for a trip to Money, a hamlet in Leflore County. There, he entered a store owned and operated by Roy Bryant, a twenty-four-year-old former soldier who was momentarily absent, and his wife, Carolyn Bryant, the twenty-one-year-old

mother of their two sons. She was five feet tall and weighed 103 pounds. Witnesses disagreed about what happened next, but apparently a couple of the adolescents began taunting Till, daring the five-foot, four-inch 160-pound Chicagoan to ask Mrs. Bryant for a date. Rather than evade the challenge, he bought some bubble gum, then, according to Mrs. Bryant's testimony, he firmly squeezed her hand and asked: "How about a date, baby?" When she immediately withdrew from him, she claimed, Till jumped between two counters to block her path, raised his hands and held her waist, reassuring her, again according to testimony that she later gave in court: "Don't be afraid of me, baby. I ain't gonna hurt you. I been with white girls before." Mrs. Bryant also testified that he used "unprintable" words. It was then that one of Till's cousins rushed in and dragged him from the store, as Mrs. Bryant ran to get a pistol. As the group drove away, she testified, Till exclaimed, "Bye, baby," and "wolf whistled" at her.

According to Roy Bryant, two days after the alleged incident, a black customer informed him of this breach of Jim Crow etiquette. Claiming later that his sense of honor had been violated, Bryant asked his half brother, J. W. "Big" Milam, a thirty-six-year-old veteran of World War II, to accompany him the next night to punish the northern visitor. Armed with pistols, Bryant and Milam drove in Milam's pickup truck to the Wrights' shack, abducted Till, and pistol-whipped him. Then, near Glendora, Till was forced to tie himself to a cotton gin fan that would weigh his body down just before he was murdered and dumped into the Tallahatchie River.

Although an indictment of whites for such a crime was very rare in Mississippi, all five lawyers practicing in the county seat of Sumner volunteered to represent the defendants pro bono, an offer that Bryant and Milam accepted. A month after the murder, perhaps seventy reporters from major newspapers and magazines covered their trial, at which the defendants were acquitted by a jury of their peers—twelve white men. Despite Mamie Till's wrenching testimony and Moses Wright's identification in court of the two abductors, the jurors needed little more than an hour to reach their decision, which sent shock waves of editorial criticism and black protests throughout the country as well as abroad. The crime and the exoneration later affected writers and musicians as important and diverse as novelists TONI MORRISON and JAMES BALDWIN (both of whom wrote plays about it), scenarist Rod Serling (who wrote a television drama), singer Bob Dylan (who wrote a song), and poet GWENDOLYN BROOKS (who wrote a ballad).

Because the victim was so young, because the infraction of the segregationist code seemed to outsiders so minor, because the culprits were freed while the U.S. Department of Justice declined to intervene, the case exposed, like no other episode, the vulnerability of the region's blacks. The sense of black precariousness in the rural South helped to spur the civil rights movement. That assault against Jim Crow was facilitated when the intensity of the southern commitment to preserve its "way of life" was revealed. The brutality of Bryant and Milam and the communal support they commanded helped to erode the arrangement of white supremacy that they believed themselves to be reinforcing. Their crime made sense only in terms of a caste system that they took for granted, and yet paradoxically the murder was especially appalling because that system was already beginning to collapse. The intricate intermingling of tradition, race, and caste was entering a phase of decomposition, heightened by the growing realization of the anachronism of such violence during the cold war struggle for the support of the emerging Third World. Till's death became notorious because it intersected the antinomies of black and white, male and female, urban and rural, North and South, old and new, and native and stranger.

FURTHER READING

The papers of William Bradford Huie, the journalist who cracked the case by paying the acquitted defendants to recount their crime in *Look* magazine, are deposited at Ohio State University.

Huie, William Bradford. *Wolf Whistle* (1959).
Whitfield, Stephen J. *A Death in the Delta* (1988).

—STEPHEN J. WHITFIELD

TINDLEY, CHARLES ALBERT (7 July 1856– 26 July 1933), Methodist minister, was born in Berlin, Maryland, the son of Charles and Ester, both slaves. He was self-educated. In 1885 he was examined for ministerial orders by the Delaware Annual Conference, a black Methodist Episcopal Conference. He was admitted on probation and assigned to the Cape May, New Jersey, church where he served for two years. In 1887 he was ordained deacon and transferred to the South Wilmington, Delaware, church. Subsequently he served as statistical secretary to Reverend Joseph R. Waters. Ordained an elder in the Delaware Conference in 1889, he was again transferred, this time to the Odessa, Delaware, charge. Between 1890 and 1900 Tindley served pastorates at Pocomoke and Pocomoke Circuits in Maryland and at Fairmount and Wilmington in Delaware, where he served historic Ezion Methodist Church. In 1900 he was appointed presiding elder of the Wilmington District. Concurrent with his term of office as presiding elder, he became pastor at Bainbridge Street Methodist Church, Philadelphia, which he served for thirty-three years. He continued to obtain an education: he attended the Brandywine Institute Theological Course, and by correspondence he took the Greek course at Boston University School of Theology.

By 1906 Tindley's church had become the premier black congregation in Philadelphia. In his sermons and with his own musical compositions, Tindley strove to provide an atmosphere of warm fellowship among the members of the middle-class congregation. Between 1901 and 1916 he published "Songs of Paradise," writing the words for thirty-three songs and the music for sixteen. East Calvary Methodist Episcopal Church, as the Bainbridge Street Church was renamed, became a center and symbol of black culture and religion in Philadelphia. Tindley himself developed strong personal friendships with important political and social leaders, including John Wanamaker and Russell H. Conwell. Tindley frequently became involved in social issues, developing a feed-the-hungry program and opposing the proliferation of movie theaters in the city.

Returning from the Delaware Annual Conference in 1920, having been defeated in his bid to be elected to the Methodist episcopacy, Tindley began to make plans to construct a massive cathedral for his congregation of more than seven thousand. Guided by the advice of John Wanamaker, the financial campaign was a success, and the new building was completed by Thanksgiving 1924. Unfortunately, the first service held at the church was dimmed by the sudden death of Tindley's wife, Annie Daisy Henry, whom he had married in 1884 and with whom he had had six children.

Tindley's personal life soon took several more unhappy turns. His secret marriage to Jenny Cotton, a widow, in 1925 infuriated the eligible women in his church who, upon discovering that he was married, called in their loans on the building program. In addition, his adult children did not accept the marriage and rebelled against their stepmother. To make matters worse, he was charged with breach of promise to marry Alice MacDonald of Newark, New Jersey, with whom he was briefly acquainted. Although the charges were dropped, the seventy-year-old clergyman's reputation was besmirched and the church's fortunes suffered. In a desperate attempt to reduce the debt, the church invited the flamboyant evangelist G. Wilson Becton to conduct services at the temple, which he did for several months in 1930, regularly receiving "consecrated dime collections." Tindley objected to this intrusion and watched the quality of his ministry erode. In the end Becton was expelled from the temple, whereupon he took his Gospel Feast Party to a nearby boxing arena and competed with Tindley for the attentions of religiously minded black Philadelphians.

Nonetheless, at his death in Philadelphia, Tindley was still the undisputed leader of the Delaware Annual Conference. His temple—which later was renamed the Tindley Temple Methodist Episcopal Church in his honor— claimed ten thousand members, with a Sunday school of two thousand pupils and seventy-two teachers. In his last year of ministry alone he raised twenty-four thousand dollars for the conference benevolence program. Owing to his famous published sermon, *Heaven's*

Christmas Tree (1915), and many published hymns and gospel songs, Tindley also was well remembered as the "Prince of Preachers." The official historian of the Delaware Annual Conference wrote of him that "his towering physique, his commanding voice, his matchless eloquence, his cogent reasoning, his inimitable style, and his unbounded faith, all combined to render him the most popular preacher of his time."

FURTHER READING

The church records of the Tindley Temple Methodist Episcopal Church in Philadelphia constitute a history of Tindley as a pastor. Other helpful materials can be found in the Eastern Pennsylvania Annual Conference Archives at St. George's United Methodist Church in Philadelphia.

Jones, Ralph H. *Charles Albert Tindley: Prince of Preachers* (1982).

Tindley, E. T. *The Prince of Preachers: The Remarkable Story of Charles Albert Tindley of Philadelphia, Pennsylvania* (1942).

Obituaries: *Philadelphia Tribune*, 27 July and 3 Aug. 1933.

—WILLIAM H. BRACKNEY

TOOMER, JEAN

(26 Dec. 1894–30 Mar. 1967), writer and philosopher, was born Nathan Pinchback Toomer in Washington, D.C., the only child of Nathan Toomer, a planter from North Carolina, and Nina Pinchback, the daughter of the Reconstruction-era senator P. B. S. PINCHBACK. Pinchback was biracial, and he could easily have passed for white. In fact, his sister urged him to do just that when she wrote, "I have nothing to do with negroes am <u>not</u> one of them. Take my advice <u>dear</u> brother and do the same" (Kerman and Eldridge, 19). Toomer's grandfather ignored that advice, went on to become, briefly, acting governor of Louisiana, and was elected to both the U.S. House of Representatives and the U.S. Senate, though he was denied entrance to both houses.

Toomer once said that it would be "libelous for anyone to refer to me as a colored man" (Rayford Logan, *Dictionary of American Negro Biography*

Novelist Jean Toomer in a pastel portrait by Winold Reiss, a German artist who helped shape the image of the "New Negro" during the Harlem Renaissance. National Portrait Gallery, Smithsonian Institution/Art Resource, NY

[1982], 598), and he felt betrayed when ALAIN LOCKE included some of his writings in *The New Negro* (1925), a book showcasing emerging black artists of the Harlem Renaissance. Unraveling the paradox of his life and work goes to the heart of the problem of race in America: Who is black, what is black culture, and who has the power to make these decisions?

Abandoned by her husband in 1895, Nina took her son to live with her parents in their stately home in Washington, D.C. Pinchback did not

want his grandson to keep either the name Nathan or the name Toomer because they belonged to his delinquent father, the family began calling him Eugene instead, after another relative. As an adult, Toomer chose the form Jean. He grew up in a neighborhood where most of the children were white, and he did not think of himself as being different until he was about nine years old, when he entered the Garnet School for colored children. Then, for the first time in his life, the pall of race separated him from those he thought were his natural associates. He did not apply himself or excel academically, though he maintained a sense of entitlement and superiority over his peers.

In 1906 Nina married Archibald Combes, an insurance salesman, and the family moved to New York, where they lived in predominantly white neighborhoods in Brooklyn and then in New Rochelle. However, when Toomer's mother died three years later, he returned to Washington to live with his grandparents, who had moved to a more modest residence in an integrated section of town. In 1910 Toomer enrolled at the M Street High School, which he described as "an aristocracy—such as never existed before and perhaps never will exist again in America—mid-way between the white and negro worlds. For the first time I lived in a colored world" (Kerman and Eldridge, 47).

Toomer saw himself as a person who could travel freely in the black world, comprehend its meaning, and imbibe its melancholy beauty, but he never claimed that world as his own, and he resisted every attempt at being claimed by it. In fact, at every juncture at which he was given the chance to indicate his racial identity (on college applications, marriage licenses, and so on), he chose to identify himself as white. This was not merely a subconscious motivation; Toomer was quite aware of his chameleon-like ability to straddle the color line. He remarked that "viewed from the world of race distinctions, I take the color of whatever group I at the time am sojourning in" (Kerman and Eldridge, 96).

Toomer's early adult years were devoid of focus. Between 1914 and 1917 he enrolled at the University of Wisconsin, Massachusetts College of Agriculture, American College of Physical Training in Chicago, University of Chicago, New York University, and City College of New York. He attempted to join the military but was rejected because of poor eyesight. For a brief time he studied privately to become a musician. Between each fleeting ambition, Toomer worked a variety of jobs: drugstore clerk, assistant librarian, fitter in a New Jersey shipyard, and car salesman. Financially, Toomer relied on his grandfather's largesse and, later, on the generosity of various women in his life.

Although he did not thrive in formal academic settings, Toomer was a voracious reader. He delved into works on Eastern religion and politics and the writings of Walt Whitman, George Bernard Shaw, and Robert Frost. While living in Greenwich Village in 1918, Toomer began writing poetry and short stories in earnest. Waldo Frank, a close friend and mentor, nurtured his literary aspirations and encouraged him to refine his talent. Destitute and desperate to make a success of writing, Toomer returned to Washington, secluded himself in a room rented by his grandfather, and devoted himself to his new craft.

An auspicious break came in the fall of 1921, when Toomer learned from one of his grandfather's visitors that the all-black Sparta Agricultural and Industrial Institute in Georgia was in need of a temporary principal. Toomer secured the position and moved to the South, where he took in the sight of blacks toiling in the soil, the sound of spirituals sung in black churches, and the drama of black life in the segregated South. This experience was artistically stimulating for Toomer, it contrasted sharply with his limited encounters with the Negro elite in Washington, and it supplied the inspiration and much of the content for his literary masterpiece.

Cane (1923) is a montage of self-contained vignettes interspersed with poetry. Each of its elements could stand alone (and several were published separately), but they fit together to form a harmonious testament to a segment of black life in the twilight between slavery and freedom. Toomer's female characters, in particular, are imbued with an aesthetic beauty and pathos that makes each of their stories compelling. This slim volume had a monumental impact, opening up new avenues of expression for Negro artists trying to find an authentic voice. It demonstrated that black folk culture could be rendered in powerful prose of a sort not often found in polemical novels and with an integrity that was lacking in the "happy darky" caricatures popular at the time. Similarly, its mosaic structure encouraged greater experimentation with form and presentation. LANGSTON HUGHES and ZORA NEALE HURSTON were so moved by *Cane* that they drove to Sparta as if they might find there a wellspring of creativity. Yet Toomer

had written this gem and walked away. A gold rush followed, as other artists eagerly mined the black experience, which until then had not been fully appreciated as a fruitful source for serious works of literature, music, and art.

When *Cane* appeared in 1923 to moderate reviews and sales among the white reading public but to enthusiastic praise in Negro publications, such as the *Crisis* and *Opportunity*, Toomer realized that a place was being set for him at the table of black writers, whereas he had hoped to be accepted as a writer without reference to race. Toomer was disappointed that Waldo Frank, whom he had asked to write the book's introduction, referred to him as a "Negro," and Toomer bluntly refused to assist his publisher in any marketing strategy that featured him as a premier black talent. However, his choice of subject matter emphasized the very connection to blackness that he had hoped to avoid. Despite the prodding of those who yearned for more works like *Cane*, Toomer devoted the next four decades to writing material that explored universal rather than racial topics. For the rest of his life, he threw himself into a world of mystics, spiritualists, and new age thinkers.

Toomer's spiritual journey ranged from Jungian psychology to Scientology. He consulted psychics, journeyed to India in search of enlightenment, and became a noted Quaker. Toomer was most captivated with the teachings of the Russian philosopher George Ivanovich Gurdjieff, who developed a system of beliefs and exercises by which one could achieve a higher consciousness he called "Unitism." In 1924 Toomer became an acolyte of this movement; he met the guru in New York and by 1929 had made several trips to France to study at Gurdjieff's Institute for Man's Harmonious Development. Back in the United States, Toomer became a teacher of Gurdjieffian metaphysics. In Harlem he attempted to recruit members of the black intelligentsia, such as AARON DOUGLAS, NELLA LARSEN, and Arna Bontemps. While speaking at a Gurdjieff gathering in Chicago, Toomer met Margery Latimer, a wealthy white writer. The two were married in 1931. Margery died within the year while giving birth to Toomer's only child, Margery.

In addition to *Cane*, Toomer wrote three unpublished novels: "The Gallowerps" (1927), "Transatlantic" (1929), and "Caromb" (1932). None of these books features black protagonists, and they were all rejected by the publishers to whom they were sent. *Essentials* (1931), a collection of aphorisms, was privately printed. In 1934 Toomer married Marjorie Content, a photographer and the daughter of an affluent Wall Street executive. They settled in Doylestown County, Pennsylvania, where Toomer continued to write essays and fiction that embodied his philosophy. The closest Toomer ever came to writing about racial issues after *Cane* was in a discursive poem called "Blue Meridian," which appeared in *The New American Caravan* (1936). This poem articulates a fantastic vision of the amalgamation of different races into a new order of being represented by the "blue" man. Toomer's play *Balo* appeared in Alain Locke's *Plays of Negro Life* (1929), and some of his early essays and short stories were featured in *Dial*, the *Crisis*, *Broom*, and the *Little Review*.

After a series of geriatric illnesses, Toomer died in 1967 in a nursing home in Bucks County, Pennsylvania, at the age of seventy-seven and in virtual obscurity. In 1969 *Cane* was reissued and has become an indispensable work in the African American literary canon. ALICE WALKER wrote in her review of *The Wayward and the Seeking* (1982), a collection of Toomer's previously unpublished work, that "*Cane* was for Toomer a double 'swan song.' He meant it to memorialize a culture he thought was dying, whose folk spirit he considered beautiful, but he was also saying goodbye to the 'Negro' he felt dying in himself. *Cane* then is a parting gift, and no less precious because of that. I think Jean Toomer would want us to keep its beauty, but let him go" (*New York Times Book Review*, 13 July 1980).

FURTHER READING

The main body of Toomer papers is located at the Beinecke Rare Book and Manuscript Library, Yale University, New Haven, Connecticut.

Jones, Robert B., ed. *Critical Essays on Jean Toomer* (1994).

Kerman, Cynthia, and Richard Eldridge. *The Lives of Jean Toomer: A Hunger for Wholeness* (1987).

McKay, Nellie Y. *Jean Toomer, Artist: A Study of His Literary Life and Work, 1894–1936* (1984).

Turner, Darwin T., ed. *The Wayward and the Seeking: A Collection of Writings by Jean Toomer* (1982).

—SHOLOMO B. LEVY

 TROTTER, WILLIAM MONROE (7 Apr. 1872– 7 Apr. 1934), newspaper publisher and civil rights activist, was born in Chillicothe, Ohio, the son of James Monroe Trotter, a politician who served as recorder of deeds under President Grover Cleveland, and former slave Virginia Isaacs. Raised among Boston's black elite and steeped in the abolitionist tradition, Trotter entered Harvard University and made history as the institution's first African American elected to Phi Beta Kappa. After graduating magna cum laude and earning his master's degree from Harvard, Trotter returned to Boston to learn the real estate business. He founded his own firm in 1899, the same year that he married Boston aristocrat Geraldine Pindell.

A turning point in Trotter's life occurred in 1901 when discrimination in his real estate business and worsening racial conditions throughout the country, and especially in the South, led to his increased militancy. In response to his frustration with segregation, disenfranchisement, and violence against blacks, Trotter founded the *Boston Guardian*, a crusading weekly newspaper. Cofounder George Forbes soon left the paper in Trotter's able hands. The *Guardian* was an overnight success that boasted a circulation of 2,500 by its first birthday. As editor and publisher, Trotter was articulate, fearless, and defiant. The *Guardian* reestablished the black press as a force in the struggle for civil rights.

Trotter's great crusade in the pages of his newspaper was a vendetta against BOOKER T. WASHINGTON. Trotter opposed Washington's complacent optimism in the face of increasingly intolerable racial conditions. He also disagreed with Washington's emphasis on manual and industrial training for blacks, with its accompanying denigration of the classical education. Trotter's opposition to Washington forced

white America to acknowledge that all of black America did not adhere to Washington's conciliatory and accommodationist views. Trotter's frustration with Washington reached its boiling point in July 1903. When Washington came to Boston for a public appearance, Trotter and some thirty associates heckled the orator and asked him several embarrassing questions. A free-for-all erupted into what became known as the Boston Riot. Washington supporters then pursued the case to its conclusion, resulting in Trotter being fined fifty dollars and imprisoned for a month. Trotter thereafter assumed the mantle of martyr.

Trotter has been credited with leading a resurgence of the protest tradition among African Americans of the early twentieth century. In 1905 he joined W. E. B. DU BOIS in founding the Niagara Movement, an early civil rights organization and precursor of the National Association for the Advancement of Colored People (NAACP). Trotter helped to push Du Bois away from research and into defiance as the avenue down which African Americans would secure equal rights. The tenacity and independence that served Trotter well as a journalist, however, hampered his work as a political leader. Personal quarrels with Du Bois created an estrangement between the two leaders. Chief among their disagreements was Trotter's insistence that a national civil rights organization had to be led and financed exclusively by African Americans. In 1908 Trotter founded the National Equal Rights League, an all-black organization that advocated militant efforts to secure racial equality. Although Trotter participated in the founding of the NAACP a year later, he would not accept the white leadership and financial support underpinning the association. As the NAACP's influence swelled, the uncompromising Trotter became isolated on the left wing of black leadership.

One of Trotter's most fiery interchanges occurred at the White House. Trotter, a political independent, supported Woodrow Wilson for president in 1912. When Wilson approved increased segregation in federal office buildings, however, the new president lost Trotter's support. The radical black leader took a delegation to the White House in 1914 and engaged Wilson in a jaw-to-jaw argument. After nearly an hour, the president ordered the vitriolic Trotter out of his office.

Trotter moved the struggle for racial equality in the direction of mass mobilization. In 1915 he experimented with picket lines and demonstrations by orchestrating a nonviolent effort to ban D. W. Griffith's epic motion picture *Birth of a Nation*. Trotter's arrest did not prevent him from leading some one thousand marchers to the State House two days later, thereby creating one of the earliest protest marches by Americans of African descent.

In 1919 Trotter announced plans to attend the Versailles Peace Conference in an attempt to have a racial equality clause adopted in the treaty. When the U.S. government denied his request for a passport, the defiant Trotter secured a job as a ship's cook and sailed to France. Although his efforts at Versailles ultimately failed, they garnered worldwide publicity—and Wilson's wrath. Trotter continued to raise his voice through the *Guardian*, doing so only by sacrificing both his own and his wife's personal wealth to finance the newspaper.

After Geraldine Trotter died in the influenza epidemic of 1918, her husband grew ever more isolated. The economic downturn of the Depression proved too overwhelming for Trotter, and he lost his newspaper early in 1934. Trotter died later that year, apparently of suicide, when he plunged from the roof of a three-story building in Boston on his sixty-second birthday.

FURTHER READING

A small collection of Trotter papers is at Boston University, and some Trotter correspondence is in the papers of W. E. B. Du Bois at the University of Massachusetts, Amherst.

Fox, Stephen R. *The Guardian of Boston: William Monroe Trotter* (1970).
　　　　　　　　—RODGER STREITMATTER

 TRUTH, SOJOURNER
(c. 1799–26 Nov. 1883), abolitionist and women's rights advocate, was born in Hurley, Ulster County, New York, the daughter of James and Elizabeth Baumfree, who were slaves. Named Isabella

Sojourner Truth, fervent abolitionist and campaigner for women's rights, in a studio photograph that she used on her visiting card. National Portrait Gallery, Smithsonian Institution/Art Resource, NY

by her parents, she took the name Sojourner Truth in 1843. As a child, Isabella belonged to a series of owners, the most memorable of whom were the John Dumont family of Esopus, Ulster County, to whom she belonged for approximately seventeen years and with whom she remained close until their migration to the West in 1849. About 1815 she married another of Dumont's slaves, Thomas, who was much older than she; they had five children. Isabella left Thomas in Ulster County after their emancipation under New York state law in 1827, but she did not marry again.

In the year before her emancipation, Isabella left her master Dumont of her own accord and went to work for the family of Isaac Van Wagenen in Hurley. When a member of Dumont's wife's family illegally sold Isabella's son into

perpetual slavery in Alabama, she took another remarkable step for a slave: she went to court and sued successfully for her son's return. She also had a conversion experience, was born again, and joined the newly established Methodist church in Kingston, where she met a Miss Grear, with whom she migrated to New York City in 1828.

In New York, Isabella worked in private households and attended both the predominantly white John Street Methodist Church and the African Methodist Episcopal Zion Church, where she briefly encountered three of her older siblings who had also migrated to New York City. She adhered to a series of unorthodox religious societies: the Methodist perfectionists led by James Latourette, the urban missionaries to prostitutes of the Magdalene Asylum, and the Sing Sing "kingdom" or commune of the prophet Matthias (Robert Matthews). The Latourettes introduced Isabella to the Magdalene Asylum, where she met Elijah Pierson, a wealthy Pearl Street merchant. While working in Pierson's household, she met Matthias in 1832. As the only black and one of two working-class members of Matthias's commune, she believed wholeheartedly in his eclectic mixture of spiritualism, millenarianism, personal anointment, temperance, and holistic health practices. She remained his follower until the commune's demise in 1835, following allegations of murder and sexual irregularity. After another of the commune's members charged her with attempted poisoning, she sued successfully for libel and cleared her name. There is no record of her activities between 1835 and 1843, when she did household work in New York City.

Isabella was deeply affected by the millenarian agitation associated with the prophesies of William Miller, who warned that the second coming of Christ would occur in 1843. In the midst of the economic hard times that followed the panic of 1837, she, too, sensed impending doom. On the first of June 1843, acting on the instructions of what she believed to be the Holy Spirit, Isabella changed her name to Sojourner Truth—which translates as itinerant preacher—and set out toward the east to preach the need to embrace Jesus. Traveling to Brooklyn, Long Island, Connecticut, and the Connecticut River Valley, she went from one Millerite camp meeting to another. By the end of the year the Millerites were facing their Great Disappointment, when the apocalypse did not occur, and Sojourner Truth looked for a place to spend the winter.

Truth settled in the Northampton Association, a utopian community dedicated to the cooperative manufacture of silk, located in what is now Florence, Massachusetts. The Northampton Association had been founded in 1842 by several idealists, including George Benson, brother-in-law of the leading white Boston abolitionist, William Lloyd Garrison. The tenor of the Northampton Association was quite liberal; blacks were allowed access, and deep convictions about antislavery and women's rights were taken for

granted. Reformers such as Garrison, the black abolitionist FREDERICK DOUGLASS, and the British antislavery member of Parliament George Thompson visited the community. Truth made her first appearance at an antislavery meeting in New York City in 1845, while she was living at the Northampton Association. When the association collapsed in 1846 and its lands were subdivided and sold to satisfy creditors, she bought a house on Park Street, paying off the mortgage with proceeds from sales of *The Narrative of Sojourner Truth*, which she had dictated to Olive Gilbert and had published in Boston in 1850.

During the 1850s Truth supported herself through sales of the *Narrative* and other mementos to reform-minded audiences. Sometime in about 1847 she uttered the words that were her most famous in the nineteenth century. Truth was in the audience at Faneuil Hall in Boston when Frederick Douglass, despairing that slavery could be abolished peaceably, began to advocate insurrection. Indicting his lack of faith in God's goodness, Truth stood up and asked, "Frederick, is God dead?" To evangelically attuned, nineteenth-century sensibilities, her trust was more appealing than his radicalism. She and Douglass both spoke at a women's rights convention in Worcester, Massachusetts, in 1850. She addressed a similar gathering of Ohio feminists in Akron in 1851, giving what today is her most famous speech. Demanding that poor and working women also be counted as women, Truth was later quoted as having posed the rhetorical question, "and ar'n't I a woman?" which would make her reputation among twentieth-century feminists.

Truth visited Harriet Beecher Stowe, author of *Uncle Tom's Cabin*, in 1852 or 1853. Stowe wrote a preface to a new edition of *The Narrative of Sojourner Truth* and took notes for the essay that most effectively publicized Truth during her lifetime. Stowe published her widely cited "Sojourner Truth, the Libyan Sibyl" in the April 1863 *Atlantic Monthly*; her title, "Libyan Sibyl," crops up in connection with Sojourner Truth throughout the rest of the century.

In 1856 Truth sold her house in Massachusetts and moved to Michigan, where she was close to her daughters

and their families, abolitionist supporters, Quakers of various sorts, spiritualists, and relatives of her Rochester friends Amy Post and Isaac Post (including Frances Titus, who edited the 1875-1878 edition of the *Narrative*). Truth also may have been in contact with a branch of Millerites who, under Ellen White, became the Seventh Day Adventists. Although she spent most of her time in Michigan in the town of Battle Creek, Truth joined what was at least her third planned community: she bought a house in 1857 and lived for several years in Harmonia, a community of progressive Friends. She continued her lecture tours throughout the 1850s. In a small town in northern Indiana in 1858, she faced down critics who doubted that so forceful an abolitionist could be a woman, by baring her breast and shaming her antagonists. In 1867 she built a house big enough for her daughters and their families on College Street in Battle Creek, making her remarkable among blacks for her real estate holdings.

During the Civil War, Truth met President Abraham Lincoln in his office in 1864 and worked with volunteers assisting southern black refugees. During her stay in Washington she went to court to appeal successfully for her rights for a third time, asking for the right to ride what had been Jim Crow streetcars. Realizing that charity was only a palliative, and appalled by the freedpeople's continuing poverty, Truth initiated an effort to find them jobs in and around Rochester, New York, and Battle Creek, Michigan, in 1867. When this task overwhelmed her, she conceived of a plan for resettling freedpeople on government lands in the West. Traveling through New England, the Northwest, and into Kansas in 1870 and 1871, she collected signatures on a petition to Congress, but Congress never allocated any land to African Americans in the West or the South. In 1879, after Truth had retired, a spontaneous migration to Kansas of black Exodusters from Texas, Louisiana, Mississippi, and Tennessee took tens of thousands out of the post-Reconstruction South in which they justifiably feared reenslavement. Truth was unable to return to Kansas in support of the Exodusters. She died in Battle Creek.

In the nineteenth century, this tall, dark-skinned, charismatic, illiterate wise-woman who dressed like a Quaker was best known as a Methodist-style itinerant preacher and religiously inspired supporter of women's rights and the abolition of slavery. A familiar figure in reform circles, she also advocated temperance and associated with spiritualists and water-cure enthusiasts. In her own day she presented herself as the quintessential slave woman. In modern times she has come to stand for the conjunction of race, class, and gender in American liberal reform and symbolizes the unintimidated, articulate black woman. Acutely intelligent although totally unschooled, Truth represents a type of inspired, naive witness that has long appealed to Americans suspicious of over-education.

FURTHER READING

The richest manuscript collection on Truth is the Family Papers of Isaac and Amy Post in the Library of the University of Rochester.

Truth, Sojourner. *Narrative of Sojourner Truth* (1884; repr. 1998).

Bernard, Jacqueline. *Journey toward Freedom: The Story of Sojourner Truth* (1967; repr. 1990).
Ortiz, Victoria *Sojourner Truth, a Self-Made Woman* (1974).
Painter, Nell Irvin. *Sojourner Truth: A Life, a Symbol* (1996).

—NELL IRVIN PAINTER

TUBMAN, HARRIET

(c. 1822–10 Mar. 1913), Underground Railroad conductor, abolitionist, spy and scout, and social reformer, was born Araminta Ross in Dorchester County on Maryland's Eastern Shore, one of nine children, to slave parents Harriet Green and Ben Ross. She took her mother's name, Harriet, around 1844. This was also about the time she married John Tubman, a free black of about thirty-two years in age. The couple had no children.

The black community in which Harriet grew up comprised a mix of free and slave, skilled and unskilled people who married one another and formed interconnected, extended families. Freemen and slaves worked together

in the fields, swamps, forests, and canals. Harriet's father worked as a skilled slave, cutting and hauling timber for his master, Anthony Thompson, a lumber supplier for the area's shipbuilding industry. A favorite of Thompson, Ross eventually won his freedom in 1840 by a provision in Thompson's will that stipulated staggered emancipation dates for all his slaves. The other family members did not fare as well. The death of Thompson's wife in 1824 effected the first family separation, when Thompson's stepson Edward Brodess inherited Harriet Ross and her children.

Under the new master the family fell upon particularly hard times. The distance between the two plantations dictated only infrequent family gatherings, while Brodess's practice of hiring out his slaves, even the younger ones, separated the children from one another and from

their mother for long periods of time. Brodess, like other slaveholders with small landholdings, commonly hired out his excess slaves or sold them in the slave market to meet expenditures. Several of Harriet Tubman's siblings were sold outside the state, though her mother was successful in saving her youngest son. With threats and cunning she hid him in the woods for a month, thus thwarting his sale into Georgia.

As a child Harriet Tubman was hired out to several masters, serving them in a variety of capacities. She worked as a house servant, cleaning house and tending children. She often encountered cruelty and beatings from her white mistresses. She was sent at a young age to trap muskrats in the marshland of Dorchester County, where she became ill from the cold and wet surroundings. In her teens she was hired out most often

Known as the "Moses of her People," Harriet Ross Tubman was a prominent abolitionist and also carried out spy missions for the Union Army during the Civil War. Library of Congress

Harriet Ross Tubman (left), one of the most daring conductors of the Underground Railroad, photographed with a group of slaves she led out of the South to freedom in the early 1860s. © Bettmann/Corbis

as a field hand. She drove oxen, carted wood, plowed, crushed flax, worked in timber gangs, and labored as hard as a man. One master to whom she was hired enjoyed displaying her physical strength to his neighbors.

From an early age Harriet made clear her unwillingness to comply with the slave system. At seven years old she hid from a slave mistress for five days after being threatened with a beating for taking a lump of sugar. An episode during her teen years shows her tenacity and foreshadows the work for which she became most well known. When a fellow slave was threatened with a beating for going to a village store without permission, Tubman was ordered to help tie him down. She refused to help, so the overseer grabbed a two-pound weight and hurled it at her. The object struck her in the head, leaving an injury that caused narcoleptic seizures throughout her life.

Before her own escape to freedom, Harriet and her siblings worried constantly about being sold into deep southern slavery. Three sisters had suffered this fate, and when her master's death in 1849 portended the same, she determined to run away. The sale of Tubman's niece, also named Harriet, and her niece's two-year-old daughter, Mary Ann, proved the signal event that pushed her and her brothers to set

out for freedom. Tubman's husband, John, refused to join them. Her brothers became fearful not long into the journey and returned, bringing Harriet back as well. Two days later she set out alone. She was probably emboldened by stories of other fugitives. Indeed, Maryland led the southern states in the number of escaped slaves. Nor was the route of escape completely unfamiliar to her. While working on timber gangs, she had learned of a world beyond slavery. In this largely male workforce she heard about and made the acquaintance of free black stevedores and seamen along the eastern seaboard. As the story of MOSES ROPER has indicated, black seamen historically constituted an important source of information linking together southern and northern black communities.

Tubman fled Maryland on foot, walking through Delaware and into Pennsylvania, traveling at night and hiding or sleeping by day. In Philadelphia and Cape May, New Jersey, she worked as a cook, maid, and laundress. However, feeling alone in her freedom, Tubman determined to have the community of her family and friends around her and saved her earnings in order to return south and rescue others. Her reputation as a liberator began in 1850 when she saved her niece Kessiah and her two children from sale in Baltimore; a few months later she returned

to free her youngest brother. During that same year, enactment of the Fugitive Slave Law necessitated extra precaution and made it more difficult to take escapees to Canada. In 1851 Tubman stole back into Maryland for her husband, only to discover that he had remarried. Despite her great disappointment, she continued her rescue work undaunted—determined "to do without him."

Around 1855 Tubman took up residence in St. Catherine's, Ontario, Canada, an area to which she delivered many others to freedom. While she resided there, the abolitionist John Brown, who called her "General," sought her out to recruit soldiers for and lead his planned slave insurrection, which collapsed with the failure of the famed attack on the federal arsenal at Harper's Ferry, West Virginia. Tubman apparently supported Brown's plan and spoke admirably of him throughout her life, though illness and a change in date prevented her participation in the raid. In 1857 Tubman accomplished the difficult feat of delivering her own elderly parents to Auburn, New York. Since they were too feeble to walk, Tubman managed her parents' travel to freedom by wagon. She settled them in a modest home on property she bought in Auburn with assistance from New York (and, later, U.S.) Secretary of State William Seward. Tubman took up residence there in 1865.

Tubman made fourteen trips back to the Eastern Shore between 1849 and 1860. Recent scholarship reveals that she directly rescued seventy to eighty slaves, some of whom were family members, and indirectly freed about fifty others through instructions she provided. She preferred traveling in the winter months when the daylight was shorter, and she solicited free blacks in Maryland to remove postings of slave runaway advertisements. She wore a variety of disguises and carried a gun to avert trouble and to prevent being betrayed by those who became weary or fearful. Tubman would give them a choice: either go forward to freedom or die. She carried paregoric to sedate babies so their crying would not give them away. Her ability to travel undetected rested upon an elaborate communication system, along with numerous strategies and routes. Her intimate knowledge of various routes and trade networks, wooded areas and waterways, enhanced her surreptitious and daring escapes, but she was also aided by an array of underground operatives—slave and free, rich and poor, white and black—who provided "safe houses" along the way.

Black churches and abolitionist friends like Thomas Garrett, WILLIAM STILL, and Lucretia Mott provided the fugitives with housing, clothing, transportation, and other resources. Tubman herself gave the greatest credit for her success to divine guidance. As a woman of deep religious faith she found inspiration, like many other enslaved African Americans, in a mixture of evangelical Protestantism and African American folk beliefs. Thus she spoke of charms, experienced spiritual visions, and attributed her ingenuity and daring success to divine handiwork. From her perspective, God's power made it possible for her to boast of never having lost a "passenger." Tubman's success in delivering people from bondage resulted in her being given the moniker "Moses" in her lifetime.

With the onset of the Civil War, Tubman threw herself into the war effort. She traveled to coastal South Carolina in May 1862 and set about nursing wounded soldiers, bondmen, and bondwomen. She also sought to help newly freed women become self-supporting by washing and cooking for the soldiers. Continuing to display ingenuity and sensitivity, Tubman relinquished the privilege of receiving army rations like whites when local blacks expressed suspicion of this. Instead, she supported herself by selling pies, cakes, and root beer she prepared in the evenings.

Tubman's nursing skills and herbal remedies became known and sought after; on one occasion an officer requested that she travel to Florida to attend to troops suffering from severe dysentery. Receiving notes and passes from army officials, she passed freely among Union forces by foot and federal transport. Tubman's plain appearance allowed her to move effortlessly among the slaves, thus making her a valuable scout and spy in Confederate territory. She obtained information about cotton storage, ammunition deposits, and

the location of black communities useful to the success of Union campaigns. She particularly admired Colonel James Montgomery, who had fought side by side with John Brown in "Bleeding Kansas," and she worked closely with him in the recruitment of black soldiers at Port Royal, South Carolina. With Montgomery's permission, she led a spying expedition up the Combahee River. The mission resulted in the capture by Montgomery's troops of large caches of material resources and the freeing of 756 slaves.

An independent and practical thinker in regard to gender conventions, Tubman sought appropriate attire for her army work. In a letter to northern friends she commented on her preference for pants or bloomers, given the difficulty of wearing a dress on scouting expeditions, especially when running. After the war she took pride in having worn "pants" and having carried a musket and other military accoutrements, which she saved as souvenirs. During 1865 Tubman served as a nurse, treating black patients at the James River contraband hospital in Virginia; near the end of the war she became matron of the Colored Hospital at Fortress Monroe.

In 1869 the unconventional Tubman married Nelson Davis, a former Union soldier twenty years her junior, though she kept her first husband's name. Like FREDERICK DOUGLASS and SOJOURNER TRUTH, Tubman raised funds for herself and her causes by selling copies of her biography, which was written by Sara Bradford. For twenty-five years Tubman wrote to the federal government in pursuit of her right to a military pension. Colonel Thomas Wentworth Higginson and General Rufus Saxton were among those who intervened unsuccessfully to obtain a government pension for her service. Ironically, two years after her husband's death in 1888 she was finally awarded a pension, receiving compensation not for her own service in the war but for her status as the widow of a black veteran.

Tubman's postbellum work focused on racial uplift efforts for elderly and destitute blacks. Seeing the connection of racial and gender oppression, she worked primarily with black women's groups and black churches, although she

did accept monetary gifts from white supporters. She was a delegate at the July 1896 meeting of the Federation of Afro-American Women in Washington, D.C. When asked to address the group, she called for assistance in providing homes for the aged. She worked primarily through her local congregation, Thompson Memorial African Methodist Episcopal (AME) Zion Church, and through the larger AME Zion denomination. In 1896 she was successful in purchasing twenty-five acres of land adjoining her home, on which she sought to build facilities for the indigent. Her meager resources delayed completion of the facility until 1903. In that year she deeded the property to AME Zion trustees. In 1911 Tubman herself entered the Harriet Tubman Home for Aged and Indigent Colored People. She died two years later.

Tubman was a well-known and much respected figure among abolitionists and women's rights advocates of her time. Frederick Douglass lauded her willingness to work without public praise. The suffragist pioneer and leader Susan B. Anthony expressed high regard for "this wonderful woman." The abolitionist William Still said she was unequaled in courage, shrewdness, and altruistic efforts to deliver others. The historian BENJAMIN QUARLES noted that "esteem for her was practically universal among blacks of her day, including high and low, young and old, male and female, and cutting across sectional lines." Later generations would continue to honor her. Formal federal recognition of Harriet Tubman as an enduring model of heroism and patriotism has included naming a ship after her in World War II, designating her home in Auburn a national historic landmark in 1974, and issuing a postage stamp bearing her image in 1978.

FURTHER READING

Bradford, Sara. *Scenes in the Life of Harriet Tubman* (1869).

Humez, Jean McMahon, ed. *Harriet Tubman: The Life and the Life Stories* (2003).

Larson, Kate Clifford. *Bound for the Promised Land: Harriet Tubman, Portrait of an American Hero* (2003).

Quarles, Benjamin. *Allies for Freedom and Blacks and John Brown* (1974).

————. "Harriet Tubman's Unlikely Leadership" in *Black Leaders of the Nineteenth Century*, eds. Leon F. Litwack and August Meier (1988).

—ROSETTA E. ROSS

TURE, KWAME. *See* Carmichael, Stokely.

TURNER, CHARLES HENRY (3 Feb. 1867–14 Feb. 1923), biologist and educator, was born in Cincinnati, Ohio, the son of Thomas Turner, a church custodian, and Adeline Campbell, a nurse. Although neither parent had attended college, Thomas Turner would eventually earn a reputation as "a well-read man, a keen thinker, and a master of debate [who] surrounded himself with several hundred choice books." Both parents, but especially the father, imparted a love of learning to young Charles. After graduating valedictorian of his high school class in Cincinnati, he proceeded to the University of Cincinnati, where he earned a BS in 1891 and an MS in 1892. His goal was to teach science and ultimately to head a technological or agricultural school for African Americans. As an undergraduate he came under the influence of Clarence Luther Herrick, a professor of biology at Cincinnati and pioneer in the field of psychobiology. When Herrick established the *Journal of Comparative Neurology* in 1891, Turner became a regular contributor; he published eight research articles and at least six abstracts in the journal between 1891 and 1901. Text and illustrations from his undergraduate thesis, "Morphology of the Avian Brain," appeared in the inaugural volume.

Turner's first teaching appointments were at the Governor Street School in Evansville, Indiana (1888–1889), and for a brief period subsequently (1889) as a substitute in the Cincinnati public schools. In 1891 he was appointed to an assistantship in the biological laboratory at the University of Cincinnati, a position he held for two years. Anxious, as he put it, to "get to work among my own people," he wrote to BOOKER T. WASHINGTON in April 1893 requesting notification of any openings at black colleges. Later that year he became professor of biology and head of the department of science and agriculture at the all-black Clark University in Atlanta, Georgia. His tenure at Clark (1893–1905) was followed by posts at other black schools: principal of College Hill High School, Cleveland, Tennessee (1906); professor of biology and chemistry at Haines Normal and Industrial Institute, Augusta, Georgia (1907–1908); and instructor in biology at Sumner High School, St. Louis, Missouri (1908–1923). Sumner, founded in 1875, was highly regarded for the caliber of its faculty, which at one time had included EDWARD BOUCHET, the first African American to receive a PhD (in Physics from Yale, 1876).

In 1907 Turner earned his PhD in Zoology (magna cum laude) at the University of Chicago. At Chicago he worked under the eminent zoologists Charles Otis Whitman, Charles Manning Child, and Frank Rattray Lillie. He was one of the earliest black Americans to earn a doctorate in the biological sciences (Alfred O. Coffin had earned one at Illinois Wesleyan University in 1889). Turner's doctoral thesis, a study of the "homing" mechanism in ants, marked a watershed in his scientific research. Earlier, his work had followed classic morphological lines—that is, examination of an organism's form and structure by means of microscopic observation in the laboratory. Following his time at Chicago, his work became more behavioral, focusing on animals in the field, in their natural habitat. His goal was to continue developing insights into elusive problems of neurology and comparative psychology—problems first introduced to him by Herrick at Cincinnati.

While teaching in St. Louis, Turner established himself as an authority on insect behavior. He was the first to fully describe a unique movement—a pattern of gyration—that certain species of ant go through when returning to their nests. This movement came to be widely known, in the scientific literature, as "Turner's circling." Turner also showed that ant movement is influenced by landmarks and light, that bees respond to color and pattern as well as odor, that wasps and burrowing bees may memorize landmarks adjacent to their nests, that ant lions lie motionless for prolonged periods out of an involuntary response to external stimuli ("terror paralysis") rather than as a self-concealment or camouflage reflex, that certain insects can hear and distinguish pitch, and that cockroaches learn by trial and error (but forget quickly). The innovative experimental techniques and ingenious devices that Turner developed to carry out his work were admired and often emulated by other scientists. His reputation for accuracy and thoroughness resulted in several invitations to contribute annual literature reviews on insect behavior, vertebrate and invertebrate behavior, tropisms, and other topics to *Psychological Bulletin* and *Journal of Animal Behavior*. Turner's seminal work, "The Homing of Ants: An Experimental Study of Ant Behavior," is in *The Journal of Comparative Neurology and Psychology* 17 (Sept. 1907): 367–434. His longest work, coauthored with C. L. Herrick, is *Synopsis of the Entomostraca of Minnesota; With Descriptions of Related Species Comparing All Known Forms from the United States, Included in the Orders Copepoda, Cladocera, Ostrocada* (1895). In all, he published over fifty scientific articles (with at least three others appearing posthumously). His work appeared in major journals, such as *Science, American Naturalist*, and *Biological Bulletin*.

Turner's research was carried out with his own resources and in his spare time. The focus of his professional life was teaching. At Sumner he inspired in his students a curiosity about the natural world that outlasted their high-school years. Also active in black civic organizations, Turner served as a director of the Colored Branch, St. Louis YMCA. He wrote occasional papers on racial issues for *The Southwestern Christian Advocate* and other publications. One article, "Will the Education of the Negro Solve the Race Problem?" in *Twentieth Century Negro Literature*, ed. D. W. Culp (1902), supported W. E. B. Du Bois's contention (in opposition to Booker T. Washington) that college or university education—not industrial training—was the best way to stimulate prosperity for blacks and to promote interracial harmony. Drawing on his work as a biologist, Turner compared human and animal "societies." He theorized, for example, that "animals are prejudiced against animals unlike themselves, and the more unlike they are the greater the prejudice," but that with humans "dissimilarity of minds is a more potent factor in causing prejudice than unlikeness of physiognomy." He advanced this theory in support of his argument for equal educational opportunity, irrespective of race.

Turner was a member of the Entomological Society of America, the Academy of Science of Illinois, and the Academy of Science of St. Louis. He held elective office in the latter organization, serving terms as secretary of the entomology section and as council member. He was twice married, first (in 1888) to Leontine Troy of Cincinnati (she died in 1894) and later to Lillian Porter of Augusta, Georgia. Following his death in Chicago, a school for the physically handicapped—the Charles H. Turner School in St. Louis—was built in his memory.

FURTHER READING

A few Turner letters survive in the Herrick papers (part of the Neurology Collections), Department of Special Collections, Kenneth Spencer Research Library, University of Kansas.

Haines, D. E. "The Contributors to Volume 1 (1891) of *The Journal of Comparative Neurology*: C. L. Herrick, C. H. Turner, H. R. Pemberton, B. G. Wilder, F. W. Langdon, C. J. Herrick, C. von Kupffer, O. S. Strong, T. B. Stowell," *Journal of Comparative Neurology* 314 (1991): 9–23.

Hayden, Robert C. "Charles Henry Turner," *Seven Black American Scientists* (1970), 68–91.

Transactions of the Academy of Sciences of St. Louis 24 (Dec. 1923), a special memorial issue in Turner's honor.

—KENNETH R. MANNING

TURNER, HENRY McNEAL

TURNER, HENRY McNEAL (1 Feb. 1834–8 May 1915), African Methodist Episcopal (AME) Church bishop and emigrationist, was born in Newberry, South Carolina, the son of Hardy Turner and Sarah Greer, free African Americans. Sarah made great efforts to obtain an education for her son, despite the state prohibition against teaching African Americans to read. In 1848, after Turner's father died and his mother remarried, he was hired as a janitor by lawyers in Abbeville, South Carolina. Recognizing Turner's intelligence, they helped him to master many subjects, including arithmetic, astronomy, geography, history, law, and theology.

From 1848 to 1851 Turner attended numerous camp meetings conducted by Methodist evangelists and underwent a powerful conversion experience. He soon joined the Methodist Episcopal Church, South, probably in 1849, and determined to undertake a ministerial career. He was licensed to preach in 1853. Subsequently, he traveled throughout the South, holding huge audiences of blacks and whites spellbound with his fluid oratory and mastery of a wide range of subjects. In 1858 he traveled to St. Louis, where he was ordained as a minister of the African Methodist Episcopal Church, then the largest black denomination.

Turner married four times and was widowed three times. In 1856 he married Eliza Ann Peacher; they had fourteen children. Each of his subsequent marriages, in 1893 to Martha DeWitt, in 1900 to Harriet Wayman, and in 1907 to Laura Lemon, was childless.

From 1858 to 1863 Turner pastored AME churches in Baltimore and Washington, D.C. He continued his education, studying Latin, Greek, and Hebrew with various ministers and auditing medical classes at Johns Hopkins University. He won renown as a powerful evangelist, producing many converts during revivals. He also became involved in many social and political activities. He helped to raise money both for Wilberforce University in Ohio, founded by the AME Church's DANIEL ALEXANDER PAYNE in 1863, and for the assistance of contrabands, the fleeing slaves who sought refuge behind Federal army lines. He befriended numerous members of Congress, including Representative Thaddeus Stevens and Senator Charles Sumner.

After President Abraham Lincoln's 1863 Emancipation Proclamation authorized the enlistment of African Americans in the Union army, Turner was instrumental in organizing the First U.S. Colored Troops, a regiment he subsequently joined as chaplain. Despite being incapacitated for several months by a bout of smallpox, Turner participated in nine battles, including those at Petersburg, Virginia, and Fort Fisher, North Carolina. He helped teach many soldiers in his regiment to read and held numerous revivals during lulls in the fighting.

In the fall of 1865 Turner was reassigned to a regiment in Atlanta, but he soon resigned his army commission to spend all of his time organizing the AME Church in Georgia. He settled in Macon, where he pastored the congregation that had recently joined the AME Church. He also served as the presiding elder for all AME churches in the state. His most difficult task was finding pastors for the churches that joined the denomination, since there were few literate black ministers. Turner solved this difficulty by encouraging ordinary African Americans to serve as ministers, often approaching strangers with the question, "Can you preach?" He also served as a prominent revivalist, converting thousands during protracted meetings.

In 1867 Turner turned to politics, helping to organize Union Leagues and the Republican Party in his state and serving as a delegate to the state constitutional convention in Atlanta. He was elected to the Georgia state legislature in 1868. Soon, however, he and twenty-three other African American legislators were expelled on account of their race—but only after Turner delivered a brilliant speech denouncing the expulsions. With the help of U.S. Senator Charles Sumner, he obtained an appointment as postmaster in Macon. He quickly came under unrelenting persecution by the white citizens of Macon and had to resign after being accused of passing bad currency and associating with a prostitute. In 1870 Turner and the other African American legislators reclaimed their seats in the Georgia legislature by order of Congress and served the remainder of their terms. He was subsequently defeated in his bid for reelection in the fall of 1870 in a disorderly election marked by considerable Democratic fraud and Ku Klux Klan violence.

Turner then retreated to Savannah, where he pastored an AME Church and compiled a new denominational hymnbook. He also served as a detective for the U.S. customs house. Elected manager of the AME publishing house in 1876, Turner moved to Philadelphia. He supported Rutherford B. Hayes for president and later visited him in Washington but criticized Hayes for removing federal troops from the South and for failing to appoint an African American to his cabinet.

Turner was long attracted to the notion of African Americans returning to Africa to "civilize" and Christianize the continent. As a result of the political repression and economic hardship suffered by many African Americans, he became a more vigorous advocate of this idea, even gaining election as an honorary vice president of the emigrationist American Colonization Society in 1876.

Turner was elected a bishop in the AME Church in 1880 and moved to Atlanta, where he continued to champion many reform causes. He denounced the U.S. Supreme Court when, in 1883, it voided much of the Civil Rights Act of 1875, declaring that the decision made it more urgent for African Americans to return to Africa. In 1885 he was the first bishop in his denomination to ordain a woman, Sarah Ann Hughes, to the ministry, but her ordination was overturned by the church two years later. His energetic advocacy of prohibition won black support for an 1885 city ordinance banning the sale of whiskey. He evangelized vigorously on behalf of the AME Church throughout the southern and western states, helping to transform it from a small denomination based mostly in the North into a truly national denomination.

Turner visited Liberia and Sierra Leone in 1891, 1893, and 1895. His most successful trip was to South Africa in 1898, where he joined the Ethiopian church led by Mangena Mokone into union with the AME Church. Turner also intensified his efforts on behalf of African emigrationism during this decade. He edited and published two monthly newspapers, *The Voice of Missions* (1893–1900) and *The Voice of the People* (1901–1904), to disseminate his views on African missions and emigration. He inspired the formation of an International Migration Society, which arranged for two shiploads of emigrants to sail to Liberia in 1895 and 1896, but complaints from the ill-cared-for emigrants prevented him from promoting any more such voyages.

Turner articulated a theology strongly based on affirming blackness and defending civil rights. He stated that "a man must believe he is somebody before he is acknowledged as somebody.... Respect black." He called for learned black scholars to retranslate the Bible in order to make it "wholly acceptable and in keeping with the higher conceptions of the black man." Protesting the idolatry of whiteness in American Christian theology, Turner declared, "God is a Negro."

After suffering a stroke in 1899, Turner lost some of his enormous vitality. As the state of Georgia prepared to disenfranchise African Americans in 1906, he stated, "Hell is an improvement on the United States where the Negro is concerned." After he commented that "to the Negro in this country, the American flag is a dirty and contemptible rag," some white Georgians wrote President Theodore Roosevelt in an unsuccessful effort to have Turner charged with treason. The embittered Turner stated that he hoped to die outside of the United States because of its denial of human rights to African Americans, and, in fact, he died in Windsor, Ontario, while traveling on church business.

Turner's significance is multifaceted and far-reaching. His black theology and political activism paved the way for twentieth-century civil rights and black nationalist movements. His African emigrationism constituted a pointed challenge to the nation's retreat from civil rights in the post-Reconstruction era. Turner, however, devoted most of his time to his church work, not to politics, and he played a large part in making the AME Church the strongest and most influential organization controlled entirely by African Americans in the latter half of the nineteenth century.

FURTHER READING

A small but fascinating collection of Turner's papers, including a Civil War diary and numerous photographs, can be found at Howard University.

Angell, Stephen W. *Bishop Henry McNeal Turner and African American Religion in the South* (1992).

Redkey, Edwin. *Black Exodus: Black Nationalist and Back-to-Africa Movements, 1890–1910* (1969).

———. *Respect Black: The Writings and Speeches of Henry McNeal Turner* (1971).
—STEPHEN W. ANGELL

 TURNER, NAT
(2 Oct. 1800?–11 Nov. 1831), abolitionist and rebel, was born on the Virginia plantation of Benjamin Turner, the child of an enslaved woman named Nancy; the name of his father, also a slave, has not been recorded. Little is known about either parent. Family tradition holds that Nancy landed in Norfolk in 1795, the slave of a refugee fleeing the revolt in Saint Domingue (Haiti). Evidence indicates that after being purchased by Turner, Nancy was used as a domestic servant. Later in life, Nat Turner insisted that his father ran away when Nat was still a boy.

Early on, blacks and whites alike came to regard Nat as unusually gifted. Upon being given a book, the boy quickly learned how to read, "a source of wonder to all in the neighborhood." As a devout Methodist, Benjamin Turner was not only aware of Nat's literacy, he even encouraged him to read the Bible, as did his paternal grandmother, Old Bridget, who Nat

An unknown nineteenth-century artist's fictionalized representation of Nat Turner (left), with others he had recruited to plan and carry out the slave rebellion that took place in Southampton County, Virginia, in August 1831. This uprising, in which over sixty white people were killed and Turner and twenty others hanged, intensified white fears and resulted in the harsher treatment of slaves. William Loren Katz Collection

later said was "very religious, and to whom I was much attached." Even assuming that some of what Turner later told the attorney Thomas R. Gray was exaggerated bravado—or that the white lawyer's editorial hand helped shape the pamphlet published as *The Confessions of Nat Turner*—there is little reason to doubt his assertion that he spent every possible childhood moment "either in prayer" or in reading books purchased for white children on nearby Southampton County farms and estates (Tragle, 306–307).

Aware of his unique abilities, young Nat "wrapped [himself] in mystery." When not doing light work in the fields, he kept to himself and "studiously avoided mixing in society." Unlike other enslaved boys, he neither played practical pranks on others nor touched liquor. Told by both his mother and grandmother that he was "intended for some great purpose," the unusually serious child devoted his limited leisure moments to "fasting and prayer." As was later said of FREDERICK DOUGLASS, whites spoke of Nat as being too clever to be raised in bondage, and Benjamin Turner once remarked that the boy

"would never be of service to anyone as a slave" (Tragle, 307–308).

In 1809 Benjamin Turner's oldest son, Samuel, purchased 360 acres two miles away. Nancy, Nat, Old Bridget, and five other slaves were loaned to Samuel to help him establish his cotton plantation, a move that became permanent the following year, when Benjamin died during a typhoid epidemic. It may have been at this point that Nat adopted the surname of Turner as a way of linking himself to his ancestral home place, rather than as an act of homage to the deceased Benjamin Turner. Although the evidence for a spouse is circumstantial, the Richmond *Constitutional Whig* later reported that Turner married a young slave woman; this may have been a woman called Cherry, who was sold to Giles Reese when Samuel died and his estate was liquidated in 1822. Turner was sold to Thomas Moore for four hundred dollars, an indication that he was regarded as a prime field hand. Despite being short of stature and a little knock-kneed, Turner's shoulders were broad and well muscled from more than a decade of hard labor.

Embittered by the forced separation from his wife, Turner turned to fasting and prayer. He avoided large spiritual gatherings on Sundays, but at night in the quarters he willingly described what he had discovered during his solitary readings of the Bible. Sometime in 1825, while working in the fields, Turner had his first vision. "I saw white spirits and black spirits engaged in battle," he later recalled, "and the sun was darkened—the thunder rolled in the Heavens, and blood flowed in streams" (Tragle, 308). Certain that he was ordained to bring about Judgment Day, Turner began to conduct religious services at Barnes's Church near the North Carolina border. Most whites scoffed, but at least one man, Etheldred T. Brantley, an alcoholic overseer on a nearby plantation, asked Turner to baptize him before an interracial crowd at Pearson's Mill Pond.

On 12 May 1828 Turner experienced his most epochal vision to date. "I heard a loud noise in the heavens," he remembered, "and the Spirit instantly appeared to me." The voice instructed Turner to take up the "yoke" of Christ, "for the time was fast approaching when

the first should be last and the last should be first" (Tragle, 310). Warned not to act until given a further sign by God, Turner was instructed to continue teaching but not to breathe a word of his plans to his family or friends.

Several months later Thomas Moore died, and Turner became the property of Thomas's nine-year-old son, Putnam. When the boy's mother married Joseph Travis, a local wheelwright, Turner and the other sixteen slaves on the Moore plantation found themselves under the supervision of yet another new master. When an eclipse of the sun took place in February 1831, Turner concluded that the time was near to act. He recruited four trusted lieutenants: Hark Travis, Nelson Williams, Henry Porter, and Sam Francis. Turner had known Hark Travis for years, as he was also a slave on the Moore plantation and now under the supervision of Joseph Travis. The five initially established 4 July as the date of the uprising, but Turner fell ill, perhaps as the result of fasting, and the target day passed. Since evidence exists that Turner was merely part of a much larger, two-state revolt, it is also possible that he was waiting for bondsmen across the border to rise first.

Turner's precise goals remain unclear. He may have planned to establish a maroon colony within the nearby Dismal Swamp, or the black evangelical may have preferred to leave the next step in his plan to God's will. But once the town of Jerusalem was within the grasp of his army, he could either fortify the hamlet and wait for word of the rising to spread across the countryside or retreat into the swamp and establish a guerrilla base in the interior. According to the *Norfolk Herald* (26 Sept. 1831), Turner later confessed that he planned to conquer "the county of Southampton [just] as the white people did in the revolution."

The rebels began around 2:00 a.m. on Monday, 22 August. Turner struck the first blow but failed to kill Joseph Travis with his hatchet. Hark finished the work, and killed the four other whites in the house, including the Travis baby in its cradle. By noon the slave army had grown to roughly seventy armed and mounted men. They had sacked fifteen houses and killed sixty whites; Turner killed one young woman, Margaret

Whitehead. As they neared Jerusalem, a column of eighteen volunteers attacked the insurgents. Turner's men waded into the group, but the tide turned when reinforcements arrived. During the fighting, six of Turner's men were wounded, and several others, too drunk to continue, abandoned the army and made their way back to the quarters. By Tuesday only twenty rebels remained. In hopes of bolstering their numbers, Turner rode for the plantation of Dr. Simon Blunt, who owned sixty bondspeople. Understanding that the revolt had failed, Blunt's slaves cast their lots with the winning side. When they attacked the rebels with clubs and pitchforks, Turner's demoralized army collapsed. Among those badly wounded was Hark Travis, who survived only to be hanged on 9 September.

For more than a month Turner hid in a crude dugout beneath a pile of fence rails near Cabin Pond and the Reese farm, although if his wife aided him there is no evidence for it. On Sunday, 30 October, as he worked to arrange the camouflage around his hiding place, Turner was accidentally discovered by Benjamin Phipps, a farmer who happened by on the way to a neighbor's. Turner was tried on 5 November by Virginia's special courts of *oyer and terminer*, segregated tribunals reserved for slave crimes; the accused man faced a series of justices rather than a judge, and no appeal was allowed except to the governor, John Floyd. The court quickly found Turner guilty, valued him at $375, and sentenced him to hang on 11 November. According to local tradition, Turner sold his body to a local doctor and used the money to buy ginger cakes as a last meal; aged residents of Southampton later confirmed to Drewry that whites "skinned [him] and made grease of the flesh" (98–102). Turner was thirty-one years old. Altogether, sixty-six men were tried. Twenty-one rebels, including Turner, were hanged, and another sixteen were transported outside the region.

Shocked by the rebellion, the Virginia legislature debated the prospect of gradual emancipation during the winter session of 1831–1832. Governor John Floyd endorsed manumission as the only way to avoid further violence, and assemblyman Thomas Jefferson Randolph submitted a plan for colonization of freed slaves based upon his grandfather's famous scheme. But in January the House of Delegates voted down the report calling for immediate emancipation and colonization by a vote of 85 to 73. Black Virginians, however, remembered Turner more fondly. As one twentieth-century resident of Southampton County put it, Nat was "God's man. He was a man for war, and for legal rights, and for freedom."

The conventional view that Turner was mentally unstable began to form immediately after his death. Southampton authorities refused to dignify his theology with the term "religion" and instead insisted that his desire to be free was "instigated by the wildest superstition and fanaticism" (*Norfolk Herald*, 4 Nov. 1831). At the height of the Jim Crow era, area whites still spoke of seeing Turner's skull, which was retained as a curiosity. Most described it as abnormal. The publication of William Styron's 1968 Pulitzer Prize–winning novel, *The Confessions of Nat Turner*, only contributed to the modern characterization of the slave leader as a dangerously irrational rebel. But rural Americans in the antebellum years would have had an equally difficult time understanding the rationalist tone of Styron's modern world. During the Jacksonian era, many Americans, white and black, devoutly believed that the end of time was near and that Christ would soon return to rule his earthly kingdom. To that extent, Turner was well within the popular millenarian religious tradition of the period and was hardly abnormal for his time.

FURTHER READING

Drewry, William S. *The Southampton Insurrection* (1900).

Greenberg, Kenneth, ed. *The Confessions of Nat Turner and Related Documents* (1996).

———, ed. *Nat Turner: A Slave Rebellion in History and Memory* (2003).

Oates, Stephen B. *The Fires of Jubilee: Nat Turner's Fierce Rebellion* (1975).

Tragle, Henry I., ed. *The Southampton Slave Revolt of 1831: A Compilation of Source Material* (1971).

—DOUGLAS R. EGERTON

V

VANDERZEE, JAMES AUGUSTUS JOSEPH

(29 June 1886–15 May 1983), photographer and entrepreneur, was born in Lenox, Massachusetts, the second of six children of John VanDerZee and Susan Elizabeth Egberts. Part of a working-class African American community that provided services to wealthy summer residents, the VanDerZees (sometimes written Van Der Zee or Van DerZee) and their large extended family operated a laundry and bakery and worked at local luxury hotels. James played the violin and piano and enjoyed a bucolic childhood riding bicycles, swimming, skiing, and ice fishing with his siblings and cousins. He received his first camera from a mail-order catalogue just before his fourteenth birthday and taught himself how to take and develop photographs using his family as subjects. He left school that same year and began work as a hotel waiter. In 1905 he and his brother Walter moved to New York City.

James was working as an elevator operator when he met a seamstress, Kate Brown. They married when Kate became pregnant, and a daughter, Rachel, was born in 1907. A year later a son, Emile, was born but died within a year. (Rachel died of peritonitis in 1927.) In addition to a series of service jobs, VanDerZee worked sporadically as a musician. In 1911 he landed his first photography-related job at a portrait studio located in the largest department store in Newark, New Jersey. Although he was hired as a darkroom assistant, he quickly advanced to photographer when patrons began asking for "the colored fellow." The following year VanDerZee's sister Jennie invited him to set up a small studio in the Toussaint Conservatory of Art, a school she had established in her Harlem brownstone. Convinced that he could make a living as a photographer, VanDerZee wanted to open his own studio, but Kate was opposed to the venture. This fundamental disagreement

Self-portrait of the photographer James VanDerZee. © Donna Mussenden VanDerZee

contributed to the couple's divorce in 1917.

VanDerZee found a better companion and collaborator in Gaynella Greenlee, a woman of German and Spanish descent who, after marrying VanDerZee in 1917, claimed to be a light-skinned African American. That same year the couple opened the Guarantee Photo Studio, later the GGG Photo Studio, on West 135th Street, next door to the Harlem branch of the New York Public

Library. This was the first of four studio sites VanDerZee would rent over the next twenty-five years. With his inventive window displays and strong word of mouth within the burgeoning African American community, VanDerZee quickly established himself as Harlem's preeminent photographer.

By the early 1920s VanDerZee had developed a distinct style of portrait photography that emphasized narrative, mood, and the uniqueness of each

Future Expectations, *c. 1926*. © Donna Mussenden VanDerZee

image. Harlem's African American citizens—couples, families, co-workers, and even family pets—had their portraits taken by VanDerZee. With a nod to Victorian photographers, he employed a range of props, including fashionable clothes and exotic costumes, and elaborate backdrops (many of which he painted himself) featuring landscapes or architectural elements. Although they appear natural and effortless, VanDerZee's portraits were deliberately constructed compositions, with sitters posed in complex and artful arrangements. "I posed everyone according to their type and personality, and therefore almost every picture was different" (McGhee). VanDerZee made every sitter look and feel

like a celebrity, even mimicking popular media images on occasion. In VanDerZee's photographs, sitters appear sophisticated, urbane, and self-aware, and Harlem emerges as a prosperous, healthy, and diverse community.

Another characteristic of VanDerZee's portrait work was his creative manipulation of prints and negatives, which included retouching, double printing, and hand painting images. In addition to improving sitters' imperfections, retouching and hand painting added dramatic and narrative details, like tinted roses or a wisp of smoke rising from an abandoned cigarette. VanDerZee often employed double printing—at times using as many as three or four negatives to make a print—to

introduce theatrical storytelling elements into his portraits.

Such attention to detail was commercial as well as artistic. VanDerZee never forgot that photography was essentially a commercial venture and that making his patrons happy and his images one of a kind helped business. He regularly took on trade work, creating calendars and advertisements and, in later years, photographing autopsies for insurance companies and identification cards for taxi drivers. But portraits, of both the living and the dead, were VanDerZee's bread and butter. Funerary photography, a practice begun in the nineteenth century and popular in some communities through the mid-twentieth century, was a major part of his business. VanDerZee's daily visits to funeral parlors culminated in his book *Harlem Book of the Dead* (1978). Harlemites of every background hired VanDerZee to document their weddings, baptisms, graduations, and businesses with portraits and on-site photographs. Organizations as diverse as the Monte Carlo Sporting Club, Les Modernes Bridge Club, the New York Black Yankees, the Renaissance Big Five basketball team, MADAME C. J. WALKER's Beauty Salon, the Dark Tower Literary Salon, and the Black Cross Nurses commissioned VanDerZee portraits. Today these photographs serve as an invaluable and unique visual record of African American life during Harlem's heyday.

In the 1920s and 1930s and into the 1940s VanDerZee photographed the African American leaders living and working in Harlem, including the entertainment and literary luminaries of the Harlem Renaissance BILL "BOJANGLES" ROBINSON, JELLY ROLL MORTON, and COUNTÉE CULLEN; the boxing legends JACK JOHNSON and JOE LOUIS; and the political, business, and religious leaders Adam Clayton Powell Sr. and ADAM CLAYTON POWELL JR., A'lelia Walker, FATHER DIVINE, and DADDY GRACE. In a move that anticipated the birth of photojournalism, VanDerZee took to documenting street life and events when he was hired by MARCUS GARVEY to create photographic public relations material for the Universal Negro Improvement Association (UNIA) in 1924. VanDerZee produced several thousand prints of UNIA parades, rallies, and the fourth international convention, including many of the most reproduced images of Garvey.

Unlike many of its competitors, Van-DerZee's studio remained profitable throughout the Depression. After World War II, however, business steadily declined, the result of the popularity of portable cameras, changing aesthetic styles, and the broader financial decline of Harlem as middle-class blacks moved away from the area. In 1945 the Van-DerZees purchased the house they had been renting on Lenox Avenue, but by 1948 they had taken out a second mortgage and by the mid-1960s were facing foreclosure. Fighting for his economic survival, VanDerZee worked primarily as a photographic restorer.

The reevaluation of VanDerZee's place in photographic history began with *Harlem on My Mind*, a ground-breaking and controversial 1969 exhibition at the Metropolitan Museum of Art. After being "discovered" by the photo researcher Reginald McGhee, VanDerZee became the single largest contributor to the exhibition, which drew seventy-seven thousand visitors in its first week. Unfortunately, the exhibition's success arrived too late to help the cash-strapped couple, and the Van-DerZees were evicted from their Lenox Avenue house the day after the exhibition closed. Gaynella suffered a nervous breakdown as a result and remained an invalid until her death in 1976.

Hoping to resurrect his finances, VanDerZee established the James Van-DerZee Institute in June 1969. With McGhee as project director, the institute published several monographs and organized nationwide exhibitions showcasing VanDerZee's photographs alongside work by young African American photographers. In the early 1970s VanDerZee became a minor celebrity, appearing on television, in film, and as the subject of numerous articles. Meanwhile, he found himself living in a tiny Harlem apartment and relying on his Social Security payments, having received little financial support from the VanDerZee Institute. Several benefactors helped VanDerZee in fund-raising and in his attempts to wrest control of his photographic collection from the VanDerZee Institute, which in 1977 moved to the Metropolitan Museum of Art.

In 1978 the majority of his photographic materials held by the Metropolitan was transferred to the Studio Museum in Harlem, and in 1981 Van-DerZee, who had saved almost every negative he had ever made, sued the museum for ownership of fifty thousand prints and negatives. The dispute was finally settled a year after VanDerZee's death, when a New York court divided the collection between the VanDerZee estate, the VanDerZee Institute, and the Studio Museum.

In 1978 VanDerZee married Donna Mussenden, a gallery director thirty years his junior who physically and spiritually rejuvenated the ninety-two-year-old photographer. Encouraged by Mussenden, VanDerZee returned to portrait photography, and in the early 1980s photographed such prominent African Americans as BILL COSBY, MILES DAVIS, EUBIE BLAKE, MUHAMMAD ALI, OSSIE DAVIS, RUBY DEE, JEAN-MICHEL BASQUIAT, and ROMARE BEARDEN.

James VanDerZee died in 1983, just shy of his ninety-seventh birthday, on the same day he received an honorary doctorate from Howard University. Although he was omitted from Beaumont Newhall's 1982 seminal volume *The History of Photography*, VanDerZee was honored in 2002 by the U.S. Postal Service with a postage stamp.

VanDerZee's photographs chronicle African American life between the wars. His images of such landmarks as the Hotel Theresa and the Manhattan Temple Bible Club Lunchroom and of the ordinary drugstores, beauty salons, pool halls, synagogues, and churches of Harlem record the unprecedented migration of black Americans from the South to the North and from rural to urban living. His portraits offer a human-scale account of the New Negro and the Harlem Renaissance and of race pride and self-determination. Documenting the vitality and diversity of African American life, VanDerZee's photographs countered existing popular images of African Americans, which historically rendered black Americans invisible or degenerate. Here, instead, are images testifying to the artistic, commercial, and political richness of the African American community.

FURTHER READING

Haskins, James. *Van DerZee: The Picture Takin' Man* (1991).

McGhee, Reginald. *The World of James Van DerZee: A Visual Record of Black Americans* (1969).

Willis, Deborah. *VanDerZee: Photographer 1886–1983* (1993).

Obituary: *New York Times*, 16 May 1983.

—LISA E. RIVO

VARICK, JAMES (1750– 22 July 1827), Methodist leader, clergyman, and race advocate, was born near Newburgh in Orange County, New York, the son of Richard Varick. The name of his mother, who was a slave, is unknown. The family later relocated to New York City. With few educational opportunities for African American children growing up in New York City at the time, Varick by some means acquired very solid learning. Around 1790 Varick married Aurelia Jones; they had three girls and four boys. While he worked as a shoemaker and tobacco cutter and conducted school in his home and Church, the ministry was clearly his first love. Having embraced Christianity in the historic John Street Methodist Church, Varick served as an exhorter and later received a preacher's license. Racial proscription in the Methodist Episcopal Church during the latter part of the 1700s and early 1800s prevented Varick, ordained a deacon in 1806, from receiving full elder's orders until 1822.

Varick emerged as a major religious leader in New York. The Methodist Episcopal Church, like other mainly white denominations in postrevolutionary America, gradually but clearly abandoned a previous stance toward African American members that was more firmly antislavery and less discriminatory than was to be the case in later years. As a result, a number of black Methodists withdrew from white-controlled congregations to form separate racial churches, some of which eventually united to form independent black denominations by the 1820s. As early as 1796 Varick led a number of African Americans out of the John Street Church and formed a separate black congregation, which in 1800 entered its first building and in 1801 incorporated as the African Methodist Episcopal Church in New York. It was commonly known as Zion

833

Church. Because of legal maneuvering involving the incorporation agreement and the persistent efforts of white ministers to have access to the Zion pulpit, the congregation continued to struggle to attain true autonomy within the Methodist Episcopal Church. Efforts to effect some type of self-governing status under the general rubric of the predominantly white denomination ultimately failed. The Methodist Episcopal Church officials in the New York area were unwilling to depart from normal denominational polity and governance, insisting that the leadership of the church should be selected by the general body.

Varick also helped to organize the John Wesley Church in New Haven, Connecticut, which later connected with Zion and other bodies to form an independent black denomination. The African Methodist Episcopal Zion Church (AMEZ) emerged between 1820 and 1824 under the leadership of Varick and others. Unwilling to remain under the governance of the Methodist Episcopal Church, Varick and his colleagues equally objected to joining the African Methodist Episcopal Church (AME), formed in 1816 and headed by Bishop RICHARD ALLEN of Philadelphia, Pennsylvania. Apparently, they found Allen's methods too autocratic and were alienated by the AME's attempt to "invade" Zion's domain by establishing congregations and seeking to win over churches to the AME in the New York City area. Varick was elected and consecrated the connection's first superintendent in 1822; he was reelected in 1824 and held the post until his death in 1827. The connection did not affix "Zion" as a part of its official church title until 1848, a move to distinguish it from its major competitor, the older AME. Denominating their chief officer as "superintendent" (although later they employed the terms "bishop" and "superintendent" interchangeably) and having him stand for election every four years, Varick and these Zionites clearly sought to differentiate themselves from the governance of both the Methodist Episcopal and the African Methodist Episcopal churches, including the goal of making provision for greater rights for the laity. Zionites in later decades, under attack from other Methodist bodies for not having an "authentic" episcopacy, began to use

the term "bishop" more frequently and, perhaps for this and other reasons, eventually began electing these officers for life terms in 1880.

Varick tirelessly labored on behalf of racial freedom and advancement. In 1808 he delivered the thanksgiving sermon in a celebration in the Zion Church marking the federal government's prohibition of the importation of slaves. He also played a prominent role in William Hamilton's New York African Society for Mutual Relief, organized in 1808. Quite possibly Varick played a role in establishing the first African American masonic lodge in New York State, the Lodge of Freemasonry, or African Lodge, begun in 1812. The Methodist leader also served as one of the first vice presidents of the New York African Bible Society, founded in 1817 and later affiliated with the American Bible Society. Varick joined a group of religious and business leaders in supporting a petition to secure voting rights for blacks at the state constitutional convention held in 1821. The group's effort met with some success. After much discussion the convention approved a limited extension of suffrage conditioned by property ownership, the payment of taxes, and age.

He fought strenuously against the effort of the American Colonization Society (formed in 1816–1817) to repatriate blacks in Africa, joining with others to establish the African Wilberforce Benevolent Society of New York and other organizations to secure racial justice. Varick, along with black leaders such as PETER WILLIAMS JR. and Richard Allen, was instrumental in helping JOHN BROWN RUSSWURM and SAMUEL CORNISH publish in March 1827 the first black newspaper, *Freedom's Journal*, which operated for one year out of the Zion Church. Bishop Varick died in New York several months after the emergence of this newspaper and eighteen days after Independence Day 1827, the deadline set by the state of New York for all of its enslaved residents to attain their freedom. While he has been neglected in scholarly circles, Varick stands in history as one of the major leaders of American religion and independent black Christianity, as well as a testimony to the key role that African American church leaders played

in effecting political and economic freedom for the entire race.

FURTHER READING

Walls. William J. *The African Methodist Episcopal Zion Church: Reality of the Black Church* (1974).

—SANDY DWAYNE MARTIN

VAUGHAN, SARAH

(27 Mar. 1924–3 Apr. 1990), jazz singer, was born Sarah Lois Vaughan in Newark, New Jersey, to Asbury Vaughan, a carpenter, and Ada Vaughan, a laundress. Her father, who played guitar for pleasure, and her mother, who sang in the choir of the local Mount Zion Baptist Church, gave their only daughter piano lessons from the age of seven. Before her teens Vaughan was playing organ in church and singing in the choir. In 1942, on a dare from a friend, she took the subway into Harlem and entered the Apollo Theatre's legendary Wednesday-night amateur contest. She won the ten-dollar first prize and a weeklong spot there as an opening act.

That engagement launched a singer who would soon develop a voice of operatic splendor and an imagination to match. Embraced early on by the pioneers of bebop, "The Divine One," as she was called, absorbed their innovations and applied them lavishly to the Great American Songbook. Gunther Schuller, the Pulitzer Prize–winning classical conductor and scholar, called Vaughan the greatest vocal artist of the twentieth century: "Hers is a perfect instrument, attached to a musician of superb instincts" (Liska, 19). Unlike her peer Carmen McRae, Vaughan was no probing interpreter of words. She communicated drama through sound, wallowing in a seemingly endless range of textures. In one drawn-out note she could change timbres repeatedly, from dulcet to husky, or make a feathery leap from bass to soprano.

After hearing her sing at the Apollo, crooner Billy Eckstine, a reigning black heartthrob of the day, took her to meet his boss, the pianist and bandleader Earl "Fatha" Hines. Soon Vaughan was sharing the bandstand with Eckstine, as well as bebop pioneers CHARLIE PARKER and DIZZY GILLESPIE, who were in Hines's band. "I thought Bird and

Sarah Vaughan, jazz singer and musician who was awarded the Grammy Lifetime Achievement Award in 1989. Library of Congress

Diz were the end," said Vaughan. "Horns always influenced me more than voices" (Gold, 13). But she borrowed a lot from Eckstine, whose voluptuous swoops and overripe vibrato turned up in Vaughan's singing.

In the summer of 1944 Eckstine left Hines to form a groundbreaking bebop orchestra and took Vaughan with him. She made her first recording, "I'll Wait and Pray," with the band on 5 December 1944. Thereafter she recorded for several small bop labels. But it was clear to George Treadwell, a handsome trumpeter with whom she shared a bill in 1946, that Vaughan's voice had commercial potential. After a brief courtship, they wed on 17 September of that year. Treadwell became her manager, investing thousands of dollars on a makeover for his wife, including a nose job, teeth straightening, and gowns.

Also in 1946, a glamorized Vaughan joined a new label, Musicraft. In 1947 her luscious cover version of Doris Day's hit "It's Magic" climbed to number eleven. The next year she covered NAT KING COLE's "Nature Boy," reaching number nine. Every year from 1947

through 1952 she won *Down Beat*'s poll as best female jazz singer; through 1959 she had twenty-six Top Forty singles.

Vaughan's straddling of jukebox pop and modern jazz tended to frustrate both worlds. She went on the defense. "I'm not a jazz singer, I'm a singer," she said, while naming a wide range of favorite colleagues, from MAHALIA JACKSON to Polly Bergen (Liska, 21). In a fruitful relationship with Columbia from 1949 to 1953, Vaughan recorded show tunes, saccharin torch songs like "My Tormented Heart," and a now-classic LP with MILES DAVIS.

In 1954 she signed a dual contract with a pop label, Mercury, and its jazz subsidiary, EmArcy. Among the jazz milestones she created is *Sarah Vaughan*, a 1954 small-group album that teamed her with a bebop wunderkind, trumpeter Clifford Brown. Vaughan gained a new trademark in 1958 when she recorded "Misty," the Erroll Garner–Johnny Burke ballad, with a twinkly, sugar-dusted arrangement credited to QUINCY JONES. Her commercial stature rose as she recorded a series of kitschy hits, notably "Broken-Hearted Melody" (1959), a country-pop

ditty with a heavy backbeat and a male chorus singing "doomp-do-doomp" behind her. "God, I hated it," she said later. "It's the corniest thing I ever did" (Liska, 21). Yet it reached number seven and lifted her into a glamorous rank of white supper clubs. Vaughan even appeared in a 1960 gangster film, *Murder Inc.*

Also in 1960 Vaughan accepted a lucrative offer from Roulette, a gangster-run rock and jazz label. Through 1963 she created some of her best-loved work at Roulette: late-night jazz with guitar and bass (*After Hours* and *Sarah + 2*) and sessions with the Benny Carter and COUNT BASIE orchestras. But she also made a series of string-laden ballad discs, and jazz purists continued to attack her. The grumbling rose during her second stint at Mercury, from 1963 to 1967. Vaughan later claimed that she quit the label, citing various grievances: she hated the pop material, the records were not promoted, and she was not getting royalties. She did not record again until 1971.

Vaughan's luck with men was not much better. Having divorced Treadwell in 1956—she claimed that all he had done for her had been for himself—Vaughan had taken on a new husband-manager in 1959: Clyde "C. B." Atkins, a former professional football player who now owned a Chicago taxi fleet. In 1961 the couple adopted a child, Deborah (now Paris Vaughan, an actress). Divorcing the violent Atkins in the 1960s, Vaughan found he had left her in heavy debt to the Internal Revenue Service. From 1970 through 1977 she had a more pleasant relationship with Marshall Fisher, a restaurateur who became her manager. But when asked in an interview about the men in her life, an angry Vaughan threatened to "throw up" (O'Connor, 96).

Vaughan's career gained new life when she signed with Mainstream, a jazz label run by Bob Shad, her producer at EmArcy. She made more blatant pop albums, along with *Live in Japan*, a double LP of Vaughan singing the standards she loved with a first-rate trio, and *Sarah Vaughan with Michel Legrand*, a sumptuous orchestral collaboration with the celebrated French composer-arranger. For the rest of her life Vaughan was a touring machine, second only to ELLA FITZGERALD as a living legend of vocal jazz. No longer did she record fluff. From 1977 through 1982 she made a series of uncompromising jazz albums for the Pablo label. These included *Send in the Clowns* (1982), Vaughan's third LP with the Count Basie Orchestra. The title song, from Stephen Sondheim's *A Little Night Music*, was her key showstopper of later years. Singing the lament of an actress who has triumphed onstage but not in love, the shy and private Vaughan gave a rare flash of autobiography. She delivered the song as a slow, emotional aria, lingering on the words, "Sure of my lines / No one is there." Returning to Columbia, she recorded the Grammy Award–winning *Gershwin Live* (1982), a symphonic program she performed for years.

By now Vaughan had ended another marriage, to trumpeter Waymon Reed. Though sixteen years her junior, he died of cancer in 1983. Vaughan herself had smoked, drunk, and snorted cocaine for decades, with little audible damage. Her 1987 album, *Brazilian Romance*, proved this. But in 1989, soon after she won a Grammy for lifetime achievement, Vaughan was diagnosed with lung cancer. That October she returned to the Blue Note jazz club, her New York headquarters of the 1980s, for what would be her final performances. On 3 April 1990, one week after turning sixty-six, she died at her home in Hidden Hills, a Los Angeles suburb.

All of Vaughan's Mercury recordings are available in four box sets; her Roulette sides are gathered in *The Complete Roulette Sarah Vaughan Studio Sessions* (Mosaic). In 1991 the Public Broadcasting System aired a television documentary on Vaughan, *The Divine One*, as part of its *American Masters* series. In 2002 singer Dianne Reeves won a Grammy for her tribute album to Vaughan, *The Calling*. Reeves explained: "I'd never heard a voice like that, that was so rich and deep and beautiful, just sang all over the place. I thought, 'You mean, there are *those* kinds of possibilities?'" (Interview with author, 2000).

FURTHER READING

Dahl, Linda. *Stormy Weather: The Music and Lives of a Century of Jazzwomen* (Limelight Editions, 1996).

Gardner, Barbara. *Down Beat*, 2 Mar. 1961.

Gavin, James. Liner note essay for *The Complete Roulette Sarah Vaughan Studio Sessions* (Mosaic Records 8-CD set)

Gold, Don. *Down Beat*, 30 May 1957.

Liska, A. James. *Down Beat*, May 1982.

Mackin, Tom. "Newark's Divine Sarah." *Newark Sunday News*, 10 Nov. 1968.

O'Connor, Rory. *New York Woman*, Apr. 1988.

"Queen for a Year." *Metronome*, Feb. 1951.

Obituary: *New York Times*, 5 Apr. 1990.

—JAMES GAVIN

VESEY, DENMARK

(c. 1767–2 July 1822), mariner, carpenter, abolitionist, was born either in Africa or the Caribbean and probably grew up as a slave on the Danish colony of St. Thomas, which is now a part of the U.S. Virgin Islands. When Denmark was about fourteen years old, the slave trader Captain Joseph Vesey purchased him to sell on the slave market in Saint Domingue (Haiti). The identity of Denmark Vesey's parents and his name at birth are unknown, but Joseph Vesey gave him the name "Telemaque." He became "Denmark Vesey" in 1800, after he purchased his freedom from lottery winnings. Vesey's family life is difficult to reconstruct. He had at least three wives and several children, including three boys—Sandy, Polydore, and Robert—and a girl, Charlotte. His first and second wives, Beck and Polly, and their children lived as slaves. His third wife, Susan, was a free woman of color.

Not suitable for sale in Haiti, Telemaque became Captain Vesey's slave and "cabin boy" and moved with him to Charleston, South Carolina, in 1783. In Charleston Vesey labored as an urban slave for nearly seventeen years. As a chandler's man and a multilingual laborer who could read and write in English and French, Denmark Vesey conducted business for his owner's trade company. He was part of a large, diverse, and stratified urban black community that outnumbered the local white population. The occupations of black Charlestonians, a mixture of slave and free persons, varied; the population included artisans, domestics, agriculturalists, and other skilled and unskilled laborers. African Americans took advantage of the city's illicit trade network as they struggled to make a living in a challenging environment, where they faced white oppression and intraracial economic competition.

In 1799, at age thirty-three, Vesey purchased his freedom, joining just over 3,100 other people of color who made up Charleston's community of free blacks. State regulations made life for free persons of color semiautonomous at best. Free blacks had white patrons and paid annual "freedom" taxes, which left them vulnerable to white control as they labored in a city determined to limit their earning potential, social standing, and political power. South Carolina slaveholders hired out laborers for the Charleston market, thus creating economic tensions among free and enslaved black laborers. Divisions mounted as distinctions were drawn between blacks and those who were of mixed race. In this complex society Vesey apprenticed under established craftsmen and became a well-known and respected carpenter. Marginalized from the free community of light-skinned blacks, Vesey readily identified with rural and urban slaves who lived an arduous life that he remembered all too well.

At the turn of the century Vesey joined a growing number of southern blacks and converted to Christianity. After a short-term membership in a segregated congregation of the Second Presbyterian Church, he became a Methodist. Inspired by RICHARD ALLEN's movement in Philadelphia, Charleston's black Methodist population, which outnumbered whites of the same faith, established their own church. By 1818 the African Methodist Church had become the centerpiece for black religious congregation and supported political and economic activism. Influenced by Old Testament teachings, Vesey grew increasingly critical of slavery and commonly spoke against the institution. He compared the African American plight to that of the Israelites and joined America's rising antislavery fervor by arguing that white slaveholders denied blacks rights that were sanctioned by God. These debates inspired a grand scheme of resistance to South Carolina's aged slavery institution.

It is not known how long Vesey planned his resistance movement. Some modern scholars and primary-source accounts maintain that his plot was detailed, well organized, and that Vesey discussed the plan at length with a small group of trusted lieutenants. His accused co-conspirators, Peter Poyas, Rolla Bennett, Monday Gell, and Jack Pritchard, were all members of the African Methodist Church. The movement sought the assassination of South Carolina's governor and Charleston's mayor, and the rebels planned to take the militia arsenal, burn the city, and slaughter white citizens. They believed that blacks from the countryside and city would join the uprising as it grew, culminating in a mass exodus to Haiti, where President Jean-Pierre Boyer had encouraged free-black American immigration. A series of confessions exposed the conspiracy and led to the arrest of 128 black men. Thirty-five of those arrested were hanged, and forty were transported for their roles as co-conspirators in the revolt. Based on confessions and testimonies, South Carolina's courts named Vesey the chief organizer of the revolt and sentenced him to execution. He was hanged on 2 July 1822.

Vesey became a martyr for the American antislavery movement and a symbol for black resistance following his alleged role as mastermind of the 1822 insurrection. His life, the revolt, and his death have raised questions about nineteenth-century race relations and black resistance. Historians still debate whether the 1822 events in Charleston represented a failed, however expertly designed, uprising or whether the alleged Vesey rebellion occurred only in the minds of whites, and was fueled by rumors and deep-rooted white fears of slave resistance. The question remains, Was Denmark Vesey falsely accused because he was a literate and outspoken free black who used his thorough knowledge of Christianity to challenge American slavery? Or did he take this spirit of protest a step further, to plan what would have been, prior to NAT TURNER's rebellion in 1830, the largest slave revolt in U.S. history?

FURTHER READING

Egerton, Douglas R. *He Shall Go Out Free: The Lives of Denmark Vesey* (1999).

Lofton, John. *Denmark Vesey's Revolt: The Slave Plot That Lit a Fuse to Fort Sumter* (1983).

Pearson, Edward A. *Designs against Charleston: The Trial Record of the Denmark Vesey Slave Conspiracy of 1822* (1999).

Robertson, David. *Denmark Vesey: The Buried Story of America's Largest Slave Rebellion and the Man Who Led It* (1999).

—TIWANNA M. SIMPSON

W

WALCOTT, DEREK

(23 June 1930–), poet, playwright, and literary and cultural critic, was born Derek Alton Walcott in the town of Castries on the Caribbean island of St. Lucia, then a British colony. It had experienced very slow Anglicization since its acquisition from the French after the Napoleonic wars. His parents, Warwick Walcott and Alix (maiden name unknown), were Methodists in a mostly Roman Catholic society. His mother was a schoolteacher and seamstress and, for many years, headmistress of the Methodist Infant School. She enjoyed acting and reciting. Walcott's father, an avid watercolorist and civil servant, died in 1931, leaving his wife to raise young Derek, his twin brother (Roderick Alton), and his sister (Pamela), who was two years older.

Derek Walcott grew up in a house filled with books and other indications of the intellectual and artistic interests of his parents. After completing elementary school under the watchful eye of his mother, he won a scholarship to secondary school at St. Mary's College in Castries in 1941. Finishing in 1947, he taught at that institution until 1950. During these early years, perhaps the single most significant influence that shaped Walcott's path as a developing poet was his sense that he should follow in his father's artistic footsteps.

When he was only fourteen years old, Walcott announced his vocational intentions by publishing his first poem, "The Voice of St. Lucia," in the local newspaper. The poem dealt with learning about God through nature rather than through the church. In effect, Walcott challenged Roman Catholic supremacy in St. Lucia. When a local priest took up the challenge and replied in verse to accuse Walcott of blasphemy, it was clear to Walcott that he must be on the right track to have excited such a response, although he was also shocked.

By nineteen years of age Walcott had self-published two books of poetry: *25 Poems* (1948), which was released quickly in a second edition, and *Epitaph for the Young: A Poem in XII Cantos* (1949). He did not have the money to publish the first collection, but somehow his mother found enough to help him, and the book was finally printed in Trinidad. Walcott sold copies in St. Lucia to friends and recovered the printing costs. One of the poems ("A City's Death by Fire") in that first volume captured the severe trauma and the multilayered significance of the destruction by fire on 19–20 June 1948 of a large part of Castries, a few days before Walcott's eighteenth birthday. In 1950, after cofounding (with Maurice Mason) the St. Lucia Arts Guild, he left St. Lucia for Jamaica on a scholarship to study for a bachelor's degree in French, Spanish, and Latin at the recently established (1948) University College of the West Indies (later University of the West Indies).

Walcott's inclination to pursue the writing of poetry and drama professionally appears to have been well established. In 1951 another collection of his work, *Poems*, was privately printed in the Caribbean. Walcott's first three books of poems can be said to belong to this apprentice period, when he was influenced by the contexts of life in St. Lucia, including learning to paint under the guidance of his father's friend Harold Simmons, and by his exposure to the work of such poets as Stephen Spender, W. H. Auden, Louis MacNeice, T. S. Eliot, Ezra Pound, William Butler Yeats, Gerard Manley Hopkins, Dylan Thomas, John Crowe Ransom, and Robert Lowell. Walcott's early poetry depended heavily on the English literary tradition.

In 1953 Walcott moved to Trinidad, and, having earned the BA degree, he taught for a few years in Grenada, St. Lucia, and Jamaica. In 1953 he also married Faye A. Moyston, with whom he had a son, Peter, but the couple divorced in 1954. In 1957 he received the Jamaica Drama Festival Prize for

his play *Drums and Colors*, and in 1958 he was commissioned to compose an epic pageant in celebration of the first time the West Indian Federal Parliament would meet. His success with that project earned him a Rockefeller grant to study the American theater in New York City, and during that time he began work on one of his notable plays, *Dream on Monkey Mountain*, based upon reflections about St. Lucia, the Caribbean search for identity, and related concerns. An important stage in Walcott's career came in 1959, when he became founder-director of the Little Carib Theatre Workshop (later the Trinidad Theatre Workshop), in Port of Spain.

It is generally understood that his breakthrough as a mature poet came with the publication of his collection *In a Green Night* in 1962, and since then he has published several impressive collections, including *Selected Poems* (1964), *The Castaway and Other Poems* (1965), *Another Life* (1973), *Sea Grapes* (1976), *The Fortunate Traveler* (1981), and *Omeros* (1990), as well as plays and essays. In 1962 he married Margaret Maillard, with whom he had two daughters, Elizabeth and Anna; the couple later divorced.

Since the 1980s Walcott has combined university teaching in the United States, primarily at Boston University, with his artistic endeavors, maintaining a steady pace of creative productivity. In 1982 he married Norline Metivier. He won a prestigious John D. and Catherine T. MacArthur Foundation grant in 1981 and, in 1992, the Nobel Prize for Literature. His Nobel address, *Antilles: Fragment of Epic Memory*, was published in 1993. Walcott divides his time between St. Lucia (where he has his home), the Caribbean, and the United States, where he continues to lecture in literature and creative writing.

FURTHER READING

Walcott, Derek. "Leaving School—VIII," *The London Magazine*, Sept. 1965.

Baer, William, ed. *Conversations with Derek Walcott* (1996).

Burnett, Paula. *Derek Walcott: Politics and Poetics* (2001).

King, Bruce. *Derek Walcott: A Carribean Life* (2000).

Thieme, John. *Derek Walcott* (1999).

—DAVID BARRY GASPAR

WALKER, ALICE MALSENIOR

(9 Feb. 1944–), writer, activist, and educator, was born in Eatonton, Georgia, the youngest daughter of Willie Lee and Minnie Lou Grant Walker, who were sharecroppers. As the youngest of eight children growing up in the South, Walker experienced her share of familial and racial tension but also a good deal of closeness between, particularly, the female members of her family, whose talents and achievements she celebrates in her novels, poems, and essays. When she was eight years old, her brother shot her in the eye with a BB gun while they were playing cowboys and Indians, causing an injury that, despite later corrective surgery, scarred her for life. The incident led Walker into the first of several recurrent episodes of self-reflection and isolation, which, although

Alice Walker, novelist, essayist, poet, and winner of the Pulitzer Prize for her novel The Color Purple *in 1983.* Corbis

desperately difficult, often resulted in the reassertion of her artistic voice.

A gifted child, Walker graduated from her high school as its valedictorian in 1961 and was awarded a scholarship to Spelman College in Atlanta. After two years she transferred to Sarah Lawrence College in New York, traveled to Africa in the summer of 1964, and graduated a year later. Her passage through adolescence and young adulthood was, like her childhood, not without its problems. Talented and idealistic but also a troubled young woman, Walker returned from Africa pregnant, though not by choice. Depression and suicidal feelings marked her final year at Sarah Lawrence. Once she had made the difficult decision to have an abortion, writing provided a refuge from self-destruction. The fruits of this period, poems later published in *Once* in 1968 and the short story "To Hell with Dying" (1967), ripened under the encouragement of the poets Muriel Rukeyser and LANGSTON HUGHES.

After college Walker went to work for the New York City welfare department. In 1967 she married the white Jewish civil rights lawyer Mel Leventhal, and the couple moved to the South to settle in Jackson, Mississippi. Both were active in civil rights—Walker canvassed for voter registration in her native Georgia and acted as a black history consultant for Head Start in Mississippi, while her husband worked for the movement as a lawyer. At the same time Walker kept on writing—at times professionally, as writer in residence at Tougaloo and Jackson State colleges, but mostly in her scarce spare time, which became scarcer still after the birth of her only child, Rebecca, on 17 November 1969.

Life in the South was not easy at this time and under these conditions. Walker wrote much later, in "Breaking Chains and Encouraging Life" (1980), published in the essay collection *In Search of Our Mothers' Gardens: Womanist Prose* (1983), about the censure she received from reviewers, not for her work but for her "lifestyle," meaning her interracial marriage. In 2000 she also published a memoir of the early years of her marriage, "To My Young Husband" in *The Way Forward Is with a Broken Heart*. Her daughter Rebecca Leventhal Walker, later still, published her own memoirs of growing up as a child of mixed descent in *Black, White* *and Jewish: Autobiography of a Shifting Self* (2001).

At the time, however, the opinions of black critics and southern whites were minor concerns compared with Walker's intensely felt commitment to an interracial movement for civil rights, black and white together in nonviolent action under the leadership of men like MARTIN LUTHER KING JR. His death in 1968 disturbed her as much as his appearance on national TV had once excited and motivated her to join the movement, as she wrote in her tribute to him, "Choice," in *In Search of Our Mothers' Gardens*.

Domestic violence and abuse, witnessed in her youth in the South, were the major themes of her very early work, such as the award-winning short story collection *In Love and Trouble* (1973), and the novel *The Third Life of Grange Copeland* (1970). But civil rights inspired the next phase of Walker's writing. Besides several essays in *In Search of Our Mothers' Gardens*, her experiences in the civil rights movement also inspired the novel *Meridian* (1976) and some of the more critical stories in the collection *You Can't Keep a Good Woman Down* (1982), where Walker took issue with black nationalism.

The early to mid-seventies was a productive period for Walker—the poetry collection *Revolutionary Petunias* (1973) won the Lillian Smith Award—but the stress of living in a tumultuous period in the South's history, and of balancing work with family life took their toll. Walker's marriage to Leventhal was dissolved in 1977. Walker then turned her attention to teaching and writing, accepting a position at Wellesley College in New England, where she designed and taught the first-ever course in black women's writing. By this time she had made a major discovery: that there existed a tradition of black women writers and artists who had found ways of expressing themselves creatively and making their presences felt in the world. She had discovered the artistry of black women like her mother and her ancestor May Poole, of indomitable spirit, who had created gardens and handed their stories down through the generations. She had discovered, notably, the writer and anthropologist ZORA NEALE HURSTON, who, like Walker, came from the South a stranger to metropolitan academe but who, while enrolled at Barnard College in New York, kept the faith with her people and was not ashamed to celebrate their creativity and wisdom.

The result of this discovery was the pathbreaking anthology *I Love Myself When I Am Laughing: A Zora Neale Huston Reader* (1979). Hurston, who had experienced some success but was forgotten by the time she reached middle age, had a profound influence on Walker. Certainly, the concept of "womanism," for which Walker has become renowned and which is often taken to mean, too simply, "black feminism," owes much to Hurston's example as a sassy, serious, sometimes outrageous but, most of all, independent-minded and proud black woman. She was a feminist before feminism was invented, like Shug in *The Color Purple* (1983).

Written in northern California, where Walker had moved in 1977 to devote herself full time to her art, with the support of Guggenheim and National Endowment for the Arts fellowships, *The Color Purple* was a turning point in Walker's career. Perhaps a radical change in living conditions made this possible: Walker was living in rural Mendocino County with her daughter and her new partner, Robert Allen. In the persona of Celie, an abused and downtrodden southern black woman who rises to her own spiritual and literal fortune through the love of Shug, a jazz singer, and a reunion with her long-lost sister, Nettie, the voice of the artist emerged fully developed in a Hurston-inspired everyday language that was both simple and poetic.

The Color Purple was a runaway success; it won the Pulitzer Prize and the National Book Award in 1983, but it also caused a good deal of controversy, especially after the film version, directed by Steven Spielberg, came out in 1985. The main source of offense in the novel was Walker's depiction of lesbianism in the relationship between Shug and Celie; in the film it was the portrayal of black men as either child molesters (Albert) or buffoons (Harpo) that attracted virulent criticism. Because the tone of such criticism was often hateful, Walker revisited, after another of those periods of self-reflection and isolation, the debate around *The Color Purple* in the memoir *The Same River Twice: Honoring the*

Difficult (1996). She commemorated in this volume the pain that criticism of *The Color Purple* had caused her, at a time when she was also suffering from Lyme disease and having relationship problems with Robert Allen.

Once again difficult times eventually produced new work, however, and in *The Temple of My Familiar* (1989) sexuality or, more accurately, sensuality and loving relationships—whether between lovers, within extended families, or in creation at large—were a major theme. Easily the longest and most challenging of Walker's novels, *The Temple of My Familiar* took the whole of world history and the kinship of humans with the natural world as its subject. Many of Walker's paganist beliefs found their expression here, as did her increasing awareness of her own bisexuality. This, and Allen's alcoholism, eventually led to a breakup in 1990; since then Walker has mostly been in relationships with women.

More than most writers, Alice Walker uses her life in her creative work, often for didactic purposes. Typical is the incident of her brother shooting her in the eye with a BB gun. Walker has often recounted this story to explain how, in apparently innocent children's games, boys learn the early scripts of masculinity: to inflict pain on those smaller and weaker than themselves, something that later in life may lead them to domestic violence. She has also harked back to the memory of her "patriarchal wound" as a connection, through identification and trauma, with women in Africa who have to suffer female genital mutilation, often at a very young age. In the 1992 film documentary *Warrior Marks*, directed by Pratibha Parmar, Walker told her own story of the injury while filming young girls who were about to be mutilated. In the accompanying book *Warrior Marks: Female Genital Mutilation and the Sexual Blinding of Women* (1993) and in the novel *Possessing the Secret of Joy* (1992), Walker sought to educate the world about the crime of female genital mutilation. Departing from fiction writers' custom, she even ended her novel with an afterword, "To the Reader," in which she gave statistics on this practice and a list for further reading.

Besides being a writer who uses her own life in her creative work, Walker thus is also an activist and an educator.

She taught at a number of universities, including Berkeley and Yale, but it is as an informal educator, an elder or grandmother, that she has come to style herself in the later works. Her womanist, environmentalist, and paganist credo was made most explicit in *Anything We Love Can Be Saved: A Writers' Activism* (1997), a book of essays and open letters on a range of issues, from wearing dreadlocks to the boycott of Cuba. The relation between the political and the personal, always a trademark of Walker's writing, remained paramount also in the pamphlet *Sent by Earth: A Message from the Grandmother Spirit after the Attacks on the World Trade Center and Pentagon* (2001).

Since the death of both her parents (her father in 1973 and her mother in 1993) and a brother (1996), Walker has reevaluated her relationship with her family. In *Anything We Love Can Be Saved* she wrote about the spiritual journey to make peace with her father and brothers at last. But the great love remained her mother; an essay entitled "My Mother's Blue Bowl" concludes the collection in tribute.

This same theme of family relations—their difficulty and the eventual forgiveness that leads to reconciliation—suffused *By the Light of My Father's Smile* (1998), a novel that is a meditation on a writer's life and death. Walker's fascination with the mortality of art and artists dates back at least to her discovery of Zora Neale Hurston, whose premature death in obscurity Walker took, in the late seventies, to be a cautionary tale about how little African American artists were valued. It seemed, however, that by the twenty-first century the Californian, bisexual, pagan, womanist Alice Walker not only was confident in her role as writer and medium but also was recognized worldwide as an elder and spiritual guide for generations to come.

FURTHER READING

Walker, Alice. *Anything We Love Can Be Saved: A Writer's Activism* (1997).
———. *The Same River Twice: Honoring the Difficult* (1996).
———. *In Search of Our Mothers' Gardens: Womanist Prose* (1983).
———. *The Way Forward Is with a Broken Heart* (2000).

O'Brien, John. "Alice Walker: An Interview" in *Alice Walker: Critical Perspectives Past and*

Present, eds. Henry Louis Gates Jr. and K. A. Appiah (1993), 326–346.

Wilson, Sharon. "A Conversation with Alice Walker" in *Alice Walker: Critical Perspectives Past and Present*, eds. Henry Louis Gates Jr. and K. A. Appiah (1993) 319–325.

—MARIA LAURET

WALKER, DAVID (1796?– 6 Aug. 1830), used-clothing dealer and political writer, was born in Wilmington, North Carolina, the son probably of a free black woman and possibly of a slave father. Almost nothing is known about either parent; only a little more is known about Walker's years in the South. Walker was born in a town where by 1800 African Americans predominated demographically over whites by more than two to one. Their influence on the town and the region was profound. Most labor—skilled or unskilled—was performed by black slaves who were the foundation of the region's key industries: naval stores production, lumbering, rice cultivation, building construction, and shipping. The Methodist church in Wilmington was largely the creation of the local black faithful. The skill and resourcefulness of the African Americans amid their enslavement deeply impressed Walker.

Sometime between 1815 and 1820 Walker left Wilmington and made the short journey south to Charleston, South Carolina. He probably decided to move because free blacks comprised a much higher percentage of the black population in Charleston than in Wilmington, had far greater economic opportunity there, and had created a number of social and benevolent organizations to serve their needs. How Walker was employed in Charleston is not known. By 1817 a number of the town's black religious leaders formed one of the first branches of the new African Methodist Episcopal church, founded in Philadelphia in 1816 by RICHARD ALLEN. Walker was probably exposed to this particular congregation and began then his deep devotion to Allen and his example of racial and religious courage. Walker must also have known of the relentless white efforts to close the church and the bitterness that these attempts engendered in many of its devout members. By 1821 these increasing attacks helped provoke several members to begin plotting a revolt against slavery in the region. This complicated plot—named after the free black carpenter who orchestrated it, DENMARK VESEY—coordinated slaves and free blacks in the city with slaves in the surrounding rice parishes to set fire to key points in the city, seize weapons caches, and murder whites indiscriminately in the confusion on a predetermined night in June 1822. However, the conspiracy was revealed very late by an informer, and all the principals were soon arrested, summarily tried, and hanged. Walker was in Charleston at least as late as 1821 and probably for this series of dramatic events in 1822 as well. This may have influenced his later efforts to link black empowerment and resistance in the South with religion.

By 1825 Walker had settled in Boston, Massachusetts, and had opened a used-clothing store near the city's wharves. In 1826 he entered the social life of the black community more fully, marrying a local woman, Eliza Butler, in February and in July becoming initiated into Prince Hall Masonry at African Lodge No. 459, North America's first black masonic lodge. Membership in this order gave Walker immediate access to most of black Boston's prominent men, and he soon became a leading political force in the community. He also affiliated with a local black Methodist congregation whose minister, Samuel Snowden, was a fiery preacher and an impassioned antislavery activist. They developed a very close friendship. In 1827 Walker championed the United States' first black newspaper, *Freedom's Journal*, and was its principal agent in Boston. Along with his fellow lodge brothers he helped organize and police several parades, or "African Celebrations," in the heart of Boston's African American community, the heavily black-settled north slope of Beacon Hill. Walker spoke at one celebration honoring the visit of an African prince, Abduhl Rahhaman, recently emancipated in the South. He also played a key role in creating the Massachusetts General Colored Association, formed no later than 1828 and one of the first avowedly black political organizations in the country. In December of that year Walker articulated its essential position: "[T]he primary object of this institution is to unite the colored population, so far, through the United States . . . and not [withhold] anything which may have the least tendency to meliorate *our* miserable condition." By early 1829, a recent inductee into the tiny club of black homeowners in Boston and his community's leading political voice, Walker prepared to undertake his greatest challenge.

On 28 September 1829 Walker published the first edition of the work for which he is best known, *Appeal to the Colored Citizens of the World*, one of the most influential black political documents of the nineteenth century. Displaying a vehemence and outrage unprecedented among contemporary African American authors, Walker's *Appeal* decried in vivid and personal terms the uniquely savage, un-Christian treatment blacks suffered in the United States, especially as slaves:

> All I ask is, for a candid and careful perusal of . . . my Appeal, where the world may see that we, the Blacks or Coloured People, are treated more cruel by the white Christians of America, than devils themselves ever treated a set of men, women and children on this earth. (i)

By depriving African Americans of secular education, the word of God, civil liberties, and any position of social responsibility, white Americans forced blacks closer and closer to the life of brutes. Indeed the most "insupportable insult" that whites hurled at blacks—expressed the most fully, Walker charged, in Thomas Jefferson's *Notes on the State of Virginia*—was that "they were not of the human family" but descended originally "from the tribes of *Monkeys* or *Orang-Outangs*." Walker feared the profound demoralization such pervasive attitudes would have on African Americans and intended the *Appeal* to be a clarion to them of their worth as humans, their noble history in Africa, and God's special love for them. Walker's *Appeal* challenged African Americans to uplift and organize themselves and cast off this oppression that, he proclaimed, God found an intolerable provocation and sinful for them to endure any longer: "[Y]our full glory and happiness . . . under Heaven, shall never be fully consummated, but with the *entire emancipation of your enslaved brethren all over the world*" (29).

By late 1829 and throughout 1830 Walker terrified white southern authorities with novel efforts to circulate his pamphlet on their turf. Relying on black and white mariners to introduce the booklet into key southern ports, and sometimes using the mail, Walker sought especially to enlist the support of educated and evangelical black leaders in these towns in reaching out to the local black masses and rallying them to the message of the *Appeal*. His plan, while never fully formulated or enacted, nevertheless bespoke one of the boldest and most extensive visions of slave empowerment and rebellion ever conceived in antebellum America. Although officials in the South had stemmed the circulation of his book by late 1830, fear of his and his associates' further subversions continued to trouble them into 1831. Several states reacted by strengthening their laws against slave literacy, the circulation of antislavery matter, and contact between transient black seamen and local black residents in ports.

Walker's work remained an inspiration for many young African Americans who, by the early 1830s, were becoming much more assertive in their calls for an end to slavery and racial discrimination. The young black activist MARIA W. STEWART summarized black Boston's reverence for him in 1831 when she referred to him in a speech as "the most noble, fearless, and undaunted David Walker." Although rumors circulated widely that Walker's death in Boston was caused by poisoning from a southern assassin, his death certificate stated the cause as consumption, the same disease from which his infant daughter Lydia Ann had died a few days earlier. David Walker was probably the father of Edwin Garrison Walker, who in 1861 became one of the first blacks admitted to the Massachusetts bar and who earned similar distinction when elected to the Massachusetts legislature in 1866. By the 1890s he had gained national prominence as the president of the Colored National League.

FURTHER READING

Aptheker, Herbert. *"One Continual Cry": David Walker's "Appeal to the Colored Citizens of the World" (1829–1830)—Its Setting and Its Meaning* (1965).

Hinks, Peter P. *To Awaken My Afflicted Brethren: David Walker and the Problem of Antebellum Slave Resistance* (1996).
—PETER P. HINKS

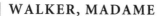

WALKER, GEORGE W.

See Williams, Bert, and George Walker.

WALKER, MADAME C. J.

(23 Dec. 1867–25 May 1919), business-woman, was born Sarah Breedlove in Delta, Louisiana, the daughter of Minerva Anderson and Owen Breedlove, sharecroppers. Her destitute parents died, leaving Sarah an orphan at seven years of age. She lived next with her sister, Louvenia, in Vicksburg, Mississippi, but life was not much better there. At the age of fourteen, she married Moses McWilliams, having one daughter, Lelia (later to call herself A'Lelia). In 1887 McWilliams was killed, and Sarah Breedlove, twenty years old, barely literate, unskilled, and with a two-year-old child, faced a desperate situation. Leaving Mississippi, she headed up the Mississippi River to St. Louis, where she became a washerwoman.

Over years of poverty, poor diet, inadequate hygiene, and labor in the steam and chemical fumes of the laundry, Breedlove, like many other black women, started to lose her hair. She began experimenting with the various chemicals she used every day, trying to find some kind of preparation that would aid in the care and grooming of the hair and skin of black women like herself and sometime between 1900 and 1905 she came up with a new hair-care formula for black women. The nature of the formula was always kept secret by her and the company, but it seems probable that the highly touted "secret ingredient" was sulphur. Some people at the time, however, claimed that Breedlove bought a product made by ANNIE TURNBO MALONE's

Entrepreneur Madame C. J. Walker built her business empire on the creation of hair products for African American women. Courtesy of A'Lelia Bundles

Poro Company, analyzed it, and then copied it.

At about the same time, Breedlove's firm also popularized an improved version of the hot comb, made out of steel to make it more useful to African Americans. With her ointment and her steel hot comb, Breedlove developed what would later be known as the "Walker System" for straightening hair, though she always insisted that her major contribution was the growing, not the straightening, of African American hair. Nonetheless, a major emphasis of the Walker System was the removal of "kinks" from the hair of black women—to straighten their hair—so it was often referred to as the "Anti-Kink Walker System."

After meeting with some success, Breedlove decided in July 1905 to move to Denver, where she took a job and began peddling her hair product in her spare time. Soon thereafter she married Charles J. Walker, a newspaperman and publicist, who gave her tips for marketing and advertising her product. The Walker business proved highly successful in Denver, largely through door-to-door marketing. As the popularity of her hair-care products grew, Madame C. J. Walker began training "agent-operators." She traveled extensively in the South and East, giving lectures and demonstrations at black clubs, homes, schools, and churches.

The Walker System became so popular in the eastern states that Walker decided it was imperative to establish an office closer to those markets. While on her travels in 1910, she stopped in Indianapolis and decided to move the headquarters there, establishing a large-scale manufacturing operation. Later she would add a training center for her salespeople, along with research and production laboratories, and another beauty school.

Walker at this time also began to organize her agents into a series of "Walker Clubs" that gave cash prizes to the clubs doing the largest amount of philanthropic work. These clubs became engines of business growth as well as community and individual uplift. Then Walker began to bring her agents together in national conventions. The first of these was held in Philadelphia in 1917, when two hundred Walker agents convened for the first meeting of the Madame C. J. Walker Hair Culturists Union of America. Coming from the deep South, the North, and the West, they met to learn new techniques, to share business experiences, and to tell their own personal success stories. At these conventions Walker would personally hand out fifty-dollar prizes to the clubs that had been most generous in supporting their churches and missionary societies. The annual meetings also became venues for the empowerment of African American women.

Walker became increasingly involved in club and philanthropic work. She joined the National Association of Colored Women, became a staunch benefactor of Bethune-Cookman College in Florida, leaving it five thousand dollars in her will, and gave sizable contributions to the NAACP. During her time in Indianapolis, she donated one thousand dollars to the YMCA and made further donations to homes for the aged and the needy. In addition, she maintained scholarships for young women at Tuskegee and gave money to Palmer Memorial Institute in Sedalia, North Carolina.

As Walker became wealthier from her hair preparation business (the firm by 1917 had business amounting to $500,000 annually), she began to invest her profits in other endeavors, particularly real estate. In 1916 she left Indianapolis to live in New York City, where she engaged in an increasingly more opulent lifestyle. She bought a four-and-a-half-acre estate in Irvington on the banks of the Hudson and built a gracious mansion with a formal Italian garden and swimming pool, costing over $350,000, called "Villa Lewaro." By this time, her health began to fail, and soon thereafter she died at her new home. She had divorced her husband in 1912.

Walker was a washerwoman until age thirty-eight; when she died thirteen years later, she left a fortune of between a half million and a million dollars, having successfully operated the largest black-owned business in the United States. Nonetheless, her cultural legacy is somewhat ambiguous. Although she served as a model of black entrepreneurship, gave pride and empowerment to a generation of African American women, and generously contributed to worthy groups and causes, the source of her fortune was a product that exploited a desire to lessen the distinctiveness of black identity. During an era in American history when poverty often seemed the inevitable lot of the descendents of slaves and the ridicule of black features was pervasive, the use of Madame C. J. Walker's Hair Grower to straighten one's hair enabled African Americans to suppose that they could look more like people of European origin. Nearly half a century would pass before the Afro would become an assertive statement of black identity.

FURTHER READING

The bulk of Walker's papers are at the Indiana Historical Society; other materials can be found in the BOOKER T. WASHINGTON Papers at the Library of Congress.

Bundles, A'Lelia. *On Her Own Ground: The Life and Times of Madam C. J. Walker* (2001).

Lowry, Beverly. *Her Dream of Dreams: The Rise and Triumph of Madam C. J. Walker* (2003).

Peiss, Kathy. *Hope in a Jar* (1998).

Obituaries: *New York Times, New York Sun, Indianapolis News,* and *St. Louis Post-Dispatch,* all 27 May 1919.

—JOHN N. INGHAM

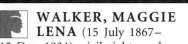

WALKER, MAGGIE LENA (15 July 1867– 15 Dec. 1934), civil rights and women's rights activist, community leader, and the nation's first woman bank president, was born in Richmond, Virginia, to Elizabeth "Lizzie" Draper, a former slave, and Eccles Cuthbert, a white writer. Unwed at the time of Maggie's birth, Lizzie Draper worked as an assistant cook in the home of Elizabeth Van Lew, an ardent abolitionist and Union spy. In 1869 Lizzie married William Mitchell, a former slave, who worked as Van Lew's butler and later as the headwaiter at the posh St. Charles Hotel. A son, Johnny, was born shortly after the family's move to downtown Richmond. In 1878 William was robbed and murdered, leaving Lizzie and her two young children without savings, insurance benefits, or financial support, circumstances that informed Maggie's adult work on behalf of the economic status of black women. Lizzie, with Maggie's help, supported her family as a laundress. "I was not born with a silver spoon in mouth," Maggie stated later, "but instead, with a clothes basket almost upon my head."

A strong voice for education, Maggie Lena Walker became the first African American female bank president. Witherspoon Collection, Valentine Museum, Richmond, Virginia

Maggie concluded her education in Richmond's segregated public schools with a call for racial justice. In 1883 at age fifteen, she organized one of the country's first African American school strikes when she led her nine high school classmates in protesting the disparity between black and white graduation ceremonies. Maggie taught school until her 1886 marriage to Armstead Walker Jr., a building contractor. Together they had three sons: Russell Eccles Talmadge, Armstead Mitchell, who died at the age of seven months, and Melvin DeWitt.

When she was fourteen Walker had joined the Grand United Order of Saint Luke, a fraternal organization founded by a former slave, Mary Prout, in Baltimore in 1867. The order, like many of the African American mutual benefit societies of its time, offered services that were generally unavailable to blacks through white agencies, including insurance policies, access to health care, and help with burials. In 1895 Walker formed the juvenile branch of the order and two years later was elected secretary of the endowment department. In 1899, having served in many positions during the previous ten years, Walker was elected right worthy grand secretary-treasurer, the order's top post.

When Walker's tenure as director began, the order was near financial ruin. Undeterred, she changed the organization's name to the Independent Order of Saint Luke (IOSL) and moved its headquarters to Richmond. In an effort to better inform the community the IOSL served, in 1902 Walker established and edited a weekly newspaper, the *Saint Luke Herald*. Through the *Herald*, which by 1925 had six thousand subscribers, Walker condemned segregation, lynching, and the lack of equal educational opportunities for black children. In 1903 Walker negotiated and supervised the construction of a four-story brick headquarters for the organization.

Walker became the first woman bank president in the United States when she founded the Saint Luke Penny Savings Bank in 1903. The black-owned bank, which had several women board members, recognized the unique situation and often limited resources of Richmond's blacks and its women in particular. Many of the bank's

first customers were washerwomen (including Walker's mother) and children who were encouraged to "turn [their] pennies into dollars." The bank's slogan, "Bring It All Back Home," encapsulated the role the bank played in securing economic self-determination for the African American community. The bank's special commitment to the "small depositor" included a strong emphasis on financing black home ownership, and by 1920 it had helped purchase more than six hundred homes. Walker's leadership saw the bank through name changes, alterations in federal banking laws, and the merging of the Saint Luke Bank with the two remaining black banks in Richmond in 1930. The resulting Consolidated Bank and Trust Co. remains open, located across the street from its original site in Richmond. It is the oldest continuously black-owned bank in the United States.

Around the turn of the century, discrimination and hostility toward blacks increased. Segregation was concretized in every facet of life, and American blacks were systematically removed from political and civil positions of power. Walker's decision in 1905 to open the Saint Luke Emporium, a black-owned department store, signaled yet another attempt at establishing a self-reliant black community. The store, which sold goods at cheaper prices than were available to blacks in white-owned stores, closed in 1912 as a result of organized opposition from Richmond's white merchants. Walker's other projects, however, continued to thrive. Under her leadership, the IOSL grew from 3,500 members in 1899 to over 100,000 members from twenty-two states by 1925.

Walker led vigorous women's suffrage and voter registration campaigns. In the 1920 elections, eighty percent of Richmond's eligible black voters were women. The increased political voice of Richmond's black women was one factor in the formation of the Virginia Black-Lily Republican Party. As a protest against attempts by the "Lily-White" (all-white) wing of the Republican Party to expel blacks from party leadership positions, the Black-Lily Party ran all-black slates of state and national candidates, including Walker herself, who ran for state superintendent in 1921.

A tireless leader and activist, Walker co-founded both the Richmond branch of the NAACP and the Colored Women's Council of Richmond, which, along with other philanthropic projects, raised money for Janie Porter Barrett's Virginia Industrial School for Colored Girls, one of two schools that Walker directed. She served on the board of the Richmond Urban League and as a member of its interracial commission, as a trustee of the Hartshorn College at Virginia Union University, and as a member of the Virginia State Federation of Colored Women, the Negro Organization Society of Virginia, and the International Council of Women of the Darker Races. Nationally, Walker sat on the executive committees of the NAACP and the National Association of Colored Women and worked as vice president of the National Association of Colored Women's Clubs.

Walker was remarkable in her unwavering focus on the importance of entrepreneurship within the black community and, in particular, on the economic lives of black women. She promoted the employment of women outside domestic service, as well as broader racial self-empowerment and "buy black" programs. Black women must rely on and credit each other, she insisted. They must "band themselves together, organize,...put their mites together, put their hands and their brains together and make work and business for themselves" (quoted in Brown, 271). The facts of her own life had taught Walker that black women must be given the skills and resources to support themselves. To this end, she worked on behalf of the National Association of Wage Earners, a women's organization that worked to expand economic opportunities for black women. In 1898 Walker played a key role in establishing the Woman's Union, a female insurance company whose motto was "The Hand That Rocks the Cradle Rules the World."

Walker artfully articulated the unique and complex position of black women. "Who is as helpless as the Negro woman?" she asked. "Who is so circumscribed and hemmed in, in the race of life, in the struggle for bread, meat and clothing as the Negro woman?" (quoted in Brown, 272). She understood that white women's expanding roles might limit opportunities for black women. She was also keenly aware of the criticism voiced by many within the black community that, by organizing, black women were staging an assault on the sanctity of the home. In word and action Walker showed that bettering the political and economic life of all African Americans necessitated tying race consciousness to the equality of women, with black men supporting the broadening of opportunities for black women.

Amid all her success, Walker endured great tragedy. In 1915 Walker's husband was accidentally shot and killed on the back porch of their house by their eldest son, Russell, who mistook his father for a burglar. Russell, who was tried and acquitted twice, never fully recovered from the incident and died in 1923. Despite confinement to a wheelchair in 1928 and other health problems resulting from diabetes and a 1907 fall that broke her kneecap, Walker remained active until her death from diabetic gangrene in 1934. In 1978 the U.S. Department of the Interior designated Walker's Richmond home a National Historic Site.

FURTHER READING

Walker's unpublished papers are available at the Maggie L. Walker National Historic Site, Richmond, Virginia.

BRAWLEY, BENJAMIN. *Negro Builders and Heroes* (1937).

Brown, Elsa Barkley. "Womanist Consciousness: Maggie Lena Walker and the Independent Order of Saint Luke" in *Unequal Sisters: A Multi-Cultural Reader in U.S. Women's History*, ed. Vicki L. Ruiz (1994).

Dabney, Wendell P. *Maggie L. Walker and the I.O. of St. Luke: The Woman and Her Work* (1927).

—LISA E. RIVO

WALLER, FATS

(12 May 1904–15 Dec. 1943), pianist, organist, singer, and composer, was born Thomas Wright Waller in New York City, the fourth of five surviving children of Edward Waller and Adeline (maiden name unknown). Edward was a Baptist lay minister, and one of young Thomas's earliest musical experiences

was playing harmonium for his father's street-corner sermons. Thomas's mother was deeply involved in music as well, and the family acquired a piano around 1910. Although Waller had formal musical instruction during his formative years, he was largely self-taught and indulged in a lot of musical experimentation.

Thomas's development as a jazz pianist really began in 1920, when, upon the death of his mother, he moved in with the family of the pianist Russell Brooks and then with the Harlem stride piano master James Price Johnson. Like his pianist contemporaries, Waller had learned some aspects of ragtime and jazz style from studying the player piano rolls of masters such as Johnson. Now his instructional experience consisted of sitting at one piano while Johnson sat at another. Johnson's earliest impression of Waller was that he "played with fervor" but that "he didn't have any swing then" (Peck, 20). At the time, young Thomas was playing quite a bit of organ and had not developed the propulsive and difficult stride left hand required of the jazz piano style of the day. Long hours

of practice, association with Johnson and other stride masters, and formal studies with the pianist Leopold Godowsky and the composer Carl Bohm at Juilliard honed Waller's skills.

By 1922 Waller had embarked on a busy career cutting piano rolls and playing theater organ at the Lincoln and Lafayette theaters. In that same year he made his debut solo recording for the Okeh label with "Muscle Shoals Blues" and "Birmingham Blues." He also began accompanying a number of vaudeville blues singers, including Sara Martin and Alberta Hunter. In 1923, through an association with the New Orleans songwriter Clarence Williams, Waller launched his own songwriting career with the publication and recording of "Wild Cat Blues."

In the mid-1920s many of Waller's instrumental compositions were recorded by the prominent Fletcher Henderson orchestra, including "Henderson Stomp," which featured a brief sixteen-bar solo by Waller as guest pianist that demonstrated his muscular technique and innovative ascending parallel tenths in his left hand. Henderson

Pianist and composer Fats Waller, whose influence can be heard in the playing of almost all the swing pianists who followed him, including COUNT BASIE. ©Bettmann/CORBIS

also recorded Waller's "Stealin' Apples" and an overblown parody of the Paul Whiteman Orchestra called "Whiteman Stomp." During this time Waller began his association with the lyricists Spencer Williams and Andy Razaf. With Razaf, Waller wrote his most enduring songs, those included in the musicals *Keep Shufflin'* (1928) and *Hot Chocolates* (1929). *Hot Chocolates*, which premiered at Connie's Inn in Harlem, moved to Broadway within a month. "Ain't Misbehavin'," a song from that show, was a signature vehicle for CAB CALLOWAY and was largely responsible for propelling the singing career of LOUIS ARMSTRONG.

Waller became a star entertainer in his own right. His large physical dimensions—which earned him the nickname "Fats"—his wit, and his extroverted personality made him a comic favorite to millions. While many fans and critics saw Waller as a mere buffoon, they failed to grasp the true genius of his humorous presentation. Often given uninspired hack songs to record, Waller transformed the material into successful performance vehicles that simultaneously offered veiled, biting commentary. Through his musical and comic ingenuity, he chided pompous, high-brow society in the song "Lounging at the Waldorf" and tainted the glib romantic sentiment of Billy Mayhew's "It's a Sin to Tell a Lie" by modifying the lyric to "If you break my heart, I'll break your jaw, and then I'll die." Much like the interlocutors of minstrelsy, he used pompous, complex word replacements, such as "your pedal extremities are colossal" in place of "your feet's too big." Waller was also able to diffuse overt racist expressions in songs like "Darktown Strutters' Ball" by referring to it as "Sepia Town."

Waller had a long-running relationship with Victor Records dating back to 1926 and had an exclusive contract with them by 1934. He recorded prolifically with his own ensembles, Fats Waller and His Rhythm, and costarred with and accompanied other artists. In addition to an exhausting and ultimately fatal road tour schedule, he had his own regular radio program on WOR in New York (1931) and WLW in Cincinnati (1932–1934). He made four "soundies," song-length music videos on film that were shown in nickelodeon arcades, and appeared in three full-length films, *King of Burlesque* (1935), *Hooray for Love* (1935), and *Stormy Weather* (1943), costarring LENA HORNE, BILL "BOJANGLES" ROBINSON, KATHERINE DUNHAM, the Nicholas Brothers, and Eddie "Rochester" Anderson.

Fats Waller's ultimate contribution to music was as a pianist. Behind the comic exterior was an uncompromising and deeply gifted keyboard artist. His most sublime piano performances were recorded in a series beginning in 1929 that included "Handful of Keys," "Smashing Thirds," and "Numb Fumblin'." These pieces continued the two-fisted, swinging, and virtuoso solo style developed by James P. Johnson and others, but they also showcased Waller's own innovations, such as a graceful melodic sense and gliding walking tenths in the left hand that presaged modern swing. His influence can be heard in almost all the swing pianists who followed him, including COUNT BASIE. Waller had a love and deep knowledge of classical music, especially Bach, and in 1928 he was the soloist premiering in James P. Johnson's *Yamekraw*, a concert work for piano and orchestra performed at Carnegie Hall. In London in 1939 Waller ventured into longer compositional forms with his *London Suite*, which was orchestrated and recorded by the Ted Heath Orchestra in 1950. Waller continued to record jazz, blues, and popular songs on his beloved pipe organ and was the first prominent artist to showcase the new Hammond electric organ in the 1930s.

In 1943 Waller's overweight condition and indulgences in food, tobacco, and liquor, combined with the exhausting pace of his career and several personal crises, including an alimony liability to Edith Hatchett, his wife of 1920–1923, that dogged him all his adult life, finally caught up with him. On a train returning to the East Coast from Hollywood after filming *Stormy Weather*, Waller died in his sleep somewhere around Kansas City. He was thirty-nine years old.

FURTHER READING

Hadlock, Richard. *Jazz Masters of the Twenties* (1965; repr. 1988).

Kirkeby, Ed. *Ain't Misbehavin': The Story of Fats Waller* (1966; repr. 1988).

Machlin, Paul S. *Stride: The Music of Fats Waller* (1985).

Peck, Seymour. "The Dean of Jazz Pianists," *PM*, 27 Apr. 1945: 20.

Shipton, Alyn. *Fats Waller: The Cheerful Little Earful* (2002).

Waller, Maurice, and Anthony Calabrese. *Fats Waller* (1977).

Discography

Posnak, Paul, compiler. *The Great Piano Solos 1929–1941* (1998).

"Thomas Wright "Fats" Waller" in *Performances in Transcription 1927–1943*, comp. Paul S. Machlin, Music of the United States of America series, vol. 10 (2001).
—DAVID JOYNER

WASHINGTON, BOOKER T. (5 Apr. 1856?–14 Nov. 1915), educator and race leader, was born on the plantation of James Burroughs, near Hale's Ford in Franklin County, Virginia, the son of an unknown white father and Jane, a slave cook owned by Burroughs. Washington was never certain of the date of his birth and showed little interest in who his father might have been. His mother gave him his first and middle names, Booker Taliaferro; he took his last name in 1870 from his stepfather, Washington Ferguson, a slave whom his mother had married. In his autobiography *Up from Slavery* (1901), he recalled the poverty of his early years as a slave on Burroughs's plantation, but because emancipation came when he was around nine, he was spared the harsher experiences of the slave system. In 1865, at the end of the Civil War, his mother moved him, his half-sister, and his half-brother to Malden, West Virginia, where her husband had found work. Young Booker was put to work packing salt from a nearby mine and later did even harder work in a coal mine.

Two women were influential in Washington's early education. The first was his mother. He displayed an intense interest in learning to read; although illiterate herself, she bought her son a spelling book and encouraged him to learn. While working in the mines, Washington also began attending a local elementary school for black youths. The other female influence was Viola Ruffner, wife of General Lewis Ruffner, owner of the mines. Probably around the age of eleven, eager to escape the brutal mine work, he secured a position

Educator and prominent African American leader Booker T. Washington as painted in 1917 by HENRY OSSAWA TANNER. State Historical Society of Iowa, Des Moines

as Viola Ruffner's houseboy. She had a prickly personality, was a demanding taskmaster, and had driven off several other boys, but in the eighteen months he worked for her he came to absorb and appreciate her emphasis on the values of hard work, cleanliness, and thrift; thereby an unlikely bond of affection and respect developed between these two people from very different backgrounds. Early on, Ruffner spotted the ambition in young Washington: "He seemed peculiarly determined to emerge from his obscurity. He was ever restless, uneasy, as if knowing that contentment would mean inaction. 'Am I getting on?'—that was his principal question" (quoted in Gilson Willetts, "Slave Boy and Leader of His Race," *New Voice* 16 [24 June 1899]: 3).

In 1872, at age sixteen, Washington entered Hampton Normal and Agricultural Institute in Hampton, Virginia; it turned out to be one of the most important steps of his life. Having overheard two miners talking about the school for young blacks, he had determined to

make his way there and set out on the five-hundred-mile trip with a small sum of money donated by family and friends, barely enough to take him partway by train. The rest of the monthlong journey was on foot or via an occasional passing wagon. He arrived with fifty cents in his pocket and asked to be admitted. Ordered to clean out a room, and sensing that this might be his entrance examination, he swept and dusted until the room was spotless and was soon a Hampton student. While there he worked as a custodian to help defray his expenses.

Hampton Institute, only four years old at the time, was a monument to its principal, General Samuel Chapman Armstrong, probably the single most influential person in Washington's life. Born of missionary parents in Hawaii, Armstrong had led black troops in the Civil War. Convinced that the future of the freedmen lay in practical and industrial education and the instilling of Christian virtues, Armstrong had founded Hampton under

the auspices of the American Missionary Association. In Booker Washington he found an extraordinarily apt and ambitious pupil. Washington not only learned agriculture, brickmasonry, and the standard academic subjects taught at Hampton, more importantly he absorbed the entire philosophy of character building and utilitarian education stressed by the handsome and charismatic Armstrong.

After graduating in 1875, Washington returned to Malden for three years to teach in a black school and to spread the Hampton philosophy. Several months spent at Wayland Seminary, a Baptist institution, in Washington, D.C., in 1878–1879 convinced the restless young Washington that he was not cut out for the ministry. In addition, his exposure to the poverty and degeneracy of lower-class urban life instilled in him a lifelong dislike of cities. This prejudice would later weaken to a degree his message to his fellow blacks to remain in the rural South, at a time when far greater job opportunities were to be found in the nation's burgeoning cities.

Somewhat adrift in the late 1870s, having rejected the ministry, law, and public school teaching as viable careers, Washington was invited back to Hampton in 1879 by General Armstrong to run the night school and later to supervise the dormitory for Indian boys, who had recently been admitted. As usual, his performance was exemplary. In the spring of 1881 Armstrong received a request from three education commissioners in Alabama to recommend a white principal for a new Negro normal school to be established in Tuskegee. He wrote a persuasive letter urging them to accept Washington instead. They agreed, and the young educator was soon on the way to what would be his life's work. On arriving in Alabama, he learned that the state legislature had appropriated two thousand dollars for salaries only. There was no land, no buildings, no campus.

Plunging into unremitting activity, Washington won over local whites in the community, began to recruit black students who were hungry for education, and held the first classes in a shanty. One of his mentors at Hampton was the school's treasurer, James F. B. Marshall, an elderly and kindly ex-general who now began coaching Washington in the arts of financial management and extracting money from wealthy white benefactors. With a two-hundred-dollar loan from Marshall, Washington purchased land outside of town for a permanent campus. Student labor erected the initial buildings of Tuskegee Institute, and student farming supplied much of the foodstuff for the dormitory kitchen. Tuskegee would grow to 2,000 acres and 100 buildings, with a faculty of nearly 200 and an endowment close to $2 million by the time of Washington's death.

In spite of Washington's national fame in years to come, Tuskegee never ceased to be his base of operations and the enterprise to which he devoted most of his time. Each morning began with a horseback ride to inspect the campus. He hired and fired faculty, admitted and expelled students, oversaw the smallest details of finances and purchasing, bought more land when he could, kept creditors at bay when he had to, and spent much time cultivating northern philanthropists for donations, at which he became extremely adept. Among the notable benefactors of Tuskegee were steel magnate Andrew Carnegie, oilman John D. Rockefeller, camera manufacturer George Eastman, and Julius Rosenwald, president of Sears, Roebuck, and Co.

In many respects Tuskegee was a "colony" of Hampton Institute, as Washington had imbibed General Armstrong's emphasis on industrial skills and character building. The vocational curriculum included some thirty-eight subjects, including printing, carpentry, cabinetmaking, and farming. Female students specialized in cooking, sewing, and other domestic skills. In addition to the standard academic subjects, from grammar and composition to history, mathematics, chemistry, and bookkeeping, strong emphasis was placed on personal hygiene and moral development and on daily chapel services. At the time of Washington's death the student body numbered more than fifteen hundred.

Unlike Hampton, however, Washington's faculty and administrative staff were all black, and many were graduates of Hampton and Fisk University. Notable among the staff were botanist and agricultural researcher GEORGE WASHINGTON CARVER and MONROE NATHAN WORK, the sociologist and bibliographer of black history and life who spent thirty-seven years at Tuskegee as head of the Records and Research Department. The highly capable Olivia Davidson, a graduate of Hampton and the Framingham State Normal School near Boston, arrived in 1881 to serve as principal of the female students and came as close as anyone to being Washington's co-superintendent. For the last eighteen years of his life, Washington's personal private secretary, factotum, and alter ego was EMMETT JAY SCOTT, an extraordinarily loyal, astute, and circumspect assistant who handled much of Washington's correspondence, supervised the Tuskegee office staff, and was privy to all of Washington's secret machinations at controlling black American politics.

Washington was married three times. His first wife, Fannie N. Smith, his sweetheart from Malden, gave birth to a child in 1883, the year after their marriage, but died prematurely the next year. In 1885 Washington married Olivia Davidson; they had two children. This too was a short marriage, for she had suffered from physical maladies for years and died in 1889. Four years later he married Margaret J. Murray (MARGARET MURRAY WASHINGTON), a Fisk graduate who had replaced Davidson as lady principal. She remained Washington's wife for the rest of his life, helping to raise his three children and continuing to play a major role at Tuskegee.

As Tuskegee Institute grew, it branched out into other endeavors. The annual Tuskegee Negro Conferences, inaugurated in 1892, sought solutions for impoverished black farmers through crop diversity and education. The National Negro Business League, founded in 1900, gave encouragement to black enterprises and publicized their successes. Margaret Washington hosted women's conferences on campus. Washington established National Negro Health Week and called attention to minority health issues in addresses nationwide.

By the mid-1880s Washington was becoming a fixture on the nation's lecture circuit. This exposure both drew attention and dollars to Tuskegee and allowed the black educator to articulate his philosophy of racial advancement. In a notable 1884 address to the National Education Association in Madison, Wisconsin, Washington touted education for blacks—"brains, property, and character"—as the key to black advancement and acceptance by white southerners. "Separate but equal" railroad and other public facilities were acceptable to blacks, he argued, as long as they really were equal. This speech foreshadowed the accommodationist racial compromises he would preach for the rest of his life. During the 1880s and 1890s Washington went out of his way to soft-pedal racial insults and attacks on blacks (including himself) by whites. He courted southern white politicians who were racial moderates, arguing that black Americans had to exhibit good citizenship, hard work, and elevated character in order to win the respect of the "better sort" of whites. Full political and social equality would result in all due time, he maintained.

The apogee of Washington's career as a spokesman for his race occurred at the opening of Atlanta's Cotton States and International Exposition in September 1895. This was one of a number of such fairs held to highlight the South's progress since the Civil War. Blacks had their own, albeit segregated, exhibit space at the exposition, and the Atlanta leaders of the affair invited Washington to give a ten-minute address. He spent much time honing the speech, sensing its symbolic importance, and was uncharacteristically nervous as 18 September approached.

Dubbed the "Atlanta Compromise," the speech was a masterpiece of tact and ambiguity intended to impress all members of the integrated audience—northern whites, southern whites, and blacks from the South. It had all been said before by Washington but never as succinctly and before such an important gathering. Though acceding realistically to the deplorable state of race relations in the United States at that time, Washington seemed to accept the existence of segregation for his people and urged them not to push for integrated facilities and other civil and political rights. "The wisest among my race understand that the agitation of questions of social equality is the extremest folly, and that progress in the enjoyment of all the privileges that will come to us must be the result of severe and constant struggle rather than of artificial forcing." He urged southern blacks to "cast down your bucket where you are"—stay in the South, gain education, and through hard work win the economic advancement that would also gain them the respect of their white neighbors. He reminded his white listeners that the blacks among them made up one-third of the South's population and that the fates of the two races were inextricably bound. The climax of the speech, which brought the audience to its feet in thunderous applause, was the memorable sentence: "In all things that are purely social we can be as separate as the fingers, yet one as the hand in all things essential to mutual progress."

The Atlanta Compromise speech unquestionably secured Washington's position as the leading spokesman for American blacks to the larger white community and particularly to the white power structure of American politics, and it was lavishly praised by white leaders. Symbolically the torch of black leadership had also been passed to a younger generation, inasmuch as FREDERICK DOUGLASS, the former slave turned abolitionist, orator, and journalist, who had been the most notable black American of his day, had died a few months before Washington spoke. Washington had tapped into the classic American myth that hard work, self-discipline, and economic independence would win for any citizen the respect of his neighbors. He conveniently ignored or chose to omit the fact that at the very time he spoke, American race relations were at their worst point since the end of the Civil War, with lynchings and other violence, grinding poverty, and legal and extralegal discrimination at the ballot box a fact of life for most American blacks. The U.S. Supreme Court's decision the very next year in *Plessy v. Ferguson* would place the fiction of "separate but equal" on segregated public facilities.

Yet the decade after 1895 was for Washington the most influential period of his life, if that influence is measured by his demand as a speaker and the power he wielded among white political leaders. In 1898 President William McKinley paid a visit to Tuskegee Institute. McKinley's successor, Theodore Roosevelt, had been a friend of Washington's for several years. The relationship between president and educator began on an inauspicious note when Roosevelt, one month after taking office in 1901, invited Washington to dinner at the White House. Although other blacks had visited the executive mansion on occasion since at least the time of Abraham Lincoln, the Roosevelt-Washington dinner set off a firestorm of outrage, especially in the southern white press. Washington was chagrined by the whole affair; Roosevelt made light of it to his southern friend but privately called it a "mistake" and never again invited minorities to the White House.

The dinner aside, the relationship between the two men was unusually close. Roosevelt regularly though privately consulted Washington on matters involving race and southern policies, and almost all of the minority political appointments Roosevelt made as president were first cleared with the Tuskegeean. Washington's relationship with Roosevelt's successor, William Howard Taft, was cooler, given Taft's greater reluctance than Roosevelt to make significant black political appointments; but Washington scored an occasional minor victory with Taft, and it was one of the many ironies of his career that while he urged ordinary blacks to eschew politics and humbly go about their daily work, he himself wielded more political power than any other black American of his day.

Washington's prolific writing also helped to spread his influence; moreover, much of the royalties from his books went into the coffers of Tuskegee. He wrote scores of articles and ten books, often with the help of ghost-writers, due to his busy schedule. Among them were *The Future of the American Negro* (1899), a collection of his articles and speeches; *The Story of My Life and Work* (1900), the first of three autobiographies; *Up from Slavery* (1901), his most critically acclaimed autobiography, translated into some eighteen languages; *Working with the Hands* (1904); *The Negro in Business* and a biography of Frederick Douglass, both in 1907; *My Larger Education* (1911), the last of the trilogy about his own life; and *The Man Farthest Down* (1912), based on a European tour.

Washington's power involved not only close relationships with influential white political leaders and industrialists but also a secret network of contacts with journalists and various organizations. He schemed with white and black Alabamians to try to keep other black schools from locating near Tuskegee. He engineered political appointments for supporters in the black community as a way of solidifying his own power base. He planted spies in organizations unfriendly to him to report on their activities and at one time even used a detective agency briefly. Despite public denials, Washington owned partial interests in some minority newspapers. This allowed him to plant stories and to influence their news coverage and editorial stands in ways beneficial to himself. Beginning in the mid-1880s, and lasting for some twenty years, he maintained a clandestine relationship with T. THOMAS FORTUNE, editor of the *New York Age*, the leading black newspaper of its day. He helped support the paper financially, was one of its stockholders, and quietly endorsed many of Fortune's militant stands for voting and other civil rights and against lynching. He also supported the Afro-American League, a civil rights organization founded by Fortune in 1887. Washington secretly provided financial and legal support for court challenges to all-white juries in Alabama, segregated transportation facilities, and disfranchisement of black voters. As black suffrage decreased nonetheless around the turn of the century, Washington struggled to keep a modicum of black influence and patronage in the Republican Party in the South. From 1908 to 1911 he played a major, though covert, role in the successful effort to get the U.S. Supreme Court to overturn a harsh Alabama peonage law under which Alonzo Bailey, a black Alabama farmer, had been convicted.

It is clear, from research in Washington's massive correspondence, that he supported the full agenda of civil and political rights put forward by Fortune, the Afro-American League, and later the National Association for the Advancement of Colored People (NAACP). But he refused to go public with such efforts, fearing, probably rightly, that to reveal his involvement would undercut if not destroy his support from white politicians and philanthropists and perhaps threaten his beloved Tuskegee. Emmett Scott was one of very few blacks who knew the full range of Washington's secret activities; certainly no whites did.

After about 1900 Washington came under increasing criticism from black opponents who questioned his measured and nonaggressive responses to legalized segregation, loss of voting rights, and violence against blacks. His critics referred disrespectfully to his enormous influence as the Tuskegee Machine. Among the most vocal were WILLIAM MONROE TROTTER, the militant editor of the *Boston Guardian*, and noted sociologist W. E. B. DU BOIS. In his *The Souls of Black Folk* (1903) Du Bois launched a strong indictment of Washington's accommodationist philosophy toward the terrible racial climate of the time. Du Bois and others also questioned Washington's emphasis on vocational and industrial education, claiming that the black race needed college-educated professionals in its fight against discrimination and injustice.

A series of setbacks after the turn of the century illustrated how little effect Washington's moderation had had in ameliorating the nation's tense racial climate. The uproar over the 1901 dinner with President Roosevelt was a harbinger of worse things to come. In September 1906 five days of frenzied racial violence rocked Atlanta, the supposedly progressive capital of the New South. After the violence subsided, at least eleven citizens, ten black and one white, were dead, many other blacks were injured, and black areas of the city experienced destruction. Washington gave his usual muted response, urging Atlanta's blacks to exercise "self-control" and not compound the lawless white behavior with violence of their own. He was, however, instrumental in bringing leaders of both races together after the riot to begin the healing process.

Also in 1906 occurred the notorious Brownsville affair. In August an undetermined group of people shot up an area of Brownsville, Texas, nearby Fort Brown, where black infantry soldiers were stationed. One white man was killed. The racial climate was already strained due to previous attacks on soldiers by local residents. Townspeople assumed that the soldiers had done the shooting in retaliation for the previous attacks. All of the black soldiers vehemently denied their involvement, however, and there was no compelling evidence or proof whatsoever of their guilt. In spite of Washington's pleas not to do so, President Roosevelt dishonorably dismissed three companies of the black troops, creating an uproar among blacks and liberal whites.

Exasperated with Washington's low-key responses in the Atlanta and Brownsville cases, his old friend Fortune finally broke with him. More serious for Washington was the founding of the NAACP in 1909. Melvin J. Chisum, a northern confidant of Emmett Scott, had infiltrated Trotter's Boston Suffrage League and later the Niagara Movement, the forerunner of the NAACP, and reported the activities of both groups back to Tuskegee. Characteristically, Washington had a spy planted at the NAACP's founding meeting. Nonetheless, he was unable to prevent the creation of the NAACP, the membership of which included blacks, sympathetic white progressives, Jews, and even a few white southerners, or to influence its agenda, which included a broad-based call for a major assault on all fronts against racial injustice and white supremacy. Washington's old nemesis Du Bois became editor of the organization's monthly magazine, the *Crisis*. Although Washington privately supported many of the goals of the NAACP, his concern was its threat to his own power within the black community.

An ugly incident that took place in New York City on the evening of 19 March 1911 illustrates how little protection was then afforded to a black person, even one as eminent as Washington, under certain circumstances. While scanning the residents' directory in the vestibule of an apartment building in search of a friend, Washington was assaulted and repeatedly struck on the head by Henry Ulrich, a white resident of the apartment. Ulrich first claimed that Washington was a burglar; the second version of his story was that the black educator was looking through the keyhole of a white woman's apartment and that he had made an improper advance toward Ulrich's wife. Washington charged him with assault, and the ensuing trial received much national publicity. Washington won considerable support from the black community, even from his critics. Ulrich's acquittal in the face of overwhelming evidence illustrated the difficulties that even a prominent black man could have with the American justice system in the early twentieth century.

Washington died of overwork and arteriosclerosis at Tuskegee, shortly after returning from New York City, where he had been hospitalized.

Assessments of Washington by his contemporaries and, later, by historians have been wide-ranging and contentious, revealing, if nothing else, his complexity and many-sidedness. In the 1960s his secret life emerged as scholars began to plumb the one million documents in his collected papers. They reveal a much more complex, manipulative, secretive, vain, and at times deceptive individual than the inspiring and benign image that Washington himself so assiduously cultivated in his own lifetime. Indeed, he likely enjoyed leading this "double life."

To most of his students and faculty at Tuskegee, and to millions of poor blacks nationwide, he was a self-made and beneficent, if stern, Moses leading them out of slavery and into the promised land. He tirelessly preached an upbeat, optimistic view of the future of his fellow blacks. "When persons ask me," he said once, "how, in the midst of what sometimes seem hopelessly discouraging conditions, I can have such faith in the future of my race in this country, I remind them of the wilderness through which and out of which a good Providence has already led us." When he also wrote that he would "permit no man, no matter what his color, to narrow and degrade my soul by making me hate him," he was undoubtedly sincere. His message to his fellow blacks that hard work, good citizenship, patient fortitude in the face of adversity, and love would ultimately conquer the hatred of the white man was appealing to the majority of whites of his time and foreshadowed the similar message of a later leader, MARTIN LUTHER KING JR.

Washington's hardscrabble "up from slavery" background made it difficult for him to communicate with his college-educated critics, such as Trotter and Du Bois. They in turn, from the comfort of their editorial offices in the North, were perhaps unable to fathom the pressures and constraints from the white community that southern educators like Washington had to deal with on a daily basis. Yet their point that the race needed lawyers and doctors as well as farmers and bricklayers was valid, and the growing crescendo of criticism against Washington on this issue made the last decade of his life probably his most difficult. The irony, of course, was that Washington was secretly supporting the campaign against legal segregation and racial violence and for full civil rights. But he was unwilling to reveal his covert role for fear that it would undercut his power base among blacks and sympathetic whites, and he was doubtlessly right.

Close analysis of Washington's autobiographies and speeches reveals a vagueness and subtlety to his message lost on most people of his time, whites and blacks alike. He never said that American minorities would forever forgo the right to vote, to gain a full education, or to enjoy the fruits of an integrated society. But he strategically chose not to force the issue in the face of the overwhelming white hostility that was the reality of American race relations in the late nineteenth and early twentieth centuries. In this sense, he did what he had to do to assure the survival of himself and the people for whom he spoke.

FURTHER READING

Most of Washington's papers are in the Library of Congress. A smaller but important collection is at Tuskegee University. The major published collection is *The Booker T. Washington Papers*, ed. Louis R. Harlan and Raymond W. Smock (14 vols., 1972–1989).

Harlan, Louis R. *Booker T. Washington: The Making of a Black Leader, 1856–1901* (1972).
———. *Booker T. Washington: The Wizard of Tuskegee, 1901–1915* (1983).
Hawkins, Hugh, ed. *Booker T. Washington and His Critics: The Problem of Negro Leadership* (1962).
Logan, Rayford W. *The Betrayal of the Negro* (1965).
Meier, August. *Negro Thought in America, 1880–1915: Racial Ideologies in the Age of Booker T. Washington* (1963).
Scott, Emmett J., and Lyman Beecher Stowe. *Booker T. Washington: Builder of a Civilization* (1916).

Obituary: *New York Times*, 15 Nov. 1915.
—WILLIAM F. MUGLESTON

WASHINGTON, DENZEL

(28 Dec. 1954–), actor and director, was born in Mt. Vernon, New York, the middle child of Denzel Washington Sr., a Pentecostal minister, and Lennis (maiden name unknown), a beautician and one-time gospel singer. Raised in a religious household in an integrated neighborhood just north of the Bronx, the Washington children were discouraged by their parents from watching television or movies. Instead, Denzel passed the time attending church, assisting his mother in the beauty parlor, and participating as a member of the Boys Club and the local YMCA. At age fourteen, when his parents divorced, Denzel helped his family make ends meet by working part-time at the local drycleaner and in his mother's barbershop.

Troubled by his parents' separation, Denzel developed a rebellious attitude and his schoolwork declined. Anxious to set him on the right path, his mother enrolled him in the largely white, private school, Oakland Academy in New Windsor, New York. His behavior problems eased as Denzel found other, more productive outlets, including playing baseball, track, football, and basketball. Off campus he played piano with a local blues band. After graduating from Oakland in 1972, Washington enrolled at Fordham University in New York City, where he began as a pre-med student, but eventually ended up as a journalism and drama major. Washington briefly dropped out of school due to poor grades, and when he returned found success on the stage. Washington played the title roles in school productions of *The Emperor Jones* and *Othello* and his onstage work was strong enough to net him an agent prior to graduation and a small part in the television movie *Wilma* (1977) about track star WILMA RUDOLPH.

In 1977 Washington finally graduated from Fordham after which he entered the acting program at the American Conservatory Theater in San Francisco, leaving the program after the first year of a three year program, in order to move to Los Angeles. Although he won minor stage roles and a small part in the television film *Flesh and Blood* (1979), Washington was financially and artistically frustrated in Los Angeles and he soon moved back to his mother's house in Mt. Vernon. Upon his return to the East Coast, Washington became reacquainted with Pauletta Pearson, an actress and singer he had met on the set of *Wilma*. The couple married in 1983 and had four children.

In 1980 Washington took a job teaching sports at a children's recreation center. Only one week before his job was to begin, Washington was cast as MALCOLM X in *When the Chickens Come Home* at Woodie King's New Federal Theater. Critics were impressed with Washington's performance, especially his willingness to physically transform himself to play the role, and he was awarded the Audelco Award for excellence in black theater.

Washington landed the lead role opposite George Segal in *Carbon Copy*, a comedic film universally panned upon its release in 1981. That same year Washington was cast as Private Peterson in the Negro Ensemble Company's off-Broadway production of Charles Fuller's play *A Soldier's Play*. Focusing on the investigation of a racially charged murder during World War II, the play won a Pulitzer Prize for Drama, an Obie Award for Best Ensemble Performance, and an Outer Circle Critics Award for Washington. Washington reprised the role in Los Angeles, remaining with the play until being cast as Dr. Phillip Chandler in the television drama *St. Elsewhere*, a role he played from 1983 to 1987.

In 1984 Washington reprised his role as Private Peterson in Norman Jewison's film adaptation of *A Soldier's Play*, renamed *A Soldier's Story*. In 1986 Washington appeared opposite Richard Gere in the Sidney Lumet film *Power* (1986) and the television movie *The George McKenna Story*, a fact-based story about a school principal in a tough inner city Los Angeles high school. The following year his performance as the martyred South African leader Steven Biko in Sir Richard Attenborough's film *Cry Freedom* (1997) earned him a NAACP Image Award and an Academy Award nomination. Proud to be recognized by his peers, Washington was nonetheless vociferous about the way the film emphasized the story of Biko's white liberal lawyer, played by Kevin Kline, at the expense of Biko. With his outspoken criticism, Washington emerged as a spokesman for increased visibility and better-quality roles for black entertainers. "The success narrows the roles you get to play, race narrows the roles you get to play," commented Washington (*Chicago Tribune*, 1 Feb. 1988).

In 1988 Washington made his Broadway debut in Ron Milner's comedy *Checkmates*. Later that year he starred in *For Queen and Country* and the Caribbean film caper *The Mighty Quinn* alongside Robert Townsend. In 1989 Washington gave a searing performance in *Glory*, a film based on the letters of Colonel Robert G. Shaw (played by Matthew Broderick in the film), leader of the Fifty-fourth Massachusetts Volunteer Infantry, the unit of African American soldiers in the Civil War established in 1863. Appearing with Morgan Freeman and Andre Braugher, Washington played Trip, a former slave who played a key role in the unit's attack on Battery Wagner, an important fortification of Charleston, South Carolina. For his performance Washington received an Academy Award for Best Supporting Actor.

In 1990 Washington emerged as a matinee idol following his work in SPIKE LEE's romance-drama *Mo' Better Blues*. He played the role of a self-absorbed jazz trumpeter, Bleek Gilliam, a character loosely based on MILES DAVIS. In 1992 Washington received the NAACP Best Actor Award for his performance in *Mississippi Masala*, a romantic drama about black and Asian relations in the American South. The same year he returned to the role of Malcolm X in Spike Lee's controversial biopic *X*. His startling performance garnered him a slew of accolades, including an Academy Award nomination, a NAACP Image Award, and the Chicago, Boston, and New York critics' awards.

Handsome and stirringly charismatic, Washington was voted one of *People*'s "Fifty Most Beautiful People in the World" in 1994. One of the highest paid

African American actors in Hollywood, he had become known for playing virtuous and heroic—if troubled—black men. Meanwhile, Washington continued to diversify as an actor, playing opposite Kenneth Branaugh and Emma Thompson in Shakespeare's *Much Ado about Nothing* (1993) and Tom Hanks in the AIDS drama *Philadelphia* (1993), and starring in the Hollywood thrillers *The Pelican Brief* (1993), *Crimson Tide* (1995), *Courage Under Fire, Fallen* (1998), and *The Siege* (1998), and *The Bone Collector* (1999). In 1995 he starred as Easy Rawlins in Carl Franklin's film adaptation of Walter Mosely's book *Devil in a Blue Dress*, about a 1940s black private investigator. The following year he again worked with a black cast in *The Preacher's Wife* (1996) and re-teamed with Lee for *He Got Game* (1998) and *Bamboozled* (2000). In 2000 he netted another Best Actor Academy Award nomination for his portrayal of wrongfully imprisoned Reuben Carter in Norman Jewison's *The Hurricane*.

In 1983 Washington married actress Pauletta Pearson. The couple have four children, and live in a house designed by PAUL REVERE WILLIAMS. Over the course of his film career, Washington maintained his public image as a devout family man, even coaching his children's sports teams. On a summer trip to South Africa in 1995, the Washingtons renewed their marriage vows in a ceremony officiated by archbishop Desmond Tutu. Washington, who has donated one million dollars to the Children's Fund of South Africa, $2.5 million to the Church of God in Los Angeles, and time and money to the Boys and Girls Club, received the WHITNEY M. YOUNG Award from the Los Angeles Urban League in 1997.

For his complex performance as a rogue cop in Antoine Fuqua's drama *Training Day* (2001), Washington became the first black actor since SIDNEY POITIER to win an Academy Award for Best Actor. The film revealed yet another side of Washington's remarkable diversity as an actor, since he was cast against type as the film's "bad guy." He emerged to great critical acclaim as a film director with *The Antwone Fisher Story* (2002), a psychological drama based on the true story of the

title character, a Sony Pictures security guard who eventually gained fame as a writer and Hollywood producer. In 2004 Washington starred in the Frank Sinatra role in Jonathan Demme's remake of *The Manchurian Candidate*.

About his career as an actor, Washington once remarked, "I'm just trying to fulfill my part of the bargain, which is to give back, to be a positive influence on others" (*Jet*, 2 Oct. 1995, 32). One of the few African American men in the film industry with the power to pick roles and "greenlight" projects, Washington has remained in firm control of the destiny of his career.

FURTHER READING

Brode, Douglas. *Denzel Washington: His Films and Career* (1996).

Davis, Thulani. "Denzel in the Swing," *American Film* (Aug. 1990).

Hill, Anne E. *Denzel Washington* (1998).

—JASON KING

 WASHINGTON, HAROLD (15 Apr. 1922– 25 Nov. 1987), politician and mayor of Chicago, was born on the South Side of Chicago, the son of Roy Lee Washington, a stockyard worker, and Bertha Jones, a domestic worker. Harold Washington attended a Benedictine boarding school in Milwaukee, Wisconsin, until the age of six. He was then enrolled in Chicago public schools but dropped out of high school after his junior year to take a job in a meat packing plant. His father, who had become an attorney and a precinct captain for the Democratic Party in Chicago's largely African American Third Ward, secured a job for Washington at the Chicago office of the U.S. Treasury Department. In 1941 he married Dorothy Finch. They had no children and divorced in 1950.

Following U.S. involvement in World War II in December 1941, Washington was drafted into the U.S. Army. He was stationed in the South Pacific with the Air Force Engineers, and he took enough correspondence courses between missions to receive his high school equivalency diploma.

After the war Washington enrolled in Roosevelt College in Chicago, an experimental new college that was one of the few in the country to be fully integrated. He excelled at Roosevelt and was the first African American elected senior class president. He graduated in 1949 with a bachelor's degree in Political Science.

After graduating from Roosevelt, Washington entered Northwestern University Law School, where he was the only African American in his class. He earned his law degree in 1952, then entered into practice with his father. When Roy Washington died the following year, Ralph Metcalfe, an alderman and Democratic party committeeman, hired the junior Washington to replace his father as captain of his precinct.

Washington quickly won favor with the Chicago Democratic machine, effectively turning out the vote for Metcalfe and other Democratic candidates. As head of the Third Ward's Young Democrats, Washington became a valued member of the Chicago Democratic Party machine for his ability to cultivate young black party leaders. In return, he was rewarded with jobs as an assistant corporation counsel for the city from 1954 to 1958 and as an arbitrator for the Illinois Industrial Commission from 1960 to 1964.

In 1964 Washington campaigned for and was elected state representative for the Third Ward. Once in office, he began to establish his independence from the Chicago political machine, then dominated by Mayor Richard J. Daley. Washington first broke with city Democratic leaders in the late 1960s, when he sponsored a bill to create a police review board with civilian participation. At the same time he began to establish himself as a civil rights advocate, further distancing himself from the white-dominated Daley machine. As a member of the state legislature he supported the Equal Rights Amendment in the 1970s, worked to strengthen the Fair Employment Practices Act, and in 1969 helped establish the Illinois Legislative Black Caucus. In 1976 Washington was elected to the state senate despite opposition from a machine candidate.

In 1977 Washington made a decisive break from the Chicago Democratic organization by campaigning for the mayoralty in the special election that followed Daley's death. Despite a drubbing in the Democratic primary, in which he received less than half the black vote, Washington vowed to carry on the fight against the machine. "I'm going to do what maybe I should have done ten or twelve years ago," he announced. "I'm going to stay outside that damn Democratic organization and give them hell." True to his word, Washington returned to the state senate and continued to push reform legislation that was well to the left of the Chicago party's wishes.

In 1980 Washington successfully challenged a machine loyalist in the election for a seat representing Chicago in the U.S. Congress. In the House of Representatives he emerged as a leading figure in the Democratic Party's embattled liberal wing. He served as secretary of the Congressional Black Caucus and sponsored legislation that extended the Voting Rights Act of 1965, making it easier for African Americans to challenge discriminatory electoral practices. On foreign policy issues, Washington sought to reverse the military buildup championed by President Ronald Reagan. He supported an end to the production of nuclear weapons, opposed U.S. military intervention in Central America, and called for a 20 percent reduction in defense spending.

During his first term in Congress, Washington was approached by several Chicago political groups that were eager to draft a black candidate for the mayoral election in 1983. Washington agreed on the condition that a massive voter registration campaign be carried out before the election. The groups undertook the challenge, adding more than 130,000 new voters, many of them African Americans. Satisfied that the electoral base was now sufficient to make his campaign viable, Washington announced his candidacy.

In the Democratic primary Washington faced the incumbent mayor Jane Byrne and State's Attorney Richard M. Daley, son of the former mayor. Washington won the primary with a plurality of 36 percent of the vote to Byrne's 34 percent and Daley's 30 percent. Washington's grassroots campaign earned him 85 percent of the votes cast by African Americans, who constituted approximately 40 percent of the electorate.

In the general election Washington's challenger was Republican Bernard Epton, an attorney and former Illinois state legislator, who capitalized on the wrath of a large segment of Chicago's white population. Washington nonetheless eked out a victory with 51.5 percent of the vote to become the city's first African American mayor. His support came overwhelmingly from black, Latino, and white liberal voters.

Washington's victory inaugurated a four-year period of factional struggle within the city council. The "Council Wars," as they came to be known, featured white opposition to Washington's attempts to reform Chicago's system of political patronage and diversify the city's political leadership. The white majority on the city council, led by Aldermen Edward Vrdolyak and Ed Burke, succeeded in blocking many of Washington's initiatives. Yet the new mayor was able to achieve passage of several laws that severely weakened the power of the white Democratic machine. His most important accomplishment was the Shakman Decree, which outlawed patronage hiring and firing of municipal employees. He successfully instituted a $1,500 limit on campaign contributions from companies with city contracts, and he added scores of women and minorities to the city administration, including Chicago's first black police chief. Washington effectively ended the system of political patronage that had dominated Chicago's governance for most of the twentieth century. Some of his critics, including television anchor Walter Jacobson and Aldermen Vrdolyak, Burke, and Richard Mell, though, charged that he only redistributed political spoils to a new elite of black and Latino politicians and bureaucrats.

In 1987 Washington was challenged by Byrne in the Democratic primary and by Vrdolyak, running as an independent, in the general election. With more than 99 percent of black voters casting their ballots for Washington, he easily outpolled his opponents, taking 54 percent of the vote in both races. Only seven months after his reelection, Washington died in Chicago.

A pivotal figure in African American politics, Washington initiated a wave of black electoral insurgency that resulted in the election of African American mayors in many of the largest cities in the United States. His success in dismantling the Chicago political machine made him a pivotal figure in the history of the city as well. Though he was a consummate politician and a product of the political system he ultimately dismantled, Washington destroyed an old system of urban governance and helped change the process as well as the face of American politics.

FURTHER READING

Dempsey, Travis J. *An Autobiography of Black Politics* (1987).

Kleppner, Paul. *Chicago Divided: The Making of a Black Mayor* (1985).

Rivlin, Gary. *Fire on the Prairie: Chicago's Harold Washington and the Politics of Race* (1992).

Obituary: *New York Times*, 26 Nov. 1987.

—THADDEUS RUSSELL

WASHINGTON, MARGARET MURRAY

(9 Mar. 1861–4 June 1925), educator and clubwoman, was born Margaret James Murray in Macon, Mississippi, near the Mississippi-Alabama border, to Lucy (maiden name unknown), a washerwoman who was possibly a slave, and James Murray, who had immigrated to the United States from Ireland. After her father's death, seven-year-old Margaret left home to live with her northern-born, white siblings, the Sanders. The Sanders, who were Quakers, taught school in their community and encouraged their little sister to pursue a career in education. Margaret's Quaker surroundings fostered in the growing girl a sense of social responsibility, community building, self-help, and obligation. Taking the advice of her siblings, she passed the qualifying exam and began teaching local schoolchildren at age fourteen.

The ambitious young woman, known to her friends and family as Maggie, quit her teaching job and entered Fisk University in Nashville, Tennessee, in 1881, at the age of twenty. She shaved four years off her age and enrolled as a part-time student, working to support herself through preparatory

Educator and clubwoman Margaret Murray Washington. Library of Congress

school and college. Her experience as a struggling, working-class student typified the lifestyle of many black clubwomen at the turn of the century, most of whom came from humble beginnings. As the children and grandchildren of slaves, these young women learned early the importance of hard work, self-respect, thrift, and community consciousness in the face of adversity.

In addition to her studies and part-time work, Maggie found time for extracurricular activities as associate editor of the *Fisk Herald* newspaper, president of a literary society, and debate team member. Her classmates at Fisk included W. E. B. Du Bois and Sterling Brown. Maggie met her future husband, Booker T. Washington, the principal of Tuskegee Normal and Industrial Institute (later Tuskegee University), on the day of her graduation from Fisk in 1889. Washington, who gave the commencement address that day, offered her a teaching job after she persistently inquired about faculty openings. Although she had already accepted a teaching position at Prairie

View College in southeastern Texas, she jumped at the chance to work alongside Washington.

Maggie Murray began her long career at Tuskegee in 1889 as an English instructor and, the following year, became lady principal and director of the Department of Domestic Service, which was later renamed Department of Girls' Industries and housed in the newly built Dorothy Hall. Murray oversaw the curriculum, which included lower-division and postgraduate courses in table setting, laundering, broom making, basketry, sewing, soap making, millinery, and cooking. Her other duties included supervising female coeds and faculty on campus, recommending faculty for merit raises, and writing letters of recommendation for job and college applicants. As dean, she organized fund-raisers and cultivated donors, including Madame C. J. Walker. Murray, whom graduates and coworkers remembered as a nurturing, yet intimidating administrator, also served on the governing committee that ran the campus in Booker T. Washington's absence.

Washington took notice of Murray's leadership skills and commitment to Tuskegee. He proposed marriage in 1891, but Murray, who already felt uneasy around children, expressed some apprehension about marrying a man twice widowed with three children. Washington, who had a daughter, Portia, from his first marriage to Fanny Smith, had married Tuskegee's cofounder, Olivia Davidson, in 1884, two years after the death of his first wife. Olivia died in 1889, following the birth of two sons, Booker Jr. and Davidson Earnest. Eventually, Murray's concerns eased, and the couple married on 12 October 1892. Years later, they took in her sister's children, Thomas and Laura Murray.

In addition to her work as wife, mother, and educator, Margaret Washington had a passion for community building. In March 1895 she and twelve other women formed the Tuskegee Women's Club, which opened a school on the Elizabeth Russell Plantation in Macon County, near Tuskegee. The rural school provided youngsters with a basic, rudimentary education; instructed wives and mothers on housekeeping and childcare; held sewing classes; and developed reading seminars for men. With the assistance of Tuskegee graduates, the school soon held both day and night classes and helped many of the tenant farmers purchase their own farms.

The Tuskegee Women's Club also established Mother's Meetings for Macon County blacks. The group, which provided day care to its participants, taught classes on etiquette, housekeeping, and childcare. Participation in the meetings swelled during the Tuskegee Institute's annual farmer's conferences, which brought five hundred southern farmers to the campus each year, but was closed to women until 1916. In 1910 the Tuskegee club women formed the Town Night School, which provided courses in carpentry, bricklaying, painting, cooking, and sewing to the men and women of Tuskegee. Over the next few years the school expanded its curriculum to cover academic subjects, including African American history.

In 1899 Washington organized the Alabama Federation of Colored Women's Clubs. Led by the activist Cornelia Bowen, the club built a center for troubled youths, a nursing home for the elderly and indigent, and libraries for black Alabamians. It raised funds for the American Red Cross, supported black troops during World War I, encouraged good health and hygiene practices in the home, and established the state's first black YWCA.

Washington also worked with activists in the national clubwoman movement. In 1895, at the invitation of the civil rights activist and journalist JOSEPHINE ST. PIERRE RUFFIN, Washington traveled to Boston to aid in the formation of what became the National Federation of Afro-American Women (NFAAW). Washington served as the organization's first president. A year later, when the NFAAW merged with the Washington Colored League, headed by MARY CHURCH TERRELL, to create the National Association of Colored Women (NACW), Washington became NACW's membership coordinator, local and state-affiliated clubs organizer, and editor of the organization's magazine, *National Association Notes*. The NACW and its affiliates protested sexism, built kindergartens, created day-care centers, and opened libraries across the country. The organization, whose membership grew from 50,000 in 1914 to 300,000 in 1920, encouraged black educators to teach African American history, lobbied for prison reform, maintained settlement houses, supported women's suffrage, and campaigned with the NAACP and Urban League against lynching.

The NACW's efforts to develop coalitions with white women's organizations were the source of tension within the organization. Terrell and CHARLOTTE HAWKINS BROWN were often at odds with Washington and Jennie Moton, the wife of ROBERT RUSSA MOTON, after Booker T. Washington's untimely death in 1915. Tempers reached new heights, and Margaret Washington and Jennie Moton were blamed by some black clubwomen when white organizers of an interracial clubwoman convention in 1920 omitted portions of a seven-point statement issued by African American activists that called, in part, for anti-lynching legislation. Washington's belief in interracial progress and cooperation was unquestionably rooted in her personal history. Similarly, her endorsement of black economic self-determination, which she viewed as both the final stage in the emancipation saga and a first step in the ongoing black civil rights struggle, was informed by her own experiences.

In her final years Washington became increasingly vocal about racial oppression in the United States and around the world. Inspired by Du Bois's newly created Pan-African Congress, Washington, NANNIE BURROUGHS, MARY MCLEOD BETHUNE, and other NACW members founded the International Council of Women of the Darker Races (ICWDR) in 1920. The ICWDR brought together women of color from across the globe in fighting sexism, racism, imperialism, and global poverty. Although she was gravely ill by the time of the ICWDR's first convention in 1922, Washington continued to work with the organization as well as with the NACW and her beloved Tuskegee students. Washington died in 1924.

FURTHER READING

Washington's papers are located in the Hollis Frissell Library, Tuskegee University, Tuskegee, Alabama.

Lane, Linda Rochell. *A Documentary of Mrs. Booker T. Washington* (2001).
Rouse, Jacqueline Ann. "Out of the Shadow of Tuskegee: Margaret Murray Washington, Social Activism, and Race Vindication," *Journal of Negro History* 81 (1996).
Shaw, Stephanie. *What a Woman Ought to Be and Do: Black Professional Women Workers during the Jim Crow Era* (1996).
—BERNADETTE PRUITT

WASHINGTON, ORA (16 Jan. 1899–28 May 1971), tennis and basketball player, was born Ora Belle Washington in Caroline County, Virginia, the daughter of John Thomas Washington, a farmer and house plasterer, and Laura Young. Ora, the fifth of nine children, attended the File School in Caroline County and the Chicago Presbyterian Training School. She lived on the family farm until she was in her teens, when she and an older sister moved to Philadelphia, where one of her aunts had settled and where many of her relatives would later go to live. The 1920 census recorded that

Washington lived as a domestic worker in a Philadelphia home.

Although Washington did not travel to Philadelphia with dreams of athletic stardom, she arrived at an opportune time for gifted African American athletes. The prosperity of the 1920s sparked a boom in many sports, and because African Americans were barred from many mainstream sporting endeavors, they developed institutions of their own. Black colleges devoted increasing amounts of time and money to athletic programs. The Washington family was part of a wave of urban African American migration that encouraged the development of recreational facilities and provided spectators for black professional organizations, such as the New York Renaissance and Harlem Globetrotter basketball teams, and the baseball teams of the Negro National League. By the 1920s African American newspapers were eager participants in a nationwide explosion in sports coverage, offering detailed accounts of both men's and women's sporting events.

At some point in the 1920s Washington began playing tennis at the YWCA in Germantown, a Philadelphia suburb. She took to the game immediately. In 1925 she marked herself as a competitor to watch by upsetting Isadore Channels, the reigning national champion of the all-black American Tennis Association (ATA). Washington captured her first ATA singles title in 1929 and remained champion through 1935. In 1936 she lost the title to the former titleholder and fellow Philadelphian Lulu Ballard but won it for a final time in 1937. She retired from serious singles competition early in 1938. Along with her singles victories, she held the national women's doubles title for twelve straight years, from 1925 to 1936, partnering with Ballard, Blanche Winston of New York, and Anita Grant of Washington, D.C. (Ashe, 448–455).

After retiring from singles, Washington continued to compete in doubles and mixed doubles, winning the ATA mixed-doubles title in 1939, 1946, and 1947. In the latter contest, she and her partner, George Stewart, defeated R. Walter Johnson and his partner, an up-and-coming young star named ALTHEA GIBSON. Gibson went on to break Washington's record of eight singles crowns by winning nine straight titles between 1947 and 1956.

Washington was a superb tennis player. While she was not especially tall, she was powerfully built, with broad shoulders and sharply defined muscles. She became well known for her forceful ground strokes, her range on the court, and her skillful work at the net. "She was dynamic to watch," one tennis fan recalled, "and her overhead game was terrific" (Young, 195). She was also respected for her mental strength. "Courage and determination were the biggest assets I had," she once explained (Young, 195).

During her prime, Washington dominated black women's tennis so completely that in 1931 the *Philadelphia Tribune* reported, "Her superiority is so evident that her competitors are frequently beaten before the first ball crosses the net" (12 Mar. 1931). She did not, however, have the opportunity to test herself against top white players. Most white tennis clubs and associations barred African Americans, and the U.S. Lawn Tennis Association refused to admit African American players to its national championship until 1950, when Althea Gibson made her debut. Washington's reign coincided with that of the championship white tennis player Helen Wills Moody, but Moody rebuffed efforts to persuade her to play against Washington.

Washington's athletic talent was also evident in her basketball play. While she always preferred tennis, she was widely regarded as the best black female basketball player of her era. Washington began her basketball career in earnest in the fall of 1930, playing with the Germantown YWCA Hornets, which was coached by Lincoln University's track coach, Joseph Rainey. After a near-perfect season, against opponents representing black colleges, YWCAs, churches, schoolteachers, and hospital nurses, the Hornets claimed the national African American woman's title. Washington, who scored more than two hundred points in the season, was the undisputed star.

By the fall of 1932 Washington had moved to the team with whom she would make her greatest mark: the Philadelphia Tribunes, sponsored by Philadelphia's dominant African American newspaper. In 1931, under the leadership of the *Tribune* circulation director and former Negro League baseball star Otto Briggs, the paper had established the team to capitalize on the growing interest in women's basketball. In the spring of 1932 the Tribunes, led by Philadelphian Inez Patterson, won a five-game championship series, beating Washington and the Hornets to claim the national title. The following year Washington joined the Tribunes and remained with the team until it was disbanded in the 1940s.

The Tribunes were consistently the dominant team in African American women's basketball, rivaling the male Tribunes in popularity. Like many African American teams of the era, they usually played by full-court "men's rules" rather than the divided court "girls' rules" that had become common among white teams. Besides playing a regular schedule of Philadelphia-area opponents, they also played outside the region. In 1934 they took trips to the Midwest, where they faced a series of white teams, and to the South, where they played African American opponents. They scheduled a second southern tour in 1938.

The Tribunes fielded many excellent players, among them Rose Wilson, Bernice Robinson, and Lil Fountaine, but Washington was almost always the featured attraction. In 1932 the *Philadelphia Tribune* sports editor Randy Dixon stated that Washington's "stamina and speed... make many male players blush with envy" (10 Jan. 1932). In 1934, when the Tribunes played the Bennett College team in Greensboro, North Carolina, the local newspaper touted Washington's tennis fame and her reputation as an "indomitable, internationally famed and stellar performer" (*Greensboro Daily News*, 9 Mar. 1932).

As in tennis, Washington and the Tribunes had few opportunities to challenge the best white teams. The Tribunes regularly played a handful of games against white northern and midwestern teams, winning some and losing others. But many of the best teams were in the South, where interracial competition was generally barred. The major national sponsor of competitive women's basketball, the Amateur Athletic Union, invited few

African American teams to its national competitions, and professional clubs such as the Tribunes were not eligible for AAU play.

Athletic talent brought little financial remuneration in Washington's era. Tennis was an amateur sport, and semiprofessional basketball paid little more. Throughout much of her athletic career, Washington supported herself with the domestic service work that was the major option for wage-earning African American women of her era. In April of 1930, as she was preparing to defend her national tennis title for the first time, she was living as a lodger in a Chicago home and was listed in the census as a hotel maid.

After the Tribunes disbanded in the 1940s, Washington stayed in Philadelphia, where many members of her extended family had settled. She never married, and in her later years she supported herself mainly by working as a housekeeper. She maintained her interest in athletics and competition for the rest of her life. Her nephew James Bernard Childs recalled that on her frequent visits to family members in Caroline County, one of her favorite spots was a family croquet court, where she played almost every afternoon.

Despite her extraordinary accomplishments, especially in the field of tennis, Washington faded quickly into obscurity. In part, she suffered the fate of many early African American athletic stars, who were overshadowed by those athletes—in Washington's case, Althea Gibson—able to take advantage of post-war cracks in racial segregation. At the same time, Washington did not fit neatly into African American tennis circles. Black tennis was an elite sport. According to the historians David Wiggins and Patrick Miller, the ATA championships "were seemingly as much a grand social gathering for the upper reaches of black society as an opportunity to determine tennis supremacy" (105). Washington, who had grown up in the rural South and who had only a high school education, did not fit this mold.

In 1939, the year after her singles retirement, Randy Dixon called for broader appreciation of Washington's achievements, writing in the *Pittsburgh Courier*, "The land at large has never bowed at Ora's shrine of accomplishment in the proper tempo.

She committed the unpardonable sin of being a plain person with no flair whatever for what folks love to call society" (21 Jan. 1939).

Washington spent her final years living with family members in Philadelphia while she contended with an extended illness. She passed away at the city's Mercy-Douglass Hospital in 1971 and was buried in Caroline County. Had Washington lived longer, her life and accomplishments might have been chronicled as part of the resurgence of interest in segregation-era African American sport that began in the 1970s. Instead, little has been written about her, and much of what has been published is inaccurate. As perhaps the greatest black female athlete of the early twentieth century, she deserves far more attention than she has received.

FURTHER READING

Ashe, Arthur R., Jr. *A Hard Road To Glory: A History of the African American Athlete, vol. 2, 1919-1945* (1993).

Grundy, Pamela, and Susan Shackelford. *A History of American Women's Basketball* (forthcoming).

Wiggins, David K., and Patrick B. Miller, eds. *The Unlevel Playing Field: A Documentary History of the African American Experience in Sport* (2003).

Young, A. S. "Doc" in *Negro Firsts in Sport* (1963).

Obituary: *Philadelphia Tribune*, 5 June 1971.

—Pamela Grundy

WATERS, ETHEL

(31 Oct. 1896–1 Sept. 1977), singer and actress, was born in a slum section of Chester, Pennsylvania, as a result of the rape at knifepoint of her twelve-year-old mother, Louisa Tar Anderson, by her white father, John Wesley Waters. She was raised by her grandmother in Chester and Philadelphia. Completing only the sixth grade, Waters could not read or write well and was unable to express herself verbally without often resorting to violence. She grew up with prostitutes, procurers, and thieves and stole in order to eat. Having begun to sing at the age of five, Waters became known as "Baby Star." In 1909, at the age of thirteen, she married Merritt

"Buddy" Purnsley, who was twenty-three. He beat her and humiliated her frequently. They separated by the time Waters was fourteen. The unhappiness of her early years is poignantly addressed in Waters's autobiography, where she writes, "I was never a child. I never felt I belonged. I was always an outsider. I was born out of wedlock" (Waters, 1).

Waters worked as a maid before she began entering singing competitions. In 1917 she made her professional debut at the Lincoln Theatre in Baltimore, Maryland, for nine dollars a week. Because of their dark skin, both Waters and Josephine Baker were rejected for the 1921 Broadway production of *Shuffle Along*. While Baker finally worked her way into the chorus and clowned her way into acceptance, Waters became bitter.

She began singing in Edmonds's Cellar in Harlem. "It was a sure enough honky-tonk, occupying the cellar of a saloon. It was the social center of what was then, and still is, Negro Harlem's kitchen. Here a tall brown-skin girl, unmistakably the one guaranteed in the song to make a preacher lay his Bible down, used to sing and dance her own peculiar numbers" (Rudolph Fisher, quoted in Krasner, 72).

Waters also toured with the Theater Owners Booking Association (TOBA), a booking agency for black performers, often referred to as "Tough on Black Actors." Performers often rehearsed

Singer and actress Ethel Waters as photographed by Carl Van Vechten in 1938. Corbis

without pay and got no money if a show closed on the road. Frequently, they were denied hot or cold running water and other amenities in their dressing rooms. More than once, Waters dressed under a staircase, without even a curtain for privacy. She endured many of the difficulties of segregated America as well as the abuse of some in management and the police. She was very poorly treated in a black wing of a hospital in Anniston, Alabama, after she sustained a leg injury in a car accident while on a TOBA tour. For much of the 1920s and all of the 1930s, Waters sang at popular nightspots and recorded. Leonard Feather observed, "It is curious that the obituaries described Waters as a blues singer, which during almost all of her career she was not. In fact, she had been the first prominent black singer on records who was not primarily associated with the blues. While BESSIE SMITH . . . [was at her peak], Waters was lending her gracious touch to pop songs of the day" (*Los Angeles Times*, 3 Sept. 1977).

Waters sang with Fletcher Henderson's and DUKE ELLINGTON's bands at the Cotton Club, the Plantation Club, and many other elegant establishments. When Earl Dancer implored Waters to leave the "colored time" and try the white clubs, she made him her manager and toured the Keith-Orpheum vaudeville circuit. In her early years Waters was tall and lean; audiences and critics dubbed her "Sweet Mama Stringbean." By 1927 she had made her Broadway debut as Miss Calico in the revue *Africana*. Following the early death of FLORENCE MILLS, Waters performed in Lew Leslie's *Blackbirds* in 1927 and 1928. Also in 1928 she married Clyde Matthews, with whom she adopted a daughter, Algretta.

All her life Waters struggled financially, even when she made good money. Generous to a fault with her men and with considerable medical expenses, Waters declared bankruptcy in 1929, at the time of the great stock-market crash. That same year she appeared in a movie, *On with the Show*, wearing a bandana and carrying a large basket of cotton, and in *Rhapsody in Blue*, a revue at the Belasco Theatre in Washington, D.C. Several New York City theaters picked up the revue in 1930, and by 1931 Waters was a star.

Irving Berlin heard her sing "Stormy Weather" at the Cotton Club and cast her in the famous Broadway revue *As Thousands Cheer*, at the Music Box in 1933. Brooks Atkinson, critic for the *New York Times*, wrote of her performance: "Ethel Waters takes full control of the audience and the show whenever she appears. Her abandon to the ruddy tune of 'Heat Wave Hits New York,' her rowdy comedy . . . and her deep-toned song about a lynching give some notion of the broad range she can encompass in musical shows" (*New York Times*, 2 Oct. 1933).

Four years out of bankruptcy, Waters became the highest-paid woman on Broadway. In 1933 she lived royally, for a season, while many stood in soup lines. She had an apartment on Harlem's "Sugar Hill," a regal wardrobe, a large earring collection, a Lincoln Town Car with a chauffeur, servants for her ten-room apartment—and a man to occupy it, though in 1934 she divorced Matthews.

In 1939, as the Depression lifted and World War II approached, Waters became one of the first African American women to star in a dramatic role on Broadway, in Dorothy and DuBose Heyward's *Mamba's Daughters*. (ROSE MCCLENDON had starred in LANGSTON HUGHES's *Mulatto* on Broadway in 1935.) Waters played Hagar, an unlettered woman on a South Carolina plantation. On opening night, she took seventeen curtain calls. Brooks Atkinson printed a lukewarm review, and many of Waters's friends took out a full-page advertisement in the *New York Times*, strongly suggesting that he return to the theater and review the play more objectively. He did. Waters also appeared in an experimental television broadcast by NBC in 1939, *The Ethel Waters Show*, which was the first ever television show to star an African American.

Following the close of *Mamba's Daughters*, Waters worked with the United Service Organization (USO), entertaining military men of color all over the world. In 1940 she starred in Lynn Root's *Cabin in the Sky* in New York City. KATHERINE DUNHAM, whose dance troupe was part of the musical, took over as choreographer when George Balanchine was fired. In *Cabin in the Sky*, Waters played a God-fearing woman whose husband, Little

Joe, gambles and enjoys the women. Hollywood made a film of *Cabin in the Sky* in 1943, again starring Waters as Petunia, with LENA HORNE replacing Dunham as Sweet Georgia Brown, the other woman. The jealousy Waters displayed on both the stage and film sets became legendary. Waters's poor judgment, violent streak, and jealousy often eclipsed her talent. During the *Cabin* productions, she lived with Eddie Mallory, a handsome trumpeter who developed an eye for other women. Nevertheless, she gave him a large portion of her savings, set him up in business, and helped sponsor his musical career.

Talley Beatty, a member of the Dunham dance company, observed that Waters removed Dunham from two dance numbers in *Cabin*, so that Waters herself could dance with the younger Archie Savage. Because Waters was better known than Dunham at the time, the producers bowed to her wishes. Waters's relationship with Mallory was in trouble, and she claimed Savage as her protégé, setting him up in her Los Angeles home, rent free, around 1943.

In 1944 Waters accused Savage of stealing ten thousand dollars in cash and thirty thousand dollars worth of jewelry, and he was convicted and sentenced to a year and a day in San Quentin Prison. Such a public display of revenge, coupled with publicity about her outbursts and language in the courtroom, did not help Waters's image in the media, which expected its female stars, at least, to show some propriety.

Waters claimed that, because of some anti-Semitic epithets she allegedly uttered on the set of *Cabin in the Sky*, she was unable to get employment for six years, except for an appearance on the *Amos 'n' Andy* radio show on NBC. In 1949, however, her fortunes turned when she secured the part of Granny Dysey Johnson, in Darryl F. Zanuck's *Pinky*, a highly touted film about passing for white, starring the white actress Jeanne Crain as Pinky, a fair-complexioned black nurse who returns to Mississippi after passing in Boston. Though Granny was ostensibly another Mammy role, Waters, like HATTIE MCDANIEL before her, gave a performance that went beyond stereotype. In 1949 Waters was nominated for an Academy Award for Best Supporting Actress for her portrayal of Granny.

In 1950 Waters took on the servant role of Berenice Sadie Browne in the stage production of Carson McCullers's *The Member of the Wedding* at New York City's Empire Theater, giving over 850 performances on the stage, followed by a road tour. The critical acclaim she received for that role, which she reprised in a film version in 1952, was the greatest of her career. In 1950 Waters began to play a maid on the *Beulah* television show. Dooley Wilson, who had portrayed Sam, the piano player, in the film *Casablanca* (1942), played her boyfriend. Television historian Donald Bogle notes that "Waters's Beulah seemed a real person, trapped in an artificial world" (Bogle, 25). She did not use dialect, and came across as much sexier than larger, older women were supposed to on television. Nonetheless, Waters left the series after two years, because she no longer wanted a "white folks kitchen comedy role" (quoted in Bogle, 25).

Being typecast in Mammy roles and her constant financial troubles marred Waters's artistic success. In a letter to Floretta Howard, her secretary, Waters wrote on 8 December 1951: "It looks as if they [the IRS] are going to make me pay an extra $4,000.... They will take $625.00 weekly.... They still don't know what I have." After Dooley Wilson's death in 1953, *Beulah* was syndicated and withdrawn. Waters's career was all but over.

Waters sought solace in religion and in 1957 began touring with the Billy Graham Crusade, singing her signature song for this period in her life, "His Eye Is on the Sparrow," which was also the title of her best-selling autobiography, which was first published in 1951. In 1959 Waters appeared in the film of William Faulkner's novel *The Sound and the Fury*, again playing a Mammy role, Dilsey. She was a favorite of President Richard Nixon and performed for him in the White House in 1971. Her tragic, though occasionally triumphant, life ended at age eighty, on 1 September 1977, in Chatsworth, California. She was a diabetic, suffered greatly from weight problems in her later years, and was living with friends, on Social Security, when she died.

FURTHER READING

Ethel Waters's letters to her secretary, Floretta Howard, are housed in the Performing Arts Section of the Library of Congress.

Waters, Ethel, with Charles Samuels. *His Eye Is on the Sparrow* (1951; repr. 1980).

Bogle, Donald. *Prime Time Blues: African Americans on Network Television* (2001).
Cherry, Randall. "Ethel Waters: The Voice of an Era" in *Temples for Tomorrow: Looking Back at the Harlem Renaissance*, ed. Geneviève Fabre and Michael Feith (2001).
Gill, Glenda E. *No Surrender! No Retreat! African American Pioneer Performers of Twentieth Century American Theater* (2000).
Krasner, David. *A Beautiful Pageant: African American Theatre, Drama and Performance in the Harlem Renaissance, 1910–1927* (2002).

Obituaries: *Chicago Tribune, New York Times, Washington Post,* and *New Orleans Picayune,* 2 Sept. 1977; *Los Angeles Times,* 2 and 3 Sept. 1977.

—GLENDA E. GILL

 ## WATERS, MUDDY

(4 Apr. 1915–30 Apr. 1983), blues singer and guitarist, was born McKinley Morganfield in Rolling Forks, Mississippi, the son of Ollie Morganfield and Bertha Jones, sharecroppers. As a small child he enjoyed playing in the swampy puddles by the family home, so he was nicknamed "Muddy Waters" by his grandmother. In time he became better known by his childhood nickname than by his family name.

When Waters was three years old, his mother died, whereupon his maternal grandmother, Della Jones, brought him to her home at Stovall's Plantation near Clarksdale. Waters attended school only through the third grade. While still a boy, he began plowing and chopping cotton at Stovall's, and in those years he took up the harmonica as his first musical instrument. In 1932 he married Mabel Berry.

The musicians best known to blacks at Stovall's and around the Mississippi Delta region in the early 1930s were guitarists, including CHARLEY PATTON, Eddie "Son" House, Willie Brown, and Robert Nighthawk (Robert McCollum). By the end of 1932 Waters had bought a guitar and began taking lessons from another teenager, Scott Bohanner. Whenever he could, Waters paid close attention to the playing of Son House, who specialized in the bottleneck style of slide guitar playing and who was even at

that time a great influence on younger musicians, including ROBERT JOHNSON. Emulating House, Waters took up the older musician's bottleneck technique and songs. Often he played weekends in a musical group with Bohanner, guitarist Percy Thomas, and fiddler Henry "Son" Simms, performing string band favorites in the style of the Mississippi Sheiks. Sometimes Waters went to Memphis, Tennessee, to hear local and visiting musicians, including the jug bands and harmonica players.

For a few months in 1939 or 1940, Waters moved to St. Louis, Missouri, but he quickly returned to Stovall's in Mississippi, working in the cotton fields and performing on weekends. Briefly he ran a roadhouse where he sometimes featured guest musicians such as Aleck Miller (also known as Sonny Boy Williamson, not to be confused with John Lee Williamson of Chicago who recorded for RCA Victor under the same nickname) and Elmore James of Helena, Arkansas, and through which he served bootleg liquor. Indeed, when Waters first met Alan Lomax of the Library of Congress in 1941, he mistook him for a government agent investigating his bootleg operation. Lomax, however, was on a field recording trip seeking guitarists who could play in the manner of Robert Johnson, who had died in 1938. Since Waters had based his "Country Blues" on the "Walking Blues" melody previously played by House and Johnson, he was allowed a lengthy interview session by Lomax, who was sufficiently impressed to record Waters with his string band shortly afterward. Later that fall Waters received a test copy of two of his solo performances, a boost to his musical confidence. Lomax returned to Stovall's the following summer and again recorded Waters in solo and band contexts.

By 1942 Waters had separated from his first wife. In December of that year he took a Stovall's resident, Sallie Ann Adams, as his second wife, and continued farming and driving a tractor. He took additional opportunities to perform, such as a couple of nights with the Silas Green of New Orleans vaudeville troupe when it was in the Clarksdale region. Forsaking the hard rural life and the racial bias against black Americans in Mississippi, Waters left

Stovall's Plantation and the Clarksdale area for Chicago in May 1943.

Initially Waters worked at menial jobs, unloading trucks or driving them; he confined his guitar playing to weekend parties. Later, as a sideman for John Lee Williamson, Waters began playing in the Chicago clubs. The urban clubs being noisier than rural juke joints, Waters realized he needed something louder than his acoustic guitar to be heard through the crowd; toward that end he acquired his first electric guitar in 1944. The following year, during a return trip to Mississippi, he met harmonicist and guitarist Jimmy Rogers, who became an important musician in Waters's first Chicago band. By this time Waters's second marriage had ended, and in the mid-1940s he married Geneva (maiden name unknown).

Waters made his first commercial records in 1946 on the labels 20th Century and Columbia as a supporting band member, and the following year he assisted pianist Sunnyland Slim during an Aristocrat Records studio date. The owners of Aristocrat, Leonard Chess and Phil Chess, noticed Waters's talent and decided to record him in a session of his own. That next session, with bassist Big Crawford, resulted in Waters's first important release, "I Can't Be Satisfied" backed with "I Feel Like Going Home." Released in 1948, the initial pressing of three thousand copies was sold out within forty-eight hours. The success of this hit paved the way for additional Aristocrat sessions with the guitar and bass format, although for club appearances Waters backed himself with a band that included Jimmy Rogers, harmonicist "Little Walter" Jacobs, and drummer "Baby Face" Leroy.

During 1950 Waters continued working in the black clubs in Chicago and in the recording studio of the Chess brothers, who by then had renamed their label Chess Records. At the same time, the Chess brothers allowed Waters to use his club band in the studio. Thus began a series of records lasting through 1960 that are now considered his most important and popular records: "Long Distance Call," "She Moves Me," "I Just Want to Make Love to You," "Still a Fool," "Standing around Crying," "I'm Your Hoochie Coochie Man," "Mannish Boy," "Nineteen Years Old," and "Got My Mojo Working." These records document Waters's command of his voice and instrument, as well as the backing performances of his best sidemen, including pianist Otis Spann, who joined Waters in 1954.

Waters's Chicago music began with his adaptation of Mississippi acoustic blues technique with bottleneck slide to the amplified electric guitar. He then fit the electric guitar in the context of amplified harmonica, piano, and drums. The songs he played were rooted in the Mississippi blues tradition, employing the standard twelve measure form and blues chord progressions. On his early records, especially in the guitar and bass format of his Aristocrat sides, Waters wrote and developed his own material. Later in the 1950s he began performing songs by another transplanted Mississippian, BIG WILLIE DIXON, a composer/bassist who was a regular session musician for Chess and other Chicago-based record labels.

Waters as bandleader was a mentor for upcoming blues musicians. "Little Walter" Jacobs enjoyed a popular solo career after scoring a hit record, "Juke," which up to that time had been the Muddy Waters Band's signature tune. Other harmonicists who followed Jacobs included Junior Wells and James Cotton. Through his death in 1970, pianist Otis Spann enjoyed several solo recordings and bookings when he was not playing behind Waters.

By the late 1950s Waters was generating international interest. In 1958 he and Otis Spann toured England with the Chris Barber band. The following spring, in April 1959, Waters played at Carnegie Recital Hall in New York, and the year after that he performed at the Newport Folk Festival, where his show was taped and released on Chess Records. Before long Waters was developing a dual career: as an acoustic guitarist for the folk revival audiences, for whom he recorded the albums *Muddy Waters Sings Big Bill* and *Folk Singer*, and as the leader of an electrically amplified band, a format imitated by British ensembles, especially the Rolling Stones (who named themselves after Waters's song "Rollin' Stone"). By the end of the 1960s Waters's influence would be heard through white American bands such as the Paul Butterfield Blues Band.

In October 1969, near the end of a successful year, Waters was in a head-on car collision that killed his driver; Waters himself was in the hospital for three months and unable to play guitar for a year. After recuperation, he resumed his tours, retaining bookings at the large festivals such as the Ann Arbor Festival and the Montreux Jazz Festival. Meanwhile, Chess Records was recording Waters two different ways: either taping his live shows with his club band (such as *Live at Mr. Kelly's* in 1972) or having him lead studio ensembles composed of young white rock and blues musicians, such as *Fathers and Sons* with Paul Butterfield and Mike Bloomfield in 1969 and *The London Muddy Waters Sessions* with Rory Gallagher in 1972.

The mid-1970s brought changes in Waters's life. During the 1950s and 1960s he lived in a brownstone on Chicago's South Side, but in 1973 he moved to Westmont, a suburb. Also in 1973 his third wife died, after some three decades of marriage. In addition, Waters took on a manager, Scott Cameron, who advised him to set up Muddy Waters Productions/Watertoons Music to protect his composing rights. Then, Cameron, Waters, and Willie Dixon sued ARC Music Corporation for the return of their respective song copyrights. The suit was settled out of court in 1976 in the musicians' favor. In the meantime, in 1975 Waters taped his last session for Chess Records and parted company with the label after twenty-eight years.

Around that time Waters deepened his acquaintanceship with Texan guitarist Johnny Winter. They began an artistic collaboration resulting in an Indian-summer series of albums for Blue Sky, a Columbia Records subsidiary, between 1976 and 1980. In the wake of the renewed acclaim these records brought, Waters toured and performed with a band that included guitarist Bob Margolin and pianist Pinetop Perkins. The band performed concerts around the world, and among the highlights were the 1977 White House staff picnic (with an introduction by President Jimmy Carter) and the 1981 Delta Blues Festival near Greenville, Mississippi. In 1979 Waters took a fourth wife, Marva Jean Brookes, and subsequently continued living in Westmont. Waters had a total of seven children with his four wives.

From 1960 on, Waters was frequently filmed and televised. Most notable was a guest appearance in *The Last Waltz* (1978), a film by Martin Scorsese of the rock group The Band. Waters died in Chicago in his sleep.

FURTHER READING

Guralnick, Peter. *Feel Like Going Home* (1971).
Obrecht, Jas. "Muddy Waters: The Life and Times of the Hoochie Coochie Man," *Blues Revue*, Dec. 1995–Jan. 1996, 24–38.
Oliver, Paul. "Muddy Waters, 1960," *Blues Unlimited Collectors' Classic*, no. 1 (1963), repr. in *Back Woods Blues* (1968), 13–19.
O'Neal, Jim, and Amy van Singel. "Muddy Waters," *Living Blues*, Mar.–Apr. 1985, 15–40.
Palmer, Robert. *Deep Blues* (1981).
Rooney, James. *Bossmen: Bill Monroe and Muddy Waters* (1971).
Welding, Pete. "An Interview with Muddy Waters," *American Folk Music Occasional*, no. 2 (1970): 2–7.

Obituary: *New York Times*, 1 May 1983.

Discography
Wight, Phil, and Fred Rothwell. *The Complete Muddy Waters Discography* (1993).
—EDWARD KOMARA

WEAVER, ROBERT CLIFTON (29 Dec. 1907–18 July 1997), government administrator, writer, and educator, was born in Washington, D.C., the second son of Mortimer Grover Weaver, a postal clerk, and Florence Weaver Freeman. Robert's grandfather, Robert Tanner Freeman, was the first African American to graduate from Harvard Dental School (in 1869), and he practiced in Washington, D.C. Robert grew up in the middle-class, integrated neighborhood of Brookland and graduated from the prestigious Dunbar High School in 1925.

Robert then enrolled at Harvard College, which his older brother, Mortimer, also attended. Among his friends in college were RALPH BUNCHE, WILLIAM HENRY HASTIE, RAYFORD W. LOGAN, and John P. Davis. Robert and his brother had intended to become lawyers and open a joint practice, but when Mortimer died suddenly at age twenty-three, Robert decided to pursue an economics degree. He received his bachelor's degree in 1929 and his master's in 1931.

Despite his credentials, Weaver was unable to secure a teaching job in a white college, and he taught briefly at North Carolina Agricultural and Technical College in Greensboro before returning to Harvard in 1932 to defend his dissertation, "The High Wage of Prosperity." In 1933, along with Harvard Law School graduate John P. Davis, Weaver founded the Negro Industrial League (NIL) to lobby the federal government for fair treatment of black workers under the National Industrial Recovery Act, passed in order to deal with the nation's economic crisis. The NIL represented black workers before the National Recovery Administration, testified at congressional hearings, and in 1934 solicited support from the NAACP, the National Urban League, and other black organizations to establish an NIL office in Washington, D.C.

Weaver's lobbying efforts brought him to the attention of Interior Secretary Harold Ickes, who in 1934 created in his department an Office on Negro Affairs and appointed Weaver as assistant to Clark Foreman, the white Atlantan chosen to run the office. Weaver joined a small but increasing number of black professionals in the federal government, a group known to some as the "Black Cabinet." While MARY MCLEOD BETHUNE was the leader of the group, Weaver provided much of the organizational direction. He fought to include blacks in projects funded by the Public Works Administration and battled racial discrimination by white southern employers.

In 1935 Weaver married Ella V. Haith, of Washington, D.C., and the couple adopted a child. Three years later Weaver became director of the office of race relations at the United States Housing Authority (USHA). Charged with overseeing the construction of public housing across the country, he focused on ensuring that blacks received employment opportunities in the construction and management of public housing. Weaver's work at USHA serves as an early model for federal affirmative action programs. So, too, did his efforts for the National Defense Advisory Commission (NDAC), where he worked to reduce racial barriers within the defense industry and supported African Americans' integration into labor unions. When

the NDAC was later incorporated into the Office of Production Management, Weaver served as the director of the Negro Training and Employment Branch and the Negro Manpower Service, where he oversaw a dramatic increase in black participation in the industrial workforce.

Despite his success in creating new opportunities for black workers, Weaver grew increasingly frustrated with the obstructionism of other federal officials, particularly in Congress. In 1944 he left the federal government to become the executive director of the Mayor's Committee on Race Relations in Chicago, which was established to prevent the eruption of racial violence that had plagued Detroit a year earlier. The committee possessed little influence, however, and he resigned less than a year later to lead the American Council on Race Relations. There, he continued to push to lower discriminatory barriers to housing in Chicago and elsewhere.

Throughout his years in the federal government, Weaver was a prolific writer, publishing at least twenty-seven articles on labor, housing, and race relations between 1933 and 1944. In 1946 he published his first book, *Negro Labor: A Problem of Today*, which examined the structure of the black labor market and the role of discrimination in limiting economic opportunities for blacks.

Weaver's second book, *The Negro Ghetto* (1948), examined the creation, growth, and current status of black urban life and was widely praised as one of the definitive studies of modern black America. The volume's research in the area of housing discrimination was used that year by the NAACP's THURGOOD MARSHALL in his brief to the U.S. Supreme Court in *Shelley v. Kraemer*, a landmark case that struck down restrictive covenants that discriminated against blacks seeking to purchase homes in certain neighborhoods. Because of his role in *Shelley*, Weaver became a leader in the fair housing movement, becoming president of the newly created National Committee against Discrimination in 1949.

Weaver moved to New York in 1949 to take the position of director of the Opportunity Fellowships Program at the John Hay Whitney Foundation. This program provided financial support to promising minority candidates pursuing advanced degrees. Among the people Weaver supported while he was director, and who went on to distinguished careers, were the economist Andrew Brimmer, the jurist A. LEON HIGGINBOTHAM, and the political scientist Martin Kilson.

Governor of New York Averill Harriman appointed Weaver deputy state housing commissioner in 1955 and, a year later, state rent administrator. As head of the state's controversial rent-control program, Weaver was the first black member of the cabinet in New York State. When Harriman left office in 1959, it was reported that Weaver would be appointed borough president of Manhattan. However, Congressman ADAM CLAYTON POWELL JR. opposed the appointment, because Weaver was not a member of Powell's political club. That year Weaver was elected chairman of the board of directors of the NAACP.

Shortly thereafter, President-Elect John F. Kennedy selected Weaver to be administrator of the Housing and Home Finance Agency (HHFA), the bureau that managed the federal government's housing programs. Weaver's nomination brought cheers from civil rights leaders, but southern members of Congress actively opposed him. After several days of grueling hearings, in which Weaver was accused of being a Communist, his nomination was approved.

Weaver quickly became the Kennedy administration's primary adviser on housing and urban affairs. He crafted and pushed through Congress the Housing Act of 1961, which expanded the nation's public housing program and provided housing for seniors. But Congress rejected the administration's proposal to elevate the HHFA to a cabinet-level Department of Urban Affairs. Kennedy's statement that he intended to appoint Weaver as secretary of the department played an important role in the failure of the initiative, because once again it engendered strong opposition from segregationists in Congress. Weaver's other major success during the Kennedy administration was the issuance of the President's Executive Order banning racial discrimination in federal housing programs. The order was of limited scope, however, and Weaver regretted that it was not more influential.

Following Kennedy's assassination, Lyndon Johnson's administration entered the White House with substantial plans for urban America. Housing and urban revitalization were important parts of Johnson's Great Society, and Weaver played a crucial role in this program. In 1965, fresh from a landslide victory, Johnson advocated the creation of the Department of Housing and Urban Development (HUD). This time the legislation passed easily. Most people expected Johnson to appoint Weaver as secretary, but Johnson delayed for more than four months, stating that he was conducting an exhaustive search. Many thought that Johnson had disgraced Weaver, and Weaver considered resigning, but in January 1966 Johnson finally nominated him. The Senate overwhelmingly approved his nomination and Weaver became the nation's first African American cabinet secretary.

As HUD secretary, Weaver spent a great deal of time speaking around the country. In the mid-1960s, as inner-city riots exposed problems of urban decay and the increasing disillusionment of young African Americans, Weaver became an important administration spokesman. He played a crucial role in the development, passage, and implementation of several major pieces of legislation, including the Model Cities Act, the Housing Act of 1968, and the Civil Rights Act of 1968. Passed at the height of the urban crisis, the Housing Act of 1968 dramatically expanded home ownership opportunities for blacks and also increased federal support for rental housing. Weaver was particularly active in the effort to pass the Fair Housing Act, which was part of the 1968 Civil Rights Act. This law, the culmination of Weaver's three decades of struggle for fairness in housing, provided federal enforcement against racial discrimination in housing.

Weaver left HUD in the fall of 1968 to become president of Baruch College, a school in the City University of New York (CUNY) system. CUNY trustees had proposed making Baruch the centerpiece of a dramatically expanded university system. A year later, however, the trustees revised their plan, and Weaver resigned in protest. Weaver spent the rest of his professional life as a distinguished professor at Hunter College. There, he mentored numerous graduate students and continued to be a prolific writer and speaker on issues of urban policy and race relations for more than twenty years. He was one of the original directors of the Municipal Assistance Corporation, the entity that was created to keep New York City out of bankruptcy in the 1970s, and he was active in many other national organizations. He died in New York City in 1997.

FURTHER READING

Weaver's papers are located at the Schomburg Center for Research in Black Culture of the New Public Library.

Gelfand, Mark. *A Nation of Cities* (1972).

Meyer, Stephen Grant. *As Long as They Don't Move Next Door: Segregation and Racial Conflict in American Neighborhoods.* (2000).

Shipp, Sigmund. "Building Bricks without Straw: Robert C. Weaver and Negro Industrial Employment, 1934–1944" in *Historical Roots of the Urban Crisis*, eds. Henry Louis Taylor Jr. and Walter Hill (2000).

Obituary: *New York Times*, 19 July 1997.

—WENDELL E. PRITCHETT

WELLS-BARNETT, IDA BELL (16 July 1862–25 Mar. 1931), anti-lynching reformer and journalist, was born Ida Bell Wells, the first of eight children born to James Wells, a carpenter, and Elizabeth Arrington, a cook, in Holly Springs, Mississippi. Her parents worked for Spires Boling, a contractor and architect, as slaves and then as free blacks until 1867, when James Wells, against the wishes of his employer, exercised his new right to vote. After returning from the polls to find his carpentry shop locked, Wells moved the family to a house nearby and went into business for himself. In Holly Springs, Ida Wells attended a freedmen's school, of which her father was a trustee, and Shaw University (now Rust College), founded by the Freedmen's Aid Society of the Methodist Episcopal Church and incorporated in 1870.

Ida Wells's early life as a "happy, light-hearted schoolgirl" (Duster, 16) was upended in 1878, when both of her parents and her infant brother died in a yellow fever epidemic that swept the Mississippi Valley that year. Wells,

Journalist and militant activist Ida B. Wells-Barnett campaigned vigorously for civil rights and to expose the horrors of lynching. Schomburg Center

who was then sixteen years of age and the oldest of the five surviving siblings, dropped out of Shaw to support her family by teaching at a rural school in Mississippi. In 1880 or 1881, her two brothers went to live with extended family members. Around that time, one of her sisters died of a disease of the spine from which she had been suffering for several years. Subsequently, Wells's widowed aunt, Fanny Wells, invited Ida and her two younger sisters to join her in Memphis. Upon her arrival in the "Bluff City," as Memphis was called, Wells took classes at LeMoyne College and taught school in Woodstock, Tennessee, ten miles outside the city; subsequently she taught in the Memphis public school system.

Wells's activist career began in earnest on 15 September 1883, when she refused to leave a first-class ladies car on the Chesapeake, Ohio, and Southwestern Railway. After the U.S. Supreme Court overturned the 1875 Civil Rights Acts in October of 1883, Wells again attempted to ride a first-class car, so that her subsequent suit against the railway could challenge the Supreme Court's decision. Although Wells won her case in the lower courts in 1884, the Tennessee Supreme Court overturned the decision in 1887.

Soon after the first court decision, Wells was asked to write about her protest for the *Living Way*, a Baptist weekly in Memphis. Her successful debut as a journalist came at a time when urbanization and the increase in black literacy rates helped propel the growth and independence of the black press. Taking the pen name of "Iola," she was soon invited to write about practical matters, black womanhood, and politics in black weeklies across the country and, occasionally, for the white dailies in Memphis. In 1887 Wells became the first woman elected as an officer of the Negro Press Association, which had been established in 1884. By 1889 she was anointed "The Princess of the Press" by her colleagues and became a co-owner of the *Free Speech and Headlight*, a militant weekly.

In 1891 a *Free Speech* editorial praising black men who set fire to buildings in Georgetown, Kentucky, in response to a lynching drew calls for the paper's extinction. In the same year, Wells was fired from her teaching position when she wrote an editorial criticizing the inadequacy of the segregated schools and the sexual exploitation of black woman teachers by white board members. With the opportunity to devote all her time to newspaper work, Wells continued writing and traveling throughout the Mississippi Valley to secure subscriptions for the paper.

When a mob murdered a close friend of Wells's and two of his associates in March 1892, Wells embarked on what became a lifelong crusade against the horrors of lynching. The victims—associated with the People's Grocery, a black-owned cooperative—were not killed for any criminal act, she editorialized, but because they took business away from a white competitor. The circumstances surrounding their deaths propelled Wells to call for a boycott of the Memphis trolleys, encourage thousands of blacks to leave Memphis for the newly opened Oklahoma Territory, and expose, as she put it, the "truth about lynching." Lynching had long been a common practice in rural America, especially in the South and West, but, beginning in the late 1880s, it began to take on a particularly racial character in the South. In 1892 alone, there were more than two hundred lynchings, most often of African Americans by whites. Southern white leaders routinely justified the practice by claiming that since emancipation black men had retrogressed to a savage state, and were raping white women. Lynching was primarily a problem in the South, but it was northern academics, at Harvard University, the University of Pennsylvania, and elsewhere, who were most responsible for promulgating theories of black retrogression.

Using the methods of investigative journalism (before there was such a category), Wells documented the fact that less than a third of black victims were even accused of rape, much less found guilty of it. Instead, she averred, it was black women who were the real victims of interracial rape and coercion. Blacks, she thought, were really being punished for their increasing militancy; for their ability to compete economically with whites; and, in particular, for the growing number of consensual relationships between black men and white women. Such assertions undermined the "scientific" racism of the period, the moral authority of white women and men, and the justification for the disenfranchisement of blacks. Her writings, replete with statistics and first-hand observation and interviews, provided the sociological framework that underpinned subsequent studies and antilynching strategies for the remainder of the twentieth century.

In 1892 Wells's campaign urged that blacks boycott the city streetcars and leave Memphis for the new territories opening in the West. Soon after, on 27 May 1892, the offices of *Free Speech* were destroyed, and Wells was exiled from the city upon the threat of death. She found refuge in Brooklyn, New York, where she wrote antilynching editorials for T. THOMAS FORTUNE's *New York Age*, widely considered the country's best black newspaper. Subsequently, her writings were compiled into a pamphlet, *Southern Horrors: Lynch Law in All Its Phases*, which was subsidized by a testimonial given to Wells by black women activists from New York, Boston, and Philadelphia. The gathering held on 5 October 1892 was the "real beginning of the club movement among colored women in this country," Wells wrote in her autobiography, *Crusade for Justice* (Wells, 81). In 1896 the movement coalesced into the National Association of Colored Women, the first secular, nationwide organization of African American women.

In 1893 Wells was invited to take her campaign to the British Isles by two editors of *Anti-Caste*, an antiracist journal published in England. She returned to the United States to protest the exclusion of blacks from the 1893 World's Columbian Exposition in Chicago and to publish a pamphlet, *The Reason Why the Colored American Is Not in the World's Columbian Exposition*, with, among others, FREDERICK DOUGLASS, an ardent supporter of her campaigns. Wells's return to the British Isles in 1894 resulted in the formation of the British Anti-lynching Committee, made up of influential journalists, members of Parliament, and such prominent figures as the duke of Argyll and the Archbishop of Canterbury. Such attention pressed important liberal figures in the United States, including the labor leader Samuel Gompers and the Women's Christian Temperance Union president Frances Willard (who had earlier opposed Wells), to lend their names to the anti-lynching cause. Upon her return, Wells continued her campaign across the United States and in 1895 published the anti-lynching pamphlet *The Red Record*.

In June of 1895 Ida Wells married Ferdinand L. Barnett, a Chicago widower who had founded the *Conservator*, the city's first black newspaper, and who, in 1896, became the first black appointed as an assistant state's attorney for Cook County. Soon after their marriage, Wells-Barnett purchased the *Conservator* from stockholders and presided over the Ida B. Wells Club, founded in 1893, which helped establish one of the first black kindergartens in the city. While remaining active in many endeavors, Wells-Barnett and her husband had four children: Charles in 1896, Herman in 1897, Ida in 1901, and Alfreda in 1904. During this period, she campaigned for Republican candidates throughout the state, cofounded the interracial Frederick Douglass Club, worked with the settlement-house founder Jane Addams to thwart calls for segregation in the Chicago public schools, enjoined an interracial delegation to the White

House to protest the lynching of a South Carolina postmaster, and mobilized protests against lynchings in her adopted state of Illinois.

In August of 1908, a riot in Springfield, Illinois—in which two blacks were lynched and businesses and homes destroyed—so alarmed a group of northern reformers that they called for the establishment of a new organization later known as the National Association for the Advancement of Colored People (NAACP). Although Wells-Barnett was one of its "Founding Forty" members, she later criticized the organization for its moderation. In response to the riot, Wells-Barnett established the Negro Fellowship League, a settlement house that provided employment and legal protection for the burgeoning number of blacks who migrated to Chicago from the South. In 1913, when women gained limited suffrage in Illinois, Wells-Barnett cofounded the first black women's suffrage club in Chicago, the Alpha Suffrage Club, which was instrumental in the election two years later of the first black city alderman, OSCAR DE PRIEST.

During World War I, both Barnetts were associated with militant protest and, like others viewed by the federal government as "radicals," were the subjects of dossiers compiled by military intelligence. In 1917, despite warnings by government authorities that she was committing treason, Wells-Barnett protested the hanging of twelve black soldiers who were court-martialed for their alleged role in a riot in Houston, Texas, where the men were stationed. Although she was not arrested, Wells-Barnett was refused a passport to attend the Versailles Peace Conference in 1919 as a delegate of the National Equal Rights League, an organization headed by the Boston editor WILLIAM MONROE TROTTER. MARCUS GARVEY's Universal Negro Improvement Association had also selected Wells-Barnett as a delegate to the Versailles Conference.

The ending of the war in Europe coincided with an upsurge in racial violence in the United States, and Wells-Barnett again played a vital role in publicizing these events. She published on-site investigations of the 1918 East St. Louis Massacre, where at least forty black people lost their lives, and also covered the even bloodier Elaine,

Arkansas, race riot the following year. The Arkansas riot was precipitated by local authorities when they attempted to break up a union meeting of black sharecroppers. Several of the farmers and a white deputy sheriff were killed in the melee, but the response by white planters and farmers was unprecedented in its barbarity. Over the course of seven days, local whites, aided and abetted by U.S. infantry troops, systematically chased down and killed more than 200 African Americans in what historian DAVID LEVERING LEWIS has described as an American pogrom. More than a thousand black sharecroppers were rounded up and packed in a stockade. Wells-Barnett, the NAACP, and other organizations engaged in a multi-year effort to defend the sharecroppers, twelve of whom were sentenced to death. Sixty-seven others were given lengthy prison terms.

But the racial violence of the era was not restricted to the South. In her hometown of Chicago in 1919, an attack and subsequent drowning of a black youth, swimming in the "white side" of a beach area, escalated into urban warfare that resulted in the death of thirty-eight people, including fifteen whites and twenty-three blacks. The Chicago riot was distinguished by the militant response of blacks who fought back and, in some cases, took the offensive. In its aftermath, Wells-Barnett urged blacks to testify against white assailants. She also became active in civic organizations formed to ameliorate race relations and, with her lawyer husband, helped defend African Americans indicted for violent crimes and murder during the uprising.

Despite her declining health in the 1920s, Wells-Barnett continued to fight discrimination and racial violence through the Ida B. Wells Club. She also remained active in politics with the Cook County League of Women's Clubs and helped to establish an early Chicago branch of A. PHILIP RANDOLPH's Brotherhood of Sleeping Car Porters and Maids. In 1930, a year before her death of uremia in Chicago, she ran unsuccessfully as an independent for a state senate seat in Illinois.

Wells-Barnett left a rich legacy of activism. She helped to establish community institutions and organizations that aided poor blacks, empowered women, and defended those unjustly accused by the legal and extra-legal systems of law. Wells-Barnett's strategies, developed through her campaign against lynching, also anticipated future political movements. Her militant activism drew upon a long tradition of African American civil disobedience and self-defense, and her political journalism challenged the prevailing racial and sexual stereotypes of her times. Her essential radicalism, which focused on the interconnections of race, class, and gender discrimination, prefigured that of later black feminist activists and writers such as ANGELA DAVIS, ALICE WALKER, and bell hooks.

FURTHER READING

The Ida B. Wells Papers, including her diary, are in Special Collections, Reggenstein Library, University of Chicago.

Duster, Alfreda M. *Crusade for Justice: The Autobiography of Ida B. Wells* (1970).

McMurry, Linda O. *To Keep the Waters Troubled: The Life of Ida B. Wells* (1998).

Obituaries: *Chicago Tribune*, 25 March 1931; *Chicago Defender*, 4 April 1931; *National Notes*, May 1931: 17; *Crisis*, June 1931: 207.
—PAULA J. GIDDINGS

 WESLEY, CHARLES HARRIS (2 Dec. 1891– 16 Aug. 1987), historian, educator, minister, and administrator, was born in Louisville, Kentucky, the only child of Matilda Harris and Charles Snowden Wesley. His father, who had attended Atlanta University and worked as a clerk in a funeral home, died when Charles Wesley was nine years old. Wesley grew up in his maternal grandparents' comfortable home, completed Louisville Central High School in two years, and entered the preparatory division of Fisk University in Nashville, Tennessee, at the age of fourteen. He later enrolled in Fisk's collegiate division, where he developed a strong interest in music. He joined the famous Fisk Jubilee Singers, which had been organized in 1867 to raise much-needed funds for the fledgling school, founded two years earlier by the American Missionary Association. The Jubilee Singers secured funds from national and international

tours to construct the university's first permanent building, Jubilee Hall, in 1875. Wesley was a baritone and sang in the group with Roland Hayes, later a renowned tenor.

Wesley excelled in the classroom, on the athletic field, and in debate and drama. He ran track, played baseball and basketball, and was quarterback of the football team. He graduated in 1911 with honors in classics and was later initiated into Phi Beta Kappa when the honor society established a chapter at Fisk in 1953. At nineteen Wesley entered Yale University with a graduate fellowship and earned a master's degree with honors in History and Economics two years later, while waiting tables to support himself. He then became an instructor of history and modern languages at Howard University and traveled to Europe, where he studied French history and language. He completed a year of law school at Howard University in 1915 and that same year married Louise Johnson of Baltimore, Maryland, with whom he had two daughters, Louise and Charlotte. Wesley's daughter Louise died in 1950, and his wife passed away in 1973.

Wesley became a minister in the African Methodist Episcopal (AME) Church and was presiding elder over all the AME churches in Washington, D.C., from 1918 to 1938. He later became a candidate for bishop but was not elected, as he refused to campaign for the position. Wesley, who had taught at Howard for seven years, took a sabbatical leave during the 1920–1921 academic year to pursue a doctoral degree in History at Harvard University, while returning regularly to Washington, D.C., to preach at several local AME churches. In 1925 he became the third African American to receive a PhD in History from Harvard, following W. E. B. DU BOIS and CARTER G. WOODSON.

Wesley rose through the ranks at Howard University, where he was promoted to professor, chaired the history department, and was director of the summer school, dean of the College of Liberal Arts, and dean of the graduate school. Together with other influential faculty, he helped persuade the board of trustees in 1926 to appoint Howard's first black president, MORDECAI JOHNSON. Wesley's first book,

based on his dissertation, *Negro Labor in the United States, 1850–1925: A Study in American Economic History*, appeared in 1927. Carter G. Woodson, who reviewed the book in *The American Historical Review* in 1927, called it "the only scientific treatment of Negro labor in the United States." Wesley refuted biased accounts of black labor, which contended that African Americans were not capable of skilled labor and that they would not work after emancipation without coercion. He revealed early labor-organizing efforts among black Americans and their struggle for economic rights after Reconstruction. Wesley concluded that labor inequality during the early twentieth century resulted more from racial prejudice and discrimination against black workers than from any innate ability among whites. His work was the first comprehensive study of African Americans as laborers rather than as slaves.

Wesley published hundreds of articles and twelve books during his career. His book *The Collapse of the Confederacy*, published in 1937 by the Association for the Study of Negro Life and History, established him as an expert in the field of southern history. The study began as an essay written for a graduate course taught by Edward Channing at Harvard. In the expanded work, Wesley suggested a revisionist thesis that the South lost the Civil War because of internal social disintegration. He became the first black historian to receive a Guggenheim Fellowship in 1930, which he used in London to study slave emancipation within the British Empire. That work influenced his pioneering publications on the role of African Americans in the fight against slavery in the United States. He sought to demonstrate that African Americans made important contributions to the struggle for their freedom. This was at a time when many mainstream historians argued that African Americans were given their freedom without much effort on their part.

During his long career, Wesley wrote extensively about the history of black fraternal organizations. He explored the group life of African Americans and what they did for themselves more than what was done to them. He published the first edition of the history of Alpha Phi Alpha, the first black college fraternity, in 1929 and became its national historian in 1941. He served as the fraternity's general president from 1932 to 1940, the longest tenure of anyone in that office.

In addition to histories of black fraternal organizations, such as the PRINCE HALL Masons, the Improved Benevolent and Protective Order of Elks, and the Sigma Pi Phi Fraternity, Wesley published *The History of the National Association of Colored Women's Clubs: A Legacy of Service*, when he was ninety-two years old. Wesley was concerned with revealing the group life of African Americans and their achievements not only within their own communities but also in the context of the broader American society. In examining how teachers of U.S. history treated African Americans, he noted that revisions had taken place in interpreting American history and stated in the journal *Social Education* in 1943 that "This need of revision is also clear in relation to the study of Negro life in the United States." He believed in a conscious effort to set the record straight and to revise the errors, omissions, and distortions about black life and culture from the African roots through slavery, Reconstruction, migration, and urbanization.

Wesley became president of Wilberforce University in 1942, an AME-affiliated school that the Methodist Episcopal Church founded in 1856 to educate African Americans from Ohio and nearby free states. The AME Church had purchased the school in 1863. He clashed with church trustees over administration of the school and was asked to resign in 1947. The state of Ohio had financially supported the Normal and Industrial Department within Wilberforce since 1887. When Wesley left Wilberforce, he presided over the separation of the state-supported unit from the university and the establishment of Wilberforce State College, which, after an acrimonious court fight, became Central State University. Wesley served as president of Central State from 1947 to 1965, when he retired.

He was soon appointed executive director of the Association for the Study of Negro Life and History (ASNLH), which had been organized in 1915 by Carter G. Woodson, who had served as a mentor to him. Wesley had been

president of ASNLH from 1950, after Woodson's death, to 1965, when he became executive director, a position that he held until 1972, when he again retired. During his tenure as executive director, he revised and republished many of Woodson's earlier works, such as *The Negro in Our History, Negro Makers of History*, and *The Story of the Negro Retold*. He also edited a ten-volume series, *The International Library of Negro Life and History*. Wesley again came out of retirement in 1974 to head the new Afro-American Historical and Cultural Museum in Philadelphia until 1976. He married Dorothy B. Porter, former head of the Moorland-Spingarn Research Center at Howard University, in 1979. Charles Harris Wesley, who at the time was known as the dean of black historians, died of pneumonia and cardiac arrest at Howard University Hospital.

FURTHER READING

Most of Charles Harris Wesley's papers are in the possession of his family. Some of his papers and publications are housed in the Archives of Dorothy Porter Wesley in Fort Lauderdale, Florida.

Conyers, James L., ed. *Charles H. Wesley: The Intellectual Tradition of a Black Historian* (1994).
Harris, Janette Hoston. "Charles Harris Wesley: Educator and Historian, 1891–1947." PhD diss., Howard University, 1975.
Meier, August, and Elliott Rudwick. *Black History and the Historical Profession, 1915–1980* (1986).

Obituary: *Washington Post*, 22 Aug. 1987.
—ROBERT L. HARRIS JR

 WEST, CORNEL
(2 June 1953–), philosopher, educator, and social critic, was born in Tulsa, Oklahoma, the son of Clifton L. West Jr., a civilian Air Force administrator, and Irene Bias, an elementary school teacher. The West family eventually settled in the segregated city of Sacramento, California. The young Cornel's childhood was at first marked by much anger and rebellion. In the third grade, when his teacher slapped him, he hit her back and was expelled. He was taught at home for six

months before being placed in a newly integrated school. At the age of eight he became a devout Christian. From then onward, the precocious Cornel became a conscientious student, and spent much of his youth reading biographies and philosophical texts from the neighborhood bookmobile and articles from the Black Panther newspaper.

West's family was Baptist, and he grew up with a sense of pride in the role of the black church in the spiritual and material survival of former slaves and their descendants. Two influential figures from his childhood were Theodore Roosevelt, a biography of whom West read at age eight, and the Danish philosopher Søren Kierkegaard, whose work he read when he was fourteen. The former inspired him to attend Harvard University and to seek a career in public life; the latter stimulated his philosophical commitment to grapple with the absurdities of modern civilization.

West studied philosophy at Harvard and later at Princeton at a time when both universities were highly influential in the development of American political philosophy. At Harvard, under the influence of the liberal philosopher John Rawls, West espoused the conviction that political institutions should be in the interest of the least advantaged members of society. West also attended many of the lectures of Peter Camejo, a Trotskyite public intellectual who used Harvard's space, and he benefited from the mentorship of Martin Kilson, the first African American professor of political science at Harvard. In 1973 West received his BA, magna cum laude, in Near Eastern Languages and Literature, reading biblical Hebrew, Old Testament Aramaic, and classical Greek. Although West's activism had begun in high school, where he served as student president and volunteered in Black Panther soup kitchens, his undergraduate years were marked by an intensification of his social commitments as he and fellow black students participated in antiwar protests and antiracist struggles.

West went to Princeton University for graduate study, because he was told by his mentors that it was the best philosophy department in the country. There he came under the influence of Richard Rorty, the

Cornel West, a leading exemplar of African American philosophical and religious thought. Marcus Halevi, 2003

most influential advocate of American pragmatist philosophy. That philosophy, built on the thought of Charles Sanders Peirce, William James, John Dewey, and Clarence Irving Lewis, asserts the importance of experience and the value of effective action in social life. West earned his MA in 1975 and completed his doctorate in 1980. His dissertation, entitled *The Ethical Dimensions of Marxist Thought*, was published by Monthly Review Press in 1991.

West was a teaching assistant while at Princeton and also an instructor in the New York federal prisons. In 1977 he joined the Union Theological Seminary in New York City, where he taught philosophy of religion and ethics. His senior colleagues at Union included James Cone, the highly regarded African American liberation theologian. While at Union, West began his preaching at Riverside Church as a lay preacher. West has taught at many institutions, including Union (1977–1984 and 1987–1988), Williams College (1982), Yale University Divinity School (1984–1987), and the University of Paris (1987). In 1988 West became Director of Afro-American Studies and Professor of Religious Studies at Princeton, before moving to Harvard in 1994, where he became the Alphonse Fletcher Jr. University Professor in 1998. He and WILLIAM JULIUS WILSON were the first African Americans to hold such professorships, Harvard's most prestigious accolade.

In 2002, after a controversial conflict with Harvard's President Lawrence

Summers, West returned to Princeton as the Class of 1943 University Professor of Religion and African American Studies. According to *The Wall Street Journal* (11 January 2002) and *The Chronicle of Higher Education* (18 January 2002), Summers had criticized West for his politics and other nonacademic work, including his rap CD *Sketches of My Culture* (Artemis Records, 2001) and his support of AL SHARPTON's presidential campaign. Summers had also derided West's scholarship as not serious, and he accused West of grade inflation and missing classes. West responded that he would not tolerate the disrespectful way Summers addressed him. The incident received much press coverage, and many editorials appeared on both sides of the dispute. However, as Glenn Louri reflected in his review of George Yancy's *Cornel West: A Critical Reader*, the many articles and growing number of books on West's scholarship attest to West's influence as a scholar. As for his activism, it is West's prerogative to have a civic life, as it is, ostensibly, for all Americans.

West's political work—marked by his concern about poverty, racism, sexism, and homophobia and by his belief in a radical participatory democracy—has led to his sometimes controversial association with many organizations and leaders, be they black nationalist, Christian, moderate Marxist, cultural leftist, or progressive. For example, West argued that he supported the Million Man March organized by

LOUIS FARRAKHAN in 1995 because the march was consistent with his own Christian values and his commitment to black liberation causes. He saw working with Farrakhan to be no more problematic than working with the many white activists with whom he has had disagreements. On another front, West and Rabbi Michael Lerner, editor of *Tikkun* magazine, collaborated on *Jews & Blacks: A Dialogue on Race, Religion, and Culture in America* (1996), in order to address the division and tension between blacks and Jews and to affirm the historical commonality of the oppression faced by both groups. Some black critics have opined that West speaks more of black anti-Semitism than he does of Jewish racism. West has also been criticized for failing to address the fact that white Jewish communities and African American communities are not on an equal playing field in American society, and he has also been criticized for overlooking the existence of African American Jews. West has also been a spokesperson for the Democratic Socialists of America, of which he remains an honorary chairperson, and an adviser to Senator Bill Bradley's presidential campaign in 2000 and to Al Sharpton's in 2004.

West's reputation as the leading exemplar of African American philosophical and religious thought was established during the late 1970s through the late 1980s. His explorations in African American philosophy and his critical engagement with contemporary problems appeared in both Christian and Marxist journals and magazines. In 1989 West became acceptable to many white scholars in philosophy and religion with the publication of *The American Evasion of Philosophy: A Genealogy of Pragmatism*, which examines the thought of mostly white philosophers and social critics, as well as that of W. E. B. DU BOIS. In 1993 he achieved national and international acclaim with the publication of *Race Matters*, which received several influential book awards. West's message of building humanistic institutions on the basis of hope, faith, and love for humanity appealed to many readers. It was also popular because of its critical and at times controversial discussion of sexual politics, racial and class conflicts, and the failures of contemporary black leadership. West's professional, intellectual march could thus be constructed as a movement from producing works that focused on black audiences at one stage, to white academic audiences at another, and then speaking to all audiences from his understanding of black America. Since 1993 West has received more than twenty honorary doctorates and awards. Interviews of him have appeared in magazines, journals, documentaries, and news programs in Africa and Europe. His popularity is also attested by his appearance in the blockbuster films *The Matrix Reloaded* and *Matrix Revolutions*, both of which appeared in 2003.

There is, however, a negative side to West's fame. For example, he often receives death threats from white supremacists and other hate groups, especially after an appearance on television. On one occasion, a gunman broke into his home and held a gun to his wife's head, and on another the West family was accosted by an assailant with a rifle. The profound love for and faith in humanity he embodies in his lectures and writings in the face of such reaction reveal much about the man. West's Christian philosophical and ethical conviction is that every human being is valuable, including his enemy. He literally loves his neighbor, including those who might hate him.

West's philosophical originality rests in his unique formulation of what he calls, in his book *Prophesy, Deliverance!* (1982), "Afro-American revolutionary Christianity." He argues that philosophy is a special type of critical writing on pressing social problems of "bondage to death, disease, and despair" (*Prophesy, Deliverance!*, 18). Such problems are a consequence of poverty and racism in American society, and they can best be addressed through three resources for African American revolutionary thought: pragmatism, Marxism, and prophetic Christianity.

West aligned himself with John Dewey's pragmatism, which he saw as making a difference through a commitment to historical criticism, and he views this pragmatism as the *American* component of African American thought. The Marxism West defends is in the tradition of democratic socialism, which rejects communism. He also draws on Antonio Gramsci's theories of "organic intellectuals,"

whose ideas reflect the interests of a particular community—which in *Prophesy, Deliverance!* is the black poor—and of "critical consciousness," which involves questioning our everyday presumptions and political assumptions. Finally, West argues for prophetic Christianity because he believes that it is the overwhelming spiritual legacy of most African Americans. He contends further that the *prophetic* aspect is expressed in the sermons of the African American clergy, many of which provide insightful criticisms of American society, as found, for example, in the thought of MARTIN LUTHER KING JR. and MALCOLM X. But more importantly, West's formulation of prophetic discourse brings pragmatism and Marxism together in the figure of the cultural critic.

Although West claims to advance three intellectual resources in the book, he in fact advances several. Existentialism emerges throughout in his reflections on black suffering. He uses French and German postmodern thought to construct a "genealogy" of modern racism in European Enlightenment thought. And African American political thought emerges in his discussion of four classical responses to racism: assimilationism, exceptionalism, marginalism, and humanism. West advocates African American humanism. His Marxism, too, is influenced by the Black Panthers' class-based black nationalist thought, which he acknowledges by giving priority to the black poor over the black middle class in both *Prophesy, Deliverance!* and *Race Matters*, in which he advocates a class-based affirmative action remedy.

Since *Prophesy, Deliverance!*, West has consistently remained an existential humanist of the pragmatist variety, a position which he defends in such scholarly works as *The American Evasion of Philosophy* and *Keeping Faith* and in popular ones as *Race Matters, The War against Parents* (1998), and his controversial hip-hop musical tribute *Sketches of My Culture* (2001). In each of these works, he presents the intellectual's task as grappling with political and spiritual absurdity and human suffering. The ongoing thesis of all these works is that African Americans should maintain hope and continue to fight for freedom

in a world in which the evidence on such matters as health and incarceration and the political disenfranchisement of black people suggests the contrary. He calls such hope in the face of seemingly hopeless situations a struggle against nihilism.

West's writings became noticeably less overtly Marxist after the fall of the Soviet Union and the Berlin Wall, but the egalitarian and humanistic spirit remains. The result is a body of work with a deep-rooted faith in the potential of American society to fulfill the promise of one day becoming a society that values people more than profits. To that end, he also continues to devote his activist work.

FURTHER READING

Cowan, Rosemary. *Cornel West: The Politics of Redemption* (2003).

Johnson, Clarence Sholé. *Cornel West and Philosophy* (2002).

Louri, Glenn C. "Review of George Yancy's *Cornel West: A Critical Reader*," *The A.M.E. Church Review* (April–June 2003).

Osborne, Peter, (ed.). *A Critical Sense: Interviews with Intellectuals* (1996).

Yancy, George, (ed.). *African American Philosophers: 17 Conversations* (1998).

———. *Cornel West: A Critical Reader* (2001).

Wood, Mark David. *Cornel West and the Politics of Prophetic Pragmatism* (2000).

—LEWIS R. GORDON

 WEST, DOROTHY
(2 June 1907–16 Aug. 1998), writer and editor, was born in Boston, Massachusetts, the only child of Rachel Pease Benson of Camden, South Carolina, and Isaac Christopher West, an enterprising former slave from Virginia who was a generation his wife's senior. Nicknamed the "Black Banana King" before his prosperous wholesale fruit business failed during the Depression, Isaac West provided his gifted daughter with a privileged, bourgeois upbringing. Dorothy's formal education began at the age of two when she took private lessons from Bessie Trotter, sister of the *Boston Guardian* editor WILLIAM MONROE TROTTER. Young Dorothy grew up in a four-story house in Boston with a large extended family made up of her mother's numerous siblings and their children. Although Dorothy

Short-story writer and novelist Dorothy West's literary career spanned eight decades. Corbis

tested at the second-grade level at age four, Rachel West insisted that her precocious daughter enter first grade at Boston's Farragut School. Years later West recalled, "When I was a child of four or five, listening to the conversation of my mother and her sisters, I would sometimes intrude on their territory with a solemnly stated opinion that would jerk their heads in my direction, then send them into roars of uncontrollable laughter.... the first adult who caught her breath would speak for them all and say 'That's no child. That's a sawed-off woman'" (West, *The Richer*). Dorothy finished her elementary education in the racist environment of the Martin School located in the city's heavily Irish Mission District, graduated from Girls' Latin School in 1923, and later took courses at Columbia University, where she studied creative writing.

Dorothy always thought of herself as a short-story writer and began her literary career at age seven when, she said, "I wrote a story about a little Chinese girl, though...I'm sure I had never seen a Chinese girl in my life" (McDowell, 267). From about age ten into her early teens, she regularly won the weekly short-story contest sponsored by the *Boston Post*. The *Post* published her first story, "Promise and Fulfillment," when Dorothy was ten, and the paper's African American short-story editor, Eugene Gordon, encouraged her

to join the Saturday Evening Quill Club, a black writers group. In response to a story submission, *Cosmopolitan*'s editor Ray Long—convinced that the writer was a forty-year-old spinster who knew nothing about love—wrote the fourteen-year-old Dorothy a scathing letter asserting that his magazine "had one Fanny Hurst and so didn't need another" (McDowell, 268). Far from discouraging her, however, this rejection had the opposite effect on Dorothy.

In 1925, shortly before turning eighteen, West entered a short-story competition sponsored jointly by the *Crisis* and *Opportunity*, the publications of the NAACP and the Urban League respectively. Her submission, "The Typewriter," tied for second place with ZORA NEALE HURSTON's "Muttsy" and was subsequently published in the July 1926 issue of *Opportunity*. West was then able to convince her family that she had the talent to launch a literary career in New York City alongside Harlem Renaissance stalwarts.

Almost immediately West's stories began to appear in print. "Hannah Byde," published in *The Messenger* (July 1926), was one of the earliest pieces of African American literature to use a jazz motif to explore the spiritual discord of urban life. Over the next few years she published "Prologue to a Life," "Funeral," and "An Unimportant Man." These early stories feature West's lifetime preoccupation with the ways in which children interact with and affect the adult world around them. They are suffused with West's characteristically ironic tone, inspired by Fyodor Dostoyevski, who, she said, "became my master, though I knew I would never write like him" (McDowell, 268). "Nine out of ten stories I write are real," West later said, of her keen observations of family, friends, and social milieus. "I change the situation, but they are something that really happened" (Dalsgard, 37).

When Hurston left New York, West and her cousin Helene Johnson, with financial help from West's father, took over her apartment. West continued to write short stories, although, for a variety of reasons, including the discontinuation of *Opportunity*'s writing contests in 1927, few were published, leaving the young writer dissatisfied with her literary prospects. In

1927 West and her new friend WALLACE THURMAN won minor roles in the stage production of *Porgy and Bess*, and her weekly earnings of seventeen and a half dollars helped keep her in New York during hard economic times. In June 1932 West sailed for the Soviet Union, along with twenty-two other African Americans including LANGSTON HUGHES, who had been commissioned to revise a movie script about black American life entitled "Black and White." When the project fell through, West—and Hughes—remained in the Soviet Union for nearly a year, until word arrived that her father had died.

A more responsible, twenty-five-year-old West returned to New York in 1933, regretful that she had not lived up to her earlier artistic promise. Only "Funeral" and "The Black Dress" were published during the 1930s, although she produced the nonfiction pieces "Ghost Story," "Pluto," "Temple of Grace," and "Cocktail Party" while working for the Depression-era Federal Writer's Project, part of the Works Progress Administration.

In 1933, in an attempt to revitalize the Harlem Renaissance movement by providing an outlet for black authors, West founded *Challenge Magazine*, of which she published five issues. Under the pseudonym of Mary Christopher, West published her own work and that of Hughes, Hurston, Arna Bontemps, CLAUDE MCKAY, COUNTÉE CULLEN, and PAULI MURRAY. The last issue appeared in June 1936, when RICHARD WRIGHT virtually took West's journal away from her. Wright wanted to shift the journal's focus toward a more socially conscious protest literature, a direction West found uncomfortable but against which she offered little resistance. As she explained later, unlike modern women, she was too passive, petite, and soft-spoken to stand up to Wright, his friends, and his lawyer, "who sent me a form to sign giving Wright the rights to something, I can't remember" (McDowell, 272). Moreover, she presumed Wright was acting as a pawn of Communists. "I was never crazy about Richard Wright because he was too timid and afraid of white people. I guess it stemmed from his southern background" (McDowell, 272).

West's own dry spell came to an end on 29 September 1940, when the *New*

York Daily News published "Jack in the Pot," a story that captured the economic and spiritual strife of the Depression. For the next twenty years she wrote two short stories per month for the *Daily News*, a job that kept her writing and able to pay her bills. In the mid 1940s West left New York and moved to Oak Bluffs, Massachusetts, on Martha's Vineyard, the summer playground of her youth. There she wrote her first novel, the semiautobiographical *The Living Is Easy* (1948). The novel, a family drama told through the eyes of young Judy Judson, includes West's examination of black middle-class social pretensions in Boston. The novel was generally well-received although, in a move that deeply affected West, *Ladies Home Journal* eventually decided against serializing the book, which it felt might offend southern readers. When the Feminist Press reprinted *The Living Is Easy* in 1982, West was introduced to a whole new generation.

In the late 1960s West began a new novel, "Where the Wild Grape Grows." Although she had financial support from a Mary Roberts Rinehart grant and a Harper and Row contract, she stopped work on the book, feeling that black revolutionary politics conflicted with her theme of miscegenation. Instead, she resigned herself to writing for the *Vineyard Gazette*, focusing on countering the impression that the only blacks on Martha's Vineyard were in work uniforms. At first her "Cottagers Corner" columns showcased prosperous and affluent black families and their prominent friends and visitors. Later, she began to write more broadly, about people, places, and island happenings, even contributing sketches to the *Gazette*'s bird column. Her last piece appeared on 13 August 1993, when she left the paper to devote herself full time to completing the novel *The Wedding*, incorporating much of the earlier "Where the Wild Grape Grows" into it.

In the early 1990s, after reading West's *Gazette* articles, Jacqueline Kennedy Onassis helped West secure a book contract for *The Wedding*. The novel, about the spiritual price of assimilation and miscegenation, was published in 1995 and became a best-seller, drawing yet another generation to the door of the woman who became known as the sole survivor

of the Harlem Renaissance. West's book, which centers on the wedding preparations of Shelby Coles, ends with a child's death and without a wedding, though Doubleday sent out review copies of the novel with an ending Dorothy West had not written. When this was discovered in the Fall of 1994, the Harvard professor of African American studies, Henry Louis Gates Jr., championed her cause, and Doubleday delayed publication until West's own final chapter could be included. Unfortunately, a number of reviewers had already published their assessments of the novel with the spurious ending. In 1998 OPRAH WINFREY produced a television adaptation of the novel starring HALLE BERRY which transformed the story into a sentimental tale in which Shelby heads down the aisle with few racial concerns and which the critic John Leonard called "Soap Oprah."

West died at age ninety-one in 1998 in Boston. Her many short stories, two prominent novels, and nonfiction articles distinguish a literary career of eight decades that, in the final analysis, reflected the many expectations, failures, and achievements of its times.

FURTHER READING

West, Dorothy. *The Dorothy West Martha's Vineyard Stories: Essays and Reminiscences by Dorothy West in the Vineyard Gazette*, ed. James Roberts Saunders and Renae Nadine Shackelford (2001).

————. *The Richer, The Poorer: Stories, Sketches, and Reminscences* (1995).

Dalsgard, Katrine. "Alive and Well and Living on the Island of Martha's Vineyard: An Interview with Dorothy West, October 29, 1988." *Langston Hughes Review* 12 (Fall 1993).

Guinier, Genii. "Interview with Dorothy West (6 May 1978)" in *Black Women Oral History Project* (1991).

McDowell, Deborah E. "Conversations with Dorothy West" in *The Harlem Renaissance Re-examined*, ed. Victor Kramer (1987).

Obituary: *New York Times*, 19 Aug. 1998.
—SALLYANN H. FERGUSON

WHARTON, CLIFTON REGINALD (11 May 1899–23 Apr. 1990), Foreign Service officer, was born in Baltimore, Maryland,

the son of William B. Wharton and Rosalind Griffin. He received an LLB cum laude from the Boston University School of Law in 1920 and an LLM in 1923 from the same institution. Wharton was admitted to the Massachusetts bar in 1920 and practiced law in Boston until 1924. In August 1924 he received a telegram appointing him as a law clerk in the Department of State. In 1924 he married Harriette Banks; they had four children before divorcing.

In January 1925 Wharton became the first black to take the new Foreign Service examination established by the 1924 Rogers Act, which had created a career Foreign Service based on competitive examinations and merit promotion. Only twenty candidates passed both the written and the oral parts of the examination. In March 1925 Undersecretary of State Joseph Grew wrote to a colleague that the twenty included "one negro, who will go at once to Liberia" (Calkin, *Women*, 72). Wharton later recalled that when he decided to take the Foreign Service exam, his prospective associates were not enthusiastic.

The lack of enthusiasm Wharton sensed also existed at the highest levels of the department. Following passage of the Rogers Act, the Executive Committee of the Foreign Service Personnel Board prepared a memorandum on how to avoid appointing women or blacks. One alternative suggested was an executive order stating that persons in those groups were not eligible to take the examination. Another was to rate such candidates so low that they could not achieve a passing mark. Secretary of State Charles Evans Hughes, however, emphatically rejected both alternatives.

Wharton was appointed a Foreign Service officer on 20 March 1925, and on 21 March he was assigned to Monrovia, Liberia. Blacks had been receiving diplomatic appointments since 1869, but such appointments were almost always to Liberia, Haiti, or small consular posts in tropical countries. Wharton was the first black in the new career Foreign Service, and his career followed the same pattern for more than half of his forty years in the Department of State.

Wharton was not sent to the new Foreign Service School for instruction as were the other new appointees. Department officials later informed him that this was because he was needed so urgently at his new post. Despite this urgency, however, they initially planned to send him and his wife to Liberia on a cargo ship. When Wharton said that he did not need the job that badly, the department officials relented and arranged for passage on an ocean liner and a passenger ship.

Wharton served as third secretary and vice consul in Liberia until December 1929. In June 1930 he became consul in Las Palmas in the Canary Islands. In July 1936 he returned to Monrovia on the first of three temporary assignments. He served alternately in Monrovia and Las Palmas until April 1942, when he was appointed consul in Antananarivo in the French island colony of Madagascar, where he also represented the wartime interests of Great Britain and Belgium.

In April 1945 Wharton was appointed a member of the U.S. maritime delegation at Ponta Delgada in the Portuguese Azores. In July of that year he became consul at Ponta Delgada, where he served for the next four years. In 1949 he married Evangeline L. Spears; they had no children. In October 1949 Wharton's career took a new path when he was named first secretary and consul in Lisbon, Portugal. In 1950 he became consul general at that post. From 1953 to 1957 he served as consul general in Marseilles, France.

When President Dwight D. Eisenhower offered him appointment as minister to Romania in February 1958, Wharton flew to Washington to talk to Deputy Undersecretary for Administration Loy Henderson to make sure that the appointment was based on merit, saying that if race were one of the criteria, he would not accept the appointment. Henderson wrote later that he had been glad to tell Wharton that "race had not been a factor" (Calkin, "A Reminiscence," 28). As minister to Romania, Wharton became the first black career Foreign Service officer to serve as chief of mission and the first black to serve as chief of mission in Europe. In 1959 he was promoted to career minister, once again the first black to achieve that honor.

Wharton became the first black ambassador to a European country when President John F. Kennedy appointed him ambassador to Norway on 2 March 1961. Democratic majority leader Mike Mansfield praised Wharton to the Senate as a "highly skillful, understanding and tactful diplomat" and quoted a *Washington Post* editorial looking forward to "a day when the appointment of a Negro so well qualified as Mr. Wharton will have ceased to be a novelty" (Calkin, "A Reminiscence"). While ambassador to Norway, Wharton also served as a delegate to the North Atlantic Treaty Organization (NATO) Ministerial Council meeting and as an alternate delegate to the sixteenth session of the UN General Assembly.

Wharton was a genuine pioneer, and his career was full of "firsts," including the first black to pass the Foreign Service exam, the first black chief of mission to a European country, the first black career minister, and the first black ambassador to a European country. Such achievements took not only superior ability but also great patience, tolerance, and persistence in the face of what was often blatant racial discrimination. For most of his career, Wharton had to fight against such discrimination alone. By the time he retired in October 1964, however, a sea change had occurred. Thanks partly to his achievements, Wharton inspired and helped to pave the way for professional careers in diplomacy for other blacks, who began to enter the Foreign Service in ever increasing numbers during the 1960s. Wharton died in Phoenix, Arizona.

FURTHER READING

Calkin, Homer L. "A Reminiscence: Being Black in the Foreign Service," *Department of State Newsletter*, no. 198 (Feb. 1978): 25–28.

———. *Women in the Department of State: Their Role in American Foreign Affairs* (1978).

Trask, David. *A Short History of the U.S. Department of State, 1781–1981* (1981).

Obituary: *New York Times*, 25 Apr. 1990.
—NINA DAVIS HOWLAND

WHEATLEY, PHILLIS

(c. 1753–5 Dec. 1784), poet and cultivator of the epistolary writing style, was born in Gambia, Africa, probably along the fertile lowlands of the Gambia River. She was enslaved as a child of seven or eight and sold in Boston to John and Susanna Wheatley on 11 July 1761. The horrors of the Middle Passage likely contributed to her persistent trouble with asthma. The Wheatleys apparently named the girl, who had nothing but a piece of dirty carpet to conceal her nakedness, after the slaver, the *Phillis*, that transported her.

The Wheatleys were more kindly toward Phillis than were most slaveowners of the time, permitting her to learn to read. The poet in Wheatley soon began to emerge. She published her first poem on 21 December 1765 in the *Newport Mercury* when she was about twelve. The poem, "On Messrs. Hussey and Coffin," relates how these two gentlemen narrowly escaped drowning off Cape Cod.

Much of her subsequent poetry deals, as well, with events occurring close to her Boston circle. Of her fifty-five extant poems, nineteen are elegies; all but the last of them are devoted to the commemoration of someone she knew personally. Wheatley herself and her career are the subjects of her last elegy. One possible explanation for her preoccupation with this genre may be that she recalled the delivery of oral laments by the women of her tribal group whose responsibility it was to make such deliveries.

In October 1770 Wheatley published an elegy that must be called pivotal to her career. The subject of this elegy is George Whitefield, evangelical Methodist minister, a close friend of Charles Wesley, and privy chaplain to Selina Hastings, countess of Huntingdon. During his career Whitefield had made seven journeys to the American colonies, where he was known as the "Voice of the Great Awakening" and as the "Great Awakener." Only a week before his death in Newburyport, Massachusetts, on 30 September 1770, Whitefield preached in Boston where Wheatley very likely heard him. As Susanna Wheatley regularly corresponded with the countess, she and the Wheatley household may well have entertained the Great Awakener. Wheatley's vivid, ostensibly firsthand account in the elegy, replete with quotes the minister is alleged to have spoken, may, then, have been based on actual acquaintance. Owing to this evangel's extreme popularity, Wheatley's deft elegy became an overnight sensation and was often reprinted.

It is almost certain that the ship that carried news of Whitefield's death to the countess also carried a copy of Wheatley's elegy. It was this elegy that brought Wheatley to the sympathetic attention of the countess. Such an acquaintance ensured that Wheatley's elegy was also reprinted many times in London, giving the young poet an international reputation. This acquaintance also ensured that Wheatley's *Poems on Various Subjects, Religious and Moral* appeared in print, not in Boston where the project was rejected for racist reasons, but in London, printed in 1773 by the English publisher Archibald Bell and financed by the countess.

Wheatley's support by Hastings and her rejection by white male–dominated Boston signaled her nourishment as a literary artist by a community of women. While Wheatley received encouragement for the writing of her poems by prominent men of Boston such as the ministers Mather Byles (nephew of Cotton Mather) and Samuel Cooper, she was taught to read the King James Bible by Susanna Wheatley and probably as well by her daughter Mary. In addition, Susanna promoted Wheatley's publication of her poems in local newspapers.

Wheatley displays in her poems a sophisticated classicism. She knew Latin well enough to craft the excellent epyllion (or short epic) "Niobe in Distress..." from book six of Ovid's *Metamorphoses*. Of Wheatley's twenty-two extant letters, seven are addressed to Obour Tanner, an African American who many have speculated may have been forced to make the journey of the Middle Passage with Wheatley; in any event, the intimacy of their relationship is self-evident from the tone and detail of Wheatley's letters to her (none of Tanner's responses are extant). Tanner must have been a close friend and probably a valuable counselor and confidante of the poet.

All these women (the countess, who encouraged and financed the publication of her *Poems*; Mary and Susanna Wheatley, who taught her to read and write; and Obour Tanner, who could empathize probably better than anyone with her condition as a slave) were much older than the poet and obviously nurtured her development. Their importance to Wheatley's development is virtually incalculable. It is not excessive to submit that without this community of women, Wheatley's poems may never have been printed. Although Anne Bradstreet's poems, Jane Turell's, and those of other women poets who preceded Wheatley were published by now, the publication of her poems through the efforts of women marks the first such occasion in the annals of American letters.

During the summer of 1773 Wheatley journeyed to England, where she assisted in the preparation of her volume for the press. While in London she enjoyed considerable recognition from such dignitaries as Lord Dartmouth, Lord Lincoln, Granville Sharp (who escorted Wheatley on several tours about London), Benjamin Franklin, and Brooks Watson, a wealthy merchant who presented Wheatley with a folio edition of Milton's *Paradise Lost* and who later became lord mayor of London. Wheatley was to have been presented at court when, due to an illness of Susanna Wheatley, she was summoned to return to Boston in August. It is significant that sometime before 18 October 1773 Wheatley was granted her freedom, according to her own testimony, "at the desire of my friends in England" (*Collected Works*, ed. Shields [1988], 170). It follows then that if Hastings had not agreed to finance Wheatley's *Poems* and if the poet had not then journeyed to London, she probably would never have been manumitted.

When the American Revolution erupted, Wheatley's patriotic feelings separated her even more from the Wheatleys. After Susanna died on 3 March 1774, Wheatley's relationship with her Loyalist former master doubtless became strained. As her position in regard to independence has often been confused with the Loyalist position of John Wheatley and his son Nathaniel, her patriotism requires underscoring. Throughout her career she repeatedly celebrated American freedom, indeed rivaling Philip Freneau's claim to the title "Poet of the American Revolution." Her two most famous revolutionary war poems are "To His Excellency General Washington" (1775), which closes with the encomium "A crown, a mansion, and a throne that shine,/With gold unfading, WASHINGTON! be thine," and "Liberty and Peace" (1784), written to celebrate the Treaty of Paris and containing the forceful line "And new-born *Rome* [i.e., America] shall give *Britannia* Law."

Another misunderstood contribution of Phillis Wheatley is her attitude toward slavery. Because major statements Wheatley made attacking the institution of slavery were recovered only in the 1970s and 1980s, she was earlier thought to have ignored the issue. In February 1774, for example, Wheatley wrote to Samson Occom: "In every human breast, God has implanted a Principle, which we call Love of Freedom; it is impatient of Oppression, and pants for Deliverance." This letter was reprinted a dozen times in American newspapers over the next twelve months. Certainly whites and blacks of Wheatley's time never questioned her attitude toward slavery.

Later in the same year Wheatley observed in a letter to John Thornton, the English philanthropist, "The world is a severe schoolmaster, for its frowns are less dang'rous than its smiles and flatteries, and it is a difficult task to keep in the path of Wisdom." This entire letter appears cast in the tone of the African American who has found her white would-be benefactor's motive to be less than philanthropic and indeed hollow or even destructive, much in the manner of the fictions of LANGSTON HUGHES, RICHARD WRIGHT, and RALPH ELLISON. In an elegy of July 1778 on the death of Major General David Wooster, who, according to Wheatley, "fell a martyr in the Cause of Freedom," Wheatley challenges the notion that whites can "hope to find/Divine acceptance with th' Almighty mind" when "they disgrace/And hold in bondage Afric's blameless race."

The year 1778 was a pivotal one for Wheatley. Soon after John Wheatley died, Phillis married John Peters, a free African American who was a jack-of-all-trades, serving in various capacities from storekeeper to advocate for African Americans before the courts. But Wheatley's fortunes began to decline. In 1779 she published a set of "Proposals" for a new volume of poems, probably in an effort to mitigate her worsening poverty. While the "Proposals" failed to

The story that Prince Whipple was the black soldier depicted in Emanuel Leutze's famous 1851 painting of George Washington Crossing the Delaware *in 1776 first appears in 1855.* Metropolitan Museum of Art

attract subscribers, they show that she had produced some three hundred pages of new poetry since the publication of *Poems* six years earlier. The volume never appeared, and, sadly, most of its poems are lost.

Wheatley's final proposal for a volume of poems in September 1784 went virtually unnoticed. This volume, whose title was to have been *Poems and Letters on Various Subjects*, would have included thirteen letters to dignitaries such as Benjamin Rush, the Earl of Dartmouth, and the Countess of Huntingdon. Once having carried a reputation of such distinction that it earned her an audience with General Washington in March 1776, Wheatley and her newborn child died alone in a shack on the edge of Boston. It is believed she died as a result of an infection from the birth.

Wheatley's end, like her beginning in America, was pitiable. Yet this genius of the pen left to the country a legacy of firsts: the first African American to publish a book, the mother of African American letters, the first woman writer whose publication was urged and nurtured by a community of women, and the first American woman author who tried to earn a living by means of her writing.

FURTHER READING

Carretta, Vincent, ed. *Phillis Wheatley: Complete Writings* (2001).
Gates, Henry Louis, Jr. *The Trials of Phillis Wheatley: America's First Black Poet and Her Encounters with the Founding Fathers* (2003).
O'Neal, Sondra A. "A Slave's Subtle War: Phillis Wheatley's Use of Biblical Myth and Symbol," *Early American Literature* 21 (1986): 144–65.
———. *Critical Essays on Phillis Wheatley* (1982).
———. "Phillis Wheatley" in *African American Writers*, ed. Valerie Smith (1991).
Robinson, William H. *Phillis Wheatley in the Black American Beginnings* (1975).
—JOHN C. SHIELDS

WHIPPLE, PRINCE

(?–1797), slave, Revolutionary War veteran, abolitionist, and jack-of-all-trades, was born, according to the historical record, in "Amabou, Africa." This location is probably Anomabu in present-day Ghana, which was known as the Gold Coast when Prince Whipple was born. The names of his parents are unknown, but oral tradition published in the mid-nineteenth century implies he was born free and maintains he was sent abroad with a brother (or cousin) Cuff (or Cuffee), but parental plans went awry and the youths were sold into slavery in North America. A collective document Whipple signed with twenty others in 1779 describes their shared experience as being "torn by the cruel hand of violence" from their mothers' "aching bosom," and "seized, imprisoned and transported" to the United States and deprived of "the nurturing care of [their] bereaved parent" (New Hampshire *Gazette*, 15 July 1780).

Prince was acquired by William Whipple, and Cuff by William's brother Joseph Whipple, white merchants in Portsmouth, New Hampshire. William Whipple's household also included Windsor Moffatt and other slaves. There are several possible reasons for the confusion about whether

Prince and Cuff were brothers or cousins: linguistic translation difficulties, uncertain community memory after their deaths, and white indifference to such distinctions in a marginalized race.

Likewise, Prince Whipple maintained that his given name reflected his actual status in Africa, although the numerous enslaved black men named Prince suggests the name was frequently given by white owners in sentimentality or mockery. If Prince's name records his African status, it represents an infrequent case of resistance to white renaming, a practice that stripped away African identity and dissociated the enslaved from both the dominant society and their own humanity. However, the persistence of Cuff's African name in a town where only a few other African names persisted lends some credence to this interpretation of Prince's name.

Nineteenth-century tradition spins an elaborate tale of Prince's participation in the American Revolution, fragments of which may be verified, disproved, or called into doubt. No documentation substantiates the claim that Prince accompanied William Whipple, a colonel in the First New Hampshire Regiment, on early revolutionary campaigns or to the Continental Congress in Philadelphia in 1776.

Documentation also argues against a tradition that Prince was with George Washington at the crossing of the Delaware River in December 1776. On that date, William Whipple was attending Congress, first in Philadelphia and then in Baltimore. Were Prince with him, it seems unlikely that William would have sent the enslaved Prince unaccompanied 130 miles to a war zone in which the enemy promised manumission in exchange for defection. The pervasive story about Prince's crossing the Delaware first appears in William C. Nell's 1855 Colored Patriots of the American Revolution, written at the height of the abolitionist movement. It is unclear whether Nell recorded an undocumented but accurate family tradition circulating among Prince's heirs or a confused family tale, or whether he symbolically attached to one individual the forgotten reality of black participation in both the Revolution and Washington's crossing. Heroic paintings of this event by the nineteenth-century artists Thomas Sully

(1819) and Emmanuel Leutze (1851) do indeed include a black man, illustrative of the lingering memory of black participation in the Revolution. New England traditions place other black men in Washington's boat, for example Prince Estabrook of Lexington (later of Ashby), Massachusetts.

Prince Whipple did, however, participate in the Revolution. He accompanied William Whipple, by then a brigadier general, on military campaigns to Saratoga, New York, in 1777 and Rhode Island in 1778. Prince was attuned to revolutionary philosophy. In 1779 he and Windsor Moffatt were among twenty enslaved men who signed a petition to the New Hampshire legislature for the abolition of slavery in the state. All the signatories were held as slaves in prominent and politically active white patriot families, and thus had ample opportunity to overhear, contemplate, and reinterpret revolutionary rhetoric. However, the petition was tabled, and slavery was not formally abolished in New Hampshire until 1857.

After the Revolution, Prince attained freedom in gradual, if unclear, stages. On Prince's marriage day, 22 February 1781, William Whipple prepared a special document that allowed Prince the rights of a freeman. The actual status conveyed by this document is obscure, as Prince was not formally manumitted until three years later, on 26 February 1784. The document may have been in response to a request from his bride's clergyman owner, who may have wished to legitimize the marriage according to his religious standards. Prince's bride, twenty-one-year-old Dinah Chase of New Castle and Hampton, New Hampshire, was manumitted by her owner on her wedding day.

In freedom, the black Whipples faced the daunting task of making a living in a context of social and economic marginalization. In his widow's obituary, Prince was remembered as "the Caleb Quotem of the old fashioned semi-monthly assemblies, and at all large weddings and dinners, balls and evening parties. Nothing could go on right without Prince." That is, he served as master of ceremonies at the Assembly House balls for white socialites. (Caleb Quotem was an eccentric, voluble character in The Review, or The Wags

of Windsor [1801], by the English playwright George Colman.) On various occasions, these balls included other black people as caterers and musicians, and it is likely that Prince's role was to bring together this supportive talent. He was "a large, well proportioned, and fine looking man, and of gentlemanly manners and deportment" (Portsmouth Journal of Literature and Politics, 22 Feb. 1846). William Whipple died one year after Prince's manumission, and his widow carved a house lot out of the back corner of the pleasure garden behind the Whipple mansion and loaned it to their former slaves. Prince and Dinah, along with Cuff, who had been manumitted in 1784, and his wife Rebecca Daverson (married on 24 August 1786) moved an old house to the lot, where they and their children lived for forty years.

Their home life was crowded. In addition to the adults and first child who occupied the house when the 1790 census was taken, others were soon born, including Prince's daughters, Esther and Elizabeth. In addition, Dinah operated the Ladies Charitable African School for black children, probably in their house, as well as working for the North Church.

Prince died in Portsmouth in 1797, Cuff in 1816. Dinah's obituary in 1846 described Prince's earlier death as "much regretted both by the white and colored inhabitants of the town; by the latter of whom he was always regarded as their prince." This reminiscence notwithstanding, Prince was not an officer of the Negro Court that held annual coronations in eighteenth-century Portsmouth. However, his signature on the abolition petition alongside those of Portsmouth's black king, viceroy, sheriff, and deputy confirms Prince's active participation in the local black community.

Prince was not buried in Portsmouth's segregated Negro Burial Ground, suggesting that it may have been closed by the 1790s. Following local tradition for black people, his grave in North Burial Ground was marked with two rough stones. Its location was later identified by a grandson, John Smith, and a more impressive stone installed. Today it is marked as that of a Revolutionary War veteran. Prince's age at death is unknown, but he was almost certainly a decade or more older than the age (forty-six) sometimes supposed.

Prince Whipple's life characterizes white Portsmouth's preference for the importation of enslaved children rather than adults, and also exemplifies his generation's participation in and advocacy for a coherent black community. The loaned residence, extended family, and his heirs' continuation in Portsmouth throughout much of the nineteenth century diverge from a local pattern of frequent changes of residence and of filial out-migration. Prince's participation in the Revolution while enslaved may have been elaborated in folk memory. But, along with CRISPUS ATTUCKS and PRINCE HALL, among others, his story reminds us of the significant African American contribution to the American struggle for independence.

FURTHER READING

Kaplan, Sidney. *The Black Presence in the Era of the American Revolution 1770–1800* (1973).

Melish, Joanne Pope. *Disowning Slavery: Gradual Emancipation and "Race" in New England, 1780–1860* (1998).

Nell, William C. *The Colored Patriots of the American Revolution* (1855).

Piersen, William D. *Black Yankees: The Development of an Afro-American Subculture in Eighteenth-Century New England* (1988).

Sammons, Mark J., and Valerie Cunningham. *Black Portsmouth* (2003).

—MARK J. SAMMONS

WHITAKER, MARK

(7 Sept. 1957–), editor and journalist, was born in Lower Merion, Pennsylvania, to Jeanne Theis Whitaker, a French professor, and Cleophus Sylvester Whitaker Jr., a political science professor. Jeanne Theis was a white native of Madagascar and the daughter of Protestant missionaries. During World War II her parents harbored Jews and other refugees and, to ensure her safety after the 1939 German occupation of France, they sent the fourteen-year-old Jeanne to live with a friend, a biology professor at Swarthmore College in Pennsylvania. She eventually became a French professor at the college.

Whitaker's parents met at Swarthmore, where Cleophus, known as Syl, was an undergraduate and Jeanne was his French professor. The unorthodox courtship between the black student and the white professor resulted in marriage but caused a stir on the small, bucolic campus. The couple left Swarthmore after Cleophus, who graduated with a degree in Political Science and later earned a doctorate in Political Science from Princeton, secured a teaching job at the University of California, Los Angeles (UCLA). He became a political science professor specializing in political development in Africa, primarily Nigeria.

With two parents employed as professors, the young Whitaker spent the first eight years of his life moving between Swarthmore, Los Angeles, Nigeria, London, Princeton, New Jersey, and Norton, Massachusetts. His father's teaching job at UCLA was followed by teaching stints at the University of Southern California, Princeton, and Rutgers. Whitaker's parents divorced when he was eight, and he and his brother returned to Norton to live with their mother. It was in Norton that Whitaker's passion for journalism began to blossom. While he was still in the seventh grade, he called a local newspaper, the *Attleboro Sun*, in a neighboring town and volunteered to cover sports. He wrote for that paper for two years and then for the newspaper at the George School, a Quaker boarding school he attended. At age fourteen, along with his brother, Paul, he spent a year in a public high school in France during their mother's sabbatical; there the boys learned to speak French.

In 1975, after completing only his junior year of high school, Whitaker enrolled in Swarthmore, the scene of his parent's unconventional courtship. Memories of the relationship lingered on campus, and Whitaker, uneasy with his "celebrity," left Swarthmore after completing a year. He moved to New Brunswick, New Jersey, to live with his father, who by then was a professor at Brooklyn College. During this period Whitaker applied to and was accepted by Harvard on a scholarship. Whitaker excelled in the Ivy League setting. He earned high grades while covering the arts and the admissions office for the prestigious Harvard *Crimson*, whose editorial board he joined. It was while working at the *Crimson* that Whitaker decided to pursue journalism as a career.

In 1977, at the age of nineteen, Whitaker was hired as a summer reporting intern at the San Francisco bureau of *Newsweek*, one of the world's most prestigious and largest newsmagazines, with a weekly circulation exceeding three million.

Over the next three summers Whitaker, working as either a *Newsweek* stringer or an intern, reported from Boston, Washington, London, and Paris. At Harvard he continued to excel academically: he was elected to Phi Beta Kappa and graduated summa cum laude in 1979. He pursued postgraduate studies in England as a Marshall scholar at Oxford University's Balliol College. In 1981 Whitaker joined *Newsweek* full time, working in the New York bureau. Over the next six years he worked in the international section and wrote cover stories from around the world, including Central America, the Falklands/Malvinas conflict, the Middle East, the Soviet Union, and South Africa.

In 1985, Whitaker married Alexis Gelber, the director of special projects at *Newsweek*, whom he met at the magazine in 1981. The couple have two children, Rachel and Matthew.

From 1987 to 1991 he served as business editor and directed coverage of the Black Monday stock market crash, insider-trading scandals, and the savings-and-loan crisis. In 1991 the shy and congenial Whitaker became assistant managing editor of *Newsweek*, just two positions removed from the top post. Under his leadership, *Newsweek* expanded its technology coverage with the launch of a monthly "Focus on Technology" section and a weekly "Cyberscope" page. The newsweekly also launched an annual newsstand magazine, *Computers & the Family*. Whitaker occasionally wrote essays on race, including a cover story, "The Hidden Race of Successful Blacks," co-authored with Ellis Cose. The article garnered awards from the Society of Professional Journalists' New York chapter and the National Association of Black Journalists. In the wake of the trial and acquittal of O. J. SIMPSON in 1995, Whitaker wrote a piece called "Whites v. Blacks," which analyzed the different reactions of African Americans and whites to the question of Simpson's guilt or innocence and to the criminal justice system more broadly.

In 1996 Whitaker was promoted to the position of *Newsweek*'s managing editor. In that capacity he directed coverage of the biggest stories of the decade, including the 1996 presidential election, resulting in an eighty-two-page special issue printed the day after the election. He also led the team that produced a special report on the death of Diana, Princess of Wales, in September 1997. That same year he assumed the role of interim editor after the editor, Maynard Parker, became incapacitated with leukemia. Whitaker oversaw the coverage of the scandal that arose concerning President Bill Clinton's relationship with the White House intern Monica Lewinsky, which earned the magazine a coveted National Magazine Award for reporting in 1999. When Parker died in October 1998, Whitaker, at age forty-one, became the first African American at the helm of one of the nation's top newsweeklies. He is also the only African American editor at one of the top one hundred general interest magazines.

Although *Newsweek* still trails its main rival *Time* by more than one million in circulation, the magazine has continued to receive national recognition under Whitaker's leadership. Most notably it received a National Magazine Award for general excellence for its coverage of the September 11, 2001, terrorist attacks on the World Trade Center. That same year Whitaker was cited for his editorial leadership by the American Society of Magazine Editors. Whitaker, who in 1999 was awarded an honorary doctorate from Wheaton College in 1999, received the 2003 Trailblazer Trumpet Award from the Turner Broadcasting Company. The award honored Whitaker for being the first African American to head a major newsweekly, though Whitaker himself has argued that his race is irrelevant to the task. "I'm proud and I'm honored to be in this position," he stated on becoming *Newsweek* editor, "but my goal is to be the very best editor of *Newsweek* that I can be, not just the best black editor" (Kuczynski, A14).

FURTHER READING

Kuczynski, Alex. "Newsweek Names Editor." *New York Times*, 11 Nov. 1998, A14.

—MAUREEN M. SMITH

 ## WHITE, AUGUSTUS AARON, III

(4 June 1936–), orthopedic surgeon and medical professor, was born in Memphis, Tennessee, the son of Augustus Aaron White, a physician, and Vivian Dandridge, a prominent teacher and librarian in the Memphis public schools. White's father died when the boy was only eight years old. The idealism that motivated White to become involved in civil rights was shaped in his boyhood, when Benjamin Hooks, also a Memphis resident and later the national chairman of the NAACP, was a family friend. As a teenager in the 1950s, White worked to register African Americans to vote at a time when many black activists feared violent reprisals for daring to challenge Jim Crow. Reflecting on his early activism, White later stated: "I reserved some energy to keeping racial issues in the front of my mind and attempting to make a contribution in terms of communication, good will, and influencing people and institutions to be more progressive and egalitarian" (White, http://www.nmf-online.org).

White attended the Mount Herman School in Massachusetts, graduating in 1953. He then entered Brown University, graduating cum laude with a BA in 1957. While still an undergraduate at Brown and a member of the football team, White became interested in the orthopedic treatment of injured athletes. Although he was a psychology major, he decided to change course and study orthopedic medicine, and graduated from Stanford University medical school in 1961. From 1960 through 1962 he received a scholarship and a clinical fellowship from the National Medical Fellowships organization, one of the nation's oldest philanthropic bodies dedicated to increasing the number of black and minority medical professionals. White completed his internship at the University of Michigan Hospital in Ann Arbor (1961–1962) and his residency in orthopedic surgery at Yale–New Haven Hospital in Connecticut (1963–1965).

From 1966 to 1968 White served as a captain and military surgeon for the U.S. Army Medical Corps in Vietnam. He recognized that he could have used graduate deferments to avoid participating in a war he did not fully support, but he chose to serve for two reasons: first, as a doctor, he was traveling to Indochina to save lives, not to end them; secondly, White felt obliged to those Americans who had fought and died in World War II to secure his freedom. White kept a diary during his time in Vietnam, and his entries reveal how he often worked around the clock, tending to the wounds of G.I.s and Vietcong sympathizers alike. In September 1966 he watched in horror as

a young boy was hit in the right hip with God knows what. It completely shattered his femur close to the joint, exploding in him, sending filth and gun powder all through his thigh, lower abdominal wall, scrotum and penis. His sciatic nerve was blown out, as was his femoral artery and 2/3 of the skin of his thigh

(Vietnam Memoirs, 19.)

Such incidents persuaded White that the war was a "misplaced, misguided effort," (19) but his commanding officer convinced him not to write a letter to President Lyndon Johnson, "respectfully asking him if it's worth it" (19). White did, however, protest the many examples of racism that he experienced during his tour of duty in Vietnam, including the occasion when he passed a U.S. army compound and demanded, successfully, that a Confederate flag be removed from display on one of the huts. White's anger at being greeted by a symbol of slavery was compounded by the disproportionate casualty rate for black soldiers at that time. Between 1965 and 1967 more than 22 percent of Americans killed in Vietnam were black, even though African Americans were only 11 percent of the U.S. population. For his efforts in commanding a MASH unit in Qui Nhon, Vietnam, White received the Bronze Star in 1967.

White developed a special interest in the biomechanical aspects of orthopedics while under the mentorship of Wayne Southwick, the chairman of Yale's orthopedic surgery department. With Southwick's help he obtained a fellowship to study this subject under a world authority at the Karolinska Institute in Sweden, where he went on to earn a DMSc degree in 1969. White then embarked on what became a lifelong intellectual and clinical crusade to expand the use of biomechanics in orthopedic medicine. He defined biomechanics as utilizing "engineering concepts and technology to scientifically and quantitatively analyze the normal and abnormal functioning of the musculoskeletal system that allows us to move about" (White, http://www.nmf- online.org). It also became evident to White that biomechanics and collaboration with engineers would advance the medical world's understanding of spinal orthopedics.

After completing his clinical training, White became an outstanding professor at Yale and Harvard medical schools. He was associate professor of orthopedic surgery at Yale from 1972 to 1976 and full professor through 1978. He then moved on to Harvard Medical School as professor of orthopedic surgery and has remained there. In addition to his teaching positions at Yale and Harvard, White held visiting professorships at eleven other colleges and universities. He was the main founder of biomechanical laboratories at both Yale and Harvard and also wrote or collaborated on more than two hundred scientific publications. The textbook he coauthored with Manohar M. Panjabi, *The Clinical Biomechanics of the Spine* (1978), was acclaimed widely both in the United States and abroad.

In addition to his teaching positions, White served on the surgical staffs of numerous hospitals in New Haven and Boston. Most notably, he was orthopedic surgeon in chief at Beth Israel Deaconess Medical Center in Boston between 1978 and 1991 and has remained there with emeritus status in orthopedic surgery since 1992. White was also an associate in orthopedic surgery at Brigham & Women's Hospital (1980–1989) and a senior associate in orthopedic surgery at Children's Hospital and Medical Center (1979–1989), both in Boston.

Throughout the late 1970s and 1980s White moved into the leadership ranks of American orthopedic surgeons. He influenced both his peers in the medical profession as well as the broader public to recognize the importance of improving the availability and quality of orthopedic surgery. In many of his writings and presentations, he emphasized that disorders of the spine are one of the most common medical problems in Western nations, affecting an estimated four-fifths of the Western

world's population at some point in the life cycle. White's popular book on this subject, *Your Aching Back: A Doctor's Guide to Relief* (1983), sold widely and generated attention throughout the national news media.

Throughout his career, White earned public recognition for his medical achievements and his commitment to racial justice. In 1980 *Ebony* magazine honored him with its award for Black Achievement in the Professions. Two years later the Ciba-Geigy Corporation chose White for its Exceptional Black Scientists Poster Series, a program which distributes posters of prominent black scientists to spur young African Americans to pursue scientific and medical careers. White has also maintained close links with his undergraduate alma mater, Brown University, serving on the university's Board of Fellows from 1981 to 1992. In the spring of 1985, when minority students challenged the administration over discriminatory conditions at Brown, White was selected to chair a committee convened by the university's president to explore the charges of institutional racism and to recommend improvements.

White has also exposed racism within the medical profession and within medical institutions and organizations. "Peer reviewed medical literature," he has noted, "documents that African Americans have higher infant mortality rates, shorter life expectancies, fewer joint replacements, and more amputations than whites" ("Justifications", 22). White believes that racially diverse medical schools and hospitals can help to end these disparities and, moreover, that "[d]iversity on clinical teams can enhance rapport between patient and physician" ("Justifications", 22). He has also highlighted a wide range of medical studies documenting the inadequate medical treatment received by racial minorities. This evidence, White argued in his 2001 Alfred R. Shands Jr. Lecture, "strongly suggests physician bias and stereotyping, however unconscious, as a cause" (Shands Lecture, 478). In reviewing the many episodes of racial violence and bias that black Americans have endured—from slavery to recent government failures to achieve health-care reform—White found a legacy of bias that "is intimately woven into the

fabric of our medical culture"(482). He then provided very specific steps his colleagues in surgery could implement to provide non-biased care. White closed his Shands lecture by remarking that "we, as physicians, can be societal leaders in facing racism clinically, not emotionally but rationally, objectively, and constructively"(482). Throughout his professional career Augustus White has exemplified such leadership.

FURTHER READING

White, Augustus A., III. "Alfred R. Shands, Jr., Lecture: Our Humanitarian Orthopaedic Opportunity." *Journal of Bone and Joint Surgery* 84-A, no. 3 (March 2002): 478–484.
———. "Justifications and Needs for Diversity in Orthopaedics." *Clinical Orthopaedics* 362 (May 1999): 22–33.
———. "Memoriam." *Brown Alumni Magazine* (May-June 1998).
———. "Vietnam Memoirs: River of Blood." *Harvard Medical Alumni Bulletin* (Spring 1993): 17–24.
Website: "Augustus A. White, III, M.D., Dr. Med. Sci.," National Medical Fellowships website, http://www.nmf-online.org/Development/scholars/1960s/augustus_white.htm

—DAVID MCBRIDE

WHITE, GEORGE HENRY (18 Dec. 1852–28 Dec. 1918), lawyer and member of Congress, was born in Bladen County, North Carolina, the son of Mary (maiden name unknown) and Wiley F. White. With one grandmother Irish and the other half American Indian, White jocularly described himself as no more than "mostly Negro." Like most black boys in the antebellum South, he had little opportunity for education. A biographical sketch in the *New York Tribune* on 2 January 1898 put it in graphic understatement, "His early studies were much interrupted because of the necessity he was under to do manual labor on farms and in the forests, and it was not until he was seventeen years old that his serious education was actually begun." After attending a combination of local schools, public and private, and saving one thousand dollars from farm work and cask making, White enrolled at Howard University.

White graduated in 1877 and returned to North Carolina. He settled in the old coastal town of New Bern, where he quickly became active in local affairs. At various times he was principal of three black schools, including the state normal school, and read enough law with Judge William J. Clark to earn his law license. In 1880 he won a seat in the state house of representatives as a Republican. After an initial defeat in 1882, he was elected to the state senate and served in the legislature of 1885. In 1886, a few weeks before his thirty-fourth birthday, he won a four-year term as district solicitor for the Second Judicial District, defeating the black incumbent and a white Democrat. Reelected to this position in 1890, he was, according to the *New York Freeman*, the only black prosecutor in the country. White prosecuted superior court cases in a six-county area, and his ability was so marked that even his political opponents occasionally praised him. Some whites resented his "presumption" and his demand to be "mistered" like other attorneys, rather than be addressed by an unadorned last name, as was customary with educated African Americans.

In 1894 White moved his home from New Bern to Tarboro so he could seek the Republican nomination in the Second Congressional District, a gerrymandered district that had elected three black congressmen since 1874. The district convention "broke up in a row," however, with both White and his brother-in-law, Henry P. Cheatham, claiming to be the regular nominee. After arbitration by the Republican National Committee, White withdrew from the race, but Cheatham was defeated in the general election, thanks partly to Republican disunity. In 1896, after another tumultuous convention, White won the Republican nomination for Congress and defeated the Democratic incumbent and a Populist nominee. Despite a statewide white supremacy campaign in 1898, he was elected to a second term.

As the only black member of Congress, White believed he spoke for all the nation's black people, not just the voters of the Second District, and he was prepared to reply spiritedly to racist pronouncements by southern congressional colleagues.

"How long must we keep quiet," he asked, "constantly sitting down and seeing our rights one by one taken away?" He introduced the first federal antilynching bill and denounced disenfranchisement and vote fraud. He also used the patronage power of his office to secure government jobs for his constituents, including some twenty black postmasters.

White supremacy zealots gave Congressman White special prominence during their struggle to defeat the Republican-Populist "fusion" in 1898 and the subsequent movement to disenfranchise North Carolina blacks. Under the editorship of Josephus Daniels, the *Raleigh News and Observer* pilloried White as a belligerent man eager "to invite the issue" of white against black. An incident at a Tarboro circus, in which White refused to surrender his seat to a white man, became an "outrage" to many Democratic journalists anxious to demonstrate the dangers of "Negro domination." In 1900, after White denied from the floor of the House that rape was the primary cause of lynching, noting as well that white men were guilty of abusing black women, Daniels fired off an editorial broadside, describing the "nigger Congressman" as "venomous, forward," and "appealing to the worst passions of his own race."

In fact, the prosperous, middle-aged black lawyer was not a fiery militant. Though some historians have portrayed White as "impetuous" or "vindictive," he was in fact a fairly conventional Republican politician, supportive of tariffs and imperialism and suspicious of civil service reform. On racial matters, he advocated caution and strict respect for the law among both black and white. In the climate of the turn of the century, however, he was considered radical merely for demanding, as he said in one speech, "all the privileges of an American citizen."

After the passage in 1900 of the state constitutional amendment disenfranchising most black voters, White decided to leave his native state. "I cannot live in North Carolina and be a man and be treated as a man," he told a northern interviewer. In a widely noticed valedictory address during his final session of Congress, he offered the black's "temporary farewell

to the American Congress," adding the prediction that "Phoenix-like he will rise up some day and come again."

Unsuccessful in seeking an appointive office, White practiced law, first in the District of Columbia, then in Philadelphia. He continued to support efforts to secure civil rights for African Americans, including lawsuits and organized protests through organizations such as the National Association for the Advancement of Colored People. An investor and visionary, he helped establish an all-black community called Whitesboro in the Cape May region of New Jersey.

White married twice, first to Fannie B. Randolph and, upon Fannie's death, to Cora Lina Cherry, daughter of Henry C. Cherry, a former legislator from Edgecombe County. White had one child in his first marriage and three children in his second marriage.

White was an active layman in the Presbyterian Church and a leader among the Colored Masons. He died in Philadelphia.

FURTHER READING

No collection of White's papers exists. A few manuscripts in his handwriting are preserved in the legislative papers and court documents of the Second Judicial District, available at the North Carolina Department of Archives and History in Raleigh, and scattered letters. White's personality is revealed in his congressional speeches and in his testimony before the Industrial Commission, *Report of the Industrial Commission*, vol. 10, 1901.

Anderson, Eric. *Race and Politics in North Carolina, 1872–1901: The Black Second* (1981).
Christopher, Maurine. *America's Black Congressmen* (1971).
Justesen, Benjamin R. *George Henry White: An Even Chance in the Race of Life* (2001).
—ERIC ANDERSON

WHITE, WALTER FRANCIS (1 July 1893–21 Mar. 1955), civil rights leader, was born in Atlanta, Georgia, to George White, a mail carrier, and Madeline Harrison, a former schoolteacher. The fourth of seven children, White, whose parents had been born in slavery, grew up entrenched in black Atlanta's leading and most respected institutions: his

family attended the prestigious First Congregational Church, and he received his secondary and collegiate education at Atlanta University, from which he graduated in 1916. (His siblings enjoyed similar religious training and educational opportunities.) With blond hair, blue eyes, and a light complexion, White was a "voluntary Negro," a person who could "pass" for white yet chose not to do so. His black racial identity was annealed by the Atlanta riot of September 1906. For three days white mobs rampaged through African American neighborhoods, destroying property and assaulting people; the thirteen-year-old White realized, as he put it in his autobiography, that he could never join a race that was infected with such toxic hatred.

Upon graduation from college, White became an executive with the Standard Life Insurance Company, one of the largest black-owned businesses of its day. Part of Atlanta's "New Negro" business elite, White was a founder of a real estate and investment company and looked forward to a successful business career. He also participated in civic affairs: in 1916 he was a founding member and secretary of the Atlanta branch of the NAACP. The branch experienced rapid growth, largely because, in 1917, it stopped the school board from eliminating seventh grade in the black public schools. White was an energetic organizer and enthusiastic speaker, qualities that attracted the attention of NAACP field secretary JAMES WELDON JOHNSON. The association's board of directors, at Johnson's behest, invited White to join the national staff as assistant secretary. White accepted, and in January 1918 he moved to New York City.

During White's first eight years with the NAACP, his primary responsibility was to conduct undercover investigations of lynchings and racial violence, primarily in the South. Putting his complexion in service of the cause, he adopted a series of white male incognitos—among the cleverer ones were itinerant patent-medicine salesman, land speculator, and newspaper reporter intent on exposing the libelous tales being spread in the North about white southerners—and fooled mob members and lynching spectators into providing detailed accounts of the recent violence.

Upon White returning to New York from his investigative trips, the NAACP would publicize his findings, and White eventually wrote several articles on the racial carnage of the post–World War I era that appeared in the *Nation*, the *New Republic*, the *New York Herald-Tribune*, and other prestigious journals of liberal opinion. By 1924 White had investigated forty-one lynchings and eight race riots. Among the most notorious of these was the 1918 lynching in Valdosta, Georgia, of Mary Turner, who was set ablaze. Turner was nine months pregnant, her womb was slashed open, and her fetus was crushed to death. White also investigated the bloody race riots that left hundreds of African Americans dead in Chicago and in Elaine, Arkansas, during the "red summer" of 1919, and the 1921 riot in Tulsa, Oklahoma, that resulted in the leveling of the black business district and entire residential neighborhoods. White's investigations also revealed that prominent and respected whites participated in racial violence; the mob that perpetrated a triple lynching in Aiken, South Carolina, in 1926, for example, included local officials and relatives of the governor.

White wrote of his undercover investigations in the July 1928 *American Mercury* and in *Rope and Faggot* (1929), a detailed study of the history of lynching and its place in American culture and politics that remains indispensable. His derring-do in narrowly escaping detection and avoiding vigilante punishment was also rendered in verse in LANGSTON HUGHES's "Ballad of Walter White" (1941).

At the same time that he was exposing lynching, White also emerged as a leading light in the Harlem Renaissance. He authored two novels. *The Fire in the Flint* (1924) was the second novel to be published by a New Negro, appearing just after JESSIE FAUSET's *There Is Confusion*. Set in Georgia after World War I and based on White's acquaintance with his native state, *The Fire in the Flint* tells the story of the racial awakening of Kenneth Harper, who pays for his new consciousness when a white mob murders him. The novel was greeted with critical acclaim and was translated into French, German, Japanese, and Russian. His second work of fiction, *Flight* (1926), set

in New Orleans, Atlanta, and New York, is both a work about the Great Migration of blacks to the North and story about "passing." *Flight*'s reviews were mixed. White's response to one of the negative reviews—by the African American poet Frank Horne, in *Opportunity* magazine—is instructive. He complained to the editor about being blindsided and parlayed his dissatisfaction into a debate over his book's merits that stretched over three issues. To White there was no such thing as bad publicity—in art or in politics. The salient point was to keep a topic—a book or a political cause—firmly in public view, which would eventually create interest and sympathy.

White's dynamism and energy was central to the New Negro movement. He was a prominent figure in Harlem's nightlife, chaperoning well-connected and sympathetic whites to clubs and dances. He helped to place the works of Langston Hughes, COUNTÉE CULLEN, and CLAUDE MCKAY with major publishers, and promoted the careers of the singer and actor PAUL ROBESON, the tenor Roland Hayes, and the contralto MARIAN ANDERSON.

When James Weldon Johnson retired from the NAACP in 1929, White, who had been looking to assume more responsibility, succeeded him. As the association's chief executive, White had a striking influence on the civil rights movement's agenda and methods. In 1930 he originated and orchestrated the victorious lobbying campaign to defeat President Hoover's nomination to the Supreme Court of John J. Parker, a North Carolina politician and jurist who had publicly stated his opposition to black suffrage and his hostility to organized labor. During the next two election cycles, the NAACP worked with substantial success to defeat senators with significant black constituencies who had voted to confirm Parker. The NAACP became a recognized force in national politics.

During Franklin Roosevelt's New Deal and Harry Truman's Fair Deal, White raised both the NAACP's public profile and its influence on national politics. White's success owed much to his special knack for organizing the more enlightened of America's white elites to back the NAACP's programs. Over the decade of the 1930s, he won the support of the majority of the Senate and House of Representatives for a federal antilynching law; only southern senators' filibusters prevented its passage. His friendship with Eleanor Roosevelt likewise gave him unparalleled access to the White House. This proved invaluable when he conceived and organized Marian Anderson's Easter Sunday 1939 concert at the Lincoln Memorial, which was blessed by the president and had as honorary sponsors cabinet members, other New Deal officials, and Supreme Court justices. As NAACP secretary and head of the National Committee against Mob Violence, White convinced President Truman in 1946 to form a presidential civil rights commission, which the following year issued its groundbreaking antisegregationist report, *To Secure These Rights*. In 1947 he persuaded Truman to address the closing rally of the NAACP's annual meeting, held at the Washington Monument; it was the first time that a president had spoken at an association event.

As secretary, White oversaw the NAACP's legal work, which after 1934 included lawsuits seeking equal educational opportunities for African Americans. He was also instrumental in convincing the liberal philanthropists of the American Fund for Public Service to commit one hundred thousand dollars to fund the endeavor, though only a portion was delivered before the fund became insolvent. After 1939 the day-to-day running of the legal campaign against desegregation rested with CHARLES HAMILTON HOUSTON and THURGOOD MARSHALL's NAACP Legal Defense Fund, but White remained intimately involved in the details of the campaign, which culminated with the Supreme Court's 1954 *Brown v. Board of Education* ruling that declared the doctrine of "separate but equal" unconstitutional.

White had married Gladys Powell, a clerical worker in the NAACP national office, in 1922. They had two children, Jane and Walter Carl Darrow, and divorced in 1948. In 1949 he married Poppy Cannon, a white woman. This interracial union provoked a major controversy within both the NAACP and black America at large, and there was widespread sentiment that White should resign. In response, White, who was always an integrationist, claimed the

right to marry whomever he wanted. He weathered the storm with the help of NAACP board member Eleanor Roosevelt, who threatened to resign should White be forced from office. Though White maintained the title of secretary, his powers were reduced, with ROY WILKINS taking over administrative duties. White continued to be the association's public spokesperson until his death on 21 March 1955. In declining health for several years, he suffered a fatal heart attack in his New York apartment.

Unlike other NAACP leaders such as W. E. B. DU BOIS and Charles Houston, Walter White was neither a great theoretician nor a master of legal theory. His lasting accomplishment lay in his ability to organize support for the NAACP agenda among persons of influence in and out of government and to persuade Americans of all races to support the cause of equal rights for African Americans.

FURTHER READING

The bulk of Walter White's papers are in the Papers of the National Association for the Advancement of Colored People, deposited at the Library of Congress in Washington, D.C., and the Walter Francis White/Poppy Cannon Papers, deposited at the Beinecke Rare Books and Manuscript Library, Yale University, New Haven, Connecticut.

White, Walter. *A Man Called White* (1948).

Cannon, Poppy. *A Gentle Knight: My Husband Walter White* (1956).
Janken, Kenneth Robert. *WHITE: The Biography of Walter White, Mr. NAACP* (2003).

Obituaries: *New York Times*, 22 Mar. 1955; *Washington Afro-American*, 26 Mar. 1955.
—KENNETH R. JANKEN

WIGGINS, THOMAS BETHUNE. *See* Blind Tom.

WILDER, DOUGLAS
(17 Jan. 1931–), Governor of Virginia, was born Lawrence Douglas Wilder in Richmond, Virginia, the son of Robert J. Wilder Sr., a door-to-door

insurance salesman, church deacon, and strict disciplinarian, and Beulah Richards, an occasional domestic and mother of ten children, including two who died in infancy. Wilder's paternal grandparents, James and Agnes Wilder, were born in slavery and married on 25 April 1856 in Henrico County, Virginia, north of Richmond. They were later sold separately, and on Sundays, James would travel unsupervised to neighboring Hanover County to visit his wife and children. According to family lore, he was so highly regarded that if he returned late, the overseer would feign punishment by beating on a saddle. Agnes Wilder, a house servant, learned to read while overhearing the lessons of a handicapped child for whom she cared. Less is known of the origins of Wilder's mother. She was raised by a grandmother and aunt in Richmond after her mother and stepfather died. Her father's identity is unknown.

Douglas (later called Doug by nonfamily members) was the next to youngest of the Wilder children and one of only two boys who survived. He was named for FREDERICK DOUGLASS, the fiery abolitionist, and PAUL LAURENCE DUNBAR, the contemplative poet. He grew up in what the family describes as "gentle poverty," surrounded by sisters and as the apple of his mother's eye. Clever and high-spirited, the young Douglas shined shoes, hawked newspapers, and teased the family that "some rich people left me here, didn't they?" "They're coming back for me, aren't they?" he would ask (Baker, 8). As a youth in segregated Richmond, Douglas had few associations with whites, other than as an elevator boy in a downtown office building and, while in college, as a waiter at private country clubs and downtown hotels.

Shortly after graduating in 1951 from Virginia Union University with a degree in chemistry, Wilder was drafted into the U.S. Army. While serving in the Seventeenth Infantry Regiment's first battalion during the Korean War, he and a comrade captured twenty North Koreans holed up in a bunker, an action that won Corporal Wilder a Bronze Star. Back in the United States, Wilder began work as a technician in the state medical examiner's office. In 1956 he enrolled in the Howard University law school, taking advantage of a state stipend encouraging African Americans to pursue advanced degrees out of state. Wilder married Eunice Montgomery in 1958, and after his graduation in 1959 they returned to Richmond, where his focus was less on dismantling segregation than on establishing a successful law practice. Over time he became known as one of the city's leading criminal trial attorneys. That record was blemished somewhat by a 1975 reprimand from the Virginia Supreme Court for "inexcusable procrastination" in a car-accident case. Wilder apologized for and did not repeat the mistake.

In 1969 Wilder entered politics by winning a special election to a state senate seat against two white opponents in a majority-white district. Arriving as the first black member since Reconstruction of a body still dominated by rural white conservatives, Wilder made waves with his maiden floor speech denouncing the state song, "Carry Me Back to Ol' Virginny." Over the next several years he pursued a legislative agenda that was liberal by Virginia standards. He fought for fair-housing laws, pushed for a national holiday honoring MARTIN LUTHER KING Jr., and opposed the reinstatement of the death penalty. Although he later claimed to have done so primarily as a courtesy, he introduced legislation calling for statehood and voting rights for the District of Columbia, whose residents are largely African American. In 1978 Wilder's marriage, which produced three children, ended in divorce.

A pivotal moment in Wilder's rise came in 1982, when a moderate Democratic legislator, Owen B. Pickett, launched his campaign for a U.S. Senate seat by invoking the name and record of Harry Flood Byrd Jr., the retiring senator and the epitome of Old Virginia. Already angry at the treatment of black lawmakers in the 1982 assembly, Wilder threatened to run as an independent if Pickett did not withdraw. Governor Charles S. "Chuck" Robb and other Democratic kingpins calculated the odds of winning without the black vote and advised Pickett to exit. He did. Wilder had demonstrated the power of black voters in Virginia. When he announced his candidacy for lieutenant governor in 1985, the white establishment fretted, but no Democrat was willing to challenge his

nomination. Benefiting from lackluster Republican opposition, Wilder ran a lively, shoestring campaign, hoarding his dollars for a final television blitz. He captured almost fifty-two percent of the vote, including support from an estimated forty-four percent of white Democrats who voted.

In the four years leading up to his 1989 race for governor, Wilder honed his trademark blend of contentiousness and charm. He quarreled with former governor Robb over politics and the present governor, Gerald Baliles. As the election approached and his chief rival for the Democratic nomination dropped out of the race, friction gave way to civility. Slight in stature, immaculately dressed, his mustache shaved, and his once bold Afro trimmed to a sedate silver cap, Wilder wooed audiences with an easy, engaging laugh and an increasingly centrist, nonthreatening message. He declined offers from JESSE JACKSON and other nationally prominent black politicians to travel to Virginia to campaign, and he deliberately avoided references to race and the historic nature of his campaign. Wilder drew support from a broad network of social acquaintances, but as in past campaigns, he kept few confidantes, relying on a small circle of advisers whose members fell in and out of grace.

Perhaps the determining event of the governor's campaign occurred on 5 July 1989, when the U.S. Supreme Court ruled in *Webster v. Reproductive Services* that states could restrict abortions beyond the limits set in 1973. Wilder deftly framed the issue as a matter of personal freedom. He trusted the women of Virginia to make the proper individual choice, he said. Wilder's opponent, former Republican Attorney General J. Marshall Coleman, attempted to soften his hard-line, antiabortion message adopted in order to win a three-way contest for the Republican nomination. But in public opinion polls, both campaigns saw women in the vote-rich Washington, D.C., suburbs swing to Wilder.

Entering the final weekend of the campaign, opinion polls showed Wilder leading Coleman by as much as eleven percentage points. As soon as the voting ended on election night, an exit survey taken by Mason-Dixon Opinion Research appeared to confirm that

margin. The celebration began. But as the evening wore on, the "landslide" turned into a cliffhanger. Wilder won by 6,741 votes of a record 1,787,131 cast. As in previous American elections involving black candidates, it appeared that many voters simply lied when asked about their vote.

In office Wilder encountered an unexpected $1.4 billion budget shortfall. By his second year, revenues lagged further. Rather than raise taxes, the option adopted by almost every other state during the recession of the early 1990s, Wilder instituted across-the-board spending cuts, laid off state workers, canceled salary increases, and insisted on holding the line on taxes. He pushed also for creation of a "rainy-day fund" to help tide the state over in future economic crises. His managing of the economic crisis was widely applauded, particularly after Virginia was cited twice in a row by *Financial World* magazine as the nation's best managed state.

Wilder also won acclaim for the passage of legislation limiting guns sales in Virginia to one per month, thereby halting extensive gun running from Virginia to the northeast, and for extensive appointments of African Americans to prominent government posts. Less lauded was his 1991 bid for the Democratic presidential nomination, a campaign that alienated many Virginia voters before his voluntary withdrawal and during which he engaged in public spats with Robb and other prominent Democrats, including some members of the legislative black caucus. An article in *U.S. News & World Report* stated that "Virginia's governor is capable of transcendent, triumphal moments and of astonishing pettiness" (13 May 1991).

Prohibited by the Virginia constitution from seeking more than one consecutive gubernatorial term, Wilder left office in January 1994. That spring he mounted a brief, independent run for Robb's U.S. Senate seat. Both money and support lagged, and Wilder withdrew. Out of office, he conducted a radio call-in show, held a distinguished professorship at Virginia Commonwealth University, and pursued various personal interests, including plans for the creation of a national slavery museum. If his later career did not match expectations prompted by his 1989 election, he nonetheless retained the distinction at the arrival of the twenty-first century of being the only black man yet elected to the high honor of governor of an American state.

FURTHER READING

Wilder's papers are housed at the L. Douglas Wilder Library at Virginia Union University and at the Library of Virginia, both in Richmond, Virginia.

Baker, Don. *Wilder: Hold Fast to Dreams* (1989).

Edds, Margaret. *Claiming the Dream: The Victorious Campaign of Douglas Wilder of Virginia* (1990).

Jeffries, Judson L. *Virginia's Native Son: The Election and Administration of Governor L. Douglas Wilder* (2002).

Yancey, Dwayne. *When Hell Froze Over: The Story of Doug Wilder: A Black Politician's Rise to Power in the South* (1990).

—MARGARET E. EDDS

WILKINS, J. ERNEST, JR.

WILKINS, J. ERNEST, JR. (27 Nov. 1923–), mathematician and engineer, was born in Chicago, the son of J. Ernest Wilkins, a prominent lawyer, and Lucile Beatrice Robinson, a school teacher with a master's degree. Wilkins developed an intense interest in mathematics at an early age, and with the encouragement and support of his parents and a teacher at Parker High School in Chicago, he was able to accelerate his education and finish high school at the age of thirteen. After graduation, he was immediately accepted by the University of Chicago, where he was the youngest student ever admitted by that institution. Within five years, Wilkins received three degrees in Mathematics, a BA in 1940, an MS in 1941, and a PhD in 1942. He was also inducted into Phi Beta Kappa in 1940 and Sigma Xi, the Scientific Research Society, in 1942. While at the university, he was university table tennis champion for three years and won the boys' state championship in 1938.

After earning his PhD from the University of Chicago, Wilkins received a Rosenwald Fellowship to carry out postdoctoral research at the Institute for Advanced Study in Princeton, New Jersey. During his stay, from October 1942 to December 1942, he worked on four papers. All were published within one year, with three appearing in the *Duke Mathematical Journal* and one in *Annals of Mathematics*.

In January 1943 Wilkins began teaching at Tuskegee Institute in Alabama, where he had accepted a position as instructor of freshmen mathematics. However, in March 1944 he was recruited to work in the Metallurgical Laboratory at the University of Chicago as part of the Manhattan Project, the United States' program to develop an atomic bomb. At the laboratory, he was given the title of "Associate Physicist" rather than "Mathematician," a designation that allowed him to receive a higher salary. Wilkins worked under Eugene Wigner, who directed the Theoretical Physics Group, which provided the theoretical basis for the design of the Hanford, Washington, fission reactor. Wilkins's duties consisted of applying his expertise in mathematics to help resolve various issues related to the understanding and design of reactors. During his stay at the Metallurgical Laboratory, Wilkins made several major contributions to the field of nuclear-reactor physics. It was in his Manhattan District reports that the concepts now referred to as the Wilkins effect, and the Wigner-Wilkins and Wilkins spectra for thermal neutrons, were developed and made quantitative.

At the completion of his duties at the Metallurgical Laboratory, Wilkins accepted a position as mathematician in the Scientific Instrument Division of the American Optical Company in Buffalo, New York. There he worked on the design of lenses for microscopes and ophthalmologic instruments. His research on "the resolving power of a coated objective" was published in the *Journal of the Optical Society of America* (1949, 1950), and was the first of a long series of publications, extending over four decades, on various problems related to apodization—methods that can be used to improve the resolving power of an optical system. In addition to the solution of several specific problems, Wilkins brought to the field of apodization a certain mathematical rigor, whose absence left many earlier results suspect.

On 22 June 1947 Wilkins married Gloria Louise Stewart; they had two children. Gloria Wilkins died in 1980. In May 1950 Wilkins moved to White Plains, New York, to accept the position

of senior mathematician at the United Nuclear Corporation. After accepting a series of increasing managerial responsibilities, he became manager of the Research and Development Division, a group of about thirty individuals in mathematics, physics, chemistry, and metallurgy doing contract work for the Atomic Energy Commission in the areas of theoretical reactor physics and shielding. Wilkins developed and applied a variety of mathematical tools to problems in these fields, and some of his methods are now presented in the standard textbooks. In addition, his work with H. Goldstein on the transport of gamma rays through various materials was the standard reference for many years and is still cited in the current literature.

Although Wilkins's work required him to provide mathematical support to the engineering staff, he discovered that many of them did not approach him for aid until their projects were substantially complete, often resulting in cost overruns. Wilkins concluded that his colleagues might respond better if he were a fellow engineer, and in 1953 he entered the Department of Mechanical Engineering at New York University. He graduated in 1957 with a BME magna cum laude and in 1960 received an MME degree. As he had hoped, his engineering colleagues at United Nuclear Corporation greatly increased their early consultations with him.

In September 1960 Wilkins accepted a position at the General Atomic Company in San Diego, California, as assistant chair of the Theoretical Physics Department. Shortly thereafter, he was promoted to assistant director of the John Jay Hopkins Laboratory, followed by further promotions to director of the Defense Science and Engineering Center and director of Computational Research. His managerial responsibilities included making sure that safety concerns were being treated seriously, insuring the progress of various technical projects, and providing both technical and policy advice to his administrative superiors. Particular programs included work on thermoelectricity, the design of high-temperature gas-cooled nuclear reactors, plasma physics as it relates to fusion reactors, and Project ORION, a program exploring the use of nuclear power to propel rockets.

In March 1970 Wilkins accepted a position at Howard University in Washington, D.C., as Distinguished Professor of Applied Mathematics and Physics. During his stay at Howard he supervised seven MS theses and four PhD dissertations. Wilkins had become a member of the American Nuclear Society in 1955; his increasing participation in the activities of the organization and his international prominence in several areas of mathematics and engineering led to his selection as national president in 1974–1975. In 1976 he was inducted into the National Academy of Engineering. The citation for this honor reads, "Peaceful application of atomic energy through contributions to the design and development of nuclear reactions."

In September 1976 Wilkins took a sabbatical leave from Howard University to go to the Argonne National Laboratory in Argonne, Illinois. As a visiting scientist, he provided mathematics consultation in reactor physics and engineering. He also continued his own research interests in apodization and "a variational problem in Hilbert space." Before Wilkins could return to Howard, he received an offer to return to industry as vice president and associate general manager for Science and Engineering at EG and G Idaho, Inc., in Idaho Falls, Idaho. He accepted this responsibility and began work in March 1977, officially resigning from the faculty at Howard in 1978. In 1978 he was promoted to deputy general manager for Science and Engineering, but he continued his position as vice president, with the responsibility of insuring the high quality of work and of representing the company in its dealings with the U.S. Department of Energy and the Nuclear Regulatory Commission.

In 1984 Wilkins retired from EG and G Idaho and returned to Argonne National Laboratory as a Distinguished Argonne Fellow. That summer he married Maxine G. Malone, who died in 1997; they had no children. At the completion of his stay at Argonne in May 1985, Wilkins went into full retirement. However, he continued to work as a consultant and adviser to a number of technical companies, professional organizations, and universities. It was during this period that Wilkins initiated a new area of research concerned with the real

zeros of random polynomials, published in the *Proceedings of the American Mathematical Society* (1988, 1991).

Wilkins's retirement ended in 1990 when he accepted the position of Distinguished Professor of Mathematics and Mathematical Physics at Clark Atlanta University in Atlanta. A major factor influencing this decision was the opportunity to collaborate with Albert Turner Bharucha-Reid, an internationally recognized mathematician, on random polynomials. Unfortunately, Bharucha-Reid died before Wilkins arrived at the university, but Wilkins continued his research, publishing over the next decade five fundamental papers on the mean number of real zeros for random hyperbolic, the French mathematician Adrien-Marie Legendre, and trigonometric polynomials. During this period he also supervised eleven MS theses in the Department of Mathematical Sciences. Wilkins retired from Clark Atlanta University in August 2003, and in September he married Vera Wood Anderson in Chicago.

J. Ernest Wilkins Jr.'s distinguished career as a research mathematician and engineer has lasted almost six decades, and his contributions to research and management have been recognized by a large number of honors and awards received throughout his life.

FURTHER READING

A complete copy of J. Ernest Wilkins Jr.'s *curriculum vita*, along with other bibliographic materials, is in the Special Collections of the Atlanta University Center of the Woodruff Library in Atlanta.

Donaldson, James. "Black Americans in Mathematics" in *A Century of Mathematics in America, Part III* (1989): 449–469.
Newell, V. K., ed. *Black Mathematicians and Their Works* (1980).
"Phi Beta Kappa at 16." *The Crisis*, Sept. 1940, 288.
Tubbs, Vincent. "Adjustment of a Genius." *Ebony*, Feb. 1958: 60–67.

—RONALD E. MICKENS

WILKINS, ROY

(30 Aug. 1901–8 Sept. 1981), reporter and civil rights leader, was born Roy Ottaway Wilkins in St. Louis, Missouri, the son of William DeWitte Wilkins, a brick kiln worker, and Mayfield Edmundson. Upon his mother's death in

Roy Wilkins in the national headquarters of the NAACP in New York City in 1963. Library of Congress

1905, Wilkins was sent with his brother and sister to St. Paul, Minnesota, to live with their aunt and uncle, Elizabeth and Sam Williams, because his mother worried that her husband could not handle raising their three children and would send them back to Mississippi. The family had fled Mississippi after an incident in which William had beaten a white man over a racial insult.

Wilkins grew up in a middle-class household in a relatively integrated neighborhood. A porter who oversaw operations in the personal car of the chief of the Northern Pacific Railroad, Sam Williams taught Wilkins the virtue of education. Stressing the importance of faith, Sam and Elizabeth also regularly took Wilkins to the local African Methodist Episcopal Church. He developed an interest in writing in high school and then went on to the University of Minnesota, where he became the first black reporter for the school's newspaper. Wilkins also served as editor of the *Saint Paul Appeal*, a weekly African American paper, and was an active member of the city's NAACP branch.

After graduating from college with honors in 1923, Wilkins became a reporter with the *Kansas City Call*. He covered the NAACP's Midwestern Race Relations Conference and was deeply inspired by JAMES WELDON JOHNSON's message stressing the need for African Americans to fight for constitutional rights. Wilkins was outraged over the widespread racism in Kansas City in housing, public accommodations, education, law enforcement, and employment, but his middle-class values of thrift and hard work also led him to look disdainfully at blacks who behaved in ways that affirmed negative white stereotypes. "A lot of the things we suffered came as wrapped, perfumed presents from ourselves," he later wrote (Wilkins, 73). Wilkins soon became secretary of the Kansas City branch of the NAACP, and in 1929 he married Aminda Badeau, a social worker who came from a prominent St. Louis family. The couple had no children.

Wilkins's writing and NAACP work soon caught the attention of WALTER WHITE, the executive secretary of the national organization, and in 1931 White persuaded Wilkins to move to New York to become his chief aide. His duties included writing, lecturing, raising money, and speaking out against racial injustice. When Will Rogers used a racial epithet four times in a radio broadcast, for example, Wilkins organized a nationwide effort to bombard the National Broadcasting Company with telegrams of protest. In 1932 he traveled to Mississippi to do an undercover investigation of the low pay and horrible working conditions suffered by African Americans working for the U.S. Army Corps of Engineers. Wilkins's findings encouraged Senator Robert Wagner of New York to hold hearings on the conditions, and as a result the workers received modest pay increases. In 1934 Wilkins became editor of the *Crisis*, the NAACP's magazine, and brought changes to the periodical that boosted its financial position and broadened its coverage. W. E. B. DU BOIS, the magazine's former editor, looked upon Wilkins and his changes with disdain, and the two would later clash over Du Bois's growing radicalism. Throughout the 1930s and 1940s Wilkins also battled Communists within the NAACP. Holding a strong faith in America's democratic promise, he disagreed profoundly with their philosophy and viewed them as politically harmful to the struggle for racial equality.

Upon Walter White's death in 1955, Wilkins was unanimously selected as the new executive secretary of the NAACP, a post he would hold for twenty-two years. Wilkins strongly believed that working through the courts for legal changes and lobbying presidents and lawmakers in Congress for civil rights legislation offered the best way to effect lasting, significant improvements for African Americans. He regularly testified before Congress on behalf of legislation, met with every president from Harry Truman through Jimmy Carter, rallied NAACP branches and other progressive organizations to support various civil rights initiatives, and appeared before Democratic and Republican conventions to urge both parties to take strong stands for racial equality. Wilkins's efforts helped produce such landmark federal laws as the 1964 Civil Rights Act, which outlawed segregation in public accommodations and employment discrimination; the Voting Rights Act of 1965; and the Fair Housing Act of 1968. Like many other civil rights leaders, Wilkins found President Lyndon Johnson to be a valuable ally. Conversely, he regularly criticized Dwight Eisenhower and John F. Kennedy for doing too little.

As direct-action protests became more prominent in the 1950s and early 1960s, Wilkins steadfastly held to his legalistic approach. He was initially skeptical about seminal protests, such as the Montgomery bus boycott and the 1963 March on Washington, though he ultimately supported them. Similarly, Wilkins and BAYARD RUSTIN urged the Mississippi Freedom Democratic Party (MFDP) to accept President Johnson's compromise offer of two at-large seats at the 1964 Democratic convention if they would moderate their demands for broader representation. The MFDP's FANNIE LOU HAMER and ROBERT P. MOSES refused to compromise, however.

Fearing that civil rights protests might turn to violence and play into the hands of the Republican presidential candidate Barry Goldwater, a staunch conservative who had opposed the 1964 Civil Rights Act, Wilkins also organized an effort among several black leaders that summer to call for a moratorium on civil rights demonstrations until after the presidential election. Wilkins often criticized MARTIN LUTHER KING JR. and groups such as CORE and SNCC, because he doubted that direct action would lead to meaningful change. "When the headlines are gone, the issues still have to be settled in court," he observed (Branch, 557). Wilkins's views also reflected his personal jealousy over the growing popularity of such groups and King. "The other organizations," he angrily commented, "furnish the noise and get the publicity while the NAACP furnishes the manpower and pays the bills" (Branch, 831). Wilkins especially feared that King and the Southern Christian Leadership Conference would erode the NAACP's financial and political strength in the South. Thus, though the two leaders often worked together, they maintained an uneasy relationship throughout the 1960s. King believed the NAACP was often too timid, while Wilkins saw King as a self-promoter. Wilkins distanced himself and the NAACP from King as the SCLC leader grew more critical of the Vietnam War.

Wilkins came under sharp attack from more radical African Americans in the mid- to late 1960s for his unwavering faith in integration, willingness to work with white allies, and confidence in American institutions. Critics also alleged that the NAACP was too timid and had no program to help African Americans economically. Wilkins bristled at these charges and fired back that Black Power was "the father of hatred and the mother of violence" (Fairclough, 320). Younger African Americans sympathetic to Black Power, Wilkins insisted, were "unfair, ungrateful, and forgetful" regarding NAACP accomplishments (*New York Times*, 9 Sept. 1981). One radical group, the Revolutionary Action Movement, even hatched plans to assassinate Wilkins in 1967, though no attempt on his life was carried out, because police raided the group's headquarters and broke up the plot.

At the same time he faced these conflicts with external rivals, Wilkins battled critics within the NAACP. A group of junior NAACP board members known as the Young Turks challenged Wilkins's positions on economic issues, race riots, and the NAACP's endorsement of Johnson in the 1964 presidential election. Supporting Johnson contradicted the organization's longstanding policy of nonpartisanship, but Wilkins saw the right-wing Republican Goldwater as a threat to recent civil rights advances. Critics also believed that Wilkins wielded too much power within the organization. The Young Turks endorsed structural changes that would give more power to local branches and would strip some authority from the national leadership. They first made their case at the NAACP's annual convention in 1965, when they came within one vote of removing Wilkins from the leadership post. The feud lasted for three years. By 1968, however, Wilkins had firmly consolidated his power and put down the rebellion. His means included co-opting some of the Turks' agenda and, at the 1968 NAACP convention in Atlantic City, calling in law enforcement officials to keep order, turning off microphones and lights when some of the Turks attempted to speak, and tabling the dissenters' proposals quickly, with little or no debate.

Wilkins continued to advocate for laws and programs to improve black life in education, housing, employment, health care, and other areas throughout the 1970s. He sharply criticized Republican presidents Richard Nixon and Gerald Ford over school desegregation, busing, and voting rights, but failing health slowed his activities somewhat. In 1969 he had suffered a second bout with cancer. Ill health forced him to retire from the NAACP in 1977, when he was replaced by Benjamin Hooks. Four years later, Wilkins died from kidney failure at New York University Medical Center. Upon hearing of Wilkins's death, JESSE JACKSON observed that he was "a man of integrity, intelligence, and courage who, with his broad shoulders, bore more than his share of responsibility for our and the nation's advancement" (*New York Times*, 9 Sept. 1981).

FURTHER READING

Roy Wilkins's papers are housed at the Library of Congress, Washington, D.C.

Wilkins, Roy, with Tom Mathews. *Standing Fast: The Autobiography of Roy Wilkins* (1982).

Branch, Taylor. *Parting the Waters: America in the King Years, 1954–1963* (1988).
Eick, Gretchen Cassel. *Dissent in Wichita: The Civil Rights Movement in the Midwest, 1954–72* (2001).
Fairclough, Adam. *To Redeem the Soul of America: The Southern Christian Leadership Conference and Martin Luther King, Jr.* (1987).

Obituary: *New York Times*, 9 Sept. 1981.
—TIMOTHY N. THURBER

WILLIAMS, BERT

(12 Nov. 1874–4 Mar. 1922), and **GEORGE WALKER** (1873–6 Jan. 1911), stage entertainers, were born, respectively, Egbert Austin Williams in Nassau, the Bahamas, and George Williams Walker in Lawrence, Kansas. Williams was the son of Frederick Williams Jr., a waiter, and Julia Monceur. Walker was the son of "Nash" Walker, a policeman; his mother's name is unknown. Williams moved with his family to Riverside, California, in 1885 and attended Riverside High School. Walker began performing "darkey" material for traveling medicine shows during his boyhood and left Kansas with Dr. Waite's medicine show. In 1893 Williams and Walker met in San Francisco, where they first worked together in Martin and Selig's Minstrels.

To compete in the crowded field of mostly white blackface performers, "Walker and Williams," as they were originally known, subtitled their act "The Two Real Coons." Walker developed a fast-talking, city hustler persona, straight man to Williams's slow-witted, woeful bumbler. Williams, who was light-skinned, used blackface makeup on stage, noting that "it was not until I was able to see myself as another person that my sense of humor developed." An unlikely engagement in the unsuccessful Victor Herbert operetta *The Gold Bug* brought Williams and Walker to New York in 1896, but the duo won critical acclaim and rose quickly through the ranks of vaudeville, eventually playing Koster and Bial's famed New York theater. During this run they added a sensational cakewalk dance finale to the act, cinching popular success. Walker performed exceptionally graceful and complex dance variations, while Williams clowned through an inept parody of Walker's steps. Aida Reed Overton, who later become a noteworthy dancer and choreographer in her own right, was hired as Walker's cakewalk partner in 1897 and became his wife in 1899. They had no children. The act brought the cakewalk to the height of its popularity, and Williams and Walker subsequently toured the eastern seaboard and performed a week at the Empire Theatre in London in April 1897.

Bert Williams and George Walker performed in WILL MARION COOK's musical In Dahomey *on the lawn of Buckingham Palace in 1902.* Museum of London

Vaudeville typically used stereotyped ethnic characterizations as humor, and Williams and Walker developed a "coon" act without peer in the industry. For the 1898 season, the African American composer WILL MARION COOK and the noted poet PAUL LAURENCE DUNBAR created *Senegambian Carnival* for the duo, the first in a series of entertainments featuring African Americans that eventually played New York. *A Lucky Coon* (1898), *The Policy Players* (1899), and *Sons of Ham* (1900) were basically vaudeville acts connected by Williams and Walker's patter. In 1901 they began recording their ragtime stage hits for the Victor label. Their popularity spread, and the 18 February 1903 Broadway premiere of *In Dahomey* was considered the first fully realized musical comedy performed by an all-black company. In 1900 Williams had married Charlotte Louise Johnson; they had no children.

Williams and Walker led the *In Dahomey* cast of fifty as Shylock Homestead and Rareback Pinkerton, two confidence men out to defraud a party of would-be African colonizers. Its three acts included a number of dances, vocal choruses, specialty acts, and a grand cakewalk sequence. Critics cited Williams's performance of "I'm a Jonah Man," a hard-luck song by Alex Rogers, as a high point of the hit show. *In Dahomey* toured England and Scotland, with a command performance at Buckingham Palace arranged for the ninth birthday of King Edward VII's grandson David. The cakewalk became the rage of fashionable English society, and company members worked as private dance instructors both abroad and when they returned home.

Williams composed more than seventy songs in his lifetime. "Nobody," the most famous of these, was introduced to the popular stage in 1905:

When life seems full of clouds and rain,
And I am filled with naught but pain,
Who soothes my thumping, bumping brain?
Nobody!

The sense of pathos lurking behind Williams's plaintive delivery was not lost on his audience. Walker gained fame performing boastful, danceable struts, such as the 1906 "It's Hard to Find a King Like Me" and his signature song, "Bon Bon Buddie, the Chocolate Drop," introduced in 1907. During this period Williams and Walker signed their substantial music publishing rights with the black-owned Attucks Music Publishing Company.

Walker, who was more business-minded than Williams, controlled production details of the 1906 *Abyssinia* and the 1907 *Bandanna Land*. Walker demanded that these "all-Negro" productions play only in first-class theaters. His hard business tactics worked, and Williams and Walker played several theaters that had previously barred black performers. In 1908, at the height of their success, the duo were founding members of The Frogs, a charitable and social organization of black theatrical celebrities. Other members included composers Bob Cole and J. Rosamond Johnson, bandleader JAMES REESE EUROPE, and writer/directors Alex Rogers and Jesse Shipp.

During the tour of *Bandanna Land*, Walker succumbed to general paresis, an advanced stage of syphilis. He retired from the stage in February 1909. Aida Walker took over his songs and dances, and the book scenes were rewritten for Williams to play alone. Walker died in Islip, New York.

Williams continued doing blackface and attempted to produce the 1909 *Mr. Lode of Koal* without Walker. His attention to business details languished, and the show failed. Williams's performances, however, received significant critical praise, and he gained stature as "an artist of pantomime" and "a comic genius." In 1910 he joined Florenz Ziegfeld's *Follies*. He told the *New York Age* (1 Dec. 1910) that "the colored show business—that is colored musical shows—is at the low ebb just now. I reached the conclusion last spring that I could best represent my race by doing pioneer work. It was far better to have joined a large white show than to have starred in a colored show, considering conditions."

Williams was aware of the potential for racial backlash from his white audience and insisted on a contract clause stating that he would at no time appear on stage with any of the scantily clad women in the *Follies* chorus. His celebrity advanced, and he became the star attraction of the *Follies* for some eight seasons, leaving the show twice, in 1913 and 1918, to spend time with his family and to headline in vaudeville. His overwhelming success prompted educator BOOKER T. WASHINGTON to quip, "Bert Williams has done more for the race than I have. He has smiled his way into people's hearts. I have been obliged to fight my way."

An Actor's Equity strike troubled Ziegfeld's 1919 edition of the *Follies*, and Williams, who had never been asked or allowed to join the union because of his African ancestry, left the show. In 1920 he and Eddie Cantor headlined Rufus and George Lemaire's short-lived *Broadway Brevities*. In 1921 the Shuberts financed a musical, *Under the Bamboo Tree*, to star Williams with an otherwise all-white cast. The show opened in Cincinnati, Ohio, but in February 1922 Williams succumbed to pneumonia, complicated by heart problems, and died the next month in New York City.

Although Williams's stage career solidified the stereotype of the "shiftless darkey," his unique talent at pantomime and the hard work he put into it was indisputable. In his famous poker game sketch, filmed in the 1916 short *A Natural Born Gambler*, Williams enacted a four-handed imaginary game without benefit of props or partners. His cache of comic stories, popularized in his solo vaudeville and Ziegfeld *Follies* appearances, were drawn largely from African American folk humor, which Williams and Alex Rogers duly noted and collected for their shows. Williams collected an extensive library and wrote frequently for the black press and theatrical publications.

The commercial success of Williams and Walker proved that large audiences would pay to see black performers. Tall and light-skinned Williams, in blackface and ill-fitting tatters, contrasted perfectly with short, dark-skinned, dandyish Walker. Their cakewalks revived widespread interest in African American dance styles. Their successful business operations, responsible for a "$2,300 a week" payroll in 1908, encouraged black participation in mainstream show business. The *Chicago Defender* (11 Mar. 1922) called them "the greatest Negro team of actors who ever lived and the most popular pair of comedy stars America has produced."

FURTHER READING

Allen, Woll. *Black Musical Theatre—From Coontown to Dreamgirls* (1989).

Charters, Ann. *Nobody: The Story of Bert Williams* (1970).

JOHNSON, JAMES WELDON. *Black Manhattan* (1930).

Rowland, Mabel. *Bert Williams: Son of Laughter* (1923).

Sampson, Henry T. *Blacks in Blackface: A Source Book on Early Black Musical Shows* (1980).

Smith, Eric Ledell. *Bert Williams: A Biography of the Pioneer Black Comedian* (1992).

Obituaries: *New York Times*, 8 Jan. 1911 (Walker) and 5 Mar. 1922 (Williams).

—THOMAS F. DEFRANTZ

 WILLIAMS, CATHAY
(Sept. 1844–?), cook, laundress, and Buffalo Soldier, was born into slavery in Independence, Missouri. Nothing is known of her parents, except that her father was reported to be a free black man. At some point in her early childhood, she went with her master's family to a farm near Jefferson City, where she toiled as a house servant until the start of the Civil War.

Probably in the summer of 1861, when she was nearly seventeen years old, Williams fled the plantation and joined the large group of escaped and newly freed slaves seeking the protection of Union troops occupying Jefferson City. Within months she was pressed into service as a laundress and cook for a Union regiment, possibly the Eighth Indiana Infantry. She maintained that position for nearly two years, accompanying the troops on campaigns in Missouri and Arkansas. In the summer of 1863 Williams found employment as a government cook in Federal-controlled Little Rock. Within a year she was a regimental laundress and cook again, purportedly working throughout the Red River campaign in Louisiana before being sent east, where she said she obtained employment as "cook and washer woman" for the staff of General Philip Sheridan during the second Shenandoah Valley Campaign in Virginia. By January 1865 Williams was back with her old regiment, traveling with them to Savannah, Georgia, until the end of the war.

After the cessation of hostilities, Williams managed to return to Missouri to reunite with her family. In November 1866, in the company of a male cousin and a "particular friend," she disguised herself as a man and enlisted in the U.S. Army in St. Louis under the alias of William Cathey. Her reasons for doing so have never been clearly delineated. She may have viewed the military as an opportunity for a decent livelihood and a semblance of respect, since as a black woman in postwar Missouri her economic prospects were dim. Her years with the Union army undoubtedly made the military seem a familiar place in which to stake her future. Or perhaps her motivation was a strong desire to accompany her cousin and her friend.

Army regulations of the time forbade the enlistment or commissioning of women as soldiers, but since recruiters did not seek proof of identity and because army surgeons often failed to fully examine enlistees, it was not very difficult for women to infiltrate the military. During the Civil War, for example, hundreds of women pretended to be men and served in both the Union and Confederate armies. Williams, however, holds the distinction of being the only known female Buffalo Soldier, and the only documented African American woman to serve in the U.S. Regulars in the nineteenth century. At least three black women served as soldiers in the Civil War: Lizzie Hoffman and another unidentified woman in the U.S. Colored Troops, and Maria Lewis, passing as a white man, in a New York cavalry regiment.

Williams, using the name William Cathey, informed the recruiting officer that she was twenty-two years old and a cook by occupation. Her enlistment papers reveal that she was illiterate at the time of her induction. The recruiting officer described Private William Cathey as five feet, nine inches tall, with black eyes, black hair, and black complexion. She was one of the tallest soldiers in her company. An army surgeon reportedly examined her upon enlistment and determined that she was fit for duty. The exam was obviously a farce or incomplete, as neither the surgeon nor the recruiter realized that she was a woman. Assigned to Company A of the segregated Thirty-eighth U.S. Infantry, Private Cathey did not have an illustrious or exciting army career. She was an average soldier, never singled out for praise or punishment, and, apparently, neither distinguished nor disgraced herself. Opinions held of Private Cathey by her fellow soldiers and officers are unknown.

From her enlistment until February 1867, Williams was stationed at Jefferson Barracks, except for one visit to a St. Louis hospital for treatment of an undocumented illness. By April 1867 Private Cathey and her company had marched to Fort Riley, Kansas, where she and fifteen others were described as "ill in quarters" for two weeks. In June 1867 her company arrived at Fort Harker, Kansas, and the following month they arrived at Fort Union, New Mexico, after a march of 536 miles. By October the company was encamped at Fort Cummings, New Mexico. It appears that Private Cathey withstood the marches as well as any man in her unit, and although she participated in her share of soldierly obligations, the company never engaged the enemy or saw any direct combat while she was a member. In January 1868 her health began to deteriorate, and she was hospitalized for rheumatism that month and again in March. In June the company marched for Fort Bayard, New Mexico, where she was admitted into the hospital in July and diagnosed with neuralgia, a catch-all term for any acute pain of the nervous system. She did not report back to duty for a month.

On 14 October 1868 Private Cathey and two others in Company A were discharged from the Thirty-eighth Infantry on a surgeon's certificate of medical disability. She had served her country for just less than two years. Although Cathey's discharge papers do not indicate that the surgeon was aware of her true sex, Williams later related that she grew tired of being a soldier and eventually confessed her true identity to obtain release from the military. Indeed, none of the records of the Thirty-eighth Infantry—including carded medical records, enlistment papers, and the muster rolls and returns of Company A, Thirty-eighth U.S. Infantry—reveal any awareness of a woman in the ranks.

Upon resuming civilian life, she traveled to Fort Union and worked as a cook until some time in 1870, when she moved to Pueblo, Colorado, and worked as a laundress for two years. She next moved to Las Animas County, Colorado, staying for a year, again working as a laundress. She finally settled, more or less permanently, in Trinidad, Colorado, making her living as a laundress, seamstress, and nurse. In 1875 Williams told her life story to a St. Louis journalist traveling in Colorado, who described her as "tall and powerfully built, black as night, muscular looking." The full newspaper article published the following year remains the only written story of her life told in her own voice. In the mid-1880s Williams moved to Raton, New Mexico, where she may have operated a boarding house. By 1889 she was back in Trinidad, hospitalized for nearly a year and a half with an undisclosed illness.

Williams was probably indigent when she left the hospital, so in June 1891 she petitioned for an "invalid pension" based upon her military service. Her sworn application gave her age as forty-one, and she declared that she was the same William Cathey who served as a private in the Thirty-eighth Infantry. She produced her original discharge certificate as proof. She claimed she was suffering deafness, contracted in the army; she referred to her rheumatism; and she declared she was eligible for the government pension because she could no longer sustain herself by manual labor. A supplemental declaration, filed the following month, contended that she had contracted smallpox at St. Louis in 1868, and, while still recovering, swam the Rio Grande on the way to New Mexico. She believed that the combined effects of smallpox and exposure led to her deafness. All of her pension papers were signed by her, as she had learned to read and to write since her time in the army more than two decades earlier.

On 8 September 1891 a medical doctor in Trinidad, commissioned by the Pension Bureau, examined Williams. Charged with providing a thorough examination of the patient and a complete description of her physical condition, the doctor described her as five feet, seven inches tall, 160 pounds, and "stout." He reported that she was not deaf and he could find no evidence of rheumatism. Most horrifying, the doctor reported that all her toes on both feet had been amputated, and she could walk only with the aid of a crutch, but he provided no explanation of the cause of amputation. Other than the loss of her toes, the doctor stated she was in good

general health and gave his opinion as "nil" on a disability rating. In February 1892 the Pension Bureau rejected her claim for an invalid pension, and Williams never received any government assistance. The bureau rejected her claim on medical grounds, but it never questioned her identity. No one appeared to doubt that William Cathey of the Thirty-eight Infantry and Cathay Williams of Trinidad were the same person.

Nothing definite is known of Williams after her pension case closed, although it is believed that she died before 1900. Where and how she lived, the date and place of her death, and her final resting place are undetermined.

FURTHER READING

Records pertaining to Cathay Williams's military service as Private William Cathey can be found at the National Archives in Washington, D.C., in Record Group 94; and her pension application file (SO 1032593), in Record Group 15.

Tucker, Phillip Thomas. *Cathy Williams: From Slave to Female Buffalo Soldier* (2002).
"Cathay Williams Story." *St. Louis Daily Times*, 2 Jan. 1876.

—DE ANNE BLANTON

 WILLIAMS, DANIEL HALE (18 Jan. 1856– 4 Aug. 1931), surgeon and hospital administrator, was born in Hollidaysburg, south central Pennsylvania, the son of Daniel Williams Jr. and Sarah Price. His parents were black, but Daniel himself, in adult life, could easily be mistaken for being white, with his light complexion, red hair, and blue eyes.

Williams's father did well in real estate but died when Daniel was eleven, and the family's financial situation became difficult. When Williams was seventeen, he and a sister, Sally, moved to Janesville, Wisconsin. Here Williams found work at Harry Anderson's Tonsorial Parlor and Bathing Rooms. Anderson took the two of them into his home as family and continued to aid Williams financially until Williams obtained his MD.

Medicine had not been Williams's first choice of a career; he had worked in a law office after high school but had found it too quarrelsome. In 1878

Janesville's most prominent physician, Henry Palmer, took Williams on as an apprentice. Williams entered the Chicago Medical College in the fall of 1880 and graduated in 1883. He opened an office on Chicago's South Side and treated both black and white patients.

Late in 1890 the Reverend Louis Reynolds, a pastor on the West Side, asked Williams for advice about his sister, Emma, who had been turned down at several nursing schools because of her color. As a result Williams decided to start an interracial hospital and a nursing school for black women. He drew on black and white individuals and groups for financial support. Several wealthy businessmen, such as meat-packer Philip D. Armour and publisher Herman H. Kohlsaat, made major contributions to the purchase of a three-story building at Dearborn and Twenty-ninth Street and its remodeling into a hospital with twelve beds. Provident Hospital and Training School Association was officially incorporated on 23 January 1891 and opened for service on 4 May of that year. The Training School received 175 applicants for its first class, and Williams selected seven for the eighteen-month course.

Provident had both white and black patients and staff members, although the lack of suitably qualified black physicians led to some problems. Williams appointed black physicians and surgeons who had obtained their medical degrees from schools such as the Rush Medical College and his own alma mater and who, in addition, had suitable experience. However, he had to deal diplomatically with some leaders of the black community who were pushing the appointment of young George Cleveland Hall, who had a degree from an eclectic school and only two years of experience (mostly in Chicago's red light district). Hall (and his equally aggressive wife) never forgave Williams for this early judgment to oppose Hall's appointment.

The hospital soon became over-crowded, but many donations—again including major contributions from Armour and Kohlsaat—resulted in the construction of a new sixty-five-bed hospital at Dearborn and Thirty-sixth streets. The new Provident opened in late 1896.

In 1893 a longtime Chicago friend of Williams, Judge Walter Q. Gresham, recently named secretary of state by President Grover Cleveland, urged Williams to seek the position of surgeon in chief at Freedmen's Hospital in Washington, D.C. This, Gresham pointed out, would bring Williams onto the national scene. Williams, believing that Provident was in good hands, finally agreed to Gresham's suggestion and in 1894 was appointed to Freedmen's where his predecessor, Charles B. Purvis, unhappy at being replaced and often with the aid of Hall, made life as difficult as possible for Williams.

Williams, nevertheless, accomplished much at Freedmen's. He reorganized the staff interracially, created an advisory board of prominent physicians for both professional and political help, and founded a successful nursing school. Williams also began an internship program, improved relationships with the Howard University Medical School, and helped establish an interracial local medical society.

Williams also worked hard on the national scene and became one of the founders of the National Medical Association in 1895. Because at the time the American Medical Association did not accept black physicians, such a national organization was a necessary part of the educational and professional growth for black health-care givers. In 1895 Williams turned down the presidency but did become vice president of the organization.

With the election in 1896 of a new U.S. president, the control of Freedmen's became involved in partisan congressional hearings. These were sufficiently upsetting for Williams, but then William A. Warfield, one of Williams's first interns at Freedmen's, accused his chief, before the hospital's board of visitors, of stealing hospital supplies. Although the congressional hearings came to no conclusion and the board of visitors exonerated Williams, he had become soured on Washington and resigned early in 1898.

In April 1898 Williams married Alice Johnson in Washington, D.C. The couple moved to Chicago, and Williams returned to his old office. There the Halls continued to undermine the Williamses' professional and social lives. Hall finally forced Williams to resign from Provident in 1912 because the latter had become an associate attending

surgeon at St. Luke's Hospital and was, therefore, "disloyal" to Provident. That this was a trumped-up charge was apparent from the fact that, since 1900, Williams had regularly had patients in up to five other hospitals at the same time.

National recognition, however, counterbalanced such sniping; in 1913 Williams was nominated to be a charter member of the American College of Surgeons, the first black surgeon to be honored in this manner. At the board of regents meeting to act on this, a surgeon from Tennessee objected because of the social implications in the South. After vigorous discussion, during which it was pointed out that "if you met him [Williams] on the street you would hardly realize that he is a Negro," Williams was accepted.

As a surgeon, Williams is best known for his stitching of a stab wound to the pericardium of Jim Cornish, an expressman, on 9 July 1893. After Williams had realized that conservative care would not be sufficient for Cornish, he searched the medical literature for reports of surgery in this area. Finding none, he nevertheless decided to perform surgery. Cornish lived for fifty years after the operation. While strictly speaking not an operation on the heart itself, this was the first successful suturing of the pericardium on record.

Perhaps more important surgically was Williams's successful suturing of a heavily bleeding spleen in July 1902, one of the earliest such operations in the United States. Williams also operated on many ovarian cysts, a condition that had not been believed to occur in black women. In 1901 he reported on his 357 such operations, almost equally divided between black and white patients.

Well aware of the lack of training opportunities available to black surgeons in the South, Williams readily accepted an invitation near the end of the century to be a visiting professor of clinical surgery at the Meharry Medical College in Nashville, Tennessee. He spent five or ten days there without pay each year for over a decade. He began operating in a crowded basement room, but by 1910 growing financial support for the college programs resulted in a separate hospital building with forty beds. Williams also operated and lectured at other schools and hospitals in the South.

In 1920 Williams built a summer home near Idlewild, Michigan, to which he and his wife moved. There Alice died of Parkinson's disease a few years later, and Williams then succumbed to diabetes and a stroke.

Williams became known for his long and successful efforts for medical care and professional training for blacks, although much of his work was multiracial. His logically developed and pioneering surgery, especially on the pericardium and the spleen, increased the possibilities and scope of surgical action.

FURTHER READING

Beatty, William K. "Daniel Hale Williams: Innovative Surgeon, Educator, and Hospital Administrator," *Chest* 60 (1971): 175–82.
Buckler, Helen. *Daniel Hale Williams: Negro Surgeon* (1954; repr. 1966).
—WILLIAM K. BEATTY

 WILLIAMS, GEORGE WASHINGTON
(16 Oct. 1849–2 Aug. 1891), soldier, clergyman, legislator, and historian, was born in Bedford Springs, Pennsylvania, the son of Thomas Williams, a free black laborer, and Ellen Rouse. His father became a boatman and, eventually, a minister and barber, and the younger Williams drifted with his family from town to town in western Pennsylvania until the beginning of the Civil War. With no formal education, he lied about his age, adopted the name of an uncle, and enlisted in the United States Colored Troops in 1864. He served in operations against Petersburg and Richmond, sustaining multiple wounds during several battles. After the war's end Williams was stationed in Texas, but crossed the border to fight with the Mexican republican forces that overthrew the emperor Maximilian. He returned to the U.S. Army in 1867, serving with the Tenth Cavalry, an all-black unit, at Fort Arbuckle, Indian Territory. Williams was discharged for disability the following year after being shot through the left lung under circumstances that were never fully explained.

For a few months in 1869 Williams was enrolled at Howard University in Washington, D.C. But with an urgent desire to become a Baptist minister, he sought admission to the Newton Theological Institution in Massachusetts. Semiliterate and placed in the English "remedial" course at the outset, Williams underwent a remarkable transformation. He became a prize student as well as a polished writer and public speaker and completed the three-year theological curriculum in two years. In 1874, following graduation and marriage to Sarah Sterret of Chicago, Williams was installed as pastor of one of the leading African American churches of Boston, the Twelfth Baptist. A year later he went with his wife and young son (their only child) to Washington, D.C. There he edited the *Commoner*, a weekly newspaper supported by FREDERICK DOUGLASS and other leading citizens and intended to be, in Williams's words, "to the colored people of the country a guide, teacher, defender, and mirror." It folded after about six months of publication.

The West beckoned, and Williams moved in 1876 to Cincinnati, where he served as pastor of the Union Baptist Church through the end of the next year. Also engaged as a columnist for a leading daily newspaper, the Cincinnati *Commercial*, he contributed sometimes autobiographical pieces on cultural, racial, religious, and military themes. He spent what spare time he had studying law in the office of Judge Alphonso Taft, father of William Howard Taft. Even before passing the bar in 1881, Williams had become deeply immersed in Republican politics—as a captivating orator, holder of patronage positions, and, in 1877, an unsuccessful legislative candidate. In 1879 the voters of Cincinnati elected him to the Ohio House of Representatives, making Williams the first African American to sit in the state legislature. He served one term, during which he was the center of several controversies, ranging from the refusal of a Columbus restaurant catering to legislators to serve him to a furor in the African American community over his support for the proposed closing of a black cemetery as a health hazard. Williams's effort to repeal a law against interracial marriage failed; he also supported a bill restricting liquor sales.

By this time Williams had developed an interest in history. In 1876

he delivered an Independence Day Centennial oration titled "The American Negro from 1776 to 1876." While in the legislature, Williams made regular use of the Ohio State Library to collect historical information. After completing his stint as a lawmaker in 1881, he devoted his full attention to writing *History of the Negro Race in America from 1619 to 1880: Negroes as Slaves, as Soldiers, and as Citizens*. Based on extensive archival research, interviews, and Williams's pioneering use of newspapers, and published in two volumes by G. P. Putnam's Sons in 1882–1883, the work was the earliest extended, scholarly history of African Americans. Comprehensive in scope, it touched on biblical ethnology and African civilization and government but gave particular attention to blacks who served in America's wars. Widely noticed in the press, Williams's *History of the Negro Race in America* was, for the most part, well received as the first serious work of historical scholarship by an African American. Williams followed it in 1887 with another major historical work, *A History of the Negro Troops in the War of the Rebellion, 1861–1865*. Drawing on his own experiences (but also on the wartime records then being published for the first time), Williams wrote bitterly of the treatment of black soldiers by white northerners as well as by Confederates. Despite disadvantages, their conduct, in his opinion, was heroic, and he concluded that no troops "could be more determined or daring." Though not as widely heralded as his earlier volumes, *A History of the Negro Troops in the War of the Rebellion* was generally well reviewed by the white and black press. Williams also planned a two-volume history of Reconstruction in the former Confederacy, but he never went beyond incorporating some of the materials he had collected for the project into his lectures in the United States and Europe. In his writings and lectures, Williams expressed an optimism based on faith in a divine power that preordained events and enlisted adherents to assist in evangelizing the rest of the world's peoples.

Williams had begun to lecture extensively early in the 1880s, and by the end of 1883 had returned to Boston, where he practiced law. He later resided

in Worcester and continued his research at the American Antiquarian Society. In March 1885 lame-duck president Chester Arthur appointed Williams minister to Haiti. He was confirmed by the U.S. Senate and sworn in during the final hours of the outgoing Republican administration, but before Williams could assume the post, Democrat Grover Cleveland appointed someone else to it.

Ever restless and aggressively ambitious, Williams turned his sights toward Africa, already an occasional subject of his writing and public speaking. He attended an antislavery conference in Brussels in 1889 as a reporter for S. S. McClure's syndicate and there met Leopold II, king of the Belgians. In the following year, without the blessing of the king but with the patronage of Collis P. Huntington, an American railroad magnate who had invested in several African projects, he visited the Congo. After an extensive tour of the country, which took him from Boma on the Atlantic coast to the headwaters of the Congo River at Stanley Falls, he had a clear impression of what the country was like and why. Having witnessed the brutal conduct and inhumane policies of the Belgians, Williams decided to speak out. He published for circulation throughout Europe and the United States *An Open Letter to His Serene Majesty, Leopold II, King of the Belgians*, thus becoming a pioneering opponent of Leopold's policies and anticipating later criticisms of Europe's colonial ventures in Africa. Among the barrage of charges against the king was that his title to the Congo was, at best, "badly clouded" because his treaties with the local chiefs were "tainted by frauds of the grossest character." He held the king responsible for "deceit, fraud, robberies, arson, murder, slave-raiding, and general policy of cruelty" in the Congo. "All the crimes perpetrated in the Congo have been done in *your* name," he concluded, "and *you* must answer at the bar of Public Sentiment for the misgovernment of a people, whose lives and fortunes were entrusted to you by the august Conference of Berlin, 1884–1885." While the attack inspired denunciations of Williams in Belgium, it was little noted in the United States, though Williams had already written a report on the Congo for President Benjamin

Harrison at the latter's request. A closer scrutiny of conditions in the Congo would come only after such "credible" persons as Roger Casement of the British foreign office and Mark Twain made charges against Leopold that echoed those of Williams.

Following his exploration of the Congo and southern Africa, Williams fell ill in Cairo, Egypt, after giving a lecture before the local geographical society (he had not been in robust health since being wounded in the army). Separated but not divorced from his wife, he subsequently went to London with his English "fiancée," Alice Fryer, intending to write a lengthy work on colonialism in Africa. There, tuberculosis and pleurisy overtook him, and he died in Blackpool. In the United States, his death was noted in the national media as well as in the black press.

To the end, George Washington Williams remained a difficult person to understand fully. To many on both sides of the racial divide he possessed a curious combination of rare genius, remarkable resourcefulness, and an incomparable talent for self-aggrandizement. Although Williams was justifiably chided during his lifetime for making inflated claims about his background, W. E. B. DU BOIS did not hesitate to pronounce him, long after his death, "the greatest historian of the race."

FURTHER READING

There are numerous Williams letters in collections of other people's correspondence, including the George F. Hoar Papers at the Massachusetts Historical Society in Boston and the Collis P. Huntington Papers at the George Arents Library at Syracuse University.

Franklin, John Hope. *George Washington Williams: A Biography* (1985).
—JOHN HOPE FRANKLIN

WILLIAMS, JOHN ALFRED (5 Dec. 1925–), novelist, journalist, and teacher, was born in Jackson, Mississippi, to John Henry Williams and Ola Mae, whose maiden name is unknown. Soon after his birth, the family returned to Syracuse, New York, where his father was a laborer and his mother a domestic. Williams attended Central High School in Syracuse, leaving in 1943 to enter the U.S. Navy. After service in the Pacific theater during World War II, he returned to Syracuse, completed high school, and, in 1947, married Carolyn Clopton; the couple had two sons, Gregory and Dennis. Williams entered Syracuse University and graduated in 1950 with a bachelor's degree in Journalism and English. He did graduate work in 1951–1952 before financial circumstances forced him to withdraw; he and Clopton also divorced in 1952.

Williams held several paid writing positions in the 1950s: he was a public relations writer in Syracuse, publicity director for Comet Press Books, editor of *Negro Market Newsletter,* a publisher's assistant, and European correspondent for both *Ebony* and *Jet* magazines. He incorporated these experiences into his first novel, *The Angry Ones* (1960), which draws mainly on his employment at Comet Press.

Williams's second novel, *Night Song* (1962), marks the start of his deep exploration of African American music, especially jazz. An account of the life of Richie "Eagle" Stokes, a fictitious saxophonist who closely resembles CHARLIE PARKER, the novel describes the opportunities and limitations that an artistically talented black man must confront in his attempt to forge meaningful art in racist America. On the strength of it, Williams was informed that he would be selected to receive the *Prix de Rome* from the American Academy of Arts and Letters.

After receiving the informal letter of congratulations that promised him the prize, the author had an interview with the director of the academy, supposedly a mere formality. Instead, after the interview, the director informed Williams that the award had been rescinded. (Williams fictionalized the events in *The Man Who Cried I Am* [1967] and recounted them in "We Regret to Inform You That," an essay reprinted in his collection *Flashbacks* [1973].) The director offered no explanation, though Williams speculated that his impending marriage to Lorrain Isaac, a white Jewish woman, was the cause. At this writing, Williams remains the only candidate to ever have had the prize retracted. Williams later married Isaac in 1965, and the couple had a son, Adam.

Williams produced another fine novel, *Sissie,* in 1963 and a compelling travelog about his exploration of America, *This Is My Country, Too,* in 1964. It was the publication of *The Man Who Cried I Am,* however, that won him international acclaim and secured his literary reputation. The novel recounts the experiences of Max Reddick, a terminally ill expatriate African American writer. As his marriage and his health deteriorate, Max pursues information left to him by a writer friend, Harry Ames. Ames, who is clearly modeled on RICHARD WRIGHT, has discovered an international plot for the subjugation of black peoples; a subset of this plot, the King Alfred Plan, is a blueprint for the annihilation of African Americans. Knowledge of King Alfred proves fatal for Max, as it has for all other blacks who have discovered it.

This novel appeared when the struggle for American racial equality was swinging away from the nonviolent resistance of the Southern Christian Leadership Conference to the more aggressive stance of the Black Power movement. Williams reflects that shift through his negative portrayal of Paul Durrell, a MARTIN LUTHER KING JR. figure whom the novelist portrays as little more than a government puppet. He intensifies that critique in his stinging biography of King, *The King God Didn't Save* (1970).

Williams's work portrays the activist as a failure whose outmoded integrationist views necessarily gave way to the militancy of the black power movement. In his introduction he argues, "So now the man is dead, and time is already proving that his philosophy began to die before he did" (23). He builds on that idea, claiming that strife is the natural outcome of white America's racist past. In telling the story of King's being hit by a brick during the Marquette Park march, for instance, Williams remarks that the minister had won the Nobel Peace Prize, an award that elsewhere in the world would have afforded him some protection. Not so in America; indeed, in Williams's view white Americans' inability to recognize and revere King "damned them to a restless racial future—which they well deserve and, in fact, have long deserved" (97). One finds a similar tone in the novel that he wrote while working on the King biography, *Sons of Darkness, Sons of Light* (1969).

At almost exactly the same time that Williams was writing these two books, he began his teaching career. Subsequent to his initial appointment as teacher and lecturer in writing at City College of the City University of New York, he has held positions at more than a dozen colleges and universities. His commencement of teaching coincided with a shift in his fiction toward a fascination with history. This did not translate into a de-emphasis on contemporary social commentary, however; rather, it provided him a means of extending his commentary through his contextualization of the present era within a larger continuum. One sees a masterly example of this in *Captain Blackman* (1972).

Grievously wounded in a Vietnam firefight, the novel's eponymous hero moves backward in time, hallucinating the entire history of African Americans' military activity up until World War II. When he emerges from his coma, he reflects on his own career, which includes World War II, the Korean War, and the Vietnam War. Although the novel ends with a somewhat fanciful call for infiltration and subversion of the American military, it provides a solidly researched, powerful commentary on the neglected contributions that African American soldiers have made to a nation that has perpetually, systematically denied them their humanity.

Captain Blackman also exhibits Williams's most striking formal achievement: a flexible chronology that embroiders a linear plot with facts, dates, and experiences that thoroughly complicate the reader's understanding of what history is and how it is constructed. This pattern demonstrates Williams's rejection of history as a monolithic, fundamentally accurate, and basically just entity. Much of his fiction identifies a plethora of intellectual-economic-racial tensions that infiltrate the telling of American history and distort the reader's perception of past (and present) events. A subsequent generation of African American writers who concern themselves with historical questions, including John Edgar Wideman, Charles Johnson, and TONI MORRISON, cite Williams as an important influence on their work.

In some of his later works, Williams applies the historical lens to more personal subjects. As Gilbert Muller notes, *!Click Song* (1982) provides a sequel to *The Man Who Cried I Am*. *!Click Song*'s narrator, Cato Caldwell Douglass, is Max Reddick's emotional and spiritual heir; nevertheless, his interest in aesthetics saves him from the destruction that political activity visits on Reddick. In *The Berhama Account* (1985), Williams effectively mixes the personal and the political, setting a love story against the backdrop of effective political action. *The Berhama Account* shows a small Caribbean nation addressing its racially inspired internal strife in the wake of a specious assassination attempt. In the midst of all this social upheaval, a cancer survivor and journalist reignites an old affair and finds personal salvation in the relationship. On many levels this plot represents a rewriting of *The Man Who Cried I Am*, with a shift in emphasis away from the annihilation plot and toward the possibility of enduring human connection.

The same is true in Williams's compelling *Clifford's Blues* (1999), which recounts the story of the gay black jazz musician Clifford Pepperidge's confinement in the Dachau Nazi concentration camp near Munich, from 1933 until 1945. (The plot of the novel is not entirely fictional; several African Americans, including the jazz singer Valaida Snow, were interned in concentration camps by the Nazis). Saved from the general camp population by his musical abilities and by a gay SS officer's sexual desire for him, Pepperidge spends his years in Dachau never fully suffering what most prisoners do and yet always remembering that he is not, cannot be, free. In the face of this, Pepperidge struggles to retain some sense of self. The emphasis on his experiences with jazz as a salvific force lends an air of hopefulness to the work. Williams tempers that hope, however, with a constant reminder that racism in America is little better than the discrimination that lands Pepperidge in Dachau initially; furthermore, by leaving the question of Pepperidge's survival unresolved, he complicates the notion that black identity and selfhood are sustainable,

no matter what resources one brings to the struggle.

The appearance of this powerful novel, almost four decades after the publication of Williams's first book, indicates that at this writing his is a vital and viable career. Furthermore, it demonstrates how his evolving approach to literature and his views about racial questions mirror shifts in the larger national populace. From an early hopeful emphasis on the chance for racial amelioration, through his strong hand in the articulation of a revolutionary black arts ethos, to a rich, subtle engagement with the issue of what black life means in America, Williams spans a range of attitudes and literary techniques that make his one of the most important American literary voices of his age.

FURTHER READING

Cash, Earl A. *John A. Williams: The Evolution of a Black Writer* (1975).
Muller, Gilbert H. *John A. Williams* (1984).
—WILLIAM R. NASH

WILLIAMS, PAUL REVERE (18 Feb. 1894– 23 Jan. 1980), architect, was born in Los Angeles, California, to Chester Stanley Williams and Lila Wright Churchill. Orphaned by the age of four, he was raised by foster parents. His foster father, Charles Clarkson, was a bank janitor. Paul was one of only a few African American students at Sentous Elementary School on Pico Street. While at Los Angeles Polytechnic High School, Paul decided to become an architect after reading about African American architect William Sidney Pittman, BOOKER T. WASHINGTON's son-in-law and a graduate of Tuskegee Institute and Drexel Institute in Philadelphia.

Paul graduated high school in 1912, and the following year he went to work for Wilbur Cook Jr., a landscape architect. Two years later he took a job as a draftsman for noted Pasadena residential architect Reginald Johnson, and in 1919 Hollywood architect Arthur Kelly hired as him a junior architect. Williams's art training had begun with evening classes from 1915 to 1920 at the Los Angeles *atelier* of the Beaux Arts Institute of Design, where he learned rendering techniques and the use of

Architect Paul Revere Williams. Schomburg Center

color. From 1916 to 1919 he attended the School of Architecture, at University of California at Los Angeles although he left before earning a degree. In 1922 Williams took a position in the office of John Austin, an architect specializing in schools and government buildings.

Williams married Los Angeles native and socialite Della Mae Givens in June 1917. They had two children, Marilyn Francis and Norma Lucille, the latter of whom became an interior designer. In 1923 Williams opened his own office at the 1400 Stock Exchange Building in downtown Los Angeles. He secured his first major construction project by promising auto industrialist Everett Lobban Cord a complete set of sketches for a house, fifteen-car garage, swimming pool, and stables within twenty-four hours. Williams won the commission for the $250,000 country house. From the 1930s to the 1950s—his most productive period—Williams's office was located on the top floor of the swank Wilshire Building in downtown Beverly Hills. Williams was the most successful African American architect of his era in a business that necessitates a delicate balance of art and commerce. In 1948 his practice grossed $140,000. His drafting room, which at the

firm's height included twenty full-time people, was an interracial mix of Chinese, German, and African American architects. Unlike James Garrott, another Los Angeles African American architect, Williams did not go out of his way to apprentice "junior" architects. With as many as thirty projects on the boards simultaneously, he needed experienced architects in order to meet production deadlines.

A competitive tennis player, Williams was lithe and muscular. His matinee-idol good looks and chic Southern California "cool" style of attire helped Williams get his foot in the door of potential white clients. Once inside, he marketed himself assiduously. Williams was a medal-winning freehand artist who rendered all the buildings he designed. He taught himself to sketch upside down (right side up to the client). An eye-catching attention-getter, the technique also positioned him on the opposite side of the table from clients, avoiding a hovering stance that made some white clients uncomfortable. Swiftly and with flair, Williams sketched design ideas before awestruck potential clients. By 1935 Williams had received commissions for close to forty houses.

During the 1930s and 1940s Williams became known as the "architect to the

stars of Hollywood," and over the years his celebrity clients included Tyrone Power, Robert Holden, ZaSu Pitts, Julie London, Lon Chaney, William Paley, Charles Cottrell, Will Hays, Desi Arnaz and Lucille Ball, Anthony Quinn, and Otto Preminger. In 1956 Williams teamed up with his daughter Norma in designing the interior of Frank Sinatra's swinging bachelor's pad, creating custom-designed chandeliers, lamps, and furniture. Williams also designed several Hollywood restaurants and lounges famous for celebrity watching: Chasen's (1936), Perino's (1949), and the Beverly Hills Hotel Polo Lounge (1959).

Williams's architectural style captured the casual, informal, Mediterranean "look" characteristic of hot, sunny climates such as Southern California's. Williams was neither an innovator nor trendsetter like Frank Lloyd Wright, whom he knew personally and admired professionally. For nonresidential buildings he generally chose an "historic" Tudor or Georgian style, applying exterior details to a functional façade. For palatial homes he used a more modernist approach. Williams described his design philosophy in *Architecture Magazine* in 1940 as "the pleasing assembly of parts and not the assembly of pleasing parts." Williams was a master of interior color coordination and was meticulous about interior architectural detailing, whether it was the joinery of a spiral grand stair or cabinetry trim.

Williams was a versatile residential architect capable of designing one-hundred-thousand-dollar country houses as well as small, practical houses for World War II veterans. A collection of his floor plans for houses costing less than five thousand dollars were compiled in two books Williams wrote in 1946: *Small Homes of Tomorrow* and *New Homes for Today*. With the publication of these books, Williams became the first African American architect to have his books distributed nationwide. Flattering profiles on Williams in *Life*, and later *Ebony*, further heightened his name recognition and attracted clients.

Over his career Williams made a profound impression on the architecture of Los Angeles. While most of his business came from wealthy white clients building homes in upscale Los Angeles neighborhoods like Beverly Hills, Pacific Palisades, and Bel Air, his firm also designed commercial real estate, schools, and public buildings. Williams's designs include the Shrine Auditorium, the Hollywood YMCA, the Los Angeles County Court House, and the MCA Building in Beverly Hills, for which he won an American Institute of Architects (AIA) award in 1939. In the 1960s Williams served as an associate architect in the design of the Los Angeles International Airport, whose futuristic look became a visual icon of its era.

In 1936, acting on a referral from a friend in the industry who was a former client of Williams, Adam Gimbel had commissioned Williams to renovate the Beverly Hills annex of the Saks Fifth Avenue department store. Williams's use of motifs more typical of residential architecture—oval recessed ceilings, bowed counters, and curvilinear display cases—was credited with increasing retail sales. Other commercial projects followed over the years, including designs for the Arrowhead Springs Hotel, the W. & J. Sloan department store, the Palm Springs Tennis Club, the Golden State Mutual Life Insurance building, and the renovation of the Ambassador Hotel. Ecumenical in pursuit of church commissions, Williams designed the First Church of Christ, Scientist, in Reno, Nevada (1939), and St. Nicholas Orthodox Church (1948) and Founders Church of Religious Science (1960), both in Los Angeles. In 1962, at the behest of television comedian and benefactor Danny Thomas, Williams volunteered to design St. Jude's Children's Hospital in Memphis, Tennessee.

Williams was well aware, however, that as an African American, he could not live in many of the neighborhoods in which he designed houses. In the July 1937 *American* magazine article "I Am a Negro," Williams conceded, "Sometimes I have dreamed of living there," referring to a client's home. "I could afford such a home. But this evening, leaving my office, I returned to my small, inexpensive home in an unrestricted, comparatively undesirable section of Los Angeles...because...I am a Negro." Williams did, however, make several contributions to the architecture of Los Angeles's African

American community, including the Second Baptist Church (1924) and the 28th Street Colored YMCA.

Williams was the first African American architect with enough government buildings in his portfolio to qualify as having a government practice. As early as 1925 Williams was commissioned to design a U.S. Post Office in Ontario, California. President Herbert H. Hoover appointed him to direct the designing of a Negro Memorial to be erected in Washington, D.C. (which was never built). In 1937, in association with Washington, D.C., African American architect Hilyard Robert Robinson, Williams designed the 274-unit Langston Terrace Public Housing, the first federally financed public housing project. Back in Los Angeles, he worked as chief architect of the Pueblo Del Rio, a housing project built in 1941. After World War II Williams and six engineers formed Allied Engineers, Inc., which was contracted in 1947 by the Defense Department to design U.S. Navy bases in Los Alamitos, Long Beach, and San Diego, California. He was also the architect for the Grave of the Unknown Sailor (1953) at Pearl Harbor.

Williams gathered an impressive list of "firsts." He was the first African American appointed to serve on the Los Angles Planning Commission, which he did beginning in 1920. In 1923 he became the first black American architect licensed in the state of California; in 1935, the first admitted to the AIA; and in 1957, the first elevated to the distinguished rank of AIA Fellow. In 1943 he was the first African American chosen to serve on a Los Angeles County grand jury, and in 1953 he became the first architect to win the NAACP's prestigious Spingarn Medal.

Paul Williams closed his office in the mid-1970s, having designed more than three thousand buildings, and gracefully transitioned into retirement. Suffering from diabetes, he died at age eighty-six in 1980. His funeral was held at the First African Methodist Episcopal Church in Los Angeles, which he had designed seventeen years earlier.

FURTHER READING

Hudson, Karen E. *Paul Revere Williams: A Legacy of Style* (1993).

—DRECK WILSON

 WILLIAMS, PETER, JR. (1780?–17 Oct. 1840), clergyman and abolitionist, was born in New Brunswick, New Jersey, the son of Peter Williams, a slave, and Mary Durham, a black indentured servant from St. Kitts. A patriot soldier during the American Revolution, his father was sexton and undertaker for John Street Methodist Church in New York City. In an unusual arrangement, the church in 1783 purchased him from his departing Loyalist master and allowed him to purchase himself over time, completing his freedom in 1796. A founder of the African Methodist Episcopal Zion Church and a tobacconist and funeral home owner, he was a leader of the small black middle class in New York City.

Williams Jr. was educated first at the African Free School and tutored privately by a white minister, Reverend Thomas Lyell, of John Street Methodist Church. He became involved in Sunday afternoon black congregations at Trinity Episcopal Church, and in 1798 he was confirmed by John Henry Hobart. Williams was licensed by the Episcopal bishop in 1812 when the fledgling black Episcopalian group elected him lay reader. In the next six years Williams organized the congregation as a separate institution, acquired land, and constructed a church costing over eight thousand dollars, much of it contributed by wealthy white Episcopalians. In 1819 the new edifice was consecrated as St. Philip's African Church. The following year the wooden church burned down. It was fully insured, however, and a new brick church was quickly constructed. Baptismal rolls indicate that the church's membership included primarily black middle-class tradesmen and female domestics. Among the young candidates for baptism were future abolitionists JAMES MCCUNE SMITH, George Thomas Downing, ALEXANDER CRUMMELL, and Charles L. Reason.

Williams was a significant figure in black New York politics. He published a speech he had delivered celebrating the close of the slave trade in 1808, *An Oration on the Abolition of the Slave Trade: Delivered in the African Church, in the City of New York.* He was a prominent member of the African Society for Mutual Relief, a benefit and burial organization. In 1817 he preached the funeral sermon after the death of his close friend, colonizationist PAUL CUFFE SR.

Despite deep reservations about the white American Colonization Society, Williams remained open to the possibility of voluntary black migration out of the United States. He favored colonization to the black republic of Haiti and visited there in 1824. In 1830 he delivered a speech at St. Philip's for the benefit of the Wilberforce colony in Canada. He also helped JOHN BROWN RUSSWURM immigrate to Liberia in 1829 under the aegis of the American Colonization Society. Williams increasingly believed, however, that blacks should remain in the United States to work for full citizenship. He eventually denounced the efforts of the American Colonization Society as racist.

Although Williams enjoyed equality in reform organizations, he was forced to accept an inferior status within the Episcopal Church, where he finally advanced to priesthood in 1826. His mentor, Bishop Henry Hobart, counseled him not to seek representation for himself or St. Philip's at the diocesan convention, even though all white clerics and churches assumed this privilege. Williams nevertheless accepted these limitations.

Williams was ubiquitous in black reform efforts in the late 1820s and 1830s. He was cofounder in 1827 of *Freedom's Journal*, the first black newspaper. A staunch believer in black education, in 1833 he helped found the Phoenix Society in New York, which enabled poor blacks to attend school, encouraged church attendance, and established a library. Williams personally assisted several young blacks, including Alexander Crummell, and frequently wrote letters of recommendation to potential white employers. Very active in the early black national convention movement, Williams was inspired by the 1831 convention to attempt to establish a manual training college in New Haven, Connecticut (the attempt was unsuccessful).

In 1833 Williams became deeply involved in the American Anti-Slavery Society as one of six black managers. In 1834 he suffered terribly for his beliefs. During early July, white mobs, angered by abolitionist efforts and competition

with blacks for jobs, and inflamed by rumors of interracial marriages, terrorized New York City blacks for three days. After hearing rumors that Williams performed an interracial marriage, a mob sacked and burned St. Philip's and its rectory. Rather than support and defend Williams, Bishop Benjamin T. Onderdonk demanded that Williams refrain from public abolitionist activity. Reluctantly, Williams acceded to Onderdonk's commands. In a moving statement, published in New York newspapers, he described childhood conversations with his father about his revolutionary war service. His father's words, he said, "filled my soul with an ardent love for the American government." Williams longed for the day when his brethren "would all have abundant reason to rejoice in the glorious Declaration of American Independence." He also expressed his lifelong love for New York City. Although his congregation supported him, acquiescence cost him much respect among younger, more militant black abolitionists. Williams continued to work for social reform and lead St. Philip's until his death in New York City.

FURTHER READING

Williams, Peter, Jr. "Response to Bishop Benjamin T. Onderdonk," *Journal of Negro History* 11 (1926): 181–85.

DeCosta, B. F. *Three Score and Ten: The Story of St. Philip's Church* (1889).
Porter, Dorothy, ed. *Early Negro Writing, 1760–1834* (1971).
Ripley, C. Peter, et al., eds. *The Black Abolitionist Papers* (5 vols., 1985–1992), especially vol. 3.

—GRAHAM HODGES

WILLIAMS, SMOKEY JOE (6 Apr. 1886–25 Feb. 1951), baseball player and manager, was born Joseph Williams in Seguin, Texas, the son of an unknown African American father and Lettie Williams, a Native American. He attended school in San Antonio, but it is not known how many years he completed. As a young boy Joe was given a baseball, which he carried with him everywhere and which he even slept with under his pillow. He pitched in the sandlots around Seguin

until 1905, when he began playing professionally with the San Antonio Black Broncos. Williams quickly became the ace of the pitching staff and in the following seasons posted records of 28–4, 15–9, 20–8, 20–2, and 32–8, all with San Antonio except 1906, when he played with Austin. In the autumn of 1909 he signed to play with the Trilbys of Los Angeles, California, which marked the first of many years that he played baseball in both summer and winter.

In 1910 Joe was recruited by Chicago Giants' owner Frank Leland, who wrote, "If you have ever witnessed the speed of a pebble in a storm you have not even seen the speed possessed by this wonderful Texan Giant" (Riley, 856). The Giants were the only black team in the semiprofessional Chicago League

Smokey Joe Williams, known as "Cyclone," whose fastball struck fear in the hearts of batters. National Baseball Hall of Fame Library, Cooperstown, N.Y.

that season. Williams then played during the 1910–1911 winter in California, where he compiled a 4–1 record with 78 strikeouts in 60 innings. After another season with the Giants, Williams made his first visit to Cuba, where he tied for the most wins, with a 10–7 record for the 1911–1912 Cuban Winter League champion Havana Reds. In the spring of 1912 he toured with the Chicago American Giants on the West Coast and defeated every Pacific Coast League team except Portland, finishing the tour with a 9–1 record.

After the 1912 tour Williams joined the New York Lincoln Giants for $105 a month; he remained with the franchise through 1923. At this point of his career he was called "Cyclone," but later in his career he would become better known as "Smokey Joe." With the Lincoln Giants, Joe joined another hard-throwing right-hander, "Cannonball" Dick Redding, and the duo pitched the Lincolns to the Eastern Championship in 1912. After the close of the 1912 regular season, Williams shut out John McGraw's National League champion New York Giants 6–0 on four hits while fanning nine. A week later he tossed another four-hit shutout, defeating Hal Chase's All-Stars, a team comprised mostly of New York Yankees. Joe was at his best against white major leaguers and compiled a lifetime 20–7 record against them. When the weather turned cold, the Lincoln Giants toured Cuba, where Joe split a pair of games with Cuban ace José Mendez. After the tour ended, Williams stayed on the island and had a 9–5 record to lead the Fe team to the 1913 Cuban Winter League championship.

After returning to the United States for the 1913 summer season, Williams jumped to the Mohawk Giants of Schenectady, New York, but the Lincoln Giants quickly paid him five hundred dollars to return, and he pitched the team to their finest season, capping the year with six victories in the championship series against RUBE FOSTER's Chicago American Giants. When the triumphant Lincoln Giants returned to New York, a large crowd was on hand at Olympic Park to welcome them home. In the fall Williams resumed his postseason performances against major leaguers. He struck out sixteen in a two-hit 9–1 win over Mike Donlin's All-Stars, fanned nine in defeating Hall-of-Famer Grover Cleveland Alexander and the Philadelphia Phillies 9–2, whiffed twelve in a 1–0 loss to Earl Mack's All-Stars, avenged that loss when he fanned fourteen to take a 7–3 win over the same team, and hurled a three-hit 2–1 victory over a white all-star team that featured Chief Bender, the Philadelphia Athletics ace pitcher.

In 1914 Williams joined the Chicago American Giants during their preseason spring barnstorming tour through the Northwest and pitched a no-hitter against Portland. Back with the Lincoln Giants for the regular season, he compiled a record of 41–3 against all levels of opposition. In the fall Williams again faced major league opposition, defeating the Philadelphia Phillies 10–4, and then fanning a dozen as he battled Hall-of-Famer Rube Marquard and the New York Giants to a 1–1 draw that was ended by darkness.

Williams suffered two injuries in 1915, a broken arm and a broken wrist, and missed much of the season, but was back in action by the fall exhibition games against major leaguers. He struck out nine in a 3–0 shutout over a combination of players from the Federal League's Buffalo and Brooklyn franchises, and fanned ten in pitching a three-hit 1–0 shutout over the National League champion Philadelphia Phillies. In the winter of 1915–1916 Williams pitched for the Chicago American Giants in California, making his last appearance on the West Coast. Later that winter he also made his final appearance in Cuba, when he joined the struggling San Francisco franchise for the second half of the season. He finished with a lifetime 22–15 record in the Cuban Winter League.

In 1917 Hilldale, a team based in the Philadelphia suburb of that name, scheduled a postseason series against major leaguers and recruited Williams to pitch. Williams rose to the occasion and defeated Connie Mack's Philadelphia Athletics 6–2, beating Athletics' ace Joe Bush, and then whiffed ten in a ten-inning 5–4 win over Rube Marquard and Chief Meyers's All-Leaguers. Joe also fanned twenty and tossed a no-hitter against John McGraw's National League champion New York Giants but lost the game 1–0 on an error. According to oral accounts, in this game Giants' star Ross Youngs gave him the nickname "Smokey Joe."

As manager of the Lincoln Giants, Williams took his team to Palm Beach, Florida, in the winter of 1917–1918 to represent the Breakers Hotel in the Florida Hotel League, where they opposed Rube Foster's Royal Poinciana team. In one memorable match-up, Williams struck out nine and tossed a two-hitter to out-duel his old rival Dick Redding 1–0. Williams continued playing and managing in the winter Florida Hotel League for several years, including a stint as manager of the Royal Poinciana team in 1926.

There was no dominant team in the East in 1918, but when Williams pitched, the Lincoln Giants were the best team. He defeated rival Brooklyn Royal Giants' ace lefthander John Donaldson 1–0 and 3–2 on successive weekends, and in the fall he continued his pitching prowess against major leaguers and fashioned an 8–0 shutout over Marquard and his All-Nationals team. On opening day 1919 the largest crowd to ever attend a game in Harlem watched Williams hurl a no-hit 1–0 masterpiece over Redding and the Brooklyn Royal Giants.

In 1922 Williams married Beatrice Johnson, a Broadway showgirl, and they had one daughter. In the spring of 1924 he became a victim of the Lincoln Giants' preference for young players and was released. He joined the Brooklyn Royal Giants and, although he was their top pitcher, was released after the season. Williams then joined the Homestead Grays in 1925 and remained with the franchise through 1932. During his years with the Grays, the nickname "Smokey Joe" was used almost exclusively, and he developed a mystique about his age, encouraging people to think that he was older than he was, that the press kept alive.

In 1929 owner Cum Posey entered the Grays in the American Negro League, and Williams, appointed captain, compiled a 12–7 record. The league folded after its only year of existence, and in the absence of an eastern league, the Grays returned to independent play. In 1930 Williams and Chet Brewer hooked up in a historic pitching duel under the Kansas City Monarchs' portable lighting system, with Joe fanning twenty-seven batters in the twelve-inning game while allowing only one hit in a 1–0 victory. At the end of the season the Grays defeated Williams's old team, the New York Lincoln Giants, in a playoff for the Eastern championship. In 1931 the Grays fielded one of the greatest teams in the history of the Negro Leagues. As an aging veteran, Williams paired with the youthful JOSH GIBSON to form an exceptional battery.

Following his retirement from baseball, Williams worked as a bartender in Harlem. In 1950 he was honored with a special day at the Polo Grounds in ceremonies before a game between the New York Cubans and Indianapolis Clowns. Less than a year later, in 1951, he died of a brain hemorrhage in New York City. In a 1952 poll conducted by the *Pittsburgh Courier*, Smokey Joe was chosen the greatest pitcher in the history of black baseball, winning over SATCHEL PAIGE by one vote. In 1999 he was elected to the National Baseball Hall of Fame in Cooperstown, New York.

FURTHER READING

Holway, John. *Black Ball Stars: Negro League Pioneers* (1988).
Peterson, Robert. *Only the Ball Was White* (1970).
Riley, James A. *The Biographical Encyclopedia of the Negro Baseball Leagues* (1994).

—JAMES A. RILEY

WILLIAMS, VENUS

(17 June 1980–), and **SERENA WILLIAMS** (26 Sept. 1981–), professional tennis players, are the fourth and fifth daughters, respectively, born to Richard Williams, a security agency owner, and Oracene Price, a nurse. Venus Ebone Starr Williams was born in Lynwood, California, and Serena Williams in Saginaw, Michigan. Both girls were homeschooled. By age ten Venus had won the under-twelve division tennis title in Southern California and was on the front page of the *New York Times* and in *Sports Illustrated*. In 1991 the family moved from Compton, California, so that Venus could accept a scholarship at Rick Macci's tennis academy in Haines City, Florida.

At the age of fourteen, in October 1994, Venus turned professional at the Bank of the West Classic in Oakland,

Serena (left) and Venus Williams work together in their Ladies Doubles match at Wimbledon, 2003. © AFP/CORBIS

California, where she nearly upset second-ranked Arantxa Sanchez Vicario. She also put in limited appearances on the circuit before making her major debut at the 1997 French Open. At the start of the 1997 season she was ranked 211th in the world. By the end of the year she had climbed to 64th. Serena, meanwhile, attended a private high school in Miami, and she, too, turned pro at age fourteen, in 1995. Although she was ranked only 304th in 1997, Serena defeated fourth-ranked Monica Seles and seventh-ranked Mary Pierce at a tournament in Chicago, in only her fifth professional tournament.

During the 1998 season Venus reached the semifinals of the U.S. Open, advanced to the quarterfinals at the Australian Open, the French Open, and Wimbledon, and won her first career singles title, the IGA Tennis Classic in Oklahoma City. Her serve was clocked that year at an unprecedented 127 miles per hour. Serena started the year ranked number 96, but climbed to number 40 after besting several higher-ranked players and losing narrowly to the world's top-ranked player, Martina Hingis. In 1999 Venus defended her Lipton title by beating Serena in the first WTA Tour final between siblings

and won her first singles title on clay, in Hamburg, Germany. That year the Williamses became the first sisters to be ranked simultaneously in the top ten and the first sisters in the twentieth century to win a Grand Slam doubles crown at the French Open. Serena continued to improve her game, winning her first singles title at an indoor tournament in Paris, France.

Serena's dramatic breakthrough came at the 1999 U.S. Open, when, seeded seventh, she upset Martina Hingis, Lindsay Davenport, and Monica Seles, the number one, two, and four seeds, respectively, to win her first career Grand Slam singles title. Serena was the first African American woman to win the singles title since ALTHEA GIBSON won the last of her five U.S. championships in 1958. She and Venus also joined forces to win the U.S. Open doubles title that year.

The year 2000 proved to be even more successful for the Williamses. Venus won her first two Grand Slam singles titles, at Wimbledon and the U.S. Open, and she and Serena won the Wimbledon doubles title. At the Olympic Games in Sydney, Australia, Venus won the singles gold medal, and when the two sisters then took the gold medal in the doubles, she became the first tennis player to win both Olympic titles since 1924.

At the 2001 U.S. Open, Venus faced her sister Serena for the title in the finals. The match was an exciting event that drew a crowd of celebrities and high television ratings, in part, at least, because the two sisters had become superstars in a sport traditionally dominated by white athletes. It was the first time since 1884 that two sisters had played each other in a Grand Slam final, and the first time that two African Americans had competed against each other in the final. Their father, Richard, had a difficult time watching the match and left before its conclusion, when Venus beat Serena, 6-2, 6-4. To cap off her banner year, Venus received the ESPY award for Outstanding Women's Tennis Performance.

Serena's first title in 2001 generated controversy when she was scheduled to face Venus in the semifinal of the State Farm Evert Cup in Indian Wells, California. When Venus withdrew from the match, rumors circulated that their father had ordered her to not play against Serena. He charged the crowd with racism, saying, "I really just think a lot of people in tennis and the business world are jealous of me. They'd rather see me sweeping the floor at the U.S. Open or picking cotton somewhere. But I'm not" (*Newsweek*, 2 July 2001). The sisters continued their winning ways and their emerging rivalry into 2002, with Serena dominating her older sister. She beat Venus for the first time since 1999 in Miami and again in the finals of the French Open, after which they became the first siblings to be ranked first and second in the world. Serena won three Grand Slam titles in 2002, Wimbledon, the French Open, and the U.S. Open, putting her in the select company of only seven women who have won three consecutive major titles. Venus won four WTA tour titles and was runner-up to Serena at Wimbledon and the U.S. Open.

Serena continued to dominate Venus in the 2003 season, besting her for the Australian title, the one Grand Slam title Serena had not been able to win. She also defeated Venus in the ladies' singles at Wimbledon, in a match that many observers viewed as a complex psychological battle. Serena appeared

initially unwilling to punish her sister's weaknesses—Venus was suffering from leg, hip, and stomach injuries—but she eventually recaptured the form that had led her to the final with some ease. Venus later revealed that she had played through great pain and would have retired from the match had her opponent been anyone other than her sister.

Venus's heroic and gracious performance in the 2003 Wimbledon final perhaps answers those critics who have suggested that the sisters default from matches too easily, especially when they play each other. But it seems likely that the dominance of the game by two sisters will continue to provoke controversy.

The role of Richard Williams, their father and coach, has also been highly controversial. Williams has been outspoken in defending his daughters from criticism, claiming that their critics are motivated by a combination of racism and jealousy. When his daughters sign endorsement deals, Williams requests that the companies donate goods to the black community. He has also criticized the WTA for being "a close-knit community that tends to embrace its own. We've never been a part of it. But then, we never planned to be a part of them either. We're a part of ourselves. People can criticize me and complain about me, but no one wants to see a tournament that Venus and Serena aren't in. We breathed life into this game, and people dislike us for it" (*Newsweek*, 2 July 2001). Richard Williams's criticisms can hardly be leveled at advertisers and the media, however, who have ensured that the Williams sisters have become the most prominent women in professional sports. In 2000 Venus signed a five-year, forty-million-dollar contract with Reebok International, the highest amount ever paid to a female athlete. She and Serena together signed a deal with Avon, making them the first athletes since Jackie Joyner-Kersee to represent the world's largest direct seller of beauty products. Avon then in the process of aggressively marketing its products to the growing global teenage market, could hardly have chosen better examples of attractive, successful young woman hood. As one Avon representative stated, "These were two very young women who were all about

empowerment and caring and sharing. Their appeal goes very far and wide" (*Advertising Age*, 22 Jan. 2001).

Despite the earlier successes of LUCY DIGGS SLOWE, ORA MAE WASHINGTON, Althea Gibson, and ARTHUR ASHE, most Americans have tended to view tennis as a white upper-class sport. Like TIGER WOODS in golf, the Williams sisters have taken it as their mission to persuade African Americans that it is their game too.

FURTHER READING

Jenkins, Sally, and David Bailey. "Double Trouble," *Women's Sports and Fitness*, Nov./Dec. 1998.

Noel, Peter, and Amanda Ward. "Fear of the Williams Sisters," *Village Voice*, 14 Nov. 2000.

Samuels, Allison. "Life with Father," *Newsweek*, 2 July 2001.

—MAUREEN M. SMITH

WILSON, AUGUST

(27 Apr. 1945–), playwright, was born Frederick August Kittel in Pittsburgh, Pennsylvania, the fourth of six children of Frederick Kittel, a German baker who emigrated to the United States at age ten, and Daisy Wilson, a cleaning woman. Frederick Kittel was an infrequent visitor to the family's two-room apartment in the city's racially mixed Hill District. As an adult, August symbolically severed ties to his father by taking his mother's maiden name, Wilson.

In 1959 David Bedford, Wilson's stepfather, moved the family to the white suburb of Hazelwood, Pennsylvania, where Wilson attended Central Catholic High School. He suffered racial taunts from other students and transferred the following year to Gladstone High School, where the greatest assault on his intelligence came from a black teacher who accused him of plagiarizing a twenty-page paper, believing that Wilson was not capable of writing such lucid prose. Confused and frustrated, Wilson dropped out of school in the ninth grade. He worked at a series of odd jobs, wandered the streets, and found solace in the public library, where he took responsibility for completing his own education, devouring the works of LANGSTON HUGHES, JAMES BALDWIN,

RICHARD WRIGHT, and the Welsh poet Dylan Thomas. With no career goal in mind, he joined the army just shy of his eighteenth birthday and was discharged a year later, unable to conform to the strict rules of the military.

Wilson's life started to come into focus on 1 April 1965, when he purchased a twenty-dollar typewriter and began to explore the written word as a critical means of self-expression and as a viable occupation. His first efforts were highly charged poems that might be appreciated for their passion, though their precise meanings could be a mystery even to their author. Wilson's aesthetic sensibilities were forged by the emerging Black Arts Movement, which identified culture as an important battleground and enlisted black artists in every medium as soldiers in the struggle for racial liberation. Just as W. E. B. DU BOIS influenced artists of his generation with the publication of "Criteria of Negro Art" during the Harlem Renaissance, Wilson and his cohorts were influenced by AMIRI BARAKA, who, in his poem "Black Art," called for "poems like fists" and urged his generation to use their creative talents to achieve collective ends. Imbued with this philosophy, Wilson drew inspiration from blues musicians such as BESSIE SMITH and visual artists such as ROMARE BEARDEN for both their cultural relevance and their aesthetic excellence.

Wilson began to establish his credentials and reputation as both an artist and an advocate for black theater by becoming a founding member of the Center Avenue Poet's Theater Workshop and, with Rob Penney in 1967, an organizer of the Black Horizon Theater Company. "Youngblood," as Wilson was called by his friends, published his first poems, "Muhammad Ali" and "For Malcolm X and Others," in *Black World* and the *Negro Digest* in 1969. In 1972 his three-year marriage to Brenda Burton, a member of the Nation of Islam with whom he had one child, ended in divorce. The following year Wilson wrote his first play, *Recycle*, exploring the painful disintegration of a marriage. *The Homecoming*, a play based on the mysterious death of the legendary blues guitarist BLIND LEMON JEFFERSON, was performed at the University of Pittsburgh's Kuntu Theater in 1976. Yet Wilson still considered himself to be primarily a poet until 1978, when he accepted an assignment in St. Paul to write children's plays for the Science Museum of Minnesota.

Writing convincing dialogue was difficult for Wilson until he was encouraged by his friend Claude Purdy at the Playwrights Center in Minneapolis to listen to the authentic voices of his characters and allow them to tell the story. In 1977, drawing on this advice, Wilson completed *Black Bart and the Sacred Hills*, a musical satire based on the infamous outlaw. In 1978 Wilson moved to St. Paul, where he met Judy Oliver, a white social worker whom he married in 1981. Wilson then wrote *Jitney* (1979), a two-act play centered on the lives of men in a gypsy cab station who confront the problems of urban renewal, the Vietnam War, and a developing generation gap. The local acclaim that *Jitney* received allowed Wilson to begin thinking of himself as a serious playwright. Later, in describing his development, Wilson said with pride, "I consider it a blessing that when I started writing plays in earnest, in 1979, I had not read Chekov. I hadn't read Ibsen. I hadn't read Tennessee Williams, Arthur Miller, or O'Neill.... It took me eight years to find my own voice as a poet. I didn't want to take eight years to find my voice as a playwright" (Lahr, 53).

Critics have not missed the irony that America's most celebrated black playwright, whose plays make millions on Broadway, are financed by white producers, and win the acclaim of New York socialites, is, in fact, an "unrepentant black nationalist" (*New York Times*, 2 Feb. 2003) who publicly champions independent black theater and supports race-specific casting. Taking note of this apparent contradiction, Henry Louis Gates Jr. opined, "The Revolution will not be subsidized" (Gates, 138). However, Wilson's entrée into the elite circles in which he now travels was made possible by the support of a black network, particularly Lloyd Richards, an influential black insider who had directed LORRAINE HANSBERRY'S *A Raisin in the Sun* in 1959. By 1982, when Wilson met him, Richards was dean of the Yale Drama School and director of the National Playwrights Conference of the Eugene O'Neill Center in Waterford, Connecticut, which invited Wilson to be one of fifteen playwrights that summer to have their work critiqued and staged. Wilson's play was *MA RAINEY's Black Bottom*, set in a recording studio in Chicago during the 1920s. The depth and complexity he weaves into a single day in the life of the audacious blues singer and her musicians elevate Wilson's exposition of racism beyond mere agitprop to a nuanced tale of exploitation, the struggle for dignity, and the dangers of uncontrolled and misdirected rage.

Richards brought Wilson and the actor Charles Dutton, who would play the lead in *Ma Rainey's Black Bottom*, to the Yale Repertory Theater, where Richards was the artistic director and their future producer, Ben Mordecai, was the managing director. Together with Wilson they further refined the play before bringing it to the Cort Theater on Broadway in 1984. It won both the New York Drama Critics' Circle Award and a Tony nomination in 1985. Richards would direct Wilson's next six plays, usually opening at the O'Neill, continuing at Yale, and traveling a circuit of local theaters on the way to Broadway, where each play in turn also won the Drama Critic's Circle Award.

Wilson and Richards next produced *Fences* (1987). Set in the 1950s and partly based on Wilson's stepfather, the play uses a sports plot to explore the physical and emotional barriers that fragment the lives of black men. *Fences* garnered a Pulitzer Prize and a Tony Award and grossed eleven million dollars. Wilson's favorite play, *Joe Turner's Come and Gone* (1988), set in 1911, explores themes of cultural dislocation and the search for identity as the main characters struggle to make the transition from slavery to freedom and have difficulty embracing an African heritage infused with occult mystery. *The Piano Lesson* (1990) turns on the dilemma of a family in the 1930s confronted with a decision to keep or sell the piano that links them with their past. This play earned Wilson a second Pulitzer and brought him together with his third wife, Constanza Romero, who designed costumes for the Yale production; they have one child. *Two Trains Running* (1992) takes place in a 1960s diner that becomes a window into the hearts and minds of its patrons, each of whom presents a slice of black life. *Seven Guitars* (1996) is ostensibly about a group of musicians in the 1940s who gather to remember the life of a blues guitarist tragically cut down on the verge of fame. Ultimately, however, their soliloquies combine to bespeak the blues of an entire people.

With the Broadway production of *Jitney* (2000), Richards was replaced by Marion McClinton, who has directed all of Wilson's subsequent plays. Wilson's break with Richards divides his career into two eras that are, nevertheless, united by an overarching objective: capturing the African American experience by devoting one play to each decade of the twentieth century. With *King Hedley II* (1999), a look at the desperate conditions and pandemic ills of the 1980s, and *Gem of the Ocean* (2002), a play set in 1904 about a man on the run who passes through a labyrinth of challenges leading to self-discovery, Wilson is poised to achieve his goal. Indeed, no playwright in history has explored so much of the African American odyssey in drama. Wilson has placed race center stage in the American theater and has advanced a philosophical discussion about the roles of history and art.

FURTHER READING

Bogumil, Mary L. *Understanding August Wilson* (1999).

Gates, Henry Louis, Jr. "The Chitlin Circuit" in *African American Performance and Theater History*, eds. Harry J. Elam Jr. and David Krasner (2001).

Lahr, John. "Been Here and Gone," *New Yorker*, 16 Apr. 2001.

Shannon, Sandra G. *The Dramatic Vision of August Wilson* (1995).

—SHOLOMO B. LEVY

 WILSON, HARRIET E.

(c. 1828?–?), servant and writer, was born Harriet Adams to parents whose names and occupations remain unidentified. Very little is known about the woman who, in 1859, published *Our Nig*, the first novel published by an African American in the United States and one of the first novels published by a black woman in any country. Harriet was probably born in 1827 or 1828 in Milford, New Hampshire, according

to her marriage record and federal census records. Although there is no record of Harriet's education, the quality of writing in *Our Nig* and the skillful use of epigraphs, including excerpts from Shelley, Byron, and Thomas Moore, indicate that she received some schooling. Evidence suggests that Harriet spent her childhood and adolescence living with and in service to the Nehemiah Hayward family. Following nineteenth-century trends in poor relief, Harriet would have been "bound out" to the Haywards as an indentured servant. After the Haywards moved to Baltimore in 1847, it appears that Harriet remained behind and supported herself until 1850, when her name appears on Milford's charity roll.

Records show that in 1851 Harriet married Thomas Wilson in Milford and that in the spring of 1852 a son, George Mason Wilson, was born in nearby Goffstown. There is no further trace of Thomas Wilson, who seems to have abandoned his wife before the birth of their son. Because Milford's charity reports for 1851–1854 are missing, there is no evidence as to whether Wilson needed financial assistance during these years. She is, however, listed on Milford's charity rolls in 1855 and 1856, and documents indicate that her son, then three years old, spent a month on the county poor farm in 1855. Charity reports for 1857–1859 list only "Harriet E. Wilson's child," suggesting that Wilson left her son behind in New Hampshire. City directories show that Wilson was most probably living in Boston during these years.

On 18 August 1859 a "Mrs. H. E. Wilson" copyrighted *Our Nig*, and the book was published several weeks later, on 5 September. Wilson states in the preface to *Our Nig* that she was motivated to write the book by financial reasons: "Deserted by kindred, disabled by failing health, I am forced to some experiment which shall aid me in maintaining myself and child.... I sincerely appeal to my colored brethren universally for patronage." Sadly, only five months after the publication of *Our Nig*, Wilson's seven-year-old son, George Mason, died of "bilious fever." Wilson reappears on Milford's 1863 charity roll, after which there is no trace of her in either Milford or Boston records. The date of her death is unknown.

Our Nig; or, Sketches from the Life of a Free Black, in a Two-Story White House, North. Showing That Slavery's Shadows Fall Even There, By "Our Nig" was printed by G. C. Rand and Avery in Boston, Massachusetts, in 1859. *Our Nig*'s protagonist is Alfrado, nicknamed Frado, the daughter of Mag, a white servant, and Jim, a free black artisan. After her father's death, Frado, then five or six years old, is abandoned by her mother and left with the Bellmonts, a white family for whom she works as an indentured servant until she is eighteen. Most of the novel describes the brutal treatment and severe deprivation Frado receives at the hands of Mrs. Bellmont and her daughter. Despite occasional attempts by the male members of the Bellmont family to protect her, Frado is treated so harshly that her health is permanently ruined. In the last pages of the book, Frado marries Samuel, a fugitive slave "lecturer" who, before deserting her, discloses "that he had never seen the South, and that his illiterate harangues were humbugs for hungry abolitionists" (128). Their son is born on the county poor farm, and Frado is forced to give him over to the county's care shortly after he is weaned. Looking for work, she travels through New England, facing contempt by racists unwilling to help, until a kind woman gives her a recipe for a home remedy, which Frado begins to sell. *Our Nig* ends with an appeal to the reader for financial assistance.

When the scholar Henry Louis Gates Jr. bought *Our Nig* at a used bookshop in 1981, he could not foresee that his fifty-dollar investment would alter African American literary scholarship, causing a literary sensation. Gates and his research team found only a handful of nineteenth- and twentieth-century references to the novel, most of which listed the author as white or male or both. But after a copyright search at the Library of Congress yielded the name "Mrs. H. E. Wilson," Gates set out to identify the novel's author and establish her race. Research confirmed, through city directories, that a "Harriet Wilson" lived in Boston during the time of *Our Nig*'s publication. They then found an 1850 census document listing Wilson's race as black. (The questionnaire's choices were "white," "black," or "mulatto.") Further historical detective work produced Wilson's 1851 marriage record and the 1860 death certificate of her son, George Mason. "Ironically," Gates explained, "George's death certificate helped to rescue his mother from literary oblivion.... The *record* of his death, *alone*, proved sufficient to demonstrate his mother's racial identity and authorship of *Our Nig*" (xiii).

Gates's reconstruction of Wilson's life, augmented by other scholars, shows the novel to be a semiautobiographical work written by Harriet E. Wilson. While the novel's fictional form allows Wilson greater narrative and creative possibilities than traditional autobiography, *Our Nig* is grounded in the economic deprivation and racism Wilson herself had experienced. Wilson borrows heavily from her own life in fashioning Frado's life, although some events, including the mixed marriage of Frado's parents, are probably fictional creations.

The complexity of *Our Nig* begins with its title. Gates was immediately drawn to Wilson's daring and ironic use of the racist epithet *"Our Nig"*: "Harriet E. Wilson allows these racist characters to name her heroine, only to *invert* such racism by employing the name, in inverted commas, as her pseudonym of authorship" (li). The descriptive phrasing of Wilson's subtitle, "in a Two-Story White House, North. Showing That Slavery's Shadows Fall Even There," highlights the book's explicit indictment of northern racism and the hypocrisy of many northern abolitionists. "My mistress was wholly imbued with *southern* principles," Wilson offers in *Our Nig*'s preface. Anticipating a hostile reaction from abolitionists, she continues, "I have purposely omitted what would most provoke shame in our good anti-slavery friends at home." By the novel's end, however, Wilson has dropped her accommodating tone: "Strange were some of her adventures. Watched by kidnappers, maltreated by professed abolitionists, who didn't want slaves at the South, nor niggers in their own houses, North. Faugh! to lodge one; to eat with one; to admit one through the front door; to sit next to one; awful!" (129). While Wilson's candor underlies the novel's daring, it also doomed sales of her book. "All the abolitionists chose to ignore *Our Nig*," Gates explains. "There were two things you couldn't do if you were a foe of slavery. One was to write

about racism in the North—and this book is all about racism in the North. Second, the man Alfrado marries is a black man pretending to be an escaped slave" (*New York Times*, 8 Nov. 1982).

Our Nig is the first representation in American fiction of an interracial marriage in which the wife is white and the husband is black. Furthermore, this unusual literary union is brought about by a black man's pity for a destitute white woman and is presented in a positive light: "He loved Mag to the last. So long as life continued, he stifled his sensibility to pain, and toiled for her sustenance long after he was able to do so" (15). Along with Wilson's fundamental reconfiguration of the theme and character of the "tragic mulatto," the novel's other characters—the brutal Bellmont women, ineffectual Bellmont men, the "fugitive slave" con artist, Samuel—are equally complex, refusing to adhere to strict literary racial or gender stereotypes.

"Wilson's achievement," Gates argues, "is that she combines the received conventions of the sentimental novel with certain key conventions of the slave narrative, then combines the two into *one new form*" (lii). *Our Nig* conforms to many of the conventions of the sentimental novel but deviates from the formula in its ambiguous ending, in which the heroine neither triumphs nor lives happily ever after. Instead, Wilson appeals directly to the reader for financial support. In the tradition of slave narratives, which often include testimonial letters from whites to help get works published, *Our Nig* appends three supporting letters attesting to the truthfulness of the narrative and pleading for the "friends of our dark-skinned brethren and sisters" to help the author by buying the book. Scholars continue to debate whether the letters are, in fact, authentic recommendations or were created by Wilson to mimic the slave narrative model.

When ALICE WALKER first encountered *Our Nig*, she "sat up most of the night reading and pondering the enormous significance of Harriet Wilson's novel *Our Nig*. It is as if we'd just discovered PHILLIS WHEATLEY—or LANGSTON HUGHES" (quoted in Wilson, vii). Since its initial publication in 1982, *Our Nig* has been canonized by its inclusion in major anthologies and classroom

curricula worldwide. Written during a critical period for African Americans marked by the DRED SCOTT decision (1857), the Fugitive Slave Act of 1850, and the Kansas-Nebraska Act (1854), *Our Nig* offers unique insights into the circumstances of a quarter-million free blacks in the North and especially into the lives of black women living in small-town New England. Before the rediscovery and verification of *Our Nig*, it was believed that the first African American–authored novel published in the United States was written after the Civil War by a man. "Harriet Wilson's novel," Gates concludes, "inaugurates the Afro-American literary tradition in a manner more fundamentally *formal* than did either WILLIAM WELLS BROWN or Frank J. Webb" (xlvi–xlvii).

FURTHER READING

Wilson, Harriet E. *Our Nig; or, Sketches from the Life of a Free Black, in a Two-Story White House, North. Showing That Slavery's Shadows Fall Even There*, ed. Henry Louis Gates Jr., with an afterword by Barbara A. White (1859; repr. 2002).

—LISA E. RIVO

WILSON, WILLIAM JULIUS (20 Dec. 1935–),

sociologist, was born in Derry Township, Pennsylvania, one of six children of Esco Wilson, a coal miner and steelworker, and Pauline Bracy. Wilson grew up in Blairsville, a small mining town outside of blue-collar Pittsburgh, and his family struggled alongside neighboring black families, all of whom experienced firsthand the slow decline of American manufacturing in the postwar era. Blairsville, Wilson later suggested, helped him realize the importance of work in organizing personal and family life, a theme that would echo in all of his writings. On graduating from high school, Wilson left for Ohio, where he attended Wilberforce University, receiving a BA in 1958. After earning an MA at Bowling Green State University in 1961, he headed west to study at Washington State University. He earned his doctorate there in 1966, a year after he received his first full time teaching position, as an assistant

Sociologist William Julius Wilson, whose book The Truly Disadvantaged *is an unflinching assessment of the causes of urban poverty.* Courtesy of Martha Stewart

professor of sociology at the University of Massachusetts at Amherst.

Although Wilson is best known for his work on urban poverty in the United States, he began his career as a comparativist, focusing in particular on race relations in South Africa under apartheid and America during the civil rights era. In the late 1960s and early 1970s he began work on *Power, Racism and Privilege* (1973), a set of essays in which he examines the relationship of race and social inequality in South Africa and the United States. Wilson married Beverly Huebner in 1971; they had two children. Wilson also had two children from a previous marriage to Mildred Hood.

In 1972 Wilson began teaching in the Department of Sociology at the University of Chicago. In doing so, he continued a long-standing tradition at the university, one that could be traced to the writings of Robert Park and E. FRANKLIN FRAZIER, of addressing American race relations. Wilson credited his arrival in Chicago for helping him to see the variegated class structure in America's black community. While the city's class-segregated black neighborhoods motivated his thinking, Chicago itself did not appear prominently in either of his first two books. This changed in the late 1970s as Wilson initiated several major research initiatives in the city.

As a young scholar, Wilson was committed to the spirit of American left—he would play a guiding role in the Democratic Socialists of America in the 1970s. However, he bucked the trend of his liberal colleagues by questioning what he felt to be the overtly polemical character of civil rights era political discourse. Looking concretely at the changing place of black Americans in U.S. society, he noticed the growing cleavages, mostly along class lines, and wondered whether this signaled a need for a new political platform. As he would remark years later in a *New Yorker* profile, "You had to live in Chicago to appreciate the changes that were taking place. I felt we had to start thinking about the black class structure.... One segment seemed to be improving, with higher incomes, better life styles, while the rest were falling further and further behind" (Remnick). Liberal-democratic policies did not take this bifurcation into account; neither did social scientists adequately capture the import of this phenomenon for American race relations.

During the late 1970s and 1980s, Wilson focused intently on the social and political implications of the changing class dynamics within the black community, questioning whether different strata of black Americans experienced daily life uniquely and thus needed different kinds of social support. He wrote *The Declining Significance of Race* (1978) as a means of specifying the unique configuration of race relations in post–civil rights era America. Numerous critics and observers have interpreted this work in terms of the growing distance it seemed to create between Wilson and segments of the black intellectual and political leadership. Many black public figures interpreted Wilson as being skeptical of government intervention in providing redress for black Americans; more extreme critics suggested that Wilson was championing the end of racism. Wilson took great pains to state that racism continued to oppress America's black community and that his argument about the diminishing impact of race was in terms of *economic* advancement, not quality of life in general. He insisted that affirmative action and government subsidies were reaching mostly middle-class blacks, not the poor who lived in depressed inner cities. In noneconomic

areas, discrimination, segregation, and outright antipathy to black Americans continued to be pressing problems that the nation needed to contend with. With this argument, Wilson had charted his own ground and faced the criticism of conservatives and liberals alike.

The Declining Significance of Race was also a significant academic achievement in terms of its mode of argumentation. Wilson had presented a historical argument about the relative weight of race and class as factors inhibiting the social advancement struggles of black Americans. Skillfully using a mix of statistical data and secondary sources, Wilson analyzed the intersection of race and class in distinct historical periods: the pre-industrial, antebellum South; early nineteenth century industrialization; the period between the World Wars; and the modern era. It would no longer be sufficient to speak of "racism" as a continuous social process. Wilson took what historians often argued—that American race relations were continuously evolving—gave it an empirically rigorous treatment, and then presented it to social scientists in such a way that they were forced to reconceptualize and analyze anew the black experience. The public reception of the work missed this important contribution, focusing instead on the title of the book and the possible fallout for black political practice.

As Wilson prepared for the writing of *The Truly Disadvantaged*, perhaps his most influential and widely held book, Chicago assumed a prominent role. His presence at the university drew a cadre of like-minded graduate students and young faculty, many of whom would move on to prominent academic careers in urban studies. Wilson supervised several empirical projects in the city's African American inner-city neighborhoods. Some were large-scale survey studies under his direct supervision, and others were solitary, often rich ethnographic investigations by his graduate students in fields as diverse as boxing, gangs, religious behavior, and domestic life. His focus on U.S. inner cities eventually helped to sponsor a rejuvenated interest in urban poverty in America's leading research institutions.

As he marshaled empirical data on the city, Wilson found himself in a new political battle. On the

903

one hand, with their writings on the supposed disfunctionality within black inner-city communities, Reagan-era intellectuals such as Charles Murray and Lawrence Mead provided fodder for an increasingly conservative public attitude towards welfare and urban inequity. Liberals challenged them—as they did in the 1960s—by suggesting that these communities were not rife with social pathology, but that black social structure was different because of the impact of racism, discrimination, and slavery. Once again, Wilson found himself challenging both views: in *The Truly Disadvantaged* (1987), he acknowledged that black Americans were growing farther from the social mainstream, but unlike conservatives, he suggested that a compromised economic opportunity structure was at the root of high crime, low marriage rates, and other indicators of nonnormative behavior.

Wilson's unflinching assessment of the conditions of inner-city communities may not have won him immediate political support, but a growing number of scholars and policymakers noted the significance of his argument. *The Truly Disadvantaged* received scholarly and popular awards and was listed as one of the fifteen notable books of 1987 by the *New York Times*. Perhaps the greatest sign of the book's reach was President Bill Clinton's admission that *The Truly Disadvantaged* had the strongest impact on his own thinking on race and urban America. In 1990 Wilson was elected as president of the American Sociological Association, the first time that an African American had held that post since E. Franklin Frazier forty-two years earlier.

In 1996 Wilson took up a post in the Kennedy School of Government at Harvard University, where he eventually became the Lewis P. and Linda L. Geyser University Professor. He continued to write prolifically on U.S. urban poverty, but his research also returned to his comparative roots. He incorporated experiences of white and Latino urban communities into his writings and worked actively to shape a research agenda on European and American urbanism, notably in *When Work Disappears: The World of the New Urban Poor* (1996).

Since the civil rights era, no author has been more influential in shaping our understanding of poverty in American society than William Julius Wilson. This description has been given to Wilson not only by scholars and policymakers, but also by a U.S. president. In his academic career, Wilson has accumulated numerous honorary doctorate degrees and awards, two of the most prestigious being a MacArthur Foundation Fellowship in 1987 and the National Medal of Science, the highest scientific honor in the United States. When he received the latter award from President Clinton in 1998, the citation praised William Julius Wilson for having "revitalized the field of urban sociology, pioneering methods of interdisciplinary social science research, advancing understanding of the interaction between the macroeconomic, social structural, cultural and behavioral forces that cause and reproduce inner city poverty".

FURTHER READING

Biographical information on Wilson can be found on the National Science foundation website, http://www.nsf.gov/od/lpa/news/media/fs_98mosvital.htm

Remnick, David. "Dr. Wilson's Neighborhood." *The New Yorker*, April 29 & May 6, 1996, 96–107.

—SUDHIR ALLADI VENKATESH

WINFREY, OPRAH

(29 Jan. 1954–), talk show host, actor, and entrepreneur, was born Oprah Gail Winfrey in Kosciusko, Mississippi, to eighteen-year old Vernita Lee, and Vernon Winfrey, a twenty-year-old soldier. Vernita intended to call the baby "Orpah," after the biblical figure, but accepted "Oprah" when the name was misspelled by a clerk. Shortly after her daughter's birth, Vernita left Mississippi for Milwaukee, Wisconsin, leaving her newborn under the watchful eye of Oprah's paternal grandparents, Hattie Mae Bullock and Earless Lee, who were pig farmers. In 1960 Oprah went to Milwaukee to join her mother, who was working as a maid and who had given birth to a second daughter, Patricia. Another child, Jeffrey, followed a few years later, and Vernita struggled to support herself and her three young children. Bright and precocious, Oprah skipped several grades in elementary school but, despite her siblings and her early academic achievements, she felt the same loneliness and isolation she had experienced in Mississippi. Her outlet became performing and public speaking. Oprah spent fourth grade with her father and his wife, Zelma, in Nashville, Tennessee, but returned to Milwaukee after the school year ended.

The traumatic events of the next several years had lifelong consequences. Vernita's Milwaukee apartment was increasingly crowded with visitors and, at one point, Oprah shared her bed with a fourteen-year-old cousin who sexually molested her. Shortly after, she was sexually abused by her father's brother. Behavioral problems soon surfaced, and while she was performing well academically—she won a scholarship to an all-white high school in suburban Milwaukee—Oprah's behavior became increasingly rebellious. By age fourteen, she was running away and stealing from her mother, and she had become sexually promiscuous. Failing to get her daughter admitted to a home for wayward teens, Vernita sent Oprah to live with Vernon and Zelma Winfrey in Nashville. A few months after her arrival, Oprah gave birth to a son, who died several weeks after delivery. She has never revealed the name of the father.

Vernon and Zelma, who had no children of their own, insisted on Oprah's obedience. Oprah, or Gail as she was known in high school, thrived under her father's strict discipline and high expectations. She excelled in school, made friends, was elected senior class president, and got a part-time job reading the news at WVOL, a predominantly black local radio station. In 1971 Oprah graduated from Nashville High School and won a local beauty pageant, Miss Fire Prevention, after which she enrolled at Tennessee State University. While in college she worked evenings as at WTVF-TV in Nashville.

In 1976, several credits shy of graduation, Winfrey left Tennessee State for a job anchoring the evening news at WJZ-TV, Baltimore's ABC affiliate. Promoting their new hire, the station peppered billboards with the question, "What's an Oprah?" WJZ management itself wasn't quite sure, and attempted a makeover, sending Winfrey to a voice coach and to a salon, where she lost her hair to a botched permanent. Having

Oprah Winfrey chats with Vice President Al Gore on The Oprah Winfrey Show *in 2000.* © *Reuters NewMedia Inc./CORBIS*

arrived with little technical training and virtually no journalistic background or education, Winfrey was ill prepared for the constraints of objective news reporting. Within a year, she was moved off the news desk to *People Are Talking*, a morning talk show where she could practice her more emotional and subjective journalistic style. In this format, Winfrey found her niche. She remained as co-host of the show until 1983, when she was hired as host of *A. M. Chicago* at WLS-TV, Chicago's ABC affiliate. Within months *A. M. Chicago*'s ratings surpassed those of the popular *The Phil Donahue Show*. Winfrey had turned a faltering show into a hit.

In 1985 *A. M. Chicago* was expanded from a half-hour to a one-hour format and re-launched as *The Oprah Winfrey Show*. That same year Winfrey starred with Danny Glover and WHOOPI GOLDBERG in Steven Spielberg's adaptation of ALICE WALKER's novel *The Color Purple*, earning both Oscar and Golden Globe nominations. Winfrey's meteoric rise began in 1986 when *The Oprah Winfrey Show* went into national syndication. Within six months the show was the highest-rated talk show and the third-highest-rated program in syndication. Within a decade, twenty-four talk shows had followed *The Oprah Winfrey Show* into national syndication.

Winfrey's syndication deal placed her in charge of her own public relations,

an indication of her savvy approach. Indeed, news stories from the mid-1980s set the tone for much of Winfrey's future press coverage, highlighting her ease on camera and her open, hands-on approach with guests and audiences. Reports also focused on the biographical details of her life, including revelations of sexual abuse, issues with regard to her weight, and the influence of such role models as SOJOURNER TRUTH and MADAME C. J. WALKER. Proof that Winfrey's celebrity was solidifying came in December 1986 when she was interviewed by Mike Wallace on *60 Minutes*. Her cameo appearance in *Throw Momma from the Train* in 1987 was the first of several films in which she played herself.

Winfrey formed Harpo Productions (Oprah spelled backwards) in 1986 and acquired ownership of *The Oprah Winfrey Show* in 1988, the same year she was named broadcaster of the year by the International Television and Radio Society. Harpo Entertainment Group, chaired by Winfrey and headquartered in an 88,000-square-foot production facility, now includes production, film, video, and print divisions. In 1989 Winfrey combined her talents by producing and starring in *The Women of Brewster Place*, a television movie based on the book by Gloria Naylor, and about which the *New York Times* commented, "There hadn't been this kind of assembly of

black actors for any TV productions since *Roots*" (12 Mar 1989). Under the umbrella "Oprah Winfrey Presents," Winfrey has produced, and occasionally starred in, the television movies *There Are No Children Here* (1993); *Before Women had Wings* (1997); *David and Lisa* (1998), starring SIDNEY POITIER; *The Wedding* (1998), based on the novel by DOROTHY WEST; *Tuesdays with Morrie* (1999); and *Amy and Isabelle* (2001).

In 1998 Winfrey returned to the silver screen in Jonathan Demme's film adaptation of TONI MORRISON's Pulitzer Prize–winning 1987 book *Beloved*. Winfrey, who produced the film, starred as Sethe, opposite Beah Richards and Danny Glover. "What I love about the story of *Beloved*," Winfrey wrote in her 1998 book *Journey to Beloved*, "is that it allows you to *feel* what slavery was like; it doesn't just intellectually *show* you the picture" (19).

Despite her various projects, *The Oprah Winfrey Show* remains the heart of Winfrey's empire. The highest-rated talk show for eighteen consecutive seasons, it has earned thirty-five Emmy awards. Each week twenty-one million American viewers watch the show, which is broadcast in 109 countries. Twenty-five thousand letters arrive at the Harpo offices each week, and the show earns $260 million a year in advertising sales.

Statistics only hint at the range and depth of Winfrey's influence on American culture. Through programs showcasing "real people" discussing heretofore "private" issues before a live audience, Winfrey and her many imitators changed both popular debates and private attitudes by introducing such new or previously ignored topics as women's empowerment, talk therapy, and new age self-help into the mainstream. Because of Winfrey, these revolutions *were* televised and, certainly, altered as a result. It seemed that the personal stories and voices of everyday Americans, especially women, were being heard for the first time. The show also engendered a revolution in television itself, changing syndication and advertising patterns, expanding the role of women in the medium, and bringing about the explosion of talk-television, which paved the way for "women's programming," celebrity brand-naming, and reality, home, and how-to TV. From the beginning, Winfrey's unique approach to broadcasting, drawing on forerunners such as Donahue and Barbara Walters, rested on her success with on-air guests and audience members. Winfrey's wit and easy, conversational style, along with her empathetic manner, endeared her to audiences. "She's like the one friend you trust," explained a woman waiting in line at *The Oprah Winfrey Show*, "the one you know has good taste" (*Los Angeles Times*, 9 Mar. 1997).

Winfrey has both fomented and served Americans' growing interest in celebrity and good taste, consistently booking top musicians, Hollywood stars, politicians, television personalities, and cultural figures on her show. Notable black figures, such as MICHAEL JORDAN, MICHAEL JACKSON, QUINCY JONES, BILL COSBY, and MAYA ANGELOU were celebrated and placed on equal footing with white stars. Such was the power of Winfrey's show that an on-air appearance often catapulted ordinary guests into the realm of minor celebrity.

Over the years, Winfrey transformed herself from a poor, female, black, and overweight outsider to the ultimate insider—rich, powerful, popular, and connected. Worldwide audiences are kept abreast of her lavish lifestyle (she owns several homes, including a fifty-million dollar estate in Montecito, California) and the machinations of her private life, especially her long-time romantic relationship with businessman Stedman Graham Jr. Tabloid reports also chronicled her often tumultuous family relationships, stemming in part from her sister's revelations of Oprah's past, and Oprah's rift with her brother, who died of AIDS in 1989.

Winfrey features two Oprah personas on her show. "Celebrity Oprah" gives audiences behind-the-scenes access to her life and celebrity friends, albeit in a carefully selected way. In 2002 she began airing a daily half-hour show, *Oprah After the Show*. "Everyday Oprah," however, struggles with the same problems as her audience. Issues of importance to Winfrey off-air, chiefly topics relating to weight, body image, and self-esteem, are consistent themes on-air. Winfrey's 15 November 1988 show, during which she revealed how she lost sixty-seven pounds on a liquid diet, won a 16.4 rating. Winfrey soon regained weight, and she shared that

fact with audiences. In the early 1990s she hired a chef and a trainer and lost seventy pounds. Winfrey parlayed her weight-loss success into a minor industry, beginning with the 1996 publication of *Make the Connection: Ten Steps to a Better Body and a Better Life*.

Most pointedly with her popular— and legally trademarked—segments "Get with the Program," "Remembering Your Spirit," and "Change Your Life TV," Winfrey uses her show as a forum for group therapy, but also as a bully pulpit. Most significantly, she took on the issues of child and sexual abuse, revealing on-air in 1990 that she had been molested as a child. The following year, she testified before Congress in support of the National Child Protection Act, which established a national database of convicted child abusers. "Oprah's Bill," as the legislation came to be known, was signed into law by President Bill Clinton in 1993.

Winfrey, who chairs The Oprah Winfrey Foundation and The Oprah Winfrey Scholars Program, brought her philanthropic endeavors to the air with the establishment of Oprah's Angel Network in 1997. When she asked viewers to send in their spare change, the show raised 3.5 million dollars. The Angel Network went on to raise a total of twelve million dollars and established the "Use Your Life Award," which provides $100,000 to individuals whose work benefits the broader community. Recently, Winfrey has shown a new interest in Africa, establishing Christmas Kindness South Africa 2002, and donating ten million dollars to build the Oprah Winfrey Leadership Academy for Girls South Africa, about which she told *TV Guide*, "I'm going to teach classes in leadership and life lessons from Chicago via satellite. I am all about girl power!" (4 Oct. 2003).

One measure of her influence was seen in 1996 when Winfrey remarked off-the-cuff during a show on mad cow disease, "It has just stopped me cold from eating another hamburger." After what the plaintiffs dubbed the "Oprah crash of 1996," which saw cattle prices plummet, a group of Texas cattle ranchers sued her. In 1998, following a jury's ruling in her favor, *Time* magazine wrote, "The winner Oprah. She's the most powerful woman in the United States. Laws be damned" (12 Jan. 1988).

If her criticism could send a market into decline, Winfrey's recommendation could also send a stock soaring. Such was the case with Oprah's Book Club, launched in 1996. Each of the book selections became instant best-sellers. In recognition of her unprecedented influence on the publishing industry, Winfrey was presented with the National Book Foundation's Fiftieth Anniversary Gold Medal.

Winfey has evolved from television personality to celebrity to media mogul to synergistic pioneer. In addition to the relationship between Oprah's Book Club and Harpo Productions, which owns the rights to many of the books selected, Winfrey has introduced a host of projects with the "Oprah" brand name. In 1995 "Oprah Online," a collaboration with AOL, debuted. Three years later she cofounded Oxygen Media Inc., a cable network offering shows inspired by *Oprah Winfrey Show* material. Another outgrowth of the show, the syndicated series *The Dr. Phil Show*, was launched in 2002. In 2000 Winfrey expanded into a new medium with the wildly successful *O, The Oprah Magazine*, co-published with Hearst Magazines. Winfrey owns a stake in Granite Broadcasting, a media company that owns eleven television stations. In 1999 Winfrey brought her entrepreneurial lessons into the classroom, co-teaching "Dynamics of Leadership" with Stedman Graham at the J. L. Kellogg Graduate School of Management at Northwestern University.

Winfrey's major honors include a George Foster Peabody Individual Achievement Award, Lifetime Achievement and Bob Hope Humanitarian Award Emmys from the National Academy of Television Arts and Sciences, and an International Radio and Television Society Foundation Gold Medal award. In 2003 *Forbes* magazine disclosed that Winfrey, the world's richest entertainer after Steven Spielberg, had become the first African American woman billionaire. Winfrey constantly tops lists of the most influential, popular, or powerful people in America. As Fran Lebowitz told *Time* magazine in 1996, "Oprah is probably the greatest media influence on the adult population. She is almost a religion" (17 June 1996).

More than a household name, or even a brand name, Oprah has become part of American language itself, as critics write about the "Oprahization" or "Oprahfication" of American culture. Although she will continue to appear each day on television, at least through the 2007–2008 season, she can rarely be found in front of a small screen; Winfrey rarely watches television, complaining, "It promotes false values" (*Life*, Sept 1997).

FURTHER READING

Mair, George. *Oprah Winfrey: The Real Story* (1994).

Lowe, Janet. *Oprah Winfrey Speaks: Insight from the World's Most Influential Voice* (1998).

—LISA E. RIVO

WONDER, STEVIE

(13 May 1950–), songwriter, singer, multi-instrumentalist, producer, and political activist, was born Steveland Judkins in Saginaw, Michigan, to Calvin Judkins and Lula Mae Hardaway, who separated early in his life. Steveland came into the world with the odds stacked firmly against him; he was poor, black, and born two months premature with a birth weight barely reaching four pounds. He spent his first fifty-two days in an incubator, resulting in the permanent loss of his eyesight. Stevie was raised largely by his mother under difficult economic and social circumstances. Calvin, a street hustler, forced his wife to work as a prostitute for a short period before the family moved from Saginaw to Detroit's Brewster Housing Projects in 1953. The couple separated shortly thereafter.

Despite his hardscrabble upbringing, Stevie never thought himself disadvantaged. With unwavering optimism, he compensated for his impairment by developing his other senses. By age five Stevie showed an aptitude for music, taking up percussion and imitating the day's top R&B artists, including Little Walter, Jimmy Reed, and the Coasters, heard on WCHB's *Sundown* show. At eight, without formal training, Stevie played piano and harmonica, sang in the Whitestone Baptist Church's gospel choir, and busked on street corners.

In 1960 one of Stevie's best friends, Gerald White, convinced his brother Ronnie White of Smokey Robinson and the Miracles to give his friend

an audition. The confident ten year old, who bragged he could "sing badder than Smokey," backed up his audacious claim with a show-stopping performance. White brought Stevie to BERRY GORDY JR., owner of Detroit's fledgling Motown label, where Stevie played every instrument in the studio. Lula signed her son's recording contract, which stipulated his earnings be held in a trust until he turned twenty-one.

Motown producer and songwriter Clarence Paul became Wonder's producer and mentor. His first two recordings, *The Jazz Soul of Little Stevie*, an all-instrumental album showcasing Wonder's instrumental virtuosity, and *A Tribute to Uncle Ray*, a homage to his idol RAY CHARLES, were held back until 1963. His first release, the 1962 single "I Call It Pretty Music (But the Old People Call It the Blues)," written by Paul, was released under the Gordy-coined moniker Little Stevie Wonder; it failed to chart.

Despite his early recordings' lack of commercial success, Wonder gave electrifying live performances. And Gordy captured Wonder's dynamism on a 1963 live recording of "Fingertips Pt 2," a seven-minute, two-sided single, complete with Wonder's inspired harmonica improvisations and an uproarious audience call and response. It became Wonder's first number-one single and the first live recording to top the charts. That track and the single "Workout Stevie Workout" propelled Wonder's album *The 12 Year Old Genius* to number one.

With a Song in My Heart, an album of treacly ballads, and *Stevie at the Beach*, an improbable surf album, predictably failed to chart. In 1965 Wonder embodied Motown's infectious pop and soul fusion with "Uptight (Everything's Alright)," a number-one single and title cut that he cowrote. The album also contained a countrified, gospel-inflected version of Bob Dylan's "Blowin' in the Wind," showcasing the sixteen-year-old's burgeoning political consciousness.

Down to Earth, released in 1967 with the un-Motown-like album cover of Wonder in a ghetto landscape, featured the number-one R&B song "I Was Made to Love Her." The summer following the album's release saw racial confrontations turn into full-scale urban riots in Newark, New York City, Cleveland, Washington, Chicago, Atlanta, and

Detroit, and in April 1968 MARTIN LUTHER KING JR. was assassinated. Wonder became more politicized, performing at benefits for the Southern Christian Leadership Conference (SCLC) in Chicago and for SCLC's Poor People's March on Washington in 1968.

From 1968 to 1970 Wonder's fame grew precipitously on the strength of four top-ten hits: "For Once in My Life," "My Cherie Amour," "Yester-Me, Yester-You, Yesterday," and "Signed, Sealed, Delivered, I'm Yours." After graduating from Michigan School for the Blind in 1969, Wonder was able to devote himself full-time to music, and he began moving beyond Motown's rigid hit-factory system, coproducing and playing most of the instruments on 1969's *Signed, Sealed, Delivered*. The record included a broader repertoire, including his inspired rendition of the Beatles' "We Can Work It Out," the socially conscious ballad "Heaven Help Us," and, especially, the title track, written with his paramour Syreeta Wright, a Motown secretary and backup singer, whom he married in 1970. The couple divorced two years later.

That same year, with his Motown contract about to expire, Wonder was granted full artistic control of *Where I'm Coming From*, the first album he produced and cowrote himself. The album contained a more cohesive political message with songs like "Think of Me as Your Soldier," expressing his opposition to the Vietnam War, and "I Wanna Talk to You," commenting on the widening generation gap.

In May 1971 Wonder turned twenty-one and received a million dollars from his Motown trust. He remained unsigned while holing up in the late JIMI HENDRIX's state-of-the-art Electric Ladyland Studio in New York. With his groundbreaking album *Music of My Mind* in hand, Wonder successfully renegotiated his Motown contract, winning complete artistic control, increased royalty rates, and his own publishing company, Black Bull.

Wonder's new artistic freedom resulted in an extraordinary burst of creativity that cemented his place as one of the twentieth century's most important musicians. The five successive albums he released in the early to mid-1970s, *Music of My Mind* (1972), *Talking Book* (1972), *Innervisions* (1973),

Fulfillingness' First Finale (1974), and *Songs in the Key of Life* (1976), represent a body of work and a creative zenith few artists ever reach.

At Electric Ladyland, Wonder delved into sound and instrument experimentation with synthesizers, Moogs, and clavinets, creating category-defying hybrids—parts jazz, R&B, rock, soul, and pop. At a session with Richie Havens, Wonder met engineers and electronic musicians Robert Margouleff and Malcolm Cecil, who became his collaborators and teachers. While *Music of My Mind* had only one single, the breezy, jazz-inflected "Superwoman (Where Were You When I Needed You)," the album's progressive music experimentation represented an enormous paradigm shift.

Following a 1972 summer tour opening for the Rolling Stones, Wonder began work, with the help of Margouleff and Cecil, on one of his most seminal recordings, *Talking Book*. The album yielded two consecutive number-one hits, the romantic, melodious "You Are the Sunshine of My Life," and the classic funk jam "Superstition," featuring Wonder's jaunty clavinet backed by bawdy horns.

Innervisions, another Wonder masterpiece, was filled with spirituality and introspection ("Visions," "Jesus Children of America," "Higher Ground"), ballads ("All in Love Is Fair," "Golden Lady"), jazz influences and psychedelia ("Too High"), political statements ("Living for the City," "He's Misstra Know It All,"), and Latin grooves ("Don't You Worry about a Thing"). Thirty years later tracks like "Higher Ground," "Living for the City," "Don't You Worry about a Thing," and "Golden Lady" remained in heavy rotation at radio stations across the globe.

On 6 August 1973, while Wonder was driving with his brother on a South Carolina highway, a log from a truck slammed into Wonder's forehead and fractured his skull. He lay in a coma for a week before regaining consciousness and was forced to stop performing until the following January. While convalescing, he met Yolanda Simmons, who became his partner and the mother of two of his children, Aisha and Keita, although they never married. In 1974 Wonder won five Grammy Awards

for *Innervisions*, including Album of the Year.

Wonder's new zeal for life on 1974's *Fulfillingness' First Finale* was evident on songs like "Smile Please," the metaphysical "Heaven Is 10 Zillion Light Years Away," the syncopated and stomping "Boogie On Reggae Woman," and the politically charged "You Haven't Done Nothin.'" The album went on to win four Grammy Awards.

Wonder's *Songs in the Key of Life* remains his veritable magnum opus, a double album featuring some of his finest work, including "Sir Duke" (a tribute to DUKE ELLINGTON), "I Wish," "Isn't She Lovely" (about his daughter Aisha), "Pastime Paradise," and "As." While detractors called the work sprawling and excessive, most saw the ambitious recording as the musical culmination of his career.

While most critics would agree that Wonder's creativity dropped off after 1980, his commercial success continued to grow. *Hotter than July* (1980) included the hit "(Master Blaster) Jammin," a tribute to Bob Marley, and "Happy Birthday," an anthem to the battle Wonder had spearheaded to make Martin Luther King's birthday a national holiday. In 1982 he had a number-one single with his duet with Paul McCartney, "Ebony and Ivory." That same year he released *Musicquarium*, a greatest hits album that produced two new hits, "That Girl" and "Do I Do." Wonder's 1984 Oscar-winning soundtrack for *The Woman in Red* featured "I Just Called to Say I Love You," his biggest-selling single. In 1989, at age thirty-nine, Wonder was inducted into the Rock and Roll Hall of Fame. Although he scored the soundtrack for SPIKE LEE's 1991 film *Jungle Fever* and released the 1995 Grammy-winning album "Conversation Peace," his output flagged in the 1990s.

Throughout the 1990s and into the new century, Wonder's legacy was enriched by the neo-soul movement, the members of which rightfully deified him, and by hip-hop, with many artists, including TUPAC SHAKUR, Wu-Tang Clan, and A Tribe Called Quest, sampling his music and introducing him to a new generation.

FURTHER READING

Horn, Martin E. *Innervisions: The Music of Stevie Wonder* (2000).

Love, Dennis, and Stacy Brown. *Blind Faith: The Miraculous Journey of Lula Hardaway, Stevie Wonder's Mother* (2002).
Swenson, John. *Stevie Wonder* (1986).

—ANDY GENSLER

 WOODS, GRANVILLE T. (23 Apr. 1856–30 Jan. 1910), mechanical and electrical engineer and inventor, was born in Columbus, Ohio. Nothing is known of Woods's parents except that they may have been named Tailer and Martha Woods. The effects of racism in Columbus, shortly before and during the Civil War, were somewhat blunted by the economic influence of a sizable African American population, which included artisans and property holders, and by growing sympathy among whites for abolitionism. Only a few years before Woods's birth, the city established a system of segregated schools for black children, which provided him an education until he was ten years old.

Like almost all American engineers during the nineteenth century, Woods obtained his technical training largely through self-study and on-the-job experience, rather than from formal schooling. Sometime after 1866 he began apprenticing as a blacksmith and machinist, probably in Cincinnati, where several decades earlier German immigrants had established a flourishing machine tool industry. Machinists considered themselves members of an elite profession, and by and large they selected only the most promising and ambitious candidates for apprenticeships. Success depended on a vivid spatial imagination, mathematical adroitness, and draftsmanship. Indeed, Woods's letters patent displayed abundant evidence of all these talents, most apparently the latter. His drawings were consistently rendered with the flair of a first-rate draftsman—presumably Woods himself.

Most of Woods's inventions were electromechanical devices and systems related to railroad technology. His interest in these fields grew out of an eclectic early experience with railroads and from dogged self-study. In November 1872 Woods moved east and was soon hired as an engineer on the St. Louis and Iron Mountain

Inventor Granville T. Woods, whose many inventions include the "third rail" that carries electricity to electric-powered trains. Ohio Historical Society

Railroad in Missouri. Given his training and youth, he likely operated lathes and drill presses in a machine shop. During his employment with Iron Mountain, he began studying electricity—at least three years before Thomas Edison patented his revolutionary lighting system. Since almost no American university provided such training, Woods had to learn about electricity from technical books and periodicals. Woods left the Iron Mountain Railroad in early 1876, and then spent two years studying at Stern's Institute of Technology. In February 1878 he signed on to the British steamer *Ironsides* as chief engineer. Two years later he returned east, where he handled locomotives for the Southern Railway, whose line ran near Danville, Kentucky.

Sometime after 1880 Woods began his career as an inventor in Cincinnati, probably only to sell one or two ideas. He chose a propitious historical moment and region. Cincinnati was home to a larger and more cohesive and prosperous African American community than that which resided in Columbus, and southwestern Ohio boasted some of the best machine shops in America. With few corporations willing to invest in their own research laboratories, independent inventors like Woods filled a niche by feeding the burgeoning appetite of those corporations for technological innovation. From the outset he made

money. His first patent, filed on 18 June 1883, was a replacement for Alexander Graham Bell's crude telephone transmitter (i.e., mouthpiece). His second invention followed almost immediately, an improved steam-boiler furnace. Significantly, he sold the transmitter to two local investors for a modest fee. This success sharply contrasted with the typical experience of a patentee during the period, when ownership of almost all inventions remained forever in the hands of their profitless inventors.

Woods resided in Cincinnati for most of the 1880s, applying for some seventeen patents while he lived there. Around 1886 he founded the Woods Electric Company. One newspaper reported Woods's intention to capitalize his new firm at one million dollars and to sell shares for fifty dollars, which suggests that he planned a large-scale factory, but if so the proposal fell through and the firm functioned only as a temporary assignee—i.e., the legal owner—for ten of his patents. The company last appears in the historical record in April 1890, as assignee on Woods's last Ohio patent.

By August 1891 Woods had relocated to the New York City area. Earlier, he had traveled extensively among large northeastern cities, probably as an engineering consultant, so he likely moved to be nearer to his work. He

lived out the remaining seventeen years of his life in New York, maintaining the vigorous pace he had established in Ohio. The U.S. Patent Office issued him twenty-eight letters patent for his New York inventions, seven of which listed a brother, Lyates, as co-inventor. Incredibly, he found assignees for all but five.

As an engineer, Woods was no revolutionary, and his inventions characteristically tackled problems associated with established technological systems. He focused primarily on inventing communications, power distribution, and control devices for electric trains, a cutting-edge technology that large cities such as New York, Boston, Philadelphia, and Washington, D.C., were increasingly adopting. In 1884 he filed a patent application for "Telegraphony," a combination telegraph and telephone system that he sold to American Bell Telephone. His "Induction Telegraph System" enabled moving railroad cars to exchange telegraph messages, which proved crucial for preventing collisions. Today his most recognizably famous idea is the "third rail," a high-current electrical conductor laid inside the two ordinary rails that guide the wheels of an electric-powered train. The Woods invention with the widest-ranging importance, though, was a method of regulating the rotational velocity of electric motors. Formerly, motors were slowed by diverting part of their electrical current to resistive elements that transformed the excess power to dangerous waste heat. Woods devised a dramatically safer tapped-inductive system that wasted far less energy. The speed of virtually almost every alternating-current electric motor today is controlled by a similar method.

Regrettably, no historian has thoroughly assessed the true technological and commercial significance of all Woods's inventions. For that matter, no one has accurately determined their number, although one reliable authority on black inventors in 1917 credited him with "upwards of 50 different inventions" (Baker, 1917). The fact that Woods sold the rights to well over half of his patents to corporations, many of which included future electrical giants like Westinghouse, General Electric, and American Bell, and one for a reported ten thousand dollars, however, indicates that he was not only a prolific inventor but also a commercially successful entrepreneur and respected engineer.

Woods died in New York City of a cerebral hemorrhage, some five years after applying for his last known patent in October 1904, and perhaps in poverty. He left a distinguished but ambiguous legacy. On one hand, he merits a place in the top tier of independent electrical inventors of the late nineteenth and early twentieth centuries. On the other hand, his position with respect to African American history must remain unfixed. Americans have admired the "Black Edison" for well over a century, but even contemporary African American writers rarely mentioned public statements on his part, except for matters of patent litigation, or when he lectured to Cincinnati audiences "on the various laws and theories that pertain to electricity and magnetism" (*Cleveland Gazette*, 7 Aug. 1886). Doubtless, white journalists, who almost entirely ignored him, deserved blame for much of the mystery surrounding Woods. But to the extent that he chose his reticence, he resembled engineers in general, who, thanks to the increasing influence of capitalism during the nineteenth century, began to adopt a hands-off approach to political and social questions, rather than risk their clients and employers. In any case, his exceptional success as an independent inventor depended on an ability to negotiate a career in an increasingly discriminatory society, and it is difficult to see how a more outspoken individual could have survived professionally in such an environment.

FURTHER READING

Baker, Henry E. "The Negro in the Field of Invention." *Journal of Negro History* II, January 1917.

Brodie, James Michael. *Created Equal: The Lives and Ideas of Black American Innovators* (1993).

Haber, Louis. *Black Pioneers of Science and Invention* (1970).

James, Portia P. *The Real McCoy: African American Invention and Innovation, 1619–1930* (1989).

Jenkins, Edward S. *To Fathom More: African American Scientists and Inventors* (1996).

—GARY L. FROST

WOODS, TIGER

(30 Dec. 1975–), golfer, was born Eldrick Woods to Earl Woods, a retired army lieutenant colonel who had been the first black baseball player at Kansas State University, and Kultida Punsawad, a native of Thailand and army secretary who met Earl when he was stationed in Thailand during the Vietnam War. Kultida chose the name Eldrick because it begins with the first initial of Earl's name and ends with the first initial of her name. The fusion of identities thus symbolized by his name would have far reaching influences on the boy's life. The sobriquet Tiger was chosen by Earl in honor of Colonel Nguyen Phong, whom Earl nicknamed Tiger because of his courage. Earl, who had three children from a previous marriage, married Kultida in 1969 while he was based at Fort Hamilton in Brooklyn, New York. He was forty-two years old and three months shy of retiring from the army when a fellow black officer invited Earl to play golf for the first time. Thus, Earl began cultivating a love for the greens that would propel his son into the world of golf.

African American golfers had played in mostly segregated venues since Reconstruction. In 1896 John Shippen became the first black golf professional when he was invited to play in the second U.S. Open Championship at the Shinnecock Hills Golf Club, but when some white golfers refused to play with an African American, Shippen was forced to pretend that he was half Shinnecock Indian in order to participate. In 1899 Dr. George Grant, a black Boston dentist, patented the first golf tee—and though he did not make any money from his invention, variations on his design revolutionized the game. Charles Sifford was the first African American to finally break the "Caucasian only" barrier when he entered the Professional Golfers Association (PGA) in 1962. The following year ALTHEA GIBSON did the same in the Ladies Professional Golfers Association (LPGA) when she put down her tennis racket and began swinging a golf club.

As an infant, Tiger was often placed in a high chair in the garage so that his father could hit golf balls into a net while at the same time watching the child. When Earl put an improvised club

into Tiger's hands, the eleven-month-old prodigy swung from his left side—as it had appeared from his perspective in the high chair. When Earl placed Tiger in the correct position, Tiger intuitively switched the club to his right, and the astonished father began to sense that his son was a natural. At the age of two Tiger made his first television appearance, on *The Mike Douglas Show*, where he demonstrated his putting (and charm) with comedian Bob Hope. Tiger was featured in *Golf Digest* magazine at the age of five and appeared on the ABC program *That's Incredible*.

Despite the early recognition of Tiger's talent, golf did not entirely consume his childhood to the exclusion of all other interests and activities. Earl was not the overbearing father of Little League infamy, trying to live vicariously through his son's playing. Kultida was an exacting disciplinarian who did not exempt the boy wonder from household chores, excuse poor academic performance, or tolerate arrogance. Nor did Tiger have to be prodded to practice; on the contrary, he enjoyed listening to subliminal tapes that told him, "You have the power to move mountains." Tiger and his family were the first black residents to move into their neighborhood in Cypress, California. Growing up in what became a diverse community, Tiger experienced a world filled with video games, rap music, and shopping malls—and though he liked *The Simpsons* more than the *Cosby Show*, he was inescapably a product of the black middle class of the 1980s. In high school he played basketball, football, and baseball and showed aptitude in each. At six feet, two inches in height, he could have pursued these more popular sports, but golf was his first love, only passion, and undeniable forte.

Kultida worked hard to make sure that his Asian identity was not overshadowed by his brown skin. She took him to Thailand when he was nine and instructed him in Buddhist traditions, which Tiger came to cherish. She taught him to be proud of his Thai ancestry even though most people were not aware of it. Exasperated by a media that referred to her son as black exclusively, she once scolded a reporter that to do so was to "deny his grandmother and grandfather. To deny me!" (*Sports Illustrated*, 27 Mar.

1995, 62). Tiger would one day tell an audience on The OPRAH WINFREY Show that he was a mixture of Caucasian, black, Indian, and Asian, which made him a "Cablinasian." This racial construction displeased some African Americans who suspected that Woods was uncomfortable being black, but it encouraged others who resented racial categories that blotted out parts of their identities, and it prompted some members of Congress to introduce a "Tiger Woods Bill" to make "mixed race" an option on the 2000 census forms. Earl was confident that Tiger could handle the social challenges that awaited him and focused instead on building Tiger's mental toughness for the pressure he would encounter in high stakes tournaments. For example, he would try to break Tiger's concentration before his son took a shot by jingling coins in his pocket, coughing, or dropping his golf bag. Tiger developed the ability to remain focused in tight situations and became a relentless competitor.

As a teenager Woods amassed a room full of trophies, including an unprecedented three consecutive U.S. Junior Amateur Championships; when he won the first one at fifteen, he became the youngest player to ever do so. In 1994 he became the youngest player to win a U.S. Amateur Championship, which he did by staging the largest comeback in tournament history. Later that year Woods enrolled at Stanford University on a golf scholarship and decided to major in economics. By the end of his freshman year he had successfully defended his U.S. Amateur title, played in his first professional major—the Masters, where he was the only amateur in the field to make the cut—and was named NCAA First Team All-America. By his sophomore year Woods had garnered a record-setting three U.S. Amateur Championships and was winning other tournaments all over the country, all while maintaining a B average. The decision to drop out of Stanford in August 1996 and become a professional golfer was a difficult one, but the forty-million-dollar endorsement deal from Nike and twenty-million-dollar deal with Titleist helped to ease the pain.

Success as a professional was not guaranteed for Woods. Like other sports, golf has seen many amateur stars fail to meet expectations when put up against seasoned veterans; others prove unable to handle the pressures and distractions that come with celebrity status. Winning even one major tournament over the course of a long professional career is quite an achievement. Woods, in comparison, became the number-one player in the world in just forty-two weeks as a pro, smashing records as he went. His first major victory was the Masters in 1997 at the Augusta National Golf Club. This exclusive all-male club in Georgia did not admit its first black member until 1990. On the final day of competition, Woods wore a red shirt, as he always does on the last day of play because his mother said that red is his lucky color of power. As he approached the final hole on that day, his ailing father was waiting to greet him, along with Lee Elder, who had been the first black golfer to play in the Masters at Augusta, doing so the year Woods was born. With this win, Woods became the first African American to win a major, and he did so by twelve strokes, the widest margin of victory in the history of that vaunted tournament.

By tradition, the winner of the Masters chooses the menu for the following year's dinner. Realizing this honor would fall to Woods, a previous Masters champion, Fuzzy Zoeller, told reporters, "Tell him not to serve fried chicken, or collard greens, or whatever the hell *they* serve" (Callahan, 61). Despite the firestorm of controversy that ensued, Woods took such comments in stride and proceeded to become golf's greatest ambassador, bringing millions of minority players to the game and attracting television viewers to the sport in numbers that rivaled baseball and basketball.

Woods went on to play on the United States teams for the Ryder Cup and the Presidents Cup. He won the PGA Championship in 1999 and from 2000 through 2001 built up a phenomenal string of victories that demonstrated his growing prowess. He opened the 2000 season by winning the Mercedes Championship and then captured the U.S. Open Championship by fifteen strokes, breaking a record that had stood since 1899. He then won the British Open at St. Andrews, Scotland, by eight strokes on the course where the modern game of golf was born, and registered the best score (19 under 269)

in the history of the British Open. With this victory Woods became the youngest player, at age twenty-four, to complete the Career Gland Slam—winning the four top tournaments over the course of one's career. Only four other players have achieved this feat. However, Woods was not finished; he won the PGA Championship again in 2000 to become the first player to win the U.S. Open, British Open, and PGA Championship in the same year. And when he won the Masters again early in 2001, Woods became the first person in history to own all the major crowns of modern golf at the same time.

When Jack Nicklaus began to establish his dominance over golf a generation earlier, Bobby Jones, a leading competitor, said of Nicklaus, "He plays a game with which I am not familiar" (Callahan, 55). Similarly, Woods unveiled a game never before seen: long off the tees, skillful on the fairways, and accurate on the putting greens. He stated that his professional goal was to surpass Nicklaus's record of eighteen major PGA titles. He delayed marriage and child rearing to pursue this quest.

When Woods met Nelson Mandela in South Africa, Mandela urged him to do something with his fame to help others. Woods subsequently established the Tiger Woods Foundation, whose goal was to help American youth through scholarships, charitable gifts, and educational programs. Woods, like his good friend MICHAEL JORDAN, chose to avoid most political issues—particularly those pertaining to race. His reticence about admitting women into the PGA or rescinding the male-only membership rules at Augusta, two controversies that erupted in 2003, disappointed those who believed that Woods had a special obligation to be outspoken on such matters. However, Woods did not relish becoming a role model, nor did he see himself becoming a champion of causes like MUHAMMAD ALI or JACKIE ROBINSON.

FURTHER READING

Callahan, Tom. *In Search of Tiger* (2003).

McDaniel, Pete. *Uneven Lies: The Heroic Story of African Americans in Golf* (2000).

Reilly, Rick. "Goodness Gracious, He's a Great Ball of Fire," *Sports Illustrated*, 27 Mar. 1995.

Strege, John. *Tiger: A Biography of Tiger Woods* (1998).

—SHOLOMO B. LEVY

WOODSON, CARTER GODWIN (19 Dec. 1875– 3 Apr. 1950), historian, was born in New Canton, Virginia, the son of James Henry Woodson, a sharecropper, and Anne Eliza Riddle. Woodson, the "Father of Negro History," was the first and only black American born of former slaves to earn a PhD in History. His grandfather and father, who were skilled carpenters, were forced into sharecropping after the Civil War. The family eventually purchased land and eked out a meager living in the late 1870s and 1880s.

Woodson's parents instilled in him high morality and strong character through religious teachings and a thirst for education. One of nine children, Woodson purportedly was his mother's favorite, and was sheltered. As a small child he worked on the family farm, and as a teenager he worked as an agricultural day laborer. In the late 1880s the Woodsons moved to Fayette County, West Virginia, where his father worked in railroad construction, and where he himself found work as a coal miner. In 1895, at the age of twenty, he enrolled in Frederick Douglass High School where, possibly because he was an older student and felt the need to catch up, Woodson completed four years of course work in two years and graduated in 1897. Desiring additional education, Woodson enrolled in Berea College in Kentucky, which had been founded by abolitionists in the 1850s for the education of ex-slaves. Although he briefly attended Lincoln University in Pennsylvania, Woodson graduated from Berea in 1903, just a year before Kentucky passed the "Day Law," prohibiting interracial education. After college Woodson taught at Frederick Douglass High School in West Virginia. Believing in the uplifting power of education, and desiring the opportunity to travel to another country to observe and experience the culture firsthand, he decided to accept a teaching post in the Philippines, teaching at all grade levels, and remained there from 1903 to 1907.

Woodson's worldview and ideas about how education could transform society, improve race relations, and benefit the lower classes were shaped by his experiences as a college student and as a teacher. Woodson took correspondence courses through the University of Chicago because he was determined to obtain additional education. He was enrolled at the University of Chicago in 1907 as a full-time student and earned a bachelor's degree and a master's degree in European History, submitting a thesis on French diplomatic policy toward Germany in the eighteenth century. Woodson then attended Harvard University on scholarships, matriculating in 1909 and studying with Edward Channing, Albert Bushnell Hart, and Frederick Jackson Turner. In 1912 Woodson earned his PhD in History, completing a dissertation on the events leading to the creation of the state of West Virginia after the Civil War broke out. Unfortunately, he never published the dissertation. He taught at the Armstrong and Dunbar/M Street high schools in Washington from 1909 to 1919, and then moved on to Howard University, where he served as dean of arts and sciences, professor of history, and head of the graduate program in history in 1919–1920. From 1920 to 1922 he taught at the West Virginia Collegiate Institute. In 1922 he returned to Washington to direct the Association for the Study of Negro Life and History full time.

Woodson began the work that sustained him for the rest of his career, and for which he is best known, when he founded the association in Chicago in the summer of 1915. Woodson had always been interested in African American history and believed that education in the subject at all levels of the curriculum could inculcate racial pride and foster better race relations. Under the auspices of the association, Woodson founded the *Journal of Negro History*, which began publication in 1915, and established Associated Publishers in 1921, to publish works in black history. He launched the annual celebration of Negro History Week in February 1926 and had achieved a distinguished publishing career as a scholar of African American history by 1937, when he began publishing the *Negro History Bulletin*.

The *Journal of Negro History*, which Woodson edited until his death, served as the centerpiece of his research program, not only providing black scholars with a medium in which to publish their research but also serving as an outlet for the publication of articles written by white scholars when their interpretations of such subjects as slavery and black culture differed from mainstream historians. Woodson formulated an editorial policy that was inclusive. Topically, the *Journal* provided coverage in various aspects of the black experience: slavery, the slave trade, black culture, the family, religion, and antislavery and abolitionism, and included biographical articles on prominent African Americans. Chronologically, articles covered the sixteenth through the twentieth centuries. Scholars, as well as interested amateurs, published important historical articles in the *Journal*, and Woodson kept a balance between professional and nonspecialist contributors.

Woodson began celebration of Negro History Week to increase awareness of and interest in black history among both blacks and whites. He chose the second week of February to commemorate the birthdays of FREDERICK DOUGLASS and Abraham Lincoln. Each year he sent promotional brochures and pamphlets to state boards of education, elementary and secondary schools, colleges, women's clubs, black newspapers and periodicals, and white scholarly journals suggesting ways to celebrate. The association also produced bibliographies, photographs, books, pamphlets, and other promotional literature to assist the black community in the commemoration. Negro History Week celebrations often included parades of costumed characters depicting the lives of famous blacks, breakfasts, banquets, lectures, poetry readings, speeches, exhibits, and other special presentations. During Woodson's lifetime the celebration reached every state and several foreign countries.

Among the major objectives of Woodson's research and the programs he sponsored through the Association for the Study of Afro-American Life and History (the name was changed in the 1970s to reflect the changing times) was to counteract the racism promoted in works published by white scholars. With several young black assistants—RAYFORD W. LOGAN, CHARLES HARRIS WESLEY, Lorenzo J. Greene, and A. A. Taylor—Woodson pioneered in writing the social history of black Americans, using new sources and methods, such as census data, slave testimony, and oral history. These scholars moved away from interpreting blacks solely as victims of white oppression and racism toward a view of them as major actors in American history. Recognizing Woodson's major achievements, the NAACP presented him its highest honor, the Spingarn Medal, in June 1926. At the award ceremony, John Haynes Holmes, the minister and interracial activist, cited Woodson's tireless labors to promote the truth about Negro history.

During the 1920s Woodson funded the research and outreach programs of the association with substantial grants from white foundations such as the Carnegie Foundation, the General Education Board, and the Laura Spellman Rockefeller Foundation. Wealthy whites, such as Julius Rosenwald, also made contributions. White philanthropists cut Woodson's funding in the early 1930s, however, after he refused to affiliate the association with a black college. During and after the Depression, Woodson depended on the black community as his sole source of support.

Woodson began his career as a publishing scholar in the field of African American history in 1915 with the publication of *The Education of the Negro Prior to 1861*. By 1947, when the ninth edition of his textbook *The Negro in Our History* (1922) appeared, Woodson had published four monographs, five textbooks, five edited collections of source materials, and thirteen articles, as well as five collaborative sociological studies. Among Woodson's major works are *A Century of Negro Migration* (1918), *A History of the Negro Church* (1921), *The Mis-Education of the Negro* (1933), and *The African Background Outlined* (1936). Covering a wide range of topics, he relied on an interdisciplinary method, combining anthropology, archaeology, sociology, and history.

Among the first scholars to investigate slavery from the slaves' point of view, Woodson studied it comparatively at institutions in the United States and Latin America. His work prefigured the concerns of later scholars of slavery by several decades, as he examined slaves' resistance to bondage, the internal slave trade and the

breakup of slave families, miscegenation, and blacks' achievements despite the adversity of slavery.

Woodson focused mainly on slavery in the antebellum period, examining the relationships between owners and slaves and the impact of slavery upon the organization of land, labor, agriculture, industry, education, religion, politics, and culture. Woodson also noted the African cultural influences on African American culture. In *The Negro Wage Earner* (1930) and *The Negro Professional Man and the Community* (1934) Woodson described class and occupational stratification within the black community. Using a sample of twenty-five thousand doctors, dentists, nurses, lawyers, writers, and journalists, he examined income, education, family background, marital status, religious affiliation, club and professional memberships, and the literary tastes of black professionals. He hoped that his work on Africa would "invite attention to the vastness of Africa and the complex problems of conflicting cultures."

Woodson also pioneered in the study of black religious history. A Baptist who attended church regularly, he was drawn to an examination of black religion because the church functioned as an educational, political, and social institution in the black community and served as the foundation for the rise of an independent black culture. Black churches, he noted, established kindergartens, women's clubs, training schools, and burial and fraternal societies, from which independent black businesses developed. As meeting places for kin and neighbors, black churches strengthened the political and economic base of the black community and promoted racial solidarity. Woodson believed that the "impetus for the uplift of the race must come from its ministry," and he predicted that black ministers would have a central role in the modern civil rights movement.

Woodson never married or had children, and he died at his Washington home; he had directed the association until his death. For thirty-five years he had dedicated his life to the exploration and study of the African American past. Woodson made an immeasurable and enduring contribution to the advancement of black history through

his own scholarship and the programs he launched through the Association for the Study of Negro Life and History.

FURTHER READING

Two small collections of Woodson's papers exist at the Library of Congress Manuscript Division and the Moorland-Spingarn Research Center at Howard University.

Goggin, Jacqueline. *Carter G. Woodson: A Life in Black History* (1993).
Meier, August, and Elliott Rudwick. *Black History and the Historical Profession, 1915–1980* (1986).
—JACQUELINE GOGGIN

WORK, MONROE NATHAN

WORK, MONROE NATHAN (15 Aug. 1866– 2 May 1945), sociologist, was born in rural Iredell County, North Carolina, the son of Alexander Work and Eliza Hobbs, former slaves and farmers. His family migrated to Cairo, Illinois, in 1866 and in 1876 to Kansas, where they homesteaded, and Work remained to help on the farm until he was twenty-three. He then started secondary school and by 1903 had received his MA in Sociology from the University of Chicago. That year he accepted a teaching job at Georgia State Industrial College in Savannah.

Living in the deep South for the first time, Work became concerned about the plight of African Americans, who constituted a majority of Savannah's population. In 1905 he answered a call from W. E. B. Du Bois to attend the conference that established the Niagara Movement, a militant black rights group that opposed BOOKER T. WASHINGTON's accommodationist approach to black advancement. While continuing to participate in the Niagara Movement, Work founded the Savannah Men's Sunday Club. It combined the functions of a lyceum, lobbying group, and civic club, engaging in such activities as petitioning the city government, opening a reading room, organizing youth activities, and conducting a health education campaign among lower-class African Americans. Quickly accepted into the city's black elite, he married Florence E. Henderson in 1904. Their marriage lasted until his death, but no children survived infancy.

In 1908 Work was offered a position at Washington's Tuskegee Institute in Macon County, Alabama. As an ally of Du Bois, Work found it difficult to accept the position, but he did. By 1908 he had begun to doubt the efficacy of protest. A streetcar boycott had not halted legalized segregation in Savannah, and the Niagara Movement had failed to expand. Work had begun to see another way to use his talents on behalf of black advancement. He was not a dynamic speaker or a natural leader, but a quiet scholar and researcher. He believed that prejudice was rooted in ignorance, and this suggested reliance on education rather than protest. In a 1932 interview Work declared that while still a student, "I dedicated my life to the gathering of information, the compiling of exact knowledge concerning the Negro." Disillusioned about the power of protest, Work believed that the resources and audience available at Tuskegee would allow him to make his skills useful: "It was the center of things relating to the Negro," he noted.

Although Washington had hired Work primarily as a record keeper and researcher for his own articles and speeches, Work used every opportunity to expand the functions of his Department of Records and Research. In 1908 he began compiling a day-to-day record of the African American experience. His sources included newspaper clippings, pamphlets, reports, and replies to his own letters of inquiry. All were organized by category and date, providing the data for the *Negro Yearbook* and the Tuskegee Lynching Report, both of which began in 1912. Each year he distributed the Tuskegee Lynching Report to southern newspapers and leaders to publicize the extent and injustice of lynch law. Under his editorship, nine editions of the *Negro Yearbook* provided information on discrimination and black progress to educators, researchers, and newspaper editorialists. In 1928 Work supplied another valuable research tool with the publication of *A Bibliography of the Negro in Africa and America*. It was the first extensive, classified bibliography of its kind.

Work did not spend all his time compiling data for others; he was also a teacher, department head, crusader, and researcher. He published over seventy articles and pamphlets. His research usually highlighted either the achievements of Africans and African Americans or the obstacles to black progress. Earlier than most black scholars, Work wrote in a positive manner about African history and culture. In a 1916 article for the *Journal of Negro History*, he declared that "Negroes should not despise the rock from which they were hewn." Work also investigated African American folktales and their African roots. Even before the Harlem Renaissance, Work celebrated the distinctiveness of African American culture. His meticulous scholarship was widely recognized in the academic community. In 1900 he became the first African American to publish an article in the *American Journal of Sociology*; the article dealt with black crime in Chicago and pointed to the lack of social services for African Americans. In 1929 he presented a paper at the American Historical Association annual meeting.

Although Work eschewed protest when he left the Niagara Movement and went to Tuskegee, he remained a quiet crusader for change. Early in his career Work developed a special interest in black health issues. In Savannah he started health education programs through the churches. He encouraged Booker T. Washington to establish National Negro Health Week in 1914. Work organized the week for seventeen years before it was taken over by the United States Public Health Service. He was also deeply concerned with the problem of lynching, and he became active in a southern-based movement to eradicate the evil. Work's estrangement from Du Bois made cooperation with the National Association for the Advancement of Colored People's antilynching campaign difficult, but Work found allies in the Atlanta-based Commission on Interracial Cooperation and the Association of Southern Women for the Prevention of Lynching. The latter groups sought to change the South through education, while the NAACP sought change through legislation. Through his contacts in the antilynching campaign, Work became actively involved in numerous interracial groups in the South.

Monroe Work overestimated the power of education to eliminate prejudice, but his numerous articles and his quiet, dignified presence in biracial professional organizations and reform groups undoubtedly helped to dispel some of the southern white stereotypes of African Americans. He accepted the constraints required to work in the deep South in order to use his abilities to change it. After his death, in Tuskegee, two of his protégés established the Tuskegee Civic Association, which brought majority rule and desegregation to Macon County. Monroe Work was one of the lesser-known figures who tilled the soil from which the civil rights movement sprouted in the 1950s and 1960s.

FURTHER READING

A small collection of Work's personal papers is kept in the Tuskegee University Archives in Alabama, and a 1932 interview by Lewis A. Jones and other biographical materials can be found among the Jessie P. Guzman papers also at Tuskegee.

McMurry, Linda O. *Recorder of the Black Experience: A Biography of Monroe Nathan Work* (1985).

—LINDA O. MCMURRY

WRIGHT, LOUIS TOMPKINS (22 July 1891–8 Oct. 1952), surgeon, hospital administrator, and civil rights leader, was born in La Grange, Georgia, the son of Ceah Ketcham Wright, a physician and clergyman, and Lula Tompkins. After his father's death in 1895, his mother married William Fletcher Penn, a physician who was the first African American to graduate from Yale University Medical School. Raised and educated in Atlanta, Wright received his elementary, secondary, and college education at Clark University in Atlanta, graduating in 1911 as valedictorian of his class. His stepfather was one of the guiding influences that led to his choice of medicine as a career.

Wright graduated from Harvard Medical School, cum laude and fourth in his class, in 1915. While in medical school he exhibited his willingness to take a strong stand against racial injustice when he successfully opposed a hospital policy that would have barred him (but not his white classmates) from the practicum in delivering babies (obstetrics) at Boston-Lying-In Hospital. Despite an early record of publications, because of restrictions based on race, Wright completed an internship during 1915–1916 at Freedmen's Hospital, the teaching hospital at the Howard University School of Medicine in Washington, D.C., one of only three black hospitals with approved internship programs at that time.

While he was an intern at Freedmen's, Wright rejected a claim in the medical literature that the Schick test for diptheria could not be used on African Americans because of their heavy skin pigmentation. A study he conducted proved the validity of the usefulness of this test on dark-skinned people and was the basis of his second published paper, "The Schick Test, with Especial Reference to the Negro" (*Journal of Infectious Diseases* 21 [1917]: 265–268). Wright returned to Atlanta in July 1916 to practice medicine. In Atlanta he launched his civil rights career as a founding member of the Atlanta branch of the NAACP, serving as its first treasurer (1916–1917).

With the onset of World War I, Wright applied for a military commission and became a first lieutenant in the U.S. Army Medical Corps. A month before going overseas in June 1918, he married Corrine M. Cooke in New York City. They had two daughters, both of whom became physicians: Jane Cooke Wright and Barbara Penn Wright.

While Wright was in France, his unit was gassed with phosgene, causing him permanent lung damage. Because his injury (for which he received a Purple Heart) imposed physical limitations, he served out the rest of the war in charge of the surgical wards at three field hospitals. As a medical officer he introduced the intradermal method for smallpox vaccination ("Intradermal Vaccination against Smallpox," *Journal of the American Medical Association* 71 [1918]: 654–657), which was officially adopted by the U.S. Army.

In 1919, when Wright settled in Harlem to start a general medical practice, Harlem Hospital, a municipal facility with a 90 percent black patient population, had no African American doctors or nurses on staff. With an assignment effective 1 January 1920 as a clinical assistant (the lowest rank) in the

Out-Patient Department, he became the first African American to be appointed to the staff of a New York City hospital. His steadfast and successful efforts during the 1920s working with hospital administrators and with city officials led gradually to appointments for other African Americans as interns and attending physicians. His push for greater opportunities for African American professionals at Harlem Hospital culminated in a reorganization mandated in 1930 by William Schroeder, commissioner of the Department of Hospitals for the City of New York. The result was the first genuine effort to racially integrate the entire medical staff of a major U.S. hospital. By then Wright had risen to the position of visiting surgeon, and in October 1934 he became the second African American to be admitted to the American College of Surgeons (established in 1913). In 1938 he was appointed to a one-year term as the hospital's director of surgery. In 1929 he had achieved yet another breakthrough, as the first African American to be appointed as a police surgeon through the city's competitive civil service examination. He retained the position until his death.

In 1935 Wright was elected chairman of the national board of directors of the NAACP, a position he held until 1952. As a civil rights leader he opposed the establishment of hospitals exclusively for black people, and in the 1940s he argued for national health care insurance; he also challenged discriminatory policies and practices of the powerful American Medical Association. In a published open letter (dated 28 Jan. 1931) in response to an offer from the Julius Rosenwald Fund to build a hospital for blacks in New York City, Wright wrote: "A segregated hospital makes the white person feel superior and the black person feel inferior. It sets the black person apart from all other citizens as being a different kind of citizen and a different kind of medical student and physician, which you know and we know is not the case. What the Negro physician needs is equal opportunity for training and practice—no more, no less."

Treating common injuries in the surgical wards of Harlem Hospital led Wright to develop, in 1936, a device for handling fractured and dislocated neck

vertebrae. In addition to this neck brace, he also designed a special metal plate to treat certain fractures of the femur. He became an expert on bone injuries and in 1937 was asked to write the chapter on head injuries for Charles Scudder's monumental textbook *The Treatment of Fractures* (1938), this being the first contribution by an African American to a major authoritative medical text.

Wright became ill with tuberculosis in 1939 and for nearly three years was confined to Biggs Memorial Hospital in Ithaca, New York. In 1939, while hospitalized, he was elected a diplomate of the American Board of Surgery. The year before, *Life* magazine had recognized him as the "most eminent Negro doctor" in the United States. In 1940 he was awarded the NAACP's prestigious Spingarn Medal for his achievements and contributions to American medicine.

In 1942, after returning to Harlem Hospital, Wright was appointed director of surgery, a position he held until his death. In 1945 he established a certified four-year residency program in surgery, a first for a black hospital. In 1948 he led a team of resident doctors in the first clinical trials of the antibiotic aureomycin with human beings. This pioneering testing at Harlem Hospital and subsequently at other hospitals paved the way for the approval of this drug and eventually other antibiotics by the U.S. Food and Drug Administration. In 1948 he established and became director of the Harlem Hospital Cancer Research Foundation, funded by the U.S. Public Health Service. Perhaps his crowning achievement was his election, that year, as president of the hospital's medical board.

Over the course of his long career at Harlem Hospital, Wright welded together into a harmonious whole the various white and black groups within the hospital. He recognized and confronted directly the problems faced by other ethnic professionals, particularly Jewish and Italian-American physicians, so that shortly before his death, at the dedication of the hospital's Louis T. Wright Library, he said, "Harlem Hospital represents to my mind the finest example of democracy at work in the field of medicine."

Wright died in New York City. His presence at Harlem Hospital and on the national civil rights scene, and his voice and actions in public and private health forums and debates, had significant consequences on American medicine in three areas: it led to a rapport between black and white doctors that generated scientific and clinical research yielding important contributions in several areas of medicine; it dispensed with myths regarding black physicians that excluded them from any hospital staff on grounds other than those related to individual competence and character; and it led to the admittance of qualified physicians who were African American into local and national medical and scientific societies.

FURTHER READING

Wright published eighty-nine scientific articles in leading medical journals: thirty-five on antibiotics, fourteen in the field of cancer, six on bone trauma, and others on various surgical procedures on the colon and the repair of gunshot wounds.

Cobb, William Montague. "Louis Tompkins Wright, 1891–1952," *Journal of the National Medical Association* 45 (Mar. 1953): 130–148.

de L'Maynard, Aubre. *Surgeons to the Poor: The Harlem Hospital Story* (1978).

Obituary: *New York Times,* 9 Oct. 1952.

—ROBERT C. HAYDEN

Richard Nathaniel Wright, author of militant protest novels Native Son *(1940) and* Black Boy *(1945).* Library of Congress

 WRIGHT, RICHARD
(4 Sept. 1908–28 Nov. 1960), author, was born Richard Nathaniel Wright in a log cabin in the backwoods of Adams County, Mississippi. He was the eldest of the two sons of Nathaniel Wright, an illiterate sharecropper, and Ella Wilson, a semi-literate schoolteacher. Since the boll weevil had ravaged the local cotton industry, the family moved to Memphis, Tennessee, and shortly afterwards, Nathaniel Wright abandoned them.

Ella Wright eked out a living by working as a servant in white households, but after a severe stroke in 1918, she was never able to work again. She and the boys went to live with her parents, Richard and Margaret Wilson, in Jackson, Mississippi. Wright's autobiographical narrative *Black Boy*

(1945) gives a vivid picture of those difficult years in his grandparents' house. There were constant arguments and violent beatings. The family resources were stretched to the limits, and his grandmother, the family matriarch, bitterly resented Richard's independent spirit. She was a devout Seventh Day Adventist who believed that all books other than the Scriptures were "Devil's Work," and pressured Wright to be "saved" by the church. Wright remained an atheist all his life.

After a year at the Negro Seventh Day Adventist School in Jackson, Wright attended the Jim Hill Primary School and, in eighth grade, the Smith Robertson Elementary School. For the first time, he came into contact with the striving black middle class, whose models were people like W. E. B. DU BOIS and BOOKER T. WASHINGTON. He blossomed and soon proved an outstanding student. In 1925 Wright was the school valedictorian. That same year, he had a short story published

in the *Southern Register,* a local African American weekly. A black high school opened in Jackson for the first time that year, but Wright could not buy books or clothes from the money he earned from odd jobs after school. In November 1925 he left behind the hostile atmosphere in his grandmother's house and took the train to Memphis to seek full-time work.

His job opportunities were severely curtailed by the color of his skin. The best he could find was work as a messenger in an optical company. One day, in the local newspaper, he came across the name H. L. Mencken. It would prove a turning point. As a black man, Wright was not able to borrow books from the public library, but he persuaded an Irish coworker to lend him his card, and he went to the library, pretending to be picking up books for this white man. He took out two books by Mencken. Wright was excited to discover that the iconoclastic Baltimore journalist and literary critic used words like a weapon. He realized he wanted nothing more than to do the same. With Mencken's *A Book of Prefaces* as his guide, Wright began to read voraciously. He was painfully aware that his formal education extended only to the eighth grade, and that famous writers, as well as their subject matter, were invariably white.

Wright left the segregated South in November 1927. For the next ten years he lived in Chicago. He was one of twelve million black people who made that journey from the rural South to the industrial North during the Great Migration of 1916–1928, and he would describe it as the most traumatic journey of his entire life. His narrative *Twelve Million Black Voices* (1941), accompanied by WPA photographs, movingly conveys the two different worlds.

Wright soon landed a job as an unskilled laborer, sorting mail on the night shift at the Chicago Post Office—the best-paying job in town for a black man. Wright brought his mother, brother, and aunt to live with him in Chicago. During the Depression, however, Wright took whatever work he could find, while also pursuing his reading and writing with extraordinary determination.

In the fall of 1933 a white friend from the post office told him about the John Reed Club, a national organization of "proletarian artists and writers" founded by the Communist Party. Wright went along and met other aspiring artists and writers—mostly sons of Jewish immigrants. Stimulated by this environment, he began to write poems, several of which were published in Communist magazines. His poem "I Have Seen Black Hands" was printed in the national weekly *The New Masses* in June 1934.

Early in 1934 Wright was pressured to join the Communist Party. Since it consciously fought racism and was one of the few places in the United States where blacks and whites mixed on an equal footing, Wright decided to do so, but from the beginning there were conflicts. He disliked being told what to do, and in his spare time, his writing was far more important to him than party work. Nevertheless, the party provided crucial support to Wright, both as an artist and as a bulwark

against racism in America. He did not leave it until 1944, when he became an outspoken anti-Communist. He was disgusted that the Communist Party put civil rights issues on hold during World War II, at a time when blacks were expected to fight in segregated armed forces, and as he explained in his famous essay, "I Tried to Be a Communist," published in the *Atlantic Monthly* in August and September 1944, while the party claimed to be democratic, it actually took its orders from Moscow.

The Works Progress Administration (WPA) was established by President Franklin Roosevelt in May 1935, with the Federal Writers Project as one of its offshoots. Wright, who by now had published two short stories and thirteen poems, was signed on to the Illinois Writers Project as a supervisor. He could hardly believe his luck. This was a thirty-hour-a-week job, and the U.S. government was paying him to write. In his spare time Wright wrote a volume of short stories, *Uncle Tom's Children* (1938), and a novel, *Lawd Today!* (1963).

Wright was influenced by Marxism and the Chicago School of Sociology, which related neurotic behavior and crime to environment, and both were important influences on the South Side group of black writers that Wright organized in 1936. Other members who became well-known writers were Frank Marshall Davis, Margaret Walker, and Theodore (Ted) Ward.

In May 1937 Wright moved to New York City. He became a friend and mentor to RALPH ELLISON, encouraged the young JAMES BALDWIN, and championed CHESTER HIMES and GWENDOLYN BROOKS. Wright was briefly the Harlem correspondent for the Communist Party newspaper *The Daily Worker*, before he was transferred to the New York Writers Project. In February 1938 his writing career took off when he won a national competition of WPA writers for his collection of short stories *Uncle Tom's Children*, which portrayed the barbarism of black life and lynching in the Jim Crow South. Harper and Brothers published the book, which won Wright national recognition.

In 1939 a Guggenheim Fellowship allowed Wright to work full-time on

his novel *Native Son* (1940). With its negative depiction of black ghetto life and its hint of interracial sex, the novel was controversial at the time and would remain so for decades to come. Promoted by the Book-of-the-Month Club, though the judges insisted on deleting nearly all allusions to interracial sexual attraction, the book sold a quarter of a million copies. Wright became the first best-selling African American writer. In 1941 the play *Native Son*, written by Wright and Paul Green and directed by Orson Welles, opened on Broadway to rave reviews. In 1945 Wright's autobiographical narrative *Black Boy*, again promoted by the Book-of-the-Month Club, sold an incredible half million copies. The original manuscript, entitled *American Hunger*, referring to the spiritual hunger of oppressed American blacks, portrayed Wright's formative years up to the beginning of the war, focusing on his experience of racism in both the deep South and in the North. The Book-of-the-Month Club insisted that he cut the second half, with its depiction of racism in the North and Wright's experiences in the Communist Party. Similarly, the judges disliked the unpatriotic title, and finally Wright changed it to *Black Boy*. The original manuscript was finally published posthumously in 1977, under its original title.

After a brief marriage to Dhimah Meidman in 1939, Wright married Ellen Poplowitz in March 1941, and their daughter Julia was born in 1942. His marriage to a white woman and the taunts that followed them when they walked together around New York and when Ellen went out with Julia reinforced Wright's desire to leave the country. He desperately wanted to expand his horizons and see the world. Encouraged by Gertrude Stein, who lived in Paris and whose work he greatly admired, Wright and his family left for Paris in May 1946. Their second daughter, Rachel, was born in Paris on 17 January 1949.

Wright was thirty-eight and in his prime when he left for Europe, but that ship voyage across the Atlantic marked a dramatic downturn in his career. For the next fourteen years he continued to write prolifically, both fiction and nonfiction. In Europe his work was celebrated by the famous existentialists Jean-Paul Sartre and Simone de Beauvoir. He was interviewed frequently and his work was widely translated. He was regarded as an important American writer and public intellectual. In the United States he was largely ignored. Even today, few Americans have heard of the titles he wrote after he left the U.S.—*The Outsider* (1953), *Savage Holiday* (1954), *Black Power* (1954), *The Color Curtain* (1956), *Pagan Spain* (1957), *White Man, Listen!* (1957), *The Long Dream* (1958), *Eight Men* (1961), and *Haiku: This Other World* (1998). Wright's exile writing had the same power, the same emotional persuasiveness. His nonfiction—a mixture of travel essay, memoir, biographical sketch, and political commentary—was in many ways ahead of its time. But in the highly conservative atmosphere of the McCarthyist 1950s, hard-hitting critiques of American racism and Western imperialism—and protest literature, in general—were no longer in vogue.

Wright's world opened up considerably after he left the United States. In 1949–1950 he spent almost a year in Argentina, where he played Bigger Thomas in the movie *Native Son.* (The film, made in an adverse political climate, with the forty-year-old Wright badly miscast as an eighteen-year old, was a financial flop.) In 1953 he visited the Gold Coast, a trip he chronicled in *Black Power.* In 1955 he attended the Bandung Conference in Indonesia, an experience he recalled in *The Color Curtain.* He spent time exploring life in Franco's Spain for the book *Pagan Spain* (1957), and he gave lectures that were collected in *White Man, Listen!* (1957).

American critics often refer to Wright's last fourteen years as his "exile" years. The term is hardly appropriate, however, since Wright's entire body of work prior to his departure for France was a passionate portrayal of what it was like to live as an exile in his native land. The prevalent view, even today, is that living abroad was bad for his writing, that it cut him off from the reality of contemporary America, from his roots, and from the anger that fueled his writing. Others claim that Wright did not lose his power in the 1950s. What changed were the

historical circumstances in which he was writing.

Wright died in Paris at the age of fifty-two. His death certificate gives a heart attack as the cause, but the circumstances of his premature death have always aroused suspicion, especially as it is known that the U.S. State Department watched him closely, throughout the 1950s. As someone who ceaselessly criticized American racism from his prominent vantage point as a black intellectual in Europe, Wright was something of a threat to the 1950s propaganda war.

Richard Wright was the first African American writer to enter mainstream American literature. A watershed figure in African American literature, he pushed back the horizons for black writers, expanding their possible subject matter. At the beginning of the twenty-first century, Wright's writing continued to provoke passionate responses, from deep admiration to vehement hostility. He is an *uncomfortable* writer. He challenges, he tells painful truths, he is a disturber of the peace. He was never interested in pleasing readers. Wright wanted his words to be weapons.

FURTHER READING

Fabre, Michel. *The Unfinished Quest of Richard Wright* (1973).
Kinnamon, Keneth, and Michel Fabre, eds. *Conversations with Richard Wright* (1993).
Rowley, Hazel. *Richard Wright: The Life and Times* (2001).
Walker, Margaret. *Richard Wright: Daemonic Genius* (1988).
Webb, Constance. *Richard Wright: A Biography* (1968).

Obituary: *New York Times,* 30 Nov. 1960.
                                        —HAZEL ROWLEY

 WRIGHT, RICHARD ROBERT, SR. (16 May 1855–2 July 1947), educator and banker, was born in Whitfield County, Georgia, the son of Robert Waddell and Harriet (maiden name unknown), both slaves. His father, of mixed African and Cherokee descent, was the coachman on a plantation where his mother was a house servant. When Richard was two years old, his father escaped to free territory. Richard and his mother were

taken by their slave owner to Cuthbert, Georgia, where she married Alexander Wright and had two children. After emancipation Harriet Wright moved with her three children to Atlanta to take advantage of the recent opening of a Freedman's Bureau School for Negroes. While Harriet supported the family by running a boarding house, Richard entered Storrs School, which was run by the American Missionary Association. In 1866 General Oliver Otis Howard, then current commissioner of the Freedmen's Bureau, visited the Sunday school at the Storrs Church and asked the students what message he should tell the children of the North about them. The young Wright stood up and said, "Tell them we are rising." This incident inspired the poem "Howard at Atlanta" by the great abolitionist John Greenleaf Whittier. Wright attended Atlanta University where he received a BA and was valedictorian of the university's first graduating class in 1876. Wright married Lydia E. Howard in 1869, and they had nine children.

After graduation from Atlanta University, Wright became the principal of a primary school in Cuthbert. In Cuthbert he helped organize local farmers into cooperatives and coordinated the state's first county fair for blacks. In 1878 he organized the Georgia State Teachers' Association (for black educators), served as its first president, and began publishing the association's *Weekly Journal of Progress,* later called the *Weekly Sentinel.* Wright represented Georgia at the 1879 National Conference of Colored Men of the United States, held in Nashville, Tennessee, which sought primarily to assist in the plight of African Americans.

In 1880 Wright was asked to set up and direct Ware High School in Augusta, Georgia, which became the state's first public high school for blacks. His political activities definitely aided his career in education. Wright was an alternate delegate in 1880 to the Republican National Convention in Chicago, a participant at the conference of the Afro-American League in Minneapolis (1881), a member of the State Republican Central Committee (1882), a special agent for the U.S. Department of the Interior Development in Alabama (1885), and a delegate for Georgia to the Republican National

Convention through 1896. In return for his political influence with the black voters, Wright was appointed by President William McKinley to the position of paymaster in the army with the rank of major during the Spanish-American War.

In October 1891 the Georgia legislature established the Georgia State Industrial College for Colored Youth in Savannah. Wright, an obvious candidate to lead the school because of his long experience in teaching and administration, remained president for thirty years, until his retirement in 1921. One of the members of his faculty was MONROE NATHAN WORK, who later wrote the well-known *Bibliography of the Negro in Africa and America*.

Wright's tenure as president was troubled by the control of an all-white board of trustees for the college that objected to higher education for blacks. Especially controversial were Wright's efforts to include classical education in the curriculum. Early in his presidency he organized the Negro Civic Improvement League in Savannah. This political organization proved to be very unpopular with the college trustees, and, under much pressure from them, Wright withdrew from the organization and politics in general. He decided to follow the emphasis placed by many black scholars and leaders of the day, such as BOOKER T. WASHINGTON, on programs of self-help and cooperative efforts with whites. It was during this time that Wright wrote *A Brief Historical Sketch of Negro Education in Georgia* (1894), which addressed his inability to obtain sufficient support for an adequate curriculum at the college.

In 1921 Wright retired as president of the Georgia State Industrial College for Colored Youth and began a new career as a banker and elder statesman. Along with a son, Richard R. Wright Jr., and a daughter, Lillian W. Clayton, Wright founded in Philadelphia in 1921 the Citizens and Southern Bank and Trust Company. Wright's reputation as an honest and well-qualified man provided the kind of stability needed to survive such economic crises as the 1929 stock market crash and the Great Depression of the 1930s. The fact that Wright managed to maintain banking operations during the Depression can be credited to both the diversity of his investment portfolio and the conservative policy of his bank.

In 1945 he attended the conference in California that organized the United Nations. A banquet was held at the conference in recognition of his long career, which included the presidency of the National Association of Presidents of A & M Colleges (1906–1919) and the presidency of the National Association of Teachers of Colored Schools (1908–1912). He helped to establish the National Freedom Day Association, supported a 1940 commemorative stamp for Booker T. Washington, and gathered information for the Georgia Archives about African Americans who fought in the First World War. In 1946, a year before his death, Wright accepted the Muriel Dobbin's Pioneers of Industry Award from the business community of Philadelphia. He died in Philadelphia.

FURTHER READING

Wright's papers are held by his family, the majority with Emanuel C. Wright of Philadelphia and others with Wright's daughter Harriet B. S. Hines of Glenarden, Maryland.

BOND, HORACE MANN. *The Black American Scholars: A Study of Their Beginnings* (1972).

Hall, Clyde W., ed. *One Hundred Years of Educating at Savannah State College, 1890–1990* (1990).

Haynes, Elizabeth Ross. *The Black Boy of Atlanta* (1952).

LOGAN, RAYFORD W. *The Betrayal of the Negro* (1965).

Meier, August. *Negro Thought in America, 1888–1915* (1963).

Obituary: *New York Times*, 3 July 1947.

—ROBERT C. MORRIS

X – Y

X, LOUIS. *See* Farrakhan, Louis Abdul.

X, MALCOLM. *See* Malcolm X.

YORK (c. 1772–before 1832), explorer, slave, and the first African American to cross the North American continent from coast to coast north of Mexico, is believed to have been born in Caroline County, Virginia, the son of an enslaved African American also named York (later called Old York), owned by John Clark, a member of the Virginia gentry and father of the famous George Rogers Clark and William Clark. York's mother is unidentified; it is likely that she, too, was a Clark family slave. A slave named Rose is sometimes listed as York's mother, but sources best identify her as his stepmother. York is believed to have been assigned while a child to William Clark as his servant and companion. Since such relationships were generally between children of about the same age, with the slave sometimes a few years younger, York may have been about two or three years Clark's junior. As the boys grew older, their roles would have become more sharply defined as master and slave. York would have learned everything necessary to serve properly as the body servant of a young Virginia gentleman. He was essentially following in his father's footsteps, since Old York was John Clark's body servant and a trusted slave. York would not have received any formal schooling and was most likely illiterate.

In March 1785 the John Clark family settled in Jefferson County, Kentucky, near Louisville. Once in Kentucky, York would have learned many of the same frontier skills as William Clark did. York probably accompanied Clark during the latter's service as a lieutenant in the U.S. Army from 1792 to 1796. A letter of 1 June 1795 by Clark mentioning that his "boy" had arrived at Fort Greenville, Ohio, might be the earliest known reference to York (Holmberg, 273, 274n). The first certain record of York is his listing in the July 1799 will of John Clark. By that will York officially became the property of William Clark.

In 1803 Clark accepted Meriwether Lewis's invitation to join him as coleader of the famous Lewis and Clark expedition (1803–1806) to the Pacific Ocean, and he took his slave with him. Thus, York was one of the earliest members of the Corps of Discovery and part of the important foundation formed in 1803 at the Falls of the Ohio, at Louisville. York was not an official member of the corps; he was carried on the rolls as Clark's servant and received no pay or land grant for his service. Nonetheless, he was an important member of the expedition, and Clark would have had little hesitation in taking him. Clark had traveled widely as a soldier and a civilian, and York almost certainly traveled with him on some, if not most, of his trips. Thus, York was an experienced traveler by land and water and possessed many of the same abilities the captains required of expedition recruits.

It was a bonus to have York present as a servant to make camp life easier for the captains. And York would have had a definite presence. Expedition-related documents provide a basic physical description of him as a large man (apparently both in height and weight), very strong, agile for his size, and very black. A personality also emerges. York was loyal, caring, and determined, and he had a sense of humor. The expedition journals also give us a basic

understanding of York's experience on the journey. The dangers and hardships of the expedition had a leveling effect on the men of the corps. While York never would have completely escaped his slave status, his participation in the daily experiences and work of the corps resulted in his acceptance as one of the group at a level he never would have enjoyed before the expedition. Additional evidence of this is York's inclusion in the November 1805 vote of expedition members regarding the location of their winter quarters. The very fact that York's opinion was sought and recorded with the others' votes reflects his acceptance and status.

An additional benefit for the corps, and a revelation to York, was realized when the explorers encountered American Indians who had never before seen a black man. Those native people almost always greeted York with awe and respect. In their cultures his uniqueness gave him great spiritual power. They also admired his enormous size, strength, and agility. The Arikara Indians named him "Big Medicine." York was consequently used to help advance the expedition. For his part, this was a new and enlightening experience. In only a couple of years he had gone from a societal and racial inferior to a position of relative equality in a primarily white group and even to being viewed by many Indians as superior to his white companions.

On 23 September 1806 the explorers arrived in St. Louis on their return from the Pacific Ocean. The men were discharged and other business taken care of before traveling eastward. On 5 November 1806 Lewis, Clark, York, and others arrived in Louisville, where York was reunited with his wife. (Only one other returning member of the expedition was married.) The names of York's wife and her owner are unknown. When York was married is not known either, though it was before October 1803, when the nucleus of the corps pushed off from the Louisville area. Nor is it known whether they had any children. There are oral traditions among some of the Indian tribes the corps visited that York left behind descendants, and Clark also made a reference in 1832 to stories he had heard that York left descendants among the Indians of the Missouri River.

Over the next year and a half Clark traveled between Louisville, St. Louis, and Virginia. York almost certainly went with him as his servant. In June 1808 Clark and his bride, Julia Hancock, moved to St. Louis to establish their permanent residence, bringing with them a number of their slaves, including York. The situation now changed for York. The years of periodic travel had meant separation from his wife, but York also knew he would be returning. Now his visits to her would be periodic and probably short. York went so far as to ask to be hired out or sold to someone in Louisville. Clark refused to grant this request and told him to forget about his wife. York persisted until Clark relented and allowed him to go for a visit, though he was angry enough to threaten to sell York or hire him out to a severe master if he tried to "run off" or failed to "perform his duty as a slave" (Holmberg, 160). A month later Clark noted that because of York's "notion about freedom and his immense services," he doubted York would ever be of service to him again (Holmberg, 183).

By spring 1809 York had returned to St. Louis, but only briefly. His attitude was no better, in Clark's opinion, and punishment failed to improve it. Clark therefore determined to keep York in Louisville. But rather than sell him, Clark hired him out for at least the next six years. In November 1815 York was still a slave, working as the wagon driver in a freight-hauling business that Clark and a nephew started in Louisville. From then until 1832 York disappears from known records.

In 1832 Clark reported to Washington Irving that he had freed York and set him up in a freight-hauling business between Nashville, Tennessee, and Richmond (Kentucky, it is believed), that York had proved a poor businessman, that he had regretted getting his freedom, and that while trying to return to Clark in St. Louis, he had died of cholera in Tennessee. A happier,

but unsubstantiated, ending has York returning to the West, where he lived in the Rocky Mountains as a chief among the Crow Indians, but despite some possible slaveholder rationalization, there is no reason to doubt the main points of Clark's statement. The possibility that York traveled deeper into slave territory upon being freed is indeed unusual. It may be that York's wife's owner had moved to Nashville and that York followed her there after being manumitted.

An assessment of his participation in the Lewis and Clark expedition shows that York made definite contributions to its success. His experience undoubtedly altered his perspective on race and his place in society. Even though doing so alienated him from Clark and brought him further hardship and unhappiness, he spoke up for the rights and freedom he believed he had earned by his years of loyal service and his role in the expedition. It is ironic that the very thing that made him a slave and inferior in white society—the color of his skin—marked him as someone to be respected and admired among many of the Indian tribes encountered on one of the most famous journeys in U.S. history.

FURTHER READING

Betts, Robert B. *In Search of York: The Slave Who Went to the Pacific with Lewis and Clark*, revised with a new epilogue by James J. Holmberg (2000).

Holmberg, James J., ed. *Dear Brother: Letters of William Clark to Jonathan Clark* (2002).
—JAMES J. HOLMBERG

YOUNG, ANDREW JACKSON, JR.

(12 Mar. 1932–), civil rights leader, United Nations ambassador, U.S. congressman, and mayor, was born in New Orleans, Louisiana, the son of Andrew Jackson Young, a dentist, and Daisy Fuller, a teacher. Young received a BS degree in Biology from Howard University in 1951 and a Bachelor of Divinity degree from Hartford Theological Seminary in Connecticut in 1955. In the same year he was ordained as a minister in the United Church of Christ. As a pastor he was sent to such places as Marion, Alabama, and Thomasville and Beachton, Georgia. During this time the civil rights movement was reaching its height under the leadership of MARTIN

LUTHER KING JR. and others who followed the nonviolent resistance tactics of Mohandas Gandhi, the pacifist who had led Indian opposition to British colonial rule. By the time of the Montgomery, Alabama, bus boycott in 1955, Young and several of his parishioners had decided to join the movement. Young himself was actively engaged in voter registration drives.

In 1957 Young returned north to serve as associate director of the Department of Youth Work of the National Council of Churches in New York City. The United Church of Christ then solicited him in 1961 to lead a voter registration drive, focusing on southern blacks who were unaware of their voting rights. Around this time he became involved with King's organization, the Southern Christian Leadership Conference (SCLC). By 1962 Young had become an administrative assistant to King, and in 1964 he was appointed SCLC's executive officer. Although Young originally opposed King's decision to support a strike by sanitation workers in Memphis, Tennessee, he finally joined and was there at the Lorraine Motel when King was assassinated on 4 April 1968.

King's death signaled the end of one phase of the civil rights movement,

Andrew Young during his tenure as Democratic congressman from Georgia, around 1972. Library of Congress

but Young soon became active in the movement's new focus on electoral politics. In 1970 Young entered the race for the Democratic nomination in Georgia's Fifth Congressional District, whose boundaries encompassed much of the southern part of metropolitan Atlanta and contained 40 percent of the area's African American population. Young's opponents were two white candidates and an African American, Lonnie King, an NAACP activist and a former leader of the Atlanta sit-in movement. Although Young was victorious in the Democratic primary, he lost the general election to the Republican challenger, Fletcher Thompson. Inclement weather on election day and a failure to energize some black voters contributed to Young's defeat.

Following that loss, Young became the chairman of Atlanta's Community Relations Commission (CRC) and fought for a better public transit system and against Atlanta's growing drug trafficking and drug use problems. These actions increased his visibility and popularity across the fifth district, and in 1972 he again sought a seat in the House. After running a more aggressive campaign, particularly in African American communities, Young received approximately 52 percent of the vote in the general election. By accomplishing this feat, even in a district that was 62 percent white, Young became the first black congressman elected from Georgia since the end of Reconstruction. Indeed, that year Young and BARBARA JORDAN were the first African Americans elected to Congress from any southern state since North Carolina's GEORGE WHITE in 1898. Young was reelected, by comfortable margins, in 1974 and 1976. During the presidential campaign of 1976, he became a strong supporter of the Democratic candidate, Jimmy Carter, a former Georgia governor.

In 1977, after Carter was elected president, he appointed Young as U.S. Ambassador to the United Nations (UN). As ambassador, Young championed African issues and visited the African continent several times. He also vehemently attacked the South African system of racial apartheid. But, after only two-and-one-half years in office, Young resigned his ambassadorial post in August 1979. This came shortly after a meeting with Zehdi Lahib Terzi, the UN observer for the Palestinian Liberation Organization (PLO). The PLO, at this time, was considered an international terrorist group by the United States government. By meeting with a PLO representative, Young violated state department rules prohibiting official contact with the Palestinian organization. Following his resignation, Young told the *Atlanta Journal* that efforts for peace in the Middle East were at a crucial and perhaps pivotal juncture, and that he had met with the PLO because a chance for peace had to be pursued.

After resigning as UN ambassador, Young returned to Atlanta and founded a consulting firm called Law International, Inc. (later GoodWorks International). The company promoted trade, especially with African nations. Seemingly satisfied with his new and financially lucrative career in business, Young, in 1981, became a reluctant candidate for mayor of Atlanta, after being urged to do so by CORETTA SCOTT KING, outgoing mayor Maynard Jackson, and others. During his campaign Young made a special effort to reach out to white businessmen, many of whom had been alienated by the affirmative action policies of the administration of Jackson, Atlanta's first black mayor. Young received 55 percent of the total vote in the election of 1981 and was reelected by a larger margin in 1985. His administrations were marked by renewed economic growth, including a revitalization of the Underground Atlanta tourist attraction, increased convention trade in the city, and a decrease in overall crime. It also was credited with a major triumph when Atlanta won the right to host the Democratic National Convention in 1988. By 1984 white business leaders were already telling publications like *Ebony* magazine that the city's reputation had improved in the boardrooms of corporate America. The Young administration, however, drew broad criticisms for its historic preservation and neighborhood revitalization policies. The city's Urban Design Commission and neighborhood activists consistently protested proposals to demolish historic buildings and housing in favor of new commercial buildings and highways—and during and after the 1988 Democratic National Convention, the administration was chastised for its rough handling of anti-abortion demonstrators.

Young's mayoral term ended in 1989, but his political aspirations remained strong. The next year he made an unsuccessful run for governor of Georgia against the state's popular lieutenant governor, Zell Miller. Remaining active in business and civic affairs, Young then led a bid by the city of Atlanta to host the 1996 summer Olympic Games. Atlanta's success in winning the bid to host the Centennial Games was largely attributed to Young's popularity and influence among African and other Third World members of the International Olympic Committee (IOC). During the pre-Olympic and Olympic period in Atlanta (a span of more than four years), Young served as cochairman of the Atlanta Organizing Committee.

After the Olympics left Atlanta, Young returned full time to his international consulting firm and continued to serve on several corporate boards, including Delta Airlines, as well as the boards of several academic and humanitarian institutions. In 1999 he returned, in a sense, to his career origins when he was elected president of the National Council of Churches.

Young's wife for forty years, Jean (a civil rights and civic activist), died in September 1994. He remarried shortly thereafter. He had fathered three children with Jean.

Unlike many of his contemporaries in the southern civil rights movement, Andrew Young's most enduring contributions came after the great legal and political battles of the 1960s had been won. Serving as a congressman, a United Nations Ambassador, and a mayor of a large American city, he affected international, national, and local policies for more than twenty-five years. In each of his roles, but particularly as UN Ambassador, he was a principal liaison between the United States and the Third World.

FURTHER READING

Young, Andrew. *An Easy Burden: The Civil Rights Movement and the Transformation of America* (1996).

———. *A Way Out of No Way: The Spiritual Memoirs of Andrew Young* (1994).

Gardner, Carl. *Andrew Young, A Biography* (1978).
Garrow, David J. *Bearing the Cross: Martin Luther King, Jr., and the Southern Christian Leadership Conference, 1955–1968* (1986).
Hornsby, Alton, Jr. *A Short History of Black Atlanta* (2003).

—ALTON HORNSBY JR.

YOUNG, COLEMAN

(24 May 1918–29 Nov. 1997), mayor, was born in Tuscaloosa, Alabama, the son of William Coleman Young, a barber and a tailor, and Ida Reese Jones Young. After his family moved to Detroit in 1923, Young grew up in the Black Bottom section of town, where his father ran a dry-cleaning and tailoring operation and also worked as a night watchman at the post office. Although Young enjoyed his early years in the then-ethnically diverse neighborhood, his family did not altogether escape discrimination. A gifted student, he was rejected by a Catholic high school because of his race, and after graduating from public Eastern High, he lost out on college financial aid for the same reason. Young became an electrical apprentice at Ford Motor Company, only to see a white man with lower test scores get the job. He then worked on Ford's assembly line but was fired for fighting a thug from Harry Bennett's Service Department who had identified Young as a union member.

After his dismissal from Ford, Young went to work for the National Negro Congress, a civil rights organization that focused on labor issues. While with the NNC, he worked at the post office and continued the fight to unionize Ford. When Henry Ford accepted a union contract, Young turned his attention to other issues such as open housing. Fired from his job in the post office for union activity, he was drafted into the army in February 1942. Young initially served in the infantry with the Ninety-second Buffalo Division before transferring to the U.S. Army Air Forces, where he underwent pilot training with the famed Tuskegee airmen. Washed out of the pilot program—an action

Young blamed on FBI interference based on his years of unionizing and associating with so-called radicals—he spent the rest of the war fighting for equal accommodations for African American servicemen on a number of military bases.

Discharged from the air forces as a second lieutenant in December 1945, Young returned to Detroit, regained his position at the post office, and resumed his union organizing activities. In January 1947 he married Marion McClellan; the couple had no children before divorcing in 1954. Shortly thereafter he married Nadine Drake; that childless marriage also ended in divorce a few years later. As a member of the United Public Workers, he soon ran afoul of Walter Reuther, whose conservative brand of anticommunist leadership within the United Auto Workers extended to the Congress of Industrial Organizations. Although Young had been elected to an executive post with the Wayne County, Michigan, chapter of the CIO, he lost his position in 1948 on account of Reuther's political machinations. Following a disastrous run for the state senate as a candidate of Henry Wallace's Progressive Party that same year, Young drifted through a series of jobs before becoming the executive secretary of the newly formed National Negro Labor Council, which achieved some successes nationwide in increasing the range and number of job opportunities for African Americans. Targeted by the federal government as a subversive group, however, the organization folded under pressure in the spring of 1956. After a few more years of drifting between jobs, Young lost a bid for Detroit's Common Council in 1960. Encouraged by the election results, he successfully gained a seat at Michigan's Constitutional Convention. Following the convention Young spent several successful years as an insurance salesman for the Municipal Credit Union League before reentering politics for good in 1964, when he gained election to the Michigan State Senate.

Young remained in the senate until 1973, where he supported open housing and school busing legislation and eventually became Democratic floor leader. In 1973 he ran for mayor of Detroit and, with substantial

union support, narrowly won a racially charged contest against former police commissioner John F. Nichols. After the election Young pledged to work together with business and labor to help turn around the badly troubled city, which was then reeling from high unemployment, rampant crime, white flight, the effects of the gasoline embargo, and the loss of its industrial base. Young presided over the 1977 opening of Renaissance Center, a downtown office-retail complex designed to revitalize the city's riverfront, and was also instrumental in building new manufacturing plants for Chrysler and General Motors. Faced with the city's possible bankruptcy, he persuaded voters to approve an income tax increase and gained wage and benefit concessions from municipal workers. Having run on a campaign of reforming the Detroit police department (long viewed as a source of oppression among African American residents), he increased the number of blacks and minorities on the force and also disbanded STRESS (Stop the Robberies, Enjoy Safe Streets), a special police decoy unit that was the focus of many complaints of brutality.

Reelected four times, Young enjoyed a particularly good relationship with President Jimmy Carter. Among the first to endorse Carter's presidential campaign in 1976, Young served as vice chairman of the Democratic National Committee between 1977 and 1981 and from 1981 until 1983 headed the United States Conference of Mayors. He fared less well under Carter's Republican successors, however, and also had to deal with long-running feuds with the local press as well as nearby suburban governments. Despite his long-held emphasis on racial cooperation, the blunt-spoken Young—who for years had a sign on his desk that read "Head Motherf**ker in Charge"—never gained the trust of many white voters, who deplored his confrontational style and his frequent overseas vacations. In addition to being the subject of federal criminal investigations, none of which resulted in any charges, Young was the target of a paternity suit by former city employee Annivory Calvert, with whom he had a son.

In declining health, Young chose not to run for reelection in 1993. He died in a Detroit hospital. Despite having to face a host of problems with resources that were limited at best, Young proved himself game in his efforts to preserve and revitalize one of America's major metropolitan centers.

FURTHER READING

Young's papers are divided between the Walter Reuther Library at Wayne State University and the African American Museum in Detroit.

Young, Coleman, with Lonnie Wheeler. *Hard Stuff: The Autobiography of Coleman Young* (1994).

Rich, Wilbur C. *Coleman Young and Detroit Politics: From Social Activist to Power Broker* (1989).

Obituaries: *Detroit Free Press*, 5 Dec. 1997; *New York Times*, 30 Nov. 1997.

—EDWARD L. LACH JR.

YOUNG, WHITNEY MOORE, JR. (31 July 1921–11 Mar. 1971), social worker and civil rights activist, was born in Lincoln Ridge, Kentucky, the son of Whitney Moore Young Sr., president of Lincoln Institute, a private African American college, and Laura Ray, a schoolteacher. Raised within the community of the private academy and its biracial faculty, Whitney Young Jr. and his two sisters were sheltered from harsh confrontations with racial discrimination in their early lives, but they attended segregated public elementary schools for African American children and completed high school at Lincoln Institute. In 1937 Young, planning to become a doctor, entered Kentucky State Industrial

College at Frankfort, where he received a BS in 1941. After graduation he became an assistant principal and athletic coach at Julius Rosenwald High School in Madison, Kentucky.

After joining the U.S. Army in 1942, Young studied engineering at the Massachusetts Institute of Technology (MIT). In 1944 he married Margaret Buckner, a teacher whom he had met while they were both students at Kentucky State; they had two children. Sent to Europe later in 1944, Young rose from private to first sergeant in the all-black 369th Anti-Aircraft Artillery Group. His experience in a segregated army on the eve of President Harry Truman's desegregation order drew Young to the challenges of racial diplomacy. In 1946, after his

Whitney Moore Young, Jr. (center), executive director of the National Urban League, meeting with President John F. Kennedy and Henry Steeger at the White House in 1962. Library of Congress

925

discharge from the army, he entered graduate study in social work at the University of Minnesota. His field placement in graduate school was with the Minneapolis chapter of the National Urban League, which sought increased employment opportunities for African American workers. In 1948 Young completed his master's degree in Social Work and became industrial relations secretary of the St. Paul, Minnesota, chapter of the Urban League. In 1950 he became the director of the Urban League chapter in Omaha, Nebraska. He increased both the Omaha chapter's membership and its operating budget. He became skilled at working with the city's business and political leaders to increase employment opportunities for African Americans. In Omaha he also taught in the University of Nebraska's School of Social Work.

In 1954 Young became dean of the School of Social Work at Atlanta University. As an administrator, he doubled the school's budget, raised faculty salaries, and insisted on professional development. In these early years after the Supreme Court's decision in *Brown v. Board of Education of Topeka, Kansas*, Young played a significant advisory role within the leadership of Atlanta's African American community. He was active in the Greater Atlanta Council on Human Relations and a member of the executive committee of the Atlanta branch of the National Association for the Advancement of Colored People (NAACP). He also helped to organize Atlanta's Committee for Cooperative Action, a group of business and professional people who sought to coordinate the social and political action of varied black interest groups and organized patrols in African American communities threatened by white violence. He took a leave of absence from his position at Atlanta University in the 1960–1961 academic year to be a visiting Rockefeller Foundation scholar at Harvard University.

In January 1961 the National Urban League announced Whitney Young's appointment to succeed Lester B. Granger as its executive director. Beginning his new work in fall 1961, Young came to the leadership of the Urban League just after the first wave of sit-in demonstrations and freedom rides had drawn national attention to new forms of civil rights activism in the South. Among the major organizations identified with the civil rights movement, the Urban League was the most conservative and the least inclined to favor public demonstrations for social change. Young was resolved to move it into a firmer alliance with the other major civil rights organizations without threatening the confidence of the Urban League's powerful inside contacts. In 1963 he led it into joining the March on Washington and the Council for United Civil Rights Leadership, a consortium initiated by Kennedy administration officials and white philanthropists to facilitate fundraising and joint planning.

In his ten years as executive director of the Urban League, Young increased the number of its local chapters from sixty to ninety-eight, its staff from 500 to 1,200, and its funding by corporations, foundations, and federal grants. After the assassination of President John Kennedy, Young developed even stronger ties with President Lyndon Johnson's administration. Perhaps Young's most important influence lay in his call for a "Domestic Marshall Plan," outlined in his book *To Be Equal* (1964), which influenced President Johnson's War on Poverty programs.

By the mid-1960s, however, the civil rights coalition had begun to fray. In June 1966 Young and ROY WILKINS of the NAACP refused to sign a manifesto drafted by other civil rights leaders or to join them when they continued the march of JAMES MEREDITH from Memphis, Tennessee, to Jackson, Mississippi. Young continued to shun the black power rhetoric popular with new leaders of the Congress of Racial Equality and the Student Nonviolent Coordinating Committee. Simultaneously, in consideration of the vital alliance with the Johnson administration, he was publicly critical of MARTIN LUTHER KING JR.'s condemnation of the U.S. pursuit of the war in Vietnam. At the administration's request, he twice visited South Vietnam to review American forces and observe elections there. Before Young left office in 1969, Lyndon Johnson awarded him the Medal of Freedom, the nation's highest civilian citation.

After Richard Nixon's inauguration in 1969, however, Young modified his earlier positions, condemning the war in Vietnam and responding to the Black Power movement and urban violence by concentrating Urban League resources on young people in the urban black underclass. He continued to have significant influence, serving on the boards of the Federal Reserve Bank of New York, MIT, and the Rockefeller Foundation and as president of the National Conference on Social Welfare (1967) and of the National Association of Social Workers (1969–1971). Subsequently, Young's successors as executive director of the Urban League, Arthur Fletcher, VERNON JORDAN, and John Jacob, maintained his legacy of commitment to the goals of the civil rights movement by sustained engagement with centers of American economic and political power.

In March 1971, while Young was at a conference on relations between Africa and the United States in Lagos, Nigeria, he suffered either a brain hemorrhage or a heart attack and drowned while swimming in the Atlantic Ocean. Former Attorney General Ramsey Clark and others who were swimming with him pulled Young's body from the water, but their efforts to revive him were to no avail.

FURTHER READING

The Whitney M. Young Jr. Papers are in the Rare Book and Manuscript Library of Columbia University; the National Urban League Papers are at the Library of Congress.

Moore, Jesse Thomas, Jr. *A Search for Equality: The National Urban League, 1910–1961* (1981).
Parris, Guichard, and Lester Brooks. *Blacks in the City: A History of the National Urban League* (1971).
Weiss, Nancy J. *Whitney M. Young Jr. and the Struggle for Civil Rights* (1990).

Obituary: *New York Times*, 12 Mar. 1971.
—RALPH E. LUKER

Entries in *African American Lives* are listed below in twenty-four categories or areas of renown. Each category is arranged chronologically by birth date. Entries with unknown birth dates have been placed within the approximate period of that person's *floruit*. Many names appear in more than one category—for example, Arthur Ashe is listed under both **Activism** and **Sports**. There is only one person whose biography appears in *African American Lives* who is not listed in any category below; the tragic life of Otabenga teaches us much, but defies classification.

Activism

Attucks, Crispus (c. 1723–1770)
Hall, Prince (1735–1807)
Cuffe, Paul (1759–1817)
Forten, James (1766–1842)
Vesey, Denmark (c. 1767–1822)
Gabriel (1776–1800)
Williams, Peter, Jr. (1780?–1840)
Henson, Josiah (1789–1883)
Steward, Austin (1793–1865)
Cornish, Samuel Eli (1795–1858)
Walker, David (1796?–1830)
Truth, Sojourner (c. 1799–1883)
Turner, Nat (1800?–1831)
Stewart, Maria W. (1803–1879)
Douglass, Sarah Mapps (1806–1882)
Pennington, James William Charles (1809–1870)
Singleton, Benjamin (1809–1892)
Remond, Charles Lenox (1810–1873)
Ruggles, David (1810–1849)
Delany, Martin Robinson (1812–1885)
Pleasant, Mary Ellen (1812?–1904)
Smith, James McCune (1813–1865)
Loguen, Jermain Wesley (c. 1813–1872)
Cinqué (c. 1814–c. 1879)
Brown, William Wells (1815–1884)
Bibb, Henry Walton (1815–1854)
Garnet, Henry Highland (1815–1882)
Reason, Patrick Henry (1816–1898)
Nell, William Cooper (1816–1874)
Caesar, John (?–1837)
Douglass, Frederick (1818–1895)
Crummell, Alexander (1819–1898)
Still, William (1821–1902)
Parker, William (1822?–?)
Tubman, Harriet (c. 1822–1913)
Gibbs, Mifflin Wistar (1823–1915)
Cary, Mary Ann Camberton Shadd (1823–1893)
Craft, William and Ellen (1824–1900)

Harper, Frances Ellen Watkins (1825–1911)
Day, William Howard (1825–1900)
Bell, James Madison (1826–1902)
Remond, Sarah Parker (1826–1894)
Paul, Nathaniel (?–1839)
Holly, James Theodore (1829–1911)
Chester, Thomas Morris (1834–1892)
Coppin, Fanny Jackson (1837–1913)
Grimké, Charlotte Forten (1837–1914)
Grimké, Archibald Henry (1849–1930)
Grimké, Francis James (1850–1937)
Brooks, Walter Henderson (1851–1945)
Parsons, Lucy (1853–1942)
Fortune, T. Thomas (1856–1928)
Washington, Booker T. (1856?–1915)
Matthews, Victoria Earle (1861–1907)
Wells-Barnett, Ida B. (1862–1931)
Terrell, Mary Eliza Church (1863–1954)
Du Bois, W. E. B. (1868–1963)
Johnson, James Weldon (1871–1938)
Trotter, William Monroe (1872–1934)
Scott, Emmett Jay (1873–1957)
Bethune, Mary Jane McLeod (1875–1955)
Burroughs, Nannie Helen (1879–1961)
Lampkin, Daisy Elizabeth Adams (1880s–1965)
Pickens, William (1881–1954)
Harrison, Hubert Henry (1883–1927)
Jones, Eugene Kinckle (1885–1954)
Garvey, Marcus (1887–1940)
Randolph, A. Philip (1889–1979)
Wright, Louis Tompkins (1891–1952)
Fauset, Crystal Bird (1893–1965)
White, Walter Francis (1893–1955)
Johnson, Charles Spurgeon (1893–1956)
Houston, Charles Hamilton (1895–1950)
Cass, Melnea Agnes Jones (1896–1978)
Garvey, Amy Euphemia Jacques (1896–1973)
Garvey, Amy Ashwood (1897–1969)

Muhammad, Elijah (1897–1975)
Alexander, Sadie Tanner Mossell (1898–1989)
Robeson, Paul (1898–1976)
Clark, Septima P. (1898–1987)
Hedgeman, Anna Arnold (1899–1990)
Nixon, Edgar Daniel (1899–1987)
Wilkins, Roy (1901–1981)
Davis, Benjamin Jefferson (1903–1964)
Baker, Ella Josephine (1903–1986)
Hastie, William Henry (1904–1976)
Marshall, Thurgood (1908–1993)
Powell, Adam Clayton, Jr. (1908–1972)
Calloway, Ernest (1909–1989)
Murray, Pauli (1910–1985)
Harrington, Oliver W. (1912–1995)
Rustin, Bayard Taylor (1912–1987)
Height, Dorothy (1912–)
Robinson, Jo Ann (1912–1992)
Parks, Rosa (1913–)
Herndon, Angelo Braxton (1913–1997)
Bates, Daisy Lee (1914–1999)
Catlett, Elizabeth (1915–)
Hamer, Fannie Lou Townsend (1917–1977)
Farmer, James (1920–1999)
Young, Whitney Moore, Jr. (1921–1971)
Motley, Constance Baker (1921–)
McKissick, Floyd Bixler (1922–1991)
Keith, Damon Jerome (1922–)
Sullivan, Leon Howard (1922–2001)
Malcolm X (1925–1965)
Evers, Medgar (1925–1963)
Abernathy, Ralph (1926–1990)
Belafonte, Harry (1927–)
King, Coretta Scott (1927–)
Forman, James (1928–)
King, Martin Luther, Jr. (1929–1968)
Hansberry, Lorraine Vivian (1930–1965)
Scottsboro Boys (1930s–)
Young, Andrew Jackson, Jr. (1932–)
Evers-Williams, Myrlie (1933–)

Blackwell, Unita Z. (1933–)
Meredith, James Howard (1933–)
Moses, Robert Parris (1935–)
Jordan, Vernon (1935–)
Cleaver, Eldridge (1935–1998)
Seale, Bobby (1936–)
Norton, Eleanor Holmes (1937–)
Edelman, Marian Wright (1939–)
Bond, Julian (1940–)
Lewis, John (1940–)
Carmichael, Stokely (1941–1998)
Robinson, Randall (1941–)
Till, Emmett Louis (1941–1955)
Jackson, Jesse L., Sr. (1941–)
Newton, Huey P. (1942–1989)
Ashe, Arthur (1943–1993)
Brown, H. Rap (1943–)
Davis, Angela Yvonne (1944–)
Mfume, Kweisi (1948–)
Sharpton, Al (1954–)

Art

Johnson, Joshua (fl. 1795–1824)
Reason, Patrick Henry (1816–1898)
Duncanson, Robert S. (1821?–1872)
Bannister, Edward Mitchell
   (c. 1826–1901)
Lewis, Edmonia (c. 1844–after 1909)
Tanner, Henry Ossawa (1859–1937)
Fuller, Meta Vaux Warrick (1877–1968)
Herriman, George Joseph (1880–1944)
Abele, Julian Francis (1881–1950)
VanDerZee, James Augustus Joseph
   (1886–1983)
Pippin, Horace (1888–1946)
Savage, Augusta (1892–1962)
Williams, Paul Revere (1894–1980)
Douglas, Aaron (1899–1979)
Barthé, Richmond (1901–1989)
Johnson, William H. (1901–1970)
Delaney, Beauford (1901–1979)
Jones, Loïs Mailou (1905–1998)
Porter, James Amos (1905–1970)
Bearden, Romare (1911–1988)
Harrington, Oliver W. (1912–1995)
Parks, Gordon, Sr. (1912–)
Catlett, Elizabeth (1915–)
Lawrence, Jacob Armstead (1917–2000)
Sleet, Moneta, Jr. (1926–1996)
Puryear, Martin (1941–)
Marshall, Kerry James (1955–)
Basquiat, Jean-Michel (1960–1988)

Aviation

Coleman, Bessie (1892–1926)
Bullard, Eugène Jacques (1895–1961)
Robinson, John C. (1903–1954)

Davis, Benjamin O., Jr. (1912–2002)
James, Daniel, Jr. (1920–1978)
Brown, Jesse Leroy (1926–1950)
Jemison, Mae (1956–)

Business

Cuffe Paul (1759–1817)
Forten, James (1766–1842)
Ruggles, David (1810–1849)
Pleasant, Mary Ellen (1812–1904)
Washington, Booker T. (1856?–1915)
Merrick, John (1859–1919)
Walker, Maggie Lena (1867–1934)
Walker, Madame C. J. (1867–1919)
Malone, Annie Turnbo (1869–1957)
Trotter, William Monroe (1872–1934)
Payton, Philip A., Jr. (1876–1917)
Barnett, Claude Albert (1889–1967)
Johnson, John (1918–)
McKissick, Floyd Bixler (1922–1991)
Sullivan, Leon Howard (1922–2001)
Gordy, Berry, Jr. (1929–)
Jones, Quincy (1933–)
Graves, Earl (1935–)
Johnson, Robert L. (1946–)
Parsons, Richard Dean (1948–)
Raines, Franklin Delano (1949–)
Chenault, Kenneth Irvine (1951–)
O'Neal, Stanley (1951–)

Dance

Lane William Henry (1825?–1852)
Robinson, Bill (1878–1949)
Mills, Florence (1895–1927)
Bubbles, John (1902–1986)
Baker, Josephine (1906–1975)
Dunham, Katherine Mary (1909–)
Ailey, Alvin (1931–1989)
Mitchell, Arthur (1934–)
Jamison, Judith (1943–)
Jones, Bill T. (1952–)

Education

Chavis, John (1763–1838)
Henson, Josiah (1789–1883)
Stockton, Betsey (c. 1798–1865)
Douglass, Sarah Mapps (1806–1882)
Pennington, James William Charles
   (1809–1870)
Payne, Daniel Alexander (1811–1893)
Crummell, Alexander (1819–1898)
Harper, Frances Ellen Watkins
   (1825–1911)
Revels, Hiram Rhoades (1827?–1901)
Langston, John Mercer (1829–1897)
Blyden, Edward Wilmot (1832–1912)

Coppin, Fanny Jackson (1837–1913)
Cardozo, Francis Louis (1837–1903)
Grimké, Charlotte Forten (1837–1914)
Brown, Hallie Quinn (1845?–1949)
Bouchet, Edward Alexander
   (1852–1918)
Albert, Octavia Victoria Rogers
   (1853–1890?)
Laney, Lucy Craft (1854–1933)
Wright, Richard (1855–1947)
Washington, Booker T. (1856?–1915)
Cooper, Anna Julia Haywood
   (1858?–1964)
Washington, Margaret Murray
   (1861–1925)
Carver, George Washington
   (c. 1864–1943)
Work, Monroe Nathan (1866–1945)
Moton, Robert Russa (1867–1940)
Du Bois, W. E. B. (1868–1963)
Hope, John (1868–1936)
Lynk, Miles Vandahurst (1871–1956)
Scott, Emmett Jay (1873–1957)
Schomburg, Arthur Alfonso
   (1874–1938)
Shepard, James Edward (1875–1947)
Woodson, Carter Godwin (1875–1950)
Burroughs, Nannie Helen (1879–1961)
Brawley, Benjamin Griffith (1882–1939)
Brown, Charlotte Eugenia Hawkins
   (1883–1961)
Slowe, Lucy Diggs (1885–1937)
Locke, Alain Leroy (1885–1954)
Delany, Sadie (1889–1999)
Savage, Augusta (1892–1962)
Johnson, Charles Spurgeon (1893–1956)
Caliver, Ambrose (1894–1962)
Mays, Benjamin E. (1894–1984)
Frazier, E. Franklin (1894–1962)
Logan, Rayford Whittingham
   (1897–1981)
Douglas, Aaron (1899–1979)
Reid, Ira De Augustine (1901–1968)
Quarles, Benjamin Arthur (1904–1996)
Bond, Horace Mann (1904–1972)
Jones, Loïs Mailou (1905–1998)
Porter, James Amos (1905–1970)
Robinson, James Herman (1907–1972)
Dunham, Katherine Mary (1909–)
Murray, Pauli (1910–1985)
Drake, St. Clair, Jr. (1911–1990)
Clark, Kenneth Bancroft (1914–)
Hutson, Jean Blackwell (1914–1998)
Franklin, John Hope (1915–)
Brooks, Gwendolyn (1917–2000)
Elders, M. Joycelyn (1933–)
Moses, Robert Parris (1935–)
Wilson, William Julius (1935–)
Lewis, David Levering (1936–)

Cole, Johnnetta Betsch (1936–)
Simmons, Ruth J. (1945–)
Jackson, Shirley Ann (1946–)
West, Cornel (1953–)

Exploration

Esteban (?–1539)
Du Sable, Jean Baptiste Pointe
 (1745?–1818)
York (c. 1772–before 1832)
Rose, Edward (?–1833?)
Beckwourth, Jim (1800?–1866?)
Sheppard, William Henry (1865–1927)
Henson, Matthew (1866–1955)
Jemison, Mae (1956–)

Invention

Temple, Lewis (1800–1854)
Rillieux, Norbert (1806–1894)
McCoy, Elijah (1843–1929)
Latimer, Lewis Howard (1848–1928)
Matzeliger, Jan Ernst (1852–1889)
Woods, Granville T. (1856–1910)
Morgan, Garrett Augustus (1877–1963)
Lee, Raphael Carl (1949–)

Journalism

Cornish, Samuel Eli (1795–1858)
Russwurm, John Brown (1799–1851)
Bell, Philip Alexander (1808?–1889)
Ruggles, David (1810–1849)
Bibb, Henry Walton (1815–1854)
Cary, Mary Ann Camberton Shadd
 (1823–1893)
Day, William Howard (1825–1900)
Chester, Thomas Morris (1834–1892)
Ruffin, Josephine St. Pierre (1842–1924)
Rudd, Daniel A. (1854–1933)
Fortune, T. Thomas (1856–1928)
Hopkins, Pauline Elizabeth (1859–1930)
Matthews, Victoria Earle (1861–1907)
Wells-Barnett, Ida B. (1862–1931)
Miller, Kelly (1863–1939)
Work, Monroe Nathan (1866–1945)
Du Bois, W. E. B. (1868–1963)
Abbott, Robert Sengstacke (1868–1940)
Trotter, William Monroe (1872–1934)
Dunbar-Nelson, Alice (1875–1935)
Bass, Charlotta (1880–1969)
Herriman, George Joseph (1880–1944)
Pickens, William (1881–1954)
Harrison, Hubert Henry (1883–1927)
Dunjee, Roscoe (1883–1965)
Barnett, Claude Albert (1889–1967)
Schuyler, George Samuel (1895–1977)
Thurman, Wallace (1902–1934)

Lacy, Sam (1903?–2003)
Thompson, Era Bell (1906–1986)
Harrington, Oliver W. (1912–1995)
Parks, Gordon, Sr. (1912–)
Johnson, John (1918–)
Rowan, Carl Thomas (1925–2000)
Sleet, Moneta, Jr. (1926–1996)
Graves, Earl, Jr. (1935–)
Whitaker, Mark (1957–)

Law

Freeman, Elizabeth (c. 1744–1829)
Scott, Dred (c. 1800–1858)
Gibbs, Mifflin Wistar (1823–1915)
Greener, Richard Theodore (1844–1922)
Grimké, Archibald Henry (1849–1930)
Plessy, Homer Adolph (1858?–1925)
Jones, Scipio Africanus (1863–1943)
Howard, Perry Wilbon (1877–1961)
Houston, Charles Hamilton
 (1895–1950)
Alexander, Sadie Tanner Mossell
 (1898–1989)
Carter, Eunice Hunton (1899–1970)
Davis, Benjamin Jefferson (1903–1964)
Hastie, William Henry (1904–1976)
Marshall, Thurgood (1908–1993)
Calloway, Ernest (1909–1989)
Murray, Pauli (1910–1985)
Carter, Robert Lee (1917–)
Coleman, William T., Jr. (1920–)
Motley, Constance Baker (1921–)
McKissick, Floyd Bixler (1922–1991)
Keith, Damon Jerome (1922–)
Higginbotham, A. Leon, Jr. (1928–1998)
Jordan, Vernon (1935–)
Edelman, Marian Wright (1939–)
Edwards, Harry Thomas (1940–)
McDonald, Gabrielle Kirk (1942–)
Thomas, Clarence (1948–)
Chenault, Kenneth Irvine (1951–)

Legend

Railroad Bill (?–1896)
Stagolee (1865–1912)

Medicine

Cesar (c. 1682–?)
Onesimus (fl. 1706–1717)
Durham, James (1762–?)
Delany, Martin Robison (1812–1885)
Smith, James McCune (1813–1865)
Crumpler, Rebecca Davis Lee
 (1831–1895)
Cole, Rebecca (1846–1922)
Williams, Daniel Hale (1856–1931)

Lynk, Miles Vandahurst (1871–1956)
Fuller, Solomon Carter (1872–1953)
Hinton, William Augustus (1883–1959)
Murray, Peter Marshall (1888–1969)
Staupers, Mabel Doyle Keaton
 (1890–1989)
Wright, Louis Tompkins (1891–1952)
Delany, Bessie (1891–1995)
Chinn, May Edward (1896–1980)
Poindexter, Hildrus Augustus
 (1901–1987)
Berry, Leonidas Harris (1902–1995)
Cannon, George Dows (1902–1986)
Drew, Charles Richard (1904–1950)
Cobb, William Montague (1904–1990)
Thomas, Vivien Theodore (1910–1985)
Lawrence, Margaret Morgan (1914–)
Jefferson, Mildred Fay (1927–)
Johnson-Brown, Hazel (1927–)
Elders, M. Joycelyn (1933–)
White, Augustus Aaron, III (1936–)
Satcher, David (1941–)
Lee, Raphael Carl (1949–)
Carson, Ben (1951–)
Jemison, Mae (1956–)

Military

Attucks, Crispus (c. 1723–1770)
Whipple, Prince (?–1797)
Hull, Agrippa (1759–1848)
Caesar, John (?–1837)
Cailloux, Andre (1825–1863)
Bowser, Mary Elizabeth (1839?–?)
Smalls, Robert (1839–1915)
Healy, Michael (1839–1904)
Williams, Cathay (1844–?)
Flipper, Henry Ossian (1856–1940)
Davis, Benjamin Oliver, Sr. (1880–1970)
Bullard, Eugène Jacques (1895–1961)
Robinson, John C. (1903–1954)
Davis, Benjamin O., Jr. (1912–2002)
Earley, Charity Adams (1917–2002)
James, Daniel, Jr. (1920–1978)
Brown, Jesse Leroy (1926–1950)
Johnson-Brown, Hazel (1927–)
White, Augustus Aaron, III (1936–)
Powell, Colin (1937–)

Music

Allen, Richard (1760–1831)
Johnson, Francis (1792–1844)
Greenfield, Elizabeth Taylor
 (c. 1817–1876)
Lane, William Henry (1825?–1852)
Blind Tom (1849–1908)
Tindley, Charles Albert (1856–1933)
Burleigh, Henry Thacker (1866–1949)

Jones, Madame Sissieretta Joyner
  (1868–1933)
Joplin, Scott (1868?–1917)
Cook, Will Marion (1869–1944)
Johnson, John Rosamond (1873–1954)
Handy, W. C. (1873–1958)
Bolden, Buddy (1877–1931)
Europe, James Reese (1880–1919)
Blake, Eubie (1883–1983)
Oliver, King (1885–1938)
Rainey, Ma (1886–1939)
Lead Belly (1888–1949)
Sissle, Noble (1889–1975)
Morton, Jelly Roll (1890–1941)
Patton, Charley (1891–1934)
Broonzy, Big Bill (1893–1958)
Bricktop (1894–1984)
Smith, Bessie (1894?–1937)
Still, William Grant (1895–1978)
Waters, Ethel (1896–1977)
Anderson, Marian (1897–1993)
Bechet, Sidney Joseph (1897–1959)
Jefferson, Blind Lemon (1897?–1929)
Armstrong, Lil (1898–1971)
Ellington, Duke (1899–1974)
Dorsey, Thomas Andrew (1899–1993)
Armstrong, Louis (1901–1971)
Waller, Fats (1904–1943)
Smith, Willie Mae Ford (1904–1994)
Basie, Count (1904–1984)
Calloway, Cab (1907–1994)
Johnson, Robert (1911–1938)
Waters, Muddy (1915–1983)
Jackson, Mahalia (1911–1972)
Holiday, Billie (1915–1959)
Dixon, "Big" Willie James (1915–1992)
Cole, Nat King (1917–1965)
Fitzgerald, Ella (1917–1996)
Horne, Lena (1917–)
Hooker, John Lee (1917–2001)
Monk, Thelonious (1917–1982)
Gillespie, Dizzy (1917–1993)
Bailey, Pearl (1918–1990)
Blakey, Art (1919–1990)
Parker, Charlie (1920–1955)
Mingus, Charles, Jr. (1922–1979)
Vaughan, Sarah (1924–1990)
King, B. B. (1925–)
Davis, Sammy, Jr. (1925–1990)
Davis, Miles (1926–1991)
Coltrane, John William (1926–1967)
Berry, Chuck (1926–)
Price, Leontyne (1927–)
Belafonte, Harry (1927–)
Kitt, Eartha Mae (1928–)
Diddley, Bo (1928–)
Gordy, Berry, Jr. (1929–)
Coleman, Ornette (1930–)
Charles, Ray (1930–)

Little Richard (1932–)
Jones, Quincy (1933–)
Brown, James (1933–)
Gaye, Marvin (1939–1984)
Franklin, Aretha (1942–)
Hendrix, Jimi (1942–1970)
Ross, Diana (1944–)
Norman, Jessye (1945–)
Wonder, Stevie (1950–)
Jackson, Michael (1958–)
Marsalis, Wynton (1961–)
Shakur, Tupac Amaru (1971–1996)

Philanthropy

Pleasant, Mary Ellen (1812–1904)
Walker, Maggie Lena (1867–1934)
Walker, Madame C. J. (1867–1919)
Malone, Annie Turnbo (1869–1957)
Dunbar-Nelson, Alice (1875–1935)
Davis, Sammy, Jr. (1925–1990)
Belafonte, Harry (1927–)
Graves, Earl (1935–)
Cosby, Bill (1937–)
Johnson, Robert L. (1946–)
Winfrey, Oprah (1954–)

Politics and Government

Russwurm, John Brown (1799–1851)
Delany, Martin Robison (1812–1885)
Gibbs, Mifflin Wistar (1823–1915)
Revels, Hiram Rhoades (1827?–1901)
Langston, John Mercer (1829–1897)
Blyden, Edward Wilmot (1832–1912)
Chester, Thomas Morris (1834–1892)
Cardozo, Francis Louis (1837–1903)
Pinchback, P. B. S. (1837–1921)
Smalls, Robert (1839–1915)
Bruce, Blanche Kelso (1841–1898)
Elliott, Robert Brown (1842–1884)
Greener, Richard Theodore (1844–1922)
Lynch, John Roy (1847–1939)
Grimké, Archibald Henry (1849–1930)
Williams, George Washington
  (1849–1891)
White, George Henry (1852–1918)
Jones, Scipio Africanus (1863–1943)
Du Bois, W. E. B. (1868–1963)
De Priest, Oscar (1871–1951)
Scott, Emmett Jay (1873–1957)
Howard, Perry Wilbon (1877–1961)
Bass, Charlotta (1880–1969)
Pickens, William (1881–1954)
Morton, Ferdinand Quintin
  (1881–1949)
Fauset, Crystal Bird (1893–1965)
Wharton, Clifton Reginald (1899–1990)
Bunche, Ralph Johnson (1904–1971)

Weaver, Robert Clifton (1907–1997)
Marshall, Thurgood (1908–1993)
Powell, Adam Clayton, Jr. (1908–1972)
Morrow, E. Frederic (1909–1994)
Bradley, Thomas (1917–1998)
Young, Coleman (1918–1997)
Brooke, Edward (1919–)
Coleman, William T., Jr. (1920–)
Washington, Harold (1922–1987)
Chisholm, Shirley (1924–)
Dinkins, David N. (1927–)
Rangel, Charles (1930–)
Wilder, Douglas (1931–)
Young, Andrew Jackson, Jr. (1932–)
Jordan, Vernon (1935–)
Jordan, Barbara (1936–1996)
Powell, Colin (1937–)
O'Leary, Hazel R. (1937–)
Norton, Eleanor Holmes (1937–)
Bond, Julian (1940–)
Lewis, John (1940–)
Brown, Ron (1941–1996)
Kelly, Sharon Pratt (1944–)
Mfume, Kweisi (1948–)
Rice, Condoleezza (1954–)

Religion

Bryan Andrew (1737–1812)
George, David (c. 1742–1810)
Jones, Absalom (1746–1818)
Varick, James (1750–1827)
Liele, George (c. 1751–1828)
Haynes, Lemuel (1753–1833)
Marrant, John (1755–1791)
Allen, Richard (1760–1831)
Cary, Lott (c. 1780–1828)
Coker, Daniel (1780?–1835?)
Williams, Peter, Jr. (1780?–1840)
Lee, Jarena (1783–?)
Henson, Josiah (1789–1883)
Elaw, Zilpha (1790–?)
Jackson, Rebecca Cox (1795–1871)
Laveaux, Marie (1801–1881)
Pennington, James William Charles
  (1809–1870)
Payne, Daniel Alexander (1811–1893)
Loguen, Jermain Wesley (c. 1813–1872)
Garnet, Henry Highland (1815–1882)
Crummell, Alexander (1819–1898)
Foote, Julia A. J. (1823?–1900)
Paul, Nathaniel (?–1839)
Holly, James Theodore (1829–1911)
Healy, James Augustine (1830–1900)
Turner, Henry McNeal (1834–1915)
Healy, Patrick Francis (1834–1910)
Tanner, Benjamin Tucker (1835–1923)
Coppin, Fanny Jackson (1837–1913)
Smith, Amanda Berry (1837–1915)

Steward, Theophilus Gould (1843–1924)
Healy, Eliza (1846–1919)
Grimké, Francis James (1850–1937)
Brooks, Walter Henderson (1851–1945)
Rudd, Daniel (1854–1933)
Tindley, Charles Albert (1856–1933)
Bragg, George Freeman, Jr. (1863–1940)
Sheppard, William Henry (1865–1927)
McGuire, George Alexander
  (1866–1934)
Demby, Edward T. (1869–1957)
Ford, Arnold Josiah (1877–1935)
Father Divine (1879?–1965)
Grace, Charles Emmanuel (1881–1960)
Michaux, Lightfoot Solomon
  (1884–1968)
Ali, Noble Drew (1886–1929)
Johnson, Mordecai Wyatt (1890–1976)
Wesley, Charles Harris (1891–1987)
Johns, Vernon Napoleon (1892–1965)
Matthew, Wentworth Arthur
  (1892–1973)
Mays, Benjamin E. (1894–1984)
Muhammad, Elijah (1897–1975)
Thurman, Howard W. (1899?–1981)
Smith, Willie Mae Ford (1904–1994)
Robinson, James Herman (1907–1972)
Powell, Adam Clayton, Jr. (1908–1972)
Burgess, John Melville (1909–2003)
Murray, Pauli (1910–1985)
Franklin, C. L. (1915–1984)
Sullivan, Leon Howard (1922–2001)
Malcolm X (1925–1965)
King, Martin Luther, Jr. (1929–1968)
Harris, Barbara (1930–)
Farrakhan, Louis Abdul (1933–)
Reverend Ike (1935–)
Jackson, Jesse L., Sr. (1941–)
Gregory, Wilton (1947–)

Science

Banneker, Benjamin (1731–1806)
Bouchet, Edward Alexander
  (1852–1918)
Carver, George Washington
  (c. 1864–1943)
Turner, Charles Henry (1867–1923)
Just, Ernest Everett (1883–1941)
Imes, Elmer Samuel (1883–1941)
Julian, Percy Lavon (1899–1975)
Nabrit, Samuel (1905–)
Hill, Mary Elliott (1907–1969)
Branson, Herman Russell (1914–1995)
Hill, Henry Aaron (1915–1979)
Amos, Harold (1918–2003)
Blackwell, David (1919–)
Wilkins, J. Ernest, Jr. (1923–)

Massey, Walter Eugene (1938–)
Jackson, Shirley Ann (1946–)

Slaves

Esteban (?–1539)
Cesar (c. 1682–?)
Onesimus (fl. 1706–1717)
Gronniosaw, James Albert Ukawsaw
  (c. 1710–c. 1773)
Hammon, Jupiter (1711–?)
Attucks, Crispus (c. 1723–1770)
Terry, Lucy (c. 1730–1821)
Hall, Prince (1735–1807)
Bryan, Andrew (1737–1812)
George, David (c. 1742–1810)
Freeman, Elizabeth (c. 1744–1829)
Equiano, Olaudah (1745?–1797)
Jones, Absalom (1746–1818)
Hammon, Briton (fl. 1747–1760)
Liele, George (c. 1751–1828)
Wheatley, Phillis (c. 1753–1784)
Allen, Richard (1760–1831)
King, Boston (1760?–1802)
Durham, James (1762–?)
Vesey, Denmark (c. 1767–1822)
Bayley, Solomon (c. 1771–c. 1839)
York (c. 1772–bef. 1832)
Hemings, Sally (1773–1835)
Whipple, Prince (?–1797)
Gabriel (1776–1800)
Coker, Daniel (1780?–1835?)
Cary, Lott (c. 1780–1828)
Grimes, William (1784?–1865?)
Henson, Josiah (1789–1883)
Mars, James (1790–?)
Steward, Austin (1793–1865)
Johnson, Joshua (fl. 1795–1824)
Horton, George Moses (1797?–1883?)
Stockton, Betsey (c. 1798–1865)
Prince, Nancy (1799–c.1856)
Truth, Sojourner (c. 1799–1883)
Beckwourth, Jim (1800?–1866?)
Turner, Nat (1800?–1831)
Scott, Dred (c. 1800–1858)
Northup, Solomon (1808–1863)
Pennington, James William Charles
  (1809–1870)
Singleton, Benjamin (1809–1892)
Thompson, John (1812–?)
Pleasant, Mary Ellen (1812?–1904)
Smith, James McCune (1813–1865)
Jacobs, Harriet (c. 1813–1897)
Loguen, Jermain Wesley (c. 1813–1872)
Cinqué (c. 1814–c. 1879)
Roper, Moses (1815–?)
Brown, William Wells (1815–1884)
Bibb, Henry Walton (1815–1854)
Garnet, Henry Highland (1815–1882)

Brown, Henry Box (1815?–?)
Greenfield, Elizabeth Taylor
  (c. 1817–1876)
Douglass, Frederick (1818–1895)
Keckly, Elizabeth Hobbs (1818–1907)
Parker, William (1822?–?)
Tubman, Harriet (c. 1822–1913)
Craft, William and Ellen (1824–1900)
Cailloux, Andre (1825–1863)
Healy, James (1830–1900)
Hughes, Louis (1832–1913)
Healy, Patrick Francis (1834–1910)
Coppin, Fanny Jackson (1837–1913)
Smith, Amanda Berry (1837–1915)
Smalls, Robert (1839–1915)
Healy, Michael (1839–1904)
Bowser, Mary Elizabeth (1839?–?)
Bruce, Blanche Kelso (1841–1898)
Williams, Cathay (1844–?)
Healy, Eliza (1846–1919)
Lynch, John Roy (1847–1939)
Blind Tom (1849–1908)
Grimké, Archibald Henry (1849–1930)
Brooks, Walter Henderson (1851–1945)
Albert, Octavia Victoria Rogers
  (1853–1890?)
Laney, Lucy Craft (1854–1933)
Love, Nat (1854–1921)
Rudd, Daniel (1854–1933)
Wright, Richard (1855–1947)
Flipper, Henry Ossian (1856–1940)
Tindley, Charles Albert (1856–1933)
Fortune, T. Thomas (1856–1928)
Washington, Booker T. (1856?–1915)
Cooper, Anna Julia Haywood
  (1858?–1964)
Merrick, John (1859–1919)
Matthews, Victoria Earle (1861–1907)
Wells-Barnett, Ida B. (1862–1931)
Jones, Scipio Africanus (1863–1943)
Carver, George Washington
  (c. 1864–1943)

Sports

Molyneaux, Tom (1784–1818)
Askin, Luther B. (1843–1929)
Murphy, Isaac (1861–1896)
Lewis, Oliver (fl. 1863–1907)
Johnson, Jack (1878–1946)
Taylor, Major (1878–1932)
Foster, Rube (1879–1930)
Slowe, Lucy Diggs (1885–1937)
Williams, Smokey Joe (1886–1951)
Washington, Ora (1899–1971)
Johnson, Judy (1899–1989)
Bell, Cool Papa (1903–1991)
Hubbard, William DeHart (1903–1976)
Lacy, Sam (1903?–2003)

Paige, Satchel (1906–1982)
Gibson, Josh (1911–1947)
Stokes, Louise (1913–1978)
Owens, Jesse (1913–1980)
Louis, Joe (1914–1981)
McLendon, Johnny (1915–1999)
Robinson, Jackie (1919–1972)
Robinson, Eddie (1919–)
Robinson, Sugar Ray (1920?–1988)
Stone, Toni (1921–1996)
Scott, Wendell (1921–1990)
Coachman, Alice (1923–)
Gibson, Althea (1927–2003)
Mays, Willie (1931–)
Liston, Sonny (1932–1970)
Aaron, Hank (1934–)
Russell, Bill (1934–)
Brown, Jim (1936–)
Chamberlain, Wilt (1936–1999)
Flood, Curt (1938–1997)
Rudolph, Wilma (1940–1994)
Ali, Muhammad (1942–)
Ashe, Arthur (1943–1993)
Smith, Tommie (1944–)
Abdul-Jabbar, Kareem (1947–)
Simpson, O. J. (1947–)
DeFrantz, Anita L. (1952–)
Payton, Walter (1954–1999)
Hyman, Flora "Flo" (1954–1986)
Griffith-Joyner, Florence (1959–1998)
Lewis, Carl (1961–)
Jordan, Michael (1963–)
Miller, Cheryl (1964–)
Woods, Tiger (1975–)
Williams, Venus (1980–)
Williams, Serena (1981–)

Theater and Film

Aldridge, Ira Frederick (1807–1867)
Johnson, James Weldon (1871–1938)
Walker, George (1873–1911)
Johnson, John Rosamond (1873–1954)
Williams, Bert (1874–1922)
Robinson, Bill (1878–1949)
Blake, Eubie (1883–1983)
Micheaux, Oscar (1884–1951)
McClendon, Rose (1884–1936)
Sissle, Noble (1889–1975)
Fetchit, Stepin (1892 or 1902–1985)
Mabley, Moms (1894?–1975)
Mills, Florence (1895–1927)
McDaniel, Hattie (1895–1952)
Waters, Ethel (1896–1977)
Robeson, Paul (1898–1976)
O'Neal, Frederick Douglass (1905–1992)
Baker, Josephine (1906–1975)
Parks, Gordon, Sr. (1912–)
Childress, Alice (1916–1994)

Horne, Lena (1917–)
Davis, Ossie (1917–)
Bailey, Pearl (1918–1990)
Dandridge, Dorothy (1922–1965)
Foxx, Redd (1922–1991)
Dee, Ruby (1924–)
Davis, Sammy, Jr. (1925–1990)
Poitier, Sidney (1927–)
Belafonte, Harry (1927–)
Kitt, Eartha Mae (1928–)
Jones, James Earl (1931–)
Parks, Gordon, Jr. (1934–1979)
Cosby, Bill (1937–)
Pryor, Richard (1940–)
Winfrey, Oprah (1954–)
Washington, Denzel (1954–)
Goldberg, Whoopi (1955–)
Lee, Spike (1957–)
Parks, Suzan-Lori (1964–)
Berry, Halle Maria (1966–)

The West

Esteban (?–1539)
du Sable, Jean Baptiste Pointe
    (1745?–1818)
York (c. 1772–bef. 1832)
Rose, Edward (?–1833?)
Beckwourth, Jim (1800?–1866?)
Williams, Cathay (1844–?)
Love, Nat (1854–1921)
Pickett, Bill (1871–1932)
Nigger Add (1892–1906?)

Writing

Gronniosaw, James Albert Ukawsaw
    (c. 1710–c. 1773)
Hammon, Jupiter (1711–?)
Terry, Lucy (c. 1730–1821)
George, David (c. 1742–1810)
Equiano, Olaudah (1745?–1797)
Hammon, Briton (fl. 1747–1760)
Wheatley, Phillis (c. 1753–1784)
Marrant, John (1755–1791)
King, Boston (1760?–1802)
Bayley, Solomon (c. 1771–c. 1839)
Lee, Jarena (1783–?)
Grimes, William (1784?–1865?)
Henson, Josiah (1789–1883)
Mars, James (1790–?)
Elaw, Zilpha (c. 1790–?)
Jackson, Rebecca Cox (1795–1871)
Walker, David (1796?–1830)
Horton, George Moses (1797?–1883?)
Prince, Nancy (1799–c.1856)
Northup, Solomon (1808–1863)
Pennington, James William Charles
    (1809–1870)
Payne, Daniel Alexander (1811–1893)
Thompson, John (1812–?)

Delany, Martin Robinson (1812–1885)
Jacobs, Harriet (1813–1897)
Roper, Moses (1815–18?)
Brown, William Wells (1815–1884)
Brown, Henry Box (1815?–?)
Nell, William Cooper (1816–1874)
Keckly, Elizabeth Hobbs (1818–1907)
Still, William (1821–1902)
Foote, Julia A. J. (1823?–1900)
Harper, Frances Ellen Watkins
    (1825–1911)
Bell, James Madison (1826–1902)
Wilson, Harriet E. (c. 1828?–?)
Hughes, Louis (1832–1913)
Smith, Amanda Berry (1837–1915)
Grimké, Charlotte Forten (1837–1914)
Steward, Theophilus Gould (1843–1924)
Brown, Hallie Quinn (1845?–1949)
Williams, George Washington
    (1849–1891)
Brooks, Walter Henderson (1851–1945)
Albert, Octavia Victoria Rogers
    (1853–1890?)
Washington, Booker T. (1856?–1915)
Chesnutt, Charles Waddell (1858–1932)
Cooper, Anna Julia Haywood
    (1858?–1964)
Hopkins, Pauline Elizabeth (1859–
    1930)
Terrell, Mary Eliza Church (1863–
    1954)
Du Bois, W. E. B. (1868–1963)
Johnson, James Weldon (1871–1938)
Dunbar, Paul Laurence (1872–1906)
Dunbar-Nelson, Alice (1875–1935)
Grimké, Angelina Weld (1880–1958)
Brawley, Benjamin Griffith (1882–1939)
Fauset, Jessie Redmon (1882–1961)
Brown, Charlotte Eugenia Hawkins
    (1883–1961)
Locke, Alain Leroy (1885–1954)
Delany, Sadie (1889–1999)
McKay, Claude (1890–1948)
Hurston, Zora Neale (1891–1960)
Larsen, Nella (1891–1964)
Delany, Bessie (1891–1995)
Johnson, Charles Spurgeon (1893–1956)
Mays, Benjamin E. (1894–1984)
Toomer, Jean (1894–1967)
Thurman, Howard W. (1899?–1981)
Brown, Sterling Allen (1901–1989)
Hughes, Langston (1902–1967)
Thurman, Wallace (1902–1934)
Cullen, Countée (1903–1946)
Thompson, Era Bell (1906–1986)
West, Dorothy (1907–1998)
Wright, Richard (1908–1960)
Petry, Ann (1908–1997)
Himes, Chester Bomar (1909–1984)

Murray, Pauli (1910–1985)
Ellison, Ralph Waldo (1913–1994)
Hayden, Robert Earl (1913–1980)
Murray, Albert (1916–)
Childress, Alice (1916–1994)
Haley, Alex (1921–1992)
Baldwin, James (1924–1987)
Williams, John Alfred (1925–)
Angelou, Maya (1928–)

Marshall, Paule (1929–)
Hansberry, Lorraine Vivian (1930–1965)
Walcott, Derek (1930–)
Morrison, Toni (1931–)
Lorde, Audre (1934–1992)
Baraka, Amiri (1934–)
Cleaver, Eldridge (1935–1998)
Lewis, David Levering (1936–)

Jordan, June (1936–2002)
Cosby, Bill (1937–)
Reed, Ishmael (1938–)
Giovanni, Nikki (1943–)
Ashe, Arthur (1943–1993)
Walker, Alice Malsenior (1944–)
Wilson, August (1945–)
Dove, Rita Frances (1952–)
West, Cornel (1953–)

AFRICAN AMERICAN PRIZEWINNERS, MEDALISTS, MEMBERS OF CONGRESS, AND JUDGES

Names in **boldface** identify entries in *African American Lives*

Spingarn Medal Winners

The Spingarn Medal is awarded annually by the NAACP for outstanding achievement by a black American

1915	**Ernest E. Just**	1960	**J. Langston Hughes**
1916	Major Charles A. Young	1961	**Kenneth B. Clark**
1917	**Harry T. Burleigh**	1962	**Robert C. Weaver**
1918	William S. B. Braithwaite	1963	**Medgar W. Evers**
1919	**Archibald H. Grimke**	1964	**Roy O. Wilkins**
1920	**W. E. B. Du Bois**	1965	**M. Leontyne Price**
1921	Charles S. Gilpin	1966	**John Harold Johnson**
1922	Mary B. Talbert	1967	**Edward W. Brooke III**
1923	**George Washington Carver**	1968	**Sammy Davis Jr.**
1924	Roland T. Hayes	1969	**Clarence M. Mitchell, Jr.**
1925	**James Weldon Johnson**	1970	**Jacob Lawrence**
1926	**Carter G. Woodson**	1971	**Leon H. Sullivan**
1927	Anthony Overton	1972	**Gordon Parks Sr.**
1928	**Charles W. Chesnutt**	1973	Wilson C. Riles
1929	**Mordecai W. Johnson**	1974	**Damon J. Keith**
1930	Henry A. Hunt	1975	**Hank Aaron**
1931	Richard B. Harrison	1976	**Alvin Ailey Jr.**
1932	**Robert Russa Moton**	1977	**Alexander P. Halcy**
1933	Max Yergan	1978	**Andrew J. Young Jr.**
1934	William T. B. Williams	1979	**Rosa L. Parks**
1935	**Mary McLeod Bethune**	1980	**Rayford W. Logan**
1936	**John Hope**	1981	**Coleman A. Young**
1937	**Walter F. White**	1982	**Benjamin E. Mays**
1938	*No award given*	1983	**Lena Horne**
1939	**Marian Anderson**	1984	**Thomas Bradley**
1940	**Louis T. Wright**	1985	**William H. Cosby Jr.**
1941	**Richard N. Wright**	1986	Benjamin L. Hooks
1942	**A. Philip Randolph**	1987	Percy E. Sutton
1943	**William H. Hastie**	1988	Frederick Douglass Patterson
1944	**Charles R. Drew**	1989	**Jesse L. Jackson**
1945	**Paul B. Robeson**	1990	**L. Douglas Wilder**
1946	**Thurgood Marshall**	1991	**Colin L. Powell**
1947	**Percy L. Julian**	1992	**Barbara C. Jordan**
1948	Channing Heggie Tobias	1993	**Dorothy I. Height**
1949	**Ralph J. Bunche**	1994	**Maya Angelou**
1950	**Charles H. Houston**	1995	**John Hope Franklin**
1951	**Mabel K. Staupers**	1996	**A. Leon Higginbotham Jr.**
1952	Harry T. Moore	1997	**Carl T. Rowan**
1953	**Paul R. Williams**	1998	**Myrlie Evers-Williams**
1954	Theodore K. Lawless	1999	**Earl G. Graves Sr.**
1955	Carl J. Murphy	2000	**Oprah Winfrey**
1956	**Jack R. Robinson**	2001	**Vernon E. Jordan Jr.**
1957	**Martin Luther King Jr.**	2002	**John Lewis**
1958	**Daisy Bates** and the Little Rock Nine	2003	**Constance Baker Motley**
1959	**Edward "Duke" Ellington**		

Nobel Prize Winners

1950	**Ralph Bunche** (Peace)	1992	**Derek Walcott** (Literature)
1964	**Martin Luther King Jr.** (Peace)	1993	**Toni Morrison** (Literature)

Pulitzer Prize Winners

1950	**Gwendolyn Brooks**	Poetry
1969	**Moneta Sleet Jr.**	Journalism (Photography)
1970	Charles Gordone	Drama
1973	*Washington Post* (team member **Roger Wilkins**)	Journalism (Public Service)
1974	*Newsday* (team member Les Payne)	Journalism (Public Service)
1975	Matthew Lewis	Journalism (Photography)
1975	Ovie Carter	Journalism
1976	**Scott Joplin**	Music (posthumous)
1977	Acel Moore	Journalism
1977	**Alex Haley**	for *Roots*
1978	James Alan McPherson	Fiction
1982	Charles Fuller	Drama
1982	John H. White	Journalism
1983	**Alice Walker**	Fiction
1984	Kenneth Cooper and Norman Lockman	Journalism
1985	Dennis Bell and Ozier Muhammad	Journalism
1986	Michel duCille (as part of team)	Journalism (Photography)
1987	**August Wilson**	Drama
1987	**Rita Dove**	Poetry
1988	Dean Baquet (as part of team)	Journalism
1988	Michel duCille	Journalism (Photography)
1988	**Toni Morrison**	Fiction
1989	Clarence Page	Journalism
1990	**August Wilson**	Drama
1991	Harold Jackson (as part of team)	Journalism
1994	**David Levering Lewis**	Biography
1994	Isabel Wilkerson	Journalism
1994	William Raspberry	Journalism
1994	Yusef Komunyakaa	Poetry
1995	Leon Dash (as part of team)	Journalism
1995	Margo Jefferson	Journalism
1995	*Virgin Islands Daily News* (for the work of Melvin Claxton)	Journalism (Public Service)
1996	E. R. Shipp	Journalism
1996	George Walker	Music
1997	**Wynton Marsalis**	Music
1998	Clarence Williams	Journalism (Photography)
1999	Angelo B. Henderson	Journalism
1999	**Duke Ellington**	Music (posthumous)
2002	**Suzan-Lori Parks**	Drama

Recipients of the Presidential Medal of Freedom

1963	**Marian Anderson**		1977	**Martin Luther King Jr.**
	Ralph Bunche		1980	Clarence M. Mitchell
	George W. Taylor		1981	**Eubie Blake**
1964	Lena F. Edwards			**Andrew Young**
	Leontyne Price		1983	**James Edward Cheek**
	A. Philip Randolph			**Mabel Mercer**
1969	**Duke Ellington**		1984	**Jackie Robinson**
	Ralph Ellison		1985	**Count Basie**
	Roy Wilkins			Jerome H. Holland
	Whitney M. Young Jr.		1988	**Pearl Bailey**
1976	**Jesse Owens**		1991	**Colin Powell**

1992	Ella Fitzgerald	
	Leon H. Sullivan	
1993	Arthur Ashe,	
	Thurgood Marshall	
	Colin Powell	
1994	Dorothy Height	
	Barbara Jordan	
1995	William T. Coleman	
	John Hope Franklin	
	A. Leon Higginbotham	

1996	James L. Farmer
	John H. Johnson
	Rosa Parks
1998	James Farmer
2000	Marian Wright Edelman
	Jesse Jackson
2002	Hank Aaron
	Bill Cosby
	Roberto Clemente

Recipients of the National Medal of Arts

1986	Gordon Parks Sr.
1987	Ella Fitzgerald
1990	Jacob Lawrence
1992	James Earl Jones
1994	Celia Cruz
1995	Ossie Davis, Ruby Dee
1997	Betty Carter
2000	Maya Angelou, Benny Carter
2001	Judith Jamison
2002	Smokey Robinson
2003	Buddy Guy

Recipients of the National Humanities Medal

1990	Henry Hampton
1993	John Hope Franklin
1994	Dorothy Porter Wesley
1995	Bernice Johnson Reagon
1996	Rita Dove.
1998	Henry Louis Gates Jr.
1999	August Wilson
2000	David C. Driskell, Ernest J. Gaines, Quincy Jones, Toni Morrison
2001	Eileen Jackson Southern
2002	Thomas Sowell

African American Members of Congress

NAME	YEARS OF SERVICE	STATE	PARTY
SENATORS			
Revels, Hiram Rhoades	1870–1871	MS	Republican
Bruce, Blanche Kelso	1875–1881	MS	Republican
Brooke, Edward W.	1967–1979	MA	Republican
Moseley-Braun, Carol	1993–1999	IL	Democratic
REPRESENTATIVES			
Rainey, Joseph H.	1870–1879	SC	Republican
Long, Jefferson Franklin	1870–1871	GA	Republican
Elliott, Robert B.	1871–1874	SC	Republican
DeLarge, Robert C.	1871–1873	SC	Republican
Turner, Benjamin S.	1871–1873	AL	Republican
Walls, Josiah T.	1871–1873 1873–1876	FL	Republican
Cain, Richard Harvey	1873–1875 1877–1879	SC	Republican
Lynch, John R.	1873–1877 1882–1883	MS	Republican
Ransier, Alonzo J.	1873–1875	SC	Republican
Rapier, James T.	1873–1875	AL	Republican
Haralson, Jeremiah	1875–1877	AL	Republican
Hyman, John A.	1875–1877	NC	Republican
Nash, Charles E.	1875–1877	LA	Republican
Smalls, Robert	1875–1879 1882–1883 1884–1887	SC	Republican
O'Hara, James E.	1883–1887	NC	Republican
Cheatham, Henry P.	1889–1893	NC	Republican
Langston, John Mercer	1890–1891	VA	Republican
Miller, Thomas E.	1890–1891	SC	Republican

Murray, George Washington	1893–1895 1896–1897	SC	Republican
White, George Henry	1897–1901	NC	Republican
DePriest, Oscar	1929–1935	IL	Republican
Mitchell, Arthur W.	1935–1943	IL	Democratic
Dawson, William L.	1943–1970	IL	Democratic
Powell, Adam Clayton, Jr.	1945–1967 1969–1971	NY	Democratic
Diggs, Charles C., Jr.	1955–1980	MI	Democratic
Nix, Robert N. C., Sr.	1958–1979	PA	Democratic
Hawkins, Augustus F.	1963–1991	CA	Democratic
Conyers, John, Jr.	1965–	MI	Democratic
Chisholm, Shirley Anita	1969–1983	NY	Democratic
Clay, William L., Sr.	1969–2000	MO	Democratic
Stokes, Louis	1969–1999	OH	Democratic
Collins, George W.	1970–1972	IL	Democratic
Dellums, Ronald V.	1971–1998	CA	Democratic
Fauntroy, Walter E.	1971–1991	DC	Democratic
Metcalfe, Ralph H.	1971–1978	IL	Democratic
Mitchell, Parren J.	1971–1987	MD	Democratic
Rangel, Charles B.	1971–	NY	Democratic
Burke, Yvonne B.	1973–1979	CA	Democratic
Collins, Cardiss	1973–1997	IL	Democratic
Jordan, Barbara C.	1973–1979	TX	Democratic
Young, Andrew J., Jr.	1973–1977	GA	Democratic
Ford, Harold E., Sr.	1975–1997	TN	Democratic
Dixon, Julian C.	1979–2000	CA	Democratic
Evans, Melvin H.	1979–1981	VI	Republican
Gray, William H., III	1979–1991	PA	Democratic
Leland, George T. "Mickey"	1979–1989	TX	Democratic
Stewart, Bennett McVey	1979–1981	IL	Democratic
Crockett, George W., Jr.	1980–1991	MI	Democratic
Dymally, Mervyn M.	1981–1993	CA	Democratic
Savage, Gus	1981–1993	IL	Democratic
Washington, Harold D.	1981–1983	IL	Democratic
Hall, Katie Beatrice	1982–1985	IN	Democratic
Hayes, Charles A.	1983–1993	IL	Democratic
Owens, Major R.	1983–	NY	Democratic
Towns, Edolphus	1983–	NY	Democratic
Wheat, Alan D.	1983–1995	MO	Democratic
Waldon, Alton R., Jr.	1986–1987	NY	Democratic
Espy, Albert M. "Mike"	1987–1993	MS	Democratic
Flake, Floyd H.	1987–1997	NY	Democratic
Lewis, John R.	1987–	GA	Democratic
Mfume, Kweisi	1987–1996	MD	Democratic
Payne, Donald M.	1989–	NJ	Democratic
Washington, Craig A.	1989–1995	TX	Democratic
Blackwell, Lucien E.	1991–1995	PA	Democratic
Collins, Barbara-Rose	1991–1997	MI	Democratic
Franks, Gary	1991–1997	CT	Republican
Jefferson, William J.	1991–	LA	Democratic
Norton, Eleanor Holmes	1991–	DC	Democratic
Waters, Maxine	1991–	CA	Democratic
Clayton, Eva M.	1992–	NC	Democratic
Bishop, Sanford D., Jr.	1993–	GA	Democratic
Brown, Corrine	1993–	FL	Democratic
Clyburn, James E.	1993–	SC	Democratic
Fields, Cleo	1993–1997	LA	Democratic
Hastings, Alcee L.	1993–	FL	Democratic
Hilliard, Earl F.	1993–	AL	Democratic

Johnson, Eddie Bernice	1993–	TX	Democratic
McKinney, Cynthia A.	1993–	GA	Democratic
Meek, Carrie P.	1993–	FL	Democratic
Reynolds, Melvin J.	1993–1995	IL	Democratic
Rush, Bobby L.	1993–	IL	Democratic
Scott, Robert C.	1993–	VA	Democratic
Thompson, Bennie G.	1993–	MS	Democratic
Tucker, Walter R.	1993–1995	CA	Democratic
Watt, Melvin L.	1993–	NC	Democratic
Wynn, Albert R.	1993–	MD	Democratic
Fattah, Chaka	1995–	PA	Democratic
Frazer, Victor O.	1995–1997	VI	Democratic
Jackson, Jesse L., Jr.	1995–	IL	Democratic
Jackson-Lee, Sheila	1995–	TX	Democratic
Watts, J. C., Jr.	1995–2002	OK	Republican
Cummings, Elijah	1996–	MD	Democratic
Millender-McDonald, Juanita	1996–	CA	Democratic
Ford, Harold E., Jr.	1997–	TN	Democratic
Kilpatrick, Carolyn Cheeks	1997–	MI	Democratic
Carson, Julia	1997–	IN	Democratic
Christian-Christensen, Donna	1997–	VI	Democratic
Davis, Danny K.	1997–	IL	Democratic
Lee, Barbara	1998–	CA	Democratic
Meeks, Gregory W.	1998–	NY	Democratic
Jones, Stephanie Tubbs	1999–	OH	Democratic
Clay, William L., Jr.	2001–	MO	Democratic

Sources: Congressional Research Service, *Black Members of the United States Congress: 1789–1997*; Congressional Quarterly, *Guide to U.S. Elections*; Congressional Quarterly, *Guide to Congress*, 1991; news reports.

Presidential Appointments of African American Judges

PRESIDENT HARRY S. TRUMAN (1945–1953)
Irvin C. Mollison — Customs Court
William Henry Hastie — 3rd Circuit

PRESIDENT DWIGHT D. EISENHOWER (1953–1961)
Scovel Richardson — Customs Court

PRESIDENT JOHN F. KENNEDY (1961–1963)
James Benton Parsons — Illinois (ND)
Wade H. McCree — Michigan (ED)
Thurgood Marshall — 2nd Circuit

PRESIDENT LYNDON B. JOHNSON (1963–1969)
A. Leon Higginbotham — Pennsylvania (ED)
Spottswood W. Robinson III — D.C.
William B. Bryant — D.C.
James L. Watson — Customs Court
Constance Baker Motley — New York (SD)
Wade H. McCree — 6th Circuit
Aubrey E. Robinson Jr. — D.C.
Spottswood W. Robinson III — D.C. Circuit
Joseph C. Waddy — D.C.
Thurgood Marshall — Supreme Court
Damon J. Keith — Michigan (ED)

PRESIDENT RICHARD M. NIXON (1969–1974)
David W. Williams — California (CD)
Barrington D. Parker, Sr. — D.C.
Lawrence W. Pierce — New York (SD)
Clifford Scott Green — Pennsylvania (ED)
Robert L. Carter — New York (SD)
Robert M. Duncan — Ohio (SD)

PRESIDENT GERALD FORD (1974–1981)
Henry Bramwell — New York (ED)
George N. Leighton — Illinois (ND)
Cecil F. Poole — California (ND)

PRESIDENT JAMES E. CARTER (1977–1981)
A. Leon Higginbotham — 3rd Circuit
Damon J. Keith — 6th Circuit
Paul A. Simmons — Pennsylvania (WD)
Robert F. Collins — Louisiana
Jack E. Tanner — Washington (WD)
Mary Johnson Lowe — New York (SD)
Theodore McMillian — 8th Circuit
Julian Abele Cook Jr. — Michigan (ED)
John G. Penn — D.C.
David S. Nelson — Massachusetts

Gabrielle Kirk McDonald	Texas (SD)
Amalya L. Kearse	2nd Circuit
Joseph Woodrow Hatchett	5th/11th Circuit
Matthew J. Perry Jr.	S. Carolina
Benjamin F. Gibson	Michigan (WD)
J. Jerome Farris	9th Circuit
Joseph C. Howard	Maryland
Nathaniel R. Jones	6th Circuit
Anne E. Thompson	New Jersey
Anna Diggs Taylor	Michigan (ED)
Alcee L. Hastings	Florida
Cecil F. Poole	9th Circuit
James T. Giles	Pennsylvania (ED)
Horace T. Ward	Georgia (ND)
Terry J. Hatter Jr.	California (CD)
Harry T. Edwards	D.C. Circuit
Odell Horton	Tennessee (WD)
Norma H. Johnson	D.C.
Clyde S. Cahill Jr.	Missouri (ED)
George W. White	Ohio (ND)
U.W. Clemon	Alabama (ND)
Thelton Eugene Henderson	California (ND)
Earl B. Gilliam	California (ND)
Myron H. Thompson	Alabama (MD)
Consuelo B. Marshall	California (CD)
George Howard Jr.	Arkansas (ED)
Richard C. Erwin	N. Carolina (MD)

PRESIDENT RONALD REAGAN (1981–1988)

Lawrence W. Pierce	2nd Circuit
John Raymond Hargrove	Maryland
Ann Claire Williams	Illinois (ND)
Henry T. Wingate	Mississippi (SD)
James R. Spencer	Virginia (ED)
Kenneth M. Hoyt	Texas (SD)
Herbert J. Hutton	Pennsylvania (ED)

PRESIDENT GEORGE BUSH (1988–1992)

Clarence Thomas	D.C. Circuit
Sterling Johnson Jr.	New York (ED)
James Ware	California (ND)
Saundra Brown Armstrong	California (ND)
Timothy K. Lewis	Pennsylvania (WD)
Fernando J. Gaitan Jr.	Missouri (WD)
Donald L. Graham	Florida (SD)
Clarence Thomas	Supreme Court
Joe Billy McDade	Illinois (CD)
Garland E. Burrell Jr.	California (ED)
J. Curtis Joyner	Pennsylvania (ED)
Carol E. Jackson	Missouri (ED)
Timothy K. Lewis	3rd Circuit

PRESIDENT WILLIAM J. CLINTON (1992–2000)

Henry Lee Adams	Florida (MD)
Wilkie D. Ferguson Jr.	Florida (SD)
Reginald C. Lindsay	Massachusetts
Charles A. Shaw	Missouri (ED)
Gary L. Lancaster	Pennsylvania (WD)
Raymond A. Jackson	Virginia (ED)

Judith W. Rogers	D.C. Circuit
Franklin D. Burgess	Washington (WD)
Michael J. Davis	Minnesota
Ancer L. Haggerty	Oregon
Audrey B. Collins	California (CD)
Deborah A. Batts	New York (SD)
Carl E. Stewart	5th Circuit
Clarence Cooper	Georgia (ND)
W. Louis Sands	Georgia (MD)
Solomon Oliver Jr.	Ohio (ND)
Raymond L. Finch	Virgin Islands
Vanessa D. Gilmore	Texas (SD)
Theodore A. McKee	3rd Circuit
Ricardo M. Urbina	D.C.
Emmet G. Sullivan	D.C.
Denise Page Hood	Michigan (ED)
Alvin W. Thompson	Connecticut
Blanche M. Manning	Illinois (ND)
Alexander Williams Jr.	Maryland
Napoleon A. Jones Jr.	California (SD)
Barrington D. Parker Jr.	New York (SD)
David H. Coar	Illinois (ND)
James Arthur Beaty Jr.	N. Carolina (WD)
Okla Jones, II	Louisiana (ED)
William H. Walls	New Jersey
Vicki Miles-LaGrange	Oklahoma (WD)
Curtis Lynn Collier	Tennessee (ED)
Wiley Y. Daniel	Colorado
Andre M. Davis	Maryland
Bernice Bouie Donald	Tennessee (WD)
R. Guy Cole Jr.	6th Circuit
Joseph A. Greenaway Jr.	New Jersey
Charles N. Clevert Jr.	Wisconsin (ED)
Henry H. Kennedy	D.C.
Eric Lee Clay	6th Circuit
Martin J. Jenkins	California (ND)
Algenon L. Marbley	Ohio (SD)
Sam A. Lindsay	Texas (ND)
Ivan L.R. Lemelle	Louisiana (ED)
Gregory M. Sleet	Delaware
Johnnie B. Rawlinson	Nevada
Stephan P. Mickle	Florida (ND)
Richard W. Roberts	D.C.
Victoria A. Roberts	Michigan (ED)
Raner C. Collins	Arizona
Ralph E. Tyson	Louisiana (MD)
Gerald Bruce Lee	Virginia (ED)
Margaret B. Seymour	South Carolina
William J. Hibbler	Illinois (ND)
Charles R. Wilson	11th Circuit
Ann Claire Williams	7th Circuit
William Joseph Haynes Jr.	Tennessee (MD)
George B. Daniels	New York (SD)
Phyllis J. Hamilton	California (ND)
Petrese B. Tucker	Pennsylvania (ED)
Laura Taylor Swain	New York (SD)
Johnnie B. Rawlinson	9th Circuit
Roger Gregory	4th Circuit

PRESIDENT GEORGE W. BUSH (2000–)

Roger Gregory	4th Circuit
Beggie B. Walton	D.C. District
Barrington D. Parker, Jr.	2nd Circuit
Julie A. Robinson	Kansas
Legrome D. Davis	Pennsylvania (ED)
Percy Anderson	California (CD)
Lavenski R. Smith	8th Circuit
Henry Edward Autry	Missouri (ED)
Morrison C. England, Jr.	California (ED)

African American Recipients of the Congressional Medal of Honor

(Arranged alphabetically by war)

Name	Rank	Service	War	State	Awarded
Barnes, William H.	PVT	Army	Civil War	MD	1865
Beaty, Powhatan	1SG	Army	Civil War	OH	1865
Blake, Robert	Contraband	Navy	Civil War	VA	1864
Bronson, James H.	1SG	Army	Civil War	OH	1865
Brown, William H.	Landsman	Navy	Civil War	MD	1864
Brown, Wilson	Boy	Navy	Civil War	MS	1864
Carney, William H.	SGT	Army	Civil War	MA	1900
Dorsey, Decatur	SGT	Army	Civil War	MD	1865
Fleetwood, Christian A.	SGT	Army	Civil War	MD	1865
Gardiner, James	PVT	Army	Civil War	VA	1865
Harris, James H.	SGT	Army	Civil War	MD	1874
Hawkins, Thomas	SGM	Army	Civil War	PA	1870
Hilton, Alfred B.	SGM	Army	Civil War	MD	1865
Holland, Milton M.	SGT	Army	Civil War	OH	1865
Kelly, Alexander	1SG	Army	Civil War	PA	1865
Lawson, John	Landsman	Navy	Civil War	PA	1864
Mifflin, James	Cook	Navy	Civil War	VA	1864
Pease, Joachim	Seaman	Navy	Civil War	NY	1864
Pinn, Robert	1SG	Army	Civil War	OH	1865
Ratcliff, Edward	1SG	Army	Civil War	VA	1865
Veal, Charles	PVT	Army	Civil War	VA	1865
Boyne, Thomas	SGT	Army	Indian Campaign	MD	1882
Brown, Benjamin	SGT	Army	Indian Campaign	VA	1890
Denny, John	SGT	Army	Indian Campaign	NY	1894
Factor, Pompey	PVT	Army	Indian Campaign	AK	1875
Greaves, Clinton	CPL	Army	Indian Campaign	MD	1879
Johnson, Henry	SGT	Army	Indian Campaign	VA	1890
Jordan, George	SGT	Army	Indian Campaign	TN	1890
McBryar, William	SGT	Army	Indian Campaign	NY	1890
Mays, Isaiah	CPL	Army	Indian Campaign	OH	1890
Paine, Adam	PVT	Army	Indian Campaign	TX	1875
Payne, Isaac	PVT	Army	Indian Campaign	AK	1875
Shaw, Thomas	SGT	Army	Indian Campaign	KY	1890
Walley, Augustus	PVT	Army	Indian Campaign	MD	1890
Wanton, George H.	PVT	Army	Indian Campaign	NJ	1899
Ward, John	SGT	Army	Indian Campaign	TX	1875
Williams, Moses	1SG	Army	Indian Campaign	LA	1896
Wilson, William O.	CPL	Army	Indian Campaign	MN	1891
Davis, John	Seaman	Navy	Interim–1881	NJ	1884
Johnson, John	Seaman	Navy	Interim–1872	PA	1872
Johnson, William	Cooper	Navy	Interim–1879	NY	1884
Noil, Joseph B.	Seaman	Navy	Interim–1872	NY	1872
Smith, John	Seaman	Navy	Interim–1880	NY	1884
Atkins, Daniel	Cook	1c Navy	Spanish American	VA	1898

Baker, Edward L.	SGM	Army	Spanish American	WY	1902
Bell, Dennis	PVT	Army	Spanish American	DC	1899
Penn, Robert	Fireman	1c Navy	Spanish American	VA	1898
Thompkins, William H.	PVT	Army	Spanish American	NJ	1899
Stowers, Freddie	CPL	Army	WWI	SC	1991
Baker, Vernon	1LT	Army	WWII	WY	1997
Carter, Edward	SSG	Army	WWII	CA	1997
Fox, John R.	1LT	Army	WWII	OH	1997
James, Willy F.	PFC	Army	WWII	MO	1997
Rivers, Ruben	SSG	Army	WWII	OK	1997
Thomas, Charles	MAJ	Army	WWII	MI	1997
Watson, George	PVT	Army	WWII	AL	1997
Charlton, Cornelius	SGT	Army	Korea	WV	
Thompson, William	PFC	Army	Korea	NY	
Anderson, James C.	PFC	USMC	Vietnam	CA	1967
Anderson, Webster	SFC	Army	Vietnam	SC	1967
Ashley Jr., Eugene	SGT	Army	Vietnam	NY	1968
Austin, Oscar P.	PFC	USMC	Vietnam	AZ	1969
Bryant, William Maud	SFC	Army	Vietnam	MI	1969
Davis, Rodney M.	SGT	USMC	Vietnam	GA	1967
Jenkins Jr., Robert H.	PFC	USMC	Vietnam	FL	1969
Joel, Lawrence	Spec/6	Army	Vietnam	NY	1965
Johnson, Dwight Hal	Spec/5	Army	Vietnam	MI	1968
Johnson, Ralph H.	PFC	USMC	Vietnam	CA	1968
Langhorn, Garfield M.	PFC	Army	Vietnam	NY	1969
Leonard, Matthew	SGT	Army	Vietnam	AL	1967
Long, Donald Russell	SGT	Army	Vietnam	KY	1968
Olive, Milton L.	PFC	Army	Vietnam	IL	1966
Pitts, Leroy Riley	CPT	Army	Vietnam	KS	1967
Rogers, Charles Calvin	Brig. Gen.	Army	Vietnam	WV	1968
Sargent, Ruppert Leon	1LT	Army	Vietnam	VA	1967
Sasser, Clarence E.	Spec/5	Army	Vietnam	TX	1968
Sims, Clifford Chester	SGT	Army	Vietnam	FL	1968
Warren Jr., John E.	1LT	Army	Vietnam	NY	1969

Page numbers in boldface refer to the main entry on the subject. Page numbers in italics refer to illustrations.

White House Conference on Aging, 15
White House Conference on Children and
 Youth (1960), 707
White House Council to Fulfill These
 Rights, 488
White House Project, 450
Whiteman, Paul, 792
White Man's Burden (film), 66
Whitemarsh Hall, designed by Julian Abele,
 7
*White on Black: The Views of Twenty-two
 White American on the Negro*
 (Thompson), 811
White Rose Travelers' Aid Society, 570
White Seal (ship), 395
White Slave Traffic Act (Mann Act), 72
Whitlock, Vivian H., 627, 628
Whitman, Charles Otis, 825
Whitman, Walt, 818
Whitney, Anne, 530
Whitney Museum of American Art (New
 York), 55, 61, 519, 691, 744
Whitney Studio Gallery, 223
Whittaker, Johnson C., 351
Whittier, John Greenleaf, 362, 918
Who Look at Me (Jordan), 485
Whoopi Goldberg (television show), 344
Wickard, Claude R., 50
Wickham, De Wayne, 508
Wideman, John Edgar, 893
Wide World of Sports (ABC), 594
Wier, Judith, 630
*Wife of His Youth and Other Stories of the
 Color Line, The* (Chesnutt), 161
Wiggins, David, 857
Wiggins, Thomas Bethune. *See* Blind Tom
Wigglesworth, Michael, 371
Wigner, Eugene, 883
Wikson, Teddy, 180
Wilberforce, Ontario, 787
 Paul Nathaniel in, 662, 663
Wilberforce University, 212, 867
 Charles Harris Wesley president of, 867
 Daniel Alexander Payne president of,
 664
 Theophilus Gould Steward at, 789
Wilbon, Michael, 508
Wilbur, Richard, 277
Wild Cat Blues (album; Sidney Bechet), 63
"Wild Cat Blues" (Clarence and Waller),
 846
Wilder, Douglas, **881–883**
Wilder, Gene, 690
Wiley, Stella, 477
Wilkins, Barron, 98
Wilkins, Ernie, 53
Wilkins, J. Ernest, Jr., **883–884**
Wilkins, Roy, *100*, 532, 881, *884*, **884–886**,
 926
 critical of Stokely Carmichael, 142

Daisy Lampkin opposing, 509
 on term "Black Power," 141
Wilkinson, J. L., 309, 648
Wilkinson, Moses, 499
Wilkinson, Robert Shaw, 572
Willard, Frances, 865
Willard, Jess, 455
William Lloyd Garrison (Bannister), 47
Williams, Adam Daniel, 501
Williams, Bert, *886*, **886–888**
 Clorindy written for, 189
 John Rosamond Johnson's collaboration
 with, 458–459
 Will Marion Cook teaming with, 189,
 189
Williams, Cathay, **888–889**
Williams, Clarence, 846
 beaten by Bessie Smith, 779
 Blue Five, 29
 helping Sidney Bechet with recordings,
 62–63
Williams, Claude, 53
Williams, Cootie
 and Duke Ellington, 272, 273
 Pearl Bailey vocalist with, 37
Williams, Daniel Hale, 74, **889–890**
Williams, Dean John T., 773
Williams, Dootsie, 310
Williams, Doug, 719
Williams, Egbert Austin. *See* Williams, Bert
Williams, Eugene. *See* Scottsboro Boys
Williams, George Washington, **890–892**
 John Hope Franklin on, 315
Williams, Hank, Jr.
 John Lee Hooker recordings with, 409
 Ray Charles recording with, 157
Williams, Hosea, 433
Williams, J. Mayo, 446
 Big Bill Broonzy introduced to, 104
Williams, Joe, 53
Williams, John, 243
Williams, John Alfred, **892–893**
Williams, John Joseph
 accompanied by Sherwood Hailey to
 Vatican I, 389
 James Healy and, 385
Williams, Julia Ward, 325
Williams, Marion, 311
Williams, Martin, 185
Williams, Mary Lou, 83
Williams, Nelson, 828
Williams, Paul, 730
Williams, Paul Revere, **893–895**
 design of Los Angeles International
 Airport, *894*
Williams, Peter, Jr., **895–896**
 assistance to James McCune Smith, 780
Williams, Richard, 899
Williams, Robert F., 58
 influence on Bobby Seale, 759

Williams, Robin, 345
Williams, Serena, *898*, **898–899**
Williams, Smokey Joe, *896*, **896–898**
Williams, Spencer
 association with Fats Waller, 847
 in *La Revue Nègre*, 40
Williams, Tony, 214
Williams, Venus, *898*, **898–899**
Williams, Walter, 284–285
Williams, Wilburn, 382
Williamson, Ansel, 533
Williamson, Fred, 653
Williamson, John Lee "Sonny Boy" (d.
 1948), 104, 861
Williamson, Sonny Boy, (d. 1965), 464, 497,
 860
Willis, Cornelia Grinnell, 442
Willis, Richard, 452, 453
Williston, J. P., 219
Willkie, Wendell, 56
Will Mastin Trio, 218
Wills, Maury, 721
"Will the Education of the Negro Solve the
 Race Problem?" (Turner), 825–826
Wilma (TV film), 852
Wilmington, Wrightsville and Onslow
 Railroad, North Carolina, 164
Wilmington Advocate (newspaper), 254
Wilson, Alice, 339
Wilson, August, **899–901**
 influence of Amiri Baraka on, 49
 James Earl Jones and, 474
Wilson, David, 632
Wilson, Dooley, 860
Wilson, Harriet E., **901–902**
Wilson, J. W., 623
Wilson, Jackie, 346, 393
Wilson, James, 146
Wilson, Llewellyn, 81
Wilson, Mary, 730
Wilson, Nancy, 552
Wilson, Rose, 857
Wilson, Sarah, 91
Wilson, Shadow, 53
Wilson, Teddy, 406
Wilson, William, 561
Wilson, William Julius, 79, 868, **902–904**,
 903
Wilson, Woodrow, 20, 364, 380, 456, 540,
 595, 614
 Archibald Grimké and, 361
 backed by Richard Greener, 352
 William Monroe Trotter's argument
 with, 819–820
Wilt's Wonder Women, 156
Wind from Nowhere, The (Micheaux), 591
Winding, Kai, 598
Windom, William, 351
Windom Resolution endorsed by Richard
 Greener, 351